HAWK's

AUTHORS' PSEUDONYMS II

A Comprehensive Reference
of
Modern Authors' Pseudonyms

Written & Compiled
by Pat Hawk

Second Edition

Pat Hawk

HAWK's

AUTHORS' PSEUDONYMS II

A Comprehensive Reference of Modern Authors' Pseudonyms

Written & Compiled
by Pat Hawk
edited by Raymond Hawk

Second Edition

ISBN: 0-9643-1851-2

DEDICATION

This publication is dedicated to my son Raymond and daughter Donna, who have provided so much editorial help in shaping this second edition; and to all the collectors, book dealers, librarians, authors, et al, who have been so helpful in gathering and providing the mass of information enabling this second edition.

INTRODUCTION

By Joe R. Lansdale
"The Kid From Nacogdoches"

Pseudonyms, or pen names as they are better known, are a strange fascination. Not only for readers who want to know who wrote what, but why a pen name anyway?

As someone who has used a few--Ray Slater, M. Dean Bayer, Richard Dale, Jack Buchannan, and others--I'll have to say the answer as to why is varied.

For one thing, it is a common thought in the industry that the writer who is too prolific is not particularly good.

I have to say, in all fairness to the industry, this is mostly correct. It is my belief that quantity makes quality--in the beginning. But in time, quantity merely makes quantity.

What happens is you get all the bad stuff out of your system by mass production, and then, the experience of having written so much begins to pay off. Quality results. But then, if the quantity approach is maintained, quality is sacrificed.

What has this to do with pen names?

This: many writers, when starting out, going through that part of the quantity stage where they have learned to put the basic elements of a story or novel together have yet learned to do it, ahem, well. Serviceable, but not very well. During this stage the material is often readable, even quirky, and possibly full of the echoes of who that writer will eventually become.

But good?

Maybe not. Exceptions to every rule, but generally, the wise writer knows this is an apprenticeship period and chooses to use pen names. This way, the writer gets paid, gets books out there, gains experience, has a resume, but the name they eventually hope to develop is not locked in with their pen name. Later, after they've written better, more successful work, they may reveal this pen name because it has little effect on their current output.

That's one reason for a pen name.

Another is mass production also leads to a lot of books or stories under one name, and finally, to make one's self look less productive, less like a machine, some authors decide a pen name is the way to go. This way, if five books appear from them in a single year they can split the production between several names, so editors, reviewers, and readers, won't see them as someone who merely turns out yard goods.

There's also this. Say a writer wants to establish themselves as a writer of crime novels, but has an idea for a series of science fiction tales. If readers have been reading this author for the crime stories, they see his or her name on other books, and they try them, and science fiction is not their cup of tea, then they may assume the writer isn't someone they want to read regularly, if at all. And publishers, editors, agents, as well as many readers, are uncertain what to do with a writer like this.

How do they market them?

What category do they fit into?

This, to my way of thinking is a narrow view on the part of readers, publishers, editors, and agents, but pretty much a true one. I know. I've written in many genres and for years that was the word I heard from editors. Choose one genre, Joe.

I didn't. I made it anyway, and I think because I fought against this sage advice.

But, had I established myself in one field, perhaps written novels under pen names, I might have found security sooner, if not happiness. Doing it that way wasn't my way, but it's the way of many, and therefore, you have another reason for pen names.

Another reason is the house name. Meaning a series like *The Red Devil Two-Handed Dog Killer*, written by Jake Rake, may in fact not be a real name, but a house name. House name means a handle given to the "author" of the books so a number of writers can be used to produce them in mass. Sometimes this is the doing of the publisher, or an editor, who comes up with a concept, then hires a writer to do the work, and if the series becomes popular, hires several writers to do the work, all of them publishing under the house name.

Another example of this subcontract work. Say a series is established by an author, but the author loses interest in the series, or sees it merely as a meal ticked so they can create other work, possibly under their own name, so they hire other writers to write for them. The work is often delivered by the creator of the series as their own, when it may in fact be the work of another, or several writers. Yet, the stories still appear under the house name.

Yet another reason is this. Sometimes it's fun to be someone else. I've even known of writers who were blocked and couldn't write under their own name, but by adopting a pen name, they were able to break the block and create. They became a new person; a writer who was fresh and didn't have the baggage of the old writer.

A variation on this is the pen name as a trick. Say an author has been around for a while. They're doing good work, but having created a number of books, none of them having delivered in any great way, editors become reluctant to publish them, or if they do publish them, they refuse to pay the author what they think they're worth.

So, the author creates a pen name, markets themselves as this name hoping to have a fresh start. Variations on this are Stephen King who wanted to see if he could build an audience under another name with different types of novels, and was well on his way with Richard Bachman, when he was discovered.

F. Paul Wilson used a pen name on his medical thriller because he felt he might be taken a bit more seriously outside of his usual stomping grounds if he were perceived as someone new. He was right. He got his biggest advance to date, and then, he revealed who he was, and the book was published as by F. Paul Wilson.

That sneaky devil.

Writers love that story.

But whatever the reason for pen names, lots of folks have used them. That being the case, readers--especially the fanatics-- want to know who wrote what.

And if anyone knows the answer to that, it's Pat Hawk.

Sure, he hasn't found out who wrote everything and under what name, but, it's close. And give him a week or two.

This book is rich with the kind of information all you literary snoops want to know.

He even found out some stuff about me.

So if you have an interest in writers and their pen names, this is your volume, pardner.

Enjoy.

Joe R. Lansdale, alias, Ray Slater, M. Dean Bayer, Richard Dale, Jack Buchannan--three times, and ....That'll do.

THANKS

A number of people have constructively contributed to the value and/or development of this document. So, thanks to the following:

- Special thanks to my son, Raymond, who reformatted the information presentation and accomplished a major portion of the edit. Also, special thanks to my daughter, Donna, who again accomplished the word processing and graphics.

- So many others have rendered advice, assistance and input as the project was updated - I hope I can remember them all:

Susan & Bill Albert
Mike Avallone
BAE (R.C. & Elwanda Holland)
Margaret Ball
Neal Barrett, Jr.
Gregory Benford
Victor Berch
Black Ace Books (Rose)
Jon L. Breen
Buck Creek Books (Nancy)
Ross Burnet
Lance Casebeer
Hugh B. Cave
Robert Colby
Glen Cook
Bill Crider
Scott Cupp
L.W. Currey
Dark Destiny (Jeff McGuire)
E & C Books
Chris Eckhoff
Harlan Ellison
Graeme Flanagan
Brad Frank
Ft. Worth Library (Marsha)
Gorgon Book (Joe & John)
Charles L. Grant
Grapevine Public Library
Art Hackathorn
Harvey Hornwood
Ryerson Johnson
Tom Johnson
Elmer Kelton
Dean R. Koontz
Marv Lachman
Joe R. Lansdale
Rex Layton
Jean Francoise Le Deist
Wendi Lee
Tom Lessor
John Lutz
John Marston Books
Ardath Mayhar
Stephen Mertz
Michael Moorcock
Wayne Mullins
Lynn Munroe Books
Will Murray
Mystery Scene
(Ed Gorman/Larry Seagriff)
Andrew J. Offutt
Pandora (Grant Thiessen)
Paperback Parade (Gary Lovisi)
Wally Pattengill
PPCC (Maurice Flanagan)
Richard S. Prather
Bill Pronzini
Robert Randisi
James Reasoner
River Oaks Books (Barbara)
Leonard Robbins
Justin Scott
Robert Silverberg
Spoon River Press (Ed)
Al Tonik
Moe Wadle
Jeffrey M. Wallmann
Donald E. Westlake

Foreword

The foundation for this reference is a database. There is no other feasible way to process/manipulate the rather significant amount of data accumulated. Considerable effort has been made in Hawk's II to present the **Authors'** section of the reference in a more useful and attractive format. In doing so we have absorbed more space, which has necessitated no longer duplicating information in the **Pseudonyms** section.

Content

I make no claim that this reference is complete or near so. However, this second publication represents a serious attempt to continue to gather and assimilate as many 20th century pseudonyms of authors as could be discovered: There are over 37,000 entries in this edition covering authors of all genres.

Pseudonyms can take on many forms, including name variations (some using a combination of names and initials) and nicknames. I have leaned toward the inclusion of many of these because many authors have resorted to this manner of obscuring gender (both ways). I have learned that even a single initial may make the difference in determining the true identity of an author. For example:

John (R.) MacDonald is Kenneth Millar
John D. MacDonald is John D(ann). MacDonald

And there are numerous instances of fine lines of identification. I have chosen to include more rather than omit some which might help you in your hunt for the truth.

This reference was never intended to be bibliographic in nature. I have added much of that kind of information - but this is only to provide help and not replace all the many excellent references of that type. This reference should serve as a roadmap or guide to those references noted.

In a work of this magnitude, there are bound to be errors, omissions, oversights, etc. I welcome input, corrections, and comments. I pledge to work towards continued improvement and periodic publication of the reference. I am always interested in any sources I may have missed. I can be reached by phone (817) 481-2077, by fax (817) 421-3289, or by mail at:

1740 Sunshine Lane
Southlake, Texas 76092-9543

ARRANGEMENT

This edition is presented in the following three sections:

AUTHOR

This section is presented in "outline" format, alphabetically by author. The author's real name is usually shown as the "Author." In some instances, the author has legally adopted a pseudonym. Examples are:

ORIGINAL	LEGALIZED PSEUDONYM
Elleson Trevor Dudley-Smith	Elleson Trevor
Charles Nutt	Charles Beaumont
Edward Hamilton Waldo	Theodore Sturgeon

In those instances, the original name is shown once as the author with the legalized name shown as a pseudo. If other pseudonyms exist, they are shown opposite the legalized pseudonym, which also appears as the author for those pseudonyms.

The author's full name is shown bold. The surname of each pseudonym is also shown bold and arrayed at the first indention. See examples 1 and 2 for complete "AUTHOR" format explanation.

Example 1

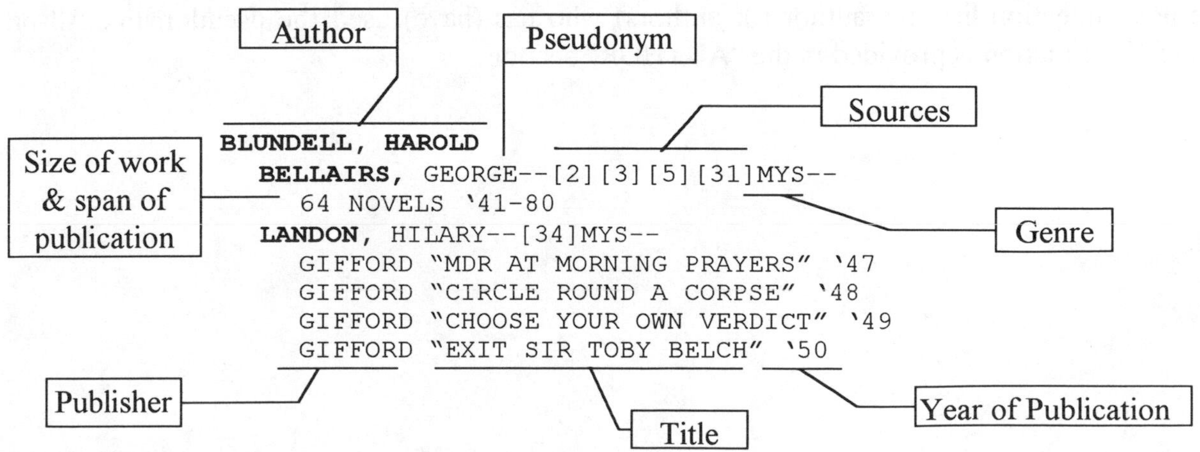

Example 2

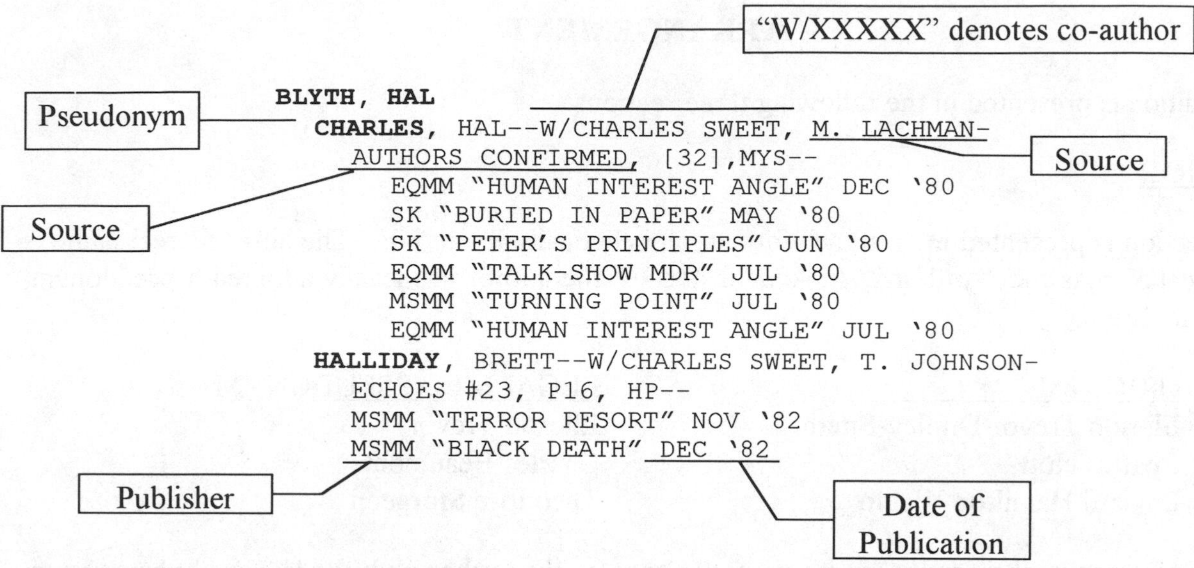

ARTICLES & COMMENTARY

Some short pieces have been included which should assist in understanding the use of pen names. Several lengthy interviews have been included (all previously published in *Books Are Everything*). There is some commentary on a selected few of many interviews, both formal and informal, conducted in the pursuit of pseudonym information.

PSEUDONYMS

Only two bits of information are provided in this section. The pseudonym is shown in full bold; the next indention lists the author (or authors) who has (have) used the pseudonym. All other related information is provided in the "AUTHOR" section.

MAJOR SOURCES

The following sources have been referenced because they have been found to be reliable in most instances. There are always a few errors in any large reference work, but other sources were omitted due to the frequency of errors or their scope of information. There is also conflict between some of these references such as spelling of names, arrangement of surname, etc. I have in each instance tried to resolve, verify and determine the most accurate information. I welcome suggestions for other sources and any useful input. Please state the provenance for your information or basis for your belief that your input is correct. If you are nominating a new source, I would appreciate some guidance on how to obtain or have access to the nominated source.

[1] *Pseudonym and Nicknames Dictionary*, edited by Jennifer Mossman, 3rd Edition.

[2] *Who's Hugh?: an SF reader's guide to pseudonyms* by Roy Robinson, 1984

[3] *Crime Fiction, 1749 - 1980: A Comprehensive Bibliography* by Allen J. Hubin, 1984 (Also a supplement which covers 1980 - 1985)

[4] *Science Fiction and Fantasy Authors: A Bibliography of First Printings of Their Fiction* by L.W. Currey, 1979

[5] *Encyclopedia of Mystery & Detection* by Chris Steinbrunner and Otto Penzler, 1976

[6] *New York Public Library Desk Reference*, 1990

[7] *Science Fiction & Fantasy Literature, 1700-1991* by R. Reginald, two volumes, 1987 and 1992

[8] *Dictionary of Literary Pseudonyms* by Frank Atkinson, 1988

[9] *Romance Readers Handbook*, 1989

[10] *Harlequin Intrigue Pseudonyms* by Victor Berch

[11] *Encyclopedia of SFI & Fantasy Through 1968* Compiled by Donald H. Tuck, 1974

[12] *Mystery Index* by Steven Olderr, 1987

[13] *Oxford Companion to Australian Literature*, 1985

[14] *A Bibliography of the Publications of N.Y. Olympia Press* by Patrick Kearney

[15] *The History of the Science Fiction Magazine* by Michael Ashley, 1976

[16] *Who's Who in Horror & Science Fiction* by Michael Ashley, Tapplinger 1978

[17] *20th Century Romance & Historical Writers,* 2nd Edition, 1990

[18] *20th Century Crime & Mystery Writers,* 3rd Edition, 1991

[19] *Encyclopedia of Frontier & Western Fiction* by John Tuska & Vicki Piekarski, McGraw Hill 1983

[20] *Oxford Companion to Spanish Literature*

[21] *The Romantic Spirit*, LAM Enterprises 1990

[22] *Hawthorn Dictionary of Pseudonyms,* 1971

[23] *The Encyclopedia of Science Fiction* by John Clute & Peter Nichols, St. Martin's Press 1993

[24] *Man of Magic & Mystery: A guide to the Work of Walter B. Gibson,* J. Randolph Cox, 1988

[25] *Twentieth Century Children's Writers,* Macmillan 1978

[26] *The Essence of Romance,* Twilight Publishing 1993 and 1994

[27] *The Mushroom Jungle: A History of Postwar Paperback Publishing* by Steve Holland, Zardoz 1993

[28] *Twentieth Century Western Writers,* 2nd Edition, St. James Press 1991

[29] *Criminal Literature in Sweden 1749-1990*, DAST Publishing 1992

[30] *Dictionary of Mexican Literature*, Greenwood Press 1992

[31] *Contemporary Authors*, Gale Research

[32] *Monthly Murders: A Checklist & Chronological Listing of Fiction of Digest Size Mystery Magazines*, compiled by Michael L. Cook, Greenwood Press 1982

[33] *Something About the Author*, Gale Research

[34] *Crime Fiction II: A Comprehensive Bibliography 1749-1990* by Allen J. Hubin, Garland 1994

[35] *The Australian Paperback Guide* by Graeme Flanagan, Gryphon Publishing 1994

[36] *Australian Crime Fiction*: A Bibliography 1857-1993 by John Loder, Thorpe 1994

[37] *Mystery, Detective & Espionage Magazines*, compiled by Michael L. Cook, Greenwood Press 1983

[38] *Contemporary Novelists*, 5th Edition, St. James Press 1991

[39] *Pseudonyme Ein Lexicon* by Jorg Weigand, Nomos Verlagsgsellschaft 1991

[40] *Bibliographie der Kriminal-Literatur: 1945-90* by Klaus-Diefer Walkhoff-Jordan, Ullstein 1991

WHAT IS A PSEUDONYM?

By Pat Hawk

The dictionary will tell you that a pen name or pseudonym is a false or assumed name. Under the most strict interpretation, all names other than your birth name [or legal name if you have had it changed] would be pseudonyms. Some purists would argue that use of nick-names, maiden names, spelling variations, etc. are not pseudonyms since they are usually not intended to hide identity. For sake of clarity, I have chosen to include all of these that make sense to help facilitate your discovery of all name variations of your "author of interest." This decision was not without agony. Many name variations are forced by the publisher, for other business reasons, according to the nature or genre of the book, and a number of reasons other than concealing the real identity of the author.

Another reason some writers use a pen name is to Anglicize their name. This is true in the case of a significant number of writers from countries that are distinctly non-Anglo and more often than not when the spelling is unusual in most English countries.

Authors often adopt pen names that take on the flavor of the genre in which they are writing. In Westerns, for example, you see "Tex" appear in a pen name. "Colt" is also incorporated in Western pen names fairly often. Even some U.S. and English writers follow this practice.

Some reasons for authors to conceal their identity are; gender, nature of written material, testing a new area of endeavor, etc. It can be a publisher's choice. Examples are the Stratemeyer Syndicate and publishers of many contemporary action or romance series. Some examples of house or publisher pseudonyms are; Nick Carter, Lee Davis Willoughby, Carter Brown, and Desmond Reid. Sometimes a pseudonym is used for collaborative efforts of two or more writers under a single name such as Ellery Queen, A.E Maxwell, Fern Michaels, Q. Patrick, James Colvin, Keith Grantland, Dan Lynch, John Cleve and Wade Miller to name a few. Where an author has had more than one story in a same issue of a magazine or digest, it has been a common practice to assign pseudonyms to all those after their first story.

A change seems to be occurring with regards to authors' use of pseudonyms. Now in many instances, pseudonyms are used not so much to obscure the authors' identity as it is to establish the equivalent of a "brand" name. Many authors are now anxious to have the ownership of a pen name known. This may be driven to some extent by the publicity required for writers to become well known and establish a reader-demand market. I recently attended a Mystery Conference to sell the first edition of this book and interview authors for the potential of new pseudonyms. It became evident over the course of the conference that attending authors perceived another benefit to this book. I'll relate two occurrences that illustrate:

> Two authors walked up to my table to see if a particular pseudonym was in the book. They were planning to co-write using this pen name if it had not been previously used. We determined it had not. I suggested we complete a data form I keep for documenting interviews and author's pen names. After providing the information needed, they then said this was the only vehicle they were aware of for registering or establishing ownership of a pseudonym. They walked away feeling confident they would not step on some other writer's pen name. They also seemed to think by having it being published in the next edition, another writer would not accidentally use the pen name they had chosen.
>
> Another author approached me and made the comment "you had better have my pseudonym in that book." We looked and it was, as luck would have it, NOT THERE. This author stomped over to a nearby dealer's table where he located several of his books published under his pen name, brought them over me and said "see THERE, and THERE, and THERE." I quickly suggested we proceed with getting his pen name entered. I did not forget to ask if he had used other pen names as well. In this instance, I believe the author wanted the pen [brand] name associated with his name in some documented fashion thus to establish his ownership.

It would seem from these two encounters and numerous conversations with authors attending, authors want a means of assuring their chosen pen name has not been previously used. They also want a vehicle or mechanism for registering or establishing ownership, they see this book as a potential vehicle to accomplish this.

With only a few exceptions, authors who have in the past preferred not to disclose their use of pseudonyms [or association with a particular pen name] are now revealing the nature and extent of their writings under pseudonyms. Such established authors as Ellison, Silverberg, Pronzini, Lansdale and Gorman have been pretty open. Their readers and collectors both appreciate this willingness to disclose their other material published. A knowledge of collectors is necessary to understand why they try to search out almost everything an "author of interest" has published. While most readers are not as tenacious, still many might want to try this other material as well.

The subject of pseudonyms is fascinating and I have begun to understand why people like Victor Berch, George Easter and Jean Francois Le Deist have devoted so much effort and time to this aspect of books.

The Pseudonym Game is Afoot

by Marvin Lachman

With the publication of the first edition of Hawk's *Author's Pseudonyms for Book Collectors,* pseudonym "junkies" were able to come out of the closet, realizing they were not alone. As the title indicates, one reason for knowing pseudonyms is the possibility of picking up a valuable book, under an obscure pseudonym, by an author who later became famous, say, Donald E. Westlake or Evan Hunter.

For those of us who write mystery reference material, there is another reason, one which is practical, if not as profitable as finding a valuable book. Any biography or bibliography of an author should include pseudonymous work, for example the books Lawrence Block wrote as <u>Paul Kavanagh</u> or <u>Chip Harrison</u>.

However, there are also reasons that are not practical. For many of us, there is the "game" of reading a work (usually it is a short story) by one author and saying, "That style reminds me of someone else" and then being proven right. The places to look are usually old pulp or digest-sized magazines. Those who wrote for these magazines had to be prolific to survive. Yet, magazines did not like to publish two stories by the same author in one issue. Therefore, authors would resort to pseudonyms. Looking at an issue of a magazine with a Bruno Fischer story might disclose a story written in a similar style but signed <u>Russell Gray</u>. That would give the discerning reader a hint, even before pseudonym information was officially disclosed.

There are other ways we can learn, including copyright information, articles in nostalgia magazines like *Echoes*, reminiscences of fellow authors, and, sometimes, private conversations, which can't even be repeated. If the practical benefits are few, there is always the satisfaction that comes with knowledge. To use the Mt. Everest analogy of climbers, we try to learn pseudonyms because they are there. And with the success of what is far-and-away the best reference source for pseudonyms, I shall continue to watch for them like a Hawk.

ROBERT SILVERBERG

Robert has written mostly SF under his own name. Four or five years ago, I stumbled onto a book by Robert written in collaboration with Eleazar Lipsky as Dan Lynch. This became the end of a string I followed which led me to a number of books written under a pseudonym by Robert and others. These discoveries were one of the key reasons I started to document pseudonyms, and look at various approaches to managing the identification and documentation of pseudonyms and their use.

As I began more in-depth research into pseudonyms, I added a considerable number of other pen names credited to Robert. I also read Robert's account of his experiences as a porno writer in Penthouse Letters ["My Life As A Pornographer"]. I decided to write Robert and verify or validate those pseudonyms I had compiled attributed to him. His response was prompt and he confirmed the validity of those I had. In retrospect, I now realize that he did not tell me of others he had used. He also chose not to answer my question about other authors who had also written adult books under pen names during the same period. 'Till now, Robert has been patient as we have traded letters so I could build an accurate list. Some of Robert's adult pen names are:

Loren Beauchamp	John Dexter
Walter Drummond	Dan Eliot
Don Elliott	Marlene Longman
Eric Rodman	L.T. Woodward MD

Laura Duchamp and Laura Du Champ were attributed by several dealers to Robert [perhaps because of the similarity to Beauchamp]. Robert denied by letter that either of these were his. Later in checking a major source for this edition, I discovered another writer, L. Timmel Duchamp, had used Laura Duchamp as a pseudonym. When initially queried, Robert did not remember Walter C. Brown, MD as one of his pen names. When he was reminded of his request of a dealer to locate books under this pseudonym to complete a collection of his books, he checked his correspondence and records, then verified this was indeed one of his pen names.

Before we think this was initially a loss of memory or dodge, we must remember that Robert admitted to having written two or more books per month during his porno phase. The publisher assigned the pseudonym and title for most adult books, and often the writer was not aware of this assignment. Books bought by the publisher were regularly retitled, and often retitled and published under yet another pen name. To further complicate authorship, a high percentage of "porn" books were formula in nature written around assigned outlines. Unless an author can match a particular book to his style or approach, these books can be difficult to attribute.

Stalking the Wild Pseudonym

by Scott A. Cupp

As a book collector, one of the many joys that you have is finding out that more work exists by a favorite writer under a variety of pseudonyms. The number of works available is increased and there exists the opportunity to find bargains on BIG NAME writers who are not yet known on a national scale under the other name. For example, when *Invasion* by Aaron Wolfe was rumored to be Stephen King, I managed to find several copies and unload them for a modest profit. Then, it was later revealed to not be King, but rather one of several pseudonyms utilized by Dean Koontz. I was hardly crushed. I saw Koontz that same year and got my personal copy of *Invasion* signed, I received a marvelous inscription "Too bad for your bank account this isn't by you-know-who." Similarly when Richard Bachman was first rumored to be King, I tracked down many copies of the books (except *Rage* which remains impossible to find). It was great! I was hunting new King titles and, no one else was competing for them. I purchased those titles for a pittance and, again, received a modest profit.

But, in addition to tracking down these pseudonyms and finding the titles, it is certainly interesting to see the wacky names that people use and the sometimes interesting connotations that can be found.

It matters not whether they range from the wacky Grendel Briarton (used by Reginald Bretnor for great shaggy dog stories) or Sue Denim (used by Lewis Shiner in some fanzine articles). The wackier and weirder name the better.

My favorite such name early on was Cordwainer Smith. CS was the name used by Paul Linebarger for his science fiction tales during the 50's and 60's. According to my Webster's, a cordwainer is a leatherworker, particularly in the area of shoes. It was unique and different and fit the stories which he created. In an unabashed piece of homage, Harlan uses the name Cordwainer Bird for screen work which he feels has been altered beyond the quality of the which he represents under his own name.

From the mystery side, I am very fond of the Ellery Queen name for a variety of reasons. First, because I love those early Challenges to the Reader. I love the fact that Dannay and Lee brought a sense of history to the mystery field and managed to get various novels considered as literature rather than "escapist trash." More than anyone, they made the mystery field respectable. Secondly, during the 60's numerous writers contributed to the Queen name for a variety of novels. Included in this group were Theodore Sturgeon, Jack Vance, and Avram Davidson - three of my personal favorite writers. One weekend in 1977 I managed to get two vastly different Ellery Queen Signatures. I received a copy of *The Detective Short Story* signed by Fred Dannay from Biblo and Tannen which had published a limited edition. Two days later, I attended a science fiction convention with Theodore Sturgeon where he signed my copy of *The Player On The Other Side* as "Ellery (THS) Queen." He was most surprised that I even knew of the work and that I had taken the time to track it down for him to sign. A similar treat was enjoyed several years later when Jack Vance signed his three EQ books for me. Avram Davidson refused steadfastly to even acknowledge that he had done the work even once it was generally known. His contract forbade claiming authorship and he held to it until his death.

Finally, I love the Queen name because of one of the EQ stories *My Queer Dean*. As a fan of "spoonerisms" I could not help but love the name and the story.

There was a time in the 70's when Phillip Jose Farmer made an industry out of writing stories that were purportedly by fictional characters. During this period he wrote as Nick Adams, Martin Eden, Lord Greystoke, Harry "Bunny" Manders, Kilgore Trout, and John H. Watson, MD among others. Perhaps his crowning achievement during this period was his story *A Scarlettin Study* by Ralph von Wau Wau, starring Ralph as a German shepherd consulting detective in the Sherlock Holmes mold. Pretty far fetched but quite a bit of fun.

But, let's look at some other names. There's Darrel T. Langert (an anagram of Randall Garrett) and James Tiptree, Jr. (used by Alice Sheldon). And Rosamond Smith (Joyce Carol Oates in a thriller mode) and B.J. Oliphant (revealed as a pseudonym of A.J. Orde which was a pseudonym of Sheri S. Tepper). And, of course, Harrison Denmark by Roger Zelazny. And Talbot Mundy the great adventurer known in real life as William L. Gribbin.

Then there are those wonderful single name guys. Guys like "Sapper" who told the exploits of Bull Dog Drummond. And Ganpat who told of lost races and cultures. And Cristabel. And the ever popular (and still writing) Anonymous who handled everything from classic literature to pseudo-Victorian erotica.

And I can't pass over Sax Rohmer. One of the all-time great names of a fun writer if you can get into the mood. Somehow, picking up *The Insidious Dr. Fu Manchu* or *Bimbashi Barouk of Egypt* by Arthur S. Ward doesn't seem nearly as exciting as picking up those same titles by SAX ROHMER.

Some people never can separate it all out. Take John Creasey with more than 25 acknowledged pseudonyms including Abel Mann (!). No one is really quite sure how many Robert Silverberg used during that apocryphal period when he was writing a book a week. More than 50 are known but there have been occasions when even Silverburg himself couldn't remember the name he used or even the title of the book.

During the pulp days there was a lot of gender bending going on with pseudonyms. Writers trying to reach the romance markets generally had to have a female name regardless of their actual status while women trying to reach the action/adventure/science fiction markets frequently utilized masculine names or hid behind initials. But, this practice continues even today. Recently Lydia Adamson, author of *The Cat Who*... mysteries was revealed to be a man trying to capture a portion of the female reading population that wouldn't read a cozy cat mystery by a man.

Forrest J. Ackerman was probably the most prolific writer at making puns from his name. In the various science fiction fan magazines he used Eeee, 4E, 4SJ, Efjay, Forijay, Jack Erman, Jack Deforest Erman among many others. When you saw these names, there was never any doubt as to the authorship of the letter or article. They were merely examples of the author's wit and punster charm.

Another favorite name was Carl Dreadstone, a house name used by Ramsey Campbell for three of the six novelizations of old Universal monster movies. The Campbell Dreadstone novels are very early in his career and, while rough, have a certain charm and flair that later developed into the Campbell style.

Did you ever wonder why Kathryn Ptacek's newsletter was entitled *The Gila Queen's Guide to Markets*? If not, it's because you've read Les Simons' *Gila*, a novel about a giant gila monster terrorizing New Mexico. Coincidentally, Ptacek is from New Mexico and has been known to sign the Simons book on occasion.

And there are those "unknown" pseudonyms. John Abbot, author of *Scimitar*, is "the pseudonym of a famous writer." People I know and trust swear that the dark author photo is of Evan Hunter (aka Ed McBain, Hunt Collins, Richard Marsten, and others). Hunter steadfastly denies this connection. And twenty years ago, the hunt for the owner of the James Tiptree, Jr. name caused much concern and debate in the science fiction press. Was it a man or was it a woman. Impassioned arguments were made each way. Alice Sheldon was finally revealed as the elusive Tiptree and the discussion moved away from the name to the quality of the work where it should have stayed all along.

These have just been some thoughts and anecdotes about some of my favorite weird (and normal) pseudonyms. For me, they are among the many things that make book collecting an exciting hobby (and obsession). There are many more stories and pseudonyms out there. I hope you have as much fun with them as I do.

A Visit with the "Grants"

The title of this piece is actually a misnomer. When I called Charles L. Grant, I was not aware that writer Kathy Ptacek was Mrs. Grant. Secondly, during our conversation I did not talk to Kathy. Charles was warm and friendly once he discovered the nature of my project. As our visit progressed, I learned Charles had written much more than the horror novels for which he is best known.

There seems to be a trait or attribute common to most of the authors I have contacted: they seem to be able to write in a number of forms or genres. My wife Mary Jo and I have both read some of Grant's books written as Lionel Fenn. They are tongue-in-cheek and very entertaining. I hope you enjoy some of the background on Charles' pseudonyms:

Felicia Andrews - Charles has used this pen name mostly for historical romance ["Mountain Witch" being the exception].
Timothy Boggs - Charles wrote "Lancelot & Blanche" as a serial in the Haggis newsletter.
Lionel Fenn - This pen name was used to write the Kent Montana series. An example is "Kent Montana and the Really Ugly Thing From Mars."
Simon Lake - This pen name was used for war and suspense.
Debora Lewis - Charles wrote gothics under this pen name.
Geoffrey Marsh - He used this pseudonym to publish pulp adventure, and SF and fantasy.

A Conversation with Harlan Ellison

I had sent a compiled list of pseudonyms to Harlan for his verification. I did not dream I would get such a terrific response which was a 30 minute conversation by phone when Harlan called just prior to his going into the hospital for heart surgery. Harlan provided a considerable amount of background on his various pseudonyms.

Derry Tiger- "Derry" was the name of a friend in the army. "Tiger" came from Derry's unbounded and largely successful pursuit of the ladies.

Paul Merchant- This was a pen name chosen by the publisher of Harlan's one admitted "dirty" book "Sex Gang." Harlan had submitted the book under "D.S." for "dirty sex." Harlan admitted to being editor for an adult book publication house in the 60's and developing the outlines for a whole stable of authors. They ground out adult books, the only material that was hot in sales at the time. Robert Silverberg and other well-known authors were part of this group. [See Robert's article in Penthouse Letters.]

Jay Charby- This was Harlan's favorite pen name and a take-off on his first wife's name [Charby] until his divorce. Thereafter, his favorite was Jay Solo.

Robert Courtney- Harlan used this pen name for magazine articles and then only a few times. Harlan stated that his friend, Charles Beaumont, was a more frequent user of this pen name [also for stories in magazines].

Wallace Edmonson-This pseudonym was chosen by the editor of Fantastic Universe from the name of the main character in Harlan's story. This was the only use of this name.

Phil "Cheech" Beldone- Harlan said he never used this pen name without the "Cheech." This pen name was only used in magazines.

Ellis Hart- Harlan informed that this pen name was used in digests such as "Guilty," "Trapped," etc.

Al[lan] Maddern-This pen name was used only once for a magazine story about hitchhiking.

I hope you enjoyed the background on these pseudonyms as much as I did my conversation with Harlan.

"JOHN CLEVE"

I have thoroughly enjoyed communicating with most authors, but Andrew J. Offutt has ranked right up there as one of the most interesting and entertaining. Compiling this reference has certainly had it's side benefits. Sure, I've enjoyed the research part of this project. However, the opportunity to become better acquainted with so many authors has been a payoff of proportions not anticipated.

A copy of his answering letter to my inquiry, illustrates the wit of Andrew J. Offutt. In addition, Andrew sent a multi-page bibliography which covered all but the most recent of his work including books published under pseudonym. Andrew even included some of his titles which were changed by the publisher. Examples follow:

Andrew's Title	Publisher's Title
Woman On Fire	Never Enough
Going Down On The Farm	Tight Fit
Love Thy Neighbor	The 8-Way Orgy
An Instinct For Incest	Ball In The Family
Breast Man	Behind Her
The Stud Farm	Farm Girl & The Hired Hand
Sex Lodge	Rear Entry

Andrew has written in a wide assortment of genre including a lot of adult fantasy, and at least two series; "the Crusades" and "Spaceways." I recommend you read some of "John Cleve" if you haven't before. If you have, bet most of you were unaware of the wide assortment of reading Andrew J. Offutt has produced. Some of his more interesting titles are:

Four On The Floor	Balling Machine
Fun With Aunt Tommy	A Miss Guided

Fan & Collector Publications

AFRAID, 857 N. Oxford Ave #4, Los Angeles, CA 90029

ARMCHAIR DETECTIVE, 129 W. 56th St., New York, NY 10019

BAE (Books Are Everything), 302 Martin Dr. Richmond, KY 40475

Black Ace Books Collector's Handbook, 1658 Griffith Park Blvd., Los Angeles, CA 90026

BOOK & MAGAZINE COLLECTOR, 45 St. Mary's Rd., Ealing, London, W5 5RQ England

CAZ - THE FANTASY COLLECTOR, 1447 Baton Rouge, LA 70802

DAST, Calle Acacia 801, Pina de Campoverde, El Pilar de La Horadada, 03190 Alicante, Spain

DEADLY PLEASURES, 408 East 200, So. Farmington, UT 84025

ECHOES, Tom Johnson, 509 E. Morris, Seymont, TX 76380

FIRSTS, P.O. Box 65166, Tucson, AZ 85728-5166

GALACTIC CENTRAL (Sci-Fi Bibliographies), P.O. Box 40494, Albuquerque, NM 87196

GOLDEN PERILS, 5 Milliken Mills Rd., Scarboro, ME 04074

LOCUS, P.O. Box 13305, Oakland, CA 94611

Lynn Munroe Sales Lists, P.O. Box 1736, Orange, CA 92668

MEAN STREETS, 214 Black Hat Rd., Blackheath, NSW, 2785 Australia

MYSTERY & DETECTIVE MONTHLY, 5601 N. 40th St., Tacoma, WA 98407

MYSTERY SCENE, P.O. Box 669, Cedar Rapids, IA 52406-0669

NEW MYSTERY MAGAZINE, The Flatiron, 175 Fifth Ave, Suite 2001, New York, NY 10010

PAPERBACK PARADE, Gryphon Publications, P.O. Box 209, Brooklyn, NY 11228-0209

PPCC, Zardoz Books, 20 Whitecroft, Dilton Marsh, Westbury, Wilts, BA13 4DJ England

PULP REVIEW, 4704 Colonel Ewell Ct., Upper Marlborough, MD 20772

PULP VAULT, 6942 N. Oleander Ave, Chicago, IL 60631

RUMBLE, Chapel House, Radway St., Bishop Steignton, South Devon, TQ149SS England

SF CHRONICLE, P.O. Box 022730, Brooklyn, NY 11202-0056

STRANGE NEW WORLDS, P.O. Box 223, Tallevast, FL 34270

THE AUSTRALIAN BOOK COLLECTOR, P.O. Box 2, Uralla, NSW, 2358 Australia

THE PULP COLLECTOR, 8417 Carrollton Parkway, New Carrollton, MD 20784

LIST OF ABBREVIATIONS

ABBREVIATION	COMMENTS
A-C	APPLETON-CENTURY
AA	AMERICAN AGENT
AACT	AIR ACTION
AAE	AMERICAN ART ENTERPRISES
AAM	ALL AMERICAN FICTION
AB	ALFRED HITCHCOCK MYS MAG
AC	ACCUSED DETECTIVE STORY
ACE	ACE PAPERBACKS
ACHD	ACE HIGH DETECTIVE
ACM	ACE MYS
ACS	ACE SPORTS
ADM	ACTION DETECTIVE MAGAZINE
ADT	AMAZING DETECTIVE TALES
ADV	ADVENTURE [GENRE]
ADVT	ADVENTURE [MAGAZINE]
ADVY	ADVENTURE YARNS
AE	ART ENTERPRISES
AGP	ASSOCIATED GENERAL PUBLICATIONS
AH	AFTER HOURS
AHMM	ALFRED HITCHCOCK MYS MAGAZINE
AL	ALL MYSTERY
ALSD	ALL STORY DETECTIVE
ALWEST	ALL WESTERN
AM	AVON MODERN SHORT STORY
AMALG	AMALGAMATED PRESS
AMRC	AMERICAN ROMANCE [CLVLD]
AMZ	AMAZING STORIES
AMZQ	AMAZING QUARTERLY
AN	ACTION NOVELS
ANCH	ANCHOR BOOKS
ANSS	ADVENTURE NOVELS & SHORT STORIES
ARC	ARCADIA
ARCPR	ARCHER PRESS
ARG	ARGOSY
ASF	ASTOUNDING SCIENCE FICTION
ASFM	AMERICAN SCIENCE FICTION MAGAZINE
ASQ	AMAZING STORIES QUARTERLY
ASS	ASTOUNDING STORIES

ABBREVIATION	COMMENTS
AST	ASTONISHING STORIES
ATHNM	ATHENEUM
AV	AVON PAPERBACKS
AVDM	AVON DETECTIVE MYSTERIES
AVFR	AVON FANTASY READER
AVGR	THE AVENGER
AVMMM	AVON MURDER MYS MONTHLY
AVWR	AVON WESTERN READER
AW	AMERICAN WEEKLY
AWS	AIR WONDER STORIES
B&MC	BOOK & MAGAZINE COLLECTORS
B&W	BROWN & WATSON
BAE	BOOKS ARE EVERYTHING
BAL	BALLANTINE BOOKS
BB	BANTAM PAPERBACKS
BBAT	BILL BARNES AIR TRAILS
BBD	BLACK BOOK DETECTIVE [BRITISH]
BBM	BLUE BOOK MAGAZINE
BC	BARCLAY
BGH	BIG HORN
BH	BEAR HUDSON
BIBL	BIBLIOGRAPHY
BJ	BLUE JAY
BL	BLOODHOUND DETECTIVE STORY MAG [BRITISH]
BLKB	BLACK BOOK DETECTIVE
BLM	BLUE MOUNTAIN
BM	BLACK MASK
BOW	BORISWOOD
BRDMN	BOARDMAN
BRNDN	BRANDON BOOKS
BS	BESTSELLER MYS MAG
BUTWH	THORNTON BUTTERWORTH
BUW	BUTTERWORTH
BW	BROWN WATSON
BZ	BIZARRE! MYS MAG
CA	CARLYLE
ca	CIRCA
CAH	CAPTAIN HAZZARD MAGAZINE
CAL	CALVERT
CAM	CAMEO BOOKS
CAN	THE CANADIAN MAGAZINE
CANY	CANYON

ABBREVIATION	COMMENTS
CAP	CRIMSON ALTAR PRESS
CARN	CARNIVAL
CBS	COWBOY STORIES
CC	CHARLIE CHAN MYS MAG
CCWWS	COMPLETE COWBOY WILD WEST STORIES
CD	CRAIG RICE CRIME DIGEST
CENT	CENTURY
CEW	CENTURY WESTERN
CF	CAPTAIN FUTURE
CG	CRAIG RICE MYS DIGEST
CH	CHASE
CHIL	CHILDREN'S BOOKS
CHM	CHARTER MYSTERY
CHP	CHAPMAN
CHSM	CHISHOLM
CJ	CRIME & JUSTICE DETECTIVE STORY MAG
CKLST	CHECK LIST
CLS	CLUES DETECTIVE
CLVLD	CLEVELAND PUBLISHING
CN	CONFLICT
CNSL	CONSUL
CNSLDT	CONSOLIDATED
CNST	CONSTABLE
CNW	COMPLETE NW NOVEL MAGAZINE
CO	COVEN 13
COL	COLUMBINE
CORW	CORONADO WESTERN [CLVLD]
CR	COPYRIGHT
CRB	CRIME BUSTERS
CRPG	COPYRIGHT PAGE
CRSL	CAROUSEL
CS	COMET STORIES
CSF	COSMIC SCIENCE FICTION
CSS	COSMIC STORIES
CURR	CURRAWONG
CWB	COMPLETE WESTERN BOOK
D&MM	DECTECTIVE & MURDER MYS
DA	DOUBLE-ACTION DETECTIVE & MYS STORIES
DAG	DOUBLE ACTION GANG
DBY	DERBY
DD	DOUBLE DETECTIVE
DE	DETECTIVE TALES-POCKET READER SERIES
DELL	DELL PAPERBACKS
DEMN	DELL MYS NOVELS MAG
DF	DETECTIVE FICTION
DFW	DETECTIVE FICTION WEEKLY
DIAM	DIAMOND
DJ	DUST JACKET

ABBREVIATION	COMMENTS
DL	DETECTIVE FILES
DLCT	DELACORTE
DLRW	DOLLAR WESTERN [CLVLD]
DM	DIME MYS MAGAZINE
DMADV	DIME ADVENTURE
DMS	DIME MYS
DMW	DIME WESTERN
DNM	DETECTIVE NOVELS MAGAZINE
DOCD	DOCTOR DEATH
DOCS	DOC SAVAGE MAGAZINE
DROM	DETECTIVE ROMANCES
DSM	DETECTIVE STORY MAGAZINE
DSR	DOC SAVAGE READER
DT	DETECTIVE TALES [BRITISH]
DYADV	DYNAMIC ADVENTURES
DYS	DR. YEN SIN
E&S	EYRE & SPOTTISWOODE
EB	ELLERY QUEEN'S MYS MAG [BRITISH]
ED	ED MCBAINS MYS BOOK
EL	EMBER LIBRARY
EM	EDGAR WALLACE MYS MAG
EP	ED MCBAINS 87th PRECINCT MYS MAG
EQMM	ELLERY QUEEN MYS MAGAZINE
ES	EDWIN SELF
EV	EVENING READER
EVB	EVERYBODY'S
EW	EDGAR WALLACE MYS MAG [BRITISH]
EX	EXECUTIONER MYS MAG
EXD	EXCITING DETECTIVE
EXJR	EXPLORER'S JOURNAL
F&SF	FANTASY & SCIENCE FICTION
FA	FANTASTIC ADVENTURES
FADM	FAST ACTION DETECTIVE & MYS STORIES
FAWES	FAMOUS WESTERN
FBD	FIREBRAND
FCS	FUTURE COMBINED W/ SCIENCE FICTION [SEE FF]
FD	FICTION HOUSE
FE	FEAR!
FEA	FAR EAST ADVENTURES
FEDA	FEDERAL AGENT
FEDS	THE FEDS
FF	THE FANTASY FAN
FFS	FUTURE FANTASY & SCIENCE FICTION [SEE FCS & FF]
FIF	FIFTEEN MYSTERY TALES
FL	FICTION LEAGUE

ABBREVIATION	COMMENTS
FLP	FOUL PLAY
FM	FANTASY MAGAZINE
FMD	FAMOUS DETECTIVES
FN	FIRST NITER
FNOV	FIVE NOVELS
FONT	FONTANA PAPERBACKS
FP	FAN PSEUDONYM
FRWY	FREEWAY PRESS
FS	FANTASTIC STORIES
FSF	MAGAZINE OF FANTASY & SCIENCE FICTION
FSQ	FOUR SQUARE BOOKS
FT	FANCIFUL TALES OF SPACE & TIME
FTGW	FIGHTING WESTERN [CLVLD]
FUF	FUTURE FICTION [SEE FCS & FFS]
FUT	FUTURA PAPERBACKS
FVSTR	FIVE STAR
FY	FANTASY
GAL	GALAXY SCIENCE FICTION
GAN	GANGSTER STORIES
GDA	GIANT DETECTIVE ANNUAL
GE	GOLD EAGLE
GGA	GOOD GIRL ART
GH	GHOST DETECTIVE
GL	GIRL FROM U.N.C.L.E. MAG
GLN	THE GALLEON
GM	GOLD MEDAL/FAWCETT
GMD	G-MEN DETECTIVE
GMN	G-MEN
GN	GOLDEN NUGGET
GOLZ	GOLLANCZ
GOSD	GOLD SEAL DETECTIVE
GP	GAYWOOD PRESS
GRAM	GRAMMERCY
GRAPH	GRAPHICS PAPERBACKS
GRD	GRANADA
GRNLF	GREENLEAF
GRSH	GRESHAM
GRY	GRAYSON
GSFN	GALAXY SF NOVELS
GU	GUILTY DETECTIVE STORY MAG
GWEST	GIANT WESTERN
HA	HAUNT OF HORROR
HAM	HAMILTON
HAMM	HAMMOND
HARB	HARBOROUGH
HGTN	HOUGHTON
HILLM	HILLMAN
HM	HEINMANN
HO	HOMICIDE DETECTIVE STORY MAG
HP	HOUSE PSEUDONYM

ABBREVIATION	COMMENTS
HRCT	HARCOURT
HRWTZ	HOROWITZ
HS	HAMILTON STAFFORD
HU	HUNTED DETECTIVE STORY MAG
HUTCH	HUTCHINSON
IASFM	ISAAC ASIMOV'S SCIENCE FICTION MAGAZINE
IM	INSPECTOR MALONE'S MYS MAG
IN	INTRIGUE MYS MAG
INPO	INTERNATIONAL POLYGONICS
INT	INTIMATE NOVELS
INTNL	INTERNATIONAL
ISFYB	INTERNATIONAL SF YEARBOOK
JCM	JOHN CREASEY MYS MAG
JENK	JENKINS
JONM	JONATHAN PRESS MYSTERY
JU	JUSTICE
JUV	JUVENILE
KE	KEYHOLE DETECTIVE STORY MAG
KEM	KEYHOLE MYS MAG
KI	KILLERS MYS STORY MAG
KNICK	KNICKERBOCKER
KWY	KAYWIN
LAN	LANCER PAPERBACKS
LEIS	LEISURE BOOKS
LIPP	LIPPINCOTT
LM	LONDON MYS MAG
LMS	LONDON MYS SELECTION
LTR	LETTER
M&L	MASON & LIPSCOMB
MA	MALCOLM'S
MACF	MACFADDEN
MAG	MAGAZINE
MAJ	MAJOR
MAMW	MAMMOTH WESTERN
MASD	MASKED DETECTIVE MAGAZINE
MASR	MASKED RIDER MAGAZINE
MB	MYS BOOK MAG
MBWE	MAX BRAND'S WESTERN
MC	MENACE
MCL	MACAULAY
MCM	THE MAGIC CARPET MAGAZINE
MCRS	MACRAE-SMITH
MD	MAMMOTH DETECTIVE
MDG	MYS DIGEST
MDL	MEDALLION
MDNR	MIDNIGHT READER
MDWD	MIDWOOD
ME	MERCURY MYS MAG

ABBREVIATION	COMMENTS
	[BRITISH]
MEMBM	MERCURY MYS BOOK MAG
MF	MYS TALES
MH	MANHUNT
MIH	MILTON HOUSE
MK	MACKILL'S MYS MAG
ML	MYS LEAGUE MAG
MLFT	MELLIFONT
MLST	MILESTONE
MM	MAMMOTH MYS
MMAG	MYSTERY MAGAZINE
MMM	MOVIE-MYS MAG
MN	MANHUNT [BRITISH]
MO	MYS MONTHLY
MOA	MODERN AGE
MOF	MODERN FICTION
MON	MONARCH PAPERBACKS
MP	MYSTERIOUS PRESS
MR	MURDER
MRW	MORROW
MS	MARVEL STORIES [SEE MSS]
MSC	MYSTERY SCENE
MSMM	MIKE SHAYNE MYS MAG
MSS	MARVEL SCIENCE STORIES
MSSNR	MESSNER
MT	MARVEL TALES
MTP	MANTRAP
MTQ	MISTIQUE
MU	MAN FROM U.N.C.L.E. MAG
MUS	MUSEUM
MUW	MUIR WATSON
MV	MIKE SHAYNE MYS MAG [BRITISH]
MW	MODERN WONDER
MWF	THE MYSTERIOUS WU FANG
MY	MYSTERIOUS TRAVELER MYS MAG
MYADV	MYS & ADV SERIES REVIEW
MYFLR	MAYFLOWER
MYH	MYSTERY HOUSE
MYS	MYSTERY FICTION
MZ	MAGAZINE OF HORROR
MacD	MacDONALD
NAL	NEW AMERICAN LIBRARY
NC	NEW CENTURY
nd	NO DATE GIVEN
NEL	NEW ENGLAND LIBRARY
NF	NEW FICTION
NH	NEW HORIZONS
NM	NEW MEDIA
NMADV	NEW MYSTERY ADVENTURES
NOV	NOVEL BOOKS

ABBREVIATION	COMMENTS
NSLM	NEWSTAND LIBRARY MAGENTA
NSWB	NEW SOUTH WALES BOOKSTALL
NTSD	NIGHTSTAND
NV	NAME VARIATION
NW	NEW WORLDS
NWD	NEW DETECTIVE
NWMM	NERO WOLFE MYS MAG
NYDL	NY DETECTIVE LIBRARY
OCSC	OCTOPUS/SCORPION
OF	OFF BEAT DETECTIVE STORIES
OLYM	OLYMPIC PRESS
OP5	OPERATOR #5
OS	ORIENTAL STORIES
PA	PHANTOM [BRITISH]
PAN	PAN PAPERBACKS
PANT	PANTHER PAPERBACKS
PAPLB	PAPERBACK LIBRARY
PCDM	POCKET DETECTIVE MAGAZINE [TROJAN]
PE	PRIVATE EYE
PEC	PUBLISHER'S EXPORT CO.
PGT	PAGEANT
PH	PHANTOM MYS MAG
PHAN	PHANTOM [U.S.]
PHANT	PHANTOM [AUSTRALIA]
PHD	PHANTOM DETECTIVE
PHN	PHOENIX PRESS
PLB	PLAYBOY
PLR	PILLAR BOOKS
PLTM	PLAYTIME
PN	PARIS NIGHTS
PNTH	PANTHEON
POCD	POCKET DETECTIVE [STREET]
POCK	POCKET BOOKS
POPFIC	POPULAR FICTION
POPLB	POPULAR LIBRARY
POW	POWELL BOOKS
PP	PAPERBACK PARADE
PPDM	POPULAR DETECTIVE MAGAZINE
PPJKS	PAPERJACKS
PPP	POPULAR PUBLIC
PPWM	POPULAR WESTERN MAG
PRD	PRIVATE DETECTIVE
PROG	PROGRESSIVE
PRZ	PRIZE PAPERBACKS
PRZW	PRIZE WESTERN
PS	PLANET STORIES
PSH	PASSING SHOW
PU	PURSUIT DETECTIVE STORY MAG
PUE	PUBLIC ENEMY
PYR	PYRAMID PAPERBACKS
R&C	RICH & COWEN
RAIN	RAINBOW

ABBREVIATION	COMMENTS
RCL	READERS CHOICE LIBRARY
RDM	RED STORY MYSTERY
RH	RINEHART
RISQ	RISQUE STORIES
RKW	RIO KID WESTERN
RMDS	RED MASK DETECTIVE STORIES
RNDM	RANDOM
ROM	ROMANCE & GOTHIC
ROMD	ROMANTIC DETECTIVE
ROMR	ROMANTIC RANGE
RP	REGULAR PUBLICATION
RPRT	REPRINTED AS
RR	RANGE RIDERS
RROM	RANCH ROMANCES
RS	REX STOUT MYS MAG
RSMM	REX STOUT MYS MONTHLY
RSMQ	REX STOUT MYS QUARTERLY
S&I	SCIENCE & INVENTION
S&SDA	STREET & SMITH DETECTIVE STORY - ANNUAL
S&SDM	STREET & SMITH DETECTIVE STORY MAG
S&SWM	STREET & SMITH WESTERN STORY MAGAZINE
S'CH	THE SAINT'S CHOICE
SA	SAINT MAG
SADM	THE SAINT DETECTIVE MAG
SAX	SECRET AGENT X
SB	STANLEY BAKER
SCLS	SOFTCOVER
SD	STARDUST
SDM	SCIENTIFIC DETECTIVE MONTHLY
SDS	STRANGE DETECTIVE STORIES
SES	SEA STORIES
SF	SCIENCE FICTION
SFD	SCIENCE FICTION DIGEST
SFDS	SURE FIRE DETECTIVE STORIES
SFM	SCIENCE FICTION [MAGAZINE]
SFQ	SCIENCE FICTION QUARTERLY
SFS	SCIENCE FICTION STORIES
SG	STRANGE
SH	SHOCK- MAG OF TERRIFYING TALES
SHD	THE SHADOW
SHDM	THE SHADOW MAGAZINE
SHDMY	THE SHADOW MYSTERY

ABBREVIATION	COMMENTS
SHS	SHORT STORIES
SI	SHOCK MYS TALES MAG
SIGN	SIGNET PAPERBACKS
SIL	SILHOUETTE
SK	SKULLDUGGERY
SKAC	SKY ACES
SKB	SKY BIRDS
SKEFF	SKEFFINGTON
SKP	THE SKIPPER
SL	SALES LIST
SLMM	SLEUTH MYS MAG
SM	SAINT'S MYS LIBRARY
SMB	SAINT MAG [BRITISH]
SMN	SMASHING NOVELS MAGAZINE
SN	STARTLING MYS STORIES
SO	SHELL SCOTT MYS MAG
SOF	SOLDIER OF FORTUNE
SONN	SONNENHEIM
SOSS	SOUTH SEA STORIES
SP	SUSPECT DETECTIVE
SPA	SPEED ADVENTURE
SPAS	SPICY ADVENTURE STORIES
SPD	THE SPIDER
SPDM	SPEED MYSTERY
SPDS	SPICY DETECTIVE STORIES
SPDW	SPIDERWEB
SPH	SPHERE PAPERBACKS
SPMS	SPICY MYSTERY
SPP	SPORTSMAN PILOT
SPSC	SPORTS SHORTS [CALVERT]
SQ	SUSPENSE, THE MYS MAG
SR	SCARAB MYS MAG
SRS	STRANGE STORIES
SRT	STRANGE TALES
SS	SHORT STORY
SSC	STIRRING SCIENCE STORIES
SSM	SHORT STORIES MAGAZINE
SSN	SUPER SCIENCE NOVELS
SSO#5	SECRET SERVICE OPERATOR #5
SSS	77 SUNSET STRIP
ST	SATURN WEB DETECTIVE STORIES
STD	STRANGE DETECTIVE STORIES
STR	SATURDAY REVIEW PRESS
STRW	STAR WESTERN
STS	STARTLING STORIES
STSY	STRATEMEYER SYNDICATE
SUD	SUPER DETECTIVE

ABBREVIATION	COMMENTS
SUFD	SURE FIRE DETECTIVE
SUH	SURREY HOUSE
SUNR	SUNDOWN READER
SUS	SUSPENSE [BRITISH]
SUSS	SUPER SCIENCE STORIES
SV	SPELLING VARIATION
SVNR	SOUVENIR
SWQ	SCIENCE WONDER QUARTERLY
SWS	SCIENCE WONDER STORIES
SX	STORY DIGEST MAG
SXB	SEXTON BLAKE
TADV	THRILLING ADVENTURE
TB	TID-BITS BOOKS
TBMM	TWO BOOK MYS MAG
TBRN	TIBURON
TCP	TALES OF CRIME & PUNISHMENT
TD	THRILLING DETECTIVE
TDA	TEN DETECTIVE ACES
TE	TERROR DETECTIVE STORY
TEDA	AEN DETECTIVE ACES
TF	TOP FICTION
TFDS	TWO-FISTED DETECTIVE STORIES
TG	TIGHTROPE!
TGL	TRUE GANG LIFE
TM	THRILLING MYS
TOF	TALES OF THE FRIGHTENED
TOW	TALES OF WONDER
TPN	TOP NOTCH
TR	TRAPPED DETECTIVE STORY MAG
TRANS	TRANSITION
TRDNT	TRIDENT
TRNPT	TRANSPORT
TRS	THRILLING RANCH STORIES
TRWE	TRIPLE WESTERN
TSB	TEN STORY BOOK
TSD	TEN STORY DETECTIVE
TSS	THRILLING SPY STORIES
TT	TERROR TALES
TW	THRILLING WESTERN
TWS	THRILLING WONDER STORIES
TXRGS	TEXAS RANGERS
UFF	UNKNOWN FANTASY FICTION [SEE UNK & UW]
UND	THE UNDERWORLD
UNDD	THE UNDERWORLD DETECTIVE
UNK	UNKNOWN [SEE UFF & UW]
UT	UNCANNY TALES [CANADIAN]

ABBREVIATION	COMMENTS
UTDBL	UP-TO-DATE BOY'S LIBRARY
UW	UNKNOWN WORLDS [SEE UFF & UNK]
VANG	VANGARD
VB	VERDICT [BRITISH]
VCDM	VERDICT CRIME DETECTION MAG
VD	VERDICT
VM	VULCAN MYSYTERIES
VT	VANTAGE
W&B	WRIGHT & BROWN
WB	WAR BIRDS
WBSTR	WEBSTER
WEAC	WESTERN ACES
WEB	WEB TERROR TALES
WEST	WESTERN FICTION
WH	WHODUNIT
WHSP	THE WHISPERER
WL	WANT LIST
WM	WEIRD MYS
WOS	WORLD STORIES
WOW	WORLD'S WORK
WP	WOMEN'S PRESS
WR	WEIRD TERROR TALES
WRDG	WRITER'S DIGEST
WRREV	WRITER'S REVIEW
WS	WONDER STORIES [SEE SW & TW]
WSB	WASHBURN
WSQ	WONDER STORIES QUARTERLY
WT	WEIRD TALES
WTR	WESTERN TRAILS
WW	WORLD WIDE
WWW	WILD WEST WEEKLY
YA	YOUNG ADULT
ZD	ZIFF-DAVIS
ZEN	ZENITH PAPERBACKS
ZGWM	ZANE GREY WESTERN MAG
ZS	ZIPPY STORIES

AUTHORS

AUTHORS

'BARNETT, PAUL LE PAGE
GRANT, JOHN--W/JOE DEVER,[7]SF--
BEAVER "LEGEND OF LONE WOLF#1-#6" '89-91

'T HART, MAARTEN
HART, MARTIN--[31]

A'BECKETT, SIR WILLIAM
MALWYN--[13]AUSTRALIAN

AALBORG, GORDON K.
KURTIS, GORDON--[35]AUSTRALIAN--HRWTZ

AALLYN, ALYSSE
CLARK, MELISSA--[9]ROM

AARON, ADOLF
L'ARRONGE, ADOLF--[39]GERMAN

AARONS, EDWARD S.
AARONS, A.A.--L. ROBBINS LTR MAR '94, PULP
AYRES, PAUL--[3][5][18][22][31]MYS--
DELL "DEAD HEAT" '50
LOOG, BUSTER--J. HOFFMANN, PP 40, P18,HP--
GERM PANTH 198 RPRT OF "DARK DESTINY"
RONN, S.--[2]
RONNS, EDWARD--V. BERCH, GM PSEUDS
PP 33,[3][5][18][22][32]MYS--34 NOVELS

AASENG, NATHAN
AASENG, NATE--[31][33]--
'SPORT ACHIEVERS' SERIES & OTHERS '84-9

AASHEIM, ASHLEY
ASHLEY, A.--[1][31]

ABARBANELL, JACOB RALPH
REVERE, PAUL--[1]
ROYAL, RALPH--[1]

ABBASI, NAJMUDDIN
ABBASI, NAJAM--[1]

ABBEY, MARILYN LORRAINE
ABBEY, LYNN--[1][7]SF--7 NOVELS '79-91
ABBY, LYNN--[1]

ABBEY, RUTH
PATTISON, RUTH--[1]

ABBOTT, AUSTIN
BENAULY--W/BENJAMIN & LYMAN ABBOTT,[1]

ABBOTT, BENJAMIN
BENAULY--W/AUSTIN & LYMAN ABBOTT,[1]

ABBOTT, EDWIN A.
SQUARE, A.--[7][11][32]

ABBOTT, LAWRENCE FRASER
FRASER, LAWRENCE--[1]

ABBOTT, LYMAN
BENAULY--W/AUSTIN & BENJAMIN ABBOTT,[1]

ABBOTT, MARY JEANNE
HEWITT, ELIZABETH--[1][9][21]ROM--
12 NOVELS

ABBOTT, MONICA & STANLEY
HOWARD, LESLEY--[3]MYS--
COWARD "INVITATION TO PARADISE" '74

ABDEL-MALEK, ANOUAR
EBN EL-NIL--[1]

ABDEL-RAHMEN, AISHA
SHATI, BENT EL--[1]

ABDU'L-BAHA
ABBAS EFFENDI--[18]MYS--NOVELS

ABEL, ALAN [IRWIN]
BRISTOL, JULIUS--[1][22][31]AMERICAN
HILL, BUNKER C.--[1]
SPENCER,[DR.] BRUCE--[1]

ABEL, JEANNE
BRONSTEIN, YETTA--[1][22][31]AMERICAN

ABELES, ELVIN
BOWLES, KERWIN--[1][31]

ABELS, HARRIETTE SHEFFER
ABELS, HARRIETTE S.--[21]ROM--7 NOVELS
SHEFFER, H.R.--[33]

ABENTE, EDUARDO PONDAL
BERGANTINOS, EL BARDO--[20]SPANISH

ABERCROMBIE, MINNIE L.J.
JOHNSON ABERCROMBIE, MIN.--[31]
JOHNSON, M.L.--[31]

ABERCROMBIE, PATRICIA B.
BARNES, PATRICIA--[9]ROM

ABERLE, KATHLEEN GOUGH
GOUGH, KATHLEEN--[1]

ABERNATHY, WILLIAM JACKS.
ABERNATHY, BILL--[31]MYS--
SFDS "TIME TO KILL" OCT '57

ABESSOR, RUDY
HENDRIK, ABBO--[39]GERMAN

ABISCH, ROSLYN KROOP
ABISCH, ROZ--[33]
MCGILLICUDDY, MR.--[1]
ROCHE, A.K.--W/BOCHE KAPLAN,[1][33]
SNIFF, MR.--[1][33]

ABOU, SAIF LAILI
SAID, LAILI--[1]

ABRAHAM, GEORGE
DOC ABRAHAM--[31]

ABRAHAMS, DORIS CAROLINE
BRAHMS, CARYL--[2][3][7][22][31][32]MYS/SF--
5 BKS W/S.J. SIMON - 1 W/NED SHERWIN,
AHMM "A BISHOP IN THE BALLET" SEPT '79
LINDEN, OLIVER--[22][29][31]

ABRAHAMSEN, CHRISTINE E.
CRISTABEL--[2][9][11][23][31]AMERICAN--
"MANALACOR OF VETTAKIN" '70
WESTCOTT, KATHLEEN--[2][3][9][11][21][23]
MYS/ROM--"BRIDE OF KILKERRAN" '74

ABRAMOVICH, SHOLEM JACOB
MENDELE, MOCHER SFORIM--[22]POLISH

ABRAMOVITZ, ANITA Z.B.
BROOKS, ANITA--[1][31]

ABRAMS, BARBARA
NEWMAN, ODETTE--[14]--
OLYM TC#438 "THE EROTIC FACULTY" '68
OLYM TC#442 "SO YOU THINK SEX IS DIRTY" '69

AUTHORS

ABRAMS, GEORGE JOSEPH
HIPP, GEORGE--[1][31]

ABRAMS, SAM
NEWMAN, FRANK--J. PRESSMAN, CNTRCLTR, BAE 21, P54,[14]-- OLMP TC#433 "BARBARA" '68

ABRASHKIN, RAYMOND
ASHLEY, RAY--[1][31][33]

ABRAVANEL, ELIZABETH
KING, ELIZABETH A.--[31]

ABSHAGEN, MARGARETE
THIELE, MARGARETE--[39]GERMAN/JUV

ABSHIRE, RICHARD
MARLOWE, TERRY--W/BILL CLAIR, LACHMAN/EASTER LIST,MYS

ACHAM, BERNARD I.F.
CHEN, JACK--[1]

ACKER, KATHY
BLACK TARANTULA, THE--[1][31]

ACKERLEY, JOE RANDOLPH
ACKERLEY, J.R.--[1]

ACKERMAN, FORREST J.
4E--[2]
4SJ--[2]
ABRAHAMS, TERRI--[2]
ACKERMONSTER--[2]
AGRICOLA, SYLVIUS--[2]
ALDEANO, SILVESTRE--[2]
ANKH-ER-MAN, PHAROAH J.--[2]
BALBOA, S.F.--[2]
BEAL, NICK--[2][11]
BENSON, BOBBY--[2]
BURKE, CARL F.--[2]HP
CARNELL, RICHARD--[2]
CHAPNICK, MORRIS--[2]
CHINWELL, WALTER--[2][11]
DEFOREST, JACQUES--[2]
DR. ACULA--[2]
ECKMAN, J. FORRESTER--[2][11]
EEEE--[2]
EFJAY--[2]
ELTON, JAMES T.--[2]HP-- [JOHN SPENCER & CO.]
ERDSTELULOV--[2]
ERMAN, JACK--[2][11]
ERMAN, JACK DEFOREST--[2]
ERMAN, JACQUES DEFOREST--[2][11][23][32]SF
ERMAYNE, LAURAJEAN--[2]
FARMINGTON, STONE T.--[2]
FARWEST--[2]
FORIJAY--[2]
FORJAK--[2]
FORSTO, MITRA--[2]
GAPERSONA, STAN--[2]
GILES, GEOFFREY--W/WALTER GILLINGS, [2][11][23]--FANT "LOST PLANET" '46
GREYSTARK, CHON--[2]
HELDING, CLAIR--[2]
KATOLIQUE, A. DEFOUT--[2]
KEPAC, COIL--[2]
KERLAY, ALLIS--[2]
LARK, J.C.--[2]
LES ANGELEANO--[2]
LORRAINE, ALDEN--[2][11][32]
MERRIT, KATARIN MARKOV--[2]
MERRITT, AIME--[2][11]
MORLEY, WILFRID OWEN--W/R.A.W. LOWNDES,[2]

ACKERMAN, FORREST J. [CONT]
NADER, OWEN & SEENA--[2]
ORNIG, GRAEG--[2]
RALPH 124E41--[2]
RHODAN, FORRY--[2]
SERVISS, GARRETT P.--[1]
STRONG, SPENCER--[2][11][32]
TOMERLIN, J.E.--[2]
TORGOIS, VERPERTINA--[2]
TORGOSI, KARLON--[2]
TRENTWORTH, FISHER--[2]
VILLETTE, ALLIS--[2]
VIRLUP, A. KVAZAU--[2]
VOYANT, CLAIR--[2][11]
WELLS, HUBERT GEORGE--[2][11][23][32]
WRIGHT, DAMON--[2]
WRIGHT, ROBERT--W/R.A.W. LOWNDES,[2][11]-- ALSO USED HIMSELF
WRIGHT, WEAVER--[2][11][23][32]

ACKERMAN, WENDAYNE
DANE, W.N.--[1][2]
MONDELLE, WENDAYNE--[11]SF

ACKERMANN, INGEBORG
BORK, TEDA--[39]GERMAN-- HAR "IM NAMEN EINER MUTTER" '62

ACKERMANN, WERNER
FIELDMAN, W.A.--[39]GERMAN
GALA, RICO--[39]GERMAN
LANDMANN, ROBERT-- [39]GERMAN

ACKWORTH, ROBERT CHARLES
ACKWORTH, ROBERT-- [21]ROMANTIC READER, 1990
ACKWORTH, ROBERTA--[21]ROM-- "NORTH COUNTRY NURSE"

ACTON, EDWARD J.
ACTON, JAY--[1][31]

ACUFF, SELMA BOYD
BOYD, SELMA--[1][31]

ADACHI, BARBARA [CURTIS]
ANTHONY, CATHERINE--[31]

ADAIR, HAZEL IRIS WILSON
HERITAGE, A.J.--[2]

ADALISA, ANNE
RAINE, ALLEN--[22]WELSH

ADAM VAN EYCK, HERBERT
WESTERKAMP, THOMAS M.--[39]GERMAN

ADAM, JULIETTE
LAMBER, JULIETTE--[1][22]
VASILI,[COMTE] PAUL--[1][22]
[LA] MESSINE--[1][22]

ADAMOVA, ELEONORA G.
ADAMIAN, NORA--[1]

ADAMS, AGNES
LOGAN, AGNES--[1]

ADAMS, ALICE BOYD
ADAMS, ALICE--[21]ROM--6 NOVELS

ADAMS, ARTHUR HENRY
JAMES, HENRY JAMES--[13]AUSTRALIAN
JAMES, JAMES--[13]AUSTRALIAN

ADAMS, BARBARA JOHNSTON
SHIELS, BARBARA--[33]

ADAMS, BERTRAM MARTIN
ADAMS, BILL--[1]PLAYTIME SLEAZE

ADAMS, BETSY
JYMES, ELIZABETH--[1]

ADAMS, CLEVE F.
CHARLES, FRANKLIN--W/ROBERT L. BELLEM, [3][5][18][29][31]MYS--
FUNK "THE VICE CZAR MURDERS" '41
SPAIN, JOHN--[3][18][29]MYS--
DUTTON "DIG ME A GRAVE" '42
DUTTON "DEATH IS LIKE THAT" '43
DUTTON "EVIL STAR" '44

ADAMS, CLIFTON H.
GANT, JONATHAN--[3][22][28][31]MYS--
ACE "NEVER SAY NO TO A KILLER" '56
AVALON "LONG VENDETTA" '63
KINKAID, MATT--[19][22][31]WEST--
AVON "HARDCASE" '53
DELL "RACE OF GIANTS" '56
RANDALL, CLAY--[1][19][22]WEST--
12 NOVELS '52-69
STACY, JAN--L. ROBBINS LTR MAR '94, PULP

ADAMS, DOROTHY
DEAN, EDNA--W/EDITH C. NORDSTROM,[34]MYS--
CARLTON "THE WAX BASKET MURDER" '86

ADAMS, DORSEY
KELLEY, DORSEY--[21][26]ROM--4 NOVELS

ADAMS, DOUGLAS
AGNEW, DAVID--W/GEORGE & GRAHAM WILLIAMS,[1][2]

ADAMS, F. RAMSAY
DANE, CARL--[1][31]

ADAMS, FRANCIS W.L.
FARRELL, AGNES--[1]

ADAMS, FRANKLIN PIERCE
F.P.A.--[22][38]AMERICAN

ADAMS, HARRIET S.
APPLETON, VICTOR--[7]HP--
STSY 'TOM SWIFT': "THE PLANET STONE"
APPLETON, VICTOR II--[1][2]HP--
STSY-TOM SWIFT
BARTON, MAY--[1]HP--STSY
DIXON, FRANKLIN W.--[1]HP--
STSY-HARDY BOYS, TED SCOTT
HOPE, LAURA LEE--[1]HP--
STSY-BOBBSEY TWINS
KEENE, CAROLYN--[1][5]HP--
STSY-NANCY DREW
THORNDIKE, HELEN LOUISE--[1]

ADAMS, HARRY [BROOKS]
AMO, TAURAATUA I--[31]

ADAMS, HELEN SIMMONS
BARNES, NANCY--[1]

ADAMS, HENRY BROOKS
SNOW, FRANCIS COMPTON--[31]

ADAMS, HENRY H.
ALLEN, HENRY--L. ROBBINS LTR MAR '94, [1][31]PULP

ADAMS, HERBERT
GRAY, JONATHAN--[3][5][22][29]MYS--
"SECRET OF BOGEY HOUSE" '24
"GOLDEN APE" '30
"CRIME IN THE DUTCH GARDEN" '30
"SAFETY LAST" '34
"THE OWL" '37

ADAMS, J.
KUPPORD, SKELTON--[2][11][23]SF--
"A FORTUNE FROM THE SKY" '03

ADAMS, LAURIE
SCHNEIDER, LAURIE--[33]

ADAMS, NORMAN
SIMPSON, LEW--[1]

ADAMS, O.L.
OLD HUTCH--[3]MYS--
STREET "DETECTIVES CLEW, OR THE TRADGEDY OF ELM GROVE" 1888

ADAMS, PETER ROBERT C.
ADAMS, PERSEUS--[1]

ADAMS, ROBERT JAMES
ADAM, ROBIN--[3]MYS--
HODDER "STALK TO KILL" '70
MACTYRE, PAUL--[2][11][23][34]MYS--
HODDER "MIDGE" '62
HODDER "FISH ON A HOOK" '63
HODDER "BAR SINISTER" '64

ADAMS, ROBERT MARTIN
KRAPP, R.M.--[22][31]AMERICAN

ADAMS, ROBERT [FRANKLIN]
ADAMSON, FRANK--[1][31]

ADAMS, SAMUEL HOPKINS
FABIAN, WARNER--[1][22][29]MYS--
SEARS FILM "THE MEN IN HER LIFE" '30

ADAMS, TRACY
EVERETT, GAIL--[9]ROM
HALE, ARLENE--[9]ROM
HALE, MARY--[9]ROM
TATE, MARY--[9]ROM
WILLIAMS, LYNN--[9]ROM

ADAMS, WALTER MARSHAM
MACAULAY, CLARENDON--[2]

ADAMS, WILLIAM
ADAMS, BILL--[7]SF--
BAL "THE UNWOUND WAY" '91

ADAMS, WILLIAM TAYLOR
ASHTON, WARREN T.--[31][33][34]--
MUSSEY "HATCHIE THE GUARDIAN SLAVE; OR, HEIRESS OF BELLVUE" 1852
BROWN, IRVING--[1][31][33]
HUNTER, CLINGHAM--[1][33]
HUNTER, CLINGHAM M.D.--[31]
MCCORMICK, BROOKS--[1][33]
OPTIC, OLIVER--W/EDWARD STRATEMEYER, [1][33]HP--STSY
WINTERTON, GAYLE--[33]

ADAMS,[FRANKLIN]
EBERHARDT, PETER--[1]

ADAMS-MANSON, PAT
HOWARD, JULIA--[9][21]ROM--
"A PASSIONATE VENTURE"

ADAMS-MANSON, PAT [CONT]
HOWARD, JULIA [CONT]
"A LASTING IMAGE"
"WORKING IT OUT"

ADAMSON, EWART
DOUGLAS, DAYLE--BAPC NWSLTR #9,[3]--
MYS HOUSE "HAUNTED HARBOR" '43

ADAMSON, FRANCES A.
GRAY, ESCA--[1]

ADAMSON, IAIAN BEATON
BEATON, CHRIS--[1]
MACADAM, IAN--[1]

ADAMSON, MARY JO
ADAMSON, M.J.--ENID SCHANTZ, DDLY
PLEASURES #3, P34
ADAMSON, YVONNE--
W/YVONNE MONTGOMERY-MYS SCENE #40, P59
DELACORTE "BRIDEY'S MOUNTAIN" '93
W/YVONNE EWEGEN & ENID SCHANTZ
DDLY PLEASURES # 3, P34
"BRIDEY'S MOUNTAIN"

ADCOCK, ALMEY ST. JOHN
MARCH, HILARY--[1]

ADCOCK, ARTHUR ST. JOHN
FLECKNOR, RICHARD--[1]
FLECNOC--[1]
RUTLAND, ARTHUR--[1]

ADCOCK, THOMAS LARRY
SANDERS, BUCK--[3]HP--
WARNER "A CLEAR & PRESENT DANGER" '81
WARNER "TRAIL OF THE TWISTED CROSS" '82

ADDIS, ERIC ELRINGTON
DRAX, PETER--[1][3][22][29]MYS--
7 HUTCHINSON NOVELS '36-9

ADDIS, HAZEL IRIS
ADAIR, HAZEL--W/RONALD MARRIOTT
[1][2][11][32]
ADDIS, H.I.--[1]
HERITAGE, A.J.--[1][2][11]

ADDISON, KATHERINE
ANSON, KATHLEEN--[1]

ADDUCI, FRANK
CARTER, NICK--[3]HP--
"TEN TIMES DYNAMITE" '80

ADELSON, JEAN
MACK, AMANDA--[9][21][26]ROM--
"MAKESHIFT MISTRESS"

ADER, PAUL [FASSET]
ALLEN, JAMES--[1][31][32]--
ST "DAUGHTERS OF HELL" AUG '58
ST "A TOUCH OF EVIL" OCT '58
OF "MY SIN - DEATH" JAN '58
OF "HELL'S WHISTLE STOP" DEC '59
ST "RESERVE MY HOT SEAT" SEPT '59
OF "HARVEST OF DOOM" MAY '59
GU "MAN WITH THE SCAR" DEC '60
TW "EYES OF MURDER" DEC '60

ADKINS, AVA VERLEA
SMITH, MARY--V. BERCH, BRNDN/BC
PSEUDS., BAE 22, P24

ADKINS, FRANK HOWARD
ST. MARS, F.--[34]MYS--
CHAMBERS "OFF THE BEATEN TRACK" '20

ADLARD, PETER MARCUS
ADLARD, MARK--[1][7][11][23]ENGLISH,SF--
"T-CITY TRIOLOGY" #3 '75
ADLARD, P.M.--[32]--
LM "ANYTHING TO OBLIGE" DEC '68

ADLER, CAROLE SCHWERDTF.
ADLER, C.S.--[7]SF--7 NOVELS

ADLER, IRVING
IRVING, ROBERT--[1][22][33]AMERICA

ADLER, JACOB
KOVNER, B.--[1][31]

ADLER, RENATA
DANIELS, BRETT--[1][31]--
ARTICLES & SHORT STORIES

ADLER, WILLIAM
DAVID, JAY--[1][31]

ADLER-GERTLER, DITTA
GERTLER, DITTA--[39]GERMAN

ADOFF, VIRGINIA HAMILTON
HAMILTON, VIRGINIA--[7]SF--
"JUSTICE CYCLE #1-3" & OTHERS

ADOMEIT, RUTH E.
PUTTER, POLLY--[1]

ADORJAN, CAROL MADDEN
KENYON, KATE--W/CANDICE F. RANSOM,[31]

ADYE, SIR JOHN
DAYE, JOHN--[1][3][29]MYS--
"WHO KILLED LORD HENRY ROLLESTONE?" '24

ADYE, TIM
ZOOL, M.H.--[23]SF--GROUP PSEUD.

AE ALBINANA, ASUNCION I.
SANDOIZ, ALBA--[30]MEXICAN--
"THE ENCHANTED JUNGLE" '45
"TAETZANI" '46

AEBY, JACQUELYN
CAREW, JOCELYN--[9][21][26][31]ROM--
4 NOVELS
GRAY, VANESSA--[9][21][26][31]ROM--
17 NOVELS

AEGERTER-HARTMANN, ELISA.
GERTER, ELISABETH--[39]GERMAN

AFRICANO, LILLIAN
ASHBY, NORA--[31]
COOK, LILA--[31]
MARCH, JESSICA--[26][31]ROM--
"ILLUSIONS"
"OBSESSIONS"
"SENSATIONS"
"EMBRACE THE FURY"
"TEMPTATIONS"

AFZALI, KARIN
LIEPELT, KARIN--[39]GERMAN/SF

AGALSTEIN, MIECZYSLAW
JASTRUN, MIECZYSLAW--[22]POLISH

AUTHORS

AGARD, ESTELLE
VIRMONNE, CLAUDE--[34]FRENCH--
BY-LINE IN FRANCE
VIRMONNE, CLAUDETTE--[34]MYS--
15 NOVELS '56-77

AGATE, JAMES
PRENTIS, RICHARD--[8]
SIR TOPAZ--[8]
WARRINGTON, GEORGE--[8]

AGHADJIAN, MOLLIE
ALLISON, MOETH--[9][21][26]ROM--4 NOVELS
ASHTON, MOLLIE--[9][21][26]ROM--3 NOVELS

AGINSKY, BERNARD W.
AGINSKY, BURT W.--[1][31]

AGISHEV, SAGIR I.
AGHISH, SAGIT--[1]
AGISH, SAGIT--[1]

AGNELLI, SUSANNA
AGNELLI, SUNI--[1]

AGNEW, EDITH J.
MARCELLINO--[1][22][31][33]AMERICAN

AGNEW, STEPHEN
ALLYNE, ROY--[1]
STEPHENS, ARTHUR--[1]
STEPHENS, KENNETH--[1]
SUMMERS, COLIN--[1]

AGNON, SHMUEL YOSEF H.
CZACZKES, SHMUEL YOSEF--[31]

AGUILAR MELANTZON, RICARD
AGUILAR, RICARDO--[31]

AGUIRRE, MAGDALENA M.
MONDRAGON, MAGDALENA--[30]MEXICAN
SEMINOFF, VERA--[30]MEXICAN

AGUTSTEIN, MIECZYSLAW
JASTRUN, MIECZYSLAW--[1]

AGUTTER, JENNIFER ANN
AGUTTER, JENNY--[31]

AHEARN, PATRICIA
FAIRCHILD, KATE--[9][21]ROM
MERIWETHER, KATE--[9][21][26]ROM--6 NOVELS
MURRAY, CAITLIN--[9][21][26]ROM--
"RISKING IT ALL"

AHERN, JEROME MORRELL
AHERN, JERRY--[7][23]SF--
GE 'DEFENDER' SERIES
GE 'SURVIVALIST' SERIES
AHERN, JERRY M.--[7]SF
CARTER, NICK--[3][7][23]HP--
CHART "TURKISH BLOODBATH" '80
CHART "DEATHLIGHT" '82
KILGORE, ALEX--V. BERCH LTR TO HUBIN
FEB '94, ALL EXCEPT "EYE FOR EYE"

AHERN, MARGARET MCCROHAN
O'CONNELL, PEG--[22][33]AMERICAN

AHERN, SHARON A[NN]
AHERN, S.A.--ECHOES 21, P14,[7]--
"THE TAKERS" W/HUSBAND, JERRY

AHERN, THOMAS FRANCIS
AHERN, TOM--[31]

AHIER, BRIAN
READ, BRIAN--[1]

AHISTROEM, GOESTA WERNER
AHLSTROM, G.W.--[31]

AHLBORN-WILKE, DIRK
WILKE, DIRK--[39]GERMAN

AHLERS, HEILWIG [M]
VON DER MEHDEN, HEILWIG--[39]GERMAN

AHLSTEDT, IVAR
KLINT, JESPER--[29]MYS--
"FORLAG" '54
TROTS "FLYKTIDIMMA" '56

AHLSTRAND, KERSTIN
KAHLE, KRISTIN--W/LARS KYHLE,[29]MYS--
"MORD FORGAVES" '56

AHN, SOO-GIL
NAM SUK--[1]

AHRENS, ANNEMARIE
BOYSEN, CORNELIA--[39]GERMAN

AICHBICHLER, WILHELMINE M
VIESER, DELORES--[39]GERMAN

AICHINGER, GERHARD
AICK, GERHARD--[39]GERMAN

AIKEN, ALBERT W.
BLAKE, REDMOND--[1]
DAVENPORT, ADELAIDE--[1]
DAVENPORT, FRANCES HELEN--[1]
PENNE, AGILE--[1]
SARA,[COL.] DELLE--[1]

AIKEN, CONRAD [P]
JEAKE, SAMUEL JR.--[1][22][31][33]SWEDISH--
LONDON CORRESPONDENT TO 'NEW YORKER'

AIKEN, JOAN
DEE, NICHOLAS--[2][11][16][32]--
SUS "MOMENT OF HAZZARD" NOV '59
LEE, ROSIE--[1][2][11][16]

AIKEN, JOHN [KEMPTON]
PAGET, JOHN--[1][2][11][23]--
"WORLD WELL LOST" '70

AIKIN, JAMES D[OUGLAS]
AIKIN, JIM--[7][23]SF--
BAL "WALK THE MOONS ROAD" '85

AIKIO, MATTI
ISAKSEN, MATHIS--[22]NORWEGIAN

AINSWORTH, CATHERINE H.
HARRIS, CATHERINE--[31]

AINSWORTH, HARRIET
CADELL, ELIZABETH--[9]ROM

AINSWORTH, MARY D. SALTER
SALTER, MARY D.--[1]

AINSWORTH, NORMA
RUEDI, NORMA PAUL--[1][22][33]AMERICAN

AINSWORTH, RUTH GALLARD
GILBERT, RUTH GALLARD A.--[31]

AINSWORTH, THOMAS HARG.
HARGRAVES, THOMAS--[31]

AINSWORTH, WILLIAM HARR.
BROWN, WILL--[33]
TICHEBURN, CHEVIOT--[33]

AIRD, ALISDAIR
FAIRLEY, ALIDAIR--[1]

AITCHISON, GEORGE
THYSON, A.C.--[1]

AITKEN, A. DONNELLY
DONNELLY, A.--[1]
SHANNON, A. DONNELLY--[1]

AITKEN, ROBERT
DOUGLAS, HUDSON--[1][2][3]MYS--
WATT "LANTERN OF LUCK" '09
WATT "MAN IN THE MIRROR" '10 & 2 MORE

AITKEN, WILLIAM RUSSELL
SCOTT, STUART--[1]

AKASS, JOHN EWART
AKASS, JON--[31]

AKENS, DAVID STRODE
LEE, S.C.--V. BERCH LTR TO HUBIN '93
"THE UNTITLED MYSTERY" '87

AKENSON, DONALD HARMAN
AKENSON, DON--V. BERCH LTR TO HUBIN '93
WALKER "THE EDGERSTON AUDIT" '88

AKIRA, KAWAKAMI
BIZAN, KAWAKAMI--[22]JAPANESE

AKMATOVA, ANNA
GORENKO, ANNA ANDREEVNA--[31]

AKS, PATRICIA
CHASE, EMILY--[31][33]

AKSENOV, VASILI PAVLOVICH
AKSENOV, VASSILY--[31]
AKSYONOV, VASSILY--[1][7]SF--
"THE ISLAND OF CRIMEA: A NOVEL" '83

AL-AMIN, JAMIL ABDULLAH
BROWN, H. RAP--[31]

AL-KHARRAT, EDWAR
FALTAS YOUSSEF, EDWAR K.--[31]

ALAILIMA, FAY C.
CALKINS, FAY--[31]

ALAIS, ERNEST W.
MILLER, LAWRENCE--[1][34]MYS--
AMALG "THE MYSTERY MAN" '10
WOLFE, CEDRIC--[1]

ALAN TURNER, V. PRUDENCE
SUMMERHAYES, PRUDENCE--[1]

ALAN, JANE
CHISHOLM, LILIAN--[9][21][26]ROM--
"SONG FOR TOMORROW"
"HEARTS GO SINGING"
"FRIEND OF THE FAMILY"
LORRAINE, ANNE--[9][21][26]ROM--5 NOVELS

ALAS Y URENA, LEOPOLDO
CLARIN--[22][31]SPANISH

ALAS Y URENA, LEOPOLDO [CONT]
ALAS, LEOPOLDO--[22]SPANISH

ALATRI, PAOLO
ROMANO, PAOLO--[1]

ALBA DE GAMEZ, CIELO CAY.
DE GAMEZ, TANA--[31]

ALBANESI, EFFIE A. MARIA
ROWLANDS, EFFIE ADELAIDE--[1][17]

ALBANO, PETER
ROBBINS, ANDREA--[9][21][26]ROM--
"THE FIRES OF OAKHEATH"

ALBERT, BURTON JR.
HEALEY, BROOKS--[1][31][33]JUV '70s

ALBERT, JERRY
ALBERT, ANDREW I.--T. JOHNSON LTR--
VM-RPRT OF 'RED MASK/RED HOOD' SERIES
4 STORIES MID '40s
RICHARDS, STANLEY--T. JOHNSON LTR--
RMDS 'RED MASK/HOOD' 4 STORIES MAR-JUL '41

ALBERT, MARVIN H.
BARONE, MIKE--[3][29][31]MYS--
"CRAZY JOE" '74
CONROY, AL--[3][31]--
LAN 75-370 "SOLDATO" '72
LAN 75-382 "DEATHGRIP" '72
LAN "BLOOD RUN" -73
CONROY, ALBERT--V. BERCH, GM PSEUDS,
PP 33,[3][31]--
GM 231 "THE ROAD'S END" '52
GM 289 "THE CHISELERS" '53
GM 676 "NICE GUYS FINISH DEAD" '57
GM 780 "THE MOB SAYS MURDER" '58
GM 806 "MURDER IN ROOM 13" '58
DELL FE B165 "MR. LUCKY" '60
CREST 349 "DEVIL IN DUNGAREES" '60
CREST S431 "THE LOOTERS" '61
MCALISTER, IAN--[3][31]--
GM "DRISCOLL'S DIAMONDS" '73
GM "SKYLARK MISSION" '73
GM "STRIKE FORCE" '74
GM "VALLEY OFASSASSINS" '75
QUARRY, NICK--V. BERCH, GM PSEUDS,
PP 33,[3]--
GM 747 "THE HOODS CAME CALLING" '58
GM 824 "TRAIL OF A TRAMP" '58
GM 938 "GIRL WITH NO PLACE TO HIDE" '59
GM 1053 "TILL IT HURTS" '60
GM 1033 "NO CHANCE IN HELL" '60
GM "SOME DIE HARD" '61
GM "THE VENDETTA" '73
ROME, ANTHONY--[1][3]AMERICAN/MYS--
POCK 1269 "MIAMI MAYHEM" '60
HALE "LADY IN CEMENT" '61
DELL FE B232 "MY KIND OF GAME" '62

ALBERT, MAX
LYKKE, TILL--[39]GERMAN
STEEN, ALBERT--[39]GERMAN

ALBERT, SUSAN W. & BILL
ADAMS, NICHOLAS--AUTHOR PROVIDED,JUV,HP--
BB "VAMPIRE'S KISS" '94
ALBERT, SUSAN WITTIG--ALBERT BIBLIO,MAY 93
SCRIBN "WITCHES' BANE"
SCRIBN "HANGMAN'S ROOT" '94
BLAKE, SUSAN--ALBERT BIBLIO, MAY 93--
BB "STEALING JOSH" 1990,HARLEQUIN,
GERMANY "LOVE IS A WILD RIVER" '90

ALBERT, SUSAN W. & BILL [CONT]
DIXON, FRANKLIN W.--ALBERT BIBLIO
MAY'93,HP--
HARDY BOYS "STREET SPIES" '88
HARDY BOYS "WITHOUT A TRACE" '88
KEENE, CAROLYN--ABERT BIBLIO, MAY '93,HP--
NANCY DREW "THIS SIDE OF EVIL"
NANCY DREW "FATAL ATTRACTION"
NANCY DREW "PLAYING WITH FIRE" '89
PAIGE, ROBIN--AUTHOR PROVIDED--
AVON "DEATH AT BISHOP'S KEEP" '94
AVON "DEATH AT GALLOWS GREEN" '95
PAYNE, NATHANIEL--ALBERT BIBLIO, MAY '93--
HARLEQUIN, GERMANY "BLOOD BROTHERS" '91
CORA VERLAG, GERMANY "QUEEN OF SWORDS" '92
"GHOSTS OF FOULKSRATH CASTLE" '92

ALBERT, SUSAN WITTIG
BLAKE, SUSAN--ALBERT BIBLIO, MAY '93--
BB 'SWEET DREAMS' #60, 84,
SPECIAL #86, 152 & 162
DELL "HAUNTED DOLLHOUSE"
NAL 'FIFTEEN' #4 & #6
FAWCETT 'SUNSET HIGH' #8
BAL 'DREAM GIRLS' #3
SCHOLASIC 'CHEERLEADERS' #19
BAL 'ROOMMATES' #1-#3
BAL 'FIRST KISS' #1
KEENE, CAROLYN--ALBERT BIBLIO,MAY '93,HP--
NANCY DREW "WHITE-WATER TERROR" &
NANCY DREW "HEART OF DANGER"
PASCAL, FRANCINE--ALBERT BIBLIO, MAY '93,HP--
BB 'SWEET VALLEY TWINS' #25, 28, 30,
32, 36, 37, 41, 43, 46, 48,49, 51,
53, 55 & #60
WITTIG, SUSAN--ALBERT BIBLIO, MAY '93--
FOUR BOOKS-ACADEMIC NON-FICTION

ALBERY, NOBUKO
MORRIS, NOBUKO--[1]

ALBICKER, JOSEF
FROMMHERZ, FLORIAN--[39]GERMAN
WILLRECHT, WALDO--[39]GERMAN

ALBINSON, JAMES P.
ALBINSON, JACK--[1][31]

ALBION, LEE SMITH
SMITH, LEE--[33]

ALBOROUGH, EDWARD MORGAN
DE BURGH, A.--[1]

ALBRECHT, FRITZ
RITTER, ROBERT--[39]GERMAN/JUV

ALBRECHT, PAUL
HARDT, HANS--[39]GERMAN/SF

ALBRIGHT, ELIZABETH A.
ALBRIGHT, BETS PARKER--[31]

ALBRITTON, CAROL
TREHEARNE, ELIZABETH--W/PATRICIA A.
MAXWELL,[9][21][26]ROM--
"STORM AT NIGHT"

ALD, ROY ALLISON
DUBALL, MICHAEL--[31]
KIHL, ARMAND--[31]
MANN, A. PHILO--[7][31]SF

ALDANI, LINO
JANDA, N.L.--[11]SF

ALDEN, ISABELLA MACDONALD
PANSY--[1][33]

ALDERFER, E. GORDON
ALDERFER, E.G.--[31]

ALDERMAN, GILLIAN
ALDERMAN, GILL--[23]ENGLISH/SF--
"GUNA #1 & #2" '89/90

ALDISS, BRIAN [WILSON]
CRACKEN, JAEL--[1][2][23]ENGLISH/SF
MEDICANT, ARCH--[1][2]ENGLISH
PICA, PETER--[1]ENGLISH
RUNCIMAN, JOHN--[1][2][23]ENGLISH/SF
SHACKLETON, C.C.--[2][11][22][23]
ENGLISH, HIST
XERXES, B.T.H.--[2]ENGLISH, SHARED PSEUD.

ALDISS, MARGARET [C]
MANSON, MARGARET--[1]

ALDOUS, ANTHONY MICHAEL
ALDOUS, TONY--[31]

ALDOUS, DONALD WILLIAM
DISCOBULUS--[1]

ALDRICH, CLARA C.T.
ALDRICH, DARRAGH--[1]

ALDRICH, EARL AUGUSTUS
LEONARD, A.B.--[1][3][22]MYS--
CLODE "THE JUDSON MURDER CASE" '33

ALDRICH, SANDRA PICKLSIM.
KAREN--[31]

ALEBY, ANDERS
ANDERSON, AL--[29]MYS--
"PERFEKT BROTT" '67

ALEKPER-ZADE, ALHUGASAN A
ALBUGASAN--[1]

ALEKSEYEV, KONSTANTIN S.
STANISLAVSKI--[22]RUSSIAN

ALEPUDELIS, ODISSEUS
ELITIS, ODISSEUS--[22]GREEK

ALESHKOVSKY, JOSEPH
ALESHKOVSKY, YUZ--[31][34]--
FARRAR "THE HAND; OR, THE CONFESSION
OF AN EXECUTIONER" '80

ALEXANDER, ALBRECHT
ALEXANDRE, ALEXANDRE--[39]GERMAN/SF

ALEXANDER, ANNA B.C.
COOKE, BARBARA--[1]

ALEXANDER, ANNA COOKE
ALEXANDER, ANNE--[31][33]CHILDREN'S BOOKS

ALEXANDER, BOYD
LACEY, JOHN--[1][31]

ALEXANDER, CHARLES W.
BRADSHAW, WELLESLY--[1]
BRADSHAW, WESLY--[1]

ALEXANDER, COLIN JAMES
JAY, SIMON--[3][11][22][31]--
COLLINS "DEATH OF A SKIN DIVER" '64
COLLINS "SLEEPERS CAN KILL" '68

ALEXANDER, DAVID
MANING, KYLE--V.BERCH LTR TO HUBIN FEB '94
REED, WILLIAM--LACHMAN/GOODE LIST[23]--
'SOLDIER OF WAR' SERIES
'PHOENIX SERIES'
"DARK MESSIAH" '87
"GROUND ZERO" '87
"METALSTORM" '88
"WHIRLWIND" '88
SIEVERT, JAN--[7]HP--
ZEBRA 'C.A.D.S.' #9 THRU #12 '90-1

ALEXANDER, ELEANOR JANE
E.A.--[1]

ALEXANDER, HAROLD LEE
ALEXANDER, ZANE--[1][31]

ALEXANDER, HORACE G[UNDY]
ALEXANDER, H.G.--[31]

ALEXANDER, JANET
MCNEILL, JANET--[1][11][31]--
HODDER-9 NOVELS '55-68

ALEXANDER, JOAN
PEPPER, JOAN--[8]

ALEXANDER, JOCELYN ANNE A
ARUNDEL, JOCELYN--[1][22][31][33]

ALEXANDER, JOSEPHINE
LORA, JOSEPHINE--[1][31]

ALEXANDER, KENNETH J.W.
ALEXANDER, KEN--[31]

ALEXANDER, MARC [ELWARD]
AYLWARD, MARCUS--[1][3]MYS--
BARKER "HARPER'S FOLLY" '84
WEIDENFELD "HARPER'S LUCK" '85
RONSON, MARK--[1][3][7][31]MYS--
HAMLYN "BLOODTHIRST" '79
HAMLYN "GHOUL" '80
HAMLYN "OGRE" '80

ALEXANDER, MARK [MARSHA]
MEADOWS, ADRIAN--V. BERCH, BRNDN/
BC PSEUDS., BAE 22, P24

ALEXANDER, MARSHA DURCHIN
ALEXANDER, MARSHA--[21]ROM--4 NOVELS

ALEXANDER, RAYMOND PACE
ALEXANDER, RAE PACE--[31][33]

ALEXANDER, ROBERT W.
ALEXANDER, R.W.--[1]
BUTLER, JOAN--[2][3][7][11][23][31]--
PAUL "SOMETHING RICH" '37
PAUL "RAPID FIRE" '39 & 39 OTHER NVLS
TEMPLE, RALPH--[1]
TEMPLE, RUTH--[8]

ALEXANDER, STANLEY WALTER
HANNIBAL--[1][31]

ALEXANDER, TRISHA
KAY, PAT--[21]ROM--
"CINDERELLA GIRL"

ALEXEYEV, SERGEY ALEXANDER
NAYDENOV, S.--[22]RUSSIAN

ALEXY, EDUARD
CYPRIAN, EDO--[39]GERMAN/JUV

ALFVEN, HANNES OLOF G.
JOHANNESON, OLOF--[2][23][31]SWEDISH/SF

ALGER, HORATIO JR.
PUTNAM, ARTHUR LEE--[33]

ALGER, LECLAIRE GOWANS
ALGER, L.G.--[33]
LEODHAS, SORCHE NIC--[2][11][31][33]
NIC LEODHAS, SORCHE--[33]
PUTMAN, ARTHUR LEE--D. LYND--
"HORATIO ALGER,JR." '61 BY FRANK GRUBER

ALGERMISSEN, JO ANN
HUDSON, ANNA--[9][21][26]ROM--
17 NOVELS

ALGIE, JAMES
LLOYD, WALLACE--[34]MYS--
DILLINGHAM "HOUSE OF GLASS" 1898
UNWIN "BERGEN WORTH" 1901

ALGOZIN, BRUCE
CARTER, NICK--[3][7][23]HP--
CHART "THE LAST SAMURAI" '82
CHART "THE DOMINICAN AFFAIR" '82

ALI KHAN, SHIRLEY
KHAN, HASSAN--[1]
KHAN, HASSINA--[31]

ALI, SCHAVI MALI
DIARA, SCHAVI M.--[31]

ALIEV, AKPER
RUKHI--[1]

ALINGTON, ARGENTINE F.
TALBOT, HUGH--[1]

ALINGTON, CYRIL A.
WESTERHAM, S.C.--[1][3][22]MYS--
McBRIDE "MIXED BAGS" '29

ALLAN, ALFRED K.
KATZ, ALFRED--[31]

ALLAN, F. CARNEY
MACDONALD, ERIC--[1]
NEISH, DUNCAN--[1]

ALLAN, JEANNE
ALLEN, JEANNE--[9][21]ROM--
"PETER'S SISTER"

ALLAN, MABEL ESTHER
ESTORIL, JEAN--[22][25][31][33]--
'DRINA DANCES' NOVELS '57-91
HAGON, PRISCILLA--[1][25][31][33]--
5 WORLD NOVELS '66-70
PILGRIM, ANNE--[1][22][25][33]--
5 ABELAIRD NOVELS

ALLAN, MARGARET
QUICK, W.T.--G. COOK, LTR AUG '93,SF--
SIGN 'DREAMS' #1-#3 '88-90
SIGN "YESTERDAY'S PAWN" '89
SIGN "THE MAMMOTH STONE"

ALLAN, TED
MAXWELL, EDWARD--[7]SF

ALLANA, GHULAM ALI
ALLANA, GHULAMALI--[31]

ALLASON, RUPERT
WEST, NIGEL--[1] V. BERCH LTR TO HUBIN '94
SECKER "THE BLUE LIST" '89

ALLBEURY, THEODORE E.
ALLBEURY, TED--[7][8][18][34]MYS--
27 NOVELS '73-90
BUTLER, RICHARD--[3][8][29][31]MYS--
DAVIES "WHERE ALL GIRLS ARE SWEETER" '75
DAVIES "ITALIAN ASSETS" '76
KELLY, PATRICK--[3][7][8][18]MYS--
GRANADA "CODEWORD CROMWELL" '80
GRANADA "LONELY MARGINS" '81

ALLDRIDGE, JOHN STRATTON
STRATTON, JOHN--[1]

ALLEGRO, JOHN MARCO
MCGILL, IAN--[8][31]

ALLEN, AGNES [B]
TRANT, ERICA--[1]

ALLEN, ARTHUR BRUCE
TRICE, BOROUGH--[1][3]MYS
"THE PYROMANIAC" '38
BIG BEN "'ORRIBLE MURDER" '42

ALLEN, BESSIE BACON
BACON, BESSIE--[1]

ALLEN, BETTY [JEANNE]
ALLEN, ELIZABETH COOPER--[31]--
DODD "MOTHER, CAN YOU HEAR ME?" '83

ALLEN, BEVERLY
HUNT, BEVERLY--[9]ROM

ALLEN, BOB
OSSLINGER, KURT--[1]

ALLEN, CATHERINE
MOORHOUSE, CATHERINE--W/DOROTHEA JENSEN,[9][21][26]ROM--
"ADRIANNA"
"LOUISA"
"DOROTHEA"

ALLEN, CECIL J.
MERCURY--[1]
VOUAGEUR--[1]

ALLEN, CHARLOTTE HALE
HALE, CHARLOTTE--[31]

ALLEN, CHARLOTTE VALE
VINCENT, CLARE--[1][17]ROM

ALLEN, D.H.
MONTGOMERY, MARIANNE--[9][21][26]ROM--
"THE PASSIONATE PRETENDER"

ALLEN, DANICE JO
DALTON, EMILY--[21][26]ROM--5 NOVELS

ALLEN, ELYSE
CRAIN, ELLEY--W/CAROL MENDENHALL,[26] ROM--"DEEP IN THE HEART"

ALLEN, EMILY JOAN
ALLEN, EMILY ANN--W/DIANE REEP,[9]ROM
REEP, DIANE--W/DIANE REEP,[9][21]ROM--
"THE BLAKEMORE TOUCH"

ALLEN, ERIC VAUGHN
ALLEN, ERIKA VAUGHAN--[1][3]MYS--
SIGN "VOICES IN THE WIND" '67

ALLEN, FELICITY
LEWIS, CATHERINE--[36]MYS--
PENG "UNABLE BY REASON OF DEATH" '89
PENG "NOT IN SINGLE SPIES" '92

ALLEN, FREDERICK G.
ALLEN, GARY--[1][31]

ALLEN, GRANT
RAYNER, OLIVE PRATT--[2][18][22][29]MYS--
"TYPEWRITER GIRL"
"ROSALBA, STORY OF HER DEVELOPMENT" 1899
WARBOROUGH, MARTIN LEACH--[2][18][22][29]--
"TOM, UNLIMITED: A STORY FOR CHILDREN" 1897
WILSON, J. ARBUTHNOT--[1][2][22]

ALLEN, HELENA GRONLUND
ALLEN, H. FREDERICKA--[1][31]

ALLEN, HENRY FRANCIS
PRUNING KNIFE--[1][2]

ALLEN, HENRY WILSON
FISHER, CLAY--JAMES CORRICK, PP 21, P49, [1][28]WEST--
16 NOVELS '51-76
HENRY, WILL--JAMES CORRICK, PP 21, P49, [23][28][31]WEST--
24 NOVELS '50-78

ALLEN, HUBERT RAYMOND
ALLEN, DIZZY--[31]
ALLEN, H.R.--[31]
GUTHRIE, DAVID--[1][31]
HELLEY, DENIS--[1]
JONES, LLEWELLYN--[1][8]

ALLEN, JAMES LOVIC JR.
ALLEN, JIM--[31]MYS--
SFDS "DIE FOR ME, PAL!" JUL '58
JAMES, ALLEN--[1][31]

ALLEN, KENNETH S.
CARTER, AVIS MURTON--[1][31][33]
SCOTT, ALISTAIR--[1][33]

ALLEN, MARION CARROLL
ALLEN, M.C.--[7]SF
ALLEN, SAM--[22][31]

ALLEN, MARY ELIZABETH
GREY, KITTY--[9][21][26]ROM--
NOVELS

ALLEN, MAXINE DALTON
ALTON, MAXINE--[1]

ALLEN, MICHAEL [DEREK]
BRADFORD, MICHAEL--[31][34]MYS--
MULLER "COUNTER-COUP" '80

ALLEN, RICHARD STANLEY
ALLEN, DICK--[7]SF--
2 NON-FICT

ALLEN, ROBERT LORING
ALLEN, LORING--[31]

ALLEN, SAMUEL WASHINGTON
VESEY, PAUL--[33]

ALLEN, SHEILA ROSALYND
O'HALLION, SHEILA--CRPG,[9][21][26]ROM--
"KATHLEEN" '88
"AMERICAN PRINCESS"
"FIRE & INNOCENCE"
"MASQUE OF HEARTS" & 2 OTHERS

ALLEN, STEPHEN V.P.W.
ALLEN, STEVE--[31]

ALLEN, TERRIL DIENER
ALLEN, T.D.--W/ARTHUR L. DIMMITZ,[1][31][33]
ALLEN, TERRY--[33]
ALLEN, TERRY D.--[1][31]

ALLEN, THOMAS BENTON
ALLEN, TOM--[31][33]

ALLEN, WILLIAM HERVEY JR.
ALLEN, HERVEY--[21]ROM--
'ANTHONY ADVERSE' SERIES
'CITY IN THE DAWN' SERIES

ALLEN,[CHARLES] GRANT B.
ALLEN, GRANT--[29]MYS--5 NOVELS 1895-17
POWER, CECIL--[2][18][22][29]MYS--
"PHILISTIA" 1884
WILSON, J. ARBUTHNOT--[23]CANADIAN/SF

ALLINGHAM, MARGERY LOUISE
MARCH, MAXWELL--[34]--
COLLINS "MAN OF DANGEROUS SECRETS" '33
COLLINS "ROGUE'S HOLLIDAY" '35
COLLINS "SHADOW IN THE HOUSE" '36

ALLISON, ERIC & MARY ANN
ALLISON, E.M.A.--[3]MYS--
DBLDY "THRU THE VALLEY OF THE DEAD"'83

ALLISON, MICHAEL F.L.
ALLEN, MIKE--[31]

ALLISON, RUTH
RICE, ALLISON--W/JANET RICE,[1][2]
ROSE, ALLISON--W/JANET ROSE,[2]

ALLISON, WILLIAM
BLINKHOOLIE--[3]MYS--
"BLAIRMOUNT" '09

ALLMENDINGER, KARL
BORUS v. MUHLAU, KARL--[39]GERMAN
NABOR, FELIX--[39]GERMAN

ALLRED, JOE
STEIN, F.N.--[2]

ALLVINE, GLENDON
SAGE, DANA--[3]MYS--
SIMON "MOON WAS RED" '44
SIMON "22 BROTHERS" '50

ALMAN, DAVID & EMILY
DAVID, EMILY--[1][22][31]AMERICAN

ALMAZAN, PASCUAL
PALOMAR, NATAL DEL--[30]MEXICAN--
ONE HISTORICAL NOVEL

ALMEDINGEN, MARTHA EDITH
ALMEDINGEN, E.M.--[7]SF--
HUTCH "STAND FAST, BELOVED CITY" '54

ALMODOVAR, PEDRO
DIFUSA, PATI--[31]

ALMQUIST, JOHN
APPLETON, VICTOR II--[7]HP--
STSY "TOM SWIFT & HIS JETMARINE"
STSY "TOM SWIFT & HIS ROCKET SHIP"

ALPERS, HANS JOACHIM
ANDREAS, JURGEN--[23][39]GERMAN/SF/JUV
DE VRIES, JORN--[39]GERMAN
FORRESTER, THORN--W/GERD MAXIMOVIC,
GERMAN/SF,HP
HERBST, DANIEL--W/R.M. HAHN, GERMAN/SF
KERN, GREGORY--[39]GERMAN,HP
KURZ, HANS--[39]GERMAN
MORRISON, MISKA--[39]GERMAN
VIETON, PETER T.--[39]GERMAN

ALPERS, MARY ROSE
CAMPION, SARAH--[8][13]AUSTRALIAN

ALPERT, HOLLIS
CARROLL, ROBERT--[3][22][31]AMERICAN/MYS--
DIAL "A DISAPPEARANCE" '75

ALPERT, RICHARD
DASS, RAM--[31]

ALPHONSO-KARKALA, JOHN B.
KARKALA, JOHN A.--[31]
KARKALA, JOHN B.A.--[31]

ALRED, MARGARET
SAUNDERS, ANNE--[9][21][26]--
"DANCING IN THE SHADOWS"
"HEATHER IS WINDBLOWN"
"CIRCLES OF FATE"

ALSOBROOK, ROSALYN
DELANEY, GINA--W/PATRICIA RAE WALLS,[9]ROM--
"WILD FURY"
"WILD DESTINY"
FRIENDS, JALYNN--W/JEAN HAUGHT,[9][21][26]
ROM--"TEXAS RAPTURE"

ALSOP, MARY O'HARA
O'HARA, MARY--[22][28][31][33]AMERICAN--
6 NOVELS '41-79
STURE-VASA, MARY--[1][28][33]AMERICAN--
CHRISTOPHER "LET US SAY GRACE" '30

ALSTON, MARY NIVEN
NIVEN, MARIAN--[1]

ALTEN, INGRID
MAWATANI, NANATA--[39]GERMAN

ALTENHOFER, LUDWIG
PETIT, VICTOR--[39]GERMAN/JUV

ALTENHOFF, WOLFGANG
WOLFF, SEBASTIAN--[39]GERMAN

ALTER, JUDITH MACBAIN
ALTER, JUDY--[31][33]

ALTER, ROBERT EDMOND
RAYMOND, ROBERT--[22][32][33]MYS--
SUS "SURVIVAL" NOV '60
SUS "CRUEL VOYAGE" APR '61
RETLA, ROBERT--[2][22][32][33]MYS--
BZ "MARINUS GHOST" NOV '65

ALTHOUSE, LAWRENCE [W]
ALTHOUSE, LARRY--[31]

ALTHUSSER, LOUIS
ALTHUSSER, L.--[31]

AUTHORS

ALTMAN, IRWIN
ALTMAN, LARRY--[1][31]

ALTMAN, LINDA JACOBS
BLACKBURN, CLAIRE--[31]
JACOBS, LINDA--[31]

ALTSHULER, HARRY
BRUNS, JOE--[31]
FAUST, ALEXANDER--[2][11]

ALTSHULLER, GENRIKH SAUL.
ALTOV, GENRIKH--[7][23]RUSSIAN/SF--
MacM "BALLAD OF THE STARS" '82

ALVAREZ, ALEJANDRO RODR.
CASONA, ALEJANDRO--[20][22][31]SPANISH

ALVAREZ, JOSE S.
CARRIZO, FABIO--[20]SPANISH

ALVAREZ, MIGUEL N. LIRA
LIRA, FELIPE--[30]MEXICAN

ALVENSLEBEN, KARL LUDWIG
ANGE, L. v.--[39]GERMAN/SF
SELLEN, GUSTAV--[39]GERMAN/SF

ALVING, FANNY
MAJA X--[29]MYS--
"JOSEFSSON PA DROTTRINGGATAN" '18

ALYWORTH, SUSAN
GALE, SHANNON--[21]ROM--
"BENEATH SIERRA SKIES"

ALZMANN, HELMUT
AHLSEN, LEOPOLD--[39]GERMAN

AMABILE, GEORGE
LOS, GEORGE--[31]

AMAMOO, JOSEPH GODSON
KAMBU, JOSEPH--[22][31]AFRICAN-ENGLISH

AMAND, MULK RAJ
MUNI, NARAD--[1]

AMANN, MARILYN MEDLOCK
STEVENS, AMANDA--[21][26]ROM--5 NOVELS

AMARILLAS, KAREN L.
AMARILLAS, SUSAN--CRPG,[26]ROM--
HARL "SNOW ANGEL"
HARL "SILVER & STEEL" '94

AMATORA,[SISTER] MARY
FLEURY, DELPHINE--[22][31]AMERICAN

AMBERGER, CARL WILHELM
WILHELM am BERGER, CARL--[39]GERMAN

AMBLER, DAIL
KARTA, NAT--S. HOLLAND, SCION CKLST,
PP 27,[34]HP--
SCION "SOME DAME" '53
SPADE, DANNY--STEVE HOLLAND, SCION CKLIST
PP 27,[22][34]MYS--32 NOVELS '50-3

AMBLER, ERIC
REED, ELIOT--W/CHARLES RODDA,
[5][22][34][36]MYS--
DBLDY "SKY TRIP" '50
DBLDY "TENDER TO DANGER" '51
DBLDY "TENDER TO MOONLIGHT" '52
COLLINS "MARAS AFFAIR" '53

AMBLER, ERIC [CONT]
MACIRE, ESOR B.--[1][22][31]

AMBROSE, ERIC [S]
RENNIE, CHRISTOPHER--[1][22]
VANCE, EDGAR--[1][22]

AMBROSE, LOTTIE F.
BIAGI, L.D.--[7][23]SF--
"CENTAURIANS" '11

AMBROSE, MICHAEL E.
BRANE, REGINALD--[2]
MOSS, DUNCAN--[2]
THACKERY, C.T.--[2]

AMBROSE, WILLIAM
HARBIN, JOEL--[2]

AMBRUS, GYOZO LASZLO
AMBRUS, VICTOR G.--[31]

AMERLING, MAJA
MERLING, MAJA--[39]GERMAN

AMERSKI, BETH
ANDERSON, BETH--[9]ROM
ANDERSON, BETT--[32]--
AHMM "CLOSED FOR THE SEASON" AUG '76
STANLEY, BETH--[9][21][26]ROM--
"COUNT ON ME"

AMES, ELEANOR MARIA
KIRK, ELEANOR--[2][32]

AMES, FRANCES H.
WATSON, FRANK--[1][22][32]AMERICAN/MYS--
TR "TAR & FEATHERS" JUN '56

AMES, JOSEPH BUSHNELL
GUNNISON, LYNN--[1]

AMES, LEE J.
DAVID, JONATHAN--[31][33]

AMES, SARAH RACHEL S.
GAINHAM, SARAH--[3][18][21][26][29][31]
MYS/ROM--11 NOVELS '56-83

AMESBURY, JAMES E.
ZORE, HYMAN--S. HOLLAND, SCION CKLST,
PP 27, P11,HP--
SCION "THE LADY IS A TRAMP" '53

AMFT, MARION JANET
REITH, MARION--[1]
SCHAELING, MARIANNE--[1]

AMIDON, WILLIAM VINCENT
AMIDON, BILL--[3][14]
ROSS, PAUL--W/NATHANIEL FREEDLAND,[34]HP--
POPLB "DYNAMITE MONSTER BOOGIE
CONCERT" '75
TAYLOR, JESSIE--[14]--
OLYMP OPS#11 "PLEASURE PRINCIPLE" '69

AMINOFF, IVAN T.E.
RADSCHA--[29]MYS - 26 BOOKS '11-18
VOX--[29]MYS "INVASIONEN" '12

AMIS, KINGSLEY W[ILLIAM]
FLEMING, IAN--A.J. HUBIN--
EQMM OCT '86--GHOSTED
MARKAM, ROBERT--[2][3][11][22]MYS--
CAPE "COLONEL SUN" '68
TANNER, WILLIAM--[1]

AUTHORS

AMLER, IRENE
AMBER, UTE--[39]GERMAN
FINCH, ARIN--[39]GERMAN
THOMAS, KATHRIN--[39]GERMAN

AMMAN, MARILYN MEDLOCK
MEDLOCK, MARILYN--[9]ROM
STEVENS, AMANDA--[9][21]ROM--
"KILLING MOON"
"THE DREAMING"

AMON, HANS-WALTER
ALKEN, INA--[39]GERMAN

AMOR, ANNE CLARK
CLARKE, ANNE--[1]

AMOROS, JUAN BATISTA
LANZA, SILVERO--[1]

AMORY, MARK
COOPER, SOPHIE--[1][31]

AMUNDSEN, ENGEBRET
JAERVEN, OSCAR--[37]NORWEGIAN/MYS--
'LYS OG SKYGGE' - 23 NVLS '25

AMUNDSEN, JOHAN FREDRIK
PAASCHE, JOHAN FREDRIK--[22]NORWEGIAN

AMY, WILLIAM LACEY
ALLAN, LUKE--[3][22][28]MYS--
"THE BEAST" '24
JARROLDS "THE WHITE CAMEL" '26
AMY, LACEY--
JENKINS "THE MANY-COLORED THREAD" '32 & OTHERS

ANAND, VALERIE
BUCKLEY, FIONA--[31]

ANASTOS, ANDREA LASONDE M
MELROSE, ANDREA LASONDE--[7]--
SEABURY PRESS "NINE VISIONS: A BOOK OF FANTASIES" '83

ANCELET, BARRY JEAN
ARCENEAUX, JEAN--[31]

ANDALORO, MICHAEL
MYKEL, A.W.--V.BERCH LTR TO HUBIN FEB'94--
ST. MARTIN'S "WIND-CHIME LEGACY" '80
ST. MARTIN'S "THE SALAMANDER GLASS" '83

ANDERMANN, BRIGITTE
ALTENAU, BRIGITTE--[39]GERMAN/JUV

ANDERS, DONNA CAROLYN
CREFELD, DONNA CAROLYN A.--[31]

ANDERS, EDITH [M] ENGLAND
ENGLAND, E.M.--[1][22][31]AUSTRALIAN
ENGLAND, EDITH--[1]AUSTRALIAN

ANDERS, LUDWIG FERDINAND
STOLLE, FERDINAND--[39]GERMAN/SF

ANDERSDATTER, KARLA M.
MARGARET, KARLA--[31][33]

ANDERSEN, JEWELL
ANDERSEN, JUEL--[1]

ANDERSEN, MARTIN
ANDERSEN NEXO, MARTIN--[1]

ANDERSEN, NILS
JOYSTON, RALF--[39]GERMAN/SF

ANDERSON, ADELINE C.
ANDERSON, CATHERINE--[9][10][21]ROM--
"REASONABLE DOUBT"
"WITHOUT A TRACE"
"SWITCHBACK"

ANDERSON, ALAN RITNER
ANDERSON, LARS--ECHOES #24--
PULP ?? UNCONFIRMED ??
ELLIS, THELMA B.--ECHOES #24--
PULP ?? UNCONFIRMED ??

ANDERSON, ANN KIEMEL
KIEMEL, ANN--[31]

ANDERSON, ARTHUR HENRY
HENRY, ARTHUR--[1]

ANDERSON, BETTY
CANYON, CLAUDIA--[1][3][22]MYS--
ARCADIA "THE JUNIOR LEAGUE MURDERS" '54

ANDERSON, BLAINE AISLINN
ANDERSON, BLAINE--[21]ROM--
"DESTINY'S KISS"
"LOVE'S SWEET CAPTIVE"

ANDERSON, CATHERINE CORL.
ANDERSON, C.C.--[33]
ANDERSON, MRS. MELVIN--[33]
CORALIE--[33]
LEE, CORA--[31][33]

ANDERSON, CHARLES
ANDERSON, CHUCK--[31]

ANDERSON, CHARLES FREER
DINAHANDBU--[1]

ANDERSON, CHESTER [V.J.]
ANDERSON, C.V.--[23]SF
BLAKE, ANDREW--W/LAURENCE JANIFER,[2]

ANDERSON, CLARENCE W.
ANDERSON, C.W.--[1]

ANDERSON, DANA
PENDER, LAURA--[9][26][34]MYS/ROM--
7 HARLEQUIN NOVELS '80s & 90s

ANDERSON, DAVID POOLE
ANDERSON, DAVE--[31][33]

ANDERSON, DENNIS
MEREK, JACK--V.BERCH LTR TO HUBIN '94--
WARNER "TARGET STEALTH" '89
CONTEMPORARY "BLACKBIRD" '90

ANDERSON, EDGAR
ANDERSON, EDGARS--[1][31]

ANDERSON, G.J.B.
CAPTAIN DANGERFIELD--[1]
FIELDING, HOWARD--[1]
LYNN, MAX--[1]

ANDERSON, GEORGE LEE
ANDERSON, SPARKY--[31]

ANDERSON, GRACE FOX
FOX, GRACE--[1][31][33]

ANDERSON, HANS CHRISTIAN
WALTER, VILLIAM CHRISTIAN--[33]

ANDERSON, HARRY WALTER
GREY, VIVIAN--[34]MYS--
EVERETT "TERROR OF THE ROAD" 1900
EVERETT "STORIES OF SCOTLAND YARD" 1906

ANDERSON, JACKSON NORTHM.
ANDERSON, JACK--[31][32]MYS--
DS "REG'LAR ARMY MAN" OCT '44

ANDERSON, JAMES NORMAN
ANDERSON, J.N.--[31]

ANDERSON, JO
BENSON, STELLA--[2][32]

ANDERSON, JOAN W.
ANDERS, JEANNE--[31]

ANDERSON, JOHN KINLOCH
ANDERSON, JOHN K.--[31]

ANDERSON, JOHN L.
ANDERSON, LONZO--[31]

ANDERSON, KAREN
KRUSE, JUNE MILLICHAMP--[1][2][11][32]

ANDERSON, LUCIA LEWIS
LEWIS, LUCIA Z.--[31][33]

ANDERSON, MADELEINE P.
PALTENGHI, MADELEINE--[1][22]AMERICAN--
CHILDREN'S BOOKS

ANDERSON, MARGARET
ANDERSON, MAGGIE--[31]

ANDERSON, MARLENE J.
LANCASTER, JOAN--[9][21][26]ROM--
"PROMISE ME RAINBOWS"
"SUMMER EYES"

ANDERSON, MRS. J.O.
BENSON, STELLA--[11]SF

ANDERSON, POUL [W]
CRAIG, A.A.--[2][11][16][23][31][33]SF
KARAGEORGE, MICHAEL--[2][11][16][23][31]SF
SANDERS, WINSTON P.--[2][11][16][23]
[29][32][33]SF

ANDERSON, ROBERT
ANDERSON, CLIFFORD--W/CLIFFORD M.IRVING &
RICHARD GARDNER,[1]

ANDERSON, ROBERT C.
COTTLE, CHARLES--[1][31]

ANDERSON, ROBERTA
MICHAELS, FERN--W/MARY KUCZKIR,
[1][3][21]MYS/ROM--
MacM "PANDA BEAR IS CRITICAL" '82

ANDERSON, ROSA
KAULITZ-NIEDECK, R.--[1]

ANDERSON, SHERWOOD
FEVER, BUCK--[1]

ANDERSON, SHIRLEY LORD
LORD, SHIRLEY--[1][21][26]ROM--
"GOLDEN HILL"
"ONE OF MY BEST FRIENDS"

ANDERSON, STELLA BENSON
BENSON, STELLA--[1]

ANDERSON, SUSAN M.
RANDALL, LINDSAY--[9][21][26]ROM--5 NOVELS

ANDERSON, UELL STANLEY
ANDERSON, U.S.--[31]--
POPLB EB-72 "HARD & FAST" '56
DUDGEON, ROBERT--J. HOFFMANN,PP 40,P18,HP--
GERM PANTH 152 RPRT OF
POPLB EB-72 "HARD & FAST"

ANDERSON, VIRGINIA
ASHE, MEGAN--[9][21][26]ROM--
"A MOUNTAIN MAN"
"THE LIGHTNING TOUCH"

ANDERSON, VIRGINIA [R.C.]
HILL, HYACINTHE--[31]

ANDERSON, WALTER TRUETT
ANDERSON, WALT--[31]

ANDERSON, WILLIAM
FORBES, ALEXANDER--[13]AUSTRALIAN

ANDERSON, WILLIAM C.
ANDERSON, ANDY--[1][2][11][23]SF

ANDERSON,[LADY] FLAVIA
PORTOBELLO, PETRONELLA--[1]

ANDERSSON, C. DEAN
DRAKE, ASA--W/NINA R. ANDERSSON,[7][26]
AVON "CRIMSON KISSES" '81
AVON "LAIR OF ANCIENT DREAMS" '72
DRAKE, ASA--[7]SF--
POPLB "HEL #1-#3" '85-86

ANDERSSON, ERIK
FURA, ERIK ASON--[29]MYS--
"DEN VIDLYFTIGA ZIGENERSKAN" '80

ANDERSSON, NINA ROMBERG
ARCHER, JANE--HAWK/ROMBERG INTRVW,[9][21]ROM--
"SILKEN SPURS & WILD WIND" & 14 MORE
DRAKE, ASA--W/C. DEAN ANDERSSON,
[7][21][26]SF--
AVON "CRIMSON KISSES" '81
AVON "LAIR OF ANCIENT DREAMS" '82
ROMBERG, NINA--[7][21]ROM/SF--
PINN "SPIRIT STALKER" '89

ANDERSSON, STIG
DAGERMAN, STIG--[1]
QROLL--[1]

ANDERTON, JOANNE GAST
ANDERTON, JOHANA GAST--[31]
ANDERTON, OHANA GAST--[1][31]

ANDONIAN, JEANNE
MAY, JANINE--[1]

ANDRADE, H.
HASKINS, DICK--[1]

ANDRE, HERBERT
ANDREW, BERT--[39]GERMAN/SF

ANDRE,[K] MICHAEL
FRETTER, T.W.--[1][31]
PUCK, Y.U.--[1]

AUTHORS

ANDREAS, WILLY
CURWILL, W.--[39]GERMAN

ANDREAS-DRANERT, PETER W.
ALEXANDER, FRITZ--[39]GERMAN
RICHTER, HANNES--[39]GERMAN

ANDREEV, VASILII D.
ANDREEV, ALEXSANDR--[1]

ANDRESEN, JOHN H[ENRY] JR
ANDRESEN, JACK--[31]

ANDRESEN, JULIA TETEL
ANDRESEN, JULIE--[1]
JOYCE, JULIA--[9][21][26][31]ROM--
"LORD LAXTON'S WILL"
JOYCE, JULIE--[1]
TETEL, JULIE--[9][21][26]ROM--8 NOVELS

ANDREVON, JEAN-PIERRE
BRUTSCHE, ALPHONSE--[1][2][11]

ANDREW, AVERY THORNE
BARNES, ELIZABETH--[21][26]ROM--4 NOVELS

ANDREW, JOHN
CHESTER, PETER--[29]MYS--
JENKINS "KILLING COMES EASY" '58
JENKINS "MURDER FORESTALLED" '60
JENKINS "THE PAY-GRAB MURDERS" '62

ANDREWS, ALLEN
COTTON, BILLY--[1]
PIERREPOINT, ALBERT--[1]

ANDREWS, BARBARA L. ROCK
ANDREWS, BARBARA--[21]ROM--19 NOVELS

ANDREWS, CECILY ISOBEL
WEST, REBECCA--[2][7][32]MYS/SF--
"HARRIET HUME: A LONDON FANTASY" '29
SUS "DELIVERANCE" JUL '59
EQMM "IF THE JOURNEY HAD NO END"APR'61

ANDREWS, CLARENCE A.
RANDALL, STEVE--[1]

ANDREWS, ELIZA FRANCES
HAY, ELZEY--[1]

ANDREWS, ELIZABETH
HAINSTOCK--[1]

ANDREWS, JAMES SYDNEY
ANDREWS, J.S.--[1]

ANDREWS, JOHN MALCOLM
MALCOLM, JOHN--[3][18]MYS--
COLLINS "A BLACK ROOM IN SOMERS TOWN"'85
COLLINS "GODWIN SIDEBOARD" '85
COLLINS "THE GWEN JOHN SCULPTURE" '85

ANDREWS, JULIE
EDWARDS, JULIE--[31][33]

ANDREWS, KEITH & CLARE
CLAIRE, KEITH--[1][2][7][31]SF--
HOLT "THE OTHERWISE GIRL" '76

ANDREWS, LUCILLA MATHEW
GORDON, DIANA--[3][17][21][26]MYS/ROM--
CORGI "A FEW DAYS IN ENDEL" '68
MARCUS, JOANNA--[9][29][34]MYS--
BARRIE "A FEW DAYS IN ENDEL" '78
HUTCH "MARSH BLOOD" '80

ANDREWS, MERVYN
CONWAY, JOHN--[35]AUSTRALIAN--
HRWTZ PB373 "THOSE WERE THE
WICKED DAYS" '68
DEL MAR, JUSTIN--[35]AUSTRALIAN--
HRWTZ PB286 "CRIMSON WAKE" '66
HRWTZ PB298 "DEVIL'S DAUGHTER" '67
HRWTZ PB327 "BUCCANEER'S BOOTY" '67
HUNT, ROGER--[35]AUSTRALIAN,HP--
HRWTZ "AUSTRALIAN ACES" '62
HRWTZ "BLOOD ON BEERSHEBA" '63
PASQUALI, SELENE--[35]AUSTRALIAN--
HRWTZ PB313 "VIRGIN OF FATU HIVA" '67

ANDREWS, PATRICK E.
LANSING, JOHN--[28][34]WAR/THRL--
20 NOVELS '83-90
LEE, PATRICK--J.R. BAKER-ECHOES#5,P7,HP--
SIX-GUN SAMURAI "BUSHIDO VENGEANCE" '81
"THE DEVIL'S BOWMAN" '81

ANDREWS, PETER J.
TORRO, PEL--S. HOLLAND, PP#39, P38--
COBRA "WHITE LIGHTNING" '57

ANDREWS, WAYNE
O'REILLY, MONTAGU--[22]AMERICAN

ANDREWS, WILLIAM L.
SETTLE, EDITH--[1][22]ENGLISH

ANDREWS,[C] ROBERT D.
DOUGLAS, ROBERT--[1][31]
HARDY, DOUGLAS--[1][31]

ANDREYEV, LEONID N.
LYNCH, JAMES--[31]

ANDRIESSEN, DAVID
POYER, D.C.--[2]

ANDRUS, L.R.
ANDRE, LEE--[1][2][11]

ANDRZEJEWSKI, JERZY
ANDRZEYEVSKI, GEORGE--[1][31]

ANGELL, BRYAN MARY DOYLE
CROMARSH, H. RIPLEY--[34]MYS--
RICHARDS "EPISODES OF MARGE" '03
WARD "SECRET OF MOOR COTTAGE" '07

ANGELL, FRANK JOSEPH
ANGELILLI, FRANK JOSEPH--[31]

ANGELO, NANCY CAROLYN H.
DE ANGELIS, NANCY--[1]

ANGER, MARTIN
FORSTER, JOACHIM--[39]GERMAN/JUV

ANGERS, FELICITE
CONAN, LURIE--[1]

ANGLOWITZ, MAURICE [MICK]
DEKKER, JOHNNY--[27][34]ENGLISH, MARTIN &
REID, WESTERN & GANGSTER NVLS '44-50

ANGOFF, CHARLES
HINTON, RICHARD W.--[2][22][31]AMERICAN--
KNOPF "ARSENAL FOR SCEPTICS" '34

ANGREMY, JEAN-PIERRE
MARLOT, RAYMOND--[1]
REMY, PIERRE-JEAN--[1][34]MYS--
MORROW "COMPARTMENT EAST" '80

AUTHORS

ANGSTMANN, AUGUSTIN
ANGSTMANN, GUSTL--[39]GERMAN

ANGUS, SYLVIA
LAZLO, KATE--[1][31]

ANGUS-BUTTERWORTH, LIONEL
BUTTERWORTH, LIONEL M.A.--[31]

ANHALT, EDWARD
HOLT, ANDREW--W.R. COX, ECHOES 22, P6, [31][32]MYS--
DT "A BIER FOR BELINDA" SEPT '61

ANNAND, ALAN
FOXX, ALEISTER--D. SKENE-MELVIN- '93 BOUCHERCON PROG, MYS--
MARKS, ALAN--D. SKENE-MELVIN- '93 BOUCHERCON PROG, MYS--
BELM "SKYRAIDERS" '79
BELM "ANTENNA SYNDROME"

ANOBILE, ULLA [K]
KAKONEN, ULLA--[1][31]

ANSCHUETZ, A.O.
RUST, ALBERT OTTO--[39]GERMAN

ANSCOMBE, GERTRUDE ELIZ.
ANSCOMBE, ELIZABETH--[31]

ANSELL, EDWARD C.T.
CRAD, JOSEPH--[8]

ANSLE, DOROTHY PHOEBE
BARNES, MARGARET CAMPBELL--[9]ROM
CONWAY, LAURA--[2][7][9][17][26][34], ENGLISH,ROM--
COLLINS "THE UNFORGOTTEN" '67
COLLINS "LONELY DREAMER"'72
COLLINS "STRANGE VISITOR" '73
COLLINS "IF THIS BE SIN" '75 & OTHER
ELSNA, HEBE--[3][7][9][17][21][26]MYS/ROM--
COLLINS "TAKE HEED OF LOVING ME" '70
HALE "STRANGE VISITOR" '56
LANCASTER, VICKY--[8][9][17][21]ROM
OLIVANE, MARY--[17]ROM--
"THE SOUL OF MARY OLIVANE" '73
SNOW, LYNDON--[3][9][17][21]ROM/MYS--
COLLINS "MOMENT OF TRUTH" '68
COLLINS "FRANCESCA" '70
COLLINS "YESTERDAY & TOMORROW" '71

ANSON, CHARLES VERNON
ANSON, CAPT.--[7]SF

ANTHEILL, GEORGE J.C.
BISHOP, STACEY--[3]MYS--
FABER "DEATH IN THE DARK" '30

ANTHONY, BARBARA
BARBER, ANTONIA--[2][8][9][11][31][33]

ANTHONY, EDWARD
EDAR--[1]
GATE, A.G.--[8]

ANTON, UWE
ASIMUFF, ISAAK--W/R.M. HAHN,[39]GERMAN/SF
BAXTER, MARK--[39]GERMAN,HP
BRAUN, CARSTEN--[39]GERMAN
COLLINS, FREDERIC--[39]GERMAN,HP
DE LORCA, FRANK--[39]GERMAN,HP
DEREK, LOGAN--W/U. VOHL,[39]GERMAN
GHOST, HENRY--[39]GERMAN,HP
LAMONT, ROBERT--[39]GERMAN,HP

ANTON, UWE [CONT]
MEUER, CARSTEN--[39]GERMAN
PALMER, L.D.--[39]GERMAN
QUINN, HENRY--W/RANIER ZUBEIL,[39]GERMAN
RADEMACHER, HEIKE--[39]GERMAN
SHOCKER, DAN--[39]GERMAN,HP
SLADE, TED--[39]GERMAN
SPIDER, JOHN--[39]GERMAN,HP
TRENTON, OLSH--[39]GERMAN,HP
USHER, H.P.--[39]GERMAN,HP
WOLFF-SASSE, HERMANN--[39]GERMAN

ANTONACCI, ROBERT J.
BARR, JENE--W/JENE BARR COHEN,[31]--
"YOUNG CHAMPIONS" SERIES-4 BOOKS '56-62

ANTONI, FRIDE [E.R.]
LENNART, MARK--[29]MYS

ANTONICK, ROBERT J.
KAMIN, NICK--[2][11][23][31]AMERICAN/SF--
"EARTHRIM" '69
"THE HEROD MEN" '71

ANTONIO, DIANE
ANTHONY, DIANE--[9][21][26]ROM--
"ONCE A LOVER"
"OUT OF A DREAM"
"SWEET INDULGENCE"
LYNDON, DIANA--[9][21][26]ROM--
"HER HEART'S DESIRE"
"MY LORD, MY LOVE"
"COUNTRY ROSE"

ANTONISEN, O. ARTHUR J.
OMRE, ARTHUR--[3][29]MYS--
APPLETON "FLIGHT" '40

ANTSCHEL, PAUL
CELAN, PAUL--[22]GERMAN

ANZENGRUBER, LUDWIG
GRUBER, LUDWIG--[39]GERMAN

APELIAN, ALBERT SOLOMON
APILENTZ--[31]

APPEL, LISELOTTE
DELION, ELISABETH CHARL.--[39]GERMAN
FORTRIDE, L.A.--[39]GERMAN/MYS

APPEL, MARTIN E[LIOT]
APPEL, MARTY--[31][33]

APPEL, WALTER
BAXTER, MARK--[39]GERMAN,HP
CAMERON, JOHN--[39]GERMAN,HP
CASTELLO, CARINA--[39]GERMAN
COOPER, STEVE--[39]GERMAN,HP
COTTON, JERRY--[39]GERMAN,HP
DALLAS, DAN--[39]GERMAN
DARK, JASON--[39]GERMAN,HP
DENVER, MARK--[39]GERMAN
ELLIOT, BRIAN--[39]GERMAN,HP
EVANS, FRANK--[39]GERMAN
EVANS, LINDA--[39]GERMAN
KENT, ROY--[39]GERMAN
KILBURN, MILES--[39]GERMAN
KOJAK--[39]GERMAN
LAMONT, ROBERT--[39]GERMAN,HP
LATIMER, HONDO--[39]GERMAN/WEST,HP
MORTON, JACK--[39]GERMAN,HP
REICHARDT, FRANK--[39]GERMAN
ROMEN, ROBERT--[39]GERMAN
SANDBERG, CORINNA--[39]GERMAN
SLADE, JACK--[39]GERMAN,HP

APPEL, WALTER [CONT]
SPIDER, JOHN--[39]GERMAN,HP
WARREN, EARL--[39]GERMAN
WARREN, LINDA--[39]GERMAN

APPIGNANESI, LISA
AYRE, JESSICA--[31]

APPLEBAUM, A.E.
APPLE, A.E.--R. SAMPSON, ECHOES #47,[37]--
DSM 'MR. CHANG' STORIES '24-6

APPLEBAUM, STAN
KEITH, ROBERT--[1][31][33]

APPLEBY, CAROL MCAFEE
MORGAN, CAROL MCAFEE--[8]

APPLEBY, KENNETH PHILIP
APPLEBY, KEN--[23]SF

APPLEGATE, KATHERINE
KENDALL, KATHERINE--[9][21][26]ROM--
"THE MIDAS TOUCH"
"FIRST & FOREVER"

APPLEMAN, JOHN ALAN
DALEY, BILL--[1]
MONTROSE, JAMES ST. DAVID--[1]

APPLEMAN, MARK JEROME
JEROME, MARK--[31]

APPLEMAN, M[ARJORIE] H.
APPLEMAN, MARGIE--[31]

APPLETON, JAMES HENRY
APPLETON, JAY--[31]

APPLEY, MORTIMER HERBERT
APPLEZWEIG, M.H.--[22][31]

APPLIN, ARTHUR
SWIFT, JULIAN--[1][22]MYS

APPS, EDWIN
WRAITH, JOHN--W/PAULINE DEVANEY,[8]

APPS, JEROLD W.
APPS, JERRY--[31]--
"LAND STILL LIVES" '70
"CABIN IN THE COUNTRY" '72

AQUINO, BENIGNO S. JR.
AQUINO, NINOY--[31]

ARAGON, LOUIS
DE ROUTISIE, ALBERT--[31]
DE SAINT ROMAN, ARNAUD--[31]
LA COLERE, FRANCOIS--[31]
LACOLERE, FRANCOIS--[31]

ARBATOV, GEORGI [A]
ARBATOV, G.A.--[31]
ARBATOV, YURI ARKADEVICH--[31]

ARCHER, GEORGE W.
BENDBOW, HESPER--[1]

ARCHER, REX
A., REX--BAPC NWSLTR #9--
COVER ARTIST FOR PAN, ARROW & PANTHER

ARCHIBALD, CATHERINE
ARCHER, CATHERINE--[26]ROM--
"ROSE AMONG THORNS"

ARCHIBALD, JOSEPH S.
ARCHIBALD, JOE--[31][32][33]MYS--
SA "THE DEFUNCT BLONDE" NOV '54
MSMM "CRIME OF HIS LIFE" MAR '59
PH "DOCTOR'S ORDERS" APR '62

ARCONE, SONYA
GOODMAN, SONYA--[1][31]

ARD, WILLIAM [THOMAS]
COX, W.R.--L. ROBBINS LTR MAR '94, PULP
HAMLIN, KEN--V. BERCH, MONARCH PSEUDS.,
BAE 9,P26--
MON 145"GUNS OF REVENGE" '60
KERR, BEN--[3][31]MYS--
POPLB 467 "SHAKEDOWN" '52
POPLB 653 "DOWN I GO" '55
POPLB 785 "DAMNED IF HE DOES" '56
POPLB 763 "I FEAR YOU NOT" '56
POPLB 803 "CLUB 17" '57
POPLB EB104 "THE BLONDE &
JOHNNY MALLOY" '58
LARGO, LOU--L. ROBBINS LTR MAR '94, PULP
MORAN,MIKE--[3][18][22][29]--
POPLB 494 "DOUBLECROSS" '53
WARD, JONAS--V. BERCH, GM PSEUDS, PP 33,
[1][19]HP, ORIGINATED & WROTE 1ST FIVE
& STARTED "BUCHANAN ON THE PROD",
ROBERT SILVERBERG FINISHED
WILLS, THOMAS--JEAN F. LE DEIST,BAE 18,P9,
V. BERCH, GM PSEUDS, PP 33
[18][22][29][34]--
LION 87 "YOU'LL GET YOURS" '52
GM 490 "MINE TO AVENGE" '55

ARDAGH, ALICE MAUD
ESPERANCE--[1]

ARDIES, TOM
TROLLEY, JACK--PUBL WEEKLY REVIEW, MYS--
"BALBOA FIREFLY" '94

ARDMORE, JANE KESNER
MORRIS, JANE--[1]

ARGLES, THEODORE EMILE
GREY, HAROLD--[13]AUSTRALIAN
PILGRIM, A--[13]AUSTRALIAN

ARGUILE, CHERYL
TEMPLE, SARAH--[21][26]ROM--
"KINDRED SPIRITS"
"LIFELINE"
"THE LIBERATION OF LAYLA"

ARGYRIS, HELEN
ARCHERY, HELEN--[26]ROM--
"THE SEASON OF LOVING"
"THE AGE OF ELEGANCE"
ARGERS, HELEN--[26]ROM--
"LADY OF INDEPENDENCE"
"CAPTAIN'S LADY"
"AN UNLIKELY LADY"
"A SCANDALOUS LADY"

ARHOSUO, URPO
ANTTALA, ESA--[29]MYS

ARKIN, ALAN [WOLF]
SHORT, ROGER--[33]

ARKLEY, ARTHUR J[AMES]
HACKETT, LEE--[1][31]

ARLANDSON, LEONE
RYLAND, LEE--[1]

ARMAGNAC, A.L.
CARTER, NICHOLAS--[3]HP

ARMBRUSTER, FRANCIS E.
ARMBRUSTER, FRANK--[31]

ARMER, FRANK
CLAYFORD, JAMES--[34]MYS,HP--
FALCON "MAN CRAZY" '51
WALLACE, ARTHUR--[3]MYS--
VALHALLA-"PASSION PULLS THE TRIGGER"'36

ARMER, KARL MICHAEL
LINDBERG, MICHAEL--[39]GERMAN/SF

ARMING, FREDRICH WILHELM
FITZ-BERTH, WILLIAM--[39]GERMAN

ARMITAGE, AUDREY
MCCALL, K.T.--W/MURIEL WATKINS,[34][35][36]
AUSTRALIAN/MYS-- 22 HRWTZ NOVELS '57-8
NORTH, GERRY--W/MURIEL WATKINS,[35][36]
HRWTZ "MEET GERRY NORTH" '59
HRWTZ "GERRY NORTH COLLECTS" '59

ARMITAGE, DOROTHY
JANES, GENE--W/MURIEL WATKINS,[35]--
HRWTZ "LADY'S FOUND WANTON" '56
HRWTZ "SHROUD FOR A SHREW" '56

ARMITAGE, GARY EDRIC
ARMITAGE, G.E.--[31]
EDRIC, ROBERT--[31]

ARMITAGE, JOHN
HIN ME GEONG--[1]

ARMITAGE, REGINALD
GAY, NOEL--[8]

ARMOUR, R. COUTTS
BRISBANE, COUTTS--[1][2][3][11]MYS--
24 AMALGAMATED NOVELS '30-40
TREMAYNE, HARTLEY--[1]
WHITLEY, REID--[1][11][34]MYS--
5 ALDINE NOVELS '27-37

ARMSTRONG, CHARLES W.
STRONG'TH'ARM, C.--[1][2]

ARMSTRONG, CHARLOTTE
VALENTINE, JO--[3][5][17][18][21]MYS/ROM--
COWARD "THE TROUBLE IN THOR" '53

ARMSTRONG, CHRISTOPHER J.
ARMSTRONG, ANTHONY C.--[31]

ARMSTRONG, DOUGLAS A.
DOUGLAS, ALBERT--[1][22][31]
TRIBUNE--[1][22]
WINDSOR, REX--[1][22]

ARMSTRONG, ELIZABETH
TYLER, A.E.--[1]

ARMSTRONG, HAROLD HUNTER
AIKMAN, HENRY G.--[1]

ARMSTRONG, JOHN BYRON
BYRON, JOHN--[1][22][31]
WILLARD, CHARLES--[1][22]

ARMSTRONG, JOSEPH CHARLES
ARMSTRONG, JOE C.W.--[31]

ARMSTRONG, KEITH F.W.
CARM, MAC--[31]
KEITH X--[31]

ARMSTRONG, RICHARD
RENTON, CAM--[1]

ARMSTRONG, TERANCE IAN F.
GAWSWORTH, JOHN--[2][11][22][23]
ENGLISH/HOR/MYS

ARMSTRONG, THOMAS
O'NEILL, NOREEN--[9][21]ROM--
"ECSTASY'S DREAM"

ARMSTRONG, TILLY
ALEXANDER, KATE--[9][21][26][31]ROM--
"FIELDS OF BATTLE"
"FRIENDS & ENEMIES"
"PATHS OF PEACE"
LANGLEY, TANIA--[9][21][26][31]ROM--
GM "DAWN" '80

ARMSTRONG, WILLIAM A.
HAZELTON, ALEXANDER--[1][22][31]
SCOTTISH-ENGLISH

ARMSTRONG, WILLIMINA L.
DOST, ZAMIN KI--V. BERCH-ECHOES #8/[34]MYS--
DBLDY "SON OF POWER" '20

ARMSTRONG-JONES, ANTONY
ARMSTRONG JONES, TONY--[31]

ARNADE, CHARLES W.
GIERSCH, JULIUS--[1][31]

ARNALDI, JEAN
ARNOLD, JEAN--[1][34]MYS--
DIAL "PRETTYBELLE" '70

ARNANDEZ, RICHARD
EDWIN, BROTHER B.--[31]

ARNAUD, ARSENE
CLARETIE, JULES--[1]

ARNAZ Y DE ACHA, DESIDERI
ARNAZ, DESI--[31]

ARNEMANN, M.F.
KUHN, OTTO--[39]GERMAN,HP

ARNESEN, DAVID D.S.
BENDOW, PETER--[29]MYS--
"MISS EVES" '28
"DET SPOKER" '35
"MED EGEN INGANG" '35

ARNESEN, DAVID DIETRICH
MUNTER, HERRMANN--[29]MYS--
BRNDN "MUNTERGOKENS DETEKTIVBYRA"
RAFFT, BJORN--[29]MYS

ARNESON, D.J.
DR. DREW--W/ANTHONY TALLARICO,[7]--
"SECRET DRAWING GUIDE TO CREATING
SPACE CREATURES" '81

ARNETT, TOM
PENDLETON, DON--[34]HP--
GE "DEATH GAMES" '85
GE "HELL'S GATE" 86
STIVERS, DICK--[34]HP--
GE "DEATH BITES" '84
GE "FIVE RINGS OF FIRE" '84"

ARNETT, TOM [CONT]
STIVERS, DICK [CONT]
GE "BLOOD GAMBIT" '86
GE "IRON GOD" '86
GE "WORLD WAR III GAME" '86
GE "DEATH RIDE" '87
GE "FIRECROSS" '87

ARNOLD, ADELAIDE VICTORIA
ARNOLD, MRS. J.O.--[1][34]MYS--
NELSON "THE MERLEWOOD MYS" '28

ARNOLD, ADLAI FRANKLIN
FRANKLIN, A.--[31]

ARNOLD, ELIZABETH
KAUMANDI, KAVITA--[1]

ARNOLD, EMILY
MCCULLY, EMILY ARNOLD--[33]

ARNOLD, FREDERICK
PIGOT, F.--[34]--
WARD "STRANGEST JOURNEY OF MY LIFE
& OTHER STORIES" 1889

ARNOLD, GAIL E.H.
HAILEY, GAIL E.--[1]

ARNOLD, HAMNS
RAY-ATKINSON, JOHN--[39]GERMAN/ADV

ARNOLD, HILDEGARD-GERTRUD
LIND, HILTRUD--[39]GERMAN/JUV

ARNOLD, IGNAZ FERDINAND
ARNOLD, THEODOR F.K.--[39]GERMAN/SF

ARNOLD, JOHAN HEINRICH
ARNOLD, HEINI--[31]

ARNOLD, JUNE DAVIS
CARPENTER--[31]

ARNOLD, LINDA
GOODWIN, HOPE--V.BERCH LTR TO HUBIN '93--
MANOR "HOME FOR THE HEART" '79

ARNOLD, MADELYN M.
DAVIDSON, MELANIE--[31]

ARNOLD, MRS. J.O.
ARNOLD, A.V.--[3]MYS--
ARNOLD "THE CLUE" '27

ARNOLD, PETER
GRAHAM, MATTHEW--[31]

ARNOLD, RICHARD
COCH-Y-BONDDHU--[1][22][31]ENGLISH

ARNOLD, TIM
PFEIFER, TILL--[39]GERMAN
TOLD, GUSTAV--[39]GERMAN

ARNOLD, WALTER
BEHREND, MARGARETE--[39]GERMAN
BERGEDORF, SYLVIA--[39]GERMAN
BLEEKER, DON--[39]GERMAN/MYS
COOPER, STANLEY--[39]GERMAN/MYS
SCOTT, HENRY C.--[39]GERMAN/MYS
VON KIRCHSTEIN, DAGMAR--[39]GERMAN,HP

ARNOLD-FORSTER, MARK
FORSTER, MARK [ARNOLD]--[31]

ARNOLDI, HENRIQUE DI
DAUTHAGE, HEINRICH--[39]GERMAN

ARNOLDOVICH, ILYA
PETROV, EVGENY PETROVICH--W/EVGENY
KATEYEV,[22]RUSSIAN

ARNOSKY, HAMES EDWARD
ARNOSKY, JIM--[31]

ARNOT, ROBIN PAGE
CADE, JACK--[1]

ARNOULD, ARTHUR
MATTHEY, A.--[34]MYS--
VIZETELLY "THE VIRGIN WIDOW" 1887

ARNOW, HARRIETTE [L]
SIMPSON, HARRIETTE--[1][33]

ARONHEIM, YOHANAN
AHARONI, YOHANAN--[1]

ARONSON, VIRGINIA
LEWIS, SYLVAN R.--[1][31]

ARP, JEAN
ARP, HANS--[31]GERMAN-FRENCH

ARQUETTE, LOIS S. DUNCAN
CARDOZ, LOIS S.--[1]
DUNCAN, LOIS--[2][7][33]SF--NOVELS '80s
KERRY, LOIS--[1][33]--CHILDREN'S BOOKS

ARRABEL, FERNANDO
ARRABEL--[1][31]--CHILDREN'S BOOKS

ARRIETA, HERNAN DIAZ
ALONE--[20]SPANISH

ARROW, JAY
BRADFORD, GORDON--[7]SF--
"THE OCCULT COXSMAN"
"ARROW" MAY BE A PSEUDONYM AS WELL

ARROWSMITH, PAT
BARTON, PAT--[31]

ARROYA, STEPHEN JOSEPH
ARROYA, SANTANA--[21]ROM--
"BRIGHT GLOWS THE DAWN"

ARTAUD, ANTONIN
LE REVELER--[31]

ARTER, WALLACE E.
KAY, WALLACE--[1]

ARTHUR, CHESTER ALAN
ARTHUR, GAVIN--[8]

ARTHUR, FRANCES BROWN
CUNNINGHAM, RAY--[8]

ARTHUR, HERBERT
ARTHUR, BURT--[8]

ARTHUR, ROBERT
FELL, ANDREW--LACHMAN LIST
HALLIDAY, BRETT--W/W. RYERSON JOHNSON,
T. JOHNSON, ECHOES #23, P16,HP--
MSMM "FATAL MESSAGE" JUN '61
HITCHCOCK, ALFRED--[2]GHOSTED
MYSTERIOUS TRAVELER--[2]
NORMAN, JAY--LACHMAN LST,[32]MYS--
MY "THE HINT" JUN '52

ARTHUR, ROBERT [CONT]
WEST, JOHN--LACHMAN LST,[32]MYS--
MY "FOUND MONEY" NOV '51
MY "WEEPING WOMAN" '52
MY "THE VANISHING PASSENGER" JUN '52

ARTHUR, RUTH M.
HUGGINS, RUTH MABEL--[8]

ARTHUR, THOMAS H.
ARTHUR, TOM--[31]

ARTIN, THOMAS
ARTIN, TOM--[31]

ARTMANN, HANS CARL
KULL, STASI--[39]GERMAN/SF

ARTZ, EMILY
FRANCIS, EMILY--W/FRANCIS POKRAS YARIV, V. BERCH LTR TO HUBIN '94, MYS--
LEIS "ELENA" '77

ARUNDALE, GEORGE SYDNEY
ARUNDALE, G.S.--[31]

ARUTIUNIAN,MKRTICH G.
ARMEN, MKRTICH--[1]

ARVAY, HEINZ
ARMSTRONG, HENRY H.--[1][31]
ARVAY, HARRY--[1][31][34]MYS--
12 WAR/INTRIGUE NOVELS '75-9
5 GHOSTED BY GIL BREWER PER BREWER LTR

ARVONEN, HELEN
WORTH, MARGARET--[2][3][7][9][29]--
AVON "RED WINE OF RAPTURE" '73

ARY, SHEILA M.L.
LITTLEBOY, SHEILA M.--[1][22][31]
ENGLISH-AMERICAN

ASBELL, BERNARD
MAX, NICHOLAS--[1][2]

ASCASUBI, HILARIO
EL GALLO, ANICETO--[20]SPANISH

ASCH, SHOLEM
ASH, SHALOM--[31]

ASCHER, CAROL
LOPATE, CAROL--[1][31]

ASCHER, SHEILA
ASCHER, STRAUS--W/DENNIS STRAUS,[7][31]SF--
TRD PRESS "LTR TO AN UNKNOWN WOMAN" '80
TREACLE PRESS "MENACED ASSASSIN" '82
TOP STORIES "RED MOON, RED LAKE" '84

ASCHMANN, ALBERTA
CLARE, FRANCIS D.--[1][31]
FRANCIS, MOTHER MARY--[31]
MARY FRANCIS--[1]

ASH, BRIAN
DORLAND, HENRY--[1][8][31]

ASH, EDWARD CECIL
BRASSET, A.D.--[1]
FIELDING, A.D.--[1]
SYNTAX--[1]

ASH, MARY KAY WAGNER
KAY, MARY--[31]

ASH, RENE LEE
LEE, A.R.--[31]

ASHABRANNER, GERARD
GARNET, G.--L. RIBBINS LTR '94, PULP
KIRBY, DAN--L. ROBBINS LTR '94, PULP

ASHBERY, JOHN [L]
BERRY, JONAS--W/LAWRENCE G. BLOCHMAN, [31]TRANSLTR--
DELL "MURDER IN MONTMARTE" '60

ASHBROOK, HARRIETTE CORA
ASHBROOK, H.--JEAN F. LE DEIST,BAE 18,P9 MARK ROSE, BAE 19,[3][22]MYS--8 NOVELS
SHANE, SUSANNAH--[1][3]MYS--5 NOVELS '41-6

ASHBY, RICHARD
DARRICK, SYBAH--[14]--
TC#431 "LOVE ON A TRAMPOLINE" '68
OLYM OPH#240 "BANNED IN HOLLYWOOD" '71

ASHBY, RUBY C.
FREUGON, RUBY--[1][5]MYS

ASHCRAFT, LAURA
ASHCRAFT, LAURIE--[31]

ASHER, SANDRA FENICHEL
ASHER, SANDY--[31]

ASHFORD, F.C.
CHARLES, FREDERICK--[8]

ASHFORD, MARGARET MARY
ASHFORD, DAISY--[1][31][33]

ASHKENAZY, IRVIN
GARNET, G.--[1][2][11]

ASHLEY, ARTHUR ERNEST
VIVIAN, FRANCIS--[2][3][22][32]ENGLISH, MYS--
JENK "BLACK ALIBI" '38 & MORE'37-56
LM "LIGHT FROM THE EAST" FEB '51

ASHLEY, FAYE
SUMMERS, ASHLEY--[9][21][26]ROM--8 NOVELS

ASHLEY, J.
MCCALL, CLINT--[35]AUSTRALIAN--
CLVLD NOVELETTE "ON THE PROD"
CLVLD "RANGE WAR"
CHISHOLM 699 "THE DRIFTER"

ASHLEY, MICHAEL RAYMOND D
ASHLEY, MIKE--[7][23][26]SF/NON-FICT/ROM--
"LADY MOLLY"
"PHILIPPA"
"THEODOSIA"

ASHMORE, BASIL NORTON
MARLIN, ROY--[1]

ASHTON, ADEN
GOEWY, EDWIN A.--[2]

ASHTON, KATHERINE
TALBOT, KATHERINE--[21]ROM

ASHTON, MARGERY VIOLET
ASHTON, VIOLET--[21]ROM--4 NOVELS

ASHTON, WINIFRED
DANE, CLEMENCE--[2][3][5][7][11][22][23][31]
HM "LEGEND" '19
"THE BABYLONS" '27

ASHTON, WINIFRED [CONT]
  DANE, CLEMENCE [CONT]
    HODDER "ENTER SIR JOHN" '28
    HODDER "PRINTER'S DEVIL" '30
    HODDER "REENTER SIR JOHN" '32
    "THE ARROGANT HISTORY OF WHITE BEN" '39

ASHTON-GWATKIN, FRANK T.A
  PARIS, JOHN--[2]

ASHTON-WARNER, SYLVIA C.
  HENDERSON, SYLVIA--[8][31]

ASHWELL, PAUL
  ASH, PAUL--[11]SF
  ASHWELL, PAULINE--MYS SCENE,JAN '93

ASHWORTH, EDWARD MONTAGUE
  ABBOTT, JOHNSTON--[1]

ASIMOV, ISAAC
  DALE, GEORGE E.--[1][2][11][31][33]--
    ASF-ONE STORY
  DR. A--MARTY SWIATKOWSKI LTR APR '93,[2]
    "THE SENSOUS DIRTY OLD MAN"
  FRENCH, PAUL--[2][4][11][18][31][33]
    JUVENILE "LUCKY STAR" STORIES '52-8
  OGDEN, H.B.--ASIMOV, IN MEMORY
    YET GREEN,[11]--
    SUPER SCIENCE "THE WEAPON" MAY '42

ASIMOV, JANET O. JEPPSON
  CEDARHOLM, JAN--[1][32]MYS--
    SA "WINTER IN THE MORGUE" MAY '66
  JEPPSON, J.O--[7][23][31]SF--
    HOUGHTON "THE LAST IMMORTAL" '80 &
    A COLLECTION OF SS

ASKA, WARABE
  MASUDA, TAKESHI--[31][33]

ASPERN-BUCHMEIER, ELISAB.
  BERNAUER, EVA MARIA--[39]GERMAN
  BUNDLER, HANS--[39]GERMAN/MYS
  COLLIN, PH.--[39]GERMAN/MYS
  FELDON, HARRY--[39]GERMAN/MYS
  GLUECK, PETER--[39]GERMAN/MYS
  GRAHAM, WILLIAM--[39]GERMAN/MYS
  HALLER, H.--[39]GERMAN/MYS
  MALTEN, MARGARETE--[39]GERMAN
  NEY, ELISABETH--[39]GERMAN
  NORDMANN, FRITZ--[39]GERMAN/MYS
  STRONG, PITT--[39]GERMAN
  STRUNZ, PETER--[39]GERMAN
  WEST, HARALD--[39]GERMAN
  WESTMANN, HARALD--[39]GERMAN
  ZECHT, BERNHARD--[39]GERMAN

ASPIEYEVSKI, ANNE LINDBERG
  LINDBERG, ANNE--
    "THE HUNKY-DORY DAIRY" '86
    "THE SHADOW ON THE DIAL" '87

ASSAEL, SOL
  MANNING, JOHN SPENCER--W/MICHAEL NAHUM,[2]

ASSELBERGS, WILLEM JAN M.
  BACKX, PIETER--[22]DUTCH
  VAN DUINKERTEN, ANTON--[22]DUTCH

ASSELINEAU, ROGER [M]
  MAURICE, ROGER--[1]

ASSENSOH, AKWASI BRETUO
  ASSENSOH, A.B.--[31]
  BRETUO, AKWASI--[31]

ASTL, JARO
  TROSSAU, BURKHARD ASTL--[39]GERMAN

ASTLEY, THEA B. MAY
  ASTLEY, THEA--[21]ROM--
    "IT'S RAINING IN MANGO"

ASTLEY, WILLIAM
  WARUNG, PRICE--[1][34]MYS--
    ROUTLEDGE "TALES OF OLD REGIME" 1897
    SWAN "HALF-CROWN BOB & TALES
    OF THE RIVERINE" 1898
    ROBERTSON "TALES OF THE ISLE
    OF DEATH" 1898

ASTON, BENJAMIN GWILLIAM
  GREY, ANTHONY--[34]MYS--
    5 BOOKS '73-90

ASTOR, GAVIN
  LORD ASTOR OF HEVER--[31]

ASWELL, MARY LOISE
  PATRICK, Q.--W/RICHARD W. WEBB,[11][34]MYS--
    FARRAR "S.S. MURDER" '33
    HARTNEY "COTTAGE SINISTER" '35

ATAKUZIEV, RAKHMATULLA
  UIGUN--[1]

ATCHESON, RICHARD
  TRESSILIAN, CHARLES--[1]

ATCHISON, SANDRA DALLAS
  DALLAS, SANDRA--[1][22][31]AMERICAN

ATCHLEY, ROBERT C.
  ATCHLEY, BOB--[31]

ATENE, RITA ANNA
  ATENE, ANN--[31][33]

ATHANAS, WILLIAM VERNE
  ATHANAS, VERN--LACHMAN LTR '93,[32]MYS--
    EQMM "A HANGING MATTER" OCT '56
    EQMM "RIDE WITH A KILLER" JAN '57
    MSMM "FLAMING SCARF" JUN '59
  ATHANAS, W.V.--[1]
  BOONE, IKE--[1][28]--
    INDIAN STORIES "BRAND OF THE RED
    WARRIOR" FALL '50
  COLSON, BILL--[1][2][11][28]WEST--SS '50-3
  SLAUGHTER, ANSON--[1][28]--
    INDIAN STORIES "DEATH TO THE WHITE
    SIOUX" FALL '50

ATHERTON, GERTRUDE [F]
  LIN, FRANK--[23][28]SF--
    "WHAT DREAMS MAY COME" 1888

ATKEY, PHILIP
  MERRIMAN, PAT--[3][5][18]MYS--
    HUTCH "NIGHT CALL" '39
  PEROWNE, BARRY--[3][5][18][32]MYS--
    27 NOVELS '32-79, DIGEST SS

ATKIN, JANE
  ADDISON, JAYNE--[26]ROM--
    "YOU MADE ME LOVE YOU"

ATKINS, ARTHUR HAROLD
  JACKSON, J.P.--[31]

ATKINS, CHESTER BURTON
  ATKINS, CHET--[31]

ATKINS, FRANCIS HENRY
ASH, FENTON--[1][2][11][23]SF
ASHLEY, FRED--[1][2]
AUBREY, FRANK--[2][3][7][23]--
JARROLDS "A STUDIO MYSTERY" 1897
MZ "SPELL OF THE SWORD" FALL '67
ST. MARS, F. JR.--[2][11]

ATKINS, FRANK JR.
ASH, FENTON--[23]SF--
SHARED PSEUD. W/FATHER
"CAUGHT BY A COMET" '10
ST. MARS, F.--[23]SF

ATKINS, JAMES G.
ATKINS, JIM--[31]

ATKINS, JANE
KEENE, SARAH--[9][21][26]ROM--4 NOVELS

ATKINS, JOHN RINGROSE
BARRY, DAN--[13]AUSTRALIAN

ATKINS, MARGARET ELIZAB.
ATKINS, MEG ELIZABETH--[7]SF--
HARPER "BY THE NORTH DOOR" '75
HARPER "SAMAIN" '76
MOORE, ELIZABETH--[1]

ATKINS, OLIVER F.
ATKINS, OLLIE--[31]

ATKINSON, B.M. JR.
DUNCAN, PETER--[3]MYS--
GM "THE TELL-TALE TART" '61

ATKINSON, DOROTHY
FIFE, DUNCAN--[1]

ATKINSON, ELEANOR [S]
MARKS, NORA--[1]

ATKINSON, FRANK
CURNOW, FRANK--[1][31]
SHALLOW, ROBERT--[1]

ATKINSON, GEORGE SCOTT
SCOTT, RALPH--[3]MYS--
HURST "THE UNKNOWN QUEST" '30

ATKINSON, HUGH
GEDDES, HUGH--[36]AUSTRALIAN/MYS--
SUN "PYJAMA GIRL CASE" '78

ATKINSON, NANCY
BENKO, NANCY--[1]

ATKINSON, TERRY
PARKER, MORTON--V. BERCH, BRNDN/
BC PSEUDS., BAE 22, P24

ATKINSON, WILLIAM WALKER
ATKINSON, W.W.--[31]

ATTENBOROUGH, BERNARD G.
RAND, JAMES S.--[3]MYS--
McLELLAN "THE STAKE" '59

ATTENHOFER, EDUARD
CHRUGEL, CHIRDONIUS--[39]GERMAN

ATTHILL, ROBERT ANTHONY
ATTHILL, ROBIN--[1]

ATTLEE, CLEMENT RICHARD
ATTLEE, C.R.--[31]

ATTRACHOVICH, KANDRAT
KRAPIVA, KANDRAT--[22]RUSSIAN

ATWATER, FREDERICK MUND
ATWATER, RICHARD TUPPER--[1]

ATWATER, PHYLLIS M.H.
FUFFMAN, PHYLLIS--[31]

ATWATER, RICHARD TUPPER
RIQ--[1][33]

ATWOOD, MARY ANN
SOUTH, M.A.--[1]

AUBERT, ROSEMARY
SNOW, LUCY--[9][21][26]ROM--
"SONG OF EDEN"
"A REDBIRD IN WINTER"
"GARDEN OF LIONS"

AUBREY-FLETCHER, HENRY L.
WADE, HENRY--[3][5][18][32]MYS--
22 NOVELS '26-57
ML "PAYMENT IN FULL" NOV '33
EQMM "SMASH & GRAB" JUL '45
BS "THE DYING FALL" JUL '59

AUCHINCLOSS, BAYARD
NEGULESCO, BRIAN--[3]MYS--
EXPOSITION "WOMAN FROM A.U.N.T." '70

AUCHINCLOSS, LOUIS S.
LEE, ANDREW--[6][22][31]AMERICAN

AUDEMARS, PIERRE
HODEMART, PETER--[18][22][29]MYS

AUEL, JEAN MARIE
AUEL, JEAN M.--[21]HISTORICAL ROM

AUERBACH, ALINE SOPHIE B.
AUERBACH, ALINE B.--[31]

AUERBACH, ARNOLD JACOB
AUERBACH, RED--[31]

AUERBACH, STEVANNE
FINK, STEVANNE AUERBACH--[31]

AUERSPERG, ANTON ALEX. v.
GRUN, ANASTASIUS--[39]GERMAN

AUGE, HENRY J. JR.
AUGE, BUD--[31]

AULT, PHILLIP HALLIDAY
AULT, PHIL--[31]

AULT, ROSIE SAIN
AULT, ROZ--[1][31][33]

AUMENTE, JOY
DARLINGTON, JOY--[9][21][26]ROM--
"FAST FRIENDS"
"THOSE VAN DER MEER WOMEN"
GARDNER, JOY--[9][21][26]ROM--
"FORTUNE'S BRIDE"

AUNG, [MAUNG] HTIN
AUNG, U. HTIN--[31][33]
FOURTH BROTHER, THE--[22][31]ENGLISH

AURANDT, PAUL HARVEY
HARVEY, PAUL--[1][31]

AUSLANDER, AUDREY WURDEMANN W.
WURDEMANN, AUDREY--[1]

AUSPITZ, KATE
BELFORT, SOPHIE--V. BERCH LTR TO HUBIN '93
ATHNM "LACE CURTAIN MURDERS" '86

AUSTER, PAUL
BENJAMIN, PAUL--RECYCLE BOOKS '93/
LACHMAN-EASTER LST '93,[34]MYS--
ALPHA-OMEGA "SQUEEZE PLAY" '82
FABER "THE NEW YORK TRILOGY" '85

AUSTIN, ALFRED
LAMIA--[1]

AUSTIN, BENJAMIN FISH
ALBARUS, HEDWIG S.--[1]
NITSUA, BENJAMIN--[1][3]MYS--
AUSTIN "MYSTERY OF ASHTON HALL" '10

AUSTIN, DEBORAH
MARSHALL, JACQUELINE--[9][21][26]ROM--
"DRASTIC MEASURES"
STIRLING, ELAINE K.--[10]

AUSTIN, JOHN LANGSHAW
AUSTIN, J.L.--[1]

AUSTIN, MARY H.
STAIRS, GORDON--[1][2][28]WEST--
MURRAY "OUTLAND" '10

AUSTIN, NANCY
NORTH, MIRANDA--W/MARY KEVERN,
[21][26]ROM--
"DESERT SLAVE"
"FOREVER PARADISE"
"SWEET LIES"

AUSTIN, NANCY LAMB
AUSTIN, R.G.--W/RITA GELMAN,[1]

AUSTIN, STANLEY
CLIFFORD, MARTIN--[1]HP
CONQUEST, OWEN--[1]HP
RICHARDS, FRANK--[1]HP

AUTH, WILLIAM ANTHONY JR.
AUTH, TONY--[31][33]

AUTY, PHYLLIS
RICHARDS, PHYLLIS--[22]ENGLISH

AVALLONE, MICHAEL
ALDEN, MICHELE--HOLLAND-AVALLONE INTRVW-CKLST,
BAE 4/BAE 5/HAWK-AVALLONE INTRVW '93--
"SCARBOROUGH WARNING"- NOT PUBLISHED
AVALLONE, MICHAEL ANGELO--[21]ROM
BLAINE, JAMES--HOLLAND-AVALLONE INTRVW/
CKLST, BAE 4/BAE 5/[2][31]--
LAN "MY SECRET LIFE WITH OLDER WOMEN"'69
CARTER, NICK--HOLLAND-AVALLONE INTRVW
CKLST ,BAE 4,P7,BAE 5,P20,[2][4][34]HP--
AWARD "THE CHINA DOLL" '64
AWARD "RUN, SPY, RUN" '64
AWARD "SAIGON" '64
AWARD "100TH ANIVERSARY ED." '75,
CONWAY, TROY--HOLLAND/AVALLONE INTRVW
CKLST, BAE 4, P7,BAE 5, P20,[2][31]HP--
PAPLB "COME ONE, COME ALL" '68
PAPLB "MAN-EATER" '68
PAPLB "HAD ANY LATELY?" '69
PAPLB "A GOOD PEACE" '69
PAPLB "BIG BROAD JUMP" '69
PAPLB "I'D RATHER FIGHT THAN SWISH"'69

AVALLONE, MICHAEL [CONT]
CONWAY, TROY [CONT]
PAPLB "BLOW YOUR MIND AFFAIR" '69
PAPLB "CUNNING LINGUIST" '69
PAPLB "ALL SCREWED UP" '70
PAPLB "PENETRATOR" '71
PAPLB "A STIFF PROPOSITION" '71
DALTON, PRISCILLA--HOLLAND-AVALLONE
INTRVW/CKLST, BAE 4, P7,BAE 5, P20
[2][3][4][31]--
PAPLB "90 GRAMERCY PARK" '65
PAPLB "SILENT SILKEN SHADOWS" '65
PAPLB "DARKENING WILLOWS" '65
DANE, MARK--HOLLAND/AVALLONE INTRVW
CKLST, BAE 4, P7, BAE 5, P20,[2][3]
[4][31][32][37]--
TF "STOP AT NOTHING" '56
TF "WHITE LEGS" AUG '57
BELM "FELICIA" '64
DE PRE, JEAN-ANNE--HOLLAND/AVALLONE
INTRVW/CKLST, BAE 4, P7,BAE 5, P20
[3][4][21][26]--
POPLB "THIRD WOMAN" '70
POPLB "A SOUND OF DYING ROSES" '71
POPLB "DIE, JESSICA, DIE!" '72
POPLB "AQUARIUS, MY EVIL" '72
POPLB "WARLOCK'S WOMAN"
FRAZER, FRED--HAWK/AVALLONE INTRVW
MAY '93,[31]--MAG ARTICLES & SHORT
STORIES-NO BOOKS
HALLIDAY, BRETT--T. JOHNSON,ECHOES #23,P16
[2]HP--MSMM "MASK OF MURDER" AUG '61
MSMM "CIVIL WAR OF MICHAEL SHAYNE" NOV '61
MSMM "NOT ENOUGH CLUES" JAN '62
MSMM "MURDER STRIKES OUT" MAR '62
MSMM "RESTLESS REDHEAD" APR '62
MSMM "MARGIN FOR TERROR" JUL '62
MSMM "FRIGHTENED TARGET" AUG '62
MSMM "GIRL CRIED MURDER" NOV '62
MSMM "GALLOWS HIGHWAY" MAR '63
MSMM "MURDER MOST WELCOME" MAY '63
MSMM "DEATH IN A THREE RING CIRCUS" JUL '63
MSMM "TEARS FOR A GENTLE OLD LADY" AUG '63
HIGHLAND, DORA--HOLLAND/AVALLONE INTRVW
CKLST, BAE 4, P7, BAE 5,P20,[2][3][4][31]-
POPLB "WARLOCK'S WOMAN" '72
POPLB "153 OAKLAND STREET" '72
POPLB "DEATH IS A DARK MAN" '73
JARRETT, AMANDA JEAN--HOLLAND/AVALLONE
INTRVW/CKLST,BAE 4,P7, BAE 5, P20,[21]--
DELL 'SOUTHERNER SERIES':
"RED ROSES FOREVER" '82
JASON, STUART--HOLLAND/AVALLONE INTRVW
CKLST, BAE 4, P7, BAE 5, P20,[3][4]HP--
PINN "BUTCHER NOVELS:#27-#35" '79-81
KARLOFF, BORIS--[2]GHOSTED
MICHAELS, STEVE--HOLLAND/AVALLONE
INTRVW/CKLST, BAE 4, P7, BAE 5, P20
[2][3][4]--
BELM "THE MAIN ATTRACTION" '63
MORGAN, MEMO--HAWK/AVALLONE INTERVW
MAY '93--ED NOONE CHAR. USED IN MAG
ART. & SHORT STORIES
NILE, DOROTHEA--HOLLAND/AVALLONE INTRVW
CKLST,BAE 4, P7, BAE 5, P20,[2][3][4]--
TWR "MISTRESS OF FARRONDALE" '65
TWR"TERROR AT DEEPCLIFF" '66
TWR "EVIL MEN DO" '66
LAN "VAMPIRE CAMEO" '68
VON "THIRD SHADOW" '72
NOON, ED--HAWK-AVALLONE INTRVW MAY'93[1][2]
MAG ART & SHORT STORIES
NOONE, EDWINA--HOLLAND-AVALLONE INTRVW
CKLST, BAE 4, P7, BAE 5, P20,[2][3][4]--
ACE "DARK CYPRESS" '65
ACE "CORRIDOR OF WHISPERS" '65
LAN "HEIRLOOM OF TRADEGY" '65

AVALLONE, MICHAEL [CONT]
NOONE, EDWINA [CONT]
BELM "VICTORIAN CROWN" '65
BELM "SECOND SECRET" '66
AWARD "EDW. NOONE'S GOTHIC SAMPLER" '66
SIGN "DAUGHTER OF DARKNESS" '66
SIGN "SEACLIFFE" '66
BEAGLE "CRAGHOLE LEGACY" '71
BEAGLE "CRAGHOLE CURSE" '72
BEAGLE "CRAGHOLE CREATURES" '72
CURTIS "CLOISONNE VASE" '72
BEAGLE "CRAGHOLE CRYPT" '72
DELL "TENDER LOVING FEAR" '83
STANTON, VANCE--HOLLAND-AVALLONE INTRVW
CKLST, BAE 4, P7, BAE 5, P20,[2]--
POPLB "K. PARTDIDGE, MASTER SPY" '71
"WALKING FINGERS" '72
CURTIS "FAT & SKINNY MURDER MYS" '72
"WHO'S LAUGHING IN THE GRAVE?" '72
STUART, SIDNEY--HOLLAND-AVALLONE INTRVW
CKLST, BAE 4, P7,BAE 5, P20,[2][3][4]--
AWARD "NIGHT WALKER" '64
BELM "YOUNG DILLINGER" '65
POPLB "BEAST WITH RED HANDS" '72
WALKER, MAX--HOLLAND-AVALLONE INTRVW
CKLST, BAE 4/BAE 5/[3][4]MYS/WAR--
POPLB "THE LAST ESCAPE" '70
WILLOUGHBY, LEE DAVIS--HOLLAND-AVALLONE
INTRVW/CKLST,BAE 4/BAE 5/[21]ROM--HP--
DELL-'MAKING OF AMERICA SERIES':
"GUNFIGHTERS" '81
"SIX-GUN APPOSTLES" '85
"ROUGH RIDERS" '83

AVEDIS, HIKMET
AVEDIS, HOWARD--[31]

AVELING, JOHN CEDRIC HUGH
AVELING, HUGH--[31]

AVENELLE, DONNE
CHARTERIS, LESLIE--W/GRAHAM WEAVER,
[34]MYS, GHOSTED--
HODDER "SAINT & TEMPLAR TREASURE" '79
KING, CHARLES--[8]

AVERILL, ESTHER [HOLDEN]
DOMINO, JOHN--[25][31][33]AMERICAN,
CHILDREN'S--"FABLE OF A PROUD PONY" '34

AVERS, ROBERTS
MUKS, ROBERTS--[1]

AVERY, HAROLD
WESTRIDGE, HAROLD--[8]

AVERY, IRA
HATHAWAY, MAVIS--[3][31]MYS--
POPLB "A SILENCE OF NIGHTINGALES" '77
POPLB "SON OF NIGHTINGALES" '77

AVERY, RUBY
BIDWELL, LITA--[31]--
HALE "A RAINBOW IN HAWAII" '91
PAGE, VICKI--[8][9][21][26]ROM--
HALE "HOUSE OF HARRON" '77 & 29 OTHERS

AVERY, SAMUEL PUTNAM
PARTINGTON, MRS.--[1]
SLICK, SAM JR.--[1]
SPAVERY--[1]

AVICE, CLAUDE-PIERRE
BARBET, PIERRE--[2][7][11][23][31]SF--
DAW "ERIDANUS #1 & 2"
"BAPHOMET #1 & 2"

AVICE, CLAUDE-PIERRE [CONT]
MAINE, DAVID--[2][11][23][31]SF
SPRIGEL, OLIVER--[1][2][11][23]SF

AVIRGAN, ANTHONY LANCE
AVIRGAN, TONY--[31]

AVRETT, ROSALIND CASE
AVRETT, ROZ--[31]

AWDRY, RICHARD CHARLES
CHARLES, RICHARD--[1][8]

AWOONOR-WILLIAMS, GEORGE
AWOONOR, KOFI--[31]GHANA

AXELRAD, NANCY
KEENE, CAROLYN--[1]HP--
STSY-DANA GIRLS

AXLERAD, SYLVIA BRODY
BRODY, SYLVIA--[31]

AYCKBOURNE, ALAN
ALLEN, ROLAND--[31]
ALLEN, RONALD--[8]

AYCOCK, ROGER DEE
DEE, ROGER--[2][7][11][23][32]MYS/SF--
PLANET STORIES "THE WHEEL IS DEATH" '49
PLANET STORIES "AN EARTH GONE MAD" '54
MM "THIRD FROM THE END" AUG '58
PH "MURDER ON SCHEDULE" MAR '62
STARR, JOHN--[1][2][11]HP

AYDT, BRUNHILD
MILLER, BRINHILD--[39]GERMAN

AYER, ALBERTA CONSTANCE
WELLS, DEE--[1]

AYKROYD, DANIEL EDWARD
AYKROYD, DAN--[31]
BLUES, ELWOOD--[31]

AYLING, KEITH
ADLON, ARTHUR--[34]MYS--
CHARIOT "THE PRINCE OF POISONERS" '60

AYLWORTH, SUSAN
GALE, SHANNON--[21][26]ROM--
"BENEATH SIERRA SKIES"

AYNES, EDITH ANNETTE
AYNES, PAT EDITH--[31]

AYRAUD, PIERRE
NARCEJAC, THOMAS--[2][3][7][18]MYS/SF--
13 NOVELS

AYREN, ARMIN
SCHIEFER, HERMANN--[39]GERMAN

AYRES, NOREEN
ASHER, SARAH--
AUTHOR PROVIDED AUG '94, POETRY

AYRES, RUBY MILDRED
AYRES, RUBY M.--[21]ROM--11 NOVELS

AYRTON GOULD, MICHAEL
AYRTON, MICHEL--[1]ENGLISH
GOULD, MICHAEL--[22]ENGLISH
GOULD, MICHEL--[1]ENGLISH

AYTOUN, WILLIAM E.
GAULTIER, BON--W/[SIR] THEODORE MARTIN,[1]

AYVAZIAN, L. FRED
FLAGG, KENNETH--[1][31]
LEVON, FRED--[31][32][34]MYS--
EQMM "HELP ME - IF YOU CAN" APR '53
DODD "MUCH ADO ABOUT MURDER" '59
WORLD "MANX CAT" '70
AHMM "FOR THE LIFE OF ME" SEPT '71

AZNAVOURIAN, VARENAGH
AZNAVOUR, CHARLES--[31]

AZOOMANIAN, RALPH SARKIS
AZOOMANIAN, RAFFI--[31]

AZRAEL, JUDITH ANNE
GREENBERG, JUDITH ANNE--[31]

AZUELO, MARIANO
BELENO--[1]

B-F VON OCHSENFELD, ANTON
HERBSTENBURGER, TONI--[39]GERMAN/JUV

BAADE, HANNI [B]
BOHLMANN, HANNI--[39]GERMAN

BAARNHEIM, E.W.
BARNES, E.W.--[1]
E.W.B.--[1]

BABCOCK, FREDERICK
MARK, MATTHEW--[8][22]AMERICAN

BABCOCK, MAURICE P.
BEA, EMPTY--[8]

BABCOCK, WINIFRED
WATANNA, ONOTO--[22]AMERICAN

BABEL, ISAAC E.
LIUTOV, KIRIL--[1]

BABER, DOUGLAS GORDON
RITSON, JOHN--[3]MYS--
BRDMN "DEATH OF A MIND" '59
BRDMN "BENEATH THE PRECIPICE" '62
BRDMN "DESPERATE VENTURE" '63
BRDMN "THE DEADLY BLUNDER" '64

BABIC, LJUBA
GJALSKA, KSAVER SANDOR--[22]CROATIAN

BABJUK, ANDREY
IRCHAN, MYROSLAV--[22]UKRAINIAN

BACA, JIMMY SANTIAGO
BACA, JOSE SANTIAGO--[31]

BACHMANN-MARTIG, SINA
MARTIG, SINA--[39]GERMAN

BACKMAN, DIANA
MARLOW, MAX--W/CHRISTOPHER NICOLE, [7]SF--
NEL "MELTDOWN" '89
NEL "THE RED DEATH" '91

BACKUS, CAROL SUZANNE
BARCLAY, SUZANNE--[26]ROM--4 NOVELS

BACKUS, JAMES GILMORE
BACKUS, JIM--[31][33]

BACKUS, JEAN LOUISE
MONTROSS, DAVID--[34]MYS--
COLLINS "CRIME ON COTE DE NEIGES" '51
COLLINS "MURDER OVER DORVAL" '52
HARL "THE BODY ON MOUNT ROYAL" '53
HALE "GAMBLING WITH FIRE" '69

BACON, CHERYL
KENT, LYNETTE--[26]ROM--
"NO ILLUSION"

BACON, DON
GIFFORD, CLARK--V. BERCH, BRNDN/BC PSEUDS., BAE 22, P24

BACON, EDWARD
BOON, FRANCIS--[31]

BACON, ELIZABETH
MORROW, BETTY--[8]

BACON, GAIL
FRAZER, MARGARET--W/MONICA PULVER, DEADLY PLEASURES #3, P34--
"THE NOVICE'S TALE" '92

BACON, JOHN B.
BRANDSTON, GARTH--V. BERCH, BRNDN/BC PSEUDS., BAE 22, P24

BACON, JOSEPHINE D.
DASKAM, JOSEPHINE DODGE--[31][33]
LOVELL, INGRAHAM--[8][22][31][33]MYS

BACON, MARGARET FRANCES
BACON, PEGGY--[31][33]

BACOT, CLAUDE
DAVIDSON, PAUL--V.BERCH LTR TO HUBIN '94, MYS-
VANTAGE "KATMANDU AFFAIR" '80

BACZEWSKI, JANICE K.J.
BARTLETT, KAY--[9][21][26]ROM--
"A SHIVER OF RAIN"
"FAMILY TIES"
JOHNSON, JANICE KAY--[9][21][26]ROM--
"SEIZE THE DAY"
"NIGHT & DAY"
"IMPERILED HEIRESS"
KIRBY, KAY--W/NORMA KAY T. JOHNSON [9][21][26]ROM--
"SUMMERTIME LOVE"
"AUTUMN BEGINNING"
STEVENS, JANICE--[9][21 ROM--
"TEST OF LOVE"
"DREAM SUMMER"
"PLAYING FOR KEEPS"

BADAWI, MOHAMED MUSTAFA
BADAWI, MUHAMMED MUSTAFA--[31]

BADE, THOMAS MICHAEL
BADE, TOM--[7]SF
MINTON, T.M.--W/ROBIN STEVENSON, [7]SF--
PINN "SWITCHBACK" '88
MINTON, T.M.--[7]--
LEIS "OFFERINGS" '86
ST. THOMAS, ROBIN--W/ROBIN STEVENSON [9][21][26]ROM--7 NOVELS

BADERI, JUNE
WILSON, JANE--[8]

BADGER, JOSEPH E.
BEAN, K.--[1]
HAZARD, HARRY--[1]

BADGER, JOSEPH E. [CONT]
HAZELTON, HARRY--[1]
ROY, RALPH--[1]

BADGLEY, JONATHAN
UNCLE JONATHAN--[1]

BAEHR, PATRICIA GOEHNER
BAEHR, PAT[RICIA]--[21]ROM--
"INDIAN SUMMER"

BAEHTHOLD, ALFRED
BERNHARD, LUDWIG--[39]GERMAN

BAEN, JAMES PATRICK
BAEN, JIM--[23]SF

BAENZIGER, HANS
BANZIGER, HANS--[31]

BAER, JUDY
KAYE, JUDY--[21][26][31][33]ROM--
"LETTERS OF LOVE"
"ARIANA'S MAGIC" & 9 OTHER NOVELS

BAER, LUCY A.
HILL, K.F.--[1]
HILL, K[ATE] F.--[3]MYS--
IVERS "SARA BROWN, DETECTIVE" '01 & OTHERS

BAETZ, WILLIAM
HILD, JACK--[34]HP--
GE 'SOB's':
"BARRABUS FIX" '88
"BARRABUS KILL" '89

BAEUMI, FRANZ H[EINRICH]
BAUMI, FRANZ H.--[31]

BAGDON, PAUL
PHILLIPS, TONY--[7]HP--
BAL 'TURBO COWBOYS' #5, #7, #8 & #10

BAGGETT, NANCY
LEE, AMANDA--W/EILEEN BUCKHOLTZ & RUTH GLICK
[9][21][31]ROM--NOVELS

BAGLEY, SIMON
BAGLEY, DESMOND--DAST,[1]

BAGNANO, PATRICK F.
BUNYON, PAT--V. BERCH, BRNDN/BC PSEUDS.
BAE 22, P24--
NSLS U103 "BIG BLUES" '60
SABER SA16 "I PEDDLE JAZZ" '60

BAGNARA, ELSIE POE
HESS, NORAH--[9][21]ROM--
"MARNA"
"WILDFIRE" & 5 OTHERS

BAGNEL, JOAN
CIPOLLA, JOAN BAGNEL--[31]

BAGNOLD, ENID
LADY OF QUALITY, A--[22][31][33]ENGLISH

BAHAR, MUHAMMAD TAQI
BAHAR, MALIK AL-SHU'ARA--[22]PERSIAN

BAHLKE, VALERIE WORTH
WORTH, VALERIE--[7]SF--
FARRAR "FOX HILL" '86

BAHR, MARY
FRITTS, MARY BAHR--[31]

BAHRS, HANS
BRUNS, HANKE--[39]GERMAN
LINDHORST, HARM--[39]GERMAN

BAIER, ANNA LEE
LEIGH, ANA--[21][26]ROM--
10 NOVELS

BAILEY, ALFRED GOLDSW.
CLAYTON, SUSAN--[31]

BAILEY, DEBRA
JAMES, DEBORAH--[26]ROM--
4 NOVELS

BAILEY, DONNA VERONICA A.
BONAR, VERONICA--[33]

BAILEY, E.J.
CRANE, PAUL--[35]AUSTRALIAN--
HRWTZ PB128 "KILLER SHARK" '62

BAILEY, ELIZABETH
BAILEY, E.M.--[21]ROM--
"THE FALLING PLACE"

BAILEY, FRANCES EVANS
WILSON, ANN--[8]

BAILEY, GEORGE T.
WOOD, VALENTINE--W. MURRAY, ECHOES #5, HP

BAILEY, GORDON
GORDON, KEITH--[8]

BAILEY, HILARY
BRAND, HILARY--[11]
GRAHAM, PIPPIN--[2]
MOORCOCK, MICHAEL--W/MICHAEL MOORCOCK
TARNELORN ARCHIVES,
SILENT COLLAB "BLACK CORRIDOR" '69

BAILEY, IRENE T.
BAILEY, TEMPLE--[8]

BAILEY, ROBERT WAYNE
BAILEY, ROBIN W.--[7]SF--
TSR "NIGHTWATCH" '90
POCK 'FROST' #1-#3 '83-6
& OTHERS

BAILEY-PRATT, CYNTHIA
BROWNE, LYDIA--[26]ROM--
"HEARTSTRINGS"

BAILIE, ALEXANDER DUKE
MURRAY, INSPECTOR--[3]MYS--
LAIRD "JOSEPH PRICKETT, SCOTLAND
YARD DETECTIVE" 1889
LAIRD "LEAGUE OF GUILT" 1892

BAIN, DONALD
LUNDY, MIKE--W/TOM KELLY, V. BERCH LTR
TO HUBIN '94,MYS--AT LEAST
"BABY FARM"

BAIN, KENNETH B.F.
FINDLATER, RICHARD--[8]

BAIR, ANN
EVANS, ANN--[26]ROM--
"FLAMINGO MOON"
HAMMOND, ANN--[26]ROM--
"SEASON OF THE HEART"

AUTHORS

BAIR, PATRICK
GURNEY, DAVID--[7][11][23]SF--
NEL "F CERTIFICATE" '68
NEL "CONJURERS" #1 & 2
NEL "EVIL UNDER WATER" '77

BAIRD, JOHN CHARLTON
BAIRD, JACK--[31]

BAIRD, MARGARET E.
BAYARD, FRED--W/JOHANNA F. JANSEN,[3]MYS--
PHOENIX "DEATH & LILACS" '48

BAIRD, ROLAND
BRENNAN, CHRISTOPHER--
W/CHRISTOPHER KININMOUTH, [1]

BAIRD, WILLIAM BRITTON
BAIRD, BILL--[31]

BAISCH, CHRISTA
BAISCH, CRIS--[39]GERMAN/JUV

BAITAILLE, DIANE
WARFIELD, SELENA--[14]--
OLYM TC#222 "THE WHIP ANGELS" '68

BAITAILLE, GEORGES
ANGELIQUE, PIERRE--[31]

BAJARD, JEAN
BAYARD, JEAN-PIERRE--[1]

BAJOG, GUNTHER
BAJOX, REDDY--[39]GERMAN
BARTON, GIL--[39]GERMAN,HP
BURNETT, PETER--[39]GERMAN,HP
CARTER, JIM--[39]GERMAN,HP
CHANNON, BILL--[39]GERMAN
COLINGS, EDDY--[39]GERMAN,HP
CONWAY, AL--[39]GERMAN,HP
FERGUSON, DAN--[39]GERMAN
GARRETT, BILL--[39]GERMAN
JACKSON, JIM--[39]GERMAN,HP
JENKINS, C.B.--[39]GERMAN,HP
LEASOR, JAMES--[39]GERMAN,HP
MARTINEZ, BENITO--[39]GERMAN,HP
MORRIS, JACK--[39]GERMAN,HP
MORTON, JACK--[39]GERMAN,HP
MURPHY, BILL--[39]GERMAN
NOLAN, FREDERICK--[39]GERMAN,HP
O'CONNOR, WILLIAM--[39]GERMAN
PATTON, GLENN--[39]GERMAN,HP
ROBERTS, H.G.--[39]GERMAN
SLADE, JACK--[39]GERMAN,HP
SPIRIT, GORDON--[39]GERMAN,HP
TUCKER, BEN--[39]GERMAN,HP
WARRICK, LON--[39]GERMAN,HP

BAJOMI, LAZAR ENDRE
ANDRE, LAZAR--[1]

BAKER, AGNES MONICA
HILL, MONICA--[1][34]MYS--
HUTCH "SMOOTH RUNS THE WATER" '36

BAKER, ALFRED THORNTON
BAKER, BOBBY--W/ROBERT G. BAKER,[31]

BAKER, ALLEN ALBERT
KANE, JACK--[31]

BAKER, ANNE
CROSS, NANCY--[9]ROM

BAKER, AUGUSTUS
BARON, ANTHONY--[1]
BARON, JOHN--[1]

BAKER, BERNHARD
TRES, L.--[39]GERMAN
Y.Z.--[39]GERMAN

BAKER, BETTY DOREEN F.
RENIER, ELIZABETH--[21][22][26]ENGLISH/ROM--
19 NOVELS

BAKER, CAROL
STEIN, BAKER--W/LANA STEIN, V. BERCH LTR
TO R. REGINALD '93, SF--
ZEBRA "UNHOLY GODDES" '81

BAKER, CHARLES WILLIAM
BAKER, BILL--[31]
BAKER, C. WILLIAM--[31]

BAKER, CHRIS
FANGORN--[2]

BAKER, CHRISTINE
WEST, CHRISTINE--[9][21]ROM

BAKER, DARLENE
LANG, HEATHER--[9][21][26]ROM--
"THORN IN MY SIDE"

BAKER, FRAN
BAKER, JUDITH--W/JUDITH NOBLE, [9][21][26]--
"WHEN LAST WE LOVED"
"LOVE IN THE CHINA SEA"
MCCOY, CATHLYN--[9][21][26]ROM--
"ON LOVE'S OWN TERMS"

BAKER, GEORGE
OLEMY, P.T.--JAMES CORRICK, BAE 3/[2]

BAKER, GORDON P.
BAKER, G.P.--[31]

BAKER, JAMES
DILLINGER, JAMES--V. BERCH LTR TO HUBIN, MYS--
SIGN "ADRENALINE" '85

BAKER, JAMES W.
BAKER, JIM--[31][33]

BAKER, JOHN GILBERT H.
BAKER, GILBERT--[31]

BAKER, LAURA NELSON
MINIER, NELSON--W/ADRIEN STOUTENBURG, [1]

BAKER, LOUISA ALICE D.
ALIEN--[34]MYS--
UNWIN "THE DEVIL'S HALF-ACRE" 1900

BAKER, MARC[EIL GENEE K.]
BAKER, MARC--[1][21]ROM
BLAIR, MARCIA--[34]MYS--
ZEBRA, 8 "FINAL" NOVELS '78-80
MILLER, MARC--[1][22][31][34]MYS--
MA "DIAL TONE" MAR '54
ARCADIA "DEATH AT THE EASEL" '56
FADM "TOMORROW'S HEADLINE" JAN '57
ARCADIA "THE PLAID SHROUD" '57
ARCADIA "DEATH IS A LIAR" '59
ARCADIA "WIDOW, WEEP FOR ME" '60
ARCADIA "ROOM, BOARD & DEATH" '60
MILLER, MARCIA--[9][21][26]ROM--
"SPOTLIGHT FOR MEGAN" & OTHER NOVELS
MILLER, MARTHA--[1]

BAKER, MARJORIE
MCMASTER, ALISON--[9][32]MYS/ROM--
LM "NOT FOR THE NERVOUS" SEPT '66

BAKER, MARY GLADYS
STUART, SHEILA--[9][21][22][26][33]
SCOTTISH/ROM--
"NO YESTERDAY"

BAKER, PAULINE H[ALPERN]
AUBER, PAUL--[31]

BAKER, RACHEL MADDUX
MADDUX, RACHEL--[11]SF

BAKER, RAY STANNARD
GRAYSON, DAVID--[22][31]AMERICAN

BAKER, REGINALD ROBIN
BAKER, R.R.--[31]
BAKER, ROBIN--[31]

BAKER, ROBERT G.
BAKER, BOBBY--W/ALFRED T. BAKER, [31]

BAKER, SUSAN CATHERINE
RICHARDS, KAY--[33]

BAKER, W.A. HOWARD
ARTHUR, WILLIAM--[1][34]MYS--
AMALG "MURDER WITH VARIETY" '57
BALLINGER, W.A, [34][41]MYS--HP
SEXTON BLAKE "EPITATH TO TREASON" '60
DEVON, NICOLA--[3]MYS--
ACE "HOUSE OF DELUSION" '69
MCNEILLY, WILFRED--[3]GHOSTED
REID, DESMOND--W/A. CAHILL & G.P. MANN
[34]MYS, HP--
AMALG "BULLETS ARE TRUMPS" '53
REID, DESMOND--W/ANTHONY DOUSE &
G.P. MANN, [34]--
AMALG "DEAD ON CUE" '62]
REID, DESMOND--W/ARTHUR MACLEAN,
[3][8]HP, REVISED--
"ANGER AT WORLD'S END"
REID, DESMOND--W/VIC HANSON, [34]HP--
AMALG "CULT OF DARKNESS" '63
AMALG "DEATH ON A HIGH NOTE" '62
REID, DESMOND--W/WILFRED G. MCNEILLY, [34]HP--
MAYFLOWER "THE SNOWMAN COMETH" '66
SAXON, PETER--W/WILFRED G. MCNEILY, [7][34]HP-
"THE TORTURER" '67
"DARK WAYS TO DEATH" '68
"HAUNTING OF ALAN MAIS" '70
SAXON, PETER--W/STEPHEN D. FRANCES [1][7][34]-
"THE DISORIENTED MAN
SAXON, PETER--W/SYDNEY J. BOUNDS, [34]HP--
AMALG "WHITE MERCENARY" '62
SAXON, PETER--BOB BRINEY, BAE 17, P9
[2][3][7]HP--
AMALG "VOODOO DRUM" '48
AMALG "DANGER AHEAD" '56
AMALG "DECOY FOR MURDER" '56
AMALG "FLIGHT INTO FEAR" '56
AMALG "FRONT PAGE WOMAN" '56
AMALG "AN ACT OF VIOLENCE" '57
AMALG "VIOLENT HOURS" '57
AMALG "LAST DAYS OF BERLIN" '57
AMALG "A CRY IN THE NIGHT" '57
AMALG "NAKED BLADE" '58
AMALG "SEA TIGERS" '58
AMALG "VIOLENT ONES" '59
AMALG "LOVELY-BUT LETHAL!" '61
AMALG "VENGEANCE IS OURS" '65
AMALG "THIS SPY MUST DIE" '67
AMALG "BLACK HONEY" '68

BAKER, W.A. HOWARD [CONT]
SAXON, PETER [CONT]
AMALG "THE KILLING BONE" '70
AMALG "VAMPIRE'S MOON" '72
WELLSLEY, JULIE--[3]MYS--
11 NOVELS ['68-73 LANCER & MAYFLOWER]
WILLIAMS, RICHARD--BOB BRINEY-BAE17/
[29][34]HP--
AMALG "HURRICANE WARNING" '60
WILLIAMS, RICHARD--W/BOB HOPKINS, G.P. MANN &
MAX MARQUIS, [34]HP--
AMALG "MURDER BY PROXY" '63
WILLIAMS, RICHARD--W/JACK T. STORY, [34]HP--
AMALG "LARGE TYPE KILLER" '60

BAKER, W.J.
CHURCHWARD, JOHN--[7][11]SF--
NEL "WHAT BECK'NING GHOST ?" '75

BAKHTIN, MIKHAIL M.
BAKHTIN, M.--[31]
BAKHTIN, M.M.--[31]
MEDVEDER, PAVEL--[1]
VOLOSHINOV, VLADIMIR--[1]

BAKKER, JAMES ORSEN
BAKKER, JIM--[31]

BAKKER, TAMARA FAYE
BAKKER, TAMMY FAYE--[31]

BALASSA, ILONA
PICHLER, ELISABETH--[39]GERMAN

BALBERNIE, ARTHUR G.
KENT, JOHN--[3]MYS--
WARD "GIVE ME LIBERTY" '39

BALCHIN, NIGEL MARTIN
SPADE, MARK--[2]

BALDWIN, BEATRICE LILLIAN
BALDWIN, BEE--[7][23]NEW ZEALAND/SF

BALDWIN, CATHY-JO LADAME
LADAME, CATHRYN--[9][21][26]ROM--
"WINTER'S HEART"
"TRAIL OF THE UNICORN"
LADD, CATHRYN--[9][21][26]ROM--
"CENTENNIAL SUMMER"
"ISLAND AUTUMN"
"TAPESTRY OF LOVE"

BALDWIN, EDWARD ROBINSON
BALDWIN, NED--[31]

BALDWIN, GORDON C.
BALDWIN, GORDO--[22][28][31][33]WEST--
AVALON "AMBUSH BASIN" '60
AVALON "WYOMING RAWHIDE" '61
GORDON, LEW--[22][28][31][33]WEST--
AVALON "POWDERSMOKE JUSTICE" '61
HALE "AMBUSH BASIN" '65

BALDWIN, JAMES
DUDLEY, ROBERT--[31][33]

BALDWIN, MERL WILLIAM JR.
BALDWIN, BILL--[7][23]AMERICAN/SF--
POPLB 'HELMSMAN' #1-#4 '85-91
BALDWIN, MERL--[23]AMERICAN/SF

BALDWIN, MICHAEL
JESSE, MICHAEL--[22][31]ENGLISH

BALDWIN, OLIVER RIDSDALE
HUSSINGTREE, MARTIN--[2][8]

BALDWIN, WILLIAM JR.
BALDWIN, BILL--[31]

BALE, PATRICIA
BALE, G.F.--W/GLADYS BALE WELLBROCK,[7]SF--
CHART "IF THOUGHTS COULD KILL" '90

BALES, JAMES E[DWARD]
BALES, JACK--[31]

BALFOUR, ARTHUR JAMES
BALFOUR, A.J.--[31]

BALFOUR, EVA
BALFOUR, HEARNDEN--W/BERYL HEARNDEN,
[3][22]MYS--
HODDER "PAPER CHASE" '27
HODDER "ENTERPRISING BURGLAR" '28
HODDER "ANYTHING MIGHT HAPPEN" '31

BALFOUR, FREDERIC H.
DERING, R.G.--[2]

BALFOUR, J. PATRICK D.
KINROSS, LORD--[31]

BALFOUR, ROBERT LOUIS
STEVENSON, ROBERT LOUIS--[5][32]MYS--
EQMM "MARKHEIM" JUL '55

BALFOUR, WILLIAM
RUSSELL, RAY--[32]MYS--
MH "SWORD OF LAERTES" OCT '59
AHMM "THE MARQUESA" FEB '69
EQMM "MAN WHO SPOKE IN RYHME" NOV '69
EQMM "ACRES OF BREAD" JAN '70
AHMM "BEFORE HE KILLS" DEC '73
RUSSELL, RAYMOND--[8]

BALL, BRIAN N[EVILLE]
BALL, B.N.--[31]
KINSEY-JONES, BRIAN--[8][29][31]

BALL, DONNA
BRADY, TAYLOR--W/[ELIZ] SHANNON HARPER
[21][26]ROM--
"KINCAIDS" SERIES
BRISTOL, LEIGH--W/[ELIZ] SHANNON HARPER
[9][21][26]ROM--
9 NOVELS
CARLISLE, DONNA--[9][21][26]ROM--
8 NOVELS
FLANDERS, REBECCA--[7][9][10][21][26]
ROM--NOVELS
"DREAMWEAVER" W/FELICIA GALLANT

BALL, DORIS BELL C.
BELL, JOSEPHINE--[3][5][21][26][32]--
HODDER "A HOLE IN THE GROUND" '71
HODDER "VICTIM" '75
LONGMANS "ALL IS VANITY" '40 & OTHERS
9 DIGEST STORIES [SA, JCM & OTHERS]

BALL, MARGARET
ASHTON, KATE--AUTHOR VERIFIED,
[9][21][26]ROM--
"SUNSET & DAWN"
FRASER, KATHLEEN--AUTHOR VERIFIED
[9][21][26]--5 NOVELS
LYNDELL, CATHERINE--AUTHOR VERIFIED--
"FLAMEWEAVER" BOOK BIO,
[9][21]ROM--10 NOVELS

BALL, NANONI PATRICIA M.H
HAMILTON, NAN--[32][34]MYS--
MSMM "INCIDENT AT THE BRIDGE" 'JUL '77
MSMM "FILE NO.348" MAY '78
EQMM "TOO MANY PEBBLES" SEPT '78
EQMM "MELTED-SUGAR GLAZE" DEC '79
AHMM "VISIT OF UNCLE USHIRO" MAY '80
WALKER "KILLER'S RIGHTS" '84
DODD "SHAPE OF FEAR" '86
MDL "TOMORROW IN KATMANDU" '86
SQUIRES, PATRICIA--[2]

BALL, SYLVIA PATRICIA
ENGLAND, E. SQUIRES--[31]

BALLANTINE, WILLIAM O.
BALLANTINE, BILL--[31]

BALTYNE, ADELAIDE
BALTYNE, GINA--[13]AUSTRALIAN

BALTYNE, R[OBERT] M.
COMUS--[31][33]

BALLARAT
CARMICHAEL, JENNINGS--[13]AUSTRALIAN

BALLARD, ERIC ALAN
ALLEN, ERIC--V. BERCH, MON PSEUDS, BAE 9,
P26,[3][32]MYS--NOVELS
JCM "STRONG-ARM MAN" SEPT '56
MSMM "NOISE IN THE NIGHT" OCT '59
MSMM "THE LADY KILLER" AUG '61
MON 345 "LIKE WILD" '63
MON 359 "ANOTHER NIGHT, ANOTHER LOVE" '63
"A CLEAR CASE OF CONSCIENCE" SEPT '63
MON 420 "LOUISA" '64
HARRISON, EDWIN--[3]MYS--
AMALG "THE FATAL HOUR" '58
AMALG "DIAMONDS CAN BE TROUBLE" '58
AMALG "KILLER'S PLAYGROUND" '59
AMALG "WITNESS TO MURDER" '59

BALLARD, JAMES GRAHAM
BALLARD, J. G.--[1]

BALLARD, W. TODHUNTER
AGAR, BRIAN--V. BERCH, MONARCH PSEUDS.
BAE 9, P26,[18]--
MON 195 "HAVE LOVE, WILL SHARE" '61
SOFTCOVER "THE SEX WEB" '67
BALLARD, P.D.--[3][22][28][31]MYS--
5 GM NOVELS '63-74
BALLARD, TODHTR. & PHOEBE--MUNROE RVW FEB '93-
CHILDREN'S
"MAN WHO STOLE A UNIVERSITY"
BALLARD, TODHUNTER--[8]
BALLARD, W.T.--[1][22][31][34]MYS--
12 NOVELS '42-84
BALLARD, WILLIS T.--L. ROBBINS LTR MAR '94
[31]PULP
BONNER, PARKER--V. BERCH, MON PSEUDS,
BAE 9, P26,[18][19][28][31]WEST--
8 NVLS '53-69
MON 452 "TOUGH IN THE SADDLE" '64
BOWIE, SAM--V. BERCH, MON PSEUDS, BAE 9, P26
[18][19][22][29][31]WEST--5 NOVELS '59-73
MON 113 "THUNDERHEAD RIDGE" '59
BRUCE, WALT--[18]MYS--
PPDM SHORT STORIES '42-4
CARTER, NICK--[1][3]HP--
AWARD "THE KREMLIN FILE" '73
D'ALLARD, HUNTER--[18][22][28][31]MYS--
AVON "THE LONG SWORD" '62
FOX, BRIAN--[19][28][31]WEST--
10 AWARD NVLS '68-73

BALLARD, W. TODHUNTER [CONT]
GRANGE, JOHN--W/ROBERT L. BELLEM, [18][37]--
SUD "DEALER IN DEATH" & OTHERS '42-3
HUNT, HARRISON--W/N. DAVIS, [3][22]MYS--
CURL "MURDER PICKS A JURY" '47
HUNTER, GEORGE--[8][31]
HUNTER, JOHN--[18][19][28][31]MYS/WEST--
15 NOVELS '54-75
KILGORE, WILLARD--[18][32]MYS--
SD "I COULD KILL YOU" FEB '48
MACNEIL, NEIL--V. BERCH, GM PSEUDS,
PP 33,[3][22][28][31]MYS--7 NVLS '58-66
RENO, CLINT--[1][19][28]HP--
"SIERRA MASSACRE" '74
"SUN MOUNTAIN SLAUGHTER" '74
SHEPHERD, JOHN--[3][22][28]--
BELM "LIGHTS, CAMERA, MURDER" '60
BELM 91-248 "DEMISE OF A LOUSE" '62
SLADE, JACK--[18][19][28]WEST, HP--
TWR "LASSITER"
TWR "BANDITO"
TWR "SABATA"
TWR "MAN FROM CHEYENNE"
TURNER, CLAY--[18][19][28]WEST--
PAPLB "GIVE THE MAN A GUN" '71
PAPLB "GOLD GOES TO THE MT" '74
PAPLB "GO WEST, BEN GOLD" '74
WALLACE, ROBERT--[3]HP--CORINTH/REGENCY

BALLINGER, WILLIAM S.
BALLINGER, BILL S.--[1][3][18][22]MYS/THRIL--
26 NOVELS '48-74
FREYER, FREDERIC--[3][5][18][29][31]MYS--
ST. MARTIN'S "THE BLACK, BLACK HEARST" '55
SANBORN, B.X.--[3][5][18][22]MYS--
DUTTON "THE DOOM-MAKER" '59
RPRTD AS ZENITH ZB-39 "THE BLONDE
ON BORROWED TIME" '60

BALLINGER, [V] MARGARET
HODGSON, MARGARET--[31]

BALLOD, CARL
ATLANTICUS--[39]GERMAN/SF

BALLOU, MATURIN M.
MURRAY, LT. M.M.--[34]MYS--
6 NOVELS 1887-9

BALOUGH, PENELOPE
FOX, PETRONELLA--[8][33]

BALSDON, [J.P.V.] DACRE
BALSDON, J.P.V.D.--[31]

BALTER, E.
COOKE, ARTHUR--W/C. KORNBLUTH, [2]HP
COOKE, ARTHUR--W/D.A. WOLLHEIM, [2]HP
COOKE, ARTHUR--W/J. MICHEL, [2]HP
COOKE, ARTHUR--W/R.A.W. LOWNDES, [2]HP

BALTERMAN, MARCIA R.
CARAFOLI, MARCI--[1]
MCGILL, MARCI--[1]
RIDLON, MARCI[A]--[1][31]

BALUCKI, MICHAL
ELPIDON--[22]POLISH

BALY, ELAINE
BROWNING, VIVIENNE--[8]

BALZAC, HONORE DE
SAINT-AUBIN, HORACE DE--[7]SF--
"THE CENTENARIAN; OR, THE TWO
BERINGHELDS" '76

BALZANO, JEANNE KOPPEL
BELL, GINA--[22][31]
BELL-ZANO, GINA--[22][31]
IANNONE, JEANNE--[31]

BALZER, UTA
ROGGENDORF, UTA--[39]GERMAN

BAMBARA, TONI CADE
CADE, TONI--[31]

BAMBERGER, HELEN R.
ARESBYS, THE--W/RAYMOND BAMBERGER,
[1][3][22]MYS--3 WASHBURN NVLS '27-30
BERGER, HELEN--[1][9][22]

BAMBERGER, HERMAN
VAMBERG, ARMIN--[1]

BAMBERGER, RAYMOND
ARESBYS, THE--W/HELEN R. BAMBERGER,
[1][3][22]MYS--3 WASHBURN NVLS '27-30

BAMFIELD, VERONICA
WOOD, MARY--[1][8][22]

BANBURY, OLIVE L.
LETHBRIDGE, OLIVE--[8]

BANCHINI, ELSA
STEINMANN, ELSA--[39]GERMAN/JUV

BANCROFT, GEORGE PLEYDELL
PLEYDELL, GEORGE--[3]MYS--
METHUEN "THE WARE CASE" '13

BANCROFT, IRIS M. NELSON
BANCROFT, IRIS--[21]ROM--5 NOVELS
BARNRIGHT, JULIA--[1][31]
BRENT, IRIS--[1][21][31]ROM--
"MY LOVE IS FREE"
"SWINGER'S DIARY"
LAYTON, ANDREA--[21][26]ROM--4 NOVELS
NELSON, INGRID--[21]ROM

BANCROFT, MARIE C.
O'CONNOR, PHILIP--[8]

BANDER, PETER
JONES, MELVILLE--[1][8]

BANDILLA, MARGRIT
AUPREE, LAURA--[39]GERMAN
BURTON, MARNIE--[39]GERMAN
WEIRING, KATJA--[39]GERMAN

BANDROWSKI, JULJUSZ
KADEN--[1]

BANDY, [EUGENE] FRANKLIN
FRANKLIN, EUGENE--[3][31]MYS--
STEIN "MURDER TRAP" '71
STEIN "MONEY MURDERS" '72
STEIN "BOLD HOUSE MURDERS" '73

BANG, MOLLY GARRETT
BANG, GARRETT--[31]

BANGS, JOHN KENDRICK
DRAKE, GASTON V.--[1]
GASTIT, HORACE DODD--[1]
GRAY, BLAKENEY--[1]
KENDRICK, JOHN--[1]
MANN, A. SUFFERAN--[1]
MORLEY, ARTHUR SPENCER--[1]
PODMORE, PERIWINKLE--[1]

BANGS, **JOHN KENDRICK [CONT]**
SMITH, T. CARLYLE--[1]
WAGS, TWA--W/FRANK D. SHERMAN, [1][2]
WITHERUP, ANNE WARRINGTON--[11]SF

BANGS, **ROBERT BABBITT**
BABBITT, ROBERT--[1][31]

BANIM, **JOHN & MICHAEL**
O'HARA FAMILY--[2][3]MYS--
CARY "GHOST HUNTER & HIS FAMILY" 1833

BANIS, **VICTOR J[EROME]**
ALEXANDER, JAN--[3][7][9][11][21][26]MYS/ROM--
19 NOVELS '70-7
BANIS, V.J.--[21]ROM--NOVELS
BANIS, VICTOR--[21]ROM--NOVELS
BENEDICT, LYNN--[2][3][9][11][21][26]MYS/ROM--
7 AVON NOVELS '73-4
JAY, VICTOR--V. BERCH, BRNDN/
BC PSEUDS., BAE 22, P24,[14]ADULT--
OLYM TC#484 "THE GAY HAUNT" '70
MONTEREY, ELIZABETH--[9][21][26]ROM--
"A WESTWARD LOVE"
SAMUELS, VICTOR--[1][2]

BANK, **THEODORE PAUL II**
BANK, TED--[31]
KIRK, TED--[31]

BANKOFF, **GEORGE ALEXIS**
BORODIN, GEORGE--[1][2]

BANKS, **ARTHUR LESLIE**
BANKS, A. LESLIE--[31]
BANKS, A.L.--[31]

BANKS, **CAROLYN**
CLIMER, NANCY--HAWK/BANKS INTRVW MAY '93
DUNCAN, LYNNE--HAWK/BANKS INTRVW MAY '93

BANKS, **ELIZABETH**
ENID--[1]
MAXWELL, MARY M.--[1]

BANKS, **HARRY**
OHON--[1]

BANKS, **JAMES HOUSTON**
BANKS, JIMMY--[31]

BANKS, **JANE**
BANKS, TAYLOR--[1][31]

BANKS, **JEFF**
RIBBER, JACK D.--[1][2]

BANKS, **JOHN**
SLADE, MICHAEL--W/JAY CLARKE, LEE CLARKE &
RICHARD COVELL, [3][7]MYS--
ALLEN "HEADHUNTER" '84
BEECH TREE "GHOUL" '87

BANKS, **LYNNE REID**
REID BANKS, LYNNE--[7]SF--8 NOVELS '76-89

BANKS, **MICHAEL A.**
GOULD, ALAN--[23]SF

BANKS, **RAYMOND E.**
BURCH, RALPH--GLEN COOK & V. BERCH LTRS '93--
WW[HUSTLER] "DUPLICATE LOVERS" '80
FREAIR, FRED--V. BERCH LTR '93--
PLANET STORIES "LIFE OF A
SALESMAN" WINT '54-5

BANKS, **SARA [J.G.H.]**
HARRELL, SARA [J] GORDON--[1][31][33]

BANNER, **CHARLA ANN L.**
LEIBENGUTH, CHARLA ANN--[31]

BANNER, **HUBERT STEWART**
VEXILLUM--[22]ENGLISH-AMERICAN

BANNISTER, **DONALD**
BANNISTER, DON--[31]

BANNISTER, **PATRICIA**
VERYAN, PATRICIA--[8][9][21][26][34]MYS/ROM--
ST. MARTIN'S "LOGIC OF THE
HEART" '90 & 22 OTHERS
MOORE, GWYNETH--[9][21][26]ROM--3 NOVELS

BANTEL, **LINDA**
SAMTER, LINDA BARTEL--W/JAMES T. FLEXNER,[31]--
POTTER "FACE OF LIBERTY:
FOUNDERS OF THE U.S." '75

BANZHAF, **ERWIN**
DONALD, FRANK--[39]GERMAN/MYS
KENNETH, GORDON--[39]GERMAN/MYS
MOREL, ED--[39]GERMAN/MYS
YALE, REX--[39]GERMAN/MYS

BAR-ZOHAR, **MICHAEL**
BARAK, MICHAEL--[29][31][34]MYS--
4 NOVELS '76-81
HASTINGS, MICHAEL--[29][31][34]MYS--
MacM "A SPY IN THE WINTER" '84
MacM "UNKNOWN SOLDIER" '86
SCRIBNER "THE DEVIL'S SPY" '88

BARACH, **ALVAN LEROY**
COIGNARD, JOHN--[8]

BARADA, **WILLIAM RICHARD**
BARADA, BILL--[31]

BARAKA, **AMIRI**
JONES, LEROI--[31]

BARANAUKAS, **ANTANAS**
BARONAS, ANTANAS--[22]LITHUANIAN

BARANIECKI, **ROBERT LEO**
HORN, LUDWIG J.--[39]GERMAN/JUV

BARASCH, **MARC IAN**
ZEIT, CALVIN--W/HENRIK DRESCHER, [1][31]--
QUILLER "TRUE PARANOID FACTS" '82
ZEIT, CALVIN--[1][18]--SIX NOVELS

BARBARA, **JOSEPH ROLAND**
BARBERA, JOE--[33]

BARBER, **DULAN F.**
FLETCHER, DAVID--[18][29][31][34]MYS--
12 NOVELS '74-89

BARBER, **DULAN F.W.**
BROOKES, OWEN--[18][31][34]MYS--
6 NOVELS '79-85
RUSH, ROBERT--[1][18][34]MYS--
FUTURA "BIRTHDAY TREAT" '81
MacDON "BIRTHDAY GIRL" '83

BARBER, **MARGARET FAIRLESS**
FAIRLESS, MICHAEL--[11][38]SF--
"THE ROADMINDER"

BARBER, STEPHEN GUY
BERNARD, GUY--[31]

BARBER, WALTER LANIER
BARBER, RED--[31]--
DBLDY "RHUBARB IN THE CATBIRD SEAT" '68

BARBERA, JOSEPH ROLAND
BARBERA, JOE--[31]

BARBERIS, FRANCO
BARBERIS--[1][31]

BARBERIS, JUAN CARLOS
KUMPA--[33]
MY--[33]

BARBERO, YVES REGIS FRAN.
FRANCOIS, YVES REGIS--[7]SF--
DBLDY "THE CTZ PARADIGM" '75

BARBIERI, ELAINE
ROME, ELAINE--[26]ROM--
"STARK LIGHTNING"

BARBILIAN, DAN
BARBU, ION--[22]RUMANIAN

BARBOLLA, BARBARA MARTYN
MARTYN, DON--[34][40]MYS--
7 HALE NOVELS '65-71
"NO GUEST AT THE VILLA" '71

BARBOUR, ANNA MARY
BARBOUR, A[NNA]MAYNARD--[1][3][29]MYS--
5 NOVELS 1897-06

BARBOUR, H.W.
VAUGHN, JASON--[34]MYS--
VANTAGE "TRAILOR PARK" '75

BARBOUR, RALPH HENRY
POWELL, RICHARD STILLMAN--[22][33]MYS

BARBROOK, ALEXANDER THO.
BARBROOK, ALEC--[31]

BARCLAY, FLORENCE L.C.
ROY, BRANDON--[1][17]ROM

BARCLAY, GEORGE
KINNOCH, R.G.B.--[1]

BARCLAY, VERA C.
BEECH, MARGARET--[1][9]ROM

BARCYNSKI, LEON ROGER
PHILLIPS, OSBORNE--[1]

BARCYNSKI, VIVIAN G.
DENNING, MELITA--[1][31]

BARCZZA, ALICJA
ORME, ALEXANDRA--[8]

BARDENS, DENNIS [C]
FAREL, CONRAD--[1][22][31]ENGLISH
ROBERTS, JULIAN--[1][22]ENGLISH

BARDEY, EMIL
ANTON, EMIL--[39]GERMAN

BARDIN, JOHN FRANKLIN
ASHE, DOUGLAS--[2][18][21][26][29][31]ROM--
PAPLB "THE LONGSTREET LEGACY" '70

BARDIN, JOHN FRANKLIN [CONT]
TREE, GREGORY--[1][3][18][29]MYS--
SCRIB "A SHROUD FOR GRANDMA" '51
SCRIB "CASE AGAINST BUTTERFLY" '51
SCRIB "CASE AGAINST MYSELF" '50
SCRIB "SO YOUNG TO DIE" '53

BARFIELD, ARTHUR OWEN
BURGEON, G.A.L.--[1][2][22][23][31]ENGLISH/SF

BARGONE, FREDERIC C.P.E.
FARRERE, CLAUDE--[2][3][7][23]BRENT--
ANO "MAN WHO KILLED" '17
DUTTON "HOUSE OF THE SECRET" '23
DUTTON "USELESS HANDS" '26
DUTTON "BLACK OPIUM" '29

BARHAM, RICHARD HARRIS
INGOLDSBY, THOMAS--[1][2][11]

BARISH, EVELYN
GREENBERGER, EVELYN BAR.--[31]

BARK, CONRAD VOSS
VOSS BARK, CONRAD--[7][31]SF--
NEL "THE BIG WAVE" '79

BARKER, ALBERT W.
KING, REEFE--[1]
MACRAE, HAWK--[1][33]

BARKER, ARTHUR JAMES
BARKER, A.J.--[1]
MUSKATEER--[1][22]ENGLISH

BARKER, C. HEDLEY
HEDLEY, FRANK--[1][3]MYS--
LIPPINCOTT "CAVALIER OF CRIME" '37
SEAFARER--[1][3]MYS--
11 WARD NOVELS '54-60

BARKER, DUDLEY
BLACK, LIONEL--[3][18][29][31]MYS--
18 NOVELS '60-81
MATTHEWS, ANTHONY--[1][3][18][29]--
IN ENGLAND ON SOME WORK
AS BY 'LIONEL BLACK'

BARKER, ELSA [M]
BARKER, E.M.--[1][31]
JORDAN, NELL--[1]

BARKER, ELVER A.
HARDING, CARL B.--[1][31]

BARKER, ILSE EVA L.
TALBOT, KATHRINE--[8]

BARKER, LEONARD NOEL
NOEL, L.--[1][2][3]MYS--
13 PAUL NOVELS '27-47

BARKER, MARY ANNE
BROOME, LADY MARY ANNE--[13]AUSTRALIAN

BARKER, MUHAMMED ABD
BARKER, M.A.R.--[7]SF--
DAW "TEKUMEL #1 " & OTHERS

BARKER, REBECCA
BARKER, BECKY--[21]ROM--
"CAPTURED BY A COWBOY"

BARKER, REGINALD C.
HARRINGTON, LEE--L. ROBBINS LTR MAR '94, PULP

BARKER, RONALD [ERNEST]
RONALD, E.B.--[3][22]MYS--
GOLZ "CAT & FIDDLE MURDERS" '54
GOLZ "DEATH BY PROXY" '56
BOARDMAN "A SORT OF MADNESS" '58

BARKER, RONNIE
WILEY, GERALD--[8]

BARKER, S. OMAR
CANUSI, JOSE--[1][22][31][33]AMERICAN
SCOTT, DAN--[1][22][28][33]AMERICAN--
CHILDREN'S
SQUIRES, PHIL--[1][11][22][33]AMERICAN

BARKER, WILL
DEMAREST, DOUG--[1][22][31][33]AMERICAN

BARKER, WILLIAM JOHN
BARKER, BILL--[31]

BARKIN, CAROL
CARROLL, ELIZABETH--W/ELIZABETH JAMES,
BARKIN CONFIRMED JAN '94--
S&S "SUMMER LOVE" '83
HASTINGS, BEVERLY--W/ELIZABETH JAMES,
[1][3]MYS--
JOVE "DON'T TALK TO STRANGERS" '80
BERK "DON'T WALK HOME ALONE" '85
BERK "WATCHER IN THE DARK" '86
POCK "DON'T CRY, LITTLE GIRL" '87
BERK "DON'T LOOK BACK" '91
BERK "HOME BEFORE DARK" '93
BERK "SOMEBODY HELP ME" '93

BARKUDARIAN, TADEOS A.
KOLUNTSEV, FEDOR--[1]

BARLETTA, PATRICIA L.
CHRISTOPHER, AMY--[26]--
"CAPTIVE KISS"
"ECSTACY'S GAMBLE"
"REBEL'S CAPTIVE"

BARLEY, MAURICE WILLMORE
BARLEY, M.W.--[31]
BARLING, CHARLES--[3][22][29][31]ENGLISH/MYS--
8 HALE NVLS '63-8

BARLING, MURIEL VERE MANT
BARRINGTON, P.V.--[3][22][29][31]ENGLISH
MYS, GM "NIGHT OF VIOLENCE" '59
BARRINGTON, PAMELA--
[3][22][29][31]ENGLISH,MYS--
GM "ACCOUNT RENDERED" '53 &
18 OTHERS '32-68

BARLING, PHILIP
BEN, PHILIP--[1]
GREET, BEN--[1]

BARLOW, JAMES HENRY S.
FORDEN, JAMES--[1][29]--
HAMILTON "THE PATRIOTS" '60
HAMILTON "THIS SIDE OF THE SKY" '64
HAMILTON "LINER" '73

BARLOW, JAMES WILLIAM
SKORPIOS, ANTARES--[1][2][11]

BARLTROP, ROBERT
COSTER, ROBERT--[31]

BARME, GEREMIE
BAI JIEMING--[31]

BARNARD, ALFRED J.
CLIFFORD, MARTIN--[1]HP
HART, LEONARD--[1]

BARNARD, AMY
BARR, MAYNARD--[1][32]MYS--
ST "LING-TSU'S EXPERIMENTS IN FEAR" MAR '63

BARNARD, ELIZABETH QUINN
QUINN, ELIZABETH--[21][26]ROM--
"ALLIANCES"
"ANY DAY NOW"

BARNARD, JUDITH
MICHAEL, JUDITH--W/MICHAEL FAIN
[1][9][21][26]ROM--7 NOVELS

BARNARD, LESLIE T.
BOGAR, JEFF--[34]MYS, HP--
HAMILTON "HOODMAN'S BAIT" '53
HAMILTON "DINAH FOR DANGER" '52
RPRTD AS LION 79 "MY GUN, HER BODY" '52
MARLOWE, GREG--[34]MYS, HP--
HAMILTON "BEHIND THE ENEMY" '52
HAMILTON "DEATH-MASK OF WAR" '52
REGAN, CASS--[34]--
HAMILTON--4 'RUSTY BROWN' NOVELS '52
STRATTON, JEFF--[34]MYS--
HAMILTON "DOUBLE TROUBLE" '52
HAMILTON "TERROR ON THE RAILROAD" '52
HAMILTON "THE MAIN HIGHWAY" '52

BARNARD, MARJORIE FAITH
ELDERSHAW, M. BARNARD--W/FLORA ELDERSHAW
[2][3][7][11][23]MYS/SF--
ANGUS "MURDER PIE" '36
ANGUS "TOMORROW & TOMORROW" '47

BARNARD, MELVILLE CLEMENT
ARID, BEN--[1][22]

BARNARD, RICHARD INNES
RICHARDS, FRANK--[1]HP

BARNARD, ROBERT
BASTABLE, ROBERT--
MYS SCENE #38, P60,
"TO DIE LIKE A GENTLEMAN" '93

BARNARD, WILHELMUS
VAN DER GRAFT, GUILLAUME--[22]DUTCH

BARNE, MARION C.
BARNE, KITTY--[1][25][31]ENGLISH, CHILDREN'S
BOOKS

BARNES, ARTHUR K.
BARNES, DAVE--W/NORBERT DAVIS, [1][2][11]SF
KENT, KELVIN--W/HENRY KUTTNER, [1][2]--
TWS "ROMAN HOLIDAY" &
TWS "SCIENCE IS GOLDEN" BOTH '39
KENT, KELVIN--[23]--
TWS - 4 STORIES '39-44

BARNES, CLARA ERNST
ERNST, CLARA--[23][31]AMERICAN/SF

BARNES, DJUNA
STEPTOE, LYDIA--[1][22]

BARNES, HALLY
BARNES, AL--[1]

BARNES, JULIAN [P]
KAVANAGH, DAN--[3][18][23][31]MYS--
CAPE "DUFFY" '80
CAPE "FIDDLE CITY" '81
CAPE "PUTTING THE BOOT IN" '85
VIKING "GOING TO THE DOGS" '87
SEAL, BASIL--[8]

BARNES, MICHAEL [L.G.]
CELLO, JOHNNY--[34]MYS--HP--
SCION "LIGHTS OUT!" '53
CLINTON, MAX--PPCC#7, P64,[34]MYS--HP--
COMYNS "NO DAME WANTS TO DIE" '52
COMYNS "NO PLACE FOR A DAME" '53
DRAYTON, RICKY--[1][2][3][29]MYS--
24 NOVELS '51-54
HANSON, FRANK--[34]MYS--
SCION "YOU'VE BEEN TUMBLED" '52
SCION "LADY BE BAD" '53
SCION "I'LL GET BY" '53
MEDUSA, KARL--[27][34]MYS--
SCION "I SPY" '51
SCION "LOW-DOWN ON G-MEN" '51
SCION "THEY KILL BY NIGHT" '52
WESLEY, ALISON--[33]
ZORE, HYMAN--[3]MYS--HP--
SCION "BLUE ORCHID" '53

BARNES, PATRICIA
ABERCROMBIE, PATRICIA B.--[8]

BARNES, RONALD GORELL
GORELL, LORD--[3][29]MYS--10 BOOKS '22-54

BARNES, STEPHEN EMORY
BARNES, STEVEN--[7][31]SF--
ACE "STREETLETHAL" '83
TOR "KUNDALINI EQUATION" '86
TOR "GORGON CHILD" '89

BARNES-SVARNEY, PATRICIA
BARNES, LOUTRICIA--[31]

BARNETT, JAMES MONROE
BARNETT, JIM--[31]MYS--
SFDS "SHE DESERVED TO DIE" APR '57
TFDS "THE TWISTED ONE" MAR '60

BARNETT, NAOMI
BACHHEIMER, NAOMI BARNETT--[1][31][33]

BARNETT, PAUL LE PAGE
BREZHNEV, DENNIS--[2]
DEVERAUX, EVE--[2][23]
GRANT, JOHN--W/DAVID LANGFORD, [7]SF--
GRAFTON "EARTHDOOM" '87
GRANT, JOHN--[2][7][23]SF--
"ARIES I" '79
"ALBION" '91

BARNEY, MAGINEL WRIGHT
ENRIGHT, MAGINEL WRIGHT--[1][33]

BARNITT, NEDDA LAMONT
LAMONT, N.B.--[1][31]
LAMONT, NEDDA--[1][31]

BARNSLEY, ALAN G.
FIELDING, GABRIEL--[8][22]ENGLISH

BARNUM, AUGUSTINE
FAX--[1]

BAROCHE, JACQUES ANTOINE
RAMUS, PIERRE--[1]

BARON, ORA WENDY
DIMSON, WENDY--[31]

BARON, OSCAR
BORDEN, ORSON T.--[1]

BARONDESS, SUE KAUFMAN
KAUFMAN, SUE--[1][22][31]AMERICAN

BAROVSKY, SHARON DALEY
DALEY, SHARON--[31]

BARR, ANTHONY
BARR, TONY--[31]

BARR, BETTY
SKIPPER, BETTY--[1]

BARR, ELIZABETH
EDWARDS, IRENE--[29]MYS--
HALE "CASTLE HERITAGE" '77

BARR, PATRICIA
HAZARD, LAURENCE--[8][32]MYS--
JCM "A CORPSE FOR CHRISTMAS"
JCM "SO KIND OF YOU, SANTA" DEC '59

BARR, PATRICIA MIRIAM
BARR, PAT--[21]ROM--
"JADE"
"KENJIRO"

BARR, ROBERT
SHARP, LUKE--[22][29][34]MYS--
NOVELS & SS COLL 1892-10
"YOUNG LORD STRANLEIGH" '23

BARRACLOUGH, JUNE [MARY]
BENN, JUNE--[31]
BENN, JUNE WEDGEWOOD--[31]

BARRADELL-SMITH, WALTER
BIRD, RICHARD--[1]

BARRATT, GLYNN [RICHARD]
BARRATT, G.R.V.--[31]
BARRETT, G.R.--[31]

BARRAUD, E.M.
JOHNS, HILARY--[8]

BARRE, JEAN
LINDSAY, LEE--[3]MYS--
WRIGHT "THREE BUCCANEERS" '34
WRIGHT "CRUSADERS SECRET" '37

BARREN, CHARLES MCKINNON
RAINHAM, THOMAS--[3][31]ENGLISH/MYS--
HURST "TOO LATE TO MEND" '57
& 8 OTHERS '57-66

BARRER-RUSSELL, GERTRUDE
BARRER, GERTRUDE--[31][33]

BARRETT, ALFRED WALTER
ANDOM, R.--[2][3][8][22][23]ENGLISH/SF--
"BUNGLINGS OF TUTT" '05
"GENIAL RASCAL" '09

BARRETT, CHARLES LESLIE
BARR, DONALD--[1]

BARRETT, DEAN
CHAR, YUM--[1][31]

BARRETT, ELIZABETH
COLLINS, CHRISTINE--[9][21][26]ROM--
"A MAN'S FANCY"
MCLEAN, CARA--[9][21][26]ROM--
"THE PERFECT MIX"

BARRETT, GEOFFREY JOHN
ANDERS, REX--[28]WEST, GRESHAM--
5 NOVELS '63-66
BARRETT, G.J.--[1]
BLAINE, JEFF--L. ROBBINS LTR MAR '94,
[28]WEST--
HALE-13 NOVELS '62-88
COLE, RICHARD--[28]ENGLISH
GORT, SAM--[28]WEST--
HALE "GUNN CAME BACK" '88
HALE "THE FASTEST GUN" '89
GREER, JACK--WEST--
HALE-4 NOVELS '88-91
KILBOURN, MATT--[28]WEST--
HALE "THREE GUNS FROM MIDNIGHT" '65
HALE "FACE THE QUICK GUN" '66
LEIGHTON, EDWARD--[7][21][23][28]SF--
HALE "A LIGHT FROM TOMORROW" '77
HALE "LORD OF THE LIGHTNING" '77
HALE "OUT OF EARTH'S DEEP" '77
HALE "LORD OF LIGHTNING" '77
MACEY, CARN--[28]WEST--
GRESHAM-4 NOVELS '64-65
RICKARD, COLE--D. WHITEHEAD-PPCC#9/[28]WEST--
THORPE "RIDERS OF THE WHITE HELL" '93
THORPE "RED BOUNTY" '94 & 20 MORE '64-91
ROYAL, DAN--[28]WEST--
HALE-24 NOVELS '65-91
SANDERS, BRETT--[28]WEST--
GRESHAM-4 NOVELS '64-66
STERN, MAX--[28]WEST--
HALE-4 NOVELS '89-91
SUMMERS, D.B.--L. ROBBINS LTR MAR'94,
[28]WEST--
HALE-17 NOVELS '65-89
SUMMERS, DENNIS--[7][23][28]--
HALE "A MADNESS FROM MARS" '76
HALE "ROBOT IN THE GLASS" '77
HALE "STALKER OF THE WORLDS" '77
WADE, BILL--[1][23][28]WEST--
35 NOVELS '65-90
WALLACE, JAMES--[7][23][28]SF--
HALE "A MAN FOR TOMORROW" '76
HALE "PLAGUE OF THE GOLDEN RAT" '76
HALE "GUARDIAN OF KRANDOR" '77

BARRETT, HARRY B.
BEMISTER, HENRY--[1][31]

BARRETT, HELEN
CHANNING, JUSTIN--W/KAREN HITZIG,
[9][21][26]ROM--
"CAROLINA WOMAN"
"SOUTHERN BLOOD"

BARRETT, HUGH G.
BELLMAN, WALTER--[1]

BARRETT, JUDITH
BARRETT, JUDI--[31]

BARRETT, MAX
BARRETT, MAYE--[1][3][9][21]--
ZEBRA "A LADY OF STANTONWYCK" '81
& 3 OTHERS

BARRETT, MONTGOMERY
BARRETT, MONTE--[1][31]

BARRETT, NEAL JR.
APPLETON, VICTOR--HAWK/BARRETT INTRVW '92,
[7]SF,HP--
STSY 'TOM SWIFT':
"ARK TWO"
"THE INVISIBLE FORCE"
CALHOUN, CHAD--R. BENOIT,CRPG, HP--
DELL 07323 "RIVER BEAUTY" '82
DIXON, FRANKLIN W.--HAWK/BARRETT
INTRVW JAN '92, HP--
STSY "HARDY BOYS"
DUNCAN, TERRENCE--R. BENOIT, HP--
POWELL'S ARMY' SERIES
DRURY, REBECCA--R. BENOIT,[21]HIST, HP--
'WOMEN AT WAR': SERIES
"VALIANT WINGS"
ELLIS, WESLEY--S. CUPP/GARDNER/R. BENOIT, HP--
'LONE STAR'SERIES:
"KANSAS TIMBER WOLVES" '83
"RENEGADE COMANCHES" '83
"DENVER MADAM" '83
"SAN ANTONIO RAID" '83
"MOUNTAIN MEN" '84
"SCHOOL FOR OUTLAWS" '85
"BUFFALO HUNTER" '85
"ALASKA GUNS" '85
"CHEROKEE STRIP" '85
HARDIN, J.D.--R. BENOIT, HP--
"COLD HEARTED LADY" '81
"BOBBIES, BAUBLES & BLOOD" '81
"HARD CHAINS, SOFT WOMEN" '81

BARRETT, NORMAN [S]
BARRETT, N.S.--[31]

BARRETT, WILLIAM CHRIST.
BROWN, MOSES--[31]

BARRETTO, LAURENCE B.
BREVOORT, LAURENCE--[1][31]

BARRICKLOW, PATTI B.
BURROUGHS, PATRICIA--[9][21][26]ROM--
5 NOVELS

BARRINGTON, HOWARD
STONE, SIMON--[1][3][8][22]MYS--
7 NOVELS '42-51

BARRON, ANN FORMAN
ERWIN, ANNABEL--[21][26][31]ROM--
"AURIELLE"
"LILIANE"

BARRON, OSWALD
LONDONER--[1]

BARROW, KENNETH
BRAITHWAITE, KENNETH JAME--[31]

BARROW, P.S.
SARBROW, CEPRE--[1][2]

BARROWS, [RUTH] MARJORIE
ALDEN, JACK--[1][8][31]
AMES, NOEL--[1][31]
BARROWS, R.M.--[1][31]
BOOJUM--[1]
DIXON, RUTH--[1][8][31]
GRAHAM, HUGH--[1][31]
PSYCHO ANN--[1]

BARRY, JOHN ARTHUR
BARRY, J.A.--[1]

BARSTOW, PHYLLIDA
HART-DAVIS, PHYLLIDA--[31]

BARTEL, ANNE-MARIE [S]
MAMPEL, ANNE-MARIE--[39]GERMAN/JUV

BARTH, CHARLES P.
BUFFALO CHUCK--[31]

BARTH, OSKAR
BARBE, TILL--[39]GERMAN
RUBIN, SEP--[39]GERMAN

BARTHEL, MANFRED
HALLER, MICHAEL--[39]GERMAN
HELLBERG, WOLFGANG--[39]GERMAN

BARTHEL-WINKLER, FRITZ
BARWIN, F.L.--W/LISA BARTHEL-WINKLER, [39]GERMAN/ADV/WEST

BARTHEL-WINKLER, LISA
BARWIN, F.L.--W/FRITZ BARTHEL-WINKLER, [39]GERMAN/ADV/WEST

BARTHOLOMEW, FRANK H.
BARTHOLOMEW, BART--[31]

BARTLE, HANIA ANNETTE
BARRY, ANDREA--[9][21][26]ROM--
"AFRICAN ENCHANTMENT"

BARTLE, L.E.
LAURENCE, RICHARD--[1][2][11]
RICHARDSON, FRANCIS--W/FRANK H. PARNELL,[1][2][11]

BARTLETT, ELSA JAFFE
JAFFE, ELSA--[31]

BARTLETT, FREDERIC CHARLE
BARTLETT, F.C.--[31]

BARTLETT, FREDERICK ORIN
CARLETON, WILLIAM [WILL]--[1]

BARTLETT, MARIE
BARTLETT, BILLIE--[1]
LEE, ROWENA--[1][9][31]ROM
LINDEN, SARA--[1][31]
RIFT, VALERIE--[1][9]ROM
SWAN, MARIE--[1]

BARTLETT, STEPHEN
SLADE, GURNEY--[1][13]AUSTRALIAN

BARTLETT, VERNON
OLDFELD, PETER--W/PER JACOBSSON, [3][22][29]MYS--
WASHBURN "DEATH OF A DIPLOMAT" '28
WASHBURN "ALCHEMY MURDER" '29

BARTON, JILLIAN
BARTON, JILL--[33]--
COLLINS "WITCHES & THE SINGING MICE" '93

BARTON, JOHN
GRUELLE, JOHNNY--[1]

BARTON, PAT
ARROWSMITH, PAT--[33]

BARTON, ROBERT EUSTACE
EUSTACE, ROBERT--[2][3][29][32]--
LONG "HUMAN BACILLUS" '07

BARTON, ROBERT EUSTACE [CONT]
EUSTACE, ROBERT [CONT]
EQMM "MAN WHO DISAPPEARED" MAY '48
MEADE, L.T.--W/ELIZABETH T. SMITH, [3]MYS--
"A MASTER OF MYSTERY" 1898
"GOLD STAR LINE"1899
"THE SANCTUARY CLUB" 1900

BARTON, WYNNE
ANDERSON, ADRIENNE--[7]SF

BARTOSCHEK, EVA [R]
RECHLIN, EVA--[39]GERMAN/JUV

BARTOSIEWICZ, EDWARD JOHN
BARTEK, E.J.--[1]

BARTZ, PATRICIA MCBRIDE
MCBRIDE, PATRICIA--[1]

BARUCH, HUGO
BILBO, JACK--[2][11][39]GERMAN/SF
BOLBO, KAPT'N--[39]GERMAN

BARUCH, MOSES
AUERBACH, BERTHOLD--[39]GERMAN
CHAUBER, THEOBALD--[39]GERMAN

BARUFELD, R.
LEIGH, VERONICA--V. BERCH LTR TO HUBIN '94

BARWICK, TONY
BARWICK, JAMES--W/DONALD JAMES, [3]MYS--
MacM "HANGMAN'S CRUSADE" '81 & OTHERS

BARZINI, LUIGI G.
SMITH, LOUIS--[31]

BASCOM, DAVID
POLTROON, MILFORD--[1]

BASE, A.H.
ARTHUR, HARRY--[1]

BASHMAK, IAKOV VASILEVICH
BASH, IAKOV VASILEVICH--[1]

BASIE, WILLIAM JAMES
BASIE, COUNT--[31]

BASIL, OTTO
HORMANN, MARKUS--[39]GERMAN

BASILE, GLORIA VITANEA
MORGAN, MICHAELA--[9][21][26]--
"MADELAINA"
"ZANZARA"

BASIT, ABDUL
BASIT, M.A.--[1]

BASKIN, MARJORIE RAWLINGS
RAWLINGS, MARJORIE KINNAN--[1]

BASNER, GERHARD
BARNER, G.F.--[39]GERMAN/WEST
DUFF, HOWARD--[39]GERMAN/WEST, HP
FREDERICK, GERALD--[39]GERMAN/WEST
PETERS, A.F. JR.--[39]GERMAN/WEST, HP
PETERS, CLAUS--[39]GERMAN/WEST
RINGO, JOHNNY--[39]GERMAN/WEST
WACO, G.F.--[39]GERMAN/WEST
WEGO, G.F.--[39]GERMAN/WEST

BASON, FREDERICK THOMAS
BASON, FRED--[31]

BASON, FREDERICK THOMAS [CONT]
GALLERITE, THE--[22][31]ENGLAND

BASS, ALTHA LEAH B.
BASS, ALTHEA--[31]

BASS, CLARA MAY
OVERY, CLAIRE MAY--[8]

BASSETT, FLORA MARJORIE
BASSETT, MARNIE--[1][13][31]AUSTRALIAN

BASSETT, RONALD LESLIE
CLIVE, WILLIAM--[1][8][31]

BASSETT, WILLIAM B.K.
DARIEN, PETER--[22][31]AMERICAN

BASSLER, THOMAS J.
BASS, T.J.--[2][4][11][23][31]SF

BASSNETT, SUSAN E[DNA]
BASSNETT-MCGUIRE, SUSAN--[31]

BASTIAN, HARTMUT
EIGK, CLAUS--[39]GERMAN/SF

BASTIN, JOHN
STURGIS, J.B.--[8]

BATAILLE, GEORGES
ANGELIQUE, PIERRE--[1][31]
AUCH, LORD--[1][31]

BATBEDAT, JEAN
LARNEUIL, MICHEL--[1]

BATCHELDER, JOHN
FORMER RESIDENT OF HUB--[2]

BATCHELOR, RICHARD A.C.
HENTON, COLLETT--[1]
MAYNE, ARTHUR--[1]

BATEMAN, F. JOHN ALFORD
PATON, JOHN--[7][23]--
HALE "LEAP TO THE GALACTIC CORE" '78
HALE "PROTEUS" '79
HALE "SEA OF RINGS" '79

BATEMAN, HENRY GIBSON
GIBSON, HENRY--[1]

BATEMAN, ROBERT MOYES
MOYES, ROBIN--[8]

BATES, BARBARA S.
CUYLER, STEPHEN--[1][22][31][33]
ROBERTS, JIM--[1][22][33]

BATES, CLIVE
IRVING, CLIVE--[1]

BATES, ELIZABETH
BATES, BETTY--[31]

BATES, HARRY ARTHUR
ARTHUR, HARRY--[1][3][22]MYS--
PAGEANT "SUMMER SHOWERS" '52
GILMOUR, ANTHONY--W/DESMOND W. HALL
[2][4][7][11][23]SF--
'HAWK CARSE' SERIES
HOLMES, A.R.--[1][2][11][23]SF
SABE, QUIEN--[2][11]
WINTER, H.G.--W/DESMOND W. HALL
[1][2][11][23]SF

BATES, HERBERT ERNEST
BATES, H.E.--[1]HIST/ROM
FLYING OFFICER X--[2][29][31]--
"THE PURPLE PLAIN" '49
GAWSWORTH, JOHN--[1][31]

BATES, SUSANNAH VACELLA
BATES SU--[31]
CHURCH, SUZANNE--[1][31]

BATESON, FREDERIK WILSE
BATESON, F.W.--[1]

BATEY, TOM
TOMKINS, JASPER--[33]

BATISTA Y ZALDIVAR, FULG.
BATISTA, FULGENCIO--[31]

BATRA, RAVEENDRA N[ATH]
BATRA, RAVI--[31]

BATT, LEON
DU BOIS, LEON--[36]AUSTRALIAN/MYS--
PERTINENT "LEGIONAIRE & OTHER STORIES" '45
FORRESTER, E.--[36]AUSTRALIAN/MYS--
PERTINENT "LEGIONAIRE & OTHER STORIES" '45
HERBERTSON, A.--[36]AUSTRALIAN/MYS--
PERTINENT "LEGIONAIRE & OTHER STORIES" '45
SINGLETON, LEONARD--[36]AUSTRALIAN/MYS--
PERTINENT "LEGIONAIRE & OTHER STORIES" '45
WARNE, LEONA--[36]AUSTRALIAN/MYS--
PERTINENT "LEGIONAIRE & OTHER STORIES" '45
WEBLEY, JONATHAN--[36]AUSTRALIAN/PERTINENT--
"MILLS OF GODS" nd
"LEGIONAIRE & OTHER STORIES" '45

BATTERBURY, ARIANE R.
RUSHKIN, ARIANE--[1]

BATTIN, BRINTON WARNER
BATTIN, B.W.--[31]
BATTIN, BUCK--[1][31]
WARNER, LEE--[7][31]SF--
POCK "INTO THE PIT" '89
POCK "IT'S LOOSE" '90

BATTISCOMBE, ESTHER G.H.
BATTISCOMBE, E. GEORGINA--[31]ENGLISH
HARWOOD, GINA--[1][31][22]

BATTISI, EUGENIO
RINALDINI, ANGIOLO--[1]

BATTLES, ROXY EDITH
BATTLES, EDITH--[21]ROM--
"SECRET OF CASTLE DRAI"

BATTYE, GLADYS STARKEY
LYNN, MARGARET--[3][8][9][21]
[26][29][31]ROM--
HODDER "TO SEE A STRANGER" '61
HODDER "WHISPER OF DARKNESS" '65
HODDER "A LIGHT IN THE WINDOW" '67
& MORE

BATY, LINDA LEA
THRASHER, L.L.--BATY LTR DEC '93--
COUNCIL OAKS BKS "CAT'S PAW, INC" '91

BAUCH, KATHE
BUCHA, KARIN--[39]GERMAN

BAUDISCH, PAUL
ROLAND, GEORGES--[39]GERMAN

BAUER, DIETER
BAUER, HEDI--[39]GERMAN/JUV

BAUER, ERWIN A.
BOURBON, KEN--[1][22][31]AMERICAN, OUTDOORS & ADVENTURE
FRANKLIN, NAT--[1][31]
HARDIN, TOM--[1][22][31]AMERICAN
NORTH, CHARLES W.--[1][22]AMERICAN
PETERS, BARNEY--[1]

BAUER, GERARD
GUERMANTES--[1]

BAUER, HERBERT
BALAZS, BELA--[22]HUNGARIAN-AUSTRIAN

BAUERLE, ADOLF-JOHANN
HORN, OTTO--[39]GERMAN/SF

BAUM, L[YMAN] FRANK
AKERS, FLOYD--[2][11][22][23][25][33]FANTASY
BANCROFT, LAURA--[1][2][23][25][33]
BARTLETT, LAURA--[8][11]
BAUM, LOUIS F.--[1][31]
BROOKS, GEORGE--[1][31]
COOKE, JOHN ESTES--[2][11][23][25][31]-- "TAMAWACA FOLKS" '07
FITZGERALD, CAPT. HUGH--[2][11][23][25][31]
FITZGERALD, HUGH--[2][11][23][25]
METCALF, SUZANNE--[2][11][33]
STANTON, SCHUYLER--[2][8][11][22][23][25][33]--
"FATE OF A CROWN" '05
"DAUGHTERS OF DESTINY" '06
VAN DYNE, EDITH--[2][8][11][22][23][25][33]

BAUM, ROBERT
JUNGT, ROBERT--[1]

BAUMANN, AMY [B] BEECHING
BARBARY, JAMES--W/JACK BEECHING,[1][23][33]
BROWN, ALEXIS--[1][31][33]

BAUMANN, MARGARET
LEES, MARGUERITE--[8][9][21][26]ROM-- 9 NOVELS

BAUMBACH, RUDOLF
BACH, PAUL--[22]GERMAN

BAUME, FREDERICK EHREN.
BAUME, ERIC--[34]MYS-- HUTCH "UNREHEARSED INCIDENT & OTHER STORIES" '48

BAUMGARDNER, CATHIE L.
LINZ, CATHIE--[9][21][26][31]ROM-- 22 NOVELS

BAUMGARTEN, SYLVIA
HALLIDAY, ENA--[9][21][26]ROM--
"LYSETTE"
"DELPHINE"
"MARIELLE"
RAWLINGS, LOUISA--[9][21][26]ROM-- 7 NOVELS

BAUMRIN, BERNARD H.
BAUMRIN, STEFAN--[1][22][31]AMERICAN
BERNARD, STEFAN--[1][22][31]AMERICAN

BAUSHER, MILDRED JORDAN
JORDAN, MILDRED--[31]

BAUSMAN, FREDERICK
AIX--[34]MYS--
DUFFIELD "ADVENTRS OF A NICE YOUNG MAN" '08
DUFFIELD "THIEVES" '11

BAVLY, DAN [ABRAHAM]
BAWLY, DAN--[31]

BAVOUSETT, GLEN B[YRON]
LOGAN, JAKE--HAWK/MCCORD/BALLAS INTRVW, HP-- BERKELEY-"SAN ANGELO SHOOTOUT" 1992
SHARPE, JON--MCCORD/BALLAS/HAWK INTRVW, HP-- NAL 'TRAILSMAN' SERIES: #96, 98, 99, 101,104, 105, 107, 109, 111, 113, 115 & 117

BAWDEN, EDWARD
E.B.--BAPC NWSLTR #9, PAN COVER ARTIST

BAWDEN, NINA MARY MABREY
KARK, NINA MARY [M]--[31]

BAX, SIR ARNOLD
O'BYRNE, DERMOT--[1]

BAXTER, CRAIG
DUNBAR, DAVID--[1][31]

BAXTER, ELIZABETH
HOLLAND, ELIZABETH--[8]

BAXTER, GORDON F. JR.
BAX--[31]

BAXTER, JOHN
BLACKSTONE, JAMES--W/JOHN BROSNAN, [2][7][23]SF-- GRAFTON "TORCHED" '86
LORAN, MARTIN--W/RON SMITH,[2][11][23][31]SF

BAXTER, LUCY C.
SCOTT, LEADER--[1]

BAXTER, MICHAEL JOHN
BAXTER, MIKE--[31]

BAXTER, STEPHEN
BAXTER, S.M.--[23]SF
BAXTER, STEVE--[23]NV/SF

BAXTER, ZENOBIA
BAXTER, ZENO--[1]

BAYARD, EVALINE
NESS, EVALINE [M]--[1]

BAYBARS, TANER
BAYLISS, TIMOTHY--[1][8][31]-- "MODERN POETRY IN TRANSLATION" '71

BAYER, ELEANORE & LEO
BAYER, OLIVER WELD--[1][3][22]MYS-- 4 NOVELS '43-47

BAYER, LINDA
BAYER-BERENBAUM, LINDA--[31]
BERENBAUM, LINDA BAYER--[31]

BAYER, OSWALD GEORG
BAYROS--[39]GERMAN

BAYER, SANDRA LEE
BAYER, SANDRA L.--[7]SF--NOVELS
BAYER, SANDY--[7][31]SF-- ALYSON "CRYSTAL #1 & #2" '88-91

BAYER, WILLIAM
ST. JOHN, LEONIE--W/NANCY HARMON, [1][8]

BAYER-BERENBAU, LINDA
BERENBAU, LINDA BAYER--[7]SF,NON-FICTION

BAYES, RONALD H[OMER]
LIEF, N.H.--[1][31]

BAYFIELD, WILLIAM J.
BLAIR, ALLAN--[1][34]MYS--34 NOVELS '30-40
CARR, GORDON--[1]
JARDINE, WARWICK--[1]HP
MAXWELL, ALLAN--[1][34]MYS--
AMALG "THE PRIEST'S SECRET" '36

BAYFIELD, WILLIAM JOHN
OSBORNE, MARK--[1]
WING, JAMES EGERTON--[1]

BAYLEY, BARRINGTON J.
AUMBRY, ALAN--[1][11][23][31]SF--
ONE STORY
BARRINGTON, MICHAEL--W/MICHAEL MOORCOCK,
[2][11][23]--ONE STORY
COLVIN, JAMES--W/MICHAEL MOORCOCK, [2]
DIAMOND, JOHN--[1][2][11][23]SF--ONE STORY
MOORCOCK, MICHAEL--J. DAVEY LTR JAN '94--
BOYS WORLD ANNUAL "TIME DROP" '65
WOODS, P.F.--[1][11][23]SF--10 STORIES
WOODS, PETER--[2][23]SF--NW "THE PATCH" '64

BAYLEY, VICTOR
SMITH, WAYLAND--[7][23]SF--
"THE MACHINE STOPS" '36

BAYLISS, JOHN CLIFFORD
BAYLISS, J.C.--[1]ENGLISH
CLIFFORD, JOHN--[1][2][22][31]ENGLISH

BAYLOR, BYRD
SCHWEITZER, BYRD BAYLOR--[1][33]

BAYLY, ADA ELLEN
LYALL, EDNA--[1][2][22]ENGLISH

BAYNES, DOROTHY JULIA
CRESTON, DORMER--[8]

BAYNTON, BARBARA
SQUEAKER'S MATE--[13]AUSTRALIAN

BEACH, ELIZABETH
AWBREY, ELIZABETH--[9][21][26]ROM--
"RECKLESS ANGEL"
STUART, ELIZABETH--[9][21][26]ROM--
"HEARTSTORM"
"WHERE LOVE DWELLS"

BEACH, THOMAS MILLER
LE CARON, HENRY--[22]ENGLISH

BEADLE, GEORGE W[ELLS]
BEADLE, G.W.--[31]

BEADLE, GWYNETH GORDON
GORDON, GLENDA--[8]

BEAGLEHOLE, JOHN CAWTE
BEAGLEHOLE, J.C.--[1]

BEAL, GWYNETH MORGAN
MORGAN, GWYNETH--[1]

BEALES, HELEN R. ABBOTT
ABBOTT, HELEN RAYMOND--[1]

BEALES, HELEN R. ABBOTT [CONT]
H.B.--[1]

BEAMISH, ANNIE O'MEARA
BEAMISH, NOEL DE VIC--[1][8][22][31]
IRISH-FRENCH
BERNARD, JOHN--[1][2][23]ENGLISH/SF

BEAN, KEITH FENWICK
FENWICK, KAY--[1][22][31]AUSTRALIAN
HARRINGTON, K.--[31]AUSTRALIAN
HARRINGTON, KAY--[1][22]AUSTRALIAN

BEAN, MABEL GREENE
GREENE, MABEL--[31]

BEAN, MYRTLE AMELIA
BEAN, AMELIA--[21]ROM--
"THE FANCHER TRAIN"

BEAR, JOAN E.
MAYHEW, ELIZABETH--[9][21][26]ROM--
"FELICIA"
"IN THE PATH OF EAGLES" & 2 OTHERS

BEARD, JAMES H.
JAMES, PHILIP--W/LESTER DEL REY, [1][2]

BEARDMORE, GEORGE CEDRIC
BEARDMORE, CEDRIC--[1][31][33]
STOKES, CEDRIC--[1][3][33]MYS--
MacD "STAFFORDSHIRE ASSASSINS" '45
WOLFENDEN, GEORGE--[1][3][33]MYS--
3 HURST NOVELS '37-42

BEARDSLEY, CHARLES N.
RADCLIFFE, JOCELYN--[3]MYS--
CURTIS "BLACKWOOD" '74
WILLOUGHBY, LEE DAVIS--[21]HP--
DELL 'MAKING OF AMERICA' SERIES:
"GOLDEN STATERS"
"BOOMERS"
"BAJA PEOPLE"

BEARNE, COLIN GERALD
BEARNE, C.G.--[1]

BEATTIE, TASMAN
HAMILTON, ALISTAIR--[3]AUSTRALIAN/MYS--
HAMLYN "THE HALO JUMP" '79
HAMLYN "HOLDING PATTERN" '81

BEATTY, JEROME
STOOKEY, AARON W.--[22]AMERICAN

BEATTY, LORRAINE
CARROLL, LORRAINE--[26]ROM--
"LEAD WITH YOUR HEART"
"THE ICE PRINCESS"

BEATTY, PATRICIA [R]
BARTHOLOMEW, JEAN--[9]ROM

BEATY, BETTY
CAMPBELL, KAREN--[3][17][29][31]MYS/ROM--
6 NOVELS '69-79
ROSS, CATHERINE--[1][8][17]ROM

BEATY, WARREN
BEATTY, WARREN--[31]

BEATY, [ARTHUR] DAVID
STANTON, PAUL--[3][23][29]MYS--
"VILLAGE OF STARS" '60
"CALL ME CAPTAIN" '59
"GUN GARDEN" '65

BEAUCHAMP, KATHLEEN M.
BERRY, MALTILDA--[8]
K.M.--[1][31]
MANSFIELD, KATHERINE--[8][22][32]MYS--
EQMM "HOW PEARL BUTTON WAS KIDNAPPED" AUG '49
EQMM "POISON" DEC '50
PETRONSKY, BORIS--[1]

BEAUCHAMP, MARY ANNETTE
CHOLMONDELEY, ALICE--[17]AUSTRALIAN/ROM
CHOLMONDELEY, MARY--[32]AUSTRALIAN/MYS--
EQMM "HAND ON THE LATCH" OCT '49
ELIZABETH--[17]AUSTRALIAN/ROM

BEAUDE, HENRI
D'ARLES, HENRI--[1]

BEAUDOIN, KENNETH LAWR.
DE CHATELLERAULT, VICTOR--[31]
DE TODANY, JAMES--[31]

BEAUMAN, SALLY
JAMES, VANESSA--[9][21][26][31]ROM--7 NOVELS

BEAUMONT, ANNE
PYATT, ROSINA--[21]ROM--6 NOVELS

BEAUMONT, CHARLES
ANMAR, FRANK--MUNROE SLS LST 20, BEAUMONT BIBL,[32]--
TE "LAUGH TILL YOU DIE" APR '57
BEAUMONT, E.J.--[1][2][11]
BEAUMONT, E.T--"HOWLING MAN" INTRO, USED EXCLUSIVELY FOR PULP ILLUSTRATIONS
COCKRELL, EUSTACE--MUNROE SLST 20, BEAUMONT BIBLIO
COURTNEY, ROBERT--HARLAN ELLISON INTRVW, HP--[ROGUE]
GRANTLAND, KEITH--W/JOHN TOMERLIN, MUNROE SLST 20, BEAUMONT BIO, BERCH, GM PSDS, PP 33,[2][11][34]--
GM 701 "RUN FROM THE HUNTER" '57
LOVEHILL, C.B.--MUNROE SLST 20, BEAUMONT BIBLIO,[1][2][11][31]--SHORT STORIES
MCNUTT, CHARLES--[8][16]
PHILLIPS, MICHAEL--MUNROE SALES LIST 20, BEAUMONT BIBLIO,[1][2][11][16]
TENNESHAW, S.M.--[1][2][32]HP--
WM "WHO SUPS WITH THE DEVIL" FALL '70

BEAUMONT, DONNA BROOKS
CLAXTON, JOHN G.--[1][2]

BEAUMONT, EDGAR
HALIFAX, CLIFFORD--[22][29][32]MYS--
MSMM "HORROR OF STUDLEY GRANGE" W/L.T. MEADE, DEC '73
HALIFAX, [DF.] CLIFFORD--[1]

BEAUMONT, HELEN
ECKERSLEY, JILL--[9][21][26]ROM--
"A LITTLE LOVING"
EMERY, DENISE--[9][21][26]ROM--
"BELLS OF UTRECHT"
"SUNRISE IN HONG KONG"
SANDERSON, JILL--[9][21][26]ROM--
"THE LEAPING FLAME"
"NEVER FORGET ME"
STANTON, ANNA--[9][21][26]ROM--
"JOURNEY'S END"

BEAVER, BEVERLY
BARTON, BEVERLY--[21][26]ROM--
"YANKEE LOVER"
"LUCKY IN LOVE" & 8 OTHER NOVELS

BEAVER, [JACK] PATRICK
BILLINGTON, JOHN--[1][31]

BEAVERBROOK, WILLIAM M.A.
AITKEN, WILLIAM MAXWELL--[31]

BEBENBURG, WALTER ERICH v
RICHARTZ, W.E.--[39]GERMAN

BECCE, EMMA [W]
VON SAWERSKY, MARIA--[39]GERMAN

BECHDOLT, JOHN ERNEST
BECHDOLT, JACK--[23][29]SF/MYS--
"DOMDA TILL DODEN" '40

BECHKO, PEGGY ANNE
BECHKO, P.A.--[28]WEST--7 NOVELS '74-84
HALLER, BILL--[8][28][31]WEST--
PINN "SIDEWINDER'S TRAIL" '76
PINN "DEAD MAN'S FEUD" '76

BECHTKE, WOLFGANG
DURIAN, WOLF--[39]GERMAN/JUV

BECHTLE-BECHTINGER, JOAC.
GUMPERT, JOACHIM S.--[39]GERMAN
SCHRECK, JOACHIM--[39]GERMAN

BECHTLE-BECHTINGER, SIBYL
DURIAN, SIBYLLE--[39]GERMAN/JUV
KAI, KIM--[39]GERMAN/JUV

BECK, EARL CLIFTON
BECK, DOC--[1][31]

BECK, ED
STORM, ERIC--[2]

BECK, ELIZA LOUISA M.
BARRINGTON, E.--[2][11][16][17][22]ROM
BECK, LILY ADAMS--[1]
MORESBY, LOUIS--[1]
MORESBY, L[OIS]--[2][11][16][17][22]ROM

BECK, FLORIAN
BECK, JOHN F.--[39]GERMAN/WEST
NOLAN, FREDERICK--[39]GERMAN/WEST, HP
SLADE, JACK--[39]GERMAN/WEST, HP

BECK, ROBERT
SLIM, ICEBERG--J. PRESSMAN, COUNTERCULTURE, BAE 21, P54,[1][3]

BECK, ROLAND STANLEY
ST. ANBECK, ROLAND--[8]

BECKE, GEORGE LEWIS
BECKE, LOUIS--[1]

BECKER, ALFRED
CHADWICK, NEAL--[39]GERMAN/WEST

BECKER, BERND
BECKSTRAT, BERND--[39]GERMAN

BECKER, CARL EDWARD C.P.
BECKER, FRECKLE--[1]

BECKER, KURT
MARTELL, GUNTER--[39]GERMAN/JUV/SF

BECKER, MARIETTA
BAKER, MARY--[39]GERMAN
BECK, M. v. d.--[39]GERMAN
KEITH, KATRIN--[39]GERMAN

BECKER, MAX O.
ALTH, MAX O.--[1]
COLLINS, HARRY C.--[1]
HARDFORTH, CARNIE--[1]

BECKER, ROLLY
BECKER, FRANZISKA--[39]GERMAN

BECKER, STEPHEN [DAVID]
DODGE, STEVE--V. BERCH-GM PSEUDS, PP 33/ [3][22][29][31]MYS, GM 456 "SHANGHAI INCIDENT" '55

BECKER, THEODORE L[EWIS]
BECKER, TED--[31]

BECKER, WILLIAM
BECKER, BILL--[31]

BECKERS, FRANS
DEMERS, FRANS--[22]DUTCH
ELSING, J.M.--[22]DUTCH

BECKERS, MICHAEL
GREEDERS, MIRIAM--[39]GERMAN

BECKETT, C.E.
LEVENAX, DAVID--[34]MYS-- HEDERWICK "PLAIN TALES OF THE CITIES & SUBURBS" '24

BECKETT, GILLIAN
BOWER, ALISON--[1]

BECKETT, KENNETH ALBERT
BOWER, KEITH--[1][31]

BECKETT, RONALD BRYMER
ANTHONY, JOHN--W/JOHN A. CIARDI, [31]
ANTHONY, JOHN--W/JOHN A. SABINI, [31]
ANTHONY, JOHN--[1][8][22][31]

BECKMAN, GUNNEL
BANCK, LUIS--[29]MYS--
"MORD I MANADSGILLET" '45
"NOBELPRISTAGARE INNEBRAND" '47

BECKMAN, KARIN
BECKMAN, KAJ--[1][31][33]

BECKMAN, LEIF
FLYNN, CHARLES--[29]MYS--
"VAGEN TILL SHIRAZ" '36
"ANN CARPENTER'S ARV" '43

BECKMANN, MARIA [N]
SCHENCK, SIBYLLE--[39]GERMAN

BECKWITH, AUDREY
FREDERICK, KATE--V. BERCH LTR TO HUBIN FEB '94, MYS--
ZEBRA "PERIWINKLE BROOCH" '88
ZEBRA "MIDNIGHT HEIRESS" '89
ZEBRA "BLACK WIND OF PENROSE ISLAND" '90

BECKWITH, BURNHAM PUTNAM
BURNHAM, JOHN--[1][31]
PUTNAM, JOHN--[1]

BEDFORD, DEBORAH LYNN
BEDFORD, DEBBIE--[9][21]ROM--4 NOVELS

BEDFORD, JESSIE
GODFREY, ELIZABETH--[3]MYS-- JARROLDS "STOLEN IDEA" 1899

BEDFORD, JOHN T.
CITY WAITER--[1]
GREENHORN, JOSEPH--[1]
ROBERT--[1]

BEDFORD-JONES, HENRY
BEDFORD, DONALD F.--W/DONALD FRIEDE & KENNETH FEARING, [1][2][11][16]
BEDFORD-FORAN, CAPT.--W/WILLIAM ROBERT FORAN, [1]
BRISSARD, MONTAGUE--[1][2][11][16]
CHASE, CLEVELAND B.--[1][2][11][16]
DE MOURANT, GEORGE SOULI--[1][2][11][16]
FERVAL, PAUL--[1][2][11][16]
FRIKELL, SAMRI--LACHMAN/COOKE LIST
GALLISTER, MICHAEL--[1][2][11][16]
GORDON, KEYNE--L. ROBBINS LTR MAR '94
H.B.J.--[23]SF
HAWKWOOD, ALLAN--[2][3][11][16][23]-- HURST "JOHN SOLOMON, INCOGNITO" '25
KEYNE, GORDON--[2][8][11][16][23]
LASSEZ, M.--[2][11][16]
PAMJEAN, LOUIS--[1]
PEMJEAN, LUCIAN--[2][11][16]
SANGERSON, MARGARET LOVE--[1][2][11][16]
SEABROOKE, DAVID--[1]
SOULI, CHARLES GEORGE--[1][2][11][16]
STUART, GORDON--[1][2][11][16]
TREVISION, TORQUAY--[1][11]SF
WHITNEY, ELLIOTT--W/HARRY L. SAYLER, [1][2][11][16]
WYCLIFFE, JOHN--[1][2][11][16]

BEDNARIK, CHARLES PHILIP
BEDNARIK, CHUCK--[31]

BEE, HELEN L.
DOUGLAS, HELEN BEE--[1][31]

BEEBE, ELSWYTH
THANE, ELSWYTH--[1][9]ROM

RAY, IRENE--[1]
SUTTON, MARGARET--[1]

BEEBY, GEORGE STEPHENSON
BEEBY, G.S.--[36]AUSTRALIAN/MYS-- A&R "A LOADED LEGACY" '30

BEECHCROFT, THOMAS OWEN
BEECHCROFT, T.O.--[1]

BEECHING, JACK
BARBARY, JACK--W/AMY [B] BEECHING BAUMANN, [1][31][33]

BEER, EDITH LYNN
HORNIK, EDITH LYNN--[1]
HORNIK-BEER, EDITH LYNN--[31]

BEER, ELOISE C.S.
BEER, LISL--[1][8][22][31]AMERICAN
DRAKE, LISL--[1][8][22][31]AMERICAN

BEER, FRITZ
ALTER, PETER--[39]GERMAN

BEER, GUSTAVE
WHEATLEY, G.W.--[39]GERMAN

BEER, NATALIE
BERNGATH, URSULA--[39]GERMAN

BEERMAN, F.
GRAY, CAROLINE--[21]ROM--
"VICTORIA'S WALK"
"WHITE RANI"

BEESTON, L.J.
CAMDEN, RICHARD--[1][8]
DAVIES, LUCIEN--[1][8]

BEETS, NIKOLAAS
HILDEBRAND--[22]DUTCH

BEETZ, DIETER
BEETZ, DIETMAR--[39]GERMAN/MYS/JUV--
"MORD AM HIRSCHLACHUFER" '82

BEEVERS, JOHN LEONARD
CLAYTON, JOHN--[31]

BEGBIE, ARUNDEL
ANDRUL--[34]MYS--
HODDER "THE WAYSIDE" '11

BEGBIE, [EDWARD] HAROLD
LEWIS, CAROLINE--W/M.H. TEMPLE & J.S. RANSOME
[2][23]SF--
"CLARA IN BUNDERTON" '02
"LOST IN BLUNDERLAND" '03

BEGIN, MENACHIM
BEGIN, MENAHEM--[31]

BEGOVIC, MILAN
DE LA MARAJA, XERES--[1]
DUSIC, STANKO--[1]

BEGUM, ROKEYA S, HOSSAIN
ROKEYA, BEGUM--[7]SF--
"SULTAN'S DREAM & SELECTIONS FROM
THE SECLUDED ONES" '88

BEHA, ERNEST
BEDE, ANDREW--[22][31]ENGLISH
ELVIN, DRAKE--[22][31]ENGLISH

BEHAN, BRENDAN
STREET, EMMETT--[8]

BEHANNA, GERTRUDE F.
BURNS, ELIZABETH--[8]

BEHM, WILHELM
BEHM, BILL--[39]GERMAN/ADV
VON FALKENBERG, FRANK--[39]GERMAN/ADV

BEHRENDT, ERWIN
NIDDEN, CHRISTOPHER--[39]GERMAN

BEHRENS-THYSELIUS, THORA
THYSELIUS, THORA--[39]GERMAN

BEIER, ULLI
AKANJI, SANGODARE--[1][31]
ARAGBABALU, OMIDIJI--[1][31]
OBUTUNDE, IJIMERE--[1]
SANGODARE AKANJI, OMIDIJI--[31]

BEILENSON, EDNA
DEAN, ELISABETH--[1][31]

BEILES, SINCLAIR
MENG, WU WU--C. ECKHOFF SLST--
OLYMP TC-75 "HOUSES OF JOY" '65

BEISSEL, RUDOLF
CORNEL, FRANK--[39]GERMAN/ADV
CORTAN, F.B.--[39]GERMAN/ADV
OTTO, OTTO--[39]GERMAN/ADV

BEITH, JOHN HAY
HAY, IAN--[2][22]SCOTTISH

BEIZER, BORIS
SHEDLEY, ETHAN I.--[3][7][23]--
VIKING "EARTH SHIP & STAR SONG" '79
VIKING "MEDUSA CONSPIRACY" '80

BEKESSY, JANOS
BEKESSY, JEAN--[34][39]GERMAN
DEEN, DONALD--[39]GERMAN/NOVELS--NON-FICTION
FERNWALD, PAUL--[39]GERMAN/NVLS--NON-FICTION
HABE, HANS--[3][31][39]GERMAN/MYS--
HARRAP "AGENT OF THE DEVIL" '58
HARRAP "THE POISONED STREAM" '69
RICHARD, FRANK--[39]GERMAN/NOVELS--
NON-FICTION
RICHLER, JOHN--[39]GERMAN/NOVELS--NON-FICTION
WOLFGANG, HANS--[39]GERMAN/NOVELS--
NON-FICTION

BEKKER, PETRUS JACOBUS
BEKKER, PIROW--[1]

BEKLEMISHEV, YURI SOLOM.
KRYMOV, YURI--[22]RUSSIAN

BELANEY, ARCHIBALD S.
BELANEY, GEORGE STANFIELD--[1]CANADIAN
GREY OWL--[1][22][31][33]CANADIAN
WA SHA-QUON-ASIN--[1][22][33]CANADIAN

BELANGOR-GILL, GEORGIANNA
DE MOTREUIL, GAETANE--[1]

BELCHEM, RONALD F.
BELCHEM, DAVID--[1][8][31]

BELCHEVA, ELISAVETA
BAGRJANA, ELISAVETA--[22]BULGARIAN
BAGRYANA, ELISAVETA--[31]

BELDEN, LOUISE CONWAY
BELDEN, GAIL--[1][31]

BELFIELD, HARRY WEDGEWOOD
DRAKE, RUPERT--[1]
GRIMSHAW, MARK--[1]
WROXHAM, CECIL--[1]

BELFOUR, HUGH J.
DORSET, ST. JOHN--[2]

BELIARD, JEAN
VIGNANT, JEAN FRANCIS--[34]MYS--
CHELSEA "THE ALPINE AFFAIR" '70

BELL, CHARLES F.M.
BELL, C.F. MOBERLY--[1]

BELL, CHARLES WENTWORTH
KILLREYNARD, EARL OF--[1]

BELL, CLARE [LOUISE]
COLEMAN, CLARE--W/M.C. EASTON,
LOCUS MAG 1/93, [23]--
JOVE "DAUGHTER OF THE REEF" '92
JOVE "SISTER OF THE SUN"

BELL, COLIN ALEXANDER
BELL, COLIN KANE--[1]

BELL, ERIC TEMPLE
BADGER, RICHARD C.--[2][11]
J.T.--[2][11]
TAINE, JOHN--[2][4][11][23]SF
TEMPLE, JAMES--[2][11]

BELL, GEORGE
BARNARTO, BART--[27]HP--EDWIN SELF
COSTELLO, PETE--[27][34]HP--EDWIN SELF
SELF "MURDER IN MINK" '52
SELF "HONEY DON'T DARE" '53
SELF "MY CUTIE'S A CORPSE" '53
VALOIS, JEAN PAUL--[27]HP--EDWIN SELF

BELL, JOHN KEBLE
HOWARD, KEBLE--[2][3][22]ENGLISH/MYS--
UNWIN "THE CHEERFUL KNAVE" '27
METHUEN, JOHN--[1]

BELL, JOYCE
COLIN, JEAN--[1][31]

BELL, LARAINE
MCDANIEL, LARAINE--[10][26]ROM--
"AGAINST ALL HOPE"

BELL, LORNA BEATRICE
BELL, BETTY--[31]

BELL, LOUISE PRICE
BRONSON, LITA--[1][31]
JEFFREY, RUTH--[1][31]

BELL, ROBERT CHARLES
BELL, R.C.--[1]

BELL, ROBERT STANLEY W.
BRETT, HAWKSLEY--[1][31][33]
OLD FAG--[1][33]

BELLAH, JAMES WARNER
BRAUNSLAU, NATHAN--V. BERCH, BRNDN/BC
PSEUDS, BAE 22, P24
FRIEDMAN, ARNOLD--V. BERCH, BRNDN/BC
PSEUDS, BAE 22, P24
NEIL, GEOFFREY--MUNROE, NUETZEL INTRVW,
BAE 25, P52--
RUBICON 1012 "SWEET KISS OF YOUTH"
NEIL, MARTIN--V. BERCH, BRNDN/BC PSEUDS,
BAE 22, P24
RAVEN, HOWARD--V. BERCH, BRNDN/BC PSEUDS,
BAE 22, P24

BELLAIRS, GEORGE
LANDON, HILLARY--J. MEYERSON--
SLST #110 "CIRCLE AROUND A CORPSE"

BELLAMY, ELIZABETH WHITF.
THORPE, KAMPA--[1]

BELLASIS, MARGARET ROSA
MARTON, FRANCESCA--[1]

BELLEFROID, MARTHA
GRONON, ROSE--[22]DUTCH

BELLEM, ROBERT LESLIE
BELLEM, R.L.--ECHOES #9--
UT "CURSE OF THE LOVELY TORSO" MAR '40
BRUCE, WALT--S. MERTZ, ECHOES #19, P10/
L. ROBBINS LTR MAR '94, PULP
CASE, JUSTIN--LACHMAN LST,[37]HP--
SPDS - PULP STORIES
CHARLES, FRANKLIN--W/CLEVE F. ADAMS,[18][34]--
"VICE CZAR MURDERS" '41
"NO WINGS ON A COP" '50
GRANGE, JOHN--W/W. TODHUNTER BALLARD,[18][37]-
UD "DEALER IN DEATH" & OTHERS '42-3
SAXON, JOHN A.--[18][32][34]GHOSTED--
MILL "HALF PAST MORTEM" '47
SW "DEATH IN A CRYSTAL CASKET" JUN '45

BELLERBY, [M.E] FRANCES
PARKER, M.E. FRANCES--[1]

BELLINGHAM, HELEN MARY D.
BEAUCLERK, HELEN--[17]ROM
DE VERE BEAUDERK, HELEN--[1]

BELLINI, TINA
FLOWERS, T.J.--[7]--
MIDWD "MOONGLOW" '74,
REPRT OF OPH#162 "NIGHT OF
THE WOLF" '69 BY S. FOREST
FOREST, SALAMBO--[14]--
OLYM OPH#122 "FIRE CHILD" '68
OLYM OPH#127 "TWIN SATYRS" '68
OLYM OPH#137 "THE YEAR OF THE COCK" '69
OLYM OPH#154 "THE ENORMOUS EXPERIENCE" '69
OLYM OPH#162 "NIGHT OF THE WOLF" '69
OLYM OPH#188 "ON MY THROBBING ENGINE" '69
OLYM OPH#198 "PAN ON A RAMPAGE" '70
OLYM OPH#204 "THE SKIN GARDEN" '70
OLYM OPH#262 "FOR THE WITCH, A STONE" '71
OLYM OPS#35 "WITCH POWER" '71
HOPPER, MAX--[14]--
OLYM TC#473 "UNORTHODOX SEX EDUCATION
OF BILLY JOE"

BELLMANN, JOHANN DIEDRICH
BELLMANN, DIETER--[39]GERMAN

BELLOC, [J] HILAIRE [P]
BELLOC, JOSEPH PETER H.--[31]
BELLOC, JOSEPH PIERRE H.--[31]
BELLOC, HILAIRE--[22]ENGLISH
BELLOC, HILARY--[1]
CHESTERBELLOC--W/G.K. CHESTERTON, [1]
H.B.--[1]

BELLOMI, ANTONIA
RANDA, LUIGI--[2]ITALY/SF,INTERNTNL SFYB,

BELLONY, ALICE
BELLONY-REWALD, ALICE--[31]

BELTON-COBB, GEOFFREY
BELL, COBDEN--[1]

BELTRAN, CAYETANO R.
ONATEYAC--[30]MEXICAN

BELYAEV, ALEXANDER
BELIAYEV, A.--[2]
BELYEV, A.--[2]

BELZ, FRED GOTTHILF
MARBACH, MICHAEL--[39]GERMAN

BEMMANN, HANS
MARTINSON, HANS--[39]GERMAN/SF

BEMME-WINGERT, HEINZ
WINGERT, HEINER--[39]GERMAN/JUV

BEN-DAVID, JOSEPH
DAVID, JOSEPH BEN--[31]

BEN-EPHRAIM, GAVRIEL
EPHRAIM, GAVRIEL BEN--[31]

BENARY-ISBERT, MARGOT
BENARY, MARGOT--[1][31][33]CHILDREN'S BOOKS
BENARY-ISBERT, M.--[31]

BENCHLEY, ROBERT CHARLES
FAWKES, GUY--[1][31]
PERRY, BRIGHTON--[1]

BENCUR, MATEJ
KAKUCHIN, MARTIN--[22]SLOVAK
KUKUCIN, MARTIN--[1]

BENDER, ARNOLD
PHILIPPO, MARK--[1]

BENDER, ERICH F.
FRANK, DR. STEFAN--[39]GERMAN

BENDIT, GLADYS WILLIAMS
PRESLAND, JOHN--[1][22]AUSTRALIAN-ENGLISH

BENEDETTI, MARIO
DAMOCLES--[31]

BENEDICT, STEVE
MARIUS--[1][2][11]

BENES, JAN
STEPKA, MILAN--[1]

BENES, VACLAV
TREBIZSKY, VACLAV BENES--[22]CZECH

BENESCH, IRMFRIED
AICHNER, FRIDOLIN--[39]GERMAN/JUV

BENFORD, GREGORY ALBERT
ALBERT, LINCOLN--W/LAURENCE LITTENBERG, [2]
BLAKE, STERLING--BENFORD VERIFIED AT ARMADILLOCON '94--
BB "CHILLER" '93
REALIST, B.A.--[2]

BENGSCH, GERHARD
ABT, TERENZ--[39]GERMAN

BENGSTON, HAKAN
WIDMARK, HAKAN--[29]MYS

BENGT-AKE, CRAS
BURELL, JOHN--[29]MYS--
"LIKKISTOR TILL SALU" '80
"DET HOGA FALLET" '81

BENITEZ, MIGUEL ANGEL OS.
ARENALES, RICARDO--[20]SPANISH
BARBA JACOB, PORFIRIO--[20]SPANISH
XIMENEZ, MAIN--[20]SPANISH

BENIUSEVICIUTE-Z, JULIJA
ZEMAITE--[22]LITHUANIAN

BENJAMIN, ARNOLD ALEX.
ALEXANDER, ARNO--[29][39]GERMAN/MYS--
7 NOVELS '33-36

BENJAMIN, CLAUDE M.E.P.
EDWARDS, MAX--[22][31]AMERICAN
GEORGE, MARION--[31]
GEORGE, MARION E.--[22]AMERICAN

BENJAMIN, EGBERT
FAIN, C.C.--[1]

BENJAMIN, LEWIS SAUL
MELVILLE, LEWIS--W/REGINALD HARGREAVES, [1][2][11] ALSO USED HIMSELF

BENJAMIN, MORTON J.
MORSE, BENJAMIN [DR.]--V. BERCH, MONARCH PSEUDS., BAE 9, P26 - ALSO ATTRIBUTED TO LAWRENCE BLOCK

BENJAMIN, WALTER
CONRAD, C.--[1]
HOLZ, DETLEV--[1]

BENK, AXEL
BENCH, FREDDY--[29]MYS--
"BITTER KAMP" '67

BENN, ANTHONY NEIL W.
BENN, TONY--[31]

BENN, STANLEY I[SSAC]
BENN, S.I.--[31]

BENNETT, C.N.
COLLIER, NORMAN--[1]

BENNETT, CONSTANCE
BENNETT, CONNIE--[9][21]ROM--6 NOVELS

BENNETT, DOROTHY
KINGSLEY, LAURA--[9]ROM

BENNETT, ERNEST NATHANIEL
BENNETT, E.N.--[31]

BENNETT, GARETH VAUGHN
BENNETT, G.V.--[31]

BENNETT, GEOFFREY MARTIN
SEA-LION--[2][3][11][22][23]SF--
"INVISIBLE SHIPS" '50
"THIS CREEPING EVIL" '50

BENNETT, GEORGE HAROLD
BENNETT, HAL--[1][3][31]MYS--
DBLDY "WAIT UNTIL EVENING" '74

BENNETT, GERTRUDE BARROWS
STEVENS, FRANCES--[2][4][23]SF--
12 FANTASY STORIES IN MAGAZINES '17-23

BENNETT, GORDON
ROMUN, ISAK--LACHMAN LIST

BENNETT, HAL
REVERE, JOHN D.--V. BERCH LTR TO HUBIN '94, MYS--
PINN "ASSASSIN" '83
PINN "VATICAN KILL" '83
PINN "BORN TO KILL" '84
PINN "STUD SERVICE" '85
PINN "DEATH'S RUNNING MATE" '85

BENNETT, HENRY STANLEY
BENNETT, H.S.--[1]

BENNETT, ISADORA
MORGAN, WESKY--[1]

BENNETT, JAY
RAND, STEVE--V. BERCH, MON PSEUDS BAE 9, P26,[1][3][29]--
MON 193 "ALL HER VICES" '61
MON 211 "SO SWEET, SO WICKED" '61

BENNETT, JEFF
BRAUN, TERRANCE--[7]SF/SEX--
"ORGY GIRL" RPRT OF "COSMIC RAPE"--
'BENNETT' ALSO A PSEUD.

BENNETT, JOHN JEROME N.
BENNETT, JEREMY--[1][31]

BENNETT, KEMYS DEVERELL
BENNETT, KEM--[1]

BENNETT, LAURA
BENNETT, LAURA GILMOUR--W/JEAN GILMOUR HARVEY, [7]--
"BY ALL THAT IS SACRED" '91
RPRTS "A WHEEL OF STARS"
HARLOW, JUSTIN--W/TINA MCKENZIE & JEAN HARVEY, [21]
HARLOWE, JUSTINE--W/JEAN HARVEY & TINA MACKENZIE, [8][26]ROM--
"JEALOSIES"
"MEMORY & DESIRES"

BENNETT, MARCIA J[OANNE]
BENNETT, M.J.--[31]

BENNETT, REGINALD G.S.
LONG, ELLIOTT--[28]WEST--
HALE, 4 NOVELS '90-91

BENNETT, ROBERT AMES
ROBINET, LEE--L. ROBBINS LTR '94,[23]SF--
"THE FOREST MAIDEN" '13

BENNETT, WILLIAM EDWARD
ARMSTRONG, WARREN--[1][11]SF

BENNETT, [ENOCH] ARNOLD
BENNETT, E.A.--[3]MYS--
GARDNER "SIDNEY YORKE'S FRIEND" '01
GWENDOLYN--[1][31]
TONSON, JACOB--[1]

BENNETTS, PAMELA
ASHFIELD, HELEN--[9][17][21][26]ROM--
13 NOVELS
JAMES, MARGARET--[3][17][21][26]ROM--
3 NOVELS--BYLINE U.S. EDITIONS

BENNIS, WESSEL JOHANNES
LUCULLUS--[1]

BENOIT, ALICE P.
MONIQUE--[1]
SINBETH, LESLY--[1]

BENSEN, D.R.
JENNIFER, SUSAN--[11]SF

BENSEN, DONALD R.
FLYNN, JACKSON--[1][31]
MASTERS, ZEKE--[1]
THATCHER, JULIA--[3][9][21]AMERICAN MYS/ROM--6 NOVELS '76-80

BENSEN, MARGARET
SHAYNE, MAGGIE--[26]ROM--
"RECKLESS ANGEL"

BENSINK, JOHN ROBERT
ROBERTSON, JOHN--[7]SF--
ZEBRA "PIPER" '87

BENSMAN, JOSEPH
BENTHAM, JAY--[31]

BENSON, ALLAN INGVALD
VALDING, VICTOR--W/JOHN V. PETERSON, [1][2][11]

BENSON, ARNOLD
KERNER, KEITH--[14]--
OLYM OPH#145 "MOTHER TONGUE" '69
OLYM OPH-182 "HAPPINESS IS A WARM PUSSY" '69
OLYM OPH#159 "THE BALL CARRIER" '69
OLYM OPH#166 "PUSSY IN BOOTS" '69

BENSON, ARTHUR CHRISTOPH.
BENSON, A.C.--[1]
CARR, CHRISTOPHER--[1]
H.L.G.--[1]
T.B.--[1]

BENSON, EDWARD FREDERIC
BENSON, E.F.--[1]
DILLY, TANTE--[1]

BENSON, FREDERICK WILLIAM
BENSON, TED--[31]

BENSON, MILDRED [A] WIRT
AUSGUSTINE, MILDRED--[31][33]
BELL, FRANK--[8][31]
CLARK, JOAN--[8][31][33]
DUNCAN, JULIA K.--[33]HP
JUDD, FRANCES K.--[33]HP
KEENE, CAROLYN--NICOLE CARROLL/C. MIERAU
MYS SCENE #39, HP--
STSY 'NANCY DREW': #1-6, #11-26
STSY 'DANA GIRLS'
PALMER, DON--[33]
WEST, DOROTHY--[8][33]
WIRT, ANN--[33]
WIRT, MILDRED A.--[33]

BENSON, SALLY
EVARTS, ESTHER--[31]

BENSON, SARA MAHALA R.S.
BENSON, SALLY--[1]
EVARTS, ESTHER--[1][33]

BENSON, VIRGINIA
BENSON, GINNY--[31]

BENTCH, KITTY
CRISS, DANI--[26]ROM--
"SHERIFF'S LADY"

BENTEIN, JEAN-MARIE G.J.
DORCHATO, JEAN--[1]
GEORGES, JEAN--[1]

BENTHAM, JOSEPHINE
MAYFIELD, SERENA--[1][3]MYS--
"STRANGER IN THE HOUSE" '72
"LONELY TERROR" '73

BENTLEY, EDMOND CLERIHEW
BENTLEY, E.C.--[1][32]MYS--
EQMM "GREEDY NIGHT" JAN '43
EQMM "MINISTERING ANGEL" SEPT '43
EQMM "GENUINE TABBARD" NOV '50
EQMM "SWEET SHOT" JUL '52
EQMM "FEEBLE FOLK" MAR '53

BENTLEY, EDMUND CLERIHEW
CLERIHEW, E.--[5][31]MYS

BENTLEY, JAMES W.B.
CLAUGHTON-JAMES, JAMES--[1]
NOSTALGIA--[1]

BENTLEY, JANICE BABB
BABB, JANICE BARBARA--[31]

BENTLEY, MARGARET
ALEXANDER, FAITH--[31]
ELLIS, KATHY--[1][31]
STEPHENS, FRANCES--[1]

BENTLEY, SARAH
DOELY, SARAH BENTLEY--[31]

BENTLEY, WILLIAM
RADFORD, JOHN P.--[3]MYS--
CANYON "GAME SHOW GIRLS" '75 & 3 MORE

BENTON, PEGGIE
BURKE, SHIFTY--[1][31]

BENTZ, HANS GEORG
HILT, GEORGE--[39]GERMAN

BENTZIEN, EVA MARIA
KOHL, EVA MARIA--[39]GERMAN/JUV

BENY, WILFRED ROY
BENY, ROLOFF--[31]

BERA, SUDHIU
SRI-RAJPUTRA--[1]

BERCKHAN, ORTRUD
RIVERA, DON--[39]GERMAN/MYS

BERCOFF, ANDRE MAURICE
CATON--[1]

BERCOVICI, ALFRED
CARTER, ALBERTA SIMPSON--[3][21][26]MYS/ROM--
POPLB "AN ADOPTED FACE" '75
POPLB "FOOL'S PROOF" '75
POPLB "WITH MALICE TOWARD ALL"
SIMPSON, ALBERTA--[3]MYS--
CURTIS "THE FALMONT HEIRESS" '73

BERCOVICI, JOSEPH
JOSEPHS, BERTRAND--[1]

BERDICZEVSKY, MICHA YOSE.
BIN GORION, M.Y.--[1][22]

BERDNYK, OLEKSANDR PAVLO.
BERDNYK, OLES--[7]SF--
BAYDA "APPOSTLE OF IMMORTALITY: UKRANIAN SCIENCE FICTION" '84

BERDOE, EDWARD
SCAPEL, AESULAPIUS--[1]

BERDYAEV, NIKOLAI ALEK.
BERDYAEV, NICOLAS--[31]

BERENDT, GERD
BERNHARDT, KLAUS--[39]GERMAN/NOVELS/JUV

BERENDT, KLAUS
FOCK, EUGEN--[39]GERMAN/NOVELS/JUV
GOBBO, LANZELOT--[39]GERMAN/NOVELS/JUV
HEYDECKER, JUPP--[39]GERMAN/NOVELS/JUV
SEBASTIAN, TILL--[39]GERMAN/NOVELS/JUV
TRASS, EUGEN--[39]GERMAN/NOVELS/JUV

BERENSON, LAURIEN
BLAIR, LAUREN--[9]ROM
BLAIR, LAURIEN--[9][21][26]ROM--4 NOVELS

BERENT, MARK
SANDBERG, BERENT--W/PER LARS SANDBERG, [3]MYS-
SIGN "BRASS DIAMONDS" '80
SIGN "HONEYCOMB BID" '81
SIGN "THE CHINESE SPUR" '83

BERENT, WACLAW
RAWICZ, WACLAW--[22]POLISH

BERESFORD, JOHN DAVYS
BEREFORD, J.D.--[1]

BERESFORD, LESLIE
PAN--[2][22][23]ENGLISH/SF

BERESFORD, MARCUS
BRANDEL, MARC--[3][7][11][22]NAME CHANGED TO "BRANDEL",MYS--7 NVLS '45-85
EQMM "IT COULD HAPPEN TO ANYONE" FEB '56
JCM "SCHEME TO DEFRAUD" MAR '58
JCM "MURDER SUSPECT" APR '61

BERG, DANIEL
MAHDEN, MAC--[29]MYS--
"MAH-JONG MORDEN"

BERG, DAVID
BERG, DAVE--[31][33]

BERG, JOHANNES M.
GOOTE, THOR--[39]GERMAN

BERGAUER, CONRAD
AUBERGER, GEORG--[39]GERMAN

BERGE, CAROL
KEEL, LAURA--[22]AMERICAN

BERGEL, HANS
BREGENZ, CURD--[39]GERMAN

BERGER, ALBERT
HOLLANDER, LESLIE--W/DIANNE NERAL, V. BERCH LTR TO HUBIN '94/MYS--
PINN "THE EXHIBIT" '81

BERGER, DORANNA
CROSS, CAITLIN--[9][21][26]ROM--4 NOVELS

BERGER, EVELYN MILLER
MILLER, EVELYN--[1]

BERGER, FRANCES TALAVERA
BERGEN, FRAN--[21]ROM--6 NOVELS
FLORES, FRANCES--[21][26]ROM--
"DESPERATE LONGINGS"
"LOVE'S WINE"

BERGER, IVAN [B]
EVANS, BENNETT--[1][31]
GROZNY, I.L.--[1][31]
LEYNARD, MARTIN--[1]

BERGER, JOSEF
DIGGES, JEREMIAH--[1][22][31][33]AMERICAN

BERGER, KARL HEINZ
HEINZ, K.--[39]GERMAN/MYS/JUV
HENRY, CHARLES P.--[39]GERMAN/MYS/JUV

BERGER, MARGOT
LANGER, BORIS--[39]GERMAN/MYS

BERGER, MEL
STONE, MIKE--V. BERCH LTR TO HUBIN '94, MYS--
DELL "ALLISON'S BABY" '88

BERGER, MELVIN H.
STEIN, DUFFY--V. BERCH LTR TO HUBIN '94, MYS--
DELL "OWLSFANE HORROR" '81
DELL "GHOST CHILD" '82
DELL "OUT IN THE SHADOWS" '84
DELL "THROUGH THE FLAMES" '86

BERGER, NOMI
WELLES, ALYSSA--[9][21][26]ROM--
"DRAGON FLOWER"

BERGER, OTTO
ROYAN, ROY--[39]GERMAN/ADV

BERGER, PETER
FRANK, AXEL--[39]GERMAN/JUV
MOUNT, PITT--[39]GERMAN/JUV

BERGFRIED, URSULA
BERNARDY, ULLA--[39]GERMAN

BERGHAMMER, SUSANNE
GREINER, SUSY--[39]GERMAN/JUV

BERGK, JOHANN ADAM
WUNDER, ERASMUS--[39]GERMAN

BERGLUND, E.P.
DE MAMMAIS, DR. PIERRE--W/WALTER C. DEBILL,[2]

BERGLUND, LARSS ERIK T.
HELGESSEN, LARS--[29]MYS--
"ISOLERINGEN" '79

BERGMAN, ERNST INGMAR
ERIKSSON, BUNTEL--[31]

BERGMAN, HJALMAR
BRATE, HOLGER--[29]MYS--
"FALSKA PAPPER" '16

BERGMAN, RICHARD T.
RICHARDS, THOMAS--[1]

BERGMAN, STEPHEN JOSEPH
SHEM, SAMUEL--V. BERCH LTR TO HUBIN '94,[34]--
ST. MARTIN'S "FINE" '85

BERGMAN, WERNER
MANN, W. BERG--[1]

BERGMANN, EDITH
MULLER-BECK, EDITH--[39]GERMAN/JUV

BERGNER, KARLHERRMANN
HERRMANN, KARL--[39]GERMAN/JUV

BERGSTROM, KAY
MILES, CASSIE--[9][10][21][26]ROM--
12 HARL NOVELS

BERK, THEODORE GEORGE
GEORGE, THEODORE--[3][29][40]MYS--
DODD "MURDER ON THE SQUARE" '71
DODD "DEADLY HOMECOMING" '72

BERKEBILE, FRED DONOVAN
DONOVAN, WILLIAM--[1][22][31][33]AMERICAN
ERNEST, WILLIAM--[1][22][31]AMERICAN
STAUFFER, DON--[1][22][33]AMERICAN

BERKMAN, EDWARD O[SCAR]
BERKMAN, TED--[31]

BERKMAN, EDWINA
REED, DANA--[7]SF--
7 LEIS NOVELS '84-90

BERKMANN, EVELYN [D]
WADE, JOANNA--[1][2][22]AMERICAN-ENGLISH

BERLAND, NANCY
LANDON, NANCY--[9][21]ROM--
"MIDNIGHT BLUE"
"SOUNDWAVES"
"ICE PALACE"

BERLYN, MICHAEL [STEVEN]
SONDERS, MARK--[7][23],SF--
ACE "BLIGHT" '81

BERMAN, ARNOLD M.
BRETONNE, ANNE-MARIE--[26][34]MYS/ROM--
4 NOVELS '75-7

BERMAN, ED
CHECK, OTTO PREMIER--[31]
DOGG, PROFESSOR R.L.--[31]

BERMANGE, MAURINE J.L.
ROSS, MAGGIE--[11]SF

BERMANN, RICHARD A.
HOLLRIEGEL, ARNOLD--[39]GERMAN

BERMANN, RICHARD ARNOLD
HOLLRIEGEL, ARNOLD--[1][2]

BERNAL, JUDITH F.
DUNN, JUDITH F.--[31]

BERNARD, FRITS
SERVATIUS, VICTOR--[39]GERMAN

BERNARD, KARL
PAOLO, PETER MARIA--[39]GERMAN/SF
WINTER, THOMAS R.--[39]GERMAN/SF

BERNARD, PATRICIA SCOT
SCOT-BERNARD, P.--[36]AUSTRALIAN/MYS--
BANTAM "SEX IS A DEADLY EXERCISE" '87

BERNDORFF, HANS-RUDOLF
VAN WERTH, RUDOLF--[39]GERMAN

BERNDT, KARL-HEINZ
BERG, KAI--[39]GERMAN
DE BARRINKH, LENTZ--[39]GERMAN
GUBANE, BERNY--[39]GERMAN
GUBEN, BERNDT--[39]GERMAN
JERSEY, JOHN--[39]GERMAN, HP
KING, JOHN B.--[39]GERMAN
PINSCHER, MICHEL--[39]GERMAN
TUREK, WILL--[39]GERMAN
VAN JOHST, J.J.--[39]GERMAN
VON BERN, H.--[39]GERMAN

BERNE, ERIC [L]
GANDALAC, LENNARD--[31]
HORSELY, RAMSBOTTOM--[31]
PINTO, PETER--[31]
ST. CYR, CYPRIAN--[31]

BERNELL, SUE
BERNE, KARIN--W/MICHAELA KARNI,[3]MYS--
POPLB "BARE ACQUAINTANCES" '85
POPLB "SHOCK VALUE" '85
BURKE, DIANA--W/MICHAELA KARNI,[9][21]ROM

BERNET, MICHAEL M.
BEN-DOV, MEIR--[31]

BERNET, MICHAEL [STEVEN]
ANONYMOUS--[14]--
OLYM OPS#3 "SEVEN EROTIC MINUTES"'70
FOSTER, SHEILA--[1][14]--
OLYM OPS#10 "SOHO WHORE" '70
OLYM OPS #20 "MAFAIR MISTRESS" '71
JADWAY, J.J.--[14]--
OLYM OPS#1 "ORIGINAL SEVEN MINUTES"

BERNHARDT, CLYDE EDRIC B.
BARRON, ED--[31]

BERNHARDT, MARCIA A.
BERNHARDT, M.A.--[1]

BERNITT-DREYER, JANNA
BERT, JO--[39]GERMAN

BERNS, ULRICH
BAUMANN, BODO--[39]GERMAN/JUV

BERNSTEIN, AL
BERN, DONALD--[2]
BERNSEN, ALBERT--[2]
RAY, ROBERT--[2]

BERNSTEIN, ALEC
BARON, [JOSEPH] ALEXANDER--[1]

BERNSTEIN, GERRY
MORRISON, G.F.--[1]

BEROV, LILI
BEJANOVA, LILIANA--[39]GERMAN

BERRIAULT, GEORGIANNA
BERRIAULT, GINA--[7]SF

BERRIGAN, EDMUND J.M. JR.
BERRIGAN, TED--[31]

BERRILL, NORMAN JOHN
BERRILL, N.J.--[1]

BERROW, CYRIL NORMAN
BERROW, N.--[36]AUSTRALIAN/MYS--
WARD "ELEVENTH PLAGUE" '53
WARD "DON'T JUMP MR. BOLAND" '54

BERRY, BARBARA J.
BERRY, B.J.--[1][31][33]

BERRY, BRYAN
DEEGAN, JON J.--VULTURES OF THE VOID, HP
GARNER, ROLF[E]--[][2][11][23][31]SF
SHELDON, ROY--VULTURES OF THE VOID, HP

BERRY, CHARLES EDWARD A.
BERRY, CHUCK--[31]

BERRY, DAVID [CHAPMAN]
BERRY, D.C.--[31]

BERRY, D[OUGLAS] BRUCE
CLEVE, JOHN--W/ANDREW J. OFFUTT,[7]--
BEE-LINE "PLEASURE US!" 1971
DOUGLAS, JEFF--W/ANDREW J. OFFUTT,[2][11]--
"BALLING MACHINE"
DRAKE, MORGAN--W/ANDREW OFFUTT,
[2][7][11][14]SF--
WARNER "GENETIC BOMB" '75

BERRY, JAMES
BERRY, JIM--[31]

BERRY, JAMES GOMER
KEMSLEY, VISCOUNT--[31]

BERRY, JANE COBB
COBB, JANE--[1][31][33]

BERRY, JOCELYN
BERRY, JO--[1]

BERRY, MARTHA EUGENIA
ST. JOHN, EUGENIA--[1]

BERRYMAN, JAMES THOMAS
BERRYMAN, JIM--[31]

BERRYMAN, JOHN
BUPP, WALTER--[23]SF--ASTOUNDING SF '60s

BERSCHEID, ELLEN
WALSTER, ELAINE HATFIELD--W/ELAINE C.
HATFIELD,[1][31]--
"INTERPERSONAL ATTRACTION" '69

BERSIANIK, LOUKY
DURAND, LUCILE--[31]

BERTELLI, LUIGI
VAMBA--[22]ITALIAN

BERTHELIUS, JENNY
LAGEVI, BO--[29]SWEDISH/MYS--
NOVELS '68-84

BERTHOLD, WILL
AMBERG, STEFAN--[39]GERMAN
DEUSEL, P.M.--[39]GERMAN
FRANKEN, BERT--[39]GERMAN
MOIRA, MARTIN--[39]GERMAN

BERTHOUD, EUGENE
BORYS, GONTRAU--[1]

BERTIE, MARIE
EMMBE--[1]

BERTIGNONO, GIOVANNI
BERTIN, JACK--[2][23]ITALIAN/SF

BERTIN, EDDY C.
BRENDALL, EDITH--[1][2][11]
GREYSUN, DORIAC--[1][2][11]

BERTIN, JOHN
BERTIN, JACK--[31]

BERTON, PIERRE
KRONIUK, LISA--[1]

BERTOU, GWILHERM
KERVERZHIOU--[22]BRETON

BERTRAM, JAMES G.
COOPER, WILLIAM--[1]

BERTRAND, MICHEL
ANGEBERT, JEAN--[1][31]
ANGEBERT, JEAN-MICHEL--[1][31]
ANGEBERT, MICHEL--[1][31]

BERZIN, MIERVALDIS I.
BIRZE, MIERVALDIS IANOV.--[1]

BESANT, [SIR] WALTER
MAURICE, WALTER--[1]
W.B.--[1]

BESEMERES, JOHN
DALY, JOHN--[1]

BESKOW, BO
MALL, VIKTOR--[1]

BESSER, CHRISTA
BURCHARDT, CHRISTA--[39]GERMAN

BESSIE, ALVAH
YOUNG, NEDRICK--[1]

BESSIERE, RICHARD
RICHARD-BESSIERE, F.--W/FRANCOIS RICHARD, [1][2][11]

BEST, CAROL ANN
ASHE, SUSAN--[1][9]ROM
DARLINGTON, CON--[9]ROM
MARTIN, ANN--[9]ROM
WAYNE, MARCIA--[9]ROM

BEST, GEOFFREY [FRANCIS]
BEST, G.F.A.--[31]

BEST, R. BRETON AMIS
AMIS, BRETON--[3][22][31]MYS--
FH "THEY WALKED IN FEAR" 46
INTNL "TERROR FARM" '47
BENTINCK, RAY--[8][34]MYS--
AMALG "DARK BANNER" '49
AMALG "MASTER OF DESTINIES" '49
AMALG "TOP SPOT FOR DANGER" '64
BEST, RAYLEIGH--[9]ROM
HADDOW, LEIGH--[8][9]ROM
HUGHES, TERRENCE--[8][9]ROM
ROBERTS, DESMOND--[8][9]ROM
WILDE, LESLIE--[8][9][32]MYS/ROM--
JCM "THE HELPING HAND" OCT '57

BEST, THARRATT GILBERT
TARASC, GILBERT--[1]

BEST, WALTER
WALDTHAUSEN, SEBASTIAN--[39]GERMAN/JUV

BEST, [E] ALLENA CHAMPLIN
BERRY, ERICK--[1][31][33]--
CHILDREN'S BOOKS
ERICK--[1]
MAXON, ANNE--[1][31][33]--CHILDREN'S BOOKS

BESTER, ALFRED
LENNOX, JOHN--[11]SF
POWELL, SONNY--[1][2][11][23]--
FSF "QUINTETS" SEPT '59

BESTON, ELIZABETH COATSW.
COATSWORTH, ELIZABETH--[1]

BESTWICK, HARRY
BEZIQUE--[1]
BUSY BEE--[1]
EGERTON, RANDOLPH--[1]

BETANCOURT, JOHN GREGORY
APPLETON, VICTOR--[23]HP--
STSY 'TOM SWIFT':
"THE UNDERSEA RAIDERS" '92
KINGSTON, JEREMY--[7][23]SF--
HARPER 'R. SILVERBERG'S TIME TOURS':
"CAESAR'S TIME LEGIONS" '91

BETHANCOURT, T. ERNESTO
PAISLEY, TOM--[33]

BETHE, HANS ALBRECHT
BETHE, H.A.--[31]

BETHELL, MARY URSULA
HAYES, EVELYN--[22]NEW ZEALAND

BETHMANN, HORST
DIETRICH, H.P.--[39]GERMAN

BETHUNE, MARY
CLOPET, LILIANE [M.C.]--[1][32]MYS--
LM "SHIPSHAPE SHILLING" DEC'49-JUN'53

BETJEMAN, [SIR] JOHN
EPSILON--[1][31]
FARREN, RICHARD M.--[31]
FARREN, RICHARD J.--[1][31]

BETZ, EVA KELLY
PETERS, CAROLINE--[1][22][33]AMERICAN

BETZ, INGRID
MARTIN, MONICA--[9][21][26]ROM--
"THE BUTTERCUP DREAM"

BETZ, JOSEF
BOY-LINDEN, ELMAR--[39]GERMAN

BEUM, ROBERT LAWRENCE
LAWRENCE, ROBERT--[31][32]MYS--
MSMM "HE'S NOT LISTENING" MAR '78
EQMM "DYING MESSAGES" AUG '78

BEUMELBURG, WERNER
MCGORGO--[39]GERMAN

BEURET-AMMANN, ESTHER
AMMANN, ESTHER E.--[39]GERMAN

BEUTTENMILLER, HERMANN
BEUTTEN, HERMANN--[39]GERMAN

BEUTTLER, EDWARD IVAN O.
BUTLER, IVAN--[2][3][7][31]MYS/SF--
PLAYBOY "DANGER INSIDE" '60

BEVAN, GLORY ISOBEL
BEVAN, GLORIA--[17]ROM
MURRAY, FIONA--[35][17]AUSTRALIAN/ROM--
HRWTZ PB277 "INVITATION TO DANGER" '66
HRWTZ PB9 "GOLD COAST AFFAIR" '67

BEVAN, TOM
BAUMFYLDE, WALTER--[1][31][33]

BEVARD, CAMILLE
HUME, MICKEY--[1]

BEVERIDGE, MERYLE SECREST
DOMAN, JUNE--[1][31]
SECREST, MERYLE--[1]

BEVIS, HERBERT URLIN
BEVIS, H.U.--[1]

BEYEA, BASIL
BENSON, B.A.--[1][31]

BEYFUSS, ERIKA
FRIES, ERIKA--[39]GERMAN

BEYLE, HENRI
STENDHAL--OXFORD COMPANION TO FRENCH LIT. 1961

BEYLIN, KAROLINA
MALISZEWSKA, MARIA--[1]
STEPHEN, CHARLES B.--[1]
WITKOWICKI, KAROL--[1]

BEYNON, JANE
LEWIS, LANGE--[1][22][34]MYS--
5 BOBBS NOVELS '43-52

BHABRA, H.S.
KABAL, A.M.--[1][34]--
ALLISON "THE ADVERSARY" '85--
ALLISON "BAD MONEY" '86

BHARTI, MA SATYA
JACOBS, JILL--[31]

BHATIA, JAMUNADEVI
BHATIA, JUNE--[1][31]
EDWARDS, JUNE--[1][31]
FORRESTER, HELEN--[1][31]
RANA, J.--[1]

BHOSALE, YESHWANTRAO
RAMALA, PRATAP ROY--[1]
ROY, RAMALA PRATAP--[1]

BIALK, ELISA
KRAUTTER, ELISA--[33]CHILDREN'S BOOKS

BIANCHI, JACQUI
DENYS, TERESA--[9][21][26]ROM--
"FLESH & THE DEVIL"
"THE SILVER DEVIL"

BIANCHI, MARTHA D.
DICKINSON, MARTHA GILBERT--[1]

BIANCHI, VIRGINIA BROWN
BROWN, VIRGINIA--[21]ROM--9 NOVELS
BROWN, MICKI--[26]ROM--
"BECAUSE OF YOU"
"ONCE A REBEL"
HARRINGTON, EMMA--W/MELINDA J. HARRISON,
[9][21][26]ROM--7 NOVELS
LYNN, VIRGINIA--[21][26]ROM--
"RIVER'S DREAM"
"CUTTER'S WOMAN" & 6 MORE

BIANCO, MARGERY WILLIAMS
WILLIAMS, MARGERY--FANT. LIT. FOR CHILDREN
& YOUNG ADULTS BY RUTH NADELMAN

BIBESCO, MARTHE LUCILE
DECAUX, LUCILE--[1][31]

BICCHIERI, THERESA F.
BUCCHIERI, THERESA F.--[1]

BICKEL, ALICE
KING, SANDRA--[39][40]GERMAN/MYS--
"GEHEIMNISSE UM LA LUZ" '69 & 3 OTHERS

BICKERS, RICHARD L.T.
CHARLES, MARK--[1][31]BROWN WATSON--
"HERE COME THE MARINES" '58
CITTADINO, ROBERT--[1][32]MYS--
EQMM "PRIDE IN ONE'S ACCOMPLISHMENT"APR '77
EQMM "MESSAGE FROM A DEAD MAN"JUL '78
CITTAFINO, RICHARDO--[1][31]--
BW "CONSCRIPT" '58
DUKES, PHILIP--[1][31]--
BW "KIDNAP" '58
HALL, RICHARD--[31]WAR--
4 HALE NOVELS '84-93
KAPUSTA, PAUL--[1][31]--
BW "AVENGING EAGLE" 58
KEENE, BURT--[1][31]--
BW "DEATH BUT NO GLORY" '58
KIRSCHNER, FRITZ--[1][31]--
BW "S.S." '58
LEFEVRE, GUI--[1][31]--
BW "WE WERE THREE" '58
LESLIE, RICHARD--[31]WAR--
15 HALE NOVELS '80-6
MUELLER, GERHARDT--[1][31]--
BW "LUFTWAFFE" '58
RICHARDS, DAVID--[1][3][31]--
DIGIT "DOUBLE GAME" '58 & 3 OTHERS
TOWNSHEND, RICHARD--[1][31]WAR--

BICKERS, RICHARD L.T. [CONT]
TOWNSEND, RICHARD [CONT]
SELF "ANGELS TWENTY-FIVE" '55
SELF "MALAYASIAN EPISODE" '56
SELF "JAPANESE ENCOUNTER" '56
SELF "TERROR IN CYPRUS" '57

BICKERSTAFF-DREW, FRANCIS
AYSCOUGH, JOHN--[3]MYS--
CHATTO "PRODIGALS & SON" '14

BICKHAM, JOHN M.
BICKHAM, JACK--[3][31]MYS--
TOR "DAY SEVEN "88
TOR "DROPSHOT" '90 & 2 MORE '67-80
CLINTON, JEFF--[7][19][23][28][31]SF--
LASER "KANE'S ODYSSEY" '76 &19 WEST '61-75
LOGAN, JAKE--[19]HP--
"HANGING JUSTICE"
MILES, JOHN--[3][22][29]MYS--
ACE "DALLY WITH A DEADLY DOLL" '61
& 4 OTHERS
SHAW, GEORGE--[1][28]

BICKLE, JUDITH BRUNDRETT
TWEEDALE, J.--[1][22]ENGLISH

BIDDLE, KATHERINE G.C.
CHAPIN, KATHERINE G.--[31]

BIDSTON, LESTER
HOTSPUR, PAUL--[1]

BIDWELL, J.S.
CHRISTIE, COLLEEN--[9][21]ROM--
"A KISS IS STILL A KISS"

BIDWELL, M. ELIZABETH
FORD, ELIZABETH--[3][17][21][26]
[31]ENGLISH/MYS--
HURST "A COUNTRY HOLIDAY" '66
& 31 OTHERS '33-76
GIBBS, MARY ANNE--[3][9][17][21]
[26][31]MYS/ROM--25 NOVELS '64-77

BIEBER, JANET LYNN P.
JOYCE, JANET--W/JOYCE A.S. THIES,[9][21][26],
ROM--16 NOVELS
JOYCE, JENNA LEE--W/JOYCE A.S. THIES,
[9][21][26]ROM--5 NOVELS

BIEDERMANN, FELIX
DOERMANN, FELIX--[1][22]AUSTRIAN

BIEGE, KARL HEINZ
MORRIS, CLYDE--[39]GERMAN/SF

BIEGER, MARCEL
SEELMANN, KURT E.--[39]GERMAN/SF

BIELECKI, CZESLAW
M.P.--[1]
POLESKI--[1]

BIELICKE, GERHARD
KERFIN, GERHARD--[39]GERMAN

BIENENGRABER, ALFRED
SIEGWART, ALFRED--[39]GERMAN

BIENES, NICHOLAS PETER
BIENES, NICK--V. BERCH LTR TO HUBIN'94, MYS--
GOULD, JUDITH--W/REA GALLAGHER,
V. BERCH LTR TO HUBIN '94,[31]MYS--
DUTTON "NEVER TOO RICH" '90

BIENSTOCK, MYRON JOSEPH
BIENSTOCK, MIKE--[1][31]

BIERACH, ALFRED
BESTE, DR. RICHARD--[39]GERMAN
LOCKHART, JOHN--[39]GERMAN/WEST

BIERBAUM, OTTO JULIUS
MOBIUS, MARTIN--[39]GERMAN

BIERCE, AMBROSE
BOWERS, MRS. J. MILTON--[11]SF
GRILE, DOD--[2][5][11][22][23][29]MYS/SF
HERMAN, WILLIAM--W/THOMAS A. HARCOURT,[1][2]
SLOBUCK, J. MILTON--[1][11]SF
URSUS--[2]

BIERMAN, JOHN
BREWSTER, DAVID--[34]MYS--
COWARD "HEARTS GROWN BRUTAL" '72

BIERMAN, JUNE
BENNETT, MARGOT--W/BARBARA TOOHEY,[8][32]--
BS "MAN WHO DIDN'T FLY" JAN '60
BENNETT, MARGARET--W/BARBARA TOOHEY,[8]

BIERMANN-RATJEN, HANS H.
RATJEN, HANS HARDER--[39]GERMAN

BIERSCHENCK, BURKHARD P.
ERFURT, PETER--[39]GERMAN
SCHENCK, BURKHARD--[39]GERMAN

BIETRIX, VINCENT
VISAN, TANCREDE DE--OXFORD COMPANION TO FRENCH LIT. 1961

BIGG, PATRICIA NINA
AINSWORTH, PATRICIA--[3][9][17][31][36]MYS/ROM--
HALE "THE DEVIL'S HOLE" '71

BIGNON, JEAN PAUL
SANDERSON, MR. DE--[2]

BIHALJI-MERIN, OTO
MERIN, PETER--[1]
THOENE, PETER--[1]

BILLAM, GEORGE
GOLDSMITH, PETER--W/JOHN B. PRIESTLEY,[18][22][29]MYS--
PLAY "SPRING TIDE" '36

BILLINGS, EDITH S.
BILLINGS, MARIS H.--[1]
WARRINGTON, MARIS--[1]

BILLS, SHARON & ROBERT
EDWARDS, SARAH--[9][21][26]ROM--
"CRYSTAL RAPTURE"
"FIRE & SAND"

BILSKY, EVA
AUNT EVA--[1]

BINDER, EARL ANDREW
BINDER, EANDO--W/OTTO BINDER,[1][2][4]
COLERIDGE, JOHN--W/OTTO BINDER,[1][2][4][22][23]SF
GARTH, WILL--W/OTTO BINDER,[1][2][23], HP [STANDARD]
GILES, GORDON A.--W/OTTO BINDER,[1][2][23]SF
O'BRIEN, DEAN D.--W/OTTO BINDER,[1][2][23]SF

BINDER, EARL ANDREW [CONT]
TUREK, IAN FRANCIS--W/OTTO BINDER,[2][3][23]MYS/SF--
CURTIS "TERROR IN THE BAY" '71
TUREK, IONE FRANCES--W/OTTO BINDER,[2][4][23]SF--

BINDER, FREDERICK MOORE
MOORE, ANDREW--[3]MYS--
APOLLO "THE SERBIAN ASSIGNMENT" '71

BINDER, JACK
PLAISTED, MAX--W/OTTO BINDER,[2]

BINDER, OTTO
BINDER, EANDO--W/EARL ANDREW BINDER,[1][2]
ALSO ALONE AFTER EARL'S DEATH
COLERIDGE, JOHN--W/EARL ANDREW BINDER,[2][22][23][31]SF
GARTH, WILL--W/EARL ANDREW BINDER,[1][2][23]HP [STANDARD]
GILES, GORDON A.--W/EARL ANDREW BINDER,[1][2][22][23]SF--TWS '37-42
O'BRIEN, DEAN D.--W/EARL ANDREW BINDER,[1][2][22][23]SF
PLAISTED, MAX--W/JACK BINDER,[2]
TUREK, IAN FRANCIS--W/EARL ANDREW BINDER,[2][23]MYS/SF--
CURTIS "TERROR IN THE BAY" '71
TUREK, IONE FRANCES--W/EARL ANDREW BINDER,[2][3][23]SF

BINDER-GASPER, CHRISTIANE
GASPARRI, CHRISTIANE--[39]GERMAN

BING, JON
CATAMARAN--[1]

BINGENHEIMER, HEINZ
BINGS, HENRY--[39]GERMAN/SF

BINGHAM, EADFRID A.
BERTON, GUY--W/GUY R. LA COSTE,[3][22]MYS--
DODD "ART THOU THE MAN?" '05

BINGHAM, EVANGELINE M.
ELLIOT, GERALDINE--[1][31]

BINGHAM, MADELEINE
MANNERING, JULIA--[1][8][22][31]ENGLISH

BINGHAM, MELINDA
BINGHAM, MINDY--[31]

BINGLEY, DAVID ERNEST
ADAMS, BART--[8][28][31]WEST--
GRESHAM "OWLHOOT RAIDERS" '66
GRESHAM "RENEGADE'S STAMPEDE" '67
HALE "COYOTE KIDS" '70
BENSON, ADAM--[8]
BINGLEY, D.E.--[28][31]MYS--
HALE "ELUSIVE WITNESS" '66
HALE "CARRIBEAN CRISIS" '66
BRIDGER, ADAM--[8][28][31]WEST--
HALE "COUNTERFEIT TRAIL" '65
HALE "GUNSMOKE GORGE" '66
HALE "RENEGADE RANGE" '69
CAMBER, ANDREW--[31]
CANUCK, ABE--[8][28][31]WEST--
HALE "RIOTING RENEGADES" '66
HALE "SILVERTOWN TRAIL" '69
HALE "HELLION'S HOSTAGE" '71
CARVER, DAVE--[8][28][31]WEST--
HALE "BAR T BRAND" '64
HALE "GUNSMOKE GAMBLER" '66
HALE "RENEGADE RIVER" '73

BINGLEY, DAVID ERNEST [CONT]
CARVER, HENRY--[1][28]
CHATHAM, LARRY--[8][28][31]WEST--
10 HALE NOVELS '63-85
CHESHAM, HENRY--[3][28]MYS--
HALE "NAPLES OR DIE" '65
HALE "SKYBORN SAPPER" '66 &
7 OTHERS '65-86
COLTMAN, WILL--[8][28][31]WEST--
GRESHAM "TORRINGTON TRAIL" '66
HALE "KILLER'S CREEK" '69
HALE "GHOST TOWN KILLER" '70
CONISTON, ED--[8][28][31]WEST--
GRESHAM "BAR X BANDIT" '65
GRESHAM "ELUSIVE RENEGADE" '67
HALE "BOULDER CREEK TRAIL" '69
DORMAN, LUKE--[8][28][31]WEST--
HALE "RENEGADE'S BLADE" '65
HALE "BUZZARD'S BREED" '66
HALE "RED ROCK RENEGADES" '70
FALLON, GEORGE--[3]MYS--
HALE "RENDEZVOUS IN RIO" '67
HORSLEY, DAVID--[8][28][31]WEST/WAR--
26 NOVELS '57-85
JEFFORD, BAT--[8][28][31]WEST--
HALE "CREEK TOWN KILLER" '66
HALE "PECOS RIVER POSSE" '68
HALE "SILVER CREEK TRAIL" '70
KINGSTON, SYD--[8][28][31]WEST--
7 HALE NOVELS '64-85
LYNCH, ERIC--[8][28][31]WEST--
GRESHAM "SOUTH FORK SHOWDOWN" '67
HALE "MURDER MESA" '68
HALE "RENEGADES RETREAT" '71
MARTELL, JAMES--[8][28][31]WEST--
HALE "LITTLE PECOS TRAIL" '65
HALE "RENEGADE TRAIL" '66
HALE "SALT CREEK SHOWDOWN" '70
HALE "COWTOWN KIDNAP"'71
NORTH, COLIN--[8][28][31]WEST--
HALE "RELUCTANT GUNMAN" ''65
HALE "TRAIL OF TRAGEDY" '66
HALE "TRAILTOWN TRICKSTER" '69
PLUMMER, BEN--[8][28][31]WEST--
HALE "GUNSMOKE COUNTRY" '64
HALE "RAILROAD RENEGADES" '65
HALE "COWTOWN KILLERS" '72
PRESCOTT, CALEB--[8][28][31]WEST--
HALE "RUTHLESS RENEGADES" '66
HALE "PECOS RIVER POSSE" '67
HALE "SIX SHOOTER JUNCTION" '70
REMINGTON, MARK--[8][28][31]WEST--
HALE "HELLION'S ROOST" '65
HALE "SILVER CITY SHOWDOWN" '66
HALE "EL YANQUI' GOLD" '69
ROBERTS, JOHN--[8][28][31]WEST--
HALE "SHOWDOWN AT THE LAZY T" '64
HALE "COLORADO GUN LAW" '66
HALE "TRAILMEN'S TRUCE" '72
ROMNEY, STEVE--[8][28][31]WEST--
HALE "GUNSMOKE LAWYER" '65
HALE "SAWBONE'S CITY" '67
HALE "SHOWDOWN CITY" '70
SILVESTER, FRANK--[8][28][31]WEST--
8 HALE NOVELS '65-86
STARR, HENRY--[8][28][31]WEST--
HALE "SHORT-TRIGGER VALLEY" '64
HALE "BORDER BRIGANDS" '65
HALE "LAWMAN'S LAMENT" '72
TUCKER, LINK--[8][28][31]WEST--
GRESHAM "RENEGADE VALLEY" '65
GRESHAM "CIRCLE M SHOWDOWN" '67
HALE "HELLION'S AT LARGE" '69
WIGAN, CHRISTOPHER--[8][28][31]WEST--
10 NOVELS '57-85
YORKE, ROGER--[8][28][31]WEST--
HALE "IRON TRAIL" '65

BINGLEY, DAVID ERNEST [CONT]
YORKE, ROGER [CONT]
HALE "GUADALUPE BANDIT" '66
HALE "OWLHOOT BANDITS" '66

BINGLEY, MARGARET [JANE]
KIRBY, MARGARET--[31][33]

BINGZHI, JIANG
DING LING--[1]CHINESE

BINNS, OTWELL
BOLT, BEN--[3][22][29]MYS--38 NOVELS '21-44

BINZEN, WILLIAM
BINZEN, BILL--[31][33]

BIONDI, DIANNA R.G.
GUEST, DIANA--[9][21][26]ROM--
"TWILIGHTS BURNING"

BIOY CASARES, ADOLFO
DAVIS, B. LYNCH--W/JORGE L. BORGES,[31]
DOMECQ, M. BUSTOS--W/JORGE L. BORGES,[23][31]
LYNCH, DAVIS--W/JORGE LUIS BORGES,[1]
MIRANDA, JAVIER--[1]
SACASTRU, MARTIN--[1]
SUAREZ LYNCH, B.--W/JORGE LUIS BORGES,[1]

BIRCH, JACK ERNEST LIONEL
FLIGHT, FRANCIES--W/VENETIA PAULINE MURRAY,[8]

BIRD, DENNIS LESLIE
NOEL, JOHN--[8]

BIRD, FLORENCE [B]
FRANCIS, ANNE--[1][31]

BIRD, FREDERIC MAYER
TIMSOL, ROBERT--[1]

BIRD, ROBERT M.
PILGRIM, PETER--[1]

BIRD, SARAH MCCABE
CATES, TORY--[9][21][26][31]ROM--
"HANDFUL OF SKY"
"CLOUD WALTZER"
"DIFFERENT DREAMS" & MORE

BIRD, VIVIAN
BEER, VIC--[1][31]

BIRD, WILLIAM HENRY F.
BLAIR, ADRIAN--[1][7][11][23]SF, HP--
CW "COSMIC CONQUEST" '53
EAGLE, JOHN--[23]SF, HP--
CURTIS "RECKLESS JOURNEY" '47
CURTIS "BRIEF INTERLUDE" '47
ELLIOTT, LEE--[2][7][11][23]SF, HP--
CURTIS "THE THIRD MUTANT '53
FLEMING, HARRY--[2][7][11][23]--
"BLAST-OFF INTO SPACE" '66
LE PAGE, RAND--[2][7][23]SF, HP--
CURTIS "WAR OF ARGOS" '52
LORRAINE, PAUL--[2][7][11][23]SF, HP--
CURTIS "TWO WORLDS" '52
LUNA, KRIS [CHRIS]--[2][7][11][23][34]SF, HP--
CURTIS "OPERATION ORBIT" '53
TOUCAN, JOHN--[2][11][23]SF

BIRD, [C] KENNETH
BLOXHAM, PETER--[3][29]MYS--
HALE "FUNERAL FOR A PHYSICIST" '66
HALE "DEATH FOR A DROPOUT" '70
FOUGASSE--[22][31]ENGLISH

BIRKENHEAD, ELIZAH
BIRKENHEAD, EDWARD--[1]

BIRKIN, CHARLES L.
LLOYD, CHARLES--[2][11][31]

BIRKSTED-BREEN, DANA
BREEN, DANA--[1][31]

BIRLA, LAKSHIMINIWAS
ACHYUT--[1]

BIRNAGE, DEREK A.W.
BIRNAGE, DIRK--[1]
WINDSOR, FRANK--[1]

BIRNBAUM, ERNST
BAUM, ERNST--[39]GERMAN/JUV
MURR, KATER--[39]GERMAN/JUV

BIRNBAUM, NATHAN
ACHER, MATHIAS--[1]

BIRNBAUM, STEPHEN NORMAN
BIRNBAUM, STEVE--[31]

BIRNER, OTTO
NOLAN, FREDERICK--[39]GERMAN/WEST, HP

BIRNEY, HERMAN HOFFMAN
KENT, DAVID--[3][22][28]MYS--
RANDOM "JASON BURN'S FIRST CASE" '41
RANDOM "A KNIFE IS SILENT" '47

BIRO, BALINT STEPHEN
BIRO, B.--[31]AS ILLUSTRATOR
BIRO, B.S.--[31]AS ILLUSTRATOR
BIRO, VAL--[8][31][33]CHILDREN'S '68-91

BIRON, GEORG
SILVESTRE, DINO--[39]GERMAN

BIRON, SIR HENRY CHARTRES
RAGGED, HYDER--[1][2]

BIRREN, FABER
LANG, GREGOR--[1][2][7][22][31]AMERICAN
LANG, MARTIN--[1][8][22][31]AMERICAN

BIRT, FRANCIS BRADLEY
BRADLEY, SHELLAND--[8]

BIRT, THEODOR
BEATUS RHENANUS--[22]GERMAN

BIRTI, HELENE
LAIR, HELENE--[39]GERMAN

BIRTILL, GEORGE ARTHUR
PENDLE, NICHOLAS--[1]

BISCH, EDITH
DE BORN, EDITH--[1]

BISCHITZKY, LEO BODRICH
BIRCH, LEO BEDRITCH--[1]

BISCHOF, HEINZ
IMM, GUNTHER--[39]GERMAN

BISCHOFF, DAVID F.
F.X., MICHAEL--[23]FANTASTIC-STORIES THAT COMPRISED THE BOOK "A PERSONAL DEMON"
GRANT, MARK--W/TIM SULLIVAN,[7][23]SF--
AVON 'MUTANTS AMOK': #1, 3 & 6" '91

BISCHOFF, DAVID F. [CONT]
GRANT, MARK--[23]SF--
AVON 'MUTANTS AMOK': #2 & 5" '91
LAMPTON, CHRIS--W/CHRISTOPHER LAMPTON,[23]SF--
"SEEKER" '76

BISCHOFF, EMIL
GURDAN, EMIL--[39]GERMAN

BISCHOFF, KARL HEINRICH
BURKLE, VEIT--[39]GERMAN

BISCHOFF, MARIANNE [E]
MCDUNN, GARRY--[39]GERMAN/SF
REINERS, CHRIS--[39]GERMAN/SF
SYDOW, MARIANNE--[39]GERMAN/SF

BISHOFF, JOSEPH E.K.
VON BOLANDER, KONRAD--[1]

BISHOFF, JULIA BRISTOL
ARNOLDY, JULIE--[1][31][33]

BISHOP, ALLISON
LURIE, ALLISON--[11]SF

BISHOP, CLAIRE HUCHET
HUCHET, CLAIRE--[1]

BISHOP, CURTIS [KENT]
BRANDON, CURT--[8][22][33][31]AMERICAN
CARROLL, CURT--[1][22][31][33]AMERICAN

BISHOP, ELIZABETH
FOSTER, SARAH--[1]

BISHOP, ISABELLA LUCY [B]
BIRD, ISABELLA--[1]
BISHOP, ISABELLA BIRD--[31]

BISHOP, JAMES ALONZO
BISHOP, JIM--[31]

BISHOP, LESLIE
TOLIVAR, ROBIN--W/PAT C. OAKSON,[9][21]ROM--
"IN LOVE'S FURY"

BISHOP, MATTHEW
ZOOL, M.H.--[23]SF,GROUP PSEUD.

BISHOP, MORRIS GILBERT
JOHNSON, W. BOLINGBROKE--[2][3][11][22][31]
AMERICAN,MYS--
KNOPF "THE WIDENING STAIN" '42

BISHOP, S. WALTER EDGAR
EDGAR, ICARUS WALTER--[1]

BISHOP, TETIANA KROITOR
BISHOP, TANIAN KROITOR--[1]
SEMKIEV, VIRYANA--[1]
SHEVCHUK, TETIANA--[1]

BISHOP, THOMAS W[ALTER]
BISHOP, TOM--[31]

BISHOP, WILLIAM HENRY
UNKNOWN--[34]MYS--
CASSELL "SERGEANT VON; OR, A LONG CHASE" 1893

BISHOP, ZEALIA BROWN
HEALD, HAZEL--[1][2]
REED, Z.B.--[2]

BISLAND, ERNEST CHARLES
BISLAND, BILKO--[31]
BISLAND, E.C.--[31]

BISSELL, ELAINE
FAULKNER, WHITNEY--[9][21][26]ROM--
"AMERICA DREAM SAGA" 4 NOVELS

BISSOONDOYAL, BASDEO
GOTAMA, RAMTA YOGI--[1]
VAMDEVA, VISHNUDAYAL--[1]
VASUDEVA, VISHNUDAYAL--[1]

BITTNER, ARCHIBALD
APPEL, H.M.--LACHMAN LST MAY '93,[11]
QB 54 "ILLICIT DESIRES" '49
UNI 22 "TAINTED PASSIONS" '51
UNI 29 "BRUTAL KISSES" '52
CURTIS, STEELE--W. MURRAY, ECHOES #5, HP
HOUSE, BRANT--W. MURRAY, ECHOES #6,P6, HP--
'SECRET AGENT X':
"PLAGUE OF THE GOLDEN DEATH"
KIMBALL, CONRAD--[11]
ROGERS, WAYNE--W. MURRAY ECHOES #47--
MSMM "EYES IN THE DARKNESS" AUG '57
DT "ISLAND OF SILVER HELL" DEC '61
STEELE, CURTIS--ECHOES #6,P6,
BAE 25,P89,[23]HP--
'OPER 5':
"THE SUICIDE BATTALION" JUL '38
"DAY OF THE DAMNED" SEP '38
"DAWN THAT SHOOK THE WORLD" NOV '38
"WHEN HELL CAME TO AMERICA" JAN '39
"INVASION FROM THE SKY" MAR '39
"WNGD HORDES OF THE YELLOW VULTURES" MAY'39
"WAR TANKS OF THE Y.V."JUL '39
"CORPSE CAVALRY OF THE Y.V." SEP '39
"ARMY FROM UNDERGROUND" NOV '39
STOCKBRIDGE, GRANT--W. MURRAY,ECHOES #6, HP--
'THE SPIDER': "THE CORPSE BROKER"

BITTNER, F. ROSANNE
SAGE, JESSIE BELL--[9]ROM

BITTON JACKSON, LIVIA E.
JACKSON, LIVIA BITTON--[31]

BITZIUS, ALBERT
GOTTHELF, JEREMIAS--[2][39]GERMAN/SF

BIXBY, JEROME L.
BIXBY, JAY LEWIS--[1]
DREXEL, JAY B.--[1][2][11][22][23]SF
HERRICK, THORNECLIFF--[1][2][11]HP--
PLANET COMICS
JANS, EMERSON--[1][11][22][31]
LEWIS, D.B.--[1][2][11][22][31]
NEAL, HARRY--[1][2][11][22][23]SF
PALEY, MORTON D.--W/SAM MERWIN JR.,[11],SF,FP
ROME, ALGER--W/ALGIS BUDRYS,[1][2][11][23]SF--
"UNDERESTIMATION" '53
RUSSEL, ALBERT--[1][1]
RUSSEL, J. [RUSSEL]--[1][11][22]
ST. VIVANT, M.--[1][22]

BIXLER, WILLIAM ALLEN
ALLENBY, ENOS WILL--[1]

BIYIDI, ALEXANDRE
BETI, MONGO--[1]
BOTO, EZA--[1][31]

BIZARDEL, YVON
LAPAQUELLERIE, YVON--[1][31]

BJARKLIND, UNNUR B.
HULDA--[1]

BJARKMAN, PETER CHRISTIAN
DOCTOR BASEBALL--[31]

BJARNE, IVAN
DAGH, EVA--[29]MYS--
"MILLIONERNAS" '15

BJERKE, ANDRE
BORGE, BERNHARD--[3][29][37]NORWEGIAN/MYS--
"DEATH IN THE BLUE LAKE" '61

BJERREGAARD, WILHEM
GREEN BAR BILL--JEAN F. LE DEIST LTR '93,[1]
HILLCOURT, WILLIAM--[1][33]

BJOERK, CHRISTINA
BJORK, CHRISTINA--[31]

BJOERNEBOE, JENS
BJORNEBOE, JENS--[31]

BJOERNSON, BJOERNSTJERNE
BJORNSON, BJORNSTJERNE--[31]

BJORILD, STEN DOUGLAS
GRIMETON, DOUGLAS--[29]MYS--
5 NOVELS '12-25

BJORNBERG, SIGNE
STARK, SIGGE--[29]MYS

BLACK, CAMPBELL
ALTMAN, THOMAS--W/JEFFREY A.CAINE,[3][7]MYS--
BB "KISS DADDY GOODBYE" '80
ARMSTRONG, CAMPBELL--[7][29][34]--
HODDER "JIG" '87
HODDER "MAZURKA" '88
HODDER "BRAINFIRE" '90
HODDER "MAMBO" '90
CAMPBELL, JEFFREY--W/JEFFREY A. CAINE,
[3][7][31]MYS/SF--
PUTNAM "THE HOMING" '80

BLACK, CLINTON
BROSSE, VANE DE--[1]

BLACK, DAVID [MACLEOD]
BLACK, D.M.--[31]

BLACK, DOROTHY
ALBERTYN, DOROTHY--[31]
BLACK, KITTY--[9][29][31]ROM--
2 BOOKS '31-8

BLACK, HAZELTON
GRAHAM, SCOTT--[3]MYS--
7 NOVELS 1885-1912

BLACK, LADBROKE LIONEL D.
DAY, LIONEL--[1][23]SF--
"BURIED WORLD" '28

BLACK, LADBROKE [L.D.]
URQHARDT, PAUL--[1][3][23][29]MYS--
23 NOVELS '07-40

BLACK, MARGARET K.
BLACK, MAGGIE--[31]
HOWARD, KATHERINE--[1]
HOWORTH, M.K.--[1][31]
HOWORTH, MARGARET--[1]

BLACK, TERRY
BISHOP, PIKE--AFRAID #17, P4, HP--
'DIAMONDBACK' WESTERN SERIES-2 BOOKS

BLACK, WINIFRED
LAURIE, ANNIE--W/ALMA S. SCARBERRY,[31]

BLACKBURN, DOUGLAS
SARD, ERASMUS--[1]

BLACKBURN, TOM W.
REPP, ED EARL--PPCC#9, P96--
GHOSTED FOR REPP IN LATE 30's

BLACKETT, VERONICA HEATH
HEATH, VERONICA--[1][31][33]

BLACKLEDGE, ETHEL H.
HALE, ALLISON--[1]

BLACKMUR, RICHARD PALMER
HOBBS, PERRY--[31]

BLACKMUR-HRDY, SARAH C.
BLAFFER, SARAH C.--[1]

BLAICK, HANS ERICH
OWLGLASS, DR.--[1]
RATATOSKR--[1]

BLAIKLOCK, EDWARD MUSGRV.
GRAMMATICUS--[22][31]NEW ZEALAND

BLAINE, MARGERY K.
BLAINE, MARGE--[31]

BLAINE, THOMAS ROBERT
BLAINE, TOM R.--[31]

BLAIR, ANDREW JAMES F.
BLAIR, HAMISH--[2][7][23]SF

BLAIR, DOROTHY
SCARLETT, ROGER--W/EVELYN PAGE,[1][3][22],
AMERICAN/MYS--5 NOVELS '30-33

BLAIR, DOROTHY SARA G.
BOLITHO, RAY D.--[1][31]

BLAIR, ERIC ARTHUR
ORWELL, GEORGE--[2][7][23][29][33]SF--
"ANIMAL FARM: A FAIRY STORY" '45
"1984" '49

BLAIR, JOHN
JOHNS, BLAIR--S. HOLLAND, SCION CKLST
PP 27, P11
LUGAR, HANS--S. HOLLAND, SCION CKLST
PP 27, P11
PATTERSON, ALISTAIR--S. HOLLAND,
SCION CK LIST, PP 27, P11

BLAIR, KATHRYN
BRETT, ROSALIND--[17][21]ROM--26 NOVELS
CONWAY, CELINE--[17][21]ROM--20 NOVELS

BLAIR, PATRICK
GURNEY, DAVID--[2][7]SF--
NEL "CONJURERS" #1 & #2 '71-6
NEL "EVIL UNDER WATER" '77

BLAIR, PAULINE CLARKE H.
CLARKE, PAULINE--[7]/FANT. LIT. FOR CHILDREN &
YOUNG ADULTS BY RUTH NADELMAN

BLAIR, PAULINE HUNTER
CLAIRE, HELEN--[8]

BLAIR, WALTER
POST, MORTIMER--[1][3]MYS--
DBLDY "CANDIDATE FOR MURDER" '36

BLAIR-FISH, W. WILFRID
BLAIR--[31]
BLAIR, WILFRID--[31]

BLAISDELL, ELINOR
BLAISDELL, ANNE--[2]

BLAISDELL, PAUL
DELL, PAUL--[1][2][11]

BLAKE, ALAN
GWINN, OMAR--[11]SF

BLAKE, ANDREA
WEALE, ANNE--[1][21]ROM--NOVELS

BLAKE, GEORGE
VAGABOND--[1]

BLAKE, JAMES HUBERT
BLAKE, EUBIE--[31]

BLAKE, JOHN WILLIAM
BLAKE, J.W.--[31]
BLAKE, JOHN W.--[31]

BLAKE, JULIAN WATSON
BLAKE, BUD--[31]

BLAKE, LESLIE JAMES
LESTER, JAMES--[1][31]
TABARD, PETER--[1]

BLAKE, LILLIAN DEVEREAUX
AESOP--[1]
TIGER LILY--[1]

BLAKE, MINDEN V.
BLAKE, MINDY--[1][31]

BLAKE, MRS. MUIRSON
DELAIRE, JEAN--[23]SF--
"AROUND A DISTANT STAR" '04

BLAKE, ROBERT W.
BLAKE, LORD--[31]

BLAKE, SALLY MIRLISS
SARA--[1][22]AMERICAN

BLAKENEY, JAY D.
DALTON, SEAN--[7]SF--
ACE "OPERATION STARHAWKS #1-#4" '90/91

BLAKESTON, OSWELL
SIMON--W/ROGER D. BURFORD,[3][8][22]MYS--
WISHART "MURDER AMONG FRIENDS" '33
WISHART "DEATH ON THE SWIM" '34
WISHART "CAT WITH A MOUSTACHE" '35

BLANC, MARIE THERESE
BENTZON, THERESE--[1]

BLANCHARD, ANGELA ORTIZ
BLANCHARD, REBECCA--[9][34]MYS--
TUDOR "NO EASY WAY OUT" '88
TUDOR "A TEAR MUST FALL" '89

BLANCO WHITE, AMBER
REEVES, AMBER--[1]

BLAND, E.A.
D, E.A.B.--[34]MYS--
CONSTABLE 42Z "RELIGIOUS TRACT SOCIETY" 1888

BLAND, EDITH N. & HUBERT
BLAND, FABIAN--[1][3]MYS--
DRANE "THE PROPHET'S MANTLE" 1889

BLAND, EDITH NESBIT
NESBIT, EDITH--[32][34]MYS--
METHUEN "DORMANT" '11
METHUEN "RED HOUSE" '02
PAUL "FEAR" '10
EQMM "NO. 17" AUG '51
EQMM "IN THE DARK" SEPT '52

BLAND, ELEANOR MILDRED
BLAND, ELEANOR TAYLOR--HAWK/BLAND
INTRVW MAY '93--
ST. MARTINS "DEAD TIME"
ST. MARTINS "SLOW BURN"

BLANDEN, CHARLES G.
BLACKBURN, LAURA--[1]
RHUDDLAU, JOHN--[1]

BLANDFORD, BRIAN E[RNEST]
BARNABUS--[31]

BLANEY, CHARLES E.
BLANEY, HARRY CLAY--[1]

BLANFORD, VIRGINIA
CREWE, SARAH--[21][26]ROM--
"GOLDEN ILLUSIONS"
"NIGHTFLAME"
"SEAFLAME"
"WINDFLAME"

BLANK, CLARISSA MABEL
BLANK, CLAIR--[33]

BLANK, MATTHIAS
BERLEPSCH, E.--[39]GERMAN
BIRKENAU, M.B.--[39]GERMAN
BRANDEIS, B.--[39]GERMAN
BURG, E.M.--[39]GERMAN
HOHENOFEN, M.B.--[39]GERMAN
VON BLANKENSEE, THEO--[39]GERMAN
WALTER, R.--[39]GERMAN
WESSLING, M. v.--[39]GERMAN

BLANKFORT, MICHAEL [S]
FORD, BRYANT--[3]MYS--
DODD "SHOW BUSINESS" '39

BLANKMEISTER, HELMUT
BLAMASIA, MAX--[39]GERMAN

BLANVALET, LOTHAR
WILLBERG, HEINO--[39]GERMAN

BLASIUS, RICHARD
BLAKE, JAMES--[39]GERMAN/ADV/WEST
IGNOTUS--[39]GERMAN
RICHARD, KARL--[39]GERMAN/ADV/WEST

BLASSINGAME, WYATT RAINEY
RAINEY, W.B.--[1][2][16][33]
RAINEY, WILLIAM B.--E.R. HAGEMANN, COMPH. INDEX BLK MASK '82,[11]

BLATCHFORD, MONTAGUE
BLONG, MONT--[1]

BLATTY, WILLIAM PETER
CLYNE, TERENCE--[1][22][31]AMERICAN

BLAU, ERIC
BLAU, MILTON--[1][31]

BLAU, JOSHUA
BLAU, YEHOSHUA--[31]

BLAUER, ETTAGALE
LAURE, ETTAGALE--[31][33]

BLAUSTEIN, ALBERT PAUL
DE GRAEFF, W.B.--W/[E]GROFF CONKLIN,[11]SF
DEGRAEFF, ALLEN--[1][2][23][31]SF

BLAUW, PIETER WILHELMUS
BLAUW, WIM--[31]

BLAYLOCK, JAMES P[AUL]
ASHBLESS, WILLIAM--W/TIMOTHY THOMAS POWERS--
JAMES SEELS-BLAYLOCK BIBLIOGRAPHY '93
BRYANT, EDWARD--[23]SF
HASTING, WILLIAM--W/TIMOTHY THOMAS POWERS--
JAMES SEELS-BLAYLOCK BIBLIOGRAPHY '93

BLAZE DE BURY, MARIE P.R.
DUDLEY, ARTHUR--[1]
FLASSAN, MAURICE--[1]

BLAZE DE BURY, YETTA
BROWN, JANE--[1]

BLEAKERSTOWE, GEORGE H.
HOWES, ROYCE B.--W/BEVANS BLY,
L. ROBBINS LTR MAR '94, PULP

BLEAKLEY, HORACE WILLIAM
TIVOLI--[1]

BLECK, WILLIAM JAMES
BLAKE, WILLIAM J.--[1]

BLEECK, G.C.
ANSTEE, M.H.--G. FLANAGAN LTR '94,
AUSTRALIAN--CLVLD SS
BRODY, HANK--G. FLANAGAN LTR '94,
AUSTRALIAN--CLVLD SS
CARTER, ACE--[36]HP--
TRNPT-ALL BUT "FUGITIVES FROM FLAME WORLD"
CORDELL, BRAD--[35]AUSTRALIAN/WEST,
CLVLD NOVELS '62-71
DELANEY, CAROL--G. FLANAGAN LTR '94--
AMRC "TEMPTATION" '56
DENBY, COLT--G. FLANAGAN LTR '94,
AUSTRALIAN--CLVLD SS
ELLIS, JOHN--G. FLANAGAN LTR '94--
AMWC "AMBUSH" '54
FTGW "FIREBRAND" '54
FTGW "RED HELLION FOR HIRE" '54
FTGW "TEXAS TORNADO" '54
DLRW "EMPTY HOLSTERS" '54
G.C.B.--G. FLANAGAN LTR '94,
AUSTRALIAN--
CURRAWONG "MEET MR. RAGGLES" '42
GORDON, CLIVE--G. FLANAGAN LTR '94,
AUSTRALIAN--
CLVLD "GLOVE HAPPY" '52
CLVLD "TOPPLING TITLE" '52
SSC "USE YOUR WHIP" '53
GROVER, MARSHALL--G. FLANAGAN LTR '94--
CORW 933 "SON OF HELLFIRE" '56

BLEECK, G.C. [CONT]
HERSCHOLT, WOLFE--[36]HP--
TRNPT "ASTEROID PERIL" '49
TRNPT "PLANET OF FIRE" '49
KENSLOW, VIC--G. FLANAGAN LTR '94,
AUSTRALIAN--CLVLD SS
KENT, LANE--[36]HP--
TRNPT-1 BOOK
LAWSON, DINK--G. FLANAGAN LTR '94,
AUSTRALIAN--CLVLD SS
LESLIE, NICOLE--G. FLANAGAN LTR '94--
AMRC "INNOCENCE OF EVE" '56
LUIGI, BELLI--[34][35][36]AUSTRALIAN--
TRNPT-ALL BUT "DEATH HAS NO WEIGHT"
MERLE, PETE--G. FLANAGAN LTR '94,
AUSTRALIAN--CLVLD SS
NELSON, JOHNNY--[35]AUSTRALIAN--
CLEVE NVLT "PAY-OFF IN LEAD" '50s
8 CLEVELAND WESTERNS
CHISHOLM 648 "TROUBLE TOWN"
CORONADA 957 "TRIGGER GUARD"
O'NEILL, C.M.--G. FLANAGAN LTR '94--
HRWTZ "CAREER GIRL JENNIFER" '60
PARKER, SHARON--G. FLANAGAN LTR '94--
AMRC "ONCE TO EVERY WOMAN" '56
WHALEN, GARY-- G. FLANAGAN LTR '94--
AGP 'WESTERN SAGA' SERIES:
"HIT THE TRAIL" '54

BLEIER, ROBERT PATRICK
BLEIER, ROCKY--[31]

BLEILER, EDWARD F.
LE VERT, LIBERTE E.--[23]SF

BLESCHKE, JOHANNA
SANZARA, RAHEL--[39]GERMAN

BLESH, RUDOLPH PICKETT
BLESH, RUDI--[31]

BLEVINS, WINFRED
BLEVINS, WIN--[26]ROM

BLEWETT, DOROTHY EMILE
PRAIZE, ANN--[1]

BLEY, WULF
HARTWIG, W.H.--[39]GERMAN

BLICK, ELSA
DANIEL, LAURENT--[1]
TRIOLET, ELSA--[1]

BLINDER, ELLIOT
ELLIOT, ASA--[31]

BLISH, JAMES B.
ATHELING, WILLIAM, JR.--[7][11][23][31]SF--
"THE ISSUE AT HAND"
EMDEN, V.K.--[2]
FROME, NILES H.--[2]
LAVERTY, DONALD--W/DAMON KNIGHT,
[2][4][11][23][31][33]SF
LYONS, MARCUS--[11][31][33]
MACDOUGAL, JOHN--W/ROBERT A.W. LOWNDES,
[11][23][31][33]--
ASF "CHAOS COORDINATED" '46
MERLYN, ARTHUR--[2][11][23]SF--
"SUNKEN UNIVERSE" '42
TORLEY, LUKE--[1][11][33]

BLISH, MRS. JAMES
LAWRENCE, J.A.--[7]SF--'STARTREK' SERIES
LAWRENCE, JUDITH ANN--[11]SF

BLISS, ALAN JOSEPH
BLISS, A.J.--[31]

BLISS, LENA EDITH
LE NOIRE, FELICIA--[1]

BLITCH, FLEMING LEE
LEE, ERIC--[1]
LEE, FLEMING--[1][32]MYS--
SA "GADGET LOVERS" JUL '67
SA "CORK TREE SYSTEM" AUG '67
SA "DEATH GAME" AUG '67
SA "DIZZY DAUGHTER" SEPT '67
SA "POWER ARTIST" OCT '67

BLIXEN-FENEKE, KAREN
BLIXEN, KAREN--[1][11]
BLIXEN, TANIA--[1]
DINESEN, TANNE--[1]
OSCEOLA--[1][22][33]
TANIA B.--[1]
TITANIA--[1]
ANDREZEL, PIERRE--[1][2][11][21][22]--
ACE "THE ANGELIC AVENGERS" '63
DINESEN, ISAK--[1][2][11][22][31]

BLOBEL-WAASEN, BRIGITTE
BLOBEL, BRIGITTE--[39]GERMAN/ADULT/MYS/JUV
BLYTON, ENID--[39]GERMAN/ADULT/MYS/JUV

BLOCH, BARBARA
EDWARDS, PHOEBE--[1][31]

BLOCH, ROBERT [A]
BOWEN, R.T.--[2]
BOWER, R.G.--[2][32]MYS--
LM "ARCHIE" DEC '62
COMBER, R.J.--[2]
FISKE, TARLETON--LESSER/HOLLAND,
STRANGE TALES, BAE 10,P12
[2][11][15][16][23][31]SF/HOR
FOLKE, WILL--[16][23][31][32]--
SH "PIN-UP GIRL" JUL '60
KE "CASE OF CLUMSY CADAVER" AUG '60
GAUER, W.H.--PPCC#3, P17--GHOSTED FOR GAUER
HAMMOND, KEITH--W/HENRY KUTTNER,[2]
HINDIN, NATHAN--W/NATHAN HINDIN,
[2][11][15][16][31]--GHOSTED
JARVIS, E.K.--PPCC#3, P17,[2][11]HP--
ZIFF-DAVIS
KANE, WILSON--PPCC#3, P17,
[2][11][16][23][32]--
WM "HUNGARIAN RHAPSODY" WINT '70
KJELGAARD, JIM--PPCC#3,P17,[2]--
GHOSTED FOR KJELGAARD
MALONE, SHERRY--PPCC#3,P17,[2][11]
SCANLON, HERBERT--[2]
SHELDON, JOHN--PPCC#3, P17,
[2][11][16][23]SF--HP
SHERIDAN, JOHN--L. ROBBINS LTR '94--PULP
YOUNG, COLLIER--PPCC#3/L. SHOUP,
BAE 18, P7,[5]--GHOSTED
DELL 8969 "THE TOD DOSSIER" '69

BLOCH, SUSANNE [E]
EMMCKE, SUSANNE--[39]GERMAN/JUV

BLOCHMAN, LAWRENCE G.
BERRY, JONAS--W/JOHN ASHBERY,[31]--
TRANSLTR DELL "MURDER IN MONTMARTE" '60
BLOCHMAN, L.G.--M. LACHMAN--PULP MYS STORIES

BLOCK, HERBERT LAWRENCE
HERBLOCK--[31]

BLOCK, LAWRENCE

ARD, WILLIAM--GHOSTED
MON 172 "BABE IN THE WOODS" '60
BLACK, LAWRENCE--MUNROE LST 24--
TFDS "DEATH BY APPOINTMENT" JUN '60
MIDWD 34-812 "BORN BAD" '67
MIDWD 34-841 "DELICATE TRAMP" '67
BLOCK, JOHN--MUNROE RVW FEB '93,[32]--
ST "THE GLORY KIDS" MAY '60-UNCONFIRMED-
SEE BAE 4/93
CHRISTOPHER, BEN--MUNROE CONVRSTN W/WESTLAKE,
BAE 21, P3,[32]--
SV "ELEPHANT BLUES" JUL '60
BEAC B487F "STRANGE EMBRACE" '62
CROFIELD, HILTON-- MUNROE LST 24,'AFTERWORD'
IN "INTRODUCING CHIP HARRISON"
FOUL PLAY 50-019, '84
CROWLEY, LIZ--HOLLAND/MUNROE REVWS FEB'93--
MON MB508 "I SELL LOVE" '60
DEXTER, JOHN--MUNROE SL #25--
MDNR 471 "SHAME DANCE"
DEXTER, JOHN--W/DONALD WESTLAKE,
MUNROE LST 24--
NTSD 1513 "NO LONGER A VIRGIN"
EMERSON, JILL--W. MULLINS-L. BLOCK CKLST,
BAE 15, P60--
ALL BOOKS HIS
EVANS, LESLEY--BAE 22,P4, MUNROE RVW FEB '93--
CREST 336 "STRANGE ARE WAYS OF LOVE" '59
GREENE, HERBERT LESLIE--V. BERCH/
MUNROE LIST 24--
'SWANK' MAG "TRAVELERS" NOV '67
MH "BUDDIES" APR '67
MH "THE PUNK" JUN '63
MH "DEATH BEGINS" SEPT '64
'SPORTSMAN' MAG "THE PIRATES" JAN '67
HARRIS, AMY--MUNROE LST 24 FEB '93--
MIDWD F203 "BIRTH OF A TRAMP" '62
MIDWD F212 "TOUCH ME GENTLY" 1962
MIDWD F265 "ALL OF ME" 1963
MIDWD 32-807 "JANITOR'S DAUGHTER" 1967
MIDWD 33-654 "PRIZE PUPIL" 1967
MIDWD 35-953 "RUNAWAY TEEN" 1968--
ALL 'AMY HARRIS' UNCONFIRMED FOR "BLOCK"
HARRISON, CHIP--W. MULLINS-L. BLOCK CK LIST
BAE 15, P60,[3]MYS--
GM 2285 "NO SCORE" '70
GM 2421 "CHIP HARRISON SCORES AGAIN" '71
GM 3029 "MAKE OUT WITH MURDER" '74
GM 3274 "TOPLESS TULIP CAPER" '75
HOLLIDAY, DON--W/HAL DRESNER,
MUNROE REVIEW FEB '93--
BDSD 1220 "CIRCLE OF SINNERS"
JOSEPHSON, LAWRENCE--MUNROE LST 24--
SOME 'JILL EMERSON' BOOKS CREDITED
TO 'JOSEPH LAWRENCE'--
LARRY'S IDEA OF FUN
KAVANAGH, JACK--MUNROE LST 24,[32]--
'WEB' STORY MAY-JUN '60
MD "KEEP IT CLEAN" DEC '58
MD "THE ENVELOPE" FEB '59
TW "KILLERS DIE HARD" SEPT '59
OF "DEATH CAN'T LOSE" NOV '59
OF "HER SHREIKS BROUGHT TERROR" JAN '60
ST "HOT DAMES SPELL TROUBLE" FEB '60
ST "YOU'LL DIE LAUGHING" MAY '60
OF "HOT FRAIL - COLD TRAIL" JUL '60
ST "AND SIN NO MORE" AUG '60
OF "THE DEAD CAN KILL" NOV '60
TFDS "MORE BODIES FOR BABY" JAN '60
TFDS "HOT DAMES ARE MURDER!" MAR '60
OF "GREEN BAIT FOR THE SHARK" JUL '59
KAVANAGH, PAUL--W. MULLINS-L. BLOCK CKLST
BAE 15, P60,[3]MYS--
WORLD "TRIUMP OF EVIL" '71
MacM "SUCH MEN ARE DANGEROUS" '69,
PUTNAM "NOT COMIN' HOME TO YOU" '74

BLOCK, LAWRENCE [CONT]

LAWRENCE, B.L.--MUNROE RVW,[32]--
GU "ONE NIGHT OF DEATH" NOV '58
TR "SWEET LITTLE RACKET" APR '59
LORD, SHELDON--W. MULLINS-L. BLOCK CK LIST
BAE 15, P60--
MIDWD 8 "CARLA" '58
MIDWD 9 "A STRANGE KIND OF LOVE" '59
MIDWD 14 "BORN TO BE BAD" '59
MIDWD 24 "69 BARROW ST." '59
MIDWD 29 "OF SHAME & JOY" '60
MIDWD 35 "KEPT" '60
MIDWD 33 "A WOMAN MUST LOVE" '60
MIDWD 40 "CANDY" '60
MIDWD 55 "21 GAY ST." '60
BEAC B387 "PADS ARE FOR PASSION" '61
BEAC B469F "HUSBAND CHASER" '62
BEAC B491F "THIRD WAY" '62
BEAC B552F "OLDER WOMAN" '62
MIDWD 34-108 "PLEASURE MACHINE"
SCL 75163 "SEX SHUFFLE"
OF "BARGAIN IN BLOOD" FEB '59
LORD, SHELDON--W/DONALD WESTLAKE
AS 'ALAN MARSHALL'--
MIDWD 41 "A GIRL CALLED HONEY" '60
MIDWD 48 "SO WILLING" '60
MORSE, DR. BENJAMIN--NOT DENIED BY BLOCK-
ALL TITLES
SHAW, ANDREW--MUNROE CONVERSATION
W/WESTLAKE, BAE 21, P2--
NTSD 1505 "CAMPUS TRAMP"
NTSD 1511 "THE ADULTERERS"
NTSD 1517 "HIGHSCOOL SEX CLUB"
NTSD 1520 "THE SIN-DAMNED"
NTSD 1526R "THE WIFE-SWAPPERS"
NTSD 1531R "SEXPOT"
NTSD 1534 "COLLEGE FOR SINNERS"
MDNR 404 "MOTEL SEX CLUB"
MDNR 402 "PASSION IN PAINT"
MDNR 408 "LUST CAMPUS" ATTRIB BY W.COONS
NTSD 1541 "TRAMP" '61
NTSD 1543 "THE TWISTED ONES"
NTSD 1546 "$20 LUST"
NTSD 1548 "GIRLS ON THE PROWL"
NTSD 1551 "LOVER"
NTSD 1553 "TRAILOR TROLLOP"
MDNR 427 "CROSSROADS OF LUST"
MDNR 431 "FLESH PARADE"
MDNR 462 "FLESH MOB"
MDNR 463 SIN SUCKER"
NTSD 1588 "SIN HELLCAT"
NTSD 1604 "BUTCH"
NTSD 1611 "PASSION ALLEY"
NTSD 1614 "LUST WEEKEND"
NTSD "THE SADIST"
NTSD 1635 "SINTIME"
MDNR 405 "LUST DAMNED" '61
MDNR 456 "HARLOT SCHOOL" '62
MDNR 477 "FLESH FOOLS" '63
WELLS, JOHN WARREN--MUNROE RVW FEB '93--
LANCER 75-029 "EROS & CAPRICORN" '65
LAN 75-041 "TABOO BREAKERS" '68
LAN 78-622 "OLDER WOMEN & YOUNGER MEN:
MRS. ROBINSON SYNDROME" '69
LAN 75-088 "SEX & THE STEWARDESS" '69
DELL 9558 "WIFE SWAP REPORT" '70
DELL 8678 "THEIR OWN THING" '72
SIGN T4155 "TRICKS OF THE TRADE" '70
DELL 8834 "3 IS NOT A CROWD" '71
DELL 0884 "BEYOND GROUP SEX" '72
LAN 447-37002 "WOMEN WHO SWING
BOTH WAYS" '71
LAN 447-78673 "MALE HUSTLER" '71
LAN 447-78719 "SEX THERAPISTS" '73
LAN 447-78442 "ANY WAY YOU WANT IT" '73
DELL 1780 "DIFFERENT STROKES" '74
DELL 5064 "LOVE AT A TENDER AGE" '74

BLOCK, LAWRENCE [CONT]
WELLS, JOHN WARREN [CONT]
DELL 8430 "SEX WITHOUT STRINGS" '74
WARNER 78-597 "TOTAL SEXUALITY" '74
LAN 78-611 "NEW SEXUAL UNDERGROUND" '68
LAN 447-78710 "DOING IT" '72
LAN 447-78698 "COME FLY WITH US" '72

BLOCK, RUDOLPH
LESSING, BRUNO--[1]

BLOCKLINGER, PEGGY O'MORE
BLOCKLINGER, BETTY--[1][31]
BOWMAN, JEANNE--[1][9][21][31]ROM--33 NOVELS
O'MORE, PEGGY--[1][9][21]ROM--22 NOVELS

BLOCKSIDGE, CHARLES W.
BAYLEBRIDGE, WILLIAM--[13]AUSTRALIAN

BLOFELD, JOHN [E.C.]
CHU FENG--[1]
CHU CH'AN--[1][31]TRANSLATIONS

BLOM, ERIC WALTER
FARR, SEBASTIAN--[1][3][22]MYS--
DENT "DEATH ON THE DOWN-BEAT" '41

BLOM, KARL ARNE
EKBLOM, PAL A.--[29]MYS--
"DU KAN INTE SJUNGA OM GRATENS FAGLAR" '77
LAGEVI, BO--[29][31]MYS, HP--
"ALLT VA DU GJORT MOT NAGON" '76
"UTAN PERSONLIGT ANSVAR" '77
"SPEL OVER TVA ZONER" '78
WERNER, THOMAS [B]--W/JANERIK LARSSON,[29]MYS-
-
"ATTENTATTET" '75
"MASSAKERN" '76

BLOMBERG, STIG
VILLNER, OLLE--[29]MYS--4 NOVELS '55-59

BLONDEL, ROGER
BRUSS, B.R.--[1][2][11]

BLOOD, MARJE
MCKENZIE, PAGE--[1][9]ROM

BLOOD, ROBERT OSCAR JR.
BLOOD, BOB--[31]

BLOOM, CHARLES
NORMAN, CHARLES--[1][32]MYS--
JCM "INTRODUCING THE COXES" OCT '61
EQMM "FINAL TOUCH" APR '62
SA "MURDERER WHO QUOTED
SHAKESPEARE" JAN '65
LM "ENCHANTRESS" JUN '65 & OTHERS

BLOOM, DANIEL HOWARD
BLOOM, DANIEL HALEVI--[1]
MOOLB, LEINAD--[1]

BLOOM, DON JACK
DONNE, JACK--[1]

BLOOM, HERMAN IRVING
BELLAMY, HARMON--[1][31]
HART, BARRY--[1][31]

BLOOM, MARK
ARCHITECHS ADVENTURE--W/RICHARD MEYER/WALTER &
LISA HUNT/EVAN JAMIESON/BILL SCAMMELL/
CHRISIVEY,[7]

BLOOM, URSULA
BURNS, SHEILA--[9][17][21][26][31]ROM
CLARE, PAULINE--[8]
ESSEX, MARY--[9][17][21][26][31]ROM--4 NOVELS
HARVEY, RACHEL--[1][9][17][31]ROM
HARVEY, URSULA--[9]ROM
MANN, DEBORAH--[1][9][17][31]ROM
PROLE, LOZANIA--W/CHARLES EADE,
[2][7][9][17][21][26]ROM/SF--10 NOVELS
SLOANE, SARA--[8][17][21]ROM--
"HEAVEN LIES AHEAD"

BLOOM, WILLIAM
W.W.--[2][7][11]

BLOOMAN, PERCY A.
PAB--ENGLISH-SOUTH AFRICAN

BLOOMBERG, MAX ARTHUR
BLOOMBERG, MARTY--[31]

BLOOMER, ARNOLD E.M.
MORE, EUSTON--[1]

BLOUET, PAUL
O'RELL, MAX--[1][22]FRENCH

BLOW, MRS R. [MARYA M.]
MANNES, MARYA--[2][11]

BLUESTEIN, DANIEL THOMAS
THOMAS, DANIEL B.--[1]

BLUESTONE, ROSE
BLUE, ROSE--[1]

BLUM, GARY
DEVON, GARY--V. BERCH LTR TO
HUBIN FEB '94,MYS--
KNOPF "LOST" '86
RANDOM "BAD DESIRE" '90

BLUM, LILLI [M]
MARTINI, LILLI--[39]GERMAN/JUV

BLUM, RICHARD H.
HARTSHORNE--[3]MYS--
HALE "MEXICAN ASSASSIN" '77
HALE "CODENAME, STARLIGHT" '78
HALE "WHISPER OF TREASON" '81

BLUMBERG, GARY
BRADLEY, MICHAEL--[1][3][31]MYS--
PAPLB "BLOOD BARGAIN" '74
PAPLB "CORSICAN CROSS" '74
PAPLB "KILL THE HACK" '74
PAPLB"SWISS SHOT" '74

BLUMBERG, RHODA L.G.
GOLDSTEIN, RHODA L.--[31]

BLUME, HORST-M.
QUIST, TORNER--[39]GERMAN
SYLVESTER, MICHAEL--[39]GERMAN

BLUMENFELD, F. YORICK
EWING, JENNY--[23]SF--
"JENNY EWING: MY DIARY" '81

BLUMENFELD-MEYER, OLGA
MEYER, OLGA--[39]GERMAN/JUV

BLUMENTHAL, GERTRUDE
BLANE, GERTRUDE--[31][33]

BLUMER, HENRY KENNETH
CORLEY, ERNEST--[22]ENGLISH
JOHNS, KENNETH--[22]ENGLISH
KENT, PHILIP--[22]ENGLISH
MARAS, KARL--[22]ENGLISH
NEWMAN, JOHN--[22]ENGLISH

BLUNCK, HANS FRIEDRICH
BLUNCK, JOHANN FRIEDRICH--[1]

BLUNDELL, HAROLD
BELLAIRS, GEORGE--[2][3][5][31]MYS--
64 NOVELS '41-80
LANDON, HILARY--[34]MYS--
GIFFORD "MURDER AT MORNING PRAYERS" '47
GIFFORD "CIRCLE ROUND A CORPSE" '48
GIFFORD "CHOOSE YOUR OWN VERDICT" '49
GIFFORD "EXIT SIR TOBY BELCH" '50

BLUNDELL, JUDITH
GARVEY, KATHLEEN--[21]ROM--
"VIDEO FEVER"
O'NEILL, JUDE--[9][21][26]ROM--
4 NOVELS

BLUNDELL, MRS. FRANCES
FRANCIS, M.E.--[34]MYS--
GRIFFITH "WHITHER?" 1892
LONGMANS "LYNCHGATE HALL" '04
LONGMANS "STORY OF MARY DUNNE" '13

BLUNDELL, V.R.
NIXON, KATHLEEN--[9]ROM

BLY, BEVANS
HOWES, ROYCE B.--W/GEORGE H. BLEAKERSTOWE,
L. ROBBINS LTR MAR '94

BLY, CAROLYN
BLY, CAROL--[31]
CAMPBELL, JOANNA--[1][31]
REYNOLDS, ANNE--[1]

BLYTH, HAL
CHARLES, HAL--W/CHARLES SWEET, M. LACHMAN-
AUTHORS CONFIRMED,[32]--
EQMM "SUDDEN DEATH" APR '80
SK "BURIED IN PAPER" MAY '80
SK "PETER'S PRINCIPLES" JUN '80
EQMM "TALK-SHOW MURDER" JUL '80
MSMM "TURNING POINT" JUL '80
EQMM "HUMAN INTEREST ANGLE" DEC '80
HALLIDAY, BRETT--W/CHARLES SWEET, T. JOHNSON-
ECHOES #23, P16, HP--
MSMM "TERROR RESORT" NOV '82
MSMM "BLACK DEATH" DEC '82
MSMM "RETURN OF BEACH BUTCHER" JAN '83
MSMM "A DIRTY BUSINESS" FEB '83
MSMM "SEARCH & DESTROY" MAR '83
MSMM "SHADOW OF DEATH" APR '83
MSMM "HUNTING OF M. SHAYNE" MAY '83
MSMM "DEADLY MEMORIES" JUL '83
MSMM "GRAVEN IMAGE" AUG '83
MSMM "HELLHOLE" SEP '83
MSMM"DEATH STALKS THE CAMPUS" OCT '83
MSMM "DEATH ON SKULL MT" NOV '83
MSMM "DEAD RINGER" JAN '84
MSMM "SANDCASTLES" FEB '84
MSMM "ALL IN A DAY'S WORK" MAR '84
MSMM "DAY OF REVENGE" APR '84
MSMM "YESTERDAY'S HERO" AMY '84
MSMM "DEVIL DUST & MURDER" JUN '84
MSMM "SHARKS" JUL '84
MSMM "SHADOWS OF THE PAST" AUG '84
MSMM "KEY OF DEATH" SEP '84
MSMM "KILLING TIME" OCT '84
MSMM "DEATH TAKES A PILGRIMAGE" NOV '84

BLYTH, HAL [CONT]
HALLIDAY, BRETT [CONT]
MSMM "DEATH TOPS CHARTS" JAN' 85
MSMM "QUICK & THE DEAD" FEB '85
MSMM "DEADLY VISIONS" MAR '85
MSMM "THY WILL BE DONE" MAY '85
MSMM "A DARK NIGHT WITH A
BLIND LADY" APR '85
MSMM "STING OF DEATH" JUN '85
MSMM "A NIGHT IN HELL" JUL '85
MSMM "WILDE WEEKEND" AUG '85]

BLYTH, HARRY
MEREDITH, HAL--[5]MYS

BLYTON, ENID
POLLOCK, MARY--[8][25][33]ENGLISH--
CHILDREN'S BOOKS

BOAKE, BARCROFT
SURCINGLE--[13]AUSTRALIAN

BOARD, PRUDENCE FOSTER T.
FOSTER, P.T.--CRPG [7]SF--
LEIS 2724 "THE VOW" '89
FOSTER, PRUDENCE--[7]SF--
POCK "BLOOD LEGACY" '89

BOARDMAN, JOHN
BLAKE, ERIC--[1][2]

BOARDMAN, THOMAS VOLNEY
BOARDMAN, TOM--[23]SF
XERXES, B.T.H.--[2]SHARED PSEUD.

BOAS, GUY HERMAN SIDNEY
G.B.--[31]

BOATFIELD, JEFFREY
JEFFRIES, JEFF--[8]

BOBADILLA, EMILIO
CANDIL, FRAY--[1][20]SPANISH

BOBADILLO Y LUNAR, EMILIO
MARMORA, DAGOBERTO--[1]

BOBILLIER, MARIE
BRENET, MICHEL--[22]FRENCH

BOBIN, DONALD E.M.
HALLIDAY, SHIRLEY--[1]
LAWSON, WARREN J.--[1]

BOBIN, JOHN WILLIAM
ANDREWS, JOHN--[34]MYS--
AMALG "MYS OF THE DOPE DEN" '39
RPRT OF "HIDDEN MENACE"
ASCOTT, ADELIE--[1][8]
ASCOTT, JOHN--[29][34]MYS--
AMALG "THE GREAT SHIPYARD MYSTERY" '31
GREENHALGH, KATHERINE--[8]
IRONSIDE, MATTHEW--[1]
NELSON, GERTRUDE--[8]
NELSON, STEVE--[1]
NELSON, VICTOR--[1]
OSBORNE, MARK--[3][29]MYS--10 NOVELS '31-40

BOBORNIKOFF, EMMANUEL
BOVE, EMMANUEL--[1]

BOBRI, VLADIMIR V.
BOBRITSKY, VLADIMIR--[31][33]
BOBRI--[33]

BOCH-SCHLIMME, EDITH
CARELL, EDITH--[39]GERMAN/MYS

BOCHENSKI, JOSEPH M.
BOCHENSKI, INNOCENTIUS M.--[31]
MICHE, JOSEF--[22]POLISH

BOCHSKANDL, MARCELLA
D'ARLE, MARCELLA--[39]GERMAN/JUV

BOCK, HAROLD I.
BOCK, HAL--[31][33]

BOCKEL, JOSEF HEINRICH
BARDA, J.H.--[39]GERMAN/SF

BOCKER, HANS WERNER
ARELLANO, PETER--[39]GERMAN/JUV

BOCKL, MANFRED
DE LAFORET, JEAN--[39]GERMAN/MYS/SF/WEST
ELLIOT, BRIAN--[39]GERMAN/SF/MYS/WEST, HP
KINSALE, FRED--[39]GERMAN/MYS/SF/WEST
NOLAN, FREDERICK--[39]GERMAN/WEST, HP
SLADE, JACK--[39]GERMAN/WEST, HP
VANDA, JOHN P.--[39]GERMAN/MYS/SF/WEST

BODART-TALBOT, JONI
BODART, JONI--[31]

BODE, WALTER
ANDERS, PAUL--[39]GERMAN

BODENHAM, HILDA ESTER
BODEN, HILDA--[8][22][31][33]ENGLISH
WELCH, PAULINE--[22][33]ENGLISH

BODENSCHATZ, HERBERT
FLOORMANN, BERT--[39]GERMAN/MYS

BODENSTEDT, HANS
BRENNECKE, HANS--[39]GERMAN
SIX, JUPP--[39]GERMAN

BODETT, THOMAS EDWARD
BODETT, TOM--[31]

BODINE, SHERRILL
LESLIE, LYNN--W/ELAINE SIMA,
[9][10][21][26][34]MYS/ROM--
HARL "STREET OF DREAMS" '90 & 3 MORE
LYNN, LESLIE--W/ELAINE SIMA,
[9][21][26][34]MYS/ROM--
LYNX "BURIED SHADOWS" '88 & 3 MORE

BODINGTON, NANCY H.
SMITH, SHELLEY--[3][11][18][22][29]MYS--
18 NOVELS '45-71

BODINGTON, STEPHEN
EATON, JOHN--[31]

BODINO, RICHARD
HILARY, RICHARD--W/HILARY CONNORS,
LACHMAN-EASTER LST,[34]MYS--
BB "SNAKE IN THE GRASSES" '87
BB "PIECES OF CREAM" '88
BB "PILLOW OF THE COMMUNITY" '88
BB "BEHIND THE FACT" '89

BODKIN, M. MACDONNELL
CROM A BOO--[1][22]MYS

BODLEY, HARLEY RYAN JR.
BODLEY, HAL--[31]

BOECKLE, FRANZ
BOCKLE, FRANZ--[31]

BOECKMAN, PATRICIA
BOECKMAN, PATTI--[26]ROM
KENNELLY, PATRICIA--[26]MAIDEN NAME

BOECKMAN, PATTI & CHARLES
BECKMAN, PATTI--[9][21][26][31]ROM--48 NOVELS

BOEGEHOLD, BETTY [DOYLE]
DOYLE, DONOVAN--[31][33]

BOEHM, DAVID ALFRED
MASTERS, ROBERT V.--[8]

BOEHNHARDT, PATRICIA
HART, ELLEN--LACHMAN/EASTER LST MAY '93,[34]MYS--
SEAL "HALLOWED MURDER" '89
"THIS LITTLE PIGGY WENT TO MURDER" '94

BOELL, HEINRICH THEODOR
BOLL, HEINRICH [THEODOR]--[31]

BOESCHE, TILLY
JEAN, EVE--[39]GERMAN/JUV
KORFF, ILKA--[39]GERMAN
TROJAN, EVE--[39]GERMAN

BOESE, DAWN C.
CARROLL, DAWN--[9][21][26]ROM--
"CODENAME:CASSONOVA"
"NAUGHTY THOUGHTS"
"BEGUILED"

BOESEN, VICTOR
HALL, JESSE--[31][33]
HARALD, ERIC--[31][33]

BOESS, JULIE
KNIESE, JULIE--[39]GERMAN

BOETTICHER, HANS
RINGELNATZ, JOACHIM--[39]GERMAN

BOEX-BOREL, JOSEPH
ROSNY, J.H. [AINE]--W/JUSTIN BOEX-
BOREL,[2][23]SF

BOEX-BOREL, JUSTIN
ROSNY, J.H. [JU]--W/JOSEPH BOEX-BOREL,
[2][23]SF

BOFILL I. MATES, JAUME
DE LIOST, GUERAU--[20]SPANISH

BOGART, ELEANOR ANNE
BOGART, E.A.--[31]

BOGART, WILLIAM G.
BROOKER, WALLACE--LACHMAN-COOKE LST,[37]MYS--
DOCS "QUEST OF DEATH"
GOULD, STEPHEN--L. ROBBINS LTR MAR '94--PULP
HALE, RUSSELL--LACHMAN LIST
HARLEY, BRUCE--W. MURRAY, ECHOES #26, HP
LANE, GRANT--[37]MYS--SHDM - SHORT STORIES
CONTINUED FISHER'S 'DOOME' &
'GARRETT' STORIES
MOFFATT, GEO. ALLAN--W. MURRAY,ECHOES #26, HP
ROBESON, KENNETH--W/LESTER DENT,[7][34]HP--
BB "THE ANGRY GHOST" '77
BB "FIRE & ICE"
BB "TUNNEL TERROR"
BB "WORLD'S FAIR GOBLIN"
BB "HEX"
BB "THE SPOTTED MEN"

BOGART, WILLIAM G. [CONT]
ROBESON, KENNETH--W/LESTER DENT & HAROLD K. DAVIS--"5 IN 1 VOL-#173-177"

BOGDANOVICH, PETER
THOMAS, DEREK--[2]

BOGEN, ALEXANDER
SCHOLTIS, AUGUST--[39]GERMAN

BOGEN, KAREN BARKER
BOGEN, K.R.--HAWK/BOGEN INTRVW NOV '93--TSR "GO QUEST YOUNG MEN" '94

BOGERSHAUSEN, KARL-HEINZ
KEMPE, KARL--[39]GERMAN
VANDREY, BORIS--[39]GERMAN

BOGGIS, DAVID
VAUGHAN, GARY--[8]

BOGGS, HELEN
GWYNNE, NELL--[8]

BOGGS, WILLIAM III
BOGGS, BILL--[31]

BOGGS, WINIFRED
BURKE, EDMUND [H]--[8][32]MYS--
LM "THE OPEN WINDOW" DEC '56
LM "THE BABE" MAR '57

BOGHANDEL, FLOR'S
CONNOR, PAT--[37]MYS--
"MESTERDETEKTIVEN: PAT CONNOR" ca '15

BOGORAZ, LLADIMIR GERM.
TAN--[22]RUSSIAN

BOGRAD, LARRY
BARROL, GRADY--[31][33]

BOGSRUD, TORVALD
BRATT, FINN--[37]NORWEGIAN,MYS--
'LYS OG SKYGGE' - 4 NOVELS '25

BOHANNAN, LAURA M. SMITH
BOWEN, ELENORE SITH--[8]

BOHLEN & HALBACH, BERNDT
ANDERS, HARRY--[39]GERMAN
HILLIG, WERNER--[39]GERMAN
LUERSSEN, MARGARETHE--[39]GERMAN

BOHLIEN, GUENTHER
RUBUNIN, LIONEL--[39]GERMAN

BOHLMAN, EDNA MCCAULL
MCCAULL, M.E.--[22]AMERICAN

BOHLMANN, ANNELIESE
JESSEN, ALF--[39]GERMAN

BOHM, ALBERT
SCHWENK, KARL EMIL--[39]GERMAN

BOHM-RAFFAY, HELMUT
BRANDTNER, HEINZ--[39]GERMAN

BOHMAN, BIRGITTA
BRENDON, KAY--[29]MYS

BOHMER, GABRIELE RENATE
BACHEM, BELE--[39]GERMAN

BOHNE, JOSEFINE
RICHTER, JOSEFINE--[39]GERMAN/JUV
TANNWEBER, MILLA--[39]GERMAN

BOHNING, WOLF RUEDIGER
BOEHNING, W.R.--[31]

BOIES, JANICE
BLAIR, ALISON--[21]ROM--
"NO CONTEST"
BOIES, JAN--[21]ROM--8 NOVELS
LOWELL, ANNE HUNTER--[21]ROM--
12 NOVELS

BOILEAU, PIERRE
LUPIN, ARSENE--W/THOMAS NARCEJAC,[40]MYS--
"LE SECRET D'EUNERVILLE" '73
"LA POUDRIERE" '74

BOILES, CHARLES LAFAYETTE
LAFAYETTE, CARLOS--[31]

BOISSARD, JANINE
ORIANO, JANINE--[40]MYS--
"B COMME BAPTISTE" '71
"MISS" '71
"OK, LEON" '72

BOJERUD, STELLAN
WINTER, HARRY--[29]MYS--
TIMBRO "OPERATION GARBO" '88
TIMBRO "GARBO II" '89

BOKUM, FANNY BUTCHER
BUTCHER, FANNY--[31]

BOLAND, BERTRAM J[OHN]
BLAKE, JUSTIN--[2]
TREVOR, JAMES--[3]MYS--
AWARD "THE SAVAGE GAME" '67
AWARD "THE SAVAGE HEIGHT" '69

BOLAY, KARL-HEINZ
DA BYOLA, UGO--[39]GERMAN
SVENSSON, SVEN--[39]GERMAN

BOLBJERG, ALFRED
PEMBERTON, RONALD--[29]MYS--
19 NOVELS '42-55

BOLDING, PER OLOF
PERSON, NIKLAS--[29]MYS--
"DRAGARBRUNNSGATAN" '58

BOLEN & HALBACH, HERTHY
ANDERS, HARRIET--[39]GERMAN

BOLEN, R. KEATING
BROOKE, JUSTIN--[34]MYS--
9 MODERN NOVELS '30s
TRAYNOR, J. RICHARD--V. BERCH LTR TO HUBIN FEB '94, MYS--
MELLIFONT "DEATH ON THE VIADUCT" '36

BOLES, HAROLD WILSON
BOLES, HAL--[8]

BOLGER, PHILIP CUNNINGHAM
CORPORAL TIM--[31]

BOLINDER, JEAN
BORGHAM, JESPER--[29]MYS--
"MANNEN MED KLUMPFOTEN" '74
LAGEVI, BO--[29]MYS, HP--
"MEDALJENS BAKSIDA" '77
"EN KRITIKERS DOD" '78

BOLINDER, JEAN [CONT]
SCHALIN, ELISABETH--[29]MYS--
"PICASSOFISKEN" '77
"STENSKEPPET" '77

BOLL, THEOPHILUS ERNEST M
BOLL, THEO--[31]

BOLLING-MORITZ, CORDULA
MORITZ, CORDULA--[39]GERMAN

BOLMER, [HENRY] KENNETH
SCOTT, CHESMAN--VULTURES OF THE VOID--
BRITISH SF MAG SHORT STORY

BOLOGNESE, DONALD ALAN
BOLOGNESE, DON--[31]

BOLSTAD, OIVIND
EDEN, MARTIN--[22]NORWEGIAN
EIKAN, THEO--[22]NORWEGIAN

BOLTON, MAISIE SHARMAN
DAVIS, STRATFORD--[3][22][31]ENGLISH,MYS--
5 NOVELS '52-63
SHARMAN, MIRIAM--[3][22]ENGLISH,MYS--
4 NOVELS '65-71

BOLUS, JAMES MICHAEL
BOLUS, JIM--[31]

BOMACK, ALAN
HILD, JACK--W/ROBIN HARDY &
JACK CANON,[34]MYS, HP--
GE 'SOB's' SERIES
"BARRABUS RUN" '83
PENDLETON, DON--[3]MYS, HP--
GE "AMBUSH ON BLOOD RIVER" '83
GE "HAMMERHEAD REEF" '86
GE "HELLFIRE CRUSADE" '86
GE "THE INVISIBLE ASSASSINS" '83
GE "TERMINAL VELOCITY" '84

BOMAN, ROBERT
ALMAN, BOB--W/LARS LAMBERT,[29]MYS--
"DEN FARLIGA KUNSKAPEN" '65
"MORDSSOMMARFESTEN" '66

BOMKE, BERNHARD
ALLISON, JIM--[39]GERMAN/WEST
DEL BERNIS, RIGOS--[39]GERMAN
FABER, IMTRAUT--[39]GERMAN
KEENE, KING--[39]GERMAN/WEST
LASH, LARRY--[39]GERMAN/WEST
RANGER, L.S.--[39]GERMAN/WEST
STUART, TONNY--[39]GERMAN/WEST
YELLING, DAN--[39]GERMAN/WEST

BONANNO, MARGARET WANDER
NORTH, RICK--[7]SF, HP--
ZEBRA "ASTRONAUTS #4 & #6"

BOND, EDWARD JARVIS
BOND, E.J.--[31]
BOND, TED--[31]

BOND, F.
BLAKESLEY, STEPHEN--[3][22][29]MYS--
BH "TERRELL IN TROUBLE" '46
FD "A CASE FOR THE CARDINAL" '46
FD "PROCTOR CASE" '46
FD "CASE OF THE ALPHA MURDERS" '47
AMALG "RIDDLE OF BLAZING BUNGALOW" '51
AMALG "MAN WITH A NUMBER" '52
AMALG "TRAIL OF THE RAIDER NO. I" '52

BOND, FLORENCE DEMAREST F
DEMAREST, ANNE--[22][34]MYS--
HILLMAN "MURDER ON EVERY FLOOR" '39
GRAMMERCY "SHE WAS HIS SECRETARY" '39

BOND, GLADYS BAKER
MENDEL, JO--[1][22][33]AMERICAN, HP--
ALBERT WHITMAN & CO.
WALKER, HOLLY BETH--[8]

BOND, GRACE
TODHUNTER, PHILIPPA--[8]

BOND, LEE
COLE, JACKSON--L. ROBBINS LTR '94--PULPS
ENDICOTT, CLEVE--L. ROBBINS LTR '94--PULP

BOND, NELSON S.
DANZELL, GEORGE--[2][11][23]SF
MAVITY, HUBERT--[2][11][23]SF

BONDY, FRITZ
SCARPI, N.O.--[39]GERMAN

BONDY, JOSEF
BOR, JOSEF--[1]

BONES, JAMES C. JR.
BONES, JIM JR.--[31]

BONEWITS, PHILIP E. I.
BONEWITS, ISAAC--[31]

BONGARTZ, HEINZ
THORWALD, JURGEN--[39]GERMAN,MYS

BONHAM, BARBARA THOMAS
NORTH, SARA--[3][9][21]MYS, HP--
PLAYBOY "JASMIN FOR MY GRAVE" '78

BONHAM, CECIL FRANCIS
BONHAM, FRANK--PPCC#9, P95,MYS & MYS
REPP, ED EARL--LACHMAN LST,PPCC#9,P95,
[31]WEST--GHOSTED LATE '30s

BONIFACE, JOSEPH XAVIER
SAINTINE, XAVIER--[22]FRENCH

BONIME, FLORENCE
CUMMINGS, FLORENCE--[31]

BONITZ, CLEMENTINE
MINDE-BONITZ, GRETE--[39]GERMAN

BONN, PATRICIA CAROLYN
BONN, PAT--[33]

BONNELL, KENNETH
LEONE, SCOTT--[2]

BONNER, GERALDINE
HARD PAN--[22]MYSTERY

BONNETT, JEANNE
DELAMARTER, JEANNE--[31]

BONSALL, CROSBY B. NEWELL
NEWELL, CROSBY--[8]

BOOKCHIN, MURRAY
HERBER, LEWIS--[31]

BOON, AUGUST
BRETON-SMITH, CLARE--[9]ROM
CALDWELL, ELINOR--[9]ROM
VERNON, CLAIRE--[9]ROM

BOON, AUGUST [CONT]
WILDE, HILARY--[9]ROM

BOON, LOUIS-PAUL
BOONTJE--[31]

BOON, VIOLET MARY
WILLIAMS, VIOLET M.--[8]

BOONE, CHARLES EUGENE
BOONE, PAT--[8][22][31]AMERICAN

BOONE, DEBORAH ANN
BOONE, DEBBY--[31]

BOORSTIN, DANIEL JOSEPH
PROFESSOR X--[8]

BOORSTIN, RUTH C. FRANKEL
BOORSTIN, RUTH F.--[31]

BOOTE, ROBERT EDWARD
ARVILL, ROBERT--[31]

BOOTH, EDWIN
BLUNT, DON--[22][28][31][34]AMERICAN,MYS--
AVALON "SHORT CUT" '62
AVALON "DEAD GIVEAWAY" '63
ARCADIA "BROKEN WINDOW" '60
ARCADIA "DEATH ON A SUMMER DAY" '60
ARCADIA "CROOKED SPUR" '60
BOOTH, REGINA--L. ROBBINS LTR '94--PULP
HAZARD, JACK--[1][22][28][31]AMERICAN
SULLIVAN, REX--L. ROBBINS LTR '94--PULP

BOOTH, GEOFFREY THORNTON
BOOTH, TED--[31]

BOOTH, HENRY SPENCER
CRAIG, COLIN--[2]

BOOTH, MAUD CHARLESWORTH
CHARLESWORTH, M.E.--[3]MYS--
PUTNAM "THE RELENTLESS CURRENT" '12

BOOTH, PHILIP ARTHUR
WERNER, PETER--[8]

BOOTH, ROSEMARY FRANCES
MURRAY, FRANCES--[3][8][21][26]ROM/MYS--
5 NOVELS

BOOTON, CATHERINE KAGE
BOOTON, KAGE--[21]ROM--
"PLACE OF SHADOWS"
"THE TOY"
"THE TROUBLED HOUSE"

BORBOLLA, BARBARA MARTYN
MARTYN, DON--[1][3]MYS--
7 NOVELS '66-71

BORCHARD, RUTH
IQUA--[22]GERMAN-ENGLISH
MEDLEY, ANNE--[8][22]GERMAN-ENGLISH

BORCHARDT, GEORG HERMANN
HERMANN, GEORG--[39]GERMAN

BORCHERS, KARL
BORGERS, CHARLES--[39]GERMAN

BORDEN, DEAL
BORDEN, LEO--[8]

BORDEN, LINDA
BORDEN, LIZZIE--[31]

BORDEN, MARY
MACLAGAN, BRIDGET--[22][31]AMERICAN-ENGLISH

BORDES, FRANCOIS
CARSAC, FRANCIS--[2][11][31]

BOREMAN, LINDA
LOVELACE, LINDA--[8]

BORG, BJOERN RUNE
BORG, BJORN--[31]

BORG, PHILIP ANTHONY JOHN
BEXAR, PHIL--[8][28]WEST--
15 JENKINS NOVELS '57-69
BORG, JACK--[8][28]WEST--
32 JENKINS NOVELS '54-75
PICKARD, JOHN Q.--[8][28]WEST--
14 WARD LOCK NOVELS '62-8

BORGES, JORGE LUIS
BUSTOS DOMECQ, H.--W/ADOLFO BIOY-CASAERES,[1]
BUSTOS DOMECQ, H[ONRIO]--[31]
BUSTOS, F[RANCISCO]--[1][31]
DAVIS, B. LYNCH--W/ADOLFO BIOY CASARES,[31]
DOMECQ, H. BUSTOS--W/ADOLFO BIOY CASARES,[31]
LYNCH, DAVIS--W/ADOLFO BIOY-CASAERES,[1]
SUAREZ LYNCH, B.--W/ADOLFO BIOY-CASAERES,[1]

BORGMAN, JAMES MARK
BOSMAN, JIM--[31]

BORGMANN, DMITRI A.
HOUDINI, MERLIN X.--[31]
UQSOR, EL--[22][31]GERMAN-AMERICAN

BORLAND, HAROLD GLEN
BORLAND, HAL--[8][22][28][31][33]
AMERICAN/WEST--3 NOVELS '57-63
WEST, WARD--[8][22][28][33]WEST--
"TROUBLE VALLEY" '34
"HALFWAY TO TIMBERLINE" '35
"RUSTLERS TRAIL" '48

BORLAND, KATHRYN KILBY
ABBOTT, ALICE--W/HELEN R. SPEICHER,
[3][9][21][26]MYS/ROM--
ACE "THE THIRD TOWER" '74
ACE "GOODBYE JULIE SCOTT" '75
LAND, JANE & ROSS--W/HELEN R. SPEICHER,
[31][33]--
SEALE "MILES & THE BIG BLACK HAT" '63
LAND, JANE--W/HELEN R. SPEICHER,[3]MYS--
BAL "TO WALK THE NIGHT" '76
DBLDY "IRENA" '79
DBLDY "THESE TIGERS' HEARTS" '79

BORLAND, WILLIAM ARMSTNG.
DIXON, BINGHAM--[22]MYSTERY

BORLASE, JAMES SKIPP
BRADLEY, J.J.G.--[36]AUSTRALIAN--BOY'S BOOKS

BORNEMAN, ERNEST [W.J.]
MCCABE, CAMERON--[3]GERMAN/MYS--
GOLZ "FACE ON THE CUTTING ROOM FLOOR" '37

BORNEMANN, EVA
GEISEL, EVA--[8]

BORNGRABER, GERTRUD
VON ROBERTUS, GERDA--[39]GERMAN

BORNSTROEM-RUNDE, UWE
BERGEN, GINA--[39]GERMAN
CHRISTIANI, SVEN DETLEV--[39]GERMAN
MORTIMER, CARROL--[39]GERMAN
SYLVESTER, HELGE--[39]GERMAN
THOMAS, ANDREA--[39]GERMAN

BORRMANN, MARTIN
BORN, MATTHIAS--[39]GERMAN

BORSON, RUTH ELIZABETH
BORSON, ROO--[31]

BORTIN, GEORGE & VIRGINIA
BORTIN, V.G.--[1][31]

BORTON, JOHN C. JR.
BORTON, TERRY--[31]

BOSANQUET, NICHOLAS F.G.
BOSANQUET, NICK--[31]

BOSANQUET, REGINALD
BOSANQUET, REGGIE--[31]

BOSCH, HENRY GERARD
HENBOS--[31]

BOSETKY, HORST
BOSET, HORST--[29]MYS
-KY--[39][40]GERMAN/MYS--
"AUS DER TRAUM" '83
-KY & CO.--[39][40]GERMAN/MYS--
"DIE KLEITTE" '83
DRAKE, JOHN--[39]GERMAN/MYS

BOSKAMP, PAUL
KAMP, FRIEDRICH--[39]GERMAN
MANSOR, A.L.--[39]GERMAN

BOSLER, COLLEEN Q.
QUINN, COLLEEN--[9][21][26]ROM--
10 NOVELS

BOSNA, VALERIE
KING, VALERIE--[9][21][26]ROM--13 NOVELS
MONTROSE, SARAH--[9][21][26]ROM--
"THE GOLDEN HEIRESS"

BOSQUET, ALAIN
BISQUE, ANATOLE--[22]RUSSIAN-AMERICAN

BOSTICCO, [ISABELL] MARY
BEY, ISABELLE--[8][31]

BOSTOCK-SMITH, COLIN
REED, SIMON--W/MARY H. DANBY,[8][31]--
"METAL MICKEY'S BOOGIE BOOK" '81

BOSTON, NOEL
BARTRAM, NOEL--[2]
BERTRAM, NOEL--[2][11]

BOSTWICK, ANGELA
WELLS, ANGELA--[9][21][26]ROM--14 NOVELS

BOSWELL, BARBARA
OSBORNE, BETSY--[9][21][26]ROM--4 NOVELS

BOSWORTH, ALLAN R.
ANDERSON, NELSE--L. ROBBINS LTR '94--PULP
BOYD, ALAMO--[8][28][31]WEST--
ARCADIA "STEEL TO THE SUNSET" '41
DEERE, PHILIP F.--L. ROBBINS LTR '94--PULP
ENDICOTT, CLEVE--L. ROBBINS LTR '94--PULP
LITCHFIELD, FRANK JOHNSON--L. ROBBINS LTR '94

BOSWORTH, ALLAN R. [CONT]
McKINLEY, DEAN--L. ROBBINS LTR '94--PULP
SQUIRES, PHIL--L. ROBBINS LTR '94--PULP

BOSWORTH, WILLAN GEORGE
BORTH, WILLAN G.--[3][22]MYS--
SELWYN "THE MONK'S BRIDGE MYSTERY" '29
LEONID--[22]MYS
WORTH, MAURICE--W/MAURICE H.B. MASH,
[1][3]MYS--
HUTCH "GOLDEN PHEASANT" '27 & 2 OTHERS

BOTHE-PELZER, HEINZ
MORRISON, HENRI--[39]GERMAN

BOTNER, PHIL
READE, JOHN--VENUS VOL., VV104

BOTSCH, CHARLOTTE
SCHALLES, LOTTE--[39]GERMAN

BOTT, HENRY
RECOUR, CHARLES--[2][11]

BOTTCHER, KARL
HILBERSDORF, KARL--[39]GERMAN

BOTTICHER, CLARISSA [L]
LOHDE, CLARISSA--[39]GERMAN

BOTTO, JAN
KRASKO, IVAN--[22]SLOVAK

BOUCOLON, MARYSE
CONDE, MARYSE--[31]

BOUDAT, MARIE-LOUISE
BELLOCQ, LOUISE--[22][31]FRENCH

BOULARAN, JACQUES
DEVAL, JACQUES--[22][31]FRENCH

BOULET, ADA
JOHN, ADA--[9][21][26]ROM--
"BY LOVE BETRAYED"

BOULGER, MRS. DOROTHY H.H
GIFT, THEO--[34]MYS--
HURST "VICTIMS" 1887

BOULTING, SYDNEY
BOULTING--[31]
COTES, PETER--[31]
NORTHCOTE--[31]

BOULTON, A. HARDING
HARDING, RICHARD--[8]

BOUMA, JOHANNES L.
CONWAY, TROY--V. BERCH, SPY SPOOF, BAE 9--
SHANNON, STEVE--[1][8][28]WEST--
CREST 189 "THE HELL-FIRE KID" 57
HAWK, ALEX--L. ROBBINS LTR '94,WEST, HP--

BOUMELHA, PENELOPE ANN
BOUMELHA, PENNY--[31]

BOUNDS, SYDNEY J.
BAKER, MARTIN L.--[2][11]
BAXTER, J.K.--P. HARBOTTLE, PP 40, P12--
BADGER CRIME #8 "BIG FRAME"
CARNE, ROGER--[2][11]
CLARKSON, W.E.--[2][11]
DIAMOND, BRETT--[34]MYS, HP--
SPNCR "A COFFIN FOR CLARA" '50

BOUNDS, SYDNEY J. [CONT]
ELLISON, EARL--[34]HP--
SPNCR "BLONDES AREN'T SO DUMB" '50
SPNCR "MINK MAKES A GOOD SHROUD" '50]
HAMMOND, PAUL--[2][11]
MADISON, RICK--[34]MYS, HP--
SPNCR "TERROR RIDES THE WEST WIND" '51
MARLOWE, REX--[34]MYS, HP--
SPNCR "HELL HATH NO FURY" '51
SPNCR "ONE WAY TICKET" '51
SPNCR "IDENTITY UNKNOWN" '52
MARSHALL, JAMES--[2][16]
REID, DESMOND--[23][34]MYS, HP--
SBL "GIRL WHO SAW TOO MUCH" '63
ROSS, JAMES--[2][11]
SAUNDERS, WES--[2][11][16]
SAXON, PETER--W/W.A. HOWARD BAKER,[34]HP--
SBL "WHITE MERCENARY" '62
SMITH, LARRY--[2][11][32]MYS--
AHMM "A VERY OBSCURE MURDER" MAY '70
SMITH, LAWRENCE--[2][11]
SYDNEY, GEORGE--[34]MYS--
SBL "COUNTDOWN FOR MURDER" '62
WALLACE, CLIFFORD--[2][11]

BOURGEOIS, CAMILLE
CAROL, ROBERT--[3]MYS--
PAPLB "ANCESTOR" '69
PAPLB "GWYNETH" '69
AWARD "THE GYPSY'S CURSE" '71
CAROL, ROBIN [ROBERT]--[21][26]ROM--
"THE ANCESTOR"
"GYPSY'S CURSE"

BOURILLON, PIERRE
HAMP, PIERRE--[22]FRENCH

BOURNE, CAROLINE
LEIGH, ELIZABETH--W/DEBBIE HANCOCK,
[21][26]ROM--
"CREOLE CARESS" & 4 OTHER NOVELS

BOURNE, RANDOLPH S.
AURELIUS--[31]
BLOOMBERG, AURELIUS--[31]
COE, MAX--[31]
JUVENIS--[31]

BOURNS, MARSHA
ALEXANDER, MARSHA--[3]MYS--
4 MAJOR NOVELS '76-79

BOURQUIN, PAUL H.J.
AMBERLEY, RICHARD--[34]MYS--
HALE "INCITEMENT TO MURDER" '68
HALE "DEAD ON THE STONE" '69
HALE "AN ORDINARY ACCIDENT" '71

BOUTELLEAU, JACQUES
CHARDONNE, JACQUES--[22]FRENCH

BOUTERWECK, OLAF
EMSCHER, HORST--[39]GERMAN/MYS/SF

BOUTLAND, DAVID
ROME, DAVID--[2][11][23][35]AUSTRALIAN--
NW "TIME OF ARRIVAL" APR '61
HRWTZ PB254 "13 TIMES DEATH" '66
HRWTZ PB299 "SANDRA" '67
HRWTZ PB308 "RUBY" '67
HRWTZ PB322 "CHRISTINE" '67
HRWTZ PB349 "WIFE SWAP" '67
HRWTZ PB359 "CLEAVER" '68
HRWTZ PB377 "CANNIBALS" '68
HRWTZ PB403 "CIRCLE" '69
HRWTZ PB431 "SQUAT" '70

BOUTLAND, DAVID [CONT]
ROME, DAVID [CONT]
HRWTZ A089 "NAKED BUG" '73
HRWTZ SP026 "SEX SCENE" '76

BOWDEN, JEAN
ANNANDALE, BARBARA--[9][21][26][31]--
3 ROM NOVELS
BARRY, JOCELYN--[1][9][31]ROM
BLAND, JENNIFER--[1][3][31]MYS--
BARKER "ACCOMPLICE" '74
BARKER "DEATH IN WAITING" '75
CURRY, AVON--[9][22][31][34]MYS--
ALLEN "DERRY DOWN DEATH" '60
ALLEN "DYING HIGH" '61
LONG "A PLACE FOR EXECUTION" '69
ACE "FETISH MURDERS" '73
MILTON "HUNT FOR DANGER" '74
MILTON "SHACK-UP"
DELL, BELINDA--[9][21][22][26][31]--
9 ROM NOVELS

BOWDEN, JOAN CHASE
BACON, JOAN CHASE--[1][31][33]
GODFREY, JANE--[1][31][33]
GRAHAM, CHARLOTTE--[1][31]
KENNY, KATHRYN--[1][31]HP

BOWDEN, SUSAN
BARRON, ELIZABETH--[26]ROM--4 NOVELS

BOWEN, ALICE
BOWEN, ALYCE--[9][21][26]--3 ROM NOVELS

BOWEN, JOHN [GRIFFIN]
BLAKE, JUSTIN--W/JEREMY BULLMORE,[8][31]

BOWEN, JOSEPH
CONCANNON, WINNIE--W/DELORIS M. TARZAN,
V. BERCH, BRNDN/BC PSEUDS,
BAE 22, P24,[11]

BOWEN, JOSHUA DAVID
BOWEN, DAVID--[33]

BOWEN, ROBERT SIDNEY
MORGAN, LT. SCOTT--[2]SHARED PSEUD.
WALLACE, ROBERT--[3][29]MYS, HP--
CROWN "MAKE MINE MURDER" '46
CROWN "MURDER GETS AROUND" '47
RICHARD, JAMES ROBERT--[33]

BOWEN, RUBIN
KAJAR--[8]

BOWEN, [IVOR] IVAN
HOGARTH, CHARLES--W/JOHN CREASEY,
[3][18][29]MYS--
SELWYN "MURDER ON LARGO ISLAND" '44

BOWEN-JUDD, SARA HUTTON
BURTON, ANNE--[3][18][29]MYS--
RAVEN "THE DEAR DEPARTED" '80
RAVEN "WHERE THERE'S A WILL" '80
CHALLIS, MARY--[3][18][29]MYS--
RAVEN "BURDEN OF PROOF" '80
RAVEN "CRIMES PAST" '80
LEEK, MARGARET--[3][18][29]MYS--
RAVEN "THE HEALTHY GRAVE" '80
RAVEN "WE MUST HAVE A TRIAL" '80
WOODS, SARA--[3][18][22]MYS--
32 NOVELS '62-84

BOWER, BERTHA MUZZY
BOWER, B.M.--[28]WEST--
NOVELS & SS '06-40

BOWER, JOHN GRAHAM
KLAXON--[2]

BOWERS, SANTHA RAMA RAU
RAU, SANTHA RAMA--[22]INDIAN-AMERICAN

BOWERS, WARNER FREMONT
FREMONT, W.B.--[31]

BOWERS, WILLIAM L.
BOWERS, BILL--W/BILL MALLARDI--[7]SF

BOWES, COLIN RICHARD
FALCONER, COLIN--[34][36]AUSTRALIAN/MYS--
HODDER "VENOM" '89
HODDER "DEATH WATCH" '91

BOWKETT, STEPHEN
GAROU, LOUIS P.--[31][33]

BOWLER, LOUIS P.
ROOINEK--[34]MYS--
HURST "AFRICAN NIGHTS" '29

BOWMAN, GERALD [MOORE]
LYNK, WARDER--[34]MYS--
AMALG "MYSTERY MAN OF MAYFAIR" '35
MAGNUS, GERALD--[8]
MOORE, GERALD--[34]MYS--
MELLIFONT "TEST OF LOVE" '32
MELLIFONT "THE DEATH KISS" '34

BOWMAN, ROBERT T.
BOWMAN, BOB--[31]

BOWSER, JIM
CARTER, NICK--[3]MYS, HP--
AWARD "DEATH OF THE FALCON" '74
AWARD "A HIGH YIELD IN DEATH" '76
WINSTON, PETER--[3]MYS, HP--
AWARD, ADJUSTERS SERIES
AWARD "THE GLASS CIPHER" '67
AWARD "DOOMSDAY VENDETTA" '68

BOWSER, PEARL
BOWSER, JOAN--[31]

BOYAJIAN, JEREL MICHAEL
BOYAJIAN, JERRY--[23]SF

BOYCE, DAVID
BOYD, DON--P. HARBOTTLE-PPCC#2,
P61 & S. HOLLAND-BOYCE CKLST,
PPCC#9, P72,[34]MYS--
BAKER "FEAR STALKS THE FOOTLIGHTS" '52
BAKER "DOLLS ARE DEADLY" '54
CALLAHAN, ROD--P. HARBOTTLE-PPCC#2, P61 &
S. HOLLAND-BOYCE CK LST,
PPCC#9,P72,[34]MYS, HP
WDL "TOO SMART TO LIVE" '51
GORDON, SPIKE--S. HOLLAND-BOYCE CKLST,
PPCC#9,[34]HP--
MOF "DON'T TEMPT THE HANGMAN" '53
GRAY, LINDA--S. HOLLAND-BOYCE CKLST,
PPCC#9--WDL "SOUTHERN HONEYMOON" '50
WDL "PRODIGAL DAUGHTER" '51
WDL "WITH THIS RING" '52
GRIFF--S. HOLLAND-BOYCE CKLST,
PPCC#9,[34]HP--
MOF "SHOOT TO LIVE" '53
M'QUADE, TEX--S. HOLLAND-BOYCE CKLST,
PPCC#9,WEST--
GANNET "WHIPCORD COUNTRY" '54
MCCOY, TRENT--P. HARBOTTLE-PPCC#2 &
S. HOLLAND-BOYCE CKLST, PPCC#9,[34]MYS--
HAM "WAKE NOT THE SLEEPING WOLF" '52

BOUCE, DAVID [CONT]
MCCOY, TRENT [CONT]
SB "QUINTON CLYDE, P.I." '52
FH "JUSTICE OF THE CANYON" '52
COOPERBKS "ILL COME QUIETLY" '52
SB "TREASURE OF THE YUKON" '53
COOPERBKS "LADY, WHAT NOW!" '53
FH "RAILROAD RENEGADE" '55
WDL "RIDERS OF THE RAFTER J" '56
FH "OUTLAWS OF THE RANGE" '56
FH "STAGECOACH TO SANTE FE" '57
FH "DYNAMITE TRAIL" '58
POWERS, JOHN--S. HOLLAND-BOYCE CKLST,
PPCC#9,[34]MYS, HP--
WDL "FRONT PAGE MURDER" '54
SAND, PETER--S.HOLLAND-SCION CKLST, PP 27 &
BOYCE CKLST,PPCC#9,[34]MYS, HP--
SCION "THE NINE O'CLOCK WALK" '51
SCION "BLUE SAGE" '52
SANDYS, PETE--S.HOLLAND-SCION CKLST, PP 27 &
BOYCE CKLST, PPCC#9,MYS, HP--
SCION "BADLANDS BUCKAROO" '54
SCION "ARIZONA BLOODSHED" '54
WARING, SONIA--S. HOLLAND-BOYCE CK LST,
PPCC#9--WDL "BRIEF MELODY" '52

BOYCE, JOHN CHRISTOPHER
BOYCE, CHRIS--[23]SF

BOYCOTT, GEOFFREY
BOYCOTT, GEOFF--[31]

BOYD, EDMOND A.D.
BOYD, ESTHER--[9][21][26]ROM--
"OMEN FOR LOVE"
"PRECIOUS PIRATE"
"BALI BREEZES"

BOYD, ELIZABETH
MACCALL, ISABEL--[9]ROM

BOYD, LYLE G. & WILLIAM C
ELLANBEE, BOYD--[1][11]SF
ELLANBY, BOYD--[1]

BOYD, MARTIN A. BECKER
MILLS, MARTIN--[8]

BOYD, ROBERT THOMPSON
BOYD, BOB--[31]

BOYD, WALDO T.
ANDERSON, TED--[1][31][33]
ANDREASSEN, KARL--[1][31]
PARKER, ROBERT--[1][33]

BOYER, GLENN G.
BOYLE, G.G.--[31]

BOYER, JEAN AUGUSTE
BOYER D'AGEN--[22]FRENCH

BOYER, RICHARD LEWIS
BOYER, RICHARD L.--[29]MYS--
HOUGHTON "BILLINGSGATE SHOAL" '82,
ON CR PAGE
BOYER, RICK--[29][31][34]MYS--
HOUGHTON "BILLINGSGATE SHOAL" '82

BOYERS, MARGARET ANNE
BOYERS, PEGGY--[31]

BOYLAND, BOYD
LODE, REX--W/WILLIAM ISAAC GOLDSTEIN,
[22]AMERICAN

BOYLE, ANN [PETERS]
BRENT, AUDREY--[9][21][26]ROM--
"SNOWFLAKES IN THE SUN"
BRYAN, ANN--[9][21]ROM--"SOMEONE TO LOVE"

BOYLE, ELEANOR VERE G.
E.V.B.--[31][33]

BOYLE, HAROLD VINCENT
BOYLE, HAL--[31]

BOYLE, JOHN HOWARD JACKSN
DAWSON, MICHAEL--[8]

BOYLE, TIMOTHY ROBERT
BOYLE, TIMM--[31]

BOYLES, CLARENCE SCOTT
BROWN, WILL C.--[8][22][31][32]MYS/WEST--
9 WEST NOVELS '55-64
PU "SUICIDE LETTER" SEPT '53
EQMM "ONE FOR THE ROAD" NOV '53

BOYLL, RANDALL
DIXON, MARK--V. BERCH LTR TO HUBIN JUNE '93, HP--
BERK "CRIME WAVE" '88

BOYNTON, WILLIAM DAVID
GARR, MULLIN--[1][14]
OLYM OPH "BIG WOMAN" '68
OLYM OPH#113 "LIGHTNING ROD" '68
OLYM OPH#118 "NAKED LADY" '68
OLYM OPH#130 "SUNDAY KIND OF LOVE" '68
OLYM OPH#138 "BIG MAN IN THE SADDLE" '69
OLYM OPH#167 "THE WAY I CAME" '69
OLYM OPH#151 "GOOD-TIME CHARLIE" '69
OLYM OPH "GO SAM SUNDAY" '70
OLYM OPH#219 "THE GREAT PERFORMANCE" '70

BOYUM, JOY GOULD
GOULD, JOY--[31]

BOZIC, SRETEN
BANUMBER--[13]AUSTRALIAN
BIRIMBIR--[13]AUSTRALIAN
WONGAR, B.--[7][13]AUSTRALIAN/SF--
DODD "NUCLEAR TRILOGY #1, 2 & #3" '83-7

BRABBINS, OLIVER G.
BRAB--BAPC NWSLTR, COVER ARTIST
FOR CORGI, FOUR SQUARE, HODDER & MORE
BRABBINS--BAPC NWSLTR #9, COVER
ARTIST FOR CORGI, FOUR SQUARE,
HODDER & MORE

BRACALE, CARLA
CASSIDY, CARLA--[26]ROM--13 NOVELS

BRACHO, MARY
SEYMOUR, ANA--[26]ROM--
"THE BANDITS BRIDE"
"ANGEL OF THE LAKE"

BRACK, WALTER
HAY, STEPHEN--[39]GERMAN/MYS/WEST

BRACKEN, CATHARINE PHILL.
BRACKEN, C.P.--[40]GERMAN/MYS--
"ROMAN RING" '68

BRACKETT, LEIGH
SANDERS, GEORGE--[3][4][11]MYS, GHOSTED--
SIMON "STRANGER AT HOME" '46

BRACKMAN, ARNOLD C.
BUNKER, CAPT. MOSS--[8]

BRADBURNE, ELIZABETH S.
LAWRENCE, E.S.--[31]

BRADBURY, BIANCA [R]
WYATT, JANE--[31][33]--
'TELL-A-TALE' BKS "ROWDY" '46
WYATT, MOLLY--[33]

BRADBURY, PARNELL
DERMOTT, STEPHEN--[8]
LYNN, STEPHEN--[8]

BRADBURY, RAY [DOUGLAS]
AMORY, GUY--[1][11]AMERICAN--FAN PSEUD.
BANAT, D.R.--[2][11][16]AMERICAN
BANKS, EDWARD--[2][11][16]AMERICAN
CORVAIS, ANTHONY--[1][11]AMERICAN--FAN PSEUD.
CUNNINGHAM, CECIL C.--[1][11]AMERICAN--
FAN PSEUD.
CUNNINGHAM, E.--[1][11]AMERICAN--FAN PSEUD.
DOUGLAS, LEONARD--[1][2][11][16]AMERICAN
ELDRED, BRIAN--[1][11]AMERICAN--FAN PSEUD.
ELLIOTT, WILLIAM--[1][2][11][16]AMERICAN
GREGORY, DANE--AUTHOR CONFIRMED,[37]MYS--
DT "ONE LUCKY CORPSE" FEB '43
DT "SAVE A GRAVE FOR ME" OCT '44
HOLLERBOCHEN--[1][11]AMERICAN--FAN PSEUD.
OMEGA--[1][11]AMERICAN--FAN PSEUD.
REYNOLDS, DON--[1][2][11][16]AMERICAN
ROGERS, DOUG--[1][11]AMERICAN--FAN PSEUD.
SPALDING, WILLIAM--[1][2]AMERICAN
SPAULDING, DOUGLAS--[11]SF
SPAULDING, LEONARD--[2][11][16][22]AMERICAN
STERLING, BRETT--[1][2][11]AMERICAN, HP--
TWS "REVERENT" '48
TREYMAINE, D. LERIUM--[1][11]AMERICAN--
FAN PSEUD.

BRADBURY, WILLIAM
SQUERENT, WILL--[3]MYS--
MacM "YOUR GOLDEN JUGULAR" '70

BRADBY, RACHEL
ANDERSON, RACHEL--[8]

BRADDON, MARY ELIZABETH
WHITE, BABINGTON--[5][18]MYS
BRADDON, M.E.--[34]MYS--
SIMPKIN "THE CONFLICT" '03
HURST "DEAD LOVE HAS CHAINS" '07
& MORE

BRADEN, THOMAS WARDELL
BRADEN, TOM--[31]

BRADFIELD, ROGER
BRADFIELD, JOLLY ROGER--[31]

BRADFORD PATIENCE A.
ANDREWES, PATIENCE--[31]

BRADFORD, BARBARA
BRADFORD, SALLY--W/SALLY SIDDON,[9][21]--
"WHEN FORTUNE SMILES"
"SPRING THAW"
"THE ARRANGEMENT"
SIDDON, BARBARA--W/SALLY SIDDON,[9][21]ROM--
"DECEIVE ME, DARLING"

BRADFORD, JOHN
HOMELY, JOSIAS--[34]MYS--
SIMPKIN "TALES OF THE MOOR" 1841

BRADFORD, MRS. MARSHALL
BUSHNELL, ADELYN--[2]

BRADLEY, EDWARD
BEDE, CUTHBERT--[34]MYS--
McLEAN "PHOTOGRAPHIC PLEASURES" 1855

BRADLEY, KATHERINE H.
FIELD, MICHAEL--W/EDITH E. COOPER,
[8][22]ENGLISH

BRADLEY, LURA LYNNETTE
BRADLEY, LURA L.--HAWK/BRADLEY INTRVW '93,
NOVELS & POETRY
BRADLEY, LYNN--HAWK/BRADLEY INTRVW '93,
PRIVATE EYE NOVELS
BRADLEY, LYNN L.--HAWK/BRADLEY INTRVW '93,
SHORT STORIES & ESSAYS
BRADLEY, LYNNE--HAWK/BRADLEY INTRVW '93,
PRIVATE EYE NOVELS
LYNNETTE--HAWK/BRADLEY INTRVW '93,POETRY

BRADLEY, MARION ZIMMER
BRADLEY, ASTARA ZIMMER--[2]
CHAPMAN, LEE--V. BERCH-MON PSEUDS, BAE 9/J.
PRESSMAN-LESBIANA, BAE 20,[2][4][17][23]--
MON MB529 "I AM A LESBIAN" '62
DEXTER, JOHN--G. THIESSEN,BAE 3,
[2][4][11][17][23]HP--LEIS
GARDNER, MIRIAM--V. BERCH-MON PSEUDS,BAE 9/J.
PRESSMAN-LESBIANA, BAE 20,[2][4][17][23]--
MON 249 "STRANGE WOMEN" '62
MON 352 "MY SISTER, MY LOVE" '63
MON 418 "TWILIGHT LOVERS" '64
GRAVES, VALERIE--[2][4][17][23]
IVES, MORGAN--V. BERCH-MON PSEUDS, BAE 9/J.
PRESSMAN-LESBIANA, BAE 20,[4][11][17][23]--
MON 335 "SPARE HER HEAVEN" '63
MORLEY, BRIAN--[1][2][11]
O'BRIEN, DEE--[1][2][11]
RIVERS, DEE--[1][2]
WELLS, JOHN JAY--W/JUANITA COULSON,
[2][11][23],SF
ZIMMER, ASTARA--[2]
ZIMMER, MARION--[2]

BRADLEY, RACHEL
ANDERSON, RACHEL--[9]ROM

BRADLEY, RODRICK
PHILLIPS, R.B.--[34]MYS--
FOUL PLAY "GUN PLAY" '87

BRADLEY, W.H.
LAIRD, ANDREW--[14]--
OLYM OPH#197 "HER BACK TO THE WALL" '70
OLYM OPH#208 "RAVISHED" '70
MACAULEY, DOUGLAS--[14]--
OLYM OPH#134 "A CERTAIN GREEK TYCOON" '69
OLYM OPH#144 "NEW KAMA SUTRA TALES"

BRADLEY, WILLIAM WARREN
BRADLEY, BILL--[31]

BRADSHAW, MRS. ALBERT S.
BRADSHAW, ANNIE [CROPPER]--[3]MYS--
CASSELL "A CRIMSON STAIN" 1885

BRADSHAW-JONES, MALCOLM
JONES, BRADSHAW--CRPG/[8][29][34]MYS--
LONG "DEATH ON A PALE HORSE" '64
LONG "DEADLY TRADE" '67 & MORE '63-70

BRADY, ESTHER WOOD
WOOD, ESTHER--[33]

BRADY, JANE FRANCES
WHITE, JANE--[1][7][8]SF--
HAMILTON "COMET: A NOVEL" '75

BRAEM, ELISABETH M.
KAISER, ELISABETH M.--[39]GERMAN

BRAEME, CHARLOTTE M.
CLAY, BERTHA M.--[3][9][22]MYS--
6 NOVELS '35-43

BRAGDON, ELSPETH MACDUFF.
ELSPETH--[22][31][33]AMERICAN

BRAGG, MABEL CAROLINE
PIPER, WATTY--[33]

BRAGG, RICHARD GEOFFREY
KENDAL, GEOFFREY--[31]

BRAGG, WILLIAM FREDERICK
BRAGG, BILL--[31]
SQUIRES, PHIL--L. ROBBINS LTR MAR '94

BRAGG, WILLIAM HENRY
BRAGG, SIR W.H.--[31]

BRAGUNIER, MORDINA FLOYD
FLOYD, MORDIE--[3]MYS--
BOUREGY "THE SECRET OF SARABAND" '61

BRAHAM, HAL
COLTON, MEL--[3][29]--
ACE D3 "BIG FIX" '52
ACE D19 "NEVER KILL A COP" '53
ACE D27 "DOUBLE TAKE" '53
RAIN 127 "BIG WOMAN" '53
PU "MURDER PAYS DOUBLE" JUL "54
HU "RING AROUND A MURDER" APR '55
HU "VICIOUS ONES" AUG '55
PU "MURDER ON ACCOUNT" MAY '55
ACE D-101 "POINT OF NO ESCAPE" '55
PU "DON'T WAIT FOR ME" SEPT '55
PU "SECOND GUESS" NOV '56
TRASK, MERRILL--[1][3]MYS--
MYH "MURDER IN BRIEF" '56

BRAHM, OTTO
ABRAHAMSOHN, OTTO--[22]

BRAIMAN, SUSAN
GETTLEMAN, SUSAN--[31]

BRAINERD, EDITH RATHBONE
RATH, E.J.--W/J.C.C. BRAINERD,[2][3][22]--
WATT "TOO MANY CROOKS" '18
NELSON "STOLEN CAR" '29

BRAINERD, JOHN WHITING
BEE, JAY--[31][33]

BRAITHWAITE, ALTHEA
ALTHEA--[8][31]

BRAKENHOFF, MARGARETHE
HOLLRIEDE, HAGDIS--[39]GERMAN/JUV

BRALY, MALCOLM
LORNING, RAY--[22]AMERICAN

BRAM, CHRISTOPHER
BRAM, CHRIS--[31]

BRAMBLEBY, AILSA
CRAIG, JENNIFER--[8]

BRAMER, JENNIE PERKINS
PERKINS, FAITH--[22]AMERICAN

BRAMESCO, NORTON J.
DAEDALUS--[31]

BRAMWELL, JAMES GUY
BYROM, JAMES--[3][22][31]MYS--
CHATTO "OR BE HE DEAD" '58
CHATTO "TAKE ONLY AS DIRECTED" '59
HM "THOU SHOULDST BE LIVING" '64

BRAND, CHARLES NEVILLE
LORNE, CHARLES--[8][22]MYS

BRAND, DEBRA
RAND, SUZANNE--[9][21]ROM--8 NOVELS

BRAND, KURT
BRACK, BUSTER--[39]GERMAN/WEST
BRAEK, BUSTER--[39]GERMAN/WEST
COTTON, JERRY--[39]GERMAN/MYS, HP
CUBA, CONNY--[39]GERMAN
DE LORCA, FRANK--[39]GERMAN, HP
JACK, GARRY--[39]GERMAN/WEST
KINGSTON, H.S.--[39]GERMAN
LAMONT, ROBERT--[39]GERMAN, HP
MARKS, T.W.--[39]GERMAN
MORTIMER, PHILIPP--[39][40]GERMAN/MYS--
"PHILIPP PFEIFT MORD" '69 & 2 OTHERS
MOSS, CHERRY--[39]GERMAN
MUNRO, C.R.--[39]GERMAN
OSTEN, I.S.--[39]GERMAN, HP
PETERS, PIT--[39]GERMAN, HP
PORTER, LEX--[39]GERMAN, HP
RIFLE, JOHN--[39]GERMAN/WEST
SCOUT, TED--[39]GERMAN/WEST
SPENCER, CLARK--[39]GERMAN
STARNE, PETER L.--[39]GERMAN
TARR, HANNO--[39]GERMAN
TORSTEN, LARS--[39]GERMAN
TURK, KAY--[39]GERMAN
VEREB, JANOS--[39]GERMAN

BRAND, WILLEM SIMON
BRANDT, WILLEM--[22]DUTCH

BRANDECKER, WALTER G.
SCHWEIZER, H.--[39]GERMAN

BRANDEL, MARC
MARCUS, BERESFORD--[29]MYS--
HARPER "RAIN BEFORE SEVEN" '45

BRANDENBERG, ALIKI L.
ALIKI--[22][31][33]--
FABER "STORY OF WILLIAM TELL" '60

BRANDENBERGER, ANNE
BRADUN, JOHANNA--[39]GERMAN

BRANDES, RHODA
RAMSAY, DIANA--[3]MYS--
COLLINS, 5 NOVELS '73-77

BRANDHORST, ANDREAS
BRAND, HORST--[39]GERMAN/SF
LAMONT, ROBERT--[39]GERMAN/SF, HP
LOCKWOOD, THOMAS--[39]GERMAN/SF
WEILER, ANDREAS--W/KARL-ULRICH BURGDORF,
[39]GERMAN/SF
WERNING, ANDREAS--[39]GERMAN/SF

BRANDLE, ALEXANDER
BRAND, B. ALEC--[39]GERMAN/ADV/JUV/SF

BRANDNER, GARY
BRAND, GARRISON--BRANDNER LTR FEB '94,[1][31]
CARTER, NICK--W/ROBERT COLBY,
BRANDNER LTR FEB '94, HP--
AWARD "DEATH'S HEAD CONSP." '73
GARRISON, PHIL--BRANDNER LTR FEB '94--
"DRESSED UP FOR MURDER"
IN ANTHOL "CLAWS & FEATHERS" '89
PITMAN "GOOD LUCK SMILING CAT" '84
PITMAN "DISAPPEARING MAN" '84
GREY, ROMER ZANE--BRANDNER LTR '94, HP--
ZGWM "TRAIL HERD TO ABILENE" JUN '72
HALLIDAY, BRETT--W/CLAYTON MATTHEWS,
BRANDNER LTR '94, HP--
MSMM "SHORT CUT TO MURDER" SEP '73
MOORE, CLAYTON--BRANDNER LTR '94,
[1][31], HP--
BERK "RIVER FALLS: WESLEY SHERIDAN" '74
MOORE, CLAYTON--W/CLAYTON MATTHEWS,[31]--
CURTIS "SATURDAY NIGHT IN MILWAUKEE" '73
QUILL, BARNABY--BRANDNER LTR '94,[31]--
GEM "HER AUNT THE WITCH" '71
YES "HER AUNT THE WITCH" '73
YES "LADY CHATTERLEY'S LOSER" '74
WILLOUGHBY, LEE DAVIS--BRANDNER LTR '94,
[1], HP--
DELL "THE EXPRESS RIDERS"
ZOLNY, NORMAN--BRANDNER LTR '94--
WHISPER "THE GREAT VITAMIN E
RIPOFF" JUN '73

BRANDON, JOHNNY
EDWARDS, FRANCIS--[31]
FRANKS, ED--[31]

BRANDON, ROBERT JOSEPH
BRANDON, ROBIN--[31]

BRANDT, ADOLF
STILLFRIED, FELIX--[22]GERMAN

BRANDT, CAROL
DENNY, CAROL--[1][31]

BRANDT, IRMENGARD
HALL, SISSY--[39]GERMAN

BRANDT, JANE LEWIS
BEYNON, JANE--[11]
LEWIS, LANGE--[11][31]SF

BRANDT, LUCILE [L.S.]
LONG, LUCILE--[1][31]

BRANDT, NATHAN HENRY JR.
BRANDT, NAT--[31]

BRANDT, PAUL
LICHT, HANS--[1]

BRANDT, PAUL MARTIN
RIGHT, P.M.--[39]GERMAN/MYS/JUV

BRANNIGAN, WILLIAM
BRANNIGAN, BILL--[31]

BRANNON, WILLIAM T.
BARRINGTON, H.W.--[1][31]AMERICAN
BOUDRAINE, WILLIAM--[1]AMERICAN
BROUSTON, WILLIAM--[1]AMERICAN
GARDNER, LAWRENCE--[1][22]AMERICAN
HAMILTON, JACK--[1][22][31]AMERICAN
HERMANNS, PETER--[1][22][31]AMERICAN
LEBERT, RANDY--[1][22][31]AMERICAN
MCGLINN, DWIGHT--[1][22]AMERICAN
OBERHOLTZER, PETER--[1][22]AMERICAN

BRANNON, WILLIAM T. [CONT]
PETERS, S.T.--[1][22]AMERICAN
RANDOLPH, JERRY--[1]AMERICAN
SWANSTROM, NILS--[1]AMERICAN
TIBBERTS, WILLIAM--[1][22][31]AMERICAN

BRANOWITZER-RODLER, MARIA
VON SONNHOF, MARIA--[39]GERMAN/JUV

BRANYAN-BROADBENT, BRENDA
BRANYAN, BRENDA--[31]

BRARD, MARGOT
KOTTE, MARGOT--[39]GERMAN

BRASH, MARGARET MAUDE
KENDALL, JOHN--[2]

BRASHLER, WILLIAM
EVERS, CRABBE--W/REINDEER VAN TIL--
DDLY PLEAS #3--"MURDER IN
WRIGLEY FIELD" '91

BRASINGTON, A. LARRY
CROSS, STEPHEN--[2]

BRAUER, DEANA
DANIELS, DANA--[9][21][26]ROM--4 NOVELS
RHEE, DENA--[9][21][26]ROM--
"AN IMMODEST PROPOSAL"
"IF EVER WE MEET"
"LESSONS OF LOVE"

BRAUN, FERNANDO MAX RICH.
BRAUN, FRANK F.--[39][40]GERMAN/MYS--
"DIE GOLDENE DREIZEHN" '50 & 5 OTHERS

BRAUN, HANNS MARIA
DIETRICH, JOHANN GOTTLIEB--[39]GERMAN

BRAUN, HANS
STEINEMANN, FRITZ--[39]GERMAN

BRAUN, MATTHEW
BURKE, WARREN--[7][34]MYS--
CHART "THE KILLING TOUCH" '83
WALKER "A TIME OF INNOCENCE" '86

BRAUN, MAURICE GILLES
BRAUN, MAURICE-GEORGES--[34]MYS--
4 NOVELS

BRAUN, REINHOLD
RUF, ADAM--[39]GERMAN

BRAUN, WILBUR
ALBERT, NED--[3][8]MYS--3 PLAYS
BLAKE, WALTER--[3]MYS--2 PLAYS
BRANDON, BRUCE--[3]MYS--1 PLAY
BRISTOL, STEPHEN--[34]MYS--
PLAY "CRIME PHOTOGRAPHER" '50
CALDWELL, FRED--[3]MYS--1 PLAY
CROSBY, MILLARD--[3]MYS--3 PLAYS
DUMKEY, RAYMOND--[3]MYS--1 PLAY
FERNWAY, PEGGIE--[8]
FLEMING, NAN--[3]MYS--1 PLAY
FORSYTHE, ANTHONY--[3]MYS--1 PLAY
GRABLE, MARSHA--[3]MYS--1 PLAY
HORNUNG, EDWIN F.--[3]MYS--1 PLAY
PARISH, JED--[3]MYS--1 PLAY
RING, BASIL--[3]MYS--1 PLAY
SNAPP, ORVILLE--[3]MYS--1 PLAY
SPRAGUE, MORTIMER--[3]MYS--1 PLAY
STONER, BERT--[3]MYS--1 PLAY
WARREN, WAYNE--[8]

BRAUND, HAROLD
BRAUND, HAL--[31]

BRAUNE, JOACHIM
RASMUS-BRAUNE, JOACHIM--[39]GERMAN/JUV

BRAUNS-LEUTZ, ILSE
HARRISON, J.L.--[39]GERMAN
LEUTZ, ILSE--[39]GERMAN
THYROW, CHRISTIANE--[39]GERMAN

BRAUNSTEIN, BINNIE SYRIL
SYRIL, BINNIE--[9][21][26]ROM--
"THE COLOR OF LOVE"
"OUT OF THE DARKNESS"
"BABY LOVE"

BRAV, STANLEY R[OSENBAUM]
BARKTON, S. RUSH--[31]

BRAWLEY, PAUL LEROY
BRAWLEY, PAUL HOLM--[31]

BRAWN, ANNA LIVIA JULIAN
LIVIA, ANNA--[7][23]IRISH-ENGLISH/SF--
"BULLDOZER RISING" '88
"SACCHARIN CYANIDE" '90

BRAWNER, HELEN
COFFIN, GEOFFREY--W/F.V.W. MASON,
[2][3][5][18][29]MYS--
DODGE "MURDER IN THE SENATE" '35
DODGE "FORGOTTEN FLEET MYSTERY" '36

BRAY, JOHN
ZOOL, M.H.--[23]SF-GROUP PSEUD.

BRAYTON, GERTRUDE E.
BRYAT, EDITH--[2]

BREBNER, PERCY [JAMES]
LYS, CHRISTIAN--[2][3][7][22]MYS--
8 NOVELS '07-24

BRECHT, EUGEN BERTHOLD F.
BRECHT, BERTOLT--[31]

BRECKENFELD, VIVIAN GURN.
BRECK, VIVIAN--[8][21][22][26][31][33]ROM--
"MAGGIE"

BREDBERG, ERNST C. JR.
ERNESTO--[29]MYS--
"DEN DODES SKUGGA" '30
MATSON, DR.--[29]MYS--
"TRIANGELBOCKERNA" '52
MCGEORGE, DR. M. ERNEST--[29]MYS--
"DODEN I CIRKUS" '52
"FLOATING COFFINS"
"LACE LEADS TO LOSE" & 2 MORE

BREEDLOVE, WILLIAM
CHRISTY, RICHARD--V. BERCH-BRNDN/BC PSEUDS,
BAE 22, P24--

BREEN, PHILLIP
MORGAN, WYNN L.--W/CHESTER KRONE,[3]MYS--
DELL "THE ICE MAN" '79

BREESE, DAVID WILLIAM
BREESE, DAVE--[31]

BREESE, EDWARD Y.
HALLIDAY, BRETT--T. JOHNSON-ECHOES#23, HP--
MSMM "NAME OF THE GAME IS MURDER" APR '70
MSMM "LOBSTER WAR" MAR '70

BREESE, EDWARD Y. [CONT]
HALLIDAY, BRETT [CONT]
MSMM "DEAD MAN'S HERITAGE" MAY '70
MSMM "DEATH WALKS HERE" JUN '70
MSMM "THOUSAND FLOWERS MURDER CASE" JUL '70
MSMM "THIS KEY UNLOCKS COFFINS" AUG '70
MSMM "TRIPLE CROSS AT HOLY CROSS" SEP '70
MSMM "BIG HOUSE BLUES" OCT '70
MSMM "DOUBLE INDEMNITY FOR A RIVER BUM" NOV '70
MSMM "DEATH HAS TWO FACES" DEC '70
MSMM "YACHT TRIP TO DEATH" JAN '71
MSMM "LADY HAS A GUN" FEB '71
MSMM "CHARGE IS MURDER" MAR '71
MSMM "DEATH IS MY PAYOFF" APR '71
MSMM "WE'RE ALL KILLERS" MAY '71
MSMM "AIRPORT MURDERS" JUN '71
MSMM "SHOOLHOUSE MURDERS" JUN
MSMM "DEATH COMES TO BREAKFAST" AUG '71
MSMM "MURDER OF A MEAN OLD MAN" SEP '71
MSMM "LANDLORD MURDER CASE" OCT '71
MSMM "DEATH WORE A BRIDAL VEIL" NOV '71
MSMM "POSTMAN BROUGHT MURDER" DEC '71
MSMM "SWEET DREAMS OF DEATH" FEB '72
MSMM "DEATH IN THE FAMILY" MAY '72
MSMM "NIGHTMARE HOUSE" JUL '72
MSMM "FAT MAN" OCT '72
MSMM "WEEKENDS ARE FOR KILLING" DEC '72
MSMM "HARMLESS KILLER" FEB '73
MSMM "DEATH IN THE CRYSTAL BALL" APR '73
MSMM "NOBODY MURDER CASE" AUG '73
MSMM "YELLOW DOG MURDER CASE" DEC '73
MSMM "MURDER IN MY FAMILY" FEB '74
MSMM "VERY RELUCTANT CORPSE" APR '74
MSMM "WHO KILLED BABY SISTER" JUN '74
MSMM "MURDER OF A GHOST" AUG '74
MSMM "LITTLE GIRL MURDER CASE" OCT '74
MSMM "TO ALL MY HEIRS" APR '75

BREETVELD, JAMES PATRICK
MANN, AVERY--[8][22][31]AMERICAN

BREHM, DORIS
DIEZ, DORIS--[39]GERMAN

BREHM, WILHELM JOHANN
VON TARNOWITZ, WILHELM--[39]GERMAN

BREHMER, ARTHUR
BLUNT, CHARLES--[39]GERMAN

BREINBERG, PETRONELLA
ASHEY, BELLA--[31][33]ALL BRITISH PUBL WRITING
TOTHAM, MARY--[31][33]--
BODLEY HEAD "DOCTOR SHAWN" - ONE STORY IN THE COLL.

BREINLINGER, ALICE BEREND
BEREND, ALICE--[22]GERMAN

BREIT, WILLIAM
JEVONS, MARSHALL--W/KENNETH G. ELZINGA, [3][31],MYS--
HORTON "MURDER AT THE MARGINS" '78
MIT "THE FATAL EQUILIBRIUM" '85

BREITBACH, JOSEPH
SALECK, JEAN-CHARLOT--[39]GERMAN

BREITENEICHNER, HANS
BRANDIN, HANS I.--[39]GERMAN/JUV

BREKKE, PAAL EMANUEL
RHODE, ARVID--[22]NORWEGIAN

BREMER, JO[ANNE]
CARROLL, JOELLYN--W/CAROL I. WAGNER, [9][21]ROM--
"RUN BEFORE THE WIND"
"A FLIGHT OF SPLENDOR"

BREMER, SVEND AAGE
HARRIGAN, CLARK--[29][37]MYS--
"MANNEN BAKOM LJUSET" '42

BREMYER, JAYNE DICKEY
DICKEY, LEE--[31]

BRENAN, EDWARD FITZGERALD
BEATON, GEORGE--[2][22][31]ENGLISH
BRENAN, GERALD--[8]

BRENNAN, JAMES HERBERT
BRENNAN, JAN--[3][7]MYS/SF--
COLLINS "GREYTHORN WOMAN" '79
DBLDY "A DREAM OF DESTINY" '80

BRENNAN, JOHN N.H.
WELCOME, JOHN--[3][18][29][31]MYS--
13 NOVELS '49-90

BRENNAN, JOSEPH [LOMAS]
GRAYSTONE, LYNN--[1][31]AMERICAN
LOMAS, STEVE--[22][31][33]AMERICAN

BRENNAN, LILLA
BLAKELY, MELISSA--[21][26]ROM--
"HOLD ME FOREVER"

BRENNECKE, JOCHEN
JANSSEN, JENS--[39]GERMAN
JENSEN, JENS--[39]GERMAN
LASS, E.G.--[39]GERMAN

BRENNEISEN, WOLFGANG
SALIK, KONRAD--[39]GERMAN

BRENNER, HANS GEORG
GRABE, REINHOLD TH.--[39]GERMAN

BRENNER, MAYER ALAN
NORTH, RICK--[7SF, HP--
ZEBRA "ASTRONAUTS #5"

BRENNER, REEVE R[OBERT]
BAR NER, R.--[31]

BRENT, HAROLD PATRICK
BRENT, HARRY--[1]

BRENT, PETER [LUDWIG]
PETERS, LUDOVIC--[2][3][7][11][18][23]MYS/SF--
"RIOT 71" '67 & 9 OTHERS

BRENT-DYER, ELINOR MARY
DYER, ELINOR MARY BRENT--[31]

BRERETON, JOHN LE GAY
GARSTANG, BASIL--[8]

BRESLAUER, HANS KARL
O'CLEANER, JAMES--[39]GERMAN
SCHNEIDER, BASTIAN--[39]GERMAN

BRESLIN, HOWARD
NIALL, MICHAEL--V. BERCH-MON PSEUDS, BAE 9 & GM PSEUDS, PP 33,[3]MYS--
GM 451 "BAD DAY AT BLACK ROCK" '54
MILL "RUN LIKE A THIEF" '62

BRESLIN, JAMES
BRESLIN, JIMMY--[31]

BRESSLAUER, HANS KARL
ROMBERG, JENNY--[39]GERMAN

BRETNOR, [A] REGINALD
BRIARTON, GRENDEL--[2][7][11][23]SF--
MIRAGE "THE COMPLEAT FEGHOOT" '75

BRETON-SMITH, CLARE
CALDWELL, ELINOR--[1]
WILDE, HILARY--[1]

BRETT, JAN [C]
BOWLER, JAN BRETT--[31][33]--
FAWCETT "LORD LAXTON'S WILL" '85

BRETT, LESLIE FREDERICK
BRETT, MICHAEL--[8]

BRETT, MARY ELIZABETH
BRETT, MOLLY--[8][22][31]ENGLISH--
CHILDRENS BOOKS

BREUCKER, OSCAR HERBERT
ARIZONA-TIGER--[39]GERMAN/WEST
ASTOR, FRANK--[39]GERMAN/MYS/SF/WEST
BLUCO, AXEL--[39]GERMAN/MYS/SF/WEST
CHITTERWICK, CAPT. OLD--[39]GERMAN/MYS/SF/WEST
CLASS, HEIN--[39]GERMAN/MYS/SF/WEST
CLURE, CLIFF--[39]GERMAN/MYS/SF/WEST
CLURE, CLIFFORD--[39]GERMAN/MYS/SF/WEST
CONNOR, TEX--[39]GERMAN/WEST
CURE, CLIFF--[39]GERMAN/MYS/SF/WEST
DUX, DENNIS--[39]GERMAN/MYS/SF/WEST
FERRER, JOE--[39]GERMAN/MYS/SF/WEST
GARBY, RALPH--[39]GERMAN/MYS/SF/WEST
HALE, RAY--[39]GERMAN/MYS/SF/WEST
HARDON, RONNY--[39]GERMAN/MYS/SF/WEST
HUNTER, TOM--[39]GERMAN/WEST
ISLAND, BERT F.--[39][40]GERMAN/MYS/SF, HP
MORAND, ERIC--[39]GERMAN/MYS/SF/WEST
NOBODY, UNUS--[39]GERMAN/SF
RANDELL, MIKE--[39]GERMAN/MYS/SF/WEST
TAGGERT, JOHN--[39]GERMAN/MYS/WEST
WEBSTER, HARRY--[39]GERMAN/MYS/SF/WEST
WOLTER, FRANK--[39]GERMAN/MYS/SF/WEST
YESTER, BURT--[39]GERMAN/MYS/SF/WEST
YPSEN, UDO--[39]GERMAN/MYS/SF/WEST

BREUER, GEORG KARL FELIX
BORST, JURGEN--[39]GERMAN/JUV
BREUER, JORG--[39]GERMAN/JUV

BREUER, GUSTAV J.
BREUER, GUSTL--[1][31]
HARDT, MICHAEL--W/GWEN L. DAVENPORT,
[1][3]MYS--
BOBBS "A STRANGER & AFRAID" '43

BREUER, SANDRA
WOOD, DEBORAH--V. BERCH LTR TO HUBIN '94--
ZEBRA "MISTRESS OF SOUNDCLIFF MANOR" '80

BREWER, DEREK STANLEY
BREWER, D.S.--[31]

BREWER, FRED
WYNN, ALFRED--[22]AMERICAN

BREWER, GIL
ARVAY, HARRY--PRONZINI LTR '94--
GHOSTED 5 ISRAELI-ARAB WAR
NOVELS FOR 'ARVAY'PER BREWER LTR
BB Q7759 "OPERATION KUWAIT" MAR '75

BREWER, GILL [CONT]
CONROY, AL--PRONZINI LTR FEB '94--
LAN 75-459 "MURDER MISSION" '73
LAN 75-433 "STRANGLEHOLD" '73
ELLSON, HAL--PRONZINI LTR JAN '94,[34]--
GHOSTED PYR "BLOOD ON THE IVY" '69
EVANS, ELAINE--[34]MYS/ROM--
LAN 74-705 "SHADOWLAND" '70
LAN 75-403 "A DARK & DEADLY LOVE" '72
LAN 78-752 "BLACK AUTUMN" '73
POPLB "WINTERSHADE" '74
FITZGERALD, ERIC--LACHMAN LST--[18][32]MYS--
PU "THE SCREAMER" SEPT '55
HU "DEATH COMES LAST" OCT '55
PU "SAUCE FOR THE GOOSE" JAN '56
HU "THE BLACK SUITCASE" FEB '56
PU "HOME-AGAIN BLUES" MAR '56
HU "ALLIGATOR" APR '56
PU "CUT BAIT" MAY '56
PU "RETURN TO YESTERDAY" JUL '56
HALLIDAY, BRETT--T. JOHNSON, ECHOES #23,P16,
HP--MSMM ?? UNCONFIRMED ??
MORGAN, BAILEY--LACHMAN LST--[18][32]--
HU "SUDDEN JUSTICE" APR '55
HU "HAMMER" OCT '55
PU "DIG THAT CRAZY CORPSE" MAR '55
PU "GIGOLO" JUL '55
PU "MY LADY IS A TRAMP" MAY '55
PU "DEATH IN BLOOM" SEPT '55
PU "SPEAK NO EVIL" NOV '55
HU "DON'T DO THAT" DEC '55
PU "WIFE SITTER" JUL '56
PU "COLD RAIN" SEPT '56
PU "WHISKEY" NOV '56
PENDLETON, DON--PRONZINI LTR JAN '94, HP--
EXECUT. SERIES-SUBMITTED A
NOVEL ? PUBLISHED ?
QUEEN, ELLERY--PRONZINI LTR JAN '94,[34]--
GHOSTED LAN "THE CAMPUS MURDERS" '69

BREYTENBACH, BREYTEN
BLOM, JAN--[31]

BREZHNEV, LEONID ILLYICH
BREZHNID, L.I.--[31]

BRIDGE, JAMES HOWARD
BRYDGES, HAROLD--[2][7]SF

BRIDGE, SUSAN
CAREY, ELISABETH--[9][21][26]ROM--3 NOVELS

BRIDGEMAN, SARAH ATHERTON
ATHERTON, SARAH--[31]

BRIDGES, HILDA [MAGGIE]
GARDINER, JOAN--[36]AUSTRALIAN/MYS--
MAGPIE "DEAD FIRES" '45
MAGPIE "OF MANY COLOURS" '45

BRIDGES, ROYAL
BRIDGES, ROY--[36]AUSTRALIAN/MYS--
HUTCH "OWL IS ABROAD" '41 & 6 OTHERS

BRIDGES, THOMAS CHARLES
BECK, CHRISTOPHER--[2][7]SF
BRIDGES, T.C.--[7]SF
BRIDGES, TOM--[8]

BRIE, ALFRED
MAXIME, A.--[39]GERMAN

BRIGGS, CAROLE S.
AYRES, CAROLE BRIGGS--[1][31]

BRIGGS, DESMOND LAWTHER
  FITZROY, ROSAMOND--[31]

BRIGGS, PHYLLIS
  BRIGGS, PHILIP--[2][7]SF

BRIGHOUSE, HAROLD
  CONWAY, OLIVE--W/JOHN WALTON,[8]

BRIGHT, MARY C.D.
  EGERTON, GEORGE--[2][7][11]SF--
    "FANTASIAS" 1897

BRIGHT, ROBERT DOUGLAS
  DOUGLAS, MICHAEL--[8][31][33]

BRIGHTFIELD, RICHARD
  BRIGHTFIELD, RICK--[31][33]--
    "MAZES" BOOKS '73-5

BRIK, JOHANNES
  BRIK, HANS THEODOR--[39]GERMAN/JUV/SF

BRINCHMANN, ALEXANDER
  ROBERTS, ROY--[3]MYS--
    HODDER "THE CRAYFISH CLUB" '31

BRINDLE, ERNEST
  BAYNE, PETER--[34]MYS--
    AMALG "SHAN CHUNG'S CONSPIRACY" '12

BRINEY, ROBERT E.
  ANDREWS, CARRIE--BRINEY INTRVW '93--POETRY
  DUANE, ANDREW--[2][11]
  ROBERTS, ED--HAWK/BRINEY INTRVW '93--
    FANFARE MAG - SHORT STORIES

BRINGEMAN, GUSTAF
  RUNE, K.G.--[29]MYS--
    "DEN RODA FJADERN" '26

BRINGLE, MARY HANFORD B.
  MORRIS, KATHLEEN--[21][26]ROM--
    "AN ELEGANT AFFAIR"
    "MARA"

BRINITZER, CARL
  USIKOTA--[22]RUSSIAN

BRINKMANN, JURGEN
  EVERTIER, PAUL--[39]GERMAN/SF
  SJOBERG, ARNE--[39]GERMAN/JUV/SF

BRINKMANN, KARL HERMANN
  HOLLE, CHRISTIAN--[39]GERMAN

BRINKMEIER, HANNELORE
  BLANK, ANNELORE--[39]GERMAN

BRINKWORTH, IAN
  BROOK, IAN--[3]MYS--
    CASSELL "THE GOLDEN BULL" '68

BRINSMEAD, HESBA FAY
  BRINSMEAD, H.F.--[8][31]
  HUNGERFORD, PIXIE--[8][31][33]

BRINTON, HENRY
  FRASER, ALEX--[3][22][31]ENGLISH/MYS--
    6 BLES NOVELS '56-61

BRIOD, BETTY [E]
  SAINT-HELIER, MONIQUE--[39]GERMAN

BRISSENDEN, ROBERT FRANC.
  BRISSENDEN, BOB--[36]AUSTRALIAN

BRISSENDEN, ROBERT FRANC. [CONT]
  BRISSENDEN, R.F.--[36]AUSTRALIAN,MYS--
    ALLEN "POOR BOY" '87
    ALLEN "WILDCAT" '91

BRISSON, CLAUDINE
  JARDINE, CLAUDINE--[1]

BRISTER, RICHARD
  GROVE, WILL O.--[1][22][31]AMERICAN
  LEWIN, C.L.--[1][22][31]AMERICAN
  RICHMOND, GEORGE--[1][8][22]AMERICAN

BRITTAIN, WILLIAM E.
  BRITTAIN, BILL--[7][31][33]--
    "COVEN TREE #1-#4" '81-90
    "ALL THE MONEY IN THE WORLD" '79 & OTHERS
  KNOX, JAMES--[1][18][32]MYS--
    EQMM "LAST WORD" JUNE '68
    EQMM "MR. LIGHTNING" JULY '66

BRITTON, MATTIE LULA C.
  COOPER, MATTIE LULA--[31]
  PATTERSON, JANE--[22]AMERICAN

BRITTON, PETER EWART
  LEMESURIER, PETER--[31]

BROADHEAD, HELEN CROSS
  CROSS, HELEN REEDER--[31][33]

BROADWELL, CLYDE
  VALLIENT, FRANCOIS DI--[2]HP--STREET & SMITH

BROCHASKA, BRUNO
  WOLFGANG, BRUNO--[39]GERMAN

BROCHET, JEAN ALEXANDRE
  BRUCE, JEAN--V. BERCH & S. HOLLAND,
    ARCH CKLST, BAE 15,[34]--
    ARCH "CORPSES GALORE" '52
    CORGI "COLD SPELL" '67
    CORGI "TOP SECRET" '67 & 13 OTHERS '51-67

BROCK, ALAN [ST. HILL]
  DEWDNEY, PETER--[3][22]MYS--
    WRIGHT "ON APPEAL" '38
    WRIGHT "ARISING FROM A ACCIDENT" '39

BROCK, GEORGE LESLIE
  BROCK, G.L.--[31]

BROCK, PATRICK WILLET
  BROCK, P.W.--[31]

BROCK, RUDOLF
  BROCK, PETER--[39]GERMAN/JUV
  KORB, PETER--[39]GERMAN/JUV

BROCKETT, LINUS PIERPONT
  HAZELTON, CAPT. JOSEPH P--[3]MYS

BROCKIES, ENID FLORENCE
  MAGRISKA, HELEN--[2]

BROD, DEBORAH C.
  BROD, D.C.--HAWK/BROD INTRVW MAY '93,[34]MYS--
    WALKER "MURDER IN STORE" '89
    WALKER "ERROR IN JUDGEMENT" '90
    WALKER "MASQUERADE IN BLUE"
    WALKER "FRAMED IN BLUE"
    WALKER "BROTHERS IN BLOOD"

BROD, RUTH HAGY
  HAGY, RUTH GERI--[31]

BRODEUR, DIANE & GREG
CAREY, DIANE--[9][21][26]ROM--4 NOVELS
GREGORY, LYDIA--[9][21][26]ROM--
"UNWILLING ENCHANTRESS"

BRODEY, JIM
FEMORA--[8]
TAYLOR, ANN--[8]

BRODIE, JOHN
GUTHRIE, JOHN--[2][11][22]NEW ZEALANDER

BRODIE, JULIAN PAUL
DENBIE, ROGER--W/ALAN B. GREEN,[3][22]--
MRW "DEATH ON LIMITED" '33
MRW "DEATH CRUISES SOUTH" '34

BRODNEY, SPENCER
BRODZKY, LEON--[13]AUSTRALIAN

BRODSKY, IOSIF ALEXANDER
BRODSKY, JOSEPH--[31]POETRY '72-6

BRODY, JANE ELLEN
BRODY, JEAN--[21][26]ROM--
"GIDEON'S HOUSE"

BRODY, JOHN
BODY, JOHN--[2]

BRODY, PETER S.
WILDERNESS, DAVID O.--[3]MYS--
PAGEANT "SINSATION OF A SINTARY" '56

BROEG, ROBERT M.
BROEG, BOB--[31]

BROEGER, ACHIM
BROGER, ACHIM--[31]

BROEKEL, RANIER LOTHAR
BROEKEL, RAY--[31][33]

BROEMEL, ROSE
EVELYN, ROSE D'--[22]MYS

BROFELT, JUHANI
AHO, JUHANI--[22]FINNISH

BROGAN, COLM
CANDIDUS--[8]

BROGAN, DENNIS WILLIAM
BARRINGTON, MAURICE--[3]MYS--
HAMILTON "STOP ON THE GREEN LIGHT" '41

BROGGER, WALDEMAR
VALENIN, PETER--[29]MYS--
"MURDEREN PLUKKER FLUESOPP" '57
"MORDAREN PLOCKAR FLUGSVAMP" '58

BROGREN, JEANNE
BROSTEN, CARLO--W/HANS-ERIK STENBERG,[29]MYS--
"MORDARE MED SILKESSTRUMPOR" '46

BROKAMP, MARILYN
LYNN, MARY--[33]

BROKAW, THOMAS JOHN
BROKAW, TOM--[31]

BROLL, WOLFGANG W.
BURNS, WILLIAM--[39]GERMAN/JUV/MYS/SF
WOLICK, PETER--[39]GERMAN/JUV/MYS/SF

BROMIGE, IRIS
TRACEY, ANN--[9]ROM

BROMMUND, CHRISTOPH
BROHM, CHRIS--[39]GERMAN/JUV

BRONDFIELD, JEROME
BRONDFIELD, JERRY--[31][33]

BRONER, ESTHER MASSERMAN
BRONER, E.M.--[38]--
HOLT RHINEHART "HER MOTHERS" '75
HOLT RHINEHART "A WEAVE OF WOMEN" '78

BRONNEN, ARNOLT
SCHELLE-NOETZEL, A.H.--[39]GERMAN

BRONNER, FERDINAND
ADAMUS, FRANZ--[39]GERMAN

BRONSON, ANTOINETTE
BRONSON, MAUREEN--W/MAUREEN WOODCOCK,
[9][21][26]ROM--5 NOVELS

BRONSTEIN, LEV DAVYDOVICH
TROTSKY, LEON--[22]RUSSIAN

BRONTE, ANN
BELL, ACTON--[6]
GERALDA, LADY--[6]
VERNON, OLIVIA--[6]
ZENOBIA, ALEXANDRIA--[6]

BRONTE, CHARLOTTE
BELL, CURRER--[2]
C.B.--[6]
DOURO, MARQUIS OF--[6]
GENIUS--[6]
WELLESLEY, LORD CHARLES--[6]

BRONTE, EMILY JANE
ALCON, R.--[6]
BELL, ELLIS--[2]

BROOK, JUDITH PENELOPE
BROOK, JUDY--[31][33]

BROOK, MARGARET F. BACON
BACON, PEGGY--[7]SF--
LITTLE "THE MAGIC TOUCH" '68

BROOKE, AVERY [ROGERS]
BENJAMIN, ALICE--[31]

BROOKE, PETER
CARSON, ANTHONY--[8]

BROOKER, BERTRAM
HERNE, HUXLEY--[3][22]MYS--
NELSON "THE TANGLED MIRACLE" '36
SURREY, RICHARD--[22]MYS

BROOKES, EWART STANLEY
TYLER, CLARKE--[8]

BROOKMAN, LAURA L.
WILSON, EDWINA H.--[8]

BROOKMAN, ROSINA FRANCESC
FRANCESCA, ROSINA--[31]

BROOKS, ANNE TEDLOCK
CARTER, ANN[E]--[9][21][31]ROM--
"HIS WORDS OF LOVE"
"FREEZE FRAME"
"PRELUDE TO SUMMER"

BROOKS, ANNE TEDLOCK [CONT]
MILBURN, CYNTHIA--[8][22]AMERICAN
MILLBURN, CYNTHIA--[8][22]AMERICAN

BROOKS, C.W. JR.
BROOKS, NED--W/DON MARTIN,[7]SF

BROOKS, COLLIN
BROOK, BARNABY--[8][22]MYS

BROOKS, EDWY SEARLES
BROWN, CALDWELL--[29]MYS--
"DEN BLONDA HAMMERSKAN" '41
"CLIFTON TAYLOR KOMMER" '42
"SCOTLAND KOR FAST" '46
"CLIFTON TAYLOR'S KUPP" '46
"C.T. OCH PIRATEN" '47
BROWNE, REGINALD--[1]
CLIFFORD, MARTIN--[1]HP
CONRAD, ROBERT W.--[1][2][22][29]
GOSFIELD, C. HEDDINGHAM--[1]
GRAY, B.--[2]
GRAY, BERKELEY--[2][3][5][22][29]MYS--
52 COLLINS NOVELS '38-69
GREAVES, NORMAN--[1]
GUNN, VICTOR--[3][5][29]MYS--
43 COLLINS NOVELS '39-65
HALSTEAD, E. SINCLAIR--[1]
HALSTEAD, S.B.--[1]
MADISON, REX--[34]MYS--
MELLIFONT "THE BLACK INQUISITOR" '43
RICHARDS, FRANK--[1]HP
ROSS, CARLTON--[1][3][29]MYS--
SWAN "THE BLACK SKULL MURDERS" '42
SWAN "RACKETEERS OF THE TURF" '47
THORNTON, EDWARD--[1]

BROOKS, ERN
ORION--[8]

BROOKS, JANICE YOUNG
BROOKS, JANET--W/JEAN BROOKS-JANOWIAK,[9]ROM
CHURCHILL, JILL--[9]ROM--
BB "GRIME & PUNISHMENT" '89
CHURCHILL, JILL--[9][31]ROM--
BB "GRIME & PUNISHMENT" '89
AVON "A FAREWELL TO YARNS" '91
AVON "A QUICHE BEFORE DYING" '93
SINGER, AMANDA--[31]--
BOUREGY "OZARK LEGACY" '75
VAYLE, VALERIE--W/JEAN BROOKS-JANOWIAK,
[9][21]ROM--
"LADY OF FIRE"
"SEAFLAME"
"ORANNA"
VAYLE, VALERIE--[31]--
SIGN "SEVENTREES" '81

BROOKS, JEREMY
MEIKLE, CLIVE--[8][22]ENGLISH

BROOKS, KANDIUS
BROOKS, KANDI--[21]ROM--
"THE REAL WORLD"
SINCLAIR, BROOKE--[21][26]ROM--
"NO HIDING PLACE"

BROOKS, MARGARET ANN
BROOKS, MAGGIE--[31]

BROOKS, RAYMOND
RIVERS, GAYLE--[8]

BROOKS, TERRENCE DEAN
BROOKS, TERRENCE D.--[7]SF--NOVELS
BROOKS, TERRY--[7]SF--NOVELS

BROOKS, VIVIAN COLLIN
MILLS, OSMINGTON--[3][22]MYS--
15 NOVELS '55-70

BROOKS-DAVIES, DOUGLAS
BROOKS, DOUGLAS--[31]

BROOKS-GUNN, JEANNE
BROOKS, JEANNE--[31]

BROOKS-JANOWIAK, JEAN
ABBEY, ANN MERTON--[9][21][26]ROM--
"CATHERINE IN THE COURT OF SIX QUEENS"
BROOKS, JANET [JEAN]--W/JANICE Y. BROOKS,
[9][21]ROM
VAYLE, VALERIE--W/JANICE Y. BROOKS,
[9][21]ROM--
"LADY OF FIRE"
"SEAFLAME"
"ORIANNA"

BROOM, JOHN
BRIGGS, JOE BOB--[7]SF--
DELACORTE "JOE BOB GOES TO
THE DRIVE-IN" '87 & SEQUEL IN '90

BROOMALL, ROBERT W.
EDWARDS, HANK--[28]WEST--
HARPER "TEXAS FEUD" '91
HARPER "WAR CLOUDS" '91

BROOMHEAD, ANN [ALLEDA]
MCCUTCHEN, ANN--[7]SF,NON-FICTION--
"NESFA INDEX YO SCIENCE FICTION"

BROPHY, DONALD FRANCIS
CHRISTOPHER, KENNETH--[31]

BROPHY, JAMES JOSEPH
BROPHY, JIM--[31]

BRORS, FRANZ
EVERTZ, FRANZ--[39]GERMAN

BROSNAN, JAMES PATRICK
BROSNAN, JIM--[31][33]

BROSNAN, JOHN RAYMOND
BLACKSTONE, JAMES--W/JOHN BAXTER,
[2][7][23]SF--
GRAFTON "TORCHED" '86
CHILDER, SIMON IAN--W/LEROY KETTLE,
[2][7][23]SF--
GRAFTON "TENDRILS" '86
CHILDER, SIMON IAN--[7]SF/HOR--
GRAFTON "WORM" '87
KNIGHT, HARRY ADAM--W/LEROY KETTLE,
[2][7][23]SF--
STAR "SLIMER" '83
STAR "FUNGUS" '85
KNIGHT, HARRY ADAM--[7]SF/HOR--
STAR "CARNOSAUR" '84
BART "WORM" '88
RAYMOND, JOHN--[2][7][34]--
HAMLYN "STARSHIP" '81
FUTURA "BLIND EYE" '85
FUTURA "BOGEYMAN" '86
FUTURA "JERICHO SCAM" '86
FUTURA "LUCKY STREAK" '86
JAVELIN "THIN ICE" '87

BROSSARD, CHANDLER
HARPER, DANIEL--[3][31]MYS--
AVON "THE WRONG TURN" '54

BROUDE, CRAIG HOWARD
HEPBURNE, MELISSA--[21][26]ROM--4 NOVELS
LENORE, LISA--[21][26]ROM--
"DANCE OF DESIRE"
"LOVE'S HOUR OF DANGER"

BROUGHTON, F. LUSK
STAFFORD, JOHN K.--[34]MYS, HP--
MAGNET #453 "CHEATING JUSTICE" '06
MAGNET #437 "KING AMONG CROOKS" '06
STARK, INSPECTOR--[34]HP--
NEW MAGNET #426 "WESTERN FERRET; OR, THE MYSTERIOUS O.E.L." '06

BROUILLARD, ANDRE
NORD, PIERRE--[40]MYS--
"QUI EST LE POLICIER" '57
"PROCES D'ESPIONNAGE" '61 & 2 OTHERS

BROUN, HEYWOOD OREN
BROUN, HOB--[31]

BROUSE, BARBARA
SCOTT, ARABY--[9][21][26]ROM--
"HEART OF THE FLAME"
"WILD SWEET WITCH"
TAYLOR, ABRA--[9][21][26]ROM--13 NOVELS

BROWER, CHARLES HENDRIC.
BROWER, CHARLIE--[31]

BROWIN, FRANCES WILLIAMS
WILLIAMS, FRANCIS B.--[22][33]AMERICAN

BROWN, A.L.
SMITH, DANA WARREN--[21]ROM--"HIGH STAKES"

BROWN, ALICE
REDFIELD, MARTIN--[22]AMERICAN

BROWN, ANTONY
FORREST, ANTONY--W/NORMAN I. MacKENZIE, [34]MYS--
LONG "SLAY ME SUDDENLY" '68

BROWN, CAROLYN S.
BROWN, CARRIE--[31]

BROWN, CROSSLAND
GRAY, A.W.--HAWK/SHUTTE INTERVIEW MAY '93

BROWN, DANIEL A.
CURZON, DANIEL--V. BERCH LTR TO HUBIN FEB '94, MYS--
IGNA "FROM VIOLENT MEN" '83

BROWN, E.
CAVENDISH--[8]

BROWN, EDWIN SCOTT
SIMEON, SCOTT--[14]--
OLYM OPH#191 "DING DONG BELL, PUSSY'S IN THE WELL" '70
OLYM OPH#263 "ROUTE OF ENTRY" '71

BROWN, ELIJAH
RALEIGH, ALAN--[3]MYS--
LONG "THE MAN IN THE CAR" '13

BROWN, FORNAN
MEEKER, RICHARD--[33]

BROWN, FORREST
BOWNE, FORD--L. ROBBINS LTR MAR '94,[31]
BROWN, RAE--[31]

BROWN, FREDRIC [WILLIAM]
GRAHAM, FELIX--[1][2][11]

BROWN, GAYLE ROGERS
ROGERS, GAYLE--[21]ROM--
"NAKOA'S WOMAN"

BROWN, GEORGE DOUGLAS
DOUGLAS, GEORGE--[8]

BROWN, GERALD J.
CORDEL, PAUL M.--[2]

BROWN, HARRY PETER M.
GREENGROIN, ARTIE--[31]

BROWN, HORACE
ALLEN, LESLIE--[1][3][29]MYS--
FIVE STAR "MURDER IN THE ROUGH" '46

BROWN, IVOR
I.B.--[8]

BROWN, JAMES D.
RYMAN, RAS--[7][23]SF--
HALE" DAY OF THE ULTRAMIND" '77
HALE "QUADRANT WAR" '76
HALE "WEAVERS OF DEATH" '81

BROWN, JOHN
BROWNING, JOHN--[8][34]MYS--
4 HALE NOVELS '70-4

BROWN JOHN, ALAN
BARRINGTON, JOHN--[8][31][33]

BROWN, JOHN J.
SHERASHEVSKI, BORIS--[8][22]CANADIAN

BROWN, JOHN MACMILLAN
SWEVEN, GODFREY--[2][23]SF--
"ARCHIPELAGO OF EXILES" '01
"LIMANORA: ISLAND OF PROGRESS" '03

BROWN, JOHN RIDLEY
CASTLE, DOUGLAS--[8]

BROWN, KAY
BACK-BACK--[8]

BROWN, L. ROWLAND
GREY, ROWLAND--[8]

BROWN, LAURENCE KRASNY
MERINGOFF, LAURENE KRASNY--[1][33]

BROWN, LAURENCE OLIVER
OLIVER, L.--[8][32]MYS--
AHMM "THE GLUTTON" NOV '66
OLIVER, LAURENCE--[8]

BROWN, LAWRENCE JR.
BROWN, LARRY--[31]

BROWN, LEON CARL
BROWN, L. CARL--[31]

BROWN, LISA G.
SMITH, DANA WARREN--[26]ROM--
"HIGH STAKES"

BROWN, LOIS ANN
DABNEY, ANN--W/NANCY JACKSON,[21][26]ROM--
"A LIFE TIME TO LOVE"
ELIOT, JESSICA--W/BARBARA LEVY,[3][9][21][26]--
DELL "HOME TO THE HIGHLANDS" '80 & 2 OTHERS

BROWN, MARGARET ELIZABETH
BROWN, MAREL--[8]

BROWN, MARGARET WISE
HAY, TIMOTHY--[31][33]
MACDONALD, GOLDEN--[33]
SAGE, JUNIPER--W/EDITH T. HURD,[22][31]--
"MAN IN THE MAN-HOLE & FIX-IT MEN" '46

BROWN, MAY
BLAKE, VANESSA--[3][21][26][31]MYS/ROM--
7 HALE NOVELS '70-74
BROWN, MANDY--[1][9][31]ROM
BROWN, MARY--[9]ROM--
"PLAYING THE JACK"

BROWN, MELISSA MATHER
MATHER, MELISSA--[34]MYS/SF--
BAL "EMELIE" '82
WATTS "DAMIAN" '86

BROWN, MORNA DORIS M.
FERRARS, E.X.--EQMM JAN 85,[5][9][18][32]--
U.S. PSEUD FOR MYS NOVELS & SS
FERRARS, ELIZABETH [X]--[3][5][9][18][31][32]
MYS--60 NOVELS '40-80 & DIGEST SS
MACTAGGART, MORNA--[18]MYS--
"TURN SIMPLE" '32
"BROKEN MUSIC" '34

BROWN, MORRIS CECIL
GOSLOVICH, MARIANNE--[31]

BROWN, PAULA
GLICK, PAULA BROWN--[31]

BROWN, REBECCA BARD
ORE, REBECCA--[7][23]--
TOR "TOM RED CLAY" #1-3 '88
TOR "ILLEGAL REBIRTH OF BILLY THE KID" '91
TOR "BECOMING ALIEN" '88
TOR "BEING ALIEN" '89
TOR "HUMAN" '90

BROWN, ROBERT CARLTON
BROWN, BOB--[31]

BROWN, ROBERT JOSEPH
BROWN, BOB--[31][33]

BROWN, ROBERT MCAFEE
ST. HERETICUS--[8]

BROWN, ROSALIE G.M.
MOORE, ROSALIE--[8][22][33]AMERICAN

BROWN, SANDRA [LYNN COX]
JORDAN, LAURA--BROWN INTRVW-DMN,
[9][17][21][26][34]--
"HIDDEN FIRES" '82
"THE SILKEN WEB"
POPLB "SLOW HEAT IN HEAVEN" '88
WARNER "BEST KEPT SECRETS" '89
RYAN, RACHEL--BROWN INTRVW-DMN,
[9][17][21][26]ROM--
"LOVE'S ENCORE" '81
"LOVE BEYOND REASON"
"ELOQUENT SILENCE"
"PRIME TIME"
"TREASURE WORTH SEEKING"
ST. CLAIRE, ERIN--BROWN INTRVW-DMN,
[9][17][21][26]ROM--14 NOVELS

BROWN, SEVELLON III
BROWN, JEFF--[31]

BROWN, SUSAN C.
ASHLEY, SUZANNE--[9][21][26]ROM--
"BITTERSWEET BETRAYAL"

BROWN, THOMAS H. JR.
BROWN, TOM--[31]

BROWN, TINA
BOOT, ROSIE--[8]

BROWN, VIRGINIA SHARPE
BROWN, GINNY--[31]

BROWN, W. P.
CARTER, NICHOLAS--[3]MYS--HP

BROWN, WENZELL
TOLMAN, GUY--LACHMAN LST,[32]MYS--
SA "THE SCAR" APR '64
SA "PURPLE JACKET" OCT '64

BROWN, WILLIAM F.
WARREN, CHRISTOPHER--V. BERCH LTR TO
HUBIN '94,[1]--
BEAUFORD "ALLAH CONSPIRACY" '81

BROWN, WILLIAM L.
BROWN, BILL--[31][33]

BROWN, WILLIAM [JAMES] C.
BROWN, JAMIESON--[1]

BROWN, ZENITH [JONES]
CONRAD, BRENDA--[3][5][8][18][31]MYS--
3 NOVELS '41-44
FORD, LESLIE--[2][3][5][11][18][29][31]MYS--
44 NOVELS '31-62
FROME, DAVID--[2][3][5][18][32]MYS--
15 NVLS '29-50
EB "MAN ON THE IRON PALINGS" DEC '53

BROWNE, CHARLES FARRAR
WARD, ARTEMUS--[1]

BROWNE, GEORGE WALDO
CARTER, NICHOLAS--[3]MYS, HP

BROWNE, HABLOT KNIGHT
PHIZ--[33]

BROWNE, HARRY T.
JOHN O' THE NORTH--[8]

BROWNE, HENRY
BROWNE, HARRY--[31]

BROWNE, HOWARD
BLADE, ALEXANDER--[1][2][11][23]HP--
ZIFF-DAVIS
BRENGLE, WILLIAM--[1][2][11]HP--
FANTASTIC ADV
CARLETON, H[UGH] B.--[1][2][11]
CHANDLER, LAWRENCE--[2][11]HP--ZIFF-DAVIS
EVANS, JOHN--MUNROE SLS LST 23,
S. HOLLAND-SCION CKLST,
PP 27,[2][5][18][23][32][37]--
BOBBS "HALO FOR SATAN" '48
MH "SO DARK FOR APRIL" FEB '53
MD "MURDER WEARS A HALO"
MD "HALO 'ROUND MY DEAD"
MD "HALO IN BLOOD"
FRANCIS, LEE--[2][11][23]HP--
FANTASTIC ADV/AMAZING
HUGGINS, ROY--[2]GHOSTED
JORGENSEN, IVAR--JEAN F. LE DEIST,
BAE 12,[2][11][23]HP--ZIFF-DAVIS

BROWNE, HOWARD [CONT]
MCGREEVEY, JOHN [W]--[11][32]HP--
DIGEST STORIES - HU, MV & PU
PHILLIPS, PETER--[1][11][32]MYS--
SU "SHE DIDN'T BOUNCE" SPR '51
POLLARD, JOHN X.--[1][11]HP--ZIFF-DAVIS
SPILLANE, MICKEY--[2]GHOSTED - ONE ITEM

BROWNE, NICHOLAS
CARTER, NICK--[3]MYS, HP--
"OPERATION STARVATION" '66
"BRIGHT BLUE DEATH" '67
"SEVEN AGAINST GREECE" '67
"THE CHINESE PAYMASTER" '67

BROWNE, NOEL
REID, DESMOND--W/G.P. MANN,[34]HP--
AMALG "SHOWDOWN IN SYDNEY" '59
REID, DESMOND--[1][34]MYS, HP--
AMALG "CONTRACT FOR A KILLER" '60

BROWNE, RICHARD ARTHUR A.
BROWNE, DIK--[31]

BROWNE, THOMAS A.
BOLDREWOOD, ROLF--[2][22][36]AUSTRALIAN--
REMINGTON "ROBBERY UNDER ARMS" 1888
MacM "IN BAD COMPANY & OTHERS" '01

BROWNING, ALICE C[ROLLEY]
BENTLEY, RICHARD--[31]

BROWNING, DAPHNE DU MAUR.
DU MAURIER, DAPHNE--[7]SF/HOR--
"THE LOVING SPIRIT" '31 & OTHERS

BROWNING, DIXIE [S.B.]
DOZIER, ZOE--W/MARY WILLIAMS,[17][21][31]--
"HOME AGAIN MY LOVE"
"WARM SIDE OF THE ISLAND"
WILLIAMS, BRONWYN--W/MARY WILLIAMS,
[7][17][21]SF/ROM--
HARL "WHITE WITCH" '88

BROWNING, GEORGE HENRY
BROWNING, GARETH H.--[1][3]MYS--
HUTCH "THE BLACK INK MYS" '27

BROWNING, LEE & ARTHUR
ARTHUR, LEE--[9][21]ROM--
"THE MER-LION"

BROWNING, PAMELA
KETTER, PAM--[9][21]ROM--
"WISH FOR TOMORROW"
"STARDUST SUMMER"
"ONE ON ONE"
ROWE, MELANIE--[9][21]ROM--
"SANDS OF XANADU"
"SEA OF GOLD"

BROWNING, WILLIAM
BROWNING, COLUMBAN--[31]--
"WOMAN'S HIGHEST FULFILLMENT" '65
"GOD REALLY LOVES US" '79

BROWNING, [Z] SINCLAIR
CARPENTER, WILLOW--[1][31]

BROWNLEE, FRANCES
DICKINSON, FRANKIE--[8]

BROWNLEY, MARGARET
DAMON, KATE--[9][21][26]ROM--
"BITTER FRUIT"
"NAPA"

BROWNLIE, NOREEN
WHITNEY, JAMISAN--[9][21][26]ROM--4 NOVELS

BROXHOLME, JOHN FRANKLIN
BROXHOLME, J.F.--[18]MYS--
FREWIN "THE WAR QUEEN" '67
KYLE, DUNCAN--[3][18][29][31]MYS/THRIL--
COLLINS "A CAGE OF ICE" '70
COLLINS " A RAFT OF SWORDS" '74 & MORE
MELDRUM, JAMES--[18][29][34]MYS--
WEIDENFELD & NICOLSON "SEMONOV IMPULSE" '75

BROXON, MILDRED DOWNEY
SKALDASPILLIR, SIGFRIOUR--[7][8]SF

BROZA-TALKE, HELGA
TALKE, HELGA--[39]GERMAN/JUV

BRUCE, JOANNA H. CAMPBELL
SIMON, JO ANN--[7][9]ROM/SF--
AVON "BELOVED CAPTAIN" '88
AVON "HOLD FAST TO LOVE"
AVON "SOJORN"
CAMPBELL, JOANNA--[21]
"THE THOROUGHBRED"
"SECRET IDENTITY"
"LOVE NOTES"

BRUCE, KENNETH
CRAYON, DIEDRICK, JR.--[2]

BRUCE-NOVOA, JUAN D.
BRUCE-NOVOA--[31]
BRUCE-NOVOA, JOHN DAVID--[31]

BRUCE-THOMAS, CAROL
VINCER, RACHEL--W/DEBRA MCCARTHY-ANDERSON,
[26]ROM--
"HOT COPY"
"PRIM AND IMPROPER"

BRUCK, LORRAINE
BRIDGES, LAURIE--[1][31][33]

BRUCKER, MEREDITH
KINGSTON, MEREDITH--[9][21][26]ROM--
5 NOVELS

BRUCKER, MEREDITH B.
LINDLEY, MEREDITH--[9][21][26]ROM--
"AGAINST THE WIND"

BRUCKNER, ELEONORE
RONECK, ELEONORE--[39]GERMAN
VON BERNFELD, ELEONORE--[39]GERMAN

BRUCKNER, MARIE
BRANDT, EVA--[39]GERMAN/JUV
LACOMBE, MARIE--[39]GERMAN/JUV

BRUDER, HERTA
ANTHES, NATAKIE--[39]GERMAN

BRUECKEL, FRANCIS J.
BRIDGE, FRANK J.--[2][11]

BRUEGEL, JOHANN WOLFGANG
BRUEGEL JOHN WOLFGANG--[31]

BRUGGEN, CAROL HOLMES
BRIDGES, EMILY--[31]

BRUGGER, WILLIAM
BRUGGER, BILL--[31]

BRUGMANN, KARL
HEINRICH, CARL JOHANN--[39]GERMAN

BRUGMANN-EBERHARDT, LOTTE
DROSTE, LOTTE--[39]GERMAN/JUV
EBERHARDT, LOTTE--[39]GERMAN/JUV

BRUHL, GUSTAV
KARA, GIORG--[22]GERMAN-AMERICAN

BRULLER, JEAN MARCEL
VERCORS--[2][3][7][11][23]FRENCH/SF/MYS--
LITTLE "YOU SHALL KNOW THEM" '53
VERCORS, J. BRULLER--[1]

BRUN, MARCEL
VILLAIN, JEAN--[39]GERMAN

BRUNCLAIR, VICTOR J.
BARDEMEYER, GEERT--[22]DUTCH
FIKKENS, J.--[22]DUTCH
LIRIO--[22]DUTCH

BRUNDAGE, JOHN HERBERT
HERBERT, JOHN--[8][31]

BRUNDLE, JOHN
JOHN, A SUFFOLK HERD BOY--[8]

BRUNER, BUREEDA
MEREDITH, ANNE--AUTHOR PROVIDED,HIST/ROM--
"LOVES TIMELESS HOPE" '94

BRUNNER, JOHN [K.H.]
BRUNNER, K. HOUSTON--[11]
CROSSTREES, HENRY, JR.--[2]ENGLISH
HOUSTON, KILIAN--[11][23]ENGLISH/SF--
"THE WANTON OF ARGUS" '63
HUNT, GILL--[2][4][7][11][23]ENGLISH/HP--
CURTIS "GALACTIC STORM" '51
LOXSMITH, JOHN--[2][11][23][31]ENGLISH/SF
SHELDON, ROY--[1]ENGLISH/HP
STAINES, TREVOR--[2][23][31]ENGLISH--
ONE STORY IN '55
WOODCOTT, KEITH--[2][4][7][23][31]SF--
ACE "I SPEAK FOR EARTH" '61
ACE "LADDER IN THE SKY" '62
ACE "PSIONIC MENACE" '63
ACE "THE MARTIAN SPHINX" '65

BRUNNER, MAURICE YAW
BOATENG, YAW MAURICE--[31]

BRUNS, FRANK
BROWN, FRANCIS--[39]GERMAN/HOR

BRUSTAT-NAVAL, FRITZ
NAVAL, FREDERIK--[39]GERMAN/JUV
TAR, JACK--[39]GERMAN/JUV

BRUSTLEIN, DANIEL
ALAIN--[8][31][33]

BRUSTLEIN, JANICE T.
JANICE--[8][31][33]

BRUSTOWIECKI, MOTEK
BRUSTO, MAX--[39]GERMAN

BRUTUS, DENNIS
BRUIN, JOHN--[8][31][33]--
"THOUGHTS ABROAD" '70

BRYANS, ROBERT HARBINSON
BRYANS, ROBIN--[22][31]IRISH
CAMERON, DONALD--[31]

BRYANS, ROBERT HARBINSON [CONT]
HARBINSON, ROBERT--[22][31]IRISH

BRYANT, BAIRD
BARON, WILLIE--[8][14]--OLYMPIA PRESS

BRYANT, DENNY
DRAKE, WINIFRED--[8]

BRYANT, EDWARD W.
TALBOT, LAWRENCE--[2][23]

BRYANT, KATHERINE CLIFTON
CLIFTON, KATHERINE POTTER--[31]

BRYANT, KATHLEEN
BRADLEY, KATE--[21]ROM--
"ANCIENT SECRET"
"SHEEP'S CLOTHING"

BRYANT, PAUL
BENTON, TAD--R.C. & ELWANDA HOLLAND
RVW JAN '93, BANNER 103

BRYANT, PAUL WILLIAM
BRYANT, BEAR--[31]

BRYANT, THOMAS ALTON
ALTON, THOMAS--[31]
BRYANT, AL--[31]

BRYDEN, WILLIAM CAMPBELL
BRYDEN, BILL--[31]

BRYER, JUDITH E.
BRYER, JUDY--[21]ROM
DRUMMOND, BRENNA--[9][21][26]ROM--
"PROUD VINTAGE"
LAWRENCE, ALLISON--[9][21][26]ROM--
"HIGHLAND LOVER"
O'BRIAN, EVE--W/ARNIE HELLER,[9][21]ROM--
"MYSTERY AT MIDNIGHT"

BRYL, IVAN A
BRYL, IANKA--[1]

BRYNING, FRANK
CORNISH, F.--[2]

BRYNNER, WITTER
MORGAN, EMANUEL--W/ARTHUR DAVIDSON FICKE,
[22]AMERICAN
MORGAN, EMANUEL--[31]

BRYSON, CHARLES
BARRY, CHARLES--[3][22]MYS--
23 NOVELS '25-51

BRYSON, DEBORAH
BRYAN, DEBORAH--[9][21][26]ROM--
"DEATHTRAP"
JOYCE, DEBORAH--W/JOYCE PORTER,
[9][10][[21][26]ROM--6 NOVELS

BRZOZOWSKI, LEOPOLD S.L.
CZEPIEL, ADAM--[22]POLISH

BR^CKENBERG, HANS
ELSTER, TOROLF--[29]MYS--
"HISTORIEN OM GOTTLOB" '41
"PROVOKATOR, FBI" '57

BUBECK, HEINRICH
BUMPERLI, LUX--[39]GERMAN

BUBER, PAULA [W]
MUNK, GEORG--[39]GERMAN

BUBNER, RUEDIGER
BUBNER, RUDIGER--[31]

BUCHAN, ANNA
DOUGLAS, O.--[8]

BUCHAN, JOHN
CADMUS & HARMONIA--W/SUSAN BUCHAN, [1][31]MYS--
HODDER "ISLAND OF SHEEP" '19
TWEEDSMUIR, BARON--[1][7]SF

BUCHAN, SUSAN
CADMUS & HARMONIA--W/JOHN BUCHAN,[1][31]MYS--
HODDER "ISLAND OF SHEEP" '19

BUCHAN, THOMAS BUCHANAN
BUCHAN, TOM--[31]

BUCHAN, [JOHN] STUART
ERSKINE, DOUGLAS--[7]SF
FOXE, JASON--[34]MYS--
WORLDWIDE "THE HAMPTON CLASSIC" '87
FOXE, PAMELA--[9][21][26]ROM--
"YOUR CHEATING HEART"
STUART, BECKY--[9][21]ROM--10 NOVELS

BUCHANAN, BETTY JOAN
SHEPHERD, JOAN--[3][22]MYS--
WSB "GIRL ON THE LEFT BANK" '53
WSB "TENDER IS THE NIGHT" '56

BUCHANAN, EILEEN-MARIE D.
BUCHANAN, MARIE--[18]MYS--
5 NOVELS
CURZON, CLAIRE--[3][31]MYS--
COLLINS "A LEAVEN OF MALICE" '79
COLLINS "SPECIAL OCCASION" '81
COLLINS "I GIVE YOU FIVE DAYS" '83
COLLINS "MASKS & FACES" '84
COLLINS "TROJAN HEARSE" '85
PETRIE, RHONA--[32][34]MYS--
9 GOLZ '64-70
EQMM "WHAT WE'RE ALL HOOKED ON" SEPT '68
EQMM "SUCH A LONG TIME AFTER" DEC '68
EQMM "PART OF THAT COLD EYE" JUL '69
EQMM "PEOPLE DEEP DYING ROUND HERE" MAR '69
SHORT STORY COLL. "COME HELL & HIGH WATER" '70

BUCHANAN, JAMES DAVID
BEYLE, HANK--[31]

BUCHANAN, JESSIE HORSTING
BUCHANAN, JESSICA--[7]SF
HORSTING, JESSIE--[7]SF--
STARLOG PRESS "STEPHEN KING AT THE MOVIES" '86

BUCHANAN, LAURA
KING, FLORENCE--[9]ROM

BUCHEISTER, PATT
PARRISH, PATT--[9][21][26]ROM--
5 NOVELS '80s

BUCHINSKAYA, NADEZHDA AL.
TEFFY--[22]RUSSIAN

BUCK, JAMES SMITH
PROPHET JAMES, THE--[2]

BUCK, PEARL [S]
SEDGES, JOHN--[1][22]AMERICAN

BUCK, WILLIAM RAY
BUCHANAN, WILLIAM--W/RUSSELL THORNDIKE, [22]AMERICAN
BUCHANAN, WILLIAM--[8]

BUCKAWAY, CATHERINE M.
BUCKAWAY, C.M.--[31]

BUCKBY, SAMUEL
BLAIR, FRANK--[8]

BUCKETTE, HILDAGARDE
ROSTOV, MARA--V. BERCH LTR TO HUBIN '94,MYS--
PUTNAM "EROICA" '77
PUTNAM "NIGHT HUNT" '79
PUTNAM "A CARELESS FEAST" '85

BUCKHOLDER, MARTA
LLOYD, MARTA--[8][21][26]ROM--
"THE LION'S SHADOWS"
"THE WINDS OF LOVE"

BUCKHOLTZ, EILEEN [G]
CHASE, SAMANTHA--W/RUTH GLICK,[9][33][34]ROM--
TUDOR "POSTMARK" '88
TUDOR "NEEDLEPOINT" '89
HOWARD, ALYSSA--W/RUTH GLICK, LOUISE TITCHENER & CAROLYN MALES,[9][21]--
"SOUTHERN PERSUASION"
LEE, AMANDA--W/RUTH GLICK & NANCY BAGGETT, [9][21][26]ROM--7 NOVELS
YORK, REBECCA--W/RUTH GLICK--[7][9][21][26] ROM/SF--12 NOVELS

BUCKINGHAM, JAMES WILLIAM
BUCKINGHAM, JAMIE--[31]

BUCKLAND, CAROL E.
BUCK, CAROL--[9][21]ROM--18 NOVELS

BUCKLAND, RAYMOND
EARLL, TONY--[1][31]
ROBAT--[1]
WELLS, JESSICA--[1]

BUCKLAND-WRIGHT, MARY
HUME, FRANCES--[8][32]MYS--
LM "BLUEBEARD'S DOLLS" FEB '52

BUCKLES, ELEANOR
YATES, ROSCOE--V. BERCH--BRNDN/BC PSEUDS, BAE 22, P24

BUCKLEY NEVILLE, HEATHER
BUCKLEY, DORIS HEATHER--[31]

BUCKLEY, FERGUS REID
CRUMPET, PETER--[8]

BUCKLEY, KATHLEEN
MAJOR, H.M.--W/SHARON JARVIS,[3][23]MYS/SF--
SIGN "ALIEN TRACE" '84
SIGN "TIME TWISTER" '84

BUCKLEY, SAMUEL
BLAIR, FRANK--[13]AUSTRALIAN

BUCKMAN, ROBERT ALEXANDER
BUCKMAN, ROB--[31]

BUCKNER, MARY DALE
DALE, DONALD--[2][11][37]MYS--
RED CIRCLE MAGS - PULP STORIES

BUDAY, GYORGY
BUDAY, GEORGE--[31]

BUDD, JOHN
PRESCOTT, JULIAN--[3]MYS--
9 NOVELS '58-66

BUDD, MAVIS
DENHAM, SALLY--[31]
WILDING, ANN--[1]

BUDD, WILLIAM JOHN
BUDD, JACKSON--[2][3][22]MYS--
JOSEPH "DARK HORSEMAN" 39
LOW "GOLD EXPRESS"47 & MORE
JACKSON, WALLACE--[3][22]MYS--
LOW "ZADDA STREET AFFAIR" '34
LOW "DIAMONDS OF DEATH" '36 & 2 MORE

BUDDEE, PAUL
RICHARDS, PAUL--[8][11]SF

BUDGETT, FRANCES ELIZAB.
DEJEANS, ELIZABETH--[34]MYS/ROM--
DBLDY "DOUBLE HOUSE" '24 & 3 MORE '17-24

BUDLONG, WARE TORREY
CROSBY, LEE--[21]ROM--
"BRIDGE HOUSE"
"DOORS TO DEATH"
HALE, JENNIFER--W/FRANK SMITH,[21]ROM--
7 NOVELS
WARE, JUDITH--[21]ROM--5 NOVELS
WINSLOW, JOAN--[21]ROM--
"GRIFFIN TOWERS"
"ROMANCE IS A RIOT"

BUDRYS, ALGIRDAS JONAS
ARGO, SAM & JANET--[2]LITHUANIAN-AMERICAN
BUDRYS, ALGIS--[1][23][31]SF
HODGKINS, DAVID C.--[1][2][11][23]SF
JANVIER, IVAN--[1][2][11][23]SF
JANVIER, PAUL--[1][2][11][23]SF
JAVLYN, GORDON--[2]
MARNER, ROBERT--[1][2][11][23]SF
MASON, FRANK--BRAD VERTER, BAE 10, P11,[2]
ROME, ALGER--W/JEROME L. BIXBY,[2][11][23]--
"UNDERESTIMATION" '53
SCARFF, WILLIAM--[1][2][11][23]
SENTRY, JOHN A.--[2][11][23][32]--
EW "THE NIGHT-WATCH" OCT '55
STROUD, ALBERT--[1][2][11][23]SF
VAN DALL, HAROLD--[1][2][11][23]SF

BUECHTING, LINDA
ADAMS, KELLY--[21]ROM--11 NOVELS
JAMISON, KELLY--[21]ROM--
"ECHOES FROM THE HEART"
"HEARTS IN HIDING"

BUEHLER, CURT FERDINAND
BUHLER, CURT F.--[31]

BUEHLER, EUGEN KARL
COLTER, JAK--[39]GERMAN

BUEHLMANN, WALBERT
BUHLMANN, WALBERT--[31]

BUELL, ROBERT KINGERY
BROTHER BOB--[31]

BUFORD, ELMER
FELTON, B.--[1]

BUGAYEV, BORIS N.
BELY, ANDREY--[8][22][31]
BELYI, ANDREI--[31]

BUGBEE, RUTH CARSON
CARSON, RUTH--[22][31]AMERICAN

BUGGIE, OLIVE M.
BUGY, OLY--[8]

BUHNEMANN, HERMANN
RUFER, WILFRIED--[39]GERMAN/JUV

BUITENKANT, NATHAN
MARK, DAVID--[8]

BUKSA, PAVEL
MICHAEL, KAREL--[40]GERMAN/MYS--
"DIE UHREN DES HERRN P."

BULAU, J.v.
VON BULOW, JOACHIM--[39]GERMAN

BULEY, BERNARD
MASTERS, BAT--[34]MYS--
ALDINE "MONEY FOR NOTHING" '23
ALDINE "A DEAD MAN'S DERBY" '23
ALDINE "AN ASCOT MYS" '23
ALDINE "STOLEN JOCKEY" '27
ALDINE "ANY PRICE BLACKMAIL" '27
ALDINE "CALCUTTA SWEEP MYS" '28
ALDINE "SWEEP SWINDLERS" '29

BULEY, BERNARD
MCRAE, ROY--[34]MYS--
POPULAR "DEATH AT THE THEATRE" '47
GRAYLING "BLACK CAT MURDER" '49

BULGYA, ALEXANDER A.
FADEYEV, A.--[31]
FADEYEV, ALEXANDER--[31]

BULK, NANCY HARWOOD
HOLMES, DEE--[21]ROM--
"BLACK HORSE ISLAND"
"RETURN OF SLADE GARNER"

BULL, BRUNO HORST
BARRY, ROLAND--[39]GERMAN/JUV

BULL, KATHERINE T.J.
THOMAS, KATE--[34]MYS--
DOXIE "AILA" 1896

BULL, LOIS
BURT, MELLVILLE--[3][22][29]MYS--
MCL "YELLOW ROBE MURDERS" '35
MCL "GLANVILLE CRYPT MURDERS" '36
WRIGHT, JUDITH GROVNER--[22]MYS

BULL, OLAF
BRADA, OLOF--[29]MYS--
"HERR SAHLES HEMLIGTEN" '14
"MIT NAVN ER KNOPH" '14
BREDA, OLAF--[29]MYS--
"HERR SALES HEMLIGHET" '14

BULL, REINA M.
R.M.B.--BAPC NWSLTR #9--
ENGLISH COVER ARTIST PULPS

BULLARD, ANN ELIZABETH
STUART, CASEY--[9][21][26]--
ZEBRA 1716 "PASSION'S FLAME" '85
ZEBRA 2115 "VELVET DECEPTION" '87
ZEBRA 2348 "BELOVED PIRATE" '88

BULLARD, ANN ELIZABETH [CONT]
STUART, CASEY [CONT]
ZEBRA 2573 "PASSION'S PRISONER" '89
& 5 OTHERS

BULLARD, ARTHUR
EDWARDS, ALBERT--[8][22]AMERICAN

BULLEID, HENRY A.V.
COLLINS, D.--[8][22][31]ENGLISH

BULLETT, GERALD WILLIAM
FOX, SEBASTIAN--[3][22][29]MYS--
CHATTO "ONE MAN'S POISON" '56
DENT "ODD WOMAN OUT" '58

BULLIET, RICHARD WILLIAMS
JACKSON, CLARENCE J.L.--[3]MYS--
HARPER "KICKED TO DEATH BY A CAMEL" '73

BULLINGER, MAUREEN
QUINN, SAMANTHA--[9][21][26]ROM--4 NOVELS

BULLINS, ED
BASS, KINGSLEY B. JR.--[31]

BULLIVANT, CECIL H[ENRY]
EVERARD, MAURICE--[34]MYS--
4 AMALG & OTHER BOY'S NOVELS '15-24
GREY, CARLTON--[34]MYS--
GIRL'S FRIEND "THE BIG STRAW HAT" '15
MILLARD, ALICE--[34]MYS--
GIRL'S FRIEND "MABELLE RIVERS,
GIRL DETECTIVE" '15

BULLMORE, JEREMY
BLAKE, JUSTIN--W/JOHN BOWEN,[8]

BULLOCK, MICHAEL HALE
HALE, MICHAEL--[8][22][31]ENGLISH--
FAVIL "TRANSMUTATIONS" '38

BULLOCK-WILSON, BARBARA
BULLOCK, BARBARA--[31]

BULMER, [HENRY] KENNETH
AKERS, ALAN BURT--[2][4][7][11][23]SF
BLAKE, KEN--[2][3][4][11]--
"PROFESSIONAL" TV SERIES - 6 BOOKS
BRANDON, FRANK--[2][11][23][31]
BULMER, H.K.--[7]SF
CLINTON, RUPERT--[1][2][11][31]
CORLEY, ERNEST--[2][4][23][31]SF/NON-FICT
FRAZIER, ARTHUR--[1][2][4][23]SF/HP
GREEN, PETER--[1][2][31]
HARDY, ADAM--[2][4][23]HP--
HORNBLOWER-LIKE SEA ADVENTURES
JOHNS, KENNETH--W/JOHN NEWMAN,[23][31]--
ARTICLES FOR NW & NEBULA
KENT, PHILIP--P. HARBOTTLE, TID-BITS CKLST,
PP#38,[7][23][33]--
TB "VASSALS OF VENUS" '54
TB "MISSION TO THE STARS" '54
TB "HOME IS THE MARTIAN" '54
TB "SLAVES OF THE SPECTRUM" '54
KRAUSS, BRUNO--[2][23][31]SF/NON-FICT
LANGHOLM, NEIL--[2][4][23][31]SF/NON-FICT
MARAS, KARL--PPCC#7,[2][4][7]SF, HP--
COMYNS "PERIL FROM SPACE"
COMYNS "ZHORANI: MASTER OF THE UNIVERSE"
NORVIL, MANNING--[2][4][7][23]SF--
3 DAW NOVELS '77-80
PIKE, CHARLES R.--[2][4][11]SF,SHARED PSEUD--
NON-FICT
PRESCOTT, DRAY--IPCS 6, PSEUD. LST,
[2][7][11][23]SF

BULMER, [HENRY] KENNETH [CONT]
QUILLER, ANDREW--[2][4][11][23]SF, HP
SCOT, CHESMAN--[1][2][11]
SHERWOOD, NELSON--[1][2][11]
SILVER, RICHARD--[1][2][4][11][23]SF, HP--
NON-FICT
STRATFORD, PHILIP--[1][2][11]
STURGEON, KENNETH--[2]
ZETFORD, TULLY--[2][4][7][11][23]SF--
'HOOK' SERIES

BULMER-THOMAS, IVOR
THOPMAS, IVOR--[8]

BULTMANN KLAUS
HANSEN, K.U.--W/WOLFGANG KEHL,[39]GERMAN/SF

BULWER-LYTTON, EDWARD G.
BULWER-LYTTON, BARON--[33]
BULWER-LYTTON, E.--[32]MYS--
WR "THE HOUSE & THE BRAIN" WINT '69-70
LYTTON, LORD--[11]SF

BUMPPO, NATHANIEL JOHN B.
BUMPPO, NATTY--[31]
DEAN, JOHN--[31]

BUMPUS, DORIS MARJORIE
ALAN, MARJORIE--[3][22]MYS--
10 NOVELS '45-56

BUMSTEAD, KATHLEEN MARY
MORGAN, ELLEN--[33]

BUNCE, LINDA SUSAN S.
LAUREN, LINDA--[31]

BUNCE, OLIVER BELL
CENSOR--[8]

BUNCH, CHARLOTTE ANNE
BUNCH-WEEKS, CHARLOTTE--[31]

BUNCH, DAVID R.
GROUPE, DARRYL R.--[2][11][31]

BUNDEY, ELLEN MILNE
DUNNE, LYELL--[8]

BUNDGEN, FRANZ-RUDOLF
CYBORG, THOMAS--[39]GERMAN/SF

BUNTE, ANNEMARIE
WIETIG, ANNEMARIE--[39]GERMAN/JUV

BUNTING, ANNE EVELYN
BOLTON, EVELYN--[31][33]
BUNTING, A.E.--[31]
BUNTING, EVE--[31][33]

BUNTING, D.G.
GEORGE, DANIEL--[8][11]

BUNYO, NOZAKI
ROBIN, KANAGAKI--[22]JAPANESE

BURACK, SYLVIA K.
KAMERMAN, SYLVIA E.--[31][33]

BURAK, LINDA [GALLINA]
MEADOWS, ALICIA--W/JOAN ZEIG,[1][9][21]ROM--
"SWEET BRAVADO"
"TENDER TORMENT"

BURANELLI, PROSPER
PROSPER, JOHN--W/JOHN C. FARRAR,[3]MYS--
DORAN "GOLD-KILLER" '22

BURBRIDGE, EDITH JOAN
COCKIN, JOAN--[1][34]MYS--
HODDER "CURIOSITY KILLED THE CAT" '47
HODDER "VILLIAINY AT VESPERS" '49
HODDER "DEADLY EARNEST" '52

BURCH, MONTE G.
GREGORY, MARK--[31]

BURCHARD, MARSHALL
BURCHARD, M.--[31]

BURCHARD, SUE
BURCHARD, S.H.--[31]

BURCHARD, WILLIAM ROBERT
BURCHARD, BILL--[28][31]WEST--
9 NOVELS '63-81

BURCHARDT, JULIUS
BARDT, JULIUS--[39]GERMAN

BURDEKIN, KATHERINE
BURDEKIN, KAY--[2][7][23]SF
CONSTANTINE, MURRAY--[2][7][23]SF--
BW "PROUD MAN" '34
BW "DEVIL, POOR DEVIL!" '34
GOLZ "SWASTIKA NIGHT" '37

BURDELEV, ALEKSEI S.
RUSETSKIE, ALEXSEI S.--[1]

BURDEN, JEAN
AMES, FELICIA--[31]

BURESCH, WOLFGANG
ORLOFF, WOLF--[39]GERMAN/JUV

BURFORD, ROGER D'ESTE
EAST, ROGER--[8][22][34]ENGLISH/MYS--
9 COLLINS NOVELS '34-63
SIMON--W/OSWELL BLAKESTON,
[3][8][22][29]ENGLISH/MYS--
3 WISHART NVLS '33-5

BURG, DAVID
DOLBERG, ALEXANDER--[8]

BURGDORF, KARL-ULRICH
BAUER, C.T.--[39]GERMAN/SF
CRAVEN, ROBERT--W/W.E. HOHLBEIN,[39]
GERMAN/SF, HP
DUNCAN, ARL--[39]GERMAN/SF
HOLLBURG, MARTIN--W/W.E. HOHLBEIN,[39]
GERMAN/SF, HP
MUNZER, HARALD--[39]GERMAN/SF
WEILER, ANDREAS--W/ANDREAS BRANDHORST,
[39]GERMAN/SF
WOLF, HENRY--W/W.E. HOHLBEIN,[39]GERMAN/SF, HP

BURGE, DORIS
EARLE, JEAN--[31]

BURGE, JERRY
WILBURN, LEN--W/GERALD W. PAGE,[2]

BURGE, M.R. KENNEDY
ELDER, EVELYN--[3][18]MYS--
METHUEN "MURDER IN BLACK & WHITE" '31
METHUEN "ANGEL IN THE CASE" '32

BURGE, M.R. KENNEDY [CONT]
KENNEDY, MILWARD--[3][5][18][22][32]MYS--
18 NOVELS '29-52
SA "PERFECT ACCIDENT" MAR '54
SA "YOU'VE BEEN WARNED" FEB '55
JCM "LOST AMBASSADOR" MAY '58
KENNEDY, ROBERT MILWARD--W/ARCHIBALD G.
MCDONELL,[3][18][22]MYS--
GOLZ "BLESTON MYSTERY" '29

BURGER, DIONIJS
BURGER, DIONYS--[23]SF

BURGER, JOHN ROBERT
BURGER, JACK--[31]

BURGER, PIXIE
PETRIE, JODRA--W/JULIA PERCIVALL,
V. BERCH LTR '93/[31]--
AWARD AQ1076 "BUSY WOMAN'S ALMANAC" '73

BURGER, ROSAYLMER
PAULL, JESSICA--W/JULIA PERCIVAL,[34]--
AWARD "DESTINATION TERROR" '68
AWARD "PASSPORT TO DANGER" '68
AWARD "RENDEZVOUS WITH DEATH" '69
WALLACE, C.H.--[3][29]MYS--
BELM B50-639 "CRASH LANDING IN
THE CONGO" '65
BELM B50-664 "TAIL WIND TO DANGER" '66
BELM B50-722 "HIGHFLIGHT TO HELL" '66
BELM B50-734 "ETA FOR DEATH" '66

BURGESS, CHRISTOPHER
JOHN, CHRISTOPHER--PPCC#5, P93--
"SAVAGE"

BURGESS, HELEN STEERS
STEERS, HELEN--[1][34]MYS--
DODD "DEATH WILL FIND ME" '47

BURGESS, JANE K.
BURGESS-KOHN, JANE--W/WILLARD K. KOHN,
[1][31]ADULT--
BEAC "THE WIDOWERS" '78

BURGESS, JOANNA
FIRESIDE, CAROLYN--[21]ROM--
"ANYTHING BUT LOVE"
"GOODBYE AGAIN"
"IN THE GRASP"

BURGESS, JUSTINE
HARRIS, JOANNA--[9][21][34]MYS/ROM--
AVON "WORLDLY INNOCENT" '89

BURGESS, MARY E.
BURGESS, SALLY--[8]

BURGESS, MARY WYCHE
BURGESS, EM--[31][33]

BURGESS, MICHAEL ROY
ALCALDE, MIGUEL--[1][31]
BURGESS, M.R.--W/R. REGINALD,[ALSO BURGESS]
"CUMULATIVE PB INDEX, 1939-1959:
BIBL. GUIDE,[7]
BURGESS, MICHAEL--W/JEFFREY ELLIOT,[2][7]--
"THE WORK OF R. REGINALD: AN
ANNOTATED BIBL. & GUIDE"
BURGESS, MIKE--[31]
CLARKE, BODEN--[1][2][23][31]SF
CLARKE, BODEN--W/JAMES HOPKINS,[7]--
"WORK OF WILLIAM F. NOLAN:
AN ANNOTATED BIBL. & GUIDE"

BURGESS, MICHAEL ROY [CONT]
COOPER, C. EVERETT--[7][11][23][31]SF--
BORGO "UP YOUR ASTEROID! A SCIENCE FICTION FANTASY" '77
DEMOTES, MICHAEL--[1][31]
DURAND, G. FORBES--[1][31]
GRAZHDANIN, MISHA--[1][31]
HARDING, PETER--[1][31]
KAPEL, ANDREW--[1][31]
LAWSON, JACOB--[1][31]
MAUZY, PETER--[31]
MILETUS, REX--[1][31]
MOBLEY, WALT--[1][31]
NIMBLE, JACK B.--[1][31]
PAINTER, DANIEL--[1][31]
R.R.--[31]
RALE, NERO--[1][31]
REGINALD, R.[ROBERT]--[2][7][11][23]SF, NON-FICT
REGINALD, REGINALD R.--[31]
SHARPE, LUCRETIA--[1][31]
SPARTICUS, TERTIUS--[1][31]
WEBB, LUCAS--[2][7][11][23]SF
WEBB, LUCAS--W/JEFFREY M. ELLIOT,[23]--
"THE ATTEMPTED ASSASINATION OF J.F. KENNEDY" '77

BURGESS, THORNTON W.
THORNTON, W.B.--[8][31][33]--
"COUNTRY LIFE IN AMERICA"

BURGHARDT, OSWALD
JURIJ, KLEN--[22]UKRAINIAN

BURGIN, G.B.
SMEE, WENTWORTH--[8]

BURGMAIER, ALBERT
ALTENBERGER, JAKOB--[39]GERMAN/SF

BURK, KATHLEEN
JEWESS, KATHLEEN--[31]

BURKE, JEAN
ESMOND, HARRIET--W/JOHN F. BURKE,[3][18]--
DELACORTE "DARSHAM'S FOLLY" '73
DELACORTE "EYE STONES" '75
GM "FLORIAN SIGNET" '77

BURKE, JOHN [FREDERICK]
BURKE, J.F.--[23][32]--
"SWIFT SUMMER" '49
AHMM "I'LL KILL YOU IN THE MORNING" OCT '77
BURKE, JONATHAN--[2][3][7][8][18][21][23][29]ROM/MYS--
LONG "WEEKEND GIRLS" '66 & 10 OTHERS
BURKE, OWEN--[18][21][26][31]MYS/ROM--
"THE FIGUREHEAD" '79
ESMOND, HARRIET--W/JEAN BURKE,[3][18]MYS--
DELACORTE "DARSHAM'S FOLLY" '73
DELACORTE "EYE STONES" '75
GM "FLORIAN SIGNET" 77
GEORGE, JONATHAN--W/GEORGE THEINER,[3][18][31]MYS--
MacM "THE KILL DOG" '70
MacM "DEAD LETTERS" '72
JOHN, J.F.--[18]MYS
JONES, JOANNA--[18][29][31]--
"NURSE IS A NEIGHBOR"
"NURSE ON THE DISTRICT"/
"THE ARTLESS FLAT HUNTER"
"THE ARTLESS COMMUTER"
MIALL, ROBERT--[2][3][7][18][23]MYS/SF--
'UFO' #1 & 2
"JASON KING"
"KILL JASON KING"

BURKE, JOHN [FREDERICK] [CONT]
MIALL, ROBERT [CONT]
"THE PROTECTORS"
"THE ADVENTURERS"
MORRIS, SARA--[18][22][29]MYS--
"A WIDOW FOR THE WINTER" '61
REID, DESMOND--W/G.P. MAN, PPCC#8,[23][34]MYS, HP--
SBL "HIGH HEELS & HOMICIDE" '58
SANDS, MARTIN--[3][18][29]MYS--
PAN "THE JOKERS" '67
PAN "MAROC 7"

BURKE, NORA
DUVAL, HENRI--[27]ENGLISH, HP--AMALG
LAMOUR, ANDRE--PPCC#5, P58,[27]HP--
CURZON "HAREM CAPTIVE" '47
CURZON "DESERT PASSION" '47
CURZON "DUSKY BRIDEGROOM" '47
LESTRANGE, PAUL--PPCC#5, P58,[27]HP--
CURZON "SLAVE TO PASSION" '48
CURZON "TARNISHED ANGEL" '48

BURKE, SOPHIE VAN E.L.
LYONS, SOPHIE--[1]
OWENS, FANNIE--[1]
WILSON, KATE--[1]
WILSON, MARY--[1]

BURKE, VINCENT & VELMA
BURKE, VEE--[31]

BURKHARDT, EVE & ROBERT
BLISS, ADAM--[3][22]MYS--
BARSE "CAMDEN RUBY MURDER" '31
MacRAE "MURDER UPSTAIRS" '34
MacRAE "FOUR TIMES A WIDOWER" '36
EDEN, ROB--[2][3][7]MYS/SF--
GROSSET "SHORT SKIRTS" '30
"THE GOLDEN GODDESS" '35
GRAM "LOVE COMES FLYING" '40 & OTHERS
JARDIN, REX--[2][22][34]MYS--
FICTION LEAGUE "THE DEVIL'S MANSION" '31

BURKHARDT, OTTO BRUNO
WELLER, FREDDY--[39]GERMAN, HP

BURKHART, KATHRYN W.
BURKHART, KITSI--[31]

BURKHOLDER, EDWIN V.
JONES, G. WAYMAN--[2]HP
MOFFATT, GEORGE ALLAN--W. MURRAY, ECHOES #17 & LACHMAN LST,[32][37]--
PD "CAMERA EVIDENCE" JUN '37
PD "LIFE OF RILEY" MAR '37
ALSO STORIES IN DS & SD DIGESTS
WALLACE, ROBERT--[3]MYS, HP--
PHD - 30's

BURKHOLTZ, HERBERT
LUCKLESS, JOHN--W/CLIFFORD [M] IRVING,[3]MYS--
SUMMIT "THE DEATH FREAK" '78

BURKI, PETER
BANDI, PETER--[39]GERMAN

BURKITT, FREDERICK EVELYN
SABEN, GREGORY--W/GERTRUDE C.S. SABEN,[1]

BURKLE, ROLF A.
CAMERON, JOHN--[39]GERMAN/MYS, HP
COTTON, JERRY--[39]GERMAN/MYS, HP
KOJAK--[39]GERMAN/MYS

BURKS, ARTHUR J.
CRITCHIE, ESTIL--[2][11][16]
MACARTHUR, BURKE--[2][11][16]
WALLACE, ROBERT--W/C.S. MONTAYNE,W. MURRAY-
ECHOES #17, HP--
PHD "BLACK BALL OF DEATH"
WHITNEY, SPENCER--[2][11][16]

BURKS, EDWARD C.
BURKS, ED--[31]

BURLAND, COTTIE A.
BURLAND, C.A.--[31][33]

BURMAN, ALICE CADDY
CADDY, ALICE--[31][33]

BURMESTER, ALBERT KONRAD
BARRING, GEO--[39]GERMAN/SF/WEST
BERGER, AXEL--[39]GERMAN/SF/WEST
LANDER, HANNS--[39]GERMAN/SF/WEST
REBERG, ALEX--[39]GERMAN/SF/WEST

BURN, HENRY PELHAM
CATANACH, J.N.--V. BERCH LTR TO HUBIN '93,MYS-
FLP "WHITE IS THE COLOR OF DEATH" '88
FLP "BRIDEPRICE" '89

BURNAND, FRANCIS COWLEY
COLVIN, CECIL--[1]

BURNE, CLENDENNIN TALBOT
HAWKES, JOHN--[8]

BURNES, [ROBERT] BRITT
BURNS, BURNSY--[1]

BURNESS, WALLACE BINNY
BURNESS, TAD--[31]

BURNETT, DAVID
PACE, PETER--[1][22]AUSTRO-AMERICAN

BURNETT, DAVID [B.F.]
BERNARN, TERRAVE--[1][22][31]AUSTRO-AMERICAN

BURNETT, HALLIE
HUTCHINSON, ANNE--[8]

BURNETT, HUGH
PHELIX--[8]

BURNETT, W.R.
BURNETT, W.R.--SEE ROBERT SILVERBERG,[2]
JOHNSON, SAINT--LES ADAMS & BUCK RAINEY--
"SHOOT-EM-UPS"
MOVIE "LAW & ORDER" '53
MONAHAN, JOHN P--V. BERCH, GM PSEUDS,
PP 33,[3][18][28]--
GM 355 "BIG STAN" '53
UPDIKE, JAMES--[1][18][28]MYS--
RANDOM "IT'S ALWAYS FOUR O'CLOCK" '56

BURNETT-SMITH, ANNIE S.
SWAN, ANNIE S.--[8]

BURNFORD, SHEILA [P.C.]
BURNFORD, S.D.--[3]MYS
LOUISBURGH, SHEILA BURNFD--[1][33]

BURNHAM, CLARA LOUISE
DOUGLAS, EDITH--[22]MYS

BURNHAM, JACK WESLEY
BURNHAM, J.W.--[31]

BURNIAUX, ROBERT
MUNO, JEAN--[7]SF--
OWL CREEK "GLOVE OF PASSION,
VOICE OF BLOOD" '86

BURNS, ALMA
DALTON, CLAIRE--[3][31]MYS--
BEAGLE "THE SECOND LIFE OF
CECILY PRIDE" '73

BURNS, BERNARD
AULD, PHILIP--[8]

BURNS, CAROL
HOLDER, SAMANTHA--W/DEBORAH JONES,
[9][21][26]ROM--
"SCANDAL IN BATH"
"TEMPORARY WIFE"
"MISS ROWLAND'S RESOLVE"

BURNS, EDSON LOUIS MILL.
CONWAY, ARLINGTON [B]--[22][31]CANADIAN

BURNS, OLIVE ANN
LARKIN, AMY--[31][33]--
LOCAL ADVICE COLUMN "ASK AMY"

BURNS, RALPH J.
BYRNE, RALPH--[31]

BURNS, RAYMOND HOWARD
BURNS, RAY--[31]

BURNS, REX RAOUL S.S.
BURNS, REX--AUTHOR PROVIDED/[18][32]--
MYS--
VIKING "AVENGING ANGEL" '83
VIKING "KILLING ZONE" '88 & MORE
EQMM "SHERMAN'S HORSE" NOV '79
SEHLER, TOM--HAWK/BURNS INTRVW '94, MYS--
VIKING "WHEN REASON SLEEPS" '91

BURNS, ROBERT MILTON C.
BURNS, SCOTT--[31]

BURNS, VINCENT GODFREY
BURNS, BOBBY--[8][31]

BURNS, [ROBERT] BRITT
BURNS, HOSS--[1]

BURNSTEIN, JOHN
GOODBODY, [MR.] SLIM--[1]

BURRAGE, ALFRED M.
EX-PRIVATE X--[2][7][8][11][16]

BURRELL, SUE
BERNE, KARIN--W/MICHAELA KARNI,[9]ROM
BURKE, DIANA--W/MICHAELA KARNI,[21][26]ROM--
"HEART OF THE MATTER"
"IMPOVERISHED HEIRESS"

BURRMEISTER, GERTRUD
BURMEISTER, GERTY-CHARL.--[39]GERMAN

BURROUGHS, EDGAR RICE
BEAN, NORMAN--[1][2][11]
BURROUGHS, TARZAN--[1]
MCCULLOCH, JOHN TYLER--[1][2][11]--
ACE "PIRATE BLOOD" '70

BURROUGHS, MARGARET TAYL.
BURROUGHS, MARGARET G.--[31]

BURROUGHS, ROBERT & MILLY
BURROUGHS, ROBERTA--[3]MYS--
GEM "THE FUGITIVE FEET" '85

BURROUGHS, WILLIAM S.
BRADLY, MR.--[22]AMERICAN
LEE, WILLIAM--D.C. PEEK-BK RVW "JUNKIE", BAE 7,[2][22][31]
LEE, WILLY--[31]AMERICAN
MARTIN, MR.--[22]AMERICAN

BURROWES, MICHAEL A.B.
BURROWES, MIKE--[31]

BURROWS, ABRAM SOLMAN
BURROWS, ABE--[31]

BURROWS, HERMANN
RAG MAN--[8]

BURSTEIN, JOHN
GOODBODY, SLIM--[31][33]

BURSTENBINDER, ELISABETH
WERNER, E.--[22]GERMAN

BURTON, ALICE ELIZABETH
KERBY, SUSAN ALICE--[2][11]
KIRBY, SUSAN ALICE--[2]

BURTON, EDWARD J.
CAREY, MICHAEL--[3][29][31]MYS--
AVON "VICE SQUAD COP" '57
AVON "THE VICE NET" '58

BURTON, FREDERICK RUSSELL
CARTER, NICHOLAS--[3]MYS, HP

BURTON, HAROLD BERNARD
BURTON, HAL--[31]

BURTON, KRISTIN
CHRISTIE, SUSANNA--W/SUSAN B. OSSANA, [9][21][26]ROM--3 NOVELS

BURTON, LEONORA
BLYTHE, LEONORA--[9][21][26]ROM--
6 NOVELS

BURTON, REBECCA
WINTERS, REBECCA--[9][21][26]ROM--
12 NOVELS

BURTON, SAMUEL HOLROYD
BURTON, S.H.--[7][31]SF--
LONGMAN "EIGHT GHOST STORIES" '78
HOLROYD, SAM--[2][7][31]SF--
NEL "TIBBS HOUSE" '77

BURTON, SARAH
WAKEFIELD, HANNAH--W/JUDY HOLLAND,[18][34]--
WMN'S PR "PRICE YOU PAY" '87
WMN'S PR "A FEB MOURNING" '91

BURY, THOMAS
TOUCHSTONE, TOM--[13]AUSTRALIAN

BUSBEE, JAMES JR.
SCOFIELD, JONATHAN--[21]ROM, HP--
DELL 'FREEDOM FIGHTER' SERIES:
"PACIFIC HELLFIRE"

BUSBY, F.M.
PEMBERTON, RENFREW--[2][11][23]--
FP--STORIES IN FANZINE "CRY"

BUSBY, PETER
DUNANT, PETER--W/SARAH DUNANT,[34]--
DEUTSCH "EXTERMINATING ANGELS" '83
DEUTSCH "INTENSIVE CARE" '86

BUSCAGLIA, FELICE LEONAR.
BUSCAGLIA, LEO F.--[31][33]

BUSCH, FRITZ OTTO
CORNELISSEN, PETER--[39]GERMAN

BUSCH, GERTRAUDE
BUSCH, MONIKA--[39]GERMAN/JUV

BUSCH, MARTA
FOLKERTS, MARTA--[39]GERMAN

BUSCHKUEHL, MATTHIAS
BUSCHKUHL, MATTHIAS--[31]

BUSCHLEN, JOHN PRESTON
PRESTON, JACK--[3]MYS--
REILLY "HEIL! HOLLYWOOD" '39

BUSE, RENEE
BENTON, ROBERT--[31]
BUSE, R.F.--[31]
KING, MICHAEL--W/MEIR [D] KAHANE,[31]

BUSH, CHARLIE CHRISTMAS
BUSH, CHRISTOPHER--[5][18][32][34]MYS--
HM "CUT THROAT" '32
CASSELL "CASE OF THE APRIL FOOLS" '33
& MORE NOVELS '20-60
SA - 5 DIGEST STORIES
HOME, MICHAEL--[3][18][22]MYS--
METHUEN "CYPRESS ROAD" '45
METHUEN "AUBER FILE" '53 & MORE

BUSH, GEORGE S[IDNEY]
PARKSMITH, GEORGE--W/PARK SMITH,[1]

BUSH, JOSEF
D'ARCANGELO, ANGELO--[14]--
OLYM TC#436 "THE HOMOSEXUAL HANDBOOK" '68
OLYM TC#465 "SOOKEY" '69
LEMERCIER, JUSTINE & JULE--W/PHOEBE WRAY, [14], JULE=JULIETTE--
OLYM TC#443 "THE TURKISH BATH" '69

BUSH, KIM OSTROM
CAITLIN, KIMBERLEIGH--[9][21][26]ROM--
"NIGHTWILDE"
"WILDWITCH"
"SKY OF ASHES"
"SEA OF FLAMES"
CATES, KIM--[26]ROM--NOVELS
CATES, KIMBERLY--[9][21][26]ROM--
"CROWN OF MIST"
"RESTLESS IS THE WIND" & OTHERS

BUSH, LAWRENCE DANA
BUSH, LARRY--[31]

BUSH, NANCY
BISHOP, NATALIE--[9][21][26]ROM--14 NOVELS

BUSH-FEKETE, MARIE ILONA
FAGYAS, MARIA--[8][21][26][29]MYS--
"COURT OF HONOR"
"DANCE OF THE ASSASSINS"
"DEVIL'S LT."

BUSHMILLER, ERNEST PAUL
BUSHMILLER, ERNIE--[31]

BUSHYHEAD, ANNE
JORDON, NICOLE--[9][21][26]ROM--7 NOVELS

BUSKIRK, RICHARD H[OBART]
AQUARIUS, QASS--[31]

BUSSENIUS, RUTH
KRAFT, RUTH--[39]GERMAN/JUV

BUSSY, DOROTHY
OLIVIA--J. PRESSMAN-LESBIANA, BAE 20,P32,[8]
BERK G74 "OLIVIA" '57

BUTENSCHON, HELENE
LEHNE, FR.--[39]GERMAN

BUTLER, ARTHUR RONALD
BUTLER, RICHARD--[8]

BUTLER, BASIL CHRISTOPHER
BUTLER, B.C.--[31]

BUTLER, ERNEST ALTON
BUTLER, BILL--[31]
SABBAH, HASSAN I--[8][31]

BUTLER, FRANCIS
POLTROON--W/ALASTAIR JOHNSTON,[1]

BUTLER, GWENDOLINE W.
MELVILLE, JENNIE--[3][7][17]MYS/SF--
JOSEPH "COME HOME & BE KILLED" '62
SIMON "TAROT'S TOWER" '78
HODDER "SUMMER ASSASSIN" '71
SIMON "DRAGON'S EYE" '76
& OTHERS

BUTLER, H.M.
BLACK, M. DANA--[22]MYS

BUTLER, JEAN ROUVEROL
ROUVEROL, JEAN--[21]ROM--
"STORM WIND RISING"

BUTLER, RAYMOND RAGAN
BUTLER, RAE--[9][21]ROM--
"ARABESQUE"

BUTLER, RICHARD
BUTLER, R.--[36]AUSTRALIAN,MYS--
LONG "SOUTH OF HELL'S GATE" '67
& 5 OTHERS

BUTLER, RICHARD AUSTIN
BUTLER, RAB--[31]

BUTLER, SAMUEL
CELLARIUS--[2]
OWEN, JOHN PICKARD--[8]

BUTLER, TERESA MARY
HOOLEY, TERESA--[9]ROM

BUTLER, WILLIAM A. VIVIAN
BUTLER, BILL--[31]
BUTLER, VIVIAN--[31]
MARRIC, J.J.--J. MEYERSON SLST SEPT '93,
[8][31]GHOSTED--
"GIDEON'S WAY" '86

BUTLER, WILLIAM FRANCIS
AN OLD SOLDIER--[2]

BUTLER, WILLIAM HUXFORD
BUTLER, BILL--[31]

BUTTERS, DOROTHY GILMAN
GILMAN, DOROTHY--[7][8][18][22][34]
AMERICAN/MYS--16 NOVELS '67-89

BUTTERS, PAUL
WILLIAMSON, PAUL--[8]

BUTTERWORTH, FRANK NESTLE
BLUNDELL, PETER--[2][7][22][34]MYS--
LAURIE "MR. POND OF BORNEO" '20

BUTTERWORTH, LIONEL MILN.
ANGUS-BUTTERWORTH, LIONEL--[1]

BUTTERWORTH, MICHAEL
CHALLONER, ROBERT--[31]
DOBSON, WILLIAM--[34]MYS--
SIGN "THE CHILD PLAYER" '81
SIGN "THE RIPPER" '81
KEMP, SARAH--[29][34][40]MYS--
COLLINS "GOODBYE, PUSSY" '79
RPRTD AS "OVER THE EDGE" IN U.S.
CENT "NO ESCAPE" '85
CENT "LURE OF THE SWEET DEATH" '86
CENT "WHAT DREAD HAND?" '87
SALISBURY, CAROLA--[1][8]

BUTTERWORTH, WILLIAM E.
BALDWIN, ALEX--[3][31]MYS--
POCK "MEN AT WAR" SERIES '85-88
BEECH, WEB--[3][31]--
GM 1212 "NO FRENCH LEAVE" '60
GM 1431 "ARTICLE 92: MURDER-RAPE" '65
GM 1467 "WARRIOR'S WAY" '65
GM 1548 "MAKE WAR IN MADNESS" '65
BLAKE, WALKER E.--V. BERCH-MON PSEUDS,
BAE 9,[22][31]--
MON 247 "HEARTBREAK RIDGE" '62
MON 279 "THE LOVED & THE LOST" '62
MON 419 "ONCE MORE WITH PASSION"'64
MON "DOING WHAT COMES NATURALLY" '65
DOUGLAS, JAMES--[1]
DUGAN, JACK--[1][3][31]MYS--
CHART 14224 "THE DEEP KILL" '84
DUGAN, JOHN KEVIN--[34]MYS--
JOVE "BADGE OF HONOR" '88
JOVE "SPECIAL OPERATIONS" '88
GRIFFEN, W.E.B.--[1][31]--
JOVE "BROTHERHOOD OF WAR" SERIES '83-6
JOVE "CORPS" SERIES '86-92
JOVE "BADGE OF HONOR" SERIES '88-92
HUGHES, EDEN--[9][21][26][31]--
SIGN AE1506 "THE SELKIRKS" '81
SIGN E9520 "THE WILTONS" '83
MITCHELL, ALLISON--[21][31]ROM--
SIGN "WILD HARVEST" '84
SIGN AE3158 "WILD HERITAGE" '85
McM. DOUGLAS, JAMES--[31]JUV/RACING--
5 PUTNAM NOVELS '67/72
SCHOLEFIELD, EDMUND O.--[22][31][33]
JUV/SPORTS--
WORLD PUBL-5 NOVELS '66-71
WILLIAMS, PATRICK J.--[1][31]JUV/RACING--
5 NOVELS '67-9

BUTTINGER, MURIEL GARDIN.
GARDINER, MURIEL--[31]--3 NON-FICT

BUTTITTA, ANTHONY
BUTTITA, TONY--[31]

BUTTON, MARGARET
LEONA--[8]

BUTTREY, DOUGLAS NORTON
BARR, DENSIL NEVE--[2][11][23]SF

BUTTS, JANE ROBERTS
ROBERTS, JANE--[7][34]MYS/SF--
PRENTICE-HALL "EDUCATION OF
OVERSOUL SEVEN" '73

BUTTS, MRS. M.F.
BARTON, FANNY M.--[1]

BUWERT, HARALD
FORRESTER, THORN--[39]GERMAN/SF, HP

BUXBAUM, MARTIN
NOLL, MARTIN--[22]AMERICAN

BUXTON, ANNE
MAYBURY, ANNE--[3][8][9][21][26]ROM--24 NOVELS
TROY, KATHERINE--[3][8][9][21][26]MYS/ROM--
MCKAY "FARRAMONDE" '68 & 8 OTHERS

BUXTON, RAYMOND
GORDON, HAVA--[34]MYS, HP--
MOF "DEAD ON ARRIVAL" '53
GORDON, SPIKE--P. HARBOTTLE-FEARN'S
THRILLERS, PP 25/[34]MYS, HP--
MOF "GALE GALLYON TAKES A HAND" '51
GRIFF--PPCC#7-HP
ROGAN, DON--[34]--
MOF "DAMES TAKE TO CRIME "50
MOF "UNHAPPY SOULS" '50
MOF "GUNMAN DIE HART" '51

BUYLE, HUBERT
HELDERENBERG, GERY--[22]DUTCH

BVUNTING, EVE
BUNTING, A.E.--[33]

BYATT, ANTONIO SUSAN D.
BYATT, A.S.--[31]ROM--
COLLIER "VIRGIN IN THE GARDEN" '78
COLLIER "STILL LIFE" '85
COLLIER "POSSESSION"
COLLIER "SHADOW OF A SUN"
COLLIER "SUGAR & OTHER STORIES"
COLLIER "THE GAME"

BYERS, AMY IRENE
BARRY, ANN--[1][8]

BYERS, CORDIA
BLAIR, CATHERINE--[26]ROM--
"DEVIL WIND"

BYFORD-JONES, WILFRED
QUAESTOR--[8]

BYINGTON, KAA
LEGRANDE, SYBIL--[9][21][26]ROM--
"SILKEN TREMORS"
STREET, OCTAVIA--[9][21][26]ROM--4 NOVELS

BYKOV, VASILY V.
BYKAU, VASILII U.--[31]

BYRD, MARTHA
HOYLE, MARTHA BYRD--[1][31]

BYRD, ROBERT JAMES
BYRD, BOBBY--[31]

BYRNE, JOHN KEYES
LEONARD, HUGH--[8]

BYRNE, STUART J.
AMARE, ROTHAYNE--[1][3][7][31]MYS/SF--
MAJOR "THE VISITATION" '72

BYRNE, STUART J. [CONT]
BLOODSTONE, JOHN--[1][2][11][23]--
"GOLDEN GODS" '57
POWELL PP205 "GODMAN!" '70
DARE, HOWARD--L. MUNROE-NUETZEL INTRVW,
BAE 25,[1][2]--
RUBICON 1011 "SWAPPING SINGLES"
KAYE, MARX--[1][2][11]HP--AMAZING

BYRNES, EDWARD GAINES
STAFFORD, JOHN K.--[34]MYS, HP--
MAGNET #461 "WHEN THIEVES FALL OUT;
OR, IN SEARCH OF A NAME" '06

BYRON, BAIRD
BARON, WILLY--C. ECKHOFF SLST,
OLYMP "PLAY MY LOVE" '60 "

BYRON, GEORGE GORDON NOEL
HORNEM, HORACE ESQ.--[31]

BYRON, ROBERT
WAUGHBURTON, RICHARD--W/CHRISTOPHER SYKES,[1]

CABALLZERO, MANUEL
ELCHAMO, JASON--[31]
ELCHAMO, SEBASTIAN--[31]
HEMEZE--[31]
HEMEZE, SEBASTIAN--[31]
JASON--[31]

CABALLERO-CALDERON, EDUA.
CABALLERO-CALDERON, E.--[31]

CABANAS, JOAQUIN R.
LUGO, J. PEREZ--[30]MEXICAN

CABELL, JAMES BRANCH
JEFFERSON, HENRY LEE--[1][2][11]
WASHINGTON, BERWELL--[1][2][11]

CABLE, GEORGE WASHINGTON
DROP SHOT--[1][31]
LAZARUS, FELIX--[1][31]

CABLE, JAMES
HUGO, GRANT--[8][31]

CABOS, LEW M.
MALLORY, C.H.--[2]

CABRAL, AMICAR
DJASSI, ABEL--[31]

CABRAL, OLGA
CABRAL, O.M.--[1][31][33]

CABRAL, WALTER A. GORDON
GORDON, GORDON--[29]MYS

CABRERA INFANTE, G.
CAIN, G.--[31]
CAIN, GUILLERMO--[1][31]
INFANTE, G. CABRERA--[31]

CABRERA, LUIS
RIBERA, LUCAS--[1]
URREA, LIC. BLAS--[1]

CABRERA, RAIMUNDO
BUENAMAR, RICARDO--[1]
C.C.--[1]

CADDEN, THOMAS SCOTT
CADDEN, TOM SCOTT--[31]

CADELL, VIOLET ELIZABETH
AINSWORTH, HARRIET--[3][17][31]
ENGLISH/ROM/MYS--
4 NOVELS '55-64

CADET, JOHN
BROWN, CHARLES--[1][31]
GREENE, FRED--[1][31]

CADIGAN, PATRICIA K.
CADIGAN, PAT--[23]SF--
"MINDPLAYERS" '87
"PATTERNS: STORIES" '89
"SYNNERS" '91

CADY, JACK [ANDREW]
FRANKLIN, PAT--[7]SF--
DIAMOND "DARK DREAMING" '91

CAESAR, RICHARD DYNELY
JAMES, DYNELY--W/WILLIAM J.C. MAYNE,
[1][8][22]ENGLISH

CAESAR, [EU]GENE [LEE]
LAREDO, JOHNNY--V. BERCH REVIEW JAN '93,
[1][22][31] AMERICAN
STERLING, ANTHONY--[1][22]AMERICAN

CAFFREY, KATE
TOLLER, KATE CAFFREY--[1]

CAFFYN, KATHLEEN M.
IOTA--[1][8]

CAHILL, A.
REID, DESMOND--W/W. HOWARD BAKER &
G.P. MANN,[34]MYS, HP--
SBL "BULLETS ARE TRUMPS" '61

CAHILL, FRANK
AGG, JOHN--[1]
CONWAY, MARK--[1]
MAKEWRIGHT, GEORGE W.--[1]
SIMPSON, MARIA--[1]

CAHILL, JOHN DENNIS
CAHILL, JACK--[31]

CAHILL, THOMAS QUINN
CAHILL, TOM--[31]

CAHN, ZVI
LAURIE, HARRY L.--[1]

CAIDIN, MARTIN [CARL V.S]
CAIDIN, MARTIN--[7]ADV/SF--
16 NOVELS

CAIN, ARTHUR H.
KING, ARTHUR--[1][31][33]

CAIN, ELLEN JACOB
JAMES, ELLEN--[21]ROM--
"HOME FOR LOVE"
"THE TURQUOISE HEART"

CAIN, JAMES MALLAHAN
CAIN, J.M.--[1]

CAIN, NICHOLAS [COLORADO]
BAXTER, ROBERT--AUTHOR BIO, HP--
GE "HEROES #3: ZEBRA CUBE" '92
CAIN, JONATHAN--AUTHOR BIO, HP--
ZEBRA 'SAIGON COMMANDOS' SERIES:
#1 THRU #12" '83/86
'GUNG HO' MAG "SAIGON BEAT" '80-82

CAIN, NICHOLAS [COLORADO] [CONT]
HAWKINS, JACK--AUTHOR BIO, HP--
BAL 'CHOPPER-1' SERIES:
#1 THRU #8 '87-88
NIK-UHERNIK--AUTHOR BIO, HP--
ZEBRA 'WAR DOGS' SERIES:
#1 THRU #4" '84-86
STIVERS, DICK--AUTHOR BIO,[34]HP--
GE "KILL ORBIT" '89
GE "NIGHT HEAT" '89
GE "COUNTERBLOW" '90
UHERNIK, NICK--AUTHOR BIO--
SOF "TOUGHEST BEAT IN THE WORLD:
AMERICAN MP IN VIETNAM"

CAIN, ROBERT OWEN
CAIN, BOB--[31]

CAINE, JEFFREY A.
ALTMAN, THOMAS--W/CAMPBELL BLACK,[3]MYS--
BB "KISS DADDY GOODBYE" '80
CAMPBELL, JEFFREY--W/CAMBELL BLACK,
[1][3][7]SF/MYS--
PUTNAM "THE HOMING" '80

CAINE, THOMAS H. HALL
CAINE, HALL--[17]ENGLISH/ROM, NOVELS

CAIRD, ALICE MONA
HATTON, G. NOEL--[1]

CAIRNCROSS, ALEXANDER K.
CAIRNCROSS, ALEC--[31]

CAIRNS, HUNTINGTON
UTLEY, RALPH--[1]

CALDER, PETER RITCHIE
RITCHIE-CALDER, PETER R.--[1]

CALDERELLA, SUSAN
BROSNAN, KATE--[34]MYS--
LEIS "A CRY IN THE NIGHT" '77

CALDERELLI, NAZARENO
CALDARELLI, VINCENZO--[22]ITALIAN

CALDERON, GEORGE
TIHOTI--[1]

CALDERON, MARY S.
MARTIN, MARY STEICHEN--[1]

CALDWELL, ERSKINE
KIRKLAND, JACK--V. BERCH,
MON PSEUDS, BAE 9--
SIGN 978 "TOBACCO ROAD" '52

CALDWELL, JANET [M] TAYLOR [H]
CALDWELL, TAYLOR--W/MARCUS REBACK,[8][11]
HOLLAND, MARCUS--[1][31]
REINER, MAX--W/MARCUS REBACK,[1][8][22]

CALDWELL, KATHRYN [S]
ALEXANDER, KATHRYN--[1][31]

CALDWELL, ROBERT
COCHRANE, ANDREW--[13]AUSTRALIAN

CALDWELL, STRATTON F.
FRANKLIN, KERRY--[31]

CALDWELL, WILLIAM A.
STYLITES, SIMEON--[1][2]

CALHOUN, CONYUS
CONYUS--[31]

CALHOUN, CORNELIA DONOVAN
BREAUX, DAISY--[1]

CALIF, RUTH
LAMMERT, CHARLOTTE--[34]MYS--
ZEBRA "MISTRESS OF FALCON COURT" '89

CALISTRO McCAULEY, PATRI.
CALISTRO, PADDY--[31]NON-FICT

CALIXTE, HERVE
PAGERY, FRANCOIS--[2]HP

CALKINS, RODELLO
HUNTER, RODELLO--[31]

CALLAHAN, CLAIRE WALLIS
COLE, ANN KILBORN--[1][22][31]AMERICAN
HARTWELL, NANCY--[1][22][31]AMERICAN

CALLARD, THOMAS HENRY
ROSS, SUTHERLAND--[1][22]ENGLISH

CALLE, PAUL
PIERRE, PAUL--[1][2][11]

CALLEN, LAWRENCE WILLARD
CALLEN, LARRY--[31][33]

CALLENDER, GEORGE
CALLENDER, RED--[31]

CALMENSON, STEPHANIE
CALDER, LYN--[31][33]

CALMER, EDGAR
CALMER, NED--[31]

CALNAN, THOMAS DANIEL
CALNAN, T.D.--[1]

CALVANO, TONY
DALVANO, TONY--V. BERCH,
BDSD CKLST, BAE 20,
BDSD1206 "SWAMP LUST" '60 -
'CALVANO' A PSEUD.

CALVERT, CAROLINE L.W.
ATKINSON, LOUISA--[1]

CALVERT, PATRICIA
FREEMAN, PETER J.--[1][31][33]

CALVERT, WILLIAM ROBINSON
CROFT, ROY--[1]
DALE, AUSTIN--[1]

CAMARA, HELDER PESSOA
HELDER, DOM--[31]

CAMDEN, PATRICIA
HOWARD, JULIA--[21]ROM--
"A PASSIONATE VENTURE"
"A LASTING IMAGE"
"WORKING IT OUT"

CAMEJO, PETER MIGUEL
CAMEJA, PEDRO--[31]
CAMEJO, PEDRO--[31]
CAMEJO, PEDRO M.--[31]

CAMENZIND, JOSEF MARIA
RIGISEPP--[39]GERMAN

CAMERON, BARBARA ANNE
HUBERT, CAM--[7][31]SF--
AVON "DREAMSPEAKER" '80
CAMERON' BECAME LEGALIZED NAME

CAMERON, DESMOND L.
CAMERON, KIP--V. BERCH, BRNDN/BC PSEUDS,
BAE 22, P24

CAMERON, DONALD A.
CAMERON, D.A.--[1][31]
CAMERON, SILVER DONALD--[1][31]
WALLACE, ROBERT--T. JOHNSON LTR JAN '94,
J. EDWARDS-ECHOES, HP--
PHD "RADIO MURDERS" APR '39

CAMERON, ELEANOR CRANSTON
FOWLE, ELEANOR CRANSTON--[31]

CAMERON, ELIZABETH D.C.
BOWEN, ELIZABETH--[1][32]MYS--
EQMM "TELLING" OCT '48

CAMERON, ELIZABETH JANE
DUNCAN, JANE--[1][22][33]SCOTTISH
SANDISON, JANET--[1]

CAMERON, KENNETH M.
BARTRAM, GEORGE--[3][7][29][31]MYS/SF--
MacM " FAIR GAME" '73
MacM "A JOB ABROAD" '75
PUTNAM "AELIAN FRAGMENT" '76
POPLB "WHITE PERIL" '77
PINN "SUNSET GUN" '83
PINN "UNDER THE FREEZE" '84
ARROW "MASTER OF SECRETS" '87
ARROW "THE SUN IS BLEEDING" '89

CAMERON, KENNETH NEILL
MADDEN, WARREN--[22]ENGLISH-AMERICAN

CAMERON, LESLIE GEORGIANA
LESLIE, ANN--[1]

CAMERON, LOU
ADAMS, JUSTIN--[1][28][31]--
DELL "CHAINS" '77
ARNOLD, L.J.--[1][22][28]
CAMERON, JULIE--[7][21][23][26]SF--
"DARKLINGS" '75
"DEVIL IN THE PINES"
"KITTEN DOWN A WELL"
CAMERON, LOUIS--[28]--INDIAN NON-FICT
CARTIER, STEVE--[1][22]
DAGMAR--V. BERCH, BAE 10,[2][7][34]
GHOSTED FOR V.R. EGNOR--
LAN 73-614 "SPY WITH THE BLUE KAZOO" '67
LAN 73-683 "SPY WHO CAME IN FROM
THE COPA" '67
EVANS, TABOR--[19][28][31]WEST, HP--
JOVE "IN BOULDER CANYON"
JOVE "GREAT TRAIN ROBBERY"
MANNING, MARY LOUISE--[26][28][34]MYS--
LITTLE "LAST CHRONICLES OF
BALLYFUNGUS" '78
MARVIN, W.R.--[1][22][28]
SCOFIELD, JONATHAN--[21]HP--
DELL 'FREED FTR' SERIES:
"ARMAGEDDON IN THE WEST"
THORNE, RAMSAY--CRPG,[1][19][28]WEST--
'RENEGADE':
"DEATH HUNTER" '80

CAMERON, LOU [CONT]
WILLOUGHBY, LEE DAVIS--[21]HP--
DELL 'WOMEN WHO WON THE WEST' SERIES:
"BELLE OF FT. SMITH"
DELL 'MAKING OF AMERICA' SERIES:
"WILDERNESS SEEKERS"
"COPPER KINGS"
"HOMESTEADERS"

CAMERON, SCOTT
COREMAN, JAY S.--[36]AUSTRALIAN/MYS--
UMBILICA "TED'S TOOL SHED" '88

CAMERON, STELLA
ABBOTT, JANE WORTH--W/VIRGINIA MYERS,
[9][21][26]ROM--
"CHOICES"
"YES IS FOREVER"
"SPIN OFF-FACES OF A CLOWN"
BRANDON, ALICIA--W/LINDA RICE,[9][21][26]ROM--
"LOVE BEYOND QUESTION"
HARL "FULL CIRCLE" '86

CAMERON, WILLIAM ERNEST
ALLERTON, MARK--[1][3][22]MYS--
8 NOVELS '08-27

CAMINO Y GALICIA, LEON-F.
LEON-FELIPE--[22]SPANISH

CAMP, CANDACE [PAULINE]
GREGORY, LISA--[9][21][26]ROM--
11 NOVELS '78-92
JAMES, KRISTIN--[9][21][26]ROM--
18 NOVELS '81-91
STEPHENS, SHARON--[9][21][26]ROM--
"THE BLACK EARL"

CAMP, DEBORAH ELAINE
BENET, DEBORAH--[9][21][26]ROM--
6 NOVELS
CAMP, DEBBIE--[21][26]ROM--
"GATEWAY TO THE HEART"
CAMP, DEBBY--[21][26]ROM--
"FACADE"
"TANDEM"
CAMP, DEBORAH--[9][21][26][34]MYS/ROM--
AVON "FALLEN ANGEL" '89 & 5 OTHERS
CAMP, DELAYNE--[9][21][26]ROM--
3 NOVELS
CAMP, ELAINE--[21]ROM--
14 NOVELS
TUCKER, DELAINE--[9][21]ROM--
"TOMORROW'S BRIDE"
TUCKER, ELAINE--[9][21]ROM--
"THEY SAID IT WOULDN'T LAST"
"STRANGE BEDFELLOWS"

CAMP, JOHN
SANDFORD, JOHN--LACHMAN-EASTER LST,
[29][34]MYS--
PUTNAM "RULES OF PREY" '89
PUTNAM "SHADOW PREY" '90

CAMP, JOSEPH SHELTON JR.
CAMP, JOE--[7][31]SF--
JUV "OH HEAVENLY DOG" '80
CAMP, JOSEPH S.--[7]SF

CAMPBELL WILL DAVIS
BRETT, DAVID--[22][31]AMERICAN

CAMPBELL, ALICE ORMAND
INGRAM, MARTIN--[8][29]MYS--
DODD "JUGGERNAUT" '28
DODD "DOKTOR SARTORIUS" '29

CAMPBELL, ANDREW
ANDREWS, JOHN--[1]

CAMPBELL, ANDREW C.
CAMPBELL, A.C.--[31]

CAMPBELL, BLANCHE
FISH, JULIAN--[1][22][31]AMERICAN

CAMPBELL, C. SAMUEL
ROANE, PETER--[1]

CAMPBELL, GABRIELLE M.V.
BOWEN, MARJORIE--[8][17][18][31]MYS/ROM--
COLLINS "WITHERING FIRE" '31
CAMPBELL, MARGARET--[18][21]MYS/ROM--
NAL "NIGHTS DARK SECRET" '75
NAL "BLANCHE FURY"
NAL "SPECTRAL BRIDE"
NAL "SPIDER IN THE CUP"
PAYE, ROBERT--[8][17][18]MYS/ROM--
LANE "DEVIL'S JIG" '30
BENN "JULIA ROSENGRAVE" '33
PREEDY, GEORGE [R]--[8][17][18]MYS/ROM--
25 NOVELS '28-52
SHEARING, JOSEPH--[17][18][32]MYS--
EQMM "CHINESE APPLE" APR '49
EQMM "BISHOP OF HELL" JUN '52
EQMM "LOVE-IN-A-MIST" NOV '48
EQMM "SCOURED SILK" AUG '51
WINCH, JOHN--[8][17][18]MYS/ROM--
COLLINS "IDLER'S GATE" '32

CAMPBELL, HANNAH
FRANKLIN, ELIZABETH--[1][22][31]

CAMPBELL, HOPE
HUGHES, VIRGINIA--[2][23][31]SF--
"LIGHT OF LILITH" '61
"LEGEND OF LOST EARTH" '63
SUMMERS, TRUE--[9][21][26]ROM--
"POPPY"
WALLIS, G. MCDONALD--[2][11][23][31]SF

CAMPBELL, H[ERBERT] J.
CARNI, ROSS--[34]MYS, HP--
HAM STFFD "AGAINST THE F.B.I." '52
DEEGAN, JON J.--[1][2][11]HP
SHELDON, ROY--[23][27]HP--
MAGDA SEQ: "MAMMOTH MAN" '52
MAGDA "TWO DAYS OF TERROR" '52
MAGDA "MOMENT OUT OF TIME" '52
MAGDA "MENACING SLEEP" '52
MAGDA 'SHINY SPEAR' SEQ:
"ATOMS IN ACTION" '53
MAGDA "HOUSE OF ENTROPY" '53

CAMPBELL, JAMES HOWARD
CAMPBELL, JIM--[31]--
"HOLD FAST:AN ILLUSTRATED
HISTORY OF SAIL" '84

CAMPBELL, JANE
EDWARDS, JANE--[26]ROM--8 NOVELS

CAMPBELL, JANET BRUCE
BRUCE, JANET--[31]

CAMPBELL, JOHN LORNE
CHANAIDH, FEAR--[1][31]

CAMPBELL, JOHN W[OOD]
MCCANN, ARTHUR--[1][2][11][23]--
MAG ARTICLES '37-38
STUART, DON A.--[1][15][23]SF--
ASS "TWILIGHT" & OTHERS NOV '34 - OCT '35

CAMPBELL, JOHN W[OOD] [CONT]
VAN CAMPEN, KARL--[2][15][23]SF--
ASS "THE IRRELEVANT" DEC '34

CAMPBELL, JOSEPH
CATHMHAOIL, SEOSAMH MAC'--[22]IRISH

CAMPBELL, JUDITH
GRANT, ANTHONY--[8]

CAMPBELL, LOUISA D.
ALEXANDER, LIZA--[31]

CAMPBELL, M.E. BAIRD
BAYARD, FRED--W/JOHANNA F. JANSEN,[1][3]MYS--
PHOENIX "DEATH & LILACS" '48

CAMPBELL, MARILYN
PALMIERI, MARINA--[26]ROM--
"DAYDREAMS"

CAMPBELL, PATRICIA J[EAN]
CAMPBELL, PATTY--[31][33]

CAMPBELL, R.O.
STAVELEY, ROBERT--[8]

CAMPBELL, RAMSAY
DREADSTONE, CARL--[16] HP

CAMPBELL, ROBERT WRIGHT
CAMPBELL, R. WRIGHT--[18][34]MYS--
8 NOVELS
CLINTON, F.G.--[3][18]MYS--
PINN "THE TIN COP" '83

CAMPBELL, RONALD GRAYSON
GRAYSON, REX--[34][36]AUSTRALIAN/MYS--
LONGMANS "SNATCH & GRAB" '38

CAMPBELL, ROSMAE WELLS
CAMPBELL, R.W.--[1][31][33]CHILDREN'S

CAMPBELL, SYDNEY GEORGE
CAMPBELL, STUART--[8]
LAWRENCE, CHESTER--[1]

CAMPBELL, THOMAS F.
CROSSCOUNTRY--[31]

CAMPBELL, WALTER STANLEY
VESTAL, STANLEY--PATRICIA LIMERICK-
NY TIMES BKRVW JUL '93,[22][34]--
"KIT CARSON: HAPPY WARRIOR OF
THE OLD WEST" '28
LITTLE "WINE ROOM MURDER" '35
"THE OLD SANTE FE TRAIL" '39
"BIG FOOT WALLACE" '42

CAMPBELL, WILL DAVIS
BRETT, DAVID--[31]

CAMPBELL, WILLIAM
CAMPBELL, WILFRED--[31]

CAMPBELL, WILLIAM MARCH
MARCH, WILLIAM--[22][32][34]MYS--
RINEHARDT "BAD SEED" '54
EQMM "BIRD HOUSE" FEB '54
EQMM "NO NICKLE & DIME STUFF" NOV '55

CAMPBELL,[ALBERT] ANGUS
CAMPBELL, ALBERT A.--[31]

CAMPBELL,[JOHN] RAMSEY
COMFORT, MONTGOMERY--[1][2][11]SF
DREADSTONE, CARL--[2][7][16]HP--
BERK "BRIDE OF FRANKENSTEIN"
BERK "DRACULA'S DAUGHTER"
BERK "WOLFMAN"
LEYTON, E.K.--S. HOLLAND-PPCC #9,[7]SF--
STAR "DRACULA'S DAUGHTER" '80
RAMSAY, JAY--[1][7]SF--
"THE CLAW" '83
UNDERCLIFFE, EARL--[1][2][11][16]

CAMPION, SARAH
ALPERS, MARY ROSE--[9]ROM

CAMPION, SIDNEY RONALD
SWAYNE, GEOFFREY--[1][22]ENGLISH

CAMPLING, FRANK KNOWLES
WOOD, ERIC--[1][34]MYS--
5 NOVELS '20-38

CAMPO, ANGEL DEL
MICROS--[20]SPANISH
TICK-TACK--[20]SPANISH

CAMPO, ESTANISLAO DEL
EL PARDO--[20]SPANISH
EL POLLO, ANASTASIO--[20]SPANISH

CAMPOS, JOSE ANTONIO
JACK THE RIPPER--[20]SPANISH

CAMPULKA, WALTER
AUE, WALTER--[39]GERMAN

CAMUS, ALBERT
BAUCHART--[1][31]
MATHE, ALBERT--[1]
SAETONE--[1]

CANADAY,JOHN
HEAD, MATTTHEW--[2][3][5][11][31]MYS--
7 NOVELS '34-55

CANADEO, ANNE
CAVALIERE, ANNE--[9][21][26]ROM--
"PERFECT TIMING"
"SQUEEZE PLAY"
"PRIVATE LESSONS"
DOUGLAS, ALYSSA--[9][21][26]ROM--
"PARADISE DAYS, PARADISE NIGHTS"
"SWEET TEMPTATION"

CANAWAY, W.H.
CANAWAY, BILL--[8]
HAMILTON, WILLIAM--[8]
HERMES--[8]

CANCIAN, FRANCIS ALEX.
CANCIAN, FRANK--[31]

CANDLISH, JASMINE CRESSW.
CRAIG, JASMINE--[21]ROM--14 NOVELS
CRESSWELL, JASMINE--[21]ROM--18 NOVELS

CANEDO, ALEJANDRO
ALEJANDRO--[1][2][11]SF

CANFIELD, SANDRA
KEAST, KAREN--[9][21][26][34]MYS/ROM--
SLH "NIGHT SPICE" '90 & 13 OTHERS
SHANE, SANDI--W/PENNY RICHARDS,
[9][21][26]ROM--
"NO PERFECT SEASON"
"SWEET BURNING"

CANNELL, CHARLES HENRY
MANN, JACK--[11]SF
VIVIAN, E. CHARLES--[2][7]--LEGALLY CHANGED TO E. CHARLES VIVIAN

CANNING, VICTOR
GOULD, ALAN--[3][5][18][31]MYS--
6 NOVELS '36-40

CANNON, HELEN
PROSPER, LINCOLN--[1]

CANNON, WILLIAM S.
CANNON, BILL--[31]

CANON, JACK
CARTER, NICK--[7][34]HP--
CHART "THE EBONY CROSS" '78
CHART "THE REDOLMO AFFAIR" '79
CHART "THE SATAN TRAP" '79
CHART "SOCIETY OF NINE " '81
CHART "THE DEATH STAR AFFAIR" '82
CHART "HIDE & GO DIE" '83
CHART "THE BUDAPEST RUN" '83
CHART "THE DEATH DEALER" '83
CHART "KREMLIN KILL" '84
CHART "ALGARVE AFFAIR" '84
CHART "OPERATION SHARKBITE" '84
CHART "ASSIGNMENT: RIO" '84
CHART "NIGHT OF THE WARHEADS" '84
CHART "TARLOV CIPHER" '85
CHART "BLOOD OF THE SCIMITAR" '85
CHART "CIRCLE OF SCORPIONS" '85
CHART "THE MACAO MASSACRE" '85
CHART "THE NORMANDY CODE" '85
CHART "BERLIN TARGET" '86
CHART "BLOOD RAID" '86
CHART "CYCLOPS CONSPIRACY" '86
CHART "SLAUGHTER DAY" '86
JOVE "SPYKILLER" '86
CHART "TARGET RED STAR" '86
CHART "THE TERROR CODE" '86
CHART "TERROR TIMES TWO" '86
CHART "TUNNEL FOR TRAITORS" '86
CHART "DEATH SQUAD" '87
CHART "KILLING GAMES" '87
JOVE "THE POSEIDON TARGET" '87
JOVE "TERMS OF VENGEANCE" '87
CHART "CROSSFIRE RED" '87
JOVE "BOLIVIAN HEAT" '88
JOVE "BLOOD TRAIL TO MECCA" '88
JOVE "CODE NAME COBRA" '88
JOVE "COUNTDOWN TO ARMAGEDDON" '88
JOVE "DEADLY DIVA" '89
JOVE "DAY OF THE ASSASSIN" '89
JOVE "HELL-BOUND EXPRESS" '89
JOVE "DRAGON SLAY" '90
HILD, JACK--W/ROBIN HARDY & ALAN BOMACK,[34]HP--
GE 'SOB's':
"BARRABUS RUN" '83

CANTOR, ELI
DOUGLAS, GREGORY A.--[7][31]SF--
ZEBRA "THE NEST" '80
ZEBRA "THE RITE" '79
RPRT AS "THE UNHOLY SMILE"

CANTWELL, LOIS
DENNISON, MILO--[7][31]SF--
TOR "BLACKSTONE'S MAGICAL ADVENTURE #1 & 2" '86

CANUTT, ENOS EDWARD
CANUTT, YAKIMA--[31]

CAP, FRIEDL[INDE]
CHIPPERS, DAVID--[39]GERMAN/SF
ROBE, ALEXANDER--[39]GERMAN/SF

CAPELLA, RAUL GARCIA
CAPELLA, RAY--[11]SF

CAPES, M. HARRIET
BROOKE, MAGDALEN--[1]

CAPESIUS, BERNHARD
BERNHARD, KARL--[39]GERMAN

CAPETO, ISABEL
CABOT, ISABEL--[3]MYS--
AVALON "MISSING WITNESS" '61
AVALON "MURDER IS A HOUSE GUEST" '62

CAPLIN, ALFRED GERALD
CAPP, AL--[2][8][11][31][33]

CAPON, ELLIOTT
O'ROURKE, ISRAEL--W/G.M. O'BRIEN,[2]

CAPP, BERNARD STUART
CAPP, B.S.--[31]

CAPPELL, CONSTANCE
MONTGOMERY, CONSTANCE--[33]

CAPPS, CARROLL M.
MACAPP, C.C.--[2][7][23]SF--
LAN "PRISONERS OF THE SKY" '69
AVON "WORLDS OF THE WALL" '69
DELL "RECALL NOT EARTH" '70
PAPLB "SUBB" '71

CAPRIANA, VINCENT
MASSEY, CHARLOTTE--[8]

CAPRIO, ELIZABETH BLAIR
CAPRIO, BETSY--[7][31]SF--
"STAR TREK: GOOD NEWS IN MODERN IMAGES" '78

CAPSTICK, ELIZABETH
SCOTT, ELIZABETH--[8]

CARAS, ROGER ANDREW
SARAC, ROGER--[1][2][11][23][33]SF--
"THE THROWBACKS" '65

CARAWAN, CAROLANNE M.
CARAWAN, CANDIE--[1][31]

CARBET, CLAUDE
CLAUDE--[1]

CARBONI, SUSAN G.
GORDON, SUSAN--[9][21][26]ROM--
"MATCH OF THE SEASON"

CARCOPINO-TUSOLI, FRANCIS
CARCO, FRANCIS--[3][22]FRENCH/MYS--
CAPE "NOOSE OF SIN" '23
COVICI "PERVERSITY '28
AV 555 "RUE PIGOLLE" '54
BERK 337 "ONLY A WOMAN" '55
BERK G81 "DEPRAVITY" '57
BERK G140 "THE FAMILY" '58
BERK D2031 "STREET OF THE LOST"

CARD, ORSON SCOTT
GREEN, BRIAN--[31]
PELLUME, NOAM D.--[23]SF
WALLEY, BRYON S.--[23]SF--SHORT WORK

CARDENA, CLEMENT
DE LAUBE--[8]

CARDIF, MAURICE
LINCOLN, JOHN--[8]

CARDINAL, ORA
CARDINAL, SISTER MARY ORA--[31]

CARDINAL, ROGER
BRIDGECROSS, PETER--[1][31]

CARDONA-HINE, ALVARO
SANFORD, URSULA--[3]MYS--
"THE POISONED ANEMONES" '74

CARDWELL, JAMES M.
JAMES, ADOBE--LACHMAN LST-
CONFRD BY HAWK/PRONZINI INTRVW--
MYS & HOR LATE '60s

CARESS, JAMES M.
CARESS, JAY--[31]

CARET, ERNESTINE GILBERT
GILBERT, ERNESTINE--[1]

CARETTE, LOUIS ALBERT
MARCEAU, FELICIEN--[1]

CAREW, JOHN MOHUN
CAREW, TIM--[8][22][31]ENGLISH

CAREW-SLATER, HAROLD JAME
CAREY, JAMES--[1]

CAREY, DIANE
GREGORY, LYDIA--[31]

CAREY, ELIZABETH
MAGOON, CAREY--W/MARIAN A.W. MAGOON,
[3][22]MYS--
FERRAR "I SMELL THE DEVIL" '43

CAREY, JOYCE
MALLORY, JAY--[8]

CAREY, MARY VIRGINIA
CAREY, M.V.--[31][33]JUV/MYS--
'THREE INVESTIGATORS' SERIES '71-87

CAREY, ROSA NOUCHETTE
LE VOLEUR--[3]MYS--4 NOVELS 1895-1900

CAREY, VERNA
CAREY, SUZANNE--[9][21][26]ROM--21 NOVELS

CAREY-BRODEUR, DIANE L.
BRODEUR, DIANE--[26]ROM

CARGILL, MORRIS
MORRIS, JOHN--W/JOHN HEARNE,[1][3][29]MYS--
COLLINS "FEVER GRASS" '69
COLLINS "CANDYWINE DEVELOPMENT" '70
CITADEL "CHECKERBOARD CAPER" '75

CARHART, ARTHUR H.
THORNE, HART--[1][22]AMERICAN
VAN SICKLE, V.A.--[3][7][22]AMERICAN/MYS--
KNOPF "THE WRONG BODY" '37

CARIVEAU, ROBERT EDWARD
CARY, ROBERT--[1]

CARL, DOUGLAS
DITTON, JAMES--[3]MYS--4 NOVELS '73-80

CARL-MARDORF, WILHELM
BUSCHKLEPPER, WILHELM--[39]GERMAN

CARLBERG, BIRGER
BERCO--[29]MYS--
"MORD I ELSKEN" '53
"MORD I MORKRUM" '54
"DODSKNIVEN" '54

CARLE, C.E.
MORGAN, MICHAEL--W/DEAN M. DORN,
[22][29][32][34]MYS--
RANDOM "NINE MORE LIVES" '47
ACE D9 "DECOY" '53
PYR 116 "HIS KIND OF WOMAN" '54

CARLETON, BARBARA
SILVER, PAT--[1]

CARLI, AUDREY
CRAIG, BETH--[1]
PATYN, ANN--[1]

CARLILE, CLARENCE
CARLILE, CLANCY--[7]SF--
MORROW "SPORE 7" '79

CARLILE, JOHN CHARLES
IRON, JOHN--[1]

CARLIN, SVEN GUSTAF
CARVIN, DAN--[29]MYS--
"SPINDELN RIVER NATET" '43

CARLISLE, FRED
MURRAY, K.F.--[1]

CARLISLE, NORMAN
OWEN, MARK--V. BERCH, GM PSEUDS,
PP 33, WEST--
GM 794 "TROUBLE AT BORRASCA RIM" '58

CARLISLE, R.H.
HAWKEYE--[8]

CARLISLE, THOMAS FISKE
KAHN, BALTHAZAR--[31]

CARLON, PATRICIA BERNADT.
CHARTERS, PATRICIA--[1]
CHRISTIE, BARBARA--[1]
CURTIS, PATRICIA--[1]

CARLSON, CAROLE C.
CARLSON, C.C.--W/HAL LINDSEY,[31]--
"LATE GREAT PLANET EARTH" '70
"SATAN IS ALIVE & WELL" '71

CARLSON, JANICE
AHSCROFT, LAURA--[9][21][26]ROM--
"HEART OF FIRE"
PRICE, ASHLAND--[9][21][34]MYS--
GM "ENEMY IN MY ARMS" '86
BART "ABDUCTION OF A ROYAL" '89
PRICE, LAURA--[9]

CARLSON, JUDITH LEE
LEE, JUDY--[1][31]

CARLSON, PATRICIA M[cEL.]
CARLSON, P.M.--[31]MYS--
3 AVON '85-6
3 BB '88-91
DBLDY "MURDER MISREAD" '90

CARLSON, RUTH [E] KEARNEY
KEARNEY, RUTH ELIZABETH--[1][31]

CARLSON, VADA F.
ROSE, FLORELLA--[1][31]

CARLSON, WADE
SIMON, GEORGE--[1]

CARLSSON, EGON
KALL, EGON--[29]MYS

CARLTON, EFFIE CROCKETT
CANNING, EFFIE--[8]

CARLTON, G.E.L.
ATKINSON, REGINALD--[1]
CARLTON, LEWIS--[1]
CLIFFORD, MARTIN--[1]HP

CARLTON, GERALD
CARLTON, LIEUT.--[3]MYS--
13 NOVELS 1902-04
WAYDE, BERNARD--[3]MYS--
22 NOVELS 1902-04

CARLTON, GRACE
GARTH, CECIL--[8]

CARLTON, LORI
LEIGH, LORI--[9][21][26]ROM--
"ON THE WINDS OF LOVE"

CARMAN, BLISS
NORMAN, LOUIS--[8]

CARMICHAEL, CLAIRE
MCNAB, CLAIRE--V. BERCH LTR TO HUBIN '94--
NAIAD "LESSON IN MURDER" '88
NAIAD "FATAL REUNION" '89
ALLEN "DEATH DOWN UNDER" '90

CARMICHAEL, HARRIET
CARMICHAEL, CARRIE--[31]

CARMICHAEL, WILLIAM EDW.
BEST, ADAM--[31]

CARNEGIE, RAYMOND ALEXDR.
CARNEGIE, SACHA--[1][31]

CARNELL, LOIS CHRISTIAN
CARNELL, LOIS C.--[21]ROM--
"SUMMER MAGIC AT SUMMERSET"
"LOVE RIDES THE WIND"

CARNELL,[EDWARD] JOHN
CARNELL, E.J.--[31]
CARNELL, JOHN--[11]SF

CARNEY, JACK
EFF, B.--[8]

CARPENTER, CARLETON
MANCHESTER, IVY--[34]MYS--
CURTIS "PINECASTLE" '73

CARPENTER, CLARENCE A.
CARPENTER, CAL--[1][31]

CARPENTER, DONALD G.
MERLINO, MERLIN MESMER--[1][2]

CARPENTER, ELIZABETH S.
CARPENTER, LIZ--[31]

CARPENTER, JOHN HOWARD
ARMITAGE, FRANK--[31]
CHANCE, JOHN T.--[31]

CARPENTER, LYNETTE
BORTON, D.B.--DEADLY PLEASURES #3--
CAT CALIBAN "ONE FOR THE MONEY" '92

CARPENTER, PATRICIA [H.E]
EVANS, PATRICIA HEALY--[1][31][33]

CARPENTIER VALMONT, ALEJO
JACQUELINE--[1][31]

CARR, ALBERT H. ZOLOTKOFF
CARR, A.H.Z.--[22][31][32]MYS--
EQMM "TRIAL OF JOHN NOBODY" NOV '50
& 15 OTHERS
CARBURY, A.B.--[31]

CARR, BARBARA I.V. COMYNS
COMYNS, BARBARA--[8]

CARR, DOROTHY STEVENSON
LAIRD, DOROTHY--[1][22][31]SCOTTISH-ENGLISH

CARR, ELIAS F.
HARI KARI--[1]

CARR, FRANK
CROSSE, LAUNCELOT--[1]

CARR, GORDON
WEST, EDGAR--[1]
WESTCOMBE, CHARLES--[1]

CARR, JAMES JOSEPH LLOYD
CARR, J.L.--[38]--8 NOVELS '63-91

CARR, JESSE CROWE JR.
CARERRA, KATHLEEN--[31]
CARR, JESS--[31]

CARR, JOHN DICKSON
DICKSON, CARR--[2][3][5][11][18]MYS--
MORROW "BOWSTRING MURDERS" '33 & OTHERS
DICKSON, CARTER--[2][5][11][18][29][31]MYS--
34 NOVELS '34-56
DIXON, CARTER--[2]
FAIRBAIRN, ROGER--[3][18][29]MYS--
HARPER "DEVIL KINSMERE" '34

CARR, MARGARET
CARROLL, MARTIN--[1][3]MYS--
8 NOVELS '67-71
KERR, CAROLE--[3][29][31]MYS--
HALE "SHADOW OF THE HUNTER" '75

CARR, PAT M.
ESSLINGER, PAT M.--[1][31]

CARR, TERRY G.
BRANDON, CARL--[1][2]
EDWARDS, NORMAN--W/TED WHITE, V. BERCH-
MON PSEUDS, BAE 9,[7][11][23]SF--
MON "INVASION FROM 2500" '64

CARR, WOODA NICHOLAS
CARR, NICK--G. JOHNSON-
'CARR' BIO IN ECHOES #1, P9
CARR, NICK--[7]SF--
"THE FLYING SPY; A HISTORY G-8" '78
THORPE, DICKSON--G. JOHNSON-
'CARR' BIO IN ECHOES #1, P9,

CARR-HARRIS, BERTHA HANNA
B.H.W.--[1]

CARRELL, LENORE K.C.G.
GREGORY, KATE--[1]

CARRIER, DICK
OLIVER, ROBERT--W/OLIVER LAWSON DICK, [8]

CARRINGTON, CHARLES EDM.
EDMONDS, CHARLES--[8][22][31]ENGLISH

CARRINGTON, GRANT
CORD, SMITHWAINER--[2]

CARRINGTON, HEREWARD
FODOR, NANDOR--[2][11]
LAVINGTON, HUBERT--[2][11]

CARRION, ALEJANDRO
CIELO, JUAN SIN--[20]SPANISH

CARRO, PATRICIA
MARKHAM, PATRICIA--[9][21]ROM--
"RIVER RAPTURE"

CARROLL, ALICE VIOLA
MARY CONSOLATA--[1]

CARROLL, CARLA-ELISABETH
VON SCHENCKENDORFF, C.E.--[39]GERMAN

CARROLL, JOY
HILL, HEATHER--[9][21][26]ROM--
"GREEN PARADISE"
"LADY MOON"

CARROLL, PERRY ORGAN
ORGAN, PERRY--[3]MYS--
HM "HOUSE ON CHEYNE WALK" '75

CARROLL, SIDNEY
LANE, KENDALL--[3]MYS--
GM 1741 "GAMBIT" '66

CARROLL, THOMAS THEODORE
CARROLL, TED--[7][31]SF

CARROLL, TOM M.
CARROLL, ST. THOMAS MARIO--[31]

CARROLL, WILLIAM JOSEPH
CARROLL, W.J.--[36]AUSTRALIAN/MYS--
EUREKA "DAVID THE AVENGER" '44
EUREKA "HUMAN SALVAGE" '44
EUREKA "STRANGE DILEMMA OF
GORDON JONES" '44
PERDUE, ANN--[36]AUSTRALIAN--
CARROLL "HUMOR OF THE GRINNING SKULL" '54?

CARSE, ROBERT
VAIL, JOHN--V. BERCH, GM PSEUDS, PP 33--
GM 309 "SWORD IN HIS HAND" '53
GM 396 "DARK THRONE" '54
GM 441 "SOW THE WILD WIND" '54
GM 476 "BLONDE SAVAGE" '55
GM 556 "HOLD BACK THE SUN" '56
RSB 13 "SEA WAIFS" '52
RSB 27 "LOVE ISN'T FOR NOW" '53

CARSJENS, GERHARD
PRESTO, C.--[39]GERMAN/MYS/WEST

CARSON, ANGELA
PETERS, SUE--[21]ROM--21 NOVELS

CARSON, BART
HARRAGAN, STEVE--PPCC#3, P18--USED IN U.S.

CARSON, XANTHUS
CARSON, KIT--[1][31]
WADE, KIT--[1]

CARSTENS, NETTA
FORTINA, MARTHA--[1][8][9]SOUTH AFRICAN/ROM
LAFFEATY, CHRISTINA--[21]ROM--
"THE RELUCTANT BRIDE"
"ZULU SUNSET"
"COUNT ANTONON'S HEIR"

CARSTENSEN, BERNICE
KENDYL, SHARICE--W/SHARRY MICHELS, [7]SF--
LEIS "TO SHARE A SUNSET" '90

CARTER, BRYAN
CARTER, NICK--[1][11]HP

CARTER, COMPTON IRVING
CARTER, JOHN L.--[8]

CARTER, CONRAD POWELL
CARTER, NICK--[1]HP

CARTER, DAVID CHARLES
BERTRAND, CHARLES--[31]
DOYLE, DAVID--[31]

CARTER, DYSON
DESMOND, WARREN--[1]

CARTER, ERNEST FRANK
GIFFIN, FRANK--[1]

CARTER, FRANCES MONET
EVANS, FRANCES--[8][31]

CARTER, JAMES EARL JR.
CARTER, JIMMY--[31]

CARTER, JOHN FRANKLIN
DIPLOMAT--[2][3][11][22]MYS--
7 NOVELS '30-34
FRANKLIN, JAY--[2][7][11][22][31]SF--
"CHAMPAGNE CHARLIE" '50
"RAT RACE" '50
UNOFFICIAL OBSERVER--[11][22]SF

CARTER, JOHN HOWARD
CARTER, NICK--[1]HP

CARTER, JOHN L.J.
IRVING, COMPTON--[1][2]

CARTER, LIN[WOOD VROOMAN]
CARTER, LIN--[1][23]SF

CARTER, MARGERY L.A.
ALLINGHAM, MARGERY--[29][32]MYS--
NOVELS--DIGEST STORIES '29-66
CARTER, M.L.--[1]
CARTER, PHILIP YOUNGMAN--[5]
MARCH, MAXWELL--[3][29]MYS--
3 COLLINS NOVELS '33-6

CARTER, PAUL A.
CARTER, PHILIP--[2][11]

CARTER, PAUL WARREN
CARTER, NICK--[1]HP

CARTER, PETE
WHITE EAGLE--L. ROBBINS LTR MAR '94

CARTER, REGINALD HERBERT
JANSON, HANK--[2]HP--GAYWOOD PRESS

CARTER, RICHARD
AINSLEY, TOM--[1][31]

CARTER, ROBERT AYRES
AYRES, ALISON--[31]

CARTER, RUBIN
CARTER, HURRICANE--[31]

CARTER, RUSSELL KELSOE
KENYON, ORR--[1]

CARTER, THOMAS
WOOD, J. CLAVERTON--[8]

CARTER, THOMAS EARL
CARTER, TOM--[31]

CARTER, VINCENT
CARTER, NICK--[1]HP

CARTER, YOUNGMAN
ALLINGHAM, MARGERY--A.J. HUBIN-
EQMM OCT 86--GHOSTED AFTER DEATH

CARTMELL, ROBERT
TARNACRE, ROBERT--[2]

CARTMILL, CLEVE
CHATERIS, LESLIE--[2][11]--GHOSTED
CORBIN, MICHAEL--[2][11][32]MYS--
SQ "THE PALMER METHOD" NOV '46
KUTTNER, HENRY--[3]MYS,GHOSTED--
HARPER "MAN DROWNING" '52
SANDERS, GEORGE--ARMCHAIR DET ART-'RICE'--
GHOSTED WITH RICE--
SIMON "CRIME ON MY HANDS" '44

CARTWRIGHT, JUSTIN
CRISPIN, SUZY--[8]
SUTTON, PENNY--[8]

CARTWRIGHT, ROSALIND DYM.
DYMOND, ROSALIND--[31]

CARUBA, ALAN
JORDAN, MONICA--[31]

CARUSO, JOSEPH
BARNWELL, J.O.--[8][28]WEST--
MacM "DEATH RIDER" '55
ALLEN "TRAIL OF A GUNFIGHTER" '62

CARY, JOYCE
CARY, ARTHUR--[8]
JOYCE, THOMAS--[8]

CARY, LOUIS FAVREAU
CARY--[31][33]

CARY, PEGGY-JEAN M.
CARY, DIANA SERRA--[31]
SERRA, DIANA--[31]

CARYL, WARREN H.
TADRACK, MOSS--V. BERCH-PIKE CKLST, BAE 18,
[3][32]MYS/ADULT--
BRNDN "SHOCKING NYMPHS" '62
BRNDN "MISTRESS OF EVIL" '66
BRNDN "HALO OF SIN" '67
MSMM "COLD FLIGHT" OCT '77
MSMM "COLD DEAL" APR '78
MSMM "COLD LAUGHTER" JUN '78

CARYL, WARREN H. [CONT]
TADRACK, MOSS [CONT]
MSMM "COLD SEA" JAN '79
MSMM "COLD GREEN LIGHT" AUG '80

CASACCIA, BIBOLINI G.
CASACCIA, GABRIEL--[31]

CASAL, JULIAN DEL
EL CONDE DE CAMORS--[20]SPANISH

CASALANDRA, ESTELLE
MARY, ESTELLE--[1]

CASALS, PAU CARLOS S.D.
CASALS, PABLO--[31]

CASE, DAVID
HOLLIDAY, DON--MUNROE REVIEW FEB '93

CASE, FRANCIS POWELL
POWELL, FRANCIS--[3]MYS--
5 NOVELS '04-11

CASE, JOHN FRANCIS
KANE, PHILIP--[1]

CASE, PEGGY C.
CASE, PEG--W/DOUGLAS PETERSON--
HAWK/CASE INTRVW '93--
PPJKS "TOTAL RECALL"
CASE, PEG--W/JOHN MIGLIORE--
HAWK/CASE INTRVW '93--
PPJKS "DEATH BLADE"

CASE, ROBERT ORMOND
REDDINGTON, LARRY--L. ROBBINS LTR MAR '94

CASE, THEODORE WILLARD
CASE, BILL--[31]

CASELEYR, CAMILLE A.M.
DANVERS, JACK--[2][3][23][36]--
HM "LIVING COME FIRST" '61
HM "END OF IT ALL" '62

CASEMENT, CHRISTINA
MACLEAN, CHRISTINA--[1]

CASEWIT, CURTIS
VERNOR, D.--[1][22][33]GERMAN-AMERICAN
WERNER, K.--[1][22][33]GERMAN-AMERICAN

CASEWIT, CURTIS [W]
GREEN, D.--[1][22][31][33]GERMAN-AMERICAN

CASEY, DANIEL J.
O'CATHASAIGH, DONAL--[1][31]--
"POETRY OF THE CUCHULAIM COUNTRY" '78

CASEY, JANE BARNES
BARNES, JANE--[1][31]

CASEY, JOHN
CASEY, JACK--[31]

CASEY, JUNE E.
ASH, MELISSA--[9][21][26]ROM--
"PROMISES IN THE SAND"
DOUGLAS, CASEY--[9][21][26]ROM--
7 NOVELS
RAVENSTOCK, CONSTANCE--[9][21][26]ROM--
"RENDEZVOUS AT GRAMMERCY"
TREVOR, JUNE--[9][21][26]ROM--
"WINGED VICTORY"
"UNTIL THE END OF TIME"

CASEY, JUNE E. [CONT]
TRIGLIA, JUNE--W/JOAN TRIGLIA,[21]

CASEY, MICHAEL & ROSEMARY
CASEY, MART--[1][8][31]

CASH, DEIRDRE
ROHAN, CRIENA--[13]AUSTRALIAN

CASH, ELLEN LEWIS BUELL
BUELL, ELLEN LEWIS--[31]

CASH, GRACE SAVANNAH
CASH, GRADY--[31]

CASH, JOHN R.
CASH, JOHNNY--[31]

CASHMORE, E. ELLIS
CASHMORE, ERNEST--[31]

CASIMIR, HENDRIK BRUGT G.
CASIMIR, H.B.G.--[31]

CASMAN, FRANCES WHITE
KEENE, FRANCES W.--[8]

CASON, MABEL EARP
BELL, EMILY MARY--[1][22][31][33]

CASPER, WILLIAM EARL JR.
CASPER, BILL JR.--[31]
CASPER, BILLY--[31]

CASS, DE-LYSLE FERREE
SMITH, ASHTON CLARK--[7]SF-GHOSTED??
"AS IT IS WRITTEN" '82

CASSAU, CARL
ADELSBERG, CARL--[39]GERMAN
BURG, CARL--[39]GERMAN
CARL, C.--[39]GERMAN
CARRES, C.--[39]GERMAN
VON FALKENBURG, CARL--[39]GERMAN
VON ILMENAU, CARL--[39]GERMAN
WOLFSHAGEN, G. v.--[39]GERMAN

CASSIDAY, BRUCE [BINGHAM]
BINGHAM, CARSON--V. BERCH-MON PSEUDS,
BAE 9,R. KOLLANDER-BAE 4,[2][3][7][11]--
MON MM-603 "GORGO" '60
BELM 203 "PAYOLA WOMAN" '60
MON 194 "RUN TOUGH, RUN HARD" '61
MON 227 "IT HAPPENED IN HAWAII" '61
MM-606 "STREET IS MY BEAT" '61
MON 283 "LOVES OF DR. DEVERE" '62
MON 372 "THE GANG GIRLS" '63
CARTER, NICK--[3]MYS, HP--
AWARD "SPANISH CONNECTION" '73
DAY, MAX--[2][22][31]--
BEACON B334 "THE RESORT" '60
DREW, MARY ANNE--[1][3][31]MYS--
AVON "THE DIABOLIST" '75
FONG, C.K.--[3]MYS--
MANOR "THE YEAR OF THE COCK" '75
MCALLISTER, ANNIE LAURIE--[3][7][11]--
BERK "HOUSE OF VENGEANCE" '76
BERK "QUEEN OF THE LOOKING GLASS" '78
MCMURDIE, ANNIE LAURIE--[1][3][7]MYS/SF--
LAN "NIGHTMARE HALL" '73
RAYMOND, ALEX--[2][7]SF--
AVON "TIME TRAPS OF MING" '74
AVON "WITCH QUEEN OF MONGO" '74
STEFFANSON, CON--[1][7][23]HP--
AVON "WITCH QUEEN OF MONGO"
AVON "TIME TRAP OF MING"

CASSIDAY, BRUCE [BINGHAM] [CONT]
STRATFORD, MICHAEL--[1][3]MYS--
AWARD "THE SNIPER" '74

CASSIDY, ROBERT JOHN
GILROONEY--[8]

CASSIDY, WILLIAM L.
SCHWABE, WILLIAM--[1]

CASSILL, RONALD VERLIN
AHERNE, OWEN--[22][31][38]--
AV T182 "AN AFFAIR TO REMEMBER" '57
AV T177 "MAN ON FIRE" '57
CASSILL, R.V.--[1][38]
WEBSTER, JESSIE--[1][22]

CASSINI IGOR LOIEWSKI
KNICKERBOCKER, CHOLLY--[31]

CASSITY, JUNE
MO, MANAGER--[8]

CASSON, FREDERICK
BEATTY, BADEN--[8]

CASSOU, JEAN
NOIR, JEAN--[1]

CASSTEVENS, JEANNE S.
SAVERY, JEANNE--[26]ROM--
"LAST OF THE WINTER ROSES"
"A SPRINGTIME AFFAIR"

CASTBERG, CHRIS
VANEK, C.S.--[14]--
OLYM TC#449 "THE SKIN BOOK" '69
OLYM TC#453 "HIDE & SEX" '69
OLYM TC#467 "THRUST" '69
OLYM TC#503 "PRIVATE & BIZARRE" '71

CASTEDO, ELENA
CASTEDO-ELLERMAN, ELENA--[31]

CASTELL, LUISE zu
ULLRICH, LUISE--[39]GERMAN

CASTELLE, FRIEDRICH
DIETMER, HANS--[39]GERMAN

CASTELLI, IGNAZ FRANZ
FATALIS, BRUDER--[39]GERMAN
KOSMAS--[39]GERMAN
ROSENFELD--[39]GERMAN
STILLE, C.A.--[39]GERMAN

CASTILLO VELAQUEZ, LUIZ A
ALBA, PATRICIO--[1]

CASTLE SMITH, MRS. G.
BRENDA--[8]

CASTLE, ANTHONY PERCY
CASTLE, TONY--[31]--
"TUESDAY AGAIN" '77
FROST, PAUL--[31]--
HODDER "APPRENTICE PRIEST"
HODDER "GOOD HEAVENS" '80

CASTLE, BRENDA
EDWARDS, RACHELLE--V. BERCH LTR
TO HUBIN '94--
HALE "DEVIL'S BRIDE" '76
HALE "SILKEN NET" '78 & MORE

CASTLE, BRENDA
FERRAND, GEORGINA--[3][21][40]MYS/ROM--
HALE "HOUSE OF GLASS" '77
HALE "GILDED CAGE" '79 & MORE

CASTLE, FRANCES MUNDY
WHITEHOUSE, PEGGY--[8]

CASTLE, FRANK
BLACKBURN, TOM W.--PPCC#9, P96--
GHOSTED NVLS ca '48
THURMAN, STEVE--V. BERCH-MON PSEUDS,
BAE 9,[18][29][34]MYS--
GRAP 96 "GUN LIGHTNING" '55
MON 142 "NIGHT AFTER NIGHT" '59
MON MA313 "BABY-FACE NELSON" '61
MM-607 "MAD DOG COLL" '61
MON 246 "LIGHTNING GUN" '62
GSB IL7-21 "SANITARIUM OF TEARS" '64
PAPLB 50-969 "HUNGRY GUN" '66

CASTLE, MARGERY SHARP
SHARP, MARGERY--[1][32]MYS--
EQMM "MAN WHO FEARED THE WATER" OCT '54
& 6 OTHERS

CASTO, JACQUELINE A.
ASHLEY, JACQUELINE--[9][21][26][34]MYS--
HARL "SECRETS OF THE HEART" '84 & OTHERS
BLACK, JACKIE--[9][21][26]ROM--
17 NOVELS
CASTO, JACKIE--[21]ROM--
"DREAMS OF DESTINY"
"DAUGHTER OF DESTINY"
"THE NEW FRONTIER"

CASTORO, LAURA ANN
BONNER, TERRY NELSON--[21][31]HP--
'AUSTRALIAN/NZ':"FREE WOMAN"
PARKER, LAURA--[7][9][21][26]ROM/SF--16 NOVELS

CASTRO, ANTONIO
CASTRO, TONY--[1][31]

CASTROVILLA, JOSEPH A.
ANTHONY, JOSEPH--V. BERCH, BRNDN/
BC PSEUDS, BAE 22, P24

CASWELL, EDWARD A.
MYSELF AND ANOTHER--[2]

CATALANI, VICTORIA
HAAS, CAROLA--[8]

CATCHPOLE, WILLIAM LESLIE
CLIFFORD, MARTIN--[1]HP
CONQUEST, OWEN--[1]HP
HAWKINS, JOHN--[1][32]MYS--
SA "YOU'LL BE THE NEXT TO DIE" JUN '53
HAWKINS, JOHN & WARD--[1][32]MYS--
EQMM, 8 STORIES ?? UNCONFIRMED ??
HOWARD, ROLAND--[1]
HUNTER, ROWLAND--[1]
RICHARDS, FRANK--[1]HP

CATE, RICHARD EDWARD N.
CATE, DICK--[31][33]

CATHER, WILELLA [S]
CATHER, WILLA--[1][31]
CATHER, WILLIAM MD--[1]

CATHERALL, ARTHUR
BALTIMORE, J.--[1][31][33]--
FICTION HOUSE "SINGAPORE SARI" '58

CATHERALL, ARTHUR [CONT]
CHANNEL, A.R.--[25][31][33]--
"TUNNEL BUSTERS" '60
"M & ICE FLOE" '61
"LITTLE SEALER" '61
CORBY, DAN--[1][25][31]--
CHILDREN'S "A SHARL ON THE SALTINGS" '59
HALLARD, PETER--[1][25][31]--
CHILDREN'S "CORAL REEF CASTAWAY" '58
MAINE, TREVOR--[1][25][31]--
"BLUE VEIL & BLACK GOLD" '61
PETERS, LINDA--[1][25][31][33]--
"REINDEER RESCUE" '66
RUTHIN, MARGARET--[1][25][31][33]--
CHILDREN'S - 11 BOOKS

CATTAUI, GEORGES
FRANCES, MICHEL--[1][31]

CATTO, MAXWELL JEFFREY
CATTO, MAX--[29][34]MYS--
9 NOVELS & 1 PLAY '49-77

CATTO, MAX[WELL J.]
FINKELL, MAX--[1][29][31]
KENT, SIMON--[3][29][31]MYS--
HUTCH "THE LIONS AT THE KILL" '59

CATTON, C. MARIE
CATTON, C.M.--[36]AUSTRALIAN/MYS--
CONDOR "CARTOON FOR CRIME" '45

CAUDILL, REBECCA
AYARS, REBECCA CAUDILL--[1]

CAULDER, COLLINE
KING, BILLI--[1][31]
NYNCH, STEPHANIE J.--[1]

CAULEY, TROY JESSIE
CAULEY, TERRY--[22][31]AMERICAN

CAULFIELD, MALACHY F.
CAULFIELD, MAX--[1][31]
HALSTOCK, MAX--[1][31]
MCCOY, MALACHY--[1]

CAUSEWAY, JANE
COOK, BARRY--[9]ROM

CAUSSE, CHARLES
MAEL, PETER/PIERRE--W/CHARLES VINCENT,[2]

CAUTE, DAVID
SALISBURY, JOHN--[8]

CAVAFISM KONSTANTINOS P.
CAVAFY, C.P.--[31]

CAVALLARO, ANN ABELSON
ABELSON, ANN--[22][33]

CAVANAGH, HELEN
CHRISTOPHER, HONEY--[9]ROM

CAVANNA, ELIZABETH ALLEN
ALLEN, BETSY--[9][22][25][33]AMERICAN/ROM
CAVANNA, BETTY--[9][22][33]AMERICAN
HARRISON, ELIZABETH--[9][21][22]AMERICAN--
4 ROM NOVELS
HEADLEY, ELIZABETH--[1][22][25][33]AMERICAN

CAVE, GEOFFREY
VACE, GEOFFREY--HAWK/CAVE INTRVW MAR '94,
STORIES PRE DEC '31, THEREAFTER WAS
'HUGH' CAVE

CAVE, HUGH B[ARNETT]
BARNETT, C.H.--HAWK/CAVE INTRVW MAR '94,
WOMAN'S HOME COMPANION "THE 75th
BABY" MAR '45
BECK, ALLEN--HAWK/CAVE INTRVW MAR '94,
[2][11][16][32]--
PD "COPPER'S BIBLE" FEB '37
BM "LONG LIVE THE DEAD" DEC '38
CASE, JUSTIN--HAWK/CAVE INTRVW MAR '94,
[2][11][16]--
SPAS "SABALI MADNESS"
SPAS "HURRICANE TRAMP"
SPAS "THE CRAWLING ONES" FEB '36
SPAS "IN THE DRAGON'S LAIR" MAR '36
SPDS "I SEE BY THE PAPERS" MAY '36
SPDS "WOMEN ARE DAMNED FOOLS" SEPT '36
SPAS "EEL TRAP" JUN '36
SPAS "YELLOW HORDE" JUL '36
SPMS "DARK NIGHT OF DOOM" JAN '36
SPMS "DOOM DOOR" 3/36
SPMS "MISTRESS OF VENGEANCE" 6/36
SPMS "SHE FROM BEYOND" 7/36
SPMS "EVIL FLAME" SEPT '36
SPMS "PREY OF THE NIGHTBORN" SEPT '36
SPMS "CULT OF THE CORPSE" OCT '36
SPMS "HURRICANE WOMAN" FEB '37
SPMS "STRANGE DEATH OF IVAN
GROMLEIGH" JUN '37
SPMS "CAVERN OF THE DAMNED" MAY '37
SPMS "TOMB FOR THE LIVING" JUN '37
SPAS "DARK TEMPLE OF TORMENT" JAN '37
SPAS "RIVER OF BLOOD" APR '37
SPAS "SHOTGUN CEREMONY" JUN '37
SPDS "DEATH TO COPS" JAN '37
SPDS "EEL POISON" AUG '37
SPDS "DEATH WEARS NO ROBE" OCT '37
SPAS "SECRET OF THE LOST CITY" AUG '37
SPAS "EEL SLIPS THROUGH" DEC '37
PRD "SLEEP BABY SLEEP" SEPT '37
SPMS "SATAN'S ALTAR" JAN '38
SPMS "HOUSE OF DEATHLESS
SHADOWS" APR '38
SPMS "DEATH'S FIERY SERPENTS" MAY '38
SPMS "ZANNIN'S PUPPETS" AUG '38
SPMS "SERVANT OF SATAN" SEPT '38
SPMS "SONG OF THE LASH" DEC '38
PRD "DESIGN FOR DEATH" JAN '38
PRD "SHE SLEPT TOO LONG" JUN '38
SPAS "BLACK OF JOE MING" APR '38
SPAS "TOMORROW YOU DIE" SEPT '38
SPAS "HELL HOLE" JAN '38
SPDS "PRISON PAY-OFF" AUG '38
ROMD "THE GORILLO WILL GET YOU" DEC '38
SPAS "EEL BAIT" JAN '38
SPAS "PRISONER OF TITUAN" APR '38
SPAS "PREY OF THE PROWLER" OCT '40
SPDS "EEL'S ERRAND" AUG '40
SPDS "THE WIDOW WEARS SCARLET" OCT '40
SPDS "LAST LAUGH" DEC '40
SPDS "ANNIE ANY MORE" MAR '41
SPDS "ON ICE" APR '41
SPDS "DEATH HAS GREEN EYES" JUN '41
SPDS"SECOND SLUG" JUN '41
SPDS "KROCK'S WIFE" OCT '41
SPMS "MONSTER FRINGE" MAY '41
SPMS "BENEATH THE VAPOR VEIL" JAN '41
SPMS "THE WHISPERERS" APR '42
SPMS "CAVERNS OF TIME" MAY '42
SPMS "SATAN'S SLOUGH" SEPT '42
SPMS "CALAVAN" DEC '42
SPMS "THING FROM THE SWAMP" FEB '42
SPMS "PURR OF A CAT" MAR '42
SPAS "VANISHING DEAD" MAY '42
SPAS "WHITE STAR OF EGYPT" NOV '42
SPDS "A PILE OF PUBLICITY" JAN '42
SPDS "EEL'S EVE" APR '42
PRD "BAD WATER" NOV '43

CAVE, HUGH B[ARNETT] [CONT
CASE, JUSTIN [CONT]
SPA "COMEBACK IN REDLING" MAR '44
SPA "SO LONG, SISTER" MAY '44
SPA "GENERAL COMES TO TOWN" JUL '44
PRD "P.D. FILE 213" MAR '44
RISQ "ERZULIE" OCT '84
RISQ "HOUSE OF DARK DESIRE" JUL '85
COLE, J.C.--HAWK/CAVE INTRVW--
PRD "HEADLINE BAIT" MAR '38-
RPRT OF "I SEE BY THE PAPERS"
D'ARCY, JACK--HAWK/CAVE INTRVW MAR '94--
FEA "MONKEY OF SIMMS"
20 STRY MAG "WATCH YOUR SLIP"
DECATUR, WILLIAM--HAWK/CAVE INTRVW '94--
SPAS "DARK OUTLAW" OCT '42-
RPRT OF "TOMORROW YOU DIE"
HANNA, PAUL--HAWK/CAVE INTRVW '94--
SPAS "DEATH BOX" FEB '42-
RPRT OF "THE CRAWLING ONES"
KNOWLES, RUPERT--HAWK/CAVE INTRVW '94--
POPFIC "YOUNG COURAGE" DEC '31
[KNOWLES PLAGIARIZED]
MAYNARD, R.T.--HAWK/CAVE INTRVW MAR '94--
SPAS "AS FOR KEEPS" DEC '42-
RPRT OF "SHOTGUN CEREMONY"
NEILSON, MAX--HAWK/CAVE INTRVW 3/94--
SPDM "CANYON OF FEAR" JAN '43-
RPRT OF "MISTRESS OF VENG."
SMITH, MAXWELL--HAWK/CAVE INTRVW 3/94--
20 STORY MAG "ISLAND ORDEAL" JUL '32
VACE, GEOFFREY--HAWK/CAVE INTRVW '94/[11][16]-
CAM "THE RED ROAD UP" AUG '34
DM "THE HOUSE OF EVIL" NOV '33
FEA "UP-RIVER FROM SANDAKAN" DEC '31
20-STORY MAG "TOO MUCH IMAGINATION" '32
WAYNE, JOHN--HAWK/CAVE INTRVW '94--
SPMS "VOODOO MADNESS" 12/42-
RPRT OF "CULT OF THE CORPSE"

CAVE, PETER [LESLIE]
CHRISTIAN, PETRA--W/CHRISTOPHER PRIEST,[2]--
ALSO USED HIMSELF
COTELO, C.S.--[34]MYS--
SIGN "WHITE LINE FEVER" '75
MAXWELL, PETER--[3][29][40]MYS--
HAMLYN "INSANITY MACHINE" '78
HAMLYN "KILL FACTOR FIVE" '79

CAVE, RODERIC K.G.J.M.
MUNRO, JAMES--[1][22]ENGLISH

CAVENDISH, RICHARD
CORNWALL, MARTIN--[1][31]

CAVERHILL, W. MELVILLE
MELVILLE, ALAN--[1][3][22]MYS--
6 NOVELS '34-37

CAVETT, RICHARD A.
CAVETT, DICK--[31]

CAVIN, RUTH BRODIE
BRODIE, SALLY--[1][33]
SOBLE, JENNIE--[1][33]

CAVOUKIAN, RAFFI
RAFFI--[33]

CAWTHORN, JAMES
JAMES, PHILIP--W/MICHAEL MOORCOCK,
J. DAVEY LTR,[2][7][11]SF--
"DISTANT SUNS"
REID, DESMOND--W/S. HALL, P. CHAMBERS &
M. MOORCOCK,[2][34]HP--
AMALG "CARRIBEAN CRISIS" '62

CAZAURAN, AUGUSTUS R.
CAREY, MATTHEW--[1]
MORAY, JOHN S.--[1]

CEBULASH, MEL
CARMENDELLA, ANTHONY--[1]
FARRELL, BEN--[1][31][33]
HARLAN, GLEN--[1][31][33]
JANSEN, JARED--[1][31][33]
MARA, JEANETTE--[1][33]

CECH, ADELE
HOLDEN, ADELE--[39]GERMAN

CEDER, GEORGIANA DORCAS
DOR, ANA--[1][22][31][33]AMERICAN

CEDERBERG, AKE
CEDELL, CHRISTIAN--[29]MYS--
NORST "MANOVER MED MORDARE" '65

CELA, CAMILLO JOSE
DON CAMILLO--[1]
VERDU, MATILDE--[1]

CELESTINO, MARTHA LAING
LAING, MARTHA--[1][31][33]

CERF, CHRISTOPHER C.
FL*M*NG, I*N--W/MICHAEL K. FRITH,[3][7]--
VANITAS V4402 "ALLIGATOR" '62 & 8 OTHERS

CERIO, CLARA
CERIO, CLARETTE--[40]MYS--
"BLUT IM CHIANTI" '79 & OTHERS

CERKEG, VLADIMIR
CEZ--[1]

CERRI, LAWRENCE J.
CORTESI, LAWRENCE--[1][31]

CERUTTI, MARIA ANTONIETTA
CERUTTI, TONI--[31]

CHABRILLAN, E. CELESTE DE
DE CHABRILLAN, CELESTE--[36]
AUSTRALIAN/MYS--
SUN "THE GOLD ROBBERS" '70

CHADWICK, CHARLES
DEVLIN, OWEN--[1]
LIFE, JOHN--[1]
STEELE, DANIEL--[1]

CHADWICK, JOSEPH L.
BARTON, JACK--[1][28]WEST--
POPLB "BRAND OF FURY" '55
POPLB "VENGEANCE RIDER" '56
VIKING "TEXAS RAWHIDER" '56
BURTON, JACK--[29]MYS
CALLAHAN, JOHN--HOLLAND RVW FEB '93,
[8][28]WEST--
AVALON "TEXAS FURY" '52
CHADWICK, JOSELYN--[3][28][29]MYS--
AV "EVIL IS THE NIGHT" '74
AV "WEB OF EVIL" '72
COLE, JACKSON--A. TONIK-COLE CKLST
"SPICY ARMADILLO", HP--
TEX RGR "DEATH RIDES THE STAR ROUTE"
TEX RGR "BLOOD ON THE SPUR" OCT '52
TEX RGR "TRAIL OF THE DESERT
WITCH" APR '53
CONROY, JANET--[21][26]ROM--
"THE HARLAN LEGACY"

CHADWICK, JOSEPH L. [CONT]
CONROY, JIM--[8][28]MYS--
DBLDY "DESTINATION REVENGE" '53
CONWAY, JOHN--V. BERCH, MON PSEUDS, BAE 9,
[3][28][29]MYS--
MON 115 "MADIGAN'S WOMAN" '59
MON 128 "HELL IS MY DESTINATION" '59
MON 148 "THIS DARK DESIRE" '60
MON 174 "LOVE IN SUBURBIA" '60
MON "REQUIEM FOR A CHASER" '60
MON 222 "A SIN IN TIME" '61
MON MA309 "THE APACHE WARS" '61
MON MA324 "THE SIOUX INDIAN WARS" '62
MON MA327 "WOMAN-BREAKER" '62
MON MA333 "THE TEXAS RANGERS" '63
MON MA349 "THE VALIANT BREED" '63
MON 561 "OCTAROON" '65
CREIGHTON, JO ANNE--
[3][21][26][28][29]ROM/MYS--
5 NOVELS '73-7
CREIGHTON, JOHN--[3][28][29]MYS--
ACE D167 "DESTROYING ANGEL" '56
ACE D247 "NOT SO EVIL AS EVE" '57
ACE D317 "THE WAYWARD BLONDE" '58
ACE D321 "TRIAL BY PERJURY" '58
ACE D333 "STRANGLEHOLD" 59
ACE D393 "EVIL IS THE NIGHT" '59
ACE D425 "A HALF INTEREST IN MURDER" '60
ACE F115 "BLONDE CRIED MURDER" '61
GRAYSON, ELIZABETH--[34]MYS--
MANOR "BY DEMONS POSSESSED" '73
MANOR "A TOKEN OF EVIL" '74
MANOR "MACRABRE MANOR" '74
HAWK, ALEX--L. ROBBINS LTR MAR '94, HP
KENDRICKS, JAMES--L. ROBBINS LTR MAR '94, HP
KIRBY, MAC--L. ROBBINS LTR MAR '94
LAYNE, JIM--L. ROBBINS LTR MAR '94

CHADWICK, PAUL
BOSTON, RALPH--W. MURRAY-ECHOES #47
HAMMOND, ELEANOR--PULP CLASSIC #22, P77--
STORIES IN 'LOVE FICTION MONTHLY'
?? UNCONF ??
HAWK, PAUL--W. MURRAY-ECHOES #47,
?? UNCONFIRMED ??
HAWKS, CHESTER--LACHMAN LST '93,
W. MURRAY, ECHOES #47--
CAH "PYTHON MEN OF LOST CITY" '38
HOUSE, BRANT--PULP CLASSIC #22/[2][3][7]HP--
SAX "CURSE OF THE WAITING DEATH" FEB '35
SAX "CITY OF THE LIVING DEAD" JUN '34
SAX "DEATH-TORCH TERROR" APR '34
SAX "SPECTRAL STRANGLER" MAR '34
SAX "SINISTER SCOURGE" JAN '35
SAX "TORTURE TRUST" FEB '34
SAX "AMBASSADOR OF DOOM" MAY '34
SAX "OCTOPUS OF CRIME" SEPT '34
SAX "HOODED HORDES" OCT '34
SAX "DEVILS OF DARKNESS" MAR '35
SAX "MONARCH OF MURDER" AUG '35
SAX "HORDE OF THE DAMNED" OCT '35
SAX "FEAR MERCHANTS" MAR '36
PULP CLASSIC#4 "BRAND OF THE
METAL MAIDEN"

CHAFETS, ZE'EV
CHAFETS, ZEV--[31]

CHAFFIN, LILLIE D.
CHAFFIN, RANDALL--[1][32]MYS--
SFDS "IT'S YOUR TURN TO DIE" FEB '58
DAY, LILA--[1]
WINSTON, LENA--[1]

CHAIJ, FERNANDO
ALCALDE, E.L.--[31]

CHALKE, HERBERT
BLACKER, HERETH--[8]

CHALKER, JACK
OWINGS, MARK--[2]--PER [23]THIS IS NOT CHALKER'S PSEUD.

CHALLANS, MARY
RENAULT, MARY--[1][21][26][33]ROM-- 11 NOVELS

CHALLON, DAVID
RAWLINGS, PETER--V. BERCH-BDSD CKLST, BAE 20-- BDSD 975 "SWINDLER'S KISS" '60

CHALMERS, FLOYD S.
DUKE, JOHN--[1][31]

CHALMERS, ISAAC
HALE, FORBES--[1]

CHALMERS, STEPHEN
CARTER, NICHOLAS--[3][29]MYS, HP

CHALONER, JOHN SEYMOUR
CHALON, JON--[1][8][31]

CHALONER, WILLIAM HENRY
CHALONER, W.H.--[31]

CHAMBERLAIN, SAMUEL
BECK, PHINEAS--[1]

CHAMBERS, AIDAN
BLACKLIN, MALCOLM--[7][8][11][31][33]-- MacM "GHOSTS FOUR" '78

CHAMBERS, DEREK HYDE
DAVID, KIRK--[34]MYS, HP-- CURTIS "BORN TO DIE" '52
HYDE, D. HERBERT--[3][29]MYS-- AMALG "DRESSED TO KILL" '59
STANDISH, PETER--[34]MYS, HP-- CURTIS "DARK SHADOW" '52

CHAMBERS, EDMUND K.
CHAMBERS, E.K.--[1]

CHAMBERS, JAMES
CLIFF, JIMMY--[31]

CHAMBERS, MARGARET ADA E.
CHAMBERS, PEGGY--[31][33]-- "WOMEN & THE WORLD TODAY" '54

CHAMBERS, MARIA CRISTINA
MENA, MARIA CRISTINA--[1]

CHAMBERS, PETER
DANIELS, PHILIP--M. LACHMAN-- JACKET "GOLDMINE-LONDON W.I." '9X

CHAMBERS, PHILIP
REID, DESMOND--W/GORDON SOWMAN--[34]HP-- AMALG "DEATH IN DOCKLAND" '62
REID, DESMOND--W/S. HILL, J. CAWTHORN & M. MOORCOCK, HP-- REVISED AMALG "CARRIBEAN CRISIS" '62
WILLIAMS, RICHARD--[1]HP

CHAMBERS, ROBERT WILLIAM
CHAMBERS, R.W.--[1]

CHAMBERS, VIRGINIA ANNE S
CHAMBERS, GINGER--[21]ROM-- 16 NOVELS

CHAMBERS,[J.D] WHITTAKER
ADAMS, CHARLES--[1]
BREEN, DAVID--[1]
CANTWELL, LLOYD--[1]
CHAMBERS, CARL--[1]
CHAMBERS, CROSLEY--[1]
CHAMBERS, JAY VIVIAN--[1]
CROSLEY, GEORGE--[1]
DWYER, ARTHUR--[1]

CHAMBLISS, JOHN
CARTER, NICK--[1][2][34]HP-- "RENDEZVOUS WITH A DEAD MAN" '48
KEITH, HARRISON--W/PHILIP CLARK, [1][2][37]MYS-- CLS "MURDER IN A BLACK FRAME" JUL '36

CHAMBLISS, WILLIAM JOSEPH
BOXMAN--[31]
CHAMBLISS, BILL--[31]

CHAMPION, D'ARCY LYNDON
CHAMPION, D.L.--A. TONIK, ECHOES #8 & ECHOES #69,[32]--
SD "4F & FLAT FEET" MAR '44
ND "WRONG WAY CORPSE" APR '51
DT "THE BIGGER THEY ARE" AUG '58
CHAMPION, TOM--T. JOHNSON-BEHIND THE MASK #22,[37]-- FEDA "EMERGENCY CALL" AUG '36
D'ARCY, JACK--[1][2][3]MYS-- USED BY OTHERS [AT LEAST HUGH B. CAVE]
JONES, G. WAYMAN--A. TONIK-ECHOES#8, [2][34]HP-- FICTION LEAGUE "ALIAS MR. DEATH" '32
WALLACE, ROBERT--J. EDWARDS-ECHOES #73,[2][3]HP-- PHD "DEATH GLOW" NOV '38

CHAMPION, RICHARD GORDON
CHAMPION, DICK--[31]

CHAMPLIN, CAROLINE L.
LLEWELLYN, CAROLINE--V. BERCH LTR TO HUBIN '94,[21]MYS/ROM--
SCRIBN "MASKS OF ROME" '88
SCRIBN "LADY OF THE LABYRINTH" '90

CHAMPLIN, EDWIN ROSS
FAIRFIELD, CLARENCE--[1]
GOSSIP, JOHN--[1]
WEST, BUXTON--[1]

CHAMPLIN, JOHN MICHAEL
CHAMPLIN, TIM--[1][28][31]BAL-- 9 NOVELS '82-90

CHAMSON, ANDRE J.
LAUTER--[1][22][31]FRENCH

CHANCE, JOHN NEWTON
CHANCE, JONATHAN--[1][23][31]SF-- "THE LIGHT BENDERS" '68
DRUMMOND, J.--[31]
DRUMMOND, JOHN--[2][3][11][18][25]MYS-- 25 SEXTON BLAKE NOVELS '44-55
LYMINGTON, JOHN--[3][7][23][29][31]--MYS/SF-- "GIVE DADDY THE KNIFE DARLING" '89 & 23 SF NOVELS
NEWTON, DAVID C.--[2][11][18][23]CHILDREN'S--
"BLACK GHOST" '47
"DANGEROUS ROAD" '48
REID, DESMOND--[2][3][11][23]HP-- SBL "ANGER AT WORLD'S END" '63

CHANCE, LISBETH L.
DANIELS, LEIGH--[9][10][21][26][34]MYS/ROM--
"ON THE RUN"
"THE BASQUE SWALLOW"
WALKER "BAJA RUN" '86
WALKER "CUTTING EDGE" '85

CHANDLER, A. BERTRAM
DUNSTAN, ANDREW--[2][11][23][31]ENGLISH-AUSTRALIAN--ONLY USED IN AUSTRALIA
GRIMES, JOHN--[2]
S.H.M.--[23]--USED IN AUSTRALIA ONLY
WHITLEY, GEORGE--[2][11][23]SF--
ASF "FAMILIAR PATTERN" '59
SES "PERMANENT CORRECTION" NOV '53

CHANDLER, BRYN
BLAKE, CHRISTINA--[1][31]

CHANDLER, JENNIFER [W]
WESTWOOD, JENNIFER--[1]

CHANEY, JOHN GRIFFITH
LONDON, JOHN GRIFFITH--[1]

CHANEY, WILLIAM HENRY
LONDON, JACK--[29]

CHANG AI-LING
CHANG, EILEEN--[1]

CHANG PIN-CHIN
DING LING--[31]

CHANG, CHEN-CHI
CHANG, CHENG-CHI--[31]
CHANG, GARMA C.C.--[31]

CHANNON, ETHEL M.
CHANNON, E.M.--J. MEYERSON SLST #110--
BENN "TWICE DEAD" '30

CHANSLOR, MARJORIE TORREY
BEVANS, TORRE--[1][22]MYS
TORREY, MARJORIE--[1][22]MYS

CHAPIN, ALENE O. DALTON
DALTON, ALENE--[31][33]

CHAPIN, ANNA ALICE
COVERDALE, HARRY--[1][3][29]MYS--
CHELSEA "SEVENTH SHOT" '24
CHELSEA "UNKNOWN SEVEN" '23
SEABROOKE, JOHN PAUL--[34]MYS, HP--
CHELSEA "SHADOW HALL" '27

CHAPIN, ANSEL
CARTER, NICK--W/DEE STUART,[3], HP--
"DEATH MESSAGE: OIL 74-2" '76
"PAMPLOMA AFFAIR" '78

CHAPLIN, CHARLES SPENCER
CHAPLIN, CHARLEY--[31]

CHAPLIN, W.W.
CHAPLIN, BILL--[31]

CHAPMAN, ELIZABETH COBB
COBB, ELIZABETH--[1]

CHAPMAN, FRANK MONROE
CHAPMAN, FRANCES--[1][31]
FOURNIER, FRANK--[1][31]
GRUMBLING GOURMET, THE--[31]
JOHNSTONE, REX--[1][31]
KATZ, STAN--[1][31]

CHAPMAN, FRANK MONROE [CONT]
MONROE, FRANK--[1]
RICE, R.B.--[1]
WOODBURY, FRANK--[1]

CHAPMAN, GEORGE W.V.
WARREN, VERNON--[1][3][22]MYS--
"STOP-OVER DANGER" '72 & 14 OTHERS '53-61

CHAPMAN, GRAHAM
PYTHON, MONTY--[31]--CO-WROTE SCREENPLAYS W/CLEESE, GILLIAM, IDLE, PALIN & T. JONES

CHAPMAN, JAMES KEITH
KEITH, HAMISH--[31]

CHAPMAN, JOHN STANTON H.
CHAPMAN, MARISTAN--W/MARY H. CHAPMAN--
[1][22][31][33]ENGLISH--
KNOPF "GLEN HAZARD" '33
CONNELL, KIRK--W/MARY H. CHAPMAN--
[1][22][31][33]ENGLISH
ISLEY, DENT--W/MARY H. CHAPMAN--
[1][22][31][33]ENGLISH
SELKIRK, JANE--W/MARY H. CHAPMAN--
[1][22]ENGLISH

CHAPMAN, MARY HAMILTON
CHAPMAN, MARISTAN--W/JOHN S.H. CHAPMAN--
[22][33]ENGLISH--
KNOPF "GLEN HAZARD" '33
CONNELL, KIRK--W/JOHN S.H. CHAPMAN,
[1][22]ENGLISH
ISLEY, DENT--W/JOHN S.H. CHAPMAN,
[1][22][33]ENGLISH
SELKIRK, JANE--W/JOHN S.H. CHAPMAN,
[1][22][33]ENGLISH

CHAPMAN, MATTHEW
RAMSAY, JACK--W/BRUCE ROBINSON, CRPG--
ACE 70345 "THE RAGE" '77

CHAPMAN, RAYMOND
NASH, SIMON--[3][22][31]ENGLISH/MYS--
5 NOVELS '62-66

CHAPMAN, STEPAN
CHAPMAN, STEVEN--[1][31]

CHAPMAN, VERA
TOOK, BELLADONNA--[1][33]

CHAPMAN-HUSTON, D.M.
MOUNTJOY, DESMOND--[1]

CHAPMAN-MORTIMER, CHARLES
MORTIMER, CHAPMAN--[1][22]SCOTTISH-SWEDISH
MORTIMER, CHARLES--[1][22]SCOTTISH-SWEDISH

CHAPPELL, GEORGE S.
TRAPROCK, WALTER E.--[1][23]SF

CHAPPELL, HELEN
BALDWIN, REBECCA--[1][21][26]ROM--12 NOVELS

CHAPPELYEAR, LAURIE
GRANT, LAURIE--[9][21]ROM--
"DEFIANT HEART"
"FOREVER LOVE"
"EMERALD FIRE" & OTHERS

CHARBONNEAU, LOUIS
JENKINS, HERBERT--[2]
YOUNG, CARTER TRAVIS--[2][11][23][28]WEST/ROM--
15 NOVELS '60-88

CHARD, JUDY
CHASE, LYNDON--[1]
GORDON, DOREEN--[1][31]

CHARKIN, PAULA
CHARKIN, PAUL--K. DILBONE-BADGER CKLST, BAE 13, P30

CHARLES, GEORGE
BOWIE, JIM--S. HOLLAND-SCION CKLST, PP 27, P11, HP
HAMPTON, MARK--S. HOLLAND-SCION CKLST, PP 27, P11
KARTA,NAT--S. HOLLAND-SCION CKLST, PP 27, P11, HP
NORWOOD, VICTOR--S. HOLLAND-SCION CKLST, PP 27, P11--GHOSTED??

CHARLES, GORDON H.
HULL, CHARLES--[1][31]

CHARLES, RICHARD
AWDRY, R.C.--[8]

CHARLES, THERESA
LANCE, LESLIE--[1]
SWATRIDGE, IRENE MAUDE--[1]

CHARLIER, ROGER H.
ROCHARD, HENRI--[1]
SCOTT, MARCO--[1]
WALLACE, ROGER--[1]

CHARLTON, HENRY BUCKLEY
CHARLTON, H.B.--[1]

CHARLTON, JOHN
CHARLTON, JACK--[31]

CHARLWOOD, DONALD ERNEST
CHARLWOOD, D.E.--[31]
CHARLWOOD, DON--[31]

CHARNOCK, JOAN PADGETT
THOMSON, JOAN--[1]

CHARNWOOD, GODFREY BENSON
BENSON, GODFREY--[1]

CHARNY, CARMI
CARMI, T.--[22][31]AMERICAN

CHARQUES, DOROTHY [T]
DOROTHY, R.D.--[1][31]

CHARRIERE, HENRI
PAPPILON, HENRI--[29]MYS--
LAFFONT "PAPPILON" '71
"BANCO" '72

CHARTERIS, MARY EVELYN
ASQUITH, LADY CYNTHIA--[11]SF

CHARTIER, EMILE-AUGUST
ALAIN--[22]OXFORD COMPANION TO FRENCH LIT. '61--FRENCH

CHARTIER-LI, ANNETTE M.
CHARTIER, DANETTE--[26]ROM--
"ALABAMA TWILIGHT"
"STOLEN FIRE"

CHARTON, JEAN
GUIREC, JEAN--[1]

CHARTRAND, JOSEPH DEMERS
DES ESCORRES, CHARLES--[1]

CHARTRIAN, ALEXANDRE
ERCKMANN-CHARTRIAN--W/EMILE ERCKMANN, MYS--
EB "MYSTERIOUS SKETCH" DEC '62
ERCKMANN-CHARTRIAN, M.M.--W/EMILE ERCKMANN,
[34]MYS--
WARD "MAN-WOLF & OTHER TALES"
"STORIES OF THE RHINE"

CHASE, ANYA SETON
SETON, ANYA--[1][21]ROM--12 NOVELS

CHASE, JOSEPHINE
WICKES, MARTHA--[3]MYS--
PENN "MYSTERY OF THE SUN DIAL COURT" '26

CHASE, LAWRENCE
CHASE, LARRY--[31]

CHASE, NAOMI FEIGELSON
FEIGELSON, NAOMI--[1][31]

CHASE, TREVETT COBURN
CHASE, KIP--[1][34]MYS--
HAMMOND "WHERE THERE'S A WILL" '61
HAMMOND "MURDER MOST INGENIOUS" '62
HAMMOND "KILLER BE KILLED" '63

CHASE, VIRGINIA
PERKINS, VIRGINIA CHASE--[8]

CHASTAIN, SANDRA
DARCY, JENNA--W/NANCY KNIGHT,[9][26]ROM--
"THE VERY BEST"
JORDAN, ALLIE--[26]ROM--
"SPIDER'S WEB"
"SWEET SEDUCTION"

CHASTAIN, THOMAS
CARTER, NICK--[3]MYS, HP--
AWARD "ASSASSINATION BRIGADE" '73

CHATER, ELIZABETH EILEEN
CHAYTOR, LEE --[31][32][34]MYS--
TRANS "A COURSE IN THE MURDER" '69
CO "ON THE STAIRS" MAR '70
SA "MISS SILLITHORPE'S HOBBY" SEPT '59
SA "INFERNAL TRIANGLE" JUL '60
SA "BROTHERHOOD OF DARKNESS" AUG '62
MOORE, LISA--[1][9][21]ROM

CHATRIAN, ALEXANDRE
ERCKMANN-CHATRAIN--W/EMILE ERCKMANN,[2]
ERCKMANN-CHATRIAN--W/EMILE ERCKMANN,[11]SF

CHATTERJI, SARATCHANDRA
CHATTERJI, SARAT CHANDRA--[31]

CHATZOPULOS, KOSTAS
VASILIKOS, PETROS--[22]GREEK

CHAUNCY, NANCEN B.M.
CHAUNCY, NAN--[1][31]

CHAUNDLER, CHRISTINE
MARTIN, PETER--[8][33]

CHAVEZ, MANUEL
CHAVEZ, ANGELICO--[31]
CHAVEZ, FRAY ANGELICO--[31]

CHAVIARAS, STRATES
HAVIARAS, STRATIS--[31]

CHAYEFSKY, SIDNEY AARON
AARON, SIDNEY--[2][31]
CHAYEFSKY, PADDY--[7][23][31]SF--
"ALTERED STATES"

CHEETHAM, JAMES HAROLD
CHEETHAM, HAL--[8][31]
CHEETHAM, J.H.--[31]

CHEEVER, HENRY P.
CARLOS, DON--[1]
SLOKUMB, SI--[1]

CHEKANI, LORETTA
CHASE, LORETTA--V. BERCH LTR TO HUBIN '94/
[21][26]MYS--
WALKER "SANDALWOOD PRINCESS" '90
CHASE, LORETTA LYNDA--[21]ROM

CHEKENIAN, ARAM HAIGAZ
HAIGAZ, ARAM--[1][31]

CHEKHOV, ANTON PAVLOVICH
CHEKHONTE, ANTOSHA--[31]

CHELTHAM-STRODE, WARREN
DOUGLAS, NOEL--[8]

CHELWOOD, TUFTON VICTOR H
BEAMISH, TUFTON VICTOR H.--[31]

CHEN, ANTHONY
CHEN, TONY--[31]

CHENEY, CHRISTOPHER ROBT.
CHENEY, C.R.--[31]

CHENEY, S. LANCER
FIELD, PETER--[19]WEST, HP--
"OUTLAW OF EAGLES NEST"

CHENEY, THEODORE ALBERT
CHENEY, TED--[31][33]--
HARCOURT "LAND OF HIBERNATING RIVERS" '68
CHENEY, THEODORE A. REES--[31]--
ACE "DAY OF FATE" '81

CHENG, JAMES K.C.
CHENG, YI--[31]

CHENG, TIEN-HSI
CHENG, F.T.--[31]

CHENNEVIERE, DANIEL
RUDHYAR, DANE--[2][7]SF

CHENNEVIERE, GEORGES
DEBILLE, GEORGE--[22]FRENCH

CHERBONNEL, ALICE
DE LA BRETE, JEAN--[22]FRENCH

CHERNENKO, KONSTANTIN U.
CHERNENKO, K.U.--[31]

CHERRY, CAROLYN JANICE
CHERRYH, C. J.--[2][4][7][23][31]SF

CHERTOK, HARVEY
CHERTOK, HAIM--[31]

CHERVOKAS, JOHN VINCENT
LEIGH, MATTHEW ANDREW--[31]

CHESBRO, GEORGE [CLARK]
CROSS, DAVID--[7][18][34]MYS/SF--
JOVE "CHANT" '86
JOVE "SILENT KILLER" '86
JOVE "CODE OF BLOOD" '87

CHESHIRE, DAVID FREDERICK
CHESTER, TOM--[8]

CHESHIRE, GIFFORD PAUL
CHESHIRE, GIFF--[8][28][32]WEST--
11 NOVELS '54-69--
DS "WHITE WATER TEST" FEB '45
DS "VIOLENCE WITH EYE SHADOW" AUG '45
DS "CUT HIS SHARE OF THAT" DEC '45
FORD, PENDLETON--[8][28]WEST--5 NOVELS '54-8

CHESHIRE, GIFFORD PAUL
MERRIMAN, CHAD--V. BERCH, GM PSEUDS, PP 33,
[28]--12 NOVELS '52-70

CHESNEY, GEORGE T.
AN EYE WITNESS IN 1925--[7]SF--
"SOCIALIST REVOLUTION OF 1888" 1884

CHESNEY, MARION G.
CHESTER, SARAH--[26][34]MYS--
TUDOR "DANCING ON THE WIND" '89
WARD, CHARLOTTE--[1]
BEATON, M.C.--[3][31]MYS--
ST. MARTIN'S "DEATH OF A GOSSIP" '85
ST. MARTIN'S "DEATH OF A CAD" '87/
CRAMPTON, HELEN--[21][26]ROM--
"MARRIAGE A'LA MODE
"MARQUIS TAKES A BRIDE"
"HIGHLAND COUNTESS"
FAIRFAX, ANN--[21][26][31]ROM--
"ANNABELLE"
"HENRIETTA"
"PENELOPE"
"MY DEAR DUCHESS"
TREMAINE, JENNIE--[26]ROM--12 NOVELS
TREMAINE, JENNY--[3][21][26]MYS/ROM--
ST. MARTIN'S "MAGGIE" '84

CHESNUTT, LINDA
HANKS, LINDSEY--W/GEORGIA PIERCE,[9][21]ROM--
"MIDNIGHT DECEPTION"
"SAVAGE SURRENDER" & MORE

CHESSER, EUSTACE
HILTON, ALEC--W/ALEX. FULLERTON,[1][31]--
CORGI "THE CONSULTANT" '68

CHESTER, ANNIE M.
MYRTLE, ANNIE--[1]

CHESTER, CHARLIE
NOONE, CARL--[3]--
NEL "SWEET CYANIDE" '76
NEL "MIND OVER MURDER" '76
NEL "EVEN THE RAINBOWS BENT" '77

CHESTER, DEBORAH ANN
BLAKENEY, JAY D.--[7][31]SF--
"ANTHI #1 & 2" '85/90
"OMCRI MATRIX" '87
"GODA WAR" '89
DALTON, SEAN--[7]SF--
"STARHAWKS #1-4" '90/91

CHESTER, TESSA ROSE
DONETTA--[31]

CHESTERMAN, JEAN
KENWARD, JEAN--[8]

CHESTERTON, ADA ELIZABETH
PROTHERO, JOLEN KEITH--[34]MYS--
MELLIFONT "DIAMOND CUT DIAMOND" '32

CHESTERTON, GILBERT KEITH
ARION--[29]MYS
CHESTERBELLOC--W/J.H.P. BELLOC,[1][23]
CHESTERTON, G.K.--[23][34]MYS--
'FATHER BROWN' STORIES & OTHERS 1905-'86
G.K.C.--[29]MYS

CHESTNUTT, EDGAR B.
SCOTT, WALTER--[1]

CHETHAM-STRODE, WARREN
HAMILTON, MICHAEL--[1][22]ENGLISH

CHETWYND, LIONEL
DION, PETER--[31]

CHETWYND-HAYES, RON
CAMPBELL, ANGUS--[2][7][11][16][31]
CLUTCHER, HANS--[2]

CHETWYND-TALBOT, EDWARD H
TALBOT, HUGH--[1]

CHEVALIER, PAUL EUGENE G.
GEORGE, EUGENE--[1][31]

CHEVALLIER, SONJA
LASSERRE, SONJA--[39]GERMAN

CHEW, RUTH
SILVER, RUTH--[1][33]

CHEYNE, JOSEPH LISTER W.
MUNROE, R.--[1]

CHEYNEY, REGINALD E.S.
BRUST, HAROLD--[18][31]MYS--
"IN PLAIN CLOTHES: FURTHER MEMOIRS OF A POLITICAL POLICE OFFICER"
CHEYNEY, PETER--[3][18]MYS--
COLLINS "DARK WANTON" '48
COLLINS "LADIES WON'T WAIT" '51 & MORE
JCM "A MATTER OF HABIT" FEB '57 & OTHERS

CHI, RICHARD HU SEE-YEE
CHIN, CHUAN--[31]

CHIBBETT, H.S.W.
HASTWA, A.--[2]

CHIBNALL, MARJORIE MCCAL.
MORGAN, MARJORIE--[8]

CHIDSEY, DONALD BARR
O'HARA, DONN--R.C. & ELWANDA HOLLAND
REVW JAN '93--
GRAPH G212 "ROGUE ROYAL" '56
STEELE, FLETCHER--L. ROBBINS
LTR MAR '94--PULP

CHILD, HERBERT
MORE, ATHERTON--[1]

CHILD, JUDITH
GREEN, JULI--W/LISA NEHER,[9][21][26]ROM--
"BENEATH A SUMMER MOON"

CHILD, LYDIA MARIA
CHILD, L. MARIA--[31][33]
CHILD, MRS.--[31][33]

CHILD, MAUREEN
CARBERRY, ANN--[26]ROM--3 NOVELS
KANE, KATHLEEN--[26]ROM--
"MOUNTAIN DAWN"
"PAPER HEARTS"
"SMALL TREASURES"

CHILD, PHILIP A.G.
WENTWORTH, JOHN--[1][8]

CHILDRESS, SUSAN
WIGGS, SUSAN--[9][26]ROM--
"EMBRACE THE DAY"

CHILDS, EDMUND BURTON
AYNSWORTH, CECIL--[1]
BLAKE, ROYSTON--[1]
BURTON, EDMUND--[2][3][11][29]MYS--
"RIDDLE OF THE CLOISTERS" '46
"ROYAL SPECIAL & OS" '47

CHILDS, ELEANOR STUART
STUART, ELEANOR--[1]

CHILDS, JAMES RIVES
FILMER, HENRY--[31]

CHILDS, MARYANNA
CHILDS, C. SAND--[1][22][31]AMERICAN
MARYANNA--[1]

CHILDS, WILLIAM HAROLD J.
CHILDS, W.H.J.--[31]

CHILSON, ROBERT DEAN
CHILSON, ROB--[23]SF--
POPLB "STAR-CROWNED KINGS" '75
POPLB "SHORES OF KANSAS" '76
POPLB "REFUGE" '88
POPLB "ROUNDED WITH SLEEP" '90

CHIN, CHARFA
SIMMS, CHARLOTTE--W/JANE KIDDER,[21]ROM--
"SILVER CARESS"

CHIN, FRANK CHEW
DE MENTON, FRANCISCO--[1][31]

CHING, JULIA CHIA-Y
KING, JOYCE--[31]

CHINMOY, SRI
GHOSE, SRI CHINMOY KUMAR--[31]

CHIPP, DONALD LESLIE
CHIPP, D.L.--[31]

CHIPPERFIELD, JOSEPH E.
CRAIG, JOHN ELAND--[22][31][33]ENGLISH--
NELSON "DOG FROM CASTLE CRAG" '52

CHISHOLM, ARTHUR MURRAY
CHISHOLM, A.M.--[31]

CHISHOLM, LILLIAN MARY
ALAN, JANE--[8]
LORRAINE, ANNE--[1]

CHISHOLM, ROBERT FERGUSON
CHISHOLM, R.F.--[31]

CHISHOLM, SAMUEL WHITTEN
CHISHOLM, SAM WHITTEN--[31]

CHITTENDEN, HIRAM MARTIN
PHUCHER, ITOTHE--[1]

CHITTENDEN, MARGARET
CARSON, ROSALIND--[21][31][33]ROM--
9 NOVELS

CHITTY, MARGARET HAZEL
WHITTON, BARBARA--[8]

CHITTY, SIR THOMAS WILES
HINDE, THOMAS--[3][31]MYS--
HODDER "DAY THE CALL CAME" 65
HODDER "GAMES OF CHANCE" '67

CHITWOOD, BILLY JAMES
CHITWOOD, B.J.--[31]

CHLEBNIKOV, VICTOR VIKTO.
CHLEBNIKOV, VELEMIR--[22]RUSSIAN

CHLOROS, ALEXANDER GEORGE
CHLOROS, A.G.--[31]
CHLOROS, ALECK GEORGE--[31]

CHOATE, GWEN PETERSON
CHOATE, R. G.--L. ROBBINS LTR MAR '94,
[22][31]AMERICAN, PULP
MICHAELS, KRISTIN--[9][21]ROM, HP--
"SHADOW OF LOVE"

CHOCHOLAK, MISHA
MISHA--[7]SF--
WORDCRAFT "PRAYERS OF STEEL" '88
"RED SPIDER, WHITE WEB" '90

CHOGYAM TRUNGPA
RINPACHE--[31]INDIA

CHOLLET, HANS-JOACHIM
WOLTER, HANS-JOACHIM--[39]GERMAN/JUV

CHOMETTE, RENE LUCIEN
CLAIR, RENE--[22][31]FRENCH

CHONG, THOMAS
CHONG--[31]
CHONG, TOM--[31]

CHOPIN, KATHERINE
CHOPIN, KATE--[31]

CHORAO, ANN MCKAY SPROAT
CHORAO, KAY--[31]

CHORLEY, RICHARD JOHN
CHORLEY, R.J.--[31]

CHOSACK, CYRIL
MACLEAN, BARRY--[8]

CHOU KUANG HU
SUYIN, HAN--[1]

CHOU, ERIC
CH'LAO, SUNG--[31]
CHOU, YU-JUI--[31]

CHOUDHURY, GOLAM WAHED
CHOUDHURY, G.W.--[31]

CHOVIL, ALFRED HAROLD
BROOK, PETER--[8]

CHOVOSTAL, SANDRA NOVY
PAUL, SANDRA--[26]ROM--
"LAST CHANCE FOR MARRIAGE"

CHRIST, ROBERT B.
BRANDMULLER, JOHANNES--[1]
FRIDOLIN--[1]
GLOPFHAISCHT--[1]

CHRISTENBERRY, JUDITH R.
CHRISTENBERRY, JUDY--[21]ROM--
"NOTORIOUS WIDOW"
"A LITTLE INCONVENIENCE"
STAFFORD, JUDITH--[21]ROM--
"THE LEMON CAKE"
"A HERO'S WELCOME"

CHRISTENSEN, JACK ARDEN
CHRISTENSEN, J.A.--[31]

CHRISTENSEN, THOMAS F.
ADELON, SVEN--[29]MYS--3 NOVELS '30-35

CHRISTENSEN, YOLANDA MAR.
CHRISTENSEN, JO IPPOLITO--[1][31]

CHRISTIAN, CURTIS WALLACE
CHRISTIAN, C.W.--[31]

CHRISTIANSSON, OLIVER
REVILO--[1]

CHRISTIE, AGATHA [M.C.]
MALLOWAN, A.C.--[1][5]MYS
WESTMACOTT, MARY--[2][5][11][21][22][26]ROM--
"THE BURDEN"
"GIANT'S BREAD"
"UNFINISHED PORTRAIT" & 2 MORE

CHRISTIE, ANN PHILIPPA P.
PEARCE, A[NN] PHILIPPA--[1]
PEARCE, PHILIPPA--[31]

CHRISTIE, ANNIE ROTHWELL
ROTHWELL, ANNIE--[1]

CHRISTIE, DOUGLAS
CAMPBELL, COLIN--[3][22]MYS--6 NOVELS '32-36
DURIE, LYNN--[3][22]MYS--
WARD "PAYDIRT" '31
WARD "THE TRIALL CASE" '32
WARD "THIS YELLOW SLAVE" '33

CHRISTIE, ERNEST
CLAY, WEALD--[1]

CHRISTIE, ROBERT
BOLTON, ALEXANDER--V. BERCH-MON PSEUDS, BAE 9--
MON 224 "LADIES OF THE DARK" '61

CHRISTIE, WILLIAM H.
WHITE, CECIL B.--[2][11]

CHRISTIE-MURRAY, DAVID
ARTHUR, HUGH--[31]--
HAMLYN "ASTROLOGY"
CHRISTIE, HUGH--[1][31]

CHRISTIN, PIERRE
LINUS--[2]

CHRISTMAS, JOYCE
PETERSON, CHRISTMAS--W/JON PETERSON,
[21]ROM--
"HIDDEN ASSETS"

CHRISTOPHER, MATTHEW F.
CHRISTOPHER, MATT--[31]MYS--
SFDS "THERE'S DEATH IN HER KISS" DEC '57
GU "BLONDE BAIT" OCT '57

CHRISTOPHER, MATTHEW F. [CONT]
MARTIN, FREDERIC--[1][31][33]JUV--
3 LITTLE BROWN BOOKS '65-8

CHRISTOPHERSEN, SOLVEIG
CHRISTOV, S.--[22]NORWEGIAN

CHRISTOPHS, BERNT
HEIDENS, PETER--[29]MYS--
"MORDANDE FAKTA" '54
"BEVINGAD DOD" '56
"SISTA RONDEN" '57 & OTHERS

CHRISTY, JOSEPH M.
CHRISTY, JOE--[31]

CHU, ARTHUR T.S.
CHU, W.R.--[31]

CHU-YUAN, CHENG
CHENG TEK-CHEUNG--[22]CHINESE-AMERICAN

CHUDNOW, YAFFA
BRYAN, JESSICA--[7]SF--
BB "ACROSS A WINE-DARK SEA" '91

CHUNG, CONSTANCE YU-HWA
CHUNG, CONNIE--[31]

CHUNG, KYUNG CHO
CHONG, KYONA-JO--[31]

CHURCH, ELSIE
PARRISH, JEAN J.--[8]

CHURCHILL, E. RICHARD
PENDLETON, DON--[3]MYS, HP--
GE "ISLAND DEATHTRAP" '83
GE "MOUNTAIN RAMPAGE" '83

CHURCHILL, ED
SCANLON, C.K.M.--W. MURRAY-ECHOES #5, HP--
GMD 'DAN FOWLER' STORIES

CHURCHILL, GAIL WINSTON
CHURCHILL, BILL--[31]

CHURCHILL, JOHN HOWARD
CHURCHILL, J.H.--[31]

CHURS, GUNTER
TRAVEN, DIANA--[39]GERMAN

CHUTE, BEATRICE JOY
CHUTE, B.J.--[31]

CHWAT, ALEKSANDER
WAT, ALEKSANDER--[7]SF--
NW UNIV PRESS "LUCIFER UNEMPLOYED" '91

CIARDI, JOHN ANTHONY
ANTHONY, JOHN--[2][11][31][33]
ANTHONY, JOHN--W/RONALD B. BECKETT,[31]

CICHANTH, ELAINE
SHELLEY, ELIZABETH--W/ELIZABETH SCHAAL,
[9][21]ROM--
"CARAVAN OF DESIRE"

CICONE, JOHN
BALLE, RICHARD--[14]--
OLYM OPH#186 "DEEPER THAN THAT" '70

CIENCIN,[MALCOLM] SCOTT
AWLINSON, RICHARD--[7]HP--
TSR 'FORGOTTEN REALMS': "SHADOWDALE"

CIENCIN,[MALCOLM] SCOTT [CONT]
AWLINSON, RICHARD--W/JAMES LOWDER,[7]HP--
TSR 'FORGOTTEN REALMS': "TANTRAS"
BARON, NICK--W/GREG COX,[7]--
'ROBERT SILVERBERG'S TIME TOURS' #5"

CIMBALO, GUY
FORVE, GUY--[21]ROM--
"ALEXANDER MCKENZIE: LONE COURAGE"

CINAR-MECK, BARBARA
MECK, BARBARA--[39]GERMAN/SF

CINQUIN, EMMANUELLE
CINQUIN, SISTER EMMANUELL--[31]

CIORAN, EMIL M.
CIORAN, E.M.--[31]

CIRNIGLIARO, JAMES N.
CIRNI, JIM--V. BERCH LTR TO HUBIN '94, MYS--
SOHO "KISS OFF" '87
SOHO "COME ON" '89

CITOVITCH, ENID
BALDRY, ENID--[8]

CIVIL, SUSAN
LEE, RACHEL--[26]ROM--9 NOVELS

CIZINSKI, JAKUB
BART, JAKUB--[22]POLISH

CLAASEN, HAROLD
POMEROY, HUB--[22]AMERICAN--SPORTS

CLAESSON, BIGI
BRENDON, KAY--[29]MYS--
TID BITS "SENSATION" '37
"MYSTERIET PA PAGE HALL" '42

CLAGETT, SUE HARRY
CLAGETT, JOHN--[1]
WAKING, ELIZABETH--[1]

CLAGUE, MARYHELEN
SNOW, ASHLEY--[9][21][26]ROM--
6 NOVELS

CLAIR, BILL
MARLOWE, TERRY--W/RICHARD ABSHIRE,
LACHMAN/EASTER

CLAIR, COLIN
NICOLI, C.L.R.--[8]

CLAIRMONT, ELVA
CORRIE, ELVA--[31]

CLAMP, HELEN M.E.
LEIGH, OLIVIA--[8][9]ROM

CLAMPETT, ROBERT
CLAMPETT, BOB--[33]

CLANCY, FRANCIS MICHAEL
CLANCY, KING--[31]

CLANCY, LAURENCE JAMES
CLANCY, LAURIE--[31]

CLANCY, THOMAS LEO JR.
CLANCY, TOM--[7][31]ADV--
PUTNAM "HUNT FOR RED OCTOBER" '85
PUTNAM "RED STORM RISING" '86
& OTHER NOVELS

CLANMORRIS, BARON
BINGHAM, JOHN MICHAEL--[29]MYS

CLAREMONT, CHRISTOPHER S.
CLAREMONT, CHRIS--[23]SF--
"FIRSTFLIGHT #1 & 2" '87-91

CLARK, ALFRED A.G.
CLARK, A.A. GORDON--[18]MYS--
EDITOR OF "ROSCOE'S CRIMINAL EVIDENCE" '52
HARE, CYRIL--[2][3][5][18]
[29][31][40]ENGLISH/MYS--
13 NOVELS & SOME SS

CLARK, BLAIR FOSTER
FOSTER, BLAIR--[7]SF--
LEIS "LOVE'S UNEARTHLY POWER" '83

CLARK, CHARLES HEBER
ADELER, MAX--[2][11][23]
QUILL, JOHN--[23]SF

CLARK, CHARLES MANNING H.
CLARK, C.M.H.--[31]

CLARK, CHARLOTTE MOORE
CLAY, CHARLES [M]--[2][32]MYS--
LM "WORSE THAN HANGING" DEC '49

CLARK, DALE
CLARK, GEORGE E.--L. ROBBINS LTR MAR '94--PULP

CLARK, DONALD HENRY
CLARK, DON--[31]

CLARK, DONALD ROWLEE
CLARK, DON--[31]

CLARK, DOROTHY [PARK]
MCMEEKIN, CLARK--W/ISABEL [M]
MCMEEKIN,[1][22]AMERICAN

CLARK, DOUGLAS M.J.
HOSIER, PETER--[1][18][31]--
"THE MIRACLE MAKERS" '71
CLARK, D.M.J.--[18][31]WAR--
DAVIES "SUEZ TOUCHDOWN: A
SOLDIER'S TALE" '64
DITTON, JAMES--[3][18][29][31]MYS--
3 NOVELS, 1 WAR NOVEL '73-80

CLARK, FREDERICK STEPHEN
DALTON, CLIVE--[31]

CLARK, GAILS
MACKEEVER, MAGGIE--[9][21]ROM--
18 NOVELS

CLARK, GAIL
SOUTH, GRACE--[9][21]ROM--
"MERRIE"

CLARK, JOHN HOWARD
CLARK, J.H.--[31]

CLARK, JOHN PEPPER
CLARK, J.P.--[31]

CLARK, JOHN RUSSELL
CLARK, J.R.--[31]

CLARK, JONATHAN CHARLES
CLARK, J.C.D.--[31]

CLARK, JUSTUS KENT
CLARK, J. KENT--[31]

CLARK, KATHY
CASSIDY, KRIS--[26]ROM--
"BORN TO BE WILD"

CLARK, LOUISE
MACDONALD, ROSLYN--[9][21]ROM-
"SECOND GENEREATION"
"TRANSFER OF LOYALTIES"
"AN INDEPENDENT LADY"

CLARK, MABEL MARGARET C.
STORM, LESLEY--[3]MYS--
HUTCH "GALLOWS-BIRD" '37
PLAY "THE DAY'S MISCHIEF" '52

CLARK, MARIA LOUISA G.
CLARK, MARY LOU--[8][31]

CLARK, MARIE CATHERINE A.
CURLING, AUDREY--[8]

CLARK, MARJORIE
RIVERS, GEORGIA--[8]

CLARK, MARY ELIZABETH
CLARK, MARGERY--W/MARGERY QUIGLEY,[1][8]

CLARK, MAVIS THORPE
CLARK, M.R.--[31][33]AUSTRALIAN--
BOY'S ADVS "HATHERLY'S FIRST FIFTEEN" '30
LATHAM, MAVIS--[31][33]AUSTRALIAN--
TEXTBOOK "FISHING" '63

CLARK, MELISSA
AALYWN, ALYSSE--[21]ROM--
"DEVLYN"

CLARK, PATRICIA D.R.
LORRIMER, CLAIRE--[8][17][29][34]MYS/ROM--
SOUVENIR "A VOICE IN THE DARK" '67

CLARK, PATRICIA D.R.
ROBINS, PATRICIA--[8][17]ROM

CLARK, PHILIP
CARTER, NICK--[1][2]HP
KEITH, HARRISON--W/JOHN CHAMBLISS,
[2][37]MYS--
CLS "MURDER IN A BLACK FRAME" JUL '36

CLARK, RICHARD WAGSTAFF
CLARK, DICK--W/BILL LIBBY,[31]

CLARK, ROSY LEE W.C.
FINLEY, SCOTT--[3][8][22]MYS--
PHOENIX "CASE OF THE BLACK SHEEP" '50

CLARK, SUSIE CHAMPNEY
ST. CLAIR, CECIL--[2]

CLARK, SYLVIA
CLARK, BLAIR--[9]ROM
FOSTER, BLAIR--[9]ROM

CLARK, THOMAS WILLARD
CLARK, TOM--[31]

CLARK, VELMA [VALMA ?]
ADAMS, FAY--V. BERCH-LESBIANA/CTR-CLTR,
BAE 22,GM PSEUDS, PP 33, ADULT--
GM 228 "APPOINTMENT IN PARIS" '52
GM 333 "TO LOVE, TO HATE" '53

CLARK, WILLIAM ARTHUR
CLARK, BILL--[31]

CLARK-KENNEDY, ARCHIBALD
CLARK-KENNEDY, A.E.--[31]

CLARKE, ARTHUR C.
O'BRIEN, E.G.--[2][11][23]SF--
1 STORY '47-51
WILLIS, CHARLES--[2][11][23]SF--
3 STORIES '47-51

CLARKE, BODEN
HOPKINS, JAMES--W/WILLIAM F. NOLAN,[7]--
"WORK OF WILLIAM F. NOLAN:
ANNOTATED BIBLIO. & GUIDE"

CLARKE, BRENDA M.L.H.
HONEYMAN, BRENDA--[9][21][31]ROM--
6 NOVELS

CLARKE, DAVID WALDO
WALDO, DAVID--[22]ENGLISH

CLARKE, DEREK ASHDOWN
CLARKE, D.A.--[31]

CLARKE, DOROTHY JOSEPHINE
SHAW, JOSEPHINE--[8]

CLARKE, GEORGE SYDENHAM
SEAFORTH, A. NELSON--[2][23]--
"THE LAST GREAT NAVAL WAR" 1891

CLARKE, GERALD
GRANT, ALAN--[2]

CLARKE, HENRY CHARLES
CLARKE, HOCKLEY--[8][31]

CLARKE, IGNATIUS IAN F.
CLARKE, I.F.--[31]
CLARKE, IAN--[31]

CLARKE, JOSEPH CALVITT
ADDISON, CAROL--[8][22]MYS

CLARKE, JANET K.
CHRISTOPHER, JANE--[9][21][26]ROM--
3 NOVELS
KENYON, JOANNA--[9][21][26]ROM--
"DANGEROUS PARADISE"
KINCAID, NELL--[9][21][26]ROM--
9 NOVELS

CLARKE, JAY
SLADE, MICHAEL--W/JOHN BANKS, JAY CLARKE
& RICHARD COVELL,[3][7]MYS--
ALLEN "HEADHUNTER" '84

CLARKE, JOHN
CLELAND, P.--[22]ENGLISH
KINGSLEY, ROBERT--[22]ENGLISH

CLARKE, JOHN CAMPBELL
CLELAND, HUGH--[31]

CLARKE, JOSEPH CALVITT
GRANT, RICHARD--[2][3][32][34]MYS--
16 NOVELS
EQMM "MR. PIKE'S HOBBY" OCT '79

CLARKE, JOSEPHINE F.M.
FITZGERALD, ERROL--[34]MYS--
MILLS "THE FAITHFUL KNAVE" '38
FITZGERALD, ERROLL--[22]MYS

CLARKE, JUDITH
CLARKE, J.--[33]AUSTRALIAN--
"HEROIC LIFE OF AL CAPSELLA" '88

CLARKE, LEE
SLADE, MICHAEL--W/JOHN BANKS, RICHARD
COVELL & JAY CLARKE--
BEECH TREE "GHOUL" '87

CLARKE, MARGARET
BUSS, HELEN M.--[31]

CLARKE, PAULINE
CLARE, HELEN--[25]ENGLISH--
5 CHILDREN'S BOOKS

CLARKE, PERCY A.
FRAZER, MARTIN--[3][29]MYS--
14 NOVELS '36-52
LANDER, DANE--[8]
LYTTON, JANE--[8]
NIELSON, VERNON--[8]
ROGERS, STEVE--[34]MYS--
AMALG "THE WOLF OF TEXAS" '39
WATSON, ST. JOHN--[34]MYS--
AMALG "MYSTERY OF THE MOOR" '34

CLARKE, REBECCA SOPHIA
MAY, SOPHIE--CAROL BILLMAN, SECRET OF
STRATEMEYER SYNDICATE,[22]AMERICAN--
LEE "THE CAMPION DIAMONDS" 1897

CLARKE, SYLVESTRE
BUFFALO CHILD LONG LANCE--[8]

CLARKE, WILLIAM JAMES
MONKSHOOD, G.F.--[3][22]MYS--
"MY LADY RUBY & JOHN BASILEON,
CHAN. OF POLAND" 1899

CLARKSON, LESLIE ALBERT
CLARKSON, L.A.--[31]

CLARO, JOSEPH,
CLARO, JOE--[7]SF/JUV--
"HERBIE SERIES" '80-2
"CONDORMAN" '81
"VOYAGERS!" '82

CLARY, SYDNEY ANN
CARR, SHERRY--[9][21][26]ROM--
"LET PASSION SOAR"
CHANCE, SARA--[9][21][26]ROM--
14 NOVELS

CLAUDE, ANNE P.F.
NANCY, A.P.F.--[1]

CLAUSEN, WENDELL VERNON
CLAUSEN, W.V.--[31]

CLAUSS, LUDWIG FERDINAND
BRANDECK, GOTZ--[39]GERMAN

CLAUVOT-GEER, URSINA
GIRUN, GIAN--[22]ROMANISH

CLAY, CASSIUS
ALI, MUHAMMAD--[31]

CLAY, JAMES
CLAY, JIM--[31]

CLAY, MICHAEL JOHN
GRIFFIN, JOHN--[3][29]MYS--
10 NOVELS '76-79

CLAYTON, RICHARD
RICHARDS, EUGENE--V. BERCH-BRNDN/BC PSEUDS, BAE 22, P24

CLAYTON, RICHARD HENRY M.
HAGGARD, WILLIAM--[2][3][5][18][29][31]ENGLISH/MYS--26 NOVELS '59-79

CLEARY, C.V.H.
DAY, HARVEY--[8]
DUNCAN, A.H.--[8]
NORRIS, P.E.--[8]

CLEATOR, PHILIP ELLABY
CLEATOR, P.E.--[31]

CLEAVER, ANASTASIA
CLEAVER, A.--[26]ROM
PETERS, NATASHA--[1][9][21]ROM--7 NOVELS

CLEAVER, DIANE
SMITH, JULIA CLEAVER--W/NICHOLS SMITH,[1]

CLEAVER, HYLTON REGINALD
CRUNDEN, REGINALD--[8]

CLEAVER, WILLIAM & VERA
CLEAVER, BILL--[31]--CHILDREN'S FICT--17 BOOKS '67-83

CLEAVES, MARGARET MAJOR
MAJOR, ANN--[9][21][26]ROM--24 NOVELS

CLEESE, JOHN [MARWOOD]
PYTHON, MONTY--[31]CO-WROTE SCREENPLAYS W/CHAPMAN, GILLIAM, IDLE, PALIN & T. JONES

CLEGG, ALEXANDER BRADSHAW
CLEGG, ALEC--[31]

CLEGG, PAUL
VALE, KEITH--[8]

CLEMENS, BRIAN
O'GRADY, TONY--[8]

CLEMENS, PAUL
CADWALLADER--[8]

CLEMENS, SAMUEL LANGHORNE
JOSH--[31]
LYCURGUS, SOLON--[1]
SLOCUM, HI--[1]
SNODGRASS, THOMAS JEFFER.--[33]
SWAIN, MARK--[1]
TWAIN, MARK [1]--[2][7][11][32]--
"TOM SAWYER"
"HUCKLEBERRY FINN" & OTHERS
EQMM "STOLEN WHITE ELEPHANT" JUL '43
SC "ADV OF SHAMROCK JONES" '45
EQMM "A MEDIEVAL ROMANCE" NOV '45
EQMM "TOM SAWYER, DETECTIVE" AUG '52
EQMM "MY FIRST INTERVIEW WITH ARTEMIS WARD" MAY '52
EQMM "MY WATCH" MAY '54
EQMM "WHAT DID POOR BROWN DO?" SEPT '55
MZ "THE UNDYING HEAD" AUG '63
TWAIN, QUARTER--[1]

CLEMENS-FOX, CAROL
FOX, ALICIA--[9][21][26]ROM--"LEGAL TENDER"

CLEMENT, ERNEST C.
CONNELL, CANDACE--[3][9][21][26]ROM/MYS--
DBLDY "RED TURRETS OF ORNE" '79
ZEBRA "ELLENA" '75

CLEMENT, GEORGE H.
HENRI, G.--[31]

CLEMENTS, ARTHUR LEO
CLEMENTS, A.L.--[31]

CLEMENTS, KAYE L.
JENNINGS, CAYLIN--W/JEANNE TRINER,[9]ROM
TRINER, JEANNE KAYE--W/JEANNE TRINER,[9]ROM

CLEMO, REGINALD JOHN
CLEMO, JACK--[8][31]

CLERY, REGINALD VALENTINE
CLERY, VAL--[31]
JANUS--[31]

CLERY, WILLIAM EDWARD
FRYERS, AUSTIN--[2][3][7]MYS/SF--
PEARSON "A PAULPER BILLIONAIRE" 1899
PEARSON "DEVIL & THE INVENTOR" 1900
PEARSON "UNCREATED MAN" '12

CLEVELAND, GEORGE
CLEVELAND, BOB--[31][33]
DICK, CAPPY--[31][33]

CLEVELAND, MARY
ALLEN, MARY--[31]

CLEVELAND, PHILIP JEROME
ADAMS, A. DON--[22][31]AMERICAN
CHUTE, RUPERT--[22]AMERICAN
CHUTE, RUPERT--[31]
FRIEND, A.--[31]AMERICAN

CLEVELY, HUGH DESMOND
CLAYMORE, TOD--PPCC#7, P58,[34]--
CASSELL "YOU REMEMBER THE CASE" '39
CASSELL "SPEEDWELL" '46
PENG 1061 "APPOINTMENT IN NEW ORLEANS" '55
PENG 1087 "REUNION IN "FLORIDA" '55

CLEVEN, KATHRYN SEWARD
CLEVEN, CATHRINE--[31][33]CHILDREN'S BKS--
BOBBS "SECRET OF KING'S FIELD" '52

CLEVIN, JOERGEN
CLEVIN, JORGEN--[31]

CLIFFORD, CHARLES
AMES, ROBERT--V. BERCH-GM PSEUDS, PP 33,[3]MYS--
GM269 "THE DEVIL DRIVES" '52
GM435 "THE DANGEROUS ONE" '55
GM518 "AWAKE & DIE" '55
CLIFFORD, L.--L. ROBBINS LTR MAR '94--PULP

CLIFFORD, GERALDINE JONC.
JONCICH, GERALDINE--[31]

CLIFFORD, HAROLD B.
FARNHAM, BURT--[22][31][33]AMERICAN

CLIFFORD, MARGARET CORT
CLIFFORD, PEGGY--[31][33]--
"ELLIOTT" '67
"TO ASPEN & BACK" '80
& OTHER CHILDREN'S BOOKS
CORT, M.C.--[31][33]--CHILDREN'S BOOKS

CLIFFORD, MARGARET CORT
CORT, MARGARET--[31]JUV--
"LITTLE OLEG" '71

CLIFFORD, MARTIN
KENIAN, PAUL ROGER--[31]

CLIMO, SHIRLEY
BEISTLE, SHIRLEY--[31]

CLINE, NORMA
KLOSE, NORMA CLINE--[8]

CLINE, SARA LOUISE
CLINE, S.L.--[31]

CLINGAN, A.B.
CHADWICK, ADRIAN--[2]

CLINGAN, C.C.
KENNEDY, EARL--[2]
SILVERBIRD, CORD--[2]

CLINTON, DANIEL JOSEPH
ROURKE, THOMAS--[3]MYS--
FARRAR "THE SCARLET FLOWER" '33

CLINTON, EDWIN M.
MORE, ANTHONY--[2][11]

CLINTON, IRIS A. CORBIN
CORBIN, IRIS--[22][31]ENGLISH-RHODESIAN

CLINTON, LLOYD DEWITT
CLINTON, D.--[31]

CLINTON-BADDELEY, V.C.
BADDELEY, V.C. CLINTON--[31]

CLISH,[LEE] MARIAN
LEE, MARIAN--[31][33]

CLITHERO, MYRTLE ELY
CLITHERO, SALLY--[31]

CLONES, NICHOLAS J.
KLONIS, N.I.--[31]

CLOPET, LILIANE M.C.
BETHUNE, MARY--[8]

CLOUGH, BRENDA WANG
CLOUGH, B.R.--[31]

CLOUTIER, CHARLES
CLOUKEY, CHARLES--[2][11]

CLOUTIER-WOJCIECH, CECILE
CLOUTIER, CECILE--[31]
DE LANTAGNE, CECILE--[31]

CLOWES, WILLIAM LAIRD
NAUTICUS--[22]ENGLISH--NAVAL

CLUNE, ANNE
CLISSMANN, ANNE--[8][31]

CLUNE, FRANCIS PATRICK
CLUNE, FRANK--[31][36]AUSTRALIAN/MYS--
INVIN "DARK OUTLAW: STORY OF
GUNMAN GARDINER" ca '45

CLUTHA, JANET P. FRAME
FRAME, JANET--[7][31]SF--
BLOOMSBURY "THE CARPATHIANS" '88

CLUTTERBUCK, RICHARD
JOCELYN, RICHARD--[8][31]

CLYDE, LEONARD WORSWICK C
BARON, PETER--[3][22]MYS--
6 NOVELS '27-31

CLYMER, ELEANOR
BELL, JANET--[25][31][33]AMERICAN--
2 CHILDREN'S BOOKS
KINSEY, ELIZABETH--[8][25][31][33]AMERICAN--
CHILDREN'S BOOKS

CLYNE, DOUGLAS
SINCLAIR, ALASDAIR--[8]

COAD, FREDERICK R.
SOSTHENES--[8]
SUTTON, I.M.--[8]

COADE, JESSIE
LESLIE, JANE--[31]

COATES, ANNA
JOSEPH, ANNE--[31]
SCOTTI, ANNA--[33]

COATES, ANTHONY
MANDEVILLE, D.E.--[8]

COATES, FREDERICK AMES
ATES, C.O.--L. ROBBINS LTR MAR '94--PULP

COATES, JOHN FRANCIS
COATES, J.F.--[31]

COATES, KENNETH STEPHEN
COATES, K.S.--[31]
COATES, KEN [S]--[31]

COBB, CLAYTON W.
PATTEN, J.--[8]

COBB, IVO GEIKIE
WEYMOUTH, ANTHONY--[3][29]MYS--
7 NOVELS & SS '34-51

COBB, RICHARD CHARLES
COBB, R.C.--[31]

COBB, WELDON J.
CARTER, NICHOLAS--[3][34]MYS, HP--
WHITMAN "A TRIPLE CRIME" '30

COBBE, FRANCIS POWER
NOSTRODAMUS, MERLIN--[2]

COBBING, BOB
CENTO--[31]

COBURN, WALTER J.
COBURN, WALT--[28]WEST--NOVELS '27-68

COCAGNAC, A.M.
WARBLER, J.M.--[33]

COCHRAN, HOWE P.
ANONYMOUS--V. BERCH--GM PSEUDS, PP 33--
"BELLE BRADLEY--HER STORY"

COCHRANE, ELIZABETH
COCHRAN, ELIZABETH--[31]
BLY, NELLIE--[3]MYS--
DILLINGHAM "MYSTERY OF CENTRAL PARK" 1889

COCHRANE, GEORGE HENRY
HERVY, GRANT--[13]AUSTRALIAN

COCHRANE, PAULINE A.
ATHERTON, PAULINE--[31]

COCHRANE, WILLIAM E.
BOULT, S. KYE--[2][7][11][23][31]SF--
BERK "SOLO KILL" '77
PAIGE, LEO--[23]SF--
FANTASY BK "HOW HIGH ON THE LADDER?" '50

COCKBURN, SARAH
CAUDWELL, SARAH--[29][34]MYS--
COLLINS "THUS WAS ADONIS MURDERED?" '81
COLLINS "SHORTEST WAY TO HADES" '84
COLLINS "SIRENS SANG OF MURDER" '89

COCKBURN,[FRANCIS] CLAUD
CORK, PATRICK--[1][31]
DREW, KENNETH--[1][31]
HELVICK, JAMES--[2][3][7][31][32]MYS--
BRDMN "BEAT THE DEVIL" '53
BRDMN "HORSES" '61
SUS "BRAVE JACK CONWAY" FEB '61
SUS "ALL LAID ON FOR BERNARD" APR '61
EQMM "TOTAL RECALL" AUG '62
PITCAIRN, FRANK--[1]

COCKCROFT, GEORGE POWERS
RHINEHART, LUKE--CRPG,[7][23]SF--
"DICE MAN" '71
"MATARI" '75
GRAFTON "ADVENTURES OF WIM" '86
DELC "LONG VOYAGE BACK" '83

COCKRELL, BARBARA
HAMILTON, KATRINA--[21]ROM--
"MOONLIGHT MASQUERADE"
HARGIS, BARBARA--[21]ROM--
"HEART SONG"

COCKS, PAMELA P.
THOMAS, DICEY--V. BERCH LTR TO HUBIN '94--
TUDOR "STATUATORY MURDER" '89

COCKSHUT, NAIDRA
GREY, NAIDRA--[3]MYS--
PUTNAM "DARK SUN, PALE SHADOWS" '73
PUTNAM "FOXGLOVE SUMMER" '76

CODDINGTON, LYNN
HAYES, ALLISON--[21]ROM--
"SPELLBOUND"

CODRESCU, ANDREI
LAREDO, BETTY--[31]

CODY, STONE
MOUNT, TOM E.--L. ROBBINS LTR '94--PULP
THORNE, KENT--L. ROBBINS LTR '94--PULP

COE, FREDERICK
COE, FRED--[31]

COERR, ELEANOR BEATRICE
HICKS, ELEANOR [B]--[8][31][33]
PAGE, ELEANOR--[8][33]

COFFEY, DANIEL
DR. SCIENCE--[31]

COFFEY, EDWARD HOPE, JR.
HOPE, EDWARD--[2]

COFFMAN, RAMON PEYTON
UNCLE RAY--[22][33]AMERICAN, JUV

COFFMAN, VIRGINIA [E]
CAMERON, KAY--[9][21]AMERICAN/ROM--
AWARD "PASSION'S REBEL"
CROSS, VICTOR--[3][17][21]AMERICAN/ROM/MYS--
AWARD "BLOODSPORT" '66
DU VAUL, VIRGINIA C.--[3][17][21][26]
[29][31]AMERICAN/ROM/MYS--
"MASQUE BY GASLIGHT"
DUVAL, JEANNE--[9][17][21][26]AMERICAN/ROM--
"LADY SERENA"
"RAVISHERS"
SAUNDERS, DIANA--[9][21][26]AMERICAN/ROM--
"PASSION OF LETTY FOX"
"TANA MAGUIRE"
STANFIELD, ANN--[9][17][21][26]ROM--
"GOLDEN MARGUERITE"
"DOXY'S MASQUE"
"ROYAL SUMMER"

COGGINS, PASCHAL HESTON
MARLOW, SIDNEY--[3]MYS--
3 NOVELS 1890-'12

COGHLAN, PEGGIE
STIRLING, JESSICA--W/HUGH C. RAE,[9][21]ROM--
15 NOVELS

COGSWELL, CORALIE NORRIS
HOWARD, CORALIE--[22][31]AMERICAN

COGSWELL, FREDERICK WILL.
COGSWELL, FRED--[31]

COGSWELL, GEORGE RAE
COGSWELL, GEORGIA--V. BERCH LTR TO HUBIN '94,
MYS--
ZEBRA "GOLDEN OBSESSION" '79

COGSWELL, THEODORE
THOMAS, COGSWELL--W/THEODORE L.
THOMAS,[11]SF

COGSWELL, THEODORE R.
CHARTERIS, LESLIE--LOCUS #389 OBIT
FOR CHARTERIS,
GHOSTED--DID NOT STATE WHICH STORIES
COGSWELL, TED--LOCUS #389 OBIT
FOR CHARTERIS

COHAN, ANTHONY ROBERT
COHAN, TONY--[7]SF--
ACROBAT BKS "NINE SHIPS: A BOOK
OF TALES" '75

COHEN, ALFRED J.
DALE, ALAN--[3]MYS--
OGILVIE "NED BACKMAN, THE NEW ORLEANS
DETECTIVE" 1887

COHEN, BEN
BURROW, RHODA--W/RHODA C.K. LEDERER,[31]--
BRIDGE BOOKS

COHEN, BERNARD HALSBAND
COHEN, BARNEY--[7]SF--
BERK "THE NIGHT OF THE TOY DRAGONS" '77
TOR "BLOOD ON THE MOON" '84

COHEN, CHESTER
CONANIGHT--W/DAMON KNIGHT,[2][11]
CONANT, CHESTER B.--[2][11]

COHEN, DAVE
COHEN, HARRY--[2]
COHN, HARRY--S. HOLLAND-VULTURES OF THE VOID--BR. SF MAG - FAN COLUMN '54

COHEN, ERIC
MENSCH, H.L.--W/DENNIS W. ETCHISON, B. LEVIN--OASIS "STUD ROW" '69

COHEN, JANET
NEEL, JANET--DDLY PLEAS. #3, P34--"INSP. MCLEISH/FRANCESCA WILSON" SERIES

COHEN, JENE BARR
BARR, JENE--W/ROBERT J. ANTONACCI,[1][31]--"YOUNG CHAMPIONS" SERIES - 4 BKS '56-62

COHEN, MALCOLM
ZOOL, M.H.--[23]SF GROUP PSEUD.

COHEN, MARTIN A.
ALBRAN, KEHLOG--W/SHELDON R. SHACKET,[1]

COHEN, MATTHEW
COHEN, MATT--[23][38]CANADIAN/SF--"KORNSONILOFF" '69 & 8 OTHERS TO '90

COHEN, MORRIS
COHEN, MIKE--[22][31]AMERICAN

COHEN, MORTON N.
MORETON, JOHN--[8][22]AMERICAN

COHEN, NORA
TARLOW, NORA--[33]--PUTNAM "AN EASTER ALPHABET" '91

COHEN, NORMAN
COHEN, NORM--[31]

COHEN, RHODA
BROWNLEIGH, ELEONORA--[9][21][26]ROM--7 NVLS
LOY, DIANA--[9][21][26]ROM--
"CHERISH THE NIGHT"
"NEW YORKERS"
"AFTERALL"

COHEN, SUSAN HANDLER
ST. CLAIR, ELIZABETH--[3][7][9][21][26]--ZEBRA "TREK OR TREAT" '80 & 9 OTHERS '74-80

COHEN, VICTOR
CALDECOTT, VERONICA--[8]

COHN, ELSE
LOTTING, EVA--[39]GERMAN

COHN, EMIL
LUDWIG, EMIL--[22]GERMAN--MAY HAVE BEEN CHANGED LEGALLY TO "LUDWIG"

COHN, OTTO JUSTINUS
JUSTINUS, OTTO--[39]GERMAN

COHN, VERA
BROIDO, VERA--[31]

COHON, BARUCH JOSEPH
COHON, BARRY--[31]

COKE, DESMOND
BLINDERS, BELINDA--[8]

COKER, CAROLYN
COLE, ALISON--[31][34]MYS--DODD "BACK TOWARD LISBON" '85

COLAKOVIC, RODOLJUB
PAVOLOVIC, IVAN--[1]
ROSENKO, MIKHAIL LENINEST--[1]
RUDI--[1]
VUKOVIC--[1]

COLBRON, GRACE ISABEL
MARCHANT, ROMANO ISABEL--[22]MYS

COLBY, ROBERT
CARTER, NICK--AUTHOR PROVIDED,[3]HP--AWARD "DEATH'S HEAD CONSPIRACY" '73

COLDSMITH, DONALD C.
COLDSMITH, DON--[28][31]WEST--19 NOVELS '80-90

COLE, ADRIAN
BRYANT, ADRIAN--[2][16]--SHARED BY COLLABORATION

COLE, EUGENE ROGER
COLE, E.R.--[31]

COLE, GEORGE & MARGARET
G.D.H.--[40]MYS--"GREAT SOUTHERN MYSTERIES" '31

COLE, GEORGE D.H.
COLE, C.--W/MARGARET I.P. COLE,[29]MYS--"MORD I SJUAN" '50
COLE, DOUGLAS--[8][32]MYS--OF "FIENDS LOVE TOO!" JUL '60
COLE, G.D.H. & M.I.--W/M.I. POSTGATE,[5][32]MYS--
ML "OWL AT THE WINDOW" NOV '33
EQMM "A LESSON IN CRIME" JUL '44
MK "DEATH ON HOLIDAY" JUL '53
POPULUS--[8]

COLE, HUGH SAMUEL DAVID
COLE, H.S.D.--[31]
COLE, SAM--[31]

COLE, JOANNA
COOKE, ANN--[1][31][33]

COLE, JOHN
LEIGHTON, J.G.--[11]SF

COLE, JOHN PETER
COLE, J.P.--[31]NON-FICT

COLE, LEONARD LESLIE
LESLEY, COLE--[31]

COLE, LESTER
COHN, LESTER--[31]
COPLEY, GERALD L.C.--[31]
STURGIS, COLIN--W/MELVIN STURGIS,[2][11]

COLE, LOIS DWIGHT
ARNETT, CAROLINE--[31][33]--
GM "MELINDA" '75
GM "CLARISSA" '76
GM "THEODORA"'77
GM "CLAUDIA" '78
GM "STEPHANIE" '79
AVERY, LYNN--[8][22][31][33]--
DUELL "CAPPY & THE RIVER" '60
DUELL "MYS OF VANISHING HORSES" '63
DUDLEY, NANCY--[8][22][31][33]AMERICAN/ROM--5 COWARD NVLS '53-7

COLE, LOIS DWIGHT [CONT]
DWIGHT, ALLAN--W/TURNEY A. TAYLOR,
[8][22][31][33]--
MacM "SPANIARD'S MARK" '32
MacM "LYNN DICKSON, CONFEDERATE" '34
MacM "DRUMS IN THE FOREST" '36
MacM "KENTUCKY CARGO" '38
DWIGHT, ALLEN--[1]AMERICAN
ELIOT, ANNE--[3][22][31][33][40]MYS--
5 NOVELS '67-74
LATTIN, ANN--[1][31]AMERICAN
TAYLOR, LOUIS DWIGHT COLE--[1]AMERICAN

COLE, MARGARET ALICE
MANNING, ROSEMARY--[8][22]ENGLISH
RENTON, JULIA--[8][22]ENGLISH
SAUNDERS, IONE--[8][22]

COLE, MARGARET P.I.
COLE, C.--W/GEORGE D.H. COLE,[29]MYS--
"MORD I SJUAN" '50

COLE, WILLIAM R.
COLE, COZY--[31]

COLE, WILLIAM SHADRACK
COLE, BILL--[31]

COLEMAN, CLAY
ADAMS, NICHOLAS--[7]HP--
HARPER "HORROR HIGH:HARD ROCK;
HEARTBREAKER; MR. POPULARITY"
HARPER "HORROR HIGH:NEW KID
ON THE BLOCK; & RESOLVED, YOU'RE DEAD"

COLEMAN, HILDA
CRAYDER, TERESA--[33]--CHILDREN'S BOOKS

COLEMAN, JOHN
DEXTER, JOHN--[11]HP
KANTO, PETER--[11]HP
VAN HELLER, MARCUS--[11]HP

COLEMAN, PATRICIA REG.
COLEMAN, PATTY R.--[31]

COLEMAN, ROBERT DAVID
COLEMAN, BOB--[31]

COLEMAN, ROBERT W.A.
INSIGHT, JAMES--[22]EGYPTIAN-ENGLISH

COLEMAN, VERNON
CHARBONNIER, MARC--[7]SF--
HALE "TUNNEL" '80

COLEMAN, WILLIAM LAWRENCE
COLEMAN, LONNIE--[8][31]

COLEMAN, WILLIAM VINCENT
COLEMAN, BILL--[31]

COLEMAN, WIN
PERRIMAN, COLE--W/PAT PERRIN--
CRPG "TERMINAL GAME"

COLEMAN-COOKE, JOHN C.
FORD, LANGRIDGE--[8]

COLERIDGE, MARY ELIZABETH
ANOCLOS--[31]
COLERIDGE, M.E.--[31]

COLES, ALBERT JOHN
STEWER, JAN--[8]

COLES, CYRIL HENRY
COLES, MANNING--W/ADELAID MANNING,
[2][3][5][11][16][22]
COLES, MANNING--[3]CYRIL W/TOM HAMMERTON--
"HOUSE AT PLUCK'S GUTTER"
"SEARCH FOR A SULTAN"
GAITE, FRANCIS--W/ADELAIDE MANNING,
[2][3][5][18][31]MYS--
5 'LATIMER' NOVELS

COLES, PHOEBE CATHERINE
FRASER, PETER--[8][31]ROM--
15 NOVELS '44-80

COLETTE, SIDONIE GABRIELL
COLETTE-- FRENCH AUTHOR'S BIOS, REF WORK

COLEY, REX
RAGGED STAFF--[8]

COLIN SMITH, RODNEY
COLLIN, RODNEY--[8]

COLLAS, FELIX EDWARD
COLLAS, PHIL--[7]SF--
STONE "THE INNER DOMAIN" '89

COLLEY, BARBARA
LOGAN, ANNE--[26]ROM--
"GULF BREEZES"
"TWIN OAKES"

COLLIE, RUTH
STITCH, WILHELMINA--[8]

COLLIER, HUGH
DALTON, MORAY--[3]MYS--
14 NOVELS '29/51

COLLIER, JAMES L.
WILLIAMS, CHARLES--[1][31][33]

COLLIER, LUCILLE ANN
COLLIER, JOHNNIE LUCILLE--[31]
COLLIER, LUCY ANN--[31]

COLLIGNON, ILSE
ARCOL, MARGUERITE--[39]GERMAN
REMY, ILLA--[39]GERMAN

COLLIGNON, JETTA
RENTZLOW, BRITTA--[39]GERMAN
SACHS, JETTA--[39]GERMAN
VON BRENCKEN, JULIA--[39]GERMAN

COLLINGS, EDWARD GEOFFREY
BLACKWELL, JOHN--[8][34]MYS--
HM "SECURITY RISK" '35

COLLINGS, I.J.
COLLINGS, JILLIE--[8]
GEORGE, VICKIE--[8]

COLLINS, ANDREW J.
AMES, EDNA--[3]MYS--
MAJOR "THE HOUSE OF SECRETS" '76
CROWELL, ANTHONY--V. BERCH-BRNDN/BC PSEUDS,
BAE 22, ADULT--
POWERS, R.T.--V. BERCH-BRNDN/BC PSEUDS, BAE
22, ADULT--
ROAN, PAUL--V. BERCH-BRNDN/BC PSEUDS, BAE 22,
ADULT--
WHITE, LORIMER--V. BERCH-BRNDN/BC PSEUDS, BAE
22, ADULT--

COLLINS, ARTHUR WORTH JR.
COLLINS, BED--[31]

COLLINS, BARBARA
ALLAN, BARBARA--W/MAX ALLAN COLLINS,
HAWK-COLLINS INTRVW MAY '93

COLLINS, CHARLES JAMES
PRIAM--[34]MYS--
WARD "DICK DIMINY" 1854

COLLINS, DALE
FENNIMORE, STEPHEN--[8]

COLLINS, DOROTHEA T.B.
BRANDE, DOROTHEA--[1]

COLLINS, FREDERICK LEWIS
LEWIS, FREDERICK--[1][3]MYS--
CLODE "THE STRANGE CASE OF MARY PAGE" '16

COLLINS, JAMES L.
MILLER, JIM--CRPG--
HARPER 100706 "BORDER MARSHALL" '93
POCK 66946 "RANGER'S REVENGE" '90
GM 12481 "GONE TO TEXAS" '84 & OTHERS

COLLINS, JOHN LAWRENCE JR
COLLINS, JOHN L.--[7]SF
COLLINS, LARRY--[7][31]SF--
S&S "MAZE: A NOVEL" '89
JONQUIL--[2]

COLLINS, KATHLEEN
KRANIDAS, KATHLEEN--[1][31]

COLLINS, MARION SMITH
COLLIN, MARION--[9]--[21]SAYS AUTHOR IS
"MARION CRIPPS COLLINS"
SMITH, MARION--[9][21]ROM--
14 NOVELS

COLLINS, MAX ALLAN
ALLAN, BARBARA--W/BARBARA COLLINS,
HAWK-COLLINS INTRVW '93
COLLINS, MAX--HAWK-COLLINS INTRVW '93--
EARLY CURTIS & PINN
RUSHING, PATRICK--HAWK-COLLINS
INTRVW '93--FUTURE WORK

COLLINS, MICHAEL
COLLINS, MICHELLE--[34]MYS--
ZEBRA "MURDER AT WILLOW RUN" '79
ZEBRA "PREMIERE AT WILLOW RUN" '80

COLLINS, MILDRED
COLLINS, JOAN--[8]

COLLINS, NANCY A.
REGALIA, NANZI--[7]SF--
DARK CARNIVAL PR "LOVE THROBBING BOB" '90

COLLINS, PATRICIA LOWERY
COLLINS, PAT--[31]

COLLINS, RANDALL
WATSON, DR. JOHN H.--[7]SF--
CROWN "CASE OF THE PHILOSOPHER'S
RING" '78

COLLINS, THOMAS HIGHTOWER
HIGHTOWER, PAUL--[31]

COLLINS, VERE HENRY
TELLAR, MARK--[8]

COLLINS, WILKIE
COLLINS, CHARLES--W/CHARLES DICKENS,
[11][32]MYS--
EW "LA TETE NOIRE" NOV '65

COLLINS-CHAPMAN, NANCY W.
COLLINS, NANCY W.--[31]

COLLIS, ARTHUR
EHRLICH, COLLIS--W/ROSANNE EHRLICH,
V. BERCH LTR TO HUBIN '94--
BAL "ATTACK" '80

COLLISON, WILSON
KENT, WILLIS--[3][22]MYS--
MCBRIDE "A WOMAN IN PURPLE PAJAMAS" '31

COLLUMS, BRENDA
CROSS, BRENDA--[1]
HUGHES, BRENDA--[1]

COLMAN, HILA
CRAYDER, TERESA--[31][33]

COLOMINAS, KATHLEEN ADELE
COLE, KAY--[31]

COLORADA CAPELLA, ANTONIO
COLORADA, ANTONIO J.--[31]

COLSTON-BAYNES, DOROTHY
CRESTON, DORMER--[31]

COLTER, ELIZABETH
COLTER, ELI--[3][11]MYS/SF--
MILL "GULL COVE MURDERS" '46
MILL "CHEER FOR THE DEAD" '47
ARCADIA "REHEARSAL FOR THE FUNERAL" '53

COLTMAN-ALLEN, V. ERNEST
DUDLEY, ERNEST--[29][32][34]MYS--
29 NOVELS '43-60
7 DIGEST STORIES [EW, JCM & LM]
LYDECKER, J.J.--[8]

COLTON, MEL
TRASK, MERRILL--[22]MYS

COLVER, ANNE
GRAFF, POLLY ANNE--[31][33]
HARRIS, COLVER--[3][22][31][33]MYS--
3 NOVELS '33-8

COLVILLE, HELEN HESTER
WYLDE, KATHARINE--[34]MYS--
OSGOOD "OUR WILLS & FATES" 1897

COMBER, LILLIAN
BECKWITH, LILLIAN--
[9][21][22][26][31]ENGLISH/ROM--
"A PROPER WOMAN"

COMBER, ROSE
STAR, ELISON--[8]

COMBUECHEN, SIGRID
COMBUCHEN, SIGRID--[31]

COMER, CORNELIA ATWOOD
PRATT, CORNELIA ATWOOD--[23]--MAIDEN &
WORKING NAME

COMFORT, ALEXANDER
COMFORT, ALEX--[31]
HORNBROOKE, OBADIAH--[8]

COMMINGS, JOSEPH
COMO, JOSEPH--[14]ADULT--
OLYM OPH#230 "THE BITCH OF BUCHENWALD" '71

COMMINGS, JOSEPH
CRAVEN, MONTE--LACHMAN-ED HOCH LST '93--
MD "DIVER & THE WITCH" MAR-APR '62
& 11 OTHERS

COMPTON, DAVID GUY
COMPTON, D.G.--[3][31]ENGLISH/MYS--
"THE PALACE '69
COMPTON, GUY--[2][3][4][11][31]ENGLISH/MYS--
6 NOVELS '62-66
LYNCH, FRANCES--[2][3][4][21][23][26]MYS/SF--
SOUVENIR "A DANGEROUS MAGIC" '78
& 4 OTHERS

COMYNS-CARR, BARBARA I.R.
COMYNS, BARBARA--[23][31]ENGLISH/SF

CONAN DOYLE, ADRIAN MALC.
DOYLE, ADRIAN M.C.--[31]

CONANT, PAUL
PAUL, GENE--[34]MYS--
LION 104 "LITTLE KILLER" '52
TRNPT "NAKED IN THE DARK" '53
LION LL158 "THE BIG MAKE" '57

CONARAIN, ALICE [NINA]
BOWYER, NINA--[8]IRISH
CONARAIN, NINA--[8]IRISH
HOY, ELIZABETH--[9][17][21][26]IRISH/ROM--
25 NOVELS

CONAWAY, JAMES C.
CONAWAY, J.C.--[21]ROM
CONAWAY, JIM--[21][34]MYS/ROM--
BELM "ANGEL POSSESSED" '74
BELM "DEADLIER THAN THE MALE" '77
BELM "THEY DO IT WITH MIRRORS" '77 & OTHERS
LYONS, LEILA--[9][21]ROM--
"BRIDGE TO TOMORROW"
"PILLARS OF HEAVEN"
"STAR QUALITY"
VALCOUR, VANESSA--[9][21]ROM--
"PLAY IT BY HEART"
QUINN, JAKE--[3]MYS--
LEIS "SHALLOW GRAVE" '74
LEIS "THE UNDERTAKER" '74
LEIS "MINDBENDERS" '75

CONDON, JOHN CARL JR.
CONDON, JACK--[31]

CONDON, MADELINE B.
HAEFER, HANNA--[8]

CONDRAY, BRUNO G.
BRACK, VEKTIS--[2][7]HP

CONE, MOLLY [L]
MORE, CAROLINE--W/MARGARET P. STRACHAN, [1][22][33]--
DIAMOND "BATCH OF TROUBLE" '63

CONE, P.C.L.
CLAPP, PATRICIA--[8][11]

CONGAR, GEORGES YVES M-J
CONGAR, MARIE JOSEPH--[31]
CONGAR, Y.M.--[31]
CONGAR, YVES--[31]
CONGAR, YVES M.-J.--[31]

CONGAR, GEORGES YVES M-J [CONT]
CONGAR, YVES M.J.--[31]
CONGAR, YVES MARIE JOSEPH--[31]

CONGRAT-BUTLER, STEFAN
BUTLER, STEFAN C.--[31]

CONIL, JEAN-EDMOND
PAGE, ALAIN--[3]MYS--
INTRNL "SO LATE, MONSIEUR CALONE" '69
INTRNL "HOOK" '69

CONKLIN,[E.] GROFF
DE GRAEFF, W.B.--W/A.P. BLAUSTEIN,[1][2][11]

CONLEY, ENID MARY
BLUNDEL, ANNE--[31]

CONLON, BEN
GRIDLEY, AUSTIN--PPCC#5-'WESTERN PULP HERO' BY N. CARR--
"PETE RICE" WEST ADV
MOFFATT, GEO. ALLAN--W. MURRAY--ECHOES #26

CONLY, ROBERT LESLIE
O'BRIEN, ROBERT C.--[2][3][7][23][33]MYS--
ATHENEUM "A REPORT FROM GRP 17" '72

CONN, CANARY DENISE
CANARY--[31]

CONN, PHOEBE
BURKE, CINNAMON--CRPG,[26]ROM--
LEIS "RAPTURE'S MIST"
LEIS 3558 "LADY ROGUE"

CONNELL, ALAN
CONN, ALAN--[2][11]

CONNELL, ETHEL
BRITT, KATRINA--[9][21]ROM--
31 NOVELS

CONNELL, SUSAN
SUMMERS, CHLOE--[26]ROM--
"NO EASY TASK"

CONNER, MICHAEL
CONNER, MIKE--[23]SF

CONNER, PATRICK REARDON
CONNER, REARDON--[8][31]
MALIN, PETER--[8]

CONNETT, EUGENE VIRGINIUS
VIRGINIUS--[22]AMERICAN

CONNIFF, JAMES C.G.
COOLWATER, JOHN--[1][31]

CONNOLLY, CYRIL VERNON
PALINURUS--[22]ENGLISH

CONNOLLY, ROBERT DUGAN JR
DUGGANS, PAT--[31]

CONNOLLY, VIVIAN
HARRIS, ANDREA--[3][31]HP--
PLAYBOY "IRISH AFFAIR" '78
PLAYBOY "A SCREAM AWAY" '79
ROSSE, SUSANNA--[9][21][26]ROM--
"DANCE ON THE TIGHTROPE"
"TO LOVE AS EAGLES"

CONNOR, JOHN ANTHONY
ANTHONY, JOHN--[8][31]

CONNOR, JOHN ANTHONY [CONT]
CONNOR, TONY--[8][22][31]ENGLISH
HARDWICK, ADAM--[22][31]ENGLISH

CONNOR, JOYCE MARY
MARLOW, JOYCE--[8]

CONNER, PATRICK REARDON
MALIN, PETER--[1][22][31]ENGLISH

CONNOR, WILLIAM NEIL
CASSANDRA--[31]

CONNORS, A.V.
KEYES, PETER--V. BERCH, BRNDN/
BC PSEUDS, BAE 22, P24

CONNORS, HILARY
HILARY, RICHARD--W/RICH BODINO, LACHMAN-
EASTER LST '93,[34]MYS--
BB "PIECES OF CREAM" '87

CONQUEST, EDWIN PARKER JR
CONQUEST NED--[31]

CONQUEST, ROBERT
ARDEN, J.E.M.--[2][11][22][31]ENGLISH

CONRAD, HAROLD
CONRAD, HAL--[31]

CONRAD, HELEN [MANAK]
HUNT, JENA--[9][21][26]ROM--
5 NOVELS
MORGAN, RAYE--[9][21][26]ROM--
15 NOVELS

CONRAD, ISAAC
CONRAD, JACK--[8]

CONRADS, DIETRICH
CONRADS, DIETER--[40]GERMAN/MYS--
"DER SCHATZ IN DER ALTEN" '76
"HALTET DEN HUNDRDIEB" '77
PERLACH, MARK--[39]GERMAN

CONROW, HERBERT
ORB, CLAY--[2]

CONROY, JOHN WESLEY
BRENNAN, TIM--[1][22][31][33]AMERICAN
MORINE, HODER--[1][2][33]AMERICAN
NORCROSS, JOHN--[1][22][33]AMERICAN

CONSIDINE, ROBERT BERNARD
CONSIDINE, BOB--[31]

CONSTABLE, TREVOR JAMES
JAMES, TREVOR--[31]

CONSTANT, ALPHONSE LOUIS
LEVI, ELIPHAS--[11]SF

CONSTANTINE, GREGORY JOHN
CONSTANTINE, GREG--[31]

CONWAY, GERARD F.
MOORE, WALLACE--[2][11][23]--
'BALZAN OF THE CAT PEOPLE' SERIES--
3 BOOKS '74-75

CONWAY, JILL KER
KER, JILL--[31]

CONWAY, ROBERT
ZERLIN, WALTER JR--V. BERCH LTR TO HUBIN '94--
FRENCH MYS PLAY '81 W/DAVID McGILLIVRAY

CONWAY, THOMAS DANIEL
CONWAY, TIM--[31]

COOK, ARLENE ETHEL
COLE, CANNON--[31]

COOK, BONNA LEE D.
DUBOIS, BONNA LEE--[9][21][26]ROM--
"LONG AGO LOVE"

COOK, DEIRDRE
CORK, DOROTHY--[21]ROM--
"THE KURRANULLA ROUND"
CORK, DERIDRE--[26]ROM--
35 NOVELS

COOK, DOROTHY MARY
CAMERON, D.Y.--[8][31]
CARLISLE, D.M.--[3][31]MYS--
BARKER "ALTHEA'S FALCON" '74
CLARE, ELIZABETH--[8][31]

COOK, FRED GORDON
CAREW, BURLEIGH--[1]
CHAVERTON, BRUCE--[1]
CLIFFORD, MARTIN--[1]HP
FOY, PETER--[1]
OWEN, VINCENT--[1]
RICHARDS, FRANK--[1]HP
SMEATON, FRED--[1]

COOK, GLEN
STEVENS, GREG--GLEN COOK LTR '92--
PEC G1205 "SWAP ACADEMY"

COOK, IDA
BURCHELL, MARY--[9][17][21][26][31]ROM--
NUMEROUS NOVELS

COOK, JAMES RICHARD
COOK, RICK--[7]SF--
BAEN "WIZARD'S BANE #1-3" '89-91
BAEN "LIMBO SYSTEM" '89

COOK, JOHN AUSGUSTINE
COOK, JACK--[31]

COOK, JOHN LENNOX
COOK, LENNOX--[31]

COOK, KENNETH
DUFFY, JOHN--[35]AUSTRALIAN, HP--
HRWTZ "THE TAKE" '63

COOK, MABEL COLLINS
COLLINS, MABEL [C]--[11][31]SF

COOK, MARJORIE GRANT
GRANT, MARJORIE--[8]
SEAFORD, CAROLINE--[8]

COOK, MICHAEL LEWIS
COOKE, MICHAEL F.R.C.S.--[1]
LEWIS, DAVID MARSHALL--[1]

COOK, P. MARGUERITE MARY
ARNOLD, MARGOT--[3][7][21][26]MYS--
PLAYBOY "EXIT ACTORS, DYING" '79
PLAYBOY "CAPE COD CAPER" '80
PLAYBOY "ZARDOK'S TREASURE" '80

COOK, RAMONA GRAHAM
GRAHAM, RAMONA--[8][22][31]AMERICAN

COOK, ROBERT [W.A.]
COOK, ROBIN--[18][31][34]ENGLISH/MYS--
6 HUTCHINSON NOVELS '62-71
RAYMOND, DEREK BAL.--P. DUNCAN-COOK INTRVW, BAPC NEWSLTR,[18][23][34]--
ALISON "HE DIED WITH HIS EYES OPEN" '84
ALISON "THE DEVIL'S HOME ON LEAVE" '85
SECKER "HOW THE DEAD LIVE" '86
SECKER "I WAS DORA SUAREZ" '90
SECKER "DEAD MAN UPRIGHT" '93

COOK, S.A.
DANCER, LACEY--[26]ROM--8 NOVELS

COOK, WILLIAM EVERETT
BROOMHAUER, CHARLIE--[28]
COOK, W.--[21]ROM--
"SABRINA KANE"
COOK, WILL--[32]MYS/WEST--
MOF "LET'S ALL GO KILL THE SCARED OLD MAN" FEB '59
SUS "A GUNMAN CAME TO TOWN" FEB '61
EVERETT, WADE--[19][28]WEST--17 NOVELS '59-68
KEENE, JAMES--PPCC #8,[19][28]WEST--
"GUNNISON'S EMPIRE" '66 & 9 OTHERS
PEACE, FRANK--PPCC #8,[28]WEST--
PERMA "EASY MONEY" '56
PERMA "BRASS BRIGADE" '56
PERMA "DRIFTER" '69
RICHARDS, WILLIAM--L. ROBBINS LTR MAR '94, HP--PULP
RIORDAN, DAN--[1][28]WEST--
RROM "BULLET RANGE" FEB '55
THOMAS, PAUL--L. ROBBINS LTR MAR '94--PULP

COOK, WILLIAM WALLACE
CARTER, NICHOLAS--[3][5]MYS, HP
EDWARDS, JOHN MILTON--L. ROBBINS LTR MAR '94,[31]
GRAYSON, DONALD--JEAN F. LE DEIST LTR '93

COOKE, C.H.
BICKERDYKE, JOHN--[8]

COOKE, DIANA
WITHERBY, DIANA--[8]

COOKE, MILLEN
BLADE, ALEXANDER--[1][2][11]HP [ZIFF-DAVIS]

COOKE, MRS. LEONARD
CONQUEST, JOAN--[2]

COOKSON, CATHERINE ANN
FAWCETT, C.--[1]
FAWCETT, CATHERINE--[9]ROM
MARCHANT, CATHERINE--[3][9][17][21][26][33]ENGLISH/ROM/MYS--
8 NOVELS '62-76
MCMULLEN, CATHERINE--[1][17][33]ROM
MCMULLEN, KATIE--[21]ROM--
"HERITAGE OF FOLLY"
"HOUSE OF MEN"

COOKSON, SYBIL ELEANOR T.
TREMAYNE, SYDNEY--[34]MYS--
FILM "THE AUCTION MART" '15

COOLBEAR, MARIAN H.
COLBERE, HOPE--[8]

COOMARASWAMY, AMANDA K.
COOMARASWAMY, A.K.--[31]

COOMBS, CHARLES IRA
COOMBS, CHICK--[31][33]--OCCASIONAL TRAVEL ARTICLES

COOMBS, JOYCE
HALES, JOYCE--[8]
SCOBEY, MARION--[8]

COONEY, MICHAEL
CONOR, GLEN--[31]

COONS, MAURICE
TRAIL, ARMITAGE--[1][3]MYS--
WHITMAN "THIRTEENTH GUEST" '29
LONG "SCARFACE" '30

COONS, WILLIAM R.
BROOKS, BARBARA--MUNROE SEPT '93 AUCT--
MIDWD S300 "SHADOW DANCE" '63
MIDWD F323 "JUST THE TWO OF US" '63
MIDWD 32-410 "HELLCAT" '64
MIDWD 34-447 "AND WHEN SHE WAS BAD" '65
MIDWD 32-451 "A SHAMELESS NEED" '65
MIDWD 34-462 "JUST YOU, JUST ME" '65
MIDWD 32-525 "TABOO" '65
MIDWD 34-548 "THE SWINGER" '65
MIDWD 34-596 "TWO TIMES TWO" '66
HOLLAND, DELL--MUNROE RVW FEB '93--
BDSD 1223 "HELLHOLE OF SIN" '62
BDSD "SIN TOWN" '62
MARSHALL, ALAN--MUNROE LST 24, HP--
NTSD 1581 "CALL ME SINNER"
SHAW, ANDREW--MUNROE RVW FEB '93, HP--
NTSD 1563 "PASSION SLAVES"
NTSD 1566 "SIN DEVIL"
NTSD 1569 "ARMY SIN GIRLS"
NTSD 1575 "HOUSE OF 7 SINS"
MDNR 409 "SLUM SINNERS"
MDNR 420 "PASSION COD"
MDNR 436 "PASSION NIGHTMARE"
NTSD 1578 "PONYTAIL TRAMP"
LEIS 603 "PASSION MADMAN"
MDNR "SIN BUM"
NTSD 1639 "LUST PAD"
NTSD 1641 "FLESH MAD"
NTSD 1647 "SIN SLUM"
PILLAR 827 "SIN MASTER"

COOPER, AGNES ROSEMARY
BELL, RAMSAY--W/MARY E.P. WELLER,[3]MYS--
HODDER "DRAGON UNDER GROUND" '37
HODDER "DANGEROUS PROMISE" '39
HODDER "LAKE OF GHOSTS" '40

COOPER, ALFRED MORTON
COOPER, MORLEY--[22][31]AMERICAN

COOPER, ALICE
FURNIER, VINCENT DAMON--[31]

COOPER, CLARENCE L.
CHESTNUT, ROBERT--[34]MYS

COOPER, COLIN SYMONS
BENSON, DANIEL--[3][8][31]MYS--
FABER "THUNDER & LIGHTNING MAN" '68
"OUTCROP" '69

COOPER, DOUGLAS
LORD, DOUGLAS--[1]

COOPER, EDITH EMMA
FIELD, MICHAEL--W/KATHARINE H. BRADLEY, [8][22]ENGLISH

COOPER, EDMUND
AVERY, RICHARD--[2][4][7][11][23]ENGLISH/SF--
CORONET 'EXPENDABLES' SERIES #1-4 '75

COOPER, ELIZABETH
ALLEN, BETTY [JEANNE]--[31]--NAME LEGALLY
CHANGED TO "ALLEN"

COOPER, EVAN
DUHRING, NATHAN--[2]

COOPER, GORDON
COLAM, LANCE--[8]

COOPER, HENRY S. FENIMORE
COOPER, HENRY S.F.--[33]

COOPER, JACQUELINE
CAROL, JACQUELINE--[31]

COOPER, JAMES FENIMORE
MORGAN, JANE--[33]

COOPER, JOHN
FINCH, JOHN--[8]
LLOYD, JOHN--[8]

COOPER, JOHN DEAN
COOPER, JEFF--[8][31]

COOPER, JOHN MURRAY
SUTHERLAND, WILLIAM--[3][22]MYS--
3 ARROWSMITH NOVELS '33-35

COOPER, KENNETH C.
COOPER, CARL--[1][31]

COOPER, MAE [KLEIN]
COOPER-KLEIN, NINA--W/GRACE KLEIN,
[22][31]AMERICAN
FAREWELL, NINA--W/GRACE KLEIN,
[1][8][22]AMERICAN--
MULLER "LILY HENRY" '60

COOPER, PARLEY J.
DAWES, DOROTHY--[1][31]
FRETAG, JOSEPH--[1][31]
FRETAG, JOSEPHINE--[1][31]
FREYTAG, JOSEPHINE--V. BERCH LTR TO HUBIN '94-
-
"AMBER PALACE" '80
MAYFIELD, JACK--[1][21]ROM--
"THE APPRAISER"
"LOVING STRANGERS"
"THE MAGNATE"
MCKINNEY, D.J.--[1]
NEBRENSKY, ALEX--[1][7]SF--
SIGN "THE UNHOLY" '82

COOPER, PENNY
CHAMBERLAIN, ENA--[31]

COOPER, RICK
SARAZEN, NICHOLAS--W/MARK DAVIS,[7]SF--
PINN "FAMILY REUNION" '90

COOPER, ROBERT ANDREW
ANDREW, ROBERT--[1]
HAYES, ALEXANDER--[1]
MATLOCK, ALEX--[1]
ROBERTSON, AMY--[1]

COOPER, SANDRA LEONORE
COOPER, SONNI--[7]SF--
STAR TREK #8
POCK 'A TIMESCAPE'

COOPER, SAUL
BENSON, RICHARD--[1]
MILNER, MICHAEL--[1][31]

COOPER, SYLVIA
JERMAN, SYLVIA PAUL--[31]

COOPER, WILLIAM
HOFF, H.S.--[31]ROM--
4 HEINEMANN NOVELS '34-46

COOPER,[C] HENRY ST JOHN
ST. JOHN, HENRY--[34]MYS--
AMALG "NOT GUILTY" '20

COOVER, JAMES BURRELL
JAMES, C.B.--[31]--
LEFTOVER PRESS "UP TO THE HILT" '75

COPE, ROBERT KNOX
COPE, JACK--[22][31][38]S. AFRICAN--
MACGIBBON "FAIR HOUSE" '55
HM "GOLDEN ORIOLE" '58 PLUS

COPE, VINCENT ZACHARY
ZETA--[22]ENGLISH

COPELAND, EDITH
COLE, DIANE--[3]MYS--
ARCADIA "MURDER AT THE WHITE TULIP" '60

COPELAND, FRANCES
FISHER, FRAN--[21]ROM--
"STAY, SWEET LOVE"

COPELAND, LEWIS
HENRY, LEWIS C.--[8]

COPELAND, VIVIAN
KEITH, VIVIAN--[26]ROM--
"WAYWARD ANGEL"

COPP, ALF E.
COPP, A.E.--[36]AUSTRALIAN/MYS--
LANE "MELBOURNE MYS" '29 [W/S.J. STUTLEY]
LANE "POISONED GLASS" '30 [W/S.J. STUTLEY]

COPP, ANDREW JAMES III
COPP, JIM--[31]

COPP, DEWITT S.
CARTER, NICK--[3]MYS, HP--
"A DIFFERENT KIND OF RAIN"
"PURSUIT OF AGENT M"
AWARD "SIX BLOODY SUMMER DAYS" '75
CHART "UNDER THE WALL" '78
PICARD, SAM--[3]--
AWARD "THE NOTEBOOKS" '69
AWARD "DEAD MAN RUNNING" '71
AWARD "MAN WHO NEVER WAS" '71

COPP, THEODORE BAYARD F.
COPP, TED--L. ROBBINS LTR MAR '94--PULP

COPPARD, ALFRED EDGAR
COPPARD, A.E.--[1][32]MYS--
EQMM "A BROADSHEET BALLAD" FEB '49

COPPEL, ALFREDO JOSE
COPPEL, ALFRED--[1][34]MYS/WAR--
MacM "THIRTY-FOUR EAST HARCOURT" '74
& OTHERS
GALAXAN, SOL--[1][2][11][23]--SF--
ASF - 1 STORY '53
GILMAN, ROBERT CHAM--[2][7][23][31]SF--
'RHADA SPACE OPERA' NOVELS '64-85

COPPEL, ALFREDO JOSE [CONT]
LEPPOC, DERFLA--[2][11][29]
MARIN, A.C.--[2][3][29]MYS--
HARCOURT "CLASH OF DISTANT THUNDER" '68
& 2 OTHERS '68-71
MARIN, ALFRED--[1][2]

COPPER, BASIL
FALK, LEE--[1][18]GHOSTED--
AV "PHANTOM & SCORPION MENACE" '72
AV "SLAVE MARKET OF MUCAR" '72
AV "STORY OF THE PHANTOM" '72

COPPER, DOROTHY
CARTER, DIANA--[8][11]
DICKENS, IRENE--[8]
GRANT, CAROL--[8]
GREEN, LINDA--[8]

COPPULA, SUSAN CARROLL
CARROLL, SUSAN--[9][21][26]ROM--
7 NOVELS
RICHARDS, SERENA--[21]ROM--
"MASQUERADE"
"RENDEZVOUS"

CORBIN, HAROLD STANDISH
COTRELL, HARVEY S.--[2]
COTTRELL, HARVEY S.--[2][11]
FAIRFIELD, HENRY W.A.--[2][11]
FLETCHER, JOHN C.--[2][11]
PROCTOR, WALTER. G.--[2]

CORBY, JANE [IRENITA]
BRIGHTON, LAURA--[3]MYS
CAREW, JEAN--[3][22]MYS--
ARCADIA "RUN, NURSE, RUN" '65
ARCADIA "SAMANTHA" '66
HOLDEN, JOANNE--[3][22]MYS--
ARCADIA "NURSE AT THE CASTLE" '65
ARCADIA "DANGEROUS LEGACY" '66

CORCORAN, BARBARA
DIXON, PAIGE--[8][31]
HAMILTON, GAIL--[31]

CORCORAN, DOROTHY
PATRICK, DE ANN--W/MARY ANN SLOJKOWSKI,
[9][26]ROM--
"KINDRED SPIRITS"
"MONTANA BRIDE"

CORDEAU, KATE MARIAN
DORMER, DANIEL--[3]MYS--
MAXWELL "MESMERIST'S SECRET" 1888

CORDES, HEINRICH
FASOLD, CHRISTIAN--[39]GERMAN

CORDES, THEODORE K.
CASE, T.--[8]
DAEDALUS--[8]
ERSKINE-GRAY--[8]

CORDTS, GEORG & RENATE
KRISTAN, GEORG R.--[39]GERMAN/MYS

COREA, GENOVETTA
COREA, GENA--[31]

COREY, WINIFRED
GRAHAM, WINIFRED--[2]

CORFE, THOMAS HOWELL
CORFE, TOM--[31][33]

CORINGTON, WILLIAM
CORIOLAN, JOHN--[14]ADULT--
OLYM TC#3232 "SEVEN WAYS FROM SUNDAY" '72

CORK, BARRY
CAUSEWAY, JANE--[8]

CORK, BARRY
DILLON, CATHERINE--V. BERCH LTR TO HUBIN '94,
MYS--
HODDER "CONSTANTINE CAY" '75

CORLEY, EDWIN RAYMOND
CORLEY, RAY--[31]
BUCHANAN, PATRICK--W/JACK MURPHY,
[3][29][31]MYS--
STEIN "A MURDER OF CROWS" '71
DODD "A REQUIEM OF SHARKS" '73 & 2 MORE
COLLINS, WILL--[1][31]
HARPER, DAVID--[3][29][31]MYS--
DODD "HIJACKED" '70
DODD "PATCHWORK MAN" '75
DODD "HANGED MEN" '76
JUDSON, WILLIAM--[3][31]MYS--
FIELDS "ALICE & ME '73
FIELDS "COLD RIVER" '75
FIELDS "KILMAN'S LANDING" '76

CORMACK, ALEXANDER J.R.
CORMACK, SANDY--[31]

CORMACK, DONALD G.
STOCKBRIDGE, GRANT--PULP #13/T. JOHNSON
LTR '94, HP--
SPIDER "LEGEND IN BLUE STEEL" '43

CORMIER, ROBERT EDMUND
FITCH, JOHN IV--[31][33]--HUMAN INTEREST
COLUMN

CORNBERG, CATHERINE GASK.
GASKIN, CATHERINE--[21]ROM--
DELL S18 "CORPORATION WIFE"

CORNELL, JEFFREY
CORNELL, J.--[31]

CORNER, EDRED JOHN HENRY
CORNER, E.J.H.--[31]

CORNETT, ROBERT
HELM, ERIC--W/KEVIN D. RANDLE--G. COOK
LTR '93,[34], HP--
PINN'"SCORPION SQUAD' SERIES:
"BODY COUNT" '84
"NHU STING" '84
"RIVER RAID" '85
"CHOPPER COMMAND" '85

CORNISH, DORIS MARY
LISLE, MARY--[8]

CORNWELL, DAVID J.M.
LECARRE, JOHN--[2][3][5][18][29][31]ENGLISH--
NUMEROUS MYS NOVELS

COROMINAS, PERE
MERCADER, ENRIQUE--[22]SPANISH CATALAN

CORRADINI, BRUNO
CORRA, BRUNO--[22]ITALIAN

CORRADOT, JEANNE E.M.J.
MAGALI--[3]MYS--11 NOVELS '69-80

CORRALL, ALICE ENID
GLASS, JUSTINE [C]--[8][22][31]ENGLISH

CORREA, MIGUEL ANGEL
BOOZ, MATEO--[20]

CORRODI-HORBER, MARGRIT
MARKWALDER, MARGA--[39]GERMAN

CORSARO, FRANCESCO ANDREA
CORSARO, FRANK--[31]

CORSER, JUDY E.
BOWEN, JUDITH--[21]ROM--
"THAT MAN NEXT DOOR"

CORSON, MARTHA
LACEY, ANNE--[9][21][26]ROM--
10 NOVELS
MICHAELS, KRISTIN--[9][21]ROM, HP--
"LOVE'S PILGRIMAGE"
"LOVE ON COURSE"

CORSON-FINNERTY, ADAM D.
FINNERTY, ADAM DANIEL--[31]
FINNERTY, DANIEL JOHN--[31]

CORTAZAR, JULIO
DENIS, JULIO--[31]

CORTE, WILHELM
OSKAR, THEODOR--[39]GERMAN

CORTEZ-COLUMBUS, ROBERT C
KENNEDY, R.C.--[8]

CORY, ANNIE SOPHIE
CORY, VIVIAN--[7]SF
CROSS, VICTORIA--[7]SF
CROSS[E], VICTORIA--[2][7][23]ENGLISH

CORY, CHARLES BARNEY
NOX, OWEN--[8]

CORY, IRENE E.
CORY, CORRINE--[31]
CORYA, I.E.--[31]

CORY, MATILDA WINIFRED G.
GRAHAM, WINIFRED--[7]SF--
"THE NEEDLEWOMAN" '11

CORYELL, JOHN RUSSELL
CARTER, NICHOLAS--[1][3][5]MYS, HP
CARTER, NICK--W/ORMAND G. SMITH,
[2][5][11]MYS, HP
CLAY, BERTHA M.--[1][2][22]
CURRIO, TYMAN--[1][23]SF--
"WEIRD & WONDERFUL STORY OF ANOTHER
WORLD" 1905
DRAYTON, LILLIAN R.--[1]
EDWARDS, JULIA--[1]
FLEMING, GERALDINE--[1][3]MYS--
6 NOVELS 1885-1910
GRANT, MARGARET--[1]
HOWARD, BARBARA--[1]
MILMAN, HARRY DU BOIS--[1]
QUARTERLY, MILTON--[1]
RUSSELL, LUCY MAY--[1]
RYAN, SGT.--[1]

COSBY, WILLIAM HENRY JR.
COSBY, BILL--[31][33]

COSENS, ABNER
WAYFARER--[8]

COSGROVE, RACHEL RUTH
ARCH, E.L.--[7][23]SF

COSTA, GABRIEL
CALLISTHENES--[8]

COSTABEL, EVA DEUTSCH
DEUTSCH, EVA C.--[31]

COSTAIN, THOMAS
HAND, PAT--LACHMAN LST '93,[32]MYS--
EQMM "SHOWDOWN" JAN '44
EQMM "ALIBI" NOV '44
EQMM "THE IMPONDERABLES" JUL '44
EQMM "ACE OF SPADES" DEC '44

COSTLEY, WILLIAM K.
COSTLEY, BILL--[31]--
'GHOST DANCE' BOOKS '78-89

COTES, PETER
NORTHCOTE--[22]ENGLISH

COTLER, GORDON
GORDON, ALEX--[3][29][31]MYS--
SIMON "THE CIPHER" '61

COTTON, KELLY P. [J.M.G.]
GAST, KELLY P.--[2][3]MYS--
DBLDY "DIL DIES HARD" '75

COTTON, LESTER
SILK, STAFFORD--[35]AUSTRALIAN--
HRWTZ PB 163 "THE BOOGLE MYS" '63

COTTON, WILLIAM
NEWBURY, WILL--V. BERCH-MON PSEUDS, BAE 9
& BRNDN/BC PSEUDS- BAE 22, ADULT--
MON 226 "CALL BOY" '61
MON 347 "CRUISE SHIP GIRLS" '63
MIDWD 32-453 "TOURIST TRAP" '65
MIDWD 32-508 "QUEEN BEE" '65
MIDWD 34-597 "PRETTY PLAYMATE" '66

COUCH, HELEN FOX
FOX, V. HELEN--[22][31]AMERICAN

COUFFER, JACK [C]
COTTER, JOHN--W/JUDITH FRANKLE,[7]SF--
BERK "NIGHTS WITH SASQUATCH" '77

COUGHLIN, PATRICIA M.
GRADY, LIZ--[9][21][26]ROM--
9 NOVELS

COUGHLIN, WILLIAM J.
KEY, SEAN A.--[3][29]MYS--
DELL "THE MARK OF CAIN" '80

COUGHRAN, LARRY C.
CRAIG, LARRY--[1][31]

COUILLARD, BEVERLEE
ROSS, BEVERLEE--[26]ROM--
"ANNABELLE"

COULET DU GARD, RENE
ALGERY, ANDRE--[31]--REVIEWS IN
FRENCH PERIODICALS
ANDUZE-DUFY, RAPHAEL--[31]--
"LES ECHOS DU MONDE"

COULSON, FELICITY W.C.
BONETT, EMERY--[3][5][31]ENGLISH/MYS--
HM "NEVER GO DARK" '40
HM "HIGH PAVEMENT" '44

COULSON, FELICITY W.C.
BONETT, JOHN & EMERY--W/JOHN H.A. COULSON,[3][5]MYS--
10 NOVELS '49-72
CARTER, FELICITY--[18]MYS--
HM "NEVER GO DARK" '40

COULSON, JOHN HUBERT A.
BONETT, JOHN--[5][22][31][34]ENGLISH/MYS--
HALE "PERISH THE THOUGHT" '84
BONETT, JOHN & EMERY--W/FELICITY W.C. COULSON,[3][5]MYS--
10 NOVELS '49-74

COULSON, JUANITA [R.W.]
WELLS, JOHN JAY--W/MARION Z. BRADLEY,[2][16][23]--
FSF "ANOTHER RIB" '63

COULSON, NOEL JAMES
COULSON, N.J.--[31]

COULSON, ROBERT
BLACK, ROBERTA--W/SANDRA MIESEL,[1]
STRATTON, THOMAS--W/EUGENE DEWEESE, J. CORRICK, BAE 4,[1][2][11]--
MU "INVISIBILITY AFFAIR" '67
MU "MIND TWISTER AFFAIR" '67

COULTER, STEPHEN
MAYO, JAMES--[3][18][29][40]MYS--
9 NOVELS '61-71

COULTON, MARY ROSE
CAMPION, SARAH--[2][3]MYS--
DAVIES "UNHANDSOME CORPSE" '38

COULTRY, BARBARA
BLACKTREE, BARBARA--[9][21][26]ROM--
"ARIEL'S SONG"

COUNSELMAN, MARY ELIZAB.
DU BOIS, CHARLES--[31]

COURCELLES, SANDRA
DAY, SAMANTHA--[9][21][26]ROM--
5 NOVELS

COURNOS, HELEN
NORTON, SYBIL--[8]

COURNOS, JOHN
COURTNEY, JOHN--[3][22]MYS--
SKEFFINGTON "GRANDMOTHER MARTIN IS MURDERED" '30
GAULT, MARK--[3][22][31]MYS--
METHUEN "FACE OF DEATH" '33

COURSE, PAMELA MARY
BECKET, LAVINIA--[1]
MANSBRIDGE, PAMELA--[1]

COURTHS-MAHLER, HEDWIG
RELHAM, HEDWIG--[39]GERMAN

COURTIER, S[IDNEY] H.
CHESTOR, RUI--[1][22][31]MYS

COURTINE, ROBERT
LA REYNIERE--[1][31]
SAVARIN--[1]

COURTNEY, NICHOLAS PIERS
HANMER, DAVINA--[1][31]

COURTNEY-BROWNE, R. DAVID
BROWNE, COURTNEY--[1][3]MYS--
HALE "THE ANCIENT POND" '67

COURY, LOUISE ANDRE
ANDREE, LOUISE--[1][31][33]
ANDREWS, LAURA--[1][31][33]
ANDREWS, LAURIE--[32]MYS--
LM "AS A MAN THINKS" MAR '64
AUNTIE DEB--[1][31][33]
AUNTIE LOUISE--[1][31][33]
CARE, FELICITY--[1][33]
MORTIMER, MARY H.--[1][33]
STRANGE, PHILLIPA--[1][33]

COUSINS, MARGARET
JOHNS, AVERY--[2][3][9][22][31]AMERICAN/MYS--
DBLDY "TRAFFIC WITH EVIL" '62
MASTERS, WILLIAM--[9][22][31][33]ROM
PARRISH, MARY--[9][22][31][33]ROM

COUTARD, WANDA L. HALE
HALE, WANDA--[31]

COUTURIER, LOUIS JOSEPH
CARROUGES, MICHEL--[31]

COUVEUR, JESSIE
TASMA--[13]AUSTRALIAN

COVARRUBIAS, BARBARA F.
FAITH, BARBARA--[1][31]MYS--
MANOR "KILL ME GENTLY, DARLING" '78
POCK "MOON KISSED" '80
POCK "SUN DANCERS" & 9 OTHERS

COVE, JOSEPH WALTER
GIBBS, LEWIS--[2][11][23]SF--
"LATE FINAL" '51
"PARABLE FOR LOVERS" '34

COVELL, RICHARD
SLADE, MICHAEL--W/JOHN BANKS, JAY & LEE CLARKE,[3]MYS--
ALLEN "HEADHUNTER" '84
ALLEN "GHOUL" '87

COVERT, ALICE LENT
DALE, MAXINE--[8]
LOWELL, ELAINE--[8]

COVILLE, BRUCE [F]
TALLIS, ROBYN--[7]SF, HP--
IVY "PLANET BUILDERS #1 & #6" '88-9

COWAN, BERTHA MUZZY B.S.
BOWER, B.M.--[3]MYS--
LITTLE "THE VOICE OF JOHNNYWATER" '23
LITTLE "THE HAUNTED HILLS" '34

COWARD, NOEL [PEIRCE]
WHITTLEBOT, HERNIA--[8][22][31]ENGLISH-SWISS

COWEN, FRANCES
HYDE, ELEANORE--[3][17][29]MYS--
HALE "SINISTER MELODY" '76
HALE "TUDOR MURDERS" '77 & OTHERS

COWEN, RONALD
COWEN, RON--[31]

COWERN, ROGER WILLIAM
PERRY, ROGER--[7]SF--
HALE "SENIOR CITIZEN" '79
HALE "ESPER'S WAR" '81
HALE "THE MAKING OF JASON" '86

COWIE, DONALD
ABBERLEY, ALDWYN--[1]
MOUNTAIN, JULIAN--[1]
PYTCHELY, R.F. ST. B.--[1]
STONE, RUFUS--[1]

COWLE, JEROME MILTON
COWLE, JERRY--[31]

COWLES, GARDNER A JR.
COWLES, MIKE--[31]

COWLISHAW, RANSON
WASH, R.--[1][8]ENGLISH
WOODROOK, R.A.--[1][8][22]ENGLISH

COWPER, FRANCIS
ROE, RICHARD--[8]

COX, ADRIAN
ZOOL, M.H.--[23]SF GROUP PSEUD.

COX, ANNE
GRAY, ANNABEL--[3]MYS--
SIMPKIN "MYSTIC NUMBER SEVEN" 1900

COX, ANTHONY BERKELEY
BERKELEY, ANTHONY--[2][3][5][18][31][32]MYS--
18 NOVELS '25-39
5 DIGEST STORIES '45-51
COX, A.B.--[5][31]MYS
ILES, FRANCIS--[2][3][5][32]MYS--
DBLDY "MALICE AFORETHOUGHT" '31
DBLDY "BEFORE THE FACT" '32
DBLDY "AS FOR THE WOMAN" '39
EQMM "DARK JOURNEY" MAY '43
EQMM "OUTSIDE THE LAW" JUN '49
EQMM "THE COWARD" JAN '53
PLATTS, A. MONMOUTH--[3][18]MYS--
LONG "CECILY DISAPPEARS" '27

COX, ARTHUR JEAN
CARGHILL, RALPH--[2][11]
COX, JEAN--[2][11]
CROSS, GENE--JEAN F. LE DEIST,
BAE 18,[2]ADULT--
EL 359 "TIGER LILLY AFFAIR" '67
DEXTER, JOHN--W/ART PLOTNIK & MILO
PERICHITCH, MUNROE LST 24--
EL 327 "SHAME TIGERS" '66
ROKESMITH, JOHN THAMES--[2]AMERICAN/SF--
ISFYB

COX, EDITH MURIEL
GOAMAN, MURIEL--[8]

COX, EUPHRASIA EMELINE
COX, LEWIS--[1][8]
PARSONS, BRIDGET--[8]

COX, FREDERICK MORELAND
COX, FRED M.--[31]

COX, H.D.
COX, DOUGLAS--[1]

COX, JOHN ROBERTS
ROBERTS, DAVID--[1][8][33]
HAVENHAND, JOHN--[1][33]
COX, JACK--[8][31][33]

COX, JULIA
JULIA--[8]

COX, MARIE-THERESE HENR.
COX, MOLLY--[31]

COX, PATRICIA BALE
BALE, G.F.--W/GLADYS B. WELLBROCK,[7][34]MYS--
CHART "IF THOUGHTS COULD KILL" '90

COX, PATRICK BRIAN
COX, P. BRIAN--[31]
STUART, KENNETH--[31]

COX, STEPHEN ANGUS D.
CARTER, NICHOLAS--[3][31]MYS, HP
STARK, INSPECTOR--[34]MYS, HP--
NEW MAGNET #389 "A DEED OF DARKNESS" '05

COX, STEPHEN R.
SLOANE, BEN--LACHMAN-GOODE LST '93,[34]MYS--
GE "BLOWN DEAD" '90
GE "HOT ZONE" '90

COX, WALLACE MAYNARD
COX, WALLY--[31]

COX, WILLIAM ROBERT
D'ARCY, WILLARD--[18][28][31][33]MYS--
"SATAN TRADES" JAN '40
FREDERIC, MIKE--[8][18][33]AMERICAN/MYS/JUV--
FRANK MERRIWELL SERIES
PARKHILL, JOHN--[18][28]MYS--
DM "SECOND HAND COFFIN" MAR '43
DM "SLIPS THAT PASS IN THE NIGHT" MAY '45
REEVE, JOEL--[8][22][28][33]AMERICAN--
BLUE BOOK SS '42-52
PHILLIPS "GOAL AHEAD" '67
ROBBINS, WAYNE--[18][28][33]MYS--
DM "THINGS IN SEARCH OF A BODY" FEB '40
SPELLMAN, ROGER G.--[8][18][28][33]
AMERICAN/WEST--
GM "TALL FOR A TEXAN" '65
WARD, JONAS--[8][18][19][28]WEST, HP--
"BUCHANAN'S WAR" '70
"A TRAP FOR BUCHANAN" '71
"BUCHANAN'S GAMBLE" '72
"BUCHANAN'S SEIGE" '72
"BUCHANAN ON THE RUN" '73
"GET BUCHANAN" '73
"BUCHANAN'S BLACK SHEEP" '85
"BUCHANAN'S STAGE LINE" '86

COX, WILLIAM TREVOR
TREVOR, WILLIAM--[3][7][21]MYS/SF--
BODLEY "ANGELS AT THE RITZ" '75
BODLEY "CHILDREN OF DYNMOUTH" '76
BODLEY "FAMILY SINS & OS" '90

COXALL, JACK ARTHUR
DAWSON, OLIVER--[8]

COXE, EDWARD D.
A FUGITIVE--[2][7]SF--
"THE FOOL KILLER"

COXE, GEORGE HARMON
COXE, GEORGE H.--[29]MYS--
KNOPF "FASHIONED FOR MURDER" '47

COXON, MURIEL
HINE, MURIEL--[1][2][11]

COY, STANLEE MILLER
CHARLES, IONA--W/CAROLYN NICHOLS,
[3][9][21][26]MYS/ROM--
POPLB "THE RELUCTANT LADY"
POPLB "WHEN ONLY THE BOUGAINVILLA
BLOOMS" '75
POPLB "GRENENCOURT" '75

COY, STANLEE MILLER [CONT]
MILLER, CISSI[E]--W/CAROLYN NICHOLS, [9][21][26]ROM-- "TISH"

COYLE, LEO PERRY
COYLE, LEE--[31]

COYNE, JOSEPH E.
BERCH, WILLIAM O.--[1][9][22][31]AMERICAN/ROM

CRABBE, CLARENCE LINDEN
CRABBE, BUSTER--[31]

CRADDOCK, WILLIAM JAMES
JAMES, WILLIAM--[1][31]

CRADOCK, JOHN
BON VIVEUR--W/PHYLLIS NAN SORTAIN CRADOCK,[8]

CRADOCK, PHYLLIS NAN S.
BON VIVEUR--W/JOHN CRADOCK,[8]
CRADOCK, FANNY--[8]
DALE, FRANCES--[1][3]MYS-- HURST "SCORPION'S SUICIDE" '42

CRAFT, KINUKO Y.
CRAFT, K.Y.--[31][33]

CRAFTS, WILBUR FISK
FISK, CALLENE--[1]
UNCLE WILL, V.M.--[1]

CRAGG, DAN
CRAGG, D.J.--[31]

CRAGO, CLARA
SCOTT, ROWENA--[14]ADULT-- OLYM TC#481 "INTO THE PLAYHOUSE" '70

CRAIG, ALEXANDER GEORGE
CRAIG, ALEC--[31]
CRAIK, ARTHUR--[1]
CRAIK, ARTHUR--[1][22][31]ENGLISH

CRAIG, EDWARD ANTHONY
CARRICK, EDWARD--[1][8][22]ENGLISH

CRAIG, EVELYN QUITA
LANGDALE, EVE--[31]

CRAIG, LILLIAN
REED, KIT--[31]--NAME LEGALLY CHANGED TO "KIT REED"

CRAIG, MARY FRANCIS S.
CRAIG, M.F.--[31][33]
CRAIG, M.S.--[8][17][21][31][33]ROM
CRAIG, MARY--[21][31][33]ROM-- 5 NOVELS
CRAIG, MARY S.--[21][31][33]ROM-- "DARK PARADISE"
CRAIG, MARY SHURA--[21]ROM--
"FORTUNE'S DESTINY"
"LYON'S PRIDE"
"PIRATE'S LANDING"
HILL, ALEXIS--[9][17][21][26][33]ROM--
SP "PASSION'S SLAVE"
SP "UNTAMED HEART"
HILL, MEREDITH--[33]
SHURA, MARY FRANCES--[3][17][21]MYS/ROM-- "THE SHOP ON TURENSDY ST." '72

CRAIG, MARY COAD
CLARK, DUNCAN MD--[1]

CRAIGIE, DOROTHY M.
CRAIGIE, DAVID--[1][2][7][11][23]SF

CRAIGIE, PEARL MARY T.
HOBBES, JOHN OLIVER--[1][8][22] AMERICAN-ENGLISH

CRAIGIE, WILLIAM A.
CRAIGIE, W.A.--[1]

CRAIK, DINAH MARIA MULOCK
MULOCK, DIANA--FANT. LIT. FOR CHILDREN & YOUNG ADULTS BY RUTH NADELMAN
MULOCK, DINA MARIA--[33]

CRAINE, EDITH JANICE
DARU, JULISKA--[1]

CRAINE, JOHN
CRANE, MANNIN--[1]

CRAINE, JOHN HENRY
JASON--[8]

CRAMB, JOHN ADAM
REVERMORT, J.A.--[2]

CRANDALL, NORMA
CHAMBERLAND, WILSON--W/WILSON MCCARTY,[1]

CRANE, JAMES GORDON
CRANE, JIM--[31]

CRANE, ROYSTON CAMPBELL
CRANE, ROY--[33]

CRANE, STEPHEN [TOWNLEY]
SMITH, JOHNSTON--[33]

CRANE, WILLIAM B.
CRANE, BILL--[31]

CRANFIELD, W.T.
CRANE, DENIS--[1]

CRANMER, HELEN WORDEN
BRUMMEL, BELLE--[1]
DIX, DOROTHY--[1]
WORDEN, HELEN--[1]

CRANNY, TITUS FRANCIS
FRANCIS, DANIEL--[1][31]

CRANSTON, METHILDE
DELORME, MICHELE--[31]

CRANSTON, RUTH
WARWICK, ANNE--[1]

CRAVEN, BARBARA C.
CATLIN, BARBARA--[9][21][26]ROM-- 3 NOVELS
CATLIN, MIRANDA--W/MARTHA R. HIX, [9][21][26]ROM-- "PRISONER OF LOVE"

CRAVEN, WESLEY EARL
CRAVEN, WES--[31]

CRAWFORD, BETTY ANNE
BENOIT, HENDRA--[7]SF-- SCHOLASTIC "PSI PATROL #2 HENDRA'S BOOK" '85
CREIGHTON, LEE--[7]SF-- ACE "TWO QUEENS OF LOCHRIN" '90

CRAWFORD, BETTY ANNE [CONT]
HURLEY, MAXWELL--[7]SF--
SCHOLASTIC "PIS PATROL #3 MAX'S BOOK" '85
LIQUORI, SAL--[7]SF--
SCHOLASTIC "PSI PATROL #1 SAL'S BOOK" '85

CRAWFORD, CHAR
JOHNSON, CHARLENE--[1]][31]

CRAWFORD, DIANNA
CRAWFORD, ELAINE--[26]ROM--
"CAPTIVE ANGEL"
"RIVER TEMPTRESS"

CRAWFORD, EVERETT LAKE
HUNTER, ANOLE--[1]

CRAWFORD, JOHN RICHARD
WALKER, J.--[8]

CRAWFORD, KAREN
MARSHALL, ANDREA--[21]ROM--
"WRITTEN IN THE STARS"
"HANDLE WITH CARE"
"AGAINST THE ODDS"

CRAWFORD, MARGARET
FORD, GARRET--W/WILLIAM L. CRAWFORD,[2][11]

CRAWFORD, PHYLLIS
TURNER, JOSIE--[8][33]

CRAWFORD, SALLIE
TROTTER, SALLIE--[8]

CRAWFORD, TERRENCE MICH.
CRAWFORD, TERRY--[31]

CRAWFORD, WILLIAM HULFISH
CRAWFORD, BILL--[31]

CRAWFORD, WILLIAM [E]
BRANDT, ROGER--[3][29][31][40]MYS--
PLAYBOY "THE DEATH CONNECTION" '76
LOGAN, DON--[1][3][31]MYS--
POCK "THE RAPIST" '76
RAWFORD, W.C.--[1][31]--
ZEBRA "RANGER KIRK" '74
PINN "RIDE TO SUNDOWN" '76
ROSS, PAUL--[3][29][31][40]MYS, HP--
MANOR "THE ASSASSIN" '74
WILLIAMS, BILL--[1][31]--
"THE CATMAN OF MAZATLAN" '71

CRAWFORD, WILLIAM L.
FORD, GARRET--W/MARGARET CRAWFORD,
[2][7][11][23]--
"SCIENCE & SOCERY" '53
PETERSON, JIM--[3][29][31][40]MYS--
PINN "SICILIAN SLAUGHTER" '73
REYNOLDS, PETER--W/AMELIA R. LONG,[34]MYS--
VISIONARY "BEHIND THE EVIDENCE" '36

CRAWFURD, OSWALD J.F
BANKS, ARCHIBALD--[1]
BRETT, GEORGE IRA--[1]
DANGERFIELD, JOHN--[1]
LATOUCHE, JOHN--[1]
SANDYS, GEORGE WINDLE--[1]
ST. KAYNE, HUMPHREY--[1]
STRANGE, JOSEPH--[1]
TURNER, ALEXANDER FREKE--[1]

CRAWLEY, TONY
DUPEA, BOBBY--[31]

CRAY, EDWARD
CRAY, ED--[31]
SKALD--[1]

CRAY, PAUL
ZOOL, M.H.--[23]SF GROUP PSEUD.

CREAGER, EUNICE WHAYNE
EMERSON, ALICE B.--[1]
HOPE, LAURA LEE--[1]

CREAGH, PATRICK
BRASIER-CREAGH, PATRICK--[31]

CREASEY, CLARENCE H.
CRESSY, EDWARD--[8]

CREASEY, JOHN
ASHE, GORDON--[2][3][7][18][29]MYS--
LONG "DEATH ON DEMAND" '39 & OTHERS '39-75
COOKE, M.E.--[3][11][18][29][31]MYS--
20 NOVELS '34-40
COOKE, MARGARET--[11][18][31]MYS--
14 NOVELS
COOPER, HENRY ST. JOHN--[11][18][31]MYS--
6 NOVELS '37-40
CREDO--[1][31]
DEANE, NORMAN--[2][3][5][29][32]--
HURST--21 NOVELS '39-54
JCM "MAN I DIDN'T KILL" APR '58
FECAMPS, ELISE--[1][18][31]ROM--
"LOVE OF HATE"
"TRUE LOVE"
"LOVES TRIUMPH"
FRAZER, ROBERT CAINE--[2][3][18][31][32]MYS--
6 NOVELS '59-62
JCM "HOLLYWOOD HOAX" OCT '61 & NOV '61
JCM "MARK KILBY TAKES A RISK" SEPT,
OCT & DEC '62
GILL, PATRICK--[3][18][29][31]MYS--
7 MELLIFONT NOVELS '37-40
HALLIDAY, MICHAEL--[2][3][5][18][29][32]MYS--
56 NOVELS '37-73
JCM "THICKER THAN WATER" JAN '60
JCM "REVENGE" FEB '62
JCM "WHEN THE WORM TURNS" MAR '62
JCM "UNSOUND MIND" APR '62
HOGARTH, CHARLES--W,[IVOR] IAN BOWEN,
[3][18][29][31]MYS--
SELWYN "MURDER ON LARGO ISLAND" '44
HOPE, BRIAN--[3][18][31]MYS--
NEWNES "FOUR MOTIVES FOR MURDER" '38
HUGHES, COLIN--[3][18][29][31]MYS--
NEWNES "TRIPLE MURDER" '40
HUNT, KYLE--[2][3][18][32]MYS--
4 ORIG NOVELS & RPRTS OF NOVELS AS
BY "MICHAEL HALLIDAY"
JCM "KILL MY LOVE" JUL '59
MANN, ABEL--[3][18][29][31]MYS--
POCK "DANGER WOMAN" '66
MANTON, PETER--[2][3][18][29]MYS--
14 NOVELS '37-54
MARRIC, J.J.--[2][3][32]MYS--
22 NOVELS '55-75
19 DIGEST STORIES
MARSDEN, JAMES--[1][11][18]JUV--
"MIDDLE WEIGHT CHAMPION" '35
MARTIN, RICHARD--[2][3][18][29]MYS--
EARL "KEYS TO CRIME" '47
EARL "VOTE FOR MURDER" '48
HODDER "ADRIAN & JONATHAN" '54
MOF "VENOM VENGEANCE" OCT '59
MATTHESON, RODNEY--[3][18][29]MYS--
FICT HOUSE "DARK SHADOW" '37
FICT HOUSE "HOUSE OF FERRARS" '37

CREASEY, JOHN [CONT]
MORTON, ANTHONY--[2][18][32][34]MYS--
NOVELS '24-70
3 DIGEST STORIES
RANGER, KEN--[1][2][18]WEST--
"ONE-SHOT MARRIOTT" '38
"ROARING GUNS" '39
REILLY, WILLIAM K.--[1][2][18]WEST--13 NOVELS
RILEY, TEX--[2][11][18]WEST--14 NOVELS
ST. JOHN, HENRY--[1][11]
WILDE, JIMMY--[1][11]
YORK, JEREMY--[2][3][18][32]MYS--
23 NOVELS & RPRTS OF
'MICHAEL HALLIDAY' NOVELS
JCM "SO SOON TO DIE" SEPT '58

CREBBIN, EDWARD HORACE
SEA-WRACK--[1][3]MYS--
"McINNESOF THE N.I.D." '41

CRECHALES, ANTHONY GEORGE
ANTHONY, GEORGE--V. BERCH-BRNDN/BC PSEUDS,
BAE 22, ADULT--
CRECHALES, TONY--[1][31]
KENT, TONY--[1][31]
TRELOS, TONY--V. BERCH-BRNDN/BC PSEUDS,
BAE 22/[1]ADULT--

CREESE, IRENE
RAY, RENE--[7]--
BK GUILD "ANGEL ASSIGNMENT" '88

CREEVEY, LUCY E.
BEHRMAN, LUCY CREEVEY--[31]

CREIGHTON, JEAN SCOTT
BORTHWICK, J.S.--KLEIN-GREAT WOMEN MYSTERY
WRITERS, MYS--
ST. MARTIN'S "CASE OF HOOK-BILLED
KITES" '82
ST. MARTIN'S "DOWN EAST MURDERS" '85
ST. MARTIN'S "STUDENT BODY" '86
ST. MARTIN'S "BODIES OF WATER" '90

CRELLIN, H.N.
ARAWIYAH, AL--[2]

CRESSWELL, DONALD
ANGEL, ROSS--S. HOLLAND-SCION CKLST,
PP 27,[27][34]MYS--
31 NOVELS '50-4
CRESSON, PIERRE--S. HOLLAND--SCION CKLST,
PP 27, P11
KARTA, NAT--S. HOLLAND-SCION CKLST,
PP 27,[3], HP--
SCION "FOOLISH VIRGIN RETURNS" '53

CRESSWELL, JASMINE ROSEM.
CRAIG, JASMINE--[9][31]

CRESWELL, HARRY B.
CRESWELL, H.B.--[1]
KARSHISH--[1]

CRESWELL, ROSEMARY
CLAREMONT, RUTH--W/COLE MANNERS,
[34][36]AUSTRALIAN/MYS--
McPHEE "TO SLEEP, TO DIE" '89

CRETIN, BERNARD JACQUES M
CERTINAGES, BERNARD--[1]

CREWS, ETHEL MAXAM
MAXAM, MIA--[9][21][26]ROM--
5 NOVELS

CREWS, JUDSON [C]
BETIS, WILLARD EMORY--[1]
DRACHLER, TRUMBULL--[1]
FARALLON, CERISE--[1]
MACADAMS, TOBIN--[1]

CRICHTON, DOUGLAS
DOUGLAS, MICHAEL--W/JOHN MICHAEL
CRICHTON,[2][11][18]--
ONE NOVEL '71

CRICHTON, ELEANOR
MCGAVIN, MOYRA--[1]

CRICHTON,[JOHN] MICHAEL
DOUGLAS, MICHAEL--W/DOUGLAS
CRICHTON,[2][11][18][29]--
ONE NOVEL '71
HUDSON, JEFFREY--[2][3][18][29][31][33]MYS--
NAL "A CASE OF NEED" '68
LANGE, JOHN--[2][3][11][18][29]MYS--
SIGN "EASY GO" '68
KNOPF "BINARY" '72 & 7 MORE

CRICHTON, KYLE SAMUEL
FORSYTHE, ROBERT--[8]

CRICHTON, LUCILLA MATTHEW
ANDREWS, LUCILLA--[8]

CRIDEN, JOSEPH
CRIDEN, YOSEF--[31]

CRIDER,[ALLEN] BILL[Y]
BANKS, CLIFF--HAWK/CRIDER INTRVW '93,
WAR, HP--
POPLB 'TUNNEL RATS' #1 '89
BUCHANAN, JACK--HAWK/CRIDER
INTRVW '93, HP--
'M.I.A.' SERIES:
JOVE "BACK FROM NAM" '89
JOVE 10032 "DESERT DEATH RAID" '89
JOVE 09678 "MIAMI WAR ZONE" '88
CARTER, NICK--W/JACK DAVIS,[3]MYS, HP--
CHART "THE COYOTE CONNECTION" '81
MCLANE, JACK--HAWK-CRIDER INTRVW '93,[7]--
ZEBRA "KEEPERS OF THE BEAST" '88
ZEBRA "REST IN PEACE" '90
ZEBRA "JUST BEFORE DEATH" '90
McKENNA, K.C.--HAWK/CRIDER INTRVW '93--
"RIVERS OF GOLD" JAN '95

CRILE, GEORGE JR.
CRILE, BARNEY--[31]

CRILE, HELGA SANDBURG
SANDBURG, HELGA--[1]

CRIPPS, LOUISE LILIAN
CRIPPS, L.L.--[1]
SAMOILOFF, LOUISE CRIPPS--[1]

CRISLER, HERBERT ORIN
CRISLER, FRITZ--[31]

CRISP, ANTHONY THOMAS
CRISP, TONY--[8][31]
WESTERN, MARK--[8]

CRISP, S.E.
CRISPIE--[8]

CRITCHETT, RICHARD CLAUDE
CARTON, RICHARD CLAUDE--[8][22]ENGLISH

CRITCHLEY, JULIAN [M.G.]
BEAUFITZ, WILLIAM--[31]

CRITCHLOW, DOROTHY
DAWSON, JANE--[8]

CRITTEN, STEPHEN HENRY
BELL, NEIL--[7]SF
SOUTHWOLD, STEPHEN--[23]--NAME ASSUMED [LEGALIZED TO DISAVOW FATHER]

CRIUCH, WILLIAM MAXWELL
CROUCH, BILL JR.--[31]

CRNJANSKI, MILOS
MILL, C.R.--[22]HUNGARIAN-ENGLISH

CROAL, FRANCES
HAMMOND, FRANCES--[1]

CROCCHIOLA, FRANCIS STAN.
STANLEY FRANCIS--[1]
STANLEY, F.--[8]

CROCKER, SAMUEL
ISLET, THEODORE OCEANIC--[1]

CROCKETT, DAVID
CROCKETT, DAVY--[31]

CROCKETT, SAMUEL R.
BERETON, FORD--[1]
CROCKETT, S.R.--[1]

CROCOMBE, LEONARD CECIL
HAMMERSLEY, CECIL--[1]

CROFT-COOKE, RUPERT
BRUCE, LEO--[3][18][31][32]MYS--
32 NVLS '37-74
SA "MURDER IN MINIATURE" MAY '55
CROFT, TAYLOR--[1][8][22]MYS

CROFTS, FREEMAN WILLS
CROFTS, F.W.--[29]MYS--
SKOGL "GREUZERTAVLAN" '58
WALLER, JOHN--[29]MYS--
JVA/VA 21 "TAVELSVINDELN" '42

CROFUT, WILLIAM E. III
CROFUT, BILL--[33]

CROISSANT, KAY
KAY, CATHERINE--W/CATHERINE DEES, [9][21][26]ROM-- 5 NOVELS
MCKENZIE, KATE--W/CATHERINE DEES,[21]ROM--
"BED AND BREAKFAST"

CROLY, HERBERT DAVID
HERBERT, WILLIAM--[1]

CROLY, JANE CUNNINGHAM
JUNE, JENNIE--[31]
JUNE, JENNY--[8][22]ENGLISH-AMERICAN
VENI VIDI--[1]

CROMIE, ALICE HAMILTON
HAMILTON, ALICE--[22][31][33]AMERICAN
MORT, VIVIAN--LACHMAN LST MAY '93,[1][22][33]

CROMPTON, ANNE
ELIOT, ANNE--[9][21][26]ROM--
5 NOVELS

CROMPTON, MARGARET NORAH
MAIR, MARGARET--[8][22][31]ENGLISH

CRONIN, ARCHIBAL JOSEPH
CRONIN, A.J.--[1]

CRONIN, BERNARD CHARLES
ADAIR, DENNIS--[3][22][36]MYS--
HUTCH "DEATH RIDES THE DESERT" '40
BOHUN, HUGH--[1]
DIXON, WALLACE--[1][22]
NORTH, ERIC--[2][3][7][36]MYS/SF--
HODDER "TOAD" '29
DOBSON "A CHIP ON MY SHOULDER" '55
DOBSON "NAME IS SMITH" '57
DOBSON "NOBODY STOPS ME" '60
FM "GREEN FLAME" JUL '50

CRONIN, BRENDAN LEO
CRONIN, MICHAEL--[3][22][29][40]MYS--
57 NOVELS '53-80
MILES, DAVID--[1][3][29]MYS--
4 NOVELS '60-4

CRONSICE, AXEL WILHELM
AXE, WILLHELM--[29]MYS--
VART HEM "SEMENOFFS TESTAMENTE" '27

CROOK, BETTE JEAN
LESLIE, SAN--[31]

CROOK, COMPTON N[EWBY]
TALL, STEPHEN--[2][7][11][23]SF--
BERK "STARDUST #1 & 2"
"PEOPLE BEYOND THE WALL"

CROOK, JOEL
J.C.--[1]

CROPP, BENJAMIN
CROPP, BEN--[31]

CROSBIE, HUGH PROVAN
CARRICK, JOHN--[3][22][29][31]SCOTTISH/MYS--
7 NOVELS '64-69

CROSBIE, SYLVIA KOWITT
KOWITT, SYLVIA--[31]

CROSBY, HARRY C. JR.
ANVIL, CHRISTOPHER--V. BERCH-MON PSEUDS, BAE 9,[2][7][23][32]--
MON 478 "DAY THE MACHINES STOPPED" '64

CROSBY, HARRY C. JR.
CROSBY, HENRY GREW--[31]
CROSBY, HENRY STURGIS--[31]

CROSBY, HARRY LILLIS
CROSBY, BING--[31]

CROSBY, JACQUELINE GART.
CROSBY, JACKIE--[31]

CROSBY, MARY PHELPS [J]
CROSBY, CARESSE--[1]
CROSBY, POLLY--[1]

CROSBY, MICHAEL [HUGH]
CROSBY, JEREMIAH--[1][31]

CROSE, SUSAN
JACKSON, LISA--[9][21][26]ROM--
32 NOVELS
MATHEWS, MICHELLE--[9][21]ROM--
"UNDER THE MISTLETOE"

CROSHER, GEOFFREY ROBINS
KESTEVEN, G.R.--[7][8][31][33]SF--
CHATTO "PALE INVADERS" '74
CHATTO "AWAKENING WATER" '77

CROSLAND, SUSAN [WATSON]
BARNES, SUSAN--[8]

CROSS, CLAIRE
CROSS, M. CLAIRE--[31]

CROSS, COLIN JOHN
WEIR, JOHN--[22]ENGLISH

CROSS, GILBERT B.
WINTERS, J.C.--[3][22][33]MYS--
AV "BERLIN FUGUE" '85
WINTERS, JON--[3][22][31][33]MYS--
AV "DRAKOR MEMORANDA" '79
AV "CATENARY EXCHANGE" '83
AV "BERLIN FUGUE" '85

CROSS, JOHN KEIR
MACFARLANE, STEPHEN--[2][16][23][31]SF--
"THE ANGRY PLANET" '45
MORELY, SUSAN--[1][2]

CROSS, RENA
CRANE, RENE--[35]AUSTRALIAN--
HRWTZ PB147 "KEY OF CORRUPTION" '63
DEE, REBECCA--[35]AUSTRALIAN, HP--
HRWTZ "NIGHT SPECIAL" '63
HRWTZ "AGENCY GIRL" '63
DUFFY, JOHN--[35]AUSTRALIAN, HP--
HRWTZ "OUTSVILLE PUB" '63
HRWTZ "INSVILLE MOB" '65
JAMES, CHRISTINE--[35]AUSTRALIAN--
HRWTZ PB161 "MODEL SCHOOL" '63
MILLER, KAREN--[35]AUSTRALIAN, HP--
HRWTZ NOVELS #2-11 '62-3
TOLHURST, GEOFFREY--[35]AUSTRALIAN--
HRWTZ PB132 "FLAT 4, KING'S CROSS" '63
HRWTZ PB135 "BIG KICK" '63
HRWTZ PB154 "BEACH BOY" '63

CROSS, ZORA BERNICE MAY
MAY, BERNICE--[1]

CROSSEN, KENDELL FOSTER
BARCLAY, BENNET--[2][3][11][18][29][37]MYS--
"SATAN COMES ACROSS" '45
CHABER, M.E.--[2][3][18][29][32][37]MYS--
"ACID NIGHTMARE" '67
"GREEN LAMA" '76
SUS "A HEARSE OF ANOTHER COLOR" MAY '60
SES "RENEGADE!" NOV '53
CROSSEN, KEN--[8][11][23][32]MYS/SF--
"MURDER OUT OF MIND" '45
FOSTER, RICHARD--N. CARR, PP 1,V. BERCH-
GM PSEUDS, PP 33,[2][3][18][23][29]MYS/SF--
DD "GREEN LAMA" STORIES
VULM 3 "LAUGHING BUDDHA MURDERS" '44
FSM 5 "INVISIBLE MEN MURDERS" '45
POPLB 667 "BLONDE & BEAUTIFUL" '55
POPLB EB 32 "GIRL FROM EAST ST." '55
GM899 "BIER FOR A CHASER" '59
GM853 "THE REST MUST DIE" '59
GM995 "TOO LATE FOR MOURNING" '60
GM "TASKENT CRISIS" '71
MONIG, CHRISTOPHER--[2][3][11][18][29][37]--
4 MYS NOVELS '56-60
RICHARD, KENT--[1][2][11][37]MYS
RICHARDS, CLAY--[3][11][18][29][31]MYS--
4 'BOBBS' NOVELS '61-4

CROSSLEY, LOUISE RODGERS
RENA--[1]

CROTHERS, JESSIE F.
WRIGHT, FRANCES J.--[1]

CROUDACE, GLYNN
MONNOW, PETER--[34]MYS--
JENKINS "FIRE OPAL" '68
JENKINS "KILLING OF ALQUIN JUDD" '69
HALE "HOODED SKULL" '72

CROUNSE, HELEN LOUISE
JACKSON, JOYCE--[1]

CROUSE, ANNE D. JORDAN
CROUSE, ANNE D.--[7]SF
JORDAN, ANNE--[7]SF--
"FIRES OF THE PAST: 13 CONTEMP.
FANTASIES ABOUT HOMETOWNS" '91

CROUTCH, LESLIE A.
FREDD, AL--[2]

CROW, DONNA FLETCHER
FLETCHER, DONNA--[21]ROM-- 16 NOVELS
PAUL, ELIZABETH--[1][33]

CROWCROFT, PETER
ALCOTT, JULIA--[1]
CROWCROFT, JANE--[1][21][26][31]ROM--
"OF LOVE INCARNATE"
"WITCH LOVE"
HORATIO, JANE--[1]
MUNTZ, JAMES--[1]
MUNTZ, JAMES Z.--L. MUNROE-NUETZEL INTRVW,
BAE 25--
RUBICON 1010 "NYMPHETTE"
ORLOFF, MAX--[1]
ROBERTS, RINALDO--[1]
VAN ZANDT, E.F.--[1]

CROWE, AMANDA COCKRELL
COCKRELL, AMANDA--[1][31]

CROWE,[BETTINA] LUM
LUM, PETER--[8][11][22][31][33]
AMERICAN-ENGLISH

CROWELL, MARY REED
EMERCE--[1]

CROWLE, EILEEN G.B.
CROWLE, PIDGEON--[1]

CROWLEY, EDWARD ALEXANDER
CROWLEY, ALISTAIR--[34]MYS--
"THE SCRUTINIES OF SIMON IFF" '87
BOLESKIN, LORD--[1]
THERION, MASTER--[1]
VEREY,[REV] C.--[1]
ABHAVANANDA--[1][8]
CARR, H.D.--[1][8]
CROWLEY, ALEISTER--[1][8]
FENIX, COMTE DE--[1][8][11]
KHAN, KHALED--[8]
PERDURABO, FRATER--[8][31]
SVAREFF, COUNT VLADIMIR--[8]

CROWN, PETER J.
LEWIS, PETE--[2]

CROWNINSHIELD, FRANCIS W.
BRUCE, ARTHUR LORING--[22]AMERICAN

CROWTHER, BRUCE [IAN]
ANSARA, MICHAEL--[31]
GRANT, JAMES--[3][29]MYS--7 NOVELS '78-80

CROWTHER, WILMA [BERYL]
GEORGE, WILMA--[1][22][31]ENGLISH

CROWTHER-HUNT, NORMAN C.
HUNT, NORMAMN C.--[31]

CROYDON, HAROLD PERCY
TRITTON, DUKE--[13]AUSTRALIAN

CROYDON, JOHN
COOPER, JOHN C.--[1][2][3]MYS--
"DEATH GRIP OF STRANGLER" '58
& 3 OTHERS [ACE & DIGIT]

CROZETTI, RUTH G.W.L.
LORING, J.M.--[1]
O'MAHONEY, RICH--[1]
WARNER-CROZETTI, R.--[1]

CROZIER, KATHLEEN M.E.
EYLES, MERLE--[1][22]MYS
TENNANT, CATHERINE--[1][22]MYS

CRUGER, JULIE GRINNELL
GORDON, JULIEN--[2][3][7]MYS/SF--
LIPPINCOTT "A DIPLOMAT'S DIARY" 1890

CRUGER, PAUL
WORTH, DAN--[1]

CRUICKSHANK, CHARLES G.
GREIG, CHARLES--[8]

CRUICKSHANK, HAROLD F.
FRASER, BERT--[1]

CRUMB, ROBERT
CRUD--[31]
CRUM THE BUM--[31]
CRUMARUMS--[31]
CRUMBUM--[31]
CRUMSKI--[31]
CRUNK--[31]
CRUSTT--[31]
CUM, R.--[31]
DICTUM, STEVE--[31]
GRUBB--[31]
GRUNGE--[31]
KRUMB--[31]
KRUMWITZ--[31]

CRUMBAKER, ALICE
BAKER, ALLISON--[9][21][26][31]ROM--
"AYSA"

CRUSE, HELOISE
HELOISE--[22]AMERICAN

CRUTTENDEN, NELLIE
WREN, JENNY--[8]

CRUZ, GILBERT RALPH
CRUZ, GILBERTO RAFAEL--[31]

CRYER, NEVILLE B.
FERN, EDWIN--[1][8]

CSALLNER, ALFRED
NOSNER, FRIEDRICH--[39]GERMAN/JUV

CUBITT, SONIA ROSEMARY
KEPPEL, SONIA--[1]

CUDLIPP, EDYTHE
ALCOTT, JULIA--[9][21][26][31]ROM--
"ISLAND OF LOVE"
"KEY TO HER HEART"
"A LONG LOST LOVE"
HORATIO, JANE--[1][31]
JORDAN, CARRIE--[1][26][31]ROM--
"RIVALS FOR LOVE"
LACHLAN, EDYTHE--[9]ROM
MONTGOMERY, BETTINA--[9][21][26]ROM--
"FAMILIAR STRANGER"
NORMAN, NICOLE--[9][21][26]ROM--
"THE FIREBIRD"
"HEATHER SONG"
NORRIS, MAUREEN--[9][21][26]ROM--
"STARRY EYED"
"SEA SWEPT"
ROBERTS, RINALDA--[1][21]ROM--
"THE FOUR MARYS"
VAN ZANDT, E.F.--[1]

CUEVAS, CLARA
DE RIVEL, ISA--[1]

CUFFE, W.U.O'C.
DESART, THE EARL OF--[23]SF--
"THE RAID OF THE DETRIMENTAL"

CULIANU, I[OAN] P[ETRU]
COULIANO, I.P.--[7]SF--
"OUT OF THIS WORLD:OTHERWORLDLY
JOURNEYS FROM GILGAMESH
TO EINSTEIN" '91

CULLEN, COUNTEE
CAT, CHRISTOPHER--[2]

CULLIFORD, PIERRE
PEYO--[33]

CULLIGAN, MATTHEW JOSEPH
CULLIGAN, JOE--[31]

CULVER, CAROL
GRACE, CAROL--[21]ROM--
"ROOM FOR NANNY"
"A TASTE OF HEAVEN"

CULVER, COLLEEN
FAULKNER, COLLEEN--[9][21][26]ROM--
12 NOVELS

CUMBERLAND, MARTEN
BEVIS, JAMES--W/B.V. SHANN,[1][31]
LAUGIER, R.--[18][22][29][31]ENGLISH/MYS
O'HARA, KEVIN--[3][18][22][29]ENGLISH--
16 MYS NOVELS '51-66

CUMES, JAMES WILLIAM C.
JAMES, C.W.--[1][31]

CUMING, EDWARD WILLIAM D.
TEMPEST, EVELYN--[1]

CUMMING, M.I.
CARNES, CAPT.--[1]

CUMMING, ROBERT DAZIEL
SKOOKUM CHUCK--[1][8]

CUMMING-SKINNER, DUGALD M
CUMMINGS, KEN--[1]
DANE, DONALD--[1]
DE BEAUREGARD, HENRI--[1]
DUNDEE, DOUGLAS--[1]
MORAY, DAVID--[1]

CUMMINGS, BARBARA
CROWLEIGH, ANN--W/JO-ANN POWER,
DDLY PLEAS. #3,[26]--
'CLIVELY CLOSE' MYSTERIES
"DEAD AS DEAD CAN BE"
"WAIT FOR THE DARK

CUMMINGS, BRUCE FREDERICK
BARBELLION, W.N.P.--[1][8][22]

CUMMINGS, GABRIELLE
WILSON, GABRIEL--W/RAY CUMMINGS,[37]--
UT - EROTIC TALES

CUMMINGS, JOHN W.
CUMMINGS, JACK--[31]--
CHART "THE VENTURE" '78

CUMMINGS, MONA A.
CUMMINGS, M.A.--[1]
CUMMINGS, MONETTE--V. BERCH LTR TO
HUBIN '94, [21]MYS/ROM--
PGT "ROYAL CONSPIRACY" '88 & OTHERS

CUMMINGS, MR. & MRS. RAY
WILSON, GABRIEL--[2]

CUMMINGS, RAY[MOND KING]
CAMPBELL, JOHN--[2][11]--
DUCHESS MAG "BRIGANDS OF THE MOON"
CUMMINGS, GABRIEL--L. ROBBINS
LTR MAR '94--PULP
CUMMINGS, RAY--[23][31][32][34]SF/MYS--
SS COLL "TALES OF SCIENTIFIC
CRIME CLUB" '79
SW "A LITTLE TOO YOUNG" APR '48
ANC 1 "THE PRINCESS OF THE ATOM" '50 & MORE
SA "LITTLE THINGS" JUL '54
SA "FATA OVERSIGHT" OCT '54
SA "PLAINEST CLUE" JUN '56
ST "REQUIEM FOR A SMALL PLANET" MAR '58
DT "SILVER COFFIN" JAN '61
PH "WRONG EVIDENCE" JAN '62
KING, RAY--[2][11]
SHOTWELL, RAY P.--[2][11]
WALLACE, ROBERT--T. JOHNSON LTR JAN '94,HP
WILSON, GABRIEL--W/GABRIELLE CUMMINGS,
L. ROBBINS LTR '94,[37]--
UT - EROTIC TALES

CUMMINS, ELIZABETH [ANN]
COGELL, ELIZABETH CUMMINS--[7]SF--
"URSULA K. LE GUIN: A PRIMARY
& SECONDARY BIBLIOGRAPHY" '83

CUMMINS, MARY WARMINGTON
MACKIE, ALICE--[8]
MELVILLE, JEAN--[1][8]
TAYLOR, SUSAN--[9][21][29]ROM--
"GIRL OF THE SEA"

CUNLIFFE, BARRINGTON W.
CUNLIFFE, BARRY--[1][31]

CUNLIFFE, DAVE
ALEXANDER, DAVID--[1]
FERKINSHAW, ALBERT--[1]

CUNLIFFE-OWEN, FREDERICK
FONTENOY, MARQUIS DE--[1]

CUNNINGHAM, ALBERT B.
DALE, ESTIL--[1][3]MYS--
DUTTON "THE LAST SURVIVOR" '52
HALE, GARTH--[1]
HALE, GARTH--[22]MYS

CUNNINGHAM, CHESTER GRANT
BODINE, J.D.--[28]WEST--
LYNX "RED BLUFF REVENGE" '89
CALHOUN, CHAD--[28]WEST--
DELL 'BRAD SPEAR' NOVELS '69-TBD
CARRINGTON, G.A.--[28]--
DELL "THE TEMPLETON MASSACRE" '90
CARTER, NICK--W/DANIEL T. STREIB,[3]HP--
AWARD "NIGHT OF THE AVENGER" '73
CODY, JESS--[28]WEST--
IN ENGLAND "GOLD TRAIN" '87
"AZTEC GOLD" '87
"DEVIL'S GOLD" '87
"THE GOLD WAGON" '89
"DIE OF GOLD" '89
"BLOODY GOLD" '89
CUNNINGHAM, CATHY--[3][7][21][26]--
"CURSE OF VALKYRIE HOUSE"
"DEMONS OF HIGHPOINT HOUSE" '73
CUNNINGHAM, CHET--[7]SF
DALTON, KIT--[28]ADULT WEST--
11 NOVELS '86-88
DERRICK, LIONEL--[3][28]HP--
PINN "PENNETRATOR" SERIES EVEN # TITLES
FLETCHER, DIRK--[1][28][31]ADULT WEST--
23 NOVELS '81-89
FLETCHER, FARIS--[21]HP--
'TEXANS' SERIES "REMEMBER THE ALAMO"
PENDLETON, DON--W/LES DANFORTH,[3]HP--
GE "COUNCIL OF KINGS" '85
PENDLETON, DON--[3]MYS,HP--
GE "CRUDE KILL" '83
GE "ORBITING OMEGA" '84
GE "SKYSWEEPER" '84
GE "BALTIMORE TRACKDOWN" '84
GE "NOTHING PERSONAL" '84
GE "KILL TRAP" '84
GE "HELLBINDER" '85
GE "RESURRECTION DAY" '86
GE "MOTOR CITY MAYHEM" '85
PHILLIPS, TONY--[7]SF,HP--
BAL "TURBO COWBOYS #1-#4"
RICHARDS, PAUL--W/DAN STREIB,[3]MYS,HP--
AWARD "MOSCOW AT HIGH NOON IS
THE TARGET" '75

CUNNINGHAM, EUGENE
CARDER, LEIGH--[1][19][28]WEST--
"BORDER GUNS" '35
"BRAVO TRAIL" '35
"OUTLAW JUSTICE" '35

CUNNINGHAM, JAN
FORREST, CHELSEY--[9][21][26]ROM--
"AN ARTIST TOUCH"

CUNNINGHAM, MARILYN
CARLOCK, LYNN--[7][31]SF/ROM--
SILHOUETTE "DAUGHTER OF THE MOON" '86
CHASE, CAROLYN--[21]ROM,HP--
'13 COLONIES' SERIES
"MARYLAND:REBEL'S KISS"

CUNNINGHAM, VIRGINIA MYRA
MUNDY, V.M.--[8]

CUNNINGHAME GRAHAM, R.B.
DON ROBERTO--[31]

CUNNINGTON, CHARLES L.
C.L.C.--[1]
OLD DOG--[1]
RUSTYFACE--[1]

CUNTZ, DIETER
BROCKHOFF, STEFAN--W/OSKAR SEIDLIN & R. PLANT,[39][40]GERMAN/MYS-- "BEGENUNG IN ZERMATT" '55

CUNYNGHAME, FRANCES J.
KINGSTEAD, JULIAN--[1]

CURL, JAMES STEVENS
KEELING, E.B.--[1][31]

CURLE, CHARLES T.W.
CURLE, ADAM--[31]

CURLE, M.O.
ORMISTON, MARGARET--[1]

CURLER, [MARY] BERNICE
DAVIS, [MARY] BERNICE--[1][31]

CURLEWIS, ETHEL S. [T]
TURNER, ETHEL--[1]

CURLING, BRYAN WILIIAM R.
JULIUS--[1][31]
CURLING, BILL--[31]
HOTSPUR--[1][31]

CURLOVICH, JOHN
PAINE, MICHAEL--[7]SF--
CHART "CITIES OF THE DEAD"
CHART "COLORS OF HELL"
CHART "OWL LIGHT"

CURNOW, ALLEN
WHIM WHAM--[8]

CURRAN, JAN GOLBERG
GOLDBERG, JAN--[1][31]

CURRAN, MONA ELISA
MERTON, GILES--[1][22]ENGLISH
MURRAY, ADRIAN--[1][22]ENGLISH
THOMAS, MERVYN--[1][22]ENGLISH

CURRAN, ROBERT
CURRAN, BOB--[31]

CURRENS, JANE
FITZ-RANDOLPH, JANE [C]--[1]

CURREY, CECIL BARR
CINCINNATUS--[31]

CURREY, L.W.
TROUT, KILGORE--W/DAVID G. HARTWELL, HARTWELL INTRVW '93,[7]-- "SF-1 BIBLIO" CA '7-

CURRIE, JOHN DESMOND
WARNER, DOUGLAS--W/ELIZABETH WARNER, [2][3][11][29][40]MYS-- 6 NOVELS '61-68

CURRIE, LADY MARY M.L.
FANE, VIOLET--[1][8][22]ENGLISH

CURRINGTON, OWEN JOSIAH
CURRINGTON, O.J.--[40]MYS--
"A BAD NIGHTS WORK" '74
"BREAK-OUT" '78

CURRUTHERS, MOYES
BATEMAN, ROBERT--[2]

CURRY, COLIN THOMAS
DOUGLAS, COLIN--[8]

CURRY, THOMAS ALBERT
BENTON, JOHN L.--[1][3][29]MYS-- 4 NOVELS '37-42
COLE, JACKSON--A. TONIK, COLE CKLST, 'SPICY ARMADILLO',HP-- TEXAS RNGR 55 STORIES '37-'51
CURRY, TOM--[28][32]WEST/MYS--
MSMM "LET'S TAKE A WALK" JUN '64
MSMM "REWARD" JUL '64
MSMM "AGING STAR" AUG '64
MSMM "YOU CAN NEVER TELL" OCT '64
MSMM "WRITTEN IN BLOOD" DEC '65
MU "BIG CAT'S CLAWS" FEB '66
GREY, ROMER ZANE--[28]WEST-- ZGWM 'BUCK DUANE' NOVELETTES
JEFFERIES, JEFF--L. ROBBINS LTR MAR '94
JEFFERS, ALBERT--[1][3][29]MYS-- MYH "SCREAM FOR MURDER" '41
JEFFERS, JEFF--[8]
MOORE, AL--L. ROBBINS LTR MAR '94--PULP
SCOTT, BRADFORD--A. TONIK, ECHOES #4,P33-- ONE OF THE LAST NOVELS ca '74
TOMPKINS, WALKER A.--[28]WEST-- POPLB "SANTE FE TRAIL" '48 PUBL IN ERROR AS BY "TOMPKINS"

CURRY, WINIFRED J.P.
PRIMROSE, JANE--[8]

CURSHAM, MARY ANN
M.A.C.--[1]

CURTIES, T.J. HORSELY
HORSELY, T.J.--[2]

CURTIS BROWM, BEATRICE
BROWN, BEATRICE C.--[31]

CURTIS, E.J.
SMITH, SHIRLEY--[1]

CURTIS, MARY HASKELL
CURTIS, MARY H. [MARY]--[21]ROM--
"KISSES FOR KATE"
"LOVE LYRICS"
"CLIFFHANGER"
HASKELL, MARY--[9][21][26]ROM--11 NOVELS

CURTIS, RICHARD [A]
ALDEN, BURT--L. MUNROE RVW FEB '93--
PIL PB801 "SIN MAKERS" '63
PB809 "SIN SELL" '63
ALDRICH, CURT--L. MUNROE RVW FEB '93-- EL 347 "BIKINI BRIDE"
DAVIS, ROBERT HART--A. TONIK, ECHOES#24,HP-- MU "VOLCANO BOX AFFAIR" NOV '67
DEXTER, JOHN--L. MUNROE SALES LIST 22-- MDNR 465 "LUST PRO" '62
LILLY, RAY--[1][3]MYS-- MANOR "THE SUNDAY ALIBI" '77
MACBRIAN, JAMES--[1][34]GHOSTED-- MON 429 "REVOLT OF ABBIE LEE" '64 FOR DAVE FOLEY
RICHARDS, CURTIS--GLEN COOK LTR AUG '93,[1][33]
STEVENS, CURTIS--W/PAUL STEVENS,[3]MYS-- DELL 3307 "GRAVY TRAIN HIT" '77
STULTIFER, MORTON--[1][33]
WARD, MELANIE--[1][33]

CURTIS, SHARON & THOMAS
JAMES, ROBIN--[9][21][26]AMERICAN/ROM--
"THE GOLDEN TOUCH"
"THE TESTIMONY"
LONDON, LAURA--[9][17][21][26][31]
AMERICAN/ROM--7 NOVELS

CURTIS, THOMAS DALE
CURTIS, TOM--[31]

CURZON, DANIEL
BROWN, DANIEL RUSSELL--[31]

CURZON-HERRICK, L. MAUD C
CAIRNES, MAYD--[1][2][7]

CUSHING, ENID LOUISE
CUSHING, ENID--W/ANDRE ALICE NORTON,
GLEN COOK LTR AUG '93--
"MAID-AT-ARMS"
DAWSON, MABEL LOUISE--[1]

CUSHING, RICHARD JAMES
CUSHING, RICHARD CARDINAL--[31]

CUSHMAN, DAN
DRUMMOND, JOHN PETER--LACHMAN LST MAY '93
LOOG, BUSTER--J. HOFFMANN, PP 40, P18,HP--
GERM PANTH 203 RPRT OF "PORT ORIENT"
MILES, YUKON--V. BERCH-GM PSEUDS, PP 33--
GM 201 "STAMPEDE" '51
STARR, JOHN--LACHMAN LST MAY '93--
CREST 529 "THE PURVEYOR" '62

CUSHMAN, JANE
SANDFORD, JANE--[3]MYS--
GM "IN SAFE HANDS" '84

CUST, BARBARA
FANSHAWE, CAROLINE--[9]ROM
WARD, KATE--[9]ROM--
"CASTLE DANGEROUS"

CUTCHEN, BILLYE WALKER
BROWN, BILLYE WALKER--[1][31]

CUTFORTH, JOHN ASHLIN
ASHLIN, JOHN--[22][31]ENGLISH

CUTHBERT, ESTELLA Y
YEREX, CUTHBERT--[1][2][7]SF

CUTHRELL, FAITH B.
BALDWIN, FAITH--[8][9][21][26]ROM
LEE, AMBER--[1]

CUTLER, IVOR
KNIFESMITH--[22][31]ENGLISH

CUTTEN, MERVYN JAMES
CUTTEN, M.J.--[31]

CUYLER, MARGERY S.
WALLACE, DAISY--[1][33]

CWALINSKI, PAUL
McDONALD, PAUL CHEROKEE--V. BERCH LTR
TO HUBIN '94, MYS--
POPLB "THE PATCH" '86
POPLB "GULF STREAM" '88

CWOJDZINSKA, SELMA
SCHROEDTER, BILLA--[39]GERMAN
WESSEL, OKTAVIA--[39]GERMAN

CZACZKES, SHMUEL YOSEF
AGNON, S.Y.--[1]
IRONI--[1]
MAZAL TOV--[1]

CZECH-JOCHBERG, ERICH
CLAM, ERNST--[39]GERMAN

CZECHOWSKI, JULIE
MOFFETT, JULIE--[26]ROM--
"FOR ALL TIME"
"TOUCH OF FIRE" & OTHERS

CZELL, CARL
MERZ, CARL--[39]GERMAN

CZERNIK, THEODOR
FELD, HEINRICH--[39]GERMAN/MYS/JUV

CZERWENKA, RUDI
WENK, RUDOLF--[39]GERMAN/JUV

CZULEGER, REBECCA
BOND, REBECCA--[9][21][26]ROM--4 NOVELS
FORSTER, REBECCA--[9][21][26]ROM--9 NOVELS

CZURA, ROMAN PETER
CURTIS, PAUL--[1][32]--
NSLM U-166 "CHAINED SEX" '60
MH "IMPULSE" FEB-MAR '67
MH "BANKER'S TRUST" NOV '64
CZURA, R.P.--[1]
DALE, ROMAN--[1]

D'ALTENA, ARNAUD DE BORC.
DE BORCHGRAVE, ARNAUD--W/ROBERT MOSS,[7]--
"THE SPIKE" '80

D'AMATO, BARBARA
BLACK, MALACAI--LACHMAN LST '93,
AUTHOR PROVIDED,[34]MYS--
3 ZEBRA NOVELS '81-90

D'AMBRE, ANNE CAROLINE
COEUR, PIERRE--[1]

D'AMBROSIO, CHARLES A.
DOLLAR INVESTOR--[31]

D'ANDREA, WILLIAM L.
WILLOUGHBY, LEE DAVIS--[21]HP--
DELL 'MAKING OF AMERICA' SERIES:
"VOYAGEURS"

D'ANGELO, LUCIANO
D'ANGELO, LOU--[1][31]

D'ANNUNZIO, GABRIELE
MINIMO, DUCA--[22]ITALIAN
DUCA MINIMO--[31]

D'APERY, HELEN B.G.
HARPER, OLIVE--[2][3][22]MYS--
17 NOVELS '03-12

D'ARCY, JACK
JONES, G. WAYMAN--[29]MYS, HP

D'ARCY-ORGA, ATES
ORGA, ATES--[1]

D'ARLEY, CATHERINE
ARLEY, CATHERINE--[8][29]MYS--
"LOCKFAGELN" '58

D'AVIGDOR, ELIM HENRY
WANDERER--[2][3]MYS--
GILBERT "WHIMS" 1889

D'AVRIL, [BARON] ADOLPH
CYRILLE--[1]

D'EASUM, CEDRIC GODFREY
D'EASUM, DICK--[31]

D'ERLANGER, FREDERIC A.
REGNAL, F.--[8]

D'ESMENARD, JEAN
D'ESME, JEAN--[2][7]SF--
"THE RED GODS" '24

D'ORS Y ROVIRA, EUGENIO
XENIUS--[20][22]SPANISH

DA CRUZ, DANIEL JR.
BALLANTINE, JOHN--[1][8][31]
CROSS, T.T.--[1][31]

DA SILVA, JOAQUIM B.C.
D'ARCOS, J. PACO--[2]

DACE, LETITIA [S]
DACE, TISH--[1][31]

DACHS, DAVID
STANLEY, DAVE--[1][8]

DAGAN, AVIGDOR
FISCHI, VIKTOR--[31]

DAGG, JILLIAN
BRIAN, MARILYN--[9][21][26]ROM--
"PASSIONS GLOW"
FAYRE, JILLIAN--[9][21][26]ROM--
"WHISPERS OF THE HEART"
WILDMAN, FAYE--[9][21][26]ROM--4 NOVELS

DAHL, CHRISTER
AHL, KENNET--W/LASSE STROMSTEDT,[29]MYS--
PRISM "GRUNDBULTEN" '74
PRISM "LYFTET" '76
PRISM "RAVSAXEN" '78
PRISM "SLUTSTSTIONEN" '80

DAHL, JURGEN
HATJE, JAN--[39]GERMAN/JUV

DAHL, LINDA
DE CAMPOS, L.--[31]

DAHL, SOREN A.
ANKER, PETER--[37]MYS,HP--
'BEDRIFTER' STORIES '42-7

DAIANOV, KADYR K.
DAIAN, KADYR--[1]

DAISNE, JOHAN
THIERY, HERMAN--[22]FLEMISH

DAKERS, ANDREW H.
STEWART, ANDREW--[1][3]MYS--
BODLEY "ONCE I WAS BLIND" '26
CASSELL "CIRCUMSTANTIAL EVIDENCE" '28

DAKERS, ELAINE KIDNER
LANE, JANE--[2][7][9][21][31][34]MYS/ROM--
"A CALL OF TRUMPETS"
"YOUNG & LONELY KING"
HALE "CONIES IN THE HAY" '57

DALE, CHERYL
EMERSON, CHERYL--[26]ROM--
SIL 19 "TREACHEROUS BEAUTIES"

DALE, MARGARET J.M.
MILLER, MARGARET J.--[1][8][22]ENGLISH

DALE, MRS. R.J.
VINTON, V.V.--[1][8]

DALE, THOMAS F.
STONECLINK--[1]

DALE-HARRIS, ROSALIND
ASHE, ROSALIND--[7][32]MYS--
HUTCH "MOTHS" '76
EQMM "LONG GLASS MAN" NOV '76
HUTCH "HURRICANE WAKE" '77
BB "STARCROSSED" '79
SPHERE "DARK RUNNER" '85
BB "LAYING OF THE NOONE WALKER" '87

DALEY, BRIAN C.
MCKINNEY, JACK--W/JAMES LUCENO,[7][23]SF-
BAL "ROBOTECH #1 THRU #13"
BAL "SENTINEL #1 THRU #7"
"KADUNG MEMORIES" '90
"EVENT HORIZON" '91
"ARTIFACT OF THE SYSTEM" '91

DALEY, MARGARET K.R.
DALEY, KATHLEEN--[21][26]ROM--
"PROMISED PORTRAIT" & MORE
DALEY, KIT--[21][26]ROM--
NUMEROUS NOVELS
MOORE, PATTI--[21][26]ROM--
"GIFT OF ORCHIDS"
RIPY, MARGARET--[21][26]ROM--
"FLAMING TREE"
"FIREBIRD" & MORE

DALEY, VICTOR
ROE, CLEEVE--[13]AUSTRALIAN

DALGLEISH, JAMES CORTEEN
DALGLEISH, JAMES--[28]HIST/ADV--
HALE--5 NOVELS '74-79
KINCAID, J.D.--[28]WEST--
HALE "JACK STONE" SERIES
5 NOVELS '89-90

DALGLEISH, OSCAR
COLLINS, ROSEMARY--[2]
MOSCA, FRANK--[2]

DALLAS, OSWALD [C.C.]
ANSON, PIERS--W/DRAYCOTT [M] DELL,[34]MYS--
COLUMBINE "THE DEATH CLUB" '40

DALLAS-DAMIS, ATHENA G.
DALLAS, ATHENA GIANAKAS--[31]

DALLMAYR, ILSE
STRASSER, HEIDI--[9][21]ROM--
"LOVE'S MEMORIES"

DALLY, ANN G.M.
MULLINS, ANN--[1][8][22]ENGLISH

DALRYMPLE-HAY, JOHN & BAB
HAY, JOHN--[1][23]AUSTRALIAN/SF--
"THE INVASION" '68

DALSACE, LIONEL
BLECK, AIMEE--[1][2][7]SF

DALTON, DOROTHY
KUEHN, DOROTHY DALTON--[31]

DALTON, GILBERT LAWFORD
CARSTAIRS, ROD--[1][8][34]MYS--
PAGET "PAULINE'S AFFAIR" '49
PAGET "TRAFFIC IN SOULS" '50
NORTON, VICTOR--[1][8][34]MYS--
AMALG "THE SKY RAIDERS" '32
AMALG "WALLY THE BOY 'TEC'" '32

DALTON, JAMES
ANONYMOUS--S. WELLS SF LIST

DALY, CARROLL JOHN
CARROLL, JOHN D.--E.R. HAGEMANN--
BM "ROARING JACK" DEC '22
FD "LANTERN IN THE MIND" AUG '53
DA "AUNT BETSY'S ARCH FIEND" '56

DALY, EDITH IGLAUER
IGLAUER, EDITH--[1][31]

DALY, MARY VIRGINIA
DALY, MARY VIRGENE--[1]

DALY, NICHOLAS
DALY, NIKI--[1][31][33]

DALZEL-JOB, PATRICK
DALZEL, PETER--[1][8][22][31]SCOTTISH

DAMBREVILLE, CLAUDE
CYPRIEN, ANATOLE--[1]

DAMBRUSKAS, JOAN ARDEN
ARDEN, NOEL--[1][31]

DAME, LAWRENCE
POMFRET, BARON--[1][22]AMERICAN

DAMIAN, FRANZ
GARNER, HANS--[39]GERMAN

DAMIO, WARD
DRURY, REBECCA--[21]HIST/ROM,HP--
'WOMEN AT WAR' SERIES:
"COURAGE AT SEA"
WILLOUGHBY, LEE DAVIS--[21]HIST/ROM,HP--
DELL 'MAKING OF AMERICA' SERIES:
"VIGILANTES"

DANA, MRS. J.M.
AUNT ADNA--[1]

DANAHER, KEVIN
DANACHAIR, CAOIMHIM O--[31]

DANBERG, DOROTHY SMITH
DANIELS, DOROTHY--JEAN F. LE DEIST,
BAE 24,[2]--NAME LEGALLY CHANGED TO
"DANIELS" W/NORMAN A.

DANBERG, NORMAN A.
DANIELS, NORMAN A.--[2]NAME LEGALLY
CHANGED-WIFE WROTE MOSTLY AS
DOROTHY DANIELS

DANBY, MARY HEATHER
REED, SIMON--W/COLIN BOSTOCK-SMITH,
[8][31]--
"METAL MICKEY'S BOOGIE BOOK" '81
REED, SIMON--W/DORIS DICKENS,[8][31]--
"QUICK QUIZ" '81
STEVENS, ANDY--W/E. STICKLEE,[8][31]--
"WORLD OF STARS" '80

DANCE, FRANCIS ESBURN X.
DANCE, FRANK E.X.--[31]

DANCO, KATHERINE LECK
DANCO, KATHY--[31]

DANCYGER, IRENE
BRIDGEMAN, IRENE--[1]
JAMES, RACHEL--[1]

DANDRIDGE, RAYMOND GARF.
DANDRIDGE, RAY G.--[31]

DANEHY, DONALD
RICHMOND, DONALD--V. BERCH LTR TO
HUBIN '94,MYS/WAR--
STEIN "THE DUNKIRK DIRECTIVE" '80

DANFORTH, ETHEL M.
DEL RAY, MARIA--[1]
HAGAR, GEORGE--[1]
VICTORIA, M.--[1]

DANFORTH, LES
PENDLETON, DON--W/CHET CUNNINGHAM,[3]HP--
GE "COUNCIL OF KINGS" '85

DANIEL PENNAC, JEAN-BERN.
NACRAY, J.-B.--W/PATRICK RAYNARD,[40]MYS

DANIEL, ANITA
ANITA--[1][33]

DANIEL, GLYN [EDMUND]
DANIEL, GLYN--[3]MYS--
GOLZ "WELCOME DEATH" '54
REES, DILWYN--[3][5][22][29]MYS--
GOLZ "CAMBRIDGE MURDERS" '45
GOLZ "WELCOME DEATH" '54

DANIEL, JULIE GOLDSMITH
GILBERT, JULIE GOLDSMITH--[1][31]

DANIEL, REBECCA
DANIEL, BECKY--[31][33]

DANIEL, YULI
ARZHAK, NIKOLAI--[2][11][23][31]RUSSIAN/SF

DANIEL, [WILLIAM] ROLAND
ANDERSON, SONIA--[1][18]ENGLISH/ROM--
28 NOVELS '53-65

DANIELL, ALBERT SCOTT
BOXWOOD, RICHARD--[22][25][31]ENGLISH--
"GREAT INVENTIONS" '61
DANIELL, DAVID SCOTT--[22][25][31]ENGLISH--
CHILDREN'S
LEWESDON, JOHN--[1][25]--
"LADYBIRD BOOK OF LONDON" '61

DANIELS, CORALIN
LUCRECE--[1]

CREASEY, JOHN
DORSETT, DANIELLE--W/NORMAN DANIELS,
[3][17][26][29][31]--
PINN "THE DUELING OAKS" '72
GRAY, ANGELA--W/NORMAN DANIELS,
[3][7][21][26][31]MYS/ROM--
10 LANCER NOVELS '71-3
KAVANAGH, CYNTHIA--W/NORMAN DANIELS,
[3][9][21][26][31]--
PYR "BRIDE OF LENORE"
"THE DECEPTION" '66

CREASEY, JOHN [CONT]
ROSS, HELAINE--W/NORMAN DANIELS, [9][21]ROM-- "NO TEARS TOMORROW" '62
SOMERS, SUZANNE--W/NORMAN DANIELS, [3][9][21][26]ROM/MYS-- 10 NOVELS '62-73
THAYER, GERALDINE--W/NORMAN DANIELS, [3][9][21][26]MYS/ROM-- AVALON "THE DARK RIDER" '61
WESTON, HELEN GRAY--W/NORMAN DANIELS, [3][17]-- PAPLB "MYSTIC MANOR" '66 PAPLB "HOUSE OF FALSE FACES" '67

DANIELS, JAMES RAYMOND
DANIELS, JIM--[31]

DANIELS, NORMAN & DOROTHY
DANIELS, DOROTHY--LACHMAN LIST MAY '93

DANIELS, NORMAN A.
BENTON, JOHN L.--[2][29][37]MYS-- DNM "MURDER BY PICTURES" JUN '39 & 22 OTHER "JERRY WADE" NVLS
BRADY, PETER--[1][31]
BROOKER, WALLACE--[2][7][29][37]-- PULP CLASSICS #16 "BREATHLESS ISLANDS" CLS & DOCS "SKIPPER" YARNS i.e. "SEA VULTURE" & "GRIM PILOT" '39-43
CARTER, NICK
ROY JAMES, BAE 22, P12,HP-- RADIO PROGRAM SCRIPTS
CLAYFORD, JAMES--ROY JAMES, BAE 22, P12-- CROW "SIDESHOW GIRL" '50
DALE, WILLIAM--JEAN F. LE DEIST, BAE 24,[18]-- GATEWAY "JOHN DOE, MURDERER" '42
DANIELS, KRISTY--W/KRISTY MONTEE,[21]ROM-- "THE DANCER" "HOT TYPE"
DANN, NORMA--[1]
DORSETT, DANIELLA--W/DOROTHY DANIELS, ROY JAMES, BAE 22-- PINN "DUELING OAKS" '72
GARTH, WILL--[2]HP--STANDARD
GOODRICH, CLIFFORD--JEAN F. LE DEIST, BAE 24, W. MURRAY,ECHOES #5,[16]HP
GRADY, PETER--JEAN F. LE DEIST, BAE 24, P8,[18]-- "TWO TRAILS TO BANNACK" '52 "MARSHALL OF WINTER GAP"
GRAY, ANGELA--W/DOROTHY DANIELS, ROY JAMES, BAE 22--10 ROM/MYS NOVELS
GREGORY, CHARLES ALAN--W. MURRAY CALL FEB '94, RANGE RIDERS MAG-- ONE STORY
JOHNSON, FRANK--W. MURRAY, ECHOES #5,[18][37]MYS-- DNM "ENTER THE CRIMSON MASK" AUG '40 DNM "TRAFFIC IN MURDER" APR '44 & 13 OTHERS
JONES, G. WAYMAN--W. MURRAY, ECHOES #5,[2][7][29]-- PHANT DET-14 NOVELS JUL '35 TO AUG '36 BLKB - 55 'BLACK BAT' STORIES JUL '39 TO JUN '53
JUDD, HARRISON--[3][29][31]MYS-- GM S1124 "SHADOW OF A DOUBT" '61
KAVANAUGH, CYNTHIA--W/DOROTHY DANIELS, R. JAMES-BAE 22-- PYR "BRIDE OF LENORE" "THE DECEPTION"
MORGAN, LT. SCOTT--JEAN F. LE DEIST-BAE 24, W. MURRAY-ECHOES #5-- AIR WAR-7 'CAPT DANGER' TALES

DANIELS, NORMAN A. [CONT]
McROBERTS, KERRY--JEAN F. LE DEIST-BAE 24, W. MURRAY-ECHOES #5-- TSS 'JEFF SHANNON' STORIES
NORMAN, DAVID--W. MURRAY '94-- GOLD SEAL DETECTIVE
RAND, KIRK--JEAN F. LE DEIST, BAE 24, P8,[16]
REED, MARK--[1][3]MYS-- RAIN "VICE COP" '52 FALC "LAY DOWN & DIE" ca'52
ROBESON, KENNETH--[1][2][11][29]MYS/SF,HP-- STREET & SMITH
ROSS, HELAINE--W/DOROTHY DANIELS, ROY JAMES-BAE 22-- "NO TEARS TOMORROW" '62
SCANLON, C.K.M.--JEAN F. LE DEIST, BAE 24, P8,W. MURRAY-ECHOES #5,HP-- MASD "MASKED DETECTIVE" STORIES GMD "DAN FOWLER" STORIES
SOMERS, SUZANNE--W/DOROTHY DANIELS, ROY JAMES-BAE 22, ROM/MYS-- 10 NOVELS
STORM, JACK--JEAN F. LE DEIST-BAE 24, W. MURRAY-ECHOES #5,HP--CLS
TALLY, JUDD--JEAN F. LE DEIST-BAE 24, W. MURRAY-ECHOES #5,[16]-- MASR "CORPSE CANYON" AUG '49 RR "THE LONG TRAIL" '49
THAYER, GERALDINE--W/DOROTHY DANIELS, ROY JAMES-BAE 22-- AVALON "THE DARK RIDER" '61
VANE, NORMAN THADDEUS--ROY JAMES, BAE 22, P12--TOWER BT50-753
WADE, DAVID--J. GERTZMAN, BAE 17,[1][34]MYS-- FALCON "COME NIGHT, COME DESIRE" '51 RAIN "BEDROOM WITH A VIEW" '52 "SHE WALKS BY NIGHT" '52 RAIN "ONLY HUMAN" '52 FALCON "RAISE THE DEVIL" '52 RAIN "WALK THE EVIL STREET" '52
WALLACE, ROBERT--ECHOES #17, P4, [3][29]MYS,HP-- CORINTH "MURDER UNDER THE BIG TOP" '65 PHD "MERCHANT OF DEATH" OCT '34 "PRINCE OF MURDER" JUL '35
WESTON, HELEN GRAY--W/DOROTHY DANIELS, R. JAMES-BAE 22, MYS-- "MYSTIC MANOR" "HOUSE OF FALSE FACES"

DANIELS, PHILIP
CHAMBERS, PETER--LACHMAN/EASTER LST MAY '93

DANIELS-HENDERSON, BETH
HENDERSON, BETH--[21]ROM-- "NIKROVA'S PASSION"

DANN, VICTORIA
GLENN, VICTORIA--[9][21][26]ROM--13 NOVELS

DANNAY, FREDERIC
NATHAN, DANIEL--[8][11][32]-- LITTLE & BROWN "GOLDEN SUMMER" '53 EQMM "BOY & THE BOOK" JUN '56 EQMM "BOY & THE LAW" OCT '56 EQMM "BOY & THE MONEY BOX" AUG '56
QUEEN, ELLERY--W/MANFRED B. LEE, [1][2][3]HP--[ORIGINATED W/LEE]
QUEEN, ELLERY JR.--W/MANFRED B.LEE, [1]AMERICAN/JUV/MYS
ROSS, BARNABY--W/MANFRED B. LEE, [2][3][32][37]MYS-- 4 NOVELS-LATER RPRTD AS BY "QUEEN" ML "DRURY LANE'S LAST CASE" OCT '33

DANNENBERGER, HERMANN
REGER, ERIK--[39]GERMAN

DANO, LINDA
FLANDERS, REBECCA--W/DONNA BALL,[26]ROM--
HARL 517 "FOREVER ALWAYS"
HARL 558 "QUINN'S WAY" & OTHERS
GALLANT, FELICIA--[1][21]ROM--
"DREAM WEAVER" W/REBECCA FLANDERS
"WHO IS DONNA BALL"

DANRIT, EMILE A.
DANRIT, CAPITAINE--[2]

DANSER, ELLEN SPENCER
CHARLES, SPENCER--W/PATRICK C. FINLEON,
V. BERCH LTR TO HUBIN '94, MYS--
BM "MYS ON THE MOUNT" '84

DANSON, FRANK CORSE
DICKSON, FRANK C.--[8]

DAOUST, PAMELA
KINCAID, KATHARINE--[9][21][26]ROM--
"CRIMSON DESIRE"
"CRIMSON EMBRACE"
"WILDLY, MY LOVE" & OTHERS

DARBOVEN, ANNA-MARIA
WAGNER, JOHANNES--[39]GERMAN

DARBY, CHRISTOPHER LOVETT
OUDEIS--[1][2]

DARBY, EDITH M.
GREENFIELD, BERNADETTE--[8]

DARBY, JEAN [KEGLEY]
DARBY, GENE--[31]
DARBY, GENE KEGLEY--[31]

DARBY, JOANNA
MARKS, JOANNA--[21][26]ROM--
"LOVE IS A LONG SHOT"
"WILD AT HEART"
"HEAT OF THE MOMENT"

DARD, FREDERIC
CHARLES, FREDERICK--JEAN F. LE DEIST,
BAE 18, P9,[40]MYS
KAPUT--[40]
KILL HIM--[40]
MILK, CORNELL--[40]
NOIR, L'ANGE--[40]
SAN ANTONIO--JEAN F. LE DEIST-BAE 18,
[3][40]MYS--
HARB "A NIGHT IN BOULOGNE" '54
DUCKWORTH "TOUGH JUSTICE" '67
DUCKWORTH "FROM A TO Z" '68
DUCKWORTH "THE STRANGLER" '68
SPHERE "CROOK'S HILL" '69
SPHERE "THUGS & BOTTLES" '69
SPHERE "STONE DEAD" '69
DUCKWORTH "KNIGHTS OF ARABIA" '69
PAPLB "HATCHET MAN" '70
JOSEPH "THE SUB KILLERS" '71

DARE, ALAN
GOODCHILD, GEORGE--[2]

DARE, MARCUS PAUL
DARE, M.P.--[1]

DAREFF, HAL
FOLEY, SCOTT--[1][8][31]

DARGAN, OLIVE TILFORD
BURKE, FIELDING--[8][22][31]AMERICAN

DARION, JOSEPH
DARION, JOE--[31]

DARK, ELEANOR
O'RANE, PATRICIA--[13]AUSTRALIAN

DARK, LAWRENCE CHARNY
DARK, LARRY--[7]SF--
"THE LITERARY GHOST: GREAT
CONTEMPORARY GHOST STORIES" '91

DARLING, JAY NORWOOD
DARLING, DING--[1]
DING, J.N.--[1][31]

DARLING, JOHN A.
MIGNON, AUGUST--[1]

DARLING, MARY KATHLEEN
DARLING, KATHY--[31][33]

DARLING, WILLIAM YOUNG
SMITH, SACHEVERELL--[1]

DARNSTADT, HELGE
BURG, CRISTEL--[39]GERMAN/JUV
HAGEN, SABINE--[39]GERMAN/JUV
THOMAS, KATHRIN--[39]GERMAN/JUV

DARRINGTON, HUGH
ROSS, JAMES--W/TONY HALLIWELL,
[1][2][23]SF--
"THE GOD KILLERS" '70
"GRAVITOR" '71

DARRINGTON, PAULA
WILLIAMS, PAULA--[9][21][26]ROM--
"A CASE FOR LOVE"
"LOVESONG"

DARROCH, SANDRA JOBSON
JOBSON, SANDRA--[1][31]

DARWIN, LEONARD
DARWIN, LEN--[31][33]

DAS, KAMALA
MADHAVIKUTTY--[8]

DAS, PRAFULLA CHANDRA
SUBHADRA-NANDAN--[1]

DASCHKOWSKI, OTTO
NAUNDORF, PETER--[39]GERMAN/JUV

DASHWOOD, ROBERT JULIAN
HILLAS, JULIAN--[1][22]ENGLISH

DAUDET, ERNEST
REYMOND, LOUIS--[1]

DAUDET, JULIE R.C.
STEEN, KARL--[1]
STERNE, KARL--[1]

DAUGHTREY, OLIVE LYDIA
EARLE, OLIVE L.--[8]

DAUKES, SIDNEY HERBERT
FAIRWAY, SIDNEY--[2][29][34]MYS--
10 PAUL NOVELS '31-47

DAUM, FRITZ
ORTWIG RAMIN, FR. D.--[39]GERMAN
ORTWIG, F.D.--[39]GERMAN

DAUMANN, RUDOLF HEINRICH
HARD, RUDOLF--[39]GERMAN/JUV/SF

DAVENPORT, GUY M.
MONTGOMERY, MAX--[31]--
LITERARY & POETRY REVIEWS

DAVENPORT, GWEN LEYS
HARDT, MICHAEL--W/GUSTAV J. BREUER,
[1][3]MYS--
BOBBS "A STRANGER & AFRAID" '43

DAVENPORT, KATHRYN
GRAVES, KELLER--W/EVELYN ROGERS,
[9][21]ROM--5 NOVELS

DAVENPORT, MARCIA
GETER, LENA--[17]ROM--
"OF LENA GEYER" '49

DAVENTRY, LEONARD JOHN
ALEXANDER, MARTIN--[8]

DAVEY, MORRIS FRANK
SARGESON, FRANK--[1]

DAVIAULT, PIERRE
HARTEX, PIERRE--[1]

DAVID, A[NN] ROSALIE
DAVID, A.R.--[31]EDITOR
"THE MANCHESTER EGYPTIAN
MUMMY RESEARCH PROJECT" '79
DAVID, ROSALIE--[31]--
"MYSTERIES OF THE MUMMIES" '79

DAVID, MARIE DE SAFFRON
DE NAVERY, RAOUL--[3]MYS--
BENZIGER "IDOLS; OR, THE SECRET OF
THE RUE CHAUSSEE D'ANTIN" 1882

DAVID, PETER [ALLEN]
PETERS, DAVID--[7][23][34]SF--
DIAM "PHOTON #1-#6"
DIAM "PSI-MAN #1-#5"
"MIND FORCE WARRIOR" '90

DAVID, RICHARD W.
DAVID, R.W.--[31]

DAVIDS, LEONARD ROBERT
DAVIDS, BOB--[31]

DAVIDSON, ALAN
LANGHOLM, A.D--[7]SF--
"BEWITCHING OF ALISON ALLBRIGHT" 79

DAVIDSON, AVRAM
QUEEN, ELLERY--LOCUS #389, P5,
[2][3][4][7]GHOSTED--
RANDOM "AND ON THE EIGHTH DAY" '64
RANDOM "THE FOURTH SIDE OF
THE TRIANGLE" '65
SIGN "THE HOUSE OF BRASS" '68

DAVIDSON, EDITH MAY
MAY, ROBERTA E.--[8]

DAVIDSON, FRANK CYRIL S.
COALFLEET, PIERRE--[8]

DAVIDSON, GEOFFREY
DUNCAN, GEORGE--[31]

DAVIDSON, HILDA RODERICK
ELLIS, HILDA RODERICK--[22][31]ENGLISH

DAVIDSON, LIONEL
LINE, DAVID--[7][18][38]JUV--
HM "UNDER PLUM LAKE" '82
HARPER "SOLDIER & ME" '65
CAPE "RUN FOR YOUR LIFE" '66
CAPE "MIKE & ME" '74
CAPE "SCREAMING HIGH" '85

DAVIDSON, MARGARET C.
COMPERE, MICKIE--[1][8][31]JUV
DAVIDSON, MICKIE--[1][8][31]

DAVIDSON, RAYMOND
DAVIDSON, R.--[31][33]

DAVIDSON, S.
ACTON, JAMES--[1]

DAVIDSON, WILLAIM
DAVIDSON, BILL--[31]

DAVIDSON, WILLIAM R.
DAVIDSON, BILL R.--[31]

DAVIES, BETTY EVELYN
WARWICK, PAULINE--[1][3][22]MYS--
CASSELL "DEATH OF A SINNER" '44

DAVIES, BLODWEN
ABBOTT, BROOK--[1]

DAVIES, COURTMAN
RANK, CLIFTON--[34]MYS--
HS "TIGERS ON TUESDAY" '51
HS "BURY HIM GENTLY" '52
HS "HOMICIDE RACKETT" '52
HS "MIND MY SHROUD" '52

DAVIES, D. JACOB
JACOB, HERBERT MATHIAS--[8]

DAVIES, DAVID MARGERISON
MARGERSON, DAVID--[8][22][32]MYS--
MSMM "CYANIDE COCKTAIL" DEC '56

DAVIES, EDITH
JAY, JOAN--[8]

DAVIES, EILEEN WINIFRED
ELIAS, EILEEN--[1][22][31]ENGLISH

DAVIES, ERNEST
MARTIN, OLIVER--[3][22][29]MYS--
HODDER "THE IRON DOOR" '23
FABER "MERMAID" '26
BENN "MIDDLE DISTANCE" '29

DAVIES, GORDON C.
DAVIES--BAPC #11--BRITISH COVER
ARTIST FOR CURTIS

DAVIES, HILDA A.
TANIS--[8]

DAVIES, HOWELL
MARVELL, ANDREW--[2][11][23]ENGLAND/SF--
"MINIMUM MAR OR TIME BE GONE" '38
"THREE MEN MAKE A WORLD" '39
"CONGRATULATE THE DEVIL" '39

DAVIES, HUNTER
ATTICUS--[31]

DAVIES, IRIS
GOWER, IRIS--[21]ROM--7 NOVELS

DAVIES, IVOR NOVELLO
NOVELLO, IVOR--[8]

DAVIES, JOAN HOWARD
DRAKE, JOAN--[1][8]
LYNGSETH, JOAN--[1][7][33]SF--
"MARTIN'S STARWARS"

DAVIES, JOHN
WHITAKER, RAY--[8]

DAVIES, JOHN CHRISTOPHER
DAVIES, CHRISTIE--[8][31]

DAVIES, JOHN E.W.
DAVIES, JASPER--[1]
MATHER, BERKLEY--[3][18][29][32][36]--
12 MYS NVLS '59-75
SUS "A DUCK IN BOMBAY" NOV '60
SUS "MOON OF THE CAT" MAR '61
EW "TROUBLED LADY" JUN '67
EQMM "BIG BITE" DEC '70
EQMM "RAJAH'S EMERALDS" APR '71
& 13 OTHERS
WESTON, JOHN--[1][31]

DAVIES, KAY HAMMOND
HAMMOND, KAY--[2]

DAVIES, LESLIE PERNELL
BERNE, LEO--[1][23][31]ENGLISH
BLAKE, ROBERT--[23][31][32]ENGLISH--
LM "DAVEY" JUN '60
LM "CROOKED SMILE" SEPT '60
LM "BLOW THAT HORN" DEC '60
LM "THE VALLEY" MAR '61
LM "SELF-MADE MAN" SEPT '61
LM "WITCH'S DAUGHTER" SEPT '62
BRIDGEMAN, RICHARD--[23][31][32]ENGLISH--
LM "FRONTIER" DEC '60
LM "LAST EVIL" SEPT '60
LM "THE MORGAN TRUST" MAR '61
LM "NOT ON SUNDAYS" NOV '61
EVANS, MORGAN--[1][23][31]ENGLISH
JEFFERSON, IAN--[23][31][32]ENGLISH/MYS--
LM "THE DOCTOR'S STORY" MAR '61
PETERS, LAWRENCE--[1][23][32]MYS--
LM "FLYING FOX" SEPT '60
LM "STORY OF LEONARD VINCENT" DEC '60
PHILIPS, THOMAS--[1][23]ENGLISH
THOMAS, G.K.--[1][23][32]ENGLISH--
LM "HAPPIEST DAYS" DEC '60
LM "MAN WHO LOST HIS PAST" MAR '61
LM "AFTER THE GREAT LIGHT" MAY '61
LM "NEW LIFE" MAR '62
VARDE, LESLIE--[2][3][18][23][29][32]--
LM "SIGHT OF BLOOD" MAR '60
LM "TELL IT TO THE DEAD" '66
LM "THE NAMELESS ONES" '67
& 17 OTHER LM SS
WELCH, ROWLAND--[18][23][32]MYS--
LM "IDOL OF BAKED CLAY" JUN '60

DAVIES, MARY CATHERINE
DAVIES, M.C--[1]

DAVIES, NAUNTON
COVERTSIDE, NAUNTON--[34]MYS--
DIGBY "SECRET OF A HOLLOW TREE" 1898

DAVIES, OLWEN B.
BOWEN, OLWEN--[11]SF

DAVIES, PAUL C.W.
DAVIES, P.C.W.--[1][31]

DAVIES, PETER
ATKINSON, ALEX--[29]MYS--
PLAY "FOUR WINDS" '54
DAVIES "EXIT CHARLIE" '55

DAVIES, SUMIKO
SUMIKO--[33]

DAVIES, THOMAS
DAVIES, TOM--[31]

DAVIES, [W] ROBERTSON
MARCHBANKS, SAMUEL--[1][31]ESSAYS-
4 COLLECTIONS '47-85

DAVIN, DANIEL MARCUS
DAVIN, DAN--[31]

DAVIS, A.W.
RICHARDS, FRANK--[1]HP

DAVIS, ADELLE
DUNLAP, JANE--[31]

DAVIS, ARTHUR HOEY
RUDD, STEELE--[1][22][34]AUSTRALIAN/MYS--
"FOR LIFE & OS" '08
"IN AUSTRALIA" '08

DAVIS, BRIAN
FFOLKES--[31]
FFOLKES, MICHAEL--[31]

DAVIS, BURTON & CLARE O.
SAUNDERS, LAWRENCE--[3][8][22]MYS--
NOVELS '31-33

DAVIS, CATHERINE
DAVIS, MILDRED--W/LUCIFER LAND,[21]ROM--
7 NOVELS

DAVIS, CHARLES A.
DOWNING, J. MAJOR--[31]

DAVIS, DIANE WICKER
DEVERS, DELANEY--[9][21][26]ROM--
4 NOVELS '59-76

DAVIS, EDITH VERZOLLES
VEZELAY, EDITH--[1]

DAVIS, EDWIN ADAMS
DAVIS, E. ADAMS--[31]

DAVIS, ELIZABETH SWITZER
JOY, ELIZABETH--[1]

DAVIS, FRANCES
ALDA, FRANCES--[8][22]

DAVIS, FREDERICK WILLIAM
CAMPBELL, SCOTT--[3][22][29]MYS--
24 NOVELS 1900-09
CARTER, NICHOLAS--[1][3][11]MYS,HP

DAVIS, FREDERICK [CLYDE]
AIKEN, CLARK--W. MURRAY-ECHOES #6,
LACHMAN LST MAY '93,[37]MYS--
GOSD [PULP STORIES '36]

DAVIS, FREDERICK [CLYDE] [CONT]
COOMBS, MURDO--[3][18][22][29]MYS--
DUTTON "A MOMENT OF NEED" '47
RANSOME, STEPHEN--[2][3][18][22][29]MYS--
22 NOVELS '39-71
STEELE, CURTIS--ECHOES #5 & 6,
PULP#13,[2][7][18][34]HP--
OP5 "MASKED INVASION" APR '34
"INVISIBLE EMPIRE" MAY '34
"YELLOW SCROURGE" JUN '34
"MELTING DEATH" JUL '34
"CAVERN OF THE DAMNED" AUG '34
"MASTER OF BROKEN MEN" SEP '34
"INVASION OF THE DARK LEGIONS" OCT '34
"GREEN DEATH MISTS" NOV '34
"LEGIONS OF STARVATION" DEC '34
"RED INVADERS" JAN '35
"LEAGUE OF WAR MONSTERS" FEB '35
"ARMY OF THE DEAD" MAR '35
"MARCH OF THE FLAME MARAUDERS" APR '35
"BLOOD REIGN OF THE DICTATOR" MAY '35
"INVASION OF YELLOW WARLORDS" JUN '35
"LEGIONS OF THE DEATH-MASTER" JUL '35
"HOSTS OF THE FLAMING DEATH" AUG '35
"INVASION OF CRIMSON DEATH CULT" SEP '35
"ATTACK OF THE BLIZZARD MEN" OCT '35
"SCOURGE OF INVISIBLE DEATH" NOV '35

DAVIS, GORDON WINTHROP
DAVIES, MELISSA--[3][21][26]MYS/ROM--
POPLB "FACE OF CHALK" '77

DAVIS, GRANIA
MAMA G.--[1][31][33]--AUTHORED COLUMN
'MAMA G' IN 'MARIN SCOOPS'
& 'PENTHOUSE LTRS'

DAVIS, GWEN
FINK, BRAT--[1][22]AMERICAN

DAVIS, GYLE
DANIELS, GIL--[11]SF

DAVIS, HAROLD A.
BROOKER, WALLACE--[37]MYS--
DOCS "IT PAYS TO FIGHT"
"CAP FURY GOES TO WAR"
"THE FOURTH MONEY"
ROBESON, KENNETH--W/LESTER DENT,
[34]MYS,HP--
BB "DUST OF DEATH" '69
BB "EXPLODING LAKE"
BB "GOLDEN PERIL" '70
BB "MENTAL WIZARD" '70
BB "LAND OF FEAR" '73
BB "SEVEN AGATE DEVILS" '73
BB "CRIMSON SERPENT" '74
BB "KING MAKER" '75
BB "PURPLE DRAGON" '78
ROBESON, KENNETH--[2][11][29][34]HP--
BB "MERCHANTS OF DISASTER" '69
BB "MUNITIONS MASTER" '71
BB "LIVING FIRE MENACE" '71
BB "GREEN DEATH" '71
BB "MOUNTAIN MONSTER" '76
BB "DEVILS OF THE DEEP" '84

DAVIS, HAROLD LENOIR
DAVIS, H.L.--[1][32]MYS--
EQMM "MURDER STORY" MAY '52

DAVIS, HOPE HALE
HALE, HOPE--[8]

DAVIS, HORACE BANCROFT
GREEN, BRYAN--[1]
RELING, JAN--[1]
WILLIS, LOWELL E.--[1]

DAVIS, HORACE CHANDLER
DAVIS, CHAN--[1]

DAVIS, HOWARD CHARLES
COBDEN, GUY--[1]

DAVIS, IAN
DALLAS, IAN--[11]SF

DAVIS, JACK
CARTER, NICK--W/BILL CRIDER,[3]MYS,HP--
CHART "COYOTE CONNECTION" '81

DAVIS, JAMES
HALL, OWEN--[2][34]MYS--
CHATTO "JETSAM" 1897

DAVIS, JAMES MADISON
DAVIS, J. MADISON--HAWK-DAVIS INTRVW '94,
MYS--
WALKER "MURDER OF FRAU SCHUTZ" '88
WALKER "WHITE ROOK" '89
WALKER "BLOODY MASKS" '90
WALKER "RED KNIGHT" '91

DAVIS, JAMES ROBERT
DAVIS, JIM--[31][33]--
COMIC STRIP "GARFIELD"

DAVIS, JOHN
DE LA SALLE, JOHN--[1]

DAVIS, JUDITH L.
TORAL, JUDITH--V.BERCH LETTER TO
HUBIN '94, MYS--
"DADDY'S GONE A-HUNTING" '83

DAVIS, JULIA
DRACO, F.--[3][8][31][33]MYS--
RINEHART "THE DEVIL'S CHURCH" '51
"CRUISE WITH DEATH" '52

DAVIS, JULIE
DAVIDSON, JULIANA--[9][21][26]ROM--
5 NOVELS

DAVIS, LAVINIA [R]
FARMER, WENDELL--[1][8][22]AMERICAN/MYS

DAVIS, LILY M. & ROSEMARY
DAVIS, ROSEMARY L.--[1][8]

DAVIS, LOIS CARLILE
LAMPLAUGH, LOIS--[8]
LAMPLUGH, LOIS--[1][2][11]

DAVIS, LOU ELLEN
BANNISTER, PAT--[3][29][31]MYS--
GM 1418 "SEVEN VOTES FOR DEATH" '64
DAVIS, ELIZABETH--[3][11][21][26]
[29][31]MYS--
SIGN "SUFFER A WITCH TO DIE" '69
SIGN "ALONG CAME A SPIDER" '70
PYR "MY SOUL TO KEEP" '70
DBLDY "THERE WAS AN OLD WOMAN" '71

DAVIS, MADELINE
GARRY, MADELINE--[9][21][26]ROM--
"MYSTERIOUS STRANGER"

DAVIS, MAGGIE S.
COOPER, M.E.--[33]
DANIELS, MAGGIE--[26]ROM--
"A CHRISTMAS ROMANCE"
DAVIS, BARBARA STEINCROHN--[33]
DAVIS, EMMA--[33]
DEAUXVILLE, KATHERINE--[26]ROM--
"BLOOD RED ROSES"
"DAGGERS OF GOLD"

DAVIS, MARK
SARAZEN, NICHOLAS--W/RICK COOPER,[7]SF--
PINN "FAMILY REUNION" '91

DAVIS, MARTHA WIRT
VAN ARSDALE, WIRT--[1][3][22]MYS--
DBLDY "PROFESSOR KNITS A SHROULD" '51

DAVIS, MARY JOHNSON
JORDAN, ROSEMARY--W/DEBORAH JORDAN,
[9][21][26]ROM--
"LOVE'S LEGACY"

DAVIS, MARY OCTAVIA
DUTZ--[31][33]

DAVIS, MILDRED WIRT
DAVIS, KATHERINE--[9]ROM--
COULD THIS BE 'MILDRED WIRT BENSON' ?

DAVIS, NICHOLAS
DAVIS, NICK--[31]

DAVIS, NORBERT
BARNES, DAVE--W/ARTHUR K. BARNES,[11]SF
HUNT, HARRISON--W/W.T. BALLARD, MUNROE
SLST #21-N. DAVIS BIBLIO,[29][34]--
CURL "MURDER PICKS THE JURY" '47

DAVIS, PATRICIA
HAMILTON, VICTORIA--V. BERCH LTR TO
HUBIN '94, MYS--
ZEBRA "A TRAITOROUS HEART" '90

DAVIS, ROBERT HART
GRANT, MAXWELL--[1][2]HP

DAVIS, ROBERT PRUNIER
BRANDON, JOE--[22][29][31]AMERICAN/MYS

DAVIS, ROGER
DAVIS--BAPC #11--BRITISH COVER ARTIST
FOR SCION
DAVIS, R.--BAPC #11--BRITISH COVER ARTIST
FOR SCION

DAVIS, RUTH ELIZABETH
DAVIS, BETTY--[31]

DAVIS, SARAH MATILDA
S.M.D.--[1]

DAVIS, SYDNEY CHARLES H.
CASQUE, SAMMY--[1][22][31]ENGLISH

DAVIS, THOMAS NEIL
DAVIS, NEIL--[31]
DAVIS, T.N.--[31]

DAVIS, TIMOTHY FRANCIS T.
CASHMAN, JOHN--[1][3][31]MYS--
HARPER "GENTLEMAN FROM CHICAGO" '73
HARPER "COOK GENERAL" '74
HARPER "KID GLOVE CHARLIE" '78

DAVIS, WILL R.
WALLACE, JOHN--[8]

DAVIS, WILLIAM F.
DAVIS, ZEKE--[34]MYS--
PAGEANT "INVITED" '59

DAVISON, GLADYS PATTON
CONDOR, GLADYN--[22][31]AMERICAN

DAVISON, JULIANNA
DAVISON, JULIE--[1]

DAVITZ, JOEL ROBERT
DAVITZ, J.R.--[31]

DAVY, CHARLES WILLIAM
AGOGAS--[1]

DAVYDOVA, MAII M.
DAVYDOVA, NATALIE--[1]

DAWES, EDNA
DANE, EVA--[9][34]MYS/ROM--
MacD ""SHADOWS IN THE FIRE" '75
MacD "A LION BY THE MANE" '77
MacD "THE VAALDORP DIAMOND" '78
DARRELL, ELIZABETH--[9][26]ROM--
"BEYOND ALL FRONTIERS"
"THE GATHERING WOLVES" & MORE
DREW, ELEANOR--[9][26]ROM--
"BURN ALL YOUR BRIDGES"
DRUMMOND, EMMA--[9][26]ROM--
"BEYOND ALL FRONTIERS"
"DRAGON OF DESTINY" & MORE

DAWES, ROBYN MASON
CUBAS, BRAZ--[31]

DAWSON, ALEC JOHN
DAWSON, A.J.--[1]

DAWSON, CHARLES KENNETH
WEST COUNTRY--[1]

DAWSON, ERNEST
ATHOS--[1]

DAWSON, GEORGE H.
DELLA, LEW--PPCC#3, P16, J. PRESSMAN-
ARCH CKLST,HP--
MLST/ARCPR "LADIES SLEEP ALONE" '51
FLAMMECHE, PIERRE--J. PRESSMAN-
ARCPR CKLST,[1]--
ARCPR "WHEN PASSION RULES" '50
ARCPR "SILKEN LURE" '51
ARCPR "SPOILED LIVES" '50
PERRELLI, NICK--V. BERCH/S. HOLLAND-
ARCPR CKLST, BAE 15,[27][34]HP--
SCION "VIRGINS DIE LONELY" '49
SCION "BODY RAN HOME" '51
SCION "SHE SURE SLIPPED" '52
STORM[E], MICHAEL--[1][27][34]MYS--
30 NOVELS [ARCH, HARB & KWY]'49-54

DAWSON, JAMES LEE
DAWSON, JIM--[31]

DAWSON, JANIS
CLARE, SAMANTHA--[31]
COLES, JANIS--[31]
CONSTANT, JAN--[31]

DAWSON, MABEL LOUISE
CUSHING, E[NID] LOUISE--[34]MYS--
ARCADIA "MURDER'S NO PICNIC" '53
ARCADIA "MURDER WITHOUT REGRET" '54
ARCADIA "BLOOD ON MY RUG" '56
ARCADIA "UNEXPECTED CORPSE" '57

DAWSON, SAMUEL EDWARD
[A] COLONIST--[1]

DAWSON, SIR GEOFFREY
GLYN, ANTHONY--[1]

DAWSON, WILLIAM HENRY
HAWTHORNE, ERNEST H.--[8]
LOWNDES, GEORGE--[8]

DAY, A. GROVE
SAXON, CARL--[1]

DAY, ALEXANDRA
DARLING, SANDRA--[31][33]

DAY, BETH [FEAGLES]
FEAGLES, ELIZABETH--[1][22][31][33]AMERICAN

DAY, DIANNE
BANE, DIANA--[26]ROM--
"EYES OF THE NIGHT"
"LOVERS OF THE GOLDEN DRUM"
SANDERS, MADELYN--[10][26]ROM--
HARL 158 "UNDER VENICE"
HARL 187 "SARABANDE"
HARL 218 "DARKNESS AT COTTONWOOD HALL"
HARL 234 "LAIRD'S MOUNT"

DAY, GEORGE
HOWARD, BRUCE--[1]

DAY, GEORGE HAROLD
QUINCE, PETER--[8][22]ENGLISH

DAY, HOWARD E.
DAY, GENE--[2]

DAY, JOHN ROBERT
CYCLOPS--[1]

DAY, SAM HOUSTON
DAY, HOUSTON--[31]--MAGAZINE FICTION

DAY-LEWIS, CECIL
BLAKE, NICHOLAS--[2][3][5][22][29][31]MYS--
26 NOVELS '38-63
NORTON, CHARLES ELIOT--[5]MYS

DAZEY, AGNES J[OHNSTON]
JOHNSTON, AGNES CHRISTINE--[31][33]--
CHILDREN'S BOOKS

DE ALBINANA, ASUNCION I.
FONSALBA, PABLO MARIA--[30]MEXICAN--
"THE CITY ON THE LAKE" '49
MAIRENA, ANA--[30]MEXICAN--
"THE EXTRAORDINARY ONES" '61

DE ALCAYAGA, LUCILA GODOY
MISTRAL, GABRIELA--[22]CHILEAN

DE ALENCAR, GERTRUDE E.L.
VON SCHWARZFELD, GERTRUDE--[22]AUSTRIAN

DE ANDREA, WILLIAM L.
DE GRAVE, PHILIP--[3][18][31]MYS--
DBLDY "UNHOLY MOSES" '85
DBLDY "KEEP THE BABY, FAITH" '86

DE ANDREA, WILLIAM L. [CONT]
WILLOUGHBY, LEE DAVIS--[7][18][21]
HIST/ROM, HP--
DELL 'MAKING OF AMERICA' SERIES:
"THE VOYAGEURS"

DE ARAUGO, TESS S.
DE ARAUGO-O'MULLANE, TESS--[31]

DE ARAUJO, JOACHIM A.B.N.
NABUCO, JOAQUIM--[22]BRAZILIAN

DE ARGUIJO, JUAN
ARCICIO--[20]SPANISH

DE ASUAJE, JUANA R.
CRUZ, SOR JUANA INEZ--[30]MEXICAN

DE AVALLE-ARCE, JUAN B.
DE MONTALVO, LUIS GALVEZ--[31]
GOYENECHE, GABRIEL--[31]

DE AYALA, RAMON PEREZ
CUEVAS, PLOTINO--[20]SPANISH

DE BALKANY, MARIE [R.Z.]
BALKA, MARIE--[31]

DE BALZAC RIDEAU, CHARLES
CHANCELLOR, JOHN--[32][34]MYS--
16 NOVELS '26-70
MH "ALIEN HERO" JAN '65

DE BANZIE, ERIC
BAXTER, GREGORY--W/JOHN S.M. RESSICH,
[2][3][22][29]MYS--
7 NOVELS '29-35

DE BAQUERO, EDUARDO GOMEZ
ANDRENIO--[20]SPANISH

DE BARY, ANNA
BUNSTON, ANNA--[1]

DE BELLET, LIANE
DE FACCI, LIANE--[8]

DE BERMANS, A.
DUBRONY, A.--[1]

DE BETS, JULIE
MCGIVENY, MAURA--[9][21]26]ROM--
HARL 674 "A GRAND ILLUSION"
"MEGAM'S FOLLY" & MORE

DE BLACAM, HUGH [A]
RODDY THE ROVER--[1]

DE BOHELIER-LEPELETIER, G
BOUHELIER, SAINT-GEORGES--[1]

DE BOINOD, BERNARD L. JACOT
JACOT, B.L.--[1][22][31][32][34]MYS--
HUTCH "FROGS DON'T GROW FEATHERS" '30
SA "APPOINTMENT IN MAYFAIR" AUG '56
& OTHER SS COLL
JACOT, BERNARD--[8]

DE BOIS, WILHELMINA
DE BOIS, HELMA--[1][31]

DE BOIS-HEBERT, GUY [MAR]
DE BOVET, MARIE ANNE--[22]FRENCH
BOVET, MARIE ANNE DE--[1]

DE BOISSY, MARQUESE T.
GUICCIOLI, [COUNTESS] T.--[1]

DE BOLOGNE, MICHELE
SYGRIANUS--[1]

DE BOLT, JOSEPH WAYNE
DE BOLT, JOE--[7]SF--NON-FICTION

DE BONIS, SOFIA MCQUAIDE
BORDEUX, VAHDAH J.--[1]

DE BOURGOGNE, JEHAN
MANDEVILLE, SIR JOHN--[2]

DE BRA, LEMUEL LAWRENCE
LAWRENCE, EDMOND--L. ROBBINS LTR MAR '94

DE BRAHM, JEANNE I.ALCANTOR
ROSMER, JEAN--[3]MYS--
LIPPINCOTT "IN SECRET SERVICE" '37

DE BRISSAC, MALCOLM
DICKINSON, PETER--FANT. LIT. FOR CHILDREN & YOUNG ADULTS, RUTH NADELMAN

DE BROGLIE, LOUIS VICTOR
DE BROGLIE, L.--[31]

DE BURY, F. BLAZE
DICKBERRY, F.--[1][2]

DE CAMP, L[YON] SPRAGUE
LYON, LYMAN R.--L. ROBBINS LTR MAR '94, [2][11][31][33]SF
WELLS, J. WELLINGTON--L. ROBBINS LTR MAR '94,[2][11][22][33]SF
WELLS, J.W.--[1][2][32]MYS--
EQMM "HIS FIRST BOW" DEC '51

DE CAMPOS, LUIS
GOLD, FRANK--[1]

DE CASTRO, GUSTAF ADOLPHE DANZIGER
DANZIGER, ADOLPHE--[1]
DANZIGER, GUSTAV A.--[1]
DE CASTRO, ADOLPHE--[2][7][11]SF--
CENTURY "PORTRAIT OF AMBROSE BIERCE" '29

DE CAUX, LEONARD HOWARD
DE CAUX, LEN--[31]

DE CHAIR, SOMERSET S.
HON MEMBER FOR X--[1][8][31]

DE CHIRICO, ANDREA
SAVINO, ALBERTO--[22]ITALIAN

DE CORMERE, MATHORON
ANCEY, GEORGES--[1]

DE COSQUEVILLE STACEY, P.
DE COSQUEVILLE, PIERRE--[8]
SHELTON, MICHAEL--[8]

DE COSTA RITCHIE, LEWIS A
BARTIMEUS--[34]MYS--
CASSELL "GREAT SECURITY" '25
RICH "A MAKE-AND-MEND" '34
RICCI, LEWIS A.--[8]
RITCHIE, LEWIS--[22]

DE COURCY-PARRY, CHARLES
DALESMAN--[1]

DE COVARRUBIAS, BARBARA F
FAITH, BARBARA--[9][21][26][31]ROM--
33 NOVELS

DE CRAYENCOUR, MARGARET
YOURCENAR, MARGARET--[1][7]SF--
"ORIENTAL TALES" '85

DE CRISTOFORO, R.J.
CRISTY, R.J.--[8][31]

DE CUELLAR, JOSE TOMAS
FACUNDO--[20]SPANISH

DE CUYPER, FRANK ROGER
ROGER, FRANK--[2]BELGIAN/SF--ISFYB

DE CYRANO, SAVINIEN
DE BERGERAC, CYRANO--[2]

DE ECHEVARRIA, MARIA F.Y.
YAN, MAXI--[20]SPANISH

DE ELOLA Y GULIERREZ, JOE
IGNOTUS--[22]SPANISH

DE FOIGNY, GABRIEL
SADEUR, JAQUES--[2]

DE FREES, MADELINE
GILBERT, SISTER MARY--[8]

DE FREITAS, MICHAEL
MICHAEL X--[8]

DE FREYNE, GEORGE
BRIDGES, VICTOR--[8]MYS--
JCM "WHITE VIOLETS" FEB '57

DE GHELDERODE, MICHEL
MARTENS, ADEMAR--[22]BELGIAN

DE GRAAF-BOUKEMA, BONNY
CHEIXAOU, ELISABETH--[22]DUTCH

DE GRAMONT, SANCHE
MORGAN, TED--[7][8]SF--
NAME LEGALLY CHANGED--NON-FICTION

DE GRAS, HENRY ERNEST
BENNEY, MARK--[1][29][34]MYS--
DAVIES "LOW COMPANY" '36
DAVIES "SCAPEGOAT DANCES" '38

DE GRAZIA, ETTORE
DE GRAZIA--[1][33]
DE GRAZIA, TED--[1][31][33]

DE GUISE, ELIZABETH M.T.
CHACE, ISOBEL--[8][17][21][26]ENGLISH/ROM--
35 NOVELS
DE GUISE, ELIZABETH--[21][26]ENGLISH/ROM--
"PURITAN WIFE"
HUNTER, ELIZABETH--[31]
RIDER, ELISE B.--[9]ROM

DE HAAN BRUGGEN, CAROLINA
ABBING, JUSTINE--[22]

DE HAMONG, LOUIS
DE HAMONG, COUNT LEIGH--[2]

DE HARTOG, JAN
ECKMAR, F.R.--[31]

DE HEREDIA, MARIE L.A.
D'HOUVILLE, GERARD--[1][22]FRENCH

DE HOSTOS, EUGENIO MARIA
DE HOSTOS, E.M.--[31]
DE HOSTOS, EUGENIO M.--[31]

DE JONG, DAPHNE
BRIGHT, LAUREY--[9][21][26]ROM--13 NOVELS
CLAIR, DAPHNE--[9][21][26]ROM--18 NOVELS
LOREL, CLAIRE--[9][21][26]ROM--
"LORD BRANDSLEY'S BRIDE"
"MISS MIRANDA'S MARRIAGE"

DE JONG, DAVID CORNEL
BREDA, TJALMAR--[8][31]

DE JOUVENEL, EDUORD BERT.
DE JOUVENEL, BERTRAND--[31]

DE KAY, CHARLES
BARNAVAL, LOUIS--[1]
ECKFORD, HENRY--[1]

DE KERPELY, THERESA
KAY, TERESA--[1][31]

DE KIEWET, CORNELIS WILL.
DE KIEWIT, CORNELIS W.--[31]

DE KIRILINE LAWRENCE, LOUISE
DE KIRILINE, LOUISE--[8][31][33]

DE KOSTROWITSKY, W.APOLL.
APOLLINAIRE, GUILLAME--[2][31]

DE KOVEN, BERNARD
DE KOVEN, BERNIE--[31]

DE KREMER, JEAN RAYMOND
FLANDERS, JOHN--[1][2][11][23]
BELGIAN/SF--ISFYB
GRAVEN, NICHOLAS--JEAN F. LE DEIST
LETTER JAN '93, BELGIAN
GRAY, JACK--JEAN F. LE DEIST
LETTER JAN '93, BELGIAN
GRAY, MARY LILIAN--JEAN F. LE DEIST
LETTER JAN '93, BELGIAN
RAY, JEAN--[2][3][11][23]SF--
BERK "GHOULS IN MY GRAVE" '65

DE LA BEDOYERE, MICHAEL
BEDOYERE, MICHAEL DE LA--[31]

DE LA CORTINA, JOSE GOMEZ
DE LA CORTINA, EL CONDE--[30]MEXICAN

DE LA COSTE, MATHILDE
GERALD, LOUISE--[1]

DE LA FOREST-DIVONNE, PHIL
SILVE, CLAUDE--[2]

DE LA HIRE, JEAN
CAZAL, COMMANDER--[2]

DE LA MARE, WALTER
RAMAL, WALTER--[2][11][33]

DE LA PASTURE DASHWOOD, E
DELAFIELD, E.M.--[8][17][22]ENGLISH/ROM--
NUMEROUS NOVELS

DE LA RAMEE, MARIE LOUISE
OUIDA--[22][33][34]ENGLISH/MYS--
CHATTO "CECIL CASTLEMAINE'S GAGE" 1867

DE LA RAMEE, MARIE LOUISE [CONT]
RAME, MARIE LOUISE--[1]

DE LA REE, GEREAUX DEFOR.
DE LA REE, GERRY--[7]SF--NON-FICTION

DE LA ROCHE ST ANDRE, ANN
SARA--[33]--2 TRANSLATIONS OF
CHILDREN'S BOOKS

DE LA VANDERA, ALONSO CA.
CONCOLORCORVO--[20]SPANISH

DE LANCEY LANDON, MELVILLE
LAN--[8]AMERICAN
PERKINS, ELI--[1][2]AMERICAN
PERKINS, ELIZABETH--[2]

DE LATOUCHE, JACQUES CHAS
DE FARNIENTE, BEAUREGARD-- C. ECKHOFF SLST--
OLYMP "ADV OF FATHER SILAS" '58

DE LAUNAY, ANDRE JOSEPH
LAUNAY, ANDRE--[8]
LAUNAY, DROO--[8]

DE LEEUW, CATEAU W.
HAMILTON, KAY--[9][22][31]ROM
LYON, JESSICA--[9][22][31]ROM

DE LIMA BARRETO, ALFONSO
BARRETO, AFONSO HENRIQUE--[31]

DE LIMA, CLARA ROSA
DRIFTWOOD, PENELOPE--[1]

DE LINT, CHARLES [H.D.H.]
AKI, TANUCKI--[2][23]SF
CUISCARD, HENRI--[2][23]SF
KEY, SAMUEL M.--[7]SF--
JOVE "ANGEL OF DARKNESS" '90
PENALURICK, JAN--[2][23]SF
SONGWEAVBER, CERIN--[23]SF
WENDELESSEN--[23]

DE LINVAL, PAUL CASSIUS
MARX, JEAN--[1]

DE LISSER, HERBERT GEORGE
DE LISSER, H.G.--[31]

DE LONG, CLAIRE
EVANS, CLAIRE--[9][21][26]ROM--
"APPOLLO'S DREAM"
"LED INTO MOONLIGHT"
"COME WINTER'S END"

DE LONG, CLAIRE [ANN]
CLAIRE, EVA--[9][21][26]ROM--
"APPALACHIAN SUMMER"
"STAR ATTRACTION"

DE LONGUEVILLE, M.THERESE
SAINT-LAMBERT, PATRICK--V. BERCH LETTER TO
HUBIN '94, MYS--
MYSTIQUE "WHEEL OF FATE" '80

DE LOS UERDES, E. ALVAREZ
DEL REY, LESTER--LEGALIZED TO 'DEL REY'

DE LOUDONIEX, PAUL
PAUL, PIERRE ET--[1]FRENCH

DE LUBICZ-MILOSZ, OSCAR W
MILOSZ--[22]FRENCH

DE MARCO, JOANNE
SAINT-CLAIRE, SYBIL--V. BERCH-BRNDN/ BC PSEUDS, BAE 22, P24
WINTERS, DEENA--V. BERCH BRNDN/ BC PSEUDS, BAE 22, P24

DE MATTOS, MRS.
HERZ-GARTEN, THEODOR--[1]

DE MAUNI, BARON ROGER
DI MONTONE, N. BRACCIO--[2]

DE MELIKOFF, JODI
MCCARTER, JODY--W/VERMILLE MCCARTER,[2]

DE MENDELSSOHN, HILDE
SPIEL, HILDIE--[1][8]

DE MESNE, EUGENE [F]
OCEAN, JULIAN--[1]

DE MESONERO ROMANO, RAMON
EL CURIOSO PARLANTE--[20]SPANISH

DE MILLE, RICHARD
COSTER, ARTHUR--[2][11]
DIMRECKIN, B. GRAYER--[1][31]
WUNDT, WILHELM--[1]

DE MORGAN, JOHN
RAGGED, HYDER--[2]

DE MUNOZ MARIN, MUNA LEE
GAYLE, NEWTON--W/MAURICE C. GUINESS, [1][34]MYS--5 SCRIBNER NOVELS '35-8

DE NEEN, DOUGLAS
DOUGLAS, DEAN--V. BERCH-GM PSEUDS, PP 33-- GM 407 "MAN DIVIDED" '54

DE PADILLA, JUAN
EL CARTUJANO--[20]SPANISH

DE PAOLA, THOMAS ANTHONY
DE PAOLA, TOMIE--[31][33]-- ADDISON HOUSE "CRISS-CROSS, APPLESAUCE" & MORE '79-91

DE PATOT, SIMON TYSSOT
BAYLE, MONSIEUR--[2]
MASSEY, JAMES--[2]

DE PEREYRA, MARIA E. Y R.
MOSKOWSKI, IVAN--[30]MEXICAN

DE PIETRO, ALBERT
LOREL, PHIL--[1]

DE QUEIROS, FRANCISCO TE.
MORENO, BENTO--[22]PORTUGUESE

DE QUINTANILLA, MARIA A.
ROMANONES, COUNTESS OF--[22]AMERICAN-SPANISH

DE REGNIERS, BEATRICE S.
KITT, TAMARA--[8][31][33]

DE RENEVILLE, MARY M.M.S.
MOTLEY, MARY--[1][22]ENGLISH

DE REYNA, DIANE DETZER
DE REYNA, JORGE--[1][2][23]SF-- "RETURN OF THE STARSHIPS" '68
DETZER, DIANE--[1][23]SF-- "THE TOMB" '58

DE LA RAMEE, MARIE LOUISE [CONT]
LUKENS, ADAM--[1][2][23]SF--
"THE SEA PEOPLE" '59
"CONQUEST OF LIFE" '60
"SONS OF THE WOLF" '61
"THE GLASS CAGE" '62
"EEVALU" '63
"ALIEN WORLD" '63
"THE WORLD WITHIN" '62

DE REYNIAC, MAURICE DRUON
DRUON, MAURICE--[7]SF-- "TISTOU OF THREE FINGERS" '58

DE RICAULT, CHARLES JOS.
HERICAULT, CHARLES D'--[22]FRENCH

DE RIDDER, ALFONS JOSEPH
ELSSCHOT, WILLEM--[1][22]FLEMISH

DE RIQUETTI MIRABEAU, SYB
GYP--[22]FRENCH

DE ROCHA, ADOLFO CORREIA
TORGA, MIGUEL--[22]PORTUGUESE

DE ROSA, PETER [C]
BOYD, NEIL--[1][8][31]

DE ROSSO, HENRY ANDREW
DE ROSSO, H.A.--[28][32]MYS/WEST-- ST "TRACK OF FEAR" MAY '61 & OVER 200 OTHERS

DE SAINT CRICQ, LORENSO
MARCOY, PAUL--[1]

DE SAMPER, SOLEDAD ACOSTA
BERTILDA--[20]SPANISH

DE SCHANSCHIEFF, JULIET D
DYMOKE, JULIET--[8][17][31]ENGLISH/ROM--
"THE ROYAL GRIFFIN"
"TWO FLAGS FOR FRANCE" & MORE

DE SELINCOURT, ANNE
SEDGEWICK, ANNE DOUGLAS--[1]

DE SHA, SANDRA DONOVAN
DONOVAN, SANDRA--[9][26]ROM--
"DECEPTION'S FIVE"
"RAPTURE'S REWARD"
"RESTLESS PASSIONS"

DE SHORN, ROY
FARGO, WES--L. ROBBINS LTR MAR '94--PULP

DE SILVA, ANGELITA H.
DE SILVA, NINA--[1]

DE SILVA, DAVID
PARASARA--[1]

DE SOUSA, JOSE OSWALD
DE ANDRADE, OSWALD--[22]BRAZILIAN

DE SOUZA FILHO, HENRIQUE
HENFIL--[31]

DE STEFANO, ANTHONY
JOHN, ANTHONY--W/JOHN S. LITTEL,[7][34]MYS--
GRAFTON "THE PREDATOR" '86
JOVE "JUDAS VOICE" '89

DE STEUCH, HARRIET HENRY
HENRY, HARRIET--[31]

DE STRATTON, ADAM
FLETA--[1]

DE TALAVERA BERGER, FRAN
BERGEN, FRAN--[9][21][26]ROM--
SIL 191 "CAPITOL AFFAIR"
SIL 29 "YEARNING OF ANGELS" & MORE

DE TALAVERA BERGER, FRAN
FLORES, FRANCES--[9][21][26]ROM--
"DESPERATE LONGINGS"
"LOVE'S WINE"

DE TARDE, ALFRED
AGATHON--W/HENRI MARSIS,[1]

DE TARDE, JEAN GABRIEL
TARDE, GABRIEL--[23]FRENCH/SF--
"UNDERGROUND MAN" 1905

DE TIRTOFF, ROMAIN
ERTE--[31]

DE TOLNAY, CHARLES E.
TOLNAI, KAROLY--[1]
TOLNAI, VAGUJHELYI KAROLY--[1]

DE TRAZ, GEORGES
FOSCA, FRANCOIS--[1]

DE TREVINO, ELIZABETH B.
BORTON, ELIZABETH--[33]--
CHILDREN'S BOOKS

DE VAUX, BARON
MARTIN, EUGENE--[1]

DE VEER, HENDRIK
MOBACHUS, VESALIUS--[22]DUTCH

DE VERE, [LADY] D.
DE'BEUCLERK, LADY--[1]

DE VOLTAIRE, FRANCIS M.A.
VOLTAIRE--[2][32]MYS--
EQMM "THE DOG & THE HORSE" OCT '54

DE VORE, MARY
DOHRN, MADELYN--W/JOAN DORNBUSH,
[9][21][26]ROM--
SIL 501 "LABOR OF LOVE"
"BEST DEFENSE" & MORE

DE VRIES, LAURA LEE
GORDON, LAURA--[26]ROM--
"DOUBLE BLACK DIAMOND"
"TERROR BY DESIGN"

DE WAAL, VIOLET MARY
IRWIN, VIOLET--[1]

DE WEINDECK, U.M.C.W.
FIGHTON, GEORGE Z.--[2][34]MYS--
HUTCH "GHOST OF PASSY" 1889

DE WILLIGEN, ELISABETH
VUYK, BEB--[1]

DE WYZEWSKI, TEODOR
WYZEWA--[22]POLISH

DE YOUNG, HENRY C.
CHUNG, HENRY--[1]

DE ZAMACOIS Y QUINTANA, E
ZAMACOIS, EDUARDO--[1]

DE ZIEL, HENRI FRANS
TREFOSSA--[1]

DEADMAN, EMMETT
DEDMON, EMMETT--[1]

DEAKIN, HILDA L.
DEAKIN, H.L.--[34]MYS--
METHUEN "SECRET OF THE COVE" '30
NELSON "SHOT THAT KILLED
GRAEME ANDREWS" '31

DEAKING, PHYLLIS A.
DACQUIN, FELICITY--[1]

DEAL, BORDEN
BORDEN, LEE--V. BERCH, GM PSEUDS, PP 33,
[22][31][34]MYS--
GM 744 "THE SECRET OF SYLVIA" '58
AVON T-520 "THE DEVIL'S WHISPER" '61
BORDEN, LEIGH--[8][31]
HER--[31]
HIM--[31]

DEALE, KENNETH EDWIN LEE
MARTIN, PAUL--[1][22][31]IRISH--
NON-FICTION, ARMS & ARMOR

DEALEY, EDWARD MUSGROVE
DEALEY, TED--[31]

DEAN, EDITH M.
MEREDITH, DEAN--[1]

DEAN, GEORGE
DOUGLAS, GEORGE--[34]MYS--
BOUREGY "CASE OF THE GREEDY RAINMAKER" '01

DEAN, JOHN EDWIN
BUMPPO, NATHANIEL J.B.--[1]
BUMPPO, NATTY--[1]

DEAN, MARGUERITE M.M.
MARSHALL, MARGUERITE M.--[1]

DEAN, MARY
MEE, MARY--[1][8]

DEAN, ROBERT GEORGE
GRISWOLD, GEORGE--[3][22][31][40]MYS--
DUTTON "A GAMBIT FOR MR. GROODE" '52
& MORE

DEARMAND, DALE
DEARMAND, DALE BURLISON--[31]

DEAVER, JEFFREY WILDS
JEFFERIES, WILLIAM--CRPG/DDLY PLEAS. #3--
AV "BLOODY RIVER BLUES" '91
AV "SHALLOW GRAVES" '92
AV "DON'T MISS THE NEXT"
AV "LOCATION SCOUT MYS"

DEBEAUBIEN, PHILIP FRANCI
HOLIDAY, HOMER--[31]

DEBELJAK, TINE
KALIN, JEREMIJA--[22]SLOVAK

DEBERRY, VIRGINIA
JOYCE, MARIE--W/DONNA GRANT,[21][26]ROM--
"EXPOSURES"

DEBILL, WALTER C. JR.
HAMMAIS, DR. PIERRE DE & DR. ERIC VON
KONNENBERG--W/E.P. **BERGLUND,**[2]

DEBILL, WALTER C. JR. [CONT]
VON KONNEBERG, DR. ERIC--W/E.P. EGLUND,[2]

DEBOLT, ADRIANA
DANE, CHRISTOPHER--[7]SF--
AAE "THE GALACTIC ARENA" '81
"RIDERS OF THE DRAGON" '81

DEBORDE, SHERRY
DENTON, ANN--AUTHOR PROVIDED--
FUTURE JUVENILE BOOKS
SCOTT, KRISTAL LEIGH--AUTHOR PROVIDED--
ZEBRA "BOUND BY ECSTASY" '91
ZEBRA "SANTE FE SURRENDER" '92
ZEBRA "LONE STAR SEDUCTION" '92

DEBRANDT, DON H.
HILDEBRANDT, DON--G. COOK LTR AUG '93

DEBROT, NICHOLAAS
DEBROT, COLA--[1]

DECKER, ANDREAS
LAMONT, ROBERT--W/W.K. GIESA,[39]GERMAN/JUV/SF

DECKER, DUANE
WAYNE, RICHARD--[1][33]

DECKER, HEINZ-BRUNO
DECK, BRUNO--[39]GERMAN/MYS
HART, HEINZ-BRUNO--[39]GERMAN/MYS
KRAFFT, HEINZ--[39]GERMAN/MYS

DECKER-VOIGT, HANS-HELMUT
MORGEN, JORG--[39]GERMAN
MORGEN, JURGEN--[39]GERMAN

DECLOS, ANNE
AURY, DOMINIQUE--[1]

DECORMIER, LOUISE
CARDIFF, SARA--W/REBECCA KAVALIER
& GLORIA KIRCHEIMER,[34]MYS--
5 NOVELS '71-9

DEE, RON
DARKE, DAVID--M. BAKER-'AFRAID' #15--
PINN "BLIND HUNGER" '93
PINN "SHADE" '94

DEE, SHERRY
FLOURNOY, SHERYL--[21][26]ROM--
SIL 371 "JASON'S TOUCH"
"RECKLESS DESIRE" & MORE

DEE, STEPHANIE
PLOWMAN, STEPHANIE--[8]

DEEGAN, FRANCIS M.
FRANCIS, D.--L. ROBBINS LTR MAR '94--PULP

DEEGAN, PAUL JOSEPH
O'REILLY, SEAN--[1][33]

DEEPING, GEORGE WARWICK
WARWICK, GEORGE--[1]

DEER, MARY J.
DEER, M.J.--W/GEORGE H. SMITH,[2][11]--
FRA F50 "A PLACE NAMED HELL" '63
FRA F66 "FLAMES OF DESIRE" '63

DEES, CATHERINE
KAY, CATHERINE--W/KAY CROISSANT,
[9][21][26]ROM--
HARL 45 "DAWN OF PASSION" & MORE

DEES, CATHERINE [CONT]
MCKENZIE, KATE--W/KAY CROISSANT,[21]ROM--
HARL 143 "BED & BREAKFAST"

DEFOE, DANIEL
PYTHAGOROLUNISTER--[2]

DEGEE, OLIVIER
TOUSSEUL, JEAN--[1][22]BELGIAN

DEGHY, GUY [S]
FROY, HERALD--W/KEITH [S]WATERHOUSE,
[1][22][31]HUNGARIAN-ENGLISH
GIBB, LEE--W/KEITH [S] WATERHOUSE,
[1][22]HUNGARIAN-ENGLISH

DEGLER, CLAUDE
ROGERS, DON--[1][2][11]

DEGLMANN, ERICA
SCHWARZ, ERICA--[39]GERMAN/JUV

DEGNER, HELMUT
ANDERS, HELMUT--[39]GERMAN

DEHMEL, KARL JULIUS
ALBINI, J.--[39]GERMAN/SF

DEIGHTON, LEONARD CYRIL
DEIGHTON, LEN--[7][31][34]SF/MYS--
HODDER "IPCRESS FILE" '62 & 17 OTHERS

DEIHL, EDNA GROFF
AUNT ESTE--[1]
FORGE, ANDRE--[1]

DEINDORFER, ROBERT GREENE
GREENE, ROBERT--[1][8][31]AMERICAN
BENDER, JAY--[8][22][31]AMERICAN
DENDER, JAY--[22]AMERICAN

DEINET, MARGARETHE
HALLER, M.--[39]GERMAN/JUV

DEITZ, THOMAS FRANKLIN
DEITZ, TOM--[7]SF--
"DAVID SULLIVAN #1-5" '86/91

DEJONG, DAVID CORNEL
BREDA, TJALMAR--[1][22]AMERICAN

DEKKER, MAURITS RUDOLF J.
PROBAZKI, BORIS--[22]DUTCH

DEL MONTE Y APONTE, DOMIN
ALMADOVAR, SANCHEZ DE--[1]
SANCHEZ DE ALMODOVAR, B.T--[1]

DEL REY, JUDY-LYNN
BENJAMIN, JUDY-LYNN--[31]

DEL REY, LESTER
ALVAREZ, JOHN--[2][23]SF
ALVAREZ, R.--LOCUS-EULOGY OF DEL
REY JUNE '93--AS PUBLISHER
ALVAREZ, RAMON--[2]
DEL REY, ALVAREZ--[1]
HALL, CAMERON--W/H. DEMPSEY OR HARRY
HARRISON,[1][2]ALSO HIMSELF
HENRY, MARION--[2][11][23][31]
JAMES, PHILIP--W/JAMES BEARD,
[1][2][11][23]ALSO HIMSELF
KAEMPFERT, WADE--[1][2][11][31]HP--
ROCKET STORIES
MARION, HENRY--[1][2][23][31]

DEL REY, LESTER [CONT]
MCCANN, EDSON--W/ FREDRIC POHL,[2][11][23]SF--
"PREFERRED RISK" '55
RAYMOND, JOHN--[11]SF
SATTERFIELD, CHARLES--W/F. POHL,[2][11][23]SF--
"BEYOND-NO MORE STARS" '54
ST. JOHN, PHILIP--[2][4][11][23][31]
VAN LHIN, ERIK--[2][4][7][11][23][33]SF--
"POLICE YOUR PLANET" '53
VINCENT, JOHN--[1][11]
WRIGHT, KENNETH--[2][4][11][23][33]

DELAFOSSE, FREDERICK M.
VARDON, ROGER--[1][8]

DELAND, MARGARETTA W.C.
DELAND, MARGARET--[31]

DELANEY, FRANCIS JR.
DELANEY, BUD--[1][31]

DELANEY, JACK
STONE, RICHARD--[1]

DELANEY, JOSEPH FRANCIS
DANE, JOEL Y.--[1][22][34]MYS--
DBLDY "CABANA MURDERS" '37
DBLDY "GRASP AT STRAWS" '38 & MORE

DELANEY, KENT
PENDLETON, DON--[34]MYS,HP--
GE "COUNTDOWN FOR CHAOS" '87

DELANEY, MARY MURRAY
LANE, MARY D.--[8][31]

DELANEY, THOMAS NICHOLAS
DELANEY, NED--[31]

DELANY, SAMUEL R.
DELANEY, CHIP--[1]
DELANEY, SAMUEL R.--[2]
STEINER, K. LESLIE--[23]SF--
"STRAITS OF MESSINA"

DELATUSH, EDITH
DE PAUL, EDITH--[7][9][21][26][31]SF/ROM--
DELL "VISCOUNT'S WITCH" '81 & MORE
MORGAN, ALYSSA--[9][26]ROM--
"WHITEWATER LOVE"
"NO OTHER LOVE"
"BECKONING HEART"
ST, GEORGE, EDITH--[9][21][26]ROM--
SIL 69 "WEST OF THE MOON"
"MIDNIGHT WINE" & MORE

DELAVAUD, MARIE COLLIN
COLMONT, MARIE--[1]

DELAY-TUBIANA, CLAUDE
BAILLEN--[31]--
"CHANEL SOLITAIRE" '71
BAILLEN, CLAUDE--[31]
DELAY, CLAUDE--[31]--
GALLINARD "PARADIZ NOIR" '76
PAUVERT "ROGER LA GRENOUILLE" '78

DELDERFIELD, RONALD F.
DELDERFIELD, R.F.--[21]ROM--19 NOVELS

DELEHANTY, RANDOLPH
DELAHANTY, RANDOLPH--[31]

DELEONI, PAUL
CHARNET, PAUL--[1]

DELF, THOMAS
MARTEL, CHARLES--[34]MYS--
WARD "DETECTIVE NOTEBOOK" 1860
WARD "DIARY OF AN EX-DETECTIVE" 1860

DELFS, RAINER
BENTEEN, JOHN--[39]GERMAN--WEST,HP
BRENNAN, MICHAEL--[39][40]GERMAN/MYS--
'KOMMISSAR X' #533 & #526
BROWN, MATT--[39]GERMAN/WEST
CRAIG, JOHN ROSCOE--[39]GERMAN/MYS/HOR
DONOVAN, CHAD--[39]GERMAN/MYS/HOR
DONOVAN, JACK--[39]GERMAN/MYS
HART, RAYMOND--[39]GERMAN/MYS
KIRBY, JOHN--[39]GERMAN,HP
LAFITTE, JEAN--[39]GERMAN,HP
MARTIN, LEE--[39]GERMAN/WEST
MARTINEZ, BENITO--[39]GERMAN,HP
MILES, JOHN--[39]GERMAN
PHILIPP, FLORIAN--[39]GERMAN
PHILIPP, FRANK--[39]GERMAN
ROSSITER, SAM--[39]GERMAN
SLADE, JACK--[39]GERMAN/WEST,HP

DELIBES SETIEN, MIGUEL
DELIBES, MIGUEL--[31]

DELINSKY, BARBARA
DRAKE, BONNIE--[9][21][26][31]ROM--
"GEMSTONE"
"SWEET EMBER" & MORE
DOUGLASS, BILLIE--[9][21][26][31]ROM--
SIL 74 "BEYOND FANTASY" & MORE

DELK, KAREN
KINGSLEY, KATE--[26]ROM--
"RANSOME OF THE HEART"
"SEASON OF STORMS"

DELK, ROBERT CARLTON
CARLTON, ALVA--[1][31]
TENNESS, GEORGE--[1]

DELL, DRAYCOT MONTAGUE
ANSON, PIERS--[1][34]MYS--
COLUMBINE "FAN TAN OF THE FRONT PAGE" '39
ANSON, PIERS--W/OSWALD [C.C] DALLAS,[34]MYS--
COLUMBINE "THE DEATH CLUB" '40
THOMPSON, STEPHEN--[1]

DELLBRIDGE, JOHN
PLUMMY--[22]MYS

DELLIGAN, WILLIAM F.
CRAIG, ROBERT--V. BERCH LTR TO HUBIN '94,
MYS--
SIGN "TRAUMA" '84
DAVIES, GWYNNETH--[3][26]MYS/ROM--
POPLB "TERROR AT DEERCLIFF HOUSE" '76
POPLB "PORTRAIT OF SUSAN" '77
ORFORD, ELLEN--[3][26]MYS/ROM--
CURTIS "MAZE" '73
CURTIS "BRIDE OF RAVEN ISLAND" '74
POPLB "THE SUTTER HOUSE" '75
TREMONTE, JULIA--V. BERCH LTR SEPT '93--
PINN "THE DEVIL'S HOUSE" '74
TREVELYAN, JULIA--V. BERCH LTR TO
HUBIN '94, MYS--
SIGN "GREYTHORNE" '74
SIGN "BLACKMOOR" '76
SIGN "THE TOWER ROOM" '79
SIGN "LANDSEND TERROR" '79

DELLILO, DON
BIRDWELL, CLEO--[1]

DELLIN, BILLIE GENELL
DALTON, GENA--[21][26]ROM--
SIL 69 "SORREL SUNSET"
"CHEROKEE FIRE" & MORE

DELMAS, LEON RENE
CHAMPLIN, VIRGINIA--[34]MYS--
OGILVIE "SHADOWED BY A DETECTIVE; OR, THE WOMAN IN WAX" 1885
DE PONT-JEST, RENE--[1][3]MYS--
5 NOVELS 1885-99

DELORME, REVE
HAUS, LADOVIE--[1]

DELOUGHERY, GRACE L.
WIEST, GRACE L.--[1][8]

DELRUE, EMIEL
VAN DER STRAETEN, EMIEL--[22]FLEMISH

DELUPIS, INGRID
DETTER, INGRID--[1][31]
DOIMI DI DELUPIS, INGRID--[1][31]

DELVES-BROUGHTON, JOSEPH.
BRYAN, JOHN--[3][29]MYS--
FABER "THE CONTESSA CAME TOO" '57
FABER "THE DIFFERENCE TO ME" '57
FABER "THE MAN WHO CAME BACK" '58

DEMARET, JAMES NEWTON
DEMARET, JIMMY--[31]

DEMBNER, S. ARTHUR
DEMBNER, RED--[31]

DEMBSKI, WERNER
DIKSEN, BERND--[39][40]GERMAN/MYS--
"DER HULLE TOD" '70
"DER VERLIERER ZAHLT" '71 & OTHERS

DEMETROPOULOS, NICHOLAS
EVANS, JEAN--[9]][21][26]ROM--
"DESIGN FOR LOVE"
EVANS, MARIANNE--[9][21]ROM--
"A SPLENDID PASSION"

DEMILLE, JAMES
ANONYMOUS--S. WELLS SF LIST
GAUL, GILBERT--[11]SF

DEMILLE, NELSON [RICHARD]
CANNON, JACK--CRPG,[34]MYS--
POCK 63208 "SNIPER"
POCK "SMACK MAN"
POCK 63213 "CANNIBAL" - ALL '89
POCK "HAMMER OF GOD" '89
POCK 63210 "NIGHT OF THE PHOENIX" '89
POCK 63211 "THE DEATH SQUAD" '90
KAY, ELLEN--[1][18][29]--
"$5 MILLION WOMAN: BARBARA WALTERS" '79
LADNER, KURT--[18][29][31]--
"HITLER'S CHILDREN" '76
MATTHEWS, BRAD--[1][18][29]--
"KILLER SHARKS: THE REAL STORY" '76

DEMING, RICHARD
CLARK, HALSEY--[18]MYS--
DELL "GRAND FINALE" '83
CRAIG, JONATHAN--L. ROBBINS LTR MAR '94--PULP
CURTIS, RICHARD HALE--[18][21]HP--
'SKYMASTER' SERIES:
"THE BARNSTORMERS"

DEMING, RICHARD [CONT]
DAVIS, ROBERT HART--A. TONIK, ECHOES #24,HP--
GL "SHEIK OF ARABY AFFAIR" DEC '66
GL "VELVET VOICE AFFAIR" DEC '66
GL "DEADLY DRUG AFFAIR" JUN '67
DEEMING, RICHARD--[1][11]
FRANKLIN, MAX--[7][18][32][33][34]MYS--
19 NVLS '53-78
12 DIGEST SS
HALLIDAY, BRETT--T. JOHNSON-ECHOES #23,HP--
MSMM "DEATH TAKES OVER" NOV '58
MSMM "LADY WORE A GUN" DEC '58
MSMM "KEEP ME OUT OF THE MORGUE" FEB '59
MSMM "TWISTED MIND" MAR '59
MSMM "INVITATION TO MURDER" MAY '59
MSMM "DEATH CREEPS SLOWLY" 8/59
MSMM "MASQUERADE FOR MURDER" NOV '59
MSMM "BULLET FOR A BLONDE" MAR '60
MSMM "DEBT OF DEATH" JUN '60
MSMM "MURDER ON JUNGLE KEY" JUL '60
MSMM "CHRONIC WIDOWER" SEP '60
MSMM "PICKUP MURDER" JAN '61
MSMM "EDGE OF THE LAW" MAR '61
MSMM "PATTERN FOR A CRIME" MAY '61
MSMM "MURDER OVER MIAMI" JUL '61
MSMM "DEATH OF A PHONY" OCT '61
MSMM "GANG KILL" DEC '61
LA VERN, SHERRY--L. ROBBINS LTR MAR '94--PULP
MARINO, NICK--LACHMAN LIST MAY '93--
PYR 159 "ONE-WAY STREET" '55
PYR G315 "CITY LIMITS" '58
MOOR, EMILY--[3][18][29][33]MYS--
BEAGLE "THE SHADOWED PORCH" '72
QUEEN, ELLERY--[2][3][18][34]MYS,HP--
DELL "DEATH SPINS A PLATTER" '62
DELL "LOSERS, WEEPERS" '66
DELL "WIFE OR DEATH" '63
DELL "COPPER FRAME" '65
DELL "SHOOT THE SCENE" '66
POPLB "WHY SO DEAD?" '66
POPLB "HOW GOES THE MURDER?" '67
POPLB "WHICH WAY TO DIE?" '67
POPLB "WHAT'S IN THE DARK?" '68
LAN "BLACK HEARTS MURDER" '70
WILLOUGHBY, LEE DAVIS--[18][21]ROM,HP--
DELL 'MAKING OF AMERICA' SERIES:
"SMUGGLERS"
"BOUNTY HUNTERS"

DEMING, ROBERT
DEMING, BOB--[29]MYS--
NYCK 281 "TRE MINUTER ATT LEVA" '49
DAVIS, ROBERT--[29]MYS--
NYCK 308 "MORDARENS NAT" '50

DEMKO, MIKOLAY
MOCZAR, MIECZYSLAW--[1]

DEMMON, CALVIN W.
DAMON, CARL--[1][2][11]

DEMOREST, STEPHAN
DEVON, D.G.--W/MICHAEL R. GROSS,[3][31]MYS--
BAL "TEMPLE KENT" '82
BAL "SHATTERED MASK" '83
BAL "PRECIOUS OBJECTS" '84

DEMPEWOLFF, RICHARD F.
DAY, MICHAEL--[1][8][22][31]AMERICAN
FREDERICK, DICK--[1][8][22][31]AMERICAN
WOLF, FREDERICK--[1][8][22]AMERICAN

DEMPSEY, HENRY MAXWELL
HARRISON, HARRY--[1][7]--
NAME CHANGED TO 'HARRISON'

DEMPSEY, WILLIAM HARRISON
DEMPSEY, JACK--[31]

DENDEL, ESTHER [S.W]
WARNER, ESTHER S.--[1]

DENENBERG, HERBERT SIDNEY
DUMPTY, HUMPTY S.--[31]

DENENHOLZ, ALMA
CLISTIER, ADELINE--[1]
DENNY, ALMA--[1]

DENHAM, AVERY S.
STRAKOSCH, AVERY--[1]

DENHAM, MARY ORR
CASWELL, ANNE--[8][9][22]AMERICAN/ROM
ORR, MARY--[8][21][22]AMERICAN/ROM--
"GRASS WIDOWS"
"TEJERA SECRETS" & MORE

DENHOLM, DAVID
FORREST, DAVID--[1][8]

DENHOLM, TERESE MARY ZITA
WHITE, ZITA--[1][22]AUSTRALIAN

DENISON, MURIEL [G]
NEWTON, FRANCES--[1]

DENNEBORG, SILVIA [G]
GUT, SYLVIA--[39]GERMAN/JUV

DENNETT, HERBERT VICTOR
DELTA--[1][22][31]ENGLISH
SYNTAX, JOHN--[1][22]ENGLISH
TENT, NED--[1][22]ENGLISH

DENNEY, DIANA
GRI--[31]
ROSS, DIANA--[1][8][31]

DENNING, ALFRED THOMPSON
DENNING, A.T.--[31]

DENNING, TROY
AWLINSON, RICHARD--[7]SF,HP--
TSR 'F.R. FANT. ADV':
"DRAGONWALL"
"PARCHED SEA"
"WATERDEEP"

DENNIS, GEOFFREY
BROWNE, BARUM--W/HILARY ST. G. SAUNDERS,
[1][3]MYS--
GOLZ "DEVIL & X.Y.Z." '31
DENT, GUY--[23]ENGLISH/SF--
"EMPEROR OF IF" '26

DENNIS, WALTER L.
MCDERMOTT, DENNIS--W/P.S. MILLER
& PAUL MCDERMOTT--
"DUEL ON THE ASTEROID" '32

DENNIS-JONES, HAROLD
HAMILTON, PAUL--[1][8][31]
HESSING, DENNIS--[1][8][31]

DENNISON, DULCIE W.C.
GRAY, DULCIE--[18][34][36]MYS--
BARKER "MURDER ON THE STAIRS" '57
BARKER "BABYFACE" '59
BARKER "MURDER IN MELBOURNE" '58 & MORE

DENNISON, ELIZABETH FREE.
CRUST, CHRISTIE--[1]

DENNISON, ENID
LLOYD, WILLSON--[8]

DENNISON, SHARON
DELACORTE, SHAWNA--[26]ROM--
"SARAH & THE STRANGER"
"BARGAIN BACHELOR, CASSIE'S LAST GOODBYE"

DENNISTON, ELINORE
ALLAN, DENNIS--[3][18][29]MYS--
GREYSTONE "HOUSE OF TREASON" '36
MILL "BRANDON IS MISSING" '40
FOLEY, RAE--[3][18][21][31]MYS/ROM--
DODD "BONES OF CONTENTION" '50
DODD "AN APE IN VELVET" '51
DODD "LAST GAMBLE" '56 & MORE
MAXWELL, HELEN K.--[3]MYS--
LITTLE "GIRL IN A MASK" '71
LITTLE "LEAVE IT TO AMANDA" '72
LITTLE "THE LIVINGSTON HEIRS" '73

DENNORE, ROBERTA
DENORRE, ROCHEL--[9][21]ROM--5 NOVELS

DENNY, FELIX
BARR, DENNIS--[1][3]MYS--
CAPE "A DOCK BRIEF" '28
JARROLDS "A ROPE BROKE" '32

DENNY, JOHN THOMAS
LEIGH, HART--[1]
WINWOOD, BRET--[1]

DENNY, NORMAN GEORGE
DALE, NORMAN--[8][31][33]

DENNYS, ELISABETH
ONSLOW, KATHERINE--[8]

DENSLOW, MARTIN VAN B.
O'QUILL, MAURICE--[1]

DENSLOW, WILLIAM W.
DENSLOW, W.W.--[1]

DENT, ANTHONY AUSTEN
APPLEGIRTH, ANTHONY--[1][31]
BUNDUKHARI--[1]
EL BUNDUKHARI--[31]
GARTHWAITE, MALABY--[1][31]
LAMPTON, AUSTIN--[1]

DENT, C.H.
FANSHAW, CECIL--[1]ENGLISH
HUDLESTON, JOHN--[1]ENGLISH
HUDLESTON, ROBERT--[1]ENGLISH

DENT, LESTER
CASH, H.O.--LACHMAN LST MAY '93--PULPS
CASH, HARMON--LACHMAN LST MAY '93,
[29][32]MYS--
SD "SMITH IS DEAD" FEB-MAR '47
GRANT, MAXWELL--[1][2][11][29]HP--
HOWE, CLIFF--LACHMAN LST MAY '93--PULPS
ROBERTS, KENNETH--[1][11][18][29]MYS
ROBESON, KENNETH--[2][3][11]HP--
ORIGINATED 'DOC SAVAGE'
& 'AVENGER' NOVELS
ROBESON, KENNETH--W/HAROLD A. DAVIS,[34]HP--
BB "EXPLODING LAKE"
BB "DUST OF DEATH" '69
BB "MENTAL WIZARD" '70
BB "GOLDEN PERIL" '70

DENT, LESTER [CONT]
ROBESON, KENNETH [CONT]
BB "LAND OF FEAR" '73
BB "SEVEN AGATE DEVILS" '73
BB "CRIMSON SERPENT" '74
BB "KING MAKER" '75
BB "PURPLE DRAGON" '78
ROBESON, KENNETH--W/W. RYERSON JOHNSON, [2][34]HP--
BB "FANTASTIC ISLAND" '66
BB "LAND OF ALWAYS-NIGHT" '66
BB "MOTION MENACE" '71
ROBESON, KENNETH--W/WILLIAM G. BOGART,[34]HP--
BB "THE ANGRY GHOST" '77
BB "FIRE & ICE"
BB "HEX"
BB "SPOTTED MEN"
BB "WORLD'S FAIR GOBLIN"
RYAN, TIM--W/EDMUND SEWARD, [2][11][18][23]MYS/SF
SCANLON, C.K.M.--LACHMAN LST MAY '93, HP--PULPS
WALLACE, ROBERT--LACHMAN LST MAY '93, BAE 25--'PHANTOM DETECTIVE' STORIES

DENT, ROXANNE
MASTERS, MELISSA--[9][21][26]ROM--
"BARBARY BOUNTY"
"BARBARY BRIDE"

DENT, THOMAS COVINGTON
DENT, TOM--[31]

DENT, W. REDNERS
REDNERS--L. ROBBINS LTR MAR '94

DENTON, JOHN
LONGLEY, JOHN--[8]

DEPASTURE, MADRIS
DUPREE, MADRIS--[26]ROM--
HARL 213 "MY LORD BEAUMONT"

DEPEW, WALTER WESTERFIELD
DEPWE, WALLY--[31]

DEPLAZE, GION
VIAL, GION--[1]

DEPPE, HETTY
LANGHARDT, HETTY--[39]GERMAN/JUV

DEPTA, SIEGMUND
SIEGMUND, HEINRICH--[39]GERMAN

DERBY, E.C.
CARTER, NICHOLAS--[3]MYS,HP--
STREET & SMITH

DEREN, ELEANORA
DEREN, MAYA--[31]

DEREVANCHUK, GORDON
DERRY, GORDON--[2]

DERFOLDY-LUX, WILHELM
LUX, HARRY--[39]GERMAN

DERIN, P.L.
LANSEL, PIEDER--[22]ITALIAN

DERLETH, AUGUST [WILLIAM]
DIVERS HANDS--[2]
GARTH, WILL--[2][11]HP--STANDARD

DERLETH, AUGUST [WILLIAM] [CONT]
GRENDON, STEPHEN--[2][4][16][18][23][31]--
"MR. GEORGE & OTHER ODD PERSONS" '63
HEATH, ELDON--[1][2][11][16]
HOLMES, KENYON--[1][2][11][16]
LE FANU, J. S[HERIDAN]--[2][11]
MASON, TALLY--[2][3][5][16][18][23]--
STACKPOLE "CONSIDER YOUR VERDICT" '37
WEST, MICHAEL--[1][2][11][16]

DERMOT, THOMAS AH.
REDCAM, TOM--[1]JAMAICAN

DERMOUT-INGERMANN, HELENA
DERMOUT, MARIA--[31]

DERN, E. PEARL GADDIS
CLAYFORD, JAMES--V. BERCH/S. HOLLAND-ARCPR, BAE 18,[9]
COURTLAND, ROBERTA--[1][8][9]
CRAIG, GEORGIA--[8][9]
DERN, EROLIE--[9]
DERN, PEGGY--[8][9]
GADDIS, PEGGY--V. BERCH/S. HOLLAND-ARCPR, BAE 15,[8][9]
JORDAN, GAIL--V. BERCH/S. HOLLAND-ARCPR, BAE 18,[8][9][26]ROM--
"GAMBLING ON LOVE"
"LOVE ON THE RUN"
KNOWLES, MARTHA--V. BERCH/S. HOLLAND-ARCPR, BAE 18--
LEE, CAROLINE [CAROLINA]--[1][8]
LINDSAY, PERRY--V. BERCH/S. HOLLAND-ARCPR, BAE 18,[8][9][26]ROM--
"DESIRE UNDER THE ROSE"
SHERMAN, GAIL--[1]
SHERMAN, JOAN [JANE]--V. BERCH/S. HOLLAND-ARCPR, BAE 18,[8][9]

DEROIN, NANCY
ROSS, NANCY--[1]

DERRICK, HENRY
DOUGLAS, GEORGE--W/MRS. GEORGE FERME,[34]--
OLIPHANT "MYS OF NORTH FORTUNE" 1895

DERRICK, NEIL
ELLIOTT, BRUCE--W/EDWARD FIELD,[21][26][32]--
"VILLAGE"
DS "JUNGLE JAZZ" JUN '44
SD "CRIME GOES TO COLLEGE" JUN '44
SD "CASE OF MELTING ARTICHOKES" JUL '44
SD "DEATH PACES THE WIDOW'S WALK" OCT '44
JU "COCKTAIL JUNGLE" JAN '56

DERRINCOURT, WILLIAM
DAY, WILLIAM--[13]

DERVEER, MAX VAN
HALLIDAY, BRETT--T. JOHNSON, INDEX TO MSMM IN ECHOES #23, HP

DES ESSAUT, M. DAVRELLE
MAITRE--[1]

DES ORMEAUX, J.J.
GARY, GENE--[11]SF

DES ROCHES, FRANCIS
FRANDERE--[1]

DES VOIGNES, JULES VERNE
OLNEY, OLIVER--[1]

DESFONTAINES, PIERRE
GULLIVER, JOHN--[2]

DESFOSSES, HELEN
COHN, HELEN DESFOSSES--[31]

DESLANDES, MADELAINE A.E.
OSSIT--[1]

DESMARAIS, OVID E.
DEMARIS, OVID--VICTOR BERCH, MONARCH PSEUDS., BAE 9, P26,[3]

DESMOND, ARTHUR
RAGNAR REDBEARD--[13]

DESNOS, ROBERT
ANDIER, PIERRE--[1]
CANCALE--[1][31]
GALLOIS, LUCIEN--[1]
GULLOIS, VALENTIN--[1]

DESROSIERS, MARIE A.T.
LE NORMAND, MICHELLE--[1]

DESSAUER, FRIEDRICH
STAB, JAKOB--[39]GERMAN

DESSAUR, CATHERINE IRMA
BURNIER, ANDREAS--[1]

DESTOUCHES, LOUIS FERDIN.
CELINE, LOUIS FERDINAND--[1][22]FRENCH

DETLEFSEN, THEA
SOMMERER, THEA--[39]GERMAN

DETTMANN, HANS EDUARD
DANN, EDWARD--[39]GERMAN

DETZER, KARL
COSTELLO, MICHAEL--[1][31]
HENDERSON, WILLIAM--[1]
WOODS, LELAND--[1]

DEUCHAR, MAUDE
TREMAINE, HERBERT--[1]

DEUTSCH, HERMAN
BAKER, HUGH--W/DONALD HUGH HIGGINS--
HOUGHTON "CARTWRIGHT IS DEAD, SIR!" '36

DEUTSCHER, ISAAC
DEUTSCH, KURT--[1]
PEREGRINE--[22][31]POLISH
SINGER, KURT D[EUTSCH]--[1]
SINGER, KURT--[1][32]MYS--
JCM "CHOCOLATE JUDGE" JUN '63
ME "JOURNEY INTO OBLIVION" FEB '64

DEUTZMAN, LAWRENCE
TRAVIS, LAWRENCE--[1]
[THE] RAMBLER--[1]

DEVANEY, PAULINE
WRAITH, JOHN--W/EDWIN APPS,[8]

DEVANEY, ROBERT
ABBOT, SANDRA--[3]
CHALMERS, GEORGETTE--V. BERCH LTR,9/93--
LEIS BK-"BIG MOUTH:CONFESSIONS OF A PORNO STAR" '75
MACIVERS, SARAH--[3]
MacF "CURSE OF RAVENSWOOD" '73
BELM "CRY OF THE WIND" '74
BELM "NIGHT WITHOUT END" '75

DEVEER, MAX VAN
HALLIDAY, BRETT--T. JOHNSON, ECHOES #23, P16, HP--
MSMM "SHADOW OF FEAR" JAN '72
MSMM "A MAN OF VIOLENCE" MAR '72
MSMM "BLOOD RUNS RED" JUN '72
MSMM ".5M DIAMOND CAPER" SEP '72
MSMM "MAFIA PAYS A RANSOM" NOV '72
MSMM "SPY WHO CAME HOME" JAN '73
MSMM "MURDER AT DONDO BEACH" MAR '73
MSMM "STRYCHNINE SMILE" MAY '73
MSMM "SNATCH A DEAD MAN" JUL '73
MSMM "DEATH STROLLS IN FLAMINGO PARK" NOV '73
MSMM "DEATH OF AN INNOCENT" JAN '74
MSMM "DOUBLE DATE WITH DEATH" MAR '74
MSMM "A PERFECT WOMAN TO MURDER" MAY '74
MSMM "DEATH RIDES THE BLACK MARKET" JUL '74
MSMM "RICH DIE, TOO" OCT '74
MSMM "CLUE OF THE PEKING MAN" SEP '74
MSMM "THREE DOLLS, THREE CASKETS" MAR '75
MSMM "TIMETABLE FOR TERROR" JUN '75
MSMM "BLEEDING SHADOWS" FEB '76
MSMM "BRONZ STATUE MURDERS" AUG '76
MSMM "A CLIMATE FOR MURDER" SEP '76

DEVERY, ELIZABETH COLEMAN
CLIFT, BETTY--[1]

DEVINE, DAVID MCDONALD
DEVINE, D.M.--[1][5][34]MYS--
COLLINS "ROYSTON AFFAIR" '64
COLLINS "FIFTH CORD" '67 & 5 MORE
DEVINE, DOMINIC--[1][3][5]
COLLINS "SLEEPING TIGER" '68
COLLINS "ILLEGAL TENDER" '70 4 MORE
MUNRO, DAVID--[1][32]MYS--
LM "REFLECTIONS ON A MIRROR" AUG '51

DEVLAN, EUGENE
FOWLER, GENE--[1]

DEVON, PAUL
DAWSON, ERASMUS--[2]

DEVOTO, BERNARD AUGUSTIN
HEWES, CADY--[8][28][31]--
HOUGHTON & MIFFLIN "WOMEN & CHILDREN FIRST" '56
AUGUST, JOHN--[34]MYS--
LITTLE "TROUBLED STAR" '39
LITTLE "RAIN BEFORE SEVEN" '40
LITTLE "ADVANCE AGENT" '41
LITTLE "WOMAN IN THE PICTURE" '44

DEVRIES, LAURA LEE
GORDON, LAURA--[26]ROM--
HARL 255 "SCARLET SEASON"
HARL 282 "TERROR BY DESIGN"

DEWAR, HUBERT STEPHEN L.
WESSEX REDIVIVUS--[8]

DEWEESE, EUGENE
DEWEESE, JEAN--[2][3][7][23][31]MYS/SF--
10 NOVELS '75-8
STRATTON, THOMAS--W/ROBERT S. COULSON, J.A. CORRICK, BAE 4,[2][3][23]MYS/SF--
MU "INVISABILITY AFFAIR '67
MU "MIND TWISTER AFFAIR" '67
THOMAS, VICTORIA--W/CONNIE KUGI,[1][21]ROM--
"GINGER'S WISH"
DEWEESE, GENE--[31]

DEWEY, ARIANE
ARUEGO, ARIANE--[31][33]

DEWEY, THOMAS B.
BRANDT, TOM--[3][5][18]MYS--
POPLB 539 "KISS ME HARD" '53
POPLB 584 "RUN BROTHER, RUN" '54
WAINER, CORD--V. BERCH-GM PSEUDS, PP 33,[5][18]--
GM 276 "MOUNTAIN GIRL" '52

DEWISME, CHARLES
VERNES, HENRI--[34]--
CORGI "CITY OF A THOUSAND DRUMS" '66
CORGI "DINOSAUR" '66
CORGI "WHITE GORILLA" '67
CORGI "TREASURE OF THE GOLCONDAS" '67
CORGI "OPERATION PARROT '68

DEWITT, EDITH OPENSHAW
DE FORREST, JULIE--[31]

DEXHEIMER, LUDWIG
TOKKO, RI--[39]GERMAN/SF

DEY, FREDERIC VAN R.
BECKMAN, ROSS--[1]
BEECKMAN, ROSS--W/DONALD FAIRDE,[11][34]MYS--
WATT "LAST WOMAN"
"PRINCESS ZARA" BOTH '09
BURR, AARON AINSWORTH--[1][11]
CARTER, NICHOLAS--[3][11][29]MYS,HP--
WHITMAN "GIDEON DREXEL'S MILLIONS" '30
CARTER, NICK--[2][3][5]HP
CLAY, BERTHA M.--[1][22][31]HP
DEY, MARMADUKE--[3][11][29][31]MYS--
STREET "THE POISONED PEN" 1890
GILMORE, MARIAN--[1][11]
ORMOND, FREDERIC--[3][11][29]MYS--
WATT "THE THREE KEYS" '09
VAN DOREN, DIRCK--[1][11]
VANARDY, VARICK--[3][11][29]MYS--
8 NOVELS & SHORT STORIES '13-20

DEY, HATTIE [H] CALHOON
DEY, HARYOT HOLT--[1]

DEYOE, CORI L.
BARKLEY, JESSICA--[9][21][26]ROM--
"MONTANA MAN"
"INTO THE SUNSET"
"FRAME-UP"

DEZORT, MIREK
ORT, MIK--[39]GERMAN/SF

DEZSERY, ENDRE ISTVAN
DEZSERY, ANDRAS--[1]

DI FRANCESCO, PHYLLIS
HARMON, ANNE--W/NIRA HERRMANN,[26]ROM--
"DESERT FLAME"
"WYOMING WILDFIRE"
HERRMANN, PHYLLIS--W/NIRA HERRMANN, [21][26]ROM--
"TWO FOR ONE"
"DESIRE'S DREAM"

DI FRANCO, ANTHONY MARIO
DEFRANCE, ANTHONY--[31][33]

DI LORENZO, EDWARD
ROMAN, VIC--V. BERCH-BRNDN/ BC PSEUDS, BAE 22, P24--

DI PAOLA LEVIN, JORGE A.
DIPI--[1]

DI PRIMA, DIANE
DARRICH, SYBAH--[1][8]--V. BERCH BELIEVES INCORRECT-SEE 'RICHARD ASHBY'

DI TROPPENBURG, ULDERICO
DE RICO, UL--[7]SF--
"THE RAINBOW GOBLINS" '78

DIAL, JOAN MAVIS R.
DEVON, ALEXANDRA--[9]ROM
KENT, KATHERINE--[9][26][31]ROM--
"DREAM TIDE"
"DRUID'S RETREAT"
"TAWNY ROSE" & OTHERS
SINCLAIR, KATHERINE--[9][21][26]ROM--
"A DIFFERENT EDEN"
"FAR HORIZONS"
"VISION OF TOMORROW"
YORK, AMANDA--[9][21][26]ROM--
"BELOVED ENEMY"
"MAN'S BEST FRIEND" & MORE

DIAMANT, GERTRUD
DAHLMANN, GERT--[39]GERMAN

DIAMANT, LINCOLN
GOYA, FRED--[1]
KLOPFINGER, HERMAN III--[1]
MCDOUGAL, STAN--[1]

DIAMOND, BARBARA B.
BENTLEY, BARBARA--[9][21][26]ROM--
"MISTRESS NANCY"

DIAMOND, GRAHAM
LESLIE, ROCHELLE--[9][21][26][31]ROM--
"TEARS OF PASSION, TEARS OF SHAME"

DIAS DA CRUZ, EDDY
REBELO, MARQUES--[1]

DIAS, PATRICK WALTER
JALAP--[1]

DIBBLE, NANCY ANN
DIBELL, ANSEN--[2][7][31]SF--
DAW 'KANTMORE'SERIES #1-3 '78-82

DIBENEDETTO, THERESA
CANTRELL, RAINE--[26]ROM--
"CALICO"
"DESERT SUNRISE"
"TARNISHED HEARTS"
MICHAELS, THERESA--[26]ROM--
"A CORNER OF HEAVEN"
"GIFTS OF LOVE"

DICHTL, RUTH [v.M.]
FISCHER, RUTH--[39]GERMAN
MODESTA--[39]GERMAN
VON MAYENBURG, RUTH--[39]GERMAN
WIEDEN, RUTH--[39]GERMAN

DICK, KAY
LANE, EDWARD--[8]
SCOTT, JEREMY--[2][3][7][23]MYS/SF--
"THE MANDRAKE ROOT" '46
"AT CLOSE OF EVE" '47
ALLEN "ANGELS IN YOUR BEER" '79
ALLEN "HUNTED" '80

DICK, OLIVER LAWSON
OLIVER, ROBERT--W/ROBERT CARRIER,[8]

DICK, PHILIP K.
PHILLIPS, RICHARD--[1][11]
VAN DYKE, MARK--[2]

DICK-HUNTER, NOEL
N.D.H.--[8]

DICK-LAUDER, GEORGE A.
LAUDER, GEORGE--[1][8][11]

DICKE, WILLIS
WYSEMAN, DEMETRIUS--[1]

DICKENS, CHARLES
COLLINS, CHARLES--W/WILKIE COLLINS,[11][32]--
EW "LA TETE NOIRE" NOV '65

DICKENS, DORIS
REED, SIMON--W/MARY H. DANBY,[8][31]--
"QUICK QUIZ" '81

DICKEY, ROBERT PRESTON
DICKEY, R.P.--[1]

DICKIE, CHARLES HERBERT--
[AN] M.P.--[1]

DICKINS, ANTHONY STEWART
DICKINS, A.S.M.--[31]

DICKINSON, ANNE HEPPLE
HEPPLE, ANNE--[1][8]

DICKINSON, DONALD PERCY
DICKINSON, DON--[31]

DICKINSON, MRS. T.P.
BENEDICT, HESTER A.--[1]

DICKINSON, PETER
DE BRISSAC, MALCOLM--[1][31]

DICKINSON, SUSAN E.
VERNON, ALDA--[1]

DICKINSON, WALTER S.
DICKINSON, RUBE--[1]

DICKINSON-WILDBERG, HEINO
WILDBERG, BODO--[39]GERMAN/SF

DICKMANN, ERNST GUNTER
DYCK, NORMAN--[39][40]GERMAN/MYS--
"DER HIMMEL SCHLPOSS DIE AUGEN" '85

DICKS, TERRANCE
BLAND, ROBIN--[2]

DICKSCHAT, OTTO
KAMP, STEFFEN--[39]GERMAN

DICKSON, GORDON R[UPERT]
SERLING, ROD--[4][7]GHOSTED--
"DEVILS & DEMONS"
"R.S.'s TRIPLE W"

DICKSON, JAMES GRIERSON
KING, HILARY--[1][3][29]MYS--
AMALG "PARTNERS IN CRIME" '51
AMALG "MAN FROM DIEPPE" '52 & MORE

DICKSON, KWESI ABOTSIA
DICKSON, K.A.--[1][31]

DICKSON, NAIDA
RICHARDSON, GRACE LEE--[1][33]

DIDIER, EUGENE LEMOINE
LEMOINE--[1]

DIEDRICH, KLAUS
ASKON, TOM--[39]GERMAN/SF
HOWARD, H.P.--W/RONALD HAHN
& HORST PUKALLUS,[39]GERMAN/SF

DIEDRICHS, EDMUND
COTTON, JERRY--[39]GERMAN/MYS,HP

DIEGO CENDOYA, GERARDO
DIEGO, GERARDO--[31]

DIEHL, W.W.
CLAY, DUNCAN--[22]AMERICAN

DIEHN, ROSMARIE
RUTTE-DIEHN, ROSEMARIE--[39]GERMAN/JUV

DIEHNEL, TABITHA ELLEN
DIEHNEL, ELLIE TATUM--[1]

DIEKENGA, I.E.
DON--[1]

DIENER, BERTHA [E]
GALAHAD, SIR--[39]GERMAN

DIENES, ZOLTAN PAUL
ZED--[1]

DIERKES, RUDOLF
KESS, ROLF--[39]GERMAN/MYS
MEYER, ED--[39]GERMAN/MYS

DIETL, FRANZ
SECUNDUS, NOE--[39]GERMAN

DIETRICH, KARL A.
JEROME, FRED G.--[39]GERMAN

DIETRICH, RICHARD V.
DIRK, R.--[31]
KIRK, R.--[31]

DIETSCH, ARTHUR
ZORRO, JOSE--[39]GERMAN

DIETSCH, WERNER
FRISCO, TOM--[39]GERMAN/WEST
HOFER, PETRA--[39]GERMAN/ADV
KALLMER, ULLRICH--[39]GERMAN/ADV
MAREK, MAX--[39]GERMAN/ADV
STIRLING, GLENN--[39]GERMAN/WEST

DIETZ, ELISABETH [H]
DIETZ, BETTY WARNER--[1][31]

DIETZ, GERTRUD
FUSSENEGGER, GERTRUD--[39]GERMAN

DIETZ, HOWARD
FRECKLES--[8]

DIEZ, MRS. M.A.
HENRY, WILLIAM--[1]

DIFFIN, CHARLES WILLARD
WILLARD, C.D.--[2][11][15]SF--
ASS "THE EYE OF ALLAH" JUN '30

DIGGS, ELLEN IRENE
DIGGS, IRENE--[31]

DIHATI, MUHAMMAD-I MAS'UD
MUHAMMAD-I MAS'UD--[22]PERSIAN

DIHKHODA, ALI AKBAR
DAKHOW--[22]RUSSIAN

DIKTY, JULIAN [C] MAY
CHAIN, JULIAN--[1][2][11]
CUNNINGHAM, BOB--[1][31]
DIKTY, JUDY--[7]SF
FALCONER, LEE [N]--[7][23][31]SF--
"A GAZETEER OF THE HYBORIAN WORLD
OF CONAN" '77
FEILEN, JOHN--[1][31]
GRANT, MATTHEW G.--[1][31]
MAY, JULIAN [C]--[2][7][23]SF--NUMEROUS NOVELS
THORNE, IAN--[7][23][33]SF--12 NOVELS
THORNE, JEAN WRIGHT--[1]
ZANDERBERGEN, GEORGE--[1]

DILCOCK, NOREEN
CHRISTIAN, JILL--[9][21][26][31]ROM--
"THE TENDER BOND"
"A SCENT OF LEMONS"
FORD, NORREY--[9][21][26][31]ROM--
"LET LOVE ABIDE"
"ONE HOT SUMMER" & MORE
WALFORD, CHRISTIAN--[1][9]ROM

DILKS, JOHN M.
LA THORNE, JEAN--[1]

DILKS, JOHN M.--
[A] TRAVELING SALESMAN--[1]

DILL, JAMES REID
J.R.D.--[1]

DILLARD, POLLY HARGIS
HARGIS, PAULINE--[9]ROM
HARGIS, POLLY--[9]ROM

DILLENBURGER, ELMY
LANG, ELMY--[39]GERMAN/JUV

DILLENBURGER, INGEBORG
BRUGGER, KARLA--[39]GERMAN/JUV

DILLON, EMILE JOSEPH
LANIN, E.B.--[1][8]

DILLON, JOHN M[YLES]--
[THE] WESTERN SPY--[1]

DILLON, LIONEL J. & DIANE
DILLON, LEO--[7]SF--
"THE ART OF LEO & DIANE DILLION" '81

DILLON, R. PATRICIA
DILLON, PATRICIA--[21]ROM--
"LOVE ALONE"

DILNOT, GEORGE
FROEST, FRANK--[8]

DIMEN, MURIEL
DIMEN-SCHEIN, MURIEL--[31]

DIMENSTEIN, CATHERINE WE.
WELLS, CATHERINE--[7]SF--
BAL "THE EARTH IS ALL THAT LASTS" '91

DIMICK, CHERYLLE LINDSEY
LINDSEY, DAWN--[3][21][26]MYS/ROM--
DBLDY "DUCHESS OF VIDEL" '78 & MORE

DIMMITZ, ARTHUR L.
ALLEN, DON B.--[1]
ALLEN, T.D.--W/TERRIL DIENER ALLEN,[1][33]

DIMOND, EDMUNDS GREY
DIMOND, E. GREY--[31]

DIMT, CHRISTINE
BUSTA, CHRISTINE--[22]AUSTRIAN

DINGES, JOHN [CHARLES]
MARSANO, RAMON--[1]

DINGLE, A. EDWARD
COTTERELL, BRIAN--[1][3]MYS--
HARRAP "SINISTER EDEN" '34
DINGLE, CAPT.--[1]
SINBAD--[2][3]MYS--
HARRAP "SPIN A YARN" '34
HARRAP "PIPE ALL HANDS" '35
HARRAP "SAILORS DO CARE" '36

DINGLER, MAX
ILGERD, N.M.--[39]GERMAN

DINGLEY, SALLY G[ARRETT]
GARRETT, SALLY--[9][21][26]ROM--
15 NOVELS

DINGWELL, JOYCE
STARR, KATE--[9][21][26]ROM--8 NOVELS

DINHOFER, ALFRED
DINO--[1][31]

DINNEEN, BETTY
NEWARK, ELIZABETH--[33]

DINNER, WILLIAM
DINNER, W. & W. MORUM--[3]MYS--
2 NOVELS & 3 PLAYS '49-64
MORUM, WILLIAM--W/SURREY SMITH,[1]
SMITH, SURREY--W/WILLIAM MORUM,[8][34]MYS--
DMN "NO TEARS FOR TEDDY" '64
BRDMN "ASTONISHED GUARDSMAN" '65
HALE "A GUN FOR DELILAH" '79

DINSDALE, TIMOTHY KAY
DINGLEBERRY, MR.--[1]

DINWIDDIE, FAYE V.L.
FOSTER, FAYE LOVE--[1]

DINWIDDY, JOHN ROWLAND
DINWIDDY, J.R.--[31]

DIPRIMA, DIANE
DUFFY, ROBERT M.--W/ALICE MOLLOY,[14]--
OLYM OPH#2222 "OF SHEEP AND GIRLS" '68

DIRAC, PAUL ADRIEN M.
DIRAC, P.A.M.--[31]

DIRKS, WILHELMINA
DIRKS, WILLY--[31][33]

DISCH, THOMAS M.
DEMIJOHN, THOM--W/JOHN SLADEK,
[2][3][4][23]MYS/SF--
DBLDY "BLACK ALICE" '68
DISCH, TOM--[31]
HARGRAVE, LEONIE--[2][3][4][23][29][31]MYS--
KNOPF "CLARA REEVE" '75
HASTINGS, VICTOR--G. COOK LTR '93,[23]--
"ALFRED THE GREAT"

DISCH, THOMAS M. [CONT]
KNYE, CASSANDRA--W/JOHN SLADEK,
[2][3][4][23][31]MYS/SF--
POPLB "HOUSE THAT FEAR BUILT" '66
NYE, CASSANDRA--G. COOK LTR '93--
BERKELEY ONLY
THORPE, DOBBIN--[1][2]

DISNEY, WALTER ELIAS
DISNEY, WALT--[33]
YENSID, RETLAW--[1][33]

DISSTON, HARRY
HILL, H.D.N.--[31]

DITMARS, RAYMOND LEE--
[THE] SNAKE MAN--[1]

DITTMARSCH, KARL
MENK, F.--[39]GERMAN/SF

DITTON, T.A. BELCHER
DITTON, T.A.B.--L. ROBBINS LTR MAR '94

DITZEN, RUDOLF WILHELM F.
FALLADA, HANS--[2][22][31][39]GERMAN/SF--
"SPARROW FARM, TALE OF A CITY CLERK.." '37

DIVER, JENNY
JONES, MRS. JANE--[1]

DIVINE, ARTHUR DURHAM
DIVINE, DAVID--[2][3][11][31][33]MYS--
5 NOVELS '53-64
RAME, DAVID--[2][3][11][22][33]
SOUTH AFRICA/MYS--

DIVINSKY, NATHAN [JOSEPH]
DIVINSKY, N.J.--[31]

DIVONO, SHARMAN
APPLETON, VICTOR--W/WILLIAM ROTSLER,[7]HP--
STSY 'TOM SWIFT':
"ASTRAL FORTRESS"
"CITY IN THE STARS"
"RESCUE MISSION"
"ALIEN PROBE"
"TERROR ON THE MOONS OF JUPITER"
"WAR IN OUTER SPACE"

DIXELIUS-BRETTNOR, HILDUR
DIXELIUS, HILDUR--[1]

DIXON, ANDREW
SACKETT, HARRY--[1]

DIXON, ARTHUR
WHYE, FELIX--[1][8]

DIXON, ELLA HEPWORTH
WYNMAN, MARGARET--[1][8]

DIXON, HENRY HALL
DRUID, THE--[22]ENGLISH

DIXON, JEAN
HARPER, MARY WOOD--[1][31]
STONE, JOSEPHINE RECT.--[7][33]SF--
ATHENEUM "THOSE WHO FALL FROM THE SUN" '78
ARGO "MUDHEAD" '80
ARGO "PRAISE ALL THE MOONS OF MORNING" '79
ARGO "GREEN IS FOR GALANX" '80

DIXON, LARRY
LACKEY, MERCEDES--W/MERCEDES LACKEY,
B. FRANK '93--
"WINDS OF FATE" '91
"WINDS OF CHANGE" '92
"WINDS OF FURY" '93

DIXON, MARJORIE [MACK]
MACK, MARJORIE--[1]

DIXON, MRS.
LESLIE, EMMA--[1]

DIXON, ROBERT MALCOLM W.
BROWN, HOSANNA--[36]AUSTRALIAN/MYS--
GOLZ "I SPY, YOU DIE" '84
GOLZ "DEATH UPON A SPEAR" '86
DIXON, R.M.W.--[36]AUSTRALIAN

DIXON, ROGER
CHRISTIAN, JOHN--[3][31]MYS--
HARWOOD "FIVE GATES TO ARMEGEDDON" '75
HARWOOD "PERSIAN DEATH TRAP" '76
LEWIS, CHARLES--[8][7][23][31]SF--
HARWOOD "THE CAIN FACTOR" '75

DIXON, SYDENHAM
VIGILANT--[1]

DIXON, THOMAS
COLE, BURT--[2][7][11][23]AMERICAN/SF--
MORROW "THE QUICK" '89

DIXON, W. WILLMOTT
THORMANBY--[3]MYS--
EVERETT "ROMANCES OF THE ROAD" '01
HEATH "THE BLACK BEAN" '13

DIXON, WILLIAM SCARTH
WANDERER--[1]

DJURICIC, ULADEN ST.
DRINCIC, SAVA--[1]
MLAD-MILTIJAD--[1]

DOANE, PELAGIE
HOFFNER, DOROTHY--[8]

DOBELL, ISABEL MARIAN B.
BARCLAY, ISABEL--[1][22][31][33]CANADIAN
DOBELL, I.M.B.--[22][31]CANADIAN

DOBER, CONRAD K.
CONRAD, CON--[8]

DOBKIN, KATHY
DOBKIN, KAYE--[21]ROM--
"DESIRE & DREAMS"
"PROMISE ME TOMORROW"
"A VALENTINE FOR BETSY"

DOBKIN, MARJORIE HOUSEP.
HOUSEPIAN, MARJORIE--[31]

DOBLER, HANSFERDINAND
BARABAN, PETER--[39]GERMAN

DOBLIN, ALFRED
POOT, LINKE--[22][39]GERMAN

DOBNER, MAEVA PARK
PARK, MAEVA--[1][32]MYS--
MH "A DEADLY NUISANCE" MAY '64
AHMM "BEAUTIFUL BLONDE" DEC '63
MH "MURDER, THOUGH IT HAVE NO
TONGUE" FEB '66 & 3 OTHERS

DOBRACZYNSKI, JAN
HOZJUSZ--[1][22][31]POLISH
KUROWSKI, EUGENIUSZ--[1][22][31]POLISH

DOBRE, ION
CRAINIC, NICHIFOR--[22]RUMANIAN

DOBREE, GLADYS MAY M.
DOBREE, VALENTINE--[1]

DOBROGEANU-GHEREA, ION
GHEREA, ION--[22]RUMANIAN

DOBSCHA, LEILA LAURENCE
LAURENCE, LEILA--HAWK/DOBSCHA INTRVW MAY '93

DOBSON, E. PHILIP
SPRING, PHILIP--[22][32]ENGLISH/MYS--
LM "BETWEEN CYPRESS & SLEEP" DEC '63
LM "DARK GLASSES" MAR '57
LM "LABYRINTH" SEPT '61 & 14 OTHERS ALL LM

DOBSON, ELINORE LUCILLE
KEISTER, ELINORE--[31]

DOBSON, JAMES
JAMES, MAC--V. BERCH-BRNDN/
BC PSEUDS, BAE 22, P24

DOBSON, JULIA LISSANT
TUGENDHAT, JULIA--[8]

DOCKWEILER, JOSEPH HAROLD
LAVOND, PAUL DENNIS--W/FREDERIK POHL,
C.M. KORNBLUTH & ROBERT LOWNDES,[1]
WHITNEY, ELLIOTT--W/FREDERICK ARNOLD
KUMMER, JR.,[11]SF
WYLIE, DIRK--[2][11][23]ALSO CO-WROTE
WITH CYRIL KORNBLUTH & FREDERIK POHL

DODD, ALLEN ROBERT
ALLEN, ROBERT--[2][3]MYS--
HODDER "CAPT. GARDINER OF THE
INTERNL. POLICE" '16

DODD, EDWARD HOWARD JR.
HILL, W.M.--[1][31]

DODD, MARGUERITE
BRAYMER, MARGUERITE--[31]

DODD, MARIA ASSUNTA I.V.
DODD, BELLA V.--[31]

DODD, WAYNE DONALD
WAYNE, DONALD--[1][8]

DODGE, ELIZABETH C.
STEDMAN--[1]

DODGE, FREDERICK
PAULDING, FREDERICK--[1]

DODGE, JOSEPHINE DASKAM
BACON, J.D.--[8]

DODGE, MARY ABIGAIL
HAMILTON, GAIL--[1][22]AMERICAN

DODGE, MARY ELIZABETH M.
J.S.--[1]
M.M.D.--[1]
STACY, JOEL--[1]

DODGE, OSSIAN E.
ORT, IVAN--[1]

DODGE, WENDELL PHILLIPS
FLETCHER, RICHARD--[1]
PHILLIPS, W.--[1]

DODGSON, CHARLES LUTWIDGE
CARROLL, LEWIS--[2][11][23][33]SF

DOEBLIN, ALFRED
BOERNE, ALFRED--[1]
DOBLIN, ALFRED--[31]
LINKE, POOT--[1]

DOEHMEL, FRIEDRICH
LEE, CONRAD--[39]GERMAN

DOEHNEL, KARL FRIEDRICH
SPITZNAGEL, D. KILIAN Z.--[39]GERMAN

DOELLERDT, ARTUR
STEENBERG, SVEN--[39]GERMAN

DOERFFLER, ALFRED
DUNN, HARRIS--[8][22][31]AMERICAN
FORD, FRED--[8][22][31]AMERICAN
THOMAS, CARL H.--[1][8][22]

DOERRIE, DORIS
DORRIE, DORIS--[31]

DOERRSCHUCK, HUBERT
SIEBENPUNKT, AMADEUS--[39]GERMAN

DOHANEY, JEAN
DOHANEY, M.T.--[31]

DOHERTY, BARBARA
FERRER, SISTER VINCENT--[31]

DOHERTY, C.L.
GRACE, C.L.--SUE FEDER/MARV LACHMAN JULY '93

DOHERTY, EDWARD JOSEPH
DOHERTY, EDDIE--[31]
O'DOHERTY, NED--W. MURRAY-ECHOES #26

DOHERTY, GEOFFREY DONALD
DOHERTY, G.D.--[1]

DOHERTY, IVY RUBY D.
HARDWICK, SYLVIA--[1][8][31]

DOHERTY, P.C.
CLYNES, MICHAEL--DEADLY PLEASURES #3,
P34--HIST MYS SERIES
GRACE, C.L.--DEADLY PLEASURES #3,
P34--HIST MYS SERIES
HARDING, PAUL--LACHMAN-EASTER LST '93,
DEADLY PLEAS. #3--HIST MYS SERIES

DOHERTY, ROBERT R.
YONGE, REMINGTON--[1]

DOHRING, KARL SIEGFRIED
HERDEGEN, HANS--[39]GERMAN
RAVENDRO, RAVI--[39]GERMAN

DOINEL, JULES
KOSTKA, JEAN--[1]

DOLAN, MIKE
MICHAELS, JACK--V. BERCH-BRNDN/
BC PSEUDS, BAE 22, P24

DOLBERG, ALEXANDER
BURG, DAVID--[1][31]

DOLBEY, ETHEL & GEOFFREY
HAWTHORNE, E.M.D.--[1][3]MYS--
HAMILTON "QUIETLY SHE LIES" '53

DOLE, NATHAN HASKELL
N.H.D.--[1]

DOLEZAL, ERICH
LINDENAU, ERIK--[39]GERMAN/SF

DOLGOFF, SAM
WIENER, SAM--[1]

DOLGOV, BORIS
DOLBOKOV--W/WAYNE WOODARD,[2][11]

DOLINSKY, MEYER
DOLINSKY, MIKE--[1][11][23][31]SF--
"MIND ONE" '72

DOLL, HANELORE
DONG, LEONIE--[39]GERMAN

DOLL, HERBERT GERHARD
COMMENT, JEAN PIERROT--[39]GERMAN
DALLMANN, EHM--[39]GERMAN
HEGEDO, HERBERT G.--[39]GERMAN
SAHDAS, GERD--[39]GERMAN
STICHLING, CASPAR--[39]GERMAN
WEIKERSHEIM, MATTHIAS--[39]GERMAN

DOLLEN, CHARLES JOSEPH
BENEDICT, JOSEPH--[22][31]

DOLLEY, REGINALD HUGH
DOLLEY, MICHAEL--[1]

DOLMATCH, THEODORE BIELEY
JOSEPHS, STEPHEN--[31]

DOLPHIN, REGINALD C.
DEVON, NICHOLAS--[1]
DEVON, NICOLA--[1][34]MYS--
ACE "HOUSE OF ILLUSION" '69
DOLPHIN, REX--[29][32]MYS--
AMALG "TROUBLE IS MY NAME" '61
EW "PHANTOM GUEST" AUG '64
EW "LAST BANDITS" SEPT '64
EW "NO MARGIN FOR ERROR" AUG '65
REID, DESMOND--[1][34]MYS,HP--
AMALG "THE WORLD SHAKERES" '60
SAXON, PETER--R.E. BRINEY-BAE 17, P9, MYS,HP--
BERK "VAMPIRES OF FINISTERE" '70
WELLSLEY, JULIE--[34]MYS,HP--
DELL "CASTLE ON THE MOUNTAIN" '72
WILLIAMS, RICHARD--[1][34]MYS,HP--
AMALG "SPEAK ILL OF THE DEAD" '63

DOLSON, FRANKLIN ROBERT
DOLSON, FRANK--[31]

DOMASCHEVITSKY, ISAIAH
BERSCHADSKY, ISAIAH--[22]RUSSIAN

DOMBROWSKI, IVAN
GRAHAM, JOHN--[1]

DOMBROWSKI, KATRINA
K.O.S.--[2]

DOMBROWSKI, THEODOR
CORMAC, BORIS--[39]GERMAN/SF/WEST
DE LORCA, FRANK--[39]GERMAN/SF/WEST,HP
JONES, EVERETT--[39]GERMAN/SF/WEST,HP
MONGO, MARCOS--[39]GERMAN/SF/WEST,HP
READ, JACK--[39]GERMAN/SF/WEST

DOMBROWSKI, THEODOR [CONT]
SKINNER, ARNO--[39]GERMAN/SF/WEST

DOMERGUE, MAURICE
DUNOYER, MAURICE--[3]1

DOMINGO, PEDRO
SANTOS, DOMINGO--[1][2]

DOMINICK, MARGARET
D.E.A.--[2][11]

DOMINIQUE, ANTOINE
PONCHARDIER, DOMINIQUE--[1]

DOMMARTIN, LEON
D'ARDENNE, JEAN--[22]BELGIAN

DONABEDIAN, BAIRJ
WESTERLY, DANIEL--[7]SF--
POCK "DEVOTION" '87

DONAHEY, MARY DICKERSON
DICKERSON, MARY A.--[1]
HALLOWAY, JANE--[1]

DONAHUE, PHILLIP JOHN
DONAHUE, PHIL--[31]

DONALD, ANABEL
GALT, SERENA--[31]

DONALD, CHARLES HILLARD
EXILE--[1]

DONALDSON, BRYN STEVENS
STEVENS, BRYN--[1]

DONALDSON, DALE C.
ALDRICH, FRANCES--[2]
CEPHUS, DELORES--[2]
DEMATHEWS, MO--[2]
DEMIC, WILLIAM--[2]
IZZO, J. JR.--[2]
KELLY, RENYARD--[2]
MALVERN, HUGH--[2]
MCTAVISH, PAULINE--[2]
PETERS, OTHELLO F.--[2]
ROSS, REBECCA--[2]

DONALDSON, FRANCIS
NEWTON, MACDONALD--[34]MYS--
BOARDMAN "TO HAVE & TO HOLD" '63

DONALDSON, MARGARET
SALTER, MARGARET LENNOX--[1]

DONALDSON, STEPHEN R.
STEPHENS, REED--[2][3][23][29]MYS/SF--
BAL "MAN WHO KILLED HIS BROTHER" '80
BAL "MAN WHO RISKED HIS PARTNER" '84
BAL "MAN WHO TRIED TO GET AWAY" '90

DONALDSON, WILLIAM
LEGRIS, JEAN-LUC--[8]
ROOT, HENRY--[8]

DONALDSON, WILLIE
CHURCH, TALBOT--[1]

DONART, ARTHUR C[HARLES]
DONAT, ANTON--[1][31]

DONCEV-KORALOV, EMIL
KORALOV, EMIL--[1]

DONDAY, AUGUSTE MARIE
O'NEDDY, PHILOTHIE--[1]

DONGES, GUNTER
ACTON, JOHN D.--[39]GERMAN/MYS
BRASTER, MIKE B.--[39]GERMAN/MYS
BRIESTER, JEFF--[39]GERMAN/WEST,HP
CARSON, GAY D.--[39]GERMAN/MYS
CILLINGH, DAN--[39]GERMAN
COLLINS, CONNY--[39]GERMAN/HOR
CONTER, JEFF--[39]GERMAN/WEST,HP
COTTON, JERRY--[39]GERMAN/MYS,HP
DE VALLON, HENRI--[39]GERMAN
DRILLING, RICHARD W.--[39]GERMAN/MYS
DRIVING, MAC--[39]GERMAN
GILLANE, MUCKY--[39]GERMAN/MYS
GOBINAL, CHESTER--[39]GERMAN
LANDING, JERRY--[39]GERMAN
LARRING, GLENN--[39]GERMAN
LONSDALE, JERRY--[39]GERMAN
VAN KESSEL, ROLF--[39]GERMAN
WENDT, JULIA--[39]GERMAN
WILDING, PAT--[39]GERMAN,HP

DONICH, CATHERINE LEIGH
LEIGH, CATHERINE--W/LINDA S. WOLTHAUSEN, [21][26]ROM--
"A PLACE FOR THE HEART"

DONICHT, MARK ALLEN
ALLEN, MARCUS--[1][31]
ALLEN, MARK--[1][31]

DONISTHORPE, IDA M.L.
PANSY--[1]

DONKERSLOOT, NICOLAAS A.
DONKER, ANTHONIE--[22]DUTCH

DONLEAVY, JAMES PATRICK
DONLEAVY, J.P.--[1]

DONN-BYRNE, BRIAN OSWALD
BYRNE, DONN--[1][8][17][32]MYS/ROM--
EQMM "A QUATRAIN OF LING TAI FU'S" MAY '48
EQMM "AN INFRINGEMENT OF THE DECALOGUE" MAY '50
NUMEROUS ROM NOVELS
O'BEIRNE, BRIAN--[1]

DONNADIEU, MARGUERITE
DURAS, MARGUERITE--[1]

DONNELLY, AUSTIN S.
BULLEN BEAR--[1][8][31]

DONNELLY, IGNATIUS
BOISGILBERT, EDMUND--[2][7][11][31]SF--
"CAESAR'S COLUMN"
"DOCTOR HUGUET: A NOVEL"

DONNELLY, THOMAS F.
BOOKWORM--[1]
POMEROY, EUGENE--[1]

DONNER, BILL
BRAND, NAT--MASK READER, MR104

DONNET, MICHAEL G.L.M.
MIKE--[1]

DONNY, JULIUS
DAHL, FRITZ--[39]GERMAN

DONOHUE, FRANK
GAYLL, ARTHUR--[13]AUSTRALIAN

DONOHUE, HAL
BARRY, TOM--[1]

DONOVAN, BONITA R.
DONOVAN, BONNIE--[1][31]

DONOVAN, GRACE WALLACE
KEON, GRACE--[34]MYS--
BENZIGER "WHEN LOVE IS STRONG" '07

DONOVAN, JOHN
HENNESSEY, HUGH--[8]

DONOVAN, LAURENCE
BROOKER, WALLACE--LACHMAN LST '93, W. MURRAY-ECHOES #47,[29][37]HP--
SKP "RED HEART PEARLS" '36
SHP "BLACK LEOPARD PRINCESS" '36
DOCS "BLACK IVORY DEATH" NOV '37
SKP "DEVILS OF THE RIVER"
SKP "BLACK DAYLIGHT"
SKP "BREATHLESS ISLAND"
SKP "CLIPPER MENACE"
SKP "GREEN PLAGUE"
CRB "DEVIL OF DIAMONDS" JUL '42
DOCS "DEATH'S PAY-OFF MAN" & 9 OTHERS
DENT, LESTER--[2]HP
DUNN, LARRY--W. MURRAY-ECHOES #47
GOODRICH, CLIFFORD--W. MURRAY-ECHOES #47, [29][37]MYS,HP--
WHSP "DEAD WHO TALKED" '36
WHSP "MURDER QUEENS"
WHSP "FOOTBALL RACKETEERS"
WHSP "MURDERS IN CRAZYLAND"
WHSP "MURDER ON THE LINE"
WHSP "LOST FACE MURDERS"
WHSP "RED HATCHETS"
WHSP "MURDER BROTHERHOOD"
WHSP "KILL THEM FIRST" & 6 OTHERS '36-7
SHD "BULLET BAIT"
SHD "BOULEVARD OF DEATH" '37-40
GRIDLEY, AUSTIN--W. MURRAY-ECHOES #47, PPCC#5,[29]MYS,HP
HARLEY, BRUCE--W. MURRAY-ECHOES #47, MYS,HP
JONES, G. WAYMAN--W. MURRAY-ECHOES #5, T. JOHNSON LTR '94, MYS,HP--
BLKB "MURDER PROPHET"
LAURENCE, DON--W. MURRAY-ECHOES #47
LAWRENCE, DON--W. MURRAY-ECHOES #47
ROBESON, KENNETH--[7][34]MYS,HP--
BB "MURDER MELODY" '67
BB "COLD DEATH" '68
BB "MAD EYES" '69
BB "HAUNTED OCEAN" '70
BB "HE COULD STOP THE WORLD" '70
BB "LAND OF LONG JUJU" '70
BB "MEN WHO SMILED NO MORE" '70
BB "MURDER MIRAGE" '72
BB "BLACK SPOT" '74
SCANLON, C.K.M.--W. MURRAY-ECHOES #47,MYS,HP
STORM, JACK--W. MURRAY-ECHOES #26 & #47, MYS,HP--
CLS "THE CRIME PROPHET" JAN '41
CRB "THE MURDER MAKER" MAY '41
WALLACE, ROBERT--[34]MYS,HP--
PD "SAMPAN MURDERS" SEPT '39
PD "MONEY MAD MURDERS" NOV '39
PD "THE CURIO MURDERS" MAR '41
PD "MURDER STALKS A BILLION" DEC '41
PD "MURDER MOON OVER MIAMI" JAN '42
PD "MURDER CUTS DIAMOND" SEPT '42
PD "DEATH TO THE LAUGHING CLOWN" OCT '42
REGENCY "BROADWAY MURDERS" '65
WAYNE, WALTER--W. MURRAY-ECHOES #47,MYS,HP

DONOVAN, PETER
P.O., D.--[1][8]

DONSON, CYRIL
CORDIS, LONNY--[1][28][31]
HARTFORD, VIN--[1][28][31]
KIDD, RUSSELL--[1][28][31]ENGLISH/WEST--
HALE "THROW A TALL SHADOW" '67
HALE "BATTLE FOR BEAR HEAD CREEK" '82
HALE "BANNER'S BACK FORM BOOT HILL" '83
MACKIN, ANITA--[1][28][31]
PINDER, CHUCK--[8][28]

DOOLEY, JANET M.
HENLEY, LIZ--W/LYDIA S. HENRY,[26]ROM--
"JUST HER TYPE"

DOOLING, DAVID JR.
DOOLING, DAVE--[31]

DOOLITTLE, HILDA
H.D.--[8][22][31]AMERICAN
HELFORTH, JOHN--[31]--
DARANTIERE "NIGHTS" '35

DORCY, MARY JEAN
BENNETT, JEAN FRANCIS--[1]
[SISTER] MARY JEAN--[1]

DORE, CLAIRE MORIN
FRANCE, CLAIRE--[1][31][22]CANADIAN
MORIN, CLAIRE--[22]CANADIAN

DORER, FRANCIS CATHERINE
DORN, FRANK--W/NANCY DORER,[7][23]SF--
"WHEN NEXT I WAKE" '79
"EAGLE SEQUENCE" '79/80

DORFMEISTER, GREGOR
GREGOR, MANFRED--[39]GERMAN

DORGAN, THOMAS ALOYSIUS
TAD--[8][22]AMERICAN

DORGELES, ROLAND
LECAVELE, ROLAND--[31]

DORLIAE, PETER GONDRO
DORLIAE, SAINT--[1][31]

DORLING, HENRY TAPRELL
TAFFRAIL--[1][3][29]MYS--
31 NOVELS '16-56

DORMAN, MICHAEL
BISHOP, JACK--[1][22]AMERICAN

DORN, DEAN M.
MORGAN, MICHAEL--W/C.E. CARLE,
[22][29][32][34]MYS--
RANDOM "NINE MORE LIVES" '47
ACE D9 "DECOY" '53
PYR 116 "HIS KIND OF WOMAN" '54
HU "THE BLONDE EYE" JUN '55

DORN, WILLIAM S.
EARLSON, IAN MALCOLM--[31]

DORNBUSH, JOAN
DOHRN, MADELYN--W/MARY DE VORE,
[9][21][26]ROM--
SIL "BEST DEFENSE"
SIL "LABOR OF LOVE" & MORE

DORNER, CLAUS S.
MAXWELL, SILVESTER--[39]GERMAN/MYS
SILVESTER, CLAUS--[39]GERMAN/MYS

DOROSLAVIC, MILUTIN
DOR, MILO--[39][40]GERMAN/MYS-
"INTERNATIONAL ZONE" '53
"UND EINER FOLGT DEM ANDEREN" '53
FEDOR--W/REINHARD FEDERMANN,[39][40]GERMAN/MYS

DORR, JULIA CAROLINE
RIPLEY, JULIA C.--[1][8]

DORRIS, MICHAEL [ANTHONY]
DORRIS, MICHAEL A.--[33]NAME VARIATION
NORTH, MILOU--W/LOUISE EDRICH,[31]--
"WOMAN" - BOOK REVIEWS

DORSAINVIL, JUSTIN C.
DORSAINVIL, J.C.--[1]

DORSEY, CHRISTINE
ELLIOTT, CHRISTINE--W/ANNE ELLIOTT,
BOOK BIO,[9][21][26]ROM--
"THE CAPTAIN'S CONQUEST"

DORSEY, HELEN
BLINN, HELEN--[1]
BLINN, JOHNA--[31]

DORSEY, SARAH ANNE
FILIA ECCLESIAE--[1]

DORST, JEAN PIERRE
D'URSTELLE, PIERRE--[22][31]FRENCH

DORTENWALD, RUDOLF
ROTH, MICHAEL--[39]GERMAN
RUDOR, JACK--[39]GERMAN

DORWORTH, ALICE GREY
LYNCH, GREY--[1]

DOS SANTOS, JOYCE AUDY
ZARINS, JOYCE AUDY--[33]

DOTSON, ROBERT CHARLES
DOTSON, BOB--[31]

DOTY, GLADYS
DOUGLASS, MARCIA KENT--[31]

DOTY, JEAN SLAUGHTER
SLAUGHTER, JEAN--[1][33]

DOTZLER, URSULA
ISBEL, URSULA--[39][40]GERMAN/MYS--
"NUR EIN FLUGELSCHLAG" '73
"DAS SCHLOSS IN NEBEL" '84

DOUARDO, AUTRAN
DOUARDO, WALDOMIRO AUTRAN--[1]

DOUBLED, VICTOR
PECCADILLE--[1]

DOUBLEDAY, NELTJE
BLANCHAN, NELTJE--[1][8]

DOUGHERTY, WILLIAM
APPLETON, VICTOR II--[7]SF,HP--
STSY 'TOM SWIFT':
HIS FLYING LAB"

DOUGHTY, BRADFORD
DENNY, BRIAN--[1][31]

DOUGHTY, CHARLES MONTAGUE
DOUGHTY, C.M.--[1]

DOUGHTY, FRANCIS W.
CARTER, NICK--[1]MYS,HP
GARNE, GASTON--[23]JUV/SF--
"AL & HIS AIRSHIP" 1903
[A] NY DETECTIVE--[1][37]MYS--
NYDL 'JAMES BRADY' STORIES 1880's

DOUGLAS, ALFRED BRUCE
BOSIE--[1]

DOUGLAS, ARCHIBALD C.
NEMO--[8]

DOUGLAS, CHARLOTTE
MALCOLM, MARINA--[26]ROM--
"SECRETS IN THE SHADOWS"

DOUGLAS, ELSA F.
NORMYX--W/GEORGE NORMAN DOUGLAS,[1][23]--
"UNPROFESSIONAL TALES" 1901

DOUGLAS, GEORGE NORMAN
NORMYX--W/ELSA F. DOUGLAS,[1][23]--
"UNPROFESSIONAL TALES" 1901

DOUGLAS, HELEN GAHAGAN
GAHAGAN, HELEN--[31]

DOUGLAS, JEFF
DOUGLAS, JEFF--W/ANDREW J. OFFUTT--
CARLYLE COMM "BALLING MACHINE"

DOUGLAS, KATHLEEN
DOUGLAS, KATE--[31]

DOUGLAS, KEITH
HATRED, PETER--[8]

DOUGLAS, LALETTE
HAMMETT, LAFAYETTE--[26]ROM--
"THE CAPTAIN'S DOXY"

DOUGLAS, MARY
TEW, MARY--[8]

DOUGLAS, MYRTLE R.
MOROJO--[1][2][11]

DOUGLAS, ROBERT K.
MEADE, L.T.--W/ELIZABETH T. SMITH,[3]MYS--
GARDNER "UNDER THE DRAGON THRONE" 1897

DOUGLASS, ELLSWORTH
WERNER, ISAIAH--[1]

DOUGLASS, PERCIVAL IAN
BEAR, I.D.--[8]
CRANE, HENRY--[8]

DOURADA, [W.F.] AUTRAN
AUTRAN DOURADA, WALDOMIRO--[31]
DOURADA, WALDOMIRO AUTRAN--[31]

DOURAS, MARION CECILIA
DAVIES, MARION--[31]

DOUSE, ANTHONY
REID, DESMOND--W/HOWARD BAKER & G.P. MANN,
[1][34]MYS,HP--
AMALG "DEAD ON CUE" '62

DOUTHWAITE, L[OUIS] C.
GOODALL, CEDRIC--[34]MYS--8 NOVELS '34-50

DOUYAN, JACQUES
ST. MOORE, ADAM--[3]MYS--
INTNL "ANGELFACE TATTERS THE KIMONA" '69

DOW, LAWRENCE T.
LAWRENCE, LARRY--[1]

DOWDELL, DOROTHY [F.K.]
MCALISTAIR, AMANDA--[1][3][29]MYS--
PLAYBOY "PRETTY ENOUGH TO KILL" '76

DOWDEN, ANNE OPHELIA TODD
TODD, ANNE OPHELIA--[1][22][33]AMERICAN

DOWDING, A.L.
RAMSDEN, LEWIS--[1][2]

DOWER, JOHN WILLIAM
DOWER, J.W.--[31]

DOWLING, ALLEN
KING, JACK--[1][31]

DOWLING, THOMAS JR.
DOWLING, TOM--[31]

DOWN, C. MAURICE
CLIFFORD, MARTIN--[1]HP
CONQUEST, OWEN--[1]HP
HOWARD, PROSPER--[1]HP
RICHARDS, FRANK--[1]HP

DOWNES, DEIRDRE K.
DOWNES, KATHLEEN--[9][21][26]ROM--
"MAN NEXT DOOR"
"CHAR'S WEB" & MORE

DOWNEY, EDMOND
ALLEN, F.M.--[2][7][11][23][32]IRISH/SF--
"LONDON'S PERIL" 1900

DOWNEY, WILLIAM LESLIE
DOWNEY, BILL--[31]

DOWNIE, MARY ALICE
HUNTER, DAWE--[33]

DOWNS, ROBERT BINGHAM
DOWNS, ROBERT B.--[31]

DOWNS, SARAH ELIZABETH F.
SHELDON, MRS. GEORGIE--[34]MYS--
STREET "MAX" 1892
HENDERSON "WELFLEET MYS" '01

DOYGLAS, LLOYD CASSEL
DOUGLAS, LLOYD C.--[31]

DOYLE, ARTHUR CONAN
DOYLE, A. CONAN--[31]
DOYLE, CONAN--[31]
DOYLE, SIR A.--[31]
DOYLE, SIR ARTHUR CONAN--[31]
WATSON, JOHN H. MD--
G. WOLFE-LOCUS REVIEW JULY '93

DOYLE, CHARLES
DOYLE, MIKE--[8][31]

DOYLE, DEBRA
ADAMS, NICHOLAS--W/JAMES D.
MACDONALD,[7]SF,HP--
HARPER "HORROR HIGH PEP RALLY"

DOYLE, DEBRA [CONT]
APPLETON, VICTOR--W/JAMES D. MACDONALD,[7][23]HP--
STSY 'TOM SWIFT':
"AQUATECH WARRIORS"
"MONSTER MACHINE"
TALLIS, ROBYN--W/JAMES D. MACDONALD,[7]SF--
"PLANET BUILDERS #2 & #5 '89

DOYLE, GERALD A.
DOYLE, JERRY--[31]

DOYLE, JAMES J.
O DUBHGHAILL, SEAMUS--[1]

DOYLE, MARTHA CLAIRE M.
JAMES, MARTHA--[1]

DOYLE, ROSINA [WHEELER]
ALCIPHRON--[1]

DRABER, UWE
WOODWARD, MEL--[39]GERMAN

DRABKIN, YAKOV D.
GUSEV, SERGEY IVANOVICH--[1]

DRACHMAN, JULIAN M.
ADAM, BEN--[1][31]
GOODALL, MELANIE--[1][31]
OCTOPUS--[1]

DRACKETT, PHILIP A.
KING, PAUL--[1][8][22][31]ENGLISH

DRACOTT, ALICE ELIZABETH
D., A.E.--[3]MYS--
SPCK "A MYSTERY AT KING'S GRANT" 1896

DRACUP, ANGELA
SIBSON, CAROLINE--[33]

DRAFFIN, PETER
SPENSER, JULIAN--[35]AUSTRALIAN--
HRWTZ PB264 "CROSS SECTION" '66
HRWTZ PB279 "CLIK!" '66
HRWTZ PB293 "SHOOTING SEQUENCE" '67
HRWTZ PB304 "SPUNGERS" '67

DRAGER, GARY
EDENS, COOPER--[1]

DRAGO, HARRY SINCLAIR
CROSS, STEWART--[1][28][31]WEST--
MACAULAY "THIS WAY TO HELL" '33
DEMING, KIRK--[19][28][31]WEST--
WARD "COLT LIGHTNING" '35
WARD "GRASS MEANS FIGHT" '38
DRAGO, SINCLAIR--[28][31]MYS/WEST--
MCL "DIVORCE TRAP" '31
MCL "GUARDIANS OF THE SAGE" '32
AMOUR PRESS "WOMEN TO LOVE: A ROMANCE OF THE UNDERWORLD" '31
ERMINE, WILL--[19][28][31]WEST--
NUMEROUS NOVELS '33-57
FIELD, PETER--[19]WEST,HP--
MRW "CANYON OF DEATH"
MRW "TENDERFOOT KID" '39
MRW "DOCTOR TWO-GUNS" '39
MRW "MAN FROM THIEF RIVER" '40
MRW "LAW BADGE" '40]
FORBES, COSMO--L. ROBBINS LTR MAR '94--PULP?
LOMAX, BLISS--[19][28][31]WEST--
NUMEROUS NOVELS '36-59
PEURONE, JOYCE--L. ROBBINS LTR MAR '94--PULP?

DRAGO, HARRY SINCLAIR [CONT]
PUTNAM, J. WESLEY--[1][28]ROM--
MCL "HIDDEN THINGS" '15
MCL "BORROWED REPUTATIONS" '24 & 2 MORE
SINCLAIR, GRANT--[1][28]ROM--
MCL "THE WOMAN THOU ART" '25
WATT "WILD FRUIT" '26

DRAGONWAGON, CRESCENT
PARSONS, ELLEN--[1][33]
ZOLOTOV, ELLEN--[1]

DRAITSER, EMIL
ABRAMOV, EMIL--[1]

DRAKE, J.B.
INGELOW, PAUL--[34]MYS--
MELBOURNE "CHRONICAL OF A CAMERA" 1892

DRAPER, BEN
ROBERTS, HOLT--[1]

DRAPER, WARWICH HERBERT
WATCHMAN--[1][2]

DRASKAU, JENNIFER
KEWLEY, JENNIFER--[1]

DREETZ, JOACHIM
BALL, KURT HERWARTH--[39]GERMAN/SF

DREFUS, JEAN-PAUL ETIENNE
LE CHANOIS, JEAN-PAUL--[31]

DRESCHER, HENRIK
ZEIT, CALVIN--W/MARC IAN BARASCH,[1][31]--
QUILLER "TRUE PARANOID FACTS" '82

DRESCHER, SANDRA
DRESCHER-LEHMAN, SANDRA--[1]

DRESCHER, WALTER
ESCHER, STEFAN W.--[39]GERMAN

DRESCHNER, HANS GUENTHER
DESCHNER, GUENTHER--[31]

DRESNER, HAL
HOLLIDAY, DON--W/LARRY BLOCK-MUNROE CONVERSE W/WESTLAKE, BAE 21, P2, MUNROE CONFIRMED W/HAL
LORD, SHELDON--MUNROE-PERICHITCH, ADULT--
BEAC "APRIL NORTH"

DRESSER, DAVIS
BAKER, ASA--R.C. HOLLAND-BAE 1, [3][5][18][28][31]MYS--
STOKES "MUM'S THE WORD FOR MURDER" '38
CARLYLE "THE KISSED CORPSE" '39
BLOOD, MATTHEW--W/RYERSON JOHNSON, V. BERCH-GM PSEUDS, PP 33, [5][18][28][29]MYS--
GM 235 "THE AVENGER" '52
GM 423 "DEATH IS A LONELY DAME" '54
CARSON, SYLVIA--[1][5]
CULVER, KATHRYN--[5][18][28][29][31]ROM--
PHN "LOVE IS A MASGUERADE" '35
CURL "TOO SMART FOR LOVE" '37
CURL "MILLION DOLLAR MADNESS" '37
CURL "GREEN PATH TO THE MOON" '38
GODWIN "ONCE TO EVERY WOMAN" '38
GRAMMERCY "GIRL ALONE" '39
DAVIS, DON L.--[32]MYS--
CJ "KILLERS ROAD BLOCK" MAR '57
KI "HOLD UP TIME-TABLE" MAR '57

DRESSER, DAVIS [CONT]
DAVIS, DON--[18][28][29][31]WEST--
MRW "RETURN OF THE RIO KID" '40
HUTCH "DEATH ON TREASURE TRAIL" '40
MRW "RIO KID JUSTICE" '41
MRW "TWO-GUN RIO KID" '41
DEBRETT, HAL--W/KATHLEEN R. DRESSER, [3][5][28]MYS--
DODD "BEFORE I WAKE" '49
DODD "A LONELY WAY TO DIE" '50
FIELD, PETER--[19]WEST,HP--
MRW "GUNS FROM POWDER VALLEY" '41
MRW "POWDER VALLEY PAYOFF" '41
MRW "TRAIL SOUTH FROM POWDER VALLEY" '42
MRW "LAW MAN OF POWDER VALLEY" '42
MRW "FIGHT FOR P.V." '42
MRW "POWDER VALLEY VENGEANCE" '43
MRW "SHERIFF ON THE SPOT" '43
MRW "SMOKING IRON" '44
MRW "MIDNIGHT ROUNDUP" '44
MRW "DEATH RIDES THE NIGHT" '44
MRW "END OF THE TRAIL" '45
MRW "ROAD TO LARAMIE" '45
MRW "POWDER VALLEY SHOWDOWN" '46
HALLIDAY, BRETT--V. BERCH--GM PSEUDS, PP 33, T. JOHNSON ECHOES #23,[2][3][5][18][28]MYS--
HOLT "DIVIDEND ON DEATH" '49
HOLT "PRIVATE PRACTICE OF MICHAEL SHAYNE" '40
HOLT "UNCOMPLAINING CORPSES" '40
HOLT "TICKETS FOR DEATH" '42
HOLT "BODIES ARE WHERE YOU FIND THEM" '42
DODD "CORPSE CAME CALLING" '42
DODD "MURDER WEARS A MUMMER'S MASK" '43
DODD "BLOOD ON THE BLACK MARKET" '43
DODD "MIKE SHAYNE'S LONG CHANCE" '43
DODD "MURDER & THE MARRIED VIRGIN" '44
DODD "MARKED FOR MURDER" '45
DELL "DEAD MAN'S DIARY & DINNER AT DUPRE'S" '45
ZD "BLOOD ON BISCAYNE BAY" '46
ZD "COUNTERFEIT WIFE" '47
DODD "BLOOD ON THE STARS" '48
DODD "A TASTE FOR VIOLENCE" '49
DODD "CALL FOR MICHAEL SHAYNE" '49
DODD "THIS IS IT, MICHAEL SHAYNE" '50
DODD "FRAMED IN BLOOD" '51
DODD "WHEN DORINDA DANCES" '51
DODD "WHAT REALLY HAPPENED" '52
"ONE NIGHT WITH DORA" '53
TORQUIL "SHE WOKE TO DARKNESS" '54
TORQUIL "DEATH HAS THREE LIVES" '55
TORQUIL "STRANGER IN TOWN" '55
TORQUIL "BLONDE CRIED MURDER" '56
TORQUIL "SHOOT THE WORKS" '57
MSMM "WEEP FOR A BLONDE CORPSE" FEB-JUN '57
TORQUIL "MURDER & THE WANTON BRIDE" '58
MSMM "TARGET: MIKE SHAYNE" APR '59
MSMM "DIE LIKE A DOG" SEP '59
MSMM "HOMICIDAL VIRGIN" OCT '60
MSMM "BODY THAT CAME BACK" DEC-FEB '63-4
SCOTT, ANTHONY--R.C. HOLLAND-BAE 1, P38, [5][28][29]ROM--
GODWIN "MARDI GRAS MADNESS" '34
GODWIN "TEST OF VIRTUE" '34
GODWIN "TEN TOES UP" '35
GODWIN "VIRGIN'S HOLIDAY" '35
GODWIN "STOLEN SIN" '36
GODWIN "LADYS OF CHANCE" '36
GODWIN "SATAN RULES THE NIGHT" '38
GODWIN "TEMPTETION" '38
SHELLEY, PETER--[1][5][29]
WAYNE, ANDERSON--[18][28][29][34]MYS--
COWARD "CHARLIE DELL" '52

DRESSER, KATHLEEN ROLLINS
DEBRETT, HAL--W/DAVIS DRESSER, [3][5][18][28][31]MYS--
DODD "BEFORE I WAKE" '49
DODD "A LONELY WAY TO DIE" '50

DRESSER, MARY
SAVAGE, MARY--[2][3]MYS--
DODD "THE COACH DRAWS NEAR" '64

DRESSER, NORINE
LATTIMORE, JESSIE--W/MONTSERRAT FONTES,[31]

DRESSLER, GLADYS M.
MCGORIAN, GLADYS--[9][21][26]ROM--
"PRINCE REGENT'S SILVER BELL"

DRESSLER, HERRMANN
CORTH, R.--[39]GERMAN

DRESSLER, JOHANNES
HELION, JO HANS--[39]GERMAN

DRESSMAN, DENNIS LEE
DRESSMAN, DENNY--[31]

DREW, CONWAY
DREW, CON--[36]AUSTRALIAN/MYS--
SHIPPING NWS "JINKER, THE GRAFTER'S MATE" '16
BKSTL "DOINGS OF DAVE" '19
"ROGUES & RUSES" '22

DREW, JANE B.
FRY, JANE--[8]

DREXLER, ROSALYN
SOREL, JULIA--[1][8]

DREYER, EILEEN
KORBEL, KATHLEEN--[9][21][26]ROM--
"HOT SHOT"
"A FINE MADNESS" & MORE

DREYSE, NIKOLAUS v.
FRANZ, WILHELM--[39]GERMAN/MYS

DREYSEL, DORE
HELLRING, EVA--[39]GERMAN
HOLST, LIANE--[39]GERMAN

DREZE, JEAN
DELARUE, JEAN--[31]

DRIBERG, THOMAS EDWARD N.
DRIBERG, TOM--[31]
HICKEY, WILLIAM--[1][31]

DRIGIN, SERGE R.
DRIGIN, S.--BAPC #11--COVER ARTIST FOR 'SCOOPS' & PULPS

DRILHON-VON ARX, KATHAR.
VON ARX, EDITH KATHARINA--[39]GERMAN/JUV

DRINKALL, GORDON DON
DEMAINE, DON--[1][22][31]ENGLISH

DRINKER, JOHN--
[A] TRADESMAN--[1]

DRIPKE, KARL-HANS
KORFF, WERNER JURGEN--[39]GERMAN

DRIVER, CHRISTOPHER
ARCHESTRATUS--[8]

DRIVER, THOMAS
UNCLE TOM'S NEPHEW--[1]

DROBIAZKO, DARIA D.
VILDE, IRINA--[1]

DROJINE, N.A.
CHRISTIAENS, ANDRE G.--[22]DUTCH

DROR, YEHEZKEL
DEROR, YEHEZKEL--[31]

DROTNING, PHILLIP T.
PHILLIPS, TOM--[1]

DROWER, ETHEL STEFANA MAY
STEVENS, E.S.--[1][22]ENGLISH

DRUCKER, HENRY MATTHEW
DRUCKER, H.M.--[31]

DRUID, DAVID
STAFFORD, JOHN K.--[34]MYS,HP--
MAGNET #359 "DARING EXPRESS MESSENGER" '04

DRUM, ROBERT F.
DRUM, BOB--[31]

DRUMMOND, ALISON
SCHAW, RUTH--[8]

DRUMMOND, CHERRY
EVANS, CHERRY--[8]

DRUMMOND, EDITH MARIE D.C
CARMAN, DULCE--[8][22][31]ENGLISH

DRUMMOND, EDITH VICTORIA
CHICHESTER--[8]
STIRLING, VEDA--[8]

DRUMMOND, HUMPHREY
AP EVANS, HUMPHREY--[1][8]

DRUMMOND, JACK
REDDER, GEORGE--[1][3]MYS--
EXPOSITION "THE FLIGHT INSTRUCTOR MURDERS" '77

DRUMMOND, PATRICK HAMILTN
SHAW, BARTON--[1]

DRURY, MAXINE COLE
CREIGHTON, DON--[1][8][31]

DRUSSAI, GAREN
KIRKHAM, MILO--[1][2][11]

DRUTEL, MARCELLE L.M.
L'AUBANELENCO--[1]

DRUYANOV, ALTER
HAEDREYI, ABGAD--[22]HEBREW

DRYHURST, MICHAEL JOHN
DARLING, V.H.--[8]

DRYMON, KATHLEEN
MCCALL, KATHLEEN--[21][26]ROM--
"IVORY ROSE"
"WINDSWEPT HEART"

DU AIME, ALBERT
WHARTON, WILLIAM--[7]SF--
"FRANKY FURBO: A NOVEL" '89

DU BOIS, EDWARD
DE SAINT-LEON, REGINALD--[2]

DU BOIS, ROCHELLE L. HOLT
HOLT, ROCHELLE L.--[31]

DU BOIS, SHIRLEY GRAHAM
GRAHAM, SHIRLEY--[31][33]

DU BOIS, THEODORA
MCCORMICK, THEODORA--[8]

DU MAURIER, GUY
PATRIOT, A.--[2]

DU PLESSIS, JOHANNES
DU PLESSIS, PHIL--[1]

DU PLOOY ERLANK, WILLEM J
EITEMAL--[22]SOUTH AFRICAN

DU SOLLE, JOHN S.
KNICKERBOCKER--[1]

DU TOIT, JACOB DANIEL
TOTIUS--[22]SOUTH AFRICAN-AFRIKAANS

DUARD, PAUL LOUIS E.
COLLINE, PAUL--[1]

DUBENSKY, HERBERT
ALDOUBY, ZVY H[ERBERT]--[1]

DUBINA, PETER
BURNETT, PETER--[39]GERMAN/WEST,HP
COOVER, WAYNE--[39]GERMAN/SF/WEST,HP
DERRINGER, PETE--[39]GERMAN/WEST
DORNER, PETER--[39]GERMAN/JUV/SF
GARNER, R.F.--[39]GERMAN/SF
KIRBY, JOHN--[39]GERMAN/SF/WEST,HP
NICHOLS, MATT--[39]GERMAN/WEST,HP
PETERS, A.F. JR.--[39]GERMAN/SF/WEST,HP
SIEGEL, STEVE--[39]GERMAN/SF/WEST,HP

DUBOC, EDOUARD
WALDMUELLER, ROBERT--[1]
WALDMULLER, ROBERT--[22]GERMAN

DUBOSE, LOUISE JONES
TELFAIR, NANCY--[22]AMERICAN

DUBOV, GWEN BAGNI
BAGNI, GWEN--[1][31]
GIELGUD, GWEN BAGNI--[1][31]

DUBREUIL, ELIZABETH L.
ANDERSON, KRISTON--[1]
BROWN, L.J.--[2][7][31]--
NTSD "A LABOR OF LUST" '68
BROWNING, L.J.--[1][31]
CAMERON, KATE--[3][7][9][21][26][31]MYS/ROM--
2 NOVELS
CAREWE, S.C.--[1][31]
DEMILLE, ALEXANDRIA--[1][31]
DODGE, DANIEL--[1][31]
DRAGON, CAROLYN--[1][31]
DUBREUIL, LINDA--[1][26]ROM
EVANS, ELLEN--[1][31]
EVANS, EMERALD--[1][31]
GRIFFEN, EDMUND--[1]
GRIFFEN, ELIZABETH L.--[7]--
SCHOLASTIC "THE SHAGGY DOG" '67
HAGEN, LINDA--[1][3][29]MYS--
BELM "IN THE EYE OF THE LAW" '79
HAGEN, LORINDA--[7][9][21][26][31]ROM/SF--
BELM "AMY JEAN" '77

DUBREUIL, ELIZABETH L.
HANLEY, ELIZABETH--[3][7][29][31]MYS/SF--
BELM "MR. PRESIDENT" '77
BELM "GUILTY AS CHARGED" '79
LINDER, D. BARRY--[7]--
GREENLEAF "LIBIDO 23" '69
LINDNER, D. BERRY--[1][31]
LINDSAY, D. BARRY--[2][11]
MAITLAND, MARGARET--W/JEFFREY WALLMAN,
[7][9][21][31]ROM--
LEIS "LOVE'S GOLDEN CIRCLE" '78
MAITLAND, MARGARET--[26]ROM--
"CHANNINGS OF EVERLEIGH"
"EAST SIDE, WEST SIDE"
"SACRED & PROFANE"
"TIDEWATER"
"UNCONQUERED"
MARK, JON--[1]
MARSHALL, CATHERINE--[1]
POWER, CATHERINE--[1]
ROYAL, D.--V. BERCH-LESBIANA/COUNTERCULTURE,
BAE 22, P5,[1]
SEATTLE, FRANK--[1]
SUMMER, BRIAN--[1]
TODD, ERIC--[1]
VAUGHN, TONI--[1]

DUCASSE, ISIDORE LUCIEN
DE LAUTREAMONT, COMTE--[2]

DUCETTE, VINCE
DANIELS, GIL--[2]
DAVIS, GYLE--[2]
KULLINGER, J.L.--[1][2]

DUCHACEK, IVO MARIA R.
CERMAK, MARTIN--[33]
DUKA, IVO--W/HELEN KOLDOVA,[2][7][23][31]SF--
MARTIN & HIS FRIEND FROM OUTER SPACE" '55

DUCHAMP, L. TIMMEL
DUCHAMP, LAURA--[7]?? COULD THIS BE THE
AUTHOR BEHIND BOTH "DUCHAMP"
& "DU CHAMP" IN ADULT PB?

DUCHESNE, ALBERT
JACQUES--[1]

DUCHI, JACOB
TAMOR, CASPIPINI--[1]

DUCKERT, MARY
HALL, ANN--[1][31]

DUCKETT, ALFRED A.
DOUGLAS, GLENN--[31]

DUCKETT, MADELAINE G.
GIBSON, MADELAINE--[9][21][26]ROM--
"RAKE'S REWARD"
"VICIOUS VISCOUNT"

DUCKETT, WILLIAM
PAGE, HENRI--[1]

DUCKWORTH, LESLIE BLAKEY
BLAKE, LESLIE--[1]
LESLEY, BLAKE--[31]
LESLIE, BLAKE--[1][31]

DUCLAUX, AGNES MARY F.
ROBINSON, AGNES MARY F.--[1]

DUCORNET, ERICA
DUCORNET, RIKKI--[31]
RIKKI--[1]

DUDDEN, ARTHUR P.
POWER, ARTHUR--[1]

DUDDINGTON, CHARLES L.
CAMPBELL, BERKELEY--[8]
NIGHTINGALE, CHARLES--[8]

DUDEVANT, AMANDINE AURORE
SAND, GEORGE--[2]

DUDLEY EDWARDS, RUTH
EDWARDS, RUTH DUDLEY--[31]

DUDLEY, BARBARA HUDSON
POWERS, BARBARA HUDSON--[1]

DUDLEY, ERNEST
COLTMAN, ERNEST VIVIAN--[22][31]ENGLISH

DUDLEY, LOUISE POWELSON
PALEN, ADELINE--V. BERCH LTR TO HUBIN FEB '94

DUDLEY, WALTER BRONSON
DUDLEY, BIDE--[1]

DUDLEY-SMITH, TREVOR
TREVOR, ELLESTON--[2][5][32]--
CHANGED TO 'TREVOR'--
LM "THE DROP" MAY '61
SEE ENTRIES UNDER 'TREVOR' PSEUDS

DUENSING, JURGEN
BAKER, VIVIAN--[39]GERMAN/SF/WEST
BLOOD, JOHN--[39]GERMAN/SF/WEST
BROWN, TERENCE--[39]GERMAN/SF/WEST
CALLAHAN, FRANK--[39]GERMAN/WEST
CIMARRON, JOHN--[39]GERMAN/WEST
DWYNN, J.C.--[39]GERMAN/SF/WEST
LAMONT, ROBERT--[39]GERMAN/SF/WEST,HP
MARTINEZ, BENITO--[39]GERMAN/SF/WEST,HP
MCKAY, CHARLES--[39]GERMAN/SF/WEST,HP
MONGO, MARCOS--[39]GERMAN/SF/WEST,HP
NOLAN, FREDERICK--[39]GERMAN/SF,HP
SHOCKER, DAN--[39][40]GERMAN/MYS, HP
SLADE, JACK--[39]GERMAN/WEST,HP

DUER, KENNETH
CHANGER, HUGH--[1]

DUFAULT, JOSEPH ERNEST N.
JAMES, WILL--RAY AUGER-BAE 14,
P3,[19][28]WEST

DUFF, CHARLES
CHERNICHEWSKI, VLADIMIR--[8]

DUFF, CHARLES ST. LAWREN.
O DUBH, CATHAL--[1][22][31]IRISH-ENGLISH

DUFF, DOUGLAS VALDER
MAINSAIL--[8]
SAVAGE, LESLIE--[1][8]
STANHOPE, DOUGLAS--[1][8]
WICKLOE, PETER--[1][8]

DUFF, JAMES P.
CARR, JAY--V. BERCH-MON PSEUDS, BAE 9, P26--
MON 221 "MY FATHER'S WIFE" '61
MON 288 "SUBURBAN LOVERS" '62
MON MB522 "CRACK-UP IN SURBURBIA" '62

DUFF, MARGARET K.
DUFF, MAGGIE--[31][33]

DUFFIELD, DOROTHY DEAN
DUFFIELD, ANNE--[1][9]ROM

DUFFUS, LOUIS GEORGE
VAGRANT--[1]

DUFFY, AGNES MARY
VOX, AGNES MARY--[8]

DUFFY, BERNARD C.
DUFFY, BEN--[31]

DUFFY, JAMES HENRY
MURPHY, HAUGHTON--PUBL PUB REL/DDLY PLEAS #3--
SIMON 5 'REUBEN FROST' NOVELS '86-90

DUFFY, MICHAEL FRANCIS
RICHARDS, FRANK--[1]HP

DUFOUR, LOUIS
UWESON, ULF--[39]GERMAN/JUV

DUGGAN, DENISE V.
EGERTON, DENISE--[1][3][29]MYS--
5 NOVELS '54-61

DUGGAN, EDMUND
EDMUNDS, ALBERT--[13]AUSTRALIAN

DUGGLEBY, JEAN COLBECK
KENNEDY, DIANA--[8]

DUGHMAN, JOHN & FREIDA
CHURCHILL, LUANNA--[3]MYS--
11 NOVELS '72-5

DUHAMEL, GEORGES
THEVENIN, DENIS--[22]FRENCH
THEVENIN, DEVIS--[31]--
"CIVILIZATION" '17

DUKAKIS, KATHARINE
DUKAKIS, KITTY--[31]

DUKE, ANITA
HEWETT, ANITA--[1][8]

DUKE, ANNA MARIE
ASTIN, PATTY DUKE--[31]
DUKE, PATTY--[31]

DUKE, DONALD NORMAN
VALENTINE, ROGER--[1][22]AMERICAN

DUKE, JAMES A.
DUKE, JIM--[31]

DUKE, VERNON
DUKELSKY, VLADIMIR--[1][31]

DUKES, [SIR] PAUL
DUKAINE, PAUL--[1]

DUKINFIELD, WILLIAM CLAUD
BOGLE, CHARLES--[8]
CRIBLECOBLIS, OTIS--[8]
FIELDS, W.C.--[8]
JEEVES, MAHATMA KANE--[8]

DULLARD, MARGARET
ST. JOHN BATHE, MARGARET--[2]

DUMARCHAIS, PIERRE
MAC ORLAN, PIERRE--[22]FRENCH

DUMKE, GLENN S.
ALLEN, JORDAN--[31]
PIERCE, GLENN--[34]MYS--
MEDALLION "KING'S RANSOM" '86

DUMMETT, [AGNES M.] ANN
CHESNEY, ANN--[31]

DUNANT, SARAH
DUNANT, PETER--W/PETER BUSBY,[34][40]-DEUTSCH
"EXTERMINATING ANGELS" '83
"INTENSIVE CARE" '86

DUNAWAY, PATTI
NOTTINGHAM, POPPY--[9][21][26][34]MYS/ROM--
5 ACE & AVON NOVELS '74-8

DUNBAR, CHARLES STUART
PARK, ELM--[1]
WISDOME, THOMAS--[1]

DUNCAN, ACTEA CAROLYN
THOMAS, CAROLYN--[1][3][22]MYS--
LIPPINCOTT "NARROW GAUGE TO MURDER" '53
& 3 MORE

DUNCAN, CAROL S.
PERRY, CAROL DUNCAN--[26]ROM--
"WINGS OF TIME"

DUNCAN, EDWARD HOWARD
DUNCAN, ROBERT [EDWARD]--[1]
SYMMES, ROBERT EDWARD--[1]

DUNCAN, ISADORA
DUNCAN, DORA ISADORA--[31]

DUNCAN, KATHLEEN
SIMMONS, CATHERINE--[1][8]
SIMMONS, KIM--[1][8]

DUNCAN, KUNIGUNDE
ISLEY, FLORA K.D.--[1]

DUNCAN, LOIS
KERRY, LOIS--[31]--
FUNK "A LOVE SONG FOR JOYCE" '58
FUNK "A PROMISE FOR JOYCE" '59

DUNCAN, LOIS S[TEINMETZ]
ARQUETTE, LOIS S.--[33]

DUNCAN, ROBERT L. & WANDA
DUNCAN, W.R.--[3][18][31]MYS--
DELACORTE "THE QUEEN'S MESSENGER" '82

DUNCAN, ROBERT LIPCOMB
ROBERTS, JAMES HALL--[2][3][18][29]MYS--
MRW "THE Q DOCUMENT" '64
MRW "FEBRUARY PLAN" '67

DUNCAN, RONALD [F.H]
MARSLAND, BISHOP OF--[1][31]
MARSLAND, MAJ. GEN.--[1]

DUNCAN, SARA JEANETTE
GRAFTON, GARTH--[8]

DUNCAN, WILLIAM MURDOCK
CASSELLS, JOHN--[2][3][18][29][31]MYS--
56 NOVELS '46-75
DALLAS, JOHN--[3][18][29][31]MYS--
JENKINS "NIGHT OF THE STORM" '61
HALE "RED ICE" 73
DUNCAN, MURDOCK--[29]MYS--
7 NOVELS '35-45
GRAHAM, NEILL--[3][18][22][29][31]MYS--
45 NOVELS '48-77
LOCKE, MARTIN--[3][18][29][31]MYS--
WARD "VENGEANCE OF MORTIMER DALY" '61

DUNCAN, WILLIAM MURDOCK [CONT]
MALLOCH, PETER--[3][18][29][31]MYS--
33 NOVELS '57-77
MARSHALL, LOVAT--[3][18][29][40]MYS--
39 NOVELS '58-74

DUNFORD, JUDITH
GOWAR, ANTONIO--W/SUSANNA MARGOLIS,[1][31]

DUNHAM, KATHERINE
DUNN, KAYE--[1][31]

DUNHAM, ROBERT
DUNHAM, BOB--[31]
YUMA, DAN--[1]

DUNK, MARGARET
DUKE, MARGARET--[8]

DUNKELMAN, BENJAMIN
DUNKELMAN, BEN--[31]

DUNKELSBUHLER, ELISABETH
SCHAIBLE, ELISABETH--[39]GERMAN

DUNKERLEY, WILLIAM ARTHUR
OXENHAM, JOHN--[2][3][8][22]MYS--
HODDER "A MAID OF THE SILVER SEA" '10
& MORE

DUNKERLY, ELSIE JEANNETTE
OXENHAM, ELSIE JEANETTE--[8]

DUNKY-SCHLAGETER, JOHANNA
SCHLAGETER, JEANNE--[39]GERMAN/JUV

DUNLEAVY, JANET EGLESTON
EGLESTON, JANET F.--[1][31]
FRANK, JANET--[1][31]

DUNLOP, AGNES MARY R.
KYLE, ELIZABETH--[3][22][31][33]
SCOTTISH/JUV/MYS--
30 NOVELS
RALSTON, JAN--[1][8][33]SCOTTISH/JUV

DUNMORE, JOHN
CALDER, JASON--[1][3][31]AUSTRALIAN--
DUNMORE "MAN WHO SHOT ROB MULDOON" '76
DUNMORE "A WREATH FOR THE SPRINGBOKS" '77
HALE "O'ROURKE AFFAIR" '79
HALE "TARGET MARGARET THATCHER" '81

DUNN, DAWN PAULINE
DUNN, PAULINE--W/SUZAN HARTZELL,[7][34]--
ZEBRA "DEMONIC COLOR" '90
PLAGIARISM OF KOONTZ "PHANTOMS"
"FLESH STEALER" '90
"THE CRAWLING DARK" '91

DUNN, DES R.
BRADY, ADAM--[35]AUSTRALIAN--
CLEVELAND
COLE, SHELDON [B]--[35]AUSTRALIAN--
CLEVELAND
CREGAN, MATT--[35]AUSTRALIAN--
CONDOR 156 "COYOTES DON'T RUST"
CONDOR 176 "GUN SCAR"
CORONADA 967 "TIME OUT FOR HANGING"
SANTE FE 301 "HOLE CARD"
SANTE FE 324 "STAKE-OUT"
SANTE FE 328 "BIG MAN'S COUNTRY"
CULP, MORGAN--[35]AUSTRALIAN--
CLEVELAND

DUNN, DES R. [CONT]
DENVER, SHAD--[35]AUSTRALIAN--
CLVD NVLT "VALLEY OF PERIL"
5 CONDOR BKS
SANTE FE - 6 BKS
14 SIERRA BKS
17 CHISHOLM BKS
6 BIG HORN BKS
CORONADA - 9 BOOKS
HALLIDAY, GUNN--[35]AUSTRALIAN--
CONDOR 164 "HEROES DIE FAST"
CONDOR 172 "HIGH STAKES"
CHISHOLM - 6 BKS
8 BIG HORN BKS
9 CORONADA BKS
SIERRA - 4 BOOKS
5 SANTE FE BOOKS
IVERSON, BRETT--[35]AUSTRALIAN--
CLVD 990 "FOOL'S FRONTIER"
CLVD 994 "HATE HOLDS A GUN"
CLVD "OUTLAW'S BIBLE"
KENT, LARRY--[35]AUSTRALIAN, SP--
CLVD-REST OF KENT BOOKS NOT WRITTEN
BY DON HARING
RENWICK, WALT--[35]AUSTRALIAN--
SIERRA 414 "GUN WHIPPED"

DUNN, ELSIE
SCOTT, EVELYN--[1]
SOUZA, ERNEST--[1]

DUNN, JAMES
CORDER, R.E.--[1][3]MYS--
MELROSE "TALES TOLD TO THE MAGISTRATE" '25

DUNN, JOSEPH ALLAN
JACKSON, EMORY--L. ROBBINS LTR MAR '94
MONTAGUE, JOSEPH--L. ROBBINS LTR MAR '94
STRONG, JOHN B.--L. ROBBINS LTR MAR '94

DUNN, KATHLEEN
GALLISON, KATE--V. BERCH LTR-HUBIN '94, MYS--
LITTLE "UNBALANCED ACCOUNTS" '86
"DEATH TAPE" '87

DUNN, MARY ALICE
FAID, MARY--[1][8]

DUNN, PHILIP M.
DUNN, SAUL--[2][7][11][23]SF--
CORONET 'STEELEYE' #1-3 '76
CORONET 'CABAL' #1 & 2 '78

DUNN, STEPHEN PORTER
DUNN, S.P.--[31]

DUNN, SUSAN W.
DRAKE, SUSAN--[26]ROM--
SIL 588 "HEAR NO EVIL"

DUNNAHOO, TERRY
TERRY, MARGARET--[1]

DUNNE, FINLEY PETER
DOOLEY, MARTIN--[8]AMERICAN
DOOLEY, MR.--[22]AMERICAN

DUNNE, JOHN WILLIAM
DUNNE, J.W.--[1]

DUNNE, MARY COLLINS
DUNNE, MARY JO--[1][31]
MOORE, REGINA--[1][33]

DUNNE, RON
DEE, WILLIAM--[35]AUSTRALIAN--
HRWTZ PB20 "NIGHTMARE OVER NADZAB" '60

DUNNE, RON
DONOVAN, RICK--[35]AUSTRALIAN--
HRWTZ SS1 "JET JOCKEY" '60
HRWTZ SS6 "WAKE OF THE JINX" '60

DUNNER, JOSEPH
GERMANICUS--[31]
ROTH, ALEXANDER--[1]

DUNNETT, ALISTAIR M.
SINCLAIR, DUNCAN--[1]
TAVIS, ALEC--[1][3]MYS--
HAMILTON "THE DUKE'S DAY" '70

DUNNETT, DOROTHY
HALLIDAY, DOROTHY--[8][17][18][29]
ENGLISHMYS/ROM--

DUNSING, DEE
MOWERY, DOROTHY--[8]

DUNSTAN, GUY MAINWARING
MORTON, GUY MAINWARING--[1][22]ENGLISH--
NAME CHANGED LEGALLY ??

DUNSTONE, MAXWELL F.
DUNSTONE, MAX--[1][32]MYS--
LM "MURDER IN OILS" OCT '54
LM "HAGDOWN MAN" JUN '75

DUNTEMAM, ELEANOR ADELE
DUNN, ELEANOR--[1]

DUNTON, EDITH KELLOGG
WARDE, MARAGRET--[1]

DUPERRAULT, DOUG
SHORT, MALCOLM--V.BERCH-BDSD BKS
CKLST, BAE 20--
BDSD 968 "ARMY TRAMP" '60,SPINE & COVER

DUPLANY, CLAUDE MARIUS
MARIUS, CLAUDE--[1]

DUPLESSIS, YVONNE
DUPLESSIS, YVES--[31]

DUPONT, ELLEN
ST. DAVID, IVY--[9][21][26]ROM--
"A DESTINY OF LOVE"
"THE SHADOW OF LOVE"
"A GIFT OF DESIRE"

DUPREY DE LA RUFFINERE, P
TEXTU--[1]

DUPREY, RICHARD ALLEN
FIELDS, ALAN--[1][3][31]--
DELL "V-J DAY" '78

DUPUY-MAZUEL, HENRI
CATALAN, HENRI--[1][3]MYS--
SHEED "SOEUR & THE EMBARRASSED LADIES"
& MORE '53-7

DURAN, BETTY
DALE, RUTH JEAN--W/JEAN STRIBBLING,
[9][21][26]ROM

DURAND, ALICE MARIE C.F.
GREVILLE, HENRY--[3][22][29]MYS--
DONOHUE "UN MYSTERE" 1890

DURAND, FRANCOIS
DE MIOMANDRE, FRANCIS--[1][2]

DURAND, LOUIS
DUGALL, H.L.--W/HENRI GALLISSION,[40]FRENCH--
MYS "UN TEMPS POUR TUER" '69

DURAND, MRS. ALBERT C.
SAWYER, RUTH--[1]

DURANTE, JAMES FRANCIS
DURANTE, JIMMY--[31]

DURATSCHEK, MARY CLAUDIA
DURATSCHEK, SISTER MARY C--[31]

DURBEN, WOLFGANG J.M.
PASDELOUP, JEAN-MARIE--[1]
WENDOLIN--[1]
WILLIBALD, GRAF--[1]

DURBRIDGE, FRANCIS H.
TEMPLE, PAUL--W/JAMES D.R. MCCONNELL,
[3][5][18][29][33]MYS--
LONG "SEND FOR P.T. AGAIN" '38
LONG "NEW OF P.T." '40
LONG "P.T. INTERVENES" '44
LONG "CASE OF THE TWISTED SCARF" '51
HODDER "THE OTHER MAN" '58
HODDER "THE SCARF" '60
HODDER "MY WIFE MELISSA" '67
HODDER "BAT OUT OF HELL" '72

DURGNAT, RAYMOND [ERIC]
GREEN, O.O.--[8][22][31]ENGLISH

DURIBREUX, GASTON
VAN WIEREN, JAN--[22]DUTCH

DURR, EDELTRAUT
BERNER, STEFFI--[39]GERMAN

DURR, FREDERICK ROLAND E.
DURR, FRED--[31]

DURRANT, RITA D.
DUBOIS, ROSEMARY--[1][31]

DURRELL, JACQUELINE S.R.
DURRELL, JACQUIE--[31]

DURRELL, LAWRENCE [G]
NORDEN, CHARLES--[1][2][22]ENGLISH
PEESLAKE, GAFFER--[1][22]ENGLISH

DURRUA, ODETTE JEANNE
JANALAINE, ODETTE--[1]
MINERVE--[1]

DURSELEN, HELGA
BRAUN, HELGA--[39]GERMAN/SF

DURST, PAUL
BANNON, PETER--[3][28][29]MYS--
JENKINS "IF I SHOULD DIE" '58
JENKINS "THEY WANT ME DEAD" '58
JENKINS "WHISPER MURDER SOFTLY" '63
CHELTON, JOHN--V. BERCH-GM PSEUDS,
PP 33,[3][28][29][31][40]MYS--
GM 524 "MY DEADLY ANGEL" '55
COCHRAN, JEFF--[1][28][31]WEST--
AV 556 "GUNS OF CIRCLE 8" '54
SHANE, JOHN--[1][28]WEST--
4 MILLS & BOON NOVELS '54-7

DUSCHEK, JOHANN
KORNFELDER, J.D.--[39]GERMAN/MYS

DUSSERE, CAROLYN THOMAS
DUSSERE, CAROL--[31]

DUTT, SHOSHER CHUNDER
BARTON, J.A.G.--[1]

DUTTA, REGINALD
DUTTA, REX--[1][31]

DUVAL, COLETTE
VIVIER, COLETTE--[1]

DUVAL, GEORGES
TABARIN--[1]

DUVAL, MARTIN PAUL A.
DE LA BRETTONE, RATIF--[1]
LORRAINE, JEAN--[1][22]FRENCH

DUVOISIN, LOUISE
FATIO, LOUISE--[1]

DUWEZ, MAURICE
DEAUVILLE, MAX--[1][22]BELGIAN

DUYSEN, PAUL
ULLER, TYLL--[39]GERMAN

DWIGGINS, ELMER
DOUGLASS, ELLSWORTH--[7][23]SF--
"THE WHEELS OF DR. GINOCHIO GYVEA"

DWORKIN, RONALD MYLES
DWORKIN, R.M.--[31]

DWORMAN, BRENDA JOYCE
JOYCE, BRENDA--[9][21]ROM--
"THE CONQUEROR"
"LOVERS & LIARS" & MORE

DWYER, JAMES FRANCIS
DIVER, JAMES FRANCIS--[1][7]MYS/SF--
"THE SPOTTED PANTHER" '13
DWYER, GALBRAITH WELCH--L. ROBBINS LTR MAR '94
TURNER, ROBERT--L. ROBBINS LTR MAR '94

DYE, CHARLES
DYE, CHARLES--W/KATHERINE MACLEAN,[2]

DYER, CHARLES [RAYMOND]
DYER, C. RAYMOND--[31]
DYER, RAYMOND--[1][3][31]MYS--
PLAY "TIME, MURDERER, PLEASE" '62
DYER, RAYMOND J.--[32]ENGLISH/MYS--
VB "SIX STORIES UP" APR '54
MH "LAST JOB" APR '62
KRASELCHIK, R.--[1][31]
STRETTON, CHARLES--[1]
STRETTON, RENSLAW--[1]

DYER, MINNIE THERESA
MYRTLE, MINNIE--[1]

DYER, WALTER ALDEN
FEARING, ALDEN--[1]

DYER-BENNET, PAMELA DEAN
DEAN, PAMELA [C]--[7]SF--
"SECRET COUNTRY #1-3" '85/91
"TARN LIN" '91

DYGASINSKI, TOMASZ ADOLF
DYGAS--[22]POLISH

DYLAN, BOB
PENNEBAKER, D.A.--J. PRESSMAN-COUNTERCULTURE, BAE 21, P54

DYMOND, MELANIE
ZOOL, M.H.--[23]SF,GROUP PSEUD.

DYNE, MICHAEL
HANNA, EVELYN--W/ETHEL FRANK,[9][21][26]ROM--
"BLAZE OF GLORY"
"STOLEN SPLENDOR" & MORE

DYSON, GEOFFREY HARRY G.
GEOFF--[1]

DZHAUARI, ADZHIE D.
ADZHIE, DZHINDI--[1]

EADE, CHARLES
PROLE, LOZANIA--W/URSULA BLOOM,[1][2][26]ROM--
10 NOVELS

EADY, LEONARD LEOPOLD
EADIE, ARLTON--[32][34]MYS--
13 FH NVLS '29-37
MZ "NAMELESS MUMMY" JUL '69
MZ "SIREN OF THE SNAKES" MAR '68

EADY, MARY ALINE
WESLEY, MARY--[1][2][7]SF--
"THE SIXTH SEAL" '69

EADY, W.T.
E., W.T.--[34]MYS--
CHAPMAN "I.D.B.; OR, ADV OF SOLOMAN DAVIS ON THE DIAMOND FIELDS" 1887

EAGAN, FRANCES W.
SEEKER, A.--[8]

EAGER, MARY ANN
EAGER, MOLLY--[31]

EAGLESTONE, ARTHUR ARCH.
DATALLER, ROGER--[8]

EAGLETON, TERENCE [F]
EAGLETON, TERRY--[31]

EAKER, IRA CLARENCE
EAKER, IRA--[31]

EAMES, HELEN MARY
MERCURY--[8]

EARDLEY-WILMOT, R. ADM
SEARCHLIGHT--[1][2][7]WAR--
"BATTLE OF THE NORTH SEA" '14

EARLE, M.A.
CARLTON, [COUSIN] MAY--[1]

EARNSHAW, PATRICIA
MANN, PATRICIA--[1]

EARP, FRANK RUSSELL
EARP, F.R.--[1]

EAST, FRED
FIELD, PETER--[19]WEST, HP--
"GAMBLER'S GOLD"
"RAVAGED RANGE"
"TRAIL FROM NEEDLE ROCK"

EAST, FRED [CONT]
MANNING, ROY--[1][28]WEST--
5 'MACRAE SMITH' NOVELS
ACE D20 "THE DESPERADO CODE" '53
ACE D192 "BEWARE OF THIS TENDERFOOT" '56
ACE D308 "DRAW AND DIE" '58
ORPET, FRED--[1][3]MYS--
ARCADIA "MURDER'S NO ACCIDENT" '54
WEST, TOM--[1][28]WEST--48 NOVELS '44-80

EASTERLING, NARENA
EASTERLING, RENE--[1][3][22]MYS--
PGT "A STRANGE WAY HOME" '52

EASTHAM, THOMAS
HARLING, THOMAS--[31]

EASTMAN, ANN HEIDBREDER
HEIDBREDER, MARGARET ANN--[1][31]

EASTMAN, CAROL
JOYCE, ADRIAN--[31]

EASTMAN, CHARLES A.
OHIYESA--[1]

EASTON, CAROL D.
LAINI, SAFISHA--[1]

EASTON, M. COLEMAN
COLEMAN, CLARE--W/CLARE L. BELL,
LOCUS MAG JAN '93,[23][26]SF--
JOVE "DAUGHTER OF THE REEF" '92
JOVE "SISTER OF SUN"

EASTON, THOMAS A[TWOOD]
ATWOOD, SAM--[23]SF--MAGAZINE STORIES
BUNDY, RALPH--[7]SF--
AQUARIUS 7 "DRUGGED SEX" '76

EASTWOOD, CHARLES CYRIL
HALE, PHILIP--[31]

EASTWOOD, HELEN B.
BAXTER, OLIVE--[3][8][9][22]MYS--
HALE "JEWEL IN THE CRYPT" '69
RAMSAY, FAY--[1][9]

EATON, BENJAMIN V.
VALENTINE, VICTOR--[2]

EATON, EDITH
SIU SIN FAR--[1]

EATON-BACK, MRS. B.
VANE, DEREK--[1][3]MYS--16 NOVELS 1893-1933

EBAN, ABBA SOLOMON
EBAN, AUBREY--[31]

EBBETT, FRANCES EVA
BURFIELD, EVA--[31][32][34]MYS--
LM "FAIR REWARD" SEPT '62
WRIGHT "LAST DAY OF SUMMER" '68
EBBETT, EVE--[31]

EBBS, ROBERT
PITCHFORD, HARRY RONALD--[8]
SEVERN, RICHARD--[8]

EBEL, HENRY
BUTSTEIN, WILLIAM--[1]

EBEL, SUZANNE
GOODWIN, SUZANNE--[8][17]ENGLISH/ROM--
"COUSINS"
"LOVERS" & MORE '78-82
SHELBOURNE, CECILY--[8][17]ROM--
"STAGE OF LOVE" '78

EBEL, WILLI
ROHDEN, ERNST--[39]GERMAN/MYS
UHLENBRUCK, DIETER--[39]GERMAN/MYS

EBENSTEIN, WILLIAM
ELWIN, WILLIAM--[31]

EBERHARDT, ANNA
WHITE, TIFFANY--[21][26]ROM--
"OPEN INVITATION"
"CHEAP THRILLS" & 3 OTHERS

EBERLE, IRMENGARDE
ALLEN, ALLYN--[1][31][33]--
WATTS "LONE STAR COWBOY" '51
CARTER, PHYLLIS ANN--[1][31][33]--
McBRIDE "THE STORY OF CLOTH" '39

EBERT, ARTHUR FRANK
ARTHUR, FRANK--[3][22][31][32]MYS--
6 NVLS '40-73
JCM "STORY TO BE READ IN THE TRAIN" JUN '63
LM "TOO LATE TO SAVE THE WOMEN" JUN '73

EBLE, DIANE
SPENCE, CYNTHIA--[33]

EBLE, THEA
TORSTEN, THEA--[39]GERMAN/JUV

EBNER-ALLINGER, JEANNIE
EBNER, JEANNIE--[1]

EBON
DOOLEY, EBON--[31]

EBSEN, CHRISTIAN
EBSEN, BUDDY--[31]

EBY, LOIS CHRISTINE
LAWSON, PATRICK--[1]

ECCLES, CHARLOTTE O.
GODFREY, HAL--[1][2][3]MYS--
JARROLDS "THE REJUVENATING OF
MRS. SEMAPHORE" 1897

ECCLESHARE, COLIN
O.P.--[8]

ECK, PHILIP R.
ROSS, PHILIP--V. BERCH LTR TO HUBIN '94, MYS--
DODD "A GOOD DEATH" '83
TOR "BLUE HERON" '85

ECKE, FELIX
WIENER, RALPH--[39]GERMAN

ECKELS, JON
AKNATON, ASKIA--[1][31]

ECKELS, ROBERT EDWARD
ROBERTS, E.E.--LACHMAN LST MAY '93,[32]MYS--
EQMM "MUG'S GAME" FEB '71
EQMM "A LITTLE RIDE IN THE CAR" FEB '72

ECKERT, HERBERT
ECKART, PETER--[39]GERMAN

ECKERT, HORST
JANOSCH--[31][39]GERMAN/JUV

ECKHARDT, ROBERT CHRIST.
ECKHARDT, BOB--[31]

ECKHARDT, ROSEMARIE
HARDECK, MARIANNE--[39]GERMAN

ECKSTROM, MICHAEL
JADE, SYMON--[7][23]SF--
PINN "STARSHIP ORPHEUS #1-3" '82-3

EDDISON, ERIC RUECKER
EDDISON, E.R.--[1]

EDDY, CLIFFORD MARTIN JR.
EDDY, C.M. JR.--[31]
HOUDINI, HARRY--[2]GHOSTED

EDE, HAROLD STANLEY
EDE, H.S.--[31]
EDE, JIM--[31]

EDELHARDT, MICHAEL
EDELHARDT, MIKE--[31]

EDELSTEIN, HYMAN
SYNGE, DON--[8]

EDELSTEIN, SCOTT
BRONSON, DONNA--[1][2]

EDEN, DOROTHY E.
PARADISE, MARY--[3][17][21][26][29]MYS/ROM--
ACE G578 "FACE OF AN ANGEL" '61
ACE G593 "SHADOW OF A WITCH" '62
ACE "THE MARRIAGE CHEST"

EDEN, ESKIL FRANS
HEDEN, BALZAR--[29]MYS--12 NOVELS '41-43

EDEN, JOHN LANCELOT
ARTAX--[1]

EDENS, COOPER
DRAGER, GARY--[33]

EDER, GEORGE JACKSON
REED, JACKSON--[21]ROM--
"RAPTURES OF LOVE"

EDGAR, ALFRED
DENVERS, JAKE--[34]MYS--
AMALG "THE COWBOY 'TEC" '24
GREGORY, H.--[34]MYS--
"SECRET OF THE TONG" '36
LYNDON, BARRE--[2][3][11]MYS--3 PLAYS '36-9
SANSOM, JOHN--W/JIMMY SANGSTER,[1][11]

EDGAR, FRANK TERRELL R.
RITCHIE, BILL--[1]

EDGAR, KENNETH FRANK
EDGAR, KEN--[31]

EDGELEY, CYRIL
RODNEY, BRYAN--[34]MYS--
WRIGHT "OWL HOOTS" '45
WRIGHT "OWL MEETS THE DEVIL" '49
WRIGHT "OWL FLIES HOME" '52

EDGHILL, ROSEMARY
BES SHAHAR, ELUKI
MARGARET BALL,[7]SF--
DAW "HELLFLOWER" '91

EDGLEY, L.
GILLIAN, MICHAEL--[40]MYS--
"WARRANT FOR A WANTON" '52
& 4 OTHERS

EDGLY, LESLIE
BLOOMFIELD, ROBERT--[3][8][22]MYS--
8 NOVELS '47-62

EDGLY, LESLIE & MARY
HASTINGS, BROOK--[1][3][22]MYS--
DBLDY "THE DEMON WITHIN" '53

EDINGTON, ARLO & CARMEN
EDINGTONS, [THE]--[1]

EDLER, TIMOTHY
EDLER, TIM--[31]

EDMISTON, HELEN [J.M.]
ROBERTSON, HELEN--[1][3][22]MYS--
4 NOVELS '55-60

EDMOND, JAMES
SALT, TITUS--[13]AUSTRALIA

EDMONDS, ARTHUR DENIS
ARTHUR, ALAN--[1][31]
DENNIS, ARTHUR--[1][31]
EDMONS, ALAN--[1][31]
GRAHAM, ELIZABETH--[1][31]

EDMONDS, HELEN WOODS
FERGUSON, HELEN--[1][2][23]--
USED UNTIL 1940
KAVAN, ANNA--[2][7][23][29]SF--
"MY MADNESS: THE SELECTED WORKS
OF ANNA KAVAN" '90

EDMONDS, IVY GORDON
DAVIS, ROBERT HART--A. TONIK-ECHOES #24, HP--
GL "BURNING AIR AFFAIR" APR '67
MU "STOLEN SPACEMAN AFFAIR" OCT '67
MU "SINISTER SATELLITE AFFAIR" DEC '67
MU "SYNTHETIC STORM AFFAIR" MAY '67
MU "MILLION MONSTERS AFFAIR" 1/68
EDMONDS, I.G.--A. TONIK-ECHOES #27,
[8][32]MYS--
SO "MURDER ON MY MIND" MAR '66
SO "I KILLED KATHY'S KILLER" SEPT '66
GORDON, GARY--[1][31]
GROSS, GENE--[8]

EDMONDS, JAMES A.
EDMONDS, JAE--[1][31]

EDMONDS, MARGARET H.
EDMONDS, MARGOT--[1][31]

EDMONDS, ROBERT H.G.
EDMONDS, ROBIN--[1][31]

EDMONDSON Y COTTON, G.C.
EDMONDSON, GARRY C.--[31]

EDMONDSON Y COTTON, JOSE
CLEVE, JOHN--W/ANDREW J. OFFUTT,[7][23]SF--
BERK "SPACEWAYS #12"
EDMONDSON, G.C.--[2][32]SF--
BERK "ALUMINUM MAN" 75
ACE "SHIP THAT SAILED TIME STREAM" #1 & 2
EQMM "STOP BEING A SUCKER" NOV '57
DA "WILL OF ANSELMO" SEPT '58
EQMM "A QUESTION OF TRANSLATION" DEC '67
GAST, KELLY P.--[2][8][11][23][31]
LOGAN, JAKE--[23]WEST, HP

EDMONDSON Y COTTON, JOSE [CONT]
MASTERSON, J.B.--[1][23]AMERICAN/WEST
MURPHY, MARIO--[1]

EDMONDSON, SYBIL
ARMSTRONG, SYBIL--[1][8]

EDMUNDSON, JOSEPH
BURTON, CONRAD--[8]
JODY, J.M.--[8]

EDON, MARGRET RICCARDA
RAE, RICCARDA--[39]GERMAN

EDRICH, LOUISE
NORTH, MILOU--W/MICHAEL DORRIS,[31]--
"WOMAN" - BOOK REVIEWS

EDRICH, LOUISE & HEIDI
LOUISE, HEIDI--[31]--
MAGAZINES - BOOK REVIEWS

EDSALL, SCHUYLER G.
BARTON, GARY--LACHMAN LST MAY '93,[37]--
CLS '42-3

EDSON, JOHN THOMAS
DENVER, ROD--[1][28][31]WEST--
B&W "ARIZONA RANGER" '62
EDSON, J.T.--[28]ENGLISH/WEST--
B&W "QUIET TOWN" '62
NOLAN, CHUCK--[1][28]

EDWARD, ANN
WEST, ANNA--[8][9]ROM--
"A RING AT THE READY"

EDWARD, FREDERIK
FRANCKEN, FRITZ--[22]DUTCH

EDWARD, JAMES
JAMES, R.--[1]

EDWARDES, MICHAEL F.H.
CASSILIS, ROBERT--[3][8]MYS--
HM "WINDING SHEET" '78
HM "ARROW OF GOD" '79
HM "MADNESS OF THE PEOPLE" '82

EDWARDS, BILL
EDWA--[31]

EDWARDS, F.H.M.
CARNAC, NICHOLAS--[34]MYS--
HM "TOURNAMENT OF SHADOWS" '78
HM "INDIGO" '82

EDWARDS, FLORENCE
EDWARDS, LAURENCE--[8]
JOLLY, SUSAN--[8]

EDWARDS, FREDERICK A.
EDWARDS, CHARMAN--[3][7][22][29]MYS/SF--
"GIVE ME A SHIP" '32
"DRAMA OF MR. DILLY" '39 & MORE
VAN DYKE, JULIUS--[3][22][29]MYS--
FORE "THE BLACK MARKET MURDERS" '45

EDWARDS, GAWAIN
PENDRAY--L. ROBBINS LTR MAR '94

EDWARDS, GEORGE G.
GRAVELEY, GEORGE--[1]

EDWARDS, HENRY JAMES
EDWARDS, HARRY--[31]

EDWARDS, HERBERT C.
EDWARDS, BERTRAM--[1][22][31][33]ENGLISH

EDWARDS, IRENE
BARR, ELIZABETH--[3][8][9][21]
[26][29]MYS/ROM--
NUMEROUS NOVELS '72-9

EDWARDS, JAMES KEITH O.
EDWARDS, JIMMY--[31]

EDWARDS, JANE CAMPBELL
CAMPBELL, JANE--[9][21][26][31][33]ROM--
"BELIEVE NO EVIL"

EDWARDS, JOHN
DENIS, JOHN--W/DENIS FROST,[7]SF--
FONTANA "GOLIATH" '87

EDWARDS, LAWRENCE
LAWRENCE, RICHARD--[2]

EDWARDS, MARIE A. LANDIS
LANDIS, MARIE--W/BRIAN HERBERT,[7][23]SF--
ROC "MEMORYMAKERS" '91

EDWARDS, MICHAEL F.H.
CASSILS, ROBERT--[31]

EDWARDS, ROBERT ALAN
EDWARDS, BOB--[31]

EDWARDS, ROBERT H.
GRANT, E. GORDON--[1]
SAPTE, W.--[1]

EDWARDS, ROSELYN
ALEXANDER, MARGE--[1][31]
EDWARDS, R.M.--[1][31]

EDWARDS, WILLIAM B.
BENET, EDUOARD--[1][22][31]AMERICAN
BRANDT, HARVEY--[1][22][31]AMERICAN
CRANBROOK, JAMES L.--[1][22][31]AMERICAN
EDUARDI, GUILLERMO--[1][22][31]AMERICAN
JOHNSON, CHARLES S.--[1][22][31]AMERICAN
JONES, [CAPT.] WILBER--[1][22][31]AMERICAN
THOMPSON, WILLIAM C.L.--[1][22]AMERICAN

EDWIN, SHARON
RIVERS, NIKKI--[26]ROM--
HARL 550 "SEDUCING SPENCER"

EFFINGER, GEORGE ALEC
DIOMEDE, JOHN K.--[2][11][23][31][32]--
HA "THE FIRST STEP" JUN '73
HA "JEWEL IN THE ASH" AUG '73
DOENIM, SUSAN--[2][11][23][31]SF--
SHORT STORIES
NIEMAND, O.--AUTHOR PROVIDED--
S&SF SHORT STORIES - ALSO OTHER
SHORT MATERIAL

EFIMOV, IGOR M.
MOSCOVIT, ANDREI--[7][34]MYS/SF--
MERCURY "JUDGEMENT DAY ARCHIVES" '88

EFROS, ISRAEL [ISAAC]
EFROT--[31]

EGAN, EDWARD WELSTEAD
MACAODHAGON, EAMON--[1][31][33]

EGAR, RAUL
GODDARD, DARLENE--V. BERCH-BRNDN/
BC PSEUDS, BAE 22, P24

EGAR, RAUL [CONT]
SHIVE, THOMAS--V. BERCH-BRNDN/
BC PSEUDS, BAE 22, P24
SLADE, TRINA--V. BERCH-BRNDN/
BC PSEUDS, BAE 22, P24

EGER, RUDOLF
HOCHGLEND, RUDOLF--[39]GERMAN
RUDOLPH, GEORG--[39]GERMAN

EGERTON, F. CHARLES G.
GRANVILLE, CHARLES--[1][3]MYS--4 NOVELS 1887-97

EGERTON, J.K.
METCALFE, FRANCIS--[1][2][11]

EGETEMEYR, PETER
FROHLAND, PETER--[39]GERMAN

EGG, MARIA
EGG-BENES, MARIA--[31]

EGGELKRAUT-GOTTANKA, HANS
GOTTANKA, HANS--[39]GERMAN/JUV

EGGERT, PAT & JAMES E.
EGGERT, JIM--[31]--
BERGANOT "NO-MORTGAGE HOME" '73

EGGERT, REINHART
REINHART, E.W.A.--[39]GERMAN

EGGERT, VERA
VON GRIMM, VERA--[39]GERMAN/JUV

EGGLESTON, EDWARD
HIGGINS, ZORASTER--[1]
LEISURELY SAUNTERER--[1]
PENHOLDER--[1]

EGGLESTON, GEORGE CARY
REBEL--[1]

EGLETON, CLIVE F.
BLAKE, PATRICK--[3][18][29][31]MYS--
BERK "ESCAPE TO ATHENA" '79
JOVE "DOUBLE GRIFFEN" '81
TARRANT, JOHN--[3][18][29]MYS--
MacD "ROMMEL PLOT" '77
"CLAUBERG TRIGGER" '78
"CHINA GOLD" '82

EGLI, WERNER J.
BARCLAY, ALEX--[39]GERMAN/MYS/WEST
COBB, WALTER J.--[39]GERMAN/MYS/WEST
FIELD, ROBERT S.--[39]GERMAN/MYS/WEST, HP
JORDAN, LEE ROY--[39]GERMAN/MYS/WEST
PRATT, HARPER--[39][40]GERMAN/MYS--
'KOMMISSAR X' SERIES #543
ULLMAN, ROBRT--[39]GERMAN/MYS/WEST, HP

EGLUND, E.P.
KONNEBERG, DR. ERIC VON--W/WALTER C. DEBILL

EHARMAN, RICHARD
MARTIN, RICHARD--[8]

EHLERS, EDITH
MIKELEITIS, EDITH--[39]GERMAN
SCHUMANN, EDZAR--[39]GERMAN

EHLY, MOREEN
EHLY, EHREN M.--[7]SF--
LEIS "OBELISK" '88
LEIS "EVIL EYE" 89
LEIS "TOTEM" '89

EHNEBOM, PAR BIRGER
POWELL, EHRSHAW--[29]MYS--
"JIMMIE BARTON'S STORSTA AFFAR" '26

EHRENBERG, GOLDA
SCOTT, CATHERINE--[8]

EHRENBORG, MRS. C.G.
TREW, CECIL G.--[8]

EHRENBURG, ILYA G.
EHRENBOURG, ILYA [G]--[31]
EHRENBURG, ILYO [G]--[31]
ERENBURG, ILYA G.--[31]

EHRENFREUD, EDMUND OTTO
TARTARUGA, U.--[39]GERMAN/MYS

EHRENZWEIG, ROBERT
LUCAS, ROBERT--[1]

EHRHARDT, PAUL GEORG
JANUS--[39]GERMAN/SF

EHRLICH, BETTINA BAUER
BETTINA--[8][31][33]

EHRLICH, JACOB WILBURN
EHRLICH, JAKE--[31]

EHRLICH, JOHN GUNTHER
DUDGEON, ROBERT--J. HOFFMANN-PP 40, P18, HP--
GERM PANTH 192
RPRT OF DELL FE B220 "SLOW BURN"
EHRLICH, JACK--[28][31]WEST--
4 DELL NOVELS '72-79 & OTHERS '58-73

EHRLICH, LEOPOLD
HICHLER, LEOPOLD--[39]GERMAN

EHRLICH, ROSANNE
EHRLICH, COLLIS--W/ARTHUR COLLIS,
V. BERCH LTR TO HUBIN '94--
BAL "ATTACK" '80

EICH, GUENTER
GUENTER, ERICH--[1][31]

EICHEN, HEINRICH
BIRKEN, HEINZ--[39]GERMAN/JUV

EICHER, [ETHEL] ELIZABETH
CRANE, EDNA TEMPLE--[1][22]AMERICAN,
HP--DELL
PAUL, EMILY--[1][22]AMERICAN
PAUL, WILLIAM--[1][22]AMERICAN

EICHHOF, JOACHIM
ANRAINER, TRAUDL--[39]GERMAN
EICHENHOF, MARTINA--[39]GERMAN
VON HOCHRIED, INA--[39]GERMAN
VON HOLTEN, LORE--[39]GERMAN

EICHHORN, JOSY
GRAF, J.--[39]GERMAN
WALDER, J.--[39]GERMAN

EICHLER, BERTEL
BERGER, LINDA--[39]GERMAN

EICHLER, ERNST
DAVID, ERNST--[1]

EIDE, EDYTHE
TIGRINA--[1][2][11]

EIDEN, PAUL
EDWARDS, PAUL--[34]MYS, HP--
PYR "ICE GODDESS" '74
PYR "DEADLY CYBORGS" '75
PYR "OPERATION WEATHERKILL" '75
PYR "POPPIES OF DEATH" '75
ROMANO, DON--[34]MYS, HP--
PYR "OPERATION: HIJACK" '74
PYR "OPERATION: LOAN SHARK" '74
STAGG, DELANO--W/MEL R. SABRE, V. BERCH-
MON PSEUDS, BAE 9,[1][8]--
MON 140 "GLORY JUMPERS" '59
TREMONT, PHILIP--W/MEL R. SABRE, V. BERCH-
MON PSEUDS, BAE 9,[1][32]--
MON 242 "EASY COME, EASY LOVE" '62
AHMM "IMPOSSIBLE ACCOMPLICE GIZMO" NOV '58
& 6 OTHERS
WINSTON, PETER--[3]MYS, HP--
AWARD "ABC AFFAIR" '67
AWARD "ASSIGNMMENT TO BAHREIN" '67

EIGENBRODT, CARL CHRIST.
EICHENHORST, GUSTAV--[39]GERMAN

EIGNER, LAURENCE JOEL
EIGNER, LARRY--[31]

EIKER, MATHILDE
EVERMAY, MARCH--[3][22]MYS--
MacM "THEY TALKED OF POISON" '38
"THIS DEATH WAS MURDER" '40

EIKERMANN, HELMUT
ERIK, JAN--[39][40]GERMAN/MYS--
"DANN EBEN MORD" '90

EILERS, KONRAD
RIESEK, ROLAND--[39]GERMAN

EILERT, RICHARD E.
EILERT, RICK--[31]

EILSHEMUS, LOUIS MICHAEL
ELSHEMUS, LOUIS M.--[1][7]SF--
"THE DEVIL'S DIARY" 1901

EINSELEN, ANNE FRANCIS
PATERSON, ANNE--[1]

EINSLE, HANS
KOENIGSWALDT, HANS--[39]GERMAN

EINSTEIN, ALBERT
BROOKS, ALBERT--[31]--
SCREENPLAY "REAL LIFE" '79

EIPELDAUER, GERTRUDE
FALLER, GERTH--[39]GERMAN

EISELE, MARTIN
BERGER, MAREIKE--[39]GERMAN/MYS/SF
BURGER, MIKE--[39]GERMAN/MYS/SF
DAMON, ROGER--W/ROLAND ROSENBAUER,
[39]GERMAN/MYS/SF
DARK, JASON--[39]GERMAN/MYS/SF, HP
DELGADO, RYDER--[39]GERMAN/MYS/SF, HP
HOLLBURG, MARTIN--W/W.E. HOHLBEIN,
[39]GERMAN/MYS/SF, HP
SHADOW, MIKE--[39]GERMAN/MYS/SF, HP
TORWEGGE, CLAUDIA--[39]GERMAN/MYS/SF

EISENBERG, ERNEST
THORNE, LUCIFER--[2]

EISENBERG, LAWRENCE B.
DICKENS, NORMAN--[1][31]
EISENBERG, LARRY--[23]SF--
"THE MYNAH MATTER" '62

EISENHARDT, RAYMOND HENRY
HENRY, E. RAY--[1]

EISENHOWER, LEROY R.
LRE--[2]

EISENKOLB, GERHARD
G.E.--[39][40]GERMAN/MYS
KRAUSE, KNUT--[39]GERMAN

EISENPROBST, FERDINAND
CARLSBOURGH, OKTAVIAN--[39]GERMAN
FEDERLI, F.--[39]GERMAN
SCHNEIDER, J.--[39]GERMAN

EISENSTADT-JELEZNOV, MIK.
ARGUS, M.K.--[8]

EISENSTAT, JANE SPERRY
SPERRY, J.E.--[1]
SPERRY, JANE--[22]AMERICAN

EISFELD, RAINER
CAINE, JEFF--[1][11]GERMAN
COOVER, WAYNE--[1][11]GERMAN
EIBEN, ROBERT W.--[39]GERMAN--
TRANSLATION
KUHN, OTTO--[39]GERMAN, HP--
TRANSLATION
REED, ALLAN--[1][11]GERMAN
ROHL, WOLF DETLEF--[1][11]GERMAN
VON EICHENBERG, ARMIN--[39]GERMAN, HP--
TRANSLATION

EISLER, EGON & OSSO
EIS, EGON & OSSO--[39][40]GERMAN/MYS--
"DIE LETZE FRAU VON LONDON" '31

EISLER, LAWRENCE
LAWRENCE, EDDIE--[31]
LAWRENCE, EDWARD--[31]

EISNER, WILLIAM ERWIN
ERWIN, WILL--[31][33]
RENSIE, WILLIS--[33]

EITZERT, ROSEMARIE
CASPARI, TINA--[39]GERMAN/JUV
JONAS, CLAUDIA--[39]GERMAN/JUV

EIZMENDI, INAKI
BASARRI--[1]

EKELOEF, [BENGT] GUNNAR
EKELOF, [BENGT] GUNNAR--[31]

EKLUND, GORDON
STEWART, ALAN W.--[2]

EKLUND, GORDON [STEWART]
STEWART, WENDELL--[2][11][23]--
ONE STORY IN SF MAGAZINE-NO TITLE KNOWN

EKSTROEM, [S] MARGARET
EKSTROM, MARGARETA--[31]

EKWENSKI, CYPRIAN O.D.
EKWENSKI, C.O.D.--[31][33]

EL-HAJJAN, MOHAMMED CHAIB
MRABET, MOHAMMED--[1][7]SF--
"THE BIG MIRROR" '77

EL-MESSIDI, KATHY GROEHN
COSSEBOOM, KATHY GROEHN--[31]

ELBERT, VIRGINIE FOWLER
FOWLER, VIRGINIE--[1]

ELBOGEN, ANDREW
BOGEN, ANDREW--LACHMAN LST MAY '93,[32]--
MSMM "BLACK POWDER"
CC "SHE WAITS"

ELBOGEN, PAUL
SCHOTTE, PAULAS--[1][40]GERMAN/MYS--
"EIN MANN VER FOLGT SICH SELBST" '53
SCHOTTE, PAULAS--[39]GERMAN/MYS

ELDERSHAW, FLORA S.P.
ELDERSHAW, M. BARNARD--W/MARJORIE
F. BARNARD,[2][3][7][23]MYS/SF--
ANGUS "MURDER PIE" '36

ELGIN, BETTY
KIRBY, KATE--[9]ROM

ELGIN, PATRICIA SUZETTE
ELGIN, SUZETTE HADEN--[23]SF--
"OZARK FANTASY TRILOGY"
"COYOTE JONES"
"NATIVE TONGUE"

ELIADES, DAVID
FORREST, DAVID--W/ROBERT FORREST-WEBB,
[2][7][34]MYS/SF--
"AFTER ME, THE DELUGE" '47
HODDER "GREAT DINOSAUR ROBBERY" '70
HODDER "THE UNDERTAKER'S DOZEN" '74

ELIASHIV, ISIDORE
MACSHOVES, BAAL--[22]

ELIOT, CHARLES
ODYSSEUS--[1]

ELIOT, G.F.
SCANLON, C.K.M.--[1][2]HP--THRILLING

ELIOT, GEORGE
EVANS, MARY ANN--[31]

ELIOT, HENRY WARE
DEAL, MASON--[1][22][34]MYS--
HOUGHTON "THE RUMBLE MURDERS" '32

ELIOT, T[HOMAS] S[TEARNS]
APTERYX--[31]
CONYBEARE, CHARLES AUGUS.--[31]
GRIMBLE, REV. CHAS. JAMES--[31]
KRUTZCH, GUS--[31]
SCHWATTZ, MURIEL A.--[31]
SPENCE, J.A.D.--[31]
TRUNDLETT, HELEN B.--[31]

ELIOT, WINSLOW
WINSLOW, ELLIE--[9][21]ROM--
"WINE DARK SEA"
"ROMAN CANDLES" & MORE

ELIZA, GODFRIED
HUEL, FRITS--[22]DUTCH

ELIZABETH, QUEEN, RUMANIA
DITO UND IDEM--[22]RUMANIAN

ELIZABETH, QUEEN, RUMANIA [CONT]
KREMNITZ, MITE--[22]RUMANIAN
SYLVA, CARMEN--[22]RUMANIAN

ELIZONDO, SERGIO D.
DOMINGUEZ, SERGIO ELIZON.--[31]

ELKAN, SOPHIE
ROEST, RUST--[1]

ELKHADEN, SAAD [E.A.]
AL-KHADIM, SA'D--[31]

ELKIN, H.V.
BENTEEN, JOHN--[28]WEST, HP--
TOWER "CUTLER" SERIES #3-6

ELKINS, CHARLOTTE
SPENSER, EMILY--[9][21][26]ROM--
"WHERE EAGLES SOAR"
"CHATEAU VILLON" & MORE

ELKINS, ELLA RUTH
BEDDOE, ELLARUTH--[31]

ELKON-HAMELCOURT, JULIETT
ELKON, JULIETTE--[1][31]

ELLACOTT, SAMUEL ERNEST
ELLACOTT, S.E.--[1]

ELLERBECK, ROSEMARY A.L.
CLARKE, KATHERINE--[1]ENGLISH-SOUTH AFRICAN
L'ESTRANGE, ANNA--[8][9][17][21][26]ROM--
"RETURN TO WUTHERING HEIGHTS"
THORNE, NICOLA--[8][9][17][21][26]ROM--
"CASHMERE"
"BIRD OF PASSAGE" & MORE
YORKE, KATHERINE--[9][17][21][26]ROM--
'ENCHANTRESS SAGA' - 3 NOVELS

ELLERMAN, ANNA WINIFRED
BRYHER--[7][17][31]ROM/SF
BRYHER, WINIFRED--[8]

ELLERMANN, ROLF
WIWJORRA, ERNST OTTO--[39]GERMAN

ELLERSIECK, MARJORIE
ELLERS, MARJII--[1][2]

ELLETT, HAROLD PINCTON
BURNABY, NIGEL--[1][3][22]MYS--
WARD "FOREST MYS" '34
WARD "SECRET OF MATCHAMS" '34
WARD "CLUE OF THE GREEN-EYED GIRL" '35
WARD "TWO DEATHS FOR A PENNY" '35

ELLICOTT, VALCOULON MEMOY
ELLICOTT, V.L.--[31]

ELLIK, RON
BRANDON, CARL--[11]SF
DAVIES, FREDRIC--W/FREDERIC LANGLEY,[2][7]SF--
MU "CROSS OF GOLD AFFAIR" '68
DAVIES, FREDRIC--W/STEVE TOLLIVER,
[1][2][23]SF--
MU "CROSS OF GOLD AFFAIR" '68

ELLIN, ELIZABETH MURIEL
ELLIN, E.M.--[1]

ELLINGER, AUGUST
HOLMS, HOLGER--[39]GERMAN
T.-E., CHARLES ROY EARL--[39]GERMAN

ELLINGER, INGEBURG
LIND, MARIA-MADDALENA--[39]GERMAN/JUV
QUEN, THORA-ELLEN--[39]GERMAN/JUV

ELLINGTON, EDWARD KENNEDY
ELLINGTON, DUKE--[31]

ELLINGTON, NORA & GEORGE
JORGENSEN, N & G--[29]MYS--
APPLETON "CIRCLE OF VENGEANCE" '30

ELLIOT, ANDREW GEORGE
MACANDREW, RENNIE--[8]

ELLIOT, CHRISTOPHER
MARRIOT, JOHN--[8]

ELLIOT, GEORGE FIELDS
SCANLON, C.K.M.--W. MURRAY-ECHOES #5,HP--
GMD "DAN FOWLER" - MOST STORIES

ELLIOT, IAN
DAVIES, COLIN--[31]

ELLIOT, JEFFREY M.
BURGESS, MICHAEL--W/ROBERT R. REGINALD,[7]--
"WORK OF R. REGINALD: AN ANNOTATED
BIBLIOGRAPHY & GUIDE"
BURGESS, MICHAEL--W/ROBERT REGINALD,[23]--
"IF J.F. KENNEDY HAD LIVED:A POLITICAL
SCENARIO" '78
WEBB, LUCAS--W/ROBERT REGINALD,[23]--
"THE ATTEMPTED ASSASINATION OF J.F.
KENNEDY" '77

ELLIOTT, ANNE
ELLIOTT, CHRISTINE--W/CHRISTINE DORSEY,
BOOK BIO,[9][21][26]ROM--
"THE CAPTAIN'S CONQUEST"

ELLIOTT, BRUCE W.
GRANT, MAXWELL--[2][11][37], HP--
SHDM "REIGN OF TERROR" & OTHERS '43-7
LIVELY, WALTER--[1][11]
STACY, BRUCE--[1]
STACY, WALTER--[1]

ELLIOTT, ELTON T.
ELLIOTT, RICHARD--W/RICHARD E. GEIS,[3][7]--
GM "SWORD OF ALLAH" '84
GM "EINSTEIN LEGACY" '86
GM "MASTER FILE" '87

ELLIOTT, ESCALUS E. III
ELLIOTT, CHIP--[1][31]

ELLIOTT, GEORGE ROY
ELLIOTT, G.R.--[1]

ELLIOTT, JAMES FRANCIS
ELLIOTT, JUMBO--[31]

ELLIOTT, KENNETH ALLAN C.
ELLIOTT, ALLAN--[31]

ELLIOTT, LESLEY
GORDON, LESLEY--[1][11]

ELLIOTT, NANCY
DANA, ERIN--[9][21][26]ROM--
"FOOTPRINTS IN THE SAND"
"FOR LOVE OF JADE"
LANGTRY, ELLEN--[9][21][26]ROM--
"THE FIERCE GENTLENESS"

ELLIOTT, NEIL
ELLIOTT, ELLEN--[21]ROM--
"HONG KONG NURSE"

ELLIOTT, ROBERT B.
ELLIOTT, BOB--[31]

ELLIOTT, ROBERT COWELL
REID, DESMOND--[34]MYS, HP--
MAYFLOWER "SOMETHING TO KILL ABOUT" '61

ELLIOTT, WILLIAM J.
LOWITT, E.L.--[2]
RETLAW, HENRY--[2]
TILLOT, W.E.--[2]
W.E./W.J.E.--[2]
WILTE, L.T.J.--[2]
WOLLETT, LEOPOLD J.--[2]

ELLIOTT-CANNON, ARTHUR
CANNON, ELLIOTT--[3][40]MYS--
HALE "BREAKAWAY" '73
HALE "A PIECE OF ACTION" '73 & MORE
FORDE, NICHOLAS--[3][40]MYS--
HALE "URGENT ENQUIRY" '73
HALE "ENGAGED IN MURDER" '77 & MORE
MARTYN, MILES--[8]

ELLIS, DAVID
DUFFY, JOHN--[35]AUSTRALIAN, HP--
HRWTZ "PASS THE BETEL NUT" '63
HRWTZ "BULLY BEEF & LACE" '63
DUNN, JOHN--[35]AUSTRALIAN--
HRWTZ PB202 "STEAK'S OFF LUV" '65

ELLIS, EDWARD S.
ADAMS, JAMES FENIMORE C.--[1]
ADAMS, [CAPT] BRUIN--[1][11]
ADAMS, [CAPT] J.F.C.--[1][31]
BELKNAP, B.H.--[1][31][33]
BELKNAP, BOYNTON--[31]
BELKNAP, BOYNTON, MD--[1][31]
BETHUNE, J.G.--[31][33][34]MYS--
McGILL "F CIPHER" 1892
CASSELL "THIRD MAN" 1893 & MORE
BRISBANE, HENRY R.--[31]
BROWN, MAHLON A.--[1][31]
CARLETON, CAPT. LATHAM C.--[31]
CARLETON, LATHAM C.--[31]
CARLETON, [CAPTAIN] L.C.--[1][31][33]
ELLIS, E.S.--[31]
EMERSON, EDWIN--[1]
FAULKNER, FRANK--[1][31]
GORDON, [COLONEL] H.R.--[1][33]
GWYNNE, OSCAR A.--[1][31]
GWYNNE, OSWALD A.--[1][31]
HAWTHORNE, [CAPTAIN] R.M.--[1][31]
HUNTER, CAPTAIN MARCY--[31]
HUNTER, GEORGE E.--[31]
HUNTER, [LIEUT.] NED--[1][31]
JAYNE, [LIEUT.] R.H.--[1][33]
LASALLE, C.E.--[1][31][33]
LASALLE, CHARLES A.--[31]
LASALLE, GEORGE E.--[1]
LISLE, SEWARD D.--[23][31][33]SF--
"MONARCH OF THE AIR" 1907
MILLBANK, [CAPT.] H.R--[1]
MULLER, BILLEX--[1][33]
RANDOLPH, GEOFFREY--[1]
RANDOLPH, [LIEUT.] J.H.--[1][33]
ROBINS, ROLLO--[1]
ROBINS, SEELIN--[1][33]
RODMAN, EMERSON--[1][33]
ST. MOX, E.A.--[1][34]MYS--
IVERS "HEART OF OAK DETECTIVE,
OR ZIG-ZAG'S FULL HAND" 1902

ELLIS, EDWARD S. [CONT]
THOMAN, EGBERT S.--[1]
WHEELER, CAPTAIN--[1][31][33]

ELLIS, FLORENCE HAWLEY
HAWLEY, FLORENCE M.--[31]

ELLIS, GIN
ELLIS, LYN--[26]ROM--
HARL 488 "DEAR JOHN..."

ELLIS, JULIE M.
BENTLEY, PATRICIA--[9]ROM
ELLIS, JOAN--V. BERCH-LESBIANA/CNTRCLTR, BAE 22,[9]--
MDWD 54 "LANA" '60
ELLIS, MARILYN--[9]ROM
LORD, ALISON--[9][31]ROM
LORD, JEFFREY--[9]SF, HP
MARINO, SUSAN--[3][7][9][21][26]MYS/SF--
AV "VENDETTA CASTLE" '71
MARVIN, RICHARD--[1][9]
MARVIN, SUSAN--[3][7][9][21][26]MYS/SF--
LAN 74-991 "SECRET OF VIA COMO" '66
MICHAELS, LINDA--[9]ROM
MONTE, JILL--[9]ROM
RICHARD, SUSAN--[34]MYS/ROM--
PAPLB "INTRUDER AT MAISON BENEDICT" '67
PAPLB "ASHLEY HALL" '67 & MORE

ELLIS, OLIVER
BRIONY, HENRY--[8]

ELLIS, PETER BERRESFORD
TREMAYNE, PETER--[2][3][7]MYS/SF--
MAGNUM "RETURN OF RAFFLES" '81
SPHERE "ZOMBIE" '81 & MORE
MACALAN, PETER--G. THIESSEN '93,[34]MYS--
ALLEN "THE CONFESSION" '85
ALLEN "KITCHENER'S GOLD" '86
ALLEN "VALKYRIE DIRECTIVE" '87
ALLEN "DOOMSDAY DECREE" '88
SEVERN "FIREBALL" '90

ELLIS, SOPHIE WENZEL
WENZEL, SOPHIE LOUISE--[11]SF

ELLIS, WILLIAM SR.
STRONG, BEN--W/EMERIC HULME-BEAMAN,[1][3]MYS--
HODDER "TRACK OF THE SLAYER" '25 & MORE

ELLIS, WILLIAM DONOHUE
GARTH, JACKSON--[1]

ELLIS-MORRIS, ESTHER
ESTELLE--[1]

ELLISON, GLENN
ELLISON, GLENN "TIGER"--[31]

ELLISON, HARLAN
ARCHER, LEE--BAE 12, P10,[1][2][23]SF, HP--
AMZ "ESCAPE ROUTE" '57
BELDONE, PHIL "CHEECH"--AUTHOR PROVIDED, BAE 12, P10,[1][2]--ARTICLES ONLY
BIRD, C.--JEAN F. LE DEIST-BAE 12,[1][2]
TYPO-NOT USED ACCORDING TO HARLAN
BIRD, CORDWAINER--PP3, P52,[1][2]
BIRD, CORTWAINER--[2]--TYPO-
NOT USED ACCORDING TO HARLAN
CHARBY, JAY--ELLISON-HAWK INTRVW,[2]
AFTER FIRST WIFE-FAVORITE UNTIL DIVORCE--
SFDS "KISSING DEAD" APR '57
SFDS "MAD DOG" AUG '57
SFDS "MURDER MAKES A PICKUP!" DEC '57

ELLISON, HARLAN [CONT]
COURTNEY, ROBERT--AUTHOR PROVIDED,[2]HP--
MINOR USE BY HARLAN-PRIMARILY USED BY CHARLES BEAUMONT
CURTIS, PRICE--AUTHOR PROVIDED,[1][2][31]
DOYLE, JOHN--AUTHOR PROVIDED,[1]
EDMONDSON, WALLACE--AUTHOR PROVIDED,[2][31]--
EDITOR CHOOSE MAIN CHARACTER NAME OF FANTASY UNIV. STORY
ELLIS, LANDON--ELLISON-HAWK INTRVW, [2][31][32]MYS--
TR "HIT & RUN" JUN '57
HARSEN, SLEY--W/HENRY SLESAR, ELLISON-HAWK INTRVW,[31][32]--
SFDS "TOO ANXIOUS TO MURDER!" APR '57
GU "HE DISAPPEARED" MAR '57
HART, ELLIS--ELLISON-HAWK INTRVW/PP3,[2][31]--
TR "TEN YEARS WITHOUT A WOMAN" DEC '56
TR "THE BIG RUMBLE" AUG '56
TR "HER NAME WAS DEATH" JUN '57
SFDS "HELL'S HOLOCAUST" APR '57
GU "HUNCHBACK" JAN '57
GU "BLIND DATE" MAR '57
GU "LOOK ME IN THE EYE, BOY" MAY '57
SFDS "THE NEED TO DIE!" AUG '57
SFDS "BUY ME THAT KNIFE" DEC '57
JARVIS, E.K.--[1][2][23]SF, HP--
AMAZING - ONE STORY
JORGENSEN, IVAR--[2][31]SF, HP--
ZIFF-DAVIS, FEW HARLAN-PRIMARILY PAUL W. FAIRMAN
JORGENSON, IVAR--JEAN F. LE DEIST, BAE 12,[1][2]SF,HP--ZIFF-DAVIS
MADDERN, AL[AN]--AUTHOR PROVIDED,[1][2][31]--
USED ONLY ONCE FOR 'HITCHIKING' STORY
MAGNUS, JOHN--AUTHOR PROVIDED,[32]GHOSTED--
CJ "DEAD WIVES DON'T CHEAT" MAR '57
MERCHANT, PAUL--AUTHOR PROVIDED--
"SEX GANG" ONLY USE-
SUBMTD AS 'D.S.'[DIRTY SEX]-EDITOR CHGD
MITCHELL, CLYDE T.--AUTHOR PROVIDED,[2]SF,HP--
FANTASTIC "THE WIFE FACTORY" '57
NOSILLE, NALRAH--AUTHOR PROVIDED,[1][2]--
FP--FANZINE
PARKER, BERT--AUTHOR PROVIDED,[1][2]
ROBERTSON, ELLIS--W/ROBERT SILVERBERG,[1][2]
ROEDER, PAT--AUTHOR PROVIDED,[1]-- GHOSTED FOR REAL PERSON ONCE WHO WANTED WRITING START
SOLO, JAY--AUTHOR PROVIDED,[2][32]--
SB "EDDIE - YOU'RE MY FRIEND" MAR '65
TIGER, DERRY--AUTHOR PROVIDED,[1][2]--
BASED ON NAME OF FRIEND IN ARMY

ELLISON, JAMES E.
BROTHER FLAVIOUS--[8][22][31]--
CHILDREN'S

ELLISON, JEROME
EMOREY, N.--[1][31]

ELLISON, JOAN AUDREY
ROBERTSON, ELSPETH--[1]

ELLISON, MARJORIE
NORRELL, MARJORIE--[21][26]ROM--27 NOVELS

ELLISON, VIRGINIA HOWELL
HOWELL, VIRGINIA TIER--[1][33]
LEONG, GOR YUN--[1][31][33]
MAPES, MARY A.--[1][33]
MUSSEY, VIRGINIA T.H.--[1][33]
SOSKIN, V.H.--[1][33]

ELLISTON, VALERIE MAE W.
WATKINSON, VALERIE--[22]AUSTRALIAN

ELLSWORTH, SALLIE BINGHAM
BINGHAM, SALLIE--[31]

ELMAN, RICHARD M.
PEARL, ERIC--[22]AMERICAN

ELMAYER-VESTENBRUGG, RUD.
BRUGG, ELMAR--[39]GERMAN

ELMORE, ERNEST CARPENTER
BUDE, JOHN--[32][34][40]MYS--
31 NOVELS '35-58
SS IN MSMM, JCM & LM

ELROD, MARK
DANIELS, MARK--HAWK/ELROD INTRVW NOV '93,
UNPUBLISHED WEREWOLF FANTASY

ELROD, PAT
ELROD, P.N.--HAWK/ELROD INTRVW NOV '93--
ACE "VAMPIRE FILES": 6 NOVELS-
LATEST IS "RED DEATH"

ELSCHNER, KATE
BRANDEL-ELSCHNER, KATE--[39]GERMAN

ELSENSOHN, EDITH M.
MARY ALFREDA--[1]

ELTING, MARY
BREWSTER, BENJAMIN--W/FRANKLIN [B] FOLSOM,[1]
COLE, DAVIS--[22][31][33]--
"THE REAL BOOK ABOUT TRAINS" '51
GORHAM, MICHAEL--W/FRANKLIN [B] FOLSOM,[1]
TATHAM, CAMPBELL--[22][31][33]--
"THE FIRST FLYING BOOK" '44

ELTON, BENJAMIN CHARLES
ELTON, BEN--[23]SF--
"STARK" '89
"GRIDLOCK" '91

ELVESTAD, SVEN CHRISTOFER
BILLER, KRISTIAN F.--W/HERMAN WILDENVEY,
[29][37]MYS--
'LYS OG SKYGGE': 28 NVLS '10-25
RIVERTON, STEIN--[22][29][37]NORWEGIAN/MYS--
'ALIBI: RIVERTON CLUB' MAG
"IRON CHARIOT" '09

ELVIN, ANNE KATHARINE S.
STEVENSON, ANNE--[29]MYS--
COLLINS "A RELATIVE STRANGER" '70

ELWARD, JAMES JOSEPH
JAMES, REBECCA--[3][9][21][31]ROM--
DBLDY "HOUSE IS DARK" '76
"STORM'S END"
"TOMORROW IS MINE"
VAN SLYKE, HELEN--[26]ROM--
UNCREDITED CO-AUTHOR OF "PUBLIC SMILES,
PUBLIC TEARS"

ELWART, JOAN FRANCES
ELWART, JOAN POTTER--[8]
TRAWLE, MARY ELIZABETH--[8]

ELWENSPOEK, CURT
GANTER, CHRISTOPH ERIK--[39]GERMAN

ELWENSPOEK, LISE-MELANIE
BRACK, MONIKA--[39]GERMAN/JUV

ELWYN, MARY
PATCHETT, M.E.--PPCC#6, P59--
"SEND FOR JOHNNY DANGER" '54?

ELWYN-JONES, PEARL BINDER
BINDER, PEARL--[1]

ELY, GEORGE HERBERT
STRANG, HERBERT--W/CHARLES JAMES
L'ESTRANGE,[1][2][11][23]--
BOY'S ADVENTURE

ELYTIS, ODYSSEUS
ALEPOUDELIS, ODYSSEUS--[31]

ELZABURU, MANUEL
AMADOR, AMERICO--[1]
MONTES, FABIAN--[1]

ELZER, MARGARETE
DUEREN, HANNA--[39]GERMAN

ELZINGA, KENNETH GERALD
JEVONS, MARSHALL--W/WILLIAM BREIT,[1][3]MYS--
HORTON "MURDER AT THE MARGIN" '78

EMANUEL, VICTOR ROUSSEAU
BRANSCOMBE, EUGENE--[2]
EGBERT, H.M.--[2][7][11]SF--
"MY LADY OF THE NILE" '23
"ERIC OF THE STRONG HEART" '25
"MRS ALADDIN" '25
EMANUEL, R.V.--L. ROBBINS LTR MAR '94
EMANUEL, V.R.--[1][23]
ROGERS, HARRY, D.D.--[2]
ROUSSEAU, V.--[23]AMERICAN--
ALL STORY WKLY "THE SEA DEMON'S" '16
ALL STORY WKLY "DRAUGHT OF ETERNITY" '18
ROUSSEAU, VICTOR--[7][23][32]MYS--
MZ "A CRY FROM BEYOND" MAR '60
MZ "CURSE OF AMEN-RA" FALL '67
SN "MEDIUM FOR JUSTICE" SPR '67
MZ "WHEN DEAD GODS WAKE" JAN '69
SEWELL, CAPT. ALBERT--[2]
TRENT, CLIVE--[1][2][11]

EMENEGGER, ROBERT
EMENEGGER, BOB--[31]

EMERSON, DONALD C.
CONGER, DONALD--[3]MYS--
LEIS "CLOSEOUT" '80

EMERSON, ERNEST
MILKY WHITE--[8]

EMERSON, HENRY OLIVER
EMERSON, H.O.--[31]
GORDON, OLIVER--[31]

EMERSON, KATHY LYNN
GORTON, KAITLYN--[9][21][26][31][33]ROM--
"CLOUD CASTLES"

EMERSON, L.W.
FIELD, PETER--AL TONIK-P.V. LST--
HOUSE "DIG THE SPURS DEEP"
HOUSE "GUNS ROARING WEST"-BOTH '53

EMERY, BESSIE
HEAD, BESSIE--[1]

EMERY, EDITH PATTOU
PATTOU, EDITH--[7]SF--
"HERO'S SONG" '91

EMMERICH, JOSEPH FRIEDR.
WEBER, LUCIAN--[39]GERMAN

EMMONS, ELIZABETH WALES
EMMONS, ELISE--[1]

EMMOTT, WILLIAM JOHN
EMMOTT, BILL--[31]

EMMRICH, CURT [KURT]
BAMM, PETER--[1][31][39]GERMAN

EMMS, DOROTHY
CHARQUES, DOROTHY--[8]

EMPRINGHAM, ANTOINETTE F.
EMPRINGHAM, TONI--[31]

EMPRINGHAM, DOUGLAS R.
ROOME, DOUGLAS DEREK--[2]

EMRICH, DUNCAN [B.M.]
MACDONALD, BLACKIE--[1][31][33]

EMRICH, LUDWIG FRIEDRICH
EMRICH, LOUIS--[39]GERMAN

EMSHWILLER, EDMUND A.
ALEXANDER, ED--[1][2][11]
EMSH--[1][2]
EMSHLER--[1][2][11]
GARS, HENRY--[1][2]
WILLER--[1][2][11]
EMSH, ED--[11]SF
EMSHWILLER, ED--[23]SF

ENCAUSSE, GERARD [A.V.]
PAPUS--[31]

ENCEL, SOLOMON
ENCEL, SOL--[31]

ENCIMER, PAUL D.
DONNE, JACK--V. BERCH-BRNDN/
BC PSEUDS, BAE 22, P24

ENDERLE, JUDITH [A] ROSS
ENDERLE, JUDITH--W/STEPHANIE G.
TESSLER,[21]ROM--14 NOVELS
GORDON, JEFFIE ROSS--W/STEPHANIE G.
TESSLER,[7][21][31]--
"A TOUCH OF GENIUS"
"A TOUCH OF MAGIC"

ENDERWITZ-BINDSEIL, ILSE
BINDSEIL, ILSE--[39]GERMAN

ENDORE, [SAMUEL] GUY
RELIS, HARRY--[1]

ENDT, PIETER
COENRAADS, EDWARD--[22]DUTCH

ENEFER, DOUGLAS STALLARD
BOGARD, DALE--[27]MYS--
WDL "HOMICIDE IN HARLEM" & 12 OTHERS '50-2
DENVER, PAUL--[34]MYS--
WDL & CONSUL, 9 NOVELS '65-75
POWERS, JOHN--[34]MYS, HP--
WDL "THE BIG SLAM" '53

ENEY, RICHARD HARRIS
ENEY, DICK--[7]SF

ENG, STEPHEN
BREDON, JOHN--[2]

ENGEL, ARTHUR JASON
ENGEL, A.J.--[31]

ENGEL, BERND
BERND, MAXIMILIAN--[39]GERMAN/SF

ENGEL, DAVID GEORG
GIL, DAVID G.--[1]

ENGEL, ELMAR
HOLBACH, JUPP--[39]GERMAN

ENGEL, HOWARD
WOOLF, F.X.--W/JANET HAMILTON,[18][34]MYS--
VIKING "MURDER IN SPACE" '85

ENGEL, LYLE KENYON
BANNON, DON--[40]AMERICAN/MYS--
"KILLER AT LARGE" '75
KENYON, LARRY--[8]
KENYON, PAUL--[8]
LORD, JEFFREY--W. MURRAY--
BLADE SERIES, PP 1,[2]SF, HP--
ORIGINATED
STANLEY, RAY--V. BERCH-LESBIANA/CNTRCLTR,
BAE 26, P5
VIGA, DIEGO--[39]GERMAN

ENGELBERG, ALAN D.
ENGEL, ALAN--[7][31]SF--
FINE "VARIANT: A NOVEL" '88
ENGEL, ALAN M.D.--[34]MYS--
FINE "VARIANT" '89

ENGELHARDT, THOMAS ALEX.
ENG--, TOM--[31]
ENGELHARDT, TOM--[31]

ENGELKES, GUSTAV G.
SCHIPPER, ULRICH--[39]GERMAN/JUV

ENGELS, MARY TATE
KEATON, COREY--W/VICKI L. THOMPSON,
[9][21][26]ROM--
"THE NESTING INSTINCT"
KENYON, CORY--W/VICKI L. THOMPSON,
[9][21][26]ROM--
"FORTUNE HUNTER"
"RUFFLED FEATHERS" & OS
MCKENNA, TATE--[9][21][26]ROM--
"CAPTIVE DESIRE"
"LEGACY OF LOVE" & MORE

ENGELSBERGER, BERTA
BERRY, ROLAND--W/JOSEF ENGELSBERGER,
[39][40]GERMAN/MYS--
'KOMMISSAR WILTON' SERIES - 16 BKS
MARTENS, FRED--W/JOSEF ENGELSBERGER,
[39][40]GERMAN/MYS--
'KOMMISSAR WILTON' SERIES - 14 BKS

ENGELSBERGER, JOSEF
BERRY, ROLAND--W/BERTA ENGELSBERGER,
[39][40]GERMAN/MYS--
'KOMMISSAR WILTON' SERIES - 16 BKS
MARTENS, FRED--W/BERTA ENGELSBERGER,
[39][40]GERMAN/MYS--
'KOMMISSAR WILTON' SERIES - 14 BKS

ENGEN, ERIKA
BERGHOFER, ERIKA--[39]GERMAN

ENGER, LEIF & LIN
ENGER, L.L.--LACHMAN/EASTER LST '93,
DLY PLEAS #3,[34]MYS--
"COMEBACK" '90
"MURDER IN WRIGLEY FIELD" '91

ENGINGER, BERNARD
SATPREM--[1]

ENGLANDER, RICHARD
ALTENBERG, PETER--[1][22][39]GERMAN

ENGLE, JOHN DAVID JR.
JOHNN, DAVID--[31]

ENGLEBERT, MICHAEL
GRAYN, MICHAEL--[2]

ENGLEHART, ROBERT WAYNE
ENGLEHART, BOB--[31]

ENGLEMAN, PAUL
FRANCIS, PAUL--[31][34]MYS--
PR "MURDER ON TOUR" [W/DICK CLARK] '89

ENGLISH, ANASTASIA MARY
MARIA--[1]

ENGLISH, DORIS S.
STATON, ANNA LLOYD--W/JUDY S. ROCKER,
[21][26]ROM--
"THE CHALLENGED HEART"

ENGLISH, JEAN ELLEN
FRENCH, ELLEN JEAN--[8]

ENGLISH, THOMAS DUNN
DONKEY, JOHN--[1]
OGDEN, CHRISTOL--[1]
PAYNE, F.M.--[1]
QUICKENS, QUARLES--[1]

ENGSTRAND, IRIS W.
WILSON, IRIS HIGBIE--[1]

ENGSTROM, BETSY LYNN G.
ENGSTROM, ELIZABETH--[7]HOR--
"WHEN DARKNESS LOVES US" '85
"BLACK AMBROSIA" '88
"LIZZIE BORDEN" '91

ENGSTROM, THEODORE WILLH.
ENGSTROM, TED W.--[31]

ENGSTROM, TOIVO ARMAS JO.
KING, DICKY--[29]MYS--
"STUDION I LAGOR" '45

ENGUIDANOS USACH, PASCUAL
VAN SMITH, S.--JEAN F. LE DEIST LTR JAN '93
WHITE, GEORGE H.--JEAN F. LE DEIST LTR JAN '93
WITTE, GEORGE H.--JEAN F. LE DEIST LTR JAN '93

ENIKEEV, AMIRKHAN N.
ENIKI, AMIRAKHAN--[1]

ENRIGHT, DENNIS JOSEPH
ENRIGHT, D.J.--[1]

ENSIGN, THOMAS
ENSIGN, TOD--[31]

ENSKAT, FRITZ
CATSEN, FREDER--[39]GERMAN/JUV

ENSLEY, W. EVANGELINE W.
WALTON, EVANGELINE--[1][7][34]MYS/SF--
ARKHAM "WITCH HOUSE" '45
"THE SWORD IS FORGED" '82

ENTON, HARRY
FREE, [MAJ.] MICKEY--[1]
GILMAN, WINONA--[1]
HARRISON, HARRY--[1]
HAYNES, HENRY HARRISON--[1]
IRONCLAD--[1]
NONAME--[1][11], HP
VERSATILE, VAL--[1]

EPHRON, DELIA
BROCK, DELIA--[1][31][33]

EPP DE HARY, ELEONORE
EPP, JOVITA--[39]GERMAN

EPP, MARGARET A.
GOOSSEN, AGNES--[1][22][31][33]CANADIAN

EPPERS, EVA
CHRISTOFF, EVA--[39]GERMAN/SF
QUINT, ROBERT--W/W.K. GIESA &
R. ZUBEIL,[39]GERMAN/SF

EPSTEIN, BERYL [WILLIAMS]
ALLEN, ADAM--W/SAMUEL EPSTEIN,[1][22]JUV--
6 BOOKS '37-44
COE, DOUGLAS--W/SAMUEL EPSTEIN,[1][22]--
NON-FICTION--2 BOOKS
STRONG, CHARLES--W/SAMUEL EPSTEIN,[1][31]--
MESSNER "STRANGER AT THE INLET" '46
WILLIAMS, BERYL--[21][22][31][33]ROM--
"NO PATTERN FOR LOVE"
"MIRACLE FROM MICROBES" '46

EPSTEIN, JOSEPH
ARISTIDES--[31]

EPSTEIN, MICHAIL S.
GOLODNYJ, MICHAIL--[22]RUSSIAN

EPSTEIN, SAMUEL
ALLEN, ADAM--W/BERYL W. EPPSTEIN,[1][22][31]--
"TIN LIZZIE" '37 & 5 JUV BOOKS
CAMPBELL, BRUCE--[22][31][33][37]MYS/ADV--
'KEN HOLT' SERIES
COE, DOUGLAS--W/BERYL W. EPPSTEIN,[1][22][31]-
-
"BURMA ROAD" '46 & NON-FICTION
STRONG, CHARLES--W/BERYL W. EPPSTEIN,
[22][31][33]--
MESSNER "STRANGER AT THE INLET" '46

ERB, UTE
SCHURRER, UTE--[39]GERMAN

ERBSCHLOE, VICTORIA LEIGH
LEIGH, VICTORIA--[26]ROM--
LVSPT 646 "TAKE A CHANCE ON LOVE"

ERCKMANN, EMILE
ERCKMANN-CHARTRIAN--W/ALEXANDRE CHARTRIAN,
[2][11]MYS--
EB "MYSTERIOUS SKETCH" DEC '62
ERCKMANN-CHARTRIAN, M.M.--W/ALEXANDRE
CHARTRIAN,[34]MYS--
WARD "MAN-WOLF & OTHER TALES" 1875

ERCOLE, VELIA
GREGORY, MARGARET--[1]

ERDMANN, FRANZ
MARNER, FRANK--[39]GERMAN, ADV

ERDMANSDORFFER, FRIEDRICH
LAURIN, FRIEDRICH--[39]GERMAN

ERDURAN, REFIK
KANATSIZ, NECATI--[2]/ISFY

ERG, DANIEL
ALLAN, JACK--[29]MYS--
"DET RODA AVENTYRET" '18

ERHOLM, ESTER
ERHOMAA, ESTER--[1]

ERICHSEN, UWE
BENDIX, GERALD--[39]GERMAN/MYS/WEST
BENTEEN, JOHN--[39]GERMAN/WEST, HP
COTTON, JERRY--[39]GERMAN/MYS, HP
HAMMOND, GIL--[39]GERMAN/MYS/WEST
JAGO, THOMAS--[39]GERMAN/MYS/WEST
LAFITTE, JEAN--[39]GERMAN/MYS/WEST, HP
MCCOY, STEVE--[39][40]GERMAN/MYS--
'KOMMISSAR X' #605, 611, 613, 621 & #624
MCKAY, ANDREW--[39]GERMAN/MYS/WEST
SHERIDAN, JIM--[39]GERMAN/WEST
SLADE, JACK--[39]GERMAN/WEST, HP
SOLO, FRANCO--[39]GERMAN/MYS/WEST, HP

ERICKSON, SABRA ROLLINS
HOLBROOK, SABRA--[22][31]AMERICAN

ERICKSON, STEPHEN M.
ERICKSON, STEVE--[7][23][31]--
"DAYS BETWEEN STATIONS" '85
"RUBICON BEACH" '86

ERICSSON, GUSTAV
BRANDT, MARTIN--[29]MYS--
"GIRIGA HANDER" '36

ERICSSON, THORE
GUNBY, PETER--[29]MYS--
BONNIERS "DE TRE VISE MANNEN" '45
"I SISTA OGONBLICKET" '46

ERIE, PAUL
D'AVOI, PAUL--[1]

ERIKSEN, BARBARA
ARTHUR, KATHERINE--[9][21][26]ROM--
HARL 3282 "RELUCTANT LOVER" & 10 OTHERS

ERIKSON, ERIK HOMBURGER
HOMBURGER, ERIK--[31]

ERIKSON, SIBYL C. ALEX.
DICK, ALEXANDRA--[3][22]MYS--
HURST "AND ONLY MAN" '44
HALE "CRIME IN THE CLOSE" '55 & MORE
ERIKSON, CHARLOTTE--[1][22]MYS
HAY, FRANCES--[1][3][22]MYS--
JENKINS "LADY WITH A ROSE" '50
JENKINS "TRAITOR'S ISLAND" '56
ERICSON, SIBYL--[34]MYS--
BOUREGY "THE CURATE'S CRIME" '46

ERIKSSON, ERIK EINER
ERIX, EINER--[29]MYS

ERIKSSON, GUSTAF RUNE
SCOTT, NICK--[29]MYS

ERIKSSON, LENNART
RENNEL, KAJ--[29]MYS--23 NOVELS '54-56

ERIKSSON, SVEN-OLOF
EIRIK, SVEN O.--[29]MYS

ERLEI, HANS JOSEF
ERLAY, DAVID--[39]GERMAN

ERLICH, BETTINA BAUER
BETTINA--[22]ENGLISH

ERNE, GIOVANNI BRUNO
ERNE, NINO--[39]GERMAN

ERNSBERGER, GEORGE
CARTER, AMANDA--[34]MYS--
ZEBRA "WRITE ME A MURDER" '79

ERNST, ADOLPH
STERN, ADOLPH--[1]

ERNST, PAUL FREDERICK
EDSON, GEORGE ALDEN--[1][2][11][16]
FREDERICKS, ERNEST JASON--
ACE "SHAKEDOWN HOTEL" '58
ACE "CRY FLOOD!" '59
FREDERICKS, ERNEST JASON--L. ROBBINS
LTR MAR '94,[32][34]--
MSMM "BLACK BADGE OF INNOCENCE" JUN '59
KELLEY, BRYAN JAMES--[37]MYS--
PUE - LEAD NOVEL DEC '35
FEDA - 'G-77' NOVEL JAN '37
MARTIN, FRANKLIN H.--[37]MYS--
FEDA - 'AGENT K-67' LEAD NOVEL, MAR '37
ROBESON, KENNETH--[2][7][11][23][34]MYS, HP--
AVENGER SERIES #1-24
STERN, PAUL FREDERICK--[1][2][11][16]--
WIERD TALES

ERNST, [LYMAN] JOHN
CHERNOFF, DOROTHY A.--[31]
CLARK, DAVID ALLEN--[31][33]

ERNSTING, WALTER
ARTNER, ROBERT--W/ULF MIEHE,[39]GERMAN/SF/WEST
CHESTER, TOM--[39]GERMAN/WEST, HP
DARLTON, CLARK--[7][11][23][31][39]GERMAN/SF--
ACE "ATLAN #2 & #5"
ACE "PERRY RHODAN #68, 73, 76, 77, 83, 86, 87, 93, 97, 103, 109, 113, 118, 121, 127, 132 & 137"
HALLER, FRANK--[39]GERMAN/SF/WEST
I., CLARKUS--[39]GERMAN/SF
MACPATTERSON, F.--[2][11][23]GERMAN
MCPATTERSON, FRED--[39]GERMAN/SF/WEST
STIRNAGEL, ALOIS--[39]GERMAN/SF/WEST
UPTON, MUNRO R.--W/W. KUMMING, W. REINECKE, W. SCHOLZ & J. SCHEIDT,[39]GERMAN/SF
VON EICHENBERG, ARMIN--[39]GERMAN/SF/WEST, HP

ERPENBECK-ZINNER, HEDDA
ZINNER, HEDDA--[39]GERMAN

ERSKINE, BARBARA
BUCHAN, KATE--[31]

ERSKINE, GLADYS SHAW
ANTONIO--[1]
DON QUIXOTE--[1]
ERSKINE, FIRTH--W/IVAN EUSTACE FIRTH, [3][22][29]MYS--
MCL "NAKED MURDERS" '33

ERSKINE, THOMAS
T.E.--[2]

ERTL, ANNELIESE
BEHRINGER, SABINE--[39]GERMAN

ERTTMANN, PAUL OSKAR
DOLLINGER, MARGARET--[39]GERMAN
DWEN, KARL--[39]GERMAN
MUNIN, HANS--[39]GERMAN
PERKINS, BILLY--[39]GERMAN

ERTTMANN, PAUL OSKAR
PITT, PAUL--[39]GERMAN
TEMBORN, KLAUS--[39]GERMAN

ERVIN-TRIPP, SUSAN MOORE
ERVIN, SUSAN--[31]

ESCHBACH, JOSEF
DELHEID, BRIGITTE--[39]GERMAN/JUV
HEUSCHEN, MONIKA--[39]GERMAN/JUV
SCHWARZER, ANNALIESE--[39]GERMAN/JUV
YORK, HELGA--[39]GERMAN/JUV

ESCHERICH, ELSA FALK
FALK, ELSA--[1][22][31]AMERICAN

ESCHKOTTER, MARLENE
BIANCA-MARIA--[39]GERMAN
GRANT, SUSAN--[39]GERMAN

ESCHMEYER, REINHART ERNST
ESHMEYER, R.E.--[31]

ESCHNER, LENA
ROCKER, FERRY--W/EBERHARD WORM, [39][40]GERMAN/MYS-- "IN EINER NEBELNACHT" '53

ESCOTT, JONATHAN
LEONARD, JASON--[18][31]MYS--
"MEET MRS. PERCY" '81
"A LITTLE WAR IN SARAWAK" '82
ESCOTT, JACK LEONARD--[18][31]MYS
SCOTT, JACK S.--[1][3]MYS--
15 NOVELS '76-86

ESCRIVA DE BALAGUER, JOSE
ESCRIVA, JOSEMARIA--[31]

ESHBACH, LLOYD ARTHUR
SPATZ, H. DONALD--[2]
SMITH, E.E. "DOC"--[23]GHOSTED--
"SUBSPACE ENCOUNTER" '83, WRITTEN FROM 'SMITH' OUTLINE
DRAKE, W. ANDERS--[1]
GAUNT, PETER--[1][31]
SCHUYLER, JUDY--[1]

ESHLEMAN, LLOYD WENDELL
GREY, LLOYD ERIC--[7]SF, NON-FICT--
"WILLIAM MORRIS, THE LIFE OF WILLIAM MORRIS"

ESLER, CAROL CLEMEAU
CLEMEAU, CAROL--[1][3][31]MYS--
SCRIBNER "THE ARIADNE CLUE" '82

ESPEY, JOHN
HIGHLAND, MONICA--W/LISA SEE & CAROLYN SEE,[8][21][26]ROM--
"LOTUSLAND"
"SHANGHAI ROAD"

ESPINASSE, ALBERT
BRESSEUR, PIERRE--[31]

ESPINASSE, MARGARET
WATTIE, MARGARET--[1]

ESPINO, FEDERICO LICSI JR
DE EXTRAMUROS, QUIXOTE--[31]

ESPINOZA, RUDOLPH LOUIS
ESPINOZA, RUDY--[31]

ESSEN, ANDERS AXEL HARALD
EJE, ANDREAS--[34]MYS--
BALE "A HORRIBLE SUSPICION" '20
EJE, ANDERS--[29]MYS--9 NOVELS '11-19
FEDJA, FELIX--[29]MYS
MALM, GUN MAJ.--[29]MYS
NARAYANA, HARI--[29]MYS
RUNARSSON, HADAR--[29]MYS

ESSEN, R^TGER THURESSON
ERIKSSON, LEIF--[29]MYS

ESSENMACHER, EUGENIA R.
RILEY, EUGENIA--[9][21]ROM--
"ANGEL FLAME"
"LAURA'S LOVE" & 9 OTHERS

ESSER, MAURITS
VANECKEREN, GERARD--[22]DUTCH

ESSEX, HARRY
RIVERA, PICO--W/OSCAR SAUL, CRPG--
DELL 1147 "THE AMIGOS" '75

ESSL, HERBERT
FENTON-BRICKS, MARK--[39]GERMAN/MYS
SEEL, JOCHEN--[39]GERMAN/MYS

ESSOE, GABOR ATTILA
ESSOE, GABE--[1]

ESTELLE, [SISTER] MARY
CASALANDRA, ESTELLE--[22]AMERICAN

ESTENSSORO, HUGO
CHARTIER, EMILIO--[31]

ESTERGREEN, MARIAN MORGAN
ESTERGREEN, M. MORGAN--[31]

ESTIVAL, IVAN LEON
ESTIVAL--[1][2][11][26]ROM--7 NOVELS

ESTLEMAN, LOREN D.
WATSON, DR. JOHN H.--[7]SF--
AS EDITOR-"DR. JEKYL & MR. HOLMES" '79
"SHERLOCK HOLMES VS DRACULA" '78

ESTRADA, PATRICIA WALLACE
WALLACE, PATRICIA--[7]SF--
AV "HOUSE OF SCORPIO" '75
POCK "THE WAND & THE STAR" '78

ESTRADA, RITA
CLAY, RITA--[9][21][26]ROM--
"YESTERDAY'S DREAMS"
"SUMMER SONG" & 5 MORE
LACY, TIRA--[9][21]ROM--
"WITH TIME & TENDERNESS"
"ONLY TO LOVE"

ESTRIDGE, ROBIN
LORAINE, PHILIP--[2][3][7][18]MYS/SF--
HODDER "ANGEL OF DEATH" '61
COLLINS "DAY OF THE ARROW" '64
YORK, ROBERT--[18]MYS--
SCRIBN "SWORDS OF DECEMBER" '78
SCRIBN "MY LORD THE FOX" '84

ESZTERHAS, JOSEPH A.
ESZTERHAS, JOE--[31]

ETCHISON, BIRDIE L[EE]
HUNTER, LEIGH--[1][31][33]
WOOD, CATHERINE--[1][33]

ETCHISON, DENNIS WILLIAM
DOVER, BEN--B. LEVIN--
OASIS "LOVES & INTRIGUES OF DAMIAN-dj" '69
ETCHINSON, DENNIS--
DARK DREAMS - P51 "THE FOG" '80
MARTIN, JACK--[7][34]SF/HOR--
ZEBRA "HALLOWEEN II" '81
JOVE "HALLOWEEN III" '82
ZEBRA "VIDEODROME: A NOVEL" '83
MENSCH, H.L.--W/ERIC COHEN, B. LEVIN--
OASIS "STUD ROW" '69

ETTER, LESTER FREDERICK
ETTER, LES--[31]

ETTIGHOFER, PAUL COELEST.
VON WACHENDORF, F. LOHR--[39]GERMAN

ETTINGER, LEOPOLD DAVID
ETTINGER, L.D.--[31]
ETTINGER, LEOPOLD D.--[31]

ETTINGHAUSEN, MAURICE
SACHS, MAURICE--[22]FRENCH

ETTLE, JOSEF
BIRKLER, HUBERTUS--[39]GERMAN

EUBANK, JAMES E.
BANKS, KELLEY--[3]MYS--
VANTAGE "TEN-THE HARD WAY" '55

EUBANKS, GENE
CODY, GENE--[1]

EULER, GUNTER
BLATTMACHER, KALL--[39]GERMAN

EULERT, DONALD DEAN
EULERT, DON [31]--[31]

EURELIUS, GUNNO
DAHLSTIERNA, GUNNO--[1]

EUSTIS, ORVILLE B.
EUSTIS, O.R.--[31]

EUWE, MACHGIELIS
EUWE, MAX--[31]

EVANOVICH, JANET
HALL, STEFFIE--[9][26]ROM--
"HERO AT LARGE"
"FOUL PLAY"
"FULL HOUSE"

EVANS, ALBERT EUBULE
TELLET, ROY--[34] LIPPINCOTT--
BLACKWOOD "A DRAUGHT OF LETHE" 1891
BLACKWOOD "PASTOR & PRELATE" 1892

EVANS, CHRIS[TOPHER D.]
CARPENTER, CHRISTOPHER--[2][7][23]SF--
ARROW "THE TWILIGHT REALM" '85
CHRISTIE, EVAN--[23]SF
DAVIES, ALWYN--[23]SF
ELLIOTT, NATHAN--[2][23]SF--
GRAFTON "HOOD'S ARMY TRILOGY" '86
'STAR PIRATES' #1-3 '87
KNIGHT, ROBERT--[7][23]SF--
STAR "PLASMID" '80
LYON, JOHN--[7][23]SF--
PANTHER "THE SUMMONING" '85

EVANS, CONSTANCE MAY
GRAY, JANE--[1][9][22][31]ROM
O'NAIR, MAIRI--[3][9][22]MYS/ROM--
MILLS "DANGEROUS LADY" '34
MILLS "BEAUTIFUL CROOK" '37

EVANS, DARDANELLA LISTER
EVANS, DEE--[1]

EVANS, DAVID
EVANS, CARADOC--[1][22]ENGLISH

EVANS, DAVID ARNOLD
ARNOLD, LEWIS--[1]

EVANS, E. EVERETT
GARDENER, HARRY J.--[2][11]
GARDENER, HENRY--[1]
VERETT, E.--[1][2]
VERETT, H.E.--W/THELMA EVANS,[1][11]

EVANS, FRANK HOWELL
DAUNT, ATHERLEY--[1]
PAYNE, CRUTCHLEY--[1]

EVANS, GEORGE
GERAINT, GEORGE--[8]

EVANS, GEORGE BIRD
BIRD, BRANDON--W/KAY H. EVANS,[32][34]MYS--
BS "WINGS OF DEATH" MAR '59
4 DODD NVLS '50-5
EVANS, HARRIS--W/KAY H. EVANS,[1][3][22]MYS--
DODD "THE PINK CARRARA" '60

EVANS, GEORGE ESSEX
CHROSTOPHUS--[22]AUSTRALIAN

EVANS, GERALD
LA SALLE, VICTOR--K. DILBONE-BADGER CKLST,
BAE 13,[2], HP--
SPENCER "BLACK SPHERE" '51

EVANS, GILLIAN ROSEMARY
EVANS, G.R.--[31]

EVANS, GLEN
EIRELIN, GLENN--[1][31]

EVANS, GLYN
IFANS, GLYN--[8]

EVANS, GWYNFIL ARTHUR
EVANS, GWYN--W/G.H. TEED, R.M. GRAYDON
& G.N. PHILIPS,[1][34]--
WRIGHT "MURDERERS MET" '34
GWYNNE, ARTHUR--[1]
WESTERN, BARRY--[1][34]MYS--
AMALG "SIGN OF THE DOUBLE FOUR" '40
AMALG "MYSTERIOUS MR. MONTAGUE" '40
AMALG "PHANTOM OF SCOTLAND YARD" '40

EVANS, GWYNNE BLAKEMORE
EVANS, G.B.--[31]
EVANS, GWYNNE B.--[31]

EVANS, HILARY
AGARD, H.E.--[1][31]MYS--
HALE "THE ASSASSIN" '65

EVANS, HUGH AUSTIN
AUSTIN, HUGH--[3][22][29]MYS--
"MURDER IN TRIPLICATE" '35
DBLDY "COCK'S TAIL MURDER" '38

EVANS, IDRISYN OLIVER
EVANS, I.O.--[1]

EVANS, JEAN
GRAHAM, RUTH--[1][31]

EVANS, JEAN BELL SHAW
SHAW, JANE--[1]

EVANS, JEAN LORNA
JACOBY, JEAN--[1]

EVANS, JOHN
BROWNE, HOWARD--[1]

EVANS, JULIE RENDEL
HOBSON, POLLY--[3][29][31]MYS--
BENN "MYSTERY HOUSE" '63
CONSTABLE "TITTY'S DEAD" '68 & MORE

EVANS, KATHLEEN
KAYE, EVELYN--[8]

EVANS, KAY & STUART
TRACEY, HUGH--[8]

EVANS, KAY HARRIS
BIRD, BRANDON--W/GEORGE B. EVANS,[32][34]MYS--
BS "WINGS OF DEATH" MAR '59
4 DODD NOVELS '50-5
EVANS, HARRIS--W/GEORGE B. EVANS,[1][22][31]--
DODD "THE PINK CARRARA" '60

EVANS, LAWRENCE WATT
WATT-EVANS, LAWRENCE--[1][7][23]SF

EVANS, MARGUERITE H.J.
BARCLAY, MARGUERITE--[1][17]ENGLISH/ROM
BARCYNSKA, COUNTESS--[1][22][34]ENGLISH/MYS--
5 SS COLL '20-30
SANDYS, OLIVER--[3][22]ENGLISH/MYS--
LONG "WOMAN IN THE FIRELIGHT" '11
"CHICANE" '12

EVANS, MATILDA JANE
FRANC, MAUD JEAN--[13]AUSTRALIA

EVANS, PAMELA
WYKHAM, HELEN--[1]

EVANS, THELMA D. HAMM
EDWARDS, HAMM--[1][2][11]
HAMM, T.D.--[1][11]
HAMM, THELMA D.--[1]
VERETT, H.E.--W/E. EVERETT EVANS,[1][11]

EVANS, WILLIAM DANIEL
ENERGLYN, LORD--[1]

EVANS, WILLIAM HARRINGTON
EVANS, BILL--[7][23]SF--
UNGER "THE GERNSBACH FORERUNNERS" '44

EVANS-JONES, ALBERT
CYNAN--[22][31]ENGLISH

EVE, REGINALD T.
CONQUEST, OWEN--[1] HP

EVELAND, WILBUR CRANE
EVELAND, BILL--[31]

EVELYN, JOHN MICHAEL
UNDERWOOD, MICHAEL--MYS SCENE #38,
[18][29][32][34]MYS--
33 NVLS '57-80
JCM "COINCIDENCE" MAR '57

EVENS, GEORGE BRAMWELL
ROMANY--[8]

EVERETT, ELIZABETH ABBEY
EVERETT, EZA--[1]
FAIRBANKS, SABRINA--[1]

EVERETT, MRS. H.D.
DOUGLAS, THEO--[2][3][11][16]MYS--
BLACKWOOD "IRAS" 1896
EVERETT "THREE MYSTERIES" '04 & MORE

EVERETT-GREEN, EVELYN
ADAIR, CECIL--[1][22][25][31]--CHILDREN'S
DARE, EVELYN--[1][6][25][31]CHILDREN'S--
"PATRICIA PENDRAGON" '11
H.F.E.--[31]
WARD, EVELYN--[1]

EVERHART, JAMES WILLIAM
EVERHART, JIM--[31]

EVERSLEY, DAVID E.C.
SMALL, WILLIAM--[8][22]GERMAN-ENGLISH

EVERSON, WILLIAM OLIVER
BROTHER ANTONIUS--[8][22][31]AMERICAN

EVERWIEN, MAX
EVER, MAC--[39]GERMAN/MYS

EVES, REGINALD T.
BRITTON, HERBERT--[1]
CLIFFORD, MARTIN--[1] HP

EWANS, GWENDOLINE W.
ASHLEY, GLADYS--[1]
WILSON, GWENDOLINE--[1]

EWART, ERNEST ANDREW
CABLE, BOYD--[3]MYS--
HUTCH "ROLLING ROAD" '23
HUTCH "A DOUBLE SCOOP" '24 & ONE MORE

EWART-BIGGS, CHRISTOPHER
ELLIOTT, CHARLES--[8]

EWEGEN, YVONNE
ADAMSON, YVONNE--W/MARY JO ADAMSON,
ENID SCHANTZ, DDLY PLEAS #3--
"BRIDEY'S MOUNTAIN"
MONTGOMERY, YVONNE--DDLY PLEAS #3--
"SCAVENGERS" '87
"OBSTACLE COURSE" '90

EWER, MONICA
CROSBIE, ELIZABETH--[8]

EWERS, HANNS HEINZ
FRANZ, ONKEL--[39]GERMAN/SF

EWING, GEORGE M.
EWING, EDGAR--[2]

EWING, JAN
ELLERY, JAN--[34]MYS--
ZEBRA "DEATH ON THE CIRCUIT" '79
ZEBRA "THE LAST SET" '79
ZEBRA "FAMILY AFFAIRS" '79
ZEBRA "HIGH STRUNG" '80

EWING, JIM
COBURN, SAM--[35]AUSTRALIAN--
CLEVELAND PUBL

EWING, JULIANA H. GATTY
GATTY, JULIANA HORATIA--[31][33]

EWING, KATHRYN
DOUGLAS, KATHRYN--[9][21][26][31][33]ROM--
"CAVENDISH PRIDE" & MORE

EWINGS, MICHAEL
ROSS, FRANK--W/COLIN NORTHWAY,[3]MYS--
MacM "DEAD RUNNER" '77
STUART, BLAIR--[34]MYS--
MacM "BLOODWEALTH" '80

EYEN, TOM
EYEN, JEROME--[31]PLAYS
SHORT, ROGER--[31]PLAYS

EVERLY, JEANETTE
GRIFFITH, JEANETTE--W/VALERIA W. GRIFFITH,
[8][22][31][33]ROM--
16 NOVELS '61-80

EYSSELINCK, JANET GAY
BURROWAY, JANET--[8]

EYSTER, WILLIAM REYNOLDS
WILBY, R. HUNT--[1]

FABBRI, NANCY RASH
HARRISON, MARY--[1]

FABER, ELSE
ARMSTRONG, JOHN--[29]MYS
ARMSTRONG, WALDO--[37]DANIS/MYS
BLAKE, STACEY--[29]MYS--
"MED DODEN OMBORD" '38
"GULDAKTIERNA" '46
BURTON, CECIL--[29]MYS--
"SIVA-SKRIGET" '56
RASTHOLF, J.--[29]MYS--
35 NOVELS '46-56
RASTHOLT, JORGEN--[29][37]DANISH/MYS--
'SUSPENSE: THE ALEXANDER SERIES' '43-50

FABER, INEZ MCALISTER
BERESFORD, ELIZABETH--[7]SF/HOR--
"HAUNTINGS: THE WOODEN GUN" '89

FABIAN, R. RUTH
ARMITAGE, EILEEN--[29]MYS--
"EN DOFT AV VIOLER" '77

FABRICIUS, SARA
SANDEL, CORA--[22]NORWEGIAN

FABRY, JOSEPH B.
FABRIZIUS, PETER--W/MAX KNIGHT,[1][31]

FACEY, GERALD
FACEY--BAPC #11--
SPENCER & BADGER COVER ARTIST
FACEY, G.--BAPC #11--
GANNET & POCK [UK]COVER ARTIST

FACKENHEIM, PAUL ERNST
COTTON, JERRY--[39]GERMAN/MYS, HP

FACKLER, ELIZABETH
FACKLER, ELI--[1][31]

FADEL, SUHEIL
SCHAMI, RAFIK--[39]GERMAN/JUV

FADIMAN, EDWIN JR.
MARK, EDWINA--J.PRESSMAN-LESBIANA,
BAE 20, P32,[1]--
BERK G44 "MY SISTER, MY BELOVED" '57

FAEHNDRICH, MARGARITA
VON KIESLING, ANGELA--[39]GERMAN

FAFUENTE ESTEFANIA, M.A.
SPRING, TONY--JEAN F. LE DEIST LTR JAN '93

FAGERBERG, SVEN
BERHGLIND, FRANCIES--[29]MYS--
"FLICKAN INUTI" '70

FAGETTE, WOODBURY WILLIAM
WOODY, WILLIAM--L. ROBBINS LTR,[34]MYS--
ACE D379 "MISTRESS OF HORROR HOUSE" '59

FAGIOLO, MARIO
DELL'ARCO, MARIO--[22]ITALIAN

FAGUE, WILLIAM ROBERT
FAITH, WILLIAM ROBERT--[31]

FAGYAS, MARIA
BUSH-FEKETE, MARY--[1]
FAY, MARY HELEN--[31]

FAHRENKOPF, ANNE
IRVING, ALEXANDER--W/RUTH FOX [HUME],
[3][33]MYS--
DODD "BITTER ENDING" '46
DODD "DEADLINE" '47
DODD "SYMPHONY IN TWO TIME" '48

FAID, MARY
DINN, MARY--[9]ROM

FAILLET, GEORGES EUGENE
FAGUS--[22]FRENCH

FAIN, MICHAEL
MICHAEL, JUDITH--W/JUDITH BARNARD,
[1][21][26]ROM-- 7 NOVELS

FAINZIBERG, ILYA ARNOLD.
ILF, ILYA--[31]

FAIRBAIRN, EDWIN
MOHOAO--[2]

FAIRBANKS, DOUGLAS SR.
THOMAS, ELTON--[2]

FAIRBURN, ARTHUR REX D.
FAIRBURN, A.R.D.--[1]

FAIRBURN, ELEANOR
CARFAX, CATHERINE--[1][3][31]MYS--
HALE "TO DIE A LITTLE" '74 & 3 MORE
GAYLE, EMMA--[1][31]
LYONS, ELENA--[1][3][31]MYS--
PIARKUS "HAUNTING OF ABBOTSGARTH" '80
NEVILLE, ANNA--[1]

FAIRCHILD, JOHN
ESTERHAZY, LOUISE J.--[8]

FAIRCHILD, WILLIAM
CRANSTON, EDWARD--[8][31]

FAIRCLOUGH, CHRIS
HAMPTON, DAVID--[1]

FAIRCLOUGH, CHRIS
HAMPTON, DAVID--[31]

FAIRDE, DONALD
BECKMAN, ROSS--W/FREDERICK V.R. DEY & KENNETH FEARING,[11]SF--
BEECKMAN, ROSS--W/FREDERIC V.R. DEY, [11][34]MYS--
WATT "LAST WOMAN" '09
WATT "PRINCESS ZARA" '09

FAIRFAX-BLAKEBOROUGH, J.F
BLAKEBOROUGH, JACK FAIRF.--[31]
HAMBLETONIAN--[31]

FAIRFIELD, RICHARD IVAN
RICH--[1]

FAIRLIE, GERARD
SAPPER--W/CYRIL MACNEILE,[8][29]MYS

FAIRMAN, PAUL W.
CHANDLER, LAWRENCE--[2]HP--ZIFF-DAVIS
CHASE, ADAM--W/STEPHEN MARLOWE, [2][11][18][23]--
"THE GOLDEN APE" '59
DANIELS, PAUL--[1][32][34]MYS--
AHMM "MAN #6" DEC '59
MH "SWITCH-BLADE" FEB '60
MSMM "THE IVORY TOWER" DEC '60
BDTM "MOTEL GIRL" '60
MAGNET "NAKED STREETS" '60
MSMM "THE DARK ROAD HOME" FEB '61
MON 233 "PLAYBOY" '61
MON 254 "COVER GIRLS "62
MON 291 "SHOW GIRLS" '62
MON 299 "RUBY" '63
MON 422 "JEALOUS" '64
DEL REY, LESTER--W/LESTER DEL REY--
"INFINITE WORLDS OF MAYBE" '66
"TUNNEL THROUGH TIME" '66
DEL RAY, LESTER--W/ALVAREZ DEL RAY,[1][2][23]--
"THE RUNAWAY ROCKET" '66
"ROCKET FROM INFINITY" '66
"SIEGE PERILOUS" '66
"THE SCHEME OF THINGS" '66
"PRISONERS OF SPACE" '68
FAIRMAN, P.W.--BLACK ACE AUCT#31--
ASF "NEVER TRUST A MARTIAN"
FAIRMAN, PAULA--W/ROBERT VAUGHAN,[21][26]--
"IN SAVAGE SPLENDOR"
FAIRMAN, PAULA--[9][26]ROM--
"FORBIDDEN DESTINY"
"STORM OF DESIRE" & 11 OTHERS
FRANCIS, LEE--[2]HP--FANTASTIC ADV/AMAZING
GARSON, CLEE--[1][2]HP--
FA "NINE WORLDS WEST" '57
JARVIS, E.K.--[1][2][23]HP--ZIFF-DAVIS
JORGENSEN, IVAR--[2][23][32][34]MYS--
MON "REST IN AGONY" '63
MON "TEN FROM INFINITY"
FA "WHOM THE GODS WOULD SLAY" '51
LEE, ROBERT [EGGERT]--[2][11][23][31] HP
LOHRMAN, PAUL--[2][11][23][31]HP--ZIFF-DAVIS- '50-3
LOVESMITH, JANET--[9][21][26][34]--
INHERIT THE SHADOWS"
"LEGACY OF FEARS"
"THE LOCK"
PAUL, F.W.--[2][11][34]ADULT/MYS--
MAGNET "PRIZE OF FLESH" '60
LAN 73-754 "ORGY AT MADAME DRACULA'S" '68
LAN 74-531 "PLANNED PARENTHOOD CAPER" '69
LAN 74-553 "LAY OF THE LAND" '69
LAN 74-591 "GIRL WITH THE POLKA-DOT BOX" '69
LAN75-168 "KING ON QUEEN" '71

FAIRMAN, PAUL W. [CONT]
POLLARD, JOHN X.--[2], HP--ZIFF-DAVIS
QUEEN, ELLERY--W/DANNAY & LEE,[2][3]MYS--
GOLZ "A STUDY IN TERROR" '66 - HOLMES SEQUENCES
SPENCER, LEONARD G.--[2]HP--ZIFF-DAVIS
STORM, MALLORY--[1][2][11][23]SF
VANCE, GERALD--[11]HP
WARREN, PAULETTE--[3][9][21][26]MYS/ROM--
18 NOVELS '65-77

FAITHFULL, GAIL
KELLER, GAIL FAITHFULL--[1][31][33]

FAKENHEIM, PAUL ERNST
ERNEST, PAUL--[39]GERMAN/MYS

FALCONER, ALEXANDER FRED.
FALCONER, A.F.--[31]

FALENSKI, FELICJAN MEDARD
FELICJAN--[22]POLISH

FALK, HERMANN
BIRD, AL--[39][40]GERMAN/MYS--
"MURDER SO REAL" '78
BIRD, ERIC ALLEN--[39]GERMAN/MYS
BIRD, ERIK ALLAN--[39]GERMAN/MYS/WEST
CASSY, WILLIAM O.--[39]GERMAN/MYS/WEST
DALTON, FRANK--[39]GERMAN/WEST
EYLL, ORGE--[39]GERMAN
FALK, ELISABETH--[39]GERMAN/MYS/WEST
KENNAN, DAN--[39]GERMAN/MYS/WEST
ORLOFF, WERA--[39]GERMAN/MYS/WEST
PATTON, GLENN--[39]GERMAN/MYS/WEST, HP
SCHWARZE, PETER--[39]GERMAN/MYS/WEST
SCOTT, HENRY O.--[39]GERMAN/MYS/WEST
TURREK, SAM--[39]GERMAN/MYS/WEST
VOLKER, HEINZ--[39]GERMAN/MYS/WEST

FALK, STEPHEN JOHN
FALK, TOBY--[31]

FALK, SUSAN MEYERS
MEYERS, SUSAN--[1]

FALKE, KONRAD
FREY, KARL--[22]SWISS

FALKENHEYN, EGON
REDZICH, CONSTANTIN--[39]GERMAN

FALLON, JOHN WILLIAM
FALLON, JACK--[31]

FALLON, M.
MALLORY, LEE--[35]AUSTRALIAN--
CLVD 953 "TEN DAYS TO SHOWDOWN"
CLVD 963 "TIN STAR HERO"
CORONADA 972 "THE PROFESSIONAL"
SIERRA 442 "SIX-GUN VENGEANCE"
SANTE FE 330 "STEEL OF THE B-BAR-C"
SHANNON, COLE--[35]AUSTRALIAN--
CLEVELAND PUBL
DEXTER, LEE--[34]--
WARREN "POLICE DETECTIVE STORIES"
"CASE OF THE BROOKLYN MOBSTER" BOTH '49

FALUDY, GYORGY
FALUDY, GEORGE--[1][31]

FANE, VIOLET
CURRIE, MARIE M.L.S.--[31]

FANG LIZHI
FANG, L.Z.--[31]

FANGK, DOROTHEA
SIEBENBRODT, DOROTHEE--[39]GERMAN/JUV

FANGMEIER, NORBERT
METLER, ALF--[39]GERMAN

FANNING, D. CHRISTOPHER
CLARE, PATRICK--[1]
DEE, JOHN--[1]
LANE, GERALD--[1]

FANTHORPE, R.L.
BALFORT, NEIL--K. DILBONE--
BADGER PSEUDS, BAE 15, P54,[1][2][31]
BARON, OTHELLO--K. DILBONE-
BADGER PSEUDS, BAE 15, P54,[1][2][11][31]
BARTON, EARL [ERLE]--K. DILBONE-
BADGER PSEUDS, BAE 15, P54,[2][23][31]--
"THE PLANET SEEKERS" '64
BARTON, LEE--K. DILBONE-
BADGER PSEUDS, BAE 15, P54,[2][7][31]SF--
BADGER "THE UNSEEN" '63
BADGER "THE SHADOW MAN" '66
BELL, THORNTON--K. DILBONE-
BADGER PSEUDS, BAE 15,[1][2][31]SF--
BADGER "SPACE TRAP" '64
BADGER "CHAOS" '64
BERTRAM, NOEL--[1][11][23][31]SF
BRETT, LEO--K. DILBONE-BADGER PSEUDS,
BAE 15,[2][23][31]SF--
18 NOVELS/COLLECTIONS
FANE, BRON--K. DILBONE-BADGER PSEUDS,
BAE 15,[2][23][31]SF-- 12 BOOKS
HOBEL, PHIL--[1][31]
JAY, MEL--[1][2][11][31]SF--
"ORBIT ONE" '66
JOHNS, MARSTON--[2][11][23][31]SF--
"THE VENUS VENTURE" '65
"BEYOND TIME" '66
KENTON, L.P.--[2][7][11][23]SF--
BADGER "DESTINATION MOON" '59
LA SALLE, VICTOR--[2][7][11][31]SF, HP--
SPENCER "MENACE FROM MERCURY"
LERTETH, OBAN--[2][31]
LERTETH, OBEN--K. DILBONE-BADGER PSEUDS,
BAE 15,[2][11]
LIONEL, ROBERT--[2][11][23]SF--
"TIME ECHO" '64
"THE FACE OF X" '65
MULLER, JOHN E.--K. DILBONE-BADGER PSEUDS,
BAE 15,[2][23]SF--
H--SPENCER '61-6
NEEF[E], ELTON T.--K. DILBONE-BADGER PSEUDS,
BAE 15,[2][23]SF
NOBEL, PHIL--K. DILBONE-BADGER PSEUDS,
BAE 15,[2][23]SF--
BADGER "THE HAND FOR GEHENNA" '64
O'FLYNN, PETER--K. DILBONE-BADGER PSEUDS,
BAE 15,[2][23]-- SPELLING VAR. O'FLINN
RAYMOND, JOHN--K. DILBONE-BADGER PSEUDS,
BAE 15,[2]SF, HP--SPENCER
ROBERTS, LIONEL--K. DILBONE-BADGER PSEUDS,
BAE 15,[2][23]SF--11 BOOKS
ROLANT, RENE--K. DILBONE-BADGER PSEUDS,
BAE 15,[2]][23]SF
SPARTACUS, DEUTERO--K. DILBONE-BADGER PSEUDS,
BAE 15,[2][23]SF
TATE, ROBIN--K. DILBONE-BADGER PSEUDS,
BAE 15,[2]
THANET, NEIL--K. DILBONE-BADGER PSEUDS,
BAE 15,[2][23]SF--
BADGER "BEYOND THE VEIL" '64
THORPE, TREBOR [TREVOR]--K. DILBONE-
BADGER PSEUDS, BAE 15,[2][23]SF--
4 NOVELS '60-4

FANTHORPE, R.L. [CONT]
TORRO, PEL--K. DILBONE-BADGER PSEUDS,
BAE 15,[2][23]SF--12 NOVELS '60-4
TRENT, OLAF--K. DILBONE-BADGER PSEUDS,
BAE 15,[2][23]SF--
BADGER "ROMAN TWILIGHT" '63
ZEIGFREID, KARL--K. DILBONE-BADGER PSEUDS,
BAE 15,[2]SF, HP--
12 SPENCER NOVELS '62-5

FANTONI, BARRY [ERNEST]
ADDIO, E.I.--[8]
FLANNEL, J.C.--[8]
GASKET, BAMBER--[8]
HARRIS, STUART--[31]
KRIN, SYLVIE--[8][31]
SLAGG, GLENDA--[8]
THRIBB, E.J.--W/RICHARD INGRAMS,[8]

FARALLA, DOROTHY W.
FARALLA, DANA--[1][31][33]
WILMA, DANA--[1][33]

FARB, STAN PETERS
FARB, PETER--[1]

FARBER, OTTO
FERLING, OTTO--[39]GERMAN

FARBER, SIGFRID
KORNTHEUR, KONRAD--[39]GERMAN/JUV

FARELY, CAROL
MCDOLE, CAROL--[1]

FARGUS, FREDERICK JOHN
CONWAY, HUGH--[2][7][29][34]MYS/SF--
"A CARDINAL SIN" 1886
"SECRET OF THE STRADEVARIOUS" '24

FARIDI, SHAH NASIRUDDIN M
FARIDI, S.N.--[31]
JAREED--[31]

FARIGOULE, LOUIS
HICKS, JOHN H.--[1]
ROMAINES, JULES--[1][7][22] FRENCH WRITERS BIO
ROMAINS, JULES--OXFORD COMPANION TO
FRENCH LIT. 1961,[1][2]

FARJEON, ANNABEL
JEFFERSON, SARAH--[33]

FARJEON, ELEANOR
CHIMAERA--[1][31][33]ENGLISH--
VERSE-LONDON DAILY HERALD
TOMFOOL--[1][22][33]ENGLISH--
CHILDREN'S-ALSO 'TIME & TIDE' VERSE

FARJEON, EVE
JEFFERSON, SARAH--[8]

FARJEON, J. JEFFERSON
SWIFT, ANTHONY--[2][3][23]MYS/SF--
HALE "MURDER AT A POLICE STATION" '43
WHITE, LEONARD--[1]

FARKAS, ALADAR A.
RAY, OSCAR--[22]HUNGARIAN-AMERICAN

FARLEY, CAROL
MCDOLE, CAROL--[33]

FARLEY, GEORGE P.
CULVER, MAJOR HENRY C.--[34]MYS--
LAIRD "PULLMAN CAR DETECTIVE" 1894

FARMER, BERNARD J.
FOX, OWEN--[22][29][31]ENGLISH/MYS--
"DEATH OF A BOOKSELLER" '56

FARMER, DEREK
ALLEN, DEREK--W/BRAM STOKER,[7]--
BARRON'S ED. "BLOOD FROM THE
MUMMY'S TOMB" '88

FARMER, HENRY
WRIGHT, FRANKLIN--[1]

FARMER, MINNIE ELIZABETH
HARRINGTON, ELIZABETH--[1]

FARMER, PHILIP JOSE
ADAMS, NICK--[2]AMERICAN
CHAPIN, PAUL--[1][2][23]/ISFYB AMERICAN
EDEN, MARTIN--[2]AMERICAN
GRANDRITH, LORD--[4]AMERICAN
GREYSTROKE, LORD--[1][2]AMERICAN
HEROVIT, JONATHAN--[2]AMERICAN
KEEN, ROD--L. ROBBINS LTR,[1][2]AMERICAN
MANDERS, HARRY "BUNNY"--[1][2][23]SF
NORFOLK, WILLIAM--L. ROBBINS LTR,[2]
SOMERS, JONATHAN SWIFT--L. ROBBINS LTR,[1][2]
TINCROWDER, LEO QUEEQUEQ--L. ROBBINS LTR,
[1][2]/ISFYB
TROUT, KILGORE--[2][4][7][23]SF--
DELL "VENUS ON THE HALF-SHELL" '75
VON ASCHENBACH, GUSTAVE--[2]
VON WAU WAU, RALPH--L. ROBBINS LTR,[2]
WATSON, JOHN H.,MD--[2][4][31][37]MYS--
ASPEN "ADVENTURES OF THE PEERLESS PEER"

FARMERS, EILEEN ELIZABETH
LANE, ELIZABETH--[1]

FARNDALE, W.A.J.
FARNDALE, JAMES--[8]

FARNILL, BARRIE
WELLINGTON, JOHN--[1][8]

FARQUHAR, JESSE CARLTON
SCOTT, JOHN-PAUL--[8]

FARR, DIANA PULLEIN-THOMP
PULLEIN-THOMPSON, DIANA--[22]ENGLISH

FARR, WILLIAM T.
FARR, BILL--[31]

FARRAR, JOHN C.
PROSPER, JOHN--W/PROSPER BURANELLI,[3]MYS--
DORAN "GOLD-KILLER" '22

FARRELL, A. CLIFFORD
ANDERSON, NELSE--L. ROBBINS LTR MAR '94, HP
DEERE, PHILIP F.--L. ROBBINS LTR MAR '94, HP
FARRELL, CLIFF--L. ROBBINS LTR AMR '94
LITCHFIELD, FRANK JOHNSON--L. ROBBINS
LTR MAR '94, HP

FARRELL, ANNE ELISABETH
ALLABEN, ANNE E.--[8]

FARRELL, BRIAN ANTHONY
FARRELL, B.A.--[31]

FARRELL, DAVID
SMITH, F.E.--[21][26]ROM--
"DARK CLIFFS"

FARRELL, FRANCIS THOMAS
FARRELL, FRANK--[31]

FARRELL, HENRY
HENRY, CHARLES--[3][40]MYS--
RANDOM "THE HOSTAGE" '59

FARRELL, JAMES THOMAS
FARRELL, JAMES T.--[31]
FOGARTY, JONATHAN TITUL.--[22]AMERICAN

FARRELL, JOHNNY
LUGAR, HANS--[29]MYS, HP--
"NIGHT RIDE"

FARRELL, MICHAEL
BURKE, MICHAEL--[8]
GULLIVER, LEMUEL--[8]

FARRIE, HUGH
WESTBURY, HUGH--[34]MYS--
MacM "FREDERICK HAZZLEDEN" 1887

FARRINGTON, DAVID P.
FARRINGTON, D.P.--[31]

FARRIS, JOHN
BRACKEEN, STEVE--[34]MYS--
MYH "BODY ON THE BEACH" '57
CREST 206 "BABY MOLL" '58
CREST 316 "DANGER IN MY BLOOD" 59
GM 1255 "DELFINA" '62
HOLT "GUARDIANS" '64

FARROW, R.
VINCENT, JOHN--[8]

FARSON, DANIEL NEGLEY
EXCELLENT, MATILDA--[1][31]

FARWELL, JANET
CROLY, ELIZABETH--[1]

FASANO, DONNA
CLAYTON, DONNA--[21][26]ROM--
"MOUNTAIN LAUREL"
"TAKING LOVE IN STRIDE"

FASSHAUER, NANCY SUSAN C.
CHATFIELD, SUSAN--[9][21][26]ROM--
MacF "BRIDE OF THE LION"
MacF "DAWNING OF DESIRE" & MORE

FAST, HOWARD [MELVIN]
CUNNINGHAM, E.V.--[2][3][18][29][40]MYS--
16 NOVELS '60-79
ERICSON, WALTER--G. LOVISI, PP 9, P44,
[2][3][11][22][31][33]MYS--
LITTLE "FALLEN ANGEL" '52
RPRTD AS ACE D17 "THE DARKNESS WITHIN" '53

FAST, JULIUS
BARNETT, ADAM--[1][31]

FATIZIECE, UNDINE
INDRANE, ILZE--[1]

FATTARSI, ANN MARIE
DANIELS, REBECCA--[26]ROM--
"FOG CITY"
"L.A. HEAT"
"L.A. MIDNIGHT"

FAUCHER, PAUL
CASTOR, PERE--[1]

FAULEY, WILBUR FINLEY
FAWLEY, WILBUR--[2][7][34]MYS/SF--
GREEN CIRCLE "SHUDDERING CASTLE" '36

FAULK, ODIE B.
PROFESSOR X--[1]

FAULKNER, ANNE IRVIN
FAULKNER, NANCY--[21][26][31][33]ROM--
POPLB "THE JUDE BOX"
CURTIS "WITCHES BREW" & MORE

FAULKNER, DOROTHEA M.
MAGILL, RORY--[1][2][11]

FAULKNER, MARY
LINDSAY, KATHLEEN--[6]

FAULKNOR, CLIFF[ORD V.]
WILLIAMS, PETE--[1][22]CANADIAN

FAURE-BIGUET, JACQUES N.
DECREST, JACQUES--[3][29][40]MYS--
"HASARD" '33
"LE RENDEZ-VOUS DU DIMANCHE SOIR" '35
& MORE

FAUST, CAMILLE
MANCLAIR, CAMILLE--[1]

FAUST, FREDERICK S.
AUSTIN, FRANK--ROBERT EASTON-MAX BRAND,
[28][31]WEST--
DODD "RETURN OF THE RANCHER" '33 & 2 MORE
BAXTER, GEORGE OWEN--ROBERT EASTON-MAX BRAND
ECHOES #76--
WSM "BLACK SNAKE & GUN" DEC '31 & 17 NOVELS
BOLT, LEE--ROBERT EASTON-MAX BRAND,
[29][31]MYS--
BRAND, MAX--ROBERT EASTON--
MAX BRAND,[2][5][7][28]WEST/MYS--
NUMEROUS NOVELS
BUTLER, WALTER C.--R. EASTON-MAX BRAND,
[3][5]--
MCL "CROSS OVER NINE" '35
MCL "NIGHT FLOWER" '36
CHALLIS, GEORGE--ROBERT EASTON--
MAX BRAND,[2][28][31]WEST/HIST--
WS "THE TYRANT" 9 JAN-13 FEB '26
BOBBS "SPLENDID RASCAL" '26
HARPER "BAIT & THE TRAP" '51 & 4 MORE
DAWSON, PETER--ROBERT EASTON-MAX BRAND,
[2][28][31]WEST--
WS "BLACK MULDOON" 30 SEPT '22
DEXTER, MARTIN--ROBERT EASTON-MAX BRAND,
[28][31]--
WS "SHERIFF LARRRABEE'S PRISONER" DEC '21
EVAN, EVIN--ROBERT EASTON-MAX BRAND,[2][31]
EVANS, EVAN--ROBERT EASTON-MAX BRAND,
[2][28][31]WEST--
11 NOVELS '33-53
FREDERICK, JOHN--ROBERT EASTON-MAX BRAND,
[2][28]WEST--
NUMEROUS SS & 3 NOVELS '20-32
FROST, FREDERICK--R. EASTON-MAX BRAND,
[2][5][31][34]MYS--
MACRAE "SECRET AGENT NUMBER ONE" '36
MACRAE "SPY MEETS SPY" '37
MACRAE "BAMBOO WHISTLE" '37
LAWTON, DENNIS--ROBERT EASTON-MAX BRAND,
[2][31]
LITTLE BOBBIE--L. ROBBINS LTR MAR '94
M.B.--L. ROBBINS LTR,[8]
MANNING, DAVID--ROBERT EASTON-MAX BRAND,
[2][28][31]WEST--
18 NOVELS '24-8
MORLAND, PETER HENRY--ROBERT EASTON-MAX BRAND,
[28][29]WEST--
WS "SQUAW BOY" JUL/AUG '25 & 13 MORE SS

FAUST, FREDERICK S. [CONT]
OWEN, HUGH--R. EASTON-MAX BRAND,[2][28]WEST--
WS "RED WELL" DEC '34 & 3 MORE SS
SILVER, NICHOLAS--R. EASTON-MAX BRAND,
[2][28]WEST--
WS "RED RIDER" JUL '24
URIEL, HENRY--R. EASTON-MAX BRAND,[2][28][29]
WARD, PETER--L. ROBBINS LTR,[2]

FAUTSKO, TIMOTHY FRANK
EMPLOYEE X--[31]

FAVORS, JEAN
MORRIS, ELIZABETH--[9][10][21][26][34]MYS--
HARL "A TEASPOON OF MURDER" '89
& ROM NOVELS IN 80's

FAWCETT, DENNIS
OWEN, RICHARD--W/DAVID NOTT, V. BERCH LTR
TO HUBIN '94--
DUTTON "EYE OF THE GODS" '78

FAWCETT, FRANK DUBREZ
BORELLI, CASS--S. HOLLAND-SCION CKLST,
PP 27, P11
DEL MARTIA, ASTRON--[1][2]HP--GAYWOOD PRESS
DUPRES, HENRI--[2][22][23][27][31]SF
FARRA, MADAME E.--[2][22][23][31]
GLEN, EUGENE--[2][22][23][27][31]
GORDON, SPIKE--[3]MYS, HP--
MOF - ALL BUT THREE BY BOYCE,
BUXTON & FEARN
GRIFF--[2][31][34]MYS, HP--
MOF "FROM DANCE HALL TO OPIUM DEN" '50
MOF "SOME RATS HAVE TWO LEGS" '50
MOF "HOT SHOT RITA" '51
MOF "GOODBYE TOMORROW" '51
MOF "BROOKLYN MOLL SHOOTS BEDMATE" '51
MOF "EASTERN MEN" '51
MOF "MURDER BY CONTRACT" '51
MOF "TOO TOUGH TO LIVE" '52
MOF "DEVIL'S DAUGHTER" '52
MOF "THAT ROOM IN CAMDEN TOWN" '52
MOF "BACK-ALLEY BLONDE" '52
MOF "CROOKED COFFINS" '52
MOF "KISS TOMORROW GOODBYE" '52
MOF"DEAD BONES TELL TALES" '53
MOF "DEMON BARBER OF BROADWAY" '53
MOF "HOSTESS" '55
LINTON, DUKE--S. HOLLAND-SCION CKLST,
PP 27,[2][3]MYS, HP--
SCION "HOLD EVERYTHING" '53
MCCANN, COOLIDGE--[2][22][23][27]SF
SAKS, ELMER ELIOT--[27][32][34]--
BEAR "INNOCENTS ON BROADWAY" '44
"CASE OF INDIANA TORTURER" '45
JCM "AMERICA'S MILLIONAIRE
MURDERER" JAN '60
SARTO, BEN--PP 29, P40,[2][23[27][34]MYS,HP--
MOF "BOWERY BIRDIE" '47
HERMIT "DYNAMITE DOLL" '47
MOF "GRAND GRAFT HOTEL" '47
MOF "JEWS' PELLIGRINI" '47
HERITAGE "SUSIE COMES TO SOHO" '47
MOF "SHE RULED WITH A ROD" '47
MILESTONE "MISS OTIS THROWS A
COME-BACK" '47
MOF "MISS OTIS GOES UP" '47
HERITAGE "TOO BAD FOR SUSIE" '48
MILESTONE "MISS OTIS HAS A DAUGHTER" '48
MOF "QUEEN OF CROOK'S HAREM" '49
MOF "REBECCA OF THE SNATCH RACKET" '49
MOF "CHICAGO DAMES" '49
BEAC "SHE TALKED WITH A GUN" '51
BEAC "CHICAGO STRIP-TEASE" '51
BEAC "CAll ME SHAMELESS" '52
BEAC "DAMES FOR HIRE" '52

FAWCETT, FRANK DUBREZ [CONT]
SARTO, BEN [CONT]
MOF "TAKE WHAT'S COMING" '52
MOF "CITY OF SIN "52
MOF "CORRUPTED WOMEN" '52
MOF "OLDEST PROFESSION" '52
MOF "MANHATTAN TERRORS" '52
MOF "FLOOZIE TAKES LAWMAN" '52
MOF "BEECH OF THE BOULEVARD" '52
MOF "TIGRESS OF BRAZIL" '52
MOF "WORTH MORE DEAD" '53
MILESTONE "MISS OTIS GOES FRENCH" '53
MILESTONE "MISS OTIS HITS BACK" '53
MILESTONE "LADY BITES" '53
MILESTONE "MISS OTIS MAKES A DATE" '53
MILESTONE "MISS OTIS MOVES IN" '53
MILESTONE "MISS OTIS PLAYS EVE" '53
MILESTONE "MISS OTIS SAYS YES" '53
MOF "MISS OTIS TAKES THE RAP" '53
MILESTONE "NO HOLDS BARRED" '53
MILESTONE "SIDEWALK FLOOZIE" '53
MILESTONE "SNAKE HIPS" '54
MILESTONE "MISS OTIS RELENTS" '54
MILESTONE "MISS OTIS PLAYS BALL" '54
MILESTONE "MISS OTIS MAKES HAY" '54
MILESTONE "MISS OTIS DESIRES" '54
MOF "THEY BURN FOR ME" '54
MILESTONE "MISS OTIS GETS FRESH" '54
MOF "DEATH RIDES THE TRAIN" '54
MOF "SINISTER WOOING" '54
MOF "STAY OUT OF MENCHIS" '58
SPENCER, HANK--[23][27][34]MYS--
MOF "VICE SQUAD" '54
STOKES, SIMPSON--[2][22][23]SF--
"AIR GOD'S PARADE" '35

FAWCETT, WILLIAM BRIAN
FAWCETT, BILL--[7][23]AMERICAN/SF--
"WAR YEARS" SERIES
"SWORD QUEST" SERIES
FAWCETT, QUINN--W/CHELSEA Y QUINN,
AV PUBL MATL, LACHMAN LST '93--
"NAPOLEON MUST DIE" '93

FAWKES, FRANK ATTFIELD
X--[2][7]

FAY, E.F.
BOUNDER, THE--[8]

FAY, JUDITH
NICHOLSON, KATE--[34]MYS--
BLES "HOOK, LINE & SINKER" '66
NICHOLSON, KATHERINE--[32][34]MYS--
LM "MURDER IN THE SUN" MAR '66

FAZZANO, JOSEPH E.
FITZGERALD, JOHN [D]--
[22][31][32]AMERICAN/MYS--
DT "MERCHANTS OF PENANCE" SEPT '51

FEAGLES, ANITA MACRAE
MACRAE, TRAVI--[33]
MACRAE, TRAVIS--[2][3][22][31]MYS--
RINEHART "TRIAL BY SLANDER" '60
HOLT "DEATH IN VIEW" '61

FEAR, WILLIAM H.
REYNOLDS, JOHN--[8]

FEARING, KENNETH
BECMAN, ROSS--W/FREDERICK V.R. DEY
& DONALD FAIRDE,[11]SF
BEDFORD, DONALD F.--W/DONALD FRIEDE
& HENRY BEDFORD-JONES,[18][31]MYS--
"JOHN BARRY" '47

FEARING, KENNETH [CONT]
JONES, H. BEDFORD--[18]GHOSTED--
CREATIVE AGE PRESS "JOHN BARRY"

FEARING, LILLIAN B.
RUSSELL, RAYMOND--[2]

FEARN, C. EATON
LANG, PETER--[1]
MACRAE, HERBERT--[1]
MERRICK, JIM--[1]

FEARN, JOHN RUSSELL
ANONYMOUS--PPCC #8, ENGLISH--
"IT CAME FROM OUTER SPACE"
"THEM"
ARMSTRONG, GEOFFREY--S. HOLLAND--
SCION CKLST, PP 27,[2][15][23][28]--
TALES OF WONDER "SUPERHUMAN" '38
AYRE, THORNTON--[2][11][15][23]SF
BENTLEY, GENE--[27][28]ENGLISH/ROM--
SCION "LOVES OF LYDIA" '54
DRAGON PRESS 4 NOVELS '55-56
BLAYNE, HUGO--[2][3][7][27][28][34]MYS--
PAUL "EXCEPT FOR ONE THING" '47
PAUL "FIVE MATCH BOXES" '48
PAUL "FLASHPOINT" '49
PAUL "WHAT HAPPENED TO HAMMOND?" '51
BR. SF MAG "THE SILVERED CAGE" '55
BOYCE, MORTON--[1][2][11]--
VARGO STATTEN SF MAG
BROWN, WHITNEY--P. HARBOTTLE-PPCC#3, P75--
BROWN WATSON "AND SO TO ETERNITY"
CAPELLIN, MARIA--P. HARBOTTLE-PPCC#3, P75--
BROWN WATSON "FOR SALE"
CARR, CONWAY--[34]MYS--
WDL "THE RATTENBURY MYS" '55
CARSON, HANK--S. HOLLAND-PPCC#3, P63--
MUW "TEXAS TERROR"
MUW "SIX GUNS"
MUW "SHOOT TO KILL"
CLIVE, DENNIS--S. HOLLAND-SCION CKLST,
PP 27,[2][15][23][28]SF--
MUW "THE VOICE COMMANDS" '42
MUW "VALLEY OF PRETENDERS" '42
COTTON, JOHN--[2][11][15][23]SF--
CROSS, POLTON--[2][11][15][23]SF--
MUW "OTHER EYES WATCHING" '46
MUW "STOCKWHIP SHERIFF" '48
DARLING, BETH--P. HARBOTTLE-PPCC#3, P75--
GANNETT PRESS "ROMANCE REMAINS"
DEL MARTIA, ASTRON--[2][7][23][27]SF, HP--
GP "THE TREMBLING WORLD" '48
GP "DARKNESS OF DAWN" '51
GP "SPACE PIRATES" '51
GP "INTERSTELLAR ESPIONAGE" '52
DENHOLM, MARK--[1][2][11]SF--
TB "WATERS OF ETERNITY" '53
DEWALL, D.--P. HARBOTTLE-PPCC#3, P75--
BW "THE SHEIK"
BW "YELLOW YASHMAX"
DODD, DOUGLAS--[1][2]VARGO STATTEN SF MAG
DREW, SHERIDAN--[1][2]VARGO STATTEN SF MAG
ELTON, MAX--[1][2]VARGO STATTEN SF MAG
FOXE, PRESTON--[2]
GLYDE, PHILIP--[2]
GORDON, SPIKE--[2][3][11][23]MYS, HP--
MOF "DON'T TOUCH ME" '53
GRAYSON, GEOFFREY--[2]
GRIDBAN, VOLSTED--S. HOLLAND-SCION CKLST,
PP 27,[2][23][27][34], HP--
SCION "MASTER MUST DIE" '53
SCION "LONELY ASTRONOMER" '54]
GRIFF--[2][34]MYS, HP--
MOF "LIQUID DEATH" '53

FEARN, JOHN RUSSELL [CONT]
HARKON, FRANZ--[23]SF--
"SPAWN OF SPACE" '51
HARTLEY, MALCOLM--[1][2]VARGO STATTEN SF MAG
HAYES, TIMOTHY--[1][2][11]WESTERNS
HOLT, CONRAD G.--P. HARBOTTLE-TID-BITS CKLST, [2][11][23][27]--
TB "COSMIC EXODUS" '53
JACKSON, NOEL--[2]
JAMES, PRESTON--[2][34]MYS--
WDL "SECRET OF THE VASE" '55
JAPP, MATTHEW W.--S. HOLLAND-SCION CKLIST, PP 27, P11,[2]
JONES, FRANK--[1][2][11][15]SF
KARTA, NAT--[1][2][27][34], HP--
DRAGON PRESS "VISION SINISTER" '54
KAYNE, MARVIN--[1][2][11]VARGO STATTEN SF MAG
LAFORGE, EDWIN--P. HARBOTTLE-PPCC#3, P75,HP--
BROWN WATSON - MOST TITLES
LE VOYEUR, PIERRE--PPCC#3, HP--SCION
LEWIS, CLIFFORD--[2][11]VARGO STATTEN SF MAG
LLOYD, HERBERT--[1][2][11]VARGO STATTEN SF MAG
LORRAINE, PAUL--[2][11]MYS, HP--
CURTIS "DARK BOUNDARIES" '53
MAGROON, VECTOR--[2]
MCCLOUD, JED--[2]
VULTURES OF THE VOID--
BRITISH SF MAG-WESTERNS
MCCOY, MICK--S. HOLLAND--
SCION CKLST, PP 27, P11,[2]
PASSANTE, DOM--[1][2][11][15]
PEARSON, ALEX O.--[2]?
RAWLE, HENRY--[2]?
ROSE, FRANCIS--[1][2][11]VARGO STATTEN SF MAG
ROSE, FRANK--[2]
ROSE, LAWRENCE F.--P. HARBOTTLE-TID-BITS CKLST, PP#38,[2][23][27]--
TB "HELL FRUIT" '53
ROSS, WARD--[1][2][11]VARGO STATTEN SF MAG
RUSSELL, JOHN--[1][2][11][23]SF--
"ACCOUNT SETTLED" '49
RUTLAND, ELIZABETH--S. HOLLAND-SCION CKLST, PP27,P. HARBOTTLE-PPCC #3, [2][27]--
BW "SUMMER FIRES"
BW "THE DEVIL'S DAUGHTER"
RYAN; TEX--PPCC#2, P63, HP--
MUW "RIDER OF RED DUST" '48
MUW "LAWLESS RANGE" '49
RYDEN, ARNOLD--P. HARBOTTLE-PPCC#3,[27]--
GANNETT PRESS "TURPIN'S SON RIDES AGAIN"
SARGENT, J.--P. HARBOTTLE-PPCC#3--
GANNETT PRESS "LOVE IS A FEVER"
SCLANDERS, DOORN--[1][2][11]WEST
SEAGAR, JOAN--[1][2][11]ROM
SHAW, BRIAN [BRYAN]--[1][2][11][23], HP--
CURTIS "Z-FORMATION" '53
SLATE, JOHN--[2][3][11][27][29]MYS--
RICH "BLACK MARIA" '44
RICH "MARIA MARCHES ON" '45
STARFORTH, ASTROEA--[2]
STATTEN, VARGO--S. HOLLAND-SCION CKLST, PP 27,[1][2][23][27]-- 44 NOVELS
STEEL, MARJORY--P. HARBOTTLE-PPCC#3, P75--
BW "DESTINY"
BW "INTERLUDE FOR MLOVE"
TARNE, ROSINA--[1][2][11]
THOMAS, K.--[1][2][11]
TITAN, EARL--S. HOLLAND-SCION CKLST, PP 27 PPCC #2,[2][11][23][27]--
SCION "ANJANI, THE MIGHTY" '51
SCION "THE GOLD OF AKADA" '51
WATERHOUSE, ARTHUR--[1][2][11]--
VARGO STATTEN SF MAG
WERNHEIM, JOHN--[1][2][11]
WILSON, G.L.--[2]

FEARN, JOHN RUSSELL [CONT]
WINIKI, EPHRAIM--[1][2][11][23]SF
WOLLF, NICK--S. HOLLAND-PPCC#3,WEST--
MUW "BULLETS AT BAR K" '49

FEARON, PERCY
POY--[8]

FEATHER, JANE
BISHOP, CLAUDIA--[9][21][26]ROM--
"IRRESISTABLE YOU"
"KISS ME ONCE AGAIN" & MORE

FEBRUARY, VERNON ALEXAND.
FEBRUARY, VERNIE A.--[31]

FECHEROLLE, MARC ALAIN
ALYN, MARC--[1]

FECHNER, GUSTAV THEODOR
MISES, DR.--[39]GERMAN

FECHTNER, WOLFGANG
BAPTIST, JEAN--[39]GERMAN/MYS/ADULT
COTTON, JERRY--[39]GERMAN/MYS, HP
DOBLING, MAXIMILIAN--[39]GERMAN/MYS/ADULT
FRANK, DR. STEFAN--[39]GERMAN/ADULT
HOLL, DR. STEFAN--[39]GERMAN/ADULT
KOLBERG, WOLFGANG--[39]GERMAN/MYS/ADULT
ROCCO, RODOLFO--[39]GERMAN/MYS/ADULT
SHANNON, ROBERT--[39]GERMAN/MYS/ADULT

FECHY, HENRIETTE
DARTEY, LEO--[3][29]MYS--
"LA VISITEUR DE MINUIT" '63 & 2 MORE

FEDDE, OVE
GUN, WALTER--[37]NORWEGIAN/MYS--
'ALIBI' & 'DETEKTIV' MAGS -
'KNUT GRIBB' STORIES
MAISTER, MAX--[37]NORWEGIAN/MYS--
'ALIBI' & 'DETEKTIV' MAGS -
'KNUT GRIBBS' STORIES

FEDDEN, HENRY ROMILLY
FEDDEN, ROBIN--[31]

FEDDERSEN, JOHANNES
VETTER, LOUIS--[39]GERMAN/MYS

FEDDERSON, CONNIE
DRAKE, CONNIE--[9][21][26]ROM--
"ANGEL'S FIRE"
FINCH, CAROL--[9][21][26]ROM--
"APACHE WIND"
"APACHE KNIGHT" & OTHERS
ROBINS, GINA--[9][21][26]ROM--
"SWEET FIRES OF SUMMER" & MORE

FEDER, ROBERT ARTHUR
ARTHUR, ROBERT--[2][3][11][31][32]MYS--
ACE D489 "SOMEONE IS WALKING OVER MY GRAVE" '61
AHMM "A COFFIN FOR MR. CASH" MAY '57
MSMM "A LESSION WELL LEARNED" JAN '65
SA "A PERFECTLY NATURAL MURDER" SEPT '56
EQMM "MIDNIGHT VISIT" MAR '48 & OTHERS

FEDERBUSH, SIMON
FEDERBUSCH, SMON--[31]

FEDERLE, ELISABETH
WALDNER, IRENE--[39]GERMAN/JUV

FEDERMANN, REINHARD
FEDOR--W/MILUTIN DOROSLAVIC,[39][40]GERMAN/MYS

FEDERONZONI, LUIGI
DE FRENZI, GIULIO--[22]ITALIAN

FEDOROV, YEVGENY K.
FYODOROV, YEVGENY K.--[31]

FEELINGS, THOMAS
FEELINGS, TOM--[31]

FEHR, RICHARD
STEELE, SHARON--W/WILLIAM MULVEY,[21]ROM--
"A DANGEROUS WOMAN"

FEHRENBACH, ANNELIESE [F]
FEY, ANNELIESE--[39]GERMAN

FEHRENBACH, THOMAS REED
FEHRENBACH, R.R.--[2]
FREEMAN, THOMAS--[1]

FEI-KAN, LI
PA-CHIN--[22]CHINESE

FEIGEL, HANS-DIETER
ROTHEN, HANS--[39]GERMAN/JUV

FEIGENBAUM, HAROLD
FRANKLIN, HAROLD--[1]

FEIKEMA, FREDERICK
MANFRED, FREDERICK F.--[1][19]WEST--
CHGD TO 'MANFRED'

FEIL, GEORG
KENT, STEFFEN--[39]GERMAN/MYS
KNOCK, CHRISTOFFER--[39]GERMAN/JUV

FEILHAUSER, OTTO M.
HABAKUK--[1]

FEINBERG, BARBARA JANE
FEINBERG, BARBARA SILBER.--[33]

FEINBERG, BEATRICE C.F.
FREEMAN, CYNTHIA--[8][17][21][26][31]ROM--
12 NOVELS

FEINMAN, JEFFREY
MARKS, PAT R.--[1]
VENTURA, JEFFREY--[1]

FEIWEL, RAPHAEL JOSEPH
FYVEL, TOSCO JOSEPH--[31]
FYVEL, TOSCO RAPHAEL--[1]
FEYVEL, T.R.--[1][8][31]

FEJMERT, ELSA
MARTIN, LOUISA--[29]MYS

FELBER, EDITH
LAYTON, EDITH--[9][21][26]ROM--
"LOVE IN DISGUISE"
"BIRD OF PARADISE" & MORE

FELBER, RON
CARTER, NICK--[3]MYS, HP--
CHART "DEATH MISSION: HAVANNA" '80
CHART "BLUE ICE AFFAIR" '85
CHART "BLOOD ULTIMATUM" '86

FELDMAN, A. FRANCE
FELDMAN, ANATOLE--M. LACHMAN LTR '93--
PULPS
FELDMAN, ANATOLE FRANCE--M. LACHMAN LTR '93--
PULPS

FELDMAN, A. FRANCE [CONT]
FIELD, TONY--W. MURRAY-ECHOES #17,[32]--
GAN "BIG NOSE" SERRANO STORIES
SG "MYS OF MARY CELESTE" MAR '52
SG "TRAGIC FATE OF STARR FAITHFULL" MAY '52
JONES, G. WAYMAN--[1][2]HOUSE PSEUD.
WALLACE, ROBERT--[3]MYS, HP--
PH "DEATH UNDER CONTRACT" & MORE

FELDMAN, ELLEN [BETTE]
RUSSELL, AMANDA--[1][21][31]ROM--
JOVE "A WOMAN ONCE LOVED" '79
VILLARS, ELIZABETH--[3][21][26][31]MYS/ROM--
DBLDY "NORMANDIE AFFAIR" '82 & MORE

FELDMAN, EUGENE P.R.
BURROUGHS, MARGARET--[8]

FELDMAN, FRED
LAWRENCE, FRED--[21][26]ROM--
'AMERICAN EXPLORERS' SERIES #1 & #14

FELDMAN, GILDA
GILLETTE, LOUISA--W/LESLIE RUGG,
[9][21][26]ROM--
"GLORIOUS TREASURE"
"RIVER TO RAPTURE" & MORE
HALE, MADELINE--W/LESLIE RUGG,[9][21]ROM--
"DAUGHTERS OF THE SUN"
"PIROUETTE"

FELDMAN, LEONARD
ELLIOT, DANIEL--[1][31]

FELDMAN, PINHAS
SADEH, PINHAS--[1]

FELDMAN, RUTH DUSKIN
DUSKIN, RUTHIE--[1][31]

FELDMAN, ZENA
COLLIER, JANE--[34]MYS--
HALE "DEADLY FEAST" '78

FELDMANN, HARRO
FREE, ROBERT H.F.--[39]GERMAN

FELKIN, MRS. ELLEN [A]
FOWLER, ELLEN THORNEYCROF--[1][7]SF

FELKL, GERTRAUD
VON HILGENDORFF, GERTRUD--[39]GERMAN

FELL, FREDERICK VICTOR
FREDERICKS, VIC--[8]

FELL, HOWARD BARRACLOUGH
BARRACLOUGH, HOWARD--[8][31]
FELL, BARRY--[31]

FELL, WILLIAM RICHMOND
RICHMOND, WILLIAM--[1]

FELLER, HANS
CARDWELL, RAY--W/HUBERT STRASSEL,
[39]GERMAN/SF

FELLINGE, HARRY LEE
FELLINGE, H.L.--[1]
FELLINGS, HENRY--[1]
FIELDINGS, HARRY LEE--[1]
LEE, HARRY--[1]

FELLMANN, MARIA
FELLMANN, FRIEDRICH M.--[39]GERMAN/JUV

FELLOWES-GORDON, IAN
COLLIER, DOUGLAS--[8][22][31]AMERICAN
GORDON, IAN--[8][22][31]AMERICAN

FELLOWS, DOROTHY ALICE
COLLYER, DORIC--[8]
HUNT, DOROTHY--[8]

FELSEN, HENRY GREGOR
VICAR, HENRY--[1]
VICKER, ANGUS--[1][22][31]AMERICAN--
DELL "FEVER HEAT" '54

FELSINGER, EDWIN
FELSMANN, ERWIN--[39]GERMAN/MYS

FELSTEIN, IVOR
STEEN, FRANK--[8]

FELTON, FREDERICK A.
ARMSTRONG, JACK--[1]

FELTON, RONALD OLIVER
WELCH, RONALD--[8][22][33]WELCH-ENGLISH

FENDELL, BOB
ROBERTS, DELL--[1]

FENELLOSA, MARY MACNEIL
MCCALL, SIDNEY--[1]

FENICHEL, CAROL HANSEN
HANSEN, CAROL--[1][31]

FENN, CAROLINE K.
MCGREW, FENN--W/JULIA MCGREW,[1][3][22]MYS--
RH "MURDER BY MAIL" '51
RH "TASTE OF DEATH" '53

FENN, GEORGE MANVILLE
MANVILLE, GEORGE--[8]

FENSCH, THOMAS
MOORE, LANDER--[1]

FENSTER, ROBERT
ENDERS, RICHARD--[3][31]MYS--
"SLOW TWITCH" '82
"TIFGT SQUEEZE" '82

FENTON, EDWARD
FOLLETT, EDWINA--[3]MYS--
POPLB "VILLA OF SCORPIONS" '75

FENTON, ROBERT L.
FENTON, JULIA--[31]
FENTON, JULIE--[34]MYS--
CONTEMP. "BLACK TIE ONLY" '90

FENTSCH-WERY, ERNA
WERY, ERNESTINE--[39][40]GERMAN/MYS
"ALS GESTOHLEN GEMELDET" '80
"EIN SCHULTER ZUM WEINERE" '87

FENWICK-OWEN, RODERIC
OWEN, RODERIC--[1]

FENWICK WAY, ELIZABETH
FENWICK, E.P.--[18][34]MYS--
GOLLANCZ NOVELS '57-73
3 NOVELS '43/45
FENWICK, ELIZABETH--[34]MYS--
11 GOLLANCZ NOVELS '57-73

FERGUSON, BRADLEY MICHAEL
FERGUSON, BRAD--[23]SF--
'STAR TREK' TIES-"CRISIS ON CENTAURI" '86
"THE WORLD NEXT DOOR" '90
"A FLAG FULL OF STARS" '91

FERGUSON, CHARLES W.
GREGORY, HILTON--[8][22][31]AMERICAN

FERGUSON, HELEN
NEVIN, EVELYN C--[8]

FERGUSON, IDA MAY
FERGUS, DYJAN--[8]

FERGUSON, JAMES D.
DRAKE, MORGAN--[7]SF--
LEIS "SACRIFICE" '90

FERGUSON, MARILYN
RENZELMAN, MARILYN--[8]

FERGUSON, PETER K.
WONDER, JAL--[1]

FERGUSON, RACHEL
COLUMBINE--[8]
RACHEL--[1]

FERGUSON, ROBERT BRUCE
FERGUSON, BOB--[31][33]

FERGUSON, WILLIAM B.M.
MORTON, WILLIAM--[1][3][22]MYS--
6 NOVELS '28-32

FERGUSON-HANNAY, DORIS
LESLIE, DORIS--[8][21][26][31]ROM--
12 NOVELS

FERH, RICHARD
STEELE, SHARON--W/WILLIAM MULVEY,[21]ROM--
"A DANGEROUS WOMAN"

FERLINGHETTI, LAWRENCE M.
FERLING--[22]AMERICAN
FERLING, LAWRENCE--[31]AMERICAN

FERME, MRS. GEORGE
DOUGLAS, GEORGE--W/HENRY DERRICK,[34]MYS--
OLIPHANT "MYS OF NORTH FORTUNE" 1895

FERNEYHOUGH, ROGER EDMUND
HART, R.W.--[8]

FERRAND, GEORGINA
CASTLE, BRENDA--[9][21]ROM--
"HARVEST OF HAPPINESS"
"WHISPERS OF FEAR"

FERRARI, GUSTAV
EISNER, STEFAN--[39]GERMAN

FERREOL, MARCEL AUGUSTE
ACHARD, MARCEL--[3][31]MYS--
"L'IDIOTE"

FERRIDGE, PHILLIPPA
WIAT, PHILIPPA--[1][34]MYS--
HALE "PHANTASMAGORIA" '88

FERRIS, ROSE MARIE
FERRIS, VALERIE--[9][21][26]ROM--
"THE HEART'S AWAKENING"

FERRIS, ROSE MARIE [CONT]
FRANCIS, ROBIN--[9][10][21][26]ROM--
"SEASON OF DREAMS"
"TAKING A CHANCE" & MORE
ROLAND, MICHELLE--[9][21][26]ROM--
"VENUS RISING"
"BELOVED STRANGE"

FERVERS, LOUISE
FERBER, LUISA--[39][40]GERMAN/MYS--
"TOD AUF SYLT" '82
"MORD IN ULM" '82 & OTHERS

FETHERSTONHAUGH, PATRICK
FETHERSTON, PATRICK--[8]

FETTER, ELIZABETH HEAD
FALSTAFF, JAKE--[1]
LEES, HANNAH--W/LAWRENCE P. BACHMAN, [3][29][31]MYS--
RNDM "DEATH IN THE DOLL'S HOUSE" '43

FETZER, HERMAN
FALSTAFF, JAKE--[1]

FEUCHTWANGER, LION
WETCHECK, J.L.--[39]GERMAN

FEURSTEIN, KATE
VON ROEDER-GNADBERG, KATE--[39]GERMAN/JUV

FEVRIER, PAUL-HUBERT B.
FUVAL, PIERRE--[1]

FEW, EUNICE BEATTY
FEW, BETTY--[8]

FEY, JEREMY
HUDSON, TED--V. BERCH-BRNDN/ BC PSEUDS, BAE 22, P24
SCHLITZ, PAUL M.--V. BERCH-BRNDN/ BC PSEUDS, BAE 22, P24

FEYLBRIEF, J.K.
VAN OUDSHOORN, J.--[22]DUTCH

FEYNMAN, RICHARD PHILLIPS
FEYNMAN, R.P.--[31]
FEYNMAN, RICHARD P.--[31]

FEZANDIE, HECTOR
MORETTE, EDGAR--[3]MYS--
STOKES "THE STURGIS WAGER" 1899

FFEULKES, MRS.
CRAVEN, MARY--[1]

FICAROTTA, NOEL
FIAROTTA, NOEL--[1][31]

FICAROTTA, PHYLLIS
FIAROTTA, PHYLLIS--[1][31]

FICHTER, GEORGE S.
KENSINGER, GEORGE--[8][31]
WARNER, MATT--[8][31]--
"YOUR WORLD, YOUR SURVIVAL" '70
ZILIOX, MARC--[8][31]

FICKE, ARTHUR DAVIDSON
KNISH, ANNE--W/WITTER BRYNNER, [1][22]AMERICAN

FICKLING, FOREST & GLORIA
FICKLING, G.G.--[31][32][34]MYS--
14 NVLS '57-72
MD "DANCING BEAR" NOV-DEC '62
MD "GIRL IN THE GREY FLANNEL SPACE SUIT" MAY-JUN '63
MD "FIFTH HEAD" JAN-FEB '63
MSMM "RED HAIRING" JUN '65

FIDLER, JAMES M.
FIDLER, JIMMIE--[31]

FIEBRANDT, H.
PAATZ, HERBERT--[39]GERMAN

FIEDLER, ARIBERT
RELL, BERT W.--[39]GERMAN/MYS

FIELD, EDWARD
ELLIOTT, BRUCE--W/NEIL DERRICK, [21][26][32]ROM--
"VILLAGE"
JU "JUNGLE JAZZ" JUN '44
SD "CRIME GOES TO COLLEGE" JUN '44
SD "CASE OF THE MELTING ARTICHOKES" JUL '44
SD "DEATH PACES THE WIDOW'S WALK" OCT '44
JU "COCKTAIL JUNGLE" JAN '56

FIELD, FRANCES FOX
FOX, FRANCES MARGARET--[31]

FIELD, FREDERICK VANDER.
FIELD, FREDERICK V.--[31]

FIELD, JULIAN OSGOOD
L., X.--[22][34]MYS--
METHUEN "AUT DIABOLUS AUT NIHIL & OTHER TALES" 1895

FIELD, M.J.
FRESHFIELD, MARK--[8]

FIELD, RICHARD TIMOTHY
FIELD, RESHAD--[1]

FIELDEN, THOMAS PERCEVAL
DE FLETIN, P.--[31]

FIELDHOUSE, WILLIAM [L]
BAINBRIDGE, CHUCK--V. BERCH TO HUBIN '94, HP--
'HARD CORPS': "BEIRUT CONTRACT"
"THE HARD CORPS"
"SLAVE TRADE"
"WHITE HEAT"
FIELDHOUSE, W.L.--[28]WEST--
TOWER "GUN LUST" '82
LEE, PATRICK--J.R. BAKER-ECHOES #3, WEST, HP--
'SIX-GUN SAMURAI':
"SUNDOWN AT GOLDEN GATE" '81
"BUSHIDO LAWMAN" '82
WILSON, GAR--W/PAUL G. NEUMAN,[34], HP--
GE "TIGERS OF JUSTICE" '83
GE "ULTIMATE TERROR" '84
GE "HARVEST HELL" '84
GE "PHOENIX IN FLAMES" '84
GE "RETURN TO ARMAGEDDEON" '84
GE 'PHOENIX' SERIES: "SEA OF SAVAGES" '85
GE "NIGHT OF THE THUGGEE" '85
GE "VIPER FACTOR" '85
GE "TOOTH & CLAW" '85
GE "NO RULES, NO REFEREE" '85
GE "WELCOME TO THE FEAST" '85
GE "HOSTAGED VATICAN" '86
GE "DOOMSDAY SYNDROME" '86
GE "TIME BOMB" '86
GE "WEEP, MOSCOW, WEEP" '87
GE "TERROR IN THE DARK" '87

FIELDHOUSE, WILLIAM [L] [CONT]
WILSON, GAR [CONT]
GE "NIGHTMARE MERCHANTS" '87
GE "FIRE STORM" '88
GE "KINGSTON CARNAGE" '88
GE "NINJA BLOOD" '88
GE "POWER GAMBIT" '88
GE "BELGRADE DECEPTION" '88
GE "CHINA COMMAND" '89
GE "GULF OF FIRE" '89
GE "JUNGLE SWEEP" '89
GE "IRON CLAYMORE" '90
GE "COLD DEAD" '90
GE "AFRICAN BURN" '90
GE "TERROR IN GUYANA" '90

FEILDING, DOROTHY
FIELDING, ARCHIBALD E.--[8][29]
FIELDING, A.--[34]MYS--28 NOVELS '24-44

FIELDING, HENRY
KEYBER, CONNY--[31]

FIELDING, MOLLY HILL
FIELD, HILL--[8]

FIELDING-HALL, HAROLD
FIELDING, H.--[34]MYS--
HARPER "PALACE TALES" 1900

FIELDS, BERT
KINCAID, D.--DDLY PLEASURES #3, MYS--
"THE SUNSET BOMBER" '86
"THE LAWYER'S TALE" '92

FIELHAUSER, OTTO M.
GLASBRENNER--[1]

FIELITZ, HANS PAUL
GROSSE, ANDREAS--[39]GERMAN
MECHLER, ULRICH--[39]GERMAN
NOACK, WERNER--[39]GERMAN

FIENHOLD, WOLFGANG
RADEBRECHT, F.--[39]GERMAN/MYS/SF
RADEBRECHT, R.--[39]GERMAN/MYS
WALLATZE, EDGAR--[40]GERMAN/MYS--
"DIE FROSCH MIT DER GLATZE" '86

FIGGE, MICHAEL
JOHNSON, JOHN--[39]GERMAN/WEST

FIGGIS, DARRELL
IRELAND, MICHAEL--[2][7][22]IRISH/SF--
"RETURN OF THE HERO"

FIGUEROA, JOHN [J] MARIA
FIGUEROA, JOHN--[31]

FIGUEROA-MERCADO, LOIDA
FIGUEROA, LOIDA--[31]

FIKSO, EUNICE CLELAND
GRIFFIN, C.F.--[22][31][32]AMERICAN/MYS--
AHMM "A DEADLY COMBINATION" JUL '77

FILEK-WITTINGHAUSEN, WER.
VON WITTINGHAUSEN, WERNER--[39]GERMAN
WITTINGHAUSEN, ARTY--[39]GERMAN

FILER, THOMAS HANFORD
BUCK, DOUG--V. BERCH-BRNDN/BC PSEUDS,
BAE 22, P24,[1]
CHISOM, SARAH--[1][2]
COLE, STARK--V. BERCH-BRNDN/BC PSEUDS,
BAE 22, P24,[1]

FILICCHIA, RALPH
MICHAELS, RALPH--[1]

FILLERON, ROGER-CHARLES
FROLLINE--[1]

FILSTRUP, E. CHRISTIAN
FILSTRUP, CHRIS--[31]

FINALY, DOROTHEA [D]
THALER, DORA--[39]GERMAN/JUV

FINCH, PHILLIP
BIRD, AL--W/LEO N. MANDEL,[34]MYS--
COWARD "MURDER SO REAL" '78

FINDLATER, RICHARD
BAIN, BRUCE--[8]

FINE, PETER HEATH
HEATH, PETER--[2][3][7][11][23]MYS/SF--
'MIND BROTHERS' SERIES '67-8
LAN 73-600 "MIND BROTHERS" '67
LAN 73-631 "ASSASSINS FOR TOMORROW" '67
LAN 73-787 "MEN WHO DIE TWICE" '68

FINEMAN, IRVING
JOSEPH, JONATHAN--[22][31]AMERICAN

FINK CLINE, BEVERLY
CLINE, BEV--[31]
CLINE, BEVERLY--[1][31]

FINK, MORTON
FINCH, MATTHEW--[22][31][34]ENGLISH/MYS--
DOBSON "EYE WITH MASCARA" '68
DOBSON "EYE SPY" '75
FINCH, MERTON--[8]ENGLISH

FINK, R.M.
ROCK, PHILIP--[29]MYS--
"DIRTY HARRY" MOVIE NOVELIZATIONS

FINKEL, GEORGE
PENNAGE, E.M.--[1][33]

FINKLESTEIN, MARK
ATKINS, JACK--[1]
HARRIS, MARK--[1]
INGRAMS, WILLIS J.--[1]
MARTHA, HENRY--[1]
WASHINGTON, ALEX--[1]
WIGGEN, HENRY J.--[1]
WRIGHT, JACK R.--[1]

FINKLESTEIN, RONI
FRENCH, JANINE--W/ANTONIO VAN-LOON,
[9][21][26]ROM--
"CANDIDATE FOR LOVE"
"RHAPSODY"
"WADINGFIELD"

FINLEON, PATRICK CHARLES
CHARLES, SPENCER--W/ELLEN S. DANSER,
V. BERCH LTR TO HUBIN '94, MYS--
BLUE MT. "MYSTERY ON THE MOUNT" '84

FINLEY, MARTHA
FARQURHARSON, MARTHA--CAROL BILLMAN-
SECRET OF STRATEMEYER SYNDICATE

FINN, EDMUND
GARRYOWEN--[13]AUSTRALIAN

FINN, RALPH LESLIE
FINN, R.L.--[1]

FINN, REGINALD P.A.W.
FINN, R. WELDON--[31]
FINN, REX WELDON--[31]

FINN, SISTER MARY PAULINA
PINE, M.S.--[8]

FINNEY, WALTER BRADEN
BRADEN, WALTER--[1]
FINNEY, JACK--[3][7][32][34]--
EQMM "WIDOW'S WALK" JUL '47
EQMM "IT WOULD'NT BE FAIR" NOV '51
VM "THE WIDOW'S WALK" NOV '56
MD "SUCH INTERESTING NEIGHBORS" MAY '57
DBLDY "FIVE AGAINST THE HOUSE" '57
DELL "HOUSE OF NUMBERS" '57
SUS "CONTENTS OF A DEAD MAN'S POCKET" OCT '58
SIMON "ASSAULT ON A QUEEN" '59
SUS "SEVEN DAYS TO LIVE" SEPT '59

FINNIGAN, JOAN
BEDARD, MICHELLE--[31]

FINNIGAN, KAREN
LOCKWOOD, KAREN--ROMANTIC TIMES MAG MAR '93, [26]ROM "HARVEST SONG"
STRATFORD, KAREN--[26]ROM--
"LAVENDER FLAME"

FINNIN, [OLIVE] MARY
HOGARTH, JOHN--[1][31]
VIGIL, LAWRENCE--[1]

FINS, ALICE
POSNER, ALICE--[1]

FIOROTTO, CHRISTINE S.
GORDON, LUCY--[9][21][26]ROM--
HARL 219 "ROYAL HARLOT"
SIL 864 "UNCAGED" & OTHERS
SPARKS, CHRISTINE--[9]ROM

FIRBANK, LOUIS
REED, LOU--[31]

FIRCHOW, EVELYN SCHERABON
COLEMAN, EVELYN SCHERABON--[31]

FIRER, BENZION
FIRER, BEN ZION--[31]

FIRTH, [FREDERICK] ANSON
ANSON, JOHN--[1][31]

FIRTH, IVAN EUSTACE
ERSKINE, FIRTH--W/GLADYS S. ERSKINE, [3][22][29]MYS--
MCL "NAKED MURDER" '33

FIRTH, JOHN RUPPERT
FIRTH, J.R.--[31]

FIRTH, MARY VIOLET
STEELE, V.M.--[34]MYS--
PAUL "SCARRED WRISTS" '35
PAUL "HUNTERS OF HUMANS" '36
PAUL "BELOVED OF ISMAEL" '37

FIRTH, NORMAN WESLEY
ACKMAN, R.A.--[2][23][27]
ACKMAN, RICE--[2][23][27]
ANSON, NET--[27]ENGLISH--
PAGET'S WESTERN #2 - SHORT STORIES

FIRTH, NORMAN WESLEY [CONT]
DUVAL, HENRI--PPCC#5,[27][34]MYS, HP--
LEWIS "THE DEVIL IN HER" '46
CURZON "SEARCH THE LADY" '46
CURZON "SHE VAMPED A STRANGLER" '46
HAMILTON "MAYFAIR NIGHTS" '46
CURZON "PASSIONATE BRUTE" '48
ELLISON, EARL--PPCC#5,[2][34]MYS, HP--
CURZON "CORPSES DON'T CARE" '46
HAMSTL "BLOOD OF THE DRAGON" '46
HAMSTL "DESERT INTRIGUE" '49
SPNCR "MISS GLORIA GETS WISE" 49
SPNCR "RITA MAKES A KILLING" '49
EVANS, JACKSON--[27][34]--
BEAR HUDSON "DEATH HAUNTS THE CHARNEL ESTATE" '46
FIRTH, N. WESLEY--[27]ENGLISH--
"SOHO GIRLS" '48
FIRTH, SHEILA A.--[27]ENGLISH--
ONE OF HIS WIFE'S NAMES
FIRTH, WESLEY--PPCC#5--
CURZON "DAMES PLAY ROUGH" '46
LEWIS "DESIRE AT MIDNIGHT" '46
HAINES, JACKSON--[27]ENGLISH--
PAGET'S WESTERN #2 - SHORT STORIES
HALWARD, LESLIE--[2][34]MYS--
BEAR HUDSON "ARREST 'ACE' LANNINGAN" '46
BEAR HUDSON "LADIES LOVE MURDER" '46
HUGHES "DAMES IN DISTRESS" '47
HENDRY, OLGA--[27]ENGLISH--
'CASTLETON' STORIES
JOHNSON, JOEL--S. HOLLAND-SCION CKLST, PP 27,[1][27]
LAMOUR, ANDRE--PPCC#5,[27], HP--
CURZON "WEST END WOMEN" '46
"PASSION FOR THREE" '48
LESTRANGE, PAUL--PPCC#5, P58,[27], HP--
CURZON "WILD WEEKEND" '48
RAINE, MAC--[27]ENGLISH--
PAGET'S WESTERN #2 - SHORT STORIES

FIRTH, VIOLET MARY
FORTUNE, DION--[2][3][7][11]MYS/SF--
DOUGLAS "SECRETS OF DR. TAVENER" '26
DOUGLAS "DEMON LOVER" '27
"WINGED BULL; A ROMANCE OF MODERN MAGIC"
DOUGLAS "GOAT-FOOT GOD" '36
DOUGLAS "SEA PRIESTESS" '38
"MOON-MAGIC" '56

FISCHACH-FABEL, RENATE
FABEL, RENATE--[39]GERMAN

FISCHER, BRUNO
GRAY, RUSSELL--G. LOVISI- INTRO-
"A MATE FOR MURDER" JUL '92, [2][32][37]MYS-- OCSC-PULP
S&SDM "A FEMALE ON SQUAD" DEC '43
LION 38 "LUSTFUL APE" '50
"THE MAID & THE MUMMY"
"DEATH CAME CALLING"
DT "DEATH COMES CRAWLING" NOV '61
DT "UNDER THE SIGN OF THE SKULL" FEB '62
UT "FRESH FIANCES FOR DEVIL'S DAUGHTER"
STORM, HARRISON--V. BERCH LTR FEB '93
STORM, JASON F.--[14]/V. BERCH LTR CONFIRMED FEB '93, ADULT--
OLYM OPH#211 "DOMINATION" '70
TRAIN, ADAM--G. LOVISI-INTRO TO "A MATE FOR MURDER" '92

FISCHER, CLAUS
BARR, CHRISTOPHER--W/HANS GAMBER, [39][40]GERMAN/MYS--
"SOLDATO, DER KILLER" '81
"ZUM STERBEN ZU SCHON" '81

FISCHER, CLAUS [CONT]
BARRY, JAMES--[39][40]GERMAN/MYS--
"RENDEZVOUS MIT DEM TOD" '79
"TAGE DER RACHE" '80
CRAMER, MARK--[39]GERMAN/MYS/WEST
FISCHER, CORNELIUS--[39]GERMAN/MYS/WEST
FISHER, KING--[39]GERMAN/JUV
JONES, EVERETT--[39]GERMAN/WEST, HP
LAFITTE, JEAN--[39]GERMAN/MYS/WEST, HP
REICH, BODO--[39]GERMAN/MYS/WEST
SOLO, FRANCO--[39]GERMAN/MYS/WEST, HP

FISCHER, ELSE
FABER, ALFRED--[39]GERMAN

FISCHER, HUGO WILHELM
FISHER, WILLIAM--[39]GERMAN

FISCHER, ILSE [R]
FISCHER, ELISABETH--[39]GERMAN
REITBOCK, ELISABETH--[39]GERMAN
REITBOCK, ILSE--[39]GERMAN

FISCHER, KARL
VISCHER, GEORG ALFRED--[39]GERMAN

FISCHER, MARTIN
MARTIN, OTTO--[39]GERMAN-- TRANSLATION

FISCHER, MATTHIAS JOSEPH
LAURENCE, ROBERT--[8]

FISCHER, ROBERT JAMES
FISCHER, BOBBY--[31]

FISCHER-ABENDROTH, WOLFD.
DE NAGY, COURTH--[39]GERMAN

FISCHL, VIKTOR
DAGAN, AVIGDOR--[39]GERMAN

FISCHMAN, HARVE
BENNETT, HARVE--[31]

FISH, LEONARD G.
CAMPBELL, DAVID--[23]SF
FYSH--[7]SF--
"PLANET WAR" '52
HALEY, CLAUDE--[7][23]SF--
"BEYOND THE SOLAR SYSTEM" '54
LA SALLE, VICTOR--[7]SF, HP--
"AFTER THE ATOM" '53
RAYMOND, JOHN--[7], HP--
"ZAMBA OF THE JUNGLE" '51
ROGERS, LANNY--[34]MYS--
SPENCER "TWO TIMES MURDER" '51
?? UNCONFIRMED ??

FISH, MILDRED T.
ALEXANDER, MEGAN--[9][21][26]ROM--
"BLOSSOMS IN THE SNOW"
"CONTRACT FOR MARRIAGE" & MORE

FISH, ROBERT L.
LAMPREY, A.C.--[5][11]
LONDON, JACK--[3][5]MYS--
GHOSTED TO FINISH "ASSASSINATION BUREAU"
PAGE, JUAN--LACHMAN LST MAY '93
PIKE, ROBERT L.--[3][5][18][32]MYS--
DBLDY "MUTE WITNESS" '63
DBLDY "THE QUARRY" '64 & MORE
EQMM "CLANCY & THE SUBWAY JUMPER" DEC '61
EQMM "CLANCY & THE PAPER CLUE" JAN '62
EQMM "CLANCY & THE SHOESHINE BOY" JUN '62
EQMM "CLANCY & THE CAT'S EYES" MAR '63

FISH, ROBERT L. [CONT]
ROBERTS, LAWRENCE--[18]MYS--
SCHOLASTIC "THE BREAK-IN" '74
SCHOLASTIC "BIG WHEELS" '77
SCHOLASTIC "ALLEY FEVER" '79

FISH, ROY
DALE, RICHARD--W/JOE R. LANSDALE,
BIBLIO-NOVA EXPRESS--
TALAN "NELLIE" WINT '84

FISHER, A. STANLEY T.
SCARROT, MICHAEL--[8]

FISHER, BARBARA
PERRY, BARBARA FISHER--[33]

FISHER, D.H.
JULOC--[34]MYS--
UNWIN 'BOARDING-HOUSE REMINISCENSES':
"PLEASURE OF LIVING W/OTHERS" 1896

FISHER, DOROTHY F.C.
CANFIELD, DOROTHEA F.--[31]
CANFIELD, DOROTHEA FRANCE--[31]
CANFIELD, DOROTHY--[8][31][33]
CANFIELD, MIRIAM--[3][9]MYS/ROM--
LAN 72-957 "TUSCANY MADONNA" '65
& 16 OTHERS
CRANSHAW, STANLEY--[31]

FISHER, DOUGLAS [GEORGE]
DOUGLAS, GEORGE--[29][34]MYS--
23 HALE NOVELS '66-80
FISHER, GEORGE--[34]MYS--
HALE "THE HOSTAGES" '76
HALE "OPERATION V.I.P." '77

FISHER, EDWARD
FISHER, A.E.--[8]

FISHER, GENE L.
LANCOUR, GENE--[2][7][9][21][26][31]ROM/SF--
'CARLISLE FAMILY SAGA' SERIES - 3 BOOKS
LANCOUR, JEANNE--[9][21][26]ROM--
'AGE OF CHILVARY' SERIES - 3 BOOKS

FISHER, GRAHAM
JOHNSON, DUFF--[34]MYS, HP--
HAM STFFD "THE CHISELLER" '50
HAM STFFD "ROCKY MOUNTAIN" '51
HAM STFFD "WENDY PICKS A WINNER" '53
MORGAN, DEAN--[3]MYS--18 NOVELS '51-3
STRUAN, FRANK--[32][34]MYS--
TB "CONTRACT MAN" '54
TB "DEADLINE-PARIS" '54
TB "FALL GUY" '54
TB "DEATH IN THE DARKNESS" '54
TB "GIRL FROM THE SEA" '54
TB "TUNNEL OF NIGHTMARE" '54
TB "MURDER IS SO UNPLEASANT" '54
TB "RUTHLESS ENEMY" '54
MSMM "THE BODY IN THE BED" JUL '62

FISHER, JOHN [O.H.]
PIPER, ROGER--[1][33]

FISHER, LOIS JEANETTE
JARRETT, JEANETTE--[22]AMERICAN

FISHER, ROBERT PERCIVAL
FISHER, BOB--[31]

FISHER, RONALD AYLMER
FISHER, R.A.--[31]

FISHER, STEPHEN GOULD
BURNS, MILTON--L. ROBBINS LTR MAR '94, HP
BURKHOLDER, EDWIN V.--L. ROBBINS LTR MAR '94--
GHOSTED ?
DUPRE, HARRISON--L. ROBBINS LTR MAR '94--
PULP
FISHER, STEVE--[32][34]MYS--
12 NVLS '35-70
9 DIGEST STORIES [EQMM, SA, SC, PD , ETC.]
GOULD, STEPHEN--[3][5][18][29]MYS--
ARCADIA "HOMICIDE JOHNNY" '40
MCL "MURDER OF THE ADMIRAL" '36
HURLEY, BRUCE--L. ROBBINS LTR MAR '94, HP
KENT, GLORIA--L. ROBBINS LTR MAR '94--
PULP
LANE, GRANT--L. ROBBINS LTR '94,
[5][32][34]MYS--
PHOENIX "SPEND THE NIGHT" '35
SW "THE ARMY KID" OCT '44
POWERS, RALPH--L. ROBBINS LTR MAR '94, HP
STORM, JACK--L. ROBBINS LTR MAR '94, HP
WHEELAN, ARTHUR--L. ROBBINS LTR MAR '94--
PULP

FISHER, VERONICA SUZANNE
VERONIQUE--[8]

FISHMAN, JACK
GILMAN, J.D.--W/DOUGLAS W. ORGILL,
[3][29][31]MYS--
SIMON "KG 200"-AS W/JOHN CLIVE

FISON, PETER
AINSWORTH, MILO--[1][3]MYS--
HAM "MURDER IS CATCHING" '59

FITCH, ROBERT BECK
FITCH, BOB--[31]

FITCHETT, W.H.
VEDETTE--[8]

FITTOCK, R.J.
BEAUMONT, WALT--[35]AUSTRALIAN--
SANTE FE 329 "DEAD MAN'S SHADOW"
BIG HORN 349 "BLOOD RIVER"
DONOVAN, LOU--[35]AUSTRALIAN--
CLEVELAND PUBL
MCCABE, CORD--[35]AUSTRALIAN--
CLEVELAND PUBL

FITZ-GERALD, S.J.A.
HANNAFORD, JUSTIN--[8]

FITZGEORGE-PARKER, MARK D
DANIEL, MARK--[7]SF--
"CHOCKY #2" '86
CARNIVAL "THE REAL GHOST BUSTERS" '88

FITZGERALD, ARLENE J.
HEATH, MONICA--[3][29][31]MYS--
20 NOVELS '67-78

FITZGERALD, BERYL
HOFFMAN, LOUISE--[8]

FITZGERALD, DESMOND
GERALD, DARYL--[8]

FITZGERALD, DOROTHY DOW
DOW, DOROTHY--[31]

FITZGERALD, LAWRENCE P.
LAWRENCE, JACK--[8][22][31]AMERICAN

FITZGERALD, PERCY H.
DYCE, GILBERT--[22]MYSTERY

FITZGERALD, SEYMOUR VESEY
S.V.F.G.--[8]

FITZHARDINGE, JOAN M.
PHIPSON, JOAN--[2][7][8][22]
[31][33]AUSTRALIAN/SF--
29 BOOKS '52-89

FITZMAURICE-KELLY, JAMES
J.F-K.--[8]

FITZPATRICK, ERNEST H.
BARNABY, HUGO--[2][7]--
"MARSHALL DUKE OF DENVER,
OR THE LABOR REVOL. OF 1920" 1895

FIXX, JAMES FULLER
FIXX, JIM--[31]

FLACK, ISAAC HARVEY
GRAHAM, HARVEY--[2]

FLACK, NAOMI JOHN W.
JOHN, NAOMI--[1][33]
SELLERS, NAOMI JOHN--[33]

FLADLAND, KATHRYN
FARLAND, KATHRYN--[9][21][26]ROM--
"MISS MONICA MARRIES"

FLAISCHLEIN, CASAR
STUART, C.F.--[39]GERMAN
STUART, CASAR--[39]GERMAN

FLAKE, OTTO
KOTTA, LEO F.--[39]GERMAN

FLAMM, GERALD ROBERT
FLAMM, JERRY--[31]

FLAMMARION, N. CAMILLE
HERMES--[31]

FLAMMONDE, PARIS
DELFANO, M.M.--[31]

FLANAGAN, ELLEN
RASKIN, ELLEN--[8]

FLANAGAN, JAMES
LONG, MYLES--[8]

FLANDER, HENRY
THURSTON, OLIVER--[1]

FLANNER, JANET
GENET--[8][31]

FLASSCHOEN, MARIE
DAY, LUCINDA--W/MARIAM SCHEIRMAN,
[9][21][26]ROM--
"GATES OF THE SUN"
"ALOHA, MY LOVE"

FLATOW, CURTH
BARETT, C.A.--[39]GERMAN

FLAVELL, CAROL WILLSEY B.
BELL, CAROL--[31]

FLECHTNER, HANS JOACHIM
HORLA, ALEXANDER--[39][40]GERMAN/MYS--
"MATT IN 13 ZUGEN" '84

FLEET, WILLIAM HENRY
THISTLETON, HON. FRANCIS--[8]

FLEETWOOD, FRANCES
FLEETWOOD, FRANK--[31]

FLEGEL, SISSI
FISCHER, FIONA--[39]GERMAN/JUV

FLEISCHER, ANTHONY
HOFMEYER, HANS--[8]

FLEISCHER, LENORE
EDWARDS, ALEXANDER--[3][29][33]MYS--
"LAST OF SHEILA" '73
"McQ" '74
"BLACK BIRD" '75
FENTY, PHILIP--[3]MYS--
GHOSTED "SUPERFLY" '72
THOMAS, ALLISON--[33]
ROOTE, MIKE--[3][29][33]MYS--
7 MOVIE NOVELIZATIONS '70-3

FLEISCHMAN, ALBERT SIDNEY
FLEISCHMAN, A.S.--[7][34]SF/MYS--
PHOENIX "STRAW DONKEY CASE" '48
PHOENIX "MURDERS NO ACCIDENT" '49
GM 181 "SHANGHAI FLAME" '51
GM 223 "LOOK BEHIND YOU LADY" '52
GM 295 "DANGER IN PARADISE" '53
ACE D57 "COUNTERSPY EXPRESS" '54
GM 368 "MALAY WOMAN" '54
GM 499 "BLOOD ALLEY" '55
GM 958 "YELLOWLEG" '60
GM "VENETIAN BLONDE" '63
"GHOST IN THE NOONDAY SUN" '65
"MIDNIGHT HORSE"
FLEISCHMAN, SID--[7][25][31]CHILDREN & SF

FLEISHMANN, HELLE
KUTHUMI--[8]

FLEISSER, MARIELUISE
HAINDL, MARIELUISE--[31]

FLEISSNER, ROLAND
EREV--[39]GERMAN-- TRANSLATION

FLEKSER, A.L.
VOLYNSKY, AKIM L'NOVICH--[22]RUSSIAN

FLEMING, AMALIA
VOUREKA, AMALIA--[1]

FLEMING, BRANDON
ANSTRUTHER, GERALD--[3][29]MYS--
PLAY "THIRD VISITOR" '50

FLEMING, IAN [LANCASTER]
ATTICUS--[31][33]

FLEMING, KATE
MCGUIRE, JENNY--W/NANCY MORGAN,[9][21][26]ROM--
"CHRISTMAS WISHES"

FLEMING, LEE
HAYMOND, GINNY--[21][26]ROM--
"SOMEONE SPECIAL"

FLEMING, MAY AGNES
CARLETON, COUSIN MAY--[34]MYS--
BRADY "LA MASQUE; OR, THE
MIDNIGHT QUEEN" 1863
EARLIE, M[AY] A[GNES]--[34]MYS--
BRADY "EULALIE; OR, THE
WIFE'S TRAGEDY" 1866

FLEMING, PETER
MOTH--[22]MYSTERY
STRIX--[22]MYSTERY

FLEMING, RONALD
FLEMING, RHODA--[8]
FRAZER, RENEE--[8]
LANGLEY, PETER--[8]

FLEMING, THOMAS JAMES
CAIN, CHRISTOPHER--[22][33]AMERICAN
JAMES, T.F.--[22][33]AMERICAN
THOMAS, J.F.--[22][33]AMERICAN

FLEMING-ROBERTS, G.T.
CHANCE, GEORGE--[2][11][37]MYS--
GH "CALLING THE GHOST" JAN '40
GH "GHOST STRIKES BACK" SPR '40
GH "MURDER MAKES A GHOST" SUM '40
GH "CASE OF THE LAUGHING CORPSE" FALL '40
GH "CASE OF FLAMING FIST" WIN '41
GH "CASE OF WALKING SKELETON" SPR '41
GH "CASE OF BLACK MAGICIAN" SUM '41
TM "CASE OF MURDEROUS MERMAID" SEPT '42
TM "CASE OF ASTRAL ASSASSIN" NOV '42
TM "CASE OF CLUMSY CAT" MAR '43
TM "CASE OF BACHELORS BONES" JUN '43
TM "CASE OF BROKEN BROOM" FALL '43
TM "CASE OF THE EVIL EYE" WIN '44
HOUSE, BRANT--PULP CLASSIC #22,
[29][34]MYS, HP--
SAX "CORPSE CALVACADE" JUN '35
SAX "LEGION OF THE LIVING DEAD" SEPT '35
SAX "GOLDEN GHOUL" JUL '35
SAX "KINGDOM OF BLUE CORPSES" DEC '35
SAX "RINGMASTER OF DOOM" NOV '35
SAX "DIVIDENDS OF DOOM" FEB '36
SAX "SUBTERRANEAN SCOURGE" JUN '36
SAX "BRAND OF THE METAL MAIDEN" JAN '36
SAX "FACELESS FURY" APR '36
SAX "CITY OF MADNESS" DEC '36
SAX "DOOM DIRECTOR" AUG '36
SAX "HORROR'S HANDICAP" OCT '36
SAX "MURDER BRAIN" MAR '37
SAX "SATAN'S SYNDICATE" AUG '37
SAX "ASSASSIN'S LEAGUE" OCT '37
SAX "SLAVES OF THE SCORPION" JUN '37
SAX "CURSE OF THE MANDARIN'S FAN" FEB '38
SAX "DEATH'S FROZEN FORMULA" FEB '37
SAX "CORPSE THAT MURDERED" JUN '38
SAX "CORPSE CONTRABAND" DEC '38
SAX "YOKE OF THE CRIMSON COTERIE" MAR '39
JONES, G. WAYMAN--[29]MYS, HP
WALLACE, ROBERT--W. MURRAY-ECHOES #17,MYS,HP--
PH "THE CRIMINAL CAESAR" APR '36

FLEMMING, NICHOLAS COIT
JAMES, STANTON--[31]

FLESCH, HANS
BRUN, VINCENT--[34][39]GERMAN/MYS--
CAPE "THE BLONDE SPIDER" '39

FLESCH, YOLANDE CATARINA
FLESCH, Y.--[31]
GREENE, YVONNE--[31][33]

FLETCHER, AARON
FLETCHER, FARRIS--[21]ROM, HP--
'TEXANS' SERIES "RAWHIDE COUNTRY"
"LONE STAR LEGACY"
SCARPETTI, FRANK--[3]MYS, HP--
BELM "ICEPICK IN THE SPINE" '75
WILLOUGHBY, LEE DAVIS--[21]ROM, HP--
DELL 'MKNG OF AMER.' SERIES:
"MT. BREED"
"FRONTIER HEALERS"

FLETCHER, ADELE
ORMISTON, ROBERTA--[22]AMERICAN

FLETCHER, BANNISTER FLIG.
FLETCHER, SIR BANNISTER--[31]

FLETCHER, CHARLIE MAY H.
SIMON, CHARLIE MAY--[22][33]AMERICAN

FLETCHER, CONSTANCE
FLEMING, GEORGE--[8][22]AMERICAN

FLETCHER, HARRY LUFT V.
FLETCHER, JOHN--[8]ENGLISH-WELCH
GARDEN, JOHN--[3][31]MYS--
JOSEPH "MURDER ISN'T PRIVATE" '47
"ALL ON A SUMMER'S DAY" '49
HEREFORD, JOHN--[8][31]ENGLISH-WELCH--
HODDER "SHEPHERD'S TUMP" '47
& 7 MORE '48-57
WADE, HENRY--[29]MYS--
CONSTABLE "THE DUKE OF YORK'S STEPS" '29

FLETCHER, HELEN JILL
LEE, CAROL--[22][31][33]AMERICAN
MOREY, CHARLES--[22][33]AMERICAN

FLETCHER, JOANNA L.G.
DEAN, CHARLOTTE--[2]

FLETCHER, JOSEPH SMITH
SMITH, JOSEPH--[29]MYS--
"DIGBY DIAMONDS" '04
"FALSE SCENT" '04
"THE MISSCHANCELLOR" '27

FLETCHER, RICHARD E.
FLETCHER, RICK--[31][33]

FLETCHER, ROBERT JAMES
ASTERISK--[22]MYSTERY

FLEUR, ANNE ELIZABETH
ELIZABETH, ANNE--[8]
LANCASTER, A.F.--[8]
SARI--[8][22]

FLEURE, HERBERT JOHN
FLEURE, H.J.--[31]

FLEURIOT, Z. MARIE ANNE
EDIANEZ, ANNA--[1]

FLEXNER, JAMES THOMAS
SAMTER, LINDA BANTEL--W/LINDA BANTEL,[31]--
POTTER 'FACE OF LIBERTY':
"FOUNDERS OF THE U.S." '75

FLEXNER, STUART BERG
FLETCHER, ADAM--[8][22]AMERICAN
MEES, STEVE--[22]AMERICAN
SANTEE, COLLIER--[22]AMERICAN

FLIEGEL, HELLMUTH
HEYM, STEFAN--[1][7]SF--
"THE WANDERING JEW" '84

FLIEGEL, HELMUTH
FLIEG, HELMUT--[39]GERMAN
HEYM, STEFAN--[39]GERMAN

FLINDT, HOMER EON
FLINT, HOMER EON--[7]SF

FLINT, CAROLYN
BURKE, LYDIA--[26]ROM--
SIL 594 "DEVIL & JESSIE WEBSTER"

FLINT, KENNETH C[OVEY]
FLYNN, CASEY--G. COOK LTR '93,[7]SF--
"THE GODS OF IRELAND #1 & 2" '91

FLINT-GOHLKE, LUCY
FLINT, LUCY--[31]

FLOCH, LOEIZ AR
GLANDOUR, MAODEZ--[22]BRETON

FLOGSTAD, KJARTAN
VILLUN, K.--[40]GERMAN/MYS--
"EIN FOR ALLE" '76

FLOREN, LEE
AUSTIN, BRETT--V. BERCH/S. HOLLAND-ARCHER,
BAE 15,[19][22][28]--
HAN 121 "RAWHIDE SUMMONS" '50
21 WEST/ROM NOVELS AT LEAST '47-69
CAMPBELL, CLIFF--C. WINTEROWD
CALL MAR '94, WEST--
SDN "GUNS OF WRATH"
DONALD, R.V.--[1][28][31]--
LASTISMAS "THE ARAB CAPTORS" '68
LASTISMAS "I, COXSWAIN" '70
FANCHON, LISA--[9][28][31]ROM/ADULT--
RPRTS BEAC B-360 AS BY "HARDING" '60
BEAC B-744X "GIRLS WANTED" '64
BEAC B-728X "MIGRANT GIRL" '64
BEAC B-843X "KEY CLUB" '65
PEC "THE KIDNAPPED VIRGIN" '68
LASTIMAS "SEX CLUB OF DON PEDRO" '69
LASTISMAS "THE GAY GIRLS" '69
GRNLF "PALACE OPF SIN" '69
GRNLF "PALACE OF LUST" '69
LASTIMAS "NAKED WHEN I FLED" '69
GRNLF GC-376 "THE PLUNDERED VIRGIN" '69
RPRTS GRNLF SAME TITLE AS BY "HARDING"
"SCANDALOUS CONFESSIONS OF AN
ENGLISH TRAVELER" '70
MACF "ALL WOMAN" '71
"MAN TRAP" '71
HALL, CLAUDIA--[9][22][28][31]--
ARCADIA "WAIT FOR THE DAY" '55
HAMILTON, WADE--[8][22][28][31]WEST--
HARL 398 "SAGEBRUSH" '57
PYR 396 "LONGHORN BRAND" '59 & M
HARDING, MATT--[9][28][31]ADULT--
BEACON B-345 "YOUNG WIDOW" '60
BEAC B-360 "MAN TRAP" '60
BEAC B-374 "THEY COULDN'T SAY NO" '61
BEAC "B-433Y "FLY GIRL" '61
BEAC B-447Y "OFFICE GAME" '61
"MATTRESS GAME" '61
BEAC B-549Y "MOTEL TRAP" '62
BEAC B-480Y "MEN ON HER MIND" 62
BEAC B-572F "THE NEAR-NUDES" '63
BEAC "THAT WILD SUMMER" '63
LAN 72-694 "SOPHIE" '63
LAN 72-694 "SOPHIE" '63
LAN 72-728 "LAS VEGAS MADAM" '64
LAN 72-728 "LAS VEGAS MADAM" '64
BEAC B-845X "CAREER SEXPOTS" '65
BEAC B-857X "MORGAN'S GIRLS" '65
BEAC B-880X "SEX BUMS" '65
CASANOVA LL206 "DESERT LUST" '67
GRNLF "PLUNDERED VIRGIN" '68
LASTIMAS "DANCING DIVA" '68
LASTIMAS "WOMEN OF LUST" '68
LASTIMAS "I, MARGO" '68
LASTIMAS "RAP SOFTLY, LOVER" '69
LASTIMAS "BOYS & WOMEN" '69
LASTIMAS "I, JONATHAN RICHARDSON" '70

FLOREN, LEE [CONT]
HARDING, MATT [CONT]
MANOR "EDGE OF GUNSMOKE" '79
HARDING, MATTHEW WHITMAN--[1][8][28]HIST--
POPLB 00521 "MUSKETS ON THE MISSISSIPPI" '74
HORTON, FELIX LEE--[8][28][31]HIST--
POPLB "WITH LONG KNIFE & MUSKET" '72
JASON, STUART--[8][28][31][34]MYS, HP--
PINN "DEADLY DOCTOR" '74
PINN "VALLEY OF DEATH" '74
KIRBY, MARK--[1][28][31]ADULT--
SOFTCOVER LIB "COLLEGE FOR SEX" '72
LANG, GRACE--[9][21][26][28][31]ROM--
"LOVE A HOSTAGE"
"NEDRA"
"SHINING MOUNTAIN"
AVALON "SINGING PINES" '69
"SPRINGBOARD TO LOVE"
NELSON, MARGUERITE--[9][21][22][28]ROM--
"AIR STEWARDESS"
"FAR ARE THE HILLS" & MORE '57-79
SMITH, LEW--[8][22][28]NON-FICT--
"THE AMERICAN DREAM" '80
9 WESTERN NOVELS '51-84
STERLING, MARIA S[ANDRA]--[9][28]ROM/HIST--
POPLB "WAR DRUM" '72
STERLING, SANDRA--[28][31]--
LAN 72-788 "ALL NIGHT LONG" '65
LASTIMAS "STRICKLAND'S WOMEN" '68
LASTIMAS "LOVE CULT" '68
LASTISMAS "THE TORTURED VIRGIN" '69
THOMAS, LEE--[9][22][24]MYS--
ARCHER "BULLETS FOR A BANKER" '48
ALSO WESTERN NOVELS '45-85
TURNER, LEN--[1][9][22]ROM/WEST--
ARCADIA "TEXAS MEDICO" '54
ARCADIA "WINTER KILL" '54
WATSON, WILL--[9][22][28]--
LION 61 "WOLF DOG RANGE" '51
HARL 396 "DOUBLE CROSS RANCH" '57
WILSON, DAVE--[1][8][22][28]

FLORES, JANIS
KIRK, RISA--[9][21][26]ROM--
"PLAYING WITH FIRE"
"UNDERCOVER AFFAIR" & MORE

FLORKE, SASKIA
VESTER, SASKIA--[39]GERMAN

FLOURNOY, SHERYL HINES
DEE, SHERRY--[9][21][26]ROM--
"MAKE NO PROMISES"
"SHARE YOUR TOMORROWS"

FLOWER, JOSEPH EDWARD
FLOWER, JOE--[31]

FLOWER, PATRICIA MARY B.
FLOWER, PAT--[18][36]AUSTRALIAN/MYS--
SMITH "WAX FLOWERS FOR GLORIA" '58
& 14 OTHERS '58-76

FLOWERDEW, HERBERT
CAY, NOWELL--[3]MYS--
DIGBY "A FOE IN THE FAMILY" '05
DIGBY "IN HOT PURSUIT" '06 & MORE

FLOYD, GILBERT
GRENFALL, JOHN--[1]
REVELL, HARRY--[1]
SHAND, CAPTAIN--[1]
STORM, DUNCAN--[1][34]MYS--
AMALG "SECRET OF THE SEAS"'16
AMALG "MAHARAJAH'S BELT" '18 & MORE

FLOYD, R.H.
FLOYD, HERBERT LEROY--[3]MYS--
HUMPHRIES "THE RUGGED TRAIL" '49

FLUCK, DIANA
DORS, DIANA--[8][31]

FLUGGE, HANS-LUDOLF
FLUGGE-KROENBERG, GERTRUD--[39]GERMAN
KOHLHAAS, MICHAEL--[39]GERMAN

FLUHARTY, VERNON L.
CARDER, MICHAEL--[8]
O'MARA, JIM--[8][28]WEST--
POCK "WALL OF GUNS" '51
POPLB 420 "TRIAL BY GUNSMOKE" '52
POPLB 465 "GUNS OF VENGEANCE" '52
POPLB 487 "QUICK TRIGGER LAW" '53
POPLB 518 "RUSTLER OF THE OWLHORNS" '53

FLYNN, DONALD ROBERT
FLYNN, DON--[31]

FLYNN, JOHN [M]
FLYNN, J.M.--V. BERCH LTR TO HUBIN '94,MYS--
ACE D313 "DEADLY BOODLE" '58
FLYNN, JAY--[32][34]MYS--
AV F156 "FIVE FACES OF MURDER" '62
GU "BADGER GAME" NOV '56
MALCOLM, JAMES--V. BERCH-BRNDN/
BC PSEUDS, BAE 22, P24

FLYNN, KAREN
FLYNT, CATRIONA--W/VIOLET LEWIS,[26]ROM--
"LOST TREASURE"
"ONE MAN'S TREASURE" & OTHERS

FLYNN, MARY
LIVINGSTONE, MARGARET--[8]

FLYNN, MICHAEL F[RANCIS]
SHEW, ROLAND--[23]SF--
ANALOG STORIES

FLYNN, SIR J.A.
OLIVER, OWEN--[8]

FLYNN, THOMAS THEODORE
FLYNN, T.T.--[28][32]MYS--
KELLY "IT'S MURDER" '50
KELLY "MURDER CARAVAN" '50
DT "REVEL OF DEATH" JAN '62
DT "PULLMAN OF MURDER" FEB '62
DT "14TH MUMMY" MAR '62

FOBEL, JAMES M.
FOBEL, JIM--[31]

FOCKE, ERNEST
PAUL, ERNEST--[3]MYS--
HALE "JEWELS IN JEOPARDY" '67
HALE "KOMESPI AFFAIR" '68 & 4 MORE

FOCKEN, HANS
RODEN, ROBERT--[39][40]GERMAN/MYS--
"GARGANO" '86
"MARUT" '88

FODDEN, SIMON R.
RITCHIE, SIMON--LACHMAN LST,[34]MYS--
SCRIBN "HOLLOW WOMAN" '86
SCRIBN "WORK FOR A DEAD MAN" '89

FODEN, FREDERICK [T]
BARONI, NICK--[27][34]MYS, HP--
WARREN "MANHATTAN HONET" '50
WARREN "BLONDE BABY" '51
WARREN "FRANCES" '51
WARREN "PAY OFF" '51
WARREN "SALLY" '51
WARREN "SHAPELY LADY" '51
WARREN "TANSY" '51
BRUCE, PAUL--[34]MYS, HP--
WARREN "NOBODY'S GIRL" '51
CAROL, JOHN--[34]MYS, HP--
WARREN "SPIN YOUR CRIME" '52
GORDON, MAX--[34]MYS, HP--
WARREN "LOOK DOWN FOR MERCY" '52
KIRK, DAVID--[27][34]MYS, HP--
WARREN "NOW WE ARE FREE" '52
WARREN "I WAS ALONE" '53
VANE, BRETT--[27][34]MYS, HP--
WARREN "PRIVATE DOLL" '50
WARREN "BABS" '51
WARREN "DOLLAR RACKETS" '51
WARREN "EASY LIVING"'51
WARREN "MARIA" '51
WARREN "NOBODY'S DAME" '51
WARREN "PATSY" '51
WARREN "DON'T MIND STELLA" '51
WARREN "GOODBYE HONEY" '53
WARREN "HE MOVED AWAY" '53
WARREN "SHE COULDN'T STAY" '53
WARREN "SUGAR PUSS" '53

FOFF, ARTHUR R[AYMOND]
LAWRENCE, A.R.--[31]
LAWRENCE, KARL--[31]

FOGARTY, JONATHAN T.
FARRELL, J.T.--[1]

FOGEL, DANIEL MARK
KAHN-FOGEL, DANIEL--[1]

FOLB, JAY
HELLER, JEFF--W/HENRY SLESAR, LACHMAN LST '93,[32]MYS--
AHMM "SPLIT-LEVEL GHOST" APR '58
AHMM "SIMON SAYS: HAND OVER YOUR FORTUNE" OCT '59
AHMM "AND SEVEN MAKES DEATH" DEC '59
AHMM "VICTIM, DEAR VICTIM" MAY '60
AHMM "DIG WE MUST" AUG '61
AHMM "REAL-REAL CRAZY" FEB '61
AHMM "TWO ACCOUNTS, ONE DEATH" MAY '61

FOLEY, ALAN
ROACH, BRONWYN--[35]AUSTRALIAN--
HRWTZ PB318 "DON'T EVER LEAVE ME" '67

FOLEY, DAVE
DUMONT, JESSIE--V. BERCH-MON PSEUDS, BAE 9,[1][23]SF--
MON 381 "I PREFER GIRLS" '63
HATCH, GERALD--V. BERCH-MON PSEUDS, BAE 9,[2][11][23]SF--
MON 354 "DAY THE EARTH FROZE" '63
MACBRIAN, JAMES--[1][34]MYS--
MON 382 "ROZ" '63
MON 429 "REVOLT OF ABBIE LEE" '64

FOLEY, PEARL
DE MAR, PAUL--[1][3][22]MYS--
HAM "GNOME MINE MYSTERY" '33

FOLEY, [CEDRIC] JOHN
SAWYER, JOHN--[22][31]ENGLISH--
FOUR SQ "D-DAY" '66
SINCLAIR, IAN--[31]--
FOUR SQ "TENPIN BOWLING" '62
FOUR SQ "BOOT IN THE STIRRUP" '74

FOLIE, FRANZ
ANSEL, FRANZ--[22]BELGIAN

FOLLETT, KENNETH [MARTIN]
FOLLETT, KEN--[7][18][34]MYS--
HARWOOD "SHAKEOUT" '75
HARWOOD "BEAR RAID" '76
MacD "STORM ISLAND" '78
MacD "TRIPLE" '79
MORROW "KEY TO REBECCA" '80
MORROW "MAN FROM ST. PETERSBURG" '82
HAM "LIE DOWN WITH LIONS" '85
MORROW "PILLARS OF THE EARTH" '89
MORROW "NIGHT OVER WATER" '91
MARTINSEN, MARTIN--[7][18][23]SF--
ABELARD "POWER TWINS & THE WORM PUZZLE" '76
MAURICE, RENE LOUIS--[18]--
FONTANA-"THE HEIST OF THE CENTURY" 1978
MYLES, SIMON--[3][18][29][40]MYS--
EVEREST "BIG NEEDLE" '74
EVEREST "BIG BLACK" '74
ROSS, BERNARD L.--[7][18][23]SF--
FUTURA "AMOKI: KING OF LEGEND" '76
FUTURA "CAPRICORN ONE" '78
STONE, ZACHARY--[3][18][29]MYS--
COLLINS "MODIGLIANI SCANDAL" '76
COLLINS "PAPER MONEY" '77

FOLMANIS, ZHANIS K.
GRIVA, ZHAN--[1]

FOLMER, JOHN KENT
FOLMAR, J. KENT--[31]

FOLSOM, FRANKLIN [B]
BREWSTER, BENJAMIN--W/MARY ELTING, [1][22][31]AMERICAN
BREWSTER, FRANKLIN--[8]AMERICAN
CUTLER, SAMUEL--W/MARY ELTING, [1][22][31][33]AMERICAN
GORHAM, MICHAEL--W/MARY ELTING, [1][22][31][33]AMERICAN
HOPKINS, LYMAN--[1][22][31][33]AMERICAN
NESBIT, TROY--[1][22][33]AMERICAN

FOLSOM, JOHN BENTLEY
FOLSOM, JACK--[31]

FONAROW, JERRY
COGANE, GERALD--[1][31]--
MAGAZINE STORIES
FARROW, J.--[1][31]--
MAGAZINE STORIES

FONTANA, JEAN PIERRE
SCOVEL, JUY--[2]

FONTES, MONTSERRAT
LATTIMORE, JESSIE--W/NORINE DRESSER,[31]

FONTEYN DE ARIAS, MARGOT
FONTEYN, MARGOT--[31]

FONZO, L.M.D.
CHANDLER, PETER--W/J.L. KORNBLUTH,[3]MYS--
AVON "BUCKS" '80

FOOT, HUGH MACKINTOSH
CARADON, LORD--[22][31]ENGLISH

FOOT, MICHAEL MACKINTOSH
CASSIUS--[1][2]

FOOTE, CAROL
ODELL, CAROL--[8]
ODELL, GILL--W/TRAVIS GILL,[8]

FOOTE, IRVING FLINT
FOOTE, BUD--[7]SF-- NON-FICT

FOOTE, MICHAEL
CATO--W/PETER D. HOWARD AND FRANK OWEN,[1][22]

FORAN, STEVE
KURTS, ALFRED--R.C. & ELWANDA HOLLAND RVW '93

FORAN, WILLIAM ROBERT
BEDFORD-FORAN, CAPT.--[1]
BELROD-FORAN, CAPT.--W/HENRY BEDFORD-JONES,[1]

FORBAT, SANDOR
WITLEY, A.F.--[1][3]MYS--
"JE SUIS INNOCENT" PRE '38

FORBERG, BEATE GROPIUS
FORBERG, ATI--[31]

FORBES, CABOTT L[OWELL]
SMITH, CHRISTOPHER MARTIN--[1]

FORBES, DELORES STANTON
DE FORBES--LACHMAN LST MAY '93,[31]
FORBES, D.F.--[1][18][22]MYS--
SHORT STORIES
FORBES, STANTON--[3][5][18][21]
[26][31]MYS/ROM--
23 NOVELS '66-75
RYDELL, FORBES--W/HELEN B. RYDELL,
[3][18][22]MYS--
DODD "ANNALISA" '59 & 3 MORE
WELLS, TOBIAS--[18][34]MYS--
DBLDY "A CREATURE WAS STIRRING" '77
& 14 MORE '66-77

FORBES, MARCELLE AZRA
MORPHY, COUNTESS--[8]

FORBES, [LADY] ANGELA
ST.CLAIR-ERSKINE, SELINA--[1]

FORBES-DENNIS, PHYLLIS
BOTTOME, PHYLLIS--[29][31][34]MYS--
FABER "ELDORADO JANE" '56
& 6 MORE '27-56
BOTTOMS, PHYLLIS--[32]MYS--
EQMM "THE LIQUEUR GLASS" MAY '45

FORBES-ROBERTSON, FRANCES
HARROD, FRANCES--[1]

FORD, CONSUELA URISARRI
URN, ALTHEA--[2]

FORD, COREY
RIDDELL, JOHN--[1][3][22]AMERICAN/MYS--
SCRIBN "JOHN RIDDELL MURDER CASE" '30

FORD, EDWARD CHARLES
FORD, WHITEY--[31]

FORD, ELIZABETH ANNE B.
FORD, BETTY--[31]

FORD, FORD MADOX
CHAUCER, DANIEL--[23][31]SF--
"THE SIMPLE LIFE LIMITED" '11
"THE NEW HUMPTY-DUMPTY" '12
HAIG, FENIL--[31]

FORD, JAMES LAWRENCE C.
FORD, COLLIER--[31]

FORD, JOHN M.
DODGE, MICHAEL J.--[2][7]SF--
POCK "STARTREK: VOYAGE TO ADVENTURE" '84

FORD, JOSEPHINE MASSYNGB.
FORD, J. MASSYNGBAERDE--[31]

FORD, MARY ELIZABETH
DIDELOT, MARIE--[1]
FORD, M.--[36]AUSTRALIAN/WEST--
CURRAWONG "HOME ON THE RANGE" '45
& 9 OTHERS
FORD, MARIE--[1][36]AUSTRALIAN
LEWIS, JON--[1][36]MYS--
CURRAWONG "CLUE OF SIX HANDKERCHIEFS" nd

FORD, ROBERT A[RTHUR] D.
FORD, ROBERT A.D.--[31]CANADIAN-- NON-FICT

FORD, T. MURRAY
LE BRETON, THOMAS--[8]
LEBRETON, THOMAS--[2]

FORD, T.W.
CLAY, WESTON--L ROBBINS LTR,[8]-- PULP
SHOTT, ABEL--L. ROBBINS LTR,[8]

FORD, WILLIAM
ST. CLAIR--[1]

FORD, WILLISTON MERRICK
MERRICK, WILLISTON--[2][7]SF

FORDE, CLAUDE MARIE
CLAUDE--[8]

FOREGGER, F.
THURN, FRITZ--[39]GERMAN

FOREMAN, LEONARD LONDON
FOREMAN, L.L.--[28]WEST-- NOVELS '41-77
FOREMAN, LEN L.--[32]MYS--
MU "THE PROWLERS" FEB '67

FOREMAN, ROBERTO
FOREMAN, BOB--W/ROBIN MOORE,[7]SF--
MANOR "TWO SATURDAY YANKEES;
& ALI IN TV LAND" '76

FOREST, HAMES H.
FOREST, JIM--[31]

FORISHA-KOVACH, BARBARA L
FORISHA, BARBARA L.--[1][31]

FORMAN, JOAN
GREENE, PAMELA--[31]

FORNER, JUAN PABLO
CECIAL, TOME--[20]SPANISH

FORREST, RICHARD S.
EVANS, LEE--[31]
WOODS, STOCKTON--[18][34]MYS--
GM "LAUGHING MAN" '80
GM "GAME BET" '81
GM "THE MAN WHO HEARD TOO MUCH" '83

FORREST, ROSAIRE
DES ORMEAUX, J.J.--LACHMAN LST MAY '93,MYS

FORREST, WILLIAM S.
FORREST, WILMA--[3][26]MYS/ROM--
GM "LAST HOPE HOUSE" '68
GM "SHADOW MANSION" '69

FORREST-WEBB, ROBERT
FORREST, DAVID--W/DAVID ELIADES,
[2][7][34]MYS/SF--
"AFTER ME, THE DELUGE" '47
HODDER "GREAT DINOSAUR ROBBERY" '70
HODDER "UNDERTAKER'S DOZEN" '74
TREMAYNE, JONATHAN--[1][31]
TREVELYAN, ROBERT--[3]MYS--
HODDER "PENDRAGON, THE MONTENEGRAN PLOT" '77
HODDER "HIS HIGHNESS COMMANDS PENDRAGON" '76
HODDER "PENDRADRAGON, ILLUSIONIST" '80
HODDER "PENDRAGON, LATE OF PRINCE ALBERT'S OWN" '75
HODDER "PENDRAGON, SEEDS OF MUTINY" '79
WEBB, BOB--[31]--
"TACKLE MOTORCYCLE & SCOOTER MAINTENANCE THIS WAY" '67
WEBB, FORREST--[1][3]MYS--
HODDER "BRANNIGAN'S LEOPARD" '73
HODDER "SNOWBOYS" '73
WEBB, ROBERT FORREST--[1]

FORRESTER, HELEN
BHATIA, JUNE--[33]
EDWARDS, JUNE--[33]
RANA, J.--[33]

FORRESTER, MARTYN JOHN
HASELDEN, JOHN--[31]

FORSSBERG, LENNART
BERG, ROLF--[29]MYS--
NOVELS '48-57

FORSNAS, V.A.
KOSKENNIEMI, V.A.--[22]FINNISH

FORSSBERG, LENNART
FRANKE, JAN--[29]MYS--21 NOVELS '53-57
RUNE, BERT--[29]MYS--
"NAGONSTANS I UNDERJORDEN" '40
VARBERGER, FRITZ--[29]MYS--
"KATT OCH RATT " '40
"KUPPEN PA M/S GILDA" '57
WIDE, LENNART--[29]MYS--33 NOVELS '52-57

FORSTER, EDWARD MORGAN
EMF--[2][31]

FORSTER, REGINALD KENNETH
KENDAL, ROBERT--[8]

FORSYTHE, ROBIN
DINGWALL, PETER--[3][22]MYS--
METHUEN "THE POISON DUEL" '34

FORTE, CHRISTINE
FORSTER, CHRISTINE--[8]

FORTIER, CORA B.
MAXINE--[8]

FORTUNE, MARY HELENA W.
W.W.--[34][36]--
CLARSON "DETECTIVE ALBUM: TALES OF AUSTRALIAN POLICE" 1871

FORWARD, ROBERT L[ULL]
LULL, SUSAN--[23]SF--
"GALILEO-I DEMAND THE STARS FOR MY CHILDREN" '79

FOSDICK, CHARLES AUSTIN
CASTLEMON, HARRY--CAROL BILLMAN, SECRET OF STRATEMEYER SYNDICATE,[8][31]

FOSTER, ALAN DEAN
LUCAS, GEORGE--[4]SF--
GHOSTED "STAR WARS" NOVELIZATION '76

FOSTER, BENNETT
LE FEVRE, WILLIAM--L. ROBBINS LTR MAR '94

FOSTER, BRAD
SIMMONS, MARK--W/JOE R. LANSDALE,
HAWK/LANSDALE INTRVW '93--
BEELINE BL5758M "MOLLIES SEXUAL FOLLIES"

FOSTER, CHARLES FREEMAN
SEALIS, HATHERLY--[3]MYS--
BROADWAY "THE VEILED LADY" '05

FOSTER, DON
SAINT-EDEN, DENNIS--[8]

FOSTER, GEORGE C.
SEAFORTH--[2][3][23]MYS/SF--
JENKINS "MISPRISON OF FELONY" '41
JENKINS "WE BAND OF BROTHERS" '39
JENKINS "CATS IN THE COFFEE" '38

FOSTER, HAROLD RUDOLF
FOSTER, HAL--[31][33]

FOSTER, JAMES ANTHONY
FOSTER, J.A.--[31]
FOSTER, TONY--[31]

FOSTER, JESS MARY MARDON
WHITE, HEATHER--[8]

FOSTER, JOANNA
DOUGHERTY, JOANNA FOSTER--[22]AMERICAN

FOSTER, LAWRENC & PAULINE
LOGAN, JESSICA--[9][21][26]ROM--
JOURNEY INTO LOVE"
"PROMISE TO POSSESS" & MORE

FOSTER, LEROY A.
O'TYNE, NICHOLAS--[1]

FOSTER, MARGARET RUMER G.
GODDEN, RUMER--[22]ENGLISH
HAYNES-DIXON, RUMER GODD.--[22]ENGLISH

FOSTER, MARGERY LAND MAY
MAY, MARGERY LAND--[1]

FOSTER, MARIAN CURTIS
MARIANA--[8][33]

FOSTER, RAYMOND KEITH
FROST, RYKER--[28]--
HALE "A FORTUNE FOR WAR" '88
HALE "THE BATTLE OF SUN VALLEY" '89
GILES, JACK--[28]WEST--
HALE, 7 NOVELS '84-87

FOSTER, WALTER BERTRAM
CARTER, NICHOLAS--[1][5][11]MYS, HP--
FOSTER, W.B.--[28]WEST/CHILDREN'S 1901-27

FOUCAR, EMILE CHARLES V.
CARR, RAY--[1][3]MYS--
BLES "LOVE IN BURMA" '28
SKEFF "RED TIGER" '29

FOULDS, ELFRIDA VIPONT
FOULDS, E.V.--[1]
VIPONT, CHARLES--[1][31][33]--
OXFORD UNIV. PRESS "BLOW THE MAN DOWN" '39
VIPONT, ELFRIDA--[2][11][31][33]JUV--

FOULKE, WILLIAM DUDLEY
DILLINGHAM, ROBERT B.--[1]

FOURNIER, HENRI ALBAN
ALAIN-FOURNIER--FRENCH AUTHORS BIOS, REF WORK,[22][31]

FOURNIER, PIERRE
GASCAR, PIERRE--[3][22][31]FRENCH/MYS--
BRAZILLER "LAMBS OF FIRE" '63

FOUTS, EDWARD LEE
LEE, EDWARD--[3][11][22]AMERICAN/MYS--
DBLDY "NEEDLE'S EYE" '41
DBLDY "A FISH FOR MURDER" '44

FOWLER, BERTRAM B.
BAYNES, JACK--[3]MYS--
CREST 195 "MEET MOROCCO JONES" '57
CREST 224 "CASE OF SYNDICATE HOODS" '57
CREST 234 "PEEPING TOM MURDERS" '58
CREST 344 "HAND OF THE MAFIA" '58
CREST 325 "MOROCCO JONES IN THE CASE OF THE GOLDEN ANGEL" '59

FOWLER, DENNIS & PENNY
FOX, LAUREN--[9][21][26]ROM--
"COUNTRY PLEASURES"
"PASSION'S DANCE" & 3 MORE

FOWLER, ERIC
MARDLE, JONATHAN--[8]

FOWLER, EUGENE DEVLAN
FOWLER, GENE--[31]
LONG, PETER--[8]

FOWLER, FRANK G.
CHASE, BORDEN--V. BERCH-GM PSEUDS, PP 33,[3][31]MYS--
HART K2 "DIAMONDS OF DEATH" '47
GM 236 "LONE STAR" '52
RPRTD AS "RED RIVER" [BB205 & BB1725]

FOWLER, HELEN ROSA H.
FOLEY, HELEN--[8][22][31]

FOWLER, HENRY WATSON
EGOMET--[8]
QUILEBET--[8]
QUILLET--[8]

FOWLER, JAMES WILEY III
FOWLER, JIM--[31]

FOWLER, KENNETH A.
BROOKER, CLARK--[8][19][28][31]WEST--
BAL "LONE GUN" '55

FOWLES, J.R.
FOWLES, JOHN--[21]ROM/LIT--9 NOVELS

FOX, CHARLES
JEREMY, RICHARD--[1]

FOX, GARDNER F.
CARTER, LINWOOD--G. COOK LTR '92--
TENTATIVE PSEUD. IN H/C ONLY ?
CHASE, GLEN--JAMES/LOVISI/ECKHOFF/COOK-FOX CKLST, PP27,[2], HP--
LEIS "CHERRY DELIGHT #1 THRU #17, #19, #22"
LEIS "CHERRY DELIGHT: ROMAN CANDLE" '75
LEIS 'NEW CHERRY DELIGHT':"GREEK FIRE" '77
LEIS "DEVIL TO PAY" '77
LEIS "MOORLAND MONSTER" '77
LEIS "WHERE THE ACTION IS" '77
LEIS "THE MAN WHO WAS GOD" '78
CONWAY, TROY--JAMES/LOVISI/ECKHOFF-FOX CKLST, PP 27,[2], HP--
COOPER, J.--G. COOK-FOX CKLST--
PAPLB "SLAVES OF THE ROMAN SWORD" '65
COOPER, JEFF--[2]
COOPER, JEFFERSON--JAMES/LOVISI/ECKHOFF/COOK-FOX CKLST, PP 27,[2]HIST--
POCK "ARROW IN THE HILL" '55
PERMA "BLOODY SEVENS" '56
CARDN C262 "SWORDSMAN" '57
POCK "QUESTING SWORD" '58
POCK "CAPTAIN SEADOG" '59
POCK "VERONICA'S VEIL" '59
PAPLB "DELILAH" '62
PAPLB "JEZEBEL" '63
PAPLB "SAPPHO OF LESBOS"
PAPLB "THIS SWORD FOR HIRE" '66
COOPER, LYNNA--JAMES/LOVISI/ECKHOFF/COOK-FOX CKLST, PP 27,[9]ROM--
BEAG "MOON CHAPEL" '73
BEAGLE "BRITTANY STONE" '74
AV "STARK ISLAND" '74
AV "FOLLY HALL" '74
SRP "HOUR OF THE HARP" '75
SRP "SUBSTITUTE BRIDE" '76
SRP "HER HEART'S DESIRE" '76
SRP "MY TREASURE, MY LOVE" '78
SRP "HIRED WIFE" '78
SIGN "FORGOTTEN LOVE" '79
SIGN "FROM PARIS WITH LOVE" '80
SIGN "HEARTS IN THE HIGHLAND" '80
SIGN "INHERIT MY HEART" '81
SIGN "AN OFFER OF MARRIAGE"
SIGN "PORTRAIT OF LOVE" '80
SIGN "STARS CRY LOVE" '82
SIGN "DEEP WATER, DEEP LOVE"
GARDNER, JEFFREY--G. COOK LTR '92,[2]--
PYR 643 "BARBARY DEVIL" '61
GARDNER, JEFFREY K.--JAMES/LOVISI/ECKHOFF/COOK-FOX CKLST, PP 27,ROM--
PYR R787 "CLEOPATRA" '62
GRAY, ROD--JAMES/LOVISI/ECKHOFF/COOK-FOX CKLST, PP 27,[2]--
TWR "LADY FOM LUST" '67
REPRTD AS "LUST BE A LADY TONIGHT"
TWR "LAY ME ODDS"
TWR "69 PLEASURES"
TWR "HOT MAHATMA"
TWR "KISS MY ASSASSIN"
TWR "TO RUSSIA WITH LUST"
TWR "LADY TAKES ALL OFF"
TWR "FIVE BEDS TO MECCA"
TWR "SOUTH OF THE BORDELLO"
TWR "POISONED PUSSY"
TWR "SOCK IT TO ME"
TWR "LADY IN HEAT"
TWR "BLOW MY MIND"
TWR "LAID IN THE FUTURE"
TWR "COPULATION EXPLOSION"
TWR "EASY RIDE"
TWR "TURNED ON TO LUST"
TWR "BIG SNATCH"
TWR "SKIN GAME"
TWR "GO FOR BROKE"
TWR "VOODOO KILL"

FOX, GARDNER F. [CONT]
HARVEY, JAMES--[7][32]--
SAME AS BY "MOONCHILD"-
'HARVEY' ON THE COVER
TF "INCIDENT IN A FLYING SAUCER" '56
FE "CONFESSION" JUL '60
MH "THE STUD" NOV '64
HUNTER, KAREN--L. ROBBINS LTR MAR '94
JAMES, BRIAN--[7]SF--
"ESCAPE ACROSS THE COSMOS"
RETIT. "STAR CHASE" ELSEVIER/
NELSON BKS '79
JENNINGS, DEAN--GLEN COOK CK LIST,[2]--
POCKET-"SAN QUENTIN STORY" 1951
TWR "VALLA:STORY OF A SEA LION" '69
SIGN "INTIM. CASEBK OF A HYPNOPTIST"
KENDRICKS, JAMES [1]--JAMES/LOVISI/ECKHOFF/
COOK-FOX CKLST, PP 27,[2]HIST--
MON 111 "SWORD OF CASANOVA" '59
MON 123 "BEYOND OUR PLEASURE" '59
MON 295 "LOVE ME TONIGHT" '59
MON 158 "ADULTERERS" '60
MON MA301 "SHE WOULDN'T SURRENDER" ''60
MA304 "THE WICKED, WICKED WOMEN" '61
KENNEDY, JOHN PENDLETON--GLEN COOK LTR '92--
LEIS "THE LANDON EXPERIMENTS"
KERN, GREGORY--JAMES/LOVISI/ECKHOFF-
FOX CKLST, PP 27
E.C. TUBB PSEUD. PER COOK/DILBONE
MACKENDRICK, LOUISA--GLEN COOK LTR '92, HP--
LEIS "A PASSION FOR HONOR" '77
LEIS "NATCHEZ" 1978
LEIS "PASSION'S THIEF" '78
LEIS "THE GLORY SEEKER" '78
MAITLAND, MARGARET--GLEN COOK LTR '92,ROM,HP--
TWR "TIDEWATER" '77
LEIS "THE UNCONQUERED" '77
TWR "EAST SIDE, WEST SIDE"
TWR "SACRED & PROFANE"
MAJORS, SIMON--JAMES/LOVISI/ECKHOFF/
COOK-FOX CKLST, PP 27,[2]--
PAPLB "THE DRUID STONE" '67
MATHEWS, KEVIN--G. COOK LTR '92, ADULT--
MIDWD F348 "THE PAGAN PRINCESS" '64
TWR "CATHERINE THE GREAT" '64
TWR "HELEN OF TROY" '65
MATTHEWS, KEVIN--JAMES/LOVISI/ECKHOFF/
COOK-FOX CKLST, PP 27,[2]HIST--
POPLB EB54 "BARBARY SLAVE" '55
POPLB EB78 "TORY MISTRESS" '56
POPLB G293 "WOMAN OF EGYPT" '58
HILL 140 "DEVIL SWORD" '60
HILL 205 "CARDBOARD LOVER" '61
AWARD "THE MINX" '69
RPRT OF "ESCAPE ACROSS THE COSMOS"
AS MANOR "TITANS OF THE UNIVERSE" '78
MORGAN, JOHN MEDFORD--JAMES/LOVISI/
ECKHOFF/COOK-FOX CKLST, PP 27--
SIGN "ROMAN & THE SLAVE GIRL" '59
PALMER, CARA--GLEN COOK LTR '92--
TWR "A HOUSE OF GOOD REPUTE"
TWR "GIRLS OF RAMROD RANCH"
PURVIS, CLEMENT--JAMES/LOVISI/
ECKHOFF-FOX CKLST, PP 27--
"STONEHEDGE SLAVES"
ROYAL, BRIAN JAMES--[23]--
RETIT. OF "ESCAPE ACROSS THE COSMOS"
AS "TITANS OF THE UNIVERSE"
SELBY, ROBIN ANNE--G. COOK LTR '92--
TWR "EASTERLY INHERITANCE"
SOMERS, BART--JAMES/LOVISI/ECKHOFF/
COOK-FOX CKLST, PP 27,[2]SF--
PAPLB "ABANDON GALAXY" '67
PAPLB "BEYOND THE BLACK ENIGMA" 65
THOMPSON, FREIDA--G. COOK LTR '92--
TWR "SECOND LADY CAMERON"

FOX, GEORGE
COREY, FRANK--[3]MYS--
BERK "BY BLOOD ALONE" '61

FOX, GILBERT THEODORE
FOX, GILL--[31]
FOX, TED--[31]

FOX [HUME], RUTH
IRVING, ALEXANDER--W/ANNE FAHRENKOPF,
[3][22][33]AMERICAN/MYS--
DODD "BITTER ENDING" '46
DODD "DEADLINE" '47
DODD "SYMPHONY IN TWO TIME" '48

FOX, MERRION FRANCES
FOX, MEM--[33]

FOX, MONA ALEXIS
BRAND, MONA--[8]

FOX, NORMAN A.
SABIN, MARK--[1][19]WEST--
GM 144 "WINCHESTER CUT" '51

FOX, ROSALINE
DENNY, ROZ--[26]ROM--
HARL "STUBBORN AS A MULE"
HARL "ISLAND CHILD"
HARL "SOME LIKE IT HOTTER"

FOX, STUART
FORBES, STEPHEN--[34]MYS--
SIGN "FALSE CROSS" '89

FOX, THEODORE J.
FOX, TED--[31]

FOX, WILLIAM
FOX, BILL--[31]

FOX-DAVIES, ARTHUR CHAS.
X.--[22]ENGLISH/MYS

FOXALL, P.A.
VINCENT, JIM--[8]

FOXE, ARTHUR NORMAN
FODA, ANN--[8][22][31]ENGLISH--
AFE PRESS "GARBO: A COMMENT ON
THE TIMES" '32
FODA, AUN--[8][22][31]ENGLISH

FOY, KENNETH RUSSELL
FRANKLIN, KEITH--[3][31]MYS--
GM "MURDER AT SHIRTTAIL FLATS" '68

FRACKMAN, NATHALINE
LEE, NATA--[31]

FRAENKAL, HEINRICH
ASSIAC--[8][22][31]GERMAN-ENGLISH
CAISSA--[22]GERMAN-ENGLISH
CINNA--[22]GERMAN-ENGLISH

FRAGNER, BENJAMIN
KLICHKA, BENJAMIN--[22]CZECH

FRANCE, RUTH
HENDERSON, PAUL--[8]

FRANCE-HAYHURST, EVANGELN
FRANCE, EVANGELINE--[8][31]

FRANCES, CLARE
HOLMES, CLARE FRANCES--[21]ROM--
"THE TRAFLAGAR ROSE"
HOLMES, FRANCES--[21]ROM--
"THE EAGLES PAWN"

FRANCES, STEPHEN D.
BRAND, HILARY--[34]MYS,HP--
COMPACT "NEWS GIRL" '63
COMPACT "BRAND T" '64
CAPELLI, ACE--PP 29, P42,[34]HP--
KAYE "GET ME HEADQUARTERS" '49
KAYE "THIS MAN IS DEATH" '49
CARSON, MUNRO--[34]MYS--
CONSUL "TO KILL OR BE KILLED" '64
CLINTEN, MAX--[27][34]ENGLISH/MYS,HP--
COMYNS "NO FLOWERS FOR THE DEAD" ca '52
CLINTON, MARK--V. BERCH RVW '93,[34]--
LAN "COME AGAIN PECKER" '73
LAN "OH! HUGH PECKER" '73
COLEMAN, STEPHEN--PPCC#7, P64,[34]--
CNSL "LADY TAKE THE CHAIR" '64
RPRT OF "CALL HER SAVAGE"
CNSL "IT'S NOT EASY TO DIE" '64
RPRT '49 KAYE BOOK
DEL MARTIA, ASTON--[2][11][23]SF,HP--
GAYWOOD PRESS "ONE AGAINST TIME" '69
FOSTER, DIRK--[27]ENGLISH
GLINTO, DARCY--[34]MYS,HP--
MORING "SNATCHED" '56
MORING "HOUNDED" '56
MORING "PROTECTION PAYOFF" '57
GRECCO, JOHNNY--PP 29,[27][29][34]MYS,HP--
KAYE "CALL HER SAVAGE" '53
JANSON, HANK--[23][27][34]HP--
WARD "WHEN DAMES GET TOUGH" '46
WARD "SCARRED FACES" '46
FRANCES "LADY, MIND THAT CORPSE" '48
FRANCES "GUN MOLL FOR HIRE" '48
FRANCES "THIS WOMAN IS DEATH" '48
FRANCES "NO REGRET FOR CLARA" '49
FRANCES "BLONDE ON THE SPOT" '49
FRANCES "SLAY-RIDE FOR CUTIE" '49
FRANCES "SMART GIRLS DON'T TALK" '49
FRANCES "SISTER, DON'T HATE ME" '49
FRANCES "LILIES FOR MY LOVELY" '49
FRANCES "SWEET HEART, HERE'S YOUR GRAVE!" '49
FRANCES "ANGEL, SHOOT TO KILL" '49
FRANCES "HONEY, TAKE MY GUN" '49
FRANCES "GUNSMOKE IN HER EYES" '49
FRANCES "BLONDE ON THE SPOT" '49
FRANCES "JANE WITH GREEN EYES" '50
FRANCES "LADY HAS A SCAR" '50
FRANCES "TORMENT FOR TRIXIE" '50
FRANCES "BRIDE WORE WEEDS" '50
FRANCES "DON'T DARE ME, SUGAR" '50
FRANCES "LADY, TOLL THAT BELL" '50
FRANCES "LOLA BROUGHT HER WREATH" '50
FRANCES "SOME LOOK BETTER DEAD" '50
FRANCES "SWEETIE, HOLD ME TIGHT" '50
NF "BROADS DON'T SCARE EASY" '51
NF "WOMEN HATE TILL DEATH" '51
FRANCES "THIS DAME DIES SOON" '51
NF "FRAILS CAN BE TOUGH" '51
FRANCES "DON'T MOURN ME, TOOTS" '51
FRANCES "HOTSY, YOU'LL BE CHILLED" '51
FRANCES "IT'S ALWAYS EVE THAT WEEPS" '51
FRANCES "DEATH WORE A PETTICOAT" '51
NF "MILADY TOOK THE RAP" '51
FRANCES "BABY, DON'T DARE SQUEAL" '51
NF "ACCUSED" '52
NF "KILL HER IF YOU CAN" '52
NF "AUCTIONED" '52
NF "CONFLICT" '52
NF "SADIE, DON'T CRY NOW" '52
NF "KILLER" 52

FRANCES, STEPHEN D. [CONT]
JANSON, HANK [CONT
NF "SKIRTS BRING ME SORROW" '52
NF "FILLY WORE A ROD" '52
NF "MURDER" '52
NF "SUSPENSE" '52
NF "TENSION" '52
NF "WHIPLASH" '52
NF½"VENGEANCE" '53
NF "TORMENT" '53
TF "SILKEN MENACE" '53
TF "CORRUPTION" '53
TF "DEADLY MISSION" '53
TF "NYLONED AVENGER" '53
TF "PERSIAN PRIDE" '53
NF "PURSUIT" '53
NF "DESERT FURY" '53
TF "UNSEEN ASSASSIN" '53
NF "AMOK" '53
MORING "TOMORROW & A DAY" '55
MORING "CONTRABAND" '55
MORING "48 HOURS" '55
MORING "FRAMED" '55
MORING "UNTAMED" '55
NF "CACTUS" '56
MORING "THEY DIE ALONE" '56
MORING "ESCAPE" '56
MORING "DEVIL'S HIGHWAY" '56
MORING "STRANGE DESTINY" '56
MORING "BIG LIE" '56
MORING "BEWITCHED" '57
MORING "AVENGING NYMPH" '58
MORING "HELLCAT" '57
MORING "ENEMY OF MAN" '57
MORING "REVOLT" '57
MORING "SINISTER RAPTURE" '57
MORING "SWEET FURY" '57
MORING "MISTRESS OF FEAR" '58
MORING "JACK SPOT" '58
MORING "KILL THIS MAN" '58
MORING "SUGAR & VICE" '58
TURTON "TORRID TEMPTRESS" '59
TURTON "WILD GIRL" '59
ROBERTS "LATE NIGHT REVEL" '61
ROBERTS "NYMPH IN THE NIGHT" '62
ROBERTS "BRAND IMAGE" '63
ROBERTS "SECOND STRING" '63
FRANCES "DAUGHTER OF SHAME" '63
KIRBY, ARTHUR--[34]MYS,HP--
AMALG "HIGH SUMMER HOMICIDE" '62
LAMONT, PETER--[34]MYS--
CONSUL "SHROUDS ARE CHEAP" '64
LINTON, DUKE--S. HOLLAND-SCION CKLST, PP 27, PPCC#7,HP--
SCION "LIPS OF DEATH" '50
SCION "CRAZY TO KILL" '50
SCION "DAMES DIE TOO" '50
SCION "ENOUGH ROPE" '50
SCION "KILL & DESIRE" '50
SCION "SHROUDS ARE CHEAP" '50
SCION "TOO LATE FOR DEATH" '50
MARKHAM, STEVE--PP 29, P42,[27][34]HP--
KAYE "IT'S NOT EASY TO DIE" '49
PARDOE, GEOFFREY--[27]ENGLISH/MYS--
"THIS IS A MYSTERY"
"TRAFFIC IN SOULS"
REID, DESMOND--[23][34]MYS,HP--
MYFLR "THE BABCOCK BOYS" '66
MYFLR "THE DEADLIER OF THE SPECIES" '66
MYFLR "DEATH WAITS IN TUCSON" '67
ROLAND, DAVID--[34]MYS--
HUTCH "RED STAR OVER LONDON" '71
RYLAND, TEX--S. HOLLAND-SCION CKLST, PP 27, P11,[27]WEST--
SCION "BUSHWHACKED" '48

FRANCES, STEPHEN D. [CONT]
SAXON, PETER--W/W.A. HOWARD BAKER, [1][34]MYS,HP--
MYFLR "DISORIENTED MAN" '66
SHELTON, LINK--[27][34]MYS--
FRANCES "DEAD MEN DON'T LOVE" '49
STEEL, DAVID--PPCC#7, P64,[27][34]MYS--
COMYNS "LOVELY BUT DEAD" '52
COMYNS "BEAUTY FOUND IN A GRAVE" '52
COMYNS "TOO TOUGH TO DEATH" '53
COMYNS "YOU'LL LIVE TO TALK" '53
CONSUL "LIPS OF DEATH" '65 & 4 OTHERS
STEPHENS, DANNY--[34]MYS--
CONSUL "NOT EVERYBODY DIED" '64
STEPHENS, MARK--[34]MYS--
CONSUL "UNLUCKY BREAK" '64
RPRT OF "NO FLOWERS FOR THE DEAD"
WILLIAMS, RICHARD--S. HOLLAND-SCION CKLST, PP 27, P11,[34]MYS--
AMALG "VENDETTA!" '61
AMALG "SOMEBODY WANTS ME DEAD" '62
AMALG "TORMENT WAS A REDHEAD" '62
MYFLR "SLAYING OF JULIAN SUMMERS" '63
MYFLR "MAN WITH THE IRON CHEST" '65
MYFLR "THE SNIPER" '65

FRANCIS, ARTHUR BRUCE C.
BRUCE, CHARLES--[8]

FRANCIS, BASIL [HOSKINS]
RHODE, AUSTEN--[1][22]ENGLISH

FRANCIS, DOROTHY BRENNER
ALDEN, SUE--[8][31]
GOFORTH, ELLEN--[8][9][21][31]ROM--
"PATH OF DESIRE"
"A NEW DAWN"
LOUIS, PAT--[8][9][21][26][31]ROM--
"TREASURE OF THE HEART"

FRANCIS, EMILE PERCY
FRANCIS, CAT--[31]

FRANCIS, GAIL KIMBERLY
COURTNEY, DAYLE--[7]SF--
"TRAIL OF BIGFOOT" '83
KIMBERLY, GAIL--[7][32]SF/MYS--
AHMM "MELANIE IS DEAD...OR IS SHE?" FEB '70
POPLB "FLYER" '75
PYR "DRACULA BEGAN" '76
PYR "STAR JEWEL" '79

FRANCIS, JAMES
GOLDTHWAITE, JAMES [A]--ROBBINS LTR '94,[32]--
DS "DEADLIER THAN A BULLET" SEPT '44
DS "MEAT" SEPT '46

FRANCIS, R.W.
FARRAR, FRANCIS--[3]MYS--
DONOHUE "THE GREAT MINE MYSTERY" 1895

FRANCIS, RADFIELD
FRANCIS, RADFORD--R.C. & ELWANDA REVW '93--
BANNER 101

FRANCIS, RICHARD
FRANCIS, RICHARD H.--[23]SF--
ADDED FICTIONAL "H" TO DISTINGUISH HIMSELF FROM DICK FRANCIS

FRANCIS, RICHARD STANLEY
FRANCIS, DICK--[18][29][32][34]MYS--
29 NVLS '62-TD
EQMM "CARROT FOR A CHESNUT" FEB '73
EQMM "THE BIG STORY" DEC '74
EQMM "NIGHTMARES" JUN '75

FRANCIS, SOPHIA L.
FRANCES, SOPHIA--[34]MYS--
2 MINERVA BOOKS ca 1800

FRANCIS, [MOTHER] MARY
CLARE, FRANCIS D.--[22]AMERICAN

FRANCISKOWSKY, HANS GUNTHER
FRANCIS, H.G.--[40]GERMAN/MYS--
"DETEKTIV CLIPPER: EIN KOFFER VOLL GELD" '80
FRANCIS, HANS G.--[39]GERMAN/MYS/SF
FRANCIS, HEINZ G.--[39]GERMAN/MYS/SF
FRANCISCO, H.G.--[39]GERMAN/MYS/SF
FRANK, GUNTHER--[39]GERMAN/MYS/SF
MERITT, CADE C.--[39]GERMAN/MYS/SF
QUOOS-RABE, R.C.--[39]GERMAN/MYS/SF
SCOTT, TED--[39]GERMAN/MYS/SF
SKY, FRANK--[39]GERMAN/MYS/SF

FRANCK, FREDERICK S.
FREDERICKS, FRANK--[8][22][31]DUTCH-AMERICAN

FRANCOIS, [JACK] MICHEL
LACLOS, MICHEL--[1]

FRANES, S.O.
WILLIAMS, RICHARD--[1]HP

FRANK, ETHEL
HANNA, EVELYN--W/MICHAEL DYNE,[9][26]ROM--
"BLAZE OF GLORY"
"STOLEN SPLENDOR" & MORE

FRANK, LOTHAR-MATHIAS
LOTHAR, FRANK M.--[39]GERMAN/MYS

FRANK, MRS. M.J.
A.L.O.M.--[8]
LADY OF MANITOBA, A--[8]

FRANK, PETER
LILL, PETER--[39]GERMAN/MYS
REUTIN, GEORG--[39]GERMAN/MYS
SCHELLER, NIKOLAUS--[39]GERMAN/MYS

FRANK, PHILIP NORMAN
CRACKERS, FRITZ--[31]HUMOR, CARTOONS

FRANK, RUDOLF
BECKER, OLGA--[31]
ENSE, WOLFGANG--[31]
FRANK, WILLIAM G.--[31]

FRANK, WALDO DAVID
SEARCH-LIGHT--[8][22]AMERICAN/MYS--

FRANKAU, JULIA DAVIS
DANBY, FRANK--[2][3][22]MYS--
TRISCHLER "COPPER CRASH" 1889
HM "SPHINX'S LAWYER" '06 & MORE

FRANKAU, MARY EVELYN A.
ATKINSON, M.E.--[31][33]

FRANKAU, PAMELA
NAYLOR, ELIOT--[1]

FRANKE, CHARLOTTE [W]
WINHELLER, CHARLOTTE--[39]GERMAN/JUV/SF

FRANKE, HERBERT W.
BOTH, SERGIUS--[2][23][39]GERMAN/SF--
"PLANET OF THE LOST" '63
PARSIVAL, PETER--[39]GERMAN/SF

FRANKEL, RUBY
BENNETT, REBECCA--[9][21][26]ROM--
"A MERRY CHASE"
CONRAD, CONSTANCE--[9][21][26]ROM--
"ON WINGS OF NIGHT"
MARSH, LILLIAN--[9][21][26]ROM--
"HIS MASQUERADE"
"FORGOTTEN BRIDE"

FRANKEN, ROSE [DOROTHY]
GRANT, MARGARET--W/WILLIAM B. MELONEY, [17][31]ROM--
"CALL BACK LOVE" '37
MELONEY, FRANKEN--W/WILLIAM B. MELONEY, [1][8][17]ROM--3 NOVELS

FRANKLE, JUDITH
COTTER, JOHN--W/JACK [C] COUFFER,[7]--
BERK "NIGHTS WITH SASQUATCH" '77

FRANKLIN, BENJAMIN V.
CHARLES, NATHANAEL--[31]--
CONTRIB TO LIT JOURNALS & JAZZ MAGS

FRANKLIN, CYNTHIA
NEVILLE, C.J.--[1][22]AMERICAN/MYS--

FRANKLIN, HAROLD L[EROY]
ALIMAYO, CHIKUYO--[31]

FRANKLIN, MADELEINE L'ENGLE
FRANKLIN, L'ENGLE--[1]
L'ENGLE, MADELEINE--[7][23][26]ROM/SF--
"LOVE LETTERS"
"OTHER SIDE OF THE SUN"

FRANKLIN, STELLA MARIA S.
BRENT, OF BIN BIN--[8][31]
FRANKLIN, MILES--[36]AUSTRALIAN/MYS--
ENDEAVOR "BRING THE MONKEY" '33

FRANKLYN, JULIAN
MAGRON, VECTOR--S. HOLLAND-SCION CKLST, PP 27, P11

FRANKS, NORMAN
ROBERT, LESLIE--[34]MYS--
KIMBER "DIPO FLIGHT" '85

FRANZ, ERICH ARTHUR
FRANC, ERIC ARTUR--[39]GERMAN
FRANCIS, E.A.--[39]GERMAN

FRANZ, ERIKA
VON RAVEN, IRIS--[39]GERMAN

FRANZEN, WILLIAM EDWARD
FRAZEN, BILL--[31]

FRANZERO, CARLO MARIA
FRANZERO, CHARLES MARIE--[31]

FRANZKE, GUNTHER
SCHWENN, GUNTHER--[39]GERMAN

FRASER, ANTHEA
CAMERON, LORNA--[8][18][31]--
"SUMMER IN FRANCE" '81
GRAHAM, VANESSA--[8][18][21][26][31]ROM--
"TIME OF TRIAL" '79
"SECOND TIME AROUND" '80
"THE STAND IN" '84

FRASER, AUGUSTA ZELIA
SPINNER, ALICE--[1]

FRASER, DOROTHY G. SPICER
SPICER, DOROTHY--[7]SF--
BAL "THE CRYSTAL BALL" '75

FRASER, DOROTHY MAY
FRASER, MAXWELL--[1][31]

FRASER, DOUGLAS
HOPE, DAVID--[31]

FRASER, ELIZABETH MARR
FRASER, BETTY--[31][33]

FRASER, GEORGE MACDONALD
ASHTON, HELEN--R. TORRENCE-FRASER IN PB, PP 22, P9, ?
WHITTLE, TYLER--R. TORRENCE-FRASER IN PB, PP 22, P9, ?

FRASER, JOHN ARTHUR
HAWKSHAW--[1][3][22]MYS-- 9 NOVELS ca1900

FRASER, RAYMOND JOSEPH
FRASER, RAY--[31]

FRASER, WALLER BROWN
WALLER, BROWN--[1]

FRASER-HARRIS, D.
GRANGE, ELLERTON--[8]

FRATER, BARBARA LAWRENCE
BAYNTON, BARBARA--[13]AUSTRALIAN

FRAZEE, [CHARLES] STEPHEN
FRAZEE, STEVE--[1][32][34]MYS/WEST NVLS--
EQMM "MY BROTHER DOWN THERE" APR '53
MH "GRAVEYARD SHIFT" MAY '53
SA "SILENCE IS LOUD" SEPT '55
PU "THE SCHEMERS" JAN '56
EQMM "ALL LEGAL & PROPER" MAR '60
MH "THE CRIME BROKER" JUN '62
JENNINGS, DEAN--D.R. MILLER-BAE 28,[1]--
PHOENIX "RANGE TROUBLE" '51
POCK 831 "SAN QUENTIN" '51

FRAZER, JAMES IAN ARBUTH.
FRAZER, SHAMUS--[7][23][32]MYS--
"A SHROUD AS WELL AS A SHIRT" '35
"BLOW, BLOW YOUR TRUMPETS '35
LM "FLORINDA" JUN '56
LM "FIFTH MASK" JUN '57
LM "YEW TREE" DEC '58

FRAZER, WINIFRED LOESCH
DUSENBURY, WINIFRED L.--[31]
FRAZER, WINIFRED DUSENB.--[31]

FRAZIER, WALTER
CLYDE COOL--[31]
FRAZIER, WALT--[31]

FRAZZETTA, FRANK
FRAZETTA, FRANK--[7][23]SF--
ART & NON-FICT
FRITZ--[33]

FREBEL, ERNST
GEORGE, WILLIAM--[39]GERMAN/SF/WEST

FREDE, RICHARD
FREDERICS, JOCKO--[8][31][34]MYS--
HOLT "EVERYBODY'S READY TO DIE" '66

FREDE, RICHARD
FREDERICS, MACDOWELL--[8][34]MYS--
COWARD "EMERGENCY PROCEDURE" '70
CROWELL "BLACK WORK" '76
MCNAB, OLIVER--[34]MYS--
HOUGHTON "HORROR STORY" '79

FREDERICHS, HANS-JURGEN
PASCAL--[39]GERMAN

FREDRIKSEN, ERIK E.
DETINE, PADRE--W/IB SPANG OLSEN,[1][33]

FREDRIKSSON, DON
LANCASTER, F. DONALD--[1][31]

FREED, MARGARET DE HAAN
DE HAAN, MARGARET--[31]

FREED, MARY KAY S.
SIMMONS, MARY KAY--[9][21]ROM--18 NOVELS

FREEDGOOD, MORTON
GODEY, JOHN--[3][5][18][29][32]MYS--
15 NVLS '48-78
MH "THE LOVERS" OCT '56
AHMM "IT'S ALL QUITE PAINLESS" AUG '57
MORTON, STANLEY--[1][18]--
"YANKEE TRADER" '47

FREEDLAND, NATHANIEL
KENYON, PAUL--[31]HP
ROSS, PAUL--W/BILL AMIDON,[3]MYS,HP--
POPLB "DYNAMITE MONSTER BOOGIE CONCERT" '75

FREEDMAN, COLE
MANSON, WILL--JEAN F. LE DEIST,
BAE 18,[34]MYS,HP--
CARAVELLE "THE MATHMATICIAN" '67

FREEDMAN, JAMES DILLET
FREEMAN, JAMES DILLET--[1][22]AMERICAN
MANN, D.J.--[1][22]AMERICAN

FREELING, NICHOLAS
NICHOLAS, F.R.E.--[3][18][29]MYS--
GOLZ "VALPARISO" '64

FREEMAN, ANNE FRANCES
HUETHER, ANNE FRANCES--[1][31]

FREEMAN, DAVID
FREEMAN, DAVE--[31]

FREEMAN, E.
FREEMAN, JACK--[1]

FREEMAN, GILLIAN
ELIZABETH, VON S.--[8]
GEORGE, ELIOT--[1]
JACKSON, ELAINE--[31]
S, ELIZABETH VON--[8]

FREEMAN, GRAYDON LAVERNE
FREEMAN, LARRY--[1][22][31]AMERICAN
THOMPSON, JAMES H.--[1][22][31]AMERICAN
WOOD, SERRY--[1][22][31]AMERICAN

FREEMAN, HAROLD WEBBER
FREEMAN, H.W.--[1]

FREEMAN, JEAN KENNY
KENNY, JEAN--[1][31]

FREEMAN, JEAN TODD
MORGAN, JUSTINA--[1]
TODD, SARAH MANNING--[1]

FREEMAN, JOHN CROSBY
GUTHRIE, HUGH--[1][31]
MCDOWELL, CROSBY--[1]

FREEMAN, JOHN [H.G.]
ANDREW, MERRY--[1]

FREEMAN, JULIA DEAN
FORREST, MARY--[1]

FREEMAN, KATHLEEN
CORY, CAROLINE--[8][9][18][31]MYS--
MacD "DOCTOR UNDERGROUND" '56
FITT, MARY--[18][31][32][34]MYS--
28 BKS '36-59
LM "CASE OF THURSDAY PHONE-CALLS" DEC '49
LM "CASE OF THE PROFESSOR'S CHAIR" FEB '50
JCM "A DUMB FRIEND" FEB "59
LM "MEET DR. FITZBROWN" DEC '50 - MAY '52
WICK, STUART MARY--[18][34]MYS--
HUTCH "AND WHERES MR. BELLAMY?" '48
HODDER "STATUE & THE LADY" '50

FREEMAN, MARY [E.W.]
FREEMAN, M.E.--[1]
WILKINS, MARY E.--[1]

FREEMAN, RICHARD AUSTIN
ASHDOWN, CLIFFORD--W/JOHN J. PITCAIRN,
[2][5][8][32][34]MYS--
TRAIN "QUEEN'S TREASURE" '75
WARD/TRAIN, 3 BKS '02-75
EQMM "ASSYRIAN REJUVENATOR" JAN '47
EQMM "ADVENTURES OF ROMNEY PRINGLE" FEB '48
FREEMAN, R. AUSTIN--[1][31][34]MYS--
HODDER "AS A THIEF IN THE NIGHT" '28 & MORE
FRIMAN, ROBERT--[29]MYS--
HODDER "THE MYSTERY OF 31 NEW INN"
PIERS, ASHDOWN--W/JOHN J. PITCAIRN,[1]

FREEMAN, WILLIAM BRADFORD
FREEMAN, BILL--[31][33]

FREEMANTLE, ANNE
LAMB, LADY CAROLINE--[21][26]ROM--
"GLENARVON"

FREEMANTLE, BRIAN [HARRY]
EVANS, JONATHAN--[3][18][29][31][40]MYS--
JOSEPH "MISFIRE" '80
"MIDAS MEN" '81 & 5 MORE '80-5
GANT, RICHARD--[8][18][31]MYS--
"SEAN CONNERY: GILT EDGE BOND" '67
MAXWELL, JOHN--[1][18][29]MYS--
CAPE "HMS BOUNTY" '77
CAPE "THE MARY CELESTE" '79
STREET, LESLIE--[1]
WINCHESTER, JACK--[8][18][29]MYS--
COWARD "SOLITARY MAN" '80
COLLINS "CHOICE OF EDDIE FRANKS" '86

FREER, MARTHA AGNES R.
LEE, AGNES--[1]

FREETHY, BARBARA
LOGAN, KRISTINA--[21][26]ROM--7 NOVELS

FREI MONTALVA, EDUARDO
FREI, EDUARDO--[1]

FREIBERG, HANS-JOACHIM
FRYBERG, JOHN--[39][40]GERMAN/MYS--
"ERFOLGSAUSSICHTEN 11%" '69

FREIDENREICH, HARRIET P.
FRIEDENREICH, HARRIET P.--[31]

FREIHOFER, LOIS DIANE
BARTH, LOIS--[34][39]MYS--
BOUREGY "RUN FROM THE RIVER" '65
LENNOX "DARK LABYRINTH" '71
LENNOX "EPITAPH FOR A TEDDY BEAR" '73

FREIRE, PAULO
FREIRE, P.--[31]

FREITAG, OTTO
ADLER, KARL--[39]GERMAN
FRIEDEBURG, OSWALD--[39]GERMAN
OTTO, FRANZ--[39]GERMAN

FRENCH, ALICE
THANET, OCTAVE--[2][3][11][22]MYS--
BOBBS "LION'S SHARE" '07

FREND, WILLIAM HUGH C.
PHILO--[1]

FRENES-RILLA, ALIX E. DU
FRENES, ALIX DU--[39]GERMAN

FRENKLE, JOAN [C] D[ENN.]
VINGE, JOAN D.--[7]SF--
SERIES & NOVELS - MARRIED NAME

FRENTZEN, JEFFREY
KETCHUM, J.--[1][31]
SANDERS, BUCK--[1][29][34]MYS,HP--
WARNER "STAR OF EGYPT" '81
WARNER "BAYOU BRIGADE" '82
SCOTT, LAUREN--[1]

FRENZ, HANNELORE
HUNEFELD, HANNE--[39]GERMAN/JUV

FREPPERT, PETER
VON DER RELL, PITER--[39]GERMAN

FRESE, DOLORES WARWICK
WARWICK, DOLORES--[22]AMERICAN

FRESHMAN, BRUCE JACK
BRELLEN, MARC--[7]SF--
LEIS "CROSSBEARERS" '88

FRETTS, BRUCE
ADAMS, NICHOLAS--[7]SF,HP--
HARPER "HORROR HIGH: SUDDEN DEATH"

FREUNDLICH, ELISABETH
LANZER, ELISABETH--[39]GERMAN

FREUNDSBERGER, HILDEGARD
FORSTER, HILDE--[39]GERMAN/JUV

FREWER, GLYN M.L.
LEWIS, MERVYN--[3][31]MYS--
HALE "DEATH OF GOLD" '70

FREWIN, LESLIE RONALD
DUPONT, PAUL--[8][22][31]AMERICAN
NICHOLLS, MARK--[1]

FREY, AKE
WINGE, PETER--[29]MYS--
4 NOVELS '55-8

FREY, ANTON
FRANK, ARMIN--[39]GERMAN

FREY, CHARLES WEISER
FINDLEY, FERGUSON--[3][22][29]MYS--
ACE D197 "COUNTERFEIT CORPSE" '56
DUELL "MY OLD MAN'S BADGE" '50
DUELL "WATERFRONT" '51
DUELL "THE MAN IN THE MIDDLE" '52
POP LIB 780 "MURDER MAKES ME MAD" '56

FREY, FRIEDRICH HERMAN
GREIF, MARTIN--[22]GERMAN

FREY, MARLYS
MAYFIELD, MARLYS--[1]

FREY, OLIVER
ILLUSTRATOR--[7]SF--
"EXCITING STORIES OF FANTASY
& THE FUTURE" '82

FREYBERG, HERMANN
EELA, H.P.--[39]GERMAN/MYS/JUV

FREYTAG, HANS-JURGEN
FREY, H.J.--[39]GERMAN/SF

FREYTAG, WILLI GUSTAV
FRYDAG, WILL--[39]GERMAN/MYS

FRICKE, HANS WERNER
FAHLBERG, H.L.--[39]GERMAN/SF

FRIDEGARD, JAN
JOHANSSON, JOHAN FRIDOLF--[22]SWEDISH

FRIDRIKSSON, THEODOR
VALUR--[1]

FRIEBEL-ROHRING, GISELA
FRIEBEL, G.--[39][40]GERMAN/MYS--
ZAU "DAS MONSTERSCHLOSS" '78
FRIEBEL, G.--[39][40]GERMAN/MYS--
"DAS MONSTERSCHLOSS" '78

FRIEDBERG, GERTRUDE
TONKONGY, GERTRUDE--[8]

FRIEDE, DONALD
BEDFORD, DONALD F.--W/HENRY
BEDFORD-JONES & KENNETH FEARING,[1]

FRIEDE, GERHARD
TALIS, GERD--[39]GERMAN

FRIEDLAENDER, PAVEL
FERLAND, PAUL-HENRI--[1]
FRIEDLAENDER, SAUL--[1]
FRIEDLAENDER, SHAUL--[1]

FRIEDLAND, RONALD LLOYD
LLOYD, RONALD--[1]

FRIEDLANDER, PETER
FRENCH, FERGUS--[8]

FRIEDLANDER, SALOMO
MYNONA--[39]GERMAN/SF

FRIEDLANDER, WALTER ANDR.
KRAFT, WALTER ANDREAS--[31]

FRIEDLI, EMILIE IDA
VAN ITH, LILY--[1][2][7]SF

FRIEDMAN, DAVID F.
FREEMAN, DAVIS--[31]

FRIEDMAN, DAVID JERROLD
GERROLD, DAVID--AUTHOR PROVIDED,[2][4][7]--
NAME LEGALLY CHANGED TO "GERROLD"

FRIEDMAN, EVE ROSEMARY
FRIEDMAN, ROSEMARY--[8]
TIBBER, ROBERT--[1]
TIBBER, ROSEMARY--[1]

FRIEDMAN, HAROLD
FRIEDMAN, HAL--[31]

FRIEDMAN, HARRY & LINDA
WISER, H. FRED--[34]MYS--
WALKER "DEADLY STAKES" '89

FRIEDMAN, JACOB HORACE
FRIEDMAN, ELIAS--[1][8]
FRIEDMAN, JOHN--[1][8]
PATER, ELIAS--[1][8]

FRIEDMAN, JOSEPHINE TROTH
FRIEDMAN, JOY TROTH--[1][31]

FRIEDMAN, MICHAELE T.
FRIEDMAN, MICKEY--[3][31]MYS--
DUTTON "HURRICANE SEASON" '83
DUTTON "FAULT TREE" '84 & MORE

FRIEDMAN, PHILIP
CHASE, PHILIP--[3]MYS--
DELL "DEADLY CRUSADE" '76
DELL "MERCHANTS OF DEATH" '76 & 2 MORE

FRIEDMAN, STUART
MANDE, ELIZABETH ERIN--[34]MYS--
POPLB "PHANTOM ROOM" '71
PYR "SPIRIT OF MELISSA NORGATE" '72
PYR "TOWER OF DARK LIGHT" '73

FRIEDMANN, EGON
FRIEDELL, EGON--[39]GERMAN/SF

FRIEDRICH, ANITA
ALEXANDER, ANNE--[39]GERMAN/JUV
KAYSER, DINAH--[39]GERMAN/JUV

FRIEDRICH, MARGOT
CARIUS, ANNE--[39]GERMAN

FRIEDRICH-FREKSA, KURT
FREKSA, FRIEDRICH--W/GERTRUD
SCHMIDT-FREKSA,[39]GERMAN/SF

FRIEDRICHS, HOLGER
CAMERON, JOHN--[39]GERMAN/MYS/WEST,HP
COTTON, JERRY--[39]GERMAN/MYS,HP
DE LORCA, FRANK--[39]GERMAN/MYS/WEST,HP
DOUGLAS, GLENN--[39]GERMAN/MYS/WEST,HP
ELLIOT, BRIAN--[39]GERMAN/MYS/WEST,HP
FREDERIC, AL--[39][40]GERMAN/MYS--
'KOMMISSAR X' -7 BKS
'PLUTONIUM POLICE' #17, #21 & #24
LAMONT, ROBERT--[39]GERMAN/MYS/WEST,HP
PALMER, ROY--[39]GERMAN/MYS/WEST
SLADE, JACK--[39]GERMAN/WEST,HP

FRIEDRICHS, HORST
ARBORG, SVEN--[39]GERMAN/MYS/WEST
BERGEN, HENRY--[39]GERMAN/MYS/WEST
CAMERON, JOHN--[39]GERMAN/MYS/WEST,HP
COOPER, STEVE--[39]GERMAN/MYS/WEST,HP
COTTON, JERRY--[39]GERMAN/MYS,HP

FRIEDRICHS, HORST [CONT]
FREDERICK, BURT--[39]GERMAN/MYS/WEST
LAMONT, ROBERT--[39]GERMAN/MYS/WEST,HP
ROYCROFT, JAMES--[39]GERMAN/MYS/WEST
SHERARD, BRIAN--[39]GERMAN/MYS/WEST
SHORT, FREDERIC--[39]GERMAN/MYS/WEST
SLADE, JACK--[39]GERMAN/WEST,HP
WHITMAN, JOHN--[39]GERMAN/MYS/WEST

FRIEND, OSCAR J[EROME]
JEROME, OWEN FOX--[2][3][7][29][37]MYS--
8 NVLS '27-58
EXD [PULP STORIES]
SERGEANT SATURN--[1][2][11]HP--
THRILLING/STARTLING/CAPT. FUTURE
SMITH, FORD--L. ROBBINS LTR '94,[28][29]WEST--
AVALON "RANGE DOCTOR" '48
"BUZZARD'S ROOST" '61

FRIENDLICH, RICHARD J.
FRIENDLICH, DICK--[31][32][33]MYS--
MB "THE OTHER FOOT" MAY '47

FRIERSON, MEADE III
HEDGE, RALPH WOLLSTONE.--[2]

FRIESEN-MIELTITZ, FELICI.
FREEMAN, RHONDA--[39]GERMAN

FRIESTADT, BENEDIKT
FREI, BRUNO--[1]

FRII-BAASTAD, BABBIS E.
BAASTAD, BABBIS FRIIS--[1][22]
[31][33]NORWEGIAN
BABBIS, ELEANOR--[1][22][31][33]NORWEGIAN
FRIIS, BABBIS--[1][22][33]NORWEGIAN

FRINDALL, WILLIAM HOWARD
FRINDALL, BILL--[31]

FRINGS, KATHLEEN HARTLEY
FRINGS, KETTI--[1]

FRISCHWASSER, HEINZ FELIX
RA'ANAN, URI--[1]
RICHARDS, MARK--[1][32]MYS--
FE "STILL LIFE" JUL '60

FRISKEY, MARGARET RICHARD
SHERMAN, ELIZABETH--[1][22][33]AMERICAN

FRISSELL, WILLIAM DONALD
MORGAN, JASON--[3]MYS--
LAN 73-785 "DEATH IS A SWINGER" '68

FRITCH, CHARLES E.
BALTHAZAR, ANGELO--V. BERCH-BRNDN/
BC PSEUDS, BAE 22, P24
BOND, GEORGE--V. BERCH-BRNDN/
BC PSEUDS, BAE 22, P24
CARLFI, CHESTER H.--V. BERCH REVIEW JAN '93
CONWAY, TROY--MIKE AVALLONE, BAE 13, P54
MOSS, PETER--V. BERCH-BRNDN/
BC PSEUDS, BAE 22, P24
SMITH, WINSTON--V. BERCH-BRNDN/
BC PSEUDS, BAE 22, P24

FRITH, MICHAEL K.
FL*M*NG, I*N--W/CHRISTOPHER C. CERF,[3][7]--
VANITAS V4402 "ALLIGATOR" '62 & 8 OTHERS
STONE, ROSETTA--W/THEODOR SEUSS GEISEL,[1]

FRITSCH, STEFFANIE
VON ALTAN, STEFFI--[39]GERMAN

FRITSCHEL, GEO[RGE] JOHN
GAUS, GEO. J.--[1]

FRITZHAND, JAMES
CARTER, NICK--[34]MYS,HP--
AWARD "SIGN OF THE COBRA" '74
AWARD "KATMANDU CONTRACT" '75
AWARD "THE LIST" '78
FITZPATRICK, JANIE--[3][21]MYS/ROM--
WARNER "THE DREAMWALKER" '75
WARNER "SERENA" '76
RAVENSWOOD, FRITZEN--[7]SF--
ZEBRA "KEI #1 & #2" ?? UNCONFIRMED ??

FROBA, KLAUS
ANATOL, ANDREAS--[39]GERMAN/MYS/JUV
CARSTEN, CHRISTIAN--[39]GERMAN/MYS/JUV
MARTIN, MATTHIAS--[39][40]GERMAN/MYS--
"DER SCHLUSSSTRICH" '86

FROBOSE, EDITHA
MEISE, EDITHA--[39]GERMAN/JUV

FROEHLICH, GUSTAV
FROHLICH, GUSTAV--[31]

FROELICH, PETER [JACK]
GAY, PETER [JACK]--[1]

FROEST, FRANK
DILLNOT, GEORGE--[29]MYS--
"DEN KIDNAPPADE BOXAREN" '41

FROHLICH, CAROLINE LILLI
FROLICH-BUME, LILLI--[1]

FROHLICH, GUSTAV
BRANDT, HEINZ--[39]GERMAN

FROHLICH, HEINZ-PETER
HOLLING, H.P.--[39]GERMAN/SF

FROHMAN, ELSA
FRITCH, ELIZABETH--[9]ROM--11 NOVELS

FROHMAN, ELSA
FROST, ELEANOR--[9][21][26]ROM--
"A PUBLIC AFFAIR"
"ELUSIVE PARADISE"

FROMENT, MATHILDE
BOURDON, MADAM--[1]

FROMMHOLZ, ALICE
GARVEN, VIOLA--[39]GERMAN
TERENZ, GABRIELE--[39]GERMAN

FROSCHL, JOSEF G.
PEPIN, F.--[39]GERMAN/ADULT

FROST, C. VERNON
CHILD, CHARLES B.--[1][5][32]MYS--
EQMM "SATAN HAS ANOTHER NAME" MAY '52
& 24 OTHER EQMM STORIES
MD "INSPECTOR IS DISCRETE" SEPT '57

FROST, DENIS
DENIS, JOHN--W/JOHN EDWARDS,[7]SF--
FONTANA "GOLIATH" '87

FROST, G.H.
STIVERS, DICK--[34]MYS,HP--
GE "ARMY OF DEVILS" '83
GE "KILL SCHOOL" '83
GE "JUSTICE BY FIRE" '83
GE "THEY CAME TO KILL" '84

FROST, G.H. [CONT]
STIVERS, DICK [CONT]
GE "SCORCHED EARTH" '84
GE "RAIN OF DOOM" '85
GE "DEATH STRIKE" '85
GE "TECH WAR" '85
GE "IRONMAN" '85
GE "FIRE & MANUEVER" '85

FROST, HELEN
NICHOLS, DAVE--[1][22]AMERICAN

FROST, J.W.
GLENELG--[8]

FROST, KATHLEEN MARGARET
MERIVALE, MARGARET--[8]

FROST, LESLEY
BALLANTINE, LESLEY FROST--[31][33]

FROST, RUSSELL E.
FROST, JACK--[1][32]MYS--
LM "NO TIGER LILLIES FOR TANYA" MAR '75

FROSTERUS, OSKAR
PAHHALA, TEUVO--[22]FINNISH

FRTEYBE, HEIDI HUBERTA
LAMBERT, KRISTIN--[1]

FRUCHTMAN, JOEL RICHARD
RICHARDS, JOEL--[7][23]SF--
AMZ "SPEEDPLAY" '80
TOR "PINDHAREE" '86

FRY, CHRISTOPHER
HARRIS, CHRISTOPHER--[8]

FRY, DANIEL
PRYE, CHRISTOPHER--V. BERCH-BRNDN/
BC PSEUDS, BAE 22, P24

FRY, EDWIN MAXWELL
FRY, [E] MAXWELL--[31]

FRY, THOMAS FREDERICK
FRY, TOM--[31]

FRYDMAN, SZAJKO
SZAJKOWSKI, ZOSA--[1]

FRYE, VERN D.
DERMOTT, VERN--[1][2]

FRYEFIELD, MAURICE P.
BROOKS, W.A.--[8]
BROOKS, WILLIAM ALLEN--[8]
HOLMES, ARNOLD W.--[8]

FTYARAS, LOUIS GEORGE
ALEXANDER, L.G.--[8]

FUCHS, ANTON
ELTEN, THOMAS--[39]GERMAN

FUCHS, JAKOB
THOMPSON, RALPH L.--[39]GERMAN

FUCHS, SONIA HUSID
SEEDO, SONIA--[1]

FUCHS, SUMMER
LISKY, I.A.--[22]

FUCINI, RENATO
NERI TANFUCIO--[1]
TANFUCIO, NERI--[22]ITALIAN

FUELOEP-MILLER, RENE
FULOP-MILLER, RENE--[31]

FUENTES MACIAS, CARLOS M.
FUENTES, CARLOS--[7]SF--4 NOVELS

FUERST, MILAN
FUEST, MILAN--[1]

FUHSE, GEORG FEODOR
LARSSEN, TIM--[39]GERMAN

FUJIWARA, MICHIKO
SAITO, MICHIKO--[33]

FULFORD, ROBERT
DELANEY, MARSHALL--[1]

FULLBROOK, GLADYS
HUTCHINSON, PATRICIA--[8]

FULLER, DOROTHY MASON
THORNE, STERLING--[1]

FULLER, EDITH JEAN
DALE, ADRIAN--[1]

FULLER, EDMUND [M]
AMICUS, CURIAE--[1][8][31][33]

FULLER, HAROLD EDGAR
FULLER, ED--[8]
FULMAN, AL--[8]

FULLER, HENRY BLAKE
PAGE, STANTON--[1][8][22]AMERICAN

FULLER, HENRY STARKEY
FEELIN', A. FELLOW--[1]

FULLER, HOYT [W]
BARROW, WILLIAM--[1][31]

FULLER, JAMES FRANKLIN
IGNOTUS--[8]

FULLER, SAMUEL MICHAEL
FULLER, SAM--[31]

FULLER, WILLIAM
DUDGEON, ROBERT--J. HOFFMAN, PP 40 MYS,HP--
GERM PANTH 164
RPRT OF DELL FE189 "TIGHT SQUEEZE"

FULLERTON, ALEXANDER F.
FOX, ANTHONY--[3][29][31]MYS--
JOSEPH "THREAT WARNING RED" '79
JOSEPH "KINGFISHER SCREAM" '80
HILTON, ALEC--W/EUSTACE CHESSER,[1][31]--
CORGI "THE CONSULTANT" '68
CORGI "WAITING FOR THE NIGHT" '69
CORGI "HEART PEOPLE" '69

FULLERTON, GAIL JACKSON
FULLERTON, GAIL PUTNEY--[31]
PUTNEY, GAIL J.--[8]

FULLERTON, GEORGIANNA
DE NAVERY, RAOUL--[1]

FULLERTON, MARY ELIZA
MANNERS, GORDON--[36]AUSTRALIAN/MYS--
JENKINS "MURDER AT CRAB APPLE CAFE" '33

FULLILOVE, MRS. E.J.
WARWICK, ELSIE--[1]

FULLJAMES, HENRY J.
AVICUS--[1]

FULLMER, RICHARD
VANDEN, DIRK--[14]ADULT--
OLYM TC#515 "ALL OR NOTHING" '71
OLYM TC#512 "ALL IS WELL" '71

FULTON, ELIZABETH G.
FULTON, LIZ--[7]SF--
BB "THE PALM DOME" '91

FUNFGELD, MARGARETE
VON OERTZEN, MARGARETE--[39]GERMAN

FUNK, THOMPSON
FUNK, TOM--[31][33]

FURGERSON, SAMUEL
HEFFERMAN, MICHAEL--[1]

FURGURSON, ERNEST BAKER
FURGURSON, PAT--[31]

FURLONG, VIVIENNE CAROLE
WELBURN, VIVIENNE--[1]

FURMAN, ELEANOR L.
FRIED, ELEANOR L.--[31]

FURMAN, GERTRUDE L.K.
KERMAN, GERTRUDE--[31]

FURNISS, LOUISE E.
CHOLLET--[1]

FURNISS, WILLIAM
DE GRASSE, WILL--[1]

FURPHY, JOSEPH
COLLINS, TOM--[1][22]AUSTRALIAN
JACK, WARRIGAL--[13]AUSTRALIAN

FURRY, ELDA
HOPPER, HEDA--[31]--
NAME LEGALLY CHANGED TO "HOPPER"

FURST, CARL
PENDLETON, DON--[34]MYS,HP--
GE "DEAD LINE" '89
GE "KILL ZONE" '89
GE "TIGHTROPE" '89
GE "KNOCKDOWN" '90
GE "DIRECT HIT" '90
GE "DOWN & DIRTY" '90

FURSTAUER, JOHANNA
BENTLEY, JOY--[39]GERMAN/HOR/ADULT
FORESTIER, JOAN--[39]GERMAN/HOR/ADULT
KELLY, BARBARA--[39]GERMAN/HOR/ADULT
MORGEN, KEITH--[39]GERMAN/HOR/ADULT
STANLEY, DR.--[39]GERMAN/ADULT
STANLEY, J.F.--[39]GERMAN/HOR/ADULT
WHITE, SYLVIA--[39]GERMAN/HOR/ADULT

FURSTENBERG, HILDE
FRIEDRICH, HANNA--[39]GERMAN
LINDEN, HANNE--[39]GERMAN

FURTHMANN, JULIUS G.
FOX, STEPHEN--[31]SCREENPLAYS
FURTHMAN, JULES--[31]SCREENPLAYS

FURTWANGLER, VIRGINIA W.
COPELAND, ANN--[31]AMERICAN--
FOUR SS COLECTIONS '78-89

FURUKAWA, TOSHI
KANZAWA, TOSHIKO--[31][33]

FUSS, KARL
UBERZWERCH, WENDELIN--[39]GERMAN

FUSSENEGGER, GERTRUD
DORN, GERTRUD--[39]GERMAN

FUSSER, ERIKA
GREGOR, NINA--[39]GERMAN

FUSTER, SERGE
CASAMAYOR--[1]

FUTCHER, JANE
BARRY, NORA--[34]MYS--
DBLDY "SHERBOURNE'S FOLLY" '78

FYFE, H.B.
MACDUFF, ANDREW--[2][11]

FYSH, FREDERICK
F.F.--[1]

FYSON, JENNY GRACE [H]
FYSON, J.G.--[1]

FYTTON ARMSTRONG, T.I.
GAWSWORTH, JOHN--[8]

GAA, EDEL
GULDEN, BARBARA--[39]GERMAN

GAATHON, ARYEH LUDWIG
GAATHON, A.L.--[31]
GRUENBAUM, LUDWIG--[31]

GABALDON WATKINS, DIANA J
GABALDON, DIANA--[7]SF--
"OUTLANDER #1" '91

GABEL, JOSEPH
GEROELY, KALMAN--[1][31]
GEROLY, KALMAN--[31]
GOMBOSSY, ZOLTAN--[1]
MARTIN, LUCIEN--[1]

GABERMAN, JUDIE ANGELL
ANGELL, JUDIE--[7]SF--
"THE WEIRD DISAPPEARANCE OF
JORDAN HALL" '87

GABLE, JACOB HENNY J.
GABLE, J. HARRIS--[1]

GABLE, MARY
MARIELLA, [SISTER]--[1]

GABRIELSON, ERNEST L.
COTRION, ANTHONY--[2]
GABRIEL, JOHN--[2]

GADD, DAVID BERNARD H.
WERATA, TOTA--[1]

GAENZI, KURT FRIEDRICH
GANZI, KURT--[31]

GAER, JOSEPH
GAER, YOSSEF--[31]

GAERHARDIE, WILLIAM
GERHARDI, WILLIAM--[23]SF--
"GERHARDI" WAS LEGALIZED

GAGE, CAROL
SHANN, RENEE--[9][21]ROM--
"CLOUD OVER THE SUN"
"GIRL IN A TRAP" & 13 MORE

GAHAGAN, MARGUERITE
GAHAGAN, MARGARET--[36]AUSTRALIAN--
NOVELLE "MURDER IN PARADISE" nd

GAIDA-GAIDAMAVICIUS, PRA.
CHAUTIER, P.--[1]
ZAIDYS, PRANAS--[1]

GAILLOT, JANE
CORIOLA--[34]MYS--
"LE TROISIEME FEMME" '53 & 3 MORE

GAINES, JACOB
GAINES, JACK--[31]

GAINES, JOE DENNIS
KANSIL, JOLI--[1]

GAINES, ROBERT
SUMMERSCALES, ROWLAND--[8]

GAINES, WILLIAM MAXWELL
GAINES, BILL--[31]

GAITSKELL, HUGH TODD N.
GAITSKELL, H.T.N.--[31]

GAJDUSEK, ROBERT ELEMER
GAJDUSEK, ROBIN--[1]

GALAND, RENE
AR C'HALAN, REUN--[1]

GALARZA, ERNESTO
GALARZA, ERNEST--[31]

GALBRAITH, ALEXANDER
WILSON, SANDY--[2][11]

GALBRAITH, F.
GEE, JEFF--[1]

GALBRAITH, GEORGIE S.
PAGE, G.S.--[1][22]AMERICAN
PATRICE, ANN--[1][22]AMERICAN
PENNINGTON, PENNY--[1][22]AMERICAN
PENNINGTON, STUART--[1][22]AMERICAN

GALBRAITH, JEAN
CORREA--[1][31]
GREEN, JUDITH--W/JUDITH G. RODRIGUEZ,[1][31]

GALBRAITH, JOHN KENNETH
EPERNAY, MARK--[2][11][22]

GALE, E.F.
FAULKNER, JOHN--[1][7]SF--
"OVERLORDS OF ANDROMEDA" '55
"UNTRODDEN STREETS OF TIME" '55

GALE, FREDERICK
WYKEHAMICUS, FRIEDRICH--[2]

GALE, LINN A.E.
ALLEN, ADAMS--[1]
WESTON, WARREN--[1]

GALE, MICHAEL ROBERT
GALE, BOB--[31]

GALECKI, TADEUSZ
STRUG, ANDRZEJ--[1]

GALES, BARBARA J.
CARROLL, ANNE KRISTIN--[1][31]

GALIARDI, SPRING
HERMANN, SPRING--[9][21]ROM--
"TAKING CHANCES"

GALICIA, L. FELIPE CAMINO
CAMINO, FELIPE--[30]MEXICAN
LEON, FELIPE--[30]MEXICAN

GALL, INA
GALL, I.--[40]GERMAN/MYS--
"AUF PUPPEN SCHIESST MAN NICHT" '61

GALL, MICHAEL
HOMER & ASSOCIATES--[14]ADULT--
OLYM TC#206 "A BEDSIDE ODYSSEY" '67
RICHARDSON, HUMPHREY--[8][14]ADULT--
OLYM TC#205 "THE SEXUAL LIFE OF
ROBINSON CRUSOE" '67

GALLAGHER, FRANK
HOGAN, DAVID--[8][34]MYS--
SHAYLOR "DARK MOUNTAIN
& OTHER STORIES" '31

GALLAGHER, RACHEL
DRAKE, KIMBAL--[1][31]

GALLAGHER, REA
GOULD, JUDITH--W/NICK BIENES, V. BERCH
LTR TO HUBIN '94--
DUTTON "NEVER TOO RICH" '90

GALLAGHER, STEPHEN
COUPER, STEPHEN--[7][23]SF--
SPHERE "PARADISE #1: DYING OF PARADISE" '78
SPHERE "PARADISE #2: ICE BELT" '82
GALLAGHER, STEVE--[7]SF
LYDECKER, JOHN--[2][7][23]SF--
TARGET 'DR. WHO' SERIES:
"AND THE WARRIORS' GATE"
"TERMINUS"

GALLAHER, MARY DOMINIC
DOMINIC, SISTER MARY--[31]

GALLARDOS MUNOZ, JUAN
CURTIS, DONALD--JEAN F. LE DEIST LTR '93
CURTIS, GARLAND--JEAN F. LE DEIST LTR '93
DAVIS, KENT--JEAN F. LE DEIST LTR '93
DE JUAN, JAVIER--JEAN F. LE DEIST LTR '93
FORRESTER, GLEN--JEAN F. LE DEIST LTR '93
GARLAND, JOHNNY--JEAN F. LE DEIST LTR '93
HARRIS, DON--JEAN F. LE DEIST LTR '93
JAVIER--JEAN F. LE DEIST LTR '93
KIRBY, DAN--JEAN F. LE DEIST LTR '93
LOGAN, FRANK--JEAN F. LE DEIST LTR '93
MADDOX, LESTER--JEAN F. LE DEIST LTR '93
SAVAGE, MARK--JEAN F. LE DEIST LTR '93
SHERIDAN, WALT--JEAN F. LE DEIST LTR '93
STARR, ADDISON--JEAN F. LE DEIST LTR '93
TURNER, ELLIOT--JEAN F. LE DEIST LTR '93

GALLERY, DANIEL V.
GALLERY, DAN--[31]

GALLICHAN, WALTER M.
BLOUNT, ANNA--[1]
MORTIMER, GEOFFREY--[1]
MORTIMER, JANUARY--[1]

GALLISON, KATHLEEN
GALLISON, KATE--[31]

GALLISSION, HENRI
DUGALL, H.L.--W/LOUIS DURAND,[40]FRENCH/MYS--
"UN TEMPS POUR TUER" '69

GALLOWAY, JAMES M.
MOORE, ANON--[1][2]

GALLOWAY, KARA
CAIL, CAROL[E]--[26][32]ROM/MYS--
"IVORY LIES"
EQMM "MRS. LAMB'S NOSE DREAMS" DEC '73
EQMM "GARDEN OF EVIL" DEC '73
EQMM "GETAWAY" AUG '74
AHMM "DEAD WEIGHT" JAN '78
EQMM "MAY THE WORST MAN WIN" OCT '78
EQMM "NIGHTCRAWLERS" JAN '79
AHMM "BLOOD FROM A TURNIP" MAY '80

GALLOWAY, PRISCILLA
PEEBLES, ANNE--[1][33]

GALLUN, RAYMOND Z.
ALLPORT, ARTHUR--[2][11][23][31]SF
CALLAHAN, JOHN--[1][31]
CALLAHAN, WILLIAM--[2][11][23]SF--
"THE MACHINE THAT THOUGHT" '39
ELSTAR, DOW--[2][15][31]SF--
ASF "AVALANCHE" DEC '35
RAYMOND, E.V.--[2][15][31]SF--
ASF "NOVI SOLIS" DEC '35

GALLUP, LUCY
DE FLUENT, AMELIE--[1]

GALOUYE, DANIEL F.
DANIELS, LOUIS G.--[2][11][23]SF--
2 STORIES '53-4

GALPIN, J.A.
BLACKSTONE, VALERIUS D.--[1][2][7]SF

GALSBY, JOHN [S]
BUFFY--[8]
EDDY, ALBERT--[8]

GALSWORTHY, JOHN
SINJOHN, JOHN--[1][2][22]ENGLISH

GALT, ALISTAIR
KERNER, KEITH--[14]ADULT--
OLYM TC#478 "GLASS CROTCH" '70

GALT, THOMAS FRANKLIN JR.
GALT, TOM--[31][33]

GALT, WILLIAM CAMPBELL
GALT, JOSEPH R.--L. ROBBINS LTR MAR '94

GALT, WILLIAM H.
NITGENOCKLE--[1]
ULRICH, CHARLES JR.--[1]

GALUB, JACK
GANT, CHUCK--[1][31]

GAMBER, HANS
BARR, CHRISTOPHER--W/CLAUS FISCHER, [39][40]GERMAN/MYS--
"SOLDATO, DER KILLER" '81
"ZUM STERBEN ZU SCHON" '81

GAMBLE, PAUL
GAMMA--[2]

GAMMAGE, WILLIAM LEONARD
GAMMAGE, BILL--[31]

GAMMON, DAVID J.
KIRBY, DALLAS--[34]MYS--
SWAN "CARNIVAL OF DEATH" '42
SWAN "DEATH AT MY HEELS" '42
SWAN "VICTOR" '43
SWAN "VICTOR VERSUS VERHASST" '43
SWAN "DEATH MAN" '43
ROBINS, FENTON--[1]

GANDER, LEONARD
MEABEY, LEONARD--[1]

GANDHI, MOHANDAS K.
GANDHI, M.K.--[31]
GANDHI, MAHATMA--[31]

GANDLEY, KENNETH ROYCE
JACKS, OLIVER --[3][29][31]MYS--
HODDER "MAN ON A SHORT LEASH" '74
HODDER "ASSASSINATION DAY" '76
HODDER "AUTUMN HEROES" '77
ROYCE, KENNETH--[3][18][29]MYS--
CASSELL "ANGRY ISLAND" '63
CASSELL "BONES IN THE SAND" '67 & 17 MORE

GANLEY, W. PAUL
DUANE, TOBY--[1][2][11]
GRIFFIN, A. ARTHUR--[2]
QUEDNAU, WALTER--[2]
WARD, OLIVER--[2]

GANN, ERNEST K.
GRAY, ANTHONY--[11]

GANNON, E.J.
DARING, VICTOR--[1]
KENT, BEVERLY--[1]

GANTNER, NEILMA
SIDNEY, NEILMA--[1][8]

GANTOS, JOHN BRYAN JR.
GANTOS, JACK--[31][33]

GANTZER, COLEEN & HUGH
DAVE, SHYAM--[3][31]MYS--
JAICO "BALLOTS FOR VIOLENCE" '72
ORIENT "GURU DOCKET" '77 & MORE

GANTZER, HUGH
KALE, ARVIND & SHANTA--[1][31]

GARAFALO, ROBERT L.
GARAFALO, REEBEE--[1]

GARAGIOLA, JOSEPH HENRY
GARAGIOLA, JOE--[31]

GARBER, ERIC
WINGS, MARY--W/MARY L. GELLER, V. BERCH LTR TO HUBIN '94/MYS--
WP "SHE CAME TOO LATE" '87
WP "SHE CAME IN A FLASH" '88

GARBER, NELLIA B.
BERG, ILA--[9]ROM

GARBUTT, JANICE D. LOVOOS
ANGELINO, MARIE--[31]

GARBUTT, JOHN L.
ALLEN, JOHN--[1]
BREARLEY, JOHN--[1][34]MYS--
AMALG "NIGHT HAWK" '32
AMALG "PHANTOM FOE" '32 & 7 MORE
CAMERON, CLIFFORD--[1]
FORSEY, PETER Q.--[1]
TEMPLAR, JOHN--[1]

GARCIA LECHA, LUIS
CARRADOS, CLARK--JEAN F. LE DEIST LTR '93
MILK, LOUIS G.--JEAN F. LE DEIST LTR '93
PARISH, GLENN--JEAN F. LE DEIST LTR '93
VON KASELLA, KONRAT--JEAN F. LE DEIST LTR '93

GARCIA SANCHEZ, EDUARDA
PASCUAL--[1]

GARCIA SANCHEZ, JESUS
GARCIA, E.--[1]

GARCIA, EDUARDA
DANIEL--[1]

GARCIA, NANCY
O'DONNELL, KATE--[9][21][26]ROM--
"DEFY THE WIND"
'FRONTIER ENCHANTRESS"

GARCZYNSKI, J.
GAR--[1]

GARD, JOYCE
REEVES, JOYCE--[1][8]

GARDINER, ALFRED GEORGE
ALPHA OF THE PLOUGH--[8]

GARDINER, DOROTHEA FRANC.
FRANK, THEODORE--[3][8][22]MYS--
BUTWH "THE LIFTED LATCH" '29

GARDINER, RICHARD
HONEYCOMBE, WILLIAM ESQ.--[1]
MERRY FELLOW, DICK--[1]

GARDNER, BENNIE WILSON
COLE, JACKSON--B.GARDNER,HP--
TX RGR "LAND OF HIDDEN LOOT" NOV '46
TX RGR "LOOT OF THE WOLF JUNE" '47
TX RGR "GOLD OF THE AZTECS" OCT '48
GARDNER, B. WILSON--LACHMAN-B. GARDNER SON OF BENNIE '93--PULPS
GARDNER, BARRY--LACHMAN/B. GARDNER SON OF BENNIE '93--PULPS
STEELE, BEN--B. GARDNER-SON OF AUTHOR '93--PULP
STEELE, GUNNISON--LACHMAN-B. GARDNER SON OF BENNIE '93--PULPS

GARDNER, DARLENE HROBAK
QUINN, JULIA--[26]ROM--
"WADE CONNOR'S REVENGE"

GARDNER, E.D.
SCHIRE--[1]

GARDNER, ERLE STANLEY
CORNING, KYLE--[1][5][11]
FAIR, A.A.--[2][3][5][18][31]MYS--
MORROW "BATS FLY AT DUSK" '42
& 28 MORE '40-70
GARDNER, E.S.--[29]MYS--
IN SWEDEN-EXAMPLE DM 12
GREEN, CHARLES M.--[1][5]MYS--
BM "SHRINKING SKELETON"
BM "SERPENT'S COILS"
BM "THE VERDICT" '23-4
GREEN, CHARLES--L. ROBBINS LTR '94,[32][37]--
BM STORY DEC '23
EQMM "COMLIMENTS OF CALIPH BERNIE" APR '56
EQMM "SERAFINA CASE" JUL '57
EQMM "A MOUSE CALLED EMILY" APR '58
EQMM "INCIDENT AT A BAR" OCT '58
EQMM "ADVENTURE OF THE TWELVE TOUCANS" OCT '61
EQMM "ONE & ONLY BERNIE" AUG '63
HOLIDAY, GRANT--M. LACHMAN-RUTH MOORE BIBLIO,[11]--
TORONTO STAR WKLY "MARRY FOR MONEY" '41
KENDRAKE, CARLETON--[3][5][18][31]MYS--
MORROW "CLEW OF THE FORGOTTEN MURDER" '35
KENNY, CHARLES J.--[3][5][18]MYS--
MORROW "THIS IS MURDER" '35
PARR, ROBERT--L. ROBBINS LTR '94,[1][5]MYS--
TILLRAY, LES--L. ROBBINS LTR '94,[1][5]MYS--

GARDNER, GERALD BROSSEAU
0 TO 0 4=7 SCRIRE--[2]

GARDNER, JEROME
GARDNER, JEREMY--[28]ROM--
FABER "SUMMER PLACE" '60
GILCHRIST, JOHN --[7][8][23]SF--
"BIRD BRAIN" '75
"OUT NORTH" '75
"LIFELINE" '76
"THE ENGLISH CORRIDOR" '76
"THE ENGENDERING" '78
TULLY, PAUL--[28]WEST--
5 HALE NOVELS '85-90

GARDNER, JOHN
AURELIUS--[1]

GARDNER, LEWIS J.
DEARBORN, ANDREW--[1]
SWIFT, LEWIS J.--[1]

GARDNER, MARIA
HUNTER, JILLIAN--[9][21][26]ROM--
"HEART OF THE STORM"
"SHADOW OF SPLENDOR"

GARDNER, MARTIN
RENDRAG, NITRAM--[1]

GARDNER, NANCY BRUFF
BRUFF, NANCY--[8][21][26]ROM--
"CIDER FROM EDEN"
"DESIRE ON THE DUNES"
"COUNTRY CLUB"
GARDNER, NANCY--[9][21]ROM--
"MIST MAIDEN"
"FIG TREE"

GARDNER, RICHARD [M]
ANDERSON, CLIFFORD--W/CLIFFORD M. IRVING & ROBERT ANDERSON,[1][31][33]
CARVER, JOHN--[1][31][33]
CUMMINGS, RICHARD--[1][8][31][33]
GARDNER, DIC--[31]
ORTH, RICHARD--[1][33]

GARDNER, WILLIAM
W.G.--[1]

GARDNER, WILLIAM HENRY
AIKEN, HENRY--[1]

GARDOS, ALICE
SCHWARZ, ALICE--[39]GERMAN/JUV

GAREIS, HERBERT
SUKRON, S.N.--[39]GERMAN/JUV

GARELICK, MAY
CLARK, GAREL--W/ETHEL M. SCOTT,[1][31]
CLARK, GAREL--[33]

GARFIELD, BRIAN F.W.
GARLAND, BENNETT--W/THEODORE V. OLSEN,[18]MYS--
MON 391 "HIGH STORM" '63
GARLAND, BENNETT--[18][19][31]WEST--
MON 292 "7 BRAVE MEN" '62
MON 415 "LAST OUTLAW" '64
AWARD AS1159 "RIO CHAMA" '68
HAWK, ALEX--[1][19]WEST,HP--
PAPLB "SAVAGE GUNS" '68
IVES, JOHN--[5][18][28][29][32][34]MYS--
EQMM "TWO-WAY STREET" AUG '78
DUTTON "FEAR IN A HANDFUL OF DUST" '78
DUTTON "MARCHAND WOMAN" '79
MALLORY, DREW--[3][5][18][28][29]MYS--
PUTNAM "TARGET MANHATTAN" '75
O'BRIAN, FRANK--[3][18][19][28][29]MYS--
BOUREGY "RIMFIRE MURDERS" '62
BAL "BUGLE & SPUR" '66
BAL "ARIZONA" '69
DELL "ACT OF PRIVACY" '75
O'BRIEN, FRANK--L. ROBBINS LTR MAR '94, WEST
WARD, JONAS--[8][19][28]WEST,HP--
GM 1926 "BUCHANAN'S GUN" '68
WYNNE, BRIAN--[1][18][19][28]WEST--
8 NOVELS '64-9
WYNNE, FRANK--[1][18][19][28]WEST--
10 NOVELS '61-6

GARFIELD, JAMES B.
EICHBERG, JAMES BANDMAN--[33]

GARFINKEL, BERNARD MAX
ALLEN, ROBERT--[1][31]
ELLIOTT, ROBERT--[1][31]

GARFINKEL, CHARLES H.
GAR, THE--[31]
GARFINKEL, CHARLEY--[31]

GARFINKLE, BERNARD
MARTIN, JANET--[1]

GARHN, JUDITH L.
GRAHN, JUDY--[31]

GARIS, HOWARD R.
APPLETON, VICTOR--[1][2][23]HP--
STSY 'TOM SWIFT':
FIRST 35 OF 38 '10-32
CHADWICK, LESTER--[31]HP--
STSY 'BASEBALL JOE'
DAVIDSON, MARION--[1][31][33]
ROCKWOOD, ROY--[7][23]SF,HP--
STSY- FIRST 6 "GREAT MARVEL" STORIES

GARLAND, A.P.
CHANTECLER--[1]

GARLAND, KATHERINE MANN.
GARDNER, KIT--[26]ROM--
"ARABESQUE"
"THE DREAM"
"THE STOLEN HEART"

GARLAND, RENE
AR C'HALAN, REUN--[31]

GARLAND, SHERRY
LAWRENCE, LYNN--[9][26][31]ROM--
"FAMILIAR TOUCH"
"DEEP IN THE HEART"

GARLAND, STEVEN
GARLAND, LAWRENCE--W/LAWRENCE TOPPMAN,[34]MYS-
OAK KNOLL "AFFAIR OF UNPRINCIPLED PUBLISHER" '83

GARLAND, [MARY] ISABEL
LORD, GARLAND --W/MINDRET LORD, [11][22][32][34][37]MYS--
DBDLY "MURDER'S LITTLE HELPER" '41
DBLDY "SHE NEVER GREW OLD" '42
DBLDY "MURDER, PLAIN & FANCY" '43
MORROW "MURDER WITH LOVE" '43
IM "TERRIBLE DETECTIVE" SEPT-OCT '45

GARLOCK, DOROTHY
GLEN, DOROTHY--[9][21][26]ROM--
"HELL RAISER"
"THE GENTLEMEN" & MORE
PHILLIPS, DOROTHY--[9][21][26]ROM--
"SING SOFTLY TO ME"
"MARRIAGE TO A STRANGER" & MORE
PHILLIPS, JOHANNA--[9][21][26]ROM--
"PASSION'S SONG"
"AMBER-EYED MAN" & MORE

GARMAN, DOUGLAS MAVIN
MAVIN, JOHN--W/[JOHN] EDGELL RICKWORD,[1]

GARN, EDWIN JACOB
GARN, JAKE--W/STEPHEN P. COHEN,[7][31]SF--
MORROW "NIGHT LAUNCH' '89

GARNER, CHARLES
CUMBERLAND, STEWART C.--[34]MYS--
LOW "VASTY DEEP" 1889
BLACKETT " A FATAL AFFINITY" & MORE
CUMBERLAND, STUART--[2]

GARNER, HUGH
WARWICK, JARVIS--M. LANTEIGNE, TOP 500, BAE 23, P48,[1]

GARNER, PHYLLIS A.
WHITNEY, PHYLLIS--[9][21][26][32]MYS/ROM--
SN "THE SILVER BULLET" SUM '70 & MORE

GARNER, ROBERTA
ASH, ROBERTA--[1][31]

GARNETT, DAVID S.
ALMANDINE, DAVID--[2]
BURKE, LEDA--[3][31]MYS--
LAURIE "DOPE-DARLING" '19
FERRING, DAVID--[7][23]SF--
"WARHAMMER SERIES #1 & #2"
GARNETT, DAV--[23]SF--
ON EARLY WORK
LEE, DAVID--[2][23][32]MYS/SF--
MH "MY PAL ISAAC" OCT '58
"DESTINY PAST" '74
WARD, HUGO A.--[2]

GARNETT, WILLIAM JOHN
GARNETT, BILL--[7][31]SF/HOR--
SPHERE "DOWN-BOUND TRAIN" '73
SPHERE "THE SHADOW" '82
SPHERE "THE CRONE" '84

GAROFALO, ROBERT L.
GAROFALO, REEBEE--[31]

GARRARD, DOROTHY
MCNAIR, CHRISTY--[35]AUSTRALIAN--
CLEVELAND
WAYNE, LOIS--[35]AUSTRALIAN--
CLEVELAND

GARRARD, JEANNE SUE
GARRARD, GENE--[1][31]

GARRAT, ALFRED
GARRAT, TEDDIE--[8]

GARRET, EDWARD PETER
GARRET, GARET--[8]

GARRETSON, JAMES E.
DARBY, JOHN--[1]

GARRETSON, VICTORIA DIANE
COX, VICTORIA--[1][31][33]

GARRETT, ALBERT EDWARD
BARNARTO, BART--[27][34]HP--
EDWIN SELF "BIG PANIC" '53
BARONI, NICK--[34]MYS,HP--
WARREN "EASY CURVES" '50
CELLO, JOHNNY--S. HOLLAND-SCION CKLST, PP 27,HP--
COSTELLO, PETE--[27]HP--
EDWIN SELF
VALOIS, JEAN PAUL--[27]HP--
EDWIN SELF

GARRETT, CLARA MAUDE
C.M.G.--[1]

GARRETT, ELLEN AMELIA
AMELIA, ELLEN--[1]

GARRETT, RANDALL [P]
AGHILL, GORDON--W/ROBERT SILVERBERG, [2][11][23]
BARRETTON, GRANDALL--[2][11][23]SF--
AMZ "ADVENTURE OF BENEDICT BREADFRUIT"
BLADE, ALEXANDER--W/ROBERT SILVERBERG, [2][23][31]HP-- ZIFF-DAVIS - ALSO ALONE
BUPP, WALTER--[1][2]--
NOT SO PER [23]
BURKE, RALPH--W/ROBERT SILVERBERG, [2][23][31]SF
GARRETT, GORDON--[2][31]
GORDON, DAVID--[2][23][31]
GREER, RICHARD--W/ROBERT SILVERBERG,[1][23]SF--
AMZ "GREAT KLANDAR RACE" '56
JORGENSEN, IVAR--JEAN F. LE DEIST, BAE 12,[1][2]HP--
ZIFF-DAVIS
JORGENSON, IVAR--W/ROBERT SILVERBERG, [2][23][31]SF-ALSO USED HIMSELF
LANGART, DARREL[L] T.--[2][4][11][23][31]SF--
"ANYTHING YOU CAN DO" '63
MACKENZIE, JONATHAN BLAKE--[2]
MCKETTRIG, SEATON--[2]
MITCHELL, CLYDE T.--W/ROBERT SILVERBERG, [2][11][23]HP

GARRETT, RANDALL [P] [CONT]
PHILLIPS, MARK--W/LAURENCE M. HARRIS
[2][3][4][23]MYS/SF--
PYR F783 "BRAIN TWISTER" '62
PYR F875 "IMPOSSIBLES" '63
PYR F909 "SUPERMIND" '63
RANDALL, ROBERT--W/ROBERT SILVERBERG,
[2][4][23][31]SF--
GNOME "THE SHROUDED PLANET" '57
GNOME "THE DAWNING LIGHT" '59
SPENCER, LEONARD G.--W/ROBERT SILVERBERG,
[2][11][23]HP
TENNESHAW, S.M.--W/ROBERT SILVERBERG,
[2][11][23]SF,HP--
AMZ "BEAST WITH 7 TAILS" '56
TINKER, JOSEPH--[11]SF
VANCE, GERALD--W/ROBERT SILVERBERG,
[2][11][23]SF

GARRETT, THOMAS SAMUEL
GARRETT, TOM--[31]

GARRETT, WENDY
HALEY, WENDY--ROMANTIC TIMES MAG MAR '93,
P99, ROM--
"SHADOW WHISPERS"

GARRETT, WINIFRED SELINA
DEAN, LYN--[3]MYS--
MELROSE "ASK NO QUESTIONS" '37
MELROSE "THE ROPE WAITS" '37

GARRISH, HAROLD J.
BELBIN, HARRY--[1]
EVEARD, WALTER--[1]
FORDWYCH, JACK--[1]
FORDWYCH, JOHN EDMUND--[1]
FOSTER, GRANT--[1]
GERRISH, GEORGE--[1]
MORELL, WALLACE--[1]

GARRISON, CHARLES M.
MACDANIEL, CHARLES--[2][3][11]MYS/SF--
VANTAGE "MURDER ON THE MOON" '68

GARRISON, WEBB BLACK
WEBSTER, GARY--[8][22][33]AMERICAN

GARRITY, JOAN THERESA
GARRITY, TERRY--[1][31]
J--[31]

GARROD, JOHN WILLIAM
CASTLE, JOHN--W/RONALD C. PAYNE,[2][29][34]--
SVNR "FLIGHT INTO DANGER" '58
W/ARTHUR HAILEY
SVNR "SEVENTH FURY" '61

GARROWAY, DAVID C.
GARROWAY, DAVE--[31]

GARSIA, CLIVE
COTTAR, GUY--[1][34]MYS--
JARROLDS "TENACITY" '27

GARSIDE, [CLIFFORD] JACK
CARTER, NICK--[34]MYS,HP--
JOVE "PRESSURE POINT" '87
JOVE "EAST OF HELL" '87
JOVE "AFGHAN INTERCEPT" '88
JOVE "ANDRPOV FILE" '88
JOVE "BLACK SEA BLOODBATH" '88
JOVE "LETHAL PREY" '88
JOVE "SANCTION TO SLAUGHTER" '89
JOVE "ARTIC ABDUCTION" '90
JOVE "SINGAPORE SLING" '90

GARSIDE, [CLIFFORD] JACK [CONT]
HILD, JACK--[31][34]MYS,HP--
GE "SOB's":
"ALASKA DECEPTION" '87
"SAKHALIN BREAKOUT" '87

GARST, DORIS SHANNON
GARST, SHANNON--[22][31][33]AMERICAN--
CHILDREN'S BOOKS
SHANNON, STEVE--L. ROBBINS LTR MAR '94--
PULP

GARSTANG, JAMES GORDON
GARSTANG, JACK--[31]

GARSTIN, A.
REID, DESMOND--[1][34]MYS,HP--
AMALG "HUNT THE LADY!" '61

GARTMAN, HEINZ
WEHR, WERNER--[1]

GARTON, DURHAM KEITH
GARTON, D.K.--JEAN F. LE DEIST-BAE 18, P9,[1]
KEYS, DURHAM--JEAN F. LE DEIST-
BAE 18, P9,[1][2]
RYAN, AL--JEAN F. LE DEIST-
BAE 18, P9,[1][2]

GARTON, JANET
MAWBY, JANET--[1]

GARTON, RAY
LOCKE, JOSEPH--[7]SF/HOR--
"THE NIGHTMARES ON ELM ST." '89

GARVEY, ERIC WILLIAM
HERNE, ERIC--[8]

GARVICE, CHARLES
GIBSON, CHARLES--[1][17]ENGLISH/ROM
HART, CAROLINE--[9][17][21]ENGLISH/ROM--25 NOVELS
HART, CAROLYN [G]--[9][21][26]ENGLISH/ROM--
4 NOVELS

GARVIN, AMELIA WARNOCK
HALE, KATHERINE--[1][22]CANADIAN

GARVIN, J.L.
CALEHAS--[8]

GARVIN, THOMAS CHRISTOPH.
GARVIN, TOM--[31]

GARWOOD, GODFREY THOMAS
THOMAS, GOUGH--[8]

GARWOOD, JUDITH
DAIN, CATHERINE--AUTHOR PROVIDED JUN '93--
JOVE "LAY IT ON THE lINE" '92
JOVE "SING A SONG OF DEATH" '93
JOVE "WALK A CROOKED MILE" '94
BERK 14328 "LAMENT FOR A DEAD COWBOY" '94

GARY, DON
CRAWFORD, LAD--V. BERCH-BRNDN/
BC PSEUDS, BAE 22, P24

GASCOIGNE, GWENDOLEN G.T.
GALTON, GWENDOLEN DOUGLAS--[34]MYS--
EDEN "LA FENTON" 1891

GASCOIGNE, TOSS
GOODMAN, JO--W/JOSEPHINE C. GOODMAN
& MARGOT TYRRELL,[7]--
PENG "DREAMTIME: 16 STORIES" '89

GASCOYNE, ARTHUR TALBOT
CECIL, LORD ROBERT--[13]AUSTRALIAN

GASKELL DENVIL, JANE
GASKELL, JANE--[1]

GASKELL, ELIZABETH C.S.
GASKELL, MRS.--[7][32]--
"MRS. GASKELL'S TALES OF MYS & HORROR" '78
EW "SQUIRE'S STORY" AUG '85

GASKO, GORDON
GORDON, NATHANIEL--[1][2][11]

GASKOIN, CHARLES JACINTH
MERRIDEW, ARTHUR--[1]

GASPAROTTI, ELIZABETH S.
SEIFERT, ELIZABETH--[8][9][21][22][26]ROM--
"ARMY DOCTOR"
"BRIGHT SCAPEL" & MORE

GASS, SHERLOCK BRONSON
DUPREE, MORRISON--[3]MYS--
DBLDY "A TAP ON THE SHOULDER" '29

GAST, EMIL
PARATUS, VICTOR--[39]GERMAN

GASTOLDI, ERNESTO
BERRY, JULIAN--[1][2]

GASTON, HENRY A.
A SPIRIT YET IN THE FLESH--[2]

GASTON, WILLIAM JAMES
BANNATYNE, JACK--[1]
GASTON, BILL--[8][32][40]MYS--
LM "MAN WHO DIED TWICE" SEPT '63
"DEEP GREEN DEATH" '63
"DRIFTING DEATH" '64
"DEATH CRAG" '65

GAT, DIMITRI [V]
CAMBRAY, C.K.--CRPG/DDLY PLEAS.#3,[34]MYS--
"WHERE IS CRYSTAL MARTIN?" '88
"PERSONAL" '90

GATCHELL, CHARLES
KING, THOROLD--[3]MYS--
McCLURG "HASHISH" 1886

GATE, A.G.
CLEO ET ANTHONY--[8]

GATER, DILYS
EDWARDS, OLWEN--[1][31]
EDWARDS, OWEN--[33]
HOLLAND, LYS--[1][31][33]
OWEN, DILYS--[1][33]
SINCLAIR, CLOVER--[1][33][34]MYS--
HALE "LALLIE" '83
WRIGHT, KATRINA--[1][33]
YOUNG, VIVIEN--[1][33]

GATES, DAVID EDGERLEY
NACNAB, JOHN--LACHMAN LST '93-
EDITOR OF AHMM '93

GATES, HELEN
GRANVILLE-BARKER, HELEN--[1]

GATTI, ARTHUR GERARD
GERARD, ANDREW--[31]
KATZ, BASHO--[31]
LANE, CHARLES--[31]

GAUGER, RICHARD C.
GAUGER, RICK--[7][23]SF--
OMNI "THE VACUUM-PACKED PICNIC" '79

GAULDEN, RAY
RAY, WESLEY--[1][22][28]WEST--
NAL "DAMARON'S GUN" '58
PAPLB "LONG DAY IN LATIGO" '65

GAULT, WILLIAM CAMPBELL
DAVIS, NORBERT--L. ROBBINS LTR MAR '94--
GHOSTED ?
DUKE, WILL--R. WILDER-PP 21, P45,
[1][3][31]MYS--
GRAPHIC 142 "FAIR PREY" '56
FOREST, DIAL--[18][29][31]MYS--
SAGA MAG "MURDEROUS PARLAY" FEB '61
GAULT, BILL--[1], WARREN GUIDE
GAULT, W.--[29]MYS--
NYCK 321 "THE BLOODY BOKHARA" '51
SCOTT, RONEY--G. LOVISI-PP9,[3][18]MYS--
DM "DEATH HAS YELLOW EYES" SEPT '42
DT "HOT ROD HOMOCIDE" JUNE '50
ACE D17 "SHAKEDOWN" '53
STERNIG, LARRY--L. ROBBINS LTR '94,[32]MYS--
SW "DAY OF THE OGRE" JUN '46
MSMM "TIME OUT FOR MURDER" OCT '80

GAUNT, ARTHUR NETTLETON
NETTLETON, ARTHUR--[1][3]MYS--
FD "SINISTER SECRET" '37

GAUTHIER-VILLARS, HENRY
WILLY--[22]FRENCH

GAUTIER, JUDITH
WALTER, JUDITH--OXFORD COMPANION
TO FRENCH LIT. 1961

GAUTIER-SMITH, PETER C.
CONWAY, PETER--[3]MYS--
FABER "A DARK SIDE ALSO" '40
FABER "UNWANTED CHILD" '41 & MORE

GAVER, REBECCA
GAVER, BECKY--[31][33]

GAVIN, WILLIAM S.
GAVIN, BILL--[31]

GAVRILESCU, ALEXANDRINA
CAZIMIR, OTTILIA--[22]RUMANIAN

GAYLE, HAROLD
GAYLE, HENRY K.--[2]

GAYLORD, OTIS HEMMINGWAY
DAWSON, PETER--V. BERCH CALL '94--
GHOSTED - LAST 8 NVLS FOR JONATHAN GLIDDEN
OTIS, G.H.--V. BERCH CALL '94--
LION L131 "BOURBON ST." '53
LION L171 "HOT CARGO" '53

GAYLORD, WILLIAM GILBERT
GAYLORD, BILLY--[31]

GAYRE, GEORGE ROBERT
GAYRE OF GAYRE, R.--[31]--
"ETHNOLOGICAL ELEMENTS OF AFRICA" '66
GAYRE OF GAYRE, ROBERT--[31]--
"HERALDIC STANDARDS & OTHER ENSIGNS" '59

GAZDAG, ERZSEBET
GAZDAG, ERZSI--[1]

GAZDAK, D.H.
BERNADETTE, ANN--W/KAREN RAY,[9][21][26]ROM--
"ECHOES OF THE HEART"

GAZDANOV, GAITO
GAZDANOV, GEORGII--[31]

GAZE, RICHARD
GALE, JOHN --[3][31]MYS--
LONG "SPARE TIME FOR MURDER" '60
LONG "SHORT REACTION" '61
LONG "DEATH BY CHALK FACE" '62

GAZLEY, ALLEN W.
BROADLUCK, CEPHAS--[1]

GBRENVIL, WILLIAM
MARTYN, WYNDHAM--[29]MYS

GEACH, CHRISTINE
DAWSON, ELIZABETH--[1][31]
LOWING, ANNE--[3][8][9][21][26][31]MYS/ROM--
HALE "BLACK MIDNIGHT" '68 & 8 MORE
NEIL, FRANCES--[8]
WILSON, CHRISTINE--[8][9][21]ROM--
"BROKEN VOWS"
"DOUBTING HEART"

GEAR, KATHLEEN [M] O'NEAL
O'NEAL, KATHLEEN M.--[7][23][26]ROM/SF--
'POWERS OF LIGHT' TRILOGY '90-1 & OTHERS

GEARON, JOHN
FLAGG, JOHN --V. BERCH--
GM PSEUDS, PP 33,[1][31][34]MYS--
GM 103 "PERSIAN CAT" '50
GM 151 "DEATH & THE NAKED LADY" '51
GM 197 "LADY & THE CHEETAH" '51
GM 282 "WOMAN OF CAIRO" '53
GM 391 "DEAR, DEADLY BELOVED" '54
GM 628 "MURDER IN MONACO" '57
GM 787 "DEATH'S LOVELY MASK" '58
GM 1135 "PARADISE GUN" '61

GEASLAND, JOHN BUCHANAN
GEASLAND, JACK--[7][31]SF--
"TWINS: A NOVEL" '77,
RPRT BY SPHERE AS "DEAD RINGERS" '88

GEBAUER, WALTER LUDOLF
DELFT, WALTER--[39]GERMAN/MYS/ADV

GEBAUER, WILLIAM
LEMOTT, JUSTIN G.T. III--W/RAYMOND MCGOWAN,[1]

GEBERT, LI
SCHIRMANN, LI--[39]GERMAN/JUV

GEBHARDT, FRIEDRICH JOHAN
OKER, EUGEN--[39]GERMAN
WISE, ROBERT A.--[2][7][23]SF--
BDG "12 TO THE MOON" '61

GECK, HEINZ
HART, H.W.--[39][40]GERMAN/MYS--
"GEISTER MORDEN NICHT" '72

GEDDES, CAROLA
FORS-WILLNER, LENA--[29]MYS--
LADY THRILLER 23 "DE TYSTA STEGEN" '81

GEE, D. EVELYN H.
LEIGH, MICAH--W/EMMA MERRITT,[9][21]ROM--
"TEXAS DREAMS"

GEE, D. EVELYN H. [CONT]
O'BANYON, CONSTANCE--[9][21][26]ROM--
"DAKOTA DREAMS"
"LAVENDER LIES" & MORE

GEE, HERBERT LESLIE
GAY, FRANCIS--[31][33]
GAY, FRANK--[32]MYS--
MH "EXPLOSIVE TRIANGLE" JAN '65
MH "THE SEDUCTION" MAY '65
MH "FRATERNITY" DEC '65
MH "PAST PERFECT" JAN-FEB '66
MH "SCANDAL ANYONE?" APR-MAY '66
GEE, H.L.--[33]

GEEN, CLIFFORD
BERKLEY, TOM--[1]

GEHMAN, BETSY HOLLAND
KLAINIKITE, ANNE--[1][22][31]AMERICAN

GEHMAN, RICHARD
CHRISTIAN, FREDERICK--[1][22][31]AMERICAN

GEHMAN, RICHARD BOYD
SCOTT, MARTIN--[2][11][22]AMERICAN

GEHMAN, RICHARD BOYD
UFFELMAN, F.C.--[1]

GEHRMANN, HORST
CAMERON, JOHN--[39]GERMAN/MYS/SF,HP
COTTON, JERRY--[39]GERMAN/MYS/SF,HP
EWERS, H.G.--[39]GERMAN/MYS/SF
PORTER, KEN--[39]GERMAN/MYS/SF

GEIER, CHESTER S.
ARCHETTE, GUY--[2][11][23]SF--
FA "FOREVER IS TOO LONG" '47
AMZ "OUTLAW IN THE SKY" '53
ARNETTE, ROBERT--[11] ?? UNCONFIRMED ??
BLADE, ALEXANDER--[1][2][23]SF,HP
COSTELLO, P.F.--[1][2][23]SF,HP
KASTEL, WARREN--[1][2][11][23]SF,HP
TENNESHAW, S.M.--[1][2][11][23]SF,HP
VANCE, GERALD--[1][2][11][23]SF,HP
WORTH, PETER--[1][2][11][23]SF,HP

GEIGER, ERICH
MICHELL, JAN--[39]GERMAN

GEIPEL, EILEEN
DEACON, EILEEN--[1][31][33]

GEIS, BERNARD & DARLENE S
STEVENS, PETER--[8][33]

GEIS, DARLENE STERN
KELLY, RALPH--[8][31][33]
LONDON, JANE--[8][33]

GEIS, GILBERT L.
LAWRENCE, GIL--[1][3]MYS--
PYR G311 "FURY WITH LEGS" '58
PYR G468 "WOMAN RACKET" '59

GEIS, RICHARD E.
COLSON, FREDERICK--[1][31]
ELLIOTT, RICHARD--W/ELTON T. ELLIOTT,
[3][7][23][34]MYS/SF--
GM "SWORD OF ALLAH" '84
GM "EINSTEIN LEGACY" '86
GM "MASTER FILE" '87
GUY, RANDY--G. COOK LTR '93-FROM "GEIS"
JACKSON, ALBINA--V. BERCH-BRNDN/
BC PSEUDS, BA [CONTE 22, P24,[1][31]

GEIS, RICHARD E. [CONT]
KUNZUR, SHEELA--V. BERCH-BRNDN/
BC PSEUDS, BAE 22, P24,[1][31]
OWEN, BOB--G. COOK LTR '93--
ON COVER OF "THE SOLDIER" -
"ROBERT N." ON TITLE PAGE
OWEN, R.N.--BLK ACE CAT#40--
BRDN 1013 "SAILOR ON THE TOWN"
BRDN 1031 "DAME IN HIS CORNER"
BRDN 1038 "CARNAL TRAP"
OWEN, ROBERT N.--V. BERCH-BRNDN/
BC PSEUDS, BAE 22, P24,[1][2]
RADWAY, ANN--V. BERCH-BRNDN/
BC PSEUDS, BAE 22, P24,[1]
SWAN, PEGGY--G. COOK LTR '93-FROM
GEIS/V. BERCH-BAE 22--
PLTM 667 "CAMPUS LUST" '64
SWENSON, PEGGY--[2][11][23]SF/ADULT--
MIDWD F110 "THE UNLOVED" '61 & MORE
TEREGO, A.L.--G. COOK LTR '93-FROM "GEIS"

GEISA, WERNER K.
TRENTON, OLSH--W/MANFRED WEINLAND,
[39]GERMAN/SF/WEST,HP
USHER, H.P.--[39]GERMAN/SF/WEST,HP

GEISEL, HELEN
PALMER, HELEN [MARION]--[1][32][33]MYS--
SB "SUICIDE PACT" MAR '56

GEISEL, THEODOR SEUSS
DR. SEUSS--[2][11][22][31][33]AMERICAN
STONE, ROSETTA--W/MICHAEL K. FRITH,[1][33]
LE SIEG, THEO--[11][22][31][33]AMERICAN

GEISER, ROBERT L.
PETERS, STEPHEN--[3][29]MYS--
DBLDY "THE PARK IS MINE" '81

GEISLER, HANS
HANSEN, STEPHAN--[39]GERMAN/MYS/WEST
JIRA, JOHANN--[39]GERMAN/MYS/WEST
ROBERTSON, JAMES--[39]GERMAN/MYS/WEST
STEPHANI, MARION--[39]GERMAN/MYS/WEST
TOURNET, JEAN JACQUES--[39]GERMAN/MYS/WEST
TREY, STEPHAN--[39]GERMAN/MYS/WEST

GEISSLER, MARGARETE
MARGRET, ANN--[39]GERMAN/JUV

GEIST, RUDOLF
NOBODY, NICK N.--[39]GERMAN

GELB, NORMAN
MALLERY, AMOS--[8]

GELFMAN, JUDITH S.
STARR, JUDY--[1]

GELHAR, AUDREY P.A.
ELLIS, AUDREY--[1]

GELINAS, ROBERT E.
EDWARDS, ROBIN--HAWK/GELINAS INTRVW '93--
PINN "PLAYERS" '93
HALL, PARIS--HAWK/GELINAS INTRVW '93--
POCK "ANTICIPATION" '93

GELINET, CLAUDE
GILTENE, JEAN--[34]MYS--
MULLER "THE CANDID KILLER" '55

GELLER, MARY LEE
WINGS, MARY--W/ERIC GARBER, V. BERCH
LTR TO HUBIN '94/MYS--
WP "SHE CAME TOO LATE" '86

GELLER, MARY LEE [CONT]
WINGS, MARY [CONT]
WP "SHE CAME IN A FLASH" '88

GELLES-COLE, SANDI
GELLES, SANDI--[31]
RAINE, NICOLE--[9][31]ROM

GELLIS, ROBERTA L.J.
DANIELS, MAX--[2][7][23][31]SF--
AVON "PASSPORT TO TERROR" '60
AVON "SPACE GUARDIAN" '78
AVON "OFF WORLD" '79
HAMILTON, PRISCILLA--[9][17][21][26]ROM--
"THE LOVE TOKEN"
JACOBS, LEAH--[8][9][17][23][31]ROM/SF--

GELMAN, RITA GOLDEN
AUSTIN, R.G.--W/NANCY L. AUSTIN,
[1][7][31][33]SF

GELMAN, WOODROW
GELMAN, WOODY--[31]

GENAZINO, URSULA
VALENTIN, URSULA--[39]GERMAN/JUV

GENBERG, KJELL E.
EARLIN, SHELL--[29]MYS--
"FASORNAS O" '77
HOGAN, BEN--[29]MYS/ROM--
"KONSPIRATORENA" '79
LAGEVI, BO--[29]MYS,HP--
BS-1 "OM SANNINGEN SKA FRAM" '76
BS-4 "FORLOREN TAR ALLT" '76
BS-17 "GYLLENE TRIANGELN" '78

GENOVESE, VINCE
THISBY--W/DONNA M. TURNER,[1]

GENSER, CYNTHIA
COMIDAS, CHINAS--[31]

GENTLEMAN, FRANCIS
LUNATIC, SIR HUMPHREY--[2]

GENTRY, BYRON B.
GALWAY, NORMAN--[22]AMERICAN

GENTZ-WERNER, PETRA
WERNER, PETRA--[39]GERMAN

GEORGE, CHARLES
PRICE, LELAND--[3]MYS--
5 PLAYS '42-7
ROWLAND, HENRY--[3]MYS--
PLAY "HEARTS & FLOWERS" '37
STERLING, DOROTHY--[3]MYS--
1 PLAY '41

GEORGE, MARY
THORNTON, ELIZABETH--[9][21][26]ROM--
"FALLEN ANGEL"
"TENDER THE STORM" & MORE

GEORGE, MARY CAROLINE H.J
JUTSON, MARY CAROLINE H.--[1][31]

GEORGE, OLGA
BOEHEIM, OLLY--[39]GERMAN

GEORGE, PETER [BRYAN]
BRYANT, PETER--[2][3][11][23]MYS/SF--
BRDMN "TWO HOURS TO DOOM" '58

GEORGE, PETER [BRYAN] [CONT]
PETERS, BRYAN--[2][3][22][29]MYS--
DIGIT "STARBUCK" '57
BRDMN "HONG KONG KILL" '58
DIGIT "SONS OF NIPPON" '61
BRDMN "THE BIG H" '61

GEORGE, ROBERT ESMONDE G.
SENACOURT, ROBERT--[8][22]NEW ZEALAND-ENGLISH

GEORGE, SIDNEY CHARLES
GEORGE, S.C.--[1]

GEORGE, STEFAN [ANTON]
DELORME, EDMUND--[1]

GEORGE, VISCOUNT WEYMOUTH
THYNN, ALEXANDER--[7]SF--
"THE KING IS DEAD" '77

GEORGE, WILLIAM FRANCIS
GEORGE, BILL--[7]SF, NON-FICT--
"EROTICSM IN THE FANTASY CINEMA" '84

GEORGES, HENRI
ARNAUD, GEORGES--[40]MYS--
"LE SALAIRE DE PEUR" '52

GEORGIEWITZ-WEITZER, DEM.
SURYA, G.W.--[39]GERMAN

GERAHTY, DIGBY GEORGE
STANDISH, ROBERT--[2][11][29][32][34]MYS--
"THE SMALL GENERAL" '45
"ELEPHANT WALK" '48
RPRTD AS "LORD & MASTER"
"FOLLOW THE SEVENTH MAN" '50
LM "AT THE VILLA JANINE" MAR '55
LM "TEST-TUBE TERROR" MAR '59
LM "VERDICT POSTPONED" APR '59
SUS "DECOY DUCK" FEB '60
LM "GOYAS GALORE" MAR '62
"THREE BAMBOOS"
"THE WINDOW HACK" '66
"A WORTHY MAN"
RPRTD AS "STORM CENTRE"
"BONIN"
"GULF OF TIME"
"GREEN FIRE" '76
"MR. ON LONG"
"SINGAPORE KATE"
LM "BUSINESS IS BUSINESS" DEC '76

GERAINT, VICTOR V.R.
CLINTON-BADDELEY, VICTOR--[29]MYS

GERARD, EDWIN FIELD
GERARDY--[13]AUSTRALIAN
TROOPER GERARDY--[8][13]AUSTRALIAN

GERARD, FRANCES
ANNALIST--[1]
WALLACE, EDGAR--[2]GHOSTED--
AFTER WALLACE'S DEATH

GERARD, JAMES WATSON
PELICAN, A.--[1]
SHELLEY, A. FISH--[1]
SOMBRE, SAMUEL--[1]

GERARD, JEAN IGNACE I.
GRANDVILLE, J.J.--[31][33]
GRANDVILLE, JEAN IGNACE I--[31][33]

GERARD, JOHN
CHERUB--[1]

GERARD-LIBOIS, JULES C.
HEINZ, G.--[31]

GERAUD, ANDRE
PERTINAX--W/CHARLES GERAULT,[22]FRENCH

GERAULT, CHARLES
PERTINAX--W/ANDRE GERAUD,[22]FRENCH

GERBER, BARBARA [LIN]
GERBER, BOBBIE--[1][31]

GERBER-HESS, MAJA
HESS, MAJA--[39]GERMAN/JUV

GERBI, ANTONELLO
FERRANTE, DON--[31]

GERGICH, MILLIE GREY
GREY, MILLIE--[9][21][26]ROM--
"SUSPICION"
"WILD BLUE YONDER"

GERHARDIE, WILLIAM ALEX.
GERHARDI, WILLIAM ALEX.--[31]

GERICKE, GABRIELE
HERZOG, GABRIELE--[39]GERMAN

GERLE, WOLFGANG ADOLF
SPAT, KONRAD--[39]GERMAN

GERMAN, ARNOLD
BRETONNE, ANNE-MARIE--[3]MYS--
POPLB "A GALLOW STANDS IN SALEM" '75
POPLB "DARK TALISMAN"'75
BERK "THE CRY OF NEPTUNE" '77

GERMANA, ALFHILD
KNUTSEN, LALLI & FRIDTJOF--[29]MYS

GERMANO, PETER B
BERTIN, JACK--[2][23][28]GHOSTED--
"INTERPLANETARY ADVENTURERS" '70
"PYRAMIDS FROM SPACE" '70
COLE, JACKSON--A. TONIK-COLE CKLST
'SPICY ARMADILLO',[31]WEST,HP--
16 COLE NOVELS '52-8
CORD, BARRY--[2][11][28][31]WEST--
38 NOVELS '48-79
HALLIDAY, BRETT--T. JOHNSON-
ECHOES #17/#23MYS,HP--
MSMM - AT LEAST ONE STORY
KANE, JAMES--[1][28][31]WEST--
9 NOVELS '60-71
SLADE, JACK--[1]WEST, HP

GERMANY, VERA JOSEPHINE
GERMANY, JO--[31]
KING, JOSIE--[9][21][26][31]ROM--
"DANCE AT YOUR WEDDING"

GERNSBACK, HUGO
BANSHUCK, GREGO--[1][2][11]
FIPS, SOCRATES--[1][11]
GASHBUCK, GRENO--[1][2][11]
HABERGOCK, GUS N.--[1][2][11]
MUNCHAUSEN, BARON--[1][11]
ULYSSES, MOHAMMED--[2][11]

GEROSA, GUIDO
GUADO, SERGIO--[31]

GERRARD, JANE
CHEKENIAN, JANE--[31]

GERRARD, JOHN
GERRARD, A.J.--[31]

GERRETSON, FREDERIK CAREL
GOSSAERT, GEETEN--[22]DUTCH

GERRITSEN, TERRY
GERRITSEN, TESS--[9][10][21]ROM--
"ADVENTURE'S MISTRESS"
"UNDER THE KNIFE" & MORE

GERRITY, DAVID JAMES
GARRITY--[3][29][31]MYS--
GM 948 "KISS OFF THE DEAD" '60
GM 1170 "CRY ME A KILLER" '61
SIGN "DRAGON HUNT" '67
SIGN "THE HOT MODS" '69
GARRITY, CALLI GORAN--[8]
GARRITY, DAVE--[31]
GORAN, CALLI--[1][22]
HARDIN, MITCH--[1][22]

GERSHATOR, DAVID
ALCHEMY, JACK--[1][31]

GERSHON, KAREN
TRIPP, KAREN--[8]

GERSHWIN, IRA
FRANCIS, ARTHUR--[31]

GERSON, NOEL B.
BURGESS, ANNE MARIE--[1][31][33]
BURGESS, MICHAEL--[1][31][33]
EDWARDS, SAMUEL--[3][9][21]
[26][29][31]MYS/ROM--
PRAEGER "CAVES OF GUERNICA" '75
& 17 MORE
GORHAM, NICHOLAS--[1]
LEWIS, PAUL--[8][9][21][26][31][33]ROM--
'HALL OF FAME' SERIES: "THE GENTLE FURY"
PHILLIPS, LEON--[3][29][33]MYS--
DBLDY "SPLIT BAMBOO" '66
HALE "FIRE IN HIS HAND" '79
HALE "PHOENIX REACTION" '80
PORTER, DONALD CLAYTON--[33]
ROSS, DANA F[ULLER]--[9][21][33]HIST--
"YANKEE"
'WAGONS WEST' SERIES & MORE
VAIL, PHILIP--[1][8][9]
VAUGHN, CARTER A.--[8][9][21][26][33]HIST/ROM--
"BRANDED BRIDE"
"FORTRESS FURY" & MORE

GERSONI, DIANE
GERSONI-STAVN, DIANE--[31]

GERSTINE, JOHN
GERSTINE, JACK--[31]

GERSTMAYER, ALFRED
WELLER, FREDY--[39]GERMAN/HP

GERSTMAYER, HERMANN
DOYAN, RALPH--[39]GERMAN/ADV/JUV
HARALD, LEO--[39]GERMAN/ADV/JUV
LIENHART, HERMANN--[39]GERMAN/ADV/JUV

GERSTNER, NICKOLAE
NICKOLAE, BARBARA--W/BARBARA PRONIN,
HAWK/GERSTNER INTRVW--
BERK "FINDERS KEEPERS" '89-91
BERK "TIES THAT BIND" '92
BERK "KISS MOMMY GOOD NIGHT" '94

GERVAIS, CHARLES HENRY
GERVAIS, C.H.--[1]
GERVAIS, MARTY--[1][31]

GERVASI, EUGENE MICHAEL
GERVASI, TOM--[31]

GESKE, MATTHIAS
TEGERN, THOMAS--[39]GERMAN/JUV

GESNER, CLARK
GORDON, JOHN--[31][33]

GESSNER, MERLYN C.
CLARK, MERLE--[1][31][33]
GESSNER, LYNNE--[1][31][33]

GETCHELL, FLORENCE B.
HALLOWELL, FLORENCE B.--[1]

GETTINGS, FRED
DAWE, FREDERICK--[31]

GETTLER, NINA
BEAUMONT, NINA--[26]ROM--
"SAPPHIRE MAGIC"
"PROMISES TO KEEP"

GETZIN, AMBER DEAN
DEAN, AMBER--[1]

GEYER, HANS-JOACHIM
TROLL, HENRY--[39]GERMAN/MYS

GEZI, KALIL ISMAIL
GEZI, KAL--[31]

GHERI, LEOPOLD
FERRERIUS, BRUDER VINZENZ--[39]GERMAN

GHNASSIA, MAURICE [J-H]
DE LUBANO, M.--[1]
MALPOTT, VIRGULE--[1][31]
MORRISS, J.H.--[1]
PICOU, ALPHONSE--[1]

GHOLSTON, HOMER N.
GHOLSTON, J.N.--[7]SF--
MANOR "THE KOIEC COROLLARY" '79

GHOSE, AMAL
ESOHG, LAMA--[31]

GIBBONS, EUELL
WILD HICKORY NUT--[1]

GIBBONS, H.H. CLIFFORD
CHESTER, GILBERT--[3][29]MYS--
69 SEXTON BLAKE NOVELS '30-68
KEMPSTER, BERT--[1]

GIBBONS, HARRY
MERRELL, BARBARA--V. BERCH LTR TO
HUBIN '94/MYS--
ZEBRA "SIGN OF DEATH" '81

GIBBONS, HARRY SCOTT
GIBBONS, HARRY S.--[21]ROM--
"THE TALL WOMAN"

GIBBONS, J. WHITFIELD
GIBBONS, WHIT--[31]

GIBBONS, ROBERT
GIBBONS, BOB--[31]--
WILDLIFE ARTICLES/BOOKS

GIBBONS, WILLIAM
CROSS, DENNIS--[2]
GIBBONS, HELEN--[1]
RICHARDS, FRANK--[1]HP--

GIBBS, CECILIA MAY
KELLY, C.M.O.--[31]

GIBBS, JAMES ATWOOD
GIBBS, JIM--[31]

GIBBS, NORAH
BOYD, PRUDENCE--[9]ROM
GARLAND, LISETTE--[9]ROM
IRELAND, NOELLE--[9]ROM
MERRILL, LYNNE--[9]ROM
RITCHIE, CLAIRE--[9]ROM
ROMAINE, DALLAS--[3][9][21][26]MYS/ROM--
BERK "MALICIOUS MADONNA" '75
BERK "SHADOW OF EVIL" '76
SHAYNE, NINA--[9]ROM
WAYNE, HEATHER--[9]ROM
WITTINGHAM, SARA--[9]ROM

GIBBS, RAPHAEL SANFORD
GIBBS, RAFE--[31]

GIBBS, WOOLCOTT JR.
GIBBS, TONY--[31][33][34]MYS--
RANDOM "DEAD RUN" '88
RANDOM "RUNNING FIX" '90

GIBBS, [CECILIA] MAY
KELLY, C.M.O.--[1]

GIBBS-SMITH, CHARLES H.
HAVARD, CHARLES--[1][22][31]ENGLISH

GIBBS-WILSON, KATHRYN B.
HAYES, WILSON--[31]

GIBERGA, OVIDIO
DR. COGGS--[1][2]

GIBERSON, DOROTHY D.
FIELD, PENELOPE--[3][9][21][26][31]MYS/ROM--
LITTLE "SOMEONE IS WATCHING" '77

GIBESON, JACQUELINE LA T.
GRANT, SABINA--[9][21][26]ROM--
"WALK IN BEAUTY"
LA TOURETTE, JACQUELINE--[7][9][11][21]ROM/SF-
"AN ANCIENT RAGE"
"POMPEII SPLENDOR" & MORE

GIBRAN, KAHLIL
JUBRAN, KHALIL JUBRAN--[22]SYRIAN-AMERICAN

GIBSON, ALFRED
ROVER--[1]

GIBSON, AMANDA M.T.
MATHIESON, UNA COOPER--[1]

GIBSON, CHARLES HAMMOND
SUDBURY, RICHARD--[1]

GIBSON, G.H.
IRONBARK--[8][13]AUSTRALIAN

GIBSON, JOE
BRIDGER, JOHN--[1][2][11]
FURTH, CARLTON--[1][2][11]
GIBSON, JOHN--[1][2]

GIBSON, LAVINIA
HOLT, ELISABETH--[39]GERMAN

GIBSON, MARALEE G.
DAVIS, MARALEE G.--[31]

GIBSON, MARY FRANCES
WINNIFRED--[1]

GIBSON, MARY W. STANLEY
STANLEY, FRANK--[1]
WOODFERN, WINNIE--[1]

GIBSON, OWEN
FLYNN, PETER--[35]AUSTRALIAN--
'FLYNN' ON COVER

GIBSON, WALTER B.
ABBINGTON, JOHN--[1]
ABBOTT, ANDREW--[24]
ABBOTT, EARL J.--[24]
ADAMS, ANDY--[1][18][31]CHILDREN'S--
"BIFF BREWSTER" & 4 MORE
ASTRO--[2]
ATKINS, DAVID--[24]
BARNUM, BILL--[24]
BLACK, ISHI--[1][18][29]MYS--
BLACKSTONE, HARRY--[24]GHOSTED--
OR COLLABORATED WITH REAL "BLACKSTONE"
BLUM, JACK I.--[24]GHOSTED--
OR COLLABORATED WITH REAL "BLUM"
BRANNON, MAJOR ROBERT--[24]GHOSTED--
OR COLLABORATED WITH REAL "BRANNON"
BROWN, DOUGLAS--[11][29][31]
BYRNES, GENE W.--[24]
CHALK, WESLEY--[24]GHOSTED--
OR COLLABORATED WITH REAL "CHALK"
CHARLOT, HARRY--[1]GHOSTED--
OR COLLABORATED WITH REAL 'CHARLOT'
CRANDALL, BRUCE--[24]
CREIGHTON, RUSS T.--[24]
CROWE, C.B.--[1][24][31]
DARRINGTON, PETER--[24]
DONOGHUE, MARTIN--[24]
DONOHUE, MARTIN--[1][24][31]--
SPELLING VAR. OF 'DONOHUE'
DUNNINGER, JOSEPH--W. MURRAY-
ECHOES#23,[24]GHOSTED--
OR COLLABORATED WITH REAL "DUNNINGER"
ELLERT, JOHN--[24]GHOSTED--
OR COLLABORATED WITH REAL "ELLERT"
FABER, MORTON--[24]
FAIRFAX, FELIX--[1][31]
FIEDENBERG, HARRY--[24]GHOSTED--
OR COLLABORATED WITH REAL "FRIEDENBERG"
GASTON, WILBUR--[1][31]
GIRARDIN, RAY--[24]GHOSTED--
OR COLLABORATED WITH REAL "GIRARDIN"
GLASS, WALTER--[24]
GOODWIN, GEORGE--[24]GHOSTED--
OR COLLABORATED WITH REAL "GOODWIN"
GRANT, MAXWELL--[1][2][7]HP--
MYS PRESS "NORGIL #1 & 2"
PYRAMID/JOVE "SHADOW SERIES:#4 THRU #23"
"CRIME ORACLE"
"TEETH OF DRAGON"
GRIFFIN, EDWARD--[24]GHOSTED--
OR COLLABORATED WITH REAL "GRIFFIN"
GROVER, MADELEINE--[24]GHOSTED--
OR COLLABORATED WITH REAL "GROVER"
HAGEN, C.J.--[24]GHOSTED--
OR COLLABORATED WITH REAL "HAGEN"
HARAH, PONJAY--[24]
HERSHFIELD, HARRY--W/HARRY HERSHFIELD,
[18][24]GHOSTED--
BART "SINS OF ROGER DIDDLEBOCK" '47

GIBSON, WALTER B. [CONT]
HOUDINI, HARRY--[2][11]GHOSTED
HOUSEMAN, JULIAN--[24]GHOSTED--
OR COLLABORATED WITH REAL "HOUSEMAN"
HOY, DAVID--[24]GHOSTED--
OR COLLABORATED WITH REAL "HOY"
HUANG, FENG--[24]
JENSEN, O.H.--[24]GHOSTED--
OR COLLABORATED WITH REAL "JENSEN"
JOHNSON, CARTER--[24]
KALBFLEISCH, E.C.--[24]GHOSTED--
OR COLLABORATED WITH REAL "KALBFLEISCH"
KAY, GILBERT--[24]
KINEJI, MABORUSHI--[1][18][29][31]
KRESGE, GEORGE "KRESKIN"--[24]GHOSTED--
OR COLLABORATED WITH REAL "KRESGE"
LACKSEY, G.A.--[24]
LEBRUN, GAUTIER--[1][31]
MASTERS, ROY--[24]--
THERE IS ALSO A REAL "ROY MASTERS"
MAURICE, ALFRED--[2]
MAYER, HERBERT--[24]GHOSTED--
OR COLLABORATED WITH REAL "MAYER"
MCCLARY, THOMAS [CALVERT]--[24][32]MYS--
27 DIGEST STORIES [MS, MU & SA]
MCDERMOT, LT. THOMAS--[24]
MICHAELS, NEIL--[24]
MONROE, DON--[24]
MULLEN, RICHARD--[24]
NADLER, THEODORE [TEDDY]--[24]GHOSTED--
OR COLLABORATED WITH REAL "NADLER"
NEALE, ARTHUR--[2]
NICHOLS, JESS--[24]
PALMER, WARREN--[24]
PERRY, BERNARD--[2]
PERRY, RUFUS--[1]
PETERS, JACK C.--[24]
PROSKAUER, JULIAN J.--[24]GHOSTED--
OR COLLABORATED WITH REAL "PROSKAUER"
RADNER, SIDNEY H.--[24]GHOSTED--
OR COLLABORATED WITH REAL "RADNER"
RAYMOND, P.L.--[1][24]GHOSTED--
OR COLLABORATED W/REAL P.L. RAYMOND
RODNEY, HENRY [HANK]--[24]GHOSTED--
OR COLLABORATED WITH REAL "RODNEY"
RUSSELL, CHARLES--[24]GHOSTED--
OR COLLABORATED WITH REAL "RUSSELL"
SEIDMAN, SY--[24]
SEWARD, PROF. ALFRED FRAN--[24]
SMITH, ROBERT RUSSELL--[24]
SULLIVAN, EDWARD S.--[24]
THE AUTHOR OF CHERRY AMES--[24]
THURSTON, HOWARD--[2][11]GHOSTED
TOMAN, ALFRED--[24]
WELDON, WALLACE--[24]GHOSTED--
OR COLLABORATED WITH REAL
"WELDON THE WIZARD"
WELLS, HELEN--[24]GHOSTED--
OR COLLABORATED WITH REAL "WELLS"
WILSON, MARK--[24]GHOSTED--
OR COLLABORATED WITH REAL "WILSON"
WINSOR, THOMAS--[24]GHOSTED--
OR COLLABORATED WITH REAL "WINDSOR"
WOODSMAN, DAVID--[24]
YOUNG, CHESLEY V.--[24]GHOSTED--
OR COLLABORATED WITH REAL "YOUNG"
YUU, HEE FOO--[24]

GIBSON, WILLIAM
MASS, WILLIAM--[1][31]--
PLAY "THE RUBY" '55

GIBSON, WILLIAM [FORD]
MINK MOLE--W/DR. ADDER [K.W. JETER],[7]SF--
"ALLIGATOR ALLEY" '89

GIBSON-JARVIE, CLODAGH
CHAPMAN, CLODAGH--[7]SF--
"NIGHT BEFORE DARK" '88
"ECHOES ANSWER" '89
GAVIN, AMANDA--[1][31]

GICHERMANN, MORDECHAI
GICHON, MORDECHAI--[1]

GIDAL, TIM NACHUM
GIDALEWITSCH, NACHUM--[31]

GIDALEWITSCH, IGNAZ
GIDAL, NACHUM--[1]
GIDAL, TIM N.--[1]
GIDALEWITSCH, NACHUM--[1]

GIDDINGS, ARTHUR F.
BAKER, ARTHUR--[3]MYS--
DUELL "THE SHORT TERM" '48

GIDDINGS, JOHN
NASH, THURLOE--[34]MYS

GIDDY, ERIC CAWOOD G.
KNIGHT, KOBOLD--[34]MYS--
HUTCH "PETER CALLED SIMON
& OTHER STORIES" '38
KNIGHT, W. KOBOLD--[1][2][11]SF--
CASSELL "DOCTOR OF SOULS" '27

GIDEON, NANCY
GIDDINGS, LAUREN--[9][21][26]ROM--
"BARTERED BRIDE"
"SWEET TEMPEST"
RANSOM, DANA--[9][21][26]ROM--
"CHARADE OF LOVE"
"PIRATE'S CAPTIVE" & MORE

GIERGIEIEWICZ, MIECZYSLA
BIELSKI, FELIKS--[31]

GIESA, W.K.
LAMONT, ROBERT--W/ANDREAS DECKER,
[39]GERMAN/JUV/SF

GIESA, WERNER K.
CARSTENS, KURT--[39]GERMAN/SF/WEST
CLOUD, TANITH--[39]GERMAN/SF/WEST
COOPER, STEVE--[39]GERMAN/SF/WEST,HP
DAMON, ROGER--[39]GERMAN/SF/WEST,HP
EWIGK, TED--[39]GERMAN/SF/WEST
HASDUR, G.--[39]GERMAN/SF/WEST
HASDUR, MERLYN G.--[39]GERMAN/SF/WEST
HASTUR, G.--[39]GERMAN/SF/WEST
NORMAN, ART--[39]GERMAN/SF/WEST
QUINT, ROBERT--W/EVA EPPERS
& RAINER ZUBEIL,[39]GERMAN/SF
QUINT, ROBERT--[39]GERMAN/SF/WEST
RYKER, MONTY G.--[39]GERMAN/SF/WEST
SARIS, RHET--[39]GERMAN/SF/WEST
SHADOW, MIKE--W/MANFRED WEINLAND,
[39]GERMAN/SF/HOR,HP

GIESEL, MANFRED-GERHARD
SELL, FRED--[39]GERMAN

GIESY, JOHN ULRICH
DUSTIN, CHARLES--[1][31]
GIESY, J.U.--L. ROBBINS LTR MAR '94

GIFFARD, HARDINGE, GOULB.
HALSBURY, EARL--[23]ENGLISH/SF

GIFFORD, FRANCIS NEWTON
FIFFORD, FRANK--[31]

GIFFORD, GRISELDA
MACDONALD, MARY--[1][31][33]

GIFFORD, JAMES NOBLE
BREWSTER, ELIOT--[1]
GORDON, LUTHER--R.C. HOLLAND, BAE 12, P6
HOWARD, WARREN--[1]
NOBLE, EMILY--[8]
SAXON, JOHN--V. BERCH-BAE 21, P20,[1]

GIFFORD, THOMAS [E]
CLARINS, DANA--[34]MYS--
BB "WOMAN IN THE WINDOW" '84
BB "QUALITY PARTIES" '85
BB "WOMAN WHO KNEW TOO MUCH" '86
MAXWELL, THOMAS--LACHMAN LST,[34]MYS--
PR "KISS ME ONCE" '86
MYS PR "SABERDENE VARIATIONS" '87
MYS PR "KISS ME TWICE" '88
MYS PR "THE SUSPENSE IS KILLING ME" '90

GIGER, HANSRUEDI
GIGER, H.R.--[7]SWISS/SF, NON-FICT

GIGGAL, KENNETH
KENNY, STAN--[29]MYS
MARLIN, HENRY--[1]
ROSS, ANGUS--[3][18][29]MYS--
LONG "LEEDS FIASCO" '75
LONG "CONGLETON LARK" '79 & 11 MORE
SAVAGE, IAN--[1]

GILABERT, ANTONIO M. Y.
GAUTISOLO, MIGUEL--[2]

GILBART-SMITH, MARCUS M.T
GILSON, HIBBART--[3]MYS--
GILL "THE UNACCEPTED DEATH" '28

GILBERT, AGNES JOAN [S]
BAER, JILL--[3][21][26][31]MYS/ROM--
PAPLB "HOUSE OF WHISPERS" '71

GILBERT, C.H.
GILBERT, BUTCH--[1]

GILBERT, GEORGE
JORDAN, GILL--[31]

GILBERT, JACK
KUNG, TOR--W/JEAN MCLEAN,[14]ADULT--
OLYM OPH#119 "FOREVER ECSTACY" '68
OLYM TC#214 "MY MOTHER TAUGHT ME" '67

GILBERT, JEAN
WANDERER--[1]

GILBERT, KENNETH
KNAPP, ELLIS G.--L. ROBBINS LTR MAR '94

GILBERT, MARILYN B.
FERSTER, MARILYN B.--[1][31]

GILBERT, ROBERT ANDREW
DUNNING, EDWARD--[31]

GILBERT, RUTH G.A.
AINSWORTH, RUTH--[1][7][22][31]SF

GILBERT, WILLIAM S.
B.--[33]
BAB--[8][31][33]
TOMLINE, F.--[22]ENGLISH
TOMLINE, F. LATOUR--[8][33]ENGLISH

GILBERT, WILLIE
BENSOL, OSCAR--[31]SCRIPTS-ANIMATED CARTOONS
MARETH, GLENVILLE--[31]--
EMBASSY SCRNPLY "SANTA CLAUS
CONQUERS THE MARTIANS" '64

GILBERT, [SISTER] MARY
DEFREES, MADELINE--[22]AMERICAN

GILBERTSON, MILDRED G.
GILBERT, NAN--[9][21][22][31][33]ROM--
"A KNIGHT CAME RIDING"
MENDEL, JO--[1][9]HP--WHITMAN

GILCHRIST, ALAN W.
COWAN, ALAN--[8][31]

GILDEN, BERT & KATYA
GILDEN, K.B.--[1][22][31]AMERICAN

GILDERDALE, MICHAEL
FLEMMING, SARAH--[8]

GILES, CARL H[OWARD]
GALE, WILLIAM C.--[31]--
PEC "THE FIGHT TO LEGALIZE NARCOTICS" '67

GILES, JANET HOLT
GARTH, JOHN--V. BERCH LTR '93--
PYR 112 "HILL MAN" '54

GILES, JOANNA ELDER
MAGILL, MARCUS--W/BRIAN M. HILL,[1][32]MYS--
LM "A NICE WALK BY THE FIELDS" JUN '64

GILES, KENNETH
DRUMMOND, CHARLES--[3][18][29]MYS--
GOLZ "STAB IN THE BACK" '70
GOLZ "A DEATH AT THE BAR" '72
MCGIRR, EDMUND--[2][3][18][29][40]MYS--
GOLZ "HERE LIES MY WIFE" '67
GOLZ "BARDEL'S MURDER" '73

GILES, RAY A.
BARRY, B.X.--[1][2][11]

GILFORD, CHARLES BERNARD
CAMPBELL, DONALD--[22][32]AMERICAN/MYS--
AHMM "WHO SHALL THE VICTIM BE?" JAN '59
FARR, DOUGLAS--[22][31][32]AMERICAN--
12 AHMM STORIES, MAY '58-MAY '61
GILFORD, C.B. --[31][32][34]MYS--
FLGSP "DEAD MAN OUT" '67
DBLDY "CROOKED SHAMROCK" '69
DIGEST STORIES [AHMM, EQMM, GU, MF,
MH, MSMM, SA, SO, SV, TG, TR & TW]
GREGORY, ELIZABETH--[22][31]AMERICAN

GILHOOLEY, JOHN
GILHOOLEY, JACK--[31]

GILKYSON, BERNICE KENYON
KENYON, BERNICE--[31]

GILL, BARTHOLOMEW
MCGARRITY, MARK--MYS SCENE #40, P12/MYS--
RAWSON "A PASSING ADVANTAGE" '80
RAWSON "NEON CAESAR" '89

GILL, T.M.
SABATTIS--[1]

GILL, TRAVISS
ODELL, GILL--W/CAROL ODELL,[1][8][22]

GILLEN, LUCY
STRATTON, REBECCA--[21][26]ROM--44 NOVELS

GILLENWATER, SHARON
HARLOW, SHARON--[26]ROM--
"COUNTRY KISS"

GILLES, DANIEL
JOHNSON, MARIGOLD--[8]

GILLESE, JOHN PATRICK
O'HARA, DALE--[1][8][22]IRISH-CANADIAN
SHARK, GILL--[1][8][22]IRISH-CANADIAN
STARR, JOHN A.--[1][8][22]IRISH-CANADIAN

GILLESPIE, A. LINCOLN JR.
GILLESPIE, LINK--[31]

GILLESPIE, A.C.
MARS, A.--[2]

GILLESPIE, ALFRED
GILL, ALAN--[1][31]

GILLESPIE, IRIS SYLVIA
ANDRESKI, IRIS--[1][31]

GILLESPIE, JOHN BIRKS
GILLESPIE, DIZZY--[31]

GILLET, PHILIPPE CLAUDE
SAINT GIL, PHILIPPE--[1]

GILLETT, HENRY MARTIN
GILLETT, H.M.--[1]

GILLETTE, JAY MICHAEL
GILLETTE, J. MICHAEL--[31]

GILLETTE, PAUL J.
CONWAY, TROY--V. BERCH--
SPY SPOOF, BAE 9, P12,

GILLETTE, VIRGINIA M.
MCLEAN, J. SLOANE--W/JOSEPHINE M. WUNSCH,[1]

GILLHAM, ELIZABETH W.
ENRIGHT, ELIZABETH--[8]

GILLHAM, WILLIAM EDWIN C.
GILLHAM, BILL--[33]

GILLIAM, TERRY [VANCE]
GILLIAN, JERRY--[31]--
PRIMARILY ILLUSTRATION WORKS
PYTHON, MONTY--[31]--CO-WROTE SCREENPLAYS
W/CHAPMAN, CLEESE, IDLE, PALIN & T. JONES

GILLIE, CHRISTOPHER
GENN, CALDER--[1][31]

GILLIES, JOHN RUSSELL
GILL, JOHN--[1][3][40]MYS--
COLLINS "THE TENNANT" '72
LAST HEROES" '72
CAPE "KIKI" '79

GILLILAN, G. HOWARD
PURDY, [CAPT.] JIM--[1]

GILLINGS, WALTER H.
GILES, GEOFFREY--W/FORREST J. ACKERMAN,
[2][11][23]SF--
"LOST PLANET" '46
HUGHES, HERBERT--[2]

GILLINGS, WALTER H. [CONT]
PARKER, VALENTINE--[2]
SHERIDAN, THOMAS--[2][11][23]SF--
TOW "MIDGET FROM MARS" '38

GILLMER, THOMAS CHARLES
GILLMER, TOM--[31]

GILLOTTI, ALBERT F.
HENEGE, THOMAS--[3]MYS--
DODD "DEATH OF A SHIP OWNER" '81
DODD "SKIM" '84

GILMAN, BRADLEY
WENTWORTH, WALTER--[1]

GILMAN, CHARLOTTE PERKINS
STETSON, CHARLOTTE PERKIN--
[23]AMERICAN/SF/HOR--
"THE YELLOW WALL PAPER"

GILMAN, DOROTHY
BUTTERS, DOROTHY GILMAN--[31]

GILMARC, DONNA
FAIRCHILD, ELISABETH--[26]ROM--
"SILENT SUITOR"
"COUNTERFEIT COACHMAN"

GILMER, ELIZABETH M.
DIX, DOROTHY--[8][9][22][31]AMERICAN/ROM--

GILMORE, CHRISTOPHER COOK
PARY, C.C.--[1]

GILMORE, DON
DAVIS, GIL--[1][31]

GILMORE, JAMES ROBERT
KIRKE, EDMUND--[1][8][22]AMERICAN

GILMORE, JOHN
HOWARD, J.T.--V. BERCH--
BRNDN/BC PSEUDS, BAE 22, P24

GILMORE, JOSEPH [LEE]
BENNETT, DANIEL--[1][31]
CARTER, NICK--[3]MYS,HP--
CHART "STRIKE OF THE HAWK" '80
CHART "WAR FROM THE CLOUDS" '80
CHART "TREASON GAME" '82
CHART "CHRISTMAS KILL" '83
CHART "OPERATION VENDETTA" '83
CHART "SAN JUAN INFERNO" '84
CHART "LAST FLIGHT TO MOSCOW" '85
CHART "ASSASSIN CONVENTION" '85
GILMAN, JAMES--[3][29][31]MYS--
MAJOR "OPERATION NAZI-USA" '76

GILMORE, RUFUS HAMILTON
HAMILTON, RUFUS--[1]

GILOTTI, ALBERT F.
HENEGE, THOMAS--[40]GERMAN/MYS--
"DRAHTSEILAKT" '84

GILROY, STEVE
FUTURE, STEVE--P. HARBOTTLE-TID-BITS
CKLST, PP#38/SF--
TB "DOOMED NATION OF THE SKIES" '53
TB "SLAVE TRADERS OF THE SKY" '54
?? UNCONFIRMED ??

GILROY, THOMAS LAURENCE
GILROY, TOM--[31]

GILSON, CHARLES [J.L.]
GILSON, BARBARA--[23][31][33]SF--
"QUEEN OF THE ANDES" '35

GILZEAN, ELIZABETH H.B.
HOUGHTON, ELIZABETH--[9][21][22][26]
[31]CANADIAN-WELCH/ROM-- 5 NOVELS
HUNTON, MARY--[9][21][22][26]
[31]CANADIAN-WELCH/ROM--
"NURSE AVERILL'S WARD"

GINDER, RICHARD
MCGLYNN, CHRISTOPHER--[1]
MONDAY, MICHAEL--[1]

GINNES, JUDITH S.
MITCHELL, PAIGE--[9][21][26]ROM--
"WILD SEED"

GINNINGS, HARRIETT W.
HARRIETT--[31]

GINZBERG, ASHER
ACHAD HAAN--[8]
HA-AM, AHAD--[22]
HAAM, ACHAD--[22]

GINZBERG, NATALIE
TOURNYINPARTE, ALESSANDRA--[1]

GIPPIUS, ZINAIDA N.
ARENSKY, ROMAN--[1]RUSSIAN
HERMANN, COMRADE--[1]RUSSIAN
HIPPIUS--[22]RUSSIAN
HIPPIUS, ZINAIDA--[1][31]RUSSIAN
KIRSHA, ANTON--[1]RUSSIAN
KRAINY, ANTON--[1]RUSSIAN
MEREZHKOVSKY, ZINAIDA--[1]RUSSIAN
PUSHCHIN, LEV--[1]RUSSIAN

GIPSON, FREDERICK BENJAM.
GIPSON, FRED--L. ROBBINS LTR MAR '94--
"HOUND DOG MAN" & OTHERS

GIRARD, HENRI GEORGES
ARNAUD, GEORGES--[3][29][31][40]MYS--
BODLEY "WAGES OF FEAR" '52
"JOURNEY PAST REPENTANCE" '53
AV "FLESH & FIRE" '58

GIRARD, JAMES PRESTON
THARP, JEFFREY--J. JOHNSON-
'FIRSTS' JUN '94, P39--
FAWCETT "KILLING IN KANSAS" '90

GIRARD, JOE
GIRARDI, JOE--[31]

GIRAUD, JEAN
GIR--[1][2]
MOEBIUS--J.M. LOFFICIER-SCIFI
ENTERTAINMENT OCT '94, P50,[2]--
ARTIST/ILLUSTRATOR

GIRAUDOUX, [H] JEAN
ANDOUARD--[31]

GIRDLESTON, A.H.
A.H.G.--[8]

GIRKOVA, LISABETTA
ELISHEVA--[22]RUSSIAN

GIRLING, ZOE
HARE, MARTIN--[1][22]IRISH

GIRON, MANUEL BUENDA TEL.
BUENDIA, MANUEL--[31]

GIRTIN, THOMAS
GIRTIN, TOM--[31]

GISCARD D'ESTAING, VALER.
GISCARD, VALERY--[31]

GITCHOFF, GEORGE THOMAS
GITCHOFF, TOM--[31]

GITTINGS, JO [G] MANTON
MANTON, JO--[1][22][33]ENGLISH

GITTLER, LEWIS F.
DE BOUT, JACQUES--V. BERCH LTR '93--
PYR 133 "PIERRE'S WOMAN" '54

GIUDICI, ANN COUPER
TUCKER, ANN--[1]
TUCKER-FETTNER, ANN--[1]

GIURLANI, ALDO
PALAZZESCHI, ALDO--[22]ITALIAN

GIVENS, JANET E[ATON]
EATON, JANET--[1][31][33]

GIVINS, ROBERT C.
TREBOR, SNIVIG C.--[1][3]MYS--
COOK CTY RVW "THE MILLIONAIRE TRAMP" 1886

GLADDEN, EDGAR NORMAN
MANSFIELD, N.--[8]

GLADNEY GLASSEROW, MARION
GLASSEROW, MARIO N.--[1][31]

GLADSON, LEE
GARDNER, LEE--[34]MYS--
AWARD "CALINA" '67
ST. JOHN, GENEVIEVE--V. BERCH LTR FEB '94,
[34]MYS--11 BELMONT NOVELS '65-71

GLADSTONE, ARTHUR M.
GLADSTONE, MAGGIE--[1][9][21][26]ROM--
9 NOVELS
NORCROSS, ELIZABETH--[1][9]ROM
NORCROSS, LISABET--[21][26]ROM--
6 NOVELS
SEBASTIAN, MARGARET--[3][9][21][26]MYS/ROM--
POPLB "BOW ST. BRANGLE" '77
POPLB "BOW ST. GENTLEMAN" '77
SEBASTIAN, MARY--[2][3][9]MYS/ROM--
WHITMORE, CILLA--[9][21][26]ROM--
3 NOVELS

GLADSTONE, JOSEPHINE
MARQUAND, JOSEPHINE--[1]

GLANZMAN, LOUIS
GLANZ, LEW--[2]

GLASBY, JOHN S.
ADAMS, JOHN--K. DILBONE-BADGER PSEUDS,
BAE 15,[2][7][23]SF--
BDG "WHEN THE GODS CAME" '60
BARTON, J.C.--S. HOLLAND-PP#39--
COBRA CS9 "PAYOFF" '60
COBRA CS12 "CORRUPT ONES" '61 ??
BAXTER, J.K.--S. HOLLAND-PP#39--
COBRA CS8 "BIG FRAME" '60
COBRA CS13 "SET UP" '62 ??

GLASBY, JOHN S. [CONT]
BOWERS, R.L.--K. DILBONE-BADGER PSEUDS, BAE 15/PP#39,[2] -- "THIS SECOND EARTH" '57
BRENT, A.D.--S. HOLLAND-PP#39-- COBRA CS10 "RACKETS INCORPORATED" '60 ??
CAMERON, BERL--W/ARTHUR O. ROBERTS, [2][11][23]HP-- WARREN "COSMIC ECHELON" '52
WARREN "SPHERO NOVA" '52
CHARTAIR, MAX--K. DILBONE-BADGER PSEUDS, BAE 15,[2][7]SF--
COLSON-HAIG, S.--[8]
CONWAY, RANDALL--K. DILBONE-BADGER PSEUDS, BAE 15,[2][11]SF--
COSMIC, RAY--[2][11]
CRAWFORD, JOHN--[2]
DAVIGNON, GRACE--[8]
DEXTER, J.B.--K. DILBONE-BADGER PSEUDS, BAE 15,[1][2][11]SF--
EADY, W.P.R.--[8]
HAMILTON, MICHAEL--K. DILBONE-BADGER PSEUDS, BAE 15,[2][11]SF--
HANSLEY, J.J.--K. DILBONE-BADGER PSEUDS, BAE 15,[2]
HENDERSON, GEORGE--[8]
LA SALLE, VICTOR--K. DILBONE-BADGER PSEUDS, BAE 15,[1]SF,HP--
SPENCER "DAWN OF THE HALF-GODS"
SPENCER "TWILIGHT ZONE"
LAYNHAM, PETER--K. DILBONE-BADGER PSEUDS, BAE 15,[2][11]
LE PAGE, RAND--W/ARTHUR O. ROBERTS, [2][11][23]SF,HP--
WARREN "SATTELITE BC" '52
WARREN "ZERO POINT" '52
WARREN "TIME & SPACE" '52
LENNARD, H.K.--K. DILBONE-BADGER PSEUDS, BAE 15,[2][11]
LORRAINE, PAUL--W/ARTHUR O. ROBERTS, [1][2]SF,HP--
WARREN "ZENITH D" '52
MAXWELL, JOHN C.--K. DILBONE-BADGER PSEUDS, BAE 15,[2][7][11][23]SF--
BDG "TIME KINGS" '58
MERAK, A.J. --K. DILBONE-BADGER PSEUDS, BAE 15/PP#39,[2][23][34]--
"MOON DUST" '52
BDG #3 "BLOOD ON MY SHADOW" '56
COBRA CS5 "TIME FOREVER" '57
COBRA CS11 "SAVAGE CITY" '57
MORTON, JOHN--K. DILBONE-BADGER PSEUDS, BAE 15,[2]
MULLER, JOHN E. --W/ARTHUR ROBERTS, [2][7]SF,HP--
SPENCER "ALIEN" '61
SPENCER "DAY OF THE BEASTS" '61
SPENCER "UNPOSSESSED" '61
NUDLEMAN, NORDYK--[8]
POWERS, J.L.--K. DILBONE-BADGER PSEUDS, BAE 15,[1][2][23]SF--
BDG "BLACK ABYSS" '60
RAW COSMIC--K. DILBONE-BADGER PSEUDS, BAE 15,[2]
THORNDYKE, ALAN--[2]
ZEIGFREID, KARL--K. DILBONE-BADGER CKLST, BAE 15,[2][7][23]SF,HP--
SPENCER "THE URANIUM SEEKERS" '53
SPENCER "DARK CENTAURI" '54

GLASER, ELEANOR DOROTHY
ZONIK, ELEANOR DOROTHY--[8]

GLASER, FRANZ
BIXBY, AX--[39]GERMAN/WEST
GLASER, FRANK--[39]GERMAN/WEST

GLASER, KURT
GLASER, COMSTOCK--[8]

GLASER, MARTHA
WILL, RUTH--[39]GERMAN

GLASER, MILTON
CATZ, MAX--[1][22][31][33]AMERICAN

GLASKIN, GERALD MARCUS
GLASKIN, G.M.--[31]
JACKSON, NEVILLE--[8][31]

GLASS, MONTAGUE MARSDEN
COSSART, THEOPHILUS--[31]

GLASS, THEODORE
THEODAMUS--[2][7]SF

GLASSBRENNER, ADOLF
BRENNGLAS, ADOLF--[39]GERMAN
BRESINGLAS, ADOLF--OXFORD COMPANION TO GERMAN LIT. '86

GLASSCO, JOHN [S]
BAYER, SYLVIA--[1][31]CANADIAN
COLMAN, GEORGE--[1][31]CANADIAN
DE SAINT LUC, JEAN--[1][31]CANADIAN
GOOCH, MARY L.--[31]-- VEGA V-8 "INCLUDED OUT" '60
GOOCH, MARY S[HOMETTE]--[31]ADULT--
BEACON B-187 "THE LUSTING BREED" '58
BEACON B-369 "CHEATING WOMAN" '60
NSTD U171 "AMOROUS DIETICIAN" '61
FABIAN Z139 "TAINTED ROSARY" '61
SABER SA23 "HUTCH CREEK GIRL" '62
GOOCH, SILAS N.--[1][22]
OKADA, HIDEKI--[1]
UNDERWOOD, MILES--C. ECKHOFF SLST-OLYMP,[1]-- ORP OB-501 "AUTHENTIC CONFESS. OF H. MARWOOD" '67

GLASSCOCK, ANNE BONNER
BONNER, MICHAEL--[1][22][31]AMERICAN, WEST-- 4 NOVELS '60-6

GLASSER, ALLEN
GLASSER, ALAN--[7]SF--
SOLAR PUB "THE CAVEMEN OF VENUS" '32
MAJOR "THE DEMON COSMOS" '80
LANGELL, SEARS--[1][2][11]SF
ZAMBOCK, GEORGE--[1][2][11]SF

GLAUER, RUDOLF
VON SEBETTENDORF, R.F.--[39]GERMAN
VON SEBOTTENDORF, RUDOLF--[39]GERMAN

GLAZAR, BOB
FIFO, RAY--[1][31]

GLAZER-MALBIN, NONA
GLAZER, NONA Y.--[31]

GLEADOW, RUPERT SEELEY
CASE, JUSTIN--[1][22][31]MYS,HP-- USED PRIMARILY BY HUGH B. CAVE

GLEASON, EUGENE FRANKLIN
GLEASON, GENE--[31]

GLEASON, ROBERT
CAIN, JACKSON--[31]

GLEICH, JOSEPH ALOIS
BLUM, ADOLPH--[39]GERMAN/SF
DELLAROSA, LUDWIG--[39]GERMAN/SF

GLEICH, JOSEPH ALOIS [CONT]
WALDEN, H.--[39]GERMAN/SF

GLEIT, JOYCE
GLADSTONE, EVE--W/HERMA WERNER,
[9][10][21][26][34]MYS/ROM--
HARL "ENIGMA" '89 & MORE

GLEMSER, BERNARD
CRANE, ROBERT--[2][7][11][23][31]SP--
"HEROES WALK BELOW" '54
FIELD, FRANK CHESTER--[11]SF
HILL, KING--[11]SF
NAPIER, GEOFFREY--[1][3]MYS--
DELL "THE WRONG BOX" '66
DELL "A DEAR HUNGARIAN FRIEND" '66
NAPIER, GERALDINE--[1][34]MYS

GLEN, DUNCAN MUNRO
FOSTER, SIMON--[8]
MUNRO, RONALD EADIE--[8]

GLENDINNING, SARA WILSON
GLENDINNING, SALLY--[31][33]

GLENN, KAREN
CARRINGTON, GLENDA--[34]MYS--
BERK "MASTER OF GREYSTONE" '77

GLENNING, RAYMOND
VALDEZ, PAUL--[36]AUSTRALIAN/MYS--
TRNPT "THE CORPSE SAT UP" nd ['50]

GLICK, CARL CANNON
CUNNINGHAM, CAPT. FRANK--[1][31][33]
HOLBROOK, PETER--[1][33]

GLICK, RUTH [BURTNICK]
CHASE, SAMANTHA--W/EILEEN BUCKHOLTZ,[9]ROM
HILL, ALEXIS--W/LOUISE TITCHENER,
[9][21][26]ROM--
"IN THE ARMS OF LOVE"
HOWARD, ALYSSA--W/EILEEN BUCKHOLTZ,
LOUISE TITCHENER & CAROLYN MALES,[9][31]ROM
JORDAN, ALEXIS HILL--W/LOUISE TITCHENER,
[9][26]ROM--
"BRIAN'S CAPTIVE"
"SUMMER STARS" & MORE
LEE, AMANDA--W/EILEEN BUCKHOLTZ,[26][31]ROM--
"GREAT EXPECTATIONS"
"LOGICAL CHOICE" & MORE
MARLOWE, TESS--W/LOUISE TITCHENER,
[9][21][26]ROM--
"INDISCREET"
YORK, REBECCA--W/EILEEN BUCKHOLTZ,
[7][9][26]ROM--
"BAYOU MOON"
"ONLY SKIN DEEP" & MORE

GLICK, VIRGINIA KIRKUS
KIRKUS, VIRGINIA--[1][31][33]

GLICKSOHN, MIKE
DUBIOUS, GARNER R.--[2]

GLIDDEN, FREDERICK D.
GLIDDEN, F.D.--[28]WEST--
COWBOY STORIES "SIX-GUN LAWYER" AUG '35
GLIDDEN, FRED--[28]--
"RETRACTION" UNIV OF MISSOURI '30
SHORT, LEW--E.J. PARENT LTR MAY '94
SHORT, LUKE--V. BERCH-GM PSEUDS,
PP 33,[1][3]MYS/WEST--
GM 159 "BARREN LAND MURDERS" '51
BB "LAST HUNT" '62 & MORE

GLIDDEN, JONATHAN H.
DAWSON, PETER--V. BERCH LTR '94,[1][28]WEST--
ALL BUT LAST 8 NOVELS WHICH WERE GHOSTED

GLIEWE, UNADA
UNADA--[8][33]

GLIKBERG, ALEXANDER MIKH.
CHERMY, SASHA--[22]RUSSIAN

GLOSSNER, HARRY
WALDEN, FRANK--[39]GERMAN/MYS

GLOTZER, ALBERT
GATES, ALBERT--[31]

GLOVER, DENNIS JAMES M.
KETTLE, PETER--[31]

GLOVER, MODWENA
SEDGEWICK, MODWENA--[1]

GLOVER, ROBERT H.
GLOVER, BOB--[31]

GLOVER-WRIGHT, GEOFFREY
WRIGHT, GLOVER--[7]SF--
"THE HOUND OF HEAVEN" '84

GLOWACKI, ALEKSANDER
PRUS, BOLESLAW--[22]POLISH

GLOWACZ, HELMUT
JONES, EVERETT--[39]GERMAN/WEST,HP
KENDALL, JOHN--[39]GERMAN/WEST

GLUBB, JOHN BAGOT
GLUBB PASHA--[31]

GLUCHOWSKI, BRUNO
PAULSEN, ROBERT--[39]GERMAN

GLUCK, ANNA [S]
VAN STEEN, PETRA--[39]GERMAN
WIED, ANN--[39]GERMAN

GLUCK, SINCLAIR
DANNING, MELROD--[3][22][29]MYS--
HODDER "MAJESTY OF THE LAW" '16

GLUSS, BRIAN
GLUZMAN, BRIAN--[31]

GLUT, DONALD F.
GLUD, DON--[1]
GRANT, DON--[1]
JASON, JOHNNY--[1][31]
MORRISON, VICTOR--[1]
RICHMOND, ROD--[1]
ROGERS, MICK--V. BERCH-LESBIANA/CNTRCLTR,
BAE 22, P5,[1]
SPEKTOR, [DR.] ADAM--[1][31]
STEELE, DALE--[1]
THORNE, BRADLEY D.--[1]

GLYNN, ANTHONY ARTHUR
GLYN, A.A.--[1]
LANTRY, MIKE--S. HOLLAND-PP#39,[34]MYS,HP--
BDG#2 "A GUNMAN CLOSE BEHIND" '56
MARTIN, ANTHONY--[1][2][11]
MULLER, JOHN E.--[2][11][23]SF,HP--
SPENCER "PLAN FOR CONQUEST" '63
REID, DESMOND--[34]MYS,HP--
AMALG "THE CORPSE CAME TOO" '61

GNAEGY, CHARLES
GRANGE, CHRIS--[31]
GREGORY, CHUCK--[31]

GNAGY, MICHAEL JACQUES
GNAGY, JOHN--[1]
GNAGY, JON--[31]

GNOLI, DOMENICO
GADDI, DARIO--[22]ITALIAN
ORSINI, GIULIO--[22]ITALIAN

GOAMAN, MURIEL
COX, EDITH--[8]

GOBEL, DIETER
BENNET, DOUGLAS--[39]GERMAN/SF

GOBELS, HUBERT
WADDEN, HELMUT--[39]GERMAN/JUV

GODDARD, GLORIA
PALMER, PAUL--[1][3]MYS--
PHOENIX "MURDER FROM HEAVEN" '39

GODDARD, NORMAN M.
BARR, NAT--[1]
CANNOR, J.R.--[1]
DARRAN, MARK--[1]
HAVILAND, [CAPT.] FERGUS--[1]
PERGARTH, PETER--[1]
RICH, HENRY K.--[1]

GODE VON AESCH, ALEXANDER
GODE, ALEXANDER--[31][33]

GODFREY, FREDERICK M.
CRONHEIM, F.G.--[8]

GODFREY, LIONEL ROBERT H.
HOLCOMBE--[8]
KENNEDY, ELLIOT--[3][31][40]MYS--
HALE "BIG LOSER" '72
HALE "BULLETS ARE FINAL" '73 & MORE
MITCHELL, SCOTT--[1][3][40]MYS--
HAM "LONELY SHROUD" '64
HALE "DEAD ON ARRIVAL" '74 & MORE

GODLEY, ROBERT
JAMES, FRANKLIN--[1][3][22]MYS--
LANTERN PRESS "KILLER IN THE KITCHEN" '47

GODWIN, ANTHONY R.J.W.
GODWIN, TONY--[31]

GODWIN, FRANCIS
GONSALES, DOMINGO--[1][2][11]SF

GODWIN, JOHN [F]
FOSTER, FREDERICK--[1][31]AUSTRALIAN--
CONTRIBUTOR TO 'MOTHER' MAGAZINE
STARK, JOHN--[1][22]AUSTRALIAN

GODWIN, MARY W.
SHELLY, NARY--[29]MYS

GOEBBLES, [PAUL] JOSEPH
GOEBBLES, JOSEF--[31]
GOEBBLES, JOSEPH PAUL--[31]

GOEBEL, GUNTHER
VAN GOEL, LOTHAR--[39]GERMAN

GOEDEL, KURT
GODEL, KURT--[31]

GOEDSCHE, HERMANN O.F.
RETCLIFFE, SIR JOHN--[39]GERMAN/ADV

GOEN, RAYBURNE WYNDHAM JR
GOEN, TEX JR.--[31]

GOERCKE, GUNTHER
MORLOCK, MARTIN--[39]GERMAN

GOERITZ, GERDA
BIRKENSTEIN, ULLA--[39]GERMAN

GOERLING, LARS
GORLING, LARS--[31]

GOETCHEUS, CAROLYN
LYNN, CAROL--[8]

GOETZ, AUSTIN B.
O'NEILL, KATHLEEN--[3]MYS--
PLAY "OUT OF THIS WORLD" '46
PLAY "THE KITTEN'S NECKLACE" '48

GOETZ, IGNACIO L.
GOTZ, IGNACIO--[31]

GOFF, JACQUELINE
RYAN, JENNA--[9][10][21][26][31]ROM--
9 HARL NOVELS '80s & '90s

GOFF, JERRY M. JR.
COQUELIN, RENEE--V. BERCH-BRNDN/
BC PSEUDS, BAE 22, P24

GOFF, JERRY M. JR.
LANE, JERRY--G. COOK LTR AUG '93--
MERIT BOOKS - ? COULD BE 'JEREMY LANE'?

GOFFSTEIN, M.B.
GOFFSTEIN, BROOKE--[33]

GOFMAN, VICTOR V.
HUFMAN--[22]RUSSIAN

GOGARTY, OLIVER ST. JOHN
GAY, OLIVER--[1]
J.R.S.--[1]
OUSELY, GIDEON--[1]

GOGGAN, JOHN PATRICK
PATRICK, JOHN--[8]

GOGOLIN, PETER
ESCH, A.--[39]GERMAN

GOHM, DOUGLAS CHARLES
O'CONNELL, ROBERT FRANK--[8]

GOHMAN, FRED JOSEPH
WEBB, SPIDER--[22]AMERICAN

GOHRE, FRANK
A.B.S.--W/ASTRID & BERNDT SCHMACHER,
[40]GERMAN/MYS--
"TIEFE SPUREN" '89

GOICOECHEA, ANA MARIA M.
MATUTE, ANA MARIA--[7]SF

GOINES, DONALD
CLARK, AL C. --[34]MYS--
HOLLH "CRIME PARTNERS" '74
HOLLH "CRY REVENGE" '74
HOLLH "DEATH LIST" '74
HOLLH "KENYATTA'S ESCAPE" '74
HOLLH "KENYATTA'S LAST HIT" '74

GOING, ELLEN MAUDE
HARDINGE, E.M.--[1]

GOITEIN, SHELOMO DOV
GOITEIN, S.D.--[31]
GOITEIN, SOLOMON DOB F.--[31]

GOLD, FLOYD
GALE, FLOYD C.--[11]

GOLD, HORACE L.
CAMPBELL, CLYDE CRANE--[2][11][23]SF-'34-5
DELL, DUDLEY--[2][11][23]SF-'51
FOSSE, HAROLD C.--[1][2][11]SF
GOLD, H.L.--L. ROBBINS,[32]MYS--
SD "I KNOW SUICIDE" JUN-JUL '47
DS "IFUGAO, I GO" AUG '48
GRAEY, JULIAN--[1][11]
GRIMM, C.--[2]
KEITH, LEIGH--[1][2][11][23]SF-'34-5
STORY, RICHARD--[1][2][11][23]SF-'43

GOLDACKER, DEBRA DIER
DIER, DEBRA--[26]ROM--
"SHADOW OF THE STORM"
"SURRENDER THE DREAM"

GOLDBERG, HARRY
GREY, HARRY--[1][34]MYS--
CROWN "THE HOODS" '52
CROWN "CALL ME DUKE" '55
SIGN "PORTRAIT OF A MOBSTER" '58

GOLDBERG, HYMAN
PENNY, PRUDENCE--[1]

GOLDBERG, LARRY
GOLDBERG, FATS--[1][31]

GOLDBERG, LEE
LUDLOW, IAN--W/LEWIS PERDUE,[3]MYS--
PINN "MAKE THEM PAY" '85
PINN ".357 VIGILANTE" '85
PINN "WHITEWASH ALL" '85

GOLDBERG, NATHAN RALPH
RALPH, NATHAN--[8]

GOLDBERG, PHYLLIS
GOLD, PHYLLIS--[31]

GOLDBERG, REUBEN LUCIUS
GOLDBERG, RUBE--[31]

GOLDBERY, EDWARD
GOLDEY--[3]MYS--
EAGLE "TRACKED BY A WOMAN:
OR THE FEMALE DETECTIVE" 1889

GOLDBOGEN, AVROM
TODD, MIKE--[2][11]

GOLDEMBERG, ROSE L.
SCHILLER, ROSE LEIMAN--[1]
TRAVEN, BEATRICE--[1]

GOLDEN, DOROTHY
DENNISON, DOROTHY--[8]

GOLDENBAUM, SALLY
MCGUIRE, MOLLY--[26]ROM--
"FOREVER YOURS"
"MY PRINCE CHARMING"
STONE, NATALIE--W/ADRIENNE STAFF,
[9][21][26]ROM--"SKY GYPSY"
"DOUBLE PLAY" & 4 MORE

GOLDENTHAL, ALLAN B.
BENARRIA, ALLAN--[1][22][31]AMERICAN

GOLDFEDER, [K] JAMES
PAHZ, CHERYL SUZANNE--[1][31]
PAHZ, JAMES ALON--[1]
PAZ, A.--[1]
PAZ, ZAN--[1]

GOLDFRANK, HELEN [C]
KAY, HELEN--[8][22][31][33]AMERICAN

GOLDFRAP, JOHN HENRY
DEERING, FREEMONT B.--[1]
FORRESTER, DEXTER J.--[1]
LAWTON, CAPT. WILBUR--[1][2]
PAYSON, [LT.] HOWARD--[1]
WEST, MARVIN--[1]

GOLDGRABER, KENNETH
RAPHAEL, [FATHER] M.--[1]
SIMMON, KENNETH--[1]

GOLDIE, KATHLEEN ANNIE
FIDLER, KATHLEEN--[1][2][7]SF--
"THE BOY WITH BRONZE AXE" '68

GOLDIE, MARY E.K. DULCIE
DEAMER, DULCIE--[1]

GOLDIE, TERRENCE W.
GOLDIE, TERRY--[31]

GOLDIN, KATHLEEN MCKINNEY
SKY, KATHLEEN--[7][8][11]SF--
LASER "BIRTHRIGHT" '75
BERK "WITCHDAME" '85 & MORE

GOLDIN, STEPHEN
STEPHENS, CHARLES--[1]

GOLDING, LOUISE
DAVIES, LOUISE--[8]

GOLDING, MORTON JAY
LLOYD, STEPHANIE--[29][31][34]MYS--
PAPLB "GRAVESWOOD" '66
MARTIN, JAY--[2][34]MYS--
LAN 73-634 "MAKE LOVE, NOT WAVES" '67
LAN 73-753 "EROTICA CAPER" '68
LAN 73-803 "FONDLE WITH CARE" '68
LAN 74-522 "SEXY EGG LOVE-IN" '69
BERK Z1905 "DIGGING THE LOVE GODDESS" '70
MICHAELS, M.M.--[1]
MORTON, PATRICIA--[3][9][21][26][29]MYS/ROM--
LAN 72-977 "MOONDUST" '65
LAN "A CHILD OF VALUE" '66
BANN B50-114 "IN THE PROVINCE
OF DARKNESS" '67
BELM "DESTINY'S CHILD" '67
LAN "CAVES OF FEAR" '68

GOLDMAN, WILLIAM
LONGBAUGH, HARRY--MUNROE SLST 21-
GOLDMAN BIBLIO,[2][34]MYS--
GM 1384 "NO WAY TO TREAT A LADY" '64
MORGENSTERN, S.--[2][7]SF--
"THE SILENT GONDOLIERS: A FABLE" '85

GOLDSCHEIDER, ALBERT
GROLLER, BALDUIN--[39]GERMAN/MYS

GOLDSMITH, CAROL EVAN
EVAN, CAROL--[1][31]

GOLDSMITH, DAVID H.
CLEVELAND, CLIFFORD S.--[1][31]

GOLDSMITH, EDITH
OLIVER, EDITH--[1]

GOLDSMITH, HOWARD
COURTNEY, DAYLE--[1][31]
SMITH, WARD--[1][33]

GOLDSMITH, JAMES CARLTON
CARLTON, JAY--[1]

GOLDSMITH, JOHN THORBURN
THORBURN, JOHN--[33]

GOLDSMITH, OLIVER
ANGELO, MICHAEL--[1]

GOLDSTEIN, ARTHUR D.
ROSS, ALBERT--[29][34][40]MYS--
RANDOM "I KNOW WHAT I WAS DOING" '74

GOLDSTEIN, FANIA
FENELON, FANIA--[1]

GOLDSTEIN, ISIDORE
ISOU, ISIDORE--[22]FRENCH

GOLDSTEIN, MORITZ
OSTEN, MICHAEL--[39]GERMAN

GOLDSTEIN, STANLEY B.
RANDALL, BOB--[34][40]MYS--
RANDOM "THE FAN" '77
SIMON "THE CALLING" '81
WARNER "THE NEXT" '81
WARNER "LAST MAN ON THE LIST" '90

GOLDSTEIN, WILLIAM ISAAC
LODE, REX--W/BOYD BOYLAND,[22]AMERICAN

GOLDSTON, ROBERT C.
CONROY, ROBERT--[1][31]
STARK, JAMES--[22][33][34]MYS--
AV "THE GREEK VIRGIN" '62

GOLDSTONE, LAWRENCE A.
TREAT, LAWRENCE--[18][29][31][32][34]MYS--
LEGALLY CHNGD TO "TREAT"--
21 MYS NVLS '40-88
DUELL "B AS IN BANSHEE" '40
HARPER "BIG SHOT" '51 & MORE
AHMM "DRESDEN ALIAS FARADAY" FEB '59
& OTHERS-CC, CD, EQMM, MSMM,
SA, S&SDM, SL

GOLDSZMIT, HENRYK
KORCZAK, JANUSZ--[31]

GOLDTHORPE, JOHN ERNEST
GOLDTHORPE, J.E.--[31]

GOLDWASSER, MATTI
GOLAN, MATTI--[1]

GOLDWORTH, EMMA
KENDALL, MAY--[23]SF

GOLLAN, ELIZA MARGARET J.
HUMPHREYS, MRS.--[29]MYS

GOLLER, CELIA MARGARET
FREMLIN, CELIA--[29][31][32][34][40]MYS/HIST--
15 NVLS '58-90
18 EQMM & LM STORIES

GOLOMSTOCK, IGOR N.
FOMIN--[31]

GOLON, SERGE & ANNE
GOLON, SERGEANNE--[1][2]

GOLSWORTHY, ARNOLD
HOLCOMBE, ARNOLD--[8]
JINGLE--[8]

GOLTZ, DIETLIND
DU MONT, DIETLIN NEVEN--[39]GERMAN/JUV

GOLUB, VLADYSLAY
GALUBOK, VLADYSLAY--[22]RUSSIAN

GOLV, LOYAL EUGENE
GOLF, LOYAL E.--[31]

GOMBERG, V.
LIDIN, VLADIMIR GHERMANO.--[22]RUSSIAN

GOMBERG, WILLIAM GILBERT
GILBERT, WILLIE--[31]

GOMPERTZ, MARTIN LOUIS A.
GANPAT--[2][3][7]MYS/SF--
HODDER "MARCHES OF HONOR" '31
HODDER "SECOND TIGRESS" '33

GOMPERTZ, MARTIN LOUIS A.
GOMPERTZ, [MAJ.] M.L.A.--[1]

GOMULICKI, WIKTOR
FANTAZY--[22]POLISH

GONDA, ADOLPHE
DORNE, PASCAL--JEAN F. LE DEIST LTR '93
GAELI, JOSETTE--JEAN F. LE DEIST LTR '93
LEE, SANDRA--JEAN F. LE DEIST LTR '93
MORAYNS, JACQUES--JEAN F. LE DEIST LTR '93
MYRIAM--JEAN F. LE DEIST LTR '93
SEVERAC, PAUL--JEAN F. LE DEIST LTR '93
WAELE, ELISABETH--JEAN F. LE DEIST LTR '93

GONDA, ALEXANDER
SEGOVIA, PHIL--[39]GERMAN

GONZALES MORALES, ANTONIO
MURPHY, ANTHONI G.--JEAN F. LE DEIST LTR '93

GONZALES, RICHARD ALONZO
GONZALES, PANCHO--[31]

GONZALES-BICOS, OLGA
BICOS, OLGA--[26]ROM--
"WHITE TIGER"
"BY MY HEART BETRAYED"
"SANTANA ROSE"

GONZALEZ, NESTOR VINCENTE
GONZALEZ, N.V.M.--[31]

GOOCH, GEORGE PEABODY
GOOCH, G.P.--[1]

GOOCH, ROBERT MILETUS
GOOCH, BOB--[31]

GOOCH, STANLEY ALFRED
GOOCH, STAN--[31]

GOOCK, ROLAND
ETTL, ALEXANDER--[39]GERMAN/SF
JAROMIN, ROLF--[39]GERMAN/SF
KORN, PETER--[39]GERMAN/SF

GOOCK, ROLAND [CONT]
LUTZ, ADRON--[39]GERMAN/SF
ROLAND, PETER--[39]GERMAN/SF

GOOD, EDWARD
OYVED, MOYSHEH--[8]

GOOD, IRVING JOHN
DOOG, K. CAJ--[22][31]ENGLISH

GOODALL, JOHN STRICKLAND
GOODALL, J.S.--BAPC #11--PAN COVER ARTIST
JGS--BAPC #11--PAN COVER ARTIST

GOODAVAGE, JOSEPH F.
GREYSTONE, ALEXANDER A.--[8]

GOODAVAGE, JOSEPH F.
SAVAGE, STEVE--[8]

GOODCHILD, GEORGE
DARE, ALAN--[2][3][22][23][29]MYS/SF--
JENKINS "ISLE OF HATE" '24
"EYE OF ABU" '27 & MORE
REID, WALLACE Q.--[1][22][29]MYS/WEST--
9 NOVELS '28-36
TEMPLETON, JESSE--[3][22][29]MYS--
WARD "BITTER TEST" '30
HURST "JAKE CANUCK" '24 & MORE

GOODE, ARTHUR RUSSELL
RUSSELL, ARTHUR--[2][36]AUSTRALIAN/MYS--
FENLAND "TRAGEDY AT CUMBERLAND PARK" '33
HAM "WOMAN OF MYS" '33
TRNPT "CROCODILE CITY" nd ['45] & 3 OTHERS

GOODE, GEORGE W.
COOLIDGE, ERWIN L.--[34]MYS--4 NOVELS 1891-6
MILLS, HARRY--[34]MYS--4 NOVELS 1895-6

GOODE, GERALD
RAINER, JEROME--[1]

GOODE, RUTH
RAINER, JULIA--[1]
SEINFEL, RUTH--[1]

GOODEN, ARTHUR HENRY
GOODEN, A.H.--L. ROBBINS LTR '94-- PULP
RIDER, BRETT--[1][28]WEST--
6 NOVELS '40-50

GOODEY, P.E.
CONDON, PATRICIA--[8]

GOODHART, ARTHUR LEHMAN
GOODHART, A.L.--[31]

GOODIS, DAVID
CLAYBURN, LOGAN--[1]
KERMIT, LANCE--[1]

GOODMAN, ABRAHAM
MANN, ABBY--[3]MYS--
AWARD "KOJAK" '74

GOODMAN, ADOLPH WINKLER
GOODMAN, A.W.--[31]

GOODMAN, GEORGE [J.W.]
GOODMAN, WINTHROP--W/WINTHROP
KNOWLTON,[8][34]MYS--
MacD "A KILLING IN THE MARKET" '58
SMITH, ADAM--W/WINTHROP KNOWLTON,[1][3]MYS--

GOODMAN, IRENE
MORGAN, DIANA--W/ALEX KAMAROFF,[9][21][26]ROM--
"AMBER DREAMS"
"OCEAN FIRES" & MORE

GOODMAN, JOSEPHINE CHARL.
GOODMAN, JO--W/TOSS GASCOIGNE
& MARGOT TYRRELL,[7]SF--
PENG "DREAM TIME: 16 NEW STORIES" '89

GOODMAN, REBECCA GRUVER
GRUVER, REBECCA--[31]

GOODMAN, RUTH
MCKINNEY, MEAGAN--[9][21][26]ROM--
"WHEN ANGELS FALL"
"LIONS & LACE" & MORE

GOODNER, MARIE B.
ADAMS, MARYE--[3]MYS--
VANTAGE "HE WOULDN'T TALK" '59

GOODOVITCH, ISRAEL MEIR
GOODOVITCH, I.M.--[31]

GOODRICH, CHARLES [H]
GOOD, CHARLES H.--[1]

GOODRICH, HENRY NEWTON
BEELZEBUB--[36]

GOODRICH, SAMUEL G.
PARLEY, PETER--CAROL BILLMAN-SECRET OF
STRATEMEYER SYNDICATE

GOODRICH-FREER, ADELA
MISS X--[2]

GOODRIDGE, MARY WILLIAMS
DUDLEY, DOROTHY--[1]
GREELEY, MARY WILLIAMS--[1]

GOODSPEED, DONALD JAMES
MCLEISH, DOUGAL--[8][34]MYS--
HOUGHTON "TRAITOR GAME" '68
HOUGHTON "VALENTINE VICTIMS" '68
REDMAYNE, JOHN--W/HERBERT FAIRLIE WOOD,[1]

GOODSTEIN, REUBEN LOUIS
GOODSTEIN, R.L.--[31]

GOODWIN, GEOFFREY
GEMINI--[8]
TELSTAR--[8]
TOPICUS--[8]

GOODWIN, HAROLD LELAND
BLAINE, JOHN--[2][7][8][23]SF--
"RICK BRANT" SCIENCE ADV SERIES
BLAINE, JOHN--W/PHILIP J. HARKINS,
[7][23][31][33]SF--
"LOST CITY" '47
"ROCKET'S SHADOW" '47
"DANGER BELOW" '68
"MAGIC TALISMAN" '90
GOODWIN, HAL--[8][22][31][33]AMERICAN
GORDON, HAL--[1][31][33]AMERICAN
SAVAGE, BLAKE--[7][8][23][33]SF--
"RICK FOSTER RIDES THE GRAY PLANET" '52

GOODWIN, HOPE
LEE, LINDA--[9][21][26]ROM--
"DESERT ROSE"

GOODWIN, JUNE
MAXON, J.G.--W/BEN SHIFF, LACHMAN-EASTER LST '93,[34]MYS--
"PROGENY" '89

GOODWIN, RICHARD NARADHOF
LAIRD, BAILEY--[31]

GOODWIN, SUZANNE
EBEL, SUZANNE--[1][8][31]
SHELBOURNE, CECILY--[1]

GOODYEAR, STEPHEN FREDRK.
TAYLOR, SAM--[8]

GOODYKOONTZ, WILLIAM F.
GOODE, BILL--[1][3]MYS--
ZIFF DAVIS "THE SENATOR'S NUDE" '47

GOOL, RESHARD
DEVAJEE, VED--[31]

GOOLD, CHRISTINE R.
ROBB, CHRISTINE--[9]ROM

GOON, FOOK MUN
FUNG, GONG--[31]CHINESE-AMERICAN

GOONETILLEKE, DEVAPRIYA C
GOONETILLEKE, D.C.R.A.--[31]

GORDON, ACTHERINE J.B.
G., K.--[34]MYS--
RANKEN "A LEGEND OF FYRIE CASTLE" ca 1870

GORDON, ALAN BACCHUS
ORDON, A. LANG--[8]

GORDON, ARCHIBALD V.D.
GORDON, ARCHIE--[31]

GORDON, CHARLES WILLIAM
CONNOR, RALPH --[25][28][31]
[34]CANADIAN/MYS/WEST--
HODDER "CORPORAL CAMERON" '12
HODDER "PATROL OF SUNDANCE TRAIL" '14

GORDON, DEBORAH
HASTINGS, BROOKE--[9]

GORDON, GILES ALEXANDER E
BOSWELL--[31]

GORDON, HENRY ALFRED
GORDON, HARRY--[1][31]

GORDON, JAMES
FOSS, JOHN--[1][22][34]MYS--
DOBSON " OF OUR TIME" '46
DOBSON "FLESH & BLOOD" '51
DOBSON "PLUSH GUILT" '53
JEEMS, PIOUP--[1]

GORDON, JAMES WILLIAM
GRAHAEM, JIM--[13]AUSTRALIAN

GORDON, JAN
GORE, WILLIAM --[3][8][22]MYS--
HARRAP "THERE'S DEATH IN THE CHURCHYARD" '34
HARRAP "MURDER MOST ARTISTIC" '37

GORDON, MARTHA STARR
STARR, MARTHA--[9][21][26]ROM--
"FROM TWILIGHT TO SUNRISE"
"BITTER FRUIT"

GORDON, MILDRED & GORDON
GORDONS, THE--[3][29][31]MYS--
22 NOVELS '50-79

GORDON, PATRICIA
HOWARD, JOAN--[11]

GORDON, RICHARD M.
PAIGE, JUAN--LACHMAN LST AUG '94,MYS

GORDON, ROBERT I.
LONDON, ANNE--[8]
LONDON, ROBERT--[8]

GORDON, ROBERT KAY
BLAKE, NORMAN--W/HEBER C. JAMIESON,[1]

GORDON, YEHUDA LEIB
Y.L.G.--[22]RUSSIAN

GORDON, [RICHARD] STUART
GORDON, RICHARD A.--[23]SF--
NW "A LIGHT IN THE SKY" '65
GORDON, STUART--[8][11][23]SF
STUART, ALEX R.--[7][8][11][23]SF--
"OUTLAWS" '72
"DEVIL'S RIDER" '73
"BIKE FRM HELL" '73

GORDON-COOKE, N.
BROMLEY, LUKE--[35]AUSTRALIAN--
CHISHOLM 697 "SWAMP RAIDERS"
REGAN, WADE--[35]AUSTRALIAN--
SIERRA 457 "CROSSFIRE"

GORE, JOHN FRANCIS
OLD STAGER--[1]

GORELL, LETHBRIDGE
BARNES, MICHAEL--S. HOLLAND-SCION CKLST, PP 27, P11
CELLO, JOHNNY--S. HOLLAND-SCION CKLST, PP 27, P11,HP
DRAYTON, RICKY--S. HOLLAND-SCION CKLST, PP 27, P11
HANSON, FRANK--S. HOLLAND-SCION CKLST, PP 27, P11
MEDUSA, KARL--S. HOLLAND-SCION CKLST, PP 27, P11
ZORE, HYMAN--S. HOLLAND-SCION CKLST, PP 27, P11,HP

GORES, JOSEPH NICHOLAS
GORES, JOE--[18][29][31][34]MYS--
8 NOVELS '69-89
21 DIGEST STRS [EQMM, MH & MSMM]

GOREY, EDWARD ST. JOHN
BLUTIG, EDUARD--[6][22][31][33]AMERICAN
DOGYEAR, DREW--[31]AMERICAN
DOWDY, MRS. REGERA--[6][8][31]][33]AMERICAN
EDGY, WARDORE--[31]AMERICAN
GEWE, RADDORY--[31][33]AMERICAN
GREWDEAD, ROY--[31]AMERICAN
GRODE, REDWAY--[6][31][33]AMERICAN
MUDE, O.--[6][33]AMERICAN
OM--[33]AMERICAN
PHYPPES, HYACINTH--[6][33]AMERICAN
PIG, EDWARD--[33]AMERICAN
WEARY, OGDRED--[6][22][33]AMERICAN
WODGE, DREARY--[6][22][33]AMERICAN
WARD, E.D.--[33]AMERICAN
WEARY, OGDRED--[33]AMERICAN
WRYDE, DOGEAR--[33]AMERICAN

GORHAM, CHARLES
DURAND, ORSON--[14]ADULT--
OLYM TC#475 "ANGEL IN THE FLESH" '69

GORHAM, JILL
ALLAN, DINA--[34]MYS--
ZEBRA "MELODY OF MURDER" '79

GORHAM, MAURICE ANTHONY C
RAULT, WALTER--[22]ENGLISH-IRISH

GORIS, JAN-ALBERT
GIJSEN, MARNIX--[22]FLEMISH

GORLITZ, WOLF-DIETER
WINZER, FELIX--[39]GERMAN

GORMAN, EDWARD [JOSEPH]
CHASE, ROBERT DAVID [1]--W/ED & LORRAINE WARREN, V. BERCH LTR TO B. BRINEY '93--
ST. MARTIN'S "TRUE HAUNTINGS FROM AN OLD NE CEMETARY" '92
FOSTER, JAKE--HAWK/GORMAN INTRVW, WEST,HP--
PINN 55817 "TWO GUNS TO YUMA" '90
ZEBRA 3453 "HELL-FOR-LEATHER RIDER" '91
ZEBRA 3636 "RAMROD REVENGE" '92
GORMAN, ED--GARY LOVISI REVIEW JAN '93
KEEGAN, CHRISTOPHER--V. BERCH CALL '94, PP#39, P38--
WALKER "RIDE INTO YESTERDAY"
McCARRICK, CHRIS SHEA--V. BERCH LTR TO B. BRINEY '93, SUSP--
DIAM "RUN TO MIDNIGHT" '92
McLENNAN, WILL--V. BERCH LTR TO B. BRINEY '93, WEST,HP--
JOVE "RAMSEY'S LAW #13" '91
RANSOM, DANIEL--ENFANTINO-GORMAN INTRVW, PP39,[34]HOR--
ZEBRA 1606 DADDY'S LITTLE GIRL" '85
ZEBRA 1862 "TOYS IN THE ATTIC" '86
ZEBRA 2186 "NIGHT CALLER" '87
ST. MARTIN'S 90947 "THE FORSAKEN" '88
ST. MARTIN'S 91584 "THE BABYSITTER" '89
ST. MARTIN'S "NIGHTMARE CHILD" '90
DELL "THE LONG MIDNIGHT" '92
DELL 20605 "THE SERPENT'S KISS" '92

GORMAN, THOMAS DAVID
GORMAN, TOM--[31]

GORNY, YOSEF
GORNI, YOSEF--[31]
GORNY, JOSEPH--[31]

GORSKI, ARTHUR
QUASIMOTO--[22]POLISH

GORSLINE, [SALLY] MARIE
CARSON, S.M.--[31][33]
GORSLINE, S.M.--[31][33]

GORZ, HEINZ
HARDEN, HARALD--[39]GERMAN/JUV
OSTEN, PETER--[39]GERMAN/JUV

GOSLING, NIGEL
BLAND, ALEXANDER--W/MAUDE LLOYD,[1][31]

GOSLING, PAULA
SKINNER, AINSLEE--[3][7][18][23]MYS/SF--
SECKER "MIND'S EYE" '80

GOSLING, VERONICA
HENRIQUES, VERONICA--[8]

GOSLING, WILLIAM FLOWER
FLEUR, WILLIAM--[8]

GOSNELL, ELIZABETH DUKE T
GOSNELL, BETTY--[31]

GOSSELIN, LOUIS LEON T.
LENOTRE, G.--[3]MYS--
COLLINS "THE WOMAN WITHOUT A NAME" '23
LENOTRE, GEORGES--[22]FRENCH

GOTHA, LESTER L.
LILIENTHAL, NORA--[2]

GOTT, KENNETH DAVIDSON
GOTT, K.D.--[31]
HOGBOTEL, SEBASTIAN--[31]

GOTTESFELD, EVELYN
GELLER, EVELYN--[31]

GOTTFRIED, THEODORE MARK
AUTEUR, HILLARY--[1][31]
BEHAN, LESLIE--[1][31]--
LAN 72-764 "MIDWAY AT MIDNIGHT" '64
LAN 72-930 "IN LOVE'S DARK CORNERS" '65
DOM 84700 "CIRCLE OF SIN" '65
FULLER, KATHLEEN--[9][21][26]ROM--
'RIVERVIEW' SERIES-4 NOVELS
GOTTFRIED, TED--[26]ROM--
"HOUSE OF DIAMOND"
"DAUGHTER OF DIAMOND"
GREGORY, HARRY--[3][9][31]MYS--
"MAN FROM MOTHER" '67
MARCO, LOU--[1]
MARK, TED--V. BERCH-"SPIES AND SIGHS", BAE 21,[1][9]ADULT/MYS--
LAN 72-918 "MAN FROM O.R.G.Y." '65
LAN 72-958 "9 MONTH CAPER" '65
LAN 72-989 "NUDE WHO NEVER" '65
LAN 72-996 "REAL GONE GIRLS" '66
LAN 73-446 "GIRL FROM PUSSYCAT" '66
LAN 73-461 "PUSSYCAT, PUSSYCAT!" '66
LAN 73-477 "DR. NYET" '66
LAN 73-485 "MY SON, THE DOUBLE AGENT" '66
LAN 73-508 "A HARD DAY'S KNIGHT" '66
LAN 73-515 "TED MARK READER" '66
LAN 73-527 "UNHATCHED EGGHEAD" '66
LAN 73-546 "NUDE WORE BLACK" '67 & MORE
ST. JAMES, BLAKELY--[1]HP--
BERK
SUMMERS, DIANA--V. BERCH LTR TO LOVISI '93,HP--
"DRUMS OF DESIRE"
THEODORE, BROTHER--W/MARVIN KAYE,[7]HOR--
PINN "BROTHER THEODORE'S CHAMBER OF HORRORS" '75
TOBIAS, KATHERINE--[3][9][21][26]MYS--
LAN 73-536 "LADY IN THE LIGHTNING" '66
LAN "SLAVE OF PASSION"

GOTTLIEB, ARTHUR
JOSEPHS, ARTHUR--[31]

GOTTLIEB, ELAINE
HEMLEY, ELAINE GOTTLIEB--[31]

GOTTLIEBSEN, RALPH JOSEPH
SCOTT, O.R.--[1]

GOTTSCHALK, LAURA RIDING
RIDING, LAURA--[8]

GOTTSHALL, FRANKLIN HEN.
BORNEMAN, H.--[31]

GOTZ, GERD
WERNER, KATHARINA--[39]GERMAN/MYS/JUV

GOUD, ANNE
ANNE-MARIEL--[31][34]MYS--
PINN "MURDER IN VENICE" '74
PINN "TIGRESS OF THE EVENING" '76 & MORE
KARINA--[1][31]

GOUDGE, EILEEN
WOODRUFF, MARIAN--[21]ROM--
"THIS MUST BE MAGIC"
"FORBIDDEN LOVE" & MORE

GOUDISS, MARIA A. D'ELIA
D'ELIA, MARIA--[1]
HARDING, MARIA--[1][31]

GOUGH, CATHERINE
MULGAN, CATHERINE--[33]

GOUGH, WILLIAM JOHN
GOUGH, BILL--[31]

GOULART, FRANCES S.
JOHNSON, C.F.--[1][31]
LENNON, HELEN M.--[1][31]
STEFFAN, SIOBHAN R.--[1]

GOULART, RONALD JOSEPH
CALHOUN, CHAD--GOULART/HAWK INTRVW '94,
[23][31]WEST,HP--
DELL 03727 "HIDDEN PRINCESS" '82
DELL 09732 "WILD DANCER" '82
DELL "MOUNTAIN QUEEN" '82
DELL "LADY RUSTLER" '82
DIXON, FRANKLIN W.--[27], HP--
POCK 'HARDY BOYS':
"DIASTER FOR HIRE' '89
"DEADLIEST DARE" '89
"CASTLE FEAR" '90
EDWARDS, R.T.--W/ED HOCH, GOULART INTRVW '94,
[23][34]MYS--
"PRIZE MEETS MURDER" '84
FALK, LEE--GOULART INTRVW '94,
[2][3][4]GHOSTED--AS 'FRANK SHAWN'
GOULART, RON--[8][31]--
SEVERAL GENRE
JAMIESON, IAN R.--GOULART INTRW '94,
[23]GHOSTED--
MYS PRESS "TRIPLE '0' SEVEN" '90
KAINS, JOSEPHINE--GOULART/HAWK INTRVW '94,
[2][7][11][18][23][34]MYS/SF--
ZEBRA "DEVIL MASK MYS" '78
ZEBRA "GREEN LAMA MYS" '79
ZEBRA "LAUGHING DRAGON MYS" '80
ZEBRA "CURSE OF THE GOLDEN SKULL" '78
ZEBRA "WHISPERING CAT MYS" '79
ZEBRA "WITCH'S TOWER MYS" '79
KEARNY, JILLIAN--GOULART/HAWK INTRVW '94,
[2][9]ROM--
WARNER "AGENT OF LOVE"
"LOVE'S CLAIMANT"
LEE, HOWARD--GOULART/HAWK INTRVW '94,
[18][23]MYS,HP--
'KUNG FU' TV
WARNER "SUPERSTITION"
WARNER "CHAINS"
MASTERS, ZEKE--GOULART/HAWK INTRVW '94,
[23]WEST,HP--
"HIGH CARD"
"LOADED DICE"
"TEXAS TWO-STEP"
"CASHING IN"

GOULART, RONALD JOSEPH [CONT]
ROBESON, KENNETH--GOULART/HAWK INTRVW '94,
[2][4][7][18][34]MYS,HP--
AVENGER SERIES #25-36
WARNER "MAN FROM ATLANTIS" '74
WARNER "RED MOON" '74
WARNER "PURPLE ZOMBIE" '74
WARNER "DR. TIME" '74
WARNER "NIGHTWITCH DEVIL" '74
WARNER "BLACK CHARIOTS" '74
WARNER "CARTOON CRIMES" '74
WARNER "DEATH MACHINE" '75
WARNER "BLOOD COUNTESS" '75
WARNER "GLASS MAN" '75
WARNER "IRON SKULL" '75
WARNER "DEMON ISLAND" '75
SHATNER, WILLIAM--GHOSTED PER GRAEME ANDREWS
ACE "TEKWAR" '89
ACE "TEKLORDS" '91
ACE "TEKLAB" '91
ACE "TEK VENGEANCE" '93
ACE "TEK SECRET" '93
ACE "TEK JUSTICE" '93
SHAWN, FRANK S.--GOULART/HAWK INTRVW '94,
[2][4]GHOSTED--
6 AVON 'PHANTOM' NOVELS:
'LEE FALK ON COVER'
AV "GOLDEN CIRCLE" '73
AV "MYSTERY OF THE SEAHORSE" '73
AV "VEILED LADY" '73
AV "GOGGLE-EYED PIRATES" '74
AV "HYDRA MONSTER" '74
AV "SWAMP RATS" '74
SILVA, JOSEPH--W/LEIN WEIN & MARV
WOLFMAN-INTRVW,[7]SF--
POCK "STALKER FROM THE STARS" '78
SILVA, JOSEPH--GOULART/HAWK INTRVW '94,
[2][4][7][23]SF--
POCK "HOLOCAUST FOR HIRE" '79
ACE "ISLAND OF DR. MOREAU" '77
STEFFANSON, CON--GOULART INTRVW '94,HP--
AVON 'FLASH GORDON' #1-3:
'ALEX RAYMOND' ON COVER: 4 TITLES
AV "LION MEN OF MONGO" '74
AV "PLAGUE OF SOUND" '74
AV "SPACE CIRCUS" '74
AV "TIME TRAP OF MING XIII" '74
3 'LAVERN & SHIRLEY'
WARNER "TEAMWORK" '76
WARNER "EASY MONEY" '76
WARNER "GOLD RUSH" '76

GOULD, ALAN
BANKS, MICHAEL A.--[7]SF--
"UNDERSTANDING SF" '82

GOULD, ALLAN MENDELL
D'EAU, JEAN--[31]
DEEP CHIN--[31]

GOULD, LOIS
BENJAMIN, LOIS--[31]

GOULDEN, JOSEPH C. [JR.]
BECKET, HENRY S.A.--[31]

GOULSON, CARLYN FLOYD
GOULSON, CARY F.--[31]--
"SEVENTEENTH CENTURY CANADA:
SOURCE STUDIES" '70

GOURDAN, ALAIN ANDRE
CHEVENY, JULIEN--[1]

GOVAN, [MARY] C.N.
ALLERTON, MARY--[3][31][33]MYS--
BOBBS "SHADOW & THE WEB" '40

GOVAN, [MARY] C.N. [CONT]
DARBY, J.N.--[3][22][31][33]MYS--
BOBBS "MURDER IN THE HOUSE WITH THE BLUE EYES" '39
MORTON, PATIENCE--[1]

GOVINDA, ANAGARIKA B.
GOVINDA, LAMA ANAGARIKA--[31]

GOW, KARYN WITMER
KARY, EILZABETH [N]--[9][21][26][34]MYS/ROM--
JOVE "MIDNIGHT LACE" '90
"LET NO MAN DIVIDE" & 2 MORE

GOWER, IRIS
DAVIES, IRIS--[9][21]ROM--
"A DAY IN SEPTEMBER"

GOWING, SIDNEY [FLOYD]
GOODWIN, DAVID--[34]MYS--
AMALG "BLACK MASK" '10
AMALG "SEALED ORDERS" '14
AMALG "DICK O' THE HIGHWAY" '14
GOODWIN, JOHN--[3][22][29]MYS--
HODDER "MAFALDA" '25
PUTNAM "THE AVENGER" '26 & MORE
TREGALLIS, JOHN--[34]MYS--
11 AMALG NOVELS '09-15

GOY, PHILLIPE
GOY, PHILIP--[2]

GOYAU, GEORGES
GREGOIRE, LEON--[22]FRENCH

GOYDER, MARGOT
NEVILLE, MARGOT--W/ANNE N.G. JOSKE, [18][22][34][36]MYS--22 MYS NVLS '43-66

GOYNE, RICHARD
BLAIR, DAVID--[1]
COURAGE, JOHN--[1][3][22]MYS--
PAUL "DREAD CAVE" '52
PAUL "A CORPSE FOR CHARLIE" '57 & MORE
RENIN, PAUL--JEAN F. LE DEIST-BAE 18, J. PRESSMAN-ARCH CKLST,[34]MYS--
HARB "BOHEMIA" '48
HARB "VAMPED" '48
HARB "KISS OF SHAME" '48
HARB "FOOLISH WOMAN" '48
HARB "SACRIFICE" '48 & 15 MORE
ARCH "FLAME" '51
ARCH "SEX" '51
ARCH "A FORTNIGHT'S FOLLY" '52
ARCH "MIDNIGHT" '52
ARCH "THE CORRESPONDENT" '52
ARCH "LIFE" '52
ARCH "LONELY WIVES" '52
ARCH "LADY OF LEICESTER SQUARE" '52
ARCH "MARRIAGE IS DIFFERENT" '52
ARCH "LOVE"
ARCH "GLAMOUR"
ARCH "WEEK-END WIVES"
ARCH "MARK AMERY'S MISTRESS" ALL '52
ARCH "DECEPTION"
ARCH "DISHONORED"
ARCH "INTRIGUE"
ARCH "LOVE GAME" ALL '52
ARCH "UNEASY VIRTUE" '52
GRAY "DOROTHY JORDAN, THE SIREN OF OLD DRURY" '53
ARCH "AT DAWN" '53
ARCH "BRUTE" '53
ARCH "CARNIOVAL KISSES" '53
ARCH "THE RETURN"
ARCH "TWO A.M."
ARCH "WOMEN I HAVE LOVED"

GOYNE, RICHARD [CONT]
RENIN, PAUL [CONT]
ARCH "WEDDING NIGHT" ALL '53
ARCH "BAIT" '53
ARCH "EAST & WEST" '53
ARCH "DANGEROUS MOMENTS" '54
ARCH "SEVENTH NIGHT" '54
STANDISH, RICHARD--[1]

GOYTORTUA, JESUS
FIDEL--[30]MEXICAN
VARDEL, CLAUDIO--[30]MEXICAN

GRAAS, FRITZ
PIMM, FRITZ--[39]GERMAN

GRABER, GEORGE ALEXANDER
CORDELL, ALEXANDER--[2][31][33][34]WELSH-ENGLISH/MYS--
GOLZ "BRIGHT CANTONESE" '67
HODDER "IF YOU BELIEVE IN THE SOLDIERS" '73
HODDER "TO SLAY THE DREAMER" '80

GRABOWSKI, Z. ANTHONY
HEYST, AXEL--[22][31]POLISH

GRACE, ANITA
FRANCIS, JEAN--[11]
PRITCHETT, ARIADNE--[40]MYS--
"GHOSTS OF KINGS" '72 & 2 OTHERS
ST. JOHN, GAIL--[3]MYS--
DELL "DUNSAN HOUSE" '69

GRACE, LAURA
MCCANN, HEATHER--[26]ROM/MYS--
"MASTER DETECTIVE"
"WHISPERS IN THE DARK"

GRACE, MARIAN
GRAE, CAMARIN--V. BERCH LTR TO HUBIN '94/MYS--
BLAZON "WINGED DANCER" '83
NAIAD "SECRET IN THE BIRD" '88
NAIAD "SLICK" '90

GRADY, JAMES [THOMAS]
SHELBY, BRIT--[31][34]MYS--
PUTNAM "GREAT PEBBLE AFFAIR" '76

GRADY, RONAN CALISTUS
MURPHY, JOHN--[3]MYS--
MacM "GUNRUNNERS" '66
SCRIBN "EL GRECO PUZZLE" '74

GRAE, IDA
DEAN, IDA--[31]

GRAEF, MARIANNE
SCHEEL, MARIANNE--[39]GERMAN/JUV

GRAF, JOHANN
GEBHARDT, HANS--[39]GERMAN
ROSNER, HANS--[39]GERMAN

GRAFFAM, ELSIE ANN
GARDNER, ELSIE ANN--LACHMAN LIST MAY '93/MYS--

GRAHAM, ALEXANDER STEEL
GRAHAM, A.S.--[31]

GRAHAM, CHARLES ROSS
MONTROSE, DAVID--[8][34]MYS--
COLLINS "CRIME ON COTE DES NEIGES" '51
COLLINS "MURDER OVER NORVAL" '52
HARL "BODY ON MT. ROYAL" '53
HALE "GAMBLING WITH FIRE" '69

GRAHAM, DALE
LEGRAEME, D.A.--[2][11]

GRAHAM, DONALD R.
GRAHAM, DON--[31]

GRAHAM, DR. JOAN
MEDICA--[8]

GRAHAM, EILEEN WILMOT
LAMOUR, ANDRE--PPCC#5, P58, HP--
CURZON "REQUEST FOR PASSION" '48
CURZON "TEMPTATION FOR EVE" '48
WILMOT, EILEEN--S. HOLLAND-SCION CKLST, PP 27, PPCC#3,[27][34]MYS--
BW "NOT A NICE MURDER" '49
MW "DESIGN FOR LIVING" '49
MW "WOMAN BETRAYED" '49
PROG "MURDER INSOLUBLE" '50

GRAHAM, ELIZABETH
PARRISH, LAURA--[21]ROM--
"LOVE'S GENTLE SEASON"
"LOVE'S QUIET CORNER"

GRAHAM, HARRY
STREAMER, COL. D.--[8]

GRAHAM, JAMES MAXTONE
ANSTRUTHER, JAMES--[8]

GRAHAM, JOYCE MAXTONE
STRUTHER, JAN--[2][22]ENGLISH

GRAHAM, LAWRENCE OTIS
GRAHAM, LARRY--[31][33]

GRAHAM, LLOYD M.
KRYPTON--[31]

GRAHAM, MAUDE FITZGERALD
GRAHAM, SUSAN--[8]

GRAHAM, PETER
BRANDON, CARL--[11]FP

GRAHAM, ROGER P.
AMES, CLINTON--[2][11][23][31]
AMES, DREW--[2]
ARNET[TE], ROBERT--[2][23][32]MYS/SF--
MSMM "THE TIGER'S TAIL" DEC '60
BAHL, FRANKLIN--[2][11][23]SF
BLADE, ALEXANDER--[1][2][11][23]SF,HP--ZIFF-DAVIS
BROWNING, CRAIG--[2][11][23]
CONRAD, GREGG--[2][23]SF
COSTELLA, P.F. --[2][11][23]SF,HP--
"SECRET OF THE FLAMING RING" '51
ZIFF-DAVIS "SPACE IS FOR SUCKERS" '58
KUMARA, SANANDANA--[1][2]
LEE, CHARLES--[1][2][11]
MANN, CHARLES--[1][2][11]
MANN, MILTON--[1][2]
MCGOWAN, D.C.--[2]
MCGOWAN, INEZ--[1][2][11][23]SF
PHILLIPS, ROG--[2][23][32]MYS--
KE "A CASE OF HOMOCIDE" JUN '60
AHMM "EGG HEAD" AUG '61
MSMM "GOOD SOUND THERAPHY" AUG '62
ROGERS, MELVA--[1][2][11][23]SF
RUPPERT, CHESTER--[1][2][11][23]SF
SAWTELLE, WILLIAM CARTER--[1][2][11][23]SF,HP--AMAZING
STEBER, A.R.--[1][2][11][23]SF,HP--ZIFF-DAVIS
VANCE, GERALD--[1][2][11][23]SF,HP--ZIFF-DAVIS
WILEY, JOHN--[1][2][11][23]SF,HP
WORTH, PETER--[1][2][11][23]SF,HP--

GRAHAM, SUSAN
SUSAN--[22]NEW ZEALAND

GRAHAM, WILLIAM FRANKLIN
GRAHAM, BILLY--[31]

GRAHAM, WILLIAM SYDNEY
GRAHAM, W.S.--[31]

GRAHAM-BARBER, LYNDA
BARBER, LINDA--[1][31][33]
BARBER, LYNDA GRAHAM--[31]

GRAHAM-CAMERON, MALCOLM
GRAHAM-CAMERON, M.--[31][33]
GRAHAM-CAMERON, MIKE--[1][31][33]

GRAINGER, ANTHONY JOHN
GRAINGER, A.J.--[31]

GRAINGER, FRANCIS EDWARD
HILL, HEADON--[2][4][5][22][34]MYS--
WARD "THE AVENGERS" '06
WARD "BROKEN SEAL" '17 & MORE

GRAINGER, JOHN HERBERT
GRAINGER, J.H.--[31]

GRAINGER, PETER
CARTUR, PETER--[2]
DANCEY, MAX--[2]
YOUNG, ROGER FLINT--[2]

GRAINGER, STEPHNEE KAY
OWEN, J. BRADLEY--V. BERCH LTR TO HUBIN '94/MYS--
LEIS "DEAD SEASON" '88

GRAMS, BORIS
GLAGLA--[39]GERMAN

GRAN, OYULV
BAGGE, BRYNJULF--[29]MYS
GRUNDT, OIVIND--[29]MYS
WINGE, STEIN--[29]MYS--
ALIBI MAG 39 "DEN OKANDE UTPRESSAREN" '47

GRANAHL, TAMARA
WHITFIELD, ISABEL--[26]ROM--
"BODIE BRIDE"
"SILVER FURY"

GRANATH, PER JOHAN W.
HANSSON, HANS--[29]MYS--
"STOCKHOLMMYSTERIER" 1895
"OCTARENS" 1897
"AFTERFUNNEN" 1897

GRANATSTEIN, JACK LAWR.
GRANATSTEIN, J.L.--[31]

GRANBECK, MARILYN
CARTER, NICK--[1][3]MYS,HP--
AWARD "ASSIGNMENT:INTERCEPT" '76
GRANT, BEN--[3][31]MYS--
MERIT "HITCHHIKE TO HELL" '63
MAJOR "ALICE DIES TWICE" '75 & MORE
HAMILTON, ADAM--W/ARTHUR MOORE,[1][3]MYS--
BERK "XANDAR" '74
BERK "WYSS PURSUIT" '75
HENDERSON, M.R.--[3][31]MYS--
DBLDY "IF I SHOULD DIE" '85
DBLDY "BY REASON OF" '86
ST. MARTINS "THE KILLING GAME" '89
HOYT, DON--W/ARTHUR MOORE,[34]MYS--
POWELL 1009N "DEATH IS A DRAG" '70

GRANBECK, MARILYN [CONT]
LAURIE, JESSICA--[34]MYS--
ZEBRA "MISTRESS OF HARROWGATE" '81
MOORE, CLAYTON--[1][3]MYS--
BERK "THE CORRUPTERS" '74
BERK "END OF RECKONING" '74
MORGAN, ALLAN--[34]MYS,HP--
AWARD "BLOOD" '74
SAXON, VAN--W/ARTHUR MOORE,[1][3]MYS--
ZEBRA "HOLLYWOOD HIT MAN" '75

GRANBERG, WILBUR JOHN
GRANBERG, W.J.--[31]

GRAND, NATALIE
HART, SUSANNAH--[9][21][26]ROM--
"NOBODY'S BABY"
"A LEGEND IN HIS OWN TIME"

GRANDET, IRENE
ANATOLE, RAY--W/JOE WEISS, SMUT PEDDLER #2--
TOGA "THE BIG DEAL"
ELITE "DANCING IN THE DARK"

GRANDT, GUIDO
BLACK, DESMOND--[39]GERMAN/HOR,HP
SHADOW, MIKE--[39]GERMAN/HOR,HP

GRANDT, MICHAEL
BLACK, DESMOND--[39]GERMAN/HOR,HP

GRANFELT, TAIVO
LAEVASTU, TAIVO--[1]

GRANGE, CYRIL
ONLOOKER--[1][22]ENGLISH
QUILL--[1][22]ENGLISH

GRANGER, BILL
GASH, JOE--[3][18][29]MYS--
HOLT "PRIESTLY MURDERS" '84
HOLT "NEWSPAPER MURDERS" '85
GRIFFITH, BILL--[3][18][29][31]MYS--
RANDOM "TIME FOR FRANKIE COOLIN" '82

GRANGER, GEORGE A.
GRANGER, GEORGIA--[9][26]ROM--
'MKNG OF AMERICA' SERIES:
"WILD & THE WAYWARD"
JARRETT, AMANDA JEAN--[21]ROM,HP--
DELL 'SOUTHERNER' SERIES:
"WHERE MY LOVE LIES DREAMING"
SCOFIELD, JONATHAN--[21]ROM,HP--
DELL 'FREED FTR' SERIES:
"MUSKETS OF '76"
WILLOUGHBY, LEE DAVIS--[21]ROM,HP--
DELL 'MKNG OF AMER' SERIES:
"WILD & THE WAYWARD"

GRANGER, MARGARET JANE
GRANGER, PEGGY--[31][33]

GRANICH, IRVING
GOLD, MICHAEL--[8][31]

GRANIT, ARTHUR
GREENBERG, ARTHUR--[31]

GRANT, CHARLES L.
ANDREWS, FELICIA--HAWK/GRANT INTRVW '93,
[7][9][21][26]ROM--
"RIVERWITCH"
"MOUNTANWITCH"
"MOONWITCH"
"RIVERRUN"
"SILVER HUNTRESS"

GRANT, CHARLES L. [CONT]
ANDREWS, FELICIA [CONT]
"THE VELVET TART"
"SEACLIFF"
BOGGS, TIMOTHY--HAWK/GRANT INTRVW '93--
"LANCELOT & BLANCHE" SERIAL IN
HAGGIS NEWS LTR.
CHARLES, STEVEN--[7][23]SF--
'PRIVATE SCHOOL' SERIES
CROIX-ROUGE--[1]
FENN, LIONEL--HAWK/GRANT INTRVW '93, SF--
'KENT MONTANA' SERIES
'QUEST FOR THE WHITE DUCK' SERIES
GRANT, C.L.--G. COOK,[34]HOR--
FSF "WHITE WOLF CALLING" APR '75
BERK "SHADOW OF ALPHA" '76
LAKE, SIMON--HAWK/GRANT INTRVW '93,
WAR/SUSPENSE--
LEWIS, DEBORAH--HAWK/GRANT INTRVW '93,
[3][9][21]MYS/ROM--
ZEBRA "LADY IN THE TAPESTRY" '77
ZEBRA "EVE OF THE HOUND" '77
ZEBRA "VOICES OUT OF TIME" '77
ZEBRA "KIRKWOOD FIRES" '78
ZEBRA "WIND AT WINTER'S END" '79
MARSH, GEOFFREY--HAWK/GRANT INTRVW '93,
[7][23]SF--
TOR 'LINCOLN BALCKTHORNE' SERIES-4BKS
RED CROSS--[1]

GRANT, DONALD
NESS, K.T.--W/WILLIAM WILSON,[8]

GRANT, DONNA
JOYCE, MARIE--W/VIRGINIA DEBERRY,[21][26]ROM--
"EXPOSURES"

GRANT, GERTRUDE
GRANT, GERALD--[1]

GRANT, HILDA KAY
GRANT, HILDA--[9]CANADIAN/ROM
GRANT, KAY--[9]CANADIAN/ROM
HILLIARD, JAN--[3][9][22]CANADIAN/MYS--
ABELARD "MORGAN'S CASTLE" '64

GRANT, JAMES MILLER
BALFOUR, GRANT--[8]

GRANT, JAMES TIMOTHY
GRANT, MAXWELL--[1]HP--

GRANT, JOAN & TRACY
MALCOLM, ANTHEA--[9][21][26]ROM--
"COUNTERFEIT MARCH"
"WIDOW'S GAMBIT" & MORE

GRANT, JOCELYN
HUXLEY, ELSPETH--L. ROBBINS LTR '94,[32]MYS--
JCM "DEMON WITH THE LONG
FINGER-NAIL" OCT '60

GRANT, JOHN
GASH, JONATHAN--[1][3][18]MYS--
COLLINS "FIREFLY GADROON" '82
"JADE WOMAN" '88 & MORE '77-91
GAUNT, GRAHAM--[3][18]MYS--
PLAY "TERMINUS" '76
COLLINS "THE INCOMER" '81

GRANT, JOHN BARNARD
GRANT, J.B.--[31]
GRANT, JACK--[31]

GRANT, KATHRYN ANN PTACEK
ATWOOD, KATHRYN--[9][21][26]ROM--
"AURORA"
"SATANS ANGELS" & 3 MORE
GRANT, KATHRYN--[7]--
ACE "LAND OF TEN THOUSAND WILLOWS
#1 THRU #3"
MAYFIELD, ANNE--[9][21][26]ROM--
"WAYWARD WIDOW"
MAXWELL, KATHLEEN--[9][21][26]ROM--
"WINTER MASQUERADE"
"THE DEVIL'S HEART"
PTACEK, KATHY--HAWK/GRANT INTRVW FEB '93-
MAIDEN NAME
SIMON, LES--[7]PENG ENCYCLOPEDIA OF HORROR
& SUPERNATURAL '86--
NAL "GILA" '81

GRANT, LADY SYBIL
SCOT, NEIL--[8]

GRANT, LOUIS THEODORE
GOLDBERG, LOUIS--[31]

GRANT, M.H.
LINESMAN--[8]
SCOLOPAX--[8]

GRANT, MAJOR A.F.
STAFFORD, JOHN K.--[34]MYS,HP--
MAGNET #443 "DEATH DEMON: OR,
A CRY FOR HELP" '06
STARK, INSPECTOR--[34]MYS,HP--
NEW MAGNET #467 "HAND IN RED: OR,
THE RAJA'S DIAMOND" '06

GRANT, MAUDE MARGARET
FRASER, ELIZABETH--[1]
PATTERSON, MARGARET--[1]
STANLEY, ALIXIE RUSSELL--[1]

GRANT, NEIL
MOUNTFIELD, DAVID--[1][33]

GRANT, NEILS JR.
NORTH, GENE JR.--[14]--
OLYM OPH#210 "QUIVERING ROSE" '70

GRANT, ROB
NAYLOR, GRANT--W/DOUG NAYLOR,[7][23]SF--
"RED DWARF #1 & #2" '89/90

GRANT, ROBERT
J.S. OF DALE--[23]SF--
"THE KING'S MEN: A TALE OF TOMORROW" '84

GRANT, STEVEN
APPLETON, VICTOR--[7][23]SF,HP--
STSY 'TOM SWIFT':
"CYBORG KICKBOXER"

GRANT, WATSON
LOVEGOOD, JOHN--[13]AUSTRALIAN

GRANT, WILLIAM
ONLOOKER--[8]

GRANVILLE-BARKER, HARLEY
BARKER, GRANVILLE--[2][31]
BARKER, HARLEY GRANVILLE--[31]

GRASDORF, REGINALD
PURDELL, REGINALD--[1]

GRASMUCK, JURGEN
BOWLES, ALBERT C.--[39]GERMAN/MYS/SF/WEST
FLOORMAN, BERT--[39]GERMAN/MYS/SF/WEST,HP
GARRETT, J.A.--[39]GERMAN/MYS/SF/WEST
GORMAN, J.A.--[39]GERMAN/MYS/SF/WEST
GRAMS, JAY--[39]GERMAN/MYS/SF/WEST
GRASSE, JURGEN--[39]GERMAN/MYS/SF/WEST
HAMMON, JEFF--[39]GERMAN/MYS/SF/WEST
KELLY, RON--[39]GERMAN/MYS/SF/WEST
MURAT, ROLF--[39]GERMAN/MYS/SF/WEST,HP
SHOCKER, DAN--[39][40]GERMAN/MYS,HP
TODD, OWEN L.--[39]GERMAN/MYS/SF/WEST

GRATIANT, GILBERT
NOUS-TERRE, JEAN--[1]
NOUS-TOUS, JEAN--[1]

GRAUTHOFF, FERDINAND H.
PARABELLUM--[2][11][23][39]GERMAN/SF
SEESTUM--[2][23][39]GERMAN/SF

GRAVELEY, G.C.
GRAYSON, DAPHNE--[8]

GRAVERSON, PAT
GRAVES, TRICIA--[1][31]

GRAVES, CHARLES PARLIN
PARLIN, JOHN--[22][31][33]AMERICAN--
"PATRIOT'S DAYS" '64

GRAVES, CLOTILDE INEZ M.
DEHAN, RICHARD--[2][8][22][34]MYS--
BUW "MAN WITH A MASK" '31

GRAVES, ROBERT VAN RANKE
BOYLE, PAUL--[1]
DOYLE, JOHN--[1][8][31]--
HOGARTH "THE MARMOSITES MISCELLANY" '25
RICH, BARBARA--W/LAURA REICHENTHAL &
SUSAN GRAVES,[2][23][31]--
"NO DECENCY LEFT" '32

GRAVES, SUSAN
BERNARD, MARLEY--[1]
RICH, BARBARA--W/LAURA REICHENTHAL &
ROBERT VAN RANKE,[1]--
"NO DECENCY LEFT" '32

GRAWOIG, SHEILA
RAESCHILD, SHEILA--[31]

GRAY, ARTHUR
INGULPHUS--[1][2]

GRAY, CLARK
COLE, JACKSON--A. TONIK-COLE CKLST
"SPICY ARMADILLO" WEST,HP--
TEX RGR "LOBO COLONEL" 'JAN '52
TEX RGR "WARPATH" 'JUNE '52

GRAY, CLEMENT
DAYBREAK--[8]

GRAY, DOROTHY KATE
HAYNES, DOROTHY KATE--[1]
HAYNES, DOROTHY K.--[8]

GRAY, ELIZABETH JANET
VINING, ELIZABETH GRAY--[33]

GRAY, GENEVIEVE S.
GRAY, JENNY--[31][33]

GRAY, GEORGE HUGH
GRAY, TONY--[1][22][31]IRISH-ENGLISH

GRAY, JOHN RICHARD
GRAY, J. RICHARD--[31]

GRAY, K.E.
GRANT, EVE--[8]

GRAY, LINDA CROCKETT
CROCKETT, CHRISTINA--[9][21][26][31]ROM--
"SONG OF A SEABIRD"
"MOMENT OF MAGIC" & MORE
CROCKETT, LINDA--[7]SF--
TOR "SANDMAN" '90

GRAY, LINDSAY RUSSELL N.
LEMON, GREY--[8]

GRAY, LORI
GRAY, MARCY--[9][21][26]ROM--
"SO EASY TO LOVR"
"BE MY WIFE"

GRAY, PATRICIA [CLARK]
CLARK, VIRGINIA--[1][31][33]
GRAY, PATSEY--[1][31][33]
POGO--[2]

GRAY, R.E.
GRAYLING, RONALD--[1]

GRAY, SIMON [J.H.]
HOLLIDAY, JAMES--[1][34]
READE, HAMISH--[1][3]MYS--
FABER "A COMEBACK FOR STARK" '68

GRAY, TERENCE J.S.
WEI WU WEI--[8]

GRAY, VIRGINIA
GRAY, GINNA--[9][21]/JEAN F. LE DEIST
LTR '93, ROM--
"IMAGES"
"WHERE ANGELS FEAR" & MORE

GRAY, WILLIAM BITTLE
GRAY, CAPTAIN BILL--[31]

GRAYBEAL, KATHRYN
GRAY, KERRIE--[21][26]ROM--
"LOVE IS A GYPSY"

GRAYDON, ROBERT MURRAY
GRAY, DON--[1]
GRAYDON, MARK--[1]
GWYN, EVANS--W/G.A. EVANS, G.H. TEED
& G.N. PHILIPS,[34]MYS--
WRIGHT "MURDERERS MET" '34
HAMILTON, MURRAY--W/GEORGE HEBER TEED,[1]
MURRAY, ROBERT--[1]
O'FLYNN, JIMMY--[1]
ROBERTS, MURRAY--[1][11]

GRAYDON, WILLIAM MURRAY
ARMITAGE, ALFRED--[1][34]MYS--
AMALG "THE TRAPPER'S SECRET" '36
GORDON, WILLIAM MURRAY--[1]
MURRAY, WILLIAM--[1]
OLLIVER, TOM--[1]

GRAYLAND, VALERIE MERLE
BELVEDERE, LEE--[3][21][26][33]MYS/ROM--
"DELL MEET A DARK STRANGER" '73
SPANNER, VALERIE--[8]
SUBOND, VALERIE--[3][21][26][33]--
BEAGLE "HEIGHTS OF HAVENREST" '72
BEAGLE "HOME OVER HELL VALLEY" '74

GRAYLORD, OTIS
DAWSON, PETER--[28]WEST, GHOSTED--
"THE SAVAGES" '59
"YANCEY" '60
"THE TEXAS SLICKS" '61
"THE HALF-BREED" '62
"BLOODY GOLD" '63
"SHOWDOWN" '64
"A PRIDE OF MEN" '66

GRAYSON, ALBERT VICTOR
ETHEL--[8]

GRAZIA, THERESA
ALDERTON, THERESA--[9][21][26]ROM--
"AN EASTER BOUQUET"
"CRIMSON DECEPTION"
"SECOND SEASON"
SINCLAIR, ALBERTA--[9][21][26]ROM--
"A HINT OF SCANDAL"
"COUSIN NANCY"

GRBICH, RONALD IVAN
WINGATE, WILLIAM --[3][40]MYS--
HUTCH "FIREPLAY" '77
HUTCH "BLOODBATH" '78
ST. MARTIN'S "SHOTGUN" '80
ST. MARTIN'S "HARDACRE'S WAY" '80
ST. MARTIN'S "CRYSTAL" '83

GREALEY, THOMAS LOUIS
SOUTHWORTH, LOUIS--[32][34]MYS--
LM "BOOMERANG" MAR '65
HALE "FELON IN DISGUISE" '66
HALE "CORPSE ON LONDON BRIDGE" '69

GREAVES, MICHAEL
CALLUM, MICHAEL--[8]

GREBANIER, MRS. B.D.N.
WINWAR, FRANCES--[2]

GREBENSCHIKOV, GEORGE V.
GREBENS, G.V.--[7]SF--
"IVAN EFREMOV'S THEORY OF SOVIET SF" '78

GREBER, JUDITH A.
ROBERTS, GILLIAN--HAWK/GREBER INTRVW '93,
[34]MYS--
SCRIBN "PHILLY STAKES" '89
SCRIBN "CAUGHT DEAD IN PHILADELPHIA" '90

GREE, ALAIN
FARGE, MONIQUE--[1][33]

GREEK, CARL GUSTAF L.
HELLEN, ANDERS--[29]MYS-- 5 NOVELS '51-77

GREEN, ALAN B. & GLADYS
BURNE, GLEN--[3][22][29][31]MYS--
DODD "MURDER TO MUSIC" '34

GREEN, ALAN [BAER]
ALAN, JACK--[1]
DENBIE, ROGER--W/JULIAN PAUL BRODIE,
[3][31]MYS--
MORROW "DEATH ON THE LIMITED" '33
& MORE

GREEN, ANITA JANE
BRYANT, ANITA--[31]

GREEN, BERNARD
GREEN, BENNY--[31]

GREEN, CHARLES
TAHNEY, C.G.--W. MURRAY-ECHOES #17, P24
BLACK MASK
TAWNY, T.V.--A. TONIK-ECHOES #8, P7
RYERSON JOHNSON CONFIRMED
WALLACE, ROBERT--[34]MYS,HP--
PHD "MASTER OF DEATH" MAR '38
PHD "MOVIE LOT MURDERS" MAY '38
PHD "YELLOW SHADOWS OF DEATH" JUL '38
PHD "MURDER AT THE CIRCUS" MAY '39
PHD "DEATH UNDER CONTRACT" AUG '39
PHD "YACHT CLUB MURDERS" JAN '39
PHD "CHAIN OF DEATH" MAR '39
PHD "MELODY MURDERS" SEPT '40

GREEN, CHARLES HENRY
SANDHURST, B.G.--[8]

GREEN, DEBORAH
ZOOK, DEBORAH--[1]

GREEN, DOROTHY [A]
AUCHTERLONIE, DOROTHY--[1][31]

GREEN, EDMUND FISK
FISKE, JOHN--[22]AMERICAN-
LEGALLY CHANGED IN 1855

GREEN, ELIZABETH SARA
TRESILIAN, LIZ--[1][31]-- 7 BOOKS '67-84

GREEN, FREDERICK LAWRENCE
GREEN, F.L.--[1]

GREEN, GRACE
REID, GRACE--[9][21][26]ROM--
"BLACK LACE"

GREEN, JAMES C.R.
GREEN, J.C.R.--[1][31]

GREEN, JEROME FREDERIC
GREEN, JERRY--[31]

GREEN, JULIAN [HARTRIDGE]
DE MAGRET, A.--W/JEAN LEGRIS, JEAN F.
LE DEIST LTR '93
DELAPORTE, THEOPHILE--[1][22][31],
FRENCH-AMERICAN
GREEN, JULIEN--[31]
IRELAND, DAVID--[1]

GREEN, KAY
DAVIS, HARLEY--[1][31]
GRANGER, GUY--[31]CHILDREN'S BOOKS--
"HUGGLEMUSH" ADVENTURES
KENT, KATIE--[31]CHILDREN'S BOOKS--
"HUGGLEMUSH" ADVENTURES
LANE, ROUMELIA--[1][31]
MAY, FLORISSA--[1]

GREEN, LALAGE ISOBEL
MARCH, HILARY--[8]
PULVERTAFT, LALAGE--[8]

GREEN, MADGE
DERBYSHIRE, JANE--[1]
HADDON, SARAH--[1]

GREEN, MYRA
PAPERNY, MYRA--JEAN F. LE DEIST LTR '93

GREEN, PETER MORRIS
DELANEY, DENIS--[3][22][31]ENGLISH/MYS--
GRYPHON "CAT IN GLOVES" '56

GREEN, RICHARD
RICHARDS, LESLIE--V. BERCH LTR
TO HUBIN '94,[1]MYS--
MANOR "PURSUE THE WIND" '75
ZEBRA "PALE GHOST AT GRAVESEND" '77
ZEBRA "LOVE'S DEADLY SILHOUETTE" '79

GREEN, ROGER
BRECKER, CORD--[35]AUSTRALIAN--
CLEVELAND
HOLLINGER, MATT--[35]AUSTRALIAN--
CLEVELAND
HOUSTON, BRAD--[35]AUSTRALIAN--
CLEVELAND
MCCABE, SUNDOWN--[35]AUSTRALIAN--
SANTE FE 421 "THE SCALPING PARTY"
ROGERS, LESLEY--[35]AUSTRALIAN--
CLEVELAND
SHELTON, COLE--[35]AUSTRALIAN--
BIG HORN 343 "HANGING TREE VALLEY"
CORONADA 978 "LAST STAGE TO DIABLO"
SIERRA 446 "FIVE BULLETS TO HELL"
CHISHOLM 681 "DIE HARD, DIE YOUNG"
CHISHOLM 682 "FOUR NOTCHES"
SANTE FE - 6 NOVELS
TAGGART, BEN--[35]AUSTRALIAN--
CLEVELAND

GREEN, ROLAND [JAMES]
CLEVE, JOHN--W/ANDREW J. OFFUTT,[7][23]SF,HP--
BERK "SPACEWAYS #15:STARSHIP SAPPHIRE" '84
HILD, JACK--[34]MYS,HP--
GE "SOB's": "BARRABUS HEIST" '89
GE "BARRABUS WAR" '89
LORD, JEFFREY --W. MURRAY-BLADE SERIES,
PP 1,[1][2][7]SF,HP--
PINN BKS #9-#29 & #31-#37

GREEN, SHEILA ELLEN
GREENWALD, SHEILA--[22][31][33]
AMERICAN--ILLUSTRATOR

GREEN, T.
RAMSEY, MICHAEL--[8]

GREEN, WILLIAM MARK
IDEN, WILLIAM--[1][31]

GREEN-PRICE, RICH DANSEY
BORDERER--[1]

GREEN-WANSTALL, KENNETH
WANSTALL, KEN--[1][22]ENGLISH

GREENAWAY, CATHERINE
GREENAWAY, KATE--[31]JUVENILE

GREENAWAY, GLADYS
MANNERS, JULIA--[1][31]

GREENBANK, ANTHONY HUNT
HUNT, NIGEL--[1][31][33]--
"PELHAM "ADVENTURES IN CANOEING" '64

GREENBERG, ARTHUR
GRANIT, ARTHUR--[1]

GREENBERG, GERALD
GREEN, GERALD--[1]

GREENBERG, IVAN
RAHV, PHILIP--[31]

GREENBERG, JACK
GREENHILL, JACK--[8]

GREENBERG, JAN
GREGORY, JILL--[1][9][21][26]ROM--
"FOREVER AFTER"
"LONE STAR LADY" & MORE
KARR, JILLIAN--W/KAREN A. KATZ,[26]ROM--
"SOMETHING BORROWED, SOMETHING BLUE"

GREENBERG, JOANNA E.G.
GREEN, HANNAH--[25][31][33]CHILDREN'S

GREENBERGER, INGRID E.
RAINER, GEORGE--[1]

GREENBILL, MARJORIE BARST
LATTA, MARGUERITE--[1]

GREENBLATT, IRA
GREEN, I.G.--[1][2][23]AMERICAN/SF--
"TIME BEYOND TIME" '71

GREENBLATT, MANUEL HARRY
GREENBLATT, M.H.--[31]

GREENE, ALVIN CARL
GREENE, A.C.--[31]
RANDOLPH, ARTHUR C.--[1]
WEAVER, MATEMAN--[1]

GREENE, CAROLYN
MONROE, CAROLYN--[26]ROM--
"A LOVING SPOONFUL"
"KISS OF BLISS"

GREENE, CHARLES JEROME
GREENE, JERRY--[31]

GREENE, JOHN WILLIAM JR.
GREENE, JOHNNY--[31]

GREENE, LOUIS MONTAGUE
GREENE, L. PATRICK--[1][34]NAME CHANGED TO
"L. PATRICK GREENE", MYS--
HAM "DEVIL'S KLOOF" '28 & MORE

GREENE, ROBERT BERNARD JR
GREENE, BOB--[31]

GREENE, ROBERT W.
ASHE, PENELOPE--W/BILLIE YOUNG,[1][31]

GREENE, SARA PRATT M.
MCLEAN, SALLY PRATT--[1]

GREENE, SIGRID
DE LIMA, SIGRID--[1]

GREENE, SIR HUGH
ELEIGH, SEBASTIAN--[8]

GREENE, SONIA HAFT DAVIS
DAVIS, SONIA--[7]SF
DAVIS, SONIA H.--[7]SF--
"THE PRIVATE LIFE OF H.P. LOVECRAFT" '85

GREENE, STEVEN
GREENE, L.L.--W/LARRY LEVINE, V. BERCH LTR
TO HUBIN '93/MYS--
SIGN "SLEEPING BEAUTY" '82
GREENE, STEVEN--W/JOHN [T]LUTZ, HAWK/LUTZ
INTERVIEW '93--
POPLB "EXILED" '82

GREENE, WARD
DUDLEY, FRANK--[1][3][22]MYS--
CAPE "RIDE THE NIGHTMARE" '30
HOUGHTON "HAVANA HOTEL MURDERS" '36
CARRICK "KING COBRA" '40

GREENER, WILLIAM OLIVER
GERRARE, WIRT--[2][3][7][22]MYS/SF--
HUTCH "RUFIN'S LEGACY" 1892
HUTCH "PHANTASMS" 1895

GREENFIELD, IRVING A.
CARLES, RIVA--[9][21][26]ROM--
"THRALL OF LOVE"
DUNCAN, BRUCE--[1][2][11][23]SF--
"MIRROR IMAGE" '68
FIELDS, VINCENT--V. BERCH LTR TO
HUBIN '94,MYS--
PPJKS "HAMMER STRIKE SOLUTION" '88
GERON, FRANK--V. BERCH LTR TO HUBIN '93/MYS--
ZEBRA "GENEVA TRANSFER" '83
ZEBRA "OPERATION ZIMMERMAN" '86
ZEBRA "THE BLOODING" '87
GRACE, ALICIA--[3][9][21][26]MYS/ROM--
LAN "HAWKSBILL MANOR" '67
LAN "ENCHANTED CIRCLE" '68 & MORE
GRACE, ANITA--[9][21][26]ROM--
ST. JOHN, GAIL--[9][21][26]ROM--
"DUNSAN HOUSE"
VERDE, CAMPO--[7][23]SF--
"SUCCUBUS" '77

GREENFIELD, JEROME
GREENFIELD, JERRY--[31]

GREENHALL, KEN[NETH R.]
HAMILTON, JESSICA--[7]SF--
ZEBRA "HELLHOUND" '77
POCK "CHILDGROVE" '82
POCK "THE COMPANION" '88
POCK "DEATHCHAIN" '91

GREENHAUS, THELMA NURENB.
NURENBERG, THELMA--[31][33]--
4 NOVELS '32-75

GREENHILL, ELIZABETH ANN
GIFFARD, ANN--[8]

GREENHOOD, [C] DAVID
SAWYER, MARK--[1][22]AMERICAN

GREENHOUGH, TERENCE
GREENHOUGH, TERRY--[7][23]--
NEL "TIME & TIMOTHY GRENVILLE" '75
NEL "THE WANDERING WORLDS" '76
NEL "THOUGHTWORLD" '77
NEL "ALIEN CONTACT" '80
LESTER, ANDREW--[1][7][23]SF--
"THE THRICE BORN" '76

GREENLAND, W. KINGSCOTE
KING, W. SCOTT--[1][3]MYS--
HODDER "BEHIND THE GRANITE GATEWAY" '02
EPWORTH "HIDDEN PATHS" '20

GREENMAN, NANCY A.
ELLIOT, LUCY--[9][21][26]ROM--
"PRIVATE PARADISE"
"SUMMER'S PROMISE" & MORE

GREENOP, FRANK S.
BEAUMONT, JESS--[35]AUSTRALIAN--
BIG HORN 324 "GUN PROUD"
CLEVE 875 "THE MIGHTY FALL"
CLEVELAND 881 "CORDITE COURAGE"

GREENOP, FRANK S. [CONT]
DUDGEON, ROBERT--[35]AUSTRALIAN--
CLEVE NVLT "SUICIDE ST." '50s
COUGAR 112 "WAKE UP & DIE"
AM DET NVL 101 "DISAPPEARING GIRL"
106 "SHADOW OF A NOOSE"
AMERICAN DETEC NOVEL 104 "DON'T BLAME THE GIRL"
13 CLEVELAND BKS
PB 506 "HUNTED DOWN"
7 'MAX STRONG' NOVELS
DUNDEE, WALT--[35]AUSTRALIAN--
BIG HORN 323 "ROPE FEVER"
SIERRA 435 "WANTED BRAND"
MARTIN, HART E.--[35]AUSTRALIAN--
CORONADA 947 "MAN FROM COCHISE"
CORONADA 951 "HORRIGAN'S HELL"
SIERRA 420 "ONE-GUN JUSTICE"
6 BIG HORN BKS
5 CONDOR BKS
SANTE FE 307 "COLORADA KILLER"
& 5 OTHER SANTE FE BKS
CLEVE NVLT "KANSAS TWISTER"
THORPE, LEE--[35]AUSTRALIAN,HP--
BIG HORN 321 "WHISTLING DEATH"

GREENOUGH, WILLIAM PARKER
DE MONTAUBAN, G.--[8]

GREENSLADE, STANLEY LAWR.
GREENSLADE, S.L.--[31]

GREENSPAN, CONSTANCE A.P.
GREENSPAN, CAPPY PETRASH--[31]

GREENSPUN, HERMAN MILTON
GREENSPUN, H.M.--[31]
GREENSPUN, HANK--[31]

GREENWOOD, A.E.
HAWTHORNE, MARX--[8]

GREENWOOD, AUGUSTUS GEOR.
ARCHER, OWEN--[8]

GREENWOOD, GEORGE A.
HOWLEY, MARK--[1]

GREENWOOD, JULIA E.C.
ASKHAM, FRANCIS--[1][22][31]ENGLISH

GREENWOOD, LILLIAN B.
AYERS, ROSE--[21][26][31]ROM--
"THE STREET SPARROWS"

GREENWOOD, T.E.
MCCABE, RORY--[8]

GREENWOOD, THOMAS
VERVAL, ALAIN--W/LAWRENCE MONTAGUE LANDLE,[1][8]

GREER, ARTHUR ELLIS
GREER, ART--[31]

GREER, GERMAINE
BLIGHT, ROSE--[8]

GREER, THOMAS
GREER, TOM--[23]IRISH-ENGLISH/SF

GREET, THOMAS YOUNG
GREET, T.Y.--[31]

GREG, PERCY
HOLDRETH, LIONEL G.--[23]ENGLISH/SF

GREGG, ANDREW K.
BAYER, HAROLD--[1][31]

GREGG, ANDREW W.
HEARN, SNEED--[1][31]
VINEGAR, TOM--[1]

GREGG, HILDA CAROLINE
GRIER, SYDNEY C.--[2]

GREGOIRE, PIERRE
STEIN, GREGOR--[39]GERMAN

GREGOR, CAROL
CUSH, CAROL GREGOR--[31]

GREGORIAN, JOYCE BALLOU
HAMPSHIRE, JOYCE G.--[31]

GREGORIAN, VARTAN
HERIAN, V.--[1][31]

GREGORY, DICK
GREGORY, RICHARD CLAXTON--[31]

GREGORY, ISABELLA A.P.
LADY GREGORY--[31]

GREGORY, JACKSON
QUIEN-SABE--[2]

GREGORY, KENNETH JOHN
GREGORY, K.J.--[31]

GREGORY, MARGARET
'ERCOLE, VELIA--[13]AUSTRAlIA

GREGORY, MARTHA
GLENN, ELIZABETH--[9][21][26]ROM--
"GONE FISHIN"
"TASTE OF LOVE" & MORE
GRAY, MARCY--V. BERCH LTR TO HUBIN '94,MYS--
SILH "SO EASY TO LOVE" '90
GREGORY, MARTY--[9]ROM

GREGORY, MARY LAWRENCE
BONNER, TERRY NELSON--[21]ROM,HP--
AUSTRALIAN/NZ:"THE PIONEERS"
EDWARDS, ESTELLE--[9][21][26]ROM--
"MOONSLIDE"
"KNAVE OF HEARTS"
GREGORY, MARY L.--[7]SF
GREGORY, MOLLIE--[7][21][26]ROM/SF--
"MAKING MR. RIGHT" '87

GREGORY, ORMOND
ROBBINS, W. WAYNE--LACHMAN/R.JONES LST MAY '93,[11]

GREGORY, RICHARD LANGTON
GREGORY, R.L.--[31]

GREGORY, THEOPHILUS S.
GREGORY, T.S.--[1]

GREIF, MARTIN
BACH, JEAN--[31]
COPLEY, FREDERICK S.--[31]
HUNTER, LEONA WESLEY--[31]
LAWRENCE, MARTIN--W/LAWRENCE GROW,[1]

GREIG-SMITH, JENNIFER M.
AMES, JENNIFER--[3][17][21][22]AUSTRALIAN/MYS--
"LOVERS IN THE DARK" '46
COLLINS "DARK CARNIVAL" '51
COLLINS "FLIGHT INTO FEAR" '53 & MORE

GREIG-SMITH, JENNIFER M. [CONT]
BARCLAY, ANN--[1][17][22]AUSTRALIAN/ROM--
GREIG, MAYSIE--[17][21][34]MYS--
COLLINS "WHISPERS IN THE SUN"
COLLINS "CLOAK & DAGGER LOVER" '55 & 23
THOMPSON, MADELINE--[1]
WARRE, MARY DOUGLAS--[17]AUSTRALIAN/ROM
WARREN, MARY DOUGLAS--[1][17][22]
[34]AUSTRALIAN/ROM/MYS--

GREILING, WALTER
GREY, WALT--[39]GERMAN

GREIMAS, ALGIRDAS JULIEN
GREIMAS, A.J.--[31]

GREINER, FRANZ
PANK, WERNER--[39]GERMAN

GREINER-MAI, HERBERT
REINER, H.G.--[39]GERMAN/JUV

GREISSER, WOLFGANG
REISER, W.G.--[39]GERMAN

GREITHER, MARGIT
BRUGGER, JOHANNA--[39]GERMAN
RIED, FRANZISKA--[39]GERMAN
ROTH, SUSANNE--[39]GERMAN
WALSER, MARGRET--[39]GERMAN

GRENANDER, MARY ELIZABETH
GRENANDER, M.E.--[31]

GRENNELL, DEAN A.
WESLEY, ART--[1][2][11]

GRENVILLE, JOHN ASHLEY S.
GRENVILLE, J.A.S.--[31]

GRENWOOD, JULIA EILEEN C.
ASKHAM, FRANCIS--[2]

GRESHAM, CLAUDE HAM. JR.
GRESHAM, GRITS--[22][31]AMERICAN

GRESHAM, ELIZABETH [F]
GREY, ROBIN--[1][3][22][31]MYS--
DUELL "PUZZLE IN PORCELAIN" '45
DUELL "PUZZLE IN PEWTER" '47

GRESSENT, ALFRED GEORGES
VALOIS, GEORGES--[1]

GRESSER, SEYMOUR
GRESSER, SY--[31]

GRETEMAN, JAMES
GRETEMAN, JIM--[31]

GREVE, FELIX PAUL B.F.
GERDEN, FREDERICK PAUL--[1][31]
GRAFE, FELIX--[1][31]
GREVE, ELSA--[1][31]
GROVE, FREDERICK PHILIP--[2][7][11]
[23][39]GERMAN-CANADIAN/SF--
NAME CHGD TO 'GROVE'
THORER, KONRAD--[1]
THORNE, EDOUARD--[1]

GREVEN, HELGA
GREVELL, JULIE--[39]GERMAN
GREVEN, JULIANE--[39]GERMAN
KERSTEN, NICOLA--[39]GERMAN
NORMA, NICOLA--[39]GERMAN
SWANHOLM, BIRGIT--[39]GERMAN

GREVEN, HELGA [CONT]
WILDERS, JULIANE--[39]GERMAN

GREY, A.W.
BROWN, CROSLAND--[7]SF--
AVON "TOMBLEY'S WALK" '91

GREY, PEARL
GREY, ZANE--[1]

GRIBBEN, JAMES
JAMES, VINCENT--[32][34]MYS--
QUALITY "MORGAN'S WIFE" '49
"RED SKY" '53
BENN "ISLAND OF THE PIT" '55
BENN "LONG RIDE OUT" '57
EQMM "WHEN TOMORROW COMES" SEPT '73

GRIBBLE, LEONARD [R]
BROWNING, STERRY--[3][18][28]WAR/WEST/MYS--
"COASTAL COMMANDOES" '46
"SANTE FE GUNSLICK" '51
CLARKE "CRIME AT CAPE FOLLY" '51
LONG "SEX MARKS THE SPOT" '54
CODY, STETSON--[8][28]WEST--
24 NOVELS '49-73
DENVER, LEE--[8][18]WEST--
7 NOVELS '77-86
GANNET, JAMES--[28]ENGLISH
GRANT, LANDON--[5][18][29][31]WEST--
10 NOVELS '35-56
GREX, LEO--[3][5][18][29][31]MYS--
SERIES NOVELS '34-69
NON-FICT '75-80
GREY, LOUIS--[3][5][18][22][29]MYS--
NICHOLSON "SIGNET OF DEATH" '34
KELSO, CHUCK--[28]ENGLISH, WEST--
7 NOVELS '52-65
LARAMEE, COLE--[28]ENGLISH, WEST
MARLOWE, PIERS--[8][28]ENGLISH
MUIR, DEXTER--[3][5][18][29]MYS--
JENKINS "SIGNET OF DEATH" '46
JENKINS "PILGRIMS MEAT MURDER" '48
JENKINS "SPECKLED SWAN" '49
JENKINS "ROSEMARY FOR DEATH" '53
SANDERS, BRUCE--[8][28][32]MYS--
JENKINS "BLONDE BLACKMAIL" '45
"DEADLY JADE" '47 & MORE
JCM "MAN WHO PREFERRED REDHEADS" DEC '60
& OTHER DIGEST SS
SHANE, STEVE--[28]ENGLISH, WEST--
4 NOVELS '55-65

GRIBBON, WILLIAM L.
GALT, WILLIAM--[11]
MUNDY, TALBOT--[2][3][7][23][29]MYS/SF--
HUTCH "BLACK LIGHT" '30
"GUNGA SAHIB" '33
A-C "OLD UGLY FACE" '40 & MANY MORE

GRIDER, DOROTHY
DOTTIG--[1][31]
FENWICK, PATTI--[1][31][33]

GRIER, BARBARA G.D.
CASEY, GLADYS--[1][31]
DAMON, GENE--[1][31]
NIVEN, VERN--[1]
STRONG, LENNOX--[1]

GRIER, ROOSEVELT
GRIER, ROSEY--[31]

GRIERSON, DAVID
STUART, IAN --[3]MYS--
HALE "END ON THE ROCKS" '81
HALE "THE GARB OF THE TRUTH" '82
HALE "THRILLING--SWEET & ROTTEN" '82
HALE "A GROWING CONCERN" '85
HALE "PICTURES IN THE DARK" '86

GRIERSON, EDWARD [D]
CROWTHER, BRIAN--[1][18][29]MYS--
"SHALL PERISH WITH THE SWORD" '49
STEVENSON, JOHN [P]--[1][18][31]MYS--
"THE CAPTAIN GENERAL" '56

GRIERSON, WALTER
ENQUIRING LAYMAN--[8]

GRIEVE, ALEX H. GLANVILLE
GLANVILLE, ALEC--[3][22]MYS--
HARRAP "BODY IN THE TRAWL" '38
JENKINS "GUNNER'S ISLAND" '49 & 3

GRIEVE, CHRISTOPHER MURRAY
DOUGLAS, C.H.--[1]
GRIEVE, C.M.--[31]
GUTHRIE, ISOBEL--[1][31]
LAIDLAW, A.K.--[1][31]
LESLIE, ARTHUR--[1]
MAC A'GHREIDHIR, G.--[1]
MACDIARMID, HUGH--[1][11][22][31]SCOTTISH
MACLAREN, JAMES--[1][31]
MODERN BURNS--[1]
PTELEON--[1]

GRIEVESON, MILDRED
FLEMING, CARDINE--[9]ROM
FLEMING, CAROLINE--[9][21]ROM--
"CAROLINE"
MATHER, ANNE--[9][21][26]ROM--
"SIROCCO"
"SANDSTORM" & MANY MORE

GRIFFEN, FRANK
ATKIN, CHARLES--[1]
FRANKLIN, GRIFF--[34]MYS--
HUGHES "PAYMENT IN LEAD" ca'49

GRIFFEN, JAMES JEFFERDS
GRIFFEN, JEFF--[31]

GRIFFIN, ANTHONY JEROME
ALTAIR--[11]

GRIFFIN, ARTHUR HAROLD
GRIFFIN, A.H.--[31]

GRIFFIN, ARTHUR J.
FRANK, LEE--[1][31]
GRIFFIN, ANNE--[9]
GRIFFIN, ANNE [J]--[9][3][26][31]MYS/ROM--
AV "OCEAN OF FEAR" '74
AV "SPIRIT OF BRYMASTER OAKS" '74
JAMES, SUSAN--[3][31]MYS--
"HYPNOTIST OF HILARY MANSION" '77
ST. MARTIN'S "FOUL DEEDS" '89

GRIFFIN, CLIFFORD STEPHEN
GRIFFIN, C.S.--[31]

GRIFFIN, FRANK
NOBLE, JOHN--[1]

GRIFFIN, GEORGE DANIEL
GRIFFIN, DAN--[31]

GRIFFIN, ROBERT JOHN T.
GRIFFIN, JONATHAN--[8][31]
THURLOW, ROBERT--[8]

GRIFFIN, THOMAS E. JR.
GRIFFIN, TOM--[31]

GRIFFIN, VIVIAN CORY
CROSSE, VICTORIA--[8]

GRIFFITH, DAVID LEWELYN W
DE TOLIGNAC, GASTON--[31]
GRIFFITH, D.W.--[31]
GRIFFITH, LAWRENCE--[31]

GRIFFITH, GUY THOMPSON
GRIFFITH, G.T.--[31]

GRIFFITH, MARIA ALINE
QUINTANILLA, MARIA ALINE--[1]
ROMANONES, COUNTESS OF--[1]

GRIFFITH, MR. & MRS. E.G.
GRIFFITH, JASON--[3][22]MYS--
STRATFORD "THE MONKEY WRENCH" '33

GRIFFITH, PERCY
CLIFFORD, MARTIN--[1]HP--

GRIFFITH, THOMAS GWYNFOR
CIFFRIW, GWYNFOR--[1][31]

GRIFFITH, VALERIE WINKLER
GRIFFITH, JEANETTE--W/JEANETTE H.
EYERLY,[1][8][22]AMERICAN--

GRIFFITH-JONES, GEORGE C.
CARNAC, LEVIN--[2][4][11][23][31]SF
GRIFFITH, GEORGE--[31]
GRIFFITH, GEORGE CHETWYND--[1][2][11][23]SF
LARA--[1][2][31]
MORICH, STANTON--[1][2]

GRIFFITH-SHAW, GRACE K.
KELLOG, GRACE--[1]

GRIFFITHS, AILEEN ESTHER
PASSMORE, AILEEN E.--[8]

GRIFFITHS, CHARLES TOM W.
BOARDMAN, CHARLES--[8]
BOLD, RALPH--[1]

GRIFFITHS, DAVID ARTHUR
GARRON, MARCO--VULTURES OF THE VOID,
[23]SF,HP--
"AZAN THE APEMAN" SERIES '50/51
HUNT, GILL--[2][11][23]SF,HP--
WARREN "VEGA" '51
WARREN "FISSION" '52
LANG, KING--[2][7][11][23]SF,HP--
WARREN "PROJECTILE WAR" '51
WARREN "GYRATOR CONTROL" '51
WARREN "ASTRO-RACE" '51
WARREN "TASK FLIGHT" '51
WARREN "ROCKET INVASION" '51
SHAW, BRIAN [BRYAN]--[1][2][11]SF,HP--
WARREN
SHAW, DAVID--[2][11][23]SF,HP--
WARREN "LABORATORY X" '50
WARREN "PLANET FEDERATION" '50
WARREN "SPACE MEN" '51
VANE, BRETT--[34]MYS,HP--
WARREN "LULU" '51

GRIFFITHS, EDITH GRACE C.
GRIFFITHS, G.D.--[31]--
WOW "MATTIE: STORY OF A HEDGEHOG" '67

GRIFFITHS, EILEEN ESTHER
PASSMORE, EILEEN ESTHER--[1]

GRIFFITHS, GORDON DOUGLAS
GRIFFITHS, G.D.--[1][31]

GRIFFITHS, JACK
GRIFFITH, JACK--[8][32]MYS--
LM "SHERLOCK HOLMES OF BABYLON" JUN '50
JCM "TWO HEADS ARE BETTER THAN ONE" FEB '60
JCM "CROCODILE CRIME" SEPT '60
JCM "IT HAPPENED IN THE DARK" SPR '63

GRIFFITHS, STEPHEN GARETH
GRIFFITHS, STEVE--[31]

GRIFFITHS, THOMAS MELVIN
GRIFFITHS, MEL--[31]

GRIGSBY, ALCANOAN O.
ADAMS, JACK--W/MARY P. LOWE,[2][7][23][32]SF--
LM "HAPPENING IN POMPEII" SEPT '80

GRILL, NANNETTE L.
CHRISTIAN, LOUISE--[1][31]

GRIMES, LEE
DODGE, FREEMONT--[1][31][33]

GRIMES, WILLIAM HENRY
GRIMES, W.H.--[31]

GRIMKE, CHARLOTTE L.F.
FORTEN, CHARLOTTE [L]--[31]

GRIMM, CHARLES JOHN
GRIMM, CHARLIE--[31]
JOLLY CHOLLY--[31]

GRIMM, CHERRY BARBARA L.
WILDER, CHERRY--[2][7][11][23][33]AUSTRALIAN--
PIATKUS "CRUEL DESIGNS" '88

GRIMMELSHAUSEN, HANS JAK.
MESSMAHL, SIGNEUR--[39]GERMAN
VON FUGSHAIM, MELCHIOR S.--[39]GERMAN
VON GREIFENSHOLM, ERICH S--[39]GERMAN
VON HARTENFELS, SIMON L.--[39]GERMAN
VON HIRSCHFELT, SAMUEL G.--[39]GERMAN
VON HUGENFELS, ISRAEL F.--[39]GERMAN
VON SEHNSTORFF, MICHAEL R--[39]GERMAN
VON SULSFORT, GERMAN S.--[39]GERMAN

GRIMSHAW, IVAN GEROULD
SACA BONA--[1]

GRIMSLEY, ANN
DARBY, LYNDAN--W/LYNNE KINNERLEY,[7]SF--
"EYE OF TIME TRILOGY #1-3" '88/89

GRIMSTEAD, HETTI
MANNING, MARSHA--[9][17][21][31]ENGLISH/ROM--
"DANCE OF SUMMER"
"MAGIC CITY" & 12 MORE

GRINDAL, RICHARD
GRAYSON, RICHARD--[3][22][29]MYS--
GOLZ "DEATH OFF STAGE" '91
& 10 MORE '55-91

GRINDEL, EUGENE
DU HALT, JEAN--[31]
ELUARD, PAUL--[22][31]FRENCH
HERVENT, MAURICE--[31]

GRINEVSKI, ALEK S.
GREEN, ALEXANDER--[1]RUSSIAN
GRIN, ALEXANDER--[22]RUSSIAN
GRIN, ALEKSANDR--[1]RUSSIAN

GRINGHUIS, RICHARD H.
DIRK--[1][31]AMERICAN
GRINGHUIS, DIRK--[1][22][31][33]AMERICAN

GRISANTE, MARY LEE
SHEPHERD, PERDITA--[9][21][26]ROM--
"MORNINGS IN HEAVEN"
"A PROMISE IN THE WIND"

GRISWOLD DEL CASTILLO, R.
DEL CASTILLO, RICHARD G.--[31]

GROENBJERG, KIRSTEN ANDR.
GRONBJERG, KIRSTEN ANDER.--[31]

GROETTRUP, BERNHARD
BERND, GROTE--[39]GERMAN

GROGAN, EMMET
WISDOM, KENNY--[1]

GROGAN, EMMETT
FASTLIFE--[1][31]

GROH, EDWIN CHARLES
GROH, ED--[31]

GROH, GEORG ARTUR
GEORGI, GEORG--[39]GERMAN

GROIA, PHILIP
GROIA, PHIL--[31]

GROMADECKI, JOSEF
GROMA, PETER--[39]GERMAN/ADV

GROMMER, HELMUT
REINHOLD, FRITZ--[39]GERMAN/MYS/JUV

GRONEWOLD, SUSAN ELLEN
GRONEWOLD, SUE ELLEN--[31]

GRONMARK, SCOTT
SCOTT, A.G.--[7]SF/HOR--
SIGNET "CHILDMARE" '81
SHARMAN, NICK--[7]SF--8 NEL NOVELS

GRONSTEDT, JOHAN
OLYMIAS--[29]MYS--
"DET HEMLIGHETSFULLA TEATERDRAMAT" 1897

GRONWALD, PETER
WARREN, BEN--[39]GERMAN/HOR/WEST

GRONWALD, WERNER
COLVIN, MORTIMER--[39]GERMAN/HOR/WEST
GROSMONT, WESTON--[39]GERMAN/HOR/WEST
MORKIM, I.B.--[39]GERMAN/HOR/WEST
WOLTER, WERNER--[39]GERMAN/HOR/WEST

GROOM, ARTHUR WILLIAM
ADAMSON, GRAHAM--[1][22][31][33]ENGLISH
ANDERSON, GEORGE--[1][31][33]ENGLISH
DU BLANC, DAPHNE--[1][31][33]ENGLISH
GRIMSLEY, GORDON--[1][31][33]ENGLISH
PEMBURY, BILL--[1][22][31]ENGLISH

GROOM, ARTHUR WILLIAM
STANSTEAD, JOHN--[1][22][33]ENGLISH
TEMPLAR, MAURICE--[1][22][33]ENGLISH
TOONDER, MARTIN--[1][22][33]ENGLISH

GROSCHE, EUGEN
GREGORIUS, GREGOR A.--[39]GERMAN

GROSHOLZ, FRANZ
FLAMBERG, FRANZ PETER--[39]GERMAN

GROSS, HENRY H.
HUNVALD, HENRY--[3]MYS--
WORLD "MASTERPIECE OF NICE MR. BREEN" '72

GROSS, LESLIE
GROSOFSKY, LESLIE--[22][31]AMERICAN

GROSS, MICHAEL ROBERT
ALEXANDER, ROBERT--[31]
DEVON, D.G. --W/STEPHAN DEMOREST,[3][31]MYS--
BAL "TEMPLE KENT" '82
BAL "SHATTERED MASK" '83
BAL "PRECIOUS OBJECTS" '84

GROSS, SHELDON HARVEY
GROSS, SHELLY--[31]

GROSS, SUSAN ELLEN
COLE, SUE ELLEN--[9][21][26]ROM--
"A DISTANT CASTLE"
"CRITIC'S CHOICE" & MORE
COLLINS, SUSANNA--[9][21][26]ROM--
FLAMMENCO NIGHTS"
"ON WINGS OF MAGIC" & MORE
DE LYONNE, SUSAN--[9][21]ROM--
"6 DAYS & 5 NIGHTS"
GROSS, SUE--[21][26]ROM--
"STEAL A RAINBOW"
"THE JEWEL OF INDIA" & OTHERS
GROSS, SUE ELLEN--[21]ROM--
"MIDNIGHT FURY"

GROSS, TERENCE
COSTINESCU, EDWARD N.--[31]

GROSSBAUM, BENJAMIN
GRAHAM, BENJAMIN--[1]

GROSSE, CARL FRIEDRICH A.
VARGAS, GRAF EDOUARD ROM.--[39]GERMAN/SF
VON GROSSE, MARQUIS--[39]GERMAN/SF

GROSSER, KARL-HEINZ
ROSSER, G.--[39]GERMAN

GROSSHANS, ROLF H.
GROSS, ROLF H.--[39]GERMAN/SF

GROSSMAN, JEAN SCHICK
GRAYSON, ALICE BARR--[31]

GROSSMAN, JOSEPHINE JUDITH
HAMILTON, ERNEST--[1][22][31]AMERICAN
JUDD, CYRIL--W/C.M. KORNBLUTH,
[2][7][22][23]SF--
"OUTPOST MARS"'52
"GUNNER CADE" '52
MERRIL, J.--[32]AMERICAN/MYS--
SM "DRY DUST" FEB '60
MERRIL, JUDITH--[1][7][32]MYS/SF--
SB "ONE TO A CUSTOMER" JUN '61
SA "MUTED HUNGER" OCT '63
SA "ONE DEATH TO A CUSTOMER" JAN '62
SHARON, ROSE--[1][2][11][22][23]AMERICAN
THORSTEIN, ERIC--[1][22]AMERICAN

GROSSMANN, HANS HUGO
CARSON, PEER--[39]GERMAN/MYS/WEST
CARTER, JEFF--[39]GERMAN/MYS/WEST
DRAKE, JOHN--[39]GERMAN/MYS/WEST,HP
DUFF, HOWARD--[39]GERMAN/MYS/WEST,HP
GIBSON, BEN--[39]GERMAN/MYS/WEST
GRANT, JOHN--[39]GERMAN/MYS/WEST
HOLM, RALF--[39]GERMAN/MYS/WEST
KELLOG, ERNEST P.--[39]GERMAN/MYS/WEST
LANE, LEX--[39]GERMAN/WEST,HP
LOYD, NORMAN--[39]GERMAN/MYS/WEST
MASON, TEX--[39]GERMAN/WEST
MCCORMICK, INSPECTOR--[39]GERMAN/MYS
MORTON, JACK--[39]GERMAN/MYS/WEST,HP
SHANNON, MARK--[39]GERMAN/MYS/WEST
SHARP, HOOKER--[39]GERMAN/MYS/WEST
TELFORD, STAN--[39]GERMAN/MYS/WEST

GROTEWOLD, CHRISTIAN S.
VENIR, A.--[39]GERMAN

GROTKOP, EDITH
GUETTE, EDITH--[39]GERMAN/JUV

GROUSSET, PASCHAL
LAURIE, ANDRE--[2][11][23]FRENCH/SF

GROVE, FREDERICK HERRIDGE
GROVE, FRED--[28][31]WEST--20 NOVELS '58-89

GROVE, HELEN HARRIET
CHRISTIAN, GEORGE--[1]

GROVE, HENRIETTE
JOUBERT, LINDA--[1]

GROVE, MARTIN
ALLAN, JANE--[34]MYS--
ZEBRA "WHO KILLED ME?" '79
ZEBRA "WHO'S NEXT?" '79
ZEBRA "WHO'S ON FIRST?" '79
GROVE, MARJORIE--[34]MYS--
ZEBRA "YOU'LL DIE....." NOVELS '78-9

GROVER, WINIFRED POWELL
DWYER, WINIFRED--[1][2]

GROVES, HARRY EDWARD
GROVES, H.E.--[31]

GROVES, JOHN WILLIAM
GROVES, J.W.--[1]

GROVES, REGINALD
GROVES, REG--[31]

GROVES, SHEILA
DURRANT, SHEILA--[8]

GROVES, WILLIAM E.
SCOTT, ERNEST--[1]

GROW, LAWRENCE
LAWRENCE, MARTIN--W/MARTIN GREIF,[1]

GRUBER, FRANK
ACRE, STEPHEN--A. HACKATHORN-GRUBER
BIBLIO,[3][5][28]MYS--
DODD "THE YELLOW OVERCOAT" '42
"SHORT STORIES" MAG 1942
ALLWORTH, RICHARD B. --HACKATHORN-GRUBER
BIBLIO--
"ARISTOCRATS OF DIRECT SELLING" '34
"TAILORING-SIDE LINE OR EXCLUSIVELY" '34
"EVERY MAN WEARS CLOTHS" '34
"BUILDING A PERMANENT SUCCESS" '34

GRUBER, FRANK [CONT]
BOSTON, CHARLES K.--HACKATHORN-GRUBER BIBLIO,[2][3][5]MYS--
REYNAL "SILVER JACKASS" '41
BRANDON, NORMAN H.--HACKATHORN-GRUBER BIBLIO-
HOLLYWOOD DIARY "THE HOLLYWOOD WRITER" '61
HOLLYWOOD DIARY "THE TELEVISION WRITER" JUNE '61
HOLLYWOOD DIARY "THE EXTRA AND THE BIT" '61
BRANT, SAM--HACKATHORN-GRUBER BIBLIO--
'THRILLING RANCH STORIES'
"THRILLING WESTERN" 1935
COLE, JACKSON--HACKATHORN-GRUBER BIBLIO--
'THRILLING WESTERN' MAG
"TREASURE TRAP" '35
'THRILLING RANCH STORIES'
'POPULAR WESTERN' MAGS 1935
CONGER, RALPH--HACKATHORN-GRUBER BIBLIO--
'DETECTIVE TALES'
'STREET & SMITH MYS' MAGS '35-41
'HOW TO SELL' STORIES '33-35
CONKLING, W.R. --HACKATHORN-GRUBER BIBLIO--
'HOW TO SELL': "HUSTLERS & SALESMEN"
"FOSTER'S NEW DEAL"
"THE PASSING OF THE ODD JOB MAN"
"YOU CAN'T KEEP A GOOD MAN DOWN"
"EX BARBER SELLS MODERN SAFETY RAZOR" '33-34
ERWIN, GEORGE C.--HACKATHORN-GRUBER BIBLIO--
"CHRISTMAS CARDS PUT ME ON MY FEET" '33
GOGGIN, WILLIAM--HACKATHORN-GRUBER BIBLIO--
"WORDS ABOUT BOOKS" '61
GUNN, TOM--HACKATHORN-GRUBER BIBLIO,[1][5]HP--
TRS "REWARD NOTICE" '35
HALSEY, STEWART N.--HACKATHORN-GRUBER BIBLIO--
HOW TO SELL "SELLING TO RENTAL OUTLETS" '34
"PROTECTION SALESMAN IS SUCCESSFUL" '34
HOWARD, LOIS--L. ROBBINS LTR '94--PULP
KERMAN, A.L.--HACKATHORN-GRUBER BIBLIO--
'HOW TO SELL' STORIES "FOWLER STAGES A COMEBACK" '34
"JACK KRAMER QUIT DIRECT SELLING" 1933
"SELLING IN THE NINETIES" 1934
LIVERMORE, OSCAR K.--HACKATHORN-GRUBER BIBLIO--
'HOW TO SELL' STORIES: "INSURANCE FOR DIRECT SALESMAN"
"LOW COST LIFE & ACCIDENT PROTECTION" '34
MAHOOD, LOIS--HACKATHORN-GRUBER BIBLIO--
"FOUR OUT OF FIVE" '33
MCBRIDE, ARTHUR--HACKATHORN-GRUBER BIBLIO--
"YOUNG MAN ON THE WAY" '61
MORRIS, MATTHEW--HACKATHORN-GRUBER BIBLIO--
"TELEVISION TOPICS" '61
POWERS, RALPH--HACKATHORN-GRUBER BIBLIO--
"SECRET AGENT-X" MAG '36
RAINEY, WILLIAM B.--HACKATHORN-GRUBER BIBLIO,HP--
SPICY MYS "HANDS OF DEATH" NOV '36
RYDER, JOHN F. --HACKATHORN-GRUBER BIBLIO--
"MAN FROM WELLS FARGO" '61
"JOHN GODDARD" '61
"PORTRAIT OF A SUCESSFUL WRITER" '61
"THE REBEL IS COMING" '61
SCANLON, C.K.M.--[1][5]HP
STOCKBRIDGE, GRANT--[1][2][5]HP-ART
HACKATHORN SAYS 'NO' ON THIS
VEDDER, JOHN K.--HACKATHORN-GRUBER BIBLIO,[2][5][34]MYS--
HOLT "LAST DOORBELL" '41

GRUBER, GISI
ALSEGGER, BARBARA MARIA--[39]GERMAN/MYS
CHARPENTIER, JULES--[39][40]GERMAN/MYS--
'KOMMISSAR WILTON' SERIES - 15 BOOKS

GRUEB, WILLY
BERG, UWE--[39]GERMAN

GRUELLE, JOHN BARTON
GRUELLE, JOHNNY--[31][33]

GRUENBAUM, ADOLF
GRUNBAUM, ADOLF--[31]

GRUENEBERG, HANS
GRUNEBERG, HANS--[31]

GRUN, ROBERT
MOERIS, ROBERT--[39]GERMAN

GRUND, CARL-JOSEPH
DORNBERG, J.C.--[39]GERMAN/WEST
FRANK, BEN--[39]GERMAN/WEST
PRICE, WILL--[39]GERMAN/WEST

GRUNDBERG, JOHN ANDREW
GRUNDBERG, ANDY--[31]

GRUNDY, JOHN BROWNSDON C.
GRUNDY, J.B.C.--[31]

GRUNERT, CARL H.
FRIEDLAND, CARL--[39]GERMAN/SF

GRUNSKY, HANS
GUNY, HANS--[39]GERMAN/SF

GUARD, DAVID
GUARD, DAVE--[31]

GUARIENTO, RONALD
PARKS, RON--[8]

GUARINO, DEBORAH
GUARINO, DAGMAR--[31][33]

GUBERN RIBALTA, JORGE
HALLORAN, MARK--JEAN F. LE DEIST LTR '93
LANUZA, PEDRO--JEAN F. LE DEIST LTR '93
O'CONNOR, W.--JEAN F. LE DEIST LTR '93
SHALTER, BRUNO--JEAN F. LE DEIST LTR '93

GUCCIONE, LESLIE DAVIS
DAVIS, LESLIE--[9][21][26][33]ROM--
"A TOUCH OF SCANDAL"
"SPLINTERED MOON"

GUDJONSSON, HALLDOR KIJAN
LAXNESS, HALLDOR--[31]

GUDOI I RICART, JOSEP
GUDOI RICART, JOSE M.--[31]
GUDOI RICART, JOSEP--[31]

GUEHENNO, JEAN MARCEL J.M
GUEHENNE, JEAN--[31]

GUELLETTE, THOMAS SIMON
TSG--[2]

GUERIN, ALEXANDRE
CHENEVIERE, JACQUES--[22]FRENCH-SWISS

GUERRA Y SANCHEZ, RAMIRO
DIPLOMATICUS--[31]

GUERRA, EVARISTO ACEVEDO
ARRIETA, FERNANDO--[20]SPANISH

GUEST, ANTHONY GORDON
GUEST, A.G.--[31]

GUEST, ENID
QUIN, SHIRLAND--[8]

GUEST, FRANCES HAROLD
SPENSER, JAMES--[3][22]MYS--
LONGMANS "LIMEY" '33
LONGMANS "THE WHEELS" '38 & MORE

GUEST, HENRY BAYLY
GUEST, HARRY--[31]

GUETERSLOH, ALBERT PARIS
KIETREIBER, ALBERT CONRAD--[31]

GUETT, DIETER
GUTT, DIETER--[31]

GUEVARA SERNA, ERNESTO
GUEVARA, CHE--[31]

GUEZENEC, ALFRED
BREHAT, ALFRED--[2]

GUGGENHEIM, MARGARET
GUGGENHEIM, PEGGY--[31]

GUGGENHEIM, WILLIAM
WILLIAMS, GATENBY--[1]

GUGGENHEIM-WIESE, URSULA
HILTON, SIBYLLE--[39]GERMAN/JUV
VON WIESE, URSULA--[39]GERMAN/JUV
WELLING, RENATE--[39]GERMAN/JUV

GUGGISBERG, CAPT SIR F.
UBIQUE--[1][2]

GUGGISBERG, CHARLES A.W.
GUGGISBERG, C.A.W.--[31]

GUGLIOTTA, BOBETTE
BIBO, BOBETTE--[1][31]

GUGOV, NIKOLA
VEZHINOV, PAVEL--[1]

GUIBOURG, GEORGES
GEORGUIS--[1][3]MYS--
STAPLES "MY FAIR LADY" '51

GUICHARDAN, ROGER
OUVARD, JACQUES--[40]MYS--
"L'ASSASSIN EST DAVS LE COUVENT" '59
"SONNEZ LES MATINES" '62

GUIEU, JIMMY
VERSEAU, DOMINIQUE--V. BERCH LTR TO
R. REGINALD '93, SF--
GROVE "YOLANDA" #1 & #2 '75-6

GUIGO, ERNEST PHILIP
HOLT, E. CARLETON--[1][22][34]MYS--
STOCKWELL "MYS AT ARDEN COURT" '54

GUILBERT,RENE
GHIL, RENE--[22]FRENCH

GUILD, LEO
SCRAM, ARTHUR N.--[1][2]

GUILEMOT, PIERRE
NEMOURS, PIERRE--[29]MYS--
VICT 180 "DINA FADERSLAND" '72

GUILER, HUGH
HUGO, IVAN--[1]

GUILEY, ROSEMARY ELLEN
FLETCHER, ADRIAN--[7][23]W/RYDER SYVERTSEN
COWROTE "GREAT BOOK OF MOVIE
MONSTERS" '83
POPLB "PSYCHIC SPAWN: A NOVEL" '87

GUILFORD, JOY PAUL
GUILFORD, J. PAUL--[31]

GUILLAUD, SUZANNE
ANDRAU, MARIANNE--[3]MYS--
MYSTIQUE "LOVE'S TESTIMONY"
MYSTIQUE "OUT OF THE NIGHT"
MYSTIQUE "A TANGLED WEB" & MORE

GUILLEMONAT, JEAN
GUIL, J.--[1][3]MYS--
STAPLES "ONE CRIME TOO MANY" '53

GUILLEN Y BATISTA, NICHOL
GUILLEN, NICHOLAS--[31]

GUILLEVIC, EUGENE
GUILLEVIC--[31]

GUIMARAES, ALFONSO H.D.C.
DE GUIMARAENS, ALPHONSUS--[22]BRAZILIAN

GUIN, WYMAN
MENASCO, NORMAN--[2][11][23]SF--
ASF "TRIGGER TIDE" '50

GUINESS, MAURICE C.
BREWER, MIKE --[1][34]MYS--
CORGI "MAN IN DANGER" '61
CORGI "MAN ON THE RUN" '62
HALE "MAN AGAINST FEAR" '66
GAYLE, NEWTON--W/MUNA LEE DE MUNOZ MARIN,
[1][22][34]MYS-- 6 NOVELS '35-8

GUINNESS, IAN OSWALD
GUINNESS, OS--[31]

GUIRDHAM, ARTHUR
EAGLESFIELD, FRANCIS--[1][31]

GULICK, GROVER C.
GULICK, BILL--[1][28][31]WEST/HIST--
15 NOVELS '50-88

GULL, C[YRIL A.E.] RANGER
INGLESBY, LEONARD CRESWEL--[1]

GUMMERT, CHARLOTTE
HOFF, ANNEGRET--[39]GERMAN
HOLLSTEIN, JOHANNES--[39]GERMAN

GUNDELFINGER, FRIEDRICH
GUNDOLF, FRIEDRICH--[22]GERMAN

GUNDY, HENRY PEARSON
GUNDY, H.P.--[31]

GUNN, DIANA MAUREEN
GUNN, ELIZABETH--[1][31]
JAMES, DIANA--[1][31]

GUNN, JAMES E.
JAMES, EDWIN--[2][11][22][23][31][33]SF--
STS "COMMUNICATIONS" '48

GUNN, JOHN ANGUS L.
HALL, B.--[8]

GUNN, STEVEN JOHN
GUNN, S.J.--[31]

GUNN, THOMSON WILLIAM
GUNN, THOM--[31]

GUNN, WILLIAM HARRISON
GUNN, BILL--[31]

GUNNARSSON, THORINN
SMITH, A.C.H.--SCOTT CUPP, GHOSTED--
"LABRYNTH"
"DARK CRYSTAL"

GUNSKE, GEORGE
GEORGE, HERBERT--[39]GERMAN

GUNSTON, WILLIAM TUDOR
GUNSTON, BILL--[31][33]--
AIRCRAFT RELATED NON-FICT

GUNTERMANN, PAUL
MANN, P. GUNTER--[39]GERMAN/MYS

GUNTHER, ALBERT EVERARD
GUNTHER, A.E.--[31]

GUNTHER, ARCH. CLAVERING
WARNEFORD, LOJNANT ROBERT--[22][29]MYS--
"MILLIONFLICKAN" 1893

GUNTHER, HANS
SEGELCKE, JOHANN PETER--[39]GERMAN

GUNTHER, HANS LUDWIG A.
ASTOR, FRANK--[39]GERMAN/ADV/MYS

GUNTHER, HEINZ
BEKKER, JENS--[39]GERMAN
BERTRAM, SILVA--[39]GERMAN/ADV/MYS
DOERNER, STEFAN--[39]GERMAN
HEIN, GUNTHER--[39]GERMAN/ADV/MYS
KONSALIK, HEINZ G.--[39][40]GERMAN/MYS--
"DAS DOPPELSPIEL" '77 & 17 OTHERS
KONTER, HEIN--[39]GERMAN/ADV/MYS
NIKOLI, BORIS--[39]GERMAN
PAHLEN, HENRY--[39][40]GERMAN/MYS--
"BEGENUNG IN TIFLIS" '76 & 3 OTHERS
VON MARROTH, BENNO--[39]GERMAN/ADV/MYS

GUNTHER, KARL HEINZ
COTTON, JERRY--[39]GERMAN/MYS,HP
ISLAND, BERT F.--[39][40]GERMAN/MYS,HP
VON HOLSTEIN, KARL--[39]GERMAN/JUV
GUENTER, C.H.--[3]MYS--
PINN "HUNTER OF MEN" '75
MANOR "DEAD IN AQABA" '77 & 5 MORE

GUNTHER, WILLY
HASELBUSCH, GUNTHER--[39]GERMAN/JUV

GUNTRIP, HENRY JAMES S.
GUNTRIP, HARRY--[31]

GUNTRUM, SUZANNE
SIMMONS, SUZANNE--[9][26]ROM--
"VELVET MORNING"
"NEVER AS STRANGERS" & MORE
SIMMS, SUZANNE--[9][26]ROM--
"ONLY THIS NIGHT"
"MOMENT OF TRUTH" & MORE

GURK, PAUL
GRAU, ERNST--[39]GERMAN/SF
GRAU, FRANZ--[39]GERMAN/SF

GURNEY, ALBERT RAMSDELL
GURNEY, A.R.--[1][31]
GURNEY, PETE--[1]
GURNEY, PETER--[31]

GURNEY, GENE
GUERNY, GENE--[31]

GURSTER, EUGENE
STEINHAUSEN, H.--[1]

GUSS, LINDA
GRANT, NATALIE--[21][26]ROM--
"IN THE KNOW"

GUSTAFSON, JAMES
GUSTAFSON, JIM--[31]

GUSTAFSON, JON
GUSTAFSON, SMITH--W/DEAN WESLEY
SMITH,[7]SF--
"THE MOSCOW MAFIA PRESENTS RAT TALES" '87

GUSTAFSON, VICTORIA E.M.
MITCHELL, V.E.--[7]SF--
"STAR TREK #51: ENEMY UNSEEN" '90

GUSTAFSSON, LISA
BRUUN, DICK--[29]MYS--
"DE HEMLIGHETSFULLA SKRIEN" '18

GUSTAFSSON, LISA
OBERG, ULLA--[29]MYS--
BONNIER "ADRIAN WENDTS ARV" '26

GUTCHEON, BETH R.
RICHARDSON, BETH--[1]

GUTHRIE, ALFRED BERTRAM
GUTHRIE, A.B.--[31]
GUTHRIE, A.B. JR.--[1][32]WEST--11 NVLS
EQMM "CLELBRATED SKUNK OF THE MOON
DANCE BAR" OCT '58
GUTHRIE, BUD--[1]

GUTHRIE, JAMES SHIELDS
CREED, DAVID--[1][3][31]MYS--
MacM "TRIAL OF LOBO ICHEKA" '71
SECKER "DEATH WATCH" '79
SECKER "THE SCARAB" '80 & MORE

GUTHRIE, NORMAN GREGOR
CRICHTON, JOHN--[1]

GUTHRIE, P.R.
PAIN, BARRY--[8][32]MYS--
EQMM "THE PROBLEM CLUB" MAY '49

GUTHRIE, THOMAS ANSTEY
ANSTEY, F.--[2][3][8][11][31]MYS--
SMITH "SALTED ALMONDS" '06
BANDOFF, HOPE--[1][2][31]
FRANCIS--[1]
JONES, WILLIAM MONARCH--[1][2][31]

GUTHRIE, WILLIAM TYRONE
GUTHRIE, T.--[31]

GUTHRIE, WOODROW WILSON
GUTHRIE, WOODY--[8][31]

GUTMAN, SIMCHA ALTER
BEN-ZION, SH.--[22]

GUTOHRLEIN, ADOLF
HUNGRY WOLF, ADOLF--[1]

GUTSTER, EUGENE
LEPEL, H.--[1]

GUTTENBERG, VIRGINIA
GRAHAM, VIRGINIA--[1][31]

GUTTERIDGE, DONALD GEORGE
GUTTERIDGE, DON--[31]

GUYONVARCH, IRENE CECILIA
PEARL, IRENE--[1][8]

GUZZO, LOUIS RICHARD
GUZZO, LOU--[31]

GWINN, CHRISTINE M.
KELWAY, CHRISTINE--[8]

GWINN, OMAR
BLAKE, ALAN--[11]

GWINN, WILLIAM R.
BANNISTER, WILLIAM--[3]MYS--
LAN "PORTRAIT OF DEATH" '66
LAN "COUNTERFEIT OF DEATH" '68
RANDALL, WILLIAM--[3][22]MYS--
MYH "DEADLY THE DARING" '58

GWYN, WILLIAM BRENT
GWYN, W.B.--[31]

GWYNN, AUDREY
THOMSON, AUDREY--[8]

GWYNN, URSULA GRACE
LEIGH, URSULA--[1]

GWYNNE, AGNES M.
GWYNNE, A.M.--[36]AUSTRALIAN/MYS--
ROBERTSON "MYS OF LAKESIDE HOUSE" '25

GWYNNE, FREDERICK HUBBARD
GWYNNE, FRED--[31]

GYE, HAROLD FREDERICK N.
GYE, HAL--[8][13]AUSTRALIAN
HACKO--[13]AUSTRALIAN
HACKSTON, JAMES--[8][13]AUSTRALIAN

GYLLENHALL, LIZA
BENNETT, LISA--[32]MYS--
MD "BEWARE OF ROOMERS" NOV-DEC '61
BENNETT, LIZA--V. BERCH LTR TO
HUBIN FEB '94/MYS--
WW "MADISON AVE. MURDER" '89
WW "SEVENTH AVE. MURDER" '90

GYMNICH, HEINZ
GYNCH, HENRY--[39]GERMAN/ADULT
MORELL, JUANA--[39]GERMAN/ADULT

HAACKE, WILMONT
LAFEUILLE, STEFAN--[39]GERMAN

HAAF, BEVERLY T.
TERRY, BEVERLY--[9][21][26]ROM--
"LOVE BANDIT"
"THIEF OF HEARTS" & MORE

HAAKE, JURGEN
MARTIN, AXEL--[39]GERMAN
MAS, CHRISTEL--[39]GERMAN
RAU, CHRISTINE--[39]GERMAN
RAU, DAVID--[39]GERMAN
STEIN, FLORIAN--[39]GERMAN

HAAPAKOSKI, HENRIK
HORNA, HENRIK--[29]MYS--
NOVELS '41-49
OUTSIDER--[29]MYS--
"KILROY HAR VARIT HAR" '48

HAARER, ALEC ERNEST
SHANWA--[8][22]ENGLISH

HAARMANN, ERNA
DARMANN, ERNA--[39]GERMAN

HAAS, BENJAMIN LEOPOLD
BARRY, KEN--V. BERCH-BAE 18, P5--
BEAC B488F "EXECUTIVE BOUDOIR" '62
BEAC B536F "THE LOVE ITCH" '62
BEAC B597F "THE BIGAMIST" '63
BENTEEN, JOHN--[1][28][31]WEST,HP--
3 DIFFERENT SERIES UNTIL '77
DOUGLAS, THORNE--[19][28][31]WEST--
4 NOVELS '73-7
"THE LOST FRAULEIN" '70
ELLIOTT, BEN--[19]WEST--
ACE F264 "CONTRACT IN CARTRIDGES" '64
ACE M126 "BROTHER BADMAN" '65
ELLIOTT, JOHN MICHAEL--[28]
HAAS, BEN--[31]
MEADE, RICHARD--[2][3][19][28]MYS/WEST--
LAN 70-012 "TWO SURGEONS" '62
& WESTERNS
DAVIES "BEYOND THE DANUBE" '67
"LOST FRAULEIN" '70
SLADE, JACK--[19]WEST,HP--
WEBSTER, SAM--V. BERCH-BAE 18, P9--
MON 234 EXECUTIVE SUITE GIRLS" '62
MON 245 "CANCEL THESE VOWS" '62
MON 268 "WIVES OF FRIENDS" '62
MON 385 "MY NEIGHBOR'S WIFE" '63
MON 404 "SOCIETY DOCTOR" '64

HAAS, CARL-HELLMUTH
KRONEN, ANDREI--[39]GERMAN

HAAS, CAROLA
CATALANI, VICTORIA--[9]ROM

HAAS, DOROTHY F.
FRANCIS, DEE--[1][22][31][33]AMERICAN

HAASE, ANN MARIE BERNAZZA
BERNAZZA, ANN MARIE--[31]

HAASSE, WILLEM HENDRIK
VAN EEMLANDT, W.H.--[22] DUTCH

HABECK, FRITZ
GORDON, GLENN--[39]GERMAN/JUV

HABERLER, LUCIA
HABERT, L.L.--[39]GERMAN

HABERMAS, JUERGEN
HABERMAS, JURGEN--[31]

HABERNIG, CHRISTINE
LAVANT, CHRISTINE--[1]

HABISREUTINGER, RUDOLPH D
PENTLAND, FRANK--[39]GERMAN
TANNER, STEPHEN--[39]GERMAN

HACHFORTH-JONES, MARGARET
DROWER, M.S.--[1]

HACIKYAN, AGOP J.
HACIKYAN, A.J.--[31]

HACKE, ERNST MAX
BAEDEKER, PEER--[39]GERMAN

HACKER, LEONARD
HACKETT, BUDDY--[31]

HACKETT, JAN MICHELE
KEROUAC, JAN--[1][31]

HACKING, ROBIN
ROBBINS, REBECCA--[26]ROM--
"LUCKY IN LOVE"
"MISCHIEVIOUS MAID"
"AN UNUSUAL INHERITANCE"

HACKL, LEOPOLD
GARRIK, PHIL M.--[39]GERMAN/MYS/WEST

HACKLEMAN, WAUNETA
MASON, VAL--[1]

HACKMANN, KARL-HEINZ
COTTON, JERRY--[39]GERMAN/MYS,HP
FORD, JERRY--[39]GERMAN/MYS

HACKNEY, RODERICK PETER
HACKNEY, ROD--[31]

HACSI, JACQUELINE
HOPE, JACQUELINE--[9][21][26]ROM--
"LOVE CAPTIVE"
LOUIS, JACQUELINE--[9][21][26]ROM--
"LOVE'S STORMY HEIGHTS"

HADDIX-KONTOS, CECILLE P.
HADDIX, CECILLE--[1][31]
KONTOS, CECILLE--[1][31]

HADES, MICKEY
HADES, PROFESSOR--[1]
MICKEY THE MAGICIAN--[1]

HADFIELD, ALAN
DALE, ROBIN--[1]

HADFIELD, ALICE M.
SMYTHE, ALICE M.--[1]

HADFIELD, VICTOR EDWARD
HADFIELD, VIC--[31]

HADFIELD,[E] CHARLES [R]
ALEXANDER, CHARLES--[1][22][31]
SOUTH AFRICAN-ENGLISH
HADFIELD, E.C.R.--[1][22][31]
SOUTH AFRICAN-ENGLISH

HADLEY, LEE
IRWIN, HADLEY--W/ANN IRWIN,[1][31][33]--
YOUNG ADULT

HAEFS, GABRIELE
NEETIX, TRAUTCHEN--[39]GERMAN

HAEFS, GISBERT
SAHM, OSKAR T.--[39]GERMAN--
TRANSLATION

HAEGERSTRAND,[S] TORSTEN
HAGERSTRAND,[S] TORSTEN--[31]

HAEGG, TOMAS
HAGG, TOMAS--[31]

HAEMMERLING, KONRAD
MORECK, CURT--[39]GERMAN

HAENSEL, HUBERT
MCMAHON, GEORGE--[39]GERMAN/MYS/SF
SIMON, IRVING--[39]GERMAN/MYS/SF

HAERING, BERNHARD
HARING, BERNHARD--[31]

HAERTLING, PETER
HARTLING, PETER--[31]

HAFT, ELLI
MANON, MADELEINE--[39]GERMAN/JUV
STEIN, BARBARA--[39]GERMAN/JUV
THORWANG, JULIANE--[39]GERMAN/JUV

HAFT, FRITJOF
COTTON, JERRY--[39]GERMAN/MYS,HP

HAFT, UWE
COTTON, JERRY--[39]GERMAN/MYS,HP

HAGA, ENOCH JOHN
GRANT, C.B.S.--[1][31]

HAGAN, CHET
JOHN, COLIN--[1][3][7][31]MYS/SF--
TWR "THE WITCHING" '82

HAGAN, MARY PATRICIA
HAGAN, PATRICIA--[21]ROM--16 NOVELS
HOWELL, PATRICIA HAGAN--[21]ROM--
"DARK JOURNEY HOME"
"WINDS OF TERROR"

HAGAN, STELLA F.
HAWKINS, JOHN--[8]

HAGBERG, DAVID [JAMES]
BANNERMAN, DAVID--[3]MYS--
ZEBRA "MAGIC MAN" '83
ZEBRA "CALL OF HONOR" '85 & 2 MORE
CARTER, NICK--[3]MYS,HP--
AWARD "SIGN OF THE PRAYER SHAWL" '76
CHART "RACE OF DEATH" '78
CHART "OPERATION:MURDO SOUND" '80
CHART "STRONTIUM CODE" '81
CHART "OUSTER CONSPIRACY" '81
CHART "APPOINTMENT IN HAIPHONG" '82
CHART "RETREAT FOR DEATH" '82
CHART "HUNTER" '82
CHART "DAMOCLES THREAT" '82
CHART "ISTANBUL DECISION" '83
CHART "PUPPET MASTER" '82
CHART "EARTHFIRE NORTH" '83
CHART "DEATH HAND PLAY" '84
CHART "DEATH ISLAND" '84
CHART "ZERO HOUR STRIKE FORCE" '84
CHART "VENGEANCE GAME" '85
CHART "DEATH ORBIT" '86
CHART "KILLING GROUND" '86
CHART "OPERATION PETROGRAD" '86
FLANNERY, SEAN--[3][29][31]MYS--
CHART "KREMLIN CONSPIRACY" '79
& 10 OTHERS
JAMES, DAVID--[7][31][32]MYS--
LM "A MATTER OF CHOICE" NOV '73
BELM "CROC" '76
PELL, ROBERT--[1][3]MYS--
PLAYBOY "THAT WINSLOW WOMAN" '77
RAMSEY, ERIC--[1][3]MYS--
PLAYBOY "KUMMERSDORF CONNECTION" '78

HAGEN, BRUNHILDE MELITTA
LOBEL, BRUNI--[39]GERMAN

HAGEN, JOHN MILTON
SHERWIN, STERLING--[1]

HAGER,[WILMA] JEAN [L]
CRANE, LEAH--[9][21][26]ROM--
"DARK ECSTACY"
KYLE, MARLAINE--[9][21][26][31]ROM--
"A SUITABLE MARRIAGE"
"A GAME OF HEARTS"
MCALLISTER, AMANDA--[1][3][9]MYS/ROM,HP--
PLAYBOY "NO NEED FOR FEAR" '76
PLAYBOY "TRUST NO ONE AT ALL" '76
PLAYBOY "DEATH COMES TO A PARTY" '77
PLAYBOY "TERROR IN THE SUNLIGHT" '78
NORTH, SARA--[3][9][21]MYS/ROM--
PLAYBOY "SHADOW OF TAMARACKS" '79
PLAYBOY "EVIL SIDE OF EDEN" '79
STEPHENS, JEANNE--[9][21][26]ROM--
"MEXICAN NIGHTS"
"MANDY'S SONG" & 24 MORE

HAGGARD, EDWARD ARTHUR
AMYAND, ARTHUR--[1]

HAGGARD, J. HARVEY
PLANET PRINCE--[1][2][11]

HAGGERTY, PATRICK EUGENE
HAGGERTY, P.E.--[31]

HAGGOVIST, ARNE
HOLIDAY, CECIL W.--[29]MYS

HAGLER, ERWIN HARRISON
HAGLER, SKEETER--[31]

HAGN, HUGO
LOWENZAHN, LEO--[39]GERMAN/JUV
REISBACHER, HERMAN--[39]GERMAN/JUV

HAGYMASSY, LAJOS
TOLNAI, LAJOS--[22] HUNGARIAN

HAHN, ANNELY [M.-B.]
LARSEN, VIOLA--[39]GERMAN

HAHN, FRIEDRICH ERNEST
HAHN, F.E.--[31]
HAHN, FRED E.--[31]
HAHN, FRED ERNEST--[31]

HAHN, GEORGE R.
MAND, CYRIL--W/RICHARD LEVIN,[1][2][11]

HAHN, GLORIA
KIM RONYOUNG--[31]

HAHN, KEN
CORD, BIRDWHANGER--[2]

HAHN, ROLF
DUBOIS, PAUL--[39]GERMAN/ADV/WEST
HANINGWAY, RALPH--[39]GERMAN/ADV/WEST
HAYN, RALPH--[39]GERMAN/ADV/WEST
STAHL, ACHIM--[39]GERMAN/ADV/WEST

HAHN, RONALD M.
ASIMUFF, ISAAK--W/UWE ANTON,[39]GERMAN/SF
BERANEK, MARTIN--[39]GERMAN/MYS/SF,HP
BLAIDE, TERENCE--[39]GERMAN/MYS/SF
CROSBY, DAVID--[39]GERMAN/MYS/SF
DELGADO, MANUEL S.--[39]GERMAN/MYS/SF
ELLIOT, BRIAN--[39]GERMAN/MYS/SF,HP
FORRESTER, THORN--[39]GERMAN/MYS/SF,HP
HARRIS, RONALD M.--[39]GERMAN/MYS/SF
HERBST, DANIEL--W/HANS J. ALPERS, GERMAN/SF

HAHN, RONALD M. [CONT]
HOWARD, H.P.--W/KLAUS DIEDRICH
& HORST PUKALLUS,[39]GERMAN/SF
KERN, GREGORY--[2][39]GERMAN/MYS/SF,
HP--[BADGER?]
LAMONT, ROBERT--[39]GERMAN/MYS/SF,HP
LINDSAY, MARK--[39]GERMAN/MYS/SF
MONROE, DANIEL--[39]GERMAN/MYS/SF
MONTAG, MARCUS--[39]GERMAN/MYS/SF
MORRISON, MISCHA--[39]GERMAN/MYS/SF,HP
OSTEN, I.S.--[39]GERMAN/MYS/SF,HP
SLADE, TED--[39]GERMAN/MYS/SF,HP
STEINER, CONRAD C.--[39]GERMAN/MYS/SF
VON NACHSTEBRECK, ELMAR--[39]GERMAN/MYS/SF

HAHN,[MONA] LYNN L.
LOWERY, LYNN--[9][21][26]ROM--
"STARFLOWER"
"LORELIE" & MORE

HAHNLEIN, IRENE
BUSCH, IRENE--[39]GERMAN/JUV

HAIDLE, MARTHA-MARIA
BOSCH, MARTHA-MARIA--[39]GERMAN/JUV

HAIG, EMILY ALICE
B.L.H.--[8]
DE LONGCLOTHES, NINON--[8]
E.H.--[8]
FIELD, ROBERT A.--[8]
HASTINGS, BEATRICE--[8]
MORNING, ALICE--[8]
TINA, BEATRICE--[8]
TRIFORMIS, D.--[8]

HAILE, HARRY GERALD
HAILE, H.G.--[31]

HAILL, ROBERT GODFREY
COOPER, JANIE--[1][35]AUSTRALIAN--
HRWTZ AO108 "CHILD OF LUST" '73
HRWTZ AO117 "TEACHER'S PET" '74
HRWTZ AO150 "TEENAGE NYMPH" '74
HRWTZ PB040 "UNNATURAL DESIRE" '74
HRWTZ PB042 "SLAVE FOR HIRE" '75
HRWTZ PB109 "SEXATHON"
HODGES, SHIRLEY M.--[35]AUSTRALIAN--HRWTZ
SATANE, PAUL--[1]
SATANE, R.P.--[35]AUSTRALIAN--
HRWTZ PB444 "HORSE" '71
SPRING, RACHEL--[35]AUSTRALIAN--
HRWTZ PB170 "MISTRESS OF MEDINA"
?? PUBLISHED ??

HAILWOOD, STANLEY MICHAEL
HAILWOOD, MIKE--[31]

HAIME, AGNES IRVINE CONS.
PERSIS--[22]ENGLISH

HAIMERL, OTTO
HEART, HARDY--[39]GERMAN/SF

HAIN, IRMA
LOOS, IRMA--[39]GERMAN

HAINDL, MARIELUISE
FLEISSER, MARIELUISE--[31][39]GERMAN

HAINES, CAROLYN
BURNES, CAROLINE--[10][21][26][34]MYS/ROM--
HARL "A DEADLY BREED" '88
HARL "FEAR FAMILIAR"'90 & MORE

HAINING, PETER
HITCHCOCK, ALFRED--[11] GHOST EDITOR

HAINING, ROBERT
ALEXANDER, ROBERT--W/MICHAEL R. LEGAT,[34]MYS--
SVNR "THE SOUL EATER" '79

HAINS, THORNTON JENKINS
GARNETT, CAPT. MAYN CLEW--[22]AMERICAN/MYS

HAIR, PAUL EDWARD HEDLEY
HAIR, P.E.H.--[31]

HAJAK, EVA-JOHANNA
REIMEVA, ESTHER--[39]GERMAN/JUV

HAJDA, NINA JANA
MANDELIK, NINA--[7]SF--
DIAM "ENTITY" '91

HAJEK, EGON
HAIN, EGON--[39]GERMAN

HAKANSSON, JAN
LAGEVI, BO--[29]MYS,HP--
BS 19 "GUMMAN I LADAN" '78
STRANGE, ERIC--[29]MYS--
"GUMMAN I LADAN" '78

HAKE, CAROLYN
DENTON, KATE--W/JEANIE LAMBRIGHT,
[9][21][26]ROM--
HARL "NO OBJECTIONS"
HARL "CROSS PURPOSES"

HALACY, DANIEL STEPHEN
HALACY, D.S. JR.--[1][31][32]MYS--
DA 2 "A GLASS OF WINE BEFORE YOU GO" '55
PU "TRIAL BY TERROR" MAY '56
PU "A REASON FOR KILLING" SEPT '56
AHMM "HARDHEADED COP" JUL '65
AHMM "TO DRAW A LINE" APR '71
HALACY, DAN--[31]

HALASZ, GYULA
BRASSAI--[31]

HALBERT, ABRAM
GANZERT, ALBERT--[39]GERMAN

HALCOMB, RUTH
S.V.--V. BERCH-BRNDN/
BC PSEUDS, BAE 22, P24

HALDANE, ROBERT ALYMER
HALDANE, R.A.--[31]
SQUARE, CHARLOTTE--[8]

HALDANE-STEVENSON, JAMES
STEVENSON, J.P.--[8]

HALDEMAN, CANDICE ETTLIN
CLEVE, JOHN--W/ANDY OFFUTT
& JACK HALDEMAN,[7]--
BERK "SPACEWAYS #11: THE ICEWORLD
CONNECTION"

HALDEMAN, HARRY ROBBINS
HALDEMAN, H.R.--[31]

HALDEMAN, JACK C.
CLEVE, JOHN--W/ANDREW J. OFFUTT
& CANDICE ETTLIN HALDEMAN,[7]
BERK "SPACEWAYS #11: THE ICEWORLD
CONNECTION"

HALDEMAN, JOSEPH WILLIAM
GRAHAM, ROBERT--[2][3][4][7][29][31]SF--
"ATTAR'S REVENGE" '75
"WAR OF NERVES" '75
HALDEMAN, JOE--[23]SF

HALE, EDWARD EVERETT
INGHAM, COLONEL FREDERIC--[31][33]
INGHAM, FREDERIC[K]--[1][2][23]SF

HALE, ETHELA RUTH
HODGEN, J.T.--[8]

HALE, F.J.
HUDSON, EDWARD S.--[7]SF--
'STAR FRONTIER TRIOLOGY' #1:
"ALIEN DEATH FLEET"

HALE, J. ANTHONY STUART
STUART, ANTHONY--[32][34]MYS--
OF "SOFT ANGEL OF MADNESS" SEPT '61
SI "VENGEANCE OF THE UNDEAD" DEC '61
SI "HORROR ISLAND" MAR '62
SI "LOVELY MAIDEN FORM HELL" MAY '62
MacD "SNAP JUDGEMENT" '77
MacD "FORCE PLAY" '80 & 4 OTHERS

HALE, KATHLEEN
MCCLEAN, KATHLEEN--[1][8]

HALE, MARIE LOUISE G.
RUTLEDGE, MARYSE--[2][3]MYS--
STOKES "SAD ADVENTURES" '24
FL "SILVER PERIL" '31

HALE, MARY ARLENE
ADAMS, TRACY--[21]ROM--
"AUGUST IN ROME"
"MOTHS & THE FLAME"
CHRISTOPHER, LOUISE--[22][31][33]AMERICAN
EVERETT, GAIL--[21][22][26][31][33]ROM--
"LOVE'S SURPRISE"
"SESARCH FOR LOVE" & MORE
KIRKLAND, WILL--[1][31][33]
TATE, MARY ANNE--[1]
WILLIAMS, LYNN--[3][21][26][29][33]MYS/ROM--
DELL "LAKE OF THE WINE" '71
DELL "WHERE IS JANE?" '72
DELL "RENDEZVOUS WITH DANGER" '74 & MORE

HALE, ROBERT DAVID
HALE, BOB--[31]

HALE, SYLVIA
BARNARD, NANCY--[8]

HALER, WILLIAM KEITH
HALER, W. KEITH--[31]

HALES, ALFRED GREENWOOD
HALES, SMILER--[1]

HALES-TOOKE, ANN M.M.
HALES, ANN--[1][31]

HALEY, JOHN J. JR.
HALEY, JACK JR.--[31]

HALEY, WENDY
GARRETT, WENDY--[26]ROM--
"ARIZONA LOVESTORM"
"LOVE'S MAGIC SPELL" & 2 MORE

HALEY, WILLIAM JOHN
EDWARDS, OLIVER--[31]
SELL, JOSEPH--[8]

HALIFAX, CLIFFORD
MEADE, L.T.--W/ELIZABETH T.M. SMITH,[34]MYS--
"TROUBLESOME WORLD" 1893
"STORIES FROM THE DIARY OF A DOCTOR" 1894-6
"WHEN THE SHOE PINCHES" 1900
"A RACE WITH THE SUN" '01

HALKIN, SHIMON
HALKIN, SIMON--[31]

HALL, ANTHONY STEWART
HALL, TONY--[31]

HALL, ASA ZADEL
EDSON, HAROLD--[1][31]--
"STANTON WHITE: A ROMANCE OF THE NEW SOUTH" '05

HALL, BENNIE CAROLINE
BENNETT, HALL--[1][22][31]AMERICAN
MARSHALL, EMILY--[1][22]AMERICAN

HALL, CAROLYN
HALSTON, CAROLE--[9][21][26]ROM--
"UNDERCOVER GIRL"
"COLLISION COURSE" & MORE

HALL, CHARLES L.
HALL, SEA LION--[1]

HALL, DESMOND W.
GILMORE, ANTHONY--W/HARRY ARTHUR BATES, [2][7][11][23]SF--
'HAWK CARSE' SERIES
HALL, D.W.--[1]
WINTER, H.G.--W/HARRY BATES,[2][11][23]SF

HALL, ELIZABETH WASON
WASON, BETTY--[1][22]AMERICAN

HALL, EMMA
ST. CLAIRE, YVONNE--[1]

HALL, FRANK RICHARDS
NABER, CHARLES R.--[1]

HALL, FREDERICK
HALL, PATRICK--[8]

HALL, GORDON LANGLEY
SIMMONS, DAWN LANGLEY--[1]

HALL, GUS
HOLLBERG, JOHN--[31]
HOWELL, JOHN--[31]

HALL, H. FIELDING
FIELDING, H.--[1]

HALL, HALBERT WELDON
HALL, H.W.--[1]

HALL, HAYWOOD
HAYWOOD, HARRY--[31]

HALL, HENRY
DIMMOCK--BAPC #11--
BRITISH COVER ARTIST FOR BADGER
FOX, H.L.--BAPC #11--
COVER ARTIST FOR COMYNS & MF

HALL, IRENE
GOUGH, IRENE--[1]

HALL, JAMES
GILES, DOUGLAS--[11]

HALL, JAMES NORMAN
GRAVEL, FERN--[1][31][33]

HALL, JOSEF WASHINGTON
CLOSE, UPTON--[1][22][31]AMERICAN

HALL, M. HELEN
MACE, HELEN--[36]AUSTRALIAN--
HAMM "DEATH OF A GOLDEN GOOSE" '65
& 3 OTHERS

HALL, MARIE BOAS
BOAS, MARIE--[8][31]

HALL, MARY BOWEN
BOWEN, MARY--[31]

HALL, NORAH E.L.
HALL, AYLMER--[1][31]

HALL, OAKLEY M.
HALL, O.M.--[1][28][31]MYS--
FARRAR STRAUS "MURDER CITY" '49
MANOR, JASON--[22][28][29][34]MYS--
VIKING "TOO DEAD TO RUN" '53
VIKING "RED JAGUAR" '54
VIKING "PAWNS OF FEAR" '55
VIKING "THE TRAMPLERS" '56

HALL, OLIVIA M.
HALL, LIBBY--[9][21][26]ROM--
"HEARTS AT RISK"
"THE PERFECT WOMAN"
PAIGE, LAURIE--[9][21][26]ROM--
"SOUTH OF THE SUN"
"MAN WITHOUT A PAST" & MORE

HALL, PARNELL
HAILEY, J.P.--HAWK/HALL INTRVW & BIBLIO '93--
FINE 'STEVE WINSLOW' COURTROOM DRAMAS:
"BAXTER TRUST" '88
"ANONYMOUS CLIENT" '89
"THE UNDERGROUND MAN" '90
"THE NAKED TYPIST" '90
"THE WRONG GUN" '91

HALL, PENELOPE C.
WILSON, PENELOPE COKER--[1]

HALL, S.
REID, DESMOND--W/M. MOORCOCK, J. CAWTHORN & P. CHAMBER,HP--
AMAL "CARRIBEAN CRISIS" '62

HALL, STEFFIE
EVANOVICH, JANET--[26]ROM--
"MANHUNT"
"WIFE FOR HIRE" & 7 MORE

HALL, STEVE
MARKHAM, RUSS--[1][2][11]

HALL, THOMAS HENRY
CAINE, HALL--[1]
HOMMY, BEG--[1]

HALL, VALERIE
PITT, VALERIE--[1]

HALL, VERNER
HUSTLE, HUGH--[8]

HALLA, ROBERT CHRISTIAN
BILLINGS, EZRA--[31]
HALLA, CHRIS--[31]

HALLACZ, KLAUS
FISCHER, FRED--[39]GERMAN

HALLAM, DOUGLAS
P.I.X.--[1]

HALLBACK, SVEN AXEL
HALL, AKE--[29]MYS--
"TIGERSTENEN" '52

HALLBING, KJELL KARL
CAMERON, WARD--[1]
MANNING, LEO--[1]
MASTERSON, LOUIS--[1]
MORGAN, LEE--[1]

HALLER, HANS
OVERLACK, JAMES--[39]GERMAN/WEST

HALLERAN, EUGENE E.
BROWARD, DONN--[1][22][31]AMERICAN--
ACE D432 "CONVENTION QUEEN" '60
HALL, EVAN--[1][22][28][31]AMERICAN--
LION LB132 "LOGAN" '56
HALLERAN, E.E.--[28]WEST/MYS--
DS "FIGHTING MAN" JAN '44
DS "EFFICIENCY, MEIN HERR!" FEB '44
SD "RULE SIX" MAY '44
SW "DEATH HAS DARK EYES" NOV '45

HALLGRIMSON, JANSSON
KAMBAN, GUDMUNDUR--[22]ICELANDIC

HALLIDAY, DOROTHY
DUNNETT, DOROTHY--[9][34]MYS/ROM--
"CHECKMATE"
"NICCOLO" & MORE

HALLIN, EMILY WATSON
HARPER, ELAINE--[9][21][31]ROM--
"BIRD OF PARADISE"
"WE BELONG TOGETHER" & MORE

HALLIWELL, DAVID WILLIAM
ARMS, JOHNSON--[31]

HALLIWELL, TONY
ROSS, JAMES--W/HUGH DARTINGTON,[1][2][23]SF--
"GOD KILLERS" '70
"GRAVITOR" '71

HALLOCK, GERARD BENJAMIN
HALLOCK, G.R.F.--[31]

HALLOWITZ, MARK W.
HALL, MARK W.--[1]

HALLOWS, N.F.
DUPLEX--W/IAN BRADLEY,[1]

HALLS, CHRIST. PETER JOHN
CONRAD, M.--[1]
CONRAD, MARCUS--[1]

HALLS, GERALDINE [M. JAY]
JAY, CHARLOTTE--[29][31][34]MYS--
COLLINS "BEAT NOT THE BONES" '52
COLLINS "ARMS FOR ADONIS" '60 & MORE
JAY, G.S.--[1][31]
JAY, GERALDINE HALLS--[34]MYS--
HALE "FEAST OF THE DEAD" '56

HALLSTEAD, WILLIAM FINN
BEECHCROFT, WILLIAM--MSC #43, P99,[3]MYS--
DODD "POSITION OF ULTIMATE TRUST" '81
DODD "IMAGE OF EVIL" '85
DODD "CHAIN OF VENGEANCE" '86
DODD "REBUILT MAN" '87
DODD "SECRET KILLS" '88
CARROLL "PURSUIT OF FEAR"
DIGEST STORIES [EQMM & AHMM]

HALLSTROEM, PER [A.L.]
HALLSTROM, PER [A.L.]--[31]

HALLSTROM, CARL
SEDOLIN, STURE--[2][11]

HALPER-SZIGETH, ERNST AL.
VAN ALPEN, ERNEST--[39]GERMAN

HALPERN, BARBARA STRACHEY
STRACHEY, BARBARA--[7]SF--
"JOURNEY'S OF FRODO: AN ATLAS OF TOLKIEN'S LORD OF THE RINGS" '81

HALPERN, FRANCES JOY
HALE, FRANCESCA--[1][31]

HALPERN, LEIVICK
GELPERIN, L.--[31]
HALPER--[31]
HALPERN, L.--[31]
LEIVICK, H.--[31]
LEIVICK, HALPER--[31]

HALPERN, MARJORIE AGOSIN
AGOSIN, MARJORIE--[7]SF--
"THE SECRET WEAVERS: STORIES OF THE FANTASTIC BY WOMEN OF ARGENTINA & CHILE"

HALPERN, OSCAR SAUL
SAUL, OSCAR--[3]MYS--
HARPER "THE DARK SIDE OF LOVE" '74

HALPIN, MARY D.
BLAKE, CHRISTINA--[3]MYS--
RAVEN "A FRAGRANCE OF DEATH" '80
RAVEN "DEADLY LEGACY" '81

HALSALL, PENNY
JORDAN, PENNY--[9][21][26]ROM--
"TIGER MAN"
"BLACKMAIL" & MORE

HALSEY, HARLAN PAGE
OLD SLEUTH--[3]MYS--
NUMEROUS NOVELS 1890-1920
PASTOR, TONY--[3]MYS--
5 NOVELS - LATE 1800's
ROCKWOOD, HARRY--[3]MYS--
"ABNER FERRET, THE LAWYER DETECTIVE"
TAYLOR, JUDSON R.--[3]MYS--
6 NOVELS - LATE 1800's

HAMANN, BARBEL
LAUBENSTEIN, VERENA--[39]GERMAN
SIMON, KATJA--[39]GERMAN

HAMBLETON, PHYLLIS MCVEAN
VANE, PHILLIPA--[8][22]MYS

HAMDEN, JOHN
MONTAGUE, ROBERT--[8]

HAMEL PEIFER, KATHLEEN
DANA, E.H.--[1][31]
DOBKIN, KATHY--[1][31]
DOBKIN, KAYE--[1]
HAMEL DOBKIN, KATHLEEN--[31]
HEMEL DOBKIN, KATHLEEN--[31]
LABRADOR, JAMES--[1][31]
LABRADOR, JUDY--[1][31]
MOODY, G.F.--[1]

HAMEL, FELIX JOHN
DE HAMEL, FELIX JOHN--[1]
HEXHAM, LIONEL J.--[1][3]MYS--
SIMPKIN "HARRY ROUGHTON: REMINISCENCES OF A REVENUE OFFICER" 1882

HAMER, GERTRUD [v.S.]
KENNICOTT, MERVYN BRIAN--[39]GERMAN

HAMERSTROM, FRANCES
WINDSOR, CLAIRE--[1][33]

HAMES, ARTHUR CAXTON
DALTON, MORAY--[3]MYS--
15 LOW NOVELS ? UNCONFIRMED ?

HAMIL, THOMAS ARTHUR
HAMIL, TOM--[33]

HAMILL, CICELY MARY H.
HAMILTON, CICELY--[23]SF
HAMILTON, MAX--[8][23]SF
RAE, SCOTT--[8][23]SF

HAMILL, PETE
MALLOY, ROBERT--[1]

HAMILTON, ALEXANDER
POOTER--[1]
SPEED, DONALD--[2][11]

HAMILTON, BRENDA
TODD, BRENDA--[26]ROM--
HARL 474 "ALL THE RIGHT MOVES"
HARL 560 "DREAMS OF GLASS"
HARL 621 "LOCKET"

HAMILTON, CHARLES H.S.
CLIFTON, HARRY--[31][33][34]MYS,HP--
ORIGINATED & PRINCIPAL AUTHOR
CLIFTON, MARTIN--[1][31][33]HP
CLIVE, CLIFFORD--[1][31][33]
COBHAM, [SIR] ALAN--[1][31][33]
CONQUEST, OWEN--[1][31][33]HP
CONWAY, GORDON--[1][31][33]
DORIAN, HARRY--[1][31][33]
DRAKE, FRANK--[1][31][33]
FOX, FREEMAN--[1][31][33]
GREENING, HAMILTON--[1][31][33]
HERBERT, CECIL--[1][31][33]
HOWARD, PROSPER--[1][31][33]
JENNINGS, ROBERT--[1][31][33]
JONES, GILLINGHAM--[1][31][33]
LLEWELYN, T. HARCOURT--[1][31][33]
MOST PROLIFIC WRITER, THE--[1][31][33]
OWEN, CLIFFORD--[1][31][33]
REDWAY, RALPH--[1][31][33]
REDWAY, RIDLEY--[1][31][33]
RICHARDS, FRANK--[2][8][11][33]HP--
ORIGINATED & PRINCIPAL AUTHOR
RICHARDS, HILDA--[1][33]
ROBBINS, RALEIGH--[1][33]
ROGERS, ROBERT--[1][33]
STANHOPE, ERIC--[1][33]
STANLEY, ROBERT--[1][33]

HAMILTON, CHARLES H.S.
TODD, PETER--[3]MYS--
MP "ADV. OF SHERLOCK HOLMES" '76
WALLACE, NIGEL--[1][33]
WYNYARD, TALBOT--[1][33]

HAMILTON, EDMOND
BLADE, ALEXANDER--[2][11][23]SF,HP--ZIFF-DAVIS
CASTLE, ROBERT--[1][2][11][23][31]SF
DAVIDSON, HUGH--[2][15][31]SF--
WT "VAMPIRE VILLAGE" NOV '32
WT "SNAKE MAN" JAN '33
WT "VAMPIRE MASTER" OCT '33
GARTH, WILL--[1][2][23][31]SF,HP--STANDARD
HAMILTON, WORLD SAVER--[1]
STERLING, BRETT--[2][4][11][23]SF,HP--
'CAPTAIN FUTURE': "THE SPACE EMPEROR" '40
'CAPTAIN FUTURE':"THE STAR OF DREED" '43
'CAPTAIN FUTURE': "MAGIC MOON" '44
'CAPTAIN FUTURE': "RED SUN OF DANGER" '44
TWS "NEVER THE TWAIN SHALL MEET" '46
TENNESHAW, S.M.--[1][2][11]SF,HP--ZIFF-DAVIS
USED ONCE
WENTWORTH, ROBERT--L. ROBBINS LTR '94, [2][23]SF

HAMILTON, ERNEST GRAHAM
GRAHAM, H.E.--[2]

HAMILTON, GAIL
GAYLE, MARGARET--[9][21][26]ROM--
"PRECIOUS INTERLUDE"
"TO CATCH THE WIND"
"ONE IN A MILLION"

HAMILTON, GERALD
WESTON, PATRICK--[8]

HAMILTON, IAIN BETRAM
CAMPBELL, ALASDAIR IAIN--[31]

HAMILTON, JANET
WOOLF, F.X.--W/HOWARD ENGEL,[18][34]MYS--
VIKING "MURDER IN SPACE" '85

HAMILTON, JOAN LESLIE
CLINE, JOAN--[31]

HAMILTON, LEIGH BRACKETT
BRACKETT, LEIGH--[1]

HAMILTON, MARGARET WOLFE
DUCHESS, THE--[29]MYS
HUNGERFORD, MRS--[29]MYS

HAMILTON, MARY AGNES A.
ICONOCLAST--[8][22]MYSTERY

HAMILTON, MARY MARGARET KAYE
HAMILTON, MOLLIE--[29][31][33][34]MYS--
KAYE, M.M.--[7][31][40]MYS/ROM/SF--
KESTREL "THE ORDINARY PRINCESS" '80
"FAR PAVILIONS"
"SHADOW OF THE MOON" & MORE
KAYE, MARY MARGARET--[8]
KAYE, MOLLIE--[31][33][34][40]MYS--
HUTCH "SIX BARS AT SEVEN" '40

HAMILTON, SIR GEORGE R.
ROSTREVOR, GEORGE--[8]

HAMILTON, STEVE & MELINDA
STEVENS, LINDA--[9][21][34]MYS--
HARL "SHADOWPLAY" '90
HARL "ONE STEP AHEAD"

HAMILTON, STEVE & MELINDA [CONT]
VAIL, LINDA--[9][21]ROM--
"FOOL'S PARADISE"
"NIGHT SHADOW" & MORE

HAMILTON-EDWARDS, GERALD
EDWARDS, GERALD H.--[31]

HAMILTON-WILKES, EDWIN
HAMILTON-WILKES, MONTY--[8]
UNCLE MONTY--[8]

HAMLING, WILLIAM L.
DEEGAN, FRANCIS M.--[2]MYS,HP--
S&SDM "THE WANT-AD MURDERS" MAR '44
FRANCIS, LEE--[2]HP--?
MCGREEVEY, JOHN [W]--[11][32]MYS,HP--
DIGEST STORIES - HU, MV & PU
TENNESHAW, S.M.--[2][23]SF,HP--
ZIFF-DAVIS - ORIGINALLY PERSONAL PSEUD.

HAMMENSKOG, STURE
LAGEVI, BO--[29]MYS,HP--
BS-2 "DODEN PA VAG" '76

HAMMERSCHMID, JOSEF
GOLLWITZER, JOSEF--[39]GERMAN

HAMMERTON, J.A.
J.A.H.--[8]

HAMMERTON, TOM
COLES, MANNING--W/CYRIL COLES,[3]MYS--
"HOUSE AT PLUCK'S GUTTER"
"SEARCH FOR A SULTAN"

HAMMETT, DASHIELL
COLLINSON, PETER--[5][22][29][37]MYS--
BM "THE ROAD HOME" DEC '22
BM "ARSON PLUS" OCT '23
DASHIELL, SAMUEL--[8]
HAMMETT, DAVID--[29]MYS--
DM-15 "VALDETS MAN" '49
DM-50 "HALSEN I SNARAN" '51
SvN-M5 "AMOR HAR ALIBI" '50
DM-5 "INLASTA BEVIS" '52
DM-44 "LEJD FOR ATT DODA" '52
NORST "MORDET I FAREWELL" '77
HAMMETT, MARY JANE--[8]

HAMMOND INNES, RALPH
HAMMOND, RALPH--[22][29][31]ENGLISH--
"COCO'S GOLD" '50
INNES, HAMMOND--[22][29][34]MYS--
JENKINS "AIR DISASTER" '37
COLLINS "BLACK TIDE" 82 & MORE

HAMMOND, GERALD [A.D.]
DOUGLAS, ARTHUR--[18][34]MYS--
MacM "THE GOODS" '85
MacM "LAST RIGHTS" '86
MacM "A VERY WRONG NUMBER" '87
MacM "A WORM TURNS" '88
HOLDEN, DALBY--[18][34]MYS--
HALE "DOLDRUM" '87

HAMMOND, JOHN HENRY JR.
JOHNSON, HENRY--[31]

HAMMOND, LAWRENCE
FRANCIS, VICTOR--[8][32]MYS--
SUS "DANGER MONEY" NOV '58
SUS "DRINK TO DANGER" MAY '59
SUS "YOU WON'T BELIEVE IT, BUT..." NOV '60
SUS "LIGHT OF VENGEANCE" APR '61

HAMMOND, MRS. J.S.
BOYD, BELLE--[1]

HAMON, LOUIS
CHEIRO--[2][8][11][14]ADULT--OLYMP

HAMPEL, BRUNO
GLOGAU, HEINZ--[39]GERMAN

HAMPLE, STUART
BROWN, TURNER JR.--W/ERIC MARSHALL,[1]

HAMPSHIRE, JOYCE BALLOU G
GREGORIAN, JOYCE BALLOU--[7]SF--
"TRE-DANA TRILOGY #1-3" '75/87

HAMPSON, ANNE
WILBY, JANE--[9][21]ROM--
"ELEANOR & THE MARQUIS"
"MAN OF CONSEQUENCES" & MORE

HAMPSON, I.E.
CARNI, ROSS--[34]MYS,HP--
HAM STFFD "THE SHOWDOWN" '52

HAMPTON, JOHN LEWIS
HAMPTON, JIM--[31]

HAMPTON, KATHLEEN
STREET, LEE--[22]AMERICAN

HAMPTON, LINDA
DAYTON, LILY--[9][21][26]ROM--
"CAUGHT IN THE MIDDLE"

HAMRICK, SAMUEL J. JR.
TYLER, W.T.--[3][29]MYS--
DIAL "MAN WHO LOST THE WAR" '80
DIAL "ANTS OF GOD" '81
HARPER "ROGUE'S MARCH" '82
HARPER "SHADOW CABINET" '84

HAMSON, CHARLES JOHN
HAMSON, C.J.--[31]

HANCHAR, PEGGY
ROBERTS, PEGGY--[26]ROM--
"JUST IN TIME"
"MRS. PERFECT"
"WHAT EVERY WOMAN KNOWS"
STEVENS, JENNIFER--[26]ROM--
'MAGNOLIA ROAD' SERIES:
"LOUISIANA HEAT"

HANCOCK, DEBBIE BARR
LEIGH, ELIZABETH--W/CAROLINE BOURNE,
[21][26]ROM--5 NOVELS

HANCOCK, HARRIE I.
WAINWRIGHT, RICHARD ASHTN--[3]MYS--
MAGNET 204 "HUNTED DOWN" '01
MAGNET 237 "KIDNAPPED MILLIONAIRE" '02

HANCOCK, MORGAN
HANCOCK, CAROL HELEN B.--[31]

HANCOCK, WILLIAM KEITH
HANCOCK, W.K.--[31]

HAND,[ANDRUS] JACKSON
CARPENTER, FRED--[31]

HANDL, JOSEPH
HOLM, HANS--[39]GERMAN

HANGEKORB, KURT
KURT, ROBERT--[39]GERMAN/JUV

HANIFIN, JOHN M.
PHINEAS--[2]

HANING, JAMES ROBERT
HANING, BOB--[31]

HANION, CAROLYN
ANDREWS, CAROLYN--[26]ROM--
HARL 498 "C.J.'S DEFENSE"

HANKINS, ARTHUR PRESTON
ARTHUR, H. PRESTON--L. ROBBINS LTR '94,
[22]MYS--
KINSBURN, EMART--[3][22]MYS--
CHELSEA "WIZARD'S SPYGLASS" '26
CHELSEA "TONG MEN & A MILLION" '27
PRESTON, ARTHUR--[22]MYSTERY
PRESTON, ARTHUR H.--L. ROBBINS LTR MAR '94

HANKINSON, CHARLES JAMES
HOLLAND, CLIVE--[2][3][8]MYS--
SCOTT "HIDDEN SUBMARINE: PLOT THAT
FAILED" '17

HANLEY, CLIFFORD L.C.
CALVIN, HENRY--[2][3][8][22][31]MYS--
HUTCH "POISON CHASERS" '71
"ITALIAN GADGET" '66

HANLEY, JACK
HARVEY, GENE--[8]

HANLEY, JAMES
BENTLEY, JAMES--[8]
SHONE, PATRIC--[8]

HANLEY, MICHAEL F. IV
HANLEY, MIKE--[31]

HANNA, DAVID
JAMES, ANTHONY--[31]
LAINE, GLORIA--[31]

HANNA, FRANCES NICHOLS
CONTENT, NIKKI--V. BERCH-GM PSEUDS,
PP 33,[3]MYS--
GM 308 "HIDEAWAY" '53
NICHOLS, FAN--V. BERCH-MON PSEUDS, BAE 9
GM PSEUDS, PP 33,[3][29]MYS--
GODWIN "SCANDAL" '37
GODWIN "PAWN" '38
GODWIN "DEADLINE FOR LOVERS" '38
FELL "POSSESS ME NOT" '46
ARCO "ONE BY ONE" '51
GM 251 "THE CAGED" '52
POPLB 483 "ASK FOR LINDA" '53
POPLB 536 "COUNT ME IN" '53
POPLB 586 "DEVIL TAKE HER" '54
POPLB 642 "I'LL NEVER LET YOU GO" '55
POPLB 706 "ANGEL FACE" '55
POPLB G231 "I KNOW MY LOVE" '58
POPLB 791 "HE WALKS BY NIGHT" '57
MON 103 "LOVE ME NOW" '58
SIMON "THE LONER" '56
"BE SILENT, LOVE" '60,
RPTD AS "GIRL IN THE DEATH SEAT"

HANNA, GEORGE W.
GENTIL, SPIRITO--[2]

HANNA, MARY T.
COLE, MARY--[31]

HANNA, NELL[IE L.]
NELL--[33]

HANNA, WILLIAM
HANNA, BILL--[31][33]

HANNAWAY, PATRICIA H.
CHARNANCE, L.P.--[31]
HANNAWAY, PATTI--[31]

HANNAY, D.
HEATH, MICHAEL--[35]AUSTRALIAN--
HRWTZ PB149 "SOLO" '78

HANNAY, JAMES OWEN
BIRMINGHAM, GEORGE A.--[3][22][29]MYS--
HODDER "FIDGETS" '27
METHUEN "FED UP" '31 & MORE

HANNAYS, KITTY
MACAW--[1]

HANO, ARNOLD
DODGE, GIL--MUNROE RVW '93,[1]--
SIGN 1414 "FLINT" '57
GANT, MATTHEW--V. BERCH-GM PSEUDS,
PP 33,[31][32][34]MYS--
GM 335 "VALLEY OF ANGRY MEN" '53
EQMM "CRATE AT OUTPOST 1" MAY '54
SIGN 1423 "MANHUNTER" '57
EQMM "HUNGRY LOOK" JAN '58
SL "USES OF INTELLIGENCE" OCT '58
MOF "WETBACK" OCT '59
MOF "TESTAMENT OF DUMMY SLOTT" APR '59
PYR G-482 "LAST NOTCH" '60
SIGN 1927 "RAVEN & THE SWORD" '61
REGY RB315 "QUEEN ST." '63
GORDON, AD--[31][32]MYS--
JU "JUSTICE IS FINE" MAY '55
JU "TWO LITTLE BULLETS" JUL '55
HELLER, MIKE--V. BERCH-GM PSEUDS,
PP 33,[34]MYS--
GM 664 "SO I'M A HEEL" '57

HANOS, DMITRI [JAMES]
BRANDON, JIM--PULP CLASSIC #22--
STORIES IN 'MASKA' & OTHER GREEK PUBS
HANOS, JIM--PULP CLASSIC #22--
STORIES IN 'MASKA' & OTHER GREEK PUBS
HANSEN, JAMES--PULP CLASSIC #22--
STORIES IN 'MASKA' & OTHER GREEK PUBS
HATTEN, JIMMY--PULP CLASSIC #22--
STORIES IN 'MASKA' & OTHER GREEK PUBS
STEEL, DOUGLAS--PULP CLASSIC #22--
STORIES IN 'MASKA' & OTHER GREEK PUBS

HANSELL, FRANZ T.
STONEBRIDGE, JOANNE--[14]--
OLYM OPH#153 "THE FAMILY JEWELS" '69
OLYM TC#439 "I'M LOOKING FOR BABY K" '69
STONEBRIDGE, JOE--[14] ADULT--
OLYM TC#501 "PRIVATE WEAPONS" '71

HANSELL, PER TORE
HARALDSSON, HARALD--[29]MYS--
"LILLI LORENT" '19
"DET STORA BEDRAGERIET" '20
"STORVINDLARNA" '20
RUSSELL, RALF--[29]MYS

HANSEN, ANNE
PETERS, ANNE--[9][21][26]ROM--
"LIKE WILDFIRE"
"NOBODY'S PERFECT" & MORE

HANSEN, ANTON
TAMMSAARE, A.H.--[1] ESTONIAN
TAMMSAARE, ANTON--[1][22] ESTONIAN

HANSEN, CARYL [HALL]
HALL, CARYL--[1][31][33]

HANSEN, CHUCK
COUNCIL OF FOUR--W/TOM WALKER, ROY HUNT, NORM METCALF, ELLIS MILLS & BOB PETERSON,[2]

HANSEN, JOSEPH
BROCK, ROSE--[3][18][21][26][31]MYS--
AV "TARN HOUSE" '71
HARPER "LONGLEAF" '74
COLTON, JAMES--V. BERCH-BRNDN/ BC PSEUDS, BAE 22,[1][3][8][14] [18][31] ADULT/MYS--
BRANDON "KNOWN HOMOSEXUAL" '68
OLYM TC#506 "THE OUTWARD SIDE" '71
OLYM TC#514 "TODD" '71
COULTON, JAMES--[1][8]

HANSEN, JURGEN
FARINA, JOHAN--[39]GERMAN

HANSEN, JURIJ
MOSKVITIN, JURIJ--[1]

HANSEN, LOUIS INGVALD
HANSEN, L. TAYLOR--[1]

HANSEN, PEGGY M.
WESTHAVEN, MARGARET--[21][26]ROM--
"SPANISH COIN"
"WIDOW FOR HIRE" & MORE

HANSEN, ROBERT
ANKER, JENS--[1][34][37] DANISH/MYS--
KNOPF "TWO DEAD MEN" '22
ANKER, JENS--[3][29]MYS--
KNOPF "TWO DEAD MEN" '22 & 5 MORE '16-43
KASSOW, GERT--[37] DANISH/MYS
OWEN, GEOFFREY--[29]MYS

HANSHEW, MARY E.
HANSHEW, HAZEL PHILLIPS--W/THOMAS W. HANSHEW,[1][5][22]MYS--
KINGSLEY, ANNA--W/THOMAS W. HANSHEW, [1][5][22]MYS--

HANSHEW, THOMAS W.
CARTER, NICHOLAS--[1][5][11]MYS,HP--
H., T.W.--[37]MYS--NYDL - PULP STORIES
HANSHEW, HAZEL PHILLIPS--W/MARY E. HANSHEW,[1][5][22]MYS
HANSHEW, T.W. [1]--[32]MYS--
EQMM "MURDER IN A EMPTY HOUSE" JUL '48
EQMM "RIDDLE OF THE SILVER" AUG '51
EQMM "THE MAN WITHOUT HEAD" MAY '53
KINGSLEY, ANNA--W/MARY E. HANSHEW, [1][5][22]MYS
KINGSLEY, CHARLOTTE MAY--[18][22][29][31]MYS--
"ARTOL'S ENGAGEMENT" '03

HANSON, ERNEST S.
DANE, DANIEL--[3]MYS--
CASSELL "VENGEANCE IS MINE" 1890

HANSON, IRENE FORSYTHE
FORSYTHE, IRENE--[31]

HANSON, MICHAEL
HEMAN, NICHOLAS--[1]

HANSON, PAMELA
DREW, JENNIFER--W/BARBARA ANDREWS,[26]ROM--
SIL 1040 "TURN BACK THE NIGHT"
ROCK, PAM--W/BARBARA ANDREWS,[26]ROM--
"LOVE'S CHANGING MOON"
"MOON OF DESIRE"

HANSON, VICTOR JOSEPH
CELLO, JOHNNY--S. HOLLAND-SCION CKLST, PP 27, P11,HP--

HANSON, VICTOR JOSEPH
CLINTEN, MAX--PPCC#7, P64,[27][34]MYS,HP--
COMYNS "DEAD WERE STRANGERS" '52
COMYNS "DON'T MAKE ME KILL" '53
COMYNS "RED, HOT & DEADLY" '53
COMYNS "SO LONG, SUCKER" '53
COMYNS "STRICTLY ILLEGAL" '53
DUDGEON, ROBERT--J. HOFFMANN-PP 40,MYS,HP--
GERM PANTH 157-RPRT OF SCION "MURDER-SO WHAT" '51
GARROWAY, PETE--[27]MYS--
"GREY USHER"
HANSEN, VERN--[7][23][28][32]MYS/HOR--
7 DIGIT NOVELS '62-64
EW "SAVAGE DEATH" AUG '64
EW "THE KNOCKER-MAN" DEC '64
HALE "SAVAGE SUNRISE" '79
HALE "MULDARE" '80
HALE "MEN ON A DUSTY STREET" '81
HALE "HANNIBAL'S JUMP" '91
HANSON, V. JOSEPH--[28]MYS--
SCION "THE MORGUE HAS GUESTS: DIARY OF A KILLER
6 WESTERN NOVELS '50-
HANSON, V.J.--[3]MYS--
AMALG "DEATH & LITTLE GIRL BLUE" '62
SCION "LEAD BITES DEEP" '50
SCION "MORGUE HAS GUESTS" '50
HANSON, VIC J.--[3]MYS--
HALE "THE END OF THE KILL" '80
HANSON, W.J.--PPCC#3, P63, WEST--
MUW "LANNIGAN'S WEST" '49
LINTON, DUKE--S. HOLLAND-SCION CKLST, PP 27,[34]MYS,HP--
SCION "TOO MANY YESTERDAYS" '51
SCION "LEND ME A ROD" '51
SCION "THAT DAME SAL" '52
SCION "WHAT DO I CARE?" '52
SCION "THEY'VE GOT ME AGAIN" '52
SCION "CALL ME AL" '52
SCION "HOW DEAD CAN YOU BE?" '52
SCION "KEEP MOVING, BUD" '52
SCION "KILLER BAIT" '53
SCION "POISON" '53
SCION "SO SWEET, SO DEAD" '53
SCION "STRIP TEASE ANGEL" '53
SCION "WHO'S SORRY NOW?" '53
SCION "SIN'S HALF MILE" '53
SCION "SWINGING CORPSE" '54
POTTER, JAY HILL--D. WHITEHEAD-PPCC#9, [28]WEST--10 NOVELS '79-93
REID, DESMOND--W/W.A. BAKER,[34]HP--
AMALG "CULT OF DARKNESS" '63
AMALG "DEATH ON A HIGH NOTE" '62
SHANNON, BRAD--S. HOLLAND-SCION CKLST, PP 27,[27][34]MYS--
SCION "BURY TH GUY" '51
SCION ""BIG SNATCH" '52
SCION "DEATH WALKS SOFTLY" '52
& 24 MORE '50-3
ZORE, HYMAN--S.HOLLAND-CION CKLST, PP 27,[34]MYS,HP--
SCION "COVER THAT CORPSE" '53
SCION "SHADOW OF SIN" '53

HANSSON, LAURA MOHR
MARHOLM, LAURA--[1][22] SWEDISH

HANSTEIN, WOLFRAM v.
BERGER, BERG--[39]GERMAN
HELL, HELLAN--[39]GERMAN

HANZELON, ROBERT M.
DE HART, ROBERT--[8]

HANZEN, KLAAS
JACOBSE, MUUS--[22] DUTCH

HARAKAS, STANLEY SAMUEL
EXETASTES--[31]

HARAY, KEITH
HARAY, STUART BLUE--[31]

HARBAGE, ALFRED B.
KYD, THOMAS--[5][32][34]MYS--
LIPP "BLOOD IS A BEGGAR" '46
LIPP "BLOOD OF VINTAGE" '47
LIPP "BLOOD ON THE BOSOM" '48
LIPP "COVER HIS FACE" '49
EQMM "HIGH COURT" OCT '53
EQMM "THE LETTER" FEB '56
EQMM "COTTAGE FOR AUGUST" AUG '57

HARBAUGH, THOMAS C.
ALCALAW, [MAJ.] G.W.--[1]
BOSTWICK, [COL.] T.B.--[1]
BRISBANE, [MAJ.] WALTER--[1]
CARTER, NICHOLAS--[1] HOUSE PSEUD.
CARTER, NICK--[1][5][11]MYS,HP--
CLAY, BERTHA M.--[1][22]
COLLIER, OLD CAP--[1][22]--
'W.I. JAMES' SERIES
GRANT, [MAJ.] A.F.--[1]
HAWKES, ISAAC--[1]
HOLMES, CAPT. HOWARD--[1][3]MYS--
IVERS "THE NEVER FAIL DETECTIVE" '20's
HOWARD, CHARLES--[1]
INMAN, ROBERT RANDOLPH--[1] ?
KENNEDY, [CAPT.] J.L.--[1]
KNOX, JACKSON--[1]
LEE, GEORGE B.--[1]
LINCOLN, HOWARD--[1]
OLD SLEUTH--[1]
SCOTT, [MAJ.] S.S.--[1]
STEADMAN, [CAPT.] DICK--[1]
WILMOT, [MAJ.] WALT--[1]
WINSTON, F.S.--[1]
WINTON, HARRY--[1]
WINTON, [CAPT.] WALT--[1]

HARBECK, ALOIS
HARB, ALOY--[39]GERMAN
LEIBACH, OSKAR--[39]GERMAN

HARBINSON, WILLIAM ALLEN
HOWARTH, JOHN--[1]

HARBINSON-BRYANS, ROBERT
BRYANS, ROBIN--[8]
CAMERON, DONALD--[8]
HARBINSON, ROBERT--[8]

HARBURG, EDGAR YIPSEL
HARBURG, YIP--[31]

HARCOURT, MELVILLE
CRITICUS--[22][31]ENGLISH

HARCOURT, THOMAS A.
HERMAN, WILLIAM--W/AMBROSE BIERCE,[1][2]

HARCOURT, WILLIAM VERNON
HISTORICUS--[1]

HARD, EDWARD W. JR.
HARD, T.W.--[1][7][31]

HARDCASTLE, MICHAEL
CLARK, DAVID--[1][31][33]

HARDEN-HICKEY, JAMES
SAINT PATRICE--[1]

HARDING, ALLISON V.
HARCRAFT, ALICE B.--[2]

HARDING, DONALD EDWARD
DAY, DONALD--[1][31]--
ESSAYS TO PERIODICALS

HARDING, DONALD EDWARD
EDWARDS, DONALD EARL--[1][31]--
POETRY TO MAGAZINES
PARRISH, EUGENE--[1][31]--
POETRY TO MAGAZINES

HARDING, HARRY
DEAN, HAYDON--[1][3]MYS--
NICHOLSON "LOVES OF BLACKSCAR" '34

HARDING, LEE [JOHN]
NYE, HAROLD G.--[2][8][23][33]AUSTRALIAN/SF

HARDING, LEO
HARDING, LEE--[2][11]

HARDING, PAUL
CLYNES, MICHAEL--M.LACHMAN-DJ, MYS--
"POISIONED CHALICE"

HARDING, WADE GARRISON
WADE, GARRISON--[34]MYS/WEST--
VANTAGE "ALIAS JOHN SMITH" '66

HARDING, WILLIAM
ROBIN, COMMODORE--[1]

HARDINGE, CHARLES WREXE
CAPSTAN--[3][22][29]MYS--
WRIGHT "BLACK MAGIC" '41
MELLIFONT "CHINESE CABINET" '41
HARDINGE, REX--[1][32]MYS--
LM "GLIMPSE OF PARADISE" JUN '64
QUINTIN, REX--[1]
WREXE, CHARLES--[1]

HARDINGE, GEORGE
MILNER, GEORGE--[3][8][32]MYS--
8 NVLS '53-85
LM "TANCARROW TREASURE" AUG '54

HARDINGHAM, L.H.
RUSSELL, BERTRAM--[2][21]ROM--
"EASY TARGET"
"NIGHT SECRETS"

HARDISON, OSBORNE B.
BENNETT, H.O.--[1]

HARDMAN, RICHARDS LYNDEN
HOWITZER, BRONSON--[22][31]AMERICAN

HARDT, HEINZ
ROBERTSON, DIRK R.--[39]GERMAN/SF
SZILLAGHY, IRMA--[39]GERMAN/SF
VON TANNMARK, ETTA--[39]GERMAN/SF

HARDTER, FRANCES
WILLIAMS, FRANCES--[9][26]ROM--5 NOVELS

HARDWICK, MOLLIE
ATKINSON, MARY--[1][17][31]ROM
DRINKROW, JOHN--[1][17]--
"THE VINTAGE MUSIC COMEDY BOOK" '74

HARDWICK, RICHARD
HONEYCUTT, RICHARD--[8]

HARDWICK, RICHARD HOLMES
HOLMES, RICK--V. BERCH-MON PSEUDS,
BAE 9,[31][31]--
MON F262 "TROPIC OF CLEO" '62
BEAC B471F "MAN CRAZY" '62
BEAC B620 "NEW WIDOW '63
MON 346 "LOVE UNDER CAPRICORN" '63
MON 557 "RIVERFRONT GIRL" '65
MON 563 "CHILD-WOMAN" '65

HARDWICK,[J] MICHAEL [D]
DRINKROW, JOHN--[8][31]--
"THE VINTAGE OPERETA BOOK" '73
HARDWICK, J.M.D.--[31]--NON-FICT

HARDY, C. COLBURN
BLAKE, JONAS--[1][31]
MUNN, HART--[1]
PECK, LEONARD--[1]

HARDY, CARLENE
FRANCIS, RICKI--[35]AUSTRALIAN--
42 HRWTZ NOVELS '70-7
FRANKLIN, ROGER--[35]AUSTRALIAN--
HRWTZ PB077 "SHARK!" '75
HRWTZ SP002 "HURRICANE" '76
FRENCH, ROSALIND--[35]AUSTRALIAN--
HRWTZ PB041 "MAN CRAZY" '75
HRWTZ SP003 "BIKE TERROR" '76
HRWTZ SP010 "STRANGE DELIGHTS" '76
HANSBERRY, CARLENE--[35]AUSTRALIAN--
HRWTZ, PB451 "SOUL SELLERS" '71
SLATER, JOHN--[35]AUSTRALIAN,HP--
HRWTZ "SADIST'S SLAVE" '73
THOMAS, JOANNA--[35]AUSTRALIAN--HRWTZ

HARDY, FRANK
FRANKLYN, ROSS--[13]AUSTRALIAN

HARDY, HENRY
DUGDALE, DOREEN--[32]MYS--
LM "THE'LL NEVER FIND YOU NOW" MAR '74
DUGDALE, ROBERT--[31]--EDITOR & PUBLISHER

HARDY, JANE
BOILEAU, MARIE--[8]

HARDY, MARJORIE
HARDY, BOBBIE--[8]

HARDY, ROBIN
HILD, JACK--W/JACK CANON & ALAN BOMACK,
[34]MYS,HP--
GE "SOB's":
"BARRABUS RUN" '83
HILD, JACK--[34]MYS,HP--
GE "EYE OF THE FIRE" '85
GE "RIVERS OF FLESH" '85
GE "SOME CHOOSE HELL" '85
GE "RED VENGEANCE" '86
GE "SOB's":
"AGILE RETRIEVAL" '86
"NO SANCTUARY" '86
"DEATH DEAL" '86
"FIRESTORM" '87

HARDY, ROBIN [CONT]
HILD, JACK [CONT]
GE "POINT BLANK" '87
GE "SKYJACK" 87
GE "KREMLIN DEVILS" '88
GE "NO SAFE PLACE" '88

HARDY, WILLIAM GEORGE
HARDY, W.G.--[1]

HARE, THOMAS WILLIAM
HARE, THOMAS BLENMAN--[31]

HARE, WALTER B.
BURNS, MARY--[8]

HARE, WILLIAM MOORMAN
HARE, BILL--[31]

HARGRAVE, JOHN
WHITE FOX--[1]

HARGREAVES, REGINALD C.
AIGUILLETTE--[1][31]
MELVILLE, LEWIS--W/LEWIS S. BENJAMIN,
[1][2][11]

HARGROVE, JAMES
HARGROVE, JIM--[31][33]

HARING, DON
ANTHONY, CLAY--[35]AUSTRALIAN--
SANTE FE 402 "THE GUN OF TOM SLADE"
BRADFORD, SAM--[35]AUSTRALIAN--
CLEVELAND
KENT, LARRY--[35]AUSTRALIAN, SP--
CLEVE - ORIGINATED & WROTE
MOST 'KENT' BOOKS
LANGLEY, WARD--[35]AUSTRALIAN--CLEVELAND

HARING, WILHELM
ALEXIS, WILLIBALD--[39]GERMAN/MYS

HARKAVY, ZVI
YERUSHALMI, GERSHON--[1]
ZVI, H.--[1]

HARKINS, PETER J.
ADAMS, ANDY--[8]
BLAINE, JOHN--W/HAROLD L. GOODWIN,
[2][7][11][23]SF--
"ROCKETS SHADOW" '47
"LOST CITY" '47
"MAGIC TALISMAN" '90

HARKNESS, EDITH MYRTELLA
SOUTHERLAND, MYRTELLA--[1]

HARKNESS, JOHN LEIGH
HARKNESS, JACK--[31]

HARKNETT, TERRY W.
CHANDLER, FRANK--[19][28][31]WEST--
GHOSTED "A FISTFULL OF DOLLARS" '72
FORD, DAVID--[1][28][31]--
NEL "CYPRUS" '73
GILMAN, GEORGE G.--[11][19][28][31]WEST--
NUMEROUS NOVELS
HAINING, PETER--[28]--
GHOSTED "THE HERO" '73
HARDY, ADAM--[8][11]HP
HARMAN, JANE--[11][28][31]--
NEL "W.I.T.C.H." '71
HEDGES, JOSEPH--[3][8][28][31]MYS--
12 SPHERE NOVELS '73-7

HARKNETT, TERRY W. [CONT]
JAMES, WILLIAM M.--W/LAWRENCE JAMES, [11][19][28]WEST--
PINN "FIRST DEATH" '74 & 6 MORE
PETERS, ALEX--[28]GHOSTED--
"THE SAVAGE" '79
"DOOMSDAY ISLAND" '79
PIKE, CHARLES R.--[11][19][28]WEST--
CHELSEA 'JUBAL CADE' SERIES-
WROTE FIRST 3
PINE, WILLIAM--[3][8][28]MYS--
CONSTABLE "THE PROTECTORS '67
RUSSELL, JAMES--[1][28]--
NEL "THE BALEARIC ISLANDS" '72
STONE, THOMAS H.--[3][28][40]MYS--
NEL "ONE HORSE RACE" '72
& 4 OTHER NVLS '72-3
STONE, THOMAS P.--[1][32]MYS--
EQMM "A TIME FOR TEA" JUL '62
TERRY, WILLIAM--[28][34]MYS--
HAMMOND "ONCE A COPPER" '65
NEL "A TOWN CALLED BASTARD" '71
NEL "HANNIE CAULDER" '71
NEL "RED SUN" '72

HARKSEN, VERENA C.
NEREV, ADELAIDE--[39]GERMAN/SF

HARLAND, HENRY
LUSKA, SIDNEY--[2][3]MYS--
CASSELL "AS IT WAS WRITTEN" 1885

HARLING, ROBERT
DREW, NICHOLAS--[8][18]MYS--
"AMATEUR SAILOR" '44

HARLOW, NANCY
LYNN, ANN--W/KAREN PARADISO,[21]ROM--
"MIDNIGHT SAFARI"
"PASSION'S CHASE" & MORE

HARMAN, RICHARD ALEXANDER
HARMAN, ALEC--[31]
HARMAN, R. ALEC--[31]

HARMENING, WILHELM CHR.
ERNINGHAM, H.F.--[39]GERMAN/ADV
HARDING, MICHAEL--[39]GERMAN/ADV
HARMS, CHRISTEL--[39]GERMAN/ADV
HARMSEN, C.W.--[39]GERMAN/ADV

HARMON, JAMES JUDSON
GREY, JUDSON--W/RON HAYDOCK,[2][11]--
EPIC "WANTON WITCH"
EPIC"TWILIGHT GIRLS"
HARMON, JIM--[7][23][31][32]MYS/SF--
CJ "LET ME ALONE" SEPT '56
TE "HOOKED CROOK" OCT '56
CJ "THE BOMB" NOV "56
CJ "LET ME WATCH YOU KILL"
EPIC "MAN WHO MADE MANIACS" '61
NM "GODZILLA BOOK" '86
HARVEY, JAMIESON--W/WILL KUHN,SMUT PEDDLER #2--
EPIC "HARLOT MASTER"
HARVEY, JIM--W/WILL KUHN,SMUT PEDDLER #2--
BOUDOIR "ABORTION MILL"
NEWTON, CLARKE--[1][2][11]
WILKINS, J.H.--W/WILL KUHN,SMUT PEDDLER #2--
PILLOW "SIN UNLIMITED"

HARMON, NANCY
ST. JOHN, LEONIE--W/WILLIAM BAYER,[1][8]--
ACE F140 "LOVE WITH A HARVARD ACCENT" '62

HARNACK-BRAUN, KATHARINA
BRAUN, KATHE--[39]GERMAN

HARNAN, TERRY
HULL, ERIC TRAVISS--[31][33][34]MYS--
DBLDY "MURDER LAYS A GOLDEN EGG" '44

HARNESS, CHARLES [L]
LOCKHARD, LEONARD--W/THEODORE L. THOMAS, [2][23], ASF

HARNISCH, LUCY
CORNEISSEN, LUCY--[39]GERMAN

HARPER, CAROL ELY
BEN, ILKE--[1][31]
GODDARD, ALFRED--[1][31]

HARPER, CHARLES
A HAWKESBURY LAD--[13]AUSTRALIAN

HARPER, EDITH
FLAMANK, E.--[8]

HARPER, EDWARD M.
MCGHEE, EDWARD--[3]MYS--
PINN "THE LAST CAESAR" '80
PINN "ORPHEUS CIRCLE" '87
PINN "HERACLES COMMANDO" '89
MOORE, ROBIN--[34]--
WROTE PINN "CHINESE ULTIMATUM" '76,
AS BY 'MOORE & EDWARD MCGHEE'

HARPER, ELIZABETH SHANNON
BRADY, TAYLOR--W/DONNA BALL,[26]ROM--
"KINCAIDS" SERIES
BRISTOL, LEIGH--[21]ROM--
"HEARTS OF FIRE"
"AMBER SKIES" & 4 MORE
BRISTOL, LEIGH--W/DONNA BALL,[9][21]ROM--
"SUNSWEPT"
"TWICE BLESSED" & MORE
HABERSHAM, ELIZABETH--W/MADELINE PORTER, [9][21][26][34]MYS--
PINN "ISLAND OF DECEIT" '77
HARPER, MADELINE--W/MADELINE PORTER, [9][21]ROM--
"LOVE DANCE"
"JADE AFFAIR" & MORE
JAMES, ANNA--W/MADELINE PORTER,[9][21][26]ROM--
"IMAGES"
"VENETIAN NECKLACE" & MORE

HARPER, FRANCES ELLEN W.
HARPER, F.E.W.--[31]
HARPER, MRS. F.E.W.--[31]
WATKINS, FRANCES ELLEN--[1]

HARPER, GEORGE WILLIAM
CALAENO--[31]--
MAGAZINE FICTION/ARTICLES

HARPER, HARRY
CLIFFORD, MARTIN--[1]HP--

HARPER, HENRY GEORGE
G., G.--[34]MYS--
LONG "HORSES I'VE KNOWN" 1897
LONG "CHASER'S LUCK" '03

HARPER, J. CLYDE
HARPER, CLYDE--L. ROBBINS LTR MAR '94

HARPER, KAREN
CAMERON, CARYN--[9][21][26]ROM--
"SILVER SWORDS"
"WILD LILLY" & 4 MORE

HARPER, KATHERINE ERNA
HARPER, KATE--[31]

HARPER, OLIVIA & KEN
ADAMS, JOLENE--[9][21][26]ROM--
"FROM THIS DAY FORWARD"
BRANDON, JOANNA--[9][21][26]ROM--
"JUST A KISS AWAY"
"SUSPICION & DESIRE" & MORE

HARPER, WILLIAM ARTHUR
HARPER, BILL--[31]

HARPUR, THOMAS WILLIAM
HARPER, TOM--[31]

HARRAH, MADGE
HARA, MONIQUE--[9][21][26][34]MYS/ROM--
"MIRROR OF DARKNESS" '86
"SHADOW OF THE CAT" '88

HARRANTH, WOLF
NEY, WOLFGANG--[1]

HARRE, HORACE ROMANO
HARRE, ROM--[1]

HARREL, LINDA
CLARE, SHANNON--[9][21[26]ROM--
"QUEEN'S RIVAL"
"SNOW BRIDE" & MORE

HARRELL, IRENE B.
AMOR, AMOS--[1][31]
WAYLAN, MILDRED--[1]

HARRER, JOSEF ROBERT
IBIUS, ROBERT--[39]GERMAN
NELL, LUKAS--[39]GERMAN

HARRIES, JOAN
KATSARAKIS, JOAN HARRIES--[1][31][33]

HARRINGTON, CURTIS
SEBASTIAN, JOHN--[11]

HARRINGTON, EVELYN DAVIS
HARRINGTON, LYN--[31]
HARRINGTON, LYNN--[31] TRAVEL & JUV

HARRINGTON, MARK R.
DE LAS CUEVAS, RAYMON--[1][22][31]AMERICAN
JISKOGO--[1][22][31]AMERICAN
TONASHI--[1][22]AMERICAN

HARRINGTON, SHARON & RICK
CRAIG, RIANNA--[9][10][21][26][34]MYS/ROM--
HARL "ON EXECUTIVE ORDERS" '86 & MORE

HARRINGTON, WILLIAM
FURST, CARL--HARRINGTON LTR FEB '94,
ADULT? BOOKS
MARKLIN, MEGAN--HARRINGTON LTR FEB '94,[31]--
POCK "THE SUMMONED" '93
ROOSEVELT, ELLIOTT--DDLY PLEAS #3, P34,
[34]MYS, GHOSTED--
ST. MARTIN'S "HYDE PARK MURDER" '85
ST. MARTINS'S "MURDER & THE
FIRST LADY" '84
& 6 OTHERS

HARRIOTT, EDWIN THOMAS
HARRIOTT, TED--[1][31]

HARRIS, ALFRED
ADDISON, GWEN--W/ARTHUR MOORE,[1][3][11]MYS--
"STORM OVER FOX HILL" '74
MOORE, HARRIS--W/ARTHUR MOORE,[2][11][23]SF--
"SLATER'S PLANET" '71
"MARROW EATERS" '72

HARRIS, ALLISON
HARRISON, ALLIE--[26]MYS/ROM--
SIL 20 "DREAM A DEADLY DREAM"
SIL 40 "DEAD RECKONING"

HARRIS, CLARE WINGER
HARRIS, MRS. F.C.--[23]SF

HARRIS, F. BRAYTON
WEST, KIRKPATRICK--[1]

HARRIS, FRANK G.
WALLACE, WAYNE--V. BERCH-BRNDN/
BC PSEUDS, BAE 22, P24

HARRIS, HERBERT
BURY, FRANK--[31][32]--
SA "DUMB FRIEND" JUL '55
SA "SNAP JUDGEMENT" MAR '56
MSMM "BAD TIMING" NOV '72
MSMM "RIGHT LINES" JUN '73
MSMM "SAFE ALIBI" SEPT '75
MSMM "BIG FIX" NOV '75
FRIDAY, PETER--[1][29][32]MYS--
MSMM "BLUFF AT GUNPOINT" DEC '72
MOORE, MICHAEL--[1][29][32]MYS--
MSMM "DUMB WITNESS" APR '76
REGAN, JERRY--LACHMAN LST '93,[29][32]MYS--
MSMM "DEATH IN THE CAMERA" MAR '73
MSMM "THIRD TIME UNLUCKY" APR '73

HARRIS, IDA FRASER
PROCTOR, IDA--[8]

HARRIS, JAMES HENRY
STAFF, JACK--[1]

HARRIS, JAMES THOMAS
HARRIS, FRANK--[1][23]ENGLISH/SF--
"TEMPLE OF THE FORGOTTEN DEAD" '24

HARRIS, JOEL CHANDLER
SKINFLINT, OBEDIAH--[1]
UNCLE REMUS--[1]

HARRIS, JOHN
HEBDEN, MARK--[3][18][29][31]MYS--
HARRAP "ERRANT KNIGHTS" '68
HARRAP "DARK SIDE OF THE ISLAND" '73
HENNESSY, MAX--[18][29][31]WAR--8 NOVELS '78-83

HARRIS, JOHN WYNDHAM P.L
HARRIS, JOHNSON--[2][4][7][23]SF--
"LOVE IN TIME" '45
BEYNON, JOHN--[2][3][4][7][23][31]MYS/SF--
NEWNES "SECRET PEOPLE" '35
NEWNES "FOUL PLAY SUSPECTED" '35
NEWNES "PLANET PLANE" '36
DRUMMOND, J.--[2]
HARRIS, JOHN BENYON--[2][7][23]SF--
"THE SECRET PEOPLE" '64
PARKES, LUCAS--[2][4][7][11][23]SF--
BAL 341K "THE OUTWARD URGE" '59
PARKES, WYNDHAM--[2][11][23]SF--
WYNDHAM, JOHN--[2][4][7][32]MYS/SF--
SU "OPERATION PEEP" SUM '51
TF "BUT A KIND OF GHOST" '56
SUS "A LONG SPOON" SEPT '60
6 NVLS '72-80

HARRIS, JOSEPH UPPER
UPPER, JOSEPH--[1]

HARRIS, JULIE K.
AYMES, ADAM--[14]ADULT--
OLYM OPH#140 "GIN & LIME STREET" '69
OLYM OPH#155 "PLEASURE ME, PLEASE" '69

HARRIS, LAURENCE MARK
BEACH, TOM--[1][2][32]--
AC "GHOSTS THAT WANTED COMPANY" JAN '56
HU "GUN" FEB '56
AC "SEAT OF HIS PANTS" MAR '56
AC "MAN WHO HID" MAY '56
BLAKE, ALFRED--[11][2][23][31] ADULT--
BEAC B596F "FAITHFUL FOR EIGHT HOURS" '63
BLAKE, ANDREW--W/CHESTER ANDERSON,[2][11][31]
HARRIS, LARRY M.--[32]MYS--
SF "GIVE ME THAT GUN" JAN '57
AHMM "WORLD'S OLDEST MOTIVE" DEC '59
TR "PUNKS IN THE PARK" FEB '62
OF "SWEET MISTRESS OF MURDER" JUL '62
TR "DEATH OF A MUGGER" MAY '62
HARRIS, LARRY MARK--[8]
JANIFER, LAURENCE M.--[2][3][23]--
OLD FAMILY NAME ADOPTED IN '63--
LAN "YOU CAN'T ESCAPE" '67 & MORE
LOGAN, WILLIAM--[2][11][32]MYS--
PU "JACK THE RABBIT" SEPT '55
HU "AFTERNOON OF A WINO" DEC '55
MH "EL REY" MAY '55
AC "BIG ONE" MAY '56
PU "REAL THING" JAN '56
SFDS ""IT'S EASY TO KILL!" APR '57
GU "BIG DEAL" NOV '57
AB "GUN WITH A HEART" JAN '58
TR "HYPNOTIST" APR '59
OF "DEAD CAN KILL" SEPT '59
TG "I NEED PROTECTION" MAY '60
PHILLIPS, MARK--W/RANDALL GARRETT,
[2][3][11]MYS/SF--
PYR F783 "BRAIN TWISTER" '62
PYR F875 "IMPOSSIBLES" '63
PYR F909 "SUPERMIND" '63
WILSON, BARBARA--[2][11][23]--
LAN 72-774 "PLEASURES WE KNOW" '64
LAN 72-949 "VELVET EMBRACE" '65

HARRIS, LIN
KERI, AMANDA--W/ARTIE STOCKTON, HAWK/
HARRIS/STOCKTON INTRVW '93,
WESTERN HIST/MYS/ROM.

HARRIS, MARION ROSE
CHARLES, HENRY--[1][31]ENGLISH
HARRIFORD, DAPHNE--[1]ENGLISH
ROGERS, KEITH--[1]ENGLISH
YOUNG, ROSE--[1][22]ENGLISH

HARRIS, MARK
INGRAM, WILLIS J.--[31]
WIGGEN, HENRY W.--[8]

HARRIS, MONICA
HARRIS, LANE--[9][21][26]ROM--
"THE DEVIL'S LOVE"

HARRIS, MRS. HERBERT
SHORT, FRANCIS--[8]

HARRIS, PAMELA
MEINIKOFF, PAMELA--[8]

HARRIS, ROBERT EUGENE P.
HARRIS, REP--[1]

HARRIS, THOMAS CUNNINGHAM
HARRIS, TOM--[31]

HARRIS, TIMOTHY [HYDE]
HARRIS, HYDE--[3]MYS--
GOLLANCZ "KYD FOR HIRE" '77

HARRIS, VALERIE
FARRANT, SARAH--[3]MYS--
HALE "TAVERN WENCH" '78
HALE "A TOUCH OF TERROR" '80 & 7 MORE

HARRIS, WILLIAM
HARPER, EDITH--[8]

HARRIS, WILLIAM F.
HARRIS, BILL--[31]

HARRIS, YVONNE L.
LACOSTE, LILLY--[31]

HARRIS,[THEODORE] WILSON
KONA WORUK--[1]

HARRIS-BURLAND, JOHN
BURLAND, HARRIS--[2][8][29]MYS--
"THE PRINCESS THORA" '04

HARRISON, AMELIA W.
COMPTON, MARGARET--[1][11]

HARRISON, CHESTER WILLIAM
COLE, JACKSON--A. TONIK-COLE CKLST
"SPICY ARMADILLO" HP--
TEX RGR "RED HARVEST ON THE RIO" APR '43
HARRISON, WILLIAM--L. ROBBINS LTR '94,
[28]MYS--
BELM "WINTER KILL" '72
HICKOK, WILL--[28][31][33]WEST--
"WEB OF GUNSMOKE" '55
"RESTLESS GUN" '59 & MORE
NEWLAND, N.M.--[34]MYS--
PHOENIX "WALK TO YOUR GRAVE" '51
WILLIAMS, COE--[1][28][33]WEST--
POPLB "GO FOR YOUR GUN" '55

HARRISON, CLAIRE [E]
EDEN, LAURA--[9][21][26][31]ROM--
"MISTAKEN IDENTITY"
"FLIGHT OF FANCY"
"SUMMER MAGIC"

HARRISON, CONSTANCE CARY
BURTON, MRS.--[1]
REFUGITTA--[1][8]

HARRISON, DAVID LEE
GRAHAM, KENNON--[31][33]

HARRISON, EDWARD HARDY
HARRISON, TED--[31][33]JUV--
MERRITT "THE LAST HORIZON" '80

HARRISON, ELLEN
HARRISON, CLAIRE--[26]ROM--12 NOVELS

HARRISON, HARRY
BARRY, DAN--S. HOLLAND-PPCC#9--
GHOSTED "FLASH GORDON" STRIP
LATE 40's-EARLY 50's
BOYD, FELIX--GORGON BOOKS/IPCS LIST,
[2][11][23]SF--
CHARTERIS, LESLIE--LOCUS #389-
OBIT CHARTERIS,[2][4][34]GHOSTED--
DBLDY "VENDETTA FOR THE SAINT" '74
DEMPSEY, HANK--[2][11][23]SF--

HARRISON, HARRY [CONT]
DEMPSEY, HENRY--[32]MYS--
SB "DEATH AT 60,000" MAY '62
SA "FUZZ-HEAD" OCT '63
SA "DEATH IN MEXICO" OCT '62
HALL, CAMERON--W/LESTER DEL REY,[2][11]
KAEMPFERT, WADE--[1][2][11][23]SF,HP--
SPACE PUBLICATIONS
RANDOM, RICK--S. HOLLAND--
PPCC#9, P50--5 NOV '57 TO JAN '59

HARRISON, J.H.
WYNYARD, JOHN--[8]

HARRISON, JAMES THOM,AS
HARRISON, JIM--[28][31]WEST--
9 BOOKS [SEVERAL COLLECTIONS OF
NOVELLAS] '71-90

HARRISON, JOHN GILBERT
GILBERT, JOHN--[8]

HARRISON, JULIA
RICHMOND, FIONA--[8]

HARRISON, MARY BENNETT
WARDEN, FRANCIS--[1]

HARRISON, MARY ST. LEGER
MALET, LUCAS--[1][2]

HARRISON, MELINDA JANE
HARRINGTON, EMMA--W/VIRGINIA BROWN,
[9][21][26]ROM--
"FAIR EXCHANGE"
"PRAIRIE PARADISE" & MORE

HARRISON, MICHAEL
DOWNES, QUENTIN--[3]MYS--
ROY "NO SMOKE NO FLAME" '52
ROY "HEADS I WIN" '53
ROY "THEY HADN'T A CLUE" '54
EGREMONT, MICHAEL--[5][7][8][11]
[23]ENGLISH/SF--
QUEENSWAY "BRIDE OF FRANKENSTEIN" '35

HARRISON, MRS. E.E.
MOTTE, NEL--[8]

HARRISON, M[ICHAEL] JOHN
CHURCHILL, JOYCE--[2][11][23][31]ENGLISH/SF--

HARRISON, PHILIP
CARMICHAEL, PHILIP--[8]

HARRISON, REGINALD CAREY
HARRISON, REX--[31]

HARRISON, RICHARD [MOTTE]
MOTTE, PETER--[3][8][22]MYS--
CASSELL "FALL CLUTCH" '56
CASSELL "FALL OF THE CURTAIN" '58

HARRISON, SUSIE FRANCES
SERANUS--[1]

HARRISON, VIRGINIA M.
SHAW, WILENE--V. BERCH-LESBIANA/
CNTRCLTR, BAE 22--
ACE D50 "MATING CALL" '54
ACE S74 "HEAT LIGHTNING" '54
ACE S80 "FEAR & THE GUILT" '54
ACE S263 "SEE HOW THEY RUN" '57
ACE D378 "OUT FOR KICKS" '59
ACE D464 "TAME THE WILD FLESH" '60
ACE D520 "ONE FOOT IN HELL" '61

HARRISON, W.G.A.
WILSON, A.G.--[1][34]MYS--
HURST "COME AWAY DEATH" '36
HURST "SPIDER BALLET" '38

HARRISON, WILLIAM C.
HARRISON, BILL--[31]

HARRON, DON[ALD]
FARQUHARSON, CHARLIE--[1][31]
ROSEDALE, VALERIE--[1]

HARROP-ALLIN, CLINTON
ALLIN, CLINTON HARROP--[31]

HART, ALEXANDRA
JACOPETTI, ALEXANDRA--[1][31]

HART, CAROLINE HOROWITZ
WINTERS, MARY K.--[8]

HART, CYRIL CHARLES
MAX, RAYMOND--[1]

HART, HARRY
FRANK, PAT--[1][2][32]MYS--
EQMM "ON EDGE" AUG '54

HART, JEFFREY
ST. GEORGE, GEOFFREY--[3]MYS--
LITTLE "THE PROTEUS PACT" '75

HART, JOHN LEWIS
HART, JOHNNY--[31] CARTOONS--
"B.C." SERIES
"WIZARD OF ID" SERIES

HART, SUSANNE
HART, SUE--[31]

HARTEL, KLAUS DIETER
VANDENBERG, PHILIPP--[1]

HARTHERN-JACOBSON, ERNST
HOYER, NIELS--[39]GERMAN

HARTHOORN, SUSANNE [W]
HART, SUSANNE--[1]

HARTIGAN, PATRICK JOSEPH
O'BRIEN, JOHN--[8][32]MYS--
EQMM "LUDWIG SOARING DOWN" JUL '71

HARTING, PIETER
DR. DIOSCORIDES--[2]

HARTLEBEN, OTTO ERICH
ERICH, OTTO--[39]GERMAN
IPSE, HENRIK--[39]GERMAN

HARTLEY, ELLEN R.
KNAUFF, ELLEN RAPHAEL--[1]

HARTLEY, LESLIE POLES
HARTLEY, L.P.--[1]B&M COLL #26, P50, ENGLISH

HARTLEY, WILLIAM
WINTERS, DANIEL--L. ROBBINS LTR MAR '94

HARTMAN, DARLENE
LANG, SIMON--[2][7][11][23]SF--
AV "SKIPJACK: ELLUVON GIFT"

HARTMAN, JAN & LORIE
LAWRENCE, SUSANNAH--[3][9][21][26]MYS/ROM--
POPLB "DQAUGHTERS OF MUSIC" '73

HARTMAN, RACHEL FRIEDA
WARD, JANICE--[1][22]AMERICAN

HARTMANN, EDITH
ZINTH, SIRMIONE--[39]GERMAN/MYS

HARTMANN, ELIZABETH
HARTMANN, BETSY--[31]

HARTMANN, FRANZ
A STUDENT OF OCCULTISM--[2]

HARTMANN, HELMUT HENRY
COTTON, JERRY--[39]GERMAN/MYS,HP
DRAKE, JOHN--[39]GERMAN/MYS/WEST
HART, HENRY--[39][40]GERMAN/MYS--
'KOMMISSAR X' SERIES
HENRY, FRED--[39][40]GERMAN/MYS, HP--
'KOMMISSAR X' SERIES
HILTON, JACK--[39]GERMAN/MYS/WEST
SEYMOUR, H[ENRY]--[2][3][8][22][29]
[39][40]GERMAN/MYS--
10 GIFFORD NOVELS '58-72
SEYMOUR, WAYNE--[39]GERMAN/MYS/WEST

HARTMANN, RUDOLF A.
GNIFFKE, RUDOLF--[31]

HARTMANN, SADAKICHI
ALLAN, SIDNEY--[1]

HARTSCH, GERHART
CAMERON, JOHN--[39]GERMAN/MYS/WEST,HP
COTTON, JERRY--[39]GERMAN/MYS,HP
DE LORCA, FRANK--[39]GERMAN/MYS/WEST,HP
GARRETT, STEVE M.--[39]GERMAN/MYS/WEST
LAMONT, ROBERT--[39]GERMAN/MYS/WEST,HP
LAREDO, KID--[39]GERMAN/WEST
LOGAN, JACK--[39]GERMAN/WEST
MALORNY, RALPH--[39][40]GERMAN/MYS--
'KOMMISSAR X' SERIES #608
MCHART, GEORGE--[39]GERMAN/MYS/WEST
SLADE, JACK--[39]GERMAN/MYS/WEST,HP

HARTSTON, WILLIAM ROLAND
BANNERMAN, ROLAND--[1][31]

HARTWELL, ALICE BOOTH
BOOTH, ALICE--[1]

HARTWELL, DAVID G.
TROUT, KILGORE--W/L.W. CURREY,
HAWK/HARTWELL INTRVW '93,[7]--
"SF-1 BIBLIO" CA '70

HARTWICK, RICHARD
HALLIDAY, BRETT--T. JOHNSON-ECHOES #23,MYS,HP-
-
MSMM ?? UNCONFIRMED ??

HARTZELL, SUSAN KATHLEEN
DUNN, PAULINE--W/DAWN P.H. DUNN
[7][34]MYS/SF--
ZEBRA "DEMONIC COLOR" '90
ZEBRA "FLESH STEALERS" '90
ZEBRA "THE CRAWLING DARK" '91
HARTZELL, SUZY--[7]SF

HARUKI, SHIMAZAKI
TOSON, SHIMAZAKI--[22]JAPANESE

HARVEY, ANNIE JANE T.
HOPE, ANDREE--[1][3][22]MYS--
WILSON "SECRET OF WARDAK COURT
& OTHER STORIES" 1894

HARVEY, FLORENCE
DONNER, GROVE--[1][2][7]

HARVEY, HARRIET
GIBNEY, HARRIET--[1][31]

HARVEY, IRENE
OSGOOD, IRENE--[1]

HARVEY, JEAN
HARLOWE, JUSTIN--W/LAURA BENNETT
& TINA MCKENZIE,[8][21]ROM--
"JEALOUSIES"
"MEMORY & DESIRE"

HARVEY, JEAN GILMOUR
BENNETT, LAURA GILMOUR--W/LAURA BENNETT,[7]SF--
"A TIME & A PLACE" '88
"A WHEEL OF STARS" '89
"BY ALL THAT IS SACRED" '91
RPRTS "A WHEEL OF STARS"

HARVEY, JOHN HENRY
BARRINGTON, JOHN H.--[34]MYS--
LANGDON "MOVING FINGER" '47
LANGDON "MURDER IN THE WHITE PIT" '47
OPERATOR 1384--[3]MYS--9 NOVELS '35-9

HARVEY, JOHN WILFRED
FARNDALE, JOHN--[1][34]MYS--
METHUEN "THE NINE NICKS" '30

HARVEY, JOHN [BARTON]
BARTON, JON--[8][28][31][34]MYS--
CORGI "KILL HITLER" '76
CORGI "FOREST OF DEATH" '77
CORGI "LIGHTNING STRIKES" '77
BRADY, WILLIAM S.--[1][8][28]MYS/WEST--
FONTANA "HAWK" SERIES-9 BKS '74-83
FONTANA "PEACEMAKER" SERIES-
3 NOVELS '81-83
COBURN, L.J.--[8][11][28][31]WEST,HP--
SPHERE "THE RAIDERS" '77
SPHERE "BLOODY SHILOH" '78
DANCER, J.B.--[2][11][28][31]WEST,HP--
CORONET "EVIL BREED" '77
CORONET "JUDGEMENT DAY" '78
CORONET "THE HANGED MAN" '79
HART, JON--[8][28][31][34] WAR--
5 MAYFLOWER NOVELS '77-80
JAMES, WILLIAM M.--[1][28]--
PINN "APACHE" SERIES - 5 NOVELS '79-83
LENNOX, TERRY--[28][31][34]MYS--
HALE "DEATH DRAWS A WILD CARD" '85
MANN, JAMES--W/LAURENCE JAMES,[8][28][31]--
NEL "END GAME" '82
MCLAGLEN, JOHN J.--[8][11][28]WEST--
CORGI- 11 NOVELS IN "HERNE THE
HUNTER" SERIES '76-83
RYDER, THOM--[8][11][28]--
NEL "AVENGING ANGEL" '75
"ANGEL ALONE" '75
SANDON, J.D.--[1][8][28]WEST--
GRANADA "GRINGOS" SERIES EVEN #s
THRU #8 '79-82
WHITE, JONATHAN--[1][8][28]ENGLISH

HARVEY, LINDA
VAIL, CHRISTINA--V. BERCH LTR TO
HUBIN '93,[34]MYS--
LAIKA "PORCELAIN DOLL DON'T BLEED" '81

HARVEY, MARGARET SUSAN J
MICHELMORE, SUSAN--[8]

HARVEY, NIGEL
WILLOUGHBY, HUGH--[1]

HARVEY, PETER NOEL
DAY, ADRIAN--[8]
PETERS, NOEL--[8]

HARVEY, WILLIAM
DENOVAN, SAUNDERS--[8]

HARVEY, WILLIAM FRYER
HARVEY, W.F.--[1]

HARVOR, ERICA ELISABETH
HARVOR, BETH--[31]

HARWELL, WILLIAM EARNEST
HARWELL, ERNIE--[31]

HARWOOD, GWEN
GEYER, FRANCIS--[13]AUSTRALIAN
KLINE, T.F.--[13]AUSTRALIAN
LEHMAN, WALTER--[13]AUSTRALIAN
STONE, MIRIAM--[13]AUSTRALIAN

HARY, WERNER ANDREAS
CASTELL, W.A.--[39]GERMAN/HOR

HARY, WILFRID A.
DE DELORCA, FRANK--[39]GERMAN/MYS/WEST,HP
HARRIS, WILL--[39]GERMAN/WEST
LAMONT, ROBERT--[39]GERMAN/MYS/SF/WEST,HP
SHADOW, MIKE--[39]GERMAN/HOR,HP
TRAVERS, W.A.--[39]GERMANMYS/SF/WEST
USHER, H.P.--[39]GERMAN/MYS/SF/WEST,HP
WILFORD, HARRY--[39]GERMAN/MYS/SF/WEST
BAXTER, MARK--[39]GERMAN/MYS/SF/WEST,HP
ELLIOT, BRIAN--[39]GERMAN/MYS/SF/WEST,HP
FISCHER, ERNO--[39]GERMAN/MYS/SF/WEST
SHOCKER, DAN--[39][40]GERMAN/MYS, HP

HARZER, KARL
DUNCAN, ROBERT--[39]GERMAN/ADV
LYNN, GODWARD--[39]GERMAN/ADV

HASEBROEK, JOHANNES PETR.
JONATHAN--[22] DUTCH

HASEK, JAROSLAV
RUFFIAN, M.--[1]

HASEK, JAROSLAV M.F.
FRANKLIN, BENJAMIN--[1][31]
HELLENHOFFERN, VOJTECH--[1][31]

HASFORD,[JERRY] GUSTAVE
GORDON, GEORGE--[1]

HASHIAN, JAMES T.
TREVANIAN--[34]MYS--
WROTE SOME 'TREVANIAN' BKS-SUSPECT
"SHIBUMI"
"SUMMER OF KATYA"

HASKIN, DOROTHY C.
CLARK, HOWARD--[1][22][31]AMERICAN

HASKINS, JAMES S.
HASKINS, JIM--[31][33]

HASLAM, NICKY
HOPPER, SAM--[8]
PARSONS, PAUL--[8]

HASLER, OTTO
A.D-n--[29]MYS--
"DET NAMNLOSA SLOTTET" 1895

HASLER-SCHONENBERGER, E.
SCHONENBERGER, ELISABETH--[39]GERMAN/JUV

HASPELS, GEORGE FRANS
COMPASSIONE--[22] DUTCH

HASSE, HENRY
PINE, E. THEODORE--W/EMIL PETAJA,
[2][11][23]SF--

HASSEBRAUK, MARIANNE
ABEL, MARIANNE--[39]GERMAN/JUV

HASSEL, SVEN
ARBING, BORGE VILLY REDS.--[29]MYS
DE L'ARBIN, BOB--[29]MYS
HAZEL, SVEN--[29]MYS
LARSEN, JORGEN--[29]MYS
PEDERSON, BORGE V.R.--[29]MYS

HASSELBLATT, DIETER
HENRICI, KARL HERBERT--[39]GERMAN/SF/JUV
SAHLSTAEDT, BERTIL E.--[39]GERMAN/SF/JUV
ZWEYDORN, PETER--[39]GERMAN/SF/JUV

HASSELBLATT, EMIL ALERIK
TRE, HERRAR--[29]MYS--
SCHILDTS "HERR COPWIETH, GENTLEMAN-DETEKTIV" '14

HASSENSTEIN, DIETER
DIETRICH, HEINZ--[39]GERMAN
MOG, JAN--[39]GERMAN

HASSLER, ADOLF OTTO
EREX--[29]MYS--
"HILA-FANGENS BRUD" & 3 OTHERS 1886-1893
FALK, VICTOR--[29]MYS--
"HVITA SLAFVINNAN" 1891
"SLOTTETS MYSTERIUM" 1911
GRIMNER--[29]MYS--
"SPOKSLOTTETS FANGE ELLER DOLDA BROTT" 1895
"HILMA ELLER VINDO ROS" '01
SEFFENZOFF, PAUL--[29]MYS

HASSLER, ERNST
HALL, ERNST--[39][40]GERMAN/MYS--
"GLOCKEN DES TODES" '63
"HOLLENFLUG" '65
"DAS OHR" '78

HASSLER, KENNETH L.
ST. CLAIR, JEANANNE--[3]MYS--
LENNOX "THE HOUSE ON VICKER'S ISLAND" '74

HASSLINGER, INGE MARIA
GRIMM, INGE MARIA--[39]GERMAN/JUV

HASSON, JAMES
DE SALIGNAC, CHARLES--[8]

HASTINGS, BROOKE
GORDON, DEBORAH--[26]ROM--
"RUNAWAY BRIDE"

HASTINGS, CHARLOTTE
WISELY, CHARLOTTE--[21][26]ROM--
"WELCOME INTRUDER"
"LOVE HAS NO PRIDE"
"PASSIONATE ENTERPRISE"

HASTINGS, HUBERT CRONIN
DE WOLFE, IVOR--[1][31]
DE WOLFE, IVY--[1][31]

HASTINGS, MACDONALD
GULLIVER, LEMUEL--[1][31]

HASTINGS, PHYLLIS DORA H.
BEDFORD, JOHN--[1][17][22]ENGLISH/ROM--
6 NOVELS
HODGE, E. CHATTERTON--[1][17][22]ENGLISH/ROM--
LAND, ROSINA--[1][17][22]ENGLISH/ROM--
MAYFIELD, JULIA--[1][17][22]ENGLISH/ROM--

HASWELL, C. JOHN D.
FOSTER, GEORGE--[1]
HASWELL, JOCK--[1][31]

HASZARD, PATRICIA MOYES
MOYES, PATRICIA--[1][32]MYS--
EQMM "DEADLOCK" DEC '79
"A SUITABLE REVENGE" JAN '80
EQMM "MOST HATED MAN IN LONDON" MAR '80
& OTHERS

HATCH, DAVID PATTERSON
KARISHKA, PAUL--[1][2]

HATCHER, ROBIN LEE
LEIGH, ROBIN--[21][26]ROM--
"THE HAWK & THE HEATHER"
"RUGGED SPLENDOR"
"WINDS OF FIRE"

HATFIELD, CLARENCE E.
CAUTION, TAKKIE--[1]

HATFIELD, ELAINE [C]
WALSTER, ELAINE--[31]
WALSTER, ELAINE HATFIELD--W/ELLEN BERSCHEID,
[1][31]--
"INTERPERSONAL ATTRACTION" '69

HATHAWAY, RONALD F.
CATTO, P.Z.--[1]
DECOVERLEY, ROGER--[1]

HATHWAY, ALAN
GOODRICH, CLIFFORD--[2][7][11][37]MYS,HP--
SHD "VAMPIRE MURDERS"
SHD "ARROWHEAD"
SHD "EX-COP"
CRB "THE WHITE MANDARINS" JUN '39
ROBESON, KENNETH--[2][7][11][34]MYS,HP--
BB "DEADLY DWARF" '68
BB "DEATH IN SILVER" '68
BB "DEVILS PLAYGROUND" '68
BB "FLAMING FALCONS" '68
BB "MINDLESS MONSTERS"
BB "MYS UNDER THE SEA" '68
BB "RUSTLING DEATH"
BB "OTHER WORLD" '68
BB "HEADLESS MEN" '84

HATIM, MUHAMMAD A.
HATEM, MOHAMED A.--[31]

HATTON, CHARLES
DIXON, GEORGE--[34]MYS--
KIMBER "DIXON OF DOCK GREEN" '60

HAUBER, JOSEPHINE C.
CHARLTON, JOSEPHINE--[9][21][26]ROM--
"BEHIND THE SCENES"
"TABLE FOR TWO"

HAUCK, LOUISE PLATT
ARCHER, LANE--[1][3][22]MYS--
PENN "MYSTERY MANSION" '31
ASH, PETER--[1][22]MYS--
LANDON, LOUISE--[1][3][22]MYS--
PENN "GREEN LIGHT" '31
PENN "STRANGE DEATH OF A DOCTOR" '33
RANDALL, JEAN--[1]

HAUEISEN, KATHRYN M.
HAUEISEN, KATHY--[31]

HAUFF, WILHELM
CLAUREN, HEINRICH--[39]GERMAN

HAUG, DORIS
BIERI, DORIS--[39]GERMAN/JUV

HAUGEN, CHRISTIAN
ANTHONY, JAMES--[29]MYS--
4 NOVELS '18-23

HAUGHEY, JULIA
GRICE, JULIA [H]--[9][21]ROM--
"EMERALD FIRE"
"SATIN EMBRACES" & MORE

HAUGHT, JEAN
FRIENDS, JALYNN--W/ROSALYN ALSOBROOK,
[9][21][26]ROM--
"TEXAS RAPTURE"
PELLICANE, PATRICIA--[9]ROM--
"CREOLE CAPTIVE"
"FRONTIER TEMPTRESS" & MORE

HAUGK, KLAUS CONRAD
CONRAD, KLAUS--[39]GERMAN

HAUPTMAN, ELAINE
COREY, GAYLE--[9][21][26]ROM--
"TOP MARKS"

HAUSCHILD, ALBIN WALDEMAR
ONWARD, MAC--[39]GERMAN/WEST

HAUSCHILD, REINHARD
LORENZ, MICHAEL--[39]GERMAN
MUHLENFELD, ULRICH--[39]GERMAN
MULLER-ROLAND, HARALD--[39]GERMAN
ULRICH, THOMAS--[39]GERMAN

HAUSER, HEINRICH
BLADE, ALEXANDER--[1][2]HP--ZIFF-DAVIS

HAUSER, MARGARET L.
HEAD, GAY--[1][22][31][33]AMERICAN

HAUSER, OTTO
DOMMA, OTTOKAR--[39]GERMAN

HAUSFELD, RUSSELL
HERSCHOLT, WOLFE--[36]AUSTRALIAN/SF--
TRNPT "MAGNETIC PERIL" '49
KENSCH, OTTO--[36]AUSTRALIAN/MYS,HP--
TRNPT "TIME HAS A DOOR" nd ('49)

HAUSHOFER, MARIE HELEN F.
HAUSHOFER, MARLEN--[7]SF--
"THE WALL" '91

HAUSLEITNER, INES HERMINE
WIDMANN, W.L.--[39]GERMAN

HAUSMAN, GERALD
HAUSMAN, GERRY--[31][33]

HAUSMAN, LEON AUGUSTUS
POE, BERNAND--[8]

HAUSMANN, WINIFRED
WILKINSON, WINIFRED--[1]

HAUSMANN, WOLFGANG L.
MANN, W.L.--[39]GERMAN/SF

HAUTALA, RICHARD ANDREW
HAUTALA, RICK--[7]HOR--8 NOVELS

HAUTMAN, PETER
HAUTMAN, PETE--J. JOHNSON-FIRSTS JUN '94--
S&S "DRAWING DEAD" '93
MURRAY, PETER--LACHMAN LTR '93,
'FIRSTS' JUN '94--
20 NON-FICTION CHILDREN'S BOOKS

HAUTZIG, ESTHER
RUDOMIN, ESTHER--[1][22][33]POLISH-AMERICAN

HAVERSTOCK, NATHAN A.
ALFRED, RICHARD--W/RICHARD C. SCHROEDER,
[1][31]

HAVIARAS, STRATIS
CHAVIARAS, STRATES--[31]

HAVIGHURST, MARION BOYD
BOYD, MARION [M]--[1][31]

HAVILL, JUANITA
HAVEL, JENNIFER--[33]

HAWES, LOUISE
SUZANNE, JAMIE--[33]

HAWES, LYNNE GUSIKOFF S.
GUSIKOFF, LYNNE--[31]--
"GUIDE TO MUSICAL AMERICA" '84
SALOP, LYNNE--[1][31]--
VANTAGE "SUISONG" '78

HAWK, MARTIN R[AYMOND]
HAWK, PAT--AUTHOR/COMPILER--
"HAWK'S AUTHORS' PSEUDONYMS II
MARTIN, PAT--AUTHOR PROVIDED,
SHORT STORIES & ESSAYS

HAWK, RAYMOND & MARTIN
RAYMOND, PAT--AUTHORS PROVIDED--
SHORT STORIES & REFERENCE COMPILATION

HAWK, RAYMOND W[ALLACE]
HAWK, RAYMOND--AUTHOR PROVIDED--
SHORT STORIES
HOUCK, RAYMOND--AUTHOR PROVIDED--
SHORT STORIES
PATRICK, MARTIN--AUTHOR PROVIDED--
SHORT STORIES
WALLACE, RAYMOND--AUTHOR PROVIDED--
SHORT STORIES

HAWKER, MARY ELIZABETH
FALCONER, LANOE--[1][2]

HAWKES, SARAH
EAGLE, SARAH--V. BERCH LTR '94,[21][26]ROM--
JOVE "BEDEVILED BARON" '94 & 3 NOVELS & SS
FALCON, SALLY--[21][26]ROM--4 NOVELS

HAWKESWORTH, ERIC
GREAT COMTE--[1][31][33]

HAWKING, STEPHEN WILLIAM
HAWKING, S.W.--[31]

HAWKINS, ALEC DESMOND
HAWKINS, A. DESMOND--[31]

HAWKINS, ANTHONY HOPE
A.H.--[8]ENGLISH
HOPE, ANTHONY--[2][3][17][22][29]MYS--
METHUEN "BEAUMAROU HOME FROM
THE WARS" '19

HAWKINS, JOHN EDWARD
HAWKINS, JACK--[31]

HAWKINS, LORETTA
CHAPMAN, RENATE--V. BERCH LTR TO
HUBIN '94,MYS--
AVALON "EVIL IN WAITING" '74
AVALON "THE WATCHER" '74
AVALON "MILMORRA HOUSE" '78
AVALON "MYSTIC ISLAND" '79 & 2 MORE

HAWKINS, MARTIN
HAWKIN, MARTIN--[1][2][23]ENGLISH--
"WHEN ADOLF CAME" '43

HAWKINS, PETER
MARAS, KARL--[1][2][11]MYS,HP--COMYNS
RAMON, BORIS--[1]

HAWLEY, DONALD THOMAS
MCDERMOTT, ROBERT--[1]

HAWS, DUNCAN
PERTINAX--[1]

HAWTHORNE, C.S.
DENTON, REGINALD--[2]

HAWTHORNE, JULIAN
HOLLINSHED, JUDITH--[1]

HAWTON, HECTOR
CURZON, VIRGINIA--[1][22][31]ENGLISH
SYLVESTER, JOHN--[1][3][29]MYS--
AMALG "MASKED DEATH" '31
LUNN "THE PHANTOM" '46
AMALG "TERROR OF TREGARWITH" '43

HAXTON, JOSEPHINE A.
DOUGLAS, ELLEN--[1][31]

HAY, JACOB
TERME, HILARY--[1]

HAY, MILLICENT V.
DE LONG, JULIE--[31]
HAY, VICKY--[31]

HAY, OSWYN ROBERT T.
HAY, GEORGE--[7]SF--
HAM "THIS PLANET FOR SALE" '51
"FLIGHT OF THE HESPER" '52 & MORE
LANG, KING--[2][7][11]SF,HP--
WARREN "TERRA!" '52
SHELDON, ROY--[2][7][11]SF,HP--
HAM "MOMENT OUT OF TIME" '52

HAYASHI, TAKASHI
KIGI, TAKATARO--[2][11]

HAYCRAFT, ANNA
ELLIS, ALICE THOMAS--[8][31]

HAYDEN, ERIC WILLIAM
RAIKES, ROBERT--[8]

HAYDEN, JULIA ELIZABETH
HAYDEN, JULIE--[31]

HAYDEN, LAURA
KENNER, LAURA--[26]ROM--
HARL 263 "SOMEONE TO WATCH OVER ME"

HAYDEN, STERLING
HAMILTON, JOHN--[31]
HAYDEN, STIRLING--[31]

HAYDEN, THOMAS EMMET
HAYDEN, TOM--[31]

HAYDOCK, RON
GREY, JUDSON--W/JIM HARMON,[1][2][11]--
EPIC "WANTON WITCH"
EPIC "TWILIGHT GIRLS"
LORD, LONNIE--SMUT PEDDLAR#2,[1]ADULT--
"APE RAPE"
SAXON, VIN--MUNROE SEPT '93 AUCT,[1]--
PEC N135 "SEX-A-REENOS" '66
PEC "CAGED LUST"
SHEPPARD, DON--V. BERCH-PIKE CKLST,
BAE 18, P47
WILDE, RITA--SMUT PEDDLER #1, P41--
RAPTURE 201 "PERVERTED LUST"

HAYDON, JUNE
BAXTER, JUDY--W/JUDITH SIMPSON,[9]ROM
DENNY, ROZ--W/JUDY SIMPSON,[21][26]--
"RED HOT PEPPER"
"ROMANCE NOTIONS"
"CINDERELLA COACH"
FOXX, ROSALIND--W/JUDY SIMPSON,
[9][21][26][31]ROM--
"RELUCTANT WARD"
"SURRENDER BY MOONLIGHT"
HAYFORD, TARIA--W/PAT RUTHERFORD,
[1][9][21]ROM--
"TRAIL OF LOVE"
LOGAN, SARA--W/JUDY SIMPSON,
[9][21][26][31]ROM--
"GAME OF HEARTS"

HAYDON, N.G.
PEMBURY, GROSVENOR--[1]

HAYDON, PERCY MONTAGUE
HAYDON, MONTY--[1]

HAYE, JAN
SHORE, JULIET--[21][26]ROM--
"PINK JACARANDA"
"TREE OF PROMISE" & MORE
VINTON, ANNE--[21][26]ROM--
"AT THE VILLA ROMA"
"DOCTOR DOWN UNDER" & MORE

HAYES, CATHERINE E.
MARKWELL, MARY--[1]
YUKON, BILL--[1]

HAYES, HERBERT E. ELTON
ELTON, H.E.--[8]

HAYES, JOHN F.
TERRENCE, FREDERICK J.--[22]CANADIAN

HAYES, JOSEPH [ARNOLD]
ARNOLD, JOSEPH H.--[18][22][29][31]MYS--
FRENCH "SNEAK DATE" '44
"WHERE'S LAURIE" '46

HAYES, MARRIJANE & JOSEPH
SHAW, FLOYD--V. BERCH LTR TO HUBIN '94/MYS--
AV 570 "DEVIL'S DAUGHTER" '54

HAYES, RALPH EUGENE
CARTER, NICK--[1][3]MYS,HP--
AWARD "ASSAULT ON ENGLAND" '72
AWARD "CAIRO MAFIA" '72
AWARD "OMEGA TERROR" '72
AWARD "BUTCHER OF BELGRADE" '73
AWARD "STRIKE FORCE TERROR" '73
AWARD "AGENT COUNTER AGENT" '73
AWARD "ASSASSIN-CODE NAME VULTURE" '74
AWARD "VATICAN VENDETTA" '74
McCURTIN, PETER--V. BERCH LTR TO
HUBIN '94/MYS,HP--
BELM "OPERATION HONG KONG" '77
BELM "BODY COUNT" '77

HAYES, THOMAS
O HAODHA, TOMAS--[1]

HAYES, WAYNE WOODROW
HAYES, WOODY--[31]

HAYLES, BRIAN
SHUBIK, IRENE--[2] GHOST EDITED

HAYMAN, SHEILA
TRIX, MO--[8]

HAYMON, SYLVIA THERESA
HAYMON, S.T.--DP #6, P27,[31]MYS--
ST. MARTIN'S "A BEAUTIFUL DEATH" '94

HAYMOND, GINNY
FLEMING, LEE--[9]

HAYNES, ALFRED H.
CHRISTIE, KEITH--[1][22][31]ENGLISH

HAYNES, BETSY
BETTS, JAMES--[1][31][33]

HAYNES, JAMES ALMAND
HAYNES, JIM--[31]

HAYNES, JOHN HAROLD
WAKE, G.B.--[8]

HAYS, ELINOR RICE
RICE, ELINOR--[1][22]AMERICAN

HAYS, JANICE NICHOLSON
LOONIE, JANICE HAYS--[8]

HAYS, LEE
CALHOUN, CHAD--CRPG, WEST,HP--
DELL 03769 "GAMBLER'S WOMAN" '82
DESMOND, HILARY--[1]
NICHOLS, SARAH--[3][9][21][26][29]MYS/ROM--
CURTIS "MOON DANCERS" '73
PLAYBOY "CHARITY" '79 & MORE

HAYS, PETER
JEFFERIES, IAN--[1][3]MYS--
CAPE "THIRTEEN DAYS" '59
CAPE "IT WASN'T ME" '61 & 2 MORE

HAYSTEAD, WESLEY
HAYSTEAD, WES--[31]--
"CHURCH COMPUTER MANUAL" '85

HAYTER, CECIL G.
BIRD, LEWIS--[1]
STEEL, HOWARD--[1]

HAYWOOD, ELIZA
EXPLORABILIS--[2]

HAYWOOD, LAURA ALICE W.
LAURANCE, ALICE--[7][32]MYS/SF--
"CASSANDRA RISING" '78
EQMM "WE INTERRUPT THIS MAGAZINE " JUL '78

HAZARD, BARBARA
LINCOLN, LILLIAN--[9][21][26]ROM--
"THEW BELLWOOD TREASURE"
"A CHANGE OF HEART"
"FINE FEATHERS"

HAZELHOFF, HENDRIK
DENDERMONDE, MAX--[22] DUTCH

HAZLETT, WILLIAM SCOTT
HAZLETT, BILL--[31]

HAZLEWOOD, REX
DELTA--[8]
KENEU--[8]

HAZZARD, MARY
DWIGHT, OLIVIA--[1][3][31]MYS--
HARPER "CLOSE HIS EYES" '61

HEADAPOHL, BETTY R.
COX, MARY ELIZABETH--[31]
HEADAPOHL, B.R.--[31]

HEADLAM, CUTHBERT M.
B.B.--[3]MYS--
MURRAY "A STRANGE DELILAH" '21

HEAL, EDITH
BARRIEN, EDITH HEAL--[1][22]
BERRIEN, EDITH HEAL--[1][22][33]
PAGE, EILEEN--[1][22][33]
PAGE, MARY--[1]
POWERS, MARGARET--[1][22][33]

HEAL, PENELOPE
ZOOL, M.H.--[23]SF--GROUP PSEUD.

HEALD, LESLIE V.
WALSBY, CHARNOCK--[1][2][31]

HEALD, TIMOTHY VILLIERS
HEALD, TIM--[31]
LANCASTER, DAVID--[8][18][31]MYS

HEALEY, BENJAMIN J.
HEALEY, B.J.--[1][18]--NON FICTION
HEALEY, BEN--[8][18][34]MYS--
HALE "STONE BABY" '74
HALE "SNAPDRAGON MURDERS" '78 & MORE
JEFFREYS, J.G.--[18][29][31][34][40]MYS--
U.S. EDITIONS OF 'STURROCK' BOOKS
STURROCK, JEREMY--[18][29][34][40]MYS--
MacM "VILLAGE OF ROGUE'S '72
MacM "WILLFUL LADY" '75 & MORE

HEALEY-KAY, PATRICK
DOLIN, ANTON--[31]

HEALY, CHRISTINE
YORKE, ERIN--W/SUSAN M. YANSICK,
[9][21][26]ROM--
HARL "HONOR PRICE" '94 & 7 OTHERS

HEARD, HENRY FITZGERALD
HEARD, GERALD--[1][2][18][23]
ENGLISH-AMERICAN/HOR
HEARD, H.F.--[7][23][31][32]ENGLISH/MYS/SF--
USED PSEUD. IN U.S. AFTER 1937
RS "ROUSING OF MR. BRADEGAR" MAY '45
EQMM "ADV OF MR. MONTALBA,
OBSEQUIST" SEPT '45
RS "CRAYFISH" JUN '46
EQMM "PRESIDENT OF THE UNITED STATES,
DETECTIVE" MAR '47
EQMM "ENCHANTED GARDEN" MAR '49
HARPER "GABRIEL& THE CREATURES" '52

HEARD, J. NORMAN
NORMAN, JOE--[1][22]AMERICAN

HEARN, JOHN
PENTECOST, MARTIN--[1]

HEARN, MARY ANN
FARNINGHAM, MARIANNE--[1][2][7]SF--
"NINETEEN HUNDRED? A FORECAST
& A STORY" 1892

HEARN,[P] LAFCADIO [T.C]
KOIZUMI, YAKUMO--[31]

HEARNDEN, BERYL
BALFOUR, HEARNDON--W/EVA BALFOUR,
[1][3][22]MYS--
HODDER "PAPER CHASE" '27 & MORE

HEARNE, ELIZABETH GOULD
HEARNE, BETSY GOULD--[7]SF--
"MEGAN #1 & 2" '77/79
"ELI'S GHOST" '87

HEARNE, G. RICHARD MANT
MANT, RICHARD--[1]

HEARNE, JOHN EDGAR C.
MORRIS, JOHN--W/MORRIS CARGILL,[3][29][40]MYS--
COLLINS "FEVER GRASS" '69
COLLINS "CANDYWINE DEVELOPMENT" '70
COLLINS "CHECKERBOARD CAPER" 75

HEARST, PATRICIA CAMPBELL
HEARST, PATTY--[31]

HEATH, HARRY EUGENE JR.
HALL, KENDALL--[31]

HEATH-MILLER, M. BLANCHE
DUNCAN, BLANCHE--[1]

HEATON, AUGUSTUS G.
SHUFFLE, RUBE--[1]

HEATON, JEN M.
CROSS, CAROLINE--[26]ROM--
SIL 810 "DANGEROUS"
SIL 851 "RAFFERTY'S ANGEL"
MAXWELL, MARY--W/MICKY K. OSBURN,[26]ROM--
"DOUBLECROSS"
"PLAYING WITH FIRE"

HEATON, THOMAS PETER S.
HEATON, TOM--[31]

HEAVEN, CONSTANCE FECHER
FECHER, CONSTANCE--[17][21][26]ROM--
"QUEEN'S DELIGHT"
"KING'S LEGACY" & MORE
FLEMING, GEORGE--[21]ROM
HEAVEN, CONSTANCE--[21]ROM--17 NOVELS

HEAVEN, CONSTANCE FECHER [CONT]
MERLIN, CHRISTINA--[26][34]MYS/ROM--
HALE "THE SPY CONCERTO" '80
HALE "SWORD OF MITTHRAS" '82

HEBBLETHWAITE, PETER
MYDDLETON, ROBERT--[1][8]

HEBEL, PETER
BAKER, SUSAN--[39]GERMAN/MYS
BAXTER, MARK--[39]GERMAN/MYS/WEST,HP
CALLAGHAN, MIKE--[39]GERMAN/MYS/WEST
CAMERON, JOHN--[39]GERMAN/MYS/WEST,HP
COTTON, JERRY--[39]GERMAN/MYS,HP
FRANK, DR. STEFAN--[39]GERMAN/MYS,HP
HELLMAN, PETE--[39]GERMAN/MYS/WEST
KOJAK--[39]GERMAN/MYS
LEVER, JAY--[39]GERMAN/MYS/WEST
MARTINEZ, BENITO--[39]GERMAN/MYS/WEST,HP
MILLETT, E.B.--[39]GERMAN/MYS/WEST
NOLAN, FREDERICK--[39]GERMAN/MYS/WEST,HP
SLADE, JACK--[39]GERMAN/WEST,HP

HEBER, GEORGE
REID, DESMOND--W/G.P. MANN,[34]HP--
AMALG "STATE OF FEAR" '61

HEBERDEN, M[ARY V.]
LEONARD, CHARLES L.--[1][3][22]MYS--
DBLDY "SECRET OF THE SPA" '44
DBLDY "EXPERT IN MURDER" '45

HEBERER, ALFRED
ENDERS, ALFRED MICHAEL--[39]GERMAN

HEBERT, PATRICIA
CHANDLER, PATRICIA--[26]ROM--
"DECEPTION DAY"

HEBRARD, FREDERIQUE
VELLE, FREDERIQUE--[1]

HEBSAKER, GRIT
SEUBERLICH, H. GRIT--[39]GERMAN/JUV

HECHT, BEN
LONG, PETER--[1][2]

HECHT, FRIEDRICH
LANGRENUS, MANFRED--[39]GERMAN/SF

HECHT, HENRI JOSEPH
MAIK, HENRI--[33]

HECKLEMANN, CHARLES N.
CAMPBELL, CLIFF--[1][28][32]WEST--
CCWWS "LAWMAN'S GUNSMOKE CRUSADE" SEPT '42
CCWWS "HOT LEAD FOR A RANGE HOG" SEPT '42
DA "THREE FOR THE KILL" '55
COLE, JACKSON--[1][28]WEST--
TADV "GATEWAY TO DOOM" FEB '43
GRIFFIN, ANDREW--[1][28]WEST--
WWW "ESCAPE TO BOOTHILL" DEC '41
WWW "SIX GUN TICKET TO HADES" MAR '42
LAWTON, CHARLES--[1][28] YOUTH/SPORTS--
5 NOVELS '37-42
MANN, CHARLES--[1][28]WEST--
RODEO ROM "RIDING FOR LOVE" FALL '43
MANN, CHUCK--[1][28]WEST--
TEX RGR "BOUNTY HUNTER" FEB '43
RODEO ROM "BRAHMA HERD" SPRG '43
MUMFORD, TEX--[28]WEST--
RODEO ROM "RODEO CLOWN" SUM '43

HECKLEMANN, CHARLES N. [CONT]
RAND, MAT--[1][28][32]--
WEST ACTION MAG "THE LAND THAT
LAW FORGOT" JUNE '40
REAL WESTERN "DEATH'S HEAD KILLER" MAY '41
WESTERN YARNS "RANGE OF DOOMED
MEN" FALL '42
DA "AMLICE AT MIDNIGHT" SEPT '58
ROURKE, JAMES--[1][28]WEST--
WESTERN YARNS "THE FASTEST GUN
IS LAW" JUNE '41
SMITH, CHARLES--[1][28]WEST--
EXCITNG WESTERN "THE BLACK
STALLION" FALL '42
WALKER, REEVE--[1][28]WEST--
EXCITING WESTERN "RAIDERS OF THE
WILDERNESS" DEC '43
EXCITING WESTERN "CHEYENNE DEATH-
TRAP" OCT '44

HECTOR, ANNE FRENCH
ALEXANDER, MRS.--[1][3][22]MYS--
UNWIN "YELLOW FIEND" '01 & 4 MORE

HECTOR, BARBARA
BARRIE, HESTER--[8]

HEDDEN, WORTH TUTTLE
WOODLEY, WINIFRED--[1]

HEDERICH, JOHANNES
OTTEN, HEINRICH--[39]GERMAN/MYS

HEDGE, CARO
D.V.S.--LORRAINE BIER-ARMADILLOCON '93
GATES, VIVIAN--LORRAINE BIER-ARMADILLOCON '93

HEELIS, BEATRIX
POTTER, BEATRIX--[8]

HEER, FRIEDRICH
GOHDE, HERMANN--[39]GERMAN

HEERBERGER, HELGE
BRENNER, ARVID--[22]SWEDISH

HEERTJE, ARNOLD
BONTEBAL, HENK--[31]

HEFFERNAN, PATRICK
O'HEFFERNAN, PATRICK--[1]

HEFTRICH, ECKHARD
MARKUS, URS--[39]GERMAN/JUV

HEGARTY, ELLEN
HEGARTY, SISTER M. LOYOLA--[31]

HEGARTY, FRANCES
FYFIELD, FRANCES--LACHMAN-EASTER
LIST '93,[31][34]MYS--
HM "A QUESTION OF GUILT" '88
HM "SHADOWS ON THE MIRROR" '89
HM "TRIAL BY FIRE" '90

HEGE, HEINRICH
GINZKEY, FRANZ KARL--[22] AUSTRIAN

HEGEDUS, ADAM
GARLAND, RODNEY--[1][34]MYS--
ALLEN "HEART IN EXILE" '53
ALLEN "TROUBLED MIDNIGHT" '54
ALLEN "WORLD WITHOUT DREAMS" '61
ALLEN "HELL & HIGH WATER" '62
ALLEN "SORCERER'S BROTH" '66

HEGELER, STEN
  BORELL, HELENE--[31]

HEGEMAN, MARY THEODORE
  SISTER MARY THEODORE--[8]

HEHL, EILEEN
  COOPER, M.E.--[21]ROM--
    "TEACHER'S PET"
    "KISS & RUN" & MORE

HEICHEN, WALTER
  EICHNER, WALTER--[39]GERMAN/SF/JUV
  EILER, HERMANN--[39]GERMAN/SF/JUV
  HELFENSTEIN, LOTHAR--[39]GERMAN/SF/JUV
  KUHNWALD, GERD--[39]GERMAN/SF/JUV
  WALTER, ERICH--[39]GERMAN/SF/JUV
  WILDING, KARL--[39]GERMAN/SF/JUV

HEIDE, FLORENCE PARRY
  ALLEN, ALEX B.--[1][31]
  MCDONALD, JAMIE--[1][33]

HEIDE, HARRY F.
  WILSON, CLARK S.--[39]GERMAN/SF

HEIDEMANN, LENI
  SORGE, BIRGIT--[39]GERMAN

HEIDEN, KANRAD
  SILBERMAN, DAVID--[1]

HEIDRICH, INGEBORG
  HEID, GWINNY--[39]GERMAN/JUV
  ILLING, CLAIRE--[39]GERMAN/JUV

HEIDSIECK, HANS
  HOFF, HARRY--[39]GERMAN/MYS/SF
  SIECK, HEIDE--[39]GERMAN/MYS/SF

HEIJERMANS, HERMAN
  FALKLAND, SAMUEL--[1][22][31]DUTCH
  HABBEMA, KOOS--[1][22][31]DUTCH
  JELAKOWITCH, IVAN--[1][22][31]DUTCH

HEILBRUN, CAROLYN GOLD
  CROSS, AMANDA--[18][31][34][40]MYS--
    MacM "JAMES JOYCE MURDER" '67
    KNOPF "POETIC JUSTICE" '70
    RANDOM "PLAYERS COME AGAIN" '90 & MORE
  HEILBRUN, CAROLYN G.--[18]MYS--

HEILESEN, EILEEN DE LYNN
  DE LYNN, EILEEN--[8]

HEIMANN, WILHELM
  BERGEN, FEDOR WILLI--[39]GERMAN

HEIMANN-HEIZMANN, GERTRUD
  HEIZMANN, GERTRUD--[39]GERMAN/JUV

HEIMS, STEVE JOSHUA
  HEIMS, STEVE PAUL--[31]

HEIN, PIET
  KUMBEL--[31] DENMARK--
    "GRUK I-20"

HEINDEL, GOTTFRIED
  MARWERT, MICHAEL--[39]GERMAN
  HOYAU, GEORGES--[39]GERMAN

HEINECKE, RUDOLF
  HEYGK, RALPH--[39]GERMAN/JUV

HEINEMANN, ERICH
  MANN, MATTHIAS--[39]GERMAN/JUV

HEINEMANN, KATHERINE
  KAKI--[31]

HEINEY, DONALD WILLIAM
  HARRIS, MACDONALD--[2][7][23][31]SF--
    ATHNM "SCREENPLAY" '82
    MRW "LITTLE PEOPLE" '86
    STORY LINE "CATHAY STORIES
      & OTHER FICTIONS" '88

HEINKEN, MATHILDE [T]
  TROTT-THOBEN, TILLY--[39]GERMAN

HEINL, NANCY GORDON
  GORDON, NANCY--[31]

HEINLEIN, ROBERT A.
  MACDONALD, ANSON--[2][22][23][33]SF--
    ASF "SIXTH COLUMN" '41
    ASF "BEYOND THIS HORIZON" '42
    ASF "BY HIS BOOTSTRAPS" '41
    ASF "WALDO" '42
  MONROE, LYLE--[2][11][22][23][33]SF--
    SOME W/ELMA WENTZ
  RIVERSIDE, JOHN--[2][11][23][33]SF
  SAUNDERS, CALEB--[2][8][11][22][23][33]SF
  YORK, SIMON--[1][2][11][33]

HEINZ, ECKHARD
  MANSFELD, MICHAEL--[39]GERMAN

HEINZ, M.R.
  RICHARDS, M.R.--[39]GERMAN/HOR

HEISS, JOHN STANGER
  ASCHE, OSCAR--[8]

HEISSENBUETTEL, HELMUT
  HEISSENBUTTEL, HELMUT--[31]

HEITNER, IRIS
  JAMES, ROBERT--[1][3][22]MYS--
    DBLDY "BOARD STIFF" '51
    DBLDY "DEATH WEARS PINK SHOES" '52

HEITZMANN, WILLIAM RAY
  HEITZMANN, WM. RAY--[33]

HEJMADI, PADMA
  PERERA, PADMA--[1]

HELAND, VICTORIA J.R.
  JANES, JOSEPHINE--[9][21][26]ROM--
    "LONDON FROLIC"

HELD, CHRISTA
  FLENSBURG, RUTH--[39]GERMAN/JUV

HELDMAN, RICHARD B.
  MARSH, RICHARD--[32][34]MYS--
    MANY NOVELS & SS COLL
    MZ "PHOTOGRAPHS" JUN '65
    MZ "A PYCHOLOGICAL EXPERIMENT" MAY '64

HELGATH, FRANC
  BAXTER, MARK--[39]GERMAN/MYS/WEST,HP
  CAMERON, JOHN--[39]GERMAN/MYS/WEST,HP
  DE LORCA, FRANK--[39]GERMAN/MYS/WEST,HP
  ELLIOT, BRIAN--[39]GERMAN/MYS/WEST
  HURRICANE, RINGO--[39]GERMAN/WEST,HP
  KOJAK--[39]GERMAN/MYS
  LAMONT, ROBERT--[39]GERMAN/MYS/WEST,HP
  NOLAN, FREDERICK--[39]GERMAN/MYS/WEST,HP

HELGATH, FRANC [CONT]
SILVA, BEN--[39]GERMAN/MYS/WEST
SLADE, JACK--[39]GERMAN/WEST,HP

HELIAS, PIERRE JACQUES M.
HELIAS, PER JAKEY--[1]

HELLAND, BEVERLY
BIRD, BEVERLY--[9][21][26]ROM--
"FOOL'S GOLD"
"RIDE THE WIND" & 6 MORE

HELLER, ALFRED
HARWELL, SUSAN--[39]GERMAN/JUV

HELLER, ARNIE
O'BRIAN, EVE--W/JUDITH E. BRYER,[9][21]ROM--
"MYSTERY AT MIDNIGHT"

HELLER, LORENZ
HALE, LAURA--[34]MYS--
RAINBOW 103 "WILD IS THE WOMAN" '51
RAINBOW 118 "KISS OF FIRE" '52
FALCON 37 "WOMAN HUNTER" '52
HELLER, LARRY--B.CRIDER-PP 1,[34]--
POPLB 760 "I GET WHAT I WANT" '56
PYR F751 "BODY OF THE CRIME" '62
GU BLOOD IS THICKER" MAR '57
HOLDEN, LARRY--B. CRIDER-PP 1,[29][34]MYS--
ETON E132 "HIDE-OUT" '53
PYR G306 "DEAD WRONG" '57
DE "OUT OF THE FRYING PAN" JAN '59
PYR G429 "CRIME COP" '59
& 14 OTHER DIGEST STORIES
LORENZ, FREDERICK--[3][32]MYS--
LION 152 "A RAGE AT SEA" '53
LION 223 "SAVAGE CHASE" '54
LION 193 "NIGHT NEVER ENDS" '54
JU "LIVING BAIT" MAY '55
JU "BIG CATCH" JUL '55
JU "BACKBITE" JAN '56
LION LL63 A PARTY EVERY NIGHT" '56
LION LL104 "RUBY" '56
LION LB144 "HOT" '56
CHARIOT CB151 "DUNGAREE SIN" '60

HELLER, RACHELLE SARA
HELLER, SHELLY--[31]

HELLMAN, HAROLD
HELLMAN, HAL--[31][33]

HELLWIG, ERNST
ALADIN, REX ALBERT--[39]GERMAN/MYS/JUV
CANDENBACH, HORST--[39]GERMAN/MYS/JUV
CLEFF, BENNO--[39]GERMAN/MYS/JUV
NYSSEN, ERNST WILHELM--[39]GERMAN/MYS/JUV

HELLYER, ARTHUR GEORGE L.
HELLYER, A.G.L.--[31]

HELMER, ROBERTA
SKYE, CHRISTINA--[26]ROM--
"THE BLACK ROSE"
"THE RUBY" & 6 MORE

HELMER, WILLIAM
NAISMITH, HORACE--[1]

HELMERICKS, HARMON R.
HELMERICKS, BUD--[1][31]

HELMS, KARL-HEINZ
VALTNA, ATS--[39]GERMAN

HELMS, ROLAND THOMAS
HELMS, TOM--[31]

HELWIG, SARAH MAGDALEN
HELWIG, MAGGIE--[31]

HELYAR, JANE P. JOSEPHINE
POOLE, JOSEPHINE--[7]SF--
"THE VIVITOR: A STORY OF SUSPENSE" '72
"THE LOVING GHOSTS" '88

HEMERY, ERIC
TAVY, PETER--[1]

HEMING, DEMPSTER E.
DEMPSTER, GUY--[8]

HEMING, JACK C.W.
WESTERN-HOLT, J.C.--[8]

HEMING, JOHN WINTON
BARTON, TEX--[35]AUSTRALIAN--
4 HRWTZ WESTERNS '46
CURRAWONG "WAR IN TUCSON" '47
CURRAWONG "KILLER GARTH, SHERIFF" '45
DE WREDER, PAUL--[1][2][23]AUSTRALIAN/SF--
"TIME MARCHED OFF" '42
HEMING, J.W.--[35]AUSTRALIAN/WEST--
HRWTZ - 3 SPORTING NOVELS '46
WINTON, VAL--[36]AUSTRALIAN

HEMINGWAY, ERNEST
HADLEY, JOHN--[8]

HEMINGWAY, JOAN
HEMINGWAY, MUFFET--[1]

HEMMING, NORA KATHLEEN
HEMMING, N.K.--[1]

HEMMING, ROY
HAMILTON, BUZZ--[1][31]

HEMPEL, CARL GUSTAVE
HEMPEL, CARL G.--[31]

HEMPEL, EVA
HOFFMANN-ALEITH, EVA--[39]GERMAN

HEMPHILL, ELIZABETH ANNE
HEMPHILL, BETTY--[31]

HEMPSTEAD, CHARLES EDWARD
CHARLES, EDWARD--[8]

HEMZELIUS, KARL-EVERT V.
GOING, MICKEL--[29]MYS--
EVERTS "MORD I ORESUND" '54

HENAGHAN, JIM
O'NEILL, ARCHIE--[1][3]MYS--
BB "DA VINCI ROSE" '73
BB "DUPLICATE STIFF" '74

HENCKELL, JURGEN
RANDEN, RONALD--[39]GERMAN
SAINT-PIERRE, LAURA--[39]GERMAN
TILMAN, TILO--[39]GERMAN

HENDER-WALLERICH, LINDA
BENJAMIN, LINDA--[26]ROM--
"TEXAS WILDCAT"
"MIDNIGHT PASSION" & MORE

HENDER-WALLERICH, LINDA
DOUGLASS, JESSICA--[26]ROM--
"ALL MY HEART CAN HOLD"
"SNOWFIRE"
"WISH ME A RAINBOW"

HENDERSON, ARCHIBALD
STEELE, ERSKINE--[8]

HENDERSON, BILL
WALTON, LUKE--[1][2][7]SF--
"THE GALAPAGOS KID: THE SPIRIT OF 1976" '71

HENDERSON, C.J.
MORGAN, ROBERT--JOHN L. FRENCH, DDLY PLEAS. #3,M. BAKER-MYS SCENE #39, MYS/HOR--PANDORA--
BERK "THE THINGS THAT ARE NOT THERE, SOME THINGS NEVER DIE" '94
'TEDDY LONDON' - SUPERNATURAL P.I. SERIES

HENDERSON, DONALD [L]
BRIDGEWATER, DONALD--[8]
LANDELS, D.H.--[1][3][22]MYS--
HURST "UNDERSTUDY" '45
HURST "HEADMASTER" '47 & 5 MORE
LANDELS, STEPHANIE--[8]
LAUGHLIN, TOM--[31]

HENDERSON, GEORGE DAVID S
HENDERSON, G.D.S.--[31]

HENDERSON, JAMES L.
CURRIER, JAY L.--[1][3][22]MYS--
MESNER "CARGO OF FEAR" '47

HENDERSON, JAMES MADDOCK
DANVERS, PETER--[8]
JORDAN, BRYN--[8]

HENDERSON, LE GRAND
HARWIN, BRIAN--[1][22][31][33]AMERICAN
LEGRAND--[8][22][31][33]AMERICAN

HENDERSON, NEDRA
MARSHALL, ALAN--MUNROE LST 24,HP--
NTSD 1518 "SIN RESORT"

HENDERSON, SYLVIA
ASHTON-WARNER, SYLVIA--[1]

HENDERSON-DANIELS, BETH
HENDERSON, BETH--[21]ROM--
"NIKROVA'S PASSION"

HENDRICKSON, DORIS E.
HENDRICKSON, EMILY--[9][21][26]ROM--
"QUEEN OF THE MAY"
"ELIZABETH'S RAKE" & MORE

HENDRY, FRANK COUTTS
SHALIMAR--[8][34]MYS--
BLACKWOOD "MINGLED YARN" '35

HENDRY, JAMES FINDLAY
HENDRY, J.F.--[1]

HENDRY, THOMAS
HENDRY, TOM--[31]

HENDRYX, JAMES BEARDSLEY
HENDRYX, HARRISON--L. ROBBINS LTR MAR '94

HENEGHAN, JAMES
BOND, B.J.--[31]

HENEGHAN, JIM
O'NEILL, ARCHIE--
BB "THE GINZBERG CIRCLE" '74
BB "HIGH BID FOR MURDER" '74

HENGSBACH, ARNO
HACH, ERIKA--[39]GERMAN/SF

HENGSTENBERG, ERNST
HERBERGER, ERIKA--[39]GERMAN

HENHAM, ERNEST GEORGE
TREVENA, JOHN--[2][22][23]ENGLISH/SF--
"FURZE, THE CRUEL" '07
"REIGN OF SAINTS" '11

HENISSART, MARTHA
DOMINIC, R.B.--W/MARY JANE LATSIS, [18][31][34]MYS--
DBLDY "THERE IS NO JUSTICE" '71
& 6 MORE
LATHEN, EMMA--W/MARY JANE LATSIS, [18][31][34]MYS--
SIMON "ASHES TO ASHES" '71
& 19 MORE TO '78

HENKE, SHIRL
HENKE, SHIRL--W/CAROL REYNARD,[9][21]ROM--
"GOLDEN LADY"
"CACTUS FLOWER" & 3 MORE

HENKEL, ILSE
BIGGERN, KATHREIN--[39]GERMAN

HENKLE, HENRIETTA
BUCKMASTER, HENRIETTA--[1]

HENLEY, ARTHUR
ERIC, KENNETH--[8][31]
HENLEY, ART--[8][31]
JONES, WEBB--[8][31]

HENLEY, ELIZABETH BECKER
HENLEY, BETH--[31]

HENNEBERG, CHARLES
CHARLES-HENNEBERG, NATHAL--[11]--
USED BY HIS WIFE AFTER HIS DEATH

HENNELL, STANFORD
HEINKEL, STANFORD--[2][34]MYS--
TRANSPORT "KING RAT" '50

HENNING, DALE LEE
HENNING, D.L.--HENNING INTRVW AUG '94--
NPI "THE DEAD CLUE" '94

HENOCH, ERNESTINE
STODELLE, ERNESTINE--[1]

HENOT, GEORGES
OHNET, GEORGES--[2][3]MYS--
9 NOVELS 1889-1903

HENREY, MADELAINE
HENREY, MRS. ROBERT--[31]
HENREY, ROBERT--[31][34]--
SEE "ROBERT HENRY"
HENRY, ROBERT--[34]MYS--
DAVIES "DELPHINE" '47

HENRI, FLORETTE
WINTERS, MARJORIE--[1]

HENRICHS, BETTY L.
DOYLE, EMILY--[9][21][26]ROM--
"A MATTER OF TRUST"
KENT, AMANDA--[9][21][26]ROM--
"THE ARDENT PROTECTOR"

HENRIES, A. DORIS BANKS
HENRIES, DORIS--[31]

HENRY, CHARLES
FARRELL, HENRY--[3][40]MYS--
HOLT "DEATH ON THE SIXTH DAY" '61
HOLT "HOW AWFUL ABOUT ALLAN" '63
RINEHART "WHAT EVER HAPPENED TO BABY JANE?" '60

HENRY, JOHN PATRICK
MACENRI, SEAGHAN--[1]

HENRY, KAREN RAYE
LONG, KARAWYNN--LOCUS #394, P5--
"ADJUSTING THE MOON" '93

HENRY, LYDIA S.
HENLEY, LIZ--W/JANET M. DOOLEY,[26]ROM--
"JUST HER TYPE"

HENRY, PAUL-MARK
BETE-NOIRE--[2]

HENRY, WILLIAM MELLORS
HENRY, BILL--[31]

HENSCHEL, WALTRAUT
ALTHAUSEN, WALTRAUT--[39]GERMAN/JUV
VILLARET, WALTRAUT--[39]GERMAN/JUV

HENSCHKE, ALFRED
KLABUND--[22][31][39]GERMAN

HENSELER, P.S.
COTTON, JERRY--[39]GERMAN/MYS,HP

HENSEY, FREDERICK GERALD
HENSEY, FRITZ--[31]

HENSLEY, DENISE E.
HOLDEN, LESLIE--W/HOLLY G. MILLER,[34]MYS--
HARVEST "COMPTON CONNECTION" '86
HARVEST "LEGACY OF LILLIAN PARKER" '86
HARVEST "CARRIBEAN CONSPIRACY" '87

HENSLEY, JOSEPH LOUIS
ADAMS, LOUIS J.A.--W/ALEXEI PANSHIN, [1][2][23]SF--
"DARK CONCEPTION" '64
HENSLEY, J.L.--[23]AMERICAN/SF
HENSLEY, JOE L.--[32]MYS--
"COLOR OF HATE" '60
MU "ONE WILL TOO MANY" SEPT '66
"DELIVER US TO EVIL" '71
"POISON SUMMER" '74
AHMM "THE CALCULATOR" DEC '79
AHMM "TRIAL TACTICS" OCT '80

HENSLEY, SOPHIA MARGARET
TRY-DAVIES, J.--[8]

HENSON, JAMES MAURY
HENSON, JIM--[31][33]

HENSTALL, DIANA
SILBER, DIANA--[26]ROM--
"CONFESSIONS"
"LATE NIGHT DANCING"

HENTGES, ALISON J.
DEVON, GEORGINA--[9][21][26]ROM--
"UNTAMED HEART" & 5 MORE
KAYE, AMBER--[26]ROM--
"ENDLESS SURRENDER"
"HAUNTED BY LOVE"
"FAERY MAGIC" & OTHERS

HENTY, GEORGE ALFRED
HENTY, G.A.--B&M COLL #26, P12, ENGLISH--
BOY'S BOOKS

HEPBURN, EDITH ALICE M.
WICKHAM, ANNA--[8]

HEPBURN, THOMAS NICOLLSET
OUN, GABRIEL--[8]

HEPPELL, MARY
CLARE, MARGUERITE--[3][8]MYS--
HALE "BLAZE AT NOON" '66
WRIGHT "BAREFOOT WITCH" '68 & 15 MORE
HEPPELL, BLANCHE--[8]

HEPPNER, WALTHER
LINDEN, INA--[39]GERMAN
VON HOLT, UTA--[39]GERMAN

HEPWORTH, JAMES MICHAEL
HEPWORTH, MIKE--[8][31]

HERAPATH, THEODORA
CAPELLE, ANNE--[8]

HERAUD, JAVIER
H.W.--[31]

HERBERT, BRIAN
LANDIS, MARIE--W/MARIE A. LANDIS EDWARDS, [7][23]SF--
ROC "MEMORYMAKERS" '91

HERBERT, DON
WIZARD, MR.--[31][33]--CHILDREN'S BOOKS

HERBERT, HELEN JEAN
HOWAT, JEAN--[33]

HERBERT, HENRY GEORGE A.
CARNARVON, EARL OF--[31]

HERBERT, HENRY WILLIAM
FORESTER, FRANK--[22][31]ENGLISH

HERBERT, JOHN
SIMPLE, PETER--[8]

HERBERT, ROBERT DUDLEY S.
ADAMS, R.D.--[8]
ALPHA CRUCIS--[8]
R.D.A.--[8]

HERBERT, SIR ALAN PATRICK
A.P.H.--[8]
HADDOCK, ALBERT--[8][22]ENGLISH

HERBERT, WALTER WILLIAM
HERBERT, WALLY--[31][33]

HERBRAND, JANICE
HERBRAND, JAN--[21]ROM--
"THE ALTHEIMER INHERITANCE"
"DANGEROUS HOUSE"
"LOST HERITAGE"

HERBRUCK, CHRISTINE COM.
COMSTOCK, CHRISTINE--[31]

HERBST, HANS
WALLENTIN, GEORG--[39]GERMAN

HERBST, RUTH
KIRSTEN-HERBST, RUTH--[39]GERMAN

HERCHENRODER, JAN
LANGREN, CHRISTIAN G.--[39]GERMAN

HERDAN, INNES
JACKSON, INNES--[31]

HERDEN, HERBERT
HELIOS, ALEXANDER--[39]GERMAN/SF

HERDER, EDELTRAUT
BERND, TRAUTE--[39]GERMAN/JUV
SANDERS, SUZETTE--[39]GERMAN/JUV
VON ALTENAU, EDITH--[39]GERMAN/JUV

HERGENHAN, LAURENCE THOM.
HERGENHAN, LAURIE--[31]

HERHAUS, ERNST
BERNEDETTI, EUGENIO--[39]GERMAN

HERING, BURKHARD
BURKHARD, HARI--[39]GERMAN/JUV

HERING, ELISABETH
ACKNER, ELISABETH--[39]GERMAN

HERING, GEO
DORN, GEORG--[39]GERMAN
ZOGENREUTH, G.H.--[39]GERMAN

HERM, GERHARD
CRAWELLS, CARL--[31]--
"A NICE OLD GENTLEMAN" '78

HERMAN, ALAN
ALLAN, TED--[7][8]--
NAME LEGALLY CHANGED TO 'TED ALLAN'

HERMAN, IRA H.
KORNEDEPLOV, MITYA--[2]

HERMAN, JEANNIE M.
HERMAN, J.B.--V. BERCH LTR TO
HUBIN '94,MYS--
MAJOR "BLACK SABBAT" '79
MAJOR "GRANDMOTHER'S HOUSE" '80

HERMAN, MICHAELA ROSSNER
ROSSNER, MICHAELA--[7]SF

HERMANN, GUNTHER
LENNOX, JOCELYN L.--[39]GERMAN

HERMANN, L.A.
ALBERT, L.--[39]GERMAN

HERMANN, NANCY A.
JEFFRIES, JESSICA--[9][21][26]ROM--
"ALL IN THE GAME"
"A CERTAIN SUNRISE" & MORE
RUSSELL, RENEE--[9]ROM
SCOTT, SAMANTHA--[9][21][26]ROM--
"AFTER THE LOVING"
"ALL IN GOOD TIME" & MORE

HERMLIN, STEPHEN
LEDER, RUDOLF--[31]

HERN,[GEORGE] ANTHONY
HOPE, ANDREW--[8][31]
POTIPHAR--W/J.F. MARRACK,[1]

HERNANDEZ, EFREN
EALLING, TILL--[30] MEXICAN--
JOURNAL "AMERICA" - HUMOROUS ARTICLES

HERNDON, NANCY R.
CHADWICK, ELIZABETH--[26]ROM--
"VIRGIN FIRE"
"WILD HUNT & MORE

HERNDON, URSULE MOLINARO
MOLINARO, URSULE--[7]--
"THE AUTOBIOGRAPHY OF CASSANDRA, PRINCESS
& PROPHETRESS OF TROY" '79

HERNHUTTER, ALBERT
AHEARNE, BURT--[2][11][31]
JARVIS, LEE--[2][11]

HERO, NUMA C.
QUIEN SABE--[11]

HEROLD, ANNEMARIE
WENDLAND, HEIDE--[39]GERMAN

HERON, EDNA
CRONIN, BEN--[2][31]

HERON-ALLEN, EDWARD
ALLEN, EDWARD HERON--[34]--
HAS USED BOTH NAME FORMS
ARONIN, BEN--[2]
BLAYRE, CHRISTOPHER--ENCYCL. OF HORROR
& SUPERNATURAL 1986,[2][7]
DRYASDUST--[16][23]
FLAVIUS--[2][16]
HALIDOM, M.Y.--[2][23]SF
WARDDEL, NORA HELEN--[2][31]

HERPIN, CLARA ADELE LUCE
PEREY, LUCIEN--[22] FRENCH

HERR, MICHAEL
M.T.C.W.--[31]

HERRICK, MARVIN THEODORE
SMITH, JOHN--W/HOYT HUDSON,[1][8]

HERRINGTON, MRS. W. LEE
FARLEY, ALAN--E.R. HAGEMANN-COMPH.
INDEX BLK MASK '82

HERRINGTON, PATRICIA M.
HERRINGTON, PAT--[31]

HERRINGTON, TERRI
HUGHES, TRACY--[9][21]ROM--
"HONORBOUND"
"EMERALD WINDOWS" & MORE

HERRMANN, DOROTHY
HERRMANN, TAFFY--[31]

HERRMANN, GERHARD
MOSTAR, GERHART HERRMANN--[39]GERMAN

HERRMANN, JEAN
VAUTRIN, JEAN--[40]MYS--
"BILLY-ZE-KICK" '74
"BLOODY MARY" '79

HERRMANN, JOSEF
CARSTENS, BERND--[39]GERMAN/MYS--

HERRMANN, NIRA
HARMON, ANNE--W/PHYLLIS DI FRANCESCO,[26]ROM--
"DESERT FLAME"
"WYOMING WILDFIRE"
HERRMANN, PHYLLIS--W/PHYLLIS DI FRANCESCO,
[21][26]ROM--
"HIDDEN FIRE"
"TWO FOR ONE"

HERRON, ELSIE ELLERINGTON
ELSEY, J.J.--[8]

HERSCHBERGER, RUTH M.
LANGSTAFF, JOSEPHINE--[31]

HERSEY, HAROLD
BUXTON, CARL--[1][2][11]HP--
STREET & SMITH
DI VAILLENT, FRANCOIS--[2]HP--
STREET & SMITH
KEMP, HARRY--[1][2][11]
KENNEDY, PHILIP--[1][2][11]HP--
KIPROY, CHARLES--[2]HP--
STREET & SMITH
LE MOYNE, ROY--[1][2][11]HP--
STREET & SMITH
LE MOYNE, SEYMOUR--[1][2]
LERROVITCH--[1][2][11]HP--
STREET & SMITH
OWENS, ALBERT--[1][2][11]HP--
STREET & SMITH
TYSON, ARNOLD--[1][2]HP--
STREET & SMITH
VERNON, VAIL--[1][2]HP--
STREET & SMITH

HERSHBERGER, HAZEL KUHNS
ALLEN, HAZEL--[31]

HERSHEY, EDWARD NORMAN
HERSHEY, ED--[31]

HERSHFIELD, HARRY
HERSHFIELD, HARRY--W/WALTER B. GIBSON,[18]MYS--
BART "SINS OF ROGER DIDDLEBOCK" '47

HERSHMAN, FLORENCE
BROWNING, DIANA--[9][21][26]ROM--
"ALL THE GOLDEN PROMISES"
HAVILAND, DIANA--[9][26]ROM--
"STOLEN SPLENDOR" & 7 MORE

HERSHMAN, MORRIS
BOND, EVELYN--[3][9][32]MYS/ROM--
LAN "LADY IN DARKNESS" '65
MSMM "BRUTUS IS AN HONORABLE MAN" JAN '66
MSMM "DARK HOUR" SEPT '69
AV "RAVEN'S EYE" '72 & MORE
ENGLISH, ARNOLD--V. BERCH & G. LOVISI
REVIEWS '93,[32][34]MYS--
GU "FALL GUY" NOV '57
MH "BET I DON'T DIE" MAY '57
SF "ONE HUSBAND TOO MANY" DEC '57
TR "GET OUT OF TOWN" DEC '57
TR "RUMBLE FOR A BLONDE" APR '58
TR "SNOWBALL IN HELL" FEB '58
MU "TIPOFF" JUN '60
ST "AS SILENT AS DOOM" JAN '61
OF "GET LOST, BUM!" JUL '60
MSMM "BAIL HEARING" MAY '65
VEGA "EDGE OF VIOLENCE" '69
HEIMER, MEL--V. BERCH-MON PSEUDS.

HERSHMAN, MORRIS [CONT]
HUNT, NORMAN--LACHMAN LST '93/MYS--
GU "KIDNAPPED" JUN '62
MSMM "ZIGZAG AUG '64
MSMM "COPS DON'T HAVE WINGS" DEC '64
LM "HANGMAN'S HELPER" DEC '64
MSMM "DEVIL'S PAYOFF" FEB '65
MSMM "COPS TAKE CHANCES" SEPT '65
LM "LETTERS FROM BARBARA" MAR '65
MSMM "WAIR FOR TROUBLE" APR '65
SO "ONCE OVER LIGHTLY" APR '66
MU "BATTERED BRIDE" OCT '66
KAVANAUGH, IAN--[9][21][26]ROM--
'THE O'DONNELL'S SAGA'
MALLORY, MARK--LACHMAN LIST '93,MYS?
ROFFMAN, SARA--[9][21][26]ROM--
"FAMILY PROUD"
ROTHMAN, SARA--[9]ROM
TEMPLETON, JANET--[9][21][26]ROM--
"LOVER'S KNOT'
"LADY FORTUNE" & MORE
VICTOR, SAM--[3][9][21]MYS--
CHART "CUBAN INFERNO" '81
CHART "WHITE HOUSE MASSACRE" '81
WEBB, LIONEL--[9][21][26]ROM--
"SPARHAWK"
"ROGUE SLAVE" & MORE
WILCOX, JESS--[26][34]MYS--
MON 151 "KILL ME, SWEET" '60
"VANITY, MY BELOVED"
WILCOX, JESSICA--[9][21][26]ROM--
"THIS WOUNDED PASSION"

HERSHMAN, NORMAN
HERRIES, NORMAN--L. ROBBINS LTR MAR '94

HERTEL, FRANCOIS
DUBE, RODOLPHE--[31]

HERTEL, JOHANN GEORG
REINLEIN, M.--[39]GERMAN

HERTER, LORETTA M.
HERTER, LORI--[7][9][21]ROM--
"SEVENTH HEAVEN"
"LOVING DECEPTION" & MORE

HERTZ, GRETE JANUS
JANUS, GRETE--[31][33]

HERTZ, JACKOLINE G.
HERTZ, JACKY--[31]

HERTZBERG, NANCY
KEESING, NANCY--[8]

HERTZIG, ERNST
HEARTING, ERNIE--[39]GERMAN/JUV

HERVE, AIME MARIE EDUOARD
VALNAY, RAOUL--[22] FRENCH

HERVE-BAZIN, JEAN PIERRE
BAZIN, HERVE--[31]

HERWEY, MICHAEL
WALLACE, MICHAEL--[29]MYS--
DM-17 "MODARENS MARKE" '50

HERZ, JEROME SPENCER
HERZ, JERRY--[31]

HERZ, PEGGY
HUDSON, PEGGY--[31]

HERZBRUCH, ARND
REITTER, NIKOLAUS--[39]GERMAN

HERZINGER, KIM ALLEN
CORTEZ-VILLON, JUAN--[31]

HERZOG, EMILE S.
HERZOG, E.--[31]
MAUROIS, ANDRE--[2][7][23][31][32]MYS--
EQMM "SUICIDE HOTEL" FEB '52
MM "MEMO FROM THE UNDERGROUND" SEPT '56
SA "TULIP BULB" NOV '63

HERZOG, JOHANN ADOLF
TRUTH, HANSEL--[39]GERMAN

HERZOG, WILHELM PETER
DUKA, PETER--[39]GERMAN/SF/JUV
HELMI, PETER--[39]GERMAN/SF/JUV

HESELTINE, PHILIP ARNOLD
WARLOCK, PETER--[8]

HESPOS, LISELOTTE
LOUIS, CARLA--[39]GERMAN

HESS, DIRK R.
CHESS, DEREK--[39]GERMAN/SF

HESS, JANICE
CARTER, JANICE--[9][10][21][26]ROM--
HARL 593 "GHOST TIGER"
"DOUBLE JEOPARDY"

HESS, JOAN E[DMISTON]
HADLEY, JOAN--HAWK/HESS INTRVW '93,[31]--
ST. MARTINS "NIGHT BLOOMING CEREUS" '86
ST. MARTINS "DEADLY ACKEE" '88
& MORE

HESS, MAGDA
MUNNICH, MAGDA--[39]GERMAN/JUV

HESSE, HERMANN
LAUSCHER, HERMANN--[22][31][33]GERMAN-SWISS
SINCLAIR, EMIL--[22][33][39]GERMAN-SWISS

HESSELS, WILLEM
HENDRIK ADRIAAN MULDER--[22] DUTCH

HESSING, JAKOB
RESSING, RON--[39]GERMAN/WEST

HETHERINGTON, KEITH JAMES
CONWAY, KEITH--[8]
DEKKER, CARL--[35]AUSTRALIAN, HP--
CALVERT - SOME OF 40 BOOKS
HAMILTON, KIRK--[35]AUSTRALIAN--
COUGAR 541 "JOHNNY REB"
SANTE FE 423 "START PRAYING!"
CLEVELAND - 55 WESTERNS
KEITH, JAMES--[8][35]AUSTRALIAN--CLVLD
MCCALL, CLINT--G. FLANAGAN LTR '94,
AUSTRALIAN/WEST--CLVLD NOVELETTES
WARING, BRETT--[35]AUSTRALIAN--
SIERRA "BEHIND THE GUN"
SANTE FE- 6 WESTERNS
CLEVELAND- 15 WESTERNS

HETMANEK, BERTA
HAYDE, BERTL--[39]GERMAN/JUV

HETTINGER, JOHN
JOHNHETT--[2]

HETZEL, PIERRE JULES
STAHL, P.J.--[22]FRENCH

HEUER, WILHELM
FELSEGG, ARCO v.--[39]GERMAN
HEUER, WILLIAM--[39]GERMAN
ILLIW-UEHRE, M.A. v.--[39]GERMAN
MORGAN, HANS--[39]GERMAN
VON STERNAU, THEO--[39]GERMAN

HEUERT, EVA
RIED, CAROLIN--[39]GERMAN

HEUMAN, WILLIAM
KILRAIN, GEORGE--L. ROBBINS LTR MAR '94, WEST--
ACE D14 "MAVERICK WITH A STAR" '53
ACE D30 "SOUTH TO SANTE FE" '53
KRAMER, GEORGE--[8][28][31][33]YOUTH--
PUTNAM "THE LEFT HANDER" '64

HEUN, KARL GOTTLIEB SAM.
CLAUREN, HEINRICH--[39]GERMAN

HEVELIN, JAMES
BARRON, RUSTY--[2]

HEVESI, LUDWIG
ONKEL TOM--[22]AUSTRO-HUNGARIAN

HEWELCKE, GEOFFREY
JEFFRIES, HUGH--[2][11]

HEWETSON, SARA
DICANT, V.L.--[8]

HEWETT, ANITA
WELLINGTON, ANNE--[8]

HEWISON, ROBERT JOHN P.
PETRIE, JOHN--[8]

HEWITT, C.P.
TWIST, PETER--[3]MYS--
ACE S107 "GILDED HIDEAWAY" "55

HEWITT, CECIL ROLPH
CECIL, R.H.--[31]
ROLPH, C.H.--[8]

HEWITT, JOHN [HAROLD]
HOWARD, JOHN--[1]

HEWITT, KATHLEEN DOUGLAS
MARTIN, DOROTHEA--[3][8]MYS--
MATHEWS "BLACK SUNSHINE" '33

HEWSON, IRENE DALE
ROSS, JEAN--[2][8]

HEYCK, HANS
LOOTHMANN, HARRO--[39]GERMAN

HEYCOCK, LESLEY
GRANT-ADAMSON, LESLEY--KLEIN-GREAT WOMEN
MYSTERY WRITERS, MYS--
SCRIBN "DEATH ON WIDOW'S WALK" '85
FABER "FACE OF DEATH" '85
FABER "GUILTY KNOWLEDGE" '86
FABER "WILD JUSTICE" '87
FABER "THREATENING EYE" '88
FABER "CURSE THE DARKNESS" '90

HEYDA, ERNST
ALBERT, ERNST--[39]GERMAN/JUV
BACH, FRANK O.--[39]GERMAN/JUV
ERGON, P.E.A.--[39]GERMAN/JUV

HEYDA, ERNST [CONT]
WALTER, ERNST--[39]GERMAN/JUV

HEYDON, JOSEPH KENTIGERN
TREVARTHEN, HAL P.--[2][11][23]SF--

HEYER, GEORGETTE
MARTIN, STELLA--[11][17][18][29]ENGLISH/MYS--
"TRANSFORMATION OF PHILIP JETTAN" '23

HEYLIGER, WILLIAM
WILLIAMS, HAWLEY--[33]

HEYMAN, EVAN LEE
BLACKWOOD, JOY ANN--[3]MYS--
POPLB "GHOST OF LOST LOVER'S LAKE" '73
HAYWORTH, EVELYN[E]--[3][21][26]MYS/ROM--
POPLB "EVIL AT BAYOU LAFORCHE" '72
POPLB "HAZZARD'S MANOR" '73
SCOFIELD, JONATHAN--[21][26]ROM,HP--
DELL 'FREED. FTR' SERIES:
"BULLETS ON THE BORDER"

HEYMANN, CLEMENS CLAUDE
HEYMANN, C. DAVID--[31]

HEYMANN, ROBERT
LADENBURG, MAX--[39]GERMAN/MYS/WEST
LEE, MAC--[39]GERMAN/MYS/WEST
RETCLIFFE, SIR JOHN--[39]GERMAN/MYS
ROBERTS, FRED--[39]GERMAN/MYS/WEST,HP

HEYMANN, ROBERT JR.
ARAND, LILO--[39]GERMAN/MYS/WEST
ARDEN, ROBERT--[39]GERMAN/MYS/WEST
BRETT, TODDY--[39]GERMAN/MYS/WEST,HP
ROBERTS, FRED--[39] GERMAM/MYS/WEST,HP

HEYMANN, THOMAS N.
HEYMANN, TOM--[31]

HEYNEN, JAMES
HEYNEN, JIM--[28]WEST--3 SHORT STORIES

HEYWARD, DOROTHY H. KUHNS
KUHNS, DOROTHY--[31]

HEYWOOD, JOSEPH T.
HEYWOOD, JOE T.--[31]

HIAASEN, CARL
SHULMAN, NEIL M.D.--F. FIORELLA LTR '94,
HERR SLS LST--
GHOSTED 2 SHULMAN BKS
SCRIBN "FINALLY..I'M A DOCTOR" '76
SCRIBN "WHAT?..DEAD AGAIN?" '79

HIBBERT, ELEANOR BURFORD
BURFORD, ELEANOR--[9][17][18]
[31]ENGLISH/MYS/ROM--
CARR, PHILLIPPA--[3][9][18][21]
[31][33]MYS/ROM--
COLLINS "WITCH FROM THE SEA" '75
& 2 MORE
FORD, ELBUR--[3][9][18][21][31][33]MYS/ROM--
LAURIE "POISON IN PIMLICO" '50 & MORE
HOLT, VICTORIA--[3][9][18][21][31][33]MYS/ROM--
COLLINS "DEMON LOVER" '82 & 31 MORE
KELLOW, KATHLEEN--[3][9][18][21][31]
[33]MYS/ROM--
HALE "DANCE MACABRE" '52
HALE "LILITH" '54 & 6 MORE

HIBBERT, ELEANOR BURFORD [CONT]
PLAIDY, JEAN--[9][18][21][26][33]ROM--
"MADAME SERPENT"
"BASTARD KING" & MANY MORE
TATE, ELLALICE--[9][18][21][29][33]ROM--
5 NOVELS

HIBBS, JOHN
BLYTH, JOHN--[8][31]

HICKEN, MARILYN E.
HICKEN, MANDY--[31]

HICKEN, UNA
KINDLER, ASTA--[2]

HICKEY, MADELYN EASTLUND
BAILEY, BETTY--[1]
DE LACY, LOUISE--[1]
EASTLUND, MADELYN--[8]
FARRINGTON, MAUDE--[1]
HICKEY, LYN--[8]
SULLIVAN, ERIC HARRISON--[1]

HICKMAN, LYNN
JONES, PLATO--[2][11]

HICKMANN, FRANZ MARIA
HIGHMAN, FRANK--[39]GERMAN/MYS

HICKS, JIMMY LYN
HICKS, J.L.--[31]
HICKS, JIM--[31]

HICKS, JOAN WILSON
WILDING, KAY--[21][26]ROM--
"RAINBOW'S END"
"STAND BY ME" & 2 OTHER NOVELS
WINDHAM, KIT--[9][21][26]ROM--
"SOUTHERN COMFORT"
"TWO FOR THE ROAD" & 2 MORE

HICKS, TYLER GREGORY
MURPHY, LOUIS J.--[8]

HIDEO, YAMANOUCHI
SATOMI--[22]JAPANESE

HIERONIMUS, EKKEHARD
GROHUS, MAXIMILIAN--[39]GERMAN

HIETZIG, A.B. WALTER
AFRICANUS, W.--[39]GERMAN/JUV

HIGDON, HAL
SMITH, LAFAYETTE--[22][33]AMERICAN

HIGGINBOTTOM, DAVID LEE
FISK, NICHOLAS--[7][23]ENGLISH/SF--
"SPACE HOSTAGES" '67
"TRILLIONS" '71

HIGGINGBOTHAM, ANNE D.
HIGGINGBOTHAM, ANNE T.--[8]

HIGGINS, CHARLES
DALL, IAN--[8]

HIGGINS, CHARLES ELI
MULIER--[2]

HIGGINS, DONALD HUGH
BAKER, HUGH--W/HERMAN DEUTSCH,[3]MYS--
HOUGHTON "CARTWRIGHT IS DEAD, SIR!" '36

HIGGINS, MARGARET
O'BRIEN, BERNADETTE--[8]

HIGGINS, RICHARD CARTER
HIGGINS, DICK--[31]

HIGGINS, ROSALYN COHEN
COHEN COHEN--[22]ENGLISH
COHEN, ROSALYN--[31]

HIGGINSON, HENRY CLIVE
THETA, ERIC MARK--[8]

HIGGINSON, WILLIAM JOHN
HIAN--[31]

HIGGONET, MARGARET R.
HALE, MARGARET--[31]

HIGGS, ALEC S.
STANSBURY, ALEC--[8]

HIGH, HOPETON
JAMES, BRIAN--[13]AUSTRALIAN

HIGHAM, FLORENCE MAY G.
EVANS, F.M.G.--[31]

HIGHAM, JONATHAN HUW
HIGHAM, JON ATLAS--[31]

HIGHAM, THOMAS FARRANT
HIGHAM, T.F.--[31]

HIGHET, GILBERT
HIGHET, HELEN--W/HELEN MACINNES,[9][31]--
"SEXUAL LIFE IN ANCIENT ROME" '34
"FRIEDRICH ENGELS" '36

HIGHSMITH, PATRICIA
MORGAN, CLAIRE--J. PRESSMAN--
LESBIANA-BAE 20, P32,[18][22]--
McCANN "PRICE OF SALT" '52

HIGHWATER, JAMAKE M.
MARKS, JASON--J. PRESSMAN-CNTRCLTR,
BAE 21,[33]--
GM 1234 "TWO SOULS, ONE BODY" '62
MARKS-HIGHWATER, J.--[33]

HIGON, ALBERT
JEURY, MICHEL--[7] ? UNCONFIRMED ?

HIGSON, PHILIP J. WILOBY.
HIGSON, PHILIP--[8]
WILLOUGHBY-HIGSON, PHILIP--[8]

HILDEBRANDT, TIM & GREG
HILDEBRANDT, BROTHERS--[7][31][33]SF--
ART BOOK

HILDEBRANDT, TIMOTHY
HILDEBRANDT, TIM--[31]

HILDGARD, HEINRICH GUSTAV
VILLARD, HENRY--[22]GERMAN-AMERICAN

HILDICK, EDMUND WALLACE
HILDICK, E.W.--[31][33]--
CHILDREN'S BOOKS
HILDICK, WALLACE--[8]

HILL, ABRAM BARRINGTON
HILL, AB--[31]

HILL, BRIAN [MERRIKEN]
MAGILL, MARCUS--W/JOANNA GILES,[32][34]MYS--
5 NVLS '29-32
LM "A NICE WALK BY THE FIELDS" JUN '64

HILL, DAVID CHARLES
HILL, DAVE--[31]

HILL, DAVID JOHN
HILL, DAVE--[31]

HILL, DOUGLAS ARTHUR
HILLMAN, MARTIN--[8][31][33]

HILL, GRACE [LIVINGSTON]
HILL-LUTZ, GRACE L.--[1]
LIVINGSTON, GRACE--[1]
MACDONALD, MARCIA--[8][17][33]ROM--
4 NOVELS '27 - '30

HILL, HARRY EGBERT
GREGORY, HYLTON--[34]MYS,HP--
AMALG "MYS OF THE RAJA'S SON" '35
AMALG "CURSE OF KALI" '35
AMALG "SECRET OF BLACKMAILED BARONET" '37
AMALG "SIGN OF THE BLACK FEATHER" '39

HILL, JOHN ALEXANDER
SKEEVER, JIM--[8]

HILL, KATHLEEN LOUISE
HILL, KAY--[31][33]

HILL, LANCE
HOWLETT, LANCE--[2]

HILL, LAWSON W.
CAXTON, R.F.--[2]
HOLDEN, MARC--[2]

HILL, LEROY DRAPER JR.
HILL, DRAPER--[31]

HILL, MARGARET [OHLER]
BENNETT, RACHEL--[8][22][31][33]AMERICAN
HILL, MEG--[31][33]
THOMAS, ANDREA--[8][22][33]AMERICAN

HILL, MARY RAYMOND
RAYMOND, LEE--[1]

HILL, MAVIS
BARRISTER, A.--[8]

HILL, MRS. E.E.
SOUTHERN CROSS--[8]

HILL, PAMELA
FISKE, SHARON--[8][17][31]ROM--
"SUMMER CYPRESS" '81

HILL, R. LANCE
HENRY, DAVID LEE--[1][31]

HILL, REGINALD [CHARLES]
MORLAND, DICK--[2][11][18][23][29]MYS--
"HEART CLOCK" '73
"ALBION! ALBION!" '74
RUELL, PATRICK--[18][29][34]MYS--
LONG "CASTLE OF THE DEMON" '71
LONG "RED CHRISTMAS" '72
HUTCH "DEATH TAKES THE LOW ROAD" '74
HUTCH "URN BURIAL" '75
METHUEN "LONG KILL" '86
METHUEN "DEATH OF A DORMOUSE" '86
METHUEN "DREAMS OF DARKNESS" '89

HILL, REGINALD [CHARLES] [CONT]
UNDERHILL, CHARLES--[1][18][29]MYS--
"THE FORGING OF FANTOM" '79
"CAPT. FANTOM" '80

HILL, ROBERT CECIL
HILL, BOB--[31]

HILL, ROBERT L.
HILL, BOB--[31]RELIGIOUS

HILL, ROY
CAPELLI, ACE--PP 29, P42,HP--
LA FONTAINE, HENRI--[27]ROM--
"CARESSED" ca 52/53

HILL, TERESA
HAYES, SALLY TYLER--[26]ROM--
"WHOSE CHILD IS THIS?"
"DIXON'S BLUFF"

HILL, THOMAS
HALLOWELL, TOMMY--[31]

HILL,[J.E.] CHRISTOPHER
HOLME, K.E.--[31] HARRAP--
"TWO COMMONWEALTHS" '45

HILLER, WILHELM
HILLER, WILLIAM--[39]GERMAN/WEST

HILLERET, ALAIN & ANDRE
ARCADIUS--[2]

HILLERMAN, ANTHONY GROVE
HILLERMAN, TONY--[19][34][40]AMERICAN/MYS--
AT LEAST 13 NOVELS '70-TD

HILLERS, HERMAN WILLIAM
HILLUS, WILHELM--[31]

HILLIER, JAMES MARTIN
HILLIER, JIM--[31]

HILLMAN, DOROTHY ANN
GALLOWAY, LAURA--[21][26]ROM--
"FORBIDDEN DELIGHT"

HILLS, ARGENTINA SCHIFANO
HILLS, TINA--[31]

HILLS, CHARLES RICHARD
HILLS, DICK--[31]

HILLS, FRANCES E.
MERCER, FRANCES--[8]

HILLS, PHILIP JAMES
HILLS, P.J.--[31]

HILLSTROM, JOSEPH
HILL, JOE--[8]

HILLYARD, MARY DOROTHEA
KELLWAY, MARY D.--[8]

HILTON, JAMES
TREVOR, GLEN--[2][3][22][29][33]MYS--
BENN "MURDER AT SCHOOL" '31

HILTON, JOHN BUXTON
GREENWOOD, JOHN--[18][34]MYS--
QUARTET "MIND OF MR. MOSLEY" '87
& 5 MORE '83-7
STANLEY, WARWICK--[8]

HILTON, JOHN DEAN
CLEVELAND, JOHN--[1][3]MYS--
ARCADIA "MINUS ONE CORPSE" '54

HILTON, MARGARET LYNETTE
HILTON, NETTE--[31][33]

HILTON, RICHARD
DIL, ZAKHMI--[22]ENGLISH

HILTON, RODNEY HOWARD
HILTON, R.H.--[31]

HILTON, THOMAS H.
BUONANNO, JOSEPH--V. BERCH-BRNDN/
BC PSEUDOS, BAE 22, P24

HILU, VIRGINIA
EINHORN, VIRGINIA HILU--[31]

HINCKLEY, HELEN
JONES, HELEN--[8]

HINCKS, CYRIL MALCOLM
COULSDON, JOHN--[1][8]
DAYLE, MALCOLM--[8]
DOYLE, MALCOLM--[1]
GEE, OSMAN--[1][8]
HINCKS, G. MALCOLM--[34]OCCASIONAL BYLINE
HOWARD, JOHN M.--[1][8]
MALCOLM, CHARLES--[1][8]
MALCOLM, RONALD--[8]

HINDEN, MICHAEL C.
BYRD, EMMETT--[1][31]
BYRD, JOHN CROWE--[1][31]

HINDENACH, ARTHUR
CAMBEL, ARTI--[39]GERMAN

HINDS,[EVELYN] MARGERY
HINDS, E.M.--[1]

HIND[E], ALFRED
ROCHDALE, THOMAS--[2][11]

HINE, ALEXANDRA
BLAKELEE, ALEXANDRA--[9][21][26]ROM--
"THE BOTECELLI MAN"

HINE, ALEXANDRA
BRENNAN, LILLA--[9]ROM

HINE, AL[FRED B.]
ARETINO, JR.--V. BERCH LTR '93--
PAPLB "ROMAN HOOKERS" '74
CARTER, NICK--[34]MYS,HP--
AWARD "OUR AGENT IN ROME IS MISSING" '73
AWARD "MASSACRE IN MILAN" '74
GIBSON, JOSEPHINE--W/SESYL JOSLIN,[1][22][31]--
"IS THERE A MOUSE IN THE HOUSE?" '65
KIRTLAND, G.B.--W/SESYL JOSLIN,[1][31]--
"ONE DAY IN ANCIENT ROME" '61
STREET, BRADFORD--[34]MYS--
DELL "GLASS BOTTOM BOAT" '66
DELL "IN LIKE FLINT" '67
BB "PRIMUS" '71

HINE, SESYLE JOSLIN
GIBSON, JOSEPHINE--W/ALFRED B. HINE,
[1][22][31]--
"IS THERE A MOUSE IN THE HOUSE?" '65
JOSLIN, SESYLE--[1][22][31]AMERICAN
KIRTLAND, G.B.--W/AL HINE,[1][22][31]AMERICAN--
"ONE DAY IN ANCIENT ROME"
SESYLE, JOSLIN--[11]

HINES, DOROTHEA
DE CULWEN, DOROTHEA--[1][8]

HINES, EARL KENNETH
HINES, FATHA--[31]

HINES, JEANNE MCNEILL
ROYAL, ROSAMOND--[21][26]ROM--
"RAPTURE"
SHERWOOD, VALERIE--[21]ROM--
15 NOVELS

HINGSTON, MARY SANDRA
BURGESS, MALLORY--[9][21][26]ROM--
"BALLENROSE"
"RIDE THE SAVAGE SEA" & MORE
FITZGERALD, CATHERINE--[9][21]ROM--
AV "PASSION SONG"

HINKEMEYER, MICHAEL T.
LARA, JAN--[7][26][31][34]MYS--
POPLB "LIMBO: A NOVEL" '88
WARNER "SOULCATCHERS" '90
ROYALL, VANESSA--[9][21][26]ROM--
"FLAMES OF DESIRE"
"FIREBRAND'S WOMAN" & MORE

HINKINS, FRANK R.
CUTTRISS, FRANK--W/R. CUTTRISS HINKINS,[1]

HINKINS, R. CUTTRISS
CUTTRISS, FRANK--W/FRANK CUTTRISS,[1]
CUTTRISS IS MAIDEN NAME

HINKLE, VERNON
ELKINS, H.V.--[1][31]

HINKSON, KATHARINE TYNAN
TYNAN, KATHARINE--[1]

HINOJOSA-SMITH, ROLAND
HINOJOSA-S, ROLAND R.--[31]
GALINDO, P.--[1][31]
HINOJOSA, ROLANDO--[31]

HINRICHS, EVERARD J.
SLOANE, ERIC--[1]

HINTON, HERBERT ALLAN
CLIFFORD, MARTIN--[1]HP
HOWARD, PROSPER--[1]HP
RICHARDS, FRANK--[1]HP

HINTON, HOWARD
MORLEY, RALPH--[1]

HINTON, MILTON JOHN
HINTON, MILT--[31]

HINTZ, LOREN E.
BAUM, LOREN--[1]

HINTZ, WERNER
WERTNER, HEINZ--[39]GERMAN/MYS

HINZ, DIANA
WHITNEY, DIANA--[9][21][26]ROM--
"STILL MARRIED"
"CAST A TALL SHADOW" & MORE

HINZELMANN, ELSA M.
HAUSER, MARGRIT--[39]GERMAN/JUV

HIPKINS, CHARLES HAMMOND
TALBOT, CARL--[1][3][22]MYS--
ELDON "LOVE IN DANGER" '34
"WHITE BADGER" '35
"CAMERON MYS" '35

HIPP, RUDIGER
ULMER, FLORIAN--[39]GERMAN/SF

HIPPISLEY COXE, ANTHONY D
LACY, CHARLES--[1][31]

HIPSCHMAN, MAY
HILLMAN, MAY--[1]

HIRAI, TARO
RAMPO, EDOGAWA--[2][11][34]MYS--
TUTTLE "JAPANESE TALES OF MYS
& IMAGINATION" '46

HIRANO-NAKANISHI, MARSHA
HIRANO, MARSHA--[1][31]
NAKANISHI, MARSHA--[1]

HIRAOKA, KIMITAKE
MISHIMA, YUKIO--[1]

HIRD, JAMES D.
BOTTSFORD, LORD--[2]

HIRD, NEVILLE
MEYER, HENRY J.--[8]

HIROSHI, KIKUCHI
KAN, KIKUCHI--[22]JAPANESE

HIROSHI, MURAI
GENSAI, MURAI--[22]JAPANESE

HIRSCH, DAVID LEON
HIRSCH, LEE--[1][34]MYS--
FELL "MURDER STEALS THE SHOW" '46

HIRSCH, DORA
FISCHEL, FLORENCE--[1]

HIRSCH, LUDWIG
HEVESI, LUDWIG--[39]GERMAN/SF

HIRSCH, PAUL
PEEL, NORMAN LEMON--[1]
VLASIC, BOB--[1][33]

HIRSCH, ROSEMARIE [S]
SCHUDER, ROSEMARIE--[39]GERMAN

HIRSCHFELD, BURT
BARRON, HUGH--[34]MYS--
PYR "FON CITY" '68
PYR "BIG SCORE" '69
PYR "GODDESS GAME" '70 & MORE

HIRSCHLER, ADOLF
HIRSCHLER, IVO--[39]GERMAN

HIRSCHMAN, ALBERT O.
HIRSCHMAN, A.O.--[31]

HIRSCHMANN, MARIA ANNE
HANSI--[31]

HIRSH, PHIL
LEMON PEEL, NORMAN--[1][33]

HIRSHFIELD, HENRY I.
MAYFIELD, M.I.--W/G.M. MATEYKO,[1][2]

HIRSHMAN, JACK
CONWAY, RUDOLF--V. BERCH-BRNDN/ BC PSEUDS, BAE 22, P24
GEORGE, STEVEN--V. BERCH-BRNDN/ BC PSEUDS, BAE 22, P24
LOWNDES, GEOFFREY--V. BERCH-BRNDN/ BC PSEUDS, BAE 22, P24

HIRST, GEORGE STANLEY
HERTZ, GEORGE--[1]

HIRST, GILLIAN JOSE C.
BAXTER, GILLIAN--[1][8]

HISCOCK, ERIC
E.H.--[8]
WHITEFRIAR--[1][8]

HISCOCK, LESLIE
MARSH, PATRICK--[2][7][22][34]MYS--
LONGMAN'S "BREAKDOWN" '53

HISCOCKS, RICHARD
SEYMOUR, EDWARD--[1]

HITCHCOCK, FRANCIS
MURDOCK, FRANK--[1]

HITCHENS, A.
HILTON, ROYCE--[35]AUSTRALIAN--
HRWTZ PB441 "79 HOURS" '71

HITCHENS, DELORES B.
BIRKLEY, DOLAN--[3][18][22][29]MYS--
SIMON "BLUE GERANIUM" '41
DBLDY "UNLOVEED" '65
BURKE, NOEL--[3][18][22][29]MYS--
DUTTON "SHIVERING BOUGH" '42
OLSEN, D.B.--[32][34]MYS--24 NVLS '38-63
SW "MISS RACHEL ON VACATION" SEPT '47
SW "MURDER WALKS A STRANGE PATH" MAR '48
SW "SNAKE DANCE" MAY '48
OLSEN, JAMES P.--L. ROBBINS LTR '94/MYS--
TB "DEAD TALK BACK" FEB '46

HITCHIN, MARTIN MEWBURN
MEWBURN, MARTIN--[1][8][22]ENGLISH

HITT, ORRIE [EDWIN]
ADDAMS, KAY--HOLLAND-HITT BIO/CKLST, BAE 21, ADULT--
BEAC B259 "QUEER PATTERNS" '59
BEAC B289 "WARPED DESIRE" '60
BEAC B308 "LUCY" '60
BEAC B358 "THREE STRANGE WOMEN" '60
BEAC B444Y "STRANGEST SIN" '61
NOV 6026 "AUTOBIO OF KAY ADDAMS" '63
NOV 6085 "MY WILD NIGHTS WITH 9 NUDISTS" '63
NOV 6088 "MY TWO STRANGEST LOVERS" '63
NOV 60103 "CHERRY" '63
NOV 6N253 "BEYOND LOVE" '64
BLACK, JOE--HOLLAND-HITT CKLST, BAE 21,ADULT--
MIDWD F225 "UNNATURAL URGE" '62
NORMANDIE, ROGER--HOLLAND-HITT CKLST, BAE 21--
KEY "RACE WITH LUST" '57
KEY "TROMENTED PASSIONS" '57
KEY "LION'S DEN" '57
VERNE, CHARLES--HOLLAND-HITT CKLST, BAE 21, ADULT--
KEY "MR. HOT ROD" '57
KEY "WHEEL OF PASSION" '57
WEAVER, NICKY--HOLLAND-HITT CKLST, BAE 21,[34]MYS--
KOZY 185 "LOVE, BLOOD & TEARS" '63
KOZY 188 "LOVE OR KILL THEM ALL" '63

HITZ, DEMI
DEMI--[1][31]--CHILDREN'S BOOKS '79-88

HITZ, ERIKA
TRAKEHNEN, ERIKA--[39]GERMAN

HITZBLECK, FRIEDRICH
LENS, CONNY--[39][40]GERMAN/MYS--
"DIE LESBE" '87
"DIE SONNENBRILLE" '87

HITZIG, KAREN
CHANNING, JUSTIN--W/HELEN BARRETT, [9][21][26]ROM--
"CAROLINA WOMAN"
"SOUTHERN BLOOD"

HIVNOR, ROBERT
ASKEW, JACK--[1][31]
PISMIRE, OSBERT--[1]

HIX, MARTHA R.
CATLIN, MIRANDA--W/BARBARA C. CRAVEN, [9][21]ROM--
"PRISONER OF LOVE"
HICKS, MARTHA--[9]ROM

HJERTSTEDT, GUNARD
KEENE, DAY--MUNROE SL #23/#25,[32]MYS--
SW "NIGHT I DIED" AUG '45
PE "BOOTY & THE BEAST" JUL '53
CJ "I'LL DIE FOR YOU" SEPT '56
SA "A BETTER MANTRAP" DEC '56
TE "DEAD DREAMS FOR SALE" FEB '57
DT "GHOST OF COCK ROBIN" AUG '58
GM 874 "TAKE A STEP TO MURDER" '59
DT "CLAWS OF THE HELL-CAT" MAR '61
DT "MR. SMITH'S FLING CORPSES" NOV '61
MSMM "FOR OLD CRIMES SAKE" DEC '64
RICHARDS, WILLIAM--MUNROE SLST #23, WARREN PB CAT, MYS--
GRAPHIC 60 "DEAD MAN'S TIDE" '53

HJORLEIFSSON, KVARAN EIN.
KVARAN, EINAR--[29]MYS

HLINKA, VOJTECH
PRAVDA, FRANTISEK--[1][22] CZECH

HLOJZY, NAGEL
JOZK, WICKOV--[1]
MULKOR, PIOTER--[1]

HOADLEY, H. ORLO
MITCHELL, GENE--[1][2][11]

HOADLEY, IRENE BRADEN
BRADEN, IRENE A.--[31]

HOAR, PETER
AMBERLEY, SIMON--[1][8]

HOAR, ROGER SHERMAN
FARLEY, RALPH MILNE--[2][4][7][11][23]SF--
8 NOVELS '46-64
GENERAL X--L. ROBBINS LTR '94,[1][2][11]SF--
ORTH, BENNINGTON--[1][2][11]SF--
PEASE, LT. JOHN--[1][2][23]SF--
AMZ - 2 STORIES

HOARE, AGNES DOROTHEA M.
HOARE, AGNES D.--[7]SF--NON-FICT
HOARE, DOROTHY M--[7]SF--NON-FICT

HOARE, ROBERT J[OHN]
KING, ADAM--[1][31][33]

HOBART, ALICE NOURSE
HOBART, ALICE TISDALE--[1][31]

HOBART, GEORGE VERE
BAUER, WRIGHT--[1]
LOTT, NOAH--[1]
MCHUGH, HUGH--[1]

HOBBS, CECIL CARLTON
HAUK, MAUNG--[31]

HOBBS, DAVID B.
TAYLOR, DAYNA--W/CORNELIA M. PARKINSON,[1]

HOBEIN, EUGEN
ARNDT, AXEL--[39]GERMAN/MYS/WEST
CARNEY, JIM--[39]GERMAN/WEST
COTTON, JERRY--[39]GERMAN/MYS,HP--
DRAKE, GLENN--[39]GERMAN/MYS/WEST
PARNASS, ROY--[39]GERMAN/MYS/WEST
SCOTT, TOM--[39]GERMAN/WEST
WILSON, HAL--[39]GERMAN/MYS/WEST

HOBER, HEINZ WERNER
COTTON, JERRY--[39]GERMAN/MYS,HP--
FALKER, JAMES--[39]GERMAN/MYS/WEST
FOSTER, JOHN--[39]GERMAN/MYS/WEST
GOLD, KING--[39]GERMAN/WEST
LANGSTER, SAM--[39]GERMAN/MYS/WEST
MULLER, HEINZ W.--[39][40]GERMAN/MYS--
"MORD-MADE IN GERMANY" '87
MULLER, HEINZ WERNER--[40]GERMAN/MYS--
"GROSSSTADT REVIER" '88
VAN ZEYCK, KARIN--[39]GERMAN/MYS/WEST

HOBHOUSE, JANET
FRASER, JANET HOBHOUSE--[31]

HOBSBAWM, ERIC JOHN ERN.
NEWTON, FRANCIS--[8][22]ENGLISH

HOBSON, B.
JAMES, BERT--[34]MYS--
STATES "THE LOSER PAYS" '25

HOBSON, BRUCE
HADITHI, MWENYE--[31][33]

HOBSON, CORALIE[VON WERN]
SALT, SARAH--[1][3][22]MYS--
DAVIES "MURDER FOR LOVE"- 2 STORIES '37

HOBSON, FRANCIS THAYER
FIELD, PETER--[19]WEST,HP--
"OUTLAWS THREE"
"DRYGULCH ADAMS"
"GRINGO GUNS"

HOBSON, HARRY
HOBSON, HANK--[3][22][31]MYS--
CASSELL "GALLANT AFFAIR" '57
CASSELL "DEATH MAKES A CLAIM" '58
CASSELL "BIG TWIST" '59
CASSELL "MISSION HOUSE MURDER" '59 & MORE
JANSON, HANK--[1][34]MYS,HP--
ROBERTS "CUTIE ON CALL" '60
ROBERTS "CROWNS CAN KILL" '61
ROBERTS "MASTER MIND" '61
ROBERTS "JANSON, GO HOME" '61
ROBERTS "MASTER MIND" '61
ROBERTS "TAKE THIS - SWEETIE" '62
ROBERTS "UNCOMMON MARKET" '62
ROBERTS "UNCOVER AGENT" '62
GOLD "ULTIMATE DETERRENT" '62
ROBERTS "TAKE THIS, SWEETIE" '62
ROBERTS "UNCOMMON MARKET" '62

HOBSON, HARRY [CONT]
JANSON, HANK [CONT]
ROBERTS "UNCOVER AGENT" '62
ROBERTS "BEAUTY & THE BEAT" '62
ROBERTS "GRAPE VINE" '62
ROBERTS "LIKE CRAZY" '62
ROBERTS "DATELINE DIANE" '62
ROBERTS "CHICAGO CHICK" '62
ROBERTS "LIKE POISON" '62
ROBERTS "LIKE LETHAL" '62
COMPACT "LOVE MAKERS" '63
ROBERTS "LOVE-IN & LAMENTATION" '63
COMPACT "FAST BUCK' '63
ROBERTS "DATELINE DARLENE" '63
COMPACT "DATELINE DEBBIE" '63
COMPACT "VISIT FROM A BROAD" '63
COMPACT "VISIT FORM A BROAD" '63
COMPACT "THAT BRAIN AGAIN" '64
COMPACT "CRIMEBEAT CRISIS" '64
COMPACT "FAN FARE" '64
COMPACT "DOCTOR FIX" '64
COMPACT "LAKE LOOT" '64
COMPACT "LIMBO LOVER" '64
COMPACT "SQUARE ONE" '64
COMPACT "MISSILE MOB" '65
COMPACT "ROXY BY PROXY" '65
COMPACT "JAZZ JUNGLE" '65
COMPACT "TAILSTING" '65
COMPACT "FLASHPOINT" '65
COMPACT "BERLIN BRIEFING" '65
COMPACT "HELLDORADA" '66
COMPACT "DARLING DELINQUENT" '66
COMPACT "ESCALATIION" '66
COMPACT "BIG H" 66
COMPACT "F.E.U.D." '66
COMPACT "MAKE MINE MINK" '66
COMPACT "LIQUOR IS QUICKER" '66
COMPACT "MAYFAIR SLAYRIDE" '66
COMPACT "PHYSICAL ATTRACTION" '66
COMPACT "RIVIERA SHOWDOWN" '66
COMPACT "LADYBIRDS ARE IN" '67
COMPACT "OPERATION OBLITERATE" '67
COMPACT "ONE-WAY SPLIT" '67
COMPACT "SAME DIFFERENCE" '67
COMPACT "CASINO STRIP" '67
COMPACT "CASINOPOLY" '67
COMPACT "DEADLY HORSE-RACE" '67
COMPACT "ZERO TAKES ALL" '67
COMPACT "ZERO TAKES ALL '67
ROBERTS "LOVE-IN & LAMENTATION" '68
COMPACT "SHALOM, MY LOVE" '68
COMPACT "SPRUNG!" '68
COMPACT "SPY IN MY BED" '69
COMPACT "GLOBE PROBE" '69
COMPACT "SPY IN MY BED" '69
GOLD "ULTIMATE DETERRENT" '70
GOLD "VILLON OF THE PIECE" '70
GOLD "VILLON OF THE PIECE" '70
GOLD "BIG ROUND BED" '70
GOLD "INFILTRATORS" '70
GOLD "LONG ARM" '70
GOLD "LAMENT FOR A LOVER" '70
GOLD "CARRIBEAN CAPER" '71
GOLD "LIZ ASSIGNATION" '71
GOLD "KAY ASSIGNATION" '71

HOBSON, LAURA K.Z.
FIELD, PETER--W/FRANCIS THAYER HOBSON,
[1]AMERICAN/WEST, HP--
QUIST, FELICIA--[1][22][31]AMERICAN
ZAMETKIN, LAURA K. HOBSON--[1][31]AMERICAN

HOBSON, THAYER
FIELD, PETER--W/LAURA K.Z. HOBSON,
[1]AMERICAN/WEST, HP

HOCH, EDWARD D.
BOOTH, IRWIN--[2][11][18][29][32]MYS--
GU "THE CHIPPY" NOV '56
TE "KILLER COP" APR '57
CIRCUS, ANTHONY--AUTHOR CNFRMD-LACHMAN LIST '93,[18][32]MYS--
EQMM "ASSIGNMENT: ENIGMA" SEPT '80
DENTINGER, STEPHEN--[2][18][23][29][32]MYS--
FADM "LAST NIGHT OF HER LIFE" MAY '57
& OTHER SS '56-7
MCMAHON, PAT--[2][18][23][29][32]MYS--
SA "THE SUITCASE" SEPT '62
SA "DAY FOR A PICNIC" NOV '63
SA "UNCLE MAX" SEPT '65
SA "AUTHENIC DEATH OF COTTON CLARK" MAY '66
MCMAHON, PATRICK--[32]MYS--
MSMM "LET'S KILL HUBBY!" APR '67
PORTER, R.E.--AUTHOR CNFRMD-LACHMAN LST '93
QUEEN, ELLERY--[2][3]MYS,HP--
LAN "BLUE MOVIE MURDERS" '72
BEST DETECT OF YR '76 "RAINDEER CLUE"
STEVENS, R.L.--[2][18][29][32]MYS--
EQMM "PHYSICIAN & THE OPIUM FIEND" 'JUL '71
& 19 OTHERS
X, MR.--AUTHOR CNFRMD-LACHMAN '93/MYS--
EQMM "WILL-O'-THE-WISP MYS" APR '71
IN 6 PARTS

HOCHHEIMER, ALBERT
JORAT, BERT--[39]GERMAN/JUV
JURAT, BERT--[1]

HOCHRAIN, HELMUT
SCHAAK, JEAN--[39]GERMAN

HOCHSTEIN, PETER
SHORT, JACKSON--V. BERCH-LESBIANA/
CNTRCLTR, BAE 22,[2]

HOCHWAELDER, FRITZ
HOCHWALDER, FRITZ--[31]

HOCKER, CHARLOTTE
MARX-LINDNER, LO--[39]GERMAN

HOCKER, KARLA
RAUTTER, CHRISTIANE--[39]GERMAN

HOCKETT, MARCIA KATHRYN
HOCKETT, KATHRYN--[21]ROM--
"ANGEL OF PASSION"
"ENDLESS ECSTACY"
"RAPTURE'S DELIGHT" & MORE

HOCKING,[MONA N.] ANNE
MESSER, MONA--[18]MYS--
METHUEN "A CASTLE FOR SALE" '30
JARROLDS "MOUSE TRAP" '31 & MORE

HODANN, VALERIE
DAUB, HANS--[39]GERMAN/SF

HODAPP, ARLENE S.
HOLLIDAY, ARLENE--[26]ROM--
"DANCER'S ANGEL"
"WILD TEXAS BLOSSOM" & OTHERS

HODDER, ALFRED
WALTON, FRANCIS--[3][5][22]MYS--
McCLURE "THE POWERS THAT PREY" 1900
W/JOSIAH F. WILLARD

HODDER-WILLIAMS, CHRIST.
BROGAN, JAMES--[2][3][11][23]MYS--
HODDER "THE CUMMINGS REPORT" '58

HODER, FRIEDRICH
HAUSEN, PETER--[39]GERMAN

HODGE, ALFRED HAROLD
HODGE, HARRY--[34]AUSTRALIAN/MYS--
ANGUS "DEATH IN THE MORNING" '38

HODGE, HORACE EMERTON
HODGE, MERTON--[8]

HODGE, PAUL WILLIAM
HODGE, P.K.--[31] NON-FICT
HODGE, P.W.--[31]

HODGE, THOMAS HOUNSELL
DEVON, H.T.--[1]

HODGES, BARBARA K.
CAMBRIDGE, ELIZABETH--[8]

HODGES, DONALD CLARK
BLAKE, JUSTIN--[1]

HODGES, DORIS MARJORIE
HUNT, CHARLOTTE--[3][7][21][26][31]MYS/SF--
ACE "A TOUCH OF MYRRH" '74
& 8 MORE '67-75

HODGKIN, ROBERT ALLASON
HODGKIN, ROBIN A.--[1]

HODGKINSON, IVAN T.
TATTERSALL, IVAN--[1][3]MYS--
CHAPMAN "SOCIETY OF NAPLES" '28

HODGSON, ELEANOR
PARKER, NORAH--[9][21][26]ROM--
"GYPSY LOVER"
"SWEET SURRENDER"
"WILD SPLENDID LOVE"
HOWARD, ELEANOR--[9][21][26]ROM--
"CLOAK OF FATE"
"FORTUNE'S CHOICE" & MORE

HODGSON, WILLIAM HOPE
HODGSON, W.H.--[1]

HODSDON, NICHOLAS EDWARD
HODSDON, NICK--[31]

HOECKER, KARLA
HOCKER, KARLA--[31]

HOEFSMIT, HENRI DIEDERICK
DE LINT, CHARLES--[7][31]SF--NOVELS

HOELLDOBLER, BERTHOLD K.
HOLLDOBLER, BERT--[31]

HOEPNER, KAPT. A.D.
HANSA--[2]

HOEST, WILLIAM P.
HOEST, BILL--[31]

HOF, ANNI [G]
GEIGER-GOG, ANNI--[39]GERMAN/JUV
GEIGER-HOF, ANNI--[39]GERMAN/JUV
MENKEN, HANNE--[39]GERMAN/JUV

HOFBAUER, ELFRIEDE
BRUCKNER, ENNE--[39]GERMAN
VON MOTTEN, FRIEDE--[39]GERMAN

HOFDORF, PIM
GEERLINK, WILL--[8]

HOFE, GUNTER
ELBERGER, BERND--[39]GERMAN

HOFF, HARRY SUMMERFIELD
COOPER, WILLIAM--[8][22][31][38]ENGLISH--
"SCENES FROM PROVINCIAL LIFE" '50
& 14 OTHERS TO '91
HOFF, H.S.--[38]--
"TRINA" '34
"RHEA" '37
"LISA" '37
"THREE MARRIAGES" '38

HOFF, MARILYN
GAYLE, MARILYN--[1][31]

HOFF, SYDNEY
HOFF, SYD--[31][32]MYS--
MSMM "REACH FOR A STAR" JUL '64

HOFFENBERG, MASON
DRAKE, HAMILTON--[8][14]ADULT--
OLYM OPH#189 "FLOWERS OF HELL" '70
OLYM OPH#207 "A FLUTTER OF LASHES" '70
PEREZ, FAUSTINO--[8][14] ADULT--
OLYM OPH2216 "UNTIL SHE SCREAMS" '68
KENTON, MAXWELL--W/TERRY SOUTHERN,[2]

HOFFMAN, ABBOTT [ABBY]
FREE--[31]--
DIAL "REVOLUTION FOR THE HELL OF IT" '68
FREED, BARRY--[31]
METESKY, GEORGE--[31]

HOFFMAN, ANDREW JAY
HOFFMAN, ANDY--[31]

HOFFMAN, ANITA
FETTAMEN, ANN--[8][31]

HOFFMAN, LISA
CANDIDA--[1][31]

HOFFMAN, MARY MARGARET
LASSITER, MARY--[31][33]

HOFFMAN, PAUL W.
CRYPTON, DR.--W/SHELDON RENAN,[7]SF--
"TREASURE: IN SEARCH OF THE
GOLDEN HORSE: A PUZZLE" '84

HOFFMAN, SHIRLEY BELL
HOFFMAN, LEE--[7]SF/WEST--
ACE "GUNFIGHT AT LARAMIE" '66
BAL "BRED TO KILL" '67
DBLDY "LOCO" '69 & OTHER WESTERNS
NESFA "IN & OUT OF QUANDRY" '82
YORK, GEORGIA--[2][28]ROM--
GM "SAVAGE KEY" '79
GM "SAVANNAH GREY" '81
GM "SAVAGE CONQUEST" '83

HOFFMANN, DONALD
ALLURED, LLOYD--[1]

HOFFMANN, ELISABETH
LANGGASSER, ELISABETH--[22]GERMAN

HOFFMANN, ERNST THEODOR W
HOFFMANN, ERNST THEODOR A--[39]GERMAN/SF

HOFFMANN, F.C.
PASSER, ARNOLD v. d.--[39]GERMAN

HOFFMANN, GUNTHER
HEIKHENHOFF, PEER--[39]GERMAN/MYS

HOFFMANN, HANS
PIERS, PETRA--[39]GERMAN/JUV
SIEGENTALER, PETER--[39]GERMAN/JUV

HOFFMANN, HORST
KENWOOD, NEIL--[39]GERMAN/SF

HOFFMANN, MARGARET JONES
HOFFMANN, KATE--[26]ROM--
HARL 456 "INDECENT EXPOSURE"
HARL 515 "LADY OF THE NIGHT" & OTHERS
HOFFMANN, PEGGY--[31][33]

HOFFMANN, OSKAR
HAMILTON, W.W.--[39]GERMAN

HOFFMANN, WALTER
KOLBENHOFF, WALTER--[39]GERMAN

HOFFMANN-HARNISCH, WOLFG.
LINDRODER, WOLFGANG--[39]GERMAN

HOFFMANNS, W.P.
SCOTT, TED--[39]GERMAN/SF,HP--

HOFFNUNG, MICHELE
GARSKOF, MICHELE HOFNUNG--[1][31]

HOFLAND, KARIN
DANIELS, KAYLA--[9][21][26]ROM--
"SPITTING IMAGE"
"HOT PROSPECT" & MORE

HOFMANN, CHARLOTTE [H]
HOCHGRUNDLER, CHARLOTTE--[39]GERMAN

HOFMANN, HELMUT W.
WOLFRAM, HELLMUT--[39]GERMAN/SF

HOFMANN, IRMELA
PAULSEN, PAULA--[39]GERMAN

HOFMANN, MARIA
GLEIT, MARIA--[39]GERMAN/JUV

HOFRICHER, PAUL
SCARPETTA, FRANK--[34]MYS,HP--
BELM "THIS ANIMAL MUST DIE" '75
STIVERS, DICK--[34]MYS,HP--
GE "CAIRO COUNTDOWN" '85
ROSSI, BRUNO--[3]MYS,HP--
LEIS "SAVAGE SLAUGHTER" '75
LEIS "SCARFACED KILLER" '75

HOFSOMMER, DONOVAN LOWELL
HOFSOMMER, DON L.--[31]

HOFSTEDE, GERARD HENDRIK
HOFSTEDE, GEERT--[31]
HOFSTEDE, GEERT H.--[31]

HOGAN, LOU RAND
RAND, LOU--[3]MYS--
PAPLB "THE GAY DETECTIVE" '65

HOGAN, ROBERT J[ASPER]
BARTON, BARRY--LACHMAN LST '93--
ALL NVLS & STORIES IN "CAPT. COMBAT" '40
CANTRELL, WADE B.--C. WINTEROWD '94,[8]WEST--
"SUNDOWN GUN" ca'51
FIELD, PETER--[19]WEST,HP--
"RETURN TO POWDER VALLEY"
"OUTLAW VALLEY"
"SHERIFF WANTED"
"BLACKSMOKE TRAIL"

HOGAN, ROBERT J[ASPER] [CONT]
GREASEBALL JOE--L. ROBBINS LTR MAR '94
JASPER, BOB--[8]

HOGAN,[ROBERT] RAY
RINGOLD, CLAY--[8][19]WEST--
ACE G727 "RETURN TO RIO FUEGO" '68

HOGARTH, GRACE W.A.
ALLEN, GRACE--[8]
GAY, AMELIA--[8][31]
WESTON, ALLEN--W/ANDRE NORTON,
[2][3][4][22]MYS--
HAMMOND "MURDERS FOR SALE" '54

HOGBEN, LANCELOT THOMAS
CALVIN, KENNETH--[8]

HOGBERG, ERIK YNGVE
WEST, OLIVER--[29]MYS
YERRICK, H.--[29]MYS

HOGBIN, HERBERT
HENRY, DANIEL JR.--[8]

HOGEL, LISA
SOBERGK, CORA--[39][40]GERMAN/MYS--
"DIE CONNERYS UND IHRE MORDER" '60

HOGELIN-BRATTSTROM, INGER
BRATTSTROM, INGER--[29]MYS--
"FALL I FARSTUN" '56

HOGG, ELIZABETH [T]
GREY, ELIZABETH--[1][22][31]ENGLISH
HOGG, BETH [T]--[1][31]

HOGG, JAMES
ETTRICK SHEPHERD--[2]

HOGG, MICHAEL
SIMPLE, PETER--[8]

HOGG, QUINTIN MCGAREL
HAILSHAM OF ST. MARYLBONE--[1]
HAILSHAM, SECOND VISCOUNT--[22]ENGLISH

HOGHRAIN, HELMUT
LIESENBERG, LEOPOLD--[39]GERMAN

HOGL, DIETRICH
HOGAN, D.C.--[39]GERMAN/SF

HOGLUND, KEN
EDWARDS, CHARLES F.--[2]
KENNETH, JOHN H.--[2]

HOGUE, OLIVER
TROOPER BLUE-GUM--[13]AUSTRALIAN

HOGUE, WILBUR OWINGS
HOGUE, DOCK--[1][22]MYS
SHANNON, CARL--[3][22][29]MYS--
PHOENIX "LADY, THAT'S MY SKULL" '47
PHOENIX "FATAL FOOTSTEPS" '48
BRDMN "MURDER ME NEVER" '51

HOHENZOLLERN, FRIEDRICH W
KAISER WILHELM II--[31]

HOHL, JOAN M.R.
LORIN, AMII--[9][21][26]ROM--
"TAWNY GOLD MAN"
"GAMBLER'S LOVE" & MORE
ROBERTS, PAULA--[9][21][26]ROM--
"COME HOME TO LOVE"

HOHLBEIN, WOLFGANG E.
COTTON, JERRY--[39]GERMAN/MYS,HP--
CRAVEN, ROBERT--W/KARL-ULRICH BURGDORF,
[39]GERMAN/SF, HP
DELGADO, RYDER--[39]GERMAN/MYS/SF/WEST,HP--
ESCHENLOH, WOLFGANG--[39]GERMAN/MYS/SF/WEST
HOLLBURG, MARTIN--W/KARL-ULRICH BURGDORF,
[39]GERMAN/SF, HP
LAMONT, ROBERT--[39]GERMAN/MYS/SF/WEST,HP--
MARKS, MICHAEL--[39]GERMAN/MYS/SF/WEST
MCCLOUD, JASON--[39]GERMAN/WEST
SMITH, ANGELA--[39]GERMAN/MYS/SF/WEST
VERNOM, JACK--[39]GERMAN/MYS/SF/WEST
WOLF, HENRY--W/KARL-ULRICH BURGDORF,
[39]GERMAN/SF, HP

HOHOFF, MARGARETE
RENARD, MADELEINE--[39]GERMAN

HOISINGTON, MAY FOLWELL
CHATTON, STACY--[1]

HOISINGTON, MAY FOLWELL
FAIR, J. MURRAY--[1]

HOKE, HELEN L.
STERLING, HELEN--[8][33]
TROY, ALAN--[8]
WATTS, HELEN L. HOKE--[33]

HOKLIN, LONN
GIDEON, JOHN--[7]SF--
JOVE "GREELY'S COVE" '91

HOLBECHE, PHILIPPA
SHORE, PHILIPPA--[8]

HOLBERG, LUDVIG
HOLBERG, LEWIS--[2]
KLIMIUS, NICHOLAS--[2][11]

HOLCROFT, MONTAGUE HARRY
HOLCROFT, M.H.--[1]

HOLDAWAY, MARJORIE F.
JAPONICA--[8]

HOLDAWAY, NEVILLE A.
TEMPLE-ELLIS, N.A.--[3][22][29]MYS--
METHUEN "MAN WHO WAS THERE" '30
HODDER "CASE IN HAND" '33 & MORE

HOLDEN, BEATRICE [P]
PECCAVI--[1]

HOLDEN, DONALD
BLAKE, WENDON--[1][31]

HOLDEN, ELIZABETH RHODA
LAWRENCE, LOUISE--[2][7][23]FANT. LIT. FOR
CHILDREN & YOUNG ADULTS, RUTH NADELMAN,
ENGLISH/SF--
"ANDRA" '71

HOLDEN, J.G.P.
REDWOOD, RALPH--[1]

HOLDEN, LISA
HOLDEN, MONIQUE--[9][26]ROM--
"TUCKERVILLE REVIVAL"

HOLDEN, MARIA
MYRTLE, NAY--[1]

HOLDEN, RAYMOND P[ECKHAM]
PECKHAM, RICHARD--[3][22][31]MYS--
MINTON "MURDER IN STRANGE HOUSES" '29

HOLDEN, WILLIAM CURRY
HOLDEN, W.C.--[31]

HOLDEN,[WILLIS] SPRAGUE
BLACK, MONTGOMERY--[1]

HOLDER, GWYNNETH
BRANFOOT, GWYNNETH--[1][31]

HOLDER, JOHN JR.
CURTIS, JACKIE--[31]--
10 PLAYS/SCREENPLAYS '67-72

HOLDER, NANCY L. JONES
CHANDLER, LAUREL--[7][9][21]ROM/SF--
SIGN "SHADES OF MOONLIGHT" '84
"BOUNDLESS LOVE" & MORE
DAVIS, WENDI--[9][21][26]ROM--
"TEACH ME TO LOVE"
"SEALED WITH A KISS" & MORE
JONES, NANCY--[9][21][26]ROM--
"JESSIE'S SONG"

HOLDING, JAMES [C.C.]
CARLISLE, CLARK--[18][31][32]MYS--
AHMM "MOST SURPRISED MAN IN THE WORLD" SEPT '60
"BUGS BUNNY'S CARROT MACHINE"
FREEMAN, JAY--[18]MYS--
WHITMAN "COUNTRY COUSINS" '64
QUEEN, ELLERY JR.--[18][33]MYS--
PUTNAM "THE PURPLE BIRD MYSTERY" '65

HOLDING, JOHN RICHARD
HAWTHORNE, J.R.H.--[13] AUSTRALIA

HOLDING, VERA ZUMWALT
ALLEN, CHESTER--[1][31]

HOLDSTOCK, ROBERT
KIRK, RICHARD--W/ANGUS WELLS,

HOLDSTOCK, ROBERT P.
BLACK, ROBERT--[2][7][32]MYS--
SQ "KING'S BIRTHDAY" DEC '46
TB "DEATH'S PASSENGER" JUN '46
SPHERE "LEGEND OF THE WEREWOLF" '76
SPHERE "THE SATANISTS" '77
SPHERE "CRY WOLF" '81
SPHERE "UNTOUCHABLES" '82
BLAKE, KEN--[2][23]SF,HP--
CARLSEN, CHRIS--[2][7][11][23][31]SF--
SPHERE 'BERSERKER' SERIES #1-3 '77-9
EISLER, STEVEN--[2][7][23]SF--
OCTOPUS "SPACE WARS: WORLDS & WEAPONS" '78
OCTOPUS "ALIEN WORLD: THE COMPLETE ILLUSTRATED GUIDE" '80
FAULCON, ROBERT--[2][7][23][31]SF--
'NIGHTHUNTER' SERIES #1-6 '87-9
KIRK, RICHARD--[2][7][11][23]SF,HP--
CORGI "RAVEN 1: SWORDMISTRESS OF CHAOS" '78
CORGI "RAVEN 2:A TIME OF GHOSTS" '78
CORGI "RAVEN 4:LORDS OF THE SHADOWS" '79

HOLDSWORTH, GLADYS BRONW.
STERN, G.B.--[1][32]MYS--
SA "A LINK IS MISSING" DEC '64

HOLENSTEIN, PETER
LENNOX, PETER--[39]GERMAN/MYS/HOR
LENOX, PETER--[39][40]GERMAN/MYS--
"MORD AM LAUFENDEN BAND" '88

HOLESCH, OSKAR
FRIEDRICH, OSKAR H.--[39]GERMAN

HOLINGER, WILLIAM JACQUES
ELLER, SCOTT--[31]

HOLKAR, MO
ZOOL, M.H.--W/NEAL TRINGHAM & IVAN TOWLSON,[7]

HOLLAND, CECELIA [A]
CARTER, ELIZABETH ELIOT--[2][11]
PRYOR, ROBERT STONE--[1]

HOLLAND, EDITH
HOLLAND, RUTH--[1][29][34]MYS--
HEINEMANN "LABURNAM GROVE" '36

HOLLAND, ELIZABETH
BAXTER, ELIZABETH--[9]ROM

HOLLAND, ISABELLE
HUNT, FRANCESCA--[8]

HOLLAND, JAMES R.
RAND, R.H.--[8]

HOLLAND, JEROME HEARTWELL
HOLLAND, BRUD--[31]

HOLLAND, JUDITH [JUDY]
WAKEFIELD, HANNAH--W/SARAH BURTON,[18][34]--
WP "THE PRICE YOU PAY" '87
WP "A FEB MOURNING" '91

HOLLAND, MARY
HOLLAND, MARTY--[32][34]MYS--
S&SDM "DOA-EAST RIVER" MAR '44
DAVIES "FALLEN ANGEL" '45
DAVIES "GLASS HEART" '46
SR "TERROR FOR TWO" JAN '51

HOLLAND, SHEILA C.
COATES, SHEILA--[1][9][17]ROM
HARDY, LAURA--[8][9][26]ROM--
SIL 76 "BURNING MEMORIES"
SIL 76 "PLAYING WITH FIRE" & OTHERS
LAMB, CHARLOTTE--[8][9][26]ROM--
"DEVIL'S ARMS"
"DARK MASTER" & MORE
LANCASTER, SHEILA--[8][9][26]ROM--
"DARK SWEET WANTON"
"MISTRESS OF FORTUNE" & OTHERS
WOOLF, VICTORIA--[9][21][26]ROM--
"SWEET COMPULSION"

HOLLAND, STEVE
MILANO, RICARDO--[27]ENGLISH--
'GAY-ETTY' MAG - SHORT STORIES
MILLE, RICHARD--[27]ENGLISH--
'GAY-ETTY' MAG - SHORT STORIES

HOLLANDER, CARLTON
STONE, EDDIE--[34]MYS--
HOLLOWAY "A VICTIM OF RAPE" '76
"STREET GAMES" '77 & 3 MORE

HOLLANDER, ZANDER
PETERS, ALEXANDER--[1][33]

HOLLEDGE, JAMES
ZOHAR, ATTILA--[35]AUSTRALIAN--
HRWTZ PB232 "KING'S CROSS BLACK MAGIC" '65

HOLLEY, MARIETTA
JEMYMA--[1][8][31]
JOSIAH ALLEN'S WIFE--[8]

HOLLIDAY, JOSEPH
BOSCO, JACK--[8][31][33]
DALE, JACK--[8][31][33]
HOLLIDAY, JOE--[31][33]

HOLLIDAY, ROBERT CORTES
HILL, MURRAY--[8]

HOLLIS, CHRISTOPHER
SOMERSET, PERCY--[8]

HOLLO, ANSELM
BIELYI, SERGEI--[1][31]
HOFMAN, ANTON--[1][31]

HOLLOWAY, ANNA
THORNET, TERESA A.--[1]

HOLLOWAY, BRENDA WILMAR
VERNEY, SARAH--[22]ENGLISH

HOLLOWAY, BRIAN W.
CAMERON, BERL--[2][11][23]SF,HP--
WARREN "DESTINATION ALPHA" '52
CHARLES, NEIL--[2][11][23]SF,HP--
WARREN "PLANET THA" '52
DALE, ADAM--[1][2]SF,HP--
WARREN "SOUTHERN EXPLORATION" '53
GRUEN, VON--[7]SF,HP--
WARREN "THE MORTALS OF RENI" '53
LANG, KING--[1][2][11] AF,HP--
WARREN "TRANS MERCURIAN" '52
LEPAGE, RAND--[1][2][11]SF,HP--
WARREN "A MEN" '52
ROMILUS, ARN--[7]SF,HP--
WARREN "BEYOND GEO" '53
SHAW, BRIAN--[7]SF,HP--
WARREN "LOST WORLD" '53
STORM, BRIAN--[1][2][11]SF,HP--
WARREN "RED STORM" '52

HOLLOWAY, ELIZABETH BRAG.
BEATTY, ELIZABETH--[3][33]MYS--
BOUREGY "THE JUPITER MISSILE MYSTERY" '60
"MURDER AT AUCTION" '61

HOLLOWAY, TERESA BRAGUNIE
MCLEOD, MARGARET VAIL--[1][22][33]AMERICAN--
YOUNG ADULTS

HOLLWERTH, HILDE
TANNER, BARBEL--[39]GERMAN

HOLLY, JOAN CAROL
HOLLY, J. HUNTER--V. BERCH-MONARCH PSEUDS,
BAE 9,[2][34]SF--
ACE G636 "ASSASSINATION AFFAIR" '61
MON 213 "GREEN PLANET" '61
MON 240"ENCOUNTER" '62
MON 260 "FLYING EYES" '62
MON 342 "RUNNING MAN" '63
ACE G1231 "TIME TWISTERS" '64
HOLLY, JOAN HUNTER--[7][23][31]SF--
LAS 22 "KEEPER" '76
LAS 55 "SHEPHERD" '77

HOLM, DONALD RAYMOJND
HOLM, DON--[31]
DENALI, PETER--[1][31]

HOLM, OSCAR WILLIAM
HOLM, BILL--[31]

HOLM, SVEN AAGE
FARMACEVTEN--[1][22][31]DANISH

HOLM, WERNER
CONRADI, PETER--[39][40]GERMAN/MYS--
"MORD IN MILIEU" '80

HOLMAN, ROBERT
HOLMAN, BOB--[31]
LAKEN, BOB--[1]

HOLMAN,[C] HUGH
HUNT, CLARENCE--[3][22][31]MYS--
PHOENIX "SMALL TOWN CORPSE" '51

HOLMBERG, ANNE
AVERY, ANNE--CRPG--
LOVE SPELL "ALL'S FAIR" '94
AVERY, ANNE--[26]ROM--
"A DISTANT STAR"
"DREAM SEEKER" '94 & OTHERS

HOLMBERG, ERIK
SVENSEN, KNUT--[29]MYS

HOLMBERG, JOHN-HENRY
BRANDON, CARL, JR.--[1][2]

HOLMBERG, NILS
MARKSMAN, A.M.--[29]MYS--
"PER STIGMAN'S AVENTYR" '45

HOLME, BRYAN
FRANCIS, CHARLES--[1][31][33]

HOLMES, BRYAN JOHN
HOLMES, B.P.--[28]ENGLISH/WEST--
14 HALE NOVELS '78-90

HOLMES, CHARLES HENRY
ADAMS, CLAYTON--[8]

HOLMES, DAVID CHARLES
CHARLSON, DAVID--[1][22][31]AMERICAN

HOLMES, DONALD JOSEPH
JOSEPH, DON--V. BERCH LTR TO HUBIN '94,MYS--
VANTAGE "SKINNERBALL!!! IN PURSUIT
OF THEM" '78

HOLMES, EMORY II
HOLMES, BUTCH--V. BERCH LTR TO
A. HUBIN '93,MYS--
HOLLOWAY "BLACK RAGE" '75

HOLMES, ERIC
LELAND, SIDNEY--L. ROBBINS LTR MAR '94

HOLMES, JOSEPH EVERETT
HOLMES, JAY--[8][31]

HOLMES, L[LEWELLYN] P.
HARDIN, DAVE--[8][19]WEST--
BAL 57 "BRANDON'S EMPIRE" '53
HOLMES, L.P.--L. ROBBINS LTR MAR '94
STUART, MATT--[8][19]WEST--
POPLB 407 "BONANZA GULCH" '52
POCK 726 "DUSTY WAGONS" '50 & MORE

HOLMES, L[LEWELLYN] P. [CONT]
WESTWOOD, PERRY--[8][19]WEST--
GM 299 "SIX-GUN CODE" '53

HOLMES, OLIVE & WYMAN
WYMAN, OLIVE--[1]

HOLMES, PEGGY
SEMLOH--[33]

HOLMES, PETER
FENWICK, PETER--[8]

HOLMES, SARA K. STONE
STONE, KATE--[1]

HOLMES, WILFRED JAY
HUDSON, ABE--[1]
HUDSON, ALEC--L. ROBBINS LTR MAR '94,[31]

HOLMES, WILLIAM KERSLEY
SERRIFILE, F.O.O.--[1]

HOLMGREN, HELEN JEAN
HOLMGREN, GEORGE ELLEN--[1][31][33]
HOLMGREN, SISTER GEORGE J--[31]

HOLMGREN, VIRGINIA C.
CUNNINGHAM, VIRGINIA--[1][31][33]

HOLMQUIST, ANN
BANNON, ANN--V. BERCH-LESBIANA/CTRCLTR,
BAE 22 & GM PSEUDS, PP 33--
GM 653 "ODD GIRL OUT" '57
GM 833 "I AM A WOMAN" '59
GM 919 "WOMEN IN THE SHADOWS" '59
GM 977 "JOURNEY TO A WOMAN" '60
GM 1066 "THE MARRIAGE" '60
GM 1224 "BEEBO BRINKER" '62

HOLMSTEN, GEORG
HOLM, PETER--[39]GERMAN
RAVENSBERG, MICHAEL--[39]GERMAN

HOLMSTROM, JOHN ERIC
GELLERT, ROGER--[8]

HOLMVIK, OYVIND
OY-VIK--[1][22]NORWEGIAN
PAPRIKA--[1][22]NORWEGIAN
SEPIA--[1][22]NORWEGIAN

HOLROYD, ETHEL MARY
COOKRIDGE, JOHN MICHAEL--[8]
MARSHALL, BEVERLEY--[8]

HOLSTON, BARBARA
HALL, ELLEN--W/ELLEN R. POLLACHER,
V. BERCH LTR TO HUBIN '94, MYS--
BB "MIDNIGHT SINS" '88

HOLT, ELIZABETH
LOVE, E.M.--V. BERCH LTR TO
R. REGINALD '93,SF--
LEIS "DRESS UP" '88

HOLT, GLEN
CAREW, S.C.--V. BERCH-BRNDN/
BC PSEUDS, BAE 22, P24
STANTON, CARL--V. BERCH-BRNDN/
BC PSEUDS, BAE 22, P24

HOLT, HENRY
HOPKINS, STANLEY--[8][29]MYS

HOLT, JOHN ROBERT
ARRE, JOHN--[1][31][32]MYS--
AHMM "NOT THE KILLER TYPE" NOV '67
GILES, ELIZABETH--[3][31]--
LAN 74-755 "CHILDREN OF THE GRIFFIN" '71
"DARKER GROWS THE NIGHT" '72
GILES, RAY--[31]--
CREST S275 "HOW TO RETIRE & ENJOY IT" '59
GILES, RAYMOND--[3][31]--
PAPLB 54-677 "NIGHT OF WARLOCK" '68
AV S361 "NIGHT OF THE VAMPIRES" '69
LAN "SHAMUS" '73

HOLT, JOHN SANDERS
PAGE, ABRAHAM--[1]

HOLT, KAARE
HOLT, KARE--[31]

HOLT, MARGARET VAN V.
HOLT, RACKHAM--[8][31][33]

HOLT, ROCHELLE LYNN
DUBOIS, ROCHELLE [L] HOLT--[1][33]

HOLT, THOMAS CHARLES LOU.
HOLT, TOM--[7][31]SF--
MacM "EXPECTING SOMEONE TALLER" '87
MacM "WHO'S AFRAID OF BEOWULF?" '88
ORBIT "FLYING DUTCH" '91

HOLT, WILL
DRURY, REBECCA--[21]ROM,HP--
'WOMEN AT WAR' SERIES:
"DARKNESS AT DAWN"

HOLTON, EDITH AUSTIN
HEATH, ELIZABETH ALDEN--[1][3][22]MYS--
CROWELL "THE AFFAIR AT TIDEWAYS" '32

HOLTON, WALTER H.
HALL, RICHARD--[1]
HOLT, RICHARD--[1]

HOLTSCHI-GRASSLE, CHARL.
BANDOL, CHARLOTTE--[39]GERMAN/JUV

HOLYER, ERNA MARIA
HOLYER, ERNIE--[1][31][33]

HOLZ, ARNO
HOLMSEN, BJARNE P.--W/JOHANNES SCHLAF,
[39]GERMAN

HOLZAPFEL, RUDOLF PATRICK
HOLZAPFEL, RUDI--[8]
HURKEY, ROOAN--[8][31]
WARD, R. PATRICK--[8]

HOLZEL, THOMAS MARTIN
HOLZEL, TOM--[31]

HOLZHAUSEN, CARL JOHAN
BLYGER--[29]MYS
C.J.H.--[29]MYS
KRABBLUND, FILIP--[29]MYS

HOLZINGER, DOROTHEA
ZEEMANN, DOROTHEA--[39]GERMAN

HOLZMAN, WILLIAM
HOLZMAN, RED--[31]

HOMAN, OLOF
  TRE, HERRAR--[29]MYS--
    SCHILDTS "HERR COPWIETH, GENTLEMAN-DETEKTIV" '14

HOMANN, WALTER
  VON BIRKENBURG, MORITZ--[39]GERMAN/SF

HOMBERG, BODO
  COLLIN, CHRISTIAN--[39]GERMAN

HOME, ALEXANDER FREDERICK
  DOUGLAS-HOME, ALEC--[1][31]

HOME, SCOTT
  MARCHMONT, ROSS--[2]

HOME, WILLIAM DOUGLAS
  DOUGLAS HOME, WILLIAM--[31]

HOME-GALL, EDWARD REGINALD
  CLIVE, CLIFFORD--[1][8]
  DALE, EDWIN--[1][8]
  HALL, RUPERT--[1][8]
  HOME-GALL, REGINALD--[8]

HOME-GALL, WILLIAM B.
  BOLINBROKE, WILLIAM--[1]
  DREW, REGINALD--[1]
  HOME, T.--[1]
  WRAY, REGINALD--[2][7][23]SF--
    "BEYOND THE NORTHERN LIGHTS" '03
    "THE DWELLER IN THE HALF-LIGHT" '23
  YOUNG, WILL--[1]

HOMERSHAM, BASIL H.
  MANNINGHAM, BASIL--[3][22]MYS--
    HALE "MOTIVE FOR MURDER" '39

HOMEWOOD, CHARLES H.
  HOMEWOOD, HARRY--[1][3][31]MYS--
    O'HARA "A MATTER OF SIZE" '75

HOMPF, ALOIS
  HOMO, [DR.] ALI--[1]

HONEY, PHILIP
  HARRISON, G.D.--[1]
  HART, PETER--[1]
  PHILLIPS, H.C.--[1]
  TAURUS--[1]

HONEYMAN, WILLIAM C.
  M'GOVAN, JAMES--[1][3][22]MYS--
    7 BOOKS 1878-1922

HONEYWELL, E.L.
  STANLEY, OLIN--[1][34]MYS--
    VANTAGE "LEGAL FIRE" '59

HONEYWELL, J. FRANK
  FRANCIS, STELLA M.--[1]

HONG, JANE FAY
  SHERIDAN, ADORA--W/EVELYN M. PAVLIK, [1][9][21]ROM--
    "THE SEASON"
    "THE SIGNET RING"

HONIG, DONALD
  MARTIN, DONALD--LACHMAN LST '93/MYS--
    18 AHMM STORIES

HONKANEN, HILJA L.V.
  ANNI, MAKITUVAN--[1]
  KARE, KAARINA--[1]
  OUTI--[1]
  PELKONEN, ELINA--[1]
  URSULA, SANNA--[1]

HONNEF, JOACHIM
  JACKSON, DAVE--[39]GERMAN/WEST
  RENO, JOHN--[39]GERMAN/WEST

HONNOR, SYLVIA CROFTS
  REDSTONE, SYLVIA--[1]

HOOD, ARCHER
  LESLIE, LILIAN--W/VIOLET PERKINS,[1][2][11]

HOOD, TORREY
  BEVANS, TORRE--[8]
  TORREY, MARJORIE--[8]

HOOD-PHILLIPS, J.H.
  HOOD, JACK--[1]

HOOF, DAVID L.
  LORNE, DAVID--[7][34]MYS/SF--
    SIGNET "SIGHT UNSEEN" '90
    AV "THE LAST PRISONER" '91

HOOK, ALFRED SAMUEL
  COLTON, A.J.--[1][3][22]MYS--
    HALE "THE COATINE CASE" '53

HOOK, H. CLARKE
  CLIFFORD, MARTIN--[1]HP
  HARVEY, ROSS--[1]
  PAINE, HAMMOND--[1]
  RICHARD, FRANK--[1]HP

HOOK, SAMUEL CLARKE
  CLARKE, [CAPT.] MAURICE--[1]
  DENE, HAMPTON--[1]
  HALE, INNIS--[1]
  HOPE, EDGAR--[1]
  LANCASTER, CAPT.--[1]
  MERRIMAN, MAURICE--[1]
  MONTEITH, OWEN--[1]

HOOKE, CHARLES W.
  CARTER, NICHOLAS--[3][34]MYS,HP--
    WHITMAN "MAN WHO STOLE MILLIONS" '30
    WHITMAN "STOLEN PAY TRAIN" '30
    WHITMAN "STOLEN RACE HORSE" '30
    WHITMAN "SECRET AGENTS OF BRAZIL" '30
  FIELDING, HOWARD--[1][3][22]MYS--
    CHELSEA "STRAIGHT CROOKS" '27
    "HIDDEN OUT" '27 & 3 MORE

HOOKER, FANNY
  HOVEN, ERNIEST--[2]

HOOKHAM, MARGARET EVELYN
  FONTEYN, MARGOT--[8]

HOOKS, GAYLOR EUGENE
  HOOKS, GENE--[31]

HOOP, EDWARD
  HENDRIKS, PAUL--[39][40]GERMAN/MYS--
    "DER TOTENIEMER" '67 & 5 OTHERS

HOOPER, ELIZABETH EDNA
  HOOPER, BETT--[1]

HOOPER, HEDLEY COLWILL
  HOOPER, PETER--[31]

HOOPER, STANLEY
BRANDON, ROY--[1]

HOOPER,[GLENDA] KAY
ROBBINS, KAY--[9][21][26]ROM--
ELUSIVE DAWN"
"KISSED BY MAGIC" & 6 MORE

HOOPES, MARY HOWARD
FINN, ANNA E.--[1]
PETERSON, MAUDE HOWARD--[1]

HOOPES, ROY
POTOMAC, PETER--[1]

HOOTEN, CHARLES
THURLAND, BILBERRY--[1]

HOOVER, HELEN D.B.
PRICE, JENNIFER--[1][8][33]

HOOVER, SARANNE
DAWSON, SARANNE--[9][21][26]ROM--
"FROM THE MIST"
"BEWITCHED" & 8 MORE
LIND, PAMELA--[9][21][26]ROM--
"PAST FORGETTING"
"SHADOW ON THE MT." & MORE

HOPE, CHARLES E. GRAHAM
PELHAM, ANTHONY--[3]MYS--
HODDER "FORTRESS OF ASHES" '36
HODDER "SUMMONS TO ADVENT." '37

HOPE, FRANCES ESSEX T.
SMITH, ESSEX--[3][22]MYS--
HUTCH "WYE VALLEY MYSTERY" '29

HOPE, HENRY
ANDOVER, HENRY--[3]MYS--
EYRE "DEATH ON PACK ROAD" '31
EYRE "DENNISDALE TRAGEDY" '36

HOPE, JESSIE
HOPE, GRAHAM--[1]

HOPE, WILLIAM EDWARD S.
DEAN, DONALD--[1]
DENVER, BRUCE--[1]
RICHARDS, FRANK--[1]
STANTON, WILL--[1][32]MYS--
EQMM "TOWN WITHOUT A STRAIGHT MAN" JUL '53
EQMM "CURSE OF STONEWALL JACKSON" JAN '54
MM "MONITORED CALL" APR '59
EQMM "YOU ARE WITH IT!" NOV '63
STANTON, WILLIAM--[1]

HOPE, WILLIAMSON
ROSS, H. WILLIAMSON--[36]AUSTRALIAN/MYS--
NC "SINGING OUTLAW" '40

HOPE-SIMPSON, JACYNTH
DUDLEY, H.--[32]MYS--
LM "BIRTHDAY PRESENT" DEC '76
DUDLEY, HELEN--[1][8][31]

HOPEGOOD, PETER
LECKIE, PETER--[13]AUSTRALIAN

HOPF, ALICE MARTHA L.
HOPF, ALICE LIGHTNER--[11]
LIGHTNER, A.M.--[7][11][22][32][33]
AMERICAN/MYS/SF--
AHMM "DEFENSE OF AGAMENON" SEPT '65
MU "THE MARS JAR" JUL '66
BB 5567 "DAY OF DRONES" '70

HOPF, ALICE MARTHA L. [CONT]
LIGHTNER, A.M. [CONT]
DUTTON "STAR CIRCUS" '77
LIGHTNER, ALICE--[2][11][31][33]

HOPFNER, KARL
ALM, HORST--[39]GERMAN

HOPKINS, ALICE K.
AKH--[2][31]

HOPKINS, ALPHONSO A.
LINTON, A.H.--[1]

HOPKINS, B.
WILLIAMS, RICHARD--[1]HP

HOPKINS, CLARK
LEE, ROY--[1][31][33]

HOPKINS, JAMES
CLARKE, BODEN--W/MICHAEL R. BURGESS,[7][23]--
"WORK OF WILL. F. NOLAN: AN ANNOTATIVE
BIBLIOGRAPHY & GUIDE"

HOPKINS, KENNETH
ADAMS, CHRISTOPHER--[3][22][33]MYS--
BRDMAN "AMATEUR AGENT" '64
BURNEY, ANTON--[1][22][33]
MANNON, WARWICK--[2][7][22][33]SF--
MARSH, PAUL--[22][32][33]MYS--
LM "THREE FEET WIDE....." MAY '61
MARSHALL, EDMUND--[1][22][33]
MEREDITH, ARNOLD--[1][22][33]ENGLISH

HOPKINS, MARGARET BRISCOE
BRISCOE, MARGARET SUTTON--[1]

HOPKINS, PAULINE MACKIE
MACKIE, PAULINE BRADFORD--[1]

HOPKINS, PRYNCE [C]
HOPKINS, PRYNS--[31]

HOPKINS, ROBERT S.
ROSTAND, ROBERT--[1][3][29]MYS--
BERK "VENGEANCE RUN" '72
WILLIAMS, RICHARD--W/HOWARD BAKER,
MAX MARQUIS & G.P. MANN,[34]MYS,HP--
AMALG "MURDER BY PROXY" '63

HOPKINS, SAM
HOPKINS, LIGHTNIN'--[31]

HOPKINS, WILLIAM BARTLETT
PEET, WILLIAM BARTLETT--[31]--
NAME LEGALLY CHGD TO "PEET"

HOPKINSON, HENRY THOMAS
HOPKINSON, TOM--[7][8][31]--
"GEORGE ORWELL" '53
PEMBROKE, THOMAS--[1][3]MYS--
BARKER "PHOTOCRIMES" '36
VINDICATOR--[1]ENGLISH

HOPP, SIGNE
ZINKEN--[8]

HOPPE, HERMANN
WOLLER, HERMANN--[39]GERMAN/JUV

HOPPE, SIGRID
STANFORD, LARA--[39]GERMAN

HOPPE, ULRICH
HALLOW, GUS--[39][40]GERMAN/MYS--
"TJACK" '87

HOPPEN-RAM, HENDERIKA W.
HOPPEN, HARRIET--[1]DUTCH
WIJNSTROOM, CHRISTY--[1]DUTCH

HOPPER, MILLARD
STREET, LEROY--J. PRESSMAN-CNTRCLTR,
BAE 21, ADULT--
PYR 122 "I WAS A DRUG ADDICT" '54

HOPSON, JANET L[OUISE]
WEINBERG, JANET HOPSON--[1]AMERICAN

HOPSON, WILLIAM L.
HOLT, TEX--[28]WEST--
ARCADIA HOUSE "HANGTREE RANGE" '52
SIMS, JOHN--[1][8]
WALLACE, ROBERT--T. JOHNSON LTR JAN '94,
HP--?? UNCONFIRMED ??

HORAN, DON
NORMAN, DONALD N.--W/NORMAN STAHL,
V. BERCH LTR TO HUBIN '94,[7]--
WARNER "THUNDER STATION" '90

HORANSKS, RUBY
HOLLAND, REBECCA--[3]MYS--
POPLB "SHADOWS ON THE BAY" '77
RAVEN "DANGER ON CUE" '80

HORBACH, MICHAEL
DONRATH, MICHAEL--[39][40]GERMAN/MYS--
"DR. LESIUS, DES TEUFELS TYRANN" '69

HORBACH, URSULA [S]
BACH, CHRISTA--[39]GERMAN
CORDES, ALEXANDRA--[39]GERMAN
MORGAN, JENNIFER--[39]GERMAN
SCHAAKE, URSULA--[39]GERMAN

HORDAHL, KURT
GLAD, PER--[29]SWEDISH/MYS
WALDOR, FRANK--[29][37]SWEDISH/MYS--
NOVELS '42-55
'KRIM-ELITEN' ADV OF KAJ HENNING '50-8

HORLER, SYDNEY
CAVENDISH, PETER--[5][11][18][29]--
"ROMEO & JULIE" '28
HERITAGE, MARTIN--[5][11][18][29]--
"HOUSE OF WINGATE" '28
HOBBS, JACK--[1]
STANDISH, O.J.--[1]

HORN, DETLEV
WINTER, DETLEV G.--[39]GERMAN/SF

HORN, ERIKA
MASUR, ERIKA--[39]GERMAN/JUV
THEBEN, ERIKA--[39]GERMAN/JUV

HORN, HOLLOWAY
WAGHORN, H.L.--[1][22]MYS

HORN, MAURICE
GRANT, KIRBY--[1]FRENCH-AMERICAN
SAUVAGE, FRANCK--[31]--
"MAN FROM HONG KONG" '59
SAUVAGE, FRANCOISE--[31][32]MYS--
MD "SCENT OF DEATH" SEPT '60

HORN, ROBERT W.
NORD, F.R.--[39]GERMAN

HORNBACK, BERT G[ERALD]
FRASCATORO, GERALD--[1][31]AMERICAN--
CONTRIBUTOR TO 'MALAHAT REVIEW'
PLUMM, NORMAN D.--[1]AMERICAN

HORNBERGER, H. RICHARD
HOOKER, RICHARD--[1][8][31]AMERICAN

HORNBUCKLE, PHYLLIS
HORN, PHYLLIS--V. BERCH LTR TO
A. HUBIN '93/MYS--
NAIAD "CHESAPEAKE PROJECT" '90

HORNBY, JOHN WILKINSON
BRENT, CALVIN--[1][8]ENGLISH
GRACE, JOSEPH--[1][8][22][31]ENGLISH
HORNBY, JOHN--[8]ENGLISH
SUMMERS, GORDON--[1][8][22]ENGLISH

HORNBY, LESLEY
TWEIGGY--[8]

HORNE, CYNTHIA MIRIAM
PILKINGTON, CYNTHIA--[1][22]ENGLISH

HORNE, GEOFFREY
NORTH, GEOFFREY--[3][32]MYS--
TB "GREEN HARVEST" JUN '46
NORTH, GIL--[3][18][22]MYS--
HALE "A CORPSE FOR KOFI KATT" '78
& 11 MORE

HORNE, HERMOD
HOGSTAD, OYVIND--[29]MYS--
"ERNA ALMS HAMND" '18

HORNE, HUGH ROBERT
MADISON, JANE--[1][22]AMERICAN

HORNE, RICHARD HENRY
FAIRSTAR, MRS.--[33]ENGLISH
HORNE, R. HENGIST--[2][23]ENGLISH/SF
O'TRIGGER, SIR LUCIUS--[33]ENGLISH
UZAIR, SALEM BEN--[31][33]ENGLISH
WATTS, EPHRAIM--[33]ENGLISH

HORNER, FREDERIK WILLIAM
FIELD, MARTYN--[1]ENGLISH

HORNER, JOHN CURWEN
HORNER, J.C.--[1][31]AUSTRALIAN

HORNER, KENRIC LANCASTER
HORNER, LANCE--[21][31]ROM--
"THE MAHOUN"
"BLACK SUN" & MORE

HORNICKLE, LAURA
KERR, LAURA--[1]

HORNIG, CHARLES D.
LESSER, DERWIN--[2][11][23]SF--WS-ONE STORY
SFM - ARTICLES

HORNIG, DOUG
CAINE, PETER--LACHMAN LST '93,[34]MYS--
ONYX "VIRUS" '89

HORNUNG, ERNEST WILLIAM
HORNUNG, E.W.--[1][29][32]ENGLISH/MYS--
SC "KNEES OF THE GODS" '45
RAFFLES--[29]MYS

HORNWOOD, HARVEY
DANZIGER, DAVID--R.C. HOLLAND-HORNWOOD BIO/CKLST, BAE 18, ADULT
DEXTER, JOHN--R.C. HOLLAND-HORNWOOD BIO/CKLST, BAE 18, ADULT,HP
GREEN, FRANCES--R.C. HOLLAND-HORNWOOD BIO, BAE 18-- WIFE'S NAME, NOT USED PER HARVEY
HAWKES, H.C.--HORNWOOD LTR DEC '92
KERSTETTER, JAMES--R.C. HOLLAND-HORNWOOD BIO/CKLST, BAE 18,[14] ADULT--
OLYM OPH#215 "CARNAL KNOWLEDGE" '70
OLYM OPH#222 "PAIN LOVERS" '70
OLYM OPH#235 "THIRD-DEGREE RAPE" '71
"PASSION'S PUPIL"
"LUST RUMBLE"
MARSHALL, ALAN--R.C. HOLLAND-HORNWOOD BIO/CKLST, BAE 18, ADULT,HP--
"SADO SWAPPERS"
ROSS, CARL--R.C. HOLLAND-HORNWOOD BIO/CKLST, BAE 18, ADULT--
"UP TIGHT"
WOOD, HARVEY--PP 20,HORNWOOD LTR DEC '92-- ARTICLES ONLY

HOROVITZ, FRANCES MARGAR.
HOOKER, FRANCES--[31]

HOROVITZ, LESLIE ALAN
HARTMAN, DANE--V. BERCH LTR TO HUBIN '93/MYS,HP--
WARNER-"DEALER IN DEATH" '83
HORVITZ, LESLIE--V. BERCH LTR TO HUBIN '93/MYS--
"BLOOD MOON" '87
LYNX "CAUSES UNKNOWN" '89 & MORE

HOROWITZ, ISRAEL A.
HOROWITZ, AL--[31]

HOROWITZ, JACOB
HARRIS, JED--[31]

HOROWITZ, SHEL ALAN
FRIEDMAN, ALAN--[1][31]
KAYE, ALAN--[1][31]

HORSCHELT, THEODOR
BOGAT, HENRY--[39]GERMAN/MYS
CARROL, MARIO--[39]GERMAN/MYS
COMBER, PIT--[39]GERMAN/MYS
COTTON, JERRY--[39]GERMAN/MYS,HP
WHITE, LOFTUS--[39]GERMAN/MYS

HORSFIELD, RICHARD HENRY
GAUNT, M.B.--[1][3]MYS--
LONG "THE LEASES OF DEATH" '37

HORSTMANN, BERNHARD
MURR, STEFAN--[39][40]GERMAN/MYS--
"AUF DEN TAG GENAU" '82 & 12 OTHERS

HORTI, MARIA
ZIMMERMANN, MARIA--[39]GERMAN

HORTON, MARIAN L.
LORRAINE, MARIAN--[9][21][26]ROM--
"ARDENT SUITOR"
"ENTERPRISING MINX"
"MISCHIEVEOUS SPINSTER"

HORTON, SUSAN
HORTON, NAOMI--[9][21][26]ROM--
"ALDY LIBERTY"
"RIVER OF DREAMS" & MORE

HORVITZ, LESLIE ALAN
HARTMAN, DANE--V. BERCH LTR TO HUBIN '94,[34]MYS,HP--
WARNER "DEATH ON THE DOCKS" '81
RIIS, DAVID ALLEN--V. BERCH LTR TO HUBIN '94/MYS--
DELL "JERUSALEM CONSPIRACY" '79

HORWICH, FRANCES R.
FRANCES, MISS--[22][33]AMERICAN

HOSELITZ, BERTHOLD FRANK
HOSELITZ, BERT F.--[31]

HOSIE, STANLEY WILLIAM
STANLEY, MICHAEL--[8]

HOSIER, HELEN KOOIMAN
KOOIMAN, HELEN W.--[1]AMERICAN

HOSKEN, ALICE C.S.
STANTON, CORALIE--W/E.C. HEATH HOSKEN,[3]MYS--
9 NOVELS 1906-24
PAUL "IRONMOUTH" '16
NUMEROUS NOVELS

HOSKEN, CLIFFORD [J.W.]
KEVERNE, RICHARD--[3][22][29]MYS--
SONSTABLE "HAVERING PLOT" '28 & MP
COLLINS "BLACK CRIPPLE" '41

HOSKEN, ERNEST CHARLES
COSTELLO, PIERRE--[1]AMERICAN
GOWER, CRAVEN--[1]ENGLISH

HOSKEN,[E.C.] HEATH
STANTON, CORALIE--W/ALICE C.S. HOSKEN,[3]MYS--
PAUL "MUZZLED OX" '11
CASSELL "DOG STAR" '13 & MORE

HOSKIN, CYRIL HENRY
GREYWHISKERS, MRS. FIFI--[7]SF--
CORGI "LIVING WITH THE LAMA" '64
KUAN-SUO, DR.--[1]
LOBSANG, T. RAMPA--[2][7][11]--
PHILOSOPHY FROM CATS POINT OF VIEW

HOSKINS, JOSEPHINE R.
HILDEGARDE--[1]AMERICAN
JACQUELINE--[1]AMERICAN

HOSKINS, ROBERT
CORREN, GRACE--R.C. HOLLAND-LASER ART/CKLST, BAE 2,[3][8][9][23]MYS/ROM--
LAN 73-862 "DARKEST ROOM" '69
LAN 74-762 "A PLACE ON DARK ISLAND" '71
LAN 75-402 "EVIL IN THE FAMILY" '72
PINN "THE ATTIC CHILD" '79
POPLB "DARK THRESHOLD" '77
POPLB "MANSION OF DEADLY DREAMS" '73
GREGORY, JOHN--[2][7][11][23]--
LEIS "LEGACY OF THE STARS" '79
HOSKINS, PHILLIP--[11]
JENNIFER, SUSAN--HOLLAND-LASER ART/CKLST, BAE 2,[2][3][8][9][21][26][31]--
AV "COUNTRY OF THE KIND" '75
AV "HOUSE OF COUNTED HATRED" '73 & MORE
JOHNSTONE, WILLIAM--G. COOK LTR AUG '93
KERR, MICHAEL--W/H.G. WELLS/J.A. CORRICK, BAE 4,[2][3][7][23]MYS/SF--
"ISLAND OF DR. MOREAU" '78
CHART "THE NIGHT RUNNERS: GEMINI RUN" '79
REDFIELD, JENNIFER--[1]AMERICAN

HOSKINS, ROBERT [CONT]
THATCHER, JULIA--[11][26]ROM/SF--
"INHERIT THE MIRAGE"
"MASK OF LOVE"
"TOWER IN THE SEA" & MORE
WILLIAMS, ROBERT--[8]
WILSON, GAR--[34]MYS,HP--
GE "ARGENTINE DEADLINE" '82
GE "FURY BOMBS" '83

HOSKYNS-ABRAHALL, CLARE C
ABRAHALL, C.H.--[1][33]ENGLISH
ABRAHALL, CLARE HOSKYNS--[1][33]ENGLISH
DRURY, CLARE MARIE--[1]ENGLISH

HOSMER, CATHERINE ANN
FOUGHT, CATHERINE ANN--V. BERCH LTR TO HUBIN '94/MYS--
NAL "RABBLE'S CURSE" '80

HOSOKAWA, WILLIAM K.
HOSOKAWA, BILL--[31]

HOSPITAL, JANETTE TURNER
JUNIPER, ALEX--LACHMAN-EASTER LST '93,[34]MYS--
PENG "A VERY PROPER DEATH" '90

HOSS, MARGIT
HEYDORN, ELLEN--[39]GERMAN, HP--

HOSSENT, HARRY
BOGAR, JEFF--[27][34]MYS,HP--
HAMILTON "BOOK A HEARSE NOW" '51
GREGORY, SEAN--[1][22][31]
HOLTON, H.B.--[1]
JOHNSON, DUFF--[34]MYS,HP--
HAM STFFD "ONE TIME CHAMPION" '51
HAM STFFD "RACING CRAZY" '52
HAM STFFD "DYNAMITE ON WHEELS" '52
O'MALLEY, KEVIN--[1]
SAVAGE, DAVID--[1][3]MYS--
JENKINS "SPY THAT GOT OFF AT LAS VEGAS" '69
STAHL, RAY--[34]MYS,HP--
HAM STAFF "NO ANSWER FROM A CORPSE" '53

HOSTOS Y BONILLA, EUGENIA
HOSTOS, E.M. DE--[31]
HOSTOS, EUGENIA M. DE--[31]

HOTCHKISS, ELLA A.
WYLDE, HAZEL--[1]AMERICAN

HOUGAN, JAMES RICHARD
HOUGAN, JIM--[31]

HOUGH, CLARA SHARPE
SHARPE, C.--[1]AMERICAN

HOUGH, JUDY TAYLOR
TAYLOR, JUDY--[33]

HOUGH, RICHARD ALEXANDER
CARTER, BRUCE--[2][7][11][23][25][31][33]ENGLISH/SF--
DENT "DEADLY FREEZE" '76
DENT "BUZZBUGS" '77
CHURCHILL, ELIZABETH--[1][2]
STRONG, PAT--[1][2]

HOUGH, STANLEY BENNETT
GORDON, REX--[2][4][18][23][31]MYS/SF--
ACE D233 "FIRST ON MARS" '57
ACE D405 "FIRST TO THE STARS" '59
F174 "FIRST THROUGH TIME" '62
ACE F416 "UTOPIA MINUS X" '66

HOUGH, STANLEY BENNETT [CONT]
HOUGH, S.B.
AV G1205 "THE TENDER KILLER" '64
STANLEY, BENNETT--[2][3][18][22]MYS--
HODDER "SEASTRUCK" '53
HODDER "ALSCOTT EXPERIMENT" '54
HODDER "GOVERNMENT CONTRACT" '56

HOULTON, PEGGY MANN
MANN, PEGGY--[31]

HOUN, AIRA
KAAL, AIRA--[1]

HOUN, FRANKLIN W.
HOU, FU-WU--[31]

HOUNSFIELD, JOAN
WHEEZY--[8]

HOURANI, ALBERT HABIB
HOURANI, A.H.--[31]

HOURS, MADELEINE
HOURS-MIEDAN, MADELEINE--[31]

HOUSE, GLORIA
KGOSITSILE, ANEB--[31]--
BROADSIDE PRESS "BLOOD RIVER: POEMS" '83

HOUSE, RICHARD CALVIN
HOUSE, R.C.--[31]
JACQUES, BEAU--[31]

HOUSEBY, SANDRA LYNN
HARTE, SAMANTHA--[3][31]MYS--
AV "SNOWS OF CRAGGMOOR" '78
PPJK "TEARS OF FLAME" '88

HOUSEMAN, JACK & PHYLLIS
HOUSEMAN, PHYLLIS--[21]ROM--
"THE VERDICT IS LOVE"

HOUSEMAN, LORNA
WESTALL, LORNA--[8]

HOUSSET, ARSENE
HOUSSAYE, ARSENE--[1]FRENCH
L'ESTOILO, PIERRE--[1]FRENCH
MOUSSE, ALFRED--[1]FRENCH

HOUSTON, DAVID
HOWARD, KEZ--[31]

HOUSTON, DOUGLAS NORMAN
GAVIN, WILLIAM--[31]

HOUTON, KATHLEEN KILGORE
KILGORE, KATHLEEN--[7]SF--
"THE GHOST-MAKER" '84

HOUWINK, ROEL
VAN ELRO, H.--[22] DUTCH

HOVELL, LUCILLE A.P.
HOVELL, LUCY A.--[31]

HOVEY, SONYA
LEVIEN, SONYA--[31]

HOVICK, ROSE LOUISE
LEE, GYPSIE ROSE--[3]MYS--
SIMON "G-STRING MURDERS" '41
SIMON "MOTHER FINDS A BODY" '42

HOVLAND, BONNIE L.
LEE, BONNIE--[3]MYS--
LENNOX "THE SHADOWS OF CLIFFSIDE" '75

HOWARD, ADAH M.
HILTON, MAUD--[1] ?? UNCONFIRMED ??

HOWARD, ALAN
McIVER, N.J.--V. BERCH LTR TO HUBIN '94/MYS--
ST. MARTIN'S "COME BACK, ALICE SMITHERENE!" '85
DBLDY "AN ASSASSIN PREPARES" '88

HOWARD, ALBERT WALDO
HOVORRE, M. AUBERRE--[2]

HOWARD, ANNA H.C.
A.H.H.--[1]AMERICAN
ELLIOT, EDITH--[1]AMERICAN
HOLYOKE, ANNA--[1]AMERICAN

HOWARD, DONALD M.
ST. JOHN, ANDREA--[9][21][26]ROM--
"NEVER LOVE A COWBOY"
"AT LONG LAST LOVE"
"PERFECT EXCHANGE"

HOWARD, DOROTHY GRAY
MILLS, DOROTHY--[1]AMERICAN

HOWARD, FELICITY
LONGFIELD, JO--[8]

HOWARD, GEOFFREY
DIXIE, MARMADUKE--[1][2]

HOWARD, GILBERT
HONIGFELD, GILBERT--[31]

HOWARD, HERBERT EDMUND
PHILMORE, R.--[3][22][29]MYS--
GOLZ "GOOD BOOKS" '36
GOLZ "DEATH IN ARMS" '39 & 5 MORE

HOWARD, HILDA GLYNN
GLYNN-WARD, H.--[1][8]ENGLISH
GLYNN-WARD, HILDA--[1][8]ENGLISH

HOWARD, JACK
STARK, INSPECTOR--[34]MYS,HP--
NEW MAGNET #406 "EYE OF GOLD; OR, A ROGUE WHO WAS STUPID" '05

HOWARD, JAMES A[RCH]
FISHER, LAINE--[3][22][29][31]MYS--
ACE D387 "FAIR PREY" '59

HOWARD, LEON A. LEE
HOWARD, LEIGH--[3][29]--
LONGMANS "BLIND DATE" '55
KRISLOV, ALEXANDER--[22][29]MYS

HOWARD, LYNETTE DELSEY
HOWARD, LYNDE--[9][21]ROM--
"ALL I EVER WANTED"
STEVENS, LYNSEY--[9][26]ROM--
HARL 1643 "TOUCHED BY DESIRE"
& 13 MORE

HOWARD, MARGHANITA LASKI
LASKI, MARGHANITA--[11]

HOWARD, MOSES L.
NAGENDA, MUSA--[1]AMERICAN

HOWARD, MUNROE
ST. CLAIR, PHILIP--[1][8]AMERICAN

HOWARD, PETER DUNSMORE
CATO--W/MICHAEL FOOTE & FRANK OWEN, [1][22][31]ENGLISH

HOWARD, ROBERT E.
ERVIN, PATRICK--[2][11][16][37]MYS--
STD "THE TOMB'S SECRET" FEB '34
HOWARD, PATRICK--[1][2][11]
TAVEREL, JOHN--[1][2][11][16]
WALSER, SAM--[1][2][11][16]
WARD, ROBERT--[1][2][11][16]

HOWARD, ROBERT WEST
CASE, MICHAEL--[8][22][31][33]AMERICAN

HOWARD, THEODORE KORNER
HOWARD, TED--[31]

HOWARD, VERNON L.
CASTLE, PAUL--[1][31][33]AMERICAN
JORDON, DON--[1][33]AMERICAN

HOWARD-ELLIS, CHARLES
AUSTRAL--[1]

HOWARTH, PAMELA
BARROW, PAMELA--[1][8][31]ENGLISH

HOWARTH, PATRICK [J.F.]
FRANCIS, C.D.E.--[1][3][22]MYS--
HAMMOND "PORTRAIT OF A KILLER" '56

HOWAT, GERALD MALCOLM D.
HENDERSON-HOWAT, GERALD--[1][8][31]ENGLISH

HOWE, CHARLES HORACE
HOWARD, CARLETON--[31]

HOWE, DORIS KATHLEEN
MUNRO, MARY--[1][8][21][26]ENGLISH/ROM--
"THIS GIRL IS MINE"
NASH, NEWLYN--W/MURIEL HOWE,[1]
STEWART, KAYE--[1][8]ENGLISH

HOWE, MARK ANTH. DE WOLFE
HOWE, M.A. DE WOLFE--[1]AMERICAN

HOWE, MURIEL
NASH, NEWLYN--W/DORIS KATHLEEN HOWE,[1]
REDMAYNE, BARBARA--[1][22]ENGLISH

HOWE, SUSANNA
THOMAS, BREE--[21][26]ROM--
"LOVE'S JOURNEY HOME"

HOWELL, BYRD
GRANGER, BYRD HOWELL--[1]AMERICAN

HOWELL, DOROTHY
PRATE, KIT--[9][21][26]ROM--
"DEFIANT ENCHANTRESS"
"WILD TEXAS WINDS"

HOWELL, DOUGLAS NAYLER
HANCOCK, ROBERT--[8]

HOWELL, HANNAH D.
DUSTIN, SARAH--[9][21][26]ROM--
"A TASTE OF FIRE"
JENNET, ANNA--[26]ROM--
"AMBER FLAME"
"PROMISED PASSION" & MORE

HOWELL, JANE L.
VANE, VIOLET--[1]

HOWELL, PATRICIA HAGAN
HAGAN, PATRICIA--[3][21][26][31]MYS/ROM--
AV "A DARK JOURNEY HOME" '72
AV "WINDS OF TERROR" '73

HOWELLS, ANNIE T.
AITIAICHE--[1]AMERICAN

HOWELLS, ROSCOE
BARN OWL--[1][31]WELSH
BROCK, BEN--[1][31]WELSH

HOWELLS, WILLIAM DEAN
HOWELLS, W.D.--[31]
TWO FRIENDS--W/JOHN JAMES PIATT,[1]

HOWINGTON, LINDA
HOWARD, LINDA--[9][21][26]ROM--
"DIAMOND BAY"
"HEARTBREAKER" & MORE

HOWITT, J. LESLIE DESPARD
DESPARD, LESLIE--[3][22][29]MYS--
HODDER "MYSTERY OF THE TOWER ROOM" '25
HODDER "AMAZING ADV. OF MR. HENRY BUTTON" '27
NASH "CRIME WITHOUT A FLAW" '31
LESLIE, JOHN--[1][22]MYSTERY

HOWL, MARCIA Y.H.
BLAYNE, SARA--[31]
HAILEY, JOHANNA--W/SHARON JARVIS, [7][9][21][23][31]ROM/SF--
ZEBRA "ENCHANTED PARADISE" '85
ZEBRA "CRYSTAL PARADISE" '87
ZEBRA "BELOVED PARADISE" '88
YORK, PAULINE--[9][21][26]ROM--
"THE TORPID DUKE"

HOWLAND, FRANCES LOUISE
WEST, KENYON--[1]AMERICAN

HOXIE, WALTER PALMER
HURLBA, ALTON--[3]MYS--
ROUTLEDGE "A FRIENDS VICTIM" 1889

HOY, CHARLOTTE
ST. JAMES, JESSICA--W/LINDA V. PALMER,[21]ROM--
"PERFECT LOVER"
"SHOWDOWN AT SIN CREEK"
"A COUNTRY CHRISTMAS"
ST. JAMES, SCOTNEY--W/LINDA V. PALMER, [9][21][26]ROM--
"HEATHER MIST"
"BY HONOR BOUND"
"DEFIANT BRIDE" & MORE

HOYER, MILDRED N.
MERRITT, SI--[1]AMERICAN

HOYLE, TREVOR
RANCE, JOSEPH--W/JUNYA SATO & RYUNOSUKE ONO, V. BERCH LTR TO HUBIN '94/MYS--
SOUVENIR "BULLET TRAIN" '80

HOYT, EDWIN P. JR.
FORBES, CABOT L.--[1][31][33]
MARTIN, CHRISTOPHER--[1]
SMITH, C. PRITCHARD--[1]
STUART, DAVID--[1]

HRDINKA, MICHAEL
COLLINS, FREDERIC--[39]GERMAN/HOR,HP
DE LORCA, FRANK--[39]GERMAN/HOR,HP
ELLIOT, BRUCE--[39]GERMAN/HOR,HP
LAMONT, ROBERT--[39]GERMAN/HOR,HP

HRDY, SARAH BLAFFER
BLAFFER, SARAH C.--[1][31]AMERICAN

HRIMAK, DENISE
MATHEWS, DENISE--W/PATRICIA J. MATHEWS, [9][21][26]ROM--
"INTIMATE STRANGERS"

HRUSCHKA, ANNI
EBENSTEIN, ERICH--[39]GERMAN

HSU, BENEDICT PEI-HSIUNG
CHUNG-YU, CHU--[31]

HSU, KENNETH JINGHWA
HSU, K.--[31]
HSU, K. JINGHWA--[31]
HSU, K.J.--[31]

HU, SHU MING
HU, SHI MING--[31]

HUANG, PARKER PO-FEI
HUANG, PO-FEI--[31]

HUBBARD, CLIFFORD LIONEL
CANIS--[8]

HUBBARD, ELBERT
FRA ELBERTUS--[8]

HUBBARD, FRANK MCKINNEY
HUBBARD, KIN--[1][8]AMERICAN
MARTIN, ABE--[1][8]AMERICAN

HUBBARD, GEORGE [BARRON]
MOORE, AMOS--[28][34]MYS--
MCL "ROYCE OF THE ROYAL MOUNTED" '32
& 16 WESTERN NOVELS

HUBBARD, L. RON
BEACHCOMBER, THE--LAYTON-HUBBARD BIBLIO '94--
'CATALINA ISLANDER'-
"THE EDNA IRENE" 11/21/46
COLT, W.R.--LAYTON-HUBBARD BIBLIO--
TEX RGRS "MAN FOR BREAKFAST" NOV '49
COLT, WINCHESTER REM.--[1][2][11][31]--
AKA 'W.R. COLT'
DALY, LT. JONATHAN--LAYTON-HUBBARD BIBLIO--
TADV "TRAIL OF THE RED DIAMONDS" JAN '35
ELRON--[1][2][31]
ENGELHARDT, FREDERICK--[2][11][16][23][31]
TM "SECOND COUNT BAKONSKI" NOV '39
TM "HERITAGE OF OSIRIS" SEP '39
ASF "GEN. SWAMP C.I.C." PTS 1&2 A-S '39
ASF "THIS SHIP KILLS" NOV '39
UK "VANDERDECKEN" DEC '39
AR "GOLDEN HEAD" N25 '39
UK "THE KRAKEN" JUN '40
AR "BIRD OF JEOPARDY" J29 '40
AR "FIFTEEN DOLLARS EVERY FRIDAY" A31 '40
TWS "HISTORY CLASS, 2133 A.D." JAN '41
ESTERBROOK, TOM--LAYTON/HUBBARD BIBL,[2][31]
F.E.--G. THIESSEN--
STATES 6 REF ATTRIBUTE THIS PSEUD
GORDON, CAPT. CHARLES--LAYTON-HUBBARD BIBLIO--
TADV "TOMB OF TEN THOUSAND DEAD" OCT '36

HUBBARD, L. RON [CONT]
HUBBARD, CAPT. L. RON--LAYTON-HUBBARD BIBLIO--
NEW MYS ADV "HELL'S LEGIONAIRE" JUL '35
'THROUGH HELL & HIGH WATER' BY MCBRIDE
SS-"IT BEARS TELLING" '41
HUBBELL, BERNARD--LAYTON-HUBBARD BIBLIO--
TPN "BUCKLEY PLAYS A HUNCH" SEPT '35
KEITH, MICHAEL--LAYTON-HUBBARD BIBLIO,[2][31]--
FNOV "BRASS KEYS TO MURDER" APR '35
FNOV "THE CHEE CHALKER" JUL/AUG '42
KELLOGG, GEORGE--LAYTON-HUBBARD BIBLIO--
FREEDOM [NEWSPPR] "JUSTICE DEPT. VS AMERICANS" MAY '75
LAFAYETTE, RENE--LAYTON-HUBBARD BIBLIO, [2][16][23][31]--
STS "CONQUEST OF SPACE" SERIES
UNKNOWN "THE INDIGESTIBLE TRITON" APR '40
ASF "ONE WAS STUBBORN" NOV '40
ASF "THE EXPENSIVE SLAVES" NOV '47
ASF "HER MAJESTY'S ABBERATION" MAR '47
ASF "GREAT AIR MONOPOLY" SEPT '47
ASF 'OLE DOC METHUSELAH' STORIES '47-50
STS "FORBIDDEN VOYAGE" JAN '49
ASF "PLAGUE" APR '49
ASF "THE CONROY DIARY" MAY '49
ASF "A SOUND INVESTMENT" JUN '49
STS "MAGNIFICENT FAILURE" MAR '49
STS "INCREDIBLE DESTINATION" MAY '49
STS "UNWILLING HERO" JUL '49
STS "BEYOND THE BLACK NEBULA" SEPT '49
STS "EMPEROR OF THE UNIVERSE" NOV '49
STS "LAST ADMIRAL" JAN '50
ASF "OLE MOTHER METHUSELAH" JAN '50
FUTURE SF [AUSTRALIAN] "FORBIDDEN VOYAGE" NOV '53
LEGIONNAIRE 148--LAYTON-HUBBARD BIBLIO
TADV "SQUAD THAT NEVER CAME BACK" MAY '35
LEGIONAIRE 14830--LAYTON-HUBBARD BIBLIO,[2]--
TADV "BLACK SULTAN WALKED TO WAR" NOV '35
MARTIN, EVE--LAYTON-HUBBARD BIBLIO
ROMR "CIRCUMSTANTIAL EVIDENCE" JUN '36
MARTIN, KEN--LAYTON-HUBBARD BIBLIO,[2]--
CBS "TOOBY" NOV '34
BBAT "CATAPULT COURAGE" NOV '35
CBS "MAYBE, BECAUSE" SEPT '34
TPN "MEDALS FOR MAHONEY" SEPT '35
TPN "THE ADVENTURE OF X" NOV '35
CBS "PLANS FOR THE BOY" JUL '35
CBS "THE BAD ONE" SEPT '35
BBAT "RAIDERS OF THE BEAM" MAR '36
CBS "HORSE & HORSE" MAY '36
ROMR "MARRIAGE FOR SPITE" APR '36
CBS "LEADUCATION" JUL '36
CBS "THE NECK SCARF" AUG '36
CBS "CANTEENS" NOV '36
CBS "SALT" AUG/SEPT '37
MORGAN,[LT.] SCOTT--[2]
TA "RILEY OF THE BENGAL LANCERS" JUN '33
TA "BROTHER OF THE TONG" AUG '33
SF "JUST PUTTERIN" JAN '34
TA "TERROR OF SIBERIA" FEB '34
TA "ORCHID OF DOOM" JUL '34
TA "TRAIL OF THE GOLD SKULLS" SEP '34
DS "STEELE JAWS" FEB '36
TA "FIRE & BLOOD" JAN '37
SF "FLAMING FOKKERS" FEB '37
SF "WINGS OF WAR" JUL '37
TA "NAZI FURY" OCT '40
AW "CAPTAIN DANGER OVER LONDON" WIN '41
AW "CAPTAIN DANGER'S NAZI HUNT" SPR '41
FS "KEEP 'EM SEPARATE" #1 '42
AW "ACE OF ACES" SPR '42
AW "BORROWED STRATEGY" SUM '42
AW "LEND-LEASE FOR RUSSIA" FAL '42
NORTHRUP, CAPT. B.A.--LAYTON-HUBBARD BIBLIO,[2]--
BBAT "FORTRESS IN THE SKY" MAY '47

HUBBARD, L. RON [CONT]
OLSEN, JAMES P.--LAYTON-HUBBARD BIBLIO--
CBS "BULLETS FOR BREAKFAST" JAN '35
RANDOLPH, BARRY--LAYTON-HUBBARD BIBLIO--
FNOV "BRANDED OUTLAW" OCT '38
ROMR "WHEN GILHOOLY WAS IN FLOWER" AUG '38
REYNOLDS, CAPT. HUMBERT--LAYTON-HUBBARD BIBLIO--
TADV "GOLDEN HELL" SEPT '36
REYNOLDS, HUMBERT--R. LAYTON LTR/ PANDORA JUNE '93
RHONE, FRANKIE--LAYTON-HUBBARD BIBLIO,[2]--
URANIA "DEATH'S DEPUTY" APR/MAY '53, PIRATE EDITION
SEABROOK, JOHN--[2]
SPECTATOR, MR.--LAYTON-HUBBARD BIBLIO--
SPORTSMAN PILOT "WASHINGTON LANGLEY DAY" MAY/JUNE '33
SPORTSMAN PILOT "SAN DIEGO FAIR MEET" SEPT '34
VON RACHEN, KURT--LAYTON-HUBBARD BIBLIO,[2][8][16][23]--
TPN "RED SAND" FEB '36
ASF "THE IDEALIST" SEPT '40
ASF "KILKENNY CATS" SEPT '40
ASF 'KILKENNEY CATS' SERIES '40-2
ASF "TRAITOR" JAN '41
ASF "MUTINEERS" APR '41
ASF "THE REBELS" FEB '42

HUBBARD, LAFAYETTE RONALD
HUBBARD, L. RON--LAYTON-HUBBARD BIBLIO,[2][8][23]

HUBBARD, RICHARD
CARTER, NICK--[3]MYS,HP--
AWARD "LIQUIDATOR" '73
AWARD "TARGET: DOOMSDAY ISLAND" '73
EYRE, MARIE--[3][40]MYS--
POPLB "BURY ME NOT AT SEA" '74
POPLB "ABSENCE" '73 & MORE
HUBBARD, REGINA--[3][40]MYS--
POPLB "CURSE OF NIGHTWIND" '75
STRATTON, CHRIS--[2][3][40]MYS--
AWARD "DEAD ON ARRIVAL" '72
POPLB "A FINE PAIR" '69 & MORE

HUBBLE, LESLIE ARTHUR B.
NOBLE, JOHN--[1]ENGLISH
WRIGHT, PHILIP--[1]ENGLISH

HUBEL, EDUARD
METSANURK, MAIT--[1] ESTONIAN

HUBELL, LOUIS W.
HUBELL, NED--[3]MYS--
POPLB "ADVENTURES OF CREIGHTON HOLMES" '79

HUBER, ARMIN OTTO
FRANK, ARMIN--[39]GERMAN/ADV
LARSEN, FRED--[39]GERMAN/ADV
STRUBBERG, ACHIM F.--[39]GERMAN/ADV

HUBER, FREDERICK VINCENT [FRED]
CARTER, NICK--[3]MYS,HP--
CHART "REICH FOUR" '79
THORNE, JED--[14] ADULT--
OLYM OPH#231 "THE BIG SPENDER" '71
THORNE, JOY--[14] ADULT--
OLYM OPH#212 "RUNNING WILD" '70

HUBER, MARY FLORENCE
HUBER, FLORENCE M.--[1]AMERICAN

HUBERT, CAM
CAMERON, BARBARA ANNE--[7]--
LEGALIZED TO "BARBARA ANNE CAMERON"

HUBERT, JAMES LEE
HUBERT, JIM--[31]

HUBLER, RICHARD GIBSON
GIBSON, HARRY CLARK--[1][8][22]AMERICAN

HUBLER-WILHELMI, CHARLOT.
WILHELMI, HELMA--[39]GERMAN/JUV

HUBNER, ELSE
DEUSE, ELSE--[39]GERMAN/JUV

HUBNER, HORST W.
CLARK, RINGO--[39]GERMAN/WEST
COOPER, STEVE--[39]GERMAN/MYS/WEST,HP
COTTON, JERRY--[39]GERMAN/MYS,HP
EISENHUTH, P.--[39]GERMAN/MYS/SF
FLYNN, CARTER--[39]GERMAN/MYS/SF/WEST
MARTINEZ, BENITO--[39]GERMAN/WEST,HP
MCKAY, CHARLES--[39]GERMAN/MYS/SF/WEST
ROSS, JAKE--[39]GERMAN/WEST
THACKERAY, NORMAN--[39]GERMAN/MYS/SF

HUBNER, JALOB
KONRAD, HERBERT--[39]GERMAN

HUBNER, PAUL FRIEDRICH
FRIEDRICH, PAUL--[39]GERMAN

HUC, PHILIPPE
DETREME, TRISTAN--[22] FRENCH

HUCH, RICARDA
HUGO, RICHARD--[1][39]GERMAN

HUCKINS, JANET
BLAYNE, SEBASTIAN--V. BERCH-GM PSEUDS,
PP 33,[3]MYS--
GM 175 "GAY GHASTLY HOLIDAY" '51
GM 325 "TERROR IN THE NIGHT" 53

HUDDLESTON, SISLEY
VERNON, PETER--[1]ENGLISH

HUDGENS, A[LICE] GAYLE
WATSON, GAYLE HUDGENS--[1]AMERICAN

HUDGINS, CATHERINE
THOMAS, KATE--[26]ROM--
SIL 1023 "TEXAS TOUCH"

HUDLESTON, GILBERT ROGER
PATER, ROGER--[8]

HUDSON, H. LINDSAY
LINDSAY, H.--[8]
LINDSAY, HARRY--[1]

HUDSON, HOYT
SMITH, JOHN--W/MARVIN THEODORE HERRICK,[1][8]

HUDSON, JANECE OLIVER
HUDSON, JANIS REAMS--[26]ROM
HUDSON, JAN--[9][21]ROM--
"WATERWITCH"
"APACHE MAGIC" & MORE
OLIVER, JAN--[9][21][26]ROM--
"THE PERFECT LOVE TEST"

HUDSON, LAVASSA V.
HUDSON, JACK--[1]AMERICAN
SHELLY, PAUL--V. BERCH-GM PSEUDS, PP 33--
GM 315 "SATURDAY'S HARVEST" '53

HUDSON, MAXINE
PARIS, FIRMIN--[1] CANADIAN

HUDSON, WILLIAM C.
CADWALADER--[1]
CARTER, NICHOLAS--[3][29]MYS,HP
GRAYDON, W.--[29]MYS
NORTH, BARCLAY--[3][22][29]MYS--4 NOVELS ca 1900

HUDSON, WILLIAM HENRY
HARFORD, HENRY--[1][8][31][33]ENGLISH
HUDSON, W.H.--[1][33]ENGLISH

HUDSON,[MARGARET] KIRSTY
MCLEOD, KIRSTY--[1][33]ENGLISH

HUEFFER, FRANZ
HUEFFER, FRANCIS--[1]
HUEPPER, FRANK--[1][32]MYS--
ST "HOT RED HONEY" AUG '60
OF "HOT TORNADO" NOV '60
MSMM "BAR FLY" DEC '60

HUEFFER, JOSEPH FORD M.
FORD, FORD MADOX--[2][3][23] LEGALLY CHGD
TO 'FORD'/MYS--

HUEFFER, OLIVER MADOX
WARDLE, JANE--[1]

HUEMER, RICHARD MARTIN
HUEMER, DICK--[7]SF

HUERLIMANN, RUTH
HURLIMANN, RUTH--[31]

HUERLIMANN-KIEPENHEUER, B
HUERLIMANN, BETTINA--[1]GERMAN
HURLIMANN, BETTINA--[31]

HUFF, CHARLES H.
DRAKE, DREXEL--[3]MYS--
LIPP "THE FALCON'S PREY" '36
LIPP "FALCON CRETINS" '37
LIPP "FALCON MEETS A LADY" '38

HUFF, DARRELL
HOUGH, DON--[8]

HUFF, TANYA SUE
HANOVER, TERRI--[31]
HUFF, T.S.--[31]

HUFF, TOM E.
HUFF, T.E.--CRPG--
"MEET A DARK STRANGER"
RPTD AS DELL 15543 "WHISPER IN
THE DARKNESS" '77
MARLOW, EDWINA--[3][9][26][29]MYS/ROM--
ACE "FALCONRIDGE" '69
PUTNAM "DANGER AT DAHLKARI" '75
BERK "MIDNIGHT AT MALLYNCOURT" '75 & MORE
PARKER, BEATRICE--[3][9][21][29]MYS/ROM--
DELL "BETRAYAL AT BLACKCREST" '71
DELL "JAMINTHA" '75 & MORE
ST. CLAIR, KATHERINE--[3][9][21][26]
[29]MYS/ROM--
BOBBS "ROOM BENEATH THE STAIRS" '75
WILDE, JENNIFER--[9][21][26]ROM--
"ANGEL IN SCARLET"
"THEY CALL HER DANA" & MORE

HUFF, URSULA
DAWSON, FRANCINE--[39]GERMAN

HUFFAKER, CLAIR
HANSEN, CECIL--[31]--
SCREENPLAYS
HANSEN, CECIL DEAN--[1]

HUFFORD, SUSAN
HUGHES, SAMANTHA--[9][26]ROM--
"A TASTE OF HEAVEN"
"DESERT SPLENDOR" & MORE

HUG, ERNST-WALTER
HUGH, R.--[39]GERMAN

HUGGETT, BERTHE
BROOK, ESTHER--[8]

HUGGINS, RUTH MABEL ARTH.
ARTHUR, RUTH M.--[7]SF--4 NOVELS '67/79

HUGHES, CHARLES J. PENN.
HUGHES, C.J. PENNETHORNE--[31]
HUGHES, JAMES PENNETHORNE--[31]

HUGHES, DENNIS [TALBOT]
ASHTON, MARVIN--[7][23]SF,HP--
WARREN "PEOPLE OF ASA" '53
BARRY, RAY--[2][11][23]SF--
"DEATH DIMENSION" '52
"BLUE PERIL" '52
"GAMMA PRODUCT" '52
"HUMANOID PUPPETS" '52
"OMINUS FOLLY" '52
BROWN, GEORGE SHELDON--[7]SF,HP--
SELF "DESTINATION MARS" '51
SELF "PLANETOID PERIL" '52
SELF "THE YELLOW PLANET" '54
CAMERON, BERL--[1][2][11]SF,HP--
WARREN "MAID OF THURO" '52
WARREN "LAST EONS" '53
CARTER, DEE--[2][11][23]SGF,HP--
WARREN "BLUE CORDON" '52
WARREN "CLOROPLASM" '52
WARREN "PURPLE ISLANDS '53
CHARLES, NEIL--[2][7][11][23]SF,HP--
WARREN "BEYOND ZOASTER" 53
WARREN "LAND OF ESA"
WARREN "TWENTY-FOUR HOURS"
WARREN "PRE-GARGANTUA" '53
WARREN "WORLD OF GOL" '52
WARREN "RESEARCH OPTA" '53
ELLIOT, LEE--[1][2][11]SF,HP--
WARREN "BIO-MUTON" '52
GARON, MARCO--PPCC#2,[23]HP--
'REX BRANDON, WHITE HUNTER' SERIES-
12 NOVELS
HEINE, IRVING--P. HARBOTTLE-TB CKLST,PP#38--
TB "DIMENSION OF ILLION" '54
HEINE, IRVING--[23]SF--
"INVASION OF ILLION" '55
HUNT, GILL--[2][7][11][23]SF,HP--
WARREN "ELEKTRON UNION" '51
WARREN "HOSTILE WORLDS"
WARREN "PLANET X" '51
WARREN "SPACE FLIGHT" '51
WARREN "SPACIAL RAY" '51
KELLAR, VON--[7][23]SF,HP--
WARREN "IONIC BARRIER" '53
KENT, BRAD--[2][11][34]MYS,HP--
WARREN "BIOLOGY A" '52
WARREN "FATAL LAW" '52
WARREN "CATALYST" '52
LANE, JOHN--[1][7][11]SF,HP--
WARREN "MAMMALIA" '53

HUGHES, DENNIS [TALBOT] [CONT]
LE PAGE, RAND--[7][23]SF,HP--
WARREN "ASTEROID FORMULA" '53
MALCOLM, GRANT--[7][23][34]SF,HP--
WARREN "RAY ELLIS IN THE GREEN
MANDARIN MYSTERY" '50
MELDE, G.R.--[23]--
"PACIFIC ADVANCE" '54
REED, VAN--[1][2][11][23]SF,HP--
WARREN "HOUSE OF MANY CHANGES" '52
REY, RUSSELL--[2][7][23]SF,HP--
WARREN "VALLEY OF TERROR" '53
ROGERSOHN, WILLIAM--[7][23]SF,HP--
BW "AMIRO" '54
BW "NORTH DIMENSION" '54]
ROMILUS, ARN--[7]SF,HP--
WARREN "BRAIN PALAEO" '53
WARREN "ORGANIC DESTINY" '53
ROYCE, E.R.--[23]SF--
"EXPERIMENT IN TELEPATHY" '54
HUGHES, DOROTHY BELLE
FLANAGAN, DOROTHY BELLE--[31]

HUGHES, EDWARD J.
HUGHES, TED--[7][23]SF--
"TALES OF THE EARLY WORLD" '88

HUGHES, GWILYM FIELDEN
ENFIELD, HUGH--[2][7][11]SF--
FONTANA "KRONOS" '72

HUGHES, IVY
HAY, CATHERINE--[8]

HUGHES, JOHN CEIROG
CEIROG--[22] WELSH

HUGHES, RICHARD HOLLAND
HUGHES, DUSTY--[31]

HUGHES, RUSSELL MERIW.
LA MERI--[31]

HUGHES, THOMAS
OLD BOY--[33]
VIATOR, VACUUS--[33]

HUGHES, VALERIE ANNE
CARRINGTON, V.--[34]MYS--
BARKER "ONE MAN'S AWE" '56

HUGHES, W.T. MAINWARING
WARING, MAIN--[1][3]MYS--
MELROSE "CLINGING SHADOWS" '36

HUGHES, WALTER LLEWELLYN
WALTERS, HUGH--[7][8][11][23][31]SF--
FABER 'CHRIS GODFREY' SERIES-
#16-24 '75-86

HUGHES, WILLIAM JESSE
DOMINIE,[THE]--[1]ENGLISH
HALLAM--[1]ENGLISH
NORTHERNER--[1][8]ENGLISH

HUGHES,[JAMES] LANGSTON
SEMPLE, JESSE B.--[1]AMERICAN

HUGI, MAURICE G.
KENT, BRAD--[2][11][23]SF,HP--
WARREN "OUT OF SILENT PLACES" '52

HUGILL, JOHN ANTHONY
CRAWFORD, ANTHONY--[8]

HUGILL, ROBERT
ELGAR, SINTON--[34]MYS--
BW "DOUBLE DEATH" '55
GILL, HUGH--[1][8]ENGLISH

HUGILL, STANLEY JAMES
HUGILL, STAN JAMES--[31]

HUGO, LEON HARGREAVES
DE VILLIERS, VICTOR--[1]SOUTH AFRICAN
HUGO, ETIENNE--[1]SOUTH AFRICAN

HUIDODRO FERNANDEZ, VINC.
HUIDODRO, VINCENTE--[31]

HULBERT, JOAN MARGERY
ROSTRON, P.R.--[1]ENGLISH
ROSTRON, PRIMROSE--[1][8]ENGLISH

HULINE-DICKENS, FRANK W.
DICKENS, FRANK--[1][31][33]ENGLISH

HULL, CHARLES
C., R.B.--[3]MYS--
DILLINGHAM "REDEEMED" 1894

HULL, EDITH MAUDE
HULL, E.M.--FIRSTS NOV '94--
DELL 174 "THE SHEIK" '47
DELL 279 "SONS OF THE SHEIK" '49
DELL 402 "CAPTIVE OF THE SAHARA" '50

HULL, JAMES
RESTLESS, JIMMY--[1]

HULL, JESSIE REDDING
HULL, JESSE REDDING--[31][33]

HULL, RICHARD
SAMPSON, RICHARD HENRY--[8]

HULLAR, LEONARD EARL
HULLAR, LINK--[7]--
"AMAZING PULP HEROES" '88

HULME BEAMAN, SYDNEY G.
HULME BEAMAN, S.G.--[1]ENGLISH, NV

HULME, ANN
GRANGER, ANN--V. BERCH LTR TO
A. HUBIN '93/MYS--

HULME, JULIET
PERRY, ANNE--M. LACHMAN-TIME MAG ART.-
21 NOV '94,MYS--
ST. MARTIN'S "CATER ST. HANGMAN" '79
ST. MARTIN'S "CALLANDER SQUARE" '80
ST. MARTIN'S "RESURRECTION ROW" '81
ST. MARTIN'S "PARAGON WALK" '81
ST. MARTIN'S "RUTLAND PLACE" '83
ST. MARTIN'S "BLUEGATE FIELDS" '84
ST. MARTIN'S "DEATH IN THE DEVIL'S
ACRE" '85
ST. MARTIN'S "CARDINGTON CRESCENT" '87
ST. MARTIN'S "SILENCE IN HANOVER CLOSE" '88
ST. MARTIN'S "BETHLEHEM ROAD" '90

HULME, THOMAS ERNEST
GRATTON, THOMAS--[1][31]
HULME, T.E.--[31]
NORTH STAFFS--[1]

HULME-BEAMAN, EMERIC
STRONG, BEN--W/WILLIAM ELLIS,[3]

HULSENBECK, RICHARD
HULBECK, CHARLES R.--[39]GERMAN

HULTKRANTZ, AAKE G.B.
HULTKRANTZ, AKE G.B.--[31]

HUMBARACI, DEMIR ARSIAN
HERVE, JEAN-LUC--[31]

HUMBERT-DROZ, JULES
CARPENTIER, CHARLES--[1][32]MYS--
MH "GOODBYE" AUG '60
MH "PAIN KILLER" APR '61
MH "GUN LOVER" APR '62
MH "DEADLY AFFAIR" OCT '61
MH "A LICENSE TO KILL" AUG '62
JEAN CHRISTOPHE--[1]
LOUIS--[1]

HUMBLOT, PIERRE
KASSAK, FRED--[3][40]FRENCH/MYS--
"PLUS AMER QUE LA MORT" '57
"VOULEZ-VOUS TUER AVEC MOI" '70

HUME, ALEXANDER BRITTON
HUME, BRIT--[1]

HUME, FERGUSON WRIGHT
HUME, FERGUS--[1]ENGLISH, NV

HUME, GEORGE HALLIBURTON
HUME, BASIL--[31]

HUMM, MARTIN J.
NATIONS, OPAL L.--[8]

HUMMEL, BERTA
HUMMEL, SISTER MARIA I.--[31][33]

HUMPEL, ELKE
MINDEN, BERTE-EVE--[39]GERMAN/JUV

HUMPHREYS, ARTHUR LEE
PENDENYS, ARTHUR--[1]ENGLISH

HUMPHREYS, ELIZA M.J.G.
GILBERT, E. JAYNE--[34]MYS--
PHILPOTT "EPISODES" '24
RITA--[3][22][29]MYS--
NEWNES "GRIM JUSTICE" '07
& 10 MORE

HUMPHREYS, M.L.
HUMPHRIES, M.L.--[2]

HUMPHREYS, MARY E. HILL
HILL, POLLY--[22][31]ENGLISH

HUMPHREYS, ROBERT ARTHUR
HUMPHREYS, ROBIN A.--[31]

HUMPHRIES, ADELAIDE
HARRIS, KATHLEEN [M]--[1][8][11][22]AMERICAN
WAY, WAYNE--[1][8][22]AMERICAN
WEST, TOKEN--[1][8][22]AMERICAN
HARRIS, KATHLEEN--[31]

HUMPHRIES, BARRY
BARRY--[8]
EVERAGE, DAME EDNA--[31]

HUMPHRIES, ELSIE MARY
FORRESTER, MARY--[1][8][31]ENGLISH

HUMPHRIES, SYDNEY
VANE, MICHAEL--[1][8]

HUMPHRYS, LESLIE GEORGE
BRACK, VEKTIS--[1][2][11][31]SF,HP--
GANNET "ODYSSEY IN SPACE" '63
CONDRAY, BRUNO G.--P. HARBOTTLE-TB CKLST, PP#38,[2][7][11][23]SF--
TB "DISSENTIZENS" '54
TB "EXILE FROM JUPITER" '55
HUMPHRIES, GEOFFREY--[1][8][31]

HUNDLEY, MRS. E.D.
GREY, FANNIE--[1]

HUNDSDORFER, GERHARD
COLLINS, FREDERIC--[39]GERMAN/HOR,HP--
DE LORCA, FRANK--[39]GERMAN/HOR,HP--
ELLIOT, BRIAN--[39]GERMAN/HOR,HP--
FARRINGTON, ANN--[39]GERMAN/HOR
HOLZNER, SEBASTIAN--[39]GERMAN/HOR,HP--

HUNGERBUHLER, EBERHARD
HUBY, FELIX--[39][40]GERMAN/MYS/JUV
"EINBRUCH IM LABOR" '77
KNOCK, CHRISTOPHER--[39]GERMAN/MYS/JUV

HUNPHREY, PAUL
MORRISON, EDWARD--[1]

HUNSBERGER, EDITH MAE
MAE, EYDIE--[1]

HUNSBURGER, H. EDWARD
CARTER, NICK--[34]MYS,HP--
CHART "PARISIAN AFFAIR" '81
FLETCHER, FARRIS--[21]ROM,HP--
'THE TEXANS' SERIES: "YELLOW ROSE"
MURPHY, WARREN--[7]MYS,HP--
'DESTROYER' SERIES: #57 & #62

HUNT, ANNA REBECCA GALE
BERWICK, CLAUDE--[8]
CANADIENNE--[8]

HUNT, BARBARA
WATTERS, BARBARA H.--[1]AMERICAN

HUNT, BERNICE KOHN
KOHN, BERNICE--[1][31]AMERICAN

HUNT, CYNTHIA WRIGHT
LINDSAY, DEVON--[9][21][26]ROM--
"CRIMSON INTRIGUE"
WRIGHT, CYNTHIA--[21][26]ROM--
"TOUCH THE SUN"
"NATALYA" & MORE

HUNT, DARRELL
NELSON, CHRIS--[8]
WEST, MARK--[8]

HUNT, DAVID CHARLES H.
HUNT, DAVE--[31]

HUNT, E. HOWARD
BAXTER, JOHN--[1][5][29][31]ADULT/SF--
PILLAR & CORINTH '54-62
AV T78 "A FOREIGN AFFAIR" '54
AV 647 "UNFAITHFUL" '55
ACE G588 "OFF-WORLDERS" '66
PAPLB 66-420 "SF IN THE CINEMA" '70
DAVIS, GORDON--J. REASONER-'ONE-SHOT EYES' PP 9, V. BERCH-GM PSEUDS, PP 33, [3][5]MYS--
GM 349 "I CAME TO KILL" '53
GM 1103 "HOUSE DICK" '61
GM 1348 "COUNTERFEIT KILL" '63
GM 1380 "RING AROUND THE ROSY" '64

HUNT, E. HOWARD [CONT]
DAVIS, GORDON [CONT]
GM 1531 "WHERE MURDER WAITS" '65
DIETRICH, ROBERT--[3][5][18][31]MYS--
PYR 128 "ONE FOR THE ROAD" '54
PYR 135 "THE CHEAT" '54
DELL FE106 "BE MY VICTIM" '56
DELL FE A141 "MURDER ON THE ROCKS" '57
DELL FE A175 "HOUSE ON Q STREET" '59
DELL FE A197 "END OF A STRIPPER" '60
DELL FE B162 "MISTRESS TO MURDER" '60
DELL FE B163 "MURDER ON HER MIND" '60
DELL FE B "STEVE BENTLEY'S CALYPSO CAPER" '61
DELL FE B203 "ANGEL EYES" '61
LAN 70-010 "CURTAINS FOR A LOVER" '61
LAN 71-311 "MY BODY" '62
DONOGHUE, P.S.--DDLY PLEAS #3,[34]MYS--
FINE "DUBLIN AFFAIR" '88
FINE "SANKOV CONFESSION" '89
EDUARDO--[1]
SALISBURY, ROBERT--[29]MYS
ST. JOHN, DAVID--[3][5][18]MYS--
SIGN "RETURN FROM VORKUTA" '65
SIGN "ON HAZZARDOUS DUTY" '65
SIGN "VENUS PROBE" '66
WEYBRIGHT "DIABOLUS" '71 & MORE

HUNT, EDGAR HUBERT
FIDELIO--[31]

HUNT, GREG
CALHOUN, CHAD--CRPG, WEST,HP--
DELL "PAINTED WOMEN" '81
DRURY, REBECCA--[21]ROM,HP--
'WOMEN AT WAR' SERIES:
"MOURNING & TRIUMP"
"WIVES & WIDOWS"
"SPLENDID VICTORY"
"MISSION TO DARKNESS"
WILLOUGHBY, LEE DAVIS--[21]ROM,HP--
DELL 'MKNG OF AMER' SERIES:
"RIVER PEOPLE"

HUNT, ISAAC
RETORT, JACK--[1] BARBADOS

HUNT, KATHERINE CHANDLER
NASH, CHANDLER--[1][8][22][34][40]MYS--
MacM "MURDER IS MY SHADOW" '60

HUNT, LINDA LAWRENCE
LAWRENCE, LINDA--[1][33]

HUNT, MARGARET RAINE
BEAUMONT, AVERIL--[1]ENGLISH

HUNT, MARY EVE
HUNT, EVE--[1]

HUNT, ROY
COUNCIL OF FOUR--W/TOM WALKER, CHUCK HANSEN, NORM METCALF, ELLIS MILLS, BOB PETERS,[2]

HUNT, WALTER & LISA
ARCHITECHS ADVENTURE--W/RICHARD S. MEYERS/ EVAN JAMIESON/BILL SCAMMELL/ MARK BLOOM 7 CHRISTINE IVEY,[7]

HUNT,[J.H.] LEIGH
HONEYCOMB, HENRY--[1]ENGLISH
SKIMPOLE, HAROLD--[1]ENGLISH
SPRAT, JOHN--[2]

HUNT-BODE, GISELE
HUNT, DIANA--[8]

HUNTER BLAIR, PAULINE C.
CLARE, HELEN--[1][31][33]ENGLISH
CLARKE, PAULINE--[1][31][33]ENGLISH

HUNTER BLAIR, PETER
BLAIR, PETER--[1][31]ENGLISH

HUNTER, ALFRED JOHN
ADDISCOMBE, JACK--[34]MYS--
GRAMOL "SECRET OF THE GRAVEYARD" '37
GRAMOL "SILK SCARF MURDERS" '37
ADDISCOMBE, JOHN--[1][34]MYS--
5 NOVELS '29-37
BRENNING, L.H.--[1][34]MYS--
CASSELL "PARISIAN LOVE" '26
CASSELL "DEATH PLOT" '31 & MORE
BRENT, FRANCIS--[1]
DAX, ANTHONY--[1][34]MYS--
WORLD'S WORK "THE MAN BEHIND" '37
DRUMMOND, ANTHONY--[1][34]MYS--
UNWIN "SCENTED DEATH" '24
GRAMOL "BLOOD MONEY" '35 & MORE
HUNTER, JEAN--[1]
HUNTER, JOHN--[8][32]MYS--
SA "SIGN OF THE SEVEN" JAN '55
MERITON, PETER--[1][34]MYS--
AMALG "MAN FROM MADRID" '43
HURST "CONSPIRACY" '45 & MORE
WORTHING, TEMPLE--[34]MYS--
GRAMOL & MOWL, 7 NOVELS '34-7

HUNTER, BLUEBELL MATILDA
GUILDFORD, JOHN--[1][3][22]MYS--
GRAYSON "DEATH DAMS THE TIDE" '32
GRAYSON "BIG BEN LOOKS ON" '33
LANCING, GEORGE--[1][2][11]

HUNTER, CHRISTINE
HUNTER, JOHN--[8]
STEER, CHARLOTTE--[8]

HUNTER, EILEEN
CLEMENTS, E.H.--[1][8]ENGLISH
LAURA--[8]

HUNTER, EVAN
ABBOTT, JOHN--LACHMAN/B. CRIDER LST '93/MYS--
"SCIMITAR" '92-DENIED BY "HUNTER"
PER SUE FEDER
CANNON, CURT--MUNROE SLST 20/V. BERCH-
GM PSEUDS. PP 33,[2][3][5][18]MYS--
GM 814 "I'M CANNON-FOR HIRE" '59
GM 743 "I LIKE 'EM TOUGH" '58 [SS COLL]
COLLINS, HUNT--MUNROE SLST 20,[3][5]
[7][23][32]--
PE "DETOUR" DEC "53
ABELAIRD "CUT ME IN" '54
PU "JOKER" JAN '55
VM "EYE-WITNESS" AUG '56
AVALON "TOMORROW'S WORLD" '56
VM "EYE-WITNESS" AUG '56 & OTHERS
BL "ATTACK" SEPT '61
BL "THE FOLLOWER" JAN '62
MH "CIRCUMSTANTIAL EVIDENCE" APR-MAY '67
EVANS, HODGE--M. SWIATKOWSKI LTR '93--
FAL 24 "THREE FOR PASSION" '52
FAL 33 "YELLOW-HEAD" '52
HANNON, EZRA--[2][3][31]MYS--
STEIN "DOORS" '75
MARSTEN, RICHARD--MUNROE SLST 20
V. BERCH-GM PSEUDS, PP 33,[2][3][5][32]MYS--
GM 415 "RUNAWAY BLACK" '54
GM 507 "MURDER IN THE NAVY" '55
HOLT "SPIKED HEEL" '56
CREST 139 "SO NUDE, SO DEAD" '56
PERM M3097 "VANISHING LADIES" '57
PERM M3117 "EVEN THE WICKED" '58

HUNTER, EVAN [CONT]
MARSTEN, RICHARD [CONT]
PENG "BIG MAN" '59
20 STRS [AC, AHMM, BL, HU, MH, MN PU & VM]
MCBAIN, ED--MUNROE SLST 20,[2][5][32][34]MYS--
NOVELS--12 DIGEST STORIES

HUNTER, GWEN F.
HUNTER, GARY--W/GARY LEVEILLE, LACHMAN-
EASTER LST '93,[34]--
WARNER "DEATH WARRANT" '90

HUNTER, HENRY
HUDSON, HARRY--[1]

HUNTER, HENRY MACGREGOR
HUNTER, MAC--[31]

HUNTER, IAN MCLELLAN
RUSH, PHILIP--W/RINGGOLD W. LARDNER JR.,[1]

HUNTER, KIM
COLE, JANET--[31]

HUNTER, MAUDE LILY
HUNTER, CHRISTINE--[1][22][31]ENGLISH--
"AGAINST ALL ODDS" '50
HUNTER, JOHN--W/W.T. BALLARD,[1][22][31]--
"MICHAEL GRAHAM, POLICE CADET" '59
STEER, CHARLOTTE--[1][22]

HUNTER, VICTORIA ALBERT
HUNTER, VICKIE--[31]
HUNTER, VICKIE MACLEAN--[1][22]AMERICAN

HUNTER, WILLIAM F.
RETNUH X--[1]AMERICAN

HUNTER, WILLIAM R.
HAGEN, BRETT--[8]

HUNTER-BLAIR, NORMA
HUNTER, ALISON--[1]ENGLISH

HUNTINGTON, E. STANTON
STANTON, EDWARD--[2]

HUNTINGTON, HELEN
LYNDE, H.H.--[8]

HUNTINGTON, THOMAS W.
FROST, MORGAN--[1]

HUNTLEY, CHESTER ROBERT
HUNTLEY, CHET--[31]

HUNZICKER, BEATRICE PLUMB
PLUMB, BEATRICE--[1][22]ENGLISH-AMERICAN

HUPPERTZ, MARGOT
MARTIN, GIGI--[39]GERMAN

HURBAN, SVETOZAR
VAJANSKY--[22] SLOVAK
VAJANSKY, SVETOZAR HURBAN--[22] SLOVAK

HURD, EDITH THATCHER
SAGE, JUNIPER--W/MARGARET W. BROWN,
[1][22][31]--
"THE MAN IN THE MAN-HOLE
& THE FIX-IT MEN" '46

HURD, FLORENCE
HILLER, FLORA--[9][21][26][31]ROM--
"LOVE'S FIERY DAGGER"

HURD, FLORENCE S.
HARROWE, FIONA--[9][21][26][31]ROM--
"BRIDGE OF FIRE"
"DARK OBSESSION" & MORE

HURLEY, DORAN
MCGREGOR--[1][22]AMERICAN

HURLEY, JOHN JEROME
CARPENTER, DUFFY--LACHMAN LST '93,[31][32]MYS--
EQMM "LAST CIGAR" JUL '76
AHMM "LAST OF THE BIG-TIME SPENDERS" NOV '76
AHMM "FIRST MOON TOURIST" DEC '76
AHMM "MIRACLE IN SMALL CLAIMS COURT" DEC '76
RAFFERTY, S.S.--[32][34]--
AVON "FATAL FLOURISHES" '79
INPO "DIE LAUGHING & OTHER MURDER SHTICK" '84
AHMM & EQMM DIGEST STORIES

HURLEY, VIC
DUANE, JIM--[1][8][22][31]AMERICAN
RICHARDS, DUANE--[1][8][22]AMERICAN

HURREN, BERNARD JOHN
GARSTON, GUY--[1][34]MYS--
MULLER "THE CHAMPAIGN MYS" '35
NOTT, BARRY--[1][8]ENGLISH

HURST, KATHRYN
BROOKS, KATE--[34]MYS--
MANOR "SECRET OF KILLER MOUNTAIN INN" '78
MANOR "MURDER IN THE LABORATORY" '79
MANOR "IMMACULATE MURDERS" '79

HURST, VIRGINIA RADCLIFFE
RADCLIFFE, VIRGINIA--[1]AMERICAN

HURT, EDWIN FRANKLIN
FRANKLIN, E.--[8]

HURT, ROLF
VON SUMAROW, ROTISLAW--[39]GERMAN

HURWITZ, RUTH [SAPIN]
SAPIN, RUTH--[1]

HURWOOD, BERNHARDT J.
KNIGHT, MALLORY T.--[2][11][23][31]--
'MAN FROM T.O.M.C.A.T.' SERIES
'INVISIBLES' SERIES
WILDE, D. GUNTHER--[1][33]
XAVIER, [FATHER]--[1][31][33]

HUSER, LAVERN CARL
BOUGH, LEE--[1][31]--
CONTRIB TO MAGS - 'ADVENTURE TRAIL' & 'SPORTS ILLUS.'
HUSER, VERNE--[31]

HUSKINSON, RICHARD KING
KING, RICHARD--[1][8]ENGLISH

HUSSERL, EDMUND GUSTAVE A
HUSSERL, E.G.--[31]

HUSSEY, TONY
GARFORTH, JOHN--CRPG/ROM--
DELL 6847 "THE PALLISERS" '75

HUSTOFT, PAUL
REED, PAUL--[1]

HUTCHCROFT, VERA
RICHTER, VERNON--[1]AMERICAN

HUTCHIN, KENNETH CHARLES
CHALLICE, KENNETH--[8][31]
FAMILY DOCTOR, A--[8]
TRAVERS, KENNETH--[8]

HUTCHINGS, WILLIAM BRUCE
HUTCHINGS, BILL--[31]

HUTCHINS, FRANCIS GILMAN
MADISON, FRANK--[1][8]AMERICAN

HUTCHINSON, ARTHUR S-M.
HUTCHINSON, A.S.M.--[1]ENGLISH--NOVELS

HUTCHINSON, BARBARA BEAT.
FEARN, ROBERTA--[8]

HUTCHINSON, HORACE GORDON
GORDON, HORATIO--[1]

HUTCHINSON, JOHN
LADYLIFT--[1]ENGLISH

HUTCHINSON, JOYCE
BAIRD, WILHELMINA--AUTHOR PROVIDED/SF--
ACE "CRASHCOURSE" '93
ACE "CLIPJOINT" '94
JAMES, KATHLEEN--AUTHOR PROVIDED/SF--
F&SF "BLIND GOD'S EYES" & 2 OTHER SS

HUTCHINSON, JULIET MARY F
PHOENICE, J.--[8]

HUTCHINSON, PATRICIA
FULLBROOK, GLADYS--[9][21][26]ROM--
"BUSH HOSPITAL"
"MAGIC MOMENT" & MORE

HUTCHINSON, RAY CORYTON
HUTCHINSON, R.C.--[1]ENGLISH--NOVELS

HUTCHINSON, ROBERT HARE
HARE, ROBERT--[2][3][22]MYS--
HURST "SPECTRAL EVIDENCE" '32
HURST "DRS. FIRST MURDER" '33
HURST "HAND OF THE CHIMPANZEE" '34

HUTCHINSON, WILLIAM
SANDS, JOHN--[1]AMERICAN

HUTCHISON, GRAHAM SETON
SETON, GRAHAM--[2][3][22]MYS--
HUTCH "EYE FOR AN EYE" '32
HUTCH "BLOOD MONEY" '34 & MORE

HUTCHISSON, W.H. FLORIO
TRIGGER, GEORGE--[1]

HUTH, MARY JOSEPHINE
HUTH, MARY JO--[31]

HUTSON, SHAUN
BISHOP, SAMUEL P.--[2][28]HOR--
STAR "SLUGS" '82
HAMLYN "THE SKULL" '82 & 18 MORE
BLAKE, NICK--[2][28]HOR--
STAR "CHAINSAW MASSACRE" '84
DICKINSON, MIKE--[2][28] JUV--
DEUTSCH "RAMBLING RAT" '85
DEUTSCH "SMUDGE" '87 & 2 MORE
HAROLD, CLIVE--[28]HOR--
ALLEN "THE UNINVITED" '79

HUTSON, SHAUN [CONT]
KRUGER, WOLF--[2][28] REPRINTS OF 5 BKS AS BY 'BISHOP'
LAMBERT, TOM--[2]
MACREADY, R.J.--[2]
NEVILLE, ROBERT--[2][7]SF-- LEIS "DEATHDAY" '89
ROSTOV, STEFAN--[2][28]-- ALLEN "SABRES IN THE SNOW" '85
TAYLOR, FRANK--[2][28]HOR-- ALLEN "UNINVITED II" '84 ALLEN "UNINVITED III" '85

HUTT, MRS. W.
BUTT, BEATRICE MARY--[1]

HUTTNER, DORALIES
DORN, LISA--[39]GERMAN/JUV

HUTTON, ANDREW NEILSON
OLYMPIC--[8]

HUTTON, AUDREY GRACE W.
HUTTON, ANN--[21]ROM-- "PASSPORT TO PERIL"
WHITNELL, BARBARA--[1][26]/ROM-- "CROSS CURRENTS" "THE RING OF BELLS" "SONG OF THE RAINBIRD"

HUTTON, VIRGINIA CAROL
HUTTON, GINGER--[1][31]AMERICAN

HUTZINGER, THERESA
VOGGENBERGER, RESA--[39]GERMAN/JUV

HUXLEY, HERBERT HENRY
STENUS--[22]ENGLISH

HUXLEY, JULIAN SORRELL
BALBUS--[8][31]
J.S.H.--[8]

HUXLEY, RENA
BRIAND, RENA--[1]AUSTRALIAN

HUXTABLE, MARJORIE
DARE, SIMON--[1][8]
STEWART, MARJORIE--[8]

HUYGEN, WILLIBRORD J.
HUYGEN, WIL--[1]

HUYGHUE, DOUGLAS S.
EUGENE--[1][8] CANADIAN

HUYSMAN, CHARLES H.G.
HUYSMAN, J.K.--[1] FRENCH
HUYSMAN, JORIS KARL--[1] FRENCH

HUZARD, ANTOINETTE DE B.
YVER, COLETTE--[1] FRENCH

HYATT, BETTY HALE
HALE, JADE--[31]

HYATT, STANLEY PORTAL
DACRE, [CAPTAIN] STANLEY--[1]ENGLISH

HYDE, ALAN
WARD, TAYLOR--[11], LACHMAN LST '93

HYDE, ANTHONY
CHASE, NICHOLAS--W/CHRISTOPHER HYDE,[1][31]-- "LOCKSLEY"

HYDE, CHRISTOPHER
CHASE, NICHOLAS--W/ANTHONY HYDE, F. FIORELLA,[1]-- "LOCKSLEY"

HYDE, DAYTON O[GDEN]
HYDE, HAWK--[1][31][33]AMERICAN

HYDE, EDMUND ERROL CLAUD
REJJE, E.--[8]

HYDE, ELIZABETH A[DSHEAD]
HYDE, E.A. WATSON--[1]ENGLISH

HYDE, LAVENDER BERYL
ASHE, ELIZABETH--[8]

HYDE, THOMAS ALEXANDER
DOUBLE, LUKE--[1] SCOTTISH

HYDEN, NILS
HEINITZ, RALF--[29]MYS-- "MR. SWANSON" '07
LIND, EINAR--[29]MYS-- "KAMPEN OM DOLLARS" '09

HYLAND, ANN
ROSS, LAURENCE--[1][8]ENGLISH
TRAILRIDER--[1][8]ENGLISH

HYLAND, M.E.F.
WYLWYNNE, KYTHE--[1][2]

HYMAN, JACKIE DIAMOND
DIAMOND, JACQUELINE--[7][9][21][26]ROM/SF-- "DREAM NEVER DIES" "FLIGHT OF MAGIC" & MORE
JADE, JACQUELINE--[9][21][31]ROM-- "A LUCKY STAR"
TOPAZ, JACQUELINE--[9][21][26]ROM-- "GOLDEN GIRL" "SWEPT AWAY" & MORE

HYMAN, SHIRLEY JACKSON
JACKSON, SHIRLEY--[1][32]AMERICAN/MYS-- EQMM "THIS IS THE LIFE" JUN '58

HYMERS, LAURA M.
WEST, LAURA M.--[8]

HYNAM, JOHN
KIPPAX, JOHN--[2][7][11][32]SF-- LM "SO MUCH IN COMMON" DEC '59 PAN "WHERE NO STARS GUIDE" '75

HYNAM, JOHN C.
FREY, JULIAN--[2]

HYND, LAVINIA LEITCH
LEITCH, LAVINIA--[1][2][11]

HYNDMAN, JANE ANDREWS
WYNDHAM, LEE--[8][33]FANTASY LIT. FOR CHILDREN & YOUNG ADULTS, RUTH NADELMAN

HYNDMAN, ROBERT UTLEY
WYNDHAM, ROBERT--[1][8][33]AMERICAN

HYNE, AILEEN
HUMPHREY, AILEEN--[26]ROM-- "THE GOLDEN SWAN" "SWEET IRIS"

HYNE, CHARLES J CUTCLIFFE
CHESNEY, WEATHERBY--[2][3][16][31]MYS-- METHUEN "FOUNDERED GALLEON" '02 & MORE

HYNE, CHARLES J CUTCLIFFE [CUNT]
HYNE, C.J. CUTCLIFFE--[1][8]
HYNE, CUTCLIFFE--[8]
JONES, ALICK--W/WETHERBY CHESNEY [ALSO HYNE],[23]SF--
METHUEN "FOUNDERED GALLEON" '02

HYNNES, LUCETTA L.
LIGHT, CAROLINE--[9][21][26]ROM--
"A GIFT IN SECRET"
"MINOR ROYALTY"

IACOCCA, LIDO ANTHONY
IACOCCA, LEE--[31]

IAKIMOV, ALEKSANDR V.
GRIN, ELMAR--[1]

IAMS, SAMUEL HARVEY JR.
IAMS, JACK--[31][34]MYS--
MRW "GIRL MEETS BODY" '47
MRW "DEATH DRAWS THE LINE" '49 & 4 MORE
MRW "INTO THIN AIR" '52
GOLZ "A CORPSE OF THE OLD SCHOOL" '55

IANNELLI, RICHARD
WAGNER, DENSON--[1]

IANNONE, JEANNE [K]
BALZANO, JEANNE--[1][31]
BELL, GINA--[1][31][33]
BELL-ZANO, GINA--[1][31]

IANNONE, RONALD VINCENT
IANNONE, RON--[31]

IBBOTT, ARTHUR PEARSON
BERTRAM, ARTHUR--[8]

IBERER, ERIKA
BEIGEL, ERIKA--[39]GERMAN/JUV

IBSEN, HENRIK [JOHAN]
BJARME, BRYNJOLF--[22][31]NORWEGIAN

ICHIKAWA, KON
CHRISTIE--[31]

ICKES, JOHANNES
MARSCHALL, HANNS--[39]GERMAN/MYS

ICKES, PAUL
BURNS, MARK--[39]GERMAN/MYS

IDE, FRANCIS OTIS [A.L.]
OGDEN, RUTH--[1]AMERICAN

IDE, HEINO
BERRY, HENRY--[39]GERMAN/MYS/WEST
COLINGS, EDDY--[39]GERMAN/MYS/WEST
GRAY, BILL--[39]GERMAN/MYS/WEST

IDE, SIMEON
THEIR WELLWISHER--[1]AMERICAN

IDELL, ALBERT E.
ROGERS, PHILLIPS--[1]

IDLE, ERIC
PYTHON, MONTY--[31]--CO-WROTE SCREENPLAYS W/CHAPMAN, CLEESE, GILLIAM, PALIN & T. JONES

IGNOTUS, PAL
IGNOTUS, PAUL--[1]HUNGARIAN-ENGLISH

IHLE, SHARON J.
CAMERON, JUNE--[26]ROM--
"GYPSY JEWEL"
MACIVER, SHARON--[21]ROM--
"DAKOTA DREAM"
"RIVER SONG"

ILEISTER, JEAN SINCLAIR
ILEISTER, CLAIR--[1]

ILGERT, BEATE
PROBSTING, BEATE--[39]GERMAN

ILIFF, GEORGE
G.I.--[1]ENGLISH

ILIFF, JOHN EDGAR
EDGEFIELD, PAUL--[1]AMERICAN

ILLNER, WOLFGANG
SERRA, RALPH--[39]GERMAN

ILLYIN, M.A.
OSORGIN, M.A.--[22]RUSSIAN

ILMER, WALTHER
MORRIS, CLAUDE--[39]GERMAN/MYS/WEST

ILOGU, EDMUND C.O.
EDILOG--[1]NIGERIAN

ILYIN, MIKHAIL A.
OSURGIN, MIKHAIL A.--[1]RUSSIAN

IMBERT-TERRY, HENRY MACHU
TERRY, HENRY MACHU--[1]

IMBODEN, DURANT
DURANT, CHERYL--[9][21][26]ROM--
"BITTERSWEET IN BERN"

IMESCH, LUDWIG
ESCH, L. IM--[39]GERMAN

INCE, MARTIN JEFFREY
BRENT, BERYL--[31]

IND, ALLISON
STANLEY, PHIL--[1][22]AMERICAN
WALLACE, RICHARD--[1][22]AMERICAN

INDERLIED, MARY ELIZABETH
EDWARDS, ELIZABETH--[31]

INDRIDASON, INDRIDI
IDAL, SVEINN--[1]ICELANDIC
SVEINSSON, ASLAKUR--[1]ICELANDIC

INFIELD, GLENN [B]
POWERS, GEORGE--[1][22]AMERICAN
RODGERS, FRANK--[1][22]AMERICAN
TOLBY, ARTHUR--[1][22]AMERICAN

INGAMELLS, F.G.
HOME GUARD--[8]

INGE, WILLIAM RALPH
INGE, W.R.--[1][31]ENGLISH--NOVELS

INGELOW, JEAN
JOHN, DON--[1]ENGLISH
ORRIS--[1][33]ENGLISH

INGHAM, HENRY LLOYD
ALLEN, CHESTER--[28]ENGLISH/WEST--
8 JENKINS NOVELS '52-57

INGHAM, MRS. W.A.
HATHAWAY, ANNE--[1]AMERICAN

INGHAMS, RICHARD REID
REID, PHILIP--W/ANDREW OSMOND,[1][3]

INGLIS, JAMES
MAORI--[1]NEW ZEALIAN

INGRAHAM, ELLEN M.
LINTNER, GRACE--[1]

INGRAHAM, PRENTISS
BURR, DANGERFIELD--[1]AMERICAN
DUNBAR, NOEL--[1]AMERICAN
ERWIN, HOWARD W.--[1]AMERICAN
GRAHAM, [LT.] PRESTON--[1]AMERICAN
HALL, [MIDSHIPMAN] TOM W.--[1]AMERICAN
INMAN, ROBERT RANDOLPH--[1]AMERICAN
KING, T.W.--[1]AMERICAN
KING, [MIDSHIPMAN] TOM W.--[1]AMERICAN
LAFITTE, [COL.] LEON--[1]AMERICAN
LAWSON, W.B.--[1]AMERICAN
OMAHUNDRO, J.B.--[1]AMERICAN
PERRY, HARRY DENNIES--[1]AMERICAN
POWELL, FRANK--[1]AMERICAN
STODDARD, [MAJ.] HENRY B.--[1]AMERICAN
TAYLOR, [CAPT.] ALFRED B.--[1]AMERICAN

INGRAM, FORREST L[EO]
VAN RIJN, IGNATIUS--[1]AMERICAN

INGRAM, JOHN H.
SALAMANCA, D.F. SE--[1]ENGLISH
SALAMANCA, DON FELIX DE--[1]ENGLISH

INGRAM, M.R. BOWEN P.
INGRAM, BOWEN--[31]ENGLISH

INGRAM, THOMAS HENRY
INGRAM, TOM--[7][31]SF--
BRADBURY PRESS "THE NIGHT RIDER" '75

INGRAM-MOORE, ERICA
MARSDEN, JUNE--[8]

INGRAMS, RICHARD REID
REID, PHILIP--W/ANDREW OSMOND,[1][8][34]MYS--
CAPE "HARRIS IN WONDERLAND" '73
THRIBB, E.J.--W/BARRY FANTONI,[1][8]ENGLISH

INGWALSON, PHOEBE C.
CONN, PHOEBE--[9][21]ROM--
"ARIZONA ANGEL"
"EMERALD FIRE" & MORE

INHOFE, SUSAN ELOISE H.
HINTON, S.E.--[1]AMERICAN

INKSTER, LEONARD
FETHALAND, JOHN--[3]MYS--
GOLZ "MURDER AT CHARTERS" '39

INNES, BRIAN
POWELL, NEIL--[1]ENGLISH

INNES, DUNCAN
D.I.--[1]SCOTTISH

INNES, ROSEMARY E.J.
JACKSON, R.E.--[1]SCOTTISH

INNES, [RALPH] HAMMOND
HAMMOND, RALPH--[18]MYS/JUV--
"COCOS GOLD" '50
"ISLE OF STRANGERS" '53
"SARACEN'S TOWER" '52

INOSUKE, TSURUYA
NAMBOKU, TSURUYA--[22]JAPANESE

INVREA, GASPARE
ZENA, REMIGIO--[22]ITALIAN

IONE, CAROLE
IONE--[31]

IONS, EDMUND S.
AUBREY, EDMUND--[3]MYS--
DODD "SHERLOCK HOLMES IN DALLAS" '80

IRANEK-OSMECKI, KAZ.
ANTONI--[1][31]POLISH
HELLER--[1][31]POLISH
MAKARY--[1][31]POLISH

IRELAND, M.J.
MAXWELL, JOSLYN--[1][2]

IRELAND, MABEL ISABEL
CROOKS, MARION--[1]AUSTRALIAN

IRELAND, SANDRA L. JONES
JONES, SANDRA L.--[31]

IRISH, BETTY M.
ARTHUR, ELISABETH--[8]

IRON, MRS. N.C.
STELLA--[1]AMERICAN, MARRIED TO NATHANIEL IRON

IRON, NATHANIEL COLV.
COLLIER, OLD CAP--[1]AMERICAN, SP
HAWKSHAW THE DETECTIVE--[1]AMERICAN

IRONSIDE, JETSKE
YETSKA--[33]

IRVIN, ROBERT W.
IRVIN, BOB--[31]

IRVINE, EDWARD JAMES
RAY, VIOLET--[1]AMERICAN

IRVINE, ROBERT RALSTONE
IRVINE, R.R. --[32][34]MYS--
POPLB "JUMP CUT" '74
EQMM "LOBSTER SHIFT" MAR '73
EQMM "ANOTHER CASE OF IDENTITY" FEB '74
EQMM "IN THE DEAD HOURS" OCT '75
POPLB "FREEZE FRAME" '76 & 3 MORE
IRVINE, ROBERT --[34]MYS--
DODDM "BAPTISM FOR THE DEAD" '88
ST. MARTIN'S "ANGEL'S SHARE" '89
ST. MARTIN'S "GONE TO GLORY" '90

IRVING, CLIFFORD MICHAEL
ANDERSON, CLIFFORD--W/ROBERT ANDERSON & RICHARD GARDNER,[1]
LUCKLESS, JOHN--W/HERBERT BURKHOLTZ, [3][29]MYS--
SUMMIT "THE DEATH FREAK" '78

IRVING, HENRY BRODRIBB
IRVING, H.B.--[1][32]ENGLISH/MYS--
JCM "AFFAIR AR SIDI MABROUK" APR '61

IRVING, JOHN TREAT
QUOD, JOHN--[8]

IRVING, NOEL
GRINGOIRE--[1]ENGLISH

IRVING, THOMAS J.
HART, GERALD--[1]AMERICAN

IRVING, WASHINGTON
AGAPIDA, FRAY ANTONIO--[33]
CRAYON, GEOFFREY--[31][33]
KNICKERBOCKER, DIEDRICH--[31][33]
LANGSTAFF, LAUNCELOT--[31][33]
OLDSTYLE, JONATHAN--[33]

IRWIN, ANNABELLE BOWEN
IRWIN, ANN--[31]
IRWIN, HADLEY--W/LEE HADLEY,[1][31][33]JUV

IRWIN, CONSTANCE F.
FRICK, C.H.--[1][22][31][33]AMERICAN
FRICK, CONSTANCE--[1][22][31][33]AMERICAN

IRWIN, DIANNE
JOYCE, JOANNA--[35]AUSTRALIAN--
HRWTZ PB325 "THE SWINGERS" '67
HRWTZ PB378 "IT'S ALRIGHT, MA,
I'M ONLY SIGHING" '68

IRWIN, H.C.
TIME, MARK--[1][2]

IRWIN, INEZ HAYNES
GILLMORE, INEZ HAYNES--[1][23]AMERICAN/SF--
HUEBSCH "JUNE JEOPARDY" '08
HUEBSCH "ANGEL ISLAND" '14

IRWIN, JOHN THOMAS
BRICUTH, JOHN--[31]

IRWIN, MARIANNE
GRANT, SARA--[21][26]ROM--
"THE SCORPIO MAN"
"A CHILD CALLED MATTHEW"

IRWIN-WILLIAMS, CYNTHIA C
IRWIN, CYNTHIA C.--[31]

ISAACS, ALAN
VALENTINE, ALEC--[1]ENGLISH

ISAACS, LEVI
ESSEX, LOUIS--[1][3]ENGLISH/MYS--
AMALG "CROOK OF CRAWFORD COURT" '30

ISAACS, MARCEL GODFREY
GODFREY, MARCEL--[1]ENGLISH
LOFTY--[1]ENGLISH

ISAACS, SUSAN S.F.
BRIERLEY, SUSAN S.--[31]

ISAKOV, M.V.
ISAKOVSKY, MICHAIL VASIL.--[22]RUSSIAN

ISBELL, SHANNON
SHANNON, ISBELL--[2]

ISBISTER, JEAN SINCLAIR
IBISTER, CLAIR--[31]AUSTRALIAN--NON-FICT

ISHIKAW, HAJIME
ISHIKAWA, HAKUHIN--[1]
ISHIKAWA, TAKUBOKU--[1]

ISLER, ELIZABETH
ISLER, BETH--[31]

ISLER, URSULA
JUCKER, IWAN--[1]SWISS

ISOGAI, HIROSHI
KO, KANZEIN--[31]JAPANESE

ISRAEL, ELMO
ELLIS, ELMO I.--[1]AMERICAN

ISRAEL, J. LEON
ISRAEL, PETER--[3][29][40]MYS--
CROWELL "HUSH MONEY" '75
CROWELL "FRENCH KISS" '76
CROWELL "STIFF UPPER LIP" '78

IUOZENAS, ALBERTUS
BALTUSHIS, IUOZAS--[1]

IVAN, GUSTAVE E.
TAVO, GUS--W/MARTHA MILLER IVAN,
[1][22]AMERICAN

IVAN, MARTHA MILLER
MILLER, MARTHA--[1][22]AMERICAN
TAVO, GUS--W/GUSTAVE E. IVAN,[1][22]AMERICAN

IVANOV, RAZUMNIK VASILY.
IVANOV-RAZUMNIK--[22]RUSSIAN

IVENS, GEORG HENRI ANTON
IVENS, JORIS--[31]

IVENS, MICHAEL WILLIAM
YORICK--[1]ENGLISH

IVES, EDWARD D[AWSON]
IVES, SANDY--[1][31]AMERICAN

IVES, MARY ALICE
OCTAVIA--[1]

IVESTER, LLOYD J.
BABBLER--[22]ENGLISH
FARMER, PETER--[22]ENGLISH
LODGER, THE--[22]ENGLISH

IVEY, CHRISTINE
ARCHITECHS ADVENTURE--W/RICHARD MEYER/
WALTER & LISA HUNT/EVAN JAMIESON/
BILL SCAMMELL/MARK BLOOM,[7]

IVEY, JAMES BURNETT
IVEY, JIM--[31]

IVISON, ELIZABETH
TOWERS, TRICIA--[1]AUSTRALIAN
WILSON, ELIZABETH--[1]AUSTRALIAN

IVORY, JAMES HARVEY T.
WALKHAM, WALTER--[7][23]SF--
"WHEN THE EARTH TREMBLED" '80

IWAMATSU, JUN ATSUSHI
YASHIMA, TARO--[1][33]JAPANESE

IWASZKIEWICZ, JAROSLAW
ELEUTER--[22]POLISH

IYENGAR, K.R.
R.R.--[1]INDIAN
RAJARAM--[1]INDIAN

IZANT, GRACE GOULDER
GOULDER, GRACE--[31]

IZBITSKY, SAMUEL
FINEMAN, A.--[1]POLISH
IZBAN, SAMUEL--[1][31]POLISH
KRANTZ, D.--[1]POLISH
LAKS, S.--[1]POLISH

JABBER, PAUL
JABBER, FUAD AMIN--[31]

JABET, GEORGE S.
WARWICK, EDEN--[1]ENGLISH

JACK, ALEX
HAPI--[1]

JACK, RONALD DYCE SADLER
JACK, R.D.S.--[31]

JACKEL, MARGARETHE
ADAM, GRETE--[39]GERMAN
ADAM-JACKEL, GRETE--[39]GERMAN

JACKLIN, ANTHONY
JACKLIN, TONY--[31]

JACKS, LAWRENCE PEARSALL
JACKS, L.P.--[1]ENGLISH

JACKS, MAURICE LEONARD
JACKS, M.L.--[1]

JACKSON, ADA ACRAMAN
AJAX--[8]

JACKSON, ANGELA & SANDRA
SANDERS, LIA [LISA]--[9][21][26]ROM--
"THE TENDER MENDING"

JACKSON, ANNA J.
JACKSON, ANNE--[31]

JACKSON, BARBARA A.G.S.
SEAGRAVE, BARBARA ANN G.--[8]

JACKSON, BARBARA W[WARD]
WARD, BARBARA--[1]

JACKSON, C. PHILIP CASTLE
CASTLE, PHILIP--[8]
HARMODIUS--[8]
P.C.--[8]

JACKSON, CAARY PAUL
JACKSON, O.B.--[1][31][33]AMERICAN
LOCHLONS, COLIN--[1][22][31][33]AMERICAN
PAULSON, JACK--[1][22][33]AMERICAN

JACKSON, CAROL
MICHAELS, PETER--[1]AMERICAN

JACKSON, DONALD DE AVILA
JACKSON, DON D.--[31]

JACKSON, EILEEN V.
COMER, LINDA--[9]ROM
MAY, HELEN--[9][21][26]ROM--
"DUEL OF LOVE"
"CHANCE OF LOVE"
"SEA-RAVEN'S BRIDE"

JACKSON, HELEN HUNT
H.H.--[19]WEST
HOLM, SAXE--[19]WEST
NO NAME--[19]WEST
VAN WINKLE, RIP--[19]WEST

JACKSON, HENRY
ARMSTRONG, HENRY--[31]

JACKSON, HENRY MARTIN
JACKSON, SCOOP--[31]

JACKSON, J. DAVID
JACKSON, DAVE--[31]

JACKSON, JOHN W.
SILENT, WILLIAM T.--[2][11][23][32]MYS--
MSMM "MEDEA" OCT '72
"LORD OF THE RED SUN" '72

JACKSON, JOSEPH [F.A]
SCOTT, CHURCHILL--[1]AMERICAN

JACKSON, KATHRYN
HUBBARD, JOAN--[8]

JACKSON, LAURA [RIDING]
GOTTSCHALK, LAURA RIDING--[31]

JACKSON, LYDIA [J]
FEN, ELISAVETA--[1][8][31]

JACKSON, MARTIN [FOREST]
ARTHUR, MARTIN [FOREST]--[1]

JACKSON, NANCY
DABNEY, ANN--W/LOIS ANN BROWN,[21][26]ROM--
"A LIFETIME TO LOVE"

JACKSON, REGINALD MARTIN.
JACKSON, REGGIE--[31]

JACKSON, SAMUEL
JACKSON, STANLEY--[1]ENGLISH

JACKSON, VINCENT EDWARD
JACKSON, BO--[31]

JACKSON, WILLIAM ARTHUR D
JACKSON, W.A. DOUGLAS--[31]

JACKSON, WINIFRED V.
BERKELEY, ELIZABETH N.--[2]

JACOB, JAMES R.
JACOB, J.R.--[31]

JACOB, NAOMI ELLINGTON
GRAY, ELLINGTON--[17][22][31]ENGLISH/ROM--
"SAFFRONED BRIDESAILS" '28

JACOB, PIERS ANTHONY [D]
ANTHONY, PIERS--[2][4][7][11]SF--
NUMEROUS NOVELS

JACOB, [CYPRIEN] MAX
DAVID, LEON--[1]FRENCH
GAELIQUE, MORVEN LE--[1]FRENCH

JACOBS, ALMA SYLVIA
BLAIR, SYLVIA--[1]AMERICAN
JACOBS, ALLEN S.--[1]AMERICAN

JACOBS, CAROLINE EMILIA
ELLIOTT, EMILIA--[1]

JACOBS, CHARLES
HUMANA, CHARLES--[8]

JACOBS, HAL
SHULMAN, NEIL, M.D.--W. HERR SLS LST '94--
GHOSTED OR WROTE W/NEIL--
SCRIBN "BACKYARD TRIBE" '94

JACOBS, HARRIET
BRENT, LINDA--[1]AMERICAN

JACOBS, HELEN HULL
HULL, H. BRAXTON--[8][22][31][33]AMERICAN

JACOBS, HOWARD
BARD OF AVONDALE--[31]

JACOBS, JILL
BHARTI, MA SATYA--[1]AMERICAN
SAFIAN, JILL--[1]AMERICAN

JACOBS, LINDA C.
AUSTIN, TOM--[1][33]
BLACKBURN, CLAIRE--[1][9][21][26][33]ROM--
"HEART ON ICE"
"RETURN ENGAGEMENT" & 2 MORE

JACOBS, SOPHIS YARNALL
YARNALL, SOPHIA--[1]AMERICAN

JACOBS, SUSAN
QUINN, SUSAN--[33]

JACOBS, WALTER DARNELL
OBOE, PETER--[1][22]AMERICAN

JACOBS, WILLIAM WYMARK
JACOBS, W.W. --[1][32]MYS--
EQMM "HIS BROTHER'S KEEPER" JUL '43
RS "IN THE LIBRARY" MAY '45
JCM "THE MONKEY'S PAW" OCT '57

JACOBSEN, HANS JACOB
BRU, HEDIN--[31]

JACOBSON, ARTHUR
JACOBSON, SPIDER--[1]ENGLISH

JACOBSON, EJLAR & EDITH
RANDOLPH, CRAIG--T. JOHNSON LTR '94,[37]--
OCSC [REWROTE PAGE'S SECOND OCTOPUS NOVEL]

JACOBSON, LOUISE HAWES
HAWES, LOUISE--[7]SF--
LODESTAR "NELSON MALONE" SERIES-
2 NOVELS

JACOBSON, STEPHEN A.
JACOBSON, STEVE--[31]

JACOBSON, SUSANNA
L*NG, L*Z*R*S--[2]

JACOBSSON, PER
OLDFIELD, PETER--W/VERNON BARTLETT,
[3][22][29]MYS--
WSB "DEATH OF A DIPLOMAT"'28
WSB "THE ALCHEMY MURDERS" '29

JACOBY, HENRY
FRANCK, SEBASTIAN--[1][31]GERMAN
MARTIN, ANDRE--[1]GERMAN

JACQUEMARD, YVES
JACQUEMARD-SENECAL--W/JEAN-M. SENECAL,[3]MYS--
COLLINS "ELEVENTH LITTLE NIGGER" '79
COLLINS "BODY VANISHES" '80

JADVIGIN, ANTON
LEVICKIJ, ANTON--[22]RUSSIAN

JAEGER, CYRIL KAREL S.
DE FONTCREUSE, MARQUIS--[1][31]ENGLISH
JAEGER, C.K.--[1]ENGLISH

JAFFEE, ELIZABETH LATIMER
JAFFE, BETSY--[31]

JAFFEE, GABRIEL
POOLE, VIVIAN--[8][22]ENGLISH

JAFFEE, HOSEA
NXELEAFRIKA, MNGUNI--[1]SOUTH AFRICA

JAFFEE, HYMAN
ALTEREGO--[1]

JAFFEE, SUSANNE
HOWARD, JILL--[1]

JAGEL, BEATRICE HAWLEY
HAWLEY, BEATRICE--[31]

JAGNINSKI, TOM
PENDLETON, DON--[3]MYS,HP--
GE "CAMBODIA CLASH" '84
GE "TIGER WAR" '84

JAGOUTZ, OLGA ELISABETH
ALT-SONNECK, OLGA ELIS.--[39]GERMAN
VON ALTENBURG, OLGA ELIS.--[39]GERMAN

JAHN, DOROTHEA
MALTEN, THEA--[39]GERMAN/JUV

JAHN, JOSEPH MICHAEL
CAMERON, J.D.--V. BERCH LTR '94,[7]SF,HP--
AV 76409 "OMEGA SUB"
AV 76050 "CITY OF FEAR" '91
CARTER, NICK--[34]MYS,HP--
CHART "CALDRON OF HELL" '81
JAHN, MIKE--[7][23][31][33]SF/WAR/THRIL
MARSHALL, H.H.--[1]
WILLOUGHBY, LEE DAVIS--[21]ROM,HP--
DELL 'MKNG OF AMERICA' SERIES: "WHALERS"

JAHN, REINHARD
KARR, HANS-PETER--[39][40]GERMAN/MYS--
"STOP DER JUWELENBANDE" '79
"STOP DEN FALSCHMUNZERN" '81

JAHNE, GERTRUD
ROTHBERG, GERT--[39]GERMAN, HP--

JAIMES FREYRE, RICARDO
FREYRE, RICARDO JAIMES--[31]

JAKES, JOHN [WILLIAM]
ARD, WILLIAM--V. BERCH PROVIDED--
MON 215 "MAKE MINE MAVIS" '61
MON 231 "AND SO TO BED" '62
MON 269 "GIVE ME THIS WOMAN" '62
BLADE, ALEXANDER--JEAN F. LE DEIST
LTR '93,[11]HP--
CARTER, NICK--M. AVALLONE-BAE 13, P8,MYS,HP--
DAVIS, ROBERT HART--A. TONIK,JEAN F. LE
DEIST LTR '93,MYS,HP--
MU "WORLD'S END AFFAIR" MAY '66
MU "MOBY DICK AFFAIR" OCT '66

JAKES, JOHN [WILLIAM] [CONT]
DAVIS, ROBERT HART [CONT]
MU "GOLIATH AFFAIR" DEC '66
MU "DEADLY DARK AFFAIR" FEB '67
MU "DOLLS OF DEATH AFFAIR" APR '67
MU "UGLY MAN AFFAIR" JUN '67
MU "MAN FROM YESTERDAY AFFAIR" SEPT '67
GRANGER, DARIUS JOHN--JEAN F. LE DEIST LTR '93,[11]
GRAY, JOHN LEE--[28]WEST--
NEW FRONTIERS VOL I "LITTLE PHIL & THE DAUGHTER OF JOY" '90
NEW FRONTIERS VOL II "SNAKEHEAD" '90
HENRY, ALAN--[2][32]MYS--
TF "SINGULAR OCCURRENCE AT STYLES" '56
AA "TRAITOR'S FLIGHT" SPRING '56
JOHNS, JACOB--LACHMAN LST '93,[32]MYS--
GU "THE BUZZARD TATTOO" JUL '56
LARGO, LOUL. ROBBINS LTR '94, PULPS,HP
PAYNE, ALAN--[2][28][32][33][34]MYS--
PU "MALICE IN WONDERLAND" MAR '55
PU "MURDER HE SAYS" '58
ACE D289 "THIS'LL SLAY YOU" '58
PAYNE, RACHEL ANN--[34]MYS--
PAPLB "GHOSTWIND" '66
PAYNE, STEPHEN--LACHMAN LST '93,[32]MYS/WEST--
ACE F238 "BRAND HIM OUTLAW" '63
AV F201 "PICK OF THE ROUNDUP"[EDITOR] '63
ACE F272 "NO JOB FOR A COWBOY" '64
ACE M114 "STAMPEDE AT FARAWAY PASS" '65
M124 "TRAIL OF VANISHING RANCHERS" '65
ACE G619 "ROOM TO SWING A LOOP" '67
MSMM "WIFE WITH A GUN" JUL '72
SCOTLAND, JAY--[2][21][28][29][33]ROM--
AV T375 "I, BARBARIAN" '59
ACE D523 "STRIKE THE BLACK FLAG" '61
ACE F146 "SIR SCOUNDREL" '62
AV F123 "VEILS OF SALOME" '62
ACE G520 "ARENA" '63
G532 "TRAITOR'S LEGEND" '63
THAMES, C.H.--JEAN F. LE DEIST LTR '93,[11]--
THIS PRIMARILY A 'STEPHEN MARLOWE' NAME
WILDER, ALLEN--JEAN F. LE DEIST LTR '93
WILLIAMS, J.X.--CONSENSUS OF RESEARCHERS--
ALL BOOKS THRU '62 ARE JAKES'

JAKSTEIN, THYRA [D]
DOHRENBURG, THYRA--[39]GERMAN--TRANSLATION

JAKUBCZYK, URSULA
KUHN, URSULA--[39]GERMAN/JUV

JAKUBOWSKI, MAXIM
STONE, CHARLOTTE--[2]

JALESKI, MARY S. STOLZ
STOLZ, MARY--[7]SF--
HARPER "CAT IN THE MIRROR" '75
GODINE "QUENTIN CORN" '85

JAMES, AL
DEXTER, JOHN--MUNROE SEPT '93 AUCT, ADULT,HP--
NTSD 1519 "MIAMI CALL GIRL" '60

JAMES, BERNARD JOSEPH
JAMES, DAKOTA--[7][23]SF--
"GREENHOUSE" '84
"MILWAUKEE, THE BEAUTIFUL" '87

JAMES, BERT
HOBSON, B.--[3]MYS--
BOOKSTALL "MYS OF THE BOXING CONTEST" '10

JAMES, CHARLES
CORONET--[8]

JAMES, CYRIL LIONEL R.
JAMES, C.L.R.--[1]TRINADADIAN
JOHNSON, J.R.--[31]TRINADADIAN

JAMES, DANIEL LEWIS
SANTIAGO, DANNY--[1][31]AMERICAN

JAMES, DAVID BURNETT S.
VIZARD, STEPHEN--[1][22]ENGLISH

JAMES, DONALD
BARWICK, JAMES--W/TONY BARWICK,[3]MYS--
MacM "HANGMAN'S CRUSADE" '80
PUTNAM "DEVIL AT THE CROSSROADS" '86
PUTNAM "KREMLIN CONTRACT" '87
DONNER, JAMES--MUNROE AUCT '93,[1]ADULT--
BEAC B782 "THAT MOTEL WEEKEND" '64

JAMES, ELIZABETH
CARROLL, ELIZABETH--W/CAROL BARKIN, JAMES LTR '94,[33]--
WANDERER' BKS "SUMMER LOVE" '83
DUVAL, KATHERINE--JAMES LTR '94,[31][33]--
PARADISE PRESS "ZIEGFIELD: THE MAN & HIS WOMEN" '78
HASTINGS, BEVERLY--W/CAROL BARKIN, BARKIN LTR,[3]MYS--
JOVE "DON'T TALK TO STRANGERS" '80
BERK "DON'T WALK HOME ALONE" '85
BERK YOUNG ADULT "WATCHER IN THE DARK" '86
POCK "DON'T CRY, LITTLE GIRL" '87
BERK "DON'T LOOK BACK" '91
BERK YOUNG ADULT "HOME BEFORE DARK" '93
BERK "SOMEBODY HELP ME" '93
LLOYD, E. JAMES--JAMES LTR FEB '94,[33]--
SHORT SUBJ FILM "LOOSE CHANGE" '72
LLOYD, JAMES--JAMES LTR FEB '94,[33]--
FEATURE FILM "BORN LOSERS" '67

JAMES, FLORENCE ALICE P.
WARDEN, FLORENCE--[3][22][29]MYS--
LONG "A DEVIL'S BARGAIN" '08
CHATTO "HEART OF A GIRL" '03 & MORE

JAMES, GEORGE WILLIAM
JAMES, BILL--[31]BASEBALL BOOKS '85-90

JAMES, GODFREY WARDEN
BROOME, ADAM--[1][3][22]MYS--
BLES "BLACK MAMBA" '36
BENN "CROWNER'S QUEST" '30 & MORE

JAMES, HEATHER
JAMES, [LADY] HEATHER
JENNER, HEATHER--[8][31]
POTTER, HEATHER--[8]

JAMES, HERBERT WENTWORTH
WENTWORTH, HERBERT--[1]ENGLISH

JAMES, J.W.G.
NORHAM, GERALD--[8]

JAMES, JOHN STANLEY
THOMAS, JULIAN--[13]AUSTRALIAN
VAGABOND--[13]AUSTRALIAN

JAMES, JORDAN
WILLIAMS, J.X.--[11]HP

JAMES, LAURENCE
AXLER, JAMES--[7]SF,HP--
GE "DEATHLANDS #2 THRU #13"]
COBURN, L.J.--[2][11][28]HP--
SPHERE "CALEB THORNE" SERIES-- #1, 3 & 5 '77-78

JAMES, LAURENCE [CONT]
DARKE, JAMES--[7]SF,HP--
SPHERE-"WITCHES #1 THRU #8"
FRASER, MARY--[28]--
SPHERE "THE FIRST SUMMER" '79
SPHERE "THE LONG WINTER" '79
SPHERE "TIME OF CHANGE" '80
FRAZIER, ARTHUR--[2][11][28]--
NEL "A LIGHT IN THE WEST" '74
NEL "VIKING SLAUGHTER" '74
GARRETT, CHARLES C.--[2][11][28]WEST--
SPHERE 'GUNSLINGER' SERIES--
#1, 3, 5, 7 & 10
GOANE, THOMAS--[28]--
HODDER "JOURNAL" SERIES--
6 NOVELS '77-78
HAIGH, RICHARD--[28]--
GRAFTON "THE FARM" '84
GRAFTON "THE CITY" '86
JAMES, WILLIAM M.--[2][11][28]--
SPHERE 'APACHE' SERIES--
#1, 3 & 5
LANGHOLM, NEIL--[2][11][28]--
SPHERE "BLOOD SACRIFICES" '75
SPHERE "SUN IN THE NIGHT" '76
MANN, JAMES--W/JOHN [B] HARVEY,[28][34]MYS--
NEL "END GAME" '81
MARVIN, JAMES W.--[28]--
CORGI 'CROW' SERIES - 8 NOVELS '79-82
MAY, JONATHAN--[2][11][28]--
SPHERE 'CONFESSIONS' SERIES-
12 NOVELS '74-80
MCLAGLEN, JOHN J.--[2][11][28]--
CORGI 'HORNE THE HUNTER' SERIES-
13 NOVELS '76-84
McPHEE, JAMES--[28]MYS--
GE "BLOOD QUEST" '91
GE "RENEGADE WAR" '91
GE "FROZEN FIRE" '91
NETTSON, KLAUS--[34]MYS/WAR--
USED AS U.S. BYLINE FOR BOOKS PUBL
AS BY 'NETZEN'
NETZEN, KLAUS--[2][3][11][28]MYS/WAR--
7 NOVELS '74-6
NOLAN, CHRISTOPHER--[2][11]
NORMAN, MICK--[11][28]MYS--
NEL "ANGELS FROM HELL" '73
NEL "ANGEL CHALLENGE" '73
NEL "GUARDIAN ANGELS" '74
NEL "ANGEL ON MY MIND" '74
QUILLER, ANDREW--[28]--
MYFLWR "THE HILL OF THE DEAD" '76
MYFLWR "BLOOD ON THE SAND" '77
QUILLER, ARTHUR--[2]

JAMES, LIONEL
INTELLIGENCE OFFICER--[2]

JAMES, L[ANA] DEAN
DEAN, LISA--W/CHERYL CURRY SAYRE AS
CHRIS CURRY,[7]SF--
POCK "WINTER SCREAM" '91

JAMES, M.R.
DANIELSON, J.D.--[1][31]AMERICAN

JAMES, MARLISE ANN
WABUN--[1]AMERICAN

JAMES, MONTAGUE RHODES
JAMES, M.R.--[1]ENGLISH
M.R.J.--[8]

JAMES, SALLY
WILSON, JOYCE--[9]ROM

JAMES, STUART
GARETH, MAX--[1]

JAMES, SYRIE A. ASTRAHAN
ASTRAHAN, SYRIE A.--[21][26]ROM--
"SONGBIRD"
"THE SKY'S THE LIMIT"

JAMES, W. MARTHA
CLARE, AUSTIN--[1][3]MYS--
LONG "CONSCIENCE OF DR. HOLT" '08
EVEREST, HOPE--[1]

JAMES, W.I.
BAXTER, YOUNG--[1][3][22]MYS--
STREET "OLD MORTALITY, KING OF
DETECTIVES" 1888
COLLIER, OLD CAP--[1] SP
JEROME, GILBERT--[34]MYS--
STREET "FILIBUSTER'S WARNING" '03
STARK, INSPECTOR--[34]MYS,HP--
NEW MAGNET #441 "RING OF IRON; OR,
SECRET OF THE UNKNOWN" '06
STEWART, DICK--[34]MYS-HP--
MAGNET #385 "SEARCH FOR A MOTIVE" '05
MAGNET #465 "AN UNHEEDE WARNING" '06

JAMES, WILLIAM MILBOURNE
T.B.D.--[1]

JAMES, [LADY] HEATHER
JENNER, HEATHER--[1]ENGLISH

JAMESON, ANNIE EDITH F.
BUCKROSE, J.E.--[1][3]MYS--
HODDER "GOOD-NATURED LADY" '27

JAMESON, MALCOLM
KEITH, COLIN--[1][2][11]AMERICAN
MACGREGOR, MARY--[1][2][11]AMERICAN

JAMESON, RAYMOND D.
DE LOI, RAIMON--[1]AMERICAN

JAMESON, ROBERT
JAMESON, ROLAND--[1]ENGLISH

JAMESON, [MARGARET] STORM
HILL, JAMES--[1][31]
LAMB, WILLIAM--[1][23][31]SF--
"THE WORLD ENDS" '37

JAMIESON, EVAN
ARCHITECHS ADVENTURE--W/RICHARD MEYER/
WALTER & LISA HUNT/BILL SCAMMELL/
MARK BLOOM/CHRISTINE IVEY,[7]

JAMIESON, HEBER CARSS
BLAKE, NORMAN--W/ROBERT KAY GORDON,[1]CANADIAN

JAMIESON, KATHLEEN FLORN.
JANES, KATHLEEN--[8]
JANES, KATHLEEN F.--[8]

JAMIESON, LELAND S.
BEEHAN, JACK ROGERS--[1]AMERICAN
SHREWSBURY, RALPH--[1]AMERICAN

JAMIESON, ROBERT JOHN
JAMIESON, BOB--[31]

JAMISON, SUSAN RAU
ROSS, SUSAN--[21][26]ROM--
"HEART"

JANAS, FRANCIS LEROY G.
BALL, ZACHARY--W/KELLY R. MASTERS, [1][22][31][33]
BREMER, LISA--[31]
GREER, FRANCESCA--[1][9][21][26][31]ROM-- "FIRST FIRE"
JANAS, FRANKIE-LEE--[21][34]MYS/ROM
O'BRIEN, SALIEE--[3][9][21][26][29]MYS/ROM-- BERK "NIGHT OF THE SCORPION" '76 & MORE

JANCE, JUDITH ANN
JANCE, J.A.--[31][34]MYS--
AV "UNTIL PROVEN GUILTY" '85
AV "TRIAL BY FURY" '86 & OTHERS

JANE, FREDERICK THOMAS
JANE, FRED T.--[23]--
MILITARY & AIRCRAFT

JANECZKO, PAUL B.
WOLNY, P.--[31][32][33]AMERICAN/MYS--
LM "ANOTHER FINAL DRINK" SEPT '77

JANES, GENE
DEKKER, CARL--[35]AUSTRALIAN, HP--
CALVERT - SOME OF 40 BOOKS
JAMES, GENE--[35]AUSTRALIAN--
'JAMES' ON COVER OF "MISSION KILL" & "RAVEN KILL"

JANNER, GREVILLE EWAN
MITCHELL, EWAN--[8][22]ENGLISH

JANSEN, ERIKA [W]
WIEDEN, ERIKA--[39]GERMAN
WILLE, EDRIKA--[39]GERMAN

JANSEN, GODFREY HENRY
JANSEN, G.H.--[31]

JANSEN, JOHANNA FREDERIKA
BAYARD, FRED--W/MARGARET E.B. CAMPBELL, [3][8]MYS--
PHOENIX "DEATH & LILACS" '48

JANSON, CHARLES WILLIAM
STRANGER, THE--[1]

JANSSON, GUNNAR
BANNISTER, WYATT--W/RUNE MANTLING,[29]MYS--
"STRIDEN OM FLYING N' " '61

JANUS, EDDA [R]
RONCKENDORFF, EDDA--[39]GERMAN

JANVIER, MARGARET T.
VANDERGRIFT, MARGARET--[1]

JANVIER, THOMAS A.
BLACK, IVORY--[1]

JAPP, ALEXANDER HAY
ALEXANDER, J.H.--[1]ENGLIAH
GRAY, E. CONDER--[1]ENGLISH
ORME, BENJAMIN--[1]ENGLISH
PAGE, H.A.--[1]ENGLISH
ROSE, A.N. MOUNT--[1]ENGLISH
SCOT, A.F.--[1]ENGLISH

JAQUES, EDWARD TYRRELL
TEARLE, CHRISTIAN--[34]MYS--
ROUTLEDGE "A LEGAL PRACTICIONER" '07

JARDINE, JACK OWEN
BARSTEAD, HARRY--[2]AMERICAN
CLARKE, P.J.--[2]AMERICAN

JARDINE, JACK OWEN [CONT]
CORY, HOWARD L.--W/JULIE JARDINE,[2][11][23]SF--
ACE "MIND MONSTERS" '66
ACE "SWORD OF LANHOR" '66
FARMER, ARTHUR--[2][11]SF--
STAR "NYMPH & THE SATYR" '62
MADDOCK, LARRY--[2][32][34]MYS--
MSMM "INNOCENT BYSTANDER" SEPT '65 [W/JULIE JARDINE]
AHMM "HONOR SYSTEM" JUN '65
MSMM "A MATTER OF TIMING" JUL '65
ACE "FLYING SAUCER GAMBIT" '66
ACE "ENERALD ELEPHANT GAMBIT" '67
ACE "GOLDEN GODDESS GAMBIT" '67
EQMM "DEATHWISH" AUG '67
MU "EVERY BODY REMEMBERS WHATSISNAME" AUG '67
ACE "TIME TRAP GAMBIT" '69

JARDINE, JULIE ANN
CORY, HOWARD L.--W/JACK O. JARDINE,[2][23]SF--
ACE "MIND MONSTER" '66
ACE "SWORD OF LANHOR" '66
HOWARD, CORRIE--W/JACK O. JARDINE,[2][32]MYS--
MSMM "INNOCENT BYSTANDER" SEPT '65

JARED, L.F.
FULLER, JARED--L. ROBBINS LTR MAR '94

JAREMKO, NESTOR
WHITE, WILLY--[2]

JARNEFELT, ARVID
KANILA, HILJA--[22]FINNISH

JARNES BERQUA, ENRIQUE
JARBER, E.--[1]SPANISH

JAROCH, FRANCES A. RANDY
JAROCH, RANDY--[31]

JARRETT, BELLA
THORNE, BELLA--[9][21][26]ROM--
"THAT ISLAND, THAT SUMMER"
"PASSIONATE SUMMER"

JARRETT, CORA [H]
KEENE, FARADAY--[3][5][22][29]MYS--
HOUGHTON "PATTERN IN BLACK & RED" '34
HOUGHTON "NIGHT OVER FITCH'S POND" '33
DAY "PECADILLOS" '49

JARRIEL, THOMAS EDWIN
JARRIEL, TOM--[31]

JARROLD, ERNEST
FINN MICKEY--[1]

JARVIS, FREDERICK G.
GORDON, FRITZ--W/ROBERT F. VAN BEEVER, [2][3][31]MYS--
AWARD "TONIGHT THEY DIE TO MENDELSSOHN" '68
AWARD "FLIGHT OF THE BAMBOO SAUCER" '68

JARVIS, SHARON [SYLVIA]
COMSTOCK, JARROD--W/ELLEN M. KOZAK,[7][23]SF--
"THE LOVE MACHINE" '84
"SCALES OF JUSTICE" '84
HAILEY, JOHANNA --W/MARCIA Y. HOWL, [7][9][21][23]ROM/SF--
ZEBRA "ENCHANTED PARADISE" '85
ZEBRA "CRYSTAL PARADISE" '87
ZEBRA "BELOVED PARADISE" '88
MAJOR, H.M.--W/KATHLEEN BUCKLEY,[3][7][31]SF--
SIGN "ALIEN TRACE" '84
SIGN "TIME TWISTER" '84

JASINSKAS, JONAS
JASMIN, J.--[1]

JASNORZEWSKA, MARIA
PAWLIKOWSKA--[22]POLISH

JASTRZEMBSKI, MARIAN
EDWARDS, MARIAN--[26]ROM--
"A YEAR & A DAY"

JAUNIERE, CLAUDE
JAUNIERE, CLAUDETTE--[3]FRENCH/MYS--
6 MYSTIQUE NOVELS '77-80

JAURAND, YVONNE
DUPLESSIS, YVES--[1][22]FRENCH

JAVITCH, DANIEL GILBERT
INMERITO--[1][31]FRENCH

JAWORSKI, FRANK ANTHONY
JAVOR, FRANK A.--[7][23][31]SF--
DAW "ELI PIKE #1 THRU #3"

JAY, AMANDA MOOR
KINSALE, LAURA--[9][21][26]ROM--
BERK "FOR MY LADY'S HEART" '93 & MORE

JAY, HARRIETT
MARLOWE, CHARLES--[34]MYS--

JAY, MARION
SPALDING, LUCILLE--[8]

JAY, RUTH INGRID
JAY, RUTH JOHNSON--[31]AMERICAN
JOHNSON, RUTH I.--[1][31]AMERICAN

JEAN, GABRIELLE LUCILE
DE MILAN, SISTER JEAN--[31]

JEAN-LOUIS, VICTOR
BAGHIO'O, JEAN-LOUIS--[1]WEST INDIAN

JEANNIN, JEAN-PAUL
CELEBERT--[1]

JEANS, HERBERT
MADDOX, MAX--[1]ENGLISH

JEBAVY, VACLAV IGNAC
BREZINA, OTAKAR--[22]CZECHOSLAVAKIAN

JEFFCOATE, SIR THOMAS
JEFFCOATE, NORMAN--[8]
JEFFCOATE, T.N.A.--[8]

JEFFERIES, GREG
COLLINS, GEOFFREY--[1]ENGLISH

JEFFERIES, IRA
MORRIS, IRA J.--[8]

JEFFERSON, XAVIER T.
JEFFERSON, OMAR XAVIER--[1][31]

JEFFERY, GRAHAM
BROTHER GRAHAM--[1][8]

JEFFERY, GRANT
TURNER, PETER PAUL--[1][22]CANADIAN

JEFFERYS, WILLIAM H.
LATTISSIONER, JOHN--[1]AMERICAN

JEFFREY, ROSA VERTNER
ROSA--[1]AMERICAN

JEFFREY-SMITH, MAY T.
AUNT MAYSIE--[1]JAMAICAN
THORNTON, MAYSIE--[1]JAMAICAN

JEFFRIES, BRUCE GRAHAM M.
BOURNE, PETER--[1][5][18][22]ENGLISH/MYS--
12 NOVELS '43-75
GRAEME, BRUCE--[2][3][5][32]MYS--
NVLS '25-80
JCM "THE EMPTY HOUSE" MAR '57
JCM "NEGATIVE CLUE" FEB '57
SA "CHECKMATE" MAY '58
GRAEME, DAVID--[2][3][5][18][31]MYS--
HARRAP "DRUMS BEAT RED" '63 & 4 MORE
GRAEME, RODERIC--W/RODERIC JEFFRIES,
[1][32][34]MYS--
JCM "A HIGH TENSION LEAD" SEPT '56
SUS "A MATTER OF LIFE & DEATH" DEC '60
LONG "BLACKSHIRT IN PERIL" '67 & MORE
HASTINGS, RODERIC--[3][18]MYS--
AV T267 "NAKED TIDE" '58

JEFFRIES, GAY
GRAEME, LINDA--[8]

JEFFRIES, RODERIC[GRAEME]
ALDING, PETER--[3][5][18]MYS--
LONG "CIRCLE OF DANGER" '68
HALE "BETRAYED BY DEATH" '82 & MORE
ASHFORD, JEFFREY--[3][5][18][31]MYS--
LONG "BENT COPPER" '71
LONG "ANGER OF FEAR" '78 & MORE
DRAPER, HASTINGS--[1][18][31]MYS
GRAEME, RODERIC --W/GRAHAM JEFFRIES,
[1][3][5][32]MYS--
JCM "A HIGH TENSION LEAD" SEPT '56
SUS "A MATTER OF LIFE & DEATH" DEC '60
HASTINGS, GRAHAM--[3][5][18]MYS--
HALE "TWICE CHECKED" '59
HALE "DEADLY GAME" '61
ROBERTS, JULIAN--[34]MYS--
WHITING "A CASE OF GIVE A DOG" '66

JEHLE, ALFONS
ELJENS, OLAF--[39]GERMAN

JEIER, THOMAS
SHERIFF BEN--[39]GERMAN/WEST
THOMAS, M.L.--[1]GERMAN
THOMAS, MARK L.--[39]GERMAN/ADV/JUV
WOOD, MARK L.--[39]GERMAN/ADV/JUV

JEKEL, P.L.
JEKEL, PAMELA--[21]ROM--
"COLUMBIA"

JELINEK, ESTELLE C.
FINE, ESTELLE--[1][31]AMERICAN

JELLEY, SYMMES W.
SMYLES, L.E.--[34]MYS--

JELLY, GEORGE OLIVER
FOSSE, ALFRED--[1]ENGLISH
HARSCH, HILYA--[1][31]ENGLISH
JELLY, OLIVER--[8]ENGLISH

JELLY, SYMMES M.
LE JEMLYS--[1][3]MYS--
3 NOVELS ca 1900

JEN, LILLIAN
JEN, GISH--[31]

JENKINS, ALAN CHARLES
BANCROFT, JOHN--[8]

JENKINS, HAROLD L.
JENKINS, HAL--[31]

JENKINS, JENNIFER
BOYLE, ROBERT--[3]MYS--
WALKER "BABY SITTER" '74
MacD "CRY RAPE" '76

JENKINS, MACGREGOR
RUSTICUS--[1]AMERICAN

JENKINS, MARIE M.
MARKINS, W.S.--[1][33]
MARY SCHOLASTICA--[1][33]
SCHOLASTICA, SISTER MARY--[33]

JENKINS, NORMAN
BROWN, GEORGE--[1]

JENKINS, RICHARD
BURTON, RICHARD--[8]

JENKINS, SARAH LUCILLE
SARGENT, JOAN--[9][21]ROM--
"RAINBOW'S END"
"HEAD IN THE CLOUDS" & 3 MORE

JENKINS, VIRGINIA C.
KNIGHT-JENKINS, VIVIAN--[26]ROM--
"PASSION'S TIMELESS HOUR"

JENKINS, WILLIAM FITZGER.
FITZGERALD, WILLIAM--[1][2][23]--
'BUD GREGORY' SERIES
JAMES, WILL F.--L. ROBBINS LTR MAR '94
JENKINS, HAL--[1]
JENKINS, WILL--L. ROBBINS LTR MAR '94
JENKINS, WILL F.--[23]SF/WEST--
HH 4 "MAN WHO FEARED" '46
HAN 62 "MURDER OF THE USA" '47
GM 126 "DALLAS" '50
GM 161 "SON OF THE FLYING Y" '51
LEE, LOUISE CARTER--[1][2]
LEINSTER, MURRAY--V. BERCH-GM PSEUDS,
PP 33,[2][23][28]SF/WEST--
"OUTLAW GUNS" '51
"TEXAS GUNSLINGER"
& 35 SF/MYS '30-69
SHAPPIRO, HERBERT--BAPC NWSLTR #9--
PEMBERTON "LOVE THROWS A LOOP" COVERS '46

JENKINS-NUTTING, LINDA
JENKINS, KATE--[9][21][26]ROM--
"ON THE WILD SIDE"
"TERMINALLY SINGLE" & MORE

JENKS, GEORGE CHARLES
CARTER, NICHOLAS--[1][3]ENGLISH/MYS,HP--
EDWARDS, JOHN MILTON--[1]ENGLISH
LAWSON, W.B.--[1][28][31]MYS--
STREET 'DIAMOND DICK' NOVELS '05-09

JENKS, KATHLEEN
STEPHENS, JENNIFER--[3]MYS--
AV "VENGEANCE OF THE CAT GODDESS" '73

JENNER, KATHERINE LEE
LEE, KATHERINE--[1]ENGLISH

JENNETT, RICHARD P.
PHILLIPS, JAMES R.--[1]AMERICAN

JENNINGS, E.C.
JAY--[8]

JENNINGS, GARY
QUYTH, GABRIEL--[7]SF--
ATHENEUM "LIVELY LIVES OF CRISPIN
MOBEY" '88

JENNINGS, JOHN [E]
BALDWIN, BATES--[1][22][31]AMERICAN
WILLIAMS, JOEL--[1][22]AMERICAN

JENNINGS, LESLIE NELSON
BROOK, A.B.--[1][22][31]AMERICAN
CARFAGNE, CYRIL--[1][22][31]AMERICAN
CARTWRIGHT, JAMES MACGRGR--[1][22][31]AMERICAN
DESPLAINES, JULIE--[1][22][31]AMERICAN
JAMES, JUDITH--[1][22][31]AMERICAN
RAYSON, PAUL--[1][22]AMERICAN

JENNINGS, LOUIS J.
DROPPER, H.--[1]

JENNINGS, MICHAEL GLENN
BRAZOS, WACO--[1][31]
KINKAID, WYATT E.--[1][31]

JENNINGS, RICHARD
W.M.--[8]

JENNISON, JOHN WILLIAM
BAILEY, GENE--PPCC#3,WEST,HP--
WARREN "GREAT PLAINS" '53
WARREN "RED RIVER" '53
WARREN "SOUTH OF RIO" '53
BARNARTO, BART--PPCC#3,[27]HP--SELF
BARONI, NICK--PPCC#3,[27]HP--
WARREN "BIG TIME GIRL" '50
WARREN "MITZI '51
WARREN "NANCY" '51
WARREN "RED DOLL" '51
BELMONT, R.--PPCC#3,HP--
CW "LINCOLN COUNTY" '54
BENSON, LEE--PPCC#3,MYS,HP--
WARREN "SANTA FE" '52
BERN, JERINE--PPCC#3,WEST,HP--
WARREN "SILVER SPURS" '52
WARREN "SILVER CITY" '52
WARREN "BLUE RENEGADE" '52
WARREN "FRONTIER BELT" '52
WARREN "COLT .38" '52
BONN, GEORGE--PPCC#3,WEST,HP--
WARREN "WELLS FARGO" '53
BOYCE, FRANK--PPCC#3,HP--
CW "MANNY" '53
CW "TENNESSEE" '53
CW "BLOCKADE" '54
BRADFORD, MATTHEW C.--PPCC#3,[7][23]SF,HP--
SELF "INVASION FROM SPACE" MAY '54
BRAUN, F.W.--PPCC#3,WEST--
ATLANTIC "THE WAY OF THE APACHE" SEPT '54
BROWNE, GEORGE SHELDON--PPCC#3,
[7]SF,HP--
SELF "THE YELLOW PLANET" '54
CARSON, ALLAN --PPCC#3,WEST,HP--
CW "NORTH OF THE ALAMO" '52
CW "EAGLE RIVER" '52
CW "MOOSE JAW" '53
CARTER, TEX--PPCC#4/WEST--
MARTIN & REID "STAGE TO ROCKVILLE" '50
& ABOUT 13 OTHERS
CHARLES, NEIL--PPCC#3,[2][[11]SF,HP--
CW "PARA ROBOT" '52
COSTELLO, PETE--PPCC#3,[27]HP--SELF

JENNISON, JOHN WILLIAM [CONT]
DAVIS, FRANCIS--PPCC#3,WEST,HP--
CW "SUN VALLEY" '53
CW "NIGHT POSSE" '53
CW "ROUGH JUSTICE" '53
CW "KID FRISCO" '53
FARO, TEX--PPCC#3,WEST,HP--
CW "RUSTLER'S GORGE" '52
CW "RANCHO NEVADA" '52
FOSTER, GERRY--PPCC#3,WEST,HP--
CW "BLACK HAWK" '52
CW "EL PASO" '52
CW "VAQUERO" '53
GARDNER, ROGER--PPCC#3,WEST,HP--
CW "OVERLAND MAIL" '54
GILBERT, BRIAN--PPCC#3,WEST,HP--
CW "MADRE GORGE" '53
CW "NEW MEXICO" '53
GOLD, KID--PPCC#3,MYS,HP--
CW "MAXIE'S ARENA" '51
CW "PAY OFF" '51
GORDON, JOHN--PPCC#3,WEST,HP--
CW "INDIAN TRAIL" '53
GREY, DEAN--PPCC#3,WEST,HP--
CW "PARDNER" '53
HUDSON, E.J.--PPCC#3,WEST,HP--
CW "INDIAN TERRITORY" '54
HUNT, GILL--PPCC#3,[2][11][23]SF,HP--
CW "STA 7" '52
CW "ZERO FIELD" '52
JERROLD, BENTLEY--PPCC#3,WEST,HP--
CW "HAWK RIDGE" '52
CW"LONE SCOUT" '52
CW "SOUTH OF YUMA" '54
KENNEDY, CLAY--PPCC#3,WEST,HP--
CW "FORT SUMMER" '54
KENNEDY, EDGAR REES--PPCC#3,[7][23]SF,HP--
ES "CONQUERORS OF VENUS" '51
ES "MYSTERY PLANET" '52
LANG, KING--PPCC#3,[2][11]SF,HP--
CW "SPACE LINE" '52
LAVELLE, MARK--VULTURES OF THE VOID,HP
MCCOY, TEX --PPCC#3,WEST,HP--
ES "BORDER RENEGADES" '51
ES "ARIZONA GUNS" '52
ES "COLORADA KILLERS" '53
ES "GUNSMOKE BREED" '54
MILLS, JOHN--PPCC#3,WEST,HP--
CW "FORAY" '54
MORGAN, D.--PPCC#3,WEST,HP--
CW "CHEROKEE" '54
NORMAN, CHET--PPCC#3,WEST,HP--
CW "ROCKY CANYON" '53
PABLO, MIGUEL--PPCC#3,HP--
CW "WHISPERING STEEL" '54
PACO, CARY--PPCC#3,WEST,HP--
CW "COMMANCHE" '52
CW "LOS GRANADOS" '52
CW "EL MORO" '52
"BORDER VALLEY" '52
"MOJAVE DESERT" '52
"COYOTE PASS" '53
PAN, GEORGE--PPCC#3,WEST,HP--
CW "GOLD CANYON" '53
CW "GOLD TOWN" '53
CW "DEEPSHAFT LOAD" '53
RUSSELL, SCOTT--PPCC#3,WEST,HP--
CW "DOUBLE DECK" '54
SANDYS, PETE--S. HOLLAND-SCION CKLST,
PP 27, PPCC#3,[27]WEST--6 NOVELS '54-5
SCLANDERS, DOORN--S. HOLLAND-SCION CKLST,
PP 27,PPCC#3,[27]WEST-- 8 NOVELS '55-6
SCOTT, CAL--PPCC#3,WEST,HP--
CW "ROUGH RIDERS" '52
CW "CHEYNEY MESA" '52
CW "SAN ROMERO" '52

JENNISON, JOHN WILLIAM [CONT]
THEYDON, JOHN--[7][23][34]SF,HP--
ARMADA "CAPT. SCARLETT #1 & #2"
ARMADA "STINGRAY #1 & #2"
ARMADA "THUNDERBIRDS #2, #3 & #5"
& MANY OTHERS
VALOIS, JEAN PAUL--VULTURES OF THE VOID,HP--
VANE, BRETT--PPCC#3,[27][34]MYS,HP--
CW "BROOKLYN DAUGHTER" '50
CW "IRENE" '51
CW "SMART GIRL" '51
YOUNG, PAUL--PPCC#3,WEST,HP--
CW "THE STORM" '53
CW "HIGH FEUD" '53
CW "SHARPSHOOTER" '54

JENS, WALTER
FREIBURGER, WALTER--[39]GERMAN

JENSEN, DOROTHEA
MOORHOUSE, CATHERINE--W/CATHERINE ALLEN,
[9][21][26]ROM--
"ADRIANNA"
"LOUISA"
"DOROTHEA"

JENSEN, ERIK B. VOLMER
RASTHOLT, JORGEN--[37]DANISH/MYS--
'SUSPENSE: THE ALEXANDER SERIES' '43-50
SOUTH, MARTIN--[37]DANISH/MYS--
BROWNING MAGAZINE

JENSEN, JEPPE
AAKJAER, JEPPE--[1]DUTCH

JENSEN, MAGGIE
BAKER, MAGGIE--[26]ROM--
"A MAN FOR THE NIGHT"

JENSEN, MAXINE DOWD
DOWD, MAXINE--[31]

JENSEN, PAULINE MARIE
LONG, ANN MARIE--[22]AMERICAN

JENYNS, ROGER SOAME
JENYNS, SOAMES--[31]

JEPSON, EDGAR [ALFRED]
CLAYMORE, TOD--[34]MYS--
CASSELL "SHIPS WITH WINGS" '48
CASSELL "NEST OF VIPERS" '48
CASSELL "WHAT ELSE COULD I DO?" '48
CASSELL "APPOINTMENT IN NEW ORLEANS" '50
CASSELL "REUNION IN FLORIDA" '52
CASSELL "DEAD MEN DON'T ANSWER" '54
CASSELL "RENDEZVOUS ON AN ISLAND" '57

JERITZA, MARIA
JEDITZKA, MARIA--[31]

JERROLD, IANTHE
BRIDGMAN, GERALDINE--[1]ENGLISH

JERSILD, PER CHRISTIAN
JERSILD, P.C.--[31]

JERV, JONOTHAN
DJARV, JOHN--[29]MYS--
"NORRLANDSTAGET PLUNDRAT I NATT" '25

JERVIS, VERA M.S.
ENGLAND, JANE--[3]MYS--
HURST "TRADER'S LICENSE" '36
HURST "FLIGHT INTO DANGER" '50 & MORE

JESCHKE, WOLFGANG
MISER, ABEL--[39]GERMAN/SF
PRAGER, HANSJORG--[39]GERMAN/SF
SENFTBAUER, E.--[39]GERMAN/SF
STANYA, F.--[39]GERMAN/SF

JESKE, COLLEEN
SHANNON, COLLEEN--[9][21][26]ROM--
"HAWK'S LADY"
"MIDNIGHT RIDER" & 2 MORE

JESSE, F. TENNYSON
FRYN--[1]ENGLISH
JESSE, TENNYSON--[31]ENGLISH/MYS--
JCM "IN DEATH THEY WERE DIVIDED" APR '57
TINKER, BEAMISH--[3][18][29]ENGLISH/MYS--
MILLS "MAN WHO STAYED AT HOME" '15

JESSUP, DEBORAH HITCHCOCK
HITCHCOCK, DEBORAH J.--[31]

JESSUP, MARY ALANE
MARK, ALANE--V. BERCH LTR TO HUBIN '94,MYS--
ACADEMY "AN ETHICAL MAN" '86

JESSUP, RICHARD
TELFAIR, RICHARD--V. BERCH-GM PSEUDS,
PP 33,[34]MYS--
GM 759 "WYOMING JONES" '58
GM 827 "DAY OF THE GUN" '58
GM 847 "BLOODY MEDALLION" '59
GM 883 "WYOMING JONES FOR HIRE" '59
GM 890 "THE CORPSE THAT TALKED" '59
GM 932 "SECRET OF APACHE CANYON" '59
GM 999 "SUNDANCE" '60
GM 1006 "SCREAM BLOODY MURDER" '60
GM 1094 "GOOD LUCK, SUCKER" '61
GM 1077 "SLAVERS" '62
DELL FE K111 "TARGET FOR TONIGHT" '62

JETER, JACQUELYN I.
JETER, JACKY--[31]

JETER, K[EVIN] W.
DR. ADDER--[7]SF--
"ALLIGATOR ALLEY" '89

JEURY, MICHEL
HIGNON, ALBERT--W/PIERRE MARLSON,
[1][2][11]FRENCH

JEWETT, JOHN HOWARD
WARNER, HANNAH--[1]

JEWETT, [T] SARAH ORNE
ELIOT, A.D.--[31]
ELIOT, ALICE [C]--[1][8][31]AMERICAN
SWEET, SARAH [C]--[1]AMERICAN

JIMENEZ [M], JUAN RAMON
JIMENEZ MANTECON, RAMON--[31]
JIMENEZ, RAMON--[31]

JIROKICHI, DEBUCHI
ENCHO--[22]JAPANESE

JOBB, JAMIE
KABIBBLE, OSH--[1][31][33]AMERICAN

JOBSON, HAMILTON
STRATHERN, WILLIAM--[18][29]MYS--
HALE "DON'T LOOK FOR ME" '81

JOCKS, YVONNE
VAUGHN, EVELYN--[26]ROM--
"WAITING FOR THE WOLF MOON"

JOEL, BARBARA
MCCAULEY, BARBARA--[26]ROM--
"HER KIND OF MAN"
"WOMAN TAMER"
"MAN FROM COUGAR PASS"

JOEL, WILLIAM MARTIN
JOEL, BILLY--[31]

JOENSSON, REIDAR
JOHSSON, REIDAR--[31]

JOERGENSEN, JOHANNES
UNICUS--[1]DANISH

JOFRIET, JAN GERARDUS
BRABANDER, GERARD DEN--[22]DUTCH

JOHANNESSON, OLOF
ALFEN, HANNES--[7]SF

JOHN, ELIZABETH BEAMON
JOHN, B.--[1][31]
JOHN, BETTY--[1][31]
SINJIN--[1]
ST. JOHN, BETH--[1][22]AMERICAN
ST. JOHN, ELIZABETH--[1]

JOHN, EUGENIE
MARLITT, E.--[1][34]MYS, SP--
DUBLIN "THE OLD MAID'S SECRET" 1871
MARLITT, E.P.--[1]

JOHN, FRIEDERIKE C.H.
MARLITT, E.--[39]GERMAN, SP

JOHN, FRIEDRICH LUDWIG
FERRER, F.L.--[39]GERMAN
SEEFELDER, ANDREAS--[39]GERMAN
WENDHOFER, TONI--[39]GERMAN

JOHN, OWEN
BOURNE, JOHN--[7][8][31][32]SF/HIST/ROM/MYS--
EW "A QUESTION OF PRIORITY" AUG '65
LM "DEATH & DECAY" DEC '66
EW "RELUCTANT DETECTIVE" APR '66
EW "EXERCISE IN TERROR" AUG '66
EW "SAD RESURRECTIONIST" FEB '67

JOHN-STEINER, VERA POLGAR
JOHN, VERA P.--[31]

JOHNS SMITH, JUNE
JOHNS, JUNE--[1]ENGLISH

JOHNS, GILBERT
STAGG, JAMES--[3][29]MYS--
AMALG "MURDER DOWN BELOW" '58
AMALG "DESERT INTRIGUE" '60 & MORE

JOHNS, WALTER T.
NEBY, AL--[8]

JOHNS, WILLIAM EARLE
EARLE, WILLIAM--[2][11][31][33]ENGLISH
EARLY, JON--P. MARRIOTT-PPCC#5,[31][33]ENGLISH
JOHNS, W.E. [CAPT.]--[1][29][33]ENGLISH/MYS
LEIGH, HOWARD--P. MARRIOTT-PPCC#5, ENGLISH

JOHNS, WILLIAM STABBACK
B.B.--W/W.M. ROGERS,[1]

JOHNSON, ANNA M.
DARLING, HOPE--[1]AMERICAN

JOHNSON, ANNABELL JONES
JOHNSON, A.--[1][22][31][33]AMERICAN
JOHNSON, A.E.--W/EDGAR RAYMOND JOHNSON, [22][31][33]--
DBLDY "THE SECRET GIFT" '61
JOHNSON, ANNABEL--[31][33]

JOHNSON, ARTHUR TYSILIO
DRAIG, GLAS--[1]

JOHNSON, BURDETTA FAYE
BEEBE, B.F.--[1][31]AMERICAN

JOHNSON, CARL E[DWARD]
JOHNSON, C. EDWARD--[31]

JOHNSON, CHARLES R.
JOHNSON, CHUCK--[31][33]

JOHNSON, CHRISTOPHER
MCINTOSH, LOUIS--[22]ENGLISH

JOHNSON, CLAUDIA ALTA T.
JOHNSON, LADY BIRD--[31]

JOHNSON, CURTIS LEE
JOHNSON, CURT--[31]
WALLEK, LEE--[1]
WHIZ, WALTER--[1]

JOHNSON, DONALD BRUCE
JOHNSTONE, D. BRUCE--[1]

JOHNSON, DONALD MCINTOSH
DE MONTFORT, GUY--[3][31]MYS--
HAMLYN "ALL THE QUEEN'S MEN" '80

JOHNSON, DUDLEY VAUGHAN
VAUGHAN, DUDLEY--[1]

JOHNSON, EARVIN JR.
JOHNSON, MAGIC--[31]

JOHNSON, EDGAR RAYMOND
JOHNSON, A.E.--W/ANNABELLE J. JOHNSON, [22][31][33]--
DBLDY "THE SECRET GIFT" '61

JOHNSON, EDITH
JOHNSON, BETSY--[21][26]ROM--
"PRIVATE WAGERS"
"WEDDING EVE"

JOHNSON, EDWARD MARHWICK
MARKWICK, EDWARD--[7][23]SF

JOHNSON, EDWIN CLARK
JOHNSON, TOBY--[1][7]SF--
LAVENDER "SECRET MATTER" '90

JOHNSON, ELLEN ARGO
ARGO, ELLEN--[9][21][26][31]ROM--
"JEWEL OF THE SEAS"
"CRYSTAL STAR"
"YANKEE GIRL"

JOHNSON, ENID
JOHNSON, E. NED--[1]
JONES, JENNIFER--W/MARGARET LANE,[3]MYS--
DBLDY "MURDER-ON-HUDSON" '37
DBLDY "DIRGE FOR A DOG" '39
CROWELL "MURDER AL FRESCO" '39

JOHNSON, EUGENE HARPER
JOHNSON, E. HARPER--[31][33]
JOHNSON, HARPER--[31][33]

JOHNSON, FORREST BRYANT
JOHNSON, FROSTY--[1][7]SF

JOHNSON, GEORGE METCALF
METCALF, GEORGE--[1]

JOHNSON, GERALD WHITE
NORTH, CHARLES--[3]MYS--
MORROW "BEWARE THE DOG" '39

JOHNSON, GRETCHEN
JENNER, SUZANNE--W/SALLY NETZEL, [9][21][26]ROM--
"MIDSUMMER"

JOHNSON, HENRY
ROBERTSON, MUIRHEAD--[3]MYS--
BARTHOLOMEW "A LOMBARD ST. MYS" 1888

JOHNSON, HENRY T.
THOMSON, NEIL--[1]

JOHNSON, HUGH
CONGREVE, GILES--[31]ENGLISH--
SUNDAY TIMES - COLUMN CONTRIBUTION

JOHNSON, JAMES ALLEN
JOHNSON, JIM--[31]

JOHNSON, JAMES WELDON
FAG, FREDERICK--[1]

JOHNSON, JAMES WILLIAM
JOHNSON, JAMES WELDON--[33]

JOHNSON, JANICE
BARTLETT, JANICE--[26]ROM--
"HOME FIELD ADVANTAGE"
"ALL THROUGH THE HOUSE"
"LIFESAVER"

JOHNSON, JERRY MACK
MACK, JERRY--[1]

JOHNSON, JOAN HELEN
JEFFERS, JO--[1][31]

JOHNSON, JOHN ARTHUR
JOHNSON, JACK--[31]

JOHNSON, JOSEPH EARL
FITZGERALD, HAL--[31]

JOHNSON, JOYCE
GLASSMAN, JOYCE--[31]

JOHNSON, KENNETH R.
JOHNSON, KEN--[23]AMERICAN/SF

JOHNSON, LESLIE J.
JOHNSON, LESLIE T.--[2]

JOHNSON, LILLIAN BEATRICE
JOHNSON, LEE--[3][40]MYS--
GIFFORD "KEEP IT SIMPLE" '63
GIFFORD "HEADS FOR DEATH" '66 & MORE

JOHNSON, MARGUERITA
ANGELOU, MAYA--[1]

JOHNSON, MARILUE CAROLYN
MARILUE--[1]

JOHNSON, MARION GEORGINA
MASSON, GEORGINA--[1][22]ENGLISH-ITALIAN

JOHNSON, MARY
RODGERS, M.J.--[9][10][21][26][34]MYS/ROM--
HARL 128 "A TASTE OF DEATH" '89 & 8 MORE

JOHNSON, MAUD LALITA
LALITA--[1][2]

JOHNSON, NANCY MARR
MARR, NANCY J.--[1][8]

JOHNSON, NORMA K. TADLOCK
KIRBY, KAY--W/JANICE BACZEWSKI,[9][21]ROM--
"SUMMERTIME LOVE"
"AUTUMN BEGINNING"
TADLOCK, NORMA--[21]ROM--
"INCA GOLD"
"TOO HOT TO HANDLE"

JOHNSON, PAMELA HANSFORD
LOMBARD, NAP--W/NEIL STEWART,[22][34]MYS--
CASSELL "TIDY DEATH" '40
SIMON "GRINNING PIG" '43

JOHNSON, PAULA JANICE
JOHNSON, JANN--[31]

JOHNSON, R.V.
JOHNSON, ROB--[8]

JOHNSON, RENATE
MARSH, ELLEN TANNER--[9][21][26]ROM--
"SCARLET & GOLD"
"IF THIS BE MAGIC" & MORE

JOHNSON, RICHARD A.
JOHNSON, DICK--[31]

JOHNSON, RONALD
CHAMBERLAIN, THEODORE--W/JONATHAN
CHAMBERLAIN WILLIAMS,[8][22]AMERICAN

JOHNSON, RUBY KELLEY
KELLEY, RUBY M.--[31]

JOHNSON, SUSAN MARIE A.
BARKIN, JILL--[21][26][34]MYS/ROM--
BERK "HOT STREAK" '90

JOHNSON, THOMAS E.
EDWARDS, JOHN--G. JOHNSON-'JOHNSON' BIO
IN ECHOES #1, P18
THOMAS, EDDY--G. JOHNSON-'JOHNSON' BIO
IN ECHOES #1, P18

JOHNSON, VICKIE
JOHNSON, VALERIE--[1]

JOHNSON, VICTOR HUGO
BELL, JOHN--[1][31]

JOHNSON, VICTOR L.
PATRICK, VICTOR--[34]MYS--
HOUSE "THREE TO MAKE MURDER" '47

JOHNSON, VIRGINIA
JOHNSON, JINNA--[31]

JOHNSON, VIRGINIA WALES
COUSIN VIRGINIA--[1]

JOHNSON, WALTER RYERSON
BLOOD, MATTHEW--W/DAVIS DRESSER, V. BERCH-
GM PSEUDS, PP 33,[3][18]--
GM 235 "AVENGER" '52
GM 423 "DEATH IS A LOVELY DAME" '54

JOHNSON, WALTER RYERSON [CONT]
HALLIDAY, BRETT--W/ROBERT ARTHUR, T. JOHNSON-
ECHOES #23,MYS,HP--
MSMM "FATAL MESSAGE" JUN '61
HALLIDAY, BRETT--T. JOHNSON ECHOES #23,
GREG GOODE-"CRIME UNDER COVER #3" MAG,
MYS,HP--
MSMM "INARTICULATE CORPSE" JUN '58
MSMM "ODDS ON MURDER" APR '60
MSMM "BODY ON THE BEACH" DEC '60
MIKE SHAYNE SERIES
HALLIDAY, BRETT--GHOSTED--
DODD "DOLLS ARE DEADLY" '60
DODD "KILLERS FROM THE KEYS" '61
JOHNSON, RYERSON--[31][34]--
WNC 69 "SOUTH TO SONORA" '46
RSB 10 "NAKED IN THE STREETS" '52
RSB 28 "MISSISSIPPI FLAME" '53
GM 459 "LADY IN DREAD" '55
ROBESON, KENNETH--W/LESTER DENT,[2][34]MYS,HP--
BB "FANTASTIC ISLAND" '66
BB "LAND OF ALWAYS-NIGHT" '66
BB "MOTION MENACE" '71
WALLACE, ROBERT--T. JOHNSON-ECHOES #17,
[3]MYS,HP--
PHD "SILENT DEATH" DEC '36
PHD "MURDER CARAVAN" JAN '37
PHD "HENCHMAN OF DEATH" MAR '37

JOHNSON, WILLIAM O.
NICHOLAS, WILLIAM--W/NICHOLAS P. THIMMESCH,[1]

JOHNSSON, [K.O.] HARALD
BERNFELDT, BENGT--[29]MYS
MILLER, MAX--[29]MYS--4 NOVELS, ALL '17
SCHIOLDBRAND, GRAN--[29]MYS--
DBLDY "DODSSKOTTETS EKO FRAN SARAJEVO
TILL BALKANS" '14
WILKINS, ROBINSON--[29]MYS--33 NOVELS '16-26

JOHNSTON, ALASTAIR
POLTROON--W/FRANCES BUTLER,[1]

JOHNSTON, ALEXANDER
SMITH, SPARTUCUS--[8]

JOHNSTON, ANNA
CARBERY, EITHNE--[22]IRISH

JOHNSTON, CHARLES
ONEIROPOLOS--[1]

JOHNSTON, GEORGE HENRY
MARTIN, SHANE--[1][3]MYS--
COLLINS "MYTH IS MURDER" '59
COLLINS "SARACEN SHADOW" '57 & 5 MORE

JOHNSTON, GEORGE HARCOURT
VANDON, GEORGE--[1]

JOHNSTON, GRACE L. KEITH
KEITH, LESLIE--[1][3]MYS--
HURST "A PLEASANT ROGUE" '02

JOHNSTON, HENRY
JOHNSTON, HANK--[31]

JOHNSTON, HUGH ANTHONY S.
FIGHTER PILOT, A--[31]
STURTON, HUGH--[33]

JOHNSTON, JILL
CROWE, F.J.--[1][31]

JOHNSTON, MABLE ANNESLEY
MARNEY, SUZANNE--[8]

JOHNSTON, NORMA
BOLTON, ELIZABETH--[1][9][33]ROM
CHAMBERS, CATHERINE E.--[1][9][33]ROM
CHAMBERS, KATE--[9]ROM
DRYDEN, PAMELA--[1][9][33]ROM
HARRIS, LAVINA--[1][9][33]ROM
ROBERTS, ADRIAN--[9]ROM
ST. JOHN, NICOLE--[7][26][34]SF--
RANDOM "GUINEVERE'S GIFT" '77
RANDOM "MEDECI RUG" '75
RANDOM "WYCHWOOD" '77

JOHNSTON, PAUL
PARIS, JUSTINE--[14]ADULT--
OLYM OPH#249 "THE HORSE MISTRESS" '71

JOHNSTON, REGINALD FLEMNG
IRVING, CHRISTOPHER--[1]
IRVING, REGINALD--[1]
LIN, SHAO-YANG--[1]
SANCTION--[1]

JOHNSTON, RICHARD MALCOLM
PERCH, PHILEMON--[1]

JOHNSTON, ROBERT THOMSON
FORSYTH, R.A.--[8]

JOHNSTON, RONALD
NELSON, MARK--[34]MYS--
MacM "THE CRUSOE TEST" '76

JOHNSTON, SUSAN T.
JOHNSTON, TONY--[1][31]AMERICAN

JOHNSTON, VELDA
JASON, VERONICA--[9][17][18][29][31]--
"SO WILD A HEART"
"NEVER CALL IT LOVE"
"WILD WINDS OF LOVE"

JOHNSTON, VELMA B.
WILD HORSE ANNIE--[1]

JOHNSTON, WILLIAM
CLAUDIA, SUSAN--[3][31]MYS--
SIGN "SEARCHING SPECTRE" '67
SIGN "MADNESS AT THE CASTLE" '66 & MORE
GARTH, ED--[3]MYS--
LAN "REVOLUTIONIST" '70
LAN "THE HOSTAGE" '71
JAY, WILLA--[3][21][26]MYS/ROM--
LAN 73-613 "A FEAR IN BORZANO" '67
SINCLAIR, HEATHER--[1][21][26]ROM--
"REMEMBERED KISS" & MORE

JOHNSTONE, CHARLES
ADEPT, AN--[1][2]

JOHNSTONE, FRANK
WILSON, ANGUS--[2]

JOHNSTONE, TED
MCDANIEL, DAVID--[2][11]

JOHNSTONE, W.H.
SAGE, RUE--[34]AUSTRALIAN/MYS--
PACKER "A RECORD MYS" '08

JOHNSTONE, WILLIAM W.
MASON, WILLIAM--V. BERCH LTR TO HUBIN '94,MYS--
ZEBRA "DAGGER" '84
ZEBRA "EAGLE DOWN" '85

JOKAI, MOR
JOKAI, MAURUS--[1][32]MYS--
EW "THE LETTERS" AUG '66

JONAS, DORIS F.
KLEIN, DORIS F.--[1][31]

JONAS, JOHANNA
JONAS-LICHTENWALLER, J.--[1]

JONAS, ROBERT
ROB-JON--[2]

JONES, A. MILES
BULLINGHAM, ANN--[8]

JONES, ADRIENNE
GREGORY, MASON--W/DORIS MEEK,[1][3][22]MYS--
ARCADIA "IF TWO OF THEM ARE DEAD" '53

JONES, ADRIENNE
MASON, GREGORY--W/DORIS MEEK,[2][3][22]MYS--
ARCADIA "WITH SOUL SO DEAD" '56

JONES, ALICE I.
JEROME, FERRIS--[1]
JOHN, ALIX--[1]
TWO WOMEN OF THE WEST--W/ELLA MARCHANT,[2]

JONES, ARTHUR LLEWELLYN
BISHOP, MORCHARD--W/OLIVER STONOR,[7]SF--
"DREAMS & VISIONS:..IMAGINATION OF ARTHUR MACHEN.." '87
MACHEN, ARTHUR--[2][32][34]MYS/HOR--
DUCKWORTH "THE TERROR" '17
EQMM "COSY ROOM" MAR '49
PERROT, GERVASE--[1]
SILURIENSIS, LEOLINUS--[1]

JONES, BARBARA L.
LEIGH, BARBARA--[26]ROM--
"TO TOUCH THE SUN"
"WEB OF LOVING LIES"

JONES, BRYAN L.
FARMER JONES--[31]

JONES, CANDY
CONOVER, JESSICA A.W.--[31]

JONES, CHARLES MARTIN
JONES, CHUCK--[31][33]

JONES, CLARA AUGUSTA
AUGUSTA, CLARA--[1][3]MYS--5 NOVELS ca 1900
STRONG, HERO--[1][3]MYS-- 3 NOVELS ca 1900
THORN, KATE--[1]

JONES, CLARENCE MEDLYCOTT
JONES, C.M.--[31]
JONES, JIMMY--[31]

JONES, CORNELIA
SOMMERS, JANE R.--[1]AMERICAN

JONES, DAVID
FITZPATRICK, WILLIAM--V. BERCH-'AFTER DARK' SERIES, BAE 27--
MacF 50-240 "TOKYO AFTER DARK" '65
MacF 60-235 "HONG KONG AFTER DARK" '66
MacF 75-298 "ISTANBUL AFTER DARK" '70

JONES, DAVID ROBERT
BOWIE, DAVID--[8][31]

JONES, DEBORAH
HOLDER, SAMANTHA--W/CAROL BURNS,
[9][21][26]ROM--
"SCANDAL IN BATH"
"TEMPORARY WIFE"
"MISS ROWLANDS RESOLVE"

JONES, DENNIS
SIMON, TED--V. BERCH LTR TO HUBIN '94/MYS--
WW "PAXOS TIGER" '89

JONES, DENNIS FELTHAM
JONES, D.F.--[1]

JONES, DIANE MCCLURE
JONES, MCCLURE--[21]ROM--
"FIX UP SERVICE"
"WHEN SEPTEMBER RETURNS"
"WHAT I KNOW ABOUT BOYS"
MATTHEWS, PHOEBE--[9][21][26]ROM--
"THE BOY ON THE COVER"
"HONEYMOON HOUSE"
"UNSUITABLE LOVERS"

JONES, DOROTHY HOLDER
JONES, DUANE--[1][22]AMERICAN

JONES, EDDIE
EDDIE--[1][2]
FANTONI, S.--[2]

JONES, EDITH NEWBALD
WHARTON, EDITH--[1][32]MYS--
EQMM "A BOTTLE OF PERRIER" DEC '48

JONES, EDWARD GERMAN
GERMAN, EDWARD--[8]

JONES, ELIZABETH B.
BROWN, BETTY--[1][31]AMERICAN

JONES, EMILY BEATRIX C.
JONES, E.B.C.--[1]
LUCAS, EMILY BEATRIX C.--[1]

JONES, EMMA GARRISON
WALRAVEN, E.G.--[1]AMERICAN

JONES, EVAN DAVID
CEITHO, DEWI--[1][31]WELCH
JONES, E.D.--[1]WELCH
RHYDDERCH, IENAN--[1]WELCH

JONES, EVERETT LEROI
BARAKA, AMIDI--[31]AMERICAN--POETRY
JONES, LEROI--[31]AMERICAN--POETRY

JONES, FELIX EDWARD AYLM.
AYLMER, FELIX--[22][31]ENGLISH

JONES, FRANCIS A.
PERIL, MILTON R.--[2][11]

JONES, FRANK H.
MENTOR--[8]

JONES, GEORGE
CLIFFE, LEIGH--[1]ENGLISH

JONES, GERALDINE
MCCAUGHREAN, GERALDINE--[1][33]

JONES, GERTRUDE WARDEN
WARDEN, GERTRUDE--[1]

JONES, GRIFFITH ROBERT
LLEYON, GUTTO--[1]WELCH

JONES, GWYNETH A.
HALAM, ANN--[1][2][7][31]ENGLISH

JONES, HARRY AUSTIN
GRAHAM, HARRY--[28]
JONS, HAL--[8][28]WEST--
MULLER "LLANO KID" '62
MULLER "MOCHITA STAGE" '64 & MORE

JONES, HELEN HINCKLEY
HINCKLEY, HELEN--[1][22][31][33]AMERICAN

JONES, J.D.F.
JORDAN, DAVID--[34]JOSEPH "NILE GREEN" '73
DEUTSCH "BLACK ACCOUNT" '75
DEUTSCH "DOUBLE RED" '81

JONES, J.G.
BLOOMER, STEVE--[1]
EARLE, AMBROSE--[1]
GORDON, GEOFREY--[1]
TREW, DIGHTON--[1]

JONES, JACK
EDMOND, JAY--[1]AMERICAN
REYNOLDS, JACK--[1][31]--
"A WOMAN OF BANGKOK"
"DAUGHTERS OF AN ANCIENT RACE"

JONES, JAMES ATHEARNE
MURGATROYD, MATTHEW--[1]

JONES, JAMES LARKIN
JONES, JACK--[1][31]ENGLISH

JONES, JAN
WELLES, CARON--[21][26]ROM--
"RAVEN'S SONG"

JONES, JEANETTE
ALLYN, JENNIFER--[1][31]

JONES, JOHN
MATHETES--[1]WELSH

JONES, JOHN ALLEN
JONES, COURTWAY--[7]--
'KING ARTHUR' #1: "IN THE SHADOW OF
THE OAK KING" '91

JONES, JOHN FINBAR
BELL, ROBIN--[31]

JONES, JOHN ROBERT
DALMAS, JOHN--[3][7][23][31]MYS/SF--
TOR "VARKAUS CONSPIRACY' '83

JONES, JOSEPH BOLITHO
MOONDYNE JOE--[13]AUSTRALIAN

JONES, JUDITH ANASTASIA
MARO, JUDITH--[8]

JONES, JUDITH PATERSON
PATERSON, JUDITH--[1]

JONES, JUSTIN
HAZEL, HARRY--[34]MYS--
MAGAZINE PUB "THREE GOLDEN BALLS; OR,
A STRING OF PEARLS" 1885

JONES, KATHLEEN EVE
ADLER, KATHLEEN--[1][31]ENGLISH

JONES, KENNETH WESTCOTT
TAUNTON, ERIC--[1]ENGLISH
WESTCOTT-JONES, K.--[1]ENGLISH

JONES, L.A.M.
CHANNING, MARK--[34]MYS--
5 HUTCHINSON BOOKS '33-7

JONES, LANGDON
PEAKE, MERVYN--[23]--
RECONSTRUCTED & COMPLETED
PEAKE'S "TITUS ALONE" '59
WESBURY, MICHAEL--[2]

JONES, LUCY M.
LUX--[22][34]MYS--
RICHARDS, "A SECRET OF THE SEA
& OTHER COLONIAL STORIES" 1899

JONES, MARTHA
JONES, MARTI--[26]ROM--
"DREAMWEAVER"
"A LOVE THROUGH TIME"
"TIME'S HEALING HEART"

JONES, MARY R.
STERLING-JONES, M.--[1]AMERICAN

JONES, MAYNARD BENEDICT
JONES, NARD--[1][28][31]MYS/WEST--
11 NOVELS '30-56

JONES, NANCY E.
LUENN, NANCY--[7]SF--
"ARTIC UNICORN" '86
"GOLDCLIMBERS" '91

JONES, NOEL
AALBEN, PATRICK--[1][3][31]MYS--
HALE "THE GRAB" '77

JONES, P.D.
DENHAM, PETER--[8]

JONES, P.F.G.
JONES, GONNER--[1][2]

JONES, PAULINE
PAUL, JOANNA--[2]

JONES, PEGGY
SIDETRACKED HOME EXECUTV.--W/PAM YOUNG,
[1]AMERICAN

JONES, RAYMOND F.
ANDERSON, DAVID--[2][11][23]SF--
"UTILITY" '44

JONES, ROBERT AMBROSE
AP IWAN, EMRYS--[22]WELSH

JONES, ROBERT MAYNARD
JONES, BOBI--[8]
PROBERT, LOWRI--[8]
SION, MARI--[8]

JONES, ROBERT PAGE
PAGE, THOMAS--W/DANIEL T. STREIB,[2]

JONES, ROBERT REYNOLDS JR
JONES, BOB--[31]

JONES, ROBERT TYRE JR.
JONES, BOBBY--[31]

JONES, RUDOLPH CLIFFORD
ROSS, JOHN--[3]MYS--9 NOVELS '36-41

JONES, RUSS
RANDOLPHE, ARABELLA--CR/[7][11]--
BERK 03508 "THE VAMPIRE TAPES" '77
YOUNGER, JACK--W/DAVID A. KRAFT,[7]SF--
MANOR "CURSE OF THE PHAROAHS" '76
CA "REST IN AGONY" '79
YOUNGER, JACK--[7][34]MYS/SF--
MANOR "CLAW" '76
MANOR "DEVLIN" '76
MANOR "CURSE OF ANUBIS" '76
CARLYLE "DEMON" '79
CARLYLE "SATAN SUBLETS" '79

JONES, SALLY ROBERTS
ROBERTS, SALLY--[1]

JONES, SHEILA MACLEOD
MACLEOD, SHEILA--[7]SF--
BODLEY HEAD "XANTHE & THE ROBOTS" '77
BODLEY HEAD "CIRCUIT-BREAKER" '78

JONES, STEPHEN GREGORY
GREGORY, STEVEN--[2][31]

JONES, STEPHEN [PHILLIP]
FALORP, NELSON P.--[1][31]

JONES, SUSAN CARLETON
CARLETON, MILECETE--[1]CANADIAN
CARLETON, S.--[11][22][34]CANADIAN/MYS--
LITTLE "LA CHANCE MINE MYSTERY" '20
CARLETON, SUSAN--[2]CANADIAN
CARLETON-MILECETE--[8]CANADIAN
MILECETE, HELEN--[1]CANADIAN

JONES, TERENCE GRAHAM P.
JONES, TERRY--[7][31]SF--
PAVILION "FAIRY TALES"
PAVILION "NICOBOBINUS"
PAVILION "SAGA OF ERIC THE VIKING"
PYTHON, MONTY--[31]--
CO-WROTE SCREENPLAYS W/CHAPMAN, CLEESE,
GILLIAM, PALIN & IDLE

JONES, THADDEUS B.
JONES, TAD--[31]

JONES, THEADOR EDWARD
JONES, TED--[31]

JONES, THOMAS W.
BUTCK, ZULIE--[1][31]AMERICAN

JONES, VERNON H.
YOUNG, RAYMOND A.--[2][11]

JONES, VIRGIL CARRINGTON
JONES, PAT--[1][22][31]AMERICAN

JONES, WILLIAM DAVID A.
JONES, BILL--[31]

JONES, [A] ARTHUR GWYNNE
CHALFONT, ALUN--[31]

JONES, [EVERETT] LEROI
BARAKA, IMAMU AMIRI--[1][6][8]AMERICAN

JONES, [MAX HIM] HENRY
MAXHIM, TRISTAN--[1]FRENCH

JONES-JACKSON, PATRICIA
JONES-JACKSON, PAT--[31]

JONES-WILSON, FAUSTINE C.
JONES, FAUSTINE CHILDRESS--[31]

JONGH, EDWARD A. DE
BARTOLOME, JOHAN--[1]

JONKOV, NIKOLA
VAPCAROV, NIKOLA--[22]BULGARIAN

JONSSON, HJALMAR NILS
JOST, HANS--[29]MYS--
AHLEN & AKERLUND "FYRA SPADER ESS" '12

JONSSON, JON
VOER, JON UR--[1]ICELANDIC

JOOST, ELISABETH
BEHM, JONNY--[39]GERMAN

JOOST, EVELYN
PETERS, EVELYN--[39][40]GERMAN/MYS --
"TRANS-EUROP-EXPRESS" '73

JOPP, HAROLD DOWLING JR.
JOPP, HAL--[31]

JORDAN, DEBORAH [DEBBIE]
DAVIS, MELANIE--W/CLAUDETTE WILLIAMS,
[21][26]ROM--
"WILD DAWN FEVER"
JORDAN, ROSEMARY--W/MARY J. DAVIS,
[9][21][26]ROM--
"LOVE'S LEGACY"

JORDAN, JAMES A.
DUGGAN, CHRIS--[34]MYS--
CRESTA "THE LAST SHOT" '60
JORDAN, J.A.--S. HOLLAND-PPCC#9,MYS--
HUGHES "COTTONWOOD GALLOWS" '49
SARTO, BEN--S. HOLLAND-PPCC#9,[34]MYS,HP--
MOF "BABY MOLL" '57
WHEATLEY, CHRIS--S. HOLLAND-PPCC#9,[34]MYS--
10 GRAY NOVELS '50-6

JORDAN, JUNE
MEYER, JUNE--[1][8][33]AMERICAN

JORDAN, MARILYN
LOCKHART, LYNN--[26]ROM--
HARL 498 "DATE WITH AN OUTLAW"
HARL 527 "NICKIE'S GHOST"

JORDAN, MILDRED ARLENE
MILLICENT--[1]

JORDAN, MRS. ARTHUR
ASTON, HELEN--[1]

JORDAN, PHILIP [F]
FRANCE, VICTOR--[1]ENGLISH

JORDAN, ROBERT FURNEAUX
PLAYER, ROBERT--[18][34]MYS--
GOLZ "INGENIUS MR. STONE" '45
GOLZ "HOMOCIDAL COLONEL" '70 & MORE

JORDAN, W.
ANDRE, W.J.--[1]

JORDAN, WILLIAM
JORDAN, BILL--[31]

JORGENSEN, J.S.
STORM, JANNICK--[1][2]

JORGENSEN, MARY VENN
VENN, MARY ELEANOR--[1][33]AMERICAN
ADRIAN, MARY--[1][33]AMERICAN

JORGENSON, ALF A.
ARNE, AARON--[2][11]

JOSCELYN, ARCHIE LYNN
ARCHER, A.A.--[28][34]MYS--
PHOENIX "THREE MEN MURDERED" '36
PHOENIX "WEEK-END MURDERS" '38

JOSCELYN, ARCHIE LYNN
ARCHER, ARCHIE ALEXANDER--L. ROBBINS
LTR MAR '94
CODY, A.R.--[8]
CODY, AL--PPCC#8,[28][31]WEST--
ARCADIA "STAR TOTER" '62
DODD "EMPTY SADDLES" '46 & MORE
HOLT, TEX--[28][31]WEST--
ARCADIA "SILENT GUNS" '63
PHOENIX "DARK CANYON" '48 & MORE
MCKENNA, EVELYN--[28][34]MYS/ROM--
PHOENIX "FIRE IN MY HEART" '36
GRAMMERCY "ENCHANTED PARK" '37
ARCADIA "CASTLE MIDNIGHT" '66
BOUREGY "CASTLE LIGHT" '76 & MORE
WESTLAND, LYNN--PPCC#8,[21][22][28]WEST--
PHOENIX "SON OF SADDLE" '36 & MANY MORE

JOSE, ARTHUR WILBERFORCE
DARE, ISHMAEL--[1][13]ENGLISH-AUSTRALIAN

JOSEPH, ARTHUR
ARTHUR, JOHN--[1]AMERICAN

JOSEPH, GEORGE ISRAEL
ST. GEORGE, JOSEPH--[34]--
HAM "DANGEROUS IMPERSONATION" '38
INVINCIBLE "CASE OF TATOOED TORSO" '50

JOSEPH, JAMES HERZ
ADAMS, LOWELL--[1][22][31][33]AMERICAN
ALZADA, JUAN SANCHEZ--[33]AMERICAN
PEREZ, WALTER--[33]AMERICAN
SANCHEZ ALZADA, JUAN--[33]AMERICAN

JOSEPH, MARIE
MOHOAO--[2]

JOSEPH, MARIE
SUE, EUGENE--[2]

JOSEPH, MICHAEL KENNEDY
JOSEPH, M.K.--[1]ENGLISH

JOSEPH, ROBERT
JOSEPH, ROBIN--[9][21][26]ROM--
"LOVE'S FERVENT FURY"

JOSEPH, ROBERT FARRAS
JOSEPH, R.F.--[21][26][31]ROM--
"THE BUCCANEER"
"DIVA, KATE'S WAY"
"ODILE"
JOSEPH, ROBERT F.--[31]

JOSEPHS, RAY
RAPHAEL, JAY--[1][22]AMERICAN

JOSHUA, ANTHONY
ANTHONY, PETER--W/PETER LEVIN SHAFFER,
[29]MYS

JOSKE, ANNE GOYDER
NEVILLE, MARGOT--W/MARGOT GOYDER, [18][34][36]AUSTRALIAN/MYS-- 22 MYS NVLS '43-66

JOTOV, DIMITAR IVANOV
ELIN-PELIN--[22]BULGARIAN
IVANOV, DIMITAR--[22]BULGARIAN
PELIN, ELIN--[22]BULGARIAN
ELIN, PELIN--[1]BULGARIAN

JOUBERT, DIRK DANIEL
JOUBERT, DIAN--[1]SOUTH AFRICAN

JOUHANDEAU, MARCEL H.
PROVENCE, MARCEL--[1]FRENCH

JOURDAIN, ELEANOR FRANCES
JOURDAIN, E.F.--[1]ENGLISH
LAMONT, FRANCES--[8]ENGLISH

JOVANOVIC, JOVAN
ZMAJ--[1]SERBIAN

JOWITT, DEBORAH
BENSON, RACHEL--[31]

JOY, WILLIAM "TED"
MURPHY, WARREN--W/WARREN MURPHY, [7]MYS/SF,HP-- 'DESTROYER' SERIES #42 "TIMBERLINE"

JOYCE, JAMES
CHANEL--[8]

JOYCE, JON LOYD
DOULOS, JAY--[31]

JOYCE, MARIANNE
SADDENS, ANNE--V. BERCH-BRNDN/ BC PSEUDS, BAE 22, P24

JOYCE, WILLIAM
JOYCE, BILL--[31][33]

JOYNER, CAROLYN
HART, CARRIE--[9][21][26]ROM-- "HARD-HEADED WOMAN"
MERRITT, JACKIE--[9][21][26]ROM-- "BABE IN THE WOODS" "RAMBLIN' MAN" & MORE

JOYNER, TIMOTHY
JOYNER, TIM--[31]

JUDD, ALFRED
JOLLING, JACK--[1]ENGLISH
POWER, NELSON--[1]ENGLISH

JUDD, FREDERICK CHARLES
COURTNEY, JOHN--[1][22]ENGLISH
LESTER-RANDS, A.--[1][22][31]ENGLISH
MILLER, G.R.--[1][22][31]ENGLISH

JUDD, HARRISON
GARRETT, TRUMAN--[8]

JUDD, MARGARET [H]
GARRETT, TRUMAN--[22][31][34]MYS-- ARCADIA "MURDER-FIRST EDITION" '56

JUDGE, M.
KESTREL, WARD--[35]AUSTRALIAN-- CLEVELAND

JUDKINS, PHILLIP EDWARD
JUDKINS, PHIL--[31]

JUDSON, EDWARD Z.C.
BUNTLINE, NED--[19][34]MYS/WEST-- 1847-89 - LAST PUBLISHED AFTER HIS DEATH IN 1886
ELDERDICE, J. RAYMOND--L. SERVER- 'DANGER IS MY BUSINESS'
HORN, R. de S.--L. SERVER- 'DANGER IS MY BUSINESS'-- "NO BACK TRAIL" JULY '32
McROBERTS, CAPT. KERRY--L. SERVER- 'DANGER IS MY BUSINESS'-- TSS "THE STOLEN GAS GUN"

JUDSON, JEANNE
HANCOCK, FRANCES DEAN--JEAN F. LE DEIST, BAE 12,[34]MYS-- AVALON "LEGACY OF FEAR" '69
THORNE, EMILY--[34]MYS-- AVALON "FLIGHT HOSTESS" '58 AVALON "AARON'S SERPENT" '62 & 3 MORE

JUDSON, RALPH
STRANGER, RALPH--[1][2][11]

JUDY, WILLIAM LEWIS
JUDY, WILL--[31]
PORT, WYMAR--[22]AMERICAN

JUENGEL, EBERHARD
JUNGEL, EBERHARD--[31]

JUENGER, ERNST
JUNGER, ERNST--[31]

JUHASZ, LESLIE ALBERT
SHEPARD, LESLIE ALBERT--[1]HUNGARIAN

JUHLING, JOH.
LOSSIUS, ROBERT--[39]GERMAN
TAYLOR, WILLIAM--[39]GERMAN

JUHNKE, JOE
SHANE, J.E.--[39]GERMAN/HOR/WEST
SHANE, YOUNG E.--[39]GERMAN/HOR/WEST

JULESBERG, ELIZABETH R.M.
MONTGOMERY, ELIZABETH--[31]-- CHILDREN'S FICT & TEXTBOOKS
MONTGOMERY, ELIZABETH R.--[1]

JULIAN, DONNA
GREY, JILLIAN--[26]ROM-- "SINS" "STAR-CROSED"

JULIEN, CHARLES-ANDRE
DELORME, ANDRE--[1][31]FRENCH

JULIEN, [CAROLA] ISOBEL
SALISBURY, CAROLA--[9][21]ROM-- "DOLPHIN SUMMER" "DARK INHERITANCE" & 4 MORE

JULIUS, EMANUEL
HALDEMAN-JULIUS, EMANUEL--[1]AMERICAN

JULYAN, LOUISE ELIZABETH
LEITH, ELIZABETH--[1]CANADIAN JOURNALIST

JUNE, HAROLD
KATELEY, WALTER--[1][2]

JUNEMAN, KAREN
DEVIN, FLANNA--[9]ROM

JUNEMANN, IGNA MARIA
MARIA, IGNA--[39]GERMAN

JUNG, ELSE
BERGHAMER, LISA--[39]GERMAN/JUV
LINDEMANN, ELSA--[39]GERMAN/JUV

JUNG, HERMANN
VON EHRENFELS-MEIR., ERIC--[39]GERMAN

JUNG, JOHANN HEINRICH
JUNG-STILLING, JOHANN H.--[39]GERMAN

JUNG, RICHARD
YOUNG, GORDON--[39]GERMAN/WEST

JUNG, ROBERT
AMBERG, LORENZ--[39]GERMAN
FORTRIDGE, ALLAN G.--[39]GERMAN
ROBERTS, L.R.--[39]GERMAN

JUNGBLUT, ALICE
GRUNER-JUNGBLUT, ALICE--[39]GERMAN

JUNGER, ERNST
JUENGER, ERNST--[23]GERMAN/SF

JUNGFER, VICTOR
JUNGHERR, VICTOR GEORG--[39]GERMAN

JUNIKE, ROLF
FISCHER, URSULA--[39]GERMAN
PETERSEN, PETRA--[39]GERMAN
RICHTER, HELGA--[39]GERMAN
RITTER, INA--[39]GERMAN
STOLL, URSULA--[39]GERMAN
VON ESCHWEG, CORNELIA--[39]GERMAN
WEBER, KARIN--[39]GERMAN
WINTER, HELGA--[39]GERMAN

JURCZYK, MARY IRENE D.
MICHAELS, IRENE--[7][9][21][26]ROM/SF--
"FRENCHMAN'S MISTRESS"

JURGENS, JAMES
SAGE, JETT--[14]ADULT--
OLYM TC-2228 "CRAZY WILD" '68
OLYM TC-429 "CRAZY WILD BREAKS LOOSE" '68

JURIN-REID, BARBARA
REID, LESLIE--[9][21][26]ROM--
"GRAND STYLE"
"LETTER OF INTENT"

JURKA, BLANCHE
YURKA, BLANCHE--[1]AMERICAN

JUSKEVICE, MILDRED H.
BLAKE, ANTONIO--[9][21][26]ROM--
"LASTING LOVE"
JAMES, SARAH--[9][21][26]ROM--
"PUBLIC AFFAIR"

JUSTIN, JENNIFER
WEST, JENNIFER--[21][26]ROM--
"EDGE OF VENUS"
"EARTH & FIRE" & 13 MORE
YUN, TAN--[22]CHINESE

JUTA, JAN
JUTA, RENE--[31]

JUTE, ANDREW
McCOY, ANDREW--V. BERCH LTR TO HUBIN '94,MYS--
SECKER "INSURRECTIONIST" '79
SECKER "BLOOD IVORY" '84
SECKER "LANCE OF GOD" '87
MCCOY, ANDREW--[7][23]SOUTH AFRICAN-AUSTRALIAN/SF--
GRAFTON "MEYERESCO HELIX" '88

KABDEBO, THOMAS
KABDEBO, TAMAS--[31][33]

KABEL, WALTHER
ABEL, W.K.--[39]GERMAN
ABELSEN, OLAF K.--[39]GERMAN
BEKAL, WALTHER--[39]GERMAN
BEL, W.K.--[39]GERMAN
BELKA, W.--[39]GERMAN
BELKA, WILLI--[39]GERMAN
BELL, W.K.--[39]GERMAN
HELD, KARL--[39]GERMAN ?? UNCONFIRMED ??
KABLER, KAPITAN WILLIAM--[39]GERMAN
KEBLA, WALTRAUD--[39]GERMAN
LEBA, W.K.--[39]GERMAN
LEBKA, WALLY--[39]GERMAN
LENSEN, W.--[39]GERMAN
NEUHOFER, W.--[39]GERMAN
NEUSCHUB, WALTHER--[39]GERMAN
SCHRAUT, MAX--[39]GERMAN
SCHUGGE, M.E.--[39]GERMAN
VON MUNDE, SWEA--[39]GERMAN
VON NEUHOF, W.--[39]GERMAN
WALTHER, KARLA--[39]GERMAN
WENDT, KATHE--[39]GERMAN
ZEHLEN, W.I.--[39]GERMAN

KACEWGARI, ROMAINE
AJAR, EMILE--[1][31]FRENCH
BOGAT, SHATAN--[1][31]FRENCH
DEVILLE, RENE--[1][31]FRENCH
GARY, ROMAIN--[2][7][23]FRENCH
GARY, ROMAINE--[1][22][31]FRENCH
KACEW, ROMAIN--[1][31]FRENCH
KACEW, ROMAN--[1][31]FRENCH
SINBALDI, FOSCO--[1]FRENCH

KACHELMEIER, GLENDA S.
SANDERS, GLENDA--[9][26]ROM--
HARL 454 "LOVER'S SECRETS"
HARL 510 "PLAYBOY MCCOY" & MORE
SANDS, GLENDA--[9][26]ROM--
SIL 337 "MOCKINGBIRD SUITE"
SIL 409 "HEART SHIFT" & MORE

KADOW, MANES
MACOKAY, A.--[39]GERMAN/SF--
WODAK, HERMANN--[39]GERMAN/SF--

KAELLBERG, STURE
KALLBERG, STURE--[31]

KAEPPLER, ADRIENNE LOIS
GATHERCOLE, ADRIENNE LOIS--[1][31]

KAESEN, MARIA
MUHLGRABNER, MARIA--[39]GERMAN

KAESTNER, ERICH
KASTNER, ERICH--[31]

KAFER, GRABRIELE
DITTMAR, GABRIELE--[39]GERMAN/JUV

KAFKA-H.-B., SOPHIE-M.
BRANDES, SOPHIE--[39]GERMAN/JUV

KAGAN, ANDREW
KANE, AARNO--[31]

KAGAN, GEORGE
LENOIR, PIERRE--[1]

KAGEY, RUDOLF H.
STEEL, KURT--[2][32][34]MYS--
10 BKS '35-43
MB "WITH INTENT TO KILL" NOV '45
SUS "UNDER THE COUNTER" JUN '60
STEEL[E], RUDOLF--[1]

KAHANE, JACK
BARR, CECIL--[8]
CARR, BASIL--[8]

KAHANE, MEIR [DAVID]
KAHANE, MARTIN--[1][31]
KING, MICHAEL--W/RENEE BUSE,[1][31]

KAHANOVITCH, PINHAS
NISTER, DER--[11]

KAHLER, HUGH [T] MACNAIR
ELPHINSTONE, MURGATROYD--[1][31]
HUGH, MACNAIR--L. ROBBINS LTR MAR '94--PULP

KAHLERT, KARL FRIEDRICH
FLAMMENBERG, LORENZ--[2][34][39]GERMAN/MYS/SF--
LANE "NECROMANCER: OR TALE OF THE
BLACK FOREST"
FLAMMERBERG, LAWRENCE--[1]
STEIN, BERNARD--[1]

KAHN, ALFRED REGINALD
BRETNOR, R.--[32]MYS--
EQMM "SPECIMEN OF THE WEEK" FEB '67
EQMM "PAPER TIGER" MAY '69
EQMM "GREATEST OF ALL WEBLEY
COLLECTORS" JUL '70
EQMM "A MATTER OF EQUINE
BALLISTICS" SEPT '71
EQMM "ACCIDENT EPIDEMIC" DEC '77
BRETNOR, REGINALD--[7]--'BRETNOR' LEGALIZED

KAHN, ELY JACQUES
KAHN, E.J. JR.--[1]

KAHN, HAROLD S.
SACKERMAN, HENRY--[1][11]

KAHN, KENNETH
HERBERT, KENNETH--V. BERCH-BRNDN/
BC PSEUDS, BAE 22, P24

KAHN, MARY
CAMERON, MIRANDA--[9][21][26]ROM--
"DESOLUTE DUKE"
"RELUCTANT ABIGAIL" & MORE
TROY, AMANDA--[9][21][26]ROM--
"DOUBLE DECEPTION"

KAHN, STEPHEN
KAHN, STEVE--[31]

KAHN, YITZHAK
BEN CHAIM--[1]
LEBENSON--[1]

KAHN-FOGEL, DANIEL MARK
FOGEL, DANIEL--[31]

KAHN-FREUND, OTTO
FREUND, OTTO K.--[31]

KAHNWEILER, DANIEL-HENRY
HENRY, DANIEL--[31]

KAIL, ROBERT
CURTIS, RICHARD HALE--[21]ROM,HP--
'SKYMASTER' SERIES:
"SEEKERS OF THE SKY"
"WIND NOR RAIN NOR DARK OF NIGHT"

KAINULAINEN, RAY
KAINEN, RAY--[14]ADULT--
OLYM TC#432 "A SEA OF THIGHS" '68
OLYM TC#441 "SPY WHO CAME" '69
OLYM TC#447 "COSMIC GASH" '69
OLYM TC#458 "HOUSES OF RISING SIN" '69
OLYM TC#469 "EARTH STATION SEX" '69
OLYM TC#482 "FUR PIE IN THE SKY" '70
OLYM OPS# "SATYR TREK" '70
KAININ, RAY--[2]
KALNEN, RAY--[1]

KAISER, HANS K.
OLIVER, RICHARD--[39]GERMAN/SF/JUV
RICHARD, R.J.--[39]GERMAN/SF/JUV

KAISER, OSCAR
VON DER GROTH, FRANZ--[39]GERMAN

KAISER, RONN & JANICE
KAISER, R.J.--DDLY PLEAS #3,[26]ROM--
"STRANGER IN MY ARMS" '93

KAISER, WALTER
GORRISH, WALTER--[1][39]GERMAN

KAKADE, GEETA M.
KINGSLEY, GEETA--[21][26]ROM--
"PROJECT VALENTINE"
"TENDER TRUCKER" & MORE

KAKONIS, THOMAS E.
KAKONIS, TOM E.--[31]

KAKU, LOUZANA
DAIR, CHRISTINA--[9][21][26]ROM--
"A WILL OF HER OWN"
"WINNING WAYS" & MORE

KALBFUSS, HEINRICH
KNIPPER, HEINZ--[39]GERMAN

KALER, JAMES OTIS
OTIS, JAMES--[1][2][33]
PERKINS, ABIGAIL--[1]
PRENTICE, AMY--[1]
WALRAVEN--[1]

KALICHMAN, CLAIRE
CALLIAM, SELMA--[1]

KALINICH, WILLIAM
DERFALL, ART--[14]ADULT--
OLYM OPH#-233 "THE BIKE FREAKS" '71

KALIS, BETTY
LAURENCE, BETHEL--LACHMAN LST '93, MYS--
EQMM "YOU ARE GOING TO DIE" AUG '56

KALISCH, A.
CRESCENDO--[8]

KALLAHNE, GUNTHER
ROBBY, ALEX--[39]GERMAN

KALLEN, KNUT HILDING
KNUTSSON, PER--[29]MYS

KALLMAN, MARY LOU
KENDALL, JACK--W/MARILYN OSER, V.BERCH LTR TO HUBIN '94, MYS--
AV "PLAYING FOR KEEPS" '89

KALMOE, ALF HALVOR
WANG, STEIN--[37]NORWEGIAN/MYS

KALMUCAZK, ROLF
DECKER, RALPH--[39]GERMAN/MYS/SF--
ADLER, JOE--[39]GERMAN/MYS/SF--
ALDEN, CLAUS--[39]GERMAN/MYS/SF--
ALDEN, THOMAS--[39]GERMAN/MYS/SF--
BERGER, RALF--[39]GERMAN/MYS/SF--
BOSTON, DON--[39][40]GERMAN/MYS--
"DIE NACKTE UND DER TOD" '72 & 12 OTHERS
BURGER, FRANK--[39]GERMAN/MYS/SF--
BURGER, FRED--[39]GERMAN/MYS/SF--
BURGER, HAL--[39]GERMAN/MYS/SF--
BURGER, HENRY--[39]GERMAN/MYS/SF--
BURGER, RALPH--[39]GERMAN/MYS/SF--
BURGER, RED--[39]GERMAN/MYS/SF--
CAIN, JOHN--[39]GERMAN/MYS/SF--
CARSON, RAY--[39]GERMAN/MYS/SF--
CARTER, HENRY--[39]GERMAN/MYS/SF--
CLAUSEN, NORBERT--[39]GERMAN/MYS/SF--
CLIFFORD, PAT--[39]GERMAN/MYS/SF--
COLLINS, CLIFF--[39]GERMAN/MYS/SF--
COLLINS, GLENN--[39]GERMAN/MYS/SF--
CONRADI, CHRISTIAN--[39]GERMAN/MYS/SF--
CORNER, CLIFF--[39]GERMAN/MYS/SF,HP--
COTTON, JERRY--[39]GERMAN/MYS,HP--
COUNT, CECIL--[39]GERMAN/MYS/SF--
DAYTON, PERRY--[39]GERMAN/MYS/SF
DEAL, SEFTON--[39]GERMAN/MYS/SF--
DELSEN, HARRY--[39]GERMAN/MYS/SF--
DEXTER, CLIFF--[39]GERMAN/MYS/SF--
DIERY, HERB--[39]GERMAN/MYS/SF--
DONNER, MIKE--[39]GERMAN/MYS/SF--
DORN, ALEC B.--[39]GERMAN/MYS/SF--
DORN, I.--[39]GERMAN/MYS/SF--
DOUGLAS, FRANK--[39]GERMAN/MYS/SF--
DUST, LIONEL--[39]GERMAN/MYS/SF--
EICH, SEBASTIAN--[39]GERMAN/MYS/SF--
FALCK, ROBERT--[39]GERMAN/MYS/SF--
FALK, HECTOR--[39]GERMAN/MYS/SF--
FALK, ROBERT--[39]GERMAN/MYS/SF--
FAROT, PIERRE--[39]GERMAN/MYS/SF--
FELLNER, CLAUS--[39]GERMAN/MYS/SF
FERRER, JEAN-PIERRE--[39]GERMAN/MYS/SF--
FERRIER, HENRI--[39]GERMAN/MYS/SF--
FLEIDEN, GEORG--[39]GERMAN/MYS/SF--
HAMMER, ROBBY--[39]GERMAN/MYS/SF--
HELDT, JORG--[39]GERMAN/MYS/SF--
HILLENBURG, MARTIN--[39]GERMAN/MYS/SF--
HILLSON, BERT--[39]GERMAN/MYS/SF--
HOFBERG, NORBERT--[39]GERMAN/MYS/SF--
HORSTEN, UDO--[39]GERMAN/MYS/SF--
JOLAS, PIERRE--[39]GERMAN/MYS/SF--
KELLOG, ROBBIE--[39]GERMAN/JUV
KELLOG, ROBERT--[39]GERMAN/MYS/SF--
KOLBER, THOMAS--[39]GERMAN/MYS/SF--
LAMBERT, FRANK--[39]GERMAN/MYS/SF--
LAMBERT, TONY--[39]GERMAN/MYS/SF--
LOEWEN, ROBERT--[39]GERMAN/MYS/SF--
MARTIN, MICHAEL--[39]GERMAN/MYS/SF--
MORENO, PHIL--[39]GERMAN/MYS/SF--
NESS, THOMAS--[39]GERMAN/MYS--
NORDEN, TIM--[39]GERMAN/MYS/SF--
ORLIK, HENRY--[39]GERMAN/MYS/SF--
ORLIK, JENS--[39]GERMAN/MYS/SF--
ORLOFF, FRANK--[39]GERMAN/MYS/SF--
OWENS, TED--[39]GERMAN/MYS/SF--
PARKER, FRED--[39]GERMAN/MYS/SF--
PAULSEN, ROBERT--[39]GERMAN/MYS/SF--

KALMUCAZK, ROLF [CONT]
PLOGAU, FRED--[39]GERMAN/MYS/SF
RANDALL, ROSS--[39]GERMAN/MYS/SF--
REIHER, ROLF--[39][40]GERMAN/MYS--
"BRUDERLEIN, KOMM STIRB MIT MIR" '72
& 2 OTHERS
REMPLE, SIMON--[39]GERMAN/MYS/SF--
SCHADEK, PETER--[39][40]GERMAN/MYS--
"DAS HORNISSENNEST" '80
SEON, SIGGI--[39]GERMAN/MYS/SF--
STEIN, CLAUS--[39]GERMAN/MYS/SF--
STERN, SEBASTIAN--[3]GERMAN/MYS/SF--
STETTNER, ERIK--[39]GERMAN/MYS/SF--
SURBANK, EVAN--[39]GERMAN/MYS/SF--
TANZER, MARTIN--[39]GERMAN/MYS/SF--
TRENK, PETER--[39]GERMAN/MYS/SF--
TURNER, ALLAN--[39]GERMAN/MYS/SF--
VENERDI, MARCELLO--[39]GERMAN/MYS/SF--
VONDREY, MARTIN--[39]GERMAN/MYS/SF--
WANK, THOMAS--[39]GERMAN/MYS/SF--
WELLS, TIM--[39]GERMAN/MYS/SF--
WELZ, MARTIN--[39]GERMAN/MYS/SF--
WELZ, STEFAN--[39]GERMAN/MYS/SF--
WELZ, THOMAS--[39]GERMAN/MYS/SF--
WILKOW, MICHAEL--[39]GERMAN/MYS/SF--
WOLF, STEFAN--[39][40]GERMAN/MYS--
"VAMPIR DER AUTOBAHN" '83
WOLFGARTEN, BERT--[39]GERMAN/MYS/SF--

KALNACH, DONAT G.
VEIIAN, ANDRIS--[1]

KALPAKIAN, LAURA ANNE
FITZGERALD, JULIET--V. BERCH LTR TO HUBIN '93, MYS--
VIKING "BELLE HAVEN" '90
GREY, CARENNA JANE--[1][31]

KALT, JEANNETTE CHAPPELL
CHAPPELL, JEANNETTE--[31]

KALTENBERGER, FRIEDERIKE
BERGER, FRANZISKA--[39]GERMAN/JUV

KALTENBOECK, JOHANNES
HOLTEN, FRITZ--[39]GERMAN

KALZ, ELFRIEDE
FRANKEN, RENATE--[39]GERMAN
HAGEN, LENI--[39[GERMAN

KAMAROFF, ALEX
MORGAN, DIANA--W/IRENE GOODMAN,[9][21][26]ROM--
"OCEAN FIRES"
"AMBER DREAMS" & MORE

KAMIEN, MARCIA
ROSE, MARCIA--W/ROSE NOVAK,[9][21][26]ROM--
"PRINCE OF ICE"
"MUSIC OF LOVE" & MORE

KAMINSKY, HOWARD & SUSAN
STANWOOD, BROOKS--[34]MYS--
MCGRAW "THE GLOW" '79
MCGRAW "THE SEVENTH CHILD" '81

KAMINSKY, MELVIN
BROOKS, MEL--[3][31]MYS--
PLAY "GET SMART" - BASED ON TV SERIES

KAMP, IRENE KITTLE
GRICE, GRIMES--[31]

KAMPF, ABRAHAM
KAMPF, AVRAM--[31]

KAMPF, HAROLD BERTRAM
KAYE, H.B.--[3][40]MYS--
GIFFORD "RED RAFFERTY" '49
GIFFORD "TOUCH OF THE SUN" '52 & MORE
KAYE, HAROLD B.--[22]MYSTERY

KANATSIZ, NECATI
KAHRAMAN, A.--[2]

KANAZAWA, MASAKATA
KANASAWA, ROGER--[31]

KANE, FRANCIS
ROBINS, HAROLD--[1]
RUBIN, HAROLD--[1]

KANE, FRANK
BOYD, FRANK--V. BERCH-MON PSEUDS, BAE 9, [1][3][31]MYS--
MON 133 "FLESH PEDDLERS" '59
GM 980 "JOHNNY STACCATO" '60

KANE, GERARD THOMAS MATT.
KANE, ROD--[31]

KANE, HENRY
MCCALL, ANTHONY--[3][11][18]MYS--
TRIDENT "OPERATION DELTA" '66
TRIDENT "HOLOCAUST" '67
MCKAY, KENNETH R.--[3][18][29]MYS--
PLBY "SHADOW OF THE KNIFE" '78
PLBY "INDECENT RELATIONS" '80
SAGOLA, MARIO J.--[3][18][29]MYS--
MacM "THE MANACLE" '78
COWARD "NAKED BISHOP" '80
STAPLETON, KATHERINE--[18][29]MYS--
ZEBRA "WITHOUT SIN AMONG YOU" '79

KANIES, GERTIE
LENZ, BEATE--[39]GERMAN

KANN, ALBRECHT PETER
ALTENBURG, PETER--[39]GERMAN/MYS/WEST
CANN, AL--[39][40]GERMAN/MYS--
'KOMMISSAR X' SERIES #394 & #399
"AFFARE SCOTT" '66
CANN, PETER--[39]GERMAN/MYS/WEST--
COTTON, JERRY--[39]GERMAN/MYS,HP--
LARAMY, FRANK--[39]GERMAN/WEST
MARK, WILLIAM--[39]GERMAN/MYS/WEST--

KANNAN, LAKSHMI
TILLY--[1]

KANNENGIESSER, GERTRUD
UENTZE, HERTHA--[39]GERMAN

KANTARIS, SYLVIA
KANTARIZIS, SYLVIA--[31]

KANTER, MARIANNE
KANTER, MARIANNE--W/RICHARD M. LIEBERMAN, [21]ROM--
"WHITE SATIN NIGHTS"

KANTOR, HARRY
IRWIN, AMY--V. BERCH-BRNDN/ BC PSEUDS, BAE 22, P24
KANTOR, HAL--[3]MYS/ADULT--
PAD "$1,000,000 BROAD" '66
PAD "EYE OF THE SNIPER" '67
PINN "VEGAS TRAP" '70
MRW "BLOWN AWAY" '80

KANTOR-BERG, FRIEDRICH
FRIEDRICH, TORBERG--[31]
TORBERG, FRIEDRICH--[39]GERMAN

KAPLAN, ANNE BERNAYS
BERNAYS, ANNE--[1][22][33]

KAPLAN, BARRY JAY
KINGSLEY, BETTINA--[2][3][29]MYS--
DELL "STAND IN" '73
DELL "BLIND CHANCE" '74 & MORE

KAPLAN, BOCHE
ROCHE, A.K.--W/ROSLYN KROOP ABISCH,[1]

KAPLAN, FRED MICHAEL
KAPLAN, FRED M.--[31]

KAPLAN, JEAN CARYL KORN
CARYL, JEAN--[1][31]

KAPLAN, M.M.
BARSHOVSKY, PHILIP--[2][11][15]SF--
WS "IMPERFECT GUESS"MAR '36
WS "ONE PREHISTORIC NIGHT" NOV '34
BARTEL, PHILIP JACQUES--[2][11][15]SF--
WS "TWENTY FIVE CENTURIES LATE" NOV '34
WS "ELIXIR OF PROGRESS" APR '35
WS "ONE HUNDRED GENERATIONS" SEPT '35
AMZ "WHEN TIME STOOD STILL" FEB '35

KAPLUN, JACOB
SPENCER, JAKE--[1]

KAPP, YVONNE
CLOUD, YVONNE--[1]

KAPPEL, GUNTER
CALETTE, FRANCOISE--[39]GERMAN/ADV/WEST--
CHAPELLE, FRANCOISER--[39]GERMAN/ADV/WEST--
CONWELL, REX--[39]GERMAN/ADV/WEST--
HIEK, PETE--[39]GERMAN/ADV/WEST--
PATRICK, FRED--[39]GERMAN/ADV/WEST--

KAPPELMAN, MURRAY MARTIN
BERLINER, ROSS--V. BERCH LTR TO HUBIN '93, MYS--
SIMON "MANHOOD CEREMONY" '78
SIGN "HIDING PLACES" '85

KAPPLER, HANNS-WALTER
HAYWARD, KEN--[39]GERMAN/ADV/WEST
HILLING, O.W.--[39]GERMAN/ADV/WEST--
KEMP, HANNES--[39]GERMAN/ADV/WEST--
KORTEN, INES--[39]GERMAN/ADV/WEST--
SCOTT, ALLAN--[39]GERMAN/ADV/WEST--
WENGEN-BERGER, K.--[39]GERMAN/ADV/WEST--

KARASEK, JOSEF JIRI LVOV.
KARASEK ZE LVOVIC, JIRI--[22]CZECH

KARIG, WALTER
DUNCAN, JULIA K.--[1]HP-- STSY
FERRIS, JAMES CODY--[1]HP--STSY
KEENE, CAROLYN--[1]HP--
STSY-'NANCY DREW' STORIES
PATRICK, KEATS--[1][3][22]MYS--
BOBBS "DEATH IS A TORY" '35

KARISNOV, MUSTAFA S.
KARIM, MUSTAI--[1]

KARK, NINA MARY MABEY
BAWDEN, NINA--[21][22][32][34]MYS/ROM--
12 NOVELS '53-87
LM "THE MADAMES" SEPT '53

KARLINS, MARVIN
BROWNE, ROBERT--[1][7][31]SF--
BAL "THE NEW ATOM'S BOMBSHELL" '80

KARLSDOTTIR, MARIA
NOVAK, HELGA M.--[39]GERMAN/JUV

KARMAN, MAL
ASH, PENELOPE--[1][31]

KARNAOOKH, GEORGE
SUMMERS, GERALD--V. BERCH-BRNDN/
BC PSEUDS, BAE 22, P24

KARNI, MICHAELA
BERNE, KARIN--W/SUE BERNELL,[3]MYS--
POPLB "BARE ACQUAINTANCES" '85
POPLB "SHOCK VALUE" '85
BURKE, DIANA--W/SUE BURRELL,[9][21]ROM--
"HEART OF THE MATTER"
"IMPOVERISHED HEIRESS"

KARNOW, MICHAEL
TARR, MICHAEL--[14]ADULT--
OLYM OPH#-226 "NEW SCHOOL FOR SEX" '71

KARO, HELENE
WENCK, LENE--[39]GERMAN

KAROLEVITZ, ROBERT F.
KAROLEVITZ, BOB--[31]

KARP, DAVID
SINGER, ADAM--[1][2]
WARE, WALLACE--[2][3][11]MYS--
DBLDY "THE CHARKA MEMORIAL" '54

KARPOV, VLADIMIR
KARPAU, ULADZIMIR--[1][31]

KARR, LEONA C.
KARR, LEE--[9][26]ROM--
SIL 3 "STRANGER IN THE MIST"
SIL 23 "TANGLED MESH" & MORE

KARRASCH, ALFRED
AMENDA, ALFRED--[39]GERMAN

KARSTEN, UWE
COTTON, JERRY--[39]GERMAN/MYS,HP--

KARU, BARUCH
KRUPNIK, BARUCH--[31]
WEINBAUM, HELEN--[1]

KASBAUER, SIXTA
BAUER, MARIA AGNES--[39]GERMAN/JUV

KASELLI, JOHAN EMANUEL
SEPTON, STANFORD--[29]MYS--
OSTROM "JAKTEN EFTER ARVTAGERSKAN" '16

KASER, ARTHUR LEROY
CAMPION, ROSE--W/RUTH PERRY & JEAN
LEE LATHAM,[1]

KASER, ARTHUR LEROY
HAYFORD, LIEUT. HARLAN--[34]MYS--
BAKER "ESPIONAGE" '40

KASHIN, CHRISTIANE
VON WIESE, CHRISTIANE--[39]GERMAN/JUV

KASNER, WILLIAM MICHAEL
MACKIN, RICK--[7][34]MYS/SF--
PINN "CHOPPER COPS #1-#4" '90-1

KASPAROV, GARY KIMOVICH
KASPAROV, G.K.--[31]
KASPAROV, GARI--[31]
KASPAROV, GARRY--[31]

KASPER, GAYLE
GAYLE, SUSAN--[21][26]ROM--
"TEMPERATURES RISING"
KAYE, GAYLE--[26]ROM--
"HARD HAT & LACE"

KASSLER, JAMIE CROY
KASSLER, J.C.--[31]

KASSON, HELEN
HALLIDAY, BRETT--T. JOHNSON-ECHOES #23,
MYS,HP--
MSMM ?? UNCONFIRMED ??]

KASSON, HELEN WEINBAUM
WEINBAUM, HELEN--[2]

KASTLE, HERBERT D.
LEE, HERBERT D'H--[1][31]

KASTNER, ERICH
BURGER, BERTHOLD--[39]GERMAN
KURTZ, MELCHIOR--[39]GERMAN
NEUNER, ROBERT--[39]GERMAN

KATAZZI, MME.
BERNARD, CAMILLE--[1]

KATCHADOURIAN, VAHE
KATCHA, VAHE--[3][11][31]MYS--
HART-DAVIS "DON'T LOOK DOWN" '62

KATCHAMAKOFF, ATANAS
SHANNON, MONICA--[8]

KATEYEV, EVGENY
PETROV, EVGENY PETROVICH--W/ILYA
ARNOLDOVICH,[22]RUSSIAN

KATKIN, PAMELA E. WEST
WEST, PAMELA--W/SAMUEL RUBENSTEIN-[7][34]MYS
ST. MARTINS "MADELEINE" '83
ST. MARTINS "YOUR'S TRULY, JACK
THE RIPPER" '87
DEL RAY "20/20 VISION" '90

KATZ, BOBBI[E]
GEORGE, BARBARA--[31]
GEORGE, EMILY--[31]
KAHN, PEGGY--[1][31]
MAISON, DELLA--[1]
REICH, ALI--[1]

KATZ, CAROL
ALLISON, PENNY--[9][21][26][31]ROM--
"KING OF DIAMONDS"
"NORTH COUNTRY NIGHTS" & MORE
CARROLL, ROSALYN--[9][21][26][31]ROM--
"ENCHANTED ENCORE"

KATZ, CYNTHIA
VICTOR, CYNTHIA--W/VICTORIA SKURNICK,
[21][26]ROM--
"CONSEQUENCES"
"RELATIVE SINS"

KATZ, HERBERT M.
GARLAND, NICHOLAS--[3]MYS--
MAREK "BUY BACK THE DAWN" '80
BERK "A CRIME OF INNOCENCE" '82

KATZ, KAREN A.
KARR, JILLIAN--W/JAN GREENBERG,[26]ROM--
"SOMETHING BORROWED, SOMETHING BLUE"

KATZ, MENKE
HIAT, ELCHIK--[8][22][31]LITHUANIAN-AMERICAN

KATZ, MYRON MEYER
KATZ, MICKEY--[31]

KATZ, SAMUEL
KATZ, SHMUEL--[1][31]

KATZ, STEVE
GAROS, STEPHANIE--[1][31]

KATZIN, OLGA
SAGITARIOUS--[1]

KATZNELSON, YEHUDA LOEB
YOGLI, BUKKI BEN--[22]

KAU, YING-MAO
KAU, MICHAEL Y.M.--[1][31]

KAUER, FRIEDL
HOFBAUER, FRIEDL--[39]GERMAN/JUV

KAUFFMAN, RUTH [H]
WRIGHT, RUTH--[1][22]MYS

KAUFFMANN, MARE
STAHL, MARE--[39]GERMAN

KAUFFMANN, STANLEY
BARRY, SPRANGER--[31]

KAUFHOLD, ?
CAMERON, WACO--[39]GERMAN/WEST
CANNON, WACO--[39]GERMAN/WEST

KAUFMAN, BOB [GARNELL]
BOMKAUF--[31]

KAUFMAN, CHAYA
DURANT, ARIEL--[1]
KAUFMAN, IDA--[1]

KAUFMAN, DAVID S.
SAMOILOV, DAVID S.--[1]

KAUFMAN, ISADORE
WEER, WILLIAM--[1]

KAUFMAN, JOHN
SWIFT, DAVID--[1][33]

KAUFMAN, LOUIS
KELLER, DAN--[3][22]MYS--
POPLB "FLEE THE NIGHT IN ANGER" '54
HALE "ONE-WAY STREET" '60

KAUFMAN, OLIVER
CRAWFORD, OLIVER--[3]MYS--
ST. MARTIN'S "THE EXECUTION" '78

KAUFMAN, WALLACE
VICKERS--[1]

KAUFMANN, CHARLOTTE
LEYKAM, CHRISTINE--[39]GERMAN
STAHL, HERBERT--[39]GERMAN

KAUKAS, BEVLYN M.
MARSHALL, BEVLYN--[9][21][26]ROM--
"GODDESS OF JOY"
"TREASURE DEEP" & MORE

KAUMEYER, DOROTHY
LAMOUR, DOROTHY--[31]

KAUNDA, KENNETH DAVID
KAUNDA, K.D.--[31]
KAUNDA, KENNETH D.--[31]

KAUS, GINA
ECKBRECHT, ANDREAS--[39]GERMAN

KAUTER, KURT
ROCAFUERTE, JOS MARIA--[39]GERMAN

KAVAFIS, KANSTANTINOS P.
KABAPHES, KONSTANTINOS P.--[31]
CAVAFY, CONSTANTINE PETER--[31]
KAVIFIS, KONSTANTINOS P.--[31]

KAVALIER, REBECCA
CARDIFF, SARA--W/LOUISE DECORMIER
& GLORIA KIRCHEIMER,[3]MYS--
RNDM "FOOL'S APPLE" '77 & MORE

KAVAN, ANNA
FERGUSON, HELEN--[2][23][31]--
PRIOR TO '40

KAVAN, JOSEF
NOR, A.C.--[22]CZECH

KAVANAGH, HERMINIE T.
TEMPLETON, HERMINIE--[1]

KAVANAGH, ROSE
RUBY--[1]
UNCLE REMUS--[1]

KAVENEY, ANDREW J.
KAVENEY, ROZ--[7] LEGALLY CHGD TO 'ROZ'--
"TALES FROM THE FORBIDDEN PLANET" '87

KAY, ERNEST
LUDLOW, GEORGE--[1][22][31]ENGLISH
RANDOM, ALAN--[1][22][31]ENGLISH

KAY, FREDERIC GEORGE
GEE, KENNETH F.--[8]
HOWARD, GEORGE--[8]

KAY, PATRICIA A.
ALEXANDER, TRISHA--[21][26]ROM--
"CINDERELLA GIRL"
"MOTHER OF THE GROOM" & MORE
PATRICK, ANN--[26]ROM--
OPENING ACT"
"HEARTS COLLIDE"
"FOR SERVICES RENDERED"

KAY, TERENCE
KAY, TERRY--[31]

KAYE, BARRINGTON
KAYE, TOM--[1]

KAYE, LLOYD S.
DREW, PATRICIA--W/JULIA PERCEVAL,[3]--
LAN "DEEP IN A DARK COUNTRY" '68
BELM "WHO IS MELODY?" '68

KAYE, MARILYN
BLAIR, SHANNON--[31][33]

KAYE, MARVIN [NATHAN]
GOODWIN, EUGENE D.--[1][31]SF--
AMZ AND F&SF STORIES
LAVINSON, JOSEPH--[1][31]SF--
AMZ AND F&SF STORIES
TERRY, SARALEE--[1][31]SF--
AMZ AND F&SF STORIES
THEODORE, BROTHER--W/THEODORE MARK GOTTFRIED,[7]--
PINN "BROTHER THEODORE'S CHAMBER OF HORRORS" '75

KAYE, PHILIP B.
ADAMS, ALGER LEROY--[1]

KAYE-KANTROWITZ, MELANIE
KAYE, MELANIE--[31]

KAYENBERGH, MARIE EMIL A.
GIRAUD, ALBERT--[22]BELGIAN

KAYSER, ANNA
HAUSERHOFF, ANNIE--[39]GERMAN

KAYSER, RONAL
CLARK, DALE--[2][32][34][37]MYS--
NSLF 37 "RED RODS"
PD "TOUGH COP" JUL '37
PD "THEY DINE WITH DEATH" AUG '37
PD "BLOOD & ORCHIDS" OCT '37
PONY 48 "NARROW CELL" '46
EQMM "CRIME LESSON" SEPT '48
EQMM "VARIOUS TRACES" JAN '49
AV MMM47 "THE BLONDE, THE GANGSTER, & THE PRIVATE EYE" '49
DF "MAKE MINE MONOXIDE" JUL '51
ACE D109 "MAMBO TO MURDER" '55
ACE D149 "A RUN FOR THE MONEY" '56
DT "MURDER MAKES THE HONEYMOON" AUG '58
DT "A GHOST IN THE HOUSE" AUG '60
DT "LOOK ALIVE - YOU'RE DEAD!" SEPT '61
EXD [PULP STORIES]
CLARKE, GEORGE E.--[2]

KAYSING, WILLIAM C.
KAYSING, BILL--[31]

KEANE, MARY NESTA S.
FARRELL, M.J.--[1][31]
KEANE, MOLLY--[1][31]
SKRINE, MARY NESTA--[1]
SKRINE, MOLLY--[1]

KEARNEY, KAY
KEANE, KAY--[35]AUSTRALIAN--
HRWTZ PB121 "THE BARBER" '62

KEATING, HENRY R.F.
HERVEY, EVELYN--A.J.HUBIN--
EQMM MAR '87,[18][31][34]MYS--
DBLDY "THE GOVERNESS" '85
DBLDY "THE MAN OF GOLD" '85
KEATING, HENRY--
WARNER "MURDER BY DEATH" '76

KEATING, LAWRENCE A.
BASSETT, JOHN KEITH--[1][22][31][33]AMERICAN
THOMAS, H.C.--[1][22][33]AMERICAN

KEATING, LEO BERNARD
KEATING, BERN--[1][31][33]

KEATLEY, SHEILA MARJORIE
AVON, MARGARET--[1]

KEATS, GWENDOLINE
ZACK--[1]

KEATS, RICHARD STEPHEN
GOODMAN, OSCAR--[1]
MARCUS, BENJAMIN--[1]

KECK, MAUDE
ORBISON, KECK--W/OLIVE ORBISON,[3][22]MYS--
WSB "KEY TO THE CASE" '29

KECKEIS, GUSTAV
MURON, JOHANNES--[39]GERMAN

KEDDELL, SCUD
ZORE, HYMAN--S. HOLLAND-SCION CKLST, PP 27, HP--
SCION "SAVAGE SIREN" '53
SCION "THIS WAS A WOMAN" '53

KEDDIE, HENRIETTA
TYTLER, SARA--[1][3]MYS--
CHATTO "THE BLACKHALL GHOSTS" 1888

KEDDIE, MARGARET MANSON
AUNTIE MARGARET--[8]

KEEGAN, MARY C.HEATHCOTT
HEATHCOTT, MARY--[9][22][31]ENGLISH/ROM--
KEEGAN, MARY CONSTANCE--[9]ROM
MERLIN, CHRISTINA--[8]
RAYMOND, MARY--[9][21][22][29][34]MYS/ROM--
COLLINS "LONG JOURNEY HOME" '67 & MORE

KEELE, KENNETH D.
CASSILS, PETER--[1][31]

KEELER, RONALD F.
KEEL, FRANK--[1][31][33]

KEELING, JILL ANNETTE
SHAW, JILL A.--[8]

KEEN, MAURICE HUGH
KEEN, M.H.--[31]

KEENAN, JAMES
BROOKS, BRUCE J.--V. BERCH-BRNDN/ BC PSEUDS, BAE 22, P24
MONTAGUE, J.J.--[34]MYS--
CANYON "CHINESE KISS" '74
CANYON "CONG KISS " '74
CANYON "FRENCH KISS" '74
CANYON "JUDAS KISS" '75
SAVAGE, J.J.--[14]ADULT--
OLYM OPH#120 "IN HOT BLOOD" '68
OLYM OPH#125 "SWEETS" '68
OLYM OPH#131 "CRESCENDO" '68
OLYM OPH#141 "YUM YUM" '69
OLYM OPH#150 "DIRTY ME" '69

KEENE, RAYMOND DENNIS
KEENE, R.D.--[31]
KEENE, RAY--[31]

KEENEY, CHARLES JAMES
KEENEY, CHUCK--[31]

KEENY, SPURGEON MILTON
KEENY, S.M.--[31]

KEESHAN, ROBERT J.
KANGAROO, CAPTAIN--[31][33]

KEEVILL, HENRY J.
ALLISON, CLAY--[22][28][31]ENGLISH/WEST--
10 NOVELS '55-64
BONNY, BILL--[22][28][31]ENGLISH/WEST--
HALE "COLORADA GUNSMOKE" '64
EARP, VIRGIL--[1][28][31]ENGLISH/WEST--
HALE "HATCHET RIDES HIGH" '64
HARDING, WES--[22][28][31]ENGLISH/WEST--
HALE "CATTLE COUNTRY" '65 & 3 MORE
MCLOWERY, FRANK--[1][22][28]ENGLISH/WEST--
BW "GUNS FOR THE SIOUX" '61 & 2 MORE
RINGO, JOHNNY--[22][28]ENGLISH/WEST--
MILLS "LONELY GUN" '54
MILLS "ACTION IN ABILENE" '66 & MORE
ALVORD, BURT--[8][28]ENGLISH/WEST--
HALE "GUNFIGHTER BREED" '65
CLAY, ALISON--[28]--
'WOMAN'S REALM' MAG "TOO MUCH FOR GRANTED" FEB '68
MOSSMAN, BURT--[1][8][28]ENGLISH/WEST--
HALE "GUNS ON EAGLE CREEK" '64
RENO, MARK--[1][8][28]ENGLISH/WEST--
GRESHAM "STAGECOACH TO FREMONT" '65
TRAVIS, WILL--[1][28]WEST--
W&B "HANGROPE TRAIL" '69
W&B "LAWMAN WITHOUT A BADGE" '68

KEGLER, HANS
REINHOLD, KARL LUDWIG--[39]GERMAN

KEHL, WOLFGANG
BUSCH, H.P.--[39]GERMAN/MYS/SF--
CRAVEN, ROBERT--[39]GERMAN/HOR,HP--
ELLMER, ARNDT--[39]GERMAN/MYS/SF--
HALL, JEREMY--[39]GERMAN/MYS/SF--
HANSEN, K.U.--W/KLAUS BULTMANN,[39]GERMAN/SF
VILLARD, HENDRIK--[39]GERMAN/MYS/SF--

KEHRER, DANIEL M[ARK]
SAVAGE, ROTH--[1]

KEHRET, MARGARET ANN
KEHRET, PEG--[7]SF--
COBBLEHILL "SISTERS LONG AGO" '90

KEIF, AUBREY
GRANT, WHITNEY--[1]

KEIGHTLEY, DAVID NOEL
KEYES, NOEL--[1][2][31]

KEILER, BARBARA
ARNOLD, JUDITH--[9][21][26]ROM--
"JACKPOT"
"TWILIGHT" & MORE
BERK, ARIEL--[9][21][26]ROM--
"HUNGRY FOR LOVE"
"TEACHER'S PET" & MORE
FREDERICK, THEA--[9][21][26]ROM--
"BELOVED ADVERSARY"

KEILLOR, GARY [EDWARD]
KEILLOR, GARRISON--[31]--
VIKING "LAKE WOBEGON DAYS" '85 & OTHERS

KEILSON, HANS
COOPER, BENJAMIN--[39]GERMAN
KAILAND, ALEXANDER--[39]GERMAN

KEILSTRUP, MARGARET
LORENS, M.K.--DDLY PLEAS #3,[34]MYS--
BB "SWEET NARCISSUS" '90
BB "DECEPTION ISLAND" '90
BB "ROPEDANCER'S FALL" '90

KEIM, FRIEDRICH
CLURE, CLIFORD--[39]GERMAN/ADV/JUV
MIMBI--[39]GERMAN/JUV
ORLANDO, CHRIS--[39]GERMAN/ADV

KEISLING, WILLIAM
KEISLING, BILL--[31]

KEITH, NANCY
KEITH, SLIM--[31]

KEITH, WILLIAM HENRY JR.
ANDREWS, KEITH WILLIAMS--[7]SF,HP--
BERK "FREEDOM'S RANGERS #1 THRU #6"
CAIN, ROBERT--[7]SF,HP--
HARPER "CYBERNARC #1 & #2"
DOUGLASS, KEITH--[7]SF,HP--
BERK "CARRIER #1 & #2"

KELLEHER, BRIAN
MALONEY, MACK--V. BERCH LTR TO R. REGINALD '93, SF--
ZEBRA 'WINGMAN' SERIES: #1-9 '87-91

KELLENBERGER, L.C.
JAMES, HENRY--[2][11][32]MYS--
MZ "THE GHOSTLY REVIVAL" SEPT '64

KELLER, BEVERLY [L]
HARWICK, B.L.--[1][31]

KELLER, DAVID H.
CECIL, HENRY--[1][2][11]
HUBELAIRE, JACOBUS--[1][2]
WORTH, AMY--[1][2][11][15]SF--

KELLER, GARY D.
EL HUITLACOCHE--[31]

KELLER, JOHN ESTEN
GATO, J.A.--[31]

KELLER, MANFRED
CAVEAU, FRED--[39]GERMAN

KELLER, MARIANNE
CARTER, MABEL--[39]GERMAN

KELLER, [Y] ETHEL MAY
KAY, BARBARA--[1]
WHITNEY, LUCIA--[1]

KELLEY, LEO P[ATRICK]
KELLEY, LEO F.--[23]AMERICAN/SF
WILLOUGHBY, LEE DAVIS--[21]ROM,HP--
DELL 'MKNG OF AMER' SERIES:
"PROPHET PEOPLE"

KELLEY, MARTHA MOTT
PATRICK, Q.--W/RICHARD W. WEBB,[2][3][11]MYS--
SWAIN "COTTAGE SINISTER" '31
SWAIN "MURDER AT THE WOMEN'S CLUB" '32

KELLEY, THOMAS P.
BANNERMAN, GENE--BAPC NWSLTR #9, [2][23]CANADIAN/SF--
BENNETT, WALLACE--[2]CANADIAN--??UNCONFIRMED??
DANYER, ROY--[2]CANADIAN--??UNCONFIRMED??
DEVLIN, ROY P.--BAPC NWSLTR #9, [2][23]CANADIAN/SF--
HALL, WAGNER--[2]CANADIAN--??UNCONFIRMED??
JAMES, HALTON--[2]CANADIAN--??UNCONFIRMED??
KANE, D.N.--[2]CANADIAN--??UNCONFIRMED??
KELLY, ZED--BAPC NWSLTR #9, CANADIAN--
AN "GUNSMOKE ON THE PLAINS" '47
AN "WESTERN GUN JUSTICE" '48

KELLEY, THOMAS P. [CONT]
LAKE, ALLEN--[2]CANADIAN--??UNCONFIRMED??
MALCOLM, SCOTT--[2]CANADIAN--??UNCONFIRMED??
MONAHAN, T.P.--BAPC NWSLTR #9, CANADIAN--
AN "RIDERS OF THE BADLANDS" '47
AN "OUTLAWS RIDE THE RANGE" '48
MONAHAN, THOMAS P.--BAPC NWSLTR #9, CANADIAN
MONTANA, ZED--BAPC NWSLTR #9, CANADIAN--
AN [JON] "SIEGE OF THE CIRCLE G" '47
AN [JON] "SIX-GUN PAYOFF!" '48
NORTH, VALENTINE--[23] SUSPECT AN ERROR--
SEE 'VALENTINE WORTH'
PERRIN, NEIL--[2]CANADIAN--??UNCONFIRMED??
REDSHAW, JAMES FRANCIS--[2]CANADIAN--??UNCNFRMD??
SCOTT, MALCOLM--[2]CANADIAN--??UNCONFIRMED??
WORTH, VALENTINE--BAPC NWSLTR #9,[2]CANADIAN

KELLIHER, DAN T.
SECRIST, KELLIHER--W/W.G. SECRIST,[3][22]MYS--
PHOENIX "MURDER MELODY" '39
MYH "MURDER MAKES BY-LINES" '41

KELLNER, ESTER
COOPER, ESTER--[1][22][31]AMERICAN

KELLOGG, JEAN [D]
JACKSON, SALLY--[1][22][31][33]AMERICAN
KELLOGG, GENE--[1][31][33]AMERICAN

KELLOGG, MARJORIE BRADLEY
KELLOGG, M. BRADLEY--[23]AMERICAN/SF--
"A RUMOR OF ANGELS" '83
"REIGN OF FIRE" '86
"THE WAVE & THE FLAME" '86

KELLOGG, VERNON L.
VERNON, MAX--[1]

KELLY, ANGELINE AGNES
HAMPTON, ANGELINE A.--[31]
KELLY, A.A.--[31]

KELLY, CHARLES E.
KELLY, COMMANDO--[31]

KELLY, DAN
CORNEY, DEBRA--[39]GERMAN

KELLY, DAVID MICHAEL
KELLY, DAVE--[31]

KELLY, DEXTER
ATLANTIS, ISADORE--[14]ADULT--
OLYM TC#496 "I FOUND IT AT THE MOVIES" '70

KELLY, ELEANOR MERCEIN
MERCEIN, ELEANOR--[1]

KELLY, ELIZABETH
KELLIER, ELIZABETH--[8]
STEVENSON, CHRISTINE--[8]

KELLY, GEORGE C.
ABSINTHE, PERE--[1]
PAYNE, HAROLD--[1][3]MYS--
PRICE "THE GILDED FLY" 1892

KELLY, GWEN NITA
HEATH, NITA--[1]

KELLY, HAROLD ERNEST
ASCHER, EUGENE--[7][23][34]MYS/SF--
EVB "GRIM CARETAKER" '44
EVB "UNCANNY ADVENTURES" '44 & MORE
MITRE "THERE WERE NO ASPER LADIES" '44
"UNCAN. ADV:5 STRANGE THRILLERS"

KELLY, HAROLD ERNEST [CONT]
CARSON, LANCE--[8]
GLINTO, DARCY--[1][29][34]MYS--
19 ROBIN HOOD NOVELS '40-53
HOLT, GORDON--[3][29]MYS--
KELLY "STABLES TO 1,000,000 POUNDS" '47
JANSON, HANK--JEAN F. LE DEIST LTR '93,
[34]MYS,HP--
"RELUCTANT HOSTESS" '61
"VENUS MAKES THREE" '61
ROBERTS "SHE SLEEPS TO CONQUER" '61
ROBERTS "TWIST FOR TWO" '62
"SAVAGE SEQUEL" '62
"VAGABOND VAMP" '62
COMPACT "HOT LINE" '63
ROBERTS "PASSION PACT" '63
COMPACT "V FOR VITALITY" '63
COMPACT "VOODOO VIOLENCE" '64
COMPACT "SEX ANGLE" '64
LOGAN, BRYN--S. CHIBNALL-PPCC#9/WEST--
'DOUBLE-SIX' NOVELS, EARLY 50's
TOLER, BUCK--[1][3][29]MYS--
MITRE "BRONSVILLE MASSACRE" '43
EVB "KILLER ON THE RUN" '46 MORE
YORKE, PRESTON--[7][34]MYS--
EVB "GAMMA RAY MURDERS" '43
EVB "ASTOUNDING CRIME" '43
EVB "CASE OF THE SWINGING SPIDER" '44
EVB "CASE OF THE STRANGLED SEVEN" '44
MITRE "DEATH ON PRIORITY 1" '45
KELLY "SPACE-TIME TASK FORCE" '53

KELLY, JAMES PLUNKETT
PLUNKETT, JAMES--[31]

KELLY, JEFFREY
KELLY, JEFF--[31][33]

KELLY, JOAN COLLINGS
SUTHERLAND, JOAN--[3]MYS--
MILLS "IN THE NIGHT" '20

KELLY, JOHN SPENCE
KELLY IAN--[31]

KELLY, JUDITH
ENGLISH, JUDITH--[9]ROM

KELLY, KAREN
LEE, KAY--[31]

KELLY, MARTHA ROSE
KELLY, MARTY--[1][31][33]

KELLY, MRS. T.
TENNANT, CARRIE--[8]

KELLY, PAULINE AGNES
BARRETT, RAINA--[31]

KELLY, TERENCE
RUSSELL, CHARLES--LACHMAN-EASTER LST '93,
[34]MYS--
DBLDY "LONG LIVE THE SPY" '87
DBLDY "SPY IS DEAD" '88

KELLY, TIM J.
BIBOLET, R.H.--[8][34]MYS--
PLAY "SHERLOCK HOLMES FIRST CASE" '76

KELLY, TOM
LUNDY, MIKE--W/DONALD BAIN, V. BERCH LTR
TO HUBIN '94--
STUART "BABY FARM" '87

KELLY, VINCENT GATTON
KELLY, VINCE--[36]AUSTRALIAN/MYS--
MAIL "LAST MINUTE CLUE" '43
MAIL "SINISTER CRIME" '44 & OTHERS

KELLY-BOOTLE, STAN
KELLY, STAN--[31]

KELMAN, ELLEN
WOODBURY, LEONORA--[9][21][26]ROM--
"GAME OF HEARTS"
"RUNAWAY COUNTESS"

KELSEY, JOAN MARSHALL
GRANT, JOAN--[2][22][31]ENGLISH

KELTON, ARYON LEWIS
KELTON, ARYAN--[1]

KELTON, ELMER
EARLY, TOM--HAWK/KELTON INTRVW '93/WEST,HP--
BERK 'SONS OF TEXAS' SERIES #1-3
HAWK, ALEX--HAWK-KELTON INTRVW/HUNT
BIBLIO/WEST,HP--
PAPLB 63-145 "SHOTGUN SETTLEMENT" '69
MCELROY, LEE--HAWK-KELTON INTRVW '93,[28]WEST-
-
DBLDY "JOE PEPPER" '75
DBLDY "LONG WAY TO TEXAS" '76
DBLDY "EYES OF THE HAWK" '81
OWENS, TOM--J. HUNT-KELTON BIBL--
GERMAN RPRT OF "BARBWIRE"
AS "DAS NARBIGE LAND" '59
STEVENS, JOHN--HAWK-KELTON INTVW '93--
RROM "YELLOW DEVIL" APR '52

KEMP, EARL
HANLON, JOHN--[2]
HANLON, JON--[2][11]

KEMP, ERNEST
THORPE, TREBOR--[2]

KEMP, PENNY
CHALMERS, PENNY--[31]

KEMP, ROY ZELL
KAY, ZELL--[31]

KEMPE, ALICE [S]
CARDOS, ALICE--[39]GERMAN

KEMPE, ANNE
PARAMENY, K.--[1]

KEMPF, PAT
HUNTER, PAT--[8]

KEMPINSKI, TOM
THOMAS, GERRARD--[8]

KEMPTON, JEAN WELCH
WELSH, JEAN-LOUISE--[33]

KENAFICK, JOSEPH
KENNEDY, JAMES--[8][32]MYS--
LM "THERE GO I" APR '52
LM "VANISHING POINT" SEPT '53
LM "POETIC INJUSTICE" OCT '54
LM "SHADOW OF THE MIND" JUN '56
LM "MORNING FOURSOME" DEC '56
JCM "MISSING OVERCOAT" APR '59

KENDALL, CARLTON
LADNEK, ODLAW--[1]

KENDALL, JULIA JAY
KINGSLEY, KATHERINE--[9][21][26]ROM--
"WILD ROSE"
"KING OF HEARTS" & MORE

KENDALL, STEPHEN
JAY, THOMAS--[1]

KENDALL, WILMORE
MONK, ALAN--[22]AMERICAN

KENDRICK, BAYNARD H.
HAYWARD, RICHARD--V. BERCH-GM PSEUDS,
PP 33,[3][18][31]MYS--
GM 242 "TRAPPED" '52
GM 479 "SOFT ARMS OF DEATH" '55

KENEALLY, THOMAS MICHAEL
KENEALLY, TOM--[36]AUSTRALIAN/MYS--
CASSELL "THE FEAR" '65
A&R "THE SURVIVOR" '69

KENEALY, JAMES P.
KENEALY, JIM--[31][33]

KENJIRO, TOKUTOMI
ROKA, TOKUTOMI--[22]JAPANESE

KENNAN, JAMES
MONTAGUE, J.J.--[3]MYS--
CANYON "CHINESE KISS" '74
CANYON "KONG KISS" '74
CANYON "FRENCH KISS" '74

KENNEALY, GERALD P.
KENNEALY, G.P.--[34]MYS--
MANOR "NOBODY WINS" '78
KENNEALY, JERRY--[34]MYS--
ST. MARTINS - 5 'POLO' NOVELS '88-90

KENNEDY, ADAM
REDGATE, JOHN--[3][31][40]MYS--
TRIDENT "KILLING SEASON" '67
CAPE "BARLOW'S KINGDOM" '68
DELACORTE "THE LAST DECATHLON" '79

KENNEDY, CHARLES JOSEPH
KENNEDY, CHUCK--[31]

KENNEDY, EDWARD MOORE
KENNEDY, TED--[31]

KENNEDY, GERALD HAMILTON
KISH, G. HOBAB--[22][31]AMERICAN

KENNEDY, GERMAINE
FRENCH, EMILY--[26]ROM--
HARL 214 "CAPTURE"

KENNEDY, H.A.
H.A.K.--[8]

KENNEDY, JOHN MCFARLAND
VERDAD, S.--[8]

KENNEDY, JOSEPH CHARLES
KENNEDY, X.J.--[7][31]--
DBLDY "NUDE DESCENDING A STAIRCASE" '61
ATHNM "THE OWLSTONE CROWN" '83

KENNEDY, MARY
EMERSON, MARY LEE--[31]

KENNEDY, NANCY MACDOUGALL
KENNEDY, NANCY [M]--[21]ROM--
"SUMMER FROST"
"VILLAGE TALE" & MORE

KENNEDY, R.A.
AUTHOR OF SPACE & SPIRIT--[23]ENGLISH/SF--
"TRIUNEVERSE: A SCIENTIFIC ROMANCE" '12

KENNEDY, TERESA A.
VICKERY, KATE--[1]
KENNEDY, T.A.--[31]

KENNETH, KEITH
HITCHCOCK, KEITH--[1]

KENNICOTT, DONALD
REEVE, JOEL--ECHOES #22, P5--
EDITOR OF BLUE BOOK

KENNINGTON, [G] ALAN
GRANT, ALAN--[22][31][34]MYS--
NICHOLSON "IT WALKS IN THE WOODS" '36
KENNINGTON, ALAN--[8][32][34]MYS--
JCM "MONEY FOR DANGER" DEC '57
JCM "DELAYED ACTION" JUL '58

KENNY, ELLSWORTH N.
NEWCOMBE, ELLSWORTH--[1][22][33]AMERICAN

KENNY, NICHOLAS NAPOLEON
KENNY, NICK--[31]

KENNY, P.D.
PAT--[1]

KENRICK, ANTHONY ARTHUR
KENRICK, TONY--[36]AUSTRALIAN/MYS--
CAPE "A TOUGH ONE TO LOSE" '72
& 8 OTHERS

KENSAKI, OGAWA
MIMEI, OGAWA--[22]JAPANESE

KENSDALE, W.E.N.
NORWOOD, ELLIOTT--[8]

KENT, ARTHUR WILLIAM C.
BOSWELL, JAMES--[1]

KENT, ARTHUR WILLIAM C.
BRADWELL, JAMES--[2][7][31]
DUBOIS, M.--[1][31]

KENT, ARTHUR WILLIAM C.
GRANADOS, PAUL--[1][31][34]MYS--
WARREN "BROADWAY CONTRABAND" '54
KAROL, ALEXANDER--[1][31]
STAMPER, ALEX--[1]
VANE, BRET--[1][34]MYS,HP--
WARREN "GARDENIA" '53

KENT, CARLETON VOLNEY JR.
KENT, BILL--[31]

KENT, ELLEN LOUISA MARG.
MARGARET--[8]

KENT, JEAN SALTER
KENT, KATHRYN--[9][21][26]ROM--
"WATERS OF EDEN"
"DRUID'S RETREAT" & MORE

KENT, JIM
BANNER, CLEVE--[35]AUSTRALIAN--
BIG HORN 345 "GUNS ALONG THE LINE"
CHISHOLM 698 "BRAND OF THE BRAVO"
CHISHOLM 700 "HELLER WITH A GUN"
CORONADA 974 "DEVIL'S SHADOW"
DOCKER, THANE--[35]AUSTRALIAN--
SIERRA 454 "DEVIL'S ACRE"
SIERRA 458 "WHEN REBELS RIDE!"
BIG HORN - 4 BOOKS
CHISHOLM - 4 BOOKS
KEMP, JULIAN--[35]AUSTRALIAN--
HRWTZ PB108 "SUMMER MADNESS"
??PUBLISHED??

KENT, JOHN WELLINGTON
KENT, JACK--[31][32][33]MYS--
MSMM "THE POISONED DART" FEB '64

KENT, LOUISE ANDREWS
TEMPEST, THERESA--[8]

KENT, ROCKWELL
HOGARTH, JR.--[31][33]

KENTON, PAUL
KENTO, NOEL--[2]

KENTON, WARREN
HALEVI, Z'EV BEN SHIMON--[1][31]

KENWARD, BETTY
JENNIFER--[8]

KENWORTHY, CHARLES J.
FRESCO, AL--[1]

KENYON, BRUCE
LEIGH, MEREDITH--[9][21][26]ROM--
"AN ELEGANT EDUCATION"
"LADY OF QUALITIES" & MORE
VIVIAN, DAISY--[1][9][21][26]ROM--
COUNTERFEIT LADY"
"FAIR GANE" & MORE

KENYON, CHARLES FREDERICK
CUMBERLAND, GERALD--[3][8]MYS--
RICHARDS "TALES OF A CRUEL COUNTRY" '19
RICHARDS "CYPRESS CHEST" '27

KENYON, MICHAEL
FORBES, DANIEL--[3][18][29][31]MYS--
"MR. BIG" '75
"THE RAPIST" '77

KENYON, MILDRED ADAMS
ADAMS, MILDRED--[1][31]

KENYON, WALTER ANDREW
KENYON, W.A.--[31]

KEOGH, LILIAN GILMORE
PATRICK, LILIAN--[22]IRISH

KEPPLER, GERTRUD
KEPLER, UTTA--[39]GERMAN

KEPPNER, GERHARD
NIELS, OLIVER--[39]GERMAN

KEREKES, TIBOR
ROTARIUS--[22]HUNGARIA-AMERICAN

KERFVE, AXEL
EHRENCLOU, ADIL--[29]MYS
AXELSSON, ERIK--[29]MYS

KERFVE, AXEL [CONT]
GRANE, GUNNAR--[29]MYS
HALLSTROM, TOR--[29]MYS
KRONDAL, ALVA--[29]MYS
KRONE, HERVOR--[29]MYS
LANGE, KURT--[29]MYS--
"EN STORSTADS SKUGGSIDOR" '04
SKRATTHULT, SVEN I--[29]MYS
SVENSKE, TOR--[29]MYS
TROLLE, BIRGER--[29]MYS
WIDE, GUSTAF--[29]MYS

KERHOUEL, GAETAN
D'OCTON, VIGNE--[22]FRENCH

KERIGAN, FLORENCE
KERRY, FRANCES--[1][31][33]

KERKOFF, JOHNSTON D.
WOLFE, PHILIP--[2]

KERMOND, EVELYN CAROLYN
CONWAY, E. CAROLYN--[1][8]

KERN, ELFIEDE
BEYVERS, ELFRIEDE--[39]GERMAN

KERN, STEVEN
LINDER, STEVEN--[1]

KERNER, FRED
FREDERICKS, FROHM--[1][22][31]CANADIAN-AMERICAN
KERN, E.R.--[1][22][31]CANADIAN-AMERICAN
KERR, FREDERICK--[1][22][31]CANADIAN-AMERICAN-

"WATCH YOUR WEIGHT GO DOWN" '63
THALER, M.N.--[1][31]CANADIAN-AMERICAN--
"IT'S FUN TO FONDUE" '68

KERNISKY, IVAN
IKER--[22]UKRAINIAN

KERNMAYR, ERICH
KERN, ERICH--[39]GERMAN

KERNMAYR, HANS GUSTL
LEONHARDT, THOMAS--[39]GERMAN

KERNMAYR, HANS GUSTL
MILLER, A.G.--[39]GERMAN

KERNMAYR, MARIE LOUISE F.
FISCHER, MARIE LOUISE--[39]GERMAN/MYS/JUV

KEROUAC, JEAN-LOUIS L.D.
INCOGNITEAU, JEAN-LOUIS--[1]
JEAN-LOUIS--[31]
KEROUAC, JACK--[1][31]BEAT--
SIGN 1619 "ON THE ROAD" '58
SIGN 1718 "DHARMA BUMS" '59
AV G1035 "MAGGIE CASSIDY" '59
AV T302 "SUBTERRANEANS" '59
AV T429 "TRISTESSA" '60
GROVE BC135 "SATORI IN PARIS" '66
KEROUAC, JOHN--[1][31]
LOUIS, JEAN--[1]

KERR, ALEX A.
KERR, ANDY--[31]

KERR, D.
COLT, RUSS--[8]

KERR, DORIS BOAKE
BOAKE, CAPEL--[8]

KERR, GRAHAM
GHALLOPING GOURMET, THE--[8][31]

KERR, JAMES LENNOX
DAWLISH, PETER--[1][25][31]JUV
KERR, LENNOX--[8]

KERSH, GERALD
ENGLAND, PIERS--P. DUNCAN-PPCC#9,[18]--
FEATURE WRITER OF 'THE PEOPLE' NEWSPAPER

KERSHAW, JOHN HUGH
D'ALLENGER, HUGH--[1][31]

KESSEL, LIPMANN
PAUL, DANIEL--[1][22]ENGLISH

KESSEL, MAURICE
DRUON, MAURICE--L. ROBBINS LTR MAR '94,[11]--
THIS IS IN CONFLICT WITH [7]

KESSELMAN-TURKEL, JUDI
K-TURKEL, JUDI--[31]
KESSELMAN, JUDI R.--[31]

KESSLER, FRANCIS PASCHAL
KESSLER, FRANK--[31]

KESSLER, HELENE
VON KALTENBERG, HANS--[39]GERMAN

KESSLER, JASCHA
ELY, FREDERICK--[22]AMERICAN

KESTIN, HELEN
VAUGHN, KATE--[1]

KETCHAM, HELEN
HAVILAND, MEG--[9][21][26]ROM--
"MISTRESS OF WYNDS"

KETCHAM, HENRY KING
KETCHAM, HANK--[31][33]

KETCHUM, PHILIP
HADRIAN, PHILIP--V. BERCH-MON PSEUDS,
BAE 9,[1]--
MON 278 "PARTY LOVERS" '62
LESLIE, MIRIAM--[1][3][28]MYS--
LAN 75-471 "CAVANAUGH KEEP" '68
SAUNDERS, CARL MCK.--[1][22]

KETCHUM, PHILIP L.
BELLAMY, JEAN--L. ROBBINS LTR '94--
LAN 74-520 "MISTRESS OF GHOSTHAVEN" '69
LAN 74-597 "GHOST OF COQUINA KEY" '69
SAUNDERS, MACK--[1][28]WEST--
GRAPHIC 140 "GUN TRAIL" '56

KETTENFEIER, PETER
ROSEGGER, PETER--[22]AUSTRIAN

KETTLE, LEROY
CHILDER, SIMON IAN--W/JOHN BROSNAN,
[2][7][23]SF--
"TENDRILS"
KNIGHT, HARRY ADAM--W/JOHN BROSNAN,
[2][7][23]SF--
"SLIMMER" '83
"CARNOSAUR" '84
"FUNGUS" '85

KETTLE, PAUL
HORNSCHU, PAUL KARL--[39]GERMAN/JUV

KETTLE, [JOCELYN] PAMELA
KETTLE, JOCELYN--[23][31]SF--
"MEMORIAL TO THE DUCHESS" '68

KETTLEHACK, GUY
CRAWFORD, DAVID--[31]

KEUNING, W.E.
KEUNING, WILLEM DE--[1]

KEVEREN, A.G.
VEREN, GILBERT--[1]

KEVERN, MARY
NORTH, MIRANDA--W/NANCY AUSTIN,[21][26]ROM--
"DESERT SLAVE"
"FOREVER PARADISE"
"SWEET LIES"

KEVIN, JOHN WILLIAM
FERRES, ARTHUR--[8][13]AUSTRALIAN

KEWES, KAROL
KAROL, K.S.--[1][22][31]POLISH-FRENCH

KEY, SAMUEL WHITTELL
KEY, UEL--[1][2]

KEY, THEODORE
KEY, TED--[31]

KEYNES, HELEN MARY
HUNTER, CLEMENTINE--[1][3][22]MYS--
HUTCH "QUEENS HAVE DIED YOUNG & FAIR" '47

KHAKETLA, BENNETT MAKALO
KHAKETLA, B.M.--[31]

KHAN, TAIDJE
BRYNNER, YUL--[31]

KHANH-GIU, TRAN
KHAI-HUNG--[22]VIETNAMESE

KHARE, NARAYAN BHASKAR
BAPU--[22][31]INDIAN

KHATENA, JOSEPH
KHATENA, JOE--[31]SINGAPORE-AMERICAN

KHLEBNIKOV, VIKTOR VLAD.
KHLEBNIKOV, VELIMIR--[31]

KHOMEINI, RUHOLLAH M.
KHOMEINI, AYATOLLAH--[31]
KHOMEINI, IMAM--[31]
KHUMEINA, RUHOLLAH--[31]

KHUBCHANDANI, LACHMAN M.
LAKHU--[31]

KICHLINE, LINDA
RAFFERTY, CARIN--[9][21][26]ROM--
"FULL CIRCLE"
"MY FAIR BABY" & MORE

KICHLINE, LINDA
RYAN, ALLYSON--[9][21][26]ROM--
"LOVE CAN MAKE IT BETTER"
"MOON & SUN" & MORE

KIDD, JAMES ROBBINS
KIDD, J. ROBY--[31]
KIDD, J.R.--[31]

KIDD, MILDRED VIRGINIA
BLISH, VIRGINIA--[1]

KIDD, WALTER EVANS
DUBLIN, CONRAD PADRAIC--[1]
PENDLETON, CONRAD--[8]
PENDLETON, CONRAD PADRAIC--[1]

KIDDER, JANE
SIMMS, CHARLOTTE--W/CHARLA CHIN,[21][26]ROM--
"SILVER CARESS"

KIEFER, TILLMAN W.
KIEFER, BILL--[31]

KIEFER, WARREN DAVID
KIEFER, MIDDLETON--W/HARRY MIDDLETON,[1]

KIEHL, CLAIRE
COLE, JUSTINE--W/SUSAN E. PHILLIPS,
[9][21][26]ROM--
"COPELAND BRIDE"

KIEHLE, JOHN ALVA
KEEL, JOHN A.--[2][7][31]SF

KIEHTREIBER, ALBERT KONR.
GUTERSLOH, ALBERT PARIS--[39]GERMAN

KIENZLE, RAYMOND N.
RAY, NICHOLAS--[8]

KIENZLE, WILLIAM X.
BOYLE, MARK--[1][31]

KIEPPER, SHIRLEY MORGAN
MORGAN, SHIRLEY--[1][31]

KIESCHNER, SIDNEY
KINGSLEY, SIDNEY--[3][22][29]MYS--
3 PLAYS '36-51

KIESTER, EDWIN JR.
REEVES, PHILIP--[1]

KILBORNE, VIRGINIA WYLIE
EGBERT, VIRGINIA WYLIE--[31]

KILBRACKEN, JOHN [R.G]
GODLEY, JOHN--[1][22]ENGLISH

KILCHENSTEIN, MARY I.
FAURE, JEAN--[9][21][26]ROM--
"BED OF ROSES"
"LONG ROAD HOME"
KIRK, MARY--[9][21][26]ROM--
"PHOENIX"
"EMBERS"
"MIRACLES"
KIRK, MARY ALICE--W/NANCY RICHARDS-AKERS,
[9][21][26]ROM--
"IN YOUR WILDEST DREAMS"

KILEY, JOHN GERALD
KILEY, JED--[1][31]

KILGORE, KATHLEEN
HOUTON, KATHLEEN--[1][31][33]

KILLOUGH, KAREN LEE
HOOD, SARAH--[1][31]
KILLOUGH, LEE--G. COOK LTR '93,[7]SF--
'BLOOD HUNT' SERIES
'MAXWELL & BRILLO' SERIES
& MORE
LEIGH, KATHY--[1]

KILLOUGH, [K] LEE

KILMER, WENDELA
VAN DER ZEE, KAREN--[9][21][26]ROM--
"WAITING"
"FANCY FREE" & MORE
VAN WIERAN, MONA--[9][21][26]ROM--
"A RHAPSOSDY IN BLUE"
"A PRINCE AMONG MEN"

KILVERT, MARGARET C.
CAMERON, MARGARET--[1]

KILWORTH, GARRY DOUGLAS
DOUGLAS, GARRY--[7][23][31]SF--
"HIGHLANDER" '86
"THE STREET" '88

KIMBALL, GRACE & RICHARD
KIMBALL, ATKINSON--[2]

KIMBERLY, GAIL
ANDRE, ALIX--[23]ROM--
"SECRET OF THE ABBEY" '80
COURTNEY, DAYLE--[23]--
YOUNG ADULT ADVENTURE

KIMBRO, JOHN M.
ALLYSON, KYM--V. BERCH-BRNDN/
BC PSEUDS, BAE 22,
[17][21][26][31][34]MYS/ROM--
BRNDN "YOU'RE A HARD MAN, JAMIE COXMAN"
BRNDN "DAISIES IN A CHAIN"
GRNLF "GAY CIRCUS"
GRNLF "BOYWATCHER"
BERK "MOON SHADOWS" '76
BRNDN "QUEER LETTERS" & MORE
ASHTON, ANN--[3][9][21][26]MYS--
DBLDY "HAUNTED PORTRAIT" '76
DBLDY "PHANTOM REFLECTION" '78
DBLDY "THREE CRIES OF TERROR" '80
DBLDY "CONCESSION" '81
BRAMWELL, CHARLOTTE--[9][17][21][34]MYS--
BEAGLE "COUSIN TO TERROR" '72
BEAGLE "STEPMOTHER'S HOUSE" '72
BEAGLE "BROTHER SINISTER" '73
JAXON, MILT--[1][31]ADULT--
GRNLF "YOUR PLACE OR OURS"
GRNLF "GOD SAVE THE SWINGERS"
GRNLF "KEEPING IT UP WITH THE JONES"
GRNLF "LIBRARIAN'S LIVING END"
GRNLF "GOING DOWN WITH THE SMITHS"
KEIMBERG, ALLYN--[1][31]ADULT--
BRNDN "PAIN LOVERS"
BRNDN "EAST OF SODOM"
KIMBRO, JEAN--[7][17][21][26][31][34]MYS--
BAL "TWILIGHT RETURN" '76
KIMBROUGH, KATHERYN--[9][11][17][21][31]
[34]MYS/ROM--49 POPLB NOVELS '72-82
LAMBEC, ZOLTAN--[1][31]ADULT--
BRNDN "REQUIEM FOR A SADIST"
MILTON, JACK--[1][31]ADULT--
BRNDN "QUEENS OF THE ROAD"
BRNDN "SWAP TIME"

KIMES, BEVERLY RAE
COX, JERI--[31]

KIMPEL-JOHNS, KAREN
JOHNS, KAREN--[9][21][26]ROM--
"BELLE GLEN"
"PROUD SURRENDER"

KINAST, LEOPOLD
REYNOLDS, LIONEL--[39]GERMAN/HOR--

KINAU, JOHANNES
FOCK, GORCH--[1][22][39]GERMAN

KINCAID, ROBIN
CLEVE, JOHN--W/ANDREW J. OFFUTT,[7]SF,HP--
BERK 'SPACEWAYS':
"ASSIGNMENT: HELLHOLE" '83
"RACE ACROSS THE STARS" '84

KINDLER, OTTO
BRANDNER, MATTHIAS--[39]GERMAN/ADV/SF--
RELDNIK, C.E.--[39]GERMAN/ADV/SF--

KINES, PAT DECKER
TAPIO, PAT DECKER--[33]

KINES, THOMAS ALVIN
KINES, TOM--[31]

KING, ALBERT
ALBION, KEN--[8][28]
BANNON, MARK--[2][7][11][23][28]SF--
HALE "WAYWARD ROBOT" '74
HALE "THE ASSIMILATOR" '74
HALE "THE TOMORROW STATION" '75
BRENNAN, WALT--[8][28]
BRENT, CATHERINE--[8][28]ROM--
HALE "SEEKING HEART" '75
HALE "DECEIVE ME NEVER" '85 & 5 MORE
BRONSON, WADE--[8][28]WEST--
HALE "POWDERSMOKE PAY-OFF" '73
HALE "FIGHTING RAMROD" '74
CLEVELAND, JIM--[8][28]WEST--
HALE "COLT THUNDER" '89
HALE "RANBO'S TREASURE" '90 & 2 MORE
CONRAD, PAUL--[2][7][23][28]SF--
HALE "EX MINUS" '74
HALE "THE SLAVE BUG" '75
HALE "LAST MAN ON KLUTH V" '75
COOPER, CRAIG--[8][28]MYS--
HALE RUNNING SCARED" '72
HALE "VALUE FOR MURDER" '72 & MORE
CREED, JOEL--[8][28]WEST--
HALE "GUNS OF COUGAR RANGE" '75
DALLAS, STEVE--[8][28]WEST--
HALE "SIX-GUN RECKONING" '90
HALE "ROGUE RANCHER" '91
DOAN, REECE--[8][28]WEST--
HALE "LAWMAN RIDING" '73
HALE "SIDEWINDER BREED" '73
DRISCOLL, ELI--[8][28]WEST--
HALE "GUN LAW IN WILLOW BASIN" '73
HALE "PISTOL BREED" '74
FORD, WALLACE--[8][28]WEST--
3 GRESHAM NOVELS '66-7
2 HALE NOVELS '89-90
FOREMAN, LEE--[8]WEST--
HALE MAGGARTY" '68
HALE "HANG-ROPE TRAIL" '67 & 6 MORE
FOSTER, EVAN--[8][28]WEST--
HALE "BAR O JUSTICE" '75
HALE "FENCE WAR" '89
GIBSON, FLOYD--[2][7][23][28]SF--
HALE "A SLIP IN TIME" '74
HALE "THE MANUFACTURED PEOPLE" '75
HALE "SHADOW OF GASTOR" '75
GIFFORD, MATT--[8][28]WEST--
HALE "LAW OF THE GUN-WOLVES" '75

KING, ALBERT [CONT]
GIRTY, SIMON--[8][28]WEST--
GRSH "LAWLESS BRAND" '66
GRSH "RAIDER'S RANGE" '66
HAMMOND, BRAD--[8][28]WEST--
HALE "COLT FEUD" '74
HALE "TROUBLE TOWN" '89 & 4 MORE
HARLAN, ROSS--[8][28]WEST--
GRSH "BOSS OF STORM VALLEY" '66
GRSH "SAVAGE SUNDOWN" '67 & MORE
HARMON, GIL--[8][28]WEST--
HALE "WILD GUNS" '72
HALE "OWLHOOT TRAIL" '89 & 5 MORE
HOFFMAN, ART--[8][28]WEST--
HALE "STORMY RANGE" '67
HALE "WOLFPACK RENEGADE" '87
HOLLAND, TOM--[8][28]WEST--
HALE ""DESPERADO TRAIL" '73
HALE "RUSTLER RANGE" '89
HALE "FUGITIVE TRAIL" '90
HOWELL, SCOTT--[2][7][23][28]SF--
HALE "MENACE FROM MAGOR" '74
HALE "PASSAGE TO OBLIVION" '75
HOYT, NELSON--[8][28]WEST--
HALE "TOWN TAMER" '62
HALE "KILLER SHERRIFF" '67 & MORE
KANE, MARK--[8][28]MYS--
HALE "RELUCTANT TRANSGRESSOR" '67
HALE "WALK OF THE DEVIL" '68
HALE "FIT TO KILL" '72
KELSEY, JANICE--[8][28]ROM--
HALE "DANGEROUS LEGACY" '69
HALE "RELUCTANT TO LOVE" '71 & 5 MORE
KIMBER, LEE--[8][28]WEST--
HALE "RENEGADE LAWMAN" '73
HALE "OUTLAW SHOOT-OUT" '73
KING, AMES--[8][28]WEST--
HALE "DESPERADO" '63
HALE "HAMMERICK" '65 & 18 MORE
KING, AMON--L. ROBBINS LTR MAR '94
KING, BERTA--[8][28]ROM--
HALE "DEAR IMPOSTER" '67
HALE "DANGEROUS QUEST" '69 & 5 MORE
KING, CHRISTOPHER--[2][7][23][28][34]SF--
HALE "WORLD OF JONAH KLEE" '76
HALE "OPERATION MORA" '74
MASON, CARL--[8][28]WEST--
HALE "TRAIL BRANDED" '73
HALE "GUNSLINGER'S WAY" '74 & 2 MORE
MULLER, PAUL--[7][23][28][34]MYS/SF--
HALE "WISTFUL WANTON" '71
HALE "FRIENDLY FIENDS" '72 & MORE
OGDEN, CLINT--[8][28]WEST--
3 GRESHAM NOVELS '66-7
HALE "STRANGER IN SAN SIMON" '89
OWEN, RAY--[8][28]MYS--
HALE "FALL GUY" '69
HALE "DATE WITH DOOM" '71 & 7 MORE
PRENDER, BART--[8][28]WEST--
HALE "GUNSMOKE IN ELKHORN" '75
RIPLEY, ALVIN--[8][28]WEST--
HALE "HOSTILE LAND" '73
HALE "RANGER JUSTICE" '89 & 4 MORE
SANTEE, WALT--[8][28]WEST--
HALE "POWDERSMOKE PASS" '64
HALE "TRAIL SOUTH TO DANGER" '64
HALE "THE RANGE HAWKS" '89
SCOTT, GROVER--[8][28]WEST--
3 GRESHAM NOVELS '66-7
2 HALE NOVELS '88-9
SHELBY, COLE--[8][28]WEST--
2 GRESHAM NOVELS '66
2 HALE NOVELS '89-90
TAGGART, DEAN--[8][28]WEST--
HALE "OUTLAW HERITAGE" '90
HALE "LAW OF THE BULLET" '74 & 4 MORE

KING, ALBERT [CONT]
TAYLOR, ELLIS [TYLER?]--[8][28]WEST--
HALE "CATAMOUNT VALLEY" '75
TYLER, ELLIS--[8][28]--
SEE THE PSEUDONYM 'ELLIS TAYLOR'
WALDRON, SIMON--[8][28]ROM/MYS--
HALE "CAUGHT IN THE MIDDLE" '72
HALE "GRAYSON AFFAIR" '75
WALLACE, AGNES--[8][28]ROM--
HALE "HEARTS IN CONFLICT" '70
HALE "DEAR DOCTOR" '73 & MORE
WETZEL, LOUIS--[8][28]WEST--
HALE "JUDAS GUN" '62
HALE "SIX-GUN FUGITIVE" '63 & 5 MORE
YARBO, STEVE--[8][28]WEST--
HALE "HARDCASE" 73'
HALE "BACK-TRAIL SHADOWS" '74 & MORE

KING, ALEXANDER HYATT
KING, ALEC HYATT--[31]

KING, BARRINGTON
KING, BARRIE--[26]ROM--
"JULIA"

KING, BRUCE ALVIN
GRANT, MARK--[7]SF,HP--
AV "MUTANTS AMOK #5-CHRISTMAS SLAUGHTER" '91
SHERRILL, KEVIN--V. BERCH LTR TO HUBIN '94, MYS--
PINN "MIDNIGHT" '89
ZOLAR--[34]--
GM 1902 "IT'S ALL IN THE STARS" '68
LAN 72-620 "DREAM BOOK" '61

KING, C. DALY
COURTNEY, ROBERT--[1][18][22]MYS--
PHELAN, JEREMIAH--[1][2][11]

KING, CHRISTINE
LOVAN, THEA--[21][26]ROM--
"PASSIONATE JOURNEY"
"BLUE SEA OF AUGUST" & MORE

KING, ELNORA
KING, DIANE--W/PAMELA WALLACE,[9][21][26]ROM--
"FRIEND OF THE HEART"
"ESSENCE OF SUMMER"

KING, FLORENCE
BUCHANAN, LAURA--[21][26][31]ROM--
BERK "THE BARBARIAN PRINCESS" '77
CYNTHIA--[1][31]ADULT
KING, VERONICA--[1][31]ADULT--
REED, EMMETT X.--[1][31]ADULT--
STAVROS, NIKO--[1][31]ADULT--
WINSTON, MIKE--[1][31]ADULT--

KING, FRANCIS HENRY
CAULDWELL, FRANK--[1][22][31]ENGLISH

KING, FRANK
CONRAD, CLIVE--[3][22][29]MYS--
MUS "THERE WAS A LITTLE MAN" '48
MUS "MONEY'S WORTH OF MURDER" '49
MUS "CRIME OF HIS LIFE" '51

KING, FRANKLIN
ADAMSON, LYDIA--V. BERCH LTR TO A. HUBIN '93, MYS--
SIGN "A CAT IN THE MANGER" '90
KING, FRANK--[34]MYS--
MAREK "DOWN & DIRTY" '78
MAREK "NIGHT VISION" '79
MAREK "RAYA" '80

KING, FRANKLIN [CONT]
KING, FRANK [CONT]
DUTTON "SLEEPING DOGS DIE" '88
DUTTON "TAKE THE D TRAIN" '90

KING, FRANKLIN ALEXANDER
KING, FRANK A.--[31]

KING, HAROLD
HAROLDSON, WILLIAM--[1][31]
HARRIS, BRIAN--[1][7][31]SF--
POCK "WORLD WAR III: A NOVELIZATION" '82

KING, JAMES CLIFFORD
FRY, PETE--[32][34]MYS--
15 BRDMN NVLS '57-70
EW "I, THE ACCUSED..." MAR '67
KING, CLIFFORD--[8]

KING, JOHN BOSWELL
BOSWELL, JOHN--[1]
KILDARE, JOHN--[1]

KING, KAY
HOLT, ELIZABETH--[8]

KING, KEITH MICHAEL
CARR, BENTLEY--[7]SF--
"TALES OF MAROTH #1" '91

KING, MARJORIE CAMERON
KING, PEGGY CAMERON--[1][31]

KING, MARY LOUISE
JOHNSON, MARY LOUISE--[1][31]

KING, PATRICIA
WILDE, KATHEY--[22]AMERICAN

KING, PAULA E. DOWNING
DOWNING, PAULA E.--[23]SF
DOWNING, PAULA E.--[7]SF--
BAL "RINN'S STAR" '90
KING, PAULA--[7][23]SF--
BAEN "MAD ROY'S LIGHT" '90

KING, RUFUS
CAMILLUS--[1]

KING, STELLA
STELLA--[2]

KING, STEPHEN [EDWIN]
BACHMAN, RICHARD--[2][3][31]MYS--
SIGN "RAGE" '77
SIGN "RUNNING MAN" '82
NAL "THINNER" '84
KING, STEVE--[31]
SWITHEN, JOHN--[1]

KING, WILLIAM BENJAMIN
KING, BASIL--[1]

KING, [R] SHERWOOD
KING, SHERRY--[1][22]MYS--

KING-BROCATO, KATHRYN
BROCATO, KATHRYN--[26]ROM--
"STORM WARNING"

KING-HALL, LUISE OLGA E.
KING-HALL, LOU--[23]SF--
"FLY ENVIOUS TIME" '44

KING-HALL, MAGDALEN
KNOX, CLEONE--[1]

KING-HALL, STEPHEN
ETIENNE--[1][22][31]ENGLISH
K-H NEWS SERVICE--[23]

KING-SCOTT, PETER EDGAR
EDGAR, PETER--[2][7][11]SF--
DIGIT "CITIES OF THE DEAD" '63

KINGHORN, ALEXANDER M.
KINGHORN, A.M.--[1]
SHARP, JAMES--[1]

KINGHORN, NORTON D.
KELVIN, NED--[34]MYS--
PAPERJACK "PEGGED FOR MURDER" '88

KINGSBURY, PHYLLIS MAY
FLOWERDEW, PHYLLIS--[1]

KINGSCOTE, ADELINA G.I.W.
CLEEVE, LUCAS--[2][3]MYS--
WHITE "WORLD'S BLACKMAIL" 1900
UNWIN "COUNSELS OF THE NIGHT" '02

KINGSLEY, CHARLES
LOT, PARSON--[33]

KININMOUTH, CHRITOPHER
BRENNAN, CHRISTOPHER--W/ROLAND BAIRD,[1][31]

KINNERLEY, LYNNE
DARBY, LYNDAN--W/ANN GRIMSLEY,[7]SF--
UNWIN "EYE OF TIME TRILOGY #1-3" '88-9

KINNES, J.
STROUD, LUKE--[35]AUSTRALIAN--
BIGHORN 334 "ANACONDA" & 35 CLEVELAND BKS

KINNEY, ELIZABETH C.
STEDMAN--[1]

KINNEY, JAMIE
SAX, ANDRE--W/STEPHEN SOITOS,[3]MYS--
CHART "SALT CAT BANK" '80
CHART "A DEATH IN THE COLONY" '80
CHART "DANCER DISAPPEARS" '82

KINNICUTT, SUSAN SIBLEY
SHELBY, SUSAN--[1]
SIBLEY, SUSAN--[1]

KINNOSUKE, NATSUME
SOSEKI--[22]JAPANESE
SOSEKI, NATSUME--[22]JAPANESE

KINROSS, PATRICK LORD
BALFOUR, PATRICK--[22]ENGLISH

KINSEY-JONES, BRIAN
BALL, BRIAN NEVILLE--[29]MYS--
BARKER "KEEGAN: NO OPTION CONTRACT" '76
& 5 MORE

KINSLEY, DANIEL ALLAN
EDWARDES, ALLEN--[1]

KINZEL, DOROTHY
KINZEL, DOTTIE--[31][33]

KIRBY, BRYAN
TYLER, JO--V. BERCH-BRNDN/
BC PSEUDS, BAE 22, P24

KIRBY, DEREK AMOS
CAPELLI, ACE--PP 29, P42, MYS,HP--
LADWICK, MARTY--[8]

KIRBY, LAURAINE
LA BAN, L.E.--V. BERCH-BRNDN/
BC PSEUDS, BAE 22, P24

KIRBY, SUSAN E.
STEPHENS, SUZANNE--[33]

KIRBY, WILLIAM
BRITTANICUS--[1]

KIRCHEIMER, GLORIA
CARDIFF, SARA--W/REBECCA KAVALIER
& LOUISE DECORMIER,[3]MYS--
RNDM "FOOL'S APPLE" '71 & MORE

KIRCHHEIM, KARL WILHELM
WARNOFRIED--[39]GERMAN

KIREEV, AKHNIAF N.
MERGEN, KIREI--[1]

KIRK, ELLEN WARNER O.
HAYES, HENRY--[1][22]AMERICAN

KIRK, IRENE
KIRK, IRINA--[1][31]

KIRK, JAMES PRIOR
PRIOR, JAMES--[1]

KIRK, RICHARD [E]
CHURCH, JEFFREY--[1][22][31]AMERICAN

KIRK, THOMAS HOBSON
THOMAS, K.H.--[1]

KIRK-GREEN, ANTHONY H.M.
CAVERHILL, NICHOLAS--[31]
H.M.S.--[1][31]
P.L.K.--[1]
YOLA, YERIMA--[1]

KIRKHAM, NELLIE
MYATT, NELLIE--[8]

KIRKHAM, REGINALD S.
CLIFFORD, MARTIN--[1]HP--
RICHARDS, FRANK--[1]HP--
VINCENT, FRANK--[1]

KIRKPATRICK, MRS. HELEN
GEMMILL--[8]

KIRKPATRICK, OLIVER A.
CANOE, JOHN--[1]

KIRKUP, JAMES
FALCONER, JAMES--[1][22][31][33]ENGLISH
JAMES, ANDREW--[1][22][31][33]ENGLISH
JUN, TERAHATA--[1]
SHIGERO TSUYNKI--[1]
SUMMERFOREST, IVY B.--[1][22]ENGLISH

KIRKWOOD, FRANCES
CRANE, FRANCES--[5][32]MYS--
EQMM "THE BLUE HAT" SEPT '46
EQMM "DEATH IN GUATEMALA" JUN '60

KIRKWOOD, JOYCE
CORLETT, JOYCE I.--[8]

KIROUAC, JOSEPH LOUIS C.
MARIE-VICTORIN, FRERE--[22]FRENCH-CANADIAN

KIRSCH, HANS CHRISTIAN
HETMANN, FREDERIK--[39]GERMAN/SF/JUV--

KIRSCHNER, ALOISIA
SCHUBIN, OSSIP--[39]GERMAN

KIRSH, ROBERT R.
BANCROFT, ROBERT--[21][31]ROM--
"CASTILIAN ROSE"
DUNDEE, ROBERT--[3][29][31]MYS--
SIGN 1768 "RESTLESS LOVERS" '60
SIGN 1980 "PANDORA'S BOX" '62
SIGN 2159 "INFERNO" '62

KIRSON, ALICE ATKINSON
ATKINSON, ALICE M.--[1]

KIRWAN, MOLLEY [M]
MORROW, CHARLOTTE--[1][22]ENGLISH

KIRWAN, THOMAS
WONDER, WILLIAM--[2]

KIRWAN-WARD, BERNARD
WARD, KIRWAN--[8]

KISH, ELEANOR MARY
KISH, ELY--[31][33]

KISNER, JACOB
KISNER, JACK--[1]
SMALLWOOD, JASON--[1]

KISNER, JAMES [MARTIN JR]
JAMES, MARTIN--[7][31][34]MYS/SF--
ZEBRA "NIGHTGLOW" '89
ZEBRA "ZOMBIE HOUSE" '90

KISSLING, DOROTHY HIGH
LANGELY, DOROTHY--[2][7][11][31]SF--

KISTIAKOWSKY, VERA
FISCHER, VERA K.--[1][31]

KISTLER, MARY
REECE, JEAN--[9][21][26]ROM--
"PRIMROSE PATH"
"DEVIL'S DARE"

KITAMURA, FEDERICA
DE CESCO, FEDERICA--[39]GERMAN

KITCHEN, HERBERT THOMAS
KITCHEN, BERT--[31][33]

KITCHIN, FREDERICK H.
COPPLESTONE, BENNET--[22][32][34]MYS--
MURRAY "LOST NAL PAPERS" '17
MURRAY "LAST OF THE GRENVILLES" '19
MURRAY "DIVERSIONS OF DAWSON" '23
RS "THE BUTLER" FEB '46

KITE, PAT
ADAMS, TRICIA--[1][26]ROM--
"BETWEEN THE SHEETS"

KITMAN, MARVIN
HIRSCH, WILLIAM RANDOLPH--W/RICHARD
R. LINGEMAN & VICTOR S. NAVASKY,[1][31]

KITTREDGE, WILLIAM
ROUNDTREE, OWEN--W/STEVEN M. KRAUZER,
[1][28]WEST--
'CORD' SERIES - 9 NOVELS '82-6

KJELGAARD, JAMES ARTHUR
KJELGAARD, JIM--L. ROBBINS LTR '94, [31][32][33]MYS--
SD "SECOND SHOT" AUG '45
EQMM "CODE OF THE UNDERWORLD" AUG '53
SA "ROLL 'EM OVER GENTLY" JUL '54
EQMM "A FAIR BET" DEC '62

KJELLBERG, PAULINE A.
FLEURY, JACQUELINE--[21][26]ROM--
"CINDERELLA BRIDE"

KLAASSEN, LEONARDUS HEND.
KLAASSEN, LEO H.--[31]

KLAASSEN, WALTER
KLASSEN, WALTER--[31]

KLABER, KURT
HELD, KURT--[39]GERMAN

KLABER, LISA [T]
TETZNER, LISA--[39]GERMAN/JUV

KLABUND
HENSCHKE, ALFRED--[31]

KLAEHR, MOGENS
TEJN, MICHAEL--[1]

KLAGES, VICTOR
WYNDHEIM, VICTOR--[39]GERMAN

KLAINER, JO-ANN & ALBERT
PETERS, L.T.--[2][3][11]MYS--
SIMON "ELEVENTH PLAGUE" '73

KLAMMER, KLAR
AMMER, K.L.--[39]GERMAN

KLAMUCZAK, ROLF
FECHNER, HELGA--[39]GERMAN/JUV

KLAR, RANDOLF
CLEAR, RALPH--[39]GERMAN/SF--

KLASS, JUDITH ALEXANDRA
KLASS, JUDY--[7]SF--
"STAR TREK #46"

KLASS, PHILIP J.
PUTNAM, KENNETH--[1][2][11]
TENN, WILLIAM--[2][4][23][32]SF--
ASF "ALEXANDER THE BAIT" '46
SU "QUICK & THE BOMB" SPR '51
SP "MURDERING MYRA" NOV '55
ASF "HUMAN ANGLE" '56
ASF "TIME IN ADVANCE" '58
ASF "SEVEN SEXES" '68
ASF "SQUARE ROOT OF MAN" '68
ASF "WOODEN STAR" '68

KLATT, CONRAD
MAHNSFELD, EUGEN--[39]GERMAN/MYS/JUV

KLAUE, LOLA SHELTON
SHELTON, LOLA--[1][22]AMERICAN

KLAUS, MICHAEL
LUKAS, MANFRED--[39]GERMAN

KLAUSNER, AMOS
OZ, AMOS--[1]

KLAVAN, ANDREW
PETERSON, KEITH--LACHMAN LST '93,[34]--
BB "RAIN" '88
BB "TRAPDOOR" '88
BB "THERE FELL A SHADOW" '88
BB "ROUGH JUSTICE" '89
DBLDY "THE SCARRED MAN" '90
TRACY, MARGARET--W/LAWRENCE KLAVAN, [29][34]MYS--
DELL "MRS. WHITE" '87

KLAVAN, LAWRENCE
TRACY, MARGARET--W/ANDREW KLAVAN,[29][34]MYS--
DELL "MRS. WHITE" '87

KLAVANS, JODIE KAY
KLAVANS, J.K.--[31]

KLEBE, CHARLES EUGENE
KLEBE, GENE--[31]

KLEFF, THEODOR
VON DIEKEN, MANFRED--[39]GERMAN/JUV

KLEIM, HEINZ F.
KUHN, OTTO--[39]GERMAN--TRANSLATION

KLEIN, AARON E.
LITTLE, A. EDWARD--[33]

KLEIN, DOROTHEE
FRANK, DR. STEFAN--[39]GERMAN, HP--
GRAF, KARIN--[39]GERMAN, HP--
JONIUS, SUSANNA--[39]GERMAN
KASTEIN, DORIT--[39]GERMAN
KASTELL, KATRIN--[39]GERMAN

KLEIN, ELIZABETH
SHAPIRO, ELIZABETH KLEIN--[1]

KLEIN, ERIKA
KLEIN-WOLKEN, ERIKA--[39]GERMAN/JUV
KORT, AMELY--[39]GERMAN/JUV
ZIEGLER-STEGE, ERIKA--[39]GERMAN/JUV--

KLEIN, FRED [FRITZ]
ELIN, FRED K.--[39]GERMAN/ADV/JUV--
WELLER, FREDDY--[39]GERMAN/ADV/JUV,HP--

KLEIN, GERARD
D'ARGYRE, GILLES--[2][11][23][31]SF--
"PLANET SURGEONS" '60
"SAILORS OF THE SUN" '61
"THE LONG JOURNEY" '64
"THE MOTE IN TIMES EYE" '75
PAGERY, FRANCOIS--[2][11][23]SF,HP--
"AMBUSHES IN SPACE" '58
STARR, MARK--[2][11][23][32]MYS/SF--
"GALACTIC AGENT" '58
MH "SALES PITCH" JUN '61

KLEIN, GERHARD
HART, DEREK--[39]GERMAN/SF--

KLEIN, GRACE
COOPER-KLEIN, NINA--W/MAE KLEIN COOPER, [22]AMERICAN
FAREWELL, NINA--W/MAE KLEIN COOPER,[1][8]

KLEIN, JOSEPH
KLEIN, JOE--[31]

KLEIN, KARL FRIEDRICH
KLEIN, CHARLES--[39]GERMAN

KLEIN, MARTIN
KATAHN, MARTIN--[1]

KLEIN, T.E.D.
VAN HELSING, KURT--[2]

KLEIN, WALTER J. JR.
KENNETH, JOHN--L. ROBBINS LTR '94

KLEINBARD, JOAN GOULD
GOULD, JOAN--[7]SF--
COWARD "OTHERBORN: A NOVEL" '80

KLEINE, ERWIN
DONATUS, GEORG--[39]GERMAN/JUV
FRIEDENHAUS, FRIEDRICH--[39]GERMAN/JUV

KLEINER, RICHARD ARTHUR
KLEINER, DICK--[31]

KLEINER-SCHONBECK, MARIA.
SCHONBECK, MARIANNE--[39]GERMAN/MYS

KLEINFIELD, NATHAN RICH.
KLEINFIELD, SONNY--[31]

KLEINHAUS, JULIUS
KAY, JAY--[1]

KLEINHOUSE, THEODORE JOHN
LITTLEJOHN, JON R.--[8]

KLEINSASSER-TESTERMAN, L.
LOGAN, CAIT--[9][21][26]ROM--
"WILD DAWN"
"GAMBLER'S LADY" & MORE
LONDON, CAIT--[9][21][26]ROM--
"PENDRAGON VIRUS"
"MIDNIGHT RIDER" & MORE

KLEINSCHMIDT, DIANNE M.
DU PRE, GABRIELLE--W/SANDRA SMITH-WARE,
[9][21][26]ROM--
"FORGET ME NOT"
"ARIANE: BELOVED CAPTIVE"

KLEINSCHMIDT, SANDRA
JAMES, SAMANTHA--[26]ROM--
"MY CHERISHED ENEMY"
"THE REBELLIOUS HEART"
JAMES, SANDRA--[9][21][26]ROM--
"GUARDIAN ANGEL"
"NORTH OF EDEN" & MORE

KLEM, KAYE WILSON
CARLETON, CATHLEEN--[21]ROM--
"RIDE HOME THE NIGHT" & 4 OTHERS

KLEMME, CHRIS
BRADY, JILL--[39]GERMAN/MYS
HANSEN, MICHAELA--[39]GERMAN/MYS
WILLIAMS, CHRIS--[39]GERMAN/MYS

KLIEMKE, ERNST
NIENKAMP, HEINRICH--[39]GERMAN

KLIMENTOV, ANDREI PLATON.
PLATANOV, ANDREI--[31]

KLIMO, VERNON
KLIMO, JAKE--[1][31]

KLINDT-JENSEN, OLE
JENSEN, OLE KLINDT--[31]

KLINE, STEPHEN EDWARD
KLINE, STEVE--[31]

KLING, BERNT
JUNG, P.R.--[39]GERMAN/SF

KLINGLER, HERMANN
ROSS, RONALD--[39]GERMAN/ADV
SANDER, SIMON--[39]GERMAN/ADV
TWELKER, THOMAS--[39]GERMAN/ADV
ULLMANN, URBAN--[39]GERMAN/ADV

KLINGLER, MARIA
BELL, MARISA--[39]GERMAN/JUV
CHRISTOPHER, JOAN--[39]GERMAN/JUV

KLIPPEL, HERMANN
FOHREN, KLAUS--[39]GERMAN/JUV

KLOBUCHAR, JAMES JOHN
KLOBUCHAR, JIM--[31]

KLOOS, WILLEM JOHAN TEOD.
G.N.--[22]DUTCH
GUIDO--[22]DUTCH
SEBASTIAAN, SR.--[22]DUTCH

KLOPFER, WILHELMINE
CORINTH, WILHELMINE--[39]GERMAN

KLOSE, ERWIN
CLOSE, ERWIN P.--[39]GERMAN

KLOSTERMEYER, ANTON
TONVUS, HEINZ--[39]GERMAN

KLUG, RONALD
KLUG, RON--[31]

KLUGER, RUTH
ALIAV, RUTH--[31]
KLUEGER, RUTH--[31]

KLUMBACH, PETER
BACH, PETER W.--[39]GERMAN/SF

KLUVER, J. WILHELM
KLUVER, BILLY--[31]

KNAACK, TWILA
COLLINS, COLETTE--[1][31]

KNAPP, CLARENCE
GLUTZ, AMBROSE--[8]

KNAUSS, ROBERT
HELDERS, MAJOR--[1][2][39]GERMAN
HELDERS, MAJOR--[39]

KNEF, HILDEGARD
NEFF, HILDEGARD--[31]

KNEIFEL, HANNS
CARR, ALEXANDER--[39]GERMAN/ADV/SF--
KELASKER, HIVAR--[39]GERMAN/ADV/SF--

KNELLER, F.C.
BRUCE, IAN--[2][11]
ELLIS, JOHN--[2][11]
FENTON, BRUCE--[2][11]SF,HP--
SPENCER
JAMES, MACK--[2][11]
JONES, MACK--[2][11]
MASON, RAY--[2][11]SF,HP--
SPENCER
MENCER, D.J.--[2][11]SF,HP--SPENCER

KNELLER, F.C. [CONT]
PATTERSON, ROD--K. DILBONE-BADGER CKLST, BAE 15,[2][32]--
SW "A DAY OFF TO DIE" JUN '47
SW "TANGO JIM'S LAST DANCE" OCT '49
ROBERTSON, JAMES--[2][11]
ROBERTSON, JOHN--[2][11]
SPALDING, NEIL J.--[2][11]
SPAULDING, NEIL J.--[2][11]
STOKES, EDWARD--[2][11]

KNIBBS, H[ENRY] H[ERBERT]
HERBERT, HENRY K.--[28]--
GENESSE PRESS "FIRST POEMS" '08

KNICKREHM, HANS
BURMESTER, DIRKS--[39]GERMAN

KNIEFEL, HANNS
BEAUFORT, SEAN--[39]GERMAN/ADV/SF

KNIGHT, ALANNA
HOPE, MARGARET--[17][21][26][31]ROM--
"QUEEN'S CAPTAIN"
"SHADOW QUEEN"
"HOSTAGE MOST ROYAL"

KNIGHT, BERNARD
PICTON, BERNARD--[1][3]ENGLISH/MYS--
JENKINS "LATELY DECEASED" '63
HALE "MISTRESS MURDER" '66 & OS

KNIGHT, CLIFFORD REYNOLDS
KNIGHT, REYNOLDS--[18]MYS--
McCLURG "TOMMY OF THE VOICES" '18

KNIGHT, DAMON
CONANIGHT--W/CHESTER COHEN,[1][2][11]
CONWAY, RITTER--[1][2]
FLEMING, STUART--[1][2][11][23][31]SF--
LAVERTY, DONALD--W/JAMES BLISH, [2][11][23][31]SF--

KNIGHT, ERIC MOWBRAY
HALLAS, RICHARD--MUNROE SLST #23, [3][31][33]MYS--
McBRIDE "YOU PLAY THE BLACK & RED COMES UP" '38

KNIGHT, ETHERIDGE
SOA, IMANU E.K.--[1]

KNIGHT, F. FRANCIS EMMA
KNIGHT, FRIDA--[1]

KNIGHT, FRANCIS EDGAR
KNIGHT, FRANK--[8][31][33]
SALTER, CEDRIC--[1][33]

KNIGHT, JOAN GEIZEY
SUMMERS, IRIS--W/MARY KUCZIR,[9][21][26]ROM--
"WHITEFIRE"

KNIGHT, KATHLEEN MOORE
AMOS, ALAN--[18][22][29][34]MYS--
DUELL "PRAY FOR A MIRACLE" '41
DBLDY "BORDERLINE MURDER" '47
DBLDY "PANIC IN PARADISE" '51
DBLDY "FATAL HARVEST" '57

KNIGHT, KATHRYN LASKY
LASKY, KATHRYN--[7]SF--
PHOENIX "HOME FREE" '85
HARCOURT "DOUBLE TROUBLE SQUARED" '91

KNIGHT, KATIE G.M.WILHELM
WILLHELM, KATE--[1][7][23]SF--
ST. MARTIN'S "CAMBIO BAY" '90
ST. MARTIN'S "CRAZY TIME" '88 & MORE

KNIGHT, MAX
FABRIZIUS, PETER--W/JOSEPH B. FABRY,[1][31]

KNIGHT, NANCY CHRISTOPHER
DARCY, JENNA--W/SANDRA CHASTAIN,[9][26]ROM--
"THE VERY BEST"
KNIGHT, KRISTIE--[26]ROM--
"GARDEN PATH"
"CAROLINA MOON" & MORE

KNIGHT, STEPHEN
DEBAL, SWAMI PUJI--[7]SF--
METHUEN "REQUIEM AT ROGANO" '79

KNIGHT, TONY
CASE, TOM--[7]SF--
CASE "COOK" '81

KNIGHT, VICK R.
TWEED, J.H.--[1]

KNIGHTLEY, D.G.
PRIOR, HARRY--[1]

KNIPE, ALDEN ARTHUR
SHEA, TIMOTHY--[1]

KNIPE, EMILIE BENSON
BENSON, THERESE--[1][3][22]MYS--
DODD "STRICTLY PRIVATE" '31
DODD "GALLANT ADVENTURESS" '33
HARPER "DEATH WEARS A MASK" '35

KNIPSCHEER, JOHANNES M.W.
FOX, JAMES--
BEACON B-204 "SURABAYA" '58, RPRT OF 'GRANT HOLMES' BK IN '56
FOX, JAMES M.--JEAN F. LE DEIST, BAE 12,[22][32][34]MYS--
COWARD "THE LADY REGRETS" '47
LITTLE "THE WHEEL IS FIXED" '51
MON 132 "SAVE THEM FOR VIOLENCE" '59
X-BOK "TERROR I LYXKLASS"'60 & MORE
HOLMES, GRANT--[18][29][34]MYS--
CASSELL "SURABAYA" '56
CASSELL "DARK CRUSADE" '65 & MORE

KNIST, F. EMMA
FALLERE, FELICIA--[1][31]

KNOBLAUCH, EDWARD
KNOBLOCK, EDWARD--[1]

KNOBLOCH, HILDA
KNOBLOCH, HANS--[39]GERMAN/JUV
OTRTHOFER, HILDA--[39]GERMAN/JUV

KNODT, JOSEF
JOTKATE, P.--[39]GERMAN
TREVERANUS, PETRUS--[39]GERMAN

KNOLES, WILLIAM [H]
ALLEN, CARTER--MUNROE-BAE 26, ADULT--
NTSD 3053 "FLESH IS MY UNDOING" RPRTS NTSD 1555
NTSD 3054 "FOR THE LOVE OF TOY" RPRTS NTSD 1557 "MALAY MISTRESS"
NTSD 4007 "TO KISS A DRAGON" RPRTS NTSD 1573 "JADE BROTHEL"
NTSD 4016 "NO EXPERIENCE NECESSARY" RPRTS NTSD 1582 "FLESH FOR HIRE"

KNOLES, WILLIAM [H] [CONT]
ALLEN, CARTER [CONT]
NTSD 4038 "THE BRUTALIZED"
RPRTS MDNR 410 "SEX RIDDLE"
NTSD 4051 "NO PRIVATE AFFAIR"
RPRTS NTSD 1601 "THE LUST GAME"
ALLISON, CLYDE--JEAN F. LE DEIST-BAE 18
MUNROE-BAE 26,[2][3]ADULT--
NTSD 1525 "THE LUSTFUL ONES" '60
MDWD 64 "MILLION DOLLAR MISTRESS" '60
NTSD 1555 "FLESH IS MY UNDOING" '61
MDWD 73 "SEX PEDDLERS" '61
NTSD 1557 "MALAY MISTRESS" '61
NTSD 1571 "SEX TRAP" '61
NTSD 1573 "JADE BROTHEL" '61
NTSD 1582 "FLESH FOR HIRE" ca '61
NTSD "1601 "LUST GAME" '62
NTSD "JAILBAIT WANTON" '62
NTSD 1632 "PASSION PRIZE" '62
NTSD 1634 "SIN TRADER" '62
BDSD 1212 "JAILBAIT" '62
BDSD 1217 "WEB OF FLESH" '62
MDNR 410 "THE SEX RIDDLE" '62
MDNR 424 "SIN KING" '62
MDNR 432 "LUST SNIPER" '62
[POSSIBLY NOT "KNOLES"]
MDNR 438 "FAST TALK SINNER" '62
MDNR 439 "SEX SPREE" '62
BERK Y705 "HAVE NUDE WILL TRAVEL" '63
NTSD 1644 "SEX, INC." '63
NTSD 1652 "MONEY BED" '63
MDNR 482 "SHAME SLAVE" '63
EMBER 927 "THE FLESH GAME"
EMBER 929 "FLESH HUNGRY" BOYH ca '63
EMBER 951 "SHAME MARKET" '64
EV "THE SIN GANG" '64
IDLE HR 410 "RAPTURE PIT" '64
LEIS 624 "SIN UNCHAINED" '64
SUNR 510 "GATEFOLD GIRLS" '64
SUNR 521 "ORGY VOYAGE" '64
NTSD 1732 "PASSION POOL" '65
NTSD 1734 "FLESH CULT" '65
EV 785 "KEY CLUB SINNERS" '65
EV 1210 "TORTURE CLUB" '65
IDLE HR 474 "SEASIDE SWAP" '65
SUNR 533 "LUSTER'S REVOLT" '65
SUNR 540 "ORGY LAIR" '65
SUNR 563 "PASSION PROFITEER" '65
IDLE HR 483 "SEXPERIMENT" '66
LEIS 1133 "SIX MONTHS TO LOVE" '66
LEIS 1137 "LEWD NUDE" '66
ALLISON, GLENN--AFTER HRS, SLEAZE ?
AMES, CLYDE--MUNROE-BAE 26,[3]ADULT--
LAN 73-607 "GROGONZOLA, WON'T YOU
PLEASE COME HOME" '67
LAN 73-286 "BANG THE DOLL SLOWLY" '68
ANDERSON, CLYDE--MUNROE-BAE 26,[1]ADULT--
PLR 832 "PASSION PLOT" '63
EMBER 908 "SIN MERCHANT" '63
EMBER 920 "LUST GAMBLE" ND ['63?]
ANDERTON, CLYDE--R.C. HOLLAND DEC '92
CRADDOCK, WILSON JR.--MUNROE-BAE 26--
SHORT STORY "THE ARTIFACT" - MAG UNKNOWN
DEXTER, JOHN--MUNROE-BAE 26, ADULT--
NTSD 1562 "SIN SONG" '61
NTSD 1594 "SIN COLONY" '62
HOLLIDAY, DON--R.C. HOLLAND DEC '92
KNOWLES, WILLIAMSON--MUNROE-BAE 26, MYS--
MD "CABIN IN THE SKY" MAY-JUN '61 ??
WILLIAMS, J.X.--MUNROE-BAE 26, ADULT--
CORINTH/HAMLYN - NO TITLES VERIFIED
WILLIAMS, MAX--MUNROE-BAE 26,--
GENT "THE CONVERTER" APR '60
ESCAPADE "TREASURE HO!" AUG '60
DUDE "DEBT OF A SALESMAN" MAR '61
IF "THE SEEDER" MAR '61

KNOLES, WILLIAM [H]
WILLIAMS, MAX [CONT]
HELP "WHAT? ANOTHER ULTIMATE
WEAPON?" APR '61
ESCAPADE "THE EDUCATION OF JEFFERSON
BURBAGE" OCT '61
HI-LIFE "STREETFIGHTING FOR FUN
& PROFIT" NOV '61
MR. "BEWARE OF PATTERNS" '61
KNIGHT "TO TAHITI - SECOND STEP" '66

KNOLL, HAROLD
THERIDION, PAUL--LACHMAN LST MAY '93

KNOLL, LUDWIG
BERGK, ALEXANDER--[39]GERMAN/MYS

KNOLL, PATRICIA F.
FORSYTHE, PATRICIA--[9]ROM
NICHOLS, CHARLOTTE--W/BARBARA WILLIAMS,
[9][21][26]ROM--
"FOR THE LOVE OF MIKE"
"EYE OF THE BEHOLDER"

KNOP, LYDIA
KATH, LYDIA--[39]GERMAN/JUV

KNORR, KLAUS EUGENE
KNORR, K.E.--[31]

KNORR, MARIAN LOCKWOOD
DEKALB, LORIMER--[31]

KNOTT, WILLIAM CECIL JR.
CAROL, BILL J.--[19][28][31][33]JUV
EARLY, TOM--J. REASONER '93,[28]WEST,HP--
BERK 'SONS OF TEXAS' SERIES #5
EVANS, TABOR--[1][19][28][31]WEST,HP--
'LONGARM' SERIES - 14 NOVELS
KNOTT, BILL--[8][19][28][31][33]JUV--
8 NOVELS '66-71
KNOTT, WILL C.--[8][28][31]
LAYNE, LAURA--[1][28][31]ROM--
ACE "NURSE JUNE'S DILEMA" '77
LOGAN, JAKE--[28]HP--
BERK "SLOCUM & CATTLE QUEEN" '83
BERK "SLOCUM & LOST DUTCHMAN MINE" '83
MITCHUM, HANK--[28]HP--
BB 'STAGECOACH STATION' SERIES:
"CHEYNNE"
"SEATTLE"
"SONORA"
"ABILENE"
"CIMARRON"
SHARPE, JON--[28]WEST,HP--
NAL 'TRAILSMAN' SERIES-13 NOVELS '84-86
ST. GIRAUD--[8]
SWIFT, BRYAN--[1][28][34]MYS,HP--
JOVE "MISSION CODE: KING'S PAWN" '81
JOVE "MISSION CODE: MINOTAUR" '81
JOVE "MISSION CODE: SPRINGBOARD" '82

KNOTT, WILLIAM KILBORN
KNOTT, BILL--[8][32]MYS--
AHMM "IT TAKES TWO" JUN '65

KNOWLES, LEO
GREGORY, JULIAN R.--[1][2]

KNOWLES, MABEL WINIFRED
LURGAN, LESTER--[2][3][23][31]SF--
GREENING "LEAGUE OF THE TRIANGLE" '11
GREENING "A MESSAGE FROM MARS" '12
EVERETT "WRESTLER ON THE SHORE " '13

KNOWLES, MABEL WINIFRED [CONT]
MAY, WYNNE--[9][21][26]ROM--
"TAMBOTI MOON"
"PINK SANDS" & MORE

KNOWLES, MICHAEL CLIVE
KNOWLES, DAVID--[1]

KNOWLTON, EDWARD ROGERS
ROGERS, KERK--[3]MYS--
MILLS "BEACH PATROL" '43
MILLS "WITH INTENT TO KILL" '44 & MORE

KNOWLTON, WINTHROP
GOODMAN, WINTHROP--W/GEORGE JEROME GOODMAN,[8]
SMITH, ADAM--W/GEORGE [J.W.] GOODMAN,[34]MYS--

KNOX, CLEO ELDON
ATOMCRACKER, BUZZ-BOLT--[2][11][23]SF--
"CONFESSIONS OF A MECHANICAL MAN" '47
BLADE, ALEXANDER--[1][2][23]SF,HP--ZIFF-DAVIS
ELDON, CLEO--[1][2][11][23]SF
OVERTON, MAX--[1][2][11][23]SF
REED, DAVID V.--W/DAVID VERN,[7]--
WFC "WHISPERING GORILLA" '50
[SOLD FOR $600 IN '93]
SHELTON, MILES--[2][11][23]SF--
AMZ & FA 'EBBTIDE JONES' STORIES '39-42
WILCOX, DON--L. ROBBINS LTR MAR '94,[23]SF

KNOX, EDMUND GEORGE V.
EVOE--[8][22][31][34]MYS--
METHUEN "FICTION AS SHE IS WROTE" '23
METHUEN "FANCY NOW" '24

KNOX, HUGH R.
KAY, H.R.--V. BERCH-BRNDN/BC PSEUDS,
BAE 22, P24,[2][3]ADULT/MYS--
BRANDON "THE DARK MANSION" '68
BRANDON "TWO GAY SLEUTHS" '68

KNOX, RONALD A.
R.A.K.--[23]SF

KNOX, WILLIAM [BILL]
KIRK, MICHAEL--[18][29][31[34]MYS--
DBLDY "OTHER PERILS" '75
DBLDY "DRAGONSHIP" '77
DBLDY "SALVAGE JOB" '79
DBLDY "CARGO RISK" '80
KNOX, BILL--[8][32]ADV/MYS--
"DRUMS OF UNGARA" '63
12 EW DIGEST STORIES '61-7
MACLEOD, ROBERT--[3][18][21][26]
[29][31]ROM/MYS--
"DARING DESTINY" & 20 MORE
WEBSTER, NOAH--[1][3][18][29]MYS--
DBLDY "A KILLING IN MALTA" '72
DBLDY "A BURIAL IN PORTUGAL" '73
DBLDY "FLICKERING DEATH" '73
AKA "A PROPERTY IN CYPRESS"
DBLDY "A WITCHDANCE IN BAVARIA" '76
DBLDY "A PAY-OFF IN SWITZERLAND" '77
DBLDY "AN INCIDENT IN ICELAND" '79

KNOX, [MARY] ELEANOR J.
SHEPARD, MARY--[33]

KNOX-JOHNSON, WILLIAM R.P
KNOX-JOHNSON, ROBIN--[1]

KNOX-MAWER, RONALD
KAY, RONALD--[31]
KNOX-MAWER, RONNIE--[31]

KNUDSEN, ROZANNE RUTH
KNUDSEN, R.R.--[1][31][33]

KNUDSON, MARGRETHE
KNUDSON, GRETA--[8]

KNUTH, PETER WALDEMAR
WOLFENBERG, PETER--[39]GERMAN

KNUTSEN, FRIDTJOF
BO, ERIK--[29]NORWEGIAN/MYS

KNUTSEN, LALLI
HILD, ALF--[29]NORWEGIAN/MYS
MARVIK, JAN--[29]NORWEGIAN/MYS
RANJE--[29]NORWEGIAN/MYS
RONSON, L.F.--[29]NORWEGIAN/MYS

KNUTSEN, LALLI & FRIDTJOF
PAN PETER--[29][37]NORWEGIAN/MYS--
'MYSTIKK' '40-5
WELLE, STEIN--[29][37]NORWEGIAN/MYS

KNUTSON, NILS
EK, EDGAR--[29]MYS--
"DOD HORIZONT" '59

KOBAYASHI, MASAKO MATSUNO
MATSUNO, MASAKO--[22]JAPANESE

KOBL, KONRAD
COLL, CONNY--[39]GERMAN/SF/WEST
KOLBL, C.H.--[39]GERMAN/SF/WEST

KOBLINSKI, HANS-JOACHIM
BRAUN, M.G.--W/FRIEDRICH TENKRAT,
[39][40]GERMAN/MYS,HP--3 NOVELS '69
FLETCHER, JOHN--[39][40]GERMAN/MYS--
"DER BOSS MACHT KLEINER FEHLER" '70

KOBUSCH, HELMUT
BROOKS, BARNEY--[39][40]GERMAN/MYS--
'KOMMISSAR X' SERIES #626
COTTON, JERRY--[39]GERMAN/MYS,HP--
DAVIES, THOMAS B.--[39]GERMAN/MYS
DUNCAN, JOHN--[39]GERMAN/ADV/WEST
MORTIMER, GLENN--[39]GERMAN/ADV/WEST
NASH, GORDON--[39]GERMAN/ADV/WEST
NOLAN, FREDERICK--[39]GERMAN/WEST,HP--
O'BRIAN, TED--[39]GERMAN/ADV/WEST

KOBY, DALE
BRITT, DEL--V. BERCH-PIKE CKLST,
BAE 18, ADULT--
PIKE 220 "SIN HOUSE" '62

KOCH, CHARLOTTE
RAYMOND, CHARLES--W/RAYMOND KOCH,[1]

KOCH, EDMUND P.
VAN EYK, PIET--[39]GERMAN

KOCH, GERHARD
COTTON, JERRY--[39]GERMAN/MYS,HP--

KOCH, KURT EMIL
BECKER, KLAUS--[1][31]
CORNEA, CAROL--[1]
DISTEL, PETER--[31]
KUCHARSKI, KASIMIR--[1]
MAROT, MARK--[1]
MONOD, RENE--[1]

KOCH, MAGDA
HALENZA, ADA--[39]GERMAN

KOCH, RAYMOND
RAYMOND, CHARLES--W/CHARLOTTE KOCH,[1]

KOCH, RICHARD
NULPE, H.C.--[39]GERMAN/SF,HP--
RICHARDS, K.--[39]GERMAN/SF

KOCHANSKI, EVA [C]
CASKEL, EVA--[39]GERMAN

KOCHER, HUGO
NECKAR, HEINRICH--[39]GERMAN/JUV

KOCHER-ERB, HEDWIG
ERB, HEDWIG--[39]GERMAN/JUV
KEMMLER, URSULA--[39]GERMAN/JUV

KOCK, FERDINAND ANTON
ANTON, FERDINAND--[39]GERMAN

KOCK, WINSTON E[DWARD]
KIRK, WAYNE--[1][31]

KOCKA, JUERGEN
KOSKA, JURGEN--[31]

KODA SHIGEYUKI
KODA ROHAN--[31]

KODELPETER, HANS E.
GORDON, REX--[39][40]GERMAN/MYS--
'KOMMISSAR X' SERIES - 6 BOOKS

KODELPETER, HANS P.
BALMORE, CEDRIC--[39]GERMAN/HOR/MYS
BRENT, GUY--[39]GERMAN/HOR/MYS
COLLINS, FREDERIC--[39]GERMAN/HOR/MYS,HP
COTTON, JERRY--[39]GERMAN/MYS,HP
DE LORCA, FRANK--[39]GERMAN/HOR/MYS,HP
ELLIOT, BRIAN--[39]GERMAN/HOR/MYS,HP
FLEMING, CHARLES--[39]GERMAN/HOR/MYS
FLEMING, PETER--[39]GERMAN/HOR/MYS

KOEBER, ELSBETH
ISENBECK, ELSBETH--[39]GERMAN

KOEBSEL, EBERHARD
LAAR, CLEMENS--[39]GERMAN

KOEFED-NIELSON, CARL
NEILSON, KOEF--[8]

KOEGEL, JOHANNES
KING, HENRY--[39]GERMAN

KOEHLER, MARGARET [H]
CHARLES, MAGGI--[9][21][26][31]ROM--
"MAGIC CRESCENDO"
"KEEP IT PRIVATE" & MORE
HUDSON, MEG--[9][21][26][31]ROM--
"RISING ROAD"
"CHANCE MEETING" & MORE
MEAD, RUSSELL--[3][9]MYS--
RAVEN "MOSES BATTLE" '80
RAVEN "THIRD ONE" '81
RAVEN "NIGHTINGALE TRIVET" '81
STANDISH, CAROLE--[9]

KOEHLER, PAUL OSWALD
INTRUS--[39]GERMAN

KOEHLER, WOLFGANG
KOHLER, WOLFGANG--[31]

KOEHN-HEINE, LALA
KOEHN, LALA--[31]

KOELSCH, WILLIAM A.
GAY, A. NOLDER--[1][31]

KOENIG, FRANZ
KONIG, FRANZ--[31]

KOENIG, FRITZ HANS
KONIG, FRITZ HANS--[31]

KOENIG, RENE
KONIG, RENE--[31]

KOENNER, ALFRED
KONNER, ALFRED--[31]

KOERNER, STEPHAN
KORNER, STEPHAN--[31]

KOERTE, MARY NORBERT
KORTE, MARY NORBERT--[31]

KOESTLER, ARTHUR
COSTLER, [DR.] A.--[1][8]

KOFALK, HARRIET
KIMBRO, HARRIET--[31]

KOFFLER, CAMILLA
YLLA--[8]

KOFOED, JOHN C.
KOFOED, JACK--[31]

KOFOED, WILLIAM H.
OSBORNE, O.O.--W/HENRY LIEFERSAND,
V. BERCH-GM PSEUDS, PP 33--
RSB 17 "QUEST" '52
GM 301 "LEAVE HER TO GOD" '53
GM 764 "RISE & FALL OF DR. CAREY" '58

KOGAN RAY, DEBORAH
KOGAN, DEBORAH--[1][31][33]
RAY, DEBORAH--[1][31][33]

KOHLENBERG, KARL FRIEDR.
FRANK, BENNO--[39]GERMAN/JUV

KOHLER, ROLF
STUART, KENNETH--[39]GERMAN/MYS

KOHLHOFER, ALEXANDER
RAXIN, ALEXANDER--[39]GERMAN

KOHLS, OLIVE N. ALLEN
ALLEN, DIXIE--[8]

KOHLS, RICHARD LOUIS
KOHLS, R.L.--[31]

KOHN, SELIGMANN
NORK, F.--W/FRIEDRICH KORN,[39]GERMAN

KOHN, WILLARD K.
BURGESS-KOHN, JANE--W/JANE K. BURGESS,[31]--
BEAC "THE WIDOWERS" '78

KOHN-BEHRENS, CHARLOTTE
REHN, VIKTORIA--[1][39][40]GERMAN/MYS--
"REICHTE AUF TONBAND"

KOHON, ETHEL [C]
DOW, ETHEL--[1]

KOHR, DIETRICH
COTTON, JERRY--[39]GERMAN/MYS,HP--
DAY, DERRICK--[39]GERMAN/ADV/MYS

KOHR, DIETRICH [CONT]
DUKE, HOBBY--[39]GERMAN/ADV/MYS
FROHLICH, SIGISMUND,--[39]GERMAN/ADV/MYS
SANDERS, PHIL E.--[39]GERMAN/ADV/MYS

KOHUT, NESTER C.
KOHUT, LES--[1][31]

KOILPILLAI, [J] CHARLES
KOILPILLAI, DAS--[31]

KOIZAR, KARL HANS
SHARK, ROLF--[39][40]GERMAN/ADV/MYS--
"DER SARG WIRD PROMPT GELIEFERT" '79

KOJIMA SHOZO
KIJIMA HAJIME--[31]

KOJUHAROV, TUDOR
CHORNY, FEDYA--[22]BULGARIAN
KOPEYKIN, CAPTAIN--[22]BULGARIAN

KOLACZYK, ANNE & EDWARD
BENSON, ANNE--[9][21][26]ROM--
"LOVE'S GENTLE SMILE"
"ESCAPE TO LOVE"
"TANGLED WEB"
BRYANT, ERIKA--[9]ROM
EDWARDS, ADRIENNE--[9][21][26]ROM--
"DESTINY'S DARLING"
"WHISTLING DIXIE" & MORE
EDWARDS, ANDREA--[9][26]ROM--
SIL 856 "MAGIC OF CHRISTMAS"
SIL 883 "JUST HOLD ON TIGHT!"
HILLARY, ANNE--[9][21][26]ROM--
"BARTERED BRIDE"
"MISMATCHED LOVERS" & MORE
JESSUP, KATHRYN--[9][21]ROM,HP--
"KAREN EVANS, MD: TRANSPLANT"

KOLASKI, BARBARA REEVES
REEVES, BARBARA--[26]ROM--
"DANGEROUS MARQUIS"
"SCANDALOUS COURTSHIP" & OTHERS

KOLATSCHEWSKY, VALERIUS
SCHAEFFNER, GEORG--[39]GERMAN

KOLB, KARL
WIEN, ALEXANDER--[39]GERMAN

KOLB, ULRIKE
SAAR, LILLI--[39]GERMAN

KOLBA, TAMARA
ST. TAMARA--[33]

KOLESNIKOV, NIKOLAI I.
PEREVALOV, NIKOLAI I--[1]

KOLFF, ROELOF COENRAAD
VAN HAREN, WOUTER--[1]

KOLLEK, THEODORE
KOLLEK, TED--[31]

KOLLER, LAWRENCE ROBERT
KOLLER, LARRY--[31]

KOLLMAR, RICHARD TOMPKINS
KOLLMAR, DICK--[31]

KOLPE, MAX
COLPET, MAX--[39]GERMAN

KOLUPAEV, VIKTOR D.
KOLUPAEV, VICTOR--[7]SF--
"HERMIT'S SWING" '80

KOMAN, VICTOR
CLEVE, JOHN--W/ANDREW J. OFFUTT,[7][23]SF,HP--
BERK "SPACEWAYS: JONUTA RISING" '83
BERK "SPACEWAYS: THE CARNADYNE HORDE" '84

KOMOROSKI, DELORES
KOMO, DELORES--V. BERCH LTR TO HUBIN '94, MYS--
CROSSING "CLIO BROWNE:
PRIVATE INVESTIGATOR" '88

KONADU, SAMUEL ASARE
ASARE, BEDIAKO--[1][31]
BEDIAKO, K.A.--[1]
BEDIAKO, KWABENA ASARE--[31]
KONADU, ASARE--[1][31]
KONADU, S.A.--[1]
SABU, FRANK--[1]

KONDO, YOJI
KOTANI, ERIC--W/ROGER ALLEN MACBRIDE,
[7][23]SF--
AV "SUPERNOVA" '91

KONIG, HANS H.
VAN DAM, HENRY--[39]GERMAN

KONIGSBERG, ALLEN S.
ALLEN, WOODY--[31]HUMOR--
"LUNATIC'S TALE" '86

KONIGSBERG, ELAINE LOBL
KONIGSBERG, E.L.--[1]

KONIGSBERG, ISADORE
KONIGSBERG, C.I.--[1]

KONINGSBERGER, HANS
KONIG, HANS--[3][31][33]DUTCH-AMERICAN/MYS--
HARCOURT "PETERSBURG-CANNES EXPRESS" '75

KONISHI, MASATOSHI
ASHOK--[1]

KONRAD, GYOERGY
KONRAD, GEORGE--[31]

KONSTAM, F.
KAYE, LORIN--W/LORIN ANDREW LATHROP,[1]

KOONTZ, DEAN R.
AXTON, DAVID--AUTHOR PROVIDED,[2][3]MYS--
LIPP "PRISON OF ICE" '76
COFFEY, BRIAN--AUTHOR PROVIDED,[2][31][34]MYS--
BOBBS "BLOOD RISKS" '73
BOBBS "SURROUNDED" '74
BOBBS "WALL OF MASKS" '75
BOBB "FACE OF FEAR" '77
DBLDY "VOICE OF THE NIGHT" '80
DWYER, DEANNA--G. THIESSEN-KOONTZ CKLST,
[2][3]MYS--
LAN "DEMON CHILD" '71
LAN "LEGACY OF TERROR" '71
LAN 75-309 "DANCE WITH THE DEVIL" '72
LAN 75-365 "CHILD OF THE STORM" '72
LAN 75-393 "DARK OF THE SUMMER" '72
DWYER, K.R.--G. THIESSEN-KOONTZ CKLST,
[2][34]MYS--
RANDOM "CHASE" '72
RANDOM "SHATTERED" '73
RANDON "DRAGONFLY" '75
SPHERE 780722 "FACE OF FEAR" '80
RPRT OF BK AS BY 'BRIAN COFFEY' '77

KOONTZ, DEAN R. [CONT]
HILL, JOHN--AUTHOR PROVIDED--
POPLB 445-00325 "LONG SLEEP" '75
KOONTZ DENIED "HEART BEEPS"
NICHOLS, LEIGH--AUTHOR PROVIDED,[2][9]SF/ROM--
POCK 46210 "KEY TO MIDNIGHT" '79
POCK "EYES OF DARKNESS" '81
POCK 43266 "HOUSE OF THUNDER" '82
POCK 43267 "TWILIGHT" '84
AV 75216 "SHADOWFIRES" '87
FONT "DOOR TO DECEMBER" '87-
RPRT OF BK AS 'RICHARD PAIGE'
NORTH, ANTHONY--AUTHOR PROVIDED,[3]MYS--
DIAL "STRIKE DEEP" '74
PAIGE, RICHARD--AUTHOR PROVIDED,[3][7]MYS--
SIGN AE3605 "DOOR TO DECEMBER" '85
WEST, OWEN--AUTHOR PROVIDED,G. THIESSEN-
KOONTZ CKLST,[3][7]MYS/SF--
JOVE S5726 "FUNHOUSE" '80
JOVE E5695 "MASKS" '81
WOLFE, AARON--G. LOVISI-PP 7,[1][7]SF--
LASER 9 "INVASION" '75

KOONTZ, GERDA & DEAN
CERRA, GERDA ANN--G. THIESSEN-KOONTZ CKLST--
LAN 75-294 "DARK HERITAGE" '71

KOOP, KATHERINE C.
LAMANCUSA, KATHERNE C.--[22][31]AMERICAN

KOOSER, THEODORE
KOOSER, TED--[31]

KOOYKER-ROMIJN, JOHANNA M
KOOIHER, LEONIE--[7][31][33]SF--
MORROW "CHRIS #1 & #2" '78-81
KOOYKER-ROMYN, JOHANNA M.--[31]

KOPELEV, LEV Z.
LEPKO, E.--[31]

KOPP, WILHELM
CONAGHER, KEN--[39]GERMAN/ADV/WEST
HARBORD, DAVIS J.--[39]GERMAN/ADV/WEST

KOPPEL, LILLIAN & SHELLEY
SHELLEY, LILLIAN--[1][9][21]ROM--
"BELLE OF BATH"
"SECRET OF HEIRESS"

KOPPENBERG, ELLEN
STEINBACH, ELLEN--[39]GERMAN

KORCZAK, JANUSZ
GOLDSZMIT, HENRYK--[31][33]

KORETSKY, JUDITH LEA
CASH-DOMINGO, LEA--LACHMAN LTR '94
EQMM INTRO JUL '94

KORINETZ, YURI I.
KORINETS, IURII I.--[1][31]

KORING-SCHETTGEN, HANNEL.
HARPER, CAROLINE--[39]GERMAN

KORMENDI, FERENC
JULIAN, PETER--[8]

KORN, FRIEDRICH
NORK, F.--W/SELIGMANN KOHN,[39]GERMAN

KORN, ILSE
HOLM, CORNELIA--[39]GERMAN/JUV

KORNAK, LUCILLE
KHORNAK, LUCILLE--[1]

KORNBLUTH, C[YRIL] M.
BALONS, EARL--[1][2]
BARCLAY, GABRIEL--[2][11][23]SF,HP--AST/SUSS
BEVAN, ALISTAIR--[1]
BURKE, CARL F.--[2]SF,HP--
COOKE, ARTHUR--[1][2][23]SF,HP--
CORWIN, CECIL--[2][11][23][31]SF--
DAVIES, WALTER C.--[2][11][23][31]SF--
EISNER, SIMON--[2][3][4][23][31]SF--
LION 109 "NAKED STORM" '52
FALCONER, KENNETH--[2][11][23][31]SF-
GOTTESMAN, S.D.--W/R.A.W. LOWNDES
& F. POHL,[2][23][31]SF--
SUSS "KING COLE OF PLUTO" '40
JUDD, CYRIL--W/JUDITH GROSSMAN,
[2][4][8][23]ADULT/SF--
BEAC 312 "SIN IN SPACE" '61
"OUTPOST MARS" '52
"GUNNER CADE" '52
KORNBLUTH, C.M.--[1][11][32]MYS--
PE "DIP DETAIL" JUL '53
MM "BLOOD ON THE CAMPUS" SEPT '60
LAVOND, PAUL DENNIS--W/J.H. DOCKWEILER,
R.A.W. LOWNDES & F. POHL [1][2]SF--
SFQ, FUTURE
MARINER, SCOTT--W/F. POHL,[2][11][23]SF--
"AN OLD NEPTUNE CUSTOM" '42
PARK, JORDAN--[2][11][23][34]MYS--
LION 135 "HALF" '53
LION 176 "VALERIE '53
LL 97 "SORORITY HOUSE" '56
PYR G368 "MAN OF COLD RAGES" '58
PEARSON, MARTIN--W/DON A. WOLHEIM,
[1][2][23]SF--
ASF "EMBASSY" '42
TOWARS, IVAR--W/RICHARD WILSON,[2][23]SF--
AS "STEPSONS OF MARS" '40
TOWERS, IVAR--W/R.A. LOWDNES, F. POHL
& RICHARD WILSON,[1][2]SF--
WYLIE, DIRK--W/J. DOCKWEILER & FREDERIK
POHL,[1][2][11]SF--
WYLIE, DIRK--W/J.H. DOCKWEILER [1][2][11]

KORNBLUTH, J.L.
CHANDLER, PETER--W/L.M.D. FONZO,[3]MYS--
AVON "BUCKS" '80

KORNER, HEINZ
MULLER, W.--[39]GERMAN
VON ROTENBURG, W.--[39]GERMAN

KORNINGEN, ANN TIZIA
LEITICH, ANN TIZIA--[39]GERMAN

KORNOELJE, CLIFFORD
DARROW, JACK--[1][2][11]SF--

KOROLENKO, VLADIMIR G.
KOROLENKO, V.G.--[31]

KORPELA, TUULA
LAUKKO, ESKO--W/MAURI SARIOLA,[29]MYS

KORSELL, JOHN
BJERKE, ONULF--[29]SWEDISH/MYS
LOIS, JOHN--[29]SWEDISH/MYS
STARK, JOHN--[37]SWEDISH/MYS--
'DETEKTIV' & 'ALIBI' MAGS-
'KNUT GRIBB' STORIES
STORM, OMAR--[29][37]SWEDISH/MYS--
'DETKTIV' MAG - 'KNUT GRIBB' STORIES
VANGEN, STYRK--[29]SWEDISH/MYS--
AM#31 "FALSKNYNTARBANDET" '48

KORTNER, PETER
HOFER, PETER--[8][31]

KORTOOMS, ANTONIUS J.
KORTOOMS, TOON--[1]

KORWIN-PIOTROWSKA, GABRL.
MASKOFF, JOZEF--[22]POLISH
ZAPOLSKA, GABRIELA--[22]POLISH

KORZENIOWSKI, JESSIE
CONRAD, JESSIE--[8]

KORZENIOWSKI, JOSEF T.K.
CONRAD, JOSEPH--[2][5][32]--
CLASSIC NOVELS & SS
SA "INN OF TWO WITCHES" JAN '59

KOS, ERIH
KOSCH, ERICH--[31]

KOSAK, CARL
CONSTANTINE, K.C.--[34]MYS--
STR "ROCKSBURG RAILROAD MURDERS" '72
STR "MAN WHO LIKED TO LOOK AT HIMSELF" '73
STR "BLANK PAGE" '74
STR "A FIX LIKE THIS" '75
GODINE "MAN WHO LIKED TO GROW TOMATOES" '82
GODINE "UPON SOME MIDNIGHTS CLEAR" '85
MYP "JOEY'S CASE" '88
MYP "SUNSHINE ENEMIES" '90

KOSHLAND, ELLEN
MCCAUGHEY, ELLEN--[1]

KOSIAK, ALEKSANDR S.
LEVADA, A.--[1]

KOSINSKI, JERZY
NOVAK, JERZY--[22]POLISH-AMERICAN
NOVAK, JOSEPH--LOCUS RVW JULY '93

KOSSAK, ZOFIA
SZCZUCKA--[22]POLISH

KOSSEZ, ROBES
KOCSIS, ROBERT--[31]

KOSSOF, HARRIET
KLASS, HARRIET--[9]ROM--

KOSTE, ROBERT FRANCIS
CUFF, BARRY--[1][31]

KOSTER-LJUNG, HANNA
MENZ, ABI--[39]GERMAN/JUV
OSTEN, FRANZISKA--[39]GERAN/JUV

KOSTLER, GISELA MARIA
ROSENBERG, GILL--[1][39]GERMAN

KOTCHEFF, WILLIAM THEODOR
KOTCHEFF, TED--[31]

KOTHNER, PAUL
BRUCKNER, DER--[39]GERMAN
NOV, J.M.--[39]GERMAN
RAPHAEL--[39]GERMAN

KOTTA, LEO F.
FLAKE, OTTO--[22]GERMAN

KOTTENRODT, W.
KOTZDE, WILHELM--[39]GERMAN

KOTULLA, ANNEMARIE
CZASCHKE, ANNMARIE--[39]GERMAN
ZASCHKE, ANNA--[39]GERMAN

KOUF, MARVIN JAMES JR.
HUNT, BOB--[31]
KOUF, JIM--[31]

KOUFAX, SANFORD
KOUFAX, SANDY--[31]

KOUMALATS, JODI
THOMAS, JODI--CRPG,[9][21]ROM--
DIAM 55773 "TENDER TEXAN" '91
DIAM "NORTH STAR" & MORE

KOURVETARIS, YORGOS A.
KOURVETARIS, GEORGE A.--[31]

KOUTOUKAS, H.M.
RIVOLI, MARIO--[31]

KOUTS, HERTHA PRETORIUS
PRETORIUS, HERTHA--[1][22]AMERICAN

KOUYOUMDJIAN, DIKRAN
ARLEN, MICHAEL--[8][22][23]SF

KOVACK, TERI S. [TERRY]
HOLLOWAY, TERESA--[9][21][32]ROM/MYS--
AHMM "OTHER MRS. NORRIS" SEPT '63
"A TOUCH OF HEAVEN"
HOLLOWAY, TESS--[9]
OLIVER, TESS--[9][21][26]ROM--
"RED, RED ROSE"
"DOUBLE OR NOTHING"
SHAPIRO, TERI--[9]ROM--

KOVACS, KATHERINE C.
COFFARO, KATHERINE--[9][21][26][34]MYS/ROM--
HARL "GENTLY INTO THE NIGHT" '85 & MORE

KOVALCHUK, MIKHAIL A.
GAKOV, VLADIMIR--[7][23]SF--
"WORLD'S SPRING" '81

KOVALENKO, DMITRII M.
KOSARIK, DMITRII M.--[1]

KOVALEV, MIKHAIL ALEXAND.
IVNEV, RYURIK--[1][22][31]RUSSIAN

KOVAR, EDITH MAE
LOWE, EDITH--[8]

KOVARIK, WILLIAM
KOVARIK, BILL--[31]

KOVARY, GEORG
CORDA, ERIC--[39]GERMAN/JUV

KOWET, DON
GELL, FRANK--[1][31]--
HARPER "BLACK BADGE: CONFESSIONS OF A CASE-WORKER" '69

KOZAK, ELLEN M.
COMSTOCK, JARROD--W/SHARON [S] JARVIS, [7][23]SF--
"LOVE MACHINE" '84
"SCALES OF JUSTICE" '84

KOZAK, JUS
JELANOV--[22]SLOVAK

KRAACK, RENATE
LUTHER, RENATE K.--[39]GERMAN

KRABBE-FLOR, LIESE-LOTTE
FLOR, CLUADE--[39]GERMAN

KRACHALOV, PEJU
JAVOROV, PEJU--[22]BULGARIAN

KRAENZEL, MARGARET POWELL
BLUE, WALLACE--[8][22][31]AMERICAN

KRAFFT, CONRAD JAMES
KRAFFT, JIM--[31]

KRAFT, DAVID ANTHONY
YOUNGER, JACK--W/RUSS JONES,[7]SF--
MANOR "CURSE OF THE PHAROAHS" '76
CA "REST IN AGONY" '79

KRAFT, ROBERT
BARKER, FRED--[39]GERMAN/ADV/SF
BAXTER, DR.--[39]GERMAN/ADV/SF
DRAKE, HARRY--[39]GERMAN/ADV/SF
LARSEN, KNUT--[39]GERMAN/ADV/SF
STARKE, R.--[39]GERMAN/ADV/SF
STRONG, HARRY--[39]GERMAN/ADV/SF
VON HAGEN, GRAF LEO--[39]GERMAN/ADV/SF
WARNER, DR--[39]GERMAN/ADV/SF

KRAFT, RUTH
BUSSENIUS-KRAFT, RUTH--[1]

KRAHNER, KARL
KARKA, B.W.--[39]GERMAN/MYS

KRAMER, ARMIN
HAWKE, HARRIET--[39]GERMAN
JONTZA, GEORG--[39]GERMAN

KRAMER, DANA
KRAMER-ROLLS, DANA--[7]SF--
"COMBAT COMMAND #1" '87
"STAR TREK: HOME IS THE HUNTER" '90

KRAMER, GERHARD
CARPEN, ROBERT--[39]GERMAN

KRAMER, JOLIE
LEIGH, JO--[26]ROM--
"SPECIAL EFFECTS"

KRAMER, KARL EMERICH
FORBAN, ANDRE--[39]GERMAN

KRAMER, KARL FRIEDRICH
FORESTIER, GEORGE--[39]GERMAN
RUSTESCH, GERHARD--[39]GERMAN

KRAMER, KATHRYN LYNN
VICKERY, KATHERINE--[9][21][26]ROM--
"FLAME OF DESIRE"
"TAME THE WILD WIND" & MORE

KRAMER, NORA
BRENT, ELEANOR--[1]

KRAMER, PETER
COTTON, JERRY--[39]GERMAN/MYS,HP--
HOOKER, P.T.--[39]GERMAN/MYS/SF
MCCOY, CLIFF--[39]GERMAN/MYS/SF
RUDERSBERG, PETER--[39]GERMAN/MYS/SF
THEODOR, PETER--[39][40]GERMAN/MYS--
'FLEDERMAUS' #334, 337 & 351

KRAMER, PETER [CONT]
TODD, W.--[39][40]GERMAN/MYS--
'KOMMISSAR X' #554 & 5 OTHERS
'PLUTONIUM POL' #19 & 23

KRAMER, ROBERTA
HART, KATE--[1][31]

KRAMER-LASSAR, EDNA E.
KRAMER, EDNA E.--[31]

KRAMISH, ARNOLD
PAINE, J. LINCOLN--[1][22]AMERICAN

KRANZLER, GEORGE G.
ISAACS, JACOB--[1][33]
KRANZLER, GERSHON--[1][31][33]

KRAPP, ERNST
SINGER, ERNEST--[39]GERMAN/MYS

KRAPP, ROBERT MARTIN
ADAMS, ROBERT MARTIN--[1][31]--
'ADAMS' LEGALIZED

KRASAUKAS, MARIONAS I.
MARUKAS, KAZIS--[1]

KRASNER, WILLIAM
KING, RANDALL--[21]ROM--
"FRANCIS PARKMAN: DAKOTA LEGEND"

KRASNEY, SAMUEL A.
CURZON, SAM--[22][29][31]AMERICAN--
MON MA318 "LEGGS DIAMOND" '62

KRASNOV, PETR
KRASSNOF, PETER N.--[1]

KRASSNER, PAUL
RUMPLEFORESKIN--[1]

KRATOCHWIL, JOSEF
BRETT, TODDY--[39]GERMAN/WEST,HP
LANE, LEX--[39]GERMAN/WEST,HP
MURRAY, GORDON W.--[39]GERMAN/WEST

KRAUS, CHARLES E.
CHARLES THE CLOWN--[31]

KRAUS, HANS PETER
KRAUS, H.P.--[31]

KRAUS, [HERMAN] ROBERT
HIPPOPOTAMUS, EUGENE H.--[1][8]
SILLY, E.S.--[33]
TUBBY, I.M.--[33]

KRAUSE, ERNST LUDWIG
CARUS, STERNE--[1][22]GERMAN

KRAUSE, EVELYNE
BRANDENBURG, EVELYNE--[39]GERMAN/SF/JUV

KRAUSE, HELGA
JLLING, HELLA--[39]GERMAN/MYS

KRAUSNICK, MICHAILL
WOLF, RAINER--[39]GERMAN/SF/JUV

KRAUSS, ROBERT G.
KRAUSS, BOB--[31]

KRAUSSE, KAY
KRAUSSE, K.--SANDRA SCOPPETTONE, A RELATIVE
OF "KRAUSSE"

KRAUTTER, ELISA BIALK
BIALK, ELISA--[22][33]AMERICAN

KRAUZER, STEVEN M.
BARON, J.W.--[1][21][28]--
PINN "BLAZE" '83
BONNER, TERRY NELSON--[21][31]ROM,HP--
AUSTRALIAN/NZ: "THE DIGGERS"
HARDING, COLE--[28]WEST--
FAR WEST "ME AND BUCK" DEC '78
LASSITER, ADAM--[28][31][34]WAR/ADV,HP--
BB "DENNISON'S WAR" '84
BB "CONTE'S RUN" '85
BB "HELL ON WHEELS" '85
BB "KING OF THE MOUNTAIN" '85
BB "TRIANGLE" '85
BB "SNOWBALL IN HELL" '86
PENDLETON, DON--[3][28]MYS,HP--
GE "BROTHERS IN BLOOD" '83
GE "DOUBLE CROSSFIRE" '82
GE "RENEGADE AGENT" '82
GE "TERRORIST SUMMIT" '82
ROUNDTREE, OWEN--W/WILLIAM KITTREDGE,
[1][28]WEST--
'CORD' SERIES '82-6

KRAVCHINSKI, SERGEI M.
STEPNIAK--[34]MYS--
HARPER "CAREER OF A NIHILIST" '89

KREBS, ALFRED
LORD, GLENN--[39]GERMAN/WEST,HP

KREBS, RICHARD JULIUS
VALTIN, JAN--[1]

KRECHNIAK, JOSEPH MARSHAL
MARSHALL, JOSEPH--[1]

KREFETZ, RUTH
MAROSSI, RUTH--[1]

KREIG, MARGARET B.
CRAIG, PEGGY--[1][31][32]MYS--
SA "MURDER AT PINEY REST" FEB '60

KREIGER, MARTHA
KNIGHT, ALLISON--[9][21][26]ROM--
"WILLOW EMBRACE"
"CAPTIVE INNOCENT" & MORE

KREIN, DANIELA
LANGENFELD, JOHANNES--[39]GERMAN/JUV

KREINER, GEORGE
BOUVERIE--[8]

KREIS, ERMA
MODENA, MARIA--[1]

KREISEL, HEINRICH
CROIXELLES, R.--[39]GERMAN

KREITMAN, MAURICE
CARR, MAURICE--[1]

KREJCI, JEROME
TAYLOR, JEROME--[1]

KREKE, CYNTIA
DAMIEN, CHRISTINE--[3]MYS--
BAL "APPLESHAW" '75

KRELLER, F.C.
PATTERSON, ROD--K.DILBONE-BADGER CKLST,
BAE 13, P30

KREMER, RUEDIGER
KREMER, RUDIGER--[31]

KREMMITZ, MARIE
ALLAN, GEORGE--[1][22]GERMAN

KRENTEL, MILDRED WHITE
MIGGY, MRS.--[1][22]AMERICAN

KRENTZ, JAYNE ANN
BENTLEY, JAYNE--[9][21][26]ROM--
"A MOMENT PAST MIDNIGHT"
"MAIDEN OF THE MORNING" & MORE
CASTLE, JAYNE--[9][21][26][34]MYS/ROM--
"GENTLE PIRATE"
"AFFAIR OF RISK" & MORE
GLASS, AMANDA--[9][7][21]ROM/SF--
"SHIELD'S LADY"
JAMES, STEPHANIE--[9][21][31]ROM--
"SERPENT IN PARADISE"
"VELVET TOUCH" & MORE
QUICK, AMANDA--[21][26]ROM--
"DANGEROUS"
"RAVISHED"
"RECKLESS"
"RENDEZVOUS"
"SEDUCTION"
"SURRENDER"
"SCANDAL"
BB "DECEPTION" '93
TAYLOR, JAYNE--[9][21][26]ROM--
"WHIRLWIND COURTSHIP"

KREPPS, ROBERT WILSON
BRANDON, BEATRICE--[3][9][21][26][31]MYS--
DODD "CLIFFS OF NIGHT" '74
DODD "COURT OF SILVER SHADOWS" '80
LOGAN, JAKE--[1][31]WEST,HP--PLAYBOY
ST. REYNARD, GEOFF--[2][11][29][32]MYS--
WM "MAKE YOURSELF A WISH" FALL '70

KRESGE, GEORGE JOSEPH JR.
KRESKIN--[31]

KRESSIG, ROLAND
GALUSSER, ROLAND--[39]GERMAN

KRETSCHMAR, BRIGITTE
HELL, LISA--[39]GERMAN

KRETSCHMER, JOHN & JOAN C
RAMSEY, LILA--V. BERCH LTR TO HUBIN '94,
MYS--
"THE BESTSELLER" '81

KRETZSCHMAR, ALEX
AMBORN, ERICH--[39]GERMAN/JUV
ALEXANDER, ALEX--[39]GERMAN/JUV

KREUGER, MARGERY [MARJ]
CARR, JAYGE--[2][11]
CARR, JAYGEE--[2]

KREUTER-TRANKEL, MARGOT
KREUTER, MARGOT--[1]
STEPHAN, AGNES--[1][39]GERMAN/JUV
TRANKEL, MARGOT--[1][39]GERMAN/JUV

KREUTZER, CATHERINE
HENRIETTE, CHRISTIANE--[39]GERMAN
LEANDER, CATHERINE--[39]GERMAN
METZNER, KATHE--[39]GERMAN

KREVITSKY, NATHANIEL I.
BEN HORAV, NAPTHALI--[1]
KRAVITZ, NATHAN--[1]

KREVITSKY, NATHANIEL I. [CONT]
KRAVITZ, NATHANIEL--[1]
KREVITSKY, NIK--[31]

KREY, LAURA LETTI
EVERETT, MARY--[1]

KRICH, ARON
KRICH, A.M.--[31]

KRICH, JOHN
PEPPER, MARTIN--[1]

KRIEGER, FRIEDA FROME
FROME, FRIEDA--[31]

KRILL, HANS RUDOLF
REIMER, HANS--[39]GERMAN/MYS

KRINGS, CARL
SOLMUND, OLAV--[39]GERMAN/JUV

KRISHNAMURTI, JIDDU
ALCYONE--[8][31]--
INDIA "AT THE FEET OF THE MASTER" '11
INDIA "EDUCATION AT SERVICE" '12

KRISTAN, GEORG & RENATE
KRISTAN, GEORG R.--[40]GERMAN/MYS--
"ANSCHLAG AUF BONN" '90

KRIZKOWSKY, HUGO
KRITZ, HUGO MARIA--[39][40]GERMAN/MYS--
"TUMULT IN 6 STOCK" '53
"MEIN FREUND, DER MORDER" '78

KROEGER, WILLY
HAGEN, ROLF--[39]GERMAN
LEE, THOMAS--[39]GERMAN

KROGZEMJU, MIKUS
AUSKELIS--[22]LATVIAN

KROHNE, HELLMUT
CROHN, PETER--[39]GERMAN/SF

KROHNKE, FRIEDRICH
KLEYMANN, KONNI--[39]GERMAN

KROHNKE, MARGARETE [K]
KUBELKA, MARGARETE--[39]GERMAN

KROKOSZ, EMILY
BRADSHAW, EMILY--[26]ROM--
"THE GIFT"
"MIDNIGHT DANCER"
"HALFWAY TO PARADISE"
CARMICHAEL, EMILY--[9][21][26]ROM--
"AUTUMN FIRE"
"CACTUS BLOSSOM"
"HEART'S"

KROLLPFEIFFER, HANNELORE
HOLTZ, HANNELORE--[39]GERMAN/JUV

KROLOW, KARL GUSTAV H.
KROEPCKE, KAROL--[31]

KRONE, CHESTER
MORGAN, WYNN L.--W/PHILLIP BREEN,[3]MYS--
DELL "THE ICE MAN" '79

KRONEMULLER, HILDA
LAWRENCE, HILDA--[1][3][29]MYS--
SIMON "BLOOD UPON THE SNOW" '44
SIMON "DEATH OF A DOLL" '47

KROPOTKIN, PIOTR ALEXEY.
BORODIN, LEVASIOV--[22]RUSSIAN

KROTKI, KAROL JOZEF
KRZYWAN, JOZEF--[31]

KROTKOV, YURI
KARLIN, GEORGE--[1]

KROUT, CAROLINE, VIRGINIA
BROWN, CAROLINE--[1]

KRUEGER, HARDY
KRUGER, HARDY--[31]

KRUEGER, LORENZ
KRUGER, LORENZ--[31]

KRUEGER, MARGERY [MARJ]
CARR, JAYGE--[7][23]SF--
"NAVIGATOR #1-3" '81-5
"LEVIATHON'S DEEP" '79

KRUEGER, WERNER
DE COTI, WERNER--[39]GERMAN

KRUELL, MARIANNE
KRULL, MARIANNE--[31]

KRUESS, JAMES
KRUSS, JAMES--[31]
POLDER, MARKUS--[1][33][39]GERMAN
RITTER, FELIX--[1][39]GERMAN

KRUEZMANN, GEORG
KREUTZENBERG, ALWIN--[39]GERMAN

KRUG, FRANZ
MORTON, JACK--[39]GERMAN/WEST,HP

KRUGER, BRUNO
COSTER, B.W.--[39]GERMAN/ADV/MYS
HARRINGTON, RICK--[39]GERMAN/ADV/MYS

KRUGER, HARRY
ANDREAS, STEPHAN--[39]GERMAN

KRUGER, INGEBORG
BURGER, MARIANNE--[39]GERMAN

KRUGER, MARY
KINGSLEY, MARY--[21][26]ROM--
"SABRINA" & 6 OTHER NOVELS
KINGSLEY, MARY--[26]ROM--
"AN INTRIGUING AFFAIR"
"SCANDAL'S LADY"
"CRYSTAL HEART"

KRULL, GEORGE
EVANS, DEAN--[32][34]MYS--
SW "A RED-HEADED DAME" FEB '48
SW "A BIER FOR ANELLO" MAY '48
MY "FLOATING FINGER" JAN '52
SU "HOT EYES" WINTER '52
GRAP 131 "THIS KILL IS MINE" '56
RPRTS "NO SLIGHTEST WHISPER" '55

KRULL, KATHLEEN
COWLES, KATHLEEN--[1][31][33]
KENNY, KATHLEEN--[1][33]
KENNY, KATHRYN--[31][33]HP
KENNY, KEVIN--[1][31]

KRUNKE, HANS-WERNER
DOHL, FRANK--[39]GERMAN

KRUSE, MAX
SIMON, KATHARINA--[39]GERMAN/SF/JUV

KRYSKO, TIMOFEI V.
VITKA, VASIL--[1]

KTISTIANSEN, ANNEMARIE S.
SELINKO, ANNEMARIE--[39]GERMAN

KUBE-MCDOWELL, MICHAEL P.
HUDSON, MICHAEL--[7]SF--
"PHOTON: THIEVES OF LIGHT" '87

KUBIAK, HANNS-KARL
KUBY, HANNS--[39]GERMAN

KUBIAK, MICHAEL
LAMONT, ROBERT--[39]GERMAN/HOR,HP
STEIN, FRANK N.--[39]GERMAN/HOR

KUBIE, NORA GOTTHEIL B.
BENJAMIN, NORA--[1][31][33]

KUBIS, PAT
SCOTT, CASEY--[1]

KUBY, ERICH
PARLACH, ALEXANDER--[39]GERMAN

KUCHARSKI, JAN EDWARD
KARJOT, JEK--[1]

KUCZKIR, MARY
MICHAELS, FERN--W/ROBERTA ANDERSON,
[3][7][9][21]MYS/ROM--
MacM "PANDA BEAR IS CRITICAL" '82
MacM "SINS OF OMISSION"
MacM "SINS OF THE FLESH"
SUMMERS, IRIS--JOAN G. KNIGHT,[9][21][26]ROM--
"WHITEFIRE"

KUEBLER-ROSS, ELISABETH
KUBLER-ROSS, ELISABETH--[31]

KUEHN, HEINZ RICHARD
KUHN, HEINZ R.--[31]

KUEHNELT-LEDDIHN, ERIK v.
CAMPBELL, FRANCIS S.--[39]GERMAN
CAMPBELL, FRANCIS STUART--[1][31]
O'LEARY, CHESTER F.--[1][39]GERMAN
VITEZOVIC, TOMISLAV--[1][39]GERMAN

KUEMMERLY, WALTER
KUMMERLY, WALTER--[31]

KUENG, HANS
KUNG, HANS--[31]

KUENSTLER, MORTON
KUNSTLER, MORTON--[31]

KUETHER, EDITH LYMAN
MALCOLM, MARGARET--[3][9][21][26][31]MYS/ROM--
DBLDY "HEADLESS BEINGS" '73

KUFER, BRUNO
SCHEERBART, PAUL--[39]GERMAN/SF

KUGELMULLER v. TESSIN, B.
VON TESSIN, BRIGITTE--[39]GERMAN

KUGI, CONNIE
THOMAS, VICTORIA--W/EUGENE DEWEESE,[1][21]ROM--
"GINGER'S WISH"

KUGLER, DIETMAR
ADAMS, KEN--[39]GERMAN/MYS/SF/WEST
BENTEEN, JOHN--[39]GERMAN/WEST,HP
BROS, WARD--[39]GERMAN/MYS/SF/WEST,HP
COOPER, STEVE--[39]GERMAN/MYS/SF/WEST,HP
FRISCO, TOM--[39]GERMAN/WEST,HP
GILMOOR, JOHN--[39]GERMAN/MYS/SF/WEST
GRAY, JOHN--JEAN F. LE DEIST LTR '93
GRAY, JOHN--[39]GERMAN/MYS/SF/WEST
GREEN, DON--[39]GERMAN/MYS/SF/WEST
GREY, JOHN--[39]GERMAN/MYS/SF/WEST
HAMBERG, STEPHAN--[39]GERMAN/MYS/SF/WEST
HAMBERG, STEVE--[39]GERMAN/MYS/SF/WEST
SLADE, JACK--[39]GERMAN/WEST,HP
STEVENSON, ALEXANDER--[39]GERMAN/MYS/SF/WEST

KUHAR, LOVRO
PREZIHOV, VORANC--[1]
VORANC, PREZIHOV--[22]SLOVAK

KUHFELD, MARY MON. PULVAR
PULVAR, MARY MONICA--[7]SF--
ST. MARTIN'S PRESS "MURDER AT WAR" '87

KUHL, BARBARA
VON STARK, BARBARA--[39]GERMAN/JUV

KUHLEMANN, PETER
NEKKEPEN, EKKE--[39]GERMAN/JUV
VON AUKAMP, PETER--[39]GERMAN/JUV

KUHLIN, SUZANNE J.
MIKELS, JENNIFER--[9][21][26]ROM--
SIL 870 "DENVER'S LADY"
SIL 929 "JAKE RYKER'S BACK IN TOWN" & MORE

KUHN, CHRISTOFFEL HERM.
MIKRO--[22]SOUTH AFRICAN-AFRIKAANS

KUHN, MARGARET E.
KUHN, MAGGIE--[31]

KUHN, WILL
HARVEY, JAMIESON--W/JAMES [JIM] HARMON,
SMUT PEDDLER #2--
EPIC "HARLOT MASTER"
HARVEY, JIM--W/JAMES [JIM] HARMON,
SMUT PEDDLER #2--
BOUDOIR "ABORTION MILL"
WILKINS, J.H.--W/JAMES [JIM] HARMON,
SMUT PEDDLER #2--
PILLOW "SIN UNLIMITED"

KUHNE, AUGUST
VAN DEWALL, JOHANNES--[22]GERMAN

KUHNE, MARIE
PEARY, MARIE AHNIGHITO--[1]
SNOW BABY--[1]

KUHNER, HERBERT
HUNT, FREDERICK--[39]GERMAN

KUHNERT, JORG
BARRYMORE, JOHN--[39]GERMAN/HOR
DEVIL, RON--[39]GERMAN/HOR
SHADOW, MIKE--[39]GERMAN/HOR,HP
USHER, H.P.--[39]GERMAN/HOR,HP

KUHNERT-SCHOSTACK, RENATE
SCHOSTACK, RENATE--[39]GERMAN

KUHNS, DOROTHY HARTZELL
HEYWARD, DOROTHY--[1]

KUITENBROUWER, LOUIS M.A.
KUYLE, ALBERT--[22]DUTCH

KULILIS, WALTER
KUBILIUS, WALTER--LOCUS #394--
LITHUANIAN-AMERICAN/SF--
LEGALIZED TO 'KUBILIUS'
KLIMARIS, J.S.--[1][2][32]MYS--
DA "CASE OF THE VANISHING CELLARS" MAY '60

KULL, ANDREW
KULL, A. STODDARD--[31]

KULSKI, WLADYSLAW WSZEBOR
COOLE, W.W.--[22][31]POLISH
KNIGHT-PATTERSON, W.M.--[8][22][31]POLISH
POLITICUS--[22]POLISH

KULYK KEEFER, JANICE
KEEFER, JANICE K.--[31]

KUMMANN, WILLIAM
NORMAN, ELIZABETH--V. BERCH LTR TO
HUBIN '94,[7]SF--
BAL "SILVER, JEWELS & JADE" '80

KUMMER, FREDERICK ARNOLD
ARNOLD, JOHN--[1][2][11][31]
FREDERICKS, ARNOLD--[3][37]MYS--
MMAG "THE COLLEGIATE DETECTIVES" '33
WATT "IVORY SNUFF BOX" '12
VAETH, MARTIN--L. ROBBINS LTR '94,[1][2][11]
WHITNEY, ELLIOTT--W/JOSEPH H. DOCKWEILER,
[1][2][11]SF

KUMMERT, WOLFGANG
RUGE, SIMON--[39]GERMAN/JUV

KUMMING, WALDEMAR
UPTON, MUNRO R.--W/W. ERNSTING, W. REINECKE,
W. SCHOLZ & J. SCHEIDT,[39]GERMAN/SF

KUMPMANN, KARL
NELSON, HEINRICH--[39]GERMAN

KUNCEWICZ, MARIA S.
KUNCEWICZOWA, MARIA--[22][31]POLISH-AMERICAN

KUNEN, JAMES SIMON
JAMES, SIMON--[1][31]

KUNHARDT, EDITH
GRUNEWALT, PINE--[31][33]
HILL, JOHNSON--[31][33]
KNAPP, EDWARD--[33]
SMITH, JESSIE--[33]
VERR, HARRY COE--[33]

KUNICZAK, W.S.
WALLIN, AMOS--[31]

KUNJUFU, JOHARI M. AMINI
AMINI, JOHARI M.--[31]

KUNKEL, KLAUS
COTTON, JERRY--[39]GERMAN/MYS,HP

KUNSTLER, MORTON
MUTZ--[33]

KUNZ-FROMEL, MARGARETE
FRIEBELUNG, MARGARETE--[39]GERMAN

KUNZE, ROLF
FORSTER, JOHN--[39]GERMAN
HAKA, ROLF--[39]GERMAN

KUNZELL, BERTA
SCHMIDT-ELLER, BERTA--[39]GERMAN/JUV

KUPERMAN, YURI
KUPER, YURI--[1][31]

KUPFERBERG, NAPHTALI
KUPFERBERG, TULI--[1][31]

KURIANSKY, JUDITH [A.B.]
DR. JUDY--[31]

KURLAND, MICHAEL
PLUM, JENNIFER--[2][3][11][21][26][33]MYS/ROM--
BELM "SECRET OF BENJAMIN SQUARE" '72

KURNITZ, HARRY
PAGE, MARCO--[2][3][5][11][18]MYS--
DODD "FAST COMPANY" '38
DODD "SHADOWY THIRD" '46
RANDOM "RECLINING FIGURE" '52

KUROWSKI, FRANZ
ALMAN, KARL--[39]GERMAN/MYS/JUV
BERNIG, HEINRICH H.--[39]GERMAN/MYS/JUV
GREIF, RUDIGER--[39]GERMAN/MYS/JUV
KAUFMANN, FRANZ K.--[39]GERMAN/MYS/JUV
KUHN, VOLKMAR--[39]GERMAN/MYS/JUV
MEEKER, JASON--[39][40]GERMAN/MYS--
"GOLDPEST" '69 & 3 OTHERS
MELLINA, GLORIA--[39]GERMAN/MYS/JUV
SCHULZ, JOH.--[39]GERMAN/MYS/JUV

KURSH, CHARLOTTE OLMSTED
OLMSTED, CHARLOTTE--[1][22]AMERICAN

KURTH, HANNS
BURGHARDT, FRIEDR.--[39]GERMAN/ADV/SF
DELACOUR, JEAN BAPTISTE--[39]GERMAN/ADV/SF
DELACOUR, MANFRED J.--[39]GERMAN/ADV/SF
FELMER, HELMUT--[39]GERMAN/ADV/SF
GABERG, GRETA--[39]GERMAN/ADV/SF
HESTER, HELEN--[39]GERMAN/ADV/SF
KOGGEN, JAN--[39]GERMAN/ADV/SF
LAFIT, GASTON--[39]GERMAN/ADV/SF
LARSEN, TOM--[39]GERMAN/ADV/SF
MERTEN, [T] K.--[39]GERMAN/ADV/SF
MEYEN, GERTRUD v.--[39]GERMAN/ADV/SF
OFFERMANN, HEINZ--[39]GERMAN/ADV/SF
OLIVES, RICARDO--[39]GERMAN/ADV/SF
PETERSEN, PETER--[39]GERMAN/ADV/SF
REIS, ERNST LUDWIG--[39]GERMAN/ADV/SF
ROTHE, GRETA--[39]GERMAN/ADV/SF
SELLNER, ERIKA--[39]GERMAN/ADV/SF
VELLER, R.A.--[39]GERMAN/ADV/SF
WEILENMANN, E.--[39]GERMAN/ADV/SF
WIEBEL, MARION--[39]GERMAN/ADV/SF
WORTH, JOHN--[39]GERMAN/ADV/SF
ZANTA, C.C.--[39]GERMAN/ADV/SF
ZIEMANN, MARTINA--[39]GERMAN/ADV/SF

KURTIS, WILLIAM HORTON
KURTIS, BILL--[31]

KURTZ, C. GORDON
GORDON, KURTZ--[3][31]MYS--6 PLAYS '34-59

KURTZ-SOLOWJEW, MERETE
VON TAACK, MERETE--[39]GERMAN/JUV

KURTZBERG, JACK
KIRBY, JACK--[11]SF

KURTZE, WERNER
COTTON, JERRY--[39]GERMAN/MYS,HP

KURUPPA, D.S.C.
CHRISTIE, STEPHEN--[3]MYS,HP--
MAYFLWR "CRASH & CARRY" '67
BAKER "SLAUGHTER IN THE SUN" '69

KURZ, CARL HEINZ
BREVIS, CARL AUGUST--[39]GERMAN/MYS/JUV

KURZ, RON
JACKSON, MARK--[1][31]

KURZ-G., MARIE-THERESE
KERSCHBAUMER, MARIE THER.--[39]GERMAN

KUSCHE, LAWRENCE DAVID
KUSCHE, LARRY--[31]

KUSCHE, LOTHAR
MANTEL, FELIX--[39]GERMAN

KUSENBERG, KURT
OHL, HANS--[1][39]GERMAN/SF

KUSKIN, KARLA SIEDMAN
CHARLES, NICHOLAS J.--[1][31]--
MacM "HOW DO YOU GET FROM HERE TO THERE?" '66
NORTON "JANE ANNE JUNE SPOON & HER VERY ADVENTUROUS SEARCH FOR THE MOON" '66

KUTHE, EUGEN
ALLAN, FRED--[39]GERMAN/ADV/MYS
UDEN, HORST--[39] GERMAN/ADV/SF

KUTTNER, HENRY
BELLIN, EDWARD--W/C.L. MOORE,[1][2][31]SF,HP--SSC
COBURN, JACK--W/C.L. MOORE,[1][2]SF--
EDMONDS, PAUL--W/C.L. MOORE,[2][11][23][31]SF--
GARDNER, NOEL--W/C.L. MOORE,[2][11][23][31]SF--
GARTH, WILL--W/C.L. MOORE,[2][5][11][23][31]SF,HP--STANDARD
GREY, WALTON--W/C.L. MOORE,[2]MYS,HP--
SPICY MYS STORIES
HALL, JAMES--W/C.L. MOORE,[1][2][11][23][31]
HAMMOND, KEITH--W/ROBERT BLOCH,[1][2][23]
HAMMOND, KEITH--W/C.L. MOORE,[1][2][11][23][31]--
STS "LORD OF THE STORM" '77
'SIGN OF THE TIME' SERIES
HASTINGS, HUDSON--W/C.L. MOORE,[2][11][23][31]
HORN, PETER--W/C.L. MOORE,[2][31]SF,HP--
FA "50 MILES DOWN" '40
KENT, KELVIN--W/A.K. BARNES & C.L. MOORE,[23][31]--
"ROMAN HOLIDAY" '39
"SCIENCE IS GOLDEN" '39
KENT, KELVIN--[23]SF--
TWS - ALONE ON SIX STORIES '39-44
KENYON, ROBERT O.--W/C.L. MOORE,[2][11][23][31]SF--
LIDDELL, C.H.--W/C.L. MOORE,[1][11][23][31]SF--
MAEPANN, HUGH--W/C.L. MOORE,[2][11][23][31]SF--
MAEPANN, K.H.--W/C.L. MOORE,[2][11][23][31]SF--
MORGAN, SCOTT--W/C.L. MOORE,[2][11][23]SF--
O'DONNELL, LAWRENCE--W/C.L. MOORE,[1][2][23]SF--
"FURY" '47
PADGETT, LEWIS--W/C.L. MOORE, PP 7,[2][3][4][5][23]MYS/SF--
BB "MURDER IN BRASS" '47
DUELL "DAY HE DIED" '47
BB 1251 'LINE TO TOMORROW" '48
ACE D69 "BEYOND EARTH'S GATES" '54
GSFN 17 "WELL OF THE WORLDS" '53
GSFN 26 "CHESSBOARD PLANET" '56

KUTTNER, HENRY [CONT]
SCANLON, C.K.M.--W/C.L. MOORE,[2]SF,HP--
THRILLING
SMITH, WOODROW WILSON--W/C.L.MOORE,[2][11][23]
STODDARD, CHARLES--W/C.L. MOORE, PP 31,[2][11][27]SF--
TADV "WATERS OF DEATH" SEPT '41
WALLACE, ROBERT--T. JOHNSON LTR '94,MYS,HP--
PD "MEDIEVAL MURDERS" JUL '42

KUTZ, CYNTHIA VAN HAZINGA
VAN HAZINGA, CYNTHIA--[21]ROM--
"GEORGIANS"
"GHOST RIVER INN" & MORE

KUYUMJIAN, DIKRAN
ARLEN, MICHAEL--[2][3][11][32]--
LEGALIZED TO "ARLEN"
HM "HELL SAID THE DUCHESS" '34
HM "CROOKED CORONET" '37
HM "FLYING DUTCHMAN" '39
11 DIGEST STORIES

KUZNETSOV, ANATOLI
ANATOL, A.--[1][31]

KWANT, REMIGUS C.
KWANT, R.C.--[1][31]
KWANT, REMY C,--[1][31]

KWOCK, LAUREEN
PETERS, CLARICE--[9][21][26]ROM--
"VANESSA"
"CONTRARY LOVERS" & MORE

KYHLE, LARS
KAHLE, KRISTINA--W/KERSTIN AHLSTRAND,[29]--
"MORD FORGAVES" '56

KYLE, DAVID A.
ACKERMAN, KYLE--[2]

KYLE, SUSAN E. SPAETH
BLAYNE, DIANA--[9][21][26]ROM--
"WAITING GAME"
"COLOR LOVE BLUE" & MORE
CURRIE, KATY--[9][21][26]ROM--
"BLIND PROMISES"
KYLE, SUSAN S.--[21]ROM--
"THE MORCAI BATTALION"
PALMER, DIANA--[9][26]ROM--
SIL 829 "SECRET AGENT MAN"
SIL 971 "KING'S RANSOM" & MORE

KYOTARO, IZUMI
KYOKA, IZUMI--[22]JAPANESE

KYUCHOUKOV, PRODAN
PETROV, IVAYLO--[1]

L'ESTRANGE, C.J.
STRANG, HERBERT--W/GEORGE H. ELY,[2][11][23]--
BOY'S ADVENTURE

L'HOTELLIER, ALF
OUTLAW, THE--[8]

L.VON SONNENBERG, JUTTA
VON SONNENBERG, JUTTA--[39]GERMAN

LA BARRE, WESTON
BALWERS, RENATO--[31]--
"PSYCHOPATHOLOGY OF DRINKING SONGS" '80
O'BRAWES, TARNEL--[31]--
"PROFESSOR WIDJOJO'S FIELD TRIP TO USANS" '80
WEARE, RALSTON B.--[31]--
"TRUTH ABOUT SHAKESPEARE" '80

LA BASTILLE, ANNE
BOWES, ANNE BASTILLE--[1][31]AMERICAN

LA COSTE, GUY ROBERT
BERTON, GUY--W/EADFRID A. BINGHAM,[3][22]MYS--
DODD "ART THOU THE MAN?" '05

LA DUE, HUBERT
MOORE, KENNETH--[1]AMERICAN

LA PALLO, A. ELISE
CHAMBERLIN, LEE--[31]

LA PIETRA, MARY
PATANNE, MARIA--[1]AMERICAN

LA SPINA, FANNY GREYE
DI SAVUTO, BARONESS--[1]AMERICAN
DI SAVUTO, BARONI--[11]
KOFOED, J.C.--[1][2][11]
PUTNAM, ISRA [EZRA]--[1][2][11][16]

LABAIGT, LAURENT
RAMEAU, JEAN--[1][22]FRENCH

LABBERTON, JOHN HENRDRIK
VAN AMEIDE, TH--[22]DUTCH

LABUCHIN, RASSOUL
MEDARD, YVES--[1]HAITIAN

LABUS, MARTA HAAKE
MCCORMICK, CLAIRE--[1][3]MYS--
WALKER "RESUME FOR MURDER" '82
WALKER "CLUB PARADISE MURDERS" '83
WALKER "MURDER IN COWBOY BRONZE" '85

LACANZA, MANUEL
BEN-EZRA, JUAN J.--[1]

LACH-SZYRMA, W.S.
LACH-SZYRMA, REV. W.S.--[23]SF
WSL-S--[1][2][23]

LACHER, HERBERT E.
RIDER, BERT--[39]GERMAN/WEST

LACHLAN, EDYTHE
ROBERTS, RINALDI [A]--[3][9]MYS--
POPLB "FOUR MARYS" '76

LACHMAN, MARVIN
LACHMAN, MARV--AUTHOR PROVIDED--
FAN MAGAZINE ARTICLES

LACKEY, MERCEDES
LACKEY, MERCEDES--W/LARRY DIXON,
B. FRANK '93,MYS--
TOR "WINDS OF FATE" '91
TOR "WINDS OF CHANGE" '92
TOR "WINDS OF FURY" '93

LACKS, CECILIA
LACKS, CISSY--[1][31]AMERICAN

LACKS, HENRIETTA
LANE, HELEN--[1]

LADANY, LASZIO
LADANY, L.--[31]

LADD, LINDA [KING]
ROTH, JILLIAN--[9][21][26]ROM--
"BITTERSWEET TEMPTATION"
"BROKEN PROMISES" & MORE

LAEDTKE, INGRID
PARKER, PAMELA--[39]GERMAN/MYS

LAENGSDORFF, JULIA V.
VIRGINIA, JULIA--[1]GERMAN

LAFARGE, ANNE
GALLANT, PHOEBE--[26]ROM--
"WITH SOMEONE LIKE YOU"

LAFFAN, KEVIN [BARRY]
BARRY, KEVIN--[31]

LAFFEATY, CHRISTINA
FORTINA, MARTHA--[8]

LAFFERTY, RAPHAEL ALOY.
LAFFERTY, R.A. --[1][7][32]AMERICAN/SF/MYS--
37 NOVELS AND COLLECTIONS
SH "BEAUTIFUL DREAMER" SEPT '60
KE "LONG TEETH" AUG '60
MZ "MAN THAT NEVER WAS" SUM '67
MZ "ULTIMATE CREATURE" NOV '67
MZ "CLIFFS THAT LAUGHED" MAR '69
EQMM "ENFANTS TERRIBLES" JUN '71
AHMM "SEVEN STORY DREAM" JUL '73
HA "GHOST IN THE CORN CRIB" JUN '73

LAFFIN, JOHN [ALFRED C.]
DEKKER, CARL--[33][34][35]MYS,HP--
CAL "SILENCE SO DEADLY" '53
CAL "DON'T BOTHER TO KNOCK" '54
CAL - 38 OTHER 'DEKKER' BOOKS
[KEITH HETHERINGTON & GENE JANES WROTE SOME]
NAPIER, MARK--[1][3][33]MYS--
ABELARD "DOORWAYS TO DANGER" '66
SABRE, DIRK--[1][3][33]MYS--
HAMMOND "MURDER BY BAMBOO" '58

LAFITTE, LOUIS
CURTIS, JEAN-LOUIS--[2][7][23]SF--

LAFONTAINE, AUGUSTUS H.J.
FREIER, GUSTAV--[39]GERMAN

LAFONTANT-MEDARD, MICHEL.
DESCHAMPS, MARGUERITE--[1]FRENCH

LAFUENTE ESTEFANIA, M.A.
ARIZONA--JEAN F. LE DEIST LTR '93
DE IRALUCE, CECILIA--JEAN F. LE DEIST LTR '93
ESTEFANIA, M.L.--JEAN F. LE DEIST LTR '93
LEWIS, DAN--JEAN F. LE DEIST LTR '93
STARR, ADDISON--JEAN F. LE DEIST LTR '93

LAFUENTE, PATRICIA
FONTAYNE, OLIVIA--[26]ROM--
"ROGUE'S REVENGE"

LAGERKVIST, PAER FABIAN
LAGERKVIST, PAR--[31]

LAGERSTROM, BERTIL AKE GEORGE
STAFFANS, K.G.--[29]MYS--
TROTS 5 "I DOD OCH LUST" '55
TROTS 10 "BRANNINGAN" '57

LAGERVIST, ULF
WIJK, KAARE--[29]MYS--
RABEN & SJOGREN "STORMDRIVEN" '76

LAGERWALL, EDNA
TRAYNOR, ALEX--[1]

LAGUERRE, ENRIQUE A.
MONTIEL, GUSTAVO--[1]
RONDA, TRISTAN--[1]
UROYAN, LUIS--[1]
YUNQUE, ALBERTO--[1]

LAHANY, KRISTIN E.E.
HORTER, KRISTIN--[1]

LAHEY, KAREN
ALBRIGHT, ELIZABETH--[9][21][26]ROM--
"A NOBLE AMBITION"

LAIDLER, GRAHAM
PONT--[8]

LAIRD, JEAN E.
DRIAL, J.E.--[1][31][33]AMERICAN
MCKEEVER, MARCIA--[1][33]AMERICAN
WAKEFIELD, JEAN L.--[1][33]AMERICAN

LAIRD, WILBUR DAVID JR.
LAIRD, DAVID--[31]

LAISING, W.K.
EDWARDS, DOLTON--[1][2]

LAIT, JACQUIN
LAIT, JACK--[1][32]--
CN "HOLLYWOOD CONFIDENTIAL"
[W/LEE MORTIMER] FALL '53

LAIZEROWITZ, MORRIS
LAZEROWITZ, MORRIS--[1]

LAJOLO, DAVIDE
ULISSE--[22] ITALIAN

LAKE, JOE BARRY
BARRY, JOE --[22][29][32][34]MYS--
MYH "THIRD DEGREE" '43
SD "LONG GONE" NOV '44
FMS 2 "THE PAY-OFF" '44
MYH "THE FALL GUY" '45
MYH "TRIPLE CROSS" '46
ARC "THE CLEAN-UP" '47
PHAN 500 "HOMICIDE HOTEL" 50
ACE D47 "KISS & KILL" '54
PHANT "GAME OF DEATH" '54
PHANT "DANGEROUS BARGAIN" '54
PHANT "NAKED VILLAINY" '59
CAREY, DONNELL--[34]MYS--
COMYNS "KISSES CAN KILL" '51
LAKE, BARRY--GARY LOVISI RVW '93--
BERK D2035 "THREE FOR THE MONEY" '60

LAKE, KENNETH R[OBERT]
BOYER, ROBERT--[1]ENGLISH
KING, ARTHUR--[1]ENGLISH
MARKET MAN--[1]ENGLISH
MENTOR--[1]ENGLISH
ROBERTS, K.--[1]ENGLISH
ROBERTS, KEN--[1]ENGLISH

LAKE, KENNETH R[OBERT] [CONT]
ROBERTS, KENNETH L.--[1][32]ENGLISH/MYS--
EQMM "THE BOTTLE MINE" JUN '63
SOUTTER, FRED--[1]ENGLISH
XENO--[1]ENGLISH

LAKE, LEONARD M.
LAKE, BABETTE ROSMOND--W/BABETTE ROSMOND,[2]

LAKER, ROSALIND
DOUGLAS, BARBARA--[34]MYS--
DBLDY "FAIR WINDS OF LOVE" '80

LAKLAN, CARLI
ALDEN, TROY--[1]
CLARKE, JOHN--[31][33]

LAKOTTA, ANNELIESE
LAKOTTA, CONSILIA MARIA--[39]GERMAN/JUV
REGIS, ANCILLA--[39]GERMAN/JUV

LAKRITZ, ESTHER
COLLINGSWOOD, FREDERICK--[1]
MARION, S.T.--[8]

LAKSO, ELAINE
ALLEN, LAINE--[9][21]ROM--
"UNDERCOVER KISSES"
"FIRE WITHIN" & MORE

LALLA, MOHAN BULCHAND
KALPANA, MOHAN--[1] INDIAN

LALLI, CELE G.
GOLDSMITH, CELE--[1]AMERICAN

LALLI, JUDY
DISCHELL, JUDY--[1][31]

LAMARSH, JULIA VERLYN
LAMARSH, JUDY--[1][31]CANADIAN

LAMB, ANTONIO
HELLERLAMB, TONI--[8]

LAMB, CHARLES
ELIA--[33]

LAMB, CHARLES BENTALL
ACHILLES--[1]ENGLISH

LAMB, ELIZABETH SEARLE
MITCHELL, K.I.--[1][8]AMERICAN

LAMB, GEOFFREY FREDERICK
BALAAM--[1][8][31]ENGLISH

LAMB, ISABEL OSTRANDER
OSTRANDER, ISABEL EGENTON--L. ROBBINS
LTR MAR '94

LAMB, WALTER
LAMB, WALLY--[31]

LAMBE, FRANK
REID, DESMOND--W/G.P. MANN,[1][34]MYS,HP--
AMALG "STAND-IN FOR MURDER" '57

LAMBERT, DAVID [COMPTON]
KENT, DAVID--[1][31][33]

LAMBERT, DEREK W.
FALKIRK, RICHARD--[3][18][29][31]MYS--
EYRE "BLACKSTONE" '72
EYRE "BEAU BLACKSTONE" '73 & MORE

LAMBERT, ELIZABETH MINNIE
LAMBERT, BETTY--[31]
LEE, BETTY--[1][31]CANADIAN
WILLIAMSON, PENELOPE--[21]CANADIAN/ROM--
"BELOVED ROGUE"
"HEARTS BEGUILED"
"A WILD YEARNING"

LAMBERT, ERIC
BRENNAND, FRANK--[1][22][31]ENGLISH
KAY, GEORGE--[1][22][31]ENGLISH

LAMBERT, F.A. HEYGATE
ARTHUR, FREDERICK--[1] WELSH

LAMBERT, HUBERT STEEL
MARLE, T.B.--[1][8]

LAMBERT, LARS
ALMAN, BOB--W/ROBERT BOMAN,[29]MYS--
"DEN FARLIGA KUNSKAPEN" '65
"MORDSOMMARFESTEN" '66

LAMBERT, LESLIE HARRISON
ALAN, A.J.--[3][11][22]MYS--
HUTCH "A.J. ALLAN'S SECOND BOOK" '33

LAMBERT, SPENCER
GRIMM, BENJAMIN--[14]ADULT--
OLYM OPH-131 "CONCEPTION OF THE BEAST" '68
OLYM TC-435 "CELEBRATION OF FLESH" 68
OLYM OPH-139 "SIR CYRIL BLACK" '69
OLYM TC-446 "NIGHTLAND SPELL" '69

LAMBERT, T.H.
LUMBERJACK--[1]ENGLISH

LAMBERT, W[ILLIAM J.] III
LAMBERT, WILLA--[9][21][26]ROM--
"LOVE'S EMERALD FLAME"
"FROM THIS BELOVED HOUR"
WILHELM, LAMBERT--G. COOK,[7]SF--
"ABORT PROJECT K" '81
"LOVE'S GOLDEN SPELL"

LAMBOT, ISOBEL [MARY]
INGHAM, DANIEL--[3][29][40]ENGLISH/MYS--
HALE "CONTRACT FOR DEATH" '72
REES, MERIEL--[1]ENGLISH
TURNER, MARY--[3][29]MYS--
GRESH "PERILOUS LOVE" '66
HALE "JUSTICE HUNT" '73 & MORE

LAMBRIGHT, JEANIE
DENTON, KATE--W/CAROLYN HAKE,[9][26]ROM--
HARL "NO OBJECTIONS"
HARL "CROSS PURPOSE"

LAMBURN, JOHN B. CROMPTON
CROMPTON, JOHN--[1][31]ENGLISH
LAMBOURNE, JOHN--[2][11][23][31]ENGLISH

LAMBURN, RICHMAL CROMPTON
CROMPTON, RICHMAL--[2][25][31][34]MYS--
HUTCH "LADIES FIRST" '29
HUTCH "SILVER BIRCH" '29
WARD "SUGAR & SPICE" '29 & MORE

LAMMLE, RUDOLF
INFUHR, HEINRICH--[39]GERMAN

LAMONT, GILVAN DERWENT
BOOMIS, CYNTHIA--V. BERCH-BRNDN/
BC PSEUDS, BAE 22, P24
LAMONT, GIL--[1]ENGLISH

LAMONT, HELEN LAMB
LAMB, HELEN B.--[31]

LAMONT, ROSETTE C.
FARMER, R.L.--[1][31]FRENCH-AMERICAN

LAMOORE, LOUIS [DEARBORN]
BURNS, TEX--G. LOVISI-PP 7,[1][31]WEST--
DBLDY 'HOPALONG CASSIDY' - 4 NOVELS '51-2
L'AMOUR, LOUIS--[1][28] WEST/HIST--
NUMEROUS NOVELS
MAYO, JIM--D.L. MAWDSLEY, PP 4,[1][28] WEST--
ACE D38 "SHOWDOWN AT YELLOW BUTTE" '53
ACE D48 "UTAH BLAINE" '54

LAMP, PETRA
TEICHERT, PETRA--[39]GERMAN/JUV

LAMPERTI, CLAUDIA J. MCK.
MCKAY, CLAUDIA--[7]SF--
"PROMISE OF THE ROSE STONE" '86

LAMPMAN, EVELYN SIBLEY
BRONSON, LYNN--[8][22][31][33]AMERICAN

LAMPP, JAMES W.
LUMPP, JAMES W.--V. BERCH LTR AUG '93,[32]MYS--
SFD "WIN WITH MURDER" FEB '57
VANEER, WILLIAM--V. BERCH LTR AUG '93,--
CROYD 42 "SCANDALS AT A NUDIST COLONY" '53
CROYD 49 "SINFUL ISLAND VACATION "'53
CROYD 52 "LOVE CULT" '53
CROYD 58 "BACK ROAD MOTEL" '54
AV T313 "DIARY OF A GEISHA GIRL" '59
AS W/KIMIKO OMURA
BEAC B385 "LUST IN PARADISE" '61
WHITTINGTON, HARRY--V. BERCH/L. MUNROE--
LAN 71-315 "LOVE CULT" '62 - NAME
IMPROPERLY ASSIGNED BY PUBLISHER

LAMPTEY, JONATHAN KWESI
J.K.--[1]GHANAIAN
UNCLE KWESI--[1]GHANAIAN

LAMPTON, CHRISTOPHER
LAMPTON, CHRIS--W/DAVID F. BISHOFF,[23][31]SF--
"SEEKER" '76

LANCASTER, A.E.
A.E.L.--[1]

LANCASTER, WILLIAM JOSEPH
COLLINGWOOD, HARRY--[1][2][23]ENGLISH/SF--

LANCE, KATHRYN
BEACH, LYNN--[7][31]SF/THRIL--
"G.I. JOE #12 & 15" '86-7
"WIZARDS, WARRIORS & YOU" '85

LAND, GEORGE THOMAS LOCK
LOCK, THOMAS--[1]AMERICAN

LANDAU, EDWIN MARIA
DEVIN, MARIUS--[1]GERMAN

LANDAU, MARK ALEC
ALDANOV, M.A.--[1][38]
ALDANOV, MARK [A]--[1][3][22]MYS--
HARRAP "THE KEY" '31
SCRIBN "FIFTH SEAL" '43 & MORE
LANDAU-ALDANOV, MARK A.--[1]

LANDAUER, ERICH
LEINSDORF, ERICH--[1]

LANDE, LAWRENCE MONTAGUE
VERVAL, ALAIN--W/THOMAS GREENWOOD,[1][8]

LANDELIUS, VALBORG
BENDER, STEN--[29]MYS--
"INGVARSSON DEBUTERAR" '46

LANDELLS, ANNE
SIBLEY, LEE--[8]

LANDELLS, RICHARD
BARON, PAUL--[8]
DRYDEN, KEITH--[8]
GAUNT, RICHARD--[8]
LANZOL, CESARE--[8]
PELHAM, RANDOLPH--[8]

LANDES-FUSS, MARIE-GISELE
LANDES, MARIE GISELE--[31]

LANDIS, ARTHUR H.
KEAVENY, JAMES R.--[2][32]MYS/SF--
CO "LET THERE BE MAGICK" SEPT '69-MAR '70

LANDIS, JILL MARIE
LANDON, JEANNE--[21]ROM

LANDON, HERMAN
COVERDALE, HARRY--[3]MYS--
CHELSEA "UNKNOWN SEVEN" '23
CHELSEA "SEVENTH SHOT" '24

LANDRY, ROBERT JOHN
LAND--[31]

LANDSBOROUGH, GORDON H.
CODY, STONE--[1]ENGLISH
G-MAN--[34]MYS--
HS "CALL IN THE FEDS" '51
HS "FBI SHOWDOWN" '52
HS "FBI SPECIAL AGENT" '52
HS "FEDERAL AGENT" '52
HEGGY, JOE P.--[34]MYS,HP--
HS "THE GRAB" '53
HS "MAKE IT NYLONS" '53
HS "POISON IVY" '53
HOLMES, L.G.--[2]ENGLISH
MCCRACKEN, MIKE--[1][34]MYS--
HS "BLACK DEATH" '51
HS "BLACK HAMMER" '51
HS "KILLER IN CANVAS JEANS" '52
HS "PROTECTION AGENT" '53
HS "DEATH SMELLS OF CORDITE" '53
HS "SPAHIS" '53

LANDSMAN, SAMUEL N.B.
LANDSMAN, SANDY--[7]SF--
ATHNM "CASTAWAYS ON CHIMP ISLAND"
ATHNM "THE GADGET FACTOR"

LANDWIRTH, HEINZ
LIND, JAKOV--[8]

LANE, ELIZABETH Y.
LANCASTER, LISA--[9][21][26]ROM--
"CAPTURE THE WIND"

LANE, HELEN
HUDSON, HELEN--[31]

LANE, KATHERINE
IKE--[1]AMERICAN

LANE, KENNETH WESTMACOTT
WEST, KEITH--[1][3]MYS--
JARROLDS "BAMBOO" '31
DICKSON "HANGING WATERS" '33
JENKINS "HOUSE THAT CHAK BUILT" '35
HALE "WIDOWS OF THE MAGISTRATE" '49
HALE "HOLLOW TUB" '51

LANE, MARGARET
JONES, JENNIFER--W/ENID JOHNSON,[3]MYS--
DBLDY "MURDER ON THE HUDSON" '37
DBLDY "DIRGE FOR A DOG" '39
CROWELL "MURDER AL FRESCO" '39
LAN, GRET--[1][34]MYS--
JENKINS "STOLEN SCAR" '25
JENKINS "RED MIRROR" '38 & MORE '25-42

LANE, MARY E.
ZAROVITCH, PRINCESS VERA--[2][7]

LANE, MARY LOUISA
EMEL--[1]AUSTRALIAN
LEE, MURIEL--[1]AUSTRALIAN

LANE, ROSE WILDER
WILDER, ROSE--[1]AMERICAN

LANE, SHEENA PORTER
PORTER, SHEENA--[1]ENGLISH

LANE, SIR RALPH NORMAN A.
ANGELL, NORMAN--[8]

LANE, THOMAS H.
LANE, FEARNLEY--PPCC#4, WEST--
"TWO-GUN SHOOTS IT OUT" '45
"CHUMS RIDE THE RANGE" '45

LANE, WILLIAM
MILLER, JOHN--[13]AUSTRALIAN
TOHUNGA--[13]AUSTRALIAN

LANE, YOTI
MAYO, MARK--[1][22] IRISH

LANES, SELMA G.
GORDON, SELMA--[1][8][31][33]

LANG, ANDREW
A WELL-KNOWN AUTHOR--[1][2]SCOTTISH
LANGWAY, HUGO--[1]SCOTTISH
LONGWAY, A. HUGE--[3][31][33]SF/MYS--
LONGMANS "MUCH DARKER DAYS" 1884

LANG, CARL GUSTAVE A.
PENKLUB--[1]

LANG, ISAAC
GOLL, IWAN--[1]FRENCH
LASSANG, IWAN--[1]FRENCH
THOR, JOHANNES--[1]FRENCH
THOR, TRISTAN--[1]FRENCH
TORSI, TRISTAN--[1]FRENCH

LANG, MIRIAM
LESLIE, MARGOT--[9][21][26]ROM--
"LOVESTRUCK"

LANG, THOMAS
MOFFUSAILLITE--[1]

LANG, VIOLA E.
BRYAN, BETH--[26]ROM--
"WHAT LUCINDA LEARNED"
"A MANAGING FEMALE"

LANGAN, RUTH
LANG, EVE--[9][21][26]ROM--
"CROSS HIS HEART"

LANGBEHN, THEO
LANG, THEO--[1][22]ENGLISH
PIPER, PETER--[22][34]MYS--
HURST "DEATH CAME IN STRAW" '45
& 4 MORE '43-57
PIPER, THEO--[1]

LANGBRIDGE, FREDERICK
KING, ALFRED FITZMAURICE--[3]MYS--
SIMPKIN "THE CLERICAL CRACKMAN" 1889

LANGDON, JOHN [F.C.]
GANNOLD, JOHN--[1][3][8]AMERICAN/MYS--
HALE "THE FIX" '72
HALE "NIGHT OF THE FOX" '74
RUSSELL, REX--[1]AMERICAN

LANGDON-DAVIES, JOHN
JAMES, JOHN--[8]
NADA, JOHN--[8]
STANHOPE, JOHN--[8]

LANGE, HANS O.
EGUISHEIM, RENE--[39]GERMAN/MYS

LANGE, JOHN FREDERICK, JR
NORMAN, JOHN--[2][7][11][23]AMERICAN/SF--
DAW 'GOR' SERIES
WARNER 'TELNARIAN HISTORIES' '91

LANGE, KARL ERNST PHILIP
GALEN, PHILIP--[39]GERMAN

LANGE, MARIA DAGMAR
LANG, MARIA--[29][34][40]SWEDISH/MYS--
HODDER "A WREATH FOR THE BRIDE" '66
HODDER "DEATH AWAITS THEE" '67
HODDER "NO MORE MURDERS" '67
"AKTA DEJ KATJA" '71
"HJALP MEJ KATJA" '72 & OTHERS

LANGENHOVEN, CORNELIS J.
ELSPET--[22] SOUTH AFRICA

LANGER, ALFONS
SCHULTZE, PAUL--[1]GERMAN

LANGFORD, DAVE
TAPPEN, ROY--[2]

LANGFORD, DAVID [ROWLAND]
GRANT, JOHN--W/PAUL LE PAGE BARNETT,[7]SF--
"EARTHDOM" '87
LOOSLEY, WILLIAM ROBERT--[7]SF--
"AN ACCOUNT OF A MEETING WITH DENIZENS
OF ANOTHER WORLD" '79

LANGFORD, JAMES R.
LANGFORD, JEROME J.--[1][31]AMERICAN

LANGFORD, SANDRA
SINCLAIR, OLIVIA--[9][21]ROM--
"ECSTACY'S TORMENT"

LANGGAESSER, ELISABETH M.
LANGGASSER, ELISABETH [M]--[31]

LANGGUTH, ARTHUR JOHN
LANGGUTH, A.J.--[1]AMERICAN

LANGHANS-MAYNC, SUSY
MAYNC, SUSY--[39]GERMAN

LANGHER, ALFONS
KOMED--[1]GERMAN

LANGLEY, F.E.
DOUGLAS, FRANK--[1]

LANGLEY, FREDERIC
DAVIES, FREDERIC--W/RON ELLIK,[2][3]MYS--
ACE "CROSS OF GOLD AFFAIR" '68

LANGLEY, ROGER
POWER, REX--[1]AMERICAN

LANGLEY, SARAH
LANGLEY, LEE--[1][3][40]MYS--
DBLDY "OSIRIS DIED IN AUTUMN" '64
DBLDY "DEAD CENTER" '68

LANGMAID, KENNETH [J.R.]
GRAHAM, PETER--[34]MYS--
HAMILTON "TIGER MARK" '28
LAING, KENNETH--[1][3]MYS--
DIAM "HOUSE OF DARKNESS" '27
JENKINS "PAYOFF" '51 & 5 MORE '27-52

LANGNER, LAWRENCE
CHILD, ALAN--BURNS MANTLE-BEST PLAYS '33-4,
[8][31]MYS--
PLAY "CHAMPAGNE"

LANIER, ALISON RAYMOND
RAYMOND, G. ALISON--[1]AMERICAN

LANIER, CLEMENT
ROBION, JEAN--[1] HAITIAN

LANIGAN, CATHERINE
WILDER, JOAN--TITPG,[21]--
AV 87262 "ROMANCING THE STONE" '84
AV 89984 "JEWEL OF THE NILE" '85

LANIGAN, RICHARD
EX JOURNALIST--[1][8]CANADIAN

LANSBERRY, PAULA VIVIEN
BATCHELOR, PAULA--[1]ENGLISH

LANSBURGH, WERNER
BRISSON, FERDINAND--[39]GERMAN

LANSDALE, JOE R.
BAYER, M. DEAN--HAWK-LANSDALE INTRVW '93--
ARTICLES IN 'CAVALIER' &
'GENTLEMAN'S COMPANION'
BUCHANAN, JACK--HAWK-LANSDALE INTRVW '93, MYS--
JOVE 'M.I.A. HUNTER' SERIES
"HANOI DEATHGRIP"
"MOUNTAIN MASSACRE"
"SAIGON SLAUGHTER"
DALE, RICHARD--W/ROY FISH-NOVA EXPR BIBLIO--
TALAN "NELLIE" WINTER '84
DALE, RICHARD--HAWK-LANSDALE INTRVW--
TALAN "HUNGRY LOINST" WINT '84
TALAN "WHAT WE FOUND IN THE MINES
THAT DAY" WINT '84
HARKER, JONATHAN--W/BILL PRONZINI & JEFFREY
WALLMAN, PRONZINI LTR '93--
BLOODRAKE #3 "HEADSTONE" '82
SIMMONS, MARK--W/BRAD FOSTER, HAWK-LANSDALE
INTRVW '93--
BL 5758M "MOLLIES SEXUAL FOLLIES"
SLATER, RAY--HAWK-LANSDALE INTRVW '93--
LEIS 2023 "TEXAS NIGHT RIDERS" '83

LANTZ, FRANCESS LIN
FRANKLIN, LANCE--[33]AMERICAN
LANTZ, FRAN--[31][33]AMERICAN
SUZANNE, JAMIE--[33]AMERICAN

LANZONI, FABIO
FABIO--W/EUGENIA RILEY, TTLPG--
AV 77046 "PIRATE" '93
AV 77047 "ROGUE" '94
AV 77048 "VIKING" '94

LAPAUZE, JEANNE LOISEAU
LESUEUR, DANIEL--[1][22]FRENCH

LAPENA-BONIFACIO, AMELIA
ITIM, TALANG--[31]

LAPIDE, PINCHAS E.
LAPIDE, PHINN E.--[31]

LAPIDUS, ELAINE
COLEMAN, LEE--[1][31]AMERICAN
PETERS, LANE--[1]AMERICAN

LAPIN, ADAM
ADAMS, BEN--[1]AMERICAN

LAPORTE, SEAN
KILGORE, ALEX--W/RAYMOND OBSTFELD, V. BERCH LTR TO HUBIN '94--
ZEBRA "EYE FOR EYE" '84

LAPP, CHARLES LEON
LAPP, CHUCK--[31]

LAPP, CHRISTIANE GERMAIN
LAGER, CLAUDE--[31][33]

LAPP, EUNICE W. BODINE
BODINE, EUNICE--[31]

LAPPIN, BERNARD WILLIAM
LAPPIN, BEN--[31]

LARAQUE, PAUL
LENOIR, JACQUES--[1]HAITIAN

LARBALESTIER, PHILIP GEO.
SCOTT, ARCHER G.--[1][8][22]MYS--

LARCHE, DOUG
GANDER, FATHER--[1]

LARCOMBE, JENNIFER GERAL.
REES, J. LARCOMBE--[8]

LARDNER, RINGGOLD W.
CLARKSON, JAMES--[1]
LARDNER, RING--[1][31][32]AMERICAN/MYS--
RS "HAIRCUT" AUG '45
EQMM "CLAUDE DIPTHONG, STUDENT OF CRIME" AUG '54
EQMM "STOP ME - IF YOU'VE HEARD THIS ONE" JAN '63
OWL EYES--[1]
RUSH, PHILIP--W/IAN MCLELLAN HUNTER,[1]--
HARL 301 "MARY READ, BUCCANEER" '54

LARGENT, R. KARL
LAWRENCE. SIMON--[7]SF/HOR--
LEIS "THE POND" '90

LARIAR, LAWRENCE
KNIGHT, ADAM--[2][3][29][31]MYS--
SIGN "GIRL RUNNING" '56
BELM "SUGAR SHANNON" '60 & 7 MORE
LAWRENCE, MICHAEL--[29][31][34]MYS--
POPLB 488 "NAKED & ALONE" '53
POPLB G354 "I LIKE IT COOL" '62
STARK, MICHAEL--[3][22][29]MYS--
CROWN "RUN FOR YOUR LIFE" '46

LARKIN, ROCHELLE R.
FAIRFIELD, DARRELL--[1][8][31]
LARKIN, R.T.--[31][34]MYS--
LAN "GODMOTHER" '71
LAN 78-703 "HONOR THY GODMOTHER" '72
LAN 78-709 "FOR GODMOTHER & COUNTRY" '72

LARKINS, WILLIAM F.
LONG, GERRY--[1][8]AUSTRALIAN

LARNED, W.L.
CARTER, NICHOLAS--[3]MYS,HP--

LARNER, JEREMY
GOUGE, ORSON--[1][22][31]AMERICAN

LAROCQUE, RUTH
STONE, OLETA--V. BERCH LTR TO HUBIN '94,MYS--
VANTAGE "THE GERANIUM CASE" '87

LARRALDE, ROMULO
BRENT, ROMNEY--[8]

LARSEN, ALF
INGELBREKT, ALF--[22]NORWEGIAN

LARSEN, ERIK
PETRONIUS--[1]AUSTRIAN

LARSEN, ERLING
BRAND, PETER--[1][22][31]AMERICAN

LARSEN, HENRY H.
LAWSON, HENRY HERTZBERG--[1]AUSTRALIAN

LARSON, DORAN
GLASGOW, JACK--[31]

LARSON, GLEN A.
YERMAKOV, NICHOLAS--W/NICHOLAS V. YERMAKOV, [7]SF--
"BATTLESTAR GLACTICA #6 & #7" '82

LARSON, MARVIN
CLAIRE, MARVIN--L. ROBBINS LTR '94,[3]MYS--
ACE D37 "THE DROWNING WIRE" '53

LARSON, ROBERTA RUBENSTN.
RUBENSTEIN, ROBERTA--[7]SF--NON-FICT

LARSON, SHIRLEY R.C.
HART, SHIRLEY--[9][21][26]ROM--
"A FATAL ATTRACTION"
"CAUGHT IN THE RAIN" & MORE

LARSON, SUSAN
MICHELLE, SUZANNE--W/BARBARA MICHELS, [9][21][26]ROM--
"ENCHANTED DESERT"
"STORMY SERENADE" & MORE

LARSSON, CARL FILIP
LARSSON I BY, CARL--[1]SWEDISH

LARSSON, JANERIK
WERNER, THOMAS [B]--W/K. ARNE BLOM,[29]MYS--
"ATTENTATET" '75
"MASSAKERN" '76

LARSSON, KARL ADOLF
ORNFJELL, STIG--[29]MYS--
36 NOVELS '44-55

LARSSON, LINDA
RAY, LINDE--[29]MYS--
FRITZES "KURIPLAN NODLANDER" '45

LARUSDOTTIR, ELINBORG
SUNNA--[1] ICELANDIC

LARUSSO, DOMINIC A.
DOMINI, JON--[1][31]AMERICAN

LASCELLES, ROBERT
PISCATOR--[1]

LASCELLES, WALTER
DOWNE, PATRICK--[1] IRISH

LASCHEVER, BARNETT D.
BARNETT, L. DAVID--[1][8][22][31]AMERICAN

LASELL, ELINOR H.
CALVERT, ELINOR H.--[31]
LASELL, FEN H.--[31][33]

LASH, WILLIAM QUINLAN
QUINLAN, WILLIAM--[8]

LASKA, PETER JEROME
LASKA--[31]

LASKER, EDWARD
MINOR, LASKER--[1]GERMAN

LASKI, MARGHANITA
RUSSELL, SARAH--[1][8][33]ENGLISH

LASKO, ELAINE
ALLEN, LAINE--[26]ROM--
"FIRE WITHIN"
"COURTING TROUBLE" & MORE

LASKOWSKI, JANINA D.
DOMANSKA, JANINA--[1] POLISH

LASKY, JESSE LOUIS JR.
LOVE, DAVID--[8]
SMEED, FRANCES--[1][8]AMERICAN

LASKY, KATHRYN
KNIGHT, KATHRYN LASKY--[31][33]

LASLETT, PETER
RUSSELL, THOMAS--[1]ENGLISH

LASLEY, JOHN WAYNE III
LASLEY, JACK--[31]

LASSALLE, CAROLINE
CAVE, EMMA --V. BERCH LTR TO HUBIN '94,[8]MYS--
COWARD "LITTLE ANGIE" '77
HM "THE BLOOD BOND" '79
COLLINS "COUSIN HENRIETTA" '81

LASSER, DAVID
PENNY, RICHARD--[1][2][11]AMERICAN

LASSWITZ, KURD
HEITER, JEREMIAS--[39]GERMAN
VELATUS, L.--[39]GERMAN

LAST, JOSEPHUS CAREL F.
LAST, JEF--[1][31]DUTCH

LATEUR, FRANK
STREUVELS, STIJN--[1][22] FLEMISH

LATHAM, ALISON & ESTHER
LATHAM, MURRAY--W/ESTHER LATHAM,[1][3]MYS--
HUTCH "ENJOY SUCH LIBERTY" '43 & 4 MORE

LATHAM, EDWARD BRYAN
BRYAN, E.--[1]ENGLISH

LATHAM, HENRY JEPSON
JEPSON, RING--[1]

LATHAM, JEAN LEE
CAMPION, ROSE--W/RUTH PERRY & ARTHUR LEROY KASER,[1]AMERICAN
GARD, JANICE--[8][31][33]AMERICAN
LEE, JULIAN--[8][31][33]AMERICAN

LATHAM, ROBIN
BISHOP, CASSANDRA--[9][21][26]ROM--
"OUTSMARTED"
"FREE SPIRIT" & 2 MORE

LATHAM, ROBIN
LYNN, ROBIN--[9][21][26]ROM--
"DREAMS OF GOLD & AMBER"

LATHBURY, MARY A.
AUNT MARY--[1]AMERICAN

LATHROP, ANNIE W.
WAKEMAN, ANNIE--[1]

LATHROP, CORNELIA
PENFIELD, CORNELIA S.P.--[1]

LATHROP, LORIN ANDREW
LORING, ANDREW--[1][22]MYS--
GAMBIER, KENYON--[1][8][22]MYS--
KAYE, LORIN--W/F. KONSTAM,[1]

LATHROP, MARY TORRANS
LENA--[1]

LATHROP, ROSE [H]
MARY ALPHONSA--[1]

LATIMER, JONATHAN [W]
COFFIN, PETER--LATIMER CKLST-PP 29, [3][5][18]MYS--
DBLDY "SEARCH FOR MY GREAT UNCLE'S HEAD" '37

LATNER, HELEN [S]
STAMBLER, HELEN--[1]AMERICAN

LATONA, BOB
CARTER, NICK--[3][29][31]MYS,HP--
AWARD "PLOT FOR THE FOURTH REICH" '77

LATSIS, EVALD M.
VILKS, EVALD--[1]

LATSIS, MARY JANE
DOMINIC, R.B.--W/MARTHA HENISSART, [3][5][18][31]MYS--
ABELARD "MURDER SUNNY SIDE UP" '68 & 6 MORE

LATSIS, MARY JANE [CONT]
LATHEN, EMMA--W/MARTHA HENISSART, [3][5][18][31]MYS--
MacM "BANKING ON DEATH" '61 & 16 MORE

LATTES, FRANCO
FORTINI, FRANCO--[22] ITALIAN

LATTIMORE, ELEANOR FRAN.
ANDREWS, ELEANOR LATTIM.--[1][31]

LATTO, THOMAS C.
DUNN, AIKEN--[1]AMERICAN

LATURNER, HANS JURGEN
TURNER, L.A.--[39]GERMAN/MYS/JUV

LAU, CHARLES RICHARD
LAU, CHARLEY--[31]

LAUDER, MARIA ELISE T.
LAUDER, TOOFIE--[1]CANADIAN

LAUE, ALEXANDER
HOOVER, CAIL--[39]GERMAN/HOR
SHOCKER, DAN--[39][40]GERMAN/MYS,HP

LAUER, HENRYK GUSTAV
BRAND, HENRYK--[1]

LAUGHLIN, TOM
CHRISTINA, FRANK & TERESA--W/DELORES TAYLOR, M. WADLE CALL '94,[31]--
AV N458 "BILLY JACK" '73
FRANK, T.C.--[31]
HENDERSON, DONALD--[31]--
MM101 "MR. BOWLING BUYS A NEWSPAPER" nd
JAMES, LLOYD E.--[31]

LAUGHLIN, VIRGINIA CARLI
CLARKE, JOHN--[1][22]AMERICAN
LAKLAN, CARLI--[1][22]AMERICAN

LAULETTA, MICHAEL
LAW, M.R.--[35]AUSTRALIAN--
CLEVELAND

LAUMER, MARCH
SEVERANCE, FELIX--[1][2][11]
XANTHUS, XAVIER--[1][2][11]

LAUMER, [JOHN] KEITH
LEBARON, ANTHONY--[2][3][11][23]SF--
"THE INVADERS" '67

LAUREL, ALICIA BAY
BAY LAUREL, ALICIA--[31]

LAURENCE, FRANCES ELSIE
FIELD, CHRISTINE--[1][8]CANADIAN

LAURENCE, JAMES
AXLER, JAMES--[23]SF--
GE "DEATHLANDS" SERIES
DARKE, JAMES--[7]SF--
SPHERE 'WITCHES' SERIES #1-7 '83-6
MAY, JONATHAN--[23]SF
MCPHEE, JAMES--[23]SF--
"SURVIVAL 2000" SEQUENCE

LAURENT, EMMANUEL
RENAULT--[1] BELGIAN

LAURENT-CELY, JACQUES
LAURENT, JACQUES--[1]FRENCH
SAINT LAURENT, CECIL--[1]FRENCH--
CROWN "THE CAUTIOUS MAIDEN" '55
"MATA HARISDOTTER" '56
VARENNE, ALBERIC--[1]FRENCH

LAURENTS, CLYDE
FREDERICKS, HARRIET--W/JAMES SMOCK,[3]MYS--
BEAGLE "THE DREAM HUNTER" '74

LAURITSEN, JOHN [P]
RED BUTTERFLY--[1]AMERICAN

LAUSSERMAYER, ROMAN
ROMAY, ROMAN--[39]GERMAN/JUV

LAUTERBACH, CHARLES
GOG, P.D.--[2]

LAUX, CONSTANCE
DEKA, CONNIE--[26]ROM--
"BRIGHT PROMISE"

LAUXMANN, LONI
NEUENKIRCH, RAINER--[39]GERMAN
TOBER, SIXT--[39]GERMAN

LAVADAN, HENRI L.E.
MANCHECOURT--[1]FRENCH

LAVADAN, LEON
GRANDLIEN, DOCTOR--[1]

LAVAGNINO-JACKY, HELENE
JACKY, HELENE--[39]GERMAN

LAVENDER, DAVID SIEVERT
CATLIN, RALPH--[8]

LAVER, JAMES
REVAL, JAMES--[8]
REVEL, JAQUES--[22]ENGLISH

LAVINE, LEWIS H.
CARLSON, LEWIS H.--[1]AMERICAN

LAVRENCIC, KARL
SYLVESTER, ANTHONY--[8]

LAVRITCH, SOPHIE B.
BENTKOWSKI, SOPHIE--[1]RUSSIAN
BENTKOWSKI-LAVRITCH, SOPH--[1]RUSSIAN
DE TRABECK, SOPHIE--[1]RUSSIAN

LAW, JULIAN SIMON
PETERSUNNE, RODDY RON--V. BERCH LTR TO HUBIN '94, MYS--
VANTAGE "SAFER THAN LIFE" '79

LAW, MICHAEL HALDANE
KREUZEMAN, MICHAEL--[1][8]

LAWLESS, BETTYCLARE H.
HAMILTON, CLARE--[31][32][34]MYS--
FA "MINIATURE MURDER" FEB '58
DA "DEAD, YOU'D BE BEAUTIFUL" NOV '58
PYR "TWILIGHT FOREST" '73
TWR "SEADRIFT HOUSE" '81

LAWLOR, PATRICK ANTHONY
BAGARAG, SHIBLI--[1][22][31]NEW ZEALANDER
LAWLOR, PAT--[31]NEW ZEALANDER
PENN, CHRISTOPHER--[1][8]NEW ZEALANDER

LAWRENCE, BESSIE
AGATHA--[1]

LAWRENCE, CHRISTOPHER G.H
ABBOTT, LAWRENCE--[1]
LYNN, ESCOTT--[1]
METCALFE, [CAPT.] W.C.--[1]

LAWRENCE, DAVID HERBERT
CHAMBERS, JESSIE--[31]AUSTRALIAN
COOLEY, BENJAMIN--[13]AUSTRALIAN
DAVIDSON, LAWRENCE H.--[1][8][31]AUSTRALIAN
DAWSON, LAWRENCE H.--[1]AUSTRALIAN
LAWRENCE, D.H.--[1][31]AUSTRALIAN

LAWRENCE, DULCIE
HAMILTON, JUDITH--[8]
MACE, MARGARET--[8]

LAWRENCE, ELIZABETH
BRADBURNE, E.S.--[8]

LAWRENCE, HAROLD G.
WANGARA, HARUN KOFI--[1]

LAWRENCE, HENRY LIONEL
LAWRENCE, H.L.--[1]

LAWRENCE, JAMES COOPER
CABOT, CALVIN QUINCY--[2][7]SF--

LAWRENCE, JAMES DUNCAN
APPLETON, VICTOR II--[7]HP--
STSY 'TOM SWIFT':
"HIS AQUATOMIC TRACKER"
"ATOMIC EARTH BLASTER"
"HIS ELECTRONIC RETROSCOPE"
"IN THE JUNGLE OF THE MAYAS"
"HIS G-FORCE INVERTER"
"HIS MEGASCOPE SPACE PROBER"
"HIS OUTPOST IN SPACE"
"HIS SKY WHEEL"
"HIS POLAR RAY DYNASPHERE"
"HIS REPELATRON SKYWAY"
"HIS SONIC BOOM TRAP"
"HIS SPACE SOLARIAN"
"HIS SPECTROMARINE SELECTOR"
"CITY OF GOLD"
"HIS SUBOCEAN GEOTRON"
"HIS 3-D TELEJECTER"
"HIS TRIPHIBIAN ATOMICAR"
"HIS ULTRASONIC CYCLOPLANE"
"ASTEROID PIRATES"
"CAPTIVE PLANETOID"
"COSMIC ASTRONAUTS"
"ELECTRIC HYDROLUNG"
"MYSTERY COMET"
"VISITOR FROM PLANET X"
"IN RACE TO MOON"
"ON THE PHANTOM SATELLITE"
LANCER, JACK--[8]HP--
STSY 'CHRISTOPHER COOL &
STSY 'TEEN AGENT'
LAWRENCE, J.D.--[31]
LAWRENCE, JIM--[23][31]AMERICAN/SF--
"MAN FROM PLANET X" SEQUENCE

LAWRENCE, JODI
KEBIN, JODY--[1][31]
KEVIN, JODI--[1][31]
LAWRENCE, JOHN--[1][31]

LAWRENCE, JUSTUS BALDWIN
LAWRENCE, JOCK--[31]

LAWRENCE, KATHLEEN
WILLOUGHBY, LEE DAVIS--[21]ROM,HP--
DELL 'WOMEN WHO WON WEST' SERIES:
"PRINCESS OF POWDER RIVER"

LAWRENCE, LOUISE
HOLDEN, ELIZABETH RHODA--[33]

LAWRENCE, LYNN
GARLAND, SHERRY--[21]ROM--
"WHERE THE CHERRY TREES BLOOM"

LAWRENCE, MARY TERESE
LAWRENCE, TERRY--[9][21][26]ROM--
"PASSION'S FLIGHT"
"THE OUTSIDER" & MORE

LAWRENCE, THOMAS EDWARD
C.D.--[8]
C.J.G.--[8]
DALE, COLIN--[1][31]
J.C.--[8]
LAWRENCE OF ARABIA--[1][22][31]
LAWRENCE, T.E.--[1][22]
ROSS, J.H.--[1][6][8]TRANSLATION--
"TWO ARABIC FOLK TALES" '37
ROSS, JOHN HUME--[1]
SHAW, T.E.--[1][6][8][22]
SHAW, THOMAS EDWARD--[1][22]--
LEGALIZED 'SHAW' IN '27

LAWRENCE, VERA BRODSKY
BRODSKY, VERA--[31]

LAWSON, ALFRED
TORROLL, G.D.--[8]

LAWSON, HORACE LOWE
LAWSON, H. LOWE--[31]
LAWSON, M.C.--[22][31]AMERICAN
SUMMERS, JOHN A.--[22]AMERICAN

LAWSON, JESSIE [K]
AIRLIE, O'HUGH--[1]

LAWSON, LOUISA
FALCONER, DORA--[13]AUSTRALIAN

LAWTON, MARION RUSSELL
LAWTON, MANNY--[31]

LAWTON, SHERMAN P.
PAXTON, DR. JOHN--[1][22]AMERICAN
PAXTON, JACK--[1][22]AMERICAN

LAXANGER, GUSTL
HOLZMAYR, SCHOLASTIKA--[39]GERMAN

LAYCOCK, GEORGE [EDWIN]
MARSHALL, JEFF--[1]

LAYMON, RICHARD
KELLY, RICHARD--[7][34]MYS/SF--
STAR "MIDNIGHT'S LAIR" '88
SPHERE "TREAD SOFTLY" '86
LAYMON, CARL--[7]SF--
DELL "NIGHTMARE LAKE" '83
WILLOUGHBY, LEE DAVIS--[21]ROM,HP--
DELL 'MKNG OF AMER' SERIES:
"THE LAWMEN"

LAYNE, ROBERT LAWRENCE
LAYNE, BOBBY--[31]

LAYTON, FRANK GEORGE
ANDREW, STEPHEN--[1][2][11]
LAYTON, F.G.--[1]

LAZARE, GERALD JOHN
LAZARE, JERRY--[31][33]

LAZARUS, ARNOLD LESLIE
ARNOLD, LESLIE--[1]
LESLIE, A.L.--[31]

LAZARUS, JACK DAVID
HOLMES, JACK D.L.--[1]

LAZARUS, LEON
CARTER, NICK--[34]MYS,HP--
CHART "JAMAICAN EXCHANGE" '79
AWARD "THE TURNCOAT" '76

LAZARUS, MARGUERITE
GASCOIGNE, MARGUERITE--[1]ENGLISH/ROM
GILBERT, ANNA--[3][9][17][21][40]MYS/ROM--
PIATKUS "THE LONG SHADOW" '83 & 8 MORE

LAZENBY, NORMAN A.
BAYES, KAY--PPCC#7,[28]ROM--
SHENSTONE "SHE WANTED ADVENTURE" '49
BLAZE, JOHN--PPCC #7,[28]WEST--
7 HALE NOVELS '90-93
CAPELLI, ACE--S. HOLLAND-PP 29,[34]MYS,HP--
STOKES "PLAY IT YOUR WAY" '53
CARSON, ALLAN--PPCC#7,[28]WEST,HP--
WARREN "APACHE COUNTRY" '52
CLARKE, W.B.--[2][11]
DALLAS, MIKE T.--PPCC#7,[28][34]MYS--
GANNET "DEATH WEARS NYLON" '54
KEN "HOT SUGAR" '53
DONNE, HAMILTON--[2][11]SF--
"WORLDS OF FAMTASY" '50
ELLISON, EARL--PPCC#7,[27][28]MYS,HP--
SPENCER "ROSALIND RUNS WILD" '50
SPENCER "UNWILLING GUEST" '52
GARFIELD, PETER--PPCC#7,[34]MYS--
SHENSTONE "DEATH AT DUNCAN HOUSE" '49
GARFIELD, SUSAN--PPCC#7 ROM--
SHENSTONE "HOLIDAY FOR LOVE" '49
GLASTON, W.B.--PPCC#7,[28]WEST--
BW "DOUBLE X RANCH" '56
GORDON, MAX--PPCC#7,[28][34]MYS,HP--
WARREN "I NEVER KILLED" '52
GULLIVER, MARTIN--[2][11]
HUGO, DON--PPCC#7,[28]ROM--
HAM "TOAST OF THE LATIN QUARTER" '49
JACKSON, J. AUSTIN--[2][11]--
'FUTURISTIC SCIENCE STORIES' APR '50
KARTA, NAT--S. HOLLAND-SCION CKLST,
PP 27,[28][34]MYS,HP--
MUW "A GUY NAMED JUDAS" '52
SCION "WE, THE CONDEMNED" '53
KLEINER, REX [ON COVER]--PPCC#7,[34]--
MOF "MIDNIGHT RENDEZVOUS" '55
'JED STORME' ON TITLE PG
LACROIX, RAMON [RAYMOND]--PPCC#7,
[28][34]MYS,HP--
MOF "RECKLESS LOVERS" '52
LAMOND, GASTON--PPCC#7,[34]MYS,HP--
CURZON "MARKED WOMAN" '46
CURZON "NO WOMAN WAS SAFE" '46
LANE, ARNOLD--PPCC#7,[28]ROM,HP--
WARREN "LOVE'S DESIRE" '50
LAZENBY, N.A.--PPCC#7, SF--
SCIENCE STORIES "NIGHTMARE PLANET"
LAZENBY, NAT--PPCC#7,[28]WEST--
GRANT HUGHES "SINGING LEAD" '49
LESTRANGE, PAUL--PPCC#7,[34]MYS,HP--
CURZON 'WAYWARD DAUGHTERS" '46

LAZENBY, NORMAN A. [CONT]
LINTON, DUKE--S. HOLLAND-SCION CKLST,
PP 27,[34]MYS,HP--
SCION "GIVE ME THE LOWDOWN" '52
LOGAN, BENNY--PPCC#7-P32,[28][34]MYS,HP--
GANNET "YA DON'T SAY" '53
MACEY, CLARK--PPCC#7,[28][34]MYS--
HOLLYFIELD "BABY, YOU'RE GRIEF!" '53
MAHONE, COLT--S. HOLLAND-SCION CKLST,
PP 27,[28]WEST--
SCION "SHERRIFF OF GREEN COULEE" '50
MISTRAL, BENGO--PPCC#7,[7][23][28]SF,HP--
GANNET "BRAINS OF HELLE" '53
MORTON, GLEN--PPCC#7,[28]WEST--
HAMILTON "COLT FEVER" '50
NORMAN, NESTA--PPCC#7-P32, ROM--
SHENSTONE "TERROR LOVE" '49
NORTON, JED--PPCC#7,[8][28]WEST--
HALE "CORRIGAN'S RANGE" '71
RAND, REX--PPCC#7, ROM--
MOF "SHE WANTED A GUY"
MOF "PLAYING WITH TIME"
MOF "SURRENDERED" '55
SCOTT, CAL--PPCC#7,[28]WEST--
WARREN "TEXAN FRONTIER" '51
SITTY, BASIL--[2][11]
STANDISH, PETER--PPCC#7,[28][34]MYS,HP--
WARREN "MITZI-STATE ENEMY" '52
STORME, JED [ON TITLE PG]--PPCC#7, MYS--
MOF "MIDNIGHT RENDEZVOUS" '55,
'REX KLEINER' ON COVER
VANE, BRETT--PPCC#7,[28][34]MYS,HP--
WARREN "ALWAYS A DAME" '50
WARREN "SUNNY" '53
VOGEL, HANS--PPCC#7,[27][28]MYS,HP--
MUW "BAD WOMEN" '50
MUW "SHAMELESS" '50
MUW "AT NIGHT I LIVE" '50
MUW "MAIN DRAG" '50
MUW "MAN TRAP" '50
MUW "LOVE FROM LOS ANGELES" '51
MUW "MIND MY INNOCENCE" '51
WEBB, PETER--PPCC#7,[28][34]MYS--
PAGET "DANCING WITH DANGER" '51
YANCEY, WES--PPCC#7,[28][35]WEST--
12 CLEVELAND NOVELS '71-74
ZORE, HYMAN--PPCC#7,[28]MYS,HP--
MUW "PASSION'S NOT FOR NOON" '50
MUW "YOU'RE MY UGLY" '51
MUW "MIND MY INNOCENCE" '51

LAZEROWITZ, ALICE AMBROSE
AMBROSE, ALICE--[1][8][31]AMERICAN

LAZUTA, EUGENE MICHAEL
AXLER, LEO--LACHMAN LST '94,CRPG--
"FINAL VIEWING"
KANE, ALEX--V. BERCH LTR TO HUBIN,[7][34]SF--
CHART "SHINGLO" '89
LAZUTA, GENE--[7]SF/HOR--
DIAM "BLOODFLIES" '90
DIAM "BLEEDER" '91
RAVEN, DANIEL--[7]SF--
ONYX "HAPPY CAGE" '89

LE BLANC, THOMAS
HOLLBURG, MARTIN--[39]GERMAN/SF,HP

LE CLAIR, THOMAS
LE CLAIR, TOM--[31]

LE COMPTE, JANE
ASHFORD, JANE--[9][21][26][34]MYS/ROM--
GM "CACHET" '84
"MIRAGE"
"FIRST SEASON" & MORE

LE FEBER, DAVID
CRONIECKSCHRIJIER--[1]DUTCH
EERFELD, B.--[1]

LE FEUVRE, AMY
DODGE, MARY THURSTON--[1]

LE FONTAINE, JOSEPH [R]
RAYMOND, JOSEPH H.--[1]AMERICAN

LE GALLIENNE, RICHARD
LOGROLLER--[8]

LE GRAND, FRANC
NOHAIN, FRANC--[1]

LE GUIN, URSULA K.
LE GUIN, U.K.--VAN COURT--
PLAYBOY MAG "STORMS"

LE QUESNE, ALFRED L.
LE QUESNE, A.L.--[31]
LE QUESNE, LAURENCE--[31]

LE RICHE, P.J.
KISH--[8]

LE ROI, DAVID DE R.
ROCHE, JOHN--[1][22]SOUTH-AFRIKAANS

LE ROY LADURIE, EMMANUEL
LADURIE, EMMANUEL LE ROY--[31]

LE ROY, LEMUEL DAVID
LE ROY, DAVE--[31]

LE ROY, MAX MARIE R.
DE MONTTESSUY, LE ROY--[1]

LE SEUR, LUCILLE
CRAWFORD, JOAN--[31]

LE SEUR, W.D.
LAON--[1]CANADIAN

LEA, ALEC
LEA, RICHARD--[1][33]CANADIAN

LEA, CONSTANCE NICHOLSON
SHORTHOUSE, REBECCA--[1]ENGLISH

LEA, TERREA
STACY, TERRY--[1][2]

LEACH, ANN
DUANE, A.S.--[1]
MCDONALD, ROBERT--[1][32]MYS--
LM "A FACE IN THE CROWD" JUN '57

LEACH, EDMUND RONALD
LEACH, E.R.--[31]

LEACH, MICHAEL
JEFFREY, CHRISTOPHER--[1][31]AMERICAN

LEADER, WILLIAM REGINALD
NASH, DANIEL--[34]MYS--
CAPE "NOT YOURS THE ISLAND" '56

LEADER, [EVELYN] BARBARA
BLACKBURN, BARBARA--[1][21]ROM--
"CITY OF FOREVER"
CASTLE, FRANCES--[1][31]
GRANT, JANE--[1][31]

LEAF, [WILBUR] MUNRO
CALVERT, JOHN--[1][8][31][33]
MUN--[8][31][33]

LEAHY, SYRELL ROGOVIN
HARRIS, LEE--V. BERCH LTR TO A. HUBIN '93,
MYS--

LEAN, FLORENCE MARRYAT C.
MARRYAT, FLORENCE--[1][3]MYS--
12 NOVELS 1871-99

LEAR, EDWARD
DERRY DOWN DERRY--[31][33]

LEASLEY, F.W.
ALMON, CASPAR--[1]AMERICAN

LEASOR, THOMAS JAMES
LEASOR, JAMES--[31]ADV/WAR--
"GREEN BEACH" & MORE
MACALLAN, ANDREW--[34]MYS--
HEADLINE "GENERATION" '90

LEATAUD, PAUL
BOISSARD, MAURICE--[22]FRENCH

LEATHAM, LOUIS S.
LOU--[1]

LEAVIS, QUEENIE DOROTHY
LEAVIS, Q.D.--[31]

LEAVY, HERBERT
LEE, TED--V. BERCH-MON PSEUDS, BAE 9,[1]--
MON 285 "THE PLEASURE IN WOMEN" '62

LEBER, EMIL
LEE, FRANK--[39]GERMAN/SF/WEST
MONTANUS, DOLF--[39]GERMAN/SF/WEST

LEBER, GERDA
HAGENAU, GERDA--[39]GERMAN/JUV

LEBER, RUDOLF
HERMLIN, STEPHAN--[39]GERMAN

LEBO, DELL
BELL, [PROF] LEO D.--[1]AMERICAN
LEBO, DELI--[1]AMERICAN

LECANTEUR, M.E.
DE PONTAUMONT--[1]

LECAVELE, ROLAND
DORGELES, ROLAND--[1][22]FRENCH
LECAVELE, L.--[1]

LECHLE, OTTO
ROLAND, OTTO--[39]GERMAN

LECKIE, PETER MARTIN
MARTIN, PETER--[2][11][23]ENGLISH/SF--
"SUMMER IN 3000: NOT A PROPHECY-A
PARABLE" '46

LECKIE, ROBERT [H]
BARLOW, ROGER--[1][22][31]AMERICAN
PORTER, MARK--[1][22]AMERICAN

LECKY, WILLIAM EDWARD H.
HIBERNICUS--[1]

LECLERC, RAYMOND P.E.
CLARYL, MICHEL--[1]

LECLERE, LEON
KLINGSOR, TRISTAN--[22]FRENCH

LECOCQ, TRACY
TRACY, MARILYN--[21][26]ROM--6 NOVELS

LECOMTE DU NOUEY, PIERRE
DU NOUEY, PIERRE LECOMTE--[31]

LECUYER, ANDREE [H]
CORTHIS, ANDRE--[1]

LED'HUY, JEAN B.A.
DAGOBERT, CHRYSOSTOME--[1]

LEDERER, ESTHER PAULINE
LANDERS, ANN--[8][22][31]AMERICAN

LEDERER, PAUL JOSEPH
CROWDER, KEN--V. BERCH LTR TO HUBIN '93,MYS--
ZEBRA "COULTER CONSPIRACY" '84
WALKER "IRON WEB" '85
WALKER "ASIAN EYES" '90
WINTERS, LOGAN--[7]SF--
TWR "SPECTROS #1 THRU #4" '81
WOLFE, ELIZABETH--[3][28]MYS--
LEIS "ICE CASTLES" '82
ACE "BOUDICEA" '80

LEDERER, RHODA C.
BARROW, RHODA--[1][31]

LEDERER, RHODA C.K.
BURROW, RHODA--W/BEN COHEN,[31]--
BRIDGE BOOKS

LEDOUX, JOHN WALTER
CALSON, ISAAC--[1][2]

LEDWIG, GERHARD
KUHN, OTTO--[39]GERMAN/TRANLATION

LEDWOCH, BERT
COTTON, JERRY--[39]GERMAN/MYS,HP--

LEE, ABBY
A.L.--[1]

LEE, ALICE LOUISE
GARLAND, JOHN--[1]

LEE, ARCHIBALD EDWARD
ESTERRE, NEVILLE D'--[1]

LEE, ARTHUR S. GOULD
GOULD, ARTHUR LEE--[2][11]

LEE, AUSTIN
AUSTWICK, JOHN--[3][22][31]MYS--
HALE "HIGHLAND HOMOCIDE" '57
HALE "HUBBERTHWAITE HORROR" '58 & MORE
CALLENDER, JULIAN--[2][3][11][22][31]MYS--
JENKINS "CORPSE TOO MANY" '65

LEE, BARBARA [MOORE]
MOORE, BARBARA--[1]

LEE, BROTHER BASIL LEO
LEE, GEORGE LESLIE--[1][31]

LEE, EDWARD EDSON
EDWARDS, LEO--[31][37]--
TUTTER BUGLE 'JERRY TODD' BOOKS '39-40
FORRESTER, LEO--[31]

LEE, ELSIE
CROMWELL, ELSIE--[9][21][34]MYS--
PAPLB "THE GOVERNESS" '69
PAPLB "IVORSTONE MANOR" '69
DANIELS, NORMAN--V. BERCH-BAE 25--
NOT A PSEUD 'DANIELS' ON COVER ONLY,
TITLE PG WAS 'LEE'
GORDON, JANE--[17][21][34]MYS--
LAN "MISTRESS OF MOUNT FAIR" '65
"SEASON OF EVIL" '65 & MORE
SHERIDAN, ELSIE--[9]ROM
SHERIDAN, LEE--W/MICHAEL SHERIDAN,
[2][3][17]MYS--
LAN 71-303 "PIT & THE PENDULUM" '61
& 2 MORE

LEE, FLEMING
BLITCH, FLEMING LEE--[31]
CHARTERIS, LESLIE--W/LESLIE C.B. YIN,
[34]GHOSTED W/SOME 'YIN'CONTENT--
HODDER "SAINT RETURNS" '69
DBLDY "SAINT ABROAD" '70
DBLDY "SAINT & PEOPLE IMPORTERS" '71
LEE, ERIC--W/GERALD W. PAGE,[31]

LEE, FRANCIS NIGEL
NIK--[1]

LEE, FRANZ JOHN T.
LESIZWE, ILIZWI--[1] SOUTH AFRICAN
LETROMACHE, MAENG--[1] SOUTH AFRICAN

LEE, HENRY BOYLE
M'CRIB, THEOPHILUS--[2]

LEE, HENRY DAVID COOK
PARIOS--[8]

LEE, JANET
LEE, JENNIE--[31]

LEE, LAWRENCE
LEE, LARRY--[31]

LEE, LINCOLN
COLLEN, NEIL--[22][31]ENGLISH

LEE, LINDA FRANCES
LEE, ALYSSA--[26]ROM--
"SWEET JASMINE"

LEE, LYDIA
LIMA, ROSE MARIE--[9][21]ROM--
"HOMELESS HEART"

LEE, MANFRED B.
QUEEN, ELLERY--W/FREDERIC DANNAY,
[1][2][3]MYS,HP--

LEE, MANFRED B.
QUEEN, ELLERY JR.--W/FREDERICH DANNAY,
[1]AMERICAN/JUV MYS
ROSS, BARNABY--W/FREDERIC DANNAY,[2][3][32]--
4 MYS NOVELS LATER RPRTD AS BY 'QUEEN'
ML "DRURY LANE'S LAST CASE" OCT '33

LEE, MANNING DE VILLEN.
HATCH, ROBERT--[8]

LEE, MARIA BERL
BERL-LEE, MARIA--[31]

LEE, MARION [V.D.M.]
LEE, BABS--W/CLARE C. SAUNDERS,[8][22][34]MYS--
SCRIBN "MEASURED FOR MURDER" '44

LEE, MARY EMILY
LEE, CECILE--[1]

LEE, MAUREEN
NORTHE, MAGGIE--[8]

LEE, NORMAN
ARMSTRONG, RAYMOND--[2][3][18][22]MYS--
LONG "MURDER OF A MARRIAGE" '60
LONG "MIDNIGHT CAVALIER" '54 & MORE
CORRIGAN, MARK--[18][22][34][36]MYS--
A&R "BIG SQUEEZE" '55
A&R"BIG BOYS DON'T CRY" '56
A&R "SYDNEY FOR SIN" '56
A&R "THE CRUEL LADY" '57
HOBART, ROBERTSON--[18][34][36]MYS--
HALE "CASE OF THE SHAVEN BLONDE" '59
HALE "DANGEROUS CARGOES" '60
HALE "BLOOD ON THE LAKE" '61
HALE "DEATH OF A LOVE" '61

LEE, PALI JAE
LEE, JAE GARDINER--[8]
LEE, POLLY JAE--[31]

LEE, SHELTON JACKSON
LEE, SPIKE--[31]

LEE, STUART
WOODS, STUART--[1]AMERICAN

LEE, SUSAN RICHMOND
YORKE, CURTIS--[1][3][29]MYS--
JARROLD "ONCE!" 1892 & 2 MORE

LEE, TOMMY L.
LEE, TOM--[31]

LEE, WAYNE CYRIL
HAVENS, STEWART--[1]AMERICAN
SHELDON, LEE--[2][11][23][31]SF--
BOUREGY "DOOMED PLANET" '67

LEE, WENDI
LEE, W.W.--HAWK-LEE INTRVW '93, WEST--
WALKER "ROGUE GOLD" '89
WALKER "RUSTLER'S VENOM" '90

LEE, WILLIAM SAUL
LEE, BILL--[31]

LEE, WILLIAM STORRS
LEE, W. STORRS--[31]

LEE, [REV] ALBERT
MASON, ADRIAN--[1]
ROMAINE, LINTON--[1]

LEE-HOSTETLER, JERI
MARSH, JERI--[33]

LEE-RICHARDSON, JAMES
DUNNE, DESMOND--[1][8] IRISH

LEECH, H.E.S.
H.E.S.L.--[1]ENGLISH

LEEMING, JILL
CHANEY, JILL--[8]

LEEMING, JOSEPH
LEEMING, JO ANN--[1][31][33]AMERICAN
SWIFT, MERLIN--[1][33]AMERICAN
ZINGARA, PROFESSOR--[1][33]AMERICAN

LEES-MILNE, JAMES
J.L.-M.--[1][31]

LEESON, ROBERT [ARTHUR]
LEESON, BOB--M. LACHMAN LTR '93--
'PRIVATE DETECTIVE' SEPT '41
LEESON, R.A.--[1][31][33]ENGLISH--
TRADE UNION EMBLEM BOOK

LEETE, FREDERICK DE LAND
DE LAND, TRACY--[1]AMERICAN

LEFER, DIANE
LARKIN, ELINOR--[9][21]ROM--
"TWICE BOUGHT BRIDE"
"LOVE'S TEMPEST"

LEFEVRE, LAURA Z.
BIRD, ZENOBIA--[1]AMERICAN

LEFEVRE, PAUL
GERALDY, PAUL--[22]FRENCH

LEFFINGWELL, ALBERT
CHAMBERS, DANA--[2][3][22][32]MYS--
10 DIAL NVLS '39-47
MB "DEATH AGAINST VENUS" MAR '46
JACKSON, GILES--[1][22][34]MYS--
DIAL "WITCH'S MOON" '41
DIAL "COURT OF SHADOWS" '43

LEFFLER, ANNE CHARLOTTE
EDGREN, A.C.--[22]SWEDISH

LEGAT, MICHAEL RONALD
ALEXANDER, ROBERT--W/ROBERT HAINING,
[31][34]MYS--
SVNR "SOUL EATER" '79

LEGER, JACK-ALAIN
HEDAYAT, DASHIELL--[1]FRENCH

LEGER, JEAN-MARC
BONES, JEAN-PAUL--[2],ISFYB, FRENCH
LEICHT, MARKUS--[2],ISFYB, FRENCH
STEEL, JACK--[2]/ISFYB, FRENCH

LEGER, RAYMOND A.
MCDONALD, RAYMOND--W/EDWARD MCDONALD,
[2][23]SF--
"MAD SCIENTIST: A TALE OF THE FUTURE" '08

LEGER, [M.-R. A.] ALEXIS
LEGER, ALEXIS--[31]FRENCH
LEGER, SAINTLEGER--[22][31]FRENCH
SAINT-JOHN-PERSE--[22]FRENCH

LEGG, W. DORR
IGNOTUS, AUCTOR--[1][2]

LEGGE, ALFRED OWEN
ONE OF HER SONS--[1]ENGLISH
STAWELL, AUGUSTUS--[1]ENGLISH

LEGMAN, GEORGE ALEXANDER
DE LA GLANNEGE, R.M.--[1]AMERICAN
DE LA GLANNEGE, ROGER-MAX--[8][31]AMERICAN
LEGMAN, G.--[1][8]AMERICAN

LEGRAND, MAURICE-ETIENNE
FRANC-NOHAIN--[22]FRENCH

LEGRIS, JEAN
DE MAGRET, A.--W/JULIE H. GREEN, JEAN F.
LE DEIST LTR '93

LEHEN, TUURE
LANGER, ALFRED--[1]
MARKUS--[1]
NEUBERG, A.--[1]

LEHMAN, HANS FRIEDRICH
USDERMARK, HANS F.L.--[39]GERMAN

LEHMAN, PAUL EVAN
EVAN, PAUL--L. ROBBINS LTR '94,[1][8]

LEHMANN, ARTHUR-HEINZ
LESTER, A.H.--[39]GERMAN
SELL, PETER--[39]GERMAN

LEHMANN, HANS FRIEDRICH
FRIEDRICHS, HANS FRANK--[39]GERMAN

LEHMANN, HANS RUDOLF
HARTMANN, LUKAS--[39]GERMAN

LEHMANN, KURT
MERZ, KONRAD--[39]GERMAN

LEHMANN, MARGARETE
HACKEBEIL, MARGARETE--[39]GERMAN

LEHMANN, R.C.
TOIL, CUNNIN--[8]

LEHMANN, RITA
CARMA, CLARISSA--[39]GERMAN

LEHMANN, RUDOLF C.
LEHMANN, R.C.--[1]GERMAN
VAGRANT--[1]GERMAN

LEHNUS, OPAL [HULL]
HULL, OPAL--[1][31]AMERICAN

LEHR, HELENE
SINCLAIR, HELENE--[9][21]ROM--
"BAYOU FOX"
"STRANGER IN MY HEART"
"TWILIGHT OF INNOCENCE"

LEHR-KOPPEL, UTA
KOPPEL, UTA--[39]GERMAN/JUV

LEHRBURGER, EGON
LARSEN, EGON--[1][2]

LEHRBURGER, PETER
LARSEN, PETER--[1]

LEHRER, JAMES CHARLES
LEHRER, JIM--[31]

LEHRER, THOMAS ANDREW
LEHRER, TOM--[31]

LEHRMANN, CHARLES CUNO
LEHRMANN, CHANAN--[31]

LEIBER, ELISABETH
ELLEN, ELLEN--[39]GERMAN

LEIBER, FRITZ REUTER JR.
LATHROP, FRANCIS--[2][29][31][39]GERMAN/MYS--

LEIBER, JERRY
GLICK, ELMO--W/MIKE STOLLER,[1]

LEIBER, STANLEY MARTIN
LEE, STAN--[2][23] NAME LEGALLY CHANGED
TO 'LEE'

LEIBL, ERNST
STERNE, BILL--[39]GERMAN

LEIBSCHER, WALT
WIEBSCHER, LALT--[2]

LEIDHOF, CHARLES
MOHR, FREDERICK--[1]

LEIDING, FRIEDA
DU BOIS, IRENE--[39]GERMAN/MYS
DU BOIS, JEAN--[39]GERMAN/MYS

LEIGH FERMOR, PATRICK M.
FERMOR, PATRICK LEIGH--[31]

LEIGH, ROBERTA
LAKE, ROZELLA--[21][26]ROM--
"CHATEAU IN PROVENCE"
"IF DREAMS COME TRUE"
LANE, ROUMELIA--[21][26]ROM--
"SECOND SPRING"
"SEA OF ZANJ" & MORE
LINDSAY, RACHEL--[21][26]ROM--
"BUSINESS AFFAIR"
"MASK OF GOLD" & MORE
SCOTT, JANEY--[21][26]ROM--
"A MELODY OF LOVE"
"MEMORY OF LOVE"
"A TIME TO LOVE"

LEIGH, STEPHEN W.
STEVENS, LEE--[23]AMERICAN/SF--
ASF - SHORT STORIES

LEIGHTON, F.S.
LERNIER, LUKE--[1]

LEIGHTON, JOHN
LIMNER, LUKE--[1]

LEIGHTON, LAUREN GRAY
GREGG, LARRY--[31]

LEIMBACH, MARTHA R.
LEIMBACH, MARTI--[31]

LEINS, ISABEL
HAMER, ISABEL--[39]GERMAN

LEIPIAR, LOUISE
REYNOLDS, L. MAJOR--[2][11][32]MYS--
MA "SECOND CHANCE" JAN '54

LEIRD, HENRY J.
PALMER, TOM--[1]

LEISK, DAVID J.
JOHNSON, CROCKETT--[2][22][23][31]AMERICAN/JUV

LEISY, JAMES FRANKLIN
ERICSON, JULIA--[31]
LYNN, FRANK--[8][22]AMERICAN

LEITE, GEORGE THURSTON
SCOTT, THURSTON--W/JODY SCOTT, V. BERCH-
LESB/CNTRCLTR-BAE 22,[3]--
HARPER "CURE IT WITH HONEY" '51

LEITHEAD, J. EDWARDS
COVERT, WILSON L.--L. ROBBINS LTR MAR '94
EDWARDS, L.J.--L. ROBBINS LTR MAR '94
HARTLEY, JAMES BUELL--L. ROBBINS LTR MAR '94
MACFARLAND, GEORGE R.--L. ROBBINS LTR MAR '94

LEITNER, HILDEGARD
STURM, DELIA--[39]GERMAN

LEITNER, RUDOLF
HUTTEN, HANS--[39]GERMAN

LEITO, ARTURO
CHOBIL--[1] CURACAON
TUYUCHI--[1] CURACAON

LELAND, CHARLES G.
BREITMANN, HANS--[1]AMERICAN
MEISTER, KARL--[1]AMERICAN
SLOPER, MACE--[1]AMERICAN

LEMAIR, HENRIETTE WILLEB.
SAIDA--[33]

LEMBERGER, LE ANN
MICHAELS, LEIGH--[9][21][26]ROM--
"DREAMS TO KEEP"
"A NEW DESIRE" & MORE

LEMIEUX, KENNETH
DOBSON, DENNIS--CRPG--
BELM B60-056 "DAMNED & THE DESTROYED" '66
'DOBSON' PUB DATE '62
ORVIS, KENNETH--[1][3]MYS--
DOBSON "CRY HALLELUJAH!" '70
HALE "DISINHERITED" '74 & MORE

LEMIEUX, MARC
BEST, MARC--[1][31]

LEMKE, KARL
MASSAN, FR.--[39]GERMAN
SCOTT, CHARLES--[39]GERMAN

LEMMON, LAURA ELIZABETH
WILSON, LEE--[1][22][34]MYS--
DODD "THIS DEADLY DROP" '46

LEMOINE, JAMES MACPHERSON
COSMOPOLITE--[1]

LEMOND, ALAN
TAHLAQUAH, DAVID--[1]AMERICAN

LENA, MARIE HOWARD
HOWARD, MARIE--[31]

LENDON, KENNETH HARRY
VAUGHAN, LEO--[1][22]CANADIAN

LENGEL, WILLIAM CHARLES
GRANT, CHARLES--[1]AMERICAN
SPENCER, WARREN--[1]AMERICAN

LENGYEL, ALFONZ
RADAN, G.T.--W/GEORGE T. RADAN,[31]--
EDITOR "THE ARCHAEOLOGY OF ROMAN
PANNONIA" '81

LENGYEL, CORNEL ADAM
ADAM, CORNEL--[1][8][22][33]AMERICAN

LENIN
LENIN, N.--[31]
LENIN, NIKOLAI--[31]
LENIN, V.I.--[31]
LENIN, VALDIMIR ILYICH--[31]
LENIN, VLADIMIR I.--[31]

LENNON, FLORENCE BECKER
BECKER, FLORENCE--[1][22]AMERICAN

LENT, BLAIR
SMALL, ERNEST--[8][31][33]JUV--
HOUGHTON "BABA YAGA" '66

LENT, D[ORA] GENEVA
DORANT, GENE--[1][22][31]CANADIAN

LENTZ, MISCHA
BACH, MICHAELA--[39]GERMAN
BEHRING, SYLVIA--[39]GERMAN

LEON, HENRY CECIL
CECIL, HENRY--[3][5][31][32]MYS--
28 BKS '48-77
EQMM "I KILLED GORDON McNAUGHTON" JULY '59
DOUGLAS, FELICITY & HENRY--[34]MYS--
FRENCH PLAY "ACCORDING TO THE EVIDENCE" '67
MAXWELL, CLIFFORD--[8][18]MYS--
"I MARRIED THE GIRL" 1960

LEONARD, ALISON
SHARMAN, ALISON--[33]

LEONARD, ELMORE
LEONARD, DUTCH--[1]AMERICAN
LONG, EMMETT--[1][31]AMERICAN

LEONARD, FLORENCE PELTIER
PELTIER, FLORENCE--[1]AMERICAN

LEONARD, GEORGE H.
COOPER, HUGHES--[2][7]ADULT/SF--
PAPLB "SEXMAX" '69

LEONARD, GRAHAM DOUGLAS
TURO, BISHOP OF--[31]

LEONARD, JAMES S.
LEONARD, J.S.--[31]

LEONARD, JOHN
CYCLOPS--[1][8]AMERICAN

LEONARD, LIONEL FREDERICK
LONSDALE, FREDERICK--[8]

LEONARD, NELLIE MABEL
STUART, FAY--[1]AMERICAN

LEONE, ADELE
AUSTEN, CHARLOTTE--[9][21][26]ROM--
"LOVE EVERLASTING"

LEOPOLD, CAROLYN CLUGSON
MICHAELS, CAROLYN LEOPOLD--[1]AMERICAN

LEOPOLD, EMMANUEL FLAVIA
LAVIGNE, MARK--[1] WEST INDIAN

LEOPOLD, GUNTHER
POTTER, RONALD--[39]GERMAN/JUV

LEOPOLD, NATHAN F.
BALLARD, MORTON D.--[1]AMERICAN
JOHNSON, GEORGE--[1][32]MYS--
HU "GRANPA'S LITTLE GAME" DEC '54
BS "I'LL TAKE CARE OF YOU" NOV '58
LANNE, WILLIAM F.--[1][22][31]PUERTO RICAN-AMERICAN
LAWRENCE, RICHARD A.--[1][22][31]PUERTO RICAN-AMERICAN

LEPKE, FRIEDA-HERTHA
LINDEN, CHRISTA--[39]GERMAN/JUV

LEPLEY, JEAN ELIZABETH
DARCY, JEAN--[1]ENGLISH

LEPOFSKY, MANFORD
LEE, MANFRED B.--[1][5] NAME LEGALLY CHANGED TO "LEE"

LERANGIS, PETER
SINGER, A.L.--[33]

LERBS-LIENAU, RENATE
LIENAU, RENATE--[39]GERMAN/JUV

LERCH, HANSRUEDI
KASCHOWSKI, FRANZ--[39]GERMAN

LERF, URS
GEIST, HANS--[39][40]GERMAN/MYS--
"COMPUTER WEINEN NICHT" '85

LERHBERGER, PETER
LARSEN, PETER--[1]

LERMAN, JACQUELINE
COLLINS, JACKIE--[3][29][40]MYS--
ALLEN "LOVEHEAD" '74
PAN "THE BITCH" '79
"LADY BOSS" '81
COLLINS "HOLLYWOOD WIVES" '83

LEROUX, S.P.D.
LEROUX, ETIENNE--[1][31][34]MYS--
ALLEN "ONE FOR THE DEVIL" '69
ALLEN "THIRD EYE" '69

LEROUX, YVES
DUPLESSIS, BERTRAND--[1]
FRONTENAC, YVES--[1]

LEROY, AMELIA CLARE
STUART, ESME--[1][3]MYS--
WHITE "ARRESTED" 1896

LEROY, HOWARD
MANSON, WILL--JEAN F. LE DEIST, BAE 18,[34]MYS,HP--
CARAVELLE "CHINESE CONUNDRUM" '67

LEROY, PETER VERNON
JOHNSON, LEROY PETER V.--[2]

LEROYER, PIERRE CHARLES
DELANOE, PIERRE--[1]

LERSKY, GEORGE JAN
JUR, JERZY--[1][31] POLISH

LES TINA, DOROTHY
VAID, SANFORD--W/A.W. TUCKER,[11]

LESHAN, LAWRENCE L[EE]
GRENDON, EDWARD--[1][22][31]AMERICAN

LESHENKOV, SERGY ANTONOV.
KLYCHKOV, SERGY--[22]RUSSIAN

LESHER, PHYLLIS
LIVINGSTON-MATTHEWS, ASEN--[1]AMERICAN

LESKO, RUTH
GARLAND, BLANCHE--[9][21][26]ROM--
"CASTLES IN THE SKY"

LESLEY, PETER
ALLEN, JOHN W. JR.--[8]

LESLIE, ANITA
LESLIE, ANNE--[31]

LESLIE, CECILE
MACADAM, EVE--[1][8][31]INDIAN-ENGLISH

LESLIE, JOANNA
BENTON, DARLA--[9][21][26]ROM--
"SPLENDOR BY THE SEA"
DARE, JESSICA--[9][21][26]ROM--
"HARVEST OF DREAMS"
"RHAPSODY"

LESLIE, JOHN RANDOLPH
LESLIE, SHANE--[1]ENGLISH

LESLIE, JOSEPHINE A.
DICK, R.A.--[1][2][11][31]ENGLISH--
"THE GHOST & MRS. MUIR" '45

LESLIE, MARY
JONES, JAMES THOMAS--[1]CANADIAN

LESLIE, MARY ISABEL
LANE, TEMPLE--[1][2] IRISH

LESLIE, MIRIAM FLORENCE
LESLIE, FRANK--[1]AMERICAN
SQUIRE, MIRIAM F.--[1]AMERICAN

LESLIE, PETER
BUCK, PETER--V. BERCH LTR TO HUBIN '93,MYS--
SIGN "DEADLY BIRDMAN" '81
SIGN "OPERATION ICICLE" '81
SIGN "PASSPORT TO PERIL" '83 & 5 MORE
MACNEE, PATRICK--[2][29][34]MYS--
GHOSTED 'AVENGER' SERIES:
"DEADLINE" '65
"DEAD DUCK" '66
PENDLETON, DON--[3]MYS,HP--
GE "ICE COLD KILL" '84
GE "DEAD EASY" '86
GE "BLOOD HEAT ZERO" '86
GE "SUDDEN DEATH" '87
GE "ANVIL OF HELL" '88
GE "HONG KONG HIT LIST" '88
GE "VENDETTA IN VENICE" '88
GE "BLOWOUT" '89
GE "DEAD MAN'S TALE" '89
GE "HELLDUST CRUISE" '90
GE "BATTLE LINES" '90

LESLIE, SIR SHANE
IONICOS, ION--[8]

LESLIE, SUSAN
ALLYN, ASHLEY--[9][21][26]ROM--
"CHANNING HALL"
GREY, EVELYN--[9][21][26]ROM--
"CAMBERLEIGH"
"MAYFAIR"

LESLIE-MELVILLE, JOHN D.
LESLIE-MELVILLE, JOCK--[31]

LESMAN, JAN WIKTOR
BRZECHWA, JAN--[22] POLISH

LESMIAN, BOLESLAW
LESMAN, B.--[22] POLISH

LESPERANCE, DAVID
DAVIDSON, GENE A.--[1][2]

LESSER, MILTON
MARLOWE, STEPHEN--V. BERCH-GM PSEUDS, PP 33,[2][3] LEGALIZED TO 'MARLOWE'

LESSER, ROGER HAROLD
DAMOR, HAKJI--[1][31]ENGLISH

LESSING, BRUNO
BLOCK, RUDOLPH--[31]

LESSING, DORIS
SOMERS, JANE--[1]ENGLISH

LESSING, WILFRED EDWARD
EDWARDS, DOLTON--[11]

LESTER, ANDREW
GREENHOUGH, TERRY--[2]/ISFYB

LESURE, THOMAS B.
BARBOUR, THOMAS L.--[1]

LETHABY, J.W.
J.W.L.--[1][2]

LETTENMAIR, JOSEF
LINGARD, J.M.--[39]GERMAN
RAUTH, RAINER--[39]GERMAN

LETTS, BARRY
LEOPOLD, GUY--W/ROBERT SLOMAN,[2]

LEUCI, ROBERT
LEUCI, BOB--[31]

LEUKEFELD, PETER
MANN, DANIEL--[39]GERMAN
WIDBORG, MICHAEL--[39]GERMAN

LEVEILLE, GARY
HUNTER, GARY--W/GWEN HUNTER, LACHMAN-EASTER LST '93,[34]MYS--
WARNER "DEATH WARRANT" '90

LEVENSON, LOUIS
DEXTER, CHARLES--[1]AMERICAN

LEVENTHAL, ALBERT RICE
RICE, ALBERT--[1]AMERICAN

LEVENTHAL, LIONEL
RUSSELL, ALAN K.--[7]SF/HOR--
"BOOK OF THE DEAD: 13 CLASSIC TALES OF THE SUPERNATURAL" '86

LEVENTHAL, RONALD
LEE, RONNY--[1]AMERICAN

LEVENTON, VLADIMIR IVAN
LEWTON, VAL--[1]RUSSIAN-AMERICAN- BELIEVE 'LEWTON' LEGALIZED IN AMERICA

LEVER, CHARLES [JAMES]
TRAMP, TILBURY--[34]MYS--
ORR "TALES OF THE TRAINS" 1845

LEVER, JULIUS W.
LEVER, J.W.--[31]
LEVER, WALTER--[31]

LEVERSON, ADA
ELAINE--[1][31]ENGLISH
SPHINX, THE--[1]ENGLISH

LEVESQUE, PAUL
LOVITT, WILL U.--[1]CANADIAN

LEVI, PETER
TIGAR, CHAD--[8]

LEVIEN, ILSE
FRAPAN-AKUMAN, ILSE--[1]GERMAN
FRAPAN-AKUNIAN, ILSE--[1][22]GERMAN

LEVIN, ABRAHAM
GEORGE, G.S.--[8]

LEVIN, BERNARD
BATTLE, FELIX--[8]
CHERRYMAN, A.E.--[8]
TAPER--[8]

LEVIN, DAVID I.
DALLIN, DAVID J.--[1]RUSSIAN

LEVIN, JANE WHITBREAD
WHITBREAD, J.R.--[1][32]MYS--
JCM "BRITAIN'S 'WILD WEST' DAYS" NOV '61
JCM "MURDER OF WOMEN" FEB '62
JCM "MURDER ON THE LINE" JAN '62
JCM "TICKETS, TRUNKS & TORSOS" MAR '62
WHITBREAD, JANE--[1]AMERICAN

LEVIN, MARCIA OBRANSKY
MARTIN, JEREMY--W/MARTIN P. LEVIN,[1][22]JUV
MARTIN, MARCIA--[1]AMERICAN

LEVIN, MARTIN P.
MARTIN, JEREMY--W/MARCIA OBRANSKY LEVIN, [1][22]JUV

LEVIN, RICHARD
MAND, CYRIL--W/GEORGE HAHN,[1][2][11]

LEVINE, BETTY K.
KRASNE, BETTY--[1][31][33]AMERICAN

LEVINE, DIANA
HENSTELL, DIANA--[3][40]MYS--
BB "THE OTHER SIDE" '84
BB "DEADLY FRIEND" '86
BB "GOOD MORNING DRAGON" '87

LEVINE, ISAAC DON
MONITOR--[1]RUSSIAN

LEVINE, LARRY
GREENE, L.L.--W/STEVEN GREENE, V. BERCH LTR TO HUBIN '93, MYS--
SIGN "SLEEPING BEAUTY" '82

LEVINE, PHILIP
POE, EDGAR--[8][22]AMERICAN

LEVINE, SEYMOUR
CLOVIS, ELMONT--V. BERCH LTR '93--
MACF MB 60-232 "TOPLESS BATHING SUIT" '65

LEVINE, WILLIAM
FORD, JEREMY--[3]MYS--
BOUREGY "MURDER LAUGHS LAST" '56
LEVINREW, WILL--[1][3][22]MYS--
ML "FOR SALE-MURDER" '32
McBRIDE "POISON PLAGUE" '29 & MORE

LEVINSKY, ELCHANAN LEIB
KAROV, RABBI--[22] HEBREW

LEVINSON, CHARLES
LEVINSON, CHIP--[1]CANADIAN

LEVINSON, LEONARD [L]
BODINE, JACK--CRPG--
HARPER 'THE PECOS KID' SERIES:
"OUTLAW HELL" '93 & OTHERS
BRADY, NICHOLAS--[31][34]MYS,HP--
LEIS "SHARK FIGHTER" '76
LEIS "INSIDE JOB" '78
CHANG, LEE--[1][31][34]MYS,HP--
MANOR "YEAR OF THE BOAR" '75
CHASE, GLEN--[1][7]SF,HP--
LEISURE-"MAN WHO WAS GOD" ??
CURTIS, RICHARD HALE--[1][21]][31]ROM,HP--
'SKYMASTER' SERIES: "EVERY MAN AN EAGLE"
DAVIS, GORDON--[1][3][31]MYS--
ZEBRA "THE GOERING TREASURE" '80
DAWSON, CLAY--[31]
DE MILLE, NELSON--[1][31][34]MYS, GHOSTED--
LEIS "TERRORISTS" '74
EDWARDS, JOSH--[31]
GALLAGHER, RICHARD--[31][32][34]MYS--
MOF "E TRAIN" DEC '58
MOF "BLIND MAN'S BLUFF" FEB '59
AWARD "DOOMSDAY COMMITTEE" '70
LAN "ONE-ARMED MURDER" '71
LAN "MURDER BY GEMINI" '71
LAN "STEWARDESS STRANGLER" '71
HASTINGS, MARCH--[1]ADULT,HP--
JONES, J. FARRAGUT--[1][31]SF,HP--
JORDAN, LEONARD--[1][29][31][34]MYS--
WARNER "OPERATION: PERFIDIA" '75
KIRK, PHILIP--[3][7][31]MYS/SF--
LEIS "CHINESE ROULETTE" '79
LEIS "DEAD FALL" '82 & 10 MORE
LEIGHTON, TED--W/WILLIAM LINK, LACHMAN
LST '93, MYS--
AHMM "SUDDENLY THERE WAS MRS. KEMP" APR '59
AHMM "HUNDRED DOLLAR BIRD'S NEST" AUG '59
AHMM "MEMORY GAME" SEPT '59
LEONARD, LEONARD L.--[1][32]MYS--
EQMM "WAGES OF INNOCENCE" MAR '47
LEVINSON, LEN--CRPG-HARPER PB
MACKIE, JOHN--[1][31]
NOVAK, ROBERT--[34]MYS,HP--
BELM "THRILL KILLERS" '74
RAWLS, PHILIP--[1][3][29]MYS,HP--
MANOR "STREETS OF BLOOD" '75
ROSSI, BRUNO--[1][29][34]MYS--
LEIS "HEADCRUSHER" '74
LEIS "NIGHT OF THE ASSASSINS" '74
LEIS "WORST WAY TO DIE" '74
SCOFIELD, JONATHAN--[1][21]ROM,HP--
DELL 'FREED FTR' SERIES:
"BAYONETS IN NO-MAN'S LAND"
TRASK, JONATHAN--[1][7]SF--
BELM/TWR "THE CAMP" '77
WILKERSON, CYNTHIA--[1][31]

LEVITCH, JOSEPH
LEWIS, JERRY--[31]--
SCREENWRITER

LEVITIN, GEORGE
LEVITINE, GEORGE--[1]RUSSIAN-AMERICAN

LEVITIN, SONIA [WOLFF]
WOLFF, SONIA--[1]

LEVITT, ISRAEL MONROE
LEVITT, I.M.--[1]AMERICAN

LEVSON, ELLIOT [HASTINGS]
LEYTON, ELLIOTT [HASTNGS]--[1]

LEVY, BARBARA
ELIOT, JESSICA--W/LOIS ANN BROWN,
[3][9][21][26]MYS/ROM--
DELL "HOME TO THE HIGHLANDS" '80 & MORE

LEVY, BRIGID A.B.
BROPHY, BRIGID--[1]ENGLISH

LEVY, CHARLES
LEE, CHARLES--[1]AMERICAN

LEVY, EDWARD J.
EDWARDS, LEE--[3][29]MYS--
PLAY "ASK ME NO QUESTIONS" '49

LEVY, JULIA ETHEL
JULIET--[8]

LEVY, NEWMAN
FLACCUS--[1][8]AMERICAN

LEVY, SOLOMAN LAZARUS
LEE, SIR SIDNEY--[1][22]ENGLISH

LEWANDOWSKI, HERBERT
VAN DOVSKI, LEE--[1][39]GERMAN/SF

LEWARS, MRS. HAROLD
SINGMASTER, ELSIE--[1]AMERICAN

LEWENSOHN, LEONE
DAVIES, FRANCES--[9][21][26]ROM--
"MYSTERIOUS EAST"
"LADY IS A CHAMP" & MORE

LEWI, CHARLOTTE ARMSTRONG
ARMSTRONG, CHARLOTTE--[11][21][32]ROM/MYS--
30 NOVELS
24 DIGEST STORIES

LEWIN, GEORG
TERZIN, GERO--[39]GERMAN

LEWIN, HANNAH-MIRIAM
MARGRAF, MIRIAM--[39]GERMAN

LEWIN, LEONARD C.
CASE, L.L.--[1][22][31]AMERICAN

LEWIN, MICHAEL
FURBER, DOUGLAS--[1][3]MYS--
DAKERS "JUST ANOTHER MURDER" '50

LEWINE, ETHEL
LEWIS, ETHEL G.--[1]AMERICAN

LEWING, ANTHONY CHARLES
BANNERMAN, MARK--[1][8][31]ENGLISH

LEWINS, C.A.
RIVERS, TEX--[1]ENGLISH/WEST

LEWIS, ALETHEA BRERETON
DEACTON, EUGENIA--[1][3]MYS--
LANE "NUNS OF THE DESERT: OR, THE
WOODLAND WITCHES" 1805

LEWIS, ALFRED HENRY
QUIN--[28]--
"THE OLD PLANTATION HOME: A STORY OF
SO. LIFE JUST AFTER THE WAR" 1899
QUIN, DAN--L. ROBBINS LTR '94,[1][5]MYS--

LEWIS, ANTHONY R.
LEWIS, TONY--[7][23]SF--
"THE BEST OF ASTOUNDING" '78

LEWIS, BRENDA RALPH
CLIFFORD, RACHEL MARK--[33]

LEWIS, CHARLES BERTRAND
QUAD, M.--[2]

LEWIS, CLIFFORD
BERRISFORD, JUDITH M.--W/JUDITH M. BERRISFORD LEWIS,[1]ENGLISH
BROOKE, KESTON--PPCC#5, P58--
LEWIS "RED IS FOR DANGER" '45
CLIFFORD, LOUISE--PPCC#5, P58--
LEWIS "HONEYMOON NIGHT" '46?
DUVAL, HENRI--PPCC#5, P58--
CURZON "TORTURED LOVE" '46
GRAYSON, ENA--PPCC#5, P58--
LEWIS "NEVER LOVE ME LESS" '45
LACEY, UNA--PPCC#5, P58--
CURZON "LEARN TO LOVE" '46
CURZON "UNWILLING BRIDE" '46
LESTRANGE, PAUL--PPCC#5, P58--
LEWIS "BLONDE SLAVES" '45
MOON, LINDA--PPCC#5, P58--
LEWIS "WE THE UNLOVED" '45
MOON, LORNA--PPCC#5, P58--
LEWIS "TOO GAY" '46

LEWIS, CLIVE STAPLES
CLERK, N.W.--[2][22][31][33]ENGLISH
HAMILTON, CLIVE--[2][11][22][23][31]ENGLISH
LEWIS, C.S.--[1][31]ENGLISH/SF-
"PERELANDRA #1-3"
"NARNIAN CHRONICLES #4-7
N.W.--[2]ENGLISH
WHILK, NAT--[1][2]ENGLISH

LEWIS, DAVID
HODGSON, D[AVID]--[1][32]ENGLISH/MYS--
JCM "THE LAST CHAPTER" DEC '62

LEWIS, DOMINIC BEVAN W.
BEACHCOMBER--[1][23]SF--
LEWIS, D.B. WYNDHAM--[1]
SHY, TIMOTHY--W/RONALD W.F. SEARLE,[1]

LEWIS, DOROTHY ROE
ROE, DOROTHY--[1]

LEWIS, E.M.
MELWOOD, MARY--[33]

LEWIS, EDWIN HERBERT
LEWIS, CALEB--[1]AMERICAN

LEWIS, ETHELREDA
BAPTIST, R. HERNEKIN--[1][22]SOUTH AFRICAN

LEWIS, HARRIET NEWELL
OLD CONTRIBUTOR--W/JULIEN WARREN LEWIS, [1]AMERICAN

LEWIS, HOWEL ELVET
ELFED--[22] WELSH

LEWIS, JACK
GREGORY, HYLTON--[34]MYS,HP--
AMALG "SECRET OF THE SACRED RUBY" '40
HOOD, STEPHEN--[1][29][34]MYS--
AMALG "CROOK FROM CHICAGO" '31
JACKSON, LEWIS--[1][3][29]MYS--
AMALG "DEATH OF MRS. PREEDY" '49
AMALG "MAN WO LEFT HOME" '49
AMALG "MAN FROM PERSIA" '51
LEWIS, PHYLIS--[1]ENGLISH

LEWIS, JEANE GILBERT
DONATHAN, JEAN ANN--[26]ROM--
SIL 858 "SINGLE MOTHER"

LEWIS, JOHN DELAWARE
SMITH, JOHN--[1]

LEWIS, JOHN NOEL CLAUDE
VENNER, J.G.--[1] WELSH

LEWIS, JOHN ROYSTON
LEWIS, J.R.--[1][8][18]--
LAW-RELATED NON-FICTION
LEWIS, ROY--[8][18][34]MYS--
COLLINS "A SECRET SINGING" '72
COLLINS "BLOOD MONEY" '73 & MORE
SPINGFIELD, DAVID--[1][8][18]--
"THE COMPANY EXECUTIVE & THE LAW"

LEWIS, JOHN WOODRUFF
CONSTELLANO, JUAN--[1]AMERICAN
LEWIS, JUAN--[1]AMERICAN

LEWIS, JUDITH BERESFORD
FARR, FIONA--[1]ENGLISH
HOPE, AMANDA--[1][31]ENGLISH
BERRISFORD, JUDITH M.--W/CLIFFORD LEWIS, [1][31]

LEWIS, JULIUS WARREN
BARRINGTON, F. CLINTON--[1]
CONSTELLANO, ILLION--[1]AMERICAN
LEWIS, LEON--[1][3]MYS--
"DIAMOND SEEKER OF BRAZIL" 1891
"MAN OF MYSTERY" ca 1900
OLD CONTRIBUTOR--W/HARRIET NEWELL LEWIS, [1]AMERICAN
PIPER, A.G.--[1]AMERICAN

LEWIS, LANGE
BEYNON, JANE--[29]MYS

LEWIS, LEO RICH
RICH, C.B.--[1]AMERICAN

LEWIS, LESLEY
LAWRENCE, LESLEY--[1][8][31]ENGLISH

LEWIS, LYDIA T.
LESBIA--[8]

LEWIS, M. CHRISTIANNA M.
ASHE, MARY ANN--[29]MYS
ASHE, MARY ANNE--[3][18][25][31][33]MYS--
"ALAS FOR HER THAT MET ME" '76
"A RING OF ROSES" & MORE
BERRISFORD, MARY--[9]ROM
BRAND, CHRISTIANNA--[3][5][7][9][21][32]MYS--
14 BKS '41-82
22 EQMM DIGEST STORIES
JONES, ANNABEL--[8][18][25][31][33]--
"THE RADIANT DOVE" '75
LEWIS, MARY--[9]ROM
ROLAND, MARY--[8][18][22][25][33]--
"THE SINGLE PILGRIM" '46
THOMPSON, CHINA--[3][5][9][18][33]MYS--
HUTCH "STARRBELOW" '58

LEWIS, MARGARET CAMERON
CAMERON, MARGARET--[1]AMERICAN

LEWIS, MILDRED D.
DE WITT, JAMES--[1][8][22]
[31]AMERICAN/JUV/CHILDREN'S

LEWIS, ORT
MARSHALL, STEVE--V. BERCH-BRNDN/
BC PSEUDS, BAE 22, P24

LEWIS, RICHARD
RADNOR, ALAN--[7][34]MYS/SF--
STAR "CASE OF THE VANISHING HOUSE" '78
ARROW "WHODUNIT?" '78
HAMLYN "THE FORCE" '79
SPHERE "RED LIGHT RED" '80
MacM "POSSESSED" '82

LEWIS, SASHA GREGORY
HARRY, M.--[1][31]

LEWIS, STEPHEN
SILLS, JENNIFER--[1]AMERICAN

LEWIS, SUSAN M HEREFORD
LEWIS, SUFORD--[7]SF--LEGALIZED TO 'SUFORD'

LEWIS, TOM
BABCOCK, NICHOLAS--[1][3][31]AMERICAN/MYS--
ATHNM "BILLY'S ARMY" '82

LEWIS, VIOLET
FLYNT, CATRIONA--W/KAREN FLYNN,[9][26]ROM--
"LOST TREASURE"
"ONE MAN'S TREASURE" & OTHERS

LEWIS, W.W.
BINNACLE--[1]AMERICAN

LEWIS, [HARRY] SINCLAIR
GRAHAM, TOM--[2][23][31]--
"HIKE &N THE AIRPLANE" '12

LEWITON, MINA
SIMON, MINA LEWITON--[31][33] CHILDREN'S BOOKS

LEWITT, SHARIANN N.
KENDALL, GORDON--W/SUSAN M. SHWARTZ,
[7][23][31]SF--
TOR "WHITE WING" '85
LEWITT, S.N.--[7][23]SF--
BERK "ANGEL AT APOGEE" '87
ACE "BLIND JUSTICE" '91
"SONGS OF CHAOS"
NORTH, RICK--[7]SF,HP--
ZEBRA "YOUNG ASTRONAUTS #1 & #3"

LEWTON, VAL
KERKOW, HERBERT--[3]MYS--
MOHAWK "THE FATEFUL STAR MURDER" '31

LEXAU, JOAN M.
NODSET, JOAN L.--[1][8][33]AMERICAN
SETH, MARIE--[1][33]AMERICAN

LEY, ARTHUR GORDON
LUTHER, MARTIN--W/ROBERT ARTHUR LEY,[2][4]
W/RAY LUTHER PER CURREY
LUTHER, RAY--[2][3][31]MYS--
BANNER "INTERMIND" '57
SELLINGS, ARTHUR--W/ROBERT A. LEY,
[2][4][23][34]MYS/SF--

LEY, ROBERT ARTHUR
LUTHER, MARTIN--W/ARTHUR GORDON LEY,[2][11]
SELLINGS, ARTHUR--W/ARTHUR GORDON LEY,
[2][23][34]

LEY, WILLIE
BROWN, JOHN--[2][11]GERMAN-AMERICAN
WILLEY, ROBERT [ROBBERT]--[2][11][22]
[33]GERMAN-AMERICAN

LEYLAND, ERIC
CLEAVER, DENIS--[8]
FELMERSHAM, MICHAEL--[8]
FIELDING, ANTHONY--[8]
GRANT, NESTA--[8]
LITTLE, SYLVIA--[8]
LODGE, JOHN--[8]
PATTERSON, DUKE--[8]
STRANGEWAY, MARK--[8]
TARRANT, ELIZABETH--[8]
WYATT, ESCOTT--[8]

LEZYNSKI, WERNER J.
SCHELLE, WERNER--[1]GERMAN

LI SHANJI
HUANZHULOUZHU--[7]SF--
"BLADES FROM THE WILLOWS" '91

LI, ANNETTE
CHARTIER, DANETTE--W/DANETTE THOMPSON,[26]ROM--
"MIDNIGHT PROMISES"

LIBBY, WILLIAM B.
LIBBY, BILL--[33]
CLARK, DICK--W/RICHARD W. CLARK,[31]

LIBERT, JEAN
KENNY, PAUL--W/GASTON VANDENPANHUISE,
[3][29]MYS--
INTNL "TANAGRA AFFAIR" '69

LICHTE, PRUDENCE BINGHAM
HOUSTON, HENRIETTA--[9][21]ROM--
"AN IMPROPER BETROTHMENT"
MARTIN, PRUDENCE--[9][21]ROM--
"MOONSTRUCK"
"WAGER ON LOVE" & MORE

LICHTENBERG, ELISABETH J.
VAN SOMEREN, LIESJE--[1][22]DUTCH-ENGLISH

LICHTENSTEIN, PETER
PETERS, LANCE--[36]AUSTRALIAN/MYS--
GRD "RED COLLAR GANG" '81
GRD "DIRTY HALF-MILE" '81
A&R "CIVILIAN WAR ZONE" '88

LICHTHEIM, GEORGE
ARNOLD, G.L.--[1][31]GERMAN

LICHTVELD, LOU A.M.
HELMAN, ALBERT--[22]DUTCH

LIDDELOW, MARJORIE JEAN
LAW, MARJORIE J.--[1][3]MYS--
CASSELL "DEATH IN THE SPRING" '65

LIDDY, JAMES [D.R.]
LYNCH, BRIAN--[1][8][22]IRISH
O'CONNOR, LIAM--[1][8][22]IRISH
REEVES, DANIEL--[1][8]IRISH

LIDES, LEONID I
LIKHODEEV, LEONID I--[1]

LIE, JONAS JR.
MAUSER, MAX--[29]MYS, STEENSKE--
"DODSDIAMANTEN RAPPORTEN OM ORLOW" '32

LIEBELER, JEAN MAYER
MATHER, VIRGINIA--[1][3][22]MYS--

LIEBER, FRANCIS
FRANZ, ARNOLD--[1]
STRANGER, [THE]--[1]

LIEBERMAN, RICHARD M.
KANTOR, MARIANNE--W/MARIANNE KANTOR,[21]ROM--
"WHITE SATIN NIGHTS"

LIEBERMAN, ROBERTA
BARRON, BOBBI--[35]AUSTRALIAN--
CLEVELAND

LIEBERS, ARTHUR
LOVE, ARTHUR--[8]

LIEBICH, AUGUSTA
MARCH, MARJORIE--[1]

LIEBMANN, RUTH E.
LAWRENCE, RAE--[1]

LIECHTI-MOSER, ROSE-MARIE
LIE, ROMIE--[39]GERMAN

LIEDER, HERWIG
HERMES--[39]GERMAN/JUV

LIEDER, HERWIG
NEUGEBAUER, RALF--[39]GERMAN/JUV

LIEFERSAND, HENRY
OSBORNE, O.O. [1]--W/WILLIAM KOFOED, V. BERCH-
GM PSEUDS, PP 33--
RSB 17 "QUEST" '52
GM 301 "LEAVE HER TO GOD" '53
GM 764 "RISE & FALL OF DR. CAREY" '58

LIEHR, HEINZ
BAR, H.H.--[39]GERMAN/ADULT
DI POSITANO, RICO--[39]GERMAN/ADULT

LIEPMAN, HEINZ
NIELSEN, JENS C.--[39]GERMAN

LIERSCH, ROLF WERNER
HENDERSON, CHESTER--[39]GERMAN/SF
LA ROCCA, ED--[39]GERMAN/SF
ZOLLER, ARNO--[39]GERMAN/SF

LIESEN, HEINZ
LISENIUS, MICHAEL--[39]GERMAN/MYS

LIESTMAN, VICKI
REVSBECH, VICKI--[33]

LIFCHITZ, BORIS
SOUVARINE, BORIS--[1]

LIFTON, WALTER MICHAEL
LIFTON, MIKE--[31]MYS--
SFDS "MARKED FOR DEATH!" DEC '57
SFDS "THE TERRIBLE PASSION" OCT '57
SFDS "THE ROOTS OF HELL" JUL '58

LIFTON-ZOLINE, PAMELA
ZOLINE, PAMELA--[7][23]AMERICAN/SF--
NW "THE HEAT DEATH OF THE UNIVERSE" '67

LIGENSA, ELFIE
MARTINI, ANDREA--[39]GERMAN
NOLDEN, SUSANNE--[39]GERMAN
VAN BERG, STEFANIE--[39]GERMAN
WINTER, CORINNA--[39]GERMAN

LIGGETT, GENEVIEVE G.
GAUNTIER, GENE--[1]AMERICAN
KELEM GIRL, THE--[1]AMERICAN

LIGHT, WALTER HERROD
HERROD, WALTER--[1]ENGLISH
WILLSON, WINGROVE--[1]ENGLISH

LIGHTHALL, WILLIAM DOUW
CHATEAUCLAIR, WILFRED--[1][8]CANADIAN

LILBURN, EILEEN ANNE C.
BIGLAND, EILEEN--[7]SF--
NON-FICT

LILIENCRON, FREDRICH A.
VON LILIENCRON, DETLEV--[1]GERMAN

LILIENTHAL, DAVID ELI
ELY, DAVID--[23][32][34]MYS--
PNTH "TROT" '63
PNTH "SECONDS" '63
DLCT "THE TOUR" '67
DLCT "TIME OUT" '68
HGTN "POOR DEVILS" '70
12 AHMM & EQMM STORIES '63-79

LILJENFORS, BENNIE MADS C
MATIASON, K.G.--[1][29]MYS--
ZIND "MORDAREN" '76
"ALSKAREN" '77
"RANAREN" '78
WILDING, STEN--[1][29]MYS--
6 ZIND NOVELS '65-74

LILLEBAKKEN, J.P.
FALKBERGET, JOHAN [P.]--[1]NORWEGIAN

LILLEY, PETER
BUCKINGHAM, BRUCE--W/ANTHONY STANSFELD,[3]MYS--
JOSEPH "THREE BAD NIGHTS" '56
"BOILED ALIVE" '57
CHANDOS, DANE--W/ANTHONY STANSFELD,[1]
CHANDOS, DANE--W/NIGEL STANSBURY-MILLETT,[1]

LILLEY, THOMAS WILLIAM
LILLEY, TOM--[34]MYS--
MacM "K SECTION " '72
MacM "PROJECTS SECTION" '70

LILLIE, GORDON W.
PAWNEE BILL--[8]

LILLY, ISABELLA PURVIS
ALLAN, ANN--[1]NEW ZEALAND
COUSIN ANN--[1]NEW ZEALAND

LIMA, JOSE LEZAMA
LEZAMA, JOSE--[1] CUBA

LIMA, ROSE MARIE
LEE, LYDIA--[9][34]MYS/ROM--
PAGEANT "THE MAGNIFICENT MIRABELLE" '88

LIMB, SUE
PORTER, SUE--[1]

LIMMING, MARY SPENCER
SPENCER, MARY--[26]ROM--
"COMING HOME PLACE"
"FIRE & ICE"
"THE VOW"

LIN, ADET J[USU]
TAN YUN--[1] CHINESE

LIN, LESLIE C.B.
CHARTERIS, LESLIE--[11]GHOSTED

LINAKER, MICHAEL
BENTEEN, JOHN--[28]ENGLISH/WEST,HP--
NORDON "BOUNTY KILLER" '75
CHRISTIAN, FREDERICK H.--[28]ENGLISH/WEST--
PINN "ANGEL" SERIES #1-5 '78
HUNTER, NEIL--[28]ENGLISH/WEST--
BLADKOMPANIET "BRAND" SERIES #1-9 '78
STAR "BODIE THE STALKER" SERIES #1-6 '79
JORDAN, MATT--[28]ENGLISH/WEST--
JENKINS "BRIGHAM'S WAY" '76
JENKINS "JACOB'S ROAD" '76
STEWART, DAN--[28]ENGLISH/WEST--
JENKINS "SAVAGE GUN" '76
JENKINS "TALMAN'S WAR" '76
WILSON, GAR--[28][34]MYS,HP--
GE "MISSILE MENACE" '88
GE "AMAZON STRIKE" '89
GE "SEARCH & DESTROY" '89
GE "MAIN OFFENSIVE" '89
GE "BARRACUDA RUN" '90
WYLER, RICHARD--[28]ENGLISH/WEST--
AVON "SAVAGE JOURNEY" '67
AVON "INCIDENT AT BUTLER'S STATION" '67
AVON "TRAVIS" '67

LINCK, MOGENS
JELLING, JORGEN--[37] DANISH/MYS

LINCKENS, PAUL H.
LINCKENS, HENDRIK P.--[39]GERMAN/SF

LINCOLN, PETER
ST. MARTIN, THOMAS--[3]MYS--
DELL "JILL" '69

LINCOLN, VICTORIA
LOWE, VICTORIA LINCOLN--[1]AMERICAN

LIND, LARRY
STIVERS, DICK--[34]MYS,HP--
GE "DEATH CODE" '88

LINDARS, FREDERICK C.
LINDARS, BARNABAS--[8]
LINDARS, BARNABUS--[1]ENGLISH

LINDBERG, GUSTAF BRYNOLF
GANDVIK, LOKE--[29]MYS--
"DETEKTIVHISTORIER FRAN UPPSALA" '15

LINDBERG, KARL SIEVERT
VEITS, ULF--[1]SWEDISH

LINDE, PAUL
ELSON, LINDE--[39]GERMAN

LINDEGARD, MAI
CHRISTIANSEN, SYNNOVE--[22]NORWEGIAN

LINDEMANN, KELVIN
HARENG, ALEXIS--[1] DANISH

LINDEN, ERIK HUGO E.
LOWO, HANS--[1]SWEDISH
RISTARE, BO--[1]SWEDISH

LINDHOLM, ANNA C.
FAY, DOROTHY--[1][3][22]MYS--
GALLEON "BLACK PEARL OF PASSION" '36

LINDHOLM, FREDRIK
PRINS, PIERRE--[29]MYS--
ASKERBERG "STOCKHOLMSDETEKTIVEN" 1893

LINDHOLM, VALDEMAR
ALLEN, TOMMY--[29]MYS--
"DEN STORA RUBELSTOLDEN" '18
FLOWER, LUCAS M.--[29]MYS--
"BRODNERA WALL" '18

LINDNER, HEDDA
KOLDEWEY, MARTINA--[39]GERMAN

LINDS, MARK PRAGER
SMITTS, MR.--[1]

LINDSAY, BARBARA
JAMES, JOSEPHINE--W/EMMA G. STERNE,[1]

LINDSAY, DAN
DANIELS, FRANK--V. BERCH-GM PSEUDS, PP 33--
GM 449 "MATING CRY" '54

LINDSAY, HAROLD ARTHUR
BOGADUCK--[1][31]AUSTRALIAN
CARRICK, A.B.--[1][31]AUSTRALIAN
EX-R.S.M.--[1][31]AUSTRALIAN

LINDSAY, JACK
MEADOWS, PETER--[1][8][22]AUSTRALIAN-ENGLISH
PRESTON, RICHARD--[1][8][22]AUSTRALIAN-ENGLISH

LINDSAY, JOHN MAURICE
BROCK, GAVIN--[22][31]--
CONTRIBUTOR TO 'SCOTTISH FIELD'
& 'SCOTTISH REVIEW'

LINDSAY, KATHLEEN
CAMERON, MARGARET--[1][8][22]SOUTH AFRICAN
DESMOND, HUGH--[34]MYS--
80 WRIGHT NOVELS '40-67 ?? UNCONFIRMED ??
RICHMOND, MARY--[7][23][34]MYS/SF--
WRIGHT "VALLEY OF DOOM" '47
"GRIM TOMORROW" '53 & MORE '33-69

LINDSAY, MAURICE
BROCK, GAVIN--[1][8]SCOTTISH

LINDSAY, NORMAN
FLACK, JAMES--[13]AUSTRALIAN

LINDSAY, RACHEL
LEIGH, ROBERTA--[1][8][17]ENGLISH/ROM
SCOTT, JANEY--[1][8][17]ENGLISH/ROM, 4 NOVELS

LINDSAY, SADI
LEDUC, CLAUDINE--[1]FRENCH

LINDSEY, HAL
CARLSON, C.C.--W/CAROLE C. CARLSON,[31]--
"LATE GREAT PLANET EARTH" '70
"SATAN IS ALIVE & WELL"

LINDSKOUG, OSSIAN
COBB, O.S.--[29]MYS--
"FALSKA SEDLAR" '30

LINDSLEY, MARY FRANCES
JAFFEE, MARY L.--[1][31]AMERICAN

LINDSTROM, SIGFRID
TRISTAN--[22]SWEDISH

LINDSTROM, TORD HUBERT
HUBERT, TORD--[29]MYS--
BONNIER "FJALLHOGA MORD" '66

LINDT, GILLIAN
GOLLIN, GILLIAN LINDT--[31]

LINEBARGER, PAUL M.A.
BEARDEN, ANTHONY--[1][11]AMERICAN
FORREST, FELIX C.--[2][4][23][31][34]MYS--
DUELL "RIA" '47
DUELL "CAROLA" '48
SMITH, CARMICHAEL--[2][3][4][23]MYS/SF--
DUELL "ATOMSK: A NOVEL OF SUSPENSE" '49
SMITH, CORDWAINER--[2][4][7][23][32]MYS/SF--
ST "MARK XI" MAY '57

LINEBARGER, PAUL M.W.
MYRON, PAUL--[1]AMERICAN

LINECAR, ARTHUR
GRIM, ANTHONY--[1]ENGLISH

LINEDECKER, CLIFFORD L.
CLIFTON, LEWIS--[1][31]

LINES, MAUREEN
FARMER, PATRICIA--[3]MYS--
POPLB "LEGEND OF PIPER'S HOLE" '73

LINFIELD, MARY B.
HIGHLAND, LAWRENCE--[1]

LING, AMY
LAWRENCE, ARIADNE--[31]

LING, MRS. H.H.
MOORE-BENTLY, MARY ANN--[23]SF--
"A WOMAN OF MARS" '01

LING, PETER
LEIGH, PETRA--[9][21][26]ROM--
"GARNET"
"CORAL"
"ROSEWOOD"

LINGEMAN, RICHARD R.
CHIGNON, NILES--[1][22][31]AMERICAN
HIRSCH, WILLIAM RANDOLPH--W/MARVIN KITMAN & VICTOR S. NAVASKY,[1][22][31]AMERICAN

LININGTON, [B] ELIZABETH
BLAISDELL, ANNE--[2][3][5][9][18][29]MYS--
HARPER "NIGHTMARE" '61
EGAN, LESLEY--[2][3][5][9][18][31]MYS--
HARPER "AGAINST THE EVIDENCE" '62
& 19 MORE '62-80
O'NEILL, EGAN--[2][5][9][18][29]MYS--
"THE ANGLOPHILE" '57
SHANNON, DELL--[2][5][9][32][34]MYS--
NOVELS '60-90
ROM "SCAPEL & THE SWORD"
CHASE "THEY CALL IT INSANE" JAN '63

LINK, WILLIAM
LEIGHTON, TED--W/LEONARD LEVINSON, LACHMAN LST '93, MYS--
AHMM "SUDDENLY THERE WAS MRS. KEMP" APR '59
AHMM "HUNDRED DOLLAR BIRD'S NEST" AUG '59
AHMM "MEMORY GAME" SEPT '59

LINN, WILLIAM JOSEPH
AMOR, PAUL FUSEY--V. BERCH LTR TO HUBIN '93, MYS--
WALKER "THE PEOPLE'S REPUBLIC" '89
LINN, BILL--V. BERCH LTR TO HUBIN '93, MYS--

LINSINGER, PERT
LACHNIT, XAVER--[39]GERMAN
LEND, PERT--[39]GERMAN
LINDNER, ELISABETH--[39]GERMAN
LINDNER, KARL--[39]GERMAN

LINSKILL, DORIS JOY
TREVOR, JOY--[1]

LINSLEY, JUDITH
BEAUMONT, MARIE--W/ELLEN RIENSTRA,[21][26]ROM--
"HALFWAY HOME"
"CATHERINE'S SONG" & OTHERS
LYNLEY, ELINOR--W/ELLEN RIENSTRA,[21][26]ROM--
"SONG OF THE BAYOU"

LINTON, ADELIN S.B.
VINTON, ALDIN--[3]MYS--
PHOENIX "MYSTERY IN GREEN" '37

LINTON, BARBARA LESLIE
AUSTIN, BARBARA LESLIE--[1]

LINZ, AMELIE SPEYER
GODIN, AMELIE--[1]

LINZNER, GORDON
ANFLEMING, IRENE--[2]

LIPEZ, RICHARD
STEVENSON, RICHARD--[3][40]MYS--
ST. MARTIN'S "DEATH TRICK" '81
ST. MARTIN'S "ON THE OTHER HAND, DEATH" '84
ST. MARTIN'S "ICE BLUES" '86

LIPKE, ERIK-ALFONS
LICHTENAU, ERIK-ALFONS--[39]GERMAN

LIPKIND, WILLIAM
WILL--[1][33]

LIPOVICH, MARK D.
MAKSIMOV, MARK D.--[1]

LIPOWITZ, LORNE
MICHAELS, LORNE--[1]

LIPP, HERBERT
HAEL, KURT--[39]GERMAN

LIPP, WOLFGANG
LISSAR, FRANK--[39]GERMAN/JUV

LIPPERT, CLARISSA START
DAVIDSON, CLARISSA START--[1][31]
[LA] MARA--[1]SP
START, CLARISSA--[1]

LIPPINCOTT, SARA JANE
GREENWOOD, GRACE--[8][31]

LIPSCHITZ, CHAIM
YERUSHALMI, CHAIM--[1] ISRAELI

LIPSCHITZ, IMRE
LAKATOS, IMRE--[1]
MOLNAR, IMRE--[1]

LIPSITZ, DEAN
LIPTON, DEAN--[1]AMERICAN

LIPSIUS, MARIE--
[LA] MARA--[1]GERMAN,SP

LIPSKY, ELEASAR
BLAINE, LAWRENCE L.--W/ROBERT SILVERBERG, [1][2]
LYNCH, DAN--W/ROBERT SILVERBERG,[2]MYS--
GM 1240 "FOUR-TIME LOSER" '62

LIPSON, GERTRUDE
CHARLES, GERDA--[1]ENGLISH

LIPTON, ROBERT
STERLING, BARRY--[1][2]

LISLE, MARY
ROGERS, MARYLYLE--[9][21][26]ROM--
"HIDDEN HEARTS"
"ENCHANTED DESIRE" & MORE

LISS, PEGGY K[ORN]
KORN, PEGGY--[1][31]AMERICAN

LISSACK, LISA
LYSSAC, LISA--[39]GERMAN/JUV

LISSENDEN, GEORGE B.
WHITSTABLE, GEORGE--[1]ENGLISH

LIST, ELLEN ERNA
VON BUCHEN, ALIX--[39]GERMAN/MYS

LIST, HORST
CARRIGAN, JOHN D.--[39]GERMAN/MYS/ADV
FRIEDRICH, HORST--[39]GERMAN/MYS/ADV
HEITER, ERNST--[39]GERMAN/MYS/ADV
LIME, HARVEY F.--[39]GERMAN/MYS/ADV
LORCA, FREDERIC H.--[39]GERMAN/MYS/ADV
SHENLEY, JOHN D.--[39]GERMAN/MYS/ADV

LIST, ILKA KATHERINE
MACDUFF, ILKA--[8]
MAIDOFF, ILKA LIST--[1][33]AMERICAN
OBOLENSKY, ILKA--[8]

LIST, JURGEN E.
COTTON, JERRY--[39]GERMAN/MYS,HP--
CUNNING, JERRY E.--[39]GERMAN/ADV/MYS
FLOYD, F. STRATFORD--[39]GERMAN/ADV/MYS
JACKSON, KELTER A.--[39]GERMAN/ADV/MYS

LISTER, LORD
RAFFLES--[29]MYS

LISTON, ROBERT
BRIGHT, ELIZABETH--[9][21][26]ROM--
"REAP THE WILD HARVEST"
"PASSION'S LEGACY" & MORE

LITCHMAN, FRANK
NIGHTINGALE, URSULA--[3][21][26]MYS/ROM,HP--
POPLB "BITTER WOODS" '73

LITTEL, JOHN S.
JOHN, ANTHONY--W/ANTHONY DE STEFANO,[7][34]--
GRAFTON "THE PREDATOR" '86
JOVE "JUDAS VOICE" '89

LITTENBERG, LAURENCE
ALBERT, LINCOLN--W/GREG BENFORD,[2]--
AUTHOR CONFIRMED

LITTLE, CECILE ENID
ASHMORE, JANE--[8]

LITTLE, CONSTANCE/GWENYTH
LITTLE, CONYTH--[34][36]MYS--
DBLDY "BLACK KANBA" '44
& ALL BUT "BLACK-HEADED PIN"

LITTLE, D.F.
WESSEX, MARTIN--[7][8][23]SF--
HALE "SLOWING DOWN PROCESS" '74
HALE "CHAIN REACTION" '76

LITTLE, MALCOLM
EL-SHABAZZ, EL-HAJI MALIK--[31]
MALCOLM X--[8]

LITTLE, PAUL HUGO
DE GRANAMOUR, A.-- C. ECKHOFF-AFTER HOURS,
PP 20, ADULT--
GRNLF GC385 "MANDARIN ORGIES" '69
DE JOURLET, MARIE--[9][21][26][31]ROM--
'WINDHAVEN SAGA' - 14 NOVELS
HARDING, KENNETH--[31]
JAMES, L.F.--[31][32]MYS--
AHMM "HANGFIRE" SEPT '79
AHMM "GUN COLLECTOR" NOV '79
AHMM "LEO BROWNE'S ARREST" JAN '80
JAMES, LEIGH FRANKLIN--[9][21][31]ROM--
'SAGA OF THE SOUTHWEST' - 8 NOVELS
KOSLOFF, MYRON--C. ECKHOFF-AFTER HOURS,
PP 20, ADULT--
FN 102 "RUNNING WILD" '63
AH 105 "QUEEN OF EVIL" '64
LITTLE, PAULA--[9][21][22][31]ROM--
"ONE TRUE LOVE"
"LOVE CONQUER'S ALL"
"LOVE IN STYLE"
MINTON, PAULA--IAN COVELL-BAE 20,[3][7][9]
[22]MYS--
LAN 72-780 "SECRET MELODY" '64 & MORE
PAUL, HUGO--IAN COVELL-BAE 20,[3][11][22]MYS--
LAN 72-936 "SMASHER" '65
LAN 74-842 "THE PROCURER" '65
LAN "RICH, HIP & DEADLY" '66
LAN 73-746 "MASTER OF THE UNDEAD" '68
LAN 75-074 "PLANTATION BREED" '69

LITTLEWOOD, ALAN
CERES--[1]ENGLISH

LITTLEWOOD, SAMUEL ROB.
LITTLEWOOD, S.R.--[1]ENGLISH

LITVINOV, IVY
LOW, IVY--[1][34]ENGLISH/MYS--
HEINEMANN "HIS MASTER'S VOICE" '30

LITWINSKI, PAUL H.
LITTLE, PAUL HUGO--[1] LEGALIZED TO 'LITTLE'

LIU E.
LIU NGO--[1]
LIU T'IEH-YUN--[1]

LIU, SYDNEY [CHIEH]
FENG, CHIN--[1][31]
HSIANG, YEH--[1][31]

LIU, WILLIAM T.
LIU, YONG--[1]

LIU, WU-CHI
HSIA, HSIAO--[8][22][31]CHINESE-AMERICAN

LIVANDAIS, AUGUSTUS
KNUTT, A.P.--[1]

LIVEN, DOUGLAS A.
X.Y.Z. CLUB--W/JOHN GODFREY SAXE
& GEORGE W. PETTES,[1]

LIVERTON, JOAN
MEDHURST, JOAN--[1][8][22]ENGLISH

LIVINGSTON, A.D.
DELANO, AL--[8]

LIVINGSTON, BERKELEY
LISTON, E.J.--[11]

LIVINGSTON, CAROLE
APHRODITE, J.--[1][31][33]AMERICAN

LIVINGSTON, DON LESLIE
GABLE, RUFE--[1]AMERICAN

LIVINGSTON, GEORGETTE
CRAWFORD, DIANE--[21][26]ROM--
"SERENGITI SUNRISE"
"SAPPHIRE ISLAND" & MORE

LIVINGSTON, HERB
BLADE, ALEXANDER--[1]MYS,HP--
ZIFF-DAVIS
HICKEY, H.B.--[1][11][32]AMERICAN/MYS--
WM "CURSE OF RA" FALL '70

LIVINGSTON, MYRAN JABEZ
LIVINGSTON, M. JAY--[1][3][7]AMERICAN/MYS/SF--
COWARD "THE PRODIGY" '78

LIVINGSTONE, BERKELEY
BARCLAY, LESTER--[1][2][11]AMERICAN
BLADE, ALEXANDER--[1][2][11][23]SF,HP--
ZIFF-DAVIS
HICKEY, H.B.--[1][2]AMERICAN
LISTON, B.E.--[1][2][11]AMERICAN
STEELE, MORRIS J.--[2][11][23]SF,HP--
ZIFF-DAVIS

LIVINGSTONE, HARRISON E.
FAIRFIELD, JOHN--[1][8][31]AMERICAN

LIXFIELD, URSULA
MARSAL, UNA--[39]GERMAN/JUV

LIZASO Y GONZALES, FELIX
LIZASO, FELIX--[1] CUBAN

LJUNGGREN, ALBERT GUSTAF
ADALBERT--[29]MYS--
3 NOVELS 1897-05

LLERENA, MARIO
NIEMOLLER, ARA--[1] CUBAN-AMERICAN

LLEWELLYN, D[AVID] W.
TAFFY--[1]ENGLISH

LLEWELLYN, STEPHEN PETER
ELLIS, MICHAEL--[34]MYS--
DAVIES "THE SCORE AT TEA-TIME" '57

LLEWELLYN-THOMAS, EDWARD
LLEWELLYN, EDWARD--[7][11][23]WELSH-
CANADIAN/SF--
"DOUGLAS CONVOLUTION #1-3" '79-83

LLEWELYN-DAVIES, RICHARD
DAVIES, RICHARD LLEWELYN--[31]

LLIRO OLIVE, JOSE MARIA
BENTON, WILLY--JEAN F. LE DEIST LTR '93--
ALTERN. SPELLING-"OLIVETE"
BILLINGS, BUCK--JEAN F. LE DEIST LTR '93--
ALTERN. SPELLING-"OLIVETE"
DIXEL, DELANO--JEAN F. LE DEIST LTR '93--
ALTERN. SPELLING-"OLIVETE"
FISHER, SAM M.--JEAN F. LE DEIST LTR '93--
ALTERN. SPELLING-"OLIVETE"
FORREST, CLARK--JEAN F. LE DEIST LTR '93--
ALTERN. SPELLING-"OLIVETE"
HARE, BURTON--JEAN F. LE DEIST LTR '93--
ALTERN. SPELLING-"OLIVETE"
HAVE, BURTON--JEAN F. LE DEIST LTR '93--
ALTERN. SPELLING-OLIVETE"
LAMBERT, RICKY C.--JEAN F. LE DEIST LTR '93--
ALTERN. SPELLING-"OLIVETE"

LLIRO OLIVE, JOSE MARIA [CONT]
LUMAS, GORDON C.--JEAN F. LE DEIST LTR '93--
ALTERN. SPELLING-"OLIVETE"
SIMMONS, RAY--JEAN F. LE DEIST LTR '93--
ALTERN. SPELLING-"OLIVETE"

LLOP SELLARES, JUAN
EYSSEN, KURT--JEAN F. LE DEIST LTR '93
GREY, JACK--JEAN F. LE DEIST LTR '93
HAMPTON, WILD--JEAN F. LE DEIST LTR '93
LOMBART, CHRISTIAN--JEAN F. LE DEIST LTR '93
MAC GAN, WALL--JEAN F. LE DEIST LTR '93
MACDONALD, SKRANTON--JEAN F. LE DEIST LTR '93
SANTOS ZAPATA, EMILIANO--JEAN F. LE DEIST
LTR '93
SIMMS, NORTON--JEAN F. LE DEIST LTR '93
SKRAN, UDO--JEAN F. LE DEIST LTR '93
STREET, HARRY--JEAN F. LE DEIST LTR '93
VAN FLEET, JOHNNY--JEAN F. LE DEIST LTR '93
VON TIPPELSKIRCH, WILHELM--JEAN F. LE DEIST
LTR '93
WEIBER, JOHN--JEAN F. LE DEIST LTR '93
WHITE, HENRY--JEAN F. LE DEIST LTR '93
WILD, HAMPTON--JEAN F. LE DEIST LTR '93
WOTMAN, JOHN--JEAN F. LE DEIST LTR '93

LLOYD, ADRIAN
DRURY, REBECCA--[21]ROM,HP--
'WOMEN AT WAR' SERIES:
"INCHON DIARY"

LLOYD, DENNIS
LLOYD OF HAMPSTEAD, BARON--[31]

LLOYD, JESSIE GEORGINA
SILVERLEAF--[13]AUSTRALIAN

LLOYD, JOHN IVESTER
BABBLER--[1]ENGLISH
FARMER, PETER--[1]ENGLISH
[THE] LODGER--[1]ENGLISH

LLOYD, JOSEPH H.
LAOIDE, SEOSAMH--[1] IRISH

LLOYD, MAUDE
BLAND, ALEXANDER--W/NIGEL GOSLING,[1][31]

LLOYD, RICHARD DAVID V. LLEWELLYN
LLEWELLYN, RICHARD--[1][3][33]MYS--
5 JOSEPH NOVELS '69-77
PLAY "POISON PEN" '38

LOADER, WILLIAM REGINALD
NASH, DANIEL--[1][8]ENGLISH

LOB, WILHELM HERMANN
SCHWAB, ANTON--[39]GERMAN
STOLP, HANNS PETER--[39]GERMAN
WELLER, PHILIPP--[39]GERMAN

LOBAUGH, ELMA K.
LOWE, KENNETH--[3][22][29]MYS--
DBLDY "HAZE OF EVIL" 53
DBLDY "NO TEARS FOR SHIRLEY MINTON" '55
DBLDY "THE CATALYST" '58

LOBB, CHARLOTTE
MACLAY, CHARLOTTE--[26]ROM--
"THE VILLAIN'S LADY"
"A GHASTLY AFFAIR"
MOORE, CHARLOTTE--[26]ROM--
SIL 975 "NOT THE MARRYING KIND"

LOBLEY, ROBERT
NONG--[8]

LOBNER-FELSKI, ERIKA
KARLOWNA, E.--[39]GERMAN

LOBO, GEORGE EDMUND
SHERRY, OLIVER--[2][3][11]MYS--
JARROLD "MANDRAKE" '29

LOBOWSKI, EDWARD
SPIRIDION--[22] POLISH

LOBSACK, WILHELM
KENNEY, FRANK--[39]GERMAN/MYS/SF
MARSON, JO--[39]GERMAN/MYS/SF

LOBSENZ, IRVING LOUIS
ANDERSEN, IAN--[1]
LONDON, R[USTY] KENT--[1]

LOCH, JOICE NANKIVELL
NANKIVELL, JOICE M.--[1]AUSTRALIAN

LOCHARD, METZ T.P.
LOCHARD, DOC--[1][31]

LOCHER-WERLING, EMILIE
MEIER, LISI--[39]GERMAN
WITZIG, ANNELIE--[39]GERMAN
WUEST, GRITLI--[39]GERMAN

LOCHTE, RICHARD S.
LOCHTE, DICK--[18][32]MYS--
EQMM "MEDFORD & SON" OCT '72

LOCK, A. CHARLES COOPER
COOPER, CHARLES--[32][34][36]AUSTRALIAN/MYS--
JACKSON "TURKISH SPY" '32 & 6 OTHERS

LOCK, FREDERICK SYDNEY
DE LOGHE, SYDNEY--[13]AUSTRALIAN

LOCKARD, FRANCES M.
F.M.--[1]AMERICAN

LOCKE, CHARLES F.
MCLOCIARD, GEORGE--[1][2][11]

LOCKE, GEORGE [W]
JATUES, AYRESOME--[7][23]SF--
"A SPECTRE-ROOM OF FANCY" 1989
WALTERS, GORDON--[1][2][11][23]SF--
SS IN '60's

LOCKE, LUCIE
PRICE, LUCIE LOCKE--[33]

LOCKE, ROBERT
BESS, CLAYTON--[31][33]

LOCKE, ROBERT DONALD
ARCOT, ROGER--[2][11][31]

LOCKE, WILLIAM JOHN
LOCKE, W.J.--[1]ENGLISH
LOCKE, WILLIAM J.--[32]MYS--
EQMM "ADV OF THE KIND MR. SMITH" AUG '50

LOCKERT, LUCIA [ALICIA UNGARO F.]
FOX, LUCIA--[1][31]
FOX-LOCKERT, LUCIA--[1][31]
UNGARO DE FOX, LUCIA--[1]
DE FOX, LUCIA UNGARO--[31]

LOCKHART, ARTHUR JOHN
PASTOR, FELIX--[8]

LOCKIE, ISOBEL
KNIGHT, ISOBEL--[8]

LOCKRIDGE, FRANCIS & DICK
RICHARDS, FRANCIS--[1][8][18]

LOCKRIDGE, HILDEGARDE [D]
DOLSON, HILDEGARDE--[1][31]AMERICAN

LOCKWOOD, FRANK
CIRCUMLIBRA--[8]

LOCKWOOD, INGERSOLL
LONGMAN, IRWIN--[1]AMERICAN

LOCKYER, ROGER WALTER
FRANCIS, PHILIP--[1][8][22][31]ENGLISH

LODER, JOHN DEVERE
COFYN, CORNELIUS--W/HILARY [A] ST. GEORGE
SAUNDERS,[3][29]MYS--
GOLZ "THE DEATH RIDERS" '35

LOEFF, FRIEDEL [H]
CARELL, GEORGIA--[39]GERMAN/MYS/JUV

LOENING, SARAH [E] LARKIN
LARKIN, SARAH--[1][31]AMERICAN

LOENNBOHM, ARMAS EINO L.
LEINO, EINO--[31]

LOENNQUIST, CARL A.
TEOFILUS--[1]SWEDISH

LOERKE, GEORG
KOPERNICUS--[39]GERMAN

LOEST, ERICH
NASS, WALDEMAR--[39]GERMAN/MYS
WALLDORF, HANS--[39][40]GERMAN/MYS--
'DER GRUNE ZETTEL" '67 & OTHERS

LOEWEN, JAMES W.
LYONS, JAMES--[1]

LOEWENGARD, HEIDI H.H.
ALBRAND, MARTHA--[3][9][29][39]MYS--
LITTLE "NO SURRENDER" '42
LITTLE "WITHOUT ORDERS" '43 & 23 MORE
HOLLAND, KATRIN--[9][22][39]ROM
LAMBERT, CHRISTINE--[8][22][29]MYS--

LOEWENTHAL, LEONARD J.A.
LOWE, ALFONSO--[1]ENGLISH

LOFFELMANN, FRANZ
BALTEN, ERIC--[39]GERMAN/MYS/ADV

LOFGREN, EMANUEL
LJUNG, TOM--[29]MYS

LOFGREN, HOLGER
COLTER, RENE--[29]MYS--
SORLINS "FALLET BLAKE" '47

LOFTIN, J.C.
ACE CLUBS--[1]

LOFTING, HUGH
DOLITTLE, DR.--[1]ENGLISH

LOFTS, NORAH [E.R.]
ASTLEY, JULIET--[3][9][17][31][33]MYS/ROM--
COWARD "FALL OF MIDAS" '75
COWARD "COPSI CASTLE" '75
CURTIS, PETER--[2][3][7][9][31][33]MYS--
MacM "DEVIL'S OWN" '60
"YOUR BEST ALONE" '43 & MORE

LOGAN, CELIA
C.L.--[1]

LOGAN, JOHN DANIEL
NOVICUS, ALOYSIUS--[1]CANADIAN

LOGAN, LILLIAN MEE
NAGOL--W/VIRGIL G. LOGAN,[17]AMERICAN

LOGAN, M.C.
VINCENT, ELLERTON--[1]

LOGAN, OLIVE
BELLE, CLARA--[1]AMERICAN
CHRONIQUESE--[1][8]AMERICAN

LOGAN, VIRGIL GLEN
NAGOL--W/LILLIAN MEE LOGAN,[17]AMERICAN

LOGUE, CHRISTOPHER
VICARION, COUNT PALMIRO--[8][33]

LOHAFER, SUSAN
KUHLMANN, SUSAN--[31]

LOHAUSEN, KARL A.
CALCUM, CARL--[39]GERMAN/SF

LOHIER, MICHEL
OUBO, IRAC--[1] WEST-INDIAN

LOHLEIN, HERBERT
ASTOR, A.--[39]GERMAN/ADV

LOHMEYER, ROLF
COTTON, JERRY--[39]GERMAN/MYS

LOHNDORFF, ERNST F.
DANDOO, PETER--[39]GERMAN/ADV

LOHR, ADOLF
FROHMUT, A.--[39]GERMAN/JUV

LOINGER, SILVIA MARY
SIMALO--[1]AUSTRIAN

LOKHVITSKAYA, NADEZHDA A.
TEFFI, NADEZHDA--[1]RUSSIAN

LOMAX, E. VICTORIA
LITTLE, BYRD--[1]

LOMAX, PHIL
LEWIS, PHIL--V. BERCH-'AFTER DARK' BAE 27--
MacF 75-231 "AMSTERDAM AFTER DARK" '69
MacF 75-264 "COPENHAGEN AFTER DARK" '69

LOMAX, WILLIAM JOSEPH
FULKE, COMMISSIONER--[1]
MAXWELL, HERBERT--[1]

LOMBARDI, GEORGINA M.
LOMBARDI, CYNTHIA--[1][22]MYSTERY

LOMBINO, SALVATORE A.
HUNTER, EVAN--MUNROE SLST 20,[2][5]--
LEGALIZED TO 'EVAN HUNTER'- OTHER PSEUDS
LISTED THERE

LOMER, SYDNEY FREDERICK M
OSWALD, SYDNEY--[8]

LOMLER, FRIEDRICH WILHELM
LAODES, FRIEDRICH--[39]GERMAN

LOMNICKA, JOSEPHINE
LOM, JOSEPHINE--[8]

LONDON, JOHN GRIFFITH
LONDON, JACK--[22][23][33]AMERICAN/ADV--
NOVELS & SHORT STORIES

LONDON, JONATHAN [PAUL]
SHERWOOD, JONATHAN--[33]

LONG POU, GENEVIEVE
HOLDEN, GENEVIEVE--[3][40]MYS--
DBLDY "DEADLIER THAN THE MALE" '61
DBLDY "VELVET TARGET" '56 & 5 MORE

LONG, AMELIA REYNOLDS
COXE, KATHLEEN BUDDINGTON--W/EDNA MCHUGH,
[1][3][22]MYS--
PHOENIX "MURDER MOST FOUL" '46
LAING, PATRICK--[3][11][22][29]MYS--
PHOENIX "STONE DEAD" '45
PHOENIX "LADY IS DEAD" '51 & 4 MORE
REYNOLDS, ADRIAN--[3][22][29]MYS--
PHOENIX "FORMULA FOR MURDER" '47
PHOENIX "LEPRECHAUN MURDERS" '50 & MORE
REYNOLDS, PETER--W/WILLIAM L. CRAWFORD,
[22][34]MYS--
VISIONARY "BEHIND THE EVIDENCE" '36
WEIR, MORDRED--[1][2][11]

LONG, FRANK BELKNAP
DAVIS, ROBERT HART--A. TONIK-ECHOES#24, MYS,HP--
MU "ELECTRONIC FRANKENSTEIN AFFAIR" JUL '67
HALLIDAY, BRETT--T. JOHNSON-ECHOES #23,
MYS,HP--
MSMM - MULTIPLE STORIES
LONG, LYDA BELNAP--[4][7][23]SF--
LAN 73-840 "TO THE DARK TOWER" '69
LAN 74-772 "WITCH TREE" '71
LONG, LYDIA BELKNAP--[2][26]ROM--
"CRUCIBLE OF EVIL"
"FIRE OF THE WITCHES" & MORE
NORTHERN, LESLIE--[2]MYS,HP--
THRILLING/STARTLING

LONG, GABRIELLE M.V.C.
BOWEN, MARJORIE--[3][7][16]MYS/SF--
BODLEY "BISHOP OF HELL" '49 & MORE
CAMPBELL, MARGARET--[2][3][7][16][21]MYS/SF--
SIGN "THE SPECTRAL BRIDE" '75
CONSTANZA, SENORA--[1]ENGLISH
LANG, HILARY--[9][21]ENGLISH/ROM
PAYE, ROBERT--[2][11][16][22]ENGLISH
PREEDY, GEORGE R.--[2][3][11][16][22]MYS--
BENN "DEVIL SNAR'D" '32
HODDER "PRIMULA" '40 & MORE
SHEARING, JOSEPH--[2][3][7][16][26]MYS/SF--
HUTCH "THE FETCH" '42
HUTCH "ABODE OF LOVE" '45 & MORE
VERE, MARGARET--[1][11]ENGLISH
WINCH, JOHN--[2][11][16][22]ENGLISH

LONG, J. EDMOND
DANVERS, MILTON--[34]MYS--
8 "DISPOSE" NOVELS 1891-7

LONG, JOHN FREDERICK LAW.
LONGSWORD, JOHN--[22]ENGLISH-GERMAN

LONG, JUDITH ELAINE
LONG, JUDY--[33]

LONG, LEONARD
LONG, SHIRLEY--[8]

LONG, LILY AUGUSTA
DOUBLEDAY, ROMAN--[3][22][29]MYS--
LITTLE "HEMLOCK AVENUE MYS" '08
& 3 MORE '08-17

LONG, RICHARD A.
ALEXANDER, RIC--[31]--
5 RELIGIOUS PLAYS '63-9

LONG, WILLIAM
CREED, WILL--[34]MYS--
FVSTR "DEATH COMES GRINNING" '46
FVSTR "DEATH WEARS A GREEN HAT" '46
YATES, PETER--[34]MYS--
FVSTR "DRESS CIRCLE MURDERS" '45
FVSTR "DEATH IN THE HANDS OF TALENT" '45
FVSTR "CURTAIN CALL FOR MURDER" '45
VULCAN "DEATH COMES TO DINNER" '45

LONG, WILLIAM JOSEPH
RABBIT, PETER--[1]

LONGHURST, PERCY WILLIAM
AGENT 55--[1]ENGLISH
HOCKLEY, LEWIS--[1]ENGLISH
KINGSTON, BRIAN--[1][34]MYS--
AMALG "YELLOW PERIL" '10
SPENCE, HUBERT--[1]ENGLISH

LONGRIGG, JANE CHICHESTER
CHICHESTER, JANE--[1][22][31]ENGLISH

LONGRIGG, ROGER [ERSKINE]
BARKER, MEGAN--[9][21][26]ROM--
"BLACK-EYED SUSAN"
BLACK, LAURA--[8][34]MYS--
HAM "GLENDRACO" '77
HAM "RAVENBURN" '78
HAM "WILD CAT" '79
HAM "STRATHGALLANT" '81
DRUMMOND, IVOR--[3][9][18][29]MYS--
JOSEPH "NECKLACE OF SKULLS" '77 & 8 MORE
ERSKINE, ROSALIND--[9][18][23][31]ROM/SF--
"PASSION FLOWER HOTEL" '62
"PASSION FLOWER IN ITALY" '64
PARRISH, FRANK--[3][18][40]MYS--
CNST "FIRE IN THE BARLEY" '77 & MORE
CNST "SNARE IN THE DARK" '82
TAYLOR, DOMINI--[3][7][18]MYS--
HAM "MOTHER LOVE" '83
HAM "GEMINI" '84
HAM "SUFFER LITTLE CHILDREN" '87
HAM "SIEGE" '89

LONGSTREET, [H] STEPHEN
BURTON, THOMAS--[8][22][31]AMERICAN
BUXTON, THOMAS--[1]AMERICAN
HAGGARD, PAUL--[1][3][31]MYS--
H-C "DEATH TALKS SHOP" '38
"DEATH WALKS ON CAT FEET" '38 & MORE
ORMSBEE, DAVID--[1][8][22]AMERICAN
WEINER, HENRI--[1][3][22]MYS--
MORROW "CRIME ON THE CUFF" '36

LONGYEAR, BARRY B[ROOKES]
ANGO, FAN D.--[1][31]AMERICAN, ?? FP ??
LONGBEARD, FREDERICK--[2][23][31]AMERICAN/SF--
RANT, TOL E.--[1]AMERICAN
RINGDALH, MARK--[1]AMERICAN
VINEST, SHAW--[1]AMERICAN

LOOFS, FRIEDRICH A.
STEINART, ARMIN--[39]GERMAN

LOOK, JANE H.
DAMON, LEE--[9][21][26]ROM--
"AGAIN THE MAGIC"
"SUMMER SUNRISE" & MORE

LOOKER, ANTONINA HANSELL
HANSELL, ANTONINA--[1][31]AMERICAN
JONES, ORLANDO--[1][31]AMERICAN
MACDONALD, NINA HANSELL--[1]AMERICAN

LOOKER, SAMUEL JOSEPH
GAME COCK--[8]
PUNDIT, EPHRAIM--[8]
WADE, THOMAS--[8]

LOOMIS, ALFRED F.
SPUN YARN--[1]

LOOMIS, NOEL [MILLER]
ALLISON, SAM--[2][11][22][28][31]WEST--
LION 183 "TROUBLE ON CRAZYMAN" '53
MILLER, BENJ[AMIN]--[2][22][23]
MILLER, FRANK--[2][11][22][23][28]WEST--
AVALON "TEJAS COUNTRY" '53
WATER, SILAS--[1][2][23]SF--
RICH & COWAN "MAN WITH ABSOLUTE MOTION" '55

LOONEY, PETER
ARCHER, FRANK--V.BERCH-BRNDN/
BC PSEUDS, BAE 22, P24
COLBY, ERIC--[3]MYS--
BRANDON "THE BOSSA NOVA BED" '67
MACINNES, ANDREW--V. BERCH-BRNDN/
BC PSEUDS, BAE 22, P24

LOOSE, KATHERINE R.
SCHOCK, GEORGE--[1]AMERICAN

LOPER, JOHN JOSEPH
LOWE, JAY JR.--[33]

LOPES, BALTAZAR
ALCANBARA, OSVALDO--[1] PORTUGUESE

LOPEZ PINILLOS, JOSE
PAEMENTO--[1] SPANISH

LOPEZ Y FUENTES, GREGORIO
FUENTES, GREGORIO LOPEZ Y--[31]

LOPEZ, DEE
NORMAN, DEE--W/NORMA WILLIAMS,[9][21][26]ROM--
"WHITE NIGHTS"

LOPEZ, ENRIQUE
LOPEZ, HANK--[1]

LOPEZ, RAFAEL
FEEL, LAZARO--[30] MEXICAN--
NEWSPAPER COLUMN "PROSAS"

LOPEZ-PORTILLO ROJAS, JOE
BEN ISSA, ISUF--[1]

LOPRESTI, LUCIA LONGHI
BANTI, ANNA--[1][22] ITALIAN

LORD, DOREEN MILDRED
IRELAND, DOREEN--[1]ENGLISH
LORD, DOUGLAS--[8]ENGLISH

LORD, GRACE VIRGINIA
CHAMPLIN, VIRGINIA--[34]TRANSLATOR--
OGILVIE "SHADOWED BY A DETECTIVE; OR, THE WOMAN IN WAX" 1885

LORD, HALKLETT
KLETT, HAROLD--[1]

LORD, JAMES
PENDLETON, DON--[34]MYS,HP--
GE "FASTBURN" '85

LORD, MINDRET
LORD, GARLAND--W/[M] ISABEL GARLAND, [22][32][34][37]MYS--
DBLDY "MURDER'S LITTLE HELPER" '41
DBLDY "SHE NEVER GREW OLD" '42
DBLDY "MURDER, PLAIN & FANCY" '43
MORROW "MURDER WITH LOVE" '43
IM "TERRIBLE DETECTIVE" SEPT-OCT '45

LORD, PHILLIPS H.
PARKER, SETH--[8]

LORD, WILLIAM WILBERFORCE
LANSTAFF, TRISTRAM--[8]

LORDE, ANDRE GERALDIN
DOMINI, REY--[8][31]

LORDING, ROWLAND EDWARD
TIVEYCHOC, A.--[8]

LORENZEN, ANNEMARIE
WEBER, ANNEMARIE--[39]GERMAN

LORENZINI, CARLO
COLLODI, CARLO--[2][22][31][33] ITALIAN--
"PINNOCHIO"

LORIMER, MAXWELL
WALL, MAX--[8]

LORING, EMILIE [B]
STORY, JOSEPHINE--[1][17][22]MYS--

LORIOT, NOELLE
ORIOL, LAURENCE--[1][3][29]MYS--
"SHORT CIRCUIT" '67
"A MURDER TO MAKE YOU GROW UP LITTLE GIRL" '68

LORRIMER, CLAIRE
ROBINS, PATRICIA--[31]ROM--
46 NOVELS '44-93
5 JUV NOVELS '45-66

LORTIE, ALAIN
SERNINE, DANIEL--[7][23]FRENCH CANADIAN/SF--
"ARGUS" SERIES
"SCORPION'S TREASURE" '90 & OTHERS

LORY, ROBERT
EDWARDS, PAUL--[34]MYS--
PYR "FIST OF FATIMA" '73
PYR "DEATH DEVILS" '74
PYR "GLYPHS OF GOLD" '74
PYR "HOLOCAUST AUCTION" '75
PYR "LAUGHING DEATH" '76

LOSEY, JOSEPH WALTON
HANBURY, VICTOR--[31]

LOTAREV, IGOR VASILYEVICH
SEVERYANIN, IGOR--[22]RUSSIAN

LOTHRINGER, ANNE & FRED
DAY, ANNE--[39]GERMAN/ADV/SF
DAY-HELVIG, ANNE--V. BERCH-ECHOES #8, [39]GERMAN/ADV/SF

LOTHROP, HARRIET M.
SIDNEY, MARGARET--C. BILLMAN-SECRET OF STRATEMEYER SYNDICATE, AMERICAN

LOTINGA, W.
LYNX, LARRY--[1]ENGLISH

LOTTICH, KENNETH V.
CONRAD, KENNETH--[1][8][22][31]AMERICAN

LOTTMAN, EILEEN [SHUBB]
BARNEY, HARRY--[1][31]
COGAN, MIKE--[31][34]MYS--
"THE PRESIDIO" '88
"BLACK RAIN '89
EVANS, JESSICA--[1]
FLUTE, MOLLIE--[7][23][31]SF--
DELL "THROUGH THE LOOKING GLASS" '76
MELLORS, SAMANTHA--[1]
WILLIS, MAUD--[21][23][34]MYS--
DELL "DEVIL'S RAIN" '75
STAR "BIONIC WOMAN" #1 & #2 '76-7

LOTTMANN, F.
FRESENUS, FRITZ--[22] EAST FRISIAN

LOUDERBACK, LEW
CARTER, NICK--[34]MYS-HP--
AWARD "OPERATIO: MOON ROCKET" '68
AWARD "DANGER KEY" '66

LOUDERBACK, LEW
KENYON, LARRY--[34]MYS--
AV "DEVIL'S RING" '67
AV "REVENGE AT INDY" '67 & 2 MORE

LOUIS, PIERRE
LOUYS, PIERRE--[22]FRENCH

LOUISE, DUCHESS OF ARGYLL
FONTENOY, MYRA--[8]

LOURENS-KOOP, ADRIANA L.K
TOUSSAINT, JACKIE--[1]DUTCH

LOUVISH, MISHA
BAR-NATAN, MOSHE--[1][31] RUMANIAN

LOUWEN, JAN
VIKING, TED--[1]DUTCH

LOVE, RICHARD
AMORY, RICHARD--[14]J. PRESSMAN SLST '93, ADULT--
GRNLF GC213 "SONG OF THE LOON" '66
OLYM TC#510 "FROST" '71
OLYM FP#2032 "WILLOW SONG" '74

LOVECRAFT, H[OWARD] P.
APPLETON, LAURENCE--[1][2][11]
BARLOW, ROBERT .H--[2]
BERKELEY, ELIZABETH N.--[2]
BICKERSTAFFE, ISAAC JR.--[1][11]
BROWNLOW, J.H.--[2]
DUNNE, JOHN T.--[1][2][11]
GENT--[1]
HOUDINI, HARRY--L.SERVER,[2][11][31]GHOSTED--
WT "IMPRISONED WITH THE PHAROAHS"
JONES, JOHN J.--[1][2][31]
LITTLEWIT, HUMPHREY--[1][11]

LOVECRAFT, H[OWARD] P. [CONT]
LOVECRAFT, H.P.--[7][32][34]MYS/HOR--
NUMEROUS STORIES-SOME DIGEST--
BZ, EM, MZ, RS & SN
MAYNWARING, ARCHIBALD--[1][2][11]
PAGET-LOWE, HENRY--[1][2][11]
PHILLIPS, WARD--[1][2]
RALEIGH, RICHARD--[1][11]
ROWLEY, AMES DORRANCE--[1][2][11]
SOFTLY, EDWARD--[1][2][11]
SWIFT, AUGUSTUS T.--[1][11]
THEOBALD--[1]
THEOBALD, LEWIS [LOUIS]--[1][2]
THEOBALDUS--[1][11]
WILLIE, ALBERT FREDERIC--[1][11]
WILLIE, FREDERICK--[1]
ZOILUS--[1][11]

LOVEJOY, CORNELIA
EVERETT, PAUL--[1]

LOVEJOY, MARY EVELYN
TRAINE, GYPSEY--[1]AMERICAN

LOVEJOY, WILLIAM H.
BOSTROM, HANK--[34]MYS--
LYNX "GABRIEL'S FLIGHT" '88
LYNX "PRESSURE POINT" '88

LOVELING, VIRGINIE
WALTER, W.E.C.--[22] FLEMISH

LOVELL, MARK
ROWLANDS, PETER--[1]ENGLISH

LOVELL-WILLIAMS, DAVID A.
LOVELL, ARTHUR--[1]ENGLISH

LOVESEY, PETER [HARMER]
LEAR, PETER--[7][29][31]--
"GOLDEN GIRL" '77
"SPIDER GIRL" '80
"SECRET OF SPANDAU" '86

LOVIN, ROGER ROBERT
BRIGHTON, WESLEY JR.--[31]
CLEMENS, ROGERS--[1][7][31]SF--
GM "THE PRESENCE" '77
DRIVER, CYNTHIA C.--[1][31]
ZWEIT, ADAM--[1]

LOVINGOOD, ALVIN
KOLE, A.K.--[1]AMERICAN

LOW, LOIS DOROTHEA
CASS, ZOE--[3][8][9][31]MYS/ROM--
RNDM "ISLAND OF SEVEN HILLS" '74
RNDM "SILVER LEOPARD" '76
ELIK "A TWIST IN THE SILK" '80
LOW, DOROTHY MACKIE--[8][9][21][31][34]MYS--
HURST "DEAR LIAR" '63
HURST "INTRUDER" '65 & 4 MORE
PAXTON, LOIS--[8][9][26][29][34]MYS--
HURST "MAN WHO DIED TWICE" '68 & 2 MORE

LOW, MARY
AUNT MARY--[1]ENGLISH

LOWDER, CHRISTOPHER
ADRIAN, JACK--[2][7]SF,HP--
GE "DEATHLAND #1" '86
BAINBRIDGE, CHUCK--V. BERCH LTR TO HUBIN '94,
MYS,HP--
JOVE 'HARD CORPS':
"DEVIL'S PLUNDER" '89

LOWDER, CHRISTOPHER [CONT]
REID, DESMOND--[34]MYS,HP--
MYFLWR "THE ABDUCTORS" '68
TEED, JACK--ECHOES #24, P31, MYS--
ZEBRA "GUNSHIP"
TEED, JACK HAMILTON--[7]SF/HOR--
MILLS & BOON "THE BLOOD OF DRACULA" '77

LOWDER, JAMES
AWLINSON, RICHARD--W/SCOTT CIENCIN--[7]SF--
'AVATOR TRILOGY' #2 '89

LOWE, CHARLOTTE
ANNABELLA--[9][21][26]ROM--
"PASSION'S PAWN"
"POLYREATH WOMAN"

LOWE, HELEN PORTER
LOWE-PORTER, H.T.--[1]ENGLISH

LOWE, MARJORIE GRIFFITHS
LOWE, MARJORIE G.--[21]ROM--
"THE SUDDEN LADY"

LOWE, MARY P.
ADAMS, JACK--W/ALCANOAN O. GRIGSBY,
[7][23][32]SF--
LM "HAPPENING IN POMPEII" SEPT '80

LOWE, PAUL EMILIUS
ARP, ASA--[34]MYS--
OTTENHEIMER "ARM OF THE UNWRITTEN LAW" '07

LOWE, SUSAN [CLAIRE] L.
DAVIDSON, ANDREA--[10][26][34]MYS/ROM--
HARL "TIGER'S DEN" '85
HARL "A SIREN'S LURE" '86 & MORE
LOWE, SUSAN L.--[21][26]ROM
RANDOLPH, ELISE--[9][26]ROM--
"SHADOW GAMES"
"HANDS OFF THE LADY" & 3 OTHERS

LOWELL, JAN & ROBERT
LOWELL, J.R.--[2][3]MYS--
DLCT "DAUGHTER OF DARKNESS" '72
NEL "SECRETS" '76 & MORE

LOWELL, JOAN
TRASK, HELEN--[1]

LOWELL, SUSAN
HUMPHREYS, SUSAN L.--[31]

LOWENKOPF, SHELLY A.
CHAMBERS, HOWARD V.--[1][31]AMERICAN--
SHERBOURNE "AN OCCULT DICT FOR THE
MILLIONS"

LOWENSTEI-W-F, WOLFRAM ZU
ZU MONDFELD, WOLFRAM--[39]GERMAN/JUV

LOWENTHAL, MAJORIE FISKE
FISKE, MAJORIE--[1]

LOWENTROUT, CHRISTINE I.S
ADAMS, NICHOLAS--[7] HOR--
"HORROR HIGH: FINAL CURTAIN" '91

LOWENTROUT, CHRISTINE I.S
SMITH, SHERWOOD--[7]SF--
"WREN TO THE RESCUE" '90
TALLIS, ROBYN--[7]SF--
IVY "PLANET BUILDERS #3, #4, #9 & #10"

LOWERY, MARILYN M.
CASTLE, PHILIPPA--[9][21][26]ROM--
"THE RELUCTANT DUKE"
"DANDY'S DECEPTION"
"THE NEW FRONTIER"

LOWNDES, MARIE [A] BELLOC
BELLOC, M.A.--[1][22][31]
BELLOC-LOWNDES, MRS.--[1]
CURTIN, PHILIP--[18][29][31]MYS--
"NOTED MURDER MYSTERY" '14

LOWNDES, ROBERT A.W.
COOKE, ARTHUR--W/E. BALTER,[2][11]
[15][23][31]SF,HP
GOTTESMAN, S.D.--W/C.M. KORNBLUTH
& FREDERIK POHL,[11][15][23][31]SF--
GREENER, CARL--[11]
GREY, CAROL--[2][11][15][23][31]SF--
GROENER, CARL--[2][11][23][31]SF--
JOSEPHS, HENRY--[11]
KENT, MALLORY--[2][11][15][23][31]SF--
LAVOND, PAUL DENNIS--W/J. DOCKWEILER,
F. POHL & C.M. KORNBLUTH,[2][11][15]
[23]SF,HP--SFQ, FUTURE
LOWNDES, DOC--[1]
LOWNDES, R.A.W.--[31]
LOWNDES, R.W.--[1]
MACDOUGAL, JOHN--W/JAMES B. BLISH,
[2][11][15][23]SF--
ASF "CHAOS COORDINATED" '46
MORLEY, WILFRED OWEN--W/FORREST J. ACKERMAN,
[1][2][11]SF--
MORRISON, RICHARD--[2][11][15]SF--
SFQ "THE DELIVERERS" WINT '42
MORRISON, ROBERT--[1][2][23]
SHERMAN, [PETER] MICHAEL--[1][2][11][23]SF--
TYLER, JAY--[2][11][32]MYS--
SN "AND THEN NO MORE" SPR '68
SN "SIGHT OF ROSES" SUM '68
WOODS, LAWRENCE--W/DONALD A. WOLLHEIM,
[2][11][15][23]SF--
WRIGHT, ROBERT--W/FOREST J. ACKERMAN,[2][11]

LOWRY, HAROLD
GREENWOOD, LEIGH--[9][21][26]ROM--
"CAPTAIN'S CARESS"
"SEDUCTIVE WAGER" & MORE

LOWRY, JOAN [CATLOW]
CATLOW, JOAN--[1]ENGLISH
CATLOW, JOANNA--[8][22[31]ENGLISH
LEA, JOAN--[1]ENGLISH

LOWRY, MINA GERTRUDE
LOY, MINA--[31] POETRY

LOWRY, ROBERT [J.C.]
CALDWELL, JAMES--[1][31]

LOWTHER, ARMSTRONG JOHN
LAIRD--[8]

LOWTHER, ELIZABETH
NORTHAN, IRENE--[26]ROM--
"THE MARRIAGE BROKERS"
"PHYLLIDA"

LOXSTON, [CHARLES] HOWARD
LOXTON, [CHARLES] HOWARD--[1]

LOZINSKI, WLADYSLAW
LUBON, W.--[22] POLISH

LU KUAN YU
LUK, CHARLES--[8]

LUAN, CARLA CAMERON
DAVID, CAY--[26]ROM--
"CRYSTAL CLEAR"
"SWEPT AWAY"

LUARD, NICHOLAS
MCVEAN, JAMES--[18][29][34]MYS--
MacD "BLOODSPOOR" '77
MacD "WHITE FALCON" '79
MacD "SEABIRD NINE" '81
MacD "TITAN" '84

LUARD, WILLIAM BLAINE
LUARD, L.--[8][34]MYS--
LANE "ALL HANDS" '33

LUBANSKI, JULES C.L.
HELDAU--[1]
STAR, JEAN--[1]

LUBARS, WALTER
GARYS, WALTER--W/GARY E. WOONTEILER,
V. BERCH LTR TO HUBIN '94, MYS--
TWR "DETONATOR" '81

LUBIN, MAURICE A.
MALU--[1] HAITIAN

LUBLINER, HUGO
BURGER, HUGO--[22]GERMAN

LUBY, KATE
O'DOWD, DARBY--[1]

LUCAS, BERYL LLEWELLYN
E.V.L.--[8]
V.V.V.--[8]

LUCAS, EDGAR ERNEST
GOODSON, BILL--[8]

LUCAS, E[DWARD] V[ERRALL]
E.V.L.--[1]ENGLISH
LUCAS, E.V.--[1]ENGLISH
WARD, E.D.--[1][7][23]SF--
"MR. PULTENEY" '10

LUCAS, FRANK LAWRENCE
LUCAS, F.L.--[1]ENGLISH

LUCAS, GERALD
LOUVIER, PIERRE--[1]SWISS
MELVIER, LARENT--[1]SWISS

LUCAS, MARY M.
LUCAS, MAYO--[21][26]ROM--
"CAMELOT JONES"
"MATTERS OF THE HEART"

LUCCHETTI, ANTHONY
PRESCOTT, JOHN--[8]

LUCCOCK, HALFORD EDWARD
STYLITES, SIMEON--[8]

LUCENO, JAMES
MCKINNEY, JACK--W/BRIAN C. DALEY,[7][23]SF--
DEL RAY "ROBOTECH #1 THRU #13"
DEL RAY "SENTINEL #1 THRU #5"
DEL RAY "EVENT HORIZON" '91
DEL RAY "ARTIFACT OF THE SYSTEM" '91
McKINNEY, JACK--V. BERCH LTR TO HUBIN '94,
MYS/SF--
DEL RAY "KADUNA MEMORIES" '90

LUCEVICH, IVAN DAMINIK.
KUPALA, JANKA--[22]RUSSIAN

LUCEY, JAMES DENNIS
JAMES, MATTHEW--[8][31]
PIERCE, MATTHEW--[8]

LUCIE-SMITH, [J] EDWARD
KERSHAW, PETER--[1]ENGLISH

LUCIOLLI, MARIO
DONOSTI, MARIO--[1] ITALIAN

LUCKENWALD, HANS
ANDERS, DEEZ--[39]GERMAN

LUCY, HENRY WILLIAM
H.W.L.--[1]
TOBY, M.P.--[1][22]ENGLISH, JOURNALIST

LUCY, THOMAS ELMORE
ELMORE, CAROLE--[1]

LUDDECKE, WERNER JORG
CRAIN, ROBERT--[39]GERMAN

LUDEMANN, HANS-ULRICH
BROWNMAN, JOHN U.--[39]GERMAN/MYS/JUV

LUDERS-KNEGTMANS, ANNEKE
MANS, ADRIENNE--[3][29]MYS--
WALKER "ON SHOES OF NIGHT" '67

LUDLUM, GEORGE
L., G.--[34]MYS--
PLAY "MYSTERIOUS MURDER; OR, WHAT'S THE CLOCK!"

LUDLUM, ROBERT
HOUSE, BRIAN--[11]
RYDER, JONATHAN--[3][18][31]MYS--
DLCT "TREVAYNE" '73
DLCT "CRY OF THE HALIDON" '74
SHEPHERD, MICHAEL--[3][18][29][31]MYS--
DIAL "ROAD TO GONDOLFO" '75

LUDOVICI, ANTHONY M.
COBBETT--[1][22][31]ENGLISH
PATERSON, HUNTLEY--[1][22]ENGLISH
VALENTINE, DAVID--[1][22]ENGLISH

LUDOVICI, LORENZ JAMES
LUDOVICI, L.J.--[1] CEYLONESE--
ALTERNATE SPELLING TO "LORENZ" IS "LAWRENCE"

LUDVIGSEN, KARL [E]
MILES, ELLIOT--[1]AMERICAN
NIELSSEN, ERIC--[1]AMERICAN

LUDWIG, HELMUT
LUTZ, HARRO--[39]GERMAN/MYS/JUV

LUDWIG, MILES ERIC
WILLIAMS, J.X.--[1]AMERICAN

LUDWIGS, CHERYL
ST. JOHN, CHERYL--[26]ROM--
"LAND OF DREAMS"
"SAINT OR SINNER" & OTHERS

LUEHRMANN, ADELE
SEABROOKE, JOHN PAUL--[34]MYS,HP--
CHELSEA "EYE WITNESS" '25
"GREEN BAG" '26
"WOMAN IN 919" '26

LUFF, STANLEY GEORGE A.
FARNASH, HUGH--[1][22][31]ANGLO-ITALIAN

LUGARD, FLORA LOUISA S.
SHAW, FLORA LOUISA--[33]

LUHAN, MABLE GANSON
LUHAN, MABLE DODGE--[1]AMERICAN

LUHAR, TRIBHUVANDAS
SUNDARAM--[1] INDIAN

LUIF, KURT
BURCETTE, JAMES R.--[39]GERMAN/SF/HOR
DAVENPORT, NEAL--[39]GERMAN/SF/HOR
DE LORCA, FRANK--[39]GERMAN/SF/HOR
HARTMANN, CLAUS--[39]GERMAN/SF/HOR
SPIELMANNS, JORG--[39]GERMAN/SF/HOR

LUK, CHARLES
LU, K'UAN-YU--[22] CHINESE

LUKAS, CHARLOTTE KOPLINKA
KOPLINKA, CHARLOTTE--[31]

LUKAS, JOSEF
SCHWEITZER, FRANK--[39]GERMAN

LUKEMAN, ALEX
DAIN, ALEX--[2][11][23]SF--
"THE BANE OF KANTHOS" '69

LUMB, EMMELINE
BRITTAIN, NOEL--[1]ENGLISH

LUMLEY, BENJAMIN
HERMES--[2]

LUMMIS, CHARLES F.
CRUSADER IN CORDUROY--[1]AMERICAN

LUMPKIN, HOUSTON FORCE
HOUSTON, DAVID--[1][7][23]SF--
"TALES OF TOMORROW" SERIES '81-2
HOWARD, KEN--[1]

LUMSDEN, JEAN
SWIFT, RACHELL--[8]

LUND, A. MORTEN
BORCH, TED--[1][22][31]AMERICAN

LUND, PHILIP REGINALD
CONFUCIUS--[1][31]NEW ZEALAND

LUNDBACK, IVAR
JARNFELDT, IVAN--[29]MYS--
BONNIER "AKTIEBOLAGET STORASENS BRUK" '38

LUNDGREN, NILS
WERNER, EDWARD--[29]--
BQ "MORD PA HAND" '53
TROTS "MOTIVET AR MORD" '58
"RADDAD FOR ATT DO" '58

LUNDGREN, PAUL ARTHUR
MCCUTCHEON, JAMES--[1]AMERICAN

LUNDHOLM, ANJA
BERKELEY, ANN--[39]GERMAN
LINDSTROM, ALF--[1]GERMAN

LUNDQUIST, SUNE
SUNESON, VIC--[40]MYS--
"MORD AR MITT MAL" '75

LUNDSTROM, EVERT
BARK, JULIUS--W/JAN MOEN,[29]MYS--
"VILA VID DENNA KALLA" '65

LUNFBERG, IVAR CARL-ALF.
WILMORE, JOHN--[29]--
T. HOLM "DOKTOR BARRY'S EXPERIMENT" '32
"ARTHUR MOLLER CONTRA RISKAN" '32

LUNN, HUGH KINGSMILL
KINGSMILL, HUGH--[2][11][23][34]ENGLISH/MYS--
JARROLDS "TABLE OF TRUTH"

LUNN, SIR ARNOLD
CROFT, SUTTON--[1][8]ENGLISH
RUBICON--[8]ENGLISH

LUPESCU, VALENTIN
HEINRICH, VALENTIN--[39]GERMAN

LUPIANO, VINCENT
SLOAN, CHRISTOPHER--V. BERCH LTR TO HUBIN '94, MYS--
ZEBRA "IN SEARCH OF EAGLES" '82
ZEBRA "THE WINGS OF DEATH" '83

LUPOFF, RICHARD A.
HAMLET, OVA--[2][23][33]SF--
FS "GOD OF THE NAKED UNICORN" AUG '76
"OVA HAMLET PAPERS" '79
LUPOFF, DICK--[33]SF--
O'DONNELL, DICK--W/DONALD ARTHUR THOMPSON, [1][33]
PASCUDNIAK, PASCAL--[1][33]AMERICAN
STEELE, ADDISON E.--G. LOVISI-PP15,[7][23][33]SF--
DELL-"BUCK ROGERS" #1 & #2 '78-9

LUPTON, LEONARD
WARWICK, CHESTER--[34]MYS--
ACE F107 "MY PAL, THE KILLER" '61

LUSTBERG, JEAN ANNE
BARTLETT, JEAN ANNE--[21][26]ROM--
'AARON BURR' SERIES:
"ANGELICA"
"THEODOSIA"
"ELIZA"

LUTGE, KARL
NORDHAUSEN, K.L.--[39]GERMAN

LUTHER, FRANK
CROW, FRANCIS LUTHER--[31]

LUTHER, OTTO JENS
REHN, JENS--[39]GERMAN/SF

LUTTWAK, EDWARD NICOLAE
IGNOTUS, MILES--[1] RUMANIAN

LUTYENS, MARY
WYNDHAM, ESTHER--[1][9][21]ROM--
"BLACK CHARLES"
"BLUE ROSE" & MORE

LUTZ, BERTHOLD
BURGER, THOMAS--[39]GERMAN/JUV

LUTZ, GILES A.
CARSON, ZEKE--[19][28] WEST
CHAFFIN, JAMES B.--[8][19][28]WEST--
POPLB G314 "GUNS OF ABILENE" '59
BELM "THE WOLFER" '68

LUTZ, GILES A. [CONT]
CURTIS, BRAD--[28]ADULT--
MIDWD F313 "MAN TRAP" '63
MIDWD F335 "ANATOMY OF A MISTRESS" '63
MIDWD "THE PLEASURE GAME" '63
F356 "FOR SERVICES RENDERED" '64
MIDWD F-385 "MAN-TAMER" '64
MIDWD 32-425 "PRIVATE PROPERTY" '64
MIDWD 32-441 "NIGHT SHIFT" '65
MIDWD 34-518 "THE PICK-UP" '65
MIDWD 32-536 "THE LOVE GODDESS" '65
MIDWD 32-580 "THE GOLDEN GREED" '65
MIDWD 32-598 "LIVE & LET LIVE" '66
MIDWD "TOO YOUNG, TOO WILD"
MIDWD "A FEMALE FEMALE"
MIDWD "THRILL CRAZY"
DONOVAN, CURT--[28]ADULT--
BEAC B437Y "LUSTING HOURS" '61
BEAC B504F "WITCH WITH BLUE EYES" '62
BEAC B630 "THE WIFE GAME" '63
EVERETT, WADE--[1][8][19]WEST--
BAL "THE WHISKY TRADERS" '68
HAWK, ALEX--[8][19][28]WEST,HP--
PAPLB "TOUGH TOWN" '69
PAPLB 63-291 "DRIFTERS LUCK" '70
PAPLB 63-355 "MEXICAN STANDOFF" '70
PAPLB 63-591 "HALF BREED" '71
INGRAM, HUNTER--[8][19]WEST--
BAL U2332 "TRESPASSERS" '65
BAL "FORT APACHE" '75 & 6 MORE
MORALES, SEBASTIAN--[19][28]WEST--
SULLIVAN, REESE--[8][19][28]WEST--
ACE "NEMESIS OF CIRCLE A" '65
ACE "BLIND TRAIL" '65 & 4 MORE
THOMPSON, GENE--[8][19][28]WEST--
GRAPH 146 "SIX-GUNS WILD" '57
AVALON "RANGE LAW" '62 & 4 MORE

LUTZ, JOHN [T]
BENNETT, JOHN--HAWK/LUTZ INTRVW '93, [18][29][32]MYS--
EX "DAY OF EVIL" JUN '75
COLLINS, TOM--AUTHOR PROVIDED,[18][29]MYS--
'BEST OF MIKE SHAYNE'- "DEATH, MY LOVE" '64
GREENE, STEVEN--W/STEVEN GREENE, HAWK/LUTZ INTRVW '93,[34]MYS--
GM 4700 "EXILED" '82
MCCLOUD, VAN--HAWK/LUTZ INTRVW '93,[32]MYS--
EX "ROOM 33" JUN '75
SHEPPARTON, PAUL--HAWK/LUTZ INTRVW '93, [32]MYS--
EX "NEXT TO THE WOMAN FROM DES MOINES" JUN '75
STRANGE, ELWIN--HAWK/LUTZ INTRVW '93,[32]MYS--
EX "ORGANIZATION MAN" JUN '75
EP "PERSONALIZED COPY" JUN '75
WILLIAMS, JOHN BARRY--W/BARRY MALZBERG & BILL PRONZINI-PRONZINI LTR,[32]--
AHMM "CHEESEBURGER" OCT '78

LUTZENBURGER, JOHANNA
ERNST, HANNA--[39]GERMAN/JUV

LUXENBURG, ROSA
JUNIUS--[31]

LUXMORE, ROBERT
FESENMEYER--[8]

LUXTON, LEONORA KATHRINE
HOWARD, NONA--[31]

LYALL, JAMES ROBERT
PATROCLUS--[8]

LYALL, KATHARINE ELIZAB.
WHITEHORN, KATHARINE--[22]ENGLISH

LYANDRES, YULIAN SEMENOV
SEMENOV, JULIAN--[31]
SEMENOV, YULIAN--[31]
SEMYNOV, JULIAN--[31]
SEMYONOV, YULIAN--[31]

LYASHCHENKO, NIKOLAY NIK.
LYASKO, NIKOLAY--[22]RUSSIAN--SHORT STORIES

LYBURN, DR. ERIC FREDERIC
DOCTOR FUTUER--[8]
TOLLER--[8]

LYKIARD, ALEXIS [C]
PIANO, CELESTE--[1] GREEK

LYLE, GWLADYS M.
MORGAN, GWLADYS M.--[1]AMERICAN

LYLE, JOHN
RENN, CHRIS--V. BERCH LTR TO HUBIN '94,MYS--
ST. MARTIN'S "THE VIOLENT AIR" '80

LYLE-SMYTHE, ALAN
CAILLOU, ALAN--[2][32][34]MYS--
DAVIES "ALIEN VIRUS" '57 & 19 MORE
CO "LEONA!" SEPT '69
CO "ODILE" JAN '70
AV "DIAMONDS WILD" '79
WEBB, ALEX--[34]MYS--
PINN "BLOOD RUN" '85
PINN "DEKKER'S DEMONS" '85

LYMAN, ALBERT ROBINSON
OLD SETTLER, THE--[1][22]AMERICAN

LYMAN, G.H.
DE LEON, STUART--[1]

LYMAN, HELEN HOYT
HOYT, HELEN--[1]AMERICAN

LYNAM, JOAN
LYNAM, SHAWN--[1] IRISH

LYNCH, HARRIET LOUISE
ST. FELIX, MARIE--[1]AMERICAN

LYNCH, JANE GASKELL
GASKELL, JANE--[2][7][11][23]SF--
PAPLB 55-693 "THE SERPENT" '68
PAPLB 55-738 "ATLAN" '68
PAPLB 64-019 "THE CITY" '68

LYNCH, JOHN A.
THAN, JOHN A.--[1]AMERICAN

LYNCH, JOHN GILBERT B.
BLOOMER, JACK--[1]ENGLISH

LYNCH, MARILYN
WARD, MELANIE--[1]AMERICAN
CRAIG, DELORES--[9][21]ROM--
"SCALPEL OF HONOR"
LORD, MOIRA--[9][21][26]ROM--
"CALENDAR OF SINNERS"
"NIGHTINGALE PARK"
VINCENT, CLAIRE--[9][21][26][34]MYS--
BERK Y752 "EMERGENCY ROOM NURSE" '63
LAN 74-581 "GARDEN OF SATAN" '69
"BELIEVING IN GIANTS"
"UNHOLY SPELL"

LYNCH, MARILYN [CONT]
WALLACE, MARY--[34]MYS--
ARCADIA "FROM THIS DEATH FORWARD" '59

LYNCH, W.
BORDEN, COLE--[35]AUSTRALIAN--
CLVLD 906 "DEVIL'S LEAGUE"
CLVLD 913 "REBEL CODE"
SANTE FE 325 "RENEGADE RANGE"
SIERRA 438 "COLT VENDETTA"
GORMAN, MARK--[35]AUSTRALIAN--
4 CONDOR BKS
3 CORONADA BKS
BIG HORN 301 "SILENT .45"
CHSM 659 "GO ON, GIT!"
CHSM 678 "CLEVE BRENNAN"
SIERRA 421 "SAND"
SIERRA 436 "BEND OF THE TRAIL"
SANTE FE 311 "YWO-GUN REBEL"
SANTE FE 312 "SAVAGE DAY"
LOGAN, DAN--[35]AUSTRALIAN--
3 CHISHOLM BKS
3 SIERRA BKS
3 SANTE FE BKS
BIG HORN 305 "OWLHOOT RIDER"
BIG HORN 314 "MONTANA MARSHALL"
CONDOR 167 "COLT FURY"
CONDOR 173 "RECKLESS RANGER"
CORW 944 "UNHOLY GUN"
CORW 956 "WOLF COLT"
SAUNDERS, WILT--[35]AUSTRALIAN--
4 CORONADA BKS
BIG HORN 309 "MAN HUNTER"
BIG HORN 326 "BUZZARDS WAITED"
CHISHOLM 660 "TEXAS TYRANT"
SANTE FE 310 "TRAIL BRAND LAW"

LYNCH-FRASER, DIANE
FRASER, DIANE L.--[31]

LYND, ROBERT
O'LONDON, JOHN--[1] IRISH
Y.Y.--[1][8][22] IRISH

LYNDON, BARRE
SANSOM, JOHN--W/JIMMY SANGSTER,[2]

LYNDS, DENNIS
ARDEN, WILLIAM--[3][5][11][18]MYS--
DODD "DEAL IN VIOLENCE" '69
DODD "DEADLY LEGACY" '73 & MORE
CARTER, NICK--[1][3][18]MYS,HP--
AWARD "N3 CONSPIRACY" '74
AWARD "TRIPLE CROSS" '76
AWARD "GREEN WOLF CONNECTION" '76
CHART "DAY OF THE MAHDI" '84
CHART "MAYAN CONNECTION" '84
CHART "EXECUTION EXCHANGE" '85
CHART "PURSUIT OF THE EAGLE" '85
CHART "WHITE DEATH" '85
CHART "THE SAMURAI KILL" '86
CHART "MASTER ASSASSIN" '86
CHART "MERCENARY MT." '86
CHART "BLOOD OF THE FALCON" '87
COLLINS, MICHAEL--J. DINAN-HARDBOILED,
PP 9,[2][3][5][18][23]MYS--
DODD "ACT OF FEAR" '67 & 13 MORE
CROWE, JOHN--[32][34]--
RDM "ANOTHER WAY TO DIE" '72
AHMM "OCCUPATIONAL HAZZARD" SEPT '72
RDM "A TOUCH OF DARKNESS" '72
DODD "BLOODWATER" '74
DODD "CROOKED SHADOWS" '75
DODD "WHEN THEY KILL YOUR WIFE" '77
DODD "CLOSE TO DEATH" '79
DALLAS, WALTER--T. JOHNSON LTR '94, MYS,
HP--MSMM

LYNDS, DENNIS [CONT]
DAVIS, ROBERT HART--A. TONIK-ECHOES #24, MYS,HP--
MU "UNSPEAKABLE AFFAIR" APR '66
MU "HOWLING TEENAGER AFFAIR" FEB '66
MU "VANISHING ACT AFFAIR" JUN '66
MU "CAT & MOUSE AFFAIR" AUG '66
MU "THRUSH FROM THRUSH AFFAIR" NOV '66
MU "GENGHIS KHAN AFFAIR" AUG '67
MU "MIND SWEEPER AFFAIR" OCT '67
CC "TEMPLE OF THE GOLDEN HORDE" MAY '74
DEKKER, CARL--[3][18][31][33]MYS--
BOBBS "WOMAN IN MARBLE" '72
DOUGLAS, JOHN--LACHMAN LST '93,JOHNSON LTR '94,[18][32]MYS--
MSMM "DEATH MY LOVE" FEB '63
GRANT, MAXWELL--AUTHOR-ECHOES#5,[2][3]MYS,HP--
BELM "RETURN OF THE SHADOW" '63
BELM "SHADOW STRIKES" '64
BELM "SHADOW BEWARE" '65
BELM "CRY SHADOW" '65
BELM "SHADOW'S REVENGE" '65
BELM "MARK OF THE SHADOW" '66
BELM "SHADOW--GO MAD" '66
BELM "NIGHT OF THE SHADOW" '66
BELM "SHADOW--DESTINATION MOON" '67
HALLIDAY, BRETT--T. JOHNSON-ECHOES #23, MYS,HP--
MSMM "FRIENDLY CORPSE" SEP '62
MSMM "GUILTY BYSTANDER" OCT '62
MSMM "MIRACLE OD MURDER" DEC '62
MSMM "FOURTH MAN" FEB '63
MSMM "DETOUR TO MURDER" MAY '63
MSMM "DEATH OF DEAD MAN" JUN '63
MSMM "POWER OF DEATH" SEP '63
MSMM "DANGEROUS SECRET" OCT '63
MSMM "CROOKS HOLIDAY" NOV '63
MSMM "MILK RUN MURDER"FEB '64
MSMM "REVENGE FOR A MASSACRE" JAN '64
MSMM "DRINK UP - AND DIE" MAR '64
MSMM "KILLER'S MASQUERADE" APR '64
MSMM "KILL WITH CARE" MAY '64
MSMM "SCREAM IN THE NIGHT" JUN '64
MSMM "A MATTER OF COURAGE" AUG '64
MSMM "A TRADEGY OF ERRORS" SEP '64
MSMM "MURDER AT FLOODTIDE" OCT '64
MSMM "DEATH IN CELL FIVE" NOV '64
MSMM "MURDER ON BERKELEY SQUARE" DEC '64
MSMM "DEAD MAN'S WALK" JAN '65
MSMM "CRUISE FOR MURDER" FEB '65
MSMM "REQUEM FOR A KILLER" MAR '65
MSMM "MAGHUL BOX" APR '65
MSMM "STRING OF PEARLS" MAY '65
MSMM "INSIDE JOB" JUN '65
MSMM "A SALESMAN DIES" JUL '65
MSMM "MOVING TARGET" AUG '65
MSMM "LOVE OR MURDER" SEP '65
MSMM "PRESSURE PLAY" OCT '65
MSMM "THE UNNECESSARY" NOV '65
MSMM "ACCENT ON MURDER" DEC '65
MSMM "SPY WHO WAS MIKE SHAYNE" JAN '66
MSMM "IN THE SHADOWS" FEB '66
MSMM "GOOD CITIZEN" MAR '66
MSMM "PATTERN WENT WRONG" APR '66
MSMM "GOTHIC MANUSCRIPT" MAY '66
MSMM "BIG FRAME" JUN '66
MSMM "A RUN OF LUCK" JUL '66
MSMM "MAN WHO NEVER FORGOT" AUG '66
MSMM "KICK OF DEATH" SEP '66
MSMM "INNOCENT VICTIM" OCT '66
MSMM "VOICE OF BLOOD" NOV '66
MSMM "AN END TO HORROR" DEC '66
MSMM "UNSEEN MAN" JAN '67
MSMM "THEIF IN THE FAMILY" FEB '67
MSMM "A REASON TO DIE" MAR '67
MSMM "HUSTLE DEATH" APR '67
MSMM "TRAIL OF A PHANTOM" MAY '67

LYNDS, DENNIS [CONT]
HALLIDAY, BRETT [CONT]
MSMM "WRONG ROOM" JUN '67
MSMM "UNDERSTUDY FOR MURDER" JUL '67
MSMM "DEAD MAN'S MESSAGE" AUG '67
MSMM "DEATH IS MY RANSOM" SEP '67
MSMM "MOMENT OF FEAR" OCT '67
MSMM "FINAL PAYOFF" NOV '67
MSMM "DIE IN HASTE" DEC '67
MSMM "TEDDY BEAR MURDERS" JAN '68
MSMM "DEATH TIMES THREE" FEB '68
MSMM "KEY TO A KILLER" MAR '68
MSMM "DEATH TRAP" APR '68
MSMM "BABY DOLL MURDERS" MAY '68
MSMM "DETAIL OF DEATH" JUN '68
MSMM "LADY WHO KISSED & KILLED" JUL '68
MSMM "AFFAIR OF DEATH" AUG '68
MSMM "DEATH IS MY MISTRESS" SEP '68
MSMM "SPIRIT OF EVIL" OCT '68
MSMM "DEADLY CONSCIENCE" NOV '68
MSMM "DEAL ME OUT OF THE MORGUE" DEC '68
MSMM "DIE LIKE A THIEF" JAN '69
MSMM "RICH MAN'S BLOOD" FEB '69
MSMM "KILL IN DARK" MAR '69
MSMM "MURDER IS MY ACCOMPLICE" APR '69
MSMM "GIRL WITH THE TORTURED EYES" MAY '69
MSMM "NIGHT WAS MADE FOR MURDER" JUN '69
MSMM "CAUSE FOR MURDER" JUL '69
MSMM "YOUTH IS FOR DYING" AUG '69
MSMM "MURDER-GO-ROUND" SEP '69
MSMM "ROAD TO NOWHERE" OCT '69
MSMM "KILLER OF THE GLADES" NOV '69
MSMM "DIE IN SILENCE" DEC '69
MSMM "A WILD YOUNG CORPSE" JAN '70
MSMM "TWAS THE NIGHT BEFORE MURDER" FEB '70
MCERLEAN, SHEILA--[3]MYS--
LAN 73-799 "AMSK OF SILENCE" '68
PENDLETON, DON--W/GAYLE STONE,[34]MYS,HP--
GE "BLOOD FEVER" '89
GE "MOVING TARGET" '89
SADLER, MARK--[32][34]MYS--
RNDM "FALLING MAN" '70
RNDM "HERE TO DIE" '71
"MIRROR IMAGE" '72
AHMM "THE CHOICE" FEB '73
RNDM "CIRCLE OF FIRE" '73
RAVEN "TOUCH OF DEATH" '81
WALKER "DEADLY INNOCENTS" '86

LYNE, CHARLES
DE CASTRO, LYNE--[8]

LYNES, DAISY ELFREDA
GLYN-FOREST, D.--[8]

LYNN, ELWYN AUGUSTUS
AUGUSTUS--[1][8]AUSTRALIAN

LYNN, MARY ELIZABETH N.
LYNN, MARY--[21]ROM
MILAN, ANGEL--[21][26]ROM--
"SNOW SPIRIT"
"SONATINA" & 8 MORE
NEIBOR, ELIZABETH--[9]ROM
NELSON, ELIZABETH--[9]ROM

LYNNE, JAMES BROOME
QUARTERMAIN, JAMES--[1][34][40]MYS--
CNST "DIAMOND HOOK" '70
CNST "MAN WHO WALKED ON DIAMONDS" '71
CNST "ROCK OF DIAMOND" '72
CNST "DIAMOND HOSTAGE" '75

LYNRAVN, NORMAN SOREN
LYNRVN, N.S.--[36]AUSTRALIAN/MYS--
A&R "MURDER ON MOUNT CAPITA" '44
[W/L.W. MARTIN]

LYNTON, HARRIET RONKEN
RONKEN, HARRIET--[1]AMERICAN

LYONS, A. NEIL
MICHAEL, ALBERT--[1] SOUTH AFRICAN

LYONS, JACQUELINE
FLYNN, VERONICA--[9][21][26]ROM--
"RACE THE WIND"
"SPUN OF GOLD" & 3 MORE

LYONS, JOHN BENIGNUS
FITZWILLIAM, MICHAEL--[8][31]

LYONS, JOHN BENIGNUS
LYONS, J.B.--[31]

LYONS, JOHN MAGUIRE
O'LAITHAIN, SESU--[1]SCOTTISH

LYONS, LUELLA B.
LA PLANTE, SANDRA--[1]AMERICAN
RIDER, JANE--[1]AMERICAN

LYPE, E.J. ANDERS
ANDERS, E.J.--[34]MYS--
PHILOSOPHICAL LIB "BEHIND THE DOOR" '66

LYS, GUNTHER
PETERSEN, KAY JENS--[39]GERMAN/MYS

LYTE, CHARLES
EWART, CHARLES--[1][31]

LYTLE, MRS. W.J.A.
BERNEY, BERYL--[8]

LYTTLE, EILEEN J.
GARRETT, EILEEN J.--[2][11]

LYTTLE, RICHARD
LANG, REX--[1]

LYTTLETON, EDITH J.
LANCASTER, G.B.--[3][8][13][22]
NEW ZEALANDER/MYS--
DORAN "THE LAW BRINGERS" '13

LYTTON, EDWARD GEORGE E.
CAXTON, PISISTRATUS--[31][33]

LYTTON, ROBERT BULWER
MEREDITH, OWEN--[2]

M'ILWRAITH, JEAN N.
FORSYTH, JEAN--[8]

M'INTOSH, JIM
MURDOCH, H.J.--VULTURES OF THE VOID--
BRITISH SF MAG "THIS PRECIOUS STONE"

MAAG, GEORG
MCMILLAN, STEVE--[39]GERMAN/WEST

MAAS, DONALD
ST. CLAIR, STEPHANIE--[9][21]ROM--
"SUMMER STORMS"

MABBOTT, THOMAS O.
HUNTER, M.O.--[8]

MABROUK, DJELLOUL
MARBROOK, DEL--[1]ALGERIAN-AMERICAN

MACALLISTER, HEATHER
ALLISON, HEATHER--[21][26]ROM--
"JACK OF HEARTS"
"DECK THE HALLS" & MORE

MACALPINE, MARGARET H.
CARMICHAEL, ANN--[1][22]SCOTTISH

MACARTHUR, D[AVID] WILSON
SINCLAIR, GAVIN--[1]SCOTTISH
WILSON, DAVID--[22][34]MYS--
JENKINS "SEARCH FOR GEOFFREY GORING" '62
JENKINS "MURDER IN MOZAMBIQUE" '63

MACAULAY, FANNIE CALDWELL
LITTLE, FRANCES--[1][8][22]AMERICAN

MACAULAY, MILDRED
CULLEN, CARTER--W/RICHARD MACAULAY, V. BERCH-
GM PSEUDS. PP 33,[3][29]MYS--
GM 210 "DON'T GET CAUGHT" '51
GM 629 "THE DEADLY CHASE" '57

MACAULAY, RICHARD
CULLEN, CARTER--W/MILDRED MACAULAY, V. BERCH-
GM PSEUDS, PP 33,[3][29]MYS--
GM 210 "DON'T GET CAUGHT" '51
GM 629 "THE DEADLY CHASE" '57

MACAULEY, CLARENDON
ADAMS, WALTER MARSHAM--[7]SF--

MACAULEY, KEN
HANN, DONALD--[35]AUSTRALIAN--
HRWTZ PB169 "MICHIKO" '63
HRWTZ "P.T. COMMAND" '63
HRWTZ PB181 "DESERTERS" '64
HRWTZ PB186 "PUT IN, TAKE OUT" '64
HRWTZ PB193 "LOVE GAME" '64
HRWTZ PB195 "YIELD TO THE FLESH" 64
HRWTZ PB197 "WE'LL ALL BE KILLED" '64
HRWTZ "P.T. MISSION" '64
HRWTZ "P.T. K" '64
HRWTZ SP8 "YELLOW WITCH" '64
HRWTZ "BATTLESHIP DECOY" '65
HRWTZ "DANGEROUS MISSION" '65
LESLEY, PAUL--[35]AUSTRALIAN--
HRWTZ PB170 "P.T. COMMAND" 63
VANCE, RAY--[35]AUSTRALIAN--
HRWTZ PB172 "P.T. 106" '64

MACAULEY, ROBIE [M]
DUMBARTON, A.--[1]AMERICAN

MACBEATH, INNIS [S]
MALONEY, TIGHE--[1]IRISH
STEWART, RATTRAY--[1]IRISH
TISSANT-BERNAC, MATHIEU--[1]IRISH

MACBETH, MADGE HAMILTON
DILL, W.S.--[1][8]CANADIAN
KNOX, GILBERT--[1][8]CANADIAN

MACBRIDE, ROGER ALLEN
KOTANI, ERIC--W/YOJI KONDO,[7]SF--
AV "SUPERNOVA" '91

MACCARTHY, SIR DESMOND
HAWK, AFFABLE--[8]

MACCHETA, BLANCHE R.
PANDORA--[1]AMERICAN
ROOSEVELT, BLANCHE--[1]AMERICAN

MACCLURE, VICTOR
CRAIG, PETER--[8][22][34]MYS--
HARRAP "CONSPIRACY ISLAND" '33

MACCORMACK, SABINE G.
OSWALT, SABINE--[1]GERMAN-AMERICAN

MACDERMOTT, JOHN R.
RYAN, J.M.--MUNROE SLST 20, BIBLIO--
GM 1671 "BROOKS WILSON LTD" '66

MACDONALD, EDWINA LE VIN
LEVIN, EDWINA--[1]AMERICAN

MACDONALD, ELIZABETH
RYAN, SABRINA--[9][21][26]ROM--
"THE FIRE IN HER EYES"

MACDONALD, GEORGE A.
DALMOCAND--[1]
KELLY, JAMES BRYAN--W. MURRAY-ECHOES #17, MYS--
FEDA 'G-MAN LYNN VICKERS' STORIES
WALLACE, ROBERT--D. HUTCHISON-ECHOES #9 & 17, MYS,HP--
PHD "MURDER CRACKS DOWN" NOV '35
PHD "DEATH-SKULL MURDERS" MAY '36
PHD "SIGN OF THE SCAR" SEPT '36
PHD "EMPIRE OF TERROR" NOV '36
PHD "TOUCH OF DOOM" FEB '37
PHD "GOLDEN KILLER" APR '37
PHD "HARVEST OF DEATH" MAY '37
PHD "BEAST-KING MURDERS" JUL '37
PHD "MINIONS OF MURDER" NOV '37
PHD "CORPSE PARADE" DEC '37
PHD "FANGS OF MURDER" JAN '38
PHD "TYCOON OF CRIME" FEB '38
PHD "MILESTONES OF MURDER" APR '38
PHD "COUNTERFEIT KILLERS" SEPT '38

MACDONALD, J. HAY
JAMBON, JEAN--[1]

MACDONALD, JAMES D.
ADAMS, NICHOLAS--W/DEBRA DOYLE,[7]SF/HOR,HP--
HARPER "HORROR HIGH:PEP RALLY"
APPLETON, VICTOR--W/DEBRA DOYLE,[7]SF,HP--
STSY 'TOM SWIFT':
"AQUATECH WARRIORS"
"MONSTER MACHINE"
TALLIS, ROBYN--W/DEBRA DOYLE,[7]SF,HP--
IVY "PLANET BUILDERS #2 & #5" '89

MACDONALD, JESSICA NORTH
NORTH, JESSICA--[11]--NOT CORRECT PER [34]

MACDONALD, JOHN D.
FARRELL, JOHN--A.J. ISOBEL-ECHOES #19,[32]MYS--
DS "THE SCARRED HAND" NOV '46
FARRELL, JOHN WADE--D. GEHERIN-MacDONALD, A. TONIK-ECHOES #19,[2][5]MYS,HP
SUSS "ALL OUR YESTERDAYS" APR '49
SUSS "DEVIL SPIN" JAN '50
HENRY, ROBERT--D. GEHERIN-MacDONALD,[5]MYS,HP
LANE, JOHN--D. GEHERIN-MacDONALD,[5]MYS,HP--
WARREN
O'HARA, SCOTT--D. GEHERIN-MacCDONALD, A. TONIK-ECHOES #19,[2][5]MYS,HP--
DS "STARTLED FACE OF DEATH" NOV '46
O'HEARN, MARIAN--LACHMAN LST '93,[37]MYS--
SI - ONE STORY
REED, PETER--D.GEHERIN-MacDONALD,A.J. ISOBEL-ECHOES #19,[2][5][32]MYS,HP--
DS "TO CUT THE CARDS" JUL/AUG '47
DS "SECOND VISITOR" NOV/DEC '47
DS "TIN SUITCASE" MAY/JUN '48
SUSS "DELUSION DRIVE" APR '49

MACDONALD, JOHN D. [CONT]
REED, PETER [CONT]
SUSS "GIFT OF DARKNESS" MAY '50
SUSS "ESCAPE TO FEAR" JUL '50
REISER, HENRY--D. GEHERIN-MacDONALD,[5]MYS,HP--
RISER, HENRY--A.J. ISOBEL-ECHOES #19,MYS--
DOCS "BONDED IN DEATH" FEB '47
DOCS "WORSE THAN MURDER" NOV/DEC '47

MACDONALD, LUCY MAUDE M.
MONTGOMERY, L.M.--[1][32]CANADIAN/MYS--
SN "HOUSE PARTY AT SMOKEY ISLAND" FALL '68

MACDONALD, MALCOLM JOHN R
ROSS-MACDONALD, MALCOLM J--[1]ENGLISH

MACDONALD, PHILIP
CORRELL, A. BOYD--[5][32]MYS--
11 SW STORIES JUN '44 - APR '47
FLEMING, OLIVER--W/RONALD MACDONALD, [5][32][34]MYS--
WARD "AMBROTOX & LIMPING DICK" '20
PALMER "THE SPANDAU QUID" '23
LAWLESS, ANTHONY--[3][5][18][31]MYS--
"MOONFISHER" '31
"HARBOUR"
PORLOCK, MARTIN--[3][5][18][23]MYS--
COLLINS "MYS AT FRIAR'S PARDON" '31
COLLINS "X v. REX" '33
STUART, W.J.--[1][7][23]SF--
"FORBIDDEN PLANET" '56
STUART, WARREN--[1]

MACDONALD, RONALD
FLEMING, OLIVER--W/PHILIP MACDONALD, [5][32][34]MYS--
WARD "AMBROTOX & LIMPING DICK" '20
PALMER "THE SPANDAU QUID" '23

MACDONALD, SUSANNE
MACFARLAND, ANNE--[8]

MACDONALD, THOMAS DOUGLAS
MACCOLLA, FIONN--[8]

MACDONALD, ZILLAH K.
ZILLAH--[1][33]CANADIAN

MACDONELL, A. GORDON
CAMERON, JOHN--[3][22][29]MYS--
METHUEN "BODY FOUND STABBED" '32
GOLZ "SEVEN STUBS" '30
GORDON, NEIL--[2][3][23][29]MYS--
"THE PROFESSOR'S POISON" '28 & 5 MORE
KENNEDY, ROBERT MILWARD--W/MILWARD R.K. BURGE,[3]MYS--
GOLZ "THE BLESTON MYS" '28

MACDONNELL, JAMES EDMOND
DARK, JAMES--[7][34][36]AUSTRALIAN/MYS--
HRWTZ "HAVOC!" '62
HRWTZ "IMPACT" '62 & 16 MORE
HOOD, MARK--[36]MYS
MACDONNELL, J.E.--[36]WAR/SEA--
PYR G450 "ENEMY IN SIGHT" '59
PYR 473 "FROGMAN!" '60 & MORE
MACNELL, JAMES--[1][22]AUSTRALIAN

MACDOUGALL, MARGARET
ARMOUR, MARGARET--[1][2]

MACE, AURELIA GAY
AURELIA--[1]

MACE, NANCY LAWSON
LANG, NANCY M.--[31]

MACEOIN, DENIS
AYCLIFFE, JONATHAN--[7]SF/HOR--
HARPER "NAOMI'S ROOM" '91
EASTERMAN, DANIEL--DDLY PLEAS #3,
[7][34]MYS/SF--
HODDER "LAST ASSASSIN" '84
DBLDY "SEVENTH SANCTUARY" '87
GRAFTON "NINTH BUDDHA" '88
GRAFTON "BROTHERHOOD OF THE TOMB" '89
GRAFTON "NIGHT OF THE SEVENTH DARKNESS" '91

MACFADDEN, BERMNARD A.
ATKINS, REV. E.C.--[23]SF--
"MY BRIDE FROM THE OTHER WORLD" '04

MACFALL, CHAMBERS H.C.
HAL, DANE--[1]ENGLISH

MACFARLANE, E. MADL. DUKE
DONNE, MAXIM--[2][3][18][23]MYS/SF--
"CLARET, SANDWICHES, & SIN" '64
"THIS BUSINESS OF BOMFOG" '67
DUKE, MADELAINE--[7]SF--
"FLASHPOINT" '82
DUNCAN, ALEX--[1][8][8][31]
VETINARY NOVELS '61-83

MACFARLANE, GEORGE GORDON
MILLER, PATRICK--[8]

MACFARLANE, JOHN
ARBORY, JOHN--[1]CANADIAN

MACG, ALASDAIR ALPIN
FEATHERSTONEHAUGH, FRANCI--[22]ENGLISH

MACGIBBON, JEAN
HOWARD, JEAN--[1][31]

MACGILL, GEORGE
DARGON--[34]MYS--
LANE "THE NAMELESS ORDER" '24

MACGILL, MARGARET
GIBBONS, MARGARET--[1]
MACGILL, MRS. PATRICK--[1]

MACGILL, PATRICK
O'GORMAN, JOHN--[1]

MACGINLEY, PETER T.
MACFHIOUNLASICH, PEADOR--[1]IRISH

MACGLASHAN, JOHN
GLASHAN, JOHN--[8]

MACGREGOR, JAMES MURDOCH
FRANCIS, GREGORY--W/FRANK H. PARNELL,
[1][2][11]
M'INTOSH, J.T.--[2][4][11][23]SF--
MCINTOSH, J.T.--HOLLAND-LASER ART/CKLST,
BAE 2,[2][3][4][7][23]MYS/SF--
ACE D113 "ONE IN 300" '55
CREST 150 "RULE OF THE PAGBEASTS" '56
PERMA M3027 "WORLD OUT OF MIND" '57
AV T249 "WORLDS APART" '58
ACE F113 "200 YEARS TO CHRISTMAS" '61
PYR 898 "THE MILLION CITIES" '63
AV S347 "SNOW WHITE & THE GIANTS" '68
LASER 24 "RULER OF THE WORLD" '76
MURDOCH, H.J.--[2][11]

MACGREGOR, JOHN
J.M.--[2]
ROB ROY--[1]ENGLISH

MACGREGOR, MARY ESTHER
KEITH, MARIAN--[1]CANADIAN

MACGREGOR, MIRIAM
PEGDEN, HELEN--[8]

MACGREGOR, PATRICIA M.J.
DRAKE, ALISON [CLAIRE]--LACHMAN-EASTER
LST '93,G. COOK LTR '93/[34]SF--
BAL "FEVERED" '88
BAL "TANGO KEY" '88
BAL "BLACK MOON" '89
BAL "LAGOON" '90
JANESHUTZ, TRISH--[7][31]SF--
BB "HIDDEN LAKE" '88
MACGREGOR, T.J.--[7][34]MYS--
BAL "DARK FIELDS" '87
BAL "KILL FLASH" '87
BAL "DEATH SWEET" '88
BAL "ON ICE" '89
BAL "KIN DREAD" '90

MACGREGOR, ROB
ROBB, T.N.--[34]MYS--
IVY "FLIP SIDE" '88
IVY "PRIVATE EYE" '88

MACHADO, PAULO SERGIO M.
ROCKET, CAPTAIN--[1] BRAZILIAN

MACHAR, AGNES MAUDE
FIDELIS--[1]CANADIAN

MACHL, OTTO
LAURAT, LUCIEN--[1]
REVO, L.--[1]

MACHLIN, MILTON
JASON, WILLIAM--[1][8]AMERICAN
ROBERTS, MACLEAN--[1][8]AMERICAN

MACHLIS, JOSEPH
SELCAMAN, GEORGE--[1] LATVIAN

MACHOL, LIBBY
MACCALL, LIBBY--[1][32]AMERICAN/MYS--
EQMM "RECIPE FOR MURDER" JAN '66
AHMM "DEATH A LA NEWBURGH" MAR '66
SA "FUNGUS SOUP" SEPT '66
EQMM "PTA MYS" OCT "66
AHMM "PERFIDY OF PROFESSOR BLAKE" NOV '70
EQMM "MRS. HENDERSON TALKS TO GOD" JUL '78

MACHUISDEAN, HAMISH
GATES, MICHAEL--[1]SCOTTISH

MACIAS, SUSAN W.
MALLERY, SUSAN--[26]ROM--
SIL 554 "TEMTING FAITH"
SIL 834 "A DAD FOR BILLIE"
SIL 898 "COWBOY DADDY"

MACIEJOWSKI, IGNACY
SEWER--[22] POLISH

MACIEL, JUDI[TH ANNE]
STEWART, JUDITH ANNE--[1]AMERICAN

MACINNES, HELEN [CLARK]
HIGHET, HELEN--W/GILBERT HIGHET,[9][31]--
"SEXUAL LIFE IN ANCIENT ROME" '34
"FRIEDRICH ENGELS" '36

MACINNES, TOM
ROY, JULIEN--[1]CANADIAN

MACINTOSH, JOAN
BLAIKE, AVONA--[1][8][31]NEW ZEALAND

MACINTYRE, F. GWYNPLAINE
APPLETON, VICTOR--[7][23]SF,HP--
STSY 'TOM SWIFT':
"THE DNA DISASTER"

MACINTYRE, JOHN
BRANDANE, JOHN--[8]

MACINTYRE, JOHN THOMAS
O'NEIL, KERRY--[34]MYS--
DBLDY "DEATH AT DAKAR" '42
REYNAL "MOONEY MOVES AROUND" '39 & 2 MORE

MACISAAC, FRED[ERIC JOHN]
KANE, KASPER--[1][34]MYS--
WHITMAN "THE GLEAMING BLADE" '39
MOORE, FRANCIS--[34]MYS--
WHITMAN "FIVE KEYS TO MYSTERY" '39
ROSS, DONALD--[1][34]MYS--
WHITMAN "ALLIGATOR RING" '45
WHITMAN "DEVIL WAS KIND" '45 & 2 MORE

MACIULIS-MACIULEVICIUS, J
MARONIS--[1][22]LITHUANIAN

MACK, ELSIE FRANCES
MOORE, FRANCES SARAH--[1][8]CANADIAN

MACKAIL, JOHN WILLIAM
MACKAIL, J.W.--[1]SCOTTISH

MACKARNESS, MATILDA ANNE
PLANCHE, MATILDA ANNE--[1]ENGLISH
SUNBEAM, SUSIE--[1]ENGLISH

MACKAY, DAVID LORING
JULIEN, DAVID--W/JOSEPHINE JULIA
MACKAY,[1]AMERICAN
MACKAY, LORING--W/JOSEPHINE JULIA
MACKAY,[1]AMERICAN

MACKAY, FULTON
MCBRIDE, AENEAS--[8]

MACKAY, HUGH LEWIS
MATHESON, HUGH--[2][3]MYS--
WINGATE "THIRD FORCE" '59
GIBBS "BALANCE OF FEAR" '61

MACKAY, JAMES [A]
ANGUS, IAN--[1][31]--
'COLLECTING' BOOKS '70's
FINLAY, WILLIAM--[1][31]--
'COLLECTING POSTAL HISTORY' '73
GARDEN, BRUCE--[1][31]--
'STAMP COLLECTING' BOOKS '67-8
WHITTINGTON, PETER--[1][31]--
'ANTIQUE' BOOKS '73-5

MACKAY, JOHN HENRY
SAGITTA--[1]GERMAN

MACKAY, JOSEPHINE JULIA
JULIEN, DAVID--W/DAVID LORING
MACKAY,[1]AMERICAN
MACKAY, LORING--W/DAVID LORING
MACKAY,[1]AMERICAN

MACKAY, LOUIS ALEXANDER
SMALACOMBE, JOHN--[8]

MACKAY, MARY
CORELLI, MARIE--[2][17][23][31]ROM/SF--
SPHERE "MIGHTY ATOM" '75 & MORE

MACKAY, MINNIE
MACKAY, MARY--[1][8][23]ENGLISH/SF

MACKAY, WILLIAM R.
RICARD, W.--[34]MYS--
LIPP "SKEIN OF LIFE" 1897

MACKAYE, DAVID & JULIA
LORING, JULES--[1]

MACKELLAR, CAMPBELL
HILARION--[34]MYS--
REMINGTON "GRAFIN RIMSKY & OTHER TALES" 1892

MACKENNA, STEPHEN
DALY, MARTIN--[22]

MACKENROTH, ALBERT
MACKS, BERT--[39]GERMAN/JUV

MACKENZIE, BASIL W.S.
AMULREE, BARON--[31]

MACKENZIE, FRANCIS S.
COMPTON, FRANCIS--[1]

MACKENZIE, G.A.
DALE, ELLIS--[1]CANADIAN

MACKENZIE, JOAN
BEDARD, MICHELLE--[1]CANADIAN
FINNIGAN, JOAN--[1][8]CANADIAN

MACKENZIE, KENNETH
MACKENZIE, SEAFORTH--[1][36]AUSTRALIAN/MYS--
CAPE "REFUGE OF A CONFESSION" '54

MACKENZIE, NAN
FAIRBROTHER, NAN--[1]

MACKENZIE, NORMAN IAN
FORREST, ANTONY--W/ANTONY BROWN,[31][34]MYS--
LONG "SLAY ME SUDDENLY" '68

MACKENZIE, SIR EDWARD
PORTSEA--[8]

MACKENZIE, TINA
HARLOWE, JUSTINE--W/JEAN HARVEY
& LAURA BENNETT,[8]ROM--
"JEALOUSIES"
"MEMORY OF DESIRES"

MACKESY, LEONORA
RIVERS, DOROTHY--[9][21][26]ROM--
"SPANISH MOONLIGHT"
"SHARLEY FOR SHORT" & MORE
STARR, LEONORA--[8][9][21][26]ROM--
"FANTAILS"
"JEMIMA"

MACKIE, ALBERT DAVID
MACNIB--[8][22]SCOTTISH

MACKIE, MARY
ANDREWS, ALEX--[9]ROM
CHARLES, CAROLINE--[9]ROM
CHRISTOPHER, CATHY--[9]ROM
CHRISTOPHER, MARY--[9][21][26]ROM--
"ROYAL WEDDING"
"DARK CONQUEROR" & MORE

MACKIE, MARY [CONT]
STEVENS, SUSAN--[9][21][26]ROM--
"IVORY INNOCENCE"

MACKINLAY, LEILA A.S.
GREY, BELINDA--[1][8][31]ENGLISH

MACKINNON, CHARLES ROY
BROWN, F.--[1]ENGLISH-WEST AFRICAN
CONTE, CHARLES--[1][9][34]MYS--
HALE "SPANISH CROWN AFFAIR" '71
HALE "FEAR OF DEATH" '72
DONALD, VIVIAN--[9][21][22][26][31]ROM--
"HAPPY ISLE"
"ROYAL SCOT" & MORE
LYNN, BARBARA--[26]ROM--
"TENDER LONGINGS"
MACALPIN, RORY--[1][9][31]ENGLISH-WEST AFRICAN/ROM--
MONTROSE, GRAHAM--[1][3][9]MYS--
HALE "A MATTER OF MOTIVE" '69
HALE "ANGEL AT ARMS" '71 & 8 MORE
ROSE, HILARY--[1][9][22]ENGLISH-WEST AFRICAN/ROM--
STUART, CHARLES--W/CHARLES S. REID, [21][22]ROM--
"CUPIDS & CORONETS"
"LADY AMBASSADOR" & MORE
STUART, CHARLES--[1][9][32]ROM--
LM "GOOD-BYE, AMELIA" SEPT '68
"EARTH INSPECTOR #11"
STUART, VIVIAN--[21]ROM--
PYR "DARKLEY'S BRIDE" '76
PYR "NEW MRS. ALDRITCH" '76
PYR "DARKNESS OF LOVE" '77
STUART-VERNON, CHARLES--[21]ROM
TORR, I.--[21]ROM--
"ALLISON COMES HOME"
"SUNDOWN" & 3 MORE
TORR, IAIN--[1][9][22]ROM--

MACKINTOSH, CRAIG
CRAIG, BRIAN--W/BRIAN M. STABLEFORD,[1][2]

MACKINTOSH, ELIZABETH
DAVIOT, GORDON--[3][18][29][31]MYS--
METHUEN "MAN IN THE QUE" '29
BENN "KIF" '29 & MORE
TEY, JOSEPHINE--[3][5][18][29][31]MYS--
DAVIES "BRAT FARRAR" '49
DAVIES "MISS PYM DISPOSES" '46 & MORE

MACKINTOSH, MAY
ROSS, REGINA--[3][29]MYS--
MacD "DEVIL DANCES FOR GOLD" '76
AV "FACE OF DANGER" '82 & MORE

MACKLEWORTH, RONALD W.
MACKLEWORTH, R.W.--[1]

MACKSEY, KENNETH J.
MACKSEY, [MAJOR] K.J.--[1]ENGLISH

MACKWORTH, CECILY
RHIANNON--[1]WELSH

MACLAINE, SHIRLEY
BEATY, SHIRLEY MACLEAN--[31]

MACLANE, MARY
[THE] BUTTE BASHKIRTEFF--[1]CANADIAN

MACLAREN, JAMES PATERSON
MEDICUS--[8]

MACLEAN, ALISTAIR STUART
STUART, IAN--[2][3][18][33]MYS--
COLLINS "DARK CRUSADER" '61
COLLINS "SATAN BUG" '62

MACLEAN, ANNE & JILL
MACLEAN, JAN--[9][21]ROM--
"AN ISLAND LOVING"
"WHITE FIRE" & 4 MORE

MACLEAN, CHARLES
KONRAD, JAMES--[1][3][31]MYS--
SPHERE "TARGET ADMIN" '77

MACLEAN, CHARLES AGNEW
CARTER, NICHOLAS--[3]MYS,HP--

MACLEAN, DONALD DUART
FRAZER, MARK PETRIVICH--[1][31]ENGLISH

MACLEAN, ELIZABETH
ROLAND, BETTY--[13]AUSTRALIAN

MACLEAN, JILL
FIELD, SANDRA--[9][26]ROM--
HARL "WALK BY MY SIDE"
HARL "OUT OF WEDLOCK" & MORE
HALEY, JOCELYN--[9][26]ROM--
HARL "LOVE WILD & FREE"
HARL "WINDS OF DESIRE" & OTHERS

MACLEAN, JOHN
RUSTLER, ROBIN--[1]SCOTTISH

MACLEAN, KATHERINE
DYE, CHARLES--[2][23][31]EX-HUSBAND'S NAME--
"SYNDROME JOHNNY" '51
"MAN WHO STALKED STARS"
MORRIS, G.A.--[1]

MACLEAN, REZIN DONALD
MACLEAN, R.D.--[1]AMERICAN

MACLEOD, CHARLOTTE [M.H.]
CRAIG, ALISA--[18][31][33][34]MYS--
AV 70331 "GRUBSTAKERS MOVE A MOUNTAIN" '81 & MORE
HUGHES, MATILDA--[1][18][31][33]--
"FOOD OF LOVE"
"HEADLINES FOR CAROLINE"

MACLEOD, ELLEN JANE [A]
ANDERSON, ELLA--[1][8][33]SCOTTISH

MACLEOD, JEAN S.
AIRLIE, CATHERINE--[9][21][22][26][31]ROM--
"RED LOTUS"
"MOUNTAIN OF STARS" & MORE

MACLEOD, JOSEPH [T.G.]
DRINAN, ADAM--[1][22][31]SCOTTISH

MACLEOD, MEVROUW SOPHIA
SOPHIA, MEVROUW--[1]SCOTTISH

MACLEOD, ROBERT
KNOX, BILL--[8]

MACLEOD, RUTH
LOWRY, NAN--[1][21]ROM--
"CRYSTAL MANNING, MATERNITY NURSE"

MACMANUS, ANNA JOHNSTON
CARBERY, ETHNA--[8]

MACMANUS, SEUMAS
MAC--[1][33]IRISH
MACMANUS, JAMES--[1][33]IRISH

MACMANUS, YVONNE
CHRISTIAN, PAULA--V.BERCH-LESBIANA/ CNTRCLTR, BAE 22--
CREST 267 "EDGE OF TWILIGHT" '59
WILKINSON, L.--[1]--
BC 7355 "HIGH-FLYING HOOKERS"
WILKINSON, LEE--[1][26]ROM--
HARL "MOTIVE FOR MARRIAGE
WILKINSON, LYDIA--V. BERCH-LESBIANA/ CNTRCLTR, BAE 22, P5

MACMILLAN, CECILE
GILMORE, CECILE--[1][31]

MACMILLAN, GEORGINA F.
FITZGERALD, ENA--[1]ENGLISH

MACMILLIAN, DOUGLAS
CARY, D.M.--[1][8]ENGLISH

MACMULLAN, CHARLES W.K.
MUNRO, C.K.--[8]

MACNIE, JOHN
THIUSEN, ISMAR--[1][2][11][23]AMERICAN/SF--

MACNIECE, LOUIS
MALONE, LOUIS--[8]

MACONACHIE, WILLIAM
CARSON, BART--[34]MYS--
HAM STFFD "DAMES SCARE EASY" '52
HAM STFFD "CUBAN HEEL" '53 & 15 MORE
HARRAGAN, STEVE--[34]MYS,HP--
UNIV "CARNEY'S BURLESQUE"
UNIV "KISS OF THE DAMNED"
UNIV "SIDESHOW GIRL"
UNIV "SIN IS A REDHEAD"
UNIV "CUBAN HEEL"
STAHL, RAY--[34]MYS,HP--
HAM STFFD "DEATH STALKS THE WILD GOOSE" '52
HAM STFFD "MURDER MAYHEM" '52

MACOWEN, ARTHUR H.
WHEELER, CHRIS--[1]

MACPEEK, WALTER G.
JUMPP, HUGO--[1][31][33]

MACPHAIL, JAMES A.
CROCKETT, JAMES--W/CORNELIA WARRINER, [1][3][22]MYS--
CROWN "LULLABY WITH LUGERS" '46

MACPHERSON, ALPIN
WILD SCOTCHMAN, THE--[13]AUSTRALIAN

MACPHERSON, JESSIE INGRAM
KENNIE, JESSIE--[1][8]SCOTTISH

MACPHERSON, MRS. A.D.L.
SEALE, SARA--[1][9][21]ROM--
"GENTLE PRISONER"
"FORBIDDEN ISLAND" & MORE

MACPHERSON, THOMAS GEORGE
PARSONS, TOM--[8][22][32][33]ENGLISH/MYS--
AHMM "A KILLING IN REAL ESTATE" NOV '59

MACQUARRIE, HECTOR
CAMERON, HECTOR--[8]

MACQUEEN, JAMES WILLIAM
EDWARDS, JAMES G.--[1][3][22]MYS--
DBLDY "PRIVATE PAVILION" '35
DBLDY "MURDER AT LEISURE" '37 & 6 MORE
MCHUGH, JAY--[1][22]AMERICAN/MYS--

MACRAE, DONALD G.
CAMPBELL, CLIVE--[1][22][31]SCOTTISH-ENGLISH

MACRORY, PATRICK
GREER, PATRICK--[8]

MACSHANE, MARY
OWEN, MARGO--[9]ROM

MACTAVISH, GEORGE
MACPHERSON, DONALD--[23]CANADIAN/SF--
"GO HOME UNICORN" '35, ?? UNCONFIRMED ??

MACVEAN, PHYLLIS
GREAVES, GILLIAN--[8]
HAMBLEDON, PHYLLIS--[1][3][40]MYS--
HALE "MURDER'S NO PICNIC" '61
HALE "DEATH OF AN UNCLE" '62 & MORE
VANE, PHILLIPPA--[3]MYS--
HAMM "PRIORITY FOR DEATH' '48
HAMM "HERE IS THE EVIDENCE" '50

MADDEN, EDWARD STANISLAUS
MADDEN, E.S.--[36]MYS--
HM "CRAIG'S SPUR" '61

MADDEN, JERRY DAVID
TRAVIS, JACK--[1]ENGLISH

MADDEN, T.E.
FIELD OFFICER--[1]ENGLISH

MADDISON, ANGELA MARY
BANNER, ANGELA--[1][8][25][31][33]ENGLISH

MADDOX, AUSTIN
MATTOX, AUSTIN--[32]MYS--
AHMM "HIPSTER WITH A MESSAGE" JAN '68
MSMM "MEASURE FOUR" AUG '69

MADEIRA, ANTONIO
BRANQUIRHO DA FONSECA, A.--[1]PORTUGUESE

MADEL, WALTER
MARL, WALTER DEN--[39]GERMAN

MADETOJA, ONERVA
O'NERVA, L.--[1]FINNISH

MADEVILLE, JIM
HILD, JACK--[34]MYS,HP--
GE 'SOB's':
"BARRABUS FALLOUT" '89

MADGETT, NAOMI LONG
LONG, NAOMI CORNELIA--[1]AMERICAN
WITHERSPOON, NAOMI LONG--[1]AMERICAN

MADHUBUTI, HAKI R.
LEE, DON L.--[31]

MADISON, JOHN RODRIGO
DOS--[1]
DOS PASSOS, JOHN--[1]
JACK--[1]

MADISON, THOMAS [A]
CAMPBELL, LUKE--[1]

MADLEE, DOROTHY [H]
HAYNES, ANNE--[1][22][31]AMERICAN
ROGERS, WADE--[1][22]AMERICAN

MADSEN, AXEL
BRION, GUY--[1][31]DANISH

MADSEN, BORGE
BAXTER, PAUL--[29]MYS--
"RUBINER DER DRAEBTE" '38
"RUBINER SOM DODADE" '42
BORG, TONY--[37]DANISH/MYS
BORG, TONNY--[29]MYS
BUCHANAN, CARL--[29]MYS--
NYCK 106 "OSAMJANS HUS" '42
BURNDALE, TOM--[29]MYS
BUTLER, ANTHONY--[29]MYS--
"DEN SYNGENDE DOLK" '38
"SJUNGANDE DOLKEN" '43
BUTLER, JOHN--[29]MYS
DEPSTER, LUIS--[29]MYS
HAMPTON, JOHN--[29]MYS
HUXLEY, ALLAN--[29]MYS
LISTER, PAUL--[29]MYS

MADSEN, [MARK] HUNTER
GILRAY, JAMES--[31]

MAENCHEN, OTTO JOHN
HELFEN, OTTO J. MAENCHEN--[31]

MAES-JELINK, HENA
JELINEK, HENA M.--[31]

MAGEE, JAMES
TAYLOR, JOHN--[1][8]IRISH

MAGEE, WILLIAM K.
EGLINTON, JOHN--[1][22]IRISH

MAGENHEIMER, CATHRYN C.
MAGENHEIMER, KAY--[8]

MAGGIO, ROSALIE
KOSKENMAKI, ROSALIE--[31]

MAGLIORE, CLEMENT
SAINT ANDE, MAGLIORE--[1] HAITIAN

MAGNER, LAURA
PARRIS, LAURA--[9][21][26]ROM--
HARL 60 "HIGH VALLEY OF THE SUN"

MAGNUS-ALLCROFT, PHILLIP
MAGNUS, PHILIP--[1][22][31]ENGLISH

MAGNUSDOTTIR, MAGNEA
KLEIFUM, [FRA] MAGNEA--[1]ICELANDIC

MAGNUSSON, GUOMUNDUR
TRAUSTI, JON--[1]ICELANDIC

MAGON, JYMN
TALLIS, ROBYN--[7]SF,HP--
IVY "PLANET BUILDERS #8" '89

MAGOON, MARIAN AUSTIN
MAGOON, CAREY--W/ELIZABETH CAREY,
[1][3][22]MYS--
FARRAR "I SMELL THE DEAD" '43

MAGOUN, FREDERICK ALEX.
WRIGHT, AMOS--[22]AMERICAN
WRIGHT, ANSON--[1]AMERICAN

MAGRAW, BEATRICE IRENE
PADESON, MARY--[1]

MAGRILL, DAVID S.
DALHEATH, DAVID--[8]

MAGRUDER, JULIA
KERR, SHERRILL--[1]

MAGUIRE, H.N.
HEGMUN, IRA--[1]

MAGUIRE, ROBERT A.J.
TAAFFE, MICHAEL--[1][8][22]ENGLISH

MAGYARI, KRIEMHILD
HILDEBRANDT, KRIEMHILD--[39]GERMAN

MAHAFFEY, BEA
BELL, GEORGE--W/RAY PALMER,[2]

MAHER, RAMONA
MAYER, AHGATHA--[1]AMERICAN

MAHMUD, MUSTAFA
MAHMOUD, MOUSTAFFA--[23] EGYPTIAN/SF

MAHN, ANNY
WOTHE, ANNY--[39]GERMAN

MAHN, KLAUS
MAHR, KURT--[7][39]GERMAN/SF--
ACE 'PERRY RHODAN' SERIES #s: 61, 64,
65, 71, 72, 74, 85, 94, 95, 98, 100,
105, 110, 114, 119, 123, 128 & 133
MAILER, CECIL O.--[39]GERMAN/SF

MAHN, TRAUTE
CAMERON, JOHN--[39]GERMAN/MYS/HOR,HP
CORNER, CLIFF--[39]GERMAN/MYS/HOR,HP
LAMONT, ROBERT--[39]GERMAN/HOR,HP
LAROCHE, REBECCA--[39]GERMAN/MYS/HOR
ROBINSON, KAY--[39]GERMAN/MYS/HOR
UHL, YVONNE--[39]GERMAN/MYS/HOR

MAHNER-MONS, EMMA
NUSS, EMMA--[39]GERMAN
NUSS, EMMERICH--[39]GERMAN

MAHNER-MONS, HANS
POSSENDORF, HANS--[2][3][29][39]
[40]GERMAN/MYS--
HUTCH "THE 77TH DAY" '37
"GERBERGASSE" '49 & 6 OTHERS

MAHONEY, DAVID
ALLEN, DAVE--[8][32]MYS--
LM "THE CAR AHEAD" DEC '78

MAHONEY, ELIZABETH
MARA, THALIA--[1]

MAHONEY, IRENE
SIMON, ANGELA--[9]ROM

MAHONY, ELIZABETH WINTHRP
WINTHROP, ELIZABETH--[1][7][33]SF--
HOLIDAY HOUSE "CASTLE IN THE ATTIC" '85

MAHONY, MARTIN FRANCIS
CATLYNE, MR. Q.C.--[1]
STRADLING, MATTHEW--[1]

MAHONY, PATRICK
O'MAHONY, PATRICK--[1]

MAHR, YVONNE
HOFMANN, JO--[40]GERMAN/MYS--
"CHERRY BRANDY MIT CHEMIE, CHERIE" '84

MAHRLEIN, GOTTLIEB
MUNRO, ARN--[39]GERMAN/SF

MAIDEN, CECIL
CECIL, EDWARD--[8]

MAIER, MANFRED
MAI, MANFRED--[39]GERMAN/JUV

MAIGROT, EMILE
HENRIOT, EMILE--[1][22]FRENCH

MAINPRIZE, DON[ALD C.]
ROCK, RICHARD--[1][22]AMERICAN

MAINWARING, DANIEL [G.H.]
HOMES, GEOFFREY--[3][5][18][31]MYS--
MRW "BUILD MY GALLOWS HIGH" '46
"FORTY WHACKS" '41 & MORE

MAIR, GEORGE B.
BOK, KOOSHTI--[1]SCOTTISH
MACDOUALL, ROBERTSON--[1][22]

MAIR, GEORGE HENRY
MAIR, G.H.--[1]

MAIS, STUART PETRE
MAIS, S.P.B.--[1]ENGLISH

MAISELS, MAXINE S.
AMISHAE-MAISELS, ZIVA--[1][31]AMERICAN

MAISELS, MISHA
AMISHAE, M.H.--[1]AMERICAN

MAISON, MARGARET M.B.
CLARE, MARGARET--[1][22][31]ENGLISH

MAITLAND, E.
AINSLE, HERBERT--[1]

MAITLAND, T.G. DOWLING
CHANDOS, HERBERT--[1]
GALE, H. WINTER--[1]
MONCK, TRISTAM K.--[1]

MAIZEL, CLARICE M.
MAIZEL, C.L.--[1][22][33]ENGLISH
MAIZEL, LEAH--[1][8][22]ENGLISH

MAJESKI, WILLIAM [BILL]
FREDERICKS, VIC--[1]AMERICAN, HP

MAJOR, ALAN P.
JOHN, DANE--[1][31]

MAJOR, AUSTIN SMALL
SMALL, AUSTIN J.--[7][23]SF--
NAME LEGALLY CHANGED TO "SMALL"

MAJOR, CHARLES
CASKODEN, [SIR] EDWIN--[1][22]AMERICAN

MAJOR, GERALDINE H.
MAJOR, GERRI--[1][31]

MAJOR, J.D.
HAYWARD, DAGNEY--[1][34]MYS--
AMALG "SECRET OF THE SILENT CITY" '11
MAJOR, DAGNEY--[1]

MAKEMSON, DON E.
WORCESTER, DONALD E.--[1]

MAKEPEACE-LOTT, STANLEY
LOTT, S. MAKEPEACE--[23]ENGLISH/SF--
"VENUS" '56

MAKGILL, [SIR] GEORGE
GRANT, FRANCIS--[1]
WAITE, VICTOR--[1]

MALACRIDA, MARCHESE
PIERMARINI--[1]ITALIAN

MALAN, RENATA MARCO
MARK ALAN, ROY--[1]ITALIAN

MALCOLM, AILEEN
MALCOLM, ALEEN--[9][26]ROM--
"THE TAMING"
"CHILDREN OF THE MIST" & 4 MORE

MALCOLM, ANTHEA
GRANT, ANNA--[26]ROM--
"DARK ANGEL"

MALCOLM, DONALD
MALCOLM, ROY--W/A.E. ROY,[2]

MALCOLM, JANE
GENTRY, JANE--[9][21][26]ROM--
"LIGHTNING STRIKES TWICE"
"A TASTE OF HONEY"

MALEK, DOREEN OWENS
MORGAN, FAYE--[9][21][26]ROM--
"TRIAL BY FIRE"

MALERICH, EDWARD P.
EASTON, EDWARD--[7][23][31]SF--
MANOR "MISCAST GENTLEMAN" '78
MANOR "PIRATE OF HITCHFIELD" '78

MALES, CAROLYN
HOWARD, ALYSSA--W/RUTH GLICK, LOUISE
TITCHENER & EILEEN BUCKHOLTZ,[9][21]ROM--
RICHARDS, CLARE--W/LOUISE TITCHENER,
[9][21][26]ROM--
"RENAISSANCE SUMMER"
RICHMOND, CLARE--W/LOUISE TITCHENER,
[9][21][26]ROM--
"PIRATE'S LEGACY"
"HAWAIIAN HEAT" & MORE

MALINOVSKY, ALEXANDER
BOGDANOV, ALEXANDER--[1][2][22][23]
RUSSIAN/SF--

MALINS, PENELOPE
HOBHOUSE, PENELOPE--[31]

MALKIND, MARGARET
NEVINS, KATE--[9][21][26]ROM--
"MIDSUMMER MAGIC"
"VENETIAN SUNRISE" & MORE

MALLALIEU, J.P.W.
PIED PIPER, THE--[8]

MALLARDI, BILL
BOWERS, BILL--W/WILLIAM L. BOWERS,[7]SF-

MALLESON, LUCY BEATRICE
EGERTON, LUCY--[1][31]
GILBERT, ANTHONY--[2][3][5][18][22][29][32]MYS--NVLS '30s-70s
EQMM "YOU CAN'T HANG TWICE" NOV '46
EQMM "WHO CARES ABOUT AN OLD WOMAN" OCT '68
KEITH, J. KILMENY--[3][18][31]MYS--
COLLINS "MAN WHO WAS LONDON" '25
COLLINS "SWORD OF HARLEQUIN" '27
MEREDITH, ANNE--[3][18][29]MYS--
COLLINS "PORTRAIT OF A MURDERER" '33
COLLINS "THREE-A-PENNY" '40

MALLETTE, GERTRUDE ETHEL
GREGG, ALAN--[1]
LARSSEN, PEDAR--[1]

MALLOCK, WILLIAM H.
MALLOCK, W.H.--[1]
MOORE, WENTWORTH--[1]

MALLOWAN, MRS. MAX
CHRISTIE, AGATHA--[21]ROM/MYS

MALMBERG, ARNE
STIGSON, ARNE--[29]MYS, BONNIER--
BONNIER "SPEL OVER DOD LINJE" '55
BONNIER "DEN RESANDES ENSAK" '57
BONNIER "MORD, MAJOR" '58

MALMBERG, CARL
TRENT, TIMOTHY--[3][33]MYS--
GODWIN "NIGHT BOAT" '34
GODWIN "ALL DAMES ARE DYNAMITE" '35
GODWIN "FALL GUY" '36

MALONE, NOLA LANGNER
LANGNER, NOLA--[31]JUV--
MacM "A HOME" '88

MALONEY, F.J. TERENCE
RUBIOS, JOSE--[1][2]
TERRY--[1][2]

MALONEY, RALPH LISTON
LISTON, JACK--[1][22][33]AMERICAN

MALRAUX, CLARA GOLDSCHMID
GOLDSCHMIDT, CLARA MALR.--[31]

MALRAUX, [G] ANDRE
BERGER, [COL.] A.--[1][31]

MALVERN, GLADYS
CORBIN, SABRA LEE--[1][31][33]
VON KLOPP, VAHRAH--[1][33]

MALVILLE, JOHN MCKIM
MALVILLE, KIM--[1]

MALY, ANTON JOHANN
STORR, ROBERT--[39]GERMAN

MALZBERG, BARRY [N]
BARRY, MIKE--[2][3][4][18][23][31]MYS/SF--
BERK "BAY PROWLER" '73
BERK "HAVANA HIT" '74 & 12 MORE
DI NATALE, FRANCINE--[2][4][14][31]ADULT--
OLYM "THE CIRCLE" '69
DUMAS, CLAUDINE--[2][4][18][31]ADULT--
MIDWD "DIARY OF A PARISIAN CHAMBERMAID" '69
JOHNSON, M.L.--[2][4]
JOHNSON, MEL--[2][4][18][23][31]MYS/SF--
KELLER, B.L.--ROBERT BENOIT--
FSF "COLD DEBT" EARLY '80s

MALZBERG, BARRY [N] [CONT]
LEE, HOWARD--[2][4]
MASON, LEE W.--[2][3][4][18][29]MYS/SF--
PLAYBOY "LADY OF A THOUSAND SORROWS" '77
O'DONNELL, K.M.--[4][18][23]SF--
LAN 74-546 "EMPTY PEOPLE" '69
AV 2394 "UNIVERSE DAY" '71 & MORE
SCHAEFFER, ROBIN--[1][2]
WATKINS, GERROLD--[2][4][14]ADULT--
OLYM TC#474 "A BED OF MONEY" '69
OLYM TC#483 "ART OF THE FUGUE" '70
WILLIAMS, JOHN BARRY--W/JOHN LUTZ & BILL PRONZINI, PRONZINI LTR,[32]MYS--
AHMM "CHEESEBURGER" OCT '78

MAMIN, DMITRI N.
MAMIN, SIBERIAK--[1]
SIBIRIAK--[1]

MAN, PITER
MANN, PETER--[7]SF--
LEIS "ULTIMATUM: PU 94" '77

MAN-SHU, SU
CHIEN, SU--[22]CHINESE

MANCE, ELIZABETH HOPE
HOPE, ELIZABETH--[1]

MANCHEE, CAROL M.
COLE, CAROL CASSIDY--[1]

MAND, EWALD
KALMUS, AIN--[22][31]ESTONIAN-AMERICAN

MANDAN, ANTONIO
MANDAN DIAZ, ANTONELLA--[1] ITALIAN

MANDEL, LEO N.
BIRD, AL--W/PHILLIP FINCH,[3]MYS--
COWARD "MURDER SO REAL" '78
DALMAS, JOHN--[1]

MANDEL, NAUM M.
KORZHAVIN, N.--[1]

MANDELKORN, EUGENIA M.
MILLER, EUGENIA--[1][22]AMERICAN

MANDELL, FRAN GARE
GARE, FRAN--[31]

MANDER, M. ROSALIE G.G.
GRYLLS, ROSALIE GLYNN--[7]SF--
NON-FICT - "MARY SHELLY: A BIO" '38

MANDEVILLE, FRANCINE
CHRISTOPHER, FRANCINE--[9][21][26]ROM--
"HOLD ON TO FOREVER"
"SWEET TOMORROWS"

MANDL, HARALD
MANDER, MATTHIAS--[39]GERMAN

MANDT, GEORGE
MEINHARDT, PETER--[39]GERMAN

MANES, STEPHEN
MURCH, MEL--W/PAUL SOMERSON,[1]
MURCH, MEL & WARD STARR--[33]
PEMSTEEN, HANS--[1][33]
STARR, WARD--W/PAUL SOMERSON,[1]
STARR, WARD & MEL MURCH--[33]
STEPHENSEN, A.M.--[1][33]

MANFRED, FREDERICK [F]
FEIKEMA, FEIKE--[8][28][31]--
WEBB "THE GOLDEN BOWL" '44

MANGAN, [J.J] SHERRY
NIALL, SEAN--[1]

MANGIONE, GERLANDO
MANGIONE, JERRE--[31]

MANGRUM, VALERIE
ELLIS, PATRICIA--[21][26]ROM--
"IPLLOW TALK"
"SWEET PROTECTOR" & 3 MORE

MANJIRO, HASEGAWA
NYOZEKAN, HASEGAWA--[22]JAPANESE

MANJON-ALONSO, MARIA T.
MANJON, MAITE--[1]

MANKOWSKA, JOYCE KELLS M.
BATTEN, JOYCE MORTIMER--[1][22][31]ENGLISH

MANLEY, MARY
EGVINARDUS--[2][7]SF,SP--

MANLEY, RUTH RODNEY KING
KING, RUTH RODNEY--[1][31]

MANLEY-TUCKER, AUDRIE
HOWARD, LINDEN--[1][3][9]MYS--
ST. MARTINS "FOXGLOVE COUNTRY" '77
"DEVIL'S LADY" '80

MANN, EDWARD BEVERLY
FIELD, PETER--[8][19][28]WEST,HP--
MRW "BOSS OF LAZY 9" '36
MANN, E.B.--[8][28]WEST--
LION 27 "DEAD MAN'S GORGE" '50 & MORE
NEBAN, HUGH--[3]MYS--
LANE "CRUCIBLE OF COURAGE" '36
STRONG, ZACHARY--[8][28]WEST--
MRW "MESA GANG" '40
SWAN "OUTLAWS AGAINST THE LAW-BADGE" '47

MANN, GEORGE PAUL
HEGGY, JOE P.--[34]MYS,HP--
HAM STAFF "TROUBLE WITH WOMEN" '54
KIRBY, ARTHUR--[34]MYS,HP--
AMALG "MAN ON THE RUN" '60
MACLEAN, ARTHUR--W/C.P. WEBB,[34]MYS--
AMALG "REDHEAD FOR DANGER" '58
MACLEAN, ARTHUR--W/E.C. TUBB,[34]MYS--
AMALG "TOUCH OF EVIL" '59
MACLEAN, ARTHUR--[34]MYS--
AMALG "BROKEN TOY" '56
AMALG "CANVAS JUNGLE" '56 & 12 MORE
REID, DESMOND--W/A. CAHILL & HOWARD BAKER,[34]MYS,HP--
AMALG "BULLETS ARE TRUMPS" '53
REID, DESMOND--W/A.L. MARTIN,[34]MYS,HP--
AMALG "ROADHOUSE GIRL" '57
REID, DESMOND--W/ANTHONY DOUSE & HOWARD BAKER,[34]MYS,HP--
AMALG "DEAD ON CUE" '62
REID, DESMOND--W/BRIAN MCARDLE,[34]MYS,HP--
AMALG "FLASHPOINT FOR TREASON" '57
REID, DESMOND--W/EDDIE PLAYER,[34]MYS,HP--
AMALG "MURDER MADE EASY" '60
REID, DESMOND--W/FRANK LAMBE,[1][34]MYS,HP--
AMALG "STAND-IN FOR MURDER" '57
REID, DESMOND--W/GEORGE HEBER,[34]MYS,HP--
AMALG "STATE OF FEAR" '61
REID, DESMOND--W/GORDON SOWMAN,[34]MYS,HP--
AMALG "HOMICIDE BLUES" '57

MANN, GEORGE PAUL [CONT]
REID, DESMOND--W/JOHN [F] BURKE,[34]MYS,HP--
AMALG "HIGH HEELS & HOMICIDE" '58
REID, DESMOND--W/LEE ROBERTS,[34]MYS,HP--
AMALG "VICTIM UNKNOWN" '57
REID, DESMOND--W/NOEL BROWNE,[34]MYS,HP--
AMALG "SHOWDOWN IN SYDNEY" '59
REID, DESMOND--W/ROSAMOND M. STORY,[34]MYS,HP--
AMALG "WITCH-HUNT!" '60
REID, DESMOND--W/VIC J. HANSON & W.H. BAKER,[34]MYS,HP--
AMALG "DEATH ON A HIGH NOTE" '62
SCHWARZ, BRUNO--[8][34]MYS--
HAM - 18 'FOREIGN LEGION' NOVELS '52-5
WILLIAMS, RICHARD--W/HOWARD BAKER, BOB HOPKINS, & MAX MARQUIS,[34]MYS,HP--
AMALG "MURDER BY PROXY" '63

MANN, JAMES ANTHONY
MANN, JIM--[7]SF--
NON-FICT

MANN, MARGARET BOYER
PENDLETON, GRACE--[21][26]ROM--
"HEARTSTRINGS"

MANN, PATRICK
WALLER, LESLIE--J. BREEN--
EQMM "THE RESTLESS ONES" OCT '60

MANNERS, CAROLE
CLAREMONT, RUTH--W/ROSEMARY CRESSWELL, [34][36]AUSTRALIAN/MYS--
MCPHEE "TO SLEEP, TO DIE" '89

MANNES, MARYA
SEC--[8][22]AMERICAN

MANNETTI, LISA
KANE, L.A.--[31][33]

MANNING, ADELAIDE [F.O]
COLES, MANNING--W/CYRIL H. COLES, [3][5][22]ENGLISH/MYS--
26 NOVELS '40-63
GAITE, FRANCIS--W/CYRIL H. COLES, [2][3][5][22]MYS--
HODDER "BRIEF CANDLES" '54 & 4 MORE

MANNING, BRUCE & MRS.
BRISTOW, GWEN--[3][5]MYS--
ML "INVISIBLE HOST" '30
ML "GUTENBERG MURDERS" '31 & MORE

MANNING, FREDERIC
PRIVATE 19022--[1]

MANNING, GWEN
BRISTOW, GWEN--[1]

MANNING, MARIE
FAIRFAX, BEATRICE--W/MARION C. MCCARROLL,[31]

MANNING, ROSEMARY JOY
DAVYS, SARAH--[1][31]AMERICAN
VOYLE, MARY--[1][22][31]AMERICAN

MANNING, WILLIAM HENRY
DEFOREST, BARRY--[1]
EDWARDS, WARREN--[1]
HALLIDAY, BEN--[1]
HOYT, W.M.--[1]
INMAN, ROBERT RANDOLPH--[1]
KENT, WARREN F.--[1]
PIERCE, JO--[1]
SR. VRAIN, [MAJ.] E.L.--[1]

MANNING, WILLIAM HENRY [CONT]
WALTERS, WARREN--[1]
WARING, MARCUS H.--[1]
WARREN, HUGH--[1]
WARREN, J.T.--[1]
WARREN, NED--[1]
WARREN, V.S.--[1]
WILTON, [CAPT.] MARK--[1]

MANNOCK, LAURA
ADAIR, SALLY--[8]
MANNOCK, JENNIFER--[8]
WHETTER, LAURA--[8]

MANNON, MARTHA & MARY E.
MANNON, M.M.--[1][3][22]MYS--
BOBBS "HERE LIES BLOOD" '42 & 2 MORE

MANOFF, RUTH
MANNING, JUNE--V. BERCH-LESBIANA/
CNTRCLTR, BAE 22, P5

MANSELL, MRS. C.B.
ST. CLAIR, EVERETT--[8]

MANSFIELD, HARRY O.
BELL, THORNTON--[2]SF,SP
BRETT, LEO--[2]SF,SP
NOBEL, PHIL--[2]SF, SP
ROLANT, RENE--[2]SF,SP
TATE, ROBIN--[2]SF, SP
TORRO, PEL--[2]SF, SP

MANSFIELD, KATHERINE
BEAUCHAMP, KATHLEEN--[9]ROM

MANSS, GISELA
MENZ, GISELA--[39]GERMAN/JUV

MANTINBAND, JAMES M.
KEYSTONE, OLIVER--[1][3][22]MYS--
PHOENIX "MAJOR CRIME" '48
PHOENIX "DEEP AS THE GRAVE" '50
PHOENIX "ARSENIC FOR THE TEACHER" '50

MANTLE, WINIFRED LANGFORD
FELLOWES, ANNE--[1][22][31]ENGLISH
LANG, FRANCES--[21][22][31]ENGLISH/ROM--
"STRANGER AT THE GATE"
"THE MARQUIS' MARRIAGE"
LANGFORD, JANE--[1][22][31]ENGLISH
MANTLE, W.--[21]ENGLISH/ROM

MANTLING, RUNE
BADGER, WAYNE--[29]MYS
BANNISTER, WYATT--W/GUNNAR JANSSON,[29]MYS--
"STRIDEN OM FLYING N' " '61

MANUEL, GEORGE
GEMEL--[1]

MANUS, JAYE W.
LYNN, SHERYL--[10][26]ROM--
"DOUBLE VISION"
"DEADLY DEVOTION"

MANVILLE, WILLIAM HENRY
FRIDAY, BILL [B]--V. BERCH, LESBIANA/
CNTRCLTR, BAE 22, P5--
BB 3919 "I LOVE YOU ALICE B TOKLAS" '68
MANVILLE, W.H.--[1]
WILLIAMS, HENRY--[1][34]MYS--
DELL "HOW TO MURDER YOUR WIFE" '65

MANY, SETH E[DWARDS]
NO, DR.--[1][31]

MANYASE, LENCHMAN T.
JOLI-OX--[1]

MAPES, VICTOR
POST, MAVERIC--[1]
SHARP, SIDNEY--[1]

MAPLES, EVELYN LUCILLE
DALBY, B.J.--[1]

MARAGAKIS, HELEN
CARR, ELENI--[9][21][26]ROM--
"FOREVER BOND"
"AND THEN THERE WAS YOU" & MORE
CARRAS, HELEN--[9][21][26]ROM--
"PASSION'S ROGUE"
"FAIR WINDS"
CARTER, HELEN--[9][21][26]ROM--
"TOUCHED BY LIGHTNING"
"CHANGE OF HEART" & 4 MORE

MARBERRY, M.M.
BREWER, JORDAN--[3]MYS--
BANNER B50-103 "GET DUMM!" '67

MARBLE, HARRIET CLEMENT
JONES, HARRIET--[1][31]

MARCEL, EUGENE
PREVOST, MARCEL--[1]

MARCHAND, FIRMIN PIERRE
MARSH, PETER--JEAN F. LE DEIST-BAE 18,[1]--
SWIFT "DEVIL'S DAUGHTER" '42

MARCHANT, ANYDA
ALDRIDGE, SARAH--[31]

MARCHANT, ELIZABETH
MARCHANT, BESSIE--B&M COLL #49, P29,ENGLISH--
BOYS & GIRLS ADVENTURE 1889-42

MARCHANT, ELLA
TWO WOMEN OF THE WEST--W/ALICE JONES,[2]

MARCHANT, REX ALAN
MARCHANT, R.A.--[1]

MARCHIONI, MARK
MARCONETTE--[2][11]

MARCUS, ANNE M.
MULKEEN, ANNE--[1]

MARCZIK, EDELTRUD
MARZIK, TRUDE--[39]GERMAN

MARDICKE, FRITZ
MARKEN, WOLFGANG--[39]GERMAN
OSTEN, LUDWIG--[39]GERMAN
SPIELMANN, WERNER--[39]GERMAN

MARDON, ALLAN
MARDON, DEIRDRE--[21][26]ROM--7 NOVELS

MAREK, KURT WILLI
CERAM, C.E.--[2][22]GERMAN
CERAM, C.W.--[31][39]GERMAN

MARGERISON, JOHN S.
GREY, GILBERT--[1]
MELLALIEU, JAMES S.--[1]

MARGL, LUDWIG
FORSTNER, LUDWIG--[39]GERMAN

MARGOLIS, SUSANNA
GOWAR, ANTONIO--W/JUDITH DUNFORD,[1][31]

MARGOLIS, VIVIENNE
EISNER, VIVIENNE--[31][33]

MARHEINEKE, MARIA
MARNEK, M.--[39]GERMAN

MARIA DEL REY, SISTER
HAGAR, GEORGE--[31]

MARIE, GERALDINE
CHRISTIE, MARIE--[33]

MARIE-ANDRE DU SC, SISTER
DORGE, JEANNE EMILE MARIE--[31]

MARIN, RICHARD ANTONY
CHEECH--[31]

MARINO, CAROLYN FITCH
TRACY, SUSAN--[1]

MARION, FREIDA
KENT, ARDEN--[1][31]
VON CASTELHUN, FRIEDL--[1]

MARITANO, ADELE
CONVERSE, JANE--[9][21][26]ROM--
"MOONLIT PATH"
"HEARTSTORM" & MORE

MARITANO, ADELE
MARTIN, KAY--V. BERCH-LESBIANA/
CNTRCLTR, BAE 22,[9]ADULT--
"VANESSA"
HILL 138 "WHISPERED SEX" '60
HILL 158 "A TASTE OF PASSION" '60
BERK G460 "ON EASY TERMS" '60
HILL 190 "PAYMENT IN SIN" '61
AV T495 "SUBURBAN WIFE" '61
PYR F701 "CRY SHAME!" '62
PYR F750 "THE DIVORCEES" '62
BELM 90-274 "NYMPH IN SUBURBIA" '63
MacF 50-163 "BACHELOR GIRL" '63

MARITANO, ADELE & GALE
GALE, ADELA--[3][9][21][26]MYS/ROM--
SIGN "GODDESS OF TERROR" '67
SIGN "ANGEL AMONG WITCHES" '69
SIGN "HARVEST OF TERROR" '69

MARITZ, MAGDALENA P.
MARITZ, EMPIE--[1]

MARK, DAVIS
SARAZEN, NICHOLAS--W/RICK COOPER,[7]SF/HOR--
PINN "FAMILY REUNION" '90

MARK, JANET MARJORIE
MARK, JAN--[31] ADULT--
CAPE "ZENO WAS HERE" '87
JUV NOVELS '76-93

MARK, PAULINE [D]
MARK, POLLY--[1][33]

MARKISH, DAVID
MAGUEN, DAVID--[1]

MARKLAND, RUSSELL
INGERSLEY, R.M.--[1]

MARKO, ZEKIAL
TRINIAN, JOHN--[3]MYS--
PYR G548 "THE BIG GRAB" '60
GM 1000 "NORTH BEACH GIRL" '60
GM 1104 "THE SAVAGE BREAST" '61
ACE F107 "SCRATCH A THIEF" '61
PYR F712 "HOUSE OF EVIL" '62
LAN 72-678 "A GAME OF FLESH" '63
GM K1449 "SANDAL ON THE SAND" '64

MARKOV, GEORGII IVANOV
ST. GEORGE, DAVID--W/DAVID A. PHILLIPS,
[1][7]SF--
SECKER "RIGHT HONORABLE CHIMPANZEE" '78

MARKOVICH, MARIA ALEXAND.
VOVCHOK, MARKO--[22]RUSSIAN

MARKS, ARLENE
FRANKLIN, EDWINA--[10][21][26][34]MYS/ROM--
HARL "NO PAIN, NO GAIN" '90

MARKS, EDITH BOBROFF
BOBROFF, EDITH--[31]

MARKS, KATHY
JUDD, CATHERINE--[26]ROM--
HARL 587 "DANCE OF DECEPTION"
HARL 603 "INDISCRETE"

MARKS, LILLIAN ALICIA
MARKOVA, ALICIA--[8]

MARKS, ROBERT WALTER
COLLETON, JOHN--[1]

MARKS, STANLEY
KING, MARTIN--[1]
MARKS, STAN--[36]AUSTRALIAN/MYS--
HALE "GOD GAVE YOU ONE FACE" '64

MARKS, WINSTON K.
KENNEY, WIN--[2][11]
WINNEY, KEN--[1][2]

MARKUN, PATRICIA MALONEY
FORREST, SYBIL--[1][22][31]AMERICAN
MALONEY, PAT--[1][22][31] AMERIACN
MARROQUIN, PATRICIO--[1][22][31]AMERICAN
O'CARROLL, RYAN--[1][31][33]AMERICAN

MARLAND, DOUGLAS
CARTER, NICK--[3]MYS,HGP--
AWARD "COUNTERFEIT AGENT" '75

MARLISS, DEANNA
MARS, DIANA--[9][21]ROM--
"SWEET TRESPASS"
"SWEET DECEPTION" &5 MORE
MOORE, DIANA--[9][21]ROM--
"BLOSSOMS IN THE WIND"
"UNFINISHED BUSINESS"

MARLOWE, ALAN STEPHEN
ALEXANDER, KYLE--[1]
KENNETH, MR.--[1]
STUART, LESLIE--[1]

MARLOWE, DAN J.
AVELLANO, ALBERT--[18][29][32]MYS--
10 DIGEST STORIES IN AHMM & MSMM
ORESNIK, A.F--W/AL NUSSBAUM, NUSSBAUM
PROVIDED-LACHMAN--DIGEST STORIES

MARLOWE, DAN J. [CONT]
SANDAVAL, JAIME--NUSSBAUM LTR,[5][32]MYS--
EQMM "ALL THE WAY HOME" SEPT '65
AHMM "ROUNDABOUT" SEPT '66
MSMM "JACKPOT" MAY '66
AHMM "BON VOYAGE" MAR '69
MSMM "DAY OF THE DEAD" MAR '69
AHMM "MONEY TREE" JAN '69
AHMM "CHARTER FLIGHT" SEPT '70
AHMM "DONOR" FEB '70
AHMM "NIGHT SHIFT" FEB '71
AHMM "MARTIN FOR THE DEFENSE" DEC '71
AHMM "JUDGE & JURY" SEPT '71
MSMM "LULLABY" FEB '73
WILSON, GAR--[34]MYS,HP--
GE 'PHOENIX' SERIES:
"GUERRILLA GAMES" '82

MARLOWE, KENNETH
KENNETH, MR.--[22]AMERICAN
STUART, LESLIE--[22]AMERICAN

MARLOWE, STEPHEN
CHASE, ADAM--W/PAUL W. FAIRMAN,
[2][18][23]MYS/SF--
"QUEST OF THE GOLDEN APE" '57
FRAZER, ANDREW--[2][3][18][29][31]MYS--
AV "FIND EILEEN HARDIN" '59
AV "FALL OF MARTY MOON" '60
GRANGER, DARIUS JOHN--[2][11][31][32]MYS--
EQMM "SMALL MURDER" APR '50
PU "SAY UNCLE" MAY '55
PU "THE TERRIBLE TRUTH" MAR '55
LESSER, MILTON--[8][18][31] BIRTH NAME
QUEEN, ELLERY--[3][34]MYS,GHOSTED--
POCK "DEAD MAN'S TALE '61
RIDGEWAY, JASON--[2][3][18]MYS--
SIGN 1504 "WEST SIDE JUNGLE" '58
PERMA M4189 "ADAM'S FALL" '60
PERMA M4209 "PEOPLE IN GLASS HOUSES" '61
PERMA M4234 "HARDLY A MAN IS NOW ALIVE" '62
POCK "THE TREASURE OF COSA NOSTRA" '66
TENNESHAW, S.M.--[2][11][23]SF,HP--
ZIFF-DAVIS - ONCE
THAMES, C.H.--[2][3][11][18][22]MYS,HP--
ACE D177 "VIOLENCE IS GOLDEN" '56
PERMA M4294 "BLOOD OF MY BROTHER" '63
THAMES, CHRISTOPHER H.--L. ROBBINS LTR '94
WILDER, STEPHEN--[1][2][31]

MARLSON, PIERRE
HIGON, ALBERT--W/MICHEL JEURY,[11]

MARMOR, ARNOLD
CARTER, NICK--[3]MYS,HP--
AWARD "PEKING/TULIP AFFAIR" '69

MARNELL, JOSEPH
KOOMOTER, ZENO--[2][11]
KOOTMER, ZENO--[1][2]

MARON, MARGARET
BROWN, MARGARET E.--LACHMAN LST '93,[32]MYS--
AHMM - 9 SS, JAN '68-FEB '74

MARQUAND, JOHN P.
FULLER, TIMOTHY--[5][34]MYS--
LITTLE "HARVARD HAS A HOMOCIDE" '36
LITTLE "REUNION WITH MURDER" '41
LITTLE "THREE THIRDS OF A GHOST" '41
LITTLE "THIS IS A MURDER, MR. JONES" '43
LITTLE "KEEP COOL, MR. JONES" '50
PHILLIPS, JOHN--[1][22][29]MYS--

MARQUARD, LEO[POLD]
BURGER, JOHN--[1][22][31]SOUTH AFRICAN

MARQUES, SUSAN LOWNDES
LOWNDES, SUSAN--[8]

MARQUIS, MAX
BARNES, EDWARD F.--[31]
WILLIAMS, RICHARD--W/HOWARD BAKER, G.P. MANN
& BOB HOPKINS,[1][34]MYS-HP--
AMALG "MURDER BY PROXY" '63

MARR, RICHARD
BURMAR--[1][3]MYS--
GARDNER "THE SMITH SLAYER" '39

MARR-JOHNSON, DIANA
MAUGHAM, DIANA--[1][22]ENGLISH

MARRACK, J.F.
PORTIPHAR--W/[GEORGE] ANTHONY HERN,[1]

MARRADI, GIOVANNI
LABRONIO, G.--[22]ITALIAN

MARRECO, ANNE
ACLAND, ALICE--[8]

MARRIOTT, JAMES WILLIAM
WRAY, ROGER--[2][3][7]MYS/SF--
JARROLDS "DWELLER IN THE HALF-LIGHT" '20
JARROLDS "RAYNER CASE" '25

MARRIOTT, RONALD
ADAIR, HAZEL--W/HAZEL IRIS ADDIS,[1][2]

MARRIOTT-WATSON, H.B.
MARRIOTT-WATSON, E.B.--[32]--
MZ "DEVIL OF THE MARSH" JAN '65
MARRIOTT-WATSON, ETHELL--[2]

MARRIS, KATHERINE
BECK, K.K.--[34]MYS--
WALKER "DEATH IN A DECK CHAIR" '84
WALKER "UNWANTED ATTENTIONS" '89 & MORE
OLIVER, MARIE--[34]MYS--
PPJKS "DEATH OF A PROM QUEEN" '84

MARRISON, LESLIE WILLIAM
DOWLEY, D.M.--[8][31]

MARROW, PAUL
ZOOL, M.H.--[23]SF,GP

MARRYAT, FREDERICK
MARRYAT, CAPT.--[11]

MARS, WITOLD TADEUSZ J.
MARS, W.T.--[33]

MARSH, DONALD
ROBERTS, MARSHALL--V. BERCH--
BRNDN/BC PSEUDS, BAE 22, P24

MARSH, JOHN
DAVIS, JULIA--[1]
ELTON, JOHN--[2][7][11][22][31]ENGLISH--
"THE GREEN PLANTATIONS" '55
HARLEY, JOHN--[2][22][31]ENGLISH
HASTINGS, HARRINGTON--W/FLORENCE
SHEPHERD,[3][31]MYS--
HUTCH "CRIMINAL SQUARE" '29
HUTCH "WAR DOG STIRS" '30
HASTINGS, HARRISON--[2]ENGLISH
LAWRENCE, IRENE--[1]ENGLISH
MARSH, JOAN--[1]ENGLISH
RICHMOND, GRACE--[1][2][21][22]ROM--
"RUN AWAY FROM LOVE"

MARSH, JOHN [CONT]
SAWLEY, PETRA--[1]ENGLISH
WARE, MONICA--[1]ENGLISH
WOODWARD, LILLIAN--[1][2][21][22]ROM--
"IN ANOTHER'S LIKENESS"

MARSH, MARGARET M.M.
MITCHELL, MARGARET--[1]

MARSHALL, ALAN JOHN
MARSHALL, JOCK--[1]

MARSHALL, ARTHUR C.
BROOKE, ARTHUR--[1]
CRANE, BERKELEY--[1]
DRUMMOND, WILLIAM--[3]MYS--
PAN "MIDNIGHT LACE" '60
CORGI "VICTIM" '61
CORGI "LIFE FOR RUTH" '63
SIGN D2436 "NIGHT MUST FALL" '64
PAPLB 53-333 "GASLIGHT" '66
STEEL, HOWARD--[1]
YORKE, CARAS--[1]

MARSHALL, ARTHUR H.
MARSHALL, ARCHIBALD--[3][23]MYS/SF--
PAUL "MYS OF REDMARSH FARM" '11
METHUEN "THE TERRORS & OTHER STORIES" '13
METHUEN "UPSIDONIA" '15
COLLINS "BIG PETER" '22

MARSHALL, CHARLES HUNT
HUNT, PETER--W/GEORGE W. YATES,[3][23]MYS--
APPLETON "MURDERS AT SCANDAL HOUSE" '33
VANGARD "MURDER AMONG THE NUDISTS" '34
VANGARD "MURDER FOR BREAKFAST" '34

MARSHALL, CHRISTOBEL
ST. JOHN, CHRISTOP. MARIE--[1]

MARSHALL, EDISON [TESLA]
HUNTER, HALL--[1][22][31]AMERICAN

MARSHALL, ELIZABETH M.
SUTHERLAND, ELIZABETH--[1]

MARSHALL, ERIC
BROWN, TURNER JR.--W/STUART HAMPLE,[1][31]

MARSHALL, EVELYN
BOURNE, LESLEY--[1][22][31][33]MYS--
MARSH, J.E.--[1][22][33]
MARSH, JEAN--[21][33][34]MYS--
HAM "SHORE HOUSE MYS" '29
"LOVING PARTNERSHIP"
LONG "MURDER NEXT DOOR" '33
LONG "DEATH STALKS THE BRIDE" '43
LONG "IDENTITY UNWANTED" '51
LONG "DEATH VISITS THE CIRCUS" '53
LONG "DEATH AMONG THE STARS" '55
LONG "DEATH AT PEAK HOUR" '57

MARSHALL, FRANCIS B.
ST. AUBYN, ALAN--[1][34]MYS--
6 NOVELS 1895-06

MARSHALL, H.P.
STARK, JONATHAN--[1]

MARSHALL, JAMES VANCE
DOONE, JICE--[1][22][31]AUSTRALIAN

MARSHALL, JAMES [EDWARD]
MARSHALL, EDWARD--[33]--
DIAL "TROLL COUNTRY" '80

MARSHALL, JOSEPH R.
MARSH, JAMES J.--[3]MYS--
McKAY "THE PEKING SWITCH" '72

MARSHALL, KATHERINE H.M.
DIVER, MAUD--[1]

MARSHALL, MARGARET
SMITH, ELVET--[8]

MARSHALL, MARGARET L.W.
WILEY, MARGARET L.--[1][22]AMERICAN

MARSHALL, MARGUERITE M.
MARCH, STELLA--[1][9][21]ROM--
"OUT OF THE SHADOWS"
"SENTIMENTAL JOURNEY"
"WRONG DOCTOR"

MARSHALL, MEL[VIN]
CORY, RAY--[1][31]
EVANS, TABOR--[19]WEST, HP--
'LONGARM' & 'LONE STAR' SERIES
MITCHELL, CARLTON--V. BERCH LTR TO
HUBIN '94,[1]MYS--
TYLER, ZEKE--[1]

MARSHALL, MICHAEL [KIM]
MARSHALL, KIM--[1][33]

MARSHALL, ROBERT
CLAIRMONT, CLAIRE--[21][26]ROM--
"A CRUEL & LOVING TOUCH"

MARSHALL, [S] CATHERINE
LESOURD, CATHERINE--[1][31]

MARSIS, HENRI
AGATHON--W/ALFRED DE TARDE,[1]

MARSTON, J.E.
JEFFREY, E. JEFFREY--[8]

MARSTON, WILLIAM MOULTON
MOULTON, CHARLES--[1]

MARTEAU, F.A.
BRIDE, JACK--[8]
RAMEAUT, MAURICE--[8]

MARTEN, JON CHISHOLM
LANARK, DAVID--[8][36]AUSTRALIAN--
"PRIMAVERA" '35

MARTENS, ANNE L.COULTER
CARLISLE, RILLA--[34]MYS--
PLAY "THE BLACK GHOST" '45
KENDALL, JANE--[34]MYS--
PLAY "THE GIRL WITH TWO FACES" '44
REYNOLDS, ANN--[34]MYS--
PLAY "HOME SWEET HOMOCIDE" '47

MARTES, JOSE ANTONIO
LAUFFER, PIERRE--[1]

MARTIN, A.L.
REID, DESMOND--W/G.P. MANN,[1][34]MYS,HP--
AMALG "ROADHOUSE GIRL" '57

MARTIN, ANN M[ATTHEWS]
MATTHEWS, ANN--[1][33]

MARTIN, ARCHIBALD EDWARD
MARTIN, A.E.--[32][36]AUSTRALIAN/MYS--
CNSLDT "COMMON PEOPLE" '44 & 7 OTHERS
EQMM "FLYING CORPSE" SEPT '48
EQMM "SCARECROW MURDERS" APR '48
EQMM "THE POWER OF THE LEAF" JUL '48

MARTIN, BASIL KINGSLEY
CRITIC--[22][31]ENGLISH

MARTIN, BRIAN P[HILIP]
RUSTICUS--[1]

MARTIN, CATHERINE DEXTER
DEXTER, CATHERINE--[7]SF--
MacM "GERTIE'S GREEN THUMB" '83
MRW "ORACLE DOLL" '85
MRW "MAZEMAKER" '89

MARTIN, CHARLES E.
M., C.E.--[33]

MARTIN, CHARLES M.
MARTIN, CHUCK--[1][28]WEST--
35 NOVELS '36-74
STARR, CLAY--L. ROBBINS LTR '94, WEST--
PRZW 32 "POWDER SMOKE BLOOD" '49

MARTIN, DAVID
HOLT, MICHAEL--[7]SF--
"DR. WHO: CRISIS IN SPACE"
SPINIFLEX--[1]

MARTIN, DEBORAH
NICHOLAS, DEBORAH--[26]ROM--
"NIGHT VISION"
"SILENT SONATA"

MARTIN, DON
BROOKS, NED--W/C.W. BROOKS JR.,[7]

MARTIN, E. LE BRETON
LEE, RAYMOND--[1]
MART, DONOVAN--[1]
SHAW, MARTIN--[1]

MARTIN, EMILY
AHERN, EMILY M.--[31]

MARTIN, GLORIA ANN
LONDON, LISA--[1]
MARTIN, G.A.--[1]
TRAMIN, A.G.--[1]
TRAMIN, ED--[1]
TRAMIN, LISA--[1]

MARTIN, HANS
NITRAM, H.--[2]
NITRAM, HANS--[39]GERMAN

MARTIN, IAN
ARLISS, JOEN--[34]MYS--
ZEBRA "SHARK BAIT AFFAIR" '79
POPLB "NIGHTMARE'S NEST" '79
ZEBRA "LADY KILLER AFFAIR" '80
POPLB "BELOVED VICTIM" '80
POPLB "SHADOW OVER SEVENTH HEAVEN"

MARTIN, JACQUES
MARINUS--[1]

MARTIN, JORGE
MARTIN, GEORGE--[1]

MARTIN, JOY
CRANDALL, JOY--[1][31]

MARTIN, JUDITH SYLVIA
MANNERS, MISS--[1]

MARTIN, JUDY
ERSKINE, ANDRA--[9][21][26]ROM--
"PRIORITY AFFAIR"

MARTIN, JUDY WELLS
ERNEST, JEANETTE--[9][21][26]ROM--
"LOVER'S LAIR"
"DEAR DOUBTER"

MARTIN, KARL
ROBER, KARL--[39]GERMAN

MARTIN, KATHLEEN KELLY
LAWRENCE, KATY [KATHY]--W/LARRY JAY MARTIN, [9][21][26]ROM--
"TIN ANGEL"
MARS, KASEY--[26]ROM--
"THE SILENT ROSE"
MARTIN, KAT--[9][21]ROM--
"CAPTAIN'S BRIDE"
"DUELLING HEARTS"
"MAGNIFICENT PASSAGE"

MARTIN, KINGSLEY
CRITIC--[8]

MARTIN, LANCE
ANCEL, MARTIN--[1]

MARTIN, LARRY JAY
LAWRENCE, KATY--W/KATHLEEN K. MARTIN, [9][21][26]ROM--
"TIN ANGEL"

MARTIN, LINCOLN WILLIAM
MARTIN, L.W.--[36]AUSTRALIAN/MYS--
A&R "MURDER ON MOUNT CAPITA" '44
[W/N.S. LYNRAVEN]

MARTIN, MALACHI
SERAFIAN, MICHAEL--[1]

MARTIN, NANCY
CURRY, ELISSA--[9][21][26]ROM--
"WINTER WILDFIRE"
"KISS ME, CAIT" & MORE

MARTIN, NELL COLUMBIA B.
BOYER, COLUMBIA--[34]MYS--
HENKLE "MOSAIC EARRING" '27

MARTIN, NETTA
ASHTON, LUCY--[8]

MARTIN, OLIVER
DAVIES, ERNEST--[3]MYS--
RIVERS "DIVES & SON" '10
"THE MOMENT" '11
"WIDOW'S NECKLACE" '13

MARTIN, PATRICIA MILES
LANE, JERRY--[1][33]ADULT--
PLAYTIME BOOKS
MILES, MISKA--[1][22][33]AMERICAN--JUV
MILES, PATRICIA A.--[1][33]AMERICAN

MARTIN, REGINALD ALEC
CAMERON, BRETT--[1]
DIXON, REX--[1]
ELIOT[T], E.C.--[2][7][11][23]SF--
'KEMLO' SERIES #1-15
'TAS' SERIES
MARTIN, REX--[1]ADULT

MARTIN, REGINALD ALEC [CONT]
MARTIN, ROBERT--[1]
MARTIN, SCOTT--[1]
MCCOY, HANK--[8]

MARTIN, RHONA
NEIGHBOUR, RHONA M.--[1]

MARTIN, ROBERT BERNARD
BERNARD, ROBERT--[3][22][31]MYS--
NORTON "DEADLY MEETING" '70
NORTON "ILLEGAL ENTRY" '72 & MORE

MARTIN, ROBERT [LEE]
ROBERTS, LEE--V. BERCH-GM PSEUDS,
PP 33,[3][22]MYS--
CURTIS "SUSPICION" '71
GM 229 "LITTLE SISTER" '52
GM 968 "DEATH OF A LADIE'S MAN" '60 & MORE

MARTIN, ROY PETER
CHARLES, HAMPTON--J. APOSTOLOU, DDLY PLEAS #3
& #4,[34]MYS--
'MISS SEETON' SERIES:--
BERK "ADVENTURESS MISS SEETON" '90
BERK "MISS SEETON AT THE HELM" '90
BERK "MISS SEETON BY APPOINTMENT" '90
MELVILLE, JAMES--[3][18][40]MYS--
SECKER "WAGES OF ZEN" '79
SECKER "CHRYSANTHEUM CHAIN" '80

MARTIN, RUSSELL W.
MARTIN, RUSS--[7]SF
MOORE, ROBERT--[14]ADULT--
OLYM OPH#179 "LADY KILLER" '69
OLYM OPH#174 "RAPES OF WRATH" '69
OLYM OPH#199 "THE TIGHTER IT GETS" '70
OLYM OPH#217 "HARD GUYS & HOSTAGES" '70
OLYM OPH#225 "THE RAPE CONSPIRACY" '71
OLYM OPH#239 "MADAM SEX THIEF" '71
VON LAMBBE, COL. SPIRO RT--[14]ADULT--
OLYM OPH#178 "FLAMES OF TORTURE" '69

MARTIN, STODDARD [H] JR.
MARTIN, CHIP--[1]

MARTIN, THOMAS HECTOR
DELLA, LEW--PPCC#3, P16,HP--
TEMPEST
MANTZ, LEW--[34]MYS,HP--
HAM STFFD "ALIAS THE MARSTRO" '52
O'HARA, SHAUN--PPCC#3, ADV--
HAM "KAZAN THE KILLER"
PERRELLI, NICK--S. HOLLAND-SCION CKLST,
PP 27,[34]MYS,HP--
TEMPEST "RITA TAKES A RIDE" '50
TEMPEST "TERROR IN TOKYO" '50
SCION "DOPE FOR DELORES" '51
TEMPEST "SOHO SALAMI" '51
SCION "SOME DAMES DON'T" '52
SCION "BLIND MURDER" '52
SCION "NOTHING TO HIDE" '52
SCION "A BLONDE FOR BURIAL" '52
MLSTN "THE FRAIL'S A PHONEY" '53
SCION "A DAME DOLES DEATH" '53
RISCO, MAX--S. HOLLAND-SCION CKLST,
PP 27,[27][34]MYS--
SCION "CORPSE AT COLLEGE" '52
MLSTN "I CAN TAKE IT" '53
MLSTN "NIGHT IS SO SHORT" '53
MLSTN "TIGER LILY" '53
MLSTN "OVER MY DEAD BODY" '53
MLSTN "RAMONA" '53
MLSTN "VISA FOR VIOLENCE" '53
SAXON, PETER--W/W. HOWARD BAKER, R.E. BRINEY-
BAE 17,[2][34]HOR,HP--
LAN "CURSE OF RATHLAW" '68

MARTIN, THOMAS HECTOR [CONT]
THOMAS, MARTIN--[2][3][32][39]MYS--
24 NVLS '57-69
PA "THE GHOST RUNS" MAY '57
PA "GENUINE ARTICLE" JUL '57
PA "MAN WHO KNEW BETTER" JUL '57
PA "TESTAMENT IN OILS" JUL '57
EW "HARVEST OF HOMOCIDE" AUG '64
EW "KILLED WITH A LOVING KISS" NOV '64
LAN 73-660 "HAND OF KANE" '67

MARTIN, TIMOTHY
TIM--[8]

MARTIN, VIOLET FLORENCE
ROSS--[8]
ROSS, MARTIN--[1][22][33]IRISH
SOMERVILLE & ROSS--W/EDITH A.O.
SOMERVILLE,[1][22]IRISH--
WORLD "THE REAL CHARLOTTE" 1894

MARTIN, W.
KINGSLEY, HAMILTON--[1]

MARTIN, WILLIAM
JAMES, FREDERICK--[31]

MARTIN, WILLIAM THORNTON
MARTIN, PETE--[1]

MARTIN, [SIR] THEODORE
GAULTIER, BON--W/WILLIAM E. AYTOUN,[1]
T.M.--[1]

MARTIN-GREEN, WILLIAM
GREEN, MARTYN--[1]

MARTINE-BARNES, ADRIENNE
BARNES, ADRIENNE MARTINE--[31]

MARTINEK, RAIMUND
MARTIN, RAIMUND--[39]GERMAN/JUV
MARTINEE, RAOUL--[39]GERMAN/JUV

MARTINETZ, VIVIAN L.
BROUSSARD, VIVIAN L.--[1][31]
MARTINETZ, V.L.--[31]

MARTINEZ RUIZ, LUIS
AHRIMAN--[1]
AZORAN--[1]
CANDIDO--[1]

MARTINEZ ZUVIRIA, GUSTAVO
WAST, HUGO--[1]

MARTINEZ, CARLOS MIGUEL
MITCHELL, CHARLES--JEAN F. LE DEIST LTR.JAN '93

MARTINEZ, HUBERTO BATIS
BATIS, HUBERTO--[30] MEXICAN

MARTINEZ-DELGADO, LUIS
LUIMARDEL--[1]

MARTING, RUTH LENORE
BAILEY, HILEA--[3][22]MYS--
DBLDY "GIVE THANKS TO DEATH" '40
DBLDY "SMILING CORPSE" '41 & MORE

MARTINI, STEVEN PAUL
MARTINI, STEVE--[31]MYS--
FINE "SIMEON CHAMBER" '88 & OTHERS

MARTINI, TERI
KING, ALISON--[3][9]MYS/ROM--
POPLB "THE DREAMER, LOST IN TERROR" '76
MARTIN, WENDY--[9][21][26]ROM--
"ISLAND MAGIC"
"LOVE'S JOURNEY"
MARTINI, THERESE--[9][26][31]ROM--
"ARUNDEL TOUCH"
"DREAMS TO GIVE"
"LOVE'S LOST MELODY"
"TO LOVE & BEYOND"

MARTINI, VIRGILIO
LETRUSCO--[1][31]

MARTINN, PAUL
PLAUT, MARTIN--[8]

MARTINS, MARIA ISABEL
BARRENO, MARIA ISABEL--[1][31]

MARTINUS, [E] FRANK
ARION, F.M.--[1]

MARTOFF, NICKOLI
MAYO, NICK--[3]MYS--
STEIN "THE BENEFIT" '80

MARTONCSIK, LASZLO
MECS, LASZLO--[22] HUNGARIAN

MARTYN, EDWARD
SIRIUS--[1][2][22]IRISH

MARTYN, WYNDHAM
GRENVIL, WILLIAM--ECHOES #23, P35,[1][22]MYS--
'ANTHONY TRENT' STORIES

MARTYR, PAULA [JANE]
LAWFORD, PAULA JANE--[33]

MARVIN, FRANCIS SYDNEY
MARVIN, F.S.--[1]

MARVIN, JOHN T.
RICHARDS, CHARLES--[1][22]AMERICAN

MARWICK, ERNEST W.
E.W.M.--[1]

MARX, ERICA ELIZABETH
MANFRED, ROBERT--[1][22][31]

MARX, MICHAEL
MICHEL, MAX--[39]GERMAN

MARX, OLGA
VALHOPE, CAROL NORTH--[22]AMERICAN

MARZINEK, WILHELM
BRIESTER, JEFF--[39]GERMAN/MYS/WEST
CHASSMAN, CHERRY--[39]GERMAN/MYS/WEST
O'BRIEN, JEFF--[39]GERMAN/MYS/WEST

MASAKAZU, TOYAMA
CHUZAN, TOYAMA--[22]JAPANESE

MASCHLANKA, ANNEMARIE
KRAPP, ANNEMARIE--[39]GERMAN/JUV

MASCHLER, TOM
CAINE, MARK--W/FREDERICK [M] RAPHAEL,[1]

MASCHWITZ, ERIC
MARVELL, HOLT--[3][5][22]MYS--
"DEATH AT BROADCASTING HOUSE" '34
RICH "DEATH OF AN EXTRA" '35
RICH "DEATH IN BUDAPEST" '37

MASETTI, PIRRO
MASTRI, PIETRO--[22] ITALIAN

MASH, MAURICE H.B.
WORTH, MAURICE--W/WILLAN G. BOSWORTH,
[1][3]MYS--
HUTCH "GOLDEN PHEASANT" '27 & 2 OTHERS

MASLIN, ALICE
CRAIG, NANCY--[31]

MASON, ARTHUR CHARLES
SCROPE, MASON--[1][3]MYS--
GARDNER "MAN WITH THE BIG HEAD" '29

MASON, BEVERLY
BISHOP, MARY--[3]MYS--
DELL "KILLRAVEN" '75
DELL "WIDOW'S WALK" '75

MASON, C.P.
SNOOKS, EPAMINONDAS--[2][11]

MASON, CHARLES
MASON, S.C.--[3][22][29]MYS--
BELL "MURDER AT BADOR" '38
WARNE "GOLD OF GABRIA" '50 & 3 MORE

MASON, CHARLES W.
MR. M____--[3]MYS

MASON, CLARENCE RAY
MASON, RAYMOND--[34]MYS--
GM 395 "AND TWO SHALL MEET" '54
GM 468 "FOREVER IS TODAY" '55
GM 589 "LOVE AFTER FIVE" '56
AHMM "MARTHA MYERS, MOVIE STAR" JAN '57
AHMM "MAN IN A HURRY" AUG '57
AHMM "PASSING OF AUNT AGATHA" JUN '58
SIGN 1641 "SHADOW & THE PEAK" '59
HILL 175 "BEDEVILED" '60
GM 1248 "SOMEONE & FELICIA WARWICK" '62

MASON, CONNIE
MILES, CARA--MASON INTRVW-DMN,[26]ROM--
AV "BEYOND THE HORIZON"
AV "LORD OF THE NIGHT"
AV "LOVE ME WITH FURY"
AV "PROMISE ME FOREVER"
AV "SURRENDER TO THE FURY"

MASON, DAVID
MARTELL, DAVID--[14]ADULT--
OLYM OPH#201 "A BEDFUL OF FLESH" '70

MASON, DOUGLAS RANKINE
DOUGLAS, R.M.--[2][11][31]ENGLISH
RANKINE, DOUGLAS--[8]ENGLISH
RANKINE, JOHN--[2][4][7][11][23]ENGLISH/SF--
"TWO'S COMPANY" '64

MASON, EDITH HELEN
MASON, HILARY--[1][3]MYS--
PAUL "TREAD WARILY" '37

MASON, EUDO COLECESTRA
MAURER, OTTO--[22]ENGLISH

MASON, F. VAN WYCK
COFFIN, GEOFFREY--W/HELEN BRAWNER, [2][3][5][18][31]MYS--
DODGE "MURDER IN THE SENATE" '35
DODGE "FORGOTTEN FLEET MYSTERY" '36
MASON, F.V.W.--[1]AMERICAN
MASON, FRANK W.--[5][18][29][33]WAR--
"Q BOATS" '43
"PILOTS' MAN YOUR PLANES" '44
"FLIGHT INTO DANGER" '46
WEAVER, WARD--[5][18][29][33]MYS/HIST--
"HANG MY WREATH" '41
"END OF THE TRACK" '43

MASON, JOHN
BROWN, JOHN MASON--[1]

MASON, JOHN HOLLIS
KEITH, JOHN--[2]

MASON, MADELAINE
MASON, TYLER--[1][22]AMERICAN
BARTLETT, DAVID--[22][31][32]AMERICAN/MYS--
LM "THE PURGATION" MAR '71

MASON, MICHAEL HENRY
BLAKE, CAMERON--[1][32]MYS--
SC "THE SPOTTED ANGEL" '45

MASON, MIRIAM EVANGELINE
SWAIN, MIRIAM--[1]

MASON, PAMELA OSTRER
KELLINO, PAMELA--[2][11]

MASON, PHILIP
WOODRUFF, PHILIP--[3][22][29]MYS--
CAPE "CALL THE NEXT WITNESS" '45
CAPE "WHATEVER DIES" '48

MASON, RONALD ALISON KELL
MASON, R.A.K.--[1]

MASON, SAMUEL
MASON, DAVID--[7][32]MYS/SF--
FE "ACCOUNT CLOSED" JUL '60

MASON, SARAH JILL
CRANE, HAMILTON--CRPG,DDLY PLEAS #3, BREEN,LACHMAN,MYS--
'MISS SEETON' SERIES

MASON, SYDNEY CHARLES
CARR, CHARLES--[2][8][11]
CARR, ELAINE--[8]
HATTON, CLIFF--[8]
HAYES, CLANTON--[8]
HENDERSON, COLT--[8]
HOLMES, CAROLINE--[8]
HORN, CHESTER--[8]
LANGLEY, JOHN--[8]
LEDGARD, JAKE--[8]
LEE, JESSE--[8]
LOMAX, JEFF--[8]
MADDERN, STAN--[8]
MAINE, MASTERLING--[8]
MANN, STANLEY--[8]
MARLOW, PHYLLIS--[8]
MASTERS, STEVE--[9]ROM
MERRICK, SPENCER--[8]
STANLEY, MARGARET--[8]

MASSA, JOHN ANDREW
MASSA, JACK--[7]SF--
BERK "MOONCROW" '79

MASSADA, IONE
LEIGH, IONE--[1]

MASSELINK, BEN
TOLIVER, GEORGE--[1]

MASSEY, ERIKA
ZASTROW, ERIKA--[1]

MASSINGHAM, HAROLD J.
H.J.M.--[1]

MASSOGLIA, MARTIN FRANK
MASSOGLIA, MARTY--[7]SF--
"CHECKLIST OF ACE SF THROUGH 1968" '69

MASTEN, MARGARET
SIMPSON, MAGGIE--W/SANDRA POOL,[26]ROM--
HARL 577 "BABY BONUS"
HARL 608 "BRINGING UP FATHER"

MASTERS, ANTHONY
TATE, RICHARD--[3][7][40]MYS/SF--
CNST "THE DONOR" '70
CNST "DEAD TRAVEL FAST" '71
CNST "EMPEROR ON ICE" '73
CNST "BIRD OF A BLODIED FEATHER" '74

MASTERS, EDGAR LEE
ATHERTON, LUCIUS--[1][31]
CHUBB, ELMER--[1][31]
FORD, WEBSTER--[1][31]
PACKETT, LUKE--[1]
PROWLER, HARLEY--[1]
WALLACE, DEXTER--[1]

MASTERS, KELLY R.
BALL, ZACHARY--W/FRANKIE-LEE JANAS, [22][31][33]

MASTERS, MILDRED
HEINZEN, MILDRED--[1][31][33]

MASTERS, WILLIAM WALTER
MASTERS, W.W.--[1]

MASTERTON, GRAHAM
LUKE, THOMAS--DARK DREAMERS INTRVW/CR, [2][7]HOR--
POCK 81769 "HELL CANDIDATE" '80
POCK 83662 "PHOBIA" '80
POCK 43302 "THE HEIRLOOM "82
STAR "CONDOR" '84

MASTON, THOMAS BUFFORD
MASTON, T.B.--[1]

MASTORAKIS, NICO
NORRIS, S.D.--[7]SF--
CHART "RECKONING" '85

MASTRANGELO, CHARLES E.
C.E.M.--[31]

MASUR, HAROLD Q.
FLEMING, GUY--G. LOVISI-MASUR INTRVW, PP 30,[1]--
HITCHCOCK, ALFRED--[2][11]MYS--
GHOSTED - AS EDITOR
JAMES, EDWARD--G.LOVISI-MASUR INTRVW, PP 30--BIO PULPCON 23--
TSD - STORY JUL '41
MASUR, H.Q.--M. LACHMAN LTR '93--
'10 DETECTIVE ACES' MAG APR '41
MASUR, HAL--G. LOVISI-MASUR INTRVW, PP 30

MASUR, HAROLD Q. [CONT]
MASUR, HAROLD A.--HANCER 3rd ED, MYS--
AV G1194 "THE BIG MONEY" '64
QUINCY, HAL--A TONIK-BIO PULPCON 23, MYS--
TSD - STORY JUL '41

MATCHA, JACK
BARCLAY, JOHN--[1][3]AMERICAN/MYS--
MON 238 "ASK FOR LOIS" '62
MITCHEL, JACKSON--[1][22]AMERICAN
TANNER, JOHN--[2][3][22]MYS--
ATHENA "GAMBLER'S GIRL" '61
BRNDN "KILLER CAME NAKED" '74

MATEYKO, G.M.
MAYFIELD, M.I.--W/H.I. HIRSHFIELD,[1][2][11]

MATHER, ANNE
FLEMING, CAROLINE--[1][8]

MATHERS, EDWARD POWYS
TORQUEMADA--[3]MYS--
GOLZ "THE TORQUEMADA PUZZLE BOOK" '34

MATHESON, DONALD H.
HARMSTON, DONALD--[8]

MATHESON, JOAN
TRANSUE, JACOB--[1][2][11]

MATHESON, RICHARD [B]
MATHIESON, RICHARD--MUNROE SLST 22-RICHARD MATHESON BIBLIO
MATHISON, RICHARD--[1]
SWANSON, LOGAN--[2][7][32]SF--
PLBY "EARTHBOUND" '82
AHMM "I'LL MAKE IT LOOK GOOD" MAR '57

MATHESON, RICHARD CHRISTOPHER
MATHESON, CHRIS--[23]SF

MATHESON, SYLVIA ANNE
MUNDY, MAX--[34]MYS--
LONG "DEATH IS A TIGER" '60
LONG "DIG FOR A CORPSE" '62 & 2 MORE

MATHEWS, ALBERT
SIOGVOLK, PAUL--[8]

MATHEWS, ELLEN B.
LYALL, DAVID--[34]MYS--
HODDER "SHIPS OF MON DESIR" '10
HODDER "CONSOLATION BUREAU" '15
MATHERS, HELEN--[34]MYS--
9 NOVELS 1882-1909

MATHEWS, EVELYN CRAW
CLEAVER, NANCY--[1][22][31]CANADIAN

MATHIESON, VOLNEY
VOLNEY, DEX--L. ROBBINS LTR '94

MATHIEU, JOSEPH P.
MATHIEU, JOE--[33]

MATHIEU, NOEL JEAN
EMMANUEL, PIERRE--[22][31]FRENCH

MATHURA, MUSTAPHA
MATURA, MUSTAPHA--[1]

MATSON, NORMAN [H]
SMITH, THORNE--[23]SF--
COMPLETED "THE PASSIONATE WITCH" '41, FOR "SMITH" AFTER HIS DEATH

MATSUBA, MOSHE
BEN-YOSEF, AVRAHAM CHAIM--[31]

MATSUO, BASHO
BASHO--[31]

MATSUO, TOKUDA
SHUSEI, TOKUDA--[22]JAPANESE

MATTHAEI, CLARA
GRAY, WALTER--[22]GERMAN-AMERICAN
HOFF, GERTRUD--[22]GERMAN-AMERICAN

MATTHEW, RUPERT O[LIVER]
OLIVER, RUPERT--[1]

MATTHEWMAN, PHYLLIS
SURREY, KATHRYN--[8]

MATTHEWS, CAROLYN SEAB.
SEABAUGH, CAROLYN--[21][26]ROM--
"BUTTERFLY AUTUMN"
"LEAN ON ME"
"CICADA SUMMER"

MATTHEWS, CLAYTON [H]
BRISCOE, PATTY[1]--W/PATRICIA MATTHEWS, [9][32][34]MYS--
MSMM "RETURN TO MURDER" DEC '74
4 NVLS '69-76
CLAY, MATTHEW--G. COOK LTR '93--
ORIGN 746 "FRENCH ALLEY" '52
CAMEO "SLUM DOCTOR" '54
GREY, ROMER ZANE--T. JOHNSON-ECHOES #5, LTR '94,[28]WEST,HP--
ZGWM 'LARAMIE NELSON' NVLTS
HALLIDAY, BRETT--W/GARY BRANDNER, T. JOHNSON-ECHOES#23, MYS,HP--
MSMM "SHORT CUT TO MURDER" SEP '73
MOORE, ARTHUR--[8][32]MYS--
22 DIGEST STORIES [AHMM, EQMM, MSMM & SA]
MOORE, CLAYTON--W/GARY BRANDNER,[31]--
CURTIS "SATURDAY NIGHT IN MILWAUKEE" '73
O'DAIR, STAN--V. BERCH-BRNDN/BC PSEUDS, BAE 22, ADULT--
BRNDN 907 "LAVENDER GIRLS" '64
BRNDN 6424 "FAMILY SEX SECRETS"
'MOONGLOW READER' BOOKS

MATTHEWS, CONSTANCE MARY
CARRINGTON, MOLLY--[1][31]

MATTHEWS, EDWIN J.
SAXON--[8]

MATTHEWS, JAMES BRANDER
MATTHEWS, BRANDER--[8]
PENN, ARTHUR--[1]

MATTHEWS, JOHN HAROLD JR.
MATTHEWS, JACK--[7]SF/HOR--
"GHOSTLY POPULATIONS: SHORT STORIES' '81

MATTHEWS, MARGARET BRYAN
GOODYEAR, SUSAN--[8]

MATTHEWS, PATRICIA [BRIS]
BRISCO, P.A.--[31][32]MYS--
MSMM "GREGORY" APR '72
MSMM "THE LAST STAMP" FEB '73
BRISCO, PATTY--W/CLAYTON MATTHEWS, [9][32][34]MYS-- 4 NVLS '69-76
MSMM "RETURN TO MURDER" DEC '74
BRISCOE, PAT A.--[1][7]SF--
POWELL "OTHER PEOPLE" '70

MATTHEWS, PATRICIA [BRIS] [CONT]
MATHEWS, DENISE--W/DENISE HRIVNAK, [9][21][26]ROM-- "INTIMATE STRANGER"
WILEY, LAURA--[9][21]ROM--
WYLIE, LAURA--[1][7][33]SF-- PINN "NIGHT VISITOR" '79
WYLIE, LAURIE--[1]

MATTHEWS, STANLEY GOODWN.
GOODWIN, MARK--[1][31]

MATTYSSEN, JOHANNES
MARYNEN, JOANNES--[1]

MATURIN, CHARLES ROBERT
MURPHY, DENNIS JASPER--[2][3][11][16]MYS--
LONGMANS "FATAL REVENGE" 1807
BRADFORD "MILESIAN CHIEF" 1812

MATUSOW, HARVEY MARSHALL
ALLENBY, GORDON--[8]
MATUSOW, MARSHALL--[8]
MULDOON, OMAR--[1]
SADBALLS, JOHN--[8]

MAUCKNER, WALTER G.
BURTON, GEORGE W.--[39][40]GERMAN/MYS-- 'KOMMISSAR X' SERIES: #517, 520, 547, 560 & #581
COTTON, JERRY--[39]GERMAN/MYS/HOR,HP
GAUTHIER, GEORGES--[39]GERMAN/MYS/HOR
MAREK, WALDO--[39]GERMAN/MYS/HOR
SHAPIRO, CORA--[39]GERMAN/MYS/HOR

MAUD, LILLIAN NANCY
PRICE, NANCY--[1]

MAUERHARDT, ROLF
ERHART, ROLF--[39]GERMAN/ADV/WEST
ERHART, WOLF--[39]GERMAN/ADV/WEST
MURAT, ROLF--[39]GERMAN/ADV/WEST
ROMMY, THOMAS--[39]GERMAN/ADV/WEST
SLADE, JACK--[39]GERMAN/WEST
THOOK, GARRY--[39]GERMAN/ADV/WEST

MAUGHAM, ROBERT CECIL R.
GRIFFEN, DAVID--[1]ENGLISH
MAUGHAM, ROBIN--[7][32][34]MYS/SF--
ALLEN "THE BARRIER" '73 & MORE
EQMM "FOLLOW THE SUN" MAR '72

MAUGHAM, W. SOMMERSET
SOMERVILLE--[1]

MAULE, HAMILTON BEE
MAULE, TEX--[8][22]AMERICAN

MAULNIER, THIERRY
TALAGRANDE, JACQUES LOUIS--[1]

MAUPASSANT, GUY DE
VALMONT, GUY DE-- OXFORD COMPANION TO FRENCH LIT. '61

MAURER, KURT
BAXTER, MARK--[39]GERMAN/HOR,HP--
COFFIN, BRUCE--[39]GERMAN/MYS/HOR/WEST
LAMONT, ROBERT--[39]GERMAN/MYS/HOR/WEST,HP--
SLADE, JACK--[39]GERMAN/MYS/HOR/WEST,HP--

MAURIAC, FRANCOIS C
FOREZ--[1][31]

MAURICE, DAVID JOHN K.
GHINE, WUNNAKYAWHTIN U O.--[1][22][31]AUSTRALIAN

MAURRAS, CHARLES-MARIE-P
GARNIER, PIERRE--[1]
MARTIN, OCTAVE--[1]
RAMEAUS, LEON--[1]
XENOPHON XIII--[1]

MAVOR, ELINOR
GOHAGEN, OMAR--[23]SF-- WORK '79/80

MAVOR, OSBORNE HENRY
BRIDIE, JAMES--[8][22]SCOTTISH
HENDERSON, MARY--[31]
KELLOCK, ARCHIBALD P.--[31]

MAX, GEORGE
FARRELL, JOHNNY--S. HOLLAND-SCION CKLST, PP 27,[34]MYS--
SCION "SUGAR, YOU'RE SWELL" '52
MILESTONE "NIGHT RIDE" '53
MILESTONE "CURVES & ANGLES" '53
LUGAR, HANS--S. HOLLAND-- SCION CKLST, PP 27, MYS,HP--
SCION "MIDNIGHT SISTER" '53

MAXENCE, ROBERT
FRANCIS, ROBERT--[22]FRENCH

MAXFIELD, KAREN
LYNN, KAREN--W/LYNN TAYLOR,[9][26]ROM--
"DUAL DESTINY"
"MIDSUMMER MOON" & MORE

MAXFIELD, PRUDENCE M.
HILL, PRUDENCE--[1]

MAXIMOVIC, GERD
BREMER, MAXIM--[39]GERMAN/SF
FORRESTER, THORN--W/HANS J. ALPERS,GERMAN/SF, HP
LUNTZ, HEINRICH--[39]GERMAN/SF

MAXTONE-GRAHAM, JAMES A.
ANSTRUTHER, JAMES--[31]

MAXTONE-GRAHAM, JOYCE
STRUTHER, JAN--[8]

MAXWELL, ANN & EVAN
LOWELL, ELIZABETH--[9][21][26]ROM--
HARL 199 "RECKLESS LOVE"
HARL "FIRE & RAIN" & OTHERS

MAXWELL, ANN [ELIZABETH]
CHARTERS, LOWELL--G. COOK LTR '93
MAXWELL, A.E.--W/EVAN MAXWELL,[3][9][23]SF--
"CHANGE" '75
"THE SINGER"
MAREK "STEAL THE SUN" '82
DBLDY "JUST ANOTHER DAY IN PARADISE" '85
SUN, ANNALISE--G. COOK LTR '93

MAXWELL, EVAN
MAXWELL, A.E.--W/ANN [E] MAXWELL, [3][9][23]MYS/SF--
"CHANGE" '75
"THE SINGER"
MAREK "STEAL THE SUN" '82
DBLDY "JUST ANOTHER DAY IN PARADISE" '85

MAXWELL, PATRICIA ANNE P.
BLAKE, JENNIFER--[3][26][31][40]MYS/ROM--
COLUMBINE "MIDNIGHT WALTZ" '85 & 24 MORE

MAXWELL, PATRICIA ANNE P. [CONT]
PATRICK, MAXINE--[9][21][26]ROM--
"LOVE AT SEA"
"BAYOU BRIDE" & MORE
PONDER, PATRICIA--[3][9][21][26]MYS/ROM--
MANOR "HAVEN OF FEAR" '77
MANOR "MURDER FOR CHARITY" '77
TREHEARNE, ELIZABETH--W/CAROL ALBRITTON,
[9][21][26]ROM--
"STORM AT MIDNIGHT"

MAXWELL, SISTER MARY
IMMACULATA, SISTER--[31]

MAXWELL, VIOLET S.
MAXWELL, C. BEDE--[8]

MAXWELL, WILLIAM BABINGTN
MAXWELL, W.B.--[1]

MAY, ELAINE
DALE, ESTHER--[8]

MAY, HENRY JOHN
SCHLOSBERG, H.J.--[22] RHODESIAN-ENGLISH

MAY, HERBERT RICHARD [D]
HARDY, MARK--[1]

MAY, JOHN
DUFFER, ALLAN--[8]

MAY, KARL FRIEDRICH
DE LA ESCOSURA, RAMON D.--[39]GERMAN/ADV
GISELA, M.--[39]GERMAN/ADV/ROM
HOHENTHAL, KARL--[1][39]GERMAN/ADV
JAM, D.--[39]GERMAN/ADV
LATREAUMONT--[1]
LATREAUMONT, PRINZ MUHAM.--[39]GERMAN/ADV
PERNER, FRITZ--[39]GERMAN/ADV
POLLMER, EMMA--[39]GERMAN/ADV/ROM
VAN DER LOEWEN, P.--[39]GERMAN/ADV
VON LINDEN, E.--[1]
VON LINDEN, ERNST--[39]GERMAN/ADV

MAY, MAJORIE
DEAN, DINAH--[21][26]ROM--
"COUNTRY COUSINS"
"FLIGHT FROM THE EAGLE"

MAY, ROBERT STEPHEN
MAY, ROBIN--[1][7][31]SF--
PUFFIN "ROBIN OF SHERWOOD & HOUNDS OF
LUCIFER" '85

MAY, WINIFRED ARNOLD
ARNOLD, WINIFRED--[1]

MAY, WINIFRED JEAN
MAY, WYNNE--[1]

MAYER, CHARLES LEOPOLD
REYAM--[22]FRENCH

MAYER, CHRISTIAN ANTON
AMERY, CARL--[39]GERMAN/SF

MAYER, DEBORAH ANNE
CHRISTENSEN, ANNA--[1][31]

MAYER, HANNELORE [K]
VALENCAK, HANNELORE--[1][39]GERMAN/SF

MAYER, HELLY
PETERSEN, HELLY--[39]GERMAN

MAYER, JANE ROTHCHILD
JAYNES, CLARE--W/CLARA G. SPIEGEL,
[1][22][31][33]

MAYER, SYDNEY LOUIS
JENNINGS, PATRICK--[1]

MAYER-TREES, HILDEGARD
MATRE, HERO--[39]GERMAN/SF

MAYERS, CARROLL
CARROLL, M.A.--LACHMAN LST '93,[32]MYS--
TR "KID-GANG INITIATION" JUN '59
TR "REAL LIFE DRAMA" AUG '60
TR "HOTEL HOMICIDE" NOV '60
GU "NO DAME CHEATS ON ME" DEC '60
TR "GIRL WHO LAUGHED" FEB '60
GU "WOMAN OF THE NIGHT" JUN '61
REYAM, LORAC--LACHMAN LST '93,[32]MYS--
TR "HIS NAME IN THE PAPER" JUN '59

MAYFIELD, MARTYS
FREY, MARTYS--[31]

MAYHAR, ARDATH F.H.
CANNON, FRANK--HAWK/MAYHAR INTRVW '93, WEST--
ZEBRA "FEUD AT SWEETWATER CREEK" '87
ZEBRA "TEXAS GUNSMOKE" '88
ZEBRA "BLOODY TEXAS TRAIL" '88
TW "SWEET INNOCENT GANG DOLL" SEPT '59 ??
CANNON, RAVENNA--[1][31][33]
HURST, ARDATH FRANCES--[1]
KILLDEER, JOHN--HAWK/MAYHAR INTRVW '93,[31]--
BB 'MOUNTAINMAN' SERIES:
"WILD COUNTRY" '92
"THE UNTAMED" '92
"BLOOD KIN" '93
"WILDERNESS RENDEZVOUS" '93
"PASSAGE WEST" '94
"FAR HORIZONS" '94
MACWILLIAMS, SARAH--HAWK/MAYHAR INTRVW '93,
[23]UNPUBLISHED--
"THE CLARRINGDON HERITAGE"
"THE GUNS OF LIVINGSTON FROST"
"DEADLY MEMOIR"

MAYLEAS, WILLIAM
SAXON, WILLIAM--[7]SF--
AVON "MINDBENDER" '89

MAYNARD, CHRISTOPHER
MAYNARD, CHRIS--[33]

MAYNE, ETHEL COLBURN
HUNTLEY, FRANCES E.--[1]

MAYNE, WILLIAM [J.C.]
COBALT, MARTIN--[7][31][33]SF--
HM "SWALLOWS" '72
JAMES, DYNELY--W/RICHARD D. CAESAR,
[8][22][31][33]ENGLISH--
DUTTON "THE GOBBLING BILLY" '59
MOLIN, CHARLES--[1][31][33]--
'DORMOUSE TALES' - 5 BOOKS

MAYNES, J. OSCAR JR.
MAYNES, DR. J.O. ROCKY--[33]
MAYNES, J.O. ROCKY JR.--[33]

MAYO, ISABELLA FYVIE
GARRETT, EDWARD--[1]
GARRETT, RUTH--[1]

MAYO, WILLIAM STARBUCK
ROMER, JONATHAN--[1]

MAYR, DALLAS WILLIAM
KETCHUM, JACK--V. BERCH LTR TO HUBIN '94, [7], MYS/SF--
WARNER "COVER" '87
BAL "OFF SEASON#1 & #2" '80/91
WARNER "GIRL NEXT DOOR" '89
BERK "SHE WAKES" '89

MAYS, CEDRIC WESLEY
MAYS, SPIKE--[1]

MAZANI, ERIC C.F.N.
MARS, E.C.--[8]

MAZROFF, DAVID
HALLIDAY, BRETT--T. JOHNSON-ECHOES #23, MYS,HP--
MSMM "TO KILL A COP" AUG '72

MAZURE, ALFRED LEONARDUS
CULLNER, LEONARD--[8]
MAZ--[1][8][34]MYS--
SPEARMAN "PIGEON PARADE" '61
SPEARMAN "CASH ON DESTRUCTION" '62
SPEARMAN "PRISCILLA DARLING" '63

MAZZA, ADRIANNA
SAVIOZZI, ADRIANNA--[31][33]--
"SOMEBODY SAW" '62

MAZZOCCO, EDWARD
MAZE, EDWARD--[8]

MCADAM, CONSTANCE
CLYDE, CONSTANCE--[8]

MCADAM, DOUG
MCADAM, PRESTON--W/JOHN PRESTON,[34]MYS--
AV "ISLAND INTRIGUE" '85
AV "ARABIAN ASSAULT" '85
AV "AFRICAN ASSIGNMENT" '85

MCALLISTER, ALISTER
ALEXANDER, HENRY--[31]
BROCK, LYNN--[3][5][18][31]IRISH/MYS--
COLLINS "FOUFINGERS" '39
COLLINS "STOAT" '40 & MORE
WHARTON, ANTHONY--[2][3][5][18][29]IRISH/MYS--
COLLINS "TWO OF DIAMONDS" '26 & 3 MORE

MCALMON, ROBERT
URQUARDT, GUY--[1]
URQUHART, GUY--[8]

MCALPINE, ROBERT W.
ANCIENT, OLIVER--[1]
BRITTLE, GATH--[1]
DHU--[1]
GREGG, GEORGE GREGORY--[1]
SONICA--[1]
UNCLE JAKE--[1]

MCARDLE, BRIAN
REID, DESMOND--W/G.P. MANN,[1][34]HP--
AMALG "FLASHPOINT FOR TREASON" '57

MCAULEY, JAMES PHILLIP
MALLEY, ERN--W/HAROLD STEWART,[1][31]

MCAULIFFE, FRANK
MALACHY, FRANK--[3][18]MYS--
PERMA M3059 "HOT TOWN" '56

MCBRIDE, ROBERT MEDILL
MEDILL, ROBERT--[1]
REID, MARSHALL--[8]

MCBROOM, R. CURTIS
DRING, NATHANIEL--[2][7][31]SF--
"THE EARTH IS YOUR SPACESHIP: STORY OF MAN" '67

MCCABE, BILL
ZARO, BUKKO BE--[2]

MCCABE, RALPH
PYRRHO--[1]

MCCAFFERTY, BARBARA TAYL.
MCCLELLAN, TIERNEY--M. LACHMAN-CRPG, MYS--
"HEIR CONDITION" '95

MCCAFFERY, LAWRENCE FLOR.
MCCAFFERY, LARRY--[7]SF NON-FICT

MCCAIG, DONALD
ASHLEY, STEVEN--[3][7][31]MYS/SF--
MCKAY "CALEB, WHO IS HOTTER THAN A $2 PISTOL" '75
DIAL "STALKING BLIND" '76
LOGAN, JAKE--KNOX BURGER INTRVW-P 33, P39, WEST,HP--
MCCAIG, SNEE--[1]

MCCAIG, EDITH
ENGREN, EDITH--W/ROBERT JESSIE MCCAIG, [1][9][21]ROM--
GM "MARCY TARRANT" '78

MCCAIG, ROBERT JESSIE
ENGREN, EDITH--W/EDITH MCCAIG,[9][21][31]ROM--
GM "MARCY TARRANT" '78

MCCALL, VIRGINIA NIELSEN
NIELSEN, VIRGINIA--[21][26][33]ROM--
"ALOHA, DEATH"
"LA SAUVAGE" & MORE

MCCALMENT, MAEBELLE [B]
LEY, BREA R.--[1]
MACK, BREARLY--[1]
MACK, MAEBELLE--[1]

MCCAMMON, ROBERT
AXTON, DAVID--J. LEGG CALL '93, MYS--
ST. MARTINS-"STOLEN THUNDER" '93

MCCANCE, JAMES LAW
MAC--[1]
MCC--[1]
MCC, J.L.--[1]

MCCANDLESS, PATRICIA A.
MONTANA, PAT--[26]ROM--
SIL 993 "ONE UNBELIEVABLE MAN"

MCCANN, HELEN
DEAN, ELINOR--[33]ROM--
HALE "FALSE ENCHANTMENT" '84
HALE "MASTER OF DRYFORD" '85

MCCARGAR, JAMES GOODRICH
FELIX, CHRISTOPHER--[31][34]MYS--
ALLEN "THREE CORNERED COVER" [W/GEORGE MARTON] '73

MCCARROLL, JAMES
DUBH, SCIAN--[8]

MCCARROLL, MARION CLYDE
FAIRFAX, BEATRICE--W/MARIE MANNING,[1][31]

MCCARTER, VERMILLE
MCCARTER, JODY--W/JODI DE MELIKOFF,[1][2][11]

MCCARTHY, CHARLES
McCARTHY, CORMAC--[31]--
6 RANDOM HOUSE NOVELS '65-92

MCCARTHY, SHAUN LLOYD
CALLAS, THEO--[18][31][34]MYS--
MULLER "CITY OF KITES" '55
"ANN & PETER IN SO. SPAIN" '59
CORY, DESMOND--[18][29][32][34]MYS--
31 NOVELS '51-77
LM "UNCONTROLLED GOODS" OCT-NOV '51
MCCARTHY, SHAUN--[18]MYS--
"LUCKY HAM" '77

MCCARTHY-ANDERSON, DEBRA
VINCER, RACHEL--W/CAROL BRUCE-THOMAS,[26]ROM--
"HOT COPY"
"PRIM AND IMPROPER"

MCCARTNEY, R.J.
SCOTT, BRUCE--[8]

MCCARTON, BENJAMIN F.
CARTER, FRANK--[1]

MCCARTY, WILSON
CHAMBERLAND, WILSON--W/NORMA CRANDALL,[1]

MCCASH, JUNE HALL
MARTIN, JUNE HALL--[1]

MCCAULEY, ELFRIEDA BABNK.
HOUSE, ANNE W.--[22][31]AMERICAN

MCCAY, BILL
APPLETON, VICTOR--[7][23]SGF,HP--
STSY 'TOM SWIFT':
"BLACK DRAGON"
"NEGATIVE ZONE"

MCCAY, WINSOR
SILAS--[33]

MCCHESNEY, MARION
CHESNEY, MARION--[7]SF--
FAWCETT "THE GHOST & LADY ALICE" '82

MCCHESNEY, MARY F.
FRANKLIN, MELISSA--[14]ADULT--
OLYM OPH#209 "NYMPHES, HORSES AND ATHLETES" '70
RAYTER, JOE--[1][22][34]MYS--
SCRIBN "VICTIM WAS IMPORTANT" '54
MILL "ASKING FOR TROUBLE" '55
MILL "STAB IN THE DARK" '55

MCCLAFFERTY, SUSAN
MACPHERSON, SELINA--[26]ROM--
"ROUGH & TENDER"
"FORBIDDEN FLAME"
"EMBRACE THE WILD DAWN"

MCCLARY, JANE STEVENSON
MCILVAINE, JANE--[22]AMERICAN

MCCLARY, THOMAS CALVERT
CALVERT, THOMAS--[23]SF
CARTER, NICK--[34]MYS,HP--
VITAL "YELLOW DISC MURDER" '48
CRAMER, MILES--[23]SF
McCLARY, T.C.--L. ROBBINS LTR MAR '94
PEREGOY, CALVIN--[2][11][23]SF--
ASF 'DR. CONKLIN' SERIES '34-5

MCCLELLAND, DIANE MARGAR.
PEARSON, DIANE--[3][21][26]][31]MYS/ROM--
BB "BRIDE OF TANCRED" '67
"CSARDAS" & MORE

MCCLELLAND, HARRIET [H]
FLEMMING, HARFORD--[1]

MCCLELLAND, RICHARD L.
LEECH, RICHARD--[1]

MCCLENDON, MARIE M.D.
DANCY, M.M.--[1]

MCCLINTOCK, MARSHALL
DUNCAN, GREGORY--[22][31][33]AMERICAN
MARSHALL, DOUGLAS--[1][22][33]AMERICAN
MCCLINTOCK, MIKE--[1][22][33]AMERICAN
STARRET, WILLIAM--[22][31][33]AMERICAN

MCCLOSKEY, [JOHN] ROBERT
DANGERFIELD, BALFOUR--[22][31][33]AMERICAN

MCCLOY, HELEN [CLARKSON]
CLARKSON, HELEN--[2][7][18][23][31]SF--
TORQUIL "THE LAST DAY" '59
DRESSER, HELEN--[31]

MCCLURE, KEN
BEGG, KEN--[34]MYS--
PLUTO "THE ANVIL AGREEMENT" '85

MCCLUSKEY, SALLY
CAMPBELL, BETHANY--[10][26][34]--
HARL "PROS & CONS" '87
"ROSES OF CONSTANT" '89
"DEAD OPPOSITES"

MCCOLLAM, JAMES G.
McCOLLAM, JIM--[31]

MCCOMAS, I.V.
SOMERVILLE, H.B.--[1]

MCCOMAS, J. FRANCIS
MARLOWE, WEBB--[2][11][23]AMERICAN/SF--
SHORT STORY "FLIGHT INTO DANGER" '46

MCCOMB, FREDERIC W.H.
HABERSHON, KEITH--[1]

MCCOMB, KATHERINE WOODS
WOODS, CONSTANCE--[1]

MCCONNELL, FRANCIS DEMAY
MCCONNELL, FRANK--[7]SF--
NON-FICT

MCCONNELL, JAMES D.R.
MCCONNELL, JAMES--[18]MYS--
"BENEDICTINE COMMAND" '81
RUTHERFORD, DOUGLAS--[18][29][33][34]MYS--
COLLINS "CREEPING FLESH" '63
COLLINS "KICK START" '73 & MORE
TEMPLE, PAUL--W/FRANCIS H. DURBRIDGE, [3][18]MYS--
HODDER "TYLER MYS" '57
HODDER "EAST OF ALGIERS" '59

MCCONNELL, JOHN L.C.
CHANDOS, JOHN--[1][31]

MCCORMACK, JAMES
PATRICK, MAX--[1]

MCCORMICK, GEORGE DONALD
DEACON, RICHARD--[8][31][33]--
"SPYCLOPEDIA" BIO ON COVER

MCCORMICK, JAMES
COMO, LYNN--[34]MYS--
HAM STFFD "ICE IN HER EYES" '52
HAM STFFD "MANHUNT" '52
HAM STFFD "STUTTERING DEATH" '53
DAGON, LERIE--S. HOLLAND-SCION CKLST, P 27, P11
DARK, JOHNNY--[34]MYS,HP--
MILESTONE - TITLES NOT KNOWN
JAMES, MAX--[34]--
HAM STFFD "DEATH IS WHERE YOU MEET IT" '51
HAM STFFD "IT DOESN'T MATTER WHEN YOUR DEAD" '51
JOHNSON, DUFF--[34]MYS,HP--
HAM STFFD "COME OUT FIGHTING" '51
HAM STFFD "DEAD DON'T RISE" '51
HAM STFFD "OPERATOR FROM CHICAGO" '50
MACK, JIM--[3]MYS--
HAM STFFD "FAUST OF THE FBI" '53
MACK, JOHNNY--[34]MYS--
PAGET "FALL GUY" '48
PAGET "FRAME UP" '49 & 5 MORE
MANTZ, LEW--[34]MYS,HP--
HAM STFFD "HIJACKER'S MORGUE" '52
HAM STFFD "THE SNATCH" '52
HAM STFFD "TRAPPED" '52
MARLOWE, GREG--[34]MYS,HP--
HAM STFFD "BURMA BATTLE" '53
HAM STFFD "ESPIONAGE" '53]
STAMPER, ALEX--[27]ENGLISH--
PANT 131 "GLORY SQUAD"
& OTHER FOREIGN LEGION ADV

MCCORMICK, MARY
MCCORMICK, ROSE M.--[1]

MCCORMICK, MERLA JEAN
SPARKS, MERLA JEAN--[1]

MCCORMICK, VICTORIA
GREEN, JANET--[32][34]MYS--
ALLEN "MURDER MISTAKEN" '53
EQMM "TALLEST MAN IN WORLD" JUN '57
TRITON "MY TURN NOW" '71
AHMM "SWEETIST VOICE IN WORLD" DEC '77
EQMM "MOST TATTOOED MAN IN THE WORLD" JUN '75

MCCORMICK, WILFRED
ALLISON, RAND--[1][22][31]AMERICAN
DUNLOP, LON--[1][31]AMERICAN

MCCORQUODALE, BARBARA H.C
CARTLAND, BARBARA--[7][9][32]ROM/SF--
LM "MURDER BY MOUTH" MAR '54
LOW, LOIS--[9]ROM

MCCOURTNEY, LORENA KNOLL
DAY, JOCELYN--[9][21][26]ROM--
"GLITTER GIRL"
"ISLAND FIRES" & MORE
MCCONNELL, LISA--[9][21][26]ROM--
"RIVER OF LOVE"
MCKAY, RENA--[9][21][26]ROM--
"BRIDAL TRAP"
"DESERT DEVIL" & MORE

MCCOWAN, THOMAS E.
McGOWAN, TOM--[31] CHILDREN'S BOOKS

MCCOY, IOLA FULLER
FULLER, IOLA--[1][22][31][33]AMERICAN/MYS--
ASE T35 "THE LOON FEATHER" nd

MCCOY, JOHN
LORD COMMISSIONER--[2]

MCCOY, MADELEINE
MACE, MERLDA--[34]--
MSSNR "MOTTO FOR MURDER" '43
MSSNR "HEADLONG FOR MURDER" '43
MSSNR "BLONDES DON'T CRY" '45

MCCOY, MARJORIE CASEBIER
CASEBIER, MARJORIE--[1][31]

MCCREADY, WARREN T.
MACHIAVELLI--[1][31]

MCCUE, LILLIAN BUENO
DE LA TORRE, LILLIAN--[3][18][29][32]MYS--
5 NVLS '46-87
EQMM "WHETCOMBE WITCH" OCT '73
DE LA TORRE-BUENO, LILIAN--[8]

MCCUE, NOELLE BERRY
MONET, NICOLE--[9][21][26]ROM--
"GUARDIAN ANGEL"
"CASEY'S SHADOW" & MORE

MCCULLEY, JOHNSTON
BRIEN, RALEY--L. ROBBINS LTR '94,[1][31]
CARTER, NICHOLAS--[1][5][11]MYS,HP--
DRAYNE, GEORGE--L. ROBBINS LTR '94,[1][2][31]
MCALPIN, GRANT--L. ROBBINS LTR '94,[1]
MORTON, MONICA--L. ROBBINS LTR '94,[1][2]
O'BRIEN, RALEY--[2]
PHELPS, FREDERIC--L. ROBBINS LTR '94,[1][2]
PIERSON, WALTER--L. ROBBINS LTR '94,[1][2]
RALEY, ROWENA--L. ROBBINS LTR '94,[1][2]
STONE, JOHN MACK--L. ROBBINS LTR '94, [2][37]MYS--
DSM "ROGUE FOR A DAY" MAR '16
STRONG, HARRINGTON--[2][3][19][29]MYS--
LLOYD "LEGAL SETTLEMENT" '22
HUTCH "HOODED STRANGER" '26
HUTCH "SPIDER'S DEN" '26
CHELSEA "BRAND OF SILENCE" '24 & MORE

MCCULLOCH, DEREK
UNCLE MAC--[1][33]

MCCULLOCH, J.H.
RAWLINGS, J.R.--[1]

MCCULLOCH, JOSEPH
MICHAELHOUSE, JOHN--[8]

MCCULLOCH, SARA[H]
URE, JEAN--[1]

MCCULLOUGH-ROBINSON, COL.
MCCULLOUGH, COLEEN--[7][23]AUSTRALIAN/SF & HIST ROM

MCCURTIN, PETER
CURRY, GENE--[28]WEST--
BELM "WILDCAT WOMAN" '79
BELM "YUKON RIDE" '81 & 5 MORE
ROSSI, BRUNO--[28]MYS,HP--
LEIS "KILLING MACHINE" '73
LEIS "STILETTO" '74 & MORE
SCARPETTA, FRANK--[28]MYS,HP--
BELM

MCCUSKER, PAUL
FREED, PAUL--V. BERCH LTR TO HUBIN '94, MYS--
BAKERS PLAY "DEATH BY CHOCOLATE" '85

MCCUTCHAN, JOHN WILSON
LOCKE, PETER--[22]AMERICAN-CANADIAN

MCCUTCHAN, PHILIP [D]
GALWAY, R.C.--[36]MYS
GALWAY, ROBERT CONNINGTON--[1][34]MYS--
HALE "TIMELESS SLEEP" '63
HALE "NEGATIVE MAN" '71 & 10 MORE '63-71
MACNEIL, DUNCAN--[18][29][31]ADV--
14 HODDER NOVELS '69-82
WIGG, T.I.G.--[1][18]--
3 DOBSON NOVELS '58-61

MCCUTCHEON, BENJAMIM F.
BRACE, BENJAMIN--[1]

MCCUTCHEON, GEORGE BARR
GREAVES, RICHARD--[1]

MCCUTCHEON, HUGH [D-M]
DAVIE-MARTIN, HUGH--[29][31][34]MYS--
HALE "GIRL IN MY GRAVE" '76
HALE "SPANIARD'S LEAP" '79 & MORE

MCDADE, CHARLES
DIXON, MARK--V. BERCH LTR TO HUBIN '93,
MYS,HP--
BERK "DEADLY FORCE" '87
BERK "SPECIAL DELIVERY" '87
BERK "HEARTLANDERS" '88
PENDLETON, DON--[34]MYS,HP--
GE "MELTDOWN" '87
GE "SPLIT IMAGE" '87
GE "TROPIC HEAT" '87
GE "FLASH POINT" '88
GE "VIETNAM FALLOUT" '88
GE "BORDER SWEEP" '88
GE "BIG KILL" '89
GE "BACKLASH" '90
GE "WHIPSAW" '90

MCDANIEL, DAVID EDWARD
JOHNSTONE, TED--[2][23][31]AMERICAN/SF--
TV TIE-INS 'MAN FROM UNCLE'
& 'THE PRISONER'

MCDAVID, RAVEN I.
DARWIN, M.B.--[1][31]
HATTERAS, OWEN III--[1][31]
PYLES, AITKEN--[1]

MCDERMOTT, BEVERLY BRODS.
BRODSKY, BEVERLY--[1]

MCDERMOTT, PAUL
MCDERMOTT, DENNIS--W/WALTER L. DENNIS
& P. SCHUYLER MILLER,[2][23]SF--
"RED SPOT ON JUPITER" '31
"DUEL ON THE ASTEROID" '32

MCDEVITT, JOHN CHARLES
MCDEVITT, JACK--[7][23]SF--
ACE "HERCULES TEXT" '86
ACE "A TALENT FOR WAR" '88

MCDONALD, BERNARD
MACDONNAILL, BRIAN--[1][2]

MCDONALD, EDWARD R.
MCDONALD, RAYMOND--W/RAYMOND LEGER,
[1][2][23]SF--
"THE MAD SCIENTIST: A TALE OF THE
FUTURE" 1908

MCDONALD, ERWIN LAWRENCE
HANKINS, CLABE--[31]

MCDONALD, JULIE
JENSEN, JULIE--[1][31]

MCDONALD, MARGARET J.
MCDONALD, JO--[8]

MCDONALD, PAULA
HERRIGAN, JACKIE--[1]

MCDONALD, RICHARD C.
HERRIGAN, JEFF--[1]

MCDONALD, TRACY
DALTON, MARK MAXWELL--L. ESTLEMAN-
MYS SC#42, P81--
MCDONALD "DOWNEAST DETECTIVES"

MCDONELL, ARCHIBALD G.
KENNEDY, ROBERT MILWARD--W/MILWARD R.K.
BURGE,[3]MYS--
GOLZ "THE BLESTON MYS" '28

MCDONNELL, MARGIE P.
MICHAELS, MARGIE--[9][21][26]ROM--
"UNTAMED DESIRE"
"BELOVED PIRATE"
"MIRAGE"

MCDONNELL, VIRGINIA B.
BARCLAY, VIRGINIA--[1][21][26]ROM--
'MID-CITY HOSPITAL' SERIES - 6 NOVELS
KIRBY, JEAN--[1][31]HP--
WHITMAN
MCDONNELL, JINNY--[1]

MCDOUGALL, E. JEAN
ROLYAT, JANE--[1]

MCDOUGALL, IAN CAMPBELL
FENNERTON, WILLIAM--V. BERCH LTR TO
HUBIN '94,MYS--
DAVIES "OLD FOX" '72
ELEK "CZECH MATE" '79 & MORE

MCDOUGALL, MARGARET
NORAH--[8]

MCDOWELL, MICHAEL
ALDYNE, NATHAN--W/DENNIS SCHUETZ,[3][31]MYS--
AV "VERMIFORM" '80 & 3 MORE '80-6
McCRAY, MIKE--V. BERCH LTR TO HUBIN '94,
MYS,HP--
DELL "THE BLACK PALM" '84
McCRAY, MIKE--W/JOHN PRESTON, V. BERCH LTR
TO HUBIN '94, MYS,HP--
DELL "COLD VENGEANCE" '84
DELL "DEADLY REUNION" '84
DELL "LOUISIANNA FIRESTORM" '85
YOUNG, AXEL--W/DENNIS SCHUETZ,[34]MYS--
AV "BLOOD RUBIES" '82
AV "WICKED STEPMOTHER" '83

MCDOWELL, MICHAEL PAUL
HUDSON, MICHAEL--[23]SF--
"PHOTON: THIEVES OF LIGHT" '87

MCDOWELL, MICHAEL PAUL
KUBE-MCDOWELL, MICHAEL P.--[7][23]SF--
LEGALIZED TO 'KUBE-MCDOWELL'

MCDOWELL, ROBERT EMMETT
MCDOWELL, EMMETT--M. LACHMAN LTR '93--
'JUNGLE STORIES' MAG, FALL '47
ACE "THREE FOR THE GALLOWS" '58
ACE "IN AT THE KILL" '60
ACE "BLOODLINE TO MURDER" '60

MCDOWELL, SYL
GUNN, TOM--HAWK/HACKATHORN INTRVW '93,
WEST,HP--
PPWM - SHORT STYORIES

MCDUFF, EILEEN MAY
MCDUFF, E.M.--[36]AUSTRALIAN/MYS--
LOTHIAN "MURDER IN THE THEATRE" '47

MCELFRESH, ELIZABETH A.
BLAIR, JENNIFER--[3][26][29]MYS/ROM--
DELL "ASSIGN. IN THE ISLANDS" '70
DELL "SKYE MANOR" '72 & MORE
CLEVELAND, JOHN--[22][29][31][34]MYS--
ARCADIA "MINUS ONE CORPSE" '54
MCELFRESH, ADELINE--[9][21][26]ROM--
"FLIGHT NURSE"
"NURSE IN YUCATAN" & MORE
SCOTT, JANE--[9][21][22]ROM--
"A NEW LOVE FOR CYNTHIA"
"NURSE FOR REBEL'S RUN"
WESLEY, ELIZABETH--[3][9][21][26]MYS/ROM--
AV "SHARON JAMES, FREELANCE
PHOTOGRAPHER" '56

MCELWAIN, DEAN
CLERMONT, SHANA--[9][21][26]ROM--
'CIVIL WAR' SAGA:
"MEMPHIS"
"NATCHEZ"

MCENVOY, C.N.
STRANGE, KEMBLE--[1]

MCEVOY, HARRY K.
MACK, KIRBY--[1][22][31]AMERICAN

MCEVOY, MARJORIE HARTE
BOND, GILLIAN--[8]ENGLISH
HARTE, MARJORIE--[21][22][26][31]ROM--
"CLOSING WEB"
"STRANGE JOURNEY" & MORE

MCEWAN, MARCIA
BARRETT, CHARLES--[35]AUSTRALIAN--
HRWTZ PB194 "ADDRESS KING'S CROSS" '64
SCOTT, JAMES--[35]AUSTRALIAN--
HRWTZ PB200 "A FESTIVAL OF SPIES" '64
HRWTZ PB204 "UNFRIENDLY RELATIONS" '65
HRWTZ PB246 "DEATH DEALER" '65
HRWTZ PB303 "MANHUNTER" '67
SEVEN, JOHN--[35]AUSTRALIAN--
HRWTZ PB210 "NIGHT IN KINGS CROSS" '65
SEVERN, JEAN PAUL--[35]AUSTRALIAN--
HRWTZ PB285 "VICE TRAP-KING'S CROSS" '66
WAYNE, MARCIA--[35]AUSTRALIAN--
HRWTZ PB201 "BEAT GIRL" '65
WAYNE, MARSHA--[35] AUSTRALIA--
HRWTZ PB219 "KING'S CROSS AFFAIR" '65
HRWTZ PB247 "DISTANT ISLAND" '65
HRWTZ PB256 "A TIME TO LOVE" '66

MCEWEN, JESSIE EVELYN
FISHER, AGNES--[1]

MCFADDEN, GERTRUDE V.
MILBROOK, JOHN--[1]

MCFAGUE, SALLIE
TE SELLE, SALLIE MCFAGUE--[1]

MCFALL, FRANCES ELIZABETH
GRAND, SARAH--[1][22]ENGLISH

MCFARLAND, DOROTHY TUCK
TUCK, DOROTHY--[1]

MCFARLANE, DAVID
TYSON, TELLO--[8]

MCFARLANE, LESLIE CHARLES
ALGER, HORATIO--[2]GHOSTED
BOWIE, JIM--[2]HP--STSY
DIXON, FRANKLIN W.--[1]JUV,HP--
STSY-'HARDY BOYS'
EDWARDS, JULIE--[2]JUV
FERRIS, JAMES CODY--[31]JUV,HP--
'X BAR X BOYS'
KEENE, CAROLYN--MCFARLANE-
GHOST OF THE HARDY BOYS/JUV--
STSY-'DANA GIRLS'
ROCKWOOD, ROY--MCFARLANE-
GHOST OF THE HARDY BOYS/JUV,HP--
STSY-'DAVE FEARLESS'
STANDISH, BURT L.--[2]MYS,HP--
STREET & SMITH - MAGAZINE STORIES
WOODS, NAT--[2]JUV,HP--STSY

MCFERRAN, DOUGLASS DAVID
FARREN, DAVID--[1][7][31]SF--

MCGARRITY, MARK
GILL, BARTHOLOMEW--[1][18][34]MYS--
8 'McGARR' NOVELS '77-89

MCGARRY, WILLIAM RUTL
SMYTHE, JAMES P.--[8]

MCGARVEY, ROBERT
WHITE, STEVE--[1][3]MYS--
WARNER 'S-COM' SERIES:
"STARS & SWASTIKAS" '81
"FIGHTING IRISH" '82
"TERROR IN TURIN" '81 & 3 MORE

MCGAUGHY, DUDLEY DEAN
COLE, JACKSON--A. TONIK-COLE CKLST "SPICY
ARMADILLO",HP--
TEX RGR "WHITE GOLD OF TEXAS" MAY '47
DEAN, DUDLEY--V. BERCH-GM PSEUDS, PP 33,
[3]MYS/WEST--
GM 318 "AMBUSH AT RINCON" '53
GM 436 "MAN FROM RIONDO" '54
GM 471 "SONG OF THE GUN" '55
GM 511 "BROKEN SPUR" '55
GM 584 "DIEHARDS" '56
GM 601 "TOUGH HOMBRE" '56
CREST 154 "SIX-GUN VENGEANCE" '56
CREST 177 "BORDER RENAGADE" '57
GM 655 "GUN IN THE VALLEY" '57
GM 882 "LAWLESS GUNS" '59
GM 912 "GUNSHY" '59
GM1014 "LILA MY LOVELY" '60
BERK "CROSS OF ROPE" '63
BERK "TRAIL OF THE HUNTER" '63
GM "GUN THE MAN DOWN" '71
DREW, LINCOLN--L. ROBBINS LTR '94,
PPCC#7, WEST--
PERMA M3063 "DIE IN THE SADDLE" '56
PERMA M3107 "YELLOW ROPE" '58

MCGAUGHY, DUDLEY DEAN [CONT]
DUDLEY, OWEN--[3]MYS--
ACE D195 "DEEP END" '56
ACE D231 "MURDER FOR CHARITY" '57
EVENS, HODGE--V. BERCH RVW '93,[34]--
RAIN 109 "HER CANDLE BURNS HOT" '51
FAL 24 "THREE FOR PASSION" '52
FAL 40 "WHIP-HAND" '52
FAL 33 "YELLOW-HEAD" '52
BEAC B443Y "TWO FACES OF PASSION" '61
EVENS, OWEN--L. ROBBINS LTR '94--
BAL 670 "CHAINLINK" '62
GREY, LOREN ZANE--PPCC#7, P82, WEST,HP--
ZGWN "LASSITER"
ZGWM "LASSITER TOUGH"
HAWK, ALEX--PPCC#7, P82, WEST,HP--
PAPLB - TITLE UNKNOWN
OWEN, DEAN--[2][3][28][32]MYS/WEST--
SW "OBIT FOR A KILLER" AUG '45
SW "A GOOD ACT" SEPT '47
ACE D12 "MAN FROM BOOT HILL" '53
POPLB 538 "POINT OF A GUN" '53
POPLB 583 "RIFLE PASS" '54
POPLB 788 "GUNPOINTER" '56
MON 104 "RAWHIDER FROM TEXAS" '58
HILL 139 "A KILLER'S BARGAIN" '60
MON 602 "BRIDES OF DRACULA" '60
MON 604 "KONGA '60
MON 605 "REPTILICUS" '60
MON 308 "SAM HOUSTON STORY" '61
MON 290 "JUICE TOWN" '62
GS IL7-41 "GIRL POSSESSED" '64
OWEN, DUDLEY--L. ROBBINS LTR '94
OWEN, EVENS--L. ROBBINS LTR '94
SANDERS, BRETT--PPCC#7, P82
SLADE, JACK--PPCC#7, P82, WEST,HP--
WYNNE, BRIAN--[28]WEST--
ACE "GUNSLICK TERRITORY" '73

MCGAURAN, JOANNA
GILPEN, JOANNA--[9][21][26]ROM--
"FIRST MATES"
"A SIMPLE I DO"
"CHANCE IT"
MCGOWAN, JAN--[9][21][26]ROM--
"SILVERSEA"
"GOLDEN LILY" & MORE
MERLIN, CHRISTIE[A]--[9][21][26]ROM--
"FOREVER EDEN"
"SNOWFLAME" & MORE

MCGAW, NAOMI B.T.
HERVEY, JANE--[1][22][31]ENGLISH

MCGEE, EMILIE R.
RICHARDS, EMILIE--[9][21]ROM--
"BAYOU MIDNIGHT"
"LADY OF THE NIGHT" & MORE

MCGEE, GWYN
SNOW, EBONI--SANTE FE NEW MEXICAN-
ARTICLE 9/23/94, MYS--
"BEGUILED" '94

MCGEOGH, ANDREW
PAUL, ADRIAN--[8]

MCGEOUGH, JOHN
MACK BRIDE, JOHNNY--[28]SCOTTISH/WEST--
4 HALE NOVELS '90-91

MCGIVERN, MAUREEN DALY
DALY, MAUREEN--[1][22][31]AMERICAN--
"MENTION MY NAME IN MOMBASA" '58

MCGIVERN, WILLIAM P.
BLADE, ALEXANDER--[1][2]SF,HP--AMZ
CHANDLER, LAWRENCE--[2]SF,HP--ZIFF-DAVIS
COSTELLO, P.F.--[2]HP--ZIFF-DAVIS-
HIS EXCLUSIVELY TILL LATE '50's
GARSON, CLEE--[2] ?
JARVIS, E.K.--[2]HP--ZIFF-DAVIS
PETERS, BILL--[2][3][5][32]MYS--
DODD "BLONDES DIE YOUNG" '52
MD "EVERYBODY HAS TO DIE" MAY '57
VANCE, GERALD--[2] ?

MCGLAMRY, BEVERLY
CAMERON, KATE--[7][9][21][26]ROM/SF--
"AS IF THEY WERE GODS"
"ORENDA"

MCGLOIN, JOSEPH THADDEUS
O'FINN, THADDEUS--[3][8][22]AMERICAN/MYS--
RINEHART "HAPPY HOLIDAY" '50

MCGONIGLE, CHERYL
BISHOP, CARLY--[10][21][26]ROM--
"FUGITIVE HEART"
"FALLING STARS" & MORE

MCGOWAN, JILL
CHAPLIN, ELIZABETH--LACHMAN LST '93, MYS--
DJ OF FIRST "CHAPLIN" BOOK "HOSTAGE
OF FORTUNE" '92

MCGOWAN, RAYMOND
LEMOTT, JUSTIN G.T. III--W/WILLIAM GEBAUER,

MCGOWEN, THOMAS E.
MCGOWEN, TOM--[33]

MCGRATH, JOAN ROSITA TORR
FORBES, ROSITA--[31]

MCGRATH, ROBERT L.
LEE, BOB--[1][31]
LEE, ROBERTA--[1][31]

MCGRAW, J.H.
JACKSON, HOWARD--[1]

MCGRAW, WILLIAM CORBIN
CORBIN, WILLIAM--[1][31][33]JUV--
12 BOOKS '52-91

MCGREGOR, ELLEN
PANTELL, S.F.--[11]SF

MCGREW, JULIA
MCGREW, FENN--W/CAROLINE K. FENN,
[22][31][34]MYS--
RH "MURDER BY MAIL" '51 & 2 MORE

MCGUINNESS, BERNARD
MCGUINNESS, BRIAN--[8]

MCGUIRE, CHERYL KREUGER
KREUGER, ELIZABETH--[26]ROM--
"A SAVING GRACE"
"FOR THE CHILDREN" & MORE

MCGUIRE, LESLIE SARAH
BRITTON, LOUISA--[1][31][33]
BURTON, LESLIE--[1][31][33]
EYRE, DOROTHY--[1][31][33]
KEYSER, SARAH--[1][31][33]
LESLIE, SARAH--[1][31][33]
ROBINSON, SHARI--[1]
STRONG, DAVID--[1][33]

MCHAM, MARCIA
MARSH, CAROL--W/CAROL ANKERSON,[26]ROM--
"THE SILVER LINK"

MCHARGUE, GEORGESS
CHASE, ALICE--[8][31][33]
USHER, MARGO SCEGGE--[33]
USHER, MARGO SEESSE--[8][11]

MCHENRY, JAMES
SECONDSIGHT, SOLOMON--[2]

MCHUGH, EDNA
COXE, KATHLEEN BUDDINGTON--W/AMELIA REYNOLDS LONG,[1][3][11]MYS--
PHOENIX "MURDER MOST FOUL" '46

MCHUGH, MAXINE DAVIS
DAVIS, MAXINE--[1][31]

MCILVAINE, CHARLES
HODGE, TOBY--[1]

MCILWAIN, DAVID
MAINE, C.E.--[1][11]MYS--
HART "WORLD'S STRANGEST CRIMES" '67
MAINE, CHARLES ERIC--V. BERCH-LESBIANA/CNTRCLTR, BAE 22,[2][3][4][7][23]ADULT/SF--
HODDER "THE ISOTOPE MAN" '57
BB 1470 "TIMELINER" '56
BAL 218 "HIGH VACUUM" '57
ACE D274 "WORLD WITHOUT MEN" '58
HODDER "COUNT-DOWN" '59
BAL 360 "FIRE PAST THE FUTURE" '59
BAL 290K "TIDE WENT OUT' '59
AV T524 "HE OWNED THE WORLD" '61
BAL U6092 "B.E.A.S.T." '67
GM 1918 "SURVIVAL MARGIN" '68
MASTERSON, WHIT--[1]MYS, SP--
RAYNER, RICHARD--[2][4][23][34]MYS--
HALE "TROUBLE WITH RUTH" '60
HALE "DARLING DAUGHTER" '61
HALE "STAND-IN FOR TROUBLE" '63
HALE "DIG DEEP FOR JULIE" '63
WADE, ROBERT--[2][11][23][31]SF--

MCILWRAITH, JEAN NEWTON
FORSYTHE, JEAN--[1]

MCINERNY, RALPH [M]
AUSTIN, HARRY--[1][31]
FITZRALPH, MATTHEW--[31]
MACKEY, ERNAN--[1][31]
MACKIN, EDWARD--LACHMAN-DJ,[34]MYS--
MacM "NOMINATIVE CASE" '90
MCKAY, ERNAN--M. LACHMAN--
'85 NEWSPAPER ART. ON "MCINERNY"
QUILL, MONICA--[1][3][18]MYS--
VANG "NOT A BLESSED THING" '81
VANG "LET US PREY" '82 & 4 MORE

MCINTOSH, KENNETH
CASEY, KENT--[2][11]
KENT, CASEY--[2]

MCINTOSH, KINN HAMILTON
AIRD, CATHERINE--[3][5][8][18][29]MYS--
COLLINS "A DEAD LIBERTY" '86
& 9 MORE '66-90

MCKAY, FESTUS CLAUDIUS
EDWARDS, ELI--[1][22][31]AMERICAN

MCKEAG, ERNEST LIONEL
BARTON, TONY--[34]MYS--
HARB "THINK FAST, SISTER" '52
BRAZA, JACQUE--[1][22][31]ENGLISH
GRIFF--P. HARBOTTLE-PP 25,JEAN F. LE DEIST-BAE 18,[3]ENGLISH/MYS,HP--
MOF "DOPE IS FOR DOPES" '49
MOF "RUB-OUT SPECIALTY" '49
MOF "RACKETS INCORPORATED" '49
MOF "ONLY MUGS DIE YOUNG" '49
MOF "TRADING WITH BODIES" '50
GRIMSHAW, MARK--[22][29][31][34]ENGLISH/MYS--
AMALG "COLWYN DANE-THE OUTLAWED DETECTIVE" '37
AMALG "SIGN OF THE GRINNING DRAGON" '38
HAYNES, PAT--[1][22][31]ENGLISH
KING, JOHN--P. HARBOTTLE-PP 25,JEAN F. LE DEIST-BAE 18,PPCC #2,[2][23][32]--
"SHUNA, WHITE QUEEN OF THE JUNGLE" '51
"SHUNA & THE LOST TRIBE" '51
TW "BADGE OF DISHONOR" SEPT '59
LACROIX, RAMON--[22][27][31][34]MYS,HP--
MOF "DANGER FOR LOVE" '47
MOF "ILLICIT CARGO" '47
MOF "HOTEL FOR SCANDAL" '47
MOF "MURDER AT LE TOUQUET" '47]
LAROCHE, RENE--[1][22][31]ENGLISH
MAXWELL, JACK--[7][23]ENGLISH/SF--
"INVADED BY MARS" '34
"TERROR FROM THE STRATOSPHERE" '37
MCKEAG, EILEEN--[1][22]ENGLISH
VANE, ROLAND--S. HOLLAND, V. BERCH-ARCH, BAE 15,[34]MYS--
ARCH "NIGHT HAUNTS OF PARIS" '49
ARCH "WHITE SLAVES OF NEW ORLEANS" '49
ARCH "SINFUL SISTERS" '50
ARCH "LADIES OF THE RED LAMP" '50
ARCH "WANTON WIFE" '50
ARCH "WOMAN WITH A PAST" '50
ARCH "GIRL FROM TIGER BAY" '50
ARCH "SIN STAINED" '50
ARCH "THIS THING CALLED SIN" '50
ARCH "VICE RACKETS OF SOHO" '51
ARCH "CLIPJOINT GIRL" '52
ARCH "AMOROUS ADVENTURESS" '52
ARCH "WOMAN OF MONTMARTRE" '52
ARCH "WILLING SINNERS" '52
ARCH "SLAVES OF PASSION" '52
ARCH "PICK-UP GIRL" '52
ARCH "WHITE SLAVES OF THE RED LAMP" '52
ARCH "WHITE SLAVE RACKET" '52
ARCH "CALL GIRLS OF NEW YORK" '53
ARCH "JUVENILE DELINQUENTS" '53

MCKEE, JANICE
MCKEE, JAN [JANICE]--[9][26]ROM--
"SWEET JUSTICE"
"MONTANA SKIES" & MORE

MCKELWAY, ST. CLAIR
HALL, J. DE P.--[22][31]AMERICAN

MCKENNA, EDWARD LAWRENCE
WINGSHOT, LEO--[1]

MCKENNA, GEORGE
ALLAN, JACK--MUNROE SEPT '93 AUCT,CRPG,ADULT--
NSL U-148 "GOOD TIME GIRL" '60
NSL U-155 "LOVE IS A GENTLE WHIP" '61
VINING, JACK--V. BERCH-BC/ BRNDN PSEUDS, BAE 22, P24

MCKENNA, MARGARET MARY
MCKENNA, MARY LAWRENCE--[1]

MCKENNA, RICHARD
APPLETON, VICTOR II--[7]SF,HP--
STSY 'TOM SWIFT'
"& HIS COSMOTRON EXPRESS"
"& HIS DYNA-4 CAPSULE"
"& THE GALAXY GHOSTS"

MCKENNA, RICHARD MILTON
MCKENNA, R.M.--[1]

MCKENZIE, C[ECIL] J[AMES]
KANE--[34][35] AUSTRALIA/MYS--
14 WEBSTER NOVELS '58-9
OWEN, MICHAEL--[35]AUSTRALIAN/WAR,HP--
HRWTZ "COMMANDO STRIKE" '58
HRWTZ "JUNGLE PATROL" '59
HRWTZ "ATTACK AT DAWN" '59
HRWTZ "TANK RAIDERS" '59
HRWTZ "BATTLE TRAP" '59
HRWTZ "MARKHAM VALLEY JUMP" '59
HRWTZ "KANGA FORCE" '59
HRWTZ "WATCH OR DIE" '60
HRWTZ "Z FORCE" '60
HRWTZ "RAPE OF RABAUL" '66
HRWTZ "BEASTS OF BUSHIDO" '67

MCKENZIE, TINA
HARLOWE, JUSTIN--W/LAURA BENNETT
& JEAN HARVEY,[21]ROM--
"JEALOUSIES"
"MEMORY & DESIRE"

MCKEONE, DIXIE
LOVELACE, JANE--[9][22][26]ROM--
"ECCENTRIC LADY"
"ROLISSA"
MCKEONE, LEE--[9]ROM

MCKEOWN, NORMAN ROBERT
GILES, NORMAN--[3][22]SOUTH AFRICAN/MYS--
COLLINS "KEERBOSKLOOF" '29
COLLINS "WHIPS OF TIME" '31

MCKIBBIN, ARCHIBALD
CLOIE, MACK--[1]

MCKIBBON, J.E.
ELLIS, JOHN--[1]
PROBYN, ELISE--[1]
PROBYN, HUGH--[32]MYS--
JCM "IN FOR GOOD" AUG '62
JCM "MIREBUE SPECIAL" OCT '62 & OTHERS
PROBYN, JOHN E--[1]

MCKILLOP, NORMAN
BEG, TORAN--[8][22][31]SCOTTISH

MCKIMMEY, JAMES
DANIELS, DEWEY--[31]
JONES, TURKEL--[31]
SWIFT, BENJAMIN--[1]

MCKISSACK, LINDSAY C.
FINLAY, WINIFRED--[7]SF/HOR--
HARRAP "BEADBONNIE ASH" '73
HARRAP "SINGING STONES" '70 & MORE

MCKISSACK, PATRICIA C.
CARWELL, L'ANN--[1][31][33]

MCKITTRICK, ANNA MARGARET
ROS, AMANDA MCKITTRICK--[1]

MCKITTRICK, DOROTHY
DORS, ALEXANDRA--[9][21][26]ROM--
"COME IN FROM THE COLD"
MACK, DOROTHY--[9][21][26]ROM--
"RAVEN SISTERS"
"LOST WALTZ" & MORE

MCLACHLAN, DAN
MCMUD, DOK--[8]

MCLAREN, J.A.
ADAMS, JOHN--[1]

MCLAREN, JACK
MCNORTH, JACK--[13]AUSTRALIAN

MCLAREN, MORAY DAVID SHAW
MURRAY, MICHAEL--[8]

MCLAUGHLIN, EMMA MAUDE
WEIR, ALICE M.--[1]

MCLAUGHLIN, FRANK
BERTOLET, PAUL--[33]

MCLAUGHLIN, PATRICIA
MCLINN, PATRICIA--[7][26]SF/ROM--
"HOOPS"
"A NEW WORLD" & 4 OTHER NOVELS

MCLAURIN, ANNE
LAURIN, ANNE--[1][31][33]

MCLEAN, ANNE [JULIA]
DIAMOND, ANN--[1]

MCLEAN, CAROLINE CRAWFORD
CRAWFORD, CAROLINE--[1]

MCLEAN, ERIC W.
RAYLE, GEOFFREY--[1]
TOWNSEND, ERIC W.--[1][34]MYS--
AMALG "RIDDLE OF THE FOREST" '32
KUNG, TOR--W/JACK GILBERT,[14]ADULT--
OLYM OPH#214 "FOREVER ECSTACY" '68
OLYM TC#214 "MY MOTHER TAUGHT ME" '67

MCLEAN, JOHN DAVID RUARI
HARDIE, DAVID--[1]

MCLEAN, KATHRYN [A]
FORBES, KARINE--[1]
FORBES, KATHRYN--[1][31][33]

MCLEARY, RENA
ALERS, ROCHELLE--[9]ROM--
"CARELESS WHISPERS"

MCLEAVE, HUGH [GEORGE]
COPELAND, RICHARD--[3][40]MYS--
MacM "NO FACE IN THE MIRROR" '80

MCLEISH, SIMON
ZOOL, M.H.--[23]SF, GP

MCLELLAN, DIANA
EAR, THE--[31]
MUMMS, HARDEE--[1]

MCLEOD, JOHN FREELAND
FREELAND, JAY--[31]

MCLEOD, SCOTT WILLARD
MCLOUD, SCOTT--[1]

MCLURE, R.
KNOWLES, THOMAS E.--[1]

MCMAHAN, IAN
COLBURN, LAURA--[34]MYS--
ZEBRA "DEATH IN A SMALL WORLD" '79
ZEBRA "DEATH OF A PRIMA DONNA" '79
ZEBRA "DEATH THRU THE MILL" '79
CURTIS, RICHARD HALE--[21]ROM,HP--
'SKYMASTER' SERIES:
"AFTER THE HAWK"
WILLOUGHBY, LEE DAVIS--[21]ROM,HP--
DELL 'MKNG OF AMERICA' SERIES:
"GAMBLERS"

MCMAHON, KAY
EMM, CATHERINE--[9][21][26]ROM--
"FORBIDDEN MAGIC"

MCMAHON, MARGARET [H]
MARKHAM, PAULINE--[1]

MCMAHON, NEIL
RHODES, DANIEL--V. BERCH LTR TO
HUBIN '94,[7]MYS/SF--
ST. MARTIN'S "NEXT, AFTER LUCIFER" '88
ST. MARTIN'S "ADVERSARY" '89
ST. MARTIN'S "KISS OF DEATH" '90

MCMEEKIN, ISABEL [M]
MCMEEKIN, CLARK--W/DOROTHY [PARK] CLARK,
[1][22][33]AMERICAN

MCMILLAN, DONALD
STUART, JOHN ROY--[8]

MCMILLAN, JAMES
CORIOLANUS--[1]

MCMORDIE, JOHN ANDREW
SHAN--[8]

MCMORDIE, TABER
CHANNING, PETER--[8]

MCMULLAN, CHARLES WALDEN
MUNRO, CHARLES KIRKPATRIC--[22]ENGLISH

MCMULLAN, KATE HALL
HALL, KATY--[31]
HALL, KATE--[1][33] GHOSTED
MCMULLAN, KATY HALL--[33]

MCMULLEN, DYSART
WOOD, VALENTINE--W. MURRAY-ECHOES #5,HP

MCMULLEN, JOSEPH CARL
CARLTON, JOSEPH--[1][3]MYS--
PLAY "LADIES IN DANGER" '45

MCMULLEN, RUTH R.
RONEY, RUTH ANNE--[1]

MCMURRAY, NANCY A.
YOWA--[1]

MCMURRY, SARAH L.
BARKER, SALLY--[31]

MCMURTRY, LARRY
RAY, OPHELIA--AUTHOR CONFIRMED--
MCCLELLAND & STEWART "DAUGHTER OF
THE TEJAS" '65

MCNAB, CLAIRE
CARMICHAEL, CLAIRE--[36]AUSTRALIAN--
YOUNG ADULTS BKS

MCNALLY, MARY ELIZABETH
O'BRIEN, DEIRDRE--[8]

MCNAMARA, BARBARA WILLARD
O'CONNER, ELIZABETH--[1][8][13]AUSTRALIAN

MCNAMARA, LENA BROOK[E]
MACK, EVALINA--[8][22][34]AMERICAN/MYS--
ARCADIA "DEATH OF A PORTRAIT" '52
ARCADIA "CORPSE IN THE COVE" '55
ARCADIA "DEATH AMONG THE SANDS" '57
ARCADIA "MURDER IN MINIATURE" '59

MCNAUGHT, ANN BOYCE
GILMOUR, ANN--[9][21][26]ROM--
"TEAM DOCTOR"

MCNEELY, JEANETTE
MACKIE, MARON--[1]
MACNEILL, JANET--[1][31]

MCNEES, PAT
MANCINI, PAT MCNEES--[1][31]

MCNEILE, HERMAN CYRIL
SAPPER--[2][3][5][7][18][32]MYS,NOVELS--
JCM "HOUSE BY THE HEADLANDS" JUN '57

MCNEILL, GEORGE
REDDOCH, JENNIFER--[3]MYS--
POPLB "A CHAIR FOR DEATH" '73
POPLB "LEGACY OF MENDOUBIA" '73
POPLB "NIGHT OF THE HELLEBORE" '74

MCNEILLIE, JOHN
NIALL, IAN--[2][3][11]MYS--
HM "VILLAGE POLICEMAN" '71

MCNEILLY, MILDRED MASTER.
DEWEY, JAMES--[1]
KELLY, GLENN--[1]

MCNEILLY, WILFRED G.
ARTHUR, WILLIAM--[11]
BAKER, W. HOWARD--[1][2][11][31]--
[34] STATES HE DID NOT USE THIS PSEUD.
BALLINGER, W.A.--W/W. HOWARD BAKER
& G.P. MANN,[34]MYS--
AMALG "LAST TIGER" '63
BALLINGER, W.A.--W/W. HOWARD BAKER,[34]MYS--
AMALG "CORPSE FOR CHRISTMAS" '62
BALLINGER, W.A.--[2][3][11][16][31]MYS,HP--
AMALG "DOWN AMONG THE AD MEN" '68
GLASSFORD, WILLIAM--[1][3][7]MYS/SF--
NEL "ALPHA-OMEGA" '77
GREGG, MARTIN--[2][3][11][16][31]MYS--
HALE "DHOW PATROL" '83
HUNTER, JOE [J]--[2][16][31]MYS--
SB 118 "CASE DEFAULTING SAILOR"
SB 320 "CASE OF STOLEN RANSOM"
LECALE, ERROL--[2][3][7][16][31]MYS--
NEL "TIGGERMAN OF TERRAHPUR" '73
NEL "CASTLEDOOM" '74
NEL "THE DEATH BOX" '74
NEL "THE SEVERED HAND" '74
NEL "ZOMBIE" '75
REID, DESMOND--W/W.A. HOWARD BAKER,[34]MYS,HP--
MYFLR "SNOWMAN COMETH" '66

MCNEILLY, WILFRED G. [CONT]
REID, DESMOND--[2][16][23][34]MYS,HP--
MYFLR "MURDER BY MOONLIGHT" '61
AMALG "MURDER'S ROCK" '61
"LET MY PEOPLE BE" '65
MYFLR "FRENZY IN THE FLESH" '66
SAXON, PETER--W/W.A. HOWARD BAKER, [7][34]MYS,HP--
MYFLR "DARKEST NIGHT" '66
MYFLR "THE TORTURER" '67
MYFLR "DARK WAYS TO DEATH" '68
MYFLR "HAUNTING OF ALAN MAIS" '70
SAXON, PETER--[2][3][7][16][23]MYS/SF,HP--
MYFLR "SATAN'S CHILD" '67
SPHERE "CORRUPTION" '68
WELLSLEY, JULIE--[11][26]ROM--
"STRANGER IN A DARK LAND"
"HOUSE MALIGN"
'FATEFUL TIDE" & MORE

MCNELLY, WILLIS E.
TABARD, GEOFFREY--[1]

MCNISH, JAMES THOMAS
MARATHON--[1]

MCPHEE, HUGH
PHEE, HUGH--[8]

MCPHERSON, HUGH [A]
MCPHERSON, HUGO--[1]

MCPHERSON, MRS. H.M.
WEST, JESSAMYN--[1]

MCQUADE, ANN AIKMAN
AIKMAN, ANN--[1][22][31]

MCQUAY, MICHAEL DENNIS
APPLETON, VICTOR--[7]SF,HP--
STSY 'TOM SWIFT':
"CRATER OF MYSTERY"
"PLANET OF NIGHTMARES"
ARNETT, JACK--[7][23][34]MYS/SF,HP--
BB "BOOK OF JUSTICE #1-#4" '89-90
CAVANAUGH, SARA--G.COOK LTR '93,[7]SF/ROM--
TIARA "A WOMAN IN SPACE" '81
CLAUDIA, SUSAN--G.COOK LTR '93, SF/HOR--
?GHOSTED? "CRADLE TO GRAVE"
HOPE, LAURA LEE--[7][23]MYS,HP--
STSY 'BOBBSEY TWINS':
"HAUNTED HOUSE MYS"
KEENE, CAROLYN--[7][23]SF,HP--
STSY "NANCY DREW GHOST STORIES 2"
MCQUAY, MICHAEL D.--[7]SF
MCQUAY, MIKE--[7][23]SF
PENDLETON, DON--[34]MYS,HP--
GE "AMERICAN NIGHTMARE" '87
GE"DEATH HAS A NAME" '86
GE "CODE OF DISHONOR" '87
GE "FIRE IN THE SKY" '88
GE "KILLING URGE" '88]

MCQUEEN, J.E.
JONES, L.Q.--[7]SF

MCQUEEN, MILDRED HARK
HARK, MILDRED--[1][22][31][33]AMERICAN

MCQUINN, DONALD E.
CHARLES, CONN ALAN--V. BERCH LTR TO HUBIN '94, MYS--
TOR "LIAR'S DICE" '85

MCSHANE, MARK
LOVELL, MARC--[18][26][34][36]MYS--
DBLDY "DREAMERS IN A HAUNTED HOUSE" '75
MANOR "GUARDIAN SPECTRE" '77 & MORE
HALE "AND THEY SAY YOU CAN'T BUY HAPPINESS" '79

MCSPADDEN, JOSEPH WALKER
WALKER, JOSEPH--[1]

MCTAGGART, SHERYL
SAGE, SHERYL--W/PENNY SAGE,[26]ROM--
"PASSIONATE SURRENDER"

MCVEIGH, M. MOLLIE HUNTER
HUNTER, MOLLIE--[2][7][8][33]SF/HOR--
HAM "A STRANGER CAME ASHORE" '75
HAM "MERMAID SUMMER" '88 & MORE

MCVICKER, CHARLES TAGGART
MCVICKER, CHUCK--[33]

MCWALTERS, GEORGE S.
PATROLMAN--[1]
VERITAS--[1]

MCWILLIAMS, JUDITH
HINES, CHARLOTTE--[9][21][26]ROM--
"HEAVEN TO KISS"
"TENDER TRAP" & MORE

MEAD, EDWARD
MEAD, SHEPHERD--[2][23]SF--
"MAGNIFICENT MCINNES" '49
"BIG BALL OF WAX" '54

MEAD, MARTHA NORBURN
NORBURN, MARTHA--[8]

MEAD, SIDNEY MOKO
MOKO--[1]

MEADOWCROFT, ERNEST [W]
WILLIAM, ARNOLD--[1]

MEAGHER, M.
MARRIOTT, BUCK--[1]

MEAKER, ELOISE
CLARK, LYDIA B[ENSON]--[3][21][26][31]MYS--
ACE "YESTERDAY'S EVIL" '74
ACE "DEMON CAT" '75
HUNTER, VALANCY--[9][21][26][31]ROM--
"DEVIL'S DOUBLE'
"THE NAMESAKE"
"REBEL HEART"
LANCASTER, LYDIA--[9][21][26][31]ROM--
"FALSE PARADISE"
"ALWAYS TOMORROW" & MORE
MCALLISTER, AMANDA--[26][34]MYS-HP-
PLB "WAITING FOR CAROLINE" '76
PLB "LOOK OVER YOUR SHOULDER" '77

MEAKER, MARIJANE [AGNES]
ALDRICH, ANN--J. PRESSMAN-LESBIANA, BAE 20,[1]ADULT--
GM 509 "WE WALK ALONE" '55
GM 727 "WE TOO MUST LOVE" '58
GM 1009 "CAROL IN A THOUSAND CITIES" '60
GM 1313 "WE TOO WON'T LAST" '63
JAMES, MARY--[31]
KERR, M.E.--V.BERCH-GM PSEUDS, PP 33, [1][11][31][33]
MEAKER, M.J.--K. BURGER-PP33,[1][33]

MEAKER, MARIJANE [AGNES] [CONT]
PACKER, VIN--J. PRESSMAN-LESBIANA,
BAE 20, V. BERCH-GM PSEUDS,PP 33,
[3][11][32][33]ADULT--
GM 222 "SPRING FIRE" '52
GM 324 "LOOK BACK TO LOVE" '53
GM 250 "DARK INTRUDER
GM 363 "COME DESTROY ME" '54
GM 426 "WHISPER HIS SIN" '54
GM 510 "THRILL KIDS" '55
EQMM "ONLY THE GUILTY RUN" NOV '55
JU "HOT SNOW" JAN '56
GM 581 "YOUNG & VIOLENT" '56
GM 624 "DARK DON'T CATCH ME" '56
GM "3 DAY TERROR" '57
GM 731 "5:45 TO SUBURBIA" '58
GM 797 "EVIL FRIENDSHIP" '58
GM 861 "TWISTED ONES" '59
GM 976 "GIRL ON THE BESTSELLER LIST" '60
GM 1074 "DAMNATION OF ADAM BLESSING" '61
GM 1146 "SOMETHING IN THE SHADOWS" '61
GM 1241 "INTIMATE VICTIM" '62
GM 1294 "ALONE AT NIGHT" '63
SIGN "HARE IN MARCH" '66
DLCT "DON'T RELY ON GEMINI" '69

MEANS, MARY
SCOTT, DENIS--W/THEODORE SAUNDERS,[3][22]MYS--
BOBBS "MURDER MAKES A VILLAIN" '55
BOBBS "BECKONING SHADOW" '56

MEARES, JOHN WILLOUGHBY
UNCUT CAVENDISH--[8]

MEARES, LEONARD F.
BARLOW, GRANT--G. FLANAGAN-MEARES INTRVW,
PPCC#8,[35]AUSTRALIAN/WEST--
COUGAR "GUN WRANGLER" '57
COUGAR "TOP GUN KID" '66
BRENNAN, WARD--G. FLANAGAN-MEARES INTRVW,
PPCC#8,[35] AUSTRAL/WEST--
22 COUGAR NOVELS '61-4
DENVER, SHAD--PPCC#2,[28]WEST--
COUGAR "STACKED DECK" '56
EVERTON, FRANK--G. FLANAGAN-MEARES INTRVW,
PPCC#8,[36]WEST--
HALE "BATTLE OF JERICHO STREET" '84
GROVER, MARSHALL--L. HULLAR-'NEVADA JIM',
PP 11,[8][13][35]AUSTRALIAN/WEST--
MACAO, MARSHALL--[14]ADULT--
OLYM FP#s "K'ING KUNG-FU #1 THRU #7" '73-4
MALLOY, LESTER--G. FLANAGAN-MEARES INTRVW,
PPCC#8,[36]WEST--
HALE "JO JO & THE PRIVATE EYE" '81
HALE "HAPPIEST GHOST IN TOWN" '81
HALE "BEWARE THE YELLOW PACKARD" '82
HALE "SO HELP ME HANNAH" '82
HALE "BULLET-PROOF TOGA" '84
MCCOY, MARSHALL--L. HULLAR-'NEVADA JIM',
PP 11,[8][13]AUSTRALIAN/WEST--
MURRELL, GLENN--G. FLANAGAN-MEARES INTRVW,
PPCC#8,[35]AUSTRALIAN/WEST--
COUGAR, 32 NOVELS '56-61
NELSON, JOHNNY--G. FLANAGAN-MEARES INTRVW,
PPCC #8,[35]WEST,SP--
COUGAR "TROUBLETOWN" '55
RAND, ROBERT E.--CC#2,[28][35]AUSTRALIAN/WEST--
COUGAR 573 "SAVAGE SUNDOWN" '55
SHARPE, SHANE E.--PPCC#2,[28][35]
AUSTRALIAN/WEST--
COUGAR "TOWN TO TAME" '64
SHAWN, CLYDE B.--G. FLANAGAN-MEARES INTRVW,
PPCC#8,[35]AUSTRALIAN/WEST--
COUGAR "JUDAS GUN" '56
CLEVE 614 "BULLET BREED"
STERLING, VAL--PPCC#2,[28]AUSTRALIAN/ROM--
HALE "THE FUTURE & PHILOMENA" '82

MEAKER, MARIJANE [AGNES] [CONT]
THORPE, LEE--G. FLANAGAN-MEARES INTRVW,
PPCC#8,[35]AUSTRALIAN/WEST--
COUGAR "DRAW CARDS" '57
BIG HORN 321 "WHISTLING DEATH"
WARING, BRETT--PPCC#2,[28]AUSTRALIAN/WEST--
COUGAR "VIOLENT GUN" '59

MEARNS, DAVID CHAMBERS
FRADDLE, FARRAGUT--[1][22][31]AMERICAN

MEASOR, CHARLES PENNELL
SCRUTATOR--[1]

MEBANE, JOHN [H]
DEVILBISS, PHILIP--[1][31]
HEARTMAN, HAROLD--[1][22][31]AMERICAN

MECKE, MARIA RENEE
DAUMAS, MARIA RENEE--[39]GERMAN

MECKEL, EBERHARD
SIXT, PETER--[39]GERMAN

MEDING, OSKAR
SAMAROW, GREGOR--[1][39]GERMAN

MEDLICOTT, MARGARET P.
PAGET, MARGARET--[1]

MEE, ARTHUR
IDRIS--[8]

MEE, HUAN
MANSFIELD--[34]MYS

MEEHAN, FRANCIS JOSEPH
SCARLET, WILL--[1]
ZACHARY, LEO--[1]

MEEK SPENCER, MARGARET [D]
MEEK, MARGARET--[1]
SPENCER, MARGARET--[1]

MEEK, CAPT. S.P.
ST. PAUL, STERNER--[2]

MEEK, DORIS
GREGORY, MASON--W/ADRIENNE JONES,
[1][3][22]MYS--
ARCADIA "IF TWO OF THEM ARE DEAD" '53
MASON, GREGORY--W/ADRIENNE JONES,
[2][3][11]MYS--
ARCADIA "WITH SOUL SO DEAD" '56

MEEK, JACKLYN O'HANLON
MATTHEWS, JACKLYN MEEK--[1][33]
O'HANLON, JACKLYN--[1][33]

MEEK, PAULINE PALMER
MCROBERTS, AGNESANN--[1]

MEEK, STERNER ST. PAUL
MEEK, S.P.--[23][32]SF--
AMZQ "MURGATROYD EXPERIMENT" '29
MZ "NASTURTIA" MAY '68
SN "THE BLACK MASS" SUMMER '68
ST. PAUL, STERNER--[11][15]SF--

MEEKER, ELOISE
CLARK, LYDIA BENSON--[7]SF--
"DEMON CAT" '75
"SEANCE FOR SUSAN" '77

MEEKER, WILLY JOHNS
JOHNS, WILLY--[1][2][7][11]SF--

MEEROPOL, ABEL
ALLAN, LEWIS--[31]

MEESKE, MARILYN
CRANNACH, HENRY--[8]

MEEUS, MARCEL
CREMER, SAMUEL--[1]

MEGAW, ARTHUR STANLEY
STANLEY, ARTHUR--[1][3]MYS--
MacD "THE MONKHURST CASE" '46

MEGGED, AHARON
A.M.--[31]

MEGROS, PHYLLIS
MEADOWS, PAULINE--[1]

MEGROZ, R.L.
CUMBERLAND, ROY--[8]
DIMDALE, C.D.--[8]

MEHAN, JOSEPH ALBERT
MARTIN, ALBERT--[1]

MEHL, ARNOLD
GERMAN, GUNTHER--[39]GERMAN/JUV

MEHTA, RUSTAM JEHANGIR
HARTMAN, ROGER--[1][22][31]INDIAN
MARTIN, R. JOHNSON--[1][22]INDIAN
MARTIN, R.J.--[1][22]INDIAN
PLUTONIUS--[1][22]INDIAN

MEIDINGER-GEISE INGEBORG
MEIDINGER-GEISE, INGE--[1]

MEIER, LINDA SUSAN
MAYER, SUZANNE--[7][21][34]MYS/SF--
HARL 139 "IN FOR LIFE" '90
MEIER, SUSAN--[7][21]ROM/SF--
"TAKE THE RISK"

MEIGHAN, DONALD CHARLES
CHARLES, DONALD--[1][31][33]

MEIGS, CORNELIA LYNDE
ALDON, ADAIR--[22][31][33]

MEILACH, DONA Z.
STANLI, SUE--[1][33]

MEINHARDT, SHELLY THACKER
THACKER, SHELLY--[26]ROM--
"SILVER & SAPPHIRES" & 3 OTHER NOVELS

MEINHOLD, WILHEIM
SCHWEIDLER, MARY--[2]

MEINZER, HELEN ABBOTT
ABBOTT, A.C.--[8]

MEIRAGURI, NICHOLAS
RUHENI, MWANGI--[1]

MEISCHKE, WOLFGANG
POSSE, G. PETER--[39]GERMAN/MYS

MEISER, EDITH
XANTIPPE--[34]MYS--
DBLDY "DEATH CATCHES UP WITH MR. KLUCK" '35
?? UNCONFIRMED ??

MEISNER, MICHAEL
BERTHIER, CHRISTIAN--[39]GERMAN/JUV
GNADE, HEINZ--[39]GERMAN/JUV

MEISSNER, HANS-OTTO
ROOS, HANS--[1]

MEISTER, FRIEDRICH
BERNER, FRIEDRICH--[39]GERMAN
MORENO, FILIPP--[39]GERMAN
VICTOR, F.M.--[39]GERMAN
VON BARUTH, FRIEDRICH--[39]GERMAN

MEISTER, KNUD
MASTERS, KAY--[37]DANISH/MYS

MELAMED, ZHAK NISSUM
DRAGOMIR, ASSENOV--[1]

MELARO, CONSTANCE LORAINE
BRUCE, MONICA--[31]

MELDAL-JOHNSEN, TREVOR B.
TREVOR, DAN--W/DAN SHERMAN,[7]HOR--
JOVE "NIGHT WHISTLERS #1" '91

MELHARDT, TRUDE
GOTIKE, MARIA--[39]GERMAN

MELIDES, NICHOLAS
MCGUIRE, NICHOLAS--[1][3]MYS--
PALLADIN "MOSQUITO SERENADE" '50

MELLEN, IDA MAY
DE MAR, ESMERALDA--[22][31]AMERICAN
OTIS, GEORGE--[22]AMERICAN

MELLETT, JOHN CALVIN
BROOKS, JONATHAN--[8]

MELLICK, HENRY GEORGE
TIMOTHY, A COUNTRY BOY--[1]

MELLING, LEONARD
LUMINUS--[1]

MELLIZO, CARLOS
CUADRADO, CARLOS MELLIZO--[31]

MELLOS, ILIAS
VENEZIS, ILIAS--[1]

MELLVIG, CARL FOLKE S.
SERNER, MAC--[29]MYS--
NUTID 12 "JAGAD AV MORDARE" '56

MELONEY, WILLIAM BROWN
GRANT, MARGARET--W/ROSE FRANKEN,[1]
MELONEY, FRANKEN--W/ROSE FRANKEN,[1][8]

MELTZER, R.
BORNEO JIMMY--[1]
MURPHY, AUDIE JR.--[1]

MELVILLE, JENNIE
BUTLER, GWENDOLINE--[9][32]ROM/MYS--
EQMM "THE SISTERHOOD" OCT '68

MENAIS, BRUNO
MENEX, YANN--[2]ISFYB, FRENCH

MENCKEN, HENRY LOUIS
ALLISON, GEORGE W.--[1]
ANDERSON, C. FARLEY--[31]
ARCHER, HERBERT WINSLOW--[1][31]
BELL, W.L.D.--[1][31]

MENCKEN, HENRY LOUIS [CONT]
BELLAMY, ATWOOD C.--[1][31]
BROWNELL, CHARLES F.--[1]
BROWNELL, JOHN F.--[1]
D'AUBIGY, PIERRE--[1][31]
DE VERDI, MARIE--[1]
DELLA TORRE, RAOUL--[1]
DRAYHAM, JAMES--[31]
DRAYHAM, WILLIAM--[1]
DRYHAM, JAMES--[1]
FINK, WILLIAM--[1][31]
GILRAY, J.D.--[1][31]
HATTERAS, AMELIA--[1][31]
HATTERAS, OWEN--W/GEORGE JEAN NATHAN,[1][31]
HENDERSON, F.C.--[1][31]
JEFFERSON, JANET--[1][31]
MCLOUGHLIN, R.B.--[1]
MENCKEN, H.L.--[1]
MORGAN, HARRIET--[1]
PEREGOY, GEORGE WEEMS--[1]
RATCLIFFE, JAMES P.--[1]
RINGMASTER--[1]
SAGE OF BALTIMORE--[1]
THOMPSON, FRANCIS CLEGG--[1]
TRIMBALL, W.H.--[1]
W.G.L.--[1]
WATSON, IRVING S.--[1]
WHARTON, JAMES--[1]
WOODRUFF, ROBERT W.--[1]

MENDELL, IRVING
DELL, AMEN--[3]MYS--
MYH "JOHNNY ON THE SPOT" '43

MENDELSOHN, FELIX JR.
MAYFAIR, FRANKLIN--[1][3]MYS--
BCA "OVER MY DEAD BODY" '65

MENDELSOHN, OSCAR
MILSEN, OSCAR--[1][22]AUSTRALIAN

MENDENHALL, CAROL
CRAIN, ELLEY--W/ELYSE ALLEN,[26]ROM--
"DEEP IN THE HEART"

MENDONCA, SUSAN V. SMITH
SINCLAIR, ROSE--[1]
SMITH, SUSAN--[7]SF--
"SAMANTHA SLADE #1-4" '87-8
"CHANGING PLACES" '86

MENDOZA ROMERO, MARIA L.
CATAY--[1]
CHINA--[1]

MENENDEZ, MIGUEL ANGEL
BRISUNO, MIGUEL--[30] MEXICAN

MENESES, ENRIQUE
CARVAJAL, RICARDO--[31]
CRAIN, JEFF--[31]

MENON, S. AUBREY CLARENCE
MENEN, AUBREY--[1][22]ENGLISH

MENTZEL, GEORG
MELTON, GEORGE--[39]GERMAN/MYS/WEST
PARKER, GEORGE--[39]GERMAN/MYS/WEST

MENZEL, DONALD H.
HOWARD, DON--[8]
MENTZEL, DONALD H.--[2]

MENZEL, RODERICH
MORAWA, MICHAEL--[1][39]GERMAN/JUV
PARMA, CLEMENS--[1][39]GERMAN/JUV

MENZER, CLARA
MENTER, A.--[39]GERMAN

MERBT, MARTIN
SELBER, MARTIN--[39]GERMAN/JUV

MERCER, CECIL WILLIAM
YATES, DORNFORD--[2][3][5][7][22][38]MYS--
25 BOOKS '22-89

MERCER, JEAN
LESTER, GENE--[1][31]

MERCER, JESSIE
SHANNON, TERRY--[1][22]AMERICAN/JUV

MERCER, JOAN BODGER
BODGER, JOAN--[1][31]

MEREDITH, DORIS R.
LOCKHART, MAX--HAWK/MEREDITH INTRVW '93, MYS--
"PRIVATE EYE: #4 NOBODY DIES IN CHINA TOWN"
MEREDITH, D.R.--HAWK/MEREDITH INTRVW '93,
[34]MYS--
BAL "MURDER BY IMPULSE" '89 & MORE

MEREDITH, KENNETH LINCOLN
MAYO, ARNOLD--[8]

MEREDITH, ROBERT C.
LUCERO, ROBERTO--[1][31]

MEREDYTH-STORMER, MARJORY
LYON, MARJORIE--[1]

MERIWETHER, ELIZABETH [A]
EDMONDS, GEORGE--[1]

MERKLINGHAUS, MICHELE
BRUCE, SHELLEY--[1][31]

MERKT, FRANKIE
RICHARDS, ANN--[9][21]ROM--
"CROSS-COUNTRY MATCH"

MERLAND, OLIVER
COLLINS, COLIN--[1][34]MYS--
GREENING "HUMAN MOLE" '09
LLOYD "STEP BY STEP" '21 & 3 MORE
GRANT, DOUGLAS--[1]
POUND, SINGLETON--[1]

MERRICK, HUGH
MEYER, H.A.--[8]

MERRILL, ANTOINETTE JUNE
MERRILL, TONI--[1]

MERRILL, HENRY TINDALL
MERRILL, DICK--[1]

MERRILL, JAMES MILFORD
OLD TIMER--[1]
PARRISH, WENDAL--[1]
REDWING, MORRIS--[3]MYS--
LAIRD "GREAT TRUNK TRADGEDY: OR SHADOWED
TO AUSTRALIA" 1888 & MORE

MERRILL, JANE
FILSTRUP, JANE--[33]
FILSTRUP, JANE MERRILL--[1][33]
MERRILL, PHIL--[1][33]

MERRIMAN, CHAD
LEIGHTON, LEE--W/WAYNE D. OVERHOLSER, [28]WEST--BAL "COLORADO GOLD" '58

MERRIMAN, EFFIE
FIFIELD, MRS. JAMES C.--[2][7]SF-- "REJUVENATED" '28

MERRIMAN, MANSFIELD
LICKS, H.E.--[1]

MERRIT, WILLIAM
WILLIAMS, LEE--[9][21]ROM-- "STARFIRE" "HEAT WAVE" & MORE
WILLIAMS, LEIGH ANNE--[9][21]ROM-- "GOLDEN DREAMS" "MAGIC HOUR" & MORE

MERRITT, ABRAHAM P.
FENIMORE, W.--M. LACHMAN-AHMM ED FEB '88-- AW "POOL OF THE STONE GOD" '23
MERRITT, A.--[7]SF-- DOREAL "WOMAN OF THE WOOD" '48

MERRITT, EMMA
BENNETT, EMMA--[9][21][26]ROM-- "RIVER ENCHANTMENT" "LOVING BRAND" & MORE
LEIGH, MICAH--W/EVELYN GEE,[9][21][26]ROM-- "TEXAS DREAMS"

MERTENS, FERNAND
GRAVEY, FERNAND--JEAN F. LE DEIST LTR '93

MERTON, THOMAS JAMES
LOUIS, FATHER M.--[22]AMERICAN

MERTZ, BARBARA GROSS
MICHAELS, BARBARA--[7][18][33][34][40]MYS-- CONGDON "BLACK RAINBOW" '82 DODD "CRYING CHILD" '71 & M
PETERS, ELIZABETH--[7][18][33][34]MYS-- DODD "CROCODILE ON THE SANDBANK" '75 & 15 MORE '69-84

MERTZ, STEPHEN
BOLAN, MACK--W/MIKE NEWTON & DON PENDLETON, [28]MYS,HP-- PINN "EXECUTIONER'S WAR BOOK" '77
BRETT, STEPHEN--HAWK-MERTZ CONV '94, [34]MYS/HOR-- MANOR "SOME DIE HARD" '79 MANOR "VAMPIRE CHASE" '79
BUCHANAN, JACK--HAWK-CRIDER INTRVW '93, [34]MYS,HP-- JOVE 'M.I.A.' SERIES: "BLOOD STORM" '86 "EXODUS FROM HELL" '86 "ESCAPE FROM NICARAGUA" '87 "INVASION U.S.S.R." '88 "CROSSFIRE KILL" '89 "L.A. GANG WAR" '90
CASE, JIM--HAWK-MERTZ CONV '94, WAR,HP-- 'CODY'S WAR' SERIES - MOST BOOKS
MERTZ, STEVE--HAWK/MERTZ FEB '94
PENDLETON, DON--[34]MYS,HP-- GE "RETURN TO VIETNAM" '82 GE "LIBYA CONNECTION" '82 GE "TUSCANY TERROR" '83 GE "BEIRUT PLAYBACK" '84 GE "DAY OF MOURNING" '84 GE "IRANIAN HIT" '84 GE "APPOINTMENT IN KABBUL" '85 GE "DIRTY WAR" '85 GE "DEAD MAN RUNNING" '86

MERWIN, SAMUEL K. JR.
BENNETT, ELIZABETH DEARE--[2][3][11][29]MYS-- DELL "GOWER COURT MANOR" '76
CLARKE, HAMMOND--V. BERCH-BRNDN/ BC PSEUDS, BAE 22, P24
CROWELL, ANTHONY--V. BERCH-BRNDN/ BC PSEUDS, BAE 22, ADULT-- BC 7009 "BODY ABUSERS"
CURSON, STANLEY [S]--[1][2]ADULT-- BRNDN 609 "LESBIAN LOVE SONG" BRNDN 612 "PASSION HILL"
DAVIDSON, ANGELA--V. BERCH LTR '93,[7]-- CRSL "FORBIDDEN MANSION" RPTS "TUNNEL OF DARKNESS"
FERRAT, JACQUES JEAN--[11]
FERRIT, JAQUES JEAN--[2][31]
HALLIDAY, BRETT--T.JOHNSON-ECHOES #23, MYS,HP-- MSMM "BRING BACK A CORPSE" SEP '56 MSMM "THE BODY WENT TO BED" OCT '56 MSMM "WHO SHOT THE DUKE" NOV '56 MSMM "MARK ME FOR MURDER" DEC '56 MSMM "CITY OF BROTHERLY DEATH" MAY '75 MSMM "MUSIC FOR MURDER" JUL '77 MSMM "SEVEN TO DIE" MAR '78 MSMM "A PATTERN FOR TERROR" APR '78 MSMM "GRIM FACE OF MURDER" AUG '78 MSMM "BURY YOU LATER" NOV '78
HAMMOND, CLARKE--V. BERCH-BRNDN/BC PSEUDS, BAE 22, ADULT-- BRNDN "SO VIOLENT MY LOVE" '66
LEE, MATT--[2][11][23][31]SF--
MERWIN, SAM JR.--[23][34][38]MYS-- DBLDY "MURDER IN MINIATURES" '40 DBLDY WHITE WINDOWS" '53 OTHERS
PALEY, MORTON D.--W/JEROME L. BIXBY,[11]FP
SATURN, SERGEANT--[1][2]HP-- 'THRILLING' 'STARTLING' 'CAPT. FUTURE' MAGS
SCOTT, CRAIG--V. BERCH-BRNDN/ BC PSEUDS, BAE 22, ADULT-- BRNDN 977 "PAHAN SEX-PURITAN SEX"
SPRAGUE, CARTER--[1][2][32]MYS-- MSMM "A PRESENT FOR PETER" SEPT '56
WINSTEAD, REBECCA NOYES--V.BERCH LTR '93,[7]SF-- CANYON "TUNNEL OF DARKNESS" '74

MERWIN, WILLIAM STANLEY
MERWIN, W.S.--[1]

MESCHKE, HILDEGARD
AHEMM, HILDE--[39]GERMAN

MESKIE, EUNICE BOARDMAN
BOARDMAN, EUNICE--[1][31]

MESKILL, JOHANNA MENZEL
MENZEL, JOHANNA--[22]GERMAN-AMERICAN

MESONERO Y ROMANOS, ROMAN
PARLANTE CURIOSO--[1]

MESROBIAN, MICHAEL
MICHAELS, GRANT--[34]MYS-- ST. MARTIN'S "A BODY TO DYE FOR" '90

MESSAGER, CHARLES
VILDRAC, CHARLES--[22]FRENCH

MESSENT, CHARLES
BARING, MAX--[1][34]MYS-- "WHIFFS FROM A SHORT BRIAR" 1896

MESSER, MONA [N. ANNE]
HOCKING, ANNE--[1][3]MYS--
PAUL "CAT'S PAW" '33
PAUL "DEATH DUEL" '33 & MORE

MESSMANN, JON [JOHN]
CARTER, NICK--[34]MYS,HP--
AWARD "14 SECONDS TO HELL" '68
AWARD "DOOMSDAY SPORE" '69
AWARD "LIVING DEATH" '69
AWARD "SEA TRAP" '69
AWARD "CARNIVAL FOR KILLING" '69
AWARD "CASBAH KILLERS" '69
AWARD "BERLIN" '69
AWARD "AMAZON" '69
AWARD "OPERATION: CHE GUEVARA" '69
AWARD "OPERATION: SNAKE" '69
AWARD "EXECUTIONERS" '70
AWARD "RED REBELLION" '70
AWARD "DEATH STRAIN" '70
AWARD "MIND KILLERS" '70
AWARD "ARAB PLAGUE" '70
MOORE, COLLEEN--[9][21][26]ROM--
"BOLD ADVENTURE"
NICOLE, CLAUDE--[3]MYS--
ARCADIA "CLIFFS OF DEATH" '68
NICOLE, CLAUDETTE--[2][3][7][21][29]MYS--
GM "BLOODROOTS MANOR" '70
PYR "HAUNTED HEART" '72 & MORE
NICOLE, CLAUDIA--[3][9][21]MYS/ROM--
PAPLB "MOONWATER" '71
RICHARDS, PAUL--W/GEORGE SNYDER,[3]MYS,HP--
AWARD "OUR SPACECRAFT IS MISSING" '70
SHARPE, JON--[28]WEST--
NAL 'TRAILSMAN' SERIES
WINDSOR, PAMELA--[9][21][26]ROM--
"AT PASSION'S TIDE"
"FORSAKING ALL OTHERS"
"REBEL'S RAPTURE"

MESSMER, OTTO
SULLIVAN, PAT--[1]

MESTA, EMILY
GISCARD, VALERIE--[9][21][26]ROM--
"PASSION'S PLEASURE"
"RAPTURE'S EMBRACE"

METCALF, NORMAN
COUNCIL OF FOUR--W/TOM WALKER, CHUCK HANSEN,
ROY HUNT, ELLIS MILLS, BOB PETERS,[2]
METCALF, NORM--[23]SF

METCALFE, FELICIA
METCALFE, WHITAKER--[3]MYS--
ARCADIA "TWO WEEKS BEFORE MURDER" '59

METHOLD, KENNETH [WALTER]
CADE, ALEXANDER--[3][31]MYS--
BLES "TURN UP A STONE" '69
KENT, ALEXANDER--[1][22]SEA ADV,HP--

METLOVA, MARIA
HATHAWAY, LOUISE--[1][2][7]SF--
"THE ENCHANTED HOUR" '40

METRESS, SEAMUS P.
METRESS, JAMES P.--[1]

METZ, KURT C.
CALHOUN, ALEXANDER--[39]GERMAN/MYS/SF/WEST

METZ, LOIS LUNT
LUNT, LOIS--[1][31]

MEULENBELT-LUBER, HENRIET
LUBER, JET--[1]

MEYER, ALFRED RICHARD
MUNKEPUNKE--[39]GERMAN

MEYER, ARTHUR EMANUEL
MANUEL, ARTHUR--[39]GERMAN

MEYER, CHARLES ROBERT
JAY, DONALD--[31]

MEYER, DAVID N. II
ST. ALCORN, LLOYD--[7]SF--
SIGN "DREAM QUEST #1 THRU #3" '87-9

MEYER, DONNA
DANIEL, MEGAN--[9][21][26]ROM--
"AMERICAN BRIDE"
"QUEEN OF HEARTS" & MORE
KINGSLEY, JOHANNA--[21][26]ROM--
"FACES"
"SCENTS"
"TREASURES"

MEYER, DOROTHY QUICK
QUICK, DOROTHY--[1]

MEYER, FRIEDRICH-ALBERT
RINGER, F.A.--[39]GERMAN/JUV

MEYER, GUSTAVE
MEYER-MEYRINK, GUSTAV--[1]
MEYRINK, GUSTAV--[39]GERMAN/SF
MEYRINK, GUSTAVE--[1][2]

MEYER, HAROLD ALBERT
MERRICK, HUGH--[1][31]--
"PILLAR OF THE SKY" '42

MEYER, HEINRICH
BARLOW, ROBERT O.--[1][31]GERMAN-AMERICAN
MEYER, H.K. HOUSTON--[1][22]GERMAN-AMERICAN

MEYER, JEAN SHEPHERD
BERWICK, JEAN--[1][33]

MEYER, JEROME SYDNEY
JENNINGS, S.M.--[8][22][31]AMERICAN

MEYER, JUTTA
MANTHEY, JUTTA--[39]GERMAN/JUV
SCHREIBER, JUTTA--[39]GERMAN/JUV

MEYER, KARL ERNEST
WILLOUGHBY, LEE DAVIS--[21]ROM,HP--
DELL 'MKNG OF AMERICA' SERIES:
"WRANGLERS"

MEYER, LEO
FRANK, LEO--[40]GERMAN/MYS--
"DAS ARCHIV" '78

MEYER, PAUL E.
SCHWERTENBACH, WOLF--[39]GERMAN/MYS

MEYER, WILHELM-FRIEDRICH
VON MEYERN, WILHELM-FR.--[39]GERMAN/SF

MEYER-BROCKMANN, HENRI
BROCKMANN, H.M.--[39]GERMAN

MEYER-ESTNER, WERNER
ELLMER, MARCUS--[39]GERMAN/MYS

MEYER-KOENIG, ERNA
REX, ARNE--[39]GERMAN

MEYERS, JUDY BLACKWELL
MEYERS, JULIE--[7]SF

MEYERS, MARTIN
SARASON, MARTIN--HAWK/MEYERS INTRVW '93--
SCHOLASTIC - TITLE NOT KNOWN

MEYERS, MARTIN & ANNETTE
MEYERS, MAAN--HAWK/MEYERS-INTRVW '93,MYS--
DBLDY "THE DUTCHMAN" '93
DBLDY "THE KINGSBRIDGE PLOT" '93
DBLDY "THE HIGH CONSTABLE" '94

MEYERS, RICHARD S.
ARCHITECHS ADVENTURE--W/WALTER & LISA HUNT/
EVAN JAMIESON/BILL SCAMMEL/MARK BLOOM
& CHRISTINE IVEY,[7]
BARKER, WADE--[23][34]MYS,HP--
WARNER 'NINJA MASTER' SERIES:
"DRAGON RISING" '85
"LION'S FIRE" '85
"SERPENT'S EYE" '85
"PHOENIX SWORD" '86
HARTMAN, DANE--[34]MYS,HP--
WARNER "FAMILY SKELETONS" '82
WARNER "HATCHET MEN" '82
WARNER "THE LONG DEATH" '82
WARNER "DUEL FOR CANNONS" '82
WARNER "DEATH IN THE AIR" '83
WARNER "THE KILLING CONNECTION" '83
MEYERS, RIC--[7][23]SF/HOR--
"FEAR ITSELF" '91
"LIVING HELL" '91
"WORST NIGHTMARE" '92
MURPHY, WARREN--[7]MYS,HP--
'DESTROYER' SERIES:
#25, #27 & #29

MEYERS, ROY [LETHBRIDGE]
LETHBRIDGE, REX--[1][11][31]
MEYERS, RAY--[23]SF--
"GIFT OF THE MANTI" '77

MEYERSTEIN, EDWARD H.H.
E.H.W.M.--[1]
MEYERSTEIN, E.H.W.--[1]

MEYN, NIELS
ANKER, PETER--[29]ROM
BETJENT, OLE NY--[29][37]SWEDISH/MYS,HP--
'BEDRIFTER' STORIES '42-7
BRISTOL, CHARLES--[29]SWEDISH/MYS
CHESTER, HAROLD--[29]SWEDISH/MYS
DANNER, KURT--[29]SWEDISH
DORPH, JAN--[29][37]SWEDISH/MYS--
'MYSTISKE MR. X' '43-4
FORSTER, JOHN D.--[29]SWEDISH/MYS
GARTNER, DAVIS--[29]SWEDISH/MYS
GRIFFITH, GEORGE--[29]SWEDISH/MYS
HARDNER, CARL--[29]SWEDISH/MYS
HARDNER, GUSTAV--[29]SWEDISH/MYS
HELLING, STEEN--[29]SWEDISH
HILL, RICH M.--[29]SWEDISH/MYS
JENKINS, JOHN--[29]MYS--8 NOVELS '45-46
JONES, RAY--[29]SWEDISH
JUUL, ERIK--[29]SWEDISH
KLINDT, ARNE--[29]SWEDISH
LESTER, JACK--[29]SWEDISH/MYS
LYKKE, ANNE--[29]SWEDISH/MYS
LYNAES, KAI--[29]SWEDISH
MILLER, JAN--[29]SWEDISH
MOLLER, NIKOLAJ--[29]SWEDISH
MORRIS, JAMES--[29]SWEDISH

MEYN, NIELS [CONT]
NELSON, REX--[29][37]SWEDISH/MYS--
KKK-MAGASINET '46
ORN, RICHARD--[29]SWEDISH/MYS
PARKER, DAVID--[29]SWEDISH
RASMUSSEN, ANDR.--[29]SWEDISH
RASMUSSEN, STYRMAND--[29]SWEDISH
SOLBER, ARNE--[29]SWEDISH/MYS
STERLING, ROBERT--[29]SWEDISH
TONDER, ERIK--[29]SWEDISH

MEYNELL, ALICE [C.G.T.]
OLDCASTLE, ALICE--[1]
PHILLIMORE, FRANCES--[1]
THOMPSON, A.C.--[1]

MEYNELL, ESTER H.
MOORHOUSE, E. HALLAM--[8]

MEYNELL, LAURENCE WALTER
BAXTER, VALERIE--[18][22][31][33]CHILDREN'S
BEDFORD, SIDNEY--[1]][34]MYS--
PAUL "THE MAN WHO ESCAPED" '40
ETON, ROBERT--[2][18][31][33] CHILDREN'S
LUDLOW, GEOFFREY--[1][34]MYS--
HARRAP "INSIDE OUT! OR MAD AS A HATTER" '34
TRING, A. STEPHEN--[18][22][33] CHILDREN'S

MEYNELL, SHIRLEY RUTH
DARBYSHIRE, SHIRLEY--[8]

MEYNELL, WILFRID
OLDCASTLE, JOHN--[1]
OLDCASTLE, JONATHAN--[1]

MIALKI, W.
MASOVIUS, WERNER--[39]GERMAN

MIANDER, HARRY NILS O.H.
PELHAM, ROCK--[29]MYS--
BONNIER "MANNER UTAN HUVUD" '26
"ULVEHUVUDS BILFARD" '27

MICHAEL, IAN
SERAFIN, DAVID--[18][29][34]MYS--
COLLINS "SATURDAY OF GLORY" '79
COLLINS "CHRISTMAS RISING" '82
COLLINS "MADRID UNDERGROUND" '82
COLLINS "BODY IN CADIZ BAY" '85

MICHAEL, MORGAN
DORN, DEAN--W/C.E. CARLE,[29]MYS

MICHAEL, PETRA & ROLF
MORRISSON, LINDA--[39]GERMAN/HOR,HP

MICHAEL, ROLF
LAMONT, ROBERT--[39]GERMAN/HOR,HP
SLADE, JACK--[39]GERMAN/WEST,HP
VON TWERNE, ERLIK--[39]GERMAN/SF

MICHAEL, SIMON
MICHAEL, PETER--W/JOEL ROSENBERG,[7]SF--
GRAFTON "THE USURPER" '88

MICHAELIS, PAUL
LUCIFER--[39]GERMAN

MICHAILDIS, KLEANTHIS
EFTALIOTIS, ARJRIS--[22] GREEK

MICHEL, JOHN B.
BELLIN, EDWARD--[2]SF,HP--
STIRRING STORIES
CONWAY, BOWEN--[1][2][11]
COOKE, ARTHUR--W/E. BALTER,[1][2][11]HP--

MICHEL, JOHN B. [CONT]
RAYMOND, HUGH--[1][2][11]
RICHARD, LOUIS--[11]
TARA, JOHN--[1][32]MYS--
FADM "HORIZON" MAR '57
WOODS, LAURENCE--W/DONALD A. WOLLHEIM, [1][2][11]

MICHEL, MILTON SCOTT
SCOTT, MILTON--[3]MYS--
PHOENIX "DEAR, DEAD HARRY" '49

MICHELL, GRACE [A]
ANGOVE, GRACE--[1]

MICHELS, BARBARA
MICHELLE, SUZANNE--W/SUSAN LARSON, [9][21][26]ROM--
"ENCHANTED DESERT"
"FANCY FREE" & MORE

MICHELS, NICHOLAS A.
MIKALOWITCH, NICHOLAI--[1][2]

MICHELS, S.C.
MICHELS, CHRISTINE--[26]ROM--
"DANGER'S KISS"
"IN FUGITIVE ARMS" & OTHERS

MICHELS, SHARRY
KENDYL, SHARICE--W/BERNICE CARSTENSEN,[7]SF--
LEIS "TO SHARE A SUNSET" '90

MICKLEWHITE, MAURICE JOE.
CAINE, MICHAEL--[8]

MIDDLETON, ELIZABETH
ANTILL, ELIZABETH--[34][36]MYS--
HAMM "MURDER IN MID-ATLANTIC" '50
HAMM "DEATH ON THE BARRIER REEF" '52

MIDDLETON, ELLIS
LEES, JOHN MORTON--[1]

MIDDLETON, HARRY
KIEFER, MIDDLETON--W/WARREN DAVID KIEFER,[1]

MIDDLETON, HENRY CLEMENT
SIMPLEX, SIMON--[8]

MIDDLETON, MAUD BARBARA
WALKER, BARBARA--[8]

MIDGETT, ELWIN
MIDGETT, WINK--[1]

MIDGLEY, AMY
CLARK, AMANDA--W/JANET O'DANIEL,[21][26]ROM--
"FLOWER OF THE SEA"
"BLUEPRINT FOR LOVE" & MORE

MIEHE, ULF
ARTNER, ROBERT--W/WALTER ERNSTING, [39]GERMAN/SF/WEST

MIELANTS, FLORENT C.A. JR
HENSEN, HERWIG--[22]DUTCH

MIELKE, FRANZ
FABIAN, FRANZ--[39][40]GERMAN/MYS--
"HEUTE NOCH WIRST DU STERBEN" '59

MIELKE, OTTO
RINK, HERMANN--[39]GERMAN/ADV/MYS
WENDELBURG, OTTO M.--[39]GERMAN/ADV/MYS

MIELKE, THOMAS R.P.
CHESTER, MICHAEL C.--[39]GERMAN/MYS/SF
CORNER, CLIFF--[39]GERMAN/HOR/SF,HP
FLOORMAN, BERT--[39]GERMAN/MYS/SF,HP
GHOST, HENRY--[39]GERMAN/HOR,HP
MARCUS, ROY--[39]GERMAN/MYS/SF
MCMAN, MARC--[39]GERMAN/MYS/SF
ORBAN, MARCUS T.--[39]GERMAN/MYS/SF
PARNELL, MIKE--[39]GERMAN/MYS/SF
TAYLOR, JOHN--[39]GERMAN/MYS/SF

MIER, EDNOR
MEARE, EDNA--[39]GERMAN

MIERS, EARL SCHENCK
MEREDITH, DAVID WILLIAM--[2][22][33][34]MYS--
KNOPF "CHRISTMAS CARD MURDERS" '51

MIESEL, SANDRA
BLACK, ROBERTA--W/ROBERT [STRATTON] COULSON,[1]

MIESS, EVA
LUBINGER, EVA--[39]GERMAN

MIHALAKIS, ULYSSES G.
HASSEN, SILAKI ALI--[2]

MIHKELSON, FRIEDEBERT
TUGLAS, FRIEDEBERT--[22] ESTONIAN

MIHOLOVICH, VERONICA
SMITH, VERONICA--V. BERCH LTR TO HUBIN '94, MYS--
ZEBRA "THUNDER CASTLE" '81

MIKES, GYORGY
MIKES, GEORGE--[1][32]MYS--
JCM "CRIME DOES PAY" MAR '58

MIKKOLA, MARIA WINTER
TALVIO, MAILA--[22] FINNISH

MIKURA, GERTRUD [F]
FERRA[-MIKURA], VERA--[39]GERMAN/JUV

MILAM, LORENZO W.
ALLWORTHY, A.W.--[8]

MILAN, VICTOR [WOODWARD]
AUSTIN, RICHARD--[7][23]SF--
'GUARDIANS' SEQ #1-16" '85-91
HUNTER, S.L.--G.COOK LR '93, SF/MYS,HP--
'STEELE' SERIES #7 & #8
LOGAN, JAKE--G.COOK LTR '93, WEST,HP--
MERRICK, VAL--G.COOK LTR '93
MORROW, VAN--G.COOK LTR '93

MILDNER, THEODOR
THEUER, MARTIN MINOR--[39]GERMAN

MILELLA, JAN
MATHEWS, JAN--[9][21]ROM--
"SHADY LADY"
"NAUGHTY & NICE" & MORE
MICHAELS, JAN--[9][10][21]ROM--
"RED DOG RUN"
"ONLY WITNESS & MORE

MILES, DORIEN KLEIN
MILES, SYLIA--W/SYLVA MULARCHY,[1][3]MYS--
BOUREGY "SHADOW OVER BEAUCLAIRE" '75 & MORE

MILES, JOHN
WILLIAMS, ARTHUR--LACHMAN LST '94--
DJ "MISSING AT TENECLOC"

MILES, KEITH
INIGO, MARTIN--DDLY PLEASURES #3, P34, SPORTS SERIES
MARSTON, EDWARD--LACHMAN-EASTER LST, DDLY PLEAS #3,[34]MYS--
BB "QUEEN'S HEAD" '88
BB "MERRY DEVILS" '89
CORGI "TRIP TO JERUSALEM" 90

MILES, SUSAN
ROBERTS, URSULA--[1]

MILKOMANE, G. ALEXIS M.
BANKOFF, GEORGE ALEXIS--[1][22][31]
BORODIN, GEORGE--[1][2][22][31]
BRADDON, GEORGE--[2][3][22][31]MYS--
FABER "MICROBE'S KISS" '40
RP "LADY DEATH" '55 & MORE
CONWAY, PETER--[3][22][31]MYS--
DAKERS "PALINDROME" '51
MacD "REVISED PROOF" '47 & MORE '40-53
REDWOOD, ALEC--[1][34]MYS--
HALE "LADY IS NOT FOOLING" '74
NH "DEADLINE MOSCOW" '78 & MORE
SAVA, GEORGE--[2][11][22][34]MYS--
HALE "COCAINE FOR BREAKFAST" '73

MILKOWSKI, ZYGMUNT FORTU.
JEZ, TEODOR TOMASZ--[1][22] POLISH

MILLAIRD, M. ALBERT
GRIMM, BARON--[1]

MILLAR, FLORENA N.
MILLAR, F.N.--J. MEYERSON SLST #110,MYS--
"GRANT'S OVERTURE" '46

MILLAR, JAMES P.M.
WHITE, G.A.--[1]

MILLAR, KENNETH
MACDONALD, JOHN--A. ANDREWS-BEFORE ACKER, PP 9,[3]MYS--
KNOPF "MOVING TARGET" '49
MACDONALD, JOHN R.--[2]
MACDONALD, JOHN ROSS--J. ANDREWS-BEFORE ACKER, PP 9,[3][5][32][37]MYS--
KNOPF "DROWNING POOL" '50
KNOPF "WAY SOME PEOPLE DIE" '51
KNOPF "IVORY GRIN" '52
KNOPF "MEET ME AT THE MORGUE" '53
KNOPF "FIND A VICTIM" '54
BB "NAME IS ARCHER" '55
BL "THE IMAGINARY BLONDE" MAY '61
MACDONALD, ROSS--J. ANDREWS-BEFORE ACKER, PP 9,[2][3][5]MYS--
KNOPF "BABAROUS COAST" '56
KNOPF "DOOMSTERS" '58
KNOPF "GALTON CASE" '59
KNOPF "FERGUSON AFFAIR" '60
KNOPF "WYCHERLY WOMAN" '61
KNOPF "ZEBRA-STRIPED HEARSE" '62
KNOPF "THE CHILL" '64
KNOPF "FAR SIDE OF THE DOLLAR" '65
KNOPF "BLACK MONEY" '66
KNOPF "INSTANT ENEMY" '68
KNOPF "GOOD-BYE LOOK" '69
KNOPF "UNDERGROUND MAN" '71
KNOPF "SLEEPING BEAUTY" '73
KNOPF "BLUE HAMMER" '76
MILLER, KENNETH--[2]

MILLAR, MINNA H. JOY
COLLIER, JOY--[1][31]

MILLARD, CHRISTIAN SCLATR
MASON, STUART--[1]

MILLARD, JOSEPH [JOHN]
MILLARD, JOE--[28]WEST--
AWARD "FOR A FEW DOLLARS MORE" '67 & MORE
WESTWOOD, N.J.--[1][2][11]

MILLAY, EDNA ST. VINCENT
BOYD, NANCY--[6][8][31]

MILLER RIIS, MAUREEN
WHITE, MAURINE--[1]

MILLER, ALBERT
MILLS, ALLAN--[8]

MILLER, ANN
LONDON, ANNE--[21]ROM--
"THE FIRST ACT"
MORGAN, LESLIE--[7][26]ROM/SF--
"SILKEN WEBS"
"AGAINST ALL ODDS"

MILLER, ANNE
ALLEN, BETSY--V. BERCH LTR '93,MYS/JUV,HP--
"THE MYSTERY OF THE RUBY QUEEN"

MILLER, BARBARA J.
AMES, LAUREL--[26]ROM--
"TELLER OF TALES"
"CASTAWAY"

MILLER, BILL
DAEMER, WILL--W/ROBERT WADE,[1][3][18]MYS--
FARREL "CASE OF THE LONELY LOVERS" '51
DANNER, WILL--W/BOB WADE, MUNROE SLST 21-WADE MILLER BIBLIO
DANNER, WILLIAM M.--[32]HOR--
MZ "GUARANTEE PERIOD" JUN '65
MASTERSON, WHIT--W/BOB WADE-MUNROE SLST 21-MILLER BIBLIO,[2][5][32][34]MYS--
7 NOVELS
EQMM "WOMEN IN HIS LIFE" JUN '58
EB "SUDDENLY IT'S MIDNIGHT" JAN '58
EQMM "SEEK HIM IN THE SHADOWS" MAR '80
MILLER, WADE--W/BOB WADE, MUNROE SLST 21-MILLER BIBL/V. BERCH-GM PSEUDS. PP 33,[3][5]MYS--
GM 108 "DEVIL MAY CARE" '50
GM 139 "STOLEN WOMAN" '50
GM 152 "KILLER" '51 & MORE
ACE D518 "NIGHTMARE CRUISE" '61
WILMER, DALE--W/BOB WADE, MUNROE SLST 21-MILLER BIBLIO,[3][5]MYS--
BB1420 "DEAD FALL" '56
GRAPH 29 "MEMO FOR MURDER" '51
PYR 132 "JUNGLE HEAT" '54

MILLER, BORIS I.
MILLER, BUZI--[1]
RITER, D.--[1]

MILLER, CHARLES DEAN
VON MUELLER, KARL--[8]

MILLER, CHARLES FRANKLIN
MILLER, CHUCK--[7][23]SF NON-FICT

MILLER, CHARLES HENRY
MULDOR, CARL DE--[8]

MILLER, CINCINNATUS H.
MILLER, JOAQUIN--[8]

MILLER, EDWARD
MILLER, EDDIE--[33]

MILLER, ELIZABETH MAXFLD.
MAXFIELD, ELIZABETH--[1]

MILLER, EMILY
PURDY--[1]

MILLER, FRANCIS TREVELYN
MEUNIER, FRANCOIS--[1]

MILLER, FREDERICK WALTER
GASCON, THE--[31]

MILLER, HARRIET MANN
GWYNFRYN--[1]
MILLER, OLIVE THORN--[1][22]AMERICAN

MILLER, HELEN HILL
HILL, HELEN--[1][22][31]AMERICAN

MILLER, HOLLY G.
HOLDEN, LESLIE--W/DENISE E. HENSLEY,
[34]MYS--
HARVEST "COMPTON CONNECTION" '86
HARVEST "LEGACY OF LILLIAN PARKER" '86
HARVEST "CARRIBEAN CONSPIRACY" '87

MILLER, HUGH
WATTS, JOHN--[7]SF--
NEL "HEAD OF STATE" '79

MILLER, J.A.
POOK, PETER--[8]

MILLER, JAMES P.
FRONTIER, TEX--[31]WEST
MILLER, J.P.--[31]

MILLER, JOHN
ARNETT, JACK--G.COOK LTR '93,MYS,HP--
BB 'BOOK OF JUSTICE' - #5
OR HIGHER, 1 BOOK

MILLER, JOHN GORDON
MILLER, JON--[8]

MILLER, JOHN GRIDER
GRIDER, JAY--[31]

MILLER, LANORA
WELZENBACH, LANORA F.--[1]

MILLER, LAURIE
GRANT, LAURIE--[26]ROM--
"BELOVED DECEIVER"
"RAVEN & THE SWANN"

MILLER, LEONARD
MERRICK, LEONARD--[1][22]ENGLISH

MILLER, LYNN
CAPTIOUS CRITIC--[8]

MILLER, LYNNE ELLEN
GOLDSMITH--[31]

MILLER, MARGARET
MILL, GARRETT--[2]

MILLER, MARGARET ROGERS
ROGERS, GARET--[34]MYS--
DIAL "SCANDAL IN EDEN" '63

MILLER, MARY
DURACK, MARY--[8]

MILLER, MARY BETH
BETH, MARY--[1][31][33]

MILLER, MARY BRITTON
BOLTON, ISABEL--[1]

MILLER, MARY ESTER
KEITH, MARION--[1]

MILLER, MIRANDA
HYMAN, MIRANDA--[23][31]SF--
"UNDER THE RAINBOW" '78

MILLER, MRS. HENRY WISE
MILLER, ALICE DUER--[1]

MILLER, NICOLE PULEO
PULEO, NICOLE--[1]

MILLER, P. SCHUYLER
MCDERMOTT, DENNIS--W/PAUL MCDERMOTT
& WALTER L. DENNIS,[1][2][23]SF--
"RED SPOT ON JUPITER" '31
"DUEL ON THE ASTEROID" '32
NIHIL--[2][11]

MILLER, RON S.
HUSTON, FRAN--[1][3][31]MYS--
DBLDY "RICH GET IT ALL" '73
MILLER, R.S.--[31]

MILLER, SANDRA
MILLER, SANDY--[7]SF

MILLER, SIGMUND [STEPHEN]
BLACKWOOD, STEPHANIE--[34]MYS--
POPLB "LAMONTANE" '72

MILLER, TERRY KENNETH
MILL, IAN ST. JOHN--[1]

MILLER, TEVIS
REARDON, JOSEPH--L. ROBBINS LTR MAR '94

MILLER, THOMAS KENT
MILLER, THOS. KENT--[7]SF--
NON-FICT

MILLER, VAL
MANNING, VAL--[1]

MILLER, VALERIE
COLE, HILARY--[9][21][26]ROM--
"ROMANCING CHARLIE"
"VIOLETS ARE BLUE" & MORE

MILLER, VICTOR [B]
BROOKE, JOSHUA--[1][31]
MCCOY, ARCH--[1]
MILLER, BROOKE--[7]SF

MILLER, WARREN
STEWART, DICK--[34]MYS,HP--
MAGNET #379 "A CRIME WITHOUT A NAME" '05
VAIL, AMANDA--[1]

MILLER, WRIGHT
NORTH, MARK--[8]

MILLET, NIGEL STAMBURG
OKE, RICHARD--[1]

MILLIES, HELMUT
GREENOW, HELM--[39]GERMAN/ADV/MYS
GRONAU, HELMUT--[39]GERMAN/ADV/MYS
MALLIEUX, HOLM--[39]GERMAN/ADV/MYS

MILLIGAN, ELSIE
BURR, ELSIE--[8]

MILLIGAN, TERENCE ALAN
MILLIGAN, SPIKE--[3][22][23][33]MYS--
WOBURN "MORE GOON SHOW SCRIPTS" '73

MILLS, ALGERNON VICTOR
LATIMER, RUPERT--[3][22]MYS--
MacD "DEATH IN REAL LIFE" '43
MacD "MURDER AFTER CHRISTMAS" '44
MILLS, A.V.--[22][34]MYS--

MILLS, DEANIE FRANCIS
MILLS, D.F.--SAOM, P54,[7]SF/HOR--
DIAM "SPELLBOUND" '91
DIAM "DEADLINE" '91

MILLS, ELLIS
COUNCIL OF FOUR--W/TOM WALKER, CHUCK HANSEN, ROY HUNT, NORM METCALF, BOB PETERSON,[2]

MILLS, HUGH [TRAVERS]
TRAVERS, HUGH--[1][3]MYS--
ELEK "MADAM AUBRY & THE POLICE" '66
ELEK "M.A. DINES WITH DEATH" '67

MILLS, JANET MELANIE A.
CHALLONER, H.K.--[8][31]

MILLSAPS, DANIEL W. III
NUKI--[1]
WEB, DAN--[1]

MILLWARD, PAMELA
MIDLING, PERSPICACITY--[8]

MILN, H. CRICHTON
CRICHTON, LOUISE--[34]MYS--
COL "CHINA ROSE" '39
COL "LESS THAN DUST" '39
COL "MANDARIN'S DAGGER" '39

MILNE, ALAN A.
MILNE, A.A.--[1][32]MYS--
EQMM "IT WAS A LONG TIME AGO" JUL '50
EQMM "IT COULD HAVE HAPPENED THAT WAY" MAY '51
EQMM "MURDER AT ELEVEN" MAR '54
& 4 OTHERS

MILNE, CHARLES
MILNE, EWART--[8]

MILNER, ALFRED VISCT.
M.--[8]

MILNER, MARION BLACKETT
FIELD, JOANNA--[8][22][31]ENGLISH

MILNES, THOMAS WRAY
JIG-SAW--[1]

MILOSZ, CZESLAW
SYRUC, J.--[31]--
"WIERSZE" '40

MILSOM, CHARLES HENRY
WESTON, WILLIAM [G]--[1][32]MYS--
TF "OLD SNAGGLEBUCK" '56

MILSTEAD, JESSICA L[EE]
HARRIS, J.L.--[32]MYS--
LM "DR. MARKHAM'S SUICIDE" SEPT '80
HARRIS, JESSICA L.--[1][31]

MILTON, GLADYS ALEXANDRA
CARLYLE, ANTHONY--[1][3][22]MYS--
MILLS "CHILDREN OF CHANCE" '23
HODDER "COCK CROW" '30

MILTON, JOHN R.
GARRARD, CHRISTOPHER--[1]
LEWIS, CARSON--[1]

MILTON, PAUL R.
BAKER, ACE--[2]
WOOD, VALENTINE--W. MURRAY-ECHOES #5,HP--

MILTON, SAUL
FLINDERS, KARL--[1][2][14]ADULT--
OLYM "THE LOVE MACHINE" '71

MIMS, EMILY
ELLIOTT, EMILY--[9][21][26]ROM--
"DELICATE BALANCE"
"JUST HIS TOUCH" & MORE

MINCIELI, ROSE LAURA
ROSS, LAURA--[31]--
KNOPF "HARLEQUIN" '68

MINDT, HEINZ R.
PATURI, FELIX R.--[1]

MINER, ENOCH NEWTON
TYPIST, TOPSIE--[1]

MINER, JANE CLAYPOOL
CLAYPOOL, JANE--[1][31][33]
LADD, VERONICA--[21][31][33]ROM--
"PROMISED KISS"
"SOME DAY MY PRINCE" & MORE

MINER, OPAL IRENE F.S.
SEVREY, OPAL IRENE--[22]AMERICAN

MINER, PETER
ELLIOTT, JANE--[3]MYS--
POPLB "DARKENING NIGHT" '75

MINER, VIRGINIA SCOTT
HOOSIER, HANK--[1]
HOOSIER, HANNAH--[1]
KAY, PHOEBE--[1]
KIPLINGER, DAVID--[1]
THATCHER, AMELIA--[1]
WILCOX, HANNAH SIMS--[1]

MINES, JEANETTE MARIE
RYAN, JEANETTE MINES--[33]

MINES, SAMUEL
FIELD, PETER--AL TONIK LST,[19]WEST,HP--
MRW "COYOTE GULCH" '36
HOUSE "RIMROCK RIDERS" '61
HOUSE "OUTLAW HERD" '62
HOUSE "COUGAR CANYON" '62

MINSKEY, BETTY JANE
TOBY, LIZ--[1][22]AMERICAN

MINTO, MARY
MACQUEEN, JAY--[8]

MINTZ, JOYCE LOIS
MADISON, JOYCE--[1][3][31]MYS--
PINN "RUN IF YOU CAN" '81

MIRACOLA, GIOVANNI
BRAGAGLIA, ANTON GIULIO--[22] ITALIAN

MIREPOIX, CAMILLE
ADASTRA--[1][31]

MIRO, FRANZ
KLEIN-ROSSEL, A.--[39]GERMAN/MYS

MIRSAIDOV, MIRMUKHSIN
MIRMUKHSIN--[1]

MIRUS, LUDMILLA
EGGER, ELLEN--[1]
MIRUS-KAUBA, LUDMILLA--[1]

MISCHWITSKY, HOLGER
VON PRAUNHEIM, ROSA--[39]GERMAN

MISHA, VIDHATA
SHRIVIDHATA--[1]

MISRAKI, PAUL
THOMAS, PAUL--[11]

MISTRIK, LUDO
ONDREJOV, LUDO--[22] SLOVAK

MITCHELL, ADRIAN
HEWITT, BEN--[1]
JONES, VOLCANO--[1][31]
MUDGEON, APEMAN--[1]
TREACLE, UNCLE--[1]

MITCHELL, CHARLOTTE G.
TWAIN, MINERVA MARK--[1]

MITCHELL, CLARE MAY
CANFIELD, CLEVE--[8]

MITCHELL, DONALD GRANT
CAIUS--[1]AMERICAN
D.G.M.--[1]AMERICAN
MARVEL, IK--[1][22]AMERICAN
TIMON, JOHN--[1]AMERICAN

MITCHELL, EDWARD CARD
CAPT. COE--W/LINCOLN SPRINGFIELD,[3]MYS--
ARROWHEAD "CORONER'S UNDERSTUDY" 1891

MITCHELL, EDWARD PAGE
MITCHELL, ALBERT PAGE--[2]

MITCHELL, GLADYS [M.W.]
HOCKABY, STEPHEN--[18][29][31][33]
ENGLISH/MYS--5 NOVELS '33-9
TORRIE, MALCOLM--[3][18][29][33]MYS--
JOSEPH "HEAVY AS LEAD" '66
JOSEPH "LATE & COLD" '67 & MORE

MITCHELL, ISAAC
NELSON, JOSEPH--[1]

MITCHELL, ISABEL
PLAIN, JOSEPHINE--[8]

MITCHELL, JAMES LESLIE
GIBBON, LEWIS GRASSIC--[2][11][22][23]
[38]SCOTTISH/SF--

MITCHELL, JAMES [W]
MCGUIRE, PATRICK O.--[34]MYS--
HAMM "A TIME FOR MURDER" '55
HAMM "FIESTA FOR MURDER" '62
??UNCONFIRMED??
MELDRUM, JAMES--[1]
MUNRO, JAMES--[2][3]MYS--
HAMM "MAN WHO SOLD DEATH" '64
HAMM "DIE RICH, DIE HAPPY" '65
HAMM "MONEY THAT MONEY CAN'T BUY" '67
JENKINS "INNOCENT BYSTANDERS" '69

MITCHELL, JOHN
BLAKE, S.P.--V. BERCH-BRNDN/
BC PSEUDS, BAE 22, P24
SLATER, PATRICK--[1]

MITCHELL, JOHN HANLON
HANLON, JOHN--[1]

MITCHELL, KIRK [JOHN]
NORST, JOEL--[23][34]MYS/SF--
ST. MARTIN'S "DELTA FORCE" '86
JOVE "LETHAL WEAPON" '87
GRAFTON "COLORS" '88
SIGN "MISSISSIPPI BURNING" '89

MITCHELL, LANGDON ELWYN
VARLEY, JOHN PHILIP--[8]

MITCHELL, MARGARET JULIA
MITCHELL, MAGGIE--[1]

MITCHELL, MARGARET [M]
BENNETT, ELIZABETH--[31]

MITCHELL, MARY
PLAIN, JOSEPHINE--[1][36]AUSTRALIAN/MYS--
BUTWH "SECRET OF THE SANDBANKS" '34
BUTWH "SECRET OF THE SNOWS" '35
BUTWH "PAZENGER PROBLEM" '36

MITRINOVIC, DMITRI
COSMOI, M.M.--[8]

MITSKEVITCH, A.P.
DNEPROV, ANATOLY--[2]

MITSUTHERU, SUDO
NANSUI, SUDO--[22]JAPANESE

MITTERMEYER, HELEN
CRISTY, ANN--[9][21][26][31]ROM--
"TORN ASSUNDER"
"MYSTIQUE" & MORE
MONTEITH, HAYTON--[9][21][26]ROM--
"JINX LADY"
"LOTUS BLOSSOM" & MORE
PAUL, DANIELLE--[9][21][26]ROM--
"CHAMELEON"

MIVART, ST. GEORGE J.
DREW, D'ARCY--[1]

MIX, KATHERINE LYON
LYON, KATHERINE--[1][31]

MIZNER, ELIZABETH HOWARD
HOWARD, ELIZABETH--[1][7][22][33]AMERICAN/SF
& HIST

MOBERLY, CHARLOTTE ANNE
MOBERLY, C.A.E.--[1]
MORISON, ELIZABETH--[8]

MOCATTA, DOROTHY ALLEN
MOCATTA, FRANCES--[1]

MOCKLER, GRETCHEN
TRAVIS, GRETCHEN--[8]

MODARESSI, ANNE TYLER
TYLER, ANNE--[7]SF

MODELL, MERRIAM
PIPER, EVELYN--[18][22][29][34][40]MYS--
ATHNM "HANO'S DOLL" '61
SIMON "THE MOTIVE" '50 & MORE

MODERWELL, HIRAM K.
MOTHERWELL, HIRAM--[1]

MODICK, KLAUS
DOMCIK, LUKAS--[39]GERMAN

MODIN, UNO
MORRIS, JACK--[29]MYS

MODROVICH, KATHLEEN C.
CARROLL, KATHLEEN--[9][21][26]ROM--
"ANGEL'S WALK"
CREIGHTON, KATHLEEN--[9][21][26]ROM--
"STILL WATERS"
"SORCERER'S KEEPER" & MORE

MOEHN, SHARON DULING
MAYNE, SHARON--[26]ROM--
"HEART TROUBLE"
"THE RIGHT MOVES"
"WINNER TAKES ALL"

MOEN, JAN
BARK, JULIUS--W/EVERT LUNDSTROM,[29]MYS--
"VILA VID DENNA KALLA" '65
LAGEVI, BO--[29]MYS,HP--
BS-6 "EN FORLORARES BROTT" '77
BS-13 "ENSAM AR SVAG" '78]

MOERSBERGER, ROSEFELICITA
ROSE, FELICITAS--[39]GERMAN

MOES, EBERHARD
MONORBY, EBERHARD--[39]GERMAN

MOFFAT, DONALD
KENYON, PAUL--[7]THRIL--
"BARONESS #8: BLACK GOLD" '75

MOFFATT, JAMES
ALLEN, RICHARD--[23][34]MYS--
NEL "SKINHEAD ESCAPES" '72
NEL "SKINHEAD FAREWELL" '74
NEL "TERRACE TERRORS" '75
LM "MAIGRET CONCENTRATES ON A CASE" SEPT '75
BARCLAY, BILL--J. DAVEY LTR '93--
"SOMEWHERE IN THE NIGHT"-
COMPLETED BY MOORCOCK
BRAND, HILARY--[34]MYS,HP--
COMPACT "PEAK OF FRENZY" '64
COMPACT "ALL OR NOTHING" '65
COMPACT "BLACK SUMMER DAY" '65
COMPACT "A FLAIR FOR AFFAIRS" '66
COMPACT "RUNNING SCARED" '66
COMPACT "STRICTLY WILD" '66
JANSON, HANK--[34]MYS,HP--
COMPACT "LAST LADY " '64
COMPACT "LOVE SECRETARIES" '64
COMPACT "PATTERN OF RAPE" '64
COMPACT "DEVIL & THE DEEP" '64
COMPACT "DISH RAN AWAY" '64

MOFFATT, JAMES [CONT]
JANSON, HANK [CONT]
COMPACT "DEPRAVITY" '64
COMPACT "ABOMINATION" '65
COMPACT "BACKLASH OF INFAMY" '65
COMPACT "CATCH ME A RENEGADE" '65
COMPACT "COUNTER-FEAT" '65
COMPACT "SWEET TALK" '65
COMPACT "MODEL IN MAYHEM" '65
COMPACT "WHY SHOULD SYLVIA?" '65
COMPACT "SWEET TALK '65
COMPACT "WHY SHOULD SYLVIA?" '65
MORE, J.J.--[8]

MOFFATT, MRS. LEN
SINCLAIR, ANNA--[11]

MOFFETT, PAULA
RICHARDS, VANESSA--[9][21][26]ROM--
"BITTERSWEET TORMENT"

MOGRIDGE, STEPHEN
STEVENS, JILL--[8]

MOHAKLELE, EZEKIAL
ESEKI, BRUNO--[1]

MOHAN, JOSEPHINE ELIZAB.
JERMONTE--[8]

MOHAN, PAMELA L. O'NEILL
O'NEILL, PAMELA--[7]SF--
"CYBORG COMMANDO #1-3" '88

MOHR, ADRIAN
VON ROEDERN, JOACHIM--[39]GERMAN

MOINEAUX, GEORGES-VICTOR
COULTELINE, GEORGES--[1][22]FRENCH

MOIR, ANGUS
ANGUS, WILLIAM--[3]MYS--
VANTAGE "MURDER IN MALLORCA" '77

MOIR, DAVID MACBETH
DELTA--[22]SCOTTISH

MOISIA, IVAN LEONTEVICH
LE, IVAN--[1]

MOJICA, JOSE
GUADALOUPE, BROTHER JOSE--[31]

MOLENES, MME. PAUL DE
BENIGNE, ANGE--[1]

MOLESWORTH, MARY L.S.
GRAHAM, ENNIS--[1][22]SCOTTISH

MOLESWORTH, VOLTAIRE
MOLESWORTH, VOL--[23][36]AUSTRALIAN/MYS/SF--
CHAP "APE OF GOD" '43
CHAP "MONSTER AT LARGE" '43
CHAP "BLINDED THEY FLY" '51
CHAP "LET THERE BE MONSTERS" '52

MOLIN, LARS
LASSE-MAJA--[29]MYS

MOLL, RUDOLF
FIALA, ERICH--[39]GERMAN
HOLM, FRED--[39]GERMAN
MAHR, RUD.--[39]GERMAN

MOLLOY, ALICE
DUFFY, ROBERT M.--W/DIANE DIPRIMA,[14]ADULT--
OLYM OPH#2222 "OF SHEEP AND GIRLS" '68

MOLLOY, EDWARD
JAMIESON, THOMAS--[8]
JONES, H.S.--[8]
WARD, HERBERT B.S.--[8]

MOLLOY, JOSEPH FITZGERALD
WILDING, ERNEST--[1]

MOLNAR, GEZAR
CZIBUS, CSABA--[1]

MOLSNER, MICHAEL
ALAMO, BILL--[39]GERMAN/WEST,HP
CAMERON, ROBERT--[39]GERMAN/MYS/WEST
DRAKE, JOHN--[39]GERMAN/MYS/WEST,HP

MOLT, ANGELA
DEL MAR, MARIA--[30] MEXICAN

MOLTKE-HANSEN, DAVID
HANSEN, PETER--[7][21][26]ROM/SF--
"CREEK RIFLES"

MOMMERS, HELMUTH W.
AROL, ROBERT--[39]GERMAN/SF
RICE, ADAM--W/ERNST VLCEK,[39]GERMAN/SF

MONAHAN, JAMES HENRY F.
KENNEDY, JAMES--[31]

MONARCH, DIANE A.J.
ABBOTT, JEANNE--[21][26]ROM--
"THE SUBSTITUTE BRIDEGROOM"
ABBOTT, JENNIE--[21]ROM--
"A WISH FOR TONIGHT"

MONCRIEFF, ROBERT HOPE
HOPE, ASCOTT R.--[1]

MONCURE, JANE BELK
WANNAMAKER, BRUCE--[33]

MONDEY, DAVID CHARLES
CHARLES, DAVID--W/CHARLES D. TAYLOR,[31]

MONGELLUZZO, GUY ANTHONY
MARCO, GUY A[NTHONY]--[1]

MONGER, IFOR DAVID
RICHARDS, PETER--[8][22]ENGLISH
MANNIGIAN, PETER--[8][22]ENGLISH

MONHOFF, JUNE HILDEGARDE
FLANNER, HILDEGARDE--[31]

MONJO, FERDINAND N.
MONJO, F.N.--[1]

MONKHOUSE, BOB
JANSON, HANK--[2]MYS,HP--
GAYWOOD

MONNINGER, JOSEPH
PATRICK, BRENNAN--CRPG,[34]MYS--
DELL 16674 "NIGHT CALLER" '81

MONNIOT, JEAN-VORLE
MARY, ANDRE--[22]FRENCH

MONRO-HIGGS, GERTRUDE
MONRO, GAVIN--[8][34]MYS--
HALE "WHO KILLED AMANDA?" '67
HALE "A BENT FOR BLACKMAIL" '67
HALE "MARKED WITH A CROSS" 68
HALE "TRIP TO ETERNITY" '70

MONROE, CAROL
DUFRECHOU, CAROL--[1][31]

MONROE, ELIZA
ROSS, MORGAN--V. BERCH LTR TO HUBIN '94, MYS--
TWR "ANY NUMBER CAN DIE!" '81

MONROE, KEITH
COCHRAN, RICE E.--[1][31]
COLOMBO, DALE--[1][22][31]AMERICAN
KEITH, DONALD--W/DONALD MONROE,
[2][22][31]AMERICAN

MONROE, KEITH & DONALD
KEITH, DONALD--[2][8][11] AMERICAN

MONSELL, MARGARET E.
IRWIN, MARGARET E.--[1]

MONSMA, HILDEGARD S.
MONS, MARTIN--[29]MYS,SAXON & LINDSTROM--
"KOMMISSARIE PERQUIN OCH PARLMORDEN" '57

MONTAGU, ASHLEY
ASHLEY-MONTAGU, MONTAGUE--[31]

MONTAGU, DRAYCOT
ANSON, PIERS--[34]MYS--
AMALG "SECRET OF THE YELLOW ROBE" '32

MONTAGU, EDWARD J.B.D.S.
DOUGLAS-SCOTT-MONTAGU, ED--[31]
MONTAGU OF BEAULIEU, 3RD--[22]ENGLISH

MONTAGUE, BRUCE [ALEX.]
ALEXANDER, BRUCE--[1]
BRUCE, MARTIN--[1]
O'TOOLE, KATE--[1]
SAVAGE, OSCAR--[1]

MONTAGUE, LODOWICK EDWARD
REES, RICHARD--[7]SF--
NON-FICT ON "ORWELL"

MONTANYE, CARLETON S.
MONTANYE, C.S.--E.R. HAGEMANN-COMP.
INDX BM '82, MYS--
SW "TRUNK IN TIMES SQUARE" APR '46
SW "MURDER IN INE EASY LESSON" APR '47
EQMM "NOT FOR A CHORUS GIRL" MAR '50
EQMM "HAWK & THE PULLET" JAN '56
PH "MONEY MEANS MURDER" APR '62
WALLACE, ROBERT--ECHOES#17,[3]MYS,HP--
PHD "BLACK BALL OF DEATH" '49

MONTANYE, HAROLD [MONTY]
EATON, GEORGE L.--C.S. VERRAL-
ECHOES #22,[2][11]--
'BILL BARNES':
"STRATOSPHERE" & OTHERS

MONTEE, KRISTY
DANIELS, KRISTY--W/NORMAN A. DANIELS,
[21][26]ROM--
"THE DANCER"
"HOT TYPE"

MONTEFIORE, CAROLINE L.
ERIC--[8]

MONTEIRO E GRILO, JOAQUIM
KIM, TOMAS--[22]PORTUGUESE

MONTELEONE, THOMAS F.
DRUMM, D.B.--V. BERCH LTR TO R. REGINALD '93, SF,HP--
DELL 'TIMETRAVELER':
"TERMINAL ROAD" '86
LO MEDICO, BRIAN T.--[1]

MONTES DE ORCA, MARCO A.
DE ORCA, MARCO ANTONIO--[31]

MONTFORT, AUGUSTE
LE BRETON, AUGUSTE--[29][31][34]MYS--
COLLINS "LAW OF THE STREETS" '57 & MORE

MONTGOMERY, CHARLOTTE B.
BAKER, CHARLOTTE--[1]

MONTGOMERY, LESLIE ALEX.
DOYLE, LYNN--CVR BLURB,[8][22]IRISH--
PENG 36 "BALLYGULLION" '08 & OTHERS

MONTGOMERY, LUCY MAUDE
MONTGOMERY, L.M.--[1]

MONTGOMERY, MAMIE ELIZAB.
WAKEFIELD, ELIZABETH--[1]

MONTGOMERY, RAYMOND A.
MOUNTAIN, ROBERT--[1][7][33]

MONTGOMERY, ROBERT BRUCE
CRISPIN, EDMUND--[2][3][5][32]MYS--
12 GOLZ & STORIES IN EQMM & MACKILLS

MONTGOMERY, RUTHERFORD G.
AVERY, A.A.--[1][28][34]MYS--
FARRAR "ANYTHING FOR A QUIET LIFE" '42
AVERY, AL--[22][28][31][33]AMERICAN--
"A YANKEE FLIER WITH THE RAF[9 VOL] '41-6
ELDER, ART--[1][22]AMERICAN
MARSHALL, E.P.--[1][22]AMERICAN
PROCTOR, EVERITT--[1]

MONTGOMERY, YVONNE
ADAMSON, YVONNE--W/MARY JO ADAMSON, MYS SCENE #40, MYS--
DLCT "BRIDEY'S MOUNTAIN" '93

MONTROSE, CATHERINE COOKE
COOKE, CATHERINE--[7]SF--
ACE "WINGED ASSASSIN #1-3" '87/89
TOR "MASK #1-3" '85/88

MOODY, SUSAN [ELIZABETH]
JAMES, SUSANNAH--MYS SCENE #38, P60,[18]MYS--
NAL "A DISTANT SHORE" '81
NAL "LUCIA'S LEGACY" '84
"LOVE OVER GOLD' '93

MOOLMAN, VALERIE
CARTER, NICK--W/MIKE AVALLONE,[3]MYS,HP--
AWARD "RUN SPY, RUN" '64
AWARD "THE CHINA DOLL" '64
AWARD "SAIGON" '65
CARTER, NICK--[3]MYS,HP--
AWARD "FRAULEIN SPY" '64
AWARD "SAFARI FOR SPIES" '64
AWARD "CHECKMATE IN RIO" '64
AWARD "A BULLET FOR FIDEL" '65
AWARD "13TH SPY" '65
AWARD "HANOI" '66
AWARD "TERRIBLE ONES" '66
AWARD "WEAPON OF NIGHT" '67

MOOLMAN, VALERIE [CONT]
LOMAN, ERIC--V. BERCH LTR '93--
GM T2637 "YOU ARE WHAT YOU DREAM" '72

MOON, ALAN
BENTLEY, PETER--[7][23]SF--
HALE "DESTINED TO SURVIVE" '77

MOON, GEORGE P.
PEMBURY, MONTAGUE--[1]

MOON, MODEAN
MODEAN, MARY--[9][21][26]ROM--
"IN NAME ONLY"
"ALL THE FLOWERS"
"HEART SONG"

MOONEY, EDWARD
MOONEY, TED--[7][23]SF--
"EASY TRAVEL TO OTHER PLANETS" '81
"TRAFFIC & LAUGHTER" '90

MOONEY, PAUL
BLACK TORNADO--[1]

MOORCOCK, MICHAEL
ALLARD, NICK--H. CAMPBELL-BAE 22--
NOT A PSEUD, CHARACTER NAME ACCDG TO 'MIKE'
BARCLAY, BILL--V. PECORARO-BAE 21, J. DAVEY LTR '93,[2][3][4][29]MYS--
COMPACT "SOMEWHERE IN THE NIGHT" '66-
BEGUN BY JAMES MOFFATT
COMPACT "PRINTER'S DEVIL" '66
WROTE REVIEWS FOR NW & GN
BARCLAY, WILLIAM--J.DAVEY LTR '94,[2]--
NW "GOLDEN BARGE" VOL 49 NO.155 OCT '65
BARCLAY, WILLIAM EWART--J. DAVEY LTR '93,[31]
COVER "SOMEWHERE IN TIME"
& "PRINTER'S DEVIL"
BARRINGTON, MICHAEL--W/BARRINGTON J. BAYLEY, J. DAVEY LTR '93,[2][23][31]SF--
NW - ONE STORY
BISHOP, K.L.--J. DAVEY LTR JAN '94
BISHOP, KEITH--J. DAVEY LTR '94--
GN "MAN WITH THE BURNING BRAIN" OCT '66
BRADBURY, ED--J. DAVEY LTR DEC '93, SF--
GN - REVIEW OF THE 'NICK ALLARD' BOOKS
BRADBURY, EDWARD P.--V. PECORARO-BAE 21, J. DAVEY LTR '93,[2][4][7]SF--
LAN 72-122 "BLADES OF MARS" '65
LAN 72-118 "WARRIORS OF MARS" '65
LAN 72-127 "BARBARIANS OF MARS" '65
BRAND, HILARY--J. DAVEY LTR '94--
REWROTE PART OF NOVEL COMPACT PUBL AS
BY "BRAND" '65-6
COLVIN, JAMES--W/B.J. BAYLEY, V. PECORARO-BAE 21,[2][4][30]SF,HP--
NW "THE WRECKS OF TIME" '65
NW "DEEP FIX" '66
COLVIN, JIM--J. DAVEY LTR '94, SF--
GN "PORTOBELLO ROAD" SEPT '66
COLVIN, WARWICK JNR.--J. DAVEY LTR '94,[23]--
NW "CORSAIRS OF THE SECOND ETHER" VOL 62, NO.218 '92
CORNELIUS, FRANK--J. DAVEY LTR JAN '94
HARRIS, ROGER--HUGH CAMPBELL--
BAE 22, P9,[2][4]
ICARUS--J. DAVEY LTR JAN '94
J.C.--J. DAVEY LTR DEC '93, SF--
NW - REVIEWS
JAMES, PHILIP--W/JAMES CAWTHORN, J. DAVEY LTR '94,[23]--
'MIKE' ORIG SERILIZED "DISTANT SUNS"
JANSON, HANK--J. DAVEY LTR '94,[2]SF,HP--
GN "GIRL WHO KILLED SULTRY CAINE" NOV '66
LUMLEY, BOB--J. DAVEY LTR JAN '94

MOORCOCK, MICHAEL [CONT]
LUMLEY, R.--J. DAVEY LTR JAN '94
LUMLEY, ROBERT--J.DAVEY LTR JAN '94
LUMLEY, ROBERT S.--J. DAVEY LTR JAN '94
MACBETH, KEN--J. DAVEY LTR '94, SF--
GN "ENVIRONMENT PROBLEM" SEPT '66
MOOROCK, MICHAEL--[2]--
WAS EDITOR'S TYPO, NOT PSEUDONYM
POWYS, EDWARD--J. DAVEY LTR '93, SF--
GN - AS FICTION EDITOR FOR SEVERAL ISSUES
R.S.L.--J. DAVEY LTR JAN '94
REID, DESMOND--W/S. HALL, J. CAWTHORNE
& P. CHAMBERS, G. COOK-BAE 22,
J. DAVEY LTR '94,PPCC#8
REID, DESMOND--[2][4][23][30][34]MYS,HP--
AMALG "CARRIBEAN CRISIS" '61
RENEGADE--JEAN F. LE DEIST LTR '93,[2]
SIMONS, HENRY--J. DAVEY LTR '94, SF--
GN "ISLAND" NOV '66
TAYLOR, J.R.--J. DAVEY LTR JAN '94
TAYLOR, JIM--J.DAVEY LTR JAN '94
TORQUEMADA--J. DAVEY LTR JAN '94
W.E.B.--J. DAVEY LTR '93, SF--
NW - REVIEWS
WISDOM, JOHN--W/JOHN WISDOM, J. DAVEY LTR '94-
-
'TARZAN ADV' SERIES"
"SIEGE OF NOOTHAR" JUN '58

MOORE, ANNIE A.W.
FORESTIER, AUBER--[1]

MOORE, ARTHUR
ADDISON, GWEN--W/ALFRED HARRIS,[1][3]MYS--
"STORM OVER FOX HILL" '74
HAMILTON, ADAM--W/MARILYN GRANBECK,[1][3]MYS--
BERK "WYSS PURSUIT" '75 & 3 MORE
HOYT, DON--W/ARTHUR MOORE,[34]MYS--
POWELL 1009N "DEATH IS A DRAG" '70
KYLE, GEOFFREY--V. BERCH-BRNDN/
BC PSEUDS, BAE 22--
BC 7104 "TEEN DEVIATE" '70
MOORE, AURORA--[9][21][26]ROM--
"RAGING HEART"
MOORE, HARRIS--W/ALFRED HARRIS,[2][11][23]SF--
"SLATER'S PLANET" '71
"MARROW EATERS" '72
ORIEL, ANTRIM--[1][2]
SAXON, VAN--W/MARILYN GRANBECK,[1][3]MYS--
ZEBRA "HOLLYWOOD HIT MAN" '75
SMITHFIELD, ARTHUR P.--V. BERCH-BRNDN/
BC PSEUDS, BAE 22, P24
VAN HELLER, MARCUS--[14]ADULT,HP--
OLYM OPH#157 "A STAR IS BORN" '69

MOORE, BERNARD
CLEVES, BERNARD--[31]

MOORE, BERTHA B.
CANNON, BRENDA--[1]
MCCURRY, BETSY--[1]

MOORE, BIRKETT
ALLEGRO--[8]

MOORE, BRIAN
BRYAN, MICHAEL--[2][3]MYS--
DELL FE88 "INTENT TO KILL" '56
DELL FEA145 "MURDER IN MAJORCA" '57
MARA, BERNARD--V. BERCH-GM PSEUDS, PP 33,
[3]MYS--
GM 402 "FRENCH FOR MURDER" '54
GM 472 "A BULLET FOR MY LADY" '55
GM 562 "THIS GUN IS FOR GLORIA" '56

MOORE, CATHERINE LUCILLE
BELLIN, EDWARD--W/HENRY KUTTNER,[2]SF,HP--
STIRRING STORIES
COBURN, JACK--W/HENRY KUTTNER,[2]SF--
EDMONDS, PAUL--W/HENRY KUTTNER,[2]SF--
GARDNER, NOEL--W/HENRY KUTTNER,[2]SF--
GARTH, WILL--W/HENRY KUTTNER,[2]SF--
GREY, WALTON--W/HENRY KUTTNER,[2]SF--
HALL, JAMES--W/HENRY KUTTNER,[2][23]SF--
HAMMOND, KEITH--W/HENRY KUTTNER,[2][23]SF--
"VALLEY OF THE FLAME" '46
STARTLING STORIES-"LORD OF THE STORM" '77
'SIGN OF THE TIME' SERIES
HASTINGS, HUDSON--W/HENRY KUTTNER,
[1][2][23]SF--
HORN, PETER--W/HENRY KUTTNER,[2]SF,HP--
ZIFF-DAVIS
KENT, KELVIN--W/HENRY KUTTNER,[2]SF--
KENYON, ROBERT O.--W/HENRY KUTTNER,[2][23]SF--
LIDDEL, C.H.--W/HENRY KUTTNER,[1][11]SF--
MAEPANN, HUGH--W/HENRY KUTTNER,[2]SF--
MAEPANN, K.H.--W/HENRY KUTTNER,[2][23]SF--
MOORE, C.L.--[1][32]MYS--
AHMM "HERE LIES..." DEC '56
MU "HELLSGARDE" NOV '67
MORGAN, SCOTT--W/HENRY KUTTNER,[2][23]SF--
O'DONNELL, LAWRENCE--[1][2][23]SF--
"CLASH BY NIGHT" '43 - OTHERS W/KUTTNER
PADGETT, LEWIS--W/HENRY KUTTNER,[1][2][23]SF--
"A GNOME THERE WAS" '50
SCANLON, C.K.M.--W/HENRY KUTTNER,[2]SF,HP--
THRILLING
SMITH, WOODROW WILSON--[2][23]SF--
STODDARD, CHARLES--W/HENRY KUTTNER,[2]SF--

MOORE, CHARLES GARRETT P.
DROGHEDA, EARL OF--[31]

MOORE, CLEMENT CLARKE
COLUMELLA--[31][33]

MOORE, DORIS LANGLEY
GENTLEWOMAN, A--[8]

MOORE, DORIS O.
MOORE, PHILIPS--W/MARY A. PHILIPS,[3]MYS--
ARCADIA "DEATH DRIVES THE LEAD CAR" '61
ARCADIA "ONCE UPON A FRIDAY" '65

MOORE, ERICA MARIA
AKIRA--[2]

MOORE, EULA & MIRIAM
MORTON, MIRIAM--[7]SF

MOORE, GEORGINA MARY G.
OSBORNE, HELENA--[3]MYS--
HODDER "JOKER" '79
HODDER "WHITE POPPY" '77 2 MORE '72-9

MOORE, HANNAH H.
MOORE, N. HUDSON--[1]

MOORE, HAROLD WILLIAM
ROOME, HOLDAR--[8]

MOORE, IDORA [M]
HAMILTON, BETSY--[1]

MOORE, ISABEL
LEE, DORIAN--[34]MYS--
SWAN "CROOKED PATHS" '43
LONG "GREEN BRACKEN" '53
& 13 MORE '43-56

MOORE, JAMES
BALFOUR, JOHN--[1][31]

MOORE, JOHN RICHARD
MOORE, DICK[IE]--[1]

MOORE, JOHN TRAVERS
TRIPP, JOHN--[1]

MOORE, JOHN TROTWOOD
TROTWOOD--[1]
TROTWOOD, JOHN--[8]

MOORE, JULIANNE RANDOLPH
MCBRIDE, JULE--[26]ROM--
HARL 500 "WILD CARD WEDDING"
HARL 519 "BABY TRAP" & OTHERS

MOORE, LILLIAN
ASHERON, SARA--[31]

MOORE, LUCILE
MUIR, LUCY--[21][26]ROM--
"THE IMPRUDENT WAGER"
"HIGHLAND RIVALRY"
"SUSSEX SUMMER"

MOORE, M. LOUISE
AL-MODAD--[2]

MOORE, MADELINE ROBERTA
HUMMEL, MADELINE--[31]

MOORE, MARIE LORENZ
MOORE, LORRIE--[1]

MOORE, MARY MCLEOD
PANDORA--[8]

MOORE, NICHOLAS
KELLY, GUY--[31]

MOORE, REGINALD CHARLES A
MOORE, CHARLES--[1]
MOORE, REG--[1]

MOORE, ROBERT LOWELL
MOORE, ROBIN--V. BERCH--
MON PSEUDS, BAE 9, P26,[3][7]MYS--
AV N134 "DEVIL TO PAY" '66 & MORE
ROBERTS, LOWELL--[1]

MOORE, ROGER E[LWOOD]
LAWSON, SUSAN--W/MARGARET WEIS,[7]SF--
"ENDLESS QUEST CRIMSON CRYSTAL
ADVENTURE #1"

MOORE, ROSALIE
BROWN, BILL--[8]
BROWN, ROSALIE--[8]

MOORE, RUTH ELLEN
GARBE, RUTH MOORE--[31]

MOORE, SPENCER
BENSON, ALBRIGHT--[14]ADULT--
OLYM OPH#203 "LASCIVIA" '70

MOORE, [JOSEPH] WARD
BRADFORD, ROBERT--[23]SHOWN AS WITH
'ROBERT BRADFORD'--
SF STORIES "CADACEUS WILD" '59

MOOREHEAD, ALBERT H.
HODGES, TURNER--[1][22][31]AMERICAN

MOORES, RICHARD ARNOLD
MOORES, DICK--[33]

MOORHOUSE, H. VANSITTART
VANSITTART, JANE--[1][22]AMERICAN

MOORHOUSE, HERBERT JOSEPH
MOORHOUSE, HOPKINS--[1][3][22]MYS--
HODDER "EVERY MAN FOR HIMSELF" '20
HODDER "GOLDEN SCARAB" '26 & MORE

MOORHOUSE, SYDNEY
LANGDALE, STANLEY--[8]
LYNDALE, SYDNEY M.--[8]

MOPP, MICHAEL
SKOOG, MALTE--[29]MYS

MORAES, FRANK ROBERT
ARIEL--[22][31] INDIAN

MORALES CABRERA, PABLO
BALSAMO, JOSE--[1]
DE LA TORRE, TIRSO--[1]

MORALES, MANUEL SOTO
YANKAS, LAUTARO--[20] SPANISH

MORAN, CARLO
BLOODGOOD, HARRY--[1]

MORANT, HARRY H.
BREAKER, THE--[8]

MORAWETZ, HEDWIG
MORA, HEDWIG--[39]GERMAN

MORAY WILLIAMS, URSULA
WILLIAMS, URSULA MORAY--[33]

MORAY, HELGA
MOREAU, HELENE--[21][26]ROM--
"ROXANA"
"ROXANA & ALEXANDER"
"A SON FOR ROXANA"

MORCK, PAAL
ROLVAAG, O.E.--[1]

MORDVINOFF, NICOLAS
NICOLAS--[33]

MOREAU, DAVID
MERLIN, DAVID--[8]

MORECAMBE, ERIC
BARTHOLOMEW, JOHN ERIC--[31]

MOREH, SHMUEL
IBRAHIM, SAMI--[31]

MOREL, HERMANN
JOST, HERMANN--[39]GERMAN/WEST/JUV

MOREL, JIMMIE L.
LONGFORD, LINDSAY--[21][26]ROM--
"CADE BOUDREAU'S REVENGE"
"JAKE'S CHILD"
"PETE'S DRAGON"

MOREN, SALLY M.
MORGAN, JANE--[1][9][21][26]ROM--
"CAROLINE'
"LORD COURTNEY'S LADY"
"LOUIS"

MORENO BERNET, MANUEL
BROWN, CHARLES--JEAN F. LE DEIST LTR '93
BROWN, MIKE--JEAN F. LE DEIST LTR '93
BROWNE, MARSHALL S.--JEAN F. LE DEIST LTR '93
SANDOVAL, ARMANDO--JEAN F. LE DEIST LTR '93

MORENO, VIRGINIA
PILE--[8]

MORETON DE CHABRIL., ELIZ
CABRILLAN, CELESTE VENARD--[1]
MOGADOR, CELESTE--[1]

MORETON, DOUGLAS ARTHUR
DOUGLAS, ARTHUR--[1][3]MYS--
MIH "DECOY MURDERS" '75
MIH "NOAH'S ARK MURDERS" '74
DOUGLAS, JOYCE--[1]

MORETTI, UGO
DRUG, VICTOR--[8]
GOUTTIER, MAURICE--[8]
SHERMAN, GEORGE--[8]

MOREWOOD, SARAH L.
HOPE, NOEL--[8]

MOREY, LEO
SUMMERS, LEO RAMON--[11]

MORGAN, ALFRED P[OWELL]
POWELL, A.M.--[33]

MORGAN, ALLEN D.
SMITH, HOGAN--[2][11]

MORGAN, ANN JANE
ANN JANE--[1]

MORGAN, BRIAN STANFORD
MORGAN, BRYAN--[8]

MORGAN, CHARLES
MENANDER--[8]

MORGAN, DELORES MILLER
MORGAN, D. MILLER--HAWK/MORGAN INTRVW '93, MYS--
'DAISY MARLOW':
"MONEY LEADS TO MURDER"
"A LOVELY NIGHT TO KILL"
"PINK WAS THE COLOR OF MURDER"

MORGAN, DIANA
BLAINE, SARA--[1]
TREMAINE, LINDA--[1]

MORGAN, FRED TROY
BLEEKER, MORDECIA--[1][31]

MORGAN, GRACE JONES
MORGAN, BASSETT--[1][32]MYS--
SN "TIGER" SPR '69

MORGAN, HELEN G.L.
MORGAN, HELEN TUDOR--[33]
MORGAN, LOUISE--[33]

MORGAN, HILDA CAMPBELL
VAUGHN, HILDA--[1][7]SF--
MacM "IRON & GOLD" '48

MORGAN, JILL M[EREDITH]
FIELDS, MORGAN--HAWK/MORGAN INTRV '93,[31]MYS--
ZEBRA "DEADLY HARVEST" '89
ZEBRA "PLAY TIME" '88
ZEBRA "SHAMAN WOODS" '90
GRIFFIN, MEG--HAWK/MORGAN INTRVW '93, MYS--
NOVELS '90's
MORGAN, J.M.--HAWK/MORGAN INTRVW '93, MYS--
PINN "DESERT EDEN" '91
PIERCE, JESSICA--HAWK/MORGAN INTRVW '93, HOR--
YOUNG ADULT

MORGAN, JUDITH A.
ADAMS, JUDITH--[1]
KRAGEN, JINX--[1][31]
MORGAN, JINX--[1]

MORGAN, MURRAY C.
MURRAY, CROMWELL--[3][22]MYS--
McKAY "DAY OF THE DEAD" '46

MORGAN, NANCY
MCGUIRE, JENNY--W/KATE FLEMING,[9][21]ROM--
"CHRISTMAS WISHES"

MORGAN, SHARON A.
FUFUKA, KARAMA--[1][31]

MORGAN, TED
DE GRAMONT, SANCHE--[31]

MORGAN, THOMAS BRUCE
DAVID, NICHOLAS--[1][22][31]AMERICAN
MORGAN, NICHOLAS--[1][22]AMERICAN

MORGAN, THOMAS C.
MUIR, JOHN--[3][22]MYS--
HUTCH "CREATURES OF SATAN" '56
HUTCH "CROOK'S TURNING" '58 & MORE

MORGAN, THOMAS P.
DAFT, TENNYSON J.--[1]

MORGAN, WILLIAM SACHEUS
WEBLEY, PELAGIAN--[1]

MORGAN-GRENVILLE, GERARD
ROSS, GEORGE--[1]

MORGANSTERN, DAN M.
MORGAN, MICHEL--[1]

MORHEIM, LOUIS
PEPPER, DAN--V. BERCH-MON PSEUDS. BAE 9,[1]--
MON MM600 "ENEMY GENERAL" '60

MORICE, DAVE
ALPHABET, MR.--[1]
HOLLAND, JOYCE--[1][31]

MORISON, JOHN
CLERGYMAN, A.--[8]

MORITZ, PAUL
DOORN, JENS--[39]GERMAN

MORKEPUTZ-ROOS, ERNA
MOOR, ERNESTINE--[39]GERMAN

MORKOVIN, BORIS V.
MORKOVIN, BELA V.--[1]

MORLAND, NIGEL
DANE, MARY--[5][18][29][34][40]MYS--
WRIGHT "DEATH TRAPS THE KILLER" '38
DE SOLA, JOHN--[1][31]

MORLAND, NIGEL [CONT]
DONAVAN, JOHN--[3][5][18][29][31]MYS--
HALE "CASE OF THE BECKONING DEAD" '38
& 5 MORE '37-52
FORREST, NORMAN--[3][5][18][29][31]MYS--
HARRAP "DEATH TOOK A PUBLISHER" '36
HARRAP "DEATH TOOK A GREEK GOD" '37
GARNETT, ROGER--[5][18][22][29][32]MYS--
8 NVLS '37-48
SS "EVE FINDS THE KILLER" '47
EW "DANGER - DEATH AT WORK" MAR '65
KIMBERLEY, HUGH--[1][31]
MCCALL, JOHN COREY--[1]
MCCALL, VINCENT--[3][5][18][29]MYS--
MARTIN "ELEVEN THRILLING MYS" '45
MARTIN "SMASH & GRAB" '46
SHEPHERD, NEAL--[3][5][18][29]MYS--
CNST "DEATH FLIES LOW" '38
CNST "DEATH WALKS SOFTLY" '38 & M

MORLEY, BLYTHE
HOPKINS, STANLEY JR.--[32][34]MYS--
HRCT "MURDER BY INCHES" '43
HRCT "PARCHMENT KEY" '44
EQMM "THE LADY HOLDING A GREEN
APPLE" FEB '47

MORLEY, LESLIE REGINALD
HUTCHINS, ANTHONY--[8]

MORNAU, WILLI
MORNAU, WILJA--[39]GERMAN

MORO, CESAR
ASIN, ALFREDO QUISPEZ--[31]
ASIN, CESAR QUISPEZ--[31]

MORPURGO, ANNA SELMA
SMITH, ARTEMIS--W/BILLIE TAULMAN, V. BERCH-
MON PSEUDS, BAE 9, ADULT--
BEAC B230 "ODD GIRL" '59
BEAC B268 "THIRD SEX" '59
MON 182 "THIS BED WE MADE" '61

MORRAH, DAVID WARDLAW JR.
MORRAH, DAVE--[33]

MORRICE, JAMES KENNETH
MORRICE, KEN--[31]POETRY--
PERGAMON "FOR ALL I KNOW" '81
PERGAMON "WHEN TRUTH IS KNOWN" '86

MORRIS, ANTHONY P.
STAFFORD, JOHN K.--[34]MYS,HP--
MAGNET #431 "SHOT FROM ABOVE" '06
STARK, INSPECTOR--[34]MYS,HP--
NEW MAGNET #477 "ROOT OF ALL EVIL" '07

MORRIS, BESSIE C.
FORFEX ET HESTA--W/ANNIE B. SPEAR,[3]MYS--
GRANT "LOST KEY: OR, THE MYS BOX" 1879

MORRIS, CHARLES [S]
ALLEN, HUGH--[1]
BALLARD, J.D.--[1]
BLAKE, REDMOND--[1]
DARE, ROLAND--[1]
FRAZIER, F.M.--[1]
INMAN, R.R.--[1]
KAINE, GEORGE S.--[1]
LYTTON, EDWARD--[1]
MURRY, WILLIAM--[1]
PASTNOR, PAUL--[1]
PIERCE, JO--[1]
PRESTON, PAUL--[1]
SOUTHARD, J.H.--[1]

MORRIS, CHARLES [S] [CONT]
TRIPP, C.E.--[3]MYS--
BCA "ACE HIGH, THE FRISCO DETECTIVE" '48
VINCENT, E.L.--[1]

MORRIS, CHRISTOPHER C.
MORRIS, CHRIS--W/JANET ELLEN MORRIS,[23]SF--
PRESCOTT, CASEY--[33][34]MYS--
ARBOR "ASSET IN BLACK" '85
STRYKER, DANIEL--W/JANE STUMP,[7][23][33]SF--
JOVE "COBRA" '91
JOVE "HAWKEYE" '91

MORRIS, DAVID
HALL, MARTYN T.--[8]

MORRIS, DAVID ST. LAWREN.
LAWRENCE, DAVID--[3]MYS--
WARD "DEAD ORCHID" '58
WARD "DEATH HAS TWO HANDS" '58

MORRIS, DEBRAH
ADAMS, PEPPER--W/PAT SHAVER,[9][26]ROM--
SIL 964 "MAD ABOUT MAGGIE"
SIL 983 "LADY WILLPOWER"
JORDAN, JOANNA--W/PAT SHAVER,[9][21][26]ROM--
"DESTINY'S DREAM"
"NEVER SAY FAREWELL" & MORE
STACEY, JO ANN--W/PAT SHAVER,[9][21][26]ROM--
"ONCE UPON A DREAM"
"TEMPTING FATE"
THOMAS, DIANNE--W/PAT SHAVER,[9][21][26]ROM--
'OUT OF THE BLUE"
"HEAVEN CAN WAIT" & MORE

MORRIS, EDWARD A.
KRAMER, KARL--HOLLAND-AVALLONE INTRVW,
BAE 4,V. BERCH-MON PSEUDS, BAE 9,[34]MYS--
POPLB 650 "FAIR GAME" '55
ACE D160 "ACTION ALONG THE HUMBOLT" '56
MON 121 "KISS ME QUICK" '59
MON 136 "NOT FOR A CURSE" '59
MON 159 "THE DEADLY SEPTEMBER" '60
MON 200 "A FLAME TOO HOT" '64

MORRIS, EDWARD P.
ZORRO--R.C. HOLLAND, BAE 25, MYS,HP--
ALSD 'DOCTOR DEATH' SHORT STORIES

MORRIS, ESTHER
DENNIS, STACEY--[26]ROM--
"REMEMBER LOVE"
"TO MOTHER WITH LOVE"

MORRIS, G. SUTHERLAND
SUTHERLAND, MORRIS--[2][3]MYS--
RICH "SEND DANGER" '34
RICH "MOUNTAIN FIRES" '37 & 3 MORE '30-7

MORRIS, GERDA
GYMIR, GERDA--[39]GERMAN
SONAMA, GERDA--[39]GERMAN

MORRIS, HOMER
CARTER, NICK--[34]MYS--
AWARD "THE Z DOCUMENT" '75

MORRIS, JAMES HUMPHREY
MORRIS, JAN--[1]

MORRIS, JAMES M.
PEPPER, K.N.--[1]
MAURICE, JACQUES--[1]

MORRIS, JANET E[LLEN]
MORRIS, CHRIS--W/CHRISTOPHER C. MORRIS,[23]SF--

MORRIS, JANET E[LLEN]
STRYKER, DANIEL--G.COOK LTR '93, MYS--
JOVE "COBRA" '91
JOVE "HAWKEYE" '91

MORRIS, JOHN
MCGAW, J.W.--[8]

MORRIS, KENNETH
APARTHUR, C.--[2]

MORRIS, KENNETH
MORUS, CENYDD--[1][2]

MORRIS, [MARGARET] JEAN
O'HARA, KENNETH--[32][34]MYS--
HU "THIRD PARTY" OCT '56
12 NVLS '58-87
SL "A WEEK-END GHOUL" DEC '58
AHMM "TOUCHE " NOV '58

MORRIS-GOODALL, VANNE
GOODALL, VANNE MORRIS--[1][31]

MORRISEY, JOSEPH LAWRENCE
RICHARDS, HENRY--[2][23]SF--
"HOUR OF THE PHOENIX" '64
SAXON, RICHARD--[2][23]SF--
"THE STARS COME DOWN" '64

MORRISON, ALISTAIR A.
LAUDER, AFFERBECK--[8][13]AUSTRALIAN

MORRISON, ARTHUR
HEWITT, MARTIN--[1]

MORRISON, CHARLES THEODRE
MORRISON, C.T.--[1]

MORRISON, CHLOE ANTHONY
MORRISON, TONI--[7]SF--
CHATTO "BELOVED" '87

MORRISON, EULA ATWOOD
ATWOOD, DRUCY--[1][31]
DELMONICO, ANDREA--[1][3][31]MYS--
ACE "CHATEAU CHAMMOND" '68
ACE "EYRIE OF AN EAGLE" '69

MORRISON, JEANETTE HELEN
LEIGH, JANET--[31]

MORRISON, LESLIE WILLIAM
DOWLEY, D.M.--[1]

MORRISON, MARGARET MACKIE
COST, MARCH--[1][2][31]
MORRISON, PEGGY--[1]

MORRISON, MARY JANE
WALLIS, PENNY--[1]

MORRISON, MICHAEL ANDREWS
CHERNILO, CAPEL--[34]MYS--
CLARKE "QUEER STORIES FROM RUSSIA" 1895

MORRISON, PATRICIA K.
KENNEALY, PATRICIA--[7][9][23]ROM/SF--
BJ 'KELTIAD' SERIES #1-3
NAL 'TALES OF ARTHUR' #1

MORRISON, PAUL FIX
FIX, PAUL--[31]

MORRISON, PEGGY
COST, MARCH--[11]

MORRISON, PHYLLIS
SINGER, PHYLIS--[1]

MORRISON, THOMAS J.
MUIR, ALAN--[3][8]MYS--
JARROLDS "DEATH COMES ON DERBY DAY" '39

MORRISON, VELMA FORD
FORD, HILDEGARDE--[22][31][33]AMERICAN

MORRISON, WILLIAM
STERLING, BRETT--[11] HP

MORRITT, HOPE
CAMERON, HOPE--[1][31]

MORROUGH, E.R.
NADARR, ABU--[1][2][11]

MORROW, HONORE MCCUE
MORROW, HONORE WILLSIE--[1]

MORROW, WILLIAM CHAMBERS
MORROW, W.C.--[1]

MORSE, ANNE C.
HEAD, ANN--[3][21][22][31]MYS--
DBLDY "ALWAYS IN AUGUST" '61
DBLDY "EVERYBODY ADORED CARS" '63

MORSE, HENRY CLIFTON IV
FOURTH, CLIFTON--[22][31]AMERICAN

MORSE, LARRY ALLEN
FAIRLEIGH, RUNA--FIRSTS NOV '94,[18][34]MYS--
AVON "AN OLD FASHIONED MYS" '83
MORSE, L.A.--CRPG,[31][34]--
WARNER 82633 "FLESH EATERS" '79
AV "THE OLD DICK" '81
AV "THE BIG ENCHILADA" '82
AV "SLEAZE" '85

MORSE, MARTHA WILSON
WILSON, MARTHA--[1]

MORSE, NANCY L.
FLEMING, DANIELLE--[9][21][26]ROM--
"PRINCE'S PASSION"

MORSE, PEGGY BOZEMAN
MORELAND, PEGGY--[9][21][26]ROM--
SIL 837 "SEVEN YEAR ITCH"
SIL 867 "BABY DOCTOR" & 2 MORE

MORTELMANS, EDWARD
MORTELMANS--PPCC #8, ENGLISH--
ARTIST FOR PAN, 4SQ, CORGI & PANTHER

MORTIMER, ARMINE KOTIN
KOTIN, ARMINE AVAKIAN--[1][31]

MORTIMER, JOHN E.
BLANDFORD, EDDIE L.--BAPC NWSLTR #9--
COVER ARTIST FOR PAN, PANTHER, BADGER
& SUPERIOR

MORTIMER, JOHN [CLIFFORD]
LINCOLN, GEOFFREY--[8][18]MYS--
BLES "NO MOURNING OF THE BAR" '57

MORTIMER, PENELOPE [R]
DIMONT, PENELOPE--[1][31]
TEMPLE, ANN--[1]

MORTON, GUY [MAINWARING]
FORREST, MARK--[1][22]ENGLISH
TRAILL, PETER--[1][22][34]ENGLISH/MYS--
GRAYSON "THE ANGEL" '34
GRAYSON "HALF MAST" '36 & MORE

MORTON, JAMES SEVERS
ELDIN, RAYMOND--[31]

MORTON, JOHN BINGHAM
BEACHCOMBER--[1][23][31]HP--
HE USED EXCLUSIVELY FOR 50 YRS
MORTON, J.B.--[1][7]

MORTON, LEE JACK JR.
JAC, LEE--[31]

MORTON, TAMMYE RING
RING, THOMASINO--[21]ROM--
"TIME-SPUN RAPTURE"
"THE PROVINCE OF DARKNESS"

MORUN, WILLIAM
SMITH, SURREY--W/WILLIAM SURREY,[8]
SMITH, SURREY--W/WILLIAM DINNER,[8][34]MYS--
BRDMN "NO TEARS FOR TEDDY" '64
BRDMN "ASTONISHED GUARDSMAN" '65
HALE "A GUN FOR DELILAH" '79

MORZFELD, ERWIN
BLAYN, ROBERT--[39]GERMAN

MOSELLY, EMILE
CHENIN, EMILE--[1][22]FRENCH

MOSER, ALMA
GRAY, ALISON--[9][21][26]ROM--
"PORTER'S DESIGNS"

MOSER, DONALD BRUCE
MOSER, DON--[33]

MOSESSON, GLORIA R.
FRENCH, KATHRYN--[1][31][33]
MILLER, DORIS R.--[1][33]

MOSHER, CHRISTOPHER TERRY
AISLIN--[31]

MOSHER, FREDERICK C.
FRITZ--[1]

MOSIMAN, BILLIE SUE
STAHL, SUE--HAWK/MOSIMAN INTRVW '93--
FUTURE

MOSKOVITZ, JACK
CALVANO, ANTHONY [TONY]--MOSKOVITZ LTR '94,
ADULT,HP--
HAMLIN'S CORINTH-GREENLEAF MID TO
LATE '60's
DEXTER, JOHN--MOSKOVITZ LTR '94, ADULT,HP--
CANDID RDR CA967 "WANTONS ON WHEELS" '69
HOGAR, JACKSON--MOSKOVITZ LTR '94, ADULT--
BRNDN PCB114 "PALESTINIAN TORMENTORS" '77
MADDEN, JACK--MOSKOVITZ LTR '94, ADULT--
BRNDN PCB117 "NAZI DEGENERATE" '77
BRNDN PCB120 "TERROR IN RHODESIA" '77
MANNING, JACK--HAWK/MOSKOVITZ INTRVW '94,
ADULT--
BRNDN 6551 "TOWN OF RAPISTS" '76
MARSHALL, ALAN--MOSKOVITZ LTR '94, ADULT,HP--
NTSTD 1952 "MAYOR'S CATHOUSE" '69
MAYNARD, JACK--MOSKOVITZ LTR '94, ADULT--
BRNDN PCB101 "CHINESE PRISONER" '76
BRNDN "ARAB VICTIM" '76
MCKAY, JOHN--MOSKOVITZ LTR '94, ADULT--
BRNDN PCB103 "HER JAPANESE TORTURERS" '76
MOSS, JACK--MOSKOVITZ LTR '94,[34]MYS--
MANOR 19228 "ARSON JOB" '78
PALEAU, ROGER--MOSKOVITZ LTR '94, ADULT--
BRNDN PCB102 "NAZI CAPTURERS" '76
TUCKER, LES--MOSKOVITZ LTR '94,PP 19,ADULT--
BEE-LINE BL364N "BIG STUD, INC" '69
BEE-LINE BL373N "GFREAKOUT PARTY" '69
BEE-LINE BL380N "EVERYNIGHT LOVER" '69
BEE-LINE BL389N "AIRLINE LESBOS" '69
BEE-LINE BL441Z "NYMPHO LIBRARIAN" '70
WILLIAMS, J.X.--MOSKOVITZ LTR '94,ADULT,HP--
HAMLIN'S CORINTH-GREENLEAF MID TO
LATE '60's

MOSKOWITZ, SAM
BAHR, ROBERT--[11] FP
MARGULIES--[4]
MARTIN, SAM--[1][2]
SHAW, ROBERT SANDERS--[11] FP
WEINER, WILLIAM M.--[11] FP
WOLLONOVER, FRED--[11] FP

MOSLER, BLANCHE Y.
EDWARD, MARIE ELAINE--[3][23]MYS--
PAPLB "AMBERLEIGH" '67
PAPLB "LENORE" '66
PAPLB "TERROR MANOR" '67

MOSLEY, OSWALD EMALD
EUROPEAN--[31]

MOSS, ROBERT
DE BORCHGRAVE, ARNAUD--W/ARNAUD PAUL DE
B. D'ALTENA,[7]SF--
"THE SPIKE" '80

MOSS, ROBERT ALFRED
MOSS, NANCY--[8][22]ENGLISH
MOSS, ROBERTA--[8][22]ENGLISH

MOSS, ROSE
JOHANNES, R.--[1][31]

MOSSER, ARNE J.
ALLWOOD, EDITH--[1]
BROWN, M.E.--[1]
HALL, B.K.--[1]
RESSOM, J. ARNE--[1]

MOSSMAN, DOW
O'QUILL, SCARLETT--[1]

MOSTYN, ANITA MARY
FIELDING, ANN MARY--[8]

MOTH-LUND, POUL
HILSO, PAUL--[29]MYS
O'BREY, KATHLEEN--[29]MYS
ZILSO, PAUL--[29]MYS--
MANY NOVELS '46-55

MOTHERAL, NANCY
SHAW, LAURA--[9]ROM--

MOTT, EDWARD SPENCER
GUBBINS, NATHANIEL--[34]MYS--
LONG "ALL THE WINNER" '03 & OTHERS
GUBBINS, NATHANIEL--[8][22]ENGLISH
SPENCER, EDWARD--[8][22]ENGLISH

MOTT, J. MOLDON
BLACKBURN, JOHN--[8][11]

MOTT, MICHAEL
ALSTON, CHARLES--[8]

MOTTRAM, RALPH HALE
MARJORAM, J.--[1]
MOTTRAM, R.H.--[1]

MOULIE, CHARLES
SANDRE, THIERRY--[1][22]FRENCH

MOULIGNEAU, MICHEL
DE GUY, LATTEUR--[1]

MOUNT, THOMAS ERNEST
CODY, STONE--L. ROBBINS LTR '94,[8]WEST
KING, OLIVER--L. ROBBINS LTR '94,[1]

MOUNTBATTEN, LORD LOUIS
MARCO--[8]

MOUNTCASTLE, CLARA H.
SIMA, CARIS--[8]

MOUNTFIELD, DAVID
GRANT, NEIL--[8]

MOUSSARD, JACQUELINE
CERVON, JACQUELINE--[31][33]

MOWAT, ROBERT CASE
MOWAT, ROBIN--[1]

MOWBRAY, W.J.
GASCOIGNE, ERIC--[1]

MOYES, PATRICIA
HASZARD, MRS.--[29]MYS
HASZARD, PATRICIA MOYES--[33]

MOYLAN, THOMAS P.
MOYLAN, TOM--[7]SF--NON-FICT

MOYNIHAN, CORNELIUS
VIVIAN--[8]

MOZHEIKO, IGOR V.
BULYCHEV, KIRILL--[7][23]SF--
"GUSLIAR WONDERS" '83
"HALF A LIFE & OTHER STORIES" '77

MPHAHLELE, EZEHIEL
EZEKI, BRUNO--[31]

MUCKLE, JOHN EDWARD
EDWARDS, JOHN--[2]

MUDDOCK, JOYCE E.P.
DONOVAN, DICK--[2][3][5][18][29][36]MYS/ROM--
51 BKS 1888-1911
MUDDOCK, J.E.--[18]MYS

MUELBAUER, PAMELA
BAUER, PAMELA--[9][21][26]ROM--
"HONEY TRAP"
"HALFWAY TO HEAVEN" & MORE

MUELLER, DOROTHY
BOWICK, DOROTHY MUELLER--[1][31]

MUELLER, JOERG
MULLER, JORG--[33]

MUELLER, JOHN HENRY
MORGAN, TOM--[39]GERMAN/ADV

MUELLER-TANNEWITZ, ANNA
JUERGEN, ANNA--[1]

MUENSTERBERG, HUGO
TERBERG, HUGO--[22]GERMAN-AMERICAN

MUESING-ELLWOOD, EDITH E.
ELLWOOD, EDITH E.--[31]

MUGGENBURG, HANS J.
STANLEY, HEXER--[39]GERMAN/HOR

MUGGESON, MARGARET ELIZABETH
DICKINSON, ELIZABETH--[1]
DICKINSON, MARGARET--[31]
JACKSON, EVERATT--[3][31]MYS--
HALE "THE ROAD TO HELL" '75

MUGICA, RAFAEL
CELAYA, GABRIEL--[20] SPANISH

MUHE, WERNER
DAMMANN, PETER--[39]GERMAN/JUV

MUHRMANN, WILHELM
ANTIBES, ARLETTE--[39]GERMAN/MYS
BERG, AJA--[39]GERMAN/MYS
DIESCHEN, R.A.--[39]GERMAN/MYS
FORSTER, WOLFGANG--[39]GERMAN/MYS
MURI, EBERHARD--[39]GERMAN
OSTERBURG, DAISY--[39]GERMAN/MYS
STEINER, JUTTA--[39]GERMAN/MYS
VAN LOON, PIT--[39][40]GERMAN/MYS--
"ICH KEME DEN MORDER" '58
VAN YZEREN-LOON, WILLEM--[39]GERMAN/MYS
VON BERNECK, ALRUN--[39]GERMAN/MYS

MUIR, BARBARA K.
KAYE, BARBARA--[9][21][22][26]ROM--
"CALL OF EDEN"
"SOUTHERN NIGHTS" & 17 MORE
KILREON, BETH--[1]

MUIR, CHARLES AUGUSTUS C.
MOORE, AUSTIN--[29]MYS

MUIR, EDWIN
MOORE, EDWARD--[1]

MUIR, FLORENCE ROMA
WILSON, ROMER--[1]

MUIR, JOHN RAMSEY BRYCE
SLACK, SOLOMAN--[2]

MUIR, KENNETH [A]
FINNEY, MARK--[1][22][31]ENGLISH

MUIR, MARIE AGNES
BLAKE, MONICA--[21][22][26][31]ENGLISH/ROM--
"HIDDEN HERITAGE"
CLYNDER, MONICA--[1][22][31]ENGLISH
KAYE, BARBARA--[1][31]ENGLISH
SCOTT, JEAN--[1][22]ENGLISH

MUIR, WARDROP OPENSHAW
LANG, STEWART--[1]

MUIR, WILHELMINA JOHNSTON
MUIR, WILLA--[8]
SCOTT, AGNES NEILL--[8]

MUIR, [C] AUGUSTUS [C]
MOORE, AUSTIN--[3][22]MYS--
HODDER "BIRDS OF THE NIGHT" '30
HODDER "HOUSE OF LIES" '32

MULARCHY, SYLVIA
MILES, SYLVA--W/DORIEN K. MILES,[1][3]MYS--
"SHADOW OVER BEAUCLAIRE" '75 & MORE

MULARCZYK, ROMAN
BRATNY, ROMAN--[1]

MULCAHY, LUCILLE BURNETT
HALE, HELEN--[1][22][31]AMERICAN

MULDER, LODEWIJK
LODEWYK--[22]DUTCH

MULER, HELMUT
MILLER, HAL--[39]GERMAN/MYS

MULGRUE, G. EDWARD
CAIRNS, PETER--[34]MYS--
DIGIT "THROW BACK THE LITTLE ONES" '64
COLOMBO, PAT--[34]MYS--
AV "THROW BACK THE LITTLE ONES" '63

MULHEARN, WINIFRED
GRANDMA--[8]

MULHOLLAND, JUDITH
DUNCAN, JUDITH--[9][21][26]ROM--
"REACH THE SPLENDOR"
"STREETS OF FIRE" & MORE

MULLALY, CHARLES
GOODWIN, FRANCIS--[1]
WINSLOW, PAUL--[1]

MULLAN, CELINA RIOS
DE LEON, ANA LISA--[21][26]ROM--
"KISS GOODNIGHT & SAY GOODBYE"
DE ZAVALA, MARISA--[21][26]ROM--
"GOLDEN FIRE"
"SILVER ICE"
SCOTT, RACHEL--[21]ROM--
"IN THE DEAD OF THE NIGHT"
"STALK A STRANGER"

MULLARKY, TAYLOR
HOLDER, BOB N.--[34]MYS--
BLUDINGUTZ "DARTS OF DEATH" '85

MULLEN, DOROTHY
MULLEN, DORE--[1][21]ROM--
"ALL WE KNOW OF HEAVEN"
"SHANGHAI BRIDGE"
"FARSIDE OF DESTINY"

MULLEN, SOPHIA
MAGAFAN, SOPHIA--[2]

MULLEN, STANLEY
BEECHER, LEE--[1][2][11]
BEECHER, STANLEY--[1][2][11]
DRUMMOND, JOHN PETER--[1][2][11]HP--
NOSGOROV, SHAN--[2]

MULLER, ARTHUR
REVOIR, AU--[29]MYS

MULLER, ARTUR
BRECHT, ARNOLT--[39]GERMAN
GEORG, REINHOLD--[39]GERMAN

MULLER, CHARLES G.
GEOFFREY, CHARLES--[1][22]AMERICAN
GILLILAND, CHARLES--[1]AMERICAN

MULLER, DOROTHEE [D]
DHAN, DOROTHEE--[39]GERMAN/JUV

MULLER, EGBERT-HANS
GROPER, REINHARD--[39]GERMAN

MULLER, ERNST
WEST, JULIAN--[2][7]SF--
"MY AFTERNOON DREAM: A SEQ ..." 1900

MULLER, ERNST LOTHAR
LOTHAR, ERNST--[39]GERMAN

MULLER, FRITZ
REINEL, FRITZ--[39]GERMAN

MULLER, GABRIELE
MILLER, GABRIELLE--[39][40]GERMAN/MYS--
"DENK NICHTS SCHLECHTES UBER TOTE" '63

MULLER, GOTTFRIED
HERZOG, PAULUS--[39]GERMAN

MULLER, HEINZ
MILES, HUGH--[39]GERMAN

MULLER, HERMANN
STEPHENS, LON--[39]GERMAN/JUV

MULLER, KLAUS
GRAFFSHAGEN, STEPHAN--[39]GERMAN/JUV

MULLER, KURT
BROOK, PERCY--[39]GERMAN/MYS/WEST
COLLINS, WILLIAM C.H.--[39]GERMAN/MYS/WEST
FENTON, JACK--[39]GERMAN/MYS/WEST
HILGENDORFF, HERMANN--[39]GERMAN/MYS/WEST
KELLY, JACK--[39]GERMAN/WEST
MUELLER, H.C.--[39]GERMAN/MYS/WEST
TEX, WILLIAM--[39]GERMAN/WEST

MULLER, MARIA
LUSSNIGG, MARIA--[39]GERMAN/JUV

MULLER, NORBERT
BERGFELD, THORSTEN--[39]GERMAN

MULLER, OTTO
GLOSA, OTTO--[39]GERMAN/MYS

MULLER, PAUL ALFRED
HEIM, HEIDE--[39]GERMAN/MYS/SF
HERMES, ROLF--[39]GERMAN/MYS/SF
HOLK, JAN--[39][40]GERMAN/MYS
ISLAND, BERT F.--[39][40]GERMAN/MYS ,HP
KEYEN, WERNER--[39]GERMAN/MYS/SF
MARKKLEEBERG, P.A.--[39]GERMAN/MYS/SF
MAURER, G.--[39]GERMAN/MYS/SF
MULLER, ALFRED--[39]GERMAN/MYS/SF
MULLER-MARKKLEEBERG, A.--[39]GERMAN/MYS/SF
MULLER-MURNAU, P.A.--[39]GERMAN/MYS/SF
MYLER, LOK--[39][40]GERMAN/MYS
STEEN, I.V.--W/HELMUT K. SCHMIDT, [39]GERMAN/MYS/SF
STOCKER, PAUL--[39]GERMAN/MYS/SF
VAN HOLK, FREDER--[39][40]GERMAN/MYS--
"DAS ENDE DES GOLFSTROMS" '52

MULLER, ROBERT
ANATOLE--[8]

MULLER, WILHELM
JOCUNDAS, FRATER--[22]GERMAN-AMERICAN

MULLER, WOLFRAM
URSPRUNG, WOLFRAM--[39]GERMAN

MULLER-GUTTENBRUN, ADAM
IGNOTUS--[22] AUSTRIAN

MULLER-GUTTENBRUNN, RODER
ARNDT, DIETRICH--[39]GERMAN
MEINHART, RODERICH--[39]GERMAN

MULLER-HARLIN, WOLFGANG
THOMAS, MANUEL--[39]GERMAN

MULLER-HESS, KATHARINA
HESS, KATHARINA--[39]GERMAN
MULLER, KATHARINA--[39]GERMAN

MULLER-JUNGBLUTH, ULRICH
JUNGBLUTH, ULRICH HERBERT--[39]GERMAN

MULLER-MAREIN, JOSEF
MOLITOR, JAN--[39]GERMAN

MULLER-REYMANN, WERNER
RYMANN, CHET--[39]GERMAN/WEST

MULLER-TANNEWITZ, ANNA
HOLM, STINE--[39]GERMAN/JUV
JURGEN, ANNA--[39]GERMAN/JUV

MULLIGAN, HUGH A.
H.A.M.--[1]

MULLIN, CHRISTOPHER JOHN
MULLIN, CHRIS--[23]ENGLISH/SF--
"A VERY BRITISH COUP" '82

MULLINS, RICHARD
WELLS, MICHAEL--[1]

MULVEY, TOM
APPLETON, VICTOR II--[7]SF,HP--
STSY 'TOM SWIFT':
"IN THE CAVES OF NUCLEAR FIRE"

MULVEY, WILLIAM
STEELE, SHARON--W/RICHARD FEHR,[21]ROM--
"A DANGEROUS WOMAN"

MULVIHILL, ROCHELLE A.
WAYNE, ROCHELLE--[9][21]ROM--
"MIDNIGHT ANGEL"
"TEXAS ECSTACY" & MORE

MUMFORD, A.H.
VIDENS--[8]

MUMFORD, RUTH
DALLAS, RUTH--[8]

MUNBY, ALAN NOEL L.
MUNBY, A.N.L.--[1]

MUNBY, ARTHUR JOSEPH
BROWN, JONES--[8]

MUNCE, RUTH HILL
HILL, RUTH LIVINGSTON--[1][22][31][33]AMERICAN

MUNCH, HELLMUT-HUBERTUS
AMBOS, HELLO--[39]GERMAN/JUV,HP
BRENDT, HAL--[39]GERMAN/MYS/WEST
HART, HANS--[39]GERMAN/MYS/WEST,HP
PETERS, PIT--[39]GERMAN/MYS,HP

MUNCH, HELLMUT-HUBERTUS [CONT]
REITERLEIN, HANNES--[39]GERMAN/MYS/WEST

MUNCHAUSEN, BORRIS v.
ALBRECHT, H.--[39]GERMAN

MUNCHOW, HEINZ
KOSSELIN, TORSTEN--[39]GERMAN/JUV

MUNCHOW, VERA
ANDERS, VERA--[39]GERMAN/JUV

MUNDAY, JOHN WILLIAM
SEELEY, CHARLES SUMNER--[1][2]

MUNDIS, HESTER JANE
ASHER, MIRIAM--[1][3][31]MYS--
"NIGHTMARE IN EDEN" '74
"BLACK WIND" '76
MORGAN, VIRGINIA--[1]
WESTMINSTER, AYNN--[1][34]MYS--
DELL "MOON IN SHADOW" '74

MUNDIS, JERROLD
CALDER, ROBERT--[3][7][31]SF/HOR--
DLCT "THE DOGS" '76
CORDER, ERIC--[31][32][34]MYS--
BZ "BAD TOMMY" JAN '66
SO "THE EXTERMINATORS" MAR '66
ALLEN "HELLBOTTOM" '74
DELL "THE BITE" '75

MUNDT, KLARA
MUHLBACH, LOUISA--[2]

MUNGER, KATY
GRAY, GALLAGHER--LACHMAN LST '93-DJ OF
FIRST 'GRAY' BOOK

MUNGO, RAYMOND
LUNAR, DENIS--[1][31]

MUNN, MARGUERITE
BRYANT, M.--[1]

MUNN, MERYL LUCILE
MAGUIRE, ANNE--[1]
NEARING, PENNY--[1]

MUNN, VELLA
FLINDT, DAWN--[9][21][26]ROM--
"POWER WITHIN"
"PRAIRIE CRY"

MUNOZ, CHARLES
CARAVAN, T.P.--[11]

MUNOZ, EUGENIO
NOEL, EUGENIO--[22]SPANISH

MUNRO, HECTOR HUGH
MUNRO, H.H.--[1][23]SF--
"WHEN WILLIAMS CAME" '14
SAKI--[2][11][23][32][34]MYS--
SC "LOST SANJAK" '45
SH "SREDNI VASHTAR" JUL '60

MUNRO, NEIL
FOULIS, HUGH--[1][22]MYS--

MUNRO, NORMAN L.
DOTSON, DAVE--[37]--
UTDBL 'DAVE DOTSON' STORIES ca 1900

MUNRO, [MACFARLAND] HUGH
FARLANE, JASON--[1]
JASON--W/G. STANNUS,[1][31][35]AUSTRALIAN--
10 WEBSTER NOVELS '58-9
WYVIS, BEN--[1]

MUNROE, ELIZABETH LEE
GRENELLE, LISA--[22][31]AMERICAN

MUNSHI, KIKI SKAGEN
MUNSHI, SKEHNAAZ--[1]
SKAGEN, KIKI--[1]

MUNSON, SHERYL MCDANEL
DANSON, SHERYL--[26]ROM--
"ALWAYS A FIANCEE"

MUNSTER, CLEMENS
SCHROEDER, MARKUS--[39]GERMAN

MUNTHE, FRANCES
COWEN, FRANCES--[1][22][31]ENGLISH
HYDE, ELEANOR--[1]ENGLISH
MINTO-COWEN, FRANCES--[1]ENGLISH

MUNTHE, GUSTAF LORENZ
GELM, ROBERT--[29]MYS--
"TORSDAGSKLUBBEN" '34

MUNTZ, [ISABELLE] HOPE
LANGLAND, WILLIAM--[1]

MURADIAN, KORLEN GRIGOR
EMIN, GEVORK--[1]

MURDOCH, JAMES
M., A.--[34]MYS--
SCOTT "WOOING OF WEBSTER & OTHER
STORIES" 1899

MURDOCK, LAURETTE P.
EUSTIS, LAURETTE--[1][31]

MURDOCK, VERA
ENGLAND, JANE--[34]MYS--
HURST "TRADER'S LICENSE" '36
HURST "SAFE CONDUCT" '42
HURST "FLIGHT INTO DANGER" '50
HURST "HOUSE OF FEARS" '51

MURFREE, MARY NOAILLES
CRADDOCK, CHARLES EGBERT--[2][3][22][31]MYS--
MacM "STORY OF DULCIE HURST" '14
DEMBRY, R. EMMET--[1][31]

MURIEL, JOHN ST. CLAIR
DEWES, SIMON--[1][3][22]MYS--
RICH "CUL-DE-SAC" '41
RICH "PANIC IN PURSUIT" '45
RICH "DEATH STALKS THE WATERWAY" '46
LINDSAY, JOHN--[1]

MURILLO, JOSEFA
TOTOLOCHE--[30]MEXICAN
XOCHITL--[30]MEXICAN

MURPHY, BEATRICE M.
CAMPBELL, BEATRICE MURPHY--[1][31]

MURPHY, CHARLOTTE A.
MURPHY, AGATHA--[3]MYS--
VANTAGE "HUSH-HUSH MURDER" '78
MURPHY, C.L.--W/LAWRENCE A. MURPHY,[1]

MURPHY, EMILY F.
CANUCK, JANEY--[1]
FERGUSON, EMILY--[8]

MURPHY, EMMETT JEFFERSON
MURPHY, PAT--[33]

MURPHY, EVERIL WORRELL
MONET, LIREVE--[2]
WORRELL, EVERIL--[2][32]MYS--
PA "HOLLOW MOON" NOV '57
SN "GRAY KILLER" SUM '69

MURPHY, IDA MARY
SPENCE, AINSLIE--[34][36]AUSTRALIAN--
PITMAN "MURDER AT MONK'S PROMISE" '44
PITMAN "MYS OF RED GUM" '46

MURPHY, JOHN [JACK]
BUCHANAN, PATRICK--W/EDWIN R. CORLEY,[34]MYS--
4 NOVELS '70-4

MURPHY, LAWRENCE A.
LAWRENCE, STEVEN C.--V. BERCH-GM PSEUDS,
PP 33,[8][28][31]WEST--
GM 667 "SADDLE JUSTICE" '57
GM 788 "BRAND OF A TEXAN" '58
AV T399 "IRON MARSHALL" '60
AV T461 "NIGHT OF THE GUNMAN" '60
AV T509 "GUN FURY" '61
GM 1643 "TEXAN COMES RIDING" '66
MURPHY, C.L.--W/CHARLOTTE A. MURPHY,
[1][28]WEST--
DIAL "BUFFALO GRASS" '66

MURPHY, LYNNE
GENTRY, GEORGINA--CRPG,[9][21][26]ROM--
ZEBRA "CHEYENNE SPLENDOR" '94 & 12 MORE

MURPHY, MABEL ANSLEY
LEE, ANNE S.--[1]

MURPHY, MICHAEL
LEWIS, HERSHELL G.--[3]MYS--
NOVEL BK "COLOR ME BLOOD RED" '64
NOVEL BKS "TWO THOUSAND MANAICS!" '64

MURPHY, MOLLIE [COCHRAN]
STRYKER, DEV--W/WARREN MURPHY, DON SANDSTROM-
DAPA-EM MAG--
TOR "DEATHRIGHT"

MURPHY, NONIE CAROL
CAROLL, NONIE--[1]

MURPHY, PATRICE ANNE
MURPHY, PAT--[23]SF--
"CHRYSALIS 5" STORY- "NIGHTBIRD AT
THE WINDAO" '79

MURPHY, THOMAS BASIL JR.
MURPHY, TOM--[21][40]MYS/ROM--
"ASPEN INCIDENT" '78 & 4 OTHERS

MURPHY, WARREN
MURPHY, WARREN--W/ROBERT J. RANDISI,
JAMES A. CORRICK--PP ARTICLE IN FUTURE
STRYKER, DEV--W/MOLLY COCHRAN, HAWK/MURPHY
INTRVW '93--
TOR "DEATHRIGHT"

MURRANKA, MARY
MCGRATH, MARY--[1]

MURRAY, A.C.
GRAY, ANDREW--[1][34]MYS--
AMALG "GAMBLER" '16
AMALG "PRIDE OF THE POLICE" '16
& 4 MORE '14-7
ZEVERIL, HUBERT--[1]

MURRAY, ADRIAN
GORDON, RICHARD--[1]

MURRAY, ANDREW NICHOLAS
ANDREWS, JOHN--[34]MYS,HP--
AMALG "PERIL PIT" '31
AMALG "TEMPLE OF FEAR" '31
AMALG "WAR IN THE DESERT" '31
AMALG "1,000,000 POUND SECRET" '33
AMALG "PERIL IN PERSIA" '33
AMALG "SECRET OF THE REEF" '33
AMALG "BEGGARS OF KASHAPORE" '38
ARNOLD, MALCOLM--[1]
DEANE, VESEY--[1]
ISLAY, NICHOLAS--[1][3]MYS--
MURRAY "A BRACE OF ROGUES" '20
MURRAY "SELICOMBE MURDER" '20

MURRAY, AUDREY ALISON
MURRAY, A.A.--[34]MYS--
BELM 213 "THE BLANKET" '60
RPRT OF A DEUTSCH BOOK '57

MURRAY, BLANCHE
MURRAY, GERALDINE--[8]

MURRAY, C. GEOFFREY
GRAY, GEOFFREY--[1]
KINGSFORD, GUY--[1]
LOXLEY, RAYMOND--[1]

MURRAY, DAVID LESLIE
MURRAY, D.L.--[1]

MURRAY, DAVID STARK
BROWN, IRWIN--[1][31]

MURRAY, EDGAR JOYCE
DREW, SIDNEY--[1][3]MYS--
AMALG "GANGSTER'S DEPUTY" '30
AMALG "FORTNIGHT OF FEAR" '31 & MORE
ROVER, MAX--[1]

MURRAY, EUSTACE C.G.
HOPE, MARK--[3]MYS--
CHAPMAN "DARK & LIGHT STORIES" 1879
SCAMPINGTON, DUKE OF--[1]
TROIS, ETOILES--[1]

MURRAY, FRANCIS EDWIN
MAIR, H. ALLEN--[8]

MURRAY, JOAN
WILDEBLOOD, JOAN--[1]

MURRAY, JOHN F.
BACKGAMMON, DAISY--[1][31]AMERICAN
CARRYAWAY, NICK--[1][31]AMERICAN
COMBS, ROBERT--[1][22][31][33]AMERICAN

MURRAY, LESLIE
LEO, BESSIE--[1]

MURRAY, LINDA CHARLTON
CHARLTON, LINDA--[31]

MURRAY, MARIE
MURRAY, ANNABEL--[9][21][26]ROM--
"LAND OF THUNDER"
"DON'T ASK WHY" & MORE

MURRAY, MAXWELL
MURRAY, MAX--[18][34]MYS--
JOSEPH "KING & THE CORPSE" 49
JOSEPH "NEAT LITTLE CORPSE" '51 & MORE

MURRAY, RICHARD
ENGLISH, RICHARD--[1][3][29]MYS--
SIMON "SUGARPLUM STAIRCASE" '47

MURRAY, RUTH HILARY
FINNEGAN, RUTH H.--[1]

MURRAY, THOMAS C.
MORGAN, STEPHEN--[22]--
"THE SERF" '20
MURRAY, T.C.--[1]

MURRAY, VENETIA PAULINE
FLIGHT, FRANCIES--W/JACK ERNEST LIONEL
BIRCH,[8]

MURRAY, WILLIAM P.
BRONZINI, BART--MURRAY LTR FEB '94, FP
CASE, JUSTIN--MURRAY LTR FEB '94,HP--
SPICY ZEPPELIN STORIES
COUNT, NOAH--MURRAY LTR FEB '94,HP--
SPICY ZEPPELIN STORIES
DANGER, PRESTON--MURRAY LTR '94,
LACHMAN LST '93--
SK "ZEPPELIN TATTOO"
DAWN, ADAM--MURRAY LTR FEB '94, FP
MURPHY, WARREN--WILL MURRAY, PP 21, P46,
[7]MYS,HP,GHOSTED--
'DESTROYER' SERIES:
#56, 63, 69 THRU #86
"ASSASSIN'S HDBK"
MURRAY, BILL--MURRAY LTR '94,[37], FP--
DSR "REFLECTIONS IN A FLAKE-GOLD EYE"
DSR "THE GIRL WHO LOVED DOC SAVAGE"
MURRAY, W.P.--MURRAY LTR FEB '94, FP
MURRAY, WILL--[7][23][32]MYS/SF--
EQMM "A QUARTER FOR CRAZY EDDIE" OCT '80
SK "BIG NOTHING" JAN '80
SK "LONG & THE SHORT OF IT" APR '80
MURRILL, RAY W.--MURRAY LTR FEB '94, FP
MURRILL, WRAY--MURRAY LTR FEB '94--
SPICY ZEPPELIN STORIES
ALSO USED AS FP
NUED, D.E.--MURRAY LTR FEB '94--
SPICY ZEPPELIN STORIES
OSORIO, GRIS--MURRAY LTR FEB '94, FP
RAINBOW, JASON--MURRAY LTR FEB '94--
SPICY ZEPPELIN STORIES
ROBESON, KENNETH--WILL MURRAY, PP 21,
ECHOES #69, MYS,HP--
"WHITE EYES"
"FRIGHTENED FISH"
"JADE OGRE"
"FLIGHT INTO FEAR"
"THE FORGOTTEN REALM"
SCHOENER, KARL--MURRAY LTR FEB '94, FP
SHANER, CARL--MURRAY LTR FEB '94, FP
SPACE, PHILLIP--MURRAY LTR FEB '94--
SPICY ZEPPELIN STORIES
SPYDER, I.M.--MURRAY LTR FEB '94, FP
TURNER, PAGE--MURRAY LTR FEB '94--
SPICY ZEPPELIN STORIES

MURRAY, WILLIAM WALDIE
ORDERLY SERGEANT--[1]

MURRAY-FORD, ALICE MAY
LE BRETON, MRS. JOHN--[1]

MURRELL, ELSIE K.
SETH-SMITH, ELSIE K.--[1]

MURRELLS, JOSEPH
TEMPLE, EDITH--[1]

MURRY, JOHN MIDDLETON
COWPER, RICHARD--[2][4][7]SF--
'BIRD OF KINSHIP' SERIES
GOLZ "CUSTODIANS & OTHER STORIES" '76
& MORE
LEMAISTRE, JOHN--[2]SF--
MURRY, COLIN--[1][4][7][23]SF--
"RECOLLECTIONS OF A GHOST" '60
"A PATH IN THE SEA" '61
"PRIVATE VIEW" '72
MURRY, COLIN MIDDLETON--[2][4][7]SF--
GOLZ "ONE HAND CLAPPING" '75
GOLZ "SHADOWS ON THE GRASS" '77

MURRY, MARY MIDDLETON
GAMBLE, MARY--[31]

MURRY, VIOLET
ARDEN, MARY--[8]

MURSELL, ARTHUR
SEARCH, JOHN--[1]

MUSCHG, HANNA
JOHANSEN, HANNA--[39]GERMAN

MUSCIANO, WALTER A.
FRAKE, WARNER--[31]

MUSE, PATRICIA [ALICE]
WALTERS, NELL--[1]

MUSEO, LAURA
TANNER, JAKE--W/STEPHEN SCHERMERHORN,
LACHMAN LST, DDLY PLEAS #3, P34--
"OLD BLACK MAGIC" '91

MUSGRAVE, DAVID & MARG
MUSGRAVE, JACQUELINE--[9][21]ROM--
"NORTHERN LIGHTS"

MUSKETT, NETTA RACHEL
HILL, ANNE--[8][9]ROM

MUSPRATT, ROSALIE HELEN
JOHN, JASPER--[2][11][16][34]MYS--
WALKER "SINISTER STORIES" '30

MUSSI, MARY
EDGAR, JOSEPHINE--[3][17][26][31]MYS--
COLLINS "DARK TOWER" '66
COLLINS "DANCER'S DAUGHTER" '68 & 9 MORE
HOWARD, MARY--[9][17][21][31]ROM--
"FIRST STAR"
"MIST ON THE HILLS" & MORE

MUSTO, BARRY
SIMON, ROBERT--[1]

MUZAKOVA, JOHANNA
SVETLA, KAROLINA--[22] CZECH

MYATT, NELLI
KIRKHAM, NELLIE--[1]

MYER-PAYSAN, DIETER
TESCH, MICHAEL--[39]GERMAN

MYERS, BARRY
DRURY, REBECCA--[21]ROM,HP--
'WOMEN AT WAR' SERIES:
"FREEDOM'S JOURNEY"
"SHIPS AFLAME"
"SUNDAY'S COURAGE"
SCOFIELD, JONATHAN--[21]ROM,HP--
DELL 'FREED FTR' SERIES:
"TURNING OF THE TIDE"
SOMMERS, JEANNE--[9][21][26]ROM--
'AMERICAN INDIAN' SERIES
'MAKING OF AMERICA' SERIES
WILLOUGHBY, LEE DAVIS--[21]ROM,HP--
DELL 'MKG OF AMER' SERIES:
"CONESTOGA PEOPLE"
"BUILDERS"
"ALSKANS"
"LAND GRABBERS"
"BUFFALO PEOPLE"
"DONNER PEOPLE"
"ROBBER BARONS"
"YUKON BREED"
"SCARLET SISTERS"
"FRONTIER DETECTIVE"
DELL 'WOMEN WHO WON THE WEST' SERIES:
"DUCHESS OF DENVER"

MYERS, FREDERIC
MYERS, F.W.H.--[1]

MYERS, HOWARD L.
FORAY, VERGE--[1][2][11]

MYERS, JUDITH BLACKWELL
BLACKWELL, JUDITH--[9][21]ROM--
"JUST LIKE JESSICA"
MYERS, JUDY [JULIE]--[9]ROM

MYERS, LEOPOLD HAMILTON
MYERS, L.H.--[1]

MYERS, MARY
MCBRIDE, MARY--[26]ROM--
"RIVERBEND"
"FLY AWAY HOME"
"FOURTH OF FOREVER"

MYERS, MARY CATHCART
BORER, MARY CATHCART--[8][32]MYS--
LM "DESERT MAGIC" APR-MAY '51
CATHCART, MARY--[1]

MYERS, PEGGY A.
WILLIAMS, ANN--[21]ROM--
"DEVIL IN DISGUISE"
"HAUNTED PAST" & 2 MORE

MYERS, PEGGY A.
WILLIAMS, PEGGY--[9]ROM--

MYERS, VIRGINIA
ABBOTT, JANE WORTH--W/STELLA CAMERON,
[9][21][26]ROM--
"CHOICES"
"YES IS FOREVER"
"SPIN OFF-FACES OF A CLOWN"

MYERS, WALTER DEAN
MYERS, WALTER M.--[31][33]--
"WHERE DOES THE DAY GO?"

MYKOLAITIS, VINCAS
PUTINAS--[22] LITHUANIAN

MYLES, SANDRA
MARTON, SANDRA--[9][21][26]ROM--
"HEART OF THE HAWK"
"EYE OF THE STORM" & MORE

MYLLER, ROLF
BROWN, DAVID--[1][33]
MILONAS, ROLF--[1][33]

NABOKOV, PETER [F]
TOWNE, PETER--[1]

NABOKOV, V.V.
BLACK SWAN OF LAC LEMAN--[1]RUSSIAN-AMERICAN
SIRIN, V.--[1][22]RUSSIAN-AMERICAN

NACHMAN, ELANA
DYKEWOMAN, ELANA--[7]LESBIANA NON-FICT

NACHT, MAX
NOMAD, MAX--[1]

NADASI, LADISLAV
JEGE--[22]SLOVAK

NADEJDE, CORNELIA
MANTU, LUCIA--[22]RUMANIAN

NADEL, AARON
MARCELLINUS, ANIMIANUS--[1][2][11]

NADOLNI-S., BARBARA
BAROL, RANA--[39]GERMAN
PETERS, HENNI--[39]GERMAN

NAFZIGER, RAY
DENVER, ROBERT DALE--L. ROBBINS LTR MAR '94

NAGAL SOKICHI
KAFU--[31]

NAGEL, HERBERT CHRISTIAN
HARDING, STEVE C.--[39]GERMAN/WEST
HOLLISTER, H.C.--[39]GERMAN/WEST
KRUGER, OVEN W.--[39]GERMAN/WEST
MILTON, TED--[39]GERMAN/WEST
TRAFT, RINGO--[39]GERMAN/WEST
VANDENBERG, JESSE C.--[39]GERMAN/WEST

NAGEL, WILLEN HENDRIK
CHARLES, J.B.--[22]DUTCH

NAGELE, ANTON
CLAVELL, STAUFFER--[1]

NAGLE-HEALY, JAMES A.
HAY, NIGEL--[1]
HEALY, JAMES H.--[1]

NAGULA, MICHAEL
CAROON, MAIK--[39]GERMAN/HOR/SF
LANDMANN, MICHAEL--[39]GERMAN/HOR/SF
SHOCKER, DAN--[39][40]GERMAN/MYS,HP

NAHA, ED
DRUMM, D.B.--[7][23]SF,HP--
DELL 'TRAVELER' SERIOES:
#1, #7, #9 THRU #11, & #13
MCGANN, MICHAEL--[7]SF,HP--
JOVE 'MARAUDERS' SERIES:
#1 THRU #7

NAHUM, MICHAEL
MANNING, JOHN SPENCER--W/SOL ASSAEL,[2]

NAIMY, MIKHAIL
NU'AIMAH, MIKHA'IL--[22]SYRIAN-AMERICAN

NAIPAUL, SHIVADHAR S.
NAIPAUL, SHIVA--[1]

NAIR, KRISHNAPILLAI K.
CHAITANYA, KRISHNA--[1]

NAISMITH, HELEN
EPPIE--[31]

NAISMITH, ROBERT STEVENS.
STEVENSON, ROBERT--[8]

NAKAE, NORIKO
UENO, NORIKO--[33]

NAKOV, ATANAS FOTINOV
NAKOVSKI, ATANAS--[1]

NAMES, LARRY
HARTE, BRYCE--HAWK/MCCORD/BALLAS INTRVW,
WEST,HP--
'CREED' SERIES: 1ST 10 BOOKS

NAMIER, JULIA
DE BEAUSABRE, JULIA M.--[1]
DE BEAUSOBRE, IULIA--[31]

NAMOVICZ, GENE INYART
INYART, GENE--[1][22]AMERICAN

NANDAKUMAR, PREMA
ASWIN--[1][22][31]INDIAN

NANNE, HENRIK
HENNER, CARL--[2]

NANOVIC, JOHN L.
LYSING, HENRY--[37]MYS--
CRB - CRIME ARTICLES '37-9

NAPIER, ELMA
GARNER, ELIZABETH--[1]

NAPIER, PRISCILLA
HUNT, PENELOPE--[1][31]
STEWART, EVE--[1]

NAPJUS, ALICE JAMES
NAPJUS, JAMES--[1]

NAPOLI, VINCENT
VINCENT--[1][2]
VINCENT, JAMES--[11]

NARAYAN, RASIPURAM K.
NARAYAN, K.--[1]

NARCEJAC, THOMAS
AYARAUD, PIERRE--[29]MYS
AYRAUD, PIERRE--[29]MYS
LUPIN, ARSENE--W/PIERRE BOILEAU,[40]MYS--
"LE SECRET D'EUNERVILLE" '73
"LA POUDRIERE" '74

NARELL, IRENA
PENZIK, IRENA--[1]

NAROGIN, MUDROOROO
JOHNSON, COLIN--[36]AUSTRALIAN/MYS--
A&R "WILD CAT FALLING" '65

NARVESTAD, JOERUND
JORGENSON, THEODORE--[1]

NASH, G. MURRAY
BLACK, PAUL--[1]

NASH, JEAN
SUTHERLAND, JEAN--[21][26]ROM--
"TIES THAT BIND"

NASH, N[ATHAN] RICHARD
NUSBAUM, N. RICHARD--[1][34]MYS--
FRENCH PLAY "INCOGNITO" '41

NASH, VAUGHAN
TWO EAST LONDENERS--W/LLEWELLYN SMITH,[8]

NASIF, MALAK HIFNI
BAHITHAT AL-BADIYAH--[22]EGYPTIAN

NASON, LEONARD HASTINGS
STEAMER--[1][22][29]MYS--
DODD "CONTACT MERCURY" '46

NASSAUER, BERNICE RUBENS
RUBENS, BERNICE--[7]SF--
"OUR FATHER" '87
"SPRING SONATA: A FABLE" '79

NASSIM, LIZA
CODY, LIZA--V. BERCH LTR '93, MYS--
COLLINS "DUPE" '81
COLLINS "BAD COMPANY" '82 & MORE

NATHAN, DANIEL
DANNAY, FREDERIC--[1][5]LEGALIZED TO
'DANNAY', MYS

NATHAN, GEORGE JEAN
DRAYHAM, WILLIAM--[1]
HATTERAS, OWEN--W/HENRY LOUIS MENCKEN,[1][31]

NATHAN, ROBERT
CONDE, NICHOLAS--W/ROBERT ROSENBLUM,
V. BERCH LTR TO HUBIN '94, MYS--
HUTCH "THE RELIGION" '82
NAL "THE LEGEND" '84
ST. LOUIS, ROBERT--V. BERCH LTR TO
HUBIN '94, MYS--
GM "BUSHIDO CODE" '81

NATHANSON, LAURA WALTHER
THORPE, J.K.--[33]

NATHENSON, JOSEPH
ST. JOHN, CHERYL--[34]MYS--
MANOR "LIBRARY OF ALEX BRANDT" '79

NATSUME, KINNOSUKE
GUDABUTSU--[1]
NATSUME, SOSEKI--[1]

NATTI, MARY LEE
KINGMAN, LEE--[1][2][31]

NAUBERT, CHRISTIANE B.E.
KRAMER, PROFESSOR--[39]GERMAN/SF
MILBILLER, PROFESSOR--[39]GERMAN/SF
MULLER, JOHANN FRIEDR. W.--[39]GERMAN/SF

NAUGHTON, WILLIAM J.F.
NAUGHTON, BILL--[31]IRISH--
BAL "ALFIE" '66 & OTHERS

NAUMAN, EILEEN
BROOKES, BETH--[9][21][26]ROM--
"UNTAMED DESIRE"
"ON WINGS OF PASSION" & MORE

NAUMAN, EILEEN [CONT]
MCKENNA, LINDSAY--[9][21][26]ROM--
"SUN WOMAN"
"TEXAS WILDCAT" & MORE

NAUMANN, MARGOT
NORMAN, PEGGY--[39]GERMAN/JUV

NAVASKY, VICTOR S.
HIRSCH, WILLIAM RANDOLPH--W/MARVIN KITMAN
& RICHARD R. LINGEMAN,[1]

NAYLOR, CHARLES
HASTINGS, VICTOR--G. COOK LTR '93, MTI--
POPLB 08134 "SUNFLOWER" '69

NAYLOR, DOUG
NAYLOR, GRANT--W/ROB GRANT,[7][23]SF--
"RED DWARF #1 & #2"

NAZEL, JOSEPH G. JR.
GOBER, DON--[3]MYS--
HOLLOWAY "BLACK COP" & 3 MORE '74-6
NAZEL, JOE--[7]SF--
HOLLOWAY "BLACK EXORCIST" '74
HOLLOWAY "SATAN'S MASTER" '74

NAZMUTDINOV, NAZAR M.
NADZHMIR, NAZAR--[1]

NAZURETH, PETER
WAKO, MDOGO--[1]

NEAL, ADELINE PHYLLIS
GREY, A.F.--[2][3][11][22]MYS--
GOLZ "MOMENTARY STOPPAGE" '42

NEAL, ANN PARKER
PARKER, ANN--[1]

NEAL, JAMES THOMAS
JAMES, THOMAS N.--[31]

NEARING, ELIZABETH CUSTER
MACVEIGH, SUE--[1][3]MYS--
HOUGHTON "GRAND CENTRAL MURDER" '39
& 3 MORE '39-41

NEARING, JOHN SCOTT
SCOTT, JOHN--[1]

NEARING, PENNY
MAGUIRE, ANNE--[21][33]ROM--
"PRIDE OF FOLLY"
"RUN BEFORE MIDNIGHT" & MORE

NEARY, PATRICK
PENDLETON, DON--[3]MYS,HP--
GE "VULTURE'S VENGEANCE" '84

NEBEHAY, RENEE
KING, RENEE--[39]GERMAN/JUV

NEBEL, GUSTAVE E.
NEBEL, MIMOUCA--[33]

NEBEL, [LOUIS] FREDERICK
HILL, GRIMES--E.R. HAGEMANN, COMPH.
INDEX BM,[18]MYS--
BM "SPOT & THE LADY" MAR '31
LEWIS, ERIC--INTRO TO "NEBEL" STORY BY
BILL PRONZINI
TURNER, ROBERT--[29]MYS--9 NOVELS '52-55

NEDERVEEN HENDRIKS, WIETK
WYTSKE--[1]

NEDIDERMAN, ANDREW
ANDREWS, V.C.--G. COOK LTR '93--
? GHOSTED OR REAL ?

NEE, BRETT DE BARY
DE BARY, BRETT--[1][31]

NEE, DAVID CHIN-KUO
NEE, DAVE--[7]SF-- NON-FICT

NEEDHAM, JOSEPH
HOLORENSHAW, HENRY--[8]

NEEPER, CAROLYN A.
NEEPER, CARY--[7][11][23]SF--
SCRIBN "A PLACE BEYOND MAN" '75

NEERSKOV, HANS KRISTIAN
KRISTIAN, HANS--[1][31]

NEETHLING, JACOBUS STEPH.
NEETHLING, J.S.--[1]
NEETHLING, KOBUS--[1]

NEGGERS, CARLA A[MALIA]
HARRELL, ANNE--[9][21][31]ROM--
"BETRAYALS"
"MINSTREL'S FIRE"
JAMES, AMALIA--[9][21][31]ROM--
"MIDSUMMER DREAMS"
"TANGLED PROMISES"
"DREAM IMAGES"

NEHER, FRANZ L.
HILTEN, PETER--[39]GERMAN/SF/JUV
NEHER, FRANK--[39]GERMAN/SF/JUV

NEHER, LISA
GREEN, JULI--W/JUDITH CHILD,[9][21][26]ROM--
"BENEATH A SUMMER MOON"

NEHLS, RUDOLF
RISSOW, NILS--[39]GERMAN

NEILD, JAMES EDWARD
J.E.N.--[8]AUSTRALIAN
JAQUES--[8]AUSTRALIAN
SLY, CHRISTOPHER--[8][13]AUSTRALIAN

NEILL, CHRISTOPHER H.D.
DOUGLAS, CHRISTOPHER--[31]

NEILLANDS, ROBIN
HUNTER, ROBIN--[34]MYS--
MacM "THE FOURTH ANGEL" '85
MacM "QUARRY'S CONTRACT" '87
MORROW "THE LONDON CONNECTION" '90

NEILS, GRANT JR.
NORTH, GENE--V. BERCH--
BRNDN/BC PSEUDS, BAE 22, P24

NEITSCH, OTTO
SANDER, FRANK--[39]GERMAN

NELMS, HENNING
TALBOT, HAKE--[2][3][11][29]MYS--
SIMON "HANGMAN'S HANDYMAN" '42
SIMON "RIM OF THE PIT" '44

NELSON, ALICE RUTH M.D.
DUNBAR-NELSON, ALICE--[31]
DUNBAR, ALICE--[31]
DUNBAR, ALICE MOORE--[31]
DUNBAR-NELSON, ALICE M.--[31]

NELSON, ETHEL FLORENCE
NELSON, NINA--[1]

NELSON, MICHAEL HARRINGT.
STRATTON, HENRY--[1][3][22]ENGLISH--
MacD "BLANKET" '59

NELSON, RADELL FARADAY
ELSON, R.N.--[1][2][31]
LORD, JEFFREY--W. MURRAY-'BLADE' SERIES,
PP 1,[2]SF,HP--
PINN "BLADE #30" '79
NELSON, R. FARADAY--[23]SF--NAME VARIATION
NELSON, R.F.--[1][23]SF--
NELSON, RAY--L. ROBBINS LTR '94,[2][7]SF--
NELSON, RAY FARADAY--[23]SF--
NAME VARIATION

NELSON, T.
BROWN, DUNCAN--[1]

NELSON, [HUGH] LAWRENCE
TRENT, PETER--[1][22][29]MYS--
RIN "THE COPPER LADY" '47

NELSON-SMITH, ALAN ROY V.
NELSON, ROY--[1]

NEMCOVA, BOZENA
NEMCOVA, BETTY--[1]

NEMESHEGYI, PETER
ALMA, PETER--[31]

NEMETH, LINELL EVANSTON
ANSTON, LINELL--[21][26]ROM--
"LADY ELIZABETH"

NEMIRO, BEVERLY ANDERSON
ANDERSON, BEVERLY--[31]
ANDERSON, BEVERLY M.--[1][31]

NEMO, L.P.
HERMON, ROPARZ--[22]BRETON

NENCKEN, HENRY LOUIS
ANDERSON, C. FARLEY--[1]

NEPVEU, ANDRE
DURTAIN, LUC--[1][22]FRENCH

NERAL, DIANNE
HOLLANDER, LESLIE--W/ALBERT BERGER,
V. BERCH LTR TO HUBIN '94, MYS--
PINN "THE EXHIBIT" '81

NERLICH, MARCEL
RYS, JAN--[39]GERMAN

NERNEY, PATRICK W.
NUDNICK--[8]

NERTH, HANS
FRITZE, OTTOKAR--[39]GERMAN

NESBIT, EDITH
BLAND, E.--[2][11][31]
BLAND, EDITH--[11]
BLAND, EDITH NESBIT--[31]
BLAND, FABIAN--W/HUBERT BLAND,[3][31][33]MYS--
DRANE "THE PROPHET'S MANTLE" 1889
BLAND, MRS. HUBERT--[2]
CARISBROOKE--[1]

NESMANSKY, FRIEDRICH
NEMOV, ALEXANDER--W/EDUARD TOPOL, [40]GERMAN/MYS-- "SCHURNALIST DIJA BRESCHNEWA" '81

NESMITH, ROBERT I.
CLARKE, [CAPT.] JAFAR--[1][31]

NESTLE, JOHN FRANCIS
FALCON--[1][31]

NETHERCLIFT, BERYL C.
MASCALL, MARGERY D.--[1]

NETO, BRAULIO F. TAVARES
TAVARES, BRAULIO--[23]BRAZILIAN/SF-- "THE BACKBONE OF MEMORY" '89

NETSCH, GUNTER
BOLDEN, JACK--[39]GERMAN/MYS
GATOW, GUNTER--[39]GERMAN/MYS
NASH, GARRY--[39]GERMAN
NEXTER, GLENN--[39]GERMAN/MYS
NORRIS, GIL--[39]GERMAN/MYS
NORTON, GERALD--[39][40]GERMAN/MYS-- "SCHREI IN DER NACHT" '59
NORTON, JOHN--[39]GERMAN/MYS
RAY, A.A.--[39]GERMAN/MYS
WILDING, PAT--[39]GERMAN/MYS,HP

NETTELL, RICHARD GEOFFREY
KENNEGGY, RICHARD--[1]

NETTZ, JULIE
JULIE--[8]

NETZEL, SALLY
JENNER, SUZANNE--W/GRETCHEN JOHNSON, [9][21]ROM-- "MIDSUMMER"

NEUBAUER, WILLIAM A.
ARTHUR, WILLIAM--[9][22][31]ADULT--
BEAC B166 "PRIVATE PLEASURES OF MARY LINTON" '58 & MORE
BENNETT, CHRISTINE--[9][21][31]ROM--
"GLORIA'S GHOST"
"WIND IN THE SAGE"
"GIRL OF BLACK ISLAND"
BLIGH, NORMAN--V. BERCH/S. HOLLAND-ARCH, BAE 15, ADULT--
BEAC B363 "THE SISTERS" '60
CARTER, RALPH--V. BERCH/S. HOLLAND-ARCH, BAE 15,[31]--
BEAC B307 "PLEASURE ALLEY" '60 & MORE
GARRISON, JOAN--[9][21][31]ROM--
"BLUE HERONS"
"SNATCH A DREAM" & MORE
HATHAWAY, JAN--[9][21][31]ROM--
"COMING OF EAGLES"
"KEY OF GOLD" & MORE
MARSH, REBECCA--[3][21][29]MYS--
ARCADIA "EMERALD RING" '64
ARCADIA "LADY DETECTIVE" '60 & MORE
NEWCOMB, NORMA--[1][9][21]ROM--
"ANGEL OF THE HILLS"
"BOSS LADY" & MORE
SEMPLE, GORDON--[1][31]ADULT--
BEAC B297 "SUMMER RESORT WOMEN" '60 & MORE

NEUBERG, VICTOR [B]
ALFRICOBAS--[1]
BENJIE--[1]
BROYLE, M.--[1]
BYRDE, RICHARD--[1]
CRAYNE, CHRISTOPHER--[1]

NEUBERG, VICTOR [B] [CONT]
EDWARDES, LAWRENCE--[1]
FRENCH, ARTHUR--[1]
PENTREATH, PAUL--[1]
PYNE, NICHOLAS--[1]
STEVENS, HAROLD--[1]
TARN, SHIRLEY--[1]
VICKYBIRD--[1]
VINCAM, FRATER OMNIA--[1]
WHITE, ROLD--[1]

NEUBERT, HELMUT
COTTON, JERRY--[39]GERMAN/MYS,HP
JONES, EVERETT--[39]GERMAN/WEST,HP
NELSON, HENRY--[39]GERMAN/MYS/WEST
NOLAN, FREDERICK--[39]GERMAN/WEST,HP
SLADE, JACK--[39]GERMAN/WEST,HP

NEUEN, RUTH
VON NEUEN, RUTH--[39]GERMAN

NEUFELD, JOHN [ARTHUR]
LEA, JOHN--[1][31]

NEUFFER, IRENE LABORDE
LABORDE, RENE--[1][31]

NEUFFER, MARTIN
GASTPAR, MICHAEL--[39]GERMAN/MYS

NEUHAUS, W.
NEWHOME, W.H.--[39]GERMAN/SF

NEUHAUS, WOLFGANG
LAMONT, ROBERT--[39]GERMAN/HOR,HP

NEUKRUG, LINDA
CASTLE, JILL--[9][21][26]ROM-- "IT HAPPENED ONE MORNING"

NEUMAN, PAUL GLEN
WILSON, GAR--W/WILLIAM FIELDHOUSE,[34]MYS,HP--
GE 'PHOENIX' SERIES:
"SEA OF SAVAGES" '85
WILSON, GAR--[34]MYS,HP--
GE 'PHOENIX' SERIES:
"BONN BLITZ" '87
"DOWN UNDER THUNDER" '86
"FAIR GAME" '87
"SLOW DEATH" '87

NEUMANN-REINHARD, LUCIE
SCHLUTOW, W.--[39]GERMAN

NEVANLINNA, SINIKKA SISKO
KALLIO, SINIKKA--[1]
KALLIO-VISAPAA, SINIKKA--[1]

NEVILL, BARRY ST. JOHN
CAREY, ANNE--[1][31]
LARNACH, RUPERT--[1][31]
VYVYAN, NIGEL--[1]

NEVILLE, BARBARA ALISON
CANDY, EDWARD--[22][29][31][34]MYS--
GOLZ "WHICH DOCTOR?" '53
GOLZ "BONES OF CONTENTION" '54
GOLZ "WORDS FOR MURDER PERHAPS" '71
GOLZ "SCENE CHANGING" '77 & MORE

NEVILLE, DEREK
SALT, JOHN--[1][32]MYS--
EW "QUIET DEATH" MAY '65
SUS "ACCORDING TO LAW" FEB '61 & 6 OTHERS
SALT, JONATHAN--[1]

NEVILLE, HUGH E. CARY
CARY, MORLAND--[3]MYS,PLAYS:
"LOVE RIDES THE RAILS" '40
"BECAUSE THEIR HEARTS WERE PURE" '52

NEVILLE, KRIS [O]
STARKE, HENDERSON--[1][2][11][23]SF--

NEVINS, FRANCIS JR.
NEVINS, MIKE--[1]

NEVINSON, HENRY WOODD
NEVINSON, H.W.--[1]

NEW, CLARENCE HERBERT
ORCUTT, STEPHEN HOPKINS--L. ROBBINS LTR MAR '94
ZANDTT, CULPEPER--L. ROBBINS LTR MAR '94

NEWBERY, JOHN
AESOP, ABRAHAM--[33]
TELESCOPE, TOM--[33]

NEWBOLD, ANNA HECKSCHER
BADEN, KATIA--[1]

NEWBOUND, BERNARD SLADE
SLADE, BERNARD--[34]MYS--
FRENCH PLAY "FATAL ATTRACTION" '86

NEWBY, GEORGE ERIC
PARKER, JAMES--[1][22]ENGLISH

NEWBY, PERCY HOWARD
NEWBY, P.H.--[1]

NEWCOMB, DUANE G.
FIRESTONE, TOM--[1][31]

NEWCOMB, KERRY
CARROL, SHANA--W/FRANK SCHAEFER, [21][26][31]ROM--
"RAVEN"
"YELLOW ROSE" & MORE
GENTRY, PETER--W/FRANK SCHAEFER, [21][26][31]ROM--
"MATANZA"
"TITUS GAMBLE" & MORE
SAVAGE, CHRISTINA--W/FRANK SCHAEFER, [21][26]ROM--
"DAWN WIND"
"TEMPEST" & MORE

NEWCOMBE, EUGENE A.
NEWCOMBE, JACK--[31]--
ARBOR "IN SEARCH OF BILLY COLE" '84
CHILDREN'S FICT

NEWELL, HOPE HOCKENBERRY
HOCKENBERRY, HOPE--[1][31][33]

NEWELL, PETER
HERSHEY, SHEAF--[1]

NEWELL, ROBERT HENRY
KERR, ORPHEUS C.--[22][31][34]MYS--
"THE CLOVEN HOOF" 1871

NEWELL, ROSEMARY
GIBSON, ROSEMARY--[1][31]

NEWHALL, MRS. LAURA E.
HALSTEAD, ADA L.--[1][3]MYS--
BANCROFT "BRIDE OF INFELICE" 1892 & MORE

NEWHALL, MURIEL
FARNSWORTH, MONA--[3]MYS--
AWARD "CASTLE THAT WHISPERED" '76
ACE "COMPANION TO EVIL" '71 & 12 MORE

NEWKIRK, CLYDE C.
NEWKIRK, NEWTON--[32][34]MYS--
LUCE "STEALTHY STEVE, THE SIX-EYED SLEUTH" '04
EQMM "ORIGIN OF THE DETECTIVE BUSINESS" OCT '51

NEWLIN, MARGARET
RUDD, MARGARET--[8]

NEWLON, [FRANK] CLARKE
CLARKE, MICHAEL--[1][31][33]

NEWMAN, ADRIEN ANN
ARPEL, ADRIEN--[1][31]

NEWMAN, BERNARD [CHARLES]
BETTERIDGE, DON--[2][3][18][23][31]MYS--
JENKINS "BALKAN SPY" '42
HALE "CONTACT MAN" '60 & MORE

NEWMAN, JAMES ROY
STRYFE, PAUL--[8]

NEWMAN, JOHN
JOHNS, KENNETH--W/KENNETH BULMER, [2][11][23]SF--
NW & NEBULA ARTICLES

NEWMAN, KENNETH E.
CLIFFORD, MARTIN--[1]HP--
CONQUEST, OWEN--[1]HP--
RICHARDS, FRANK--[1]HP--

NEWMAN, KIM [JAMES]
DEWITT, ADDISON--[1][31]
YEOVIL, JACK--[7][23]SF--
'DARK FUTURE' SERIES:
"DEMON DOWNLOAD" #1-3
'WARHAMMER' SERIES:
"BEASTS IN VELVET"
"DRACHENSFELS"

NEWMAN, LEONARD HUGH
BUTTERFLY FARMER--[1]

NEWMAN, LYN LLOYD
IRVINE, LYN--[8]

NEWMAN, MONA ALICE JEAN
FITZGERALD, BARBARA--[1][9]ROM--
NEWMAN, BARBARA--[8]
STEWART, JEAN--[1][9][21]ROM--
"WHERE LOVE COULD NOT FOLLOW"

NEWMAN, TERENCE
O'CONNOR, DERMOT--[8]

NEWNHAM, DON
EDEN, MATTHEW--[8]

NEWQUIST, ROY
STERLAND, CARL--[1][2]

NEWSOME, ARDEN J.
SEBASTIAN, JEAN--[1]

NEWSONS, ALBERT
BANDS, PAUL--[1]

NEWTON, DWIGHT BENNETT
BENNETT, DWIGHT--B. BRENNER-BENNETT
INTRVW/BIBLIO, BAE 19,[28]WEST--
DBLDY - 15 NOVELS '51-81
PERMA M-3023 "TOP HAND" '55
PERMA M-3045 "THE AVENGER" '56
COLE, JACKSON--A. TONIK-COLE CKLST
"SPICY ARMADILLO",HP--
TEX RGR "LAND OF THE VIOLENT MEN"
TEX RGR "STEEL RAILS FOR TEXAS"
TEX RGR "PANHANDLE FREIGHT"
TEX RGR "THE BARBED BARRIER"
HARDIN, CLEMENT--B. BRENNER-BENNETT
INTRVW/BIBLIO, BAE 19,[1]--
ACE, 12 NOVELS '54-71
JASON, KEN--[28]WEST--
WSS "POWDERSMOKE PROVIDENCE" JUN '48
WSS "WAY OF THE WILD" JUN '49
CWB "THE MARSHALL THEY LAUGHED AT" FEB '52
LAWSON, JOHNNY--[28]WEST--
CWB "FOR A GUN & A SILVER STAR" JAN '50
LOGAN, FORD--B. BRENNER-BENNETT
INTRVW/BIBLIO, BAE 19,[1][28]WEST--
BAL 87 "FIRE IN THE DESERT" '54
MITCHUM, HANK--B. BRENNER-BENNETT
INTRVW/BIBLIO, BAE 19, WEST,HP--
BB 'STAGECOACH' SERIES:
#1, 2, 4, 6, 11, 13, 20 & #26 '82-86
NEWTON, D.B.--B. BRENNER-BENNETT
INTRVW/BIBLIO, BAE 19, WEST--
"RANGE FEUD" '53
SAND, DAVE--[28]WEST--
.44 WESTERN "NEVER TOO OLD TO
FIGHT" MAR '43
TEMPLE, DAN--B. BRENNER-BENNETT INTRVW/
BIBLIO, BAE 19,[1][28]WEST/ADULT--
RROM "MISSOURI PASSAGE" JUN '54
POPLB EB-37 "OUTLAW RIVER" '55
POPLB 783 "MAN FROM IDAHO" '56
POPLB "BULLET LEASE" '57
BEAC B-533F "THE LOVE GODDESS" '62
MON 423 "GUN & STAR" '64

NEWTON, ELIZABETH
VASE, GILLAN--[1][3]MYS--
REMINGTON "A GREAT MYS SOLVED" 1878

NEWTON, H. CHANCE
GAWAIN--[8]

NEWTON, MICHAEL
BOLAN, MACK--W/DON PENDLETON & STEVEN
MERTZ,[28]HP--
PINN "EXECUTIONER'S WAR BOOK" '77
CANNON, JOHN--[1][3][31]MYS--
CAROUSEL "DEATH CRUISE" '80
CAROUSEL "WEB OF TERROR" '80
KOZLOW, MARK--[28]
CAROUSEL "MAN IN THE GOLD HILLS" '81
CAROUSEL "RANGE WAR NOBODY WON" '81
KOZLOW, MARK J.--[31]
MALONE, PAUL--M. LACHMAN,G. GOODE
LIST '93,[28]MYS--
GE "TRIGGER PULL" '91
GE "BORDER WAR" '91
GE "THE UNDERTAKER'S WIND" '91
NEWTON, MIKE--[34]MYS--
CAROUSEL "THE SATAN RING" '78
PENDLETON, DON--W/STEPHEN MERTZ,[3][7]HP--
GE "CLEVELAND PIPELAND" '78
GE "COMMAND STRIKE" '78
PENDLETON, DON--[34]HP--
GE "TENNESSEE SMASH" '78
GE "VIOLENT STREETS" '82
GE "PARAMILITARY PLOT" '82
GE "PARADINE'S GAUNTLET" '83
GE "DOOMSDAY DISCIPLES" '83

NEWTON, MICHAEL [CONT]
PENDELTON, DON [CONT]
GE "VIOLENT STREETS" "83
GE "PRAIRIE FIRE" '84
GE "BLOOD DUES" '84
GE "ARIZONA AMBUSH"
GE "PARAMILITARY PLOT" '84
GE "HOLLYWOOD HELL" '85
GE "MISSOURI DEATHWATCH" '85
GE "BONE YARD" '85
GE "HOLLYWOOD HELL" '85
GE "SHOCKWAVES" '85
GE "SOLD FOR SLAUGHTER" '85
GE "TRIAL" '86
GE "DEFENDERS & BELIEVERS" '86
GE "FLIGHT 741" '86
GE "ROGUE FORCE" '87
GE "RUN TO GROUND" '87
GE "ASSAULT ON ROME" '87
GE "TIME TO KILL" '87
GE "ETERNAL TRIANGLE" '87
GE "LINE OF FIRE" '88
GE "FIERY CROSS" '88
GE "FLESH & BLOOD" '88
GE "COLD JUDGEMENT" '88
GE "NIGHT KILL" '89
GE "HAITIAN HIT" '89
GE "FATAL ERROR" '90
GE "BLOOD RUN" '90
GE "ASSAULT" '90
ROBINSON, VINCE--[1][3]MYS--
CAROUSEL "TERROR AT BOULDER DAM" '81
CAROUSEL "DEATH ET SEA" '81
CAROUSEL "DEADLY GAME" '81
CAROUSEL "KILLER STALK" '82

NEWTON, WILLIAM [SIMPSON]
GRIFF--[34]MYS,HP--
MOF "COME & GET ME" '49
MOF "DAMES DON'T FORGET" '49
MOF "STIFFS CAN'T SQUEAL" '50
MOF "BULLETS FO SNOOPERS" '53
JANSON, HANK--[8]
MITCHAM, GILROY--[1][34]MYS--
DOBSON "FULL STOP" '57
DOBSON "MAN FROM BAR HARBOR" '58
DOBSON "DEAD RECKONING" '60
DOBSON "UNCERTAIN JUDGEMENT" '61
MORELLI, SPIKE--V. BERCH/S. HOLLAND, ARCH,
BAE 15,[34]MYS--
ARCH "YOU'LL NEVER GET ME" '50
KWY "COFFIN FOR A CUTIE" '51
ARCH "TAKE IT & LIKE IT" '51
LEIS "THIS WAY TO HELL" '52
LEIS "DEATH FOR A DOLL" '52
HARB "MORE THAN KISSES" '52
HARB "SORRY FOR YOU, BEAUTIFUL" '52
HARB "DEAL ME OUT" '52
HARB "NO PLACE FOR ME" '52
HARB "GIVE IT TO ME STRAIGHT" '53
NEWTON, MACDONALD--[1][34]MYS--
BRDMN "TO HAVE & TO HOLD" '63
ROSS, GENE--V. BERCH/S. HOLLAND-ARCH CKLST,
BAE 15,J. PRESSMAN,[34]MYS--
ARCH "TWO SMART DAMES" '49
ARCH "THIS WAY FOR HELL" '50
ARCH "LADY, THROW ME A CURVE" '50
ARCH "YOU'RE DEAD MY LOVELY" '50
ARCH "STEP UP, SUCKER" '53
ARCH "CORPSE IN THE BOUDOIR" '53
SARTO, BEN--[34]MYS,HP--
MOF "I'LL GET BY" '48
MOF "THERE'S ALWAYS A DAME" '49
MOF "TAKE OVER, ANGEL" '55
SPENCER, HANK--[34]MYS,HP--
MOF "THE GALLOWS ARE HIGH" '53
MOF "THE CRASH OUT" '56

NEYLAND, JAMES [E]
JAMESON, JUDITH--[1][31]
ROMERO, GERRY--[1]

NGAGOYEANES, NICHOLAS
GAGE, NICHOLAS--[3][29][31]MYS--
BERK "BONES OF CONTENTION" '74

NGHIEM XUAN VIET
XUAN VIET--[1]

NGUGI, J.T.
NGUGI, WA THIONGIO--[8]

NGUYEN DINH HOA
HOA, NGUYEN-DINH--[31]

NGUYEN NGOC HUY
HUY, NGUYEN NGOC--[31]

NGUYEN, TUONG TAN
NHAT, LINK--[1]

NIAL, CHRISTINA RUT
LANI, CHRISTINA--[29]MYS--
BONNIER "MORD I PARIS" '60

NIANCI, XU
JUEWO, DONGHAI--[2]

NIBOYET, [J.A] PAULIN
FORTUNIS--[1]

NICHOLS, CAROLYN
CHARLES, IONA--W/STANLEE M. COY,
[3][9][21]MYS--
"RELUCTANT LADY"
POPLB "WHEN ONLY THE BOUGAINVILLA
BLOOMS" '75
POPLB "GRENENCOURT" '75
MILLER, CISSIE--W/STANLEE M. COY,[9]ROM

NICHOLS, CELIA FAWN
NAZARIAN, NIKKI--[1]

NICHOLS, DALE WILLIAM
DE POLMAN, WILLEM--[22][31]AMERICAN

NICHOLS, GEORGE HERBERT F
QUEX--[1]

NICHOLS, JEANETTE
JEANETTE--[2]

NICHOLS, MARY EUDORA
BROWN, EVE--[8]

NICHOLS, NINA DE VINCI
TREE, CORNELIA--[1]

NICHOLS, REBECCA S. REED
CLEAVELAND, KATE--[1]
ELLEN--[1]

NICHOLS, THOMAS
ASMODEUS--[1]
NICHOLS, T. NICKLE--[1]

NICHOLSON, DAVID
ROC, JOHN--[22]ENGLISH

NICHOLSON, JOAN
CRAIG, ALISON--[8]
WEIR, JONNET--[8]

NICHOLSON, MARGARET B.L.
YORKE, MARGARET--[3][18][29][40]MYS--
HALE "CHINA DOLL" '61
HUTCH "HAND OF DEATH" '81 & 9 MORE

NICHOLSON, VIOLET
HOPE, LAWRENCE--[8]

NICKEL, ROLAND
ROLAND, NIC--[39]GERMAN

NICKEL, RUTH
NOORDEN, RUTH--[39]GERMAN
SVENSON, BOB--[39]GERMAN

NICKEL, TH.
FUTURUS--[39]GERMAN/SF

NICKELS, SAMUEL H.
BENNETT, KENT--L. ROBBINS LTR MAR '94

NICKENS, CATHERINE A.
REYNOLDS, CATHERINE--[21]ROM--
"A THOROUGHLY COMPROMISED BRIDE"

NICKERSON, ELIZABETH
NICKERSON, BETTY--[33]

NICKL, BARBARA ELISABETH
SHROEDER, BINETTE--[33]

NICKSON, ARTHUR [THOMAS]
HODSON, ARTHUR--[1][8]
PETERS, ROY--[1][8]
SAUNDERS, JOHN--[1][8]
WINSTAN, MATT--[1][8]

NICKSON, HILDA
PRESSLEY, HILDA--[1]
PRESTON, HILLARY--[1]

NICOL, ERIC [P]
JABEZ--[1][31]--
RYERSON "SENSE & NONSENSE" '48

NICOLAEFF, ARIADNE
MOORE, NICHOLAS--[8]

NICOLAS, WALTRAUD
CORDES, IRENE--[39]GERMAN/JUV

NICOLE, CHRISTOPHER ROBIN
ADAMS, DANIEL--[9][21][26]ROM--
"BROTHERS & ENEMIES"
"DEFIANT LOVE"
ARLEN, LESLIE--[9][18][21][26]MYS/ROM--
'BARODIN' SAGA:
"LOVE & HONOR"
"RAGE & DESIRE" & 4 MORE
CADE, ROBIN--[3][9][18][29]MYS--
CASSELL "THE FEAR DEALERS" '74
GRANGE, PETER--[9][18][26]MYS--
"THE TUMULT AT THE GATE" '70
"THE GOLDEN GODDESS" '73
GRAY, CAROLINE--[18][34]MYS/ROM--
JOSEPH "THIRD LIFE" '88
SEVERN "SHADOW OF DEATH" '89 & MORE
LOGAN, MARK--[9][18][21][26]MYS/ROM--
"TRICOLOR"
"GUILLOTINE"
"BRUMAIRE"
"DECEMBER PASSION"
"CAPTAIN'S WOMAN"
"FRENCH KISS"

NICOLE, CHRISTOPHER ROBIN [CONT]
MARLOW, MAX--W/DIANA BACKMAN,[7]SF--
NEL "MELTDOWN" '91
NEL "THE RED DEATH" '89
MCKAY, SIMON--[9][18][21]MYS/ROM--
"SEAS OF FORTUNE" '84
"THE RIVALS" '85
NICHOLSON, C.R.--[1][18]MYS--
CORGI "THE FRIDAY SPY" '80
NICHOLSON, CHRISTINA--[9][18][21]MYS/ROM--
CORGI "SAVAGE SANDS" '78
CORGI "QUEEN OF PARIS" '79 & MORE
NICHOLSON, ROBIN--[1][18]MYS--
JOVE "A PASSION FOR TREASON" '81
RPRT OF CORGI "THE FRIDAY SPY" '80
SAVAGE, ALAN--[18]--
FUTURA "OTTOMAN" '90
YORK, ALISON--[9][18][21]MYS/ROM--
"FIRE & THE ROPE" '79
"SCENTED SWORD" '80 & MORE
YORK, ANDREW--[3][9][18][29]MYS--
HUTCH "THE CAPTIVATOR" '73
HUTCH "PREDATOR" '68 & 10 MORE

NICOLL, H. MAURICE D.
SWAYNE, MARTIN [LUTRELL]--[1][2][23]SF--
"THE BLUE GERM" '18

NICOLL, WILLIAM ROBERTSON
CLEAR, CLAUDIUS--[8][22]SCOTTISH
WACE, W.E.--[8]

NICOLSON, JOHN URBAN
KING OF THE BLACK ISLES--[22]MYS

NIEBERGALL, ERNST ELIAS
STREFF, ERNST--[39]GERMAN

NIEDRIG, KURT-HEINZ
HUMILIS, HILAR--[39]GERMAN

NIEHAUS, WERNER
COTTON, JERRY--[39]GERMAN/MYS,HP
SOMMERS, FRANK--[39][40]GERMAN/MYS--
"STIRB - WIE ICH WILL" '68

NIELSEN, BENT ROSENKILDE
DON BENITO--[1]

NIELSEN, HELEN [B]
GILES, KRIS--[5][22][29][31][32]MYS--
AHMM "A FAIRLY INDESTRUCTABLE
FATHER" FEB '60

NIELSEN, ISAK
SADAR, SAHIB--[29]MYS

NIELSEN, JEAN SARVER
SARVER, HANNAH--[1][22]AMERICAN

NIELSEN, JULIUS
GUSTAVE, JULES--[29]MYS--
"LUFTPIRATERNA" '14

NIEMOJEWSKI, ANDRZEJ
LAMBRO--[22]POLISH

NIENABER, PETRUS JOHANNES
DE VILLIERS, RYNO B.--[1]
ROUSSEAU, J.J.--[1]
VAN NIEKERK, I.R.--[1]

NIESE, CHARLOTTE
BURGER, LUCIAN--[22]GERMAN

NIEUWENHUYS, ROBERT
BRETON, DE NIJS, E.--[22]DUTCH

NIGG, JOSEPH EUGENE
NIGG, JOE--[31]

NIGGEMANN, GUNTER
THOMPSON, FRED--[39]GERMAN/WEST,HP

NIGHTINGALE, ANNE REDMON
REDMON, ANNE--[1][7][34]MYS--
SECKER "SECOND SIGHT" '87

NIIHARA, RYUNOSUKE
AKUTAGAWA, RYUNOSUKE--[1]

NIKOLAISEN, SHIRLEY
NICHOLSON, SAM--[7][11]SF--
ACE "CAPTAIN EMPIRICAL" '79
BERK "THE LIGHT BEARER" '80

NILAND, ROSINA RUTH PARK
PARK, RUTH--[7]SF--
"PLAYING BEATIE BOW" '80
"MY SISTER SIF" '86
"THINGS IN CORNERS" '89
"SWORDS, CROWNS & RINGS"

NILSON, ANNABEL RHODA
NILSON, BEE--[1]

NILSSON, SVEN-ERIK
MAGNUSSON, ORWAR--[29]MYS--
TIDENS "LUMP OCH LIK" '56
HARD, BORJE--[29]MYS--
29 NOVELS '52-57

NILSSON, USHA SAKSENA
PRIYAMVADA, USHA--[1]

NISBET, ULRIC
CALLAWAY, HUGH--[8]

NISOT, MAVIS ELIZABETH
PENMARE, WILLIAM--[2][3][18][22]MYS--
HODDER "BLACK SWAN" '28
HODDER "SCORPION" '29
HODDER "MAN WHO COULD STOP WAR" '29

NITSCH, HELEN ALICE [M]
OWEN, CATHERINE--[1]

NITZSCHE, KARL-WILLY
KNURRHAHN, KARL--[39]GERMAN

NIVEN, LAURENCE VAN COTT
NIVEN, LARRY--[7][23][32]MYS/SF--
EQMM "DEADLIER WEAPON" JUN '68
AHMM "$16,940" FEB '74

NIXON, ALLAN
ALLAN, NICK--V. BERCH-BRNDN/
BC PSEUDS, BAE 22, P24
ROMANO, DON--W/ROBERT H. TURNER,[3]MYS,HP--
PYR "OPERATION PORNO" '73
PYR "OPERATION COCAINE" '74
PYR "OPERATION HIT MAN" '74

NIXON, JOAN LOWERY
ELLEN, JAYE--[31]

NIXON, KATHLEEN IRENE
NIXON, K.--[1]

NKETIA, JOSEPH H. KWABENA
KWABENA NKETIA, J.H.--[31]

NOBISSON, JOSEPHINE
BRIDE, NADJA--[9][21][26]ROM--
"HIDE & SEEK"
WOOD, NURIA--[21][26]ROM--
"WITH NO REGRETS"
"THE FAMILY PLAN"

NOBLE, HAROLD
EDWARDS, HAL--V. BERCH-BRNDN/
BC PSEUDS, BAE22, ADULT--
BC 7486 "BOTTOMS UP NIECES"
OAKLAND, HARRY--V. BERCH-BRNDN/
BC PSEUDS, BAE 22, ADULT--
BRNDN 6474 "COCKSURE GRADUATE"

NOBLE, JOHN [A]
JAN--[1][31]
LOOKOUT--[1][31]

NOBLE, JUDITH
BAKER, JUDITH--W/ELIZABETH BAILEY,[21]ROM
BAKER, JUDITH--W/FRAN BAKER,[26]ROM--
"WHEN LAST WE LOVED"
"LOVE IN THE CHINA SEA"

NOCK, ALBERT JAY
HISTORICUS--[8]
JOURNEYMAN--[8]

NODER, ANTON ALFRED
DE NORA, A.--[39]GERMAN/SF

NOEL, ANTANIELLE ANNYN
NOEL, RUTH S.--[7]

NOEL, RUTH HELEN SWYCAF.
NOEL, ATANIELLE ANNYN--[7]LEGALIZED TO
'ANTANIELLE ANNYN'

NOEL-BAKER, PHILIP JOHN
BAKER, PHILIP JOHN NOEL--[31]

NOFFKE, FRITZ
PARKER, WILL[IAM]--[39]GERMAN

NOGLY, HANS
WESTA, THOMAS--[39]GERMAN

NOHRA, AUDREY
STAINTON, AUDREY--V. BERCH LTR TO
HUBIN '94, MYS--
HOLT "SWEET ROME" '82

NOHSTROM, FRANS HOLGER
C, MR.--[29]MYS

NOLAN, FREDERICK
CHRISTIAN, FREDERICK H.--[1][8]
ROCKFERN, DANIELLE--[28]
HAMLYN "FIELD OF HONOUR" '89
SEVERN, DONALD--[28]MYS/WAR--
LYNX "A TIME TO DIE" '89
LYNX "ALERT STATE BLACK" '89

NOLAN, JEANETTE COVERT
TUCKER, CAROLINE--[1][22][31][33]CHILDREN'S

NOLAN, WILLIAM F.
ANMAR, FRANK--[2][11][18][23][31]][37]MYS,SP--
CHASE "DEATH DRAG" MAY '64
CAHILL, MIKE--[1][8][11]AMERICAN
DUNCAN, TERANCE--LACHMAN LST '93,
[18]MYS/WEST,HP--
ZEBRA "POWELL'S ARMY: RIO RENEGADES" '89

NOLAN, WILLIAM F. [CONT]
EDWARDS, F.E.--[2][18][22][23][37]MYS--
CHASE "STRIPPERS HAVE TO DIE" MAY '64
HOPKINS, JAMES--W/BODEN CLARKE,[7][23]
NON-FICT--
"WORK OF WILL. F. NOLAN: ANNOT. BIBL.
& GUIDE"
PHILLIPS, MICHAEL--[1][22]
SEVERN, DONALD--LACHMAN-EASTER LST '93,
[34]MYS--

NOLAN, [VIOLET] CYNTHIA
REED, CYNTHIA--[1]

NOLL, LOU BARKER
NOLL, BINK--[22]AMERICAN

NOLL, MARTIN DAVID
BUXBAUM, MARTIN--[1]

NOLL-WERDENBERG, HEIDI
WERDENBERG, HEIDI--[39]GERMAN

NOLLETT, LOIS S.
DELMORE, DIANA--[9][21]ROM--
"ANTHEA"
"CASSANDRA"
"MELISSANDE" & MORE
STEWART, LOIS--V. BERCH LTR TO HUBIN '94,
[21][26]MYS/ROM--
ZEBRA "DARK RENDEZVOUS AT DUNGARIFF" '89
ZEBRA "AN INDEPENDENT LADY" & OTHERS

NOLTE, HELMUT
ETLON, TUMLEH--[39]GERMAN/WEST

NOLTING-HAUFF, WILHELM
BARNEWOLD, ERNST--[39]GERMAN

NONHEBEL, CLARE
JAMES, MONICA--[1][31]
LINDSAY, M.--[1][32]MYS--
EQMM "THE GARNET RING" NOV '44
LINDSAY, MARY--[1]

NOON, BRIAN
KURDSEN, STEPHEN--[31]

NOONAN, ROBERT
TRESSAL, ROBERT--[8]
TRESSELL, ROBERT--[1]

NOOREN, BORJE
ANDREVS, CHARLES--[29]MYS
ANDREWS, CHARLES--[29]MYS

NORA, DR. JAMES
CONAN, ALLAN--[34]MYS--
LIST "THE PSI DELEGATION" '89

NORBERG, MARCIA K.
KAUFFMAN, M.K.--[21]ROM

NORDAY, MICHAEL
DAMON, RAY--[2]

NORDEN, ERIC
MARNAIS, PHILIP--V. BERCH-'AFTER DARK' SERIES,
BAE 27, ADULT--
MacF 50-398 "SAIGON AFTER DARK" '67

NORDHAUSEN, RICHARD
CALIBAN--[22]GERMAN

NORDSTROM, EDITH C.
DEAN EDNA--W/DOROTHY ADAMS,[34]MYS--
CARLTON "WAX BASKET MURDER" '86

NORGATE, WALTER
LE GRYS, WALTER--[8]

NORMAN, AMES
AMES, NORMA--[1][34]MYS--
AVON "MY PATH BELATED" '70
AVON "WHISPER IN THE FOREST" '72

NORMAN, BARBARA
MAKANOWITSKY, BARABRA--[1][31]

NORMAN, C.H.
STANHOPE OF CHESTER--[8]

NORMAN, GERALDINE [L]
KEEN, GERALDINE--[1][31]

NORMAN, NOEL WILSON
KAYE, LOUIS--[13]AUSTRALIAN

NORRIS, BENJAMIN F. JR.
NORRIS, FRANK--[1][22][28]AMERICAN

NORRIS, CAROLYN B.
KARRON, KRIS--[9][21][26]ROM--
"THE RAINBOW CHASE"
NORRIS, CAROL[YN]--[21][26]ROM--
"HIDEAWAY"
"ISLAND OF SILENCE" & MORE

NORTH, DAVID
STIVERS, DICK--[34]MYS,HP--
GE "DUELLING MISSILES" '90

NORTH, WILLIAM
RADD, RALPH--[1]
VANNER, JOHN--[1]

NORTH-MONTFORT, GRACE M.
NORTH, CAROL--[1]
NORTH, GRACE MAY--[1]

NORTHAM, LOIS EDGELL
NELSON, LOIS--[8]

NORTHCOTT, WILLIAM CECIL
MILLER, MARY--[1][22][33]ENGLISH
TEMPLE, ARTHUR--[1][33]ENGLISH

NORTHCROFT, DRORTHEA
FORD, D.M.--[1]

NORTHCROFT, GEORGE J.H.
NORTH, LIONEL--[1]

NORTHMORE, ELIZABETH F.
STUCLEY, ELIZABETH--[1]

NORTHRUP, EDWIN FITCH
PSEUDOMAN, AKKAD--[1][2][11][23]SF--
"ZERO TO EIGHTY" '37

NORTHWAY, COLIN
ROSS, FRANK--W/MICHAEL EWINGS,[34]MYS--
MacM "DEAD RUNNER" '77
ROSS, FRANK--[34]MYS--
MacM "GOLDSHIP" '81
MacM "SIXTY-FIFTH TAPE" '79

NORTON, ALICE MARY
NORTON, ANDRE ALICE--[2][7]--
LEGALIZED TO "ANDRE ALICE NORTON"

NORTON, ALICE MONTGOMERY
SLATER, ELIZABETH ANNE--[1]

NORTON, ALICE WHITSON
BARRY, ALICE MONTGOMERY--[1]

NORTON, ANDRE ALICE
CUSHING, ENID--W/ENID L. CUSHING,
G. COOK LTR '93, ADULT--
"MAID-AT-ARMS"
NORTH, ANDRE--[1][11]
NORTH, ANDREW--[2][4][9][23][33]SF--
"PEOPLE OF THE CRATOR"
NORTON, ANDRE--[2][3][9][11][33]MYS/SF--
HRCT "AT SWORD'S POINT" '54
GM "VELVET SHADOWS" '77
CREST "SNOW SHADOW" '79 & MORE
WESTON, ALLEN--W/GRACE ALLEN HOGARTH,
[2][3][11][33]MYS--
HAMMOND "MURDERS FOR SALE" '54

NORTON, CHARLES LEDYARD
COGSWELL, E.--[1]
D'ESTRIAN, P.--[1]

NORTON, EDITH ELIZABETH A
DUNN, ELIZA--[1]
KENT, KARLENE--[1]

NORTON, FRANK R.B.
NORTON, BROWNING--[1][32][33]MYS--
EB "THE PANTHER" JUN '53

NORTON, MARJORIE
ELLISON, MARJORIE--[8][9]ROM
NORRELL, MARJORIE--[9][21]ROM--

NORTON, OLIVE MARION
NEAL, HILARY--[1][9][21][26]ROM--
"FACTORY NURSE"
"CHARGE NURSE" & MORE
NOON, T.R.--[1][9]ENGLISH
NORTON, BESS--[1][9][21][26]ROM--
"A NURSE IS BORN"
NORWAY, KATE--[1][9][21][26]ROM--
"PAPER HALO"
"DEDICATION JONES" & MORE

NORTON, PHILIP
SMITH, ARTEGALL--[2][23]SF--
"SUB SOL, OR UNDER THE SUN: MISSIONARY
ADV IN THE GREAT SAHARA" 1889

NORTON, ROGER HOWARD
BLACKMAN, ROBERT C.--L. ROBBINS LTR '94,
[11][32]MYS--
DS "SCARLET JUSTICE" MAY '44
NEWMAN, ROBERT--[11]

NORVICK
CIV--[2]

NORWAY, NEVIL SHUTE
SHUTE, NEVIL--[2][7][22]ENGLISH-AUSTRALIAN--
CASSELL "SO ORDAINED" '28
CASSELL "LONELY ROAD" '32
HM "NO HIGHWAY" '48
"SLIDE RULE" '54 & MORE

NORWOOD, VICTOR [G.C.]
ADAMS, CHUCK--S. HOLLAND-BAPC #11, WEST--
SPENCER "KID FROM CRIPPLE CREEK" '51
BANTON, COY--BAPC #11,[28][31]WEST--
HALE "BLOOD ON THE SAGE" '66
HALE "GUNSMOKE JUSTICE" '66

NORWOOD, VICTOR [G.C.] [CONT]

BAXTER, S.V.--S. HOLLAND-BAPC #11--
WANDERING STAR
BAXTER, SHANE--S. HOLLAND-BAPC #11, ADULT--
BOUDOIR
BAXTER, SHANE V.--BAPC #11,[14][28][31]--
OLYM OPH#181 "BABBLING WITH ECSTACY" '69
HALE "SHADOW OF A GUNHAWK" '66
HALE "TEXAN" '67
OLYM OPH#273 "VIRGIN & MONSTER" '70
GRNLF GC353 "MISSION: SINPOSSIBLE" '68
BOWIE, JIM--S. HOLLAND-BAPC #11,[28][31]WEST--
SCION "TRIGGER MUSIC" & OTHERS '51-4
BRAND, CLAY--[28][31]WEST--
HALE "COLT COURAGE" '65
HALE "POWDERSMOKE" '66
HALE "LATIMER'S LAST RIDE" '67
BRAND, VICTOR--S. HOLLAND-BAPC #11,[8]
CALVERT, PAMELA--S. HOLLAND-BAPC #11--
WANDERING STAR
CLEVINGER, PAUL--S. HOLLAND-BAPC #11,[8]
CODY, WALT--BAPC #11,[28]WEST--
HALE "REAP THE WILD WIND" '66
HALE "BLACK DAY AT EAGLE ROCK" '68
COLTER, SHANE--S. HOLLAND-BAPC #11,
WANDERING STAR
COLTER, SHAYNE--S. HOLLAND-BAPC #11,
[28][31]WEST--
HALE "HALFWAY TO HELL" '66
CORTEEN, CRAIG--[8]
CORTEEN, WES--S. HOLLAND-BAPC #11,
[28][31]WEST--
HALE "GUN CHORE" '66
DANGERFIELD, CLINT--S. HOLLAND-BAPC #11,
[28][31]WEST--
HALE "CROSSFIRE" '65
DANGERFIELD, L.D.--S. HOLLAND-BAPC #11,
WANDERING STAR
DANGERFIELD, PAUL--S. HOLLAND-BAPC #11,
WANDERING STAR-- ??UNCONFIRMED??
DARK, JOHNNY--[3][28][31]MYS--
MLST "SNAKE WALK" '51
MLST "DAME ON THE LAM" '52
MLST "VENOM" '53
MLST "FIG LEAVES FOR A LADY" '53
MLST "SQUEALER" '54
MLST "A GUY MUST LIVE" '54
DESTRY, VINCE--[28][31]--
HALE "TRAIL'S END" '65
HALE "THE GLORY TRAIL" '67
HALE "A BADGE & A GUN" '70
EVANS, VICTOR G.--S. HOLLAND-BAPC #11,
WANDERING STAR
FARGO, DOONE--S. HOLLAND-BAPC#11,[28][31]WEST--
HALE "DEATH VALLEY" '66
HALE "KILLER'S CODE" '66
FARRADAY, CHET--S. HOLLAND-BAPC #11,
WANDERING STAR-- WEST
FENTON, MARK--S. HOLLAND-BAPC #11,[8]
FISHER, WADE--S. HOLLAND-BAPC #11[28][31]WEST--
HALE "RANGER GUN LAW" '63
GEARING-THOMAS, G.--S. HOLLAND-BAPC #11,
[28][31]--
SPORTING & POLITICAL ARTICLES
HAMPTON, MARK--BAPC #11,[28][34]MYS--
SCION "RAW DEAL FOR DAMES" '52
SCION "THAT'S HER PROBLEM" '52
SCION "I DON'T SCARE EASY" '52
SCION "KILLER TAKE ALL" '53
JANSON, HANK--BAPC #11[34][28]MYS,HP--
ROBERTS "BLOOD BATH" '62
ROBERTS "GO WITH A JERK" '62
ROBERTS "KILL ME FOR KICKS" '62
COMPACT "PLAYGIRL" '63
COMPACT "SENSUALITY" '63
COMPACT "TOP TEN" '64
COMPACT "WILL-POWER" '64

NORWOOD, VICTOR [G.C.] [CONT]

KARTA, NAT--BAPC #11,[28][34]MYS,HP--
SCION "BROTHER RAT" '52
SCION "CLIMAX" '53]
M'GROOM, HECTOR--S. HOLLAND-BAPC #11,
WANDERING STAR--
SCION
MCCORD, WHIP--S. HOLLAND-BAPC #11,[28]WEST--
HALE "HELLFIRE RANGE" '66
MCCOY, ROSEANNA--S. HOLLAND-BAPC #11,
WANDERING STAR
NORWOOD, V.G.C.--S. HOLLAND-BAPC #11,
[28]WEST--
BARKER "VENGEANCE VALLEY" '66
CORGI "MAN ALONE"
RAND, BRETT--S. HOLLAND-BAPC #11,[28]WEST--
HALE "CODE OF THE LAWLESS" '67
REGAN, BRAD--AUTHOR PROVIDED,[1][28]MYS--
GANNET "RAW DEAL FOR DAMES" '52
RIGAN, BRAD--BAPC #11,[34]MYS--
GANNET "I'LL TAKE THE BODY" '53
GANNET "KILLER TAKE ALL '53
KEN "DROP DEAD SUCKER" '53
RUSSELL, SHANE--BAPC #11,[28][34]WEST--
HALE "BOUNTY TRAIL" '63
HALE "GUN TRAIL & BOOT HILL" '63
HALE "GUN TRAIL TO BOOT HILL" '64
HALE "LOBO BREED" '65
SARTO, BEN--BAPC #11,[34]MYS,HP--
MOF "SWAMP FEVER" '57
SHANE, MARK--S. HOLLAND-BAPC #11,
[3][28]MYS--
COMYNS "LADY BITES THE DUST" '52
COMYNS "DEATH AT HER FINGERS" '53
COMYNS "HONEY AIN'T SO SWEET" '53
COMYNS "JAIL & FAREWELL" '53
COMYNS "OBSESSION TO KILL" '53
COMYNS "THEY KILL TO LIVE" '53
COMYNS "BORROWED TIME" '53
BARKER "CROSSFIRE" '53
BARKER "CHANGO" '55
BARKER "VENGEANCE VALLEY" '55
SHANE, RHONDO--S. HOLLAND-BAPC #11,[28]WEST--
HALE "THE GUN HELLION" '67
SHANE, V. BAXTER--L. ROBBINS LTR MAR '94
SHANE, VICTOR--S. HOLLAND-BAPC #11,[8]
STEELE, BLUE--S. HOLLAND-BAPC #11,
WANDERING STAR
STRANGE, DILLON--S. HOLLAND-BAPC #11,[28]--
GEMS & PROSPECTING ARTICLES
THAXTER, NIGEL--S. HOLLAND-BAC #11,
WANDERING STAR
TRESSIDY, JIM--S. HOLLAND-BAPC #11,[1][28]
TYRONE, PAUL--S. HOLLAND-BAPC #11,[1][28]--
GEMS & PROSPECTING ARTICLES
WILLARD, PORTMAN--S. HOLLAND-BAPC,[1][28]--
GEM & PROSPECTING ARTICLES

NORWOOD, WARREN C.
NORWOOD, WARREN G.--[23]SF--
"G" WAS PUBLISHER'S ERROR

NOSTLINGER, CHRISTINE
NOESTLINGER, CHRISTINE--[33]

NOTLEY, FRANCES ELIZA M.
DERRICK, FRANCES--[1]

NOTREDAME, MICHEL DE
NOSTRADAMUS--[11]

NOTT, DAVID
OWEN, RICHARD--W/DENNIS FAWCETT, V. BERCH
LTR TO HUBIN '94, MYS--
"EYE OF THE GODS"

NOTTKE-AXT, MARIA
AXT, MARIA--[39]GERMAN/JUV

NOURSE, ALAN E.
DR. X--[1][31][33]
EDWARDS, AL--[31][33][32]MYS--
AHMM "THE BIG CHILL" JUN "58

NOVA, CRAIG
CARTER, NICK--[3]MYS,HP--
AWARD "DR. DEATH" '75
AWARD "THE NICHOVEV PLOT" '76

NOVACHOVITCH, LIPPE BENZ.
BEN-NEZ--[1]
BENEDICT, LEOPOLD--[1]
GHETTO POET--[1]
WINCHEVSKY, MORRIS--[1][22]LITHUANIAN-AMERICAN,NAME "WINCHEVSKY" LEGALIZED

NOVACK, GEORGE [EDWARD]
WARDE, WILLIAM F.--[1]

NOVAK, C. DAN ZACHARIA
ZACHARIA, DAN--[8]

NOVAK, KAREL
NOVY, KAREL--[22]CZECH

NOVAK, ROSE
ROSE, MARCIA--W/MARCIA S. KAMIEN,
[9][21][26]ROM--
"PRINCE OF ICE"
"CONNECTIONS" & MORE

NOVELLA, DON
SARDUCCI, GUIDO--[1]
TOTH, LAZLO--[1]

NOVELLI, ENRICO
YAMBO--[22]ITALIAN

NOVELLI, FLORENCE
FORD, FLORENCE--[31]

NOVIKOV, OLGA
OK--[8]

NOVITSKI, PAUL DAVID
ALPAJPURI--[2]

NOVOMISKI, MOISHE
OLGIN, M.J.--[22]HEBREW

NOWACZYNSKI, ADOLF
NEUWERT--[22]POLISH
PRZYJACIEL--[22]POLISH

NOWAK, MARITTE
RONSMAN, M.M.--[1]

NOWAKOWSKI, ZYGMUNT
TEMPKA, ZYGMUNT--[22]POLISH

NOWELL, ELIZABETH CAMERON
CAMERON, ELIZABETH--[22][31][33]
CLEMONS, ELIZABETH--[22][31][33]

NOWELL, HARRIETT P.
MANNERING, MAY--[1]

NOWICKI, ZBIGNIEW
NIENACKI, ZBIGNIEW--[1]

NOWLAN, PHILLIP FRANCIS
PHILLIPS, FRANK--[1][2]

NUCCIO, MARSHA L.
GAMBLE, M.L.--[10][21][26][34]MYS/ROM--
"WHEN MURDER CALLS"
HARL "DIAMOND OF DECEIT" '90 & MORE

NUCERA, MARISA LONETTE
MARISA--[22]AMERICAN

NUELLE, HELEN SHEARMAN
NUELLE, HELEN [SHEARMAN]--[21]ROM

NUETZEL, CHARLES A.
ALLEN, MARK--V. BERCH-NUETZEL CKLST,
BAE 25, ADULT--
BL436 "HOT PANTS KAREN" '70
ANDREWS, BLAKE--MONROE RVW '93, ADULT--
POWELL PP-185 "COME TO ME BABY" '69
ANONYMOUS--V. BERCH-NUETZEL CKLST, BAE 25--
DOVE DB108 "LUST IDOL"
RPRTS "TROPIC OF PASSION"
HEART HV103 "JUNGLE LUST"
RPRTS "TROPIC OF PASSION"
AUGUSTUS, ALBERT JR.--V.BERCH-NUETZEL CKLST,
BAE 25,[31]--
POW PP175 "GOLD LUST" '69
REWRTS ANCH WL109
POW PP189 "THE SLAVES OF LOMORRO" '69
BELMONT, JACK--BERCH-NUETZEL CKLST, BAE 25--
POW PP132 "TAKE ME, I'M YOURS" '69
REWRTS EPIC 120
BLAKE, ALEX--NUETZEL/MUNROE/BERCH, BAE 25--
EPIC 105 "LOVE ME TO DEATH" '61
SCORPION 108 "NOBODY LOVES A TRAMP" '64
ALL STAR AS47 "ORGY FOR 3" '65
RAPTURE RB409 "FAMILY MISTRESS" '65
BLAKE, FREDRIC--V. BERCH-NUETZEL CKLST,
BAE 25--
POW PP122 "ON THE MAKE" '69
RWRTS EPIC 131
BLAKE, J.D--BERCH/MUNROE, BAE 25, ADULT--
PEC G1121-"HOLLYWOOD STUD" '66
RPRTS EPIC 106
PEC N146 "NEON JUNGLE" '66
RPRTS EPIC 108
PEC N147 "PASSION CLUB" '66
RPRTS EPIC 111
RAPT 217 "EXECUTIVE PAD" '67
RAPT 220 "JUNGLE LUST" '67
CHARLES, REX--BERCH/MUNROE-NUETZEL CKLST,
BAE 25--
PRIVATE EDIT 301 "NYMPHO MODELS" '65
DAVIDSON, JOHN--BERCH/MUNROE-NUETZEL CKLST,
BAE 25--
EPIC 101 "HOT CARGO" '61
EPIC 108 "BODIES FOR SALE" '61
EPIC 120 "PASSIONATE TRIO" '61
EPIC 123 "TWO TIMING TART" '61
PIKE 204 "APPOINTMENT WITH TERROR" '61
REPRTS PIKE 1314 "A DATE WITH VIOLENCE"
BOUDOIR 104 "SEX IS MY BUSINESS" '62
EPIC 131 "MOTEL MISTRESS" '62
EPIC 142 "TROPIC OF PASSION" '62
'ALEC RIVERE' ON TITLE PAGE
UPTOWN 702 "BLUES FOR A DEAD LOVER" '62
UPTOWN 705 "WOMAN TRAP" '62
ANCH WL106 "NEVER IN HER ARMS" '65
ANCH WL109 "SEX ON FIRE" '65
ANCH WL116 "MISTRESS OF THE DAMNED" '65
DAVIS, CARSON--BERCH/MUNROE-NUETZEL CKLST,
BAE 25--
VENICE BOOKS VB266 "TAPED SEX
HISTORIES" '67
CLASS LIB CL40 "SUBURB SEX CLUB '68
CLASS LIB CL50 "BITCHES IN HEAT" '68
VB351 "CONFESSIONS OF A MAN OF
PLEASURE" '68-BY 'TOM X' W/CARSON DAVIS

NUETZEL, CHARLES A. [CONT]
DAVIS, CARSON [CONT]
CLASS PUB CP502 "DIARY OF A SHRIKE" '68
BY 'KAREN X'- EDITED BY DAVIS
VB359 "EXTRA-MARITAL TRAP" '68
VB385 "TORMENTED SEXUALS" '68
CLASS PUB CP512 "PLURAL SEX" '68
CP507 "AC DC" '68
CP529 "ORGY SEEKERS" '69
NEW FACT LIB NL1027 "CONFIDENTIALLY YOURS" '69
NL1034 "SEXUAL LIBERALS" '69
VB 394 "CONFESSIONS OF LITTLE SUSAN" '69
BY 'SUSAN'- EDITED BY DAVIS
NL1042 "SEX HIGH" '69
NL1069 "MARRIAGE TRAP" '69
RAM RS1004 "SEX FILE" '69
CLASS PUB CP519 "THE LESBIAN URGE" '69
VENICE VB474 "NEW BREED" '70
GRIFFON GB802 "SEX USA" '71
DAVIS, FRED--BERCH/MUNROE-NUETZEL, BAE 25--
POW PP169 "BORN TO BE LOVED" '69
RPRTS PE 350
DAVIS, JAY--BERCH/MUNROE-NUETZEL CKLST, BAE 25--
EPIC 111 "SIN SOCIETY" '61
SCORPION 101 "WILD SPREE" '64
IMPERIAL 738 "SINNERS HOLLIDAY" '65
DONALDSON, JACK--BERCH/MUNROE-NUETZEL CKLST, BAE 25--
POW PP177 "SEX BASH" '69
RWRTS PE 301
ENGLISH, CHARLES--BERCH/MUNROE-NUETZEL CKLST, BAE 25--
SCORPION 104 "LOVERS 2075" '64
EWING, FRANK--BERCH/MUNROE-NUETZEL CKLST, BAE 25--
POW PP144 "BABY-FACED HARLOT" '69
RPRTS RAPT 409 "FAMILY MISTRESS"
FRANKLIN, DONALD--BERCH-NUETZEL CKLST, BAE 25--
NITE LITE 219 "SHOW BIZ STUD" '65
PEC G1118 "SPOTLIGHT SEX" '66
PEC N139 "PLAYGIRL'S STUD" '66
RAPTURE 218 "STAR BITCH" '67
FRANKLYN, DONALD--BERCH/MUNROE-NUETZEL CKLST, BAE 25--
POW PP111 "BLOWOUT" '68
FREDRICS, GEORGE--BERCH-NUETZEL CKLST, BAE 25,[2]--
POW PP163 "CONSIDER YOURSELF DEAD" '69
REWRTS PIKE 204 "APPOINTMENT WITH TERROR" & IMP 738 "SINNERS HOLLIDAY"
POW PP171 "OPERATION NIGHTMARE" '69
RWRTS SCORP 102 "WANTONS OF BETRAYAL" & ANCH WL116 "MISTRESS OF THE DAMNED"
BCA 015 STORY-"A VERY CULTURED TASTE"
JACKSON, HOWARD--BERCH/MUNROE CKLST, BAE 25--
POW PP116 "JEAN" '68
RPRTS FRA F62 "ILLICIT BED"
JANTZEN, FRITZ--BERCH/MUNROE-NUETZEL CKLST, BAE 25--
EUROPA 1101 "BERLIN BED" '63
JOHNSON, DAVID--V.BERCH-NUETZEL CKLST, BAE 25--
POW PP112 "BODY MERCHANTS" '68
RPRTS "HOT CARGO"
SCORPION 106 "JUNGLE NYMPH" '64
KELLEM, RAY--BERCH-NUETZEL CKLST, BAE 25--
SPD SV103 "ROADHOUSE SIN"
PIRATES "MOTEL MISTRESS"
LAMBERT, HAL--BERCH/MUNROE-NUETZEL CKLST, BAE 25--
PIKE 211 "3 PARTS EVIL" '62
PIKE 804 "ONE HUNDRED DOLLAR GIRL" '63
REPRTS PIKE 311 "3 PARTS EVIL"

NUETZEL, CHARLES A. [CONT]
MACDONALD, FRANK--BERCH/MUNROE-NUETZEL CKLST, BAE 25--
PEC SPECIAL 17 "EROS CULT" '67
MACDONALD, FRED--BERCH/MUNROE-NUETZEL CKLST, BAE 25--
PILLOW 109 "RED LIGHT CAMPUS" '62
FRA F62 "ILLICIT BED" '63
SCORP 107 "WITH PASSIONS BURNING" '64
ANCH WL105 "BISEXUAL BEDS" '65
ANCH WL110 "SEX CULT MURDERS" '65-TITLE PAGE SHOWS 'DAVID JOHNSON' AS AUTHOR
ANCH WL114 "PARLEY IN PASSION" '65
POW PP107 "NYMPHO" '68
PP150 "KRISTA" '69
REWRTS "BERLIN BED"
MACDONALD, FREDA--BERCH/MUNROE-NUETZEL CKLST, BAE 25--
RAPTURE 302 "HER LESBIAN HALF" '63"
NITM 115 "PASSIONS OF HATE" '64
REMICK, BRANT--BERCH-NUETZEL CKLST, BAE 25--
SPDV 105 "CORPORATE SIN"
RPRTS "SEX IS MY BUSINESS"
RIVERE, ALEC--BERCH-NUETZEL CKLST, BAE 25,[2]--
EPIC 142 "TROPIC OF PASSION"
ON TITLE PG ONLY
PIKE 101 "LOST CITY OF THE DAMNED" '61
RPRTS PIKE 801 "NYMPHOS BE DAMNED" '62
SCORPION 102 "WANTONS OF BETRAYAL" '64
RIVERS, STU--BERCH/MUNROE-NUETZEL CKLST, BAE 25--
EPIC 106 "CASTING COUCHERS" '61
SCORP 103 "HOLLYWOOD NYMPH" '64
SCORP 105 "SEX QUEEN" '64
POW PP139 "SEX KITTENS" '69
RWRTS PE 350 "HOT STUD LOVER" '65
TURNER, JACK--BERCH/MUNROE-NUETZEL CKLST, BAE 25--
BL 449Z "EXECUTIVE WIFE SWAPPERS" '70
WEST, JAY--BERCH/MUNROE-NUETZEL LST, BAE 25--
PEC N145 "BIKINI GIRL" '66
RPRTS "WOMAN TRAP"
WILDE, RITA--BERCH/MUNROE-NUETZEL CKLST, BAE 25--
PEC FL16 "2-WAY STREET" '67
"HER LESBIAN HALF"

NUGENT, JOHN PEER
EXALL, BARRY--[1][22][31]AMERICAN

NUGENT, NANCY
HAWKE, NANCY--[31]

NUGENT, RICHARD BRUCE
BRUCE, RICHARD--[31]

NUGMANOV, KAMIL
IASHEN, KAMIL--[1]

NUNN, WILLIAM CURTIS
CURTIS, WILL--[1][22][31]AMERICAN
TWIST, ANANIAS--[1][22]AMERICAN

NURETDINOV, ZAKI S.
ZAKI, NURI--[1]

NURNBERGER, WOLDEMAR
SOLITAIRE, M.--[39]GERMAN

NURSE, MALCOLM IVAN MERE.
PADMORE, GEORGE--[8]

NUSSBAUM, ALBERT F.
AVELLANO, ALBERT--AUTHOR PROVIDED-LACHMAN--
WROTE SOME STORIES ATTRIB TO 'DAN MARLOWE'
FREDERICK, LEE--[31]
MARTIN, ALBERTO N.--AUTHOR PROVIDED-
LACHMAN, MYS--
MSMM "CAT-ALYST" APR '70
AHMM "LESSON" JUN '70
AHMM "ONE GOOD WORD" APR '70
AHMM "PEACE WORK" MAY 70
& 5 OTHER AHMM STORIES
MARTIN, CARL--AUTHOR PROVIDED-LACHMAN
LST '93-EQMM EDITOR INTRO--
NUMEROUS STORIES
NUSSBAUM, AL--[31]
ORESHNIK, A.F.--AUTHOR PROVIDED-
LACHMAN LST '93, MYS--
AHMM "BAD JOKE" OCT '71
MSMM "EXPERT" JUN '71
AHMM "TAKE-OVER" JUL '72
MSMM "BREAKING INTO THE BIG TIME" MAR '72
MSMM "KRIS KRINGLE CAPER" JAN '76
& 8 OTHER AHMM STORIES
SANDAVAL, JAIME--AUTHOR PROVIDED-LACHMAN--
WROTE SOME STORIES ATTRIBUTED
TO 'DAN MARLOWE'

NUSSER, JAMES L.
LIVINGSTON, JACK--V. BERCH LTR TO
HUBIN '94, MYS--
ST. MARTIN'S "DIE AGAIN, MACREADY" '84
& MORE

NUTBROWN, MAURICE
DENBIGH, MAURICE--[1]

NUTT, CHARLES LEROY
BEAUMONT, CHARLES--[2][7][32][34]LEGALIZED
TO 'BEAUMONT'- COLL OF SS
MH "I'LL DO ANYTHING" NOV '55
MD "THE MURDERERS" SEPT '58
MD "THE TRIGGER" JAN '59
SH "OPEN HOUSE" SEPT '60

NUTT, DAVID
BRAND, DAVID--[8]

NUTT, LILY CLIVE
ARDEN, CLIVE--[1][2][31]

NUTTALL, ANTHONY
ALLYSON, ALAN--[8]
BARDSLEY, MICHAEL--[8]
CURTIS, SPENCER--[8]
LENTON, ANTHONY--[8]
TRACEY, GRANT--[8]
TRENT, LEE--[8]
WELLS, TRACEY--[8]

NUTTALL, JEFF
CHURCH, PETER--[1][31]
HOMOSAP--[31]
MOMORUS--[1]

NUTTALL-SMITH, MARGARET E
FORTNUM, PEGGY--[31]

NUTTING, MARY OLIVIA
BARRETT, MARY--[1][32]MYS--
EQMM "SILVER SALTCELLAR" MAY '70
EQMM "DEATH OUT OF SEASON" FEB '71
EQMM "DEJA VU" JUL '72
EQMM "JOSEPHINE RIDER SAID" MAY '72
AHMM "ONE FOR THE CROW" MAR '73
EQMM "MAN IN THE LEATHER JACKET" NOV '73

NUTZ, WALTER
COTTON, JERRY--[39]GERMAN/MYS,HP

NYBERG, MARIANNE
THORBY, MARIANNE--[29]MYS--
SODERSTROM "VIN MED DODLIG BISMAK" '60

NYE, MIRIAM MAURINE H.B.
BAKER, MIRIAM HAWTHORN--[31]

NYE, NELSON C[ORAL]
CAMPBELL, CLIFF--C. WINTEROWD
CALL '94, WEST,HP--
COLT, CLEM--[1][28]WEST--
PHOENIX "FIDDLE-BACK RANCH" '44
PHOENIX "RENEGADE COWBOY" '44
ARCADIA "GUNSLICK MOUNTAIN" '45
QUALITY PRESS "BREED OF THE CHAPARRAL" '49
PHOENIX PRESS & 21 OTHER NOVELS '38-55
DENVER, DRAKE C.--[28]WEST--
W&B "THE STAR PACKERS" '38
W&B "NO WIRE RANGE" '39
PHOENIX--8 NOVELS '40-46
W&B "LONG ROPE" '49
ROCKINGHAM, MONTAGUE--[1]

NYGREN, KERSTIN
BERG, AL--[29]MYS
BERGFORS, AL--[29]MYS--
TROTS "DOD MODELL" '58

NYLEN, INGEBORG
WALLIS, JOHN--[29]MYS--
37 NOVELS '34-45

NYSTRAND, FOLKE
REUTER, JAN--[29]MYS--
HOK "PRINS KARNEVAL OCH DODEN" '61"

O SIOCHAIN, P.A.
SHEEHAN, PATRIC AUGUSTINE--[22]IRISH

O'BRIEN, CLIFFORD EDWARD
O'BRIEN, LARRY CLINTON--[1][2]

O'BRIEN, CONOR CRUISE
O'DONNELL, DONAT--[1][6]

O'BRIEN, CYRIL C.
WILSON, CRANE--[1]

O'BRIEN, DAN
A COURT BAILIFF--[2]

O'BRIEN, DAVID WRIGHT
BLADE, ALEXANDER--[1][2][11][23]SF,HP--
ZIFF-DAVIS
CABOT, JOHN YORK--[1][2][11][23]SF--
CAMERON, BERL--[1][2]SF,HP--
WARREN "PHOTOMESIS" '52
WARREN "BLACK INFINITY" '52
DENNIS, BRUCE--[1][2][11][23]SF--
FARNSWORTH, DUNCAN--[1][2][11][23]SF--
GARSON, CLEE--[2][11][23]HP--ZIFF-DAVIS
LE PAGE, RAND--[1][2]SF,HP--
WARREN "BLUE ASP" '52
LUNA, KRIS--[1][2]SF,HP--
WARREN "STELLA RADIUM EXCHANGE" '52
SHAW, BRIAN--[1][2][23]SF,HP--
WARREN "SHIPS OF VERO" '52
VARDON, RICHARD--[1][2][11][23]SF--

O'BRIEN, EDWARD JOSEPH H.
MIDDLETON, ARTHUR--[1]

O'BRIEN, G.M.
O'ROURKE, ISRAEL--W/ELLIOTT CAPON,[2]

O'BRIEN, HOWARD ALLAN FRANCIS
RICE, ANNE--[7][31]--
LEGALIZED TO 'ANNE' ABOUT '47

O'BRIEN, HOWARD VINCENT
PERRIN, CLYDE--[1][22]MYS--

O'BRIEN, MARIAN P.
BRYAN, MAVIS--[1][31]

O'BRIEN, MARY
SCOTT, JULIA--[1]

O'CALLAGHAN, MAXINE
OWENS, MARISSA--HAWK/O'CALLAGHAN INTRVW '93--
ROMANTIC SUSPENSE

O'CASEY, EILEEN REYNOLDS
CASEY, EILEEN--[31]

O'CASEY, SEAN
GREEN CROW, THE--[8]

O'CONNELL, FREDERICK W.
CONALL, CEARNACH--[1][34]MYS--
GILL "THE FATAL MOVE & OTHER STORIES" '24

O'CONNELL, KAREN
MORLAND, LYNETTE--[9][21][26]ROM--
"IRISH EYES"
"MAGIC CITY" & MORE

O'CONNER, BARRETT WILL'BY
WILLOUGHBY, BARRETT--[1]

O'CONNOR HOWE, JOSEPHINE
HOWE, JOSEPHINE M.O.--[31]

O'CONNOR, JOHN WOOLF
O'CONNOR, JACK--[28]WEST--
2 NOVELS '30-38

O'CONNOR, KAREN
SWEENEY, KAREN O'CONNOR--[33]

O'CONNOR, MARY CATHARINE
FARRELL, CATHARINE--[22][31]AMERICAN

O'CONNOR, PATRICK JOSEPH
FIACC, PADRAIC--[8][31]

O'CONNOR, RICHARD
ARCHER, FRANK--[31][33][34]--
DBLDY "MALABANG PEARL" '64
DBLDY "OUT OF BLUE" '64
DBLDY "WIDOW WATCHERS" '65
GM 1816 "TURQUOISE SPIKE" '67
BRNDN "NAKED CRUSADER" '72
BURKE, JOHN--[1][31][33]--
SIGN 2172 "300 SPARTAN" '62
AV S304 "PRIVILEDGE" '67
WAYLAND, PATRICK--[1][34]MYS--
DBLDY "COUNTERSTROKE" '64
DBLDY "DOUBLE DEFECTER" '64
DBLDY "WAITING GAME" '65

O'CONNOR, THOMAS POWER
T.P.--[8]
TAY PAY--[22]IRISH

O'CUILLEANAIN, EILIS D.
DILLON, EILIS--[1]

O'DANIEL, JANET
CLARK, AMANDA--W/A.M. MIDGLEY,[21][26]ROM--
"BLUEPRINT FOR LOVE"
"FLOWER OF THE SEA" & MORE
JANET, LILLIAN--W/LILLIAN RESSLER,[1]

O'DELL, J.W.
TYLER, MARTIN WALLACE--V. BERCH LTR '93--
LEIS "TIDAL WAVE" '75

O'DONNELL, PETER
BARNES, JOHN--[1]
BRENT, MADELEINE--[26][34]ENGLISH/MYS/ROM--
"GOLDEN URCHIN"
"MERLIN'S KEEP" & MORE
McINTOSH, J.T.--[34]GHOSTED--
MULLER "TAKE A PAIR OF PRIVATE EYES" '68

O'DONOGHUE, ELINOR MARY
ODDIE, E.M.--[8][34]MYS--
CASSELL "SLITTING OF MR. CRISPE'S NOSE" '46

O'DONOHOE, NICHOLAS BENJ.
O'DONOHOE, NICK--[7]SF--
TSR "TOO, TOO SOLID FLESH" '89

O'DONOVAN, JEREMIAH
O'DONOVAN, GERALD--[1]

O'DONOVAN, MICHAEL
O'CONNOR, FRANK--[1][22]IRISH

O'DWYER, DAISY MAY
BATES, DAISY--[13]AUSTRALIAN

O'FAOLAIN, JULIA
MARTINES, JULIA--[1]

O'FARRELL, WILLIAM
GREW, WILLIAM--[1][3][18]MYS--
DBLDY "DOUBLES IN DEATRH" '53
GRAP 105 "MURDER HAS MANY FACES" '55

O'FARRELLY, AGNES
NI FHAIRCHEALLAIGH, UNA--[1]

O'FERRALL, ERNEST
KODAK--[8]

O'GRADY, ELIZABETH ANNE
SCOLLAN, E.A.--[1]

O'GRADY, JAMES STANDISH
CLIVE, ARTHUR--[1]
NETTERVILLE, LUKE--[1][2]

O'GRADY, JOHN PATRICK
CULOTTA, NINO--[1][31]AUSTRALIAN/HUMOR
O'GRADA, SEAN--[1]AUSTRALIAN

O'GREEN, JENNIFER M.R.
MITCHELL, JENNIFER--[9]ROM
ROBERSON, JENNIFER--[7][9]SF--
"SMOKETREE"

O'HARA, GERRY
CHRISTIE, MICHELLE--[9][21][26]ROM--
"TRISTAIN'S LAIR"
"FOREVER LOVE"
"KING OF THE CASTLE"
MICHAELS, MICHELLE--[9]ROM--

O'HARA, JOHN [H]
DELANEY, FRANEY--[1]

O'HARRIS, LEE
O'HANNEGAN, LARRY--[1]

O'HEFFERMAN, PATRICK
HEFFERMAN, PATRICK--[31]

O'KEEFE, LAURENCE
HALLEY, LAURENCE--[31][34]MYS--
CAPE "SIMULTANEOUS EQUATIONS" '75

O'KELLY, JOHN J.
O CEALLAIGH, SEAN--[1]
O CEALLAIGH, THOMAS--[1]

O'LAIMHIN, J. MARTI LAVEN
LAVEN, J.C. MARTI--[21]ROM
LAVEN, MARTI--[9][21][26]ROM--
"A MATTER OF REVENGE"

O'LEARY, LIAM
O'LAOGHAIRE, LIAM--[1]

O'LEARY, PETER
O'LOAGHAIRE, PEADAR--[1]

O'MAHONY, CHARLES K.
ELLIS, JULIAN--[1]
KINGSTON, CHARLES--[1][32][34]MYS--
26 NVLS '21-45
JCM "WAITER AT LAW" NOV '59

O'MALLEY, MARY DOLLING
BRIDGE, ANN--[2][3][7][17][21][31]MYS--
"NIGHTSHADE"
"PEKING PICNIC" & MORE

O'MALLEY, MICHAEL
O'MAILLE, MICHAEL--[1]

O'MANT, HEDLEY P.A.
CLIFFORD, MARTIN--[1]HP--
CONQUEST, OWEN--[1]HP--
HAWKE, [CAPT.] ROBERT--[1]
OWEN, HEDLEY--[1]
RICHARDS, FRANK--[1]HP--
SCOTT, HAMILTON--[1]
SCOTT, HEDLEY--[1][3]MYS--
AMALG "MYS OF MISSING REFUGEE" '39
AMALG "SUSPECTED SIX" '38 & MORE
X.--[34]MYS--
AMALG "BROTHERHOOD OF THE WHITE FEATHER" '28

O'MARA, JOHN
O'MARA, JON--[35]AUSTRALIAN--
HRWTZ SP132 "SEASON FOR SIN" '78
WEIL, JERRY--[35]AUSTRALIAN--
HRWTZ NAL2 "A REAL COOL CAT" '67
HRWTZ NAL6 "DAUGHTER OF EVIL" '67
HRWTZ AO16 "HEAT" '71
HRWTZ AO7 "THE DARK SIDE OF LOVE" '71

O'MARA, TIMOTHY JOSEPH
O'MARA, PAT--[1]

O'MEARA, KATHLEEN
RAMSAY, GRACE--[1][34]MYS--
HARPER "NARKA THE NIHILIST" '87

O'NEAL, CHARLES
O'NEAL, BLACKIE--[1]
PAYNE, CHARLOTTE--[21][26]ROM--
"LORD OF THE RIVER"

O'NEAL, REGINA
O'NEAL, REGGIE--[1]

O'NEAL, WILLIAM B.
WOODS, JACK--CRPG--
PAGEANT "WOLFFILE" '88

O'NEILL, HERBERT CHARLES
STRATEGICUS--[8]

O'NEILL, MARY AGATHA
GAULE, BEATRICE--[1]

O'NEILL, ROSE CECIL
LATHAM, O'NEILL--[8]

O'NOLAN, BRIAN
AN BROC--[8]
BARNABAS, BROTHER--[1]
DOE, JOHN JAMES--[1]
KNOWALL, GEORGE--[1][8][11][23]
NA GCOPALEEN, MYLES--[1][8][11][23]
NA GOPALEEN, MYLES--[1][2][23]SF
O'BLATHER, COUNT--[1]
O'BRIEN, FLANN--[1][2][3][8][34]MYS--
WALKER "THIRD POLICEMAN" '67

O'RIORDAN, CONAL O'CONN.
CONNELL, NORREYS--[8][22]IRISH

O'ROURKE, FRANK
CONNOR, KEVIN--[8][28][31]--
JEFFERSON HOUSE "NEW DEPARTURE" '62
O'MALLEY, FRANK--[1][2][28]--
RANDOM "BEST GO FIRST" '50
O'MALLEY, PATRICK--[3][8]MYS--
MILL "AFFAIR OF THE BLUE PIG" '65
& 6 MORE '61-5

O'SHAUGHNESSY, MARJORIE
SHAW, ADELAIDE--[8]

O'SHEA, PATRICK J.
PUTNAM, KATE--W/KATE PUTNAM OSGOOD,[1]

O'SUILLEABHAIN, SEAN
O'SULLIVAN, VINCENT--[11]

OAK, PURUSHATTAM NAGESH
ARMARNATH--[1]
HANSRAJ BHATIA--[1]
PENO--[1]
UTTAM--[1]

OAKES, ELIZABETH
HALFENSTEIN, ERNEST--[1]

OAKES, VIRGINIA
OAKES, VANYA--[1]

OAKESHOTT, EDNA
PETERS, JOCELYN--[8]

OAKLEY, ERIC GILBERT
CAPON, PETER--[1][22][31]ENGLISH
GRAPHO--[1][22][31]ENGLISH
GREGSON, PAUL--[1][22][31]ENGLISH
SCOTT-MORLEY, A.--[8]

OAKSEY, JOHN GEOFFREY T.
AUDAX--[1][31]
MARLBOROUGH--[1]

OAKSON, PAT C.
TOLIVAR, ROBIN--W/LESLIE BISHOP,[9][21]ROM--
AV "IN LOVE'S FURY"

OANA, KATHERINE D.
OANA, KAY D.--[33]

OATES, JOYCE CAROL
FERNANDES, CAROL--[1]
SMITH, ROSAMOND--EQMM OCT '92,[34]MYS--
SIMON "LIVES OF TWINS" '87
ABRAHAMS "SOUL MATE" '89
DUTTON "NEMESIS" '90
DUTTON "SNAKE EYES" '92

OBENCHAIN, ELIZA CAROLINE
HALL, ELIZA CALVERT--[8]

OBER, NORMAN
WAYNE, RICK--V. BERCH LTR TO HUBIN '94,MYS--
MAG PRODUCTIONS "PLAY ROUGH!" '52

OBERDORF, CHARLES DONNELL
DONNELLY, ESMOND--[31]

OBERMEIER, SIEGFRIED
DE SCOTT, CARL--[39]GERMAN

OBERNEDER, FRIEDRICH
BERNEDER, O.--[39]GERMAN/JUV

OBERST, FREDERICK
ERICKSON, TOR--V. BERCH-BRNDN/
BC PSEUDS, BAE 22, P24

OBRECHT, JAS
CARLTON, JAY--[31]
FIVE, BILLY--[31]
FLEMING, REID--[31]
HOOPER, BIFF--[31]

OBREGON, IGNACIO M. O. Y
ACACIO, IPANDRO--[30]MEXICAN

OBRIST-STRENG, SIBYLLE
STEVENS, SIBYLLE--[39]GERMAN

OBSTFELD, RAYMOND
BISHOP, PIKE--[1][31]
FROST, JASON--[2][3][7][31]MYS,HP--
ZEBRA 'WARLORD' #1-6
"INVASION U.S.A."
KILGORE, ALEX--W/SEAN LAPORTE, V. BERCH LTR
TO HUBIN '94, MYS--
"EYE FOR EYE"
PENDLETON, DON--[3]MYS,HP--
GE "BLOODSPORT" '82
GE "FLESH WOUNDS" '83
GE "SAVANNAH SWINGSAW" '85
STEVENS, CARL--[3][29]MYS,HP--
GE "CENTAUR CONSPIRACY" '83
GE "RIDE OF THE RAZORBACK" '84]

OBUKHOVA, LIDIIA ALEKS.
OBUKHOVA, LYDIA--[7]SF--

OCHS, ARMIN
OCH, ARMIN--[39][40]GERMAN/MYS--
"DER DON VON ZURICH" '80 & 2 OTHERS

OCHSNER, NEAL
QUINT, NEAL--[34]MYS--
ZEBRA "AN AMERICAN SPY STORY" '89

ODAGA, ASENATH BOLE
KITUOMBA--[31][33]

ODELL, CAROL
ODELL, GILL--W/TRAVISS GILL,[1][8][22]ENGLISH

ODELL, WILLIAM
CARTER, NICK--[34]MYS-HP--
CHART "ASIAN MANTRAP" '78
CHART "NOWHERE WEAPON" '79
CHART "ULTIMATE CODE" '75

ODER, ARNOLD B.
ODINTSOV, ARNOLD BORISOV.--[1]

ODGERS, SALLY FARRELL
FARRELL, SALLY--[33]

ODIER, DANIEL
DELACORTA--[3][31][40]FRENCH/MYS--
SUMMIT "DIVA" '83
SUMMIT "LUNA" '84 & 3 MORE

ODOM, MEL[VIN LEWIS III]
ARNETT, JACK--G. COOK LTR '93, MYS,HP--
'BOOK OF JUSTICE' SERIES-2 BOOKS
?#5 & #6?
NORWOOD, WARREN C.--W/WARREN C. NORWOOD,[23],
COMPLETED FROM OUTLINE "TIME POLICE
#1-#3" '88-89
PENDLETON, DON--[34]MYS,HP--
GE "DEVIL FORCE" '87
GE "DEATH WIND" '89
GE "WAR BORN" '89
GE "ICE WOLF" '89
GE "WILD CARD" '90
GE "SIEGE" '90
WW "STONEY MAN #3"

OEDEMANN, GEORG
ARTUR, GEORG--[39]GERMAN/ADV/JUV

OEHLE, SOPHIE
SCHEFFLER, FRIEDEL--[39]GERMAN

OEHMKE, THOMAS HAROLD
PLAIN, WARREN--[1]

OELRICHS, BLANCHE MARIE L
STRANGE, MICHAEL--[1]

OELZE, HEDWIG MARIE
ROHDE, HEDWIG--[39]GERMAN

OERTEL, FRIEDRICH W.P.
HORN, W.O. v.--[39]GERMAN

OESTERREICH, AXEL EUGEN v
VON AMBESSER, AXEL--[39]GERMAN

OESTMAN, NAN INGER
INGER, NAN--[1]

OFFARD, CECIL
THORNTON, HAROLD--[1]

OFFERGELD, FRIEDHELM
INNSBRUCKER, MICHAEL--[39]GERMAN

OFFORD, LENORE GLEN
DURRANT, THEO--W/OTHERS,[18][31]MYS--
"MARBLE FOREST" '51
REPRT AS POPLB-"THE BIG FEAR"

OFFUTT, ANDREW J.
ANDREWS, JAY--AUTHOR PROVIDED--
VENICE "GANG SWAP"
"SEDUCTRESS"
"W.O.M.A.N."

OFFUTT, ANDREW J. [CONT]
ANDREWS, OPAL--AUTHOR PROVIDED--
SH "CELLAR OF DEGRADATION"
SH "CHAMBER OF PLEASURES"
SH "HER BROTHER LOVES BEST"
SH "MY DARLING NEPHEW"
SH "A LOVING FAMILY"
SH "FUN WITH AUNT TOMMY"
SH "LIKE A RABBIT"
SH "CHAIN ME AGAIN"
ANONYMOUS--AUTHOR PROVIDED--
VENICE "A MISS GUIDED"
BERRY, D. BRUCE--W/DOUGLAS B. BERRY, AUTHOR PROVIDED,[7]SF--
WARNER "GENETIC BOMB" '75
BROWN, JOE--AUTHOR PROVIDED--
VENICE "FOUR ON THE FLOOR"
CLEVE, JOHN--AUTHOR PROVIDED--
BRANDON, MIDWOOD, CARLYLE, BERKLEY & GROVE PRESS - 46 BKS
CLEVE, JOHN--W/D. BRUCE BERRY, AUTHOR PROVIDED,[7]SF--
BEE-LINE "PLEASURE US!" '71
CLEVE, JOHN JR.--AUTHOR PROVIDED--
'SPACEWAYS' SERIES
CLEVE, JOHN--W/ROLAND [J] GREEN, AUTHOR PROVIDED,[7]SF--
'SPACEWAYS' #15: "STARSHIP SAPPHIRE"
CLEVE, JOHN--W/ROBIN KINCAID, AUTHOR PROVIDED,[7]SF--
BERK 'SPACEWAYS'SERIES: #14 & #18
CLEVE, JOHN--W/VICTOR KOMAN, AUTHOR PROVIDED,[7]SF--
BERK 'SPACEWAYS' SERIES: #13 & #17
CLEVE, JOHN--W/GEORGE W. PROCTOR, AUTHOR PROVIDED[7]SF--
BERK 'SPACEWAYS' SERIES: #5, #7 & #10
CLEVE, JOHN--W/DWIGH V. SWAIN,[7]SF--
BERK 'SPACEWAYS'SERIES: #16
"PLANET MURDERER" '84
CLEVE, JOHN--W/G.C. EDMONDSON, AUTHOR PROVIDED,[7]SF--
BERK 'SPACEWAYS' SERIES: #12
CLEVE, JOHN--W/CANDICE & JACK HALDEMAN,[7]SF--
BERK 'SPACEWAYS': "ICEWORLD CONNECTION" '83
CORY, JACK--AUTHOR PROVIDED--
CA "BELLY TO BELLY"
CA "HIGH SCHOOL SWINGERS"
CA "DIFFERENT POSITIONS"
CA "8-WAY ORGY"
DENIS, JOHN--AUTHOR PROVIDED--
GROVE "PALACE OF VENUS"
MIDWD "SEX DOCTOR"
MIDWD "S AS IN SENSUOUS"
MIDWD "NEVER ENOUGH"
MIDWD "LOSING IT"
MIDWD "TIGHT FIT"
DOUGLAS, JEFF--W/JEFF DOUGLAS, AUTHOR PROVIDED, ADULT--
CA "BALLING MACHINE"
FAWKES, FARRAH--[11]
FOWLER, DREW--AUTHOR PROVIDED, ADULT--
VENICE "VIRGIN ISLE"
GILES, BAXTER--[11]
HAMLIN, ROSCOE--AUTHOR PROVIDED, ADULT--
"PLEASURE BENT"-RPRTS "BEHIND HER" DONE WITHOUT HIS OK
KREBB, JEREMY--AUTHOR PROVIDED--
1 BOOK - TITLE NOT KNOWN
MARSHALL, ALAN--AUTHOR PROVIDED, ADULT--
VENICE "BONDAGE BABES"
VENICE "SWAPPER TOWN"
MOREHEAD, JEFF--AUTHOR PROVIDED, ADULT--
CA - 21 BOOKS- 1 A RPRT AS BY 'ROSCOE HAMLIN'

OFFUTT, ANDREW J. [CONT]
WILLIAMS, J.X.--AUTHOR [PROVIDED, ADULT--
VENICE "SEX TOY"
VENICE "SEX PILL"
WINTER, TURK--AUTHOR PROVIDED, ADULT--
CA "A GIRL WITH TASTE"
CA "ASKING FOR IT"
CA "A DEGRADED HEROIN"
CA "SUBMISSION OF CLAUDINE"
CA "SLAVEWORLD"
CA "FAMILY BONDS"
CA "BEG FOR IT"
CA "FORMULA FOR SEX"
CA "A WEEK IN SAVANNAH"
WOODSON, JEFF--W/JEFF WOODSON, AUTHOR PROVIDED, ADULT--
CA "FIRES DOWN BELOW"

OGAN, GEORGE & MARGARET
CASTLE, LEE--[1][31][33]
KEEFER, CATHERINE--[1][31]
OGAN, M.G.--[1][32][33]MYS--
AHMM "LATE BRIDE" JUL '69
MSMM "WIFE KILLER" AUG '71
CC "NIGHT VOICE" FEB '74
EX "HELL SHIP" AUG '75
EP "MAN OVERBOARD" MAY '75
STOWE, ROSETTA--[1][9][21]ROM--
"CANNONS & ROSES"
"OUTLAW HEART

OGDEN, CHARLES KAY
OGDEN, C.K.--[1]

OGDEN, MEGAN
LINDHOLM, M[EGAN]--[2]

OGILVEY, ARTHUR JAMES
A.J.O.--[1][2]

OGLESBY, JOSEPH
FIRES, ALICIA--[1][31]
KAIN, MALCOLM--[1][31]
MULESKO, ANGELO--[1]
VALE, LEWIS--[1]
WOODSON, JEFF--[1]

OGNALL, LEOPOLD HORACE
CARMICHAEL, HARRY--[3][18][22][29]ENGLISH/MYS--
COLLINS "FLASHBACK" '64 & MORE
COLLINS "DEATH TRAP" '70
HOWARD, HARRY--[8][31]
HOWARD, HARTLEY--[2][18][29][34][40]MYS--
COLLINS "DEAD DRUNK" '74 & MORE '51-79

OHL, MAUDE
ANDREWS, ANNULET--[1]

OHLROGGE, ANNE K. STUART
STUART, ANNE--[7][9][10][26]ROM/SF--
HARL "BEWITCHING HOUR" '86
HARL "BLUE SAGE" & MORE

OHRLANDER, GUNNAR
GORMANDER, DOKTOR--[39]GERMAN

OLAUSSON, RUNE ERLAND
ALM, MONICA--[1]

OLBRICH, HANS
COTTON, JERRY--[39]GERMAN/MYS,HP

OLCOTT, ANTHONY & MARTHA
BRILL, TONI--V. BERCH LTR TO HUBIN '94,MYS--

OLD COYOTE, ELNORA A.
OLD COYOTE, SALLY--[8]
WRIGHT, ELNORA A.--[8]
WRIGHT, SALLY--[8]

OLD, PHYLLIS MURIEL ELIZ.
SHIEL-MARTIN--[8]

OLDEN, MARC
BONNER, TERRY NELSON--[21]ROM,HP--
'AUSTRALIAN/NZ' SERIES:
"THE UNVANQUISHED"
HAWKES, ROBERT--[3][29][40]MYS--
SIGN "DEATH SONG" '75
SIGN "KILL FOR IT" '75 & 7 MORE '73-5

OLDFIELD, CLAUDE H.
HOUGHTON, CLAUDE--[2][3][22][23]MYS/SF--
"NEIGHBORS" '27
HUTCH "CLOCK TICKS" '54 & MORE '27-56

OLDMEADOW, ERNEST JAMES
DOWNMAN, FRANCIS--[8][23]SF--
"THE TOWN TOMORROW: FIVE & TWENTY BROADCASTS" '37

OLDMEADOW, ERNEST JAMES
OLDMEADOW, E.J.--[1]

OLDS, ELIZABETH FAGG
FAGG, ELIZABETH--[31]

OLEA, MARIA FLORENCIA
VARAS, FLORENCIA--[1]

OLEHEWITZ, L.M.
VERNE, JULES--[32]MYS--
ST "ETERNAL ADAM" MAR '57
TR "ORDEAL OF DR. TRIFULGAS" JUL '57

OLEKSY, WALTER
OLESKY, WALTER--[33]

OLENDORF, WILLIAM
OLENDORF, BILL--[31]--
TOURIST PR, ARCHITECTURE

OLENIUS, ELSA VICTORIA
BERGIUS, ELSA BRITT--[1]

OLEPHANT, MRS.
DUNSMUIR, AMY--[1]

OLEYAR, RITA BALKEY
BALKEY, RITA--[1][9][26]ROM--
"TEARS OF GLORY"
"PRINCE OF PASSION" & 5 MORE

OLIPHANT, MARGARET
OLIPHANT, MRS.--[11]

OLIVEN, FRITZ
RIDEAMUS--[39]GERMAN

OLIVER, AMY ROBERTA
ONIONS, BERTA--[8][9]ROM
RUCK, AMY ROBERTA--[1]
RUCK, BERTA--[1][31]

OLIVER, DORIS M.
HUGHES, ALISON--[8]

OLIVER, FREDERICK S.
PHYLOS THE TIBETIAN--[2][31]

OLIVER, GEORGE
ONIONS, OLIVER--[2][11][22]MYS--

OLIVER, GERTRUDE KENT
CARR, KENT--[1]

OLIVER, JOHN RATHBONE
ROLAND, JOHN--[1][34]MYS--
BLACKWOOD "ADVENTURES OF A CIGARETTE" '15

OLIVER, PATRICIA
FONTAYNE, OLIVIA--[26]ROM--
"LADY SAMANTHA'S CHOICE"
"RELUCTANT DUCHESS"
"SCANDALOUS WAGER"

OLIVER, SIMEON
NUTCHUK--[1]

OLIVER, SYMMES CHADWICK
OLIVER, CHAD--[23]WEST/SF--
PYR "GIANTS IN THE DUST" '76
CROWN "UNEARTHLY NEIGHBORS" '84 &MORE

OLIVER-SMITH, MARTHA BAC.
BACON, MARTHA--[7]SF--
ATLANTIC MONTHLY "MOTH MANOR" '78

OLIVEROS TOVAR, MIGUEL
BRONKO, MIKE--JEAN F. LE DEIST LTR '93
KANATA, JAY--JEAN F. LE DEIST LTR '93
LUGAR, KEITH--JEAN F. LE DEIST LTR '93
LUGER, KEITH--JEAN F. LE DEIST LTR '93
ROMANO, MIGUEL--JEAN F. LE DEIST LTR '93

OLJELUND, THEA
ROOS, REBECCA--[29]MYS

OLLESSON, OLLE
UNENGE, JAN--[29]MYS

OLNER, ARNE
AXE, SVERKER--[29]MYS--
4 BOOKS '33-34

OLNERS, ARNE
AXE, SVEN--[29]MYS
OLNERS, KJENNE--[29]MYS--
DOLLAR BK #16 "NATTKLUBBMORDET" '56
OLNERS, SAM--[29]MYS--
DOLLAR BK #26 "GIFTSPEGELN" '57
SALDONS, PER--[29]MYS

OLSEN, ALFRED JOHANNES
OLSEN, BOB--[2][11][23]SF--
AMZ "FOUR DIMENSIONAL ROLLER"

OLSEN, IB SPANG
DETINE, PADRE--W/ERIK E. FREDRIKSEN [1][31][33]

OLSEN, JOHN EDWARD [JACK]
RHOADES, JONATHAN--[22]AMERICAN

OLSEN, THEODORE VICTOR
GARLAND, BENNETT--W/BRIAN W. GARFIELD, [18]WEST--
MON 391 "HIGH STORM" '63
STARK, JOSHUA--[16][22][28]WEST/ADULT--
DBLDY "BREAK THE YOUNG LAND" '64
STORM, CHRISTOPHER--[1][22][28]ADULT--
BEAC B683X "YOUNG DUKE" '63
BEAC B745X "THE SEX REBELS" '64
BEAC B852 "CAMPUS MOTEL" '65

OLSEN, THEODORE VICTOR [CONT]
WILLOUGHBY, CASS--[1][28]ADULT--
BEAC "AUTUMN PASSION" '66

OLSEN, THOMAS CARL M.
MORRELL, JOHN--[1]

OLSHESKI, GAIL
HENLEY, GAIL--[1]

OLSON, EUGENE E.
NORMAN, ERIC--[11]
STEIGER, BRAD--[1][2][32]MYS--
GU "NERVOUS HOODLUM" MAY '59
TR "MAKE LOVE & DIE" MAY '61
TR "WIFE SWAP PARTY" AUG '61
AHMM "SUNTAN" NOV '64
AHMM "TEACHER OF THE YEAR" APR '65
SA "DANGLING BUTTON" JUL '66
[W/JERRY TWEDT]
SA "SYDELLE" APR '67

OLSON, HERBERT VINCENT
OLSEN, HERB--[8]

OLSSON, JAN OLOF
JOLO--[29]MYS--
BONNIER "DE TRE FRAN HAPARANDA" '67
BONNIER "DE TRE MOT PETROGRAD" '73
BONNIER "EVIGA FOLJESLAGARE" '79

OLTMAN, VANESSA
GRANT, VANESSA--[9][26]ROM--
"TAKEOVER AMN"
"AWAKENING DREAMS" & OTHERS

OLWITZ-TITZE, EVELYN
HAGEN, EVELYN--[39]GERMAN/JUV

OMAN, CAROLA MARY A.
LENANTON, C.--[1][22][33]
LENANTON, CAROLA MARY A.O--[1]

ONADIPE, [N] KOLAWOLE
KOLON, NITA--[31]
ONADIPE, KOLA--[31]

ONEAL, ELIZABETH
ONEAL, ZIBBY--[1][33]

ONIONS, OLIVER
OLIVER, GEORGE--[1][3][7]--
LEGALIZED TO 'OLIVER'

ONO, RYUNOSUKE
RANCE, JOSEPH--W/TREVOR HOYLE & JUNYA SATO,
V. BERCH LTR TO HUBIN '94, MYS--
SOUVENIR "BULLET TRAIN" '80

OOSTERMAN, GORDON
EASTMAN, G. DON--[31]

OPATOVSKY, JOSEPH
OPATOSHU, JOSEPH--[1]

OPDYCKE, JOHN BAKER
OPDYKE, OLIVER--[1]

OPENSHAW, G.H.
GALE, JOHN--[1]
SHAW, DICK--[1]
SHAW, DUSTIN--[1]
STERN, DUNCAN--[1]

OPFERMANN, HANS-CARL
ARUBA, FERDINAND--[39]GERMAN/JUV

OPPENHEIM, E. PHILLIPS
PARTRIDGE, ANTHONY--[3][5][18][29]MYS--
HODDER "GHOSTS OF SOCIETY" '08
WARD "PASSERS-BY" '11 & MORE

OPPENHEIM, JOAN
FLEISCHER, JANE--[31]

OPPENHEIM, JOANNE
JASSEM, KATE--[31]

OPPENHEIM, RALPH
WALLACE, ROBERT--A. TONIK-ECHOES #17,HP--

OPPENHEIMER, CARLOTA
CARLOTA--[8]

OPPENHEIMER, FRANCIS J.
OPP, FRANCIS--[1]

OPPENHEIMER, JOEL LESTER
AQUARIAN--[22]
HAMMER, JACOB--[31]

OPPERMANN, HERMANN
HARRIS, RINGO--[39]GERMAN/WEST

ORAGE, ALFRED JAMES
A.R.O.--[8]

ORBISON, OLIVE
ORBISON, KECK--W/MAUDE KECK,[1][3][22]MYS--
WSB "KEY TO THE CASE" '29

ORD, IRENE
FAIRFAX, KATE--[9][21][26]ROM--
"SWEETFIRE"

ORD, LEWIS REDMON
ONE OF THE BUNGLERS--[1]

ORD-HUME, ARTHUR W.J.G.
HUME, ARTHUR W.J.G.--[31]

ORDE-WARD, F.W.
WILLIAMS, F. HARALD--[8]

ORGA, IRFAN
RIZA, ALI--[8]

ORGAN, JOHN
ASHLEY, GRAHAM--[1][22][31]ENGLISH
FARRELL, DESMOND--[1][22][31]ENGLISH

ORGEL, DORIS
ADELBERG, DORIS--[1][31]][33]

ORGILL, DOUGLAS [W]
GILMAN, J.D.--W/JACK FISHMAN,[29][31][34]MYS--
SVNR "KG 200" '77

ORIOLO, JOSEPH
ORIOLO, JOE--[33]

ORLAND, CLAUDE
ROY, CLAUDE--[22]FRENCH

ORLOFF, A.H.
HENRY, ALAN--V. BERCH-GM PSEUDS, PP 33,WEST--
GM 344 "WAGONNTRAIN WOMAN '53

ORLOVITZ, GIL
CLUBB, STACEY--JACK MOSKOVITZ-PP 19, P6,[1]ADULT--
SCLS 95159 "TRAP OF LESBOS" '70
BEAC 827 "YOUNG LUST"
BEAC 1043 "HOT BLOOD OF YOUTH"

ORLOWSKI, JERZY HENRYK
ORLEV, URI--[1]

ORME, EVE
DAY, IRENE--[8]

ORME, K.
CLIFFORD, MARTIN--[1]HP--

ORMES, ZELDA J.
ORMES, JACKIE--[33]

ORMHAUG, ELLA GRIFFITHS
WESTERHAM, JULIA--[3]MYS--
"WEB OF MURDER" '70

ORN, WERNER AUGUST
SELMERGEDETH, HARALD--[29]MYS--
"MIN FORSTA BRAGD" '04
"INSPEKTORN PA SITTALA" '20

ORNILF, GUNNAR
BORG, BERTIL--[29]MYS
BJERKE, ANNA--[29]MYS
DEBBS, LEO--[29]MYS--
ANDERSON "RANMORDETS MYSTERIUM '16
FORSMAN,, GUNNER--[29]MYS

ORNULF, HILDING KONSTANT.
BROG, BERTIL--[29]MYS
HARRIS, TOM--[29]MYS--
DBLDY "DEN SISTA CHEKEN" '18
DBLDY "SPADER DAM" '18
ORNULF, GUNNAR--[29]MYS
PARKER, FRED--[29]MYS--
11 NOVELS '18-22
TRAHNA, EBBA--[29]MYS
TROTTE, THURE--[29]MYS

ORR, ALICE HARRON
ALLISON, ELIZABETH--[9][21][26]ROM--
"DANCE OF DESIRE"
STARR, MORGANA--[9][21]ROM--
"NOTHING SHORT OF A MIRACLE"

ORR, KATHLEEN [KATHY]
GARNER, KATHLEEN--[9]ROM
ORR, KATHY [KATHLEEN]--[9][21]ROM--
"SEDUCTIVE DECEIVER"
"DRIFTER'S REVENGE" & MORE
SPENCER, CATHERINE--[9][21][26]ROM--
HARL 296 "FIRES OF SUMMER"
HARL 910 "A LASTING KIND OF LOVE" & MORE

ORRMONT, ARTHUR
HUNTER, ANSON--V. BERCH-MON PSEUDS, BAE 9,[1]ADULT--
MON MA325 "KING OF FREE LOVERS" '62

ORSAT, JEAN-FRANCOIS
D'ASTOR, JEAN--[3]MYS--
"LE GOELAND" '69
"LE PIEGE D'OR" '62 & MORE

ORSZAGH, PAVOL
HVIEZDOSLAV--[22]SLOVAK

ORTEA, FRANCISCO CARLOS
FRANCK, DR.--[1]

ORTEGA, ISABEL
LEONARD, PHYLLIS--[9][21][26]ROM, 6 NOVELS
LEONARD, PHYLLIS G.--[9][21][26]ROM--
"MARIPOSA"
"TARNISHED ANGEL" & MORE

ORTH, JOHN
CUMMINGS, RICHARD--[1]

ORTH, RICHARD MAURICA
GARDNER, RICHARD--[1][7]--
LEGALIZED TO 'GARDNER'--
POCK "MANDRILL" '75

ORTHOFER, PETER
HAGEL, JAN--[39]GERMAN
LA POINTE, PIERROT--[39]GERMAN
NEBEL, CASPAR--[39]GERMAN

ORTIZ DE MONTELLANO, B.
ORTIZ DE MONTELLANO--[1]

ORTIZ, ELIZABETH LAMBERT
LAMBERT, ELIZABETH--[1][31]

ORTMAN, E. JAN
ORTMAN, ELMER JOHN--[1]

ORTNER, TONI
ORTNER-ZIMMERMAN, TONI--[31] 9 BOOKS '74-80

ORTON, JAMES
ALSTOK--[1]

ORTON, JOHN KINGSLEY
ORTON, JOE--[3][7]MYS/SF--
BLOND "HEAD TO TOE" '71
METHUEN "ORTON DIARIES" '86
WELTHORPE, EDNA--[8]

ORTON, THORA MARGARET
COLSON, THORA--[1]

ORWID, WLADYSLAW
DANILOWSKI, GUSTAW--[22]POLISH

ORWIG, SARA
LOGAN, DAISY--[9][21][26]ROM--
"RECKLESS LONGING"
"SOUTHERN PLEASURES"
"SWEET BLISS"

ORZECHOWSKI, PETER
DROZZA, PETER--[39]GERMAN

OSBERT, REUBEN
OSBORN, REUBEN--[8]

OSBORN, LINCOLN
OSBORN, LYNN--[34]MYS--
AY "EASY MONEY" '26

OSBORNE, CHARLES H.C.
HUMFREY, C.--[1][22][31]ENGLISH

OSBORNE, DOROTHY G. YEO
ARMOUR, GLADYS--[1][8]
ARTHUR, GLADYS--[31]

OSBORNE, JESSIE HILL
FORD, JESSIE [HILL]--[9][21][26]ROM--
"BURNING WOMAN"
"THE RAIDER" & 3 MORE

OSBORNE, MARGARET ELLEN
OSBORNE, MAGGIE--[1][21]ROM--
"ALEXA"
"YANKEE PRINCESS" & MORE
ST. GEORGE, MARGARET--[9][26]ROM--
HARL 142 "WINTER MAGIC"
HARL 325 "AMERICAN PIE" & OTHERS

OSBURN, MICKY K.
MAXWELL, MARY--W/JEN M. HEATON,[26]ROM--
"DOUBLECROSS"
"PLAYING WITH FIRE"

OSENBURG, RICHARD
LAULER, MICHAEL--[1][2][11]

OSER, MARILYN
KENDALL, JACK--W/MARY L. KALLMAN, V. BERCH
LTR TO HUBIN '94, MYS--
AV "PLAYING FOR KEEPS" '89

OSGOOD, KATE PUTNAM
PUTNAM, KATE--W/PATRICK J. O'SHEA,[1]

OSLER, ERIC RICHARD
DICK, T.--[3]MYS--
LONG "DARK BEFORE DAWN" '35

OSMAN, ANDREW [P.K.]
REID, PHILIP--W/RICHARD INGRAMS,
[8][29][34]MYS--
CAPE "HARRIS IN WONDERLAND" '73

OSMUN, THOMAS EMBLY
AYRES, ALFRED--[1]

OSOFISAN, FEMI
LAUNKA, OKINBA--[31]

OSORIO, MIGUEL ANGEL
BARBA-JACOB, PORFIRIO--[22]COLOMBIAN

OSSANA, SUSAN B.
CHRISTIE, SUSANNA--W/KRISTIN BURTON,
[9][21][26]ROM--
"CLOSE ENCOUNTER"
"EDEN'S TEMPTATION" & MORE

OSSENBRINK, WILHELM
BOELE, WILHELM--[39]GERMAN

OSSOLI, SARAH MARGARET F.
FULLER, MARGARET--[31][33]

OSTEN-SACKEN, KLAUS v DER
WOLFF, KLAUS--[39]GERMAN/JUV

OSTER, JERRY
PERRY, MAX--LACHMAN-EASTER LIST '93, MYS--

OSTERGAARD, GEOFFREY
GERARD, GASTON--[8]

OSTLERE, GORDON STANLEY
GORDON, RICHARD--[1][3][31]MYS--
HM "MEDICAL WITNESS" '71 & MORE

OSTLERE, MARY
GORDON, MARY--[8]

OSTMAN, NAN & PETER
INGER, PETER--[29]MYS--
NORST "MORDANDE RECENSION" '53

OSTRANDER, ISABEL EGENTON
BURNS, WILLIAM J.--[3]MYS--
WATT "THE CREVICE" '15
CHIPPERFIELD, ROBERT FOX--[1]
CHIPPERFIELD, ROBERT ORR--[2][3][11]
[22][29]MYS--6 NOVELS '19-24
FOX, DAVID--[2][3][7][22][29]MYS--
McBRIDE "MAN WHO CONVICTED HIMSELF' '20
& 2 MORE
GRANT, DOUGLAS--[3][22][29]MYS--
WATT "BOOTY" '19
WATT "ANYTHING ONCE" '20 & 3 MORE

OSTWALD, THOMAS
WATSON, DR. JOHN--[39]GERMAN/MYS/JUV

OSTY, LUCIEN PIERRE JEAN
LARTEGUY, JEAN--[1]

OSUSKY, STEFAN
ARGUS--[31]

OTT, VIRGINIA
OTT, MAGGIE GLENN--[1]

OTT-KLUGE, HEIDELORE
KLUGE, HIDELORE,--[39]GERMAN/SF

OTTARSON, FRANKLIN A.
BAYARD--[1]

OTTEN, CAROLE CARD
CARLYLE, TENA--W/ELLEN LYLE TABER, ROM--
"BRIDE OF THE NIGHT"
"CAPTIVE TREASURE"
"RUNAWAY HEART"

OTTESON, THEA TAUBER
BANK-JENSEN--[22]DANISH

OTTILIE LUISE, PAULINE
CARMEN, SYLVIA--[31]

OTTO, HERMANN
LAUTERBACH, HERMANN O.--[39]GERMAN

OTTUM, ROBERT K.
OTTUM, BOB--[7][23]SF--
"ALL RIGHT, EVERYBODY OFF THE PLANET" '72

OUROUSSOW, EUGENIE
LEHOVICH, EUGENIE O.--[31]

OURSLER, GRACE P.
MACY, DORA--[1][3]MYS--
"BRETANO'S NIGHTMARE" '30
PERKINS, GRACE--[1][11]

OURSLER, WILL[IAM C.]
GALLAGHER, GALE--W/MARGARET SCOTT,
[3][22][31]MYS--
"I FOUND HIM DEAD" '47
"CHORD IN CRIMSON" '49
MARINO, NICK--[3][31]MYS--
HOLT "ONE-WAY STREET" '52

OURSLER, [C] FULTON
ABBOTT, ANTHONY--[2][3][5][18]MYS--
8 NOVELS '30-43
FOUNTAIN, ARNOLD--V. BERCH RVW '93,
FRIKELL, SAMRI--[2][11]

OURTNEY, NICHOLAS PIERS
HANMER, DAVINA--[1][31]

OUSELEY, GIDEON JASPER R.
DISCIPLE OF THE MASTER, A--[8]
THEOSOPHO & ELLORA--[2]

OUST, GAIL
TURNER, ELIZABETH--[9][21][26]ROM--
"SWEET POSSESSION"
"FORBIDDEN FIRES" & MORE

OUSTABASIDAS, PETER
P.I., O.--[13]AUSTRALIAN

OUTLAW-SHALLIT, LOUISE L.
ASHBY, JULIET--[21][26]ROM--
"ONE MAN FOREVER"
"MIDNITE LOVER"
"DREAMS OF PASSION"
CANADAY, LEE--[21][26]ROM--
"VICTIM OF LOVE"

OVED, M.
GOOD, EDWARD--[22]

OVERHOLSER, WAYNE D.
DANIELS, JOHN S.--[22][28][31]WEST--
13 NOVEWLS '52-69
LEIGHTON, LEE--W/CHAD MERRIMAN,[1][28]WEST--
BAL "COLORADO GOLD" '58
LEIGHTON, LEE--W/LEWIS B. PATTEN,
[19][22][28]WEST--
BAL "TOMAHAWK" '58
LEIGHTON, LEE--[1][31]
MORGAN, MARK--[1][8][28]--
LION 136 "FIGHTING MAN" '53
POWELL, EMMETT J.--HAWK/BRINEY INTRVW '93--
RAINE, WILLIAM MACLEOD--[19][28]WEST--
COMPLTD - HODDER "HIGH GRASS VALLEY" '55
AFTER RAINE'S DEATH
ROBERTS, WAYNE--[1][28]WEST--
BB 1925 "SILENT RIVER" '60
STEVENS, DAN J.--V. BERCH-MON PSEUDOS,BAE 9,
[16][22][28]WEST--
LION 50 "OREGON TRUNK" '50
AVALON "WILD HORSE RANGE" '51
PERMA M3033 "BLOOD MONEY" '56
MON 383 "HANGMAN'S MESA" '59
& 10 OTHERS '50-73
WAYNE, JOSEPH--W/LEWIS B. PATTEN,[28]WEST--
DELL "THE GUN & THE LAW"
DELL "SHOWDOWN AT STONY CREEK"

OVERY, JILLIAN P.J.
MARTIN, GIL--L. ROBBINS LTR MAR '94,[8]
OVERY, MARTIN--L. ROBBINS LTR MAR '94,[8]

OVSTEDAL, BARBARA
DOUGLAS, BARBARA--[3][9][17][31]MYS--
"FAIR WIND OF LOVE"
LAKER, ROSALIND--[3][9][26]MYS/ROM--
HALE "FAIR WINDS OF LOVE" '74
HALE "SMUGGLER'S BRIDE" '76
PAUL, BARBARA--[9][17][32][34]MYS--
MO "THE FAVOR" JUL '76
MacD"CURSE OF HALEWOOD" '76
MacD "THE FRENCHWOMAN" '77 & 2 OTHERS
"A WILD CRY OF LOVE" '78

OWAIN, OWAIN
HERCO--[1]
HUMPHREYS, JOHN--[1]

OWBRIDGE, EILEEN
ARBOR, JANE--[17]ROM

OWEN, FRANK
ABNER, GERALD--[1]
BRAITHWAITE, RAYMOND--[1]
CATO--W/PETER D. HOWARD & MICHAEL FOOTE,
[1][22]ENGLISH
KENT, RICHARD--[1][2][16]
TOM, HUNG LONG--[1][2][11][16]
WILLIAMS, ROSWELL--[1][2][16]

OWEN, GARNET
OLIVER, GAY--[1]

OWEN, HARRY COLLINSON
ADDISON, HUGH--[1][2][11][22][23]--
"BATTLE OF LONDON" '23
COLLINSON, OWEN--[1]

OWEN, JACK
DYKES, JACK--[1][31]

OWENS, IRIS
DAIMLER, HARRIET--C. ECKHOFF SLST,
[8][14]ADULT--
OLYM TC-61 "WOMAN" '65
OLYM TC-2217 "THE WOMAN THING" 68
OLYM OB#502 "DARLING" '68
OLYM TC-2218 "THE ORGANIZATION" '68

OWENS, THELMA
GRAFTON, ANN--[1][31]

OWENS, VIRGINIA STEM
ADAMS, EUGENIA--[1]

OXFORD SFI GROUP
ZOOL, M.H.--[7]SF--
SHARED BY WRITERS IN GROUP

OXLEY, DOROTHY [ANNE]
BROWN, DOROTHY--[1][31]

OXLEY, GILLIAN
VINE, KERRY--[9][21][26]ROM--
"ALPINE IDYLL"

OXLEY, WILLIAM
HARDY, JASON--[31]

OXMAN, PHILIP
PEACHUM, THOMAS--[8][14]ADULT--
OLYM TC#301 "THE WATCHER & THE WATCHED" '67

OZAKI, MILTON K.
SABER, ROBERT O.--[22][34]--
HAN 96"BLACK DARK MURDERS" '49
HAN 108 "AFFAIR OF THE FRIGID BLONDE" '50
HAN 124 "SCENTED FLESH" '51
HAN 130 "DOVE" '51
JUBILEE "TOO CUTE TO KILL"
PHAN 502 "DEADLY LOVER" '51
PHAN 510 "MURDER DOLL" '52
PHAN 512 "NO WAY OUT" '52
ORIGN 722 "CITY OF SIN" '52
PHAN "MURDER HONEYMOON" ca '53
GRAP 90 "TOO YOUNG TO DIE" '54
PHAN "MARKED FOR MURDER" ca '55
PHAN "MODEL FOR MURDER" ca '55
GRAP 99 "SUCKER BAIT" '55
GRAP 111 "A DAME CALLED MURDER" '55
GRAP 123 "A TIME FOR MURDER" '56
SHANE, MARK--PPCC#7,[34]MYS--
MORING "BORROWED TIME" '55
RPRT OF "NO WAY OUT" '52

OZBEKHAN, ANNE BINKLEY
BINKLEY, ANNE--[1]
RAND, ANNE--[1]"

PAALBORG, PAUL B.
BRADFORD, LAURA--[21][26]ROM--
"PLAYERS"

PAANANEN, ELOISE KATHER.
ENGLE, ELOISE--[31]

PACHTER, HENRY M.
RABASSEIRE, HENRY--[22]GERMAN-AMERICAN

PACHTER, JOSH
THORPE, CHARLES J.--LACHMAN LIST '93,MYS--

PACKER, JOY
LADY PACKER--[22]SOUTH AFRICAN

PADGETT, RON
DANGERFIELD, HARLAN--[8]
VEITCH, TOM--[8]

PADLEY, ARTHUR
WINN, PATRICK--[8][32]MYS--
SUS "REFLECTION OF ANGER" MAR '61
SUS "RUNAWAY" APR '61

PADLEY, WALTER
MARCUS, AURELIUS--[8]

PAFFRATH, ALFRED
FORSTER, A.W.P.--[39]GERMAN

PAGAZA, ARCADIO
MEONIO, CLEARCO--[30]MEXICAN

PAGE, EVELYN
SCARLETT, ROGER--W/DOROTHY BLAIR,
[3][22]AMERICAN/MYS--5 NOVELS '30-2

PAGE, GERALD W.
GRINDLE, CARLETON--[2][11][16][31]
JONES, HAROLD--[1][31]
LEE, ERIC--[1][31]
PEMBROKE, KENNETH--[1][2][11][16]
TIFTON, LEO--[1][2]
WILBURN, LEN--W/JERRY BURGE,[2]

PAGE, GROVER JR.
MCGINNIS, K.K.--[22]AMERICAN

PAGE, JAMES KEENA JR.
PAGE, JAKE--[3]MYS--
BOBBS "SHOOT THE MOON" '79

PAGE, NORVELL W[OOTEN]
CRAIG, RANDOLPH--[2][7][23][37]SF--
NWP "CITY CONDEMNED TO HELL" '39
NWP "SATAN'S INCUBATOR" '39
OCSC "CITY CONDEMNED TO HELL" FEB '39
& OTHER 'SKULL KILLER' STORIES
POGE, N. WOOTEN--[11][37]MYS--
DETECTIVE TALES - APR '36
STOCKBRIDGE, GRANT--JAMES-PULP #13-
PB DETECTIVE, PP 31,[2][3][7][23]MYS,HP--
SPD "WINGS OF BLACK DEATH" DEC '33
SPD "BUILDER OF THE BLACK EMPIRE" OCT '34
SPD "CORPSE CARGO" JUL '34
SPD "CITY OF FLAMING SHADOWS" JAN '34
SPD "MAD HORDE " MAY '34
SPD "PRINCE OF THE RED LOOTERS" AUG '34
SPD "REIGN OF THE SILVER TERROR" SEPT '34
SPD "DEATH'S CRIMSON JUGGERNAUT" NOV '34
SPD "RED DEATH RAIN" DEC '34

PAGE, NORVELL W[OOTEN] [CONT]
STOCKBRIDGE, GRANT [CONT]
SPD "SATAN'S DEATH BLAST" JUN '34
SPD "EMPIRE OF DOOM" FEB '34
SPD "CITADEL OF HELL" MAR '34
SPD "DEATH REIGN OF VAMPIRE KING" NOV '35
SPD "HORDES OF RED BUTCHER"JUN '35
SPD "CITY DESTROYER" JAN '35
SPD "PAIN EMPEROR" FEB '35
SPD "OVERLORD OF THE DAMNED" OCT '35
SPD "FLAME MASTER" MAR '35
SPD "SLAVES OF THE CRIME MASTER" APR '35
SPD "REIGN OF THE DEATH FIDDLER" MAY '35
SPD "KING OF THE RED KILLERS" SEPT '35
SPD "DRAGON LORD OF THE UNDERWORLD" JUL '35
SPD "MASTER OF DEATH MADNESS" AUG '35
SPD "EMPEROR OF THE YELLOW DEATH" DEC '35
SPD "MAYOR OF HELL" JAN '36
SPD "SLAVES OF THE MURDER
SYNDICATE" FEB '36
SPD "CHOLERA KING" APR '36
SPD "GREEN GLOBES OF DEATH" MAR '36
SPD "SLAVES OF THE DRAGON" MAY '36
SPD "LEGIONS OF MADNESS" JUN '36
SPD "LABORATORY OF THE DAMNED" JUL '36
SPD "SATAN'S SIGHTLESS LEGIONS" AUG '36
SPD "COMING OF THE TERROR" SEPT '36
SPD "DEVIL'S DEATH DWARFS" OCT '36
SPD "MAN WHO RULED IN HELL" JUL '37
SPD "MACHINE GUNS OVER THE WHITE
HOUSE" SEPT '37
SPD "MASTER OF FLAMING HORDE" NOV '37
SPD "GREY HORDE CREEPS" MAR '38
SPD "LEGIONS OF ACCURSED LIGHT" JAN '38
SPD "CITY OF WHISPERING DEATH" APR '38
SPD "EMPEROR FROM HELL" JUL '38
SPD "CITY THAT PAID TO DIE" SEPT '38
SPD "SPIDER AT BAY" OCT '38
SPD "SCOURGE OF BLACK LEGIONS" NOV '38
SPD "CLAWS OF GOLDEN DRAGON" JAN '39
SPD "SILVER DEATH RAIN" MAR '39
SPD "KING OF THE FLESHLESS LEGIONS" MAY '39
SPD "RULE OF MONSTER MEN" JUN '39
SPD "SPIDER & SLAVES OF HELL" JUL '39
SPD "SPIDER & FIRE GOD" AUG '39
SPD "SPIDER & EYELESS LEGIONS" OCT '39
SPD "SPIDER & FACELESS MEN" NOV '39
SPD "SATAN'S MURDER MACHINES" DEC '39
SPD "HELL'S SALES MGR" FEB '40
SPD "SLAVES OF THE LAUGHING DEATH" MAR '40
SPD "SPIDER & WAR EMPEROR" MAY '40
SPD "JUDGEMENT OF THE DAMNED" JUN '40
SPD "PIRATES FROM HELL" AUG '40
SPD "COUNCIL OF EVIL" OCT '40
SPD "SPIDER & HIS HOBO ARMY" NOV '40
SPD "SPIDER & JEWELS OF HELL" DEC '40
SPD "HARBOR OF NAMELESS DEAD" JAN '41
SPD "SPIDER & SLAVE DOCTOR" FEB '41
SPD "SPIDER & SONS OF SATAN" MAR '41
SPD "SLAVES OF BURNING BLADE" APR '41
SPD "DEVIL'S PAYMASTER" MAY '41
SPD "BENEVOLENT ORDER OF DEATH" JUN '41
SPD "MURDER'S BLACK PRINCE" JUL '41
SPD "SPIDER & SCARLET SURGEON" AUG '41
SPD "SPIDER & DEATHLESS ONE" SEPT '41
SPD "SATAN'S SEVEN SWORDSMAN" OCT '41
SPD "VOLUNTEER CORPSE BRIGADE" NOV '41
SPD "CRIME LABORATORY" DEC '41
SPD "DEATH & THE SPIDER" JAN '42
SPD "MURDER'S LEGIONAIRES" FEB '42
SPD "GENTLEMAN FROM HELL" MAR '42
SPD "SLAVES OF THE RING" APR '42
SPD "SPIDER & DEATH PIPER" MAY '42
SPD "REVOLT OF THE UNDERWORLD" JUN '42
SPD "RETURN OF THE RACKET KINGS" JUL '42
SPD "FANGS OF THE DRAGON" AUG '42
SPD "HELL ROLLS ON THE HIGHWAY" SEPT '42

PAGE, NORVELL W[OOTEN] [CONT]
STOCKBRIDGE, GRANT [CONT]
SPD "ARMY OF THE DAMNED" OCT '42
SPD "SECRET CITY OF CRIME" FEB '43
SPD "ZARA: MASTER OF MURDER" NOV '42
SPD "SPIDER & FLAME KING" DEC '42
SPD "HOWLING DEATH" JAN '43
SPD "RECRUIT FOR SPIDER LEGION" MAR '43
SPD "SIPDER & MAN FROM HELL" JUN '43
SPD "CRIMINAL HORDE" AUG '43
SPD "SPIDER & HELL'S FACTORY" OCT '43

PAGE, PATRICIA KATHLEEN
CAPE, JUDITH--[2][7][31]SF--
"THE SUN & THE MOON" '44
IRWIN, P.K.--[8][31]

PAGE, THOMAS
WALKER, THOMAS P.--[3]MYS--
SEAVIEW "RECALL" '79

PAGE, WALTER HINES
WORTH, NICHOLAS--[8][22]AMERICAN

PAGE, WILLIAM REESE
PAGE, BILL--[7]SF--
NON-FICT

PAGET, FRANCES EDWARD
WILLIAM CHURN OF STAFFDSH--FANT. LIT. FOR CHILDREN & YOUNG ADULTS, RUTH NADELMAN

PAGET, GEORGE CHARLES H.V
ANGLESEY, MARQUESS OF--[1][22]ENGLISH-NORTH WELSH

PAGET, VIOLET
LEE, VERNON--[2][7][22][34]ENGLISH/SF--
UNWIN "PENELOPE BRANDLING" '03
GROVE "SNAKE LADY & OTHER STORIES" '54

PAGNINI, ANTONIO LUCA
ELEUTERO--[22]ITALIAN

PAHZ, CHERYL SUZANNE
GOLDFEDER, CHERYL--[31][33]
PAZ, ZAN--[33]

PAHZ, JAMES ALON
GOLDFEDER, JAMES--[31]
GOLDFEDER, JIM--[31][33]
PAZ, A.--[33]

PAIMISANO, LUIGI
PALM, GENE--[2]

PAINE, HARRIET ELIZA
CHESTER, ELIZA--[1]

PAINE, LAURAN BOSWORTH
AINSBURY, RAY--[1][28]--
WORLD "WHEN THE MOON RAN WILD" '62
AINSBURY, ROY--[1][23][28]SF-
AINSWORTH, RAY--[1]
AINSWORTHY, ROY--[1][7][28]SF--
HALE "FOCOLOR" '73
ALLEN, CLAY--[1][28]WEST--
13 HALE NOVELS '65-90
ALMONTE, ROSA--[1][28]ROM--
HALE "LOVE IN THE CLOUDS" '67
ANDREWS, A.A.--[1][28]WEST--
17 HALE NOVELS '63-88
ARCHER, DENNIS--[28][31]WEST--
HALE "CANNON'S LAW" '78
HALE "VERMILLION HILLS" '78
HALE "JUNNIPER RANGE" '79
HALE "CLOUD PRAIRIE" '87
ARMOUR, JOHN--[3][28][29]MYS/WEST--
MYS-5 HALE NOVELS '69-76
WEST-5 HALE NOVELS '81-90
ASHBY, CARTER--[28][31]WEST--
HALE "PINE RIDGE" '80
HALE "TIMBER TRAIL" '82
HALE "TENINO" '83
BARTLETT, KATHLEEN--[1][21][28][31]ROM--
HALE "LOVERS IN AUTUMN" & 7 MORE '68-78
BATCHELOR, REG.--[3][28][29]MYS/WEST--
MYS-9 HALE NOVELS '67-74
WEST-5 HALE NOVELS '79-83
BECK, HARRY--[1][28]WEST--
15 HALE NOVELS '65-79
BEDFORD, KENNETH--[3][28][29]MYS/WEST--
HALE "MATHMATICS OF MURDER" '69
HALE "MERCHANT OF MENACE" '67
WEST-7 HALE NOVELS '78-90
BENTON, WILL--[1][28]WEST--
25 HALE NOVELS '61-83
BISHOP, MARTIN--[28][31]WEST--
4 HALE NOVELS '80-89
BOND, LEWIS--[28][31]WEST--
HALE "OHLAND'S RAIDERS" '79
HALE "BLACK ROCK" '82
BONNER, JACK--[28][31]WEST--
10 HALE NOVELS '79-88
BOSWORTH, FRANK--PPCC#7,[3][28][29]MYS/WEST--
HALE "MURDER NOW, PAY LATER" '69
HALE "THE NAVAJO TRAIL" & MORE '64-87
BOVEE, RUTH--[1][28]ROM--5 HALE NOVELS '67-74
BRADFORD, WILL--[1][28]WEST--
25 HALE NOVELS '62-87
BRADLEY, CONCHO--[1][28]WEST--
19 HALE NOVELS '64-86
BRADSHAW, BUCK--[28][31]WEST--
6 HALE NOVELS '84-87
BRENNAN, WILL--[1][28]WEST--
19 HALE NOVELS '63-87
BURNHAM, CHARLES--[28][31]WEST--
4 HALE NOVELS '80-87
CARREL, MARK--[2][3][7][11][23][28][32]MYS/WEST/SF--
"BANNISTER'S Z-MATTER" '73
WEST-10 HALE NOVELS '50-90
MYS-5 HALE NOVELS '65-75
SF "UNDERGROUND MEN" '75
DA "NIGHT IS FOR KNIFING" '54
CARTER, NEVADA--[1][28]WEST--
15 HALE NOVELS '63-86
CASSIDY, CLAUDE--[1][28][31]WEST--
10 HALE NOVELS '63-78
CLARK, BADGER--[1]WEST--
7 HALE NOVELS '76-78
CLARKE, RICHARD--[1][28]WEST/ROM--
WEST-7 HALE NOVELS '80-89
ROM-HALE "IDENTITY OF A LOVER" '69
CLARKE, ROBERT--[3][28][29]MYS--
6 HALE NOVELS '69-72
CUSTER, CLINT--[1][28]WEST--
8 HALE NOVELS '64-86
DANA, AMBER--[1][28]ROM--
13 HALE NOVELS '69-81
DANA, RICHARD--[3][28]MYS/WEST--
HALE "DEATH OF A MILLIONAIRE" '69
HALE "MURDERER'S MOON" '69
HALE "LONG RIDE" '80
HALE "MANDAN VALLEY" '81
HALE "SHADOW VALLEY" '82
DAVIS, AUDREY--[1][28]ROM--
4 HALE NOVELS "68-76

PAINE, LAURAN BOSWORTH [CONT]
DREXLER, J.F.--[3][28][29]MYS--
HALE "ANONYMOUS ASSASSIN" '68
HALE "FIRE ANT" '75
HALE "UNSUSPECTING VICTIM" '76
DUCHESNE, ANTOINETTE--[1][28]ROM--
HALE "DECISION TO LOVE" '68
HALE "LOVE IS THE ENEMY" '68
HALE "LOVE IS A TRIANGLE" '67
DURHAM, JOHN--[28][32]WEST/MYS--
23 HALE NVLS '63-82
MYS--EQMM "TIGER" DEC '62
FISHER, MARGOT--[1][28]ROM--
"THE MALTESE MOON" '68
FLECK, BETTY--[1][28]ROM--
6 HALE NOVELS '67-70
FLYNN, GEORGE--[28][31]WEST--
HALE "TITUSVILLE COUNTRY"
& 3 OTHERS '79-90
FOSTER, HARRY--[28][31]WEST--
4 HALE NOVELS '79-89
FROST, JONI--[1][28]ROM--
HALE "THE GIRL IN THE BLUE" '68
HALE "TO FACE THE SUN" '68
GLENDENNING, DONN--[1][28]WEST--
7 HALE NOVELS '63-77
GLENN, JAMES--[1][28]WEST--
13 HALE NOVELS '62-78
MERIT 506 "DAMNED!" '60
GORDON, ANGELA--[1][28]ROM--
20 HALE NOVELS '68-90
GORMAN, BETH--[1][21][26]ROM--
6 HALE NOVELS '67-74
HARRISON, FRED--D. WHITEHEAD-PPCC #8,[28]WEST--
HALE "THE LITTLE COUNTRY" & 4 MORE
HART, FRANCIS--[1][28]ROM--
8 HALE NOVELS '67-74
HARTLEY, TRAVIS--[28][31]WEST--
HALE "LONGLAND RANGE" '80
HALE "SHAWNEE COUNTRY" '80
HALE "BRONC BUSTER" '82
HAYDEN, JAY--[1][28]WEST--
7 HALE NOVELS '64-77
HILL, ROGER--[28][31]WEST--
5 HALE NOVELS '79-86
HOLT, HELEN--[1][28]ROM--
5 HALE NOVELS '68-73
HOUSTON, WILL--[1][28]WEST--
17 HALE NOVELS '64-86
HOWARD, ELIZABETH--[1][28]ROM--
HALE "LOVE HAS TWO FACES" '68
HOWARD, TROY--[3][7][23][28][29]SF/WEST/MYS--
MYS-4 HALE NOVELS '68-73
WEST-8 HALE NOVELS '78-87
SF "KERNEL OF DEATH" '73
HALE "MISPLACED PSYCHE" '73
HALE "BLACK LIGHT" '68
HUNT, JOHN--[28][32]WEST--
29 HALE NOVELS '63-90
LM "LIFE AFTER DEATH" SEPT '73
INGERSOL, JARED--[3][28][29][31]MYS--
HALE "MAN WHO STOLE HEAVEN" '71
& 14 MORE '68-75
KELLEY, RAY--[1][28]WEST--
14 HALE NOVELS '64-78
KELLY, RAY--PPCC#8,[1]WEST--
HALE "SHENANDOAH"
KETCHUM, CLIFF--[1][28][31]WEST--
4 HALE NOVELS '77-92
KETCHUM, FRANK--[28][31]WEST--
6 HALE NOVELS '78-88
KETCHUM, JACK--[1][28]WEST--
10 HALE NOVELS '64-81
KILGORE, JOHN--[3][29]MYS/WEST--
HALE "SOME DIE YOUNG" '70
HALE "MURDER TO MUSIC" '72

PAINE, LAURAN BOSWORTH [CONT
KILGORE,JOHN [CONT]
WEST-19 HALE NOVELS '61-87
KIMBALL, FRANK--[28][31]WEST--
HALE "SAGINAW HILLS" '81
KIMBALL, RALPH--[28][31]WEST--
HALE "BUCKEYE" '80
HALE "MANNING" '81
HALE "THE BUSHWHACKER" '89
KOEHLER, FRANK--PPCC#7,[28][31]WEST--
HALE "TROUBLE VALLEY" '82
HALE "BUFFALO RANGE" '85
HALE "FOUR CORNERS"
LEWELLYN, LEW--PPCC#7, P83--
"THE BURNT HILLS"
LIGGETT, HUNTER--[1][3][28]MYS/WEST--
MYS-4 HALE NOVELS '69-75
WEST-HALE "THE RAGHEADS" '80
LUCAS, J.K.--[1][3][28]MYS--
HALE "HAIGHT IS THE KILLER" '69
HALE "THE BORN SURVIVOR" '75
LYON, BUCK--PPCC#8, P34,[1][28]WEST--
HALE "CASTLE CRAGS" & 7 OTHERS '67-83
MARTIN, BRUCE--[1][28]WEST--
8 HALE NOVELS '63-78
MARTIN, TOM--[1][28]WEST--
12 HALE NOVELS '63-77
MORGAN, ANGELA--[1][28]ROM--
HALE "TWO LOVES FOR SUE" '74
MORGAN, ARLENE--[21][28]--
HALE "TEN DAYS TO REMEMBER" '67
HALE "STARFIRE" '74
HALE "A TIME FOR LOVERS" '74
MORGAN, FRANK--[1][28]WEST/ROM--
WEST-5 HALE NOVELS '78-87
ROM-HALE "A FORTUNE FOR LOVE" '71
MORGAN, JOHN [1]--[1][3][28]MYS/WEST--
MYS-9 HALE NOVELS '69-74
HALE "WINDRIVEN HILLS" '80
& 3 OTHERS '81-90
MORGAN, VALERIE--[1][28]ROM--
HALE "THE IDES OF LOVE" '68
HALE "THE LOVERS" '81
O'CONNOR, BERT--[28]WEST--
HALE "MORGAN VALLEY" '80
O'CONNOR, CLINT--[1][28]WEST--
9 HALE NOVELS '64-84
PAINE, L.B.--[40]AMERICAN/MYS
PINDELL, JON--[8]
RHODES, LELAND--[28]WEST--
HALE "DANGER TRAIL"
HALE "EAGLE MOUNTAIN RANGE"
HALE "MORNING GUN" '81-82
SHARP, HELEN--[1][21][28]ROM--
12 HALE NOVELS '68-73
SLAUGHTER, JIM--[1][28]WEST--
24 HALE NOVELS '64-89
ST. GEORGE, ARTHUR--PPCC#8, P34,[28]ROM/WEST--
HALE "A RACE WITH LOVE" '69
WEST-HALE "IDAHO"
STANDISH, BUCK--[1][28]WEST--
24 HALE NOVELS '63-86
STUART, MARGARET--[1][28]ROM--
HALE "APRIL IS OUR TIME" '68
HALE "A DOCTOR IN EXILE" '69
THOMAS, BRUCE--[28]WEST--
7 HALE NOVELS '79-87
THOMPSON, BUCK--[1][28]WEST--
10 HALE NOVELS '75-86
THOMPSON, RUSS--[1][28]WEST--
24 HALE NOVELS '63-92
THORN, BARBARA--[1][28]ROM--
10 HALE NOVELS '64-73
UNDINE, P.F.--[1][28]

PAINE, LESLIE HAROLD W.
PAINE, NICKY--[1]

PAINE, RUTH DARBY
DARBY, RUTH--V. BERCH LTR TO HUBIN '93,MYS--
DBLDY "BEAUTY SLEEP" '41
DBLDY "IF THIS COULD BE MURDER" '41
& 2 MORE

PAINTING, NORMAN
MILNA, BRUNO--[8]

PAIRAULT, PIERRE
WUL, STEFAN--[2][7][23]SF--
"THE TEMPLE OF THE PAST" '73
"NIOURK" '57

PALACIOUS, PEDRO BONIFACI
ALMAFUERTE--[20]SPANISH

PALAMOUNTAIN, ALAN
ILE, TASMAN--[3][29]MYS--
"SHANGHAI NIGHTS" '29

PALAZZESCHI, ALDO
GIULANI, ALDO--[31]

PALAZZO, ANTHONY D.
PALAZZO, TONY--[33]

PALENCIA, ELAINE FOWLER
BLAKE, LAUREL--[9][21][26]ROM--
"STORMY PASSAGE"
"INTO THE WHIRLWIND" & MORE

PALESCANDOLO, FRANK
PALEY, FRANK--[1][3]MYS--
CROWN "RUMBLE ON THE DOCKS" '53

PALESTRANT, SIMON S.
EDWARDS, STEPHEN--[1][22][31]AMERICAN
STEVENS, S.P.--[1][22][31]AMERICAN
STRAND, PAUL E.--[1][22]AMERICAN

PALICKAR, STEPHEN J.
CARR, STEPHEN [J]--[1][32]MYS--
SA "MENACE OF DARKNESS" JAN '62
STEPHENS, S.J.--[1]

PALIN, MICHAEL EDWARD
PYTHON, MONTY--[31]CO-WROTE SCREENPLAYS
W/CHAPMAN, CLEESE, GILLIAM, T. JONES
& IDLE

PALL, ELLEN JANE
HILL, FIONA--[1][9][21][26]ROM--
"AUTUMN ROSE"
"LOVE CHILD" & MORE

PALLANT, NORMAN C.
CROUCH, CHARLES ALBAN--[1][2]
JALLANT, NORMAN C.--[2]

PALLENBERG, CORRADO
ORSI, ROBERT--V. BERCH-'AFTER DARK' SERIES,
BAE 27, ADULT--
MacF 50-146 "ROME AFTER DARK" '62

PALLISER, IRIS
WRAY, I.--[34]MYS--
METHUEN "VYE MURDER" '30
METHUEN "MURDER - AND ARIADNE" '31

PALMCRANTZ, GOSTA
SEGERCRANTZ, GOSTA--[29]MYS--
13 NOVELS '17-48

PALMER, ANNA CAMPBELL
ARCHIBALD, MRS. GEORGE--[1]

PALMER, BERNARD
RUNYAN, JOHN--[1][28][33]

PALMER, CECIL
LUDLOW, JOHN--[8][32]MYS--
LM "LITTLE MAN'S DIARY" SEPT '55

PALMER, CLAUDE
ALLISTER, CLAUDE--[1]

PALMER, EDGAR POOLE JR.
PALMER, PETE--[1]

PALMER, EDWARD VANCE
DALY, RANN--[1]

PALMER, ELSIE PAVITT
PALMER, PETER--[1][22]AMERICAN

PALMER, JOHN LESLIE
BEEDING, FRANCIS--W/HILARY SAUNDERS,
[3][18][32]MYS-- 34 NVLS '25-42
EQMM "CONDEMNED" JUN '49
HADDON, CHRISTOPHER--[3][18][22][29]MYS--
GOLZ "UNDER THE LONG BARROW" '39
PALMER, JOHN--[3]MYS--
"MAN IN A PURPLE GOWN"
RPRTS BOOK AS BY 'HADDON'
PILGRIM, DAVID--W/HILARY SAUNDERS,
[18][22][34]ENGLISH/MYS--
MacM "EMPEROR'S SERVANT" '46

PALMER, JOHN WILLIAMSON
COVENTRY, JOHN--[8]

PALMER, LINDA VARNER
ST. JAMES, JESSICA--W/CHARLOTTE HOY--
[21][26]ROM--
"PERFECT LOVER"
"SHOWDOWN AT SIN CREEK"
"A COUNTRY CHRISTMAS"
ST. JAMES, SCOTNEY--W/CHARLOTTE HOY--
[9][21][26]--
"NORTHERN FIRE"
"NORTHERN STAR"
"DEFIANT BRIDE"
"HEATHER MIST"
"HIGHBLAND HEARTS" & 4 MORE
VARNER, LINDA--[9][21][26]ROM--
"HEART RUSTLER"
'LUCK OF THE IRISH" & MORE

PALMER, MADELYN
PETERS, GEOFFREY--[34][36]AUSTRALIAN/MYS--
WARD "EYE OF A SERPENT" '64
WARD "CLAW OF A CAT" '64
WARD "WHIRL OF A BIRD" '65
WARD "TWIST OF A STICK" '66
WARD "FLICK OF A FIN" '67
WARD "MARK OF A BUOY" '67
WARD "CHILL OF A CORPSE" '68

PALMER, P.K.
PARNELL, KEITH--[1][2][11]

PALMER, PAMELA LYNN
LEIGH, PALMER--[31]

PALMER, PAUL
DOWNING, CENTURY--[8]

PALMER, RAYMOND A.
BELL, GEORGE--W/BEA MAHAFFEY,[2]
GADE, HENRY--[1][2][11][23]SF,HP--
ZIFF-DAVIS
IRWIN, G.H.--[1][2][11]SF,HP--
ZIFF-DAVIS
PATTON, FRANK--[1][2][11][23]SF,HP--
AMAZING
PELKIE, J[OE] W[ALTER]--[1][2][11][23]SF--
QUITMAN, WALLACE--[1][2][11]SF,HP--
STEBER, A[LFRED] R.--[1][2][11][23]SF,HP--
ZIFF-DAVIS
STEELE, MORRIS J.--[1][2][11][23]SF,HP--
ZIFF-DAVIS
WEBSTER, ROBERT N.--[1][2][11][23]SF--
FIRST ISSUE OF 'OTHER WORLDS' MAG '49
WINTERS, RAE--[1][2][11][23]SF--

PALMER, THOMAS
PALMER, TOM--[7]SF--
NOR & FIELDS "DREAM SCIENCE" '90

PALMER, [CHARLES] STUART
ORCHARDS, THEODORE--[2][11]
STEWART, JAY--[3][18][29]MYS--
MILL "BEFORE IT'S TOO LATE" '50

PALMER, [N] HUMPHREY
KOI HAI--[31]

PALMER-ARCHER, LAURA M.
BUSHWOMAN--[8]

PALMISANO, LUIGI
PALM, GENE--[2][7][11]SF

PALTOCK, ROBERT
R.S.--[2]

PANAITESCU, D.
PERPESSICIUS--[22]RUMANIAN

PANAS, RUDCENKO
MYRNYJ, PANAS JAKOVICH--[22]UKRAINIAN

PANCENKO, PETRO JOSYPOV.
PANC, PETRO JOSYPOVICH--[22]UKRAINIAN
PANCH, PETR--[1]

PANGBORN, EDGAR
HARRISON, BRUCE--[2][3][11][23][29]MYS--
DUTTON "A-100: A MYSTERY STORY" '30

PANIKKAR, K. MADHAVA
CHANAKYA--[1]
PUTRA, KERALA--[1]

PANIZZA, OSKAR
ANDREE, LOUIS--[39]GERMAN/SF
DETTMER, HANS--[39]GERMAN/SF
PUBLIUS--[39]GERMAN/SF

PANNETON, PHILIPPE
RINGUET--[1][22]FRENCH-CANADIAN

PANOV, NIKOLAI N.
TUMANNYI, DIR--[1]

PANOWSKI, EILEEN JANET T.
THOMPSON, EILEEN--[8][22][33]AMERICAN

PANSHIN, ALEXEI
ADAMS, LOUIS J.A.--W/JOE L. HENSLEY,
[2][11][23]SF--
"DARK DECEPTION" '64

PANTING, ARNOLD CLEMENT
ARNOLD, CLEMENT--[1]

PANTING, JAMES HARWOOD
HEATHCOTE, CLAUD--[1]

PANY, LEONORE
NEUERT, H.--[39]GERMAN

PAPAZOGLOU, ORANIA
ANDREWS, NICOLA--[9][21][26]ROM--
"FORBIDDEN MELODY"
"RECKLESS DESIRE" & 2 MORE
HADDAM, JANE--LACHMAN/EASTER LIST '93,
[34]MYS--
BB "NOT A CREATURE WAS STIRRING" '90
PAAR, ANGELICA--V. BERCH LTR TO HUBIN '94,
MYS--
"WATCHER IN THE GARDEN" '89
PARIS, ANN--LACHMAN,[9][21][26][34]MYS/ROM--
"ARROWHEART" '88
"GRAVEN IMAGE" '87

PAPE, DONNA LUGG
PAPE, D.L.--[31]CHILDREN'S BOOKS

PAPICH, MARGERY
LAYNE, MARION MARGERY--W/MARION WOOLF
& LAYNE TORKELSON,[34]MYS--
DODD "THE BALLOON AFFAIR" '81

PAPINI, GIOVANNI
FALCO, GIAN--[1][31]

PAPPAS, ANGELOS
PAPPAZISIS, EVANGELOS--[2][7]SF--

PAPPAS, GEORGE S.
JUSTIFICUS--[8]

PARADIS, CATARINA ALB. i
CATALA, VICTOR--[22]SPANISH/CATALAN

PARADIS-SCHLANG, ILKA
VON BELLINGEN, BARBARA--[39]GERMAN/SF

PARADISO, KAREN
LYNN, ANN--W/NANCY HARLOW,[21][26]--
"MIDNIGHT SAFARI"
"SLAVE OF MY HEART"
"PASSION'S CHASE"

PARANYA, FLORENCE J.
PETERSON, CARRIE--[26]ROM--
SIL 22 "SECRETS OF SEBASTIAN BEAUMONT"

PARCELL, NORMAN HOWE
FAIRLEIGH, CHRISTOPHER--[1]
NICHOLSON, JOHN--[2][32][34]MYS--
STOCKWELL "COSTELLO-PSYCHIC
INVESTIGATOR" '54
MD "THE WRETCHES CAVE" MAY '60
PERCIVAL, NORMAN--[1]

PARDOE, GEOFFREY
CAPELLI, ACE--PP 29, P42, MYS,HP--
FOSTER, DIRK--PP 29,[34]MYS--
GAYWOOD "PAM SLIPPED UP" '52
JANSON, HANK--B&M #18, MYS,HP--
NF "AUCTIONED" '52
TF "PERSIAN PRIDE" '53
NF "PURSUIT" '53
NF "AMOK" '53
NF "KILLER" '52
NF "VENGEANCE" '53
NF "ACCUSED" '52

PARDOE, ROSEMARY A.
ALLEN, MARY ANN--[2][7]SF--
CAP "THE ANGRY DEAD" '86

PARES, MARION STAPYLTON
CAMPBELL, JUDITH--[1][22][31]ENGLISH
GRANT, ANTHONY--[7][23][31]SF--
"THE MUTANT" '80

PARGETER, EDITH [MARY]
BENEDICT, PETER--[18]MYS--
"DAY STAR" '37
CARR, JOLYON--J. BREEN-EQMM 6/93,[34]--
JENK "MURDER IN THE DISPENSARY" '38
JENK "FREEDOM FOR TWO" '39
JENK "DEATH COMES BY POST" '40
JENK "MASTERS OF THE PARACHUTE MAIL" '40
PETERS, ELLIS--[2][3][18][21][29]ENGLISH/MYS--
COLLINS "DEATH MASK" '59 & 19 MORE '60-80
REDFERN, JOHN--J. BREEN-EQMM JUN '93,
[18][34]MYS--
JARROLDS "VICTIM NEEDS A NURSE" '40

PARIKH, RASIKLAL C.
MUSIKARA--[1]

PARISH, MARGARET CECILE
PARISH, PEGGY--[33]

PARISH, MARGARET HOLT
HOLT, MARGARET--[22]AMERICAN

PARK, CHARLES CARROLL
GRAY, CARL--[1]

PARK, W[ILLIAM] B[RYAN]
PARK, BILL--[31][33]JUV

PARKER, DAVID L.
PARKER, DEE--[1]

PARKER, ELIZABETH [C]
CHANDLER, BESSIE--[1]

PARKER, HERSHEL
WILLIS, SAMUEL--[1]

PARKER, JOHN
J.P.--[1]

PARKER, JOHN THOMAS
PARKER, TOM--[31]--
NON-FICT '83-90

PARKER, KAREN BLAIR
BLAIR, KATHRYN--W/MARY K. SCAMEHORN,
[9][21][26]ROM--
"GOLDEN ROSE"
"ENCHANTING ISLAND" & MORE

PARKER, ROSA ABBOTT
ABBOTT, ROSA--[1]

PARKES, FRANK KOBINA
DOMPO, KWESI--[1]

PARKES, JAMES WILLIAM
HADHAM, JOHN--[1][31]

PARKES, TERENCE
LARRY--[8][31]

PARKHILL, FORBES
MARTINEZ, J.D.--[8]
VLOTO, OTTO--[8]

PARKHILL-RATHBONE, JAMES
RATHBONE, JAMES--[2]

PARKINSON, CORNELIA M.
TAYLOR, DAY--W/SHARON SALVATO,[9][21][26]ROM--
"BLACK SWAN"
"MOSS ROSE" & MORE
TAYLOR, DAYNA--W/DAVID B. HOBBS,[1]

PARKINSON, ROGER
HOLDE, MATTHEW--[1][31]

PARKS, GEORGINA
GABRIELLE--[1]

PARKS, TIMOTHY HAROLD
MCDOWELL, JOHN--[34]MYS--
HODDER "CARA MASSIMINA" '90

PARMER, JESS NORMAN
PARMER, J.N.--[1]

PARNELL, FRANK H.
FRANCIS, GREGORY--W/JAMES M. MACGREGOR,
[1][2][11]ALSO USED HIMSELF
RICHARDSON, FRANCIS--W/L.E. BARTLE,[1][2][11]

PARR, HARRIET
LEE, HOLME--[34]MYS--
SMITH ELDER "MAUD TALBOT" 1854

PARR, JULIAN F.
RAGATZY, ANTON--[1][2][11]

PARR, LUCY
CARROLL, LAURA--[31][33]

PARR, OLIVE KATHARINE
CHASE, BEATRICE--[1][3]MYS--
LONGMANS "PATRICIA LANCASTER'S REVENGE" '28

PARRIS, JOHN
LASCELLES, ALISON--[8]

PARROTT, KATHERINE URSULA
P., K.U.--[3]MYS--
CAPE "GENTLEMAN'S FATE" '31

PARRY, ALBERT
LECLERC, VICTOR--[31]

PARRY, DAVID HAROLD
BLAKE, [CAPT.] WILTON--[1]
PIKE, MORTON--[1][34]MYS--
LLOYD "UNDER THE SHADOW OF NIGHT" '21

PARRY, HUGH JONES
CROSS, JAMES--[3][22][29][32]MYS--
SW "MURDER IN ACT II" MAR '45
& 10 OTHER SW STORIES
MESSNER "ROOT OF EVIL" '57
MESSNER "DARK ROAD" '59
GM "GRAVE OF HEROES" '61
RANDOM "TO HELL FOR HALF-A-CROWN" '67

PARRY, MARGARET G.
GLYN, MEGAN--[8]

PARRY, MICHEL P.
CASSABA, CARLOS--[2][7][11][16]SF--
CORGI "ROOTS OF EVIL: BEYOND THE SECRET
LIFE OF PLANTS" '76
FURY, NICK--[1][2][16]
LEE, STEVE--[1][11]

PARRY, MICHEL P. [CONT]
LOVECRAFT, LINDA--[2][7][11][16]SF--
CORGI "DEVIL'S KISSES" '76
CORGI "MORE DEVIL'S KISSES" '77
PENDRAGON, ERIC--[2][7][11][16]SF--
STAR "SAVAGE HEROES: TALES OF SOCERCERY & BLK MAGIC" '77

PARRY-DRIXNER, WILLY
DRAXNER, WILL--[39]GERMAN/MYS/SF/WEST
DREYER, HARRY--[39]GERMAN/MYS/SF/WEST
DRIXNER, WILL--[39]GERMAN/MYS/SF/WEST
PARRY, HANS-HEINZ--[39]GERMAN/MYS/SF/WEST
PARRY, PERCY--[39]GERMAN/MYS/SF/WEST
PETERS, HANS-HEINZ--[39]GERMAN/MYS/SF/WEST

PARSONS, ANTHONY
NICHOLLS, ANTHONY--[1]

PARSONS, B.
HUNT, MAURICE--[1]
YOUNG, WARWICK--[1]

PARSONS, CHARLES P.
CRAVEN HILL--[8]

PARSONS, EDWARD
ONLOOKER--[1]

PARSONS, ELMER M.
RACE, PHILIP--V. BERCH-GM PSEUDS. PP 33,MYS--
GM 796 "SELF-MADE WIDOW" '58
GM 888 "KILLER TAKE ALL" '59
HILL 179 "JOHNNY COME DEADLY" '60

PARSONS, H.F. DOLLAND
DOLLAND, JOHN--[3]MYS--
LONGMANS "A GENTLEMAN HANGS" '40

PARSONS, [SIR] RICHARD
HAYTHORNE, JOHN--[34]MYS--
ANDERSON "MANDRAKE IN GRANADA" '84
& MORE '68-85

PARTCH, VIRGIL FRANKLIN
VIP--[33]

PARTINGTON, CHARLES
COLVIN, JAMES--[2]HP--??UNCONFIRMED??

PARTON, SARA PAYSON W.
FERN, FANNY--[31]

PARTRIDGE, EDWARD BELLAMY
BAILEY, THOMAS--[1][2]

PARTRIDGE, ERIC

PARTRIDGE, ERIC [H]
DENISON, CORRIE--[31]
VIGILANS--[6]

PARTRIDGE, KATE MARGARET
PARTRIDGE, SYDNEY--[8]

PARTRIDGE, [SIR] BERNARD
GOULD, BERNARD--[1]

PARULSKI, GEORGE R.
BRIAN, ALAN B.--[1][31]
TAYLOR, GEORGE--[1]

PASCALE, RICHARD TANNER
JOHNSON, RICHARD TANNER--[31]

PASCOE, IRENE M.
HALEY, ANDREA--[9][21][26]ROM--
ZEBRA "VELVET SHADOWS OF JUSTIN WOOD" '82

PASHKO, STANLEY
NORMAN, STEVE--[1][33]
ROBBINS, TONY--[1][33]

PASLEY, VIRGINIA SCHMITZ
SCHMITZ, VIRGINIA--[1]

PASSAILAIGUE, TOMAS E.B.
BETHANCOURT, T. ERNESTO--[7]--
"DOG DAYS OF ARTHUR CAINE" '76
"ODIN #1 & 2" '77
"YESTERDAY #1 & 2" '78-84

PASSES-PAZOLSKI, ALAN
PASSES, ALAN--[7]SF--
ALLEN "BIG STEP" '77

PASSINGHAM, KENNETH
SLACK--[1][2]

PASSINI, GRETE [v. U]
VON URBANITZKY, GRETE--[39]GERMAN

PASTOR, BEN
PASTOR, VERBENA--M. LACHMAN-EQMM ED INTRO, MYS--
EQMM "HARDOIN & THE MONSTERS" AUG '94

PATCHETT, MARY O. ELWYN
BRUCE, DAVID--[1]
PATCHETT, M.E.--[1]

PATERSON, A.J. BLAIR
GRIFF--P. HARBOTTLE-PP#25,[34]MYS,HP--
MOF "CURVES CAN CAST SHADOWS" '53
MOF "MAIN STREET MORGUE" '53
MOF "POISONOUS ANGEL" '53
MOF "NIGHT PATROL" '53
JOHNS, BLAIR--S. HOLLAND-SCION CKLST, PP 27,[34]MYS--
MOF "NAKED SOULS" '56 & 6 MORE '54-5
LUGAR, HANS--[27][34]MYS,HP--
SCION "APPOINTMENT WITH DESIRE" '53
SCION "HARVEST FOR HARPIES" '53
SCION "DEATH BY APPOINTMENT" '54
SCION "MARBLE HEART" '54
SARTO, BEN--[34]MYS,HP--
MOF "DISILLUSIONED" '52
MOF "VIPER'S BROOD" '54
MOF "DREAD" '55
MOF "EASTSIDE EXPOSURE" '55
MOF "FEAR" '55
MOF "HOUSE OF SIN" '56
SPENCER, HANK--[34]MYS,HP--
MOF "FLESH GAME" '54
MOF "GENTLEMAN'S RELISH" '54
MOF "NO FACE FOR A KILLER" '54
MOF "SHROUD FOR A REDHEAD" '56

PATERSON, ANDREW BARTON
BANJO--[1][22]
PATERSON, A.B.--[1]
PATERSON, BANJO--[1]

PATERSON, WILLIAM ROMAINE
SWIFT, BENJAMIN--[3][32]MYS--
6 NOVELS 1897-17
AHMM "WITH A LITTLE BIT OF LUCK" FEB '71
AHMM "NIGHT CALL" MAR '71
AHMM "SWEET, SWEET REVENGE" DEC '71

PATON WALSH, GILLIAN H.M.
PATON WALSH, JILL--[1][31]

PATRICK, DAVID GEORGE
ENGLING, RICHARD--[7]SF--
NAL "BODY MORTGAGE" '89

PATRICK, JOHNSTONE G.
FORWARD, LUKE--[22][31]SCOTTISH-AMERICAN
STAR-MAN'S PADRE--[22]SCOTTISH-AMERICAN

PATRICK, KEATS
KARIG, WALTER--[8]

PATRICK, SUSAN M.
GREY, SALIITHA--[2]

PATRY, M.
WILLIAMS, PATRY--W/D. WILLIAMS,[1]

PATSAUQ, MARKOOSIE
MARKOOSIE--[1]

PATTEE, DAVID
DAVIS, PAT--[1][2][11]

PATTEN, CLINTON A.
ROCK, JAMES--[1]

PATTEN, GILBERT
STANDISH, BURT L.--PPCC#8,[2][3]MYS,HP--
STREET & SMITH 'FRANK MERRIWELL'-3 NOVELS

PATTEN, J.A.
COBB, CLAYTON W.--[34]MYS--
STREET "MOUNTAINEER DETECTIVE" 1889

PATTEN, LEWIS B.
AUTREY, GENE--[19]WEST,GHOSTED--
"GHOSTRIDERS"
"GENE AUTREY & ARAPAHO WAR DRUMS"
BOWIE, JIM--[19]WEST,HP--
"ADVENTURES OF JIM BOWIE"
FORD, LEWIS--L. ROBBINS LTR '94, WEST--
POP LB - 3 NOVELS '54-7
LEIGHTON, LEE--W/WAYNE D. OVERHOLSER,
[19][28]WEST--
BAL "TOMAHAWK" '58
LEIGHTON, LEN--[1]WEST
PENDLETON, FORD--L. ROBBINS LTR '94
WAYNE, JOSEPH--W/WAYNE D. OVERHOLSER,[28]WEST-
-
DELL "GUN & THE LAW"
DELL "SHOWDOWN AT STONY CREEK"

PATTEN, WILLIAM GEORGE
BELL, EMERSON--[1]
BELLWOOD, HERBERT--[1]
DANGERFIELD, HARRY--[1]
MCLAREN, GORDON--[1]
PATTEN, GIL--[1]
PATTEN, GILBERT--[1]
PATTEN, WYOMMING BILL--[1]
ST. DARE, JULIAN--[1]
STANDISH, BURT L.--[1]HP--
STREET & SMITH
WILDER, WILLIAM WEST--[1]

PATTERSON, ARTHUR W.
DAVIDSON, WILDER BRISTOL--[1]

PATTERSON, CHARLOTTE
BUIST, CHARLOTTE--[1][31]

PATTERSON, ELEANOR MEDILL
GIZYCKA, ELEANOR M.--[31]

PATTERSON, HARRY
FALLON, MARTIN--[3][18][31]MYS--
ABELARD "TESTAMENT OF CASPAR SCHULTZ" '62
ABELARD "YEAR OF THE TIGER" '63
ABELARD "KEYS OF HELL" '65
LONG "MIDNIGHT NEVER COMES" '66
LONG "DARK SIDE OF THE STREET" '67
LONG "A FINE NIGHT FOR DYING" '69
GRAHAM, JAMES--[3][18][31]MYS--
MacM "A GAME FOR HEROES" '70
MacM "WRATH OF GOD" '71
MacM "KHUFRA RUN" '72
MacM "BLOODY PASSAGE" '74
HIGGINS, JACK--[3][18][22][31]MYS--
HODDER "EAST OF DESOLATION" '68
HODDER "IN THE HOUR BEFORE MIDNIGHT" '69
HODDER "NIGHT JUDGEMENT" '70
COLLINS "LAST PLACE GOD MADE" '71
COLLINS "SAVAGE DAY" '72
COLLINS "A PRAYER FOR THE DYING" '73
COLLINS "EAGLE HAS LANDED" '75
COLLINS "STORM WARNING" '76
COLLINS "DAY OF JUDGEMENT" '78
COLLINS "SOLO" '80
COLLINS "LUCIANO'S LUCK" '81
COLLINS "EXOCET" '83
COLLINS "CONFESSIONAL" '85
COLLINS "NIGHT OF THE FOX" '86
COLLINS "A SEASON IN HELL" '89
HM "COLD HARBOR" '90
MARLOWE, HUGH--[1][3][18]MYS--
ABELARD "SEVEN PILLARS TO HELL" '63
ABELARD "PASSAGE BY NIGHT" '64
ABELARD "A CANDLE FOR THE DEAD" '66
PATTERSON, HENRY--[8]

PATTERSON, ISABELLA INNIS
PATTERSON, INNIS--[8]

PATTERSON, PETER
TERSON, PETER--[8]

PATTERSON, VIRGINIA
GAINES, GARY--[1]

PATTINSON, JAMES
RYDER, JAMES--[8]

PATTINSON, LEE
DEE, REBECCA--[35]AUSTRALIAN--
HRWTZ "DOCTOR'S DAUGHTER" '62
HRWTZ "DOCTOR'S SEARCH" '63
FARR, CAROLINE--[35]AUSTRALIAN,HP--
HRWTZ GM1 "THE INTRUDER" '66
HOLLAND, ROSEMARY--[8]
LESTER, TERI--[35]AUSTRALIAN--
HRWTZ '67-9
MAXWELL, ANN--[8][11]
MILLER, ELLEN--[8]
MITCHELL, KERRY--[35]AUSTRALIAN,HP--
HRWTZ "CRUISE NURSE" '64
NICHOLS, PAMELA--[35]AUSTRALIAN--
HRWTZ PB135 "ESCAPE TO ROMANCE" '77

PATTINSON, NANCY EVELYN
ASQUITH, NAN--[1][9][17][21]ROM--
"THE CHANGING STARS"
BROOME, SUSANNAH--[9][21][26]ROM--
"AMULET OF FORTUNE"
"PEARL PAGODA"

PATTISON, ANDREW SETH P.
SETH, ANDREW--[8]

PATTISON, BETTY ANN
CARLSON, ELIZABETH--[26]ROM--
"BEST OF ALL"
YORK, VICKIE--[9][10][21]ROM--
"TOP SECRET AFFAIR"
"MORE THAN A HUNCH"

PATTISON, DOROTHY W.
SISTER DORA--[1]

PATTISON, OLIVE RUTH
ABBEY, RUTH--[3][9][21][26][29]MYS/ROM--
"BRIDGE OF TEARS"
"EVIL AT NUNNERT MANOR" & MORE

PATTON, DAVID LEWIS
LEWIS, DAVID--[3]MYS--
PINN "ANDROMEDA ASSIGNMENT" '76
PINN "OMEGA ASSIGNMENT" '76

PATTON, JAMES BLYTHE
WHITE, EDMUND--[1]

PATTON, LEAH & CLIFF
TEMPLE, LEAH--[7]SF--
ZEBRA "FATAL ANALYSIS" '88

PATTON, SARAH
ENGLISH, GENEVIEVE--[9][21][26]ROM--
"THE FRENCH CONFECTION"

PATTY, ANN
ANDREWS, V.C.--MYS SCENE #40--
GHOSTED OR REWROTE BOOKS FOR 'ANDREW NEIDERMAN'

PAUKER, JOHN
GRIFFITHS, ROBERT L. III--[1]
ORDWAY, ROGER--[1]
ROWLEY, THOMAS--[1]
SOMES, JETHRO--[1]

PAUL, AILEEN
PHILLIPS, AILEEN PAUL--[1]

PAUL, ELLIOT [H]
RUTLEDGE, BRETT--[3][18][22][29]MYS--
RANDOM "DEATH OF LORD HAW HAW" '41

PAUL, JAMES
KOCSIS, J.C.--[31][33]

PAUL, JUDITH EDISON
EDISON, JUDITH--[31]

PAUL, MAURY
BENEDICT, BILLY--[8]
KNICKERBOCKER, CHOLLY--[8]
MADISON, DOLLY--[8]
STUYVESANT, POLLY--[8]

PAUL, PAULA G.
PAUL, PAULA--[10]ROM--
HARL "SILENT PARTNER"
HARL "NIGHT OF THE JAGUAR" & 3 MORE

PAULY, MARGARETE
BERG, AJA--[39]GERMAN

PAUSACKER, JENNIFER
PAUSACKER, JENNY--[7]SF--
ANGUS & ROBERTSON "FAST FORWARD" '89

PAVEY, DON
ADAIR, JACK--[1]

PAVLENKO, PETR ANDREVITCH
PAVLENKO, PIOTR--[1]

PAVLIK, EVELYN MARIE
SHERIDAN, ADORA--W/JANE FAY HONG, [1][9][21]ROM--
"THE SEASON"
"THE SIGNET RING"

PAVLOVITCH, PAUL
AJAR, EMILE--[1]

PAVSHICH, VLADIMIR
BOR, MATEJ--[22]SLOVAK

PAWLE, GERALD STRACHAN
ATTICUS--[31]

PAWLEY, JEAN MAKINS
CARDWELL, ANN--[34]MYS--
ARCADIA "CRAZY TO KILL" '41
ARCADIA "MURDER AT CALAMITY HOUSE" '47

PAWLEY, MARTIN EDWARD
NOBLE, CHARLES--[1][8]
SPADE, RUPERT--[1][8]

PAXSON, ETHEL
GOULD, LETTIE--[31]

PAXTON, JOHN
CHERRILL, JACK--[1]

PAYELLE, RAYMOND GERARD
HERIAT, PHILIPPE--[1][22][31]FRENCH

PAYES, RACHEL COSGROVE
ARCH, E.L.--[2][3][9][23][29][31]MYS--
AVALON "DEATH STONE" '64
AVALON "FIRST IMMORTALS" '65
COSGROVE, RACHEL--[9][21][23][26]ROM--
"THE CANDY STRIPERS"
COSGROVE, RACHEL R.--[9]ROM
KAYE, JOANNE--[9][21][26]ROM--
"TO LOVE AGAIN"
"SATIN & STARS" & MORE

PAYNE, CHARLES J.
SNAFFLES--[8]

PAYNE, DONALD GORDON
CAMERON, IAN--[2][7][11][22][23]ENGLISH/SF--
"LOST ONES" '61
HODDER "WHITE SHIP" '75
MRW "MOUNTAINS AT THE BOTTOM OF THE WORLD" '72
GORDON, DONALD--[2][3][23][29]MYS/SF--
HODDER "STAR-RAKER" '62
HODDER "FLIGHT OF THE BAT" '63
HODDER "GOLDEN OYSTER" '67
HODDER "LEAP IN THE DARK" '70
MARSHALL, JAMES VANCE--[2][11][22][23][33]ENGLISH/SF

PAYNE, EILEEN MARY
MANSELL, C.R.--[8]

PAYNE, HAZEL BELLE
GAY, GREER--[1]

PAYNE, L.R.
STIVERS, DICK--W/NORMAN WINSKI,[3][29]MYS,HP--
GE "THE HOSTAGED ISLAND" '84
STIVERS, DICK--W/LARRY POWELL,[34]MYS,HP--
GE "TEXAS SHOWDOWN" '82

PAYNE, L.R. [CONT]
STIVERS, DICK--W/NORMAN WINSKI,[34]MYS,HP--
GE "HOSTAGED ISLAND" '82
STIVERS, DICK--[34]MYS,HP--
GE "TOWER OF TERROR" '82

PAYNE, PIERRE S. ROBERT
CARGOE, RICHARD--[1][23][31]
DEVON, JOHN ANTHONY--[1][23][31]
HORNE, HOWARD--[1][23][31]
PAYNE, ROBERT--[1][8]
TIKHONOV, VALENTIN--[1][23]
YOUNG, ROBERT--[1][2][23]SF--
"WAR IN THE MARSHES" '38

PAYNE, ROBERT LYLE
FROST, G[RAHAM]--V. BERCH LTR TO
HUBIN '94, MYS--
"RECON STRIKE" '87

PAYNE, RONALD CHARLES
CASTLE, JOHN--W/J.W. GARROD,[2][3][11][29]MYS-
-
SVNR "SEVENTH FURY" '61

PAZ, MAGDALEINE
MARX, MAGDALEINE--[8]

PAZOLSKI, ALAN
PASSES, ALAN--[23]ENGLISH/SF--
NW "SPOOR" '69
PASSES-PAZOLSKI, ALAN--[23]ENGLISH/SF--
"BIG STEP" '77

PEACH, EDWARD
OPHIEL--[1]

PEARCE, BRIAN LEONARD
FARNSBOROUGH--[1]
HUSSEY, LEONARD--[1]
REDMAN, JOSEPH--[1]

PEARCE, CHARLES E.
DUNN, DETECTIVE--[1][3][29]MYS--
PAUL "BEAUTIFUL DEVIL" '23
PAUL "A QUEEN OF CROOKS" '24
PAUL "THE RED MILL MYSTERY" '25

PEARCE, CHARLES LOUIS
FAIRBANKS, NAT--[1][34]MYS--
AMALG "THE MYSTERY MAKER" '21

PEARCE, DONALD
PEARCE, DONN--[34]MYS--
SCRIBN "COOL HAND LUKE" '65

PEARCE, MELVILLE CHANING
NICODEMUS--[8]

PEARCE, RAYMOND
MAPLESDEN, RAY--[8]

PEARL, JACQUES BAIN
BLAKE, STEPHANIE--[7][9][17][21][26]ROM--
PLAYBOY "SECRET SINS" '80 & 14 OTHERS
PEARL, JACK--[1][21][34]MYS/WAR/ROM, NOVELS
STEVENS, TRISHA--V. BERCH LTR '93, ADULT--
POCK "HOOKER FOR A DAY" '75

PEARLMAN, MAURICE
PEARLMAN, MOSHE--[1]

PEARLSTEIN, HOWARD J.
RUSH, JOSHUA--[1]

PEARSE, PATRICK HENRY
MACPIARAIS, PADRAIC--[1]
PEARSE, PADRAIC--[1]

PEARSON, ALEC GEORGE
LINLEY, JULIAN--[1]
SCOTT, [CAPT.] RUSSELL--[1]

PEARSON, KATHARINE
GORDON, KATHARINE--[8]

PEARSON, MILO LORENZ
PEARSON, LON--[1]

PEARSON, RIDLEY
MCCALL, WENDELL--LACHMAN LST '93,[34]MYS--
ST. MARTIN'S "DEAD AIM" '88
ST. MARTIN'S "AIM FOR THE HEART" '90

PEARSON, T.E.
NORTH, PEARSON--[1]

PEARSON, W.T.
PENGREEP, WILLIAM--[8]

PEARY, DANNIS
PEARY, DANNY--[7]--
CULT MOVIES
CULT MOVIE STARS

PECHEY, ARCHIBALD THOMAS
CROSS, MARK--[1][3][22]MYS--
WARD "MARK OF FOUR" '36
WARD "DESPERATE STEPS" '37 & 43 MORE '34-61
VALENTINE--[1][3][22]MYS--
WARD "STRANGE EXPERIMENT" '37
WARD "UNSEEN HAND" '24 & 2 MORE '24-37

PECHOVA, ELISKA
KRASNOHORSKA, ELISKA--[22]CZECH

PECK, GEORGE W.
BIGLY, CANTELL A.--[11]

PECK, LEONARD
BRAIN, LEONARD--[1][3]MYS--
COWARD "IT'S A FREE COUNTRY" '65
HALE "A CASE OF IDENTITY" '71

PECK, WINIFRED FRANCES
KNOX, WINIFRED FRANCES--[1]

PECKOLICK, ABE
PECK, ABE--[1]

PECSOK, MARY BODELL
BODELL, MARY--[1][22][31]AMERICAN

PEDERSON, KNUT
HAMSUN, KNUT--[1][22][31]NORWEGIAN
HAMSUND, KNUT PEDERSON--[31]

PEDERSON, RACHEL FIELD
FIELD, RACHEL--[21]ROM--
"ALL THIS & HEAVEN TOO"
"AND NOW TOMORROW"

PEDERSON, SVEN
HASSEL, SVEN--[1]

PEDLAR, ANN
STAFFORD, ANN--[8]

PEDLER, ANNE I. STAFFORD
STAFFORD, ANNE--[1][8]

PEDLER, CHRISTOPHER M.H.
PEDLER, KIT--[7][11][23]SF--
DF "DOOM WATCH: THE WORLD IN DANGER"
DF "DYMASTER MENACE"

PEDLER, JOHN B.S.
TORR, DOMINIC--[1][3]MYS--
BARKER "DIPLOMATIC COVER" 65
CAPE "TREASON LINE" '68

PEDNEAU, DAVE
ELIOT, MARC--[7]SF--
BAL "HOW DEAR THE DAWN" '87
HAWKS, LEE--[7]SF--
BAL "NIGHT, WINTER, AND DEATH" '90

PEDRICK, JEAN
KEFFERSTAN, JEAN--[1][31]

PEDRICK-HARVEY, GALE
PEDRICK, GALE--[8]

PEDRIERA, ANTONIO A.
ASSUR BANI PAL--[1]

PEEBLES, JAMES E.
KENNAWAY, JAMES--[2][23]SCOTTISH

PEEBLES, MARY LOUISE
PALMER, LYNDE--[1]

PEEL, COLIN D[UDLEY]L
GREY, LINDSEY--[1]

PEEL, FREDERICK
SLINGSBY, RUFUS--W/CHARLES SIDDLE,
[1][3][22]MYS--
LONG "MURDERS AT HIGHBRIDGE" '29

PEEL, HAZEL MARY
HAYMAN--[1][31]
PEEL, WALLIS--[1]

PEEL, JOHN [RONALD]
ADAMS, NICHOLAS--[7]SF,HP--
HARPER "I.O.U." '91
HARPER "SANTA CLAWS" '91
NORTH, RICK--[7]SF,HP--
ZEBRA "READY FOR BLASTOFF" '90

PEEPLES, SAMUEL A.
BASS, FRANK--[28]WEST--
DODD "THE ANGRY LAND" '58
WARD, BRAD--[1][28]WEST--
10 NOVELS '52-8

PEERS, EDGAR ALLISON
TRUSCOTT, BRUCE--[1]

PEET, WILLIAM BARTLETT
PEET, BILL--[31][33]CHILDREN'S BOOKS

PEFFER, SAM
PEFF--BAPC #11, PPCC #8, P13, ENLISH--
ARTIST FOR PAN, DIGIT, PANTHER & ARROW

PEGLER, [JAMES] WESTBROOK
PEGLER, BUD--[1]
PEGLER, PEG--[1]
PEGLER, WESTY--[1]
PEGLER, WRONG WESTBROOK--[1]

PEHLEN, KARL
TOBBY, TIM--[39]GERMAN/WEST

PEIFER, KATHLEEN HAMEL
DOBKIN, KAYE--[7]SF--
DELL "THE QUEEN OF HEARTS" '82

PEIRCE, J.F.
AD HOC--EQMM DEC '80, MYS--

PEIS, GUNTER
ALEXANDER, GUNTER--[39]GERMAN/JUV

PEISER, MARIA LILLI
PALMER, LILLI--[3][21][26]MYS--
"RED RAVEN"
WEIDENFELD "A TIME TO EMBRACE" '80
WEIDENFELD "NIGHT MUSIC" '82
GRAFTON "WHEN THE NIGHTBIRD CRIES" '89

PELADIN, JOSEPH [JOSEPHINE]
PALADAN, JOSEPHINE--[1]
PELADAN, MERODACK SAR--[22]FRENCH
SAR--[1]

PELAEZ, FRANCISCO
TARIO, FRANCISCO--[30]MEXICAN

PELFREY, JUDITH
DANIELS, JUDITH--[9][21][26]ROM--
"THE SUN ALWAYS RISES"
DANIELS, RHETT--[9][21][26]ROM--
"OVERTURE OF THE HEART"
LIVINGSTONE, MARK J.--W/MICHAEL R. PHILLIPS,
[7]SF--
"THE PEACEMAKER" '90

PELLECCHIA, KATRINKA B.
BLICKLE, KATRINKA--[21][26]ROM--
"NORTH SEA MISTRESS"
"DARK BEGININGS" & MORE

PELLETIER, ALEXIS
LUIGI--[1]
ST. AIME, GEORGES--[1]

PELLIGRIN, FRANK E.
PELL, FRANKLYN--[1][3][22]MYS--
DODD "HANGMAN'S HILL" '46

PELLOWSKI, MICHAEL JOSEPH
MICHAELS, SKI--[33]

PELLY, WILLIAM DUDLEY
PELLY, SMELLY--[1]

PELOT, PIERRE
SURAGLE, PIERRE--[1][2]ISFYB

PELTON, BEVERLY JO
JENSEN, JO--[1][31]

PELTON, ROBERT W.
ARTHUR, TIFFANY--[1][31]
MARTIN, LEVIN--[1]
MARTIN, ROBERT W.--[1]
MILTON, MARK--[1]
NOTLEP, ROBERT--[1]
SONERO, DEVI--[1]

PELTONEN, CARLA F.
ERICKSON, LYNN--W/MOLLY SWANTON,
[10][21][26][34]MYS/ROM--
NUMEROUS NOVELS '80's

PELTONEN, JUHO VIHTORI
LINNANKOSKI, JOHANNES--[22]FINNISH

PEMBER, WILLIAM L.
MONMOUTH, JACK--[1][3]MYS--
JARROLDS "DONOVAN CASE" '55
HALE "NOT READY TO DIE" '60 & 3 MORE

PEMBER-DEVEREUX, MARGARET
DEVEREUX, ROY--[8]

PEMBERTON, MARGARET
CARLISLE, CARNS--[31]

PENDLETON, DON[ALD E.]
BOLAN, MACK--W/STEVEN MERTZ & MIKE NEWTON, [28]MYS,HP--
PINN "THE EXECUTIONER'S WAR BOOK" '77
BRITAIN, DAN--[2][7][11][18][23]SF--
PINN "THE GODMAKERS" '70
GREGORY, STEPHAN--PINN "THE HUNTRESS" '66
NEVA "MADAME MURDER" '67
PINN "THE INSATIABLES" '67
PINN "THE SEX GODDESS" '67
BRNDN "COLOR HER ADULTRESS" '67
PEC "THE SEXY SAINTS" '67
PEC "THE HOT ONE" '67
GRNLF "ALL LOVERS ACCEPTED" '68

PENDOWER, THOMAS CURTIS H
CARSTAIRS, KATHLEEN--[18][28][31]ROM--
GRESHAM "IT BEGAN IN SPAIN"
GRESHAM "THIRD TIME LUCKY"
GRESHAM "SHADOWS OF LOVE"
CURTIS, TOM--[18][22][28][29]WEST--
6 PAUL NOVELS 53-57 & 3 LONG NOVELS '57-59
DOWER[S], PENN--[18][22][28][29][31]WEST--
11 LONG NOVELS '52-64
HOWARD, HELEN--[8]
JACOBS, T.C.H. [1]--[2][3][18][28][29][32]MYS--
49 NOVELS '30-72
JCM "IN THE SURGERY" FEB '62
JACOBS, T.C.H. [2]
EW "MONSTER OF DUSSELDORF" NOV '64
PENDER, LEX--[1][22][28]
PENDER, MARILYN--[1][18][22][28]ROM--
5 GRESHAM NOVELS '60-66
PENDOWER, JACQUES--[28]MYS--
22 HALE NOVELS '59-74
PENN, ANNE--[18][22][28]ROM--
GRESHAM "DANGEROUS DELUSION" '60
GRESHAM "PROVE YOUR LOVE" '61
GRESHAM "MYSTERY PATIENT '66
STAGG, ANNE--[1]
STAGG, JAMES--W/JAMES STAGG,[34]MYS--
AMALG "PANIC IN THE NIGHT" '57

PENDRAY, GEORGE EDWARD
EDWARDS, GAWAIN--[2][7][11]SF--
"THE EARTH TUBE" '29

PENKALA, ALICE
ANTON, ROBERT--[39]GERMAN
BRUCKNER, BERTA--[39]GERMAN
MEINERT, ANNALIESE--[39]GERMAN

PENN, AUDREY
ZELLAN, AUDREY PENN--[1]

PENNANEN, LEA A.
PIKKUMOLLIAINEN, LEENA--[1]

PENNELL, ELIZABETH
GREEDY WOMAN--[1]

PENNER, MANOLA J.
ALEXANDER, JEAN--[8]

PENNEY, ANNETTE CULLER
CULLER, ANNETTE LORENA--[1][31]

PENNINGTON, DAVID ALEXAN.
DAUD, DAVID--[7]SF--
BK GUILD 'STARMAKER' #1:
"THE PULSE OF ETERNITY" '91

PENNINGTON, JACQUELINE E.
LANDRESS, ELEE--[21]ROM--
"WIND SONG"
"LOVE'S DESIGN"
"DESTINATION UNKNOWN"

PENNINGTON, ROD
STIVERS, DICK--[34]MYS,HP--
GE "LETHAL TRADE" '89

PENNY, FANNY EMILY FARR
PENNY, F.E.--[34]MYS--
PENNY, MRS. FRANK--[34]MYS--
METHUEN "A FOREST OFFICER" 1900
SONN "ROMANCE OF A NAUTCH GIRL" 1888

PENROSE, GORDON
ZED, DR.--[31][33]

PENTELOW, JOHN NIX
CLIFFORD, MARTIN--[1]MYS,HP--
HUNTINGTON, HARRY--[1][34]MYS--
AMALG "THE SMUGGLER'S SECRET" '21
NORTH, JACK--[1][32][34]MYS--
AMALG "HAYGARTH DETECTIVE" '11
AMALG "THE KIDNAPPER" '23
AMALG "JOHNNY MACK, DETECTIVE" '23
LM "SEARCH FOR ARMANDO" DEC '57
RANDOLPH, RICHARD--[1]
RICHARDS, FRANK--[1]MYS,HP--
RYLE, RANDOLPH--[1]
WEST, JOHN--[1]

PENWARDEN, HELEN
SMITH, JESSICA--[8]

PENZLER, OTTO
ADLER, IRENE--[1][31]--
"BALLOONING: HIGH & WILD" '76
FERRIER, LUCY--[1][31][33]--
"DIVING THE GREAT BARRIER REEF" '76
GREGORY, STEPHEN--[1][31][33]--
"BOBSLEDDING: DOWN THE CHUTE" '76
"RACING TO WIN:SALT FLATS" '76
MILVERTON, CHARLES A.--[1][31][33]

PEOPLE, GRANVILLE CHURCH
CHURCH, GRANVILLE--[1][3][22]MYS--
MILL "BOMBS BURST ONCE" '41
MILL "RACE WITH THE SUN" '44

PEPPER, CURTIS G.
PEPPER, BILL--[1]

PEPPER, FRANK S.
COLWYN, STEWART--[31][33]
MARSHALL, JOHN--[1]
WILTON, HAL--[1][33]

PEPPER, JOAN ALEXANDER W.
ALEXANDER, JOAN--[3][9][32]MYS--
HM "ONE SUNNY DAY" '74
AHMM "GREEN IS UNLUCKY" JAN '79

PERCEVAL, JULIA
DREW, PATRICIA--W/LLOYD S. KAYE,[3]--
LAN "DEEP IN A DARK COUNTRY" '68
BELM "WHO IS MELODY?" '68

PERCEVAL, JULIA [CONT]
PAULL, JESSICA--W/ROSAYLMER BURGER,[1][3]MYS--
AWARD "PASSPORT TO DANGER" '68
AWARD "DESTINATION: TERROR" '68
AWARD "RENDEZVOUS" '69
AWARD "RENDEZVOUS WITH DANGER '69
WALLACE, C.H.--W/ROSAYLMER BURGER,[3]MYS--
BELM B50-639 "CRASH LANDING IN THE CONGO" '65
BELM B50-664 "TAIL WIND TO DANGER" '66
BELM B50-722 "HIGHFLIGHT TO HELL" '66
BELM B50-734 "ETA TO HELL" '66
PETRIE, JODRA--W/PIXIE BURGER, V. BERCH LTR '93--
AWARD AQ1076 "BUSY WOMAN'S ALMANAC" '73

PERDIGUERO PEREZ, FERNAND
PIN, OSCAR--[1]

PERDUE, LEWIS
LUDLOW, IAN--W/LEE GOLDBERG,[34]MYS--
PINN "MAKE THEM PAY" '85
PINN ".357 VIGILANTE" '85
PINN "WHITEWASH" '85

PEREIRA, HAROLD BERTRAM
ASKARI, HUSAINI MUHAMMAD--[22][31] INDIAN-ENGLISH
YEATES, MABEL--[22]INDIAN-ENGLISH

PEREIRA, JOSE MARIA D.R.
REGIO, JOSE--[22]PORTUGUESE

PERELMAN, SIDNEY JOSEPH
DYMOV, OSIP ISIDOROVICH--[22]RUSSIAN
NAMLEREP, SIDNEY--[8]
PERELMAN, S.J.--[1][32]MYS--
EQMM "FAREWELL, MY LOVELY APPETIZER" JUL '45
EQMM "NESSELRODE TO JEOPARDY" OCT '52
EQMM "SAUCIER'S APPRENTICE" DEC '61
EQMM "DANGER IN THE DRAIN" JUN '64
[EL] SID--[1]

PERELMANN, ELIEZER
BEN YEHUDA--[22]HEBREW

PEREZ BLASCO, JULIO
CATANZARO, W.--JEAN F. LE DEIST LTR '93
DEL OLMO, JULIO--JEAN F. LE DEIST LTR '93
STERLING, KAREL--JEAN F. LE DEIST LTR '93

PEREZ GALDOS, BENITO
GALDOS, BENITO PEREZ--[31]

PEREZ-VENERO, MIRNA
PIERCE, MIRNA--[9][21][26]ROM--
"PANAMA FLAME"
"PANAMA GLORY"

PERHSON, HOWARD
KING, DAVID--[19][32]MYS--
LM "A JUGGLE OF WINE" SEPT '67
LOGAN, JAKE--[19]WEST,HP--
"RIDE, SLOCUM, RIDE"
"SLOCUM'S GOLD"
WESTON, MATT--[19]WEST

PERICHITCH, MILO
DEXTER, JOHN--W/ART PLOTNIK & GENE CROSS, MUNROE RVW '93, ADULT--
EL 327 "SHAME TIGERS" '66
LORD, SHELDON--MUNROE RVW FEB '93,ADULT--
BEAC B574F "FEVER IN THE SUN" '63
BEAC B603F "BEDROOM ROUTE" '63
BEAC B636F "A SPECIAL KIND OF LOVE" '63

PERICHITCH, MILO [CONT]
LORD, SHELDON [CONT]
BEAC B659X "THE SISTERHOOD" '63
BEAC B674X "MARTA" '63
BEAC B680F "THE RIVALS" '63
BEAC B704X "SEX IS A WOMAN" '64
MILLER, MARCUS--MUNROE REVIEW '93, ADULT--
NTSD 1851 "BROADWALK"
PENN, MICHAEL--MUNROE REVIEW '93
PERRY, L.J.--V. BERCH-BRNDN/BC PSEUDS, BAE 22--TWO TITLES
WILLIAMS, J.X.--MUNROE REVIEW '93

PERKERSON, MEDORA F.
FIELD, MEDORA--[1]

PERKINS, DEBORAH
GREY, SAMANTHA--[21][26]ROM--
"MARK OF ZORRO"

PERKINS, KENNETH
HALE, RANDOLPH--L. ROBBINS LTR MAR '94
KNIGHT, KIM--L. ROBBINS LTR C. WINTEROWD CALL '94
NIGHT, KIM--L. ROBBINS LTR C. WINTEROWD CALL '94
PHILLIPS, KING--L. ROBBINS LTR '94,[1]

PERKINS, PETER
COTTON, JERRY--[39]GERMAN/MYS,HP

PERKINS, VIOLET LILLIAN
LESLIE, LILIAN--W/ARCHER HOOD OR ARTHUR LESLIE,[1][2][11]

PERKINS, VIRGINIA CHASE
CHASE, VIRGINIA LOWELL--[1][31]

PERLBERG, CHARLEY W.
MEEK, JOSEPH--CRPG, ADULT/WEST,HP--
PINN 'MOUNTAIN JACK PIKE': #13-15 '93

PERLMAN, JESS
GRAY, PHILIP--[31]

PERREARD, SUZANNE L.B.
BUTLER, SUZANNE--[1][31][33]

PERREAU-SAUSSINE, GERALD
MILES, PETER--[1]
MILES, RICHARD--[1][3]MYS--
PYR "ANGEL LOVES NOBODY"
PYR "MOONBATHERS"
"THAT COLD DAY IN THE PARK" '74

PERRIN, FORREST V.
CARTER, NICK--[3]MYS,HP--
AWARD "BEIRUT INCIDENT" '74

PERRIN, PAT
PERRIMAN, COLE--W/WIN COLEMAN, CRPG--
"TERMINAL GAME"

PERRY, CHARLES
EL ROPO, SMOKESTACK--[31]

PERRY, CLAIR WILLARD
PERRY, CLAY--[8]

PERRY, DICK
WINFIELD, DICK--[1][2][7][11]--
PAPLB "DOOLIE'S PRIVATE GODDESS" '64

PERRY, ELEANOR [R.B.]
BAYER, ELEANOR--[1][31]
BAYER, OLIVER WELD--[1][31]

PERRY, GEORGETTE
PERRIWILS, G.W.--W/WILLIAM J. WILSON,[2]

PERRY, JAMES BLACK
WEIR, LOGAN--[1]

PERRY, MARTIN HENRY
MARTYN, HENRY--[1]

PERRY, MICHALANN
BLYTHE, MEGAN--[9][21][26]ROM--
"SATIN CHAINS"

PERRY, MONTANYE
LAMBERT, MARION--[1]

PERRY, RITCHIE JOHN ALLEN
ALLEN, JOHN--[3][18]MYS/ADULT--
HALE "COPACABANA STUD" '79
HALE "UPTIGHT" '79

PERRY, ROBERT
MARQUIS, DON--[8][32]MYS--
EQMM "IRON HAND IN THE VELVET GLOVE" AUG '54

PERRY, RUTH
CAMPION, ROSE--W/ARTHUR LEROY KASER & JEAN LEE LATHAM,[1]

PERRY, RUTH FULLER
FULLER, RUTH--[31]

PERRY, STEVE
FLINT, DICK--[34]MYS--
DIME NOVELS "PREDATOR" '90
PEEL, JESSE--[23]SF--
GALAXY "WITH CLEAN HANDS" '77

PERSHALL, MARY
SHELLEY, SUSAN--[9][21][26]ROM--
"LOVE'S ENCHANTMENT"

PERSHING, KAREN
PERCY, KAREN--[21][26]ROM--
"THE HOME STRETCH"
"LOVE COUNTS"
"IN TOO DEEP"
PRICE, KERRY--[9][21][26]ROM--
"FRENCHMAN'S KISS"
"A DASH OF SPICE"
"TOUCH OF MIDNIGHT"

PERSKE, BETTY
BACALL, LAUREN--[8]

PERTHES, HANS
THES, P.R.--[39]GERMAN

PERUS, FRANCOISE
CUEVA, FRANCOISE--[1]
PERUS-CUEVA, FRANCOISE--[1]

PESCHKE, HANS
BROWN, W.--[39]GERMAN/SF,HP
HANSEN, PETER--[39]GERMAN/SF
KERN, GREGORY--[39]GERMAN/SF
PATTON, HARVEY--[39]GERMAN/SF
PEARSON, HARVEY--[39]GERMAN/SF
WILDEN, HARRY F.--[39]GERMAN/SF

PESCOLLER, HEINRICH
BROWN, HARRY--[39]GERMAN/WEST
HARDING, TEX--[39]GERMAN/WEST

PESHKOV, ALEXEI M.
CHLAMYDA, JEHUDIIL--[1][31]
GORKI, MAKSIM--[22]RUSSIAN
GORKY, MAXIM--[1][22]RUSSIAN

PESLER-ADAM, DORA
PEAD, D.--[39]GERMAN/MYS
ARTHUS, TH.--[39]GERMAN/MYS
NIEMANN, DORA--[39]GERMAN/MYS

PESSOA, FERNANDO [A.N.]
ANON, CHARLES ROBERT--[31]
CAEIRO, ALBERTO--[22][31]PORTUGUESE
DE CAMPOS, ALVARO--[22][31]PORTUGUESE
DE TEIVE, BARON--[31]
REIS, RICARDO--[22]PORTUGUESE

PETAJA, EMIL
PINE, E. THEODORE--W/HENRY HASSE, [2][11][23]SF--
SWANZA, H.J.--[2]

PETER, ALICE [J]
JURGENSEN, HELKE--[39]GERMAN

PETERKIEWICZ, JERZY
PIETRKIEWICZ, JERZY--[23]SF

PETERS, ARTHUR A.
PETERS, FRITZ--[8]

PETERS, CHARLES FRANCIS
FRANCIS, CHARLES--[34]MYS--
HALE "ASK A RIVER" '64

PETERS, HERMANN
CAINE, STAFF--[39]GERMAN/MYS/SF
COTTON, JERRY--[39]GERMAN/MYS,HP
CURTIS, JOHN--[39]GERMAN/MYS/SF
MESCALERO, JEFF--[39]GERMAN/MYS/SF
PORTER, NEIL--[39]GERMAN/MYS/SF
SCOTT, TED--[39]GERMAN/MYS/SF
STRANGER, BERT--[39]GERMAN/MYS/SF

PETERS, MAUREEN
BLACK, MAUREEN--[9]ROM
BLACK, VERONICA--[3][9][21][26]ROM/MYS--
"FAIR KILMENY"
"MOONFLEETS" & 13 MORE '69-80
DARBY, CATHERINE--[3][7][21]ROM/MYS--
"SING ME A MOON"
"FALCON'S CLAW" & 17 MORE '75-9
LAW, ELIZABETH--[21][26][34]MYS/ROM--
WALKER "THE SEALED KNOT" '89 & 3 MORE
LLOYD, LEVANAH--[1][9]ROM
ROTHMAN, JUDITH--[1][3][9]MYS/ROM--
HALE "WITH MURDER IN MIND" '75
WHITBY, SHARON--[7][8]SF--
HALE "CHILDREN OF THE RAINBOW" '83
HALE "THE SAVAGE WEB" '82
WHITLEY, SHARON--[1][9]ROM

PETERS, ROBERT LOUIS
BRIDGE, JOHN--[8]

PETERSEN, GWENN BOARDMAN
BOARDMAN, GWENN R.--[1][31]

PETERSHAM, MAUD SYLVIA F.
FULLER, MAUD--[31]

PETERSHAM, P.M.
PETERSHAM, MISKA--[1]

PETERSILEA, CARLYLE
VON HIMMEL, ERNST--[2]

PETERSON, BOB
COUNCIL OF FOUR--W/TOM WALKER, CHUCK HANSEN, ROY HUNT, NORM METCALF, ELLIS MILLS,[2]

PETERSON, CORINNA
COCHRANE, CORINNA--[1]

PETERSON, DOUGLAS
CASE, PEG--W/PEGGY C. CASE, HAWK/CASE INTVW '93, MYS--
PPJKS "TOTAL RECALL"

PETERSON, ESTER [ALLEN]
ALLEN, RUTH--[1][31][33]

PETERSON, GWENN BOARDMAN
BOARDMAN, GWENN R.--[33]

PETERSON, HARALD ALFRED
BERGSTEDT, HARALD ALFRED--[22]DANISH

PETERSON, JOHN VICTOR
VALDING, VICTOR--W/ALLAN INGVALD BENSON, [1][2][11]

PETERSON, JON
PETERSON, CHRISTMAS--W/JOYCE CHRISTMAS, [21]ROM--
"HIDDEN ASSETS"

PETERSON, KAJ HARALD L.
MUNK, KAJ--[22]DANISH

PETERSON, MARGARET [ANN]
GREEN, GLINT--[22][34]MYS--
HUTCH "DEVIL SPIDER" '32
HUTCH "POISON DEATH '33 & 2 MORE

PETERSON, ROBERT E.
SAYA, PETER--[1][22]AMERICAN

PETERZEN, ELISABETH
SKAFTE, KATRIN & ERIK--[40]MYS--
"LAUTER GANZ NORMALIE MANNER" '90

PETHICK, PHILIP M.
VANE, BRETT--[34]MYS,HP--
WARREN "MISS PINK PAYS OFF" '50

PETIOT, HENRI JULES C.
DANIEL-ROPS, HENRI--[1][22][31]FRENCH
ROPS, DANIEL--[1][22]FRENCH

PETRATUR, JOYCE
VERETTE, JOYCE--[1][9][21][26]ROM--
"DESERT FIRES"
"LION & THE LOTUS" & 9 MORE

PETRIE, RHONA
DUELL, EILEEN-MARIE--[8]

PETROCELLI, ORLANDO R.
DYER, BRIAN--W/BRIAN ROTHERY,[1][31]--
MASON & LIPSCOMB "SAGA OF A CELTIC QUEEN"
DYER, BRIAN--[31]MYS--
PINN "MATCH SET" '77
MANOR "WAYWARD HEART" '78
MANOR "FIVE DAYS TO PARADISE" '78

PETRONE, JANE MUIR
MUIR, JANE--[1][22]AMERICAN

PETROV, STEPAN G.
SKITALETS--[1][22]RUSSIAN

PETRY, ERNEST
WIDOC, E.N.--[39][40]GERMAN/MYS--
"EIN GESICHT WIE TAUSEND ANDERE" '58

PETTERSON, H. BERTIL
MALM, MARGARETHA--[1]

PETTERSON, JULIUS
REGIS, JULIUS--[1][3][29]MYS--
AHLEN & AKERLUND "DET BLA SPARET" '12
HOLT "NO 13 TORONI" '22
HOLT "THE COPPER HOUSE" '23

PETTERSSON, JULIUS
REGIS, JUL.--[29]MYS--

PETTES, GEORGE W.
X.Y.Z. CLUB--W/JOHN GODFREY SAXE & DOUGLAS A. LIVEN,[1]

PETTIT, AUBREY L. JR
PETTIT, MIKE--V. BERCH LTR TO HUBIN '94,MYS--
MEDIA PUB "A NEED TO KILL" '90

PETTIT, CHARLES
RESURGAM--[1]

PETTY, ALAN
JUDD, ALAN--V. BERCH LTR TO HUBIN '94, MYS--
HUTCH "TANGO" '89

PEYTON, KATHLEEN WENDY
HERALD, KATHLEEN--W/MICHAEL PEYTON,[1][31][33]
PEYTON, K.M.--W/MICHAEL PEYTON,[1][7][33]SF--
"A PATTERN OF ROSES" '72

PEYTON, MICHAEL
HERALD, KATHLEEN--W/KATHLEEN WENDY PEYTON, [1][31][33]
PEYTON, K.M.--W/KATHLEEN WENDY PEYTON, [1][7][33]SF--
"A PATTERN OF ROSES" '72

PFAEFFLI, CARINA
TAUSCHECK, CARINA--[39]GERMAN/JUV

PFAFF, BRIGITTE
KELLER, BRIGITTE--[39]GERMAN

PFALZGRAF, FLORENCE L.
LEIGHTON, FLORENCE--[3][22]MYS--
ARCH "AS STRANGE A MAZE" '35

PFANDLER, MARCEL
NOLDREN, MARK--[39]GERMAN/JUV
RENOLD, MARTIN--[39]GERMAN/JUV

PFEFFER, HEINRICH
BELL, OTTO--[39]GERMAN
BENALTI, ALEXANDER--[39]GERMAN
BERYLL, THOMAS--[39]GERMAN
DARRY, HARRY--[39]GERMAN
MORGAN, MAX--[39]GERMAN
MURGEL, MUSAGET--[39]GERMAN
THOMAS, MANFRED--[39]GERMAN
WENDEL, OTTOKAR--[39]GERMAN

PFEIFFER, C. BOYD
FLETCHER, SCOTT--[1]

PFEIFFER-BELLI, ERICH
HELT, ANDREAS--[39]GERMAN

PFEIL, DONALD J.
ARROW, WILLIAM--[2][7][11][23]SF,HP--
BAL "ESCAPE FROM TERROR LAGOON" '76
AWARD "RETURN TO THE PLANET OF THE APES 2" '76
DONALDSON, P.J.--V. BERCH-BRNDN/BC PSEUDS, BAE 22, P24

PFEIL, JOHN FREDERICK
PFEIL, FRED--[23]SF--
"GOODMAN 2020" '86

PFERDEKAMP, WILHELM
NOLDEN, ARNOLD--[39]GERMAN/JUV

PFERSMANN VON EICHTHAL, R
EICHTHAL, RUDOLF--[39]GERMAN

PFISTERER, SALLY
LAURENCE, ANNE--[21][26]ROM--
"ALWAYS SAY YES"
MARTIN, SALLY--[26]ROM--
"NUMBERED KISSES"
"THE RELUCTANT BRIDEGROOM"

PFLAUM, GEORGE A.
ST. CLAIR, ERIC--[11]

PFLAUM, SUSANNA WHITNEY
CONNOR, SUSANNA PFLAUM--[31]

PFOUTZ, SHIRLEY ECLOV
ECLOV, SHIRLEY--[1][31]

PFRAGNER, JULIUS
GENNER, JULIUS--[39]GERMAN/JUV

PFRETZCHNER, HERBERT
KYLLBURG, HERBERT--[39]GERMAN/JUV

PHARR, ROBERT D.
WASHINGTON C.--[1]

PHEGLEY, ANNA
HOLLISTER, RAINE--[26]ROM--
"EXCEPTION TO THE RULE"

PHELON, MIRA M. & W.P.
THE PHELONS--[2]

PHELPS, ELIZABETH STEWART
NORTH, LEIGH--[1]

PHELPS, GEORGE H.
TANGENT, PATRICK Q.--[2]

PHILBRICK, WILLIAM RODMAN
DANTZ, WILLIAM R.--[7][34]MYS/SF--
AVON "PULSE" '90
MORROW "THE SEVENTH SLEEPER" '91

PHILIPP, ELLIOT ELIAS
EMBEY, PHILIP--[8][22][31]ENGLISH
HAVIL, ANTHONY--[8]
TEMPEST, VICTOR--[8][22]ENGLISH

PHILIPP, JULIUS
HERGESELL, PHILIPP--[39]GERMAN

PHILIPS, GEORGE NORMAN
EVANS, GWYN--W/G.A. EVANS, G.H. TEED & R.M. GRAYDON,[34]MYS--
WRIGHT "MURDERERS MET" '34

PHILIPS, GEORGE NORMAN [CONT]
EVANS, GWYN--[34]MYS,GHOSTED--
WRIGHT "DEATH SPEAKING" '34
??UNCONFIRMED ??
FREMLIN, VICTOR--[1]
SKENE, ANTHONY--[3]MYS--
AMALG "DEATH TRAP" '30
AMALG "CROOK TOWN" '32
& 30 MORE '30-48

PHILIPS, JUDSON P.
BENTLEY, HUGH--[29]MYS--
ONLY USED IN SWEDEN
OWEN, PHILIP--[1][3][18]MYS--
BERKSHIRE "MYSTERY AT A COUNTRY INN" '79
PENTECOST, HUGH--[2][3][5][11][18]MYS--
54 BOOKS [SOME SS COLL.] '39-80
NUMEROUS DIGEST STORIES

PHILIPS, MARY ALICE
MOORE, PHILIPS--W/DORIS O. MOORE,[3]MYS--
ARCADIA "DEATH DRIVES THE LEAD CAR" '61
TOWER "ONCE UPON A FRIDAY" '65

PHILIPSOHN, MARTIN
WELTEN, HEINZ--[39]GERMAN

PHILIPSON, ALAN
HILD, JACK--[34]MYS,HP--
GE "BUTCHERS OF EDEN" '84
GE "GULAG WAR" '85
GE "JIHAD" '86
GE 'SOB's':
"BARRABUS STING" '88
"BARRABUS STRIKE" '88
GE "PLAINS OF FIRE" '84
GE "RED HAMMER" '85
GE "VULTURES OF THE HORN" '86

PHILLIFENT, JOHN T.
COLSON, DOROTHEA--[1]
JOHNSON, ALAN--[1]
RACKHAM, JOHN--P. HARBOTTLE-TB CKLST, PP#38, [2][11][23]SF--
'SPACE PUPPET' SERIES '54
'CHAPPIE JONES' STORIES
TB "SPACE PUPPET" '54
TB "MASTER WEED" '54
TB "JUPITER EQUILATERAL" '54
TB "ALIEN VIRUS" '55

PHILLIPS, ALAN MEYRICK K.
PHILLIPS, MICKEY--[22]ENGLISH

PHILLIPS, ALEXANDER FORBE
FORBES, ATHOL--[1]

PHILLIPS, ANNE GARVEY
DYE, ANNE G.--[31]

PHILLIPS, BLUEBELL S.
ARTHUR, GEORGE--[31]
GRIGGS, MARY--[31]

PHILLIPS, CHARLES WALTER
PROUT, DENTON--[13]AUSTRALIAN

PHILLIPS, DAVID ATLEE
ST. GEORGE, DAVID--W/GEORGI MARKOV, [1][7][23]SF--
"THE RIGHT HONORABLE CHIMPANZEE" '78

PHILLIPS, DAVID GRAHAM
GRAHAM, JOHN--[1][31]

PHILLIPS, DENNIS JOHN A.
CHALLIS, SIMON--[8][18][34]MYS--
HALE "DEATH ON A QUITE BEACH" '68
CHAMBERS, PETER--V. BERCH-MON PSEUDS,
BAE 9,[2][3][29]MYS--
36 HALE NOVELS '61-89
CHESTER, PETER--[18][29][34]MYS--
JENKINS "MURDER FORSTALLED" '60
JENKINS "TRAITORS" '64
& 3 MORE
DANIELS, PHILIP--[7][18][34]MYS/SF--
HALE "DRACULA MURDERS" '83 & 12 MORE '79-86
PHILLIPS, D.J.--[31]
PHILLIPS, DENNIS--[18]MYS--
"REVENGE, INC." '70

PHILLIPS, DORIAN M.
DORIAN, PHILIP--[34]MYS--
DORRANCE "THE STREAKER MURDERS" '76

PHILLIPS, ELIZABETH LOU.
PHILLIPS, BETTY LOU--[33]

PHILLIPS, ELIZABETH M.A.
PHILLIPS, BETTY--[1]

PHILLIPS, GEORGE NORMAN
NORMAN, PHILIP--[1]

PHILLIPS, GERALD WILLIAM
HUNTINGDON, JOHN--[1][22][34]MYS--
HOLT "THE SEVEN BLACK CHESSMEN" '28

PHILLIPS, GORDON
LUCIO--[8]

PHILLIPS, HORACE
DUKE, DEREK--[1]
HOPE, WALTER--[1]
STANTON, MARJORIE--[1]

PHILLIPS, HOWARD
RIVAS, GUILLERMO--[1]

PHILLIPS, HUBERT
CALIBAN--[8]
DOGBERRY--[8]
NINESPOT--[8]

PHILLIPS, HUGH
HUGHES, PHILLIP--[1]

PHILLIPS, IRVING W.
PHILLIPS, IRV--[33]
SABUSO--[33]

PHILLIPS, JAMES ATLEE
ATLEE, PHILIP--R. JAMES-'BEAUTIFUL LADY'
BAE 18,[29][34]MYS--
GM 1321 "GREEN WOUND" '63 & 22 MORE

PHILLIPS, JAMES R.
MCLAUGHLIN, BILL--[1]

PHILLIPS, JAMES W.
EBLIS, J. PHILIP--[31]

PHILLIPS, JILL META
LATIMER, JOANNA--[31]--
"STAR" CONTRIBUTOR
PHILLIPS, JILL M.--[21]ROM--
"THE RAIN MAIDEN"

PHILLIPS, JOHN BERTRAM
PHILLIPS, J.B.--[1]

PHILLIPS, KATHLEEN
COLE, ANNETTE--W/BARBARA A. STEINER,[1]
D'ANDREA, KATE--W/BARBARA A. STEINER,[1]

PHILLIPS, MAURICE J.
PHILLIPS, MAC--[1][22]AMERICAN

PHILLIPS, MICHAEL J.
LIVINGSTONE, MARK J.--W/JUDITH PELLA,[7]SF--
"THE PEACEMAKER" '90

PHILLIPS, NORMAN
ANGLEMAN, JACK--V. BERCH-BRNDN/BC PSEUDS,
BAE 22, P24

PHILLIPS, OLGA SOMECH
OLGA--[1]

PHILLIPS, PATRICIA SONIA
PHILLIPS, PAT--[21]ROM--
"LADY OF THE MOOR"
"MEDITERRANEAN ADVENTURE" & 2 MORE
PHILLIPS, SONIA--[21][26]ROM--
"BEATRICE"
"GIRL IN THE YELLOW DRESS"
"VENETIAN SPRING"

PHILLIPS, PAULINE ESTHER
VAN BUREN, ABIGAIL--[22]AMERICAN--
ADVICE COLUMNIST

PHILLIPS, STELLA
KENT, STELLA--[31]

PHILLIPS, SUSAN E.
COLE, JUSTINE--W/CLAIRE KIEHL,[9][21][26]ROM--
"THE COPELAND BRIDE"

PHILLIPS, WATTS
BALFOUR, F.--[34]MYS--NO TITLES KNOWN

PHILLIPS-BIRT, DOUGLAS
ARGUS--[1][22]ENGLISH
HEXTALL, DAVID--[1][22][31]ENGLISH
HOGARTH, DOUGLAS--[1][22][31]ENGLISH

PHILLPOTTS, ADELAIDE
ROSS, MARY ADELAIDE EDEN--[1]

PHILLPOTTS, EDEN
HEXT, HARRINGTON--[2][3][5][11][18][23]MYS--
MacM "THE MONSTER" '25 & 3 MORE'22-5

PHILO, GORDON
FORSYTE, CHARLES--V. BERCH LTR TO HUBIN '93
MYS--
CASSELL "DIVING DEATH" '62
& 4 MORE '61-80

PHILPOT, JOSEPH HENRY
LAFARGUE, PHILIP--[2][23]SF/ROM--
"THE FORSAKEN WAY: A ROMANCE" 1900

PHILPOTT, ALEXIS ROBERT
PANTOPUCK--[8]

PHILSTRAND, RAGNAR
ROBINSON--[29]MYS

PHYSICK, EDWARD HAROLD
VISIAK, E.H.--[2][23]SF--
"THE HAUNTED ISLAND" '10
"MEDUSA: A STORY OF MYSTERY" '29

PIANKA, PHYLLIS TAYLOR
AMES, WINTER--[9][21][26]ROM--
"EMERALD BAY"

PIATT, JOHN JAMES
TWO FRIENDS--W/WILLIAM DEAN HOWELLS,[1]

PIAZZI, ADRIENNE
HANOUM, LEILA--[1]

PICARD, DOROTHY YOUNG
CROMAN, DOROTHY YOUNG--[1]

PICCIRILLI, THOMAS EDWARD
PICCIRILLI, TOM--[7]SF--
BR. POCK "DARK FATHER" '90

PICHLER, ERNST
SAHARIEN--[39]GERMAN/SF

PICK, KARL
DELMONT, JOSEPH--[7][23][39]GERMAN/SF--
"THE SUBMARINE CITY" '30

PICK, ROBERT
RICHTER, VALENTIN--[1]

PICKART, JOAN ELLIOTT
ELLIOTT, ROBIN--[9][21][26]ROM--
"BETTING MAN"
"SILVER SANDS" & 10 MORE

PICKEN, MARY BROOKS
JOAN, MARY--[1]
MADISON, MARY--[1]
MCCLEARY, ELEANOR--[1]
WELLS, JANE WARREN--[1]

PICKER, RITA
SULTAN, MARTINA--[9][21][26]ROM--
"WHEN LIGHTNING STRIKES"

PICKERING, EILEEN MARION
FALCON, MARK--[28]WEST--
HALE "RELUCTANT OUTLAW" '79
HALE "YELLOW BANDANNA" '79
HALE "LIGHTNING HITS GLORY TOWN" '80

PICKERING, ROBERT EASTON
PICKERING, R.E.--[34]MYS--
GOLZ "HIMSELF AGAIN" '66
RPRT AS "UNCOMMITTED MAN" IN U.S.

PICKERING, STEPHEN
BEN AVRAHAM, CHOFETZ C.--[1][31]

PICKLER, EBERHARD
PAYER, ERIK N.--[39][40]GERMAN/MYS--
"EIN KOPF KEHRE ZURUCK" '50 & OTHERS

PICKLES, M. ELIZABETH
BURGOYNE, ELIZABETH--[1][22][31]ENGLISH

PICTON, NINA
DEARBORN, LAURA--[1][2]

PIDGEON, WILLIAM EDWIN
W.E.P.--[13]AUSTRALIAN

PIERCE, EDITH GRAY
GRAY, MARIAN--[31][33]

PIERCE, FRANK RICHARDSON
RANGER, SETH--L. ROBBINS LTR MAR '94

PIERCE, GEORGIA
HANKS, LINDSEY--W/LINDA CHESNUTT,
[9][21][26]ROM--
"OUTLAW LOVER"
"SAVAGE SURRENDER" & 4 MORE

PIERCE, JOHN LEONARD
BRAMLETT, JOHN--[1][3]MYS--
GM 1483 "TROUBLE-TEXAS STYLE "65
GM "DEVIL IN BROAD DAYLIGHT" '67

PIERCE, JOHN ROBINSON
COUPLING, J.J.--[2][11][22][23][31]SF--
ROBERTS, JOHN--[1][2][11][23]SF--

PIERCE, MARY CUNNINGHAM
CUNNINGHAM, MARY--[1][8]

PIERCE, WILLIAM LUTHER
MACDONALD, ANDREW--[7]SF--
VANG "THE TURNER DIARIES" '78
VANG "HUNTER: A NOVEL" '89

PIERSON, JOHN H.G.
HAND, JOHN--[31]--
"THE CIRCLING BEAST" [POEMS] '41

PIESTRE, PIERRE ETIENNE
CORMON, EUGENE--[22]FRENCH

PIETRKIEWICZ, JERZY
PETERKIEWICZ, JERZY--[1][2][11]

PIETRUSCHINSKI, HORST
HARDER, BEN--[39]GERMAN/ADV/JUV

PIETSCH, JOSEF
FLAM, COSMUS--[39]GERMAN

PIETSCHMANN, RICHARD JOHN
MILLER, RICHARD--[1]
PARISH, TOWNSEND--[1]

PIGGOTT, WILLIAM C.
WALES, HUBERT--[1][2][3]MYS--
CENTURY "BROCKLEBANK RIDDLE" '14
LONG "BLUE FLAME" '18

PIJET, GEORG W.
PINKPANK, PETER--[39]GERMAN/JUV

PIKE, MARY HAYDEN G.
LANGDON, MARY--[1]
MAY, IDA--[1]
STORY, SYDNEY A. JR.--[1]

PIKE, ROBERT MARVIN
PIKE, BOB--L. MUNROE--
NUETZEL INTRVW, BAE 25--
PUBLISHER & NOVELS
STRICK, MARV--L. MUNROE-NUETZEL INTRVW,
BAE 25--
PIKE 102 "BEATNIK BALL" '61
STRICK, MARVIN--[1]

PIKE, WILLIAM ERNEST
CONQUEST, OWEN--[1]HP
JAMES, ERNEST--[1]
RICHARDS, FRANK--[1]HP

PILCHER, ROSAMUNDE
FRASER, JANE--[9][21][26]ROM--
"BRIDGE OF CORVIE"
"DEAR TOM" & 4 MORE

PILE, D.W.
WEBBER, STAWFORD--[1]

PILKINGTON, BETTY
ALTSTERLUND, BETTY--[31]

PILLAI, N.N.
OMCHERY--[1]

PILLEY, PHIL
LINDLEY, GERARD--[8]

PILOTIN, MICHAEL
SPRIEL, STEPHEN--[2][11]

PILZ, ROLF
LENNAR, ROLF--[39]GERMAN/JUV

PINCHERLE, ALBERTO
MORAVIO, ALBERTO--[2][7][22][32]ITALIAN/MYS--
EQMM "ONLY THE DEATH OF A MAN" OCT '67
& NOVELS

PINCHIN, FRANK J[AMES]
DAGMAR, PETER--[7][23]SF--
DIGIT "ALIEN SKIES" '62
DIGIT "ONCE IN TIME" '63
DIGIT "SANDS OF TIME" "63
DIGIT "SPYKOS 4: STRNGE LIFE FORMS ON UNEXPLORED PLANETS" '62
DIGIT "TWO EQUALS ONE" '82

PINCHOT, ANN KRAMER
KULICK, JOHN--[31]

PINCKNEY, BARBARA B.P.
PINCKNEY, CALLAN--[1]

PINE, LESLIE GILBERT
MOORSHEAD, HENRY--[1][22]ENGLISH

PING-CHIH, CHIANG
TING-LING--[22]CHINESE

PINHEIRO, PAULO H.B.
BARBARA, PAULO HENRIQUE--[1]

PINIANSKI, PATRICIA
GRIFFITH, ROSLYNN--W/LINDA SWEENEY,[26]ROM--
"HEART OF THE JAGUAR"
"PRETTY BIRDS OF PASSAGE" & OS
MCKENNA, ROSE ANNE--[9][21]ROM--
"A CHANGE OF HEART"
PATRICK, LYNN--W/LINDA SWEENEY,[7][21][26]ROM--
"MISTLETOE MAGIC"
"MERMAID'S TOUCH" & 10 MORE
PATRICK, ROSLYN--W/LINDA SWEENEY,[26]ROM--
"PRINCESS ROYALE"
ROSE, JEANNE--W/LINDA SWEENEY,[26]ROM--
"BELEIVING IN ANGELS"
ROSEMOOR, PATRICIA--[9][10][21][26]ROM--
"DEATH SPIRAL"
"CRIMSON HOLIDAY" & 13 MORE

PINKERT, ERNST FRIEDRICH
ERNST, FRIEDRICH--[39]GERMAN
FRIEDRICH, ERNST--[39]GERMAN
VON DETTEN, LEONORE--[39]GERMAN

PINKERTON, A. FRANK A.
PINKERTON, FRANK--[3]MYS--
6 NOVELS [ca. 1900]
RYAN, DETECTIVE PATRICK--[3]MYS--
LAIRD "A DARING HORSE THIEF" 1890

PINKNEY, [JERRY] BRIAN
PINKNEY, J. BRIAN--[33]

PINKWATER, DANIEL MANUS
DUCK, CAPTAIN--[1]
LOME, MIKE--[1]
PINKWATER, D. MANUS--G. COOK LTR '93
PINKWATER, DANIEL M.--G. COOK LTR '93
PINKWATER, MANUS--G. COOK,[23]SF/THRIL--
"WINGMAN" '75
TRESS, ARTHUR--[1]

PINNIX, HANNAH COURTNEY
KERR--[1]

PINTER, HAROLD
BARON, DAVID--[31]

PINTO, JACQUELINE HARRIS
BLAIRMAN, JACQUELINE--[1]

PIOTROWSKY, ANDREW
HUNT, STOKER--[31]

PIPER, DAVID TOWRY
TOWRY, PETER--[8]

PIPER, EVELYN
MODELL, MIRIAM--R.C. & ELWANDA RVW '93,[8]--
BB 425 "MY SISTER, MY BRIDE" '49

PIPER, HORACE BEAM
PIPER, H. BEAM--[7]SF--
'FUZZIES' SERIES
'FEDERATION' SERIES

PIPKIN, DENICE
GREENLEA, DENICE--[21][26]ROM--
"THE MASQUER"
"FORTUNE SEEKER" & 4 MORE

PIRANDELLO, STEFANO
LANDI, STEFANO--[22]ITALIAN

PIRIE-GORDON, HARRY
PIRIE-GORDON, C.H.C.--[1]
PROSPERO & CALIBAN--W/FREDERICK ROLFE,[2]

PIRWITZ, HORST
SCHREIBER, RAINER--[39]GERMAN/JUV

PISCINI, INGRID
FRITSCH, INA--[39]GERMAN/JUV

PISCULESCU, GRIGORE
GALACTION, GALA--[22]RUMANIAN

PISERCHIA, DORIS
SELBY, CURT--AFRAID #18,[2][7][23]SF/HOR--
DAW "THE SPINNER" '80
DAW "THE FLUGER" '80
DAW 'BLOOD COUNTRY" '81
DAW "I, ZOMBIE" '82

PISTORIUS, PIETER
HENDRIKS, P.G.--[1]

PITCAIRN, JOHN JAMES
ASHDOWN, CLIFFORD--W/R. AUSTIN FREEMAN, [2][29][32][34]MYS--
EQMM "ASSYRIAN REJUVENATOR" JAN '47
EQMM "ADVENTURES OF ROMNEY PRINGLE" FEB '48
TRAIN "QUEEN'S TREASURE" '75
WARD/TRAIN - 3 OTHER BKS '02-75
PIERS, ASHDOWN--W/RICHARD FREEMAN,[1]

PITCHER, EVELYN G.
GOODENOUGH, EVELYN--[22][31]AMERICAN

PITCHER, GLADYS
ADAMS, BETSY--[2]AMERICAN
WENTWORTH, BARBARA--[22]AMERICAN
WESTON, ANN--[22]AMERICAN

PITT, STAN[LEY]
JAIS, SAFONE--[2][35]AUSTRALIAN--
PRIMARILY A COVER ILLUSTRATOR

PITT-AIKENS, TOM
AIKENS, TOM PITT--[31]

PITTARD, HELENE [D]
ROGER, NOELLE--[1][2][23]SF--
"THE NEW ADAM" '26
"HE WHO SEES" '35

PITTIONI, HANS
WOHLMUTH, HANS--[39]GERMAN

PITTOCK, JOAN [H]
WESSON, JOAN--[1]

PIZZUTI, CAROLYN
ZANE, CAROLYN--[26]ROM--
SIL 1011 "WIFE NEXT DOOR"
SIL 1035 "WIFE IN NAME ONLY"

PLACE, MARIAN T.
WHITE, DALE--[1][22][33]AMERICAN/JUV
WHITINGER, R.D.--[1][22][33]JUV

PLAGAKIS, JIM
DORE, CHRISTY--[9][21][26]ROM--
"PASSIONATE AWAKENING"

PLANT, RICHARD
BROCKHOFF, STEFAN--W/OSKAR SEIDLIN & DIETER CUNTZ,[39][40]GERMAN/MYS--
"BEGENUNG IN ZERMATT" '55

PLATH, SYLVIA
LUCAS, VICTORIA--[8][22]AMERICAN

PLATT, CHARLES [M]
BARCLAY, WILLIAM--J. DAVEY LTR '93,[2]NW-
WROTE OBITUARY OF JAMES COLVIN
CANTWELL, ASTON--[23][31]SF/ADULT--
"TEASE FOR TWO" '83
"DOUBLE DELIGHT" '83
CLARKE, ROBERT--RUCKER INTRVW, PP 11,[7]--
AVON "LESS THAN HUMAN" '86
PRENTISS, CHARLOTTE--W/WILLIAM BRAME, [23][26]ROM--
"CHILDREN OF THE ICE"
"PEOPLE OF THE MESA"
"LOVE'S SAVAGE EMBRACE" '81
ST. JAMES, BLAKELY--[1][2][11][23]SF,HP--
PLAYBOY "CHRISTINE ENCHANTED"

PLATT, EDWARD
TRENT, PAUL--[3][29]MYS--
WARD "AIR BANDITS" '35
WARD "CRAVEN MYS" '29 & 58 MORE'13-46

PLATT, KIN
CARR, KIRBY--[3][7]MYS/SF--
CANYON "GIRLS WHO CAME TO MURDER" '74
CANYON "LET ME KILL YOU SWEETHEART" '74
CANYON "WHO KILLED YOU, CINDY CASTLE?" '74
MAJOR "DON'T BET ON LIVING, ALICE" '75
MAJOR "YOU DIE NEXT, JILL BABY" '75
MAJOR "YOU'RE HIRED, YOUR DEAD" '75

PLATT, KIN [CONT]
CARR, KIRBY [CONT]
CANYON "HITMAN #4" '75
MAJOR "IMPOSSIBLE SPY" '76
YORK, WESLEY SIMON--[1][2]

PLATTE, HEINZ ERICH
ARNEMANN, FRED--[39]GERMAN

PLATTEN, WILL
FACIUS, ESTHER--[39]GERMAN
JOSSA, HANS-MARTIN--[39][40]GERMAN/MYS--
"LIEBE, LUST & LEICHEN" '88

PLATTS, BERYL
SEATON, BERYL--[1]

PLAUT, ALLENE TALMEY
TALMEY, ALLENE--[1]

PLAWIN, PAUL
GODLY, J.P.--[1][31]
STEELE, DIRK--[1]

PLAYER, EDDIE
REID, DESMOND--W/G.P. MANN,[1][34]MYS,HP--
AMALG "MURDER MADE EASY" '60

PLEHN, HEINZ
LEHNERT, H.P.--[39]GERMAN

PLENK, ELEONORA
PFNISS, MARIA--[39]GERMAN

PLES, SALLY R.
REID, SALLY HELEN--HAWK/PLES INTRVW '93, MYS--
ZEBRA "UNDERTOW"

PLIEKSANS, JAN
RAINIS, JAN--[22]LATIVIAN

PLIMMER, CHARLOTTE
DENIS, CHARLOTTE--W/DENIS PLIMMER,[1][31]

PLIMMER, DENIS
DENIS, CHARLOTTE--W/CHARLOTTE PLIMMER,[1][31]

PLIMPTON, GEORGE [AMES]
PLIMPTON, PRUFROCK--[1]

PLOGSCHTIES, H.
BJERREGAARD, HENNING--[39]GERMAN/MYS

PLOMER, WILLIAM C.F.
D'ARFEY, WILLIAM--[8][22]SOUTH AFRICAN
PAGAN, ROBERT--[8]SOUTH AFRICAN

PLOOG, ILSE
WINDMULLER, ILSE--[39]GERMAN/JUV

PLOSSNER, JUTTA
ANDERSON, MELISSA--[39]GERMAN
FRANK, DR. STEFAN--[39]GERMAN

PLOTNIK, ARTHUR
DEXTER, JOHN--W/MILO PERCHITCH & GENE CROSS, MUNROE RVW '93, ADULT--
EL 327 "SHAME TIGERS" '66
HOLLIDAY, DON--MUNROE RVW '93, ADULT--
WILLIAMS, A.P.--MUNROE RVW '93, ADULT--
BEAC B731X "TUTOR FROM LESBOS" '64

PLOTZE, HASSO
COLT, KING--[39]GERMAN/WEST
COTTON, JERRY--[39][40]GERMAN/MYS,HP

PLOTZE, HASSO [CONT]
FALKENHAIN, JENS--[39][40]GERMAN/MYS--
"ARTZ UN DAMOND" '68 & 8 OTHERS
HECHT, HASSO--[39][40]GERMAN/MYS--
"BIS DICH DER TEUFEL HOLT" '73 & 4 OTHERS
WELLS, FRANK--[39]GERMAN/WEST

PLUCKROSE, HENRY ARTHUR
COBBETT, RICHARD--[8][31][33]

PLUFF, BARBARA LITLEFIEL
CLAYTON, BARBARA--[1][22][31]AMERICAN

PLUMLEY, ERNEST F.
CLEVEDON, JOHN--[8]

PLUMMER, CLARE [E]
EMSLEY, CLARE--[1][9][17]ENGLISH/ROM--
PENARTH, WYM--[1]

PLUMMER, ROGER S.
SHERMAN, ROGER--[3]MYS--
APOLLO "BEWARE OF THE CAT" '71

PLUMMER, T. ARTHUR
SARNE, MICHAEL--[3][22][29]MYS--
PAUL "THE SCARLET SAINT" '32 & MORE

PLUMPIAN, PAUL
DEFOWE, WALTER--V. BERCH-BRNDN/BC PSEUDS,
BAE 22, P24

PLUNKETT, ANNIE E.
NELSON, ANNIE GREENE--[1]

PLUNKETT, EDWARD JOHN M.D
DUNSANY, LORD--[2][7][11][23][32]SF--
EQMM-11 STORIES MAR '51-JAN '65
NOVELS

PLUNKETT, SUSAN IRENE F.
COON, SUSAN--[7][23]SF--
AVON 'LIVING PLANET' SERIES:
#1-4 '80-2

POAGE, SCOTT T.
SCOTT, P.T.--[1]

POCHE, KLAUS
LENNERT, NIKOLAUS--[39][40]GERMAN/MYS--
"WENN EIN MARQUIS SCHON PLANE MACHT" '65
NIKOLAUS, GEORG--[39]GERMAN

POCOCK, [HENRY] ROGER [A]
POCOCK, H.R.A.--[28]WEST, NON-FICT
POCOCK, ROBERT--[1][28]WEST--
LITTLE BROWN "CURLY: A TALE OF THE
ARIZONA DESERT" '05

POCOCK, TOM
ALLCOT, GUY--[8]

PODIVINSKA, JARMILA
GLAZAROVA, JARMILA--[22]CZECH

POETSCHKUS, HORST
HAMMER, FRED--[39]GERMAN/WEST

POEWE, KARLA
CESARA, MANDA--[31]

POGGEL, MARY
AVE--[1]
MARY SALESIA [SISTER]--[1]

POGGI, EMIL J.
POGGI, JACK--[1]

POGONY, JEAN COULTER
COULTER, CATHERINE--[9][21][34]ROM--
ONYX "CALYPSO MAGIC" '88
NAL "FALSE PRETENSES" '88& MORE

POHL, FREDERIK
ANDREWS, ELTON V.--[1][2][11][31]
DE COSTA, HENRY--[11]SF,FP--
FLEUR, PAUL--[1][2][11][23][31]SF--
GOTTESMAN, S.D.--W/C.M. KORNBLUTH
& R.A.W. LOWNDES,[11][23][31]SF--
GREGOR, LEE--W/MILTON A. ROTHMAN,[1][2][31]
HOWARD, WARREN F.--[2][11][23][31]--
1 STORY '40-1
LASLY, WALT--[4][11]
LAVOND, PAUL DENNIS--W/DIRK WYLIE,
[2][11][23]SF,HP--
LAVOND, PAUL DENNIS--W/R.A.W. LOWNDES,
C.M. KORNBLUTH & JOSEPH H. DOCKWEILER,
[1][23]SF
MACCREIGH, JAMES--[2][23][32]MYS--
SW "MURDER'S MILLION" AUG '47
SW "MURDER STRIKES THREE" SEPT '47
MARINER, SCOTT--W/C.M. KORNBLUTH,[1][11][23]SF
MASON, ERNEST--[11]
MASON, ERNST--[1][2][11][23]SF
MCCANN, EDSON--W/ALVAREZ DEL REY,
[1][2][11][23]--
"PREFERRED RISK"
MCCREIGH, JAMES--L. ROBNBINS LTR '94,[1][11]
PARK, JORDAN--W/C.M. KORNBLUTH,[1][11]--
LION 135 "HALF" '53
LION 176 "VALERIE" '53
LION LL97 "SORORITY HOUSE" '56
PYR G368 "MAN OF COLD RAGES" '58
SATTERFIELD, CHARLES--W/ALVAREZ DEL REY,
[2][11][23]SF--
USED HIMSELF ON 3 MAG STORIES
STACY, DONALD--[2][4] MAY HAVE COLLABORATED
UNDER THIS PSEUD.
WILSON, DIRK--[1]
WYLIE, DIRK--W/DIRK WYLIE,[2][11]
WYLIE, DIRK--W/J. DOCKWEILER & CYRIL
KORNBLUTH,[1][2][11]
WYLIE, DIRK--[23]SF--
AST - 1 SHORT STORY '40/41
ZWEIG, ALLEN--[11]SF,FP--

POHLE, ROBERT W. JR.
FARNSWORTH, JAMES--[1][31]
LEE, DEVON--[9][21][31]ROM--
MacF "DARK INTRIGUE"
MILLER, E.F.--[1]

POHLMAN, MAX EDWARD
BENJAMIN, CLAUDE--[1]
EDWARD, MAX--[1]
GEORGE, MARION E.--[1]

POINDEXTER, CLARENCE A.
DEXTER, AL--[31]

POIRIER, LOUIS
GRACQ, JULIEN--[1][22]FRENCH

POKATSKY, HORST
PHOOKY, FRED H.--[39]GERMAN/MYS/WEST

POLAKOW, VALERIE [S]
SURANSKY, VALERIE POLAKOW--[1]

POLAND, DOROTHY ELIZABETH
FARELY, ALISON--[1][31]
HAMMOND, JANE--[1][31]

POLIAKOFF, VLADIMIR
AUGUR--[8]

POLITELLA, DARIO
GRANITE, TONY--[1][22][31]AMERICAN
STEWART, DAVID--[1][22]AMERICAN

POLITZER, HEINRICH
POLITZER, HEINZ--[1]

POLLACHER, ELLIN RENEE
HALL, ELLEN--W/BARBAR HOLSTON, V. BERCH LTR TO HUBIN '94, MYS--
BB "MIDNIGHT SINS" '88

POLLACK, RICHARD A.
POLLACK, RACHEL [GRACE]--[7][23]SF--
LEGALIZED TO "RACHEL"--
BERK "GOLDEN VANITY" '80
BERK "ALQUA DREAMS" '87
BERK "UNQUENCHABLE FIRE" '88

POLLAK, FELIX
ANSELM, FELIX--[31]

POLLAK, SIDNEY
POLLARD, SIDNEY--[1]

POLLAND, MADELEINE A.
ADRIEN, FRANCES--[1]

POLLARD, ALBERT F.
POLLARD, A.F.--[1]

POLLARD, ALFRED WILLIAM
POLLARD, A.W.--[1]

POLLARD, JAMES
MOPOKE--[13]AUSTRALIAN

POLLERO, RHONDA
ROBERTS, KELSEY--[26]ROM--
HARL 248 "LEGAL TENDER"
HARL 276 "STOLEN MEMORIES" & MORE

POLLEY, JUDITH ANNA
HAGAR, JUDITH--[9][21][26][31]ROM--
HALE "SHADOW OF THE EAGLE" '82 & 8 MORE
KENT, HELEN--[9][21][31]ROM--
LUELLEN, VALENTINA--[9][21][26][31]ROM--
"KING'S CAVALIER"
"FRANCESCA" & 19 MORE
STEWART, JUDITH--[9][21][26]ROM--
"THE LAIRD'S FRENCH BRIDE"

POLLITZ, EDWARD A. JR.
CHRISTIAN, NICK--[34]MYS--
SIGN "HOMICIDE ZONE 4" '78
SIGN "INTENSIVE FEAR" '80
TOR "RONIN" '86

POLLOCK, ALICE
OLDEST AUTHORESS--[1]

POLLOCK, COURTENAY
MAXWELL, EDWARD--[1]

POLLOCK, EDITH CAROLINE
THORN, ISMAY--[8]

POLLOCK, IDA
BARRIE, SUSAN--[21][26]ROM--
"MOUNTAIN"
"ROYAL PURPLE" & MORE
BEAUFORT, JANE--[21][26]ROM--
"A NIGHTINGALE IN THE SYCAMORE"
"DANGEROUS LOVE"
BURGHLEY, ROSE--[21][26]ROM--
'A QUALITY OF MAGIC"
"HIGHLAND MIST" & MORE
CHARLES, ANITA--[21][26]ROM--
"KING OF THE CASTLE"
"WHITE ROSE OF LOVE" & MORE
KENT, PAMELA--[21][26]ROM--
"CITY OF PALMS"
"DESERT GOLD" & MORE
ROWAN, BARBARA--[21][26]ROM--
"LOVE IS FOREVER"
"MOUNTAIN OF DREAMS" & MORE
WHISTLER, MARY--[21][26]ROM--
"ENCHANTED AUTUMN"
"PATHWAY OF ROSES" & MORE

POLLOCK, JOHN HACKETT
AN PHILBIN--[1][2]

POLLOCK, THEODORE MARVIN
POLLOCK, TED--[40]MYS--
"THE RAINBOW MAN" '79

POLLOTTA, NICHOLAS ANGELO
POLLOTTA, NICK--[7]SF--
ACE "BUREAU 13 #1" '91

POLOMSKI, GEORG
POLO, GEORG--[39]GERMAN/MYS

POLONSKY, ABRAHAM C.
HOGARTH, EMMETT--W/MITCHELL A. WILSON, [3][8][22][29]MYS--
SIMON "THE GOOSE IS COOKED" '40

POLSBY, NELSON W.
CLUN, ARTHUR--[1][31]--
MAG/PERIODICAL CONTRIBUTIONS

POLTORATSKY, N.P.
PETROVSKY, N.--[1]

POLVIANDER, ANNI K.
HEINO, KYLLIKKI--[1]
POLVA, ANNI--[1]

POLWARTH, GWENDOLINE M.
POLWARTH, G. MARCHANT--[8]

POLYDOOR, KAREL MARIA
DE MONT, POL--[22]FLEMISH

POMEROY, JOHN H.
WHITTON, DANIEL--[11]

POND, FREDERICK E.
RED WING--[1]
WILDWOOD, WILL--[1]

POND, GEORGE EDWARD
QUILIBET, PHILIP--[1]

POND, PAUL
JONES, PAUL--[1]

POND, S.T.R.
REAY, TREVACE--[1]

PONNIER, LOTTE
BETKE, LOTTE--[39]GERMAN/JUV

PONSONBY, DORIS ALMON
RYBOT, DORIS--[1][22]ENGLISH
TEMPEST, SARAH--[1][34]MYS--
HURST "A WINTER OF FEAR" '67

PONSONBY, FREDERICK E.N.
TENTH EARL OF BESSBOROUGH--[22]ENGLISH

POOL, SANDRA
SIMPSON, MAGGIE--W/MARGARET MASTEN,[26]ROM--
HARL 577 "BABY BONUS"
HARL 608 "BRINGING UP FATHER

POOLE, FREDERICK KING
HARRIS, ANDREW--[31]V. BERCH-'AFTER DARK'
BAE 27--
MacF 60-340 "BANGKOK AFTER DARK" '68
MacF 75-241 "TAPEI AFTER DARK" '69
MacF 75-410 "MANILA AFTER DARK" '71

POOLE, GRAY JOHNSON
GRAY, BETSY--[1][31]

POOLE, PEGGY
ROCHE, TERRY--[1][33]

POOLE, REGINALD H.
GREGORY, H[YLTON]--[34]MYS--
AMALG "GREAT TRUNK MYSTERY" '39
HEBER, AUSTIN--[1]
HEBER, REGINALD--[1]
POOLE, MICHAEL--[1][3][22]MYS--
AMALG "KING'S SECRET" '20
AMALG "PRISON BREAKERS" '20 & MORE
THOMAS, ANTHONY--[1][34]MYS--
ALDINE "BLACK EAGLE'S TRAIL" '26
ALDINE "BLACK EAGLE MYS" '26 & 2 MORE
VALENTINE, HENRY--[1]

POOLE, RHODA JANSSEN
JANSSEN, KRISTA--[26]ROM--
"A HEART POSSESSED"
"RIDE THE WIND"

POOR, AGNES BLAKE
PRESCOTT, DOROTHY--[1]

POORTVLIET, MARIEN
POORTVLIET, RIEN--[1][7][33]--
"THE BOOK OF THE SANDMAN AND THE
ALPHABET OF SLEEP" '89

POPE, CHARLES HENRY
STARCROSS, ROGER--[1]

POPE, F.W.
HULBERT, LLOYD--[1]

POPE-HENNESSY, JOHN W.
POPE-HENNESSY, J.W.--[1]

POPESCU, CHRISTINE
KEIR, CHRISTINE--[1][22][31]ENGLISH
PULLEIN-THOMPSON, CHRIST.--[1][22][31]ENGLISH

POPHAM, PETER NICHOLAS H.
DE LOUNE, HENRY--[31]

POPOV, ALEXANDER
VICKERS, AL--[23]SF--
"PROVINCE FIVE" '91

POPOV, ALEXANDER SERAFIM.
SERAFIMOVICH, ALEXANDER--[22]RUSSIAN COSSACK

POPP, AUGUSTIN
WALDECK, HEINRICH SUSO--[39]GERMAN

POPPE, KARL HEINZ
HEINZ, KARL--[39]GERMAN/WEST
KEEN, ROBERT--[39]GERMAN/WEST

PORCARI, CONSTANCE KWOLEK
KWOLEK, CONSTANCE--[1][31]

PORCHE, PAULINE
PORCHE, SIMONE [BRENDA]--[1]
SIMONE--[1]
SIMONE, MADAME--[1]

PORGES, ARTHUR
ARTHUR, PETER--[1][2][11][23]SF
ROGERS, PAT--[2][11][23][32]MYS/SF--
FE "NIGHTQUAKE" MAY '60

PORGES, IRWIN
JAMESON, KEITH--V. BERCH-MON PSEUDS,
BAE 9,[2]--
MON K65 "SOS THE WORLD'S GREAT
SEA DISASTERS" '62

PORN, ALICE
ALI-MAR--[8]

PORSCH, F.E.
PETERSON, INGO--[39]GERMAN

PORTAAS, HERMAN
WILDENVEY, HERMAN--[22]NORWEGIAN

PORTADIN, GARY
GARRETT, PETER M.D.--V. BERCH LTR TO
HUBIN '93, MYS--
WALKER "THERAPIST" '89

PORTAL, V.E.
BANNISDALE, V.E.--[1]

PORTE, BARBARA ANN
PORTE-THOMAS, BARBARA ANN--[33]

PORTEOUS, RICHARD SYDNEY
STANDBY--[13]AUSTRALIAN

PORTER, BARBARA CONNEY
CONNEY, BARBARA--[8]

PORTER, CALLIE RUSSELL
M.T.F.--[1]
PORTER, KATHERINE ANNE--[1][28]WEST--
LITTLE BROWN "SHIP OF FOOLS" '62

PORTER, EDWARD
HARVEY, LYON--[8]

PORTER, ELEANOR [H]
STUART, ELEANOR--[1]

PORTER, FREDERICK
WATSON, FREDERICK--[1]

PORTER, GIL
RAYMOND, RICK--V. BERCH-BRNDN/BC PSEUDS,
BAE 22, ADULT--
PLTM 666 "AC-DC SEX" & MORE

PORTER, HAROLD E.
HALL, HOLWORTHY--[1][3][22]AMERICAN/MYS--
BOBBS "WHAT HE LEAST EXPECTED" '17

PORTER, JOYCE
JOYCE, DEBORAH--W/DEBORAH BRYSON,
[9][21][26][34]MYS/ROM--
HARL "KALEIDESCOPE" & 5 MORE

PORTER, LANCELOT
HEWATSON, BOB--[1]

PORTER, LINN BOYD
ROSS, ALBERT--[1][2][34]MYS--
DILLINGHAM "HIS FOSTER SISTER" 1896
DILLINGHAM "STRANGER THAN FICTION" 1900

PORTER, MADELINE
HABERSHAM, ELIZABETH--W/SHANNON HARPER,
[21][26][34]MYS--
PINN "ISLAND OF DECEIT" '77
HARPER, MADELINE--W/SHANNON HARPER,
[9][21][26]ROM--
"JADE AFFAIR"
"KEEPSAKES" & MORE
JAMES, ANNA--W/SHANNON HARPER,[9][21][26]ROM--
"SAPPHIRE HILL"
"VENETIAN NECKLACE" & MORE

PORTER, MAURICE
MOUTHPIECE--[8]

PORTER, WILLIAM SYDNEY
AMERICAN MAUPASSANT--[1]
BLISS, JAMES L.--[1]
CLARK, HOWARD--[1]
DOWD, T.B.--[1]
HENRY, OLIVER--[1][31][33]
HENRY,O.--[2][3][5][11][22][28]--
SS PRIMARILY - 13 BOOKS '04-48
PARKER, WILL S.--[1]
PETERS, S.H.--[1][33]

PORTERFIELD, KAY
KIMBROUGH, COLLEEN--[9][21][26]ROM--
"SWEPT OFF HER FEET"

PORTWAY, CHRISTOPHER [J]
OCTOBER, JOHN--[1][7][23]SF--
HALE "THE ANARCHY PEDDLERS" '76

POSADA, JOSE M. ALVAREZ
AMIEVA, CELSO--[30]MEXICAN

POSNER, DAVID LOUIS
BOURCHIER, JULES--[8]

POSNER, JACOB D.
DEAN, GREGORY--[1][3][22]MYS--
HILLMAN-CURL "MURDER ON STILTS" '39
& 2 MORE '33-9

POSNER, RICHARD
CRAIG, JONATHAN--[1]
FOSTER, IRIS--[1][3][29]MYS--
LAN "MOORWOOD LEGACY" '72
LAN "CRIMSON MOON" '73 & 3 MORE
MITCHELL, ERICA--[1]
MURRAY, BEATRICE--[3][21][26][29]MYS/ROM--
DELL "DARK SONATA" '71
RICHARDS, ALAYNA--[1]
TODD, PAUL--[1][3][29]MYS--
WARNER "BLOOD ALL OVER" '75
WINE, DICK--[1]

POSSELT, ERIC
PALMER, EDGAR A.--[8]

POST, HENRY
SPOT, RYHON--[1]

POST, JERRY BENJAMIN
POST, J.B.--[1]

POSTGATE, M.I.
COLE, G.D.H. & M.I.--W/GEORGE D.H. COLE,
[5][32]MYS--
ML "OWL AT THE WINDOW" NOV '33
EQMM "A LESSON IN CRIME" JUL '44
MK "DEATH ON HOLIDAY" JUL '53

POSTL, KARL ANTON
SEALSFIELD, CHARLES--[39]GERMAN/ADV
SIDONS, C.--[39]GERMAN/ADV

POSTMA, MAGDALENA J.
POSTMA, MINNIE--[1]

POTEET, ARDIA
MCKINNEY, GEORGIA--[9]ROM

POTHECARY, RAYMOND
FORD, QUINTON--[1]

POTOCNIK, CAPTAIN
NOORDUNG, HERMANN--[1][2][11]

POTTER, GEORGE WILLIAM
WITHERS, E.L.--[3][22]MYS--
DBLDY "THE BIRTHDAY" '62
DBLDY "HEIR APPARENT" '61 &3 MORE '57-62

POTTER, JACQUELINE
IRELAND, JANE--[9][21][26]ROM--
"SILVER ENCHANTMENT"
"LOVE NOTES"

POTTER, JOANNA
HARVEY, CAROLINE--[1][8]
TROLLOPE, JOANNA--[1][8]

POTTER, KATHLEEN JILL K.
KINDER, KATHLEEN--[1][3][31]MYS--
COLLINS "THE RAVEN & THE DOVE" '79

POTTER, MARGARET [N]
BETTERIDGE, ANNE--[3][9][21][22]ROM/MYS--
"SIROCCO"
"CHAINS OF LOVE" & 6 MORE '70s
EVANS, MARGARET--[9][21]ROM--
MELVILLE, ANNE--[1][9][21][26]ROM--
'LORRIMER' SAGA - 4 NOVELS
NEWMAN, MARGARET--[1]

POTTER, ROBERT
EASTERLY, ROBERT--[1][2][23]SF--
"THE GERM GROWERS: AN AUSTRALIAN STORY
OF ADV & MYS" 1892
WILBRAHAM, JOHN--[1][2]

POTTHOFF, MARGOT MARIA
LUNDBEERG, KAI--[1][39]GERMAN/JUV

POTTLE, JULIET W.T.
TOMPKINS, JULIET WILBOR--[1]

POTTS, RUTH
PALMER, RACHEL--[9][21][26]ROM--
"LOVE BEYOND DESIRE"
"NO SWEETER SONG"

POTVIN, DEMASE
SAINTE FOY--[1]

POTYKA, LIN
RITTER, LINA--[39]GERMAN/JUV

POUND, EZRA LOOMIS
ADKINS, M.D.--[8]
ATHELING, WILLIAM--[1][2][22][31]
DIAS, B.H.--[8]
HALL, JOHN--[8]
JANUS, HIRAM--[8]
LLEWMYS, WESTON--[8]
SAUNDERS, ABEL--[8]
VENISON, ALFRED--[22]AMERICAN
VON HELMHOLTZ, BASTIEN--[8]

POURNELLE, JERRY
CURTIS, WADE--[2][3][4][11][23]MYS/SF--
BERK "RED HEROIN" '69
BERK "RED DRAGON" '71

POVLITZ, ROBERT E.
BURTON, ROBERT E.--[1]

POWE, BRUCE
PORTAL, ELLIS--[2][11][23]SF--
"KILLING GROUND: THE CANADIAN CIVIL WAR" '68

POWELL, BRIAN S.
BRIAN--[1]

POWELL, ERIC
RUSHOLM, PETER--[8]

POWELL, GEOFFREY STEWART
ANGUS, TOM--[31]

POWELL, JAN HAMILTON
HAMILTON, AUDREY--[9]ROM--
"LOVE MAKES THE DIFFERENCE"
HAMILTON, CELESTE--[21][26]ROM--
"A FINE SPRING RAIN"
"TORN ASSUNDER" & 12 MORE
POWELL, NEELY--[9]ROM

POWELL, LARRY
BRENT, R.L.--[3][29]MYS--
AWARD "THE LIQUIDATOR" '74
AWARD "CONTRACT FOR A KILLING" '74
AWARD "THE COCAINE CONNECTION" '74
AWARD "INVITATION TO A STRANGLING" '75
CARTER, NICK--[3]MYS,HP--
AWARD "THE CODE" '73
STIVERS, DICK--W/L.R. PAYNE,[34][29]MYS,HP--
GE "TEXAS SHOWDOWN" '82

POWELL, OSCAR REGINALD
FAIRFAX, DICK--[1]

POWELL, RICHARD PITTS
KIRK, JEREMY--[1][31]

POWELL, TALMAGE
DAVIS, ROBERT HART--A. TONIK-ECHOES #24, [18][29]MYS,HP--
MU "HUNGRY WORLD AFFAIR" JUNE '67
HENRY, ROBERT--LACHMAN LST '93, [18][29][32]MYS--
SD "MURDER STILL TO COME" JUN '44
SD "LITTLE BIT HARDER" AUG '44
SD "I AIN'T SO DUMB" DEC '46
SD "FIXED SMILE OF DEATH" JAN '47

POWELL, TALMAGE [CONT]
LAMB, MILTON T.--LACHMAN LST '93,[18]MYS--
TDA "YOUR NUMBER IS UP" JUN '43
TDA "CRIME GETS A HEAD" SEPT '43
TSD "CRIME DOESN'T PAY" NOV '43
DE "BLOOD MONEY" NOV '45
DM "HOME TO KILL" FEB '46
DM "LADIES KILLER" DEC '46
TDA "RHAPSODY IN BLOOD" SEPT '47
TSD "HOST TO HOMOCIDE" DEC '47
DE "THE DEADLY PAST" OCT '48
DE "DANGEROUS MISSION" NOV '48
DE "CURTAIN CALL FOR ROBERTO" DEC '48
FIF "WITH THIS BLOOD" FEB '50
LEIGH, DAVE--LACHMAN LST '93,[18][29][32]MYS--
MR "THE DEADLY DRUNK" DEC '56
MH "PAYMENT IN FULL" DEC '56
SA "BODY IN THE BATHROOM" JAN '58
TG "DIME A DEATH" JUN '60
TG "ALL NIGHT SUCKER" APR '60
MCCREADY, JACK--V. BERCH-MON PSEUDS, BAE 9, [3][18][29]MYS--
MON 229 "THE RAPER" '62
QUEEN, ELLERY--[3][18]MYS,HP--
POCK "MURDER WITH A PAST" '63
POPLB "BEWARE THE YOUNG STRANGER" '65
POPLB "WHERE IS BIANCA?" '66
POPLB "WHO SPIES, WHO KILLS?" '66
SANDS, DAVE--LACHMAN LST '93,[29]MYS--
MSMM "THE CRIMSON TRAIL" FEB '58
FIF "UNHOLY NIGHT" FEB '59
TALMAGE, ANNE--[3][18][21][26][29]MYS--
PRESTIGE "DARK OVER ARCADIA" '71

POWELL, [DAVID] FRANK
SURGEON SCOUT--[1]
WHITE BEAVER--[1]

POWELL-SMITH, VINCENT
ELPHINSTONE, FRANCIS--[1][31]
JUSTICIAR--[8][31]
ORBIS, VICTOR--[1]
SANTA MARIA--[1]

POWELY, MRS. A.A.
GENE, MARTA--[8]

POWER, JO-ANN
CROWLEIGH, ANN--W/BARBARA CUMMINGS-ROM TIMES MAG, MAR '93,[26]ROM--
"DEAD AS DEAD CAN BE"
"WAIT FOR THE DARK"

POWER, MARGUERITE A.
HONORIA N.--[1]

POWER, NORMAN S.
KRATOS--[1][31]

POWER, RICHARD
DE PAOR, RISTEARD--[1][31]

POWER, SIR D'ARCY
D'A.P.--[8]

POWER-WATERS, BRIAN
CAPTAIN X--[1][31]

POWERS, JOHN F.
POWERS, J.F.--[1]

POWERS, JOHN J.
POWERS, JOHN R.--[1]

POWERS, MARTHA [JEAN]
PAXTON, JEAN--[9][21][26]ROM--
"DIVIDED LOYALTY"

POWERS, PAUL S.
GRIFFIN, ANDREW A.--L. ROBBINS LTR MAR '94
STEVENS, WARD M.--L. ROBBINS LTR '94
'WESTERN PULP HERO' BY N. CARR--

POWERS, RICHARD M.
GORMAN, TERRY--[1][2]

POWERS, TIM[OTHY THOMAS]
ASHBLESS, WILLIAM--W/JAMES P. BLAYLOCK,
J. SEELS-BLAYLOCK BIBLIO '93
HASTING, WILLIAM--W/JAMES P. BLAYLOCK,
J. SEEL-BLAYLOCK BIBLIO '93

POWLEY, FAITH HINCKLEY
JAYNE, FAITH--[1]

POWLEY, FLORENCE MARY P.
POMEROY, FLORENCE MARY--[22]ENGLISH

POWYS, JOHN COWPER
POWYS, J.C.--[1]

POWYS, THEODORE FRANCIS
POWYS, T.F.--[1]

POYER, DAVID C.
ANDRIESSEN, DAVID--[7][23][31]SF--
STARBLAZE "STAR SEED" '82
POYER, D.C.--[23][32]MYS/SF--
MSMM "TOO MUCH AT STAKE" JUL '78
MSMM "BOXED IN" AUG '78
MSMM "EYE OF DESTRUCTION" JAN '79

POYER, JOSEPH JOHN
POYER, JOE--[7]SF--
ASF "MISSION RED CLASH" '65
ATHENEUM "TUNNEL WAR" '79

POYNTER, JAMES WILLIAM
INDICATOR--[1]

POZZESSERE, HEATHER G.
DRAKE, SHANNON--[9][21][26][34]MYS/ROM--
CHART "ONDINE" '88
CHART "PRINCESS OF FIRE" & 9 MORE
GRAHAM, HEATHER--[7][9][21][26]ROM/SF--
DELL "EVERY TIME I LOVE YOU" '88 & 34 MORE
POZZESSERE, GRAHAM--[21]ROM

PRABHUPADA, A.C. BHAK.
BHAKTIVEDANTA SWAMI, A.C.--[31]

PRADO [CALVO], PEDRO
ANDOVAR--[31]

PRAED, CAROLINE MARY-PR.
PRAED, MRS. CAMPBELL--[36]AUSTRALIAN/MYS
PRAED, ROSA--[36]AUSTRALIAN/MYS--
CASSELL "MYS WOMAN" '13 & OTHERS

PRAFER, HANS GEORG
CARSTEN, WILM--[39]GERMAN/JUV
FRANZ, GUNTER--[39]GERMAN/JUV

PRAGNELL, FESTUS
PARNELL, FRANCIS--[2][11][23]ENGLISH/SF--
'WONDER STORIES' - 1 STORY FIRST ISSUE '38

PRAMBERGER, ROMUALD
ELFENAU, W.--[39]GERMAN

PRANCE, JUNE E.
SHAW, ELIZABETH--[1]

PRASNIEWSKI, MARGARET
KIRK, MARGARET [P]--[21][26]ROM--
"ALWAYS A STRANGER"
"GYPSY"

PRATHER, RICHARD S.
KNIGHT, DAVID--PRATHER LTR '93/LUPOFF-
PRATHER INTRVW-PP 16,[3][18]MYS--
GRAP 48 "PATTERN FOR MURDER" '52
POCK 1120 "DRAGNET CASE NO. 561" '56
RING, DOUGLAS--PRATHER LTR '93
LUPOFF-PRATHER INTRVW, PP 16,[3][18]MYS--
LION "THE PEDDLER" '52

PRATNEY, WILLIAM ALFRED
FREEMAN, BJORN--[31]
PRATNEY, WINKIE--[7]SF--
BIBLE VOICE "STAR WARS, STAR TREK,
& 21ST CENTURY CHRISTIANS" '78

PRATT, AGNES ROTHERY
EDWARDS, AGNES--[1]
ROTHERY, AGNES EDWARDS--[1]

PRATT, DENNIS
CRISP, QUENTIN--[1][3]MYS--
METHUEN "CHOG" '79

PRATT, ELEANOR BLAKE
ATKINSON, ELEANOR BLAKE--[1]
BLAKE, E.A.--[1][22]MYS
BLAKE, ELEANOR--[22][34]MYS--
McBRIDE JADE GREEN CATS" '31
McBRIDE "DEATH DOWN EAST" '40

PRATT, ELIZABETH STUART
STUART, ELIZABETH--[21]ROM--
"THE SHAKING SHADOW"

PRATT, ELLA ANN
SHEPHERD, DOROTHEA ALICE--[1]

PRATT, INGA STEPHENS
STEPHENS, I.M.--[1][2][11]

PRATT, JAMES NORWOOD
BANNISTER, SALLY--[1][31]

PRATT, JOHN
WINTON, JOHN--[8][22]ENGLISH

PRATT, LEONARD E.
SMITH, FENTON--[1]

PRATT, RHONA OLIVE
O'HARRIS, PIXIE--[1][13]AUSTRALIA

PRATT, THEODORE
BRACE, TIMOTHY--[1][3][22]MYS--
DUTTON "MURDER GOES FISHING" '36
& 3 MORE '36-9

PRATT, WILLIAM HENRY
KARLOFF, BORIS--[2][11]GHOSTED

PRATT, [MURRAY] FLETCHER
AINSBURY, RAY--[11]
FLETCHER, GEORGE U.--[2][4][7][11][16]SF--
LANCER "WELL OF THE UNICORN" '67
LESTER, IRVIN--[2][11][23]SF--
AMZ "THE OCTOPUS CYCLE" '28
RUBY, B.F.--[1][2][11]

PRAZ, MARIO
ALCIBIADE--[31]

PREBBLE, JOHN E. CURTIS
CURTIS, JOHN--[1][31][22]ENGLISH

PREBBLE, MARJORIE CURTIS
COMPTON, ANN--[1][22][31]ENGLISH
CONWAY, DENISE--[1][22][31]ENGLISH
CURTIS, MARJORIE--[1][3][22]ENGLISH/MYS--
HALE "DEW IN THE MORNING" '75

PREINERSTORFER, ALOIS
PEN, ALFRA--[39]GERMAN/MYS
PERTH, ALY--[39]GERMAN/MYS
PERTH, JACK--[39]GERMAN/MYS

PREIS, ELISABETH
KAUT, ELLIS--[39]GERMAN/JUV

PREISSNER, CARL
KAST, PETER--[39]GERMAN

PRESBERG, MIRIAM GOLDSTEN
GILBERT, MIRIAM--[1][22][31][33]AMERICAN

PRESLAND, JOHN
BENDIT, GLADYS--[8]

PRESSBURGER, EMERIC
IMRIE, RICHARD--[31]

PRESSER, ARLYNN LEIBER
LEIBER, VIVIAN--[26]ROM--
"CASEY'S FLYBOY"
"GOODY TWO-SHOES"
"HER OWN PRINCE CHARMING"

PRESSER, JANICE
GREENE, JANICE PRESSER--[1][31]

PRESSER, [G] JACOB
DRUKKER, J.--[1][31]
VAN DAM, J.--[1]
VAN WAGENINGEN, J.--[1]

PRESSMAN, LOUIS H.
BLADE, ALEXANDER--[1]MYS,HP--
ZIFF-DAVIS

PREST, THOMAS PECKET
BOS--[2]

PRESTON, FAYRENE
CONLEE, JAELYN--[9][21][26]ROM--
"SATIN & STEEL"

PRESTON, HARRY
CARTWRIGHT, VANESSA--[26][31]ROM--
MacF "WINE OF LOVE" '78
MacF "APPOINTMENT IN ANTIBES" '78 & 5 MORE
CRANDALL, NELSON--V. BERCH-BRNDN/BC PSEUDS,
BAE 22, ADULT--
FULTON, WARD--V. BERCH-BRNDN/BC PSEUDS,
BAE 22, ADULT--
BC 7277 "GHETTO INCEST"
BC 7419 "SEX: THE BLACKMAILER'S WEAPON"
BRNDN 6497 "SORORITY SEX FREAK"
HARRIMAN, PRESTON--V. BERCH-BRNDN/BC PSEUDS,
BAE 22, ADULT--
BC 7473 "NEICE & UNCLE INCEST"
STERN, MATT--V. BERCH-BRNDN/BC PSEUDS,
BAE 22, ADULT--

PRESTON, JAMES
JAMES, RONALD--[1]

PRESTON, JOHN
HILD, JACK--[31][34]MYS,HP--
GE 'SOB's':
"BARRABUS CREED" '88
"BARRABUS RAID" 88
"PACIFIC PAYLOAD" '88
MCADAM, PRESTON--W/DOUG MCADAM,[34]MYS--
AV "ISLAND INTRIGUE" '85
AV "ARABIAN ASSAULT" '85
AV "AFRICAN ASSIGNMENT" '85
McCRAY, MIKE--W/MICHAEL McDOWELL,
BERCH LTR TO HUBIN '94,MYS,HP--
DELL "COLD VENGEANCE" '84
DELL "DEADLY REUNION" '84
DELL "LOUISIANNA FIRESTORM" '85
McCRAY, MIKE--BERCH LTR TO HUBIN '94,MYS,HP--
DELL "AKBAR CONTRACT"
DELL "RED MAN CONTRACT"
DELL "CONTRACT: TERROR SUMMIT" '86
DELL "SAMURAI CONTRACT" '87

PREUSS, GERDA
VON KRIES, GERDA--[39]GERMAN/JUV

PREUTE, MICHAEL
BERNDORF, JACQUES--[39][40]GERMAN/MYS--
"EIFEL BLUES" '89

PREVOST BATTERSBY, H.F.
PREVOST, FRANCIS--[1]

PRICE, BARBARA ANN ELLV.
ELLVINGER, BARBARA ANN P.--[31]

PRICE, BEVERLY JOAN
RANDELL, BEVERLY--[1]

PRICE, E. HOFFMAN
DALY, HAMLIN--[2][3][11][16][23]SF--
FALCON "CASE OF THE CANCELLED
REDHEAD" ca'52

PRICE, EDWIN WATHER
RINGWOOD--[1]

PRICE, EMERSON FIELD
HANLEY, HUGH--[1]

PRICE, EVADNE
SMITH, HELEN ZENNA--[1]

PRICE, FRANK J.
CONWAY, FAULKNER--[1]

PRICE, GEORGE [H]
PRICE, RHYS--[1]

PRICE, J.L.
UPFIELD, ARTHUR C.--W/DOROTHY STRANGE,[18]--
COMPLETED "LAKE FROME MONSTER"
AFTER UPFIELD'S DEATH

PRICE, JEREMIE
LANE, MARVYN--[8]

PRICE, MARJORIE
PECK, MAGGIE--[9][21][26]ROM--
"MOONLIGHT ON THE BAY"
PRINCE, MARGOT--[9][21][26]ROM--
"MAN WHO CAME TO STAY"
"RUN TO RAPTURE"

PRICE, OLIVE
CHERRYHOLMES, ANNE--[1][31][33]
WEST, BARBARA--[1][33]

PRICE, ROBERT
DREW, MORGAN--[1][31]

PRICE-BROWN, JOHN
BOHN, ERIC--[1]
PRICE-BROWN--[8]

PRICE-MARS, JEAN
MARS, JEAN PRICE--[1]

PRICHARD, HESKETH VERNON
HERON, H.--[2][16][22]ENGLISH/MYS

PRICHARD, KATE O'BRIEN
HERON, E.--[2][16][22]ENGLISH/MYS
PRICHARD, K.--[1]

PRICTHETT, VICTOR SAWDON
PRITCHETT, V.S.--[1]

PRIDVOROV, EFIM ALEXEYE.
BEDNY, DEMYAN--[22]RUSSIAN

PRIESS, KARL-HEINZ
MARTINEZ, BENITO--[39]GERMAN/SF/WEST,HP
MCKAY, CHARLES--[39]GERMAN/SF/WEST,HP
PREECE, CHARLES M.--[39]GERMAN/SF/WEST
PRIEST, CARL--[39]GERMAN/SF/WEST
SLADE, JACK--[39]GERMAN/WEST,HP

PRIEST, CHRISTOPHER [M]
CHRISTIAN, PETRA--W/PETER CAVE,[2]
MACKENZIE, GORDON--[2]
NOVAK, JOHN LUTHER--[23]SF
WEDGELOCK, COLIN--[2][23]SF

PRIESTLEY, CLIVE RYLAND
RYLAND, CLIVE--[3][22]MYS--
GRY "MURDER ON THE CLIFF" '34
HUTCH "SO DEATH CAME" '38 & 20 MORE

PRIESTLEY, JOHN BOYNTON
GOLDSMITH, PETER--W/GEORGE BILLAM,
[18][22][29]ENGLISH/MYS--
PLAY "SPRING TIDE" '36
JOLLY JACK--[1]
PRIESTLEY, J.B.--[1][32]MYS--
EQMM "AN ARABIAN NIGHT IN
PARK LANE" MAR '47
EQMM "WHAT A LIFE!" MAY '51
PAN "SALT IS LEAVING" '66 & MORE

PRILEY, MARGARET HUBBARD
HUBBARD, ANNE MARGARET--[1][31]

PRIME, CECIL THOMAS
PRIME, C.T.--[1]

PRIMM, TRACYE
MORGAN, TRACY--[26]ROM--
"MICHAEL'S WIFE"

PRIMMER, PHYLLIS
FREDRICKS, P.C.--[8]

PRINCE, DANIEL C.
CARTER, NICK--[3]MYS,HP--
CHART "HAWAII" '79

PRINCE, JACK HARVEY
AQUILLO, DON--[1]
CLINTON, JON--[1][31][33]
PRINCE, J.H.--[1]
WARDELL, DEAN--[1][33]

PRING-MILL, ROBERT D.F.
DUGUID, ROBERT--[1][22][31]ENGLISH

PRINGLE, ELIZABETH WATIES
PENNINGTON, PATIENCE--[1]

PRINGLE, LAURENCE, P.
EDMUND, SEAN--[1][33]

PRINS, ARY
COOPLANDT, A.--[22]DUTCH

PRINS, JACOB WINKLER
BRANDT, KASPAR--[22]DUTCH

PRIOR, MOLLEY
ROSCOE, JANET--[9]ROM--
"THE TROUBLED SUMMER"

PRITCHARD, JOHN LAURENCE
LAURENCE, JOHN--[2][3][22]MYS--
LONG "MYS MONEY" '30
LOW "RIDDLE OF WRAYE" '36 & 13 MORE '24-38

PRITCHARD, JOHN WALLACE
WALLACE, IAN--PPCC #4,[2][7][11][23]SF--
DAW 'CROYD' #1-3
'PAN-SAGITARIUS' #1-3
"EVERY CRAZY WIND" '58
PUTNAM "DEATHSTAR VOYAGE" '69
McCALL "PURLOINED PRINCE" '71
POPLB "SIGN OF THE MUTE MEDUSA" '77

PRITCHARD, WILLIAM THOMAS
DEXTER, WILLIAM--[1][2][11]SF--
PAPLB "WORLD IN ECLIPSE" '66
PAPLB "CHILDREN OF THE VOID" '66

PROBST, ALFRED
PRESTON, FRED--[39]GERMAN/WEST

PROCASSION, MICHAEL
CRISTOFER, MICHAEL--[8]

PROCHASKA, BRUNO
WOLFGANG, BRUNO--[39]GERMAN

PROCTOR, GEO[RGE] W[YATT]
CLEVE, JOHN--W/ANDREW J. OFFUTT,[7][23]SF--
'SPACEWAYS' SERIES: #5, #7 & #10"
ELOUS, MARV--W/ROBERT E. VARDEMAN,[7]--
"PLEASURE PLANET"
RETIT. "SEXUAL COQUETTE" BEE-LN '85
GED, CAER--[7]SF--
'ORPHEUS' SERIES:
"COMING OF CORMAC" '74
GEORGE, EDWARD--W/ROBERT E. VARDEMAN,[2][7]SF--
KAHN, OBIE--W/ROBERT E. VARDEMAN,[7]SF--
"PLEASURE PLANET"
RETIT. "INTERGALACTIC ORGY"
MOUNDS, MONICA--W/ROBERT E. VARDEMAN,[7]--
"PLEASURE PLANET"
RETIT. "OUTER SPACE EMBRACE" BL '78
ONN, CARRIE--W/ROBERT E. VARDEMAN,[7]--
"PLEASURE PLANET"
RETIT. "JANET'S SEX PLANET" BL '80
SPARKROCK, FRED--W/ROBERT E. VARDEMAN,[7]--
"PLEASURE PLANET"
RETIT. "PLAYING WITH DESIRE" BL '80
TANNER, CLAY--CRPG, WEST-- SERIES
WYATT, LEE--[7]SF--
'ORPHEUS' SERIES:
"THE FLESH HUNTERS" '74

PROCTOR, RICHARD H.
FIVE OF CLUBS--[1]

PROCTOR, RICHARD W.
SYLVAN--[1]

PROFFITT, JOSEPHINE MOORE
DEE, SYLVIA--[2][7][11]SF

PRONIN, BARBARA
NICKOLAE, BARBARA--W/NIKOLAE GERSTNER,
HAWK/PRONIN BIBLIO, MYS--
McGRAW "FINDERS KEEPERS" '89
BERK "TIES THAT BIND" '92
BERK "KISS MOMMY GOODNIGHT" '94

PRONZINI, WILLIAM JOHN
DANCER, RUSSELL--PRONZINI LTR & BAE INTRVW--
'CHIC' - MAGAZINE FICTION
DAVIS, ROBERT HART--PRONZINI LTR & BAE INTRVW,
MYS,HP--
MU "PILLARS OF SALT AFFAIR" DEC '67
DAVIS, ROBERT HART--W/JEFF WALLMANN,
ECHOES#24, MYS,HP--
CC "PAWNS OF DEATH" AUG '74
DAVIS, WILLIAM--W/JEFFREY WALLMANN,
PRONZINI BAE INTRVW, ADULT--
TBRN LLP201 "POLAROID CLUB I" '70
TBRN LLP203 "POLAROID CLUB II" '70
DREXEL, J.V.--HAWK/PRONZINI BAE INTRVW--
SHORT STORIES IN ANTHOLOGIES
FOXX, JACK--PRONZINI LTR '93,[32][34]--
MSMM "LITTLE OLD LADIES CAN BE
DANGEROUS" SEPT '69
AHMM "METHOD OF OPERATION" JUN '69
MSMM "ESCAPE" MAY '69
AHMM "CLINCHER" OCT '69
AHMM "RIGHT MOVE" MAR '70
MSMM "YOU'RE SAFE HERE" APR '70
AHMM "ONE OF THOSE DAYS" OCT '70
AHMM "ROADBLOCK" MAY '71
ZGWM "TAGGART'S GOLD" DEC '71
MSMM "THE DUEL" APR '72
AHMM "SUICIDE NOTE" MAY '72
BOBBS "JADE FIGURINE" '72
CC "INCIDENT IN THREE CROSSINGS" MAY '74
BOBBS "DEAD RUN" '75
BOBBS "FREEBOOTY" '76
BOBBS "WILDFIRE" '78
MSMM"YOUR CHOICE" APR '76
GRAYSON, ROGER--W/JEFF WALLMANN,
PRONZINI INTRVW BAE 29, ADULT--
TBRN LLP135 "COMPANY PARTY" '69
GREY, ROMER ZANE--W/JEFFREY WALLMANN,
PRONZINI LTR,HP--
ZGWM "DANGER RIDES DOLLAR WAGON" MAR '70
GUNNY, THE--PRONZINI LTR, WEST--
ZGWM "THE GUN FANNER" APRIL '73
HALLIDAY, BRETT--W/JEFFREY WALLMANN,
ECHOES #23, MYS,HP--
MSMM "DANGER: MIKE S. AT WORK" APR '72
HARKER, JONATHAN--W/JOE R. LANSDALE
& JEFFREY WALLMANN, PRONZINI LTR--
'BLOODRAKE' #3
"HEADSTONE" JUN '82
JAMES, VIOLA--W/JEFF WALLMANN, HAWK/PRONZINI
BAE INTRVW MAR '94, ADULT--
TBRN -CAN'T REMEMBER TITLES
JEFFREY, WILLIAM--W/JEFFREY WALLMANN,
PRONZINI LTR, WEST--
AHMM "FIRE HAZZARD" APR '70
AHMM "DAY OF THE MOON" JUN '70
AHMM "SHELL GAME" JUN '70
MSMM "MONDAY IS THE DULLEST DAY" JUL '70
MSMM "RETRIBUTION" AUG '70
EQMM "THE FACSIMILE SHOP" SEPT '70
MSMM "MURDER IS NO MAN'S FRIEND" NOV '70
AHMM "A CASE FOR QUIET" AUG '71
AHMM "THE ISLAND" AUG '72
AHMM "A RUN OF BAD LUCK" MAR '72

PRONZINI, WILLIAM JOHN [CONT]
JEFFREY, WILLIAM [CONT]
AHMM "TEN MILLION DOLLAR HIJACK" JAN '72
MSMM "I WANT A LAWYER" MAR '73
AHMM "A SLIGHT CASE OF SUSPICION" SEPT '73
MSMM "O'FLAHERTY'S WAKE" SEPT '75
TWR 51674 "DUEL AT GOLD BUTTES" '81
LEIS 2017 "BORDER FEVER" '83
HALE "DAY OF THE MOON" '83
JENSEN, PETER--W/JEFFREY WALLMANN,
PRONZINI LTR, ADULT--
TBRN LLP161 "A MOTHER'S LOVE '69
TBRN LLP181 "THREE'S A SANDWICH" '69
TBRN RWS109 "VIRGIN COUPLE" '70
MARLOWE, ASTON--W/JEFFREY WALLMANN,
PRONZINI LTR, ADULT--
TBRN LLP212 "RAJAH" '70
MOUNTBATTEN, RICHARD--W/JEFFREY WALLMANN,
INTRVW-BAE 29, ADULT--
TBRN LLP159 "SPELL OF THE BEAST" '69
PRONZINI, BILL--AUTHOR CONFIRMED,
[7]MYS/SF/WEST-- NUMEROUS NOVELS & STORIES
RENAULT, RICK--W/JEFFREY WALLMANN,
PRONZINI LTR--
BEAVER "DEATH ON FOUR WHEELS" NOV '68
BEAVER "DEEP SIX" NOV '81
ROBERTS, GRANT--W/JEFF WALLMAMN,
INTRVW BAE 29, ADULT--
TBRN LLP167 "RELUCTANT COUPLE" '69
TBRN RWS111 "WAYWARD WIVES" '70
TBRN RWS114 "COUPLE AFTER COUPLE" '70
SAXON, ALEX--PRONZINI LTR, MYS--
POCK 77657 "A RUN IN DIAMONDS" '73
TOWNSEND, MARK--W/JEFF WALLMANN,
INTRVW BAE 29, ADULT--
TBRN LLP104 "WHITE CAPTIVE" '69
VAN DORNE, R.--W/JEFFREY WALLMANN,
INTRVW BAE 29, ADULT--
TBRN RWS129 "A DESOLATE COVE" '70
WATSON, ELIZABETH--W/JEFFREY WALLMANN,
INTRVW BAE 29, ADULT--
TBRN LLP244 "TEACHER'S REWARD" '68
WILLIAMS, AGNES--W/JEFFREY WALLMANN,
INTRVW BAE 29--
TBRN LLP168 "PLAYHOUSE FOR SWINGERS" '69
WILLIAMS, JOHN BARRY--W/JOHN LUTZ
& BARRY MALZBERG, PRONZINI LTR,[32]MYS--
AHMM "CHEESEBURGER" OCT '78

PROSCH, T.
ASTARION, THEODOR--[39]GERMAN

PROSSER, HAROLD LEE
PINOAK, JUSTIN WILLARD--[1]

PROTHEROE, CYRIL
LEPAGE, RAND--[2][11][23]SF,HP--
WARREN "BEYOND THESE SUNS" '52

PROTHEROE, ERNEST
HENLEY, P.A.--[1]

PROUST, [V-L-G-E] MARCEL
ANTOINE, MARC--[1][31]
DOMINIQUE--[1][31]
ECHO--[1][31]
HORATIO--[1][31]

PROUT, GEOFFREY
SPENCER, ROLAND--W/FRANCIS ALISTER WARWICK,[1]
VALENTINE, HENRY--W/FRANCIS ALISTER
WARWICK,[1]

PROUTING, FREDERICK JAMES
ARGUS--[1]
BROWN, VANDYKE--[1]
VERITE SANS PEUR--[1]

PROVENCE, MARCEL
JOUHANDEAU, MARCEL--[22]FRENCH

PROVOST, GAIL LEVINE
LEVINE-FREIDUS, GAIL--[33]

PROWELL, SANDRA WEST
MEANS, EVIL--HAWK/PROWELL INTRVW '93,MYS--
'A PHOEBE SIEGEL' MYSTERY

PROWSE, RICHARD ORTON
PROWSE, R.O.--[1]

PRUDE, AGNES GEORGE
DE MILLE, AGNES--[1][31]

PRUDHOMME, RENE FRANCOIS
PRUDHOMME, SULLY--[22]FRENCH

PRUSHINSKI, ALEXANDER V.
GARUN, ALES'--[22]RUSSIAN

PRUSSIA, PRINCE GEORGE OF
CONRAD, GEORG.--[22]GERMAN

PUDDEPHA, DEREK
QUILL--[8]

PUECHNER, BARBARA
DUNCAN, TERENCE--REASONER '94,WEST,HP--
ZEBRA 'POWELL'S ARMY':
"UNCHAINED LIGHTNING" '87
& #2 & 3

PUECHNER, RAY
HADDO, OLIVER--HAWK/B. PUECHNER
INTRVW FEB '93,[1][31]
PEEKNER, RAY--HAWK/B. PUECHNER
INTRVW FEB '93
TIGER, JACK--HAWK/B. PUECHNER
INTRVW FEB '93,[1][31]
VICTOR, CHARLES B.--HAWK/B.PUECHNER
INTRVW FEB '93,[1][32]MYS--
MSMM "FALL GUY" OCT '72

PUGH, DANA RAE
LINDEN, DEANNA--[9][21][26]ROM--
"AIR DANCER"

PUGH, ROGER
ROGERS, BEN--[1]

PUHL, WILFRIED ERNEST
ERNST, WILLIE--[39]GERMAN
ERNEST, BILL--[39]GERMAN
FRIEDMANN, WILL--[39]GERMAN
POOL, BILL--[39]GERMAN

PUHLE, JOACHIM
DEMON, ROY--[39]GERMAN/SF
LE, JOHN--[39]GERMAN/SF
PAHL, JOACHIM--[39]GERMAN/SF
SANDOW, GERD--[39]GERMAN/SF
SANDOW, GERT--[39]GERMAN/SF
SANDOW, J.B.--[39]GERMAN/SF
SCHORN, L.B.--[39]GERMAN/SF
SCOTT, TED--[39]GERMAN/SF,HP--

PUIG Y DE LA PUENTE, FRAN
ROSAS, JULIO--[1]

PUKALLAS, HORST
KERN, GREGORY--[39]GERMAN/SF
ROBERT, HENRY--[39]GERMAN/SF
ROLAND, HENRY--[39]GERMAN/SF
HOWARD, H.P.--W/KLAUS DIEDRICH
& RONALD HAHN,[39]GERMAN/SF
KERN, GREGORY--[2]HP [BADGER OR SCION ?]

PULLAN, RU
BARRIC, WYNNE--[35]AUSTRALIAN--
HRWTZ PB56 "DESK WIFE" '60
DURAND, CASS--[35]AUSTRALIAN--
3 CLEVELAND BKS
3 BIG HORN BKS
3 CORONADA BKS
CHISHOLM 676 "SHADOW GUN"
CONDOR 179 "RANSOM A TOWN"
SIERRA 440 "JUNCTION FALLS SHOWDOWN"
SIERRA 444 "SAGA OF A TALL MAN"
EASTON, PAUL--[35]AUSTRALIAN--
COUGAR 108 "BLONDE V.I.P."
& 11 OTHER 'COUGARS'
HARDIN, LUKE--[35]AUSTRALIAN--
15 CLEVELAND BKS
CONDOR 178 "DEVIL TAKE TWO"
CORONADA 968 "RAMPAGE IN HELLTOWN"
RAND, LEW--[35]AUSTRALIAN--
CONDOR 177 "HUNTIN' TROUBLE"
CONDOR 180 "LARAMIE SHOOT-OUT"
CORONADA 966 "YELLOWSTONE SHOWDOWN"
SANTE FE 327 "RANSOM THE LAW"
SIERRA 443 "HIGH TRAIL HELLION"
CHISHOLM 679 "GUN BALLOT"

PULLE, LEOPOLDO
CASTELNUOVO, LEO DI--[22]ITALIAN

PULLEIN-THOMPSON, CHRISTINE
KEIR, CHRISTINE--[8][33]
THOMPSON, CHRISTINE PULL.--[33]

PULLEIN-THOMPSON, DENNIS
CANNAN, DENIS--[8][34]MYS--
PLAY "THE POWER & THE GLORY" '59

PULLEIN-THOMPSON, DIANA
THOMPSON, DIANA PULLEIN--[33]

PULLEIN-THOMPSON, JOANNA
CANNAN, JOANNA--[1][3][31]MYS--
GOLZ "DEATH AT THE DOG" '40
GOLZ "FRIGHTENED ANGELS" '36 & MORE

PULLEIN-THOMPSON, JOSEPHINE
MANN, JOSEPHINE--[1][31][34]MYS--
CORONET "A PLACE WITH TWO FACES" '72
THOMPSON, JOSEPHINE--[33]

PULLEN, GEORGE
CULPEPER, MARTIN--[8]

PULLING, ALBERT VAN SILER
PULLING, PIERRE--[1]

PULLING, CHRISTOPHER D.
DRUCE, CHRISTOPHER--[1][22][31]ENGLISH

PULS, DIERK
GERHARD, DIERK--[39]GERMAN

PULSFORD, NORMAN GEORGE
TREVOR, A.C.--[3][22]MYS--
HARRAP "DEATH HAUNTS THE LOUNGE" '36

PULVER, MARY MONICA
FRAZER, GAIL--MYS SCENE #43, P93, MYS--
"THE BISHOP'S TALE" '93
FRAZER, MARGARET--W/GAIL BACON,
DDLY PLEAS #3, P34,MYS--
"THE NOVICE'S TALE" '92

PUMILIA, [JOSEPH L.] JOE
MOAMRATH, M.M.--W/BILL WALLACE,[2][11]

PUNCHARD, CONSTANCE HOLME
HOLME, CONSTANCE--[7]SF--
CHAPMAN & HALL "HE-WHO-CAME" '30

PUNNETT, IVOR
SIMMONS, PETER--[8]

PUNNETT, IVOR & MARGARET
SIMONS, ROGER--[3][22][29][40]MYS--
BLES "DEATH ON DISPLAY" '68
BLES "REEL OF DEATH" '70 & 14 MORE

PUNSHON, ERNEST ROBERTSON
HALKET, ROBERTSON--[34]MYS--
BENN "WHERE EVERY PROSPECT PLEASES" '33
NICHOLSON "DOCUM. EVEDENCE" '36
PUNSHON, E.R.--[36]MYS--
WARD "EARTH'S GREAT LORD" 1901

PUPPA, GEORG
HUBECK, JORG--[39]GERMAN

PURACAL, JOHN T.
PURCAL, JOHN T.--[1]

PURCELL, J.S.
STAPLETON, MAURICE--[1]

PURCELL, VICTOR W.W.S.
BUTTLE, MYRA--[1]

PURCHASE, ELSPETH [S]
SANDYS, ELSPETH--[1][21]ROM--
"THE BURNING DAWN"

PURDOM, CHARLES B.
PURDOM, C.B.--[1]

PURDOM, THOMAS EDWARD
PURDOM, TOM--[23]SF--
FANU "GRIEVE FOR A MAN" '57
FANU "I WANT THE STARS" '64

PURDY, ALFRED W.
PURDY, AL--[31]

PURDY, ANNE S.
HOBBS, ANNE--[31]

PURDY, JENNIE BOUTON
SHUBAEL--[3]MYS--
ABBEY "THE DARK STAIN" '03

PURDY, KEN WILLIAM
PRENTISS, KARL--[1]

PURKART, WALTER
TRANK, WERNER--[39]GERMAN/MYS

PURNELL, IDELLA
STONE, IDELLA PURNELL--[1]
STONE, IKEY--[1]

PURNER, INGE
MUHLHOFER, INGE[BORG]--[39]GERMAN/JUV

PURRMANN, CHRISTEL
DORPAT, CHRISTEL--[39]GERMAN

PURVES, FREDERICK
LLOYD, JOSEPH M.--[8]

PURVIANCE, CHERYL LYNN
PRICE, LYNN [LINDA]--[9]ROM--
"DARE TO DREAM"
SPENCER, CHERYL--[9][21][26]ROM--
"FORTUNE'S BRIDE"

PUSCH, EDITH
BACH, BARBI--[39]GERMAN/HOR
BUSCH, BARBARA--[39]GERMAN/HOR
DESMOND, CAROL--[39]GERMAN/HOR
DORNBERG, MICHAELA--[39]GERMAN/HOR
JANKA, JUDITH--[39]GERMAN/HOR
LINZ, MARIA--[39]GERMAN/HOR
MARTIN, CAROLA--[39]GERMAN/HOR

PUSCH, HARALD
TOOLE, PETER--[39]GERMAN/SF

PUSCHEL, WALTER
SCHELL, WALTER--[39]GERMAN

PUTHOSTE, ROGER
THERIVE, ANDRE--[22]FRENCH

PUTMAN, EILEEN
WINWOOD, EILEEN--[26]ROM--
"NOBLE DECEPTION"
"WORDS OF LOVE"
"A WORTHY ENGAGEMENT"

PUTNAM, GEORGE PALMER
BEND, PALMER--[1]

PUTNAM, MARY LOWELL
COLVIL, EDWARD--[1]

PUTZ, PAUL
PAULY, NICK--[39]GERMAN/ADV/WEST
TEXAS-REITER--[39]GERMAN/WEST
THOMPSON, FRED--[39]GERMAN/WEST,HP

PUYEAR-ALERDING, KATHY
ALERDING, KATHY--[9][21][26]ROM--
"CALLING THE SHOTS"
"BENDING THE RULES"
"WITH OPEN ARMS"

PUZO, MARIO
CLERI, MARIO--V. PECORARO--
BAE 21, P19,[3][29]MYS--
BANN B50-112 "SIX GRAVES TO MUNICH" '67

PYATT, ROSINA
BEAUMONT, ANNE--[21]ROM--
"THAT SPECIAL TOUCH"
"ANOTHER TIME, ANOTHER LOVE"

PYKARE, NINA ANN COOMBS
COOMBS, ANN--[21][26][31]ROM--
"THE FIRE WITHIN"
COOMBS, NINA--[9][21][26]ROM--
"SUN SPARK"
"FORBIDDEN JOY" & 3 MORE
PEMBERTON, NAN--[21][26]ROM--
"LOVE'S DELUSION"
PORTER, NINA--[21][26]ROM--
"DESIGN FOR LOVE"
"REVERSAL OF FORTUNES" & 6 MORE

PYKARE, NINA ANN COOMBS [CONT]
POWERS, NORA--[9][21][31]ROM--
"TIME STANDS STILL"
"AFFAIRS OF THE HEART" & 10 MORE
PRYOR, NATALIE--[9]ROM--
PYKARE, NINA--[9][21]ROM--
"LADY INCOGNITA"
"SCANDALOUS SEASON" & 10 MORE
TOWERS, REGINA--[9][21][26]ROM--
"RAKE'S COMPANION"

PYKE, JOHN
WESTLAW, STEVEN--[8][36]MYS--
HODDER "MYS OF LOMBARDY CHAMBERS" '26
HODDER "WHITE PERIL" '26

PYKE, LILLIAN MAXWELL
MAXWELL, ERICA--[8]

PYLES, DANNY
DENNISON, PAULA--V. BERCH-BRNDN/BC PSEUDS, BAE 22, ADULT--
HARKINS, STERLING--[3]MYS--
BRNDN "THE BUTCHER KNIFE KILLINGS" '74

PYNN, KATHLEEN
O'BRIEN, KATHLEEN--[9][21][26]ROM--
HARL "WHITE MIDNIGHT"
HARL "DREAMS OF FIRE" & 2 MORE

QUANDT, ERNST
ECKER, ERNST L.--[39]GERMAN

QUEEN, ELLERY
SMITH , ELLERY--[5]--
FICT PSEUD. USED FOR CHARACTER OF 'QUEEN' IN "CALAMITY TOWN"

QUEISER, HANS R.
STEINER, ROBERT O.--[39]GERMAN/SF

QUENNELL, PETER COURTNEY
P.Q.--[1]

QUENTIN, DOROTHY
BEVERLY, LINDA--[8]

QUIBELL, AGATHA HUNT
PEARCE, A.H.--[1]

QUICK, ANNABELLE
MACMILLAN, ANNABELLE--[31]--
CHILDREN'S BOOKS

QUIGLEY, AILEEN
ARMITAGE, AILEEN--[9][21][26]ROM--
"HAWKSMOOR"
FABIAN, RUTH--[8][9][21][26]ROM--
POPLB "A SCENT OF VIOLETS"
LINDLEY, ERICA--[26][34]ROM/MYS--
SIGN "BELLADONNA" '78
SIGN "DEVIL IN CRYSTAL" '77 & MORE

QUIGLEY, MARGERY
CLARK, MARGERY--W/MARY E. CLARK,[1][8]

QUILLER-COUCH, ARTHUR
A, Q-C--[8]ENGLISH
Q--[2][3][11][22]ENGLISH--
CASSELL "I SAW THREE SHIPS & OTHER WINTER TALES" 1892

QUIN-HARKIN, JANET
JOHNS, JANETTA--[31]

QUINLAN, STERLING C.
QUINLAN, RED--[1][22]AMERICAN

QUINN, CHELSEA Y
FAWCETT, QUINN--W/WILLIAM B. FAWCETT, AV PUB MTL/LACHMAN LST '93,MYS--
AV "NAPOLEON MUST DIE" '93

QUINN, ELISABETH
ADAMS, DALE--[1][31][33]
QUINN, VERNON--[1][33]
VEQUIN, CAPINI--[1][33]

QUINN, SEABURY
LUGAR, HANS--S. HOLLAND-SCION CKLST, PP 27,[34]MYS,HP--
SCION "SIX FOOT DEEP" '50
SCION "COME OUT WITH YOUR HANDS UP!" '51
SCION "THIS SIDE UP" '52
SCION "DOUBLE OR QUITS" '52
SCION "HANDLE WITH CARE" '52
SCION "KILLER'S END" '52
SCION "LADY CAN LOSE" '52
SCION "LEAVE IT TO ME" '52
SCION "LINE UP" '52
SCION "ONE-WAY TICKET" '52
NORMAN, ROB--S. HOLLAND, SCION CKLST, PP 27,[34]MYS--
SCION "BAD DIE YOUNG" '51
SCION "DON'T GIVE ME THAT" '52
PARADISE, LUKE--S. HOLLAND, SCION CKLST, PP 27,[34]MYS--
SCION "SCAR ON A CORPSE" '51
SCION "TOUGH ASSIGNMENT" '51
SCION "CORPSE WORE NYLON" '52
TAYLOR, SNIP--S. HOLLAND, SCION CKLST, PP 27,[34]MYS,HP--
SCION "BLACK ANGEL" '50
SCION "LET'S GO" '52
WHITE, LEONARD--[2]

QUINN, SUSAN
JACOBS, SUSAN--[1][31]

QUINTANELLA, LUIS
TANIYA, KYN--[1]

QUINTANILLA, MARIA A.G.D.
COUNTESS OF ROMANONES--[31]

QUINTER, A.S.
O'QUINN, ALLEN--V. BERCH, GM PSEUDS, PP 33--
GM 281 "SWAMP BRAT" '53
GM 399 "A WOMAN FOR HENRY" '54
GM 463 "STRANGER IN MY BED" '55

QUINTO, CAROLE
CARMICHAEL, JEANNE--[26]ROM--
HARL "MADCAP JOHNNY"
HARL "A TOUCH OF BLACKMAIL" & 3 MORE
MICHELS, CAROL--[26]ROM--
"CHARADE OF HEARTS"

QUINTON, JOHN P.
MACBRIDE, MELCHIOR--[2]

QUIRK, JOHN EDWARD
Q, JOHN--[34]MYS--
AV S176 "BUNNIES" '65
AV S177 "SURVIVOR" '65
AV N133 "HARDWINNERS" '66
SIGN "TOURNAMENT" '66

QUIROGA, HORACIO [S]
EYNHARDT, GUILLERMO--[1][31]

QUITTENTON, BERTRAM
QUIZ, ROLAND JR.--[1]

QUITTENTON, RICHARD M.H.
QUIZ, ROLAND--[1]

QUOIREZ, FRANCOISE
SAGAN, FRANCOISE--[21][31][32]ROM--
16 NVLS '54-85
EQMM "A CRAVING FOR VIOLENCE" AUG '64

QVARNSTROM, INGRID
STAHLFELDT, STINA--[29]MYS--
GEBERS "FALLET FINLAY" '42

RA'ANAN, URI
FRISCHWASSER-RA'ANAN, H.F--[31]

RAABE, WILHELM
CORVINUS, JAKOB--[22][39]GERMAN

RABBETS, THOMAS G.
ST. EBBAR--[8]

RABBIT, JAMES FRANCIS
JAMES, R. FRANCIS--[34]MYS--
MACAULEY "HIGH, LOW & WIDE OPEN" '35

RABE, ANN C.
DEGAN, VON--[2]
DEGEN, VAN--[2]
VON RABE, BARONESS ANN--[31]

RABE, PETER
MACCARGO, J.T.--G. LOVISI-RABE CKLST, PP 25,[34]MYS,HP--
BELM "A FINE DAY FOR DYING" '75
BELM "ROUND TRIP TO NOWHERE" '75
MALAPONTE, MARCO--V. BERCH-BAE 18,G. LOVISI-RABE CK LIST, PP 25--
BEAC B615F "HER HIGH SCHOOL LOVER" '63
BEAC B639F "NEW MAN IN THE HOUSE" '63

RABEN, HANS-JURGEN
GREENE, MILES--[39]GERMAN/HOR

RABER, HANS
NAAGGI, TILLA--[39]GERMAN

RABINOVITCH, M.
BEN AMI--[22]RUSSIAN-YIDDISH

RABINOVITCH, SHOLEM
ALEICHEM, SHOLOM--[31]

RABL, HANS
KRIESTEN, HANS--[39]GERMAN

RABORG, FREDERICK A.
ASHMORE, LEWIS--[1][31]
BALDWIN, DICK--[1][31]
BRONSON, WOLFE--[1]
KERN, CANYON--[1][31]
MAYFAIR, BERTHA--[1]

RABY, DEREK GRAHAM
DERRICK, GRAHAM--[31]

RACHMAN, STANLEY JACK
DURAC, JACK--[1]

RADAN, GEORGE T.
RADAN, G.T.--W/ALFONZ LENGYEL,[31]--
EDITOR "THE ARCHAEOLOGY OF ROMAN PANNONIA" '81

RADCLIFFE, [H] GARNETT
TRAVERS, STEPHEN--[1][22][29]ENGLISH/MYS

RADE, PAUL MARTIN
MARTIN, PAUL--[22]GERMAN

RADETZBY VON RADETZ, CTS.
HARDING, BERTITA--[8]

RADFORD, RICHARD F.
CRITCHLEY, LYNN--[1]
LYNDON, AMY--[9][21][31]ROM--
"ONE WHITE ROSE"
"OPAL MOON"
"TOURNAMENT OF LOVE"

RADFORD, RUTH LORAINE
BAILEY, MATILDA--[1][31][33]
FORD, MARCIA--V. BERCH-MON PSEUDS, BAE 9, [31][33]ROM--
HARL 342 "NANCY CRAIG, RN" '55
MON 251 ISLAND NURSE" '62
MON 277 "DIXIE DOCTOR" '62
MON 287 "PRELUDE TO LOVE" '62

RADIMSKY, LADISLAW
DEN, PETR--[31]

RADLEIN, JOHANNES
JOHANNES, OTTO MARTIN--[39]GERMAN

RADNOR, JODE
O'DONNELL, JODI--[26]ROM--
SIL 1021 "A MAN TO REMEMBER"

RADVANYI, NETTY REILING
SEGHERS--[1]
SEGHERS, ANNA--[1][22][29][34][39]GERMAN/MYS--
"LITTLE "TRANSIT" '40
"SEVENTH CROSS" 42
REILING, NETTY--[1]

RADWANER, LEOPOLD
POLDYS, CAROL--[39]GERMAN

RADWANSKI, PIERRE A.
AL-VAN-GAR--[1][31]
CHOCHLIK--[1][31]
O'KEY--[1]

RADZIWILL, ANNA INGE
RAUER, INGE--[39]GERMAN

RADZIWILL, CATHERINE
VASSILI, [COUNT] PAUL--[1]

RADZYMINSKA, JOZEFA
MIECZYSLAWA--[1]

RAE, HUGH C[RAWFORD]
ALBANY, JAMES--[18][29]MYS--
PAN "DEACON'S DAGGER" '82
PAN "WARRIOR CASTE" '82
PAN "MAILED FIST" '82
PAN "CLOSE COMBAT" '83
PAN "MARCHING FIRE" '83
PAN "LAST BASTION" 84
PAN "BRONEO STORY" '84
CRAWFORD, ROBERT--[18][29][31][34] SCOTTISH/MYS--
CNST "WHIPHAND" '72 & 4 MORE '69-72
HOUSTON, R.B.--[3][18][29][31]SCOTTISH/MYS--
HALE "TWO FOR THE GRAVE" '72
MCGRATH, MORGAN--[1]SCOTTISH

RAE, HUGH C[RAWFORD] [CONT]
STERN, STUART--W/S. UNGAR,[7][18][29][34]SF--
FUTURA "MINOTAUR FACTOR" '77
FUTURA "POISON TREE" '78
STIRLING, JESSICA--W/PEGGIE COGHLAN,[18][21][29]SCOTTISH--
"GATES OF MIDNIGHT" & 14 MORE '74-90

RAE, MARGARET DORIS
RAE, DORIS--[8]

RAEF, LAURA G. CAUBLE
RAEF, LAURA C.--[21]ROM, 6 NOVELS

RAESCHILD, SHEILA
BONNER, TERRY NELSON--[21][31]ROM,HP--
'AUSTRALIAN/NZ' SERIES:
"THE DEFIANT"
GRAWOIG, SHEILA--[31]
JURNAK, SHEILA--[31]

RAFFALOVITCH, GEORGE
SANDS, BEDWIN--[1]

RAFFETY, GORDON EDWARD
GRAY, JOHN--[1]

RAG, MILFORD ANDERSON
RAE, RUSTY--[1]

RAGDALE, TALLULAH
RAGSDALE, LULAH--[1]

RAGEN, NAOMI
ERLINE, N.T.--[31]

RAGG, THOMAS MURRAY
THOMAS, MURRAY--[1][3][22]MYS--
JENKINS "INSP. WILKINS SEES RED" '34
& 2 MORE '32-5

RAGLAN, FITZROY
RAGLAN, BARON--[1]
RAGLAND, LORD--[32]MYS--
LM "NO SUCH FOLK" FEB '50
SOMERSET, FITZROY RICHARD--[1]

RAGOSTA, MILLIE J.
RANDOLPH, MELANIE--[9][21][26]ROM--
"HEART FULL OF RAINBOWS"

RAHMAN, G. ARTHUR
MCKRACKEN, JAMES A.--[2]

RAHN, WOLFGANG
BAXTER, MARK--[39]GERMAN/MYS/HOR,HP--
CONELLI, CLARK--[39][40]GERMAN/MYS--
`KOMMISSAR X' SERIES #607, #620 & #627
DANGER, BRYAN--[39]GERMAN/MYS
DUNHILL, JOE--[39]GERMAN/WEST
FRISCO, TOM--[39]GERMAN/WEST,HP--
MAVERICK, RANDY--[39]GERMAN/WEST
MONGO, MARCUS--[39]GERMAN/HOR/WEST,HP--
MORTMAIN, MORTIMER--[39]GERMAN/HOR/MYS
SLADE, JACK--[39]GERMAN/WEST,HP--
THACKERY, NORMAN--[39]GERMAN/HOR/MYS/WEST,HP--

RAHNER, RAYMOND W.
RAYNER, RAY--[1]

RAHT, CARLYSLE GRAHAM
ORR, FRANKLIN--L. ROBBINS LTR MAR '94

RAINE, WILLIAM MACLEOD
MACLEOD, AUSTIN--[19]WEST

RAINEY, BILL S.
RAINEY, BUCK--[1]

RAINEY, RICH[ARD]
FROST, JASON--[7]SF,HP--
ZEBRA 'WARLORD' SERIES:
"#6 KILLER'S KEEP" '87
HILD, JACK--[34]MYS,HP--
GE 'SOB's' SERIES:
"BARRABUS FIRE" '89
"BARRABUS THRUST" '89
"BARRABUS SWEEP" '90

RAINONE, CHRISTOPHER
HAWTHORNE, VIOLET--[3][21][26][29]ROM/MYS--
LAN "DIARY OF EVIL" '73
BAL "IDENTICAL STRANGERS" '75
BAL "SWEET DEADLY PASSION" '76

RAKNES, OLA
ARNOLD, CARL--[31]

RALEIGH-KING, ROBIN VICT.
GRAHAM, ROBIN--[8]
KING, ROBIN--[8]

RALSTON, ALBERT B.
BLACK, TREVOR--LACHMAN LST '93,[32]MYS--
EQMM "AN INCIDENT AT DEVIL'S ROCK" FEB '71
MSMM "THE ALLIANCE" DEC '72
MSMM "MY BROTHER" OCT '72
AHMM "REPEATED STORY" FEB '72

RALSTON, ALMA
PAYNE, ALMA SMITH--[1]

RALSTON, GILBERT A.
ALEXANDER, GIL--[1][31]

RAMAGE, BRUCE
ROMAN, PETER--[35]AUSTRALIAN--
HRWTZ PB051 "SERVANT OF PLEASURE" '75
HRWTZ PB099 "SERVANT OF SEX" '75
HRWTZ SP051 "SEX SYMBOL" 77
HRWTZ SP143 "NAKED & NUDE" '78
HRWTZ SP187 "NOT BEFORE MIDNIGHT" '79

RAMAGE, JENNIFER
MASON, HOWARD--[3][22][29]MYS--
JOSEPH "BODY BELOW" '55
HALE "JAIL BAIT" '59 & 3 MORE '51-55

RAMBAM, CYVIA
RAMBAM, MYRIAM--[1]
RAMBERG, MYRIAM--[1]
RAMBERT, MARIE--[1]

RAMBAUT, A. BEATRICE
ROMNEY, A.B.--[1]

RAMEY, BEN H.
HOLLIS, H.H.--[2][11]

RAMIN, TEREY DALY
RAMIN, TERESE--[9][21]ROM--
"WATER FROM THE MOON"
"ACCOMPANING ALICE"

RAMIREZ, ALICE
ALEXANDER, SERENA--[9][21][26]ROM--
"RAPTURE REGAINED"
ARKHAM, CANDICE--[3][7][21][26]ROM/MYS--
"ANCIENT EVIL"
"WAYWARD ANGEL" & 5 MORE '73-7
TINY ALICE--[1][2]

RAMIREZ, JOSE AUGUSTIN
AGUSTIN, JOSE--[30]MEXICAN

RAMIREZ, MEDARDO FIGUEROA
FIGUEROA, MEDARDO--[7]SF

RAMIREZ, THOMAS P.
PHILLIPS, TOM--V. BERCH-MON PSEUDS, BAE 9, ADULT--
MON 212 "BEYOND ALL DESIRE" '61
MON 228 "BED SHEET JUNGLE" '61
MON 273 "SORORITY GIRLS" '62
MON 451 "ALL ABOUT AMY" '64
WILSON, GAR--W/REX SWENSON,[29][34]MYS,HP--
GE "ASWAN HELLBOX" '83
WILSON, GAR--[34]MYS-HP--
GE "ALANTIC SCRAMBLE" '84
GE "KOREAN KILLGROUND" '84
GE "WHITE HELL" '83

RAMP, JAMES
AMES, WOODFORDE--[1]

RAMSAY, ALLAN
ZERO--[8]

RAMSAY-LAYE, ELIZABETH
MASSARY, ISABEL--[8]

RAMSDEN, HARTLEY
RAMSDEN, E.H.--[1]

RAMSKILL, VALERIE PATRIC.
BROOKE, CAROL--[1][22][31]ENGLISH

RANADE, KAREN BLANK
BLANK, KAREN--[7]SF--
"THE BOSKONE 9 FOLK-SONG BOOK" '72

RANCE, JANET MAY
GRAHAM, JANET--[1][32]MYS--
EQMM "THE FOLLOWER" JUN '77

RAND, ANNE BINKLEY
BINKLEY, ANNE--[3]MYS--
HARCOURT "WHAT SHALL I CRY" '68

RAND, C.H.
HAZELTON, MABEL--[1]

RANDALL, A.E.
HOPE, JOHN FRANCIS--[8]

RANDALL, FLORENCE ENGEL
RANDALL, FLORENCE E.--[21]ROM--
"THE PLACE OF SAPPHIRES"

RANDAZZO, MARY CALLAHAN
CALLAHAN, MARY--[31]

RANDERS, NICHOLAS
GRABOWSKY, NICHOLAS--[7]HOR--
"HALLOWEEN #4" '88

RANDI, JAMES
AMAZING RANDI, THE--[31]

RANDISI, ROBERT J.
BAINES, LEW--RANDISI INTRVW '93, WEST,HP--
SERIES - TITLES NOT MENTIONED
CARTER, NICK--[3][18]MYS,HP--
CHART "PLEASURE ISLAND" '81
CHART "CHESSMASTER" '82
CHART "MENDOZA MANUSCRIPT" '82
CHART "GREEK SUMMIT" '83
CHART "DECOY HIT" '83

RANDISI, ROBERT J. [CONT]
CARTER, NICK [CONT]
CHART "CARRIBEAN COUP" '84
CUTTER, TOM--HAWK INTRVW/J. CORRICK, PP 15, WEST-- AV - 7 NOVELS '83-5
FORTUNE, SPENCER--HAWK INTRVW '93--
'BEAVER' P.I. SHORT STORIES
HILD, JACK--HAWK INTRVW '93,HP--
GE 'SOB's' SERIES:TITLES NOT MENTIONED
LAKE, ROBERT--HAWK INTRVW '93--
TRADITIONAL WESTERNS
LEDD, PAUL--HAWK INTRVW '93, WEST,HP--
SERIES - TITLES NOT MENTIONED
LONGLEY, W.B.--HAWK INTRVW/J. CORRICK, PP 15,[3]MYS--
PPJKS "DEATH'S ANGEL" '85
PPJKS "MIRACLE OF REVENGE" '85
MEEK, JOSEPH--J. CORRICK-PP 15, WEST,HP--
PINN 'MT. JACK PIKE'SERIES: #1-4 '88-90
MURPHY, WARREN--W/WARREN MURPHY- GHOSTED--
'DESTROYER' SERIES: #40, 43 & 58
RANDALL, JOSHUA--HAWK INTRVW '93, WEST--
'BOUNTY HUNTER' SERIES: 5 NOVELS '87-8
ROBERTS, J.R.--LOVISI & CORRICK-PP 4 & PP 15, WEST,HP--
'GUNSMITH' SERIES: #1-26
SHARPE, JON--HAWK INTRVW '93, WEST,HP--
SERIES - TITLES NOT MENTIONED
STANTON, REX--HAWK INTRVW '93, ADULT--
'BEAVER' - 4 SHORT STORIES
WESTON, COLE--HAWK INTRVW '93, WEST,HP--
IVY 'RYDER' SERIES: TITLES NOT MENTIONED

RANDLE, KEVIN [DOUGLAS]
BOLAN, MACK--G. COOK LTR '93, MYS,HP--
'EXECUTIONER' SERIES: TITLES NOT KNOWN
HELM, ERIC--W/ROBERT CORNETT,[34]MYS,HP--
PINN "BODY COUNT" '84
"NHU STING" '84
HELM, ERIC--W/ROBERT CORNETT, G. COOK LTR '93,[34]MYS,HP--
PINN 'SCORPION SQUAD' SERIES:
'VIETNAM GROUND ZERO' SERIES:
FIRST 23 BOOKS
'SUPER 5'- 4 BOOKS
MACKENZIE, STEVE--[7][34]THRIL,HP--
AV 'SEALS'SERIES: #7 & #10" '88
PENDLETON, DON--[34]MYS,HP--
GE "WARRIOR'S REVENGE" '88

RANDOLPH, GEORGIANNA ANN
LEE, GYPSIE ROSE--A. ANDREWS-PP 6, R.C. HOLLAND-BAE 24,[3][5]MYS--
GHOSTED "G-STRING MURDERS" '43
GHOSTED "MOTHER FINDS A BODY" '44
LIPTON, MRS. LAWRENCE--[29]--
REF INDICATES THIS WAS RANDOLPH'S MARRIED NAME
MALONE, RUTH E.--[18][32]MYS--
MSMM "DEATH OF A PSYCHIATRIST" AUG '59
MALONE, RUTH--[18][32]MYS--
MSMM "DEATH OF A LIGHT-HEARTED LADY" NOV '59
SA "DEADLY INSULT" JAN '62
RICE, CRAIG--[3][5][32][37]MYS--
SIMON "CORPSE STEPS OUT" '40
LAN "BUT THE DOCTOR DIED" '67
SIMON "BIG MIDGET MURDERS" '42
BOBBS "TELEFAIR" '42 & MORE NOVELS
NUMEROUS DIGEST, PULP & SCREEN WORK
SANDERS, DAPHNE--[5][29][34]MYS--
DIAL "TO CATCH A THIEF" '43
SANDERS, GEORGE--W/CLEVE CARTMILL, V. BERCH-BAE 25, GHOSTED--
ASE R-15 "CRIME ON MY HANDS" '45
VENNING, MICHAEL--[5][18][29][32][34]MYS--

RANDOLPH, GEORGIANNA ANN [CONT]
VENNING, MICHAEL [CONT]
COWARD "MAN WHO SLEPT ALL DAY" '42
COWARD "MURDER THROUGH THE LOOKING GLASS" '43
COWARD "JETHRO HAMMER" '44
EQMM "HOW NOW, OPHELIA" JUN '47

RANDOLPH, LOWELL KING
RAN, KIP--[8]

RANDOLPH, VANCE
BOOKER, ANTON S.--[1][31]

RANDS, WILLIAM BRIGHTLY
BROWNE, MATTHEW--[31]
HOLBEACH, HENRY--[31][33]
TALKER, T.--[33]

RANGER-GULL, C[YRIL A.E.]
GULL, RANGER--[23]ENGLISH/SF--
"THE SOUL STEALER" '06
"THE ENEMIES OF ENGLAND" '15
"THE AIR PIRATE" '19
"THE CITY IN THE CLOUDS" '21
RANGER-GULL, C.--[23]ENGLISH/SF/HOR--
"BLACK HONEY" '13
THORNE, GUY--[2][3][23][29]MYS/SF--
WARD "CHARIOTEER" '07
JACK "CRUISER ON WHEELS" '15

RANK, HEINER
HEINDORF, HEINER--[39]GERMAN/SF
PETERMANN, A.G.--[39][40]GERMAN/MYS--
"DIE HUNDE BELLEN NICHT MEHR" '59
& 2 OTHERS

RANKEN, GEORGE
WALKER, W.H.--[13]AUSTRALIAN

RANKIN, HUGH
DOAK--[11]

RANKIN, RUTH DELONE IRV.
DELEONE, RUTH--[1][31]

RANNEY, AGNES V.
REEVES, RUTH ELLEN--[1][33]

RANSFORD, OLIVER
WYLCOTES, JOHN--[8]

RANSOM, CANDICE F.
KENYON, KATE--W/CAROL M. ADORJAN,[31][33]

RANSOM, WILLIAM MICHAEL
HERBERT, FRANK--[23]SF--
ASF "SONGS OF A SENTIENT FLUTE" '79
RANSOM, BILL--[7]SF--
ACE "JAGUAR" '90

RANSOME, CANDICE F.
OSBURN, JESSE--[21]ROM--
"NIGHTSHADE"
"BLACKBIRD KEEP"
"MARIGOLD BEACH"

RANSOME, J. STAFFORD
LEWIS, CAROLINE--W/HAROLD BEGBIE & M.H. TEMPLE,[2][23]SF--
"CLARA IN BUNDERTON"
"LOST IN BLUNDERLAND" '03

RANSOME, JAY ELLIS
ADAMS, HENRY T.--[1][22][31]

RANSOME, L.E.
CHESTER, ELIZABETH--[8]
CLIFFORD, MARTIN--[1]HP
HAYES, IVOR--[1]
MELBORNE, IVOR--[1]
MELBOURNE, IDA--[8]
NORMAN, VICTOR--[1]
RANSOME, BARBARA--[8]
RICHARDS, FRANK--[1]HP
STIRLING, STELLA--[8]
STIRLING, TOM--[1]

RANZETTA, LUAN
RANZETTA, V.--[23]SF--
"THE UNCHARTED PLANET" '61

RANZINI, ADDIS DURNING
AMES, ELINOR--[1][31]
DURNING, ADDIS--[1][31]

RAPER, JULIUS ROWAN
RAPER, JACK--[1]

RAPHAEL, CHAIM
DAVEY, JOCELYN--[3][18][29][31]MYS--
CHATTO "A KILLING IN HATS" '65
& 6 MORE '56-88
RAPHAEL, RAB--[1]

RAPHAEL, FREDERICK [M]
CAINE, MARK--W/TOM MASCHLER,[1][31]

RAPHAELA, CORNELIUS [N]
HERNANDEZ, VICTOR P.--[1]

RAPISARDA, ANTONIO
ANIANTE, ANTONIO--[22]ITALIAN

RAPPAPORT, SOLOMON SAMUEL
AN-SKI, SH. A.--[22]RUSSIAN-YIDDISH
ANSKY, S.--BURNS MANTLE BEST PLAYS '25-6,[1][2][11]MYS--
PLAY "THE DYBUK"
RAPPAPORT, SEMEN A.--[1]

RAPUZZI, G.L.
GRAY, WOODY--[1][2][11]
RENNA, G.--[1][2][11]

RASCH, CARLOS
IGGENSEN, IGOR--[39]GERMAN/SF
MOSS, JERRY--[39]GERMAN/SF

RASCHGOLSKI, HILLEL
BABLI, HILLEL--[22]HEBREW

RASENBERGER-KOCH, ERIKA
WILDE, KARIN--[39]GERMAN

RASH, DORA EILEEN AGNEW
WALLACE, DOREEN--[2][11][22][23]ENGLISH--
"FORTY YEARS ON" '58

RASH, NANCY
HARRISON, MARY--[31]

RASKALNIKOV, FEDOR F.
PETROV--[1]

RASLEY, ALICIA TODD
TODD, ELIZABETH--[9][21][26]ROM--
"THE EARL'S INTRIGUE"
VENET, MICHELL--[9][21][26]ROM--
"THE RELUCTANT LADY"

RASMUSSEN, ALYSSE
LEMERY, ALYSSE--[21][26]ROM--
"TWILIGHT DAWN"
"WISHING STAR"
"WINTER'S END"

RASOF, HENRY
CARTER, NICK--W/STEPHEN WILLIAMSON,[3]MYS,HP--
CHART "DUBROVNIK MASSACRE" '81

RASPE, RUDOLF ERICH
MUNCHAUSEN, KARL F.H.F. v--[39]GERMAN/SF

RASSAERTS, URSULA
ROH, URSULA--[39]GERMAN/JUV

RATCLIFF, RUTH
JENA, RUTH MICHAELIS--[31]

RATCLIFFE, PATRICIA
KING, TERI--[1]

RATHBORNE, ST. GEORGE
ADAMS, HARRISON--[1][28]JUV,HP--
STSY 'THE PIONEER BOYS OF THE
OHIO' BKS '12-28
ALLEN, HUGH--[1][28]--
NOVELIST PUBL "BATTLESMOKE; OR,
WAR CORRESP. AMONG GUERILLAS" 1883
[A] PRIVATE DETECTIVE--[1]
BURTON, ANDY--[1]
CARTER, HERBERT--[1]
CARTER, NICHOLAS--[3]HP
CLIFTON, OLIVER LEE--[1][28]--
BARSE & HOPKINS 'CAMPFIRE BOYS AT LOG
CABIN BEND' BKS '23-26
DALE, DASH--[1]
DUNCAN, DUKE--[1][28]--
"HEAD HUNTER" 1878
"HUNTED DETECTIVE" 1880
"PITTSBURG LANDING" 1883
EDWARDS, WARD--[1]
FORBES, ALECK--[1][28]--
"FREDERICKBURG" 1883
"THE COLOR BEARER" 1893
HOWARD, JACK--[1]
KEENE, LIEUT.--[1][28]--
ADV, CHICAGO PICTORIAL--
5 NOVELS 1878-80
LANGLEY, JOHN PRENTICE--[1]
LAWSON, W.B.--[1]
LESLIE, LAWRENCE--[1]
MANLY, MARLINE--[3][28]MYS/WEST--
40 NOVELS 1871-95
MERRICK, DR. MARK--[3][28]MYS--
STREET "THE GREAT TRAVERS CASE" 1890
MILLER, WARNE--[1][28]MYS--
"SILAS QUIRK, THE DIAMOND
DETECTIVE" CA.1900
OLD BROADBRIM--[1]
ROBERTSON, ALEX--[1]
SHARPE, JACK--[1]
ST. GEORGE, HARRY--[1][28]WEST/FRONTIER--
16 NOVELS 1878-84
STAFFORD, JOHN K.--[34]MYS,HP--
MAGNET #410 "SHADOWED ROUND THE WORLD" '05
STARK, INSPECTOR--[34]MYS,HP--
NEW MAGNET #459 "REVEALED BY LIGHTNING" '06
STEWART, DICK--[34]MYS,HP--
MAGNET #433 "THE HUMAN CAT" '06
MAGNET #418 "THE MAN WHO HID" '05
STEWART, GORDON--[1]
TAYLOR, NED--[28]
TRAVERS, COL J.M.--[28]WEST/MYS--
20 NOVELS 1881-90
TRAVERS, [COL.] J.M.--[1]

RATHBORNE, ST. GEORGE [CONT]
YOUNG BROADBRIM--[1]

RATHER, DEBORAH A.R.
JAMES, ARLENE--RATHER INTRVW, DMN,
[9][21][26]ROM--
"STRANGE BEDFELLOWS"
"PRIVATE GARDEN" & MORE

RATHJEN, CARL HENRY
RUSSELL, CHARLOTTE--[3][21]MYS/ROM--
LAN 75-364 "DARK MUSIC" '72
RUSSELL, CLINTON--[1]

RATHMANN, OSWALD
HALLER, ERNST--[39]GERMAN/JUV

RATIGAN, ELEANOR ELDRIDGE
WHARTON, VIRGINIA--[22]AMERICAN

RATTRAY, HENRIETTA BARB.
JEHAN, NOOR--[1]

RATZLAFF, NELL MARR DEAN
DEAN, NELL MARR--[9][21][26]ROM--
"NURSE KELLY'S CRUSADE" & MORE
MARR, ANNE--[9][21][26]ROM--
"SWEETER THAN WINE"
ROBERTS, VIRGINIA--[9][21]ROM--
"BEAUTY BY DIANE"
"NURSE KAY"
"STUDIO NURSE"

RAUBENHEIMER, GEORGE HARD
HARDING, GEORGE--[1]

RAUCINA, THOMAS FRANK
ANICAR, TOM--[31]
RACINA, THOM--[7]SF--
NEL "BLIZZARD" RETIT. OF "THE GREAT
LOS ANGELES BLIZZARD" '77
RACINE, JOHN--V. BERCH-BRNDN/BC PSEUDS,
BAE 22, ADULT--
SAXON, GRANT TRACY--V. BERCH LTR '93--
WARNER "THE HAPPY HUSTLER: MY OWN
STORY" '75
WELLS, LISA--[1][3]MYS--
ACE "MAGDA" '81

RAUDIVE-MAURINA, ZENTA
MAURINA, ZENTA--[1]

RAUSCH, ALBERT
BENRATH, HENRY--[39]GERMAN

RAUSCH, ANNEGRET [H]
HUGER, A.R.--[39]GERMAN/JUV

RAUSCH, LOTHAR
COTTON, JERRY--[39]GERMAN/MYS,HP--
ESCHBACH, LOTHAR--[39]GERMAN/MYS
FRANK, DR. STEFAN--[39]GERMAN/MYS

RAUSCHNIK, GOTTFRIED PET.
ROSENWALL, PH.--[39]GERMAN/SF

RAVEN, ACHIM
SCHOLZ, FERDINAND--[39]GERMAN

RAVEN, NINETTE HELENE J.
JEANTY, NINETTE HELENE--[31]

RAVENSCROFT, JOHN R.
RAVENSCROFT, ROSANNE--[8]

RAVINES, EUDOCIO
MONTERDO, JORGE--[1]

RAWKINS, ADA
REUBENS, AIDA--[27]ENGLISH/50's
ROSA, VICKI--[27]ENGLISH/50's

RAWLE, HENRY
RETLAW, HENRY--[2]?

RAWLEY, CALLMAN
RAKOSI, CARL--[8]

RAWLINS, EUSTACE
EUSTACE, ROBERT--[11][22][36]

RAWSON, ALBERT L.
RADMUS, G.--[1]

RAWSON, CLAYTON
MERLINI, [THE] GREAT--[11][18][22][29]MYS--
6 NOVELS '38-42
TOWNE, STUART--[2][3][5][18][29][37]MYS--
"DEATH FROM NOWHERE" - 2 NOVELETTES
RDM "GHOST OF THE UNDEAD" '40
RDM "DEATH OUT OF THIN AIR" '40
RDM "CLAWS OF SATAN" '40
RDM "THE ENCHANTED DAGGER" '40
WARREN, FRANK--[29]MYS--
SWEDISH NOVEL MAG #17 "LEVA FARLIGT" '52

RAY, ANNA CHAOIN
HOWARD, SIDNEY--[1]

RAY, DEWITT GRINNELL
GRAY, WIDETT--[1]

RAY, JAMES RALPH
AMES, JIM--[1]

RAY, JOHN PHILIP
LOVEGROVE, PETER--[3]MYS--
CASSELL "THE VON STAHMER JIGSAW" '80
LOVEGROVE, PHILIP--[1]

RAY, KAREN
BERNADETTE, ANN--W/D.H. GAZDAK,[9][21][26]ROM--
"ECHOES OF THE HEART"

RAY, NANCY LOUISE
HUNT, NAN--[1][31]

RAYER, FRANCIS G.
DEEGAN, JON J.--VULTURES OF THE VOID,HP
DELRAY, CHESTER--[7][23]SF--
"REALM OF THE ALIENS" '46
LONGDON, GEORGE--[1][2][11]
SCOTT, MILDRED--[11]
SCOTT, MILWARD--[2]
WORCESTER, ROLAND--[2][11]

RAYMON, ROSSITER W.
GRAY, ROBERTSON--[1]

RAYMOND, BENN
MCNAIR, RON--[35][36]AUSTRALIAN--
ANCHOR 133 "BLUE MURDER"

RAYMOND, GEORGE LANSING
WARREN, WALTERS--[1]

RAYMOND, RENE BRABAZON
CHASE, JAMES HADLEY--J. DINAN--
"HARDBOILED", PP 9,[2][3][5][7][18]MYS--
HALE "SAFER DEAD" '54 & MORE NOVELS
SUS "WORLD IN MY POCKET" JAN-MAR '59

RAYMOND, RENE BRABAZON [CONT]
CHASE, JAMES HADLEY [CONT]
HALE "CADE" '66
HALE "A CAN OF WORMS" '79
DOCHERTY, JAMES L.--[3][5][18][22][29]MYS--
RICH "HE WON'T NEED IT NOW" '39
GRANT, AMBROSE--[2][3][5][18][29]MYS--
EYRE "MORE DEADLY THAN THE MALE" '46
MARSHALL, RAYMOND--[2][3][5][18]MYS--
JARROLDS "BLONDES' REQUIEM" '45
HALE "HIT & RUN" '58 & MORE
RAYMOND, RENE--[18]MYS--

RAYMOND, WALTER
COBBLEIGH, TOM--[8]

RAYNARD, PATRICK
NACRAY, J.-B.--W/JEAN-BERN. DANIEL PENNAC,
[40]MYS

RAYNAUD, OLIVIER
NOLANE, RICHARD D.--[2]FRENCH, ISFYB/SF
SEABURY, DON A.--[2]FRENCH, ISFYB/SF

RAYNER, AUGUSTUS ALFRED
HALL, WHYTE--[3][22]MYS--
HARRAP "DEATH & A CLOCK" '36
& 3 MORE '36-46

RAYNER, CLAIRE B.
BRANDON, SHEILA--[1][9][31]ROM
CHETWYND, BERRY--[1][31]
LYNTON, ANN--[1][9][31]ROM
MARTIN, RUTH--[1][9][31]ROM,HP--
SAXE, ISOBEL--[1]

RAYNES, FREDERICA R.R.
CASTWEAZLE, ELEANOR--[1]

RAZZI, JAMES
RAZZI, JIM--[7]SF/THRIL--
BAL "FIND YOUR FATE-JUNIOR
TRANSFORMERS #5" '86

REACH, JAMES
ABBOTT, BRUCE--[1][22]AMERICAN
BREMER, WARD--[1][22]AMERICAN
MACROSS, ROSS--W/TOM B. TAGGART, V. BERCH-
GM PSEUDS, PP 33,[3]MYS--
MACROSS, ROSS [2]--W/TOM B. TAGGART--
GM 386 "THE BEAUTIFUL & THE DEAD" '54
MANNING, HILDA--[1][3][22]AMERICAN/MYS--
2 PLAYS '42-50
MANNING, ROY--[8]AMERICAN
RAND, JOHN--[1][3]MYS--
3 PLAYS '38-47
RESSIEB, GEORGE--[1][22]
SUTTON, THOMAS--[1][22]
WEST, TOM--[1][22]WEST-NUMEROUS NOVELS
WILLIAMS, PETE--[1][3]MYS--
PLAY "OVER MY DEAD BODY" '50
WILLIAMS, RICHARD--[1][22]

READ, ANTHONY
FERGUSON, ANTHONY--[8]

READ, JAMES
BACON, JEREMY--[8]

READ, JOHN
PHILLIPS, TONY--[7]SF,HP--
BAL 'TURBO COWBOYS' SERIES: #6 & #9" '89

READ, JOHN HINTON
READ, JAN--[1]

READ, LORNA
STANDISH, CAROLINE--[9][21][26]ROM--
"SWEET TEMPTATION"

READE, FRANCES LAWSON
LANGWORTHY, YOLANDE--[1]

REAGAN, THOMAS B.
REAGAN, THOMAS--[3]MYS--
PUTNAM "BLOOD MONEY" '70
HAMM "BIG FALL" '67 & 4 MORE '64-70
THOMAS, JIM--[1][3][40]MYS--
McCALL "CROSS PURPOSES" '71

REAHM, THELMA L.
PALMER, LEW--V. BERCH-BRNDN/BC PSEUDS,
BAE 22, ADULT--

REAMES, TARA LEE
QUINN, TARA TAYLOR--[26]ROM--
HARL 567 "YESTERDAY'S SECRETS"
HARL 600 "DARE TO LOVE" & OTHERS

REAMY, THOMAS EARL
REAMY, TOM--[7][23]SF--
"BLIND VOICES" '78
"SAN DIEGO LIGHTFOOT SUE & OTHER
STORIES" '79
FSF "TWILLA" '74

REANEY, JAMES CRERAR
SPOONBILL--[1]

REARDON, DAN
CARTER, NICK--[3]MYS,HP--
CHART "THE TARANTULA STRIKE" '80
ROSSI, BRUNO--V. BERCH LTR TO
HUBIN '94, MYS,HP--
"MAFIA DEATH WATCH"

REASONER, JAMES & LIVIA
AUSTIN, JIM--INTRVW BAE 26, WEST,HP--
BERK "FURY" '92
BERK "BLOOD RANSOM" '92
BERK "RIVER WAR" '93
BERK "LAST CHANCE CANYON" '93
BERK "NEVADA GUNS" '95
HALLIDAY, BRETT--INTRVW BAE 26, MYS,HP--
MSMM "YESTERDAY'S ANGEL" SEP '80
MSMM "MAYHEM IN THE MAGIC CITY" OCT '80
MSMM "ALL THE FACES OF FEAR" DEC '80
MSMM "STALKER OF BISCAYNE BAY" MAY '81
MSMM "BOOK OF THE DEAD" JUL '82
JAMES, LIVIA-- INTRVW BAE 26, ROM--
FAWCETT 12410 "THE EMERALD LAND" '83

REASONER, JAMES M.
DUNCAN, TERENCE--AUTHOR PROVIDED, WEST,HP--
ZEBRA `POWELL'S ARMY':
2285 "ROBBER'S ROOST" '88
"ROCKY MOUNTAIN SHOWDOWN" '88
"RED RIVER DESPERADOS" '88
EARLY, TOM--INTRVW BAE 26, WEST,HP--
BERK 'SONS OF TEXAS' SERIES:
"THE DEFIANT" '93
EVANS, TABOR--INTRVW BAE 26, WEST,HP--
JOVE 'LONGARM' SERIES: #178, #185 & #192
FOSTER, JAKE--AUTHOR PROVIDED, WEST,HP--
ZEBRA "HELL FOR LEATHER RIDER" '91
ZEBRA "RAMROD REVENGE" '91
GRANT, WILLIAM--INTRVW BAE 26, WEST,HP--
LYNX 'FARADAY' SERIES: "#1 IRON HORSE" '88
HALLIDAY, BRETT--INTRVW BAE 26, MYS,HP--
MSMM "DEATH IN XANADU" DEC '78
MSMM "TWICE AS DEADLY" JUN '79
MSMM "LADY FROM THE GRAVE" SEP '79

REASONER, JAMES M. [CONT]
HALLIDAY, BRETT [CONT]
MSMM "PHOENIX GAMBIT" DEC '79
MSMM "MURDER BY THE BAY" FEB '80
MSMM "PAYOFF IN BLOOD" MAR '80
MSMM "BEDLAM FILE" MAY '80
MSMM "MURDER IN PARADISE" JUN '80
MSMM "ENCORE FOR DEATH" JUL '80
MSMM "VIPER CONSPIRACY" AUG '80
MSMM "KILLER'S EVE" NOV '80
MSMM "BLACK LOTUS" JAN '81
MSMM "ODDS ON DEATH" FEB '81
MSMM "THREE STRIKES - YOU'RE DEAD" MAR '81
MSMM "FIT FOR A CORPSE" APR '81
MSMM "BYLINE FOR MURDER" JUN '81
MSMM "MIDNIGHT WIND" AUG '81
MSMM "KILLER'S CRUISE" SEP '81
MSMM "FULL MOON MEANS MURDER" OCT '81
MSMM "DEATH IN THE DAILIES" DEC '81
MSMM "BEAUTIFUL BUT BAD" JAN'82
MSMM "DOOMSDAY ISLAND" FEB '82
MSMM "HAVOC IN HIGH PLACES" MAR'82
MSMM "DEADLY QUEEN" APR '82
MSMM "MEDICI CASKET" MAY '82
MSMM "ASSASSINATION OF MICHAEL
SHAYNE" JUN '82
MSMM "DEADLY VISITOR" AUG '82
MSMM "DEATH IN TEXAS" SEP '82
MSMM "MURDER FROM BEYOND THE GRAVE" OCT '82
MSMM "FISHING FOR MURDER" DEC '84]
HART, MATTHEW S.--INTRVW BAE 26, WEST,HP--
BB 'CODY'S LAW' SERIES:
#1-#6, #8, #9, #11, #12"
JAMES, M.R.--INTRVW BAE 26, MYS--
MSMM "GRAVEYARD SHIFT" NOV '78
LADD, JUSTIN--INTRVW BAE 26, WEST,HP--
POCK 'ABILENE'SERIES: #1-16 '88-90
MASON, R.--INTRVW BAE 26,[32]MYS--
MSMM "OLD COLLEGE TRY" NOV '78
MITCHUM, HANK--INTRVW BAE 26, WEST,HP--
BB 'STAGECOACH STATION' SERIES:
"PECOS" '87
"PANHANDLE" '87
"TAOS" '87
"DEATH VALLEY" '88
"BONANZA CITY" '88
"WILD WEST" '91
"THE LAST FRONTIER" '91
ROSS, DANA FULLER--INTRVW BAE 26,WEST,HP--
BB 'FRONTIER TRIOLOGY': #1-3 '92-3
RUTLEDGE, ADAM--INTRVW BAE 26, HIST,HP--
BB 'PATRIOTS' SERIES: #1-6 '92-4

REASONER, LIVIA & JAMES
WASHBURN, L.J.--INTERVW BAE 26, MYS--
MSMM "SINGER AT DAWN" OCT '80

REASONER, LIVIA J.W.
WASHBURN, L.J.--INTRVW BAE 26,[32]MYS--
`WASHBURN' IS LIVIA'S MAIDEN NAME----
TOR 51041 "WILD NIGHT" '87
POCK 67187 "EPITAPH" '90 & OTHERS--
MSMM "THE LORD PROVIDES" JUN '80--
WASHBURN, LIVIA J.--INTRVW BAE 26--
3 "LUCAS HALLAM" MYS
6 WESTERN NOVELS

REAVES, JAMES MICHAEL
REAVES, J. MICHAEL--[23]SF
REAVES, MICHAEL--[23]SF

REAVIS, CHERYL
RICHARDS, CINDA--[9][21][26]ROM--
"FIRE UNDER HEAVEN"
"DILLON'S PROMISE" & 3 MORE

REBACK, MARCUS
CALDWELL, TAYLOR--W/JANET TAYLOR CALDWELL, [1][8][11]
REINER, MAX--W/JANET TAYLOR CALDWELL,[1][8]

REBCZEK, FRANZ
KERNEGGER, HANNES--[39]GERMAN

REBNER-CHRISRIAN, DORIS
CHRISTIAN, DORIS--[39]GERMAN/JUV
KIRCHMAYR, CHRISTA--[39]GERMAN/JUV
TORRIS, CHRISTIANE v.--[39]GERMAN/JUV

RECHNITZER, F.E.
RECHNITZER, REX--ECHOES #17, P9--
SKYFIGHTERS MAR '38

RECHT, CAMILLUS
CHRISTENSEN, C.--[39][40]GERMAN/MYS--
MYS "EIN PARTIE SCHACH" '52 & OTHERS

REDD, JOANNE
WILDE, LAUREN--[9][21][26]ROM--
ZEBRA 1802 "REBEL HEART" '86
ZEBRA 2375 "CAPTIVE LOVE" '88
ZEBRA 2679 "TENDER BETRAYAL" '89
ZEBRA 3411 "PASSIONS THUNDER" '91
ZEBRA "SWEET TEXAS WILDFIRE" '92
ZEBRA SWEET SAVAGE SPLENDOR" '93 & 5 OTHERS

REDDAWAY, W. BRIAN
ACADEMIC INVESTOR--[22]

REDDING, KENNETH SHIELS
SARR, KENNETH--[1]

REDDING, ROBERT HULL
BEETON, MAX--[31]
DENVER, WALT--[31]

REDGATE, JOHN
KENNEDY, ADAM--LACHMAN LST '93,[34]MYS--
TRDNT "KILLING SEASON" '67
DLCT "LAST DECATHLON" '79

REDMAN, BEN RAY
LORD, JEREMY--[3][22][31]MYS--
DBLDY "BANNERMAN CASE" '35
DBLDY "SIXTY-NINE DIAMOND" '40

REDMAN, WILLIAM XAVIER
SCARLET, WILL--[8]

REDMAYNE, MARY PRIESTLEY
RODNEY, M.--[1]

REDMON, LOIS
ROGERS, RACHEL--[8]

REDMOND, BRENDA C.
GAYLE, B.--[34]MYS--
VANTAGE "RENA" '77

REECE, ALYS [TRACY]
WINGFIELD, SUSAN--[1]

REED, ALEXANDER WYCLIF
HARLEQUIN--[1][22][31]NEW ZEALANDER

REED, BLAIR
RING, ADAM--[1][3][22]MYS--
CROWN "KILLERS PLAY ROUGH" '46

REED, DAVID V.
HORNE, PETER--[23]SF,HP--
FA - 2 STORIES

REED, EDWARD CHARLES
BRANGWYN, CHARLES--[1]

REED, ELIZABETH STEWART
STEWART, ELIZABETH GREY--[1][22]AMERICAN

REED, ISHMAEL
COLEMAN, EMMETT--J. PRESSMAN-CNTRCLTR, BAE 21,[1]--

REED, LILLIAN CRAIG
HYDE, SHELLEY--G. COOK LTR '93,[7][23][31][33]--
POCK "SAVAGE STAIN" '82
POCK "BLOOD FEVER" '82
REED, KIT--[2][7][11][23][32]MYS/SF--
EQMM "THE PERFECT PORTRAIT" JUL '68
GOLZ "KILLER MICE" '76
BERK "MAGIC TIME" '80
DBLDY "FORT PRIVILEDGE" '85 PLUS

REED, MYRTLE
GREEN, OLIVE--[1]

REED, PETER HUGH
D'ESTERRE, NEVILLE--[1]
GIRARD, PAUL--[1]

REED, ROBERT
TOUZALIN, ROBERT--[23]SF--
LRHPA "MUDPUPPIES" '86

REED, ZEALIA BROWN
BISHOP, ZEALIA B.--[11]

REED-MARR, P.J.
MARR, REED--V. BERCH-GM PSEUDS, PP 33--
GM 576 "CATCH A FALLING STAR" '56

REED-SMITH, IDA
WARRINGTON, DAN--[1]

REEDER, DAVE
YOUNG, KAREN--[2]

REEDER, RUSSELL P. JR.
REEDER, COL. RED--[8][33]

REEDS, F. ANTON
RIKER, ANTHONY--[1][2][11]

REEHANY, AMIN
AR-RAIHANT--[22]SYRIAN-AMERICAN

REEMAN, DOUGLAS [EDWARD]
KENT, ALEXANDER--[1][31]SEA ADV,HP--
MOST TITLES

REEP, DIANE
ALLEN, EMILY ANN--W/EMILY JO ALLEN,[9]
REEP, DIANE--W/EMILY JO ALLEN,[9][21]ROM--
"THE BLACKMORE TOUCH"

REES, ARTHUR JOHN
WATSON & REES--W/JOHN REAY WATSON,[29]MYS--
LANE "MYSTERY OF THE DOWNS" '18

REES, CLAIR FRANCIS
BORDEN, BOB--[31]

REES, CORALIE CLARKE
CLARKE, CORALIE--[13]AUSTRALIAN

REES, ELLA GWENDOLEN
RHYS, JEAN--B&M COLL #18, P46,ENGLISH/ROM

REES, HELEN CHRISTINA E.
OLIVER, JANE--[2][7][21][22]ENGLISH/ROM--
"LION & THE ROSE"
"SUNSET AT NOON" & 4 MORE

REES, JOAN
AVERY, JUNE--[1][31]
BEDFORD, ANN--[1][31]
STRONG, SUSAN--[1]

REES, JOAN BOWEN
RHYS, JOAN--[1]

REESE, CHARLOTTE PAUL
PAUL, CHARLOTTE--[21][26]ROM--
"PHOENIX ISLAND"
"WILD VALLEY" & 5 MORE

REESE, HELOISE BOWLES
HELOISE--[31]

REESE, JOHN [HENRY]
CARPENTER, JOHN JO--[1][28]--
S&S "SIGNAL GUNS AT SUNUP" '50 & SS
KENNEDY, CODY JR.--[21][26][28]ROM--
"THE CONQUERING CLAN"
"THIS WILD LAND"
"THE WARRIOR FLAME"

REESE, ROBERT A.
REESE, BOB--[33]

REESE, WILHELM F.C.
OSTEN, LUDWIG--[39]GERMAN/MYS/SF
REESE, WILLY--[39]GERMAN/MYS/SF
RENNER, PIT--[39]GERMAN/MYS/SF
VON OSTEN, RENATE--[39]GERMAN/MYS/SF
VON RIENZIEHAUSEN, BORCH.--[39]GERMAN/MYS/SF

REEVE, ARTHUR, B.
CREATOR OF CRAIG KENNEDY--[1]

REEVE-JONES, ALAN EDMOND
ALLEN, EDMUND--[1]
LUNCHBASKET, ROGER--[1]

REEVES, JOHN MORRIS
REEVES, JAMES--[1]

REEVES, JOYCE
GARD, JOYCE--[8][25][31][33]--FANT. LIT.
CHILDREN & YOUNG ADULTS, RUTH NADELMAN

REEVES, JUDSON
SEPTAMA, ALDARA--[2][11]

REEVES, LAWRENCE F.
LYFICK, WARREN--[1][31][33]
SEEVER, R.--[1][33]

REGAN, JOHN WILLIAM
QUINPOOL, JOHN--[1]

REHFELD, FRANK
ASLIN, SAMANTHA--[39]GERMAN/ADV/SF
ATKINS, JESSICA--[39]GERMAN/ADV/SF
COOPER, STEVE--[39]GERMAN/ADV/SF
CRAVEN, ROBERT--[39]GERMAN/ADV/SF
HOLZNER, SEBASTIAN--[39]GERMAN/ADV/SF
THYS, FRANK--[39]GERMAN/ADV/SF
WINKLER, DIETER--[39]GERMAN/ADV/SF

REHM, WARREN S.
NEMO, OMEN--[2]

REHN, GOTTFRIED
DAMANN, GUSTAV--[39]GERMAN

REIBER, JOHN N.
NEY, JOHANNES--[2]

REICHENTHAL, LAURA
GOTTSCHALK, LAURA RIDING--[1][22]AMERICAN
JACKSON, LAURA [RIDING]--[1][22]AMERICAN
RICH, BARBARA--W/ROBERT VON RANKE GRAVES,[2]
RICH, BARBARA--W/SUSAN GRAVES,[1]
RIDING, LAURA--[22]AMERICAN
RING, LAURA--[1]

REICHERT, MIRIAM ZUCKER
REICHERT, MICKEY ZUCKER--[7]SF--
DAW 'BIFROST GUARDIANS' SERIES: #1-5 '88-91

REICHNITZER, F.E.
MORGAN, LT. SCOTT--[2]HP--

REID BANKS, LYNNE
BANKS, LYNNE REID--[31]

REID, CHARLES [STUART]
DAVIDSON, JOHN--[1][31]
MARTIN, FRANCIS--[1]
STUART, CHARLES--W/CHARLES ROY MacKINNON,
[21]ROM--
"CUPIDS & CORONETS"
"LADY AMBASSADOR" & MORE

REID, DANIEL P. JR.
DANIEL, LEE--[31]

REID, ELA
SEN, ELA--[1]

REID, FRANCES P.
ALLISON, MARIAN--[1][22][31]

REID, HELEN GRACE
CARLISLE, HELEN GRACE--[1]

REID, JAMES MACARTHUR
WALKINSHAW, COLIN--[1][22]SCOTTISH

REID, JOHN
TOULMIN, DAVID--[8]

REID, JOHN COWIE
CALIBAN--[1][31]

REID, JOHN T.H.
HOWARD, TOM--[34]MYS--
RASTAR "HEALTH FARM MURDERS" '85
RASTAR "BEACH-FRONT MURDERS" '85
RASTAR "LAST GENERATION" '86
RASTAR "HOWARD'S PRICE" '87
RASTAR "ALL POSSIBLE AVENUES" '87

REID, PHILLIPA
SISE, ANNIE--[8]

REID, SARAH ADDINGTON
ADDINGTON, SARAH--[1]

REID, VICTOR STAFFORD
REID, V.S.--[1]

REID, WHITELAW
AGATE--[8]

REID, [THOMAS] MAYNE
BEACH, CHARLES--[31][33]
BEACH, CHARLES S.--[1][2]

REID, [THOMAS] MAYNE [CONT]
CANNIBAL, JACK--[1]
POOR SCHOLAR--[1]

REIF, IRENE
HOOP, CECIL J.--[39]GERMAN

REIFENBERG, ELISE
TERGIT, GABRIELE--[39]GERMAN

REIFF, H. VOLKER
CANE, TERRY--[39]GERMAN/SF

REILE, LOUIS ANTHONY
CURRAN, JOHN--[1]

REILLY, BERNARD JAMES
YORKE, ANTHONY--[1]

REILLY, HELEN [KIERNAN]
ABBEY, KIERNAN--[3][18][29]MYS--
SCRIBN "RUN WITH THE HARE" '41
SCRIBN "AND LET THE COFFIN PASS" '42
MCMULLEN, MARY--[1][3]MYS--
DBLDY "BAD-NEWS MAN" '86
HARPER "STRANGLE HOLD" '57
& 12 MORE '51-86

REIMANN, GERO
MEIER-KNILBENDORFF, RALF.--[39]GERMAN/SF

REIMESCH, FRITZ HEIN
SCHAFFER, MICHEL--[39]GERMAN

REINECKE, WALTER
RIEGL, CARL--[39]GERMAN/SF
UPTON, MUNRO R.--W/W. ERNSTING, W. KUMMING, W. SCHOLZ & J. SCHEIDT,[39]GERMAN/SF

REINECKER, HERBERT
BERG, AXEL--[39]GERMAN/MYS
DUHRKOPP, HERBERT--[39]GERMAN/SF
YOUNG, EDWARD--[1][22][33]AMERICAN

REINGOLD, CARMEL B.
ELLIS, ALEXANDRA--[9][21]ROM--
"THE LAST CARNIVAL"
"ROMANY PASSIONS"

REINHARD, HANS GEORG
GEORG, HANS--[39]GERMAN
GORDON, HANS--[39]GERMAN
HARD, HEDWIG--[39]GERMAN
HARDT, HELMUT--[39]GERMAN
WARREN, HANS--[39]GERMAN,HP

REINHARD, WILHELM PETER
CARR, PETER--[39]GERMAN
FRANKLIN, E.A.--[39]GERMAN
HAGEN, FRITZ--[39]GERMAN
HERFURTH, ALICE--[39]GERMAN
PUCK, PETER--[39]GERMAN
WARREN, HANS--[39]GERMAN,HP
WARREN-HOLM, HANS--[39]GERMAN

REINHOLD, KARL LUDWIG
KEGLER, HANS--[39]GERMAN

REINOWSKI, HANS J.
REINOW, HANS--[39]GERMAN

REINTSCH, INGEBORG
TETZNER, INGEBORG R.--[39]GERMAN/JUV

REIS, KURT
CAROLYI, STEPHAN--[39]GERMAN/JUV
COSTELLO, CONTE--[39]GERMAN/JUV
MARKUS, MARIO--[39]GERMAN/JUV
RITTER, KURT--[39]GERMAN/JUV
VON ORLOWSKI, AXEL--[39]GERMAN/JUV

REISCH-NOWAK, CHRISTINE
FRANK, DR. STEFAN--[39]GERMAN,HP
WARD, LINDA--[39]GERMAN

REISS, BARBARA EVE
EVE, BARBARA--[31]

REIT, SEYMOUR
REIT, SY--[1][33]

REITCI, JOHN GEORGE
O'CONNELL, STEVE--LACHMAN LST '93, MYS--
AHMM "DEATH, TAXES, AND..." FEB '60
AHMM "9 FROM 12 LEAVES 3" NOV '60
AHMM "PUT TOGETHER A MAN" MAY '61
AHMM "QUIET EYE" AUG '61
"REMAINS TO BE SEEN" JUN '61
"KILL THE TASTE" JUN '64
RITCHIE, JACK--[18][34]MYS--
DELL 6381 "A NEW LEAF & OTHER STORIES" '71
SO. IL. UNIV. PRESS "ADVENTURES OF HENRY TURNBUCKLE" '87
ST. MARTIN'S "LITTLE BOXES OF BEWILDERMENT" '89 & MANY UNCOLLECTED SS

REITCI, RITA KROHNE
RITCHIE, RITA--[3][7][32]MYS--
CAROUSEL "SHADOW OF THE PYRAMID" '80
MAJOR "GRIP OF FEAR"
BZ "A MATTER OF THE MIND" JAN '66

REITER, VICTORIA KELRICH
HEMINGS, T.J.--[31]

REITMAN, BOB
ROBBINS, BURCH--V. BERCH-BRNDN/BC PSEUDS, BAE 22, ADULT--

REIZ, YITZCHOK
NADIR, MOISHE--[1]ISRAELI

REIZENSTEIN, ELMER
RICE, ELMER--[2][32]MYS--
EQMM "CONCIENCE" APR '46
RICE, ELMER L.--[2][3][11][23]AMERICAN, LEGALIZED TO "RICE"--MYS PLAYS

REKAI, KATI
KATI--[31]

RELLERGERD, HELMUT
CAMERON, JOHN--[39]GERMAN/MYS/WEST,HP
CORNER, CLIFF--[39]GERMAN/HOR/MYS,HP
COTTON, JERRY--[39]GERMAN/MYS,HP
DANGER, DAMION--[39]GERMAN/MYS
DARK, JASON--[39][40]GERMAN/MYS,HP
DENVER, JOHN--[39]GERMAN/WEST
GELLER, RED--[39]GERMAN/MYS/WEST
JONES, EVERETT--[39]GERMAN/WEST,HP
LAMONT, ROBERT--[39]GERMAN/HOR
LE JOHN, KEVIN--[39]GERMAN/MYS/WEST
MORRIS, DAVE--[39][40]GERMAN/MYS--
`KOMMISSAR X' #561, 567, 568, 580, 584, 589 & #606
MORTON, JACK--[39]GERMAN/MYS/WEST
PRESCOTT, JIM--[39]GERMAN/MYS/WEST
SLADE, JACK--[39]GERMAN/WEST,HP
SOLO, FRANCO--[39]GERMAN/MYS/WEST,HP

REMAR, FRITS
DAHL, JOHN--[29]MYS

REMARD, ERICH PAUL
REMARQUE, ERICH MARIA--[1][39]GERMAN

REMI, GEORGES
HERGE--[1][31][33]

REMINGTON, ELLA-CARRIE
ALDEN, CARELLA--[31]

REMOFF, HEATHER T[REXLER]
FOWLER, HEATHER T.--[1][31]

REMPT, JAN DIRK
DE JONG VAN HAGE, T.P.M.--[1]

REMUS, MICHAEL
O'HARA, DAN--[39]GERMAN/WEST
SUMMER, MIKE--[39]GERMAN/WEST

REMY, CAROLINE
SEVERINE--OXFORD COMPANION TO FRENCH LIT. 1961,[22]FRENCH

RENA, SARAH MARY
RENA, SALLY--[1][3]MYS--
WEIDENFELD "PAINLESS DEATH" '81

RENAN, SHELDON
CRYPTON, DR.--W/PAUL W. HOFFMAN,[7]SF--
WARNER "TREASURE:IN SEARCH OF A GOLDEN HORSE:A PUZZLE"

RENARD, JOSEPH
FITZBANCROFT, TERENCE--[14]ADULT--
OLYM OPH#114 "MY SISTER MY SIN" '68
OLYM TC#500 "SHAPE OF DESIRE" '71

RENAUD, RON
COE, ROSS ANTON--[7]SF--
PINN 'WARRIOR OF VENGEANCE' SERIES: #1 & 2 '82
GERARD, RON L.--V. BERCH LTR TO HUBIN '94,MYS--
PPJKS "DEADLY AIMS" '86
PPJKS "DEADLY SIGHTS" '87
STIVERS, DICK--[34]MYS,HP--
GE "COWBOY'S REVENGE" '87
GE "CLEAR SHOT" '88
GE "COLD STEEL" '88
GE "FINAL RUN" '88
GE "RED MENACE" '88
GE "STRIKE FORCE" '88
GE "BLOOD MARK" '89
GE "DEAD ZONE" '89
GE "WHITE FIRE" '89
HEATH, CHARLES--[3]MYS--
DELL "A-TEAM" '84
DELL "SMALL BUT DEADLY WARS" '84
& 4 MORE '83-5

RENDELL, RUTH [B]
VINE, BARBARA--A.J. HUBIN-EQMM MAR '87, [18][29][34]MYS--
VIKING "DARK-ADAPTED EYE" '86
VIKING "A FATAL AVERSION" '87
VIKING "HOUSE OF STAIRS" '89
VIKING "GALLOWGLASS" '90
VIKING "KING SOLOMON'S CARPET" '91

RENERIUS, HANS-EVERT
RENE, HANS EVERT--[1]

RENERTZ, KAJ
BOHUS, KAJ--[29]MYS--
"FALLET ESSBERG" '38
STERNER, WILLIAMS--[29]MYS--
DM#29 "GIFTSMUGGLARNA" '38

RENFREW, A.
PATTERSON, SHOTT--[8]

RENFROE, MARTHA KAY
WREN, M.K.--CRPG,[2][3][7]SF--
'PHOENIX LEGACY': #1-3 '81
CONTEMP/MYS NOVELS '73-90

RENICH, HELEN T.
RENICH, JILL--[1]

RENN, THOMAS EDWARD
STRIKE, JEREMY--[2][11][23]SF--
"A PROMISING PLANET" '70

RENNART, RICHARD SCOTT
SCOTT, RICHARD--[33]

RENNAU, JOACHIM
BROWNE, K.W.--[39]GERMAN/SF/WEST
CANE, HURRY--[39]GERMAN/SF/WEST
GRANT, CHARLIE--[39]GERMAN/SF/WEST
GRAY, JIM--JEAN F. LE DEIST LTR '93, [39]GERMAN/SF/WEST
GREY, JIM--[39]GERMAN/SF/WEST
RAMIN, MONIKA--[39]GERMAN/SF
RANDALL, J.R.--[39]GERMAN/SF/WEST
RANDALL, ROLF--[39]GERMAN/SF/WEST
RENN, ROLF--[39]GERMAN/SF/WEST
RENNAU, ROLF--[39]GERMAN/SF/WEST
WHITE, JAMES S.--[39]GERMAN/SF/WEST

RENNER, KARL
SPRINGER, RUDOLF--[1][22]AUSTRIAN
SYNOPTICUS--[1][22]AUSTRIAN

RENNERT, MAGGIE
NUNLEY, MAGGIE RENNERT--[1]

RENNIE, JAMES ALAN
CLELAND, MORTON--[1][22][31]SCOTTISH
DENVER, BOONE--[1][22][31]SCOTTISH
MAC FEE, MAXWELL--[1][22][31]SCOTTISH

RENSHAW, LISA M.
WINTERS, MALORI--[9][11]ROM

RENTOUL, T. LAURENCE
GAGE, GERVAIS--[8]

REOCH, J.S.
GILBERT, BEN--[35]AUSTRALIAN--
HRWTZ PB400 "STOP FOR THE RED LIGHT" '69

REPP, ED EARL
BUCKNER, BRADNER--[1][2][11][23]WEST--
PULP '29-49
CODY, JOHN--[1][2][11][28]WEST--
GODWIN "EMPTY HOLSTERS" '36
FIELD, PETER--[1][2][11][19]WEST,HP--
"MUSTANG MESA"

REPPERT-RAUTEN, LOTHAR v.
RAUTEN, L.C.--[39]GERMAN/MYS/JUV

RES, CLAIR [FRANCIS]
BORDEN, BOB--[1]
RHYS, FRANK--[1]

RESIDE, W.J.
RAESIDE, JUKS--[8]

RESNICH, SYLVIA [S]
PAUL, SHERI--[1]

RESNICK, LAURA
LEONE, LAURA--[9][21][26]ROM--
"ULTERIOR MOTIVES"
"BANDIT KING" & 8 MORE

RESNICK, MICHAEL DIAMOND
RESNICK, MIKE--[7][23][33]AMERICAN/SF PLUS

RESNICK, SYLVIA [SAFRAN]
PAUL, SHERI--[1]

RESSICH, JOHN S.M.
BAXTER, GREGORY--W/ERIC DE BANZIE, [2][3][22]MYS--
CASSELL "BLUE LIGHTNING" '26
& 6 MORE '26-34

RESSLER, ALICE
WAYNE, ALICE--[1]

RESSLER, LILLIAN
JANET, LILLIAN--W/JANET O'DANIEL,[1]

RESTIF, NICHOLAS-ANNE-ED
DE LA BRETONNE, RESTIF--[2]

RETCHKIN, NORMAN
ST. CLAIR, MIKE--[3]MYS--
BB "DADDY'S GONE A' HUNTING" '69

RETCLIFF, JOHN
FELIX, CHARLES--[3]MYS--
SAUNDERS "NOTTING HILL MYSTERY" 1865
TINSLEY "RAM SASS" 1875 & MORE

RETTKE, MARIAN POPE
DEVON, ANNE--[9][21][26]ROM--
"WIDOW OF BATH"
"ROGUE'S LADY"
"DEFIANT MISTRESS"
DEVON, MARIAN--V. BERCH LTR TO HUBIN '94, [21][26]MYS/ROM--
CREST "MISS OSBORN MISBEHAVES" '90 &M

REUBEL-CIANI, THEO
COLLINS, INSPEKTOR--[39][40]GERMAN/MYS--
"INSPEKTOR COLLINS: DIE DRITTE SPUR" '60
ROVALI, CARLO--[39]GERMAN/MYS/JUV

REUTER, EALPH
MILLS, EDDIE--[39]GERMAN/MYS/SF/WEST

REUTER, JOSEF
BARRAN, RALPH--[39]GERMAN/MYS/SF/WEST

REUTER, RALPH
BARRAN, ROLF--[39]GERMAN/MYS/SF/WEST
CARTER, JIM--[39]GERMAN/MYS/SF/WEST,HP--
CHESTER, TOM--[39]GERMAN/MYS/SF/WEST,HP--
ELLERHORST, PETRA--[39]GERMAN/MYS/SF/WEST
GREV, WILLIAM--[39]GERMAN/MYS/SF/WEST
LORETTA, JOSCHI--[39]GERMAN/MYS/SF/WEST
MACMADISON--[39]GERMAN/MYS/SF/WEST
PARRY, ROCK--[39]GERMAN/WEST
RENAULD, PIERRE--[39]GERMAN/MYS/SF/WEST
RUITER, JAN--[39]GERMAN/MYS/SF/WEST
VARANI, MARIO--[39]GERMAN/MYS/SF/WEST

REXHAUS, GUNTHER
HAYES, REX--[39]GERMAN/WEST
REGAN, REX--[39]GERMAN/WEST

REY, PIERRE
MASTERS, DOUG--V. BERCH LTR TO HUBIN '94, MYS--
CHART "THE BEAST" '85
"DEVIL'S CLAW" '85 & MORE

REYBURN, WALLACE [M]
SCOTT, WILLIAM--[1]

REYERSBACH, HANS AUGUSTO
REY, HANS AUGUSTO--[1]
UNCLE GUS--[1][8][22][33]

REYHER, REBECCA HOURWICH
REYHER, BECKY--[33]

REYLE, WILHELM
VAN REY, E.W.--[39]GERMAN

REYMERS, ELISABET
BJORKHEM, ANN--[29]MYS

REYMONT, WLADYSLAW S.
REYMONT, LADISLAS--[1]

REYNA, RUTH
ABBOTT, EVELYN--[1]
ABBOTT, ORRINA--[1]
ANA, RAY--[1]

REYNARD, CAROL
HENKE, SHIRL--W/SHIRL HENKE,[9][21]ROM--
"GOLDEN LADY"
"MOON FLOWER" & 4 MORE

REYNOLDS, DALLAS MCCORD
BELMONT, BOB--[2]GHOSTED
COLLINS, CLARK--[1][2][11][23][31]SF
HARDING, TODD--[2][11][23]--1 NON-SF
MALLORY, MARK--[2][11][23][31]SF/MYS--
TF "MAN WHO STOLE HIS BODY" AUG '57
MH "GIRL FRIEND" SEPT '57
TR "POISON WITH THE DOLLS" OCT '57
MCCORD, GUY--[1][2][11][23]SF
REYNOLDS, MACK--[3][4][7][11][32]MYS/SF--
NOVELS
KI "MIXED DRINK MURDER" JAN '57
TF "DEAD END" AUG '57
MSMM "TALE FROM TANGIER" MAR '61
MSMM "LITTLE BARBED BANDERILLAS" NOV '61
REYNOLDS, MAXINE--[2][3][4][23]SF--
BEAGLE "HOME OF THE INQUISITOR" '72
"HOUSE IN THE KASBAH" '72
ROSS, DALLAS--[1][2][11][23]SF

REYNOLDS, GERTRUDE M.R.
REYNOLDS, BAILLIE--[7]SF--
"THE RELATIONS & WHAT THEY RELATED:
A SERIES OF WIERD STORIES" ''02
REYNOLDS, MRS. BAILLIE--[34]MYS
ROBINS, G.M.--[1]

REYNOLDS, HELEN MARY G.C.
DICKSON, HELEN--[1][22][31][33]CANADIAN
REYNOLDS, DICKSON--[1][22][33]CANADIAN

REYNOLDS, JOHN EDMUND
EDMUNDS, BRENT--[34]MYS--
LAURIE "A GUN IN MY BACK" '55
LAURIE "RIDE A DEAD HORSE" '55
LAURIE "SPIDERS IN THE NIGHT" '56
LAURIE "BEWARE THE CRIMSON CORD" '56
DEXTER, ROSS--[8]

REYNOLDS, KATHLEEN N.
REYNOLDS, KAY--[7]SF--
'ROBOTECH ART' 1 & 2 '86-7 -
'1' WAS WITH ARDITH CARLTON

REYNOLDS, THEODORE A
REYNOLDS, TED--[7][23][32]IASFM/SF--
MSMM "IDENTIFICATION IN RED" JUN '57
"BOARDER INCIDENT" '77
"TIDES OF GOD" '89

REYNOLDS, WALTER DOTY
LORD PRIME--[1][2]

RHEIN, EDUARD
HELLBORN, KLAUS--[39]GERMAN/JUV
HELLMER, KLAUS--[39]GERMAN/JUV
HORSTER, HANS-ULRICH--[39][40]GERMAN/MYS--
"BRIEFE AUF DEM JERSETTS" '86
HULSEN, ADRIAN--[39]GERMAN/JUV

RHOADES, CORNELIA HARSEN
RHOADES, NINA--[1]

RHOADES, JUDITH GRUBMAN
DILLING, JUDITH--[31]

RHODES, EUGENE MANLOVE
HIRED MAN ON HORSEBACK--[1]
NOVELIST OF CATTLE KINGDOM--[1]

RHODES, EVAN
LANE, ALLISON--V. BERCH LTR TO HUBIN '94,
MYS--
JOVE "REVELATIONS" '81

RHODES, WILLIAM H[ENRY]
CAXTON--[11][23]SF--
"THE CASE OF SUMMERFIELD" 1907

RHONDDA, MARGARET HAIG
MACKWORTH--[1]

RHYNNE, JULIA A.
HAMILTON, LUCY--[9][21][26]ROM--
"EMMA'S WAR"
"TAKING SIDES" & 10 MORE

RICCI, LEWIS ANSELM DA C.
BARTIMEUS--[8]

RICE, ALICE C. HEGAN
HEGAN, ALICE CALDWELL--[33]

RICE, ANNE
RAMPLING, ANNE--PLAYBOY INTERVIEW FEB '93,[2]--
"EXIT TO EDEN"
"BELINDA"
ROQUELAIRE, A.N.--PLAYBOY INTRVW FEB '93,
[2][7]--
DUTTON "CLAIMING OF SLEEPING BEAUTY" '83
DUTTON "BEAUTY'S PUNNISHMENT" '84
DUTTON "BEAUTY'S RELEASE" '85

RICE, BRIAN K.
VIGILANS--[1]

RICE, DESMOND CHARLES
MEIRING, DESMOND--[1][22][34]SOUTH AFRICAN-
VENZUELAN/MYS--
HODDER "BRINKMAN" '64
CNST "PRESIDENT PLAN" '74
SECKER "WILCATTER" '87
"A TALK WITH THE ANGELS" '85

RICE, DOROTHY MARY
BORNE, DOROTHY--[1][22][31]IRISH-ENGLISH
VICARY, DOROTHY--[1][22]IRISH-ENGLISH

RICE, HOWARD ALLAN FRANCES O'BRIEN
RICE, ANNE--[7]PLAYBOY INTERVIEW FEB 93--
NAME CHGD IN '47

RICE, JANE
AUSTIN, MARY--[1][2][11]
RICE, ALLISON--W/RUTH ALLISON,[1][2]

RICE, JOAN
HALLAM, JAY--[8]

RICE, LINDA
BRANDON, ALICIA--W/STELLA CAMERON,
[9][21][26][34]ROM--
HARL "LOVE BEYOND QUESTION"
"FULL CIRCLE"

RICE, LINDA & WALTER
WALTERS, LINDA--[9][21][26][34]MYS/ROM--
HARL "DRAGON'S EYE" '87
HARL "DEAD RECKONING" '88

RICE, PATRICIA
RICE, PAT--[26]ROM--
NUMEROUS NOVELS

RICH, EDITH J.R.
ISAACS, EDITH J.R.--[1]

RICH, H. THOMSON
LEIGH, DR. HENRY--[2]

RICH, MARY LOU
GRAY, SUZANNA--[26]ROM--
"MOUNTAIN MAGIC"

RICHARD, FRANCOIS
RICHARD-BESSIERE, F.--W/RICHARD BESSIERE,
[1][2][11]

RICHARD, SUSAN
ELLIS, JULIE--[26]ROM--
"COMMITMENT"
"LASTING TREASURES"
"THE ONLY SIN"

RICHARDS, ALLEN
ROSENTHAL, RICHARD A.--[8]

RICHARDS, DALE
WELLS, BARRY--[7]SF--
FSQ "DAY THE EARTH CAUGHT FIRE" '61

RICHARDS, DICK
WELLS, BARRY--[1][2]

RICHARDS, FRANK
CLIFFORD, MARTIN--[2]HP--
'GEM' MAGAZINE-CREATED PSEUD.

RICHARDS, JAMES
CLADPOLE, JIM--[8]

RICHARDS, JAMES MAUDE
RICHARDS, J.M.--[31]

RICHARDS, JONATHAN
LEWIS, CANELLA--[3][7][21][26]ROM--
BERK "SENSITIVE ENCOUNTER"
BERK "MUSIC OF AQUARIUS" BOTH '77

RICHARDS, KELVIN BARRY
RICHARDS, KEL--[36]AUSTRALIAN/MYS--
HODDER "CASE OF DISAPPEARING CORPSE" '90
HODDER "CASE OF THE SECRET ASSASSIN" '92
HODDER "SECOND DEATH" '93

RICHARDS, LAWRENCE O.
RICHARDS, LARRY--[31]RELIGIOUS

RICHARDS, PENNY
CHARLES, CHRISTY--[9]ROM
MATTHEWS, BAY--[9][21][26]ROM--
"ROSES & REGRETS"
"AMARILLO BY MORNING" & 9 MORE

RICHARDS, RONALD CHARLES
SADDLER, ALLEN--[1][33]
SADLER, K. ALLEN--[1][3]MYS--
"GILT EDGE" '66
"GREAT BRAIN ROBBERY" '66
"TALKING TURKEY" '68

RICHARDS, ROSS
MEAD, MATT--[1][29][34]MYS,HP--
HALE "DEATH SEEKERS" '64
MYFLR "MURDER ON THE MONTE" '66
MYFLR "STARCROSSED" '67
REID, DESMOND--[1][29][34]MYS,HP--
MYFLWR "DEATH ON THE SPIKE" '66
"DEAD RESPECTABLE" '67
MYFLWR "THE SLAVE BRAIN" '67
SAXON, PETER--R.E. BRINEY-BAE 17, MYS,HP--
LAN "THROUGH THE DARK CURTAIN" '68
WELLSLEY, JULIE--[34]MYS,HP--
LAN "WINE OF VENGEANCE" '69

RICHARDS, SARA LIPPINCOTT
LIPPINCOTT, SARA--[1]
STEIN, J.J.--[1]

RICHARDS, TAD
CURTIS, RICHARD HALE--[21]ROM,HP--
'SKYMASTER' SERIES:
"TO SOAR WITH EAGLES"
WILLOUGHBY, LEE DAVIS--[21]ROM,HP--
DELL 'MAKING OF AMERICA' SERIES:
"CANADIENS"
'WOMEN WHO WON THE WEST' SERIES:
"TEMPEST OF TOMBSTONE"

RICHARDS, TAD & JONATHAN
MCGILL, NANCY--V. BERCH LTR TO HUBIN '94,MYS--
ACE "CAVE OF THE MOON" '79

RICHARDS-AKERS, NANCY
KIRK, MARY ALICE--W/MARY KILCHENSTEIN,
[9][21]ROM--
"IN YOUR WILDEST DREAMS"
"PROMISES"

RICHARDSON, ALAINA W.
HAWTHORNE, ALAINA--[9][21][26]ROM--
"OUT OF THE BLUE"

RICHARDSON, ANTHONY T.S.C
CURRIE, THOMAS STEWART--[1]
WYNNTON, PATRICK--[34]MYS--
HODDER "BLACK TURRET" '25
HODDER "LOST MARK" '29 & 6 MORE '25-33

RICHARDSON, DARRELL C.
RICH, D. COLEMAN--[1][2][11]

RICHARDSON, EILEEN
SHANE--[8]

RICHARDSON, ETHEL FLOREN.
RICHARDSON, HENRIETTA--[1]
RICHARDSON, HENRY HANDEL--[1]

RICHARDSON, GLADWELL G.
BLACKSNAKE, GEORGE--ECHOES#19,[28]--
6 MULLER NOVELS '50-57
"STRANGE TALES FROM BLACKWOOD" '50
CLARKSON, ORMAND--A. TONIK-ECHOES #19,
[28][31]WEST--
10 WARD LOCK NOVELS '36-41
COLE, BUCK--A. TONIK-ECHOES #19,[28]WEST--
LANE "BIG TRACKS" '56
COLEMAN, BUCK--[31]
COLSON, LARAMIE--A. TONIK-ECHOES #19,
[28][31]WEST--3 R&C NOVELS '56-7
& 1 LONG BK '58
HAINES, JOHN--ECHOES#19,[28]--
W&B "THIN GUNMAN" '41
W&B "SIX-SHOOTER SHERIFF" '42
HAINES, JOHN S.--A. TONIK-ECHOES #19,WEST--
JAMES, CARY--A. TONIK-ECHOES #19,[28]WEST--
JENKINS "GUNSLICK RAMROD" '55
JENKINS ".45 KID" '55
JONES, CALICO--A. TONIK-ECHOES #19,
[28]WEST--11 NOVELS '51-9
KENT, PETE--A. TONIK-ECHOES #19,[28]WEST--
5 NOVELS '37-56
KILDARE, MAURICE--A. TONIK-ECHOES #19,
[28][31]WEST--9 NOVELS '38-59
KILDARESON, MAURICE--A. TONIK-ECHOES #19, P11
MAXWELL, GRANT--ECHOES #19,[28]WEST--
"ACTION AT TIMBERLANE" '56
"TEXAS TROUBLE" '57
MCADAMS, CHARLES--A. TONIK-ECHOES #19,
[28]WEST--
BARKER "RATTLE YOUR SPURS" '55
O'RILEY, WARREN--A. TONIK-ECHOES #19,
[28]WEST--5 NOVELS '51-8
PARKER, FRANK--A. TONIK-ECHOES #19, P11
SHARPE, FRANKLIN--A. TONIK-ECHOES #19, P11
SINCLAIR, BOWER--L. ROBBINS LTR MAR '94
TETON, DON--A. TONIK-ECHOES #19, P11
WARNER, FRANK--A. TONIK-ECHOES #19,
[28]WEST--12 NOVELS '42-59
WINSLOWE, JOHN--[28]WEST--
7 WARD LOCK NOVELS '39-53
WINSLOWE, JOHN R.--A. TONIK-ECHOES #19,
[8][28]WEST--10 NOVELS '36-56

RICHARDSON, HENRIETTA
RICHARDSON, HENRY HANDEL--[22]AUSTRALIAN

RICHARDSON, JAMES NATHANL
RICHARDS, NAT--[3]MYS--
ASHLEY "OTIS DUNN: MANHUNTER" '74

RICHARDSON, JOHN
JOHNSON, RICHARD--[31]

RICHARDSON, MARY KATHLEEN
NORTON, S.H.--[8]

RICHARDSON, MAURICE
LANE, RICHARD--M. LACHMAN-PER EQMM NOV'53-
SHORT STORIES

RICHARDSON, MIDGE TURK
TURK, MIDGE--[1]

RICHARDSON, ROBERT S.
LATHAM, PHILIP [PHILLIP]--[2][11][23][29]SF--
WINSTON "MISSING MEN ON SATURN" '53

RICHARTZ, HELMUTH
BRETT, TODDY--[39]GERMAN/WEST,HP--
HARPER, TOM--[39]GERMAN/WEST
MCRITCHIE, HAL--[39]GERMAN/WEST

RICHELSON, GERALDINE
LEANDER, ED--[1][31][33]

RICHESON, CENA GOLDER
RICHARDS, CYNDI--[21]ROM--
"LOVE IS WHERE YOU FIND IT"

RICHEY, DAVID
DAVEY, JOHN--[1][31]
JOHNSON, RICHARD--[1][31]

RICHLEY, MARGARET
RICH, HARRIET--[21][26]ROM--
"BRIDE OF BELVALE"

RICHMAN, AL
MORTON, JOSEPH--[1]
RICHMOND, AL--[1]

RICHMOND, CINDY PACKARD
PACKARD, CINDY--[1]

RICHMOND, E. JOHNSON
JOHNSON, EFFIE--[1]
RICHMOND, E.J.--[1]

RICHMOND, ROALDUS F.
COLE, JACKSON--A. TONIK-COLE CKLST "SPICY ARMADILLO",WEST,HP--
'TEX RGR'- 22 STORIES '52-'57
RICHMOND, ROE--[1][32][34]MYS--
AA "SCIENTIFIC APPROACH" NOV '53
PU "RELUCTANT HUNTER" MAY '56
MSMM "ASSIGNMENT AT LAS VEGAS" OCT '57
TR "WEB OF EVIL" AUG '62
LEIS "KELLEWAY'S LUCK" '81

RICHTER, ALFRED
RICHTER, ANDREAS IGEL--[39]GERMAN

RICHTER, ELISABETH
GAST, LISE--[39]GERMAN/JUV

RICHTER, ERNST H.
BROWN, WILLIAM--[1][2][11][39]GERMAN/SF
TERRIDGE, ERNEST--[1][2][11][39]GERMAN/SF

RICHTER, EUGEN
RICHTER, EUGENE--[1]

RICHTER, FERNANDE
FERN, EDNA--[22]GERMAN-AMERICAN

RICHTER, FRITZ WALDEMAR
FEXTER, DONALD O.--[29]MYS--7 NOVELS '17-19

RICHTER, HANS
LAHR, MAXIMILIAN--[39]GERMAN/SF/JUV

RICHTER, HANS PETER
JUGE, J.P.--[39]GERMAN/JUV

RICHTER, JOHANN PAUL F.
PAUL, JEAN--[39]GERMAN/SF

RICHTER, JOSEFINE
LEDNER, ERNST--[39]GERMAN

RICHTER, ROSEMARIE
SPRUNG, RENATE--[39]GERMAN

RICHTER, WOLFGANG
WOLF, ROMAN--[39]GERMAN/SF

RICHTER-FRICH, OVRE
FREEMAN, RITA--[29]MYS
NORMAN, REIDAR--[29]MYS
SERVANS--[29]MYS--
ERICHSENS "HANDELSSPION SERVANS" '17

RICHTER-TERSIK, OSWALD
STONE, KASSI--[39]GERMAN/SF

RICKARD, MRS. VICTOR
RICKARD, JESSIE LOUISA--[3]MYS--
CAPE "BLINDFOLD" '22
HODDER "EMPTY VILLA" '29 & 26 MORE '11-50

RICKE, EDELTRAUT
HERKEN, CLARA--[39]GERMAN/JUV

RICKETT, FRANCIS
KERRIGAN, KATE LOWE--[1][31]
WINSLOW, MARTHA--[1]

RICKS, PATRICIA W.B.
WYNN, PATRICIA--[9][21][26]ROM--
"SOPHIE'S HALLOO"
"LORD TOM" & 2 MORE

RICKWORD, [JOHN] EDGELL
MAVIN, JOHN--W/DOUGLAS M. GARMAN,[1][31]--
WISHART "CHARLES BAUDELAIRE: A BIO" '28

RICO, DON
FONTAINE, PAULA--V. BERCH-BRNDN/BC PSEUDS, BAE 22, ADULT--
ST. MICHAELS, DONELLE--[3]MYS--
LAN 72-110 "THE PRISONER" '66

RIDDELL, CHARLOTTE ELIZABETH
HAWTHORNE, RAINEY--[2][11][16]IRISH
RIDDELL, MRS. J.H.--[1][7]SF
TRAFFORD, F.G.--[2][11][16][22]IRISH

RIDDLE, BETSY
VON HUTTEN, BETTINA--[1][17]ROM

RIDDLESTON, CHARLES H.
DRONGO, LUKE--[8]

RIDDOLLS, BRENDA HARK
ENGLISH, BRENDA H.--[1]

RIDEAU, CHARLES DE BALZAC
CHANCELLOR, JOHN--[1][22][34]MYS--
HUTCH "STOLEN GOLD" '32
HUTCH "DARK GOD "27 & 13 MORE '11-69

RIDELL, WILLIAM RENWICK
WILLIAMS, RENDALL--[1]

RIDGE, WILLIAM PETT
SIMPSON, WARWICK--[8][34]MYS--
LEADENHALL "EIGHTEEN OF THEM-SINGULAR STORIES" 1894

RIDGWAY, JAMES M.
RIDGWAY, JIM--[7]SF--
NON-FICT

RIDLEY, JAMES
MORELL, CHARLES--[2]

RIDLON, MARCI
CARAFOLI, MARCI--[33]
MGGILL, MARCI--[33]

RIECK, ERIKA
ELTEN, EVA--[39]GERMAN
MARTEN, MARION--[39]GERMAN

RIEDEL, CURT
RECKE, CONRAD--[39]GERMAN

RIEDMAN, SARAH R.
GUSTAFSON, SARAH R.--[31][33]--
CHILDREN'S BOOKS

RIEFE, ALAN
HARDIN, J.D.--[1][31]WEST,HP--
LOGAN, JAKE--[1]WEST,HP--
PLAYBOY
RIEFE, A.R.--[9][21][26]ROM--
'FORTUNE WEST' SERIES: - 4 NOVELS
RIEFE, BARBARA--[3][7][21][26]MYS--
PLBY "THIS RAVAGED HEART" '77 & 16 MORE

RIEGEL, WILHELM MICHAEL
MORIN, MICHEL--[39][40]GERMAN/MYS--
"KOLLEGE MORDER" '60
"DIE RUFMORD-GMBH" '60

RIELAU, URSULA
STEINBERG, JILL--[39]GERMAN

RIEMER, GEORGE
POOLE, SETH--[1]
SCHIRMERHORN, CLINT--[1]

RIENSTRA, ELLEN
BEAUMONT, MARIE--W/JUDITH LINSLEY,[21]ROM--
"CATHERINE'S SONG"
LYNLEY, ELINOR--W/JUDITH LINSLEY,[21]ROM--
"SONG OF THE BAYOU"

RIESCHEL, PAUL
BREIT, FRANK--[39]GERMAN/WEST

RIFKIN, SHEPARD
LOGAN, JAKE--[1][28]WEST,HP--
PLBY "ACROSS THE RIO GRAND" '75
PLBY "SLOCUM'S WOMAN" '76
PLBY "SLOCUM'S RAGE" '79
MICHAELS, DALE--[1][22][28]AMERICAN--
"THE WARRING BREED" '73

RIGDON, CHARLES
SCOTT, ANTONIA--[3]MYS--
"FALCON'S ISLAND" '73

RIGG, HENRY H. KILBURN
KILBURN, HENRY--[31]
RIGG, H.K.--[31]

RIGG, JENNIFER
SCOTT, GENEVIEVE--[3]MYS--
GOLLANCZ "THE WATER HORSE" '74

RIGHETTI, CARLO
ARRIGHI, CLETTO--[22]ITALIAN

RIGNEY, JAMES OLIVER JR.
JORDAN, ROBERT--B. FRANK,[7][31]SF--
'CONAN' SERIES
TOR 'WHEEL OF TIME' SERIES: #1-6
LUNG, CHANG--[31]
O'NEAL, REAGAN--CRPG,[9][21][26]ROM--
'FALLON CHRONICLES'-3 NOVELS '80-1
O'REILLEY, JACKSON--[21][26]ROM--
'AMERICAN INDIAN' SERIES:
"CHEYENNE RAIDERS"

RIGONI, ORLANDO JOSEPH
AMES, LESLIE--W/WILLIAM E.D. ROSS,[29]MYS--
HALE "SINISTER LOVE" '84
AMES, LESLIE--[3][21][29][31]MYS/ROM--
LENOX "ANGRY WIND" '70
ARCADIA "HILL OF ASHES" & MORE
BELL, CAROLYN--[1]
WESLEY, JAMES--[1]

RIGSBY, HOWARD [VECHEL]
HOWARD, MARK--[1][22][31]AMERICAN--
DELL "A TIME FOR PASSION" '60
HOWARD, VECHEL--V. BERCH-GM PSEUDS, PP 33,
[34]WEST/MYS--
GM 685 "SUNDOWN AT CRAZY HORSE" '57
GM 789 "TALL IN THE WEST" '58
GM 854 "MURDER WITH LOVE" '59
GM 878 "MURDER ON HER MIND" '59
GM 943 "STAGE TO PAINTED CREEK" '59
GM 1121 "THE LAST SUNSET" '61

RIKER, LEIGH
BARTLEY, LEIGH--[1][31]

RIKHOFF, JAMES C.
CORNWALL, JIM--[22][31]AMERICAN
FARGO, JOE--[22][31]AMERICAN
KINCAID, ALAN--[22][31]AMERICAN

RILEY, EUGENIA
FABIO--W/FABIO LANZONI, TTLPG--
AV 77046 "PIRATE" '93
AV 77047 "ROGUE" '94
AV 77048 "VIKING" '94

RILEY, JAMES WHITCOMB
JOHNSON, BENJAMIN F. OF BOO--[31]
JOHNSON, BENJAMIN F.--[8][33]

RILEY, JUDITH [A] MERKLE
MERKLE, JUDITH A.--[31]

RILEY, L.W.
HUNT, ROGER--[35]AUSTRALIAN/WAR,HP--
HRWTZ "REBEL COLONEL" '58

RILEY, RICHARD ANTHONY
RILEY, DICK--[7]SF--
NON-FICT

RILEY, STELLA
BLYTHE, JULIET--[9][21][29]ROM/MYS--
"LUCIFER'S CHAMPION"
"THE PARFAIT KNIGHT"

RILEY, WILLIE
LEIGH, W. RYE--[1]

RIMBAULT, EDWARD FRANCIS
NAVA, FRANZ--[1]

RIMEL, DUANE [W]
BIGGS, PETER--[1][31]
LEGGETT, ERIC--[1][31]
LEMIR, ANDRE--[1][31]
WELDEN, REX [D]--NOBLE LIB
PLAYTIME BOOKS
PEC "TIME SWAP" '69
WELDON, REX--V. BERCH-BRNDN/BC PSEUDOS,
BAE 22,[2][11]ADULT--
NOV 60115 "PECULIARLY PASSIONATE PAIR" '63
BRNDN 945 "LOVE ME WILD" '65
PEC 1148 "ROUND ROBIN" '68

RING, ELIZABETH
SCOTT, MERISSA--[1]

RING, LOTHAR
MARSCHALL, RUDOLF--[39]GERMAN
SCHAFFER, E.--[39]GERMAN

RINGGOLD, GENE
LAWRENCE, KENNETH G.--[1][31]
MATTEO, P.B. JR.--[1]

RINGGOLD, JACOB
RODISSI--[34]MYS--
ANTON "LORD JACQUELIN BIRKNEY, THE WHITECHAPEL TERROR" 1889

RINGI, KJELL ARNE S.
S-RINGI, KJELL--[1][33]

RINJIRO, TAKAYAMA
CHOGYU, TAKAYAMA--[22]JAPANESE

RINKOFF, BARBARA
RICH, JEAN--[1]

RINTARO, MORI
OGAI, MORI--[22]JAPANESE

RINTELEN, FRITZ MARTIN
VLOTHO, FRIEDRICH--[39]GERMAN

RINZLER, CAROL EISEN
EISEN, CAROL G.--[1][31]

RIPS, ERVIN M.
FARNUM, K.T.--[1][31]
LORNQUEST, OLAF--[1][7]SF--
PINN "MOONLOVERS" '75

RIQUELME, DANIEL
CONCHALI, INOCENCIO--[20]SPANISH

RISENHOOVER, CARMEL C.
RISENHOOVER, C.C.--B. CRIDER-DDLY PLEAS #3--
McLENNAN "BLOOD BATH" '87
McLENNAN "CHILD STALKER" '87 & MORE

RISO, ALF
ISLAND, RICE--[29]MYS

RISTER, CLAUDE
BILLINGS, BUCK--L. ROBBINS LTR '94,[8]
HOLT, TEX--L. ROBBINS LTR '94,[8]
MARSHALL, JAMES--L. ROBBINS LTR MAR '94

RITCHIE, BALFOUR
BALDWIN, BASIL--[1]

RITCHIE, BARBARA
ARDEN, BARBIE--W/ADRIEN P. STOUTENBURG,[1]

RITCHIE, CLARE
HEATH, SHARON--[1][8]

RITCHIE, L. EDWIN
LEWIS, VOLTAIRE--[8]

RITCHIE, LEWIS
BARTIMEUS--[22]ENGLISH

RITCHIE, RUTH
JULINE, RUTH BISHOP--[1][31]

RITCHIE, [HARRY] WARD
QUINCE, PETER LUM--[1]

RITCHIE-CALDER, PETER R.
CALDER, RITCHIE--[31]

RITHCHILD, DOROTHY
PARKER, DOROTHY--[1]

RITHWEILER, DOROTHY
SCOFIELD, JONATHAN--[1]

RITSOS, YANNIS
RITSOS, GIANNES--[31]GREEK

RITTER, MADGE REINHARDT
REINHARDT, MADGE--V. BERCH LTR TO HUBIN '94, MYS--
BACK ROW "THE UNCLEAN BIRD" '86

RITTER, VERA
BLACHSTADT, CV.--[39]GERMAN/JUV
SCHULTZ, CACILE--[39]GERMAN/JUV

RITTER, WOLFPETER
CATLIN, JOHN--[39]GERMAN/WEST
COTTON, JERRY--[39]GERMAN/MYS,HP--
LYKOFF, PIERRE--[39]GERMAN/MYS/SF/WEST
TERRID, PETER--[39]GERMAN/MYS/SF/WEST
WYNES, PATRICIA--[39]GERMAN/MYS/SF/WEST
WYNES, PATRICK--[39]GERMAN/MYS/SF/WEST

RITTMANN, CHARLOTTE
BERG, CHARLOTTE--[39]GERMAN

RITTNER, TADEUSZ
CZASKA, TOMASZ--[22]POLISH

RITZ, DAVID
LANSING, JESSICA--[9][21][26]ROM--
"IN THE NAME OF LOVE"
PEARL, ESTER E[LIZ]--[9][21][31]ROM--
"DEEPER THAN SHAME"
"JERUSALEM THE PASSIONATE" '80

RIVETT, EDITH CAROLINE
CARNAC, CAROL--[3][5][18][29]MYS--
MacD "CLUE SINISTER" '47 & 22 MORE '36-67
LORAC, E.C.R.--[2][3][5][18][29][32]MYS--
NOVELS '32-59
MK "DEATH AT THE BRIDGE TABLE" OCT '52
MK "REMEMBER TO RING TWICE" SEPT '52
MK "CHANCE IS A GREAT THING" JAN '53
MK "PERMANENT POLICEMAN" APR '53
SA "A BIT OF WIRE-PULLING" OCT '55
RIVETT, CAROL--[18]MYS--
"OUTER CIRCLE"
"TIME REMEMBERED"

RIVOLI, MARIO
KOUTOUKAS, H.M.--[33]
MARASMUS, SEYMOUR--[33]

ROA BASTOS, AUGUSTO [A]
BASTOS, AUGUSTO [A] ROA--[31]

ROACH, ROBERT
JORGENSSON, A.K.--[1][2]

ROAN, TOM
REBEL, ADAM--[1][28]ADULT--
BEAC B107 "STABLE BOY" '54

ROARK, GARLAND
GARLAND, GEORGE--[28][31]WEST--
"DOUBTFUL VALLEY" '51
"BIG DRY" '53 & MORE '51-73

ROBARCHEK, PEG
BRETT, KATHERYN--[9][21]ROM--
"THE GENUINE ARTICLE"
SUTHERLAND, PEG--[21][26]ROM--
"THE GENUINE ARTICLE"

ROBB, INEZ [C]
RANDOLPH, NANCY--[1]

ROBBIN, [J] LUNA
PALLIDINI, JODI--[1]

ROBBINS, CLARENCE AARON
ROBBINS, C.A.--[1]
ROBBINS, TOD--[2][3][22]MYS--
OGILVIE "MYSTERIOUS MARTIN" '12
LANE "UNHOLY THREE" '17 MORE

ROBBINS, DAVID LAWRENCE
CAMERON, J.D.--V BERCH LTR '94,[7][23]SF,HP--
AV 76206 "COMMAND DECISION" '91
AV 76321 "BLOOD TIDE"
AV 76492 "DEATH DIVE"
AV 76493 "RAVEN RISING" ALL '91
THOMPSON, DAVID--CRPG--
LEIS 'WILDERNESS' SERIES:
"#13 MOUNTAIN MANHUNT" '93

ROBBINS, JANE [BORSCH]
CARTER, JANE ROBBINS--[31]

ROBBINS, JUNE
JULIE--[31]
JULIE OF COLORADA SPRINGS--[8][31]

ROBBINS, ROB
GREGORY, DANE--B. PRONZINI INTRO-DF 156--
DE 101 "DEAD MEN LAUGH LAST" '48
DE 110 "TELL HER THAT YOU SAW ME" '48
DF 156 "HEAR THAT MOURNFUL SOUND" MAY '51
DT "DEATH WINDS THE CLOCK" JAN '62

ROBBINS, THOMAS EUGENE
ROBBINS, TOM--[7]SF--
BB "JITTERBUG PERFUME" '84
BB "SKINNY LEGS AND ALL" '90

ROBBINS-CARTER, JANE [B]
ROBBINS, JANE--[1]

ROBBINS-MOWRY, DOROTHY B.
ROBBINS, DOROTHY B.--[1]

ROBERSON, JENNIFER
MITCHELL, JAY--[1][33]

ROBERSON, JENNIFER
O'GREEN, JENNIFER--[1][21][26][33]ROM--
"ROYAL CAPTIVE"
O'GREEN, JENNIFER ROBERS.--[33]

ROBERT, DEREK
WEIL, BARRY--[34]MYS--
BOBBS "DOSSIER IX" '69

ROBERT, ELLI
BENSEN, BETTINA--[39]GERMAN

ROBERT, MARIELIS
HOBERG, MARIELIS--[39]GERMAN/JUV
ROBERT, MATI--[39]GERMAN/JUV

ROBERTS, ANN LEWIS
CLWYD, ANN--[8]

ROBERTS, ARTHUR GUY
CLIFFORD, GUY--[1][3]MYS--
METHUEN "MICHAEL INTERVENES" '27

ROBERTS, ARTHUR O.
CAMERON, BERL--W/JOHN S. GLASBY,
[1][11]HP--WARREN
LE PAGE, RAND--W/JOHN S. GLASBY,
[1][11]HP--WARREN
LORRAINE, PAUL--W/JOHN S. GLASBY,
[1][11]HP--WARREN
MEGO, AL--[1]

ROBERTS, CARL ERIC [B]
BECHHOFER, C.E.--[1]
EPHESIAN--[22][34]MYS--
"ABC'S TEST CASE" '36
"ABC SOLVES FIVE" '37
"ABC INVESTIGATES" '37

ROBERTS, CECIL EDRIC M.
BERESFORD, RUSSELL--[1]
MORNINGTON, EDOR--[1]

ROBERTS, DAVID
CAPELLI, ACE--PP 29, P42,HP--

ROBERTS, DOREEN
KENT, ROBERTA--[34]MYS--
DIMENOVEL "HOT PURSUIT" '90
KINGSBURY, KATE--MELINDA HELFER/LACHMAN '93,
MYS--
"ROOM WITHOUT A CLUE" '93

ROBERTS, DOROTHY JAMES
MORTIMER, PETER--[3][22]AMERICAN/MYS--
MYH "IF A BODY KILL A BODY" '46

ROBERTS, E.N.
NEWMAN, ERNEST--[8]

ROBERTS, EDNA
FINLAY, MICHAEL--[1]
HILTON, JOSEPH--[1]
OWEN, RICHARD--[1]

ROBERTS, EDWARD DRYHURST
DRYHURST, EDWARD--[31]

ROBERTS, ELIZABETH K.
ROBERTS, EDITH--[1]

ROBERTS, ERIC
ROBIN--[22]ENGLISH

ROBERTS, GEORGE EDWARD T.
GOODRIDGE ROBERTS, THEODR--[1]

ROBERTS, IRENE W.
CARR, ROBERTA--[1][9][22][31]ENGLISH/ROM--
HARLE, ELIZABETH--[1][9][22]ENGLISH/ROM
ROBERTS, I.M.--[8]ENGLISH
ROBERTS, IVOR--[1][9][22]ENGLISH/ROM
ROWLAND, IRIS--[1][9][22]ENGLISH/ROM
SHAW, IRENE--[3][9]ENGLISH/MYS--
WRIGHT "MURDERER'S MANSION" '68

ROBERTS, JAMES
HORTON, ROBERT J.--[8]

ROBERTS, JANE
BUTTS, JANE ROBERTS--[1]

ROBERTS, JANET LOUISE
BRONTE, LOUISA [LUISA]--[2][3][7][9][21][26][29]ROM/MYS--14 NOVELS '70s
DANTON, REBECCA--[3][9][21][26][29]ROM/MYS--7 NOVELS '70s
KAYE, PAMELA--V. BERCH-BRNDN/BC PSEUDS BAE 22, ADULT--
RADCLIFFE, JANETTE--[3][21][26][29]ROM/MYS--DELL "BLUE-EYED GYPSY" '74
"GENTLEMAN PIRATE" '75 & MORE

ROBERTS, JOE
HILD, JACK--[34]MYS,HP--GE 'SOB's': "BARRABUS EDGE" '88
"BARRABUS HIT" '89

ROBERTS, JOHN GAITHER
PAUL, ROBERT--[33]

ROBERTS, JOHN MADDOX
RAMSEY, MARK--G. COOK LTR AUG '93

ROBERTS, JOHN S[TORM]
ANTHONY, JOHN--[1]
LLOYD, JANE--[1]
MWAMBA, PAL--[1]
STORM, ANTHONY--[1]

ROBERTS, KEITH
STRINGER, KEITH--[11]

ROBERTS, KEITH [J.R.]
BEVAN, ALISTAIR--[1][2][11][23]SF--SEVERAL EARLY STORIES IN SCIENCE FANTASY
KINGSTON, JOHN--[1][2][11]
STRINGER, DAVID--[1][2][11]

ROBERTS, KENNETH [L]
VAN LOOT, CORNELIUS O.--[1]

ROBERTS, LEE
LESLIE, ROBERT--[1]
REID, DESMOND--W/G.P. MANN,[1][34]HP--AMALG "VICTIM UNKNOWN" '57

ROBERTS, MARK
LEE, PATRICK--J.R. BAKER-ECHOES #3,HP--"SIX-GUN SAMURAI" '80
"KAMIKAZE JUSTICE" '81

ROBERTS, MARK K.
DERRICK, LIONEL--W/CHET CUNNINGHAM, [3][7]MYS,HP--PINN 'PENETRATOR' SERIES - ODD #s

ROBERTS, SONYA LESLIE
TREVOR, CHARLOTTE--[1]

ROBERTS, SUZANNE
MARATH, LAURIE--[9][21][26]ROM--"WINGS OF MORNING"
MARATH, SPARROW--[1]

ROBERTS, THOMAS SACRA
LAWRENCE, THOMAS--[1][31][32]MYS--LM "AN AMERICAN IN PARIS" OCT '54

ROBERTS, URSULA
MILES, SUSAN--[8]

ROBERTS, W. ADOLPHE
ENDICOTT, STEPHEN--[3]MYS--MOHAWK "MAYOR HARDING OF NY" '31
METEOR "STRANGE CAREER OF BISHOP STERLING" '32

ROBERTS, W.A.
WOOD, VALENTINE--W. MURRAY-ECHOES #5,HP--

ROBERTS, WILLIAM
CECIL, HUGH MORTIMER--[31]
NEWMAN, ERNEST--[1]

ROBERTS, WILLO DAVIS
HOLDEN, JOANNE--[26]ROM--"DANGEROUS LEGACY"
"WHERE THE HEART IS" & 4 MORE

ROBERTS-JONES, PHILLIPE J
JONES, PHILLIPE--[1]

ROBERTSHAW, [JAMES] DENIS
GAUNT, MICHAEL--[1][31]

ROBERTSON, ALICE A.
DAVID, K.--[1]
ST. LUZ, BERTHE--[1][2][7]SF

ROBERTSON, COLIN
COOPER, COLIN--[40]MYS--"MURDER IN THE MORNING" '57
"DEMON'S MOON" '51 & 4 OTHERS
REID, DESMOND--[1][34]MYS,HP--AMALG "DEADLY PERSUASION" '61

ROBERTSON, CONSTANCE N.
SCOTT, DANA--[1][3][22]MYS--FARRAR "FIVE FATAL LETTERS" '37

ROBERTSON, EILEEN A.
ROBERTSON, E. ARNOT--[2][23]ENGLISH/SF--"FOUR FRIGHTENED PEOPLE" '31
"THREE CAME UNARMED" 29

ROBERTSON, ELEANOR
ROBERTS, NORA--LACHMAN LIST '93,[21]ROM--"THIS MAGIC MOMENT"
"NIGHT MOVES" & MANY MORE

ROBERTSON, FRANK CHESTER
CRANE, ROBERT--L. ROBBINS LTR '94,[2][22][31]SP/WEST--19 NEWNES NOVELS '34-66
FIELD, FRANK CHESTER--[2][22][31]WEST--CURL "THE ROCKY ROAD TO JERICHO" '35
HILL, KING--[2][22][31]AMERICAN/WEST--

ROBERTSON, H. RICHARDSON
RICHARDSON, HENRY HANDEL--FOREWORD TO "THE FORTUNES OF RICHARD MAHONY" '41

ROBERTSON, JAMES LOGIE
HALIBURTON, HUGH--[22]SCOTTISH

ROBERTSON, JAMES ROBIN
CONNELL, JOHN--[8]

ROBERTSON, JENNIFER SIN.
ROBERTSON, JENNY--[7]SF/HOR--"FEAR IN THE GLEN" '84

ROBERTSON, JOHN HENRY
CONNELL, JOHN--[1][2]

ROBERTSON, KEITH CARLTON
KEITH, CARLTON--[3][22][31][33][40]AMERICAN/MYS--DBLDY "CRAYFISH DINNER" '66
& 5 MORE '58-68

ROBERTSON, LILLIAN MAY
STEUART, GLEN--[1][3]MYS--
LONG "THE GLASS FISH" '35
LONG "THE EVIL THAT MEN DO" '37

ROBERTSON, MARGERY ELLEN
THORP, MODWENA--[1]
THORPE, ELLEN--[1]

ROBERTSON, SIGURDUR
ALFUR, UTANGAROS--[1]

ROBERTSON, SUSAN E.
HAYNESWORTH, SUSAN--[9][21][26]ROM--
"O'DANIEL'S PRIDE"

ROBERTSON, THOMAS ANTHONY
TOMASITO, DON--[22]MEXICAN

ROBERTSON, WALTER GEORGE
WERRERSON, TALBOT--[8]

ROBERTSON, WILLIAM
STRATHEARN-HAY--[8]

ROBEY, TIMOTHY LESTER
TOWNSEND, TIMOTHY--[8]

ROBINETT, STEPHEN [A]
HAHN, STEVE--[23]SF--
USED IN CANADIAN PUBLICATION OF
"MINDWIPE" '76
HALLUS, TAK--[2][23][31]SF--
ASF "MINI-TALENT" '69
ASF "MINDWIPE" '69
ASF "STARGATE" '74

ROBINS, DENISE
CHESTERTON, DENISE--[1][8][31]
FRENCH, ASHLEY--[9][21][31]ROM--
GRAY, HARRIET--[9][21][31]ROM--
RICH "BRIDE OF DOOM" '56
HAMILTON, HERVEY--[1][8][31]
KANE, JULIA--[9][21][31]ROM
WRIGHT, FRANCESCA--[9][21][26]ROM--
"THE LOVES OF LUCRETIA"
"SHE DEVIL"

ROBINS, ELIZABETH
RAIMOND, C.E.--[8][22]AMERICAN

ROBINSON, BRUCE
RAMSAY, JACK--W/MATTHEW CHAPMAN, CRPG, MYS--
ACE 70345 "THE RAGE" 77

ROBINSON, CHAILLE HOWARD
KIRBY, JEAN--[1][22]HP--
WHITMAN & CO.
ROBINSON, KATHLEEN--[1][21][22]AMERICAN/ROM--
"RUNAWAY HEART"
"WHEN DEBBIE DARED" & 2 MORE

ROBINSON, CHARLES M. III
CHARLESTON, ROBERT E.--[1][31]

ROBINSON, DAVID
ROBINSON, BUDD--[1]

ROBINSON, DEREK
ROBSON, DIRK--[1]

ROBINSON, EDWIN MEADE
ROBINSON, TED--[1]

ROBINSON, FRANK M.
BENJI, THOMAS--[1][31]
COURTNEY, ROBERT--HAWK/BRINEY INTRVW '93,
[1]HP-- NO TITLES KNOWN
WALSH, JAMES--[1]

ROBINSON, H.
MADEOC--[8]

ROBINSON, HERBERT SPENCER
HESPRO, HERBERT--[31]

ROBINSON, IRENE
MANNING, JO--[9][21][26]ROM--
"CHERISHED DESTINY"

ROBINSON, JAN M.
FLOOD, FLASH--[1][33]

ROBINSON, JILL
SCHARY, JILL--[1]
ZIMMER, JILL SCHARY--[1]

ROBINSON, JO ANN OOIMAN
OOIMAN, JO ANN--[1]

ROBINSON, JOAN M.G.T.
THOMAS, JOAN GALE--[1][22][33]
ENGLISH/CHILDREN'S BOOKS

ROBINSON, JULIEN LEWIS
VEDEY, JULIAN--[8]

ROBINSON, LEWIS [GEORGE]
LIMNELIUS, GEORGE--[1][3][22]MYS--
BENN "THE MEDBURY FORT MURDER" '29
BLES "TELL NO TALES" '31
RAHA, GEORGE--[1][22]

ROBINSON, LISA
RHODES, LAURA--[1]

ROBINSON, LOUIE JR.
WYATT, JAMES--[1]

ROBINSON, LYNDA S.
ROBINSON, SUZANNE--CRPG--
BB "LADY VALIANT"
BB "LADY DEFIANT"
BB "LADY HELLFIRE"
BB "LADY GALLANT"
BB 29576 "LADY DANGEROUS" '94

ROBINSON, PATRICIA C.
DUVAL, MARGARET--[1][31]
MACOMBER, DARIA--W/FERDINAN STEVENSON,
[3][31][40]MYS-
"A CLEARING IN THE FOG"
"RETURN TO OCTAVIA"

ROBINSON, PAUL
ROBINSON, SPIDER--[4][7][23]SF--
DELL "ANTINOMY" '80
'CALLAHAN'S CROSSTIME SALOON' SERIES: #1-4
HOLT 'MINDKILLER' SERIES: #1 & 2 '82-7
BERK "TELEMPATH" '76 & MORE
WTATT, B.D.--[1][2][23]SF--
EARLY STORIES

ROBINSON, RICHARD B.
LEADERMAN, GEORGE--[1][3][22]MYS--
HURST "DEATH IN PURSUIT" '35
HURST "DOOR WAS VIOLENCE" '35

ROBINSON, ROBERT CHARLES
CHARLES, RAY--[31]

ROBINSON, ROXANA [BARRY]
BARRY, ROXANA--[31]

ROBINSON, SHEILA M.
RADLEY, SHEILA--LACHMAN LST '93,
[8][18][34]MYS--
CNST "THIS WAY OUT" '89 & 6 MORE '81-90
ROWAN, HESTER--LACHMAN LST '93,
[8][18][34]MYS--
COLLINS "OVERTURE IN VENICE" '75
COLLINS "THE LINDEN TREE" '77
COLLINS "SNOWFALL" '78

ROBINSON, WILLIAM I.
ESPINOZA, GUILLERMO--[31]

ROBISON, NANCY LOUISE
JOHNSON, NATALIE--[33]

ROBLES, ANTONIO
ANTONIORROBLES--[11]

ROBSON, NORMAN
CARNI, ROSS--[34]MYS,HP--
HAM STFFD "NO TIME FOR CORPSES" '52
ROBB, JOHN--[2][3][27]MYS--
HAM STFFD "SPACE BEAM" '51
"I SHALL AVENGE" '54 & 15 MORE '42-55

ROBY, MARY LINN
BRADSTREET, VALLERIE--[1][9][21][26]ROM--
"THE FORTUNE WHEEL"
"THE IVORY FAN"
D'ARCY, PAMELA--[1][9][21][26]ROM--
"MAGIC MOMENT"
"ANGEL IN THE HOUSE" & 3 MORE
GREY, GEORGINA--[9][21][26]ROM--
"FASHION'S FROWN"
"BELLE OF BRIGHTON" & 9 MORE
PRYOR, PAULINE--[9][21][26]ROM--
"THE FAINT-HEARTED FELON"
WELLES, ELIZABETH--[3][21][26][29]MYS/ROM--
"SEAGULL CRAG" '77
WILSON, MARY--[3][9][21][26][29]MYS/ROM--
"THE CHANGELING"
"WIND OF DEATH"

ROCHE, ARTHUR SOMERS
MACHAYE, ERIC--[1][22]MYS

ROCHE, THOMAS
YES TOR--[8]

ROCHEFORT, JULIAN
STEVENS, CHRISTOPHER--[1]

ROCHESTER, GEO[RGE] E.
BERESFORD, JOHN--[1]
CHATHAM, FRANK--[1]
FRAZER, ALLISON--[1]
FURZE, BARTON--[1]
GAUNT, JEFFREY--[3][29]MYS--
ELDON "THE HAUNTED MAN" '51
HALE, MARTIN--[1]
KENT, ELIZABETH--[1]
ROCHE, ERIC--[1]
ROCHE, HESTER--[1]
SMITH, HAMILTON--[1]
WEST, MARY--[1]

ROCHSTROH, ERNST
MERTEN, GERDA--[39]GERMAN

ROCK, FRANK
HURCH, CHARLES--[14]ADULT--
OLYM OPS#26 "THE FEEL-IT BOOK" '71

ROCKER, JUDY S.
STATON, ANNA LLOYD--W/DORIS S. ENGLISH,
[21]ROM--
"THE CHALLENGED HEART"

ROCKEY, HOWARD
BRYCE, RONALD--[22]MYS
PANBOURNE, OLIVER--[3][22]MYS--
"THE VARANOFF TRADITION" '26

ROCKLIN, ROSS L.
CENTE, H.F.--[2][11][31]
ROCKLYNNE, ROSS--[2][3][7][11][23]MYS/SF--
ASF "MAN OF IRON" '35
SMITH, CARLTON--[1]

RODD, KATHLEEN TENNANT
TENNANT, KYLIE--[1][22][33]AUSTRALIAN

RODDA, [P] CHARLES
HOLT, GAVIN--[3][32][36]AUSTRALIAN/MYS--
HODDER "DARK LADY" '33
& 37 MORE NOVELS '28-65
ML "DRUMS BEAT AT NIGHT" NOV/DEC '33
& JAN '34
JCM "WAIT TILL I DIE" APR '58
JCM "SKULL IN THE RUBBLE" MAY '58
LOW, GARDNER--[3][29][36]MYS--
GOLZ "INVITATION TO KILL" '37
REED, ELIOT--[36]MYS--
COLLINS "CHARTER TO DANGER" '53
COLLINS "PASSPORT TO PANIC" '58
REED, ELIOT--W/ERIC AMBLER,
[29][34][36]AUSTRALIAN/MYS--
DBLDY "SKY TRIP" '50
DBLDY "TENDER TO DANGER" '51
DBLDY "TENDER TO MOONLIGHT" '52
COLLINS "MARAS AFFAIR" '53

RODDENBERRY, EUGENE WES.
RODDENBERRY, GENE--[33]

RODDICK, BARBARA M.
MASON, HILARY--[9][21][26]ROM--
"MORISCO"

RODDICK, ELLEN
MEADE, ELLEN--[1]

RODDY, LEE
BANNER, RACHEL--[33]

RODECAPE, MARJORIE FOSTER
RATHER, LOIS--[7]SF/HOR--
NON-FICT "BITTERSWEET: AMBROSE BIERCE
& WOMEN" '75

RODEFER, STEFEN
CALAIS, JEAN--[31] TRANSLATION OF "VILLON"

RODELL, MARIE F.
RANDOLPH, MARION--[2][3][18]MYS--
HOLT "BREATH NO MORE" '40
HOLT "THIS'LL KILL YOU" '40
HOLT "GRIM GROWS THE LILLIES" '41

RODERUS, FRANK
EARLY, TOM--J. REASONER '93, WEST,HP--
BERK 'SONS OF TEXAS' SERIES: #4

RODGERS, ANNE MARIE
WINSTON, ANNE MARIE--[26]ROM--
SIL 809 "CHANCE AT A LIFETIME"
SIL 827 "UNLIKELY EDEN"

RODNEY, GEORGE BRYDGES
BRYDGES, GEORGE--L. ROBBINS LTR MAR '94

RODRIAN, IRENE
COTTON, JERRY--[39]GERMAN/MYS,HP--

RODRIGO, ROBERT
RODNEY, BOB--[22]ENGLISH/SPORTS

RODRIGUEZ, CHRISTINE M.G.
GENTRY, CHRISTINE--[7]SF--
"WHEN SPIRITS WALK" '88

RODRIGUEZ, DENNIS
MARKFIELD, RALPH--V. BERCH--
BRNDN/BC PSEUDS, BAE 22, ADULT--
QUINN, JOHN--[3][29]MYS--
PINN "KILL SQUAD" '83
PN "CRYSTAL KILL" '84 & 4 MORE '82-5

RODRIGUEZ, JUDITH G.
GREEN, JUDITH--W/JEAN GALBRAITH,[8][31]

RODZIEWICZOWNA, MARIA
ZMOGAS--[22]POLISH

ROE, ERIC
ROE, TIG--[8]

ROE, F. GORDON
CRITICUS--[1][22][31]ENGLISH
F.G.R.--[1][22]ENGLISH
RHODE, WINSLOW--[1][22]ENGLISH
UNCLE GORDON--[1][22]ENGLISH

ROE, IVAN
SAVAGE, RICHARD--[2][23][29][34]MYS--
"MURDER GOES TO SCHOOL" '46
JARROLDS "MURDER FOR FUN" '47
JARROLDS "HORRIBLE HAT" '49
JARROLDS "POISON & THE ROOT" '50
JARROLDS "SALAMANDER TOUCH" '52
WARD "WHEN THE MOON DIED" 55
MUS "LIGHTNINGS EYE" '57
MUSEUM "STRANGERS MEETING" '57
MUSEUM "INNOCENTS" '58

ROE, M.S.
HICKS, DAISY--[9]ROM
THOMPSON, JONATHAN H.--[9]ROM
THOMSON, DAISY--[9]ROM

ROE, WILLIAM JAMES
CERVUS, G.I.--[1][3][23]SF/MYS--
LIPP "WHITE FEATHERS" 1885
GENONE, HUDOR--[1][2][23]SF

ROECKEN, KURT WALTER
FREED, CECIL V.--[39]GERMAN/MYS/SF
GORDON, ROBERT S.--J. HOFFMANN-PP 40,MYS,HP--
GERM PANTH 180 "DAS TOTEMHEMD HAT KEINE TASCHEN"
PANTH 186 "DAS HAUS AM HALBEN WEGE" '61
MICHAEL, ANTHONY--[39]GERMAN/MYS/SF
ROCK, C.V.--J. HOFFMANN-PP 40,[1]MYS,HP--
GERM PANTH 171 "BEI LEBENDIGEM LEIBE" '60
STERLING, EDGAR T.--[39]GERMAN/MYS/SF--
WALTER, HENRY--[1][39][40]GERMAN/MYS--
"DAS GRAB IM MICHIGAN-SEE" '60

ROEHRICH, WILLIAM
ROERICH, WILLIAM--[1]

ROELVAAG, OLE EDVART
MORCK, PAAL--[1]
ROELVAAG, O.E.--[1]

ROESSNER-HERMAN, MICHAELA
ROESSNER, MICHAELA--[7]SF--
BB "WALKABOUT WOMAN" '88

ROETHKE, THEODORE
ROTHBERG, WINTERSET--[8]

ROFFEY, MAUREEN
LODGE, MAUREEN ROFFEY--[1][33]

ROGER, MAE DURHAM
DURHAM, MAE--[1][33]

ROGERS, CHUCK
STIVERS, DICK--[34]MYS,HP--
GE "FALL BACK & KILL" '68
GE "SHOT TO HELL" '85
GE "CAJUN ANGEL" '86
GE "HARD KILL" '86
GE "GHOST TRAIN" '87
GE "HIT & RUN" '87
GE "MIAMI CRUSH" '87

ROGERS, DALE EVANS
EVANS, DALE--[31]

ROGERS, ELEANOR WOODS
WOODS, ELEANOR--[9][21]ROM--
"HIGH STAKES"
"TRIPLE THREAT" & 27 MORE

ROGERS, ELIZABETH J.
SWAN, REBECCA--[9][21]ROM--
"LOVE'S PERFECT ISLAND"
"CHASE THE WIND"

ROGERS, EVELYN
GRAVES, KELLER--W/KATHRYN DAVENPORT,
BOOK BIO,[9][21][26]ROM--
"VELVET VIXEN" & 4 MORE

ROGERS, FRED MCFEELY
MISTER ROGERS--[33]

ROGERS, LEE
BARRETT, JEAN--[9]ROM

ROGERS, MARIAN H. JACKSON
JACKSON, MARIAN J.A.--V. BERCH LTR TO
HUBIN '94,[31]MYS--
PINN "ARABIAN PEARL" '90
PINN "PUNJAB'S RUBY" '90

ROGERS, PATRICIA
WELLES, PATRICIA--[9][21][26]ROM--
"SARA'S GHOST"
WELLES, RACHEL--[9][21][26]ROM--
"FIRE IN THE EAST"

ROGERS, PAUL [PATRICK]
HARDWICK, HOMER--[1][31]

ROGERS, ROBERT LEE
BARRETT, JEAN--[21][26]ROM--
"RING OF GOLD"
"HEAT"
"FIREBIRD" & 2 MORE
ROGERS, LEE--[21]ROM--
"ALL THESE SPLENDID SINS"

ROGERS, ROSEMARY
GRAYSON, MARINA--[9][14][21]ADULT--
OLYM OPH#242 "MAGNIFICENT ANIMALS" '71

ROGERS, RUTH
ALEXANDER, RUTH--[1][3]MYS--
RCL "BLACKMAIL" '29
RCL "ROME EXPRESS" '32 & 3 MORE '26-36

ROGERS, SAMUEL SHEPARD
SHEPARD, SAM--[8]

ROGERS, THOMAS PERCY
ROGERS, JOHN--[1]

ROGERS, W.M.
B.B.--W/WILLIAM STABBACK JOHNS,[1]

ROGERS, WAYNE
APPEL, H.M.--L. ROBBINS LTR '94--
THIS IS A 'BITTNER' PSEUD PER
LACHMAN & [11]
KIMBALL, CONRAD--L. ROBBINS LTR MAR '94
STEELE, CURTIS--PULP #13, MYS,HP--
'OP5':
"SUICIDE BATTALION" JUL '38
"DAY OF DAMNED" SEPT 38
"DAWN THAT SHOOK THE WORLD" NOV '38
"WHEN HELL CAME TO AMERICA" JAN '39
"INVASION FROM THE SKY" MAR '39
"WINGED HORDES OF YELLOW VULTURE" MAY '39
"WAR TANKS OF Y. VULTURE" JUL '39
"CORPSE CAVALRY OF Y. VULTURE" SEPT '39
"ARMY FROM UNDERGROUND" NOV '39
STOCKBRIDGE, GRANT--PULP #13,MYS,HP--
SPD "SLAVES OF THE BLACK MONARCH" AUG '37
SPD "CITY THAT DARED NOT EAT" OCT '37
SPD "SATAN'S SWITCHBOARD" DEC '37
SPD "CITY OF LOST MEN" FEB '38
SPD "WHEN THOUSANDS SLEPT IN HELL" MAY '38
SPD "SATAN'S SHACKLES" JUN '38
SPD "DEVIL'S CANDLESTICKS" AUG '38
SPD "WITHERING DEATH" DEC '38
SPD "SONG OF DEATH" FEB '39
SPD "BLIGHT OF THE BLAZING EYE" APR '39
SPD "CORPSE BROKER" SEPT '39

ROGERS, WILLIAM GARLAND
ROGERS, W.G.--[1]

ROGERSON, JAMES
HAMILTON, ROGER--[8]

ROGLER, AUGUST
MORE, ANDREAS--[39]GERMAN/JUV

ROGOW, LEE
ELLIS, CRAIG--[1][2][11][23]SF,HP--
AMAZING

ROHAN, MAURICE DESMOND
DOWNES, QUENTIN--[34]MYS--
WINGATE "NO SMOKE, NO FLAME" '52
WINGATE "HEADS I WIN" '53
ARCO "THEY HADN'T A CLUE" '54
EGREMONT, MICHAEL--[34]MYS--
RCL "BRIDE OF FRANKENSTEIN" '35
HARRISON, MICHAEL--[32][34]MYS--
HOME "DARKENED ROOM" '52
MYCROFT "EXPLOITS OF CHEVALIER DUPIN" '68
DUTTON "I, SHERLOCK HOLMES" '77
17 DIGEST STORIES [EQMM & LM] '50s-70s

ROHAN, MICHAEL SCOTT
ROHAN, MIKE SCOTT--[23]--
NAME VARIANT, SF--
"RUN TO THE STARS" '82
SCOT, MICHAEL--W/ALLAN SCOTT,[1][2][7]SF--
NEL "THE ICE KING" '86

ROHDE, ROBERT H.
DUDGEON, ROBERT--J. HOFFMANN-PP 40, MYS,HP--
GERM PANTH 177
RPRT OF CHELSEA "HUNTED DOWN" '28

ROHDE, WILLIAM L.
CARTER, NICK--[3]MYS,HP--
AWARD "AMSTERDAM AWARD" '68
AWARD "JUDAS SPY" '68
AWARD "HOOD OF DEATH" '68
AWARD "RHODESIA" '68
AWARD "HUMAN TIME BOMB" 69

ROHEN, EDWARD
CONNORS, BRUTON--[1][31]

ROHLFS, ANNA KATHARINE
GREEN, ANNA KATHARINE--L. ROBBINS LTR '94,
[1][32]MYS--
EQMM "THE BLUE WASH MYS" JAN '51
ROHLFS, MRS. CHARLES--[1]

ROHR, PAULA M.
SUMMERS, FAYE--[21][26]ROM--
"STORM SPELL"
"WINTERHALL"

ROHR, WOLF DETLEF
CAINE, GEFF--[1][2]
CAINE, JEFF--[39]GERMAN/MYS/SF
COOVER, WAYNE--[1][2]
COOVER, WAYNE--[39]GERMAN/MYS/SF
REED, ALLAN--[1][2]
REED, ALLAN--[39][40]GERMAN/MYS--
"DEI GRUNE KRANKHEIT" '58
VAN BERGEN, DETLEF--[39]GERMAN/MYS/SF

ROHRBACH, PETER THOMAS
CODY, JAMES P.--[3][29][32]MYS--
4 BERK NOVELS '74-5
AHMM "BOGUS HIJACK" DEC '70
CC "A PAYMENT FOR MURDER" FEB '74
MSMM "AGENT TO THE SECOND POWER" DEC '74

ROHRLICH, RUBY
LEAVITT, RUBY R.--[31]
ROHRLICH-LEAVITT, RUBY--[1]

ROITHMAIER, EMILIE
ERTLER, FRITZI--[39]GERMAN,

ROITMAN, VOLF & SHELLEY S
ASHLEY, SHELLEY--V. BERCH LTR TO
A. HUBIN '93, MYS--
PIATKUS "SECRET BABY" '90

ROJANKOVSKY, FEODOR S.
ROJAN--[33]

ROKUYA, TAYAMA
KATAI, TAYAMA--[22]JAPANESE

ROLAND, DONALD
CORDELL, MELISSA--[3]MYS--
MANOR "BOND OF EVIL" '77
MANOR "SHADES OF PERIL" '77

ROLDOS AGUILERA, JAIME
AGUILERA, JAIME ROLDOS--[31]

ROLEINE, ROBERTA
ROLEINE, ROBERTE--[3]MYS--
FRENCH BYLINE - 9 NOVELS '65-76

ROLFE, EDWIN
FULLER, LESTER--[8]

ROLFE, FREDERICK [W]
CORVO, BARON--[2][11][16][22][31]ENGLISH
FREDERICK, BARON CORVO--[23]SF
PROSPERO & CALIBAN--W/HARRY PIRIE-GORDON, [1][2][11][16]ENGLISH
ROLFE, FATHER--[1]ENGLISH

ROLFE, MARO ORLANDO
OLD DETECTIVE--[1]
ROBIE, ANNE A.--[1]
ROLFE, SERGEANT--[1]
ROLKER, A.W.--[1]

ROLLE-BERG, RAMONA
BRADLEY, RAMONA--[26]ROM--
"HOT ARTIC NIGHTS"
RYDELL, SIERRA--[26]ROM--
"ON MIDDLE GROUND"

ROLLINS, KATHLEEN
DEBRETT, HAL--W/DAVIS DRESSER,[1]--
MARRIED NAME 'KATHLEEN ROLLINS DRESSER'

ROLLINS, MONTGOMERY
HAY, TIMOTHY--[1]

ROLLINS, WILLIAM STACY
STACY, O'CONNOR--[2][3][11][29]MYS--
MCL "MURDER AT CYPRESS HALL" '33
THAYER, URANN--[2][11][32]MYS--
SN "THE WHITE DOMINO" WINT '69

ROMAINE, LAWRENCE B.
WEATHERCOCK, THE--[1][22]AMERICAN

ROMAINS, JULES
FARIGOULE, LOUIS--[31]

ROMANO, DEANE LOUIS
CAIRO, JON--[1][31]

ROMANOFF, ALEXANDER N.
ABDULLAH, ACHMED--[1][3][32]MYS--
13 NOVELS '15-33
EQMM "HONORABLE GENTLEMAN" MAR '51
EQMM "A SIMPLE ACT OF PIETY" MAY '52
DURANI, NADIR KHAN--[1]
NADIR, A.A.--[1]

ROMANOV, CONSTANTINE
K.R.--[22]RUSSIAN

ROMANOW, DANIEL DAVID
ROMAN, DANIEL--[1]

ROMBRO, JACOB
KRANTZ, PHILIP--[1]

ROMERO, PATRICIA W.
CURTIN, PATRICIA ROMERO--[31]

ROMHILD, HELMUT
SLADE, JACK--[39]GERMAN/MYS/WEST
CAMERON, JOHN--[39]GERMAN/MYS/WEST

ROMLEY, FREDERICK J.
ROMLEY, DEREK--[8]

ROMMEL, ALBERTA
VERHAGEN, BRITTA--[39]GERMAN/JUV

RONAL, PETER
MORGAN, MAYBETH--[3]MYS--
ACE "DARKNESS AT BROMLEY HALL" '75

RONALD, DAVID WILLIAM
WILLIAMS, D.--[1]

RONALD, JAMES
WALES, KIRK--[3][29][40]MYS--
"MURDER IN THE FAMILY" '36

RONALDS, MARY TERESA
SHERIDAN, TERESA--[1]

RONN, YUVAL
IONEL--[7]SF

RONNING, PAMELA
JERROLD, PAMELA--[21][26]ROM--
"THE OTHER MOTHER"

RONZONE, BENJAMIN ANTHONY
BARON--[3]MYS--
ROXBURGH "THE MARQUIS OF MURRAY HILL" '09

ROOKE, DAPHNIE [MARIE]
POINTON, ROBERT--[1][33]

ROOME, GERALD ANTHONY
LESLIE, COLIN--[8]

ROOP, CONSTANCE BETZER
ROOP, CONNIE--[33]

ROOS, AUDREY & WILLIAM
ROOS, KELLEY--[3][18][22]MYS--
DELL "SCENT OF MYS" '59
DODD "NECESSARY EVIL" '65 & MORE '42-71

ROOS, AUDREY [KELLEY]
KELLEY, AUDREY--[1]

ROOS, ELNA
ROLAND, STEPHEN--[29]MYS--
"MORDET I PARK HOTEL" '41

ROOS, ERNST
JOHNSSON, JOHN STEWART--[29]MYS--
DM#41 "DEN FORSVUNNA BAJONETTEN" '39

ROOS, WILLIAM
RAND, WILLIAM--[1][3][18]MYS--
DRAMITIZATION OF EQ'S "FOUR HEARTS"

ROOSEVELT, ROBERT BARNWLL
BARNWELL--[1]
ZELL, IRA--[1]

ROPER, LAURA WOOD
WOOD, LAURA N.--[1][33]

ROPER, LESTER
LESTER, SAMANTHA--[9][21]ROM--
"DUKE'S WARD"
"BRASH AMERICAN" & 2 MORE

ROPER, RONNALIE J.
HOWARD, RONNALIE ROPER--[1][31]

ROPER, SUSAN BRONTHRON
BRAND, SUSAN--[3][21][26]ROM/MYS--
SIMON "SHADOWS ON THE TOR" '77

ROPER, WILLIAM L.
FRY, DAVID--[1][31]
SPARKMAN, WILLIAM--[1]

ROPES, ARTHUR REED
ROSS, ADRIAN--[2][22]ENGLISH

ROQUEBRUNE, ROBERT
LAROQUE DE ROQUEBRUNE, R.--[31]

RORVIK, DAVID MICHAEL
DAVIDSON, MICHAEL--[31]
FARADAY, M.M.--[7][31]SF--
BB "THE SHARING" '82

ROSAN, SHIRA
ROZAN, S.J.--MWA DIRECTORY '93-4, MYS--

ROSANOV, MIKHAIL G.
OGNEV, N.--[1]

ROSAS, REBECCA BOADO
PAISLEY, REBECCA--CR,[21][26]ROM--
"BAREFOOT BRIDE" & 5 OTHERS

ROSCHMANN, KURT
ROMAN, FRIEDRICH--[39]GERMAN

ROSCOE, JOHN
ROSCOE, MIKE--W/MICHAEL RUSO,[3][29]MYS--
CROWN "RIDDLE ME THIS, CLOWN" '52 & 2 MORE
CROWN "SLICE OF HELL" '54
ACE "MIDNIGHT EYE" '58

ROSE, ALFRED
READE, ROLF S.--[1]

ROSE, ALVIN EMANUEL
PRUITT, ALAN--[1][3][22]MYS--
ZD "THE RESTLESS CORPSE" '47
HAN 135 "TYPED FOR A CORPSE" '51

ROSE, CAMILLE DAVIED
DAVIED, CAMILLE--[31]

ROSE, CARL
CROS, EARL--[33]

ROSE, CHARLES E.
EDDY, CHARLES--[1]

ROSE, DOROTHY VIOLET F.
CARRINGTON, DOROTHY--[1]

ROSE, EVELYN GITA
DAVIS, GITA--[8]

ROSE, GEORGE
SKETCHLEY, ARTHUR--[2][3]MYS--
ROUTLEDGE "MRS. BROWN ON THE TICKBORN
CASE" 1872

ROSE, GRAHAM
GRAHAM, JOHN--[8]

ROSE, IAN
DRACHMAN, WOLF--[8]
ROSE, ROBERT--[8]

ROSE, JANE
ROSE, ALLISON--W/RUTH ALLISON,[2]

ROSE, JOHN HOLLAND
ROSE, J.H.--[1]

ROSE, KEN
STIVERS, DICK--[34]MYS,HP--
GE "MEAN STREETS" '89
GE "CULT WAR" '90
GE "HOSTILE FIRE" '90
GE "SHADOW WARRIOR" '90

ROSE, MARTHA EMILY
LEE, CHARLES C.--[1]

ROSE, MARY H.
MAIZIE--[8][9]

ROSE, NANCY A.
SWEETLAND, NANCY ROSE--[8]

ROSE, PHYLLIS
JANTSANG, TANI--[2]

ROSE, SHARON
BAINBRIDGE, SHARON--[26]ROM--
"BLOOD & ROSES"
FARRADAY, ALICIA--[26]ROM--
"THE SUITABLE SUITOR"

ROSE, WENDY
EDWARDS, BRONWEN ELIZAB.--[1][31][33]
KLANSHENDEL, CHIRON--[1][31][33]

ROSEGGER, PETRI KETTENFR.
KETTENFEIER, PETRI--[1]
MALSER, HANS--[1]
P.K.--[1]
ROSEGGER, P.K.--[1]
ROSEGGER, PETER--[1]

ROSEN, MICHAEL
LANDGRAVE OF HESSE--[1]

ROSEN, WINIFRED
CASEY, WINIFRED ROSEN--[33]

ROSENBAUER, ROLAND
SHADOW, MIKE--[39]GERMAN/HOR,HP--
SHOCKER, DAN--[39][40]GERMAN/MYS,HP
SPIDER, JOHN--[39]GERMAN/HOR,HP--
USHER, H.P.--[39]GERMAN/HOR,HP--

ROSENBAUM, ALISSA
RAND, AYN--DENNIS BOHN '93
"AYN RAND" BY JAMES BAKER '87

ROSENBAUM, BEVERLY KATZ
BRYAN, BEVERLY--[26]ROM--
"WHAT FRIENDS ARE FOR"

ROSENBAUM, HERCEL
DRZEWIECKI, HENRY K.--[1]

ROSENBERG, DOROTHY
CROMAN, DOROTHY YOUNG--[1][31][33]

ROSENBERG, ELINOR BLAISDL
BLAISDELL, ANNE--[1]
BLAISDELL, ELINOR--[1]

ROSENBERG, ELSA
ASPAZIA--[22]LATVIAN

ROSENBERG, ETHEL [C]
CLIFFORD, ETH--[1][31][33]
PENN, RUTH BONN--[1][33]

ROSENBERG, HENRIETTA
KEATING, WALTER S.--[8]

ROSENBERG, JOEL
MICHAEL, PETER--W/SIMON MICHAEL,[7]SF--
GRAFTON "THE USURPER" '88

ROSENBERG, MICHAEL
MEEROPOL, MICHAEL--[1]

ROSENBERG, NANCY SHERMAN
SHERMAN, NANCY--[1][33]

ROSENBERG, NANCY TAYLOR
TAYLOR, NANCY--AUTHOR PROVIDED

ROSENBERG, WILLIAM S.
ROSE, BILLY--[2][11][32]MYS--
EQMM "DETECTIVE STORY" JUN '51
EQMM "D.O.A." JAN '52
EQMM "BEYOND ALL DOUBT" OCT '60
EQMM "OLD PSYCHO-O-MAGEE" OCT '61

ROSENBERGER, JOSEPH
CARTER, NICK--[3]MYS,HP--
CHART "THUNDERSTRIKE IN SYRIA" '79
CHANG, LEE--[3][29]MYS,SP--
MANOR - 6 NOVELS
ALL BUT "YEAR OF THE BOAR" '73-8

ROSENBLATT, FRED
DREYFUS, FRED--[1][31]

ROSENBLUM, ROBERT J.
CONDE, NICHOLAS--W/ROBERT NATHAN,
V. BERCH LTR TO HUBIN, MYS--
NAL "RELIGION" '83
NAL "THE LEGEND" '84
MAXXE, ROBERT--[3][7]MYS/SF--
DBLDY "ARCADE" '84

ROSENDORFFER, HERBERT
TOGESEN, VOBBER--[39]GERMAN

ROSENER, INGE
DRY, ILONA--[39]GERMAN/JUV

ROSENFELD, ALEXANDER F.L.
RODA RODA, ALEXANDER F.L.--[22]SLAVIK

ROSENFELD, FRIEDRICH
FELD, FRIEDRICH--[39][40]GERMAN/MYS--
"SPUK IM BERGHOTEL" '65
"MANN MIT DER GELBEN KRAWETTE" '6

ROSENFELD, LOUIS ZARA
ZARA, LOUIS--[1]

ROSENFELD, LULLA
ADLER, LULLA--[1][31]

ROSENFELD, SANDOR FRIEDR.
AABA AABA--[39]GERMAN
RODA, ALEXANDER RODA--[39]GERMAN

ROSENFIELD, JUDITH
ARCANA, JUDITH--[1]

ROSENHEIMER, ARTHUR
KNIGHT, ARTHUR--[1]

ROSENKRANTZ, LINDA
BYRD, C.L.--[1][31]
DAMIANO, LAILO--[1]

ROSENMEYER, ALAN OTTO
ROSS, ALAN O.--[1]

ROSENQUIST, FINGAL
VON SUDORF, FINGAL--[8]

ROSENRAUCH, HEINZ ERIC
ROSEN, HAIIM B.--[1]

ROSENTHAL, ALAN
TALKIN, GIL--[1]

ROSENTHAL, ANDREW
WARREN, ANDREW--W/WARREN [S] TUTE,[1]

ROSENTHAL, MACHA LOUIS
ROSENTHAL, M.L.--[1]

ROSENTHAL, MICHAEL D.H.
ROSS, MICHAEL D.H.--[8]

ROSENTHAL, NORMAN
WARD, STEVE--L. ROBBINS LTR MAR '94

ROSENTHAL, RICHARD A.
RICHARDS, ALLEN--[3][22][40]MYS--
MacM "TO MARKET, TO MARKET" '61

ROSENUS, ALAN [H]
MIDDLEBROOK, DAVID--[1]

ROSEWATER, FRANK
MAYOE, MARIAN & FRANKLIN--[1][2]

ROSEYEAR, JOHN
CIRCUS, JIM--[1][31]

ROSKAM, KAREL LODEWIJK
DUTCHMAN, KALAMU--[1]

ROSKOLENKO, HARRY
DE BALLARD, JEAN--V. BERCH-BAE 27-
'AFTER DARK' SERIES, ADULT--
MacF 60-248 "PARIS AFTER DARK" '66
MacF 75-273 "FRENCH RIVIERA AFTER DARK" '69
HAIGHT, JAMES T.--W/JEANNE THWAITE, V. BERCH-
BAE 27-'AFTER DARK' SERIES,[31]ADULT--
MacF 95-167 "SAN FRANCISCO AFTER DARK" '71
ROSS, ALLEN V.--V. BERCH-BAE 27-
'AFTER DARK' SERIES, ADULT--
MacF 60-314 "BOMBAY AFTER DARK" '68
ROSS, COLIN--[1][22]ADULT--
BEAC B196 "THE MISTRESS" '58
LAN 72-634 "SEASON OF LOVE" '62
MacF 60-268 "N.Y. AFTER DARK" '66

ROSLER, K. HERBERT
WOLF, ALEXANDER--[39]GERMAN/JUV

ROSMAN, ALICE GRANT
ROSNA--[8]

ROSMOND, BABETTE
ARROWAY, FRANCIS M.--[31]
CAMPION, BABETTE--[31]
LAKE, BABETTE ROSMOND--[2]
ROSMOND, B.--BILL PRONZINI INTRO TO
PULP STORIES

ROSS, A. JOSEPH
ROSS, JOE--[7]SF--
NON FICT "THE NESFA HYMNAL"
EDITED AS BY '79

ROSS, ALBERT HENRY
MORISON, FRANK--[1][2]

ROSS, CHARLES
FRANCIS, JAMES--[8]

ROSS, CLARE ROMANO
ROMANO, CLARE--[33]

ROSS, DON
DANA, ROSE--[1][22]SP W/DANIEL ROSS, MYS--
HALE "BROODING MIST" '67
GILMER, ALICE--[1][22]
RANDOLPH, ELLEN--[1][22]SP W/DANIEL ROSS

ROSS, DON [CONT]
ROBERTS, DON--[1][22]
ROSS, MARILYN--[1][22]SP W/DANIEL ROSS
ROSSITER, JANE--W/W.E. DANIEL ROSS, [32]MYS/ROM--
SB "DEATH IN THE GARDEN" JUL '64

ROSS, EULALIE STEINMETZ
STEINMETZ, EULALIE--[1][22]AMERICAN

ROSS, FRANK [X] JR.
FRANK, R. JR.--[1][31][33]

ROSS, ISAAC
ROSS, GEORGE--[8]

ROSS, JO ANN
ROBB, JO ANN--[9][21][26]ROM--
"TOUCH THE SUN"
"WOLFE'S PREY" & 8 MORE
ROBBINS, JO ANN--[9][21][26]ROM--
"WINNING SEASON"

ROSS, MARILYN HEIMBERG
HEIMBERG, MARILYN MARKHAM--[1][31]

ROSS, STANLEY RALPH
DONEM, SUE--[31]

ROSS, W.W. EUSTACE
E.R.--[8]

ROSS, WILLIAM E. DANIEL
AMES, LESLIE--W/ORLANDO J. RIGONI,[29]MYS--
HALE "SINISTER LOVE" '84
AMES, LESLIE--[9][11][21][26]ROM--
"ANGRY WIND"
"HUNGRY SEA" & 6 MORE
BROOKS, LAURA FRANCES--[3][29]MYS--
ACE "THE OLD EVIL HOUSE" '75
CARTER, MARILYN--[9][21][26]ROM--
"THE RELUCTANT DEBUTANTE"
COLBY, ALICE--[8]
COLBY, LYDIA--[3]MYS--
PLAYBOY "TOUCH OF EVIL" '77
DANA, ROSE--W/DON ROSS,[3][9][21][29]MYS--
HALE "BROODING MIST" '67
DANIELS, JAN--[1][3][11]MYS--
HALE "BRIDE FOR ARUNDEL" '66
DANIELS, JANE--[8]
DORSET, RUTH--[9][21][31]ROM--
"HOTEL NURSE"
"BEHIND HOSPITAL WALLS" & 4 MORE
GILMER, ANN--W/DON ROSS,[9][26][31][32]MYS--
SA "APRIL IN PARIS" MAR '64 & 11 NOVELS
LESLIE, MIRIAM--[9][21][26]ROM--
"CAVANAUGH KEEP"
MCCORMACK, CHARLOTTE--[8][11]
RANDALL, DIANA [DIANE]--[3][9][21][26]MYS/ROM--
JOVE "DRAGON LOVER" '81
RANDOLPH, ELLEN--[3][21][26]MYS/ROM--
"RUSHDON LEGACY" & MORE
RANDOLPH, JANE--[8]
ROBERTS, DAN--PPCC#8/PPCC#9,[1]WEST--
"DUREZ CITY BONANZA" '65 & 13 MORE
ROSS, CLARISSA--[2][3][7][26]MYS/ROM--
"ISTANBUL NIGHTS"
"CHINA SHADOW" & 48 MORE '66-78
ROSS, DAN--[3][7][9][11][26]MYS/ROM--
"FOGBOUND"
"MURDER AT CITY HALL" & 9 MORE '63-7
ROSS, DANA--[3][7][9][26]MYS/ROM--
"DEMON OF THE DARKNESS
"LODGE SINISTER" & 5 MORE

ROSS, WILLIAM E. DANIEL [CONT]
ROSS, MARILYN--[2][3][7][26]MYS/ROM--
"GHOST & THE GARNET"
"AMETHYST TEARS" & MORE '66-78
ROSS, W.E. DAN--AHMM FEB 57, P41,[32]MYS--
MANY DIGEST STORIES [AHMM, LM, MD, MSMM, MU & SA]
ROSS, W.E.D.--[7][8][21]ROM/SF--
"GHOST OF OAKLAND"
"NIGHTWAY ALLEY" & MORE
ROSSITER, JANE--W/DON ROSS, [9][21][26][32]MYS/ROM--
SB "DEATH IN THE GARDEN" JUL '64 & NOVELS
STEELE, TEX--D. WHITEHEAD-PPCC#9,[8]WEST--
WILLIAMS, ROSE--[9][21][26]ROM--
"AIRPORT NURSE"
"A BRIDGE FOR JUDITH"
"NURSE IN NASSAU"

ROSS, WILLIAM STEWART
SALADIN--[1]

ROSS, Z. HELEN G.
ARRE, HELEN--[28][31][34]MYS--
ARCADIA "GOLDEN SHROUD" '58
ARCADIA "WRITE IT MURDER" '56 & MORE
ILES, BERT--[22][28][31][34]MYS--
ARCADIA "MURDER IN MINK" '56
ROSS, Z.H.--[1][28]--
BOBBS - 4 NOVELS

ROSS-MACDONALD, MALCOLM J
MACDONALD, MALCOLM--[8][21]ROM--
"ABIGAIL"
"A NOTORIOUS WOMAN" & 10 MORE
ROSS, MALCOLM--[8][21]ROM--
"THE DUKES"

ROSSEN, STEVE
MACCONNELL, COLUM--W/MITCHELL SMITH, V. BERCH LTR TO R. REGINALD '93, SF--
LEIS "TARK & THE GOLDEN TIDE" '77

ROSSET, BENJAMIN CHARLES
OZY--[22]RUSSIAN-IRISH

ROSSETTI, CHRISTINA GEO.
ALLEYN, ELLEN--[31][33]

ROSSI, JEAN BAPTISTE
JAPRISOT, SEBASTIEN--[3][18][29][40] FRENCH/MYS--
SIMON "TRAP FOR CINDERELLA" '64
& 5 MORE '62-78

ROSSI, SANNA MORRISON B.
BARLOW, SANNA MORRISON--[1][31]

ROSSITER, JOHN
ROSS, JONATHAN--[3][18]MYS--
CNST "DEAD EYE" '83
CNST "A TIME FOR DYING" '89 & 4 MORE

ROSSMAN, JOHN F.
ROSS, IAN--[1][7][11]SF--
SIGN 'MINDMASTERS' SERIES:
"AMAZONS" '76
"RECYCLED SOULS" '76

ROSSNER, ROBERT
ROSS, IVAN T.--[1][3][40]MYS--
SIMON "MURDER OUT OF SCHOOL" '60
DBLDY "TEACHER'S BLOOD" '64 & MORE

ROSTEN, LEO [CALVIN]
ROSS, LEONARD Q.--[1][3][29]MYS--
CENT "DARK CORNER" '45
CENT "SLEEP MY LOVE" '47

ROTH, ARTHUR JOSEPH
HOY, NINA--[1][31][33]
MARA, BARNEY--[1][33]
MCGURK, SLATER--[3][33]MYS--
MacM "GRAND CENTRAL MURDERS" '64
MacM "BIG DIG" '68 & MORE
POMEROY, PETE--[1][33]

ROTH, CHRISTIAN
BRDLBRMPFT--[1]

ROTH, HOLLY
BALLARD, K.G.--[2][3][5][18]MYS--
BRDMN "TRIAL BY DESIRE" '60
DBLDY "COAST OF FEAR" '57 & MORE
MERRILL, P.J.--[2][3][5][18]MYS--
HRCT "THE SLENDER THREAD" '59

ROTH, JERRY
JOTH, J.--[14]ADULT--
OLYM OPS#38 "LADY DICK" '71
OLYM TC#470 "JYROS" '69

ROTH, SAMUEL
LOCKRIDGE, NORMAN-- JAY A. GERTZMAN-
BAE 21, P18,[1][31]--
CREST 141 "SEX WITHOUT TEARS" '56

ROTH-KAPELLER, INGRID
PUGANIGG, INGRID--[39]GERMAN

ROTHCHILD, SYLVIA
ROSSMAN, EVELYN--[1]

ROTHENBURG, WALTER
ROSSA, BARBA--[39]GERMAN
WERO--[39]GERMAN

ROTHERRAY, GEOFFREY NEVL.
ROOKE, DENNIS--[8]

ROTHERY, BRIAN
DYER, BRIAN--W/ORLANDO R. PETROCELLI,[1][31]--
M&L "SAGA OF A CELTIC QUEEN"

ROTHFIELD, OTTO
ROTHFELD, OTTO--[34]MYS--
SIMPKIN "INDIANA DUST" '09

ROTHMAN, CHARLES WARREN
ROTHMAN, CHUCK,--[7]SF--
POPLB "STAROAMER'S FATE" '86
IASFM "THE MONJI DESERTERS" '82

ROTHMAN, MILTON A.
GREGOR, LEE--W/FREDERIC POHL,[2][11][23],
ALSO USED HIMSELF

ROTHMANN, MARIA ELIZABETH
M.E.R.--[22]AFRIKAANS

ROTHMULLER, ARON MARKO
KINOR, JEHUDA--[31]

ROTHROCK, KENNETH
ROCKWELL, KEITH--V. BERCH-BRNDN/BC PSEUDS,
BAE 22, ADULT--
BRNDN 6391 "HARD MAN"
ROCKWOOD, KARL--V. BERCH-BRNDN/BC PSEUDS,
BAE 22, ADULT--

ROTHROCK, KENNETH
ROLAND, KENT--V. BERCH-BRNDN/BC PSEUDS,
BAE 22, ADULT--
BC 7359 "CHERRY PICKERS"
BC 7485 "SWIVEL HIPS"

ROTHSTEIN, ANDREW
ROEBUCK, C.M.--[1]

ROTHSTEINER, ALOIS
STEINER, ALEXIS--[39]GERMAN/JUV

ROTHWEILER, JOAN & PAUL
WILLOUGHBY, LEE DAVIS--[21]ROM,HP--
DELL 'MAKING OF AMERICA' SERIES:
"BARBARY COASTERS"

ROTHWEILER, PAUL R.
CURTIS, RICHARD HALE--[1][31]
RYERSON, JAMES PAUL--[1]
SCOFIELD, JONATHAN--[8][21]ROM,HP--
DELL 'FREED. FTR' SERIES:
"THE KING'S CANNON"

ROTHWELL, HENRY TALBOT
TALBOT, HENRY--[1]

ROTSLER, WILLIAM
APPLETON, VICTOR--W/SHARMAN DIVONO,[7]SF,HP--
STSY 'TOM SWIFT'SERIES:
"ASTRAL FORTRESS"
"CITY IN THE STARS"
"RESCUE MISSION"
"ALIEN PROBE"
"TERROR ON THE MOONS OF JUPITER"
"WAR IN OUTER SPACE"
ARROW, WILLIAM--[1][2]SF,HP--
BAL 'RETURN TO THE PLANET OF THE APES'
SERIES: #1 & 3
BOHASSIAN, GREGOR--[11]
BOONE, BARNEY--[11]
BRACKETT, WARING--[11]
CARSE, SHANNON--[11]
CONRAD, LOGAN--[11]
GARTH, ANDREW--[11]
HALL, JOHN RYDER--[2][7][23]SF--
"FUTUREWORLD" '76
"EYE OF THE TIGER" '77
HALL, RYDER JR.--[2]
HELLER, CORD--[11]
HILLIARD, LATHAM--[11]
HOLLAND, LINDA--[11]
HOLT, HARMONY--[11]
KORDA, LOTHAR--[11]
MALCOLM, HONEY--[11]
MARKHAM, HORD--[11]
MCCORD, CLAY--[11]
MILES, HOWARD SCOTT--[11]
RANDALL, CLINT--[11]
SORENSEN, BEVERLY--[11]
WARING, BETH--[11]
WESTFLAG, FLETCHER--[11]

ROTTENSTEINER, FRANZ
LANSKY, IRENE--[39]GERMAN/TRANSLATOR

ROTTER, ELIZABETH N.W.
MATTHEWS, LAURA--[1][26]ROM--
"LADY NEXT DOOR"
"VISCOUNT & THE HOYDEN" & 14 MORE
WALKER, ELIZABETH--[21][26]ROM--
NUMEROUS NOVELS
WALKER, ELIZABETH NEFF--[21][26]ROM--
NUMEROUS NOVELS

ROUBICZEK, PAUL [ANTON]
ROBERT, PAUL A.--[1]

ROUGIER, GEORGETTE
HEYER, GEORGETTE--[21][32]MYS/ROM-59 NOVELS
SUS "NIGHT AT THE INN" AUG '58

ROUMANOUSKY, N.K.
CHORNY, KUZMA--[22]RUSSIAN

ROUND, WILLIAM M.F.
PENNOT, PETER--[1]
VEVAY, PAUL--[1]

ROURKE, JAMES F.A.
HOLLIS, JIM--W/HOLLIS S. SUMMERS,[3]MYS--
HARPER "TEACH YOU A LESSON" '55

ROURKE, LOUIS MUSGRAVE
DICKERSON-WATKINS, L.--[1]

ROUSSEAU, LEON
STRYDOM, LEN--[8]

ROUTSCHEK, HELMUT
KROGER, ALEXANDER--[39]GERMAN/SF--

ROUTSONG, ALMA
MILLER, ISABEL--[1]

ROWAN, MARIE
ROWAN, M.M.--[28]WEST--5 HALE NOVELS '85-91

ROWAN-HAMILTON, SYDNEY O.
ORME, ROWAN--[1]

ROWBOTHAM, SHEILA
TURNER, SHEILA--[1]

ROWCROFT, CHARLES
SEEDY, ALFRED--[1]

ROWE, HELEN CRESSWELL
CRESSWELL, HELEN--[7][11]SF--
"THE WILKES" '70
"WINTER OF THE BIRDS" '75
"THE SECRET WORLD OF POLLY FLINT" '82
"MOONDIAL" '87

ROWE, JENNIFER JUNE
RODDA, EMILY--[7]SF--
"PIGS MIGHT FLY" '86
"BEST KEPT SECRET" '88
"FINDERS KEEPERS" '90

ROWE, JOHN GABRIEL
AUSTIN, MORTIMER--[1]
BRIGHT, JAMES--[1]
DUNSTAN, GREGORY--[1]
FERRIS, ARTHUR--[1]
GABRIEL, JOHN--[1]
LEWIS, CHARLES--[1]
RANSOME, CHARLES A.--[1]
ROWE, ALICE E.--[1]
WALTERS, T.B.--[1]

ROWE, MARGARET [KEVIN]
TERESA MARGARET, [SISTER]--[1]

ROWE, MRS. GEORGE F.
GIRARD, KATE--[1]

ROWE, MYRA
JORDAN, MAGGIE--[9][21]ROM--

ROWE, RICHARD
POSSUM, PETER--[13]AUSTRALIAN

ROWE, VIVIAN C[LAUDE]
HOOTON, CHARLES--[1][31]

ROWE, W.
BINGHAM, [MAJOR] ARTHUR--[1]

ROWLAND, DONALD S.
ADAMS, ANNETTE--[28]--
GRESHAM "ISLAND OF DECISION"
"DOCTOR OF THE HEART"
"HEART HEALER" ALL '68
BASSETT, JACK--[1][28]WEST--
8 HALE NOVELS '66-87
BAXTER, HAZEL--[1][28][31]ROM--
6 GRESHAM NOVELS '68-70
BENTON, KARLA--[1][28][31]ROM--
5 HALE NOVELS '71-73
BERRY, HELEN--[1][31]ROM--
6 GRESHAM NOVELS '68-70
BRANT, LEWIS--[1][28][31]WEST--
17 HALE NOVELS '64-83
BRAY, ALISON--[1][31]ROM--
7 GRESHAM NOVELS
2 HALE NOVELS '68-79
BRAYCE, WILLIAM--[1][28][31]WEST--
GRESHAM "RANGE HOG" '66
BROCKLEY, FENTON--[2][7][11][23][28][31]SF--
HALE "STAR QUEST" '74
BRONSON, OLIVER--[1][28][31]WEST--
GRESHAM "CATTLEMAN'S CREED" '65
BUCHANAN, CHUCK--[1][28][31]WEST--
HALE "BRAVE STAR" '66
CALEY, ROD--[1][28][31]WEST--
GRESHAM "LONESOME VALLEY" '66
HALE "TOUGH COUNTRY" '82
CARLTON, ROGER--[1][28][31]SF--
HALE "BEYOND TOMORROW" '75
HALE "STAR ARROW" '75
CLEVE, JANITA--[1][28][31]ROM--
5 HALE NOVELS '71-73
COURT, SHARON--[1][28][31]ROM--
5 HALE NOVELS '71-72
CRAIG, VERA--[9][21][26][31]ROM--
4 GRESHAM NOVELS
3 HALE NOVELS '69-79
CRAILLE, WESLEY--[1][28][31]WEST--
HALE "HELL-BENT" '66
DELANEY, JOHN--[1][28][31]WEST--
3 MEWS NOVELS
2 NEL NOVELS '76-78
DRYDEN, JOHN--[1][28][31]WEST--
7 HALE NOVELS '65-74
FENTON, FREDA--[1][28][31]ROM--
6 GRESHAM NOVELS '68-69
FIELD, CHARLES--[1][28][31]WEST--
5 HALE NOVELS '64-84
GARNER, GRAHAM--[7][11][28][31]SF--
HALE "SPACE PROBE" '74
"STARFALL MUTA" '75
"RIFTS OF TIME"
KROLL, BURT--[1][28][31]WEST--
14 HALE NOVELS '66-81
LANGLEY, HELEN--[1][28][31]ROM--
GRESHAM "WHERE THE HEART LIES" '68
LANSING, HENRY--[1][28][31]WEST--
GRESHAM "BLEAK RANGE" '66
LANT, HARVEY--[1][28][31]WEST--
14 HALE NOVELS '66-83
LYNN, IRENE--[1][28][31]ROM--
5 GRESHAM NOVELS '68-80
MADISON, HANK--[1][28][31]WEST--
16 HALE NOVELS '66-84

ROWLAND, DONALD S.
MASON, CHUCK--[1][28]WEST--
18 HALE NOVELS '66-81
MCHUGH, STUART--[1][28]WEST--
5 HALE NOVELS '66-87
MORGAN, G.J.--[1][28]WEST--
FUTURA "HELL ON WHEELS"
"BORDER FURY"
"TRAIL OF DEATH" ALL '75
MORGAN, GLEBE--[1][28]WEST--
BELM "THE RAIL ROGUES" '80
MURRAY, EDNA--[9][21][28]ROM--
GRESHAM "NURSE IN DANGER"
9 MORE GRESHAM '68-70
PAGE, LORNA--[1][28]ROM--
6 GRESHAM NOVELS
2 HALE NOVELS '68-70
PATTERSON, OLIVE--[1][28]ROM--
5 GRESHAM NOVELS '68-71
PORTER, ALVIN--[1][28]WEST--
HALE NOVELS '66-82
RANDOM, ALEX--[2][7][11][23][28]SF--
HALE "STAR CLUSTER SEVEN" '74
HALE "CRADLE OF STARS" '75
HALE "DARK CONSTELLATION" '75
RIMMER, W.J.--[1][28]WEST--
HALE "THE SIDEWINDERS" '66
RIX, DONNA--[1][28]ROM--
8 HALE NOVELS '71-79
ROCKWELL, MATT--[1][28]WEST--
GRESHAM "TRIGGER HELP" '66
ROSCOE, CHARLES--[1][28]WEST--
8 HALE NOVELS '64-82
ROSSETTI, MINERVA--[1][28][34]MYS/ROM--
LENNOX HILL "HEIRESS TO CRAG CASTLE" '73
& MORE
SCOTT, NORFORD--[1][2]WEST--
13 HALE NOVELS '65-87
SCOTT, VALERIE [X]--[1][21][28]ROM--
HALE "SURROGATE WIFE" & 9 MORE HALE '71-79
SEGUNDO, BART--[1][28]WEST--
HALE "BOSS OF BORDER COUNTRY" '64
SHANE, BART--[1][28]WEST--
MAGREAD "IRON RAILS" '79
MAGREAD "RAILS WEST" '80
MAGREAD "RAILHEAD" '80
SHAUL, FRANK--[1][28]WEST--
6 HALE NOVELS '64-83
SPURR, CLINTON--[1][28]WEST--
19 HALE NOVELS '64-82
STARR, ROLAND--[2][7][11][23][28]SF--
HALE 'OMINA' SEQ: 3 BKS
1 LENNOX HILL '70-76
STEVENS, J.D.--[1][28]WEST--
4 HALE NOVELS '64-65
SUFFLING, MARK--[7][11][23][28]SF--
HALE "PROJECT OCEANUS" '75
HALE "SPACE CRUSADER" '75
TALBOT, KAY--[1][28]ROM--
7 GRESHAM NOVELS '68-70
TRAVERS, WILL--[1][28]WEST--
6 HALE NOVELS '64-84
VINE, SARAH--[1][28]ROM--
W&B "OVERSEAS NURSE" '69
VINSON, ELAINE--[1][28]ROM--
5 HALE NOVELS '71-73
WALTERS, RICK--[1][28]WEST--
GRESHAM "GUNSMOKE PASS" '66
WEBB, NEIL--[1][28]WEST--
16 HALE NOVELS '64-83

ROWLAND, MARCUS L.
LEE, MARK--[2]

ROWLAND-BROWN, LILIAN
ROWLAND, GREY--[1]

ROWLAND-ENTWISTLE, A.T.
BRIQUEBEC, JOHN--[1][33]
CLARKE, LEA--[31]
ELLIS, ANYON--[1][31][33]
ENTWISTLE, THEODORE ROWL.--[31]
HALL-CLARKE, JAMES--[1][31][33]
HENRY, T.E.--[1][31][33]
LAWRENCE, J.T.--[1][31][33]

ROWLANDS, CECIL
RALEIGH, CECIL--[3]MYS--
PAUL "SINS OF SOCIETY" '09

ROWLANDS, EFFIE
ALBANESI, MADAME--PPCC#4, P19

ROWSE, ALFRED LESLIE
ROWSE, A.L.--[1]

ROXLO, CONRADO NALE
CHAMICO--[20]SPANISH

ROY, ARCHIBALD EDMISTON
MALCOLM, ROY--W/DONALD MALCOLM,[2]
ROY, ARCHIE--[7][23]SF--
LONG "DEADLIGHT" '68
LONG "CURTAINED SLEEP" '69
LONG "ALL EVIL SHED AWAY" '70
LONG "SABLE NIGHT" '73
LONG "DARK HOST" '76
LONG "DEVIL IN THE DARKNESS" '78

ROY, EWELL PAUL
BONNETTE, VICTOR--[22][31]AMERICAN
LEMOINE, ERNEST--[22][31]AMERICAN

ROYDE-SMITH, NAOMI
SMITH, NAOMI G.--[40]MYS

ROZANOV, MICHAIL GRIGORV.
OGNEV, NIKOLAY--[22]RUSSIAN

RUBAHN, HORST-GUNTER
FAINE, CLAUDE--[39]GERMAN/SF--
KRUSE, IRIS--[39]GERMAN/SF--

RUBEL, JAMES LYON
HAYES, TIMOTHY--[1][8]
MACRAE, MASON--[1][8]

RUBEN, WILLIAM S.
SHANNON, FRED--[2][7][11][23]SF--
TWR "WEIGHTLESS IN GAZA" '70

RUBENACKER, THOMAS
ASHER, RODERICK--[39]GERMAN/HOR

RUBENSTEIN, SAMUEL L.
WEBER, RUBIN--W/ROBERT G. WEAVER,[1][3]MYS--
HARPER "GRAVEMAKER'S HOUSE" '64
WEST, PAMELA [ELIZABETH]--W/PAMELA W. KATKIN, [34]MYS--
ST. MARTINS "MADELEINE" '83
ST. MARTINS "YOURS TRULY, JACK THE RIPPER" '87
DEL RAY "20/20 VISION" '90

RUBENSTEIN, STANLEY JACK
AR, ESJAY--[8]

RUBIA BARCIA, JOSE
DE ROXAS, JUAN BARTOLOME--[31]--
"YRES en UNO:..." '40

RUBIN, CHARLES J.
BUZZLE, BUCK--[1][31]

RUBIN, CYNTHIA ELYCE
ALPLAUS, N.Y.--W/JEROME RUBIN,[1][31]

RUBIN, GAIL
BERENY, GAIL RUBIN--[1]

RUBIN, HAROLD
ROBBINS, HAROLD--[3][29]MYS--
KNOPF "NEVER LOVE A STRANGER" '48
MYFLWR "STILETTO" '69& MORE

RUBIN, JACOB A.
ODEM, J.--[22]AUSTRIAN-AMERICAN

RUBIN, JEROME
ALPLAUS, N.Y.--W/CYNTHIA ELYCE RUBIN,[1][31]

RUBINGTON, NORMAN
DEL PIOMBO, AKBAR--V. BERCH-PP 21/C. ECKHOFF SLST,[14]ADULT--
CITADEL "BOILER MAKER" '61
CITADEL "FUZZ AGAINST JUNK" '61
CITADEL "HERO MAKER" '61
OLYM TC-202 "COSIMO'S WIFE, OR THE VENGEANCE OF A DUKE" '67
OLYM TC-209 "WHO PUSHED PAULA?" '67
OLYM TC-204 "DOUBLE-BELLIED COMPANION" '67
OLYM TC-462 "HOUSE IN LODZ" '69
OLYM TC-491 "INTO THE HAREM" '70
OLYM OPS-25 "EROTIC TOOL" '71
PAIGE, LESLIE--[3]MYS--
BELM "A HOUSE POSSESSED"'74
BELM "QUEEN OF HEARTS" '74 & MORE

RUCH, HANS
GALL, ROBERT--[39]GERMAN

RUCHLIS, HYMAN
BARROW, GEORGE--[8]

RUCKER, RUDOLF VON BITTER
RUCKER, RUDY--[7][23]SF--
ACE "SEX SPHERE" '84
ACE "SOFTWARE" '82
AV "WETWARE" '88

RUD, ANTHONY M.
ANTHONY, R.--[2]

RUDAHL, SHARON
SATIVA, MARY--J. PRESSMAN--
CNTRCLTR, BAE 21,[14]ADULT--
OLYM TC#450 "ACID TEMPLE BALL" '69
OLYM OPS#23 "THE LOVER'S CRUSADE" '71

RUDAT, RICHARD J.
TJORNSEN, ALF--[39]GERMAN/SF,HP--

RUDEEN, ANNE & LOUISA
ELLIS, LEIGH--[7][9][21][26]SF/ROM--
AV "THE QUICK" '82
"GREEN LADY"
"TESSA OF DESTINY"

RUDHYAR, DANE
CHENNEVIERE, DANIEL--[31]

RUDNICK, PAUL
GELMAN-WAXNER, LIBBY--DEADLY PLEASURES #2, P4--
MOVIE REVIEW COLUMN IN "PREMIERE"

RUDNYCKYJ, JAROSLAV
BIJ-BIJCHENKO--[8]

RUDOLF, CURTIS D.
CURTIS, DONALD--[1]

RUDOLPH, LEE [N]
CUMMINGS, ANN--[1][31]

RUE, ROSINA F.
HART, NICOLE--[21]ROM--6 NOVELS

RUELLAN, ANDRE
DUPONT, KURT--[1][2][11]
LOUVIGNY, ANDRE--[1][2][11]
STEINER, KURT--[1][2][11]
VIGAN, LUC--[1][2][11]
WARGAR, KURT--[1][2][11]

RUGG, LESLIE
GILLETTE, LOUISA--W/GILDA FELDMAN,[9][26]ROM--
"GOLRIOUS TREASURE"
"RIVER TO RAPTURE" & MORE
HALE, MADELINE--W/GILDA FELDMAN,[9]ROM

RUGGEBERG, ANNELIES [B]
BOER, ANNELIES--[39]GERMAN/JUV

RUHEN, CARL
BAILEY, MARTHA--[35]AUSTRALIAN--
HRWTZ PB059 "SEX PARLOUR" '75
BENTLEY, MICHAEL--[35]AUSTRALIAN--
HRWTZ A0020 "WIFE SWAP PARTY" '71
BOURKE, TERRY--[35]AUSTRALIAN--
HRWTZ PB150 "CROCODILE" '78
HRWTZ PB156 "LITTLE BOY LOST" '78
BRAND, PETER--[35]AUSTRALIAN--
HRWTZ A044 "SENSOUS CRUISE" '73
HRWTZ A072 "ORGY" '73
HRWTZ A0131 "BIKIES' LUST" '74
HRWTZ PB078 "DEVIL'S OUTRIDERS" '75
HRWTZ PB080 "NIGGER STUD" '75
HRWTZ PB094 "BIKIE GIRL" '75
HRWTZ SP059 "ROGUE BLACK" '77
DIETRICH, WOLF--[35]AUSTRALIAN--
HORWITZ A024 "NAKED VAMPIRES" '71
FARR, CAROLINE--[35]AUSTRALIAN,HP--
HORWITZ/NAL-SIGNET - 5 NOVELS '78-80
HARRIS, MARK--[35]AUSTRALIAN--
HRWTZ A079 "SWINGING PARTNERS" '73
HRWTZ A080 "PIRAHHAS" '73
HRWTZ A0107 "SOCIETY STUD" '73
HRWTZ A0130 "GAY WAY" '74
HRWTZ PB096 "SEX FANS" '75
HRWTZ SP052 "BAR STUD" '76
HRWTZ SP058 "ORGY FARM" '77
HART, ALISON--[35]AUSTRALIAN--
2 SIGN BOOKS IN U.S.
HOPGOOD, ALAN--[35]AUSTRALIAN--
HRWTZ A0125 "ALVIN PURPLE" '74
LAW, SIMONE--[35]AUSTRALIAN--
HRWITZ A028 "SWAPPING PARTNERS" '72
HRWTZ A037 "WIFE SWAP INCORPORATED" '72
HRWTZ A038 "LESBIAN LOVE SLAVE" '72
HRWTZ A043 "NAKED VOYEUR" '73
HRWTZ A051 "GIRL FRIENDS" '73
HRWTZ PB029 "PORNO GIRLS" '74
HRWTZ PB079 "EROTIC CONFESSIONS OF MADAME LASH" '75
HRWTZ SP009 "THE SENSUAL SET" '76
RIDER, SAMANTHA--[35]AUSTRALIAN--
HRWTZ SP178 "THE PERFECT OH" '78
SLATER, JOHN--[35]AUSTRALIAN,HP--
HRWTZ "BEACH HOUSE CAPTIVE" '72
HRWTZ "SLAVE TERROR" '72
STEELE, SAMANTHA--[35]AUSTRALIAN--
HRWTZ A0132 "SEX SLAVE" '74
HRWTZ A0149 "WIFE SWAP ORGY" '74
HRWTZ PB063 "SEX BEACH" '75

RUHEN, CARL [CONT]
STEELE, SAMANTHA [CONT]
HRWTZ SP001 "BEACH PARTY" '76
HRWTZ SP035 "TERROR CRUISE" '76

RUIZ, JOSE MARTINEZ
AZORIN--[22]SPANISH

RUKAVINA-MORL, LEA
VON MORL, LEA--[39]GERMAN

RUKUJZO, RON
RUKUZA, E.W.--V. BERCH LTR TO HUBIN '94,MYS--
POPLB "WEST COAST TURNAROUND" '90

RULE, ANN
STACK, ANDY--[1]--
SEE SIGNET AE5477

RULER, ALEXANDER JOHN
ALEXANDER, JOHN--[1]

RUMBALL, CHARLES
DELORNE, CHARLES--[2]

RUMBOLD-GIBBS, HENRY
GIBBS, HENRY--[1][18][31]MYS--
JARROLDS "BAMBOO PRISON" '61
& 18 MORE '43-63
HARVESTER, SIMON--[34]MYS/ADV--
JARROLDS "CAT'S CRADLE" '52
& 43 MORE '42-74
SAXON, JOHN--[1]

RUMMEL, LOUIS JACKSON
CRAWFORD, HANK--[31]

RUMPFF, HEINRICH
IBACH, LUTZ W.--[39]GERMAN/MYS

RUNBECK, MARGARET LEE
MCKINLEY, KAREN--[8]

RUNCIMAN, JAMES C.S.
RUNCIMAN, STEVEN--[1]

RUNDLE, ANNE
BELL, GEORGIANNA--[1]
LAMONT, MARIANNE--[1][9][21][31]ROM--
MANNERS, ALEXANDRA--[2][3][9][21][31]MYS/ROM--
PUTNAM "SINGING SWANS" '75 & 2 MORE
MARSHALL, JOANNE--[3][9][21][26]MYS/ROM--
COLLINS "LAST ACT" '76
AV "WILD BOAR WOOD" '73 & 2 MORE
SANDERS, JEANNE--[1][9]ROM

RUNGE, LUISE LILY
VON BRANDT, LUISE--[39]GERMAN

RUNNEQUIST, AKE
AQVIST, RUNE--[29]MYS

RUNYON, ALFRED DAMON
RUNYON, DAMON--C. JACKSON-B&MC FEB '94,
[8][32]MYS--
15 DIGEST STORIES [EQMM, VB, SA & MM]

RUNYON, CHARLES W.
QUEEN, ELLERY--LACHMAN LST '94
FRANCIS M. NEVINS
WEST, MARK--[1][22]ADULT--
BEAC B421 "OFFICE AFFAIR" '61
BEAC B468 "OBJECT OF LUST" '62
BEAC B768X "HIS BOSS'S WIFE" '64

RUOGIER, MRS. GEORGE R.
HEYER, GEORGETTE--[29]MYS

RUPERT, RAPHAEL RUDOLPH
TATRAY, ISTVAN--[22]HUNGARIAN-IRISH

RUPP, AUGUSTUS
RAVEN, ANTHONY--[7]SF/HOR--
"THE OCCULT LOVECRAFT" 1975

RUPPERT, WALTER
PERTRUP, BERT--[39]GERMAN

RUPPRECHT, OLIVIA
RUSH, MALLORY--[26]ROM--
HARL "THE EROGENOUS ZONE"

RURIC, PETER
CAIN, PAUL--[1]

RUSH, MARK
CONWAY, NORMAN--[3]MYS--
CANYON "OMEGA OPERATION" '74
CANYON "OPERATION: ALPHA DEATH" '75

RUSH, NOEL
GARNETT, DAVID S.--[8]

RUSK, JAMES JR.
JAMES, HARRISON--M. WADLE '94,[34]MYS--
GROVE GP-0118 "ABDUCTION" '74
RPRT OF "BLACK ABDUCTOR"

RUSKIN, JOHN
GRADUATE OF OXFORD, A--[31]
KATAPHUSIN--[31]
PHUSIN, KATE--[1]

RUSO, MICHAEL
ROSCOE, MIKE--W/JOHN ROSCOE,[3][29]MYS--
CROWN "RIDDLE ME THIS, CLOWN" '52 & 2 MORE
CROWN "SLICE OF HELL" '54
ACE D273 "MIDNIGHT EYE" '58

RUSS, LAVINIA FAXON
FAXON, LAVINIA--[31][33]

RUSS, PETER
HEIMBORN, CARL--[39]GERMAN

RUSSELL, C.
CLIFFORD, MARTIN--[1]HP--
WOOD, GEOFFREY--[1]

RUSSELL, EDITH
KRANZ, EDITH--[39]GERMAN/JUV

RUSSELL, ELIZABETH MARY
ELIZABETH--[1]

RUSSELL, ERIC FRANK
CRAIG, WEBSTER--[2][11][15][23][31]SF--
KENT, BRAD--[23]SF--ONE STORY
MUNROE, DUNCAN H.--[2][11][23]SF--
WILDE, NIALL[E]--[2]

RUSSELL, ETHEL HARRIMAN
BORDEN, ETHEL--[1]

RUSSELL, G. OSCAR
RUSSELL, OSCAR GEORGE--[1]

RUSSELL, GEORGE WILLIAM
A.E.--[1][23][31]SF
ONLOOKER--[1]
RUSSELL, G.W.E.--[1]

RUSSELL, HANORA MARY
LEFY, NORA--[1]
LEVY, NORMA--[1]
RUSSELL, NORMA--[1]

RUSSELL, HENRY GEORGE
MINICAM--[8]

RUSSELL, JAMES
RUSSELL, JIM--[33]

RUSSELL, JOHN
THRICE, LUKE--[1][22]MYS--

RUSSELL, LINDSAY PATRICIA
QUINN, ETHEL--[1]

RUSSELL, MARTIN [JAMES]
ARNEY, JAMES--[3][18]MYS--
HALE "A VIEW TO RANSOM" '83
LESTER, MARK--[3][18][29][31]MYS--
HALE "TERROR TRADE" '76

RUSSELL, NORMA HULL LEWIS
HODGSON, NORMA--[1][22][31]ENGLISH

RUSSELL, RAY
RENCELAW, BRIAN--[1][1][2]
THORNE, ROGER--[1][2][11]

RUSSELL, ROY
GRESHAM, ANTONY--[31]

RUSSELL, SHIRLEY
KING, STEPHANIE--[8]
VERNON, MARJORIE--[8]

RUSSELL, SYBIL
GRAY, JANET--[9][21][26]ROM--
"HEARTS ARE WILD"

RUSSELL, URSULA D'IVRY
D'IVRY, URSULA--[8]

RUSSELL, VIRGINIA FAINE
FAINE, DJINN--[11][32]MYS--
SA "HAIR TRIGGER" JAN '62

RUSSELL, WALTER
O'CONNOR, LYNN--W/PAT MIALOCQ,[14]ADULT--
OLYM FP/2021

RUSSELL, WILLIAM
ENGLISH DETECTIVE--[1]
FRENCH DETECTIVE--[1]
INSPECTOR, F--[1][34]MYS--
SHARP, GUSTAVUS--[34]MYS--
CORNISH "CONFESSIONS OF AN ATTORNEY" 1852
WARNEFORD, LIEUTENANT--[34]MYS--
WARD "MUTINY OF SATURN & SEA STORIES"
BROWN "TALES OF THE COAST GUARD"
WARNER, WARREN--[34]MYS--
BROWN "EXPERIENCE OF A BARRISTER" 1856
WATERS--[1][5][34]MYS--
WARD "GAME OF LIFE" 1857 & 11 MORE
WATERS, C.--[1]
WATERS, THOMAS--[1]

RUSSELL, WILLIAM CLARK
BOOTH, MRS. LETITIA--[1]
MOSTYN, SYDNEY--[1]
SEAFARER--[1]

RUSSELL, WINIFRED BRENT
STAIR, VIRGINIA--[1][2]

RUSSENBERGER, MAX
LENZ, MAX WERNER--[39]GERMAN

RUSSI, LUCIANO
ELLERRE--[1]

RUSSO, ALBERT
ROVIN, ALEX--[1]

RUSTAMNASADE, SULIEMAN
RUSTAM, SULIEMAN--[1]
SULIMAN, RUSTAM--[1]

RUSTERHOLTZ, WINSOME LUCY
TURVEY, WINSOME--[8]

RUTGERS VAN DER LOEFF, AN
BAS, RUTGER--[1][31][33]

RUTHERFORD, EDWARD JAMES
RUTHERFORD, WARD--[1]

RUTHERFORD, PAT
HAYFORD, TANIA--W/JUNE HAYDON,[1]

RUTLEDGE, EDWARD WILLIAM
RUTLEDGE, DOM DENYS--[22]ENGLISH

RUTLEDGE, NANCY
BRYSON, LEIGH--[3][22][29]MYS--
HAN 60 "THE GLOVED HAND" '47

RUTT KAY, ARNOLD
SO, BERNAT--[1]

RUTT, RICHARD
TAE-YONG, RO--[22]ENGLISH

RUTTER, EILEEN JOYCE
CHANT, JOY--[1][7][31]SF--
ALLEN "GREY MANE OF MORNING" '83
UNWIN "WHEN VOIHA WAKES" '83

RYALL, WILLIAM BOLITHO
BOLITHO, WILLIAM--[1][22]ENGLISH

RYAN, DOROTHY [BARGER]
MILLER, DOROTHY--[1]

RYAN, ELIZABETH ANNE
RYAN, BETSY--[33]

RYAN, GEORGE
ANDREWS, SPIKE--V. BERCH LTR TO
A. HUBIN '93, MYS--
WARNER "TOWER OF BLOOD" '83
WARNER "CULT OF THE DAMNED" '83
WARNER "KIDNAP HOTEL" '83
WILLOUGHBY, LEE DAVIS--[21]ROM,HP--
DELL 'MKNG OF AMERICA' SERIES:
"SOLDIERS OF FORTUNE"

RYAN, JOHN D.
ERNEST, [BROTHER]--[1]

RYAN, JOHN FERGUS
THAMES, JACK--[1]

RYAN, MARAH ELLIS
MARTIN, ELLIS--[1]

RYAN, NAN HENDERSON
RYAN, NAN [NANCY]--[9][21]ROM

RYAN, PAUL WILLIAM
FINNEGAN, ROBERT--[3][22][29][31]MYS--
SIMON "BANDAGED NUDE" '46
SIMON "LYING LADIES" '46
SIMON "MANY A MONSTER" '48
QUIN, MIKE--[1][18][22]MYS--
"THE BIG STRIKE" '49
"ASHCAN THE M-PLAN" '38 & MORE

RYAN, WALTER C.
STORM, MICHAEL--V. BERCH LTR TO HUBIN '94, MYS--
MYH "CRY, TIGER!" '48
MYH "EDGE OF DANGER" '57
MYH "CHINA CANE" '59

RYAN, WILLIAM PATRICK
O'RIAIN, LIAM P.--[1]

RYBARCZYK, MARIO
LADIS, MARIO--[39]GERMAN

RYDBERG, ERNIE
BROUILLETTE, EMIL--[8]
MCCARY, REED--[8]

RYDELL, HELEN B.
RYDELL, FORBES--W/D.F. STANTON FORBES,[3]MYS--
4 NOVELS '59-63

RYDELL, WENDY
RYDELL, WENDELL--[8][33]

RYDEN, ERNEST EDWIN
AUGUSTSON, ERNEST--[31]

RYDER, EILEEN
GERARD, ELAINE--[1][31]

RYDER, MICHAEL LAWSON
LAWSON, MICHAEL--[8][31]
RYDER, M.L.--[31]

RYDER, VERA
COOK, VERA--[8]
MORTIMER, JUNE--[8]

RYDZYNSKI, MARIE R.
NICOLE, MARIE--[3][9][10][21][26]MYS/ROM--
HARL "THICK AS THIEVES" '85
"CODE NAME: LOVE" '85
CHARLES, MARIE--[9][21][26]ROM--
"SMOULDERING EMBERS"
"SCENES FROM THE HEART" & MORE
FERRARELLA, MARIE [R]--[9][26]ROM--
NAME LEGALLY CHANGED TO "FERRARELLA" ?
MICHAEL, MARIE--[9][21][26]ROM--
"IRRESISTABLE FORCES"
"NO WAY TO TREAT A LOVER" & MORE

RYHLICK, FRANK
RILEY, FRANK--[1][11]

RYNAS, STEPHEN A.
ARNETTE, STEPHEN--[11]
ARR, STEPHEN--[2]

RYNNE, ALICE
CURTAYNE, ALICE--[8]

RYWELL, MARTIN
HEMMINGWAY, TAYLOR--[1][22][31]AMERICAN
SEARS, DEANE--[1][22]AMERICAN

RZAEV, RASUL IBRAGIM
RASUL, RZA--[1]

SABEN, GERTRUDE C.S.
SABIN, GREGORY--W/FREDERICK EVELYN BURKITT,[1]

SABIN, LOUIS
BAINS, LARRY--[1][31][33]
BRANDT, KEITH--[1]
SANTREY, LOUIS--[1]

SABINE, WILLIAM HENRY
WHITE FRIAR--[1]

SABINI, JOHN ANTHONY
ANTHONY, JOHN--W/RONALD B. BECKETT,[1][22][31]

SABOTT, EDMUND
STOHR, PETRA--[39]GERMAN

SABRE, MEL R.
STAGG, DELANO--W/PAUL EIDEN, V. BERCH-MON PSEUDS, BAE 9,[1][8]--
MON 140 "GLORY JUMPERS" '59
MON 210 "BLOODY BEACHES" '61

SACCOMOMONO, MARYANNE
EARLITON, ROBERT--V. BERCH-BRNDN/BC PSEUDS, BAE 22, ADULT--

SACHER-MASOCH, LEOPOLD
ARAND, CHARLOTTE--[39]GERMAN/ADULT
VAN RODENBACH, ZOE--[39]GERMAN/ADULT

SACHS, JUDITH
CHASE, EMILY--[31][33]
DIAMOND, PETRA--[9][21][26][31]ROM--
"PLAY IT AGAIN, SAM"
"CONFIDENTIALLY YOURS" & MORE
DIAMOND, REBECCA--[31][33]
SAAL, JOCELYN--[33]
SARASIN, JENNIFER--[33]
SAXON, ANTONIA--[33]

SACHSE, WILLI RICHARD
BIG BEN--[39]GERMAN
MURR, JAN--[39]GERMAN
SNUT, HEIN--[39]GERMAN

SACKVILLE-WEST, VITA MARY
NICHOLSON, VICTORIA MARY--[1]
SACKVILLE-WEST, V.--B&M COLL #33, P12, ENGLISH/CHILDREN'S BOOKS '19-55
SACKVILLE-WEST, VITA--[21]ROM--
"CHALLENGE"
"THE EDWARDIANS"

SADGROVE, SIDNEY HENRY
TORRANCE, LEE--[8]

SADLER, CHRISTINE
COE, CHRISTINE SADLER--[31]

SADLER, CLARICE LAURENCE
LAURENCE, CLARICE--[1]

SADLER, GEOFFREY WILLIS
CALHOUN, WES--[28]WEST--
HALE "CHULO" '88
HALE "AT MUERTO SPRINGS" '89
HALE "TEXAS NIGHTHAWKS" '90
SADLER, GEOFF--[28]WEST
SADLER, JEFF--[28]WEST--
14 HALE NOVELS '81-90

SADLER, M.T.H.
SADLEIR, MICHAEL--[1]

SAFFORD, LESLIE A.
CAMPBELL, CAROLINE--[9][21][26]ROM--
"LOVE MASQUE"

SAFIR, BILL
SAFIRE, BILL--[1]

SAGE, BERNARD JANIN
CENTZ, P.C.--[1]

SAGE, PENNY
SAGE, SHERYL--W/SHERYL MCTAGGART,[26]ROM--
"PASSIONATE SURRENDER"

SAHER, PETER J.
MASTERO STORYTELLER--V. BERCH LTR TO HUBIN '94, MYS--
VANTAGE "WELCOME TO THE TORTURE CHAMBER" '82

SAINSBURY, NOEL E.
RICHARDS, HARVEY D.--[1]
WAYNE, DOROTHY--[1]

SAINT INNOCENT, MARQUIS
KAHLER, WOODLAND--[8]

SAINT, DORA JESSIE
READ, MISS--[1][22][33]ENGLISH

SAINT-DENIS, MICHEL JACQ.
DUCHESNE, JACQUES--[22][31]FRENCH-ENGLISH

SAINT-HILAIRE, P.B.
PAVITRA--[8]

SAIT, FAIK
ABASIYANIK, SAIT FAIK--[1]

SAKHARNOV, SVYATOSLAV
SAKHARNOV, S.--[33]

SAKLATVALA, BERAM
MARSH, HENRY--[8]

SALA, CHARLES
KLEIN, KARL--[1][31]
LEPETIT, CHARLES--[1][31]

SALAAM, KALAMU YA
FERDINAND, VALLERY III--[31]

SALAWAY, RALPH
FRAY, AL--[34]MYS--
GRAP 118 "AND KILL ONCE MORE" '55
DELL FE A146 "DICE SPELLED MURDER" '57
DELL FE A167 "BUILT FOR TROUBLE" '58
"COME BACK FOR MORE" '58
"DAMES GAME" '60

SALE, RICHARD [B]
ROBESON, KENNETH--[2]HP--
[STREET & SMITH]
ST. JOHN, JOHN--[1][22]AMERICAN

SALERNO, ANN
HURLEY, ANN--[9][21][26]ROM--
"HEARTS IN EXILE"
"A FAIR BREEZE" & MORE

SALESKI, KATHLEEN
SALESKI, BUFFY--[1]

SALLASKA, GEORGIA MYRTLE
BENEDICT, MYRTLE--[1]

SALLIS, SUSAN DIANA
MEADMORE, SUSAN--[33]

SALMON, ANNIE ELIZABETH
ASHLEY, ELIZABETH--[1][31][33]
MARTIN, NANCY--[1][33]

SALMON, GERALDINE GORDON
SARASIN, J.G.--[1][3][22]MYS--
HUTCH "CASPIAN SONG" '35
HUTCH "THE CORSAIR" '51 & 38 MORE '23-58

SALMON, P.R.
PANLAKE, RICHARD--[8]

SALMONSON, JESSICA AMANDA
KERR, JOSIAH--[2]
LEAN, PATRICK--[2]
LONG, JOY--[2]
SALMONSON, [JESSIE] AMOS--[2]ORIGINAL NAME

SALMONSON, JESSIE AMOS
SALMONSON, JESSICA AMANDA--[7]NAME LEGALLY CHANGED TO "JESSICA AMANDA", SF

SALOLA, EEERO
DIOGENES--[1]
LAURI--[1]
LAURI, PIKKU--[1]

SALOMON-DANIGER, MARGOT
DANIGER, MARGOT--[39]GERMAN

SALSBURY, NATE
IRELAND, BARON--[8]

SALTER, ALAN
REEVES, SAM--HAWK/WILLIAM LOVE INTRVW '93, MYS--NOVELS

SALTER, DONALD P.M.
PODMARSH, ROLLO--[1]

SALTUS, EDGAR EVERTON
VERELART, MYNDART--[1]

SALVA, SALOMON DE LA
CAMINO, JUAN DEL--[30]MEXICAN

SALVATO, SHARON ANNE
RAYMOND, ALICE--[7]SF--
CHART "THE PACT" '90
TAYLOR, DAY--W/CORNELIA M. PARKINSON, [9][21][26]ROM--
"BLACK SWAN"
"MOSS ROSE" & 2 MORE

SALZMAN, JOSEPH
LAERTES, JOSEPH--[1][31]
MICHAELS, JOE--[1]
ROBERTS, JOE--[1]

SALZMANN, FELIX
SALTEN, FELIX--[22]HUNGARIAN

SALZMANN, SIEGMUND
FINDER, MARTIN--[1][33]
SALTEN, FELIX--[2][33][39]GERMAN

SAMACHSON, JOSEPH
MILLER, JOHN--[22][29][33][34]MYS--
HALE "MURDER OF A PROFESSOR" '37
MORRISON, WILLIAM--[2][11][22][33]AMERICAN
STERLING, BRETT--[2][33]SF,HP--
CF "WORLDS TO COME" '43
CF "DAYS OF CREATION" '44

SAMALMAN, ALEXANDER
GARTH, WILL--[7][23]SF,HP--
"DR. CYCLOPS" '40

SAMARAKIS, ANTONIS
KYPRIANOS, IOSSIF--[1][31]

SAMBROT, WILLIAM
AYES, ANTHONY--[1][2][11][23]SF--
AYES, WILLIAM--[1][2][11][23]SF--
"ISLE OF FEAR & OTHER SF" '63

SAMDBERG, IZOLD I.
ZVEREV, ILIA--[1]

SAMMAN, FERN
POWELL, FERN--[8]

SAMMIS, JOHN
RUSSELL, PATRICK--[1][33]

SAMPLINER, LOUIS H.
BLADE, ALEXANDER--[1][2][11]SF,HP--
ZIFF-DAVIS

SAMPSON, EMMA K. SPEED
BAUM, L. FRANK--[33]GHOSTED
SANDERSON, MARGARET LOVE--[33]
SPEED, NELL--[1]

SAMPSON, RICHARD HENRY
HULL, RICHARD--[2][3][5][8][11][18][29][32]MYS--15 NOVELS '34-53
EQMM "MRS. BRIERLY SUPPLIES THE EVEIDENCE" APR '52

SAMS, JESSIE BENNETT
SAMS, VEANIE--[1]

SAMUEL, BARBARA
WIND, RUTH--[21][26]ROM--
"STRANGERS ON A TRAIN"
"JEZEBEL'S BLUES" & 3 MORE

SAMUEL, YESHUE
SAMUEL, ATHANASIUS--[1]

SAMUELS, PHILIP FRANCIS
SAMUELS, BACON--[1]

SAMUELSON-SANDVID, DOROT.
DORFY--[8]

SAMUELSSON, STURE
KAGG, PETER--[29]MYS

SAMWAYS, GEORGE R.
CLIFFORD, MARTIN--[1]HP--
CONQUEST, OWEN--[1]HP--
LINLEY, MARK--[1]
MASTERS, PAUL--[1]
PROCTOR, PAUL--[1]
RICHARDS, FRANK--[1]HP--
RICHMOND, GEORGE--[1]

SANBORN, DUANE
BRADLEY, DUANE--[8]

SANCHEZ, MORALES NARCISCO
ALETES--[1]
ANTEO--[1]
NARSANMOR--[1]

SANCTUARY, BRENDA
CAMPBELL, BRIDGET--[1]

SANDBERG, ALGOT GUSTAF O.
BATH, KARL--[29]MYS
CHAMFORD, FELIX--[29]MYS--
"GREVE FERSTENS SPANKSROR" '16

SANDBERG, CARL [AUGUST]
MILITANT--[33]
SANDBERG, CHARLES--[31]--
"JOSEFFY"

SANDBERG, DANNIS
NORNE, THOMAS--[29]MYS

SANDBERG, KERSTIN
SAND, KIRSTIN--[29]MYS--
GEBERS "HAR LIGGER EN HUND BEGRABEN" '56
"STILLA FLYTER AN..." '57

SANDBERG, PETER LARS
SANDBERG, BERENT--W/MARK BERENT,[3]MYS--
SIGN "BRASS DIAMONDS" '80
SIGN "HONEYCOMB BID" '81
SIGN "THE CHINESE SPUR" '83

SANDBLAD-HANESON, E.C.S.
TORPARE, TORD--[1]

SANDBORN, DUANE
BRADLEY, DUANE--[1][33]

SANDBURG, CARL [AUGUST]
MILITANT--[22]AMERICAN
PHILLIPS, JACK--[1][22][31][33]AMERICAN
SANDBURG, CHARLES A.--[1][22][31]AMERICAN--
"YOU & YOUR JOB"

SANDELL, ULLA
WILHELMSON, FRANCESKA--[29]MYS--
BONNIER "LOJTNANT JURGS SABEL" '45

SANDERFORD, NELL MARY
DUNN, NELL--[1][31]

SANDERLIN, OWENITA [H]
KENNEY, KATHRYN--[1][31]

SANDERS, CLINTON R.
LATEEF, TOLEN S.--[31]

SANDERS, DOROTHY LUCIE
DEAN, SHELLEY--[1][8]AUSTRALIAN
WALKER, LUCY--[8][9][13]AUSTRALIAN/ROM--
"TO DREAM OF EVIL"

SANDERS, HARLAN
COLONEL SANDERS--[31]

SANDERS, JAMES EDWARD
HOBART, BLACK--[22][31]AMERICAN
SANDERS, ED--[31]

SANDERS, JOHN
COMER, RALPH--[1][2][11]SF--

SANDERS, LAWRENCE
ANDRESS, LESLIE--[18][29][34]MYS--
PUTNAM "CAPER" '80
UPTON, MARK--[7][23][34]MYS/SF--
COWARD "DREAM LOVER" '78
COWARD "DARK SUMMER" '79

SANDERS, LEONARD M. JR.
THOMAS, DAN--[1][2][11][23]SF--
"THE SEED" '68

SANDERS, RICHARD
SANDERS, RICARDO--[39]GERMAN/ADV

SANDERS, WILLIAM
SUNDOWN, WILL--[7]SF--
POPLB "POCKETS #1 POCKETS OF RESISTANCE" '90
POPLB "POCKETS #2 HELLBOUND TRAIN" '90

SANDERSON, H.P.
CARR, JOAN--[1][2]

SANDERSON, IVAN TERENCE
ROBERTS, TERENCE--[1][2][32]MYS--
SA "BLACK MYS" APR '62
SA "BLACK MERCURY" JUN '63
SA "BLACK GENII" AUG '66
SA "BLACK ALLIES" MAR '67

SANDERSON, SABINA WARREN
FAWCETT, MARION--[31]

SANDERSON, [R] DOUGLAS
BRETT, MARTIN--[1][22][34]MYS--
DODD "DARKER TRAFFIC" '54
POPLB "FLEE FRO TERROR" '57 & 3 MORE
DOUGLAS, MALCOLM--[8][29][34][40]MYS--
GM 477 "PREY BY NIGHT" '55
GM 539 "RAIN OF TERROR" 56
GM 614 "DEADLY DAMES" '56
GM 654 "PURE SWEET HELL" '57
GM 776 "MURDER COMES CALLING" '58

SANDES, JOHN
ORIEL--[8]

SANDFIELD, LAURENCE
MANDERS, JOHN F.--[2]
MONTAGUE, MERYL ST. JOHN--[2]

SANDFORD, CHRISTOPHER
VON DANSDORF, CHRYSILLA--[8]

SANDFORD, MATTHEW
MATT--[8]

SANDIFER, LINDA PROPHET
SANDIFER, LINDA P.--[21]ROM--
"HEART OF THE HUNTER"
"TYLER'S WOMAN"
"PRIDE'S PASSION"

SANDLIN, JOANN S. DE L.
DE LORA, JOANN S.--[31]

SANDMAN, PETER M.
DAVID, WILLIAM--[1][31]

SANDOZ, MARI[E SUSETTE]
MACUMBER, MARI--[1][33]

SANDS, CHRIST. N. JOHNST.
JOHNSTON, CHRISTOPHER N.--[3]MYS--
"MAJOR OWEN & OTHER TALES" '09

SANDS, LEO GEORGE
CRAIG, LEE--[8][22][31]AMERICAN
HELMI, JACK--[8][22][31]AMERICAN
HERMAN, JACK--[8]AMERICAN
MEURON, SKIP--[8]AMERICAN
HELMI, JACK--[31]

SANDSTROM, EVE K.
STORM, ELIZABETH--[10][21][26][34]MYS/ROM--
HARL 93 "FIRING LINE" '88

SANDWINA, ALFRED HEYMANN
SANDOR, ALFRED--[1]

SANDYS, STEPHEN
SANDY, STEPHEN--[1]

SANFORD, ANNETTE [S]
CARROLL, MARY--[9][21][26]ROM--
"DIVIDE THE WIND"
"MIDNIGHT SUN" & MORE
DOMINIQUE, MEG--[9][21][31]ROM--
SAND CASTLES"
"REBEL HEART" & MORE
SHORE, ANNE--[9][21][26]ROM--
"FARAWAY LAND"
"VALLEY OF THE BUTTERFLIES" & MORE
ST. JOHN, LISA--[9][21][26]ROM--
"GOSSAMER MAGIC"
"STARFIRE"
STARR, ANNE--[9][21][26]ROM--
"A TIME FOR LOVING"
"COME KISS A STRANGER" & MORE

SANGSTER, JIMMY
SANSOM, JOHN--W/ALFRED EDGAR,[1][2]][11]

SANKE, MARGIT
FRANK, DR. STEFAN--[39]GERMAN/HP--
VON JOSTEN, JUTTA--[39]GERMAN

SANOJO, ANA TERESA PARRA
DE LA PARRA, TERESA--[22]VENEZUELAN

SANS, MARTHA
LORING, JENNY--[9][21][26]ROM--
HARL 388 "INTERLUDE"
"CHEYENNE HERO"
SAWYER, LEE--[9][21][26]ROM--
"TIME REMEMBERED"

SANSON, KIRK
PENDLETON, DON--[34]MYS,HP--
GE "SUDAN SLAUGHTER" '89
GE "TWISTED PATH" '89
GE "WHITE LINE WAR" '90

SANTESSON, HANS STEFAN
BOND, STEPHEN--LACHMAN LST '93,[32]MYS--
SA "I KNOW YOU'D DO THE SAME FOR ME" SEPT '56
SA "IT IS NOT POSSIBLE" MAR '57
SA "CHINATOWN EVENING" SEPT '67
O'QUINN, VITHALDAS--[2]
O'QUINN, VITHALDAS H.--[1][11]
SANTESSON, H.S.--[1]
STEPHENS, JOHN--LACHMAN LST '93,[32]MYS--
PE "VENGEANCE" JUL '53
SA "ST. PETERSBURG" MAR '63
SB "DEATH IS MY BROTHER" APR '61
SA "TEMPTATION OF A MARQUIS" DEC '64
SA "MISS CLARISSA & THE RAINCOAT" AUG '66

SANTORI, HELEN
ERSKINE, HELEN--[9][21][26]ROM--
"FORTUNES OF LOVE"

SANTOS, HELEN
GRIFFITHS, HELEN--[1]

SAPIEYEVSKI, ANNE LINDBERG
FEYDE, ANNE--[1]
FEYDY, ANNE LINDBERG--[7]SF--
SEE "ANNE LINDBERG"
LINDBERG, ANNE--[1][7][33]SF--
'PINEAPPLE PLACE' #1 & 2 '82-8
"BAILEY'S WIDOW" '84

SARFATTI, MARGHERITA
CIDIE--[22]ITALIAN
EL SERENO--[22]ITALIAN

SARG, ANTHONY FREDRICK
SARG, TONY--[33]

SARGENT, GENEVIEVE
GINGER--[8]

SARGIDZHAN, AMIR
BORODIN, SERGEY PETROVICH--[22]RUSSIAN

SARIOLA, MAURI
LAUKKO, ESKO--W/TUULA KORPELA,[29]MYS

SARJEANT, W.A.S.
SWITHIN, ANTHONY-- GRANT THIESSEN CONFIRM W/AUTHOR

SARLE, CHARLES SPENSER
AMORY, ARTHUR R.--[1]

SARMIENTO, FELIX RUBEN G.
DARIO, RUBEN--[20][31]SPANISH

SAROYAN, WILLIAM
GORYAN, SIRAK--[6][22][31][33]AMERICAN

SARTE, JEAN-PAUL
GULLEMIN, JACQUES--[1][31]

SARTON, [ELEANOR] MAY
SARTON, ELEANOR MARIE--[1]

SASEEN, SHARON [DILLON]
DILLON, SHARON SASEEN--[31][33]

SASS, EUGEN v.
TOVARDS, JOHN--[39]GERMAN

SASSE, GERHARD
ELM, JONATHAN--[39]GERMAN/MYS--
HARDEN, FRED--[39]GERMAN/MYS--
WAGNER, HARRY--[39]GERMAN/MYS--

SASSOON, SIEGFRIED [L]
ANONYMOUS--[31]POETRY '06-16
KAIN, SAUL--[1][31]--
RICHMOND "THE DAFFODIL MURDER, BEING THE CHANTRY PRIZE POEM" '13
LYRE, PINCHBECK--[1][31]--
DUCKWORTH "POEMS" '31
S.S.--[8][31]--
GOLDEN HEAD PRESS "AN ADJUSTMENT" '55
SASHUN, SIGMUND--[1]
TAK YUSSUF HOFF--[1]

SASULY, RICHARD
FURTH, ALEX--[1][31]

SATERNAS, MARTA
CORAY, M.--[39]GERMAN

SATHER, JULIA COLEY D.
DUNCAN, JULIA COLEY--[1][31]

SATHERLEY, DAVID
WHITELAND, SATHERLEY--W/JAMES WHITEHAND,[8]

SATO, JUNYA
RANCE, JOSEPH--W/TREVOR HOYLE & RYUNOSUKE ONO, V. BERCH LTR TO HUBIN '94, MYS--
SVNR "BULLET TRAIN" '80

SATTER, MARLENE Y.
BARWOOD, LEE--[2]

SAUER, MURIEL STRAFFORD
STRAFFORD, MURIEL--[22]AMERICAN/MAGAZINE & NEWSPAPER

SAUL, MILTON
FLINDERS, KARL--[14]ADULT--
OLYM OPS#32 "MAKING THE PRESIDENT" '71
OLYM OPH#183 "TWELVE INCHES" '69
OLYM OPH#194 "TWELVE INCHES PLUS" '70
OLYMOPH#196 "TO SEDUCE AN ARMY" '70
OLYM OPH#190 "TWELVE INCHES WITH A VENGEANCE" '70
OLYM TC#487 "WIFE INTO WANTON" '70
OLYM TC#508 "UP DADDY" '71
OLYM OPS#24 "LOVE MACHINERY" '71
OLYM OPH #237 "TWELVE INCHES AROUND THE WORLD" '71
OLYM OPS#24 "THE LOVE MACHINERY" '71
OLYM TC#516 "THE BOY AVENGERS" '72

SAUL, OSCAR
RIVERA, PICO--W/HARRY ESSEX, CRPG--
DELL 1147 "THE AMIGOS" '75

SAUNDERS, ANN LOREILLE
COX-JOHNSON, ANN--[1][31]

SAUNDERS, CICELY
STRODE, MARY--[8]

SAUNDERS, CLARE CASTLER
LEE, BABS--W/MARION V.D.M. LEE,[34]MYS--
SCRIBNER "MEASURED FOR MURDER" '44

SAUNDERS, HILARY A.
BEEDING, FRANCIS--W/JOHN PALMER, [3][5][18][32]MYS--34 NVLS '25-43
EQMM "CONDEMNED" JUL '49
BROWNE, BARUM--W/GEOFFREY DENNIS, [7][18][31][34]MYS--
GOLZ "DEVIL & X.Y.Z." '31
COFYN, CORNELIUS--W/JOHN DEVERE LODER, [18][29][31][34]MYS--
GOLZ "DEATH RIDERS" '35
PILGRIM, DAVID--W/JOHN LESLIE PALMER, [18][22][34]MYS--
MacM "EMPEROR'S SERVANT" '46

SAUNDERS, JEAN
SUMMERS, ROWENA--[9][21][26]ROM--
"CLAY COUNTRY"
"KILLIGREW CLAY"
"SAVAGE MOON"

SAUNDERS, JEAN INNES
BLAKE, SALLY--[1][9][31]ROM--
INNES, JEAN--[9][21][26][31]ROM--
"SILVER LADY"
"TROPICAL FIRE" & MORE

SAUNDERS, MARGARET BELL
BELL, MARGARET--[1][8]

SAUNDERS, MARGARET MARSH.
SAUNDERS, MARSHALL--[8]

SAUNDERS, SUSAN
HUGHES, SARA--[1][33]

SAUNDERS, THEODORE
SCOTT, DENIS--W/MARY MEANS,[3][22]MYS--
BOBBS "MURDER MAKES A VILLAIN" '44
"BECKONING SHADOW" '46

SAUNDERS, WILLIAM
SUNDOWN, WILL--GARY LOVISI REVIEW '93

SAUPE, DIETER
CAMERON, JOHN--[39]GERMAN/MYS/HOR,HP
DE LORCA, FRANK--[39]GERMAN/MYS/HOR
ELLIOT, BRUCE--[39]GERMAN/MYS/HOR
LAMONT, ROBERT--[39]GERMAN/HOR

SAURA [ATARES], CARLOS
ATARES, CARLOS SAURA--[31]

SAUSER-HALL, FREDERIC
CENDRARS, BLAISE--[1][31]FRENCH--
NOVELS & POEMS

SAUTEL, MAUREEN ANN
MCGINN, MAUREEN ANN--[1]

SAUVAGEAU, JUAN
LAVOIX, JEAN--[1]

SAVAGE, ETHEL MAE DELL
DELL, ETHEL M.--[1]

SAVAGE, LESLIE H. JR
SAVAGE, THOMAS--L. ROBBINS LTR '94--
SIGN 728 "LONA HANSON" '49
BB 1608 "THE PASS" '57
SAVAGE, LES JR.--[1][28]WEST--
GM 111 "WILD HORSE" '50
DELL FE23 "TERESA" '54
GM 411 "BLACK HORSE CANYON" '54
DELL FE37 "LAST OF THE BREED" '54
DELL FE65 "RETURN TO WARBOW" '55
ASE 1239 "TREASURE OF THE BRASADA" nd
BAL 181 "HANGTOWN" '56 & MORE
STEWART, LOGAN--V. BERCH-GM PSEUDS, PP 33,
[1]WEST--
GM 137 "WARBONNET PASS" '50
GM 182 "THEY DIED HEALTHY" '51
GM 193 "THE TRAIL" 51
GM 243 "SECRET RIDER" '52
GM 327 "SAVAGE STRONGHOLD" '53
GM 367 "RAILS WEST" '54
SUTTER, LARABIE--V. BERCH-GM PSEUDS,
PP 33,[28]WEST--
GM 255 "THE WHITE SQUAW" '52

SAVAGE, MILDRED [SPITZ]
BARRIE, JANE--[1][31]

SAVAGE, TERESA
MCGEE, T.D.--[1]

SAVANE, VIRGILE
SALAVINA--[1]

SAVERY, CONSTANCE W.
CLOBERRY, ELIZABETH--[1]
RYCON--[1]

SAVERY, HENRY
STUKELEY, SIMON--[13]AUSTRALIAN

SAVI, ETHEL WINIFRED B.
SAVI, E.W.--[1]

SAVILE, FRANK [MACKENZIE]
ELIVAS, KNARF--[23]SF--
"BEYOND THE GREAT SOUTH WALL"

SAVILL, ROY
STACEY, PAUL--[1]

SAVINKOV, BORIS VIKTOR.
ROPSHIN--[22]RUSSIAN
ROPSHIN, V.--[1]

SAWKINS, RAYMOND [H]
BERNARD, JAY--[29][31][34]MYS--
HRCT "THE BURNING FUSE" '70
FORBES, COLIN--[11][29][31][34]MYS--
COLLINS "TRAMP IN ARMOR" '69
COLLINS "TARGET FIVE" '73
COLLINS "YEAR OF THE GOLDEN APE" '74
COLLINS "TERMINAL" '84
COLLINS "DEADLOCK" '88
COLLINS "GREEK KEY" '89
PAN "SHOCKWAVE" '90
RAINE, RICHARD--[1][3]MYS--
DENT "BOMBSHELL" '70
HM "NIGHT OF THE HAWK" '68 & 1 MORE

SAWYER, CORINE HOLT
RICKERT, CORINE HOLT--[1][22]AMERICAN

SAWYER, EUGENE TAYLOR
CARTER, NICHOLAS--[1][3][5][11]MYS,HP--
COLLIER, OLD CAP--[1]SP

SAWYER, JOHN & NANCY
ABBEY, CHRISTINA--[9][21][26]ROM--
"PATTERN FOR LOVING"
"TIME FOR TRUSTING"
BUCKINGHAM, NANCY--[3][17][26]MYS/ROM--
HALE "HEART OF MARBLE" '67
"QUEST FOR ALEXIS" '74 & 17 MORE
JOHN, NANCY--[9][17][21][26]ROM--
"OUTBACK SUMMER"
"MOONGATE WISH" & 16 MORE
LONDON, HILARY--[9][21][26]ROM--
"SCENT OF GOLD"
QUEST, ERICA--[9][17][34]MYS/ROM--
DBLDY "SILVER CASTLE" '78
DBLDY "OCTOBER CABARET" '79
DBLDY "DESIGN FOR MURDER" '81
DBLDY "DEATH WALK" '88
DBLDY "COLD COFFIN" '90

SAWYER, WALTER LEON
STANDISH, WINN--[1]

SAXBY, [HENRY] MAURICE
SAXBY, H.M.--[33]

SAXE, JOHN GODFREY
X.Y.Z. CLUB--W/DOUGLAS A. LIVEN & GEORGE
W. PETTES,[1]

SAXEGAARD, ANNIK
BRATT, BERTE--[39]GERMAN/JUV

SAXON, GLADYS RELYEA
BORDEN, M.--[1][22][31]AMERICAN
SEYTON, MARION--[1][22]AMERICAN

SAXON, RICHARD
RICHARDS, HENRY--[11]

SAXON, SOPHIA
JARRETT, KAY--[8]

SAXTON, JOSEPHINE
HOWARD, JAY--[2]

SAYER, NANCY MARGETTS
BRADFIELD, NANCY--[1]

SAYER, WALTER WILLIAM
QUIROULE, PIERRE--[1][3]MYS--
NELSON "PAINTED DEATH" '35
NELSON "HATED EIGHT" '38 & 15 MORE
SAYER, WAL--[1]

SAYERS, DOROTHY L[EIGH]
LEIGH, JOHANNA--[1][22][29]ENGLISH
RALLENTANDO, H.P.--[1]

SAYERS, JAMES DENSON
BARDWELL, DENVER--[1][28]WEST--
FWN 5 "COYOTE HUNTER" nd
GWN 10 "PRAIRIE FIRE" nd
WNMnn "GUNSMOKE IN SUNSET VALLEY" nd
JAMES, DAN--[1][8][28]WEST--
FWN 7 "STRANGER AT STORM RANCH" nd
FWN 10 "GUN THUNDER ON THE RIO" nd
PYR 269 "GUNSMOKE MESA" '57
WNMnn "RANCHO BONITO" nd

SAYLER, HARRY L.
LAMAR, ASHTON--[1]
SAYLER, H.L.--[1]
STUART, GORDON--[1]
WHITNEY, ELLIOTT--W/HENRY BEDFORD-JONES,[1]

SAYLES, EDWIN BOOTH
SAYLES, TED--[1]

SAYRE, CHERYL CURRY
CURRY, CHRIS--W/L. DEAN JAMES,[7]SF--
POCK "WINTER SCREAM" '91

SBURNIK, YAKOFF
ORAN, JACK--[1]

SCAFIDEL, JAMES R.
JARRETT, AMANDA JEAN--[21]ROM,HP--
DELL 'SOUTHERNER' SERIES:
"THE PASSION & THE FURY"
PHILLIPS, LYN--[7][21]SF/ROM--
DELL "TOMB OF THE SHROUD" '83
TOR "THE GAME" '82
"IF THE FLESH BE WILLING"
RAYMOND, JAMES--[21][26]ROM--
'AMERICAN EXPLORER' SERIES:
"LEWIS & CLARK, NORTHWEST GLORY"
SCOFIELD, JONATHAN--[21]ROM,HP--
DELL 'FREED FTR' SERIES:
"FAR SHORES OF DANGER"
WILLOUGHBY, LEE DAVIS--[21]ROM,HP--
DELL'MAKING OF AMER' SERIES:
"SOONERS"
"ASSASSINS"
DELL 'MAKING OF THE CITIES'SERIES:
"BATON ROUGE"

SCAIFE, ARTHUR HODGKIN
BILIR, KIM--[3]MYS--
PROVINCE "THREE LETTERS OF CREDIT
& OTHER STORIES" 1894

SCALES, LISA
NICHOLS, JANE--[9]ROM

SCALLY, MARY PAULINE
SCALLY, M.A.--[1]
SCALLY, [SIS]MARY ANTHONY--[1]

SCAMEHORN, MARY KATHRYN
BLAIR, KATHRYN--W/KARE B. PARKER,[9][21]ROM--
"HOME IS THE SAILOR"
"DANCING IN THE AISLES" & MOR

SCAMMEL, MICHAEL
LE MARQUE, MICHEL--[14]ADULT--
OLYM-TRANSLATOR OF "MOSCOW NIGHTS" ALSO
SUSPECTED TO BE "VLAS TENIN"

SCAMMELL, BILL
ARCHITECHS ADVENTURE--W/RICHARD MEYER
WALTER & LISA HUNT/EVAN JAMIESON/
MARK BLOOM/CHRISTINE IVEY,[7]

SCANNELL, JOHANNES PETRUS
SCANNELL, JAN--[1]

SCANTLIN, BEA
STEWART, RUTH--[9][21][26]ROM--
"ASK ME NO SECRETS"

SCANTREL, FELIX-ANDRE-YVE
SUARES, ANDRE--[22]FRENCH

SCARBERRY, ALMA SIOUX
FAIRFAX, BEATRICE--[31]HP
LAURIE, ANNIE--W/WINIFRED BLACK,[31]

SCARBOROUGH, CHARLES B.
SCARBOROUGH, CHUCK--[7]SF--
COWARD "THE MYRMIDON PROJECT" '81

SCARBOROUGH, GEORGE
PHILIPS, PAGE--[29]MYS--
MCL "AT BAY" '16

SCARF, MAGGIE
SCARF, MAGGI--[1][33]

SCARNE, JOHN
ORLANDO, PIETRO--[1]
VIRTUOUS, CARD SHARK--[1]

SCARRY, PATRICIA [M]
ROY, LIAM--[1][22][31][33]CANADIAN--
CHILDREN'S BOOKS
SCARRY, PATSY--[31][33]CHILDREN'S BOOKS

SCARRY, RICHARD JR.
SCARRY, HUCK--[1][33]

SCHAAF, MARILYN B.G.
GOFFSTEIN, M.G.--[1]

SCHAAKE, ERICH
BROCK, PETER--[39][40]GERMAN/MYS--
"DER BLONDE KHAN" '81
"DER BULLE" '81
TRAVIS, GORDON--[39][40]GERMAN/MYS--
"DER DUKE" '88

SCHAAL, ELIZABETH
SHELLEY, ELIZABETH--W/ELAINE CACHANTH,
[9][21]ROM--
"CARAVAN OF DESIRE"

SCHACHNER, NATHAN
CORBETT, CHAN--[2][11][23][31]SF-- PULP
GLAMIS, WALTER--[2][11][23][31]SF--PULP
SCHACHNER, NAT--L. ROBBINS LTR '94,[31]
[32]MYS--
WR "THE DEAD-ALIVE" WINT '69 [W/ZAGAT]

SCHACHTEL, ROGER BERNARD
FORRESTER, MARIAN--[31][33]

SCHACHTERLE, NANCY [L]
LAING, ANNE C.--[1][31]

SCHADE-HADICKE, JOSEFINE
SCHONERMARK, J.--[39]GERMAN

SCHADLICH, GOTTFRIED
NOXIUS, FRED--[39][40]GERMAN/MYS--
"DER GEISTERPFAD" '66
"KENN WORT SCHWARZER BRUMMER" '68
NOXIUS, FRIED--[39]GERMAN/JUV
SUIXON, G.F.W.--[39]GERMAN/JUV

SCHAEF, CONRAD C.
CHESTER, ROY--[39]GERMAN/SF
SHEPHERD, CONRAD--[39]GERMAN/SF

SCHAEFER, FRANK
CARROL, SHANA--W/KERRY NEWCOMB,
[9][21][26][31]ROM--
"RAVEN"
"YELLOW ROSE" & 3 MORE
GENTRY, PETER--W/KERRY NEWCOMB,
[9][21][26][31]ROM--
"MATANZA"
"TITUS GAMBLE" & MORE
SAVAGE, CHRISTINA--W/KERRY NEWCOMB,
[9][21][26]ROM--
"TEMPEST"
"DAWN WIND" & MORE

SCHAEFER, HILDEGARD
GARDENER, HILDE--[1]

SCHAETZEL, WENDY
LESKO, WENDY--[31]

SCHAFER, MAX
ALA, JOHN--[39]GERMAN/JUV
SILL, PETER--[39]GERMAN/JUV

SCHAFER, ROBERT
LAUREEN, PATRICIA--[39]GERMAN/JUV

SCHAFFER, JUTTA [W]
WESTPHAL, JUTTA--[39]GERMAN

SCHAKOVSKOY, ZINAIDA
CROISE, JACQUES--[1][22]RUSSIAN-FRENCH

SCHALDENBRAND, MARY
ALOYSIUS, SISTER MARY--[31]

SCHAMSKI, TAMMY
LEIGH, TAMARA--[26]ROM--
"WARRIOR BRIDE"
"PAGAN BRIDE"
"SAXON BRIDE"

SCHARF, MARIAN
CARROLL, MALISSA--W/CAROL I. WAGNER,
[9][21]ROM--
"MATCH MADE IN HEAVEN" & MORE

SCHARLEMANN, DOROTHY H.
SHARON, DONNA HAYE--[1]

SCHATTNER, E.
CHURCH, EMMA--[9][21][26]ROM--
"HEART REMEMBERS"
"SAPPHIRE SECRETS"
GRAHAM, ELIZABETH--[9][21][26]ROM--
"DANGEROUS TIDE"
"THIEF OF COPPER CANYON" & MORE

SCHATTSCHNEIDER, PETER
LOIKAJA, THOMAS--[39]GERMAN/SF

SCHATZ, EDWARD R.
EDWARDS, BOB--[39]GERMAN/SF
ROBERTI, EDUARDO--[39]GERMAN/SF
WARD, ROB--[39]GERMAN/SF

SCHATZLER-PERASINI, GEBH.
PERA, IRA--[39]GERMAN
RENE, GASTON--[39]GERMAN
ROBERTS, MARK--[39]GERMAN

SCHAUBELT, FRANZ JOSEPH
JOSEPH, FRANZ--[1][7][31]SF--
"STAR FLEET TECHNICAL MANUAL" '75

SCHAUER, HERBERT
BAUER, BERT--[39]GERMAN/MYS

SCHAUFFLER, MARGARET WID.
WIDDEMER, MARGARET--[1]

SCHAUMANN, JOCHEN
ISELER, JO--[39]GERMAN/MYS

SCHAUMMBURG, PAUL
BURG, PAUL--[1][21]GERMAN

SCHAUWECKER, EVA
KARX, PETER--[39]GERMAN/JUV
KARZ, EVA--[39]GERMAN/JUV

SCHECHTER, HAROLD
HARRALD, JON A.--W/GORMELY SEMEIKS,
V. BERCH LTR TO HUBIN '94, MYS--

SCHECTER, WILLIAM
WILLIAMS, CHESTER--[1]

SCHECTER, WINIFRED MORRIS
MORRIS, WINIFRED--[7]SF--
ATHNM "WITH MAGICAL HORSES TO RIDE" '85

SCHEER, KARL-HERBERT
DE CHALON, PIERRE--[39]GERMAN/MYS/SF
KERSTEN, ROGER--[39]GERMAN/MYS/SF
SCHEER, K.H.--[23]SF--
'PERRY RHODAN':#62, 67, 78, 80, 88, 92,
99, 108, 112, 117, 126 & 136
TURBOJEW, ALEXEJ--[1][2][11]

SCHEFFAUER, HERMAN GEORGE
ORCHELLA, R.L.--[22]GERMAN-AMERICAN

SCHEIN, RUTH ROBBINS
ROBBINS, RUTH--[1]

SCHEIRMAN, MARIAM
DAY, LUCINDA--W/MARIE FLASSCHOEN,
[9][21][26]ROM--
"GATES OF THE SUN"
"ALOHA, MY LOVE"

SCHELL, ROLFE F.
SCHELL, BURNY--[1]

SCHELLER, ALEKSANDRO K.
MIKHAILOV, A.--[1]

SCHEMM, MILDRED WALKER
WALKER, MILDRED--[33]

SCHENCK, ANITA A.
ALLEN, ANITA--[21][26][31]ROM--
"FALSE FACE OF DEATH"
"SPELL OF GHOTI"
"THUNDER ROCK"

SCHENCK, BARBARA
MCALLISTER, ANNE--[9][26]ROM--
HARL 1620 "CALL UP THE WIND"
"COWBOYS DON'T CRY" & OTHERS

SCHENK, JOYCE
LAWRENCE, AMY--[21]ROM--
"ANDREA"
"BLUES FOR CASSANDRA"
"COLOR IT LOVE"
"MADLY IN LOVE"
STEWART, JO--[21]ROM--
"THE LOVE VOTE"
"THE LOVE CONTEST"

SCHEPP, CHRISTIAAN LOUIS
PRINS, JAN--[22]DUTCH

SCHERE, JEAN K. & MONROE
HOWARD, JESSICA--[9][21]ROM--
"SAVAGE EMBRACE"
"PRAIRIE FLAME"
"TRAITOR'S WIFE"

SCHERE, MONROE
SUMMERHILL, J.K.--[1]
WINTER, ABIGAIL--[1][3][26]ROM--
DELL "OLIVIA'S STORY" '76
"THE SMILING DRAGON"

SCHERER, JEAN-MARIE MAUR.
CORDIER, GILBERT--[31]

SCHERMERHORN, DUANE R.
MARCOTT, JAMES--[1][3][29]MYS--
SIMON "WHISPERING CARAVANS" '74
GM "HARD TO KILL" '75

SCHERMERHORN, STEPHEN
TANNER, JAKE--W/LAURA MUSEO, LACHMAN-
EASTER LST/DDLY PLEAS #3, MYS--
"OLD BLACK MAGIC" '91

SCHERR, MARIE
CHER, MARIE--[1][2]

SCHEUTZ, TORSTEN V.
MARKLAND, PETER--W/ALLAN SCHULMAN,[29]MYS--
RABEN & SJORGEN "JAKT I ROD DIMMA" '54

SCHEVE, LIDA CLARA
BLAKE, MARGARET--[1]

SCHIAPARELLI, ELSA
SCHIAP--[1]

SCHICKEL, JULIA WHEDON
WHEDON, JULIA--[1]

SCHICKELE, PETER
BACH, P.D.Q.--[31]

SCHIER, NORMA
CANOY, E. ALDON--M. LACHMAN--
EQMM "ADVENTURE OF THE SOLITARY
BRIDE" FEB '93
CANTREE, WALTER--[32]MYS--
EQMM "F AS IN FRAUD" JUL '70
GRAINGERHILL, AMY M.--[32]MYS--
EQMM "MR. COPABLE, CRIMINOLOGIST" AUG '67
GREENSTOCK, H.T.--M. LACHMAN, MYS--
EQMM "INCREDUALITY OF BR.
FANEWORTH" AUG '94
HAIGS, NORMA--[32]MYS--
EQMM "IF HANGMAN TREADS" AUG '65

SCHIER, NORMA [CONT]
JORRICKS, HANDON C.--[32]MYS--
EQMM "HOCUS-POCUS AT DRUMIS TREE" APR '66
LOBSTER, RIF H.--M. LACHMAN, MYS--
EQMM "ADVENTURE OF THE BOING!
RITUAL" FEB '93
MCNEISH, NEIL--[32]MYS--
EQMM "LAMENT FOR A SCHOLAR" JUN '67
REQUEL, LEYNE--[32]MYS--
EQMM "DYING MESSAGE" JUL '66
RUSETT, O.X.--[32]MYS--
EQMM FRIGHTENED MAN" JAN '70
STAR, CATHY HAIG--[32]MYS--
EQMM "TECCOMSHIRE FEN" NOV '65
STOREY, RHODA LYS--[32]MYS--
EQMM "SIR ORDWEY VIEWS THE BODY" APR '67

SCHIFF, BEN
MAXON, J.G.--W/JUNE GOODWIN, LACHMAN-
EASTER LST '93,[34]MYS--
"PROGENY" '89

SCHIFF, SYDNEY
HUDSON, STEPHEN--[1][22]ENGLISH

SCHIFFMAN, MEIR
BEN HORIN, MEIR--[1]

SCHILLER, CRAIG
SCHILLER, MAYER--[1]

SCHILLER, HENRY CARL
GREY, ANTHONY--[1]

SCHIMEK, GAYLE MALONE
DANIELS, JOLEEN--[9][21][26]ROM--
"INHERITANCE"
"AGAINST ALL ODDS" & MORE

SCHIMMEL, ANNEMARIE BRIG.
KIRATI, CEMILE--[31]

SCHIOLER, CARSTEN
VESPER, TERRA--[2]ISFYB

SCHISGALL, OSCAR
COLE, JACKSON--[1][22][31][33]WEST,HP--
HARDY, STUART--[1][31][33]

SCHLAF, JOHANNES
HOLMSEN, BJARNE P.--W/ARNO HOLZ,[39]GERMAN

SCHLAPBACH-OBERHANSLI, T.
OBERHANSLI, TRUDI--[1]

SCHLEICHER, GISELA
ST. CYR, MELANIE--[39][40]GERMAN/MYS--
"EIN OPFER FUR TARANIS" '84

SCHLEIN, MIRIAM
WEISS, MIRIAM--[33]

SCHLICK, F.
APRIL, JACK--L. ROBBINS LTR '94, WEST--
PYR G239 "FEUD AT FIVE RIVERS" '57

SCHLIEPER, WALTHER
SCHEER, MAXIMILLIAN--[1]

SCHLINK, KLARA
BASILEA, [MOTHER]--[1]
SCHLINK, [MOTHER] BASILEA--[1]

SCHLITZ, LAURA AMY
CHESHIRE, CHLOE--[26]ROM--
"A GYPSEY AT ALMACK'S"

SCHMACHER, ASTRID & BERND
A.B.S.--W/FRANK GOHRE,[40]GERMAN/MYS--
"TIEFE SPUREN" '89
A.B.S.--[39][40]GERMAN/MYS--
"DEJA VU" '88
"DOUBLE FEATURE" '87

SCHMIDT, ANNA
SHORR, ANNE--[9][21]ROM--
HARL "FOR ALL TIME"

SCHMIDT, ANTON FRANZ
DIETZENSCHMIDT--[22]GERMAN

SCHMIDT, CLAIRE HARMAN
HARMAN, CLAIRE--[31]

SCHMIDT, DAN
GARRETT, FRANK--[34]MYS--
AV 'KILLSQUAD' - 10 BOOKS '86-8
KELLERMAN, DAN--[3]MYS--
PINN "BLOODRUN" '85
PINN "HELLRIDER" '85
PENDLETON, DON--[34]MYS,HP--
GE "BLOOD & THUNDER" '86
GE "BLACK DICE" '87
GE "BLOOD OF THE LION" '88
GE "CIRCLE OF STEEL" '88
GE "DEVIL'S HORN" '87
GE "TROJAN HORSE" '88

SCHMIDT, DOROTHEA MARIA
JANNAUSCH, DORIS--[39][40]GERMAN/MYS--
"BLAUER RAUCH" '70 & 6 OTHERS

SCHMIDT, EDUARD
BASS, EDUARD--[1][22]GERMAN
CLAUDIUS, EDUARD--[1]
EDSCHMID, KASIMIR--[1][22][31]GERMAN

SCHMIDT, HELMUT K.
STEEN, I.V.--W/PAUL A. MULLER,
[39]GERMAN/MYS/SF

SCHMIDT, JAMES NORMAN
NORMAN, JAMES--[2][3][18][22][33]MYS--
ZD "NIGHTWALKERS" '46
MRW "MURDER, CHOP CHOP" '42 & MORE

SCHMIDT, JO
JUSTICE, ANN--[26]ROM--
"SARA'S FAMILY"
"TWILIGHT MIST"

SCHMIDT, OTTO ERNST
ERNST, OTTO--[1][22]

SCHMIDT, RUTH
SCOFIELD, LEE--[26]ROM--
"A SLENDER THREAD"
"TAMING MARIAH" & OTHERS

SCHMIDT, WILHELM
SCHMIDTBONN, WILHELM--[22]GERMAN

SCHMIDT, WILHELMINA ANGE.
CORSARI, WILLY--[22]DUTCH

SCHMIDT, WILLY
GERHOLD, GERMAN--[1]

SCHMIDT-ELGERS, PAUL
ELGERS, PAUL--[39][40]GERMAN/MYS--
"DIE KATZE MIT DEM BLAUEN AUGEN" '81

SCHMIDT-FREKSA, GERTRUD
FREKSA, FRIEDRICH--W/KURT FRIEDRICH-FREKSA,
[39]GERMAN/SF

SCHMITT, HEINRICH
ARNAU, FRANK--[1][31]

SCHMITZ, ETTORE
SVEVO, ITALO--[1][22]ITALIAN

SCHMITZ, WALTER
FABER, WALTER--[39][40]GERMAN/MYS--
"DIE SPIELBANK MAFIA" '80
PLAY "MAMMON" '80

SCHMOCK, HELEN H.
BELL, STEVE--[1]ADULT--
NSNS U176 "VENUS OF LESBOS" '61
CLOUTIER, HELEN H.--[1]

SCHNECK, STEPHEN
BITE, BEN--[1][22][31]AMERICAN
FITE, MACK--[1][22][31]AMERICAN
KITE, LARRY--[1][22]AMERICAN[31]
KNIGHT, JAMES--[1][22][31]AMERICAN
LITE, JAMS--[1][22][31]AMERICAN
SPIT, SAM--[1][22]AMERICAN

SCHNEIDER, ANNA
SEQUOIA, ANNA--[1]

SCHNEIDER, B.V.H.
HUMPHREYS, B.V.--[8]

SCHNEIDER, DANIEL EDWARD
TAYLOR, DANIEL--[8]

SCHNEIDER, ELIZABETH [S]
COLCHIE, ELIZABETH SCHNE.--[1][31]

SCHNEIDER, HEINRICH EMIL
SARTORIUS, E.--[22]GERMAN-AMERICAN

SCHNEIDER, ISADORE
I.S.--[1][7]SF--
"DOCTOR TRANSIT" '25

SCHNEIDER, LEONARD ALFRED
BRUCE, LENNY--[31]

SCHNEIDER, LINA WELLER
BERG, WILHELM--[1]

SCHNEIDER, MONICA MARIA
OLIVER, FRANCES--[8]

SCHNEIDER, MYRA
GROVELANDS, SARAH--[31]

SCHNEIDER, UTTA [D]
DENELLA, UTTA--[39][40]GERMAN/MYS--
"DER SCHWARZE SPIEGEL" '87
DOHL, STEFAN--[39][40]GERMAN/MYS--
"DER MOND IM SEE" '75

SCHNITTKIND, HENRY THOMAS
THOMAS, HENRY--[1][2]

SCHNITZLER, ARTHUR
ANATOL--[1]

SCHOCK, PAULINE
BOYD, PAULINE--[1][31][33]

SCHODER, JUDITH
SHAY, LACEY--W/SHARON S. SHEBAR, [9][21][31]ROM--
WALLABY "LOVING ENEMY" '83

SCHOEB, ERIKA
DE WITT, DENISE--[1]
LEVI, ARISTOTLE--[1]
VON GRAU, WERNHER--[1][2]

SCHOEFFEL, FLORENCE B.
GILMAN, WENONA--[1][34]MYS--
WESTBROOK "CURSE OF POCAHONTAS" '12

SCHOENEBECK, WILLI
SPENCER, ELIOT--[39][40]GERMAN/MYS,HP--
`KOMMISSAR X' #550

SCHOENFELD, EUGENE L.
DR. HIP--[31]
DR. HIPPOCRATES--[31]
POCRATES, DR. HIP--[8]

SCHOENWEISS, SALLY
REID, MARGARET ANN--[21]ROM--
'CHARLSTON' SAGA: "WHITE LIES"

SCHOEPFLIN, HARL VINCENT
VINCENT, HARL--[2][7][37]MYS/SF--
EXD [PULP STORIES]
STARMONT FACSIMILE FICT #13 '91

SCHOFIELD, ALFRED TAYLOR
COURTENAY, LUKE THEOPHIL.--[7]SF--
"TRAVELS IN THE INTERIOR, OR THE WONDERFUL ADVENTURES OF LUKE & BELINDA"

SCHOFIELD, MICHAEL
WESTWOOD, GORDON--[1]

SCHOFIELD, SYLVIA ANNE
MATHESON, SYLVIA A.--[1]
MUNDY, MAX--[1][32][34]MYS--
LONG "DEATH IS A TIGER" 60
LONG "DIG FOR A CORPSE" '62
LONG "PAGAN PAGODA" '65
EW "A BANDIT FOR CHRISTMAS" DEC '65
EW "WHAT THE WELL DRESSED MURDERER" FEB '65
EW "IT COULD BE ..." JUN '65
LONG "DEATH CRIES OLE" '66
EW "NO TASTE OF HONEY" AUG '66
EW "LEMON LAUGH" MAR '67

SCHOLEFIELD, ALAN
JORDAN, LEE--BK BIO,[8][31][33][34]MYS--
HODDER "CAT'S EYES" '81
CORONET "CRISS-CROSS" '84
MacM "DEADLY SIDE OF THE SQUARE" '88
MacM "CHAIN REACTION" '89
MacM "TOY CUPBOARD" '89
SCHOLEFIELD, A.T.--[33][34]MYS--
MacM "DIRTY WEEKEND" '90

SCHOLZ, WINFRIED
ISLAND, BERT F.--[39][40]GERMAN/MYS,HP
SHOLS, W.W.--[2][39][40]GERMAN/MYS--
`KOMMISSAR X' #407, 433, 493, 507, 534 & 556
UPTON, MUNRO R.--W/W. ERNSTING, W. KUMMING, W. REINECKE & J. SCHEIDT,[39]GERMAN/SF

SCHOMAKER, MARY Z.
ZIMMETH, MARY--[1]

SCHOMBERG, DONNA
SAUCIER, DONNA--[9][21][26]ROM--
"AMETHYST FIRE"

SCHOMBURG, ALEX
XELA--[2]

SCHONESTEIN, DAVID
STEUNE, GEORGES--[1]

SCHONFELD, DR. HERMAN
BELCAMPO--[2]

SCHONFIELD, HUGH JOSEPH
FIELDING, HUBERT--[8]
HEGESIPPUS--[8][22][31]ENGLISH

SCHOONMAKER, ANN
BOYD, ANN S.--[1][31]

SCHOPFER, JEAN
ANET, CLAUDE--[1][2][22]

SCHORB, EDWIN MARSH
MARSH, EDWIN--[1]
MCGRATH, DOYLE--[1]

SCHORR, MARK
ELLIS, SCOTT--[18][31][34]MYS--
ST. MARTIN'S "THE BORZOI CONTROL" '86

SCHOSBERG, PAUL A.
ALLYN, PAUL--[1][31][22]

SCHOW, DAVID J.
GRAVE, STEPHEN--S. CUPP '93, R. BENOIT,MYS--
'MIAMI VICE' TV TIE-IN SERIES: #1-12
LOWENBRUCK, OLIVER--R. BENOIT--
'TWILIGHT' MAG - SHORT STORY
McCONNELL, CHAN--HAWK/CUPP INTRVW/BENOIT, MYS--SHORT STORIES

SCHRAGER, JEANNE HART
HART, JEANNE--[31]

SCHRECK, EVERETT M.
MORRILL, RICHARD--[1]

SCHREIBER, HERMANN O.L.
BASSERMANN, LUJO--[1][8][31]TRAVEL BKS-AUSTRIA
BUEHNAU, LUDWIG--[1][31]TRAVEL BKS-AUSTRIA

SCHREINER, GEORGE F.
SCHREINER, LEE--[1]

SCHREINER, OLIVE [E.A.]
IRON, RALPH--[1][22][31]ENGLISH

SCHREMPP, ELIZABETH K.
COURT, KATHERINE--[9][21][26][34]MYS/ROM--
"WHISPER, WHISPER"
"BUT DON'T GO ALONE"
"MASK OF LOVE"

SCHRODER, FREDERIK CORN.
ROOSDORP, FRITS--[22]DUTCH

SCHRODER, RAINER M.
DENVER, JEFF--[39][40]GERMAN/MYS--
"SUPERSTAR: DER HEROIN KRIEG" '78
HARGROVE, MARION--[39][40]GERMAN/MYS--
"THE SERPENTS TOOTH" '71

SCHROEDER, RICHARD C.
ALFRED, RICHARD--W/NATHAN A. HAVERSTOCK,[1]

SCHUBART, FANNIE KILBOURN
KILBOURNE, FANNIE--[1]

SCHUBE, PURCELL G.
MEE--[8]

SCHUBERT, JOHN D.
MORLAND, CATHERINE--[34]MYS--
PINN "LEGACY OF WINTERWYCK" '76

SCHUCHMAN, JOAN
BRENNER, ISABEL--[1][31]
JONES, MIRIAM--[1][31]
JONES, ZELDA--[1][31]

SCHUCK, FREDERICK H.P.
SCHUCK, F.H.P.--[1]

SCHUCK, MARILYN D.
RICE, MOLLY--[26]ROM--
"WHERE THE RIVER RUNS"
"CHANCE ENCOUNTER"

SCHUETZ, DENNIS
ALDYNE, NATHAN--W/MICHAEL MCDOWELL,[3][31]MYS--
AV "VERMILION" '80
BAL "CANARY" '86 & MORE '80-6
YOUNG, AXEL--W/MICHAEL McDOWELL,[34]MYS--
AV "BLOOD RUBIES" '82
AV "WICKED STEPMOTHER" '83

SCHULER, CANDACE L.
DARWIN, JEANETTE--[9][21][26]ROM--
"A CHERISHED ACCOUNT"
SPENCER, CANDACE--[21][26]ROM--
"BETWEEN FRIENDS"

SCHULKERS, ROBERT FRANC
HAWKINS, SEKATARY--[1]

SCHULMAN, ALLAN
MARKLAND, PETER--W/TORSTEN V. SCHEUTZ,[29]MYS--
RABEN & SJORGEN "JAKT I ROD DIMMA" '54

SCHULMAN, LESTER MARTIN
MARTIN, LES--[1][7]SF--
'INDIANA JONES' SERIES
'FRANKENSTEIN' SERIES

SCHULTE, ELAINE L.
YOUNG, ELAINE L.--[1][33]

SCHULTZ, FREDERICK WALTER
WALKER, FREDERICK--[1]

SCHULTZ, JAMES WILLARD
ANDERSON, W.B.--[1][31]
APIKUNI--[1][31]

SCHULTZ, JANET
SINCLAIR, TRACY--[9][26]ROM--
"A CHANGE OF PACE"
SIL 868 "MARRY ME, KATE" & OTHERS
STUART, JAN--[9][21][26]ROM--
"RISK WORTH TAKING"
"ENCORE OF DESIRE"
"NO GREATER LOVE"

SCHULTZ, MARION C.
CLARKE, MARION--[9][21][26]ROM--
"JADE PAGODA"
"SUMMER HOUSE"
"MASTER OF BRENDAN'S ISLE"

SCHULTZ, MARY
LOGAN, LEANDRA--[21][26]ROM--
"DILLON AFTER DARK"
"JOYRIDE" & MORE

SCHULTZ, PEARLE HENDRKSN.
PERSHING, MARIE--[9][21][26][31]ROM--
"FIRST A DREAM"
"MAYBE TOMORROW"
"HANDFUL OF STARS"

SCHULTZ, WENDY ADRIAN
WEES, WENDY ADRIAN--[2]

SCHULZE, DALLAS
HAMLIN, DALLAS--[9][21][26]ROM--
"ANOTHER EDEN"
"PRISONER IN HIS ARMS" & MORE

SCHULZE, HERTHA
WELLINGTON, KATE--[9][21][26]ROM--
"A DELICATE BALANCE"

SCHULZE-GALLERA, DR. S.
EXZELSIOR--[2]

SCHUMANN, MAURICE
SIDOBRE, ANDRE--[1]

SCHUTZ, JOSEPH W.
SCHOLL, JERRY--[1][23]AMERICAN/THRILLERS

SCHUTZE, GLADYS H.
LESLIE, HENRIETTA--[1]
MENDL, GLADYS--[1]

SCHUYLER, GEORGE S[AMUEL]
BROOKS, SAMUEL I.--[23]SF, PULP

SCHUYLER, KEITH C.
BRADLEY, BRIAN K.--[1]

SCHWAB, LINDA J.
MAXWELL, EMILY--[21][26]ROM--
"THE WICKED COUNT"
"AN EASTER DISGUISE" & MORE

SCHWABACHER, HENRI SIMON
DUVERNOISE, HENRI--[1]

SCHWALBERG, CAROL[YN E.S]
BOLLING, HAL--[1][31]
JENKINS, PHYLLIS--[1][31]
LA FONTAINE, BLANCHE--[1][31]
LEVY, LORELEI--[1][31]
SHORTER, CARL--[1]
STEIN, CHARLES--[1]
ULLMAN, BARBARA--[1]

SCHWARTZ, ANNE POWERS
POWERS, ANNE--[1][21][33]ROM--
"IRON MASTER"
"THOUSAND FIRES" & MORE

SCHWARTZ, BETTY
BLACK, BETTY--[1][31]

SCHWARTZ, FRANCES
SYLVIN, FRANCES--W/SYLVIA S. SEAMAN,[1]

SCHWARTZ, JOOST VAN DER P
MAARTENS, MAARTEN--[34]MYS--
REMINGTON--
"SIN OF JOOST AVELINGH" 1889

SCHWARTZ, PAULA REIBEL
MANSFIELD, ELIZABETH--[21][26][34]MYS/ROM--
BERK "MY LORD MURDERER" '78
BERK "PHANTOM LOVER" '79
MANSFIELD, LIBBY--[21][26]ROM--
"UNEXPECTED HOLIDAY"
MANSFIELD, PAUL H.--[3]MYS--
COLLINS "FINAL EXPOSURE" '57
REIBEL, PAULA--[21][26]--
"A MORNING MOON"

SCHWARTZ, [MAYER] MARCEL
LOYSON-BRIDET--[1]

SCHWARZ, JACOB
SCHWARZ, JACK--[1]

SCHWARZMANN, LEV ISAAKOV.
SHESTOV, LEV--[22]RUSSIAN

SCHWEISS, V.M.
MCKNIGHT, JENNA--[26]ROM--
HARL 512 "ALLIGATOR ALLEY"
539 "BRIDE, BATACHELOR & THE BABY"

SCHWEITZER, DARRELL
BUTLER, THEODORE [TED]--[1][2][31]--
CONTRIBUTER TO MAGAZINES
VREEB, ARTEMIS--[2]

SCHWEIZER, MARC
GENEROSO, MARC-ANTOINE--[1]
GENEVIEVE, PIERRE--[1]
LARISTA, PEPE--[1]
LAURAC, SERGE--[1]

SCHWINDT, EDELTRAUT
SCHWARZ, ALEXANDRA--[39]GERMAN
SCHWINDT, BARBARA--[39][40]GERMAN/MYS--
"WER IST CAROLINE CROSS" '77

SCIASCIA, LEONARDO
EINAUDI, GIULIO--[29]MYS

SCITHERS, GEORGE
FALKON, FELIX LANCE--G. COOK LTR '93
WURF, KARL--[2][11][23]SF--
IF "TO SERVE MAN" '76

SCLATER, RUTH LEIGH
LEIGH, RUTH--[1]

SCOBIE, STEPHEN ARTHUR C.
WAVERLEY, JOHN--[8]

SCOFIELD, NORMA M.C.
CARTWRIGHT, N.--[1][31]

SCOLTOCK, JACK
ZEBRA, A.--[33]

SCOPPETTONE, SANDRA
EARLY, JACK--DDLY PLEAS #3,[34]MYS--
PUTNAM "SOME UNKNOWN PERSON" '76
"SUCH NICE PEOPLE" '80
WATTS "A CREATIVE KIND OF KILLER" '84
WATTS "RAZZAMATAZZ" '85
DUTTON "DONATO & DAUGHTER" '88

SCORTIA, THOMAS N.
KURZ, ARTHUR R.--[1][31]
MCDOW, GERALD--[1]
NICHOLS, SCOTT--[1][2]

SCOTLAND, JAMES
EMERSON, RONALD--[1][31]--
CITIZENS THEATRE - REVIEWS
LITTLE, KENNETH--[1][31]--
ABOUT 200 RADIO PROGRAMS

SCOTT, ADRIENNE
WILLIAMS, LAURIE--[9]ROM

SCOTT, ALEXANDER LESLIE
BILLINGS, BUCK--J. SCOTT LTR '94, A. TONIK-
ECHOES #4, MUNROE-BAE 21, WEST--
HARL 226 "OWL HOOT TRAIL" '53
COLE, JACKSON--A. TONIK-COLE CKLST "SPICY
ARMADILLO",HP--
TX RGR - 55 STORIES '36-'51
PYR - 20 NOVELS '60-4
HOLT, TEX--A. TONIK-ECHOES #4,WEST,HP--
LESLIE, A.--J. SCOTT LTR '94,A. TONIK-
ECHOES #4,[8]WEST--
LESLIE, A. SCOTT--J. SCOTT LTR '94,A. TONIK-
ECHOES #4, MUNROE-BAE 21, WEST--
PYR 26 "ARIZONA RANGER" '51
PYR 36 "TOMBSTONE TRAIL" '51
PYR 44 "STRANGER IN BOOTS" '52
PYR 61 "THE TEXAN" '52
LESLIE, SCOTT--J. SCOTT LTR '94
MUNROE-BAE 21, WEST--
PYR G5635 "THE TEXAN" '60
SCOTT, BRADFORD--J. SCOTT LTR '94,
A. TONIK-ECHOES #4, PP 4, MUNROE-
BAE 21, WEST--
SCOTT, LES--J. SCOTT LTR '94, MUNROE-
BAE 21, ADULT--
BEAC B156 "TWILIGHT WOMEN" '57
BEAC B179 "GIRL IN THE BLACK CHEMISE" '58
SCOTT, LESLIE--J. SCOTT LTR '94, A. TONIK-
PP 4, WEST--
NSLF 102 "PICK-UP" '50
ACE DIO "BRAZOS FIREBRAND" '53
ACE D22 "BADLANDS MASQUERADER" '53
PYR 302 "TOMBSTONE SHOWDOWN" '57

SCOTT, ALLAN
SCOT, MICHAEL--W/MICHAEL SCOTT ROHAN,
[1][2][23]SF--
NEL "ICE KING" '86

SCOTT, ANNA
JOSEPH, ANNE--[7]SF--
ZEBRA "GRANDFATHER" '91

SCOTT, ANNA [K]
MARSTON, MILDRED--[1]

SCOTT, ARIANA
ADLER, ELIZABETH--[26]ROM--
"LEONIE"
"INDICRETION" & MORE

SCOTT, CORA ANNETT
ANNETT, CORA--[1][22][31][33]

SCOTT, DELORAS
SCOTT, LISA--[21]ROM

SCOTT, ELISE AYLEN
AYLEN, ELISE--[1]

SCOTT, ETHEL MCCULLOUGH
CLARK, GAREL--W/MAY GARELICK,[1]

SCOTT, EVELYN
SOUZA, ERNEST--[1][3][22]MYS--
CAPE "BLUE RUM " '30

SCOTT, G. FORRESTER
HALSHAM, JOHN--[1]

SCOTT, GENEVIEVE
RIGG, JENNIFER--[9]ROM

SCOTT, GERALDINE EDITH
MITTON, G.E.--[1]

SCOTT, HELEN MYERS
MELDRUM, HELEN MYERS--[1]

SCOTT, HILDA R.
SMITH, HARRIET--[8]

SCOTT, HUGH STOWELL
MERRIMAN, HENRY SETON--[3][22][29]MYS--
BENTLEY "SUSPENSE" 1890
SMITH "WITH EDGED TOOLS" 1894 & MORE

SCOTT, JAMES GEORGE
YOE, SHWAY [SCHWAY]--[1]

SCOTT, JEREMY
DICK, KAY--[2]

SCOTT, JODY
SCOTT, THURSTON--W/GEORGE THURSTON LEITE,
[1][3][22]MYS--
HARPER "CURE IT WITH HONEY" '51

SCOTT, JOHN
BARBAROSSA--[1]

SCOTT, JOHN ANTHONY
SCOTT, TONY--[33]

SCOTT, JOHN DICK
GAIR, MALCOLM--[3][40]MYS--
COLLINS "BAD DREAM"
"SCHULTZ MONEY" '60 & 4 MORE '57-62

SCOTT, JOHN F.
BONES, BRUDDER--[1]

SCOTT, JOHN ROBERT
FALKLAND--[1]

SCOTT, JOHN W. ROBERTSON
SCOTT, J.W. ROBERTSON--[1]

SCOTT, JUSTIN [BLAZER]
BLAZER, J.S.--SCOTT LTR '94,[3][29][31]MYS--
BOBBS "DEAL ME OUT" '73
BOBBS "LEND A HAND" '75

SCOTT, LATAYNE COLVETT
COLVETT, LATAYNE--[1][31]

SCOTT, LILY K.
BRADFORD, LILY--J. SCOTT LTR '94--
WIFE OF 'A. LESLIE SCOTT' & MOTHER
OF 'JUSTIN SCOTT'

SCOTT, MARGARET
GALLAGHER, GALE--W/WILL OURSLER,[3][29]MYS--
COWARD "I FOUND HIM DEAD" '47
COWARD "CHORD IN CRIMSON" '49

SCOTT, MARIAN GALLAGHER
OLIVER, GAIL--[1][3][22][29]MYS--
MacM "COWARD "THE MOON SAW MURDER" '37
WOLFFE, KATHERINE--[22][34]MYS--
DBLDY "TALL MAN WALKING" '36
MORROW "ATTIC ROOM" '42
FVSTR "DEATH'S LONG SHADOW" '46

SCOTT, MARY E.
GRAHAM, JEAN--[8]

SCOTT, PEG O'NEILL
O'NEILL, SCOTT--[1][2][23]SF--
"MARTIAN SEXPOT" '63
WERPER, BARTON--W/PETER T. SCOTT,
[2][7][11][23]HP--
GOLD STAR 'TARZAN':"& THE SNAKE PEOPLE" '64

SCOTT, PETER
BRADLEY, MATT[HEW]--V. BERCH-BRNDN/BC PSEUDS,
BAE 22, ADULT--
JADE 202 "LESBIAN LAND" '63
JADE 205 "BALZAC '64 VOL I" '63
JADE 206 "BALZAC '64 VOL II" '63
CARTER, EDIE--V. BERCH-BRNDN/BC PSEUDS,
BAE 22, ADULT--

SCOTT, PETER DALE
GREENE, ADAM--[1][31]
SPROSTON, JOHN--[1]

SCOTT, PETER T.
WERNER, GEORGE--[3]MYS--
GOLD STAR "ONE HELLUVA BLOW" '64
WERPER, BARTON--W/PEG O'NEILL SCOTT,
[1][2][23]SF,HP--
GOLD STAR 'TARZAN' SERIES #1, 2, 4 & #5

SCOTT, REGINALD T. MAITLAND
MAITLAND, REGINALD T.--[1]
SCOTT, R.T.M.--ECHOES, R. JAMES,[18]MYS--
PULP WORK

SCOTT, ROBERT
BLUE WOLF--[1][2]HP--
GOLD STAR

SCOTT, ROBERT T. MAITLAND
HOUSE, BRANT--PULP CLASSIC #22, P86,HP--
SAX "CLAWS OF THE CORPSE CULT" APR '38
SCOTT, MAITLAND--PULP CLASSIC #22, P86--
STORIES IN SAX, DM, TT & SDS
SCOTT, R.T.M.--PULP CLASSIC #22, P86--
STOCKBRIDGE, GRANT--R. JAMES-PP 31,
R. SAMPSON-ECHOES #3--
SPD "THE SPIDER STRIKES" OCT '33
SPD "THE WHEEL OF DEATH" NOV '33

SCOTT, ROSE LAURE
BUCKLEY, EUNICE--[8]

SCOTT, SUSAN HOLLOWAY
JARRETT, MIRANDA--[26]ROM--
"STEAL THE STARS"
"COLUMBINE"
"SPINDRIFT"

SCOTT, VINCENT E.
CARTER, NICHOLAS--[3]MYS,HP--

SCOTT, W.H.
SCOTT, WILL--[8][32]MYS--
EQMM "CLUE IN BLUE" FEB '50
EQMM "A WISH FOR A CIGAR" OCT '53
EQMM "SHABBY MAN & THE NABOB" SEPT '61
WATT, WILLIAM--[1][5]MYS--

SCOTT, WALTER [SIR]
CLEISHBOTHAM, JEBEDIAH--[31][33]
SCOTT, DIXON--[1]

SCOTT, WILLIAM NEVILLE
SCOTT, BILL--[7]SF--
OXFORD UNIV. PRESS 'BOORI' #1 & #2 '78-80

SCOTT, WILLIAM RALPH
HILL, WELDON--[1][3]MYS--
McKAY "A MAN COULD GET KILLED THAT WAY" '67

SCOTT, WINIFRED MARY
WYNNE, PAMELA--[1]

SCOTT, [PETER] HARDIMAN
FIELDING, PETER--[34]MYS--
EVANS "TEXT FOR MURDER" '51

SCOTT-DRENNAN, LYNNE
SCOTT, AMANDA--[1][9][26]ROM--
"HIGHLAND FLING"
"LADY HAWK'S FOLLY" & OTHERS

SCOTT-GILES, CHARLES WIL.
GILES, C.W. SCOTT--[31]
SCOTT-GILES, C.W.--[31]

SCOTT-HANSEN, OLIVE
MURRELL, SHIRLEY--[8]

SCOTT-JAMES, ROLFE ARNOLD
SCOTT-JAMES, R.A.--[1]

SCOTTI, LITA
AIMES, ANGELICA--[9]ROM--
"DAUGHTER OF DESIRE"
"DIVIDED HEART"
"SAMANTHA"
"FRANCESCA"

SCRIBNER, KIMBALL
KINBALL, CAPTAIN KIM--[33]

SCRIMGEOUR, GARY JAMES
SCRIMGEOUR, G.J.--[21]ROM--
"A WOMAN OF HER TIMES"

SCROGGIE, MARCUS GRAHAM
CATHODE RAY--[8]

SCUDDER, HORACE ELISHA
FELLOW, R.--[1]
JAMES, S.T.--[1]

SCUDDER, MILDRED LEE
LEE, MILDRED--[1][22][31]AMERICAN

SCULLY, WILLIAM CHARLES
WITWATERSRAND--[1]

SCUTT, JOCELYNNE ANNETTE
CHAN, MELISSA--[36]AUSTRALIAN/MYS--
SPINIFEX "TOO RICH" '91
ARTEMIS "ONE TOO MANY" '93

SEALEY, LEONARD G.W.
BRITT, GEORGE--[1]

SEAMAN, EKLIZABETH C.
BLY, NELLIE--[8][22]

SEAMAN, LUCY
ROBBE, MICHELE--[9][21]ROM--
"WALKING ON AIR"
ROBBE, MICHELLE--G. COOK LTR '93

SEAMAN, SIR OWEN
NAUTICUS--[8]
O.S.--[8]

SEAMAN, SYLVIA S.
SYLVIN, FRANCIS--W/FRANCES SCHWARTZ,[1]

SEARLE, KATHRYN ADRIENNE
KATHRYN--[31][33]

SEARLE, M.E.
EIRENE--[8]
M.E.S.--[8]

SEARLE, RONALD W.F.
SHY, TIMOTHY--W/DOMINIC BEVAN W. LEWIS,[1]

SEARLES, LIN
COLE, JACKSON--A. TONIK-COLE CKLST "SPICY ARMADILLO",HP--
TEX RGR "GUNMAN'S LEGION" AUG '57

SEARLS, HENRY HUNT JR.
COSTIGAN, LEE--[3][29]MYS--
POCK 1256 "NEVER KILL A COP" '59
GM 1186 "THE NEW BREED" '62
GRAY, ANTHONY--COVER DISCLOSURE,[34]MYS--
PUTNAM "THE PENETRATORS" '65
SEARLS, HANK--[7][11][23][34]MYS/SF--
BAL "SOUNDING" '82
BERK "FIREWIND" '82 & MORE

SEARS, ALFERD FRANCIS
INCA-PABLO-OZOLLA--[2]

SEARS, RUTH MCCARTHY
MCCARTHY, JANE--[3][29]MYS--
REEMPLOY "THE DARK DECEPTION" '75

SEAVER, RICHARD
MOLE, OSCAR--[8]

SEAWELL, MOLLY ELLIOT
DAVIS, FOXCROFT--[8]
FOXHALL--[1]
SYDNEY--[1]

SEBENTHAL, ROBERTA E.
DAVIS, HARRY--C. ECKHOFF-PP 12,[3]--
GREENBERG "MY BROTHER'S WIFE" '56
"PORTRAIT OF RENE" '56
KRUGER, PAUL--C. ECKHOFF-PP 12,[32][34]MYS--
DELL FE A160 "A BULLET FOR A BLONDE" '58
ACE D425 "DIG HER A GRAVE" '60
MSMM "LAY-AWAY PLAN" AUG '60
NSLS U164 "BEDROOM ALIBI" '61
GM 1323 "MESSAGE FROM MARISE" '63
SIMON "WEEP FOR WILLOW GREEN" '66
SIMON "WEAVE A WICKED WEB" '67
SIMON "FINISH LINE" '68
SIMON "IF THE SHROUD FITS" '69
SIMON "COLD ONES" '72
SIMON "BRONZE CLAWS" '72

SEBESTYEN, OUIDA
SEBESTYEN, IGEN--[1][33]

SEBLEY, FRANCES RAE
JEFFS, RAE--[8]

SEBREY, MARY ANN
WHITLEY, MARY ANN--[1]

SECCOMBE, THOMAS
T.S.--[8]

SECRIST, W.G.
SECRIST, KELLIHER--W/DAN T. KELLIHER, [1][3]MYS--
MYH "MURDER MELODY" '39
MYH "MURDER MAKES BY-LINES" '41

SEDDON, KEITH
CHRISTCHILD, RAVAN--[2]

SEDERQUEST, MARY F.F.
GRANGER, KATHERINE--[9][21][26]ROM--
"WANTON WAYS"
"PRIVATE LESSONS" & 12 MORE
RANSOM, KATHERINE--[9][21][26]ROM--
"WISH ON A STAR"
"COME FLY WITH ME" & 3 MORE

SEDGEMORE, BRIAN CHARLES
FORTHEMONEY, JUSTINIAN--[8]

SEDLEY, ARTHUR O.L.
CAROLAN, R.--[1]

SEDMAK, PAVLE
BEVK, FRANCE--[22]SLOVAK

SEDURO, VLADIMIR
HLYBINNY, VLADIMIR--[1][31]

SEE, CAROLYN & LISA
HIGHLAND, MONICA--W/JOHN ESPEY,[8][21][26]ROM--
"LOTUS LAND"
"SHANGHAI ROAD"

SEED, CECILE EUGENIE
SEED, JENNY--[1]

SEED, SHEILA TURNER
TURNER, SHEILA R.--[33]

SEEDO, SONIA
FUCHS, SONIA--[8]

SEELEY, FRANCIS RAE
JEFFS, RAE--[1]

SEELY, NORMA YVONNE
NORMAN, YVONNE--[9][21][34]MYS--
AVALON "TREASURE OF SEACLIFF MANOR" '77
"LEAVES ON THE WIND"

SEFERIADES, GIORGOS [S]
SEFERIS, GEORGE--[31]GREEK--
ATHENS "STROPHE" '31
SEPHERIADES, GEORGIOS--[31]GREEK

SEGALL, DON
AUGUST, LEO--[2][3][11]MYS--
AWARD "SUPERDOLL" '69

SEGEL, JUDITH
MITCHELL, [JUDITH] PAIGE--[1]

SEGER, MAURA
BATES, JENNY--[9][21][26]ROM--
"DAZZLED"
"GUILDED SPRING"
FITZGERALD, MAEVE--[9][21][26]ROM--
"ONCE & FOREVER"
HASTINGS, LAURA--[26]ROM--
"PERCHANCE TO DREAM"
"FORTUNE'S TIDE" & 3 MORE
JENNINGS, SARA--[9][21][26]ROM--
"GAME PLAN"
"REACH FOR THE STARS" & 2 MORE

SEGER, MAURA [CONT]
MACNEIL, ANNE--[9][21][26]ROM--
"A MIND OF HER OWN"
WINSLOW, LAUREL--[9][21][26]ROM--
"CAPTURED IMAGES"
"HEART SONGS"

SEGRE, DAN V[ITTORIO]
BAUDUC, R.--[31]

SEGRE, DINO
PITIGRILLI--[22]ITALIAN

SEHLER, RAOUL STEPHEN
BURNS, REX--LACHMAN/EASTER LST '93--
'BURNS' NAME OF STEPFATHER, SEE FOR HIS PSEUDS

SEIBEL, WERNER
LEBIES, RENE--[1]

SEIBERT, CATHERINE
LORD, ALEXANDRA--W/PATRICIA A. WILLIAMS, [9][21]ROM--
"A HARMLESS RUSE"

SEID, RUTH
SINCLAIR, JO--J. PRESSMAN-LESBIANA, BAE 20, [1]ADULT--
PERMA P169 "SING AT MY WAKE" '52
LAN 72-602 "WASTELAND" '61

SEIDE, DIANE
SEIDNER, DIANE--[1]

SEIDICK, KATHRYN A.
KASEY, MICHELLE--[9][21][26]ROM--
"A FINAL FARCE"
"A DIFFICULT DISGUISE" & MORE
MICHAELS, KASEY--[9][21][26]ROM--
"PRIDE OF THE PEACOCK"
"TIMELY MATRIMONY" & MORE

SEIDLIN, OSKAR
BROCKHOFF, STEFAN--W/DIETER CUNTZ & R. PLANT, [39][40]GERMAN/MYS--
"BEGENUNG IN ZURMATT" '55

SEIFFERT, MARJORIE A.
CYPHER, ANGELA--[1]

SEIGNOBOSC, FRANCOISE
FRANCOISE--[1][31][33]

SEITZ, EBERHARD
SHERWOOD, HENRY--[39][40]GERMAN/MYS--
"TEUFEL IM LANGEN KLEID" '57

SEJOUR-MAGLIORE, FRANCIS
MAGLIORE, FRANCIS L.--[1]

SEKAXSU PETAKWONEXNAJUNK.
IRON THUNDERHORSE--[31]

SELCAMM, GEORGE
MACHLIS, JOSEPH--[8]

SELDES, GILBERT VIVIAN
BLUPHOCKS, LUCIEN--[1][22][31]AMERICAN
CAULIFLOWER, SEBASTIAN--[1][22][31]AMERICAN
JOHNS, FOSTER--[3][22][31]MYS--
DAY "VICTORY MURDERS" '27
DAY "SQUARE EMERALD" '28
SHAW, VIVIAN--[1]

SELLAR, ROBERT JAMES B.
CHALFONT, PETER--[1]

SELLENGER, JOHN
HUNTER, MICHAEL--[35]AUSTRALIAN--
HRWTZ PB372 "KING'S CROSS CRIMS" '68
HRWTZ "A HELLUVA WAY TO FIGHT A WAR" '68
HRWTZ PB162 "TIMES OF DISCONTENT" '79

SELLERS, CON[NIE LESLIE]
ADAM, DON--[1]
ADAMS, RICH--[1]
ADONIS, MICHAEL--[1]
ARANA, RIC[K]--[1][7][34]MYS/ADULT--
GRNLF AB1672 "TURNING AUNTIE ON" '73
CHALLENGE "SILENT SEDUCERS" '67
POWELL PP-187 "BIG DANO" '69
POWELL PP-125 "WOMAN ON HER BACK" '69
BANNION, DELLA--[1]
BATES, NORMAN--[1]
BEAR, JOE--[1]
CAMPBELL, FRED--[1]
CARRE, CHUCK--[1]
CELLINI, CAL--[1]
CONNAUGHTON, SAM--[1]
CONNERS, SELWYN--[1]
CONNISTON, SAM--[1]
COTTON, JERRI--[1]
CRANE, ROBERT--[29][31][34]MYS,SP--
PYR 1012 "THE SERGEANT & THE QUEEN" '64
PYR "SGT CORBINS WAS" '64
"OPERATION VENGEANCE" '65
"STRIKEBACK" '65
"PARADISE TRAP" '67
PYR "TONGUE OF TREASON" '67
PAPILLON "TIME RUNNING OUT" '74
DENNING, LAURENCE--[1]
DEVRIES, CON--[1]
DILLI, RICK--[1]
DOWNS, BILL--[1]
ELIOT, C.S.--[1]
GENRTY, ARTHUR--[1]
HALL, MARCIA--[1]
HAWK, JACK--[1]
HERMAN, LOUIS--[1]
HIGGENS, MARTYN--[1]
HURST, BRIAN--[1]
JACOBS, STEVEN--[1]
LANG, JIM--[1]
LARK, JODY--[1]
LINSLEY, LADD E.--[1]
MADDEN, DICK--[1]
MENASCO, JOHN--[1]
MITCHELL, JACK--[1]
MORAN, JUDY--[1]
NOCENI, EARL--[1]
POWERS, DICK--[1]
RAINTREE, LEE--W/ANTHONY WILSON,[1][9][21]ROM--
"BED OF STRANGERS"
"DALLAS" & MORE
ROTH, KAREN--[1]
ROTH, ROBERT--[1]
SANDS, LEONARD--[1]
SELLERS, CON--[1][21]ROM--
"KEEPERS OF THE HOUSE"
"LAST FLOWER"
"MARILEE
SWEET CAROLINE"
SELLERS, CONNIE--[1]ADULT--
NSLS U120 "PRIVATE WORLD" '59
NOV 5019 "WILLING WOMEN" '60
SELLERS, MARY--[1]
SELWYN, CHUCK--[1]
SHANNON, LEONARD--[1]
SIMBEAUX, L.L.--[1]
STANTON, CHUCK--[1]

SELLERS, CON[NIE LESLIE] [CONT]
STEELE, CHARLES--[1]
TRENT, LAWRENCE--[1]
TRENT, LEO--[1]
TULLY, TOM--[1]
WARD, TOM--[1]

SELLICKS, LESLIE
LESLIE, EDWARD--[1][3]MYS--
JENKINS "RED SLAYER" '29
JENKINS "SEVENTH ENTANGLEMENT" '30
JENKINS "WHITE MAN'S PRESTIGE" '39

SELMAN, ELSIE EMILY
TAYLOR, SELMAN--[1]

SELTZER, CHARLES ALDEN
HOPKINS, HIRAM--[1]
KAYE, STEPHEN--L. ROBBINS LTR MAR '94

SELTZER, LEON E[UGENE]
LEIGH, EUGENE--[1]

SEMEIKS, GORMELY
HARRALD, JON A.--W/HAROLD SCHECHTER,
V. BERCH LTR TO HUBIN '94, MYS--

SEMPELL, CHARLOTTE
KLENBORT, CHARLOTTE--[31]

SEMPHILL, ERNEST
COLES, DETECTIVE INSPECT.--[1][34]MYS--
AMALG "THE WAR LORD" '09
GALE, ALAN--[1]
MICHAEL, JOHN--[1]
MICHAEL, PAUL--[1][32]MYS--
JCM "HOWARD KILLED THIRTEEN IN TWELVE
MINUTES" MAR '64
STORM, MICHAEL--[1]
STORM, RUPERT--[1]

SEMPLE, DUGALD
WHEELHOUSE--[1]

SEMPRUN, JORGE
SANCHEZ, FEDERICO--[1]

SEN GUPTA, PRANATI
GUPTA, PRANATI SEN--[31]

SENA, JANEANNE
JORDAN, JANEANNE--[26]ROM--
"THE SCHEME OF THINGS"
"KENTON'S COUNTESS"

SENARENS, LUIS P.
BURLEIGH, CECIL--[2][11]
CLYDE, KIT--[1][2][11]
DOUGHTY, FRANK--[1][2][11]
EARLE, W.J.--[1][2][11]
GARNE, GASTON--[1][2][11]
HOWARD, CAPTAIN [POLICE]--[1][2][11]
NONAME--[1][2][11][23]SF--
FRANK TOUSEY "FRANK READE, JR."
TOUSEY "JACK WRIGHT" TALES
SENARENS, LU--[1]
SPARLING, NED--[1][2][11]

SENDER BARAYON, RAMON
BARAYON, RAMON SENDER--[31]

SENECAL, JEAN-MICHAEL
JACQUEMARD-SENECAL--W/YVES JACQUEMARD,[3]MYS--
COLLINS "BODY VANISHES" '80
"ELEVENTH LITTLE NIGGER"

SENGHOR, LEOPOLD SEDAR
DIAMANO, SILMANG--[31]
KAYMOR, PATRICE MAGUILENE--[31]

SENIOR, ISABEL JANET C.S.
PLEYDELL, SUSAN--[22]ENGLISH

SENTJURC, IGOR
VON PERCHA, IGOR--[39][40]GERMAN/MYS--
"VERGANGEN IST DER TRAUM" '81

SERAFIMOV, SERATIM N.
SEVERNYAK, SERAFIM--[1]

SERAFINA, TINA
KNIGHT, SALI--[21][26]ROM--
"STARLIT SURRENDER"

SERAFINOWICZ, LESZEK JO.
LECHON, JAN--[22]POLISH

SERAILLIER, ANNE
ROGERS, ANNE--[8]

SERANO, JOE
SAVAGE, ADRIAN--[7]SF/HOR--
"UNHOLY COMMUNION" '88
BR. POCK "BLAKE HOUSE" '90

SEREBRIAKOFF, VICTOR
SERRY, VICTOR--[1]

SERENYI, GITTA
SERENY, GITTA--[3]MYS--
GOLZ "THE MEDALLION" '57

SERGE, VICTOR
KIBALCHICK, VIKTOR--[1]

SERGEANT, [E.F.] ADELINE
ADELINE--[1]
SARGEANT, ADELINE--[1][3]MYS--
SPELLING VARIATION

SERGHI BOGDAN, CELLA
SERGHI, CELLA--[1]

SERNER, MARTIN GUNNAR
HELLER, FRANK--[1][22][29][34]SWEDISH/MYS--
CROWELL "GRAND DUKE'S FINANCES" '24
& 7 MORE '23-7

SERRA, ART
ART, ARRES--LACHMAN LST '93,[32]MYS--
GU "KILL NIGHT" SEPT '59

SERVADIO, GAIA
MOSTYN-OWEN, GAIA--[8]

SERWICHER, KURT
KAZNAR, KURT--[8][31]

SETH, RONALD [S]
CHARTHAM, ROBERT--[1][31]

SETH-SMITH, LESLIE JAMES
BRABAZON, JAMES--[1][31]

SETHI, NARENDRA KUMARMES
SETHI, DENIS--[1]

SETON-WATSON, ROBERT W.
VIATOR, SCOTUS--[1]

SETTERBORG, GABRIEL
CRANE, ERIC--[1][2][11]

SEUFFERT, MURIEL
FAULKNER, MARY--[8]
SEUFFERT, MUIR--[8]

SEVERN, WILLIAM IRVING
SEVERN, BILL--[31][33]ALL HIS WRITING '56-90
& CHILDREN'S BOOKS

SEVERSON, ELLEN DODGE
PORATH, ELLEN--LOCUS JAN '94--
'DRAGONLANCE' SAGAS:
"THE MEETING"
"HEDRICK THE THEOCRAT" '93

SEVERSON, K.D.
GIDEON, ROBIN--[9][26]ROM--
"PASSION'S BANDIT"
"ROYAL RAPTURE" & 6 MORE

SEVILLA, CHARLES
SHOONOVER, WINSTON--DDLY PLEASURES #3,
P34, MYS--
"WILKES: HIS LIFE & CRIMES" '92

SEWALL, ROBERT
ABBOTT, BRUCE--[8]
LAMONT, WOOD C.--[8]

SEWARD, WILLIAM W. JR.
RIVES, LEIGH--[1][22]AMERICAN

SEWART, ALAN
NASH, PADDER--[1][34]MYS--
HALE "GRASS" '82
HALE "COUP DE GRASS" '83 & 6 MORE'82-6
WELL, ALAN STEWART--[1][34]MYS--
HALE "CANDICE IS DEAD" '84
HALE "WHERE LIONEL LIES" '84 & 2 MORE

SEWELL, BROCARD
JEROME, JOSEPH--[1][31]

SEYDEL, MILDRED [W]
SEYDELL, MILDRED--[1]

SEYMOUR, ARTHUR JAMES
SEYMOUR, A.J.--[1]

SEYMOUR, DOROTHY JANE Z.
JOHNSON, ELEANOR--[1][31]

SEYMOUR, FREDERICK HENRI
LORD GILHOOLEY--[1][2]

SEYMOUR, LEE EDWARD
LEE, EDWARD--[7]SF/HOR--
DIAM 'COVEN': #1 & #2
PINN "GHOULS" '88
STRAKER, PHILIP--V. BERCH LTR TO HUBIN '94,
MYS--
ZEBRA "NIGHT DATE" '82
ZEBRA "NIGHT LUST" '82

SEYMOUR, MARJORIE F.
CYNTHIA--[1]
PLANE, ANNIE--[1]

SEYMOUR, WILLIAM NAPIER
NAPIER, WILLIAM--[1]

SGARLATO, NICO
CASTELLANO, FRANCO--[1]

SHACKET, SHELDON R.
ALBRAN, KEHLOG--W/MARTIN A. COHEN,[1][31]

SHACKLETON BAILEY, DAVID
BAILEY, D.R. SHACKLETON--[31]
BAILEY, DAVID R.--[1]

SHACKLETON, DORIS [C]
FRENCH, DORIS--[1][31]

SHACKLETON, EDITH
HEALD, EDITH--[8]

SHACOCHIS, ROBERT G.
SHACOCHIS, BOB--[7]SF--
"THE NEXT NEW WORLD: STORIES" '89

SHADI, DOROTHY CLOTELLE C
CLARKE, DOROTHY CLOTELLE--[1][31]

SHAFFER, ANTHONY & PETER
ANTONY, PETER--[5][18][31][32][34]MYS--
EVANS "WOMAN IN THE WARDROBE" '51
EVANS "HOW DOTH THE LITTLE CROCODILE?" '52
LM "BEFORE & AFTER" JUN '53

SHAGINYAN, MARIETTA S.
DOLLAR, JIMMY--[1][31]
DOLLAR, JIM--[39]GERMAN/SF

SHAHANI, RANJEE
RANJEE--[1]

SHAHEEN, LEIGH
HASKELL, LEIGH--[21][26]ROM--
"THE PARAGON BRIDE"
"THE VENGEFUL VISCOUNT"

SHAKARJIAN, VICTORIA
GREGORY, VERONICA--[9][21][26]ROM--
"HEART'S POSSESSION"

SHALEEN, LEIGH
HUDSON, HARRIET L.--[9][21][26]ROM--
"IN SEARCH OF LOVE"
ZAYNE, VALERIE--[9][21][26]ROM--
"SILVER DAWN"

SHALKOVITZ, ARIEH LEIB
BEN-AVIGDOR--[22]HEBREW

SHALLENBERGER, SHARON MC.
MCCAFFREE, SHARON--[21][26]ROM--
"NOW & FOREVER" & 4 OTHER NOVELS

SHALLITT, JOSEPH
BRADY, MATT--V. BERCH--
GM PSEUDS, PP 33,[34]MYS--
GM 376 "TAKE YOUR LAST LOOK" '54

SHAMBROOK, RONA [GREEN]
RANDALL, RONA--[1][3]MYS/ROM--
COLLINS "GLENRANNOCH" '73
COLLINS "DRAGONMEDE" '74 & 21 MORE
STANDAGE, VIRGINIA--[9][21][26]ROM--
"GOLDEN REBEL"

SHAMIR, MOSHE
KELLER, ASAPH--[1]
OFFERE, M.--[1]
SHAMGAR--[1]

SHAMLU, AHMAD
BAMDAD, A.--[31]

SHANAHAN, MARGARET MARY
MARLOWE, MARY--[36]AUSTRALIA/MYS--
ENDEAVOR "PSALMIST AT DAWN" '34

SHANK, LINDA
CUTTER, LEELA--V. BERCH LTR TO HUBIN '94, MYS--
ST. MARTIN'S "MURDER AFTER TEA TIME" '81
ST. MARTIN'S "WHO STOLE STONEHENGE?" '83
ST. MARTIN'S "DEATH OF THE PARTY" '85

SHANKMAN, SARAH
STOREY, ALICE--LACHMAN LST, DDLY PLEAS. #3,
[34]MYS--
"FIRST KILL ALL THE LAWYERS" '88
"THEN HANG ALL THE LAWYERS" '89

SHANKS, WILLIAM F.G.
GORE, MARY--[1]

SHANN, B.V.
BEVIS, JAMES--W/MARTEN CUMBERLAND,[1]

SHANN, RENEE
GAYE, CAROL--[1][31]
PENT, KATHERINE--[8]

SHANNON, DORIS
GIROUX, E.X.--[1][3][31]MYS--
ST. MARTIN'S "A DEATH FOR A DANCER" '90
& 7 MORE '84-90

SHANNON, KATHLEEN
WAVERLY, SHANNON--[21][26]ROM--
"NO TRESPASSING"
"NEW LEASE ON LOVE" & 2 MORE

SHANNON, MARY JANE
SHANNON, LYTLE--[1]

SHANNON, MIKE
HOWARD, BILL--[31]

SHANNON, TERRY
PAYZANT, JESSIE MERCER K.--[33]

SHAPIRO, JULIAN L.
SANFORD, JOHN B.--[1]

SHAPIRO, KAREN
SEBASTIAN, ANNIE--[37]MYS--
SPDW "VERDICT" WIN '82

SHAPOVALOV, LEV S.
OVALOV, LEV S.--[1]

SHAPPIRO, BUDD
ARTHUR BURT & BUDD--[19]WEST--NUMEROUS NOVELS

SHAPPIRO, HERBERT ARTHUR
ARTHUR, BERT--C. WINTEROWD '94--
EDITOR ERROR ON A 'BLACK CAT WESTERN' STORY
ARTHUR, HERBERT--[1]
CAMPBELL, CLIFF--C. WINTEROWD '94, WEST,HP--
HERBERT, ARTHUR--[1]

SHARAM, NORMAN
STEED, NEVILLE--V. BERCH LTR TO HUBIN '94,
MYS--
WEIDENFELD "DIE-CAST" '87 & MORE

SHARE, MARIE-LOUISE
MARIE-LOUISE--[2]

SHARKEY, JOHN MICHAEL
ABBOT, RICK--[1][34]FRENCH/MYS--
3 PLAYS '80-7
CHANDLER, MARK--V. BERCH LTR TO
G. BRADLEY '93, MYS--
FERRIS, MONK--V. BERCH LTR TO G. BRADLEY '93
MYS--2 FRENCH PLAYS '84

SHARKEY, JOHN MICHAEL [CONT]
JOHNSON, MIKE--[1][2][3]MYS--
3 FRENCH PLAYS '78-89
SHARKEY, JACK--[1][32]MYS--
AHMM "DEADLY SHADE OF BLUE" MAY '62
WM "NO HARM DONE" WINT '70
WM "THE ARM OF ENMOND" SPR '71

SHARKEY, MRS. EMMA A.B.
COLLINS, MRS. E. BURKE--[1][34]MYS--
MUNRO "LILLIAN'S VOW; OR, MYSTERY OF RALEIGH HOUSE" 1889
STREET "A DEBT OF VENGEANCE" 1890

SHARMAT, MARJORIE WEINMAN
ANDREWS, WENDY--[33]

SHAROT, ANGELA
LANSBURY, ANGELA--[8]

SHARP, ETHEL
DUFF, BELDON--HAWK/BRINEY INTRVW '93, MYS--
DBLDY "CENTRAL PARK MURDER" '29
DBLDY "ASK NO QUESTIONS" '30

SHARP, HENRY
AINSWORTH, OLIVER--[1]

SHARP, IAN
JUDGE, THE--[8]

SHARP, JACK
STAFFORD, JOHN K.--[34]MYS,HP--
MAGNET #381 "A MILLIONAIRE'S CRIME" '05

SHARP, LUKE
BARR, ROBERT--L. ROBBINS LTR '94,[32]MYS--
EQMM "ABSENT-MINDED COTERIE" MAY '50
MSMM "DOOM OF LONDON" SPR '67
SN "A GAME OF CHESS" SUM '67

SHARP, ROBERT GEORGE
DEEGAN, JON J.--[1][2][3][23]MYS,HP--
'GROWLER' SERIES '51-3
'TIME TRAVEL' TRILOGY '52-4
HAM STD "RECONNOITRE KRELLIG II" '51
"UNDERWORLD OF ZELLO" '52
HAM STD "BEYOND THE FOURTH DOOR" '54
'INTER X' SERIES
STORME, MICHAEL--[34]MYS,GHOSTED--
ARCH "MAKE MINE A CORPSE" '50

SHARP, WILLIAM
BROOKS, W.H.--[1]SCOTTISH-AUSTRALIAN
MACLEOD, FIONA--[2][8][13][22]
SCOTTISH-AUSTRALIAN
SIWAARMILL, H.P.--[1]SCOTTISH-AUSTRALIAN
TIREBUCK, W.--[1]SCOTTISH-AUSTRALIAN

SHARPLES, ALFRED
PLOWSHARE, JOHN--[1]

SHARPLES, RICHARD MILNE
MILNE, RICHARD--[34]MYS--
WDL "HOUR OF JUSTICE" '54

SHARROCK, MARIAN EDNA
DORMIE, M.A.--[1]

SHASTRI, PRITHVINATH
MANUGUPTA--[1]
MOHAN, P. NATH--[1]
NAJAM--[1]
VASISTHA, MOHAN--[1]

SHATTUCK, DORA [RICHARDS]
SHATTUCK, RICHARD--[1][3]MYS--
MRW "SNARK WAS A BOJUM" '41
SIMON "HALF-HAUNTED SALON" '45 & 2 MORE

SHAUQI, AHMAD
SHAUKI, AHMAD BEY--[22]EGYPTIAN-ARAB
SHAUKI, AHMED--[22]EGYPTIAN-ARAB

SHAVER, PAT
ADAMS, PEPPER--W/DEBRAH MORRIS,[9][21][26]ROM--
"IN HOT PURSUIT"
"OLD BLACK MAGIC"
JORDAN, JOANNA--W/DEBRAH MORRIS,
[9][21][26]ROM--
NEVER SAY FAREWELL"
"DESTINY'S DREAM"
STACEY, JO ANN--W/DEBRAH MORRIS,
[9][21][26]ROM--
"ONCE UPON A DREAN"
"TEMPTING FATE"
THOMAS, DIANNE--W/DEBRAH MORRIS,
[9][21][26]ROM--
"HEAVEN CAN WAIT"
"OUT OF THE BLUE" & MORE

SHAVER, RICHARD S.
AMHERST, WES--[1][2][11][31]
BENSON, EDWIN--[1][2][11]
BLADE, ALEXANDER--[1][2][11]HP--ZIFF-DAVIS
DEXTER, EDWIN--[1][2][11]
DEXTER, PETER--[1][2][11]
DORET, RICHARD--[2][11]
DOROT, PETER--[1]
DORSET, RICHARD--[1][2]
ELCLAIR, MOLLIE--[1][2][11]
ENGLISH, RICHARD--[1][2][11]
IRWIN, G.H.--[1][2][11]HP--ZIFF-DAVIS
LOHRMAN, PAUL--[1][2][11][23]SF,HP--
ZIFF-DAVIS
PATTON, FRANK--[1][2][11]HP--AMAZING
RAYCRAFT, STAN--[1][2][11]
SHARPE, RICHARD D.--[1][2][11]

SHAW, BYNUM G.
GILLETTE, BOB--[1]

SHAW, CAPT. JOSEPH T.
HARPER, MARK--E.R.HAGEMANN, COMPH. INDEX
BLK MASK,[37]MYS--
CRB 'CASS MANNING' NVLTS '39

SHAW, CHARLES
SINGER, BANT--[1][34][36]AUSTRALIAN/MYS--
COLLINS "YOU'RE WRONG, DELANY" '53
COLLINS "DON'T SLIP, DELANEY" '54
COLLINS "HAVE PATIENCE, DELANEY" '54
& 1 OTHER

SHAW, FELICITY
MORICE, ANNE--[1][32][34]MYS--
25 NOVELS '70-90
AHMM "FALSE ALARM" AUG '79
AHMM "RISE & FALL OF SARAH MERRION" JAN '80
AHMM "EXTRA MAN" OCT '80

SHAW, FRANK H.
CLEVELAND, FRANK--[1]
GUTHRIE, ARCHIBALD--[1]
HAMMERTON, GRENVILLE--[1]
HUBERT, FRANK--[1]

SHAW, GEORGE BERNARD
DI BASSETTO, CORNO--[8][31]
G.B.S.--[8][31]

SHAW, HENRY WHELLER
BILLINGS, JOSH--[31]

SHAW, JANE
GILLESPIE, JANE--[8]

SHAW, JANET
BEELER, JANET--[31][33]

SHAW, LAWRENCE TAYLOR
DESTINY, ARCHIBALD--[1][2][11]
SHAW, LARRY T.--[7][23]SF
THOR, TERRY--[1][2][11][23]SF--

SHAW, PATRICIA
SHAW, P.B.--HAWK/SHAW INTRVW '93, MYS--
WALKER - POLICE PROCEDURAL

SHAW, ROBERT
SHAW, BOB--[23]IRISH/SF

SHAW, RUFUS JR.
SHAW, SUGARWOLF--[1]

SHAW, STANLEY GORDON
DARE, CAPTAIN--[1]
GORDON, S.S.--[1]
GORDON, STANLEY--[1]
HERITAGE, JOHN--[1]
STRANGE, HARRY--[1]
WALLACE, GORDON--[1][34]MYS--
AMALG "ON THE TRAIL OF JUSTICE" '20

SHAW, THELMA
SHAW, DAWN--[1]
SHAW, T.D.W.--[1]

SHAW, WILLIAM HARLAN
HARLAN--[31]

SHAW, [COLIN] HOWARD
HOWARD, COLIN--[3]MYS--
HALE "KILLING NO MURDER" '72

SHEA, CORNELIUS
AUTHOR, WRECK OF GLAUCAS--[23]SF
RAYMOND, P.K.--[23]SF--
"THE ENCHANTED EMERALD" 1902

SHEA, JOHN GERALD
FITZGERALD, JACK--[1][22][31]AMERICAN

SHEA, MICHAEL [S.M.]
SINCLAIR, MICHAEL--[3][23]MYS/SF--
SIGN "HOW TO STEAL A MILLION" '66
SIGN "DOLLAR COVENANT" '73

SHEA, PATRICK
LAUGHLIN, P.S.--[8][31]

SHEA, ROBERT [J]
EULENSPIEGEL, ALEXANDER--[1][31]
GLASS, SANDRA--[1][31]

SHEA, SHIRLEY
FOSTER, MARION--[31][32][34]MYS--
AHMM "SYSTEM FOR SUCKERS" NOV '65
FBD "MONARCHS ARE FLYING" '87

SHEARD, VIRGINIA [S]
SHEARD, VIRNA--[1]

SHEARER, SONIA M.
SHANE, NEVIS--[1]

SHEATS, MARY BONEY
BONEY, MARY LILY--[1][31]

SHEBAR, SHARON S.
SHAY, LACEY--W/JUDITH SCHODER,
[9][21][31][33]ROM--
WALLABY "LOVING ENEMY" '83

SHECKLEY, ROBERT
BARBEE, PHILLIPS--[1][2][11][31]
LANG, NED--[1][2][31]
O'DONNEVAN, FINN--[1][2][11]

SHEEAN, DIANA
FORBES-ROBERTSON, DIANA--[31]

SHEEDY, ALEXANDRA ELIZABETH
SHEEDY, ALLY--[1][33]

SHEEHAN, PERLEY POORE
REGARD, PAUL--[1]

SHEEHAN, VALERIE HARMS
HARMS, VALERIE--[1]

SHEEHY, EDNA
DEAN, CAROLE--[26]ROM--
"CALIFORNIA MAN"
"JUST ONE KISS"
"ONE TOUGH COOKIE"

SHEFFEY, ASA
HAYDON, ROBERT [EARL]--[1]

SHEIL, MATTHEW PHIPPS
SHEIL, M.P.--[1]

SHEILDS, JAMES
O'SHEEL, SHAEMAS--[1]

SHEINFELD, LESLIE A.
FIELD, LESLIE A.--[1]

SHEIOLDS, GEORGE OLIVER
COQUINA--[1]

SHEKERJIAN, REGINA TOR
TOR, REGINA--[1][33]

SHELDON, ALICE H. BRADLEY
BRADLEY, ALICE--[1][11]
SHELDON, ALICE--[23]SF--
NEW YORKER "THE LUCKY ONES" '46
SHELDON, RACCOONA--[1][2][11][23]SF--
SHORT STORIES
TIPTREE, JAMES JR.--[2][4][7][23]SF--
"WOMEN MEN DON'T SEE" '73
TOR "GIRL WHO WAS PLUGGED IN" '89
& MORE

SHELDON, CHARLES MONROE
SHELDON, C.M.--[1]

SHELDON, ELEANOR BERNERT
BERNERT, ELEANOR H.--[1][31]

SHELDON, GILBERT
COLWALL, JAMES--[1][3]MYS--
CASSELL "THE COOMBSBERROW MYS" 1890

SHELDON, MURIEL
BATHERMAN, MURIEL--[31][33]

SHELDON, PETER
GADDES, PETER--[1][31]

SHELDON, WALTER J.
HARDIN, J.D.--[1][31]WEST,HP--
JAMES, WALTER S.--[1][31]
KENNEDY, GEORGE--[3]MYS,GHOSTED--
AV "MURDER ON HIGH" '84
AV "MURDER ON LOCATION" '83
SHELDON, WALT--[32][34]MYS--
SW "EMPEROR'S EYE" JUN '47
SP "FOG HIDES FEAR" AUG '56
MSMM "DEAD MAN'S CAT" NOV '56
SA "JOHNNY PRINGLE, DETECTIVE" AUG '56
MH "OEDIPUS" MAY '56
MM "QUIET HELL" APR '58
MD "MAKE ME AN ANGEL" APR '59
EQMM "ALWAYS KEEP RUNNING" FEB '61
SD "DATE WITH A WIDOW" OCT '64
WALKER, SHEL--[1][29][34]MYS--
LION 112 "MAN I KILLED" '52
PHOENIX "TOKYO ESCAPADE" '55
WALTERS, SELDON--[2][11]SF--
WALTERS, SHELLY--[1][34]MYS--
MCKAY "THE DUNES" '74

SHELL, VIRGINIA LAW
LAW, VIRGINIA W.--[1][31]

SHELLABARGER, SAMUEL
ESTEVEN, JOHN--[3][11][22][29]MYS--
DBLDY "VOODOO" '30
MOA "GRAVEYARD WATCH" '38 & 5 MORE
LORING, PETER--[3][22][29]MYS--
MCRS "GRIEF BEFORE NIGHT" '38
MCRS "MISS RONNING STONE" '39

SHELLENBERGER, SHARON
MCCAFFREE, SHARON--[9]ROM

SHELLEY, PERCY BYSSE
A GENTLEMAN OF OXFORD--[2]

SHELLEY, RICHARD MICHAEL
SHELLEY, RICK--[7]SF--
ROC 'VAYAN MEMOIR' SERIES:
#1 & 2 '90-1

SHELTON, RICHARD BARKER
HANNIGAN, FRANCIS J.--L. ROBBINS LTR MAR '94
OXFORD, JOHN BARTON--L. ROBBINS LTR MAR '94
SHELTON, BARKER--L. ROBBINS LTR MAR '94

SHEN CONGWEN
BI SHANG-GUAN--[31]
CHEN JIA--[31]
HUAN YUE--[31]

SHENNAN, VICTORIA
SANGSTER, ANN--[1]

SHEPARD, LESLIE ALBERT
JUHASZ, LESLIE A.--[31]

SHEPHERD, DONALD LEE
KEVERN, BARBARA--[3][17][31]MYS--
PINN "DARK EDEN" '73
PINN "DEVIL'S VINEYARD" '75 & 2 MORE

SHEPHERD, FLORENCE
HASTINGS, HARRINGTON--W/JOHN MARSH,[1][3]MYS--
HUTCH "CRIMINAL SQUARE" '29
HUTCH "WAR DOG STIRS" '30

SHEPHERD, JEAN
EWING, FREDERICK R.--W/THEODORE STURGEON,[11]--
BAL 165 "I, LIBERTINE" '56

SHEPHERD, MORGAN
JOHN-MARTIN--[2]

SHEPHERD, ROBERT HENRY W.
WISHART, HENRY--[22]SOUTH AFRICAN

SHEPHERD, WILLIAM JAMES
JAMES, PEREGRINE--[1]

SHEPPARD, JOHN HAMILTON G
CREEK, NATHAN--[8]

SHEPPARD, LANCELOT C.
CAPEL, ROGER--[1][22][31]ENGLISH

SHEPPARD, S. ROSSITER
MILTON, MARK--[1]
RICHARDS, FRANK--[1]HP--

SHERER, MICHAEL L.
TRUEBLOOD, THOMAS--V. BERCH LTR TO HUBIN '94, MYS--
CSS "A HIDDEN TREASURE" '85

SHERIDAN, ELSIE LEE
CROMWELL, ELSIE--[8]
GORDON, JANE--[8]
LEE, ELSIE--[1][7][8][11]
SHERIDAN, LEE--[11]

SHERIDAN, H.B.
SHERRY, GORDON--[3]MYS--
2 PLAYS '37-47

SHERIDAN, MICHAEL
SHERIDAN, LEE--W/ELSIE LEE,[1][3][29]MYS--
LAN "PIT & THE PENDULUM" '61

SHERIDAN, PHIL R.
P.R.S.--D. HERRICK-ECHOES #7, P28--
WIZARD MAG

SHERMAN, CHRIS
CLUTCHPIN, STANISLAUS--[2]

SHERMAN, CORDELIA CAROLN.
SHERMAN, DELIA--[7]SF--
ACE "THROUGH A BRAZEN MIRROR" '89

SHERMAN, DANIEL MICHAEL
TREVOR, DAN--W/TREVOR MELDAL-JOHNSEN,[7]SF--
JOVE 'NIGHT WHISTLERS' #1 '91
WILLIAMSON, SHERMAN--W/ROBIN WILLIAMSON, LACHMAN-EASTER LST '93,[34]MYS--
NEL "THE GLORY TRAP" '77

SHERMAN, ELEANOR RAE
FLEURIDAS, ELLIE RAE--[1][22][31]AMERICAN

SHERMAN, FRANK DEMPSTER
CARMEN, FELIX--[1]
WAGS, TWA--W/JOHN FREDERICK BANGS,[2]

SHERMAN, JORY [T]
ANVIC, FRANK--[1][7][11][31]COVER BYLINE SHOWS "FRANK ANVIC"
DENVER, WALT--[1][31]
MARTIN, CORT--[1]
MITCHUM, HANK--[1]
SHERMAN, CHARLOTTE A.--[1][34]MYS--
MAJOR "THE SHUTTERED ROOM" '75
TARRANT, WILMA--[1]

SHERREN, WILKINSON
FAY, NICHOLS--[1]

SHERRIFF, ROBERT CEDRIC
SHERRIFF, R.C.--[1]

SHERROD, BARBARA
NEIL, BARBARA--[21][26]ROM--
"BELLA"
"MASK OF WHITE SATIN" & MORE

SHERTZER, LINDA K.
PRYCE, MELINDA--[21][26]ROM--
"THIEF OF HEARTS"
"TIDES OF LOVE" & 4 MORE

SHERWOOD, MARGARET POLLOK
HASTINGS, ELIZABETH--[1]

SHERWOOD, MARY
A YOUNG LADY--[2][7]SF--

SHERWOOD, ROBERT EMMET
PERCY, BRIGHTON--[1]
SHERWOOD, R.E.--[1]
SHERWOOD, ROBERT E.--[32]MYS--
EQMM "EXTRA! EXTRA!" JAN '50

SHETTERLY, EMMA BULL
BULL, EMMA--[7]SF--
ACE "WAR FOR THE OAKS" '87
ACE "FALCON" '89
ACE "BONE DANCE: A FANT..." '91

SHEVCHENKO, ARKADY N.
ARKADYEV, N.--[31]

SHEVCHUK, TETIANA
BISHOP, TANIA KROITOR--[1]
SEMKIW, VIRLYANA--[1]

SHEWRING, WALTER
FRANCIS, HAYWARD--[1]

SHIAO, C.J.
STIVERS, DICK--[34]MYS,HP--
GE "AMAZON SLAUGHTER" '83

SHIBANO, TAKUMI
KOZUMI, REI--[23]JAPANESE/SF, SS

SHIBANO, TAKUMI
REI, KOSUMI--[1][2][11]SF--

SHIEL, MATTHEW PHIPPS
HOLMES, GORDON--W/LOUIS TRACY,[2][3][5]--
"FELDISHAM MYSTERY" '10
"HOUSE AROUND THE CORNER" '14
SHIEL, M.P.--[23][34]SF--
RICHARDS "HERE COMES THE LADY" '28
RICHARDS "BLACKBOX" '31 & MORE

SHIELDS, DINAH
CLARE, JANE--[9][21][26]ROM--
"OLD LOVE"
"NEW LOVE"

SHIELDS, MRS. S.A.
FROST, S. ANNIE--[1]

SHIFFERT, EDITH [M]
MARCOMBE, EDITH MARION--[1]

SHIFFMAN, JANIS LADEN
LADEN, JANIS--[9][21][26]ROM--
"BEWITCHING MINX"
"GILDED CAGE"
"MOONLIGHT VEIL"

SHIGEYUKI, KODA
ROHAN, KODA--[1]

SHIMSHELEVITZ, AARON
REUBENI, AARON--[1]HEBREW

SHINE, DEBORAH
ADAMS, EDITH--[1][33]
BRIGHT, SARAH--[1][31][33]
HARRIS, ROBIN--[1][33]
SLIER, DEBBY--[33]

SHINE, DENNIS FRANCIS J.
SHANNON, FRANK--[2]

SHINKLE, JAMES D.
SHINKLE, TEX--[1]

SHIPLEY, JOSEPH TWADDELL
GOLIARD, ROY--[1][31]

SHIPLEY, MIRIAM ALLEN [D]
DE FORD, MIRIAM ALLEN--[1]

SHIPMAN, NATALIE
ARTHUR, PHYLLIS--[8]

SHIPPEY, THOMAS A.
SHIPPEY, TOM--[23]SF

SHIRAS, WILMAR H.
HOWES, JANE--[1][2][23]SF--
ASF "SLOW DAWNING" '46
ASF "IN HIDING" '48

SHIRLEY, EDITH
AUSTRALIA JANE--[8]

SHIRLEY, JOHN
CUTTER, TOM--R. BENOIT, MYS,HP--
'PSYCHO SOLDIERS' SERIES
DRUMM, D.B.--[7][23]SF,HP--
DELL 'TRAVELER' SERIES: #2-6 & 8 '84-6

SHIRLEY, RALPH
IRETON, ROLLO--[31]

SHIRO, SHIBA
SANSHI, TOKAI--[22]JAPANESE

SHIRREFFS, GORDON DONALD
DONALDS, GORDON--[16][22][28]WEST--
AVALON "ARIZONA JUSTICE" '56
AVALON "TOP GUN" '57
FLYNN, JACKSON--[16][22][28][31][33]WEST--
AWARD "SHOOTOUT" '74
AWARD "DUEL AT DODGE CITY" '74
AWARD "CHEYENNE VENGEANCE" '75
GORDON, STEWART--[16][22][28][31][33]WEST--
AVALON "GUNSWIFT" '56
MACLEAN, ART--[1]

SHIVELEY, THORNTON
LEE, THORNE--[32][34]MYS--
DS "WOMAN IN THE ATTIC" JUL '47
DUELL "MONSTER OF LAZY HOOK" '49
ABELAIRD "SUMMER SHOCK" '56
& 16 OTHER `DOC SAVAGE' STORIES

SHIVER, SHIRLEY T.
FAY, SHIRLEY ANN--[1][32]MYS--
AHMM "DON'T FORGET TO WRITE" MAY '62
AHMM "EXPERT" MAR '63
SA "MUD IN THE DEVIL'S EYE" JAN '64
SA "IN FRENCH COIN" MAR'67

SHIVER, SHIRLEY T. [CONT]
FAYE, SHIRLEY--[26]ROM--
"BACK OF BEYOND"
"FACE TO FACE"

SHIVPURI, GOPI KRISHNA
KRISHNA, GOPI--[31]INDIAN--NON-FICT

SHNAIDER, JULIA
KRAVCHENKO, ULIANA--[22]UKRAINIAN

SHNAYERSON, MICHAEL
BEAHAN, MICHAEL--[21][26]ROM,HP--
'AMER. EXPLORERS' SERIES:
"JOHN FREMONT, CALIFORNIA BOUND"

SHOLL, ANNA MCCLURE
CORSON, GEOFFREY--[1][22]MYS

SHOMAKER, DIANNA
MCDONALD, DIANNA--[1]

SHORE, LARRY
DE MEXICO, N.R.--D. NELSON-ELLISON INTRO TO
"ANGRY CANDY" '89, BEAT--
UNI 19 "MARIJUANA GIRL" '51
SUSN 1 "STRANGE PURSUIT" '51
IN 15 "PRIVATE CHAUFFEUR" '52

SHORT, CHRISTOPHER
CHARTERIS, LESLIE--[34]MYS,GHOSTED--
DBLDY "SAINT & THE HAPSBURG NECKLACE" '76

SHORT, ELEANOR [T.K.]
KINKEAD, ELEANOR TALBOT--[1]

SHORTER, ALYWARD
JENSI, MUGANWA NSIKU--[31]

SHORTT, CHARLES RUSHTON
RUSHTON, CHARLES--[1][32][34]MYS--
JENKINS "ANOTHER CRIME" '34 & MORE
LM "DEEP DRAWER" SEPT '79

SHRAKE, EDWIN
SHRAKE, BUD--[28]WEST--
"WILLIE NELSON: AN AUTOBIOGRAPHY"
W/WILLIE NELSON '88
SHRAKE, BUDD--[28]--
PLAY "NIGHTWING" W/STEVE SHAGAN
PLAY "TOM HORN" W/THOMAS McGUANE

SHREFFLER, KIM
RICHARDS, DENISE--[26]ROM--
"DEADLY COINCIDENCE"
"A FAMILY AFFAIR"
"HANNAH'S HERO"

SHRIVER, HARRY C.
HORNBLOWER, HARRY C.--[1][31]

SHROYER, FREDERICK
FREYER, ERICK--[2]

SHU CH'ING-CH'UN
LAO SHE--[31]

SHU, AUSTIN CHI-WEI
CHI-WEI--[31]

SHU-JEN, CHOU
CH'O, CHOU--[31]
HSUN, LU--[31]
LUSIN--[22]CHINESE--
SHORT STORIES

SHUBIN, SEYMOUR
RICHARDS, AL--[1]

SHULL, MARGARET ANNE W.
SHULL, PEG--[1]
WINDOR, ANNIE--[1]

SHULMAN, FAY GRISSOM S.
FAY, STANLEY--[31]
GRISSOM, FAY--[31]

SHULMAN, IRVING
RAWSON, TABOR--[34]MYS--
SIGN "I WANT TO LIVE" '58

SHULMAN, SANDRA DAWN
MONTAGUE, LISA--[9][21][26]ROM--
"LADY OF DARKNESS"
"FORTUNE'S FOLLY"
"EMPEROR'S JEWELS"

SHULTZ, GLADYS DENNY
GARDNER, ANNE--[1][31]

SHUMAN, MALCOLM KARL
KARL, M.S.--LACHMAN-EASTER LST '93,[34]MYS--
LEIS "MOBIUS MAN" '82
DODD "KILLER'S INK" '88
ST. MARTINS "DEATH NOTICE" 90
SHUMAN, M.K.--[31][34]MYS--
BEAUFORT "FRENCHMAN'S BLOOD" '87
ST. MARTIN'S "MAYA STONE MURDERS" '89
ST. MARTIN'S "CAESAR CLUE" '90

SHUMSKY, ZENA FELDMAN
COLLIER, JANE--[1][34]MYS--
HALE "DEADLY FEAST" '78
COLLIER, ZENA--[1][32]MYS--
AHMM "TRIAL BY NIGHT" JAN '74
HAMPSON, ZENA--[1]

SHURLY, ERNEST WILLIAM
HASLER, MARTIN--[1]

SHUSHTARY, JOHN
CANNING, JOHN--[1]

SHUTE, EVAN VERE
JAMESON, VERE--[1]

SHUTE, WALTER
ANDREWS, JOHN--[34]MYS,HP--
AMALG "THE MAN WHO DEFIED THE WORLD" '32
EDWARDS, JOHNSON--[1]
EDWARDS, WALTER--[3][29]MYS--
AMALG "MR. X FROM SCOTLAND YARD" '39
& 14 MORE
MAXWELL, GORDON--[1]
WENTWORTH, CHARLES--[1]HP--

SHUTTE, JAMES E.
DERTOLLE, JAIME--HAWK/SHUTTE INTERVIEW '93

SHWARTZ, SUSAN MARTHA
KENDALL, GORDON--W/SHARIANN LEWITT,[7][23]SF--
TOR "WHITE WING" '85

SIBERT, WILLA
CATHER, WILLA--[1]

SIBLEY, INEZ K.
PENNIBB--[1]

SICKLE, MILTON VAN
ALEXANDER, MARSHA--V. BERCH-BRNDN/BC PSEUDS, BAE 22, ADULT--
BC 7489 "FIRST TASTE OF INCEST"
BRNDN 2047 "THIS BURNING FLESH"
BRNDN 6301 "SENSOUS CHILD BRIDE"
EASTWOOD, THOMAS--V. BERCH-BRNDN/BC PSEUDS, BAE 22, ADULT--
BC 7349 "INSATIABLE CO-EDS"

SICKLEMORE, RICHARD
S., R. ESQ.--[34]MYS--
MINERVA "NEW MONK" ca1800

SIDDLE, CHARLES
SLINGSBY, RUFUS--W/FREDERICK PEEL, [1][3][22]MYS--
LONG "MURDERS AT HIGHBRIDGE" '29

SIDDON, SALLY
BRADFORD, SALLY--W/BARBARA BRADFORD, [9][21][26]ROM--
"THE ARRANGEMENT"
"SPRING THAW" & MORE
SIDDON, BARBARA--W/BARBARA BRADFORD, [9][21][26]ROM--
"DECEIVE ME DARLING"

SIDEBOTTHAM, PETER
SURD, ABE--[2]

SIDGWICK, CECILY
DEAN, MRS. ANDREW--[1]

SIDIS, WILLIAM JAMES
FOLUP, FRANK--[1]

SIDNEY, SAMUEL
BUSHMAN, A--[13]AUSTRALIAN

SIDNEY-FRYER, DOANLD
FRYER, DONALD S.--[31]

SIEBENSTADT, INGEBURG
WITTGEN, TOM--[39][40]GERMAN/MYS--
"DIE FALSCHE MADONNA" '82

SIEBER, SAM DIXON
KERR, NORMAN D.--[1][22][31]AMERICAN

SIEBOND, VALERIE
GREYLAND, VALERIE--[9]ROM

SIEGBAHN, BO
PHANDERSON, BO--[29]MYS--
BONNIER "EN GALAKVALL PA" '70

SIEGEL, BENJAMIN
BENN, MATTHEW--[1][31]

SIEGEL, DORIS
WELLS, SUSAN--[1][3]MYS/ROM--
SIMON "FOOTSTEPS IN THE AIR" '40
SIMON "WITCHES POND" '47 & 2 MORE

SIEGEL, JEROME
KENTON, BERNARD J.--[1][2][11]

SIEGEL, MARY-ELLEN KULKIN
KULKIN, MARY-ELLEN--[31]

SIEGEL, NORABELLE ROTH
NASH, NOREEN--[21]ROM--
"BY LOVE FULFILLED"

SIEGENTHAL, DEBORAH
SIMMONS, DEBORAH--CRPG,[21][26]ROM--
AV "FORTUNE HUNTER"
AV "HEART'S MASQUERADE" '89

SIEGL, HELEN
SIEGEL, HELEN--[33]

SIEGLER, EUGENE
RELGIS, EUGENE--[1]

SIENKIEWICZ, HENRYK
LITWOS--[22]POLISH

SIEPMANN, MARY
WESLEY, MARY--[8]

SIEURIN, SVEN
NORTON, RICHARD--[29]MYS--
"OLJE-LIGAN" '41
AM 33 "MYSTIK I BERGSLAGEN" '46

SIEVEKING, LANCELOT DE G.
SIEVEKING, L. DE GIBERNE--[23]SF
SIEVEKING, LANCE--[1][23][32]MYS--
EQMM "THE BOOKHAWKER" APR '54

SIGFUSDOTTIR, LARA MARGAR
SIGFUSDOTTIR, GRETA--[1]

SILBER, DIANA
HENSTELL, DIANA--[7][31][34]MYS--
BB "OTHER SIDE" '8
BB "DEADLY FRIEND" '85
BB "NEW MORNING DRAGON" '87

SILBERBERG, LESLIE F.
STONE, LESLIE F.--[1][11]--
AKA LESLIE F. RUBENSTEIN

SILBERMAN, ALEX
RECK, ALEXANDER--[14]ADULT--
OLYM TC#456 "COLORS ROAR BY" '69

SILBERSCHLAG, EISIG
STRONG, ERIC--[1]

SILBERSTEIN, JAY JEHIEL
ZIF, JAY JEHIEL--[1]

SILVANI, ANITA
A.F.S.--[2][31]

SILVERBERG, KAREN HABER L
HABER, KAREN--[7][23]SF--
FSF "MADRE DE DIOS" '88

SILVERBERG, ROBERT
AGHILL, GORDON--W/RANDALL GARRETT, [1][2][23][31]
ARNETTE, ROBERT--[2][11][23][31][33]HP--ZIFF-DAVIS
BEAUCHAMP, LOREN--SILVERBERG LTR & WL '93, ADULT--
MDWD 7 "LOVE NEST" '58
MDWD 18 "CONNIE" '59
MDWD 21 "UNWILLING SINNER" '59
MDWD 27 "ANOTHER NIGHT, ANOTHER LOVE" '59
MDWD 30 "MEG" '60
MDWD "NURSE CAROLYN" '60
MDWD "SIN ON WHEELS" '61
MDWD 86 "THE FIRES WITHIN" '61
MDWD F102 "AND WHEN SHE WAS BAD" '61
MDWD F145 "STRANGE DELIGHTS" '62
MDWD 148 "SIN A LA CARTE" '62
MDWD F206 "CAMPUS SEX CLUB" '62
MDWD F226 "WAYWARD WIDOW" '62

SILVERBERG, ROBERT [CONT]

BETHLEN, T.D.--[1][2][23][31]
BLACK, EDGAR--J. HOUSE-BAE 25--
MON K56 "SIR WINSTON CHURCHILL" '61
BLADE, ALEXANDER--W/RANDALL GARRETT,
[2][11][23][31]SF,HP-- ZIFF-DAVIS
BLAINE, LAWRENCE L.--W/ELEAZAR LIPSKY,
BAE 17,[2]WEST--
"FRONTIER LAWYER"
BROWN, DR. WALTER C.--SILVERBERG LTR/WL
TO MUNROE '93, ADULT--
MON MB515 "THE SINGLE GIRL" '61
BURKE, RALPH--W/RANDALL GARRETT,[2][23][31]SF--
BURNETT, W.R.--W/W.R. BURNETT,[2]GHOSTED--
COMPLETED "ROUND THE CLOCK AT VOLARI'S"
CHALLON, DAVID--MUNROE RVW '93, ADULT--
BDSD 803 "SUBURBAN SIN CLUB" '59
BDSD 808 "CAMPUS LOVE CLUB" '59
BDSD 820 "FRENCH SIN PORT" '59
BDSD 821 "THIRST FOR LOVE" '59
CHARIOT CB-193 "MAN MAD" '60
CHAR CB129 "UNTAMED" '60
[SHOWS "RICK WENTWORTH" ON COVER]
BDSD 961 "SUBURBAN AFFAIR" '60
BDSD 973 "CAMPUS HELLCAT" '61
CHAPMAN, WALKER--[2][31][33]--
BOBBS-MERRILL "KUBLA KHAN: LORD OF
XANADU" '66 & 3 OTHERS
CLARK, V.S.--MUNROE RVW '93, ADULT--
CHARIOT CB-175 "COMPANY GIRL" '61
CLINTON, DIRK--BAE 17,[2][32]MYS--
TR "VICIOUS BABYSITTER" JUN '59
TR "MAN IN A CHEAP HOTEL" DEC '59
GU "YOU DON'T OWN ME" MAR '60
GU "SEE YOU IN HELL" JUN '60
TR "GIRL FROM HIS PAST" AUG '60
TR "REAL TOUGH BREAK" MAY '60
GU "I CAN'T DIE NOW" MAR '61
TR "THE KIDNAPPED BEAUTY" MAY '61
COOK, ROY--[2][31]--
LIPP "LEADERS OF LABOR" '66
DERN, DANIEL P.--COPYWRITE RECORDS--
"YES SIR THAT'S MY" '78
DEXTER, JOHN--MUNROE RVW '93, ADULT,HP--
DRUMMOND, WALTER--[2][31]--
REGY RB301 "PHILOSOPHER OF EVIL" '62
REGY RB318 "HOW TO SPEND MONEY" '63
ELIOT, DAN--[2][31]
ELLIOTT, DON--BAE 17,[2][31]--
VARIATION AS 'DAN ELIOT'
SILVERBERG WL 7 AUG '93, ADULT--
IH470 "ALTERNATE WIFE"
IH482 "SIN PEEPER"
IH489 "COUSIN-LOVER"
IH492 "THE PAIN LUSTERS"
IH493 "TEASER"
IH501 "CAMPUS TRAMP"
SUNR 519 "PICKUP"
SR589 "LUST CAT"
CB524 "REGISTERED NYMPHO"
LEIS # "THE LUSTING FLESH"
[BOB UNCERTAIN OF TITLE]
EB723 "SIN COUNSELLOR"
ER742 "LUST SPREE"
SR557 "FLESH BOARDER"
EB944 "FLESH TAKER"
ER1249 "SIN KITTEN"
ER714 "LUST LEAGUE"
ER1258 "PASSION BARONS"
NB1751 "SIN SISTERS"
NB1829 "ALL THE BEST BEDS"
NTSD 1501 "LOVE ADDICT '59
NTSD 1504 "GANG GIRL" '59
NTSD 1508 "SUMMERTIME AFFAIR" '60
NTSD 1509 "PARTY GIRL" '60
NTSD 1512 "NAKED HOLIDAY" '60

SILVERBERG, ROBERT [CONT]

ELLIOT, DON [CONT]
NTSD 1516 "SIN ON WHEELS" '60
NTSD 1521 "PASSION TRAP" '60
NTSD 1528 "THE LECHER" '60
NTSD 1529 "FLESH PEDDLERS" '60
NTSD "BACKSTAGE SINNER" '61
NTSD "LUST GODDESS" '61
"SIN CRUISE" '61
MDNT "KEPT MAN" '62
MDNT "SHAME HOUSE" '62
EMBR "SIN HELLION" '63
NTSD "SIN SERVANT" '63
EVNG "BEATNIK WANTON" '64
EVNG "FLESH BRIDE" '64
LEIS "FLESH PRIZE" '64
EMBR "FLESH TAKER" '64
LEIS "SIN WARPED" '64
EVNG "SWITCH TRAP" '64
IDHR "NUDIE PACKET" '65
SNDN "YOUNG WANTON" '65
REED "JUNGLE STREET" '73
REED "DEPRAVITY TOWN" '73
GREER, RICHARD--W/RANDALL GARRETT,
[2][23][31]HP--
AMZ "GREAT GANDAR RACE" '56
HAMILTON, FRANKLIN--[2][31]HIST--
DIAL "1066" '63
DIAL "THE CRUSADES" '65
DIAL "CHALLENGE FOR A THRONE: THE WAR
OF THE ROSES" '67
HOLLANDER, PAUL--[2][31]HIST--
PUTNAM "THE LABORS OF HERCULES" '65
PUTNAM "SAM HOUSTON" '68
JARVIS, E.K.--[2][23][31]SF,HP--ZIFF-DAVIS
JORGENSEN, IVAR--W/RANDALL GARRETT,BAE 17,
[2][4][23][31][33]SF,HP--
AVALON "STARHAVEN" '58
KASTEL, WARREN--[2][23][31]SF,HP--
ZIFF-DAVIS '57
KNOX, CALVIN M.--BAE 17,[2][4][31][32]SF--
DA "LADY WITH A .38" SUM '57
ACE D-291 "LEST WE FORGET THEE, EARTH" '58
DA "HOT HEIRESS" SEPT '58
DA "SNATCH ME, SWEETHEART" NOV '58
DA "DOOMSDAY BOOK MURDERS" MAR '59
ACE D358 "PLOT AGAINST EARTH" '59
F253 "ONE OF OUR ASTEROIDS IS MISSING" '64
LONGMAN, MARLENE--[2]ADULT--
NTSD 1523 "LESBIAN LOVE" '65
NTSD 3023 "TAINTED ONE" '73
LYNCH, DAN--W/ELEAZAR LIPSKY,[2]MYS--
GM 1240 "FOUR TIME LOSER" '62
MALCOLM, DAN--[1][2][32]MYS--
GU "RUSSIAN ROULETTE" JUL '58
TR "DEATHTRAP OF DESIRE" APR '58
GU "LET HIM SWEAT" NOV '58
GU "ONE NIGHT OF VIOLENCE" MAR '59
TR "TOO EASY PICKUP" APR '59
TR "WIZARD WITH A SWITCHBLADE" FEB '59
TR "ONE GIRL TOO MANY" DEC '59
TR "PAWNBROKER" AUG '60
TR "SWEET LITTLE RACKET" NOV '60
GU "COLD CALCULATED MURDER" MAR '60
TR "PLAY IT COOL" FEB '60
TR "GIRL IN THE THUNDERBIRD" MAY '60
TR "DEATH BEHIND THE DOOR" MAY '61
GU "BEATNIK WIFE" SEPT '61
TR "MURDER OF A BEATNIK" NOV '61
TR "STAG MOVIE MURDER" FEB '62
GU "THE JUDGE'S MISTRESS" MAR '62
MARTIN, WEBBER--[1][2][23][31]SF--
MCKENZIE, RAY--[1][2][11]SF--
MERRIMAN, ALEX--[2][32]--
TR "I'LL BE GLAD WHEN YOU'RE DEAD" DEC '59
GU "HOTROD HELCATS" JUN '60
GU "BLONDE & THE BRUTE" MAY '59

SILVERBERG, ROBERT [CONT]
MITCHELL, CLYDE T.--W/RANDALL GARRETT,
[2][23][31]SF,HP--ZIFF-DAVIS
NELSON, MILDRED--BAE 17,[2]--
"TASTE OF POWER"
OSBORNE, DAVID--[2][4][11][23][31]SF--
AVALON "ALIENS FROM SPACE" '58
AVALON "INVISIBLE BARRIERS" '58
OSBORNE, GEORGE--[2][11][23][31]SF--
RANDALL, ROBERT--W/RANDALL GARRETT,
[2][4][31]SF--
GNOME "SHROUDED PLANET" '57
GNOME "DAWNING LIGHT" '59
ROBERTSON, ELLIS--W/HARLAN ELLISON,[1][2][31]
ROBINSON, LLOYD--[2][31]--
DBLDY "THE HOPEFULS: TEN PRESIDENTIAL
CANDIDATES" '66
DBLDY "THE STOLEN ELECTION: HAYES VS.
TILDEN" '68
RODMAN, ERIC--[1][2][32]MYS--
TR "DOUBLECROSSER'S DAUGHTER" DEC '58
TR "DRUNKEN SAILOR" OCT '58
GU "GROWN-UP KID GANG" JUL '58
GU "BIG TOUGH KIDS" JAN '59
TR "DEATH OF A GIGOLO" FEB '59
GU "HOLLYWOOD HOMOCIDE" JUL '59
TR "KILL THAT BABE" DEC '59
TR "HARD-HEARTED WOMAN" MAY '60
TR "MIAMI WOMAN" AUG '60
TR "TOO EXPENSIVE A WOMAN" FEB '61
TR "MAN WITH MY FACE" AUG '61
TR "CRIME OF PASSION" MAY '61
RYAN, MARK--MUNROE RVW '93,[32]MYS/BEAT--
TR "COOL CATS" OCT '59
BDSD 807 "TWISTED LUSTS" '59
BDSD 813 "STREETSOF SIN" '59
TR "RUMBLE FOR A REDHEAD" DEC '59
GU "BOY WITH A GUN" JUN '60
TR "MOTEL GIRL" MAY '60
BDSD 957 "COMPANY GIRL" '60
GU "BEATNIK KILLER" SEPT '60
GU "DEATH OF A B-GIRL" DEC '60
GU "DEATH OF A GAMBLER" MAR '61
GU "NEVER TRUST A STRIPPER" JUN '61
BDSD 957 "SAVAGE LOVE" '61
BDSD 980 "ILLICIT AFFAIR" '61
SEBASTIAN, LEE--[2][11][31][33]--
HOLT "RIVERS" '66
HOLT "THE SOUTH POLE" '68
SPENCER, LEONARD G.--W/RANDALL GARRETT,
[2][23][31]SF,HP--
AMZ "BEAST WITH 7 TAILS" '56
TENNESHAW, S.M.--W/RANDALL GARRETT,
[2][23][31]SF,HP--ZIFF-DAVIS
THORNTON, HALL--[2][11][23][31]SF--
VANCE, GERALD--W/RANDALL GARRETT,
[2][23][31]HP-- ZIFF-DAVIS
VINCENT, STAN--MUNROE RVW '93, ADULT--
CHARIOT CB-129 "UNTAMED" '60
CHARIOT "THE HOT BEAT"
WARD, JONAS--[2][28]WEST--
COMPLTD GM "BUCHANAN ON THE PROD" '60
FOR WILLIAM ARD
WATSON, RICHARD F.--[2][32]MYS--
GU "WINDOW PEEPER" SEPT '59
GU "KEEP AWAY FROM MY DAUGHTER" MAR '59
GU "BLOOD IN THE STREETS" MAY '59
OF "BLOODY SATURDAY!" MAR '59
WENTWORTH, RICK--MUNROE RVW '93, ADULT--
CHARIOT CB129 "UNTAMED"
[BY 'DAVID CHALLON' ON INSIDE]
WOODWARD, L.T. MD--SILVERBERG LTR TO
MUNROE 7 AUG '93--
MON MB507 "SEX & THE ARMED SERVICES" '60
MON MB511 "SEX FIEND" '61
MON MB516 "SEX & HYPNOSIS" '61
MON MB521 "SEX IN OUR SCHOOLS" '62

SILVERBERG, ROBERT [CONT]
WOODWARD, L.T. MD [CONT]
MON MB530 "VIRGIN WIVES" '62
MON MB538 "YOU & YOUR SEX LIFE" '63
MON S10 "THE HISTORY OF SURGERY" '63
LAN 74-821 "TWILIGHT WOMEN" '63
LAN 73-445 "SEX & THE DIVORCED WOMAN" '64
LAN 74-835 "SADISM" '64
MON MB547 "MASOCHISM" '64
LAN 75-019 "SOPHISTICATED SEX TECHNIQUES
IN MARRIAGE" '67

SILVERSTEIN, ALVIN
BUXTON, RALPH--[33]
RHINE, RICHARD--[33]

SILVERSTEIN, ALVIN & VIRG
DR. A--[31][33]

SILVERSTEIN, SHEL[BY]
UNCLE SHELBY--[1][33]

SILVETTE, HERBERT
DOGBOLT, BARNABY--[2][7][11]SF--
DUTTON "EVE'S SECOND APPLE" '46
DUTTON "GOOSE'S TALE" '47

SIM, KATHARINE [T]
NURAINI--[1][22]ENGLISH

SIMA, ELAINE
LESLIE, LYNN--W/SHERRILL BODINE,
[9][10][21][26]ROM--
"STREET OF DREAMS"
"DEFY THE NIGHT"
LYNN, LESLIE--W/SHERRILL BODINE,
[9][21][26]ROM--
"DUKE'S DECEIT"
"A SOLDIER'S HEART" & 2 MORE

SIMENON, GEORGES [J.C.]
ARAMIS--[1]
BOBETTE--[1][29][31]
BRULLS, CHRISTIAN--[5][29][31]MYS--
CARAMAN, GEORGES--[1]
D'ANTIBES, GERMAIN--[1][21][29]
D'ISLY, GEORGES--[1][29][31]MYS--
DERSONNE[S], JACQUES--[1][29][31]MYS--
DOORSAGE, JEAN--[1][29][31]MYS
DORASAN, LUC--[1][29][31]MYS--
DOSSAGE, JEAN--[29][31]MYS
DU PERRY, JEAN--[5][29][31]MYS--
GEORGES, GEORGE--[1][29]
GUT, GOM--[1][29][31]
KIM--[1][29][31]MYS--
KOSTA, VICTOR--[29][34][40]MYS--
LA DESHABILLEUSE--[1][31]
LE COQ, MONSIEUR--[1][31]
PERTUIS, MAURICE--LACHMAN LTR-'BIO OF SIMENON'
BY FENTON BRESLER '83, P52
PLICK ET PLOCK--[1][29]
POUM ET ZETTE--[1][29]
SANDOR, JEAN--[1][29]
SIM, GEORGES--[5][29]MYS--
VIALIO, G.--[1]
VIALIS, GASTON--[1][29]
VIOLIS, G.--[29]MYS

SIMMONDS, MICHAEL CHARLES
ESSEX, FRANK--[1]
SIMMONDS, MIKE--[8]

SIMMONS, BARBARA BROOKS
BROOKS, BARBARA--[33]

SIMMONS, DAWN LANGLEY
HALL, GORDON LANGLEY--[31]

SIMMONS, J.S.A.
CROMIE, STANLEY--[8]
MONTGOMERY, DEREK--[8]

SIMMONS, STEVE
CARTER, NICK--[3]MYS,HP--
CHART "AND NEXT THE KING" '80

SIMMONS, TRANA
CHASE, CAROLYN--[21]ROM,HP--
'13 COLONIES' SERIES: "FRONTIER R."

SIMMONS, WILLIAM MARK
SIMMONS, WM. MARK--[7]SF--
POPLB "IN THE NET OF DREAMS" '90

SIMON, JOSEPH H.
SIMON, JOE--[33]

SIMON, KATHERINE DRAYTON
MAYRANT, DRAYTON--[1][22]AMERICAN
MAYSI, KADRA--[1][22]AMERICAN

SIMON, LIONEL
STUART, LYLE--[1]

SIMON, MINA LEWITON
LEWITON, MINA--[1]

SIMON, MORRIS
SIMON, MADELAINE--[7]SF--
TSR 'HEARTQUEST' #2
& 4 '83 - ?? UNCONFIRMED ??

SIMON, PAUL
KANE, PAUL--[31]

SIMON, ROBERT ALFRED
REYNOLDS, LIGGET--[1][22]MYS

SIMONDS, PETER
GREAVES, RICHARD--[1][34]MYS--
DORRANCE "CASE OF CONSTABLE SHIELDS" '40

SIMONE-ROSSNEY, SONIA
SIMONE, SONIA--[26]ROM--
"SCANDALOUS"

SIMOS, MIRIAM
STARHAWK--[1]

SIMPSON, ANTHONY MCVAY
WARREN, TONY--[8]

SIMPSON, BERTRAM L.
WEALE, [B] PUTNAM--[8][22]ENGLISH

SIMPSON, CARLA
SIMPSON, PAMELA--W/PAMELA WALLACE,
[7][21][34]MYS/SF--
BB "PARTNERS IN TIME" '90

SIMPSON, COLIN
JANSON, HANK--[34]MYS,HP--
"BID FOR BEAUTY" '66
COMPACT "THE YOUNG WOLVES" '67
COMPACT "HELL BROOD" '67
COMPACT "CRUNCH" '68
COMPACT "MICRO KILL" 68
COMPACT "TAKE TWO BLONDES" '68
COMPACT "CAT'S PAW" '69
COMPACT "COVERING FIRE" '69
COMPACT "TWILIGHT TIGRESS" '70

SIMPSON, COLIN [CONT]
JANSON, HANK [CONT]
GOLD "TWILIGHT TIGRESS" '70
COMPACT "FRAME & FORTUNE" '70
COMPACT "GRASS WIDOW" '71

SIMPSON, DORIS
COHEN, ANTHEA--[18][34]MYS--
QUARTET "ANGEL DUST" '89
QUARTET "FALLEN ANGEL" '84 & 7 MORE '82-9

SIMPSON, EVAN JOHN
JOHN, EVAN--[8]

SIMPSON, JAMES ALLEN
LAKE, M.D.--HAWK/SIMPSON INTRVW '93,[34]--
AV "AMENDS FOR MURDER" '89
AV "COLD COMFORT" '90
SIMPSON, ALLEN--HAWK/SIMPSON INTRVW '93, MYS--
SIMPSON, J.A.--HAWK/SIMPSON INTRVW '93, MYS--

SIMPSON, JOHN HAMPSON
HAMPSON, JOHN--[1]

SIMPSON, JUDITH [JUDY]
BAXTER, JUDY--W/JUNE HAYDON,[9]ROM
DENNY, ROZ--W/JUNE HAYDON,[21][26]--
"RED HOT PEPPER"
"ROMANCE NOTIONS"
"CINDERELLA COACH"
FOXX, ROSALIND--W/JUNE HAYDON,[9][21][31]ROM--
"FLAME AGAINST THE WIND"
"RELUCTANT WARD" & MORE
LOGAN, SARA--W/JUNE HAYDON,[1][9][21][31]ROM--
"GAME OF HEARTS"

SIMPSON, KEITH
BAILEY, GUY--[8]

SIMPSON, MARY
WEEROONA--[13]AUSTRALIAN

SIMPSON, MYRTLE L.
EMSLIE, M.L.--[1][31][33]

SIMPSON, RUTH MARY
RASEY, RUTH M.--[1]

SIMPSON, T.M. ALBERT
ALBERT, T.M.--[34]MYS--
ALBERT "TALES OF AN ULSTER DETECTIVE" '89

SIMPSON, WILLIAM
BLOT, THOMAS--[1][2][7][23]SF--

SIMS, DENISE NATALIE
SIMS, D.N.--[1]

SIMS, GEORGE CARROL
CAIN, PAUL--MUNROE SLST 23,[18][29][34]MYS--
DBLDY "FAST ONE" '33
DBLDY "SEVEN SLAYERS" '46
RURIC, PETER--MUNROE SLST 23,[18]MSY--
"TASTING MACHINE" '49
PLAYS

SIMS, GEORGE ROBERT
DAGONET--[8][22]ENGLISH

SIMSON, ERIC ANDREW
KIRK, LAURENCE--[2][32][34]MYS--
EQMM "ONLY GHOSTS STAY YOUNG" FEB '52
EQMM "TWO OF A KIND" OCT '52

SINCLAIR, CLOVER
GATER, DILYS--[34]MYS--

SINCLAIR, KATHLEEN HENR.
KNIGHT, BRIGID--[8]

SINCLAIR, MARJORIE JANE
EDEL, MARJORIE--[31]

SINCLAIR, MARY AMELIA
SINCLAIR, MAY--[1]
SINCLAIR, PULIAN--[1]

SINCLAIR, MIRANDA JANE
SEYMOUR, MIRANDA--[7][21][26]ROM/SF--
"VAMPIRE OF VERDONIA"
"CT. MANFRED"
"RELUCTANT DEVIL"
"DAUGHTER OF THE SHADOWS"
"THE GODDESS"
"MEDEA"

SINCLAIR, OLGA ELLEN
DANIELS, OLGA--[31]
CLARE, ELLEN--[8][31]

SINCLAIR, SONIA
GRAHAM, SONIA--[31]

SINCLAIR, UPTON BEALL
FITCH, CLARKE--[1][22][31][33]AMERICAN
FITCH, ENSIGN CLARK USN--[2]HP--
STREET & SMITH
GARRISON, FREDERICK--[1][2][22][31]
[33]AMERICAN
STIRLING, ARTHUR--[1][33]AMERICAN

SINCLAIR-WOOD, R.
SAVAGE, RICHARD--[35]AUSTRALIAN--
HRWTZ PB300 "LONG COLD REVENGE" '67
SAVIC, RANN--[35]AUSTRALIAN--
HRWTZ PB240 "TEENAGE RUNAWAY" '65

SINGER, ISAAC BASHEVIS
BASHEVIS, ISAAC--[8][31][33]
WARSHOFSKY, ISAAC--[8][33]

SINGER, ISRAEL JOSHUA
SINGER, I.J.--[1]

SINGER, JAMES HYMAN
SINGER, BURNS--[8]

SINGER, JANE SHERROD
SHERROD, JANE--[1][33]

SINGER, ROCHELLE
SINGER, SHELLEY--[7][34]MYS--
ST. MARTIN'S "SUICIDE KING" '88
ST. MARTIN'S "FREE DRAW" '84 & MORE

SINGER, RONALD
HUNTER, MARGARET--[9][21][26]ROM--
"LOVE'S SECRET JOURNEY"
MARLOWE, DELPHINE--[9][21][26]ROM--
"BONNAIRE"

SINGER, SALLY M.
JAMISON, AMELIA--[9][21][26][34]MYS/ROM--
POPLB "LAIRDS OF TURIFF HALL" '74

SINGH, GOPAL
DARDI--[8]

SINGLETON, BETTY
REENS, MARY--[1]
RUTLAND, DODGE--[1]

SINIAVSKII, ANDREI D.
TERTZ, ABRAM--[1][2][11]

SINITSKY, TED
SENNETT, TED--[1]

SINNOTT, LINDA
CARLTON, KATE--[26]ROM--
"KIDNAPPED"

SIROTA, MICHAEL BARRY
SIROTA, MIKE--[7]SF--
'BERBOA' #1 & 2 '78
'DANNUS' #1-5 '78
'RO-LAN' #1-4 '80-81

SITTENFELD, KONRAD
ALBERTI, KONRAD--[22]GERMAN

SIZEMORE, CHRISTINE COSTNER
LANCASTER, EVELYN--[31]
SIZEMORE, CHRIS COSTNER--[31]

SIZEMORE, DEBORAH LIGHTF.
LIGHTFOOT, D.J.--HAWK/SIZEMORE INTRVW '93,
WEST--
"TRAIL FEVER: THE LIFE OF A TEXAS
COWBOY" '93

SIZER, LAURENCE
LAURIER, DON--[8]

SIZER, MONA
JAMES, DEANA--[9][26]ROM--
"BELOVED ROGUE"
"SEEK ONLY PASSION" & MORE
ALL BUT "MASK OF JADE"

SKARDA, PATRICIA LYN
ST. CLAIR, CLOVIS--[1]

SKEELS, VERNON H.
ROSSITER, OSCAR--[1][2][7][11][23]SF--
"TETRASOMY TWO" '74

SKELTON, ALICE & CLEMENT
CLEMENTS, ABIGAIL--[3]MYS--
GM "MISTRESS OF THE MOOR" '74
GM "CHRISTABEL'S ROOM" '75
GM "HIGHLAND FINE"

SKELTON, C. LISTER
SKELTON, C.L.--[21]ROM--
"BELOVED SOLDIERS"
"IMPERIAL WAR"

SKELTON, GLADYS
PRESLAND, JOHN--[2]

SKENE-MELVIN, DAVID
HILL, LEW--[1]

SKIDELSKY, SIMON JASHA
SIMON, S.J.--[2][32][34]MYS--5 NOVELS
EQMM "AND THEN THERE WAS ONE" JUL '78

SKINNER, CONRAD ARTHUR
MAURICE, MICHAEL--[2][3][22][23]MYS/SF--
"NOT IN OUR STARS" '23
LOW "FRAIL GHOST" '35 & MORE

SKINNER, GLORIA DALE
CAMERON, CHARLA--[26]ROM--
"DIAMOND DAYS"
"GLORY NIGHTS"
"SULTRY NIGHTS"

SKINNER, JUNE M. O'GRADY
CARLEON, A.--[8]
O'GRADY, ROHAN--
DIAL "BLEAK NOVEMBER" '70
"CURSE OF THE MONTROLFES"
"MASTER OF MONTROLFE HALL"
MacM "O'HOULIHAN'S JEST" '61
MacM "PIPIN'S JOURNAL" '62
MACM "LET'S KILL UNCLE" '63

SKINNER, MICHAEL
DE MARQUAND, ALIX--[3][28]MYS/ROM--
LAN 72-998 "SO MANY MIDNIGHTS" '66
LAN "HOUSE ON SOMBER LAKE" '68
HYDE, CYNTHIA--[28][34]MYS--
AV "HOUSE OF SINISTER SHADOWS" '72
SPAIN, NICHOLAS--[28][34]ADULT--
KOZY "WINE, WOMEN & BULLETS" '63
KOZY 189 "NAME YOUR VICE"
SWANSON, MARK--[28]--
PAPLB "FURY" '69

SKLAR, RICHARD [LAWRENCE]
APPLETON, VICTOR II--[7]SF,HP--
STSY 'TOM SWIFT':
"& HIS GIANT ROBOT" '54

SKOBELEV, ALEXANDER SERGE
NEVEROT, ALEXANDER--[22]RUSSIAN

SKOV, DAVID A.
MCLEAN, DAVIDA--[2]
MCS, DEWI--[2]
VOSK, D.M.--[2]

SKRINE, AGNES HIGGINSON
O'NEILL, MOIRA--[8]

SKUES, GEORGE EDWARD
SEAFORTH--[8]

SKUJINS, ZIGMUNDS
SINUSS, Z.--[1]
SKOTE, Z.--[1]
ZIGIS--[1]

SKURDENIS-SMIRCICK, JULIN
SKURDENIS, JULIEN V.--[1]

SKURNICK, VICTORIA
VICTOR, CYNTHIA--W/CYNTHIA KATZ,[21][26]ROM--
"CONSEQUENCES"
"RELATIVE SINS"

SLADE, JACK
BENTEEN, JOHN--[28]WEST,HP--
'SUNDANCE' SERIES '78 & ON

SLADEK, JOHN
DEMIJOHN, THOM--W/THOMAS M. DISCH,
[2][3][4][23]MYS/SF--
DBLDY "BLACK ALICE" '68
KNYE, CASSANDRA--W/THOMAS M. DISCH,
[2][3][4][23]MYS/SF--
"HOUSE THAT FEAR BUILT" '66
"CASTLE & THE KEY" '67
TILMS, RICHARD A.--[2][23]SF--
"JUDGEMENT OF JUPITER" '80
VOGH, JOHN--[2][23]SF--
"ARACHNE ARISING: 13TH SIGN OF THE
ZODIAC" '77
"COSMIC FACTOR" '78

SLADEN, DOUGLAS
ST. BARBE--[1]
WHEELTON, BROOKE--[1]

SLADEN, NORMAN ST. BARBE
BULLINGHAM, RODNEY--[1][22][31]ENGLISH
MONTCLAIR, DENNIS--[1][22]ENGLISH

SLANCIKOVA, BOZENA
TIMRAVA--[22]SLOVAK

SLANEY, GEORGE WILSON
WODEN, GEORGE--[3][8][22]ENGLISH/MYS--
HUTCH "MUNGO" '32
HUTCH "PUZZLED POLICEMAN" '49 & MORE
WOUIL, GEORGE--[1]

SLATER, ERNEST
GWYNNE, PAUL--[1][2][8]

SLATER, FRANCIS CAREY
VAN AVOND, JAN--[1]

SLATER, FRANCIS CHARLOTTE
BANCROFT, F.--[22]SOUTH AFRICAN

SLATER, JAMES
CAPITALIST--[8]

SLATER, JAMES DERRICK
SLATER, JIM--[33]

SLATER, JOHN HERBERT
SECUTOR--[1]

SLATER, LEONARD
CAPELLI, ACE--PP 29, P42, MYS,HP--

SLATER, MONTAGUE
JOHNS, RICHARD--[8][34]MYS--
DOBSON "MAN WITH A BACKGROUND OF
FLAMES" '54

SLATTERY, RAY
BENT, JAMES--[35]AUSTRALIAN--
HRWTZ PB146 "CITY OF TORTURE" '63
BENT, JAMES F.--[32][35]MYS--
SD "BLACK MEAT & RED" SEPT '44
GUNN, FRANK F.--[35]AUSTRALIAN--
HRWTZ PB165 "TIGER'S MYS" '63
HUNT, ROGER--[35]AUSTRALIAN,HP--
HRWTZ "SAVAGE ATTACK" '62
HRWTZ "JAPS AT 8 O'CLOCK" '63
MILLER, KAREN--[35]AUSTRALIAN,HP--
HRWTZ "SURGEON AT SEA" '61
MITCHELL, KERRY--[35]AUSTRALIAN,HP--
HRWTZ "SURGEON AT SEA" '61
O'HARA, FRANK--[35]AUSTRALIAN--
HRWTZ "SPIN" '62
HRWTZ "BACK STRAIGHT" '63
SLATER, JOHN--[35]AUSTRALIAN,HP--
HRWTZ - 1st 77 NOVELS '62-72
"VICTOR'S PRIZE" '73
WEST, TERRY--[35]AUSTRALIAN--
HRWTZ "WOMEN IN BONDAGE" '69
HRWTZ "MODEL KILLER" '69
HRWTZ "THE TRAPPER" '70
HRWTZ "SLAVE QUARTERS" '70

SLATTERY, SHEILA
WILLIAMS, ROSEANNE--[9][26]ROM--
HARL 460 "HOT DATE"
HARL 504 "A TRUE BLUE KNIGHT"

SLAUGHTER, FRANK GILL
TERRY, C.V.--[1][22]AMERICAN/ROM--
CARD C197 "BUCCANEER SURGEON" '55
PERMA M4057 "DARIEN VENTURE" '56
PERMA M4100 "GOLDEN ONES" '58
PERMA M4165 "DEADLY LADY OF MADAGASCAR" '60

SLAVITT, DAVID RYTMAN
BENJAMIN, DAVID--[31]--
PUTNAM "THE IDOL" '79
LAZARUS, HENRY--[31]--
FAWCETT "THAT GOLDEN WOMAN" '76
MEYER, LYNN--[31]--
RANDOM "PAPERBACK THRILLER" '75
ROBBINS, HENRY--[1]
SUTTON, HENRY--[2][3][7][11][31]MYS/SF--
GROSSET "THE SACRIFICE" 78 & 5 MORE '67-80

SLESAR, HENRY
CHANDLER, LAWRENCE--[2]HP--
ZIFF-DAVIS
HARSON, SLEY--W/HARLAN ELLISON, ELLISON INTRVW,[2][32]MYS--
SFDS "TOO ANXIOUS TO MURDER!" APR '57
GU "HE DISAPPEARED" MAR '57
HELLER, JEFF--W/JAY FOLB, LACHMAN LST '93, [32]MYS--
AHMM "SPLIT-LEVEL GHOST" APR '58
AHMM "SIMON SAYS: HAND OVER YOUR FORTUNE" OCT '59
AHMM "AND SEVEN MAKES DEATH" DEC '59
AHMM "VICTIM, DEAR VICTIM" MAY '60
AHMM "DIG WE MUST" AUG '61
AHMM "REAL, REAL CRAZY" FEB '61
AHMM "TWO ACCOUNTS, ONE DEATH" MAY '61
JORGENSEN, IVAR--JEAN F LE DEIST-BAE 12, [2]HP--ZIFF-DAVIS
LESLIE, O.H.--[2][18][23][29][31][32]MYS--
27 DIGEST STORIES [AHMM & EQMM]
MITCHELL, CLYDE T.--[2]HP--ZIFF-DAVIS
SABER, LEE--[2]
SLEASAR, HENRY--[32]MYS--
SFDS "KISSING DEAD" CO-WROTE WITH HARLAN ELLISON, APR '57
STREET, JAY--[1]
VANCE, GERALD--[2]HP--

SLIGO, JOHN
BEAUFORD, TOM--[34][36]NEW ZEALANDER/MYS--
PENG "WHAT EVER HAPPENED TO ROSIE DUNN?" '89
"THE CONCERT MASTERS"

SLOANE, WILLIAM MILLIGAN
MILLIGAN, WILLIAM--[2][4]

SLOCUM, EDWARD MARK
EDWINSON, EDMUND--[8]

SLOGGETT, NELLIE
CORNWALL, NELLIE--[1][8][31][33]
ENYS, SARAH L.--[1][31][33]
TREGARTHEN, ENYS--[1][33]

SLOJKOWSKI, MARY ANN
HAMMOND, MARY ANN--[9][21][26][31]ROM--
"LAND OF GOLD" '84
PATRICK, DE ANN--W/DOTTI CORCORAN, [9][21][26]ROM--
"KINDRED SPIRIT"
"MONTANA BRIDES"

SLOMAN, ROBERT
LEOPOLD, GUY--W/BARRY LETTS,[2]

SLONIMSKI, ANTONI
PRO-ROK--[22]POLISH

SLOSBERG, MYRON
SLOSBERG, MIKE--[1]

SLOTE, ALFRED
GARNET, A.H.--[33]

SLOTKIN, JOSEPH
SPIES, OLIVER--[1][2][11]
TOLZ, NICK--[1][2][11]

SLOTTMAN, LEONA
BAKER, CARLOTTA--PPCC#5--
LEWIS "LOVE IS SO EXCITING" '47

SLUNG, LOUIS SHEAFFER
SHEAFFER, LOUIS--[1][8]

SLUSSER, GEORGE EDGAR
ANSTEY, EDGAR--[1][31]

SMALL, AUSTIN J.
SEAMARK--[2][3][22][23][32]MYS--
EQMM "QUERY" AUG '49
HODDER "AVENGING RAY" '30 & 9 MORE

SMALL, GEORGE
S., G.G.--[37]MYS-- NYDL-PULP STORIES

SMALL, LASS
HUGHES, CALLY--[9][21][26]ROM--
"CUPID'S REVENGE"
"NEVER TOO LATE" & 4 MORE

SMART, HAWLEY
STAFFORD, JOHN K.--[34]MYS,HP--
MAGNET #479 "BACK FROM THE GRAVE" '07
STARK, INSPECTOR--[34]HP--
NEW MAGNET #420 "NYTROGLYCERIN LEAGUE; OR, A COWARDLY CRIME" '05

SMART, VIOLA
KEATS, VIOLA--[1]

SMEATON, WILLIAM HENRY
SMEATON, OLIPHANT--[1]

SMEDS, BJORN
GRONBERG, ERIK--[29]MYS
RONNBECK, ROLAND--[29]MYS--
GRESHAM "GESTAPO I SVERIGE" '45

SMIDOVICH, VIKENTY VIK.
VERESAYEV, VIKENTI--[22]POLISH-RUSSIAN

SMILEY, CHARLES WESLEY
CASCDANANDA, ANAGARACA--[1]

SMILEY, VIRGINIA K.
EWING, TESS--[9][21][26]ROM--
"STARBURST"

SMILIE, ELTON R.
SMILE, R. ELTON--[1][2]

SMIT, JOHN-PAUL
HARLAND, PAUL--[2]

SMITH WOODS, DOROTHY BER.
MOORE, BERYL--[1]

SMITH, A. DE HERRIES
FINBAR, OWEN--[1]

SMITH, ADA BEATRICE
BRICKTOP--[31]

SMITH, ALFRED ALOYSIUS
HORN, ALFRED ALOYSIUS--[1]
HORN, TRADER--[1]

SMITH, AMANDA JOAN MacK.
MACKAY, AMANDA--V. BERCH LTR TO HUBIN '94, MYS--
McKAY "DEATH IS ACADEMIC" '76
LITTLE "DEATH ON THE ENO" '81

SMITH, ANTHONY CHARLES
SMITH, ACH--[1]

SMITH, ARTHUR DOUGLAS H.
GRANT, ALLEN--[1]

SMITH, ARTHUR JAMES M.
SMITH, A.J.M.--[1]

SMITH, BARBARA C.
CAMERON, BARBARA--[9][21][26]ROM--
"METAL MISTRESS"
"STAR RIDE"

SMITH, BARBARA HERRNSTEIN
HERRNSTEIN, BARBARA--[8][22][31]AMERICAN

SMITH, BERNARD
CAMPBELL, HARRY--[1]
HEATH, BERNARD--[1]
MARTIN, IVOR--[1]
SMITH, JACK--[1]
WILLIAMS, FRED J.--[1]

SMITH, C.U.
CROWBATE, OPHELIA MAE--[1][31]

SMITH, CATHERINE R.
ADAMS, ANGELA--[1]
ANDREWS, VICKIE--[1]

SMITH, CECIL HOWARD III
HOWARD, CECIL--[31]

SMITH, CECIL LEWIS T.
FORESTER, C.S.--[1][32]ADV--
'HORNBLOWER' NVLS & MORE
9 MYS/ADV DIGEST STORIES [EQMM, SA & MD]
FORESTER, CECIL SCOTT--[1]

SMITH, CHARLES H.
BORE, [DR.] HELLE--[1]

SMITH, CHARLES HENRY
ARP, BILL--[1][8][22][31]

SMITH, CLARK ASHTON
BUXTON, CARL--[2]MYS,HP--
STREET & SMITH
DE CASSERES, BENJAMIN--[11]
GAYLORD, TIMAEUS--[2]

SMITH, CONSTANCE ISABEL
REID, ELEANOR--[22]MYS

SMITH, DAVID MACLEOD
DUNBAR, EDWARD--[1][31]
MARINER, DAVID--[2][3][23][40]MYS--
HALE "A SHAKLETON CALLED SHEILA" '70 & 7 MORE
SMITH, D. MacLEOD--CRPG--
PINN 220469 "THE LAST BRIDGE" '74

SMITH, DAVID [J.D.]
CORNWELL, SMITH--[1][31]

SMITH, DAVID [L]
GRAHAM, JOHNSTON--[1]

SMITH, DAY TOTTON
LECLAIRE, DAY--[21][26]ROM--
"JINXED"
"TO CATCH A GHOST"
"ONCE A COWBOY" & MORE

SMITH, DEAN WESLEY
GUSTAFSON, SMITH--W/JON GUSTAFSON,[7]SF--
"THE MOSCOW MOFFIA PRESENTS RAT TALES" '87

SMITH, DEBORAH
LEIGH, JACKIE--[9][21][26]ROM--
"NO HOLDS BARRED"
"PROUD SURRENDER"
LENNOX, JACQUELINE--[9][21][26]ROM--
"FORCE OF HABIT"

SMITH, DONALD TAYLOR
SMITH, DON--[34]MYS--27 NOVELS '51-78
TAYLOR, DUNCAN--[34]ADULT--
BEAC B-205 "RED CURTAIN" '59

SMITH, DOROTHY GLADYS
ANTHONY, C.L.--[2][8][11][22][31][33]
PERCY, CHARLES HENRY--[1][33]
SMITH, DODIE--[3][7][8][33]MYS/SF--
ALLEN "GIRL FROM THE CANDLE-LIT BATH" '78

SMITH, DOROTHY WHITEHILL
TRENT, MARTHA--[1]

SMITH, DOROTHY [S]
SMITH, SARAH STAFFORD--[1]

SMITH, EDGAR
MASON, MICHAEL--[8][11][26]ROM--

SMITH, EDWARD ELMER
SMITH, DOC--[1]
SMITH, DR. EDWARD E.--M. LACHMAN LTR '93--
STARTLING STORIES - JUL '50
SMITH, E.E.--[1][7]SF--NUMEROUS WORKS

SMITH, EDWARD ERNEST
LINDALL, EDWARD--[3][8][13][35]AUSTRALIAN/MYS--
HM "FIRES OF KIWAI" '68 & 12 MORE '59-75

SMITH, EDWARD H.
BLAIR, EDWARD H.--[1]

SMITH, EDWARD PERCY
PERCY, EDWARD--[3]MYS--PLAYS '36-55

SMITH, ELAINE C.
LANE, KAMI--[9][21][26]ROM--
"FANTASY LOVER"

SMITH, ELIZABETH S.
CHESTER, ELIZABETH S.--[1]
HONEYBEE--[1]

SMITH, ELIZABETH THOMASIN
MEADE, L.T.--W/ROBERT K. DOUGLAS, [2][3][32]MYS--
GARDNER "UNDER THE DRAGON THRONE" 1897
MEADE, L.T.--W/ROBERT E. BARTON,[3]--
"GOLD STAR LINE" 1899
"A MASTER OF MYSTERIES" 1898
"THE SANCTUARY CLUB" 1900
"THE LOST SQUARE" 1902
MEADE, L.T.--W/ROBERT EUSTACE--
"BROTHERHOOD OF THE SEVEN KINGS" 1899
MEADE, L.T.--W/CLIFFORD HALIFAX,[34]--
"A RACE WITH THE SUN" '01
"TROUBLESOME WORLD" 1893
"STORIES FROM DIARY OF A DOCTOR" 1894-96

SMITH, ELIZABETH THOMASIN [CONT]
MEAD, L.T. [CONT]
"WHERE THE SHOE PINCHES" 1900
MEADE, L.T.--
EQMM "MAN WHO DISSAPPEARED" MAY '48
& NUMEROUS BOOKS

SMITH, ELLEN HART
REVELL, LOUISA--[3]MYS--
7 MacM NOVELS '47-60

SMITH, ERNEST BRAMAH
BRAMAH, ERNEST--[2][3][5][32]MYS--
7 BKS '14-72
5 DIGEST STORIES [EQMM & SA]

SMITH, EVELYN E.
LYONS, DELPHINE C.--[2][23][29][31][34]MYS--
PYR R-1266 "FLOWER OF EVIL" '65
LAN 72-932 "HOUSE OF FOUR WINDOWS" '65
LAN 75-355 "DEPTHS OF YESTERDAY" '66
LAN 74-929 "VALLEY OF SHADOWS" '68
LAN 74-654 "PHANTOM AT LOST LAKE" '70

SMITH, F. JOSEPH
SMITH, F.J.--[31][32]MYS--
TR "SHOOT HIM LIKE A DOG" DEC '58
TR "ONE DOLL TOO MANY" AUG '58
TR "VINDICTIVE WOMAN" OCT '58
OF "SHAKE THE LADY DOWN" SEPT '59

SMITH, FANNY
MANETTI, FANNY--[1]

SMITH, FLORENCE MARGARET
SMITH, STEVIE--[1][8][21]ROM--
"OVER THE FRONTIER"
"NOTES ON YELLOW PAPER & MORE

SMITH, FRANCES C.
SMITH, JEAN--[1][8][33]

SMITH, FRANCIS
DEAN, S.F.X.--[3][18]MYS--
WALKER "SUCH PRETTY TOYS" '82
WALKER "BY FREQUENT ANGUISH" '82 & MO

SMITH, FRANCIS DENNIS
SMITH, FRANC

SMITH, FRANK ELLIS
CRAIG, JONATHAN--V. BERCH- LESBIANA/
CNTRCLTR,BAE 22, V. BERCH-GM PSEUDS,
PP 33,[32][34]--
FALC 36 "JUNKIE" '52
CROY 47 "REDHEADED SINNERS" '53
LION 206 "ALLEY GIRL" '54
GM 531 "DEAD DARLING" '55
GM 582 "MORGUE FOR VENUS" '56
GM 645 "CASE OF THE COLD COQUETTE" '57
GM 669 "SO YOUNG, SO WICKED" '57
GM 702 "CASE OF THE BEAUTIFUL BODY" '57
GM 716 "COME NIGHT, COME EVIL" '57
GM 784 "CASE OF THE PETTICOAT MURDER" '58
GM 872 "CASE OF NERVOUS NUDE" '59
GM 930 "CASE OF THE VILLAGE TRAMP" '59
GM 1065 "CASE OF LAUGHING VIRGIN" '60
GM 1396 "CASE OF SILENT STRANGER" '64
GM 1706 "CASE OF BRAZEN BEAUTY" '66
MANY DIGEST STORIES
HALE, JENNIFER--W/WARE TORREY [BUDLONG],
[3][21]ROM--
LAN "RAVENRIDGE" '71 & 5 MORE

SMITH, FREDERICK ESCREET
FARRELL, DAVID--[22][29][31][34]MYS--
GRESHAM "THE OTHER COUSIN" '62
SMITH, F.E.--[31]TITLE PAGE--
PAPLB "DARK CLIFFS" '65
RPRT OF "OTHER COUSIN" '62

SMITH, FREDERICK W. FURN.
BIRKENHEAD, LORD--[31]

SMITH, FREDERICK W. ROBIN
FURNEAUX, ROBIN--[1][8][31]

SMITH, G.M.
GREY, STEELE--[8]

SMITH, GARY
MOORE, RUDIN--[7]SF--
"ULTRA-VUE & SELECTED PERIPHERAL
VISIONS" '87

SMITH, GEORGE
L.L.--[1]
LOVECHURCH, LEONARD--[1]
SMITH, CLYDE--[1][8]

SMITH, GEORGE H[ARMON]
MCCURTIN, PETER--J. CORRICK-PP 36,HP--
USED ON ADV & WEST SERIES BY BELM,
TWR, DELL & LEIS
SCARPETTA, FRANK--J. CORRICK-PP 36--
BELM 'MARKSMAN' SERIES - TITLES NOT KNOWN
SMITH, GEORGE H.--J. CORRICK-PP 36--
NSLF 503 "GEORGEOUS DEVIL" '59
NSLF 507 "SATAN'S MATE" '59
NSLS U-112 "WHIP OF PASSION" '59
NSLS U-115 "DARK DESIRE" '59
NSLS U-131 "SWAMP BREED" '60
NVL 5005 "SWAMP LUST" '60
NVL 5008 "DELTA DOLL" '60
NVL 5010 "BAYOU BABE" '60
NVL 5012 "SADIST ON THE LOOSE" '60
NVL 5023 "HOT STUFF" '60
NVL 5017 "THE GOLDEN HUSSY" '60
NVL 5020 "BRUTAL ECSTASY" '60
NVL 5026 "HUGE HUGE HUGE HUNGER" '60
NVL 5029 "HOT JAZZ" '60
NVL 6011 "BACKWOODS HUSSIES" '62
NVL 6013 "THIRST FOR LOVE" '62
NVL 6021 "FARMER'S DAUGHTER" '62
NVL 6029 "TORRID TRAMPS" '62
DOLDBL 950 "LASH OF DESIRE" '62
RPRTS NWSTD U-112 "WHIP OF PASSION"
NVL 6040 "FEVER HOT WOMAN" '62
NVL 6045 "CARNAL CAGE" '62
NVL 6080 "TITINE" '63
NVL 6047 "SHOCKING SHE-ANIMAL" '62
NVL 60101 "FEMALE IN HEAT"
AKA "HOT STUFF" '63
NVL 6059 "EROTIC ORGY!" '62
NVL 6067 "3 IN BED" '63
NVL 6N236 "TATAN" '63
NVL 6N237 "DICEY MAE" '64
NVL 6N248 "SWEATER GIRL" '64
NVL 7N705 "THE FARMER'S OTHER DAUGHTER" '63
NVL 7N759 "LILLIT" '65

SMITH, GEORGE H[ENRY]
TREHUNE, MORGAN--C.ECKHOFF-PP 37, ADULT--
MDWD 195-21 "EROTICA SATANICA" '71
AUGUST, JEREMY--V. BERCH-BRNDN/BC PSEUDS,
BAE 22, ADULT--
BRNDN 1047 "FOUR BED WILDCAT" '66
BRNDN 2062 "NOVICE SEX QUEENS" '68
AUGUST, JERRY--ADULT--PLAYTIME BOOKS
BELLMORE, DON--G. COOK-PP 40, ADULT,HP--
NTSD NB1864 "LEOPARD LUST"

SMITH, GEORGE H[ENRY] [CONT]
CAMRA, ROSS--J. CORRICK-PP 36, ADULT--
EPIC 144 "ASSAULT" '62
DEER, M.J.--W/MARY J. DEER,[1][2]ADULT--
FRA F50 "A PLACE NAMED HELL" '63
FRA F66 "FLAMES OF DESIRE" '63
DEVLIN, GEORGE--G. COOK LTR '93, ADULT--
MDWD 61-765 "BLONDE VIXEN"
MDWD "HUNGRY YEARS"
DEXTER, JOHN--G. COOK-PP 40, ADULT,HP--
SNDN RDR SR556 "ORGY BUYER"
HADLEY, ROBERT--LOVISI/SMITH INTRVW-PP 36--
BL "BEDTIME BETSY"
MEDCO "SEX CLUBS UNDERGROUND"
MDWD 37-140 "CAMPUS ROUND HEELS" '68?
MDWD 35-154 "THE SEX SEEKERS" '68
MDWD 34-961 "SCHOOL TEASE" '68
MDWD 37-279 "NIGHT AFTER NIGHT" '69
MDWD 38-335 "AN INTIMATE LIFE" '69
MDWD 125-5 "LOVE COMMUNE" '69
MDWD 35-196 "THE OTHER WAY" '69
MDWD 37-217 "JET BLACK SEX" '69
MDWD 35-237 "TEACH ME HOW" '69
MDWD 195-2 "PUCKER POWER" '70
BL 676 "GIRL'S BOARDING SCHOOL" '70
MDWD 195-11 "SKIN FLICK STUD" '70
BL 744 "INCEST SWINGERS" '71
MDWD 195-41 "WICKED BODIES" '71
BL 949 "LESLIE'S PRIVATE LESSONS" '73
BL "CAMPUS SEX SCENE" '74
MDWD 60400 "THE VELVET TOUCH" '74
BL "BOY'S SEX MASCOT" '75
BL "CINDY'S TENDER TOUCH" '75
MDWD 35-241 "HIGH SCHOOL STUD" '69
BRNDN 944 "TWO TIMES FOR LOVE" '65
HENRY, GEORGE--G. COOK-PP 40--
AWARD "ATHEISM: THE CASE AGAINST GOD"
HUDSON, JAN--W/CLANCY O'BRIEN, C. ECKHOFF-PP 37, ADULT--
PENDLM 247 "THE MULTI-SEX CROWD"
HUDSON, JAN--V. BERCH-PIKE CKLST, BAE 16, [1][2]ADULT--
PIKE 205 "LOVE CULT" '61
EPIC 113 "SATAN'S DAUGHTER" 61
EPIC 102 "PASSIONS WEB" '61
PIKE 217 "LOVE GODDESS" '62
PIKE 802 "VIRGIN MISTRESS" '62
RPRT OF PIKE 203
EPIC 125 "SORORITY SLUTS" '62
BOUDOIR 103 "GIRLS AFIRE" '62
PILLOW 103 "HELL'S HIGHWAY" '62
FRA F24 "STRANGE HAREM" '62
PLAYTIME 644 "THE VIRTUOUS HARLOTS" '63
INTIMATE 721 "THE HOTEST PARTY IN TOWN" '63
GRNLF GC214 "HELLS ANGELS" '66
GRNLF GC220 "THOSE SEXY SAUCER PEOPLE" '67
PENDLM 215 "KING OF THE TEEN-AGE ORGIES" '67
PENDLM 227 "THE DYKES" '68
NEL "THE NEW BARBARIANS" '73
NEL 2545 "BIKERS AT WAR" '76
LOVESWEPT #293 "WATER WITCH" '88
BEAC B-894X "THE LOVE MAKERS" '65
JASON, JERRY--V. BERCH-PIKE CKLST, BAE 16, [1][2]ADULT--
NITETIME NT92 "PSYCHO MAKERS" '64
BOUDOIR 1027 "SEXODUS" '63
TRIUMP 343 "THE VIRGIN AGENT" SEPT '69
BRNDN 662 "LESBIAN TRIANGLE"
BRNDN 616 "COUNTRY CLUB LESBIAN" '63
O'BRIEN, CLANCY--C. ECKHOFF, PP 37,[2]ADULT--
BL 707 "PUSSY POWER" '71
O'BRIEN, CLANCY--W/JAN HUDSON, C. ECKHOFF-PP 37, ADULT--
PENDLM 247 "THE MULTI-SEX CROWD"
QUEEN, ELLERY--LOVISI/SMITH INTRVW-PP 36,HP--
EQMM ARTICLE

SMITH, GEORGE H[ENRY] [CONT]
ROBINSON, ALAN--LOVISI/SMITH INTRVW/ C. ECKHOFF-PP 37, ADULT--
LEIS LB672 "WILDCAT" '65
SMITH, GEORGE--LOVISI/SMITH INTRVW & CKLST-P 36, ADULT--
EPIC 103 "THE YEAR OF TERROR" '61
SMITH, GEORGE H.--LOVISI/SMITH CKLST-P 36, ADULT--
EPIC 110 "SCOURGE OF THE BLOOD CULT" '61
PIKE 208 "BARONESS OF BLOOD" '61
PIKE 203 "COMING OF THE RATS" '61
PIKE 210 "PRIVATE HELL" '62
PIKE 216 "SOFT LIPS ON BLACK VELVET" '62
RPRTD PIKE 1315 "BEAUTIFUL BUT BRUTAL" '64
MON 388 "DOOMSDAY WING" '63
MON 464 "THE UNENDING NIGHT" '64
PLTM 681 "STRIP ARTIST" '64
BELM B50-699 "THE FOUR DAY WEEKEND" '66
BRNDN 1137 "NAKED TO HER ENEMIES" '67
PYR T1793 "WHO IS RONALD REAGAN?" '68
SIGN P4098 "WITCH QUEEN OF LOCHLANN" '69
BRNDN "THE GIRL FROM S.I.N."
MNLT RDR 103 "THE YEAR OF LOVE"
RPRTS EPIC 103 AS BY "GEORGE SMITH"
ACE 42900 "KAR KABALLA" '69
LAN447-33005 "MARTIN LUTHER KING JR" '71
DOMINION PUBL "THE VIRGIN AGENT" 'ND
DAW 215 "SECOND WAR OF THE WORLDS" '76
DAW 298 "THE ISLAND SNATCHERS" '78
PLAYBOY AMER. FREEDOM SERIES:
#1 THRU #3" '80
16602, 16603 & 16765
SMITH, GEORGE HUDSON--J. CORRICK-PP 36, [1][2][11]--EARLY SHORT STORIES
SMITH, JAN--[1][2][11]SF--
PLANET STORIES "NARAKAN RIFLES"
STANDISH, HOLT--LOVISI/SMITH INTRVW-PP 36, ADULT--
"JAILBAIT GIRLS"
STRYKER, HAL--LOVISI/SMITH INTRVW-PP 36, [3][23]MYS--
PINN "NYPD 2025" '85
'HAWKEYE' SERIES '91
STRYKER, HANK--C. ECKHOFF-PP 37, ADULT--
BL 822 "EASY LAY!" '72
SUMMERS, DIANA--LOVISI/SMITH INTRVW-PP 36, [2][9][26][21]ADULT--
PLAYBOY 16450 "WILD IS THE HEART" '78
PLAYBOY 16502 "LOVE'S WICKED WAYS" '79
PLAYBOY 169650 "FALLEN ANGEL" '81
CHART 20548 "EMPEROR'S LADY" '84
DELL 14614 "LOUISIANA" '84
DELL 14672 "A REBEL'S PLEASURE" '86
TREHUNE, MORGANA-- LOVISI/SMITH INTRVW-PP 36--
MDWD "EROTICA SATANICA" '70
WARREN, ROY--G. COOK LTR '93--
HEART VOL 105 "SPACE SEX" nd - PIRATED
WILLIAMS, J.X.--C. ECKHOFF-PP 37, ADULT--
LTHRLIB LL708 "BLACK MASS MINX" '67
EVNG RDR ER1246 "DAUGHTERS OF SAPPHO"

SMITH, GEORGE O.
LONG, WESLEY--[1][2][11][23][31]

SMITH, GOLDWIN
BYSTANDER, A--[8]

SMITH, GUY NEWMAN
GUY, JONATHAN--AUTHOR PROVIDED,JUV--
MACRAE "BADGER ISLAND" '93
MACRAE "RAK" '94
MACRAE "PYNE" '95
NEWMAN, GAVIN--AUTHOR PROVIDED, HOR--
PIATKUS "THE HANGMAN" '94
SMITH, GUY N.--AUTHOR PROVIDED, [7]ENGLISH/FANT/HOR--NOVELS '75-TD

SMITH, H. EVERARD
EVERARD, HENRY--[8]

SMITH, HAZEL G. LITTFIELD
LITTLEFIELD, HAZEL--[7]SF--
"LORD DUNSANY, KING OF DREAMS: A PERSONAL PORTRAIT" '59

SMITH, HELEN ZENNA
PRICE, EVADNE--[3][8][22][29]MYS--
LONG "DIARY OF A RED-HAIRED GIRL" '32
& MORE NOVELS/PLAYS

SMITH, HILDEGARDE ANGELL
ANGELL, HILDEGARDE--[1]

SMITH, HOWARD VAN
SOMMERS, DAVID--[1]

SMITH, IAIN CRICHTON
MAC A'GHOBHAINN, IAIN--[1]
MAC A'GHOBHAINN, SEAMUS--[1]

SMITH, ISADORE L.L.
LEIGHTON, ANN--[1][31]

SMITH, JAMES T.
COULTER, ADAM--V. BERCH-BRNDN/BC PSEUDS, BAE 22, ADULT--
NVL 5051 "SAVAGE PASSIONS" '61
FABIAN 158 "RAPE OF EDEN" '62
FRA 26 "GOLDEN LUST" '62
FRA 56 "DEBAUCHEE" '63
BOUDOIR 1402 "FOUR TO GO-GO-GO!"

SMITH, JANE S.
SMITH, J.C.S.--[3]MYS--
ATHNM "JACOB'S FIRST CASE" '80

SMITH, JANICE DAVIS
DAVIS, JUSTINE--[9][21][26]ROM--
"ANGEL FOR HIRE"
"HUNTER'S WAY" & MORE

SMITH, JEANIE OLIVER
OLIVER, TEMPLE--[1]

SMITH, JENNIFER
CRUSIE, JENNIFER--KLEIN-GREAT WOMEN MYSTERY WRITERS, MYS--

SMITH, JOAN
GALLANT, JENNIE--[9][21][26]ROM--
"BLACK DIAMOND"
"OLIVIA" & 5 MORE

SMITH, JOHN
SMITH, C. BUSBY--[8]

SMITH, JOSHUA
BELLINI, SIGNOR--[2][11]

SMITH, JUDITH SPAETH M.
MCNAUGHT, JUDITH-- SMITH INTRVW--
DMN "TENDER TRIUMPH" '84
DMN "DOUBLE STANDARDS" '84 & OTHERS

SMITH, JULIA [MARY WYLIE]
WYLIE, JONATHAN--W/MARK J.A. SMITH,[7]--
CORGI 'UNBAL EARTH' TRIL: #1-3
CORGI 'SERVANTS OF ARK' #1-3

SMITH, KAREN ROSE
SUTHERLAND, KARI--[26]ROM--
"WISH ON THE MOON"

SMITH, KATHARINE GREY
GREY, KATHARINE--[1]

SMITH, KAY NOLTE
GILLIAN, KAY--[1][31]

SMITH, KENN
SMITH, ROBIN LEIGH--[21][26]ROM--
"PASSAGE TO GLORY"

SMITH, L.H.
WILLIAMS, SPEEDY--[2][7][11]SF--
"JOURNEY THROUGH SPACE TO A MARTIAN SATELLITE & BACK" '58

SMITH, LAURA ROUNDTREE
JUNE, CAROLINE SILVER--[1]

SMITH, LE ROI TEX
OOGAM, LE ROI--[1]
UGAMA, LE ROI--[1]
WELCH, CHARLES SCOTT--[1]

SMITH, LENA K[ENNEDY]
KENNEDY, LENA--[1][31]
SMITH, L.K.--[7]SF--
BIZARRE LIBR. "SERPENT LADY" '77
?? UNCONFIRMED ??

SMITH, LILLIAN M.
WARNER, LEIGH--[8]

SMITH, LILY
WANDERER--[8]

SMITH, LINELL NASH
CHENAULT, NELL--[22][31]AMERICAN/CHILDREN'S--
"PARSIFAL THE POODLE" '60
NASH, LINELL--[31][33]CHILDREN'S--
"THE CHRISTMAS THAT ALMOST WASN'T" '57

SMITH, LLEWELLYN
TWO EAST LONDENERS--W/VAUGHAN SMITH,[8]

SMITH, LOIS
CHADWICK, CLEO--[9][21]ROM--
"SCARLET SPINSTER"

SMITH, LORA [ROBERTS]
ROBERTS, LEIGH--[9][21][26]ROM--
"WISHING POOL"
"SIREN SONG" & 6 MORE

SMITH, LYNNE A.
CHRISTOPHER, PAULA--[9][21][26]ROM--
"THE DREAMING POOL"
LYNSON, JAN--[26]ROM--
"CAPTAIN RAKEHELL"
"DUKE'S DOWNFALL"
LYNSON, JANE--[21]ROM--
"CAPT. RAKEHELL"
MICHAELS, LYNN--[9][26]ROM--
"SECOND SIGHT"
"MOLLY & THE PHANTOM" & MORE

SMITH, MARGARET RUTH
SERANNE, ANN--[8]

SMITH, MARGUERITE
SINCLAIR, ELIZABETH--[26]ROM--
SIL 606 "JENNY'S CASTLE"

SMITH, MARJORIE SEYMOUR
FEARN, ELENA--[8]

SMITH, MARK [JONATHAN A.]
WYLIE, JONATHAN--W/JULIE M. W. SMITH,[7]SF--
CORGI 'UNBAL EARTH' TRIL #1-3
CORGI 'SERVANTS OF ARK' #1-3

SMITH, MARLEE
ALEX, MARLEE--[1]

SMITH, MARTIN
MARTIN, DAVID--[35]AUSTRALIAN--
HRWTZ PB300 "BOY FOR HIRE"
?? PUBLISHED ??

SMITH, MARTIN WILLIAM
CARTER, NICK--[1][3][7][18]MYS,HP--
AWARD "CODE NAME: WEREWOLF" '73
AWARD "INCA DEATH SQUAD" '73
AWARD "THE DEVIL'S DOZEN" '73
LOGAN, JAKE--K. BURGER-PP 33,[1][18]WEST,HP--
"NORTH TO DAKOTA" '76
"RIDE FOR REVENGE" '77
QUINN, MARTIN--[18][29]--
BAL "ADVENTURE OF A WILDERNESS FAMILY" '76
QUINN, SIMON--[3][18][23][29]MYS--
DELL 'INQUISITOR' SERIES:
"HUMAN FACTOR" '74 & 6 MORE
SMITH, MARTIN--[18]--
TWR "THE INDIANS WON" '70
SMITH, MARTIN CRUZ--[1][18][34]MYS--
NORTON "NIGHTWING" 77
RNDM "GORKY PARK" '81 & MORE

SMITH, MARY
DREWERY, MARY--[1]
RADHA--[1]

SMITH, MARY ELLEN
SMITH, MIKE--[1][33]

SMITH, MARY J. DEER
DEER, M.J.--W/GEORGE H. SMITH,[1][2]ADULT--
FRA F50 "A PLACE NAMED HELL" '63
FRA F66 "FLAMES OF DESIRE" '63

SMITH, MARY PRUDENCE [W]
THORNE, P.--[1]

SMITH, MARYN LANGER
LANGER, MARYN--[21][26]ROM--
"WAIT FOR THE SUN"
"MOON FOR A CANDLE"
"DIVIDE THE JOY"

SMITH, MILBURN
MILBURN, ELLEN--[3]MYS--
BELM "WINGS OF DARKNESS" '75

SMITH, MITCHELL
LE BEAU, ROY--[31]
MACCONNELL, COLUM--W/STEVE ROSSEN, V. BERCH
LTR TO R. REGINALD '93/SF--
LEIS "TARK & THE GOLDEN TIDE" '77

SMITH, NANCY T.
FITZGERALD, AMBER--[9][21][26]ROM--
"RELUCTANT LOVER"
"SUSPICIOUS HEART" & MORE

SMITH, NICHOLS
SMITH, JULIA CLEAVER--W/DIANE CLEAVER,[1]

SMITH, NORMA E.
BLUENOSE--[1]

SMITH, NORMAN EDWARD M.
SHERATON, NEIL--[1][3]MYS--
HALE "AFRICAN TERROR" '57
HALE "CAIRO RING" '58
HALE "CLEAR SKY ABOVE" '59
HALE "THEY FOUND A WAY BACK" '60
HALE "PRINCESS & THE PILOT" '61
SHORE, NORMAN--[1][3]MYS--
HALE "LONELY RUSSIAN" '72
HALE "HONG KONG NIGHTSTOP" '73
HALE "RUSSIAN HI-JACK" '75

SMITH, ORMAND G.
CARTER, NICK--W/JOHN R. CORYELL,[2][5]MYS,HP--

SMITH, PARK
PARKSMITH, GEORGE--W/GEORGE S[IDNEY] BUSH,[1]

SMITH, PATRICK DAVID
SMITH, PATRICK D.--[21]ROM--
"A LAND REMEMBERED"

SMITH, REGINALD DONALD
MANNING, MARTIN--[1]
MARTIN, OLIVER--[1]

SMITH, RICHARD MORRIS
STANLEY, T. LLOYD--[1]

SMITH, RICHARD REIN
BOND, RAY--[1]ADULT--SHIELD BOOK
CASTLE, DAMON--[1][7][23][31]SF--
"STARBRIGHT" '83
COLLINS, CINDY--[1][31]
CROSSAN, DARRYL--[1][31]
DAVIS, CLIFF--[1][31]
DAVIS, JIM--[1][31]
GREEN, ROBERT--[1][31]
LANE, SHERRY--[1][31]
REIN, RICHARD--[1][14]ADULT--OLYM
REINSMITH, RICHARD--[3][32]MYS--
MSMM "HOW TO KILL A HOSTAGE" APR '80
TWR "BLONDE TARGET" '80
TWR "BURY THE PAST" '80
TWR "AN EXTRA BODY" '80
TWR "FIVE & DIME MURDERS" '80
SMITH, RICHARD E.--[11]
STRADLEY, MARK--[1]
TAYLOR, ANN--V. BERCH-BRNDN/BC PSEUDS,
BAE 22,[1][14]ADULT--
OLYM OPH#116 "LOVE & LUST" '68
OLYM OPH#146 "IN & OUT" '69
TAYLOR, BRAD--[1]
TOWER, DIANA--[3][7][21][26]MYS/SF--
BAL "RED LION" '74
BEAGLE "DARK DIAMOND" '75 & MORE
WALTERS, CHAD--[1]

SMITH, ROBERT
CHATTAN, ROBERT--[1]

SMITH, ROBERT CHARLES
CHARLES, ROBERT--[32][34]MYS--
HALE "NIGHTWORLD" '84 & MORE
LM "DEATH DEALS THE CARDS" JUN '63
LEADER, CHARLES--[23][31][34]MYS--
HALE "GOLDEN LURE" '67
HALE "DRAGON ROARS" '70 & 15 MORE '66-77

SMITH, ROBERT EDWARD
BRUTE, Q.--[1]

SMITH, ROBERT KIMMEL
MARKS, PETER--[31][32][33]MYS--
MH "THE ASSASSIN" APR '62
CARROLL "SKULLDUGGERY" '87 & MORE

SMITH, ROBERT PETER
MORWOOD, PETER--[7]SF--
'BOOK OF YEARS' #1-4 '83-89
'PRINCE IVAN' #1 '90

SMITH, RON
LORAN, MARTIN--W/JOHN BAXTER,[1][2][11][23]SF--

SMITH, RONALD GREGOR
BROWNE, SAM--[1][22][31]SCOTTISH
MAXWELL, RONALD--[1][22]SCOTTISH

SMITH, RUSSELL
ROSSI, BRUNO--[3]MYS,HP--
LEIS "TRIGGERMAN" '75
SCARPETTA, FRANK--[34]MYS,HP--
BELM "DIE, KILLER, DIE" '75
SMITHSON, I.--[14]ADULT--
OLYM TCP#008 "SEX ON DOCTOR'S ORDERS" '71

SMITH, RUTH ALANA
BRYAN, EILEEN--[9][21][26]ROM--
"RUN FOR THE ROSES"
"CROSSFIRE" & MORE
SMITH, ALANA--[9][21][26]ROM--
"WHENEVER I LOVE YOU"

SMITH, SANDRA LEE
LEE, SANDRA--[9][21][26]ROM--
"OVER THE RAINBOW"
"LOVE LESSONS" & MORE

SMITH, SARAH
STRETTON, HESBA--[1]

SMITH, SEBA
DOWNING, MAJOR JACK--[31]

SMITH, SHIRLEY M[AE]
OVESEN, ELLIS--[1][31]--5 NOVELS & POETRY

SMITH, SIDNEY WALLACE
BRODIE, GORDON--[8]

SMITH, STEVE
FLEMING, JANE--[3][21]MYS/ROM--
BERK "HAWTHORN WOOD" '75

SMITH, SURREY
MORUM, WILLIAM--W/WILLIAM DINNER,[1]

SMITH, SUSAN VERNON M.
ENFIELD, CARRIE--[1][31][33]
MENDONCA, SUSAN--[1][7]SF
SINCLAIR, ROSE--[1]
VERNON, SUSAN--[33]

SMITH, TERENCE LORE
LORE, PHILIPS--[3][40]MYS--
PLAYBOY "LOOKING GLASS MURDERS" '80
"BEHIND CLOSED DOORS" '80
SATURDAY REV PRESS "WHO KILLED THE
PIE MAN?" '75
SMITH, CHARLES MERRILL--[34]--
COMPLETED PUTNAM "REV. RANDOLLPH
& THE SPLENDID SAMARITAN"
UPON DAD'S DEATH

SMITH, THOMAS
MIDNITE, CAPT.--[13]AUSTRALIAN

SMITH, WALTER CHALMERS
KNOTT, HERMANN--[8]
ORWELL--[8]

SMITH, WALTER JAMES
SMITH, W.J.--[1]

SMITH, WALTER [W]
SMITH, RED--[31]SPORTS STORIES & COLUMNS

SMITH, WARREN B.
SHEARER, JOHNNY--V. BERCH-BRNDN/BC PSEUDS,
BAE 22, ADULT--
BRNDN 954 "SODOM, USA!"

SMITH, WILLARD L.
LAURENCE, WILL--V. BERCH-MON PSEUDS,
BAE 9,[1]--
MON 330 "THE GO GIRLS" '63
MON 558 "THE DESPOILER" '64

SMITH, WILLIAM DALE
ANTHONY, DAVID--[31][34]MYS--
COLLINS "THE ORGANIZATION" '70
COLLINS "LONG HARD CURE" '79 & 3 MORE

SMITH, WILLIAM J.
HALL, STEPHANIE--[3][21][26]MYS/ROM--
POPLB "WHISPER IN THE DUST" '76
POPLB "QUEEN OF COINS" '75 & MORE

SMITH, WILLIAM JOSEPH T.
FERRAR, GUL--[1]

SMITH, WILLIAM SCOTT
DOUGLAS, SCOTT--[31]

SMITH, [EDGAR] DENNIS
HATHI--[1]

SMITH-WARE, SANDRA
DU PRE, GABRIELLE--W/DIANNE M. KLEINSCHMIDT,
[9][21][26]ROM--
"FORGET ME NOT" & MORE

SMITHELLS, ANABEL DOREEN
BOSCAWEN, LINDA--[1]

SMITHELLS, ROGER [W]
CASH, SEBASTIAN--[1][22][31]ENGLISH

SMITHERS, LEONARD
NEANISKOS--[8]

SMITS, THEODORE R.
SMITS, TEO--[1][33]

SMITTER, ELIOTT-BURTON
HADLEY, LEILA--[8]

SMOCK, JAMES
FREDERICKS, HARRIET--W/CLYDE LAURENTS,
[3][11]MYS--
BEAGLE "THE DREAM HUNTER" '74

SMOKE, STEPHEN L.
BARKER, WADE--[34]MYS,HP--
WARNER "VENGEANCE IS HIS" '81
CAINE, HAMILTON T.--[3]MYS--
CHART "CARPENTER, DETECTIVE" '80

SMOLAR, BORIS
LEWIS, BEN--[1]

SMRECZYNSKI, FRANCISZEK
ORKAN, WLADYSLAW--[22]POLISH

SMREK, JAN
CHIETEK, JAN--[22]SLOVAK

SMYTH, JOSEPH HILTON
ANONYMOUS--V. BERCH--
GM PSEUDS, PP 33--
"I, MOBSTER"
HILTON, JOSEPH--V. BERCH--
GM PSEUDS, PP 33,[29]--
GM 278 "THAT FRENCH GIRL" '52
GM475 "ANGELS IN THE GUTTER" '55
AV T178 "BEYOND MOMBASA" '57
AV T230 "CRY BABY KILLER" '58
LAN 70-050 "PRESIDENT'S AGENT" '63
LAN 75-398 "SHIP OF THE DAMNED" '72
LEBARON, JOSEPH--V. BERCH-BRNDN/BC PSEUDS, BAE 22, ADULT--

SNEDDON, ROBERT W.
SHADOW, MARK--[2][11]

SNEDECKER, CAROLINE D.P.
OWEN, CAROLINE DALE--[33]

SNELL, E.L.
ELLISON, ELLIS--[1]
ELLSEN, ELLIS--[1]

SNELL, GAY CAMERON
CAMERON, GAY--[26]ROM--
HARL 264 "HIS BROTHER'S KEEPER"

SNELL, ROY JUDSON
O'HARA, DAVID--[1]

SNELLING, O.F.
FREDERICK, OSWALD--[22][27]--
"BOOK OF BOXING"

SNEVE, VIRGINIA D. HAWK
DRIVING HAWK, VIRGINIA--[1][31][33]

SNIDER, JOHN H.
KNIGHT, TAYLOR C.--[1]

SNIPES, DEBORAH
SCOTT, DEBORAH--[3]MYS--
ACE "DEATHBED OF ROSES" '76
SCOTT, MARIANNE DE JAY--[3]MYS--
LAN "DRAMBUIE HOUSE" '72
LAN "VAN DYNE COLLECTION" '73

SNITZER, ARTHUR
ANATOL--[31]

SNODGRASS, MELINDA
HARRIS, MELINDA--[9][21][26]ROM--
"CRESCENDO"
"WIND'S EMBRACE"
"ONCE MORE WITH FEELING"
MCKENZIE, MELINDA--[7][9][21][26]SF/ROM--
SIGN "MAGIC TO DO: PAUL'S STORY" '85
& MORE ROMANCE

SNODGRASS, W.D.
GARDONS, S.S.--[8][31]
MCCONNELL, WILL--[8]
PRUTKOV, KOZMA--[8]

SNOW, CHARLES H[ORACE]
AVERILL, H.C.--[16][22][28]WEST--
W&B 30 NOVELS '38-66
"OF EARTH & HIGH HEAVEN" '85
BALLEW, CHARLES--[3][16][22][28]WEST/MYS--
W&B "RIMFIRE DETECTIVE" '36 & MORE '32-67
COLE, ROBERT--L. ROBBINS LTR,[28]WEST--
HALE "VENGEANCE TRAIL" '56
HALE "HANGMAN'S TREE" '57
DILLARD, JAMES--L. ROBBINS LTR '94,[28]WEST--
5 MULLER NOVELS '57-63
FORREST, ALLEN--[28]WEST--
CORGI "WHEELS ROLL WEST" '56
CORGI "APACHE TRAIL" '57
CORGI "INDIAN FIGHTER" '58
HARDY, RUSS--[1][22][28]WEST--
43 HAMMOND NOVELS '46-63
HARLOW, JOHN--[28]WEST--
LONG "NEVADA COWBOY" '57
LONG "DEAD MAN'S MINE" '58
LONG "TRAIL INTO MEXICO" '58
LEE, RANGER--[16][22][28]WEST--
2 HALE
2 GREYSTONE
2 PHOENIX
42 COLLINS NOVELS '37-62
MARSHALL, GARY--[16][22][28]WEST--
61 W&B NOVELS '34-56
SMITH, WADE--[16][22][28]WEST--
36 COLLINS NOVELS '42-62
WARDLE, DAN--[16][28]WEST--
W&B "TWENTY & ONE" '54
W&B "FIVE BARS OF GOLD" '55
W&B "SPEAR FOR A TIGER" '56
WILLS, CHESTER--[22][28]WEST--
29 COLLINS NOVELS '47-63

SNOW, CHARLES PERCY
SNOW, C.P.--[1][34]MYS--
HM "DEATH UNDER SAIL" '32
MacM "A COAT OF VARNISH" '79 & MORE

SNOW, DONALD CLIFFORD
FALL, THOMAS--[1][31][33]

SNOW, HELEN FOSTER
WALES, NYM--[1][2]SF--
"FABLES & PARABLES FOR THE MID-CENTURY" '52

SNOWDEN, JAMES
SNOWDEN, KEIGHLEY--[1]

SNYDER, EUGENE VINCENT
SNYDER, E.V.--[1][23]SF--
"ECODEATH" '72
SNYDER, GENE--[7][23]SF--
PLAYBOY "DARK DREAMING" '81
PLAYBOY "MIND WAR" '80
PLAYBOY "OGDEN ENIGMA" '81
CHARTER "TOMB SEVEN" '85
JOVE "SIGMA PROJECT" '88

SNYDER, GEORGE
CARTER, NICK--[3]MYS,HP--
AWARD "DEFECTOR" '69
AWARD "CAMBODIA" '70
AWARD "JEWEL OF DOOM" '70
AWARD "MOSCOW" '70
AWARD "TIME CLOCK OF DEATH" '70
AWARD "ICE BOMB ZERO" '71
AWARD "MARK OF COSTRA NOSTRA" '71
MORGAN, PATRICK--[34][36]MYS--
MacF 'OPERATION HANG TEN' SERIES: '70-1
RICHARDS, PAUL--W/DANIEL T. STRIEB,[34]MYS,HP--
AWARD "PRESIDENT HAS BEEN KIDNAPPED" '71
RICHARDS, PAUL--W/JON MESSMAN,[34]HP--
AWARD "OUR SPACESHIP IS MISSING" '70

SNYDER, HARRY
STERLING, HANK--[1]

SNYDER, LOUIS L.
NORDICUS--[1]

SNYDER, MARILYN
BURKE, MAGGIE--[31]

SOBCZYK, RUDOLF
ROMBERG, HANS--[40]GERMAN/MYS--
"MUCK ODER DER EHRLICH DIEB" '61

SOBELSOHN, KARL
RADEK, KARL BERNARDOVICH--[22]RUSSIAN

SOBOTTA, KURT
KURT, K.S.--[1]
STRAUB, OTTO--[1]

SOCKHANSKAYA, NADEZHDA S.
KOKHANOVSHAYA--[22]RUSSIAN

SODERBERG, BENGT
BERGMAN, JOAKIM--[29]MYS--
"MIDSOMMERNATTSMORD" '67

SODERBURG, PERCY MEASDAY
ARCHER, S.E.--[1][31]
MEASDAY, GEORGE--[1][22]ENGLISH
SEEBORD, G.R.--[1][22]ENGLISH
UNDERHILL, PETER--[1][22]ENGLISH

SODERHIELM, HENNING
TRE, HERRAR--[29]MYS--
SCHILDTS "HERR COPWIETH, GENTLEMAN-DETEKTIV" '14
WIKSTROM, LENNART--[29]MYS--
BONNIER "GULDGRUVAN" '16
BONNIER "MANGMILJONAREN" '20

SODERSTROM, OLE
WIKSTROM, LENNART--[29]MYS--
BONNIER "DUBBELMANNER" '18

SOERENSEN, SVEND OTTO
OTTO, SVEND--[33]
S., SVEND OTTO--[33]
SORENSEN, SVEND, OTTO--[33]

SOHL, GERALD ALLEN
BUTLER, NATHAN--[2][4][7][11]SF--
GM "KAHEESH" '83
KING, ROBERT--[7]SF--
MOUNTJOY, ROBERTA [JEAN]--[9][21][26]ROM--
"NIGHT WIND"
"BLACK THUNDER"
SOHL, JERRY--HOLLAND-LASER ART/CKLST, BAE 2,[11][32]MYS--
SP "LAUGHING DEPUTY" JUN '56
MH "CHANGE FOR A C-NOTE" JUL '56
SP "DREAM DOLL" AUG '56
SULLIVAN, SEAN MEI--[2][3][4][11]MYS/SF--
BAL "SUPER MAN CHU" '74 ??RELEASED??

SOHOMONJAN, EGISE
CARENC, EGISE--[22]ARMENIAN

SOITOS, STEPHEN
SAX, ANDRE--W/JAMIE KINNEY,[34]MYS--
CHART "A DEATH IN THE COLONY" '80
CHART "SALT CAT BANK" '80
CHART "DANCER DISAPPEARS" '82

SOKICHI, NAGAI
KAFU, NAGAI--[1][22]JAPANESE

SOKOL, WILLIAM
SOKOL, BILL--[33]

SOKOLOFF, NATALIE B.
SCOTT, NATALIE ANDERSON--[1]

SOKOLOV, ALEXANDER V.
SOKOLOV, SASHA--[1]

SOLBERT, ROMAINE
SOLBERT, RONNI--[1][31][33]--
"A FEW FLIES & I" '69

SOLER, ANTONIO ROBLES
ANTONIORROBLES--[2][11]

SOLLERS, PHILLIPPE
JOYAUX, PHILLIPPE--[31]

SOLOMON, ABBA
EBAN, ABBA--[1]
EBAN, AUDREY--[1]

SOLOMON, JANIS LITTLE
GELLINEK, JANIS LITTLE--[31]

SOLOMON, SAMUEL
BRITINDIAN--[8][31]
MOOLSON, MELUSA--[8]
SIDNEY, SAMUEL--[34]MYS--
LONGMAN "GALLOPS & GOSSIPS IN THE BUSH OF AUSTRALIA" 1854

SOLOW, MARTIN
NELSON, PETER--[1]

SOMAN, SHIRLEY CAMPER
CAMPER, SHIRLEY--[22][31]AMERICAN

SOMER, DERK
SAISON, JACQUES--V. BERCH-BRNDN/BC PSEUDS, BAE 22, ADULT--

SOMERLOTT, ROBERT
CARSON, ROBERT--[32][33]MYS--
EQMM "CODE OF THE UNDERWORLD" SEPT '56
NORTH, JESSICA--[9][21][26][34]MYS/ROM--
COWARD "LEGEND OF THE THIRTEENTH PILGRIM" '69
RANDOM "HIGH VALLEY" '73
RANDOM "RIVER RISING" '75
COWARD "MASK OF THE JAGUAR" '81

SOMERSET FRY, P.G.R. PLA.
FRY, PLANTAGENET SOMERSET--[31]

SOMERSET, HENRY HUGH A.F.
DUKE OF BEAUFORT--[31]

SOMERSON, PAUL
MURCH, MEL--W/STEPHEN MANES,[1]
STARR, WARD--W/STEPHEN MANES,[1]

SOMERVILLE, EDITH A.O.
GRAHAM, VIVA--[8]IRISH
HERRING, GUILLES--[8][22][31]IRISH
SOMERVILLE & ROSS--W/VIOLET F. MARTIN, [1][22][34]IRISH/MYS--
WARD "THE REAL CHARLOTTE" 1894

SOMMERSCALES, ROWLAND
GAINES, ROBERT--[3]MYS--
HM "DAYBREAK AT DEEST" '51
MacD "CRUEL DEADLINE" '60 & 6 MORE

SONTUP, DANIEL
CLARKE, JOHN--V. BERCH--MON PSEUDS, BAE 9,[31][32]MYS--
LM "PINKIE" SEPT '57
MON 250 "LOLITA LOVERS" '62
DANIELS, TOPSON--LACHMAN LST '93,[32]MYS--
TR "THE SQUEALER" APR '58

SONTUP, DANIEL [CONT]
DANIELS, TOPSUN--LACHMAN LST '93,[32]MYS--
GU "LADY KILLER" JUL '58
SAUNDERS, DAVID--[1][3][29]MYS--
BELM "M-SQUAD" '62
SONTUP, DAN--[31]

SOOMRO, M.I.
MUNSHI--[1]

SOREIL, [JOSEPH] ARSENE
DELAISNE, JEAN--[1]

SOREL, MARILYN MEESKE
LANSDALE, NINA--[3][9][21][26]MYS/ROM--
ARBOR "WHITE ISLAND" '75

SOREL-CAMERON, JAMES R.
CAMERON, JAMES SOREL--[31]

SORENSON, ERIK
DICKSON, BOB--[29]MYS--
ZETT "BOWERY-MYSTERIET" '19

SOROKIN, PITIRIM ALEXAND.
TCHAADAIEFF--[22]RUSSIAN-AMERICAN

SORRELS, ROY
MCCLURE, ANNA--[9][21][26]ROM--
"CHAMSON D'AMOUR"
"PASSION'S HUE"

SORTOR, JUNE ELIZABETH
SORTOR, TONI--[1][33]

SOULEN, HENRY J.
ZAULA, ONDREK--L. ROBBINS LTR '94

SOULES, JEAN GEORGES
ABELLIO, RAYMOND--[22]

SOUSTER, [HOLMES] RAYMOND
HOLMES, JOHN--[1][31][33]
HOLMES, RAYMOND--[1][31][33]

SOUTAR, GWENDOLINE AMY
DEANE, SONIA--[1]

SOUTER, HELEN GREIG
AUNT KATE--[8]

SOUTHARD, HELEN FAIRBARN
FAIRBARN, HELEN--[22][31]AMERICAN

SOUTHER, HUGH
SUTHERLAND, ROY--[1]

SOUTHERLAND, KATHERINE V.
VIRDEN, KATHERINE--[1]

SOUTHERN, TERRY
KENTON, MAXWELL--W/MASON HOFFENBERG,[1][2][31]

SOUTHEY, ROBERT
ESPRIELLA, DON MANUEL A.--[31][33]

SOUTHWOLD, STEPHEN
BELL, NEIL--[7][23][34]MYS--
GOLZ "DISTURBING AFFAIR OF NOEL BLAKE" '32
EYRE "DARK PAGE" '51
GREEN, STEPHEN--[23]SF
LAMBERT, S.H.--[1][2][23]SF
MARTENS, PAUL--[16][34]MYS--
COLLINS "DEATH ROCKS THE CRADLE" '33
COLLINS "TRUTH ABOUT MY FATHER" '34
MILES--[2][11][16][22][23]SF--

SOUTHWORTH, JOHN VAN D.
SOUTHERN, JACK--[1]

SOWERBY, A. LINDSAY
MCRAE, LINDSAY--[1][22]ENGLISH

SOWMAN, GORDON
CAPELLI, ACE--PP 29, P42, MYS,HP--
REID, DESMOND--W/G.P. MANN,[34]MYS,HP--
AMALG "HOMICIDE BLUES" '57
REID, DESMOND--W/P. CHAMBERS,[34]MYS,HP--
AMALG "CONFLICT WITHIN" '60
AMALG "DEATH IN DOCKLAND" '62
REID, DESMOND--[1][34]MYS,HP--
AMALG "CONFLICT WITHIN" '60
WINGRAVE, JOSH--[34]MYS,HP--
KAYE "THE BIG SIN" '54

SPALDING, KEITH
SPALT, KARL HEINZ G.--[8]

SPALT, KARL HEINZ
SPALDING, KEITH--[1]

SPANGENBERG, JUDITH DUNN
DUNN, JUDY--[1][31][33]

SPARER, LAURIE A. TAYLOR
TAYLOR, L.A.--[7]SF--
ST. MARTIN'S "THE BLOSSOM OF ERDA" '86

SPARK, MURIEL SARAH
CAVALLO, EVELYN--[31]

SPARKIA, ROY [BERNARD]
CAINE, MITCHELL--[1][31]

SPARRE, CHRISTIAN
VILLER, FREDRIK--[29][34]MYS--
DBLDY "BLACK TORTOISE" '01
& OTHERS 1897-1912

SPARROW, LAURA
GRIFFIN, JOCELYN--[21][26]ROM--
"WHITE WAVE"
"BATTLE WITH DESIRE"
"BELOVED INTRUDER" & MORE
HALFORD, LAURA--[21][26]ROM--
"SEASWEPT"

SPARROW, MALCOLM W.
MOINEAU, MAX--[1]

SPARSHOTT, FRANCIS EDWARD
KENT, CROMWELL--[31]
SPARSHOTT, F.E.--[1]

SPAULDING, HENRY D.
SPRING, DAN--[1]

SPAULDING, RUTH
JAY, MARION--[1][31]
SPAULDING, LUCILE--[1]

SPAULDING, SAMUEL C.
CARTER, NICHOLAS--[34]MYS,HP--
STREET "ADDER'S BROOD; OR, SPAWN OF SATAN" '17
STREET "AMPHITHEATER PLOT; OR, WORSE THAN DEATH" '18
STREET "ANGEL OF DEATH; OR, WORSE FIEND IN THE WORLD" '13
STREET "BOLTS FROM BLUE SKIES; OR, NICK CARTER'S CHANCE DISCOVERY" '14
STREET "BURDEN OF PROOF; OR, A SHREWD RASCAL" '16

SPAULDING, SAMUEL C. [CONT]
CARTER, NICHOLAS [CONT]
STREET "CASE OF ,MANY CLUES; OR, A HAND WITH FANGS" '16
STREET "CASE OF THE TWO DOCTORS; OR, CLEVEREST CROOK IN AMERICA" '12
STREET "A CLUE FROM THE UNKNOWN; OR, A LONG DISTANCE TRAIL" '16
STREET "CLUTCH OF DREAD; OR, NICK CARTER'S STEADY HAND" '13
STREET "A CONSPIRACY OF RUMORS; OR, BETWEEN DARK & DAWN" '16
STREET "A CRIME IN PARADISE; OR, NICK CARTER'S INDIAN GUIDE" '14
STREET "DANGER OF FOLLY; OR, PERILS OF EVIL WAYS" '15
STREET "DEVIL'S SON" '11
STREET "DAY OF RECKONING; OR, WHEN CLEWS ARE SCARCE" '13
STREET "DEADLY SCARAB; OR, AN INGENIOUS CRIMINAL" '12
STREET "DEATH IN LIFE; OR, A WEIRD CRIME" '18
STREET "THE GRAFTERS" '14
STREET "DOOMED TO FAILURE; OR, NICK CARTER ON TOP" '13
STREET "A DUEL OF BRAINS; OR, NICK CARTER'S QUICK DECISION" '13
STREET "FOR A PAWNED CROWN; OR, WHEN TRAILS CROSSED" '17
STREET "FOR SAKE OF REVENGE; OR, END OF A SPECTACULAR CAREER" '13

SPEAR, ANNIE B.
FORFEX ET HESTA--W/BESSIE C. MORRIS,[3]MYS--
"LOST KEY: OR THE MYS BOX"

SPEARS, RAYMOND S.
SMILEY, JIM--[1]

SPECK, GERALD EUGENE
KEPPS, GERALD--[8]
SCIENCE INVESTIGATOR--[8]
STONE, EUGENE--[8]

SPECTOR, CAROLINE
CHASE, CAROLINE--AUTHOR PROVIDED--
EDITOR OF 'AMAZING' MAG & TSR 'DUNGEONS & DRAGONS'

SPECTOR, ROBERT DONALD
SPECTOR, ROBERT D.--[21]ROM--
"THE CANDLE & THE TOWER"

SPEED, FREDERICK MAURICE
DEEPS, FREDERICK--[31]
HAFFNER, J. LILLIWHITE--[31]
SPEED, F. MAURICE--[31]

SPEER, JACK
BRISTOL, JOHN A.--[1][2][11]

SPEICHER, HELEN ROSS
ABBOT, ALICE--W/KATHRYN K. BORLAND,[3][26]MYS--
ACE "THIRD TOWER" '74
ACE "GOODBYE JULIE SCOTT" '75
LAND, JANE & ROSS--W/KATHRYN K. BORLAND, [31][33]--
SEALE "MILES & THE BIG BLACK HAT '63

SPELMAN, MARY
LOCKWOOD, MARY--[1][33]
TOWNE, MARY--[1][7][33]SF--
"GOLDEN ROD" '77
"PAUL'S GAME: A NOVEL" '83

SPENCE, W. JOHN DUNCAN
BOWDEN, JIM--[28][31]WEST--
26 HALE NOVELS '60-88
COOPER, HANNAH--[1][28][31]--
HALE "TIME WILL NOT WAIT" '83
FORD, KIRK--[1][28][31]WEST--
HALE "TRAIL TO SEDALIA" '67
HALE "FEUD RIDERS" '74
ROGERS, FLOYD--[1][28]WEST--
6 HALE NOVELS '64-79
SPENCE, BILL--[28]WAR--
HALE "BOMBER'S MOON" '81
SPENCE, DUNCAN--[1][28]--
BW "DARK HELL" '59

SPENCER, FLOYD & PAULA
BAYNE, SPENCER--[34]MYS--
HARPER "MURDER RECALLS VAN KILL" '39
HARPER "TURNING SWORD" '41
DUTTON "AGENT EXTRAORDINARY" '42

SPENCER-CHURCHILL, LAURA
DUCHESS OF MARLBOROUGH--[31]

SPENCER-MEEK, MARGARET
MEEK, MARGARET--[1]

SPENDER, JEAN MAUDE
SPENDER, J.M.--[36]AUSTRALIAN/MYS--
DYMOCKS "CHARGE IS MURDER" '33
E&S "DEATH COMES IN THE NIGHT" '38
E&S "FOLL MOON FOR MURDER" '48 & 3 OTHERS
HALE "MURDER ON THE PROWL" '60

SPENDER, JOHN ALFRED
GREVILLE, MINOR--[1]
PHILISTINE--[1]
SPENDER, J.A.--[1]

SPENDER, LYNNE
JARON, LOU--[1][31]

SPENDER, STEPHEN
S.H.S.--[8]

SPENSER, EMMA JANE
LEIGH, VICTORIA--[26]ROM--
"BEWITCHED"
"SECRET KEEPER" & MORE

SPERO, LEOPOLD
HOPE, CECIL--[1]

SPERRY, HENRY TREAT
HOWARD, PAUL--[11]

SPEWACK, BELLA
COHEN, BELLA--[31]

SPEWACK, SAMUEL
ABBOTT, A.A.--[1][22]

SPICER, BART & BETTY COE
BARBETTE, JAY--[29][31][34]MYS--
DODD "FINAL COPY" '50
DODD "DEADLY DOLL" '58 & 2 MORE

SPICKLER, CHARLES A.
BROGAN THE SCRIBE--[1][2]

SPIEGEL, CLARA GATZERT
JAYNES, CLARE--W/JANE R. MAYER, [1][22][33]AMERICAN

SPIEGELMAN, ART
CUTRATE, JOE--[31]
FLOOGLEBUCKLE, AL--[31]
GRANT, SKEETER--[31]

SPIELMANN, MARION H.A.
M.H.S.--[1]
SPIELMANN, M.H.--[1]

SPIELMANN, PETER JAMES
NIGHTRATE, EMIL--[1]

SPILLANE, FRANK MORRISON
SPILLANE, MICKEY--[2][32][34]MYS--
28 BKS '47-73
BL "EVERYBODY'S WATCHING ME" JAN-APR '53
BL "THE PICKPOCKET" DEC '61
BL "GIRL BEHIND THE HEDGE" OCT '61
MH "I CAME TO KILL YOU" JAN '64
BZ "LADY SAYS DIE" JAN '66
IN "SEVEN YEAR KILL" JAN '66

SPILLSBURY, JULIAN
TEMPEST, JOHN--[7]SF--
HARPER "VISION OF THE HUNTER" '89

SPILLUS, ELIZABETH JANE
BOTT, ELIZABETH--[1]

SPINELLI, GRACE
SPINELLI, MARCOS--[8]

SPIRER, HERBERT F.
SITZFLEISCH, VLADIMIR--[1]

SPIRO, EDWARD
COOKRIDGE, E.H.--[1][31]

SPIRT, DIANA LOUISE
LEMBO, DIANA L.--[31]

SPITTELER, CARL
TANDEM, CARL FELIX--[1][22]SWISS

SPLINE, TRICIA
INDRA--LORRAINE BIER-ARMADILLOCON '93
LEWTAN, MEG--LORRAINE BIER-ARMADILLOCON '93

SPOELSTRA, CORNELIUS
DOOLARD, A. DEN.--[22]DUTCH

SPOONER, JOHN D.
BRUTUS--[1][31]

SPOONER, PETER ALAN
MELLOR, MICHAEL--[8]
PETERS, ALAN--[8]
RENNIE, JACK--[8]
UNDERWOOD, KEITH--[8]

SPRAGUE, ALICE INGRAM ORR
ORR, A.--[7]SF--
'WORLD IN AMBER': #1 & 2 '85-6

SPRAKE, LESLIE
MIDDLE WALLOP--[1]

SPRATLING, WALTER NORMAN
SPARLING, W.--[8]

SPRATT, PHILLIP
DESMOND--[1]

SPRIGG, C. ST. JOHN
CAUDWELL, CHRISTOPHER--[1][5][22]ENGLISH

SPRIGGE, ELIZABETH
SQUIRE, MIRIAM--[33]

SPRING, GERALD MAX
BODWELL, RICHARD--[1][3]MYS--
VANTAGE "MYS OF FERNRIDGE MANOR" '74

SPRING, HOWARD
R.H.S.--[8]

SPRINGER, MARILYN HARRIS
HARRIS, MARILYN--[1][7][31][33]

SPRINGER, ROBERT
STEIN, ADAM--[1]

SPRINGFIELD, LINCOLN
CAPT. COE--W/EDWARD C. MITCHELL,[3]MYS--
"CORONER'S UNDERSTUDY" 1891

SPRINGS, ELLIOTT WHITE
GISH, JOE--[1]

SPROAT, IAIN MACDONALD
PENN, RICHARD--[8]

SPROULE, HOWARD
SPROULE, WESLEY--[8]

SPROULL, MARIE
MICHAELS, ELIZABETH ANN--[26]ROM--
"FROM A SILVER HEART"
"DESTINY'S WILL"
"A JEWEL SO RARE"
SHERWOOD, ELIZABETH--[26]ROM--
"FROM A SILVER HEART"
"VIRGINIA EMBRACE"

SPRY, THEODORE JAMES
WHITE, PALMER--[1][3]MYS--
CHAPMAN "CIRCLE OF CONFUSION" '30
CHAPMAN "MYSTERY ISLAND" '30

SQUIBBS, H.W.Q.
QUIRK--[8]

SQUIRE, JOHN COLLINS
AFFABLE HAWK--[1]ENGLISH
EAGLE, SOLOMON--[1][2][22]ENGLISH
SQUIRE, J.C.--[1][22]ENGLISH

SQUIRES, FREDERICK
THUMBTACK, TOM--[1]

SRIVASTAVA, DHANPAT RAI
CHAND, MUNSHI PREM--[31]
CHAND, PREM--[31]
PREMANCANDA--[1]
RAI, NAVAB--[1]

SROOG, ARNOLD
RODIN, ARNOLD--V. BERCH-GM PSEUDS, PP 33--
GM 232 "WOMAN SOLDIER" '52
GM "MOMENT OF TRUTH" '53
WILLIAMS, DAVID--V. BERCH-LESBIANA/
CNTRCLTR, BAE 22, ADULT--
IN 32 "BASEMENT GANG" '53
UGE 5 "BULLS, BLOOD & PASSION" '53
CROY 31 "ARMY MISTRESS" '53

ST. BRUNO, ALBERT FRANCIS
BRUNO, FRANK--[1][31]

ST. CLAIR, BYRD HOOPER
HOOPER, BYRD--[1][31][33]

ST. CLAIR, LEONARD
DE GRAFFE, RICHARD--[31]

ST. CLAIR, MARGARET
HAZEL, WILLIAM--[1][2][11]
HAZZARD, WILTON--[1][2][11][23]SF--1 STORY '52
SEABRIGHT, IDRIS--[1][2][11][23]SF--FSF '50-9

ST. JOHN, CHERYL
NATHENSON, JOSEPH--[3]MYS--
MANOR "RADNITZ" '79
MANOR "SEE NAPLES & DIE" '79

ST. JOHN, NICOLE
CHAMBERS, CATHERINE E.--[31]
CHAMBERS, KATE--[31]
DRYDEN, PAMELA--[31]
HARRIS, LAVINIA--[31]

ST. JOHN, PERCY BOLLNGBRK
BOONE, HENRY L.--[1]
BROUGHAM, J.T.--[1]
CAVENDISH, HARVEY--[1]
FREEMAN, J.L.--[1]
HOPE, ESTHER--[1]
MCKEEN, CAPT.--[1]
PERIWINKLE, PAUL--[1]
ST. JOHN, P.B.--[1]
ST. JOHN, WARREN--[1]

ST. JOHN, WYLLY FOLK
FOX, ELEANOR--[1][31][33]
LARSON, EVE--[1][31][33]
PIERCE, KATHERINE--[1][33]
VINCENT, MARY KEITH--[1][33]
WILLIAMS, MICHAEL--[1][33]

STAAL, CYRIL
WILLS, GEOFFREY--[1]

STABLEFORD, BRIAN M.
CRAIG, BRIAN--W/CRAIG MCKINTOSH,[2][7][23]SF--
SCI/FANT. "BEYOND TIME'S AEGIS" '65
CRAIG, BRIAN--[7][23]SF--
'GAMES WORKSHOP' BOOKS '89-91
GW BOOKS 'DARK FUTURE':
"GHOST DANCERS"
'MINSTREL ORFEO': #1-3
STABILE, STICKUM--[1]

STABLER, JAMIE LATHAM
WOODVILLE, JENNIE--[1]

STABLES, [WILLIAM] GORDON
STABLES, DR. GORDON, RN--[23]
CHILDREN'S FICTION

STACK, NICHOLETE MEREDITH
HILL, EILEEN--[1][31]
KENNY, MARILYN--[1]HP--
MEREDITH, NICHOLETE--[1][21][22]ROM--
"MILESTONE SUMMER"
KENNY, KATHRYN--[22][31]AMERICAN/HP

STACKEL-TREUTLEIN, FREDA
GENTER, HARRY--[39][40]GERMAN/MYS--
"DIE FREUDIN DES ARTEZ" '64
"TODLICHER FASCHING" '65

STACKHOUSE, MARY AGNES
MARY ANGELITA--[1]

STACPOOLE, H. DEVERE
DE SAIX, TYLER--[1][3][29]MYS--
UNWIN "MAN WITHOUT A HEAD" '08
UNWIN "VULTURE'S PREY" '09

STACTON, DAVID DEREK
BOYD, CARSE--[1][31]
CLIFTON, BUD--[3][29][31]MYS--
ACE D330 "MUSCLE BOY" '58
ACE D270 "D FOR DELINQUENT" '58
PYR G364 "THE BAD GIRLS" '58
ACE D383 "MURDER SPECIALIST" '59
PYR G410 "POWER GODS" '59
ACE D501 "LET HIM GO HANG" '61
DEREKSON, DAVID--[1][31]
WEST, DAVID--[3][29]MYS--
EYRE "WISH ME DEAD" '60

STACY, JAN
SARGENT, CRAIG--[7][23]SF--
POPLB 'LAST RANGER': #2-10 '88
SIEVERT, JOHN--W/RYDER SYVERTSEN,[7]SF--
ZEBRA 'C.A.D.S.': #1 '85
STACY, RYDER--W/RYDER SYVERTSEN,[7][23]SF--
ZEBRA 'DOOMSDAY WARRIOR': #1-4 '84-5

STACY, KATHY
STACY, EILEEN--[21]ROM--
"JUST LIKE A DREAM"

STACY, WALTER
ELLIOTT, BRUCE--WELLS SF LST--
BELM "ASYLUM EARTH" '68
CURTIS "RIVET IN GRANDFATHER'S NECK" '70

STADENER, INGEGERD
GAVELL, LILLEVI--[29]MYS--
"MYSTERIET MED DE BLAMARKTA SMALBENER" '60
POLONI, HELENA--[29]MYS--
BONNIER "MORD I BARM" '56
BONNIER "MANGA TUNGOR SMA" '60

STADLEMAN, SARA LEE
HARRIS, SARA LEE--[31]
STADLEMAN, S.L.--[31]

STADLER, JILL
BARNETT, JILL--[21][26]ROM--
"BEWITCHING"
"JUST A KISS AWAY" & 2 MORE

STAFF, ADRIENNE
STONE, NATALIE--W/SALLY GOLDENBAUM,[9][21]ROM--
"DOUBLE OLAY"
"SKY GYPSIE" & 4 MORE

STAFFORD, JO LEE
MORRISON, JO--[21][26]ROM--
"ALWAYS"
"AN IMPERFECT HERO"

STAFFORD, LINDA
CRYING WIND--[1][31]
LOVEQUIST, GWENDOLYNN--[1]

STAFFORD, MURIEL
SAUER, MURIEL S.--[8]

STAGG, JAMES
JOHNS, GILBERT--[1][34]MYS--
AMALG "THIEF OF CLUBS" '61
AMALG "VOTE FOR VIOLENCE" '61
REID, DESMOND--[1][34]MYS,HP--
AMALG "MURDER COMES CALLING!" '60

STAGG, JOHN REGINALD
BARNETT, JOHN--[1][34]MYS--
WARD "TRADER CARSON" '14
HARTE, OLIVER--[1]

STAHL, FRED ALAN
FEUR, D.C.--[31]

STAHL, LE ROY
SHELDON, GEORGE E.--[1][22]AMERICAN
WOOD, KIRK--[1][22]AMERICAN

STAHL, NORMAN
NORMAN, DONALD N.--W/DON HORAN,[7]SF--
WARNER "THUNDER STATION: A NOVEL" '90

STAHLSTROM, ROLLE
TILLMAN, ROLLE--[29]MYS--
BONNIER "AN LEVER LIKET"

STAHR, FANNY [LEWALD]
LEWALD, FANNY--[1]

STAICAR, THOMAS EDWARD
STAICAR, TOM--[7]SF--
NON-FICT

STAINBACK, MACKLIN
FLEMING, MACKLIN--[1]

STAMMEL, HEINZ-JOSEF
HAGEN, CHRISTOPHER--[1]
LOCKHART, T.C.--[1]

STAMP, ROGER GRESHAM
MINGSTON, R. GRESHAM--[1][2]
MINGSTON, R.G.--[11]

STANCIOFF, PANAIT
CERNA, PANAIT--[22]RUMANIAN

STANCLIFFE, ELAINE
STONE, ELISA--[21]ROM--
"A SHARED LOVE"

STANDARD-CRONK, PATTI
STANDARD, PATTI--[21]ROM--
"PRETTY AS A PICTURE"

STANDING BEAR, LUTHER
STANDING BEAR, CHIEF--[31]

STANEV, NIKOLA [S]
STANEV, ERUILIAN--[1]

STANFIELD, RICHARD H.
WAINWRIGHT, DAVID--[1]

STANFORD, JOHN KEITH
ISSCHAR--[1][22][31]ENGLISH

STANFORD, MURIEL S. SPARK
SPARK, MURIEL--[7]SF--NON-FICT

STANFORD, SALLY
BUSBY, MABEL JANICE--[31]
GUMP, SALLY--[31]

STANFORD, TERRY
KARTA, NAT--S. HOLLAND-SCION CKLST, PP 27,
[3]MYS,HP--
SCION "SINISTER LOVELY" '53

STANG, JUDIT
STANG, JUDY--[33]CANADIAN
VARGA, JUDY--[1][22][33]CANADIAN

STANGELAND, KATHARINA
MICHAELIS, KARIN--[1]

STANIER, MAIDA E. KERR
CULEX--[31]

STANIFORTH, JOHN WILLIAM
ANDREWS, JOHN--[34]MYS--
AMALG "SILVER DWARF" '38
AMALG "MISSING HEIR" '38
AMALG "DEAD MAN'S SECRET" '39
SCOTT, MAXWELL--[1][34]MYS--
29 AMALG NOVELS '06-24

STANISLAVSKY, CONSTANTIN
ALEXEYEV, CONSTANTIN [S]--[31]

STANLEY, DIANE
ZUROMISKIS, DIANE--[1][33]

STANLEY, FAY GRISSOM
FAY, STANLEY--[1]
GRISSOM, FAY--[3]MYS--
POPLB "PORTRAIT IN JIGSAW" '75

STANLEY, GEORGE EDWARD
HOPE, LAURA LEE--[31]MYS,HP--
STSY 'BOBSY TWINS':
"CASE OF RUNAWAY MONEY" '87
"MYSTERY ON THE MISSISSIPPI" '88
MILLS, ADAM--[31]JUV--
'TWIN CONNECTION' SERIES '89
SIMONS, STUART--[31]JUV--
'MINI-MYS' SERIES - SHORT STORIES '77

STANLEY, NORA K.B.S.
STRANGE, NORA K.--[1]

STANNARD, DAVID
HOLT, ARAM--[14]ADULT--
OLYMPIC PRESS
MATTHEWS, WEBB--[14]ADULT--
OLYM OPH#192 "EROS RISING '70
VAN HELLER, MARCUS--[14]ADULT--
OLYM OPH#106 "JAILBIRDS IN THE
BACKSEAT" '68
OLYM OPH#164 "GONE WITH THE WHIP" '69
OLYM OPH#221 "SADO-SHIP" '70

STANNARD, HENRIETTA ELIZ.
WHYTE, VIOLET--[1]
WINTER, JOHN STRANGE--[1][3]MYS--
WHITE "A MYS OF MAYFAIR" '08
& 11 MORE, 1885-1910

STANNARD, JOHN D.S.
SPOTSWOOD, JOHN--[1]

STANNARD, RUSSELL
MALLINSON, RUSSELL--[1]

STANNARD, WILLIAM JOHN
SANDARS, HARRY--[1]

STANNUS, [J] GORDON [D]
ANTHONY, GORDON--[1][31]
JASON--W/HUGH MUNRO,[31][35]AUSTRALIAN--
10 WEBSTER NOVELS '58-9

STANSBURY-MILLETT, NIGEL
CHANDOS, DANE--W/PETER LILLEY,[1][22]MYS--

STANSFELD, ANTHONY
BUCKINGHAM, BRUCE--W/PETER LILLEY,[3][22]MYS--
JOSEPH "THREE BAD NIGHTS" '56
JOSEPH "BOILED ALIVE" '57
CHANDOS, DANE--W/PETER LILLEY,[1][22]

STANTON, CATHY
CLARE, CATHRYN--[9][21][26]ROM--
SIL 558 "SUN & SHADOW"
SIL 599 "ANGEL & THE RENEGADE" & MORE

STANTON, JEANNE M.
MICHAELS, ELIZABETH--[7][26]ROM/SF--
"TOLLIN'S DAUGHTER"
"THE CYNIC" & MORE

STANTON, MARY
BISHOP, CLAUDIA--M. LACHMAN-CRPG--
BERK "A TASTE FOR MURDER" '94

STANTON-HOPE, W.E.
HOPE, STANTON--[8]

STAPLEBROEK, MARLYS
NICHOLS, SUZANNE--[9][21][26]ROM--
"RINGS OF GOLD"
"SATIN WHISPERS"

STAPLES, MARJORIE CHARLT.
REDWOOD, ROSALINE--[1]

STAPLES, REGINALD THOMAS
BREWSTER, ROBIN--[8]
BRIDGES, HOWARD--[1][31]
SINCLAIR, JAMES--[1][21]ROM--
"CANISE THE WARRIOR"
"WARRIOR QUEEN"
STEVENS, R.T.--[21][26][34]MYS--
SOUVENIR "FLIGHT FROM BUCHAREST" '77
SEVERN "HOSTAGE" '85
SEVERN "SHADOWS IN THE AFTERNOON" '83

STAPLES, SUZANNE FISHER
FISHER, SUZANNE--[31]

STAPLETON, DOROTHY & DOUG
STAPLETON, D & D--[1][3][22]MYS--
ARCADIA "LATE FOR THE FUNERAL" '53
ARCADIA "THE CRIME, THE PLACE & THE GIRL" '53
ARCADIA "CORPSE & ROBBERS" '54
STAPLETON, D.--[22]MYS

STARBIRD, KAYE
JENNISON, C.S.--[1][22][31][33]AMERICAN

STARDUST, ALVIN
FENTON, SHANE--[31]

STARES, JOHN EDWARD S.
ROWE, STEPHEN--[1]
SPENCER, EDWARD--[1]

STARFELT, VIVEKA
FRANCK, MONICA--[29]MYS--
BONNIERS "MORD I MAJ" '55

STARK, CLAUDE ALAN
MWANGA--[1]

STARK, DELBERT R.
NORWOOD, JOHN--[1][3][22]MYS--
WARD "NO TIME TO LAUGH" '56

STARK, DEREK RAYMOND
NORWOOD, JOHN--[8]

STARK, PESACH
STRYJKOWSKI, JULIAN--[1]

STARKEY, JAMES SULLIVAN
O'SULLIVAN, SEUMAS--[8][22]IRISH

STARR, CEWCILY
BOYAJIAN, CECILY--[31]

STARR, H.W.
ZORRO--L. ROBBINS LTR MAR '94, HP

STARR, HELEN UPSHAW
UPSHAW, HELEN--[3]MYS--
DODD "RETURN OF JENNIFER" '64

STARR, RICHARD H.
ESSEX, CAPTAIN--[1]
ESSEX, RICHARD--[29][32][34][40]MYS--
JENK "SLADE OF THE YARD" '32
EW "HONESTY IS THE BEST..." JUN '65
JENK "MURDER IN THE BANK" '36
GODWIN, FRANK--[1]
O'DARE, KERRY--[1]
RICHARDS, STELLA--[8]

STARR, S[TEPN.] FREDERICK
SCHWARTZ, S.--[1]
VALERAN, A.B.--[1]

STARTS, NANCY
LAWRENCE, NANCY--[21][26]ROM--
"DELIGHTFUL DECEPTION"

STATON-BEVAN, WILLIAM N.
ABBEY, STATON--[8]

STAUDERMAN, ALBERT P.
PHILLIPS, ALAN--[1]][31]AMERICAN

STAYNES, JILL
STACEY, SUSANNAH--W/MARGARET STOREY, LACHMAN-EASTER LST '93,[34]MYS--

STAYNOVA, ANNA
KAMENOVA, ANNA--[1]

STEAD, THISTLE Y.
HARRIS, THISTLE Y.--[1][31]

STEARN, JOHN THEODOR
STERN, JOHN--[8]

STEARNS, ALBERT
THORPE, FRED--[7][23]SF--
S&SDM "THROUGH THE EARTH: OR JACK NELSON'S INVENTION" '09

STEARNS, EDGAR FRANKLIN
FRANKLIN, EDGAR--[2][7][23][32][34]MYS--
WATT "MR. HAWKIN'S HUMOROUS ADVENTURES" '04
WATT "IN & OUT" '17
PD "MR. BATEY & THE GHOST" JAN '37
PD "THE HOT-TEMPERED HUSSY" SEPT '37
STEARNS, ALBERT--[1]
STEARNS, E.F.--ECHOES #24, ENGLISH

STEARNS, HAROLD EDMUND
DOYLE, HAROLD EDMUND--[1][31]
LUTETIUS--[1][31]
PICKEM, PETER--[1]

STEARNS, MYRON MORRIS
AMID, JOHN--[1]
MORRIS, MYRON--[1]

STEARNS, PETER N.
SHARD, DIANA--[1]

STEBEL, S[IDNEY] L[EO]
BERGSON, LEO--[1][3][31]MYS--
GM "THE WIDOWMASTER" '67

STEED, MABEL A.
HUGHES, M. ALISON--[1][22]MYS--

STEEGMULLER, FRANCIS
KEITH, DAVID--[3][22][29][31]MYS--
DODD "A MATTER OF IODINE" '40
DODD "BLUE HARPSICHORD" '49 & MORE
STEELE, BYRON--[1][2][22]MYS--

STEEL, RUDOLPH HORNADAY
KAGEY, RUDOLF--[1]
STEEL, KURT--[1]

STEELE, FRANCESCA MARIA
DALE, DARLEY--[3]MYS--
HUTCH "VILLAGE BLACKSMITH" 1892

STEELE, FRED I.
STEELE, FRITZ--[1]

STEELE, HARWOOD ELMES R.
STEELE, HOWARD--[8][28]--
UNWIN "CLEARED FOR ACTION" '14
VERSE

STEELE, JACK & HELEN
STEELE, JACLEN--V. BERCH-GM PSEUDS, PP 33, [3]MYS--
GM 221 "FORBIDDEN ROOM" '52

STEELE, MARY QUINTARD G.
GAGE, WILSON--[2][11][31][33]

STEELE, PATRICIA M.V.
JOUDRY, PATRICIA--[8]

STEELE, ROBERT V.P.
THOMAS, LATELY--[8]

STEELEY, ROBERT DEREK
CARTER, NICK--[3]MYS,HP--
CHART "TROUBLE IN PARADISE" '78
CHART "ISRAELI CONNECTION" '82
JARRETT, AMANDA JEAN--[21]ROM,HP--
DELL 'SOUTHERNERS' SERIES:
"THIS TRAITOR MOON"

STEEMAN, S.S. ANDRE
STEEMAN, A.S.--[40]GERMAN/MYS--
"DES CIERGES AU DIABLE" '65

STEEN, MALCOLM HAROLD
STEEN, MIKE--[1]

STEEN, MARGUERITE
DRYDEN, LENNOX--[1][31]
NICHOLSON, JANE--[1]

STEFANESCU, BARBU
DELAVRANCEA, BARBU--[22]RUMANIAN

STEFANSSON, MAGNUS
ARNARSON, ORN--[22]

STEFFAN, ALICE JACQUELINE
STEFFAN, JACK--[8][22]AMERICAN

STEFFANSSON, JON
GJALLANDI, PORGILS--[22]ICELANDIC

STEFFENS, ARTHUR JOSEPH
ANDREWS, JOHN--[34]MYS,HP--
AMALG "BURIED MILLIONS" '32
AMALG "MAN WITH TWO LIVES" '37
COOPER, FREEMONT--[1]
DEE, DARE--[1]

STEFFENS, ARTHUR JOSEPH [CONT]
GLYN, HARRISON--[1]
HALE, CLEMENT--[1]
HARDY, A.S.--[34]MYS--
AMALG "SECRETS OF THE RACECOURSE" '15
AMALG "CONVICT 66" '33 & 10 MORE
HARDY, ARTHUR S.--[1][8]
HARDY, ARTHUR SHERBURNE--[32]MYS--
EQMM "THE SILVER PENCIL" MAR '44
LEIGH, [CAPT.] ARTHUR--[1]
WALTERS, W.G.--[1]
WENTWORTH, CHARLES--[1]HP--

STEGEMAN, JANET ALLAIS
BRITTON, KATE--[1][31][33]

STEGER, SHELBY
LOOMIS, RAE--[1]

STEIN, AARON MARC
BAGBY, GEORGE--[3][5][18][31]MYS--
DBLDY "BLOOD WILL TELL" '50
DBLDY "BETTER DEAD" '78 & MORE
STONE, HAMPTON--[18][22][34]MYS--
18 SIMON NVLS '48-72
MH "MAN WHO HAD TOO MUCH TO LOSE" NOV '54
ED "MOURNERS AT THE BEDSIDE" '61
ME "GIRL WHO KEPT KNOCKING THEM DEAD" JUL '63

STEIN, BEN
HACKER, BURT--[1]

STEIN, FRIEDA
BIRKNER, FRIEDA--[40]GERMAN/MYS--
"DER PANTOFFEL IN DER DACHRINNE" '80

STEIN, GERTRUDE
TOKLAS, ALICE B.--[8]

STEIN, HENRY EUGENE
STINE, HANK--[1][11][23]SF--
"SEASON OF THE WITCH" '68
"THRILL CITY" '69
WHYTE, SIBLEY--[1]

STEIN, J.H.
DIXON, DON--[1]

STEIN, JESS
KAMEN, ISAI--[1][31]

STEIN, LANA
STEIN, BAKER--W/CAROL BAKER, V. BERCH LTR TO REGINALD '93, SF--
ZEBRA "UNHOLY GODDESS" '81

STEINBECK, JOHN [E]
GLASSCOCK, AMNESIA--[1][31]--
"COLLECTED POEMS OF AMNESIA GLASSCOCK" '35

STEINBERG, AARON Z.
AVRELIN, M.--[1][31]

STEINBRUNNER, PETER CHRIS
CHRISTIAN, COLIN--[11][31]
CHRISTIAN, PETER--[1][31]
STEINBRUNNER, CHRIS--[1]

STEINDLER, ROBERT A.
TREMAINE, BOB--[1][22]AUSTRIAN-AMERICAN

STEINER, BARBARA [A]
AINSLEY, ALIX--[31][34]MYS--
ZEBRA "HOUSE OF WHISPERING ASPENS" '85
ZEBRA "ECHOES OF LANDRE HOUSE" '87
COLE, ANNETTE--W/KATHLEEN PHILLIPS,[1][31][33]
D'ANDREA, KATE--W/KATHLEEN PHILLIPS, [1][31][33]
DANIEL, ANNE--[31][33]

STEINER, GEROLF
ANDERICH, JUSTUS--[1][31]
STUMPKE, HARALD--[1][2][11]
WIEDERUMP, TROTZHARD--[1]

STEINKE, ANN E.R.
CHRISTOPHER, BETH--[1][31]
REYNOLDS, ANNE--[9][21][26]ROM--
"SAILBOAT SUMMER"
"JEFF'S NEW GIRL"
REYNOLDS, ELIZABETH--[9][21][26]ROM--
"AN OCEAN OF LOVE"
"THE PERFECT BOY"
"STOLEN KISSES"
WILLIAMS, ANNE--[9][21][26]ROM--
"THE RARE GEM"

STEMPLE, JANE H. YOLEN
YOLEN, JANE--[7]SF--
'PIT DRAGONS' #1-3 '82-87
'GREAT ALTA' #1 & 2 '88-90 & OTHERS

STEMPNITSKY, ISAY
STEMP, ISAY--[1]

STENBERG, HANS-ERIK
BROSTEN, CARLO--W/JEANNE BROGREN,[29]MYS--
"MORDARE MED SILKESSTRUMPOR" '46

STENSTREEM, RUTH
BABSON, MARION--[3]
LACHMAN/EASTER LIST, MYS--
26 NOVELS '71-85

STEPHEN, ADRIAN LESLIE
STRANGE, MARK--W/KARIN STEPHEN, RACHEL STRACHEY & MARJORIE STRACHEY,[34]--
FABER "MIDNIGHT" '27

STEPHEN, JOYCE ALICE
THOMAS, J. BISSELL--[1]

STEPHEN, JUDY
TEHUDI, STEPHEN N.--[1]

STEPHEN, KARIN COSTELLOE
STRANGE, MARK--W/ADRIAN STEPHEN, RACHEL STRACHEY & MARJORIE STRACHEY,[34]--
FABER "MIDNIGHT" '27

STEPHEN, LESLIE
DON, A.--[31]

STEPHENS, BARBARA
SEYMOUR, SAMANTHA--[9]ROM
SOUTH, BARBARA--[9][21]ROM--
"A TOAST TO LOVE"

STEPHENS, CHARLES A.
STEPHENS, KIT--[1]
BAGBY, STEPHEN--[1][2]

STEPHENS, DONALD RYDER
SINDERBY, DONALD--[1][2]

STEPHENS, DOREEN
BENEDICT, RACHEL--[9]ROM
BEVERLY, JANE--[9]ROM--
"JOURNEY TO DESTINY"
STEPHENS, KAY--[9]ROM--
SIL 300 "THE FELSTEAD COLLECTION"

STEPHENS, EVE
ANTHONY, EVELYN--[8]

STEPHENS, HENRIETTA H.
BUCKMASTER, HENRIETTA--[2][3][7][29]MYS--
HRCT "THE WALKING TRIP" '72

STEPHENS, JAMES
ESSE, JAMES--[1][31]

STEPHENS, LAWRENCE STERNE
LAWRENCE, STEPHEN--[1][2]

STEPHENS, ROSEMARY
CARSWELL, LESLIE--[1][31]

STEPHENSON, ANDREW M.
AMES--[1][2]

STEPHENSON, JOHN E.D.
MACSTIOFAIN, SEAN--[1]

STEPHENSON, LYNNE REID B.
REID BANKS, LYNNE--[7]SF--
'OMRI' #1-3 '80-89
"MAURA'S ANGEL" '84
"FAIRY REBEL" '85 & OTHERS

STERLING, WARD
ZORRO--L. ROBBINS LTR '94, HP--

STERN, ALFRED
ALSTERN, FRED--[31]

STERN, DAVID
STIRLING, PETER--[2][22][34]MYS--
PHOENIX "STOP PRESS--MURDER!" '47

STERN, ELIZABETH G.
MORTON, ELEANOR--[1]
MORTON, LEAH--[1]

STERN, FREDERICK MARTIN
MARTIN, FREDERICK--[8]

STERN, JAMES
ST. JAMES, ANDREW--[1][22]MYS

STERN, JAY B[ENJAMIN]
KOHAVI, Y.--[31]
LOMOSIA, ANDREW--[1]

STERN, MARIE
MASHA--[1]

STERN, MARTHA ECCLES D.
DODD, MARTHA--[31]

STERN, PHILIP VAN DOREN
STORME, PETER--[11][22][33][34]MYS--
SIMON "THING IN THE BROOK" '37

STERN, SUSAN
SACKETT, SUSAN--[9][21][26]ROM--
"EMERALD ANGEL"
"ISLAND CAPTIVE" & 9 MORE
SAVOY, SUZANNE--[9][21][26]ROM--
"MORE THAN EVER"

STERNBACH, RICHARD MICHL.
STERNBACH, RICK--[7]SF--NON-FICT

STERNE, EMMA GELDERS
BROWN, EMILY--[1][22][31]AMERICAN
JAMES, JOSEPHINE--W/BARBARA LINDSAY, [1][22][31][33]AMERICAN

STEUSSY, MARTHA JANE
STEUSSY, MARTI--[7]SF--
BAL 'FOREST' #1 & 2 '87-8

STEVENS, AUSTIN N.
AUSTIN, STEPHEN--[1]
NASH, ENO--[1]

STEVENS, BRYNA
DONALDSON, BRYNA--[31]

STEVENS, CHARLES M.
QUONDAM--[2]

STEVENS, CLARENCE A.
STEVENS, GUS--V. BERCH-BRNDN/BC PSEUDS, BAE 22, ADULT--
BRNDN 985 "THING ABOUT SUSAN"
OLYM OPH#160 "SNOW JOB" '69
OLYM OPH#171 "LOVE ME, LOVE MY DOG" '69
OLYM OPH#184 "THE HANDYMAN" '69
OLYM OPH#202 "NON-STOP LOVER" '70
OLYM OPH#248 "GAMES IN ROOM 401" '71
OLYM TCP#2338 "SIGRID'S BEAUTIFUL FRAME" '72

STEVENS, FRANCES ISTED
STEVENS, FAE HEWSTON--[1][22]AUSTRALIAN

STEVENS, FRANCES M.R.
HALE, CHRISTOPHER--[3][22][29]MYS--
DBLDY "GHOST RIVER" '37
DBLDY "DEADLY DITTO" & MORE '35-49

STEVENS, FRANKLIN
FRANKLIN, STEVE--[31][34][40]MYS--
DBLDY "MALCONTENTS" '70
"CHICKENS IN THE AIRSHAFT" '72

STEVENS, HENRY CHARLES
GARRY, STEPHEN--[8]
MANN, JOHN--[8]

STEVENS, JANE GREENGOLD
GREENGOLD, JANE--[1][31]

STEVENS, JOHN
HATFIELD, FRANK--[1][2][7]SF--
"THE REALM OF LIGHT" '08

STEVENS, LAWRENCE STERNE
LAWRENCE--[11]

STEVENS, PAUL
STEVENS, CURTIS--W/RICHARD A. CURTIS,[34]MYS--
DELL 3307 "GRAVY TRAIN HIT" '74

STEVENS, SERITA DEBORAH
COLE, JENNIFER--[33]
MACDONNELL, MEGAN--[9][21][31][33]ROM--
"A DREAM FOREVER"
STEVENS, SHIRA--[9][26]ROM "DECEPTIVE DESIRES"

STEVENS, SHANE
RIDER, J.W.--SW MYS CON/CONFRMD BY JOHN LEGG-CR, MYS--
ARBOR "JERSEY TOMATOES" '86
ARBOR "HOT TICKET" '87

STEPHENS, SHANE--[32]MYS--
MSMM "A MATTER OF TIME" MAY '63
??UNCONFIRMED??

STEVENS-ARROYO, ANTONIO M
ARROYO, ANTONIO M. STEVEN--[31]

STEVENSON, ANDY
STEPHENS, ANN--V. BERCH-BRNDN/BC PSEUDS, BAE 22, ADULT--
BRNDN 966 "SEX OFFENSE"

STEVENSON, ANNE
ELVIN, ANNE K. STEVENSON--[29]MYS

STEVENSON, DOROTHY EMILY
STEVENSON, D.E.--[1][34]ROM/MYS--
FARRAR "CROOKED ADAM" '42
FONT "GERALD & ELIZABETH" '69
FONT "HOUSE OF THE DEER" & 9 OTHERS

STEVENSON, FERDINAN
MACOMBER, DARIA--W/P.C. ROBINSON,[3]MYS--
HALE "RETURN TO OCTAVIA" '67
HALE "A CLEARING IN THE FOG" '70

STEVENSON, FLORENCE
COLT, ZANDRA--[9][21][26]ROM--
"CACTUS ROSE"
"SPLENDID SAVAGE"
CURZON, LUCIA--[1][9][21][26]ROM--
"QUEEN OF HEARTS"
"AN ADVERSE ALLIANCE" & MORE
FAIRE, ZABRINA--[9][11][21][26]ROM--
"LADY BLUE"
"PRETTY KITTY" & 8 MORE
FITZGERALD, ELLEN--[9][21][26]ROM--
"LORD CALIBAN"
"PLAYER KNIGHT" & 15 MORE
FRAZIER, PAMELA--[9][21][26]ROM--
"WILLFUL WIDOW"
"DARING DECEPTION" & 4 MORE

STEVENSON, JAMES PATRICK
RADYR, TOMOS--[8]

STEVENSON, JOHN
CARTER, NICK--[3][7]MYS/SF,HP--
CHART "DAY OF THE DINGO" '80
CHART "GOLDEN BULL" '81
CHART "Q-MAN" '81
DENNING, MARK--[3][29]MYS--
PYR "SHADES OF GRAY" '76
PYR "DIE FAST, DIE HAPPY" '76
JOVE "BEYOND THE PRIZE" '78
JACKSON, STEPHEN--[1][2]
ROSSI, BRUNO--[3]MYS,HP--
LEIS "HIT MAN" '74
LEIS "LAS VEGAS VENGEANCE" '75
VAN HELLER, MARCUS--[14]ADULT,HP--
OLYM OPHIR #3 "ADAM & EVE" 61
?? UNCONFIRMED ??
OLYM OPH#246 "LOINS OF AMON" '71
OLYM OPH#254 "CRUEL LIPS" '71

STEVENSON, PHILIP EDWARD
LAWRENCE, LARS--[3]MYS--
INTERNATIONAL "THE HOAX" '61

STEVENSON, ROBERT LOUIS
NORTH, CAPTAIN GEORGE--[33]

STEVENSON, ROBIN
MINTON, T.M.--W/THOMAS M. BADE,[7]SF--
"SWITCHBACK" '88
ST. THOMAS, ROBIN--W/TOM BADE,[9][21][26]ROM--
"APPEARANCES"
"SENSATION" & 5 MORE

STEVENSON, WILLIAM
CHEN HWEI--[1][22][31]ENGLISH

STEWARD, DONALD WILLIAM
ANONYMOUS--[34]MYS--
10 AMALGAMATED NOVELS '27-40
STEELE, DERWENT--[34]MYS--
5 MODERN NOVELS ca'35
STUART, DONALD--[34]MYS--
38 AMALGAMATED NOVELS '30-40
VANE, NIGEL--[34]MYS--6 MODERN NOVELS ca'35
VERNER, GERALD--[34]MYS-- 82 NOVELS 33-67

STEWARD, SAMUEL M[ORRIS]
ANDROS, PHIL--[1][31]
CAVE, THOMAS--[1][31]
KRAMER, TED--[1][31]
MCANDREWS, JOHN--[1]
SPARROW, PHILIP--[1]
STAMES, WARD--[1]
YOUNG, PHILIP--[1]

STEWART, AGNES CHARLOTTE
STEWART, A.C.--[1]

STEWART, ALFRED WALTER
CONNINGTON, J.J.--[2][5][18][23][29][32]
[34]MYS/SF--
GOLZ "BOAT HOUSE RIDDLE" '31
& MORE '26-47
EW "THE THINKING MACHINE" JUL '66
CONNINGTON, JOHN JERVIS--[22]MYS

STEWART, DOROTHY MARY
ELGIN, MARY--[3][17]MYS/ROM--
HODDER "VISABILITY NIL" '64
HODDER "RETURN TO GLENSHAEL" '65 & MORE

STEWART, HAROLD
MALLEY, ERN--W/JAMES PHILLIP MCAULEY,[1]

STEWART, HARRIS BATES JR.
BENTHIC, ARCH E.--[31]--
COMPASS "THE ID OF SQUID" '70

STEWART, JAMES L.
GRANGER, STEWART--[8]

STEWART, JOHN INNES M.
INNES, MICHAEL--[2][5][11][18][22][29][32]MYS-
NOVELS '37-80 & DIGEST SS
STEWART, J.I.M.--[18][34]MYS--
GOLZ "AN OPEN PRISON" '84

STEWART, JOHN W.
COLE, JACK--[1][31][33]

STEWART, KENNETH
STEWART, COCHRANE--[1]

STEWART, KENNETH LIVINGST
LIVINGSTON, KENNETH--[3][22][32]MYS--
RICH "CLOZE PAPERS" '36
METHUEN "DODD CASES" '37
EQMM "THE MISSING MOTIVE" JAN '49

STEWART, LINDA
CARTER, NICK--[3]MYS,HP--
AWARD "PEKING DOSSIER" '74
AWARD "JERUSALEM FILE" '75
STEWART, KERRY--[3][7][40]MYS--
BERK "RUBY" '78
JOVE "THE CONCORDE" '79
STEWART, SAM--[1][3]MYS--
DELL "THE BIG RIP-OFF" '76
DELL "FUN WITH DICK & JANE" '77

STEWART, NEIL
LOMBARD, NAP--W/PAMELA JOHNSON,[22][34]MYS--
CASSELL "TIDY DEATH" '40
SIMON "GRINNING PIG" '43

STEWART, TERRY
LAFOREST, SERGE--[34]MYS--
INTNL "THE INTRUDER" '69

STEWART, WALTER
ELGIN, MARY--[21][26]ROM "A MAN FROM THE MIST"
"HIGHLAND MASQUERADE"
"WOOD & THE TREES"

STEWART, WILLIAM THOMAS
STEWART, W.T.--[36]AUSTRALIAN/MYS--
NC "GAFF LEE, DETECTIVE" '40
CURRAWONG "YELLOW SPIES" '42

STICKLAND, LOUISE ANNIE B
SOMERS, J.L.--[8]

STICKLAND, M.E.
STAND, MARGUERITE--[8]

STICKLEE, E.
STEVENS, ANDY--W/MARY H. DANBY,[8][31]--
"WORLD OF STARS" '80

STIDWORTHY, JOHN
HOWARD, JOHN--[33]

STIFF, DOROTHY AILEEN
KENDAL, JUNE--[1]

STILES, GEORGE
DENBOW, WILLIAM--V. BERCH LTR TO HUBIN '94,
MYS--
BELM "CHANDLER" '77

STILSON, CHARLES BILLINGS
WILSON, CHARLES--[29]MYS

STIMSON, FREDERIC JESUP
J.S. OF DALE--[2][22][23]AMERICAN

STINE, GEORGE HARRY
CORREY, LEE--[2][7][23][31][34]SF--
"AND A STAR TO STEER HER BY" '53
BAL "STARDRIVER" '80
WHYTE, SIBLEY--[2]

STINE, HENRY EUGENE
JORGENSON, ALLEN--[31]
STINE, HANK--[3][11][23]MYS/SF--
ACE 'THE PRISONER': "A DAY IN THE LIFE
OF" '70
"SEASON OF THE WITCH" '68
"THRILL CITY" '69
WHYTE, SIBLEY--[1]

STINE, JEAN MARIE-- LOCUS JAN '94--
FUTURE WORK

STINE, ROBERT L.
AFFABEE, ERIC--[7]SF--
'WIZARDS, WARRIORS & YOU' #2 & 16
'FIND YOUR FATE-G.I. JOE' #1 & 5
BLUE, ZACHARY--[31]
STINE, JOVIAL BOB--[1][7][33]
STINE, R.L.--[31]

STINE, WHITNEY WARD
MCLEISH, GAREN--[1]
PEAL[E], CONSTANCE F.--[9][21][26]ROM--
"GIVE US FOREVER"
WARD, JONATHAN--[1]

STIRLING, ANNA MARIA D.W.
PICKERING, PERCIVAL--[1][22]ENGLISH
STIRLING, A.M.W.--[1]

STIRLING, JESSICA
CROSBY, CAROLINE--[26]ROM--
"THE HALDANES"

STIRLING, STEPHEN MICHAEL
STIRLING, S.M.--[23]FRENCH-CANADIAN/SF--
'FIFTH MILLENIUM FASTASY' SEQ

STITT, JAMES M.
BRUNSWICK, JAMES--[1]

STITZ-ULRICI, ROLF
CORBETT, REX--[40][39]GERMAN/MYS--
"THE DIAMOND OF SOHO" '57
KORDA, HANS--[39]GERMAN/SF
RODOS, HANS--[39]GERMAN/JUV
ULRICI, ROLF--[39][40]GERMAN/MYS--
"DIE DIAMANTEN VON SOHO" '79 & OTHERS

STIVENDER, ED
JALAN, EDI LEE--[31]

STIVENS, DALLAS GEORGE
STIVENS, DAL--[7][32]MYS/SF--
SA "A PUSHOVER" SEPT '56
SA "MR. HEED DIDN'T GAMBLE" FEB '57
MSMM "MAGICIAN'S WALK" AUG '57
ANGUS "WIDE ARCH" '58
ANGUS "SELECTED STRS" '69
WILD & WOOLLEY "UNICORN & OTHER TALES" '76

STIVERS, DICK
PENDLETON, DON--[3]MYS,HP--
GE "STONEY MAN DOCTRINE" '84

STIVERS, MARK
DISROBESON, KIN I.--[1][2]

STOBBS, J. LOUIS NEWCOMBE
NEWCOMBE, LOUIS--[1]

STOBERSKI, ZYGMUNT JULIAN
BORONIECKI, MIROSLAV--[1]
STEBELSKI, JULIAN--[1]

STOBO, EDWARD JOHN
ALETHEIA--[1]

STOCKENBERG, ANTOINETTE
HALE, ANTOINETTE--[9][21][26]ROM--
"TROUBLE IN PARADISE"
"ISLAND OF DESIRE"
HARDY, ANTOINETTE--[9][21][26]ROM--
"FIT TO BE LOVED"
HOOS, SUZANNE--[26]ROM--
"BENEATH A RESTLESS SEA"
"MISTRESS OF THE MUSE" & 2 MORE

STOCKFORD, LELA E.
HAMILTON-SYOCKFORD, JOAN--[1]

STOCKING, KATHLEEN
FLAMBEAU, BLOSSOM--[31]

STOCKLEY, CYNTHIA
WEBB, LILIAN JULIAN--[22]RHODESIAN

STOCKTON, ARTIE
KERI, AMANDA--W/LIN HARRIS, HAWK/
STOCKTON/HARRIS INTRVW '93--
WESTERN HIST/MYS/ROMANCE

STOCKTON, FRANCIS R.
FORT, PAUL--[1][33]
LEWEES, JOHN--[1][33]
MOFFIT, JACK--[5][32]MYS--
EQMM "THE NECKLACE" FEB '46
EQMM "LADY & THE TIGER" SEPT '48
STOCKTON, F.R.--[1]
STOCKTON, FRANK R.--[7][32]MYS/SF--
EQMM "LADY OR THE TIGER?" MAR '53
EQMM "DISCOURAGER OF HESITANCY" MAR '53
SIGN "FAIRY TALES OF FRANK STOCKTON" '90

STOCKWELL, GRACE
STOCKWELL, GAIL--[3]MYS--
MacM "DEATH BY INVITATION" '37
MacM "ENBARASSED MURDERER" '38 & MORE

STODDARD, CHARLES WARREN
PEPPERPOD, PIP--[22]AMERICAN
PEPPERWOOD, PIP--[8]

STODDARD, JANE T.
LORNA--[1]

STODDARD, WILLIAM OSBORN
FORREST, COLONEL CHRIS--[8]

STOE, M.
BAZAGONOV, M.S.--[8]

STOFFER, EDITH G.
ROSS, DEBORAH--[8]

STOIL, MICHAEL JON
AUGUSTINE, ERICH--[31]

STOKELY, WILMA D.
DYKEMAN, WILMA--[1]

STOKER, ABRAHAM
ALLEN, DEREK--W/DEREK FARMER,[7]SF/HOR--
"BLOODS FROM THE MUMMY'S TOMB" '88
STOKER, BRAM--[5][7][21][29][33]HOR--
"DRACULA" 1897

STOKER, ALAN
EVANS, ALAN--[3][31][40]MYS--
CASSELL "BANNON" '68
HALE "BIG DEAL" '71 & MORE '66-71

STOKES, COLEMAN
ADAMS, NICHOLAS--[7]SF/HOR,HP--
HARPER 'HORROR HIGH' #1-5
COLEMAN, CLAY--[7]SF/HOR,HP--
HARPER 'ESCAPE FROM LOST ISLAND' #1-6

STOKES, FRANCIS W.
EVERTON, FRANCIS--[1][3][22]MYS--
COLLINS "MURDER AT PLENDERS" '30
COLLINS "INSOLUBLE" '34 & MORE '27-36

STOKES, GEOFFREY
ESTRAGON, VLADIMIR--[31]--
VIKING "WAITING FOR DESSERT" '82

STOKES, MANNING LEE
CARTER, NICK--[3][7]MYS,HP--
AWARD "EYES OF THE TIGER" '65
AWARD "ISTANBUL" '65
AWARD "WEBB OF SPIES" '66
AWARD "SPY CASTLE" '66
AWARD "DRAGON FLAME" '66
AWARD "KOREAN TIGER" '67
AWARD "DEVIL'S COCKPIT" '67
AWARD "ASSIGNMENT:ISRAEL" '67
AWARD "DOUBLE IDENTITY" '67
AWARD "FILTHY FIVE" '67
AWARD "MISSION TO VENICE" '67
AWARD "RED GUARD" '67
AWARD "GOLDEN SERPENT" '67
AWARD "TEMPLE OF FEAR" '68
AWARD "MACAO" '68
AWARD "RED RAYS" '69
AWARD "COBRA KILL" '69
AWARD "BLACK DEATH" '70
EDWARDS, PAUL--[3]MYS,HP--
PYR "BRAIN SCAVENGERS" '73
PYR "GREEN GODDESS" '75
PYR "SILVERSKULL" '75
PYR "NEEDLES OF DEATH" '76
PYR "VALLEY OF VULTURES" '76
LORD, JEFFREY--W. MURRAY-'BLADE' SERIES,
PP 1,[17]SF,HP-- ZIFF-DAVIS #1-8
LUDWELL, BERNICE--[1][22][29]MYS--
MANNING, LEE--[1]ADULT--
POPLB 341 "SEASON FOR PASSION" '51
MARLOWE, MARCH--[3]MYS--
ARCADIA "F.B.I. GIRL" '59
STANTON, KEN--[3]MYS,HP--
MANOR 'AQUANAUTS' #10 & 11 '74
STOKES, MANNING--[1]ADULT--
BEAC B-276 "TRIANGLE OF SIN" '59
BEAC B-409F "GIRL ON A COUCH" '61
WELLES, KERMIT--V. BERCH LTR AUG '93--
VENUS 128 "SHE HAD WHAT IT TAKES" '51
CAM 307 "SIN PREFERRED" '51
VENUS 144 "THE INNOCENT WANTON" '52
VENUS 178 "WILD SISTER" '52
ORIGN 704 "GAMBLER'S GIRL" '52
ORIGN 710 "SEE NO EVIL" '52
CAMEO 310 "PLEASURE BOUND" '52
CARN 925 "RECKLESS" '53
ACE D-332 "BLOOD ON BOOT HILL" '58
BDSD 812 "REFORMATORY WOMEN" '59
BDSD 818 "WILD WANTON" '59
PYR G563 "BLOOD ON BOOT HILL" '60
WESTLEY, KIRK--V. BERCH LTR AUG '93--
CAMEO 338 "SHANTY BOAT GIRL" '52
RPRTS CAMEO 307
CARN 949 "MAN-CHASER" '54
RPRT CAM 310

STOKES, RALPH
CAPELLI, ACE--PP 29, P42, MYS,HP

STOKESBERRY, BOB
CARTER, NICK--[3]MYS,HP--
CHART "TROPICAL DEATHPACK" '79

STOKOE, E[DWARD] G[EORGE]
CLOS, CHARLES--[28]WAR--
BW "CALL IT EXPERIENCE" '59
DANER, PAUL--[28]WEST--
BW "END OF THE TRAIL" '54
DEXTER, ROSS--[28]WEST--
BW "CARSON'S KILLER" '55
PETERS, BRIAN--[28]WEST--
BW "STARBUCK" '57
STARK, JOHN--[28]WAR--
BW "MARINE COMMANDO" '59

STOLK, ANTONIE
AVARIUS--[31]
BRUBAKER, CAROL--[31]

STOLL, DENNIS G.
CRAIG, DENYS--[8][22][31]ENGLISH

STOLLER, MIKE
GLICK, ELMO--W/JERRY LEIBER,[1]

STOLPER, ALICE
PEPPLER, ALICE STOLPER--[1]

STONE, ANDREW
STONE, ANDY--[7]SF--
DBLDY "SONG OF THE KINGDOM" '79

STONE, BARBARA HASKINS
HASKINS, BARBARA--[31]

STONE, CARL
ARLEN, SCOTT--[14]ADULT--
OLYM TC#490 "BAD NEWS BILLY BLACK" '70
OLYM OPH#195 "GREEDY POLLY" '70
OLYM OPS#19 "EVERYBODY LOVES A ENUCH" '71
OLYM OPS#37 "PANTING FOR OSCAR" '71

STONE, ELISA
STANCLIFFE, ELAINE--[9]ROM

STONE, ELNA
DANIEL, ELNA WORRELL--[1][31]

STONE, ENA MARGARET
O'RANDA, JACK--[1]
SANDOWN, MARGARET--[1]

STONE, EUGENIA
STONE, GENE--[1][33]

STONE, GAYLE
PENDLETON, DON--W/DENNIS LYNDS,[34]MYS,HP--
GE "BLOOD FEVER" '89
GE "MOVING TARGET" '89

STONE, GRACE ZARING
VANCE, ETHEL--[3][29]MYS--
LITTLE "ESCAPE" '39
LITTLE "REPRISAL" '42
HARPER "SECRET THREAD" '48

STONE, IRVING
TANNENBAUM, IRVING--[6]

STONE, KAREN
YOUNG, KAREN--[9][21][26]ROM--
"DEBT OF LOVE"
"BEYOND SUMMER" & 11 MORE

STONE, KATE MARGARET
PATRIGE, SYDNEY--[13]AUSTRALIAN

STONE, PATTY [PATTI]
PATRICK, LEAL--[1][22]AMERICAN

STONE, RODNEY
HUNTER, MATTHEW--[31]

STONEBRAKER, FLORENCE
BRANCH, FLORENZ--[34]ADULT--
PHOENIX "BEDROOM AGENT" '40
KNICK NO#6 "UNWILLING VIRGIN" '46
KNICK NO#11 "PICK-UP GIRL" '46
KNICK NO#16 "UNFAITHFUL" '46
KNICK NO#28 "PLEASURE AFTER HOURS" '46
PRZ66 "FLESHPOTS" '47
CENT 93 "FLESHPOTS" '47
CENT 114 "PASSION'S PROGRAM" 48
CENT 123 "PAST FOLLY" '50
DB 12 "BORROWED HUSBAND" '50
UNI 7 "MALE FOR SALE" '51
UNI 17 "SCANDOLOUS AFFAIR" '51
GRIF "LOVE SIREN" nd
IN 24 "WHIPPING ROOM" '52
IN 39 "DR. BRETON'S WIFE" '53
BEAC B-322 "INTIMATE PHYSICIAN" '60
SHEPARD, FERN--[34]--
ARCADIA "METER MAID" '59
AV F186 "NIGHT NURSE" '63
LAN 73-622 "PSYCHIATRIC NURSE" '67
STUART, FLORENCE--[8]--
ACE D557 "HOPE WEARS WHITE" '62
AV F166 "HAPPINESS HILL" '63
LAN 70-080 "THE NEW NURSE" '65

STONEHAM, C. THURLEY
THURLEY, NORGROVE--[3][8][22][29]MYS--
PAUL "DEVIL'S STEPS" '47
PAUL "BAMBOO ELEPHANT" '56 & MORE '47-59

STONEHOUSE, JOHN [T]
LUND, JAMES--[3]MYS--
CALDER "THE ULTIMATE" '76

STONEHOUSE, PATRICIA ETHL
RUSSELL, LINDSAY--[8][13]AUSTRALIAN

STONIER, GEORGE
FANFARLO--[1]
GURNARD, JOSEPH--[1]
WHITEBAIT, WILLIAM--[8]

STONOR, OLIVER
BISHOP, E. MORCHARD--[1][22][31]ENGLISH
BISHOP, EVELYN MORCHARD--[1][22]ENGLISH
BISHOP, MORCHARD--W/ARTHUR MACHEN,[7]--
"DREAMS & VISIONS:..IMAGINATION OF ARTHUR MACHEN.." '87
BISHOP, MORCHARD--[2][7][22][31]ENGLISH

STOPES, MARIE [C] CARM.
FAY, ERICA--[31]

STOPPELMAN, FRANS
STOPPELMAN, FRANCIS--[1]

STOREY, MARGARET
STACEY, SUSANNAH--W/JILL STAYNES, LACHMAN-EASTER LST '93,[34]MYS--

STOREY, VICTORIA CAROLYN
MARTIN, VICKEY--[1][21]ROM--
"OBEY THE MOON"
"THE BOY NEXT DOOR"

STORM, HYEMEYOHSTS
GOLDEN SILVER--[31]

STORMS, ANDRE
CASTELOT, ANDRE--[1]

STORR, CATHERINE [COLE]
ADLER, IRENE--[1][22][31]ENGLISH--
CRESSET "FREUD FOR JUNG" '63
LOURIE, HELEN--[1][22][31][33]ENGLISH--
"A QUESTION OF ABORTION" '62

STORY, JACK TREVOR
HARDING, BRETT--[34]MYS/WEST--
6 HAMILTON NOVELS '54-5
4 MILESTONE NOVELS 53-4
REID, DESMOND--[23]SF/MYS,HP--
'SEXTON BLAKE' SERIES - TITLES UNKNOWN
RIOTI, REX--[34]MYS--
MILSTONE "SCARLET WIDOW" '53
WILLIAMS, RICHARD--W/W.A. HOWARD BAKER, [34]MYS,HP--
AMALG "LARGE TYPE KILLER" '60

STORY, ROSAMOND MARY
JESKINS, RICHARD--[1]
LEE, CHARLES H.--[1]
LINDSAY, JOSEPHINE--[1][34]MYS--
MYFLWR "A HOUSE IS JUST A HOUSE" '67
REID, DESMOND--W/G.P. MANN,[1][34]MYS,HP--
AMALG "WITCH-HUNT!" '60
ROSS, KATHLEEN--[34]MYS--
MYFLWR "THE WOUNDED HEART" '67
TRACY, CATHERINE--[1]
WOODS, ROSS--[1]

STOTT, DOROTHY M.
STOTT, DOT--[33]

STOTT, MARY
JAQUES--[8]

STOTTER, MICHAEL JAMES
STOTTER, MIKE--[28]WEST--
HALE "McKINNEY'S REVENGE" '90
HALE "TOMBSTONE SHOWDOWN" '91

STOUTENBURG, ADRIEN [P]
ARDEN, BARBIE--W/BARBARA RITCHIE, [22][31][33]AMERICAN
KENDALL, LACE--[22][31][33]AMERICAN
MINIER, NELSON--W/LAURA NELSON BAKER, [1][22][33]AMERICAN

STOWE, D.A.
GORDON--BAPC #11--
COVER ARTIST FOR AUTHENIC, PAN & PANTHER

STOWE, HARRIET E. BEECHER
CROWFIELD, CHRISTOPHER--[31][33]

STOWE, MRS. H.M.
ELEVE--[2][7]SF--
"THE ELIXIR OF LIFE; OR ROBERT'S PILGRIMAGE" 1890

STOWERS, WALTER G.
STOWERS, SANDRA--[1]

STRACH, JOSEPH GEORGE
REED, WALLACE--V. BERCH LTR TO HUBIN '94, MYS--
PHOENIX "TIME TO KILL" '40
PHOENIX "MARKED FOR MURDER" '41
"NO SIGN OF MURDER" '50 & MORE '40-57

STRACHAN, GLADYS ELIZAB.
BILL--[8]

STRACHAN, J. GEORGE
GEORGE, JAY--[1][31]

STRACHAN, MARGARET P.
MOORE, CAROLINE--W/MOLLY [L] CONE, [1][22][33]AMERICAN-- DIAL "BATCH OF TROUBLE" '63

STRACHEY, JOHN ST. LOE
S.L.S.--[2]

STRACHEY, MARJORIE COLV.
STRANGE, MARK--W/RACHEL STRACHEY, ADRIAN & KARIN STEPHEN,[34]MYS-- FABER "MIDNIGHT" '27

STRACHEY, RACHEL COSTELL.
STRANGE, MARK--W/MARJORIE STRACHEY, ADRIAN & KARIN STEPHEN,[34]MYS-- FABER "MIDNIGHT" '27

STRAGE, MARK
HAZLITT, JOSEPH--[1][31]
QUICK, PHILIP--[1]

STRAITON, EDWARD CORNOCK
STRAITON, EDDIE--[31]--VETERNARIAN BOOKS
VET, T.V.--[8]

STRAKER, J[OHN] F[OSTER]
ROSSE, IAN--[8][18]MYS-- NEL "THE DROOP" '72

STRANGE, DOROTHY
UPFIELD, ARTHUR C.--W/J.L.PRICE,[18]MYS-- COMPLETED "LAKE FROME MONSTER" AFTER 'UPFIELD'S' DEATH

STRANGE, THOMAS OLIVER
CHRISTIAN, FREDERICK H.--L. ROBBINS LTR '94
RAND, MATT--L. ROBBINS LTR MAR '94--
BELM 91-267 "GUN-HELL AT BIG BEND" '62
BELM 90-273 "IT HAPPENED IN A TOWN NAMED LAWLESS" '62
BELM 90-279 "SEVEN SECONDS TO SUNDOWN" '63
BELM 90-284 "SHOOT-OUT AT SPLIT ROCK" '63
BELM 90-291 "SHERIFF OF HANGMAN'S GULCH" '64
STRANGE, OLIVER--[28]WEST-- NEWNES 'SUDDEN' SERIES - 12 NOVELS '30-50

STRANGELAND, KATHARINA M.
MICHAELIS, KARINA--[38]DANISH

STRANKS, CHARLES JAMES
HILLYER, RICHARD--[1]

STRASBERG, DAOMA WINSTON
WINSLOW, DORIAN--[1][2][3][7]MYS/SF-- "THE SORÇERORS" '73
WINSTON, DAOMA--[7][32]MYS/SF--
SA "CIRCLES IN THE SKY" SEPT '66
PAPLB "VAMPIRE CURSE" '71
LAN "SEMINAR IN EVIL" '72

STRASSEL, HUBERT
CARDWELL, RAY--W/HANS FELLER,[39]GERMAN/SF
WALKER, HUGH--[2][7]SF-- DAW 'MAGIRA' #1-3 '78-9

STRASSER, TODD
RHUE, MORTON--[1]
SILVANUS, P.W.--[1]

STRASSMAN, TONI
GILMAN, LASALLE--[2]

STRATEMEYER, EDWARD
ABBOTT, [MANAGER] HENRY--[1][22][33]
ADAMS, HARRISON--[1][22]HP--STSY
ALGER, HORATIO JR.--[5]GHOSTED,HP--S&SM
ALLEN, CAPT. QUINCY--C. BILLMAN-SECRET OF STRATEMEYER SYND--'OUTDOOR CHUMS'
APPLETON, VICTOR--[1][2][7]HP-- STSY 'DON STURDY': "IN THE PORT OF LOST SHIPS"
APPLETON, VICTOR II--[11][22][23]HP-- STSY 'TOM SWIFT'
BARNUM, RICHARD--[1][22]HP--STSY
BARNUM, THEODORE--[31]
BARTLETT, PHILIP A.--[1][22]HP-- STSY
BARTON, MAY HOLLIS--[1][2][22]HP-- STSY 'BOOKS FOR GIRLS'
BEACH, CHARLES AMORY--[1][22]HP-- STSY
BELL, EMERSON--[31]
BONEHILL, [CAPT.] RALPH--[1][11]HP-- STSY 'BOY HUNTERS'
BOWIE, JIM--[1][22][31]HP--S&SM
CALKINS, FRANKLIN--[1][22][33]
CARR, ANNIE ROE--C. BILLMAN-SECRET OF STRATEMEYER SYND 'NAN SHERWOOD'
CARSON, [CAPT.] JAMES--[1][22][33]HP-- STSY
CARTER, NICHOLAS--[3]MYS,HP--STSY
CHADWICK, LESTER--[1][22]HP-- STSY 'BASEBALL JOE'
CHAPMAN, ALLEN--[1][22]HP--
STSY 'DAREWELL CHUM' SERIES
STSY 'BOYS OF BUSINESS'
STSY 'RADIO BOYS'
STSY 'RAILROAD'
CHARLES, LOUIS--[1][22][31][33]
COOPER, JAMES A.--[1][22][33]
COOPER, JOHN R.--[1][22]HP-- STSY 'MEL MARTIN BASEBALL' SERIES
DALY, JIM--[1][22][31][33]
DAVENPORT, SPENCER--[1][22][33]
DAWSON, ELMER A.--[1][22][24]HP--
STSY 'RAYSON FOOTBALL' STORIES
STSY 'BUCK & LARRY' STORIES
DIXON, FRANKLIN W.--[1][2][22]HP--
STSY 'HARDY BOY' SERIES
STSY 'TED SCOTT FLYING STORIES' SERIES
DUNCAN, JULIA K.--[1][22]HP-- STSY 'DORIS FORCE' SERIES
EDISON, THEODORE--[1][31]
EDWARDS, JULIE[A]--[1][22][31]
EMERSON, ALICE B.--[1][22]HP--
STSY 'RUTH FIELDING'
STSY 'BETTY GORDON'
FERRIS, JAMES CODY--[1][2][22]HP-- STSY 'X BAR X BOYS'
FORBES, GRAHAM B.--[1][22]HP--
STSY 'BOYS OF COLUMBIA HIGH'
STSY 'FRANK ALLEN'
FORD, ALBERT LEE--[1][22][31][33]
GORDON, FREDERICK--[1][22]HP--
STSY 'UP & DOING'
STSY 'FAIRVIEW BOYS'
HAMILTON, RALPH--[1][31]
HAMILTON, ROBERT W.--[1][22]
HARDY, ALICE DALE--[1][22]HP--
STSY 'FLYAWAYS'
STSY 'RIDDLE CLUB'
HARKAWAY, HAL--[1][22][31][33]
HAWLEY, MABEL C.--[1][22]HP-- STSY 'FOUR LITTLE BLOSSOMS'
HENDERLEY, BROOKS--[1][22]HP-- STSY 'YMCA BOYS'
HICKS, HARVEY--[1][22][31][33]
HILL, GRACE BROOKS--[1][22]HP-- STSY 'CORNER HOUSE GIRLS'
HOPE, LAURA LEE--[1][2][22]HP-- STSY 'BOBBSEY TWINS'

STRATEMEYER, EDWARD [CONT]
HOPE, LAURA LEE [CONT]
STSY 'OUTDOOR GIRLS'
STSY 'BLYTHE GIRLS'
STSY 'BUNNY BROWN'
STSY 'MAKE BELIEVE STORIES'
STSY 'SIX LITTLE BUNKERS'
HUNT, FRANCIS--[1][22][33]HP--
STSY 'MARY & JERRY'
STSY 'MYSTERY STORIES'
JAMES, CAPTAIN LEW--[31]
JUDD, FRANCES K.--[1][22]HP--
STSY 'KAY TRACEY'
KEENE, CAROLYN--[1][5][22]HP--
STSY 'NANCY DREW'
STSY 'DANA GIRLS'
LANCER, JACK--C. BILLMAN-SECRET OF STRATEMEYER SYND,HP--
STSY 'CHRIS T. COOL'
LAWSON, W.B.--[1]?
LOCKE, CLINTON W.--[1][22]HP--
STSY 'PERRY PIERCE'
LONG, HELEN BEECHER--[1][22]HP--
STSY 'DO SOMETHING' SERIES
STSY 'MYS' SERIES
MACKENZIE, [DR.] WILLARD--[1][2][22][33]
MARLOWE, AMY BELL--[1][2][22]HP--
STSY 'BOOK FOR GIRLS'
MARTIN, EUGENE--[1][22]HP--STSY
MASON, HARRY--[22]HP--STSY
MOORE, FENWORTH--[1][22][33]HP--
STSY 'JERRY FORD WONDER'
MORRISON, GERT W.--[1][33]HP--
STSY 'GIRLS OF CENRAL HIGH'
OPTIC, OLIVER--W/WILLIAM TAYLOR ADAMS,[1][33]
PENROSE, MARGARET--[1][22][33]HP--
STSY 'DOROTHY DALE'
STSY 'CAMPFIRE'
STSY 'MOTOR GIRLS'
STSY 'RADIO GIRLS'
RIDLEY, NAT JR.--[1][22][33]HP--
STSY 'NAT RIDLEY DETECTIVE STORIES'
ROCKWOOD, ROY--[1][2][11][22]HP--
STSY 'BOMBA'
STSY 'DEEP SEA'
STSY 'DAVE DASHAWAY'
ROE, HARRY MASON--[1][22]HP--STSY
SCOTT, DAN--[1][22][33]HP--
STSY 'BRETT KING'
SHELDON, ANN--[1][22]HP--
STSY 'LINDA CRAIG'
SPERRY, RAYMOND JR.--[1][22]HP--
STSY 'WHITE RIBBON BOYS'
'LARRY DEXTER'
ST. MYER, NED--[1][2][22][33]
STEELE, CHESTER K.--[1][3][22][33]MYS--
6 NOVELS '11-28
STONE, ALAN--[22]HP--
STSY 'TOLLIVER' SERIES
STONE, RAYMOND--[1][22][33]HP--
STSY 'TOMMY TIPSTER' SERIES
STONE, RICHARD A.--[22]HP--STSY
STRAYER, E. WARD--[1][2][22][33]
THORNDYKE, HELEN LOUISE--[1][22]HP--
STSY 'HONEY BUNCH'
WARNER, FRANK A.--[1][22]HP--
STSY 'BOBBY BLAKE & BOB CHASE'
WEBSTER, FRANK V.--C. BILLMAN-SECRET OF STRATEMEYER SYND,[1][22]--
STSY 'WEBSTER' SERIES
WEST, JERRY--[1][22][33]HP--STSY
WHEELER, JANET D.--[1][22]HP--
STSY 'BILLIE BRADLEY'
WHITE, RAMY ALLISON--[1][22]HP--
STSY 'SONNY BOY' SERIES FOR BOYS

STRATEMEYER, EDWARD [CONT]
WINFIELD, ALLEN--[1]?
WINFIELD, ARTHUR M.--[1][2][22][33]HP--
STSY 'ROVER BOYS'
STSY 'PUTNAM HALL'
WINFIELD, EDNA--[1][22][33]
WOODS, NAT--[1][22][33]HP--S&SM
YOUNG, CLARENCE--[1][2][22]HP--
STSY 'MOTOR BOYS'
STSY 'JACK RANGER'
STSY 'RACER BOYS'

STRATTON, GENEVA GRACE
PORTER, GENE STRATTON--[1]
STRATTON-PORTER, GENE--[1]

STRATTON, JOHN THEODORE
SPAIN, TERRY--[3]MYS--
POPLB 500 "TIME TO KILL" '53

STRATTON, JOHN THEODORE
STRATTON, TED--[34]MYS--
GM 443 "WILD BREED" '54
PUTNAM "TOURIST TRAP" '75

STRATTON, MONICA DICKENS
DICKENS, MONICA--[7][32]--
EQMM "TO REACH THE SEA" SEPT '65
COLLINS "CRY OF A SEAGULL" '86
'THE MESSENGER' SERIES #1-3 '85-6

STRATTON, REBECCA
GILLEN, LUCY--[1][9][21][31]ROM--
"STORM EAGLE"
"PRETTY WITCH" & 35 MORE

STRATTON-PORTER, GENE
PORTER, GENE--[22]AMERICAN/NOVELS, NATURE

STRAUB, MARGARET ROGERS
QUICK, DOROTHY--[2][11]

STRAUBING, HAROLD [ELK]
BENNET, RUTH--[31]

STRAUCH, KATINA PARTHEMS
ALEXIS, KATINA--[3][7][31]MYS/HOR--
PINN "YOUNG BLOOD" '82

STRAUS, DENNIS
ASCHER, STRAUS--W/SHEILA ASCHER,[1][7][31]
TREACLE PRESS "MENACED ASSASSIN" '82
TOP STORIES "RED MOOD, RED LAKE" '84

STRAUS, RALPH
FORBES, ROBERT--[32][34]MYS--
PD "THE DEVIL KNIFE" DEC '36
FORBES, ROBERT ERSTONE--[1][3]MYS--
CHAPMAN "THE TRANSACTIONS OF OLIVER PRINCE" '24

STRAUSS, M. LUCILLE J.
JACKSON, LUCILLE--[31]

STRAUSSLER, TOM
BOOT, WILLIAM--[8][31]--
"INTRODUCTION 2" - SHORT STORIES
"SCENE" - REVIEWER
STOPPARD, TOM--[3]MYS--
FABER "THE REAL INSPECTOR HOUND" '68

STRAYER, SARA BARKER
WILSON, MARGERY--[31]

STREATFIELD, [MARY] NOEL
SCARLETT, SUSAN--[1][8][33]

STREET, ARTHUR GEORGE
BRIAN, JAMES--[1]
STREET, A.G.--[1]

STREET, CECIL JOHN C.
BURTON, MILES--[3][5][11][18][22][29]MYS--
COLLINS "A CRIME IN TIME" '55
"FOUND DROWNED" '56
F.O.O.--[18][22][29]MYS--
"WITH GUNS" '16
"WORLDLY HOPE" '17 & MORE
I.O.--[18]--
PHILIP ALLAN "THE ADMINISTRATION OF IRELAND" '21
RHODE, JOHN--[2][3][5][18][29]MYS--
COLLINS "BLOODY TOWER" '38
BLES "FATAL POOL" '60 & MORE
STREET, C.J.C.--[1][18]NON-FICTION
X.X.--[1]

STREET, GEORGE SLYTHE
STREET, JAY--[1][32]MYS--
AHMM "MAKE ME AN OFFER" DEC '58
AHMM "A VERY SPECIAL KILLER" JAN '59
AHMM "MAN IN THE TELEPHONE BOOTH" JUN '59
AHMM "LTR FROM A VERY WORRIED MAN" JUL '59
AHMM "LAST ESCAPE" JUL '60
AHMM "THE PAINLESS METHOD" OCT '61
AHMM "FAITH HEALING" JAN '62

STREIB, DANIEL T.
CARTER, NICK--W/CHET CUNNINGHAM,[3]HP--
AWARD "NIGHT OF THE AVENGER" '73
COLTER, FRANK--[3]MYS--
BELM "GANG WARS" '75
BELM "KILLERS FOR HIRE" '75
CRUZ, MARK--[3]MYS--
MANOR "DEAD END" '75
MANOR "DEAD WRONG" '75
MANOR "KILL SQUAD" '75
MANOR "VOYAGE OF DEATH" '75
CURTIS, RICHARD HALE--[21]ROM,HP--
'SKYMASTER' SERIES: "THE AVIATRIX"
GRANDVILLE, LOUISE--[9][21][26]ROM--
"WINTER'S WISH"
"AUTUMN MORNING
"CASTLES IN THE SKY"
JONES, J. FARAGUT--[1]
PAGE, THOMAS--W/ROBERT PAGE JONES,[1][2]
RICHARDS, PAUL--W/CHET CUNNINGHAM,[3]HP--
AWARD "MOSCOW AT HIGH NOON IS THE TARGET" '73
RICHARDS, PAUL--W/GEORGE SNYDER,[34]HP--
AWARD "PRESIDENT HAS BEEN KIDNAPPED" '71
ROSS, PAUL--[34]MYS,HP--
POPLB "HITCHHIKE KILLER" '72
POPLB "VALLEY OF DEATH" '72]
ROSS, PAUL--[3]MYS,HP--
POPLB "THE HITCHHIKE KILLER" '72
POPLB "VALLEY OF DEATH" '72
SCOFIELD, JONATHAN--[1][21]HP--
DELL 'FREED FTR' SERIES:
"TOMAHAWKS & LONG RIFLES"
"VOLUNTEERS FOR GLORY"
STRIBE, DAN--[31][32]MYS--
SFDS "DON'T RESCUE ME!" JUL '58
STRIEB, DAN--[21]ROM
WILLOUGHBY, LEE DAVIS--[21]ROM,HP--
DELL 'MKNG OF AMERICA' SERIES:
"TRAIL BLAZERS"
WILSON, GAR--[34]MYS,HP--
GE 'PHOENIX' SERIES:
"RIM OF FIRE" '89
"SHOW OF FORCE" '88

STRETE, CRAIG [KEE]
C.S.--[23]SF--
"TIMEDEER" '74
FALCONER, SOVEREIGN--[7]SF--
DBLDY "TO MAKE DEATH LOVE US" '87

STRETTON, HESBA
SMITH, SARAH--[22]NOVELS & JUV

STRIBBLING, JEAN
DALE, RUTH JEAN--W/BETTY DURAN,[9][26]ROM--
"ONE MORE CHANCE"
"SHOWDOWN" & 7 MORE

STRIBLING, THOMAS S.
STRIBLING, T.S.--[1][32]MYS--
EQMM "THE CABLEGRAM" FALL '41
NW "THE SHADOW" JUN '54
SA "MURDER AT FLOWTIDE" MAR '55
& 23 OTHERS

STRICH, CHRISTIAN
DE SAINT-GALL, AUGUSTE A.--[31]
FRIEDRICH, ANTON--[31]
GALL, AUGUSTE A. DE ST.--[31]
JOUVET, JEAN--[31]

STRICKLAND, MARGOT
WORTH, MARGARET--[1]

STRICKLAND, WILLIAM BRADLEY
BRADLEY, WILL--[23]SF--
"ARK LIBERTY" '92
STRICKLAND, BRAD--[23]SF-- '88-91
STRICKLAND, BRADLEY--[23][32]MYS--
EQMM "THE THIRD GRAVE" SEPT '66

STRIEBECK, NANCY
STREEBECK, NANCY--[1]

STRIEBER, [LOUIS] WHITLEY
BARRY, JONATHAN--[7]SF--
TOR "CATMAGIC" '86 AS BY 'JONATHAN BARRY' & WHITLEY STREIBER

STRIKER, FRAN
MIDDLETON, DON--L. HULLAR & T. JOHNSON-ECHOES #20--
"GOLPHER CREEK GUNMAN" '45

STRINDBERG, JOHAN AUGUST
ULF, HAERVED--[1]

STRINGER, JOHN ARBUTHNOTT
STRINGER, ARTHUR--[29]MYS

STRIVEN, WILLIAM
ST. IVEN, W.--[34]MYS--
DRANE'S "STATION-TO-STATION STORIES" '26

STROMBERG, SIGGE NATANAEL
WALL, CHRISTIAN--[29]MYS--
AHLEN & AKERLUND "HEMLIGHETEN PA ALMNAS" '22

STROMEYER, CAROLYN
THORNTON, CAROLYN--[9]ROM--
"BY THE BOOK"
"MAIL ORDER BRIDE" & 12 MORE

STROMSTEDT, LASSE
AHL, KENNET--W/CHRISTER DAHL,[29]MYS--
PRISM "GRUNDBULTEN" '74
PRISM "LYFTET" '76
PRISM "RASAXEN" '78
PRISM "SLUTSTATIONEN" '80

STRONG, AMELIA FRANCIS
DILKE, LADY--[1]

STRONG, ANNALOUISE
ANISE--[8]

STRONG, CHARLES STANLEY
BARTLETT, NANCY--[1][28]ROM--
GRAMMERCY "EMBASSY BALL" '38
KEATS, MYRON--[1]
MCCLELLAN, WILLIAM--[1][28]--
PHOENIX "WATERFRONT WAITRESS" '37
"CALL GIRL" '39
"DANCE STUDIO" '40
MCKAY, KELVIN--[1][3]MYS--
PHOENIX "MURDER AT BARCLAY HOUSE" '37
MCLELLAN, WILLIAM B.--[28]WEST--
WORLD'S WORK "TOWN TAMER" '52
REGAN, LARRY--L. ROBBINS LTR '94,[28]WEST--
4 FOULSHAM NOVELS '54-60
STANLEY, CHUCK--[1][28]WEST--
74 NOVELS '40-65
STODDARD, CHARLES--[2][3][28]MYS--
'MALLOY' SERIES
"CARIBOU PATROL"
"GOLDEN ARROW" & MORE '36-47
STURDY, CARL--[1][28]ROM--
5 PHOENIX NOVELS '37-43

STRONG, CHRISTINA
CORDAIRE, CHRISTINA--[26]ROM--
"PRIDE'S FOLLY"
"DARING ILLUSION" & OTHERS

STRONG, GEORGE A.
HENDERSON, MARC ANTHONY--[1]

STRONG, JEREMY
STRONG, J.J.--[1][33]

STRONG, JUNE
GREENE, SARA--[31]

STRONGMAN, MIKE
CUSTER, TEX--[36]AUSTRALIAN/WEST--
CURRAWONG "THE GUN SHADOW"
'STRONGMAN' MAY BE PSEUD.

STROTHER, DAVID HUNTER
CRAYON, PORTE--[31]

STROTHER, PAT WALLACE
CLOUD, PATRICIA--[9][21][26]ROM--
"THIS WILLING PASSION"
LATNER, PAT WALLACE--[31]
LORD, VIVIAN--[9][21][26]ROM--
"ONE MORE SUN"
"SUMMER KINGDOM" & 3 MORE
WALLACE, PAT--[7][9][21][26]ROM/SF--
"STAR RISE"
"SILVER FIRE" & 7 MORE
WEST, PAT--[9][21][26]ROM--
"A WIFE FOR ROMANCE"
"UNDER THE SIGN OF SCORPIO"

STROUP, WILLIAM
HOWARD, BOB--V. BERCH-BRNDN/BC PSEUDS,
BAE 22, ADULT--

STROVER, DOROTHEA
TINNE, DOROTHEA--[1][22]ENGLISH
TINNE, E.D.--[1][22]ENGLISH

STRUBBERG, FRIEDRICH ARMAND
ARMAND--[22]GERMAN
FARNWALD--[22]GERMAN

STRUBE, HERMANN
BURTE, HERMANN--[22]GERMAN

STRUBE, WILHELM
WENDLAND, MARTIN--[39][40]GERMAN/MYS--
"MIT FALSCHER MUNZE" '78

STRUNG, NORMAN
BARKEE, ASOUFF--[1][31]
MILLER, CONRAD--[1]
YAEGER, BARTD--[1]

STRUNK, GORDON
BENJAMIN, JACK--V. BERCH-BRNDN/BC PSEUDS,
BAE 22, ADULT--
BC 7179 "ORAL BRIDES"
BC 7044 "SAVVY SECRETS OF A TEEN SEX SWINGER"
BC 7121 "SUBURBAN SWAPPERS"
BC 7329 "SEXUALLY AGGRESSIVE HUSBAND"

STRUNSKY, SIMEON
PATIENT OBSERVER, THE--[8]

STRUTTON, WILLIAM HAROLD
STRUTTON, BILL--[7]SF--
"DR. WHO: AND THE ZARBI" '65
RPRTD "DR. WHO: THE WEB PLANET" '91

STUART, DONALD
STEELE, DERWENT--[18]MYS--
"THE BLACK GANGSTER" '34
"PHANTOM SLAYER" '35
"PURPLE PLAGUE" '35
"AVENGERS" '35
STUART, GERALD--[18]MYS--
"THERES NO ESCAPE" [RADIO PLAY] '64
STUART, RONALD--[1]
VANE, NIGEL--[18]MYS--
"DEVIL'S DOZEN" '34
"THE MENACE OF LI-SIN" '34
"VENGEANCE OF LI-SIN" '35
"VEILS OF DEATH" '35
"MIDNIGHT GANG" '36
VERNER, GERALD--[3][7][18][29]MYS--
WB "ALIAS THE GHOST" '33
WB "THE BLACK SKULL" '33
WB "THE VAMPIRE MEN" '41 & 11 MORE

STUART, DORIS
CARTER, NICK--W/ANSEL CHAPIN,[3]MYS,HP--
AWARD "DEATH MESSAGE: OIL 74-2" '76
AWARD "PAMPLONA AFFAIR" '78
DARLING, JOAN--[21][26]ROM--
"MAN AROUND THE HOUSE"
"CAROLINA MOON"
"TYLER'S FOLLY"
SEARIGHT, ELLEN--[21][26]ROM--
"GOLDEN INTERLUDE"
STUART, DEE--[21]ROM--
"SCARLET LILY"
"WINGS OF MORNING" & MORE

STUART, DOROTHY MARGARET
D.M.S.--[8]

STUART, HECTOR A.
CALIBAN--[8]

STUART, IAN
GRAY, MALCOLM--JEAN F. LE DEIST LTR '93,
[18]MYS--
EQMM "ENTER MISS GRINDLE" FEB '90

STUART, JESSICA JANE
JUERGENSMEYER, JANE STU.--[31]

STUART, MORNA
CAMPBELL, C.J.--[1]

STUART, PENELOPE
WISDOM, PENELOPE--[9][21][26]ROM--
"STARLIGHT"

STUART, VIOLET VIVIAN F.
ALLEN, BARBARA--[9][21][22][26][31]ROM--
HARL "GAY GORDONS"
HARL "SOMEONE ELSE'S HEART"
FINLAY, FIONA--[1][22]ENGLISH
LONG, WILLIAM STUART--[9][21][26][31]ROM--
'AUSTRALIANS' SERIES - 12 BOOKS
STUART, ALEX--[9][21][22][26]ROM--
"QUEEN'S COUNSEL"
"ISLAND FOR SALE" & 8 MORE
STUART, ROBYN--[9][21][26]ROM--
"BUCCANEER'S LADY"
STUART, V.A.--[1]ENGLISH/HIST
STUART, VIVIAN--[9][21][26]ROM--
"PILGRIM HEART"

STUART, WILLIAM LISTLE
DUDGEON, ROBERT--J. HOFFMANN, PP 40, P18,HP
GERM PANTH 149
RPRT OF AVON 186 "NIGHT CRY"

STUART-HEATON, PETER
HEATON, PETER--[8]

STUART-JERVIS, CHARLES
COYSH, EDWARD--[8]

STUBBS, HARRY CLEMENT
CLEMENT, HAL--[2][3][4][7][11][23]SF--
"NEEDLE" '50
"GNOME" '53 & OTHERS
RICHARD, GEORGE--[1][23]DF--

STUBBS, JEAN
DARBY, EMMA--[8]
MARCH, EMMA--[8]

STUBER, STANLEY IRVING
ERAMUS, M. NOTT--[1][22][31]

STUCHA, PETER
PARAGRAPH--[1]
VETERAN--[1]

STUDDERT, ANNIE LOUISE
RIXON, ANNIE [LOUISA]--[1][36]AUSTRALIAN--
STUDDERT "CAPTAIN THUNDERBOLT" nd

STUDDERT-KENNEDY, W.G.
KENNEDY, GERALD STUDDERT--[31]

STUDEBAKER, DONALD VALEN.
DECLES, JON--[2][7][11]SF--
ACE "PARTICOLORED UNICORN:
AN ENTERTAINMENT" '87
POWELL, MASON--[7]SF--
ALTERNATE PRESS "THE BRIG" '84

STUMP, JANE [BARR]
STRYKER, DANIEL--W/CHRISTOPHER MORRIS,
[7]THRIL--
JOVE "COBRA" '91
"HAWKEYE" '91

STUMPE, JOHANNES
PESTUM, JO--[39][40]GERMAN/MYS--
"DER KATER SPIELT PIK-AS" '68
ALSO JUV & SF

STURE-VASA, MARY
O'HARA, MARY--[8]

STURGEON, THEODORE
CHARTERIS, LESLIE--LOCUS #389-
OBIT FOR CHARTERIS--
GHOSTED--
"THE DARKER DRINK" '47
EWING, FREDERICK R.--W/JEAN SHEPHERD,
[2][4][23]--
BAL 165 "I, LIBERTINE" '56
HUNTER, E. WALDO--[1][2][11][23][31]SF--
QUEEN, ELLERY--[2][3][4]MYS,GHOSTED--
RANDOM "PLAYER ON THE OTHER SIDE" '63
WALDO, E. HUNTER--[1][23]SF--
WATSON, BILLY--[1][2][11][23]SF--

STURGEON, WINA
MOORE, CORY--[1]

STURGES, MARY D'ESTE
VIRAKAM, SOROR--[8]

STURGIS, MELVIN
STURGIS, COLIN--W/LES COLE,[1][2][11]

STURT, GEORGE
BOURNE, GEORGE--[1]

STURTZEL, HOWARD ALLISON
ANNIXTER, PAUL--[2][11][31][33]

STURTZEL, JANE LEVINGTON
ANNIXTER, JANE--[1][31][33]CHILDREN'S
COMFORT, JANE LEVINGTON--[1][31][33]

STUTLEY, SYDNEY JAMES D.
STUTLEY, S.J.--[36]AUSTRALIAN/MYS--
"TIPPERARY" '18
LANE "MELBOURNE MYS" '29 [W/A.E. COPP]
LANE "POISONED GLASS" '30 [W/A.E. COPP]

STUTZMAN, ESTHER FRIESNER
FRIESNER, ESTHER [1]--[7]SF--
ACE 'DEMONS' #1-3 '88-90
ACE 'GNOME' #1 '91
POPLB 'HARLOT'S RUSE' '86
'CHRONICLE OF TWELVE KINGDOMS' #1-3 '85-7
'NEW YORK' #1-3 '86-9

STYLES, FRANK SHOWELL
HOWELL, S.--[33]

STYLES, [FRANK] SHOWELL
CARR, GLYN--[3][18][29]MYS--
BLES "MURDER OF AN OWL" '56
BLES "FAT MAN'S AGONY" '69 & MORE
HOWELL, S[HOWELL]--[1][18][31]MYS--
5 NOVELS '46-8

SUBLETTE, WALTER EDWARDS
EDWARDS, S.W.--[31]

SUCHARITKUL, SOMTOW PAP.
SOMTOW, S.P.--[2][7][23]THAI/SF--
"STARSHIP & HAIKU" '81
BAL 'AQUILIAD' #1-3
DONNING 'VALENTINE' #1
AV 'RIVERRUN' #1
SOMTOW, S.V.--[2]

SUCHOW, SHERMAN MERRILL
MOUNT, CHARLES MERRILL--[1]

SUCKERT, CURZIO
MALAPARTE, CURZIO--[1]

SUDDABY, WILLIAM DONALD
GRIFF, ALAN--[2][23]--
"HOUSE OF DESOLATION" '34
"VILLAGE FANFARE OR MAN FROM THE FUTURE" '34

SUDFELD, MAX SIMON
NORDAU, MAX SIMON--[22]GERMAN

SUEO, IWAYA
SAZANAMI, IWAYA--[22]JAPANESE

SUFRIN, MARK
WILLOUGHBY, LEE DAVIS--[21]ROM,HP--
DELL 'MKNG OF AMERICA' SERIES: "NIGHTRIDERS"

SUGAR, BERT RANDOLPH
BROOKS, JOHN--[1][31]
DAVIS, SUZANNE--[1][31]

SUJATA, ANAGARIKA
CURRY, WINDELL--[31]

SUKARNO, AHMED
KARNO, BROTHER--[1]
KARNO, BUNG--[1][31]

SULLIVAN, EDMUND
NAGLE, ARTHUR--[1]

SULLIVAN, EDWARD ALAN
MURRAY, SINCLAIR--[8][23]CANADIAN/SF--
BLES "CRUCIBLE" '25
LOW "MONEY SPINNERS" '36 & 10 MORE

SULLIVAN, ELEANOR
DE HAHN, JULIA--ED HOCH '91 BOUCHERCON PROGRAM, MYS--
GRAVIROS, RUTH--LACHMAN LST '93, MYS--
LORE, ELANA--[7]--
ALFRED HITCHCOCK'S "A CHOICE OF EVILS" & "FATAL ATTRACTIONS" '83 ?UNCONF?
VAN NESS, LIKA--LACHMAN LST '93, MYS--

SULLIVAN, MARION F.
BROOKS, JAMES M.--[8]

SULLIVAN, SHEILA
BATHURST, SHEILA--[23][31]ENGLISH/SF--
CRITICISM

SULLIVAN, THOMAS JOSEPH
SULLIVAN, TOM--[33]

SULLIVAN, TIMOTHY ROBERT
GRANT, MARK--W/DAVID BISCHOFF,[7]SF--
'MUTANTS AMOK': #1 "MUTANTS AMOK" '91
SHADWELL, THOMAS--W/ARTHUR B. COVER & G. BETANCOURT,[7]--
SILVERBERG'S TIME TOURS "DINOSAUR TRKS"
SULLIVAN, TIM--[7]SF--
AV "COLD SHOCKS" '91
AV "MARTIAN VIKING" '91
AV 'V ' SERIES

SULLIVAN, TONY
RILEY, LEN--[35]AUSTRALIAN--
HRWTZ PB315 "KING'S CROSS RACKET" '67

SUMINGTON, DAVID
HALLIDAY, JAMES--[1]

SUMMERFIELD, JOANNE
GINSBERG, JOANNE--[1][31]

SUMMERS, A. WELBOURNE
STELLIER, KILSYTH--[3]MYS--
GALE "TAKEN BY FORCE" 1893

SUMMERS, AUGUSTUS MONTAG.
SUMMERS, REY--[1]

SUMMERS, ETHEL NELSON
SUMMERS, ESSIE--[1]

SUMMERS, HOLLIS [S]
HOLLIS, JIM--W/JAMES F.A. ROURKE, [3][22]AMERICAN/MYS--
HARPER "TEACH YOU A LESSON" '55
HOLLIS, JIM--W/LOUIS P. TRIMBLE, [1][22]AMERICAN/WEST--

SUMMERS, J.C.
SUMMERS, BLUE PETER--[1]

SUMMERSCALES, ROWLAND
GAINES, ROBERT--[1][3]MYS--
MacD "CRUEL DEADLINE" '60
JOSEPH "NAME IS JUDAS" '66 & 6 MORE '51-66

SUMMERTON, MARGARET
ROFFMAN, JAN--[3][9][21][26][29]MYS/ROM--
BLES "LIKELY TO DIE" '64
DBLDY "ASHES IN AN URN" '66

SUMNER, ADA
RHOME, ADA--[9]ROM
STEWARD, ADA--[21][26]ROM--
"A WALK IN PARADISE"
"HOT WIND IN EDEN" & 6 MORE

SUMNER, DAVID [W.K.]
KAISER, BILL--[1][31]

SUNNERS, WILLIAM
KEITH, LEE--[1][22]AMERICAN
SATTERLY, WESTON--[1][22]AMERICAN

SUPRANER, ROBYN
BLAKE, OLIVE--[1][31][33]
FROST, ERICA--[1][31][33]
WARREN, ELIZABETH--[1][33]

SUR, ATUL KRISHNA
CHANDRAVATI--[1]
YAMA--[1]

SURMELIAN, LEON
VANDOR, CYRIL--[1]

SURREY, KATHRYN
MATTHEWMAN, PHYLLIS--[9]ROM

SUSSMAN, CORNELIA SILVER
JESSEY, CORNELIA--[3][22][31][33]AMERICAN/MYS--
NOONDAY "THE TREASURY OF DARKNESS" '53

SUSSMAN, SUSAN
RISSMAN, ART--[1][33]
RISSMAN, SUSAN--[1][33]

SUTCLIFFE, HALLIWELL
QUILP, JOCELYN--[7]SF

SUTCLIFFE, JANICE
KAISER, JANICE--[26]ROM--
HARL 597 "YANQUI PRINCE"
HARL 462 "BETRAYAL" & OTHERS

SUTHERLAND, DOUGLAS
NASH, NORMAN--V. BERCH-'AFTER DARK' SERIES,
BAE 27, ADULT--
MacF 60-259 "LONDON AFTER DARK" '66

SUTHERLAND, JEAN
NASH, JEAN--[9]ROM

SUTHERLAND, ROBERT GARIOC
GARIOCH, ROBERT--[8]

SUTPHEN, RICHARD C.
RICHARDS, TODD--[1]

SUTTLES, SHIRLEY
CONGER, LESLIE--[1][22]AMERICAN

SUTTON, DAVID A.
ODDEY, JAMES D.--[2]

SUTTON, EUGENIA
SUTTON, JEAN--[1]

SUTTON, JEFFERSON HOWARD
GALE, CHRISTOPHER--V. BERCH-MON PSEUDS,
BAE 9,[1]--
MON 225 "TROPIC FURY" '61
SUTTON, JEFF--[1]
SUTTON, JEFFERSON H.--G. COOK LTR '93, SF--
"THE MISSILE LORDS"

SUTTON, MARGARET BEEBE
RAY, IRENE--[33]

SUTTON, MAURICE LOUIS
SUTTON, STACK--[22][28]AMERICAN/WEST--
6 NOVELS '63-90

SUTTON, PHYLLIS MARY
RICHES, PHYLLIS--[8]

SUTTON, RACHEL IRENE B.
RAY, IRENE--[1][33]CHILDREN'S
SUTTON, MARGARET--[1]
SUTTON, MARGARET BEEBE--[1]
SUTTON, RACHEL B.--[8]

SUTTON, [ERIC] GRAHAM
MARSDEN, ANTONY--[1][34]MYS--
JARROLDS "SUTTER'S FOLLY" '27
LOW "SWOONING VENUS" '32 & 8 MORE

SVEDELID, OLOV
FROST, MARTIN--[29]MYS--
FORUM "FARVAL, MR. PRESIDENT" '75

SVEE, SALLY
LE ROY, IRENE--[9][21][26]ROM--
"NOTHING TO HIDE"

SVEINSSON, SOLVEIG
RIVERS, RONDA--[8]

SVENSON, ANDREW E.
DIXON, FRANKLIN W.--[1]HP--
STSY 'HARDY BOYS'
STSY 'TED SCOTT'
STONE, ALAN--[1]HP--
STSY 'TOLLIVER ADVENTURE'
WEST, JERRY--[1]HP--
STSY 'HAPPY HOLLISTERS'

SVENSON, JON STEFAN
NONNI--[1]

SVERDIN, HANNAH GRAD
GOODMAN, HANNAH GRAD--[31]

SWADESH, FRANCES LEON
QUINTANA, FRANCES--[1]
LEON, FRANCES--[1][31]

SWAFFORD, JOHNNY C.
LUGMAN, ABDULLAH--[1]
NIG, CAPT'N--[1]

SWAIN, DWIGHT V[REELAND]
BLADE, ALEXANDER--HAWK/JOYE SWAIN INTRVW '93
MYS,HP--TITLES NOT KNOWN
CARTER, NICK--HAWK/JOYE SWAIN INTRVW '93,
[3][31]MYS,HP--
CHART "THE PEMEX CHART" '79
CLEVE, JOHN--W/ANDREW J. OFFUTT,J. SWAIN,
[7]SF,HP--
BERK 'SPACEWAYS':
"PLANET MURDERER" '84
SOUTH, CLARK--HAWK/JOYE SWAIN INTRVW '93,
[2][23][31]--
PULP/MAG - EARLY SHORT STORIES

SWAIN, EDMUND GILL
SWAIN, E.G.--[1]

SWALLOW, NORMAN
LEATHER, GEORGE--[1][31]

SWANN, ANNIE S.
LYALL, DAVID--[1]
ORCHARD, EVELYN--[8]

SWANN, DONALD [I]
TABLET, HILDA--[31]WALES-ENGLISH

SWANN, FRANCIS
PHILLIPS, JEAN--[3]MYS--
LAN 72-967 "GREENWOOD" '65
LAN 73-567 "HERMIT'S ISLAND" '67
LAN 74-647 "DAY OF DARK MEMORY" '70
AV "HOUSE OF DARKNESS" '71

SWANSON, DAN
NORTH, JAMES--[1]

SWANSON, HAROLD NORLING
SCOTT, KERRY--[1]

SWANTON, MOLLY B.
ERIKSON, LYNN--W/CARLA PELTONEN,[10][34]MYS--
HARL "ARENA OF FEAR" '86
"GENTLE BETRAYAL"

SWANZEY, CHARLEEN
SWANSEA, CHARLEEN--[1]
WHISNANT, CHARLEEN--[1]

SWARTZ, HARRY
MORENO, MARTIN--[1]
VALCOE, H. FELIX--[1]

SWARTZ, MARIA HELGA
MARTINSON, MOA--[22]SWEDISH

SWATRIDGE, CHARLES J.
CHARLES, THERESA--W/IRENE SWATRIDGE,
[3][17][31]MYS/ROM--
CASSELL "BURNING BEACON" '56 & 11 MORE
LANCE, LESLIE--[3][9][26]MYS/ROM--
LOW "DARK STRANGER" '46
PYR "THE BRIDE OF EMERSHAM" '67
ACE "THE HOUSE IN THE WOODS" '73

SWATRIDGE, IRENE M.M.
CHANDOS, FAY--[9][17][21][22][31]ENGLISH/ROM--
"HIBISCUS HOUSE"
MOSSOP, IRENE--[1][9][17]ENGLISH/ROM

SWATRIDGE, IRENE M.M.
STORM, VIRGINIA--[1][9][17][22]ENGLISH/ROM
TEMPEST, JAN--[3][17][26]MYS/ROM--
MILLS "HOUSE OF THE PINES" '46
MILLS "WINTER OF FEAR" '67 & MORE

SWAYZE, CAROLYN NORMA
MOYER, CAROLYN--[34]MYS--
BOUREGY "SECRET OF BOURKE'S MANSION" '77

SWEDIN, NILS-AXEL
KALIX, AXEL--[29]MYS--
TOMASS "DODEN FLYTTAR IN" '56

SWEENEY, CHARLES
SWEENEY, R.C.H.--[1]

SWEENEY, LINDA
GRIFFITH, ROSLYNN--W/PATRICIA PINIANSKI,
[26]ROM--
"HEART OF THE JAGUAR"
"PRETTY BIRDS OF PASSAGE"
PATRICK, LYNN--W/PATRICIA PINIANSKI,[7]--
DELL "DOUBLE OR NOTHING" '85
DELL "MORE THAN A DREAM" '85
PATRICK, ROSLYN--W/PATRICIA PINIANSKI,[26]ROM--
"PRINCESS ROYALE"
ROSE, JEANNE--W/PATRICIA PINIANSKI,[26]ROM--
"BELIEVING IN ANGELS"

SWEET, CHARLES
CHARLES, HAL--W/HAL BLYTH, LACHMAN LST-
AUTHORS CONFIRMED,[32]MYS--
EQMM "SUDDEN DEATH" APR '80
SK "BURIED IN PAPER" MAY '80
SK "PETER'S PRINCIPLES" JUN '80
EQMM "TALK-SHOW MURDER" JUL '80
MSMM "TURNING POINT" JUL '80
EQMM "HUMAN INTEREST ANGLE" DEC '80
HALLIDAY, BRETT--W/HAL BLYTH,T. JOHNSON-
ECHOES #23, MYS,HP--
MSMM "TERROR RESORT" NOV '82
MSMM "TERROR RESORT" DEC '82
MSMM "RETURN OF THE BEACH BUTCHER" JAN '83
MSMM "A DIRTY BUSINESS" FEB '83
MSMM "SEARCH & DESTROY" MAR '83
MSMM "SHADOW OF DEATH" APR '83
MSMM "HUNTING OF MIKE SHAYNE" MAY '83
MSMM "DEADLY MEMORIES" JUL '83
MSMM "GRAVEN IMAGE" AUG '83
MSMM "HELLHOLE" SEP '83
MSMM "DEATH STALKS THE CAMPUS" OCT '83
MSMM "DEATH ON SKULL MT" NOV '83
MSMM "DEAD RINGER" JAN '84
MSMM "SANDCASTLES" FEB '84
MSMM "ALL IN A DAY'S WORK" MAR '84
MSMM "DAY OF REVENGE" APR '84
MSMM "YESTERDAY'S HERO" '84
MSMM "DEVIL DUST & MURDER" JUN '84
MSMM "SHARKS" JUL '84
MSMM "SHADOWS OF THE PAST" AUG '84
MSMM "KEY OF DEATH" SEP '84
MSMM "KILLING TIME" OCT '84
MSMM "DEATH TAKES A PILGRIMAGE" NOV '84
MSMM "DEATH TOPS THE CHARTS" JAN '85
MSMM "QUICK & THE DEAD" FEB '85
MSMM "DEADLY VISIONS" MAR '85
MSMM "THY WILL BE DONE" MAY '85
MSMM "A DARK NIGHT WITH A BLIND
LADY" APR '85
MSMM "STING OF DEATH" JUN '85

SWEET, CHARLES [CONT]
HALLIDAY, BRETT [CONT]
MSMM "A NIGHT IN HELL" JUL '85
MSMM "WILDE WEEKEND" AUG '85

SWEET, HAROLD G.
KEVIN, LLOYD--V. BERCH-MON PSEUDS, BAE 9,ROM--
MON 286 "HER CHEATING HEART" '62

SWEET, JOHN
KIM--[8]

SWEETLAND, NANCY A[NN]
ROSE, NANCY A.--[1][33]

SWENSON, REX
WILSON, GAR--W/THOMAS P. RAMIREZ,[3]MYS,HP--
GE "ASWAN HELLBOX" '83

SWETENHAM, VIOLET HILDA
DRUMMOND, VIOLET HILDA--[8]

SWICEGOOD, THOMAS L.P.
LOVE, CHARLES K.--[1][31]
STIERWELL, JAY--[1]

SWIETOCHOWSKI, ALEKSANDER
OKONSKI, WLADYSLAW--[22]POLISH

SWIFT, CAROLYN RUTH
LENZ, CAROLINE RUTH S.--[1][31]

SWIFT, HELEN C[ECILIA]
LACROIX, LOUISE--[1][31]

SWIFT, JONATHAN
BICKERSTAFF, ISAAC--[31][33]
DRAPIER, M.B.--[31]
DREPIER, M.B.--[33]
GULLIVER, LEMUEL--[2]
WAYSTAFF, SIMON--[33]

SWIFT, PATRICK
HAHON, JAMES--[1][31]

SWINFORD, BETTY [J.W]
HAYNES, LINDA--[22][31][33]AMERICAN
PORTER, KATHRYN--[1][22][33]AMERICAN
SWINFORD, BOB--[1][22][33]AMERICAN
WELLS, JUNE--[1][22][33]AMERICAN

SWINNERTON, FRANK ARTHUR
PURE, SIMON--[1]

SWINTON, ERNEST DUNLOP
FATHER OF THE TANK--[1]
LUK-OIE, OLE--[2]
OLE-LUK-OIE--[1]
SWINTON, E.D.--[1]

SWINTON, SIR EDWARD
FORETHOUGHT, BACKSIGHT--[2]

SWOBODA, FAYE
ADAMS, FAYE--[26]ROM--
"ROSEBUD"

SWYCAFFER, JEFFERSON P.
COURT, HAROLD--[1][31]

SYKES, CHRISTOPHER
WAUGHBURTON, RICHARD--W/ROBERT BYRON,[1]

SYKES, ROOSEVELT
BRAGG, BOBBY--[31]

SYLVESTER, JANET HART
DIEBOLD, JANET--[31]
DIEBOLD, JANET OLINE--[31]

SYLVESTRE, J. JEAN GUY
BRUNEAU, JEAN--[31]

SYMANSKI, RICHARD
SZYMANSKI, RICHARD--[1]

SYMINGTON, DAVID
HALLIDAY, JAMES--[8][31]

SYMMES, JOHN CLEVES
SEABORN, CAPT. ADAM--[2][11]

SYMONDS, EMILY MORSE
PASTON, GEORGE--[1]

SYMONDS, FRANCIS A.
DANESFORD, EARLE--[1]
STEEL, HOWARD--[1]HP

SYMONS, ALPHONSE JAMES ALBERT
SYMONS, A.J.A.--BK & MAG COLLECTORS FEB '94
[1]--
"QUEST OF THE CORVO"
SYMONS, ALBERT JAMES A.--[1]

SYMONS, DOROTHY GERALDINE
GROVES, GEORGINIA--[8][31][33]

SYNGE, ALLEN
LEOPOLD, CHRISTOPHER--[31]

SYNGE, JOHN M.
SYNGE, J.M.--[1]

SYVERTSEN, RYDER [OTTO]
SIEVERT, JAN--W/JAN STACY,[7][23]SF,HP--
ZEBRA 'C.A.D.S.' #1 '85
SIEVERT, JAN--[7][23]SF,HP--
ZEBRA 'C.A.D.S.' #2-8
STACY, RYDER--W/JAN STACY,[7][23]SF,HP--
ZEBRA 'DOOMSDAY WARRIOR':" #1-4 '84-5
STACY, RYDER--[7][23]SF,HP--
ZEBRA 'DOOMSDAY WARRIOR': #5-11 & #13-18

SZALATNYAY, JOZEFNE
DENES, ZSOFIA--[1]

SZOT, WALTER
SCOTT, TARN--W/PETER G. TARNOR, V. BERCH-
GM PSEUDS, PP 33--
GM 668 "DON'T LET HER DIE" '57
HILL "SEX MARKS THE SPOT" '60

SZTYRMER, LUDWIK
BOMBA, GERWAZY--[22]POLISH
SZTYRMER, ELEONORA--[22]POLISH

SZUDEK, AGNES SUSAN F.
MCCAFFREY, MARY--[1][33]

SZYDLOWSKI, MARY V.
SZYDLOW, JARL--[1][7][23]SF--
MANOR "THE ARK" '78
VIGILIANTE, MARY--[1][7][23]SF--
'AFTERMATH' SERIES '79-80

TABER, ANTHONY SCOTT
ANTHONY--[31]

TABER, CLARENCE WILBUR
JOB, MODERN--[8]

TABER, ELLEN LYLE
CARLYLE, TENA--W/CAROLE C. OTTEN,
[21][26]ROM--
"BRIDE OF THE NIGHT"
"CAPTIVE TREASURE"
"RUNAWAY HEART"

TABOR, DEE
HOLLIDAY, DELORES--V. BERCH LTR TO HUBIN '93
MYS--
MTQ "SEVENTH GATE" '81
HARL "BLUE HOUSE" '86

TABORI, PAL
HEFNER, PAUL--[1][31]
STAFFORD, PETER--[2][23][34]MYS--
"WILD WHITE WITCH" '73
NEL "MAN WHO LOVED TO BLOWUP TRAINS" '74
STEVENS, CHRISTOPHER--[1]
TABORI, PAUL--[7][11][23][32]LEGALLY CHNGD
TO "PAUL"
LOW "THE FRONTIER" '50
LOW "THE TALKING TREE" '50
SA "BLACK & WHITE" MAR '57
AHMM "AN INTERLUDE FOR MURDER" 'AUG '58
PYR G624 "THE GREEN RAIN" '61
EW "BEFORE THE FACT" JUN '65 & 6 OTHERS

TACHE, JEAN CHARLES
LEMAGE, GASPARD--[1]
MEPLATS, ISIDORE--[1]

TADAO, MASAMUNE
HAKUCHO, MASAMUNE--[22]JAPANESE

TAGGART, TOM [BARNARD]
MACROSS, ROSS--W/JAMES REACH, V. BERCH-
GM PSEUD, PP 33,[3]MYS--
GM 386 "BEAUTIFUL & THE DEAD" '54
SPALDING, JOSEPH--[3]FRENCH--
PLAY "SPIDER ISLAND" '42

TAGGER, THEODOR
BRUCKNER, FERDINAND--[22]GERMAN

TAGORE, SAUMYEND
NARAYAN--[1]

TAHOURDIN, BARBARA KER W.
WILSON, BARBARA KER--[7]SF--
HODDER "A HANDFUL OF GHOSTS:13 EERIE
TALES OF AUSTRALIAN WRITERS"

TAIEB, HELIANE
VERLANGER, JULIA--[2][11]

TAIT, DOROTHY
FAIRBAIRN, ANN--[1]
STUART, JAY ALLISON--[1]

TAIT, E. MARGARET
IRONSIDE, JOHN--[1][3][22]MYS--
NELSON "JACK OF CLUBS" '31
MLFT "BLACKMAIL" '38 & 6 MORE '10-45

TAIT, GEORGE B.
BARCLAY, ALAN--[2][7][11][23]SF--
HALE "NO MAGIC CARPET" '76
HALE "CITY & THE DESERT" '76 & 2 MORE

TAKAJIAN, PORTIA
JOHNSTON, PORTIA--[31][33]
ROACH, PORTIA--[33]
WIESNER, PORTIA--[33]

TALBOT, CAROL TERRY
TERRY, CAROL--[1]

TALBOT, CHARLENE JOY
ALDEN, ELIZABETH--[9][21]ROM--
"NO SENSE OF HUMOR"
"NEVER SAY NEVER"
LEE, LUCY--[9][25][26]ROM--
"HEART'S FURY"
"THE RITE OF LOVE"
"HEART'S PARADISE"

TALBOT, KATHERINE
ASHTON, KATHERINE--[9]ROM

TALBOT, MARY WHITE
WHITE, MARY--L. ROBBINS LTR '94

TALBOT, TOBY
JOSEPHS, REBECCA--[31]

TALESE, GAETANO
GOLDBERG, HYMAN--[1]
TALESE, GAY--[1]

TALIAFERRO, BOOKER
WASHINGTON, BOOKER T.--[1]

TALIAS, ANGELA DUNTON
ALEXIE, ANGELIE--[21][26]ROM--
"VELVET THORN"
"SOMETIMES A STRANGER" & 2 MORE

TALIFERO, GERALD
STORMEROW--[33]JUV

TALLARICO, ANTHONY
DR. DREW--W/D.J.ARNESON,[7]SF--
"SECRET DRAWING GUIDE TO CREATING SPACE CREATURES" '81
TALLARICO, TONY--[7]SF--
WATERMILL "MONSTER MADNESS" '80 & 5 MORE

TALLMAN, SHIRLEY BENNETT
ROSS, ERIN--[9][21][26]ROM--
"SECOND HARVEST"
"CARNIVAL MADNESS" & 8 MORE

TAMAI, KATSUNORI
HINO, ASHIHEI--[22]JAPANESE

TAMARIN, SHIRLEY ASTOR
GLUBOK, SHIRLEY--[1]

TAMES, RICHARD LAWRENCE
LAWRENCE, JAMES--[8]

TAMEZO, KOSUGI
TENGAL, KOSUGI--[22]JAPANESE

TAMKUS, DANIEL
KEY, L.J.--V. BERCH LTR TO HUBIN '94, MYS--
DELL "THE SPAWN" '83

TAMMINGA, FREDERICK WILL.
WILLIUS, T.F.--[33]

TANN, JENNIFER
BOOTH, GEOFFREY--[1][31]

TANNAHILL, REAY
LAINE, ANNABEL--V. BERCH LTR TO HUBIN '94 MYS--
DBLDY "RELUCTANT HEIRESS' '78
MacM "DEATH AMONG STRANGERS" '87

TANNENBAUM, IRVING
STONE, IRVING--[1]

TANNER, ED EVERETT III
DENNIS, PATRICK--[1][22][31]AMERICAN
ROWANS, VIRGINIA--[1][22]AMERICAN

TAPSELL, ROBERT FREDERICK
TAPSELL, R.F.--[21]ROM--
"THE YEAR OF THE HORSETAILS"

TARASSOV, LEV
TROYAT, HENRI--[22]FRENCH

TARDIVEAX, RENE MARIE
BOYLESVE, RENE--[1][22]FRENCH

TARKINGTON, BOOTH
CORBURTON, JOHN--[1]
VAN LOOT, CORNELIUS O.--[1]
WOODFORD, CECIL--[1]

TARNOR, PETER G.
SCOTT, TARN--W/WALTER SZOT, V. BERCH-GM PSEUDS, PP 33, MYS--
GM 668 "DON'T LET HER DIE" '57
HILL "SEX MARKS THE SPOT" '60

TARSIS, VALERII I.
VALERIY, IVAN--[1]

TASCA, ANGELO
LEROUX, ANDRE--[1]
RIENZI--[1]
ROSSI, A.--[1]
SERRA--[1]
VALLE--[1]

TASHLIN, FRANK
TISH TASH--[1]

TASHMUKHAMEDOV, MUSA
EIBEK--[1]

TATARA, ELLEN LEE M.
MAGNER, LEE--[9][21][26]ROM--
"TORCH SONG"
"MUSTANG MAN" & 12 MORE

TATE, GEORGE
ARMSTRONG, GEORGE--[8]

TATE, VELMA
DAVENPORT, FRANCINE--[1][3]MYS--
ACE "THE SECRET OF THE BAYOU" '66
TAYLOR, VALERIE--V. BERCH, LESBIANA/CNTRCLTR, BAE 22,[1]ADULT--
UGE 8 "FORBIDDEN FRUIT" '53
BEAC B116 "HIRED GIRL" '54
CREST 187 "WHISPER THEIR LOVE" '57
CREST 290 "GIRLS IN 3-B" '59
MDWD F329 "RETURN TO LESBOS" '63
MDWD F346 "A WORLD WITHOUT MEN" '63
MDWD 32-427 "JOURNEY TO FULFILLMENT" '64
YOUNG, NACELLA--[1]

TATHAM, LAURA
MARTIN, JOHN--[1][22]ENGLISH
PHIPPS, MARGARET--[1][22]ENGLISH

TATSUNOSUKE, HASEGAWA
FUTABATEI, SHIMEI--[22]JAPANESE

TATTERSALL, MURIEL JOYCE
WAUD, ELIZABETH--[1][22]ENGLISH, CHILDREN'S BOOKS

TAULMAN, BILLIE
SMITH, ARTEMIS--W/ANNA S. MORPURGO, V. BERCHMON PSEUDS, BAE 9, ADULT--
BEAC B230 "ODD GIRL" '59
BEAC B268 "THIRD SEX" '59
MON 182 "THIS BED WE MADE" '61

TAURASI, JAMES V. SR.
STANNARD, LANE--[1][2][11]
VINCENT, J. HARRY--[1][2][11]

TAVELUDI, P.
POLITIS, KOSMAS--[22]GREEK

TAVES, ISABELLA
MUNRO, CHRISTY--[1]

TAYLOR, ANDREW JOHN ROBERT
TAYLOR, JOHN ROBERT--[33]

TAYLOR, ANN
GILBERT, ANN--[31][33]
JUVENILIA--[31][33]
LADY, A--[31][33]

TAYLOR, BARBARA G.
DESMARAIS, BARBARA G.--[31]

TAYLOR, BERT LESTON
B.L.T.--[8]

TAYLOR, C. LINDSAY
CULLINGFORD, GUY--[18][29][32][34]MYS--
HAMM "POST MORTEM" '53 & 8 MORE '53-68
DIGEST SS

TAYLOR, CHARLES DOONAN
CHARLES, DAVID--W/DAVID C. MONDEY,[31]
CHARLES, DAVID--[34]MYS--
TOR "SHADOWS OF VENGEANCE" '88

TAYLOR, DAN CAMBRIDGE
ST. JAMES, IAN
HM "KILLING ANNIVERSARY" '84
COLLINS "COLD DAWN" '87

TAYLOR, DEEMS
SMEED--[8]

TAYLOR, DELORES
CHRISTINA, FRANK & TERESA--W/TOM LAUGHLIN, M. WADLE CALL '94--
AV N458 "BILLY JACK" '73

TAYLOR, DON CAMBRIDGE
ST. JAMES, IAN--V. BERCH LTR TO HUBIN '94
MYS--
COLLINS "MONEY STONES" '80
HM "BALFOUR CONSPIRACY" '81
HM "WINNER HARRIS" '82

TAYLOR, ELISABETH D.
MCNEILL, ELISABETH--[7][26]ROM/SF--
"LARK RETURNING" '88
"A GARDEN OF BRIARS"

TAYLOR, FREDERICK
BALLINSLOE--[34]MYS--
VICKERS "CONFESSIONS OF A HORSE COPER" 1861

TAYLOR, GEORGE
HAUSRATH, A.--OXFORD COMPANION TO GERMAN LIT. 1986

TAYLOR, HOWARD LANGDON
TAYLOR, TIM--[1]

TAYLOR, JACK
GRAY, JONATHAN--[1][34]MYS--
HUTCH "UNTIMELY SLAIN" '47

TAYLOR, JANELLE [W]
ALEXANDER, BRANDI--[9]ROM
TAYLOR, DIANNE--[9]ROM

TAYLOR, JOHN A.
COPPE, ALBIEZER--[1][31]
DUPIN, AUGUST DUPONT--[1]
WARD, CHARLES DEXTER--[1]

TAYLOR, JOHN M[AXWELL]
ALLEN, RICHARD C.--[31]

TAYLOR, KAMALA
MARKANDAYA, KAMALA--[1]

TAYLOR, KAREN MALPEDE
MALPEDE, KAREN--[1]

TAYLOR, KATHERINE
HAMLINE, DAVID--[13]AUSTRALIAN

TAYLOR, KEITH
MORE, DENNIS--[2][11]AUSTRALIAN
INTERNATIONAL SFYB

TAYLOR, LOIS D. COLE
ARNETT, CAROLINE--[9][17][21][26]AMERICAN/ROM--
"CHRISTINE"
"STEPHANIE" & 4 MORE
DUDLEY, NANCY--[9][17]AMERICAN/ROM--4 NOVELS
DWIGHT, ALLAN--W/TURNEY A. TAYLOR, [9][17]AMERICAN/ROM--
MacM "LYNN DICKSON, CONFEDERATE" '34
ELIOT, ANNE--[17]AMERICAN/ROM--
5 NOVELS '67-74
LATTIN, ANNE--[9][17]AMERICAN/ROM--3 NOVELS
AVERY, LYNN--[9][17]AMERICAN/ROM--
"MYSTERY OF THE VANISHING HORSES" '63

TAYLOR, LYNN
LYNN, KAREN--W/KAREN MAXFIELD,[9][21][26]ROM--
"DUAL DESTINY"
"SCOTTISH MARRIAGE" & 3 MORE

TAYLOR, MARGARET STEWART
COLLIER, MARGARET--[1][31]

TAYLOR, MARY ANN
BOWE, KATE--[9][21][26]ROM--
"LOVE'S GLITTERING WEB"
"HORIZONS"
MCANDREW, CASS--[9][21][26]ROM--
"PRIMITIVE GLORY"

TAYLOR, PAULA [WRIGHT]
LAKE, HARRIET--[1][31][33]

TAYLOR, PHILIP N. WALKER
COSTELLO, PAUL--[34]MYS--
CASSELL "BLUE DIAMOND" '62
CASSELL "MORTGAGE FOR MURDER" '60
& 3 MORE 57-62
TAYLOR, WALKER--[34]--
HODDER "ADMIRAL'S SPY" '41
EYRE "SPYLIGHT" '43
EYRE "SPYROCKET" '44

TAYLOR, PHOEBE ATWOOD
DANA, FREEMAN--[3][18]MYS--
RANDOM "MURDER AT NY WORLDS FAIR" '38

TAYLOR, PHOEBE ATWOOD [CONT]
TILTON, ALICE--[2][3][18][32]MYS--
NORTON "COLD STEAL" '39
NORTON "HOLLOW CHEST" '41 & 6 MORE '37-47

TAYLOR, R.L.
BUTLER, CALVIN--[35]AUSTRALIAN--
HRWTZ PB164 "THE BOLTER" '79
HUNTER, MICHAEL--[35]AUSTRALIAN-- HRWTZ
MCCAIG, MORGAN--[35]AUSTRALIAN--
HRWTZ PB152 "PASSIONATE DYNASTY" '78
SLATER, JOHN [1]--[35]AUSTRALIAN,HP--
HRWTZ "ISLAND HELL" '72
SLATER, JOHN
HRWTZ "DESERT ISLAND" '73
HRWTZ "LOVE CAGE" '73
WESCOTT, SERENA LOUISE--[35]AUSTRALIAN--
HRWTZ PB136 "RAPE OF OAK GROVE" '77
HRWTZ PB159 "BLACK SIN" '78

TAYLOR, RICHARD
CRONUS, DIODORUS--[31]
HALL, STUART--[35]AUSTRALIAN--
HRWTZ PB428 "THE RAPIST" '70
HRWTZ PB439 "THE OPERATOR" '70
HRWTZ PB408 "ONE TOO MANY" '70
HRWTZ PB409 "DUSKY INNOCENT" '70
HRWTZ PB446 "THE SET-UP" '70
HRWTZ PB455 "THE RUBICON" '71
STEELE, MONTE--V. BERCH-BRNDN/BC PSEUDS, BAE 22, ADULT--
BDSD 1229 "JUNGLE OF LUST" '62
BDSD 1246 "PASSIONATE CHEAT" '63
BDSD 1251 "SEX-MOVIE QUEEN" '63
PLTM 624 "CLIPJOINT CUTIE"
PLTM 635 "BACHELOR APPARTMENT"
PLTM 647 "SUCKER BAIT"
PLTM 664 "LOVE CHAMP"

TAYLOR, ROLAND
GILL, STANLEY--[8]

TAYLOR, RONALD WILLIAM
TAYLOR, R.W.--[31]--
GOLD STAR "WHIPLASH" '64
TAYLOR, RON W.--[31]

TAYLOR, SAM S.
ZANE, LEHI--V. BERCH-GM PSEUDS, PP 33,[34]MYS--
GM 264 "BRENDA" '52

TAYLOR, STEPHANA VERE
BENSON, S. VERE--[8]

TAYLOR, THEODORE
LANG, T.T.--[31]

TAYLOR, THOMAS HILHOUSE
TAYLOR, TOSO--[8][36]MYS--
INGLIS "EUCHRED" 1885

TAYLOR, TURNEY ALLAN
DWIGHT, ALLAN--W/LOIS D. COLE,[9][17][31]--
MacM "LYNN DICKSON, CONFEDERATE" '34
MacM "DRUMS IN THE FOREST" '36
MacM "KENTUCKY CARGO" '38 & 6 OTHERS

TAYLOR, W.T.
BREDON, JOHN--[1]
GREGORY, DAVE--[1]
WHITEHOUSE, ARCH--[1]

TAYNTOR, CHRISTINE B.
PREBLE, AMANDA--[9][21][26]ROM--
"HALF-HEART"

TCHATSKY, SHMUEL YOSEPH
AGNON, SHEMUEL JOSEPH--[22]

TCHICAYA, GERALD FELIX
FELIX-TCHICAYA, GERALD--[31]

TCHUDI, STEPHEN N.
JUDY, STEPHEN--[31][33]
JUDY, STEPHEN N.--[31][33]

TEAGUE, GEORGE HERBERT
GALWAY, HERBERT--[1]

TEAGUE, JOHN JESSOP
GERARD, MORICE--[1][2][3][22]MYS--
HODDER "BEACON FIRES" '15
HODDER "DANES ABBEY" '18 & MORE

TEAGUE, ROBERT
TEAGUE, BOB--[33]

TEAGUE, RUTH [T. MILLS]
MILLS, RUTH--[3]MYS--
KENDALL "LEADING LADY" '36

TEDDER, LORNA
SHELLY, LAUREN--[26]ROM--
SIL 582 "A MAN CALLED REGRET"

TEE-VAN, HELEN DAMROSCH
DAMROSCH, HELEN--[31]
DAMROSCH, HELEN THERESE--[33]

TEED, CYRUS REED
CHESTER, LORD--[2][7]

TEED, GEORGE HAMILTON
BRITTANY, LEWIS--[1]
EVANS, GWYN--[34]--
AMALG "CLUE OF MISSING LINK"
CONTAINS "MYS OF PAINTED SLIPPERS"
BY 'TEED'
GWYN, EVANS--W/G.A. EVANS, R.M. GRAYDON & G.N.PHILIPS,[34]MYS--
WRIGHT "MURDERERS MET" '34
HAMILTON, GEORGE--[1]
KINGSLAND, PETER--[34]MYS--
AMALG "THE GOLDEN SECRET" '34
TEED, HAMILTON--[3]MYS--
AMALG 'SEXTON BLAKE' SERIES
AMALG 'GRANT RUSHTON' SERIES

TEED, GEORGE HEBER
HAMILTON, MURRAY--W/ROBERT MURRAY GRAYDON,[1]

TEER, BARBARA
ALLISTER, BARBARA--[9][21][26]ROM--
"A LOVE MATCH"
"MIDNIGHT BRIDE" & MORE

TEGNER, HENRY
NORTHUMBIAN GENTLEMAN--[8][22]ENGLISH
RUFFLES--[8][22]ENGLISH

TEIGE, LUDVIG
BERG, STIG--[29]MYS--
"DODSRESON" '40
"DODSREISON" '45
FOLKESEN, SVEIN--[29]MYS

TEILHARD DE CHARDIN, MARI
DE CHARDIN, PIERRE TEILH.--[31]

TEILHET, DARWIN L.
FIELDING, WILLIAM H.--V. BERCH--
GM PSEUDS, PP 33,[3]MYS--
GM 202 "THE UNPOSSESSED" '51
GM 272 "TAKE ME AS I AM" '52
GM 430 "BEAUTIFUL HUMBUG" '54
FISHER, CYRUS T.--[2]

TEILHET, HILDEGARDE TOLMN
TOLMAN, HILDEGARDE--[1][3][29]MYS--
LITTLE "HERO BY PROXY" '42

TEITELBAUM, MICHAEL
MICHAELS, JOANNE LOUISE--[33]
MICHAELS, NEAL--[33]
NEAL, MICHAEL--[33]
WATSON, B.S.--[33]

TELENGA, SUZETTE
YORKE, SUSAN--[3][36]AUSTRALIAN--
MacD "TIME & THE PLACE" '60
FARRAR "AGENCY HOUSE, MALAYA" '62

TELFER, DARIEL
FORREST, CALEB--[1][31]

TELLER, NEVILLE
OWEN, EDMUND--[1]

TEM, STEVE RASNIC
RASNIC, STEVE--[2]--
'TEM' WAS LEGALLY ADDED TO NAME

TEMPEST, MARGARET MARY
MEARS, LADY--[31][33]

TEMPLE, M.H.
LEWIS, CAROLINE--W/HAROLD BEGBIE
& J. STAFFORD RANSOME,[1][2][23]--
"CLARA IN BLUNDERTON"
"LOST IN BLUNDERLAND" '03

TEMTE, MYRNA
THOMAS, MOLLY--[9][21][26]ROM--
"REBEL HEART"

TENDRON, MARCEL
ELDER, MARC--[22]FRENCH

TENFJORD, JOHANNE MARIE
HOLM, HANNEBO--[1]

TENKRAT, FRIEDRICH
BRAUN, M.G.--W/HANS-JOACHIM KOBLINSKI,
[39][40]GERMAN/MYS,HP--3 NOVELS '69
DARK, JASON--[39][40]GERMAN/MYS,HP
FORD, BRIAN--[39][40]GERMAN/MYS--
'KOMMISSAR X' SERIES- 13 BOOKS
HENRY, FRED--[39][40]GERMAN/MYS,HP--
'KOMMISSAR X' SERIES
KAREN, ANNE--[39][40]GERMAN/MYS--
"IRGENDWANN IN EINEN ANDEREN" '83

TENNANT, EMMA C.
AYDY, CATHERINE--[1][2][23]SF--
"THE COLOR OF RAIN" '64

TENNANT, NORA JACKSON
JACKSON, NORA--[22][31]ENGLISH

TENNOW, DOROTHY
HOFFMAN, D.T.--[1]
TENNOV, DOROTHY--[1]

TENNYSON, MARGARET
FORREST, CAROL--[8]

TEODORESCU, ION N.
THEO, ION--[1]

TEPPER, SHERI S.
EBERHART, SHERI S.--CRPG, SF--
GALAXY "LULLABY, 1990" DEC '63
HORLAK, E.E.--G. THIESSEN '93,[7][31]SF--
BB "STILL LIFE " '89
OLIPHANT, B.J.--G. THIESSEN '93,[34]MYS--
GM "DEAD IN THE SCRUB" '90
"UNEXPECTED CORPSE" '90
ORDE, A.J.--G. THIESSEN '93,[7][34]MYS--
DBLDY 'J. LYNX' SERIES:
"A LITTLE NEIGHBORHOOD MURDER" '89
"DEATH & THE DOGWALKER" '90

TEPPERMAN, EMILE C.
CLEMENS, ANTHONY--PULP CLASSIC #22, P78--
PULP STORIES
COLE, JORDAN--PULP CLASSIC #22, P78--
PULP STORIES
HOUSE, BRANT--W. MURRAY-ECHOES#6,
PULP CLASSIC#22, HOR,HP--
SAX "HAND OF HORROR" AUG '34
SAX "SERVANTS OF THE SKULL" NOV '34
SAX "THE MURDER MONSTER" DEC '34
SAX "TALONS OF TERROR" APR '35
ROBESON, KENNETH--[2][11][37]MYS,HP--
CLS 'AVENGER' - 5 STORIES '42-3
STEELE, CURTIS--ECHOES#6,[2][7][11]HP--
OP5 "RAIDERS OF THE RED DEATH" DEC '35
OP5 "WAR DOGS OF GRN DESTROYER" JAN '36
OP5 "ROCKETS FROM HELL" FEB '36
OP5 "WAR MASTERS FROM ORIENT" MAR '36
OP5 "CRIME'S REIGN OF TERROR" APR '36
OP5 "DEATH'S RAGGED ARMY" JUN '36
OP5 "PATRIOT'S DEATH BATALION" AUG '36
OP5 "BLOODY FORTY-FIVE DAYS" OCT '36
OP5 "AMERICA'S PLAGUE BATTALION" NOV '36
OP5 "LIBERTY'S SUICIDE LEGIONS" JAN '37
OP5 "SIEGE OF THE THOUSAND
PATRIOTS" FEB '37
OP5 "PATRIOT'S DEATH MARCH" MAR '37
OP5 "REVOLT OF THE LOST LEGIONS" MAY '37
OP5 "DRUMS OF DESTRUCTION" JUL '37
OP5 "ARMY WITHOUT A COUNTRY" SEP '37
OP5 "BLOODY FRONTIERS" NOV '37
OP5 "COMING OF MONGOL HORDES" JAN '38
OP5 "SIEGE THAT BROUGHT BLACK
DEATH" MAR '38
OP5 "REVOLT OF THE DEVIL MEN" MAY '38
STOCKBRIDGE, GRANT--PULP #13,[2][7]HP--
SPD "CITY OF DREADFUL NIGHT" NOV '36
SPD "RETURN OF THE SNAKE MEN" DEC '36
SPD "DICTATOR OF THE DAMNED" JAN '37
SPD "MILLTOWN MASSACRES" FEB '37
SPD "SATAN'S WORKSHOP" MAR '37
SPD "SCOURGE OF THE YELLOW FANGS" APR '37
SPD "DEVIL'S PAWNBROKER" MAY '37
SPD "VOYAGE OF THE COFFIN SHIP" JUN '37
SPD "MAN FROM HELL" APR '40
SPD "DICTATOR'S DEATH MERCHANTS" JUL '40
SPD "MASTER OF THE NIGHT DEMONS" SEPT '40
WALLACE, ROBERT--T. JOHNSON LTR '94,MYS,HP--
PHD "HAMMERS OF DOOM" SEPT '37
PHD "WEB OF MURDER" FEB '39
WIRT, W.--[37]MYS--
ACE G-MAN 'SUICIDE SQUAD' STORIES '39-43

TER BALKT, HERMAN H.
AOS, FOEL--[1]
DE BALKER, HABAKUK II--[1]

TERAMOND, EDMOND G.
DE TERAMOND, GUY--[1][3]MYS--
APPLETON "MYSTERY OF LUCIEN DELORME" '15

TERHUNE, MARY VIRGINIA
HARLAND, MARION--[8][22]AMERICAN

TERKEL, LOUIS
TERKEL, STUDS--[8]

TERNI, FAUSTA CIALENTE
CIALENTE, FAUSTA--[1][22][31]ITALIAN

TERRALL, ROBERT
GONZALES, JOHN--V. BERCH--
GM PSEUDS, PP 33,[3][29]MYS--
GM 204 "DEATH FOR MR. BIG" '51
RSB 23 "MAGNIFICENT MOLL" '52
GM 1064 "END OF A J.D." '60
GM 1228 "SOMEONE'S SLEEPING IN MY BED" '62
GM 1293 "FOLLOW THAT HEARSE" '63
GM 1541 "THE ART OF LOVE" '65
HALLIDAY, BRETT--[1][34]MYS,GHOSTED--
DELL "ARMED...DANGEROUS.." '56
DODD "FIT TO KILL" '58
DODD "TARGET: MIKE SHAYNE" '59
DODD "MURDER TAKES NO HOLIDAY" '60
"MURDER IN HASTE" '61
DELL "VIOLENT WORLD OF M.S." '65
DELL "NICE FILLIES FINISH LAST" '65
DELL "MERMAID ON THE ROCKS" '67
DELL "GUILTY AS HELL" '67
DELL "SO LUSH, SO DEADLY" '68
DELL "VIOLENCE IS GOLDEN" '68
DELL "LADY, BE BAD" '69
DELL "SIX SECONDS TO KILL" '70
DELL "FOURTH DOWN TO DEATH" '70
DELL "I COME TO KILL YOU" '71
DELL "KILL ALL THE YOUNG GIRLS" '73
DELL "LAST SEEN HITCHHIKING" '74
DELL "MILLION DOLLAR HANDLE" '76
DELL "WIN SOME, LOSE SOME" '76
KYLE, ROBERT--[1][3][29]MYS--
DELL "GOLDEN URGE" '54
DELL "CROOKED CITY" '54 & 7 MORE '54-64
ROBERTS, MACLENNAN--[1]--
DELL FE-96 "GREAT LOCOMOTIVE CHASE" '56
DELL FE B105 "MOSES & THE TEN COMMANDMENTS" '56
CO-WRITTEN W/PAUL ILTON
DELL FE B113 "SEA AVENGER" '57
CO-WRITTEN W/JACK BEATER

TERRITO, MARY JO
BELMONT, KATHERYN [KATE]--[9][21][26]ROM--
"NIGHT MUSIC"
"THAT CERTAIN SMILE" & 3 MORE
FAIRFAX, GWEN--[9][21][26]ROM--
"LOVER IN DISGUISE"

TERRY, MAY
KENDRICK, TERRY--[3]MYS--
DORRANCE "ONE TOO MANY" '77

TERSTEGGE, MABEL ALICE
GEORGIANNA, SISTER--[31]

TESSENDORF, KENNETH C.
TESSENDORF, K.C.--[33]JUVENILE

TESSIER, ERNEST MAURICE
DEKOBRA, MAURICE--[2][3][22]FRENCH/MYS--
"THE STREET OF PAINTED LIPS"
& OTHERS '18-62

TESSLER, STEPHANIE GORDON
GORDON, JEFFIE ROSS--W/JUDITH R. ENDERLE, [7][21][31]--
"A TOUCH OF GENIUS" '86
"A TOUCH OF MAGIC" '87

TETERNIKOV, FEDOR K.
SOLOGUB, FEDOR--[2][7][22][23][32]RUSSIAN--
"SWEET SCENTED NAME & OTHER FAIRY STORIES" '15
"THE CREATED LEGEND" '16
MZ "WHITE DOG" MAR '69

TETLEY, EDITH MADELINE
WEETWOOD, E.M.--[8]

TETSUO, KUNIKIDA
KUNIKIDA, DOPPO--[22]JAPANESE

TETTMAR, BETTY EILEEN
SPENCE, BETTY E.--[8]

TETZNER, RUTH
HALLARD, RUTH--[1]

TEVIS, WALTER STONE
TEVIS, WALTER S.--[23]AMERICAN/SF--
GAL-"THE IFTH OF OOFTH" '57

TEW, MARY
DOUGLAS, MARY--[9]ROM

THACKER, CATHY GILLEN
GILLEN, CATHY--[9][21][26]ROM--
"ISLAND OF DESIRE"

THACKERAY, WILLIAM MAKEP.
PENDENNIS, ARTHUR ESQ.--[33]
SOLOMONS, IKEY ESQ. JR.--[33]
TITMARSH, MICHAEL ANGELO--[33]

THACKREY, THEODORE OLIN
STED, RICHARD--V. BERCH LTR TO HUBIN '94, MYS--
SIMON "THEY ALL BLEED RED" '54

THALER, MICHAEL C.
THALER, MIKE--[33]

THARAUD, CHARLES & ERNEST
THARAUD, JEROME & JEAN--[22]FRENCH

THATCHER, PHYLLIS
HARDCASTLE, CATHERINE--[21][26]ROM--
"IN THE ARMS OF A STRANGER"

THAULOW, HARALD
HELL, JON--[29]MYS--
"TILL HERR POLITIMESTEREN" '40

THAYER, EMMA REDINGTON L.
THAYER, LEE--[18][34]MYS--
DODD "BLOOD ON THE KNIGHT" '52
DODD "DUSTY DEATH" '66 & MORE '19-66

THAYER, ERNEST LAWRENCE
PHIN--[33]

THAYER, TIFFANY E.
DOE, JOHN--[3][22][29]AMERICAN/MYS--
DAY "EYE-WITNESS!" '31
ELLSWORTH, ELMER JR.--[8][22]AMERICAN
KING, O.B.--HAWK/BRINEY INTRVW '93, MYS--
DBLDY "FIVE MILLION IN CASH" '32

THAYER, WILLIAM ROSCOE
HERMES, PAUL--[1]

THEE, MARK
GDANSKI, MAREK--[1][31]

THEINER, GEORGE
GEORGE, JONATHAN--W/JOHN [F] BURKE,
[18][29][34]MYS--
MacM "KILL DOG" '70
MacM "DEAD LETTERS" '72

THEODORACOPULOS, PETER
TAKI--[8]

THEODORESCU, ION
ARGHEVI, TUDOR--[22][31]HUNGARIAN

THEROUX, PAUL EDWARD
SLAUGHTER, DOCTOR--B&M COLL #49,
AMERICAN-ENGLISH--
HODDER "HALF MOON STREET" '84

THESLOF, GEORGE HENRIK
BRUMMEL & CO--[29]MYS--
HOK "SKELETTGATAN" '29

THIBAUDEAU, COLLEEN
MORRIS, M.--[1]

THIBAULT, JACQUES ANATOLE
FRANCE, ANATOLE--[2][7][11][22]
[23]FRENCH/SF/FANT--7 NOVELS 1891-36
GEROME--[31]

THIBAULT, MARALEE G.
DAVIS, MARALEE G.--[22]AMERICAN

THIENES, THOMAS L.
NESS, TOM T.--[3]MYS--
PHOENIX "SHORT OF MURDER" '48

THIES, JOYCE ANN S.
JOYCE, JANET--W/JANET BIEBER,[9][21][26]ROM--
"WINTER LADY"
" RARE BREED" & MORE
JOYCE, JENNA LEE--W/JANET BIEBER,
[9][21][26]ROM--
"WINTER'S FIELD"
"CROSS ROADS" & MORE
SCOTT, MELISSA--[9][21][26]ROM--
"TERRITORIAL RIGHT"

THIJM, KAREL JAN L.A.
VAN DEYSSEL, LODEWIJK--[22] DUTCH

THIMBLETHORPE, J. SYLVIA
THORPE, SYLVIA--[3][9][21][29]MYS--
RICH "SMUGGLER'S MOON" '55
& 27 ROMANCE NOVELS

THIMMESCH, NICHOLAS P.
NICHOLAS, WILLIAM--W/WILLIAM O. JOHNSON,[1]

THIRKELL, ANGELA
PARKER, LESLIE--[8][13]AUSTRALIAN

THISTED, VALDEMAR ADOLPH
ROWEL, M.--[2]

THISTLE, MEL[VILLE W.]
BOHR, THEOPHILUS--[1][31]

THODY, PHILIP MALCOLM W.
FRENCH, DON--[1]
GRAVEYARD, ALOYSIUS--[1]

THOLE, CAROLUS A.M.
THOLE, KAREL--[2]

THOM, WILLIAM A. STRANG
MORRISON, J. STRANG--[8]

THOMA, LUDWIG
SCHLEMIHL, PETER--[22]GERMAN

THOMAS, BREE
HOWE, SUSANNAH--[9]ROM--
"FEVER MOON"
"MASQUERADE"
"SNOW FLAME"

THOMAS, CHARLES
TREVELYAN, PERCY--[8]

THOMAS, CORNELIUS D.
T.N.T.--[1][22]AMERICAN
THOMAS, NEAL--[1][22]AMERICAN

THOMAS, CRAIG [DAVID]
GRANT, DAVID--[3][7][29][31]MYS--
HOLT "MOSCOW 500" '79
HOLT "EMERALD DECISION" '80

THOMAS, CURTIS
KINNEY, THOMAS--[3][22]MYS--
DBLDY "DEVIL TAKE THE FOREMOST" '47

THOMAS, DONALD
SELWYN, FRANCIS--[3]MYS--
DEUTSCH "CRACKSMAN ON VELVET" '74
& MORE '74-81

THOMAS, E.
BLUEMANTLE, BRIDGET--[2]

THOMAS, EDWARD LLEWELLYN
GORDON, DON--[8]

THOMAS, ERNEST LEWIS
VAUGHN, RICHARD--[1]

THOMAS, EUGENE
GREY, DONALD--[8][22]MYS
LYNCH, WILLIAM--[40]GERMAN/MYS--
"DER UNHEIMLICHE FREMDE" '32

THOMAS, GORDON
GORDON, TOM--[1][31]ENGLISH
JAMES, BRIAN--[1][22]ENGLISH
STREET, ROBERT--[1][22]ENGLISH

THOMAS, JEANETTE GRISE
GRISE, JEANETTE--[1][31]

THOMAS, JOHN ORAM
ORAM, JOHN--[2][3][11][29]MYS--
ACE 'MAN FROM U.N.C.L.E.':
"THE COPENHAGEN AFFAIR" '65

THOMAS, JOHN PETER
THOMAS, PIRI--[1]

THOMAS, MARY
THOMAS, TAY--[8]

THOMAS, MARY ALICE
EUSTACE, ALICE--[1]

THOMAS, MONA GAY
WILSON, GAYLE--[26]ROM--
HARL 211 "HEART'S DESIRE"

THOMAS, P.J.
THOMAS, PENELOPE--[26]ROM--
"THIEF OF HEARTS"
"MASTER OF BLACKWOOD" & MORE

THOMAS, PETER
PEDERAK, SIMON--[1]

THOMAS, PETER & DONNA
PAPERMAKER, PETER--[7]--
GDBKPR "TALE OF CARA-SOU & HIS MAGIC WORD" '79
"THREE CEDARS:SS COLL." '78

THOMAS, PHILIP EDWARD
EASTAWAY, EDWARD--[8][22][31]ENGLISH

THOMAS, R. MURRAY
ROBERTS, TOM--[22]AMERICAN

THOMAS, REG
PRESTON, JANE--[8]

THOMAS, REGINALD GEORGE
DUVAL, HENRI--PPCC#5,[27]ROM,HP--
CURZON "PASSION'S VICTIM" '47
CURZON "PICK-UP FOR LOVE" '48
LAMOUR, ANDRE--[27]ENGLISH,HP--AMALG
LESTRANGE, PAUL--[27]ENGLISH,HP-- AMALG
NELSON, BARDY--[1]
PURLEY, JOHN--[1][3]MYS--
AMALG "MANSION ON THE MOOR" '43
STORM, IVAN--[1]
STUART, MICHAEL--[1]
WILSON, REG--[1]

THOMAS, ROBERT RICHARD
HOWERD, GARETH--[8]

THOMAS, RONALD WILLS
BOGAR, JEFF--[22][29][34]MYS--
HAM "UNDERCURRENT" '53
HAM "PAY-OFF FOR PAULA" '52
HAM "LADY, PASS MY GAT" '52
HAM "FIREZONE" '54
HAM "CONCRETE CURTAIN" '54
HAM "LAND PIRATE" '55
HAM "PAINTED ON A DONKEY CART" '55
HAM "PINK FILM" '55
HAM "THE SPEED QUEENS" '55
CADELL, JAMES--[1][22][29]MYS
WILLS, RONALD--[3][22][29]MYS--
WINGATE "BIG FISH" '51
WINGATE "BLACK WEAVER" '52 & MORE '51-54

THOMAS, ROSS [ELMORE]
BLEECK, OLIVER--[2][3][18][29]MYS--
MRW "HIGHBINDERS" '74
MRW "PROCANE CHRONICLE" '72 & 3 MORE '70-6

THOMAS, SARA SALLY
JACKSON, SARA--W/DAVID J. WINGROVE,[31]

THOMAS, STANLEY C.
WYANDOTTE, STEVE--[8][32]MYS--
AHMM "AN ILL WIND" APR '66

THOMAS, THEODORE L.
LOCKHARD, LEONARD--W/CHARLES HARNESS, [2][23]SF--
THOMAS, COGSWELL--W/THEODORE COGSWELL,[11]SF--
THOMAS, TED--[23]SF

THOMAS, THOMAS T[HURSTON]
WREN, THOMAS--[7][23]SF--
BAEN "THE DOOMSDAY EFFECT" '86

THOMAS, WALTER DILL JR.
DILL, WALTER--[8]

THOMAS, WILLIAM GEORGE
MONCRIEFF, WILLIAM THOMAS--[13]AUSTRALIAN

THOMAS, [W] MILES [W]
BARON OF REMENHAM--[31]

THOMASHOWER, DOROTHY
THOMAS, DOROTHY--[8]

THOMPSON, A.M.
DANGLE--[8]

THOMPSON, ALFIE
DANIELS, VAL--[21][26]ROM--
"SILVER BELLS"

THOMPSON, ALLYN
SHANNON, BESS--[21][26]ROM--
"GOING, GOING, GONE"

THOMPSON, ANTHONY ALLERT
ALBAN, ANTONY--[1][2][10][11]

THOMPSON, ARIADNE
VAN MATRE, PAZ--[1]

THOMPSON, ARTHUR L. BELL
CLIFFORD, FRANCIS--[3][18][29][32]MYS--
HODDER "NAKED RUNNER" '66
HODDER "BLINDSIDE" '71
CC "TURN & TURN ABOUT" AUG '74
& 14 MORE '55-74

THOMPSON, ARTHUR LEONARD
THOMPSON, A.L.B.--[31]

THOMPSON, AUGUSTO GOEMINE
HALMAR, AUGUSTO D'--[22] CHILEAN

THOMPSON, CHARLES J.S.
THOMPSON, CHESWICK J.--[1]

THOMPSON, DANETTE
CHARTIER, DANETTE--W/ANNETTE LI,[26]ROM--
"MIDNIGHT PROMISES"

THOMPSON, DON[ALD ARTHUR]
O'DONNELL, DICK--W/RICHARD A. LUPOFF,[1]

THOMPSON, EDWARD ANTHONY
LEJEUNE, ANTHONY--[3][18][40]MYS--
MacD "MR. DIABLO" '60
MacD "GLINT OF SPEARS" '63 & MORE '59-67

THOMPSON, ELIZABETH ALLEN
ALLEN, ELIZABETH--[1][31]

THOMPSON, ELLEN PERRONET
PERONNE--[1]

THOMPSON, ERNEST EVAN S.
SETON, ERNEST THOMPSON--[1][22]
ENGLISH-CANADIAN
THOMPSON, WOLF--[1]

THOMPSON, EUGENE ALLEN
THOMPSON, GENE--[7]SF--
RANDOM "LUPE" '77

THOMPSON, GEORGE SELDEN
SELDEN, GEORGE--[2][7][22][33]AMERICAN--
'TUCKER & HARRY' #2 & 3

THOMPSON, GRACE E.
HOPE, CAMILLA--[1][3]MYS--
LONG "MOON OF JOY" '27
LONG "CURIOUSLY PLANNED" '28
LONG "LONG SHADOWS" '28

THOMPSON, HARLAN HOWARD
HOLT, STEPHEN--[1][22][31][33]AMERICAN

THOMPSON, HUNTER S.
DUKE, RAOUL--[1]AMERICAN
OWL, SEBASTIAN--[1][22]AMERICAN

THOMPSON, J.W.M.
QUINCE, PETER--[8]

THOMPSON, JAMES W.
ELETHEA, ABBA--[31]

THOMPSON, JAMES [MYERS]
THOMPSON, JAMES--M. LANTEIGNE-'ANOTHER THOMPSON'-PP 9, P42
THOMPSON, JIM--[3][29][32]MYS--
LION 99 "BAD BOY" '53
LION 108 "A SWELL LOOKING BABE" '54
MM "BELLBOY" FEB '56
MM "PROWLERS IN THE PEAR TREES" MAR '56
EQMM "FLAW IN THE SYSTEM" JUL '56
AHMM "CELLINI CHALICE" DEC '56
MM "MURDER CAME ON THE MAYFLOWER" NOV '56
SIGN "WILD TOWN" '57
AHMM "FRIGHTENING FRAMMIS" FEB '57
SH "FOREVER AFTER" MAY '60
GM 1502 "TEXAS BY THE TAIL" '65
EQMM "EXACTLY WHAT HAPPENED" APR '67& MORE
WILLINGHAM, CALDER--W/CALDER WILLINGHAM, [18]WAR--
SCRNPLAY/NOVEL "PATHS OF GLORY"

THOMPSON, JANE MAUDE [I]
IRELAND, MAUDE--[1]

THOMPSON, JEAN M.
JACK FROST LADY--[1]

THOMPSON, JESSE JACKSON
THOMPSON, J.J.--[1]

THOMPSON, JOAN LEE
HENRY, JOAN--V. BERCH LTR TO HUBIN '94, MYS--
DBLDY "YIELD TO THE NIGHT" '54

THOMPSON, JOHN H.
HEADON, JOHN--[1]
JOHNS, THOMPSON--[1]

THOMPSON, MARGARET CURTIS
THOMPSON, MAGGIE--[7]--
SF COLLECTIBLES GUIDE PUBL '89

THOMPSON, MARMADUKE
MARMADUKE, T.--[1]

THOMPSON, MRS. ALFRED H.
PALMER, LUCILE--[3]MYS--
SARGENT "CAT-EYE" '49

THOMPSON, MURIEL STUART
STUART, MIRANDA--[1][3]MYS--
HODDER "DEAD MEN SING NO SONGS" '39

THOMPSON, PAULA & MARCELA
FLINDT, DAWN--[9]ROM--
"POWER WITHIN"
"PRAIRIE CRY" & MORE

THOMPSON, PAULA & MARCELA [CONT]
MUNN, VELLA--[10]MYS--
HARL 6 "FIREDANCE"
HARL "TOUCH A WILD HEART" & MORE
THOMPSON, PAMELA--[3][9][21][26]MYS/ROM--
HARL "RAINBOW RIBBON" '84
HARL "THE WELLSPRING"

THOMPSON, PHYLLIS [HOGE]
HOGE, PHYLLIS--[31]--
"ARTICHOKE & OTHER POEMS" '69
MORGAN, PHYLLIS--[8]
ROSE, PHYLLIS--[8]

THOMPSON, RALPH J.
RAOUL--[34]MYS--
TORCHSTREAM "FORTUNE SPINS AUBURN" '46

THOMPSON, RICHARD
HOLMS, G. RANDOLPH--V. BERCH LTR TO HUBIN '94, MYS--
VT "HOUNDS OF VATICAN, OR HOLME'S LAST BOW" '86

THOMPSON, ROBERT
DRURY, REBECCA--[21]ROM,HP--
'WOMEN AT WAR'SERIES:
"SISTERS OF BATTLE"

THOMPSON, RUTH PLUMLY
BAUM, L. FRANK--[31][33]GHOSTED--

THOMPSON, STEPHANIE PARIS
BALDWIN, STEVIE--[1]

THOMPSON, THOMAS [TOMMY]
APPELL, GEORGE C.--C. WINTEROWD CALL '94, [32]MYS--
JU "GIFT WRAPPED" MAY '55
KERMIT, LANCE--C. WINTEROWD CALL '94, WEST,HP--

THOMPSON, VICKI L.
KEATON, COREY--W/MARY T. ENGELS, [9][21][26]ROM--
"THE NESTING INSTINCT"
KENYON, CORY--W/MARY T. ENGELS,[9][21][26]ROM--
"RUFFLED FEATHERS"
"SHEER DELIGHT" & 3 MORE

THOMPSON, WILLIAM TAPPAN
JONES, MAJOR JOSEPH--[31]

THOMPSON-MORAGA, GARY A.
THOMPSON, GARY--[7]SF/HOR--
LEIS "CHUMASH" '86

THOMSEN, FREIDA
MACKENDRICK, LOUISE--[21][26]ROM,HP--
"SECOND LADY CAMERON"
[SHARED AT LEAST W/GARDNER F. FOX]

THOMSON, ARTHUR
ATOM--[2]

THOMSON, ARTHUR ALEX.
THOMSON, A.A.--[1]

THOMSON, CHRISTINE C.
ALEXANDER, DAIR--[1][2][11][34]MYS--
HALE "PENELOPE'S DAUGHTER" '75
CAMPBELL, MOLLY--[1][2][11]
HARTLEY, CHRISTINE--[1][2][11]
RICHARDSON, FLAVIA--[1][2][11]

THOMSON, DAISY HICKS
PETERSON, SIMONE--[1]
ROE, M.S.--[1]
THOMSON, D.H.--[21]ROM--
"ITALIAN FOR LOVE"
THOMSON, JONATHAN H.--[1]

THOMSON, DAVID L.
DAVIDSON, T.L.--[1][3][29]MYS--
METHUEN "MURDER IN THE LABORATORY" '29

THOMSON, DEREK S.
MACTHOMAS, RUARAIDH--[8]

THOMSON, GEORGE MALCOLM
MACDONALD, AENEAS--[22] SCOTTISH-ENGLISH

THOMSON, JAMES
B.V.--[31]

THOMSON, MORTIMER
DOESTICKS, Q.K. PHILANDER--[31]

THOMSON, NORMAN
NORMAN, EARL--[3]MYS--
BERK "KILL ME IN TOKYO" '58
BERK "KILL ME IN ATAMI" '62 & 7 MORE '58-76

THOMSON, ROBERT
CHISHTI, HAKIM M.--[31]

THOMSON, WILLIAM
A MAN IN THE MOON--[2]

THORIS, LARS
BRENMAN, CLAES--[29]MYS--
"MANNEN SOMM KALLADE SIG WALL" '78

THORLEIFSON, ALEX
THORNE, ALEXANDRA--[26]ROM--
"INTIMATE STRANGERS" & 4 OTHER NOVELS

THORN, JOHN
JONES, SANFORD W.--[33]

THORNDIKE, RUSSELL
BUCHANAN, WILLIAM--W/WILLIAM RAY BUCK,
[22]AMERICAN

THORNE, BLISS KIRBY
THORNE, B.K. TED--[22]AMERICAN
VANDAL, CAMERON--[22]AMERICAN

THORNE, ISABEL MARY
VILLIERS, ELIZABETH--[8]

THORNE, SABINA
JOHNSON, SABINA THORNE--[31]

THORNETT, ERNEST BASIL C.
PENNY, RUPERT--[3][29]MYS--
COLLINS "TALKATIVE POLICEMAN" '36
COLLINS "POLICEMAN'S HOLIDAY" '37 & MORE

THORNTON, EMMA SHORE
THORNTON, JERRY--[1]

THOROLD, WILLIAM JAMES
BARRON, LOUIE--[1]

THORP, JOSEPH
T.--[8]

THORPE, GEORGE
THORPE, E.G.--[1]

THORPE, JOHN
CAMPBELL, DUNCAN--[8]
CENTAUR--[8]
SCOTT, DOUGLAS--[8]

THORSON, DELOS RUSSELL
CHRISTIAN, KIT--W/SARA W. THORSON,[3][22]MYS--
DUTTON "DEATH & BITTERS" '43

THORSON, SARA WINFREE
CHRISTIAN, KIT--W/DELOS R. THORSON,[3][22]MYS--
DUTTON "DEATH & BITTERS" '43

THORVALL, KERSTIN
THORVALL-FALK, KERSTIN--[1]

THORWALD, JURGEN
BONGARTZ, HEINZ--[31]

THUNSTROM, GORAN
MORK, PAUL BADURA--[29]MYS--
BONNIER "HALLONFALLET KANSKE ENDECKARE" '67

THURLO, AIMEE S.
DUVAL, AIMEE--[9][21][26]ROM--
"HALFWAY THERE"
"AFTER THE RAIN" & 10 MORE
MARTEL, AIMEE--[9][21][26]ROM--
"THE FIRES WITHIN"
"HERO AT LARGE"

THURLOW, DAVID MICHAEL
MACGOWAN, JONATHAN--[34]MYS--
HALE "CHARGE IS RAPE" '78
HALE "DEATH AT THE GAMES '80
HALE "NATURE OF THE BEAST" '85

THURLOW-CRAIG, CHARLES W.
CRAIG, WILLIAM--[23]SF--
"PLAGUE OVER LONDON" '39

THURMAN, WALLACE HENRY
CASEY, PATRICK--[31]

THWAITE, JEANNE
HAIGHT, JAMES T.--W/HARRY ROSKOLENKO,
V. BERCH-'AFTER DARK' SERIES, BAE 27,[31]--
MacF 95-167 "SAN FRANCISCO AFTER DARK" '71

THYNN, ALEXANDER GEORGE
THYNNE, ALEXANDER--[34]MYS--
ALLEN "THE CARRY-COT" '72

TIBBETTS, JOHN CARTER
KETCH, JACK--[31]

TICHBORNE, HENRY
SUNDOWNER--[8]

TICHENOR, VIVIAN H.
HARRIS, VIVIAN--[9][21][26]ROM--
"A WORTHY CHARADE"

TIDD, DIANE
HART, CATHERINE--CRPG,[9][21][26]ROM--
AV 76876 "IRRESISTIBLE" '94
AV 76878 SPLENDOR" '93 & MORE

TIECK, JOHANN LUDWIG
LEBERECHT, PETER--[2][11][16]

TIERNAN, FRANCIS C.
REID, CHRISTIAN--[1]

TIERNEY, JOHN LAWRENCE
JAMES, BRIAN--[8][13][34]AUSTRALIAN--
ANGUS "COOKABUNDY BRIDGE & OTHER STORIES" '46
"BUNYIP OF BARNEY'S ELBOW" '56
ANGUS "BIG BURN" '65

TIFFANY, E.A.
SAMUELS, E.A.--[1]

TIGGES, JOHN THOMAS
ESSEX, WILLIAM--[7]SF--
LEIS "FROM BELOW" '89
LEIS "THE PACK" '87
LEIS "SLIME" '88

TILBURN, E.O.
NED, NEVADA--[3]WEST/MYS-- 5 NOVELS 1888-1901
OLIVER, DR. N.T.--[3]WEST/MYS--
8 NOVELS 1889-1900

TILBURNE, A.R.
TILBURNE, LEE--[2]

TILEY, VALERIE
GRIFFITH, MORGAN--[2]

TILLETT, DOROTHY S.
STRANGE, JOHN STEPHEN--[2][3][18][29]MYS--
DBLDY "MURDER AT WORLD'S END" '43
"STRNGLER FIG" '30 & MORE

TILLEY, E.D.
TILLEY, GENE--[8]

TILLOTSON, JOSEPH W.
FUQUA, ROBERT--[1][2][11][23]

TILLY, RONALD SUGDEN
SIMPSON, RONALD--V. BERCH--
MON PSEUDS, BAE 9,[34]MYS--
MON 185 "EVE'S APPLE" '61
MON 219 "MAKE EVERY KISS COUNT" '61
MON 413 "END OF A DIPLOMAT" '64
MON 562 "RETURN OF COLONEL PHO" '65

TILLYARD, EUSTACE M.W.
TILLYARD, E.M.W.--[1]

TILMAN, HAROLD WILLIAM
TILMAN, H.W.--B&M COLL #71, P69,
ENGLISH/ADVENTURE--
CAMBRIDGE PRESS '37-77

TILSLEY, FRANK
X.Y.Z.--[8]

TILSLEY, PETER
HADDON, PETER--[1]

TILTMAN, HUGH HESSELL
DAVENPORT, TEX--[1]
HESSELL, HENRY--[1]

TILTMAN, RONALD FRANK
FRASER, RONALD--[22][31]ENGLISH

TILTON, MADONNA ELAINE
TILTON, RAFAEL--[1][33]

TIMMS, EDWARD VIVIAN
DANE, ZEL--[31]
TIMMS, E.V.--[26][31]ROM--
"SCARLET FRONTIER"
"VALLEYS BEYOND"
"BECKONING SHORE"& 7 MORE

TIMSON, KEITH
DE WINTERS, DANIELLE--[9][21][26]ROM--
"PASSIONATE REBEL"

TINA, DOROTHY LES
TINA--[2] ?

TINDALL, WILLIAM YORK
YORICK, A.P.--[8]

TINE, ROBERT
DRAKE, JACK--LACHMAN/GOODE LST '93, MYS--
HARDING, RICHARD--[3][7][23]MYS--
HALE "GAY DECEPTION" '67
PINN 'OUTRIDER SURVIVALIST' SEQ '84-5
"RED HEAT" '86
"BEVERLY HILLS COP II" '87

TINSLEY, THEODORE
GRANT, MAXWELL--[2][11][37]MYS,HP--
SHDM "PARTNERS OF PERIL" '36
SHDM "FIFTH NAPOLEON"
SHDM "DEATH'S HARLEQUIN"
& 20 PLUS OTHERS

TIPPETTE, GILES
YOUNG, WILSON--THIESSEN RVW '93,[1][28]WEST--
DELL "AUSTIN DAVIS" '75
DELL "THE SUNSHINE KILLERS" '75
DELL "HARD LUCK MONEY" '82

TIRBUTT, HONORIA
PAGE, EMMA--[1][3]MYS--
HALE "MISSING WOMAN" '80
COLLINS "COLD LIGHT OF DAY" '83 3 MORE

TITCHENER, LOUISE
HILL, ALEXIS--W/RUTH GLICK,[9][21][26]ROM--
"IN THE ARMS OF LOVE"
HOWARD, ALYSSA--W/RUTH GLICK, EILEEN BUCKHOLTZ & CAROLYN MALES,[21]ROM--
"SOUTHERN PERSUASION"
"LOVE IS ELECTED"
JORDAN, ALEXIS HILL--W/RUTH GLICK,
[9][21][26]ROM--
"SUMMER STARS
"STOLEN PASSION" & 6 MORE
RICHARDS, CLARE--W/CAROLYN MALES,[9][21]ROM--
"RENAISSANCE SUMMER"
RICHMOND, CLARE--W/CAROLYN MALES,[9][21]ROM--
"RUNNAWAY HEART"
"BRIDE'S INN"
"PIRATE'S LEGACY
SILVERLOCK, ANNE--[9][21][26]ROM--
"FANTASY LOVER"
"CASANOVA'S MASTER" & 4 MORE
SILVERWOOD, JANE--[9][21][26]ROM--
"TENDER TRAP"
"EYE OF THE JAGUAR" & MORE
MARLOWE, TESS--W/RUTH GLICK,[21][26]ROM--
"INDISCREET"

TITLE, ELSIE
TYLER, ALISON--[9][21][26][34]--
DELL "CHASE THE SUN" '87
DELL "TEMPTING ANGEL" & 25 MORE

TITTERTON, WILLIAM R.
TITTERTON, W.R.--[1]

TITUS, CORAL HOYLE
HOYLE, CORAL--[9][21][26]ROM--
"VIRGIN HEART"
"ART OF THE HUNT" & 2 MORE

TITUS, EVE
LORD, NANCY--[8][31][33]CHILDREN'S BKS--
McGRAW "MY DOG AND I" '58

TOBILEVICH, IVAN KARPOV.
KARPENKO-KARYJ, IVAN--[22] UKRAINIAN

TOBIN, JEAN HOLLOWAY
HOLLOWAY, JEAN--[31]

TOBIN, LEE ANN
FAVOR, ERIKA--[21][26]ROM--
"MOUNTAIN HOME"

TOD, OSMA GALLINGER
COUCH, OSMA PALMER--[1][22][31]AMERICAN
GALLINGER, OSMA COUCH--[1][22][31]AMERICAN

TODD, BARBARA EUPHAN
BOWER, BARBARA--[1][31]
EUPHAN--[1][31]

TODD, HERBERT EATON
TODD, H.E.--[1]

TODD, JOHN M.
FOX, JOHN--[1][31]

TODD, MARGARET
TRAVERS, GRAHAM--[1]

TODD, RUTHVEN CAMPBELL
CAMPBELL, R.T.--[2][3][23][31]SF/MYS--
"OVER THE MOUNTAIN" '39
"LOST TRAVELER" '43 & 8 OTHERS

TOERNUDD, MARGIT
NIININEN, MARGIT--[1]

TOFANI, LOUISE E.
THEOPHANY--[8]

TOFTE, ARTHUR
ANDERSSON, NIC--[1]
BABCOCK, FLORENCE--[1]
BOLES, NICK--[1]

TOGLIATTI, PALMIRO
CORRENTI, MARIO--[31]
ERCOLI, ERCOLE--[31]

TOKOMBAEV, AALY
BALKA--[1]

TOKUTARO, OZAKI
KOYO, OZAKI--[22]JAPANESE

TOLKIEN, JOHN RONALD R.
J.R.R.T.--[1]
TOLKIEN, J.R.R.--[1]
TOLLEIS--[1]

TOLLEMACHE, DAVID
LOVELL, MARK--[1]

TOLLET, GUNNAR
STENHAGEN, JAN-JORAN--[29]MYS--
WORLD WIDE "DATADYRKARNA" '82

TOLLIVER, STEVE
DAVIES, FREDRIC--W/RON ELLIK,[2][23]MYS--
'MAN FROM 'UNCLE':
"CROSS OF GOLD AFFAIR" '68

TOLNAY, THOMAS
TOLNAY, TOM--[7]SF--
WALKER "CELLULOID GANGS" '90

TOLPOLBERG, EDMON
TOPOL, EDWARD--V. BERCH LTR TO HUBIN '94,MYS--
QUARTET "SUBMARINE U-137" '83
MaCD "RED GAS" '86

TOLSTOY, LEV NIKOLALEVICH
TOLSTOY, LEO--[1][32]MYS--
EQMM "EXPENSE OF JUSTICE" APR '63
EQMM "MAN OF GOD" OCT '67

TOMALIN, RUTH
LEAVER, RUTH--[1]

TOMERLIN, JOHN E.
GRANTLAND, KEITH--W/CHARLES BEAUMONT,
V. BERCH-GM PSEUD, PP33,[3]--
GM 701 "RUN FROM THE HUNTER" '57

TOMKINS, JANE H.
HARRISON, JENNIE--[1]

TOMKINS, JULIA MARGUERITE
NEILSON, MARGUERITE--[1][7][21]SF--
WINGATE "BRIDE OF ALBERBURN" '76
WINGATE "DARK PATH"

TOMLIN, ERIC
STUART, FREDERICK--[8]

TOMLINSON, HENRY MAJOR
TOMLINSON, H.M.--[1]

TOMLINSON, JOSHUA LEONARD
LINSON--[8]

TOMPKINS, WALKER A.
ANDERSON, NELSE--L. ROBBINS LTR '94
CARLETON, SCOTT--L. ROBBINS LTR '94
COLE, JACKSON--A. TONIK-COLE CKLST
"SPICY ARMADILLO",WEST,HP--
TEX RGR - 29 STORIES '47-'58
DEELE, PHILIP F.--L. ROBBINS LTR '94, HP
DUNNING, HAL--L. ROBBINS LTR MAR '94, HP
GRIFFIN, ANDREW A.--L. ROBBINS LTR '94
WALKER, REEVE--L. ROBBINS LTR '94
WALLACE, TRENT--L. ROBBINS LTR '94
WOOD, VALENTINE--W. MURRAY-ECHOES #5,HP--

TONKIN, C.B.
PLEDGER, P.J.--[8]

TOOHEY, BARBARA
BENNETT, MARGARET--W/JUNE BIERMANN,[8]
BENNETT, MARGOT--W/JUNE BIERMAN,[32]MYS--
BS "MAN WHO DIDN'T FLY" JAN '60

TOOKE, LOUISE MATHEWS
MATHEWS, LOUISE--[33]

TOOKER, RICHARD [PRESLEY]
LEMKE, HENRY E.--[2]
TOOKER, DICK PRESLEY--[23]AMERICAN/SF--
WT "PLANET PARADISE" '24

TOOMBS, JANE [JENKE]
DRURY, REBECCA--[21]ROM,HP--
'WOMEN AT WAR' SERIES:
"BLUE GLORY"
"SAVAGE BEAUTY"

TOOMBS, JANE [JENKE] [CONT]
STUART, DIANA--[9][21][26]ROM--
"MOON POOL"
"LEADER OF THE PACK" & 4 MORE
SUMNER, OLIVIA--[26]ROM--
"A TRIFLING AFFAIR"
"AN IMPROPER ALLIANCE" & 4 MORE
WILLOUGHBY, LEE DAVIS--[21]ROM,HP--
DELL 'MAKING OF AMERIC' SERIES:
"CREOLES"
"OUTLAWS"

TOOMBS, JOHN
CURTIS, RICHARD HALE--[21]ROM,HP--
'SKYMASTER' SERIES: "BIRDS OF WAR"
KENT, FORTUNE--[3][7][21][31][40]ROM/SF--
BAL "THE OPAL LEGACY" '75 & OTHERS
KENT, PAUL--[7]SF--
BB "THE CRIB" '87
SCOFIELD, JONATHAN--[1][21]HP--
'FREED. FIGHTERS':
"STORM IN THE SOUTH"
WILDE, JOCELYN--[1][9][21][26]ROM--
"BRIDE OF THE BAJA"
"MISTS OF PASSION" & 2 MORE
WILLOUGHBY, LEE DAVIS--[1][21]ROM,HP--
DELL 'MKNG OF AMERICA':
"FORTY NINERS"
"TEXANS"
"BORDER BREED"
"TEXAS RANGERS"
DELL 'WOMEN WHO WON THE WEST' SERIES:
"FLAME OF VIRGINIA CITY"

TOOMER, NATHAN P.
TOOMER, EUGENE--[1]
TOOMER, JEAN--[1]
TOOMER, N[ATHAN] JEAN--[1]

TOONA-ELIN, ELIN[-KAI]
GOTTSCHALK, ELIN TOONA--[1][31]
LEE, ANDREA--[31]

TOOTHMAN, CATHERINE ANN
CLARE, CATHLEEN--V. BERCH LTR '94,[26]ROM--
"CLARISSA"
"FELICIA"
"MISTRESS OF MISHAP"
AV 77432 "TOURNAMENT OF HEARTS" '94

TOPEROFF, SAM
POTTER, FAITH--[1]

TOPOL, EDUARD
NEMOV, ALEXANDER--W/FRIEDRICH NESMANSKY,
[40]GERMAN/MYS--
"SCHURNALIST DIJA BRESCHNEWA" '81

TOPPMAN, LAWRENCE
GARLAND, LAWRENCE--W/STEVE GARLAND,[34]MYS--
OAK KNOLL "AFFAIR OF THE UNPRINCIPLED
PUBLISHER" '83

TORBETT, HARVEY D.L.
DEE, HENRY--[1][22][31]ENGLISH
ISIS--[1][22]ENGLISH

TORDAY, URSULA
ALLARDYCE, PAULA--S. WOOLFOLK-PAPLB CKLST,
BAE 8,[3][9][21]][22]ROM/MYS--
MacF "WITCHES SABBATH '61
& 16 OTHER NOVELS
BLACKSTOCK, CHARITY--[2][3][7][9][29]
[31]ROM/MYS--
"GHOST TOWN"
"DEWEY DEATH" & 14 MORE '56-80

TORDAY, URSULA [CONT]
BLACKSTOCK, LEE--[31][34]MYS--
DBLDY "WOMAN IN THE WOODS" '58
DBLDY "ALL MEN ARE MURDERERS" '58
KEPPEL, CHARLOTTE--[3][9][21][26]ROM/MYS--
HODDER "MADAM, YOU MUST DIE" '75 & 3 MORE

TORKELSON, LAYNE
LAYNE, MARION MARGERY--W/MARION WOOLF
& MARGERY PAPICH,[34]MYS--
DODD "THE BALLOON AFFAIR" '81

TOROK, LOU
CONVICT WRITER, THE--[31]

TORRES-LEVIN, TERESKA [S]
ARCHARD, GEORGE--[1]
TORRES, TERESKA--[1]

TORREY [BUDLONG], WARE
CROSBY, LEE--[3][22][29]MYS--
DUTTON "TERROR BY NIGHT" '38
BELM "BRIDGE HOUSE" '65 & 3 MORE
HALE, JENNIFER--W/FRANK SMITH,[21]ROM--
"PORTRAIT OF EVIL"
"STORMHAVEN" & 5 MORE
PADGET, MEG--[3]MYS--
LAN 72-979 "HOUSE OF STRANGERS" '65
WARE, JUDITH--[3]MYS--
PAPLB "QUARRY HOUSE" '65
SIGN "A TOUCH OF FEAR" '68 & 4 MORE '65-69
WINSLOW, JOAN--[3][29]MYS--
ACE "GRIFFIN TOWERS" '66

TORREY, THERESE V. HOHOFF
HOHOFF, TAY--[31]

TORSVAN, BRUNO TRAVEN
CROVES, HAL--[31]
FEIGE, HERMANN ALBERT O.M--[31]
MARUT, RET--[39]GERMAN
TRAVEN, B.--[2][7][29][32][39]MYS--
POCK 455 "TREASURE OF SIERRA MADRE" '48
MH "EFFECTIVE MEDICINE" AUG '54
MH "TIN CAN" SEPT '54
AC "HIS WIFE'S LEGS" JUL '56
SA "CEREMONY SLIGHTLY DELAYED" OCT '57
"CREATION OF THE SUN & THE MOON" '77 & MORE

TOTH, PAMELA
ROTH, PAMELA--[9][21]ROM--
"TOO MANY WEDDINGS"

TOTTEN, GEORGE O. III
TAO MULIAN--[1]

TOURGEE, ALBION WINEGER
HENRY, EDGAR--[2]

TOURNACHON, FELIX
NADAR--[22]FRENCH

TOURNIER, JACQUES
SAINT-ALBAN, DOMINIQUE--V. BERCH LTR TO
HUBIN '94, MYS--
ST. MARTIN'S "DEJU-VU" '78

TOVELL, RUTH MASSEY
MASSEY, RUTH--[1]

TOWER, STELLA [MARY H.]
WOLSELEY, FAITH--[34]MYS--
MURRAY "WHICH WAY CAME DEATH" '36
MURRAY "SCREENED" '37
CRISP "OLD MRS. WARREN" '45

TOWERS, MAXWELL
RABBIE--[1]

TOWLE, MRS. A.E.
LAWRENCE, MARGERY--[2][11]

TOWLSON, IVAN
ZOOL, M.H.--[7][23]GP

TOWNEND, PETER [R.G.]
GASCOIGNE, PETER--[1][3][29]MYS--
COLLINS "ZERO ALWAYS WINS" '61

TOWNLEY, HOUGHTON
PRESTON, WALFORD--[1]

TOWNLEY-PARKER, CAROLINE
TOWNLEY, CAROL--[1]

TOWNSEND, DORIS M.
CLELLAND, CATHERINE--[1][31]
MCFERRAN, ANN--[1]
MCFERRAN, DORIS--[1]

TOWNSEND, GEORGE ALFRED
GATH--[8]

TOWNSEND, JOAN
POMFRET, JOAN--[1]

TOWNSEND, LARRY
WATSON, J.--[14][34]ADULT--
OLYM TC#511 "SEXUAL ADVENTURES OF SHERLOCK HOLMES" '71

TOWNSEND, MARY ASHLEY
ASHLEY, MARY--[8]
XARIFFA--[8]

TOWNSEND, THOMAS L.
LEE, TAMMIE--[21][26][31][33]ROM--
'LEATHER & LACE' SERIES:
"TEXAS WILDFLOWER"
TOWNSEND, TOM--[33]

TOYNBEE, ROSALIND
MURRAY, ROSALIND--[1]

TOYNE, CLARICE JOY
ARMIDO--[1]

TOZER, ALFRED B.
CARTER, NICHOLAS--[3]HP--
STAFFORD, JOHN K.--[34]MYS,HP--
MAGNET #688 "IN AFTER YEARS: A CRIME THAT COULDN'T BE SOLVED" '11
STEWART, DICK--[34]MYS,HP--
MAGNET #690 "THE HUMAN QUESTION MARK: OR, THE MAN OF MYS" '11

TOZER, BASIL JOHN JOSEPH
VILLAIN, REGARDANT--[1]

TRABIA-BRANCIFORTE, GIUS.
LANZA DEL VASTO, JOSEPH J--[22]ITALIAN-FRENCH

TRACHMAN, MURIEL KARLIN
KARLIN, MURIEL S.--[1][31]

TRACY, ANN BROMFIELD
HIS SISTER--[1]

TRACY, DON[ALD FISKE]
FULLER, ROGER--[2][3][7][11]MYS/SF--
PERMA "SON OF FLUBBER" '63 & OTHERS

TRACY, LOUIS
HOLMES, GORDON--W/M.P. SHIEL,[3][29]MYS--
"FELDISHAM MYSTERY" '10
"HOUSE AROUND THE CORNER" '14
HOLMES, GORDON--[3][29]MYS--
LAURIE "ARNCLIFFE PUZZLE" '06
CASSELL "LATE TENANT" '07 & MORE

TRACY, MARIE D.
ABBOTT, MARGOT--[26]ROM--
"THE INNOCENT HOUR"
ADAMS, AUDRA--[9][21][26]ROM--
"BLUE CHIP BRIDE"
"PEOPLE WILL TALK" & MORE

TRACY, ROGER SHERMAN
HODGE, T. SHIRBY--[2][23]SF--
"WHITE MAN'S BURDEN: A SATIRICAL FORECAST" '15

TRAHEY, JANE
ERLANGER, BABA--[1][31][33]

TRAIN, ARTHUR
LENCY, C.--[1]

TRAINA, DANIELLE STEEL
STEEL, DANIELLE--[21]ROM--
"FULL CIRCLE"
"KALEIDOSCOPE"
"MESSAGE FROM NAM" & 24 MORE

TRALINS, [SANDOR] ROBERT
BIXBY, RAY Z.--[1][31]
KING, NORMAN A.--[1]
LAURANCE, ALFRED D.--[1][31]
MILES, KEITH--[1][2][11][23]SF--
"DRAGON'S TEETH" '73
PALLETTE 102 "FOR LUST OR LOVE"
O'SHEA, SEAN--[2][3][23]MYS--
BEAC B904X "WHISPER" '65
BELM B50-707 "WHAT A WAY TO GO" '66
BELM B50-760 "OPERATION BOUDOIR" '67
BELM B50-798 "INVASION OF THE NYMPHOMANIACS" '67
BELM B50-769 "WIN WITH SIN" '67
BELM B50-782 "NYMPH ISLAND AFFAIR" '67
BELM B50-834 "TOPLESS KITTIES" '68
O'TOOLE, REX--[1]--
BELM B75-211 "CHEATING & INFIDELITY AMERICAN STYLE" '68
SYDNEY, CYNTHIA--[1]
TOOLE, REX--[1]
TRACY, LELAND--[1]
TRAINER, RUSSELL--[1][7][23]ADULT--
BEAC B510F "WARDEN'S WIFE" '62
BEAC B595 "LONESOME WIDOW" '63
NOV 6068 "UNBELIEVABLE 3 & 1 ORGY" '63
PAPLB 54-473 "LOLITA COMPLEX" '67
MDWD F307 "NO WAY BACK" '63
MDWD F361 "LOVE STARVED" '64
MDWD F378 "HIS DAUGHTER'S FRIEND" '64
MDWD 32-480 "TROUBLE-MAKER" '65
BRNDN 1163 "THREE MEN FOR LIBBY D"
BRNDN 6431 "VIOLENCE OF ADULTERY"
BRNDN "SEX, JEALOUSY & CONFLICT"
TRAINOR, RICHARD--[1]ADULT--
CLLB 13 "JEALOUS LOVER"
TRAINOR, SANDY--[7]--
PLEASURE BOOKS-"FUTURE SEX" 1979
?? UNCONFIRMED ??
TRAINOR, STARR--[7][23]--
PLEASURE BOOKS-"PLEASURE PLANET" 1979
?? UNCONFIRMED ??
TRALINS, BIG BOB--MUNROE RVW '93
TRALINS, BOB--[1]--

TRALINS, [SANDOR] ROBERT [CONT]
TRALINS, BOB
BELM B50-704 "THE MISS FROM SIS" '66
BELM B50-745 "RING A DING UFO" '67
NOV 5046 "TORRID ISLAND" '61
NOV 5050 "PRIMITIVE ORGY" '61
NOV 5059 "5 WILD DAMES" '61
NOV 5073 "SEDUCTIVE SALON" '62
NOV 5077 "HIRED NYMPHO" '62
NOV 6062 "INCREDIBLE ORGY" '62
BEAC 904 "WHISPER" '65
NOV 6064 "COLOSSAL CARNALITY" '60
TRAUBE, RUY--[1]--
BELM B75-209 "THE SEDUCTION ART" '68
VERDON, DOROTHY--[1]

TRALOW, JOHANNES
LOW, HANNES--[1]

TRAN BICH LAN
NGUYEN SA--[1]

TRANQUILLI, SECONDO
SILONE, IGNAZIO--[1][22][40]ITALIAN/MYS--
"UNA MANCIATA DI MORE" '85

TRANSUE, JACOB
MATHESON, JOAN--[11]

TRANTER, NIGEL [G]
TREDGOLD, NYE--[1][22] SCOTTISH

TRASK, KATE NICHOLS
TRASK, KATRINA--[8]

TRASK, MRS. S.
CLARA AUGUSTA--[1]

TRAUGOTT, ELIZABETH CLOSS
CLOSS, ELIZABETH--[31]

TRAUTMAN, JACKIE
DALTON, JACKIE--[34]MYS--
LYNX "DARK LULLABY" '88
"FORBIDDEN TREASURE"

TRAVERS, STEPHEN
RADCLIFFE, GARNETT--[2][32]MYS--
SUS "PIT OF SCREAMS" NOV '58

TRAYNOR, PAGE & ANTHONY
ANTHONY, EVELYN--[9][21][34]ROM--
ZEBRA "BALLET OF FEAR" '79
ZEBRA "BALLET OF DEATH" '79

TREAT, LAWRENCE
LORD, GORDON--LACHMAN LST '94
CONTENTO & GREENBERG, MYS--
AHMM "TIME & TIDE" MAY '57

TRECKER, JANICE LAW
LAW, JANICE--[1][31]

TREDEZ, ALAIN
TREZ--[22]FRENCH
TREZ, ALAIN--[33]

TREDEZ, DENISE [LAUGIER]
TREZ, DENISE--[22][33]FRENCH

TREDGOLD, NYE
TRANTER, NIGEL [GODWIN]--[3][29]MYS--
WARD "FAIR GAME" '50
HODDER "CABLE FROM KABUL" '68
& 36 MORE '37-68

TREDINNICK, WILLIAM JR.
KANEMAN, SOL--[2]
TAROKATH, CARMUTH--[2]
TREDINICK, BILL & KANEMAN--[2]

TREISTER, BERNARD WILLIAM
ST. JAMES, BERNARD--[34]MYS--
HARPER "APRIL THIRTEENTH" '78
"WITCH" '79
DBLDY "SEVEN DREAMERS" '82

TREMAINE, F. ORLIN
BEALE, ANNE--[2][11]
FREDERICK, ORLIN--[1][2][23]SF--
WEIRD TALES "THE THROWBACK" '26
LANE, ARTHUR--[1][2][11]
PAINE, GUTHRIE--[1][2][11]
SAND, WARREN B.--[1][2][11]
SANTOS, ALFRED--[1][2][11]
VAN LORNE, WARNER--[2][11]SP--1 STORY

TREMAINE, NELSON
VAN LORNE, WARNER--[1][2][11]SP--
ALL BUT 1 STORY

TREMBLAY, ERNEST A. II
DRURY, REBECCA--[21]ROM,HP--
'WOMEN AT WAR' SERIES:
"TEARS & LAUGHTER"

TREML, LAJOS
TAMAS, LAJOS--[1]

TRENERY, GLADYS GORDON
PENDARVES, G.G.--[2][7][11][32]MYS--
BR FANT SOC "DEVILS GRAVEYARD" '88
MZ "DARK STAR" MAY '68
MZ "WHISTLING CORPSE" FALL '70
MZ "ALTAR OF MELEK TAOS" FEB '71

TRENITE, GIJSBERT J.N.
CHARIVARIUS--[22]DUTCH

TRENT, ANN
BLYTHE, JOYCE--[1]
CARLTON, ANN--[1]
CROSSE, ELAINE--[1]
DESANA, DOROTHY--[1]
SERNICOLI, DAVIDE--[1]

TRENT, DAN & LYNDA
TRENT, DANIELLE--[9][21][26]ROM--
"WINTER ROSES"
TRENT, LYNDA--[9][21][26]ROM--
"BLACKHAWK"
"ANOTHER RAINBOW" & 36 MORE

TRENT, PAUL
KAYE, WILMOT--[1]

TREVATHAN, ROBERT E.
ROBERTS, TREV--[28]WEST--
7 ARCADIA NOVELS '59-67

TREVELYAN, GEORGE OTTO
BROUGHTON, H.--[1]

TREVELYAN, KATHARINE
GOETSCH-TREVELYAN, KATHR.--[31]

TREVES, VIRGINIA
CORDELIA--[1]

TREVINO, ELIZABETH B.
BORTON, ELIZABETH--[1][31][33]

TREVOR, ELLESTON
BLACK, MANSELL--[2][3][18][29]MYS--
HODDER "DEAD ON COURSE" '51
HODDER "SINISTER CARGO" '51 & MORE
BURGESS, TREVOR--[2][18][23]MYS--
HUTCH "A SPY AT MONK'S COURT" '49
HUTCH "THE MYSTERY OF THE MISSING BOOK" '50
HUTCH "RACING WRAITH" '53
DUDLEY, TREVOR--[11]
DUDLEY-SMITH, T.--[18]--4 NOVELS '43-8
CHILDRENS' BOOKS
FITZALAN--[1]
FITZALAN, ROGER--[2][18][31][33]ROM--
DAVIES "A BLAZE OF ARMS" '67
RPRTD AS BY 'ADAM HALL' PYR '72
HALL, ADAM--[3][7][18]MYS--
COLLINS "PEKING TARGET" '81
COLLINS "SCORPION SIGNAL" '79
& 9 MORE '63-79
NORTH, HOWARD--[1][2][3]MYS--
COLLINS "EXPRESSWAY" '73
RATTRAY, SIMON--[1][2][3]MYS--
BRDMN 'ADAM HALL' BOOKS IN ENGLAND
SAND, GEORGE--[2]
SCOTT, WARWICK--[3][18][33]--
DAVIES "IMAGE IN THE DUST" '51
DAVIES "DOOMSDAY" '52
DAVIES "NAKED CANVAS" '54
SMITH, CAESAR--[3][5][11][23]SF/HOR--
WINGATE "HEATWAVE" '57
SMITH, T.D.--[1]

TREVOR, LUCY MERIOL
TREVOR, MERIOL--[21]ROM--
"FORTUNATE MARRIAGE"
"WANTON FIRES"
"SUN WITH A FACE"

TREWIN, J.C.
J.C.T.--[8]

TRIBICH, SUSAN
BLUMENTHAL, SUSAN--[31]

TRIEGEL, LINDA J.
KIDD, ELIZABETH--[21][26][34]ROM--
WARNER "SWEET SECRETS" '88

TRIEM, PAUL ELLSWORTH
ELLSWORTH, PAUL--[1][22]AMERICAN

TRIFONOV, GEORGII E.
DEMIN, MIKHAIL--[1]
DYOMIN, MIKHAIL--[1]

TRIGG, HARRY DAVIS
CLARK, PARLIN--[31]

TRIGLIA, JOAN
TRIGLIA, JUNE--W/JUNE E. CASEY,[21]ROM--
"BOUND BY BLOOD"

TRIMBLE, BARBARA MARGARET
BLAKE, MARGARET--[3][18][29]MYS--
HALE "FLIGHT FORM FEAR" '73
HALE "COURIER TO DANGER" '73 & 6 MORE
GILL, B.M.--[3][18]MYS--
HODDER "TWELFTH JUROR" '84
HODDER "SEMINAR FOR MURDER" '85 & 7 MORE
GILL, BARBARA--[29]MYS
GILMOUR, BARBARA--[31]

TRIMBLE, BETTY JOANN C.
TRIMBLE, BJO--[7]SF--
'STARTREK' NON-FICT BOOKS

TRIMBLE, CHLOE MARIA
GARTNER, CHLOE--[8]

TRIMBLE, JACQUEL. WHITNEY
WHITNEY, J.L.H.--[3][22]AMERICAN/MYS--
ACE "WHISPER OF SHADOWS" '65

TRIMBLE, JOHN
BLAKE, ROGER--V. BERCH-BRNDN/BC PSEUDOS,
BAE 22,[3]ADULT--
AE "CAPER AT CANAVERAL" '63
COMET "STRIPPED FOR MURDER" '63
'MARK SADE' ON CVR

TRIMBLE, LOUIS P.
BROCK, STUART--[2][3][28][29]MYS/WEST--
MILL "DEATH IS MY LOVER" '48
MILL "JUST AROUND THE CORONER" '48
BOUREGY "RAILTOWN SHERIFF" '49
ACE D23 "BRING BACK HER BODY" '53
AVALON "DOUBLE-CROSS RANCH" '54
AVALON "ACTION AT BOUNDARY PEAK" '55
AVALON "WHISPERING CANYON" '55
AVALON "FORBIDDEN RANGE" '56
GRAPH 136 "KILLER'S CHOICE" '56
HOLLIS, JIM--W/HOLLIS [S] SUMMERS,[1]AMERICAN
ROURKE, JAMES--[1]AMERICAN
TRAVIS, GERRY--[2][3][28]MYS--
PHOENIX "TARNISHED LOVE" '42
AVALON "THE BIG BITE" '57
AVALON "A LOVELY MASK FOR MURDER" '56
MYH "A LOVELY MASK FOR MURDER" '56
MYH "BIG BITE" '57

TRIMMER, ERIC J.
JAMESON, ERIC--[8][31]
LAWSON, DR. PHILIP--[8]

TRINCHIERI, CAMILLA
CRESPI, CAMILLA T.--HAWK/TRINCHIERI
INTRVW '93, MYS--
CRESPI, TRELLA [TRILLA]--HAWK/TRINCHIERI
INTRVW '93, MYS--
'TROUBLE WITH...' NOVELS

TRINER, JEANNE
JENNINGS, CAYLIN--W/KAYE L. CLEMENTS,[9]ROM
TRINER, JEANNE KAYE--W/KAYE L. CLEMENTS,[9]ROM

TRINGHAM, NEAL
ZOOL, M.H.--[7][23] GROUP PSEUD.

TRIPLETT, WILLIAM SAMUEL
BULL, SGT. TERRY--[2][7]

TRIPP, H. ALKER
HOE, LEE--[8]

TRIPP, KAREN
GERSHON, KAREN--[31]

TRIPP, KATHLEEN
LOEWENTHAL, KAREN--[8]

TRIPP, MILES [BARTON]
BRETT, JOHN MICHAEL--[3][29][31]MYS--
BARKER "A PLAGUE OF DRAGONS" '65
BARKER "A CARGO OF SPENT EVIL" '66
BRETT, MICHAEL--[3][18][22][29]MYS--
GM 1360 "DIECAST" '63
BRETT, SIMON--[29]MYS--
MacM "A SHOCK TO THE SYSTEM" '84
LETT, ANTHONY--[29]MYS

TRIPPE, PETER
PETERS, GEOFFREY--[8]

TRIVELPEACE, LAUREL
MARKS, HANNAH K.--V. BERCH LTR TO HUBIN '94,[1]MYS-- "TRIAD" '80

TROCCHI, ALEXANDER
DE LAS LUNAS, CARMENCITA--[8][14]ADULT--OLYM
HARRIS, FRANK--[14]ADULT,GHOSTED-- OLYM-"MY LIFE & LOVES"
LENGEL, FRANCES--J. PRESSMAN-LESBIANA, BAE 20, C. ECKHOFF SLST,[1][14]ADULT-- GRNLF "CARNAL DAYS OF HELEN SEFERIS" '67 OLYM OB-504 "HELEN & DESIRE" '68

TROGDON, WILLIAM
LEAST HEAT MOON, WILLIAM--[1][31]

TROKE, MOLLY
BOURNE, HESTER--[3][9][21][29]MYS-- HURST "SPANISH HOUSE" '62 HURST "RED RAINCOAT" '70 & 4 MORE '64-71

TRONCHE, PHILIPPE
CURVAL, PHILIPPE--[2][7][23]FRENCH/SF-- "BRAVE OLD WORLD"

TRONCOSCO DE LA CONCHA, M
BUSCON, JUAN--[1]

TRONG-TRI, NGUYA
MAC-TU, HAN--[22] VIETNAMESE

TROTMAN, JACK H. & PALMA
PENN, JOHN--[3]MYS-- COLLINS "ACCIDENT PRONE" '87 & 4 MORE '82-9

TROTMAN, PALMA HARCOURT
HARCOURT, PALMA--LACHMAN/EASTER LST '93, MYS-- COLLINS "DOUBLE DECEIT" '90 & 16 MORE '74-90

TROTTA, GERALDINE
TROTTA, GERI--[34]MYS-- DODD "VERONICA DIED MONDAY" '52 BRDMN "DEAD AS DIAMONDS" '56

TROTTER, GRACE V.
PASCHAL, NANCY--[1][33]

TROUBETZKOI, PRINCESS
RIVES, AMELIA--[8]

TROUVE, ROGER
KARL, ROGER--[1][31]

TROWBRIDGE, JOHN TOWNSEND
CREYTON, PAUL--[8][22]AMERICAN

TROYER, BYRON L.
HAMILTON, DAVE--[1][31]

TRUAX, RHODA
WYNGARD, RHODA--[8]

TRUDEAU, GARRETSON BEEKM.
TRUDEAU, GARRY B.--[33]

TRUEBRIDGE, BENJAMIN A.
VREPONT, BRIAN--[13]AUSTRALIAN

TRUESDELL, SUSAN G.
TRUESDELL, SUE--[33]

TRULOCK, CAMILO JOSE CELA
CELA, CAMILO JOE--[1]

TRUMAN, MARCUS GEORGE
BECKETT, MARK--[1][3][22]MYS-- ELDON "TEA TIME TRADGEDY" '35 ELDON "BULLET IN THE CORNICE" '37 & MORE

TRUMAN, RUTH
TRUDIX, MARTY--[1]

TRUMBO, DONALD [DALTON]
ABBOTT, DR. JOHN--[8]
DEMAINE, C.F.--[8]
DOYLE, EMMET--[8]
FINCHER, BETH--[8]
FLEXMAN, THEODORE--[8]
JACKSON, SAM--[8][31]
RICH, ROBERT--R.C. HOLLAND, BAE 1, P6

TRUMBULL, ANNIE ELLIOT
ELIOT, ANNIE--[1]

TRUMPER, HUBERT BAGSTER
BAGSTER, HUBERT--[1][22][31]

TRUSS, [LESLIE] SELDON
SELDON-TRUSS, LESLIE--[1]
SELMARK, GEORGE--[3][8][22][29][40]MYS-- CASSELL "MURDER IN SILENCE" '39

TSATSOS, IOANNA
TSATSOS, JEANNE--[1]

TSCHERNEK, VIKTOR
BERGAUER, JOHANNES--[1]

TSCHIFFELY, AIME FELIX
TSCHIFFELY, A.F.--[1]

TSERKOVSKI,TSANKO
BAKALOV--[22] BULGARIAN

TSHIAMALA, KABASELE
JEEF, KALLE--[31]
KABASELE, JOSEPH--[31]

TSUNEHARU, NAKAMURA
KICHIZO, NAKAMURA--[22]JAPANESE

TSUNENORI, MASAOKA
SHIKI, MASAOKA--[22]JAPANESE

TSUSHIMA, SHUJI
DAZAI, OSAMU--[1][31]

TSVETAEVA, MARINA [I]
EFRON, MARINA IVANOVNA T.--[31]

TUAN, LUCY H.C.
CHEN JO-HSI--[31]

TUBB, E.C.
ADAMS, CHUCK--[2][4][11][28][31]WEST,HP-- SPENCER "TRAIL BLAZERS" '56
ALLEN, STUART--[2][28]HP-- NEBULA-2 STORIES
ARMSTRONG, ANTHONY--[1][2][28]
BAIN, TED--[1][2][11][28]
BEECHAM, ALICE--[1][2][28]
BLAKE, ANTHONY--[1][2][11][28]
BRONSON, L.T.--[2][11][28]HP-- WORLDS OF FANTASY
BURTON, RAYMOND L.--K. DILBONE-BADGER PSEUDS, BAE 15,[2][11]-- ALSO SUPERNATURAL STORIES
CAREY, JULIAN--[1][2][11][28]
CARPENTER, MORLEY--[1][2][11][28]
CARY, JUD--[2][11][28][31]HP-- SPENCER "SANDS OF DESTINY" '55

TUBB, E.C. [CONT]
CARY, JUDY--[2][4]
CARY, JULIAN--[2][28]
CLARKSON, J.F.--[2][4][11][28][31]HP--
SPENCER "MEN OF THE LONG RIFLE" '55
DALE, NORMAN--[1][2][11][28]
DEEGAN, JOHN J.--VULTURES OF THE VOID,HP--
ENNIS, ROBERT D.-- K. DILBONE-BADGER PSEUDS,
BAE 15,[2][11][28]HP--
SUPERNATURAL STORIES
EVANS, JAMES--[2][28]
FARROW, JAMES T.--[2][4][11][28][31]HP--
SPENCER "VENGEANCE TRAIL" '56
FENNER, JAMES R.--[2][4][11][28][31]HP--
SPENCER "COLT VENGEANCE" '57
GODFREY, R.H.--[1][2][11][28]
GRAHAM, CHARLES S.--[2][4][11][28][31]HP--
SPENCER "WAGON TRAIL" '57
GRAY, CHARLES--[1][2][11]
GREY, CHARLES--[2][11][23][28][31]SF--
6 MILESTONE NOVELS
2 MERIT NOVELS '53-54
"DYNASTY OF DOOM" '53
"TORMENTED CITY" '53
"I FIGHT FOR MARS" '53
"SPACE HUNGER" '53
"THE HAND OF HAVOC" '54
"THE EXTRA MAN" '54
GRIDBAN, VOLSTED--S. HOLLAND-SCION CKLST,
PP 27,[2][4][23][31]HP--
SCION "ALIEN UNIVERSE" '52
SCION "REVERSE UNIVERSE" '52
SCION "DE BRACY'S DRUG" '53
MLST "PLANETOID DISPOSALS LTD" '53
MLST "FUGITIVE OF TIME" '53
NW "NO SHORT CUTS"
GUTHRIE, ALAN--[1][2][11][28]
HALEY, CLAUD--VULTURES OF THE VOID--
ARC PRESS "BEYOND THE SOLAR SYSTEM" '54
HILL, D.W.R.--[2][28]
HOLT, GEORGE--[1][2][11][28]
HUNT, GILL--[2][4][11][23][28][31]SF,HP--
WARREN "PLANETFALL" '51
INNES, ALAN/ALLAN--[1][2][11][28][31]
JACKSON, E.F.--[2][4][11][28][31]HP--
SPENCER "COMANCHE CAPTURE" '55
KENT, GORDON--[1][2][11][28]
KERN, GREGORY--K. DILBONE-BADGER PSEUDS,
BAE 15,[7][23][28][31]HP--
DAW - 18 NOVELS '73-83
DAW "CAP KENNEDY #14 THRU #17" '73/76
LAMONT, DUNCAN--[1][2][11]
LANG, KING--[11][23][28][31]HP--
WARREN "SATURN PATROL" '51
LANTRY, MIKE--[3][11][27][28][31]HP--
SPENCER "ASSIGNMENT NEW YORK" '55
LAWRENCE, P.--[11][28][31]WEST,HP--
SPENCER "DRUMS OF THE PRAIRIE" '56
LAWSON, CHET--[11][28][31]WEST,HP--
SPENCER "MEN OF THE WEST" '56
LLOYD, NIGEL--[2][28]
LLOYD, ROBERT--[2][28]
LOMAS, FRANK T.--[2][28]
LOWAM, RON--[2][28]
MACLEAN, ARTHUR--W/G.P. MANN,
[23][28][34]MYS,HP--
FLEETWAY/AMALG "TOUCH OF EVIL" '59
MADDOX, CARL--P. HARBOTTLE-TID-BITS CKLST,
PP#38,[2][23][28]--
TB "LIVING WORLD" '54
TB "MENACE FROM THE PAST" '54
MARTYN, PHILLIP--[1][2][11][28]
MASON, JOHN--K. DILBONE-BADGER PSEUDS,
BAE 15,[2][11][28]HP--
SUPERNATURAL STORIES
MAY, COLIN--[2]

TUBB, E.C. [CONT]
MOULTON, CARL--[1][2][11][28]
NEAL, GAVIN--[1][2][11]
POWERS, L.C.--K. DILBONE-BADGER PSEUDS,
BAE 15,[2][4][11][28]HP--SPENCER
POWERS, M.L.--[2][11][28]WEST,HP--
SPENCER "SCOURGE OF THE SOUTH" '56
RICHARDS, EDWARD--[2][11][28]HP--
SCHOFIELD, PAUL--[1][2][11][28]WEST,HP--
SPENCER "THE FIGHTING FURY" '55
SEABRIGHT, JOHN--[1][2][11][28][31]--
NEBULA STORIES
SHAW, BRIAN/BRYAN--[2][4][11][23][28]SF,HP--
WARREN "ARGENTIS" '52
SHELDON, ROY--[11][23][28]SF,HP--
PANT 109 "THE METAL EATER" '54
STANTON, JAMES S.--K. DILBONE-BADGER PSEUDS
BAE 15,[2]HP--SPENCER
STEVENS, JOHN--[2][4][11]WEST,HP--
SPENCER "QUEST FOR QUANTRELL" '56
STORM, ERIC--[1][2][11][28]SP--
SUTTON, ANDREW--K. DILBONE-BADGER PSEUDS,
BAE 15,[2][11][28]HP--SPENCER
THOMSON, EDWARD--[2][4][11][23][28]--
FUTURA 'IMPERIAL ROME' SERIES:
"ATILUS THE SLAVE" '75
"ATILUS THE GLADIATOR" '75
"GLADIATOR" '78
WAINWRIGHT, KEN--[1][2][11][28]
WEIGHT, FRANK--[1][2][11][28]
WEST, DOUGLAS--[1][2][11][28]
WILDING, ERIC--[1][2][11][28]
WINNARD, FRANK--[1][2][11][28]

TUCCI, NICCOLO
STRAVOLGI, BARTOLOMEO--[8]

TUCHOLSKY, KURT
HAUSER, KASPAR--[22]GERMAN
PANTER, PETER--[22]GERMAN
TIGER, THEOBALD--[22]GERMAN
WROBEL, IGNAZ--[22]GERMAN

TUCKACHNISKY, CARL
TIKTIN, CARL--[1]

TUCKER, AGNES KENT C.
CARRUTH, AGNES K.--[1]

TUCKER, AMY
SAUNDERS, AMY ELIZABETH--[26]ROM--
"FOREVER"
"WILD SUMMER ROSE"
"SWEET SUMMER STORM"

TUCKER, BEVERLEY
SIDNEY, EDWARD WILLIAM--[2]

TUCKER, GEORGE
ATTERLEY, JOSEPH--[2][11][23]SF--

TUCKER, GEORGINA
TUCKER, GINA--[1]

TUCKER, HERBERT
H.T.--[1]

TUCKER, IRWIN ST. JOHN
FRIAR TUCK--[31]

TUCKER, JOHN F.
NEWKIRK, FOSTER--[1]

TUCKER, JOY
STREET, KELLY--[21][26]ROM--
"VIRGIN & THE UNICORN" & 3 MORE

TUCKER, ROBIN
NIBOR, KAY--[1]

TUCKER, RUTH B.
MCINTYRE, HOPE--[9][21][26]ROM--
"MOON ON EAST MOUNTAIN"

TUCKER, SUE LONG
MICHAELS, KRISTIN--[21]ROM,HP--
"FORECAST FOR LOVE"

TUCKER, WILLIAM JOSEPH
SCORPIO--[8]

TUCKER, [ALLAN] JAMES
CRAIG, DAVID--[2][23][31][34]MYS/SF--
'ROY RICKMAN' SERIES:
CAPE "ALIAS MAN" '68
MacM "A DEAD LIBERTY" '74 & 11 MORE '68-76
JAMES, BILL--LACHMAN/EASTER LST '93,[34]MYS--
CNST "YOU'D BETTER BELIEVE IT" '85
CNST "LOLITA MAN" '86
CNST "HALO PARADE" '87 & 3 MORE

TUCKER, [ARTHUR] WILSON
PONG, HOY PING--[1][2][11]SF--
TUCKER, BOB--[2][7][11][23]SF--
SSN "INTERSTELLAR WAY STATION" '41
VAID, SANFORD--W/DOROTHY LES TINA,
P. STEPHENSON, TUCKER INTRVW-
BAE 19,[2][11]--
VAID, SANFORD--W/DOROTHY LES TINA,[11]

TUDEER, ERIK
UDDE, T.--[29]MYS--
SCHILDTS "STRANDHUGG TILL DODS" '83

TUITE, DANIEL R.
BARROWS, PHILIP--[14]ADULT--
OLYM TC#211 "WHORES, QUEERS AND OTHERS" '67

TUITE, HUGH
SPENCER, CAPT.--[1]
TRELAWNEY, HUBERT--[1]

TULEJA, THADDEUS V.F.
MACAO, MARSHALL--[2][3][7]MYS/SF--
FRWY "KAK-ABDULLAH CONSPIRACY" '73
FRWY "DEVIL'S TRIANGLE" '74
FRWY "MARK OF THE VULTURE" '74

TULL, ANTHONY
PARKER, ANTHONY--[1]

TULLBERG, SIGURD
CARLSSON, SIGURD--[29]MYS
WOOD, STANLEY--[29]MYS--
EKLUNDS "MORDET I FRIMARKSKLUBBEN" '44
"FORLOVNING MED GIFT"

TULLETT, DENIS JOHN
DEE, JOHN--[8]
MELMOTH--[8]
SUTTON, JOHN--[8]

TULLOCK, W.W.
BOOKTASTER--[1]
BRIDGE, BONAR--[1]
GOOSEQUILL, GREGORY--[1]
HILL, ARTHUR--[1]
ORION--[1]

TUMAS, JUOZAS
VAIZGANTAS--[22]LITHUANIAN

TUMAY, PAULETT
HARVEY, PAULETT--[31]

TUNIS, ELIZABETH
DELANCEY, ELIZABETH--CRPG,[26]ROM--
DIAMOND 851 "TOUCH OF LACE" '93
DIAMOND "SEA OF DREAMS"

TUNLEY, ROUL
BOYD, EDWARD--[8]

TUOHY, FRANK
TUOHY, JOHN FRANCIS--[22]ENGLISH

TUONG-LONG, NGUYEN
DAO, HOANG--[22] VIETNAMESE

TUPINIER, AUGUSTIN JOSEPH
BARAUDE, H.--[2]

TURBAYNE, JOHN
SEYMOUR, JOHN--[1]

TURCO, LEWIS PUTNAM
COURT, WESLI--[1][31]

TURNBULL, ANN [C]
NICOL, ANN--[1][33]

TURNBULL, DORA AMY D.
DELTA--[1][22]
WENTWORTH, PATRICIA--[3][5][22][29]MYS--
HODDER "BLACK CABINET" '25
"CASE CLOSED" '37 & MORE '23-58

TURNER, COLIN
MACKENZIE, COLIN--[34]MYS--
PYR "PENDRAGON TAPES" '73

TURNER, DONNA M.
THISBY--W/VINCE GENOVESE,[1]

TURNER, ERNEST SACKVILLE
LANG, RUPERT--[1][31]
TURNER, E.S.--[31]

TURNER, FLORENCE
TURNER, F.H.--[14]ADULT--
OLYM OPH#255 "THE NAKED AND THE NUDE" '71

TURNER, HARVEY S.
HILL, SAM--[3]MYS--
VANTAGE "THE NODDING TOWERS" '66

TURNER, JUDY
SAXTON, JUDITH--[1]

TURNER, J[OHN] V[ICTOR]
BRADY, NICHOLAS--[22][29][34]MYS,HP--
BLES "FAIR MURDER" '33
HALE "COUPONS FOR DEATH" '44
HUME, DAVID--[22][29][34][40]MYS--
COLLINS "HEADS YOU LIVE" '39
COLLINS "FIVE ACES" '40 & 33 MORE

TURNER, LIDA LARRIMORE
LARRIMORE, LIDA--[8]

TURNER, LINDA RAY
RAYE, LINDA--[9][21][26]ROM--
"MADE IN HEAVEN"
"TEMPTRESS" & 2 MORE

TURNER, PHILIP WILLIAM
CHANCE, STEPHEN--[3][31][40]MYS--
BODLEY "SEPTIMUS & THE SPY RING" '79
& 3 MORE '71-79

TURNER, ROBERT H.
CALHOUN, ERIC--[1][31]
CARROLL, RAY--L. ROBBINS LTR '94
COOK, MERCER B.--[1][3][29]MYS--
CHALLENGE "IN HOT BLOOD" '66
KLEIN, K.K.--[1][14][31]ADULT--
OLYM TC#437 "THE SEX OF ANGELS" '68
LAWSON, STEVE--[1][31]
LEE, PARKER--[1][31]
MORGAN, ROBERT--[1]
MURRAY, KEN--[1][32]MYS--
KE "SWAN SONG" APR '60
ROBERTS, LISA--[1][21]ROM--
"A DREAM TO SHARE"
ROMANO, DON--W/ALLAN NIXON,[1][3]MYS-HP--
PYR "OPERATION PORNO" '73
PYR "OPERATION COCAINE" '74"
PYR "OPERATION HIT MAN" '74
SAVOY, MARK--[1]
THOMPSON, MIKE--V. BERCH-BRNDN/BC PSEUDS,
BAE 22, ADULT--
THOMPSON, TOBY--V. BERCH-BRNDN/BC PSEUDS,
BAE 22, ADULT--
WOOD, GLEN--L. ROBBINS LTR '94

TURNER, WILLIAM PRICE
TURNER, BILL--[3]MYS--
CNST "SOLDEN'S WOMEN" '72
CNST "HOT FOOT" '73 & 4 MORE '67-73

TURNGREN, ANNETTE
HOPKINS, A.T.--[3][22][31][40]MYS--
RINEHART "HAVE A LOVELY FUNERAL" '54

TURTLEDOVE, HARRY
IVERSON, ERIC G.--[2][7][23]SF/HOR--
TWR 'GERIN' SERIES:
"WEREBLOOD" '79
"WERENIGHT" '79

TURTON-JONES, EDITH C.B.
GILLESPIE, SUSAN--[8][31]

TUSAROVA, MARIE
MAJEROVA, MARIE--[22] CZECH

TUTE, WARREN [S]
WARREN, ANDREW--W/ANDREW ROSENTHAL,[1]

TUTTIETT, MARY GLEED
GRAY, MAXWELL--[1][3]MYS--
LONG "UNCONFESSED" '11
GREY, MAXWELL--[3]MYS--
APPLETON "AN INNOCENT IMPOSTER
& OTHER STORIES" 1893

TUTTLE, GENE VAN
VAN, GENE--L. ROBBINS LTR '94

TUTTLE, WILBUR COLEMAN
COLEMAN, W.C.--[19]WEST
COLEMAN, WILLIAM C.--[19]WEST
TUTTLE, W.C.--[19][28][32]WEST--
POPLB 46 "SINGING RIVER" '46
HILL 2 "TUMBLING RIVER RANGE" '48
HILL 5 "BLUFFER'S LUCK" '48
POPLB 149 "HIDDEN BLOOD" '48
MSMM "ANTELOPE HAVE LEGS" 'JUN '58
MSMM "PAYDAY" OCT '58 & MORE NOVELS

TWADDLE, SUSAN BOWDEN
BARRON, ELIZABETH--[9][21]ROM--
"VISCOUNT'S WAGER"
"ELUSIVE COUNTESS" & MORE
BOWDEN, SUSAN--[9][21][26]ROM--
"TOUCHED BY TJHORNS"
"RETURNING" & MORE

TWELLS, J.
BREX--[2]

TWIGGS, JAMES
JAMESON, TWIGGS--[1][2]

TWISLETON-W-F, RICHARD N.
FIENNES, RICHARD--[31]

TWITCHETT, CAROL COSGROVE
COSGROVE, CAROL ANN--[31]

TWYMAN, HAROLD WILLIAM
CARTWRIGHT, A.--[1][34]MYS,HP--
AMALG "THE FAKIR'S SECRET" '36

TWYMAN, HAROLD WILLIAM
FORGE, JOHN--[1]
MURRAY, ROBERT--[1]
RICHARDS, FRANK--[1]HP--

TYBERGIAN, SONIA
TYBERG, SON--[2] ISFYB

TYERS, KATHLEEN L.M.
TYERS, KATHY--[7]SF--
'FIREBIRD' SEQUENCE: '87-91

TYLER, J.E. ANTHONY
TYLER, J.E.A.--[7]SF--
TOLKIEN RELATED NON-FICT
TYLER, TONY--[7]SF

TYLER-WHITTLE, MICHAEL
OLIVER, MARK--[1]
WHITTLE, TYLER--[1][21]ROM--
"SOME ANCIENT GENTLEMEN"
"WIDOW OF WINDSOR" & 4 MORE

TYNAN, KATHARINE
HINKSON, KATHARINE TYNAN--[31]

TYRRELL, MARGOT
GOODMAN, JO--W/JOSEPHINE C. GOODMAN
& TOSS GASCOIGNE,[7]SF--
"DREAM TIME:NEW STORIES 16 AUTH."

UBERTIS, CORINNA TERESA G
TERESAH--[22]ITALIAN

UDALL, JAN BEANEY
BEANEY, JAN--[31][33]NON-FICTION--
"YOUNG EMBROIDERER" '66
BEANEY, JANE--[31]

UERDES, RAMON Y ALVAREZ
DEL REY, LESTER--LEGALIZED

UHR, ELIZABETH
STERN, ELIZABETH--[8]

ULLAH, SALAMAT
SALAMATULLAH--[22] INDIAN

ULLICA, JORGE
ARCE, JULIO G.--[31]

ULLMAN, ALAN
ALAN, SANDY--[31]

ULLMAN, JAMES MICHAEL
IVORY, MARTIN--LACHMAN LST '93,[32]MYS--
EQMM "RIPE FOR PLUCKING" MAY '63
EQMM "KING OF THE MAIL ORDER MYS" AUG '78

ULLMAN, NATACHA
STEWART, NATACHA--[1]

ULLYETT, KENNETH
BENTLEY, W.J.--[8]

ULMER, ROBERT EUGENE
ULMER, ROGER EUGENE--[2]

ULYANOV, VLADIMIR ILICH
LENIN, N.--[22]RUSSIAN

UNDERWOOD, MAVIS EILEEN
KILPATRICK, SARAH--[3][31]MYS--
DBLDY "WAKE ALL THE DEAD" '70

UNETT, JOHN
PRESTON, JAMES--[8][22]ENGLISH

UNGAR, S.
STERN, STUART--W/HUGH C. RAE,[34]MYS--
FUTURA "MINOTAUR FACTOR" '77
FUTURA "POISON TREE" '78

UNGER, MAURICE ALBERT
MUNGER, AL--[22]AMERICAN

UNGERER, [JEAN] THOMAS
UNGERER, TOMI--[33]

UNIACKE, EVELYN CATHERINE
CLARK, CATHERINE--[1]

UNICKEL, MARTHA
NICKELS, MERYL--[21][26]ROM--
"LOVE'S LYING EYES"
SAWYER, MERYL--[9][21][26]ROM--
"BLIND CHANCE"
"MIDNIGHT IN MARAKESH"
"NEVER KISS A STRANGER"

UNNERSTAD, EDITH ALICE
TOTTERMAN, ALICE--[29]MYS--
WW "FALLET BENGTSSON" '33
WW "FALLET MALO" '34

UNSWORTH, LILIAN
HYLTON, SARA--V. BERCH LTR TO HUBIN '93,
MYS--
HUTCH "CAPRICE" '80
HUTCH "CARADINE CHAIN" '81
HUTCH "CRIMSON FALCON" '83
CENT "WHISPERING GLADE" '85 & MORE

UNWIN, DAVID STORR
SEVERN, DAVID--[2][11][22][33]ENGLISH

UPCHURCH, BOYD BRADFIELD
BOYD, JOHN--[2][3][4][7][23][31]SF--
GOLZ "LAST STARSHIP FROM EARTH" '68
UPCHURCH, BOYD--[7]--SEE "JOHN BOYD"

UPFIELD, ARTHUR C.
HAWKE, JESSICA--[36]AUSTRALIAN/MYS--
HM "FOLLOW MY DUST" '57
SILENT COLLAB W/HAWKE

UPHAM, GRACE LE BARON
LE BARON, GRACE--[1]

UPPER, GLORIA
DOUGLAS, GLORIA--[9][21]ROM--
"WINNING HEARTS"

UPSHALL, HELEN
CURTIS, SUSANNAH--[9][21][26]ROM--
"MONK'S RETREAT"

UPSON, DOROTHY BARBARA
FAWCETT, BARBARA--[1]
FURNESS, ELIZABETH--[1]

UPSON, NORMA
KIMBALL, NANCY--[1][31]

UPTON, GEORGE PUTNAM
PICKLE, PEREGRINE--[8]

UPWARD, EDWARD FALAISE
CHALMERS, ALLEN--[8]

URCH, ELIZABETH
BROGAN, ELISE--[1][31]

URE, JEAN
COLIN, ANN--[1][31][33]
GREGORY, JEAN--[1][31][33]
MCCULLOCH, SARA[H]--[9][21][26][33]ROM--
"NOT QUITE A LADY"

URELL, WILLIAM FRANCIS
FRANCIS, WILLIAM--[3][22][29]MYS--
GRN PUB 1 "ROUGH ON RATS" '45
GRN PUB 4 "BURY ME NOT" '45
GRN PUB 12 "KILL OR CURE" '45
SIGN 742 "KILL OR CURE" '49
SIGN 865 "I.O.U. MURDER" '51
LION 123 "DON'T DIG DEEPER" '53
LUCAS, CURTIS--[34]MYS--
LION 80 THIRD WARD, NEWARK" '52
LION 91 "SO LOW, SO LONELY" '52
LION 162 "ANGEL" '53
UGE 8 "FORBIDDEN FRUIT" '53
LION LL14 "LILA" '55

URHAUSEN, MARY K.
RIPLEY, KAREN--V. BERCH LTR TO HUBIN '94,
MYS/SF--
DEL REY 'PRISONER OF DREAMS' SERIES:
"PRISONER OF DREAMS" '89
"TENTH CLASS" '91
SOLO 'INDIANA JONES' SERIES

URIE, MARY LE BARON [A]
LE BARON, MARIE--[1]

URIS, AUREN
PAUL, AUREN--[1][2]

URISTA, ALBERTO H.
ALURISTA--[1][31]

URNER, NATHAN DANE
BAINBRIDGE, BRYANT--[1]
BRENTFORD, BURKE--[1][3]MYS--
S&SM "GOLD DUST DARRELL; OR THE WIZARD
OF THE MINES" 1890
CAMPBELL, BARTLEY--[1]
CLANCOOL, CLARENCE--[1]
COURTENEY, CARL--[1]
GILDERSLEEVE, PROFESSOR--[1]
LOOKER, O.N.--[1]
MENTOR--[1]

URNER, NATHAN DANE [CONT]
MINTURN, EDWARD--[1]
NORTH, INGOLDSBY--[1]
SILINGSBY, MAURICE--[1]
URBAN, SEPTIMUS--[1]

URQUHARDT, MACGREGOR
HART, MAX--[8]
MACGREGOR, RICHARD--[7][23]SF--

USHER, FRANK HUGH
FRANKLIN, CHARLES--[22][29][32][34]MYS--
JCM "WRITING TO MUSIC" APR '57
EW "TEA PARTY" FEB '65
CHP "DON'T GO TO CEUTA" '70
HALE "KGB IS HERE" '72
& 39 MORE HALE '46-72
LESTER, FRANK--[3][29][31]ENGLISH/MYS--
HALE "BAMBOO GIRL" '61
HALE "HIDE MY BODY" '61 & MORE
LESTER, FRANK B.--[32]MYS--
JCM "CASE OF THE WATERY GRAVE" JUN '61

USHER, SHAUN
SCOTT, JEFFREY--[1][3][32]MYS--
HALE "TRUST THEM & DIE" '69
AHMM, EQMM, EW & LM STORIES

USHER, [JOHN] GRAY
BORELLI, CASS--S. HOLLAND-SCION CKLST, PP 27, MYS,HP-- SCION
GARROWAY, PETE--S. HOLLAND-SCION CKLST, PP 27, MYS,HP--
MLST "A DAME TOO MANY" '52
MLST YES, SUGAR" '52
SCION "HIGH STEPPING JEZEBEL" '53
GRAY, CHRIS[TOPHER]--[8]
LINTON, DUKE--S. HOLLAND-SCION CKLST, PP 27,[3]MYS,HP--
SCION "SINNER" '53

USPENSKII, PETR
OUSPENSKY, P.D.--[11]

UTLEY, STEVEN
DALE, SEPTIMUS--HAWK/UTLEY INTRVW '93,[2]-- SHORT MATERIAL
HOLT, BRUCE--HAWK/UTLEY INTRVW '93,[2]-- SHORT MATERIAL

UTTLEY, ALICE JANE T.
UTTLEY, ALISON--[1][33]

UZQUIANO, LINDA STEELE
STEELE, LINDA--V. BERCH LTR TO REGINALD '93, [9]SF--
DAW "IBIS" '85

VACHETTE, EUGENE
CHAVETTE, EUGENE--[1][3]MYS--
BONNER "MYSTERY OF HOTEL BRICHET" 1894

VACZEK, LOUIS CHARLES
HARDIN, PETER--[22][31][34]MYS--
SCRIBN "FRIGHTENED DOVE" '51
HARPER "HIDDEN GRAVE" '55

VADAKIN, JAMES CHARLES
GOREN, CHARLES H[ENRY]--[31]

VAHEY, JOHN G. HAZLETTE
CLANDON, HENRIETTA--[1][3][22]MYS--
BLES "INQUEST" '33
BLES "GHOST PARTY" '34 & 5 MORE '33-38

VAHEY, JOHN G. HAZLETTE [CONT]
HASLETTE, JOHN--[1][3]MYS--
DIGBY "CRAVEN BALL" '10
LOW "THE MESH" '12 & 5 MORE '10-16
LANG, ANTHONY--[1][3]MYS--
MELROSE "THE CRIME" '27
MELROSE "DARING DIANA" '29 & 3 MORE '27-30
LODER, VERNON--[1][3]MYS--
COLLINS "TWO DEAD" '34
COLLINS "DEAF-MUTE MURDERS" '36
& 20 MORE '28-38
MOWBRAY, JOHN--[1][3]MYS--
COLLINS "MEGREVE MYS" '41
COLLINS "RADIO MYS" '41 & 4 MORE '22-41
PROUDFOOT, WALTER--[1][3]MYS--
HUTCH "ARREST" '33
HUTCH "CONSPIRACY" '33 & 2 MORE '31-33
TIMOTHY, ARTHUR--[22]MYS
TIMOTHY, ARTHUR N.--[1]

VAIL, MRS. LAURENCE
BOYLE, KAY--[2]

VAIRASSE, DENIS
SIDEN, CAPTAIN--[2]

VALDEZ, PAUL
VOLDEZ, PAUL--[2]

VALE, HENRY EDMOND THEOD.
BLEDLOW, JOHN--[22][31]ENGLISH

VALENTI, JUSTINE
MAX, BARBARA--[21]ROM--
"LOVE ISLAND"
"WHISPERS OF LOVE"
VICTOR, VANESSA--[21][26]ROM--
"DINNER FOR TWO"

VALIDOR, BATYR K.
VALID, BATYR--[1]

VALIGURSKY, ED
REMBACK, WILLIAM--[1][2]

VALLEAU, EMILY
HEARN, EMILY--[31]

VALLEE, HUBERT PRIOR
VALLEE, RUDY--[8]

VALLEE, JACQUES
SERIEL, JEROME--[1][2][11]

VALLETTE, MARGUERITE
RACHILDE--[22]FRENCH

VALLS-RUSSELL, JOSEPH L.
ALAN, RAY--[1][3][29]MYS--
JOSEPH "MY BONNIE LIES UNDER THE SEA" '63
COLLINS "BEIRUT PIPELINE" '80

VALUE, BARBARA ANN
FITZGERALD, BARBARA--[31]

VAN ANROOY, FRANCINE
ANROOY, FRAN VAN--[31]--
CHILDREN'S BOOKS
VAN ANROOY, FRANS--[33]

VAN ARNAM, DAVE
ARCHER, RON--W/THEODORE E. WHITE,[1][7]SF--
PYR "LOST IN SPACE" '67

VAN ARNAM, DAVID G.
VAN ARNAM, DAVE--[23]AMERICAN/SF

VAN ATTA, WINFRED L.
RYERSON, LOWELL--[1][22]MYS

VAN BEEVER, ROBERT F.
GORDON, FRITZ--W/FREDERICK G. JARVIS,[3]MYS--
AWARD "FLIGHT OF THE BAMBOO SAUCER" '67
AWARD "TONIGHT THEY DIE TO MENDELSSOHN" '68

VAN BRIGGLE, M. FRANCES J
JESSUP, FRANCES--[22][31]AMERICAN

VAN BRUGGEN, JAN R.L.
KLEINJAN--[22]SOUTH AFRICAN

VAN BRUNT, [HOWELL] LLOYD
VAN BRUNT, H.L.--[31]--POEMS '68-80

VAN CALCAR-SCHIOTLING, E.
VAN CALCAR, ELISE--[22] DUTCH

VAN COOK, JERRY
PENDLETON, DON--[34]MYS,HP--
GE "CUTTING EDGE" '90

VAN CORSTANJE, CHARLES
VAN CORSTANJE, AUSPICIUS--[1]

VAN DE GOHM, RICHARD
GOHM, D.C.--[1]
GOHM, DOUGLAS--[1]
O'CONNELL, R.F.--[1]

VAN DE WETERING, JANWILL.
LEGRU, SEIKO--LACHMAN LST '93,DDLY
PLEAS #4 '94,MYS--
AHMM 'INSP. SAITO' STORIES '78-85

VAN DEN BOGARDE, DEREK J.
BOGARDE, DIRK--[31]

VAN DEN EYNDE, ANTOON
BRULIN, TONE--[22] DUTCH

VAN DER BOURG, WERNER
DUVART, RENE--[39]GERMAN

VAN DER MERWE, ISAK WILL.
BOERNEEF--[22] SOUTH AFRICA [AFRIKAANS]

VAN DER ZANT, JOHAN WILH.
ANDREUS, HANS--[22] DUTCH

VAN DER ZEE, BARBARA B.
GRIGGS, BARBARA--[1]

VAN DEURS, GEORGE
SHEPARD, STRATTON--[8]

VAN DEUSEN, ALONZO
CAPITALIST, A.--[2][7]SF--

VAN DEVENTER, EMMA MURD.
LYNCH, LAWRENCE L.--[3][5][22][29]MYS--
LONG "A SEALED VERDICT" '10
LAIRD "A BLIND LEAD" '12 & MORE

VAN DOOREN, INGRID
DOOREN, INGRID V.--[31]

VAN DOORNICK, FRITZHEINZ
KUHN, OTTO--[39]GERMAN--
TRANSLATION

VAN DROME, CECILE
ALDINE, FRANCE--[22]BELGIAN

VAN DROOGENBROECK, JAN
FERGUTT, JAN--[22] FLEMISH

VAN EEDEN, FREDERIK
PARADIJS, CORNELIS--[22] DUTCH

VAN ERMENGEM, FREDERIC
HELLENS, FRANZ--[1][22] BELGIAN

VAN ESSEN, W.
SERJEANT, RICHARD--[8]

VAN EYSS, EDGAR
ELIS, EGON--[40]GERMAN/MYS--
"DUELL IN DUNKEL" '58

VAN FLEET, CHARLES
FLEET, CHARLES--V. BERCH LTR TO
HUBIN '94, MYS--
RAVEN "A PLACE LIKE HESSBERG" '80

VAN GELDER, LAWRENCE
CARTER, NICK--[3]MYS,HP--
AWARD "MAN WHO SOLD DEATH" '74
CHART "DEADLY DOUBLES" '78

VAN GROENINGEN, AUGUST P.
VAN OEVERE, WILLIAM--[22] DUTCH

VAN HAAFTEN, JULIA
HAAFTEN, JULIA V.--[31]

VAN HEESE, DIETHARD
SPIDER, JOHN--[39]GERMAN/HOR

VAN HERP, JACQUES
JANSEN, MICHEL--[2]

VAN HISE, DELLA
ALLED--LORRAINE BIER-ARMADILLOCON '93
FAGAN BLACK, ALEXIS--LORRAINE BIER-
ARMADILLOCON '93
NAV ESIH, ALLED--LORRAINE BIER-
ARMADILLOCON '93

VAN HORN, DALE R.
COVINGTON, CHESTER--[1]
DALE, V.R.--[1]
DALTON, HOWARD--[1]
ENGEL, DEL--[1]
LINCOLN, E.R.--[1]
RICHARD, BILL--[1]
ROOD, JACK--[1]
VANCE, GALE--[1]
VIRGINIA, DAISY--[1]

VAN ITERSON, SINY ROSE
VAN ITERSON, S.R.--[1]

VAN KAMPEN, OSCAR
BANANA, AZIJN--[1]

VAN LAERHOVEN, ROBERT V.F
ASHMIND, KIM--[1]

VAN LEEUWE, JAN
VAN HEELU, JAN--[22]

VAN LEPENDAAL, WILLEM
VAN DER, WILLEM--[22] DUTCH

VAN LIERDE, JOHN
VAN LIERDE, PETER C.--[1]

VAN LOGHEM, MARTINUS G.L.
FIORE DELLA NEVE--[1]
NEVE, FIORE DELLA--[22] DUTCH

VAN LOOY, JACOBUS
BROUWER, A.--[22]DUTCH
VAN HOREN, THEO--[1]DUTCH

VAN LOWE, ERICH
CONTE, SAL--V. BERCH LTR TO REGINALD '93,SF--
LEIS "CHILD'S PLAY" '86
LEIS "THE POWER" '89

VAN NAME, E.J.
VANNY, JIM--[1][2][11]

VAN NUYS, JOAN
ESSEX, MARIANNA--[9][11[21]ROM--
"TORRENT OF LOVE"
"LOVE CAME COURTING"

VAN OORT, JAN
DULIEU, JEAN--[1][31]

VAN ORDEN, WILLIAM H.
JAMES, POLICE CAPTAIN--[34]MYS--
S&SM "REVENUE DETECTIVE" 1889 & MORE

VAN POORTVLIET, BARBARA
SPECHT, BARBARA--[39]GERMAN/JUV

VAN RENSBURG, ROELOG J.J.
VAN RENSBURG, JACO--[1]
VAN RENSBURG, ROELF--[1]

VAN RJNDT, PHILIPPE
MICHAELS, PHILIP--[3][7][29]MYS/SF--
AV "GRAIL" '82
AV "COME FOLLOW ME" '83

VAN RYSSELBERGHE, MARIA
SAINT-CLAIR, M.--[22] BELGIAN

VAN SAHER, LILLA
ANONYMOUS--R.C./ELWANDA HOLLAND
REVW '93, ADULT--
BEAC 152 "ADAM & TWO EVES" '57

VAN SCHAILK-WILLING, JEAN
VAN LOENE, GABRIELLE--[1]

VAN SCHEVICHAVEN, J.
IVANS--[40]GERMAN--
MYS "DE MAN UIT FRANKRIJK" '17

VAN SCHREINER, HARRY
VAN, HARRY--[2]

VAN SILLER, HILDA
SILLER, HILDA--[1]
SILLER, VAN--[3][18][22]MYS--
RS "IN THE NIGHT" '47
LIPP "LAST RESORT" '51 & 20 MORE '43-74

VAN SLYKE, HELEN
ASHTON, SHARON--[3][21][26][31]MYS/ROM--
DBLDY "THE SANTA ANA WIND" '74

VAN SMITH, HOWARD
SOMMERS, DAVID--[22]AMERICAN

VAN STOCKUM, HILDA
MARLIN, HILDA--[1]

VAN TIJN, MIJNJE L.
VAN TIJN, MAARJE--[1]

VAN TIL, REINDEER
EVERS, CRABBE--W/WILLIAM BRASHLER, DDLY
PLEAS #3, MYS--
"MRD IN WRIGLEY FIELD" '91 & MORE

VAN TRICHT, ELISABETH E.
DE JONG-KEESING, ELISAB.--[1]

VAN TUYL, ROSEALTHEA
VAN TUYL, ZAARA--[1][2][7]SF

VAN VLIERDAN, BERNARD F.
KEMP, BERNARD--[22] DUTCH

VAN VOGT, ALFRED ELTON
HULL, E. MAYNE--[4]
VAN VOGT, A.E.--F.J. ACKERMAN-VOGT'S LIT.
AGENT-INTRO. TO "MONSTERS"

VAN VOGT, EDNA MAYNE
HULL, E. MAYNE--[1][11]

VAN WEDDINGEN, MARTHE
DUMAS, CLAIRE--[1][31][34]MYS--
BAL "THE STRANGER" '77

VAN WIE, PATRICIA
KEELYN, PATRICIA--[26]ROM--
HARL 590 "KEEPING KATIE"

VAN WORMER, JOSEPH EDWARD
VAN WORMER, JOE--[33]

VAN ZANDT, EDMUND
PENDLETON, TOM--[1][3]MYS--
McGRAW "HODAK" '69

VAN ZELLER, CLAUDE HUBERT
BROTHER CHOLERIC--[8][31]
VENNINGS, HUGH--[2][7][11][23]SF--
"THE END: A PROJECTION, NOT A PROPHECY" '47

VAN ZWIENEN, ILSE C.K.
KOEHN, ILSE--[31][33]

VAN ZWIENEN, JOHN
SCOFIELD, JONATHAN--[21]ROM,HP--
DELL 'FREED. FTR' SERIES:
"GUNS AT TWILIGHT"
WILLOUGHBY, LEE DAVIS--[21]ROM,HP--
DELL 'MKNG OF AMERICA' SERIES:
"FUGITIVES"

VAN'T SANT-VAN BOMMEL, A.
VAN'T SANT, MIEN--[1]

VAN-LOON, ANTONIO
FRENCH, JANINE--W/RONI FINKELSTEIN,
[9][21][26]ROM--
"RHAPSODY"
"WADINGFIELD" & MORE

VANCE, GERALD
VENCE, GERALD--[2]

VANCE, JOHN HOLBROOK
HELD, PETER--[2][3][4][18]MYS--
MYH "TAKE MY FACE" '57
HOLBROOK, JACK--[8]
HOLBROOK, JOHN--[2][5][18][23]MYS/SF--
QUEEN, ELLERY--[2][3][4][18]MYS,HP--
MA "FIRST STAR I SEE TONIGHT" MAR '54
POCK "THE FOUR JOHNS" '64
POCK "A ROOM TO DIE IN" '65
POCK "MADMAN THREAT" '66

VANCE, JOHN HOLBROOK [CONT]
VANCE, JACK--[3][7][18][23]SF/MYS--
HILL 41 "DYING EARTH" '47
BAL 167 "TO LIVE FOREVER" '56 +
WADE, ALAN--[2][3][18][23][29][40]MYS--
MYH "ISLE OF PERIL" '57

VANCE, PHILO
FORD, COREY--[5][32]MYS--
EQMM "ONE ON THE HOUSE" DEC '46
SA "PAPER TRAIL" NOV '54

VANCE, WILLIAM E.
CASSIDY, GEORGE--[8][28][31][32]MYS/WEST--
PU "TIME TO CRY" JUL '54
MC "CLEANUP MAN" JAN '55
HU "THE MURDERED MISTRESS" FEB '55
NORDON "KING OF THE MOUNTAIN" '80

VANCEL, DORIS
THOMAS, DORIS--[1][2][11]

VANCURA, ANTONIN
MAHEN, JIRI--[22]CZECH

VANDENPANHUISE, GASTON
KENNY, PAUL--W/JEAN LIBERT,[3][29]MYS--
INTERNTL "THE TANAGRA AFFAIR" '69

VANDERBILT, CORNELIUS JR.
LANE, R.--[1]

VANDERBILT, HEIDI
CARLSON, LILLY--EQMM MAR 87

VANDERGRIFF, AOLA
BROWN, KIT--[9][21][26]ROM--
"ALYSSA DEANNE" & 2 MORE

VANDERVEEN, BARELD H.
VANDERVEEN, BART H.--[1]

VANDYOPADHYAYA, S.B.
BANERJEA, S.B.--[34]MYS--
LONGMANS "TALES OF BENGAL" '10
GAY "INDIAN DETECTIVE STORIES" '11

VANGEON, HENRI
GHEON, HENRI--[22]FRENCH

VANN, GERALD
OKE, SIMON--[8]

VANZWEINEN, ILSE C. KOEHN
KOEHN, ILSE--[1]

VARDEMAN, ROBERT E.
APPLETON, VICTOR--[7]SF,HP--
STSY 'TOM SWIFT':
"GATEWAY TO DOOM"
CARTER, NICK--[3][7]MYS,HP--
CHART "DOCTOR DNA" '82
CHART "SOLAR MENACE" '81
CHART "EIGHT CARD STUD" '80
CHART "EARTH SHAKER" '82
CHART "KALI DEATH CULT" '83
CHART "NORWEGIAN TYPHOON" '82
CHART "OUTBACK GHOSTS" '83
CHART "YUKON TARGET" '83
ELOUS, MARV--W/GEORGE W. PROCTOR[7]--
ORPHEUS "PLEASURE PLANET"
RPRTD "SEXUAL COQUETTE" BEE-LN
GEORGE, EDWARD--W/LEE WYATT,[2]--
COLLAB WAS WITH 'PROCTOR' OR 'GERROLD'
GEORGE, EDWARD [E]--W/GEORGE W. PROCTOR,
[2][7][11][23]--

VARDEMAN, ROBERT E. [CONT]
GEORGE, EDWARD E. [CONT]
ORPHEUS SERIES "PLEASURE PLANET" '74
HALE, ROBERT--AUTHOR PROVIDED, WEST
KAHN, OBIE--W/GEORGE W. PROCTOR,[7]--
"PLEASURE PLANET"
RPRTD "INTERGALACTIC ORGY" LNITE LIB
KENYON, PAUL--[11] ?? KNOWN PSEUD OF
DONALD MOFFATT ??
LOGAN, JAKE--G COOK LTR '93, WEST,HP--
TITLE UNKNOWN
MORAN, DANIEL--G. COOK LTR '93, SF--
TOR "THE FLAME KEY" '87
MOUNDS, MONICA--W/GEORGE PROCTOR,[7][23]--
"PLEASURE PLANET"
RPRTD "OUTER SPACE EMBRACE" BL '78
ONN, CARRIE--W/GEORGE PROCTOR,[7][23]--
"PLEASURE PLANET"
RPRTD "JANET'S SEX PLANET" BL '80
SPARKROCK, FRED--W/GEORGE PROCTOR,[7][23]--
"PLEASURE PLANET"
RPRTD "PLAYING WITH DESIRE" BL '86

VARGA, JENO [EUGEN]
PAULOWSKI, E.--[1]

VARLEY, JOHN [H]
BOEHM, HERB--[2][11]

VARLINSKY, DEBORAH
LE VARRE, DEBORAH--[9][21][26]ROM--
"CAPTIVE MISTRESS"

VARNUM, ZOE SHIPPEN
SHIPPEN, ZOE--[1]

VARTANIAN, BYRON
BARTON, BYRON--[1]

VASEK, VLADIMIR
BEZRUC, PER--[22] CZECH
SUK, RATIBOR--[22] CZECH

VASILEVSKA, LUDMYLA
DNIPROVA, CHAIKA--[22]RUSSIAN-UKRAINIAN

VASILEVSKAYA, VANDA
WASSILEWSKA, WANA--[22] POLISH

VASILIU, GEORGE
BACOVIA, GEORGE--[22][31] RUMANIAN

VASILIU, GHEORGHI
BACOVIA, G.--[31]

VASILOPOULOS, FREDA
VASILOS, FREDA--[9][21][26]ROM--
"MOON MADNESS"
"SUMMER WINE"
VASILOS, TINA--[9][10][21][26]ROM--
"WOLF'S PREY"
"CRY OF THE PEACOCK" &4 MORE

VASSI, FRED
VASSI, MARCO--[14]ADULT--
OLYM OPS#5 "GENTLE DEGENERATES" '70
OLYM TC#486 MIND BLOWER" '70
OLYM OPS#27 "THE SALINE SOLUTION" '71
OLYM OPS#53 "CONTOURS OF DARKNESS" '72

VASSILEV, HRISTO PETKOV
VASSILEV, ORLIN--[1]

VAUGHAN, JANE
VAUGHAN, VIVIAN--[9]ROM

VAUGHAN, LADY AURIEL R.M.
MALET, ORIEL--[1][2][11]

VAUGHAN, OWEN
RHOSCOMYL, OWEN--[2]

VAUGHAN, ROBERT
SCOFIELD, JONATHAN--[21]ROM,HP--
DELL 'FREED FTR' SERIES:
"JUNGLEFIRE"
WILLOUGHBY, LEE DAVIS--[21]ROM,HP--
DELL 'WOMEN WHO WON THE WEST' SERIES:
"LOST LADY OF LARAMIE"
DELL 'MKNG OF AMER' SERIES:
"HEARTS DIVIDED"
"RANCHERS"
"RAIDERS"
DELL 'MKNG OF AMER' SERIES:
"FAR ISLANDERS"
"WARRIORS OF THE CODE"
FAIRMAN, PAULA--W/PAUL W. FAIRMAN,
[9][21][26]ROM--
"IN SAVAGE SPLENDOR"

VAUGHAN, ROBERT R.
JACK, J.W.--GRANT THIESSEN CONFIRM W/AUTHOR
MOORE, PAULA--[9][21][26]ROM--
"LOVE PIRATE"
"SAVAGE RAPTURE" & MORE

VAUGHAN, VIRGINIA MASON
CARR, VIRGINIA MASON--[31]

VAUGHN WILLIAMS, URSULA
WOOD, URSULA--[1]

VAUGHN, OWEN
RHOSCOMYL, OWEN--[1]

VAUTIER, GHISLAINE
FRANK, HELENE--[1][31][33]

VAUX, PATRICK
NAVARCHUS--W/JAMES WOODS,[1]
NAVARCHUS--W/LIONEL YEXLEY,[2]

VAYSSE, CHARLES
FENNEL, CONNIE--[1]

VECCHI, OMERO
FOLGORE, LUCIANO--[22]ITALIAN

VEER LEE, MARION VAN DER
LEE, BABS--W/CLARE C. SAUNDERS,[3]MYS--
SCRIBN "MEASURED FOR MURDER" '44
LEE, BABS--[3]MYS--
SCRIBN "A MODEL IS MURDERED" '42
SCRIBN "PASSPORT TO OBLIVION" '43

VEGENOR, SVERRE
BRANNER, CARL--[29]MYS--
"DODEN PA BESOK" '37
CAMBRE, EINAR--[29]MYS--
DM#35 "MANNEN MED HOKANSIK" '35
"DEN DOLDA SKATTEN" '35
TERJE, SEVED--[29]MYS--
DM#1 "UTPRESSAREN" '37
DM#39 "DROMTJUVEN" '39
DM#10 "BRANDGATAN PA STEENSHUS" '41

VEIGELSBERG, HUGO
IGNOTUS--[22] HUNGARIAN

VEILLER, MARGUERITE
VALE, MARTIN--[3]MYS--
PLAY "THE TWO MRS. CARROLLS" '36

VEILLON, BARBARA LANTIER
MORGAN, KRISTIN--[26]ROM--
"LOVE CHILD"
"FIRST COMES BABY"
"WHO'S THAT BABY"

VEITCH, THOMAS
KENTIGERN, JOHN--[8]

VEITCH, TONY
COLLIER, J. COBB--[35]AUSTRALIAN
CLVLD "BUZZARDS FLY LOW"
CLVLD "ROPE TO SPARE"
CLVLD "RETURN OF THE PRODIGAL"
CLVLD "TARNISHED SPUR"

VEITCH, TONY
KESTREL, DAN--[35]AUSTRALIAN--
CLEVELAND
MCLURE, SCOTT--[35]AUSTRALIAN--
28 CLVLD '50s & 60s
SANTE FE "MAN TRAIL"
COUGAR 119 "SUNFISH KID"
129 "BLOOD BROTHER"
355 "WALK THE SKY"

VELEY, CHARLES
TAYLOR, ANTHONY--V. BERCH LTR TO
HUBIN '94, MYS--
JOVE "HOUR OF THE SCORPION" '82

VELIKOVSKY, IMMANUEL
OBSERVER--[1]

VENABLE, CLARK
CLARKE, COVINGTON--[1][2]

VENABLE, MARILYN
VENABLE, LYN--[1][11]

VENABLES, TERRY
YUILL, P.B.--W/GORDON M. WILLIAMS,
[3][18][23]ENGLISH/MYS--
'MICRONAUTS' SERIES '77-81

VENE-CAVANAGH, PAUL
CAVANAGH, PAUL--[1]

VENNARD, ALEXANDER VINDEX
BOWYANG, BILL--[8]
REID, FRANK--[8]

VENNING, COREY
HYDE, TRACY ELLIOT--[1]

VENTURA, CHARLES
DAVIS, ROBERT HART--A. TONIK-ECHOES #24
MYS,HP--
GL "MESMERIZING MIST AFFAIR" AUG '67

VENTURO, BETTY LOU BAKER
BAKER, BETTY--[1][7]SF--
MacM "SAVE SIRRUSHANNY! ALSO...." '78
MacM "SEVEN SPELLS TO FAREWELL"

VENTZEL, ELENA
GREKOVA--[1]

VERE-HODGE, CONRAD C.R.
DE VERE, V.C.--[7]SF--
"MOTTO EXCELSIOR #1-3" '88/90
MASON, ROGER--[7]SF--
'MOTTO EXCELSIOR': #4 '91

VERGE, LISA ANN
ST. PIERRE, LISANN--[9][21][26]ROM--
"DEFIANT ANGEL"

VERHAGE, JOHANNES W.C.
VAN GREVELINGEN, H.--[22] DUTCH

VERLAG, FRANZ SCHNEEKLUTH
DANELLA, UTTA--[21]ROM--
"THOSE VON TALLIEN WOMEN"

VERMEULEN, EDWARD
OOM WARDEN--[22] FLEMISH

VERMILYE, KATE
JORDAN, KATE--[1]

VERN, DAVID
BLADE, ALEXANDER--[1][2]HP--
ZIFF-DAVIS - ORIGINAL AUTHOR
ELLIS, CRAIG--[1][2][11][23]SF,HP--AMZ
HORN, PETER--[1][2][11][23]SF,HP-- ZD
REED, DAVID V.--W/CLEO ELDON KNOX,[7]--
WFC nn "THE WHISPERING GORILLA" '50
REED, DAVID V.--[3][7][11][23]SF--
GRN DRGN "I THOUGHT I WOULD DIE" '46
GALX "MURDER IN SPACE" '54
WOODRUFF, CLYDE--[1][2][11][23]SF--1 STORY

VERNER, CHRISTOPHER STU.
CHASE, LESLEY--[8]

VERNON, GEORGE S.G.
GEORGE, VERNON--[2][3]MYS--
STOCKWELL "HAMISH MONROE'S EXPERIMENT" '35

VERNON, KATHLEEN R.
DIXON, LESLEY--[9]ROM
VERNON, KAY [R]--[9][21]ROM--
"PHANTOM OF FONTHILL PARK" & MORE

VERRAL, CHARLES S [CHUCK]
EATON, GEORGE L.--[2][11][22][31][33]
CANADIAN-AMERICAN

VERRILL, A[LPHEUS] HYATT
AINSBURY, RAY--[2][10][23]AMERICAN/SF--
"WHEN THE MOON RAN WILD" '62

VERSACE, MARIE TERESA R.
RIOS, TERE--[2][11][31][33]CHILDREN'S BOOKS

VERWER, JOHANNA ELISABETH
JOHANSON, ELISABETH--[1]
VERWER, HANS--[1]

VERY, ALICE N.
BROWN, ALICE VERY--[31]

VESENGI, PAUL E.
BOD, PETER--[1][31]

VESEY, ERNEST BLAKEMAN
LEWIS, ERNEST--[8]

VESTAL, HERMAN BEESON
BEESON--[1][2]
S.A.M.--[1][2]

VESTAL, JEANNE
GOODSPEED, J.M.--V. BERCH LTR '93--
XEROX "CASE OF THE CRUNCHY PEANUT BUTTER"
"RANSOME NOTE" '75

VETSCH, JAKOB
MUNDAS, JAKOB--[1]

VEYSEY, ARTHUR HENRY
VESEY, ARTHUR H[ENRY]--[34]MYS--
APPLETON "CLOCK & THE KEY" '05
APPLETON "CASTLE OF LIES" '06

VEZZANI, FLORA
NEMI, ORSOLA--[22]ITALIAN

VIALL, PATRICIA F.
SINCLAIR, REBECCA--[21][26]ROM--
"MONTANA WILDFIRE"
"PRAIRIE ANGEL" & MORE

VIAN, BORIS
RAVI, BISON--[1]
SCHMUERZ, ADOLPH--[1]
SULLIVAN, VERN--[23]FRENCH/SF--
"S'IRAI CRACHER SUR VOS TOMBES" '46
SULLIVAN, VERNON--[1][3][11]MYS--
AUDUBON "I SPIT ON YOUR GRAVE" '71
VISI, BARON--[1]

VIARD, FELIX
SAINT ROBERT--[1]

VIARD, HENRI LOUIS LUC
WARD, HENRY--[1][2][11][23]

VIAUD, LOUIS MARIE
LOTI, PIERRE--[22]FRENCH

VICKERS, ANTOINETTE L.
FRANCHI, EDA--[1][31]
NINA V.--[1]

VICKERS, ROY
DURHAM, DAVID--[2][3][5][18][29]MYS--
HODDER "EXPLOITS OF FIDELITY DOVE" '24
& 5 OTHERS '23-39
KYLE, EGLETON--[2][11]SF--
KYLE, SEFTON--[3][5][18][28][29]MYS--
JENK "RED HAIR" '33
JENK "SILENCE" '35 & 20 MORE '24-43
SPENCER, JOHN--[3][18][22][29][31]MYS--
HODDER "THE WHISPERING DEATH" '32

VICTOR, JOAN BERG
BERG, JOAN--[31][33]

VICTOR, MRS. M.V.
CUSHMAN, CORRINE--[1]
EDWARDS, ELEANOR LEE--[1]
GRAY, WALTER T.--[1]
KENNEDY, ROSE--[1]
LEGRANDE, LOUIS MD--W/ORVILLE J. VICTOR,[1]
PEABODY, MRS. MARK--[1]
REGESTER, SEELEY--[5][34]MYS--
BEADLE "DEAD LETTER" 1866
BEADLE "FIGURE EIGHT" 1869

VICTOR, ORVILLE J.
LEGRANDE, LOUIS MD--W/MRS. M.V. VICTOR,[1]

VIDAL, [E] GORE LUTHER
BOX, EDGAR--[2][3][5][18][31]MYS--
DUTTON "DEAD BEFORE BEDTIME" '53
DUTTON "DEATH LIKES IT HOT" '54
EVERARD, KATHERINE--G. THIESSEN '93, ADULT--
PYR 23 "CRY SHAME!" '50
HARGRAVE, LEONIE--[1]
KAY, CAMERON--V. BERCH-GM PSEUDS, MYS--
GM 311 "THIEVES FALL OUT" '53
VIDAL, GORE--[1][7][18]

VIENS, CAROL
DANIELS, CAROL--[9][21][26]ROM--
"VALLEY OF DREAMS"

VIERECK, GEORGE SYLVESTER
FOUR CORNERS, GEORGE--[1][31]
VIERECK, G.S.--[1]

VIEUX, MARIE
COLIBRI--[1]

VIGG, PELLE
ERIKSEN, ANDREAS--[22] NORWEGIAN

VIGNE, PAUL
KERHOUEL, GAETAN--[1]
VIGNE, D'OCTON--[1]

VIGUERS, RUTH HILL
HILL, RUTH A.--[22][31][33]AMERICAN

VIKSNINS, GEORGE JURIS
KENECOTT, G.J.--[31]

VILDE, EDUARD
WILDE, EDWARD--[22] ESTONIAN

VILE, DELORES HOLLIDAY
HOLLIDAY, DELORES--[21][26]ROM--
"SEVENTH GATE"
"THE BLUE HOUSE"
"GREYSTONE SHADOWS"

VILENKIN, NIKOLAY MAXIM.
MINSKY, N.--[22]RUSSIAN

VILES, WALTER
BEAUMONT, BENCHLEY--[1]

VILLASENOR, GERVASIO GAL.
GALLARDO, GERVASIO--[7]SF--
BAL "THE FANTASTIC WORLD OF GERVASIO GALLARDO" '76

VILLIARD, PAUL
DEGROS, J.H.--[31][33]

VILLIERS, DAVID HUGH
BUCKINGHAM, DAVID--[1][3]MYS--
MacD "THE WIND TUNNEL" '59
MacD "THE CLIFF FACE" '60

VILOTT-SALSITZ, RHONDI A.
INGRID, CHARLES--[7][23][34]MYS/SF--
DAW 'SAND WARS': #1-6 '87-90
DAW 'MARKED MAN': #1 & 2 '89-91
DAW 'PATTERNS OF CHAOS' #1 '91
VILOTT, RHONDI--[7][23]SF--'84/85
SALSITZ, R.A.V.--[7][23]--
NAL 'DRAGONS': #1-3 '85-90
"UNICORN DANCER"
"DAUGHTER OF DESTINY" '88

VINCENS, MME. CHARLES
ARVEDE, BARINE--[1]

VINCENT, CHARLES
MAEL, PETER/PIERRE--W/CHARLES GAUSSE,[1][2]

VINCENT, FELIX
FELIX--[31]

VINCENTNATHAN, LYNN
DUBOIS, SALLY--[9][21][26]ROM--
"THE MARRIAGE SEASON"

VINCIGUERRA, FRANCESCA
WINWAR, FRANCES--[1]

VINES-HAINES, BEVERLY
CASSIDY, BECCA--[9][21]ROM--
"LUCKY STAR"
WEST, JAMIE--[9][21]ROM--
"A FLAME IN THE MOUNTAINS"

VINEY, JANE
NEVILLE, ANNE--[9][21][26]ROM--
"GOLD IN HER HAIR"
"VOICES OF LOVING"
"INNOCENT DECEPTION"

VINING, CHARLES A.M.
R.T.L.--[8]

VINNING, ELIZABETH GREY
GRAY, ELIZABETH JANET--[1][22][31]AMERICAN CHILDRENS

VINSON, REX THOMAS
KING, VINCENT--[2][7][11][23]SF--
FUTURA "TIME SNAKE & SUPERCLOWN" '76

VINTER, HELEN
SMITH, NAOMI--[8]

VINTER, MICHAEL
GIBBARD, T.S.J.--[7]SF--
HALE "VANDALS OF ETERNITY" '74
"TOROLD CORE" '80
"STARSEED MISSION" '80

VISER, LON
KEVIN, PETER--V. BERCH--BRNDN/
BC PSEUDS, BAE 22, ADULT--
SHORE, VALERY--V. BERCH LTR TO HUBIN '94,MYS--
MAJOR "FINAL PAYMENT" '79

VISHER, HELEN [C] CARUSI
LOMBARD, HELEN--[1]

VISSER, WILLEM J.C.
KLINICUS--[1]
PSIGOLOOG--[1]
VISSER, WILLIE--[1]

VITEK, DONNA JEAN K.
ALEXANDER, DONNA--[9][21][26][31]ROM--
"NO TURNING BACK"
"IN FROM THE STORM" & 2 MORE

VITRINGA, ANNES JOHAN
HOLLAND, JAN--[22] DUTCH
VAN ONDERE, JOCHEM--[22] DUTCH

VIVELO, JACQUELINE J.
VIVELO, JACKIE--[7][33]SF--
"A TRICK OF LIGHT: STORIES TO BE READ AT DUSK" '87

VIVIAN, E[VELYN] CHARLES
CANNELL, CHARLES--[2][22][23][29]MYS--
LANE "AND THE DEVIL" '31
HODDER "PASSIONLESS QUEST" '26 +
CANNELL, CHARLES HENRY--[1][2][3][7]--
"VIVIAN" WAS LEGALIZED
MANN, JACK--[2][3][23][29]MYS--
WRIGHT "ONE TRAGIC NIGHT" '30
WRIGHT "WITH INTENT TO KILL" '36

VIVIAN, HERBERT
A WELL-KNOWN AUTHOR--[7]SF/ROM--
LONG "THE MASTER SINNER: A ROMANCE" '01

VLADIMIROV, IVAN EGORROV.
VOLNOV, IVAN--[22]RUSSIAN

VLAJKOV, TODOR GENCOV
VESELIN--[22] BULGARIAN

VLASTO, JOHN ALEXANDER
ALEXANDER, JOHN--[1][3][22]MYS--
LOW "HOUSE OF SHAYLE" '33
LOW "MURDER AT THE ECLIPSE" '34
REMENHAM, JOHN--[2][3][11][22]MYS--
SKEFF "ARSENIC" '30
SKEFF "FOG" '29 & 10 MORE '28-48

VLCEK, BARTOS
JAVOR, J.--[22] CZECH

VLCEK, ERNST
RICE, ADAM--W/HELMUTH W. MOMMERS,[39]GERMAN/SF

VOELKER, JOHN DONALDSON
TRAVER, ROBERT--[3][29][32]MYS--
ST. MARTIN'S "ANATOMY OF A MURDER" '57
SUS "INTRUDER" NOV '60 AND MORE

VOGAU, BORIS ANDREYEVICH
PILNYAK, BORIS--[1]
PILNYAK, BORIS ANDREYEVIC--[22]RUSSIAN

VOGEL, HARRY BENJAMIN
KINVER, RICHARD--[1]

VOGENITZ, DAVID GEORGE
GEORGE, DAVID--[1][31]

VOHL, U.
DEREK, LOGAN--W/UWE ANTON,[39]GERMAN

VOIGT, ERNA
VOIGT-ROTHER, ERNA--[33]

VOIGT, GUDRUN
VOIGT, JO [IO]--[39][40]GERMAN/MYS--
"DER TODFEIND"

VOIGT, GUDRUN & KARL
GRAY, GEORGE P.--[39][40]GERMAN/MYS--
'FLEDERMAUS' - 19 BOOKS

VOITNOVICI, ALEXANDRU
VOITIN, AL--[1]

VOLK, GEORGE
KIDDE, JANET--[3]MYS--
JOVE "THE PROPHETRESS" '78

VOLK, GORDON
KNOTTS, RAYMOND--[1][22]MYS
SUSSEX, GORDON--[1][22]MYS

VOLKMAN, DONALD
CUTTER, FRANK--[14]ADULT--
OLYM TC#498 "SHOOT - THE MOVIE STAR" '70

VOLKOFF, VLADIMER
BARBARE, RHOLF--[1]
DULOUP, VICTOR--[1][31]

VOLLEAU, ADOLPHE
REVEL--[1]

VOLOSEVICH, GEORGII N.
VLADIMOV, GEORGII N.--[1]

VOLYANSHAYA, GALINA EVG.
NIKOLAEVA, GALINA EVGENEV--[22]RUSSIAN

VOM SCHEIDT, JURGEN
UPTON, MUNRO R.--W/W. ERNSTING, W. KUMMING, W. REINECKE & W. SCHOLZ,[39]GERMAN/SF

VON ALMEDINGEN, MARTHA E.
ALMEDINGEN, E.M.--[22][25][33]ENGLISH CHILDREN'S

VON ANTAL, ADELE SOPHIA C
WALLIS, A.S.C.--[22]DUTCH

VON BADENFELD, EDUARD
SILESIUS, EDUARD--[39]GERMAN

VON BAYER, KARL ROBERT E.
BYR, ROBERT--[1][22]AUSTRIAN-MILITARY NOVELS

VON BEHRENS, BERTHA
HEIMBURG, WILHELMINE--[39]GERMAN

VON BLANKENSEE, THEO
BLANK, MATHIS--[29]MYS--
"FORSEGLADE LAPPAR" '07
"LOSTA GATOR" '09
"VEDERGALLNING" '16 & OTHER

VON BLOCK, BELA [W]
BLACK, JONATHAN--[3]MYS--
MORROW "RIDE THE GOLDEN TIGER" ' 76
CHAMBERTIN, ILYA--W/SYLVIA VON BLOCK,[1][31]
ENDFIELD, MERCEDES--[3]MYS--
BB "LUCKY PIERRE" '75
BB "ON THE BRINK" '75
HENNESSEY, CAROLINE--W/SYLVIA VON BLOCK, [1][31]
LA BARR, CREIGHTON--[1][31]
LUCCHESI, ALDO--[1][31]
MCGINNIS, E.L.--[3]MYS--
BELM "THE STRASSBURG COLLECTION" '69
MEURICE, BLANCA--[1]
PADGETT, DESMOND--[1]
RANDOLPH, GORDON--W/SYLVIA VON BLOCK,[1]
SHOMRONI, REUVEN--[1]
SPRAGUE, W.D.--W/SYLVIA VON BLOCK, V. BERCH--
BEDSIDE CKLST, BAE 20, ADULT--
CHARIOT CB138 "SEX BEHAVIOR OF AMERICAN SECRETARY" '60
MDWD F91 "SEX BEHAVIOR OF AMERICAN HOUSEWIFE" '61
MDWD 154 "LESBIAN IN OUR SOCIETY" '62
LAN 73-420 "SEXUAL BEHAVIOR OF AMERICAN NURSES" '63 & MORE
VERNON, LEE M.--[1]

VON BLOCK, SYLVIA
BEAUMONT, BEVERLY--[1][31]
CHAMBERTIN, ILYA--W/BELA VON BLOCK,[1][31]
CLIFFORD, THEODORE--[1][31]
HENNESSEY, CAROLINE--W/BELA VON BLOCK,[1][31]
RANDOLPH, GORDON--W/BELA VON BLOCK,[1]
SPRAGUE, W.D.--W/BELA VON BLOCK, V. BERCH-
BEDSIDE CKLST, BAE 20,[1]ADULT--
MDWD 154 "LESBIAN IN OUR SOCIETY" '62
LAN 73-420 "SEXUAL BEHAVIOR OF AMERICAN NURSES" '63 & MORE

VON BLUCHER, HUBERTUS
CORELL, H.B.--[39]GERMAN, ADULT

VON BLUCHER, RUTH
VON HOHENBERG, LIANE--[39]GERMAN

VON BORN, ERIC
FINN, ERIK--[29]MYS, 5 NOVELS '38-44

VON BOSELAGER, ADA
COMITTI, GIOCONDA--[39]GERMAN
REGA, FRANCESCA--[39]GERMAN

VON BRANDENSTEIN, RUTH O.
VON OSTAU, RUTH--[39]GERMAN

VON BREDEN, CHRISTIANE F.
CHRISTEN, ADA--[22]AUSTRIAN

VON BROCKDORFF, GERTRUD
STENDAL, GERTRUD--[39]GERMAN

VON BULOW, VICCO
LORIOT--[39]GERMAN

VON BUTTLAR-BRANDENFEL, J
BUTTLAR, JOHANNES--[1]

VON CONRING, FRIEDRICH
GEORG, JUSTUS--[39]GERMAN

VON CUBE, ALEXANDER
DOMIN, MICHAEL--[39]GERMAN

VON CZIFFRA, GEZA
ANDEN, RICHARD--[39][40]GERMAN/MYS
ANTHONY, ALBERT--[39][40]GERMAN/MYS
PIRAT, FRITZ--[39]GERMAN
TRENCK, PETER--[39][40]GERMAN/MYS

VON DEDENROTH, EUGEN H.
HERRMANN, EUGEN--[39]GERMAN
PITAWALL, ERNST--[39]GERMAN
WENDELIN, R.--[39]GERMAN

VON DER BRUGGEN, VENDLA
VON LANGENN, VENDLA--[39]GERMAN

VON DER HEYDEN, FRIEDRICH
HELD, FRANZ--[39]GERMAN

VON DODERER, HEIMITO
DODERER, HEIMITO--[31]

VON DRIGALSKI, ELISABETH
DILL, LIESBET--[39]GERMAN

VON EICHENDORFF, JOSEPH
FLORENS--[39]GERMAN

VON EINEM, CHARLOTTE
INGRISCH, LOTTE--[39]GERMAN
TUVARI, TESSA--[39]GERMAN

VON EINSIEDEL, WALTRAUD I
RUTTING, BARBBARA--[39]GERMAN/JUV

VON ELTZ, LIESELOTTE [H]
HOFFMANN, LIESELOTTE--[39]GERMAN

VON ENDE, RICHARD CHAFFEY
ENDE, RICHARD CHAFFEY V.--[31]

VON ENGEL, SABINE
VON BRITZEN, ANGELA--[39]GERMAN

VON ESCHENBACH, WOLFRAM
ESCHENBACH, WOLFRAM V.--[31]

VON ESCHSTRUTH, MATHILDE
VON DER EICHEN, M.--[39]GERMAN
V. ESCHEN, M.--[39]GERMAN

VON ESCHSTRUTH, NATALY
VON KNOBELDORFF-B, NATALY--[39]GERMAN

VON ETZSCH, WOLF
ELBWART, WILM--[39]GERMAN

VON FABER, BOEHL
CABALLERO, FERNAN--[20] SPANISH

VON GAGERN, KURT
GAFRAN, KURT--[39]GERMAN

VON GATTERBURG, JULIANA
VON STOCKHAUSEN, JULIANA--[39]GERMAN

VON GAUDECKER, HANS
WOLDECK, HANS--[39]GERMAN/JUV

VON GELDERN, EGMONT C.
COLERUS, EGMONT--[39]GERMAN/SF

VON GERHARDT, DAGOBERT
VON AMYNTOR, GERHARD--[22][39]GERMAN

VON GOLSSENAU, ARNOLD F.V
RENN, LUDWIG--[22][39]GERMAN

VON HALLER, HILDEGARD
DIESSEL, HILDEGARD--[39]GERMAN/JUV

VON HANSTEIN, OTFRID
TREBONIUS, R.--[39]GERMAN/MYS/SF
VON HOHENFELS, GUENTHER--[39]GERMAN/MYS/SF
ZEHLEN, OTTO--[39]GERMAN/MYS/SF

VON HEYMER, L.
VON REHREN, LUDMILLA--[39]GERMAN

VON HILDEBRAND, DIETRICH
OTT, PETER--[22]ITALIAN-AMERICAN

VON HINDEBURG, A.B. MARIE
HAY, MARIE--[1][3]MYS--
PUTNAM "THE EVIL VANGARD" '23

VON HIRSCH, TRYGVE EINAR.
STAHLE, STEIN--[29]MYS--
TELL "AANDEMASKEN" '43

VON HOFMANNSTHAL, HUGO
LEVIS--[39]GERMAN/SF
LORIS--[39]GERMAN/SF
MELIKOW--[39]GERMAN/SF
MORREN, THEOPHIL--[39]GERMAN/SF

VON HOLLENIA, ALEXANDER
LERNET-HOLENIA, ALEXANDER--[39]GERMAN/SF

VON HORVATH, OEDOEN
VON HORVATH, ODON--[31]

VON HOYER, GALINA
RACHMANOWA, ALJA--[39]GERMAN

VON HULSEN, ILSE
REICKE, ILSE--[39]GERMAN/MYS/JUV

VON IHERING, GEORG ALBR.
RING, GEORG--[39]GERMAN/JUV

VON INGENHEIM, LUCIANO
ZUCCOLI, LUCIANO--[22]ITALIAN

VON INGERSLEBEN, EMILIE
VON ROTHENFELS, EMMY--[1]GERMAN

VON JANTSCH-STREERBACH, A
VON STREERBACH, ALBERT--[39]GERMAN

VON JEZEWSKI, STANISLAUS
FLAKENHORST, C. v.--[39]GERMAN

VON KAMER, BOGISLAV
ANDERS, RALPH--W/JESCO VON PUTTKAMER, [39]GERMAN/SF

VON KARDORFF, HUBERTA S.
VON WITZLEBEN, UTA--[39]GERMAN/JUV

VON KASCHNITZ-W., MARIE L
KASCHNITZ, MARIE LUISE--[39]GERMAN/SF--

VON KLIMBURG, HANS-ULRICH
GERNOT, JURGEN--[39]GERMAN/MYS--
THINN, AXEL--[39]GERMAN/MYS

VON KOBLINSKI, HANS-JOACH
ANDREAS, BERT--[39]GERMAN, ADULT/MYS/WEST
ANDREAS, J.H.--[39]GERMAN, ADULT/MYS/WEST
BAXTER, MARK--[39]GERMAN, ADULT/MYS/WEST,HP
CAMERON, JOHN--[39]GERMAN, ADULT/MYS/WEST,HP
COTTON, JERRY--[39]GERMAN/MYS,HP
DE LORCA, FRANK--[39]GERMAN, ADULT/MYS/WEST,HP
ELLIOT, BRIAN--[39]GERMAN, ADULT/MYS/WEST,HP
KELLOG, JIM--[39]GERMAN, ADULT/MYS/WEST,HP
KOJAK--[39]GERMAN/MYS,SP
KOLIN, GUNNAR--[39]GERMAN, ADULT/MYS/WEST
LAMONT, ROBERT--[39]GERMAN/MYS/WEST
MARTINEZ, BENITO--[39]GERMAN/MYS/WEST,HP
MCBROWN, JOE--[39]GERMAN/MYS/WEST
NOLAN, FREDERICK--[39]GERMAN/MYS/WEST,HP
OLSON, ANGIE--[39]GERMAN, ADULT/MYS/SF/WEST
SLADE, JACK--[39]GERMAN/WEST,HP--
VON KIRCHSTEIN, DAGMAR--[39]GERMAN/ADULT/MYS, WEST,HP
WAYNE, J.H.--[39]GERMAN/WEST
ZELLER, LIESL--[39]GERMAN, ADULT/HOR

VON KRIESCH, AUGUSTE
VON LENZBURG, A.--[39]GERMAN

VON LAGERSTROEM, KAMILLA
CORVIN, CELIA--[39][40]GERMAN/JUV--
"DER SILBERNE LEUCHTER" '57

VON LOEWIS OF M., ERIKA
LEFFLAR, ERIKA--[39]GERMAN

VON LOSSOW, ELSE
VON HOLLANDER-LOSOW, ELSE--[39]GERMAN

VON MEDEM, IDA
VON DUROW, JOACHIM--[39]GERMAN

VON MELGUNOFF, ALEXANDER
HAEM, A.--[39]GERMAN
MORRIS, DAN--[39]GERMAN

VON MICHALEWSKY, NIKOLAI
ANDERS, BO--[39]GERMAN, ADV/SF
BRANDIS, MARK--[39]GERMAN, ADV/SF
KARELIN, VICTOR--[39]GERMAN, ADV/SF
NORDEN, NICK--[39]GERMAN, ADV/SF

VON MOELLWITZ, GINO F.
FORST, GINO--[39]GERMAN

VON OCHSENFELD, ANTON B-F
HERBSTENBURGER, TONI--[39]GERMAN/JUV

VON OMPTEDA, GEORG
EGESTORFF, GEORG--[22][39]GERMAN

VON OTTO, ELISABETH
CAELESTES, JUNIOR--[39]GERMAN/SF

VON PUTTKAMER, JESCO
ANDERS, RALPH--W/BOGISLAV VON PUTTKAMER, SF

VON REITZENSTEIN, FRAN.
VON NEMMERSDORF, FRANZ--[1]

VON REZNICEK, FELICITAS
FELIX, PAUL--[39]GERMANMYS/JUV

VON RIMANOCZY, CHARLES A.
ELAND, CHARLES--[3]MYS--
HALE "DOSSIER CLOSED" '70
HALE "DESPERATE SEARCH" '71
HALE "GOLD HIJACK" '73

VON ROMMEL, THEODORE
VON GOLDMAR, JON--[39]GERMAN/JUV
VON ROM, THE--[39]GERMAN/JUV
VON ROMMEL, THEA--[39]GERMAN/JUV

VON ROSENBERG, IRINA
SABUROWA, IRINA--[39]GERMAN

VON RUDLOFF, ALFRED FELIX
RUDLOFF, LEO--[1]

VON RUMMEL, MARIANNE [Z]
VON ZIEGLER, MARIANNE--[39]GERMAN/JUV

VON SCHWARTZ, MARIE E.
MELENA, ELPIS--[1]

VON STORCH, ANNE B.
MALCOLMSON, ANNE--[1][31][33]CHILDREN'S

VON WODTKE, CHARLOTTE B.J
JOHNSON, CHARLOTTE BUEL--[31]

VON WOHL, LUDWIG
DE WOHL, LOUIS--[1][8]

VON ZITZEWITZ, HOOT
HOOT--[2]

VON ZOBELTITZ, HANNS
VON SPIELBERG, HANNS--[1]

VON WODKE, CHARLOTTE B.J
JOHNSON, CHARLOTTE BUEL--[1]

VONNEGUT, KURT JR.
FERDINAND--[1]

VOORHIS, HORACE JEREMY
VOORHIS, JERRY--[1]

VOORT, H. VOL
MULTOND--. DE LAET-PPCC#9, P131,DUTCH--
200-300 NOVELS

VOS, ANNA BEYERA
MINNAAR-VOS, ANNA--[1]

VOS-DAHMER VON BUCHOLZ, T
VOS, TONNY--[1]

VOSBEIN, BARBARA
BENJAMIN, NIKKI--[9][21][26]ROM--
"BEST MEDICINE"
"EMILY'S HOUSE" & 3 MORE

VOSS, VIVIAN
VEE, ROGER--[8]

VOSS, WILLI
PLESS, E.W.--[39][40]GERMAN/MYS--
"DER FAHNDER" '85
"GEL" '85
"ASPHALT" '89

VOYNICH, ETHEL L.B.
VOYNICH, E.L.--[1]

VRUGT, J.P.
BLAMAN, ANNA--[1][22] DUTCH

VUGTEVEEN, VERNA AARDEMA
AARDEMA, VERNA--[1][31]--
FOLK TALES '60-92

VULLIAMY, COLWYN EDWARD
ROLLS, ANTHONY--[3][5][22]MYS--
BLES "LOBELIA GROVE" '32
BLES "SCARWEATHER" '34 & 2 MORE '32-34
TEG, TWM--[8]

WACE, M.A.
GOLDEN GORSE--[8]

WADDELL, CHARLES CAREY
CAREY, CHARLES--[3][22][29]MYS--
DODD "THE VAN SUYDEN SAPPHIRES" '05

WADDELL, EVELYN MARGARET
COOK, LYN--[1][31]

WADDELL, MARTIN
SEFTON, CATHERINE--[7][8][33]FANTASY LIT. FOR CHILDREN & YOUNG ADULTS, RUTH NADELMAN

WADDELL, SAMUEL
MAYNE, RUTHERFORD--[8][22]IRISH

WADDINGTON, MIRIAM
MERRITT, E.B.--[1]

WADE, ROBERT [BOB]
DAEMER, WILL--W/BILL MILLER,[1][3][31]MYS--
FARRELL CASE OF THE LONELY LOVERS" '51
DANNER, WILL--W/BILL MILLER, MUNROE SLST 21-WADE MILLER BIBLIO, MYS--
MASTERSON, WHIT--W/BILL MILLER,MUNROE SLST 21-W. MILLER BIBLIO,[2][3][32]MYS--7 NOVELS
EB "SUDDENLY IT'S MIDNIGHT" JAN '58
EQMM "WOMEN IN HIS LIFE" JUN '58
MILLER, WADE--W/BILL MILLER, MUNROE SLST 21-MILLER BIB/V. BERCH-GM PSEUDS, PP 33, MYS--
WILMER, DALE--W/BILL MILLER,[3]MYS--
"MEMO FOR MURDER" '51
"DEAD FALL" '54
"JUNGLE HEAT" '54

WADE, ROSALIND HERSCHEL
CARR, CATHARINE--[1][22][31]ENGLISH

WADE, THOMAS W.
CARTER, BRONSON D.--[2][11]
LA SALLE, VICTOR--[7]SF,HP--
SPENCER "ASSAULT FROM INFINITY"
SPENCER "SEVENTH DIMENSION"
SPENCER "SUNS IN DUO"
LEROYD, RAYMOND--[2][11]
MARTIN, JOHN R.--[2][11]
ROBERTSON, VINCENT--[2][11]
SLOAN, JOHN--[2][11]
WADE, T.W.--[7]SF--
DIGIT "THE WORLD OF THEDA" '62
RPRT "THE UNKNOWN WORLD"
WADE, TOM--[7]SF

WADE, THOMAS W. [CONT]
WADEY, VICTOR--[7]SF--
DIGIT "A PLANET NAMED TERRA" '62
DIGIT "THE UNITED PLANETS" '62
ZEIGFREID, KARL--K. DILBONE-BADGER CKLST, BAE 13,[2]SF,HP--
SPENCER "BEYOND THE GALAXY"
SPENCER "CHAOS IN ARCTURUS"
SPENCER "CHARIOT INTO TIME"

WADELTON, MAGGIE JEANNE
OWEN, MAGGIE--[1]
WADELTON, MAGGIE-OWEN--[1][7]SF--
"SARAH MANDRAKE" '46

WADLEIGH, JOHN
LANGE, OLIVER--V. BERCH LTR TO HUBIN '94,MYS--
STEIN "INCIDENT AT LA JUNTA" '73
SEAVIEW "RED SNOW" '78
STEIN "DEVIL AT HOME" '86
DUTTON "MAKING IT" '89

WADSWORTH, MARY REBECCA
BRANDYWINE, REBECCA--[9]ROM

WAECHTER, GEORGE P.L.
WEBER, VEIT--[34]MYS--
JOHNSON "WOLF, OR THE TRIBUNAL OF BLOOD" 1806

WAGENKNECHT, EDWARD [C]
FORREST, JULIAN--[1][31]

WAGER, WALTER [HERMAN]
HERMANN, WALTER--[1][3]MYS--
AV "OPERATION INTRIGUE" '56
KONG, KING--[7]SF--
'KING KONG' SERIES:
"MY SIDE" '76
TIGER, JOHN--[1][3]MYS--
'I SPY' SERIES
'MISSION IMPOSSIBLE' SERIES
WILLOUGHBY, LEE DAVIS--[21]ROM,HP--
DELL 'MKNG OF AMER' SERIES:
"WILDCATTERS"
"CARIBBEANS"

WAGMAN, FRANS OSCAR
STIG, STURE--[29]MYS--
'SHERLOCK HOLMES' NOVELLETTES
& HISTORICAL '08-10

WAGMANN, ADAM
WAZYK, ADAM--[1]

WAGNER, ALICE
DEISS, JAY--[40]GERMAN/MYS--
"DROGEN UND DOLLARS" '57

WAGNER, CAROL I.
CARROLL, JOELLYN--W/JO BREMER,[9][21][26]ROM--
"RUN BEFORE THE WIND"
"A FLIGHT OF SPLENDOR"
CARROLL, MALISSA--W/MARIAN SCHARF, [9][21][26]ROM--
"MATCH MADE IN HEAVEN"
CARROLL, MARISA--W/MARIAN SCHARF,[21][26]ROM--
NUMEROUS NOVELS
CARROLL, MARISSA--W/MARIAN SCHARF,[9][26]ROM--
"NATURAL ATTRACTION"
"REMEMBERED MAGIC" & 12 MORE

WAGNER, CHARLES PETER
EPAFRODITO--[31]

WAGNER, HARALD
BENNETT, GORDON--[29]MYS
COBRA--[29]MYS
SLANGE, LENNART--[29]MYS--5 NOVELS '14-17

WAGNER, MARGARET DALE
WAGNER, PEGGY--[8]

WAGNER, SHARON [BLYTHE]
KEENE, CAROLYN--[21]ROM--
'RIVER HEIGHTS' #1-7
STEPHENS, BLYTHE--[21][26]ROM--
"WAKE TO DARKNESS"
"GIFT OF MISCHIEF"
"RAINBOW DAYS"
STEPHENS, CASEY--[21][26][29][34]--
ZEBRA "PORTERFIELD LEGACY"
"SHADOWS OF FIELDCREST MANOR" '80

WAHL, THOMAS PETER
CAEDMON, FATHER--[22][31]AMERICAN

WAHLOO, PER
WAHLOO, PETER--[1][23]SWEDISH/SF

WAIFE-GOLDBERG, MARIE
WAIFE, MARIE--[1]

WAINHOUSE, AUSTYN
AUDIART--[8]
CASAVINI, PIERALESANDRO--C. ECKHOFF SLST,[8]--
OLYM TC-49 "BEDROOM PHILOSOPHERS" '65

WAINWRIGHT, GORDON RAY
GORDON, RAY--[8][31]

WAINWRIGHT, JOHN [W]
RIPLEY, JACK--[3][18][29]MYS--
HAM "PIG THAT GOT UP & WALKED SLOWLY
AWAY" '71 & MORE '71-72

WAKEMAN, FREDERIC EVANS
WAKEMAN, EVANS--[8]

WAKEVAINEN, CLARA A.
WEST, CAROL--[1][3]MYS--
VANTAGE "LAUGHING MALEFACTOR" '65

WALBROOK, LOUISE
GORDON--C ECKHOFF SLST--
NEL "THE DEMON'S FEAST"

WALDO, EDWARD HAMILTON
STURGEON, THEODORE--[1][2][11][23][32]MYS/SF--
LEGALIZED TO 'STURGEON'--
NOVELS & DIGEST STORIES [MSMM, MV, EQMM,
SA, SH, SU & MU]

WALDRON, CORBIN A.
CAL, DAKOTA--[8]

WALDRON, MARION PATTON
PATTON, MARION--[1]

WALDRON-SHAH, DIANE L.
WALDRON, D'LYNN--[1][22]AMERICAN

WALES, HUGH GREGORY
WADE, HERBERT--[22]AMERICAN

WALFRIDSSON, WILLY
HELMUTH, WILLIAM--[29]MYS--
DM#11 "FLYGANDE X: ET" '41

WALGREN, OTTO ROLF
ROLF, O.--[29]MYS--
GREBERS "KRING TVA STELETTOS" '28

WALKER, CLIFTON REGINALD
DIXON, RICHARD--[2]

WALKER, DAVID ESDAILE
ESDAILE, DAVID--[8]

WALKER, EDITH
TRAFFORD, JEAN--[8]
WALKER, JEAN BROWN--[8]

WALKER, ELIZABETH NEFF
MATTHEWS, LAURA--[9][21]ROM--
"ALICIA" ONLY
ROTTER, ELIZABETH--[9]ROM--
"PAPER TIGER"
"SEASONS OF LOVE"

WALKER, EMILY KATHLEEN
ASH, KATHLEEN--[9]ROM--
"BEYOND PRIDE"
ASH, PAULINE--[1][9]ROM--
"SEASIDE HOSPITAL"
"MUCH LOVED NURSE"
BARRY, EILEEN--[9]ROM
DEVON, SARAH--[1][9]ROM
DURHAM, ANNE--[1]
ELLIS, LOUISE--[1]
FOSTER, DELIA--[9]ROM
LAWSON, CHRISTINE--[9]ROM
LESTER, JANE--[2][9]ROM
MAYNE, CORA--[9]ROM
MURRAY, JILL--[1][9]ROM
TILBURY, QUENNA--[1][9]ROM
TREEVES, KATHLEEN--[1][9]ROM
VINCENT, HEATHER--[9]ROM
VINCENT, HONOR--[9]ROM
WINCHESTER, KAY--[1][9]ROM

WALKER, IRMA [R.R.]
HARRIS, ANDREA--[3][21][26]ROM/MYS--
PLB "A SCREAM AWAY"
PLB "WINDFALL" & OTHERS
WALKER, IRA--[3][22]--
ABELARD "SOMEONE'S STOLEN NELLIE GREY" 63
ABELARD "MAN IN THE DRIVERS SEAT" '64
WALKER, RUTH--[9][21][26]ROM--
"AIR FORCE WIVES"
"WINGS"

WALKER, JAMES BRAZELTON
WALKER, BRAZ--[1]

WALKER, JOHN
THIRLMERE, ROWLAND--[8]

WALKER, KENNETH FRANCIS
GIFFORD-JONES, W.--[31]

WALKER, KENNETH MACFARLD.
MACFARLANE, KENNETH--[8][22]ENGLISH

WALKER, LOIS ARVIN
ADAMS, CANDICE--[9][21][26]ROM--
"STEAL AWAY"
"FASCINATION" & 11 MORE
ASHLEY, REBECCA--[9][21][26]ROM--
WILLFUL WIDOW"
"LADY FAIR" & 11 MORE
MYLES, SABRINA--[9][21][26]ROM--
"FREEDOM TO LOVE"

WALKER, LUCY
SANDERS, DOROTHY LUCY--[8]

WALKER, MARGARET
ALEXANDER, MARGARET--[9]ROM

WALKER, PETER N[ORMAN]
ARNCLIFFE, ANDREW--[1][3][31]MYS--
HALE "MURDER AFTER THE HOLIDAYS" '85
CORAM, CHRISTOPHER--[1][3][31]MYS--
HALE "A CALL TO DIE" '69
HALE "DEATH ON THE MOTORWAY" '73 & MORE
FERRIS, TOM--[1][3][31]MYS--
HALE "ESPIONAGE FOR A LADY" '69
MANTON, PAUL--[1]
RHEA, NICHOLAS--[3]MYS--
HALE "CONSTABLE ON THE HILL" '79
& 9 MORE '79-TO DATE

WALKER, R.
R.P.--[2]

WALKER, ROBERT WAYNE
CAINE, GEOFFREY--[7][31][33]SF,HP--
DIAM 'ABRAHAM STROUD' #1 & 2 '91
HALE, GLEN--[7][31][33]SF--
"DR. O" '91
ROBERTSON, STEPHEN--[33][34]MYS--
PINN "DECOY" '89
PINN "BLOOD TIES" '89 & 2 MORE '89-90

WALKER, ROWLAND
BLAIR, ANTHONY--[1]
KENWORTHY, HUGH--[1]
OLIVER, ROY--[8]

WALKER, STELLA ARCHER
ARCHER-BATTEN, S.--[8]

WALKER, T. MICHAEL
WHITE ELK, MICHAEL--[1]

WALKER, TOM
COUNCIL OF FOUR--W/CHUCK HANSEN, ROY HUNT,
NORM METCALF, ELLIS MILLS, BOB PETERSON,[2]

WALKER, W. SYLVESTER
COO-EE--[8]

WALKER, WILLIAM
CRINGLE, TOM--[1]

WALKERLEY, RODNEY L.
ATHOS--[1][22][31]ENGLISH
VITESSE, GRANDE--[1][22]ENGLISH

WALL, BARBARA
LUCAS, BARBARA--[1][31]

WALL, JOHN W.
SARBAN--[2][7][11][23]ENGLISH/SF--

WALL, JUDITH H.
HENRY, ANNE--[9][21][26]ROM--
"GLORY RUN"
"BELOVED DREAMER" & 8 MORE

WALL, ROBERT EMMET JR.
WALL, ROBERT E.--[21]ROM--
'THE ARCADIANS'
'THE CANADIANS' SERIES- 7 NOVELS

WALLACE, ALEXANDER FIELD.
FIELDING, A.W.--[31]
FIELDING, XAN--[31]

WALLACE, BILL
MOAMRATH, M.M.--W/JOE PUMILIA,[2]

WALLACE, DAVID
WALLECHINSKY, DAVID--[1]

WALLACE, EDGAR
ANSTRUTHER, JOHN--SAMPSON-YESTERDAY'S
FACES VOL 3
SMITH, E. GRAHAM--SAMPSON-YESTERDAY'S
FACES VOL 3

WALLACE, ELIZABETH VIRG.
WALLACE, BETTY--[8]

WALLACE, ELWYN
DUNCAN, GELIE--[35]AUSTRALIAN--HRWTZ

WALLACE, FLOYD L.
WALLACE, F.L.--[1][32]MYS--
MH "STILL SCREAMING" JUL '56
EQMM "DRIVING LESSON" AUG '57

WALLACE, HELEN
ROY, GORDON--[1]

WALLACE, HENRY
CHALOM, JOHN--[1]
O'DREAMS, JOHN--[1]
UNCLE HENRY--[8]

WALLACE, JOHN
AINTREE--[3][22][36]AUSTRALIAN/MYS--
CRIME BK "BEAUTY WINS" '39
CRIME BK "DEAD 'UN WINS" '40
GRANTHAM, GERALD--[3][22][36]AUSTRALIAN--
POP PUB "DOPE RUNNERS" '40
POP PUB "MYSTERY OF THE S.S TIMOR" '41
TEXAS RANGER--[22][36]AUSTRALIAN/WEST--
PPP "CROSS B" '40
PPP "TRAIL OUTLAWS" '41

WALLACE, LEWIS ALEXANDER
OXON, M.B.--[8]

WALLACE, MARY
LYNCH, M.C.--[3][32]MYS--
MSMM "CAPTIVE CORPSE" OCT '60
LM "UNFORSEEN ELEMENT" MAR '75
LYNCH, MIRIAM--[1][3][29][40]MYS--
PAPLB "BLACKTOWER" '66
LAN "RIVERWOOD" '71 & 35 MORE '56-79
LYNCH, MIRIAM C.--[1][32]MYS
MSMM "DARK CORNER" FEB '60
MSMM "LITTLE ROOM" AUG '60
AHMM "SCOTT FREE" AUG '62
AHMM "SUCH HAPPY PEOPLE" DEC '62
VINCENT, CLAIRE--[3][29][4]MYS--
ARCADIA "PINK CASTLE" '59
ARCADIA "SPELLBOUND" '66
ARCADIA "GARDEN OF SATAN" '70

WALLACE, PAMELA D.
KING, DIANE--W/ELNORA KING,[9][21][26]ROM--
"BELIEVE IN MAGIC"
"ESSENCE OF SUMMER" & 2 MORE
SIMPSON, PAMELA--W/CARLA SIMPSON,
[7][26][34]MYS/SF--
BB "PARTNERS IN TIME" '90
"SEDUCED"

WALLACE, PENELOPE
HALCROW, PENELOPE--[8]

WALLACE, RICHARD H. EDGAR
WALLACE, EDGAR--L. ROBBINS LTR MAR '94,
[11][32][34]ADV/MYS--MANY NOVELS
NUMEROUS DIGEST STORIES [EM, EQMM, EW,
JCM, DT, MY, SA & SB]

WALLACE, RUBY ANN
DEE, RUBY--[31]

WALLACE, WILLIAM KEITH
WALLACE, BILL--[32][33]MYS--
MSMM "THE FIXER" APR '71

WALLACE-CLARKE, GEORGE
HILL, ROWLAND--[1][31]
JAFFA, GEORGE--[1][31]

WALLACE-CRABBE, ROBIN
WALLACE, ROBERT--LACHMAN LST '93, BAE 25,
GOLZ BK BIO,[36]--
GOLZ "TO CATCH A FORGER" '88
COLLINS "PAYDAY" '89
GOLZ "AN AXE TO GRIND" '89
GOLZ "PAINT OUT" '90
GOLZ" GOANNA"
GOLZ "FERAL PALIT"
GOLZ "FINGER PLAY" '91
A&R "FLOOD RAIN" '91
HARPER "ART RAT" '93

WALLACH, IRA
ROBERTS, LILLIAN--[3]MYS--
PAPLB "RAFFERTY & THE GOLD DUST TWINS" '75

WALLACH, LEAH
RANDALL, ELIOT--[14]ADULT--
OLYM TC#445 "ISLE OF GLADNESS" '69

WALLENGREN, AXEL
FAKIR, FALSTAFF--[22]

WALLER, JOHN FRANCIS
SLINGSBY, JONATHAN FREDE--[1][22][34]IRISH--
WARD "THE DEAD BRIDAL" 1856

WALLER, LESLIE
CODY, C[HARLES] S.--[2][3][22][31]MYS--
WW "THE WITCHING HOUR" '52
ACE S108 LIE LIKE A LADY" '55
MANN, PATRICK--[1][3][31]MYS--
DLCT "DOG-DAY AFTERNOON" '73
PUTNAM "THE VACANCY" '73 & MORE
SPIELBERG, STEPHEN--[11]GHOSTED--

WALLER, MARY ELLA
WALLER, M.E.--[1]

WALLERICH, LINDA H.
BENJAMIN, LINDA--[9][21]ROM--
"MIDNIGHT DESIRE"
"TEXAS WILDCAT"
DOUGLASS, JESSICA--[9][21]ROM--
"SNOWFIRE"
"WISH ME A RAINBOW"

WALLEY, DAVID GORDON
TOOMBS, HARRY--[1]

WALLING, ROBERT ALFRED J.
WALLING, R.A.J.--[1]

WALLINGTON, VIVIENNE
DUKE, ELIZABETH--[26]ROM--
HARL "OUTBACK LEGACY"

WALLIS, GEORGE C.
HEATH, ROYSTON--[1][2][23]ENGLISH/SF--
"A CORSAIR IN THE SKY" '12
STANTON, JOHN--[1][2][11]ENGLISH/SF--
WALLIS, B.--[1][2][23]ENGLISH/SF--
WALLIS, B. & G.C.--[2][23]ENGLISH/SF--
AMZ "THE WORLD AT BAY" '28

WALLIS, GERALDINE MCDONALD
CAMPBELL, HOPE--[1][7]SF--
MacM "LOOKING FOR HAMLET: A HAUNTING AT DEEPING LAKE" '87
HUGHES, VIRGINIA--[1]
MCDONALD, KATHY--[1]
WELLS, HELEN--[1]

WALLIS, HENRY MARRIAGE
HILLIERS, ASHTON--[1][3]MYS--
METHUEN "THE WALBURY CASE" '23

WALLIS, PETER
YORK, PETER--[8]

WALLMANN, JEFFREY M.
BAXTER, PHYLLIS--INTRVW BAE 29,[31]ADULT,HP--
TBRN SRS-1003 "HOMEWORK AT TEACHERS" '72
CARTER, NICK--INTRVW BAE 29,[31][34]MYS-HP--
AWARD "ICE TRAP TERROR" '74
"HOUR OF THE WOLF" '75
CUTTER, TOM--INTRVW BAE 29,[31]WEST,HP--
AV 89531 'TRACKER': "OKLAHOMA SCORE" '85
DASILVA, LEON--INTRVW BAE 29,[31]ADV,HP--
LEIS "GREEN HELL" '76
LEIS 4372K "BREAKOUT IN ANGOLA"'77
DAVIS, ROBERT HART--W/BILL PRONZINI, ECHOES#24, MYS,HP--
MU "PILLARS OF SALT AFFAIR" DEC '67
CC "PAWNS OF DEATH" AUG '74
DAVIS, WILLIAM--W/BILL PRONZINI, INTRVW BAE 29, ADULT,HP--
TBRN LLP201 "POLAROID CLUB I" '70
TBRN LLP203 "POLAROID CLUB II" '70
DOUGLAS, AMANDA HART--INTRVW BAE 29, [31]ROM,HP--
LEIS "JAMAICA" '78
ELLIS, WESLEY--INTRVW BAE 29,[31]WEST,HP--
JOVE - 116 BOOKS '82-90
EVANS, TABOR--INTRVW BAE 29, WEST,HP--
'LONGARM' SERIES
GOERING, HELGA--INTRVW BAE 29,[31]ADULT,HP--
TBRN BSS/677-T "PIANO TEACHER" '73
GOODE, ALICIA--INTRVW BAE 29, ADULT,HP--
SURREE SC256 "FOUR-WAY FRENZY" '77
GRAHAM, CARLOTTA--INTRVW BAE 29,[31]ADULT,HP--
FINDLANDIA FBS-1221 "PROWL CAR GIRL" '73
GRANBY, MILTON--INTRVW BAE 29,[31]ADULT,HP--
TBRN BSS/686-T "LADY DENTIST" '73
GRAYSON, ROGER--W/BILL PRONZINI, INTRVW BAE 29, ADULT,HP--
TBRN LLP135 "COMPANY PARTY" '69
GREY, ROMER ZANE--W/BILL PRONZINI, INTRVW BAE 29, WEST,HP--
BELM 51509 "KING OF THE OUTLAW HORDE"
ZGWM "DANGER RIDES DOLLAR WAGON" MAR '70
HALLIDAY, BRETT--W/BILL PRONZINI, ECHOES#23, MYS,HP--
MSMM "DANGER: MIKE SHAYNE AT WORK" APR '72
HARKER, JONATHAN--W/BILL PRONZINI & JOE LANSDALE, INTRVW BAE 29--
BLOODRAKE #3 "HEADSTONE" 'JUN '82
HEFLIN, DONALD--INTRVW BAE 29,[31]ADULT,HP--
TBRN SRS-1022 "TEACHER'S EXPOSURE" '73
JAMES, VIOLA--W/BILL PRONZINI, INTRVW BAE 29, ADULT--
TBRN - TITLES NOT REMEMBERED
JEFFREY, WILLIAM--W/BILL PRONZINI, INTRVW BAE 29, WEST--
AHMM "FIRE HAZZARD" APR '70
AHMM "DAY OF THE MOON" JUN '70
AHMM "FACSIMILE SHOP" SEPT '70
AHMM "SHELL GAME" JUN '70
MSMM "RETRIBUTION" AUG '70
AHMM "MONDAY IS THE DULLEST NIGHT" JUL '70
MSMM "MURDER IS NO MAN'S FRIEND" NOV '70

WALLMANN, JEFFREY M. [CONT]
JEFFREY, WILLIAM [CONT]
AHMM "A CASE FOR QUIET" AUG '71
AHMM "THE ISLAND" AUG '72
AHMM "TEN MILLION DOLLAR HIJACK" JAN '72
AHMM "A RUN OF BAD LUCK" MAR '72
MSMM "I WANT A LAWYER" MAR '73
AHMM "A SLIGHT CASE OF SUSPICION" SEPT '73
TWR 51674 "DUEL AT GOLD BUTTE" '81
LEIS 2017 "BORDER FEVER" '83
JENSEN, PETER--W/BILL PRONZINI--
INTRVW BAE 29, ADULT,HP--
TBRN LLP161 "A MOTHER'S LOVE" '69
TBRN LLP181 "THREE'S A SANDWICH" '70
TBRN RWS109 "VIRGIN COUPLE" '70
JENSEN, PETER--INTRVW BAE 29,[31]AFDULT-HP--
TBRN RWS123 "HER HONOR THE JUDGE" '70
TBRN LLP218 "BLACKMAILED MOTHER I" '70
TBRN LLP220 "BLACKMAILED MOTHER II" '70
TBRN "RAVISHED" '71
TBRN LLP248 "FATHER & SON" '71
KAINE, MYRA--INTRVW BAE 29, ADULT,HP--
TBRN SRS-1001 "TEACHING TEACHER" '72
MAITLAND, MARGARET--W/ELIZABETH L. DUBREUIL,
[7][31]ROM,HP--
LEIS 557TK "LOVE'S GOLDEN CIRCLE" '78
MAITLAND, MARGARET--INTRVW BAE 29,[31]ROM,HP--
LEIS "COME SLOWLY, EDEN"
LEIS "TRIAL"
LEIS "HOW DEEP THE CUP"
LEIS "SUNDAY SEDUCER"
MANN, GEOFFREY M.--INTRVW BAE 29, ADULT,HP--
TBRN LLP366 "SENATOR'S SECRETARY" '74
MARLOWE, ASTON--W/BILL PRONZINI, INTRVW
BAE 29, ADULT,HP--
LLP212 "RAJAH" '70 & OTHERS
MASTERSON, LOUIS--INTRVW BAE 29, WEST,HP--
CORGI 09764 "BLOODY EARTH" '75
CORGI 09794 "NEW ORLEANS GAMBLE" '75
MCELROY, WINSTON--INTRVW BAE 29, ADULT,HP--
TBRN LLP210 "GANG INITIATION" '70
MINER, MATTHEW--INTRVW BAE 29,[31][32]--
"ENEMY LEGION"
MSMM "THERE'S ALWAYS A FLAW" DEC '70
MSMM "FUMMIGATOR" NOV '71
MOUNTBATTEN, RICHARD--W/BILL PRONZINI, INTRVW
BAE 29,ADULT,HP--
TBRN LLP159 "SPELL OF THE BEAST" '69
RENAULT, RICK--W/BILL PRONZINI, INTRVW BAE 29--
BEAVER "DEATH ON FOUR WHEELS" NOV '68
BEAVER "DEEP SIX" NOV '81
RESKIND, JOHN--INTRVW BAE 29,[31]ADULT,HP--
TBRN "UNHOLY MASTER" '69
TBRN "PARKSBURG SAGA [6 VOL]" '70
TBRN LLP276 "CAESAR CONQUERS" '72
TBRN LLP274 "CAESAR'S REVENGE" '72
TBRN LLP272 "CAESAR COMES HOME" '72
ROBARD, JACKSON--INTRVW BAE 29,[31]ADULT,HP--
TBRN RWS181 "PRESENT FOR TEACHER" '72
TBRN RWS207 "TEACHER'S LOUNGE" 72
TRBN BSS632T "PASSIONATE TEACHER" '72
ROBERTS, GRANT--W/BILL PRONZINI, INTRVW
BAE 29, ADULT,HP--
TBRN LLP167 "RELUCTANT COUPLE" '69
TBRN RWS111 "WAYWARD WIVES" '70
TBRN RWS114 "COUPLE AFTER COUPLE" '70
ROBERTS, GRANT--INTRVW BAE 29,[31]ADULT,HP--
TBRN LLP195 "NAKED CIRCLE" '70
TBRN RWS118 "FOUR ON ONE" '70
RYDER, CLIFTON--INTRVW BAE 29, ADULT,HP--
TBRN RWS 236 "BOY'S DEPARTMENT" '73
SAXON, BILL--INTRVW BAE 29,[31]ADULT,HP--
TBRN RAS1404 "JUNKYARD RAPE" '72
TBRN RAS1415 "THE TERRORIST" '72
SHARPE, JON--INTRVW BAE 29, ADULT,HP--
SIGN AE4931 'TRAILSMAN':
"TRAPPER RAMPAGE" '87

WALLMANN, JEFFREY M. [CONT]
SHELDON, SCOTT--INTRVW BAE 29,[31]MYS--
FUTURA "THE IKON" '77
SIMMONS, BLAKE--INTRVW BAE 29,[31]ADULT,HP--
TBRN SRS1005 "FACULTY ADVISOR" '73
SINCLAIR, GRACE--INTRVW BAE 29,[31]ADULT,HP--
TBRN "MOTHER'S SHARE" '71
ST. GERMAIN, GREGORY--INTRVW BAE 29,
[31]MYS,HP--
SIGN AE1827 "RESISTANCE: NIGHT & FOG" '82
SIGN "MAGYAR MASSACRE" '82
TOWNSEND, MARK--W/BILL PRONZINI, INTRVW
BAE 29,[31]ADULT,HP--
TBRN LLP104 "WHITE CAPTIVE" '69
TOWNSEND, MARK--INTRVW BAE 29,[31]ADULT,HP--
TBRN LLP328 "TEENAGE TEASER" '73
VAN DORNE, R.--W/BILL PRONZINI, INTRVW
BAE 29,[31]ADULT,HP--
TBRN RWS129 "DESOLATE COVE" '70
VICTORINE, OMAR--INTRVW BAE 29, ADULT,HP--
TBRN RAS1405 "VIOLATED" '73
WALLMANN, JEFFREY N.--COVER ERROR--
TWR 51528 "DEATH TREK" '80
WATSON, ELIZABETH--W/BILL PRONZINI, INTRVW
BAE 29, ADULT,HP--
TBRN LLP244 "TEACHER'S REWARD" '68
WILLIAMS, AGNES--W/BILL PRONZINI,INTRVW
BAE 29,HP--
TBRN LLP168 "PLAYHOUSE FOR SWINGERS" '69
WILSON, CAROLE--INTRVW BAE 29,[31]ADULT,HP--
TBRN LLP227 "KAREN & MOTHER" '71

WALLNER, CHRISTIAN J.
WINKLER, JOHANNES--[1]

WALLOP, LUCILLE FLETCHER
FLETCHER, LUCILLE--
[22][29][31][32]AMERICAN/MYS--
SC "NIGHT MAN" '46

WALLS, IAN GASCOIGNE
GREENFINGER, MR.--[1]
LINDSAY, DAVID--[1]

WALMSLEY, ARNOLD ROBERT
ROLAND, NICHOLAS--[1][2][11]

WALMSLEY, HAINES
WALMSLEY, BUCK--[1]

WALMSLEY, LEO
MARCH HARE--[1]

WALPOLE, HORACE
HILL, STRAWBERRY--[1]
MARALTO, ONAPHRIO--[1]
MARSHALL, WILLIAM--[1][2]
TYDEUS--[1]
ULTIMUS, ROMANORAM--[1]

WALRAFEN, CONRAD KURT
CONTY, JEAN-PIERRE--[34]MYS--
CTY PR "CANAL STREET" '54
SUZUKI "A BIG SECRET" '69

WALSH, DAVID JOHN
ST. DAVID, JOHN--[1][3]MYS--
AUTHOR "VANISHING OF IRA BOUCK" '36

WALSH, GILLIAN PATON
PATON WALSH, JILL--[7]SF--
MacM "A CHANCE CHILD" '78
MacM "THE GREEN BOOK" '81
VIKING "TORCH" '87

WALSH, JAMES MORGAN
CAREW, JOHN [JACK]--[8][36]AUSTRALIAN
HILL, H. HAVERSTOCK--[2][3][23][36]SF--
HODDER "ANNE OF THE FLYING GAP" '26
HODDER "SPOIL OF THE DESERT" '27
HODDER "THE GOLDEN ISLE" '28
HODDER "GOLDEN HARVEST" '29
HODDER "SECRET OF THE CRATOR" '30
AMZ "TERROR OUT OF SPACE" '34
MADDOCK, STEPHEN--[2][3][11][29]
[36]AUSTRALIAN/MYS--
25 COLLINS NOVELS '33-52
WALSH, J.M.--[1][23][36]AUSTRALIAN--
HAM "MYS OF CRYSTAL SKULL" '29
RPRTS AS BY `WHITE'
WHITE, GEORGE M.--[2][3][11][29]
[36]AUSTRALIAN/MYS--
HAM "MYS OF THE CRYSTAL SKULL" '26

WALSH, JAMES P[ATRICK]
BREATNAC, SEAMUS--[1][31]

WALSH, MARY
LAVIN, MARY--[1]

WALSH, R.F.
CARTER, NICHOLAS--[3]MYS,HP--

WALSH, SHEILA
LEYTON, SOPHIE--[1][8]

WALSH, V.P.
WALSH, KELLY--[9][21]ROM--
"RUSSIAN NIGHTS"
"A PRIVATE AFFAIR"

WALSHE, DOUGLAS
CARR, ADAMS--[1]

WALSTON, MARIE
WALSTON, JOSEPH--[1]

WALTARI, MIKA [T]
NAUTICUS--[1]
RITVALA, M.--[1]

WALTER, DOROTHY BLAKE
BLAKE, KATHERINE--[3][21]--
REYNAL "MY SISTER, MY FRIEND" '65
STEIN "NIGHT STANDS AT THE DOOR" '74
BLAKE, KAY--[1][22][31]AMERICAN
ROSS, KATHERINE--[1][22]AMERICAN
WALTER, KATHERINE--[8]
WALTER, KAY--[8]

WALTERS, J.
OWEN, NORMAN--[1]

WALTERS, J. DONALD
KRIYANANDA--[31]
KRIYANANDA, S.--[31]
KRIYANANDA, SRI--[31]
KRIYANANDA, SWAMI--[31]

WALTERSCHEID, EDWARD C.
WALTERSCHEID, WALTER C.--[2]

WALTHER, THOMAS A.
WALTHER, TOM--[33]

WALTMAN, WILLIAM JOHN
WALTIMORE, IAIN--[1]

WALTON, BRYCE
FRANKLIN, PAUL--[2][11][23]
[32]AMERICAN/MYS/SF--
PU "THE DUEL" SEPT '55
O'HARA, KENNETH--[1][2][23]AMERICAN--
GHOSTED--
AH & HU MAGS
SANDS, DAVE--[2][11][23][32]MYS--
MV "CRIMSON TRAIL" FEB '58
MV "UNHOLY NIGHT" MAR '58

WALTON, HARRY
COLLIER, HARRY--[1][2][11]
FLETCHER, HARRY--[2]

WALTON, JOHN
CONWAY, OLIVE--W/HAROLD BRIGHOUSE,[8]

WALTON, ROBERTA F. SMITH
SMITH, BOBBI--[9][21]ROM--
"BAYOU BRIDE"
"DESERT HEART"

WALTZ, JEAN JACQUES
HANSI--[1]

WALWORTH, JEANETTE R.
ATOM, ANNE--[1]
HADERMAN, JANET H.--[1]
HADERMAN, JEANETTE--[1]

WALZ, AUDREY BOYERS
BONNAMY, FRANCIS--[22][32][34]MYS--
8 NOVELS '31-51
EQMM "LOADED HOUSE" DEC '50

WAN-YING, HSIEH
PING-HSIN--[22]CHINESE

WANDREI, HOWARD E.
COLEY, ROBERT--[1][2][11][23]SF--
GARRON, ROBERT A. [1]--[2][11][32][34]MYS--
"SPICY DETECTIVE ENCORES #3" '87
TB "LEAGUE OF BALD MEN" JUN '46
GRAHAM, HOWARD W.--L. ROBBINS LTR '94,
[1][2][11]
GUERNSEY, H.W.--[2][11][23][32]MYS/SF--
PD "MONKEY WRENCH" APR '37
PD "MURDER CAN WAIT" JUN '37
PD "PINEAPPLE FOR BREAKFAST" AUG '37
MY "PLAY WITH FIRE" JAN '52
VON DREY, HOWARD--L. ROBBINS LTR '94,
[1][2][11]

WANG, HUI-MING
H.M.W.--[31]

WANGDI, MANGYAL
TIGER OF THE SNOWS--[1]

WANGDI, NAMGYAL
NORGAY, TENZING--[1]

WANNAN, JOHN FEARN
FEARN, JOHN--[8]

WANNON, WILLIAM FIELDING
WANNON, BILL--[7]--
"AUSSIE HORROR STORIES" '83

WARBURG, JAMES PAUL
DURFEE, JOHN--[1]
HERRICK, WALLACE--[1]
JAMES, PAUL--[31]
JANUS, PAUL--[1]
PAUL, JAMES--[8]

WARBURG, SANDOL STODDARD
STODDARD, SANDOL--[1][33]

WARD, ARTHUR HENRY S.
FUREY, MICHAEL--[2][3][5][23][29][31]MYS--
JARROLDS "WULFHEIM" '50
ROHMER, SAX--V. BERCH-GM PSEUDS, PP 33,
[2][3][7][32]MYS/SF--49 BOOKS '13-57
JCM "FIRES OF BAAL" APR '57
SA "BREATH OF ALLAH" NOV '59 & OTHERS
WARD, A. SARSFIELD--[1]

WARD, B.
MISTRAL, BENGO--[7]SF,HP--
GANNET "PIRATES OF CEREBUS" '53-

WARD, BILL
CAVAL, PATRICE--C. ECKHOFF-AFTER HRS,
PP 20, ADULT--
AFTER HRS 161 "OUT OF ACTION" '67
MARSHALL, BILL--C. ECKHOFF-AFTER HOURS,
PP 20, ADULT--

WARD, CANDACE
O'BRIEN, LEE--[3]MYS--
POPLB "SWEET WILLIAM IS DEAD" '75
POPLB "WHEN SHE WAKES" '75

WARD, DON
TRACY, POWERS--[22][32]AMERICAN/MYS--
MSMM "THE WAY IT HAPPENED" AUG '58

WARD, EDWARD
WARD, B.--VULTURES OF THE VOID,[7]--
WORLDS OF FANTASY "AFTERMATH"
?? UNCONFIRMED ??

WARD, ELIZABETH CAMPBELL
ALLEN, E.C.--[3][31]MYS--
PYR "THE LAGUNA CONTRACTS" '73
WARD, E.C.--[34]MYS--
ST. MARTIN'S "A NICE LITTLE BEACH TOWN" '89
WARD, ELIZABETH C.--[34]MYS--
WALKER "COAST HIGHWAY 1" '83

WARD, ELIZABETH HONOR
LESLIE, WARD S.--[1][22][31]ENGLISH

WARD, ELIZABETH REBECCA
INCHFAWN, FAY--[1]

WARD, FREDERICH
THUNDERBOLT, CAPT.--[13]AUSTRALIAN

WARD, HAROLD
STARR, H.W.--E.R. HAGEMANN-COMPH. INDEX
BLK MASK, '82
STERLING, WARD--E.R. HAGEMANN-COMPH. INDEX
BLK MASK, '82
ZORRO--[2][7][28][34]--
CORINTH "GRAY CREATURES" '66
CORINTH "SHRIVELING MURDERS" '66
CORINTH "12 MUST DIE" '66

WARD, JOHN C.
MAC AN BHARD, SENGHAN--[1]

WARD, LEW
WARE, L.L.--[34]MYS--
PLAY "GYP THE HEIRESS; OR, THE DEAD
WITNESS" 1892

WARD, LYNDA C.M.
JEFFRIES, JULIA--[9][21][26]ROM--
"THE CHADWICK RING"
"THE CLERGYMAN'S DAUGHTER"

WARD, MARION INEZ
FOX, MARION--[1]

WARD, MARY JOSEPHINE
WARD, MAISIE--[1]

WARD, PHILIP
GREENFIELD, DARBY--[1]

WARD, RICHARD HERON
WARD, R.H.--[1]

WARD, ROBERT M.
CASSIDY, S.J.--V. BERCH LTR TO HUBIN '94, MYS--
JOVE "THE ALTAR BOY" '82

WARD, ROBERT SPENCER
KING, EVAN--[1]

WARD, ROSE ELIZABETH
KNOX, LISBETH--[1]
ROHMER, ELIZABETH SAX--[2][3][11]MYS--
MYH "BIANCA IN BLACK" '58

WARD, STUART
ADAMS, MARY--[1]
ONYX--[1]
PHELPS, ELIZABETH STUART--[1]

WARD-THOMAS, EVELYN B.P.S
ANTHONY, EVELYN--[22][31][34]ENGLISH/MYS--
HUTCH "DEFECTOR" '80
"LEGEND" '69 & 19 MORE '67-83
STEPHENS, EVE--[1]

WARDE, BEATRICE L.
BEAUJON, PAUL--[2][7][23]SF--
WARDE "SHELTER IN BEDLAM" '37

WARDROP, DAVID
KROGE, SUDS--[1]

WARE, EUGENE FITCH
IRONQUILL--[8][22]AMERICAN

WARE, WILLIAM
X.--[1]

WARLOMONT, MAURICE
WALLER, MAX--[22] BELGIAN

WARNER, ANNA BARTLETT
LOTHROP, AMY--[1]

WARNER, ELIZABETH
WARNER, DOUGLAS--W/JOHN D. CURRIE,
[2][3][29][40]MYS--
CASSELL "DEATH OF A BOGEY" '62 & 5 MORE

WARNER, G. GEOFFREY JOHN
JOHNS, GEOFFREY--[1][31]

WARNER, KENNETH LEWIS
MOREL, DIGHTON--[2][11][22][34]MYS--
SECKER "MOONLIGHT RED" '60

WARNER, REGINALD ERNEST
WARNER, REX--[1][7]SF--

WARNER, SUSAN BOGERT
WETHERELL, ELIZABETH--[8][22]
AMERICAN/CHILDREN'S

WARNER-CROZETTI, RUTH G.
CROZETTI, R. WARNER--[31]

WARNLOF, ANNA-LISA
COQUE--[29]MYS--
"DEN LYCKA'LEK" '56

WARREN, DAVID
FEATHERSTONE, D.--[1][31]

WARREN, ED & LORRAINE
CHASE, ROBERT DAVID--W/ED GORMAN, V. BERCH
LTR TO BRINEY '93, MYS--
ST. MARTIN'S "TRUE HAUNTING'S FROM AN OLD NEW ENGLAND CEMETARY" '92

WARREN, EDWARD PERRY
RAILIE, ARTHUR LYON--[8]

WARREN, ELIZABETH AVERY
WARREN, BETSY--[21][33]ROM--
"SONG WITHOUT WORDS"

WARREN, GEORGE
CARTER, NICK--[3][7]MYS,HP--
CHART "VULCAN DISASTER" '76
CHART "DOOMSDAY SPORE" '79
CHART "SUICIDE SEAT" '80
HALLIDAY, BRETT--T. JOHNSON-ECHOES #23, MYS,HP--
MSMM "MEXICAN PAYOFF" MAR '77

WARREN, JOHN BYRNE L.
LANCASTER, WILLIAM--[22]ENGLISH
PRESTON, GEORGE F.--[22]ENGLISH

WARREN, J[OHN] RUSSELL
COVERACK, GILBERT--[3][22]MYS--
HURST "TIME FOR A MURDER" '41
HURST "MAGPIE MURDER" '42
HURST "ATS MYSTERY" '43

WARREN, LINDA
WEST, FRANCES--[9][21][26]ROM--
"HONKY TONK ANGEL"
"WHITE HEAT" & 2 MORE

WARREN, PAT
COX, PATRICIA--[9][21][26]ROM--
"FOREVER FRIENDS"
"FOREVER CHOICE"
"DAYS & KNIGHTS"

WARREN, PATRICIA NELL
KILINA, PATRICIA--[31]

WARREN, PETER WHITSON
WHITSON--[1]

WARREN, ROBERT PENN
WARREN, RED--[1]

WARREN, SAMUEL
WARNER, WARREN--[1][3][22]MYS--
BROWN "THE EXPERIENCES OF A BARRISTER" 1856

WARREN, WENDY
CHANDLER, LAURYN--[26]ROM--
SIL 981 "ROMANTICS ANONYMOUS"
SIL 1033 "OH, BABY!"

WARREN, WILLIAM BOND
WARREN, BILL--[7]AMERICAN/SF--NON-FICT

WARREN, WILLIAM STEPHEN
WARREN, BILLY--[33]

WARRINER, CORNELIA
CROCKETT, JAMES--W/JAMES A. MacPHAIL, [3][22]MYS--
CROWN "LULLABY WITH LUGERS" '46

WARRINER, THURMAN
KERSEY, JOHN--[3][18][29]MYS--
CASSELL "NIGHT OF THE WOLF" '68
TROY, SIMON--[3][18][29][32][40]MYS--
COLLINS "ROAD TO RHUINE" '52
& 11 GOLZ NVLS '55-70
EQMM "ONCE A POLICEMAN" OCT '69
EQMM "LIQUIDATION FILE" AUG '70

WARSHAW, JERRY
WARSH--[33]

WARTSKI, MAUREEN A.C.
CRANE, M.A.--[31][33]
FRANCIS, SHARON--[9][21][26]ROM--
"HOT TIME"
"EARTHLY SPLENDOR" & 4 MORE
JORDAN, LAURA--MELINDA HELFER '93,ROM--
THIS PREVIOUSLY USED BY SANDRA BROWN
LEIGH, CYNTHIA--MELINDA HELFER AUG '93,ROM--
"SILKEN TIGER"
SHANNON, EVELYN--[9][21][26]ROM--
"TWO FOR THE ROAD"
SHORE, FRANCINE--[9][21][26]ROM--
"FLOWER OF DESIRE"
"GOLDEN MAIDEN" & 3 MORE
SINCLAIR, CYNTHIA--[9][21][26]ROM--
"WINTER BLOSSOM"
"BELOVED ENEMY" & 4 MORE
WARD, REBECCA--MELINDA HELFER '93,[26],ROM--
"FAIR FORTUNE"
"WILD ROSE" & 7 MORE

WARWICK, ALAN ROSS
ROSS, ALAN--[1][33]
SIDNEY, FRANK--[1][33]

WARWICK, FRANCIS ALISTAIR
CLIFFORD, MARTIN--[1]HP--
JARDINE, WARWICK--[1][3][29]MYS--
AMAL "CROOK'S LOOT" '32
AMALG "DOOMED MEN" '32 & 30 MORE '32-61
SIDNEY, FRANK--[1]
SPENCER, ROLAND--W/GEOFFREY PROUT,[1]
SYDNEY, FRANK--[1]
VALENTINE, HENRY--W/GEOFFREY PROUT,[1]

WARWICK, SIDNEY
DRAYSON, A.W.--[1]
SIDNEY, FRANK--[1]

WASCJLEWSKI, JAN
MERLIN, JAN--[1]

WASHBURN, MARK
FREY, JAMES N.--[7]SF--
ZEBRA "THE ELIXIR" '86
ZEBRA "U.S.S.A.: A NOVEL" '87
ZEBRA "CIRCLE OF DEATH" '88

WASHINGTON, ELSIE
WELLES, ROSALIND--[9][21]ROM--
"ENTWINED DESTINIES"

WASHINGTON, GLADYS JOSEPH
CURRY, GLADYS J.--[31]

WASHINGTON, M. BEAUCHAMP
BEATON, ANNE--[1][22][31]ENGLISH
BEAUCHAMP, PAT--[1][22][31]ENGLISH
WASHINGTON, PAT BEAUCHAMP--[1][22]ENGLISH

WASHINGTON, SOLOMAN
GLADDEN, WASHINGTON--[8][22]AMERICAN

WASSEFALL, ADELL
PRYOR, ADEL--[1]

WASSERSUG, DR. JOSEPH
BRADFORD M.D., ADAM--[2][11][22][31]AMERICAN

WASYLEWSKI, STANISLAW
BURY, JAN--[22] POLISH

WATERHOUSE, KEITH [S]
FROY, HERALD--W/GUY [S] DEGHY,
[1][22][31]ENGLISH
GIBB, LEE--W/GUY [S] DEGHY,[1][22]ENGLISH

WATERS, HAROLD A.
WATERS, CHRIS--[1]

WATERS, JOHN
WARNER, JACK--[8]

WATERS, ROBERT E.
EMMETT, ROBERT--V. BERCH LTR TO HUBIN '93,
MYS--
SIGN "BEAT A DISTANT DRUM" '81
& 4 MORE '81-2

WATERS, ROSEMARY ELIZAB.
HORSTMANN, ROSEMARY--[8]

WATERSTON, WILLIAM
R.C.W.--[1]

WATFORD, JOEL ALBERT
ESSEX, JON--[1]

WATJEN, CAROLYN L.T.
STAFFORD, CAROLINE--[1][21][34]MYS/ROM--
SIMON "HOUSE OF EXMOOR" '75
"MOIRA" '76 & 2 MORE '75-9

WATKINS, ALAN CLARENCE
WATKINS, A.C.--[36]AUSTRALIAN

WATKINS, ALEX
LINKLATER, J[OSEPH] LANE--M. LACHMAN,
[22][34]MYS--
SW "THE THREAT" DEC '45
DS "FAST TRACK FOR MURDER" JUN '46
SW "BLACK BULL" APR '47
MILL "BLACK OPAL" '47
SD "PLASTICS MURDER" JUN '47
MN "THREE TALL MEN" APR '54 & MORE

WATKINS, ALLAN
OWEN, MICHAEL--[35]AUSTRALIAN,HP--
HRWTZ "JUNGLE RED" '64

WATKINS, ARTHUR T.L.
WATKINS, A.T.L.--[1]ENGLISH
WATKYN, ARTHUR--[1][22][34]ENGLISH/MYS--
3 PLAYS '58-65

WATKINS, MURIEL
JANES, GENE--W/AUDREY ARMITAGE,[35]--
HRWTZ "LADYS FOUND WANTON" '56
HRWTZ "SHROUD FO A SHREW" '56
MCCALL, K.T.--W/AUDREY ARMITAGE,
[34][35][36]MYS--
HRWTZ "CAVIAR TO KILL" '58 & 21 MORE '57-8
NORTH, GERRY--W/AUDREY ARMITAGE,[35][36]--
HRWTZ "MEET GERRY NORTH"
HRWTZ "GERRY NORTH COLLECTS" '59

WATKINS-PITCHFORD, D.J
B.B.--[1][2][11][22][31]ENGLISH
TRAHERNE, MICHAEL--[1][2][22][33]ENGLISH

WATKINSON, BRENDA F.
WATSON, FRANCES--[2]

WATNEY, BERNARD MARTYN
DOLLEY, MARCUS J.--[1]

WATNEY, JOHN B.
ROBERTS, ANTHONY--[1][22][34]ENGLISH/MYS--
GIFFORD "SCHEME FOR ONE" '45

WATSON, ADAM
SCIPIO--[8]

WATSON, ALBERT ERNEST
WATSON, ANDREW--[8]

WATSON, ELLIOT GRANT
LOVEGOOD, JOHN--[8]

WATSON, EVELYN MABEL
PALMER, HALLECK--[1]

WATSON, JACK CHARLES WAU.
CHRYSTIE, EDWARD M.--[8]

WATSON, JAMES WREFORD
WREFORD, JAMES--[8]

WATSON, JANE WERNER
BEDFORD, A.N.--[1]][31][33]AMERICAN
BEDFORD, ANNIE NORTH--[1][22][31][33]AMERICAN
HILL, MONICA--[1][22][31][33]AMERICAN
JASNER, W.K.--[1][31][33]AMERICAN
NAST, ELSA RUTH--[1][22][33]AMERICAN
WERNER, ELSA JANE--[1][33]AMERICAN
WERNER, JANE--[1][33]AMERICAN

WATSON, JOHN
KARTA, NAT--PPCC#3,[27][34]HP--
MUIR WATSON "EAT ME IF YOU MUST" '49
MUIR WATSON "MERRY VIRGIN" '49
MACLAREN, IAN--[1][22] SCOTTISH-AMERICAN
VOGEL, HANS--[27]ENGLISH,HP
ZORE, HYMAN--[27]ENGLISH,HP

WATSON, JOHN REAY
WATSON & REES--W/ARTHUR JOHN REES,[29]MYS--
LANE "MYS OF THE DOWNS" '18

WATSON, JULIA
DE VERE, JANE--[17][21][26]WELSH-ENGLISH/ROM--
"SCARLET WOMAN"
FITZGERALD, JULIE [JULIA]--[17][21][26]
WELSH-ENGLISH/ROM--
"JADE MOON"
"FIREBIRD" & 26 MORE
HAMILTON, JULIA--[17][21][26]
WELSH-ENGLISH/ROM--
"SON OF YORK"
"ANNE OF CLEVES" & 2 MORE

WATSON, LEWIS H.
HARRISON, LEWIS--[3]MYS--
RAND "A STRANGE INFATUATION" 1890
WELCH "NOT TO THE SWIFT" 1891

WATSON, MARY [FRANCES]
TUBALCAIN--[1]
TURNER, LYNN--[9][21][26]ROM--
"MYS TRAIN"
"LASTING GIFT" & 8 MORE

WATSON, MRS. ROBERT A.
CROMARTY, DEAS--[1]

WATSON, PAULINE
POLA--[33]

WATSON, SELWYN VICTOR
SELWYN--[1][3]MYS--
HODDER "OPERATION BALLERINA" '53

WATSON, VIRGINIA CRUSE
WEST, ROGER--[1]

WATSON, WILLIAM LORIMER
LORIMER, ADAM--[1]

WATT, ALEXANDER PETER F.
FRASER, PETER--[8]

WATT, DONALD
CAMERON WATT, DONALD--[1]

WATT, ELSIE GOWANS
GOWANS, ELSA--[1]

WATT, ESME VIOLET
JEANS, ANGELA--[1]

WATT, JOHN F.
KNELLER, FRANK--VULTURES OF THE VOID--
WORLDS OF FANT. '50
MASON, RAY--VULTURES OF THE VOID--
WORLDS OF FANT. '50
MENCET, D.R.--VULTURES OF THE VOID--
WORLDS OF FANT. '50
WATT, JON--S, HOLLAND-SCION CKLST,
PP 27,[34]MYS--
SCION "YOU'RE DEAD RIGHT" '50

WATTERS, BARBARA HUNT
HUNT, BARBARA--[7][31]SF

WATTERS, PATRICIA
EDWARDS, PATRICIA--[21][26]ROM--
"SWEET PROMISED LAND"

WATTERSON, JOHN WILLIAM
COWLEY, RAMSAY--[1]

WATTS, EDGAR JOHN PALMER
PALMER, JOHN--[1][3]MYS--
HODDER "CAVES OF CLARO" '64
HODDER "CRETAN CIPHER" '65
HODDER "ABOVE & BELOW" '67
HODDER "SO MUCH FOR GENNARO" '68

WATTS, HELEN L. HOKE
HOKE, HELEN [L]--[7][31]HOR--
WATTS "MONSTER, MONSTERS, MONSTERS" '75
& MORE '75-84

WATTS, MABEL PIZZEY
LYNN, PATRICIA--[1][31][33]

WATTS, PETER CHRISTOPHER
CHISHOLM, MATT--[19][28]WEST--
PANT "HODGE" '58
PANT "JOE BLADE" '59 & 92 MORE '58-81

WATTS, PETER CHRISTOPHER
JAMES, CY--[19][28]WEST--
PANT "BRASADA GUNS" '61
PANT "BLOOD CREEK" '65 & 19 MORE '61-71
JONES, LUKE--[8][28]WEST--
CNSL "BRASADA" '62
CNSL "THREE CANYONS TO DEATH" '61
MacKINLOCH, DUNCAN--[1][28]HOR--
PANT "ISLAND OF HELL" '61
OWEN, TOM--[1][28]HOR--
PANT "DREAD & THE GLORY" '59
PANT "CIRCUS OF HORROR" '60
WATTS, PETER--[28]--
HODDER "OUT OF YESTERDAY" '50
CORGI "THE LONG NIGHT THROUGH" '62
CORGI "SCREAM & SHOUT" '66

WATTS, WALTER THEODORE
WATTS-DUNTON, THEODORE--[1]

WATTS, [ANNA] BERNADETTE
BERNADETTE--[1][31][33]

WAUGH, ALEXANDER RABAN
WAUGH, ALEC--[29]MYS-"ISLAND IN THE SUN" '56
"FUEL FOR THE FLAME" '60
"MULE ON THE MINURET"

WAUGH, AUBERON
DE ST. CRISPIAN, CRISPIN--[8]

WAUGH, CAROL-LYNN ROESSEL
ROESSEL-WAUGH, C.C.--W/CHARLES G. WAUGH,
[1][33]

WAUGH, CHARLES G.
ROESSEL-WAUGH, C.C.--W/CAROL-LYNN
ROESSEL WAUGH,[1][33]

WAUGH, HILLARY B.
GRANDOWER, ELISSA--[18][26][29]
[34]ENGLISH/MYS/ROM--
"SEAVIEW MANOR" & 3 MORE '76-80
TAYLOR, H. BALDWIN--[3][18][29]MYS--
"DUPLICATE" '64
"TRIUMVERATE" '66
"TROUBLE WITH TYCOONS" '67
WALKER, HARRY--[5][18][29][34]ENGLISH/MYS--
ARCADIA "CASE OF THE MISSING GARDNER" '54

WAX, ROSALIE AMELIA H.
HANKEY, ROSALIE A.--[31]

WAY, ELIZABETH FENWICK
FENWICK, E.P.--[3]--
FARRAR "INCONVENIENT CORPSE" '43
FARRAR "MURDER IN HASTE" '44
FARRAR "TWO NAMES FOR DEATH" '45
FENWICK, ELIZABETH--[1][3]MYS--
HARPER "MAKE-BELIEVE MAN" '63
GOLZ "A NIGHT RUN" '61 & MORE '57-73

WAY, ROBERT E.
BLACK, DAVID--[1][31]

WAYDE, BERNARD
COLLIER, OLD CAP--[1][22]MYS--
'W.I. JAMES' SERIES

WAYE, ELLEN JEANNE
JOSE, ELLEN J.--[1]

WAYMAN, DOROTHY G.
GEOFFREY, THEODATE--[31]

WAYMAN, TONY RUSSELL
CARDUI, VAN--[1][31]
CARDUI, VANESSA--[1][31]
RAHMAN, ABDUL--[1]

WAYNE, CHARLES STOKES
HAZELTINE, HORACE--[2][3][11]MYS--
McCLURG "THE SABLE LORCHA" '12

WAYNE, KYRA PETROVSKAYA
PETROVSKAYA, KYRA--[1][33]

WEAKLEY, JAMES
BENNET, JOHN--[11]

WEALE, ANNE
BLAKE, ANDREA--[9][21]ROM--
"SEPTEMBER IN PARIS"
"NIGHT OF HURRICANE"
WILSON, ANNE--[9]ROM

WEATHERBY, WILLIAM JOHN
PERRY, WILL--[3][40]MYS--
PYR "DEATH OF AN INFORMER" '73
PYR "HOME IN THE DARK" '76
DODD "MURDER AT THE U.S. SENATE" '76
DODD "KREMLIN WATCHER" '78 & MORE '73-8
WEATHERBY, W.J.--[21][34]MYS/ROM--
"CHARIOTS OF FIRE"
"THE MOONDANCERS"
BB "GOLIATH" '81
BB "CORONATION" '90
RPRTS OF 4 BKS AS BY `WILL PERRY'

WEATHERLY, MAX
AVERY, ANDERSON--V. BERCH-MON PSEUDS,
BAE 9, ADULT--
MON 274 "ADULTERESS" '62

WEATHERS, PHILIP JOSEPH
SHERWOOD, MICHAEL--[1]

WEATHERS, WINSTON
PALMER, TOBIAS--[1]

WEATHERSTONE, JUNE IRENE
COLLINS, JUNE--[1]

WEAVER, BERTRAND
HUNTER, PAUL--[22]AMERICAN

WEAVER, GERTRUDE RENTON
COLMORE, G.--[1][7][34]MYS/SF--
HURST "WHISPERS"
HURST "A BROTHER OF THE SHADOW" '26
DUNN, GERTRUDE--[1][2][7]SF--
"UNHOLY DEPTHS" '26
"MARK OF THE BAT;A TALE OF VAMPIRES
LIVING & DEAD" '28
"AND SO FOREVER" '29

WEAVER, GRAHAM
CHARTERIS, LESLIE--W/DONNE AVENELLE,[34]MYS--
GHOSTED--
HODDER "SAINT & TEMPLAR TREASURE" '79

WEAVER, GUSTINE COURSON
LADY GUSTINE--[1]
TEXAS DOLL LADY--[1]

WEAVER, HARRIET SHAW
WRIGHT, JOSEPHINE--[8]

WEAVER, JUDITH
CHAPEL, ASHLEY--[9]ROM
MCBRIDE, HARPER--[9][21][26]ROM--
"GENTLEMEN IN PARADISE"
"TENDER TORMENT"

WEAVER, KATHERINE GREY D.
WEAVER, KITTY--[1]

WEAVER, ROBERT G.
WEBER, RUBIN--W/SAMUEL L. RUBENSTEIN,
[1][3]MYS--
HARPER "THE GRAVEMAKER'S HOUSE" '64

WEBB, ANNE
REEVE, CHRISTOPHER--[3]MYS--
COLLINS "GINGER CAT" '29
JARROLDS "EMERALD KISS" '32 & 6 MORE '29-48

WEBB, ARTHUR PATTERSON
SIMPKIN--[1]

WEBB, AUGUST CAESAR
WEBB, A.C.--[1]

WEBB, BLANCHE A.
DRAPER, BLANCE A.--[2][7]SF--
"THE GREAT AWAKENING" '53

WEBB, C.P.
MACLEAN, ARTHUR--W/G.P. MANN,[34]MYS--
AMALG "REDHEAD FOR DANGER" '58

WEBB, CHARLES HENRY
PAUL, JOHN--[8][22]AMERICAN

WEBB, DOROTHY ANNA
MARCH, JERMYN--[1][3][22]MYS--
HURST "RUST OF MURDER" '24
HURST "DEAR TRAITOR" '25 & 2 MORE '25-9

WEBB, EDWARD MERYON
MERYON, EDWARD--[36]AUSTRALIAN/MYS--
NSWB "AT HOLLAND'S TANK" '22

WEBB, ETHEL
ROCK, DALBY--[1]

WEBB, GODFREY EDWARD C.
ENGLAND, NORMAN--[1]
GODFREY, CHARLES--[1]

WEBB, JACK RANDOLPH
FARR, JOHN--[18][22][31][34]MYS--
"THE BIG SIN" '52
"NAKED ANGEL" '53
"DAMNED LOVELY" '54
"DON'T FEED THE ANIMALS" '55
"BROKEN DOLL" '55
ACE S159 "SHE SHARK" '56
"BAD BLONDE" '56
"BRASS HALO" '57
ACE D235 "LADY & THE SNAKE" '57
ACE D301 "DEADLY COMBO" '58
"DEADLY SEX" '59
"DELICATE DARLING" '59
"ONE FOR MY DAME" '61
"MAKE MY BED SOON" '63
FRIDAY, JOE--[1]
GRADY, TEX--[18][22][29][31]MYS/WEST--
DUTTON "HIGH MESA" '54

WEBB, JEAN FRANCIS III
BROWN, ROSWELL--M. LACHMAN LST '93,
L. ROBBINS LTR,[31][33][37]MYS--
SHDM - STORIES
HAMILL, ETHEL--[1][22][31][33]AMERICAN
KAVANAUGH, IAN--[1][31]HP--DELL
MORRISON, ROBERTA--[3][21][26][29][40]MYS--
PAPLB "TREE OF EVIL" '66 & OTHERS
SCANLON, C.K.M.--W. MURRAY-ECHOES #5, MYS,HP--
GMD 'DAN FOWLER' STORIES
WILLOUGHBY, LEE DAVIS--[1][8][21]ROM,HP--
'MAKING OF AMERICA' SERIES:
"THE CAJUNS"

WEBB, LILIAN JULIAN
STOCKLEY, CYNTHIA--[1]

WEBB, MAGGIE
LEE, SAMANTHA--[7]SF--
ORBIT "CHILDE ROLAND" '89

WEBB, MARTHA [ANNE] G.
MARTIN, LEE--[34]MYS--
MSMM "NIGHTMARE EDGES" FEB '61
ST. MARTIN'S "TOO SANE A MURDER" '84
WINGATE, ANNE--AUTHOR CONFIRMED, MYS--
WALKER "DEATH BY DECEPTION" '88
WALKER "EYE OF ANNA" '90

WEBB, MARY HAYDN
ROSS, LEAH--[1]

WEBB, REGINALD CYRIL
HEADE, REGINALD--[27]ENGLISH--COVER ARTIST
WEBB, CY--[27]ENGLISH--COVER ARTIST
WEBB, CYRIL--[27]ENGLISH--COVER ARTIST

WEBB, RICHARD WILSON
BARRICK, W.--W/HUGH C. WHEELER,[29]MYS--
"DAMEN I PURPURHATTEN" '45
PATRICK, Q.--W/HUGH C. WHEELER, B. BRINEY,
BAE 9,[2][3][5]--8 MYS NVLS '33-41
PATRICK, Q.--W/MARY L. ASWELL,[3][5]MYS--
HARNEY "GRINDLE NIGHTMARE" '35
FARRAR "S.S. MURDER" '33
PATRICK, Q.--[34]MYS--
FARRAR "MURDER AT CAMBRIDGE" '33
PATRICK, Q.--W/MARTHA M. KELLEY,[2][3][5]MYS--
SWAIN "COTTAGE SINISTER" '31
SWAIN "MURDER AT THE WOMEN'S CLUB" '32
QUENTIN, PATRICK--W/HUGH C. WHEELER,
BOB BRINEY, BAE 9, P6,[2][3][5]MYS
STAGGE, JONATHAN--W/HUGH C. WHEELER,
[2][3][5][18][32]MYS--9 NOVELS '37-46
MB "DEATH, MY DARLING DAUGHTERS" JAN '46

WEBB, RUTH ENID B.M.
MORRIS, RUTH--[1][22]AUSTRALIAN

WEBB, SHARON LYNN
WEBB, RON--[23][32]SF--
AHMM "DUMB CANE" JUL '62
MD "A CERTAIN AMOUNT OF POLISH" SEPT '62
FSF "ATOMIC REACTION" '63
AHMM "THE PERSONAL TOUCH" MAY '63
AHMM "INNOCENT GESTURE" JAN '64
FSF "GIRL WITH THE 100 PROOF EYES" '64

WEBB, THOMAS CHARLES P.
ANGELO, TONY--V. BERCH/S. HOLLAND-ARCH CKLST,
BAE 15,J. PRESSMAN,[34]ADULT/MYS--
ARCH "SINNER'S SHROUD" '50
ARCH "SATAN'S SISTER" '51
HARB "HONEY, HOLD THAT SCREAM" '52

WEBB, VICTORIA
LEE, MARTIN--[1]

WEBB, WILLIAM THOMAS
WEBB, W.T.--[1]

WEBBE, GALE DUDLEY
COLE, STEPHEN--[8][22][31]AMERICAN

WEBBER, ANNE MARIE
HENNING, KATJA--[1]

WEBBER, EBBERT T.
WEBBER, BERT--[1][31]--
NON-FICTION

WEBBER, HULDA
KATZ, HILDA--[1]

WEBER, NANCY
HARMISTON, OLIVIA--[1][31]
ROSE, JENNIFER--[1][21][26]ROM--
"SHAMROCK SEASON"
"A TASTE OF HEAVEN" & 6 MORE
WEST, LINDSAY--[1][7]SF--
ACE "EMPIRE OF ANTS" '77

WEBSTER, ALICE JANE C.
WEBSTER, JEAN--[1][33]

WEBSTER, DAVID ENDICOTT
STRONGBLOOD, CASPER--[1]

WEBSTER, EDITH SMITH
SMITH, EDITH LILLIAN--[1]

WEBSTER, JENNIE ELLIS B.
BURDIC, JEANNE ELLIS--[1]

WEBSTER, NOSTRA H.
STERNE, JULIAN--[1][34]MYS--
BOSWELL "SECRET OF THE ZODIAC" '33

WEBSTER, OWEN
PILGRIM, ADAM--[8]

WEDGE, FLORENCE
WAYNE, FRANCIS--[1][22]CANADIAN

WEDGWOOD, CECILY V.
WEDGWOOD, [DAME] C.V.--[1]

WEED, TRUMAN A.W.
WELLINGTON, ANDREW--[1]

WEEKES, A[GNES] R[USSELL]
PRYDE, ANTHONY--[1][34]MYS--
DODD "PURPLE PEARL" '22
DODD "ROWFOREST" '27 & MORE

WEEKLY, MAURICE ARDEN
ARDEN, RICE--[2]

WEEKS, CONSTANCE T.
TOMKINSON, CONSTANCE--[1][22]CANADIAN-ENGLISH

WEES, FRANCIS SHELLEY
SHELLY, FRANCES--[1][33]

WEGENER, MANFRED
WAYER, FRED M.--[39][40]GERMAN/MYS--
`KOMMISSAR X' - 16 BKS
`FLEDERMAUS' #336

WEHEN, JOY DEWEESE
WADE, JENNIFER--[1][34]MYS--
COWARD "THE SINGING WIND" '77

WEHMEYER, LILLIAN [M] B.
BIERMANN, LILLIAN--[31]

WEI, JI
SHI, MUI--[2]

WEI, REX YUE-TIEN
WILLIAMS, REX--[1]

WEIDEMEYER, JOHN WILLIAM
MONTCLAIR, J.W.--[1]

WEIDNER, E.H.
WEIR, EVANGELINE--[2]

WEIGHTMAN, ARCHIBALD JOHN
STUART, ALAN--[8][32]MYS--
LM "THE GREY LADY OF GLENGARRION" MAR '55
LM "NO COMPANY AT CORRIE KEEP" JUN '55

WEIL, JERRY
ADIRONDACK, LESLIE--[14]ADULT--
OLYM TC#459 "ELECTRIC SENSATION" '69
OLYM TC#497 "CAMPUS SLEEP-IN" '70

WEILL, RENE
COOLUS, ROMAIN--[22]FRENCH

WEIMAN, BARBARA OWENS
OWENS, BARBARA--EQMM DEC '92,[32]MYS--
EQMM "CLOUD BENEATH THE EAVES" JAN '78
EQMM "A LITTLE PIECE OF ROOM" DEC '79

WEIN, LEONARD NORMAN
WEIN, LEN--W/DAVID HOUSTON,[7]SF--
TOR 'SWAMP THING' #1 '82
WEIN, LEN--W/RON J. GOULART & MARV WOLFMAN, [7]SF--
POCK "STALKER FROM THE STARS" '78

WEINBAUM, HELEN
KASSON, HELEN [W]--LACHMAN LST,[32]--
MSMM "MUSICAL DOLL" JUL '59
AHMM "OBJECT ALL SUBLIME" DEC '64

WEINBAUM, STANLEY G.
JESSELL, JOHN--[2][11][23]SF--
"THE ADAPTIVE ULTIMATE" '35
STANLEY, MARGE--[2][11][23]SF/ROM--
"THE LADY DANCES" '34

WEINBERG, LAWRENCE E.
WEINBERG, LARRY--[7][33]SF--
11 NOVELS '80-86

WEINBERGER, MOSHE
CARMILLY, MOSHE--[1]

WEINER, MARGERY
LAKE, SARAH--[8]

WEINER, STEWART
LEBREO, STEWART--[1][31]
WEINER, SKIP--[1]

WEINERT, ALOIS
WEINERT-WILTON, LOUIS--[39][40]GERMAN/MYS--
"DIE WEISSE SPINNE" '29
"DIE KONIGIN DER NACHT" '30

WEINHOUSE, BETH
LAWRENCE, MELINDA--[31]

WEINLAND, MANFRED
SHADOW, MIKE--W/WERNER K. GEISA, [39]GERMAN/SF/HOR,HP
TRENTON, OLSH--W/WERNER K. GEISA, [39]GERMAN/SF/WEST,HP

WEINMAN, BENZION
BEN-ZION--[31]

WEINRAUCH, HERSCHEL
VINOKUR, GRIGORY--[1][22]RUSSIAN-AMERICAN

WEINRICH, ANNA KATHARINA
AQUINAS, SISTER MARY--[8][31]

WEINSTEIN, AARON
WYN, A.A.--[1][2]

WEINSTEIN, LOUIS
BARROW, JACKSON--LACHMAN LST '93-PER EQMM--
PULP STORIES

WEINSTEIN, NATHAN W.
IRONIC PROPHET--[1]
WEST, NATHANIEL--[1][2][7]SF--4 BOOKS
WEST, PEP--[1]

WEINSTEIN, SOL
PUMPERNICKLE--[22]AMERICAN

WEINSTOCK, HELEN
LEWIS, FRANCINE--[1][31]
WELLS, HELEN--[1][31] NAME LEGALIZED TO 'WELLS'

WEINTRAUB, WIKTOR
QUIDAM--[1]
THEATES--[1]

WEIR, ROSEMARY
BELL, CATHERINE--[1]
GREEN, R.--[8]

WEIRICH, BOB
DONNIGAN, DREGS--[1]

WEIS, MARGARET [EDITH]
BALDWIN, MARGARET--[1][31][33]

WEISENBORN, GUENTHER
FOERSTER, EBERHARD--[1]
MUNK, CHRISTIAN--[1]

WEISER, MARJORIE P.K.
KATZ, MARJORIE P.--[1]][31][33]

WEISGARD, LEONARD JOSEPH
GREEN, ADAM--[31][33]CHILDREN'S BOOKS

WEISINGER, MORT
GARTH, WILL--[1][2][11][23]SF,HP--
STANDARD
GERIS, TOM ERWIN--[1][2][11]
RECTEZ, IAN--[1][2][11]
SATURN, SERGEANT--[1][2][11]SF,HP--
THRILLING/STARTLING/CAPT. FUTURE

WEISKOP, GRETE
WEDDING, ALEX--[1]

WEISMAN, JOAN
SAVAGE, JOAN--[1]

WEISS, ALBERT MARIA
VON DER CLANA, HEINRICH--[22]GERMAN

WEISS, DAVID
HALIVNI, DAVID--[31]
HALIVNI, DAVID WEISS--[31]

WEISS, EHRICH
HOUDINI, HARRY--[2][11]-- GHOSTED

WEISS, HENRY GEORGE
FLAGG, FRANCIS--[2][7][23][32]SF--
AMZ "MACHINE-MAN OF ARDATHIA" '27
AMZ "NIGHT PEOPLE" '47
MZ "DISTORTION OUT OF SPACE" JUN '65
SN "BY THE HANDS OF THE DEAD" SPR '70
SN "THE SMELL" SUM '70

WEISS, IRVING J.
DI MARCO, GINO--[31]
FORIO, ROBERT--[22][31]AMERICAN

WEISS, JOE
ANATOLE, RAY--SMUT PEDDLER #2, ADULT--
ELITE "WILDCAT HUNT"
TOGA "DAUGHTER OF APHRODITE"
ANATOLE, RAY--W/IRENE GRANDET, SMUT PEDDLER #2--
TOGA "BIG DEAL"
ELITE "DANCING IN THE DARK"
ANDREA, GUY--SMUT PEDDLER #2, ADULT--
KEY "TORMENTED VENUS"
KEY "PASSION PEN"
BOYER, PAM--W/PAM BOYER, SMUT PEDDLER #2, ADULT--
KEY "ARTISTRY IN PASSION" '57
BOYER, PAMELA--SMUT PEDDLER #2, ADULT--
KEY "BLONDE FLAME"
KEY "SHE WOLF"
BROOKS, WILLIAM--SMUT PEDDLER #2, ADULT--
KEY "GIRL GANGS"
DAUPHINE, CLAUDE--SMUT PEDDLER #2,ADULT--
ELITE "ROAMIN' CIRCUS" '59
TOGA "GLAMOUR INCORP." '59
TOGA "DEVIL'S JOKER" '59
ELITE "ROAMIN' CARNIVAL" '60
DAUPHINE-AUMONT--SMUT PEDDLER #2, ADULT--
TOGA "SMART COOKIE" '59
ELITE "FATAL CHARM"
DU PRES, HENRY--SMUT PEDDLER #2, ADULT--
KEY "LOVE IN THE FACE OF DEATH"
MIRBEAU, KEN--SMUT PEDDLER #2, ADULT--
TOGA "BOHEMIAN SET"
ELITE "THE FRANTIC ONES" '60
MIRBEAU-FRANCOIS--SMUT PEDDLER #2, ADULT--
TOGA "CURTAIN CALLS"
NORDAY, MICHAEL--SMUT PEDDLER #2,ADULT--
VIXEN "ON WITH THE DANCE" '54
VIXEN "DESOLATE SANDS" '55
VIXEN "STAGE FOR FOOLS" '55
NORMANDIE, ROGER--SMUT PEDDLER #2, ADULT--
KEY "THE LION'S DEN" '57
KEY "RUN FOR COVER"
PHILIPPE, EDOUARD--SMUT PEDDLER #2, ADULT--
KEY "THE PLAYTHING" '56
KEY "THE RUNAWAYS"
PRIMITIF, GEORGES--SMUT PEDDLER #2, ADULT--
TOGA "MR. WITCH DOCTOR"
SADEN, MAURICE--SMUT PEDDLER #2, ADULT--
KEY "PAGAN HONEYMOON"
KEY "SHE WOLF"
SULLIVAN, VERNON--SMUT PEDDLER #2, AFDULT--
KEY "DARK HUNTER"

WEISS, MORRIS S.
HIGGINGS, INK--[1][31]
SIRROM, WES--[1]

WEISS, [PAUL] SHANDOR
RAINBOW-WIND, SHANDOR--[1]

WEISSMAN, JACK
ANDERSON, GEORGE--[1][22][31]

WELBROCK, GLADYS BALE
BALE, G.F.--W/PATRICIA B. COX,[34]MYS--
CHART "IF THOUGHTS COULD KILL" '90

WELCH, ANN COURTENAY E.
DOUGLAS, ANN C.--[1][31]
EDMONS, ANN C.--[1][31]

WELCH, COLIN
SIMPLE, PETER--[8]

WELCH, EDGAR L.
GAY, J. DREW--[2][7][23]SF--
"MYSTERY OF THE SHROUD: A TALE OF SOCIALISM" '87
GRIP--[2][7][23]SF--2 NOVELS

WELCH, TIMOTHY L.
CAKE, PATRICK--[1][3][31]MYS--
PROTEUS "THE PRO-AM MURDERS" '79

WELCHER, ROSALIND
SLAVIC, ROSALIND WELCHER--[1]

WELDON, A.E.
MACNAMARA, BRINSLEY--[8][34]MYS--
TALBOT "SOME CURIOUS PEOPLE" '45

WELDON, JOHN
MACNAMARA, BRINSLEY--[1][22][31]IRISH

WELFORD, SUE
KELLY, FIONA--[33]MYS--
HODDER 'MYS CLUB' SERIES

WELLBROCK, GLADYS BALE
BALE, G.F.--W/PATRICIA BALE COX,[7][34]MYS/SF--
CHART "IF THOUGHTS COULD KILL" '90

WELLEN, EDWARD [P]
FELDER, PAUL--[1][31][32]--
MSMM "RUB THE WRING WAY" MAY '70
EX "FIGHT FIRE WITH FIRE" OCT '75
GELLERT, LEW--[1][31][32]MYS--
MSMM "DARK MOTIVE" JUN '70
MSMM "BIG DIFFERENCE" DEC '70
KILLIAN, LARRY--[1][31][32]MYS--
MSMM "RECOIL" MAY '71

WELLER, DOROTHY
BERNARD, DOROTHY ANN--[9][21][26]ROM--
"DELICATE DIMENSIONS"
"DESTINY'S TOUCH" & 4 MORE
HALE, DOROTHEA--[9][21][26]ROM--
"A WOMAN'S PEROGATIVE"
"FLIGHT OF FANCY"

WELLER, GEORGE [ANTHONY]
WHARF, MICHAEL--[33]

WELLER, MARY E.P.
BELL, RAMSEY--W/AGNES COOPER,[3]--
HODDER "DRAGON UNDER GROUND" '37
HODDER "DANGEROUS PROMISE" '39
HODDER "THE LAKE OF GHOSTS" '40

WELLES, CARON
JONES, JAN--[9]ROM

WELLES, MARGERY MILLER
MILLER, MARGERY--[1]

WELLMAN, BERT
LAW-ABIDING REVOLUTIONIST--[2]

WELLMAN, MANLY WADE
BARCLAY, GABRIEL--[2][11][23]SF,HP--
ASTONISHING/SUPER SCIENCE STORIES
COTTON, JOHN--[1][2][11][16]
CROW, LEVI--XENOPHILE #2 APR '74, [2][11][16][23]--
'AMERICAN INDIAN LIFE' SERIES:
"YOUNG-MAN-WITH-SKULL-AT-HIS-EARS"
"WARRIOR IN DARKNESS"
"THE HAIRY THUNDERER"
ELM, M.W.--L. ROBBINS LTR MAR '94

WELLMAN, MANLY WADE [CONT]
ELM, MICHAEL W.--L. ROBBINS LTR '94--
OF "AND SLAY NO MORE!" JAN '62
FERNEY, MANUEL--[1][2][11][16]
FIELD, GANS T.--[2][4][11][16][23]SF--
WEIRD TALES 'JUDGE PURSUIVANT'
SERIES '38-41
'JOHN THUNSTONE' SERIES '83-5
"THE BLACK DRAMA' '46
GARTH, WILL--[1][2][11]SF,HP--STANDARD--
NOT SO ACCORDING TO [23]
MALONE, EDWARD DUNN--G. LOVISI RVW '93,SP
PEREZ, JUAN--[1][2][11][23]
WALLACE, ROBERT--T. JOHNSON LTR '94,HP--
WATSON, JOHN H. MD--G. LOVISI RVW '93,SP
WELLS, HAMPTON--[1][2][11][16]
WELLS, WADE--[1][11][16]
WHITELY, T.K.--[2]

WELLMAN, MRS. MANLEY WADE
GARFIELD, FRANCIS--[11]

WELLMAN, WADE
MALONE, EDWARD DUNN--G. LOVISI RVW '93,SP
WATSON, JOHN H. MD--G. LOVISI RVW '93,SP
WELLMAN, WADE--W/MANLEY WADE WELLMAN
[HIS FATHER],[8]

WELLS, ANGUS
BRADY, WILLIAM S.--[28]--
FONTANA 'HAWK' SERIES- 7 NOVELS '79-83
'PEACEMAKER' SERIES- 7 NOVELS
DANCER, J.B.--[2][11][28]WEST--
CORONET 'LAWMAN' SERIES- 3 NOVELS '77-80
EVANS, IAN--[2][7][11][23][28]SF--
CORGI "STARMAIDENS" '77
GARRETT, CHARLES C.--[2][11][28]WEST--
SPHERE 'GUNSLINGER' SERIES-5 NOVELS '78-80
KIRK, MATTHEW--[28]WEST--
GRANADA 'CLAW' SERIES - 6 NOVELS '83-4
KIRK, RICHARD--W/ROBERT P. HOLDSTOCK,
[2][7][23]SF--
CORGI 'RAVEN'SERIES:
"SWORDMISTRESS OF CHAOS" '78
"THE FROZEN GOD" '78
"A TIME OF DYING"
MUIR, JAMES A.--[2][11][23][28]WEST--
SPHERE 'BREED' SERIES-22 NOVELS '76-85
PIKE, CHARLES R.--[2][11][23][28]WEST--
'JUBAL CADE' SERIES - 12 MYFLR NOVELS
7 GRANADA NOVELS
QUILLER, ARTHUR--[2]--
SHARED PSEUD.
SANDON, J.D.--[28]WEST--
GRANADA 'GRINGO' SERIES-5 NOVELS '79-82

WELLS, BASIL [EUGENE]
ELLERMAN, GENE--[2][11][23]AMERICAN/SF--
4 STORIES

WELLS, CAROLYN
WRIGHT, ROWLAND--[3][18][22][29]ENGLISH/MYS--
DODD "DISAPPEARANCE OF KIMBALL WEBB" '20

WELLS, CHARLES HARDING
WELLS, CHARLIE--[29]MYS--
ABELARD "LET THE NIGHT CRY" '53
SIGN 1225 "THE LAST KILL" '55
WELLS, CHUCK--[29][32]MYS--
SFDS "THE COUNTERFEIT MURDERER!" JUL '58

WELLS, GEOFFREY H[ARRY]
WEST, GEOFFREY--[7]--
"H.G. WELLS: A SKETCH FOR A PORTRAIT" '30

WELLS, H.G.
B.B.--[2]
BLISS, REGINALD--[2][4][8][22][23]SF--
"BOON" '15
BROWN, SEPTIMUS--[2]
CRABTREE, JANE--[2]
D.P.--[2]
GLOCKENHAMMER, WALKER--[1][2]
S.B.--[2]
S.S.--[2]
SHOCKENHAMMER, WALTER--[2]
SMITH, SOSTHENES--[1][2]
TYRO--[2]
WELLS, H.S.--[2]
WHEELS, H.G.--[2]

WELLS, HERBERT GEORGE
WELLS, H.G.--[1][32--NOVELS
DIGEST STORIES [EQMM, MZ, SA & SN]

WELLS, LEE EDWIN
COLE, JACKSON--A. TONIK-COLE CKLST "SPICY
ARMADILLO",HP--
TEX RGR "THE DEVIL'S MILL" JAN '47
POOLE, RICHARD--L. ROBBINS LTR '94,[8]
RICHARDS, LEE--V. BERCH-GM PSEUDS, PP 33,
[34]MYS--
GM 495 "HELL STRIP" '55
GM 671 "LUSTY CONQUEST" '57
ACE D424 "SHOOT-OUT AT THE WAY STATION" '60
CHARIOT CB145 "MERCENARY LOVER" '60
BEAC B581F "SEXECUTIVES" '63
BEAC B628F "EAGER BEAVERS" '63
BEAC B706X "PUNKS" '64

WELLS, PATRICIA RAE
DELANEY, GINA--W/ROSLYN ALSOBROOK,
[9][21][26]ROM--
"WILD FURY"
"WILD FLAME"
"WILD SPLENDOR"

WELLS, WINIFRED
CAMERON, CLARE--[18]MYS

WELSH, CHARLES
MCIVOR, IVOR BEN--[1]

WELSH, KEN
BERKELEY, TAYLOR--[35]AUSTRALIAN--
HRWTZ PB346 "GIRL IN THE GILDED CAGE" '67
HRWTZ PB376 "LEGEND OF THE HOLOCAUST" '67
HRWTZ PB392 "BROTHERS OF EVIL" '69
BREYDOR, BILL--[35]AUSTRALIAN--
HRWTZ CAP10 "YOU OUGHTA SEEN US" '69
CARSTAIRS, CHRIS--[35]AUSTRALIAN--
HRWTZ CAP9 "CASTAWAY COMMANDOS" '68
HRWTZ CAP10 "ZERO HEROES" '69
L.A.C. BREYDOR, B.--[35]AUSTRALIAN--
HRWTZ CAP3 "THANK GOD THERE'S AN ARMY" '67
HRWTZ CAP6 "FLYING IS FOR THE BIRDS" '67
MASON, ANDREW--[35]AUSTRALIAN--
HRWTZ "TO THE ENDS OF HELL" '67
HRWTZ "WINGS OF DEATH" '60

WELSH, MARY FLYNN
FLYNN, MARY--[1][33]

WELTY, SUSAN
WELTY, S.F.--[1][33]

WELZENBACH, LANORA
MILLER, LANORA--[7][26]SF/ROM--
"THE DEVIL'S DICE"
"QUICKTHORN"
"THE HOUSE ON WOLF TRAIL"

WENDER, DOROTHEA
WENDER, THEODORA--M. LACHMAN-CRPG, MYS--
AV "KNIGHT MUST FALL" '85
AV "MURDER GETS A DEGREE" '86

WENGROVSKY, CHARLES
WENGROV, CHARLES--[1]

WENKART, HENNY
WENKART, HENRI--[1]

WENTZ, ELMA
MONROE, LYLE--W/ROBERT A. HEINLEIN,[11]SF--

WENZ, PAUL
WARREGO, PAUL--[13]AUSTRALIAN

WERLBERGER, HANS
KADES, HANS--[34][39][40]GERMAN/MYS--
"MENSCHEN IM ZWIELICHT" '59
"AUF DER SONNENSEITE" '70
ANGUS "THE HOUSE OF CRYSTAL" '57

WERMESKERKE-JUNIUS, SOPH.
VAN WOULDE, JOHANNA--[22]DUTCH

WERNBERG, HJALMAR
BJORNSSON, RUDOLF--[29]MYS--
3 BOOKS 1896-1902
SARDOUX, LEON--[29]MYS--
WEIJMERS "DEN GLADDA ANKAN" '07

WERNER, ELSA JANE
BEDFORD, A.N.--[8]
BEDFORD, ANNIE NORTH--[8]
HILL, MONICA--[8]
NAST, ELSA RUTH--[8]
WERNER, JANE--[8]

WERNER, EYVIND OLOF
JOHNSON, EYVIND--[7]SF--
"DREAMS OF ROSES & FIRE"

WERNER, HERMA
COWEN, EVE--[1][31][33]
GLADSTONE, EVE--W/JOYCE GLEIT,
[10][26][29][33]ROM/MYS--
"ENIGMA"
"GHOSTWRITER" & 14 MORE
JARRETT, ROXANNE--[9][21][26][33]ROM--
"IN NAME ONLY"
PINNER, JOMA--[1][33]

WERNER, MORRIS ROBERT
WERNER, M.R.--[1]

WERNER, PATRICIA BARNES
WERNER, PATRICIA--[9][10][26]ROM--
"CHEROKEE BRIDE" & MORE

WERNER, VICTOR EMILE
DALLAS, VINCENT--[1]

WERNER, VIVIAN
JACKSON, STEPHANIE--[1][31]
LESTER, JOHN--[1][31]

WERNICK, SAUL
CARTER, NICK--[3]MYS,HP--
AWARD "AZTEC AVENGER" '74
AWARD "FANATICS OF AL ASAD" '76
AWARD "GALLAGHER PLOT" '76
AWARD "SNAKE FLAG CONSP" '76
AWARD "REVENGE OF THE GENERALS" '78
JULIAN, ROBERT--[3]MYS--
RAVEN "MURDER IN FOCUS" '81

WERNICK, SAUL [CONT]
PENDLETON, DON--[3]MYS,HP--
GE "THE NEW WAR" '81

WERREMEIER, FRIEDHELM
WITTENBOURG, JACOB--[39][40]GERMAN/MYS--
"TAXI NACH LEIPZIG" '70

WERT, LYNETTE L.
LE MON, LYNN--[9][21][26][31]ROM--
"SUNRISE TEMPTATION"
"THIS REBEL HUNGER"

WERTENBACKER, LAEL TUCKER
TUCKER, LAEL--[1]

WERTENBAKER, G. PEYTON
PEYTON, GREEN--[1][2][11]

WERTHEIMER, FREDERICK I.
WERTHAM, FREDERIC--[1][7]SF--
"WORLD OF FANZINES: A SPECIAL FORM OF
COMMUNICATION" '73

WERTHEIMER, LEO
BRUNNER, CONSTANTIN--[22]GERMAN

WERTMULLER, LINA
BROWN, GEORGE--[31]--
"RITA LA ZANZARA" '66

WESANDER, BJOERN K.
COX, P[ATRICK] BRIAN--[1]
STUART, KENNETH--[1]
TANTRIST--[1]

WESCHCKE, CARL L.
GNOSTICUS--[1]

WESLAGER, CLINTON ALFRED
WESLAGER, C.A.--[1]

WESLEY, JOSEPH
STECHER, L.J.--[2]

WESOLOWSKY, JOAN
VINCENT, JOAN--[9][21]ROM--
"THOMASINA"
"CURIOUS ROGUE" & MORE

WESSOLOWSKI, HANS W.
WESSO, [H.W]--[2][11]

WEST, ANTHONY
MACGRIAN, MICHAEL--[1]

WEST, BETTY
BOWEN, BETTY [MORGAN]--[1][22][33]AMERICAN

WEST, CHARLES CONVERSE
BARNABAS--[1][31]

WEST, CHASSIE
MCGILL, JOYCE--[26]ROM--
"A LOVING TOUCH"
"THROUGH LOOKING GLASS"
"UNFORGIVEABLE"

WEST, EMILY GOVAN
PAYNE, EMMY--[1][33]
WEST, EMMY--[1][33]

WEST, FRANCIS HORNER
WEST, FRANK H.--[31]NON-FICT--5 BOOKS '49-81

WEST, G.A.
KAP-O-KASLO--[8]

WEST, GERTRUDE IDA
WEST, TRUDY--[1]

WEST, JENNIFER
JUSTIN, JENNIFER--[9]ROM--
"PASSION'S VICTORY"

WEST, JOANN
WAYNE, JOANNA--[26]ROM--
HARL 288 "DEEP IN THE BAYOU"

WEST, JOYCE [T]
GILBERT, MANU--[1][31]

WEST, MORRIS L.
EAST, MICHAEL [1]--[29][31][36]AUSTRALIAN--
HM "McCREARY MOVES IN" '58
DELL A169 "THE CONCUBINE" '58
DELL K102 "NAKED COUNTRY" '61
MORRIS, JULIAN--[1][31]AUSTRALIAN

WEST, REBECCA
ANDREWS, CICILY FAIRFIELD--[31]

WEST, UTA
ATCHESON, LOUISE--[14]ADULT--
OLYM OPS#22 "THE PARTY" '71, PER CRPG
AUDEN, RENEE--[1][7][14]ADULT--
OLYM OPS#22 "THE PARTY" '71, ON COVER

WEST, WALLACE
BARLOW, ROGER--[1][2]

WEST-WATSON, KEITH C.
CAMPBELL, KEITH--[1][3][22]MYS--
MacD "BORN BEAUTIFUL" '51 & 7 MORE '41-54

WESTBERG, SIGURD
MARK, ARTHUR--[29]MYS--
GEBERS "SPOKCENTRALEN" '20

WESTCOTT-JONES, KENNETH
JONES, K. WESCOTT--[31]

WESTHEIMER, DAVID
SMITH, Z.Z.--[3][29][33]MYS--
SIGN "A VERY PRIVATE ISLAND" '63

WESTIN, JEANNE EDDY
WESTIN, JEAN--[21]ROM--
"LOVE & GLORY"

WESTLAKE, DONALD [EDWIN]
ALLAN, JOHN B.--W. MULLINS-WESTLAKE CKLST,
BAE 20[1]--
MON K55 "ELIZABETH TAYLOR" '61
CHRISTOPHER, BEN--L. MUNROE--
'77 SUNSET STRIP' MAG "ELEPHANT
BLUES" SUM '60
CLARK, CURT--W. MULLINS-WESTLAKE CKLST,
BAE 20,[2][23]SF--
ACE F421 "ANARCHOS" '67
COE, TUCKER--W. MULLINS-WESTLAKE CKLST,
BAE 20,[2][5]MYS--
RNDM "KINDS OF LOVE" '66
RNDM "MURDER AMONG CHILDREN" '68
RNDM "WAX APPLE" '70
RNDM "A JADE IN ARIES" '71
RNDM "DON'T LIE TO ME" '72
CULVER, TIMOTHY J.--W. MULLINS-WESTLAKE CKLST
BAE 20,[2][23][34]MYS--
EVANS "EX-OFFICIO" '70

WESTLAKE, DONALD [EDWIN] [CONT]
CUNNINGHAM, J. MORGAN--W. MULLINS-WESTLAKE
CKLST, BAE 20,[2]HUMOR--
SIGN Q5425 "COMFORT STATION" '73
DEXTER, JOHN--W/LAWRENCE BLOCK, MUNROE
LST 24, ADULT--
NTSD 1513 "NO LONGER A VIRGIN"
ELLIOTT, DON--H. ELLISON LTR JUL '94--
EMB EL306 "THE SINS OF SEENA" '65
HOLT, SAM--R.C. HOLLAND-BAE 20,[32]MYS--
OF "RUMBLE BAIT!" FEB '59
TW "TERROR QUEEN" JUL '59
TW "DEATH WEARS A BIKINI" SEPT '59
OF "SCRAMBLE MY BRAINS" NOV '59
TFDS "REQUIEM FOR A TRAMP!" JAN '60
HOLT, SAMUEL--R.C. HOLLAND-WESTLAKE BIO,
BAE 20,[34]MYS--
TOR "I KNOW A TRICK OR TWO" '86
TOR "ONE OF US IS WRONG" '86
TOR "WHAT I TELL YOU THREE TIMES IS
FALSE" '87
TOR "FOURTH DIMENSION IS DEATH" '89
MARSHALL, ALAN--W/LAWRENCE BLOCK AS
'SHELDON LORD'--
MDWD 41 "A GIRL CALLED HONEY" '60
MDWD 48 "SO WILLING" '60
MARSHALL, ALAN--R.C. HOLLAND-WESTLAKE CKLST
BAE 20, ADULT,HP--
MDWD 15 "ALL MY LOVERS" '59
STAG SP186 "ALL MY LOVERS" ?
MDWD 20 "MAN HUNGRY" '59
MDWD 22 "SALLY" '59
MDWD 28 "ALL THE GIRLS WERE WILLING" '60
MDWD 31 "WIFE NEXT DOOR" '60
MDWD 36 "VIRGIN'S SUMMER" '60
MDWD 51 "ALL ABOUT ANNETTE" '60
BDSD 1202 "OFF LIMITS"
BDSD 1211 "WARPED ONES"
BDSD 1218 "SIN DRIFTER"
MDWD F259 "CRUEL TOUCH" '63
MDWD 149 "APPRENTICE VIRGIN" '62
SALACIOUS, GRACE--MUNROE RVW '93--
'ESCAPADE' MAG "MATING PLACE" AUG '58
SHAW, ANDREW--ELECTRIC SHEEP SLST '92--
? UNCONFIRMED ?
STARK, RICHARD--W. MULLINS-WESTLAKE CKLST,
BAE 20,[2][23][32][34]MYS--
MD "THE LAST GHOST" NOV-DEC '59
MD "DOWN-PAYMENT FOR MURDER" SEPT-OCT '60
AHMM "CURIOUS FACTS PRECEEDING MY
EXECUTION" SEPT '60
AHMM "JUST A LITTLE PRACTICAL JOKE" MAR '61
PERMA M4272 "HUNTER" '62
MH "THE OUTFIT" APR '63
"MAN WITH THE GETAWAY FACE" '63
PERMA M4298 "MOURNER" '63
PERMA M4292 "OUTFIT" '63
POCK 35014 "SCORE" '64
POCK 50149 JUGGER" '65
POCK 50220 "HANDLE" '66
POCK "SEVENTH" '66
MacM "DAMSEL" '67
GM 1803 "RARE COIN SCORE" '67
GM 1861 "GREEN EAGLE SCORE" '67
MacM "DAME" '67
GM 1949 "BLACK ICE SCORE" '68
GM 2037 "SOUR LEMON SCORE" '69
MacM "BLACKBIRD" '69
RNDM "SLAYGROUND" '71
WORLD "LEMON'S NEVER LIE" '71
RNDM "DEADLY EDGE" '71
RNDM "PLUNDER SQUAD" '72
RNDM "BUTCHER'S MOON" '74
WEST, EDWIN--W. MULLINS-WESTLAKE CKLST,
BAE 20, ADULT--
MON 165 "YOUNG & INNOCENT" '60
MON 189 "CAMPUS DOLL" '61

WESTLAKE, DONALD [EDWIN] [CONT]
WEST, EDWIN [CONT]
MON 199 "BROTHER & SISTER" '61
MON 232 "STRANGE AFFAIR" '62
MON 334 "CAMPUS LOVERS" '63

WESTMARLAND, ETHEL LOUISA
COURTNEY, CHRISTINE--[8]
ELLIOTT, ELLEN--[8]

WESTMORELAND, REG
CONWAY, WARD--[1]

WESTMORELAND, VERA GERTR.
ELYSIAN, ANNE--[8]

WESTON, NIGELLA
MIXON, VERONICA--[9]ROM

WESTPHAL, ARNOLD CARL
CHILDREN'S SHEPHERD, THE--[31][33]

WESTPHAL, WILMA ROSS
WEST, NANCY RICHARD--[1]

WESTWATER, AGNES MARTHA
EARLEY, MARTHA--[31]

WESTWOOD, JENNIFER
CHANDLER, JENNIFER--[31]

WETHERBY, EARLENE ADKINS
ADKINS, ERLE--V. BERCH LTR JAN '94, WEST--
HARPER "KILLING REVENGE" '94

WETHERELL, JUNE
FRAME, PATRICIA--[1]

WETHERELL-PEPPER, JOAN A.
ALEXANDER, JOAN--[1][22][31]ENGLISH
PEPPER, JOAN--[1][32]--
LM "BREAD & BUTTER SISTER" JUN '53
LM "HOUSE DOWN THE LANE" AUG '54

WETTERBERG, CARL ANTON
ONKEL, ADAM--[22]SWEDISH

WEVERKA, ROBERT
McMAHON, ROBERT--[1][3]MYS--
GM "THE WIDOWMASTER" '67
[W/S.L. STEBEL AS LEO BERGSON]

WEXLER, JEROME
DELMAR, ROY--[1][31][33]

WEYGAND, JAMES LAMAR
INDIANA, KID--[1]
JAMES. WESTBROOK--[1]

WEYMOUTH, ELIZABETH G.
WEYMOUTH, LALLY--[1]

WHALEY, BARTON STEWART
BARTON, S.W.--[3][7][23]MYS--
MRW "THE LAST PRESIDENT" '80 [W/M. KURLAND]

WHALLEY, DOROTHY
COWLIN, DOROTHY--[1][22][31]ENGLISH
WELL-WISHER TO KING & CITY--[1]

WHARMBY, MARGOT
WINN, ALISON [O.]--[1]

WHARTON, ANNABEL JANE
EPSTEIN, ANN WHARTON--[31]

WHARTON, MICHAEL
SIMPLE, PETER--[8]

WHARTON, WILFRED G.
JOHNSON, DUFF--[34]MYS,HP--
HAM STFFD "THE COME BACK" '52

WHEALLER, CYNTHIA
RICHARDSON, EVELYN--[21][26]ROM--
"EDUCATION OF LADY FRANCIS"
"MISS CRESSWELL'S LONDON TRIUMPH"

WHEAR, [DR.] RACHAEL
LOW, RACHAEL--[1]

WHEARLEY, BOB
EARLEY, FRAN--[9][10][21]ROM--
"RANSOM IN JADE"
"MOVING TARGET" & MORE

WHEAT, CAROLYN
BENNETT, CORINTHA--[9][21][26]ROM--
"JEMIMA DANCER"

WHEAT, PATTE
MAHAN, PAT--[1][31]
MAHAN, PATTE WHEAT--[1][31]
WHEAT-LIEBER, PATTE--[1]

WHEATLEY, HENRY BENJAMIN
WHEATLEY, H.B.--[1]

WHEELAHAN, PAUL
BONNARD, ADAM--[35]AUSTRALIAN--
CLVLD - 4 `HORATIO FABLE' BKS, LATE '60s
CLAY, E. JEFFERSON--[35]AUSTRALIAN--
CLEVELAND
DODGE, EMERSON--[35]AUSTRALIAN--
18 CLEVELAND BKS
BIG HORN 335 "REBEL LOOK BACK"
SANTE FE 326 "NEVER RIDE BACK"
SANTE FE 429 "DAM IT, YOU'RE TROUBLE"
SIERRA 495 "FAST TRAIL TO BOOTHILL"
JEFFERSON, BEN--[35]AUSTRALIAN--
SANTE FE 408 "COYOTE"
MCKINLEY, BRETT--[35]AUSTRALIAN--
12 CLEVELAND BKS
6 SANTE FE BKS

WHEELER, HUGH C.
BARRICK, W.--W/RICHARD W. WEBB,[29]MYS--
"DAMEN I PURPURHATTEN" '45
PATRICK, Q.--W/RICHARD WILSON WEBB,
[2][11][18][22]MYS--7 NOVELS '36-52
QUENTIN, PATRICK--W/RICHARD W. WEBB,
[2][11][18][34]MYS--16 NOVELS '36-65
STAGGE, JONATHAN--W/RICHARD W. WEBB,[2][11]
[18][32][34]MYS--9 NOVELS '36-49
MB "DEATH, MY DARLING DAUGHTERS" JAN '46

WHEELER, MARY JANE
FOWLER, MARY JANE--[1][31]
SIMONSON, MARY JANE--[1]

WHEELER, WILBER
REELHEW, RIBLEW--E.R. HAGEMANN-COMP. INDEX
BLK MASK, '82

WHEELER, [C] GRILEY
GRILEY, CHARLES--[1][31]

WHEELER-NICHOLSON, MALCO.
EATON, GEORGE L.--C. VERRAL-ECHOES #22--
"HAWKS OF THE GOLDEN CRATER" FEB '34
& 5 BILL BARNE'S STORIES

WHEELOCK, MARTHA E.
ALINDER, MARTHA WHEELOCK--[31]

WHEEN, FRANCIS
HOUSE, PATRICIA--[8]

WHELAN, GERALDINE
MELLING, O.R.--[7]SF--
VIKING "THE SINGING STONE" '86
VIKING "FALLING OUT OF TIME" '89

WHELAN, JEROME BERNARD
BRIEN, R.N.--[8]

WHELAN, JOHN
O'FAOLAIN, SEAN--[8]

WHELPTON, [GEORGE] ERIC
LYTE, RICHARD--[1][22][31]FRENCH-ENGLISH
PARRY, JOHN--[1][22]FRENCH-ENGLISH

WHEWAY, JOHN W.
ARMITAGE, HAZEL--[8]
ARMITAGE, VINCENT--[1]
RICHARDS, HILDA--[1]

WHIBLEY, CHARLES
THERSITES--[8]

WHICHER, FRANK
HILTON, MAUDE--[1]

WHISENAND, VALERIE
ADAMS, KASEY--[9][21][26]ROM--
"WINTER'S PROMISE"
"EVER SINCE EVE" & MORE
WHISENAND, VAL--[21]ROM--
"TREASURE HUNTERS"
"GIVEAWAY GIRL"

WHISH, VIOLET E.
SWIFT, STELLA--[8]

WHISHAW, FRED[ERICK J.]
SWAN, EDGAR--[34]MYS--
LONG "LUCK OF THE CZAR" '08

WHISTLER, PENELOPE
EVANS, MARGIAD--[8]

WHISTLER, REGINALD JOHN
WHISTLER, REX--[33]

WHITAKER, PETER
PROTEUS--[8]

WHITAKER, RODNEY W.
LE CAGAT, BENAT--[1][29]MYS
MORAN, J-L--[29]MYS
MORAN, J.L.--[1]
SEARE, NICHOLAS--[1][8][18][29]MYS--
"RUDE TALES & GLORIOUS" '83
TREVANIAN--[3][18]MYS--
CROWN "EIGER SANCTION" '72
CROWN "LOO SANCTION" '73
HRCT "MAIN" '76
CROWN "SHIBUMI" '79
WHITAKER, ROD--[18]MYS--
"THE LANGUAGE OF FILM" '70
SCREENPLAY "EIGER SANCTION" '75

WHITAKER, ROGERS E.M.
FRIMBO, E.M.--[31]

WHITBY, ANTHONY CHARLES
LESSER, ANTHONY--[8]

WHITCOMBE, RICK TRADER
QUILTY, RAFE--[7]SF

WHITE, ALAN
FRASER, JAMES--[3][18][29]MYS--
JENK "EVERGREEN DEATH" '68
JENK "DEADLY NIGHTSHADE" '70 & MORE
WHITNEY, ALEC--[3][18][29]MYS--
ALLEN "EVERY MAN HIS PRIZE" '68
ALLEN "TRIPLE ZERO" '71 & MORE '68-77

WHITE, CAROL
CHASE, EMILY--[1][31]
STANLEY, CAROL--[1]

WHITE, CELIA
TUSTIN, ELIZABETH--[1]

WHITE, CHARLES WILLIAM
WHITE, MAX--[1]

WHITE, CHARLOTTE
COLE, MARIANNE--[9][21][26]ROM--
"GENTLE AWAKENING"
"SHINING PROMISE"
DALE, JENNIFER--[9][21][26]ROM--
"TENDER RHAPSODY"
"REMEMBER MY LOVE"
"FROST FIRE"

WHITE, CONSTANCE
HOWARD, CONSTANCE--[1]

WHITE, ELWYN BROOKS
E.B.W.--[1]
WHITE, ANDY--[1]
WHITE, E.B.--[1]
WHITE, EN--[1]

WHITE, FRANK JAMES
STEWART-HARGREAVES, E.H.I--[8]

WHITE, GEORGIA ATWOOD
ATWOOD, DASCOMB--[1]

WHITE, GERTRUDE MASON
WAKEFIELD, R.I.--[1][34]MYS--
DODD "YOU WILL DIE TODAY!" '53

WHITE, HERBERT OLIVER
MARTYN, OLIVER--[3][9][22]MYS--
MORROW "THE MAN THEY COULDN'T HANG" '33

WHITE, JOHN IRWIN
JOHNS, WHITEY--[31]

WHITE, JUDE GILLIAM
DEVEREAUX, JUDE--[7][9][21][31]SF--
POCK "THE MAIDEN" '88
"A KNIGHT IN SHINING ARMOR" '89 & MORE

WHITE, KATHARINE S.
K.S.W.--[1]

WHITE, LIONEL
BLANCO, L.W.--HAWK/GEORGE KELLY INTERVIEW, MAY 93, "SPYKILL", CONF. BY MARV LACHMAN
CARTER, NICK--W/VALERIE MOOLMAN,[3][29]MYS,HP--
AWARD "MIND POISONERS" '66

WHITE, OSMAR [E.D.]
DENTRY, ROBERT--[31][34]MYS--
WREN "ENCOUNTER AT KHARMEL" '71

WHITE, PAUL HAMILTON H.
JUNGLE DOCTOR--[22][31]AUSTRALIAN

WHITE, PAULINE ARNOLD
ARNOLD, PAULINE--[8]

WHITE, PHYLLIS D. JAMES
JAMES, P.D.--[29][32][34]ENGLISH/MYS--
NOVELS '62-TD
EQMM "MOMENT OF POWER" JUL '68
EQMM "MURDER" OCT '70

WHITE, RANDY
RAMM, CARL--V. BERCH LTR TO HUBIN '94, MYS--
DELL "L.A. WARS" '84
"DENVER STRIKE" '86 & MORE
STRIKER, RANDY--V. BERCH LTR TO HUBIN '94, MYS--
SIGN "DEADLIEST SEX" '81
"DEEP SIX" '81 & MORE

WHITE, RICHARD
AGILE, ROGER--C. ECKHOFF SLST,[14]ADULT--
OLYM TC-434 "BISHOP'S GAMBOL" '68

WHITE, RICHARD ALAN
CABRAL, ALBERTO--[1][31]

WHITE, RUTH C.
MILLER, RUTH WHITE--[1][33]

WHITE, SARA ELIZABETH
WHITE, SALLY JOY--[1]

WHITE, STANHOPE
BANA, DAN--[1]
SABIAD--[1]

WHITE, STANLEY
KRULL, FELIX--[3][8][22][29][31]MYS--
WARD "THE VILLAGE PUB MURDERS" '62
PETO--[1][22]
PETO, JAMES--[1][22]
WHITE, JAMES DILLON--[22][29][34]MYS--
HUTCH "A SPREAD OF SAIL" '75
HM "QUIET RIVER" '53 & MORE '52-79

WHITE, TERI
LEWIS, STEPHEN--[34]MYS--
ALYSON "COWBOY BLUES" '85

WHITE, TERRENCE H.
ASTON, JAMES--[1][2][4][31][33]

WHITE, THEODORE EDWIN
ARBOGAST, DONALD K.--[2]
ARCHER, RON--[2][4][7][11][23][31]SF--
PYR X1679 "LOST IN SPACE" '67
W/DAVE VAN ARNUM
EDWARDS, J.--[2]
EDWARDS, NORMAN--W/TERRY CARR, V. BERCH-MON PSEUDS, BAE 9,[2][4][23]SF--
MON 453 "INVASION FROM 2500" '64
JOHNSTONE, WILLIAM C.--[2]SF,HP--AMAZING
WHITE, TED--[7][8][23]SF--

WHITE, TRENTWELL MASON
TRANT, MARTIN--[1]

WHITE, VICTOR H.
BERARD, RALPH--L. ROBBINS LTR '94,[32]MYS--
SW "MURDER HAPPENS AT BREAKFAST" AUG '44
SW "REST IN PEACE" JUN '46
SW "CRESCENDO OF DEATH" OCT '47
JASON, KEN--L. ROBBINS LTR MAR '94

WHITE, VICTOR H.
TWICE, VINCENT--L. ROBBINS LTR MAR '94

WHITE, WILLIAM
SPINOSSIMUS--[33]

WHITE, WILLIAM A.P.
BOUCHER, ANTHONY--[2][3][7]MYS/SF--
"THE COMPLEAT WEREWOLF & OTs" '69
"FAR & AWAY" '55
DURRANT, THEO--[3]--
PART OF GROUP OF CALIF. WRITERS
HOLMES, H.H.--[2][3][5][7][32]MYS--
DUELL "ROCKET TO THE MORGUE" '42
"NINE TIMES NINE" '40
EQMM "THE STRIPPER" MAY '45
MB "VACANCY WITH CORPSE" FEB '46
MUDGETT, HERMAN W.--[2][11][22][23]
WHITE, PARKER--[2][11]

WHITE, WILLIAM HALE
RUTHERFORD, MARK--[1][22]ENGLISH
SHAPCOTT, REUBEN--[1]ENGLISH

WHITE, WILLIAM ROBINSON
WHITE, ROBIN--[1]

WHITEFIELD, JOHN HUMPHREY
PILIO, GERONE--[8][22]ENGLISH

WHITEHALL, HAROLD
FRITZ--[1][31]

WHITEHAND, JAMES
WHTIEHAND, SATHERLEY--W/DAVID SATHERLEY,[8]

WHITEHEAD, DAVID [HENRY]
BRIDGES, BEN--[28]WEST--
HALE - 13 NOVELS '86-91
LOGAN, MATT--[28]WEST--
HALE "TANNER'S GUNS" '91
WHITEHEAD, JANET--[28]ROM--
HALE "YOURS FOR ETERNITY" '91
HALE "PATTERNS IN THE SNOW" '91

WHITEHEAD, KATE
OXLEY, KATE--[1]

WHITEHOUSE, ARTHUR G.T.
EATON, GEORGE L.--W. MURRAY-ECHOES #20,SP--
'BILL BARNES' STORIES AFTER
C.S. VERRAL QUIT
WHITEHOUSE, ARCH[IBALD]--[22][34]MYS--
HAM "WINGS OF ADVENTURE" '36
WOW "CRIME ON A CONVOY CARRIER" '43

WHITEHOUSE, JEANNE
PETERSON, JEANNE WHITEH.--[33]

WHITEING, RICHARD
ALB--[1]
SPROUT, MR.--[1]
THORNE, WHYTE--[1]

WHITELOCK, LOUISE C.
CLARKSON, L.--[1][2][3]MYS--
WHITE "SHADOW OF JOHN WALLACE" 1884

WHITEMAN, WILLIAM MERED.
TURNER, C. JOHN--[8]

WHITEMORE, HUGH JOHN
GALLUP, RALPH--[31]

WHITFIELD, RAOUL
DECOLTA, RAMON--[5][18]MYS--
BM 'JOE GAR' STORIES
FIELD, TEMPLE--[3][18]MYS--
FARRAR "FIVE" '31
FARRAR "KILLER'S CARNIVAL" '32

WHITFORD, JOAN
FORD, BARRY--[1]
OLDHAM, HUGH R.--[1]

WHITLOCK, RALPH
COUNTRYMAN, THE--[1][31][33]
REYNOLDS, JOHN--[1][33]
REYNOLDS, MADGE--[1][33]

WHITMAN, SYDNEY
CARROLL, SYDNEY [W]--[1][32]MYS--
SUS "COFFEE FOR ONE" DEC '58

WHITNEY, CAROL A.
CARROLL, MARGARET--[26]ROM--
"PRAIRIE LIGHT"

WHITNEY, JULIE
YULYA--[8]

WHITNEY, MARIE LOUISE S.H
WHITNEY, MARYLOU--[1]

WHITNEY, WALTER LANGDON
LANG, DON--[1]

WHITON, JAMES NELSON
BOLO, SOLOMON--[1]
BOYLAN, BOYD--[1][31]

WHITSON, JOHN HARVEY
CARTER, NICK--[5][11]MYS,HP--
GARLAND, LUKE--[1]
HAZELTON, CAPT.--[1]
HAZELTON, COL.--[1]
MERRIWELL, FRANK--[1]
SEWELL, ARTHUR--[1]
SIMS, LT. A.K.--[1][28]WEST--
21 BEADLE & ADAMS NOVELS 1888-95
STANDISH, BURT L.--[1]
STEEL, ADDISON--[1]
STEEL, ROBERT--[1]
STEVENS, MAURICE--[1]
WILLIAMS, RUSSELL--[1]

WHITTAKER, FREDERICK
POYNTZ, LAUNCE--[1]

WHITTEN, WILFRED
O'LONDON, JOHN--[1]

WHITTET, GEORGE SORLEY
JOK--[1]
KERR, JOHN O'CONNELL--[1]
MONKLAND, GEORGE--[1]

WHITTINGHAM, RICHARD
DAVID, ANDREW--[31]--
CHILDREN'S BKS
PAIGE, DAVID--[31]--
CHILDREN'S BKS

WHITTINGTON, HARRY
CARTER, ASHLEY--HOLLAND-WHITTINGTON BIO, CKLST, BAE 9,[21][28]ROM--
19 NOVELS '75-86
DAVIS, ROBERT HART--A. TONIK-ECHOES #24,HP--
MU "GHOST RIDERS AFFAIR" JUL '66
MU "BEAUTY & BEAST AFFAIR" MAR '66

WHITTINGTON, HARRY [CONT]
DAVIS, ROBERT HART [CONT]
MU "BRAINWASH AFFAIR" SEPT '66
MU "LIGHT KILL AFFAIR" JAN '67
EVANS, TABOR--[18][28]WEST,HP--
JOVE 'LONGARM' SERIES:
"LONGARM" '78
"TEXAS RANGERS" '79
"THE WENDIGO" '79
"AVENGING ANGELS" '79
"THE HATCHETT MEN" '79
"ON THE BORDER" '79
"IN THE INDIAN NATION" '80
"THE LOGGERS" '80
"THE HI-GRADERS" '81
"THE GOLDEN LADY" '81
"THE BLUE NORTHER" '81
"THE NESTERS" '81
"ON THE HUMBOLT" '81
"IN LINCOLN CTY" '82
"IN SILVER CITY" '82
"IN BOULDER CANYON" '82
"IN THE BIG THICKETT" '82
"THE LONE STAR VENGEANCE" '83
"THE LONE STAR RESCUE" '85
HARRISON, WHIT--R.C. HOLLAND-WHITTINGTON BIO, CKLST, BAE 9,[3][18][28]ADULT--
ORIG 714 "BODY & PASSION" '52
VENUS 153 "SAILOR'S WEEKEND" '52
ORIG 718 "SAVAGE LOVE" '52
ORIG 742 "SHANTY ROAD" '52
PHAN 508 "SWAMP KILL" '52
PHAN 511 "VIOLENT NIGHT" '52
POPLB "NATURE GIRL" '52
VENUS 158 "GIRL ON PAROLE" '53
VENUS 161 "ARMY GIRL" '53
ZEN ZB-35 "MAN CRAZY" '60
BEAC 350 "STRIP THE TOWN NAKED" '60
BEAC 392 "ANY WOMAN HE WANTED" '60
BEAC 416 "A WOMAN POSSESSED" '61
HOLLAND, KEL--K. MILLET, BAE 12,[18][28][29]ADULT--
BEAC B682X "STRANGE YOUNG WIFE" '63
BEAC B714 "TEMPTED" '64
MOSSIG, HANK A.--J. HOFFMANN-PP 40, MYS--
GERM PANTH 200
RPRT OF "MOURN THE HANGMAN"
MYERS, HARRIET KATHRYN--R.C. HOLLAND-WHITTINGTON BIO/CKLST, BAE 9, [21][28][29]ROM--
ACE D543 "SMALL TOWN NURSE" '62
ACE D564 "PRODIGAL NURSE" '63
NRE, HITTIER--B. CRIDER INTRVW '93--
GREENLEAF - TITLE UNKNOWN
PALMER, JOE--[29]--
X-BOK #27 "MODARENS ANSIKTE"
PHILLIPS, STEVE--[1][31]
SHEPARD, SHEP--V. BERCH--
BDSD BKS CKLST, BAE 20, ADULT--
BDSD 802 "NAKED LUST" '59
SHEPHERD, SHEP--[32]MYS--
JU "PEPPER IN HIS TRACKS" JAN '56
SHEPPARD, SHEP--V. BERCH--
BDSD BKS, BAE 20, ADULT--
NV 953 "EXOTIC SINNER" '59
STEPHENS, SUZANNE--R. JAMES-PP 40, P57
STEVENS, BLAINE--[26][28][29]ROM--
JOVE "THE OUT LANDERS" '79
JOVE "ISLAND OF KINGS" '81
JOVE "EMBRACE THE WIND" '82
STUART, CLAY--K. MILLET-BAE 12, [18][28][29]ADULT--
BEAC B698X "HIS BROTHERS WIFE" '64
WELLS, HONDO--[18][28]WEST--
ACE "PRAIRIE RAIDERS" '63
NAL "SHADOW AT NOON" '77 RPTS PYR 169

WHITTINGTON, HARRY [CONT]
  WHITE, HARRY--K. MILLET-BAE 12, [18][28][32]WEST--
    PYR 169 "SHADOW AT NOON" '55
    SF "YOU CAN'T KILL LUCK" JAN '57
  WHITNEY, HALLAM--R.C. HOLLAND-WHITTINGTON BIO, CKLST, BAE 9,[28][29]ADULT--
    ORIG 723 "BACKWOODS HUSSY" '52
    CARN 923 "SINNERS CLUB" '53
    CARN 931 "BACKWOODS SHACK" '53
    ORIG 731 "SHACK ROAD" '53
    ORIG 737 "CITY GIRL" '54
    ACE S-153 "THE WILD SEED" '56
  WHITTIER, HENRI--R. JAMES-PP 40, P57

WHITTINGTON-EGAN, RICHARD
  BARRINGTON, NICHOLAS--[1]
  CURZON, CHARLES--[1]
  DOUGHTY, NIGEL--[1]

WHYTE, DONALD
  SENNACHIE--[1]

WHYTE, HENRY
  FIOUN--[1]

WIATR, LINDA CATHERINE
  COLLINS, LAUREL--[9][21][26]ROM--
    LEIS "DARK SURRENDER" '88 & 4 MORE

WIBBERLEY, LEONARD [P.O.]
  HOLTON, LEONARD--[3][5][18][29]MYS--
    DODD "MIRROR OF HELL" '72
    DODD "DEVIL TO PAY" & MORE '60-77
  O'CONNOR, PATRICK--[2][5][11][18][22]MYS--
    CHILDRENS FICTION
  WEBB, CHRISTOPHER--[1][2][18]
    CHILDRENS FICTION

WICHERS, HERMAN P. SCHON.
  BELCAMPO--[22][23]DUTCH/SF

WICKER, RANDOLFE HAYDEN
  HAYDEN, C. GERVIN--[31]

WICKER, THOMAS GREY
  CONNOLLY, PAUL--V. BERCH-GM PSEUDS, PP 33,[2][3][31]MYS--
    GM 188 "GET OUT OF TOWN" '51
    GM 224 "TEARS ARE FOR ANGELS" '52
    GM 500 "SO FAIR, SO EVIL" '55
  WICKER, TOM--[31]

WICKHAM, JEAN
  GORDON, JEAN--[1]

WICKHAM, JOHN
  WILSDEN, CLEMENSFORD--[1]

WICKING, GEORGE WALTER
  WICKING, G.W.--[36]AUSTRALIAN/MYS--
    A&R "GLORY BOX MYS" '36
    WRIGHT "BALES OF TROUBLE" '37
    A&R "MYSTERIOUS VALLEY" '38
    BATCHELOR "GALLEONS GOLD" '40

WICKS, KATHARINE G.
  GIBSON, KATHARINE--[1]

WICKSTEED, MARGARET HOPE
  HOPE, MARGARET--[8]

WICKSTROM, VICTOR HUGO
  SWAHN, CHRISTER--[29]MYS--
    FRITZES "ENHOSPITALSHISTORIA" 1883

WIDDEMER, IRENE
  WARD, IRELAND--[1]

WIDDEMER, MABEL CLELAND
  CLELAND, MABEL--[1][22][33]AMERICAN
  LUDLUM, MABEL CLELAND--[1][22][31][33]AMERICAN

WIDGERY, JEAN-ANNE
  WIDGERY, JAN--[8]

WIDNER, ARTHUR L.
  LAMBERT, ARTHUR--[1][2][11]

WIEDENBECK, EMILIE AGNES
  MABLE, PETER--[8]

WIEDER, ROBERT S.
  SHANNON, ROBERT--[1]

WIEGAND, URSULA
  SONNTAG, USCHI--[1]

WIEHE, EVELYN M.C. MORD.
  MORDAUNT, ELEANOR--[1][22]MYS
  MORDAUNT, ELINOR--[22][34]MYS--
    HUTCH "AND THEN __?" '27
    HUTCH "DEATH IT IS & OTHER STORIES" '39
  RIPOSTE, A.--[1][22]MYS

WIEMER, SUSANNE
  KEVIN, KELLY--[39][40]GERMAN/MYS--
    \`PLUTONIUM POLICE' SERIES
    \`KOMMISSAR X' SERIES

WIENER, FRANZ
  DE CROISSET, FRANCIS--[22]FRENCH

WIENER, NORBERT
  NORBERT, W.--[2][11][23]SF--
    FSF "MIRACLE OF THE BROOM CLOSET" '52
    "CROSSROAD IN TIME: SS-THE BRAIN" '53

WIENER, THOMAS G.
  WINNER, THOMAS G.--[1]

WIER, STUART AUSTIN
  AUSTIN, STUART--[1]

WIERSMA, STANLEY M.
  BUNING, SIETZE--[1][31]

WIESEL, ELIEZER
  WIESEL, ELIE--[1]

WIESLER, ROLF
  WILLIS, TED--[29]MYS

WIETE, ROBIN LEANNE
  GRAYSON, LEANNE--[26]ROM--
    "REBEL WIND"

WIGGINS, DAVID
  PRIESTLEY, ROBERT--[8]

WIGGLESWORTH, MARTIN
  WORTH, MARTIN--[8]

WIGGS, SUSAN
  CHILDRESS, SUSAN--[21]ROM--
    "EMBRACE THE DAY"

WIGHT, JAMES ALFRED
  HERRIOT, JAMES--B&M COLL #71,[6][31][33]--
    VETERINARY STORIES

WIGNALL, ANNE
ACLAND, ALICE--[1][31]
MARRECO, ANNE--[1]

WIGNALL, T[REVOR] C.
DENE, ALAN--[1]
REES, DAVID--[1]

WIGNELL, EDNA
WIGNELL, EDEL--[7]SF--
WALTER McVITTY BKS ""ESCAPE BY DELUGE" '89

WILBER, RICHARD ARNOLD
WILBER, RICK--[7]SF--NON-FICT

WILBY, BASIL LESLIE
KNIGHT, GARETH--[7][8][31]SF--NON-FICT

WILCOCK, EVELYN
DEWAR, EVELYN--[34]MYS--
BLES "PERFUMES OF ARABIA" '73
BLES "A DYING BUSINESS" '74

WILCOX, COLLIN
COLLINS, JEFFREY--[1]
WICK, CARTER--[18][29][34]MYS--
SAT REVW "FACELESS MAN" '75
RAVEN "DARK HOUSE, DARKROAD" '81

WILCOX, HARRY
DERBY, MARK--[3][22][32]MYS--
COLLINS "MALAYAN ROSE" '51
COLLINS "BIG WATER" '53
SUS "MAN WHO SOLD SILENCE" AUG '58
SUS "KEY TO THE FUTURE" MAY '59
SUS "DEATH FROM A FRIEND" JUL '59
COLLINS "THE TIGRESS" '59 & 8 MORE '51-61
SUS "HIGH TERROR" JUL '70

WILD, DORA MARY
BROOME, DORA--[8]

WILD, REGINALD
EDWARDS, LEONARD--[8]

WILDE, JANE FRANCESCA S.
LADY WILDE--[11]

WILDENVEY, HERMAN
BILLER, KRISTIAN--W/SVEN ELVESTAD,[29]MYS

WILDING, PHILIP
FRASER, JEFFERSON--[1][8]ENGLISH
HAYNES, JOHN ROBERT--[2][7][11][23]ENGLISH/SF--
"THE SCREAM FROM OUTER SPACE" '55
MARSHALL, LLOYD--[1][8]ENGLISH
RUSSELL, ERLE--[1][8]ENGLISH
STANTON, BORDEN--[1][8]ENGLISH
STEWART, LOGAN--[1]ENGLISH
STUART, LOGAN--[1][8]ENGLISH

WILDMAN, CORINNA
CUNLIFFE, CORINNA--[9][21][26]ROM--
"HAND OF FORTUNE"
"PLAY OF HEARTS"
"UNSUITABLE CHAPERONE"

WILES, DOMINI
VAN HASSEN, AMY--[3]MYS--
NEL "MENACE" '81

WILEY, CARL A.
SAUNDERS, RUSSELL--[1][2]

WILHELM, LAMBERT
LAMBERT, WILLIAM J. III--[11]

WILHELM, TERRI LYNN
LINDSEY, TERRI--[26]ROM--
"GOING MY WAY"
LYNN, TERRI--[26]ROM--
"UNCOMMON STOCK"
"VALENTINE'S SUMMER"

WILHELMSSON, YNGVE M.
ARMAS, RICHARD--[29]MYS

WILHITE, BETTIE MARIE
AUGUST, ELIZABETH--[9][21][26]ROM--
"WILD HORSE CANYON"
"A SMALL FAVOR" & 16 MORE
DOUGLAS, ELIZABETH--[9][21][26]ROM--
"AN EXQUISITE DECEPTION"
"VIRGINIA BRIDE"
PAGE, BETSY--[9][21][26]ROM--
"PERFECT FRAME"
"WYOMIAN" & 3 MORE

WILKES, W.
EVELYN, A.W.--[1]

WILKES-HUNTER, RICHARD
ASHTON, FIONA--[35]AUSTRALIAN--
HRWTZ PB140 "WRITTEN IN THE STARS" '77
BALLARD, DEAN--[1][22][31]AUSTRALIAN
BRODY, MARC--[1][3][29][31]AUSTRALIAN-NOT SO ACCRDNG TO G. FLANNAGAN [PP 25, P48]
CONRAD, TOD--[3][29][31][35]AUSTRALIAN--
WEBSTER "RAWHIDE VIXEN" '58
WEBSTER "COLONEL & THE CORPSE" '58
WEBSTER "KANE & MISS ABEL" '58
CRANE, ALEX--[3][29][31]AUSTRALIAN--
HRWTZ "BUSHMAN" '59
HRWTZ "ONE NIGHT OF FEAR" '59
DARK, JAMES--[35]AUSTRALIAN/MYS,HP--
HRWTZ "SPY FROM THE GRAVE" '64
DOUGLAS, D.--[8]AUSTRALIAN
DOUGLAS, DIANA--[35]AUSTRALIAN--
HRWTZ PB141 "NURSE CHADWICK'S SORROW" '77 & OTHERS IN U.S.
DOUGLAS, SHANE--[22][31][35]AUSTRALIAN--
ABOUT 70 HRWTZ NOVELS '60s-80s
DUNN, JAMES--[1][31][35]AUSTRALIAN--
HRWTZ PB164 "LAWRENCE OF ARABIA" '63
DUNN, JAMES A.--[31][32]MYS--
MH "A REASONABLE DOUBT" OCT '62
FARR, C.--[8]AUSTRALIAN
FARR, CAROLINE--[34][35]AUSTRALIAN/ROM,HP--
HRWTZ/SIGN - 39 NOVELS '66-80
GORDON, PETER--[22][31][35]AUSTRALIAN--
HRWTZ "COMMANDO SORTIE" '63
GRAY, ADRIAN--[8][22][35]AUSTRALIAN/ADULT--
HRWTZ - 7 MEDICAL NOVELS '71-3
HART, ALISON--[35]AUSTRALIAN--
HRWTZ AH01 "GIRLS IN TROUBLE" '76
HRWTZ AH02 "NO WAY BACK" '77
HUNT, ROGER--[35]AUSTRALIAN/WAR--
HRWTZ "OPERATION GUNSIGHT' '61
HUNTER, R.--[35]AUSTRALIAN--
HRWTZ PB29 "DOCTOR'S AFFAIR" '60
HRWTZ PB67 "STUDENT NURSE" '60
HUNTER, R. WILKES--[35]AUSTRALIAN/MYS--
HRWTZ/KING "FIVE DAYS TO KILL" '55
DNTNDT "A FOOL FROM DOWN UNDER" '50s
HRWTZ PB54 "INNOCENT SAVAGE" '60
HRWTZ PB188 "PLEASURE ISLAND" '64
HRWTZ PB191 "ISLE OF FREE LOVE" '64
HUNTER, R.W.--[35]AUSTRALIAN--
HRWTZ PB168 "MATA" '63
HRWTZ PB174 "TIKAI" '64

WILKES-HUNTER, RICHARD [CONT]
HUNTER, R.W. [CONT]
HRWTZ PB176 "CHETA" '64
HUNTER, WILKES--[35]AUSTRALIAN--
HRWTZ MN2 "THE DEVIL'S DOSSIER" '59
LESTER, TERI--[35]AUSTRALIAN--HRWTZ '67-9
MITCHELL, KERRY--[1][22]AUSTRALIAN,HP--
HRWTZ ? TITLES ?
MORLEY, KELL--[35]AUSTRALIAN--CLVLD
O'NEILL, C.M.--[1][22][35]AUSTRALIAN--
HRWTZ SS2 "FLIGHT INTO ROMANCE" '60
HRWTZ SS3 "CAREER GIRL JENNIFER" '60
HRWTZ SS5 "ROCK `n' ROLL ROMANCE" '60
OWEN, MICHAEL--[35]AUSTRALIAN/WAR,HP--
HRWTZ "THE COASTWATCHERS" '65
ROSS, BRADLEY--[35]AUSTRALIAN--
HRWTZ MN1 "NO MARGIN FOR TERROR" '59
HRWTZ MN4 "THE SOFT TOUCH" '59
SANDERS, KENT--[1][22]AUSTRALIAN
SHULBERG, ALAN--[1][22][35]AUSTRALIAN--
WEBSTER 'RIOT' SERIES - 3 OR MORE
TITLES '59
WATERS, LUCY--[35]AUSTRALIAN--
HRWTZ PB139 "DARK FIRES" '77

WILKINS, GINA
FERRIS, GINA--[9][21][26]ROM--
"LADY BEWARE"
"IN FROM THE RAIN" & 8 MORE

WILKINS, MARGARET
MOORE, MARGARET--[26]ROM--
"WARRIOR'S HEART"
"A WARRIOR'S QUEST"
"CHINA BLOSSOM"

WILKINS, MARILYN R.
WILKINS, MARNIE--[1][33]

WILKINS, MARY H.L.
CALHOUN, MARY--[1][11][31]

WILKINS, MARY [E]
FREEMAN, MARY E. WILKINS--[7]HOR--
"COLLECTED GHOST STORIES" '74

WILKINSON, A.G.
DESOR, RENE--[8]

WILKINSON, CHERRY
ADAIR, CHERRY--[26]ROM--
HARL 492 "THE MERCENARY"

WILKINSON, IRIS G.
HYDE, ROBIN--[1][22] NEW ZEALANDER

WILKINSON, JOHN DONALD
IRONMASTER, MAXIMUS--[22]ENGLISH

WILKINSON, LORNA H.K.
DEANE, LORNA--[1][22][31]ENGLISH

WILKINSON, LOUIS U.
MARLOW, LOUIS--[1][2][23]SF--
"DEVIL IN CRYSTAL" '44

WILKINSON, PERCY FRANCIS
WILKINSON, TIM--[1]

WILKINSON, RICHARD HILL
BROCKE, JULIAN--[3]MYS--
PLAY "THOMAS SHELTON'S GHOST" '36
HAYFORD, EUGENE--[1][3]MYS--
PLAY "ONE HORRIBLE NIGHT" '39
OTT, E. HARRISON--[1][3]MYS--
PLAY "MYSTERY OF CRAZY CANYON RANCH" '40

WILKINSON, RICHARD HILL [CONT]
PRAY, PAUL--[1][34]MYS--
PLAY "GHOST IN THE BELFREY" '41

WILKINSON, RONALD
THORN, RONALD SCOTT--[1][3][22]ENGLISH/MYS--
HALE "EXPERIMENT WITH EROS" '67
HM "TWIN SERPENTS '65

WILKS, BRIAN
HUGHES, SAM--[31]

WILKS, MICHAEL THOMAS
THOMAS, MICHAEL--[1]
WILKS, MIKE--[33]

WILLANS, ANGELA
GRANT, MARY--[8]

WILLARD, CAROLINE MCCOY
PENN, RACHEL--[1]

WILLARD, JOSHUA FLYNT
FLYNT, JOSHUA--[1][3][22]AMERICAN/MYS--
3 NOVELS 1900-04

WILLARD, TOM
DOLAN, BILL--[1][7][23]SF/THRIL--
'AKRIKORPS' #1 & 2
DOLAN, WILLIAM--[1][23][32]--
AHMM "THE HARD SELL" NOV '67

WILLEFORD, CHARLES [RAY]
CHARLES, WILL--[3][29]WEST--
LENOX "HOMBRE FROM SONOMA" '71
SANDERS, W. FRANKLIN--W/W. FRANKLIN SANDERS,
MUNROE SL#25--
GM 1087 "WHIP HAND" '61-UNCREDITED COLLAB

WILLEMS, J. RUTHERFORD
LASSEN-WILLEMS, JAMES--[31]

WILLENS, DORIS
KAPLAN, DORIS--[31]

WILLERBEY, LEONARD
O'CONNOR, PATRICK--[2]

WILLETT, BROT. FRANCISCUS
PREMONT, BROT. JEREMY--[22]AMERICAN
PRIMM, BROT. ORRIN--[22]AMERICAN

WILLETT, EDWARD
BRENT, CARL--[1]
HENDERSON, J. STANLEY--[1]

WILLETT, FRANCISCUS
BOND, IAN--[1][22]
MCKERN, PAT--[8]

WILLETT, JINCY
KORNHAUSER, JINCY--[31]

WILLETTS, RONALD F.
WILLETTS, R.F.--[1]

WILLIAMS, ALEXANDER [H]
HAZARD, FORRESTER--[1][3]MYS--
LIPP "THE HEX MURDER" '36

WILLIAMS, ANITA
FERGUSON, MAGGIE--[26]ROM--
HARL 284 "LOOKS ARE DECEIVING"

WILLIAMS, ARTHUR
TISTE, R.--[2]

WILLIAMS, BARBARA
NICHOLS, CHARLOTTE--W/PATRICIA KNOLL, [21][26]ROM--
"FOR THE LOVE OF MIKE"
"EYE OF THE BEHOLDER"
WILSON, BARBARA--[33]

WILLIAMS, BERNIE
HITT, ORRIE--M. AVALLONE-BAE 4,PP 32, GHOSTED--TITLES NOT KNOWN

WILLIAMS, CAROL ELIZABETH
FENNER, CAROL--[8]

WILLIAMS, CLAERWEN
LANG, MAUD--[1]

WILLIAMS, CLAUDETTE
DAVIS, MELANIE--W/DEBBIE JORDAN, [9][21][26]ROM--
"WILD DAWN FEVER"

WILLIAMS, CLYDE C.
WILLIAMS, SLIM--[33]

WILLIAMS, COLIN
WELLAND, COLIN--[1]

WILLIAMS, D.F.
WILLIAMS, PATRY--W/M. PATRY,[1][8]

WILLIAMS, DAVID RHYS
GAN, INDEX--[1]

WILLIAMS, DORIAN
LORINER--[8]
PIED PIPER--[1]

WILLIAMS, DOROTHY JEANNE K.
CASTELL, MEGAN--[21][26][28]ROM/WEST--
POCK "QUEEN OF A LONELY COUNTRY" '80
CREASEY, JEANNE--[8]
CRECY, JEANNE--[3][28][31]MYS/ROM--
BERK "LIGHTNING TREE" '73
NAL "WINTER KEEPER" '75 & MORE
FOSTER, JEANNE--[9][21][26][28]MYS/ROM--
'FRONTIER WOMEN' SAGA-3 NOVELS & OTHERS
MICHAELS, KRISTIN--[9][21][28]ROM,HP--
NAL "TO BEGIN WITH LOVE" '75
NAL "A SPECIAL KIND OF LOVE" '76
NAL "SONG OF THE HEART" '77
NAL "ENCHANTED JOURNEY" '77
NAL "VOYAGE TO LOVE" '78
NAL "MAGIC SIDE OF THE MOON" '81
RHYS, MEGAN--[1][33]
ROWAN, DEIRDRE--[3][26][28]MYS/ROM--
GM "DRAGON'S MOUNT" '73
GM "RAVENSGATE" '76 & 3 MORE '73-6
STUART, MEGAN--[9]ROM
WILLIAMS, J.R.--[1][28][33] CHILDRENS BOOKS--
"HORSE TALKER" '61 & 4 MORE
WILLIAMS, JEANNE--[21][28]ROM/WEST--
"CAVE DREAMERS"
"BRIDE OF THUNDER" & 11 MORE

WILLIAMS, EDWARD FRANCIS
FRANCIS-WILLIAMS, BARON--[1][23][31]SF--
WILLIAMS, FRANK--[23]SF--
"THE RICHARDSON STORY" '51

WILLIAMS, EDWARD JOHN
FARRER, E. MAXWELL--[8]

WILLIAMS, EDWIN ALFRED
DE CAIRE, EDWIN--[3][22]MYS--
HODDER "DEATH AMONG THE WRITERS" '52
HODDER "UMGASI DIAMONDS" '54
MOODIE, EDWIN--[1][22]

WILLIAMS, EIRLYS O.
TREFOR, EIRLYS--[1][22] WELSH

WILLIAMS, ELISEUS
EIFION, WYN--[22] WELSH

WILLIAMS, ELMA MARY
OXFORD, JANE--[1]

WILLIAMS, ERIC CYRIL
WILLIAMS, E.C.--[1]

WILLIAMS, ERNEST NEVILLE
WILLIAMS, E.N.--[1]

WILLIAMS, FERELITH ECCLES
ECCLES--[33]

WILLIAMS, GEORGE
AGNEW, DAVID--W/DOUGLAS ADAMS,[1][2]

WILLIAMS, GEORGE VALENTINE
VALENTINE, DOUGLAS--[18][29][34]MYS--
JENK "MAN WITH THE CLUBFOOT" '18
JENK "THE SECRET HAND..." '18
VEDETTE--[1][22][29]MYS

WILLIAMS, GERALYN DAWSON
DAWSON, GERALYN--AUTHOR PROVIDED, ROM--
"TEXAN'S BRIDE"
"CAPTURE THE NIGHT"
"TEMPTING MORALITY"

WILLIAMS, GILBERT M.
WOLFE, MICHAEL--[1][3]MYS--
HARPER "MAN ON A STRING" '73
HARPER "PANAMA PARADOX" '77 & MORE '73-7

WILLIAMS, GORDON M.
YUILL, P.B.--[3][18]MYS--
MacM "BORNLESS KEEPER" '74
YUILL, P.B.--W/TERRY VENABLES, [3][18][23]MYS/SF--
MacM "HAZLE PLAYS SOLOMON" '74 & 2 MORE
'MICRONAUTS' SERIES '77-81

WILLIAMS, GRAEME
DENT, DENIS--[1]

WILLIAMS, GRAHAM
AGNEW, DAVID--W/DOUGLAS ADAMS,[1][2]

WILLIAMS, GUY RICHARD O.
GUINNESS, OWEN--[8]
WOOLLAND, HENRY--[8]

WILLIAMS, HAROLD
AFTEREM, GEORGE--[2][34]MYS--
CUPPLES "SILKEN THREADS" 1885

WILLIAMS, HENRY LLEWELLYN
MIZZEN, MATT--[34]MYS--
DEWITT "BINNACLE JACK; OR, THE CAVERN OF DEATH" & 2 OTHERS

WILLIAMS, HERBERT
H.W.--[2]

WILLIAMS, JACK LEWIS
ARTFAB--[1]
ISAMBARD--[1]

WILLIAMS, JAY
DELVING, MICHAEL--[18][31][33][34]MYS--
SCRIBN "BORED TO DEATH" '75
SCRIBN "CHINESE EXPERT" '77 & 5 MORE

WILLIAMS, JOHN A.
GREGORY, J. DENNIS--[1][31]

WILLIAMS, JOHN BABINGTON
BRAMPTON, JAMES--[1]

WILLIAMS, JONATHAN CHAMBERLAIN
CHAMBERLAIN, THEODORE--W/RONALD JOHNSON, [22]AMERICAN

WILLIAMS, KATHLEEN F.
STEVENSON, KATE--[26]ROM--
SIL 576 "A PIECE OF TOMORROW"

WILLIAMS, KATHRYN VINSON
VINSON, KATHRYN--[1]

WILLIAMS, LAURIE
SCOTT, ADRIENNE--[21][26]ROM--
"PRIDE & PROMISES"

WILLIAMS, LEIGH ANNE
WILLIAMS, LEE--[21]ROM--
"PILLOW TALK"
"HEAT WAVE" & 12 MORE

WILLIAMS, LINDA V.
GRANT, LINDA--LACHMAN LST '93,[34]MYS--
AV "RANDOM ACCESS MURDER" '88
SCRIBN "BLIND TRUST" '90

WILLIAMS, LIZA
LERHMAN, LIZA--[1][31]

WILLIAMS, LOUISE BONINO
BONINO, LOUISE--[31]

WILLIAMS, LUCITA SQUIER
SQUIER, LUCITA--[1]

WILLIAMS, M.H.
STAFFORD, JOHN K.--[34]MYS,HP--
MAGNET #351 "SMUGGLERS AT ODDS" '04
MAGNET #387 "UNDER THE SURFACE" '05
STEWART, DICK--[34]MYS,HP--
MAGNET #424 "BELROX MYS: OR, CHASE OF A CLEVER DETECTIVE" '05

WILLIAMS, MARCIA
FALKENDER, BARONESS MARCI--[31]

WILLIAMS, MARGARET W.
ERSKINE, MARGARET--[3][18][26]MYS/ROM--
HAM "I KNEW MacBEAN" '48
"FATAL RELATIONS" '55 & 18 MORE
WILLIAMS, WETHERBY--[8]

WILLIAMS, MARY
HARVEY, MARIANNE--[9][21][26]ROM--
"WILD ONE"
"GYPSY FIRES" & 3 MORE
WILLIAMS, BRONWYN--W/DIXIE [S.B.] BROWNING, [7][21]SF--
"WHITE WITCH" '88
"DANDELION"
"STORMWALKER"

WILLIAMS, MEURIG MON
CARRINGTON, MICHAEL--[1]

WILLIAMS, NATHAN WINSLOW
DALLAS, RICHARD--[3][29]MYS--
PUTNAM "A MASTER HAND" 1903

WILLIAMS, NED
HARBIN, ROBERT--[1]

WILLIAMS, NORMA
NORMAN, DEE--W/DEE LOPEZ,[9][21][26]ROM--
"WHITE NIGHTS"
NORMAN, WYNN--[21]ROM--
WILLIAMS, WYNN--[21][26]ROM--
"STARRY NIGHTS"
"ONE BREATHLESS MOMENT"
"BEWITCHING NIGHTS"

WILLIAMS, PATRICIA A.
LORD, ALEXANDRA--W/CATHERINE SEIBERT, [9][21]ROM--
"A HARMLESS RUSE"

WILLIAMS, PEGGY EILEEN A.
EVANS, MARGIAD--[8]

WILLIAMS, RICHARD V.
ROWLEY, RICHARD--[1][2]

WILLIAMS, ROBERT MOORE
BROWNING, JOHN S.--[1][2][11][23]AMERICAN/SF
HARMON, H.H.--[2][11][23][31]AMERICAN/SF
JARVIS, E.K.--[1][2][11]SF,HP--ZIFF-DAVIS
MOORE, ROBERT--[2][11][23]AMERICAN/SF--
ASF "ZERO AS A LIMIT" '37
STORM, RUSSELL--[1][2][11][23]AMERICAN/SF

WILLIAMS, ROBERT PAUL
WILLIAMS, TAD--[7]SF--
DAW 'MEMORY, SORROW & THORN' #1 & 2 '88-90
"TAILCHASER'S SONG" '85

WILLIAMS, ROSWELL
HUNG LONG TOM--[11]
KENT, RICHARD--[11]
OWEN, FRANK--LACHMAN LST '93,[11][32]MYS--
AV "PALE PINK PORCELAIN" '47

WILLIAMS, SHERLEY
WILLIAMS, SHIRLEY--[1]

WILLIAMS, SIDNEY
AUGUST, MICHAEL--M. BAKER-MYS SCENE #39, MYS--ZEBRA SUSPENSE NOVEL

WILLIAMS, THOMAS ANDREW
ANDREAS, THOMAS--[31]

WILLIAMS, THOMAS LANIER
WILLIAMS, TENNESSEE--[2][7][11][32]SF--
SUS "THE VINE" OCT '60
"THE KNIGHTLY QUEST: A NOVELLA & FOUR STORIES" '66

WILLIAMS, VIVIAN CLAUD C.
V.C.C.W.--[1]

WILLIAMS, WALTER JON
WILLIAMS, JON--HAWK/WILLIAMS INTRVW '93, [23]SF--
'PRIVATEER' SERIES-5 NVLS '81-TD

WILLIAMS, WILLIAM H.
BRODY, MARC--G. FLANAGAN-PP 25,[34][36]MYS--
HRWTZ - 79 NOVELS '55-60
WILLIAMS, BILL--G. FLANAGAN-PP#25,
[35][36]AUSTRALIAN/MYS

WILLIAMSON, ALICE M.L.
ALLISON, WILLIAM--[34]MYS--
DBLDY "A SECRET OF THE SEA" '20 3 MORE--
?? UNCONFDIRMED ??
D'ALPENS, MARGUESA--[22]MYS
D'ALPINS, MARCHIONESS--[34]MYS--
HODDER "HOUSE OF THE LOST COURT" '08
DE CRESPIGNY, CHARLES--W/CHARLES N.
WILLIAMSON,[1][22]
DE SAVALLO, DONA TERESA-- W/CHARLES N.
WILLIAMSON,[1][3][22][29]
McCLURE "THE HOUSE OF THE LOST COURT" '08
REVERE, M.P.--[1][22]
STUYVESANT, ALICE--W/CHARLES N.
WILLIAMSON,[3][22]MYS--
WILLIAMSON, A.M.--[1]
WILLIAMSON, MRS. HARCOURT--[3][22]MYS

WILLIAMSON, CHARLES N.
DE CRESPIGNY, CHARLES--W/ALICE WILLIAMSON,
[1][22]
DE SAVALLO, DONA TERESA--W/ALICE M.L.
WILLIAMSON,[1][3][22][29]
McCLURE "THE HOUSE OF THE LOST COURT" '08
REVERE, M.P.--W/ALICE M.L. WILLIAMSON,[1]
STUYVESANT, ALICE--W/ALICE WILLIAMSON,
[1][3][22]MYS
WILLIAMSON, C.N.--[1]

WILLIAMSON, CHESTER C.
WILLIAMSON, CHET--[7]HOR--
TOR - 6 NOVELS '86-90

WILLIAMSON, CLAUDE C.
HOPE, FELIX--[1][22][31]ENGLISH

WILLIAMSON, ELLEN DOUGLAS
DOUGLAS, ELLEN--[1][22][31]AMERICAN/MYS--
BOUREGY "MOON OF VIOLENCE" '60

WILLIAMSON, ETHEL
CARDINAL, JANE--[1][2]
VEHEYNE, CHERRY--[1]

WILLIAMSON, GEOFFREY
HASTINGS, ALAN--[1][22][31]ENGLISH

WILLIAMSON, GERALD NEAL
SHOCK, JULIAN--[1][7]SF--
ZEBRA "EXTRATERRESTRIAL" '82
WILLIAMSON, J.N.--[1][7][34]MYS/HOR--
36 NOVELS '79-91

WILLIAMSON, HENRY
BANK, W. DANE--[1]
HEATH, W. SHAW--[1]

WILLIAMSON, HUGH ROSS
ROSSITER, IAN--[22]ENGLISH

WILLIAMSON, J.C.
DJIN DJIN--[13]AUSTRALIAN

WILLIAMSON, JOHN STEWART
SONDERLAND, NILS O.--[2]
STEWART, WILL--[2][4][7][11][15]SF--
ASF "COLLISION ORBIT" JUL '42
ASF "OPPOSITES REACT" JAN '43
'SEETEE' #1 & 2 '50-1

WILLIAMSON, JOHN STEWART [CONT]
WILLIAMSON, JACK--L. ROBBINS LTR '94,
[7][32][34]MYS/SF--17 NOVELS & NON-FICT
MZ "WOLVES OF DARKNESS" NOV '67

WILLIAMSON, LYDIA BUCKLN.
SORACE, RICHARD--[8]

WILLIAMSON, ROBIN
WILLIAMSON, SHERMAN--W/DAN M. SHERMAN,
LACHMAN-EASTER LST '93, MYS--
NEL "THE GLORY TRAP" '77

WILLIAMSON, SHARON
WILSON, SHAWN--HAWK/WILLIAMSON INTRVW '93,
MYS--
PLAY "DIPLOMATIC IMUNITY"
PLAY "MORE THAN TRIVIAL PURSUIT"

WILLIAMSON, STEPHEN
CARTER, NICK--W/HENRY RASOF,[3]MYS,HP--
CHART "THE DUBROVNIK MASSACRE" '81

WILLIAMSON, THAMES ROSS
DAGONET, EDWARD--[8]
DRAGPNAT, EDWARD--[1]
FLEMING, WALDO--[1]
MORGAN, DE WOLFE--[1]
SALTAR THE MONGOL--[8]
SMITH, S.S.--[1]
TRENT, GREGORY--[1]

WILLINGHAM, CALDER
WILLINGHAM, CALDER--W/JAMES M. THOMPSON,[18]
SCREENPLAY/NOVEL "PATHS OF GLORY"

WILLIS, CONSTANCE ELAINE
WILLIS, CONNIE--[7]SF--
BLUEJAY "FIRE WATCH" '85
BB "LINCOLN'S DREAMS" '87

WILLIS, CORINNE D.
DENNING, PATRICIA--[1][31]

WILLIS, EDWARD HENRY
BISHOP, GEORGE--[29]MYS--
"BITTE, LASST DIE BLUMEN LEBEN"
BISHOP, JOHN--[18]MYS--
PLAY "SABOTAGE" '43
WILLIS, TED--[18]MYS

WILLIS, ERNEST LISTER H.
BARNARTO, BART--[27]HP--SELF
COSTELLO, PETE--[27]HP--SELF
ELLISON, EARL--[27][34]HP--
SPNCR "MIDNIGHT ALIBI" '52
"CORRUPT CITY" '53
"PAID IN FULL '53
KING, ROSCOE--PPCC#3,[34]MYS--
MUIR WATSON "PARDON MY GUN" '49
LAVELLE, MARC--[34]MYS--
SELF "CURVES SPELL DEATH" '52
SELF "DAME WITHOUT SHAME" '52
SELF "PARIS AFTER DARK" '52
SELF "PAY-OFF FOR DESIRE" '52
SELF "REEFER GIRL" '52
SELF "CALL ME SUGAR" '53
SELF "LADY, BEWARE" '53
LISLE, MICHAEL--[34]MYS--
TEMPEST "I'LL HIRE THE HEARSE" '49
MADISON, RICK--[34]MYS,HP--
SPENCER "HIT THE JACKPOT" '52]
PERELLI, NICK--S, HOLLAND-SCION CKLST,
PP 27,[34]MYS,HP--
SCION "TWO DAMES TOO MANY" '52
VALOIS, JEAN PAUL--[27]HP--SELF

WILLIS, ERNEST LISTER H. [CONT]
VAN LODEN, EARL--[11]
VAN LODEN, ERLE--[2][7][11]SF
WILLIS, LISLE--S, HOLLAND--
SCION CKLST, PP 27, P11,[2]

WILLIS, GEORGE ANTHONY A.
A.A.--[8]
A.A. OF PUNCH--[22]MYS
ARMSTRONG, ANTHONY--[2][3][5][7][23]
[31]MYS/SF--19 NOVELS & PLAYS '27-72

WILLIS, MAUDE
LOTTMAN, EILEEN--[11]

WILLIS, TED
DIXON, GEORGE--[31]

WILLIS, WALT
BRYAN, WALTER--[1][2]

WILLMAN, MARIANNA
CLARK, MARIANNE--[9][21][26]ROM--
"APACHE TEARS"
"HOPE THERE BE DRAGONS"
CLARK, SABINA--[1][9][21][26]ROM--
"AN ARTFUL LADY"

WILLOUGHBY, ELAINE M.
MACMANN, ELAINE--[1][31]

WILLOUGHBY-HIGSON, PHILIP
HIGSON, P.J.W.--[8]

WILLS, BETTY JO
WILLS, ANN MEREDITH--W/MARALYS WILLS,
[21][26]ROM--
"TEMPEST & TENDERNESS"
"MOUNTAIN SPELL"

WILLS, FINGAL O'FLAHERTIE
C.3.3--[31]
WILDE, OSCAR--[31]

WILLS, GARY ANTHONY A.
ROMAN, WILLIAM--[1]

WILLS, MARALYS
WILLS, ANN MEREDITH--W/BETTY JO WILLS,
[9][21][26]ROM--
"TEMPEST & TENDERNESS"
"MOUNTAIN SPELL"

WILLS, RONALD THOMAS
CADELL, JAMES--[29]MYS

WILLSON, MITCHELL A.
HOGARTH, EMMETT--W/ABRAHAM POLANSKY,[8]

WILMOT, ANTHONY
RAOUL, ANTHONY--[1]

WILMOT, FRANK LESLIE T.
FURNEY, MAURICE--[8][13]AUSTRALIAN
MAURICE, FURNLEY--[1][22]AUSTRALIAN

WILMOT, JAMES R.
STEWART, FRANCIS--[1][22]MYS
TREVOR, RALPH--[1][22][34]MYS--
WRIGHT "HIGH SPY" '42
WRIGHT "MURDER IN SILK" '37
& 29 MORE '37-42

WILNER, JUDE
RANDAL, JUDE--[26]ROM--
"JUST ONE OF THOSE GUYS"
"NORTHERN MANHUNT"

WILSON, ALBERT W.
WILSON, YATES--[1]

WILSON, ALEC
ULSTER IMPERIALIST--[8]

WILSON, ALEXANDER [D.C.]
SPENCER, GEOFFREY--[3][22]MYS--
LAURIE "CONFESSIONS OF A SCOUNDREL" '33

WILSON, ANDREW J.
SILVONIUS, A.J.--[2]

WILSON, ARTHUR
DALRY--[8]

WILSON, AUGUSTA JANE
EVANS, AUGUSTA JANE--[1]

WILSON, BARBARA
GRAYSON, LAURA--[1]

WILSON, BARBARA & PAMELA
SUMMERVILLE, MARGARET--[9][21][26]ROM--
"HIGHLAND LADY"
"TOWN TANGLE" & 13 MORE

WILSON, BRENDA LEE E.
HIMROD, BRENDA--[21][26]ROM--
"HER SISTER'S MAN"
LANE, MEGAN--[21][26]ROM--
"TROUBLE WITH MAGIC"
"GYPSY RENEGADE" & 8 MORE
TRENT, BRENDA--[21][26]ROM--
"RISING STAR"
"HUNTER'S MOON" & 19 MORE
WILSON, B.L.--[21]ROM--
"THE MASSEUSE"

WILSON, BUDGE
WILSON, MARJORIE--[33]

WILSON, CAMILLA JEANNE
WILSON, CAMMY--[1]

WILSON, CAROL
WILSON, CARYL--[26]ROM--
"TONIGHT & FOREVER"

WILSON, DEREK ALAN
PRESTON, HUGH--[1]

WILSON, DESEMEA
PATRICK, DIANA--[1]

WILSON, DORIS MARIE
PERRI, LESLIE--[1][2][11]

WILSON, DOROTHY JEAN
WILSON, JAYE--[1]

WILSON, ELLEN
EVANS, LAUREL--[9][26]ROM--
"BUILT TO LAST"
"TIMELESS RITUALS" & 4 MORE

WILSON, FRANCES ENGLE
WILSON, FRAN--[21]ROM--
"AMBER WINE"
"AFTER AUTUMN" & 5 MORE

WILSON, FRANK PERCY
WILSON, F.P.--[1]

WILSON, F[RANCIS] PAUL
ANDREWS, COLIN--M. BAKER/WILSON INTRVW-
MYS SCENE #39, MYS--
"THE SELECT"

WILSON, G.L.
FALKLAND, FRANK--[1]

WILSON, GUTHRIE EDWARD
PAOLOTTI, JOHN--[1]

WILSON, HALSEY WILLIAM
WILLIAMS, HAROLD WORKMAN--[31]--
"TOASTER'S HANDBOOK" '14
WILSON, H.W.--[31]

WILSON, HELEN
WILSON, HOLLY--[8]

WILSON, HELEN HELGA
MAYNE, H.H.--[1]

WILSON, J ANTHONY BURGESS
BURGESS, ANTHONY--[2][3][7][23]ENGLISH/MYS/SF-
-
HM "A CLOCKWORK ORANGE" '62 & MORE
KELL, JOSEPH--[2][22][31][34]ENGLISH/MYS--
DAVIES "ONE HAND CLAPPING" '61
WILSON, JOHN BURGESS--[8]

WILSON, JAMES ANDREW
WILSON, SNOO--[8]

WILSON, JAMES GRANT
GRANT, ALLAN [ALLEN]--[1]

WILSON, JOAN HOLT
HOLT, JOAN--[31]

WILSON, JOHN
STRIPPER--[8]

WILSON, JOYCE
JAMES, SALLY--[21][26]ROM--
"CLANDESTINE AFFAIR"
"PETRONRLLA'S WATERLOO"
"HEIR TO ROWANLEA"

WILSON, JOYCE M.
STRANGER, JOYCE--[1][22][33]ENGLISH--
WILDLIFE

WILSON, LIONEL
BLACKTON, PETER--[1][31][33]
ELLIS, HERBERT--[1][31][33]
SALZER, L.E.--[1][33]

WILSON, MARGARET C.
STEWART, MARGARET--[1]

WILSON, MARGARET [W]
AN ELDERLY SPINSTER--[31]

WILSON, MARIE BEATRICE
MARIE, JEANNE--[1][3][29]MYS--
LENNOX "BLACK FOR A BRIDE" '73
LENNOX "ARROW OF TERROR" '73
LENNOX "WAIT FOR ME WENDY" '74

WILSON, MARILLA
NORTH, MARILLA--[1]

WILSON, MARY REILLY
MCMULLEN, MARY--[32][34][40]MYS--
19 DBLDY NOVELS '51-86
EQMM "HER HEART'S HOME" MAY '77
REILLY, MARY--WILSON IS MARRIED NAME

WILSON, MAY
NORTH, ANISON--[1]

WILSON, MILES
M.W.--[2]

WILSON, NELLY
WILSON, JUSSEN--[1]

WILSON, NORMAN SCARLYN
NORMAN, W.S.--[1]
WEBB, ANTHONY--[1][34]MYS--
JENK "BILL BLUNDERS THROUGH" '40
& 10 HARRAP NOVELS '37-47

WILSON, OSCAR
JASON, STUART--HANCER,HP--
LAN 75-095 "BLACK HERCULES" '69

WILSON, RENEE
ROSZEL, RENEE--[9][21][26]ROM--
"LEGENDARY LOVER"
"DEVIL TO PAY" & 10 MORE

WILSON, RICHARD
CROSS, JAY--[2]
HALIBUT, EDWARD--[2][11][23]SF--
"COURSE OF EMPIRE" '56
TOWERS, IVAR--W/C.M. KORNBLUTH,
[1][2][11]SF,HP--
AST "STEPSONS OF MARS" '40
TOWERS, IVAR--[23]SF,HP--
AST "MAN WITHOUT A PLANET" '42

WILSON, ROBERT EDWARD
GATHERIDGE, R. EDWARD--[31]

WILSON, ROBERT MCNAIR
WYNNE, ANTHONY--[3][22][29][40]AMERICAN/MYS--
HUTCH "BLUE VERSUVIOUS" '30 & MORE '25-50

WILSON, ROBIN SCOTT
SCOTT, ROBIN--[2][23][31]SF--

WILSON, ROGER HARRIS
HARRIS, ROGER--[1][22]AMERICAN

WILSON, SANDRA
HEATH, SANDRA--[8][21][26][31]ROM--
"OPERA DANCER"
"PILFERED PLUME" & 27 MORE

WILSON, STANLEY KIDDER
PLINY THE YOUNGEST--[22]MYS

WILSON, VIVA
VIVA--[8]

WILSON, WILLIAM
NESS, K.T.--W/DONALD GRANT,[8]

WILSON, WILLIAM J.
PERRIWILS, G.W.--W/GEORGETTE PERRY,[2]

WILSON, [ALAN] DORIC
ALDON, HOWARD--[31]

WILTON, CHARLES EDWARD
ANGIO-AUSTRAL--[8]

WILTON-ELY, JOHN
ELY, JOHN WILTON--[31]

WILTSHIRE, DAVID
BEDFORD, JOHN--[7][34]MYS--
HALE "OPERATION TRIGEMINAL" '78
HALE "GENERAL DIED TOGETHER" '80
HALE "NEMISIS CONCERTO" '82
HALE "MOMENT IN TIME" '83
HALE "TITRON MADNESS" '84

WIMHURST, CECIL G.E.
BRENT, NIGEL--[1][3][22]MYS--
MULLER "GOLDEN ANGEL" '58
MILLER "LEOPARD DIED TOO" '57
& 7 MORE '53-60

WIMMER, MAX
WHYMER, MAC--[39][40]GERMAN/MYS--
"DIE SECHS TABATIEREN"

WIMMERMARK, KERSTEN
IDSTROM, NILS--[29]MYS

WINANS, KATHARINE B.
BRUSH, KATHARINE--[1][32]MYS--
EQMM "SILK HAT" OCT '47

WINCH, MARIE ELIZABETH A.
WINCH, EVELYN M.--[1][22]MYS

WINCH, WILL
STAFFORD, JOHN K.--[34]MYS,HP--
MAGNET #471 "ONLY A BULLETT: OR, A TRIPLE CRIME" '06
STEWART, DICK--[34]HP--
MAGNET #445 "SKELETON CLEW: OR, OUT OF THE DEAD PAST" '06

WINCHELL, PRENTICE
COLLANS, DEV--[1][18][29]MYS--
GHOSTED "I WAS A HOUSE DETECTIVE" '54
DE BEKKER, JAY--[3][18][29]ADULT/MYS--
BEAC 108 "GUTTER GANG" '54
BEAC 110 "KEYHOLE PEEPER" '55
DEAN, SPENCER--V. BERCH-GM PSEUDS, PP 33, [3][18][29]MYS--
DBLDY "MERCHANT OF MURDER" '59 & 8 MORE
JONES, G. WAYMAN--[29]MYS,HP--
SCANLON, C.K.M.--L. ROBBINS LTR '94, MYS,HP--
ST. CLAIR, DEXTER [1]--V. BERCH-GM PSEUDS, PP 33,[3][18][29]MYS--
GM 195 "MANTRAP" '51
GM 1312 "THE LADY'S NOT FOR LIVING" '63
GM 155 "SARATOGA MANTRAP" '51
STERLING, STEWART [1]--ECHOES #5,[3][18][29][32]MYS--18 NVLS '46-60
DE "BLOOD FEEDS THE FLAMES" '48
PE "BIG DEAL" JUL '53
BLKB "HOT, WILLING & DEADLY" '55
MM "DEAD RIGHT" FEB '56
MSMM "MURDER COMES TO THE PLAZA ROYAL" AUG '57
SA "CORPSE DOCTOR" MAR '62
STOCKBRIDGE, GRANT--PULP #13, JOHNSON LTR '94, MYS,HP--
SPD "WHEN SATAN COMES TO TOWN" OCT '43
WALLACE, ROBERT--T. JOHNSON LTR '94, MYS,HP--

WINCHESTER, CLARENCE
ORNIS--[1]
TANNER-RUTHERFORD, C.--[1]

WINCHEVSKY, MORRIS
BEN-NEZ--[22]LITHUANIAN-AMERICAN
BARRIE, MONICA--[7][9][21][26]ROM/SF--
POCK "QUEEN OF KNIGHTS" '85 & 18 MORE
DALTON, JENIFER--[9][21][26]ROM--
"RUN ON THE WIND"
"WHISPERS OF DESTINY"
DAVIDS, MARILYN--[9][21][26]ROM--
"A LOVE SO FRESH"

WIND, DAVID MILTON
BARRIE, MONICA--[7][9][21][26]ROM/SF--
POCK "QUEEN OF KNIGHTS" '85 & 18 MORE
DALTON, JENIFER--[9][21][26]ROM--
"RUN ON THE WIND"
"WHISPERS OF DESTINY"
DAVIDS, MARILYN--[9][21][26]ROM--
"A LOVE SO FRESH"
MILTON, DAVID--[34]MYS--
DUTTON "HYTE MANUEVER" '88
PINN "AS PEACE LAY DYING" '90
PINN "A CONSPIRACY OF MIRRORS" '91
WIND, DAVID--[26]ROM--
"QUEEN OF HEARTS"

WINDER, MAVIS ARETA
ARETA, MAVIS--[1][31]
WINDER, MAVIS--[8]
WYNDER, MAVIS ARETA--[1]

WINDSOR, BESSIE W.W.S.S.
DUCHESS OF WINDSOR--[31]

WINDSOR, LINDA
COVINGTON, LINDA--[26]ROM--
"TEXAS LOVESTORM"
"WILD TORY ROSE" & MORE

WINDSOR, PATRICIA FRANCES
DANIEL, COLIN--[1][7][8][31]SF--
DELL 'TWILIGHT': #9 "DEMON TREE" '83

WINER, DEBORAH GRACE
GRACE, DEBORAH--[31]

WING, FRANCES
SCOTT, FRANCES V.--[1][22]AMERICAN

WING, JANET [JANICE]
BARBER, LEONORA--[9][21][26]ROM--
" A BLUEPRINT FOR RAPTURE"

WING, WILLIS KINGSLEY
BRYAN, MICHAEL--[3]MYS--
DELL FE 88 "INTENT TO KILL" '56
DELL FE A145 "MURDER IN MAJORCA" '57

WINGATE, LISA
ASHMORE, APRIL--CRPG,[26]ROM--
ZEBRA "TENDER TEXAS TOUCH"
ZEBRA "AUTUMN'S TENDER FIRE"
ZEBRA "HEARTSONG" '93

WINGATE, [MARTHA] ANNE G.
MARTIN, LEE--[SEE MARTHA [ANNE] G. WEBB]

WINGFIELD DIGBY, GEORGE F
DIGBY, GEORGE WINGFIELD--[31]

WINGROVE, DAVID JOHN
JACKSON, DANIEL--[31]
JACKSON, SARA--W/SARA S. THOMAS,[31]

WINKWORTH, DEREK W.
5029--[8]

WINNER, VIOLA HOPKINS
HOPKINS, VIOLA--[1][31]

WINNINGTON, RICHARD
ROSS, JOHN--[8]

WINSHIP, ELIZABETH
BETH--[1][31]

WINSKI, NORMAN
STIVERS, DICK--W/L.R. PAYNE,[34]MYS,HP--
GE "THE HOSTAGED ISLAND" '83

WINSLOW, PAULINE GLEN
SHERIDAN, JANE--[1]

WINSON, J.W.
WILDWOOD--[1]

WINSTEAD, REBECCA NOYES
DAVIDSON, ANGELA--[34]MYS--
CAROUSEL "THE FORBIDDEN MANSION" '81

WINSTED, HULDAH L.
DAKOTAN--[1]

WINSTEN, STEPHEN
SCOFIELD, JONATHAN--[21]ROM,HP--
DELL 'FREED FTR' SERIES: "FRONTIER WAR"
WILLOUGHBY, LEE DAVIS--[21]ROM,HP--
DELL 'WOMEN WHO WON THE WEST' SERIES:
"DODGE CITY DARLING"

WINSTON, ROBERT A.
FOX, COL. VICTOR J.--[1][3]MYS--
FREEDOM PRESS "THE PENTAGON CASE" '58

WINSTON, SARAH
LORENZ, SARAH E.--[1][31]

WINTER, BEVIS [PETER]
BOCCA, AL--S, HOLLAND-SCION CKLST, PP 27,
PPCC #3,[3][27][31]MYS--33 NOVELS '50-4
CAGNEY, PETER--PPCC #3,[3][27][29][32]MYS--
JENK "HEAR THE STRIPPER SCREAM" '60
JENK "NO DIAMONDS FOR A DOLL" '61
JENK "A GRAVE FOR MADAM" '61
MSMM "MURDERERS MAKE MISTAKES" JUN '60
COBURN, SAMMY--S. HOLLAND-SCION CKLST, PP 27,
[27][34]MYS--
SCION "HOT CARGO" '50
SCION "UNEASY STREET" '50
SCION "YOU CAN'T DIE HERE" '50
SCION "SHOWDOWN" '51
SCION "LADY PAYS" '51
SCION "DON'T TEMPT ME" '51
SCION "DEATH WARRANT" '52
SCION "BRUNETTES ARE NO BETTER" '52
HILL, BENNET--[8][34]MYS--
WARREN "DIAMOND CRIME DETECTIVE" '50
SHAYNE, GORDON--PPCC #3,[22][29][34]MYS--
JASMIT "AND SO TO DEATH" '52
JASMIT "TICKET TO ETERNITY" '54
ZORE, HYMAN--S, HOLLAND-SCION CKLST, PP 27,
[34]ENGLISH/MYS,HP--
SCION "IT'S A SIN" '53

WINTER, C.H.
RIVERINA--[8]

WINTER, ELIZABETH C.
CASTELAR, ISABELLA--[1]

WINTER, LESLIE
STROM, LESLIE WINTER--[1]

WINTER, PATRICK
ST. GERMAIN, GREGORY--V. BERCH LTR TO
HUBIN '94, WAR,HP--
SIGN - TILE NOT KNOWN

WINTERBOTHAM, RUSS[EL] R.
ADDY, TED--V. BERCH-MON PSEUDS, BAE 9,[1]MYS--
MON MA323 "DUTCH SCHULTZ STORY" '62
AUNT PEGGY--[11]
BOND, J. HARVEY--[2][3][11][23][29]MYS--
ACE D279 "BYE-BYE BABY" '58
ACE D301 "MURDER ISN'T FUNNY" '58
ACE D349 "KILL ME WITH KINDNESS" '59
ACE D483 "IF WISHES WERE HEARSES" '61
"THE OTHER WORLD" '63
BOTHAM, R.R.--[2][11]SF--
BRADFORD, SIMON--[11]
HADLEY, FRANKLIN[T]--V. BERCH-MON PSEUDS,
BAE 9,[2][11][23]SF--
MON 431 "PLANET BIG ZERO" '64
WINTER BOTTOM, RUSS--[11]
WINTER, R.R.--[1][33]

WINTERFELD, HENRY
MICHAEL, MANFRED--[1][33]

WINTERMUTE, EDWIN H.
DEEVER, BRIAN--L. ROBBINS LTR MAR '94

WINTERS, BERNICE
WINTERS, BAYLA--[1]

WINTERS, CATHERINE [MARY]
GORDON, MARY EBBITT--[1][31]

WINTERS, JANET LEWIS
LEWIS, JANET--[1][22]AMERICAN

WINTERTON, FRANCIS DERYK
HOBSON, FRANCIS--[34]MYS--
EYRE "DEATH ON A BACK BENCH" '59

WINTERTON, PAUL
BAX, ROGER--[3][5][18][29]MYS--
SKEFF "RED ESCAPADE" '40
HUTCH "CAME THE DAWN" '49 & 4 MORE
GARVE, ANDREW--[3][5][18][29][32]MYS--
30 NOVELS '50-78
7 DIGEST SS
SOMERS, PAUL--[3][5][18][29]MYS--
COLLINS "BEGINNER'S LUCK" '58
COLLINS "BROKEN JIGSAW" '61 & 2 MORE

WINTHROP, BUD ROBERT
FLANAGAN, BUD--[8]

WINTLE, ALFRED DANIEL
COBB, MICHAEL--[1][2][3]MYS--
SELWYN "COLD HARBOR" '39
SELWYN "SHOLTO BUD" '32 MORE '29-39

WINTLE, ANNE
ELLIS, OLIVIA--[1][31]
FRANCIS, ANNE--[1][31]

WINTLE, FRANK EDWARD
RUTHERFORD, EDWARD--[1]

WINTLE, JUSTIN [B]
BEECHUM, JUSTIN--[1][31]

WINTRINGHAM, TOM
GRACCHUS--[8]

WIREN, SVEN G. CARL-AXEL
CLARK, MILTON--[29]MYS--
"AFFAREN MALINOWSKY" '43

WIRT, WINOLA WELLS
FRAZIER, SARAH--[31]

WIRTANEN, ATOS KASIMIR
FINN, HUCK--[1]
MUSKETOEREN--[1]
SAWYER--[1]

WISE, ARTHUR
MCARTHUR, JOHN--[2][22]ENGLISH--
"DAYS IN THE HAY" '60
"HOW NOW BROWN COW" '62
SWIFT, BRIAN--[34]MYS,HP--
JOVE "MISSION CODE: SYMBOL" '81
JOVE "MISSION CODE: ACROPOLIS" '82

WISE, ERNEST GEORGE
GEORGE, ERNEST--[34]MYS--
GOLZ "BELLE" '29

WISE, JAMES WATERMAN
ANALYTICUS--[31]

WISEBERG, MARIAN ALICE
MOUNTAIN, ALICE--[1]

WISEMAN, ANN [S]
DENZER, ANN WISEMAN--[1][31][33]

WISEMAN, DAVID
JULIAN, JANE--[31]

WISLER, GENE CHARLES
WISLER, G.C.--[21]ROM--
"SUNRISE"

WISLER, G[ARY] CLIFTON
McLENNAN, WILL--[28]WEST--
JOVE "THE RAMSEYS" '89
JOVE "RAMSEY'S LUCK" '89
JOVE "MATT RAMSEY" '89

WISNER, WILLIAM L.
WISNER, BILL--[33]

WITCOMBE, RICK
MARKER, CLARE--[8]

WITHERS, CARL A.
NORTH, ROBERT--[1][33]
WEST, JAMES--[1][33]

WITHERSPOON, IRENE MURRAY
MURRAY, IRENE--[1]

WITMOND-BERKHOUS, ANNA C.
VAN BERKEN, TINE--[22]DUTCH

WITT, OTTO
KING, SAM--[29]MYS--
AHLEN & AKERLUND "ANDEFOTOGRAFIET" '14

WITT, SHIRLEY HILL
THUNDERCLOUD, KATHERINE--[1][33]

WITTE, GLENNA FINLEY
FINLEY, GLENNA--[3][22][26]MYS--
ARCADIA "DEATH STRIKES OUT" '57
& 41 ROM NOVELS

WITTER, SUZANNE E.
ELIZABETH, SUZANNE--[26]ROM--
"WHEN DESTINY CALLS"

WITTERMANS, ELIZABETH
PINO, E.--[22]INDONESIAN-AMERICAN

WITTLIN, THADDEUS ANDREW
KARNIEWSKI, JANUSZ--[31]

WITTON, EILEEN
BENNETT, JANICE--[21][26]ROM--
"HOLLY BROOCH"
"FOREVER IN TIME" & 11 MORE
BENNETT, JANICE N.--[21][26]ROM--
"CASTLE ON THE RIVER"
"HAUNTED"
"PIONEERS"
"HOUSE OF ATHENA"

WODEHOUSE, PELHAM GRENV.
BROOKE-HAVEN, P.--[31]
GRENVILLE, PELHAM--[1][31][33]
PLUM, J.--[1][33]
POWYS, STEPHEN--[8]
WEST, C.P.--[1]
WILLIAMS, J. WALKER--[1][33]
WINDHAM, BASIL--[1][33]
WODEHOUSE, P.G. [1]--[1][32][34]MYS--
JENK "HOT WATER" '32
JENK "PIGS HAVE WINGS" '52 & MORE
SA "MR. MULLINER, PRIVATE DET." SEPT '54
EQMM "JEEVES & THE STOLEN VENUS" AUG '59
& 6 OTHER DIGEST STORIES

WOHL, BURTON
HILLS, BALDWIN--[1][2]

WOHL, JAMES P[AUL]
COLTRANE, JAMES--[1][34]MYS--
BOBBS "TALON" '78

WOHLMUTH, ED
DAVID, ED--[31]

WOJCIECHOWSKA, MAIA T.
LARKIN, MAIA--[31]
MARKIN, MAIA--[31]
RODMAN, MAIA--[22][31][33]POLISH-AMERICAN--
3 CHILDREN'S BOOKS '52-80

WOJHOSKI, BARBARA M.
PACE, LAUREL--[10][26][34]ROM--
HARL 247 "BLOOD TIES"
"DESTINY'S PROMISE"
"WINDS OF DESTINY"
WOJHOSKI, B.--[21]ROM--
"DECEPTION BY DESIGN"

WOLF, MIRIAM BREDOW
BREDOW, MIRIAM--[22][31]AMERICAN

WOLF, SARAH [ELIZABETH]
WOLF, S.K.--[34]MYS--
S&S "HARBINGER EFFECT" '89
IVY "LONG CHAIN OF DEATH" '91
S&S "MACKINNON'S MACHINE" '91

WOLF, SUSAN WHITTLESEY
TYLER, ANTONIA--[9][21][26]ROM--
"THIS SHINNING HOUR"

WOLFE, CHARLES KEITH
HENDRICKS, KAW--[1][31]

WOLFE, LOIS
WYETH, GILLIAN--[9][21][26]ROM--
"DARE I LOVE?"

WOLFE, RON
WINTERS, MICK--W/JOHN [S] WOOLEY,[7]SF/HOR--
BERK "FULL MOON" '89

WOLFE, THOMAS CLAYTON
HUNGRY GULLIVER--[1]

WOLFF, CARL
CAROLUS--[1]

WOLFF, CECIL DRUMMOND
WALDO, CEDRIC DANE--[1][2][7]SF--
"THE BAN OF THE GUBBE" 1896

WOLFF, VIRGINIA
MARTELL, CLAUDIA--[1]

WOLFF, WILLIAM DEAKIN
MARTINDALE, SPENCER--[1]

WOLFGANG, OTTO
HILL,TOM--[1]
ROY, PERCY GORDON--[1]

WOLFSON, VICTOR
DODGE, LANGDON--[3][22]MYS--
DBLDY "MIDSUMMER MADNESS" '50

WOLK, GEORGE
GANT, NORMAN--[34]MYS--
LAN 75-047 "CHANE" '68
LAN 75-053 "BLACK VENGEANCE" '68
LAN 75-070 "SLAVE EMPIRE" '69
LAN 74-683 "BURN" '70
GRAAT, HEINRICH--[1][2]
KIDDE, JANET--[7][11]SF--
JOVE "THE PROPHETESS" '78
PARRISH, BARNEY--[7]SF--
PLAYBOY "THE CLOSED CIRCLE: A NOVEL" '76
WATT, SEBASTIAN--[21]ROM--
"NATCHEZ KINGDOM"

WOLLHEIM, DONALD A.
COOKE, ARTHUR--W/E. BALTER ET AL,
[2][15][23]SF,HP--COMET STORIES
GORDON, MILLARD VERNE--[1][2][15][23]SF--
FUTURE FANTASY & SCIFI
GRINNELL, DAVID--[23][31][33][32]MYS/SF--
6 NOVELS ALONE
1 W/LIN CARTER
MZ "THE FEMININE FRACTION" NOV '64
MZ "THE GARRISON" APR '65
LAVOND, PAUL DENNIS--[2]SF,HP--SFQ/FUTURE
PEARSON, MARTIN--[2][15][23]SF--
ASF "EMBASSY" '42
"POGO PLANET"
'AJAX CALKINS' SERIES
ST "OBSERVATION PLATFORM" OCT '57
WARLAND, ALLEN--[2][15][23]SF--
SCIFI QUARTERLY "BABY DREAMS" WINT '41-2
WELLS, BRAXTON--[1][2]
WOODS, LAWRENCE--W/JOHN B. MICHEL,
[2][15][23]SF--
SCIFI QTRLY "EARTH DOES NOT REPLY" SUM '41
WOODS, LAWRENCE--W/R.A.W. LOWNDES,
[2][3][15][23]SF--
"BLACK FLAMES" '41
WOODS, LAWRENCE--[23]AMERICAN/SF--
"STRANGE RETURN" '41
X.--[2][15]SF--
SSC "!!!" APR '41

WOLTHAUSEN, LINDA S.
LEIGH, CATHERINE--W/CATHERINE L. DONICH,
[21][26]ROM--
"A PLACE FOR THE HEART"

WOLVERTON, JOHN DAVID
WOLVERTON, DAVE--[7]SF--
BB "ON MY WAY TO PARADISE" '89
BB "SERPENT CATCH" '91

WOMACK, DAVID A.
BUCHAN, DAVID--[1][31]
YATES, DAVID O.--[1]

WOOD, ANNA COGSWELL
RIDGEWAY, ALGERNON--[1]

WOOD, CHRISTOPHER [H]
DIXON, ROSIE--[1][31]
GRAPE, OLIVER--[1][31]
LEA, TIMOTHY--[1][31]
MAY, JONATHAN--[8]
SUTTON, PENNY--[1]

WOOD, CLEMENT
DUBOIS, ALAN--[1][22]MYS

WOOD, EDGAR ALLARDYCE
WOOD, KERRY--[8][33]

WOOD, EDWARD D. JR.
BATES, NORMAN--MUNROE RVW '93
BLUE, SHERI--G. THIESSEN '93
EDWARDS, WOODROW--MUNROE RVW '93
EVERETT, KATHLEEN--MUNROE RVW '93
JASON, N.V.--MUNROE RVW '93
JENSEN, V.N.--G. THIESSEN '93
LENNON, FRANK--MUNROE REVIEW, FEB 93
LEONARD, FRANK--MUNROE RVW '93
MERRILL, MANDY--MUNROE RVW '93
MOREAU, EMIL--MUNROE RVW '93
NICHOLS, JASON--MUNROE RVW '93
PETERS, DR. T.K.--MUNROE RVW '93
QUINN, JOHN--MUNROE RVW '93
SPENCER & WEST--MUNROE RVW '93
TRENT, DICK--L. MUNROE SLST 20-ED WOOD JR. BIBLIO--
TRENT, DICK--L. MUNROE-NUETZEL INTRVW-
BAE 25, ADULT--
POW PP-129 "MAMA'S DIARY" '69
WADE, CARLSON--SMUT PEDDLER #2, ADULT--
EUROPA 517 "HOMOSEXUAL GENERATION"
RPRTS "ME DY IN DRAG?"
WESTERMIER, DAVID L.--MUNROE RVW '93
WILLIAMS, J.X.--MUNROE RVW '93
WORTHY, KEN--SMUT PEDDLER #2, ADULT--
COVER OF EUROPA 571 - SEE CARLSON WADE

WOOD, EDWARD JOHN
BARNAO, JACK--LACHMAN-EASTER LST '93,
[18][34]MYS--
SCRIBN "HAMMERLOCKE" '86
SCRIBN "LOCKESTEP" '88
`COLD BLOOD' SS COLL- STORY "THAT WAS NO LADY" '89
WOOD, TED--[18][34]MYS--
SCRIBN "FOOL'S GOLD" '86
SCRIBN "CORKSCREW" '87 & 5 MORE '83-90

WOOD, ELLEN PRICE
LUDLOW, JOHNNY--[1]
WOOD, MRS. HENRY--[1]

WOOD, FERNEY
ROSMANITH, OLGA L. [1]--V. BERCH-LESBIANA/
CTRCLTR, BAE 22/GM PSEUDS-PP 33,
[34]ADULT/MYS--
CASSELL "SIGNATURE TO A CRIME" '38
MURRAY "PASSENGER LIST" '40
MURRAY "STORM CLOUD OVER VIENNA" '40
GM 273 "UNHOLY FLAME" '52
LION 200 "LONG THRILL" '54
POPLB EB68 "DON'T SAY NO" '56

WOOD, GRACE ASHLEY
ANCILLA--[8]

WOOD, HERBERT FAIRLIE
REDMAYNE, JOHN--W/DONALD JAMES GOODSPEED,[1]

WOOD, H[ARRY] F[REEMAN]
WARD, WILLIAM--[34]MYS,HP--
WESTBROOK "PASSENGER FROM SCOTLAND
YARD" '08
WOOD, H.F. WILBER--[34]MYS--
SISLEY'S "UNDER MASKS" '08

WOOD, J.G.
FORREST, GEORGE--B&M COLL #79--
ROUTLEDGE - 4 BOY'S BOOKS

WOOD, JAMES PLAYSTEAD
BRIAVELS, JAMES S.--[22]AMERICAN
SOUDLEY, HENRY--[1][22][33]AMERICAN
ST. BRIAVELS, JAMES--[1][33]AMERICAN

WOOD, JAMES [A.F]
FRASER, STUART--[1][31]
MCLEOD, FINLAY--[8]
STUART, GORDON--[8]

WOOD, JOHN JAMES O'HARA
DEE, R.K.--[8]

WOOD, JULIA AMANDA
LEE, MINNIE MARY--[1]

WOOD, LILLIAN CATHERINE
CYMRY BACH--[8]

WOOD, PATRICIA E.W.
ROSS, PATRICIA--[8]

WOOD, ROBERT PAUL
WOOD, ROBIN--[7]SF--
DONNING "THE PEOPLE OF PERN" '88

WOOD, SABINE W.
FISHER, JACOB--[34]MYS--
WINSTON "MAN WHO SAW WRONG" '13

WOOD, SARA BARD F.
FIELD, SARA BARD--[1]
GLICKSOHN, SUSAN WOOD--[23]AMERICAN/SF

WOOD, TONYA [TONIA]
COREY, RYANNE--[26]ROM--
"VALENTINA ST. HUSTLE"
"LEATHER & LACE"
"THE STRANGER"
RYAN, COURTNEY--[9][21][26]ROM--
"TEMPORARY ANGEL"
"BEST OF STRANGERS" & 7 MORE

WOOD, VIOLET
WOOD, QUALITY--[1]

WOOD, [SAMUEL] ANDREW
CROSS, THOMSON--[1]
RAVENGLASS, HAL--[1]
TEMPLE, ROBIN--[2][3][7][22][23]SF--
BLACKIE "AZTEC TEMPLE" '55
& 14 MYS NOVELS '32-46
WOOD, S. ANDREW--[34]MYS

WOOD-SEYS, ROLAND ALEXAN.
CUSHING, PAUL--[1][34]MYS--
BLACKWOOD "BLACKSMITH OF VOE" 1888
MacM "GREAT CHIN EPISODE" 1893

WOOD-SMITH, NOEL
CLIFFORD, MARTIN--[1]HP--
CONQUEST, OWEN--[1]HP--
RICHARD, FRANK--[1]HP--
TAYLOR, NORMAN--[1]
TERRY, NOEL--[1]

WOODARD, WAYNE
BOK, HANNES--[2][4][7][11]SF--
3 BOOKS ABOUT ART
DOLBOKOV--W/BORIS DOLGOV,[2][11][16]
MERRITT, A.--[23]SF,GHOSTED--
"THE BLACK WHEEL" '47
"THE FOX WOMAN & THE BLUE PAGODA" '46

WOODCOCK, E. PAGE
UNCLE REG--[8]

WOODCOCK, MAUREEN
BRONSON, MAUREEN-- W/ANTOINETTE BRONSON,
[9][21][26]ROM--
"BLIND FAITH"
"RAGTIME DAWN" & 3 MORE

WOODERIDGE, KATHLEEN M.
PARTRIDGE, KATHLEEN--[1]

WOODFORD, [I] CECIL
BARRIE, JANE--[1]
DOUGLAS, KIM--[1]
GOFF, MADELEINE--[8]
LEE, VERONICA--[1]

WOODHAM-SMITH, CECIL
GORDON, JANET--[8]

WOODHOUSE, CHRISTOPHER M.
WOODHOUSE, C.M.--[1]

WOODHOUSE, MARTIN C.
CHARLTON, JIM--[34]MYS--
MacM "THE REMINGTON SET" '76
CHARLTON, JOHN--[1][29][31][40]MYS

WOODLAND, EVA [EVE]
DE LYN, NICOLE--[9][21][26]ROM--
"FIRE & ICE"
"ENCHANTMENT" & 3 MORE
LINDSAY, NICOLE--[9]ROM

WOODMAN, THOMAS
QUILTER, EDDIE--[1]

WOODRICH, MARY NEVILLE
NEVILLE, MARY--[1][31][33]CHILDREN'S

WOODROFFE, JOHN
AVALON, ARTHUR--[1][31]

WOODROW, TERRY
BLUEJAY--[7]SF--
"IT'S TIME: A NUCLEAR NOVEL" '85

WOODRUFF, JUDY
VAN GIESON, JUDITH--HAWK/WOODRUFF INTRVW '93, [34]MYS--
WALKER "NORTH OF THE BORDER" '88
HARPER "RAPTOR" '90 & MORE

WOODRUFF, JULIA L.M.C.
JAY, MRS. W.L.M.--[3]MYS--
WARD "HOLDEN WITH THE CORDS" 1876

WOODS, CLEE
FORREST, LEE--[1][31]
PARK, D.W.--[1]
WARBRIDGE, C.W.--[1]

WOODS, FREDERICK
IVES, LAWRENCE--[1][31]

WOODS, JAMES
NAVARCHUS--W/PARTICK VAUX,[1]
YEXLEY, LIONEL--[1]

WOODS, MARGERY
CAINE, REBECCA--[9][21]ROM--
"SUMMER OF SURRENDER"
"PAGAN HEART"
"CHILD OF TAHITI"
HILTON, MARGERY--[8][9][21]ROM--
"GIRL CRUSOE"
"SNOW BRIDE" & 21 MORE

WOODS, MRS. J.C.
WOODROFFE, DANIEL--[1][2]

WOODS, OWEN SPENCER
WOODS, JONAH--[1]

WOODS, SHERYL ANN
KIRK, ALEXANDRA--[9][21][26][31]ROM--
"SAND CASTLES"
"IMAGES OF LOVE"
SHERRILL, SUZANNE--[9][21][26]ROM--
"RESTORING LOVE"
"DESIRABLE COMPROMISE"
WOODS, SHERRYL--[9]ROM--
"A KISS AWAY"
"SAFE HARBOR"

WOODS, SUSAN [JOAN]
GLICKSOHN, SUSAN WOOD--[7][23]SF--
NON-FICT

WOODSON, JEFF
WOODSON, JEFF--W/ANDREW J. OFFUTT--
CARLYLE COMM "FIRES DOWN BELOW"

WOODSON, JOHN WADDIE JR.
WOODSON, JACK--[33]

WOODWARD, EDWARD E.
GRIERSON, JANE--[1][22]MYS

WOODWARD, GRACE STEEL
DOANE, MARIAN S.--[1][22][31]AMERICAN

WOODWARD, TENA GARRISON
GARRISON, ANET--[1]

WOODY, REGINA JONES
DEVI, NILA--[31]

WOOLACOTT, LESLIE LOVAL
WEST, V.C.--[36]AUSTRALIAN/MYS--
CURR "THE GARAGE SKELETON" '41

WOOLEY, JOHN [S]
LESLIE, ROBERT B.--[1][31]
SEVERS, JEROME--[1]
WINTERS, MICK--W/RON WOLFE,[7]SF/HOR--
BERK "FULL MOON" '89

WOOLF, MARION
LAYNE, MARION MARGERY--W/MARGERY PAPICH & LAYNE TORKELSON,[34]MYS--
DODD "BALLOON AFFAIR" '81

WOOLFOLK, JOANNA MARTINE
MARTINE--[1][7]ADULT--
PLEASURE BKS "DANCE OF LOVE" '79
RPRTD "DANCE OF DESIRE"

WOOLFOLK, JOSHUA PITTS
ANONYMOUS--SMUT PEDDLER #2, ADULT--
SIGNATURE "DOWN & DOWN & DOWN" '52
BRITT, SAPPHO HENDERSON--[1][22]AMERICAN
FORDWOOD, JACK--RYERSON JOHNSON LTR '94--
'BREEZY' & `FILM FUN' TYPE MAGS
JACKWOOD, JIM--RYERSON JOHNSON LTR '94--
`BREEZY' & `FILM FUN' TYPE MAGS
KENNEDY, HOWARD--[1][22]AMERICAN/MYS--
ER "LADY KILLER" '33
SAYRE, GORDON--[1][22]AMERICAN
WOODFORD, JACK--JEAN F. LE DEIST-BAE 18, [2][3][11][22]MYS--
"FIND THE MOTIVE" '32
CARLYLE "FIVE FATAL DAYS" '33
WOODFORD PRESS "TEMPTRESS" '46
WOODFORD PRESS "HOOF HEARTED" '51
SIGNATURE PRESS "BUNDLE OF CURVES" '52
WOODFORD, JILL--RYERSON JOHNSON LTR APR '94,
`BREEZY' & `FILM FUN' TYPE MAGS

WOOLFOLK, WILLIAM
LYON, WINSTON--[1][34]MYS--
"CRIMINAL COURT" '66
2 SIGNET BATMAN NOVELS '66

WOOLLEY, CATHERINE
THAYER, JANE--[1][33]

WOOLMAN, DAVID S.
VAIDON, LAWDOM--[1]

WOOLRICH, CORNELL HOPLEY
ANONYMOUS--F.M. NEVINS JR/M. LACHMAN--
MYS PULP STORY "THE NIGHT I DIED"
HOPPLEY, GEORGE--[2][3][5]MYS--
RINEHART "FRIGHT" '50
FARRAR "NIGHT HAS A THOUSAND EYES" '45
IRISH, WILLIAM--[2][5][32][34]MYS--
24 BOOKS '42-56
16 DIGEST SS
WOOLRICH, CORNELL--[1][2]

WOOLRICH, DANIEL
HOLMES, GEOFFREY--[1][2][11]

WOOLSEY, MARY HALE
HALE, EUGENIA--[1]
HALE, MARY--[1]
SNOW, TERRY--[1]

WOOLSEY, SARAH CHAUNCY
COOLIDGE, SUSAN--[1][22][31]AMERICAN--
STORIES FOR GIRLS

WOOLSON, CONSTANCE F.
MARCH, ANNE--[1]

WOONTEILER, GARY E.
GARYS, WALTER--W/WALTER LUBARS, V.BERCH LTR TO HUBIN '94, MYS--
TWR "DETONATOR" '81

WORBOYS, ANN[ETTE I.]
EYRE, ANNETTE--[9][21][26]ROM--
"GIVE ME YOUR LOVE"
"MAGNOLIA ROOM"
"VENITIAN INHERITANCE"
MAXWELL, VICKY--[3][21][26]MYS/ROM--
COLLINS "HIGH HOSTAGE" '76
"CHOSEN CHILD" '73 & MORE '73-7
WORBOYS, ANNE E. EYRE--[1]

WORDEN, FRAN
HENRY, FRAN WORDEN--[1]

WORDINGHAM, JAMES A.
DARE, MICHAEL--[8]

WORKMAN, JAMES
DARK, JAMES--[1][2][35]AUSTRALIAN--
HRWTZ PB116 "IMPACT" '62
HRWTZ PB124 "HAVOC" '62
HRWTZ PB129 "TERRIFYING STORIES" '63
HRWTZ PB 138 "HORROR TALES" '63
HRWTZ PB141 "SWEET TASTE OF VENOM" '63
HOLLEGE, JAMES--[35]AUSTRALIAN,GHOSTED--
HRWTZ PB131 "CLEOPATRA OF EGYPT" '65
KAIN, VICTOR--[35]AUSTRALIAN--
HRWTZ PB126 "THE MAD SURGEON" '62

WORKMAN, KAREN
MILLER, KAREN--[35]AUSTRALIAN,HP--
HRWTZ ?? TITLE(s) ??]

WORLEY, DOROTHY
LENNOX, SUSAN--V. BERCH--
MON PSEUDS, BAE 9, ROM--
MON 208 "DOCTOR'S CHOICE" '61

WORLEY, FREDERICK U.
BENEFICE--[2]

WORM, EBERHARD
ROCKER, FERRY--W/LENA ESCHNER, [39][40]GERMAN/MYS--
"IN EINER NEBELNACHT" '53

WORMSER, RICHARD [E]
CARTER, NICK--[2][11][34]MYS,HP--
VITAL "MURDER UNLIMITED" '45
VITAL "DEATH HAS GREEN EYES" '46
VITAL "EMPIRE OF CRIME" '46
VITAL "PARK AVENUE MURDER" '46
FRIEND, ED--[7][28][29][34]MYS/WEST--
DELL "GREEN HORNET IN THE INFERNAL LIGHT" '66
LAN 73-200 "CORPSE IN THE CASTLE" '70
GM 1732 "ALVAREZ KELLY" '66
GM 1911 "SCALPHUNTERS" '68
TEMPO 5302 "HIGH CHAPARRAL: COYOTE GOLD" '69

WORNER, PHILIP A.I.
INCLEDON, PHILIP--[1][8]
SYLVESTER, PHILIP--[1][8]

WORNUM, MIRIAM
DENNIS, EVE--[1][8]

WORRELL, EVERIL
CABRAL, O.M.--[1][2][16]
MONETT, LIREVE--[8][11][16]

WORSLEY, T.C.
LISTER, RICHARD--[8]

WORTHINGTON-STUART, BRIAN
MEREDITH, PETER--[22][34]MYS--
WARD "CROCODILE MAN" '51
WARD "DENZIL EMERALDS" '54 & 6 MORE '49-54
STUART, BRIAN--[3][22][32]MYS--
WARD "SERPENT'S FANG" '51
LM "COL. CHINSTRAP'S GHOST STORY" MAR '54
WARD "CASE IS ALTERED" '55 & 6 MORE '48-55

WORTHLEY, R.G.
VIOLA--[8]

WORTHY, BRIAN JOHNSON
JOHNSON, BRIAN--[8]

WORTIS, EDWARD IRVING
AVI--CRPG,[7]SF--
COLLIER 41511 "WOLF RIDER" '86 & 4 MORE

WORTS, GEORGE FRANK
BRENT, LORING--[22][34]MYS--
CHELSEA "WHO DARES?" '27
HODDER "RETURN OF GEORGE WASHINGTON" '28

WOSMEK, FRANCES
BRAILSFORD, FRANCES--[31]

WOTHERSPOON, RALPH
WOON--[1]

WRAITH, W.J.
ALEXANDER, WALTER--[8]

WRAY, PHOEBE
LEMERCIER, JUSTINE & JULE--W/JOSEF BUSH, [14] ADULT--
OLYM TC-443 "TURKISH BATH" '69

WRAY, W. FITZWATER
KUKLOS--[1]

WREN, PERCIVAL CHRISTOP.
WREN, P.C.--[1][32]--
"BEAU GESTE"
EQMM "DIRTY DOG'S CLUB" JUL '43
EQMM "NO CORPSE - NO MURDER" JAN '44

WRIGHT, ANNA MARIA L.P.
ROSE, ANNA PERROT--[33]

WRIGHT, ARLETA
RICHARDSON, ARLETA--[1]

WRIGHT, BETTY REN
REVENA--[1][33]

WRIGHT, DAPHNE
COOPER, NATASHA--LACHMAN/EASTER LST '93, [34]MYS--
SIMON "FESTERING LILIES" '90

WRIGHT, DONALD K.
WRIGHT, DON--[21]ROM--
"THE CAPTIVES"
"THE WOODSMAN"

WRIGHT, ELINOR BRUCE
LYON, ELINOR--[1]

WRIGHT, ELSIE N.
GRAYSON, [CAPT.] J.J.--[1][22]AMERICAN/MYS

WRIGHT, ENID M.
MEADOWCROFT, ENID LAMONTE--[1][22]
[33]AMERICAN/JUV

WRIGHT, EUGENE ALDEN
WRIGHT, GENE--[7]HOR--
NON-FICT

WRIGHT, EVAN
GRAHAM, DAVID--[7]SF--
HALE "DOWN TO A SUNLESS SEA" '79
HALE "SIDEWALL" '82

WRIGHT, FARNSWORTH
HARD, FRANCIS--[1][2][11]

WRIGHT, FAYE
MATA, DAYA--[1]

WRIGHT, GEORGE T.
WRIGHT, TED--[8]

WRIGHT, GILBERT MUNGER
LEBAR, JOHN--W/HARRY B. WRIGHT,[1][2]SF--
"THE DEVIL'S HIGHWAY" '32

WRIGHT, GUIER & GREGORY
GREGORY, GUY--[7]SF--
BB "HEROES OF ZARA KEEP" '82

WRIGHT, HARRY BELL JR.
LEBAR, JOHN--W/GILBERT M. WRIGHT,[1][2]SF--
"THE DEVIL'S HIGHWAY" '32

WRIGHT, JOHN
WRIGHT, WADE--[34][40]MYS--
HALE "BLONDE TARGET" '66
HALE "HADES HELLO" '73 & 8 MORE '64-73

WRIGHT, LAN
STRICKLAND, JEROME--[11]

WRIGHT, LAUREANA
DE KLEINHANS, LAUREANA W.--[30] MEXICAN

WRIGHT, LIONEL PERCY
STRICKLAND, JEROME--[2]ENGLISH
WRIGHT, LAN--[1][2][23]ENGLISH/SF--
NEW WORLD "OPERATION EXODUS" '52

WRIGHT, LUCRETIA
KNIGHT, ALICIA--[9][10][21][26]ROM--
"CRESCENT CARNIVAL"
"ETERNAL FLAME"

WRIGHT, MABEL OSGOOD
BARBARA--[1][2]
RUSSELL, SARAH--[1]

WRIGHT, MARJORY BEATRICE
PILGRIM--[8]

WRIGHT, MARY MAUDE
DUNN, MARY--[23]ENGLISH/SF
LORRAINE, LILITH--[2][7][11][23]SF--

WRIGHT, MARY PAMELA
BAWN, MARY--[1][22][31]ENGLISH

WRIGHT, MARY PATRICIA
NAPIER, MARY--[1][34]MYS--
BB "THE WAITING" '80
COLLINS "FORBIDDEN PLACES" '81
HUTCH "STATE OF FEAR" '84
BODLEY "POWERS OF DARKNESS" '90 & MORE

WRIGHT, NOEL
WORTH, NIGEL--[2][3][7]MYS/SF--
"ARMS OF PHAEDRA" '24 & MORE '23-7

WRIGHT, PATRICIA
THAYER, PATRICIA--[26]ROM--
"JUST MAGGIE"

WRIGHT, R.L. GERARD
BRISTOWE, EDWIN--[8]

WRIGHT, RONALD SELBY
RADIO PADRE--[8]

WRIGHT, SCOTT
SCOTT, ANNJEANETTE--[3][21][26]MYS--
POPLB "CASTLE FOR THE LEFT HAND" '76
POPLB "COUNT OF VON RHEEDEN CASTLE" '76

WRIGHT, SEWELL PEASLEE
ANDREWS, THOMAS--L. ROBBINS LTR '94,
[2][11][31]
CAMERON, LEIGH--L. ROBBINS LTR '94,[2][11]
SPENCER, PARKE--L.ROBBINS LTR '94,[2][11]
WRIGHT, S.P.--L. ROBBINS LTR '94

WRIGHT, SIDNEY FOWLER
FOWLER, SYDNEY--[7][23][34]MYS--
RICH "ADVENTURE OF BLUE ROOM" '45
HARRAP "BELL ST MURDERS" '31
SEYMOUR, ALAN--[2][18][23]SF--
"SCENES FROM THE MORTE D'ARTHUR" '19
WINGRAVE, ANTHONY--[2][4][7][11][23]SF--
"VENGEANCE OF GWA" '35

WRIGHT, STEPHEN WILLIAM
WRIGHT, STEVE--[36]MYS--
PAN "LOVE, AVALON" '90
PAN "A DROP IN THE OCEAN" '91
PAN "A BREAK IN THE TRAFFIC" '92

WRIGHT, TERRANCE M.
ARMSTRONG, F.W.--[7][31][34]SF/HOR--
TOR 'CHANGING' #1 & 2 '85-7

WRIGHT, WATKINS E.
WILLIAMS, WRIGHT--R.C. & ELWANDA RVW '93,
ADULT--
BEAC B143 "SHOCK TREATMENT" '57
BEAC B167 "PLAY FOR PAY" '58
BEAC B170 "SIDE STREET" '58

WRIGHT, WILLARD H.
VAN DINE, S.S.--[5][18][29][34]MYS--
SCRIBN "SCARAB MURDER CASE" '30
& 12 MORE '26-50

WRIGHT-FRIERSON, VIRGINIA
WRIGHTFRIERSON--[33]

WROCZ, JOSEPH
ROSS, JOSEPH--[2][11][23]SF--
"WRZOS"

WRONKER, LILI CASSELL
CASSELL, LILI--[31][33]
CASSELL-WRONKER, LILI--[33]

WU, NELSON I.
LU-CH'IAO--[22]CHINESE-AMERICAN

WUNDERER, RICHARD JR.
DARK, JASON--[39][40]GERMAN/MYS,HP

WUNSCH, JOSEPHINE M.
MCLEAN, J. SLOAN--W/VIRGINIA M. GILLETTE,[1]

WUOLIJOKI, HELLA MARIA
TERVAPAA, JUHANI--[22]FINNISH

WURMBRAND, RICHARD
MOSES, RUBEN--[8]

WURTS[Z], JANICE
WURTS, JANNY--[7]SF--
ACE 'CYCLE OF FIRE' #1-3 '84-8

WYATT, JOHN
PARKER, JOHN--[1]

WYATT, LEE
GED, CAER--[2]

WYBRANIEC, PETER F.
LEONHART, RAPHAEL W.--[2]

WYCHERLEY, RICHARD N.
MURRAY, GILBERT--[1]

WYETH, NEWELL CONVERS
WYETH, N.C.--[1]

WYLER, ROSE
THAYER, PETER--[33]
THAYER, ROSE--[8]

WYLIE, FRANCIS E.
WYLIE, JEFF--[1]

WYLIE, IDA ALEXA ROSS
WYLIE, I.A.R.--[1]

WYLIE, PHILIP
HOMESLEY, LEATRICE--[2][4]

WYLLIE, JAMES MCLEOD
BARRAS SEER--[8]

WYMAN, WALTER F.
CHAPMAN, JOHN--[1][32]MYS--
SUSPENSE MAG "THE DEATHLESS ONES" SPR '51
JOHNSON, H.B.--[1]
MAXWELL, HERBERT M.--[1]
WITHERSPOON, J.J.--[1]

WYND, OSWALD [MORRIS]
BLACK, GAVIN--[2][22][29][34]MYS--
COLLINS "COLD JUNGLE" '69
COLLINS "BITTER TEA" '73 MORE '62-79

WYNDHAM LEWIS, D.B.
BEACHCOMBER--[8]
SHY, TIMOTHY--[8]

WYNDHAM, LEE
HYNDMAN, JANE LEE--[22]RUSSIAN-AMERICAN

WYNNE-TYSON, ESME
AMANDA--[31]
DE MORNY, PETER--[8][31]
DIOTIMA--[31]

WYNNE-TYSON, JON
FOUREST, MICHEL--[1][22][31]ENGLISH
PITT, JEREMY--[1][22][31]ENGLISH

YABES, LEOPOLDO Y.
CHRISTIAN, A.B.--[1][31]
IBARRA, CHRISOSTOMO--[1][31]
SILANGAN, MANUEL--[1]

YAFFE, RICHARD
CHANAN, BEN--[31]

YAGER, JAN
BARKAS, J.L.--[31]
BARKAS, JANET--[31]

YAKOVETIC, JOSEPH SANDY
YAKOVETIC, JOE--[33]

YAKOVLEV, ALEKSANDR I.
HERZEN, ALEKSANDR--[1]
ISKANDER--[1]

YAKUBOVICH, PETER FILIP.
MELSHIN, L.--[22]RUSSIAN

YANCHEVETSKY, VASILY
YAN, V.--[22]RUSSIAN

YANEZ, AUGUSTIN
DELGADILLO, MONICO--[1]

YANEZ, JOSE DONOSO
DONOSO, JOSE--[7]SF--
KNOPF "OBSCENE BIRD OF NIGHT" '73
"SACRED FAMILIES: 3 NOVELLAS" '77

YANOSUKE, NAKAZATO
KAISAN, NAKAZATO--[22] JAPANESE

YANOW, SHERRY
HUNTER, HILARY--[26]ROM--
HARL 496 "COOPER'S LAST STAND"

YANSICK, SUSAN MCGOVERN
YORKE, ERIN--W/CHRISTINE HEALY,[9][21][26]ROM--
HARL "HONOR PRICE" '94 & 7 OTHERS

YAP, DIOSDADO M.
DOC--[1]

YARBRO, CHELSEA QUINN
BONNER, TERRY NELSON--[31]ROM,HP--
'AUSTRALIAN/NZ' SERIES]
PRYOR, VANESSA--[9][21][23][26]ROM/SF--
"A TASTE OF WINE" '82
"CRUSADER'S TORCH"

YARDE, JEANNE B.F.T.
HUNTER, JOAN--[9][21][26]ROM--
"ROXANNA"
"CAVALIER'S WOMAN" & 2 MORE
MONTAGUE, JEANNE--[3][26]MYS/ROM--
CENT "CLOCK TOWER" '83
CENT "MIDNIGHT MOON" '85 & 3 MORE

YARDUMIAN, MIRYAM
MIRYAM--[8]

YARIV, FRANCIS POKRAS
FRANCIS, EMILY--W/EMILY ARTZ, V. BERCH LTR
TO HUBIN '94, MYS--
LEIS "ELENA" '77

YATES, ALAN GEOFFREY
BROWN, CARTER--JEAN F. LE DEIST-BAE 18,
[3][7][18][35][36]AUSTRALIAN/MYS,HP--
MOST EARLY BKS
MSMM "PAY NOW - KILL LATER!" JUL '66
BROWN, PETER CARTER--[3][18][36]
AUSTRALIAN/MYS--
BYLINE ON SOME EARLY `CARTER BROWN' BKS
CARTER-BROWN, PETER--[3][18][36]
AUSTRALIAN/MYS--
BYLINE ON SOME EARLY `CARTER BROWN' BKS

YATES, ALAN GEOFFREY [CONT]
CONRAD, TEX--[13][35][36]AUSTRALIAN/WEST
CONWAY, TOD--[1][23][35][36]AUSTRALIAN/WEST
CONWAY, TOM--[31]
MACKELLAR, SINCLAIR--[34]MYS--
RAVEN "PROMPT FOR MURDER" '81
SINCLAIR, DENNIS--[34][36]MYS--
SIGN "TEMPLE DOGS GUARD MY FATE" '69
VALDEZ, PAUL--[13][34][35][36]AUSTRALIAN--
TRNPT "HYPNOTIC DEATH" '49
TRNPT "FATAL FOCUS" '50
TRNPT "CELLULOID SUICIDE" '51
TRNPT "KILL HIM GENTLY" '51
TRNPT "KILLER BY NIGHT" '51
TRNPT "FLIGHT INTO HORROR" '51
TRNPT "GHOSTS DON'T KILL" '51
TRNPT "MURDER GIVES NOTICE" '51
TRNPT "SATAN' SABBATH" '51
TRNPT "TIME THIEF" '51
TRNPT "YOU CAN'T KEEP MURDER OUT" '51
TRNPT "CROOK WHO WASN'T THERE" '52
TRNPT "FELINE FRAME-UP" '52
TRNPT "MANAIC MURDERS" '52
TRNPT "MURDER I DON'T REMEMBER" '52
TRNPT "THERE'S NO FUTURE IN MURDER" '52
YATES, A.G.--[1][18]AUSTRALIAN/MYS--
"COLD DARK HOURS" '58
YATES, ALAN--JEAN F. LE DEIST-BAE 18,[3][35]AUSTRALIAN--
HRWTZ "COLD DARK HOURS" '58
ADM "FAREWELL, MY LADY OF SHALOTT!" '50s
YATES, PETER--[23]AUSTRALIAN

YATES, ELIZABETH
MCGREAL, ELIZABETH--[1]

YATES, GEORGE WORTHINGTON
HUNT, PETER--W/CHARLES H. MARSHALL, [22][34]MYS--
VANGARD "APPLETON MURDERS AT SCANDAL HOUSE" '33
VANGARD "MURDER AMONG THE NUDISTS" '34
VANGARD "MURDER FOR BREAKFAST" '34

YATES, LIONEL [PEEL]
ROE, OWEN--[34]MYS--
LONGMANS "BY THE BROWN BAG" W/HONOR URSE '13

YATES, RAYMOND F.
HALL, BORDEN--[1][31][33]
PIONEER--[1][33]

YATRON, MICHAEL
SOREL, BYRON--[1]

YAUKEY, GRACE S.
SPENCER, CORNELIA--[1][33]

YBARRA, THOMAS R.
YBARRA, T.R.--[1]

YEAKLEY, MARJORIE HALL
BLAIR, LUCILE--[1][31]
HALL, MARJORY--[29][31][33]MYS--
DELL "ROSAMUNDA" '74
MORSE, CAROL--[1][33]

YEATMAN, ROBERT JULIAN
YEATMAN, R.J.--[1]

YEATS-BROWN, FRANCIS C.C.
YEATS-BROWN, F.C.--[1]

YELLOTT, BARBARA LESLIE
JORDAN, BARBARA LESLIE--[1]

YEN-PING, SHEN
MAO-TUN--[22]CHINESE--
NOVELIST & SHORT STORIES

YEN-PING, SHIN
DUN, MAO--[31]

YERGER, ROBERT
STANLEY, BOB--[14]ADULT--
OLYM OPH#214 "FORTUNE STICK" '70
VAN HELLER, MARCUS--[14]ADULT,HP--
OLYM OPH#185 "APE" '69

YERKE, T. BRUCE
FASSBINDER, CARLTON J.--[1][2][11]
YERKE, T,B,--[1]

YERKOVICH, ANTHONY
GRAVE, STEPHEN--V. BERCH LTR TO HUBIN '94 MYS--
AT LEAST "FLORIDA BURN"

YERMAKOV, NICHOLAS VALENTINE
HUNTER, S.L.--[7][23]SF--
BERK 'STEELE' SERIES:
"FUGITIVE STEELE" '91
"MOLTEN STEELE" '91
MASTERS, J.D.--V. BERCH LTR TO HUBIN '94, [7][23]MYS/SF--
CHART 'STEELE' SERIES-6 NOVELS '89-90
YERMAKOV, NICHOLAS--W/GLEN, A. LARSON,[7]SF--
HAWKE, SIMON--[2][7][34] LEGALIZED IN '84 MYS/SF--
POPLB "WIZARD OF WHITECHAPEL" '88 & MORE

YERXA, LEROY
ARNO, ELROY--[2][11][23]SF
BLADE, ALEXANDER--[2][11][23]SF,HP--ZIFF-DAVIS
CASEY, RICHARD--[2][11][23]SF,HP-- ZIFF-DAVIS
FRANCIS, LEE--[2][11]SF,HP--
FANTASY ADVENT./AMAZING
L.Y.--[23]SF--
"DEATH RIDES AT NIGHT" '42

YEVTUSHENKO, YEVGENY A.
EVTUSHENKO, EVGENIL A.--[31]

YEXLEY, LIONEL
NAVARCHUS--W/PATRICK VAUX,[2]

YIN, LESLIE CHARLES B.
CHARTERIS, LESLIE--[2][3][18][23] LEGALIZED IN '26, MYS--
'SAINT' BOOKS & STORIES
TAYLOR, BRUCE--[1]

YIRKA, BARBARA
BARBOUR, ANNE--[26]ROM--
"A PRESSING ENGAGEMENT"
"A TALENT FOR TROUBLE"
"KATE & THE SOLDIER"
"LADY LIZA'S LUCK"

YOCKEY, FRANCIS PARKER
VARANGE, ULICK--[8]

YODER, JUDITH
YATES, JUDITH--[9][21][26]ROM--
"A TEMPTING MAGIC"
"STARS IN HER EYES"

YOGII, HARBHAJAN SINGH K.
BHAJAN, YOGI--[31]

YONEMATSU, MORITA
SOHEI, MORITA--[22] JAPANESE

YONGE, CHARLOTTE MARY
AUNT CHARLOTTE--[8]

YORINKS, ARTHUR
YAFFE, ALAN--[1][33]

YORKE, HENRY VINCENT
GREEN, HENRY--[2][7][22][23][31]ENGLISH/SF

YORKE, MARGARET ELIZABETH
ABBEY, MARGARET--[9][21][26]ROM--
"FRANCESCA"
"GIRDLE OF AMBER" & 7 MORE
MAKEPEACE, JOANNA--[9][21][26]ROM--
"TEMPTATION'S TRIUMPH"
YORK[E], ELIZABETH--[9][21]ROM--
"THE MEDEA LEGEND"
"RIDER ON A PALE HORSE"

YOSELOFF, THOMAS
YOUNG, THOMAS--[8]

YOUD, CHRISTOPHER [S]
CHRISTOPHER, JOHN--G. COOK-BAE 13,[2][3][7][23][25][32]MYS/SF--
NVLS & DIGEST STORIES
FORD, HILARY--G. COOK-BAE 13,[2][25][26][29][34]MYS/SF--
HAM "SARNIA" '74
MacM "CASTLE MALINDINE" '75
HAM "BRIDE FOR BEDIVERE" '76 & 3 MORE
GODFREY, WILLIAM--[2][4][11][31][33]SF--
GRAAF, PETER--[2][3][29][31]MYS--
JOSEPH "DAUGHTER FAIR" '58
DAVIES "GULL'S KISS" '62 & 4 MORE
NICHOLS, PETER--[2][3][4][11][33]MYS--
HOLT "PATCHWORK OF DEATH" '65
RYE, ANTHONY--[2][4][11][33]
VINE, WILLIAM--[1][2][11]
YOUD, C.S.--[1]
YOUD, SAMUEL--[4]

YOUNG, AGNES
YOUNG, AGATHA--[8]

YOUNG, AHDELE CARRINE
YOUNG, CARRIE--[31]AUTOBIO
SS COLL
COOKBOOK

YOUNG, ANDREW S.N.
YOUNG, A.S.--[1]
YOUNG, DOC--[1]

YOUNG, BILLIE
ASHE, PENELOPE--W/ROBERT W. GREENE,[1][31]

YOUNG, CHESLEY VIRGINIA
BARNES, C.V.--[8]
BARNES, CHESLEY VIRGINIA--[1]

YOUNG, DOROTHEA BENNETT
BENNETT, DOROTHEA--[22][29]SWISS/MYS--
COWARD "THE JIG SAW MAN" '76

YOUNG, EMILY HILDA
YOUNG, E.H.--[1]

YOUNG, ENA
CARR, KERRY--[9]ROM
JOYCE, JANE--[9]ROM

YOUNG, ERIC BRETT
LEACROFT, ERIC--[1][22]MYS

YOUNG, ERNEST A[VON]
CARTER, NICHOLAS--[34]MYS,HP--
CLINCH, CAPT.--[34]MYS--
STREET "PERTH AMBOY MYSTERY" 1901
GILCRAFT--[8]
MCKENZIE, DONALD J.--[34]MYS--
STREET "UNDER HIS THUMB: OR, RIVAL DETECTIVE'S CLUES" 1889
STREET MAGNET #76 "FACE TO FACE: OR, THE GRAND PARK MYS" 1899
STREET MAGNET #104 "A PAST MASTER OF CRIME: OR, DETECTIVE BUSH'S CLEVER WORK" 1899
STREET MAGNET #110 "WORKING MAN DETECTIVE: OR, A CRIME AGAINST THE POOR" 1899
STREET MAGNET #119 "REPORTER DETECTIVE" 1899
STREET MAGNET #187 "WALL STREET WONDER" 1901
STREET MAGNET #200 "DETECTIVE AGAINST DETECTIVE: OR, SOLVING A STREET CAR MYS" 1901
ROCKWOOD, HARRY--[1][3][22]MYS,HP--
STSY - 21 NOVELS 1882-1900

YOUNG, FRED W.
ARNOLD, FRANK--[1]
NEWCOMBE, COLIN--[1]
SCOTT, HEDLEY--[1]
WYATT, BEN--[1]
YOUNG, FRANK W.--[1]

YOUNG, GEORGE MALCOLM
YOUNG, G.M.--[1]

YOUNG, GORDON [RAY]
RICHMOND, HUGH--[1][28]--
COWARD "MR. BEAMISH" '40
STEWERT, PAUL--L. ROBBINS LTR MAR '94
YOUNG, GORDON R.--L. ROBBINS LTR MAR '94

YOUNG, JAMES MAXWELL
YOUNG, JIM--[7]SF--
POCK "FACE OF THE DEEP" '79

YOUNG, JANET & ROBERT
RANDALL, JANET--[1][8][22][33]MYS--
YOUNG, BOB--[8]
YOUNG, JAN--[8][33]

YOUNG, KIM RON
HAHN, GLORIA--[1]

YOUNG, MARTHA
SHEPPARD, ELI--[1]

YOUNG, MARY ELIZABETH R.
HAWORTH, MARY--[31]

YOUNG, MARY JO
NOLAN, JENNY--[9][21][26]ROM--
"SUMMER LACE"

YOUNG, MARY LOU DAVES
LAWRENCE, MARY--[31]

YOUNG, NEDRICK
DOUGLAS, NATHAN--[8]

YOUNG, NOEL
ELDER, LEON--[1][31]

YOUNG, PAM
SIDETRACKED HOME EXECUTV.--W/PEGGY JONES,[1]

YOUNG, PATRICIA HELENA
ROSS, HELENA--[1]

YOUNG, PERCY MARSHALL
MARSHALL, PERCY--[1][22][33]ENGLISH

YOUNG, PHYLLIS BRETT
YOUNG, KENDAL--[8][34][40]MYS--
ALLEN "THE RAVINE" '61

YOUNG, RICHARD
MACNAUGHTAN, RICHARD--[34]MYS--
FENLAND "PREPARATORY SCHOOL MURDER" '34

YOUNG, ROBERT
HILL, RABIN--[8]

YOUNG, ROBERT W.
YOUNG, BOB--[33]

YOUNG, SANDRA
HARRIS, SANDRA--[9]ROM
WILSON, ABIGAIL--[9]ROM
YOUNG, BRITTANY--[9][21][26]ROM--
"KARAS CUP"
"WHITE ROSE" & 21 MORE

YOUNG, VERNON
HALES, NORMAN--[1][31]

YOUNGBERG, NORMA IONE
WINFIELD, LEIGH--[1][22]AMERICAN

YOUNGER, ELIZABETH HELY
HELY, ELIZABETH--[29][34]MYS--
HM "DOMINANT THIRD" '59
HM "LONG SHOT" '63 & 3 MORE '59-65

YOUNGER, WILLIAM A.
MOLE, WILLIAM--[22][29][34]MYS--
EYRE "LOBSTER GUERILLAS" '53
"SKIN TRAP" '56 & 3 MORE '52-7

YOXALL, HARRY W.
PARTINGTON, F.H.--[22]ENGLISH

YU-HO ECKE, BETTY TSENG
YU-HO, TSENG--[22]CHINESE

YU-T'ANG, LIN
YUTANG, LIN--[23]CHINESE-AMERICAN/SF

YUVACHOV, DANIIL IVANOVIC
KHARMS, DANIIL--E. BURNS-NY TIMES BK
RVW SEPT 25 '94, MYS--
"INCIDENCES" '94

YUZO, TSUBOUCHI
SHOYO--[22]JAPANESE
SHOYO, TSUBOUCHI--[22]JAPANESE

YVELIN, ALBERT
SAXO-NORMAN--[1]

ZACH, CHERYL [BYRD]
COLE, JENNIFER--[9][21][31][33]ROM--
"THE KISS"
"ON THIN ICE" & MORE

ZACHARIA, IRWIN
IRWIN, SARITA--[7]SF/HOR--
AMER. ART ENTERPRISES "TO LOVE A
VAMPIRE" '82

ZACHARY, ELIZABETH
WILLOUGHBY, LEE DAVIS--[21]ROM,HP--
DELL 'MKNG OF AMERICA' SERIES:
"LAND RUSHERS"
ZACHARY, ELIZABETH--W/HUGH ZACHARY,
[2]CRPG, ROM--
"BLAZING VIXEN"
"DYNASTY OF DESIRE"

ZACHARY, HUGH
DEXTER, JOHN--[1][31]HP--
DRURY, REBECCA--[21]ROM,HP--
'WOMEN AT WAR' SERIES: "DESERT BATTLE"
"BITTER VICTORY"
FORMAN, GINNY--J.A. CORRICK-BAE 3, BAE 18,
[2][11]SF--
GORMAN, GINNY--[1][31]
HUGHES, ELIZABETH--W/ELIZABETH ZACHARY,
JEAN F. LE DEIST-BAE 18,[2][11]SF--
HUGHES, ZACH--J.A. CORRICK-BAE 3, BAE 18,
[2][3][7][23]MYS/SF--
SIGN "PRESSURE MAN" '80 & MORE
HUGHES, ZACHARY--[3][31]MYS--
JOVE "ADLON LINK" '81
JOVE "FIRES OF PARIS" '81
JOVE "FORTRESS LONDON" '81
JOVE "TOWER OF TREASON" '82
INNES, EVAN--[7]SF--
BB 'AMERICA 2040': #1-5 '86-8
KANE, PABLO--J.A. CORRICK-BAE 3, BAE 18,
[2][11][14][31]ADULT--
OLYM OPH#206 "A DICK FOR ALL SEASONS" '70
KANTO, PETER--J.A. CORRICK-BAE 3, BAE 18,
[2][14][23][31]ADULT--
OLYM OPH#123 "WORLD WHERE SEX WAS BORN" '68
OLYM TC#452 "COUPLING GAME" '69
OLYM OPH#176 "GREEN THUMB & SILVER
TONGUE" '69
OLYM TC#472 "NAKED JOY" '69
OLYM TC#485 "SEXPO DANISH STYLE" '70
"ROSY CHEEKS"
PILGRIM, DERRAL--J.A. CORRICK-BAE 3,
BAE 18,[2][11]--
RANGELEY, E.R.--[1]
RANGELY, OLIVIA--J.A. CORRICK-BAE 3,
BAE 18,[2][11]
VAN HELLER, MARCUS--J.A. CORRICK-BAE 3,
BAE 18,[1][2][14]ADULT--
OLYM OPH#148 "NEST OF VIXENS" '69
ZACHARY, ELIZABETH--W/ZACHARY, ELIZABETH
JEAN F. LE DEIST-BAE 18,[1][11]ROM--
"BLAZING VIXEN"
"DYNASTY OF DESIRE"

ZACHERLE, JOHN C.
ZACHERLEY--[1][2][7][11]

ZAFFO, GEORGE J.
STEWART, SCOTT--[1][8][33]

ZAGAT, ARTHUR LEO
ALZEE, GRENDON--[1][2][11]
CONYERS, LATHAM--[1][2][11]
HOUSE, BRANT--PULP CLASSIC #22, MYS,HP--
SAX "PLAGUE OF THE GOLDEN DEATH" DEC '37
YORKE, ANTON--[1][2][11]

ZAGNONI, ROSA
MARINONI, ROSA ZAGNONI--[2]

ZAHAVA, IRENE
LEVINSON, IRENE--[1][31]

ZAHM, JOHN AUGUSTINE
MOZANS, H.J.--[1]

ZAIDENBERG, ARTHUR
AZAID--[1][31]

ZAKO, ANDON
CAJUPI--[22] ALBANIAN

ZALBERG, DANIEL
DANIEL, S.--[8]

ZALLER, ANGELIKA BITA
BITA, LILI--[1][31]

ZAMBRENO, MARY FRANCES
TALLIS, ROBYN--[7][33]SF,HP--
IVY "CHILDREN OF THE STORM" '89

ZANE, LEHI
TAYLOR, SAM S.--[32][34]MYS--
DUTTON "SLEEP NO MORE" '49
DUTTON "NO HEAD FOR HER PILLOW" '52
DUTTON "SO COLD, MY BED" '53
PHANT "HOLIDAY IN HELL" ca '54
MH "STATE LINE" SEPT '54
MH "GENERAL SLEPT HERE" APR '55
SA "DIG IT, BROTHER" MAY '56
BL "SUMMER IS A BAD TIME" NOV '61
BL "A CLEAR PICTURE" MAR '62

ZANGWILL, ISRAEL
BARONESS VON S.--[1]
BELL, J. FREEMAN--[1]
MARSHALLIK--[1]

ZANGWILL, LOUIS
Z.Z.--[1][34]MYS--
CHATTO "A NINETEENTH CENTURY MIRACLE" 1897

ZAPP, ARTHUR
TERANUS--[2]

ZARCHY, HARRY
LEWIS, ROGER--[8][33]

ZARIF, MARGARET MIN'IMAH
JONES, MARGARET BOONE--[33]

ZATLIN, PHYLLIS
BORING, PHYLLIS ZATLIN--[1][31]
ZATLIN-BORING, PHYLLIS--[1]

ZATLYN, EDWARD
CHALLOT, DEAN--V. BERCH-BRNDN/BC PSEUDS, BAE 22, ADULT--

ZAVALA, ANN
POPE, ANN--[9][26]ROM--
"GOLD FEVER"
POPE, LEE--[9]ROM

ZAWADSKY, PATIENCE
DAY, PATIENCE--[34]MYS--
HARTMAN, PATIENCE--[1][31]
LYNN, BECKY--[1][31]

ZAWIDOSKI, GREGORY
BURGESS, MASON--[7]SF/HOR--
LEIS "BLOOD MOON" '86
LEIS "CHILD OF DEMONS" '85
LEIS "GRAVEYARD" '87

ZDEREK, MARILEE
EARLE, MARILEE--[1][31]

ZEBROWSKI, JERZY TADEUZ
ZEBROWSKI, GEORGE [THAD.]--[7]SF--
NAME ANGLICIZED--
NUMEROUS WORKS ALONE & WITH OTHERS

ZECK, GERALD ANTHONY
ZECK, GERRY--[33]
ZUPA, G. ANTHONY--[1][33]

ZEHNDER, MEINRAD
MARTIN, ANTHONY--[8]

ZEIG, JOAN
MEADOWES, ALICIA--W/LINDA BURAK,[9][21]ROM--
"SWEET BRAVADO"
"TENDER TORMENT" & MORE

ZEIGER, HENRY A.
PETERSON, JAMES--[1][22][34]AMERICAN/MYS--
DELL "ARRIVIDERCI, BABY!" '66

ZEIGERMAN, GERALD
GERALD, ZIGGY--[1][31]

ZEIGLE, KATE M.
STEWART, CATHERINE--[1]

ZEIGLER, MEL
VALLEY, MEL--V. BERCH LTR '93, MYS--
PAPLB "MAGNUM FORCE" '74

ZEITLIN, ISRAEL
TIEMPO, CESAR--[20] SPANISH

ZEKOWSKI, ARLENE
BERNE, ARLENE--[1]
JANS, ZEPHYR--[1][31]

ZELAZNY, ROGER
DENMARK, HARRISON--[1][11][23][33]SF--
AMZ - STORIES '62-7

ZELENSKI, TADEUSZ
BOY--[22]POLISH

ZELVER, PATRICIA [F]
FARRELL, PATRICIA--[1][31]

ZEMAN, ANTONIN
STASEK, ANATAL--[22]CZECH

ZEMAN, KAMIL
OLBRACHT, IVAN--[22]CZECH

ZENO GANDIA, MANUEL
DE LA CASA, JUAN--[1]
DEL MONTE, FILOMENA--[1]
MOLENDO, GASPAR--[1]
OMEGA--[1]
SARMIENTO, CAMILO--[1]

ZERKHAUSEN, HENRY L.
ELLISON, HENRY LEOPOLD--[1]

ZEROMSKI, STEFAN
KATERLA, JOZEF--[1][22] POLISH
ZYCH, MAURYCY--[1][22]

ZETTERBORG, GABRIEL
DEVINE, DAVID--[29]MYS--

ZETTERLUND, GOSTA
ROWE, MARTIN--[29]MYS--
FREGATT 15 "FORSTA STRIDEN" '76
FREGATT 19 "GRYM FAGENSKAP" '76
FREGATT 20 "FORRADEN" '77

ZETTERSTROM, HANS HARALD
Z, HASSE--[22]SWISS

ZEVIN, ISRAEL JOSEPH
TASHRAK--[1][22]RUSSIAN-AMERICAN
YIDDISH MARK TWAIN--[1][22]RUSSIAN-AMERICAN

ZHANG JIE
CHANG CHIEH--[31]
CHANG CHIEN--[31]
JIE, ZHANG--[31]

ZHISHAN, YE
ZHI, YU--[2]

ZHUCHENKOV, YAR
SLAVUTYCH, YAR--[1]

ZIEGENFUSS, ALAN JOHN
WARREN, ALAN--[7]SF--
STARMONT HOUSE "ROALD DAHL" '88
WARREN, ALAN J.--[1][32]MYS--
MSMM "IN THE CARDS" JUL '80

ZIEGLER, ALAN
BONA, MERCY--[1][31]

ZIEGLER, EDWARD WILLIAM
TYLER, THEODORE--[2][11][23]SF--
"MAN WHOSE NAME WOULDN'T FIT, OR
CASE CARTWRIGHT CHICKERING" '68

ZILLBERG, VENYAMIN ALEX.
KAVERIN, VENYAMIN--[1][22]RUSSIAN

ZILLIACUS, KONNI
COVENANTER--[8]
DIPLOMATICUS--[8]
VIGILANTES--[8]
WILLIAMS, ROTH--[8]

ZIM, SONIA BLEEKER
BLEEKER, SONIA--[8][31]

ZIMM, LOUISE HASBROUCH
HASBROUCH, LOUISE SEYMR.--[1]

ZIMMER, EGON MARIA
BERGIUS, C.C.--[34]MYS--
BARKER "THE NOBLE FORGER" '62

ZIMMER, MAUDE FILES
BAIRD, MAUDE F.--[8]
FILEMAN, NAN--[8]

ZIMMERMAN, ROBERT ALLEN
DYLAN, BOB--[1][8]--
"TARANTULA" '71
KNOPF "WRITINGS & DRAWINGS" '73

ZIMMERMAN, WERNER
DOUGLAS, DRAKE--[2][7]SF/HOR--
"HORROR" '66

ZINBERG, LEONARD S.
APRIL, STEVE--[1][18]MYS--27 DIGEST STORIES
"ROUTE 13" '54
LACY, ED--V. BERCH-LESBIANA/CNTRCLTR,
BAE 22,[3][5][11][18][32]MYS/ADULT--
29 MYS NOVELS '51-69
OF "LESS LIVES THAN A CAT" MAR '59
ST "GHOST BEAT" JAN '61
ST "SO YOUNG TO DIE" MAY '61
OF "BIG BRAINS - BIG DOUGH!" SEPT '59
& OTHERS

ZINBERG, LEN--[18]MYS--
AV 6 "STRANGE DESIRE" '48
"HOLD WITH THE HARES" '48
LION 29 "WALK HARD, TALK LOUD" '50
AV T93 "WHAT D'YA KNOW FOR SURE?" '55

ZINER, FLORENCE
BENNETT, ALICE--[31]
ZINER, FEENIE--[1]

ZINGLERSEN, Z.
WAYNE, H.--[37]DANISH/MYS

ZINSSER, HANS
R.S.--[8]

ZIONOVIEV, ALEKSANDR A.
ZINOVIEV, ALEXANDER--[7]SF--
BODLEY HEAD "THE YAWNING HEIGHTS" '79

ZIRKELBACH, THELMA
MICHAELS, LORNA--[7][26]ROM--
"SEASON OF LIGHT"
"BLESSING IN DISGUISE"
"A MATTER OF PRIVILEDGE"
ALEXANDER, THELMA--[26]ROM--
KISMET 153 "A MAN OF A FEW WORDS"

ZITELMANN, KONRAD
TELMANN, KONRAD--[22]GERMAN

ZIYADAH, MARIE
COPIA, ISIS--[22]SYRO-EGYPTIAN
MAYY--[22]SYRO-EGYPTIAN

ZMICHOWSKA, NARCYZA
GABRYELLA--[22]POLISH

ZOLF, LARRY
JADED OBSERVER--[1][31]

ZOLL, DONALD ATWELL
WINSLOW, DONALD--[8][22]AMERICAN

ZOLLINGER, GULIEIMA
GLADWIN, WILLIAM Z.--[1][31][33]

ZOLOTOW, CHARLOTTE [S]
ABBOTT, SARA--[1][31][33]
BOOKMAN, CHARLOTTE--[1][31][33]

ZONIK, ELEANOR DOROTHY
GLASER, ELEANOR DOROTHY--[8][22][31]ENGLISH

ZORNES, JEANNE DOERING
DOERING, JEANNE--[1][31]

ZORZA, VICTOR
KREMINOLOGIST--[8]

ZUBEIL, RAINER
QUINT, ROBERT--W/EVA EPPER & WERNER K.
GIESA,[39]GERMAN/SF
QUINN, HENRY--W/UWE ANTON,[39]GERMAN

ZUBER, MARY E.L.
ROWLANDS, LESLEY--[8]

ZUCCARI, ANNA RADIUS
NEERA--[1][22]ITALIAN

ZUCH, STAN[LEY ALFRED]
GOOCH, STAN[LEY ALFRED]--[1]

ZUCKER, DORIS MAE B.
HILL, DEE--[1][22][31]
HILL, DEVRA Z.--[1][31]
MYLES, DEVERA--[1][22]

ZUCKERMANN, LYDIA
LAMBERT, LYDIA--[30]MEXICAN
LAPOUSE, MICHELIN--[30]MEXICAN

ZUKAUSKAS, ANTANAS
VIENUOLIS--[22]LITHUANIAN

ZULAWSKI, JULIUSZ
J.Z.--[1]

ZUPRINGER, JEREMY JAMES
PASCALL, JEREMY--[7]SF--
CHARTWELL "KING KONG STORY" '87
EBURY "GOD: THE ULTIMATE AUTOBIOGRAPHY" '87
EBURY "SATAN: KISS & TELL MEMOIRS" '88

ZURHORST, CHARLES [S]
STEWART, CHARLES--[1]

ZUROY, MICHAEL
MICHAEL, Z.M.--[1][32]MYS--
GU "WE WON'T STEAL ANYMORE" DEC '61

ZUVIRIA, GUSTAVO MARTINEZ
WAST, HUGO--[22] ARGENTINIAN

ZWEIG, STEFAN
BRANCH, STEPHEN--[1]

ZWIBAK, JACQUES
SEDYCH, ANDREI--[1]

ZWINGELBERG, MARK
MANLEY, MARK--V. BERCH LTR TO
REGINALD '93, SF--
CHART "BLOOD SISTERS" '85
POPLB "THROWBACK" '87
POPLB "SOCEROR: A NOVEL" '88
ZEBRA "DEVIL'S COIN" '90

ZYSKIND, BRUNO
JASIENSKI, BRUNO--[1][22]POLISH

PSEUDONYMS

PSEUDONYMS

'ERCOLE, VELIA
GREGORY, MARGARET

-KY
BOSETZKY, HORST

-KY & CO.
BOSETZKY, HORST

0 TO 0 4=7 SCRIRE
GARDNER, GERALD BROSSEAU

4E
ACKERMAN, FORREST J.

4SJ
ACKERMAN, FORREST J.

5029
WINKWORTH, DEREK W.

A COLONIST
DAWSON, SAMUEL EDWARD

A COURT BAILIFF
O'BRIEN, DAN

A FUGITIVE
COXE, EDWARD D.

A GENTLEMAN OF OXFORD
SHELLEY, PERCY BYSSE

A HAWKESBURY LAD
HARPER, CHARLES

A MAN IN THE MOON
THOMSON, WILLIAM

A NY DETECTIVE
DOUGHTY, FRANCIS W.

A PRIVATE DETECTIVE
RATHBORNE, ST. GEORGE

A SPIRIT YET IN THE FLESH
GASTON, HENRY A.

A STUDENT OF OCCULTISM
HARTMANN, FRANZ

A TRADESMAN
DRINKER, JOHN

A TRAVELING SALESMAN
DILKS, JOHN M.

A WELL-KNOWN AUTHOR
LANG, ANDREW
VIVIAN, HERBERT

A YOUNG LADY
SHERWOOD, MARY

A, Q-C
QUILLER-COUCH, ARTHUR

A., REX
ARCHER, REX

A.A.
WILLIS, GEORGE ANTHONY A.

A.A. OF PUNCH
WILLIS, GEORGE ANTHONY A.

A.B.S.
GOHRE, FRANK

A.B.S.
SCHMACHER, ASTRID & BERND

A.D-n
HASLER, OTTO

A.E.
RUSSELL, GEORGE WILLIAM

A.E.L.
LANCASTER, A.E.

A.F.S.
SILVANI, ANITA

A.H.
HAWKINS, ANTHONY HOPE

A.H.G.
GIRDLESTON, A.H.

A.H.H.
HOWARD, ANNA H.C.

A.J.O.
OGILVEY, ARTHUR JAMES

A.L.
LEE, ABBY

A.L.O.M.
FRANK, MRS. M.J.

A.M.
MEGGED, AHARON

A.P.H.
HERBERT, SIR ALAN PATRICK

A.R.O.
ORAGE, ALFRED JAMES

AABA AABA
ROSENFELD, SANDOR FRIEDR.

AAKJAER, JEPPE
JENSEN, JEPPE

AALBEN, PATRICK
JONES, NOEL

AALYWN, ALYSSE
CLARK, MELISSA

AARDEMA, VERNA
VUGTEVEEN, VERNA AARDEMA

AARON, SIDNEY
CHAYEFSKY, SIDNEY AARON

AARONS, A.A.
AARONS, EDWARD S.

AASENG, NATE
AASENG, NATHAN

ABASIYANIK, SAIT FAIK
SAIT, FAIK

ABBAS EFFENDI
ABDU'L-BAHA

ABBASI, NAJAM
ABBASI, NAJMUDDIN

ABBERLEY, ALDWYN
COWIE, DONALD

ABBEY, ANN MERTON
BROOKS-JANOWIAK, JEAN

ABBEY, CHRISTINA
SAWYER, JOHN & NANCY

ABBEY, KIERNAN
REILLY, HELEN [KIERNAN]

ABBEY, LYNN
ABBEY, MARILYN LORRAINE

ABBEY, MARGARET
YORKE, MARGARET E.

ABBEY, RUTH
PATTISON, OLIVE RUTH

ABBEY, STATON
STATON-BEVAN, WILLIAM N.

ABBING, JUSTINE
DE HAAN BRUGGEN, CAROLINA

ABBINGTON, JOHN
GIBSON, WALTER B.

ABBOT, ALICE
SPEICHER, HELEN ROSS

ABBOT, RICK
SHARKEY, JOHN MICHAEL

ABBOT, SANDRA
DEVANEY, ROBERT

ABBOTT, A.A.
SPEWACK, SAMUEL

ABBOTT, A.C.
MEINZER, HELEN ABBOTT

ABBOTT, ALICE
BORLAND, KATHRYN KILBY

ABBOTT, ANDREW
GIBSON, WALTER B.

ABBOTT, ANTHONY
OURSLER, [C] FULTON

ABBOTT, BROOK
DAVIES, BLODWEN

ABBOTT, BRUCE
REACH, JAMES
SEWALL, ROBERT

ABBOTT, DR. JOHN
TRUMBO, DONALD [DALTON]

ABBOTT, EARL J.
GIBSON, WALTER B.

ABBOTT, EVELYN
REYNA, RUTH

ABBOTT, HELEN RAYMOND
BEALES, HELEN R. ABBOTT

ABBOTT, JANE WORTH
CAMERON, STELLA
MYERS, VIRGINIA

PSEUDONYMS

ABBOTT, JEANNE
MONARCH, DIANE A.J.

ABBOTT, JENNIE
MONARCH, DIANE A.J.

ABBOTT, JOHN
HUNTER, EVAN

ABBOTT, JOHNSTON
ASHWORTH, EDWARD MONTAGUE

ABBOTT, LAWRENCE
LAWRENCE, CHRISTOPHER G.H

ABBOTT, MARGOT
TRACY, MARIE D.

ABBOTT, ORRINA
REYNA, RUTH

ABBOTT, ROSA
PARKER, ROSA ABBOTT

ABBOTT, SARA
ZOLOTOW, CHARLOTTE [S]

ABBOTT, [MANAGER] HENRY
STRATEMEYER, EDWARD

ABBY, LYNN
ABBEY, MARILYN LORRAINE

ABDULLAH, ACHMED
ROMANOFF, ALEXANDER N.

ABEL, MARIANNE
HASSEBRAUK, MARIANNE

ABEL, W.K.
KABEL, WALTHER

ABELLIO, RAYMOND
SOULES, JEAN GEORGES

ABELS, HARRIETTE S.
ABELS, HARRIETTE SHEFFER

ABELSEN, OLAF K.
KABEL, WALTHER

ABELSON, ANN
CAVALLARO, ANN ABELSON

ABERCROMBIE, PATRICIA B.
BARNES, PATRICIA

ABERNATHY, BILL
ABERNATHY, WILLIAM JACKS.

ABHAVANANDA
CROWLEY, EDWARD ALEXANDER

ABISCH, ROZ
ABISCH, ROSLYN KROOP

ABNER, GERALD
OWEN, FRANK

ABRAHALL, C.H.
HOSKYNS-ABRAHALL, CLARE C

ABRAHALL, CLARE HOSKYNS
HOSKYNS-ABRAHALL, CLARE C

ABRAHAMS, TERRI
ACKERMAN, FORREST J.

ABRAHAMSOHN, OTTO
BRAHM, OTTO

ABRAMOV, EMIL
DRAITSER, EMIL

ABSINTHE, PERE
KELLY, GEORGE C.

ABT, TERENZ
BENGSCH, GERHARD

ACACIO, IPANDRO
OBREGON, IGNACIO M. O. Y

ACADEMIC INVESTOR
REDDAWAY, W. BRIAN

ACE CLUBS
LOFTIN, J.C.

ACHAD HAAN
GINZBERG, ASHER

ACHARD, MARCEL
FERREOL, MARCEL AUGUSTE

ACHER, MATHIAS
BIRNBAUM, NATHAN

ACHILLES
LAMB, CHARLES BENTALL

ACHYUT
BIRLA, LAKSHIMINIWAS

ACKERLEY, J.R.
ACKERLEY, JOE RANDOLPH

ACKERMAN, KYLE
KYLE, DAVID A.

ACKERMONSTER
ACKERMAN, FORREST J.

ACKMAN, R.A.
FIRTH, NORMAN WESLEY

ACKMAN, RICE
FIRTH, NORMAN WESLEY

ACKNER, ELISABETH
HERING, ELISABETH

ACKWORTH, ROBERT
ACKWORTH, ROBERT CHARLES

ACKWORTH, ROBERTA
ACKWORTH, ROBERT CHARLES

ACLAND, ALICE
MARRECO, ANNE
WIGNALL, ANNE

ACRE, STEPHEN
GRUBER, FRANK

ACTON, JAMES
DAVIDSON, S.

ACTON, JAY
ACTON, EDWARD J.

ACTON, JOHN D.
DONGES, GUNTER

AD HOC
PEIRCE, J.F.

ADAIR, CECIL
EVERETT-GREEN, EVELYN

ADAIR, CHERRY
WILKINSON, CHERRY

ADAIR, DENNIS
CRONIN, BERNARD CHARLES

ADAIR, HAZEL
ADDIS, HAZEL IRIS
MARRIOTT, RONALD

ADAIR, JACK
PAVEY, DON

ADAIR, SALLY
MANNOCK, LAURA

ADALBERT
LJUNGGREN, ALBERT GUSTAF

ADAM, BEN
DRACHMAN, JULIAN M.

ADAM, CORNEL
LENGYEL, CORNEL ADAM

ADAM, DON
SELLERS, CONNIE LESLIE

ADAM, GRETE
JACKEL, MARGARETHE

ADAM, ROBIN
ADAMS, ROBERT JAMES

ADAM-JACKEL, GRETE
JACKEL, MARGARETHE

ADAMIAN, NORA
ADAMOVA, ELEONORA G.

ADAMS, A. DON
CLEVELAND, PHILIP JEROME

ADAMS, ALGER LEROY
KAYE, PHILIP B.

ADAMS, ALICE
ADAMS, ALICE BOYD

ADAMS, ANDY
GIBSON, WALTER B.
HARKINS, PETER J.

ADAMS, ANGELA
SMITH, CATHERINE R.

ADAMS, ANNETTE
ROWLAND, DONALD S.

ADAMS, AUDRA
TRACY, MARIE D.

ADAMS, BART
BINGLEY, DAVID ERNEST

ADAMS, BEN
LAPIN, ADAM

ADAMS, BETSY
PITCHER, GLADYS

PSEUDONYMS

ADAMS, BILL
ADAMS, BERTRAM MARTIN
ADAMS, WILLIAM

ADAMS, CANDICE
WALKER, LOIS ARVIN

ADAMS, CHARLES
CHAMBERS, [J.D] WHITTAKER

ADAMS, CHRISTOPHER
HOPKINS, KENNETH

ADAMS, CHUCK
NORWOOD, VICTOR [G.C.]
TUBB, E.C.

ADAMS, CLAYTON
HOLMES, CHARLES HENRY

ADAMS, DALE
QUINN, ELISABETH

ADAMS, DANIEL
NICOLE, CHRISTOPHER ROBIN

ADAMS, EDITH
SHINE, DEBORAH

ADAMS, EUGENIA
OWENS, VIRGINIA STEM

ADAMS, FAY
CLARK, VELMA [VALMA ?]

ADAMS, FAYE
SWOBODA, FAYE

ADAMS, HARRISON
RATHBORNE, ST. GEORGE
STRATEMEYER, EDWARD

ADAMS, HENRY T.
RANSOME, JAY ELLIS

ADAMS, JACK
GRIGSBY, ALCANOAN O.
LOWE, MARY P.

ADAMS, JAMES FENIMORE C.
ELLIS, EDWARD S.

ADAMS, JOHN
GLASBY, JOHN S.
MCLAREN, J.A.

ADAMS, JOLENE
HARPER, OLIVIA & KEN

ADAMS, JUDITH
MORGAN, JUDITH A.

ADAMS, JUSTIN
CAMERON, LOU

ADAMS, KASEY
WHISENAND, VALERIE

ADAMS, KELLY
BUECHTING, LINDA

ADAMS, KEN
KUGLER, DIETMAR

ADAMS, LOUIS J.A.
HENSLEY, JOSEPH LOUIS
PANSHIN, ALEXEI

ADAMS, LOWELL
JOSEPH, JAMES HERZ

ADAMS, MARY
WARD, STUART

ADAMS, MARYE
GOODNER, MARIE B.

ADAMS, MILDRED
KENYON, MILDRED ADAMS

ADAMS, NICHOLAS
ALBERT, SUSAN W. & BILL
DOYLE, DEBRA
FRETTS, BRUCE
LOWENTROUT, CHRISTINE I.S
MACDONALD, JAMES D.
PEEL, JOHN [RONALD]
STOKES, COLEMAN
COLEMAN, CLAY

ADAMS, NICK
FARMER, PHILIP JOSE

ADAMS, PEPPER
MORRIS, DEBRAH
SHAVER, PAT

ADAMS, PERSEUS
ADAMS, PETER ROBERT C.

ADAMS, R.D.
HERBERT, ROBERT DUDLEY S.

ADAMS, RICH
SELLERS, CONNIE LESLIE

ADAMS, ROBERT MARTIN
KRAPP, ROBERT MARTIN

ADAMS, TRACY
HALE, [MARY] ARLENE

ADAMS, TRICIA
KITE, PAT

ADAMS, WALTER MARSHAM
MACAULEY, CLARENDON

ADAMS, [CAPT] BRUIN
ELLIS, EDWARD S.

ADAMS, [CAPT] J.F.C.
ELLIS, EDWARD S.

ADAMSON, FRANK
ADAMS, ROBERT [FRANKLIN]

ADAMSON, GRAHAM
GROOM, ARTHUR WILLIAM

ADAMSON, LYDIA
KING, FRANKLIN

ADAMSON, M.J.
ADAMSON, MARY JO

ADAMSON, YVONNE
EWEGEN, YVONNE
MONTGOMERY, YVONNE
ADAMSON, MARY JO

ADAMUS, FRANZ
BRONNER, FERDINAND

ADASTRA
MIREPOIX, CAMILLE

ADDAMS, KAY
HITT, ORRIE [EDWIN]

ADDINGTON, SARAH
REID, SARAH ADDINGTON

ADDIO, E.I.
FANTONI, BARRY [ERNEST]

ADDIS, H.I.
ADDIS, HAZEL IRIS

ADDISCOMBE, JACK
HUNTER, ALFRED JOHN

ADDISCOMBE, JOHN
HUNTER, ALFRED JOHN

ADDISON, CAROL
CLARKE, JOSEPH CALVITT

ADDISON, GWEN
HARRIS, ALFRED
MOORE, ARTHUR

ADDISON, HUGH
OWEN, HARRY COLLINSON

ADDISON, JAYNE
ATKIN, JANE

ADDY, TED
WINTERBOTHAM, RUSS[EL] R.

ADELBERG, DORIS
ORGEL, DORIS

ADELER, MAX
CLARK, CHARLES HEBER

ADELINE
SERGEANT, [E.F.] ADELINE

ADELON, SVEN
CHRISTENSEN, THOMAS F.

ADELSBERG, CARL
CASSAU, CARL

ADEPT, AN
JOHNSTONE, CHARLES

ADIRONDACK, LESLIE
WEIL, JERRY

ADKINS, ERLE
WETHERBY, EARLENE ADKINS

ADKINS, M.D.
POUND, EZRA LOOMIS

ADLARD, MARK
ADLARD, PETER MARCUS

ADLARD, P.M.
ADLARD, PETER MARCUS

ADLER, C.S.
ADLER, CAROLE SCHWERDTF.

ADLER, ELIZABETH
SCOTT, ARIANA

ADLER, IRENE
PENZLER, OTTO
STORR, CATHERINE [COLE]

ADLER, JOE
KALMUCZAK, ROLF

ADLER, KARL
FREITAG, OTTO

ADLER, KATHLEEN
JONES, KATHLEEN EVE

ADLER, LULLA
ROSENFELD, LULLA

ADLON, ARTHUR
AYLING, KEITH

ADONIS, MICHAEL
SELLERS, CONNIE LESLIE

ADONY, RAOUL
LAUNAY, ANDRE [J]

ADRIAN, JACK
LOWDER, CHRISTOPHER

ADRIAN, MARY
JORGENSEN, MARY VERN

ADRIEN, FRANCES
POLLAND, MADELEINE A.

ADZHIE, DZHINDI
DZHAUARI, ADZHIE D.

AESOP
BLAKE, LILLIAN DEVEREAUX

AESOP, ABRAHAM
NEWBERY, JOHN

AFFABEE, ERIC
STINE, ROBERT L.

AFFABLE HAWK
SQUIRE, JOHN COLLINS

AFRICANUS, W.
HIETZIG, A.B. WALTER

AFTEREM, GEORGE
WILLIAMS, HAROLD

AGAPIDA, FRAY ANTONIO
IRVING, WASHINGTON

AGAR, BRIAN
BALLARD, W. TODHUNTER

AGARD, H.E.
EVANS, HILARY

AGATE
REID, WHITELAW

AGATHA
LAWRENCE, BESSIE

AGATHON
DE TARDE, ALFRED
MARSIS, HENRI

AGENT 55
LONGHURST, PERCY WILLIAM

AGG, JOHN
CAHILL, FRANK

AGHILL, GORDON
GARRETT, RANDALL [P]
SILVERBERG, ROBERT

AGHISH, SAGIT
AGISHEV, SAGIR I.

AGILE, ROGER
WHITE, RICHARD

AGINSKY, BURT W.
AGINSKY, BERNARD W.

AGISH, SAGIT
AGISHEV, SAGIR I.

AGNELLI, SUNI
AGNELLI, SUSANNA

AGNEW, DAVID
ADAMS, DOUGLAS
WILLIAMS, GRAHAM

AGNON, S.Y.
CZACZKES, SHMUEL YOSEF

AGNON, SHEMUEL JOSEPH
TCHATSKY, SHMUEL YOSEPH

AGOGAS
DAVY, CHARLES WILLIAM

AGOSIN, MARJORIE
HALPERN, MARJORIE AGOSIN

AGRICOLA, SYLVIUS
ACKERMAN, FORREST J.

AGUILAR, RICARDO
AGUILAR MELANTZON, RICARD

AGUILERA, JAIME ROLDOS
ROLDOS AGUILERA, JAIME

AGUSTIN, JOSE
RAMIREZ, JOSE AUGUSTIN

AGUTTER, JENNY
AGUTTER, JENNIFER ANN

AHARONI, YOHANAN
ARONHEIM, YOHANAN

AHEARNE, BURT
HERNHUTTER, ALBERT

AHEMM, HILDE
MESCHKE, HILDEGARD

AHERN, EMILY M.
MARTIN, EMILY

AHERN, JERRY
AHERN, JEROME MORRELL

AHERN, JERRY M.
AHERN, JEROME MORRELL

AHERN, S.A.
AHERN, SHARON A[NN]

AHERN, TOM
AHERN, THOMAS FRANCIS

AHERNE, OWEN
CASSILL, RONALD VERLIN

AHL, KENNET
DAHL, CHRISTER
STROMSTEDT, LASSE

AHLSEN, LEOPOLD
ALZMANN, HELMUT

AHLSTROM, G.W.
AHISTROEM, GOESTA WERNER

AHO, JUHANI
BROFELT, JUHANI

AHRIMAN
MARTINEZ RUIZ, LUIS

AHSCROFT, LAURA
CARLSON, JANICE

AICHNER, FRIDOLIN
BENESCH, IRMFRIED

AICK, GERHARD
AICHINGER, GERHARD

AIGUILLETTE
HARGREAVES, REGINALD C.

AIKEN, CLARK
DAVIS, FREDERICK [CLYDE]

AIKEN, GINNY
ANIKIENO, GINNY

AIKEN, HENRY
GARDNER, WILLIAM HENRY

AIKENS, TOM PITT
PITT-AIKENS, TOM

AIKIN, JIM
AIKIN, JAMES D[OUGLAS]

AIKMAN, ANN
MCQUADE, ANN AIKMAN

AIKMAN, HENRY G.
ARMSTRONG, HAROLD HUNTER

AIMES, ANGELICA
SCOTTI, LITA

AINSBURY, RAY
PAINE, LAURAN BOSWORTH
PRATT, [MURRAY] FLETCHER
VERRILL, A[LPHEUS] HYATT

AINSBURY, ROY
PAINE, LAURAN BOSWORTH

AINSLE, HERBERT
MAITLAND, E.

AINSLEY, ALIX
STEINER, BARBARA [A]

AINSLEY, TOM
CARTER, RICHARD

AINSWORTH, HARRIET
CADELL, VIOLET ELIZABETH

AINSWORTH, MILO
FISON, PETER

PSEUDONYMS

AINSWORTH, OLIVER
SHARP, HENRY

AINSWORTH, PATRICIA
BIGG, PATRICIA NINA

AINSWORTH, RAY
PAINE, LAURAN BOSWORTH

AINSWORTH, RUTH
GILBERT, RUTH G.A.

AINSWORTHY, ROY
PAINE, LAURAN BOSWORTH

AINTREE
WALLACE, JOHN

AIRD, CATHERINE
MCINTOSH, KINN HAMILTON

AIRLIE, CATHERINE
MACLEOD, JEAN S.

AIRLIE, O'HUGH
LAWSON, JESSIE [K]

AISLIN
MOSHER, CHRISTOPHER TERRY

AITIAICHE
HOWELLS, ANNIE T.

AITKEN, WILLIAM MAXWELL
BEAVERBROOK, WILLIAM M.A.

AIX
BAUSMAN, FREDERICK

AJAR, EMILE
KACEWGARI, ROMAINE
PAVLOVITCH, PAUL

AJAX
JACKSON, ADA ACRAMAN

AKANJI, SANGODARE
BEIER, ULLI

AKASS, JON
AKASS, JOHN EWART

AKENSON, DON
AKENSON, DONALD HARMAN

AKERS, ALAN BURT
BULMER, [HENRY] KENNETH

AKERS, FLOYD
BAUM, L[YMAN] FRANK

AKH
HOPKINS, ALICE K.

AKI, TANUCKI
DE LINT, CHARLES

AKIRA
MOORE, ERICA MARIA

AKNATON, ASKIA
ECKELS, JON

AKSYONOV, VASSILY
AKSENOV, VASILI PAVLOVICH

AKUTAGAWA, RYUNOSUKE
NIIHARA, RYUNOSUKE

AL-KHADIM, SA'D
ELKHADEN, SAAD [E.A.]

AL-MODAD
MOORE, M. LOUISE

AL-VAN-GAR
RADWANSKI, PIERRE A.

ALA, JOHN
SCHAFER, MAX

ALADIN, REX ALBERT
HELLWIG, ERNST

ALAIN
BRUSTLEIN, DANIEL
CHARTIER, EMILE-AUGUST

ALAIN-FOURNIER
FOURNIER, HENRI ALBAN

ALAMO, BILL
MOLSNER, MICHAEL

ALAN, A.J.
LAMBERT, LESLIE HARRISON

ALAN, JACK
GREEN, ALAN [BAER]

ALAN, JANE
CHISHOLM, LILLIAN MARY

ALAN, MARJORIE
BUMPUS, DORIS MARJORIE

ALAN, RAY
VALLS-RUSSELL, JOSEPH L.

ALAN, SANDY
ULLMAN, ALAN

ALAS, LEOPOLDO
ALAS Y URENO, LEOPOLDO

ALB
WHITEING, RICHARD

ALBA, PATRICIO
CASTILLO VELAQUEZ, LUIZ A

ALBAN, ANTONY
THOMPSON, ANTHONY ALLERT

ALBANESI, MADAME
ROWLANDS, EFFIE

ALBANY, JAMES
RAE, HUGH C[RAWFORD]

ALBARUS, HEDWIG S.
AUSTIN, BENJAMIN FISH

ALBERT, ANDREW I.
ALBERT, JERRY

ALBERT, ERNST
HEYDA, ERNST

ALBERT, L.
HERMANN, L.A.

ALBERT, LINCOLN
BENFORD, GREGORY ALBERT
LITTENBERG, LAURENCE

ALBERT, NED
BRAUN, WILBUR

ALBERT, SUSAN WITTIG
ALBERT, SUSAN W. & BILL

ALBERT, T.M.
SIMPSON, T.M. ALBERT

ALBERTI, KONRAD
SITTENFELD, KONRAD

ALBERTYN, DOROTHY
BLACK, DOROTHY

ALBINI, J.
DEHMEL, KARL JULIUS

ALBINSON, JACK
ALBINSON, JAMES P.

ALBION, KEN
KING, ALBERT

ALBRAN, KEHLOG
COHEN, MARTIN A.
SHACKET, SHELDON R.

ALBRAND, MARTHA
LOEWENGARD, HEIDI H.H.

ALBRECHT, H.
MUNCHAUSEN, BORRIS v.

ALBRIGHT, BETS PARKER
ALBRIGHT, ELIZABETH A.

ALBRIGHT, ELIZABETH
LAHEY, KAREN

ALBUGASAN
ALEKPER-ZADE, ALHUGASAN A

ALCALAW, [MAJ.] G.W.
HARBAUGH, THOMAS C.

ALCALDE, E.L.
CHAIJ, FERNANDO

ALCALDE, MIGUEL
BURGESS, MICHAEL ROY

ALCANBARA, OSVALDO
LOPES, BALTAZAR

ALCHEMY, JACK
GERSHATOR, DAVID

ALCIBIADE
PRAZ, MARIO

ALCIPHRON
DOYLE, ROSINA [WHEELER]

ALCON, R.
BRONTE, EMILY JANE

ALCOTT, JULIA
CROWCROFT, PETER
CUDLIPP, EDYTHE

ALCYONE
KRISHNAMURTI, JIDDU

PSEUDONYMS

ALDA, FRANCES
DAVIS, FRANCES

ALDANOV, M.A.
LANDAU, MARK A

ALDANOV, MARK ALEX
LANDAU, MARK A

ALDANOV, MARK [A]
LANDAU, MARK A

ALDEANO, SILVESTRE
ACKERMAN, FORREST J.

ALDEN, BURT
CURTIS, RICHARD [A]

ALDEN, CARELLA
REMINGTON, ELLA-CARRIE

ALDEN, CLAUS
KALMUCZAK, ROLF

ALDEN, ELIZABETH
TALBOT, CHARLENE JOY

ALDEN, JACK
BARROWS, [RUTH] MARJORIE

ALDEN, MICHELE
AVALLONE, MICHAEL

ALDEN, SUE
FRANCIS, DOROTHY BRENNER

ALDEN, THOMAS
KALMUCZAK, ROLF

ALDEN, TROY
LAKLAN, CARLI

ALDERFER, E.G.
ALDERFER, E. GORDON

ALDERMAN, GILL
ALDERMAN, GILLIAN

ALDERTON, THERESA
GRAZIA, THERESA

ALDINE, FRANCE
VAN DROME, CECILE

ALDING, PETER
JEFFRIES, RODERIC [GRAEME]

ALDON, ADAIR
MEIGS, CORNELIA LYNDE

ALDON, HOWARD
WILSON, [ALAN] DORIC

ALDOUBY, ZVY H[ERBERT]
DUBENSKY, HERBERT

ALDOUS, TONY
ALDOUS, ANTHONY MICHAEL

ALDRICH, CURT
CURTIS, RICHARD [A]

ALDRICH, DARRAGH
ALDRICH, CLARA C.T.

ALDRICH, FRANCES
DONALDSON, DALE C.

ALDRIDGE, SARAH
MARCHANT, ANYDA

ALDRITCH, ANN
MEAKER, MARIJANE AGNES

ALDYNE, NATHAN
MCDOWELL, MICHAEL
SCHUETZ, DENNIS

ALEICHEM, SHOLOM
RABINOVITCH, SHOLEM

ALEJANDRO
CANEDO, ALEJANDRO

ALEPOUDELIS, ODYSSEUS
ELYTIS, ODYSSEUS

ALERDING, KATHY
PUYEAR-ALERDING, KATHY

ALERS, ROCHELLE
MCLEARY, RENA

ALESHKOVSKY, YUZ
ALESHKOVSKY, JOSEPH

ALETES
SANCHEZ, MORALES NARCISCO

ALETHEIA
STOBO, EDWARD JOHN

ALEX, MARLEE
SMITH, MARLEE

ALEXANDER, ALEX
KRETZSCHMAR, LAEX

ALEXANDER, ANNE
ALEXANDER, ANNA COOKE
FRIEDRICH, ANITA

ALEXANDER, ARNO
BENJAMIN, ARNOLD ALEX.

ALEXANDER, BRANDI
TAYLOR, JANELLE [W]

ALEXANDER, BRUCE
MONTAGUE, BRUCE [ALEX.]

ALEXANDER, CHARLES
HADFIELD, [E] CHARLES [R]

ALEXANDER, DAIR
THOMSON, CHRISTINE C.

ALEXANDER, DAVID
CUNLIFFE, DAVE

ALEXANDER, DONNA
VITEK, DONNA JEAN K.

ALEXANDER, ED
EMSHWILLER, EDMUND A.

ALEXANDER, FAITH
BENTLEY, MARGARET

ALEXANDER, FRITZ
ANDREAS-DRANERT, PETER W.

ALEXANDER, GIL
RALSTON, GILBERT A.

ALEXANDER, GUNTER
PEIS, GUNTER

ALEXANDER, H.G.
ALEXANDER, HORACE G[UNDY]

ALEXANDER, HENRY
MCALLISTER, ALISTER

ALEXANDER, J.H.
JAPP, ALEXANDER HAY

ALEXANDER, JAN
BANIS, VICTOR J[EROME]

ALEXANDER, JEAN
PENNER, MANOLA J.

ALEXANDER, JOAN
WETHERELL-PEPPER, JOAN A.

ALEXANDER, JOHN
RULER, ALEXANDER JOHN
VLASTO, JOHN ALEXANDER

ALEXANDER, KATE
ARMSTRONG, TILLY

ALEXANDER, KATHRYN
CALDWELL, KATHRYN [S]

ALEXANDER, KEN
ALEXANDER, KENNETH J.W.

ALEXANDER, KYLE
MARLOWE, ALAN STEPHEN

ALEXANDER, L.G.
FTYARAS, LOUIS GEORGE

ALEXANDER, LIZA
CAMPBELL, LOUISA D.

ALEXANDER, MARGARET
WALKER, MARGARET

ALEXANDER, MARGE
EDWARDS, ROSELYN

ALEXANDER, MARSHA
ALEXANDER, MARSHA DURCHIN
BOURNS, MARSHA
SICKLE, MILTON VAN

ALEXANDER, MARTIN
DAVENTRY, LEONARD JOHN

ALEXANDER, MEGAN
FISH, MILDRED T.

ALEXANDER, MRS.
HECTOR, ANNE FRENCH

ALEXANDER, P.
ALEXANDER, PAUL

ALEXANDER, R.W.
ALEXANDER, ROBERT W.

ALEXANDER, RAE PACE
ALEXANDER, RAYMOND PACE

PSEUDONYMS

ALEXANDER, RIC
LONG, RICHARD A.

ALEXANDER, ROBERT
GROSS, MICHAEL ROBERT
HAINING, ROBERT
LEGAT, MICHAEL RONALD

ALEXANDER, RUTH
ROGERS, RUTH

ALEXANDER, SERENA
RAMIREZ, ALICE

ALEXANDER, THELMA
ZIRKLEBACK, THELMA

ALEXANDER, TRISHA
KAY, PATRICIA A.

ALEXANDER, WALTER
WRAITH, W.J.

ALEXANDER, ZANE
ALEXANDER, HAROLD LEE

ALEXANDRE, ALEXANDRE
ALEXANDER, ALBRECHT

ALEXEYEV, CONSTANTIN [S]
STANISLAVSKY, CONSTANTIN

ALEXIE, ANGELIE
TALIAS, ANGELA DUNTON

ALEXIS, KATINA
STRAUCH, KATINA PARTHEMS

ALEXIS, WILLIBALD
HARING, WILHELM

ALFEN, HANNES
JOHANNESSON, OLOF

ALFRED, RICHARD
HAVERSTOCK, NATHAN A.
SCHROEDER, RICHARD C.

ALFRICOBAS
NEUBERG, VICTOR [B]

ALFUR, UTANGAROS
ROBERTSON, SIGURDUR

ALGER, HORATIO
MCFARLANE, LESLIE CHARLES

ALGER, HORATIO JR.
STRATEMEYER, EDWARD

ALGER, L.G.
ALGER, LECLAIRE GOWANS

ALGERY, ANDRE
COULET DU GARD, RENE

ALI, MUHAMMAD
CLAY, CASSIUS

ALI-MAR
PORN, ALICE

ALIAV, RUTH
KLUGER, RUTH

ALIEN
BAKER, LOUISA ALICE D.

ALIKI
BRANDENBERG, ALIKI L.

ALIMAYO, CHIKUYO
FRANKLIN, HAROLD L[EROY]

ALINDER, MARTHA WHEELOCK
WHEELOCK, MARTHA E.

ALKEN, INA
AMON, HANS-WALTER

ALLABEN, ANNE E.
FARRELL, ANNE ELISABETH

ALLAN, ANN
LILLY, ISABELLA PURVIS

ALLAN, BARBARA
COLLINS, BARBARA
COLLINS, MAX ALLAN

ALLAN, DENNIS
DENNISTON, ELINORE

ALLAN, DINA
GORHAM, JILL

ALLAN, FRED
KUTHE, EUGEN

ALLAN, GEORGE
KREMMITZ, MARIE

ALLAN, JACK
ERG, DANIEL
MCKENNA, GEORGE

ALLAN, JANE
GROVE, MARTIN

ALLAN, JOHN B.
WESTLAKE, DONALD [EDWIN]

ALLAN, LEWIS
MEEROPOL, ABEL

ALLAN, LUKE
AMY, WILLIAM LACEY

ALLAN, NICK
NIXON, ALLAN

ALLAN, SIDNEY
HARTMANN, SADAKICHI

ALLAN, TED
HERMAN, ALAN

ALLANA, GHULAMALI
ALLANA, GHULAM ALI

ALLARD, NICK
MOORCOCK, MICHAEL

ALLARDYCE, PAULA
TORDAY, URSULA

ALLBEURY, TED
ALLBEURY, THEODORE E.

ALLCOT, GUY
POCOCK, TOM

ALLED
VAN HISE, DELLA

ALLEGRO
MOORE, BIRKETT

ALLEN, ADAM
EPSTEIN, BERYL [WILLIAMS]
EPSTEIN, SAMUEL

ALLEN, ADAMS
GALE, LINN A.E.

ALLEN, ALEX B.
HEIDE, FLORENCE PARRY

ALLEN, ALLYN
EBERLE, IRMENGARDE

ALLEN, ANITA
SCHENCK, ANITA A.

ALLEN, BARBARA
STUART, VIOLET VIVIAN F.

ALLEN, BETSEY
HARRISON, ELIZABETH C.
CAVANNA, ELIZABETH ALLEN
MILLER, ANNE

ALLEN, BETTY [JEANNE]
COOPER, ELIZABETH

ALLEN, CAPT. QUINCY
STRATEMEYER, EDWARD

ALLEN, CARTER
KNOLES, WILLIAM [H]

ALLEN, CHESTER
HOLDING, VERA ZUMWALT

ALLEN, CLAY
PAINE, LAURAN BOSWORTH

ALLEN, DAVE
MAHONEY, DAVID

ALLEN, DEREK
FARMER, DEREK
STOKER, ABRAHAM

ALLEN, DICK
ALLEN, RICHARD STANLEY

ALLEN, DIXIE
KOHLS, OLIVE N. ALLEN

ALLEN, DIZZY
ALLEN, HUBERT RAYMOND

ALLEN, DON B.
DIMMITZ, ARTHUR L.

ALLEN, E.C.
WARD, ELIZABETH CAMPBELL

ALLEN, EDMUND
REEVE-JONES, ALAN EDMOND

ALLEN, EDWARD HERON
HERON-ALLEN, EDWARD

ALLEN, ELIZABETH
THOMPSON, ELIZABETH ALLEN

ALLEN, ELIZABETH COOPER
ALLEN, BETTY [JEANNE]

PSEUDONYMS

ALLEN, EMILY ANN
ALLEN, EMILY JOAN
REEP, DIANE

ALLEN, ERIC
ALLEN-BALLARD, ERIC

ALLEN, ERIKA VAUGHAN
ALLEN, ERIC VAUGHN

ALLEN, F.M.
DOWNEY, EDMOND

ALLEN, GARY
ALLEN, FREDERICK G.

ALLEN, GRACE
HOGARTH, GRACE W.A.

ALLEN, GRANT
ALLEN, [CHARLES] GRANT B.

ALLEN, H. FREDERICKA
ALLEN, HELENA GRONLUND

ALLEN, H.R.
ALLEN, HUBERT RAYMOND

ALLEN, HAZEL
HERSHBERGER, HAZEL KUHNS

ALLEN, HENRY
ADAMS, HENRY H.

ALLEN, HERVEY
ALLEN, WILLIAM HERVEY JR.

ALLEN, HUGH
MORRIS, CHARLES [S]
RATHBORNE, ST. GEORGE

ALLEN, JAMES
ADER, PAUL [FASSET]

ALLEN, JEANNE
ALLAN, JEANNE

ALLEN, JIM
ALLEN, JAMES LOVIC JR.

ALLEN, JOHN
GARBUTT, JOHN L.
PERRY, RITCHIE JOHN ALLEN

ALLEN, JOHN W. JR.
LESLEY, PETER

ALLEN, JORDAN
DUMKE, GLENN S.

ALLEN, LAINE
LAKSO, ELAINE

ALLEN, LESLIE
BROWN, HORACE

ALLEN, LORING
ALLEN, ROBERT LORING

ALLEN, M.C.
ALLEN, MARION CARROLL

ALLEN, MARCUS
DONICHT, MARK ALLEN

ALLEN, MARK
DONICHT, MARK ALLEN
NUETZEL, CHARLES A.

ALLEN, MARY
CLEVELAND, MARY
ALLEN, MARY ANN
PARDOE, ROSEMARY A.

ALLEN, MIKE
ALLISON, MICHAEL F.L.

ALLEN, RICHARD C.
TAYLOR, JOHN M[AXWELL]

ALLEN, RICHARD
MOFFATT, JAMES

ALLEN, ROBERT
DODD, ALLEN ROBERT
GARFINKEL, BERNARD MAX

ALLEN, ROLAND
AYCKBOURNE, ALAN

ALLEN, RONALD
AYCKBOURNE, ALAN

ALLEN, RUTH
PETERSON, ESTER [ALLEN]

ALLEN, SAM
ALLEN, MARION CARROLL

ALLEN, STEVE
ALLEN, STEPHEN V.P.W.

ALLEN, STUART
TUBB, E.C.

ALLEN, T.D.
ALLEN, TERRIL DIENER
DIMMITZ, ARTHUR L.

ALLEN, TERRY
ALLEN, TERRIL DIENER

ALLEN, TERRY D.
ALLEN, TERRIL DIENER

ALLEN, TOM
ALLEN, THOMAS BENTON

ALLEN, TOMMY
LINDHOLM, VALDEMAR

ALLEN, WOODY
KONIGSBERG, ALLEN S.

ALLENBY, ENOS WILL
BIXLER, WILLIAM ALLEN

ALLENBY, GORDON
MATUSOW, HARVEY MARSHALL

ALLERTON, MARK
CAMERON, WILLIAM ERNEST

ALLERTON, MARY
GOVAN, [MARY] C.N.

ALLEYN, ELLEN
ROSSETTI, CHRISTINA GEO.

ALLIN, CLINTON HARROP
HARROP-ALLIN, CLINTON

ALLINGHAM, MARGERY
CARTER, MARGERY L.A.
CARTER, YOUNGMAN

ALLISON, CLAY
KEEVILL, HENRY J.
ALLISON, CLYDE
KNOLES, WILLIAM [H]

ALLISON, E.M.A.
ALLISON, ERIC & MARY ANN

ALLISON, ELIZABETH
ORR, ALICE HARRON

ALLISON, GEORGE W.
MENCKEN, HENRY LOUIS

ALLISON, GLENN
KNOLES, WILLIAM [H]

ALLISON, HEATHER
MACALLISTER, HEATHER

ALLISON, JIM
BOMKE, BERNHARD

ALLISON, MARIAN
REID, FRANCES P.

ALLISON, MOETH
AGHADJIAN, MOLLIE

ALLISON, PENNY
KATZ, CAROL

ALLISON, RAND
MCCORMICK, WILFRED

ALLISON, SAM
LOOMIS, NOEL [MILLER]

ALLISON, WILLIAM
WILLIAMSON, ALICE M.L.

ALLISTER, BARBARA
TEER, BARBARA

ALLISTER, CLAUDE
PALMER, CLAUDE

ALLPORT, ARTHUR
GALLUN, RAYMOND Z.

ALLURED, LLOYD
HOFFMANN, DONALD

ALLWOOD, EDITH
MOSSER, ARNE J.

ALLWORTH, RICHARD B.
GRUBER, FRANK

ALLWORTHY, A.W.
MILAM, LORENZO W.

ALLYN, ASHLEY
LESLIE, SUSAN

ALLYN, JENNIFER
JONES, JEANETTE

ALLYN, PAUL
SCHOSBERG, PAUL A.

ALLYNE, ROY
AGNEW, STEPHEN

PSEUDONYMS

ALLYSON, ALAN
NUTTALL, ANTHONY

ALLYSON, KYM
KIMBRO, JOHN M.

ALM, HORST
HOPFNER, KARL

ALM, MONICA
OLAUSSON, RUNE ERLAND

ALMA, PETER
NEMESHEGYI, PETER

ALMADOVAR, SANCHEZ DE
DEL MONTE Y APONTE, DOMIN

ALMAFUERTE
PALACIOUS, PEDRO BONIFACI

ALMAN, BOB
BOMAN, ROBERT
LAMBERT, LARS

ALMAN, KARL
KUROWSKI, FRANZ

ALMANDINE, DAVID
GARNETT, DAVID S.

ALMEDINGEN, E.M.
VON ALMEDINGEN, MARTHA E.

ALMON, CASPAR
LEASLEY, F.W.

ALMONTE, ROSA
PAINE, LAURAN BOSWORTH

ALONE
ARRIETA, HERNAN DIAZ

ALOYSIUS, SISTER MARY
SCHALDENBRAND, MARY

ALPAJPURI
NOVITSKI, PAUL DAVID

ALPERS, MARY ROSE
CAMPION, SARAH

ALPHA CRUCIS
HERBERT, ROBERT DUDLEY S.

ALPHA OF THE PLOUGH
GARDINER, ALFRED GEORGE

ALPHABET, MR.
MORICE, DAVE

ALPLAUS, N.Y.
RUBIN, CYNTHIA ELYCE
RUBIN, JEROME

ALSEGGER, BARBARA MARIA
GRUBER, GISI

ALSTERN, FRED
STERN, ALFRED

ALSTOK
ORTON, JAMES

ALSTON, CHARLES
MOTT, MICHAEL

ALT-SONNECK, OLGA ELIS.
JAGOUTZ, OLGA ELISABETH

ALTAIR
GRIFFIN, ANTHONY JEROME

ALTENAU, BRIGITTE
ANDERMANN, BRIGITTE

ALTENBERG, PETER
ENGLANDER, RICHARD

ALTENBERGER, JAKOB
BURGMAIER, ALBERT

ALTENBURG, PETER
KANN, ALBRECHT PETER

ALTER, JUDY
ALTER, JUDITH MACBAIN

ALTER, PETER
BEER, FRITZ

ALTEREGO
JAFFEE, HYMAN

ALTH, MAX O.
BECKER, MAX O.

ALTHAUSEN, WALTRAUT
HENSCHEL, WALTRAUT

ALTHEA
BRAITHWAITE, ALTHEA

ALTHOUSE, LARRY
ALTHOUSE, LAWRENCE [W]

ALTHUSSER, L.
ALTHUSSER, LOUIS

ALTMAN, LARRY
ALTMAN, IRWIN

ALTMAN, THOMAS
BLACK, CAMPBELL
CAINE, JEFFREY A.

ALTON, MAXINE
ALLEN, MAXINE DALTON

ALTON, THOMAS
BRYANT, T[HOMAS] ALTON

ALTOV, GENRIKH
ALTSHULLER, GENRIKH SAUL.

ALTSTERLUND, BETTY
PILKINGTON, BETTY

ALURISTA
URISTA, ALBERTO H.

ALVAREZ, JOHN
DEL REY, LESTER

ALVAREZ, R.
DEL REY, LESTER

ALVAREZ, RAMON
DE LOS UERDES, E. ALVAREZ

ALVORD, BURT
KEEVILL, HENRY J.

ALYN, MARC
FECHEROLLE, MARC ALAIN

ALYWARD, MARCUS
ALEXANDER, MARC [ELWARD]

ALZADA, JUAN SANCHEZ
JOSEPH, JAMES HERZ

ALZEE, GRENDON
ZAGAT, ARTHUR LEO

AMADOR, AMERICO
ELZABURU, MANUEL

AMANDA
WYNNE-TYSON, ESME

AMARE, ROTHAYNE
BYRNE, STUART J.

AMARILLAS, SUSAN
AMARILLAS, KAREN L.

AMAZING RANDI, THE
RANDI, JAMES

AMBER, UTE
AMLER, IRENE

AMBERG, LORENZ
JUNG, ROBERT

AMBERG, STEFAN
BERTHOLD, WILL

AMBERLEY, RICHARD
BOURQUIN, PAUL H.J.

AMBERLEY, SIMON
HOAR, PETER

AMBORN, ERICH
KRETZSCHMAR, ALEX

AMBOS, HELLO
MUNCH, HELLMUT-HUBERTUS

AMBROSE, ALICE
LAZEROWITZ, ALICE AMBROSE

AMBRUS, VICTOR G.
AMBRUS, GYOZO LASZLO

AMELIA, ELLEN
GARRETT, ELLEN AMELIA

AMENDA, ALFRED
KARRASCH, ALFRED

AMERICAN MAUPASSANT
PORTER, WILLIAM SYDNEY

AMERY, CARL
MAYER, CHRISTIAN ANTON

AMES
STEPHENSON, ANDREW M.

AMES, CLINTON
GRAHAM, ROGER P.

AMES, CLYDE
KNOLES, WILLIAM [H]

AMES, DREW
GRAHAM, ROGER P.

PSEUDONYMS

AMES, EDNA
COLLINS, ANDREW J.

AMES, ELINOR
RANZINI, ADDIS DURNING

AMES, FELICIA
BURDEN, JEAN

AMES, JENNIFER
GREIG-SMITH, JENNIFER M.

AMES, JIM
RAY, JAMES RALPH

AMES, LAUREL
MILLER, BARBARA J.

AMES, LESLIE
RIGONI, ORLANDO JOSEPH
ROSS, WILLIAM E. DANIEL

AMES, NOEL
BARROWS, [RUTH] MARJORIE

AMES, NORMA
NORMAN, AMES

AMES, ROBERT
CLIFFORD, CHARLES

AMES, WINTER
PIANKA, PHYLLIS TAYLOR

AMES, WOODFORDE
RAMP, JAMES

AMHERST, WES
SHAVER, RICHARD S.

AMICUS, CURIAE
FULLER, EDMUND [M]

AMID, JOHN
STEARNS, MYRON MORRIS

AMIDON, BILL
AMIDON, WILLIAM VINCENT

AMIEVA, CELSO
POSADA, JOSE M. ALVAREZ

AMINI, JOHARI M.
KUNJUFU, JOHARI M. AMINI

AMIS, BRETON
BEST, R. BRETON AMIS

AMISHAE, M.H.
MAISELS, MISHA

AMISHAE-MAISELS, ZIVA
MAISELS, MAXINE S.

AMMANN, ESTHER E.
BEURET-AMMANN, ESTHER

AMMER, K.L.
KLAMMER, KLAR

AMO, TAURAATUA I
ADAMS, HARRY [BROOKS]

AMOR, AMOS
HARRELL, IRENE B.

AMOR, PAUL FUSEY
LINN, WILLIAM JOSEPH

AMORY, ARTHUR R.
SARLE, CHARLES SPENSER

AMORY, GUY
BRADBURY, RAY [DOUGLAS]

AMORY, RICHARD
LOVE, RICHARD

AMOS, ALAN
KNIGHT, KATHLEEN MOORE

AMULREE, BARON
MACKENZIE, BASIL W.S.

AMY, LACEY
AMY, WILLIAM LACEY

AMYAND, ARTHUR
HAGGARD, EDWARD ARTHUR

AN BROC
O'NOLAN, BRIAN

AN ELDERLY SPINSTER
WILSON, MARGARET [W]

AN EYE WITNESS IN 1925
CHESNEY, GEORGE T.

AN M.P.
DICKIE, CHARLES HERBERT

AN OLD SOLDIER
BUTLER, WILLIAM FRANCIS

AN PHILBIN
POLLOCK, JOHN HACKETT

AN-SKI, SH. A.
RAPPAPORT, SOLOMON SAMUEL

ANA, RAY
REYNA, RUTH

ANALYTICUS
WISE, JAMES WATERMAN

ANATOL
SCHNITZLER, ARTHUR

ANATOL, A.
KUZNETSOV, ANATOLI

ANATOL, ANDREAS
FROBA, KLAUS

ANATOLE
MULLER, ROBERT

ANATOLE, RAY
GRANDET, IRENE
WEISS, JOE

ANCEL, MARTIN
MARTIN, LANCE

ANCEY, GEORGES
DE CORMERE, MATHORON

ANCIENT, OLIVER
MCALPINE, ROBERT W.

ANCILLA
WOOD, GRACE ASHLEY

ANDEN, RICHARD
VON CZIFFRA, GEZA

ANDERICH, JUSTUS
STEINER, GEROLF

ANDERS, BO
VON MICHALEWSKY, NIKOLAI

ANDERS, DEEZ
LUCKENWALD, HANS

ANDERS, E.J.
LYPE, E.J. ANDERS

ANDERS, HARRIET
BOLEN & HALBACH, HERTHY

ANDERS, HARRY
BOHLEN & HALBACH, BERNDT

ANDERS, HELMUT
DEGNER, HELMUT

ANDERS, JEANNE
ANDERSON, JOAN W.

ANDERS, PAUL
BODE, WALTER

ANDERS, RALPH
VON KAMER, BOGISLAV
VON PUTTKAMER, JESCO

ANDERS, REX
BARRETT, GEOFFREY JOHN

ANDERS, VERA
MUNCHOW, VERA

ANDERSDATTER, KARLA [M]
BILLINGS, KARLA M.C.

ANDERSEN NEXO, MARTIN
ANDERSEN, MARTIN

ANDERSEN, IAN
LOBSENZ, IRVING LOUIS

ANDERSEN, JUEL
ANDERSEN, JEWELL

ANDERSON, ADRIENNE
BARTON, WYNNE

ANDERSON, AL
ALEBY, ANDERS

ANDERSON, ANDY
ANDERSON, WILLIAM C.

ANDERSON, BETH
AMERSKI, BETH

ANDERSON, BETT
AMERSKI, BETH

ANDERSON, BEVERLY
NEMIRO, BEVERLY ANDERSON

ANDERSON, BEVERLY M.
NEMIRO, BEVERLY ANDERSON

ANDERSON, BLAINE
ANDERSON, BLAINE AISLINN

PSEUDONYMS

ANDERSON, C. FARLEY
MENCKEN, HENRY LOUIS

ANDERSON, C.C.
ANDERSON, CATHERINE CORL.

ANDERSON, C.V.
ANDERSON, CHESTER [V.J.]

ANDERSON, C.W.
ANDERSON, CLARENCE W.

ANDERSON, CATHERINE
ANDERSON, ADELINE C.

ANDERSON, CHUCK
ANDERSON, CHARLES

ANDERSON, CLIFFORD
ANDERSON, ROBERT
GARDNER, RICHARD [M]
IRVING, CLIFFORD MICHAEL

ANDERSON, CLYDE
KNOLES, WILLIAM [H]

ANDERSON, DAVE
ANDERSON, DAVID POOLE

ANDERSON, DAVID
JONES, RAYMOND F.

ANDERSON, EDGARS
ANDERSON, EDGAR

ANDERSON, ELLA
MACLEOD, ELLEN JANE [A]

ANDERSON, GEORGE
GROOM, ARTHUR WILLIAM
WEISSMAN, JACK

ANDERSON, J.N.
ANDERSON, JAMES NORMAN

ANDERSON, JACK
ANDERSON, JACKSON NORTHM.

ANDERSON, JOHN K.
ANDERSON, JOHN KINLOCH

ANDERSON, KRISTON
DUBREUIL, ELIZABETH L.

ANDERSON, LARS
ANDERSON, ALAN RITNER

ANDERSON, LONZO
ANDERSON, JOHN L.

ANDERSON, MAGGIE
ANDERSON, MARGARET

ANDERSON, MELISSA
PLOSSNER, JUTTA

ANDERSON, MRS. MELVIN
ANDERSON, CATHERINE CORL.

ANDERSON, NELSE
BOSWORTH, ALLAN R.
FARRELL, A. CLIFFORD
TOMPKINS, WALKER A.

ANDERSON, RACHEL
BRADBY, RACHEL

ANDERSON, SONIA
DANIEL, [WILLIAM] ROLAND

ANDERSON, SPARKY
ANDERSON, GEORGE LEE

ANDERSON, TED
BOYD, WALDO T.

ANDERSON, U.S.
ANDERSON, UELL STANLEY

ANDERSON, W.B.
SCHULTZ, JAMES WILLARD

ANDERSON, WALT
ANDERSON, WALTER TRUETT

ANDERSSON, NIC
TOFTE, ARTHUR

ANDERTON, CLYDE
KNOLES, WILLIAM [H]

ANDERTON, JOHANA GAST
ANDERTON, JOANNE M. GAST

ANDIER, PIERRE
DESNOS, ROBERT

ANDOM, R.
BARRETT, ALFRED WALTER

ANDOUARD
GIRAUDOUX, [H] JEAN

ANDOVAR
PRADO [CALVO], PEDRO

ANDOVER, HENRY
HOPE, HENRY

ANDRAU, MARIANNE
GUILLAUD, SUZANNE

ANDRE, ALIX
KIMBERLY, GAIL

ANDRE, LAZAR
BAJOMI, LAZAR ENDRE

ANDRE, LEE
ANDRUS, L.R.

ANDRE, W.J.
JORDAN, W.

ANDREA, GUY
WEISS, JOE

ANDREAS, BERT
VON KOBLINSKI, HANS-JOACH

ANDREAS, J.H.
VON KOBLINSKI, HANS-JOACH

ANDREAS, JURGEN
ALPERS, HANS JOACHIM

ANDREAS, STEPHAN
KRUGER, HARRY

ANDREAS, THOMAS
WILLIAMS, THOMAS ANDREW

ANDREASSEN, KARL
BOYD, WALDO T.

ANDREE, LOUIS
PANIZZA, OSKAR

ANDREE, LOUISE
COURY, LOUISE ANDRE

ANDREEV, ALEXSANDR
ANDREEV, VASILII D.

ANDRENIO
DE BAQUERO, EDUARDO GOMEZ

ANDRESEN, JACK
ANDRESEN, JOHN H[ENRY] JR

ANDRESEN, JULIE
TETEL, JULIE

ANDRESKI, IRIS
GILLESPIE, IRIS SYLVIA

ANDRESS, LESLIE
SANDERS, LAWRENCE

ANDREUS, HANS
VAN DER ZANT, JOHAN WILH.

ANDREVS, CHARLES
NOOREN, BORJE

ANDREW, BERT
ANDRE, HERBERT

ANDREW, MERRY
FREEMAN, JOHN [H.G.]

ANDREW, ROBERT
COOPER, ROBERT ANDREW

ANDREW, STEPHEN
LAYTON, FRANK GEORGE

ANDREWES, PATIENCE
BRADFORD PATIENCE A.

ANDREWS, A.A.
PAINE, LAURAN BOSWORTH

ANDREWS, ALEX
MACKIE, MARY

ANDREWS, ANNULET
OHL, MAUDE

ANDREWS, BARBARA
ANDREWS, BARBARA L. ROCK

ANDREWS, BLAKE
NUETZEL, CHARLES A.

ANDREWS, CAROLYN
HANION, CAROLYN

ANDREWS, CARRIE
BRINEY, ROBERT E.

ANDREWS, CHARLES
NOOREN, BORJE

ANDREWS, CICILY FAIRFIELD
WEST, REBECCA

ANDREWS, COLIN
WILSON, F[RANCIS] PAUL

ANDREWS, ELEANOR LATTIM.
LATTIMORE, ELEANOR FRAN.

PSEUDONYMS

ANDREWS, ELTON V.
POHL, FREDERIK

ANDREWS, FELICIA
GRANT, CHARLES L.

ANDREWS, J.S.
ANDREWS, JAMES SYDNEY

ANDREWS, JAY
OFFUTT, ANDREW J.

ANDREWS, JOHN
BOBIN, JOHN WILLIAM
CAMPBELL, ANDREW
MURRAY, ANDREW NICHOLAS
SHUTE, WALTER
STANIFORTH, JOHN WILLIAM
STEFFENS, ARTHUR JOSEPH

ANDREWS, KEITH WILLIAMS
KEITH, WILLIAM HENRY JR.

ANDREWS, LAURA
COURY, LOUISE ANDRE

ANDREWS, LAURIE
COURY, LOUISE ANDRE

ANDREWS, LUCILLA
CRICHTON, LUCILLA MATTHEW

ANDREWS, NICOLA
PAPAZOGLOU, ORANIA

ANDREWS, OPAL
OFFUTT, ANDREW J.

ANDREWS, ROBERT D.
ANDREWS, C.R. DOUGLAS HA.

ANDREWS, SPIKE
RYAN, GEORGE

ANDREWS, THOMAS
WRIGHT, SEWELL PEASLEE

ANDREWS, V.C.
NEDIDERMAN, ANDREW
PATTY, ANN

ANDREWS, VICKIE
SMITH, CATHERINE R.

ANDREWS, WENDY
SHARMAT, MARJORIE WEINMAN

ANDREZEL, PIERRE
BLIXEN-FINEKE, KAREN

ANDRIESSEN, DAVID
POYER, DAVID C.

ANDROS, PHIL
STEWARD, SAMUEL M[ORRIS]

ANDRUL
BEGBIE, ARUNDEL

ANDRZEYEVSKI, GEORGE
ANDRZEJEWSKI, JERZY

ANDUZE-DUFY, RAPHAEL
COULET DU GARD, RENE

ANET, CLAUDE
SCHOPFER, JEAN

ANFLEMING, IRENE
LINZNER, GORDON

ANGE, L. v.
ALVENSLEBEN, KARL LUDWIG

ANGEBERT, JEAN
BERTRAND, MICHEL

ANGEBERT, JEAN-MICHEL
BERTRAND, MICHEL

ANGEBERT, MICHEL
BERTRAND, MICHEL

ANGEL, ROSS
CRESSWELL, DONALD

ANGELILLI, FRANK JOSEPH
ANGELL, FRANK JOSEPH

ANGELINO, MARIE
GARBUTT, JANICE D. LOVOOS

ANGELIQUE, PIERRE
BATAILLE, GEORGES

ANGELL, HILDEGARDE
SMITH, HILDEGARDE ANGELL

ANGELL, JUDIE
GABERMAN, JUDIE ANGELL

ANGELL, NORMAN
LANE, SIR RALPH NORMAN A.

ANGELO, MICHAEL
GOLDSMITH, OLIVER

ANGELO, TONY
WEBB, THOMAS CHARLES P.

ANGELOU, MAYA
JOHNSON, MARGUERITA

ANGIO-AUSTRAL
WILTON, CHARLES EDWARD

ANGLEMAN, JACK
PHILLIPS, NORMAN

ANGLESEY, MARQUESS OF
PAGET, GEORGE CHARLES H.V

ANGO, FAN D.
LONGYEAR, BARRY B[ROOKES]

ANGOVE, GRACE
MICHELL, GRACE [A]

ANGSTMANN, GUSTL
ANGSTMANN, AUGUSTIN

ANGUS, IAN
MACKAY, JAMES [A]

ANGUS, TOM
POWELL, GEOFFREY STEWART

ANGUS, WILLIAM
MOIR, ANGUS

ANGUS-BUTTERWORTH, LIONEL
BUTTERWORTH, LIONEL MILN.

ANIANTE, ANTONIO
RAPISARDA, ANTONIO

ANICAR, TOM
RAUCINA, THOMAS FRANK

ANISE
STRONG, ANNALOUISE

ANITA
DANIEL, ANITA

ANKER, JENS
HANSEN, ROBERT

ANKER, PETER
DAHL, SOREN A.
MEYN, NIELS

ANKH-ER-MAN, PHAROAH J.
ACKERMAN, FORREST J.

ANMAR, FRANK
BEAUMONT, CHARLES
NOLAN, WILLIAM F.

ANN JANE
MORGAN, ANN JANE

ANNABELLA
LOWE, CHARLOTTE

ANNALIST
GERARD, FRANCES

ANNANDALE, BARBARA
BOWDEN, JEAN

ANNE-MARIEL
GOUD, ANNE

ANNETT, CORA
SCOTT, CORA ANNETT

ANNI, MAKITUVAN
HONKANEN, HILJA L.V.

ANNIXTER, JANE
STURTZEL, JANE LEVINGTON

ANNIXTER, PAUL
STURTZEL, HOWARD ALLISON

ANOCLOS
COLERIDGE, MARY ELIZABETH

ANON, CHARLES ROBERT
PESSOA, FERNANDO [A.N.]

ANONYMOUS
BERNET, MICHAEL [STEVEN]
COCHRAN, HOWE P.
DALTON, JAMES
DEMILLE, JAMES
FEARN, JOHN RUSSELL
NUETZEL, CHARLES A.
NUETZEL, CHARLES A.
OFFUTT, ANDREW J.
SASSOON, SIEGFRIED [L]
SMYTH, JOSEPH HILTON
STEWARD, DONALD WILLIAM
VAN SAHER, LILLA
WOOLFOLK, JOSHUA PITTS
WOOLRICH, CORNELL HOPLEY

ANRAINER, TRAUDL
EICHHOF, JOACHIM

ANROOY, FRAN VAN
VAN ANROOY, FRANCINE

ANSARA, MICHAEL
CROWTHER, BRUCE [IAN]

ANSCOMBE, ELIZABETH
ANSCOMBE, GERTRUDE ELIZ.

ANSEL, FRANZ
FOLIE, FRANZ

ANSELM, FELIX
POLLAK, FELIX

ANSKY, S.
RAPPAPORT, SOLOMON SAMUEL

ANSON, CAPT.
ANSON, CHARLES VERNON

ANSON, JOHN
FIRTH, [FREDERICK] ANSON

ANSON, KATHLEEN
ADDISON, KATHERINE

ANSON, NET
FIRTH, NORMAN WESLEY

ANSON, PIERS
DALLAS, OSWALD [C.C.]
DELL, DRAYCOT MONTAGU

ANSTEE, M.H.
BLEECK, G.C.

ANSTEY, EDGAR
SLUSSER, GEORGE EDGAR

ANSTEY, F.
GUTHRIE, THOMAS ANSTEY

ANSTON, LINELL
NEMETH, LINELL EVANSTON

ANSTRUTHER, GERALD
FLEMING, BRANDON

ANSTRUTHER, JAMES
MAXTONE-GRAHAM, JAMES A.

ANSTRUTHER, JOHN
WALLACE, EDGAR

ANTEO
SANCHEZ, MORALES NARCISCO

ANTHES, NATAKIE
BRUDER, HERTA

ANTHONY
TABER, ANTHONY SCOTT

ANTHONY, ALBERT
VON CZIFFRA, GEZA

ANTHONY, C.L.
SMITH, DOROTHY GLADYS

ANTHONY, CATHERINE
ADACHI, BARBARA [CURTIS]

ANTHONY, CLAY
HARING, DON

ANTHONY, DAVID
SMITH, WILLIAM DALE

ANTHONY, DIANE
ANTONIO, DIANE

ANTHONY, EVELYN
STEPHENS, EVE
TRAYNOR, PAGE & ANTHONY
WARD-THOMAS, EVELYN B.P.S

ANTHONY, GEORGE
CRECHALES, ANTHONY GEORGE

ANTHONY, GORDON
STANNUS, [J] GORDON [D]

ANTHONY, JAMES
HAUGEN, CHRISTIAN

ANTHONY, JOHN
BECKETT, RONALD BRYMER
CIARDI, JOHN ANTHONY
CONNOR, JOHN ANTHONY
ROBERTS, JOHN S[TORM]
SABINI, JOHN ANTHONY

ANTHONY, JOSEPH
CASTROVILLA, JOSEPH A.

ANTHONY, PETER
JOSHUA, ANTHONY

ANTHONY, PIERS
JACOB, PIERS ANTHONY [D]

ANTHONY, R.
RUD, ANTHONY M.

ANTIBES, ARLETTE
MUHRMANN, WILHELM

ANTILL, ELIZABETH
MIDDLETON, ELIZABETH

ANTOINE, MARC
PROUST, [V-L-G-E] MARCEL

ANTON, EMIL
BARDEY, EMIL

ANTON, FERDINAND
KOCK, FERDINAND ANTON

ANTON, ROBERT
PENKALA, ALICE

ANTONI
IRANEK-OSMECKI, KAZ.

ANTONIO
ERSKINE, GLADYS SHAW

ANTONIORROBLES
SOLER, ANTONIO ROBLES

ANTONY, PETER
SHAFFER, ANTHONY & PETER

ANTTALA, ESA
ARHOSUO, URPO

ANVIC, FRANK
SHERMAN, JORY [T]

ANVIL, CHRISTOPHER
CROSBY, HARRY C. JR.

AOS, FOEL
TER BALKT, HERMAN H.

AP EVANS, HUMPHREY
DRUMMOND, HUMPHREY

AP IWAN, EMRYS
JONES, ROBERT AMBROSE

APARTHUR, C.
MORRIS, KENNETH

APHRODITE, J.
LIVINGSTON, CAROLE

APIKUNI
SCHULTZ, JAMES WILLARD

APILENTZ
APELIAN, ALBERT SOLOMON

APOLLINAIRE, GUILLAME
DE KOSTROWITSKY, W.APOLL.

APPEL, H.M.
BITTNER, ARCHIBALD
ROGERS, WAYNE

APPEL, MARTY
APPEL, MARTIN E[LIOT]

APPELL, GEORGE C.
THOMPSON, THOMAS [TOMMY]

APPLE, A.E.
APPLEBAUM, A.E.

APPLEBY, KEN
APPLEBY, KENNETH PHILIP

APPLEGIRTH, ANTHONY
DENT, ANTHONY AUSTEN

APPLEMAN, MARGIE
APPLEMAN, M[ARJORIE] H.

APPLETON, JAY
APPLETON, JAMES HENRY

APPLETON, LAURENCE
LOVECRAFT, H[OWARD] P.

APPLETON, VICTOR
ADAMS, HARRIET S.
BARRETT, NEAL JR.
BETANCOURT, JOHN GREGORY
DIVONO, SHARMAN
DOYLE, DEBRA
GARIS, HOWARD R.
GRANT, STEVEN
MACDONALD, JAMES D.
MACINTYRE, F. GWYNPLAINE
MCCAY, BILL
MCQUAY, MICHAEL DENNIS
ROTSLER, WILLIAM
STRATEMEYER, EDWARD
VARDEMAN, ROBERT E.

APPLETON, VICTOR II
ADAMS, HARRIET S.
ALMQUIST, JOHN
DOUGHERTY, WILLIAM
MULVEY, TOM
SKLAR, RICHARD [LAWRENCE]
STRATEMEYER, EDWARD
LAWRENCE, JAMES DUNCAN
MCKENNA, RICHARD

APPLEZWEIG, M.H.
APPLEY, MORTIMER HERBERT

APPS, JERRY
APPS, JEROLD W.
APRIL, JACK
SCHLICK, F.

APRIL, STEVE
ZINBERG, LEONARD S.

APTERYX
ELIOT, T[HOMAS] S[TEARNS]

AQUARIAN
OPPENHEIMER, JOEL LESTER

AQUARIUS, QASS
BUSKIRK, RICHARD H[OBART]

AQUILLO, DON
PRINCE, JACK HARVEY

AQUINAS, SISTER MARY
WEINRICH, ANNA KATHARINA

AQUINO, NINOY
AQUINO, BENIGNO S. JR.

AQVIST, RUNE
RUNNEQUIST, AKE

AR C'HALAN, REUN
GALAND, RENE

AR, ESJAY
RUBENSTEIN, STANLEY JACK

AR-RAIHANT
REEHANY, AMIN

ARAGBABALU, OMIDIJI
BEIER, ULLI

ARAMIS
SIMENON, GEORGES [J.C]

ARANA, RIC[K]
SELLERS, CONNIE LESLIE

ARAND, CHARLOTTE
SACHER-MASOCH, LEOPOLD

ARAND, LILO
HEYMANN, ROBERT JR.

ARAWIYAH, AL
CRELLIN, H.N.

ARBATOV, G.A.
ARBATOV, GEORGI [A]

ARBATOV, YURI ARKADEVICH
ARBATOV, GEORGI [A]

ARBING, BORGE VILLY REDS.
HASSEL, SVEN

ARBOGAST, DONALD K.
WHITE, THEODORE EDWIN

ARBOR, JANE
OWBRIDGE, EILEEN

ARBORG, SVEN
FRIEDRICHS, HORST

ARBORY, JOHN
MACFARLANE, JOHN

ARCADIUS
HILLERET, ALAIN & ANDRE

ARCANA, JUDITH
ROSENFIELD, JUDITH

ARCE, JULIO G.
ULLICA, JORGE

ARCENEAUX, JEAN
ANCELET, BARRY JEAN

ARCH, E.L.
PAYES, RACHEL C.

ARCHARD, GEORGE
TORRES-LEVIN, TERESKA [S]

ARCHER, A.A.
JOSCELYN, ARCHIE LYNN

ARCHER, ARCHIE ALEXANDER
JOSCELYN, ARCHIE LYNN

ARCHER, CATHERINE
ARCHIBALD, CATHERINE

ARCHER, DENNIS
PAINE, LAURAN BOSWORTH

ARCHER, FRANK
LOONEY, PETER
O'CONNOR, RICHARD

ARCHER, HERBERT WINSLOW
MENCKEN, HENRY LOUIS

ARCHER, JANE
ANDERSSON, NINA ROMBERG
ROMBERG, NINA

ARCHER, LANE
HAUCK, LOUISE PLATT

ARCHER, LEE
ELLISON, HARLAN

ARCHER, OWEN
GREENWOOD, AUGUSTUS GEOR.

ARCHER, RON
VAN ARNAM, DAVE
WHITE, THEODORE EDWIN

ARCHER, S.E.
SODERBURG, PERCY MEASDAY

ARCHER-BATTEN, S.
WALKER, STELLA ARCHER

ARCHERY, HELEN
ARGYRIS, HELEN

ARCHESTRATUS
DRIVER, CHRISTOPHER

ARCHETTE, GUY
GEIER, CHESTER S.

ARCHIBALD, JOE
ARCHIBALD, JOSEPH S.

ARCHIBALD, MRS. GEORGE
PALMER, ANNA CAMPBELL

ARCHITECHS ADVENTURE
BLOOM, MARK

ARCHITECHS ADVENTURE [CONT]
HUNT, WALTER & LISA
IVEY, CHRISTINE
JAMIESON, EVAN
MEYERS, RICHARD S.
SCAMMELL, BILL

ARCICIO
DE ARGUIJO, JUAN

ARCOL, MARGUERITE
COLLIGNON, ILSE

ARCOT, ROGER
LOCKE, ROBERT DONALD

ARD, WILLIAM
BLOCK, LAWRENCE
JAKES, JOHN [WILLIAM]
WILLIS, THOMAS

ARDEN, BARBIE
RITCHIE, BARBARA
STOUTENBURG, ADRIEN [P]

ARDEN, CLIVE
NUTT, LILY CLIVE

ARDEN, J.E.M.
CONQUEST, ROBERT

ARDEN, MARY
MURRY, VIOLET

ARDEN, NOEL
DAMBRUSKAS, JOAN ARDEN

ARDEN, RICE
WEEKLY, MAURICE ARDEN

ARDEN, ROBERT
HEYMANN, ROBERT JR.

ARDEN, WILLIAM
LYNDS, DENNIS

ARELLANO, PETER
BOCKER, HANS WERNER

ARENALES, RICARDO
BENITEZ, MIGUEL ANGEL OS.

ARENSKY, ROMAN
GIPPIUS, ZINAIDA N.

ARESBYS, THE
BAMBERGER, HELEN R.
BAMBERGER, RAYMOND

ARETA, MAVIS
WINDER, MAVIS ARETA

ARETINO, JR.
HINE, AL[FRED B.]

ARGERS, HELEN
ARGYRIS, HELEN

ARGHEZI, TUDOR
THEODORESCU, ION

ARGO, ELLEN
JOHNSON, ELLEN ARGO

ARGO, SAM & JANET
BUDRYS, ALGIRDAS JONAS

PSEUDONYMS

ARGUS
OSUSKY, STEFAN
PHILLIPS-BIRT, DOUGLAS
PROUTING, FREDERICK JAMES

ARGUS, M.K.
EISENSTADT-JELEZNOV, MIK.

ARID, BEN
BARNARD, MELVILLE CLEMENT

ARIEL
MORAES, FRANK ROBERT

ARION
CHESTERTON, GILBERT KEITH

ARION, F.M.
MARTINUS, [E] FRANK

ARISTIDES
EPSTEIN, JOSEPH

ARIZONA
LAFUENTE ESTEFANIA, M.A.

ARIZONA-TIGER
BREUCKER, OSCAR HERBERT

ARKADYEV, N.
SHEVCHENKO, ARKADY N.

ARKHAM, CANDICE
RAMIREZ, ALICE

ARLEN, LESLIE
NICOLE, CHRISTOPHER ROBIN

ARLEN, MICHAEL
KUYUMJIAN, DIKRAN

ARLEN, SCOTT
STONE, CARL

ARLEY, CATHERINE
D'ARLEY, CATHERINE

ARLISS, JOEN
MARTIN, IAN

ARMAND
STRUBBERG, FRIEDRICH ARM.

ARMARNATH
OAK, PURUSHATTAM NAGESH

ARMAS, RICHARD
WILHELMSSON, YNGVE M.

ARMBRUSTER, FRANK
ARMBRUSTER, FRANCIS E.

ARMEN, MKRTICH
ARUTIUNIAN, MKRTICH G.

ARMIDO
TOYNE, CLARICE JOY

ARMITAGE, AILEEN
QUIGLEY, AILEEN

ARMITAGE, ALFRED
GRAYDON, WILLIAM MURRAY

ARMITAGE, EILEEN
FABIAN, R. RUTH

ARMITAGE, FRANK
CARPENTER, JOHN HOWARD

ARMITAGE, G.E.
ARMITAGE, GARY EDRIC

ARMITAGE, HAZEL
WHEWAY, JOHN W.

ARMITAGE, VINCENT
WHEWAY, JOHN W.

ARMOUR, GLADYS
OSBORNE, DOROTHY [G] YEO

ARMOUR, JOHN
PAINE, LAURAN BOSWORTH

ARMOUR, MARGARET
MACDOUGALL, MARGARET

ARMS, JOHNSON
HALLIWELL, DAVID WILLIAM

ARMSTRONG JONES, TONY
ARMSTRONG-JONES, ANTONY

ARMSTRONG, ANTHONY
TUBB, E.C.
WILLIS, GEORGE ANTHONY A.

ARMSTRONG, ANTHONY C.
ARMSTRONG, CHRISTOPHER J.

ARMSTRONG, CAMPBELL
BLACK, CAMPBELL

ARMSTRONG, CHARLOTTE
LEWI, CHARLOTTE ARMSTRONG

ARMSTRONG, F.W.
WRIGHT, TERRANCE M.

ARMSTRONG, GEOFFREY
FEARN, JOHN RUSSELL

ARMSTRONG, GEORGE
TATE, GEORGE

ARMSTRONG, HENRY
JACKSON, HENRY

ARMSTRONG, HENRY H.
ARVAY, HEINZ

ARMSTRONG, JACK
FELTON, FREDERICK A.

ARMSTRONG, JOE C.W.
ARMSTRONG, JOSEPH CHARLES

ARMSTRONG, JOHN
FABER, ELSE

ARMSTRONG, RAYMOND
LEE, NORMAN

ARMSTRONG, SYBIL
EDMONDSON, SYBIL

ARMSTRONG, WALDO
FABER, ELSE

ARMSTRONG, WARREN
BENNETT, WILLIAM EDWARD

ARNARSON, ORN
STEFANSSON, MAGNUS

ARNAU, FRANK
SCHMITT, HEINRICH

ARNAUD, GEORGES
GIRARD, HENRI GEORGES

ARNAZ, DESI
ARNAZ Y DE ACHA, DESIDERI

ARNCLIFFE, ANDREW
WALKER, PETER N[ORMAN]

ARNDT, AXEL
HOBEIN, EUGEN

ARNDT, DIETRICH
MULLER-GUTTENBRUNN, RODER

ARNE, AARON
JORGENSON, ALF A.

ARNEMANN, FRED
PLATTE, HEINZ ERICH

ARNETT, CAROLINE
COLE, LOIS DWIGHT

ARNETT, JACK
MCQUAY, MICHAEL DENNIS
MILLER, JOHN
ODOM, MEL[VIN LEWIS III]

ARNETTE, ROBERT
GEIER, CHESTER S.
SILVERBERG, ROBERT

ARNET[TE], ROBERT
GRAHAM, ROGER P.

ARNETTE, STEPHEN
RYNAS, STEPHEN A.

ARNEY, JAMES
RUSSELL, MARTIN [JAMES]

ARNO, ELROY
YERXA, LEROY

ARNOLD, A.V.
ARNOLD, MRS. J.O.

ARNOLD, CARL
RAKNES, OLA

ARNOLD, CLEMENT
PANTING, ARNOLD CLEMENT

ARNOLD, FRANK
YOUNG, FRED W.

ARNOLD, G.L.
LICHTHEIM, GEORGE

ARNOLD, HEINI
ARNOLD, JOHAN HEINRICH

ARNOLD, JEAN
ARNALDI, JEAN

ARNOLD, JOHN
KUMMER, FREDERICK ARNOLD

ARNOLD, JOSEPH H.
HAYES, JOSEPH [ARNOLD]

ARNOLD, JUDITH
KEILER, BARBARA

ARNOLD, L.J.
CAMERON, LOU

ARNOLD, LESLIE
LAZARUS, ARNOLD LESLIE

ARNOLD, LEWIS
EVANS, DAVID ARNOLD

ARNOLD, MALCOLM
MURRAY, ANDREW NICHOLAS

ARNOLD, MARGOT
COOK, P. MARGUERITE MARY

ARNOLD, MRS. J.O.
ARNOLD, ADELAIDE VICTORIA

ARNOLD, PAULINE
WHITE, PAULINE ARNOLD

ARNOLD, THEODOR F.K.
ARNOLD, IGNAZ FERDINAND

ARNOLD, WINIFRED
MAY, WINIFRED ARNOLD

ARNOLDY, JULIE
BISHOFF, JULIA BRISTOL

ARNOSKY, JIM
ARNOSKY, HAMES EDWARD

AROL, ROBERT
MOMMERS, HELMUTH W.

ARONIN, BEN
HERON-ALLEN, EDWARD

ARP, ASA
LOWE, PAUL EMILIUS

ARP, BILL
SMITH, CHARLES HENRY

ARP, HANS
ARP, JEAN

ARPEL, ADRIEN
NEWMAN, ADRIEN ANN

ARQUETTE, LOIS S.
DUNCAN, LOIS S[TEINMETZ]

ARR, STEPHEN
RYNAS, STEPHEN A.

ARRABEL
ARRABEL, FERNANDO

ARRE, HELEN
ROSS, Z. HELEN G.

ARRE, JOHN
HOLT, JOHN ROBERT

ARRIETA, FERNANDO
GUERRA, EVARISTO ACEVEDO

ARRIGHI, CLETTO
RIGHETTI, CARLO

ARROW, WILLIAM
PFEIL, DONALD J.
ROTSLER, WILLIAM

ARROWAY, FRANCIS M.
ROSMOND, BABETTE

ARROWSMITH, PAT
BARTON, PAT

ARROYA, SANTANA
ARROYA, STEPHEN JOSEPH

ARROYO, ANTONIO M. STEVEN
STEVENS-ARROYO, ANTONIO M

ART, ARRES
SERRA, ART

ARTAX
EDEN, JOHN LANCELOT

ARTFAB
WILLIAMS, JACK LEWIS

ARTHUR BURT & BUDD
SHAPPIRO, BUDD

ARTHUR, BERT
SHAPPIRO, HERBERT ARTHUR

ARTHUR, BURT
ARTHUR, HERBERT

ARTHUR, ELISABETH
IRISH, BETTY M.

ARTHUR, FRANK
EBERT, ARTHUR FRANK

ARTHUR, FREDERICK
LAMBERT, F.A. HEYGATE

ARTHUR, GAVIN
ARTHUR, CHESTER ALAN

ARTHUR, GEORGE
PHILLIPS, BLUEBELL S.

ARTHUR, GLADYS
OSBORNE, DOROTHY G. YEO

ARTHUR, H. PRESTON
HANKINS, ARTHUR PRESTON

ARTHUR, HARRY
BASE, A.H.
BATES, HARRY ARTHUR

ARTHUR, HERBERT
SHAPPIRO, HERBERT ARTHUR

ARTHUR, HUGH
CHRISTIE-MURRAY, DAVID

ARTHUR, JOHN
JOSEPH, ARTHUR

ARTHUR, KATHERINE
ERIKSEN, BARBARA

ARTHUR, LEE
BROWNING, LEE & ARTHUR

ARTHUR, MARTIN [FOREST]
JACKSON, MARTIN [FOREST]

ARTHUR, PETER
PORGES, ARTHUR

ARTHUR, PHYLLIS
SHIPMAN, NATALIE

ARTHUR, ROBERT
FEDER, ROBERT ARTHUR

ARTHUR, RUTH M.
HUGGINS, RUTH MABEL ARTH.

ARTHUR, TIFFANY
PELTON, ROBERT W.

ARTHUR, TOM
ARTHUR, THOMAS H.

ARTHUR, WILLIAM
BAKER, W.A. HOWARD
MCNEILLY, WILFRED G.
NEUBAUER, WILLIAM A.

ARTHUS, TH.
PESSLER-ADAM, DORA

ARTIN, TOM
ARTIN, THOMAS

ARTNER, ROBERT
ERNSTING, WALTER
MIEHE, ULF

ARTUR, GEORG
OEDEMANN, GEORG

ARUBA, FERDINAND
OPFERMANN, HANS-CARL

ARUEGO, ARIANE
DEWEY, ARIANE

ARUNDALE, G.S.
ARUNDALE, GEORGE SYDNEY

ARUNDEL, JOCELYN
ALEXANDER, JOCELYN ANNE A

ARVAY, HARRY
ARVAY, HEINZ
BREWER, GIL

ARVEDE, BARINE
VINCENS, MME. CHARLES

ARVILL, ROBERT
BOOTE, ROBERT EDWARD

ARZHAK, NIKOLAI
DANIEL, YULI

ASARE, BEDIAKO
KONADU, SAMUEL ASARE

ASCHE, OSCAR
HEISS, JOHN STANGER

ASCHER, EUGENE
KELLY, HAROLD ERNEST

ASCHER/STRAUS
ASCHER, SHEILA
STRAUS, DENNIS

ASCOTT, ADELIE
BOBIN, JOHN WILLIAM

PSEUDONYMS

ASCOTT, JOHN
BOBIN, JOHN WILLIAM

ASH, FENTON
ATKINS, FRANCIS HENRY
ATKINS, FRANK JR.

ASH, KATHLEEN
WALKER, EMILY KATHLEEN

ASH, MELISSA
CASEY, JUNE E.

ASH, PAUL
ASHWELL, PAUL

ASH, PAULINE
WALKER, EMILY KATHLEEN

ASH, PENELOPE
KARMAN, MAL

ASH, PETER
HAUCK, LOUISE PLATT

ASH, ROBERTA
GARNER, ROBERTA

ASH, SHALOM
ASCH, SHOLEM

ASHBLESS, WILLIAM
BLAYLOCK, JAMES P[AUL]
POWERS, TIM[OTHY THOMAS]

ASHBROOK, H.
ASHBROOK, HARRIETTE CORA

ASHBY, CARTER
PAINE, LAURAN BOSWORTH

ASHBY, JULIET
OUTLAW-SHALLIT, LOUISE L.

ASHBY, NORA
AFRICANO, LILLIAN

ASHCRAFT, LAURIE
ASHCRAFT, LAURA

ASHCROFT, LAURA
CARLSON, JANICE

ASHDOWN, CLIFFORD
FREEMAN, RICHARD AUSTIN
PITCAIRN, JOHN JAMES

ASHE, DOUGLAS
BARDIN, JOHN FRANKLIN

ASHE, ELIZABETH
HYDE, LAVENDER BERYL

ASHE, GORDON
CREASEY, JOHN

ASHE, MARY ANN
LEWIS, M. CHRISTIANNA M.

ASHE, MARY ANNE
LEWIS, M. CHRISTIANNA M.

ASHE, MEGAN
ANDERSON, VIRGINIA

ASHE, PENELOPE
GREENE, ROBERT W.
YOUNG, BILLIE

ASHE, ROSALIND
DALE-HARRIS, ROSALIND

ASHE, SUSAN
BEST, CAROL ANN

ASHER, MIRIAM
MUNDIS, HESTER JANE

ASHER, RODERICK
RUBENACKER, THOMAS

ASHER, SANDY
ASHER, SANDRA FENICHEL

ASHER, SARAH
AYRES, NOREEN

ASHERON, SARA
MOORE, LILLIAN

ASHEY, BELLA
BREINBERG, PETRONELLA

ASHFIELD, HELEN
BENNETTS, PAMELA

ASHFORD, DAISY
ASHFORD, MARGARET MARY

ASHFORD, JANE
LE COMPTE, JANE

ASHFORD, JEFFREY
JEFFRIES, RODERIC[GRAEME]

ASHLEY, A.
AASHEIM, ASHLEY

ASHLEY, ELIZABETH
SALMON, ANNIE ELIZABETH

ASHLEY, FRED
ATKINS, FRANCIS HENRY

ASHLEY, GLADYS
EWANS, GWENDOLINE W.

ASHLEY, GRAHAM
ORGAN, JOHN

ASHLEY, JACQUELINE
CASTO, JACQUELINE A.

ASHLEY, MARY
TOWNSEND, MARY ASHLEY

ASHLEY, MIKE
ASHLEY, MICHAEL RAYMOND D

ASHLEY, RAY
ABRASHKIN, RAYMOND

ASHLEY, REBECCA
WALKER, LOIS ARVIN

ASHLEY, SHELLEY
ROITMAN, VOLF & SHELLEY S

ASHLEY, STEVEN
MCCAIG, DONALD

ASHLEY, SUZANNE
BROWN, SUSAN C.

ASHLEY-MONTAGU, MONTAGUE
MONTAGU, ASHLEY

ASHLIN, JOHN
CUTFORTH, JOHN ASHLIN

ASHMIND, KIM
VAN LAERHOVEN, ROBERT V.F

ASHMORE, APRIL
WINGATE, LISA

ASHMORE, JANE
LITTLE, CECILE ENID

ASHMORE, LEWIS
RABORG, FREDERICK A.

ASHOK
KONISHI, MASATOSHI

ASHTON, ANN
KIMBRO, JOHN M.

ASHTON, FIONA
WILKES-HUNTER, RICHARD

ASHTON, HELEN
FRASER, GEORGE MACDONALD

ASHTON, KATE
BALL, MARGARET

ASHTON, KATHERINE
TALBOT, KATHERINE

ASHTON, LUCY
MARTIN, NETTA

ASHTON, MARVIN
HUGHES, DENNIS [TALBOT]

ASHTON, MOLLIE
AGHADJIAN, MOLLIE

ASHTON, SHARON
VAN SLYKE, HELEN

ASHTON, VIOLET
ASHTON, MARGERY VIOLET

ASHTON, WARREN T.
ADAMS, WILLIAM TAYLOR

ASHTON-WARNER, SYLVIA
HENDERSON, SYLVIA

ASHWELL, PAULINE
ASHWELL, PAUL

ASIMUFF, ISAAK
ANTON, UWE
HAHN, RONALD M.

ASIN, ALFREDO QUISPEZ
MORO, CESAR

ASIN, CESAR QUISPEZ
MORO, CESAR

ASKARI, HUSAINI MUHAMMAD
PEREIRA, HAROLD BERTRAM

PSEUDONYMS

ASKEW, JACK
HIVNOR, ROBERT

ASKHAM, FRANCIS
GREENWOOD, JULIA E.C.

ASKON, TOM
DIEDRICH, KLAUS

ASLIN, SAMANTHA
REHFELD, FRANK

ASMODEUS
NICHOLS, THOMAS

ASPAZIA
ROSENBERG, ELSA

ASQUITH, LADY CYNTHIA
CHARTERIS, MARY EVELYN

ASQUITH, NAN
PATTINSON, NANCY EVELYN

ASSENSOH, A.B.
ASSENSOH, AKWASI BRETUO

ASSIAC
FRAENKAL, HEINRICH

ASSUR BANI PAL
PEDRIERA, ANTONIO A.

ASTARION, THEODOR
PROSCH, T.

ASTERISK
FLETCHER, ROBERT JAMES

ASTIN, PATTY DUKE
DUKE, ANNA MARIE

ASTLEY, JULIET
LOFTS, NORAH [E.R.]

ASTLEY, THEA
ASTLEY, THEA B. MAY

ASTON, HELEN
JORDAN, MRS. ARTHUR

ASTON, JAMES
WHITE, TERRENCE H.

ASTOR, A.
LOHLEIN, HERBERT

ASTOR, FRANK
BREUCKER, OSCAR HERBERT
GUNTHER, HANS LUDWIG A.

ASTRAHAN, SYRIE A.
JAMES, SYRIE A. ASTRAHAN

ASTRO
GIBSON, WALTER B.

ASWIN
NANDAKUMAR, PREMA

ATARES, CARLOS SAURA
SAURA [ATARES], CARLOS

ATCHESON, LOUISE
WEST, UTA

ATCHLEY, BOB
ATCHLEY, ROBERT C.

ATENE, ANN
ATENE, RITA ANNA

ATES, C.O.
COATES, FREDERICK AMES

ATHANAS, VERNE
ATHANAS, WILLIAM VERNE

ATHANAS, W.V.
ATHANAS, WILLIAM VERNE

ATHELING, WILLIAM
POUND, EZRA LOOMIS

ATHELING, WILLIAM, JR.
BLISH, JAMES B.

ATHERTON, LUCIUS
MASTERS, EDGAR LEE

ATHERTON, PAULINE
COCHRANE, PAULINE A.

ATHERTON, SARAH
BRIDGEMAN, SARAH ATHERTON

ATHOS
DAWSON, ERNEST
WALKERLEY, RODNEY L.

ATKIN, CHARLES
GRIFFEN, FRANK

ATKINS, CHET
ATKINS, CHESTER BURTON

ATKINS, DAVID
GIBSON, WALTER B.

ATKINS, JACK
FINKLESTEIN, MARK

ATKINS, JESSICA
REHFELD, FRANK

ATKINS, JIM
ATKINS, JAMES G.

ATKINS, MEG ELIZABETH
ATKINS, MARGARET ELIZAB.

ATKINS, OLLIE
ATKINS, OLIVER F.

ATKINS, REV. E.C.
MACFADDEN, BERMNARD A.

ATKINSON, ALEX
DAVIES, PETER

ATKINSON, ALICE M.
KIRSON, ALICE ATKINSON

ATKINSON, ELEANOR BLAKE
PRATT, ELEANOR BLAKE

ATKINSON, LOUISA
CALVERT, CAROLINE L.W.

ATKINSON, M.E.
FRANKAU, MARY EVELYN A.

ATKINSON, MARY
HARDWICK, MOLLIE

ATKINSON, REGINALD
CARLTON, G.E.L.

ATKINSON, W.W.
ATKINSON, WILLIAM WALKER

ATLANTICUS
BALLOD, CARL

ATLANTIS, ISADORE
KELLY, DEXTER

ATLEE, PHILIP
PHILLIPS, JAMES ATLEE

ATOM
THOMSON, ARTHUR

ATOM, ANNE
WALWORTH, JEANETTE R.

ATOMCRACKER, BUZZ-BOLT
KNOX, CLEO ELDON

ATTERLEY, JOSEPH
TUCKER, GEORGE

ATTHILL, ROBIN
ATTHILL, ROBERT ANTHONY

ATTICUS
DAVIES, HUNTER
FLEMING, IAN [LANCASTER]
PAWLE, GERALD STRACHAN

ATTLEE, C.R.
ATTLEE, CLEMENT RICHARD

ATWATER, RICHARD TUPPER
ATWATER, FREDERICK MUND

ATWOOD, DASCOMB
WHITE, GEORGIA ATWOOD

ATWOOD, DRUCY
MORRISON, EULA ATWOOD

ATWOOD, KATHRYN
GRANT, KATHRYN ANNE P.

ATWOOD, SAM
EASTON, THOMAS A[TWOOD]

AUBER, PAUL
BAKER, PAULINE H[ALPERN]

AUBERGER, GEORG
BERGAUER, CONRAD

AUBREY, EDMUND
IONS, EDMUND S.

AUBREY, FRANK
ATKINS, FRANCIS HENRY

AUCH, LORD
BATAILLE, GEORGES

AUCHTERLONIE, DOROTHY
GREEN, DOROTHY [A]

AUDAX
OAKSEY, JOHN GEOFFREY T.

PSEUDONYMS

AUDEN, RENEE
WEST, UTA

AUDIART
WAINHOUSE, AUSTYN

AUE, WALTER
CAMPULKA, WALTER

AUEL, JEAN M.
AUEL, JEAN MARIE

AUERBACH, ALINE B.
AUERBACH, ALINE SOPHIE B.

AUERBACH, BERTHOLD
BARUCH, MOSES

AUERBACH, RED
AUERBACH, ARNOLD JACOB

AUGE, BUD
AUGE, HENRY J. JR.

AUGUR
POLIAKOFF, VLADIMIR

AUGUST, ELIZABETH
WILHITE, BETTIE MARIE

AUGUST, JEREMY
SMITH, GEORGE H[ENRY]

AUGUST, JERRY
SMITH, GEORGE H[ENRY]

AUGUST, JOHN
DEVOTO, BERNARD AUGUSTINE

AUGUST, LEO
SEGALL, DON

AUGUST, MICHAEL
WILLIAMS, SIDNEY

AUGUSTA, CLARA
JONES, CLARA AUGUSTA

AUGUSTINE, ERICH
STOIL, MICHAEL JON

AUGUSTSON, ERNEST
RYDEN, ERNEST EDWIN

AUGUSTUS
LYNN, ELWYN AUGUSTUS

AUGUSTUS, ALBERT JR.
NUETZEL, CHARLES A.

AULD, PHILIP
BURNS, BERNARD

AULT, PHIL
AULT, PHILLIP HALLIDAY

AULT, ROZ
AULT, ROSIE SAIN

AUMBRY, ALAN
BAYLEY, BARRINGTON J.

AUNG, U. HTIN
AUNG, [MAUNG] HTIN

AUNT ADNA
DANA, MRS. J.M.

AUNT CHARLOTTE
YONGE, CHARLOTTE MARY

AUNT ESTE
DEIHL, EDNA GROFF

AUNT EVA
BILSKY, EVA

AUNT KATE
SOUTER, HELEN GREIG

AUNT MARY
LATHBURY, MARY A.
LOW, MARY

AUNT MAYSIE
JEFFREY-SMITH, MAY T.

AUNT PEGGY
WINTERBOTHAM, RUSS[EL] R.

AUNTIE DEB
COURY, LOUISE ANDRE

AUNTIE LOUISE
COURY, LOUISE ANDRE

AUNTIE MARGARET
KEDDIE, MARGARET MANSON

AUPREE, LAURA
BANDILLA, MARGRIT

AURA
GALE, WILLIAM

AURELIA
MACE, AURELIA GAY

AURELIUS
BOURNE, RANDOLPH S.
GARDNER, JOHN

AURY, DOMINIQUE
DECLOS, ANNE

AUSGUSTINE, MILDRED
BENSON, MILDRED [A] WIRT

AUSKELIS
KROGZEMJU, MIKUS

AUSTEN, CHARLOTTE
LEONE, ADELE

AUSTIN, BARBARA LESLIE
LINTON, BARBARA LESLIE

AUSTIN, BRETT
FLOREN, LEE

AUSTIN, FRANK
FAUST, FREDERICK S.

AUSTIN, HARRY
MCINERNY, RALPH [M]

AUSTIN, HUGH
EVANS, HUGH AUSTIN

AUSTIN, J.L.
AUSTIN, JOHN LANGSHAW

AUSTIN, JIM
REASONER, JAMES & LIVIA

AUSTIN, MARY
RICE, JANE

AUSTIN, MORTIMER
ROWE, JOHN GABRIEL

AUSTIN, R.G.
AUSTIN, NANCY LAMB
GELMAN, RITA GOLDEN

AUSTIN, RICHARD
MILAN, VICTOR [WOODWARD]

AUSTIN, STEPHEN
STEVENS, AUSTIN N.

AUSTIN, STUART
WIER, STUART AUSTIN

AUSTIN, TOM
ALTMAN, LINDA JACOBS

AUSTRAL
HOWARD-ELLIS, CHARLES

AUSTRALIA JANE
SHIRLEY, EDITH

AUSTWICK, JOHN
LEE, AUSTIN

AUTEUR, HILLARY
GOTTFRIED, THEODORE MARK

AUTH, TONY
AUTH, WILLIAM ANTHONY JR.

AUTHOR OF SPACE & SPIRIT
KENNEDY, R.A.

AUTHOR, WRECK OF GLAUCAS
SHEA, CORNELIUS

AUTRAN DOURADA, WALDOMIRO
DOURADA, [W.F.] AUTRAN

AUTREY, GENE
PATTEN, LEWIS B.

AVALLONE, MICHAEL ANGELO
AVALLONE, MICHAEL

AVALON, ARTHUR
WOODROFFE, JOHN

AVARIUS
STOLK, ANTONIE

AVE
POGGEL, MARY

AVEDIS, HOWARD
AVEDIS, HIKMET

AVELING, HUGH
AVELING, JOHN CEDRIC HUGH

AVELLANO, ALBERT
MARLOWE, DAN J.
NUSSBAUM, ALBERT F.

AVERILL, H.C.
SNOW, CHARLES H[ORACE]

AVERY, A.A.
MONTGOMERY, RUTHERFORD G.

PSEUDONYMS

AVERY, AL
MONTGOMERY, RUTHERFORD G.

AVERY, ANDERSON
WEATHERLY, MAX

AVERY, ANNE
HOLMBERG, ANNE

AVERY, JUNE
REES, JOAN

AVERY, LYNN
COLE, LOIS DWIGHT

AVERY, RICHARD
COOPER, EDMUND

AVI
WORTIS, EDWARD IRVING

AVICUS
FULLJAMES, HENRY J.

AVIRGAN, TONY
AVIRGAN, ANTHONY LANCE

AVON, MARGARET
KEATLEY, SHEILA MARJORIE

AVRELIN, M.
STEINBERG, AARON Z.

AVRETT, ROZ
AVRETT, ROSALIND CASE

AWBREY, ELIZABETH
BEACH, ELIZABETH

AWDRY, R.C.
CHARLES, RICHARD

AWLINSON, RICHARD
DENNING, TROY
CIENCIN, [MALCOLM] SCOTT
LOWDER, JAMES

AWOONOR, KOFI
AWOONOR-WILLIAMS, GEORGE

AWOONOR-WILLIAMS, GEORGE
AWOONOR, KOFI

AXE, SVEN
OLNERS, ARNE

AXE, SVERKER
OLNER, ARNE

AXE, WILLHELM
CRONSICE, AXEL WILHELM

AXELSSON, ERIK
KERFVE, AXEL

AXLER, JAMES
JAMES, LAURENCE

AXLER, LEO
LAZUTA, EUGENE MICHAEL

AXT, MARIA
NOTTKE-AXT, MARIA

AXTON, DAVID
KOONTZ, DEAN R.
MCCAMMON, ROBERT

AYARAUD, PIERRE
NARCEJAC, THOMAS

AYARS, REBECCA CAUDILL
CAUDILL, REBECCA

AYCLIFFE, JONATHAN
MACEOIN, DENIS

AYDY, CATHERINE
TENNANT, EMMA C.

AYERS, ROSE
GREENWOOD, LILLIAN B.

AYES, ANTHONY
SAMBROT, WILLIAM

AYES, WILLIAM
SAMBROT, WILLIAM

AYKROYD, DAN
AYKROYD, DANIEL EDWARD

AYLEN, ELISE
SCOTT, ELISE AYLEN

AYLMER, FELIX
JONES, FELIX EDWARD AYLM.

AYMES, ADAM
HARRIS, JULIE K.

AYNES, PAT EDITH
AYNES, EDITH ANNETTE

AYNSWORTH, CECIL
CHILDS, EDMUND BURTON

AYRAUD, PIERRE
NARCEJAC, THOMAS

AYRE, JESSICA
APPIGNANESI, LISA

AYRE, THORNTON
FEARN, JOHN RUSSELL

AYRES, ALFRED
OSMUN, THOMAS EMBLY

AYRES, ALISON
CARTER, ROBERT AYRES

AYRES, CAROLE BRIGGS
BRIGGS, CAROLE S.

AYRES, PAUL
AARONS, EDWARD S.

AYRES, RUBY M.
AYRES, RUBY MILDRED

AYRTON, MICHEL
AYRTON GOULD, MICHAEL

AYSCOUGH, JOHN
BICKERSTAFF-DREW, FRANCIS

AZAID
ZAIDENBERG, ARTHUR

AZNAVOUR, CHARLES
AZNAVOURIAN, VARENAGH

AZOOMANIAN, RAFFI
AZOOMANIAN, RALPH SARKIS

AZORAN
MARTINEZ RUIZ, LUIS

AZORIN
RUIZ, JOSE MARTINEZ

B.
GILBERT, WILLIAM S.

B.B.
HEADLAM, CUTHBERT M.
JOHNS, WILLIAM STABBACK
ROGERS, W.M.
WATKINS-PITCHFORD, D.J
WELLS, H.G.

B.H.W.
CARR-HARRIS, BERTHA HANNA

B.L.H.
HAIG, EMILY ALICE

B.L.T.
TAYLOR, BERT LESTON

B.V.
THOMSON, JAMES

BAASTAD, BABBIS FRIIS
FRII-BAASTAD, BABBIS E.

BAB
GILBERT, WILLIAM S.

BABB, JANICE BARBARA
BENTLEY, JANICE BABB

BABBIS, ELEANOR
FRII-BAASTAD, BABBIS E.

BABBITT, ROBERT
BANGS, ROBERT BABBITT

BABBLER
IVESTER, LLOYD J.
LLOYD, JOHN IVESTER

BABCOCK, FLORENCE
TOFTE, ARTHUR

BABCOCK, NICHOLAS
LEWIS, TOM

BABLI, HILLEL
RASCHGOLSKI, HILLEL

BABSON, MARION
STENSTREEM, RUTH

BACA, JOSE SANTIAGO
BACA, JIMMY SANTIAGO

BACALL, LAUREN
PERSKE, BETTY

BACH, BARBI
PUSCH, EDITH

BACH, CHRISTA
HORBACH, URSULA [S]

PSEUDONYMS

BACH, FRANK O.
HEYDA, ERNST

BACH, JEAN
GREIF, MARTIN

BACH, MICHAELA
LENTZ, MISCHA

BACH, P.D.Q.
SCHICKELE, PETER

BACH, PAUL
BAUMBACH, RUDOLF

BACH, PETER W.
KLUMBACH, PETER

BACHEM, BELE
BOHMER, GABRIELE RENATE

BACHHEIMER, NAOMI BARNETT
BARNETT, NAOMI

BACHMAN, RICHARD
KING, STEPHEN [EDWIN]

BACK-BACK
BROWN, KAY

BACKGAMMON, DAISY
MURRAY, JOHN F.

BACKUS, JIM
BACKUS, JAMES GILMORE

BACKX, PIETER
ASSELBERGS, WILLEM JAN M.

BACON, BESSIE
ALLEN, BESSIE BACON

BACON, J.D.
DODGE, JOSEPHINE DASKAM

BACON, JEREMY
READ, JAMES

BACON, JOAN CHASE
BOWDEN, JOAN CHASE

BACON, MARTHA
OLIVER-SMITH, MARTHA BAC.

BACON, PEGGY
BROOK, MARGARET F. BACON

BACOVIA, G.
VASILIU, GHEORGHI

BACOVIA, GEORGE
VASILIU, GEORGE

BADAWI, MUHAMMED MUSTAFA
BADAWI, MOHAMED MUSTAFA

BADDELEY, V.C. CLINTON
CLINTON-BADDELEY, V.C.

BADE, TOM
BADE, THOMAS MICHAEL

BADEN, KATIA
NEWBOLD, ANNA HECKSCHER

BADGER, RICHARD C.
BELL, ERIC TEMPLE

BADGER, WAYNE
MANTLING, RUNE

BAEDEKER, PEER
HACKE, ERNST MAX

BAEHR, PAT[RICIA]
BAEHR, PATRICIA GOEHNER

BAEN, JIM
BAEN, JAMES PATRICK

BAER, JILL
GILBERT, AGNES JOAN [S]

BAGARAG, SHIBLI
LAWLOR, PATRICK ANTHONY

BAGBY, GEORGE
STEIN, AARON MARC

BAGBY, STEPHEN
STEPHENS, CHARLES M.

BAGGE, BRYNJULF
GRAN, OYULV

BAGHIO'O, JEAN-LOUIS
JEAN-LOUIS, VICTOR

BAGLEY, DESMOND
BAGLEY, SIMON

BAGNI, GWEN
DUBOV, GWEN BAGNI

BAGRJANA, ELISAVETA
BELCHEVA, ELISAVETA

BAGRYANA, ELISAVETA
BELCHEVA, ELISAVETA

BAGSTER, HUBERT
TRUMPER, HUBERT BAGSTER

BAHAR, MALIK AL-SHU'ARA
BAHAR, MUHAMMAD TAQI

BAHITHAT AL-BADIYAH
NASIF, MALAK HIFNI

BAHL, FRANKLIN
GRAHAM, ROGER P.

BAHR, ROBERT
MOSKOWITZ, SAM

BAI JIEMING
BARME, GEREMIE

BAILEY, BETTY
HICKEY, MADELYN EASTLUND

BAILEY, D.R. SHACKLETON
SHACKLETON BAILEY, DAVID

BAILEY, DAVID R.
SHACKLETON BAILEY, DAVID

BAILEY, E.M.
BAILEY, ELIZABETH

BAILEY, GENE
JENNISON, JOHN WILLIAM

BAILEY, GUY
SIMPSON, KEITH

BAILEY, HILEA
MARTING, RUTH LENORE

BAILEY, MARTHA
RUHEN, CARL

BAILEY, MATILDA
RADFORD, RUTH LORAINE

BAILEY, ROBIN W.
BAILEY, ROBERT WAYNE

BAILEY, TEMPLE
BAILEY, IRENE T.

BAILEY, THOMAS
PARTRIDGE, EDWARD BELLAMY

BAILLEN
DELAY-TUBIANA, CLAUDE

BAILLEN, CLAUDE
DELAY-TUBIANA, CLAUDE

BAIN, BRUCE
FINDLATER, RICHARD

BAIN, TED
TUBB, E.C.

BAINBRIDGE, BRYANT
URNER, NATHAN DANE

BAINBRIDGE, CHUCK
FIELDHOUSE, WILLIAM [L]
LOWDER, CHRISTOPHER

BAINBRIDGE, SHARON
ROSE, SHARON

BAINES, LEW
RANDISI, ROBERT J.

BAINS, LARRY
SABIN, LOUIS

BAIRD, BILL
BAIRD, WILLIAM BRITTON

BAIRD, JACK
BAIRD, JOHN CHARLTON

BAIRD, MAUDE F.
ZIMMER, MAUDE FILES

BAIRD, WILHELMINA
HUTCHINSON, JOYCE

BAISCH, CRIS
BAISCH, CHRISTA

BAJOX, REDDY
BAJOG, GUNTHER

BAKALOV
TSERKOVSKI,TSANKO

BAKER, ACE
MILTON, PAUL R.

BAKER, ALLISON
CRUMBAKER, ALICE

PSEUDONYMS

BAKER, ARTHUR
GIDDINGS, ARTHUR F.

BAKER, ASA
DRESSER, DAVIS

BAKER, BETTY
VENTURO, BETTY LOU BAKER

BAKER, BILL
BAKER, CHARLES WILLIAM

BAKER, BOBBY
BAKER, ALFRED THORNTON
BAKER, ROBERT G.

BAKER, C. WILLIAM
BAKER, CHARLES WILLIAM

BAKER, CARLOTTA
SLOTTMAN, LEONA

BAKER, CHARLOTTE
MONTGOMERY, CHARLOTTE B.

BAKER, G.P.
BAKER, GORDON P.

BAKER, GILBERT
BAKER, JOHN GILBERT H.

BAKER, HUGH
DEUTSCH, HERMAN
HIGGINS, DONALD HUGH

BAKER, JIM
BAKER, JAMES W.

BAKER, JUDITH
BAKER, FRAN
NOBLE, JUDITH

BAKER, MAGGIE
JENSEN, MAGGIE

BAKER, MARC
BAKER, MARC[EIL GENEE K.]

BAKER, MARTIN L.
BOUNDS, SYDNEY J.

BAKER, MARY
BECKER, MARIETTA

BAKER, MIRIAM HAWTHORN
NYE, MIRIAM MAURINE H.B.

BAKER, PHILIP JOHN NOEL
NOEL-BAKER, PHILIP JOHN

BAKER, R.R.
BAKER, REGINALD ROBIN

BAKER, ROBIN
BAKER, REGINALD ROBIN

BAKER, SUSAN
HEBEL, PETER

BAKER, VIVIAN
DUENSING, JURGEN

BAKER, W. HOWARD
MCNEILLY, WILFRED G.

BAKHTIN, M.
BAKHTIN, MIKHAIL M.

BAKHTIN, M.M.
BAKHTIN, MIKHAIL M.

BAKKER, JIM
BAKKER, JAMES ORSEN

BAKKER, TAMMY FAYE
BAKKER, TAMARA FAYE

BALAAM
LAMB, GEOFFREY FREDERICK

BALAZS, BELA
BAUER, HERBERT

BALBOA, S.F.
ACKERMAN, FORREST J.

BALBUS
HUXLEY, JULIAN SORRELL

BALDRY, ENID
CITOVITCH, ENID

BALDWIN, ALEX
BUTTERWORTH, WILLIAM E.

BALDWIN, BASIL
RITCHIE, BALFOUR

BALDWIN, BATES
JENNINGS, JOHN [E]

BALDWIN, BEE
BALDWIN, BEATRICE LILLIAN

BALDWIN, BILL
BALDWIN, MERL WILLIAM JR.
BALDWIN, WILLIAM JR.

BALDWIN, DICK
RABORG, FREDERICK A.

BALDWIN, FAITH
CUTHRELL, FAITH B.

BALDWIN, GORDO
BALDWIN, GORDON C.

BALDWIN, MARGARET
WEIS, MARGARET [EDITH]

BALDWIN, MERL
BALDWIN, MERL WILLIAM JR.

BALDWIN, NED
BALDWIN, EDWARD ROBINSON

BALDWIN, REBECCA
CHAPPELL, HELEN

BALDWIN, STEVIE
THOMPSON, STEPHANIE PARIS

BALE, G.F.
COX, PATRICIA BALE
WELLBROCK, GLADYS BALE

BALES, JACK
BALES, JAMES E[DWARD]

BALFORT, NEIL
FANTHORPE, R.L.

BALFOUR, A.J.
BALFOUR, ARTHUR JAMES

BALFOUR, F.
PHILLIPS, WATTS

BALFOUR, GRANT
GRANT, JAMES MILLER

BALFOUR, HEARNDEN
BALFOUR, EVA
HEARNDEN, BERYL

BALFOUR, JOHN
MOORE, JAMES

BALFOUR, PATRICK
KINROSS, PATRICK LORD

BALKA
TOKOMBAEV, AALY

BALKA, MARIE
DE BALKANY, MARIE [R.Z.]

BALKEY, RITA
OLEYAR, RITA BALKEY

BALL, B.N.
BALL, BRIAN N[EVILLE]

BALL, BRIAN NEVILLE
KINSEY-JONES, BRIAN

BALL, KURT HERWARTH
DREETZ, JOACHIM

BALL, ZACHARY
JANAS, FRANCIS LEROY G.
MASTERS, KELLY R.

BALLANTINE, BILL
BALLANTINE, WILLIAM O.

BALLANTINE, JOHN
DA CRUZ, DANIEL JR.

BALLANTINE, LESLEY FROST
FROST, LESLEY

BALLANTYNE, GINA
BALLANTYNE, ADELAIDE

BALLARD, DEAN
WILKES-HUNTER, RICHARD

BALLARD, J.D.
MORRIS, CHARLES [S]

BALLARD, J.G.
BALLARD, JAMES GRAHAM

BALLARD, K.G.
ROTH, HOLLY

BALLARD, MORTON D.
LEOPOLD, NATHAN F.

BALLARD, P.D.
BALLARD, W. TODHUNTER

BALLARD, TODHTR. & PHOEBE
BALLARD, W. TODHUNTER

BALLARD, TODHUNTER
BALLARD, W. TODHUNTER

BALLARD, W.T.
BALLARD, W. TODHUNTER

BALLARD, WILLIS T.
BALLARD, W. TODHUNTER

BALLE, RICHARD
CICONE, JOHN

BALLEW, CHARLES
SNOW, CHARLES H[ORACE]

BALLINGER, BILL S.
BALLINGER, WILLIAM S.

BALLINGER, W.A.
BAKER, W.A. HOWARD
MCNEILLY, WILFRED G.

BALLINSLOE
TAYLOR, FREDERICK

BALMORE, CEDRIC
KODELPETER, HANS P.

BALONS, EARL
KORNBLUTH, C[YRIL] M.

BALSAMO, JOSE
MORALES CABRERA, PABLO

BALSDON, J.P.V.D.
BALSDON, [J.P.V.] DACRE

BALTEN, ERIC
LOFFELMANN, FRANZ

BALTHAZAR, ANGELO
FRITCH, CHARLES E.

BALTIMORE, J.
CATHERALL, ARTHUR

BALTUSHIS, IUOZAS
IUOZENAS, ALBERTUS

BALWERS, RENATO
LA BARRE, WESTON

BAMDAD, A.
SHAMLU, AHMAD

BAMM, PETER
EMMRICH, CURT [KURT]

BANA, DAN
WHITE, STANHOPE

BANANA, AZIJN
VAN KAMPEN, OSCAR

BANAT, D.R.
BRADBURY, RAY [DOUGLAS]

BANCK, LUIS
BECKMAN, GUNNEL

BANCROFT, F.
SLATER, FRANCIS CHARLOTTE

BANCROFT, IRIS
BANCROFT, IRIS M. NELSON

BANCROFT, JOHN
JENKINS, ALAN CHARLES

BANCROFT, LAURA
BAUM, L[YMAN] FRANK

BANCROFT, ROBERT
KIRSH, ROBERT R.

BANDI, PETER
BURKI, PETER

BANDOFF, HOPE
GUTHRIE, THOMAS ANSTEY

BANDOL, CHARLOTTE
HOLTSCHI-GRASSLE, CHARL.

BANDS, PAUL
NEWSONS, ALBERT

BANE, DIANA
DAY, DIANNE

BANERJEA, S.B.
VANDYOPADHYAYA, S.B.

BANG, GARRETT
BANG, MOLLY GARRETT

BANIS, V.J.
BANIS, VICTOR J[EROME]

BANIS, VICTOR
BANIS, VICTOR J[EROME]

BANJO
PATERSON, ANDREW BARTON

BANK, TED
BANK, THEODORE PAUL II

BANK, W. DANE
WILLIAMSON, HENRY

BANK-JENSEN
OTTESON, THEA TAUBER

BANKOFF, GEORGE ALEXIS
MILKOMANE, G. ALEXIS M.

BANKS, A. LESLIE
BANKS, ARTHUR LESLIE

BANKS, A.L.
BANKS, ARTHUR LESLIE

BANKS, ARCHIBALD
CRAWFURD, OSWALD J.F

BANKS, CLIFF
CRIDER, [ALLEN] BILL[Y]

BANKS, EDWARD
BRADBURY, RAY [DOUGLAS]

BANKS, JIMMY
BANKS, JAMES HOUSTON

BANKS, KELLEY
EUBANK, JAMES E.

BANKS, LYNNE REID
REID BANKS, LYNNE

BANKS, MICHAEL A.
GOULD, ALAN

BANKS, TAYLOR
BANKS, JANE

BANNATYNE, JACK
GASTON, WILLIAM JAMES

BANNER, ANGELA
MADDISON, ANGELA MARY

BANNER, CLEVE
KENT, JIM

BANNER, RACHEL
RODDY, LEE

BANNERMAN, DAVID
HAGBERG, DAVID [JAMES]

BANNERMAN, GENE
KELLEY, THOMAS P.

BANNERMAN, MARK
LEWING, ANTHONY CHARLES

BANNERMAN, ROLAND
HARTSTON, WILLIAM ROLAND

BANNION, DELLA
SELLERS, CONNIE LESLIE

BANNISDALE, V.E.
PORTAL, V.E.

BANNISTER, DON
BANNISTER, DONALD

BANNISTER, PAT
DAVIS, LOU ELLEN

BANNISTER, SALLY
PRATT, JAMES NORWOOD

BANNISTER, WILLIAM
GWINN, WILLIAM R.

BANNISTER, WYATT
JANSSON, GUNNAR
MANTLING, RUNE

BANNON, ANN
HOLMQUIST, ANN

BANNON, DON
ENGEL, LYLE KENYON

BANNON, MARK
KING, ALBERT

BANNON, PETER
DURST, PAUL

BANSHUCK, GREGO
GERNSBACK, HUGO

BANTI, ANNA
LOPRESTI, LUCIA LONGHI

BANTON, COY
NORWOOD, VICTOR [G.C.]

BANUMBER
BOZIC, SRETEN

BANZIGER, HANS
BAENZIGER, HANS

BAPTIST, JEAN
FECHTNER, WOLFGANG

BAPTIST, R. HERNEKIN
LEWIS, ETHELREDA

PSEUDONYMS

BAPU
KHARE, NARAYAN BHASKAR

BAR NER, R.
BRENNER, REEVE R[OBERT]

BAR, H.H.
LIEHR, HEINZ

BAR-NATAN, MOSHE
LOUVISH, MISHA

BARABAN, PETER
DOBLER, HANSFERDINAND

BARADA, BILL
BARADA, WILLIAM RICHARD

BARAK, MICHAEL
BAR-ZOHAR, MICHAEL

BARAKA, AMIDI
JONES, EVERETT LEROI

BARAKA, IMAMU AMIRI
JONES, [EVERETT] LEROI

BARAUDE, H.
TUPINIER, AUGUSTIN JOSEPH

BARAYON, RAMON SENDER
SENDER BARAYON, RAMON

BARBA JACOB, PORFIRIO
BENITEZ, MIGUEL ANGEL OS.

BARBARA
WRIGHT, MABEL OSGOOD

BARBARA, PAULO HENRIQUE
PINHEIRO, PAULO H.B.

BARBARE, RHOLF
VOLKOFF, VLADIMER

BARBAROSSA
SCOTT, JOHN

BARBARY, JACK
BEECHING, JACK

BARBARY, JAMES
BAUMANN, AMY [B] BEECHING

BARBE, TILL
BARTH, OSKAR

BARBEE, PHILLIPS
SHECKLEY, ROBERT

BARBELLION, W.N.P.
CUMMINGS, BRUCE FREDERICK

BARBER, ANTONIA
ANTHONY, BARBARA

BARBER, LEONORA
WING, JANET [JANICE]

BARBER, LINDA
GRAHAM-BARBER, LYNDA

BARBER, LYNDA
GRAHAM-BARBER, LYNDA

BARBER, LYNDA GRAHAM
GRAHAM-BARBER, LYNDA

BARBER, RED
BARBER, WALTER LANIER

BARBERA, JOE
BARBERA, JOSEPH ROLAND

BARBERIS
BARBERIS, FRANCO

BARBET, PIERRE
AVICE, CLAUDE-PIERRE

BARBETTE, JAY
SPICER, BART & BETTY COE

BARBOUR, ANNE
YIRKA, BARBARA

BARBOUR, A[NNA] MAYNARD
BARBOUR, ANNA MARY

BARBOUR, THOMAS L.
LESURE, THOMAS B.

BARBROOK, ALEC
BARBROOK, ALEXANDER THO.

BARBU, ION
BARBILIAN, DAN

BARCLAY, ALAN
TAIT, GEORGE B.

BARCLAY, ALEX
EGLI, WERNER J.

BARCLAY, ANN
GREIG-SMITH, JENNIFER M.

BARCLAY, BENNET
CROSSEN, KENDELL FOSTER

BARCLAY, BILL
MOFFATT, JAMES
MOORCOCK, MICHAEL

BARCLAY, GABRIEL
KORNBLUTH, C[YRIL] M.
WELLMAN, MANLY WADE

BARCLAY, ISABEL
DOBELL, ISABEL MARIAN B.

BARCLAY, JOHN
MATCHA, JACK

BARCLAY, LESTER
LIVINGSTONE, BERKELEY

BARCLAY, MARGUERITE
EVANS, MARGUERITE H.J.

BARCLAY, SUZANNE
BACKUS, CAROL SUZANNE

BARCLAY, VIRGINIA
MCDONNELL, VIRGINIA B.

BARCLAY, WILLIAM
MOORCOCK, MICHAEL
PLATT, CHARLES [M]

BARCLAY, WILLIAM EWART
MOORCOCK, MICHAEL

BARCYNSKA, COUNTESS
EVANS, MARGUERITE H.J.

BARD OF AVONDALE
JACOBS, HOWARD

BARDA, J.H.
BOCKEL, JOSEF HEINRICH

BARDEMEYER, GEERT
BRUNCLAIR, VICTOR J.

BARDSLEY, MICHAEL
NUTTALL, ANTHONY

BARDT, JULIUS
BURCHARDT, JULIUS

BARDWELL, DENVER
SAYERS, JAMES DENSON

BARETT, C.A.
FLATOW, CURTH

BARING, MAX
MESSENT, CHARLES

BARK, JULIUS
LUNDSTROM, EVERT
MOEN, JAN

BARKAS, J.L.
YAGER, JAN

BARKAS, JANET
YAGER, JAN

BARKEE, ASOUFF
STRUNG, NORMAN

BARKER, A.J.
BARKER, ARTHUR JAMES

BARKER, BECKY
BARKER, REBECCA

BARKER, BILL
BARKER, WILLIAM JOHN

BARKER, E.M.
BARKER, ELSA [M]

BARKER, FRED
KRAFT, ROBERT

BARKER, GRANVILLE
GRANVILLE-BARKER, HARLEY

BARKER, HARLEY GRANVILLE
GRANVILLE-BARKER, HARLEY

BARKER, M.A.R.
BARKER, MUHAMMED ABD

BARKER, MEGAN
LONGRIGG, ROGER [ERSKINE]

BARKER, SALLY
MCMURRY, SARAH L.

BARKER, WADE
MEYERS, RICHARD S.
SMOKE, STEPHEN L.

BARKIN, JILL
JOHNSON, SUSAN MARIE A.

BARKLEY, JESSICA
DEYOE, CORI L.

BARKTON, S. RUSH
BRAV, STANLEY R[OSENBAUM]

BARLEY, M.W.
BARLEY, MAURICE WILLMORE

BARLING, CHARLES
BARLING, MURIEL VERE MANT

BARLOW, GRANT
MEARES, LEONARD F.

BARLOW, ROBERT .H
LOVECRAFT, H[OWARD] P.

BARLOW, ROBERT O.
MEYER, HEINRICH

BARLOW, ROGER
LECKIE, ROBERT [H]
WEST, WALLACE

BARLOW, SANNA MORRISON
ROSSI, SANNA MORRISON B.

BARN OWL
HOWELLS, ROSCOE

BARNABAS
WEST, CHARLES CONVERSE

BARNABAS, BROTHER
O'NOLAN, BRIAN

BARNABUS
BLANDFORD, BRIAN E[RNEST]

BARNABY, HUGO
FITZPATRICK, ERNEST H.

BARNAO, JACK
WOOD, EDWARD JOHN

BARNARD, NANCY
HALE, SYLVIA

BARNARTO, BART
BELL, GEORGE
GARRETT, ALBERT EDWARD
JENNISON, JOHN WILLIAM
WILLIS, ERNEST LISTER H.

BARNAVAL, LOUIS
DE KAY, CHARLES

BARNE, KITTY
BARNE, MARION C.

BARNER, G.F.
BASNER, GERHARD

BARNES, ADRIENNE MARTINE
MARTINE-BARNES, ADRIENNE

BARNES, AL
BARNES, HALLY

BARNES, C.V.
YOUNG, CHESLEY VIRGINIA

BARNES, CHESLEY VIRGINIA
YOUNG, CHESLEY VIRGINIA

BARNES, DAVE
BARNES, ARTHUR K.
DAVIS, NORBERT

BARNES, E.W.
BAARNHEIM, E.W.

BARNES, EDWARD F.
MARQUIS, MAX

BARNES, ELIZABETH
ANDREW, AVERY THORNE

BARNES, JANE
CASEY, JANE BARNES

BARNES, JOHN
O'DONNELL, PETER

BARNES, LOUTRICIA
BARNES-SVARNEY, PATRICIA

BARNES, MARGARET CAMPBELL
ANSLE, DOROTHY PHOEBE

BARNES, MICHAEL
GORELL, LETHBRIDGE

BARNES, NANCY
ADAMS, HELEN SIMMONS

BARNES, PATRICIA
ABERCROMBIE, PATRICIA B.

BARNES, STEVEN
BARNES, STEPHEN EMORY

BARNES, SUSAN
CROSLAND, SUSAN [WATSON]

BARNETT, ADAM
FAST, JULIUS

BARNETT, C.H.
CAVE, HUGH B[ARNETT]

BARNETT, JILL
STADLER, JILL

BARNETT, JIM
BARNETT, JAMES MONROE

BARNETT, JOHN
STAGG, JOHN REGINALD

BARNETT, L. DAVID
LASCHEVER, BARNETT D.

BARNEWOLD, ERNST
NOLTING-HAUFF, WILHELM

BARNEY, HARRY
LOTTMAN, EILEEN [SHUBB]

BARNRIGHT, JULIA
BANCROFT, IRIS M. NELSON

BARNUM, BILL
GIBSON, WALTER B.

BARNUM, RICHARD
STRATEMEYER, EDWARD

BARNUM, THEODORE
STRATEMEYER, EDWARD

BARNWELL
ROOSEVELT, ROBERT BARNWLL

BARNWELL, J.O.
CARUSO, JOSEPH

BAROL, RANA
NADOLNI-S., BARBARA

BARON
RONZONE, BENJAMIN ANTHONY

BARON OF REMENHAM
THOMAS, [W] MILES [W]

BARON, ANTHONY
BAKER, AUGUSTUS

BARON, DAVID
PINTER, HAROLD

BARON, J.W.
KRAUZER, STEVEN M.

BARON, JOHN
BAKER, AUGUSTUS

BARON, NICK
CIENCIN, [MALCOLM] SCOTT

BARON, OTHELLO
FANTHORPE, R.L.

BARON, PAUL
LANDELLS, RICHARD

BARON, PETER
CLYDE, LEONARD WORSWICK C

BARON, WILLIE
BRYANT, BAIRD

BARON, WILLY
BYRON, BAIRD

BARON, [JOSEPH] ALEXANDER
BERNSTEIN, ALEC

BARONAS, ANTANAS
BARANAUKAS, ANTANAS

BARONE, MIKE
ALBERT, MARVIN H.

BARONESS VON S.
ZANGWILL, ISRAEL

BARONI, NICK
FODEN, FREDERICK [T]
GARRETT, ALBERT EDWARD
JENNISON, JOHN WILLIAM

BARR, CECIL
KAHANE, JACK

BARR, CHRISTOPHER
FISCHER, CLAUS
GAMBER, HANS

BARR, DENNIS
DENNY, FELIX

BARR, DENSIL NEVE
BUTTREY, DOUGLAS NORTON

BARR, DONALD
BARRETT, CHARLES LESLIE

BARR, ELIZABETH
EDWARDS, IRENE

BARR, JENE
ANTONACCI, ROBERT J.

BARR, JENE
COHEN, JENE BARR

BARR, MAYNARD
BARNARD, AMY

BARR, NAT
GODDARD, NORMAN M.

BARR, PAT
BARR, PATRICIA MIRIAM

BARR, ROBERT
SHARP, LUKE

BARR, TONY
BARR, ANTHONY

BARRACLOUGH, HOWARD
FELL, HOWARD BARRACLOUGH

BARRAN, RALPH
REUTER, JOSEF

BARRAN, ROLF
REUTER, RALPH

BARRAS SEER
WYLLIE, JAMES MCLEOD

BARRATT, G.R.V.
BARRATT, GLYNN [RICHARD]

BARRENO, MARIA ISABEL
MARTINS, MARIA ISABEL

BARRER, GERTRUDE
BARRER-RUSSELL, GERTRUDE

BARRETO, AFONSO HENRIQUE
DE LIMA BARRETO, ALFONSO

BARRETT, CHARLES
MCEWAN, MARCIA

BARRETT, G.J.
BARRETT, GEOFFREY JOHN

BARRETT, G.R.
BARRATT, GLYNN [RICHARD]

BARRETT, JEAN
ROGERS, ROBERT LEE

BARRETT, JUDI
BARRETT, JUDITH

BARRETT, MARY
NUTTING, MARY OLIVIA

BARRETT, MAYE
BARRETT, MAX

BARRETT, MONTE
BARRETT, MONTGOMERY

BARRETT, N.S.
BARRETT, NORMAN [S]

BARRETT, RAINA
KELLY, PAULINE AGNES

BARRETTON, GRANDALL
GARRETT, RANDALL [P]

BARRIC, WYNNE
PULLAN, RU

BARRICK, W.
WEBB, RICHARD WILSON
WHEELER, HUGH C.

BARRIE, HESTER
HECTOR, BARBARA

BARRIE, JANE
SAVAGE, MILDRED [SPITZ]
WOODFORD, [I] CECIL

BARRIE, MONICA
WIND, DAVID MILTON

BARRIE, SUSAN
POLLOCK, IDA

BARRIEN, EDITH HEAL
HEAL, EDITH

BARRING, GEO
BURMESTER, ALBERT KONRAD

BARRINGTON, E.
BECK, ELIZA LOUISA M.

BARRINGTON, F. CLINTON
LEWIS, JULIUS WARREN

BARRINGTON, H.W.
BRANNON, WILLIAM T.

BARRINGTON, JOHN
BROWNJOHN, ALAN

BARRINGTON, JOHN H.
HARVEY, JOHN HENRY

BARRINGTON, MAURICE
BROGAN, DENNIS WILLIAM

BARRINGTON, MICHAEL
BAYLEY, BARRINGTON J.
MOORCOCK, MICHAEL

BARRINGTON, NICHOLAS
WHITTINGTON-EGAN, RICHARD

BARRINGTON, P.V.
BARLING, MURIEL VERE MANT

BARRINGTON, PAMELA
BARLING, MURIEL VERE MANT

BARRISTER, A.
HILL, MAVIS

BARROL, GRADY
BOGRAD, LARRY

BARRON, BOBBI
LIEBERMAN, ROBERTA

BARRON, ED
BERNHARDT, CLYDE EDRIC B.

BARRON, ELIZABETH
TWADDLE, SUSAN BOWDEN

BARRON, HUGH
HIRSCHFELD, BURT

BARRON, LOUIE
THOROLD, WILLIAM JAMES

BARRON, RUSTY
HEVELIN, JAMES

BARROW, GEORGE
RUCHLIS, HYMAN

BARROW, JACKSON
WEINSTEIN, LOUIS

BARROW, PAMELA
HOWARTH, PAMELA

BARROW, RHODA
LEDERER, RHODA C.

BARROW, WILLIAM
FULLER, HOYT [W]

BARROWS, PHILIP
TUITE, DANIEL R.

BARROWS, R.M.
BARROWS, [RUTH] MARJORIE

BARRY
HUMPHRIES, BARRY

BARRY, ALICE MONTGOMERY
NORTON, ALICE WHITSON

BARRY, ANDREA
BARTLE, HANIA ANNETTE

BARRY, ANN
BYERS, AMY IRENE

BARRY, B.X.
GILES, RAY A.

BARRY, CHARLES
BRYSON, CHARLES

BARRY, DAN
ATKINS, JOHN RINGROSE
HARRISON, HARRY

BARRY, EILEEN
WALKER, EMILY KATHLEEN

BARRY, J.A.
BARRY, JOHN ARTHUR

BARRY, JAMES
FISCHER, CLAUS

BARRY, JOCELYN
BOWDEN, JEAN

BARRY, JOE
LAKE, JOE BARRY

BARRY, JONATHAN
STRIEBER, [LOUIS] WHITLEY

BARRY, KEN
HAAS, BENJAMIN LEOPOLD

BARRY, KEVIN
LAFFAN, KEVIN [BARRY]

BARRY, MIKE
MALZBERG, BARRY [N]

PSEUDONYMS

BARRY, NORA
FUTCHER, JANE

BARRY, RAY
HUGHES, DENNIS [TALBOT]

BARRY, ROLAND
BULL, BRUNO HORST

BARRY, ROXANA
ROBINSON, ROXANA [BARRY]

BARRY, SPRANGER
KAUFFMANN, STANLEY

BARRY, TOM
DONOHUE, HAL

BARRYMORE, JOHN
KUHNERT, JORG

BARSHOVSKY, PHILIP
KAPLAN, M.M.

BARSTEAD, HARRY
JARDINE, JACK OWEN

BART, JAKUB
CIZINSKI, JAKUB

BARTEK, E.J.
BARTOSIEWICZ, EDWARD JOHN

BARTEL, PHILIP JACQUES
KAPLAN, M.M.

BARTH, LOIS
FREIHOFER, LOIS DIANE

BARTHOLOMEW, BART
BARTHOLOMEW, FRANK H.

BARTHOLOMEW, JEAN
BEATTY, PATRICIA [R]

BARTHOLOMEW, JOHN ERIC
MORECAMBE, ERIC

BARTIMEUS
DE COSTA RITCHIE, LEWIS A

BARTLETT, BILLIE
BARTLETT, MARIE

BARTLETT, DAVID
MASON, MADELEINE

BARTLETT, F.C.
BARTLETT, FREDERIC CHARLE

BARTLETT, JANICE
JOHNSON, JANICE

BARTLETT, JEAN ANNE
LUSTBERG, JEAN ANNE

BARTLETT, KATHLEEN
PAINE, LAURAN BOSWORTH

BARTLETT, KAY
BACZEWSKI, JANICE K.J.

BARTLETT, LAURA
BAUM, L[YMAN] FRANK

BARTLETT, NANCY
STRONG, CHARLES STANLEY

BARTLETT, PHILIP A.
STRATEMEYER, EDWARD

BARTLEY, LEIGH
RIKER, LEIGH

BARTOLOME, JOHAN
JONGH, EDWARD A. DE

BARTON, BARRY
HOGAN, ROBERT J[ASPER]

BARTON, BEVERLY
BEAVER, BEVERLY

BARTON, BYRON
VARTANIAN, BYRON

BARTON, EARL [ERLE]
FANTHORPE, R.L.

BARTON, FANNY M.
BUTTS, MRS. M.F.

BARTON, GARY
EDSALL, SCHUYLER G.

BARTON, GIL
BAJOG, GUNTHER

BARTON, J.A.G.
DUTT, SHOSHER CHUNDER

BARTON, J.C.
GLASBY, JOHN S.

BARTON, JACK
CHADWICK, JOSEPH L.

BARTON, JILL
BARTON, JILLIAN

BARTON, JON
HARVEY, JOHN [BARTON]

BARTON, LEE
FANTHORPE, R.L.

BARTON, MAY
ADAMS, HARRIET S.

BARTON, MAY HOLLIS
STRATEMEYER, EDWARD

BARTON, PAT
ARROWSMITH, PAT

BARTON, S.W.
WHALEY, BARTON STEWART

BARTON, TEX
HEMING, JOHN WINTON

BARTON, TONY
MCKEAG, ERNEST LIONEL

BARTRAM, GEORGE
CAMERON, KENNETH M.

BARTRAM, NOEL
BOSTON, NOEL

BARWICK, JAMES
BARWICK, TONY
JAMES, DONALD

BARWIN, F.L.
BARTHEL-WINKLER, FRITZ
BARTHEL-WINKLER, LISA

BARWOOD, LEE
SATTER, MARLENE Y.

BAS, RUTGER
RUTGERS VAN DER LOEFF, AN

BASARRI
EIZMENDI, INAKI

BASH, IAKOV VASILEVICH
BASHMAK, IAKOV VASILEVICH

BASHEVIS, ISAAC
SINGER, ISAAC BASHEVIS

BASHO
MATSUO, BASHO

BASIE, COUNT
BASIE, WILLIAM JAMES

BASILEA, [MOTHER]
SCHLINK, KLARA

BASIT, M.A.
BASIT, ABDUL

BASON, FRED
BASON, FREDERICK THOMAS

BASS, ALTHEA
BASS, ALTHA LEAH B.

BASS, EDUARD
SCHMIDT, EDUARD

BASS, FRANK
PEEPLES, SAMUEL A.

BASS, KINGSLEY B. JR.
BULLINS, ED

BASS, T.J.
BASSLER, THOMAS J.

BASSERMANN, LUJO
SCHREIBER, HERMANN O.L.

BASSETT, JACK
ROWLAND, DONALD S.

BASSETT, JOHN KEITH
KEATING, LAWRENCE A.

BASSETT, MARNIE
BASSETT, FLORA MARJORIE

BASSNETT-MCGUIRE, SUSAN
BASSNETT, SUSAN E[DNA]

BASTABLE, ROBERT
BARNARD, ROBERT

BASTOS, AUGUSTO [A] ROA
ROA BASTOS, AUGUSTO [A]

BATCHELOR, PAULA
LANSBERRY, PAULA VIVIEN

BATCHELOR, REG.
PAINE, LAURAN BOSWORTH

PSEUDONYMS

BATEMAN, ROBERT
CURRUTHERS, MOYES

BATES SU
BATES, SUSANNAH VACELLA

BATES, BETTY
BATES, ELIZABETH

BATES, DAISY
O'DWYER, DAISY MAY

BATES, H.E.
BATES, HERBERT ERNEST

BATES, JENNY
SEGER, MAURA

BATES, NORMAN
SELLERS, CONNIE LESLIE
WOOD, EDWARD D. JR.

BATESON, F.W.
BATESON, FREDERIK WILSE

BATH, KARL
SANDBERG, ALGOT GUSTAF O.

BATHERMAN, MURIEL
SHELDON, MURIEL

BATHURST, SHEILA
SULLIVAN, SHEILA

BATIS, HUBERTO
MARTINEZ, HUBERTO BATIS

BATISTA, FULGENCIO
BATISTA Y ZALDIVAR, FULG.

BATRA, RAVI
BATRA, RAVEENDRA N[ATH]

BATTEN, JOYCE MORTIMER
MANKOWSKA, JOYCE KELLS M.

BATTIN, B.W.
BATTIN, BRINTON WARNER

BATTIN, BUCK
BATTIN, BRINTON WARNER

BATTISCOMBE, E. GEORGINA
BATTISCOMBE, ESTHER G.H.

BATTLE, FELIX
LEVIN, BERNARD

BATTLES, EDITH
BATTLES, ROXY EDITH

BAUCHART
CAMUS, ALBERT

BAUDUC, R.
SEGRE, DAN V[ITTORIO]

BAUER, BERT
SCHAUER, HERBERT

BAUER, C.T.
BURGDORF, KARL-ULRICH

BAUER, HEDI
BAUER, DIETER

BAUER, MARIA AGNES
KASBAUER, SIXTA

BAUER, PAMELA
MUELBAUER, PAMELA

BAUER, WRIGHT
HOBART, GEORGE VERE

BAUM, ERNST
BIRNBAUM, ERNST

BAUM, L. FRANK
SAMPSON, EMMA K. SPEED
THOMPSON, RUTH PLUMLY

BAUM, LOREN
HINTZ, LOREN E.

BAUM, LOUIS F.
BAUM, L[YMAN] FRANK

BAUMANN, BODO
BERNS, ULRICH

BAUME, ERIC
BAUME, FREDERICK EHREN.

BAUMFYLDE, WALTER
BEVAN, TOM

BAUMI, FRANZ H.
BAEUMI, FRANZ H[EINRICH]

BAUMRIN, STEFAN
BAUMRIN, BERNARD H.

BAWDEN, NINA
KARK, NINA MARY MABEY

BAWLY,DAN
BAVLY, DAN [ABRAHAM]

BAWN, MARY
WRIGHT, MARY PAMELA

BAX
BAXTER, GORDON F. JR.

BAX, ROGER
WINTERTON, PAUL

BAXTER, DR.
KRAFT, ROBERT

BAXTER, ELIZABETH
HOLLAND, ELIZABETH

BAXTER, GEORGE OWEN
FAUST, FREDERICK S.

BAXTER, GILLIAN
HIRST, GILLIAN JOSE C.

BAXTER, GREGORY
DE BANZIE, ERIC
RESSICH, JOHN S.M.

BAXTER, HAZEL
ROWLAND, DONALD S.

BAXTER, J.K.
BOUNDS, SYDNEY J.
GLASBY, JOHN S.

BAXTER, JOHN
HUNT, E. HOWARD

BAXTER, JUDY
HAYDON, JUNE
SIMPSON, JUDITH [JUDY]

BAXTER, MARK
ANTON, UWE
APPEL, WALTER
HARY, WILFRIED A.
HEBEL, PETER
HELGATH, FRANC
MAURER, KURT
RAHN, WOLFGANG
VON KOBLINSKI, HANS-JOACH

BAXTER, MIKE
BAXTER, MICHAEL JOHN

BAXTER, OLIVE
EASTWOOD, HELEN B.

BAXTER, PAUL
MADSEN, BORGE

BAXTER, PHYLLIS
WALLMANN, JEFFREY M.

BAXTER, ROBERT
CAIN, NICHOLAS [COLORADO]

BAXTER, S.M.
BAXTER, STEPHEN

BAXTER, S.V.
NORWOOD, VICTOR [G.C.]

BAXTER, SHANE
NORWOOD, VICTOR [G.C.]

BAXTER, SHANE V.
NORWOOD, VICTOR [G.C.]

BAXTER, STEVE
BAXTER, STEPHEN

BAXTER, VALERIE
MEYNELL, LAURENCE WALTER

BAXTER, YOUNG
JAMES, W.I.

BAXTER, ZENO
BAXTER, ZENOBIA

BAY LAUREL, ALICIA
LAUREL, ALICIA BAY

BAYARD
OTTARSON, FRANKLIN A.

BAYARD, FRED
CAMPBELL, M.E. BAIRD
JANSEN, JOHANNA FREDERIKA

BAYARD, JEAN-PIERRE
BAJARD, JEAN

BAYER, ELEANOR
PERRY, ELEANOR [R.B.]

BAYER, HAROLD
GREGG, ANDREW K.

BAYER, M. DEAN
LANSDALE, JOE R.

PSEUDONYMS

BAYER, OLIVER WELD
BAYER, ELEANORE & LEO
PERRY, ELEANOR [R.B.]

BAYER, SANDRA L.
BAYER, SANDRA LEE

BAYER, SANDY
BAYER, SANDRA LEE

BAYER, SYLVIA
GLASSCO, JOHN [S]

BAYER-BERENBAUM, LINDA
BAYER, LINDA

BAYES, KAY
LAZENBY, NORMAN A.

BAYLE, MONSIEUR
DE PATOT, SIMON TYSSOT

BAYLEBRIDGE, WILLIAM
BLOCKSIDGE, CHARLES W.

BAYLISS, J.C.
BAYLISS, JOHN CLIFFORD

BAYLISS, TIMOTHY
BAYBARS, TANER

BAYNE, PETER
BRINDLE, ERNEST

BAYNE, SPENCER
SPENCER, FLOYD & PAULA

BAYNES, JACK
FOWLER, BERTRAM B.

BAYNTON, BARBARA
FRATER, BARBARA LAWRENCE

BAYROS
BAYER, OSWALD GEORG

BAZAGONOV, M.S.
STOE, M.

BAZIN, HERVE
HERVE-BAZIN, JEAN PIERRE

BEA, EMPTY
BABCOCK, MAURICE P.

BEACH, CHARLES
REID, [THOMAS] MAYNE

BEACH, CHARLES AMORY
STRATEMEYER, EDWARD

BEACH, CHARLES S.
REID, [THOMAS] MAYNE

BEACH, LYNN
LANCE, KATHRYN

BEACH, TOM
HARRIS, LAURENCE MARK

BEACHCOMBER
HUBBARD, L. RON
LEWIS, DOMINIC BEVAN W.
MORTON, JOHN BINGHAM
WYNDHAM LEWIS, D.B.

BEADLE, G.W.
BEADLE, GEORGE W[ELLS]

BEAGLEHOLE, J.C.
BEAGLEHOLE, JOHN CAWTE

BEAHAN, MICHAEL
SHNAYERSON, MICHAEL

BEAL, NICK
ACKERMAN, FORREST J.

BEALE, ANNE
TREMAINE, F. ORLIN

BEAMISH, NOEL DE VIC
BEAMISH, ANNIE O'MEARA

BEAMISH, TUFTON VICTOR H.
CHELWOOD, TUFTON VICTOR H

BEAN, AMELIA
BEAN, MYRTLE AMELIA

BEAN, K.
BADGER, JOSEPH E.

BEAN, NORMAN
BURROUGHS, EDGAR RICE

BEANEY, JAN
UDALL, JAN BEANEY

BEANEY, JANE
UDALL, JAN BEANEY

BEAR, I.D.
DOUGLASS, PERCIVAL IAN

BEAR, JOE
SELLERS, CONNIE LESLIE

BEARDEN, ANTHONY
LINEBARGER, PAUL M.A.

BEARDMORE, CEDRIC
BEARDMORE, GEORGE CEDRIC

BEARNE, C.G.
BEARNE, COLIN GERALD

BEATON, ANNE
WASHINGTON, M. BEAUCHAMP

BEATON, CHRIS
ADAMSON, IAIAN BEATON

BEATON, GEORGE
BRENAN, EDWARD FITZGERALD

BEATON, M.C.
CHESNEY, MARION G.

BEATTY, BADEN
CASSON, FREDERICK

BEATTY, ELIZABETH
HOLLOWAY, ELIZABETH BRAG.

BEATTY, WARREN
BEATY, WARREN

BEATUS RHENANUS
BIRT, THEODOR

BEATY, SHIRLEY MACLEAN
MACLAINE, SHIRLEY

BEAUCHAMP, KATHLEEN
MANSFIELD, KATHERINE

BEAUCHAMP, LOREN
SILVERBERG, ROBERT

BEAUCHAMP, PAT
WASHINGTON, M. BEAUCHAMP

BEAUCLERK, HELEN
BELLINGHAM, HELEN MARY D.

BEAUFITZ, WILLIAM
CRITCHLEY, JULIAN [M.G.]

BEAUFORD, TOM
SLIGO, JOHN

BEAUFORT, JANE
POLLOCK, IDA

BEAUFORT, SEAN
KNIEFEL, HANNS

BEAUJON, PAUL
WARDE, BEATRICE L.

BEAUMONT, ANNE
PYATT, ROSINA

BEAUMONT, AVERIL
HUNT, MARGARET RAINE

BEAUMONT, BENCHLEY
VILES, WALTER

BEAUMONT, BEVERLY
VON BLOCK, SYLVIA

BEAUMONT, CHARLES
NUTT, CHARLES LEROY

BEAUMONT, E.J.
BEAUMONT, CHARLES

BEAUMONT, E.T
BEAUMONT, CHARLES

BEAUMONT, JESS
GREENOP, FRANK S.

BEAUMONT, MARIE
LINSLEY, JUDITH
RIENSTRA, ELLEN

BEAUMONT, NINA
GETTLER, NINA

BEAUMONT, WALT
FITTOCK, R.J.

BECHDOLT, JACK
BECHDOLT, JOHN ERNEST

BECHHOFER, C.E.
ROBERTS, CARL [E.B.]

BECHKO, P.A.
BECHKO, PEGGY ANNE

BECK, ALLEN
CAVE, HUGH B[ARNETT]

BECK, CHRISTOPHER
BRIDGES, THOMAS CHARLES

PSEUDONYMS

BECK, DOC
BECK, EARL CLIFTON

BECK, HARRY
PAINE, LAURAN BOSWORTH

BECK, JOHN F.
BECK, FLORIAN

BECK, K.K.
MARRIS, KATHERINE

BECK, LILY ADAMS
BECK, ELIZA LOUISA M.

BECK, M. v. d.
BECKER, MARIETTA

BECK, PHINEAS
CHAMBERLAIN, SAMUEL

BECKE, LOUIS
BECKE, GEORGE LEWIS

BECKER, BILL
BECKER, WILLIAM

BECKER, FLORENCE
LENNON, FLORENCE BECKER

BECKER, FRANZISKA
BECKER, ROLLY

BECKER, FRECKLE
BECKER, CARL EDWARD C.P.

BECKER, KLAUS
KOCH, KURT EMIL

BECKER, OLGA
FRANK, RUDOLF

BECKER, TED
BECKER, THEODORE L[EWIS]

BECKET, HENRY S.A.
GOULDEN, JOSEPH C. [JR.]

BECKET, LAVINIA
COURSE, PAMELA MARY

BECKETT, MARK
TRUMAN, MARCUS GEORGE

BECKMAN, KAJ
BECKMAN, KARIN

BECKMAN, PATTI
BOECKMAN, PATTI & CHARLES

BECKMAN, ROSS
DEY, FREDERIC VAN R.
FAIRDE, DONALD

BECKSTRAT, BERND
BECKER, BERND

BECKWITH, LILLIAN
COMBER, LILLIAN

BECMAN, ROSS
FEARING, KENNETH

BEDARD, MICHELLE
FINNIGAN, JOAN
MACKENZIE, JOAN

BEDDOE, ELLARUTH
ELKINS, ELLA RUTH

BEDE, ANDREW
BEHA, ERNEST

BEDE, CUTHBERT
BRADLEY, EDWARD

BEDFORD, A.N.
WATSON, JANE WERNER

BEDFORD, ANN
REES, JOAN

BEDFORD, ANNIE NORTH
WATSON, JANE WERNER

BEDFORD, DEBBIE
BEDFORD, DEBORAH LYNN

BEDFORD, DONALD F.
BEDFORD-JONES, HENRY
FEARING, KENNETH
FRIEDE, DONALD

BEDFORD, JOHN
HASTINGS, PHYLLIS DORA H.
WILTSHIRE, DAVID

BEDFORD, KENNETH
PAINE, LAURAN BOSWORTH

BEDFORD, SIDNEY
MEYNELL, LAURENCE WALTER

BEDFORD-FORAN, CAPT.
BEDFORD-JONES, HENRY
FORAN, WILLIAM ROBERT

BEDIAKO, K.A.
KONADU, SAMUEL ASARE

BEDIAKO, KWABENA ASARE
KONADU, SAMUEL ASARE

BEDNARIK, CHUCK
BEDNARIK, CHARLES PHILIP

BEDNY, DEMYAN
PRIDVOROV, EFIM ALEXEYE.

BEDOYERE, MICHAEL DE LA
DE LA BEDOYERE, MICHAEL

BEE, JAY
BRAINERD, JOHN WHITING

BEEBE, B.F.
JOHNSON, BURDETTA FAYE

BEEBY, G.S.
BEEBY, GEORGE STEPHENSON

BEECH, MARGARET
BARCLAY, VERA C.

BEECH, WEB
BUTTERWORTH, WILLIAM E.

BEECHAM, ALICE
TUBB, E.C.

BEECHCROFT, T.O.
BEECHCROFT, THOMAS OWEN

BEECHCROFT, WILLIAM
HALLSTEAD, WILLIAM FINN

BEECHER, LEE
MULLEN, STANLEY

BEECHER, STANLEY
MULLEN, STANLEY

BEECHUM, JUSTIN
WINTLE, JUSTIN [B]

BEECKMAN, ROSS
DEY, FREDERIC VAN R.
FAIRDE, DONALD

BEEDING, FRANCIS
PALMER, JOHN LESLIE
SAUNDERS, HILARY A.

BEEHAN, JACK ROGERS
JAMIESON, LELAND S.

BEELER, JANET
SHAW, JANET

BEELZEBUB
GOODRICH, HENRY NEWTON

BEER, LISL
BEER, ELOISE C.S.

BEER, VIC
BIRD, VIVIAN

BEESON
VESTAL, HERMAN BEESON

BEETON, MAX
REDDING, ROBERT HULL

BEETZ, DIETMAR
BEETZ, DIETER

BEG, TORAN
MCKILLOP, NORMAN

BEGG, KEN
MCCLURE, KEN

BEGIN, MENAHEM
BEGIN, MENACHIM

BEHAN, LESLIE
GOTTFRIED, THEODORE MARK

BEHM, BILL
BEHM, WILHELM

BEHM, JONNY
JOOST, ELISABETH

BEHREND, MARGARETE
ARNOLD, WALTER

BEHRING, SYLVIA
LENTZ, MISCHA

BEHRINGER, SABINE
ERTL, ANNELIESE

BEHRMAN, LUCY CREEVEY
CREEVEY, LUCY E.

BEIGEL, ERIKA
IBERER, ERIKA

PSEUDONYMS

BEISTLE, SHIRLEY
CLIMO, SHIRLEY

BEJANOVA, LILIANA
BEROV, LILI

BEKAL, WALTHER
KABEL, WALTHER

BEKESSY, JEAN
BEKESSY, JANOS

BEKKER, JENS
GUNTHER, HEINZ

BEKKER, PIROW
BEKKER, PETRUS JACOBUS

BEL, W.K.
KABEL, WALTHER

BELANEY, GEORGE STANFIELD
BELANEY, ARCHIBALD S.

BELBIN, HARRY
GARRISH, HAROLD J.

BELCAMPO
SCHONFELD, DR. HERMAN
WICHERS, HERMAN P. SCHON.

BELCHEM, DAVID
BELCHEM, RONALD F.

BELDEN, GAIL
BELDEN, LOUISE CONWAY

BELDONE, PHIL "CHEECH"
ELLISON, HARLAN

BELENO
AZUELO, MARIANO

BELFORT, SOPHIE
AUSPITZ, KATE

BELIAYEV, A.
BELYAEV, ALEXANDER

BELKA, W.
KABEL, WALTHER

BELKA, WILLI
KABEL, WALTHER

BELKNAP, B.H.
ELLIS, EDWARD S.

BELKNAP, BOYNTON
ELLIS, EDWARD S.

BELKNAP, BOYNTON, MD
ELLIS, EDWARD S.

BELL, ACTON
BRONTE, ANN

BELL, BETTY
BELL, LORNA BEATRICE

BELL, C.F. MOBERLY
BELL, CHARLES F.M.

BELL, CAROL
FLAVELL, CAROL WILLSEY B.

BELL, CAROLYN
RIGONI, ORLANDO JOSEPH

BELL, CATHERINE
WEIR, ROSEMARY

BELL, COBDEN
BELTON-COBB, GEOFFREY

BELL, COLIN KANE
BELL, COLIN ALEXANDER

BELL, CURRER
BRONTE, CHARLOTTE

BELL, ELLIS
BRONTE, EMILY JANE

BELL, EMERSON
PATTEN, WILLIAM GEORGE
STRATEMEYER, EDWARD

BELL, EMILY MARY
CASON, MABEL EARP

BELL, FRANK
BENSON, MILDRED [A] WIRT

BELL, GEORGE
MAHAFFEY, BEA
PALMER, RAYMOND A.

BELL, GEORGIANNA
RUNDLE, ANNE

BELL, GINA
BALZANO, JEANNE KOPPEL

BELL, J. FREEMAN
ZANGWILL, ISRAEL

BELL, JANET
CLYMER, ELEANOR

BELL, JOHN
JOHNSON, VICTOR HUGO

BELL, JOSEPHINE
BALL, DORIS BELL C.

BELL, MARGARET
SAUNDERS, MARGARET BELL

BELL, MARISA
KLINGLER, MARIA

BELL, NEIL
CRITTEN, STEPHEN HENRY
SOUTHWOLD, STEPHEN

BELL, OTTO
PFEFFER, HEINRICH

BELL, R.C.
BELL, ROBERT CHARLES

BELL, RAMSAY
COOPER, AGNES ROSEMARY
WELLER, MARY E.P.

BELL, ROBIN
JONES, JOHN FINBAR

BELL, STEVE
SCHMOCK, HELEN H.

BELL, THORNTON
FANTHORPE, R.L.
MANSFIELD, HARRY O.

BELL, W.K.
KABEL, WALTHER

BELL, W.L.D.
MENCKEN, HENRY LOUIS

BELL, [PROF] LEO D.
LEBO, DELL

BELL-ZANO, GINA
BALZANO, JEANNE KOPPEL

BELLAIRS, GEORGE
BLUNDELL, HAROLD

BELLAMY, ATWOOD C.
MENCKEN, HENRY LOUIS

BELLAMY, HARMON
BLOOM, HERMAN IRVING

BELLAMY, JEAN
KETCHUM, PHILIP L.

BELLE, CLARA
LOGAN, OLIVE

BELLEM, R.L.
BELLEM, ROBERT LESLIE

BELLIN, EDWARD
KUTTNER, HENRY
MICHEL, JOHN B.
MOORE, CATHERINE LUCILLE

BELLINI, SIGNOR
SMITH, JOSHUA

BELLMAN, WALTER
BARRETT, HUGH G.

BELLMANN, DIETER
BELLMANN, JOHANN DIEDRICH

BELLMORE, DON
SMITH, GEORGE H[ENRY]

BELLOC, HILAIRE
BELLOC, [J] HILARY [P]

BELLOC, HILARY
BELLOC, [J] HILARY [P]

BELLOC, JOSEPH PETER H.
BELLOC, [J] HILAIRE [P]

BELLOC, JOSEPH PIERRE H.
BELLOC, [J] HILAIRE [P]

BELLOC, M.A.
LOWNDES, MARIE [A] BELLOC

BELLOC-LOWNDES, MRS.
LOWNDES, MARIE [A] BELLOC

BELLOCQ, LOUISE
BOUDAT, MARIE-LOUISE

BELLONY-REWALD, ALICE
BELLONY, ALICE

BELLWOOD, HERBERT
PATTEN, WILLIAM GEORGE

PSEUDONYMS

BELMONT, BOB
REYNOLDS, DALLAS MCCORD

BELMONT, JACK
NUETZEL, CHARLES A.

BELMONT, KATHERYN [KATE]
TERRITO, MARY JO

BELMONT, R.
JENNISON, JOHN WILLIAM

BELROD-FORAN, CAPT.
FORAN, WILLIAM ROBERT

BELVEDERE, LEE
GRAYLAND, VALERIE MERLE

BELY, ANDREY
BUGAYEV, BORIS N.

BELYEV, A.
BELYAEV, ALEXANDER

BELYI, ANDREI
BUGAYEV, BORIS N.

BEMISTER, HENRY
BARRETT, HARRY B.

BEN AMI
RABINOVITCH, M.

BEN AVRAHAM, CHOFETZ C.
PICKERING, STEPHEN

BEN CHAIM
KAHN, YITZHAK

BEN HORAV, NAPTHALI
KREVITSKY, NATHANIEL I.

BEN HORIN, MEIR
SCHIFFMAN, MEIR

BEN ISSA, ISUF
LOPEZ-PORTILLO ROJAS, JOE

BEN YEHUDA
PERELMANN, ELIEZER

BEN, ILKE
HARPER, CAROL ELY

BEN, PHILIP
BARLING, PHILIP

BEN-AVIGDOR
SHALKOVITZ, ARIEH LEIB

BEN-DOV, MEIR
BERNET, MICHAEL M.

BEN-EZRA, JUAN J.
LACANZA, MANUEL

BEN-HORAV, NAPTHALI
KRAVITZ, NATHANIEL

BEN-NEZ
NOVACHOVITCH, LIPPE BENZ.
WINCHEVSKY, MORRIS

BEN-YOSEF, AVRAHAM CHAIM
MATSUBA, MOSHE

BEN-ZION
WEINMAN, BENZION

BEN-ZION, SH.
GUTMAN, SIMCHA ALTER

BENALTI, ALEXANDER
PFEFFER, HEINRICH

BENARRIA, ALLAN
GOLDENTHAL, ALLAN B.

BENARY, MARGOT
BENARY-ISBERT, MARGOT

BENARY-ISBERT, M.
BENARY-ISBERT, MARGOT

BENAULY
ABBOTT, AUSTIN
ABBOTT, BENJAMIN
ABBOTT, LYMAN

BENCH, FREDDY
BENK, AXEL

BEND, PALMER
PUTNAM, GEORGE PALMER

BENDBOW, HESPER
ARCHER, GEORGE W.1]

BENDER, JAY
DEINDORFER, ROBERT GREENE

BENDER, STEN
LANDELIUS, VALBORG

BENDIT, GLADYS
PRESLAND, JOHN

BENDIX, GERALD
ERICHSEN, UWE

BENDOW, PETER
ARNESEN, DAVID D.S.

BENEDICT, BILLY
PAUL, MAURY

BENEDICT, HESTER A.
DICKINSON, MRS. T.P.

BENEDICT, JOSEPH
DOLLEN, CHARLES JOSEPH

BENEDICT, LEOPOLD
NOVACHOVITCH, LIPPE BENZ.

BENEDICT, LYNN
BANIS, VICTOR J[EROME]

BENEDICT, MYRTLE
SALLASKA, GEORGIA MYRTLE

BENEDICT, PETER
PARGETER, EDITH [MARY]

BENEDICT, RACHEL
STEPHENS, DOREEN

BENEFICE
WORLEY, FREDERICK U.

BENET, DEBORAH
CAMP, DEBORAH ELAINE

BENET, EDUOARD
EDWARDS, WILLIAM B.

BENIGNE, ANGE
MOLENES, MME. PAUL DE

BENJAMIN, ALICE
BROOKE, AVERY [ROGERS]

BENJAMIN, CLAUDE
POHLMAN, MAX EDWARD

BENJAMIN, DAVID
SLAVITT, DAVID RYTMAN

BENJAMIN, JACK
STRUNK, GORDON

BENJAMIN, JUDY-LYNN
DEL REY, JUDY-LYNN

BENJAMIN, LINDA
WALLERICH, LINDA H.

BENJAMIN, LOIS
GOULD, LOIS

BENJAMIN, NIKKI
VOSBEIN, BARBARA

BENJAMIN, NORA
KUBIE, NORA GOTTHEIL B.

BENJAMIN, PAUL
AUSTER, PAUL

BENJI, THOMAS
ROBINSON, FRANK M.

BENJIE
NEUBERG, VICTOR [B]

BENKO, NANCY
ATKINSON, NANCY

BENN, JUNE
BARRACLOUGH, JUNE [MARY]

BENN, JUNE WEDGEWOOD
BARRACLOUGH, JUNE [MARY]

BENN, MATTHEW
SIEGEL, BENJAMIN

BENN, S.I.
BENN, STANLEY I[SSAC]

BENN, TONY
BENN, ANTHONY NEIL W.

BENNET, DOUGLAS
GOBEL, DIETER

BENNET, JOHN
WEAKLEY, JAMES

BENNET, RUTH
STRAUBING, HAROLD [ELK]

BENNETT, ALICE
ZINER, FLORENCE

BENNETT, CHRISTINE
NEUBAUER, WILLIAM A.

BENNETT, CONNIE
BENNETT, CONSTANCE

PSEUDONYMS

BENNETT, CORINTHA
WHEAT, CAROLYN

BENNETT, DANIEL
GILMORE, JOSEPH [LEE]

BENNETT, DOROTHEA
YOUNG, DOROTHEA BENNETT

BENNETT, DWIGHT
NEWTON, DWIGHT BENNETT

BENNETT, E.A.
BENNETT, [ENOCH] ARNOLD

BENNETT, E.N.
BENNETT, ERNEST NATHANIEL

BENNETT, ELIZABETH
MITCHELL, MARGARET [M]

BENNETT, ELIZABETH DEARE
MERWIN, SAMUEL K. JR.

BENNETT, EMMA
MERRITT, EMMA

BENNETT, G.V.
BENNETT, GARETH VAUGHN

BENNETT, GORDON
WAGNER, HARALD

BENNETT, H.O.
HARDISON, OSBORNE B.

BENNETT, H.S.
BENNETT, HENRY STANLEY

BENNETT, HAL
BENNETT, GEORGE HAROLD

BENNETT, HALL
HALL, BENNIE CAROLINE

BENNETT, HARVE
FISCHMAN, HARVE

BENNETT, JANICE
WITTON, EILEEN

BENNETT, JANICE N.
WITTON, EILEEN

BENNETT, JEAN FRANCIS
DORCY, MARY JEAN

BENNETT, JEREMY
BENNETT, JOHN JEROME N.

BENNETT, JOHN
LUTZ, JOHN [T]

BENNETT, KEM
BENNETT, KEMYS DEVERELL

BENNETT, KENT
NICKELS, SAMUEL H.

BENNETT, LAURA GILMOUR
BENNETT, LAURA
HARVEY, JEAN GILMOUR

BENNETT, LISA
GYLLENHALL, LIZA

BENNETT, LIZA
GYLLENHALL, LIZA

BENNETT, M.J.
BENNETT, MARCIA J[OANNE]

BENNETT, MARGARET
BIERMANN, JUNE
TOOHEY, BARBARA

BENNETT, MARGOT
BIERMAN, JUNE
TOOHEY, BARBARA

BENNETT, RACHEL
HILL, MARGARET [OHLER]

BENNETT, REBECCA
FRANKEL, RUBY

BENNETT, WALLACE
KELLEY, THOMAS P.

BENNEY, MARK
DE GRAS, HENRY ERNEST

BENOIT, HENDRA
CRAWFORD, BETTY ANNE

BENRATH, HENRY
RAUSCH, ALBERT

BENSEN, BETTINA
ROBERT, ELLI

BENSOL, OSCAR
GILBERT, WILLIE

BENSON, A.C.
BENSON, ARTHUR CHRISTOPH.

BENSON, ADAM
BINGLEY, DAVID ERNEST

BENSON, ALBRIGHT
MOORE, SPENCER

BENSON, ANNE
KOLACZYK, ANNE & EDWARD

BENSON, B.A.
BEYEA, BASIL

BENSON, BOBBY
ACKERMAN, FORREST J.

BENSON, DANIEL
COOPER, COLIN SYMONS

BENSON, E.F.
BENSON, EDWARD FREDERIC

BENSON, EDWIN
SHAVER, RICHARD S.

BENSON, GINNY
BENSON, VIRGINIA

BENSON, GODFREY
CHARNWOOD, GODFREY BENSON

BENSON, LEE
JENNISON, JOHN WILLIAM

BENSON, RACHEL
JOWITT, DEBORAH

BENSON, RICHARD
COOPER, SAUL

BENSON, S. VERE
TAYLOR, STEPHANA VERE

BENSON, SALLY
BENSON, SARA MAHALA R.S.

BENSON, STELLA
ANDERSON, JO
ANDERSON, STELLA BENSON

BENSON, TED
BENSON, FREDERICK WILLIAM

BENSON, THERESE
KNIPE, EMILIE BENSON

BENT, JAMES
SLATTERY, RAY

BENT, JAMES F.
SLATTERY, RAY

BENTEEN, JOHN
DELFS, RAINER
ELKIN, H.V.
ERICHSEN, UWE
HAAS, BENJAMIN LEOPOLD
KUGLER, DIETMAR
LINAKER, MICHAEL
SLADE, JACK

BENTHAM, JAY
BENSMAN, JOSEPH

BENTHIC, ARCH E.
STEWART, HARRIS BATES JR.

BENTINCK, RAY
BEST, R. BRETON AMIS

BENTKOWSKI, SOPHIE
LAVRITCH, SOPHIE B.

BENTKOWSKI-LAVRITCH, SOPH
LAVRITCH, SOPHIE B.

BENTLEY, BARBARA
DIAMOND, BARBARA B.

BENTLEY, E.C.
BENTLEY, EDMOND CLERIHEW

BENTLEY, GENE
FEARN, JOHN RUSSELL

BENTLEY, HUGH
PHILIPS, JUDSON P.

BENTLEY, JAMES
HANLEY, JAMES

BENTLEY, JAYNE
KRENTZ, JAYNE ANN

BENTLEY, JOY
FURSTAUER, JOHANNA

BENTLEY, MICHAEL
RUHEN, CARL

BENTLEY, PATRICIA
ELLIS, JULIE M.

PSEUDONYMS

BENTLEY, PETER
MOON, ALAN

BENTLEY, RICHARD
BROWNING, ALICE C[ROLLEY]

BENTLEY, W.J.
ULLYETT, KENNETH

BENTON, DARLA
LESLIE, JOANNA

BENTON, JOHN L.
CURRY, THOMAS ALBERT
DANIELS, NORMAN A.

BENTON, KARLA
ROWLAND, DONALD S.

BENTON, ROBERT
BUSE, RENEE

BENTON, TAD
BRYANT, PAUL

BENTON, WILL
PAINE, LAURAN BOSWORTH

BENTON, WILLY
LLIRO OLIVE, JOSE MARIA

BENTZON, THERESE
BLANC, MARIE THERESE

BENY, ROLOFF
BENY, WILFRED ROY

BERANEK, MARTIN
HAHN, RONALD M.

BERARD, RALPH
WHITE, VICTOR H.

BERCH, WILLIAM O.
COYNE, JOSEPH E.

BERCO
CARLBERG, BIRGER

BERDNYK, OLES
BERDNYK, OLEKSANDR PAVLO.

BERDYAEV, NICOLAS
BERDYAEV, NIKOLAI ALEK.

BEREFORD, J.D.
BERESFORD, JOHN DAVYS

BERENBAUM, LINDA BAYER
BAYER, LINDA

BEREND, ALICE
BREINLINGER, ALICE BEREND

BERENY, GAIL RUBIN
RUBIN, GAIL

BERESFORD, ELIZABETH
FABER, INEZ MCALISTER

BERESFORD, JOHN
ROCHESTER, GEO[RGE] E.

BERESFORD, RUSSELL
ROBERTS, CECIL EDRIC M.

BERETON, FORD
CROCKETT, SAMUEL R.

BERG, AJA
MUHRMANN, WILHELM
PAULY, MARGARETE

BERG, AL
NYGREN, KERSTIN

BERG, AXEL
REINECKER, HERBERT

BERG, CHARLOTTE
RITTMANN, CHARLOTTE

BERG, DAVE
BERG, DAVID

BERG, ILA
GARBER, NELLIA B.

BERG, JOAN
VICTOR, JOAN BERG

BERG, KAI
BERNDT, KARL-HEINZ

BERG, ROLF
FORSSBERG, LENNART

BERG, STIG
TEIGE, LUDVIG

BERG, UWE
GRUEB, WILLY

BERG, WILHELM
SCHNEIDER, LINA WELLER

BERGANTINOS, EL BARDO
ABENTE, EDUARDO PONDAL

BERGAUER, JOHANNES
TSCHERNEK, VIKTOR

BERGEDORF, SYLVIA
ARNOLD, WALTER

BERGEN, FEDOR WILLI
HEIMANN, WILHELM

BERGEN, FRAN
DE TALAVERA BERGER, FRAN

BERGEN, GINA
BORNSTROEM-RUNDE, UWE

BERGEN, HENRY
FRIEDRICHS, HORST

BERGER, AXEL
BURMESTER, ALBERT KONRAD

BERGER, BERG
HANSTEIN, WOLFRAM v.

BERGER, FRANZISKA
KALTENBERGER, FRIEDERIKE

BERGER, HELEN
BAMBERGER, HELEN R.

BERGER, LINDA
EICHLER, BERTEL

BERGER, MAREIKE
EISELE, MARTIN

BERGER, RALF
KALMUCZAK, ROLF

BERGER, [COL.] A.
MALRAUX, [G] ANDRE

BERGFELD, THORSTEN
MULLER, NORBERT

BERGFORS, AL
NYGREN, KERSTIN

BERGHAMER, LISA
JUNG, ELSE

BERGHOFER, ERIKA
ENGEN, ERIKA

BERGIUS, C.C.
ZIMMER, EGON MARIA

BERGIUS, ELSA BRITT
OLENIUS, ELSA VICTORIA

BERGK, ALEXANDER
KNOLL, LUDWIG

BERGMAN, JOAKIM
SODERBERG, BENGT

BERGSON, LEO
STEBEL, S[IDNEY] L[EO]

BERGSTEDT, HARALD ALFRED
PETERSON, HARALD ALFRED

BERHGLIND, FRANCIES
FAGERBERG, SVEN

BERK, ARIEL
KEILER, BARBARA

BERKELEY, ANN
LUNDHOLM, ANJA

BERKELEY, ANTHONY
COX, ANTHONY BERKELEY

BERKELEY, ELIZABETH N.
JACKSON, WINIFRED V.
LOVECRAFT, H[OWARD] P.

BERKELEY, TAYLOR
WELSH, KEN

BERKLEY, TOM
GEEN, CLIFFORD

BERKMAN, TED
BERKMAN, EDWARD O[SCAR]

BERL-LEE, MARIA
LEE, MARIA BERL

BERLEPSCH, E.
BLANK, MATTHIAS

BERLINER, ROSS
KAPPELMAN, MURRAY MARTIN

BERN, DONALD
BERNSTEIN, AL

BERN, JERINE
JENNISON, JOHN WILLIAM

BERNADETTE
WATTS, [ANNA] BERNADETTE

BERNADETTE, ANN
GAZDAK, D.H.
RAY, KAREN

BERNARD, CAMILLE
KATAZZI, MME.

BERNARD, DOROTHY ANN
WELLER, DOROTHY

BERNARD, GUY
BARBER, STEPHEN GUY

BERNARD, JAY
SAWKINS, RAYMOND [H]

BERNARD, JOHN
BEAMISH, ANNIE O'MEARA

BERNARD, MARLEY
GRAVES, SUSAN

BERNARD, ROBERT
MARTIN, ROBERT BERNARD

BERNARD, STEFAN
BAUMRIN, BERNARD H.

BERNARDY, ULLA
BERGFRIED, URSULA

BERNARN, TERRAVE
BURNETT, DAVID [B.F.]

BERNAUER, EVA MARIA
ASPERN-BUCHMEIER, ELISAB.

BERNAYS, ANNE
KAPLAN, ANNE BERNAYS

BERNAZZA, ANN MARIE
HAASE, ANN MARIE BERNAZZA

BERND, GROTE
GROETTRUP, BERNHARD

BERND, MAXIMILIAN
ENGEL, BERND

BERND, TRAUTE
HERDER, EDELTRAUT

BERNDORF, JACQUES
PREUTE, MICHAEL

BERNE, ARLENE
ZEKOWSKI, ARLENE

BERNE, KARIN
BURRELL, SUE
KARNI, MICHAELA

BERNE, LEO
DAVIES, LESLIE PERNELL

BERNEDER, O.
OBERNEDER, FRIEDRICH

BERNEDETTI, EUGENIO
HERHAUS, ERNST

BERNER, FRIEDRICH
MEISTER, FRIEDRICH

BERNER, STEFFI
DURR, EDELTRAUT

BERNERT, ELEANOR H.
SHELDON, ELEANOR BERNERT

BERNEY, BERYL
LYTLE, MRS. W.J.A.

BERNFELDT, BENGT
JOHNSSON, [K.O.] HARALD

BERNGATH, URSULA
BEER, NATALIE

BERNHARD, KARL
CAPESIUS, BERNHARD

BERNHARD, LUDWIG
BAEHTHOLD, ALFRED

BERNHARDT, KLAUS
BERENDT, GERD

BERNHARDT, M.A.
BERNHARDT, MARCIA A.

BERNIG, HEINRICH H.
KUROWSKI, FRANZ

BERNSEN, ALBERT
BERNSTEIN, AL

BERRIAULT, GINA
BERRIAULT, GEORGIANNA

BERRIEN, EDITH HEAL
HEAL, EDITH

BERRIGAN, TED
BERRIGAN, EDMUND J.M. JR.

BERRILL, N.J.
BERRILL, NORMAN JOHN

BERRISFORD, JUDITH M.
LEWIS, CLIFFORD
LEWIS, JUDITH BERRISFORD

BERRISFORD, MARY
LEWIS, M. CHRISTIANNA M.

BERROW, N.
BERROW, CYRIL NORMAN

BERRY, B.J.
BERRY, BARBARA J.

BERRY, CHUCK
BERRY, CHARLES EDWARD A.

BERRY, D. BRUCE
OFFUTT, ANDREW J.

BERRY, D.C.
BERRY, DAVID [CHAPMAN]

BERRY, ERICK
BEST, [E] ALLENA CHAMPLIN

BERRY, HELEN
ROWLAND, DONALD S.

BERRY, HENRY
IDE, HEINO

BERRY, JIM
BERRY, JAMES

BERRY, JO
BERRY, JOCELYN

BERRY, JONAS
ASHBERY, JOHN [L]
BLOCHMAN, LAWRENCE G.

BERRY, JULIAN
GASTOLDI, ERNESTO

BERRY, MALTILDA
BEAUCHAMP, KATHLEEN M.

BERRY, ROLAND
ENGELSBERGER, BERTA
ENGELSBERGER, JOSEF

BERRYMAN, JIM
BERRYMAN, JAMES THOMAS

BERSCHADSKY, ISAIAH
DOMASCHEVITSKY, ISAIAH

BERT, JO
BERNITT-DREYER, JANNA

BERTHIER, CHRISTIAN
MEISNER, MICHAEL

BERTILDA
DE SAMPER, SOLEDAD ACOSTA

BERTIN, JACK
BERTIGNONO, GIOVANNI
GERMANO, PETER B

BERTIN, JOHN
BERTIGNONO, GIOVANNI

BERTOLET, PAUL
MCLAUGHLIN, FRANK

BERTON, GUY
BINGHAM, EADFRID A.
LA COSTE, GUY ROBERT

BERTRAM, ARTHUR
IBBOTT, ARTHUR PEARSON

BERTRAM, NOEL
BOSTON, NOEL
FANTHORPE, R.L.

BERTRAM, SILVA
GUNTHER, HEINZ

BERTRAND, CHARLES
CARTER, DAVID CHARLES

BERWICK, CLAUDE
HUNT, ANNA REBECCA GALE

BERWICK, JEAN
MEYER, JEAN SHEPHERD

BERYLL, THOMAS
PFEFFER, HEINRICH

BES SHAHAR, ELUKI
EDGHILL, ROSEMARY

BESS, CLAYTON
LOCKE, ROBERT

BEST, ADAM
CARMICHAEL, WILLIAM EDW.

BEST, G.F.A.
BEST, GEOFFREY [FRANCIS]

BEST, MARC
LEMIEUX, MARC

BEST, RAYLEIGH
BEST, R. BRETON AMIS

BESTE, DR. RICHARD
BIERACH, ALFRED

BETE-NOIRE
HENRY, PAUL-MARK

BETH
WINSHIP, ELIZABETH

BETH, MARY
MILLER, MARY BETH

BETHANCOURT, T. ERNESTO
PASSAILAIGUE, TOMAS E.B.

BETHE, H.A.
BETHE, HANS ALBRECHT

BETHLEN, T.D.
SILVERBERG, ROBERT

BETHUNE, J.G.
ELLIS, EDWARD S.

BETHUNE, MARY
CLOPET, LILIANE M.C.

BETI, MONGO
BIYIDI, ALEXANDRE

BETIS, WILLARD EMORY
CREWS, JUDSON [C]

BETJENT, OLE NY
MEYN, NIELS

BETKE, LOTTE
PONNIER, LOTTE

BETTERIDGE, ANNE
POTTER, MARGARET [N]

BETTERIDGE, DON
NEWMAN, BERNARD [CHARLES]

BETTINA
EHRLICH, BETTINA BAUER

BETTS, JAMES
HAYNES, BETSY

BEUTTEN, HERMANN
BEUTTENMILLER, HERMANN

BEVAN, ALISTAIR
KORNBLUTH, C[YRIL] M.

BEVAN, ALISTAIR [CONT]
ROBERTS, KEITH [J.R.]

BEVAN, GLORIA
BEVAN, GLORY ISOBEL

BEVANS, TORRE
CHANSLOR, MARJORIE TORREY
HOOD, TORREY

BEVERLY, JANE
STEPHENS, DOREEN

BEVERLY, LINDA
QUENTIN, DOROTHY

BEVIS, H.U.
BEVIS, HERBERT URLIN

BEVIS, JAMES
CUMBERLAND, MARTEN
SHANN, B.V.

BEVK, FRANCE
SEDMAK, PAVLE

BEXAR, PHIL
BORG, PHILIP ANTHONY JOHN

BEY, ISABELLE
BOSTICCO, [ISABELL] MARY

BEYLE, HANK
BUCHANAN, JAMES DAVID

BEYNON, JANE
BRANDT, JANE LEWIS
LEWIS, LANGE

BEYNON, JOHN
HARRIS, JOHN WYNDHAM P.L.

BEYVERS, ELFRIEDE
KERN, ELFIEDE

BEZIQUE
BESTWICK, HARRY

BEZRUC, PER
VASEK, VLADIMIR

BHAJAN, YOGI
YOGII, HARBHAJAN SINGH K.

BHAKTIVEDANTA SWAMI, A.C.
PRABHUPADA, A.C. BHAK.

BHARTI, MA SATYA
JACOBS, JILL

BHATIA, JUNE
BHATIA, JAMUNADEVI
FORRESTER, HELEN

BI SHANG-GUAN
SHEN CONGWEN

BIAGI, L.D.
AMBROSE, LOTTIE F.

BIALK, ELISA
KRAUTTER, ELISA BIALK

BIANCA-MARIA
ESCHKOTTER, MARLENE

BIBO, BOBETTE
GUGLIOTTA, BOBETTE

BIBOLET, R.H.
KELLY, TIM J.

BICKERDYKE, JOHN
COOKE, C.H.

BICKERSTAFF, ISAAC
SWIFT, JONATHAN

BICKERSTAFFE, ISAAC JR.
LOVECRAFT, H[OWARD] P.

BICKHAM, JACK
BICKHAM, JOHN M.

BICOS, OLGA
GONZALES-BICOS, OLGA

BIDWELL, LITA
AVERY, RUBY

BIELSKI, FELIKS
GIERGIEIEWICZ, MIECZYSLA

BIELYI, SERGEI
HOLLO, ANSELM

BIENES, NICK
BIENES, NICHOLAS PETER

BIENSTOCK, MIKE
BIENSTOCK, MYRON JOSEPH

BIERI, DORIS
HAUG, DORIS

BIERMANN, LILLIAN
WEHMEYER, LILLIAN [M] B.

BIG BEN
SACHSE, WILLI RICHARD

BIGGERN, KATHREIN
HENKEL, ILSE

BIGGS, PETER
RIMEL, DUANE [W]

BIGLAND, EILEEN
LILBURN, EILEEN ANNE C.

BIGLY, CANTELL A.
PECK, GEORGE W.

BIJ-BIJCHENKO
RUDNYCKYJ, JAROSLAV

BILBO, JACK
BARUCH, HUGO

BILIR, KIM
SCAIFE, ARTHUR HODGKIN

BILL
STRACHAN, GLADYS ELIZAB.

BILLER, KRISTIAN
WILDENVEY, HERMAN

BILLER, KRISTIAN F.
ELVESTAD, SVEN CHRISTOFER

BILLINGS, BUCK
LLIRO OLIVE, JOSE MARIA

BILLINGS, BUCK [CONT]
RISTER, CLAUDE
SCOTT, ALEXANDRE LESLIE

BILLINGS, EZRA
HALLA, ROBERT CHRISTIAN

BILLINGS, JOSH
SHAW, HENRY WHELLER

BILLINGS, MARIS H.
BILLINGS, EDITH S.

BILLINGTON, JOHN
BEAVER, [JACK] PATRICK

BIN GORION, M.Y.
BERDICZEVSKY, MICHA YOSE.

BINDER, EANDO
BINDER, EARL ANDREW
BINDER, OTTO

BINDER, PEARL
ELWYN-JONES, PEARL BINDER

BINDSEIL, ILSE
ENDERWITZ-BINDSEIL, ILSE

BINGHAM, CARSON
CASSIDAY, BRUCE [BINGHAM]

BINGHAM, JOHN MICHAEL
CLANMORRIS, BARON

BINGHAM, MINDY
BINGHAM, MELINDA

BINGHAM, SALLIE
ELLSWORTH, SALLIE BINGHAM

BINGHAM, [MAJOR] ARTHUR
ROWE, W.

BINGLEY, D.E.
BINGLEY, DAVID ERNEST

BINGS, HENRY
BINGENHEIMER, HEINZ

BINKLEY, ANNE
OZBEKHAN, ANNE BINKLEY R.

BINNACLE
LEWIS, W.W.

BINZEN, BILL
BINZEN, WILLIAM

BIRCH, LEO BEDRITCH
BISCHITZKY, LEO BODRICH

BIRD, AL
FALK, HERMANN
FINCH, PHILLIP
MANDEL, LEO N.

BIRD, BEVERLY
HELLAND, BEVERLY

BIRD, BRANDON
EVANS, GEORGE BIRD
EVANS, KAY HARRIS

BIRD, C.
ELLISON, HARLAN

BIRD, CORDWAINER
ELLISON, HARLAN

BIRD, ERIC ALLEN
FALK, HERMANN

BIRD, ERIK ALLAN
FALK, HERMANN

BIRD, ISABELLA
BISHOP, ISABELLA LUCY [B]

BIRD, LEWIS
HAYTER, CECIL G.

BIRD, RICHARD
BARRADELL-SMITH, WALTER

BIRD, ZENOBIA
LEFEVRE, LAURA Z.

BIRDWELL, CLEO
DELLILO, DON

BIRIMBIR
BOZIC, SRETEN

BIRKEN, HEINZ
EICHEN, HEINRICH

BIRKENAU, M.B.
BLANK, MATTHIAS

BIRKENHEAD, EDWARD
BIRKENHEAD, ELIZAH

BIRKENHEAD, LORD
SMITH, FREDERICK W. FURN.

BIRKENSTEIN, ULLA
GOERITZ, GERDA

BIRKLER, HUBERTUS
ETTLE, JOSEF

BIRKLEY, DOLAN
HITCHENS, DELORES B.

BIRKNER, FRIEDA
STEIN, FRIEDA

BIRMINGHAM, GEORGE A.
HANNAY, JAMES OWEN

BIRNAGE, DIRK
BIRNAGE, DEREK A.W.

BIRNBAUM, STEVE
BIRNBAUM, STEPHEN NORMAN

BIRO, B.
BIRO, BALINT STEPHEN

BIRO, B.S.
BIRO, BALINT STEPHEN

BIRO, VAL
BIRO, BALINT STEPHEN

BIRZE, MIERVALDIS IANOV.
BERZIN, MIERVALDIS I.

BISHOP, CARLY
MCGONIGLE, CHERYL

BISHOP, CASSANDRA
LATHAM, ROBIN

BISHOP, CLAUDIA
FEATHER, JANE
STANTON, MARY

BISHOP, E. MORCHARD
STONOR, OLIVER

BISHOP, EVELYN MORCHARD
STONOR, OLIVER

BISHOP, GEORGE
WILLIS, EDWARD HENRY

BISHOP, ISABELLA BIRD
BISHOP, ISABELLA LUCY [B]

BISHOP, JACK
DORMAN, MICHAEL

BISHOP, JIM
BISHOP, JAMES ALONZO

BISHOP, JOHN
WILLIS, EDWARD HENRY

BISHOP, K.L.
MOORCOCK, MICHAEL

BISHOP, KEITH
MOORCOCK, MICHAEL

BISHOP, MARTIN
PAINE, LAURAN BOSWORTH

BISHOP, MARY
MASON, BEVERLY

BISHOP, MORCHARD
JONES, ARTHUR LLEWELLYN
STONOR, OLIVER

BISHOP, NATALIE
BUSH, NANCY

BISHOP, PIKE
BLACK, TERRY
OBSTFELD, RAYMOND

BISHOP, SAMUEL P.
HUTSON, SHAUN

BISHOP, STACEY
ANTHEILL, GEORGE J.C.

BISHOP, TANIA KROITOR
BISHOP, TETIANA KROITOR

BISHOP, TANIAN KROITOR
BISHOP, TETIANA KROITOR

BISHOP, TOM
BISHOP, THOMAS W[ALTER]

BISHOP, ZEALIA B.
REED, ZEALIA BROWN

BISLAND, BILKO
BISLAND, ERNEST CHARLES

BISLAND, E.C.
BISLAND, ERNEST CHARLES

BISQUE, ANATOLE
BOSQUET, ALAIN

BITA, LILI
ZALLER, ANGELIKA BITA

BITE, BEN
SCHNECK, STEPHEN

BIXBY, AX
GLASER, FRANZ

BIXBY, JAY LEWIS
BIXBY, JEROME L.

BIXBY, RAY Z.
TRALINS, [SANDOR] ROBERT

BIZAN, KAWAKAMI
AKIRA, KAWAKAMI

BJARME, BRYNJOLF
IBSEN, HENRIK [JOHAN]

BJERKE, ANNA
ORNULF, GUNNAR

BJERKE, ONULF
KORSELL, JOHN

BJERREGAARD, HENNING
PLOGSCHTIES, H.

BJORK, CHRISTINA
BJOERK, CHRISTINA

BJORKHEM, ANN
REYMERS, ELISABET

BJORNEBOE, JENS
BJOERNEBOE, JENS

BJORNSON, BJORNSTJERNE
BJOERNSON, BJOERNSTJERNE

BJORNSSON, RUDOLF
WERNBERG, HJALMAR

BLACHSTADT, CV.
RITTER, VERA

BLACK SWAN OF LAC LEMAN
NABOKOV, V.V.

BLACK TARANTULA, THE
ACKER, KATHY

BLACK TORNADO
MOONEY, PAUL

BLACK, BETTY
SCHWARTZ, BETTY

BLACK, D.M.
BLACK, DAVID [MACLEOD]

BLACK, DAVID
WAY, ROBERT E.

BLACK, DESMOND
GRANDT, GUIDO
GRANDT, MICHAEL

BLACK, EDGAR
SILVERBERG, ROBERT

BLACK, GAVIN
WYND, OSWALD [MORRIS]

BLACK, ISHI
GIBSON, WALTER B.

BLACK, IVORY
JANVIER, THOMAS A.

BLACK, JACKIE
CASTO, JACQUELINE A.

BLACK, JOE
HITT, ORRIE [EDWIN]

BLACK, JONATHAN
VON BLOCK, BELA [W]

BLACK, KITTY
BLACK, DOROTHY

BLACK, LAURA
LONGRIGG, ROGER [ERSKINE]

BLACK, LAWRENCE
BLOCK, LAWRENCE

BLACK, LIONEL
BARKER, DUDLEY

BLACK, M. DANA
BUTLER, H.M.

BLACK, MAGGIE
BLACK, MARGARET K.

BLACK, MALACAI
D'AMATO, BARBARA

BLACK, MANSELL
TREVOR, ELLESTON

BLACK, MAUREEN
PETERS, MAUREEN

BLACK, MONTGOMERY
HOLDEN, [WILLIS] SPRAGUE

BLACK, PAUL
NASH, G. MURRAY

BLACK, ROBERT
HOLDSTOCK, ROBERT P.

BLACK, ROBERTA
COULSON, ROBERT
MIESEL, SANDRA

BLACK, TREVOR
RALSTON, ALBERT B.

BLACK, VERONICA
PETERS, MAUREEN

BLACKBURN, BARBARA
LEADER, [EVELYN] BARBARA

BLACKBURN, CLAIRE
ALTMAN, LINDA JACOBS

BLACKBURN, JOHN
MOTT, J. MOLDON

BLACKBURN, LAURA
BLANDEN, CHARLES G.

BLACKBURN, TOM W.
CASTLE, FRANK

BLACKER, HERETH
CHALKE, HERBERT

BLACKLIN, MALCOLM
CHAMBERS, AIDAN

BLACKMAN, ROBERT C.
NORTON, ROGER HOWARD

BLACKSNAKE, GEORGE
RICHARDSON, GLADWELL G.

BLACKSTOCK, CHARITY
TORDAY, URSULA

BLACKSTOCK, LEE
TORDAY, URSULA

BLACKSTONE, HARRY
GIBSON, WALTER B.

BLACKSTONE, JAMES
BAXTER, JOHN
BROSNAN, JOHN RAYMOND

BLACKSTONE, VALERIUS D.
GALPIN, J.A.

BLACKTON, PETER
WILSON, LIONEL

BLACKTREE, BARBARA
COULTRY, BARBARA

BLACKWELL, JOHN
COLLINGS, EDWARD GEOFFREY

BLACKWELL, JUDITH
MYERS, JUDITH BLACKWELL

BLACKWOOD, JOY ANN
HEYMAN, EVAN LEE

BLACKWOOD, STEPHANIE
MILLER, SIGMUND [STEPHEN]

BLADE, ALEXANDER
BROWNE, HOWARD
COOKE, MILLEN
GARRETT, RANDALL [P]
GEIER, CHESTER S.
GRAHAM, ROGER P.
HAMILTON, EDMOND
HAUSER, HEINRICH
JAKES, JOHN [WILLIAM]
KNOX, CLEO ELDON
LIVINGSTON, HERB
LIVINGSTONE, BERKELEY
MCGIVERN, WILLIAM P.
O'BRIEN, DAVID WRIGHT
PRESSMAN, LOUIS H.
SAMPLINER, LOUIS H.
SHAVER, RICHARD S.
SILVERBERG, ROBERT
SWAIN, DWIGHT V[REELAND]
VERN, DAVID
YERXA, LEROY

BLAFFER, SARAH C.
HRDY, SARAH BLAFFER

BLAIDE, TERENCE
HAHN, RONALD M.

BLAIKE, AVONA
MACINTOSH, JOAN

BLAINE, JAMES
AVALLONE, MICHAEL

PSEUDONYMS

BLAINE, JEFF
BARRETT, GEOFFREY JOHN

BLAINE, JOHN
GOODWIN, HAROLD LELAND
HARKINS, PETER J.

BLAINE, LAWRENCE L.
LIPSKY, ELEASAR
SILVERBERG, ROBERT

BLAINE, MARGE
BLAINE, MARGERY K.

BLAINE, SARA
MORGAN, DIANA

BLAINE, TOM R.
BLAINE, THOMAS ROBERT

BLAIR
BLAIR-FISH, W. WILFRID

BLAIR, ADRIAN
BIRD, WILLIAM H.F.

BLAIR, ALISON
BOIES, JANICE

BLAIR, ALLAN
BAYFIELD, WILLIAM J.

BLAIR, ANTHONY
WALKER, ROWLAND

BLAIR, CATHERINE
BYERS, CORDIA

BLAIR, DAVID
GOYNE, RICHARD

BLAIR, EDWARD H.
SMITH, EDWARD H.

BLAIR, FRANK
BUCKBY, SAMUEL
BUCKLEY, SAMUEL

BLAIR, HAMISH
BLAIR, ANDREW JAMES F.

BLAIR, JENNIFER
MCELFRESH, ELIZABETH A.

BLAIR, KATHRYN
PARKER, KAREN BLAIR
SCAMEHORN, MARY KATHRYN

BLAIR, LAUREN
BERENSON, LAURIEN

BLAIR, LAURIEN
BERENSON, LAURIEN

BLAIR, LUCILE
YEAKLEY, MARJORIE HALL

BLAIR, MARCIA
BAKER, MARC[EIL GENEE K.]

BLAIR, PETER
HUNTER BLAIR, PETER

BLAIR, SHANNON
KAYE, MARILYN

BLAIR, SYLVIA
JACOBS, ALMA SYLVIA

BLAIR, WILFRID
BLAIR-FISH, W. WILFRID

BLAIRMAN, JACQUELINE
PINTO, JACQUELINE HARRIS

BLAISDELL, ANNE
LININGTON, [B] ELIZABETH
ROSENBERG, ELINOR BLAISDL

BLAISDELL, ELINOR
ROSENBERG, ELINOR BLAISDL

BLAKE, ALAN
GWINN, OMAR

BLAKE, ALEX
NUETZEL, CHARLES A.

BLAKE, ALFRED
HARRIS, LAURENCE MARK

BLAKE, ANDREA
WEALE, ANNE

BLAKE, ANDREW
ANDERSON, CHESTER [V.J.]
HARRIS, LAURENCE MARK

BLAKE, ANTHONY
TUBB, E.C.

BLAKE, ANTONIO
JUSKEVICE, MILDRED H.

BLAKE, BUD
BLAKE, JULIAN WATSON

BLAKE, CAMERON
MASON, MICHAEL HENRY

BLAKE, CHRISTINA
CHANDLER, BRYN
HALPIN, MARY D.

BLAKE, E.A.
PRATT, ELEANOR BLAKE

BLAKE, ELEANOR
PRATT, ELEANOR BLAKE

BLAKE, ERIC
BOARDMAN, JOHN

BLAKE, EUBIE
BLAKE, JAMES HUBERT

BLAKE, FREDRIC
NUETZEL, CHARLES A.

BLAKE, J.D.
NUETZEL, CHARLES A.

BLAKE, J.W.
BLAKE, JOHN WILLIAM

BLAKE, JAMES
BLASIUS, RICHARD

BLAKE, JENNIFER
MAXWELL, PATRICIA ANNE P.

BLAKE, JOHN W.
BLAKE, JOHN WILLIAM

BLAKE, JONAS
HARDY, C. COLBURN

BLAKE, JUSTIN
BOLAND, BERTRAM J[OHN]
BOWEN, JOHN [GRIFFIN]
BULLMORE, JEREMY
HODGES, DONALD CLARK

BLAKE, KATHERINE
WALTER, DOROTHY BLAKE

BLAKE, KAY
WALTER, DOROTHY BLAKE

BLAKE, KEN
BULMER, [HENRY] KENNETH
HOLDSTOCK, ROBERT P.

BLAKE, LAUREL
PALENCIA, ELAINE FOWLER

BLAKE, LESLIE
DUCKWORTH, LESLIE BLAKEY

BLAKE, LORD
BLAKE, ROBERT W.

BLAKE, MARGARET
SCHEVE, LIDA CLARA

BLAKE, MARGARET
TRIMBLE, BARBARA MARGARET

BLAKE, MINDY
BLAKE, MINDEN V.

BLAKE, MONICA
MUIR, MARIE AGNES

BLAKE, NICHOLAS
DAY-LEWIS, CECIL

BLAKE, NICK
HUTSON, SHAUN

BLAKE, NORMAN
GORDON, ROBERT KAY
JAMIESON, HEBER CARSS

BLAKE, OLIVE
SUPRANER, ROBYN

BLAKE, PATRICK
EGLETON, CLIVE F.

BLAKE, REDMOND
AIKEN, ALBERT W.
MORRIS, CHARLES [S]

BLAKE, ROBERT
DAVIES, LESLIE PERNELL

BLAKE, ROGER
TRIMBLE, JOHN

BLAKE, ROYSTON
CHILDS, EDMUND BURTON

BLAKE, S.P.
MITCHELL, JOHN

BLAKE, SALLY
SAUNDERS, JEAN INNES

BLAKE, STACEY
FABER, ELSE

BLAKE, STEPHANIE
PEARL, JACQUES BAIN

BLAKE, SUSAN
ALBERT, SUSAN W. & BILL
ALBERT, SUSAN WITTIG

BLAKE, VANESSA
BROWN, MAY

BLAKE, WALKER E.
BUTTERWORTH, WILLIAM E.

BLAKE, WALTER
BRAUN, WILBUR

BLAKE, WENDON
HOLDEN, DONALD

BLAKE, WILLIAM J.
BLECK, WILLIAM JAMES

BLAKE, [CAPT.] WILTON
PARRY, DAVID HAROLD

BLAKEBOROUGH, JACK FAIRF.
FAIRFAX-BLAKEBOROUGH, J.F

BLAKELEE, ALEXANDRA
HINE, ALEXANDRA

BLAKELY, MELISSA
BRENNAN, LILLA

BLAKENEY, JAY D.
CHESTER, DEBORAH ANN

BLAKES, STERLING
BENFORD, GREGORY ALBERT

BLAKESLEY, STEPHEN
BOND, F.

BLAMAN, ANNA
VRUGT, J.P.

BLAMASIA, MAX
BLANKMEISTER, HELMUT

BLANCHAN, NELTJE
DOUBLEDAY, NELTJE

BLANCHARD, REBECCA
BLANCHARD, ANGELA ORTIZ

BLANCO, L.W.
WHITE, LIONEL

BLAND, ALEXANDER
GOSLING, NIGEL
LLOYD, MAUDE

BLAND, E.
NESBIT, EDITH

BLAND, EDITH
NESBIT, EDITH

BLAND, EDITH NESBIT
NESBIT, EDITH

BLAND, ELEANOR TAYLOR
BLAND, ELEANOR MILDRED

BLAND, FABIAN
BLAND, EDITH N. & HUBERT
NESBIT, EDITH

BLAND, JENNIFER
BOWDEN, JEAN

BLAND, MRS. HUBERT
NESBIT, EDITH

BLAND, ROBIN
DICKS, TERRANCE

BLANDFORD, EDDIE L.
MORTIMER, JOHN E.

BLANE, GERTRUDE
BLUMENTHAL, GERTRUDE

BLANEY, HARRY CLAY
BLANEY, CHARLES E.

BLANK, ANNELORE
BRINKMEIER, HANNELORE

BLANK, CLAIR
BLANK, CLARISSA MABEL

BLANK, KAREN
RANADE, KAREN BLANK

BLANK, MATHIS
VON BLANKENSEE, THEO

BLATTMACHER, KALL
EULER, GUNTER

BLAU, MILTON
BLAU, ERIC

BLAU, YEHOSHUA
BLAU, JOSHUA

BLAUW, WIM
BLAUW, PIETER WILHELMUS

BLAYN, ROBERT
MORZFELD, ERWIN

BLAYNE, DIANA
KYLE, SUSAN E. SPAETH

BLAYNE, HUGO
FEARN, JOHN RUSSELL

BLAYNE, SARA
HOWL, MARCIA Y.H.

BLAYNE, SEBASTIAN
HUCKINS, JANET

BLAYRE, CHRISTOPHER
HERON-ALLEN, EDWARD

BLAZE, JOHN
LAZENBY, NORMAN A.

BLAZER, J.S.
SCOTT, JUSTIN [BLAZER]

BLECK, AIMEE
DALSACE, LIONEL

BLEDLOW, JOHN
VALE, HENRY EDMOND THEOD.

BLEECK, OLIVER
THOMAS, ROSS [ELMORE]

BLEEKER, DON
ARNOLD, WALTER

BLEEKER, MORDECIA
MORGAN, FRED TROY

BLEEKER, SONIA
ZIM, SONIA BLEEKER

BLEIER, ROCKY
BLEIER, ROBERT PATRICK

BLESH, RUDI
BLESH, RUDOLPH PICKETT

BLEVINS, WIN
BLEVINS, WINFRED

BLICKLE, KATRINKA
PELLECCHIA, KATRINKA B.

BLIGH, NORMAN
NEUBAUER, WILLIAM A.

BLIGHT, ROSE
GREER, GERMAINE

BLINDERS, BELINDA
COKE, DESMOND

BLINKHOOLIE
ALLISON, WILLIAM

BLINN, HELEN
DORSEY, HELEN

BLINN, JOHNA
DORSEY, HELEN

BLISH, VIRGINIA
KIDD, MILDRED VIRGINIA

BLISS, A.J.
BLISS, ALAN JOSEPH

BLISS, ADAM
BURKHARDT, EVE & ROBERT

BLISS, JAMES L.
PORTER, WILLIAM SYDNEY

BLISS, REGINALD
WELLS, H.G.

BLITCH, FLEMING LEE
LEE, FLEMING

BLIXEN, KAREN
BLIXEN-FENEKE, KAREN

BLIXEN, TANIA
BLIXEN-FENEKE, KAREN

BLOBEL, BRIGITTE
BLOBEL-WAASEN, BRIGITTE

BLOCHMAN, L.G.
BLOCHMAN, LAWRENCE G.

BLOCK, JOHN
BLOCK, LAWRENCE

BLOCK, RUDOLPH
LESSING, BRUNO

BLOCKLINGER, BETTY
BLOCKLINGER, PEGGY O'MORE

BLOM, JAN
BREYTENBACH, BREYTEN

BLONG, MONT
BLATCHFORD, MONTAGUE

BLOOD, BOB
BLOOD, ROBERT OSCAR JR.

BLOOD, JOHN
DUENSING, JURGEN

BLOOD, MATTHEW
DRESSER, DAVIS
JOHNSON, WALTER RYERSON

BLOODGOOD, HARRY
MORAN, CARLO

BLOODSTONE, JOHN
BYRNE, STUART J.

BLOOM, DANIEL HALEVI
BLOOM, DANIEL HOWARD

BLOOMBERG, AURELIUS
BOURNE, RANDOLPH S.

BLOOMBERG, MARTY
BLOOMBERG, MAX ARTHUR

BLOOMER, JACK
LYNCH, JOHN GILBERT B.

BLOOMER, STEVE
JONES, J.G.

BLOOMFIELD, ROBERT
EDGLY, LESLIE

BLOT, THOMAS
SIMPSON, WILLIAM

BLOUNT, ANNA
GALLICHAN, WALTER M.

BLOXHAM, PETER
BIRD, [C] KENNETH

BLUCO, AXEL
BREUCKER, OSCAR HERBERT

BLUE WOLF
SCOTT, ROBERT

BLUE, ROSE
BLUESTONE, ROSE

BLUE, SHERI
WOOD, EDWARD D. JR.

BLUE, WALLACE
KRAENZEL, MARGARET POWELL

BLUE, ZACHARY
STINE, ROBERT L.

BLUEJAY
WOODROW, TERRY

BLUEMANTLE, BRIDGET
THOMAS, E.

BLUENOSE
SMITH, NORMA E.

BLUES, ELWOOD
AYKROYD, DANIEL EDWARD

BLUM, ADOLPH
GLEICH, JOSEPH ALOIS

BLUM, JACK I.
GIBSON, WALTER B.

BLUMENTHAL, SUSAN
TRIBICH, SUSAN

BLUNCK, JOHANN FRIEDRICH
BLUNCK, HANS FRIEDRICH

BLUNDEL, ANNE
CONLEY, ENID MARY

BLUNDELL, PETER
BUTTERWORTH, FRANK NESTLE

BLUNT, CHARLES
BREHMER, ARTHUR

BLUNT, DON
BOOTH, EDWIN

BLUPHOCKS, LUCIEN
SELDES, GILBERT VIVIAN

BLUTIG, EDUARD
GOREY, EDWARD ST. JOHN

BLY, CAROL
BLY, CAROLYN

BLY, NELLIE
COCHRANE, ELIZABETH J.

BLYGER
HOLZHAUSEN, CARL JOHAN

BLYTH, JOHN
HIBBS, JOHN

BLYTHE, JOYCE
TRENT, ANN

BLYTHE, JULIET
RILEY, STELLA

BLYTHE, LEONORA
BURTON, LEONORA

BLYTHE, MEGAN
PERRY, MICHALANN

BLYTON, ENID
BLOBEL-WAASEN, BRIGITTE

BO, ERIK
KNUTSEN, FRIDTJOF

BOAKE, CAPEL
KERR, DORIS BOAKE

BOARDMAN, CHARLES
GRIFFITHS, CHARLES TOM W.

BOARDMAN, EUNICE
MESKIE, EUNICE BOARDMAN

BOARDMAN, GWENN R.
PETERSEN, GWENN BOARDMAN

BOARDMAN, TOM
BOARDMAN, THOMAS VOLNEY

BOAS, MARIE
HALL, MARIE BOAS

BOATENG, YAW MAURICE
BRUNNER, MAURICE YAW

BOBETTE
SIMENON, GEORGES [J.C]

BOBRI
BOBRITSKY, VLADIMIIR

BOBRITSKY, VLADIMIR
BOBRI, VLADIMIR V.

BOBROFF, EDITH
MARKS, EDITH BOBROFF

BOCCA, AL
WINTER, BEVIS [PETER]

BOCHENSKI, INNOCENTIUS M.
BOCHENSKI, JOSEPH M.

BOCK, HAL
BOCK, HAROLD I.

BOCKLE, FRANZ
BOECKLE, FRANZ

BOD, PETER
VESENGI, PAUL E.

BODART, JONI
BODART-TALBOT, JONI

BODELL, MARY
PECSOK, MARY BODELL

BODEN, HILDA
BODENHAM, HILDA ESTER

BODETT, TOM
BODETT, THOMAS EDWARD

BODGER, JOAN
MERCER, JOAN BODGER

BODINE, EUNICE
LAPP, EUNICE W. BODINE

BODINE, J.D.
CUNNINGHAM, CHESTER GRANT

BODINE, JACK
LEVINSON, LEONARD [L]

BODLEY, HAL
BODLEY, HARLEY RYAN JR.

BODWELL, RICHARD
SPRING, GERALD MAX

BODY, JOHN
BRODY, JOHN

BOECKMAN, PATTI
BOECKMAN, PATRICIA

BOEHEIM, OLLY
GEORGE, OLGA

BOEHM, HERB
VARLEY, JOHN [H]

BOEHNING, W.R.
BOHNING, WOLF RUEDIGER

BOELE, WILHELM
OSSENBRINK, WILHELM

PSEUDONYMS

BOER, ANNELIES
RUGGEBERG, ANNELIES [B]

BOERNE, ALFRED
DOEBLIN, ALFRED

BOERNEEF
VAN DER MERWE, ISAK WILL.

BOGADUCK
LINDSAY, HAROLD ARTHUR

BOGAR, JEFF
HOSSENT, HARRY
BARNARD, LESLIE T.
THOMAS, RONALD WILLS

BOGARD, DALE
ENEFER, DOUGLAS STALLARD

BOGARDE, DIRK
VAN DEN BOGARDE, DEREK J.

BOGART, E.A.
BOGART, ELEANOR ANNE

BOGAT, HENRY
HORSCHELT, THEODOR

BOGAT, SHATAN
KACEWGARI, ROMAINE

BOGDANOV, ALEXANDER
MALINOVSKY, ALEXANDER

BOGEN, ANDREW
ELBOGEN, ANDREW

BOGEN, K.R.
BOGEN, KAREN BARKER

BOGGS, BILL
BOGGS, WILLIAM III

BOGGS, TIMOTHY
GRANT, CHARLES L.

BOGLE, CHARLES
DUKINFIELD, WILLIAM CLAUD

BOHASSIAN, GREGOR
ROTSLER, WILLIAM

BOHLMANN, HANNI
BAADE, HANNI [B]

BOHN, ERIC
PRICE-BROWN, JOHN

BOHR, THEOPHILUS
THISTLE, MEL[VILLE W.]

BOHUN, HUGH
CRONIN, BERNARD CHARLES

BOHUS, KAJ
RENERTZ, KAJ

BOIES, JAN
BOIES, JANICE

BOILEAU, MARIE
HARDY, JANE

BOISGILBERT, EDMUND
DONNELLY, IGNATIUS

BOISSARD, MAURICE
LEATAUD, PAUL

BOK, HANNES
WOODARD, WAYNE

BOK, KOOSHTI
MAIR, GEORGE B.

BOLAN, MACK
MERTZ, STEPHEN
NEWTON, MICHAEL
PENDLETON, DON[ALD E.]
RANDLE, KEVIN [DOUGLAS]

BOLBO, KAPT'N
BARUCH, HUGO

BOLD, RALPH
GRIFFITHS, CHARLES TOM W.

BOLDEN, JACK
NETSCH, GUNTER

BOLDREWOOD, ROLF
BROWNE, THOMAS A.

BOLES, HAL
BOLES, HAROLD WILSON

BOLES, NICK
TOFTE, ARTHUR

BOLESKIN, LORD
CROWLEY, EDWARD ALEXANDER

BOLINBROKE, WILLIAM
HOME-GALL, WILLIAM B.

BOLITHO, RAY D.
BLAIR, DOROTHY SARA G.

BOLITHO, WILLIAM
RYALL, WILLIAM BOLITHO

BOLL, HEINRICH [THEODOR]
BOELL, HEINRICH THEODOR

BOLL, THEO
BOLL, THEOPHILUS ERNEST M

BOLLING, HAL
SCHWALBERG, CAROL[YN E.S]

BOLO, SOLOMON
WHITON, JAMES NELSON

BOLOGNESE, DON
BOLOGNESE, DONALD ALAN

BOLT, BEN
BINNS, OTWELL

BOLT, LEE
FAUST, FREDERICK S.

BOLTON, ALEXANDER
CHRISTIE, ROBERT

BOLTON, ELIZABETH
JOHNSTON, NORMA

BOLTON, EVELYN
BUNTING, ANNE EVELYN

BOLTON, ISABEL
MILLER, MARY BRITTON

BOLUS, JIM
BOLUS, JAMES MICHAEL

BOMBA, GERWAZY
SZTYRMER, LUDWIK

BOMKAUF
KAUFMAN, BOB [GARNELL]

BON VIVEUR
CRADOCK, JOHN
CRADOCK, PHYLLIS NAN S.

BONA, MERCY
ZIEGLER, ALAN

BONAR, VERONICA
BAILEY, DONNA VERONICA A.

BOND, B.J.
HENEGHAN, JAMES

BOND, E.J.
BOND, EDWARD JARVIS

BOND, EVELYN
HERSHMAN, MORRIS

BOND, GEORGE
FRITCH, CHARLES E.

BOND, GILLIAN
MCEVOY, MARJORIE HARTE

BOND, IAN
WILLETT, FRANCISCUS

BOND, J. HARVEY
WINTERBOTHAM, RUSS[EL] R.

BOND, LEWIS
PAINE, LAURAN BOSWORTH

BOND, RAY
SMITH, RICHARD REIN

BOND, REBECCA
CZULEGER, REBECCA

BOND, STEPHEN
SANTESSON, HANS STEFAN

BOND, TED
BOND, EDWARD JARVIS

BONEHILL, [CAPT.] RALPH
STRATEMEYER, EDWARD

BONES, BRUDDER
SCOTT, JOHN F.

BONES, JEAN-PAUL
LEGER, JEAN-MARC

BONES, JIM JR.
BONES, JAMES C. JR.

BONETT, EMERY
COULSON, FELICITY W.C.

BONETT, JOHN
COULSON, JOHN HUBERT A.

BONETT, JOHN & EMERY
COULSON, FELICITY W.C.
COULSON, JOHN HUBERT A.

BONEWITS, ISAAC
BONEWITS, PHILIP E. I.

BONEY, MARY LILY
SHEATS, MARY BONEY

BONGARTZ, HEINZ
THORWALD, JURGEN

BONHAM, FRANK
BONHAM, CECIL FRANCIS

BONINO, LOUISE
WILLIAMS, LOUISE BONINO

BONN, GEORGE
JENNISON, JOHN WILLIAM

BONN, PAT
BONN, PATRICIA CAROLYN

BONNAMY, FRANCIS
WALZ, AUDREY BOYERS

BONNARD, ADAM
WHEELAHAN, PAUL

BONNER, ELIZABETH
ANDERSEN, LINDA

BONNER, JACK
PAINE, LAURAN BOSWORTH

BONNER, MICHAEL
GLASSCOCK, ANNE BONNER

BONNER, PARKER
BALLARD, W. TODHUNTER

BONNER, TERRY NELSON
CASTORO, LAURA ANN
GREGORY, MARY LAWRENCE
KRAUZER, STEVEN M.
OLDEN, MARC
RAESCHILD, SHEILA
YARBRO, CHELSEA QUINN

BONNETTE, VICTOR
ROY, EWELL PAUL

BONNY, BILL
KEEVILL, HENRY J.

BONTEBAL, HENK
HEERTJE, ARNOLD

BOOJUM
BARROWS, [RUTH] MARJORIE

BOOKER, ANTON S.
RANDOLPH, VANCE

BOOKMAN, CHARLOTTE
ZOLOTOW, CHARLOTTE [S]

BOOKTASTER
TULLOCK, W.W.

BOOKWORM
DONNELLY, THOMAS F.

BOOMIS, CYNTHIA
LAMONT, GILVAN DERWENT

BOON, FRANCIS
BACON, EDWARD

BOONE, BARNEY
ROTSLER, WILLIAM

BOONE, DEBBY
BOONE, DEBORAH ANN

BOONE, HENRY L.
ST. JOHN, PERCY BOLLNGBRK

BOONE, IKE
ATHANAS, WILLIAM VERNE

BOONE, PAT
BOONE, CHARLES EUGENE

BOONTJE
BOON, LOUIS-PAUL

BOORSTIN, RUTH F.
BOORSTIN, RUTH C. FRANKEL

BOOT, ROSIE
BROWN, TINA

BOOT, WILLIAM
STRAUSSLER, TOM

BOOTH, ALICE
HARTWELL, ALICE BOOTH

BOOTH, GEOFFREY
TANN, JENNIFER

BOOTH, IRWIN
HOCH, EDWARD D.

BOOTH, MRS. LETITIA
RUSSELL, WILLIAM CLARK

BOOTH, REGINA
BOOTH, EDWIN

BOOTH, TED
BOOTH, GEOFFREY THORNTON

BOOTON, KAGE
BOOTON, CATHERINE KAGE

BOOZ, MATEO
CORREA, MIGUEL ANGEL

BOR, JOSEF
BONDY, JOSEF

BOR, MATEJ
PAVSHICH, VLADIMIR

BORCH, TED
LUND, A. MORTEN

BORDEN, BOB
REES, CLAIR FRANCIS

BORDEN, COLE
LYNCH, W.

BORDEN, ETHEL
RUSSELL, ETHEL HARRIMAN

BORDEN, LEE
DEAL, BORDEN

BORDEN, LEIGH
DEAL, BORDEN

BORDEN, LEO
BORDEN, DEAL

BORDEN, LIZZIE
BORDEN, LINDA

BORDEN, M.
SAXON, GLADYS RELYEA

BORDEN, ORSON T.
BARON, OSCAR

BORDERER
GREEN-PRICE, RICH DANSEY

BORDEUX, VAHDAH J.
DE BONIS, SOFIA MCQUAIDE

BORE, [DR.] HELLE
SMITH, CHARLES H.

BORELL, HELENE
HEGELER, STEN

BORELLI, CASS
FAWCETT, FRANK DUBREZ
USHER, [JOHN] GRAY

BORER, MARY CATHCART
MYERS, MARY CATHCART

BORG, BERTIL
ORNILF, GUNNAR

BORG, BJORN
BORG, BJOERN RUNE

BORG, JACK
BORG, PHILIP ANTHONY JOHN

BORG, TONNY
MADSEN, BORGE

BORG, TONY
MADSEN, BORGE

BORGE, BERNHARD
BJERKE, ANDRE

BORGERS, CHARLES
BORCHERS, KARL

BORGHAM, JESPER
BOLINDER, JEAN

BORING, PHYLLIS ZATLIN
ZATLIN, PHYLLIS

BORK, TEDA
ACKERMANN, INGEBORG

BORLAND, HAL
BORLAND, HAROLD GLEN

BORN, MATTHIAS
BORRMANN, MARTIN

BORNE, DOROTHY
RICE, DOROTHY MARY

BORNEMAN, H.
GOTTSHALL, FRANKLIN HEN.

BORNEO JIMMY
MELTZER, R.

BORODIN, GEORGE
MILKOMANE, G. ALEXIS M.

BORODIN, LEVASIOV
KROPOTKIN, PIOTR ALEXEY.

BORODIN, SERGEY PETROVICH
SARGIDZHAN, AMIR

BORONIECKI, MIROSLAV
STOBERSKI, ZYGMUNT JULIAN

BORSON, ROO
BORSON, RUTH ELIZABETH

BORST, JURGEN
BREUER, GEORG KARL FELIX

BORTH, WILLAN G.
BOSWORTH, WILLAN GEORGE

BORTHWICK, J.S.
CREIGHTON, JEAN SCOTT

BORTIN, V.G.
BORTIN, GEORGE & VIRGINIA

BORTON, D.B.
CARPENTER, LYNETTE

BORTON, ELIZABETH
DE TREVINO, ELIZABETH B.

BORTON, TERRY
BORTON, JOHN C. JR.

BORUS v. MUHLAU, KARL
ALLMENDINGER, KARL

BORYS, GONTRAU
BERTHOUD, EUGENE

BOS
PREST, THOMAS PECKET

BOSANQUET, NICK
BOSANQUET, NICHOLAS F.G.

BOSANQUET, REGGIE
BOSANQUET, REGINALD

BOSCAWEN, LINDA
SMITHELLS, ANABEL DOREEN

BOSCH, MARTHA-MARIA
HAIDLE, MARTHA-MARIA

BOSCO, JACK
HOLLIDAY, JOSEPH

BOSET, HORST
BOSETKY, HORST

BOSIE
DOUGLAS, ALFRED BRUCE

BOSMAN, JIM
BORGMAN, JAMES MARK

BOSTON, CHARLES K.
GRUBER, FRANK

BOSTON, DON
KALMUCZAK, ROLF

BOSTON, RALPH
CHADWICK, PAUL

BOSTROM, HANK
LOVEJOY, WILLIAM H.

BOSTWICK, [COL.] T.B.
HARBAUGH, THOMAS C.

BOSWELL
GORDON, GILES ALEXANDER E

BOSWELL, JAMES
KENT, ARTHUR WILLIAM C.

BOSWELL, JOHN
KING, JOHN BOSWELL

BOSWORTH, FRANK
PAINE, LAURAN BOSWORTH

BOTH, SERGIUS
FRANKE, HERBERT W.

BOTHAM, R.R.
WINTERBOTHAM, RUSS[EL] R.

BOTO, EZA
BIYIDI, ALEXANDRE

BOTT, ELIZABETH
SPILLUS, ELIZABETH JANE

BOTTOME, PHYLLIS
FORBES-DENNIS, PHYLLIS

BOTTOMS, PHYLLIS
FORBES-DENNIS, PHYLLIS

BOTTSFORD, LORD
HIRD, JAMES D.

BOUCHER, ANTHONY
WHITE, WILLIAM A.P.

BOUDRAINE, WILLIAM
BRANNON, WILLIAM T.

BOUGH, LEE
HUSER, LAVERN CARL

BOUHELIER, SAINT-GEORGES
DE BOHELIER-LEPELETIER, G

BOULT, S. KYE
COCHRANE, WILLIAM E.

BOULTING
BOULTING, SYDNEY

BOUMELHA, PENNY
BOUMELHA, PENELOPE ANN

BOUNDER, THE
FAY, E.F.

BOURBON, KEN
BAUER, ERWIN A.

BOURCHIER, JULES
POSNER, DAVID LOUIS

BOURDON, MADAM
FROMENT, MATHILDE

BOURKE, TERRY
RUHEN, CARL

BOURNE, GEORGE
STURT, GEORGE

BOURNE, HESTER
TROKE, MOLLY

BOURNE, JOHN
JOHN, OWEN

BOURNE, LESLEY
MARSHALL, EVELYN

BOURNE, PETER
JEFFRIES, BRUCE GRAHAM M.

BOUVERIE
KREINER, GEORGE

BOVE, EMMANUEL
BOBORNIKOFF, EMMANUEL

BOVEE, RUTH
PAINE, LAURAN BOSWORTH

BOVET, MARIE ANNE DE
DE BOIS-HERBERT, GUY

BOWDEN, JIM
SPENCE, W. JOHN DUNCAN

BOWDEN, SUSAN
TWADDLE, SUSAN BOWDEN

BOWE, KATE
TAYLOR, MARY ANN

BOWEN, ALYCE
BOWEN, ALICE

BOWEN, BETTY [MORGAN]
WEST, BETTY

BOWEN, DAVID
BOWEN, JOSHUA DAVID

BOWEN, ELENORE SITH
BOHANNAN, LAURA M. SMITH

BOWEN, ELIZABETH
CAMERON, ELIZABETH D.C.

BOWEN, JUDITH
CORSER, JUDY E.

BOWEN, MARJORIE
LONG, GABRIELLE M.V.C.

BOWEN, MARY
HALL, MARY BOWEN

BOWEN, OLWEN
DAVIES, OLWEN B.

BOWEN, R.T.
BLOCH, ROBERT [A]

BOWER, ALISON
BECKETT, GILLIAN

BOWER, B.M.
COWAN, BERTHA MUZZY B.S.

BOWER, BARBARA
TODD, BARBARA EUPHAN

BOWER, KEITH
BECKETT, KENNETH ALBERT

BOWER, R.G.
BLOCH, ROBERT [A]

PSEUDONYMS

BOWERS, BILL
BOWERS, WILLIAM L.
MALLARDI, BILL

BOWERS, MRS. J. MILTON
BIERCE, AMBROSE

BOWERS, R.L.
GLASBY, JOHN S.

BOWES, ANNE BASTILLE
LA BASTILLE, ANNE

BOWICK, DOROTHY MUELLER
MUELLER, DOROTHY

BOWIE, DAVID
JONES, DAVID ROBERT

BOWIE, JIM
CHARLES, GEORGE
MCFARLANE, LESLIE CHARLES
NORWOOD, VICTOR [G.C.]
PATTEN, LEWIS B.
STRATEMEYER, EDWARD

BOWIE, SAM
BALLARD, W. TODHUNTER

BOWLER, JAN BRETT
BRETT, JAN [C]

BOWLES, ALBERT C.
GRASMUCK, JURGEN

BOWLES, KERWIN
ABELES, ELVIN

BOWMAN, BOB
BOWMAN, ROBERT T.

BOWMAN, JEANNE
BLOCKLINGER, PEGGY O'MORE

BOWNE, FORD
BROWN, FORREST

BOWSER, JOAN
BOWSER, PEARL

BOWYANG, BILL
VENNARD, ALEXANDER VINDEX

BOWYER, NINA
CONARAIN, ALICE [NINA]

BOX, EDGAR
VIDAL, [E] GORE LUTHER

BOXMAN
CHAMBLISS, WILLIAM J.

BOXWOOD, RICHARD
DANIELL, ALBERT SCOTT

BOY
ZELENSKI, TADEUSZ

BOY-LINDEN, ELMAR
BETZ, JOSEF

BOYAJIAN, CECILY
STARR, CEWCILY

BOYAJIAN, JERRY
BOYAJIAN, JEREL MICHAEL

BOYCE, CHRIS
BOYCE, JOHN CHRISTOPHER

BOYCE, FRANK
JENNISON, JOHN WILLIAM

BOYCE, MORTON
FEARN, JOHN RUSSELL

BOYCOTT, GEOFF
BOYCOTT, GEOFFREY

BOYD, ALAMO
BOSWORTH, ALLAN R.

BOYD, ANN S.
SCHOONMAKER, ANN

BOYD, BELLE
HAMMOND, MRS. J.S.

BOYD, BOB
BOYD, ROBERT THOMPSON

BOYD, CARSE
STACTON, DAVID DEREK

BOYD, DON
BOYCE, DAVID

BOYD, EDWARD
TUNLEY, ROUL

BOYD, ESTHER
BOYD, EDMOND A.D.

BOYD, FELIX
HARRISON, HARRY

BOYD, FRANK
KANE, FRANK

BOYD, JOHN
UPCHURCH, BOYD BRADFIELD

BOYD, MARION [M]
HAVIGHURST, MARION BOYD

BOYD, NANCY
MILLAY, EDNA ST. VINCENT

BOYD, NEIL
DE ROSA, PETER [C]

BOYD, PAULINE
SCHOCK, PAULINE

BOYD, PRUDENCE
GIBBS, NORAH

BOYD, SELMA
ACUFF, SELMA BOYD

BOYER D'AGEN
BOYER, JEAN AUGUSTE

BOYER, COLUMBIA
MARTIN, NELL COLUMBIA B.

BOYER, PAM
WEISS, JOE

BOYER, PAMELA
WEISS, JOE

BOYER, RICHARD L.
BOYER, RICHARD LEWIS

BOYER, RICK
BOYER, RICHARD LEWIS

BOYER, ROBERT
LAKE, KENNETH R[OBERT]

BOYERS, PEGGY
BOYERS, MARGARET ANNE

BOYLAN, BOYD
WHITON, JAMES NELSON

BOYLE, G.G.
BOYER, GLENN G.

BOYLE, HAL
BOYLE, HAROLD VINCENT

BOYLE, KAY
VAIL, MRS. LAURENCE

BOYLE, MARK
KIENZLE, WILLIAM X.

BOYLE, PAUL
GRAVES, ROBERT VAN RANKE

BOYLE, ROBERT
JENKINS, JENNIFER

BOYLE, TIMM
BOYLE, TIMOTHY ROBERT

BOYLESVE, RENE
TARDIVEAX, RENE MARIE

BOYSEN, CORNELIA
AHRENS, ANNEMARIE

BRAB
BRABBINS, OLIVER G.

BRABANDER, GERARD DEN
JOFRIET, JAN GERARDUS

BRABAZON, JAMES
SETH-SMITH, LESLIE JAMES

BRABBINS
BRABBINS, OLIVER G.

BRACE, BENJAMIN
MCCUTCHEON, BENJAMIM F.

BRACE, TIMOTHY
PRATT, THEODORE

BRACK, BUSTER
BRAND, KURT

BRACK, MONIKA
ELWENSPOEK, LISE-MELANIE

BRACK, VEKTIS
CONDRAY, BRUNO G.
HUMPHRYS, LESLIE GEORGE

BRACKEEN, STEVE
FARRIS, JOHN

BRACKEN, C.P.
BRACKEN, CATHARINE PHILL.

BRACKETT, LEIGH
HAMILTON, LEIGH BRACKETT

BRACKETT, WARING
ROTSLER, WILLIAM

BRADA, OLOF
BULL, OLAF

BRADBURNE, E.S.
LAWRENCE, ELIZABETH

BRADBURY, ED
MOORCOCK, MICHAEL

BRADBURY, EDWARD P.
MOORCOCK, MICHAEL

BRADDON, GEORGE
MILKOMANE, G. ALEXIS M.

BRADDON, M.E.
MAXWELL, MARY ELIZABETH B

BRADDON, MARY E.
MAXWELL, MARY ELIZABETH B

BRADEN, IRENE A.
HOADLEY, IRENE BRADEN

BRADEN, TOM
BRADEN, THOMAS WARDELL

BRADEN, WALTER
FINNEY, WALTER BRADEN

BRADFIELD, JOLLY ROGER
BRADFIELD, ROGER

BRADFIELD, NANCY
SAYER, NANCY MARGETTS

BRADFORD M.D., ADAM
WASSERSUG, DR. JOSEPH

BRADFORD, GORDON
ARROW, JAY

BRADFORD, LAURA
PAALBORG, PAUL B.

BRADFORD, LILY
SCOTT, LILY K.

BRADFORD, MATTHEW C.
JENNISON, JOHN WILLIAM

BRADFORD, MICHAEL
ALLEN, MICHAEL [DEREK]

BRADFORD, ROBERT
MOORE, [JOSEPH] WARD

BRADFORD, SALLY
BRADFORD, BARBARA
SIDDON, SALLY

BRADFORD, SAM
HARING, DON

BRADFORD, SIMON
WINTERBOTHAM, RUSS[EL] R.

BRADFORD, WILL
PAINE, LAURAN BOSWORTH

BRADLEY, ALICE
SHELDON, ALICE H. BRADLEY

BRADLEY, ASTARA ZIMMER
BRADLEY, MARION ZIMMER

BRADLEY, BILL
BRADLEY, WILLIAM WARREN

BRADLEY, BRIAN K.
SCHUYLER, KEITH C.

BRADLEY, CONCHO
PAINE, LAURAN BOSWORTH

BRADLEY, DUANE
SANBORN, DUANE

BRADLEY, J.J.G.
BORLASE, JAMES SKIPP

BRADLEY, KATE
BRYANT, KATHLEEN

BRADLEY, LURA L.
BRADLEY, LURA LYNNETTE

BRADLEY, LYNN
BRADLEY, LURA LYNNETTE

BRADLEY, LYNN L.
BRADLEY, LURA LYNNETTE

BRADLEY, LYNNE
BRADLEY, LURA LYNNETTE

BRADLEY, MATT[HEW]
SCOTT, PETER

BRADLEY, MICHAEL
BLUMBERG, GARY

BRADLEY, RAMONA
ROLLE-BERG, RAMONA

BRADLEY, SHELLAND
BIRT, FRANCIS BRADLEY

BRADLEY, WILL
STRICKLAND, WILLIAM BRAD.

BRADLY, MR.
BURROUGHS, WILLIAM S.

BRADSHAW, ANNIE [CROPPER]
BRADSHAW, MRS. ALBERT S.

BRADSHAW, BUCK
PAINE, LAURAN BOSWORTH

BRADSHAW, EMILY
KROKOSZ, EMILY

BRADSHAW, WELLESLY
ALEXANDER, CHARLES W.

BRADSHAW, WESLY
ALEXANDER, CHARLES W.

BRADSTREET, VALLERIE
ROBY, MARY LINN

BRADUN, JOHANNA
BRANDENBERGER, ANNE

BRADWELL, JAMES
KENT, ARTHUR WILLIAM C.

BRADY, ADAM
DUNN, DES R.

BRADY, JILL
KLEMME, CHRIS

BRADY, MATT
SHALLITT, JOSEPH

BRADY, NICHOLAS
LEVINSON, LEONARD [L]
TURNER, J[OHN] V[ICTOR]

BRADY, PETER
DANIELS, NORMAN A.

BRADY, TAYLOR
BALL, DONNA
HARPER, SHANNON

BRADY, WILLIAM S.
WELLS, ANGUS
HARVEY, JOHN [BARTON]

BRAEK, BUSTER
BRAND, KURT

BRAGAGLIA, ANTON GIULIO
MIRACOLA, GIOVANNI

BRAGG, BILL
BRAGG, WILLIAM FREDERICK

BRAGG, BOBBY
SYKES, ROOSEVELT

BRAGG, SIR W.H.
BRAGG, WILLIAM HENRY

BRAHMS, CARYL
ABRAHAMS, DORIS CAROLINE

BRAILSFORD, FRANCES
WOSMEK, FRANCES

BRAIN, LEONARD
PECK, LEONARD

BRAITHWAITE, KENNETH JAME
BARROW, KENNETH

BRAITHWAITE, RAYMOND
OWEN, FRANK

BRAM, CHRIS
BRAM, CHRISTOPHER

BRAMAH, ERNEST
SMITH, ERNEST BRAMAH

BRAMLETT, JOHN
PIERCE, JOHN LEONARD

BRAMPTON, JAMES
WILLIAMS, JOHN BABINGTON

BRAMWELL, CHARLOTTE
KIMBRO, JOHN M.

BRANCH, FLORENZ
STONEBRAKER, FLORENCE

BRANCH, STEPHEN
ZWEIG, STEFAN

BRAND, B. ALEC
BRANDLE, ALEXANDER

BRAND, CHRISTIANNA
LEWIS, M. CHRISTIANNA M.

PSEUDONYMS

BRAND, CLAY
NORWOOD, VICTOR [G.C.]

BRAND, DAVID
NUTT, DAVID

BRAND, GARRISON
BRANDNER, GARY

BRAND, HENRYK
LAUER, HENRYK GUSTAV

BRAND, HILARY
BAILEY, HILARY
FRANCES, STEPHEN D.
MOORCOCK, MICHAEL
MOFFATT, JAMES

BRAND, HORST
BRANDHORST, ANDREAS

BRAND, MAX
FAUST, FREDERICK S.

BRAND, MONA
FOX, MONA ALEXIS

BRAND, NAT
DONNER, BILL

BRAND, PETER
LARSEN, ERLING
RUHEN, CARL

BRAND, SUSAN
ROPER, SUSAN BRONTHRON

BRAND, VICTOR
NORWOOD, VICTOR [G.C.]

BRANDANE, JOHN
MACINTYRE, JOHN

BRANDE, DOROTHEA
COLLINS, DOROTHEA T.B.

BRANDECK, GOTZ
CLAUSS, LUDWIG FERDINAND

BRANDEIS, B.
BLANK, MATTHIAS

BRANDEL, MARC
BERESFORD, MARCUS

BRANDEL-ELSCHNER, KATE
ELSCHNER, KATE

BRANDENBURG, EVELYNE
KRAUSE, EVELYNE

BRANDES, SOPHIE
KAFKA-H.-B., SOPHIE-M.

BRANDIN, HANS I.
BREITENEICHNER, HANS

BRANDIS, MARK
VON MICHALEWSKY, NIKOLAI

BRANDMULLER, JOHANNES
CHRIST, ROBERT B.

BRANDNER, MATTHIAS
KINDLER, OTTO

BRANDON, ALICIA
CAMERON, STELLA
RICE, LINDA

BRANDON, BEATRICE
KREPPS, ROBERT WILSON

BRANDON, BRUCE
BRAUN, WILBUR

BRANDON, CARL
CARR, TERRY G.
ELLIK, RON
GRAHAM, PETER

BRANDON, CARL, JR.
HOLMBERG, JOHN-HENRY

BRANDON, CURT
BISHOP, CURTIS [KENT]

BRANDON, FRANK
BULMER, [HENRY] KENNETH

BRANDON, JIM
HANOS, DMITRI [JAMES]

BRANDON, JOANNA
HARPER, OLIVIA & KEN

BRANDON, JOE
DAVIS, ROBERT PRUNIER

BRANDON, NORMAN H.
GRUBER, FRANK

BRANDON, ROBIN
BRANDON, ROBERT JOSEPH

BRANDON, ROY
HOOPER, STANLEY

BRANDON, SHEILA
RAYNER, CLAIRE B.

BRANDSTON, GARTH
BACON, JOHN B.

BRANDT, EVA
BRUCKNER, MARIE

BRANDT, HARVEY
EDWARDS, WILLIAM B.

BRANDT, HEINZ
FROHLICH, GUSTAV

BRANDT, KASPAR
PRINS, JACOB WINKLER

BRANDT, KEITH
SABIN, LOUIS

BRANDT, MARTIN
ERICSSON, GUSTAV

BRANDT, NAT
BRANDT, NATHAN HENRY JR.

BRANDT, ROGER
CRAWFORD, WILLIAM [E]

BRANDT, TOM
DEWEY, THOMAS B.

BRANDT, WILLEM
BRAND, WILLEM SIMON

BRANDTNER, HEINZ
BOHM-RAFFAY, HELMUT

BRANDYWINE, REBECCA
WADSWORTH, MARY REBECCA

BRANE, REGINALD
AMBROSE, MICHAEL E.

BRANFOOT, GWYNNETH
HOLDER, GWYNNETH

BRANGWYN, CHARLES
REED, EDWARD CHARLES

BRANNER, CARL
VEGENOR, SVERRE

BRANNIGAN, BILL
BRANNIGAN, WILLIAM

BRANNON, MAJOR ROBERT
GIBSON, WALTER B.

BRANQUIRHO DA FONSECA, A.
MADEIRA, ANTONIO

BRANSCOMBE, EUGENE
EMANUEL, VICTOR ROUSSEAU

BRANT, KYLIE
BAHNSEN, KIMBERLY

BRANT, LEWIS
ROWLAND, DONALD S.

BRANT, SAM
GRUBER, FRANK

BRANYAN, BRENDA
BRANYAN-BROADBENT, BRENDA

BRASIER-CREAGH, PATRICK
CREAGH, PATRICK

BRASSAI
HALASZ, GYULA

BRASSET, A.D.
ASH, EDWARD CECIL

BRASTER, MIKE B.
DONGES, GUNTER

BRATE, HOLGER
BERGMAN, HJALMAR

BRATNY, ROMAN
MULARCZYK, ROMAN

BRATT, BERTE
SAXEGAARD, ANNIK

BRATT, FINN
BOGSRUD, TORVALD

BRATTSTROM, INGER
HOGELIN-BRATTSTROM, INGER

BRAUN, CARSTEN
ANTON, UWE

BRAUN, F.W.
JENNISON, JOHN WILLIAM

BRAUN, FRANK F.
BRAUN, FERNANDO MAX RICH.

BRAUN, HELGA
DURSELEN, HELGA

BRAUN, KATHE
HARNACK-BRAUN, KATHARINA

BRAUN, M.G.
KOBLINSKI, HANS-JOACHIM
TENKRAT, FRIEDRICH

BRAUN, MAURICE-GEORGES
BRAUN, MAURICE GILLES

BRAUN, TERRANCE
BENNETT, JEFF

BRAUND, HAL
BRAUND, HAROLD

BRAUNSLAU, NATHAN
BELLAH, JAMES WARNER

BRAWLEY, PAUL HOLM
BRAWLEY, PAUL LEROY

BRAY, ALISON
ROWLAND, DONALD S.

BRAYCE, WILLIAM
ROWLAND, DONALD S.

BRAYMER, MARGUERITE
DODD, MARGUERITE

BRAZA, JACQUE
MCKEAG, ERNEST LIONEL

BRAZOS, WACO
JENNINGS, MICHAEL GLENN

BRDLBRMPFT
ROTH, CHRISTIAN

BREAKER, THE
MORANT, HARRY H.

BREARLEY, JOHN
GARBUTT, JOHN L.

BREATNAC, SEAMUS
WALSH, JAMES P[ATRICK]

BREAUX, DAISY
CALHOUN, CORNELIA DONOVAN

BRECHT, ARNOLT
MULLER, ARTUR

BRECHT, BERTOLT
BRECHT, EUGEN BERTHOLD F.

BRECK, VIVIAN
BRECKENFELD, VIVIAN G.

BRECKER, CORD
GREEN, ROGER

BREDA, OLAF
BULL, OLAF

BREDA, TJALMAR
DEJONG, DAVID C[ORNEL]

BREDON, JOHN
ENG, STEPHEN
TAYLOR, W.T.

BREDOW, MIRIAM
WOLF, MIRIAM BREDOW

BREEN, DANA
BIRKSTED-BREEN, DANA

BREEN, DAVID
CHAMBERS, [J.D] WHITTAKER

BREESE, DAVE
BREESE, DAVID WILLIAM

BREGENZ, CURD
BERGEL, HANS

BREHAT, ALFRED
GUEZENEC, ALFRED

BREIT, FRANK
RIESCHEL, PAUL

BREITMANN, HANS
LELAND, CHARLES G.

BRELLEN, MARC
FRESHMAN, BRUCE JACK

BREMER, LISA
JANAS, FRANCIS LEROY G.

BREMER, MAXIM
MAXIMOVIC, GERD

BREMER, WARD
REACH, JAMES

BRENAN, GERALD
BRENAN, EDWARD FITZGERALD

BRENDA
CASTLE SMITH, MRS. G.

BRENDALL, EDITH
BERTIN, EDDY C.

BRENDON, KAY
CLAESSON, BIGI

BRENDT, HAL
MUNCH, HELLMUT-HUBERTUS

BRENET, MICHEL
BOBILLIER, MARIE

BRENGLE, WILLIAM
BROWNE, HOWARD

BRENMAN, CLAES
THORIS, LARS

BRENNAN, CHRISTOPHER
BAIRD, ROLAND
KININMOUTH, CHRITOPHER

BRENNAN, JAN
BRENNAN, JAMES HERBERT

BRENNAN, LILLA
HINE, ALEXANDRA

BRENNAN, MICHAEL
DELFS, RAINER

BRENNAN, TIM
CONROY, JOHN WESLEY

BRENNAN, WALT
KING, ALBERT

BRENNAN, WARD
MEARES, LEONARD F.

BRENNAN, WILL
PAINE, LAURAN BOSWORTH

BRENNAND, FRANK
LAMBERT, ERIC

BRENNECKE, HANS
BODENSTEDT, HANS

BRENNER, ARVID
HEERBERGER, HELGE

BRENNER, ISABEL
SCHUCHMAN, JOAN

BRENNGLAS, ADOLF
GLASSBRENNER, ADOLF

BRENNING, L.H.
HUNTER, ALFRED JOHN

BRENT, A.D.
GLASBY, JOHN S.

BRENT, AUDREY
BOYLE, ANN [PETERS]

BRENT, BERYL
INCE, MARTIN JEFFREY

BRENT, CALVIN
HORNBY, JOHN WILKINSON

BRENT, CARL
WILLETT, EDWARD

BRENT, CATHERINE
KING, ALBERT

BRENT, ELEANOR
KRAMER, NORA

BRENT, FRANCIS
HUNTER, ALFRED JOHN

BRENT, GUY
KODELPETER, HANS P.

BRENT, HARRY
BRENT, HAROLD PATRICK

BRENT, IRIS
BANCROFT, IRIS M. NELSON
NIELSON, INGRID

BRENT, LINDA
JACOBS, HARRIET

BRENT, LORING
WORTS, GEORGE FRANK

BRENT, MADELEINE
O'DONNELL, PETER

BRENT, NIGEL
WIMHURST, CECIL G.E.

BRENT, OF BIN BIN
FRANKLIN, STELLA MARIA S.

PSEUDONYMS

BRENT, R.L.
POWELL, LARRY

BRENT, ROMNEY
LARRALDE, ROMULO

BRENTFORD, BURKE
URNER, NATHAN DANE

BRESINGLAS, ADOLF
GLASSBRENNER, ADOLF

BRESLIN, JIMMY
BRESLIN, JAMES

BRESSEUR, PIERRE
ESPINASSE, ALBERT

BRETNOR, R.
KAHN, ALFRED REGINALD

BRETNOR, REGINALD
KAHN, ALFRED REGINALD

BRETON, DE NIJS, E.
NIEUWENHUYS, ROBERT

BRETON-SMITH, CLARE
BOON, AUGUST

BRETONNE, ANNE-MARIE
BERMAN, ARNOLD M.

BRETT, DAVID
CAMPBELL, WILL D[AVIS]

BRETT, GEORGE IRA
CRAWFURD, OSWALD J.F.

BRETT, HAWKSLEY
BELL, ROBERT STANLEY W.

BRETT, JOHN MICHAEL
TRIPP, MILES [BARTON]

BRETT, KATHERYN
ROBARCHEK, PEG

BRETT, LEO
FANTHORPE, R.L.
MANSFIELD, HARRY O.

BRETT, MARTIN
SANDERSON, [R] DOUGLAS

BRETT, MICHAEL
BRETT, LESLIE FREDERICK
TRIPP, MILES [BARTON]

BRETT, MOLLY
BRETT, MARY ELIZABETH

BRETT, ROSALIND
BLAIR, KATHRYN

BRETT, SIMON
TRIPP, MILES [BARTON]

BRETT, STEPHEN
MERTZ, STEPHEN

BRETT, TODDY
HEYMANN, ROBERT JR.
KRATOCHWIL, JOSEF
RICHARTZ, HELMUTH

BRETUO, AKWASI
ASSENSOH, AKWASI BRETUO

BREUER, GUSTL
BREUER, GUSTAV J.

BREUER, JORG
BREUER, GEORG KARL FELIX

BREVIS, CARL AUGUST
KURZ, CARL HEINZ

BREVOORT, LAURENCE
BARRETTO, LAURENCE B.

BREWER, D.S.
BREWER, DEREK STANLEY

BREWER, JORDAN
MARBERRY, M.M.

BREWER, MIKE
GUINESS, MAURICE C.

BREWSTER, BENJAMIN
ELTING, MARY
FOLSOM, FRANKLIN [B]

BREWSTER, DAVID
BIERMAN, JOHN

BREWSTER, ELIOT
GIFFORD, JAMES NOBLE

BREWSTER, FRANKLIN
FOLSOM, FRANKLIN [B]

BREWSTER, ROBIN
STAPLES, REGINALD THOMAS

BREX
TWELLS, J.

BREYDOR, BILL
WELSH, KEN

BREZHNEV, DENNIS
BARNETT, PAUL LE PAGE

BREZHNID, L.I.
BREZHNEV, LEONID ILLYICH

BREZINA, OTAKAR
JEBAVY, VACLAV IGNAC

BRIAN
POWELL, BRIAN S.

BRIAN, ALAN B.
PARULSKI, GEORGE R.

BRIAN, JAMES
STREET, ARTHUR GEORGE

BRIAN, MARILYN
DAGG, JILLIAN

BRIAND, RENA
HUXLEY, RENA

BRIARTON, GRENDEL
BRETNOR, [A] REGINALD

BRIAVELS, JAMES S.
WOOD, JAMES PLAYSTEAD

BRICKTOP
SMITH, ADA BEATRICE

BRICUTH, JOHN
IRWIN, JOHN THOMAS

BRIDE, JACK
MARTEAU, F.A.

BRIDE, NADJA
NOBISSON, JOSEPHINE

BRIDGE, ANN
O'MALLEY, MARY DOLLING

BRIDGE, BONAR
TULLOCK, W.W.

BRIDGE, FRANK J.
BRUECKEL, FRANCIS J.

BRIDGE, JOHN
PETERS, ROBERT LOUIS

BRIDGECROSS, PETER
CARDINAL, ROGER

BRIDGEMAN, IRENE
DANCYGER, IRENE

BRIDGEMAN, RICHARD
DAVIES, LESLIE PERNELL

BRIDGER, ADAM
BINGLEY, DAVID ERNEST

BRIDGER, JOHN
GIBSON, JOE

BRIDGES, BEN
WHITEHEAD, DAVID [HENRY]

BRIDGES, EMILY
BRUGGEN, CAROL HOLMES

BRIDGES, HOWARD
STAPLES, REGINALD THOMAS

BRIDGES, LAURIE
BRUCK, LORRAINE

BRIDGES, ROY
BRIDGES, ROYAL

BRIDGES, T.C.
BRIDGES, THOMAS CHARLES

BRIDGES, TOM
BRIDGES, THOMAS CHARLES

BRIDGES, VICTOR
DE FREYNE, GEORGE

BRIDGEWATER, DONALD
HENDERSON, DONALD [L]

BRIDGMAN, GERALDINE
JERROLD, IANTHE

BRIDIE, JAMES
MAVOR, OSBORNE HENRY

BRIEN, R.N.
WHELAN, JEROME BERNARD

BRIEN, RALEY
MCCULLEY, JOHNSTON

BRIERLEY, SUSAN S.
ISAACS, SUSAN S.F.

BRIESTER, JEFF
DONGES, GUNTER
MARZINEK, WILHELM

BRIGGS, JOE BOB
BROOM, JOHN

BRIGGS, PHILIP
BRIGGS, PHYLLIS

BRIGHT, ELIZABETH
LISTON, ROBERT

BRIGHT, JAMES
ROWE, JOHN GABRIEL

BRIGHT, LAUREY
DE JONG, DAPHNE

BRIGHT, SARAH
SHINE, DEBORAH

BRIGHTFIELD, RICK
BRIGHTFIELD, RICHARD

BRIGHTON, LAURA
CORBY, JANE [IRENITA]

BRIGHTON, WESLEY JR.
LOVIN, ROGER ROBERT

BRIK, HANS THEODOR
BRIK, JOHANNES

BRILL, TONI
OLCOTT, ANTHONY & MARTHA

BRINSMEAD, H.F.
BRINSMEAD, HESBA FAY

BRION, GUY
MADSEN, AXEL

BRIONY, HENRY
ELLIS, OLIVER

BRIQUEBEC, JOHN
ROWLAND-ENTWISTLE, A.T.

BRISBANE, COUTTS
ARMOUR, R. COUTTS

BRISBANE, HENRY R.
ELLIS, EDWARD S.

BRISBANE, [MAJ.] WALTER
HARBAUGH, THOMAS C.

BRISCO, P.A.
MATTHEWS, PATRICIA [BRIS]

BRISCO, PATTY
MATTHEWS, PATRICIA [BRIS]

BRISCOE, MARGARET SUTTON
HOPKINS, MARGARET BRISCOE

BRISCOE, PAT A.
MATTHEWS, PATRICIA [BRIS]

BRISCOE, PATTY
MATTHEWS, CLAYTON [H]

BRISSARD, MONTAGUE
BEDFORD-JONES, HENRY

BRISSENDEN, BOB
BRISSENDEN, ROBERT FRANC.

BRISSENDEN, R.F.
BRISSENDEN, ROBERT FRANC.

BRISSON, FERDINAND
LANSBURGH, WERNER

BRISTOL, CHARLES
MEYN, NIELS

BRISTOL, JOHN A.
SPEER, JACK

BRISTOL, JULIUS
ABEL, ALAN [IRWIN]

BRISTOL, LEIGH
BALL, DONNA
HARPER, ELIZABETH SHANNON

BRISTOL, STEPHEN
BRAUN, WILBUR

BRISTOW, GWEN
MANNING, BRUCE & GWEN
MANNING, GWEN

BRISTOWE, EDWIN
WRIGHT, R.L. GERARD

BRISUNO, MIGUEL
MENENDEZ, MIGUEL ANGEL

BRITAIN, DAN
PENDLETON, DON[ALD E.]

BRITINDIAN
SOLOMON, SAMUEL

BRITT, DEL
KOBY, DALE

BRITT, GEORGE
SEALEY, LEONARD G.W.

BRITT, KATRINA
CONNELL, ETHEL

BRITT, SAPPHO HENDERSON
WOOLFOLK, JOSHUA PITTS

BRITTAIN, BILL
BRITTAIN, WILLIAM E.

BRITTAIN, NOEL
LUMB, EMMELINE

BRITTANICUS
KIRBY, WILLIAM

BRITTANY, LEWIS
TEED, GEORGE HAMILTON

BRITTLE, GATH
MCALPINE, ROBERT W.

BRITTON, HERBERT
EVES, REGINALD T.

BRITTON, KATE
STEGEMAN, JANET ALLAIS

BRITTON, LOUISA
MCGUIRE, LESLIE SARAH

BROADLUCK, CEPHAS
GAZLEY, ALLEN W.

BROCATO, KATHRYN
KING-BROCATO, KATHRYN

BROCK, BEN
HOWELLS, ROSCOE

BROCK, DELIA
EPHRON, DELIA

BROCK, G.L.
BROCK, GEORGE LESLIE

BROCK, GAVIN
LINDSAY, [JOHN] MAURICE

BROCK, LYNN
MCALLISTER, ALISTER

BROCK, P.W.
BROCK, PATRICK WILLET

BROCK, PETER
BROCK, RUDOLF
SCHAAKE, ERICH

BROCK, ROSE
HANSEN, JOSEPH

BROCK, STUART
TRIMBLE, LOUIS P.

BROCKE, JULIAN
WILKINSON, RICHARD HILL

BROCKHOFF, STEFAN
CUNTZ, DIETER
PLANT, RICHARD
SEIDLIN, OSKAR

BROCKLEY, FENTON
ROWLAND, DONALD S.

BROCKMANN, H.M.
MEYER-BROCKMANN, HENRI

BROD, D.C.
BROD, DEBORAH C.

BRODEUR, DIANE
CAREY-BRODEUR, DIANE L.

BRODIE, GORDON
SMITH, SIDNEY WALLACE

BRODIE, SALLY
CAVIN, RUTH BRODIE

BRODSKY, BEVERLY
MCDERMOTT, BEVERLY BRODS.

BRODSKY, JOSEPH
BRODSKY, IOSIF ALEXANDER

BRODSKY, VERA
LAWRENCE, VERA BRODSKY

BRODY, HANK
BLEECK, G.C.

BRODY, JEAN
BRODY, JANE ELLEN

BRODY, MARC
WILKES-HUNTER, RICHARD
WILLIAMS, WILLIAM H.

BRODY, SYLVIA
AXLERAD, SYLVIA BRODY

BRODZKY, LEON
BRODNEY, SPENCER

BROEG, BOB
BROEG, ROBERT M.

BROEKEL, RAY
BROEKEL, RANIER LOTHAR

BROG, BERTIL
ORNULF, HILDING KONSTANT.

BROGAN THE SCRIBE
SPICKLER, CHARLES A.

BROGAN, ELISE
URCH, ELIZABETH

BROGAN, JAMES
HODDER-WILLIAMS, CHRIST.

BROGER, ACHIM
BROEGER, ACHIM

BROHM, CHRIS
BROMMUND, CHRISTOPH

BROIDO, VERA
COHN, VERA

BROKAW, TOM
BROKAW, THOMAS JOHN

BROMLEY, LUKE
GORDON-COOKE, N.

BRONDFIELD, JERRY
BRONDFIELD, JEROME

BRONER, E.M.
BRONER, ESTHER MASSERMAN

BRONKO, MIKE
OLIVEROS TOVAR, MIGUEL

BRONSON, DONNA
EDELSTEIN, SCOTT

BRONSON, L.T.
TUBB, E.C.

BRONSON, LITA
BELL, LOUISE PRICE

BRONSON, LYNN
LAMPMAN, EVELYN SIBLEY

BRONSON, MAUREEN
BRONSON, ANTOINETTE
WOODCOCK, MAUREEN

BRONSON, OLIVER
ROWLAND, DONALD S.

BRONSON, WADE
KING, ALBERT

BRONSON, WOLFE
RABORG, FREDERICK A.

BRONSTEIN, YETTA
ABEL, JEANNE

BRONTE, LOUISA [LUISA]
ROBERTS, JANET LOUISE

BRONZINI, BART
MURRAY, WILLIAM P.

BROOK, A.B.
JENNINGS, LESLIE NELSON

BROOK, BARNABY
BROOKS, COLLIN

BROOK, ESTHER
HUGGETT, BERTHE

BROOK, IAN
BRINKWORTH, IAN

BROOK, JUDY
BROOK, JUDITH PENELOPE

BROOK, PERCY
MULLER, KURT

BROOK, PETER
CHOVIL, ALFRED HAROLD

BROOKE, ARTHUR
MARSHALL, ARTHUR C.

BROOKE, CAROL
RAMSKILL, VALERIE PATRIC.

BROOKE, JOSHUA
MILLER, VICTOR [B]

BROOKE, JUSTIN
BOLEN, R. KEATING

BROOKE, KESTON
LEWIS, CLIFFORD

BROOKE, MAGDALEN
CAPES, M. HARRIET

BROOKE-HAVEN, P.
WODEHOUSE, PELHAM GRENV.

BROOKER, CLARK
FOWLER, KENNETH A.

BROOKER, WALLACE
BOGART, WILLIAM G.
DANIELS, NORMAN A.
DONOVAN, LAURENCE
DAVIS, HAROLD A.

BROOKES, BETH
NAUMAN, EILEEN

BROOKES, OWEN
BARBER, DULAN F.W.

BROOKS, ALBERT
EINSTEIN, ALBERT

BROOKS, ANITA
ABRAMOVITZ, ANITA Z.B.

BROOKS, BARBARA
COONS, WILLIAM R.
SIMMONS, BARBARA BROOKS

BROOKS, BARNEY
KOBUSCH, HELMUT

BROOKS, BRUCE J.
KEENAN, JAMES

BROOKS, DOUGLAS
BROOKS-DAVIES, DOUGLAS

BROOKS, GEORGE
BAUM, L[YMAN] FRANK

BROOKS, JAMES M.
SULLIVAN, MARION F.

BROOKS, JANET
BROOKS, JANICE YOUNG

BROOKS, JANET [JEAN]
BROOKS-JANOWIAK, JEAN

BROOKS, JEANNE
BROOKS-GUNN, JEANNE

BROOKS, JOHN
SUGAR, BERT RANDOLPH

BROOKS, JONATHAN
MELLETT, JOHN CALVIN

BROOKS, KANDI
BROOKS, KANDIUS

BROOKS, KATE
HURST, KATHRYN

BROOKS, LAURA FRANCES
ROSS, WILLIAM E. DANIEL

BROOKS, MAGGIE
BROOKS, MARGARET ANN

BROOKS, MEL
KAMINSKY, MELVIN

BROOKS, NED
BROOKS, C.W. JR.
MARTIN, DON

BROOKS, SAMUEL I.
SCHUYLER, GEORGE S[AMUEL]

BROOKS, TERRENCE D.
BROOKS, TERRENCE DEAN

BROOKS, TERRY
BROOKS, TERRENCE DEAN

BROOKS, W.A.
FRYEFIELD, MAURICE P.

BROOKS, W.H.
SHARP, WILLIAM

BROOKS, WILLIAM
WEISS, JOE

BROOKS, WILLIAM ALLEN
FRYEFIELD, MAURICE P.

BROOME, ADAM
JAMES, GODFREY WARDEN

BROOME, DORA
WILD, DORA MARY

BROOME, LADY MARY ANNE
BARKER, MARY ANNE

BROOME, SUSANNAH
PATTINSON, NANCY EVELYN

BROOMHAUER, CHARLIE
COOK, WILLIAM EVERETT

BROPHY, BRIGID
LEVY, BRIGID A.B.

BROPHY, JIM
BROPHY, JAMES JOSEPH

BROS, WARD
KUGLER, DIETMAR

BROSNAN, JIM
BROSNAN, JAMES PATRICK

BROSNAN, KATE
CALDERELLA, SUSAN

BROSSE, VANE DE
BLACK, CLINTON

BROSTEN, CARLO
BROGREN, JEANNE
STENBERG, HANS-ERIK

BROTHER ANTONIUS
EVERSON, WILLIAM OLIVER

BROTHER BOB
BUELL, ROBERT KINGERY

BROTHER CHOLERIC
VAN ZELLER, CLAUDE HUBERT

BROTHER FLAVIOUS
ELLISON, JAMES E.

BROTHER GRAHAM
JEFFERY, GRAHAM

BROUGHAM, J.T.
ST. JOHN, PERCY BOLLNGBRK

BROUGHTON, H.
TREVELYAN, GEORGE OTTO

BROUILLETTE, EMIL
RYDBERG, ERNIE

BROUN, HOB
BROUN, HEYWOOD OREN

BROUSSARD, VIVIAN L.
MARTINETZ, VIVIAN L.

BROUSTON, WILLIAM
BRANNON, WILLIAM T.

BROUWER, A.
VAN LOOY, JACOBUS

BROWARD, DONN
HALLERAN, EUGENE E.

BROWER, CHARLIE
BROWER, CHARLES HENDRIC.

BROWN, ALEXIS
BAUMANN, AMY [B] BEECHING

BROWN, ALICE VERY
VERY, ALICE N.

BROWN, BEATRICE C.
CURTIS BROWN, BEATRICE

BROWN, BETTY
JONES, ELIZABETH B.

BROWN, BILL
BROWN, WILLIAM L.
MOORE, ROSALIE

BROWN, BILLYE WALKER
CUTCHEN, BILLYE WALKER

BROWN, BOB
BROWN, ROBERT CARLTON
BROWN, ROBERT JOSEPH

BROWN, CALDWELL
BROOKS, EDWY SEARLES

BROWN, CAROLINE
KROUT, CAROLINE, VIRGINIA

BROWN, CARRIE
BROWN, CAROLYN S.

BROWN, CARTER
YATES, ALAN GEOFFREY

BROWN, CHARLES
CADET, JOHN
MORENO BERNET, MANUEL

BROWN, CROSLAND
GREY, A.W.

BROWN, DANIEL RUSSELL
CURZON, DANIEL

BROWN, DAVID
MYLLER, ROLF

BROWN, DOROTHY
OXLEY, DOROTHY [ANNE]

BROWN, DOUGLAS
GIBSON, WALTER B.

BROWN, DR. WALTER C.
SILVERBERG, ROBERT

BROWN, DUNCAN
NELSON, T.

BROWN, EMILY
STERNE, EMMA GELDERS

BROWN, EVE
NICHOLS, MARY EUDORA

BROWN, F.
MACKINNON, CHARLES ROY

BROWN, FRANCIS
BRUNS, FRANK

BROWN, GEORGE
JENKINS, NORMAN
WERTMULLER, LINA

BROWN, GEORGE SHELDON
HUGHES, DENNIS [TALBOT]

BROWN, GINNY
BROWN, VIRGINIA SHARPE

BROWN, H. RAP
AL-AMIN, JAMIL ABDULLAH

BROWN, HARRY
PESCOLLER, HEINRICH

BROWN, HOSANNA
DIXON, ROBERT MALCOLM W.

BROWN, IRVING
ADAMS, WILLIAM TAYLOR

BROWN, IRWIN
MURRAY, DAVID STARK

BROWN, JAMIESON
BROWN, WILLIAM [JAMES] C.

BROWN, JANE
BLAZE DE BURY, YETTA

BROWN, JEFF
BROWN, SEVELLON III

BROWN, JOE
OFFUTT, ANDREW J.

BROWN, JOHN
LEY, WILLIE

BROWN, JOHN MASON
MASON, JOHN

BROWN, JONES
MUNBY, ARTHUR JOSEPH

BROWN, KIT
VANDERGRIFF, AOLA

BROWN, L. CARL
BROWN, LEON CARL

BROWN, L.J.
DUBREUIL, ELIZABETH L.

BROWN, LARRY
BROWN, LAWRENCE JR.

BROWN, M.E.
MOSSER, ARNE J.

BROWN, MAHLON A.
ELLIS, EDWARD S.

BROWN, MANDY
BROWN, MAY

BROWN, MAREL
BROWN, MARGARET ELIZABETH

BROWN, MARGARET E.
MARON, MARGARET

BROWN, MARY
BROWN, MAY

BROWN, MATT
DELFS, RAINER

BROWN, MICKI
BROWN, VIRGINIA

BROWN, MIKE
MORENO BERNET, MANUEL

BROWN, MOSES
BARRETT, WILLIAM CHRIST.

BROWN, PETER CARTER
YATES, ALAN GEOFFREY

BROWN, RAE
BROWN, FORREST

BROWN, ROSALIE
MOORE, ROSALIE

BROWN, ROSWELL
WEBB, JEAN FRANCIS III

BROWN, SEPTIMUS
WELLS, H.G.

BROWN, TERENCE
DUENSING, JURGEN

BROWN, TOM
BROWN, THOMAS H. JR.

BROWN, TURNER JR.
HAMPLE, STUART
MARSHALL, ERIC

BROWN, VANDYKE
PROUTING, FREDERICK JAMES

BROWN, VIRGINIA
BIANCHI, VIRGINIA BROWN

BROWN, W.
PESCHKE, HANS

BROWN, WHITNEY
FEARN, JOHN RUSSELL

BROWN, WILL
AINSWORTH, WILLIAM HARR.

BROWN, WILL C.
BOYLES, CLARENCE SCOTT

BROWN, WILLIAM
RICHTER, ERNST H.

BROWNE, BARUM
DENNIS, GEOFFREY
SAUNDERS, HILARY A.

BROWNE, COURTNEY
COURTNEY-BROWNE, R. DAVID

BROWNE, DIK
BROWNE, RICHARD ARTHUR A.

BROWNE, GEORGE SHELDON
JENNISON, JOHN WILLIAM

BROWNE, HARRY
BROWNE, HENRY

BROWNE, HOWARD
EVANS, JOHN

BROWNE, K.W.
RENNAU, JOACHIM

BROWNE, LYDIA
BAILEY-PRATT, CYNTHIA

BROWNE, MARSHALL S.
MORENO BERNET, MANUEL

BROWNE, MATTHEW
RANDS, WILLIAM BRIGHTLY

BROWNE, REGINALD
BROOKS, EDWY SEARLES

BROWNE, ROBERT
KARLINS, MARVIN

BROWNE, SAM
SMITH, RONALD GREGOR

BROWNELL, CHARLES F.
MENCKEN, HENRY LOUIS

BROWNELL, JOHN F.
MENCKEN, HENRY LOUIS

BROWNING, COLUMBAN
BROWNING, WILLIAM

BROWNING, CRAIG
GRAHAM, ROGER P.

BROWNING, DIANA
HERSHMAN, FLORENCE

BROWNING, GARETH H.
BROWNING, GEORGE HENRY

BROWNING, JOHN
BROWN, JOHN

BROWNING, JOHN S.
WILLIAMS, ROBERT MOORE

BROWNING, L.J.
DUBREUIL, ELIZABETH L.

BROWNING, STERRY
GRIBBLE, LEONARD [R]

BROWNING, VIVIENNE
BALY, ELAINE

BROWNLEIGH, ELEONORA
COHEN, RHODA

BROWNLEY, MEGAN
BROWNLEY, MARGARET

BROWNLOW, J.H.
LOVECRAFT, H[OWARD] P.

BROWNMAN, JOHN U.
LUDEMANN, HANS-ULRICH

BROXHOLME, J.F.
BROXHOLME, JOHN FRANKLIN

BROYLE, M.
NEUBERG, VICTOR [B]

BRU, HEDIN
JACOBSEN, HANS JACOB

BRUBAKER, CAROL
STOLK, ANTONIE

BRUCE, ARTHUR LORING
CROWNINSHIELD, FRANCIS W.

BRUCE, CHARLES
FRANCIS, ARTHUR BRUCE C.

BRUCE, DAVID
PATCHETT, MARY O.E.

BRUCE, IAN
KNELLER, F.C.

BRUCE, JANET
CAMPBELL, JANET BRUCE

BRUCE, JEAN
BROCHET, JEAN ALEXANDRE

BRUCE, LENNY
SCHNEIDER, LEONARD ALFRED

BRUCE, LEO
CROFT-COOKE, RUPERT

BRUCE, MARTIN
MONTAGUE, BRUCE [ALEX.]

BRUCE, MONICA
MELARO, CONSTANCE LORAINE

BRUCE, PAUL
FODEN, FREDERICK [T]

BRUCE, RICHARD
NUGENT, RICHARD BRUCE

BRUCE, SHELLEY
MERKLINGHAUS, MICHELE

BRUCE, WALT
BALLARD, W. TODHUNTER
BELLEM, ROBERT LESLIE

BRUCE-NOVOA
BRUCE-NOVOA, JUAN D.

BRUCE-NOVOA, JOHN DAVID
BRUCE-NOVOA, JUAN D.

BRUCKNER, BERTA
PENKALA, ALICE

BRUCKNER, DER
KOTHNER, PAUL

BRUCKNER, ENNE
HOFBAUER, ELFRIEDE

BRUCKNER, FERDINAND
TAGGER, THEODOR

BRUEGEL JOHN WOLFGANG
BRUEGEL, JOHANN WOLFGANG

BRUFF, NANCY
GARDNER, NANCY BRUFF

BRUGG, ELMAR
ELMAYER-VESTENBRUGG, RUD.

BRUGGER, BILL
BRUGGER, WILLIAM

BRUGGER, JOHANNA
GREITHER, MARGIT

BRUGGER, KARLA
DILLENBURGER, INGEBORG

BRUIN, JOHN
BRUTUS, DENNIS

PSEUDONYMS

BRULIN, TONE
VAN DEN EYNDE, ANTOON

BRULLS, CHRISTIAN
SIMENON, GEORGES [J.C]

BRUMMEL & CO
THESLOF, GEORGE HENRIK

BRUMMEL, BELLE
CRANMER, HELEN WORDEN

BRUN, VINCENT
FLESCH, HANS

BRUNEAU, JEAN
SYLVESTRE, J. JEAN GUY

BRUNNER, CONSTANTIN
WERTHEIMER, LEO

BRUNNER, K. HOUSTON
BRUNNER, JOHN [K.H.]

BRUNO, FRANK
ST. BRUNO, ALBERT FRANCIS

BRUNS, HANKE
BAHRS, HANS

BRUNS, JOE
ALTSHULER, HARRY

BRUNSWICK, JAMES
STITT, JAMES M.

BRUSH, KATHARINE
WINANS, KATHARINE B.

BRUSS, B.R.
BLONDEL, ROGER

BRUST, HAROLD
CHEYNEY, REGINALD E.S.

BRUSTO, MAX
BRUSTOWIECKI, MOTEK

BRUTE, Q.
SMITH, ROBERT EDWARD

BRUTSCHE, ALPHONSE
ANDREVON, JEAN-PIERRE

BRUTUS
SPOONER, JOHN D.

BRUUN, DICK
GUSTAFSSON, LISA

BRYAN, ANN
BOYLE, ANN [PETERS]

BRYAN, BETH
LANG, VIOLA E.

BRYAN, BEVERLY
ROSENBAUM, BEVERLY KATZ

BRYAN, DEBORAH
BRYSON, DEBORAH

BRYAN, E.
LATHAM, EDWARD BRYAN

BRYAN, EILEEN
SMITH, RUTH ALANA

BRYAN, JESSICA
CHUDNOW, YAFFA

BRYAN, JOHN
DELVES-BROUGHTON, JOSEPH.

BRYAN, MAVIS
O'BRIEN, MARIAN P.

BRYAN, MICHAEL
MOORE, BRIAN
WING, WILLIS KINGSLEY

BRYAN, WALTER
WILLIS, WALT

BRYANS, ROBIN
BRYANS, ROBERT HARBINSON

BRYANT, ADRIAN
COLE, ADRIAN

BRYANT, AL
BRYANT, THOMAS ALTON

BRYANT, ANITA
GREEN, ANITA JANE

BRYANT, BEAR
BRYANT, PAUL WILLIAM

BRYANT, EDWARD
BLAYLOCK, JAMES P[AUL]

BRYANT, ERIKA
KOLACZYK, ANNE & EDWARD

BRYANT, M.
MUNN, MARGUERITE

BRYANT, PETER
GEORGE, PETER [BRYAN]

BRYAT, EDITH
BRAYTON, GERTRUDE E.

BRYCE, RONALD
ROCKEY, HOWARD

BRYDEN, BILL
BRYDEN, WILLIAM CAMPBELL

BRYDGES, GEORGE
RODNEY, GEORGE BRYDGES

BRYDGES, HAROLD
BRIDGE, JAMES HOWARD

BRYER, JUDY
BRYER, JUDITH E.

BRYHER
ELLERMAN, ANNA WINIFRED

BRYHER, WINIFRED
ELLERMAN, ANNIE WINIFRED

BRYL, IANKA
BRYL, IVAN A

BRYNNER, YUL
KHAN, TAIDJE

BRYSON, LEIGH
RUTLEDGE, NANCY

BRZECHWA, JAN
LESMAN, JAN WIKTOR

BUBNER, RUDIGER
BUBNER, RUEDIGER

BUCCHIERI, THERESA F.
BICCHIERI, THERESA F.

BUCHA, KARIN
BAUCH, KATHE

BUCHAN, DAVID
WOMACK, DAVID A.

BUCHAN, KATE
ERSKINE, BARBARA

BUCHAN, TOM
BUCHAN, THOMAS BUCHANAN

BUCHANAN, CARL
MADSEN, BORGE

BUCHANAN, CHUCK
ROWLAND, DONALD S.

BUCHANAN, JACK
CRIDER, [ALLEN] BILL[Y]
LANSDALE, JOE R.
MERTZ, STEPHEN

BUCHANAN, JESSICA
BUCHANAN, JESSIE HORSTING

BUCHANAN, LAURA
KING, FLORENCE

BUCHANAN, MARIE
DUELL, EILEEN-MARIE

BUCHANAN, PATRICK
CORLEY, EDWIN RAYMOND
MURPHY, JOHN [JACK]

BUCHANAN, WILLIAM
BUCK, WILLIAM RAY
THORNDIKE, RUSSELL

BUCK, CAROL
BUCKLAND, CAROL E.

BUCK, DOUG
FILER, THOMAS HANFORD

BUCK, PETER
LESLIE, PETER

BUCKAWAY, C.M.
BUCKAWAY, CATHERINE M.

BUCKINGHAM, BRUCE
LILLEY, PETER
STANSFELD, ANTHONY

BUCKINGHAM, DAVID
VILLIERS, DAVID HUGH

BUCKINGHAM, JAMIE
BUCKINGHAM, JAMES WILLIAM

BUCKINGHAM, NANCY
SAWYER, JOHN & NANCY

BUCKLEY, DORIS HEATHER
BUCKLEY NEVILLE, HEATHER

BUCKLEY, EUNICE
SCOTT, ROSE LAURE

BUCKLEY, FIONA
ANAND, VALERIE

BUCKMAN, ROB
BUCKMAN, ROBERT ALEXANDER

BUCKMASTER, HENRIETTA
STEPHENS, HENRIETTA H.

BUCKNER, BRADNER
REPP, ED EARL

BUCKROSE, J.E.
JAMESON, ANNIE EDITH F.

BUDAY, GEORGE
BUDAY, GYORGY

BUDD, JACKSON
BUDD, WILLIAM JOHN

BUDE, JOHN
ELMORE, ERNEST CARPENTER

BUDRYS, ALGIS
BUDRYS, ALGIRDAS JONAS

BUEHNAU, LUDWIG
SCHREIBER, HERMANN O.L.

BUELL, ELLEN LEWIS
CASH, ELLEN LEWIS BUELL

BUENAMAR, RICARDO
CABRERA, RAIMUNDO

BUENDIA, MANUEL
GIRON, MANUEL BUENDA TEL.

BUFFALO CHILD LONG LANCE
CLARKE, SYLVESTRE

BUFFALO CHUCK
BARTH, CHARLES P.

BUFFY
GALSBY, JOHN [S]

BUGY, OLY
BUGGIE, OLIVE M.

BUHLER, CURT F.
BUEHLER, CURT FERDINAND

BUHLMANN, WALBERT
BUEHLMANN, WALBERT

BUIST, CHARLOTTE
PATTERSON, CHARLOTTE

BULL, EMMA
SHETTERLY, EMMA BULL

BULL, SGT. TERRY
TRIPLETT, WILLIAM SAMUEL

BULLEN BEAR
DONNELLY, AUSTIN S.

BULLINGHAM, ANN
JONES, A. MILES

BULLINGHAM, RODNEY
SLADEN, NORMAN ST. BARBE

BULLOCK, BARBARA
BULLOCK-WILSON, BARBARA

BULMER, H.K.
BULMER, [HENRY] KENNETH

BULWER-LYTTON, BARON
BULWER-LYTTON, EDWARD G.

BULWER-LYTTON, E.
BULWER-LYTTON, EDWARD G.

BULYCHEV, KIRILL
MOZHEIKO, IGOR V.

BUMPERLI, LUX
BUBECK, HEINRICH

BUMPPO, NATHANIEL J.B.
DEAN, JOHN EDWIN

BUMPPO, NATTY
BUMPPO, NATHANIEL JOHN B.
DEAN, JOHN EDWIN

BUNCH-WEEKS, CHARLOTTE
BUNCH, CHARLOTTE ANNE

BUNDLER, HANS
ASPERN-BUCHMEIER, ELISAB.

BUNDUKHARI
DENT, ANTHONY AUSTEN

BUNDY, RALPH
EASTON, THOMAS A[TWOOD]

BUNING, SIETZE
WIERSMA, STANLEY M.

BUNKER, CAPT. MOSS
BRACKMAN, ARNOLD C.

BUNSTON, ANNA
DE BARY, ANNA

BUNTING, A.E.
BUNTING, ANNE EVELYN

BUNTING, EVE
BUNTING, ANNE EVELYN

BUNTLINE, NED
JUDSON, EDWARD Z.C.

BUNYON, PAT
BAGNANO, PATRICK F.

BUONANNO, JOSEPH
HILTON, THOMAS H.

BUPP, WALTER
BERRYMAN, JOHN
GARRETT, RANDALL [P]

BURCETTE, JAMES R.
LUIF, KURT

BURCH, RALPH
BANKS, RAYMOND E.

BURCHARD, BILL
BURCHARD, WILLIAM ROBERT

BURCHARD, M.
BURCHARD, MARSHALL

BURCHARD, S.H.
BURCHARD, SUE

BURCHARDT, CHRISTA
BESSER, CHRISTA

BURCHELL, MARY
COOK, IDA

BURDEKIN, KAY
BURDEKIN, KATHERINE

BURDIC, JEANNE ELLIS
WEBSTER, JENNIE ELLIS B.

BURELL, JOHN
BENGT-AKE, CRAS

BURFIELD, EVA
EBBETT, FRANCES EVA

BURFORD, ELEANOR
HIBBERT, ELEANOR BURFORD

BURG, CARL
CASSAU, CARL

BURG, CRISTEL
DARNSTADT, HELGE

BURG, DAVID
DOLBERG, ALEXANDER

BURG, E.M.
BLANK, MATTHIAS

BURG, PAUL
SCHAUMMBURG, PAUL

BURGEON, G.A.L.
BARFIELD, ARTHUR OWEN

BURGER, BERTHOLD
KASTNER, ERICH

BURGER, DIONYS
BURGER, DIONIJS

BURGER, FRANK
KALMUCZAK, ROLF

BURGER, FRED
KALMUCZAK, ROLF

BURGER, HAL
KALMUCZAK, ROLF

BURGER, HENRY
KALMUCZAK, ROLF

BURGER, HUGO
LUBLINER, HUGO

BURGER, JACK
BURGER, JOHN ROBERT

BURGER, JOHN
MARQUARD, LEO[POLD]

BURGER, LUCIAN
NIESE, CHARLOTTE

BURGER, MARIANNE
KRUGER, INGEBORG

BURGER, MIKE
EISELE, MARTIN

BURGER, RALPH
KALMUCZAK, ROLF

BURGER, RED
KALMUCZAK, ROLF

BURGER, THOMAS
LUTZ, BERTHOLD

BURGESS, ANNE MARIE
GERSON, NOEL B.

BURGESS, ANTHONY
WILSON, J ANTHONY BURGESS

BURGESS, EM
BURGESS, MARY WYCHE

BURGESS, M.R.
BURGESS, MICHAEL ROY

BURGESS, MALLORY
HINGSTON, MARY SANDRA

BURGESS, MASON
ZAWIDOSKI, GREGORY

BURGESS, MICHAEL
BURGESS, MICHAEL ROY
GERSON, NOEL B.
ELLIOT, JEFFREY M.

BURGESS, MIKE
BURGESS, MICHAEL ROY

BURGESS, SALLY
BURGESS, MARY E.

BURGESS, TREVOR
TREVOR, ELLESTON

BURGESS-KOHN, JANE
BURGESS, JANE K.
KOHN, WILLARD K.

BURGHARDT, FRIEDR.
KURTH, HANNS

BURGHLEY, ROSE
POLLOCK, IDA

BURGOYNE, ELIZABETH
PICKLES, M. ELIZABETH

BURKE, CARL F.
ACKERMAN, FORREST J.
KORNBLUTH, C[YRIL] M.

BURKE, CINNAMON
CONN, PHOEBE

BURKE, DIANA
BURRELL, SUE
KARNI, MICHAELA

BURKE, EDMUND [H]
BOGGS, WINIFRED

BURKE, FIELDING
DARGAN, OLIVE TILFORD

BURKE, J.F.
BURKE, JOHN [FREDERICK]

BURKE, JOHN
O'CONNOR, RICHARD

BURKE, JONATHAN
BURKE, JOHN [FREDERICK]

BURKE, LEDA
GARNETT, DAVID S.

BURKE, LYDIA
FLINT, CAROLYN

BURKE, MAGGIE
SNYDER, MARILYN

BURKE, MICHAEL
FARRELL, MICHAEL

BURKE, NOEL
HITCHENS, DELORES B.

BURKE, OWEN
BURKE, JOHN [FREDERICK]

BURKE, RALPH
GARRETT, RANDALL [P]
SILVERBERG, ROBERT

BURKE, SHIFTY
BENTON, PEGGIE

BURKE, VEE
BURKE, VINCENT & VELMA

BURKE, WARREN
BRAUN, MATTHEW

BURKHARD, HARI
HERING, BURKHARD

BURKHART, KITSI
BURKHART, KATHRYN W.

BURKHOLDER, EDWIN V.
FISHER, STEPHEN GOULD

BURKLE, VEIT
BISCHOFF, KARL HEINRICH

BURKS, ED
BURKS, EDWARD C.

BURLAND, C.A.
BURLAND, COTTIE A.

BURLAND, HARRIS
HARRIS-BURLAND, JOHN

BURLEIGH, CECIL
SENARENS, LUIS P.

BURMAR
MARR, RICHARD

BURMEISTER, GERTY-CHARL.
BURRMEISTER, GERTRUD

BURMESTER, DIRKS
KNICKREHM, HANS

BURNABY, NIGEL
ELLETT, HAROLD PINCTON

BURNDALE, TOM
MADSEN, BORGE

BURNE, GLEN
GREEN, ALAN B. & GLADYS

BURNES, CAROLINE
HAINES, CAROLYN

BURNESS, TAD
BURNESS, WALLACE BINNY

BURNETT, PETER
BAJOG, GUNTHER
DUBINA, PETER

BURNETT, W.R.
BURNETT, W.R.
SILVERBERG, ROBERT

BURNEY, ANTON
HOPKINS, KENNETH

BURNFORD, S.D.
BURNFORD, SHEILA [P.C.]

BURNHAM, CHARLES
PAINE, LAURAN BOSWORTH

BURNHAM, J.W.
BURNHAM, JACK WESLEY

BURNHAM, JOHN
BECKWITH, BURNHAM PUTNAM

BURNIER, ANDREAS
DESSAUR, CATHERINE IRMA

BURNS, BOBBY
BURNS, VINCENT GODFREY

BURNS, BURNSY
BURNES, [ROBERT] BRITT

BURNS, ELIZABETH
BEHANNA, GERTRUDE F.

BURNS, HOSS
BURNS, [ROBERT] BRITT

BURNS, MARK
ICKES, PAUL

BURNS, MARY
HARE, WALTER B.

BURNS, MILTON
FISHER, STEPHEN GOULD

BURNS, RAY
BURNS, RAYMOND HOWARD

BURNS, REX
BURNS, REX RAOUL S.S.

BURNS, REX RAOUL S.S.
SEHLER, RAOUL STEPHEN

BURNS, SCOTT
BURNS, ROBERT MILTON C.

BURNS, SHEILA
BLOOM, URSULA

BURNS, TEX
LAMOORE, LOUIS [DEARBORN]

BURNS, WILLIAM
BROLL, WOLFGANG W.

BURNS, WILLIAM J.
OSTRANDER, ISABEL EGENTON

BURR, AARON AINSWORTH
DEY, FREDERIC VAN R.

BURR, DANGERFIELD
INGRAHAM, PRENTISS

BURR, ELSIE
MILLIGAN, ELSIE

BURROUGHS, MARGARET
FELDMAN, EUGENE P.R.

BURROUGHS, MARGARET G.
BURROUGHS, MARGARET TAYL.

BURROUGHS, PATRICIA
BARRICKLOW, PATTI B.

BURROUGHS, ROBERTA
BURROUGHS, ROBERT & MILLY

BURROUGHS, TARZAN
BURROUGHS, EDGAR RICE

BURROW, RHODA
COHEN, BEN
LEDERER, RHODA C.K.

BURROWAY, JANET
EYSSELINCK, JANET GAY

BURROWES, MIKE
BURROWES, MICHAEL A.B.

BURROWS, ABE
BURROWS, ABRAM SOLMAN

BURT, MELLVILLE
BULL, LOIS

BURTE, HERMANN
STRUBE, HERMANN

BURTON, ANDY
RATHBORNE, ST. GEORGE

BURTON, ANNE
BOWEN-JUDD, SARA HUTTON

BURTON, CECIL
FABER, ELSE

BURTON, CONRAD
EDMUNDSON, JOSEPH

BURTON, EDMUND
CHILDS, EDMUND BURTON

BURTON, GEORGE W.
MAUCKNER, WALTER G.

BURTON, HAL
BURTON, HAROLD BERNARD

BURTON, JACK
CHADWICK, JOSEPH L.

BURTON, LESLIE
MCGUIRE, LESLIE SARAH

BURTON, MARNIE
BANDILLA, MARGRIT

BURTON, MILES
STREET, CECIL JOHN C.

BURTON, MRS.
HARRISON, CONSTANCE CARY

BURTON, RAYMOND L.
TUBB, E.C.

BURTON, RICHARD
JENKINS, RICHARD

BURTON, ROBERT E.
POVLITZ, ROBERT E.

BURTON, S.H.
BURTON, SAMUEL HOLROYD

BURTON, THOMAS
LONGSTREET, [H] STEPHEN

BURY, FRANK
HARRIS, HERBERT

BURY, JAN
WASYLEWSKI, STANISLAW

BUSBY, JONATHAN
ALLEN, ERIC

BUSBY, MABEL JANICE
STANFORD, SALLY

BUSCAGLIA, LEO F.
BUSCAGLIA, FELICE LEONAR.

BUSCH, BARBARA
PUSCH, EDITH

BUSCH, H.P.
KEHL, WOLFGANG

BUSCH, IRENE
HAHNLEIN, IRENE

BUSCH, MONIKA
BUSCH, GERTRAUDE

BUSCHKLEPPER, WILHELM
CARL-MARDORF, WILHELM

BUSCHKUHL, MATTHIAS
BUSCHKUEHL, MATTHIAS

BUSCON, JUAN
TRONCOSCO DE LA CONCHA, M

BUSE, R.F.
BUSE, RENEE

BUSH, CHRISTOPHER
BUSH, CHARLIE CHRISTMAS

BUSH, LARRY
BUSH, LAWRENCE DANA

BUSH-FEKETE, MARY
FAGYAS, MARIA

BUSHMAN, A
SIDNEY, SAMUEL

BUSHMILLER, ERNIE
BUSHMILLER, ERNEST PAUL

BUSHNELL, ADELYN
BRADFORD, MRS. MARSHALL

BUSHWOMAN
PALMER-ARCHER, LAURA M.

BUSS, HELEN M.
CLARKE, MARGARET

BUSSENIUS-KRAFT, RUTH
KRAFT, RUTH

BUSTA, CHRISTINE
DIMT, CHRISTINE

BUSTOS DOMECQ, H.
BORGES, JORGE LUIS

BUSTOS, F[RANCISCO]
BORGES, JORGE LUIS

BUSY BEE
BESTWICK, HARRY

BUTCHER, FANNY
BOKUM, FANNY BUTCHER

BUTCK, ZULIE
JONES, THOMAS W.

BUTLER, ANTHONY
MADSEN, BORGE

BUTLER, B.C.
BUTLER, BASIL CHRISTOPHER

BUTLER, BILL
BUTLER, ERNEST ALTON
BUTLER, WILLIAM A. VIVIAN
BUTLER, WILLIAM HUXFORD

BUTLER, CALVIN
TAYLOR, R.L.

BUTLER, GWENDOLINE
MELVILLE, JENNIE

BUTLER, IVAN
BEUTTLER, EDWARD IVAN O.

BUTLER, JOAN
ALEXANDER, ROBERT W.

BUTLER, JOHN
MADSEN, BORGE

BUTLER, NATHAN
SOHL, GERALD ALLEN

BUTLER, R.
BUTLER, RICHARD

BUTLER, RAB
BUTLER, RICHARD AUSTIN

BUTLER, RAE
BUTLER, RAYMOND RAGAN

BUTLER, RICHARD
ALLBEURY, THEODORE E.
BUTLER, ARTHUR RONALD

BUTLER, STEFAN C.
CONGRAT-BUTLER, STEFAN

BUTLER, SUZANNE
PERREARD, SUZANNE L.B.

BUTLER, THEODORE [TED]
SCHWEITZER, DARRELL

BUTLER, VIVIAN
BUTLER, WILLIAM A. VIVIAN

BUTLER, WALTER C.
FAUST, FREDERICK S.

BUTSTEIN, WILLIAM
EBEL, HENRY

BUTT, BEATRICE MARY
HUTT, MRS. W.

BUTTERFLY FARMER
NEWMAN, LEONARD HUGH

BUTTERS, DOROTHY GILMAN
GILMAN, DOROTHY

BUTTERWORTH, LIONEL M.A.
ANGUS-BUTTERWORTH, LIONEL

BUTTITA, TONY
BUTTITTA, ANTHONY

BUTTLAR, JOHANNES
VON BUTTLAR-BRANDENFEL, J

BUTTLE, MYRA
PURCELL, VICTOR W.W.S.

BUTTS, JANE ROBERTS
ROBERTS, JANE

BUXBAUM, MARTIN
NOLL, MARTIN DAVID

BUXTON, CARL
HERSEY, HAROLD
SMITH, CLARK ASHTON

BUXTON, RALPH
SILVERSTEIN, ALVIN

BUXTON, THOMAS
LONGSTREET, [H] STEPHEN

BUZZLE, BUCK
RUBIN, CHARLES J.

BYATT, A.S.
BYATT, ANTONIO SUSAN D.

BYKAU, VASILII U.
BYKOV, VASILY V.

BYR, ROBERT
VON BAYER, KARL ROBERT E.

BYRD, BOBBY
BYRD, ROBERT JAMES

BYRD, C.L.
ROSENKRANTZ, LINDA

BYRD, EMMETT
HINDEN, MICHAEL C.

BYRD, JOHN CROWE
HINDEN, MICHAEL C.

BYRDE, RICHARD
NEUBERG, VICTOR [B]

BYRNE, DONN
DONN-BYRNE, BRIAN OSWALD

BYRNE, RALPH
BURNS, RALPH J.

BYRNES, GENE W.
GIBSON, WALTER B.

BYROM, JAMES
BRAMWELL, JAMES GUY

BYRON, JOHN
ARMSTRONG, JOHN BYRON

BYSTANDER, A
SMITH, GOLDWIN

C, MR.
NOHSTROM, FRANS HOLGER

C., R.B.
HULL, CHARLES

C.3.3
WILLS, FINGAL O'FLAHERTIE

C.B
BRONTE, CHARLOTTE

C.C.
CABRERA, RAIMUNDO

C.D.
LAWRENCE, THOMAS EDWARD

C.E.M.
MASTRANGELO, CHARLES E.

C.J.G.
LAWRENCE, THOMAS EDWARD

C.J.H.
HOLZHAUSEN, CARL JOHAN

C.L.
LOGAN, CELIA

C.L.C.
CUNNINGTON, CHARLES L.

C.M.G.
GARRETT, CLARA MAUDE

C.S.
STRETE, CRAIG [KEE]

CABALLERO, FERNAN
VON FABER, BOEHL

CABALLERO-CALDERON, E.
CABALLERO-CALDERON, EDUA.

CABLE, BOYD
EWART, ERNEST ANDREW

CABOT, CALVIN QUINCY
LAWRENCE, JAMES COOPER

CABOT, ISABEL
CAPETO, ISABEL

CABOT, JOHN YORK
O'BRIEN, DAVID WRIGHT

CABRAL, ALBERTO
WHITE, RICHARD ALAN

CABRAL, O.M.
CABRAL, OLGA
WORRELL, EVERIL

CABRILLAN, CELESTE VENARD
MORETON DE CHABRIL., ELIZ

CADDEN, TOM SCOTT
CADDEN, THOMAS SCOTT

CADDY, ALICE
BURMAN, ALICE CADDY

CADE, ALEXANDER
METHOLD, KENNETH [WALTER]

CADE, JACK
ARNOT, ROBIN PAGE

CADE, ROBIN
NICOLE, CHRISTOPHER ROBIN

CADE, TONI
BAMBARA, TONI CADE

CADELL, ELIZABETH
AINSWORTH, HARRIET

CADELL, JAMES
THOMAS, RONALD WILLS

CADIGAN, PAT
CADIGAN, PATRICIA K.

CADMUS & HARMONIA
BUCHAN, JOHN
BUCHAN, SUSAN

CADWALADER
HUDSON, WILLIAM C.

CADWALLADER
CLEMENS, PAUL

CAEDMON, FATHER
WAHL, THOMAS PETER

CAEIRO, ALBERTO
PESSOA, FERNANDO [A.N.]

CAELESTES, JUNIOR
VON OTTO, ELISABETH

CAGNEY, PETER
WINTER, BEVIS [PETER]

CAHILL, JACK
CAHILL, JOHN DENNIS

CAHILL, MIKE
NOLAN, WILLIAM F.

CAHILL, TOM
CAHILL, THOMAS QUINN

CAIDIN, MARTIN
CAIDIN, MARTIN [CARL V.S]

CAIL, CAROL[E]
GALLOWAY, KARA

CAILLOU, ALAN
LYLE-SMYTHE, ALAN

CAIN, BOB
CAIN, ROBERT OWEN

CAIN, CHRISTOPHER
FLEMING, THOMAS JAMES

CAIN, G.
CABRERA INFANTE, G.

CAIN, GUILLERMO
CABRERA INFANTE, G.

CAIN, J.M.
CAIN, JAMES MALLAHAN

CAIN, JACKSON
GLEASON, ROBERT

CAIN, JOHN
KALMUCZAK, ROLF

CAIN, JONATHAN
CAIN, NICHOLAS [COLORADO]

CAIN, PAUL
SIMS, GEORGE CARROL

CAIN, ROBERT
KEITH, WILLIAM HENRY JR.

CAINE, GEFF
ROHR, WOLF DETLEF

CAINE, GEOFFREY
WALKER, ROBERT WAYNE

CAINE, HALL
CAINE, THOMAS H. HALL
HALL, THOMAS HENRY

CAINE, HAMILTON T.
SMOKE, STEPHEN L.

CAINE, JEFF
EISFELD, RAINER
ROHR, WOLF DETLEF

CAINE, MARK
MASCHLER, TOM
RAPHAEL, FREDERICK [M]

CAINE, MICHAEL
MICKLEWHITE, MAURICE JOE.

CAINE, MITCHELL
SPARKIA, ROY [BERNARD]

CAINE, PETER
HORNIG, DOUG

CAINE, REBECCA
WOODS, MARGERY

CAINE, STAFF
PETERS, HERMANN

CAIRNCROSS, ALEC
CAIRNCROSS, ALEXANDER K.

CAIRNES, MAYD
CURZON-HERRICK, L. MAUD C

CAIRNS, PETER
MULGRUE, G. EDWARD

CAIRO, JON
ROMANO, DEANE LOUIS

CAISSA
FRAENKEL, HEINRICH

CAITLIN, KIMBERLEIGH
BUSH, KIM OSTROM

CAIUS
MITCHELL, DONALD GRANT

CAJUPI
ZAKO, ANDON

CAKE, PATRICK
WELCH, TIMOTHY L.

CAL, DAKOTA
WALDRON, CORBIN A.

CALAENO
HARPER, GEORGE WILLIAM

CALAIS, JEAN
RODEFER, STEFEN

CALCUM, CARL
LOHAUSEN, KARL A.

CALDARELLI, VINCENZO
CALDERELLI, NAZARENO

CALDECOTT, VERONICA
COHEN, VICTOR

CALDER, JASON
DUNMORE, JOHN

CALDER, LYN
CALMENSON, STEPHANIE

CALDER, RITCHIE
RITCHIE-CALDER, PETER R.

CALDER, ROBERT
MUNDIS, JERROLD J.

CALDWELL, ELINOR
BOON, AUGUST
BRETON-SMITH, CLARE

CALDWELL, FRED
BRAUN, WILBUR

CALDWELL, JAMES
LOWRY, ROBERT [J.C.]

CALDWELL, TAYLOR
CALDWELL, JANET TAYLOR
REBACK, MARCUS

CALEHAS
GARVIN, J.L.

CALETTE, FRANCOISE
KAPPEL, GUNTER

CALEY, ROD
ROWLAND, DONALD S.

CALHOUN, ALEXANDER
METZ, KURT C.

CALHOUN, CHAD
BARRETT, NEAL JR.
CUNNINGHAM, CHESTER GRANT
HAYS, LEE
HUNT, GREG
GOULART, RONALD JOSEPH

CALHOUN, ERIC
TURNER, ROBERT H.

CALHOUN, MARY
WILKINS, MARY H.L.

CALHOUN, WES
SADLER, GEOFFREY WILLIS

CALIBAN
NORDHAUSEN, RICHARD
PHILLIPS, HUBERT
REID, JOHN COWIE
STUART, HECTOR A.

CALISTRO, PADDY
CALISTRO McCAULEY, PATRI.

CALKINS, FAY
ALAILIMA, FAY C.

CALKINS, FRANKLIN
STRATEMEYER, EDWARD

CALLAGHAN, MIKE
HEBEL, PETER

CALLAHAN, FRANK
DUENSING, JURGEN

CALLAHAN, JOHN
CHADWICK, JOSEPH L.
GALLUN, RAYMOND Z.

CALLAHAN, MARY
RANDAZZO, MARY CALLAHAN

CALLAHAN, ROD
BOYCE, DAVID

CALLAHAN, WILLIAM
GALLUN, RAYMOND Z.

CALLAS, THEO
MCCARTHY, SHAUN LLOYD

CALLAWAY, HUGH
NISBET, ULRIC

CALLEN, LARRY
CALLEN, LAWRENCE WILLARD

CALLENDER, JULIAN
LEE, AUSTIN

CALLENDER, RED
CALLENDER, GEORGE

CALLIAM, SELMA
KALICHMAN, CLAIRE

CALLISTHENES
COSTA, GABRIEL

CALLUM, MICHAEL
GREAVES, MICHAEL

CALMER, NED
CALMER, EDGAR

CALNAN, T.D.
CALNAN, THOMAS DANIEL

CALSON, ISAAC
LEDOUX, JOHN WALTER

CALVANO, ANTHONY [TONY]
MOSKOVITZ, JACK

CALVERT, ELINOR H.
LASELL, ELINOR H.

CALVERT, JOHN
LEAF, [WILBUR] MUNRO

CALVERT, MARY
CALVERT, MARY H. DANBY

CALVERT, PAMELA
NORWOOD, VICTOR [G.C.]

CALVERT, THOMAS
MCCLARY, THOMAS CALVERT

CALVIN, HENRY
HANLEY, CLIFFORD L.C.

CALVIN, KENNETH
HOGBEN, LANCELOT THOMAS

CAMBEL, ARTI
HINDENACH, ARTHUR

CAMBER, ANDREW
BINGLEY, DAVID ERNEST

CAMBRAY, C.K.
GAT, DIMITRI [V]

CAMBRE, EINAR
VEGENOR, SVERRE

CAMBRIDGE, ELIZABETH
HODGES, BARBARA K.

CAMDEN, RICHARD
BEESTON, L.J.

CAMEJA, PEDRO
CAMEJO, PETER MIGUEL

CAMEJO, PEDRO M.
CAMEJO, PETER MIGUEL

CAMERON WATT, DONALD
WATT, DONALD

CAMERON, BARBARA
SMITH, BARBARA C.

CAMERON, BARBARA ANNE
HUBERT, CAM

CAMERON, BERL
GLASBY, JOHN S.
HOLLOWAY, BRIAN W.
HUGHES, DENNIS [TALBOT]
O'BRIEN, DAVID WRIGHT
ROBERTS, ARTHUR O.

CAMERON, BRETT
MARTIN, REGINALD ALEC

CAMERON, CARYN
HARPER, KAREN

CAMERON, CHARLA
SKINNER, GLORIA DALE

CAMERON, CLARE
WELLS, WINIFRED

CAMERON, CLIFFORD
GARBUTT, JOHN L.

CAMERON, D.A.
CAMERON, DONALD [A]

CAMERON, D.Y.
COOK, DOROTHY MARY

CAMERON, DONALD
BRYANS, ROBERT HARBINSON

CAMERON, ELIZABETH
NOWELL, ELIZABETH CAMERON

CAMERON, GAY
SNELL, GAY CAMERON

CAMERON, HECTOR
MACQUARRIE, HECTOR

CAMERON, HOPE
MORRITT, HOPE

CAMERON, IAN
PAYNE, DONALD GORDON

CAMERON, J.D.
JAHN, JOSEPH MICHAEL
ROBBINS, DAVID LAWRENCE

CAMERON, JAMES SOREL
SOREL-CAMERON, JAMES R.

CAMERON, JOHN
APPEL, WALTER
BURKLE, ROLF A.
FRIEDRICHS, HOLGER
FRIEDRICHS, HORST
GEHRMANN, HORST
HARTSCH, GERHART
HEBEL, PETER
HELGATH, FRANC
MACDONELL, A. GORDON
MAHN, TRAUTE
RELLERGERD, HELMUT
ROMHILD, HELMUTH
SAUPE, DIETER
VON KOBLINSKI, HANS-JOACH

CAMERON, JULIE
CAMERON, LOU

CAMERON, JUNE
IHLE, SHARON J.

CAMERON, KATE
DUBREUIL, ELIZABETH L.
MCGLAMRY, BEVERLY

CAMERON, KAY
COFFMAN, VIRGINIA [E]

CAMERON, KIP
CAMERON, DESMOND L.

CAMERON, LEIGH
WRIGHT, SEWELL PEASLEE

CAMERON, LORNA
FRASER, ANTHEA

CAMERON, LOUIS
CAMERON, LOU

CAMERON, MARGARET
KILVERT, MARGARET C.
LEWIS, MARGARET CAMERON
LINDSAY, KATHLEEN

CAMERON, MIRANDA
KAHN, MARY

CAMERON, ROBERT
MOLSNER, MICHAEL

CAMERON, SILVER DONALD
CAMERON, DONALD [A]

CAMERON, WACO
KAUFHOLD, ?

CAMERON, WARD
HALLBING, KJELL KARL

CAMILLUS
KING, RUFUS

CAMINO, FELIPE
GALICIA, L. FELIPE CAMINO

CAMINO, JUAN DEL
SALVA, SALOMON DE LA

CAMP, DEBBIE
CAMP, DEBORAH ELAINE

CAMP, DEBBY
CAMP, DEBORAH ELAINE

CAMP, DEBORAH
CAMP, DEBORAH ELAINE

CAMP, DELAYNE
CAMP, DEBORAH ELAINE

CAMP, ELAINE
CAMP, DEBORAH ELAINE

CAMP, JOE
CAMP, JOSEPH SHELTON JR.

CAMP, JOSEPH S.
CAMP, JOSEPH SHELTON JR.

CAMPBELL, A.C.
CAMPBELL, ANDREW C.

CAMPBELL, ALASDAIR IAIN
HAMILTON, IAIN BETRAM

CAMPBELL, ALBERT A.
CAMPBELL, [ALBERT] ANGUS

CAMPBELL, ANGUS
CHETWYND-HAYES, RON

CAMPBELL, BARTLEY
URNER, NATHAN DANE

CAMPBELL, BEATRICE MURPHY
MURPHY, BEATRICE M.

CAMPBELL, BERKELEY
DUDDINGTON, CHARLES L.

CAMPBELL, BETHANY
MCCLUSKEY, SALLY

CAMPBELL, BRIDGET
SANCTUARY, BRENDA

CAMPBELL, BRUCE
EPSTEIN, SAMUEL

CAMPBELL, C.J.
STUART, MORNA

CAMPBELL, CAROLINE
SAFFORD, LESLIE A.

CAMPBELL, CLIFF
FLOREN, LEE
NYE, NELSON C[ORAL]
SHAPPIRO, HERBERT ARTHUR
HECKLEMANN, CHARLES N.

CAMPBELL, CLIVE
MACRAE, DONALD G.

CAMPBELL, CLYDE CRANE
GOLD, HORACE L.

CAMPBELL, COLIN
CHRISTIE, DOUGLAS

CAMPBELL, DAVID
FISH, LEONARD G.

CAMPBELL, DONALD
GILFORD, CHARLES BERNARD

CAMPBELL, DUNCAN
THORPE, JOHN

CAMPBELL, FRANCIS S.
KUEHNELT-LEDDIHN, ERIK v.

CAMPBELL, FRANCIS STUART
KUEHNELT-LEDDIHN, ERIK v.
VON KUEHNELT-LEDDIH, ERIK

CAMPBELL, FRED
SELLERS, CONNIE LESLIE

CAMPBELL, HARRY
SMITH, BERNARD

CAMPBELL, HOPE
WALLIS, GERALDINE MCDONL.

CAMPBELL, JANE
EDWARDS, JANE CAMPBELL

CAMPBELL, JEFFREY
BLACK, CAMPBELL
CAINE, JEFFREY A.

CAMPBELL, JIM
CAMPBELL, JAMES HOWARD

CAMPBELL, JOANNA
BLY, CAROLYN
BRUCE, JOANNA H. CAMPBELL

CAMPBELL, JOHN
CUMMINGS, RAY[MOND KING]

CAMPBELL, JUDITH
PARES, MARION STAPYLTON

CAMPBELL, KAREN
BEATY, BETTY

CAMPBELL, KEITH
WEST-WATSON, KEITH C.

CAMPBELL, LUKE
MADISON, THOMAS [A]

CAMPBELL, MARGARET
LONG, GABRIELLE M.V.C.

CAMPBELL, MOLLY
THOMSON, CHRISTINE C.

CAMPBELL, PATTY
CAMPBELL, PATRICIA J[EAN]

CAMPBELL, R. WRIGHT
CAMPBELL, ROBERT WRIGHT

CAMPBELL, R.T.
TODD, RUTHVEN CAMPBELL

CAMPBELL, R.W.
CAMPBELL, ROSMAE WELLS

CAMPBELL, SCOTT
DAVIS, FREDERICK WILLIAM

CAMPBELL, STUART
CAMPBELL, SYDNEY GEORGE

CAMPBELL, WILFRED
CAMPBELL, WILLIAM

CAMPER, SHIRLEY
SOMAN, SHIRLEY CAMPER

CAMPION, BABETTE
ROSMOND, BABETTE

CAMPION, ROSE
KASER, ARTHUR LEROY
LATHAM, JEAN LEE
PERRY, RUTH

CAMPION, SARAH
ALPERS, MARY ROSE
COULTON, MARY ROSE

CAMRA, ROSS
SMITH, GEORGE H[ENRY]

CANADAY, LEE
OUTLAW-SHALLIT, LOUISE L.

CANADIENNE
HUNT, ANNA REBECCA GALE

CANARY
CONN, CANARY DENISE

CANAWAY, BILL
CANAWAY, W.H.

CANCALE
DESNOS, ROBERT

CANCIAN, FRANK
CANCIAN, FRANCIS ALEX.

CANDENBACH, HORST
HELLWIG, ERNST

CANDIDA
HOFFMAN, LISA

CANDIDO
MARTINEZ RUIZ, LUIS

CANDIDUS
BROGAN, COLM

CANDIL, FRAY
BOBADILLA, EMILIO

CANDY, EDWARD
NEVILLE, BARBARA ALISON

CANE, HURRY
RENNAU, JOACHIM

CANE, NANCY
COHEN, NANCY J.

CANE, TERRY
REIFF, H. VOLKER

CANFIELD, CLEVE
MITCHELL, CLARE MAY

CANFIELD, DOROTHEA F.
FISHER, DOROTHY F.C.

CANFIELD, DOROTHEA FRANCE
FISHER, DOROTHY F.C.

CANFIELD, DOROTHY
FISHER, DOROTHY F.C.

CANFIELD, MIRIAM
FISHER, DOROTHY F.C.

CANIS
HUBBARD, CLIFFORD LIONEL

CANN, AL
KANN, ALBRECHT PETER

CANN, PETER
KANN, ALBRECHT PETER

CANNAN, DENIS
PULLEIN-THOMPSON, DENNIS

CANNAN, JOANNA
PULLEIN-THOMPSON, JOANNA

CANNELL, CHARLES
VIVIAN, E[VELYN] CHARLES

CANNELL, CHARLES HENRY
VIVIAN, E[VELYN] CHARLES

CANNIBAL, JACK
REID, [THOMAS] MAYNE

CANNING, EFFIE
CARLTON, EFFIE CROCKETT

CANNING, JOHN
SHUSHTARY, JOHN

CANNON, BIOLL
CANNON, WILLIAM S.

CANNON, BRENDA
MOORE, BERTHA B.

CANNON, CURT
HUNTER, EVAN

CANNON, ELLIOTT
ELLIOTT-CANNON, ARTHUR

CANNON, FRANK
MAYHAR, ARDATH F.H.

CANNON, JACK
DEMILLE, NELSON [RICHARD]

CANNON, JOHN
NEWTON, MICHAEL

CANNON, RAVENNA
MAYHAR, ARDATH F.H.

CANNON, WACO
KAUFHOLD, ?

CANNOR, J.R.
GODDARD, NORMAN M.

CANOE, JOHN
KIRKPATRICK, OLIVER A.

CANOY, E. ALDON
SCHIER, NORMA

CANTREE, WALTER
SCHIER, NORMA

CANTRELL, RAINE
DIBENEDETTO, THERESA

CANTRELL, WADE B.
HOGAN, ROBERT J[ASPER]

CANTWELL, ASTON
PLATT, CHARLES [M]

CANTWELL, LLOYD
CHAMBERS, [J.D] WHITTAKER

CANUCK, ABE
BINGLEY, DAVID ERNEST

CANUCK, JANEY
MURPHY, EMILY F.

CANUSI, JOSE
BARKER, S. OMAR

CANUTT, YAKIMA
CANUTT, ENOS EDWARD

CANYON, CLAUDIA
ANDERSON, BETTY

CAPE, JUDITH
PAGE, PATRICIA KATHLEEN

CAPEL, ROGER
SHEPPARD, LANCELOT C.

CAPELLA, RAY
CAPELLA, RAUL GARCIA

CAPELLE, ANNE
HERAPATH, THEODORA

CAPELLI, ACE
FRANCES, STEPHEN D.
HILL, ROY
KIRBY, DEREK AMOS
LAZENBY, NORMAN A.
PARDOE, GEOFFREY
ROBERTS, DAVID
SLATER, LEONARD
SOWMAN, GORDON
STOKES, RALPH

CAPELLIN, MARIA
FEARN, JOHN RUSSELL

CAPITALIST
SLATER, JAMES

CAPITALIST, A.
VAN DEUSEN, ALONZO

CAPON, PETER
OAKLEY, ERIC GILBERT

CAPP, AL
CAPLIN, ALFRED GERALD

CAPP, B.S.
CAPP, BERNARD STUART

CAPRIO, BETSY
CAPRIO, ELIZABETH BLAIR

CAPSTAN
HARDINGE, CHARLES WREXE

CAPT. COE
MITCHELL, EDWARD CARD
SPRINGFIELD, LINCOLN

CAPTAIN DANGERFIELD
ANDERSON, G.J.B.

CAPTAIN X
POWER-WATERS, BRIAN

CAPTIOUS CRITIC
MILLER, LYNN

CARADON, LORD
FOOT, HUGH MACKINTOSH

CARAFOLI, MARCI
BALTERMAN, MARCIA R.

CARAMAN, GEORGES
SIMENON, GEORGES [J.C]

CARAVAN, T.P.
MUNOZ, CHARLES

CARAWAN, CANDIE
CARAWAN, CAROLANNE M.

CARBERRY, ANN
CHILD, MAUREEN

CARBERY, EITHNE
JOHNSTON, ANNA

CARBERY, ETHNA
MACMANUS, ANNA JOHNSTON

CARBURY, A.B.
CARR, ALBERT H.Z.

CARCO, FRANCIS
CARCOPINO-TUSOLI, FRANCIS

CARDER, LEIGH
CUNNINGHAM, EUGENE

CARDER, MICHAEL
FLUHARTY, VERNON L.

CARDIFF, SARA
DECORMIER, LOUISE
KAVALIER, REBECCA
KIRCHEIMER, GLORIA

CARDINAL, JANE
WILLIAMSON, ETHEL

CARDINAL, SISTER MARY ORA
CARDINAL, ORA

CARDOS, ALICE
KEMPE, ALICE [S]

CARDOZ, LOIS S.
ARQUETTE, LOIS S. DUNCAN

CARDUI, VAN
WAYMAN, TONY RUSSELL

CARDUI, VANESSA
WAYMAN, TONY RUSSELL

CARDWELL, ANN
PAWLEY, JEAN MAKINS

CARDWELL, RAY
FELLER, HANS
STRASSEL, HUBERT

CARE, FELICITY
COURY, LOUISE ANDRE

CARELL, EDITH
BOCH-SCHLIMME, EDITH

CARELL, GEORGIA
LOEFF, FRIEDEL [H]

CARENC, EGISE
SOHOMONJAN, EGISE

CARERRA, KATHLEEN
CARR, JESSE CROWE JR.

CARESS, JAY
CARESS, JAMES M.

CAREW, BURLEIGH
COOK, FRED GORDON

CAREW, JEAN
CORBY, JANE [IRENITA]

CAREW, JOCELYN
AEBY, JACQUELYN

CAREW, JOHN [JACK]
WALSH, JAMES MORGAN

CAREW, S.C.
HOLT, GLEN

CAREW, TIM
CAREW, JOHN MOHUN

CAREWE, S.C.
DUBREUIL, ELIZABETH L.

CAREY, ANNE
NEVILL, BARRY ST. JOHN

CAREY, CHARLES
WADDELL, CHARLES CAREY

CAREY, DIANE
BRODEUR, DIANE & GREG

CAREY, DONNELL
LAKE, JOE BARRY

CAREY, ELISABETH
BRIDGE, SUSAN

CAREY, JAMES
CAREW-SLATER, HAROLD JAME

CAREY, JULIAN
TUBB, E.C.

CAREY, M.V.
CAREY, MARY VIRGINIA

CAREY, MATTHEW
CAZAURAN, AUGUSTUS R.

CAREY, MICHAEL
BURTON, EDWARD J.

CAREY, SUZANNE
CAREY, VERNA

CARFAGNE, CYRIL
JENNINGS, LESLIE NELSON

CARFAX, CATHERINE
FAIRBURN, ELEANOR

CARGHILL, RALPH
COX, ARTHUR JEAN

CARGOE, RICHARD
PAYNE, PIERRE S. ROBERT

CARISBROOKE
NESBIT, EDITH

CARIUS, ANNE
FRIEDRICH, MARGOT

CARL, C.
CASSAU, CARL

CARLEON, A.
SKINNER, JUNE M. O'GRADY

CARLES, RIVA
GREENFIELD, IRVING A.

CARLETON, CAPT. LATHAM C.
ELLIS, EDWARD S.

CARLETON, CATHLEEN
KLEM, KAYE WILSON

CARLETON, COUSIN MAY
FLEMING, MAY AGNES

CARLETON, H[UGH] B.
BROWNE, HOWARD

CARLETON, LATHAM C.
ELLIS, EDWARD S.

CARLETON, MILECETE
JONES, SUSAN CARLETON

CARLETON, S.
JONES, SUSAN CARLETON

CARLETON, SCOTT
TOMPKINS, WALKER A.

CARLETON, SUSAN
JONES, SUSAN CARLETON

CARLETON, WILLIAM [WILL]
BARTLETT, FREDERICK ORIN

CARLETON, [CAPTAIN] L.C.
ELLIS, EDWARD S.

CARLETON-MILECETE
JONES, SUSAN CARLETON

CARLFI, CHESTER H.
FRITCH, CHARLES E.

CARLILE, CLANCY
CARLILE, CLARENCE

CARLISLE, CARNS
PEMBERTON, MARGARET

CARLISLE, CLARK
HOLDING, JAMES [C.C.]

CARLISLE, D.M.
COOK, DOROTHY MARY

CARLISLE, DONNA
BALL, DONNA

CARLISLE, HELEN GRACE
REID, HELEN GRACE

CARLISLE, RILLA
MARTENS, ANNE L.C.

CARLOCK, LYNN
CUNNINGHAM, MARILYN

CARLOS, DON
CHEEVER, HENRY P.

CARLOTA
OPPENHEIMER, CARLOTA

CARLSBOURGH, OKTAVIAN
EISENPROBST, FERDINAND

CARLSEN, CHRIS
HOLDSTOCK, ROBERT P.

CARLSON, C.C.
CARLSON, CAROLE C.
LINDSEY, HAL

CARLSON, ELIZABETH
PATTISON, BETTY ANN

CARLSON, LEWIS H.
LAVINE, LEWIS H.

CARLSON, LILLY
VANDERBILT, HEIDI

CARLSON, P.M.
CARLSON, PATRICIA M[cEL.]

CARLSSON, SIGURD
TULLBERG, SIGURD

CARLTON, ALVA
DELK, ROBERT CARLTON

CARLTON, ANN
TRENT, ANN

CARLTON, JAY
GOLDSMITH, JAMES CARLTON
OBRECHT, JAS

CARLTON, JOSEPH
MCMULLEN, JOSEPH CARL

CARLTON, KATE
SINNOTT, LINDA

CARLTON, LEWIS
CARLTON, G.E.L.

CARLTON, LIEUT.
CARLTON, GERALD

CARLTON, ROGER
ROWLAND, DONALD S.

CARLTON, [COUSIN] MAY
EARLE, M.A.

CARLYLE, ANTHONY
MILTON, GLADYS ALEXANDRA

CARLYLE, TENA
OTTEN, CAROLE CARD
TABER, ELLEN LYLE

CARM, MAC
ARMSTRONG, KEITH F.W.

CARMA, CLARISSA
LEHMANN, RITA

CARMAN, DULCE
DRUMMOND, EDITH MARIE D.C

CARMEN, FELIX
SHERMAN, FRANK DEMPSTER

CARMEN, SYLVIA
OTTILIE LUISE, PAULINE

CARMENDELLA, ANTHONY
CEBULASH, MEL

CARMI, T.
CHARNY, CARMI

CARMICHAEL, ANN
MACALPINE, MARGARET H.

CARMICHAEL, CARRIE
CARMICHAEL, HARRIET

CARMICHAEL, CLAIRE
MCNAB, CLAIRE

CARMICHAEL, EMILY
KROKOSZ, EMILY

CARMICHAEL, HARRY
OGNALL, LEOPOLD HORACE

CARMICHAEL, JEANNE
QUINTO, CAROLE

CARMICHAEL, JENNINGS
BALLARAT

CARMICHAEL, PHILIP
HARRISON, PHILIP

CARMILLY, MOSHE
WEINBERGER, MOSHE

CARNAC, CAROL
RIVETT, EDITH CAROLINE

CARNAC, LEVIN
GRIFFITH-JONES, GEORGE C.

CARNAC, NICHOLAS
EDWARDS, F.H.M.

CARNARVON, EARL OF
HERBERT, HENRY GEORGE A.

CARNE, ROGER
BOUNDS, SYDNEY J.

CARNEGIE, SACHA
CARNEGIE, RAYMOND ALEXDR.

CARNELL, E.J.
CARNELL, [EDWARD] JOHN

CARNELL, JOHN
CARNELL, [EDWARD] JOHN

CARNELL, LOIS C.
CARNELL, LOIS CHRISTIAN

CARNELL, RICHARD
ACKERMAN, FORREST J.

CARNES, CAPT.
CUMMING, M.I.

CARNEY, JIM
HOBEIN, EUGEN

CARNI, ROSS
CAMPBELL, H[ERBERT] J.
HAMPSON, I.E.
ROBSON, NORMAN

CAROL, BILL J.
KNOTT, WILLIAM CECIL JR.

CAROL, JACQUELINE
COOPER, JACQUELINE

CAROL, JOHN
FODEN, FREDERICK [T]

CAROL, ROBERT
BOURGEOIS, CAMILLE

CAROL, ROBIN [ROBERT]
BOURGEOUS, CAMILLE

CAROLAN, R.
SEDLEY, ARTHUR O.L.

CAROLL, NONIE
MURPHY, NONIE CAROL

CAROLUS
WOLFF, CARL

CAROLYI, STEPHAN
REIS, KURT

CAROON, MAIK
NAGULA, MICHAEL

CARPEN, ROBERT
KRAMER, GERHARD

CARPENTER
ARNOLD, JUNE DAVIS

CARPENTER, CAL
CARPENTER, CLARENCE A.

CARPENTER, CHRISTOPHER
EVANS, CHRIS[TOPHER D.]

CARPENTER, DUFFY
HURLEY, JOHN JEROME

CARPENTER, FRED
HAND, [ANDRUS] JACKSON

CARPENTER, JOHN JO
REESE, JOHN [HENRY]

CARPENTER, LIZ
CARPENTER, ELIZABETH S.

CARPENTER, MORLEY
TUBB, E.C.

CARPENTER, WILLOW
BROWNING, [Z] SINCLAIR

CARPENTIER, CHARLES
HUMBERT-DROZ, JULES

CARR, A.H.Z.
CARR, ALBERT H. ZOLOTKOFF

CARR, ADAMS
WALSHE, DOUGLAS

CARR, ALEXANDER
KNEIFEL, HANNS

CARR, ANNIE ROE
STRATEMEYER, EDWARD

CARR, BASIL
KAHANE, JACK

CARR, BENTLEY
KING, KEITH MICHAEL

CARR, CATHARINE
WADE, ROSALIND HERSCHEL

CARR, CHARLES
MASON, SYDNEY CHARLES

CARR, CHRISTOPHER
BENSON, ARTHUR CHRISTOPH.

CARR, CONWAY
FEARN, JOHN RUSSELL

CARR, ELAINE
MASON, SYDNEY CHARLES

CARR, ELENI
MARAGAKIS, HELEN

CARR, GLYN
STYLES, [FRANK] SHOWELL

CARR, GORDON
BAYFIELD, WILLIAM J.

CARR, H.D.
CROWLEY, EDWARD ALEXANDER

CARR, J.L.
CARR, JAMES JOSEPH LLOYD

CARR, JAY
DUFF, JAMES P.

CARR, JAYGE
KREUGER, MARGERY [MARJ]

CARR, JAYGEE
KREUGER, MARGERY [MARJ]

CARR, JESS
CARR, JESSE CROWE JR.

CARR, JOAN
SANDERSON, H.P.

CARR, JOLYON
PARGETER, EDITH [MARY]

CARR, KENT
OLIVER, GERTRUDE KENT

CARR, KERRY
YOUNG, ENA

CARR, KIRBY
PLATT, KIN

CARR, MAURICE
KREITMAN, MAURICE

CARR, NICK
CARR, WOODA NICHOLAS

CARR, PETER
REINHARD, WILHELM PETER

CARR, PHILLIPPA
HIBBERT, ELEANOR BURFORD

CARR, RAY
FOUCAR, EMILE CHARLES V.

CARR, ROBERTA
ROBERTS, IRENE W.

CARR, SHERRY
CLARY, SYDNEY ANN

CARR, STEPHEN [J]
PALICKAR, STEPHEN J.

CARR, VIRGINIA MASON
VAUGHAN, VIRGINIA MASON

CARRADOS, CLARK
GARCIA LECHA, LUIS

CARRAS, HELEN
MARAGAKIS, HELEN

CARRE, CHUCK
SELLERS, CONNIE LESLIE

CARREL, MARK
PAINE, LAURAN BOSWORTH

CARRES, C.
CASSAU, CARL

CARRICK, A.B.
LINDSAY, HAROLD ARTHUR

CARRICK, EDWARD
CRAIG, EDWARD ANTHONY

CARRICK, JOHN
CROSBIE, HUGH PROVAN

CARRIGAN, JOHN D.
LIST, HORST

CARRINGTON, DOROTHY
ROSE, DOROTHY VIOLET F.

CARRINGTON, G.A.
CUNNINGHAM, CHESTER GRANT

CARRINGTON, GLENDA
GLENN, KAREN

CARRINGTON, MICHAEL
WILLIAMS, MEURIG MON

CARRINGTON, MOLLY
MATTHEWS, CONSTANCE MARY

CARRINGTON, V.
HUGHES, VALERIE ANNE

CARRIZO, FABIO
ALVAREZ, JOSE S.

CARROL, MARIO
HORSCHELT, THEODOR

CARROL, SHANA
NEWCOMB, KERRY
SCHAEFER, FRANK

CARROLL, ANNE KRISTIN
GALES, BARBARA J.

CARROLL, CHRISTINA
HENDERSON, MARILYN RUTH

CARROLL, CURT
BISHOP, CURTIS [KENT]

CARROLL, DAWN
BOESE, DAWN C.

CARROLL, ELIZABETH
BARKIN, CAROL
JAMES, ELIZABETH

CARROLL, JOELLYN
BREMER, JO[ANNE]
WAGNER, CAROL I.

CARROLL, JOHN D.
DALY, CARROLL JOHN

CARROLL, KATHLEEN
MODROVICH, KATHLEEN C.

CARROLL, LAURA
PARR, LUCY

CARROLL, LEWIS
DODGSON, CHARLES LUTWIDGE

CARROLL, LORRAINE
BEATTY, LORRAINE

CARROLL, M.A.
MAYERS, CARROLL

CARROLL, MALISSA
SCHARF, MARIAN
WAGNER, CAROL I.

CARROLL, MARGARET
WHITNEY, CAROL A.

CARROLL, MARISA
WAGNER, CAROL I.

CARROLL, MARISSA
WAGNER, CAROL I.

CARROLL, MARTIN
CARR, MARGARET

CARROLL, MARY
SANFORD, ANNETTE [S]

CARROLL, RAY
TURNER, ROBERT H.

CARROLL, ROBERT
ALPERT, HOLLIS

CARROLL, ROSALYN
KATZ, CAROL

CARROLL, ST. THOMAS MARIO
CARROLL, TOM M.

CARROLL, SUSAN
COPPULA, SUSAN CARROLL

CARROLL, SYDNEY [W]
WHITMAN, SYDNEY

CARROLL, TED
CARROLL, THOMAS THEODORE

CARROLL, W.J.
CARROLL, WILLIAM JOSEPH

CARROUGES, MICHEL
COUTURIER, LOUIS JOSEPH

CARRUTH, AGNES K.
TUCKER, AGNES KENT C.

CARRYAWAY, NICK
MURRAY, JOHN F.

CARSAC, FRANCIS
BORDES, FRANCOIS

CARSE, SHANNON
ROTSLER, WILLIAM

CARSON, ALLAN
LAZENBY, NORMAN A.
JENNISON, JOHN WILLIAM

CARSON, ANTHONY
BROOKE, PETER

CARSON, BART
MACONACHIE, WILLIAM

CARSON, GAY D.
DONGES, GUNTER

CARSON, HANK
FEARN, JOHN RUSSELL

CARSON, KIT
CARSON, XANTHUS

CARSON, LANCE
KELLY, HAROLD ERNEST

CARSON, MUNRO
FRANCES, STEPHEN D.

CARSON, PEER
GROSSMANN, HANS HUGO

CARSON, RAY
KALMUCZAK, ROLF

CARSON, ROBERT
SOMERLOTT, ROBERT

CARSON, ROSALIND
CHITTENDEN, MARGARET

CARSON, RUTH
BUGBEE, RUTH CARSON

CARSON, S.M.
GORSLINE, [SALLY] MARIE

CARSON, SYLVIA
DRESSER, DAVIS

CARSON, ZEKE
LUTZ, GILES A.

CARSON, [CAPT.] JAMES
STRATEMEYER, EDWARD

CARSTAIRS, CHRIS
WELSH, KEN

CARSTAIRS, KATHLEEN
PENDOWER, THOMAS CURTIS H

CARSTAIRS, ROD
DALTON, GILBERT LAWFORD

CARSTEN, CHRISTIAN
FROBA, KLAUS

CARSTEN, WILM
PRAFER, HANS GEORG

CARSTENS, BERND
HERRMANN, JOSEF

CARSTENS, KURT
GIESA, WERNER K.

CARSWELL, LESLIE
STEPHENS, ROSEMARY

CARTER, ACE
BLEECK, G.C.

CARTER, ALBERTA SIMPSON
BERCOVICI, ALFRED

CARTER, AMANDA
ERNSBERGER, GEORGE

CARTER, ANN[E]
BROOKS, ANNE TEDLOCK

CARTER, ASHLEY
WHITTINGTON, HARRY

CARTER, AVIS MURTON
ALLEN, KENNETH S.

CARTER, BRONSON D.
WADE, THOMAS W.

CARTER, BRUCE
HOUGH, RICHARD ALEXANDER

CARTER, DEE
HUGHES, DENNIS [TALBOT]

CARTER, DIANA
COPPER, DOROTHY

CARTER, EDIE
SCOTT, PETER

CARTER, ELIZABETH ELIOT
HOLLAND, CECELIA [A]

CARTER, FELICITY
COULSON, FELICITY W.C.

CARTER, FRANK
MCCARTON, BENJAMIN F.

CARTER, HELEN
MARAGAKIS, HELEN

CARTER, HENRY
KALMUCZAK, ROLF

CARTER, HERBERT
RATHBORNE, ST. GEORGE

CARTER, HURRICANE
CARTER, RUBIN

CARTER, JANE ROBBINS
ROBBINS, JANE [BORSCH]

CARTER, JANICE
HESS, JANICE

CARTER, JEFF
GROSSMANN, HANS HUGO

CARTER, JIM
BAJOG, GUNTHER
REUTER, RALPH

CARTER, JIMMY
CARTER, JAMES EARL JR.

CARTER, JOHN L.
CARTER, COMPTON IRVING

CARTER, LIN
CARTER, LIN[WOOD VROOMAN]

CARTER, LINWOOD
FOX, GARDNER F.

CARTER, M.L.
CARTER, MARGERY L.A.

CARTER, MABEL
KELLER, MARIANNE

CARTER, MARILYN
ROSS, WILLIAM E. DANIEL

CARTER, NEVADA
PAINE, LAURAN BOSWORTH

CARTER, NICHOLAS
ARMAGNAC, A.L.
BROWN, W. P.
BROWNE, GEORGE WALDO
BURTON, FREDERICK RUSSELL
CHALMERS, STEPHEN
COBB, WELDON J.
COOK, WILLIAM WALLACE
CORYELL, JOHN RUSSELL
COX, STEPHEN ANGUS D.
DAVIS, FREDERICK WILLIAM
DERBY, E.C.
DEY, FREDERIC VAN R.
FOSTER, WALTER BERTRAM
HANSHEW, THOMAS W.
HARBAUGH, THOMAS C.
HOOKE, CHARLES W.
HUDSON, WILLIAM C.
JENKS, GEORGE CHARLES
LARNED, W.L.
MACLEAN, CHARLES AGNEW
MCCULLEY, JOHNSTON
RATHBORNE, ST. GEORGE
SAWYER, EUGENE TAYLOR
SCOTT, VINCENT E.
SPAULDING, SAMUEL C.
STRATEMEYER, EDWARD
TOZER, ALFRED B.
WALSH, R.F.
YOUNG, ERNEST A[VON]

CARTER, NICK
ADDUCI, FRANK
AHERN, JEROME MORRELL
ALGOZIN, BRUCE
AVALLONE, MICHAEL
BALLARD, W. TODHUNTER

CARTER, NICK [CONT]
BOWSER, JIM
BRANDNER, GARY
BROWNE, NICHOLAS
CANON, JACK
CARTER, BRYAN
CARTER, CONRAD POWELL
CARTER, PAUL WARREN
CARTER, VINCENT
CARTER, [JOHN] HOWARD
CASSIDAY, BRUCE [BINGHAM]
CHAMBLISS, JOHN
CHAPIN, ANSEL
CHASTAIN, THOMAS
CLARK, PHILIP
COLBY, ROBERT
CONON, JACK
COPP, DEWITT S.
CORYELL, JOHN RUSSELL
CRIDER, [ALLEN] BILL[Y]
CUNNINGHAM, CHESTER GRANT
DANIELS, NORMAN A.
DAVIS, JACK
DEY, FREDERIC VAN R.
DOUGHTY, FRANCIS W.
FELBER, RON
FRITZHAND, JAMES
GARSIDE, [CLIFFORD] JACK
GILMORE, JOSEPH [LEE]
GRANBECK, MARILYN
HAGBERG, DAVID [JAMES]
HARBAUGH, THOMAS C.
HAYES, RALPH EUGENE
HINE, AL[FRED B.]
HUBBARD, RICHARD
HUBER, FREDERICK V [FRED]
HUNSBURGER, H. EDWARD
JAHN, JOSEPH MICHAEL
JAKES, JOHN [WILLIAM]
LATONA, BOB
LAZARUS, LEON
LOUDERBACK, LEW
LYNDS, DENNIS
MARLAND, DOUGLAS
MARMOR, ARNOLD
MCCLARY, THOMAS CALVERT
MESSMANN, JON [JOHN]
MOOLMAN, VALERIE
MORRIS, HOMER
NOVA, CRAIG
ODELL, WILLIAM
PERRIN, FORREST V.
POWELL, LARRY
PRINCE, DANIEL C.
RANDISI, ROBERT J.
RASOF, HENRY
REARDON, DAN
ROHDE, WILLIAM L.
ROSENBERGER, JOSEPH
SIMMONS, STEVE
SMITH, MARTIN WILLIAM
SMITH, ORMAND G.
SNYDER, GEORGE
STEELEY, ROBERT DEREK
STEVENSON, JOHN
STEWART, LINDA
STOKES, MANNING LEE
STOKESBERRY, BOB
STREIB, DANIEL T.
STUART, DORIS
SWAIN, DWIGHT V[REELAND]
VAN GELDER, LAWRENCE
WALLMANN, JEFFREY M.
WHITE, LIONEL
WHITSON, JOHN HARVEY
WILLIAMSON, STEPHEN
VARDEMAN, ROBERT E.

CARTER, NICK [CONT]
WARREN, GEORGE
WERNICK, SAUL
WORMSER, RICHARD [E]

CARTER, PHILIP
CARTER, PAUL A.

CARTER, PHILIP YOUNGMAN
CARTER, MARGERY L.A.

CARTER, PHYLLIS ANN
EBERLE, IRMENGARDE

CARTER, RALPH
NEUBAUER, WILLIAM A.

CARTER, TEX
JENNISON, JOHN WILLIAM

CARTER, TOM
CARTER, THOMAS EARL

CARTER-BROWN, PETER
YATES, ALAN GEOFFREY

CARTIER, STEVE
CAMERON, LOU

CARTLAND, BARBARA
MCCORQUODALE, BARBARA H.C

CARTON, RICHARD CLAUDE
CRITCHETT, RICHARD CLAUDE

CARTUR, PETER
GRAINGER, PETER

CARTWRIGHT, A.
TWYMAN, HAROLD WILLIAM

CARTWRIGHT, JAMES MACGRGR
JENNINGS, LESLIE NELSON

CARTWRIGHT, N.
SCOFIELD, NORMA M.C.

CARTWRIGHT, VANESSA
PRESTON, HARRY

CARUS, STERNE
KRAUSE, ERNST LUDWIG

CARVAJAL, RICARDO
MENESES, ENRIQUE

CARVER, DAVE
BINGLEY, DAVID ERNEST

CARVER, HENRY
BINGLEY, DAVID ERNEST

CARVER, JOHN
GARDNER, RICHARD [M]

CARVIN, DAN
CARLIN, SVEN GUSTAF

CARWELL, L'ANN
MCKISSACK, PATRICIA C.

CARY
CARY, LOUIS FAVREAU

CARY, ARTHUR
CARY, JOYCE

CARY, D.M.
MACMILLIAN, DOUGLAS

CARY, DIANA SERRA
CARY, PEGGY-JEAN M.

CARY, JUD
TUBB, E.C.

CARY, JUDY
TUBB, E.C.

CARY, JULIAN
TUBB, E.C.

CARY, MORLAND
NEVILLE, HUGH E. CARY

CARY, ROBERT
CARIVEAU, ROBERT EDWARD

CARYL, JEAN
KAPLAN, JEAN CARYL KORN

CASACCIA, GABRIEL
CASACCIA, BIBOLINI G.

CASALANDRA, ESTELLE
ESTELLE, [SISTER] MARY

CASALS, PABLO
CASALS, PAU CARLOS S.D.

CASAMAYOR
FUSTER, SERGE

CASAVINI, PIERALESANDRO
WAINHOUSE, AUSTYN

CASCDANANDA, ANAGARACA
SMILEY, CHARLES WESLEY

CASE, BILL
CASE, THEODORE WILLARD

CASE, JIM
MERTZ, STEPHEN

CASE, JUSTIN
BELLEM, ROBERT LESLIE
GLEADOW, RUPERT SEELEY
MURRAY, WILLIAM P.
CAVE, HUGH B[ARNETT]

CASE, L.L.
LEWIN, LEONARD C.

CASE, MICHAEL
HOWARD, ROBERT WEST

CASE, PEG
CASE, PEGGY C.
PETERSON, DOUGLAS

CASE, T.
CORDES, THEODORE K.

CASE, TOM
KNIGHT, TONY

CASEBIER, MARJORIE
MCCOY, MARJORIE CASEBIER

CASEY, EILEEN
O'CASEY, EILEEN REYNOLDS

CASEY, GLADYS
GRIER, BARBARA G.D.

CASEY, JACK
CASEY, JOHN

CASEY, KENT
MCINTOSH, KENNETH

CASEY, MART
CASEY, MICHAEL & ROSEMARY

CASEY, PATRICK
THURMAN, WALLACE HENRY

CASEY, RICHARD
YERXA, LEROY

CASEY, WINIFRED ROSEN
ROSEN, WINIFRED

CASH, GRADY
CASH, GRACE SAVANNAH

CASH, H.O.
DENT, LESTER

CASH, HARMON
DENT, LESTER

CASH, JOHNNY
CASH, JOHN R.

CASH, SEBASTIAN
SMITHELLS, ROGER [W]

CASH-DOMINGO, LEA
KORETSKY, JUDITH LEA

CASHMAN, JOHN
DAVIS, TIMOTHY FRANCIS T.

CASHMORE, ERNEST
CASHMORE, E. ELLIS

CASIMIR, H.B.G.
CASIMIR, HENDRIK BRUGT G.

CASKEL, EVA
KOCHANSKI, EVA [C]

CASKODEN, [SIR] EDWIN
MAJOR, CHARLES

CASONA, ALEJANDRO
ALVAREZ, ALEJANDRO RODR.

CASPARI, TINA
EITZERT, ROSEMARIE

CASPER, BILL JR.
CASPER, WILLIAM EARL JR.

CASPER, BILLY
CASPER, WILLIAM EARL JR.

CASQUE, SAMMY
DAVIS, SYDNEY CHARLES H.

CASS, ZOE
LOW, LOIS DOROTHEA

CASSABA, CARLOS
PARRY, MICHEL P.

CASSANDRA
CONNOR, WILLIAM NEIL

CASSELL, LILI
WRONKER, LILI CASSELL

CASSELL-WRONKER, LILI
WRONKER, LILI CASSELL

CASSELLS, JOHN
DUNCAN, W. MURDOCH

CASSIDY, BECCA
VINES-HAINES, BEVERLY

CASSIDY, CARLA
BRACALE, CARLA

CASSIDY, CLAUDE
PAINE, LAURAN BOSWORTH

CASSIDY, GEORGE
VANCE, WILLIAM E.

CASSIDY, KRIS
CLARK, KATHY

CASSIDY, S.J.
WARD, ROBERT M.

CASSILIS, ROBERT
EDWARDES, MICHAEL F.H.

CASSILL, R.V.
CASSILL, RONALD VERLIN

CASSILS, PETER
KEELE, KENNETH D.

CASSILS, ROBERT
EDWARDS, MICHAEL F.H.

CASSIUS
FOOT, MICHAEL MACKINTOSH

CASSY, WILLIAM O.
FALK, HERMANN

CASTEDO-ELLERMAN, ELENA
CASTEDO, ELENA

CASTELAR, ISABELLA
WINTER, ELIZABETH C.

CASTELL, MEGAN
WILLIAMS, DOROTHY JEANNE

CASTELL, W.A.
HARY, WERNER ANDREAS

CASTELLANO, FRANCO
SGARLATO, NICO

CASTELLO, CARINA
APPEL, WALTER

CASTELNUOVO, LEO DI
PULLE, LEOPOLDO

CASTELOT, ANDRE
STORMS, ANDRE

CASTLE, BRENDA
FERRAND, GEORGINA

CASTLE, DAMON
SMITH, RICHARD REIN

CASTLE, DOUGLAS
BROWN, JOHN RIDLEY

CASTLE, FRANCES
LEADER, [EVELYN] BARBARA

CASTLE, JAYNE
KRENTZ, JAYNE ANN

CASTLE, JILL
NEUKRUG, LINDA

CASTLE, JOHN
PAYNE, RONALD CHARLES
GARROD, JOHN WILLIAM

CASTLE, LEE
OGAN, GEORGE & MARGARET

CASTLE, LINDA
CROCKETT, LINDA

CASTLE, PAUL
HOWARD, VERNON L.

CASTLE, PHILIP
JACKSON, C. PHILIP CASTLE

CASTLE, PHILIPPA
LOWERY, MARILYN M.

CASTLE, ROBERT
HAMILTON, EDMOND

CASTLE, TONY
CASTLE, ANTHONY PERCY

CASTLEMON, HARRY
FOSDICK, CHARLES AUSTIN

CASTO, JACKIE
CASTO, JACQUELINE A.

CASTOR, PERE
FAUCHER, PAUL

CASTRO, TONY
CASTRO, ANTONIO

CASTWEAZLE, ELEANOR
RAYNES, FREDERICA R.R.

CASWELL, ANNE
DENHAM, MARY ORR

CAT, CHRISTOPHER
CULLEN, COUNTEE

CATALA, VICTOR
PARADIS, CATARINA ALB. i

CATALAN, HENRI
DUPUY-MAZUEL, HENRI

CATALANI, VICTORIA
HAAS, CAROLA

CATAMARAN
BING, JON

CATANACH, J.N.
BURN, HENRY PELHAM

CATANZARO, W.
PEREZ BLASCO, JULIO

CATAY
MENDOZA ROMERO, MARIA L.

CATE, DICK
CATE, RICHARD EDWARD N.

CATES, KIM
BUSH, KIM OSTROM

CATES, KIMBERLY
BUSH, KIM OSTROM

CATES, TORY
BIRD, SARAH MCCABE

CATHCART, MARY
MYERS, MARY CATHCART

CATHER, WILLA
CATHER, WILELLA [S]

CATHER, WILLIAM MD
CATHER, WILELLA [S]

CATHMHAOIL, SEOSAMH MAC'
CAMPBELL, JOSEPH

CATHODE RAY
SCROGGIE, MARCUS GRAHAM

CATLIN, BARBARA
CRAVEN, BARBARA C.

CATLIN, JOHN
RITTER, WOLFPETER

CATLIN, MIRANDA
CRAVEN, BARBARA C.
HIX, MARTHA R.

CATLIN, RALPH
LAVENDER, DAVID SIEVERT

CATLOW, JOAN
LOWRY, JOAN [CATLOW]

CATLOW, JOANNA
LOWRY, JOAN [CATLOW]

CATLYNE, MR. Q.C.
MAHONY, MARTIN FRANCIS

CATO
FOOTE, MICHAEL
HOWARD, PETER DUNSMORE
OWEN, FRANK

CATON
BERCOFF, ANDRE MAURICE

CATSEN, FREDER
ENSKAT, FRITZ

CATTO, MAX
CATTO, MAXWELL JEFFREY

CATTO, P.Z.
HATHAWAY, RONALD F.

CATTON, C.M.
CATTON, C. MARIE

CATZ, MAX
GLASER, MILTON

CAUDWELL, CHRISTOPHER
SPRIGG, C. ST. JOHN

CAUDWELL, SARAH
COCKBURN, SARAH

CAULDER, INGLATH
COOPER, INGLATH

CAULDWELL, FRANK
KING, FRANCIS HENRY

CAULEY, TERRY
CAULEY, TROY JESSIE

CAULFIELD, MAX
CAULFIELD, MALACHY F.

CAULIFLOWER, SEBASTIAN
SELDES, GILBERT VIVIAN

CAUSEWAY, JANE
CORK, BARRY

CAUTION, TAKKIE
HATFIELD, CLARENCE E.

CAVAFY, C.P.
CAVAFISM KONSTANTINOS P.

CAVAFY, CONSTANTINE PETER
KAVAFIS, KONSTANTINOS P.

CAVAL, PATRICE
WARD, BILL

CAVALIERE, ANNE
CANADEO, ANNE

CAVALLO, EVELYN
SPARK, MURIEL SARAH

CAVANAGH, PAUL
VENE-CAVANAGH, PAUL

CAVANAUGH, SARA
MCQUAY, MICHAEL DENNIS

CAVANNA, BETTY
CAVANNA, ELIZABETH ALLEN
HARRISON, ELIZABETH C.

CAVANNA, ELIZABETH ALLEN
HARRISON, ELIZABETH C.

CAVE, EMMA
LASSALLE, CAROLINE

CAVE, THOMAS
STEWARD, SAMUEL M[ORRIS]

CAVEAU, FRED
KELLER, MANFRED

CAVENDISH
BROWN, E.

CAVENDISH, HARVEY
ST. JOHN, PERCY BOLLNGBRK

CAVENDISH, PETER
HORLER, SYDNEY

CAVERHILL, NICHOLAS
KIRK-GREEN, ANTHONY H.M.

CAVETT, DICK
CAVETT, RICHARD A.

CAXTON
RHODES, WILLIAM H[ENRY]

CAXTON, PISISTRATUS
LYTTON, EDWARD GEORGE E.

CAXTON, R.F.
HILL, LAWSON W.

CAY, NOWELL
FLOWERDEW, HERBERT

CAZAL, COMMANDER
DE LA HIRE, JEAN

CAZIMIR, OTTILIA
GAVRILESCU, ALEXANDRINA

CECIAL, TOME
FORNER, JUAN PABLO

CECIL, EDWARD
MAIDEN, CECIL

CECIL, HENRY
KELLER, DAVID H.
LEON, HENRY CECIL

CECIL, HUGH MORTIMER
ROBERTS, WILLIAM

CECIL, LORD ROBERT
GASCOYNE, ARTHUR TALBOT

CECIL, R.H.
HEWITT, CECIL ROLPH

CEDARHOLM, JAN
ASIMOV, JANET O. JEPPSON

CEDELL, CHRISTIAN
CEDERBERG, AKE

CEIROG
HUGHES, JOHN CEIROG

CEITHO, DEWI
JONES, EVAN DAVID

CELA, CAMILO JOE
TRULOCK, CAMILO JOSE CELA

CELAN, PAUL
ANTSCHEL, PAUL

CELAYA, GABRIEL
MUGICA, RAFAEL

CELEBERT
JEANNIN, JEAN-PAUL

CELINE, LOUIS FERDINAND
DESTOUCHES, LOUIS FERDIN.

CELLARIUS
BUTLER, SAMUEL

CELLINI, CAL
SELLERS, CONNIE LESLIE

CELLO, JOHNNY
BARNES, MICHAEL [L.G.]
GARRETT, ALBERT EDWARD
GORELL, LETHBRIDGE
HANSON, VICTOR JOSEPH

CENDRARS, BLAISE
SAUSER-HALL, FREDERIC

CENSOR
BUNCE, OLIVER BELL

CENTAUR
THORPE, JOHN

CENTE, H.F.
ROCKLIN, ROSS L.

CENTO
COBBING, BOB

CENTZ, P.C.
SAGE, BERNARD JANIN

CEPHUS, DELORES
DONALDSON, DALE C.

CERAM, C.E.
MAREK, KURT WILLI

CERAM, C.W.
MAREK, KURT WILLI

CERES
LITTLEWOOD, ALAN

CERIO, CLARETTE
CERIO, CLARA

CERMAK, MARTIN
DUCHACEK, IVO MARIA R.

CERNA, PANAIT
STANCIOFF, PANAIT

CERRA, GERDA ANN
KOONTZ, GERDA & DEAN

CERTINAGES, BERNARD
CRETIN, BERNARD JACQUES M

CERUTTI, TONI
CERUTTI, MARIA ANTONIETTA

CERVON, JACQUELINE
MOUSSARD, JACQUELINE

CERVUS, G.I.
ROE, WILLIAM JAMES

CESARA, MANDA
POEWE, KARLA

CEZ
CERKEG, VLADIMIR

CH'LAO, SUNG
CHOU, ERIC

CH'O, CHOU
SHU-JEN, CHOU

CHABER, M.E.
CROSSEN, KENDELL FOSTER

CHACE, ISOBEL
DE GUISE, ELIZABETH MARY

CHADWICK, ADRIAN
CLINGAN, A.B.

CHADWICK, CLEO
SMITH, LOIS

CHADWICK, ELIZABETH
HERNDON, NANCY R.

CHADWICK, JOSELYN
CHADWICK, JOSEPH L.

CHADWICK, LESTER
GARIS, HOWARD R.
STRATEMEYER, EDWARD

CHADWICK, NEAL
BECKER, ALFRED

CHAFETS, ZEV
CHAFETS, ZE'EV

CHAFFIN, JAMES B.
LUTZ, GILES A.

CHAFFIN, RANDALL
CHAFFIN, LILLIE D.

CHAIN, JULIAN
DIKTY, JULIAN [C] MAY

CHAITANYA, KRISHNA
NAIR, KRISHNAPILLAI K.

CHALFONT, ALUN
JONES, [A] ARTHUR GWYNNE

CHALFONT, PETER
SELLAR, ROBERT JAMES B.

CHALK, WESLEY
GIBSON, WALTER B.

CHALLICE, KENNETH
HUTCHIN, KENNETH CHARLES

CHALLIS, GEORGE
FAUST, FREDERICK S.

CHALLIS, MARY
BOWEN-JUDD, SARA HUTTON

CHALLIS, SIMON
PHILLIPS, DENNIS JOHN A.

CHALLON, DAVID
SILVERBERG, ROBERT

CHALLONER, H.K.
MILLS, JANET MELANIE A.

CHALLONER, ROBERT
BUTTERWORTH, MICHAEL

CHALLOT, DEAN
ZATLYN, EDWARD

CHALMERS, ALLEN
UPWARD, EDWARD FALAISE

CHALMERS, GEORGETTE
DEVANEY, ROBERT

CHALMERS, PENNY
KEMP, PENNY

CHALOM, JOHN
WALLACE, HENRY
CHALONER, JOHN SEYMOUR

CHALONER, W.H.
CHALONER, WILLIAM HENRY

CHAMBERLAIN, ENA
COOPER, PENNY

CHAMBERLAIN, THEODORE
JOHNSON, RONALD
WILLIAMS, JONATHAN CHAMB.

CHAMBERLAND, WILSON
CRANDALL, NORMA
MCCARTY, WILSON

CHAMBERLIN, LEE
LA PALLO, A. ELISE

CHAMBERS, CARL
CHAMBERS, [J.D] WHITTAKER

CHAMBERS, CATHERINE E.
JOHNSTON, NORMA
ST. JOHN, NICOLE

CHAMBERS, CROSLEY
CHAMBERS, [J.D] WHITTAKER

CHAMBERS, DANA
LEFFINGWELL, ALBERT

CHAMBERS, E.K.
CHAMBERS, EDMUND K.

CHAMBERS, GINGER
CHAMBERS, VIRGINIA ANNE S

CHAMBERS, HOWARD V.
LOWENKOPF, SHELLY A.

CHAMBERS, JAY VIVIAN
CHAMBERS, [J.D] WHITTAKER

CHAMBERS, JESSIE
LAWRENCE, DAVID HERBERT

CHAMBERS, KATE
JOHNSTON, NORMA
ST. JOHN, NICOLE

CHAMBERS, PEGGY
CHAMBERS, MARGARET ADA E.

CHAMBERS, PETER
DANIELS, PHILIP
PHILLIPS, DENNIS JOHN A.

CHAMBERS, R.W.
CHAMBERS, ROBERT WILLIAM

CHAMBERTIN, ILYA
VON BLOCK, BELA [W]
VON BLOCK, SYLVIA

CHAMBLISS, BILL
CHAMBLISS, WILLIAM JOSEPH

CHAMFORD, FELIX
SANDBERG, ALGOT GUSTAF O.

CHAMICO
ROXLO, CONRADO NALE

CHAMPION, D.L.
CHAMPION, D'ARCY LYNDON

CHAMPION, DICK
CHAMPION, RICHARD GORDON

CHAMPION, TOM
CHAMPION, D'ARCY LYNDON

CHAMPLIN, TIM
CHAMPLIN, JOHN MICHAEL

CHAMPLIN, VIRGINIA
DELMAS, LEON RENE
LORD, GRACE VIRGINIA

CHAN, MELISSA
SCUTT, JOCELYNNE ANNETTE

CHANAIDH, FEAR
CAMPBELL, JOHN LORNE

CHANAKYA
PANIKKAR, K. MADHAVA

CHANAN, BEN
YAFFE, RICHARD

CHANCE, GEORGE
FLEMING-ROBERTS, G.T.

CHANCE, JOHN T.
CARPENTER, JOHN HOWARD

CHANCE, JONATHAN
CHANCE, JOHN NEWTON

CHANCE, SARA
CLARY, SYDNEY ANN

CHANCE, STEPHEN
TURNER, PHILIP WILLIAM

CHANCELLOR, JOHN
DE BALZAC RIDEAU, CHARLES

CHAND, MUNSHI PREM
SRIVASTAVA, DHANPAT RAI

CHAND, PREM
SRIVASTAVA, DHANPAT RAI

CHANDLER, BESSIE
PARKER, ELIZABETH [C]

CHANDLER, FRANK
HARKNETT, TERRY W.

CHANDLER, JENNIFER
WESTWOOD, JENNIFER

CHANDLER, LAUREL
HOLDER, NANCY L. JONES

CHANDLER, LAURYN
WARREN, WENDY

CHANDLER, LAWRENCE
BROWNE, HOWARD
FAIRMAN, PAUL W.
MCGIVERN, WILLIAM P.
SLESAR, HENRY

CHANDLER, MARK
SHARKEY, JOHN MICHAEL

CHANDLER, PATRICIA
HEBERT, PATRICIA

CHANDLER, PETER
FONZO, L.M.D.
KORNBLUTH, J.L.

CHANDOS, DANE
LILLEY, PETER
STANSBURY-MILLETT, NIGEL

CHANDOS, DANE [CONT]
STANSFELD, ANTHONY

CHANDOS, FAY
SWATRIDGE, IRENE M.M.

CHANDOS, HERBERT
MAITLAND, T.G. DOWLING

CHANDOS, JOHN
MCCONNELL, JOHN L.C.

CHANDRAVATI
SUR, ATUL KRISHNA

CHANEL
JOYCE, JAMES

CHANEY, JILL
LEEMING, JILL

CHANG CHIEH
ZHANG JIE

CHANG, CHENG-CHI
CHANG, CHEN-CHI

CHANG, EILEEN
CHANG AI-LING

CHANG, GARMA C.C.
CHANG, CHEN-CHI

CHANG, LEE
LEVINSON, LEONARD [L]
ROSENBERGER, JOSEPH

CHANGER, HUGH
DUER, KENNETH

CHANNEL, A.R.
CATHERALL, ARTHUR

CHANNING, JUSTIN
BARRETT, HELEN
HITZIG, KAREN

CHANNING, MARK
JONES, L.A.M.

CHANNING, PETER
MCMORDIE, TABER

CHANNON, BILL
BAJOG, GUNTHER

CHANNON, E.M.
CHANNON, ETHEL M.

CHANT, JOY
RUTTER, EILEEN JOYCE

CHANTECLER
GARLAND, A.P.

CHAPEL, ASHLEY
WEAVER, JUDITH

CHAPELLE, FRANCOISER
KAPPEL, GUNTER

CHAPIN, KATHERINE G.
BIDDLE, KATHERINE G.C.

CHAPIN, PAUL
FARMER, PHILIP JOSE

CHAPLIN, BILL
CHAPLIN, W.W.

CHAPLIN, CHARLEY
CHAPLIN, CHARLES SPENCER

CHAPLIN, ELIZABETH
MCGOWAN, JILL

CHAPMAN, ALLEN
STRATEMEYER, EDWARD

CHAPMAN, CLODAGH
GIBSON-JARVIE, CLODAGH

CHAPMAN, FRANCES
CHAPMAN, FRANK MONROE

CHAPMAN, JOHN
WYMAN, WALTER F.

CHAPMAN, LEE
BRADLEY, MARION ZIMMER

CHAPMAN, MARISTAN
CHAPMAN, JOHN STANTON H.
CHAPMAN, MARY HAMILTON

CHAPMAN, RENATE
HAWKINS, LORETTA

CHAPMAN, STEVEN
CHAPMAN, STEPAN

CHAPMAN, WALKER
SILVERBERG, ROBERT

CHAPNICK, MORRIS
ACKERMAN, FORREST J.

CHAPPELL, JEANNETTE
KALT, JEANNETTE CHAPPELL

CHAR, YUM
BARRETT, DEAN

CHARBONNIER, MARC
COLEMAN, VERNON

CHARBY, JAY
ELLISON, HARLAN

CHARDONNE, JACQUES
BOUTELLEAU, JACQUES

CHARIVARIUS
TRENITE, GIJSBERT J.N.

CHARKIN, PAUL
CHARKIN, PAULA

CHARLES THE CLOWN
KRAUS, CHARLES E.

CHARLES, ANITA
POLLOCK, IDA

CHARLES, CAROLINE
MACKIE, MARY

CHARLES, CHRISTY
RICHARDS, PENNY

CHARLES, CONN ALAN
MCQUINN, DONALD E.

CHARLES, DAVID
MONDEY, DAVID CHARLES
TAYLOR, CHARLES DOONAN

CHARLES, DONALD
MEIGHAN, DONALD CHARLES

CHARLES, EDWARD
HEMPSTEAD, CHARLES EDWARD

CHARLES, FRANKLIN
ADAMS, CLEVE F.
BELLEM, ROBERT LESLIE

CHARLES, FREDERICK
ASHFORD, F.C.
DARD, FREDERIC

CHARLES, GERDA
LIPSON, GERTRUDE

CHARLES, HAL
BLYTH, HAL
SWEET, CHARLES

CHARLES, HAMPTON
MARTIN, ROY PETER

CHARLES, HENRY
HARRIS, MARION ROSE

CHARLES, IONA
COY, STANLEE MILLER
NICHOLS, CAROLYN

CHARLES, J.B.
NAGEL, WILLEN HENDRIK

CHARLES, LOUIS
STRATEMEYER, EDWARD

CHARLES, MAGGI
KOEHLER, MARGARET [H]

CHARLES, MARIE
RYDZYNSKI, MARIE R.

CHARLES, MARK
BICKERS, RICHARD L.T.

CHARLES, NATHANAEL
FRANKLIN, BENJAMIN V.

CHARLES, NEIL
HOLLOWAY, BRIAN W.
HUGHES, DENNIS [TALBOT]
JENNISON, JOHN WILLIAM

CHARLES, NICHOLAS J.
KUSKIN, KARLA SIEDMAN

CHARLES, RAY
ROBINSON, ROBERT CHARLES

CHARLES, REX
NUETZEL, CHARLES A.

CHARLES, RICHARD
AWDRY, RICHARD CHARLES

CHARLES, ROBERT
SMITH, ROBERT CHARLES

CHARLES, SPENCER
DANSER, ELLEN SPENCER
FINLEON, PATRICK CHARLES

CHARLES, STEVEN
GRANT, CHARLES L.

CHARLES, THERESA
SWATRIDGE, CHARLES J.

CHARLES, WILL
WILLEFORD, CHARLES [RAY]

CHARLES-HENNEBERG, NATHAL
HENNEBERG, CHARLES

CHARLESTON, ROBERT E.
ROBINSON, CHARLES M. III

CHARLESWORTH, M.E.
BOOTH, MAUD CHARLESWORTH

CHARLOT, HARRY
GIBSON, WALTER B.

CHARLSON, DAVID
HOLMES, DAVID CHARLES

CHARLTON, H.B.
CHARLTON, HENRY BUCKLEY

CHARLTON, JACK
CHARLTON, JOHN

CHARLTON, JIM
WOODHOUSE, MARTIN C.

CHARLTON, JOHN
WOODHOUSE, MARTIN C.

CHARLTON, JOSEPHINE
HAUBER, JOSEPHINE C.

CHARLTON, LINDA
MURRAY, LINDA CHARLTON

CHARLWOOD, D.E.
CHARLWOOD, DONALD ERNEST

CHARLWOOD, DON
CHARLWOOD, DONALD ERNEST

CHARNANCE, L.P.
HANNAWAY, PATRICIA H.

CHARNET, PAUL
DELEONI, PAUL

CHARPENTIER, JULES
GRUBER, GISI

CHARQUES, DOROTHY
EMMS, DOROTHY

CHARTAIR, MAX
GLASBY, JOHN S.

CHARTERIS, LESLIE
AVENELLE, DONNE
COGSWELL, THEODORE R.
HARRISON, HARRY
LEE, FLEMING
LIN, LESLIE C.B.
SHORT, CHRISTOPHER
STURGEON, THEODORE
WEAVER, GRAHAM
YIN, LESLIE CHARLES B.

CHARTERS, LOWELL
MAXWELL, ANN [ELIZABETH]

CHARTERS, PATRICIA
CARLON, PATRICIA BERNADT.

CHARTHAM, ROBERT
SETH, RONALD [S]

CHARTIER, DANETTE
CHARTIER-LI, ANNETTE M.
LI, ANNETTE
THOMPSON, DANETTE

CHARTIER, EMILIO
ESTENSSORO, HUGO

CHASE, ADAM
FAIRMAN, PAUL W.
MARLOWE, STEPHEN

CHASE, ALICE
MCHARGUE, GEORGESS

CHASE, BEATRICE
PARR, OLIVE KATHARINE

CHASE, BORDEN
FOWLER, FRANK G.

CHASE, CAROLINE
SPECTOR, CAROLINE
CUNNINGHAM, MARILYN

CHASE, CAROLYN
SIMMONS, TRANA

CHASE, CLEVELAND B.
BEDFORD-JONES, HENRY

CHASE, EMILY
AKS, PATRICIA
SACHS, JUDITH
WHITE, CAROL

CHASE, GLEN
LEVINSON, LEONARD [L]
FOX, GARDNER F.

CHASE, JAMES HADLEY
RAYMOND, RENE BRABAZON

CHASE, KIP
CHASE, TREVETT COBURN

CHASE, LARRY
CHASE, LAWRENCE

CHASE, LESLEY
VERNER, CHRISTOPHER STU.

CHASE, LORETTA
CHEKANI, LORETTA

CHASE, LORETTA LYNDA
CHEKANI, LORETTA

CHASE, LYNDON
CHARD, JUDY

CHASE, NICHOLAS
HYDE, ANTHONY
HYDE, CHRISTOPHER

CHASE, PHILIP
FRIEDMAN, PHILIP

CHASE, ROBERT DAVID
GORMAN, EDWARD [JOSEPH]
WARREN, ED & LORRAINE

CHASE, SAMANTHA
BUCKHOLTZ, EILEEN [G]
GLICK, RUTH [BURTNICK]

CHASE, VIRGINIA LOWELL
PERKINS, VIRGINIA CHASE

CHASSMAN, CHERRY
MARZINEK, WILHELM

CHATEAUCLAIR, WILFRED
LIGHTHALL, WILLIAM DOUW

CHATERIS, LESLIE
CARTMILL, CLEVE

CHATFIELD, SUSAN
FASSHAUER, NANCY SUSAN C.

CHATHAM, FRANK
ROCHESTER, GEO[RGE] E.

CHATHAM, LARRY
BINGLEY, DAVID ERNEST

CHATTAN, ROBERT
SMITH, ROBERT

CHATTERJI, SARAT CHANDRA
CHATTERJI, SARATCHANDRA

CHATTON, STACY
HOISINGTON, MAY FOLWELL

CHAUBER, THEOBALD
BARUCH, MOSES

CHAUCER, DANIEL
FORD, FORD MADOX

CHAUNCY, NAN
CHAUNCY, NANCEN B.M.

CHAUTIER, P.
GAIDA-GAIDAMAVICIUS, PRA.

CHAVERTON, BRUCE
COOK, FRED GORDON

CHAVETTE, EUGENE
VACHETTE, EUGENE

CHAVEZ, ANGELICO
CHAVEZ, MANUEL

CHAVEZ, FRAY ANGELICO
CHAVEZ, MANUEL

CHAVIARAS, STRATES
HAVIARAS, STRATIS

CHAYEFSKY, PADDY
CHAYEFSKY, SIDNEY AARON

CHAYTOR, LEE
CHATER, ELIZABETH EILEEN

CHECK, OTTO PREMIER
BERMAN, ED

CHEECH
MARIN, RICHARD ANTONY

CHEETHAM, HAL
CHEETHAM, JAMES HAROLD

CHEETHAM, J.H.
CHEETHAM, JAMES HAROLD

CHEIRO
HAMON, LOUIS

CHEIXAOU, ELISABETH
DE GRAAF-BOUKEMA, BONNY

CHEKENIAN, JANE
GERRARD, JANE

CHEKHONTE, ANTOSHA
CHEKHOV, ANTON PAVLOVICH

CHELTON, JOHN
DURST, PAUL

CHEN HWEI
STEVENSON, WILLIAM

CHEN JIA
SHEN CONGWEN

CHEN JO-HSI
TUAN, LUCY H.C.

CHEN, JACK
ACHAM, BERNARD I.F.

CHEN, TONY
CHEN, ANTHONY

CHENAULT, NELL
SMITH, LINELL NASH

CHENEVIERE, JACQUES
GUERIN, ALEXANDRE

CHENEY, C.R.
CHENEY, CHRISTOPHER ROBT.

CHENEY, TED
CHENEY, THEODORE ALBERT

CHENEY, THEODORE A. REES
CHENEY, THEODORE ALBERT

CHENG TEK-CHEUNG
CHU-YUAN, CHENG

CHENG, F.T.
CHENG, TIEN-HSI

CHENG, YI
CHENG, JAMES K.C.

CHENIN, EMILE
MOSELLY, EMILE

CHENNEVIERE, DANIEL
RUDHYAR, DANE

CHER, MARIE
SCHERR, MARIE

CHERMY, SASHA
GLIKBERG, ALEXANDER MIKH.

CHERNENKO, K.U.
CHERNENKO, KONSTANTIN U.

CHERNICHEWSKI, VLADIMIR
DUFF, CHARLES

CHERNILO, CAPEL
MORRISON, MICHAEL ANDREWS

PSEUDONYMS

CHERNOFF, DOROTHY A.
ERNST, [LYMAN] JOHN

CHERRILL, JACK
PAXTON, JOHN

CHERRYH, C. J.
CHERRY, CAROLYN JANICE

CHERRYHOLMES, ANNE
PRICE, OLIVE

CHERRYMAN, A.E.
LEVIN, BERNARD

CHERTOK, HAIM
CHERTOK, HARVEY

CHERUB
GERARD, JOHN

CHESHAM, HENRY
BINGLEY, DAVID ERNEST

CHESHIRE, CHLOE
SCHLITZ, LAURA AMY

CHESHIRE, GIFF
CHESHIRE, GIFFORD PAUL

CHESNEY, ANN
DUMMETT, [AGNES M.] ANN

CHESNEY, MARION
MCCHESNEY, MARION

CHESNEY, WEATHERBY
HYNE, CHARLES J CUTCLIFFE

CHESS, DEREK
HESS, DIRK R.

CHESTER, ELIZA
PAINE, HARRIET ELIZA

CHESTER, ELIZABETH
RANSOME, L.E.

CHESTER, ELIZABETH S.
SMITH, ELIZABETH S.

CHESTER, GILBERT
GIBBONS, H.H. CLIFFORD

CHESTER, HAROLD
MEYN, NIELS

CHESTER, LORD
TEED, CYRUS REED

CHESTER, MICHAEL C.
MIELKE, THOMAS R.P.

CHESTER, PETER
ANDREW, JOHN
PHILLIPS, DENNIS JOHN A.

CHESTER, ROY
SCHAEF, CONRAD C.

CHESTER, SARAH
CHESNEY, MARION G.

CHESTER, TOM
CHESHIRE, DAVID FREDERICK
ERNSTING, WALTER
REUTER, RALPH

CHESTERBELLOC
BELLOC, [J] HILARY [P]
CHESTERTON, GILBERT KEITH

CHESTERTON, DENISE
ROBINS, DENISE

CHESTERTON, G.K.
CHESTERTON, GILBERT KEITH

CHESTNUT, ROBERT
COOPER, CLARENCE L.

CHESTOR, RUI
COURTIER, S[IDNEY] H.

CHETWYND, BERRY
RAYNER, CLAIRE B.

CHEVENY, JULIEN
GOURDAN, ALAIN ANDRE

CHEYNEY, PETER
CHEYNEY, REGINALD E.S.

CHI-WEI
SHU, AUSTIN CHI-WEI

CHICHESTER
DRUMMOND, EDITH VICTORIA

CHICHESTER, JANE
LONGRIGG, JANE CHICHESTER

CHIEN, SU
MAN-SHU, SU

CHIETEK, JAN
SMREK, JAN

CHIGNON, NILES
LINGEMAN, RICHARD R.

CHILD, ALAN
LANGNER, LAWRENCE

CHILD, CHARLES B.
FROST, C. VERNON

CHILD, L. MARIA
CHILD, LYDIA MARIA

CHILD, MRS.
CHILD, LYDIA MARIA

CHILDER, SIMON IAN
BROSNAN, JOHN RAYMOND
KETTLE, LEROY

CHILDREN'S SHEPHERD, THE
WESTPHAL, ARNOLD CARL

CHILDRESS, SUSAN
WIGGS, SUSAN

CHILDS, C. SAND
CHILDS, MARYANNA

CHILDS, W.H.J.
CHILDS, WILLIAM HAROLD J.

CHILSON, ROB
CHILSON, ROBERT DEAN

CHIMAERA
FARJEON, ELEANOR

CHIN, CHUAN
CHI, RICHARD HU SEE-YEE

CHINA
MENDOZA ROMERO, MARIA L.

CHINWELL, WALTER
ACKERMAN, FORREST J.

CHIPP, D.L.
CHIPP, DONALD LESLIE

CHIPPERFIELD, ROBERT FOX
OSTRANDER, ISABEL EGENTON

CHIPPERFIELD, ROBERT ORR
OSTRANDER, ISABEL EGENTON

CHIPPERS, DAVID
CAP, FRIEDL[INDE]

CHISHOLM, A.M.
CHISHOLM, ARTHUR MURRAY

CHISHOLM, LILIAN
ALAN, JANE

CHISHOLM, MATT
WATTS, PETER CHRISTOPHER

CHISHOLM, R.F.
CHISHOLM, ROBERT FERGUSON

CHISHOLM, SAM WHITTEN
CHISHOLM, SAMUEL WHITTEN

CHISHTI, HAKIM M.
THOMSON, ROBERT

CHISOM, SARAH
FILER, THOMAS HANFORD

CHITTERWICK, CAPT. OLD
BREUCKER, OSCAR HERBERT

CHITWOOD, B.J.
CHITWOOD, BILLY JAMES

CHLAMYDA, JEHUDIIL
PESHKOV, ALEXEI M.

CHLEBNIKOV, VELEMIR
CHLEBNIKOV, VICTOR VIKTO.

CHLOROS, A.G.
CHLOROS, ALEXANDER GEORGE

CHLOROS, ALECK GEORGE
CHLOROS, ALEXANDER GEORGE

CHOATE, R.G.
CHOATE, GWEN PETERSON

CHOBIL
LEITO, ARTURO

CHOCHLIK
RADWANSKI, PIERRE A.

CHOGYU, TAKAYAMA
RINJIRO, TAKAYAMA

CHOLLET
FURNISS, LOUISE E.

CHOLMONDELEY, ALICE
BEAUCHAMP, MARY ANNETTE

PSEUDONYMS

CHOLMONDELEY, MARY
BEAUCHAMP, MARY ANNETTE

CHONG
CHONG, THOMAS

CHONG, KYONA-JO
CHUNG, KYUNG CHO

CHONG, TOM
CHONG, THOMAS

CHOPIN, KATE
CHOPIN, KATHERINE

CHORAO, KAY
CHORAO, ANN MCKAY SPROAT

CHORLEY, R.J.
CHORLEY, RICHARD JOHN

CHORNY, FEDYA
KOJUHAROV, TUDOR

CHORNY, KUZMA
ROUMANOUSKY, N.K.

CHOU, YU-JUI
CHOU, ERIC

CHOUDHURY, G.W.
CHOUDHURY, GOLAM WAHED

CHRISTCHILD, RAVAN
SEDDON, KEITH

CHRISTEN, ADA
VON BREDEN, CHRISTIANE F.

CHRISTENBERRY, JUDY
CHRISTENBERRY, JUDITH R.

CHRISTENSEN, ANNA
MAYER, DEBORAH ANNE

CHRISTENSEN, C.
RECHT, CAMILLUS

CHRISTENSEN, J.A.
CHRISTENSEN, JACK ARDEN

CHRISTENSEN, JO IPPOLITO
CHRISTENSEN, YOLANDA MAR.

CHRISTIAENS, ANDRE G.
DROJINE, N.A.

CHRISTIAN, A.B.
YABES, LEOPOLDO Y.

CHRISTIAN, C.W.
CHRISTIAN, CURTIS WALLACE

CHRISTIAN, COLIN
STEINBRUNNER, PETER CHRIS

CHRISTIAN, DORIS
REBNER-CHRISRIAN, DORIS

CHRISTIAN, FREDERICK
GEHMAN, RICHARD
LINAKER, MICHAEL
NOLAN, FREDERICK
STRANGE, THOMAS OLIVER

CHRISTIAN, GEORGE
GROVE, HELEN HARRIET

CHRISTIAN, JILL
DILCOCK, NOREEN

CHRISTIAN, JOHN
DIXON, ROGER

CHRISTIAN, KIT
THORSON, DELOS RUSSELL
THORSON, SARA WINFREE

CHRISTIAN, LOUISE
GRILL, NANNETTE L.

CHRISTIAN, NICK
POLLITZ, EDWARD A. JR.

CHRISTIAN, PAULA
MACMANUS, YVONNE

CHRISTIAN, PETER
STEINBRUNNER, PETER CHRIS

CHRISTIAN, PETRA
CAVE, PETER [LESLIE]
PRIEST, CHRISTOPHER [M]

CHRISTIANI, SVEN DETLEV
BORNSTROEM-RUNDE, UWE

CHRISTIANSEN, SYNNOVE
LINDEGARD, MAI

CHRISTIE
ICHIKAWA, KON

CHRISTIE, AGATHA
MALLOWAN, MRS. MAX

CHRISTIE, BARBARA
CARLON, PATRICIA BERNADT.

CHRISTIE, COLLEEN
BIDWELL, J.S.

CHRISTIE, EVAN
EVANS, CHRIS[TOPHER D.]

CHRISTIE, HUGH
CHRISTIE-MURRAY, DAVID

CHRISTIE, KEITH
HAYNES, ALFRED H.

CHRISTIE, MARIE
MARIE, GERALDINE

CHRISTIE, MICHELLE
O'HARA, GERRY

CHRISTIE, STEPHEN
KURUPPA, D.S.C.

CHRISTIE, SUSANNA
BURTON, KRISTIN
OSSANA, SUSAN B.

CHRISTINA, FRANK & TERESA
LAUGHLIN, TOM
TAYLOR, DELORES

CHRISTOFF, EVA
EPPERS, EVA

CHRISTOPHER, AMY
BARLETTA, PATRICIA L.

CHRISTOPHER, BEN
BLOCK, LAWRENCE
WESTLAKE, DONALD [EDWIN]

CHRISTOPHER, BETH
STEINKE, ANN E.R.

CHRISTOPHER, CATHY
MACKIE, MARY

CHRISTOPHER, FRANCINE
MANDEVILLE, FRANCINE

CHRISTOPHER, HONEY
CAVANAGH, HELEN

CHRISTOPHER, JANE
CLARKE, JANET K.

CHRISTOPHER, JOAN
KLINGLER, MARIA

CHRISTOPHER, JOHN
YOUD, CHRISTOPHER [S]

CHRISTOPHER, KENNETH
BROPHY, DONALD FRANCIS

CHRISTOPHER, LOUISE
HALE, MARY ARLENE

CHRISTOPHER, MARY
MACKIE, MARY

CHRISTOPHER, MATT
CHRISTOPHER, MATTHEW F.

CHRISTOPHER, PAULA
SMITH, LYNNE A.

CHRISTOV, S.
CHRISTOPHERSEN, SOLVEIG

CHRISTY, JOE
CHRISTY, JOSEPH M.

CHRISTY, RICHARD
BREEDLOVE, WILLIAM

CHRONIQUESE
LOGAN, OLIVE

CHROSTOPHUS
EVANS, GEORGE ESSEX

CHRUGEL, CHIRDONIUS
ATTENHOFER, EDUARD

CHRYSTIE, EDWARD M.
WATSON, JACK CHARLES WAU.

CHU CH'AN
BLOFIELD, JOHN [E.C.]

CHU FENG
BLOFELD, JOHN [E.C.]

CHU, W.R.
CHU, ARTHUR T.S.

CHUBB, ELMER
MASTERS, EDGAR LEE

CHUNG, CONNIE
CHUNG, CONSTANCE YU-HWA

CHUNG, HENRY
DE YOUNG, HENRY C.

CHUNG-YU, CHU
HSU, BENEDICT PEI-HSIUNG

CHURCH, EMMA
SCHATTNER, E.

CHURCH, GRANVILLE
PEOPLE, GRANVILLE CHURCH

CHURCH, JEFFREY
KIRK, RICHARD [E]

CHURCH, PETER
NUTTALL, JEFF

CHURCH, SUZANNE
BATES, SUSANNAH VACELLA

CHURCH, TALBOT
DONALDSON, WILLIE

CHURCHILL, BILL
CHURCHILL, GAIL WINSTON

CHURCHILL, ELIZABETH
HOUGH, RICHARD ALEXANDER

CHURCHILL, J.H.
CHURCHILL, JOHN HOWARD

CHURCHILL, JILL
BROOKS, JANICE YOUNG

CHURCHILL, JOYCE
HARRISON, M[ICHAEL] JOHN

CHURCHILL, LUANNA
DUGHMAN, JOHN & FREIDA

CHURCHWARD, JOHN
BAKER, W.J.

CHUTE, B.J.
CHUTE, BEATRICE JOY

CHUTE, RUPERT
CLEVELAND, PHILIP JEROME

CHUZAN, TOYAMA
MASAKAZU, TOYAMA

CIALENTE, FAUSTA
TERNI, FAUSTA CIALENTE

CIDIE
SARFATTI, MARGHERITA

CIELO, JUAN SIN
CARRION, ALEJANDRO

CIFFRIW, GWYNFOR
GRIFFITH, THOMAS GWYNFOR

CILLINGH, DAN
DONGES, GUNTER

CIMARRON, JOHN
DUENSING, JURGEN

CINCINNATUS
CURREY, CECIL BARR

CINNA
FRAENKEL, HEINRICH

CINQUIN, SISTER EMMANUELL
CINQUIN, EMMANUELLE

CIORAN, E.M.
CIORAN, EMIL M.

CIPOLLA, JOAN BAGNEL
BAGNEL, JOAN

CIRCUMLIBRA
LOCKWOOD, FRANK

CIRCUS, ANTHONY
HOCH, EDWARD D.

CIRCUS, JIM
ROSEYEAR, JOHN

CIRNI, JIM
CIRNIGLIARO, JAMES N.

CITTADINO, ROBERT
BICKERS, RICHARD L.T.

CITTAFINO, RICHARDO
BICKERS, RICHARD L.T.

CITY WAITER
BEDFORD, JOHN T.

CIV
NORVICK

CLADPOLE, JIM
RICHARDS, JAMES

CLAGETT, JOHN
CLAGETT, SUE HARRY

CLAIR, DAPHNE
DE JONG, DAPHNE

CLAIR, RENE
CHOMETTE, RENE LUCIEN

CLAIRE, EVA
DE LONG, CLAIRE [ANN]

CLAIRE, HELEN
BLAIR, PAULINE HUNTER

CLAIRE, KEITH
ANDREWS, KEITH & CLARE

CLAIRE, MARVIN
LARSON, MARVIN

CLAIRMONT, CLAIRE
MARSHALL, ROBERT

CLAM, ERNST
CZECH-JOCHBERG, ERICH

CLAMPETT, BOB
CLAMPETT, ROBERT

CLANCOOL, CLARENCE
URNER, NATHAN DANE

CLANCY, KING
CLANCY, FRANCIS MICHAEL

CLANCY, LAURIE
CLANCY, LAURENCE JAMES

CLANCY, TOM
CLANCY, THOMAS LEO JR.

CLANDON, HENRIETTA
VAHEY, JOHN G. HAZLETTE

CLAPP, PATRICIA
CONE, P.C.L.

CLARA AUGUSTA
TRASK, MRS. S.

CLARE, AUSTIN
JAMES, W. MARTHA

CLARE, CATHLEEN
TOOTHMAN, CATHERINE ANN

CLARE, CATHRYN
STANTON, CATHY

CLARE, ELIZABETH
COOK, DOROTHY MARY

CLARE, ELLEN
SINCLAIR, OLGA ELLEN

CLARE, FRANCIS D.
ASCHMANN, ALBERTA
FRANCIS, [MOTHER] MARY

CLARE, HELEN
HUNTER BLAIR, PAULINE C.

CLARE, JANE
SHIELDS, DINAH

CLARE, MARGARET
MAISON, MARGARET M.B.

CLARE, MARGUERITE
HEPPELL, MARY

CLARE, PATRICK
FANNING, D. CHRISTOPHER

CLARE, PAULINE
BLOOM, URSULA

CLARE, SAMANTHA
DAWSON, JANIS

CLARE, SHANNON
HARREL, LINDA

CLAREMONT, CHRIS
CLAREMONT, CHRISTOPHER S.

CLAREMONT, RUTH
CRESWELL, ROSEMARY
MANNERS, CAROLE

CLARETIE, JULES
ARNAUD, ARSENE

CLARIN
ALAS Y URENA, LEOPOLDO

CLARINS, DIANA
GIFFORD, THOMAS [E]

CLARK, A.A. GORDON
CLARK, ALFRED A.G.

CLARK, AL C.
GOINES, DONALD

CLARK, AMANDA
MIDGLEY, AMY

PSEUDONYMS

CLARK, AMANDA
O'DANIEL, JANET

CLARK, BADGER
PAINE, LAURAN BOSWORTH

CLARK, BILL
CLARK, WILLIAM ARTHUR

CLARK, BLAIR
CLARK, SYLVIA

CLARK, C.M.H.
CLARK, CHARLES MANNING H.

CLARK, CATHERINE
UNIACKE, EVELYN CATHERINE

CLARK, CHRISTIE
CRAIG, CHRISTIE

CLARK, CURT
WESTLAKE, DONALD [EDWIN]

CLARK, D.M.J.
CLARK, DOUGLAS M.J.

CLARK, DALE
KAYSER, RONAL

CLARK, DAVID
HARDCASTLE, MICHAEL

CLARK, DAVID ALLEN
ERNST, [LYMAN] JOHN

CLARK, DICK
CLARK, RICHARD WAGSTAFF
LIBBY, WILLIAM B.

CLARK, DON
CLARK, DONALD HENRY

CLARK, DUNCAN MD
CRAIG, MARY COAD

CLARK, GAREL
GARELICK, MAY
SCOTT, ETHEL MCCULLOUGH

CLARK, GEORGE E.
CLARK, DALE

CLARK, HALSEY
DEMING, RICHARD

CLARK, HOWARD
HASKIN, DOROTHY C.
PORTER, WILLIAM SYDNEY

CLARK, J. KENT
CLARK, JUSTUS KENT

CLARK, J.C.D.
CLARK, JONATHAN CHARLES

CLARK, J.H.
CLARK, JOHN HOWARD

CLARK, J.P.
CLARK, JOHN PEPPER

CLARK, J.R.
CLARK, JOHN RUSSELL

CLARK, JOAN
BENSON, MILDRED [A] WIRT

CLARK, LYDIA B[ENSON]
MEAKER, ELOISE

CLARK, M.R.
CLARK, MAVIS THORPE

CLARK, MARGERY
CLARK, MARY ELIZABETH
QUIGLEY, MARGERY

CLARK, MARIANNE
WILLMAN, MARIANNA

CLARK, MARY LOU
CLARK, MARIA LOUISA G.

CLARK, MELISSA
AALLYN, ALYSSE

CLARK, MERLE
GESSNER, MERLYN C.

CLARK, MILTON
WIREN, SVEN G. CARL-AXEL

CLARK, PARLIN
TRIGG, HARRY DAVIS

CLARK, RINGO
HUBNER, HORST W.

CLARK, SABINA
WILLMAN, MARIANNE

CLARK, TOM
CLARK, THOMAS WILLARD

CLARK, V.S.
SILVERBERG, ROBERT

CLARK, VIRGINIA
GRAY, PATRICIA [CLARK]

CLARK-KENNEDY, A.E.
CLARK-KENNEDY, ARCHIBALD

CLARKE, ANNE
AMOR, ANNE CLARK

CLARKE, BODEN
BURGESS, MICHAEL ROY
HOPKINS, JAMES

CLARKE, CORALIE
REES, CORALIE CLARKE

CLARKE, COVINGTON
VENABLE, CLARK

CLARKE, D.A.
CLARKE, DEREK ASHDOWN

CLARKE, DOROTHY CLOTELLE
SHADI, DOROTHY CLOTELLE C

CLARKE, GEORGE E.
KAYSER, RONAL

CLARKE, HAMMOND
MERWIN, SAMUEL K. JR.

CLARKE, HOCKLEY
CLARKE, HENRY CHARLES

CLARKE, I.F.
CLARKE, IGNATIUS IAN F.

CLARKE, IAN
CLARKE, IGNATIUS IAN F.

CLARKE, J.
CLARKE, JUDITH

CLARKE, JOHN
LAKLAN, CARLI
LAUGHLIN, VIRGINIA CARLI
SONTUP, DANIEL

CLARKE, KATHERINE
ELLERBECK, ROSEMARY A.L.

CLARKE, LEA
ROWLAND-ENTWISTLE, A.T.

CLARKE, MARION
SCHULTZ, MARION C.

CLARKE, MICHAEL
NEWLON, [FRANK] CLARKE

CLARKE, P.J.
JARDINE, JACK OWEN

CLARKE, PAULINE
HUNTER BLAIR, PAULINE C.

CLARKE, RICHARD
PAINE, LAURAN BOSWORTH

CLARKE, ROBERT
PAINE, LAURAN BOSWORTH
PLATT, CHARLES [M]

CLARKE, W.B.
LAZENBY, NORMAN A.

CLARKE, [CAPT.] JAFAR
NESMITH, ROBERT I.

CLARKE, [CAPT.] MAURICE
HOOK, SAMUEL CLARKE

CLARKSON, HELEN
MCCLOY, HELEN [CLARKSON]

CLARKSON, J.F.
TUBB, E.C.

CLARKSON, JAMES
LARDNER, RINGGOLD W.

CLARKSON, L.
WHITELOCK, LOUISE C.

CLARKSON, L.A.
CLARKSON, LESLIE ALBERT

CLARKSON, ORMAND
RICHARDSON, GLADWELL G.

CLARKSON, W.E.
BOUNDS, SYDNEY J.

CLARO, JOE
CLARO, JOSEPH,

CLARYL, MICHEL
LECLERC, RAYMOND P.E.

CLASS, HEIN
BREUCKER, OSCAR HERBERT

CLAUDE
CARBET, CLAUDE

CLAUDE
FORDE, CLAUDE MARIE

CLAUDIA, SUSAN
JOHNSTON, WILLIAM
MCQUAY, MICHAEL DENNIS

CLAUDIUS, EDUARD
SCHMIDT, EDUARD

CLAUGHTON-JAMES, JAMES
BENTLEY, JAMES W.B.

CLAUREN, HEINRICH
HAUFF, WILHELM
HEUN, KARL GOTTLIEB SAM.

CLAUSEN, NORBERT
KALMUCZAK, ROLF

CLAUSEN, W.V.
CLAUSEN, WENDELL VERNON

CLAVELL, STAUFFER
NAGELE, ANTON

CLAXTON, JOHN G.
BEAUMONT, DONNA BROOKS

CLAY, ALISON
KEEVILL, HENRY J.

CLAY, BERTHA M.
BRAEME, CHARLOTTE M.
CORYELL, JOHN RUSSELL
DEY, FREDERIC VAN R.
HARBAUGH, THOMAS C.

CLAY, CHARLES [M]
CLARK, CHARLOTTE MOORE

CLAY, DUNCAN
DIEHL, W.W.

CLAY, E. JEFFERSON
WHEELAHAN, PAUL

CLAY, JIM
CLAY, JAMES

CLAY, MATTHEW
MATTHEWS, CLAYTON [H]

CLAY, RITA
ESTRADA, RITA

CLAY, WEALD
CHRISTIE, ERNEST

CLAY, WESTON
FORD, T.W.

CLAYBURN, LOGAN
GOODIS, DAVID

CLAYFORD, JAMES
ARMER, FRANK
DANIELS, NORMAN A.
DERN, E. PEARL GADDIS

CLAYMORE, TOD
CLEVELY, HUGH DESMOND
JEPSON, EDGAR [ALFRED]

CLAYPOOL, JANE
MINER, JANE CLAYPOOL

CLAYTON, BARBARA
PLUFF, BARBARA LITLEFIEL

CLAYTON, DONNA
FASANO, DONNA

CLAYTON, JOHN
BEEVERS, JOHN LEONARD

CLAYTON, SUSAN
BAILEY, ALFRED GOLDSW.

CLEAR, CLAUDIUS
NICOLL, WILLIAM ROBERTSON

CLEAR, RALPH
KLAR, RANDOLF

CLEATOR, P.E.
CLEATOR, PHILIP ELLABY

CLEAVELAND, KATE
NICHOLS, REBECCA S. REED

CLEAVER, A.
CLEAVER, ANASTASIA

CLEAVER, BILL
CLEAVER, WILLIAM & VERA

CLEAVER, DENIS
LEYLAND, ERIC

CLEAVER, NANCY
MATHEWS, EVELYN CRAW

CLEEVE, LUCAS
KINGSCOTE, ADELINA G.I.W.

CLEFF, BENNO
HELLWIG, ERNST

CLEGG, ALEC
CLEGG, ALEXANDER BRADSHAW

CLEISHBOTHAM, JEBEDIAH
SCOTT, WALTER [SIR]

CLELAND, HUGH
CLARKE, JOHN CAMPBELL

CLELAND, MABEL
WIDDEMER, MABEL CLELAND

CLELAND, MORTON
RENNIE, JAMES ALAN

CLELAND, P.
CLARKE, JOHN

CLELLAND, CATHERINE
TOWNSEND, DORIS M.

CLEMEAU, CAROL
ESLER, CAROL CLEMEAU

CLEMENS, ANTHONY
TEPPERMAN, EMILE C.

CLEMENS, ROGERS
LOVIN, ROGER ROBERT

CLEMENT, HAL
STUBBS, HARRY CLEMENT

CLEMENTS, A.L.
CLEMENTS, ARTHUR LEO

CLEMENTS, ABIGAIL
SKELTON, ALICE & CLEMENT

CLEMENTS, E.H.
HUNTER, EILEEN

CLEMO, JACK
CLEMO, REGINALD JOHN

CLEMONS, ELIZABETH
NOWELL, ELIZABETH CAMERON

CLEO ET ANTHONY
GATE, A.G.

CLERGYMAN, A.
MORISON, JOHN

CLERI, MARIO
PUZO, MARIO

CLERIHEW, E.
BENTLEY, EDMUND CLERIHEW

CLERK, N.W.
LEWIS, CLIVE STAPLES

CLERMONT, SHANA
MCELWAIN, DEAN

CLERY, VAL
CLERY, REGINALD VALENTINE

CLEVE, JANITA
ROWLAND, DONALD S.

CLEVE, JOHN
BERRY, D[OUGLAS] BRUCE
EDMONDSON Y COTTON, JOSE
GREEN, ROLAND [JAMES]
HALDEMAN, CANDICE ETTLIN
HALDEMAN, JACK C.
KINCAID, ROBIN
KOMAN, VICTOR
OFFUTT, ANDREW J.
PROCTOR, GEO[RGE] W[YATT]
SWAIN, DWIGHT V[REELAND]

CLEVE, JOHN JR.
OFFUTT, ANDREW J.

CLEVEDON, JOHN
PLUMLEY, ERNEST F.

CLEVELAND, BOB
CLEVELAND, GEORGE

CLEVELAND, CLIFFORD S.
GOLDSMITH, DAVID H.

CLEVELAND, FRANK
SHAW, FRANK H.

CLEVELAND, JIM
KING, ALBERT

CLEVELAND, JOHN
HILTON, JOHN DEAN
MCELFRESH, ELIZABETH A.

CLEVEN, CATHRINE
CLEVEN, KATHRYN SEWARD

CLEVES, BERNARD
MOORE, BERNARD

CLEVIN, JORGEN
CLEVIN, JOERGEN

CLEVINGER, PAUL
NORWOOD, VICTOR [G.C.]

CLIFF, JIMMY
CHAMBERS, JAMES

CLIFFE, LEIGH
JONES, GEORGE

CLIFFORD, ETH
ROSENBERG, ETHEL [C]

CLIFFORD, FRANCIS
THOMPSON, ARTHUR L. BELL

CLIFFORD, GUY
ROBERTS, ARTHUR GUY

CLIFFORD, JOHN
BAYLISS, JOHN CLIFFORD

CLIFFORD, L.
CLIFFORD, CHARLES

CLIFFORD, LOUISE
LEWIS, CLIFFORD

CLIFFORD, MARTIN
AUSTIN, STANLEY
BARNARD, ALFRED J.
BROOKS, EDWY SEARLES
CARLTON, G.E.L.
CATCHPOLE, WILLIAM LESLIE
COOK, FRED GORDON
DOWN, C. MAURICE
EVES, REGINALD T.
GRIFFITH, PERCY
HARPER, HARRY
HINTON, HERBERT ALLAN
HOOK, H. CLARKE
KIRKHAM, REGINALD S.
NEWMAN, KENNETH E.
O'MANT, HEDLEY P.A.
ORME, K.
PENTELOW, JOHN NIX
RANSOME, L.E.
RICHARDS, FRANK
RUSSELL, C.
SAMWAYS, GEORGE R.
WARWICK, FRANCIS ALISTAIR
WOOD-SMITH, NOEL

CLIFFORD, PAT
KALMUCZAK, ROLF

CLIFFORD, PEGGY
CLIFFORD, MARGARET CORT

CLIFFORD, RACHEL MARK
LEWIS, BRENDA RALPH

CLIFFORD, THEODORE
VON BLOCK, SYLVIA

CLIFT, BETTY
DEVERY, ELIZABETH COLEMAN

CLIFTON, BUD
STACTON, DAVID DEREK

CLIFTON, HARRY
HAMILTON, CHARLES H.S.

CLIFTON, KATHERINE POTTER
BRYANT, KATHERINE CLIFTON

CLIFTON, LEWIS
LINEDECKER, CLIFFORD L.

CLIFTON, MARTIN
HAMILTON, CHARLES H.S.

CLIFTON, OLIVER LEE
RATHBORNE, ST. GEORGE

CLIMER, NANCY
BANKS, CAROLYN

CLINCH, CAPT.
YOUNG, ERNEST A[VON]

CLINE, BEV
FINK CLINE, BEVERLY

CLINE, BEVERLY
FINK CLINE, BEVERLY

CLINE, JOAN
HAMILTON, JOAN LESLIE

CLINE, S.L.
CLINE, SARA LOUISE

CLINTEN, MAX
FRANCES, STEPHEN D.
HANSON, VICTOR JOSEPH

CLINTON, D.
CLINTON, LLOYD DEWITT

CLINTON, DIRK
SILVERBERG, ROBERT

CLINTON, F.G.
CAMPBELL, ROBERT WRIGHT

CLINTON, JEFF
BICKHAM, JOHN M.

CLINTON, JON
PRINCE, JACK HARVEY

CLINTON, MARK
FRANCES, STEPHEN D.

CLINTON, MAX
BARNES, MICHAEL [L.G.]

CLINTON, RUPERT
BULMER, [HENRY] KENNETH

CLINTON-BADDELEY, VICTOR
GERAINT, VICTOR V.R.

CLISSMANN, ANNE
CLUNE, ANNE

CLISTIER, ADELINE
DENENHOLZ, ALMA

CLITHERO, SALLY
CLITHERO, MYRTLE ELY

CLIVE, ARTHUR
O'GRADY, JAMES STANDISH

CLIVE, CLIFFORD
HAMILTON, CHARLES H.S.
HOME-GALL, EDWARD REG.

CLIVE, DENNIS
FEARN, JOHN RUSSELL

CLIVE, WILLIAM
BASSETT, RONALD LESLIE

CLOBERRY, ELIZABETH
SAVERY, CONSTANCE W.

CLOIE, MACK
MCKIBBIN, ARCHIBALD

CLOPET, LILIANE [M.C.]
BETHUNE, MARY

CLOS, CHARLES
STOKOE, E[DWARD] G[EORGE]

CLOSE, ERWIN P.
KLOSE, ERWIN

CLOSE, UPTON
HALL, JOSEF WASHINGTON

CLOSS, ELIZABETH
TRAUGOTT, ELIZABETH CLOSS

CLOUD, PATRICIA
STROTHER, PAT WALLACE

CLOUD, TANITH
GIESA, WERNER K.

CLOUD, YVONNE
KAPP, YVONNE

CLOUGH, B.R.
CLOUGH, BRENDA WANG

CLOUKEY, CHARLES
CLOUTIER, CHARLES

CLOUTIER, CECILE
CLOUTIER-WOJCIECH, CECILE

CLOUTIER, HELEN H.
SCHMOCK, HELEN H.

CLOVIS, ELMONT
LEVINE, SEYMOUR

CLUBB, STACEY
ORLOVITZ, GIL

CLUN, ARTHUR
POLSBY, NELSON W.

CLUNE, FRANK
CLUNE, FRANCIS PATRICK

CLURE, CLIFF
BREUCKER, OSCAR HERBERT

CLURE, CLIFFORD
BREUCKER, OSCAR HERBERT
KEIM, FRIEDRICH

CLUTCHER, HANS
CHETWYND-HAYES, RON

CLUTCHPIN, STANISLAUS
SHERMAN, CHRIS

CLWYD, ANN
ROBERTS, ANN LEWIS

CLYDE COOL
FRAZIER, WALTER

CLYDE, CONSTANCE
MCADAM, CONSTANCE

CLYDE, KIT
SENARENS, LUIS P.

CLYNDER, MONICA
MUIR, MARIE AGNES

CLYNE, TERENCE
BLATTY, WILLIAM PETER

CLYNES, MICHAEL
DOHERTY, P.C.
HARDING, PAUL

COALFLEET, PIERRE
DAVIDSON, FRANK CYRIL S.

COATES, J.F.
COATES, JOHN FRANCIS

COATES, K.S.
COATES, KENNETH STEPHEN

COATES, KEN [S]
COATES, KENNETH STEPHEN

COATES, SHEILA
HOLLAND, SHEILA C.

COATSWORTH, ELIZABETH
BESTON, ELIZABETH COATSW.

COBALT, MARTIN
MAYNE, WILLIAM [J.C.]

COBB, CLAYTON W.
PATTEN, J.A.

COBB, ELIZABETH
CHAPMAN, ELIZABETH COBB

COBB, JANE
BERRY, JANE COBB

COBB, MICHAEL
WINTLE, ALFRED DANIEL

COBB, O.S.
LINDSKOUG, OSSIAN

COBB, R.C.
COBB, RICHARD CHARLES

COBB, WALTER J.
EGLI, WERNER J.

COBBETT
LUDOVICI, ANTHONY M.

COBBETT, RICHARD
PLUCKROSE, HENRY ARTHUR

COBBLEIGH, TOM
RAYMOND, WALTER

COBDEN, GUY
DAVIS, HOWARD CHARLES

COBHAM, [SIR] ALAN
HAMILTON, CHARLES H.S.

COBRA
WAGNER, HARALD

COBURN, JACK
KUTTNER, HENRY
MOORE, CATHERINE LUCILLE

COBURN, L.J.
HARVEY, JOHN [BARTON]
JAMES, LAURENCE

COBURN, SAM
EWING, JIM

COBURN, SAMMY
WINTER, BEVIS [PETER]

COBURN, WALT
COBURN, WALTER J.

COCH-Y-BONDDHU
ARNOLD, RICHARD

COCHRAN, ELIZABETH
COCHRANE, ELIZABETH

COCHRAN, JEFF
DURST, PAUL

COCHRAN, RICE E.
MONROE, KEITH

COCHRANE, ANDREW
CALDWELL, ROBERT

COCHRANE, CORINNA
PETERSON, CORINNA

COCKIN, JOAN
BURBRIDGE, EDITH JOAN

COCKRELL, AMANDA
CROWE, AMANDA COCKRELL

COCKRELL, EUSTACE
BEAUMONT, CHARLES

CODY, A.R.
JOSCELYN, ARCHIE LYNN

CODY, AL
JOSCELYN, ARCHIE LYNN

CODY, C[HARLES] S.
WALLER, LESLIE

CODY, GENE
EUBANKS, GENE

CODY, JAMES P.
ROHRBACH, PETER THOMAS

CODY, JESS
CUNNINGHAM, CHESTER GRANT

CODY, JOHN
REPP, ED EARL

CODY, LIZA
NASSIM, LIZA

CODY, STETSON
GRIBBLE, LEONARD [R]

CODY, STONE
LANDSBOROUGH, GORDON H.
MOUNT, THOMAS ERNEST

CODY, WALT
NORWOOD, VICTOR [G.C.]

COE, CHRISTINE SADLER
SADLER, CHRISTINE

COE, DOUGLAS
EPSTEIN, BERYL [WILLIAMS]
EPSTEIN, SAMUEL

COE, FRED
COE, FREDERICK

COE, MAX
BOURNE, RANDOLPH S.

COE, ROSS ANTON
RENAUD, RON

COE, TUCKER
WESTLAKE, DONALD [EDWIN]

COENRAADS, EDWARD
ENDT, PIETER

COEUR, PIERRE
D'AMBRE, ANNE CAROLINE

COFFARO, KATHERINE
KOVACS, KATHERINE C.

COFFEY, BRIAN
KOONTZ, DEAN R.

COFFIN, BRUCE
MAURER, KURT

COFFIN, GEOFFREY
BRAWNER, HELEN
MASON, F. VAN WYCK

COFFIN, PETER
LATIMER, JONATHAN [W]

COFYN, CORNELIUS
LODER, JOHN DEVERE
SAUNDERS, HILARY A.

COGAN, MIKE
LOTTMAN, EILEEN [SHUBB]

COGANE, GERALD
FONAROW, JERRY

COGELL, ELIZABETH CUMMINS
CUMMINS, ELIZABETH [ANN]

COGSWELL, E.
NORTON, CHARLES LEDYARD

COGSWELL, FRED
COGSWELL, FREDERICK WILL.

COGSWELL, GEORGIA
COGSWELL, GEORGE RAE

COGSWELL, TED
COGSWELL, THEODORE R.

COHAN, TONY
COHAN, ANTHONY ROBERT

COHEN COHEN
HIGGINS, ROSALYN COHEN

COHEN, ANTHEA
SIMPSON, DORIS

PSEUDONYMS

COHEN, BARNEY
COHEN, BERNARD HALSBAND

COHEN, BELLA
SPEWACK, BELLA

COHEN, HARRY
COHEN, DAVE

COHEN, MATT
COHEN, MATTHEW

COHEN, MIKE
COHEN, MORRIS

COHEN, NORM
COHEN, NORMAN

COHEN, ROSALYN
HIGGINS, ROSALYN [COHEN]

COHEN-STRATYNER, BARBARA
COHEN, BARBARA NAOMI

COHN, HARRY
COHEN, DAVID

COHN, HELEN DESFOSSES
DESFOSSES, HELEN

COHN, LESTER
COLE, LESTER

COHON, BARRY
COHON, BARUCH JOSEPH

COIGNARD, JOHN
BARACH, ALVAN LEROY

COLAM, LANCE
COOPER, GORDON

COLBERE, HOPE
COOLBEAR, MARIAN H.

COLBURN, LAURA
MCMAHAN, IAN

COLBY, ALICE
ROSS, WILLIAM E. DANIEL

COLBY, ERIC
LOONEY, PETER

COLBY, LYDIA
ROSS, WILLIAM E. DANIEL

COLCHIE, ELIZABETH SCHNE.
SCHNEIDER, ELIZABETH [S]

COLDSMITH, DON
COLDSMITH, DONALD C.

COLE, ALISON
COKER, CAROLYN

COLE, ANN KILBORN
CALLAHAN, CLAIRE WALLIS

COLE, ANNETTE
PHILLIPS, KATHLEEN
STEINER, BARBARA [A]

COLE, BILL
COLE, WILLIAM SHADRACK

COLE, BUCK
RICHARDSON, GLADWELL G.

COLE, BURT
DIXON, THOMAS

COLE, C.
COLE, GEORGE D.H.
COLE, MARGARET P.I.

COLE, CANNON
COOK, ARLENE ETHEL

COLE, CAROL CASSIDY
MANCHEE, CAROL M.

COLE, COZY
COLE, WILLIAM R.

COLE, DAVIS
ELTING, MARY

COLE, DIANE
COPELAND, EDITH

COLE, DOUGLAS
COLE, GEORGE D.H.

COLE, E.R.
COLE, EUGENE ROGER

COLE, G.D.H. & M.I.
COLE, GEORGE D.H.
POSTGATE, M.I.

COLE, H.S.D.
COLE, HUGH SAMUEL DAVID

COLE, HILARY
MILLER, VALERIE

COLE, J.C.
CAVE, HUGH B[ARNETT]

COLE, J.P.
COLE, JOHN PETER

COLE, JACK
STEWART, JOHN W.

COLE, JACKSON
BOND, LEE
CHADWICK, JOSEPH L.
CURRY, THOMAS ALBERT
GARDNER, BENNIE WILSON
GERMANO, PETER B.
GRAY, CLARK
GRUBER, FRANK
HARRISON, CHESTER WILLIAM
HECKLEMANN, CHARLES N.
MCGAUGHY, DUDLEY DEAN
NEWTON, DWIGHT BENNETT
RICHMOND, ROALDUS F.
SCHISGALL, OSCAR
SCOTT, ALEXANDER LESLIE
SEARLES, LIN
TOMPKINS, WALKER A.
WELLS, LEE EDWIN
GRAY, CLARK

COLE, JANET
HUNTER, KIM

COLE, JENNIFER
STEVENS, SERITA DEBORAH
ZACH, CHERYL [BYRD]

COLE, JORDAN
TEPPERMAN, EMILE C.

COLE, JUSTINE
KIEHL, CLAIRE
PHILLIPS, SUSAN E.

COLE, KAY
COLOMINAS, KATHLEEN ADELE

COLE, MARIANNE
WHITE, CHARLOTTE

COLE, MARY
HANNA, MARY T.

COLE, RICHARD
BARRETT, GEOFFREY JOHN

COLE, ROBERT
SNOW, CHARLES H[ORACE]

COLE, SAM
COLE, HUGH SAMUEL DAVID

COLE, SHELDON [B]
DUNN, DES R.

COLE, STARK
FILER, THOMAS HANFORD

COLE, STEPHEN
WEBBE, GALE DUDLEY

COLE, SUE ELLEN
GROSS, SUSAN ELLEN

COLEMAN, BILL
COLEMAN, WILLIAM VINCENT

COLEMAN, BOB
COLEMAN, ROBERT DAVID

COLEMAN, BUCK
RICHARDSON, GLADWELL G.

COLEMAN, CLARE
BELL, CLARE [LOUISE]
EASTON, M. COLEMAN

COLEMAN, CLAY
STOKES, COLEMAN

COLEMAN, EMMETT
REED, ISHMAEL

COLEMAN, EVELYN SCHERABON
FIRCHOW, EVELYN SCHERABON

COLEMAN, LEE
LAPIDUS, ELAINE

COLEMAN, LONNIE
COLEMAN, WILLIAM LAWRENCE

COLEMAN, PATTY R.
COLEMAN, PATRICIA REG.

COLEMAN, STEPHEN
FRANCES, STEPHEN D.

COLEMAN, W.C.
TUTTLE, WILBUR COLEMAN

COLEMAN, WILLIAM C.
TUTTLE, WILBUR COLEMAN

PSEUDONYMS

COLERIDGE, JOHN
BINDER, EARL ANDREW
BINDER, OTTO

COLERIDGE, M.E.
COLERIDGE, MARY ELIZABETH

COLERUS, EGMONT
VON GELDERN, EGMONT C.

COLES, DETECTIVE INSPECT.
SEMPHILL, ERNEST

COLES, JANIS
DAWSON, JANIS

COLES, MANNING
COLES, CYRIL HENRY
HAMMERTON, TOM
MANNING, ADELAIDE [F.O]

COLETTE
COLETTE, SIDONIE GABRIELL

COLEY, ROBERT
WANDREI, HOWARD E.

COLIBRI
VIEUX, MARIE

COLIN, ANN
URE, JEAN

COLIN, JEAN
BELL, JOYCE

COLINGS, EDDY
BAJOG, GUNTHER
IDE, HEINO

COLL, CONNY
KOBL, KONRAD

COLLANS, DEV
WINCHELL, PRENTICE

COLLAS, PHIL
COLLAS, FELIX EDWARD

COLLEN, NEIL
LEE, LINCOLN

COLLETON, JOHN
MARKS, ROBERT WALTER

COLLIER, DOUGLAS
FELLOWES-GORDON, IAN

COLLIER, HARRY
WALTON, HARRY

COLLIER, J. COBB
VEITCH, TONY

COLLIER, JANE
SHUMSKY, ZENA FELDMAN

COLLIER, JOHNNIE LUCILLE
COLLIER, LUCILLE ANN

COLLIER, JOY
MILLAR, MINNA H. JOY

COLLIER, LUCY ANN
COLLIER, LUCILLE ANN

COLLIER, MARGARET
TAYLOR, MARGARET STEWART

COLLIER, NORMAN
BENNETT, C.N.

COLLIER, OLD CAP
HARBAUGH, THOMAS C.
IRON, NATHANIEL COLV.
JAMES, W.I.
SAWYER, EUGENE TAYLOR
WAYDE, BERNARD

COLLIER, ZENA
SHUMSKY, ZENA FELDMAN

COLLIN, CHRISTIAN
HOMBERG, BODO

COLLIN, MARION
COLLINS, MARION SMITH

COLLIN, PH.
ASPERN-BUCHMEIER, ELISAB.

COLLIN, RODNEY
COLIN SMITH, RODNEY

COLLINE, PAUL
DUARD, PAUL LOUIS E.

COLLINGS, JILLIE
COLLINGS, I.J.

COLLINGSWOOD, FREDERICK
LAKRITZ, ESTHER

COLLINGWOOD, HARRY
LANCASTER, WILLIAM JOSEPH

COLLINS, BED
COLLINS, ARTHUR WORTH JR.

COLLINS, CHARLES
COLLINS, WILKIE
DICKENS, CHARLES

COLLINS, CHRISTINE
BARRETT, ELIZABETH

COLLINS, CINDY
SMITH, RICHARD REIN

COLLINS, CLARK
REYNOLDS, DALLAS MCCORD

COLLINS, CLIFF
KALMUCZAK, ROLF

COLLINS, COLETTE
KNAACK, TWILA

COLLINS, COLIN
MERLAND, OLIVER

COLLINS, CONNY
DONGES, GUNTER

COLLINS, D.
BULLEID, HENRY A.V.

COLLINS, FREDERIC
ANTON, UWE
HRDINKA, MICHAEL
HUNDSDORFER, GERHARD
KODELPETER, HANS P.

COLLINS, GEOFFREY
JEFFERIES, GREG

COLLINS, GLENN
KALMUCZAK, ROLF

COLLINS, HARRY C.
BECKER, MAX O.

COLLINS, HUNT
HUNTER, EVAN

COLLINS, INSPEKTOR
REUBEL-CIANI, THEO

COLLINS, JACKIE
LERMAN, JACQUELINE

COLLINS, JEFFREY
WILCOX, COLLIN

COLLINS, JOAN
COLLINS, MILDRED

COLLINS, JOHN L.
COLLINS, JOHN LAWRENCE JR

COLLINS, JUNE
WEATHERSTONE, JUNE IRENE

COLLINS, LARRY
COLLINS, JOHN LAWRENCE JR

COLLINS, LAUREL
WIATR, LINDA CATHERINE

COLLINS, MABEL [C]
COOK, MABEL COLLINS

COLLINS, MAX
COLLINS, MAX ALLAN

COLLINS, MICHAEL
LYNDS, DENNIS

COLLINS, MICHELLE
COLLINS, MICHAEL

COLLINS, MRS. E. BURKE
SHARKEY, MRS. EMMA A.B.

COLLINS, NANCY W.
COLLINS-CHAPMAN, NANCY W.

COLLINS, PAT
COLLINS, PATRICIA LOWERY

COLLINS, ROSEMARY
DALGLEISH, OSCAR

COLLINS, SUSANNA
GROSS, SUSAN ELLEN

COLLINS, TOM
FURPHY, JOSEPH
LUTZ, JOHN [T]

COLLINS, WILL
CORLEY, EDWIN RAYMOND

COLLINS, WILLIAM C.H.
MULLER, KURT

COLLINSON, OWEN
OWEN, HARRY COLLINSON

COLLINSON, PETER
HAMMETT, DASHIELL

COLLODI, CARLO
LORENZINI, CARLO

COLLYER, DORIC
FELLOWS, DOROTHY ALICE

COLMAN, GEORGE
GLASSCO, JOHN [S]

COLMONT, MARIE
DELAVAUD, MARIE COLLIN

COLMORE, G.
WEAVER, GERTRUDE RENTON

COLOMBO, DALE
MONROE, KEITH

COLOMBO, PAT
MULGRUE, G. EDWARD

COLONEL SANDERS
SANDERS, HARLAN

COLORADA, ANTONIO J.
COLORADA CAPELLA, ANTONIO

COLPET, MAX
KOLPE, MAX

COLSON, BILL
ATHANAS, WILLIAM VERNE

COLSON, DOROTHEA
PHILLIFENT, JOHN T.

COLSON, FREDERICK
GEIS, RICHARD E.

COLSON, LARAMIE
RICHARDSON, GLADWELL G.

COLSON, THORA
ORTON, THORA MARGARET

COLSON-HAIG, S.
GLASBY, JOHN S.

COLT, CLEM
NYE, NELSON C[ORAL]

COLT, KING
PLOTZE, HASSO

COLT, RUSS
KERR, D.

COLT, W.R.
HUBBARD, L. RON

COLT, WINCHESTER REM.
HUBBARD, L. RON

COLT, ZANDRA
STEVENSON, FLORENCE

COLTER, ELI
COLTER, ELIZABETH

COLTER, FRANK
STREIB, DANIEL T.

COLTER, JAK
BUEHLER, EUGEN KARL

COLTER, RENE
LOFGREN, HOLGER

COLTER, SHANE
NORWOOD, VICTOR [G.C.]

COLTER, SHAYNE
NORWOOD, VICTOR [G.C.]

COLTMAN, ERNEST VIVIAN
DUDLEY, ERNEST

COLTMAN, WILL
BINGLEY, DAVID ERNEST

COLTON, A.J.
HOOK, ALFRED SAMUEL

COLTON, JAMES
HANSEN, JOSEPH

COLTON, MEL
BRAHAM, HAL

COLTRANE, JAMES
WOHL, JAMES P[AUL]

COLUMBINE
FERGUSON, RACHEL

COLUMELLA
MOORE, CLEMENT CLARKE

COLVER, ANNE
HARRIS, POLLY ANNE COLVER

COLVETT, LATAYNE
SCOTT, LATAYNE COLVETT

COLVIL, EDWARD
PUTNAM, MARY LOWELL

COLVIN, CECIL
BURNAND, FRANCIS COWLEY

COLVIN, JAMES
BAYLEY, BARRINGTON J.
PARTINGTON, CHARLES
MOORCOCK, MICHAEL

COLVIN, JIM
MOORCOCK, MICHAEL

COLVIN, MORTIMER
GRONWALD, WERNER

COLVIN, WARWICK JNR.
MOORCOCK, MICHAEL

COLWALL, JAMES
SHELDON, GILBERT

COLWYN, STEWART
PEPPER, FRANK S.

COMBER, PIT
HORSCHELT, THEODOR

COMBER, R.J.
BLOCH, ROBERT [A]

COMBS, ROBERT
MURRAY, JOHN F.

COMBUCHEN, SIGRID
COMBUECHEN, SIGRID

COMER, LINDA
JACKSON, EILEEN V.

COMER, RALPH
SANDERS, JOHN

COMFORT, ALEX
COMFORT, ALEXANDER

COMFORT, JANE LEVINGTON
STURTZEL, JANE LEVINGTON

COMFORT, MONTGOMERY
CAMPBELL, [JOHN] RAMSEY

COMIDAS, CHINAS
GENSER, CYNTHIA

COMITTI, GIOCONDA
VON BOSELAGER, ADA

COMMENT, JEAN PIERROT
DOLL, HERBERT GERHARD

COMO, JOSEPH
COMMINGS, JOSEPH

COMO, LYNN
MCCORMICK, JAMES

COMPASSIONE
HASPELS, GEORGE FRANS

COMPERE, MICKIE
DAVIDSON, MARGARET C.

COMPTON, ANN
PREBBLE, MARJORIE CURTIS

COMPTON, D.G.
COMPTON, DAVID GUY

COMPTON, FRANCIS
MACKENZIE, FRANCIS S.

COMPTON, GUY
COMPTON, DAVID GUY

COMPTON, MARGARET
HARRISON, AMELIA W.

COMSTOCK, CHRISTINE
HERBRUCK, CHRISTINE COM.

COMSTOCK, JARROD
JARVIS, SHARON [SYLVIA]
KOZAK, ELLEN M.

COMUS
BALLANTYNE, R[OBERT] M.

COMYNS, BARBARA
CARR, BARBARA I.V. COMYNS
COMYNS-CARR, BARBARA I.R.

CONAGHER, KEN
KOPP, WILHELM

CONALL, CEARNACH
O'CONNELL, FREDERICK W.

CONAN, ALLAN
NORA, DR. JAMES

CONAN, LURIE
ANGERS, FELICITE

CONANIGHT
COHEN, CHESTER
KNIGHT, DAMON

CONANT, CHESTER B.
COHEN, CHESTER

CONARAIN, NINA
CONARAIN, ALICE [NINA]

CONAWAY, J.C.
CONAWAY, JAMES C.

CONAWAY, JIM
CONAWAY, JAMES C.

CONCANNON, WINNIE
BOWEN, JOSEPH

CONCHALI, INOCENCIO
RIQUELME, DANIEL

CONCOLORCORVO
DE LA VANDERA, ALONSO CA.

CONDE, MARYSE
BOUCOLON, MARYSE

CONDE, NICHOLAS
NATHAN, ROBERT
ROSENBLUM, ROBERT J.

CONDON, JACK
CONDON, JOHN CARL JR.

CONDON, PATRICIA
GOODEY, P.E.

CONDOR, GLADYN
DAVISON, GLADYS PATTON

CONDRAY, BRUNO G.
HUMPHRYS, LESLIE GEORGE

CONELLI, CLARK
RAHN, WOLFGANG

CONFUCIUS
LUND, PHILIP REGINALD

CONGAR, MARIE JOSEPH
CONGAR, GEORGES YVES M-J

CONGAR, Y.M.
CONGAR, GEORGES YVES M-J

CONGAR, YVES
CONGAR, GEORGES YVES M-J

CONGAR, YVES M.-J.
CONGAR, GEORGES YVES M-J

CONGAR, YVES MARIE JOSEPH
CONGAR, GEORGES YVES M-J

CONGER, DONALD
EMERSON, DONALD C.

CONGER, LESLIE
SUTTLES, SHIRLEY

CONGER, RALPH
GRUBER, FRANK

CONGREVE, GILES
JOHNSON, HUGH

CONISTON, ED
BINGLEY, DAVID ERNEST

CONKLING, W.R.
GRUBER, FRANK

CONLEE, JAELYN
PRESTON, FAYRENE

CONN, ALAN
CONNELL, ALAN

CONN, PHOEBE
INGWALSON, PHOEBE C.

CONNAUGHTON, SAM
SELLERS, CONNIE LESLIE

CONNELL, CANDACE
CLEMENT, ERNEST C.

CONNELL, JOHN
ROBERTSON, JAMES ROBIN
ROBERTSON, JOHN HENRY

CONNELL, KIRK
CHAPMAN, JOHN STANTON H.
CHAPMAN, MARY HAMILTON

CONNELL, NORREYS
O'RIORDAN, CONAL O'CONN.

CONNER, MIKE
CONNER, MICHAEL

CONNER, REARDON
CONNER, PATRICK REARDON

CONNERS, SELWYN
SELLERS, CONNIE LESLIE

CONNEY, BARBARA
PORTER, BARBARA CONNEY

CONNINGTON, J.J.
STEWART, ALFRED WALTER

CONNINGTON, JOHN JERVIS
STEWART, ALFRED WALTER

CONNISTON, SAM
SELLERS, CONNIE LESLIE

CONNOLLY, PAUL
WICKER, THOMAS GREY

CONNOR, KEVIN
O'ROURKE, FRANK

CONNOR, PAT
BOGHANDEL, FLOR'S

CONNOR, RALPH
GORDON, CHARLES WILLIAM

CONNOR, SUSANNA PFLAUM
PFLAUM, SUSANNA WHITNEY

CONNOR, TEX
BREUCKER, OSCAR HERBERT

CONNOR, TONY
CONNOR, JOHN ANTHONY

CONNORS, BRUTON
ROHEN, EDWARD

CONOR, GLEN
COONEY, MICHAEL

CONOVER, JESSICA A.W.
JONES, CANDY

CONQUEST NED
CONQUEST, EDWIN PARKER JR

CONQUEST, JOAN
COOKE, MRS. LEONARD

CONQUEST, OWEN
AUSTIN, STANLEY
CATCHPOLE, WILLIAM LESLIE
DOWN, C. MAURICE
EVE, REGINALD T.
HAMILTON, CHARLES H.S.
NEWMAN, KENNETH E.
O'MANT, HEDLEY P.A.
PIKE, WILLIAM ERNEST
SAMWAYS, GEORGE R.
WOOD-SMITH, NOEL

CONRAD, BRENDA
BROWN, ZENITH [JONES]

CONRAD, C.
BENJAMIN, WALTER

CONRAD, CLIVE
KING, FRANK

CONRAD, CON
DOBER, CONRAD K.

CONRAD, CONSTANCE
FRANKEL, RUBY

CONRAD, GEORG.
PRUSSIA, PRINCE GEORGE OF

CONRAD, GREGG
GRAHAM, ROGER P.

CONRAD, HAL
CONRAD, HAROLD

CONRAD, JACK
CONRAD, ISAAC

CONRAD, JESSIE
KORZENIOWSKI, JESSIE

CONRAD, JOSEPH
KORZENIOWSKI, JOSEF T.K.

CONRAD, KENNETH
LOTTICH, KENNETH V.

CONRAD, KLAUS
HAUGK, KLAUS CONRAD

CONRAD, LOGAN
ROTSLER, WILLIAM

CONRAD, M.
HALLS, CHRIST. PETER JOHN

CONRAD, MARCUS
HALLS, CHRIST. PETER JOHN

CONRAD, PAUL
KING, ALBERT

CONRAD, ROBERT W.
BROOKS, EDWY SEARLES

CONRAD, TEX
YATES, ALAN GEOFFREY

CONRAD, TOD
WILKES-HUNTER, RICHARD

CONRADI, CHRISTIAN
KALMUCZAK, ROLF

CONRADI, PETER
HOLM, WERNER

CONRADS, DIETER
CONRADS, DIETRICH

CONROY, AL
ALBERT, MARVIN H.
BREWER, GIL

CONROY, ALBERT
ALBERT, MARVIN H.

CONROY, JANET
CHADWICK, JOSEPH L.

CONROY, JIM
CHADWICK, JOSEPH L.

CONROY, ROBERT
GOLDSTON, ROBERT C.

CONSIDINE, BOB
CONSIDINE, ROBERT BERNARD

CONSTANT, JAN
DAWSON, JANIS

CONSTANTINE, GREG
CONSTANTINE, GREGORY JOHN

CONSTANTINE, K.C.
KOSAK, CARL

CONSTANTINE, MURRAY
BURDEKIN, KATHERINE

CONSTANZA, SENORA
LONG, GABRIELLE M.V.C.

CONSTELLANO, ILLION
LEWIS, JULIUS WARREN

CONSTELLANO, JUAN
LEWIS, JOHN WOODRUFF

CONTE, CHARLES
MACKINNON, CHARLES ROY

CONTE, SAL
VAN LOWE, ERICH

CONTENT, NIKKI
HANNA, FRANCES NICHOLS

CONTER, JEFF
DONGES, GUNTER

CONTY, JEAN-PIERRE
WALRAFEN, CONRAD KURT

CONVERSE, JANE
MARITANO, ADELE

CONVICT WRITER, THE
TOROK, LOU

CONWAY, AL
BAJOG, GUNTHER

CONWAY, ARLINGTON [B]
BURNS, EDSON LOUIS MILL.

CONWAY, BOWEN
MICHEL, JOHN B.

CONWAY, CELINE
BLAIR, KATHRYN

CONWAY, DENISE
PREBBLE, MARJORIE CURTIS

CONWAY, E. CAROLYN
KERMOND, EVELYN CAROLYN

CONWAY, FAULKNER
PRICE, FRANK J.

CONWAY, GORDON
HAMILTON, CHARLES H.S.

CONWAY, HUGH
FARGUS, FREDERICK JOHN

CONWAY, JOHN
ANDREWS, MERVYN
CHADWICK, JOSEPH L.

CONWAY, KEITH
HETHERINGTON, KEITH JAMES

CONWAY, LAURA
ANSLE, DOROTHY PHOEBE

CONWAY, MARK
CAHILL, FRANK

CONWAY, NORMAN
RUSH, MARK

CONWAY, OLIVE
BRIGHOUSE, HAROLD
WALTON, JOHN

CONWAY, PETER
GAUTIER-SMITH, PETER C.
MILKOMANE, G. ALEXIS M.

CONWAY, RANDALL
GLASBY, JOHN S.

CONWAY, RITTER
KNIGHT, DAMON

CONWAY, RUDOLF
HIRSHMAN, JACK

CONWAY, TIM
CONWAY, THOMAS DANIEL

CONWAY, TOD
YATES, ALAN GEOFFREY

CONWAY, TOM
YATES, ALAN GEOFFREY

CONWAY, TROY
AVALLONE, MICHAEL
BOUMA, JOHANNES L.
FOX, GARDNER F.
FRITCH, CHARLES E.
GILLETTE, PAUL J.

CONWAY, WARD
WESTMORELAND, REG

CONWELL, REX
KAPPEL, GUNTER

CONYBEARE, CHARLES AUGUS.
ELIOT, T[HOMAS] S[TEARNS]

CONYERS, LATHAM
ZAGAT, ARTHUR LEO

CONYUS
CALHOUN, CONYUS

COO-EE
WALKER, W. SYLVESTER

COOGAN, BEATRICE
ROBINS-CLARK, PATRICIA D.

COOK, BARRY
CAUSEWAY, JANE

COOK, JACK
COOK, JOHN AUSGUSTINE

COOK, LENNOX
COOK, JOHN LENNOX

COOK, LILA
AFRICANO, LILLIAN

COOK, LYN
WADDELL, EVELYN MARGARET

COOK, MERCER B.
TURNER, ROBERT H.

COOK, RICK
COOK, JAMES RICHARD

COOK, ROBIN
COOK, ROBERT [W.A.]

COOK, ROY
SILVERBERG, ROBERT

COOK, VERA
RYDER, VERA

COOK, W.
COOK, WILLIAM EVERETT

COOK, WILL
COOK, WILLIAM EVERETT

COOKE, ANN
COLE, JOANNA

COOKE, ARTHUR
BALTER, E.
KORNBLUTH, C[YRIL] M.
LOWNDES, ROBERT A.W.
MICHEL, JOHN B.
WOLLHEIM, DONALD A.

COOKE, BARBARA
ALEXANDER, ANNA B.C.

COOKE, CATHERINE
MONTROSE, CATHERINE COOKE

COOKE, JOHN ESTES
BAUM, L[YMAN] FRANK

COOKE, M.E.
CREASEY, JOHN

COOKE, MARGARET
CREASEY, JOHN

COOKE, MICHAEL F.R.C.S.
COOK, MICHAEL LEWIS

COOKRIDGE, E.H.
SPIRO, EDWARD

COOKRIDGE, JOHN MICHAEL
HOLROYD, ETHEL MARY

COOLE, W.W.
KULSKI, WLADYSLAW WSZEBOR

COOLEY, BENJAMIN
LAWRENCE, DAVID HERBERT

COOLIDGE, ERWIN L.
GOODE, GEORGE W.

COOLIDGE, SUSAN
WOOLSEY, SARAH CHAUNCY

COOLUS, ROMAIN
WEILL, RENE

COOLWATER, JOHN
CONNIFF, JAMES C.G.

COOMARASWAMY, A.K.
COOMARASWAMY, AMANDA K.

COOMBS, ANN
PYKARE, NINA ANN COOMBS

COOMBS, CHICK
COOMBS, CHARLES IRA

COOMBS, MURDO
DAVIS, FREDERICK [CLYDE]

COOMBS, NINA
PYKARE, NINA ANN COOMBS

COON, SUSAN
PLUNKETT, SUSAN IRENE F.

COOPER, BENJAMIN
KEILSON, HANS

COOPER, C. EVERETT
BURGESS, MICHAEL ROY

COOPER, CARL
COOPER, KENNETH C.

COOPER, CHARLES
LOCK, A. CHARLES COOPER

COOPER, COLIN
ROBERTSON, COLIN

COOPER, CRAIG
KING, ALBERT

COOPER, ESTER
KELLNER, ESTER

COOPER, FREEMONT
STEFFENS, ARTHUR JOSEPH

COOPER, HANNAH
SPENCE, W. JOHN DUNCAN

COOPER, HENRY S.F.
COOPER, HENRY S. FENIMORE

COOPER, HENRY ST. JOHN
CREASEY, JOHN

COOPER, HUGHES
LEONARD, GEORGE H.

COOPER, J.
FOX, GARDNER F.

COOPER, JAMES A.
STRATEMEYER, EDWARD

COOPER, JANIE
HAILL, ROBERT GODFREY

COOPER, JEFF
COOPER, JOHN DEAN
FOX, GARDNER F.

COOPER, JEFFERSON
FOX, GARDNER F.

COOPER, JOHN C.
CROYDON, JOHN

COOPER, JOHN R.
STRATEMEYER, EDWARD

COOPER, LYNNA
FOX, GARDNER F.

COOPER, M.E.
DAVIS, MAGGIE S.
HEHL, EILEEN

COOPER, MATTIE LULA
BRITTON, MATTIE LULA C.

COOPER, MORLEY
COOPER, ALFRED MORTON

COOPER, NATASHA
WRIGHT, DAPHNE

COOPER, SONNI
COOPER, SANDRA LEONORE

COOPER, SOPHIE
AMORY, MARK

COOPER, STANLEY
ARNOLD, WALTER

COOPER, STEVE
APPEL, WALTER
FRIEDRICHS, HORST
GIESA, WERNER K.
HUBNER, HORST W.
KUGLER, DIETMAR
REHFELD, FRANK

COOPER, WILLIAM
BERTRAM, JAMES G.
HOFF, HARRY SUMMERFIELD

COOPER-KLEIN, NINA
COOPER, MAE [KLEIN]
KLEIN, GRACE

COOPLANDT, A.
PRINS, ARY

COOVER, WAYNE
DUBINA, PETER
EISFELD, RAINER
ROHR, WOLF DETLEF

COPE, JACK
COPE, ROBERT KNOX

COPELAND, ANN
FURTWANGLER, VIRGINIA W.

COPELAND, RICHARD
MCLEAVE, HUGH [GEORGE]

COPIA, ISIS
ZIYADAH, MARIE

COPLEY, FREDERICK S.
GREIF, MARTIN

COPLEY, GERALD L.C.
COLE, LESTER

COPP, A.E.
COPP, ALF E.

COPP, JIM
COPP, ANDREW JAMES III

COPP, TED
COPP, THEODORE BAYARD F.

COPPARD, A.E.
COPPARD, ALFRED EDGAR

COPPE, ALBIEZER
TAYLOR, JOHN A.

COPPEL, ALFRED
COPPEL, ALFREDO JOSE

COPPLESTONE, BENNET
KITCHIN, FREDERICK H.

COQUE
WARNLOF, ANNA-LISA

COQUELIN, RENEE
GOFF, JERRY M. JR.

COQUINO
SHIELDS, GEORGE OLIVER

CORALIE
ANDERSON, CATHERINE CORL.

CORAM, CHRISTOPHER
WALKER, PETER N[ORMAN]

CORAY, M.
SATERNAS, MARTA

CORBETT, CHAN
SCHACHNER, NATHAN

CORBETT, REX
STITZ-ULRICI, ROLF

CORBIN, IRIS
CLINTON, IRIS A. CORBIN

CORBIN, MICHAEL
CARTMILL, CLEVE

CORBIN, SABRA LEE
MALVERN, GLADYS

CORBIN, WILLIAM
MCGRAW, WILLIAM CORBIN

CORBURTON, JOHN
TARKINGTON, BOOTH

CORBY, DAN
CATHERALL, ARTHUR

CORD, BARRY
GERMANO, PETER B.

CORD, BIRDWHANGER
HAHN, KEN

CORD, SMITHWAINER
CARRINGTON, GRANT

CORDA, ERIC
KOVARY, GEORG

CORDAIRE, CHRISTINA
STRONG, CHRISTINA

CORDEL, PAUL M.
BROWN, GERALD J.

CORDELIA
TREVES, VIRGINIA

CORDELL, ALEXANDER
GRABER, GEORGE ALEXANDER

CORDELL, BRAD
BLEECK, G.C.

CORDELL, MELISSA
ROLAND, DONALD

CORDER, ERIC
MUNDIS, JERROLD J.

CORDER, R.E.
DUNN, JAMES

CORDES, ALEXANDRA
HORBACH, URSULA [S]

CORDES, IRENE
NICOLAS, WALTRAUD

CORDIER, GILBERT
SCHERER, JEAN-MARIE MAUR.

CORDIS, LONNY
DONSON, CYRIL

COREA, GENA
COREA, GENOVETTA

CORELL, H.B.
VON BLUCHER, HUBERTUS

CORELLI, MARIE
MACKAY, MARY

COREMAN, JAY S.
CAMERON, SCOTT

COREY, FRANK
FOX, GEORGE

COREY, GAYLE
HAUPTMAN, ELAINE

COREY, RYANNE
WOOD, TONYA [TONIA]

CORFE, TOM
CORFE, THOMAS HOWELL

CORINTH, WILHELMINE
KLOPFER, WILHELMINE

CORIOLA
GAILLOT, JANE

CORIOLAN, JOHN
CORINGTON, WILLIAM

CORIOLANUS
MCMILLAN, JAMES

CORK, DERIDRE
COOK, DERIDRE

CORK, DOROTHY
COOK, DEIRDRE

CORK, PATRICK
COCKBURN, [FRANCIS] CLAUD

CORLETT, JOYCE I.
KIRKWOOD, JOYCE

CORLEY, ERNEST
BLUMER, [HENRY] KENNETH

CORLEY, RAY
CORLEY, EDWIN RAYMOND

CORMAC, BORIS
DOMBROWSKI, THEODOR

CORMACK, SANDY
CORMACK, ALEXANDER J.R.

CORMON, EUGENE
PIESTRE, PIERRE ETIENNE

CORNEA, CAROL
KOCH, KURT EMIL

CORNEISSEN, LUCY
HARNISCH, LUCY

CORNEL, FRANK
BEISSEL, RUDOLF

CORNELISSEN, PETER
BUSCH, FRITZ OTTO

CORNELIUS, FRANK
MOORCOCK, MICHAEL

CORNELL, J.
CORNELL, JEFFREY

CORNER, CLIFF
KALMUCZAK, ROLF
MAHN, TRAUTE
MIELKE, THOMAS R.P.
RELLERGERD, HELMUT

CORNER, E.J.H.
CORNER, EDRED JOHN HENRY

CORNEY, DEBRA
KELLY, DAN

CORNING, KYLE
GARDNER, ERLE STANLEY

CORNISH, F.
BRYNING, FRANK

CORNWALL, JIM
RIKHOFF, JAMES C.

CORNWALL, MARTIN
CAVENDISH, RICHARD

CORNWALL, NELLIE
SLOGGETT, NELLIE

CORNWELL, SMITH
SMITH, DAVID [J.D.]

CORONET
JAMES, CHARLES

CORPORAL TIM
BOLGER, PHILIP CUNNINGHAM

CORRA, BRUNO
CORRADINI, BRUNO

CORREA
GALBRAITH, JEAN

CORRELL, A. BOYD
MACDONALD, PHILIP

CORREN, GRACE
HOSKINS, ROBERT

CORRENTI, MARIO
TOGLIATTI, PALMIRO

CORREY, LEE
STINE, GEORGE HARRY

CORRIE, ELVA
CLAIRMONT, ELVA

CORRIGAN, MARK
LEE, NORMAN

CORSARI, WILLY
SCHMIDT, WILHELMINA ANGE.

CORSARO, FRANK
CORSARO, FRANCESCO ANDREA

CORSON, GEOFFREY
SHOLL, ANNA MCCLURE

CORSON-FINNERTY, ADAM D.
FINNERTY, ADAM DANIEL

CORT, M.C.
CLIFFORD, MARGARET CORT

CORT, MARGARET
CLIFFORD, MARGARET CORT

CORTAN, F.B.
BEISSEL, RUDOLF

CORTEEN, CRAIG
NORWOOD, VICTOR [G.C.]

CORTEEN, WES
NORWOOD, VICTOR [G.C.]

CORTESI, LAWRENCE
CERRI, LAWRENCE J.

CORTEZ-VILLON, JUAN
HERZINGER, KIM ALLEN

CORTH, R.
DRESSLER, HERRMANN

CORTHIS, ANDRE
LECUYER, ANDREE [H]

CORVAIS, ANTHONY
BRADBURY, RAY [DOUGLAS]

CORVIN, CELIA
VON LAGERSTROEM, KAMILLA

CORVINUS, JAKOB
RAABE, WILHELM

CORVO, BARON
ROLFE, FREDERICK [W]

CORWIN, CECIL
KORNBLUTH, C[YRIL] M.

CORY, CAROLINE
FREEMAN, KATHLEEN

CORY, CORRINE
CORY, IRENE E.

CORY, DESMOND
MCCARTHY, SHAUN LLOYD

CORY, HOWARD L.
JARDINE, JACK OWEN

CORY, HOWARD L.
JARDINE, JULIE ANN

CORY, JACK
OFFUTT, ANDREW J.

CORY, RAY
MARSHALL, MEL[VIN]

CORY, VIVIAN
CORY, ANNIE SOPHIE

CORYA, I.E.
CORY, IRENE E.

COSBY, BILL
COSBY, WILLIAM HENRY JR.

COSGROVE, CAROL ANN
TWITCHETT, CAROL COSGROVE

COSGROVE, RACHEL
PAYES, RACHEL C.

COSMIC, RAY
GLASBY, JOHN S.

COSMOI, M.M.
MITRINOVIC, DMITRI

COSMOPOLITE
LEMOINE, JAMES MACPHERSON

COSSART, THEOPHILUS
GLASS, MONTAGUE MARSDEN

COSSEBOOM, KATHY GROEHN
EL-MESSIDI, KATHY GROEHN

COST, MARCH
MORRISON, MARGARET MACKIE
MORRISON, PEGGY

COSTELLA, P.F.
GRAHAM, ROGER P.

COSTELLO, CONTE
REIS, KURT

COSTELLO, MICHAEL
DETZER, KARL

COSTELLO, P.F.
GEIER, CHESTER S.
MCGIVERN, WILLIAM P.
GRAHAM, ROGER P.

COSTELLO, PAUL
TAYLOR, PHILIP N. WALKER

COSTELLO, PETE
BELL, GEORGE
GARRETT, ALBERT EDWARD
JENNISON, JOHN WILLIAM
WILLIS, ERNEST LISTER H.

COSTELLO, PIERRE
HOSKEN, ERNEST CHARLES

COSTER, ARTHUR
DE MILLE, RICHARD

COSTER, B.W.
KRUGER, BRUNO

COSTER, ROBERT
BARLTROP, ROBERT

COSTIGAN, LEE
SEARLS, HENRY HUNT JR.

COSTINESCU, EDWARD N.
GROSS, TERENCE

COSTLER, [DR.] A.
KOESTLER, ARTHUR

COSTLEY, BILL
COSTLEY, WILLIAM K.

COTELO, C.S.
CAVE, PETER [LESLIE]

COTES, PETER
BOULTING, SYDNEY

COTRELL, HARVEY S.
CORBIN, HAROLD STANDISH

COTRION, ANTHONY
GABRIELSON, ERNEST L.

COTTAR, GUY
GARSIA, CLIVE

COTTER, JOHN
COUFFER, JACK [C]
FRANKLE, JUDITH

COTTERELL, BRIAN
DINGLE, A. EDWARD

COTTLE, CHARLES
ANDERSON, ROBERT C.

COTTON, BILLY
ANDREWS, ALLEN

COTTON, JERRI
SELLERS, CONNIE LESLIE

COTTON, JERRY
APPEL, WALTER

COTTON, JERRY [CONT]
BRAND, KURT
BURKLE, ROLF A.
DIEDRICHS, EDMUND
DONGES, GUNTER
ERICHSEN, UWE
FACKENHEIM, PAUL ERNST
FECHTNER, WOLFGANG
FRIEDRICHS, HOLGER
FRIEDRICHS, HORST
GEHRMANN, HORST
GUNTHER, KARL HEINZ
HACKMANN, KARL-HEINZ
HAFT, FRITJOF
HAFT, UWE
HARTMANN, HELMUT HENRY
HARTSCH, GERHART
HEBEL, PETER
HENSELER, P.S.
HOBEIN, EUGEN
HOBER, HEINZ WERNER
HOHLBEIN, WOLFGANG E.
HORSCHELT, THEODOR
HUBNER, HORST W.
KALMUCZAK, ROLF
KANN, ALBRECHT PETER
KARSTEN, UWE
KOBUSCH, HELMUT
KOCH, GERHARD
KODELPETER, HANS P.
KOHR, DIETRICH
KRAMER, PETER
KUNKEL, KLAUS
KURTZE, WERNER
LEDWOCH, BERT
LIST, JURGEN E.
LOHMEYER, ROLF
MAUCKNER, WALTER G.
NEUBERT, HELMUT
NIEHAUS, WERNER
NUTZ, WALTER
OLBRICH, HANS
PERKINS, PETER
PETERS, HERMANN
PLOTZE, HASSO
RAUSCH, LOTHAR
RELLERGERD, HELMUT
RITTER, WOLFPETER
RODRIAN, IRENE
VON KOBLINSKI, HANS-JOACH

COTTON, JOHN
FEARN, JOHN RUSSELL
WELLMAN, MANLY WADE

COTTRELL, HARVEY S.
CORBIN, HAROLD STANDISH

COUCH, OSMA PALMER
TOD, OSMA GALLINGER

COULIANO, I.P.
CULIANU, I[OAN] P[ETRU]

COULSDON, JOHN
HINCKS, CYRIL MALCOLM

COULSON, N.J.
COULSON, NOEL JAMES

COULTELINE, GEORGES
MOINEAUX, GEORGES-VICTOR

COULTER, ADAM
SMITH, JAMES T.

COULTER, CATHERINE
POGONY, JEAN COULTER

COULTON, JAMES
HANSEN, JOSEPH

COUNCIL OF FOUR
HANSEN, CHUCK
HUNT, ROY
METCALF, NORMAN
MILLS, ELLIS
PETERSON, BOB
WALKER, TOM

COUNT, CECIL
KALMUCZAK, ROLF

COUNT, NOAH
MURRAY, WILLIAM P.

COUNTESS OF ROMANONES
QUINTANILLA, MARIA A.G.D.

COUNTRYMAN, THE
WHITLOCK, RALPH

COUPER, STEPHEN
GALLAGHER, STEPHEN

COUPLING, J.J.
PIERCE, JOHN ROBINSON

COURAGE, JOHN
GOYNE, RICHARD

COURT, HAROLD
SWYCAFFER, JEFFERSON P.

COURT, KATHERINE
SCHREMPP, ELIZABETH K.

COURT, SHARON
ROWLAND, DONALD S.

COURT, WESLI
TURCO, LEWIS PUTNAM

COURTENAY, LUKE THEOPHIL.
SCHOFIELD, ALFRED TAYLOR

COURTENEY, CARL
URNER, NATHAN DANE

COURTLAND, ROBERTA
DERN, E. PEARL GADDIS

COURTNEY, CHRISTINE
WESTMARLAND, ETHEL LOUISA

COURTNEY, DAYLE
FRANCIS, GAIL KIMBERLY
GOLDSMITH, HOWARD

COURTNEY, JOHN
COURNOS, JOHN
JUDD, FREDERICK CHARLES

COURTNEY, ROBERT
BEAUMONT, CHARLES
ELLISON, HARLAN
KING, C. DALY
ROBINSON, FRANK M.

COUSIN ANN
LILLY, ISABELLA PURVIS

COUSIN VIRGINIA
JOHNSON, VIRGINIA WALES

COVENANTER
ZILLIACUS, KONNI

COVENTRY, JOHN
PALMER, JOHN WILLIAMSON

COVERACK, GILBERT
WARREN, J[OHN] RUSSELL

COVERDALE, HARRY
CHAPIN, ANNA ALICE
LANDON, HERMAN

COVERT, WILSON L.
LEITHEAD, J. EDWARDS

COVERTSIDE, NAUNTON
DAVIES, NAUNTON

COVINGTON, CHESTER
VAN HORN, DALE R.

COVINGTON, LINDA
WINDSOR, LINDA

COWAN, ALAN
GILCHRIST, ALAN W.

COWEN, EVE
WERNER, HERMA

COWEN, FRANCES
MUNTHE, FRANCES

COWEN, RON
COWEN, RONALD

COWLE, JERRY
COWLE, JEROME MILTON

COWLES, KATHLEEN
KRULL, KATHLEEN

COWLES, MIKE
COWLES, GARDNER A JR.

COWLEY, RAMSAY
WATTERSON, JOHN WILLIAM

COWLIN, DOROTHY
WHALLEY, DOROTHY

COWPER, RICHARD
MURRY, JOHN MIDDLETON

COX, A.B.
COX, ANTHONY BERKELEY

COX, DOUGLAS
COX, H.D.

COX, EDITH
GOAMAN, MURIEL

COX, FRED M.
COX, FREDERICK MORELAND

COX, JACK
COX, JOHN ROBERTS

COX, JEAN
COX, ARTHUR JEAN

COX, JERI
KIMES, BEVERLY RAE

COX, LEWIS
COX, EUPHRASIA EMELINE

COX, MARY ELIZABETH
HEADAPOHL, BETTY R.

COX, MOLLY
COX, MARIE-THERESE HENR.

COX, P. BRIAN
COX, PATRICK BRIAN

COX, PATRICIA
WARREN, PAT

COX, P[ATRICK] BRIAN
WESANDER, BJOERN K.

COX, VICTORIA
GARRETSON, VICTORIA DIANE

COX, W.R.
ARD, WILLIAM [THOMAS]

COX, WALLY
COX, WALLACE MAYNARD

COX-JOHNSON, ANN
SAUNDERS, ANN LOREILLE

COXE, GEORGE H.
COXE, GEORGE HARMON

COXE, KATHLEEN BUDDINGTON
LONG, AMELIA REYNOLDS
MCHUGH, EDNA

COYLE, LEE
COYLE, LEO PERRY

COYSH, EDWARD
STUART-JERVIS, CHARLES

CRABBE, BUSTER
CRABBE, CLARENCE LINDEN

CRABTREE, JANE
WELLS, H.G.

CRACKEN, JAEL
ALDISS, BRIAN [WILSON]

CRACKERS, FRITZ
FRANK, PHILIP NORMAN

CRAD, JOSEPH
ANSELL, EDWARD C.T.

CRADDOCK, CHARLES EGBERT
MURFREE, MARY NOAILLES

CRADDOCK, WILSON JR.
KNOLES, WILLIAM [H]

CRADOCK, FANNY
CRADOCK, PHYLLIS NAN S.

CRAFT, K.Y.
CRAFT, KINUKO Y.

CRAGG, D.J.
CRAGG, DAN

CRAIG, A.A.
ANDERSON, POUL [W]

CRAIG, ALEC
CRAIG, ALEXANDER GEORGE

CRAIG, ALISA
MACLEOD, CHARLOTTE [M.H.]

CRAIG, ALISON
NICHOLSON, JOAN

CRAIG, BETH
CARLI, AUDREY

CRAIG, BRIAN
MCINTOSH, CRAIG M.
STABLEFORD, BRIAN M.

CRAIG, COLIN
BOOTH, HENRY SPENCER

CRAIG, DAVID
TUCKER, [ALLAN] JAMES

CRAIG, DELORES
LYNCH, MIRIAM

CRAIG, DENYS
STOLL, DENNIS G.

CRAIG, GEORGIA
DERN, E. PEARL GADDIS

CRAIG, JASMINE
CRESSWELL, JASMINE ROSEM.

CRAIG, JENNIFER
BRAMBLEBY, AILSA

CRAIG, JOHN ELAND
CHIPPERFIELD, JOSEPH E.

CRAIG, JOHN ROSCOE
DELFS, RAINER

CRAIG, JONATHAN
DEMING, RICHARD
POSNER, RICHARD
SMITH, FRANK ELLIS

CRAIG, LARRY
COUGHRAN, LARRY C.

CRAIG, LEE
SANDS, LEO GEORGE

CRAIG, M.F.
CRAIG, MARY FRANCIS S.

CRAIG, M.S.
CRAIG, MARY FRANCIS S.

CRAIG, MARY
CRAIG, MARY FRANCIS S.

CRAIG, MARY S.
CRAIG, MARY FRANCIS S.

CRAIG, MARY SHURA
CRAIG, MARY FRANCIS S.

CRAIG, NANCY
MASLIN, ALICE

CRAIG, PEGGY
KREIG, MARGARET B.

CRAIG, PETER
MACCLURE, VICTOR

CRAIG, RANDOLPH
PAGE, NORVELL W[OOTEN]

CRAIG, RIANNA
HARRINGTON, SHARON & RICK

CRAIG, ROBERT
DELLIGAN, WILLIAM F.

CRAIG, VERA
ROWLAND, DONALD S.

CRAIG, WEBSTER
RUSSELL, ERIC FRANK

CRAIG, WILLIAM
THURLOW-CRAIG, CHARLES W.

CRAIGIE, DAVID
CRAIGIE, DOROTHY M.

CRAIGIE, W.A.
CRAIGIE, WILLIAM A.

CRAIK, ARTHUR
CRAIG, ALEXANDER GEORGE

CRAILLE, WESLEY
ROWLAND, DONALD S.

CRAIN, ELLEY
ALLEN, ELYSE
MENDENHALL, CAROL

CRAIN, JEFF
MENESES, ENRIQUE

CRAIN, ROBERT
LUDDECKE, WERNER JORG

CRAINIC, NICHIFOR
DOBRE, ION

CRAMER, MARK
FISCHER, CLAUS

CRAMER, MILES
MCCLARY, THOMAS CALVERT

CRAMPTON, HELEN
CHESNEY, MARION G.

CRANBROOK, JAMES L.
EDWARDS, WILLIAM B.

CRANDALL, BRUCE
GIBSON, WALTER B.

CRANDALL, JOY
MARTIN, JOY

CRANDALL, NELSON
PRESTON, HARRY

CRANE, ALEX
WILKES-HUNTER, RICHARD

CRANE, BERKELEY
MARSHALL, ARTHUR C.

CRANE, BILL
CRANE, WILLIAM B.

CRANE, DENIS
CRANFIELD, W.T.

CRANE, EDNA TEMPLE
EICHER, [ETHEL] ELIZABETH

CRANE, ERIC
SETTERBORG, GABRIEL

CRANE, FRANCES
KIRKWOOD, FRANCES

CRANE, HAMILTON
MASON, SARAH JILL

CRANE, HENRY
DOUGLASS, PERCIVAL IAN

CRANE, JIM
CRANE, JAMES GORDON

CRANE, LEAH
HAGER, [WILMA] JEAN [L]

CRANE, M.A.
WARTSKI, MAUREEN A.C.

CRANE, MANNIN
CRAINE, JOHN

CRANE, PAUL
BAILEY, E.J.

CRANE, RENE
CROSS, RENA

CRANE, ROBERT
GLEMSER, BERNARD
ROBERTSON, FRANK CHESTER
SELLERS, CONNIE LESLIE

CRANE, ROY
CRANE, ROYSTON CAMPBELL

CRANNACH, HENRY
MEESKE, MARILYN

CRANSHAW, STANLEY
FISHER, DOROTHY F.C.

CRANSTON, EDWARD
FAIRCHILD, WILLIAM

CRAVEN HILL
PARSONS, CHARLES P.

CRAVEN, MARY
FFEULKES, MRS.

CRAVEN, MONTE
COMMINGS, JOSEPH

CRAVEN, ROBERT
BURGDORF, KARL-ULRICH
HOHLBEIN, WOLFGANG E.
KEHL, WOLFGANG
REHFELD, FRANK

CRAVEN, WES
CRAVEN, WESLEY EARL

CRAWELLS, CARL
HERM, GERHARD

CRAWFORD, ANTHONY
HUGILL, JOHN ANTHONY

PSEUDONYMS

CRAWFORD, BILL
CRAWFORD, WILLIAM HULFISH

CRAWFORD, CAROLINE
MCLEAN, CAROLINE CRAWFORD

CRAWFORD, DAVID
KETTLEHACK, GUY

CRAWFORD, DIANE
LIVINGSTON, GEORGETTE

CRAWFORD, ELAINE
CRAWFORD, DIANNA

CRAWFORD, HANK
RUMMEL, LOUIS JACKSON

CRAWFORD, JOAN
LE SEUR, LUCILLE

CRAWFORD, JOHN
GLASBY, JOHN S.

CRAWFORD, LAD
GARY, DON

CRAWFORD, OLIVER
KAUFMAN, OLIVER

CRAWFORD, ROBERT
RAE, HUGH C[RAWFORD]

CRAWFORD, TERRY
CRAWFORD, TERRENCE MICH.

CRAY, ED
CRAY, EDWARD

CRAYDER, TERESA
COLMAN, HILA

CRAYNE, CHRISTOPHER
NEUBERG, VICTOR [B]

CRAYON, DIEDRICK, JR.
BRUCE, KENNETH

CRAYON, GEOFFREY
IRVING, WASHINGTON

CRAYON, PORTE
STROTHER, DAVID HUNTER

CREASEY, JEANNE
WILLIAMS, DOROTHY JEANNE

CREATOR OF CRAIG KENNEDY
REEVE, ARTHUR, B.

CRECHALES, TONY
CRECHALES, ANTHONY GEORGE

CRECY, JEANNE
WILLIAMS, DOROTHY JEANNE

CREDO
CREASEY, JOHN

CREED, DAVID
GUTHRIE, JAMES SHIELDS

CREED, JOEL
KING, ALBERT

CREED, WILL
LONG, WILLIAM

CREEK, NATHAN
SHEPPARD, JOHN HAMILTON G

CREFELD, DONNA CAROLYN A.
ANDERS, DONNA CAROLYN

CREGAN, MATT
DUNN, DES R.

CREIGHTON, DON
DRURY, MAXINE COLE

CREIGHTON, JO ANNE
CHADWICK, JOSEPH L.

CREIGHTON, JOHN
CHADWICK, JOSEPH L.

CREIGHTON, KATHLEEN
MODROVICH, KATHLEEN C.

CREIGHTON, LEE
CRAWFORD, BETTY ANNE

CREIGHTON, RUSS T.
GIBSON, WALTER B.

CREMER, SAMUEL
MEEUS, MARCEL

CRESCENDO
KALISCH, A.

CRESPI, CAMILLA T.
TRINCHIERI, CAMILLA

CRESPI, TRELLA [TRILLA]
TRINCHIERI, CAMILLA

CRESSON, PIERRE
CRESSWELL, DONALD

CRESSWELL, HELEN
ROWE, HELEN CRESSWELL

CRESSWELL, JASMINE
CANDLISH, JASMINE CRESSW.

CRESSY, EDWARD
CREASEY, CLARENCE H.

CRESTON, DORMER
COLSTON-BAYNES, DOROTHY

CRESWELL, H.B.
CRESWELL, HARRY B.

CREWE, SARAH
BLANFORD, VIRGINIA

CREYTON, PAUL
TROWBRIDGE, JOHN TOWNSEND

CRIBLECOBLIS, OTIS
DUKINFIELD, WILLIAM CLAUD

CRICHTON, JOHN
GUTHRIE, NORMAN GREGOR

CRICHTON, LOUISE
MILN, H. CRICHTON

CRICHTON, LUCILLA
ANDREWS, LUCILLA MATHEW

CRIDEN, YOSEF
CRIDEN, JOSEPH

CRILE, BARNEY
CRILE, GEORGE JR.

CRINGLE, TOM
WALKER, WILLIAM

CRIPPS, L.L.
CRIPPS, LOUISE LILIAN

CRISLER, FRITZ
CRISLER, HERBERT ORIN

CRISP, QUENTIN
PRATT, DENNIS

CRISP, TONY
CRISP, ANTHONY THOMAS

CRISPIE
CRISP, S.E.

CRISPIN, EDMUND
MONTGOMERY, ROBERT BRUCE

CRISPIN, SUZY
CARTWRIGHT, JUSTIN

CRISS, DANI
BENTCH, KITTY

CRISTABEL
ABRAHAMSEN, CHRISTINE E.

CRISTOFER, MICHAEL
PROCASSION, MICHAEL

CRISTY, ANN
MITTERMEYER, HELEN

CRISTY, R.J.
DE CRISTOFORO, R.J.

CRITCHIE, ESTIL
BURKS, ARTHUR J.

CRITCHLEY, LYNN
RADFORD, RICHARD F.

CRITIC
MARTIN, BASIL KINGSLEY

CRITICUS
HARCOURT, MELVILLE
ROE, F. GORDON

CROCKETT, CHRISTINA
GRAY, LINDA CROCKETT

CROCKETT, DAVY
CROCKETT, DAVID

CROCKETT, JAMES
MACPHAIL, JAMES A.
WARRINER, CORNELIA

CROCKETT, LINDA
GRAY, LINDA CROCKETT

CROCKETT, S.R.
CROCKETT, SAMUEL R.

CROFIELD, HILTON
BLOCK, LAWRENCE

CROFT, ROY
CALVERT, WILLIAM ROBINSON

CROFT, SUTTON
LUNN, SIR ARNOLD

CROFT, TAYLOR
CROFT-COOKE, RUPERT

CROFTS, F.W.
CROFTS, FREEMAN WILLS

CROFUT, BILL
CROFUT, WILLIAM E. III

CROHN, PETER
KROHNE, HELLMUT

CROISE, JACQUES
SCHAKOVSKOY, ZINAIDA

CROIX-ROUGE
GRANT, CHARLES L.

CROIXELLES, R.
KREISEL, HEINRICH

CROLY, ELIZABETH
FARWELL, JANET

CROM A BOO
BODKIN, M. MACDONNELL

CROMAN, DOROTHY YOUNG
ROSENBERG, DOROTHY

CROMARSH, H. RIPLEY
ANGELL, BRYAN MARY DOYLE

CROMARTY, DEAS
WATSON, MRS. ROBERT A.

CROMIE, STANLEY
SIMMONS, J.S.A.

CROMPTON, JOHN
LAMBURN, JOHN B. CROMPTON

CROMPTON, RICHMAL
LAMBURN, RICHMAL CROMPTON

CROMWELL, ELSIE
LEE, ELSIE

CRONHEIM, F.G.
GODFREY, FREDERICK M.

CRONIECKSCHRIJIER
LE FEBER, DAVID

CRONIN, A.J.
CRONIN, ARCHIBAL JOSEPH

CRONIN, BEN
HERON, EDNA

CRONIN, MICHAEL
CRONIN, BRENDAN LEO

CRONUS, DIODORUS
TAYLOR, RICHARD

CROOKS, MARION
IRELAND, MABEL ISABEL

CROPP, BEN
CROPP, BENJAMIN

CROS, EARL
ROSE, CARL

CROSBIE, ELIZABETH
EWER, MONICA

CROSBY, BING
CROSBY, HARRY LILLIS

CROSBY, CARESSE
CROSBY, MARY PHELPS [J]

CROSBY, CAROLINE
STIRLING, JESSICA

CROSBY, DAVID
HAHN, RONALD M.

CROSBY, HENRY GREW
CROSBY, HARRY C. JR.

CROSBY, HENRY STURGIS
CROSBY, HARRY C. JR.

CROSBY, JACKIE
CROSBY, JACQUELINE GART.

CROSBY, JEREMIAH
CROSBY, MICHAEL [HUGH]

CROSBY, LEE
TORREY [BUDLONG], WARE

CROSBY, MILLARD
BRAUN, WILBUR

CROSBY, POLLY
CROSBY, MARY PHELPS [J]

CROSLEY, GEORGE
CHAMBERS, [J.D] WHITTAKER

CROSS, AMANDA
HEILBRUN, CAROLYN GOLD

CROSS, BRENDA
COLLUMS, BRENDA

CROSS, CAITLIN
BERGER, DORANNA

CROSS, CAROLINE
HEATON, JEN M.

CROSS, DAVID
CHESBRO, GEORGE [CLARK]

CROSS, DENNIS
GIBBONS, WILLIAM

CROSS, GENE
COX, ARTHUR JEAN

CROSS, HELEN REEDER
BROADHEAD, HELEN CROSS

CROSS, JAMES
PARRY, HUGH JONES

CROSS, JAY
WILSON, RICHARD

CROSS, M. CLAIRE
CROSS, CLAIRE

CROSS, MARK
PECHEY, ARCHIBALD THOMAS

CROSS, NANCY
BAKER, ANNE

CROSS, POLTON
FEARN, JOHN RUSSELL

CROSS, STEPHEN
BRASINGTON, A. LARRY

CROSS, STEWART
DRAGO, HARRY SINCLAIR

CROSS, T.T.
DA CRUZ, DANIEL JR.

CROSS, THOMSON
WOOD, [SAMUEL] ANDREW

CROSS, VICTOR
COFFMAN, VIRGINIA [E]

CROSS, VICTORIA
CORY, ANNIE SOPHIE

CROSSAN, DARRYL
SMITH, RICHARD REIN

CROSSCOUNTRY
CAMPBELL, THOMAS F.

CROSSE, ELAINE
TRENT, ANN

CROSSE, LAUNCELOT
CARR, FRANK

CROSSE, VICTORIA
GRIFFIN, VIVIAN CORY

CROSSEN, KEN
CROSSEN, KENDELL FOSTER

CROSSTREES, HENRY, JR.
BRUNNER, JOHN [K.H.]

CROSS[E], VICTORIA
CORY, ANNIE SOPHIE

CROUCH, BILL JR.
CRIUCH, WILLIAM MAXWELL

CROUCH, CHARLES ALBAN
PALLANT, NORMAN C.

CROUSE, ANNE D.
CROUSE, ANNE D. JORDAN

CROVES, HAL
TORSVAN, BRUNO TRAVEN

CROW, FRANCIS LUTHER
LUTHER, FRANK

CROW, LEVI
WELLMAN, MANLY WADE

CROWBATE, OPHELIA MAE
SMITH, C.U.

CROWCROFT, JANE
CROWCROFT, PETER

CROWDER, KEN
LEDERER, PAUL JOSEPH

CROWE, C.B.
GIBSON, WALTER B.

CROWE, F.J.
JOHNSTON, JILL

CROWE, JOHN
LYNDS, DENNIS

CROWELL, ANTHONY
COLLINS, ANDREW J.
MERWIN, SAMUEL K. JR.

CROWFIELD, CHRISTOPHER
STOWE, HARRIET E. BEECHER

CROWLE, PIDGEON
CROWLE, EILEEN G.B.

CROWLEIGH, ANN
CUMMINGS, BARBARA
POWER, JO-ANN

CROWLEY, ALISTAIR
CROWLEY, EDWARD ALEXANDER

CROWLEY, LIZ
BLOCK, LAWRENCE

CROWTHER, BRIAN
GRIERSON, EDWARD [D]

CROZETTI, R. WARNER
WARNER-CROZETTI, RUTH G.

CRUD
CRUMB, ROBERT

CRUM THE BUM
CRUMB, ROBERT

CRUMARUMS
CRUMB, ROBERT

CRUMBUM
CRUMB, ROBERT

CRUMPET, PETER
BUCKLEY, FERGUS REID

CRUMSKI
CRUMB, ROBERT

CRUNDEN, REGINALD
CLEAVER, HYLTON REGINALD

CRUNK
CRUMB, ROBERT

CRUSADER IN CORDUROY
LUMMIS, CHARLES F.

CRUSIE, JENNIFER
SMITH, JENNIFER

CRUST, CHRISTIE
DENNISON, ELIZABETH FREE.

CRUSTT
CRUMB, ROBERT

CRUZ, GILBERTO RAFAEL
CRUZ, GILBERT RALPH

CRUZ, MARK
STREIB, DANIEL T.

CRUZ, SOR JUANA INEZ
DE ASUAJE, JUANA R.

CRYING WIND
STAFFORD, LINDA

CRYPTON, DR.
HOFFMAN, PAUL W.
RENAN, SHELDON

CUADRADO, CARLOS MELLIZO
MELLIZO, CARLOS

CUBA, CONNY
BRAND, KURT

CUBAS, BRAZ
DAWES, ROBYN MASON

CUEVA, FRANCOISE
PERUS, FRANCOISE

CUEVAS, PLOTINO
DE AYALA, RAMON PEREZ

CUFF, BARRY
KOSTE, ROBERT FRANCIS

CUISCARD, HENRI
DE LINT, CHARLES

CULEX
STANIER, MAIDA E. KERR

CULLEN, CARTER
MACAULAY, MILDRED
MACAULAY, RICHARD

CULLER, ANNETTE LORENA
PENNEY, ANNETTE CULLER

CULLIGAN, JOE
CULLIGAN, MATTHEW JOSEPH

CULLINGFORD, GUY
TAYLOR, C. LINDSAY

CULLNER, LEONARD
MAZURE, ALFRED LEONARDUS

CULOTTA, NINO
O'GRADY, JOHN PATRICK

CULP, MORGAN
DUNN, DES R.

CULPEPER, MARTIN
PULLEN, GEORGE

CULVER, KATHRYN
DRESSER, DAVIS

CULVER, MAJOR HENRY C.
FARLEY, GEORGE P.

CULVER, TIMOTHY J.
WESTLAKE, DONALD [EDWIN]

CUM, R.
CRUMB, ROBERT

CUMBERLAND, GERALD
KENYON, CHARLES FREDERICK

CUMBERLAND, ROY
MEGROZ, R.L.

CUMBERLAND, STEWART C.
GARNER, CHARLES

CUMBERLAND, STUART
GARNER, CHARLES

CUMMINGS, ANN
RUDOLPH, LEE [N]

CUMMINGS, FLORENCE
BONIME, FLORENCE

CUMMINGS, GABRIEL
CUMMINGS, RAY[MOND KING]

CUMMINGS, JACK
CUMMINGS, JOHN W.

CUMMINGS, KEN
CUMMING-SKINNER, DUGALD M

CUMMINGS, M.A.
CUMMINGS, MONA A.

CUMMINGS, MONETTE
CUMMINGS, MONA A.

CUMMINGS, RAY
CUMMINGS, RAY[MOND KING]

CUMMINGS, RICHARD
GARDNER, RICHARD [M]
ORTH, JOHN

CUNLIFFE, BARRY
CUNLIFFE, BARRINGTON W.

CUNLIFFE, CORINNA
WILDMAN, CORINNA

CUNNING, JERRY E.
LIST, JURGEN E.

CUNNINGHAM, BOB
DIKTY, JULIAN [C] MAY

CUNNINGHAM, CAPT. FRANK
GLICK, CARL CANNON

CUNNINGHAM, CATHY
CUNNINGHAM, CHESTER GRANT

CUNNINGHAM, CECIL C.
BRADBURY, RAY [DOUGLAS]

CUNNINGHAM, CHET
CUNNINGHAM, CHESTER GRANT

CUNNINGHAM, E.
BRADBURY, RAY [DOUGLAS]

CUNNINGHAM, E.V.
FAST, HOWARD [MELVIN]

CUNNINGHAM, J. MORGAN
WESTLAKE, DONALD [EDWIN]

CUNNINGHAM, MARY
PIERCE, MARY CUNNINGHAM

CUNNINGHAM, RAY
ARTHUR, FRANCES BROWN

CUNNINGHAM, VIRGINIA
HOLMGREN, VIRGINIA C.

CURE, CLIFF
BREUCKER, OSCAR HERBERT

CURLE, ADAM
CURLE, CHARLES T.W.

CURLING, AUDREY
CLARK, MARIE CATHERINE A.

CURLING, BILL
CURLING, BRYAN WILLIAM R.

CURNOW, FRANK
ATKINSON, FRANK

CURRAN, BOB
CURRAN, ROBERT

CURRAN, JOHN
REILE, LOUIS ANTHONY

CURRIE, KATY
KYLE, SUSAN E. SPAETH

CURRIE, MARIE M.L.S.
FANE, VIOLET

CURRIE, THOMAS STEWART
RICHARDSON, ANTHONY T.S.C

CURRIER, JAY L.
HENDERSON, JAMES L.

CURRINGTON, O.J.
CURRINGTON, OWEN JOSIAH

CURRIO, TYMAN
CORYELL, JOHN RUSSELL

CURRY, AVON
BOWDEN, JEAN

CURRY, CHRIS
SAYRE, CHERYL CURRY

CURRY, ELISSA
MARTIN, NANCY

CURRY, GENE
MCCURTIN, PETER

CURRY, GLADYS J.
WASHINGTON, GLADYS JOSEPH

CURRY, TOM
CURRY, THOMAS ALBERT

CURRY, WINDELL
SUJATA, ANAGARIKA

CURSON, STANLEY [S]
MERWIN, SAMUEL K. JR.

CURTAYNE, ALICE
RYNNE, ALICE

CURTIN, PATRICIA ROMERO
ROMERO, PATRICIA W.

CURTIN, PHILIP
LOWNDES, MARIE [A] BELLOC

CURTIS, BRAD
LUTZ, GILES A.

CURTIS, DONALD
GALLARDOS MUNOZ, JUAN
RUDOLF, CURTIS D.

CURTIS, GARLAND
GALLARDOS MUNOZ, JUAN

CURTIS, JACKIE
HOLDER, JOHN JR.

CURTIS, JEAN-LOUIS
LAFITTE, LOUIS

CURTIS, JOHN
PETERS, HERMANN
PREBBLE, JOHN E. CURTIS

CURTIS, MARJORIE
PREBBLE, MARJORIE CURTIS

CURTIS, MARY H. [MARY]
CURTIS, MARY HASKELL

CURTIS, PATRICIA
CARLON, PATRICIA BERNADT.

CURTIS, PAUL
CZURA, ROMAN PETER

CURTIS, PETER
LOFTS, NORAH [E.R.]

CURTIS, PRICE
ELLISON, HARLAN

CURTIS, RICHARD HALE
DEMING, RICHARD
KAIL, ROBERT
LEVINSON, LEONARD [L]
MCMAHAN, IAN
RICHARDS, TAD
ROTHWEILER, PAUL R.
STREIB, DANIEL T.
TOOMBS, JOHN

CURTIS, SPENCER
NUTTALL, ANTHONY

CURTIS, STEELE
BITTNER, ARCHIBALD

CURTIS, SUSANNAH
UPSHALL, HELEN

CURTIS, TOM
CURTIS, THOMAS DALE
PENDOWER, THOMAS CURTIS H

CURTIS, WADE
POURNELLE, JERRY

CURTIS, WILL
NUNN, WILLIAM CURTIS

CURVAL, PHILIPPE
TRONCHE, PHILIPPE

CURWILL, W.
ANDREAS, WILLY

CURZON, CHARLES
WHITTINGTON-EGAN, RICHARD

CURZON, CLAIRE
BUCHANAN, EILEEN-MARIE D.

CURZON, CLARE
DUELL, EILEEN-MARIE

CURZON, DANIEL
BROWN, DANIEL A.

CURZON, LUCIA
STEVENSON, FLORENCE

CURZON, SAM
KRASNEY, SAMUEL A.

CURZON, VIRGINIA
HAWTON, HECTOR

CUSH, CAROL GREGOR
GREGOR, CAROL

CUSHING, ENID
CUSHING, ENID LOUISE
NORTON, ANDRE ALICE

CUSHING, E[NID] LOUISE
DAWSON, MABEL LOUISE

CUSHING, PAUL
WOOD-SEYS, ROLAND ALEXAN.

CUSHING, RICHARD CARDINAL
CUSHING, RICHARD JAMES

CUSHMAN, CORRINE
VICTOR, MRS. M.V.

CUSTER, CLINT
PAINE, LAURAN BOSWORTH

CUSTER, TEX
STRONGMAN, MIKE

CUTLER, SAMUEL
FOLSOM, FRANKLIN [B]

CUTRATE, JOE
SPIEGELMAN, ART

CUTTEN, M.J.
CUTTEN, MERVYN JAMES

CUTTER, FRANK
VOLKMAN, DONALD

CUTTER, LEELA
SHANK, LINDA

CUTTER, TOM
RANDISI, ROBERT J.
SHIRLEY, JOHN
WALLMANN, JEFFREY M.

CUTTRISS, FRANK
HINKINS, FRANK R.
HINKINS, R. CUTTRISS

CUYLER, STEPHEN
BATES, BARBARA S.

CYBORG, THOMAS
BUNDGEN, FRANZ-RUDOLF

CYCLOPS
DAY, JOHN ROBERT
LEONARD, JOHN

CYMRY BACH
WOOD, LILLIAN CATHERINE

CYNAN
EVANS-JONES, ALBERT

CYNTHIA
KING, FLORENCE
SEYMOUR, MARJORIE F.

CYPHER, ANGELA
SEIFFERT, MARJORIE A.

CYPRIAN, EDO
ALEXY, EDUARD

CYPRIEN, ANATOLE
DAMBREVILLE, CLAUDE

CYRILLE
D'AVRIL, [BARON] ADOLPH

CZACZKES, SHMUEL YOSEF
AGNON, SHMUEL YOSEF H.

CZASCHKE, ANNMARIE
KOTULLA, ANNEMARIE

CZASKA, TOMASZ
RITTNER, TADEUSZ

CZEPIEL, ADAM
BRZOZOWSKI, LEOPOLD S.L.

CZIBUS, CSABA
MOLNAR, GEZAR

CZURA, R.P.
CZURA, ROMAN PETER

D'A.P.
POWER, SIR D'ARCY

D'AGYRE, GILLES
KLEIN, GERARD

D'ALLARD, HUNTER
BALLARD, W. TODHUNTER

D'ALLENGER, HUGH
KERSHAW, JOHN HUGH

D'ALPENS, MARGUESA
WILLIAMSON, ALICE M.L.

D'ALPINS, MARCHIONESS
WILLIAMSON, ALICE M.L.

D'ANDREA, KATE
PHILLIPS, KATHLEEN
STEINER, BARBARA [A]

D'ANGELO, LOU
D'ANGELO, LUCIANO

D'ANTIBES, GERMAIN
SIMENON, GEORGES [J.C]

D'ARCANGELO, ANGELO
BUSH, JOSEF

D'ARCOS, J. PACO
DA SILVA, JOAQUIM B.C.

D'ARCY, JACK
CAVE, HUGH B[ARNETT]
CHAMPION, D'ARCY LYNDON

D'ARCY, PAMELA
ROBY, MARY LINN

D'ARCY, WILLARD
COX, WILLIAM ROBERT

D'ARDENNE, JEAN
DOMMARTIN, LEON

D'ARFEY, WILLIAM
PLOMER, WILLIAM C.F.

D'ARGYRE, GILLES
KLEIN, GERARD

D'ARLE, MARCELLA
BOCHSKANDL, MARCELLA

D'ARLES, HENRI
BEAUDE, HENRI

D'ASTOR, JEAN
ORSAT, JEAN-FRANCOIS

D'AUBIGY, PIERRE
MENCKEN, HENRY LOUIS

D'AVOI, PAUL
ERIE, PAUL

D'EASUM, DICK
D'EASUM, CEDRIC GODFREY

D'EAU, JEAN
GOULD, ALLAN MENDELL

D'ELIA, MARIA
GOUDISS, MARIA A. D'ELIA

D'ESME, JEAN
D'ESMENARD, JEAN

D'ESTERRE, NEVILLE
REED, PETER HUGH

D'ESTRIAN, P.
NORTON, CHARLES LEDYARD

D'HOUVILLE, GERARD
DE HEREDIA, MARIE L.A.

D'ISLY, GEORGES
SIMENON, GEORGES [J.C]

D'IVRY, URSULA
RUSSELL, URSULA D'IVRY

D'OCTON, VIGNE
KERHOUEL, GAETAN

D'URSTELLE, PIERRE
DORST, JEAN PIERRE

D, E.A.B.
BLAND, E.A.

D., A.E.
DRACOTT, ALICE ELIZABETH

D.E.A.
DOMINICK, MARGARET

D.G.M.
MITCHELL, DONALD GRANT

D.I.
INNES, DUNCAN

D.M.S.
STUART, DOROTHY MARGARET

D.P.
WELLS, H.G.

D.V.S.
HEDGE, CARO

DA BYOLA, UGO
BOLAY, KARL-HEINZ

DABNEY, ANN
BROWN, LOIS ANN
JACKSON, NANCY

DACE, TISH
DACE, LETITIA [S]

DACQUIN, FELICITY
DEAKING, PHYLLIS A.

DACRE, [CAPTAIN] STANLEY
HYATT, STANLEY PORTAL

DAEDALUS
BRAMESCO, NORTON J.
CORDES, THEODORE K.

DAEMER, WILL
MILLER, BILL[Y]
WADE, ROBERT [BOB]

DAFT, TENNYSON J.
MORGAN, THOMAS P.

DAGAN, AVIGDOR
FISCHL, VIKTOR

DAGERMAN, STIG
ANDERSSON, STIG

DAGH, EVA
BJARNE, IVAN

DAGMAR
CAMERON, LOU

DAGMAR, PETER
PINCHIN, FRANK J[AMES]

DAGOBERT, CHRYSOSTOME
LED'HUY, JEAN B.A.

DAGON, LERIE
MCCORMICK, JAMES

DAGONET
SIMS, GEORGE ROBERT

DAGONET, EDWARD
WILLIAMSON, THAMES ROSS

DAHL, FRITZ
DONNY, JULIUS

DAHL, JOHN
REMAR, FRITS

DAHLMANN, GERT
DIAMANT, GERTRUD

DAHLSTIERNA, GUNNO
EURELIUS, GUNNO

DAIAN, KADYR
DAIANOV, KADYR K.

DAIMLER, HARRIET
OWENS, IRIS

DAIN, ALEX
LUKEMAN, ALEX

DAIN, CATHERINE
GARWOOD, JUDITH

DAIR, CHRISTINA
KAKU, LOUZANA

DAKHOW
DIHKHODA, ALI AKBAR

DAKOTAN
WINSTED, HULDAH L.

DALBY, B.J.
MAPLES, EVELYN LUCILLE

DALE, ADAM
HOLLOWAY, BRIAN W.

DALE, ADRIAN
FULLER, EDITH JEAN

DALE, ALAN
COHEN, ALFRED J.

DALE, AUSTIN
CALVERT, WILLIAM ROBINSON

DALE, COLIN
LAWRENCE, THOMAS EDWARD

DALE, DARLEY
STEELE, FRANCESCA MARIA

DALE, DASH
RATHBORNE, ST. GEORGE

DALE, DONALD
BUCKNER, MARY DALE

DALE, EDWIN
HOME-GALL, EDWARD REG.

DALE, ELLIS
MACKENZIE, G.A.

DALE, ESTHER
MAY, ELAINE

DALE, ESTIL
CUNNINGHAM, ALBERT B.

DALE, FRANCES
CRADOCK, PHYLLIS NAN S.

DALE, GEORGE E.
ASIMOV, ISAAC

DALE, JACK
HOLLIDAY, JOSEPH

DALE, JENNIFER
WHITE, CHARLOTTE

DALE, MAXINE
COVERT, ALICE LENT

DALE, NORMAN
DENNY, NORMAN GEORGE
TUBB, E.C.

DALE, RICHARD
FISH, ROY
LANSDALE, JOE R.

DALE, ROBIN
HADFIELD, ALAN

DALE, ROMAN
CZURA, ROMAN PETER

DALE, RUTH JEAN
DURAN, BETTY
STRIBBLING, JEAN

DALE, SEPTIMUS
UTLEY, STEVEN

DALE, V.R.
VAN HORN, DALE R.

DALE, WILLIAM
DANIELS, NORMAN A.

DALESMAN
DE COURCY-PARRY, CHARLES

DALEY, BILL
APPLEMAN, JOHN ALAN

DALEY, KATHLEEN
DALEY, MARGARET K.R.

DALEY, KIT
DALEY, MARGARET K.R.

DALEY, SHARON
BAROVSKY, SHARON DALEY

DALGLEISH, JAMES
DALGLEISH, JAMES CORTEEN

DALHEATH, DAVID
MAGRILL, DAVID S.

DALL, IAN
HIGGINS, CHARLES

DALLAS, ATHENA GIANAKAS
DALLAS-DAMIS, ATHENA G.

DALLAS, DAN
APPEL, WALTER

DALLAS, IAN
DAVIS, IAN

DALLAS, JOHN
DUNCAN, W. MURDOCH

DALLAS, MIKE T.
LAZENBY, NORMAN A.

DALLAS, RICHARD
WILLIAMS, NATHAN WINSLOW

DALLAS, RUTH
MUMFORD, RUTH

DALLAS, SANDRA
ATCHISON, SANDRA DALLAS

DALLAS, STEVE
KING, ALBERT

DALLAS, VINCENT
WERNER, VICTOR EMILE

DALLAS, WALTER
LYNDS, DENNIS

DALLIN, DAVID J.
LEVIN, DAVID I.

DALLMANN, EHM
DOLL, HERBERT GERHARD

DALMAS, JOHN
JONES, JOHN ROBERT
MANDEL, LEO N.

DALMOCAND
MACDONALD, GEORGE A.

DALRY
WILSON, ARTHUR

DALTON, ALENE
CHAPIN, ALENE O. DALTON

DALTON, CLAIRE
BURNS, ALMA

DALTON, CLIVE
CLARK, FREDERICK STEPHEN

DALTON, EMILY
ALLEN, DANICE JO

DALTON, FRANK
FALK, HERMANN

DALTON, GENA
DELLIN, BILLIE GENELL

DALTON, HOWARD
VAN HORN, DALE R.

DALTON, JACKIE
TRAUTMAN, JACKIE

DALTON, JENIFER
WIND, DAVID MILTON

DALTON, KIT
CUNNINGHAM, CHESTER GRANT

DALTON, MARK MAXWELL
MCDONALD, TRACY

DALTON, MORAY
COLLIER, HUGH
HAMES, ARTHUR CAXTON

DALTON, PRISCILLA
AVALLONE, MICHAEL

DALTON, SEAN
BLAKENEY, JAY D.
CHESTER, DEBORAH ANN

DALVANO, TONY
CALVANO, TONY

DALY, HAMLIN
PRICE, E. HOFFMAN

DALY, JIM
STRATEMEYER, EDWARD

DALY, JOHN
BESEMERES, JOHN

DALY, LT. JONATHAN
HUBBARD, L. RON

DALY, MARTIN
MACKENNA, STEPHEN

DALY, MARY VIRGENE
DALY, MARY VIRGINIA

DALY, MAUREEN
MCGIVERN, MAUREEN DALY

DALY, NIKI
DALY, NICHOLAS

DALY, RANN
PALMER, EDWARD VANCE

DALZEL, PETER
DALZEL-JOB, PATRICK

DAMANN, GUSTAV
REHN, GOTTFRIED

DAMIANO, LAILO
ROSENKRANTZ, LINDA

DAMIEN, CHRISTINE
KREKE, CYNTIA

DAMMANN, PETER
MUHE, WERNER

DAMOCLES
BENEDETTI, MARIO

DAMON, CARL
DEMMON, CALVIN W.

DAMON, GENE
GRIER, BARBARA G.D.

DAMON, KATE
BROWNLEY, MARGARET

DAMON, LEE
LOOK, JANE H.

DAMON, RAY
NORDAY, MICHAEL

DAMON, ROGER
EISELE, MARTIN

DAMON, ROGER
GIESA, WERNER K.

DAMOR, HAKJI
LESSER, ROGER HAROLD

DAMROSCH, HELEN
TEE-VAN, HELEN DAMROSCH

DAMROSCH, HELEN THERESE
TEE-VAN, HELEN DAMROSCH

DANA, AMBER
PAINE, LAURAN BOSWORTH

DANA, E.H.
HAMEL PEIFER, KATHLEEN

DANA, ERIN
ELLIOTT, NANCY

DANA, FREEMAN
TAYLOR, PHOEBE ATWOOD

DANA, RICHARD
PAINE, LAURAN BOSWORTH

DANA, ROSE
ROSS, DON
ROSS, WILLIAM E. DANIEL

DANACHAIR, CAOIMHIM O
DANAHER, KEVIN

DANBY, FRANK
FRANKAU, JULIA DAVIS

DANBY, MARY
CALVERT, MARY H. DANBY

DANCE, FRANK E.X.
DANCE, FRANCIS ESBURN X.

DANCER, J.B.
HARVEY, JOHN [BARTON]
WELLS, ANGUS

DANCER, LACEY
COOK, S.A.

DANCER, RUSSELL
PRONZINI, WILLIAM JOHN

DANCEY, MAX
GRAINGER, PETER

DANCO, KATHY
DANCO, KATHERINE LECK

DANCY, M.M.
MCCLENDON, MARIE M.D.

DANDOO, PETER
LOHNDORFF, ERNST F.

DANDRIDGE, RAY G.
DANDRIDGE, RAYMOND GARF.

DANE, CARL
ADAMS, F. RAMSAY

DANE, CHRISTOPHER
DEBOLT, ADRIANA

DANE, CLEMENCE
ASHTON, WINIFRED

DANE, DANIEL
HANSON, ERNEST S.

DANE, DONALD
CUMMING-SKINNER, DUGALD M

DANE, EVA
DAWES, EDNA

DANE, JOEL Y.
DELANEY, JOSEPH FRANCIS

DANE, MARK
AVALLONE, MICHAEL

DANE, MARY
MORLAND, NIGEL

DANE, W.N.
ACKERMAN, WENDAYNE

DANE, ZEL
TIMMS, EDWARD VIVIAN

DANELLA, UTTA
VERLAG, FRANZ SCHNEEKLUTH

DANER, PAUL
STOKOE, E[DWARD] G[EORGE]

DANESFORD, EARLE
SYMONDS, FRANCIS A.

DANGER, BRYAN
RAHN, WOLFGANG

DANGER, DAMION
RELLERGERD, HELMUT

DANGER, PRESTON
MURRAY, WILLIAM P.

DANGERFIELD, BALFOUR
MCCLOSKEY, [JOHN] ROBERT

DANGERFIELD, CLINT
NORWOOD, VICTOR [G.C.]

DANGERFIELD, HARLAN
PADGETT, RON

DANGERFIELD, HARRY
PATTEN, WILLIAM GEORGE

DANGERFIELD, JOHN
CRAWFURD, OSWALD J.F.

DANGERFIELD, L.D.
NORWOOD, VICTOR [G.C.]

DANGERFIELD, PAUL
NORWOOD, VICTOR [G.C.]

DANGLE
THOMPSON, A.M.

DANIEL
GARCIA, EDUARDA

DANIEL, ANNE
STEINER, BARBARA [A]

DANIEL, BECKY
DANIEL, REBECCA

DANIEL, COLIN
WINDSOR, PATRICIA FRANCES

DANIEL, ELNA WORRELL
STONE, ELNA

DANIEL, GLYN
DANIEL, GLYN [EDMUND]

DANIEL, LAURENT
BLICK, ELSA

DANIEL, LEE
REID, DANIEL P. JR.

DANIEL, MARK
FITZGEORGE-PARKER, MARK D

DANIEL, MEGAN
MEYER, DONNA

DANIEL, S.
ZALBERG, DANIEL

DANIEL-ROPS, HENRI
PETIOT, HENRI JULES C.

DANIELL, DAVID SCOTT
DANIELL, ALBERT SCOTT

DANIELS, BRETT
ADLER, RENATA

DANIELS, CAROL
VIENS, CAROL

DANIELS, DANA
BRAUER, DEANA

DANIELS, DEWEY
MCKIMMEY, JAMES

DANIELS, DOROTHY
DANBERG, DOROTHY SMITH
DANIELS, NORMAN & DOROTHY

DANIELS, FRANK
LINDSAY, DAN

DANIELS, GIL
DAVIS, GYLE
DUCETTE, VINCE

DANIELS, JAN
ROSS, WILLIAM E. DANIEL

DANIELS, JANE
ROSS, WILLIAM E. DANIEL

DANIELS, JIM
DANIELS, JAMES RAYMOND

DANIELS, JOHN S.
OVERHOLSER, WAYNE D.

DANIELS, JOLEEN
SCHIMEK, GAYLE MALONE

DANIELS, JUDITH
PELFREY, JUDITH

DANIELS, KAYLA
HOFLAND, KARIN

DANIELS, KRISTY
DANIELS, NORMAN A.
MONTEE, KRISTY

DANIELS, LEIGH
CHANCE, LISBETH L.

DANIELS, LOUIS G.
GALOUYE, DANIEL F.

DANIELS, MAGGIE
DAVIS, MAGGIE S.

DANIELS, MARK
ELROD, MARK

DANIELS, MAX
GELLIS, ROBERTA L.J.

DANIELS, NORMAN
LEE, ELSIE

DANIELS, NORMAN A.
DANBERG, NORMAN A.

DANIELS, OLGA
SINCLAIR, OLGA ELLEN

DANIELS, PAUL
FAIRMAN, PAUL W.

DANIELS, PHILIP
CHAMBERS, PETER
PHILLIPS, DENNIS JOHN A.

DANIELS, REBECCA
FATTARSI, ANN MARIE

DANIELS, RHETT
PELFREY, JUDITH

DANIELS, TOPSON
SONTUP, DANIEL

DANIELS, TOPSUN
SONTUP, DANIEL

DANIELS, VAL
THOMPSON, ALFIE

DANIELSON, J.D.
JAMES, M.R.

DANIGER, MARGOT
SALOMON-DANIGER, MARGOT

DANILOWSKI, GUSTAW
ORWID, WLADYSLAW

DANN, EDWARD
DETTMANN, HANS EDUARD

DANN, NORMA
DANIELS, NORMAN A.

DANNAY, FREDERIC
NATHAN, DANIEL

DANNER, KURT
MEYN, NIELS

DANNER, WILL
MILLER, BILL[Y]
WADE, ROBERT [BOB]

DANNER, WILLIAM M.
MILLER, BILL[Y]

DANNING, MELROD
GLUCK, SINCLAIR

DANRIT, CAPITAINE
DANRIT, EMILE A.

DANSON, SHERYL
MUNSON, SHERYL MCDANEL

DANTON, REBECCA
ROBERTS, JANET LOUISE

DANTZ, WILLIAM R.
PHILBRICK, WILLIAM RODMAN

DANVERS, JACK
CASELEYR, CAMILLE A.M.

DANVERS, MILTON
LONG, J. EDMOND

DANVERS, PETER
HENDERSON, JAMES MADDOCK

DANYER, ROY
KELLEY, THOMAS P.

DANZELL, GEORGE
BOND, NELSON S.

DANZIGER, ADOLPHE
DE CASTRO, GUSTAF A.D.

DANZIGER, DAVID
HORNWOOD, HARVEY

DANZIGER, GUSTAF A.
DE CASTRO, GUSTAF A.D.

DAO, HOANG
TUONG-LONG, NGUYEN

DARBY, CATHERINE
PETERS, MAUREEN

DARBY, EMMA
STUBBS, JEAN

DARBY, GENE
DARBY, JEAN [KEGLEY]

DARBY, GENE KEGLEY
DARBY, JEAN [KEGLEY]

DARBY, J.N.
GOVAN, [MARY] C.N.

DARBY, JOHN
GARRETSON, JAMES E.

DARBY, LYNDAN
GRIMSLEY, ANN
KINNERLEY, LYNNE

DARBY, RUTH
PAINE, RUTH DARBY

DARBYSHIRE, SHIRLEY
MEYNELL, SHIRLEY RUTH

DARCY, JEAN
LEPLEY, JEAN ELIZABETH

DARCY, JENNA
CHASTAIN, SANDRA
KNIGHT, NANCY CHRISTOPHER

DARDI
SINGH, GOPAL

DARE, ALAN
GOODCHILD, GEORGE

DARE, CAPTAIN
SHAW, STANLEY GORDON

DARE, EVELYN
EVERETT-GREEN, EVELYN

DARE, HOWARD
BYRNE, STUART J.

DARE, ISHMAEL
JOSE, ARTHUR WILBERFORCE

DARE, JESSICA
LESLIE, JOANNA

DARE, M.P.
DARE, MARCUS PAUL

DARE, MICHAEL
WORDINGHAM, JAMES A.

DARE, ROLAND
MORRIS, CHARLES [S]

DARE, SIMON
HUXTABLE, MARJORIE

DARGON
MACGILL, GEORGE

DARIEN, PETER
BASSETT, WILLIAM B.K.

DARING, VICTOR
GANNON, E.J.

DARIO, RUBEN
SARMIENTO, FELIX RUBEN G.

DARION, JOE
DARION, JOSEPH

DARK, JAMES
MACDONNELL, JAMES EDMOND
WILKES-HUNTER, RICHARD
WORKMAN, JAMES

DARK, JASON
APPEL, WALTER
EISELE, MARTIN
RELLERGERD, HELMUT
TENKRAT, FRIEDRICH
WUNDERER, RICHARD JR.

DARK, JOHNNY
MCCORMICK, JAMES
NORWOOD, VICTOR [G.C.]

DARK, LARRY
DARK, LAWRENCE CHARNY

DARKE, DAVID
DEE, RON

DARKE, JAMES
JAMES, LAURENCE

DARLING, BETH
FEARN, JOHN RUSSELL

DARLING, DING
DARLING, JAY NORWOOD

DARLING, HOPE
JOHNSON, ANNA M.

DARLING, JOAN
STUART, DORIS

DARLING, KATHY
DARLING, MARY KATHLEEN

DARLING, SANDRA
DAY, ALEXANDRA

DARLING, V.H.
DRYHURST, MICHAEL JOHN

DARLINGTON, CON
BEST, CAROL ANN

DARLINGTON, JOY
AUMENTE, JOY

DARLTON, CLARK
ERNSTING, WALTER

DARMANN, ERNA
HAARMANN, ERNA

DARRAN, MARK
GODDARD, NORMAN M.

DARRELL, ELIZABETH
DAWES, EDNA

DARRICH, SYBAH
DI PRIMA, DIANE

DARRICK, SYBAH
ASHBY, RICHARD

DARRINGTON, PETER
GIBSON, WALTER B.

DARROW, JACK
KORNOELJE, CLIFFORD

DARRY, HARRY
PFEFFER, HEINRICH

DARTEY, LEO
FECHY, HENRIETTE

DARU, JULISKA
CRAINE, EDITH JANICE

DARWIN, JEANETTE
SCHULER, CANDACE L.

DARWIN, LEN
DARWIN, LEONARD

DARWIN, M.B.
MCDAVID, RAVEN I.

DASHIELL, SAMUEL
HAMMETT, DASHIELL

DASILVA, LEON
WALLMANN, JEFFREY M.

DASKAM, JOSEPHINE DODGE
BACON, JOSEPHINE D.

DASS, RAM
ALPERT, RICHARD

DATALLER, ROGER
EAGLESTONE, ARTHUR ARCH.

DAUB, HANS
HODANN, VALERIE

DAUD, DAVID
PENNINGTON, DAVID ALEXAN.

DAUMAS, MARIA RENEE
MECKE, MARIA RENEE

DAUNT, ATHERLEY
EVANS, FRANK HOWELL

DAUPHINE, CLAUDE
WEISS, JOE

DAUPHINE-AUMONT
WEISS, JOE

DAUTHAGE, HEINRICH
ARNOLDI, HENRIQUE DI

DAVE, SHYAM
GANTZER, COLEEN & HUGH

DAVENPORT, ADELAIDE
AIKEN, ALBERT W.

DAVENPORT, FRANCES HELEN
AIKEN, ALBERT W.

DAVENPORT, FRANCINE
TATE, VELMA

DAVENPORT, NEAL
LUIF, KURT

DAVENPORT, SPENCER
STRATEMEYER, EDWARD

DAVENPORT, TEX
TILTMAN, HUGH HESSELL

DAVEY, JOCELYN
RAPHAEL, CHAIM

DAVEY, JOHN
RICHEY, DAVID

DAVID, A.R.
DAVID, A[NN] ROSALIE

DAVID, ANDREW
WHITTINGHAM, RICHARD

DAVID, CAY
LUAN, CARLA CAMERON

DAVID, ED
WOHLMUTH, ED

DAVID, EMILY
ALMAN, DAVID & EMILY

DAVID, ERNST
EICHLER, ERNST

DAVID, JAY
ADLER, WILLIAM

DAVID, JONATHAN
AMES, LEE J.

DAVID, JOSEPH BEN
BEN-DAVID, JOSEPH

DAVID, K.
ROBERTSON, ALICE A.

DAVID, KIRK
CHAMBERS, DEREK HYDE

DAVID, LEON
JACOB, [CYPRIEN] MAX

DAVID, NICHOLAS
MORGAN, THOMAS BRUCE

DAVID, R.W.
DAVID, RICHARD W.

DAVID, ROSALIE
DAVID, A[NN] ROSALIE

DAVID, WILLIAM
SANDMAN, PETER M.

DAVIDS, BOB
DAVIDS, LEONARD ROBERT

DAVIDS, MARILYN
WIND, DAVID MILTON

DAVIDSON, ANDREA
LOWE, SUSAN [CLAIRE] L.

DAVIDSON, ANGELA
MERWIN, SAMUEL K. JR.
WINSTEAD, REBECCA NOYES

DAVIDSON, BILL
DAVIDSON, WILLAIM

DAVIDSON, BILL R.
DAVIDSON, WILLIAM R.

DAVIDSON, CLARISSA START
LIPPERT, CLARISSA START

DAVIDSON, GENE A.
LESPERANCE, DAVID

DAVIDSON, HUGH
HAMILTON, EDMOND

DAVIDSON, JOHN
NUETZEL, CHARLES A.
REID, CHARLES [STUART]

DAVIDSON, JULIANA
DAVIS, JULIE

DAVIDSON, LAWRENCE H.
LAWRENCE, DAVID HERBERT

DAVIDSON, MARION
GARIS, HOWARD R.

DAVIDSON, MELANIE
ARNOLD, MADELYN M.

DAVIDSON, MICHAEL
RORVIK, DAVID MICHAEL

DAVIDSON, MICKIE
DAVIDSON, MARGARET C.

DAVIDSON, PAUL
BACOT, CLAUDE

DAVIDSON, R.
DAVIDSON, RAYMOND

DAVIDSON, T.L.
THOMSON, DAVID L.

DAVIDSON, WILDER BRISTOL
PATTERSON, ARTHUR W.

DAVIE-MARTIN, HUGH
MCCUTCHEON, HUGH [D-M]

DAVIED, CAMILLE
ROSE, CAMILLE DAVIED

DAVIES
DAVIES, GORDON C.

DAVIES, ALWYN
EVANS, CHRIS[TOPHER D.]

DAVIES, CHRISTIE
DAVIES, JOHN CHRISTOPHER

DAVIES, COLIN
ELLIOT, IAN

DAVIES, ERNEST
MARTIN, OLIVER

DAVIES, FRANCES
LEWENSOHN, LEONE

DAVIES, FREDERIC
LANGLEY, FREDERIC

DAVIES, FREDRIC
ELLIK, RON
TOLLIVER, STEVE

DAVIES, GWYNNETH
DELLIGAN, WILLIAM F.

DAVIES, IRIS
GOWER, IRIS

DAVIES, JASPER
DAVIES, JOHN E.W.

DAVIES, LOUISE
GOLDING, LOUISE

DAVIES, LUCIEN
BEESTON, L.J.

DAVIES, M.C
DAVIES, MARY CATHERINE

DAVIES, MARION
DOURAS, MARION CECILIA

DAVIES, MELISSA
DAVIS, GORDON WINTHROP

DAVIES, P.C.W.
DAVIES, PAUL C.W.

DAVIES, RICHARD LLEWELYN
LLEWELYN-DAVIES, RICHARD

DAVIES, THOMAS B.
KOBUSCH, HELMUT

DAVIES, TOM
DAVIES, THOMAS

DAVIES, WALTER C.
KORNBLUTH, C[YRIL] M.

DAVIGNON, GRACE
GLASBY, JOHN S.

DAVIN, DAN
DAVIN, DANIEL MARCUS

DAVIOT, GORDON
MACKINTOSH, ELIZABETH

DAVIS
DAVIS, ROGER

DAVIS, AUDREY
PAINE, LAURAN BOSWORTH

DAVIS, B. LYNCH
BIOY CASARES, ADOLFO
BORGES, JORGE LUIS

DAVIS, BARBARA STEINCROHN
DAVIS, MAGGIE S.

DAVIS, BETTY
DAVIS, RUTH ELIZABETH

DAVIS, CARSON
NUETZEL, CHARLES A.

DAVIS, CHAN
DAVIS, HORACE CHANDLER

DAVIS, CLIFF
SMITH, RICHARD REIN

DAVIS, DON L.
DRESSER, DAVIS

DAVIS, DON
DRESSER, DAVIS

DAVIS, E. ADAMS
DAVIS, EDWIN ADAMS

DAVIS, ELIZABETH
DAVIS, LOU ELLEN

DAVIS, EMMA
DAVIS, MAGGIE S.

DAVIS, FOXCROFT
SEAWELL, MOLLY ELLIOT

DAVIS, FRANCIS
JENNISON, JOHN WILLIAM

DAVIS, FRED
NUETZEL, CHARLES A.

DAVIS, GIL
GILMORE, DON

DAVIS, GITA
ROSE, EVELYN GITA

DAVIS, GORDON
LEVINSON, LEONARD [L]
HUNT, E. HOWARD

DAVIS, GYLE
DUCETTE, VINCE

DAVIS, H.L.
DAVIS, HAROLD LENOIR

DAVIS, HARLEY
GREEN, KAY

DAVIS, HARRY
SEBENTHAL, ROBERTA E.

DAVIS, J. MADISON
DAVIS, JAMES MADISON

DAVIS, JAY
NUETZEL, CHARLES A.

DAVIS, JIM
DAVIS, JAMES ROBERT
SMITH, RICHARD REIN

DAVIS, JULIA
MARSH, JOHN

DAVIS, JUSTINE
SMITH, JANICE DAVIS

DAVIS, KATHERINE
DAVIS, MILDRED WIRT

DAVIS, KENT
GALLARDOS MUNOZ, JUAN

DAVIS, LESLIE
GUCCIONE, LESLIE DAVIS

DAVIS, MARALEE G.
GIBSON, MARALEE G.
THIBAULT, MARALEE G.

DAVIS, MAXINE
MCHUGH, MAXINE DAVIS

DAVIS, MELANIE
JORDAN, DEBORAH [DEBBIE]
WILLIAMS, CLAUDETTE

DAVIS, MILDRED
DAVIS, CATHERINE
DAVIS, MILDRED

DAVIS, NEIL
DAVIS, THOMAS NEIL

DAVIS, NICK
DAVIS, NICHOLAS

DAVIS, NORBERT
GAULT, WILLIAM CAMPBELL

DAVIS, PAT
PATTEE, DAVID

DAVIS, R.
DAVIS, ROGER

DAVIS, ROBERT
DEMING, ROBERT

DAVIS, ROBERT HART
CURTIS, RICHARD [A]
DEMING, RICHARD
EDMONDS, IVY GORDON
JAKES, JOHN [WILLIAM]
LONG, FRANK BELKNAP
LYNDS, DENNIS
POWELL, TALMAGE
PRONZINI, WILLIAM JOHN
VENTURA, CHARLES
WALLMANN, JEFFREY M.
WHITTINGTON, HARRY

DAVIS, ROSEMARY L.
DAVIS, LILY M. & ROSEMARY
DAVIS, ROSEMARY

DAVIS, SONIA
GREENE, SONIA HAFT DAVIS

DAVIS, SONIA H.
GREENE, SONIA HAFT DAVIS

DAVIS, STRATFORD
BOLTON, MAISIE SHARMAN

DAVIS, SUZANNE
SUGAR, BERT RANDOLPH

DAVIS, T.N.
DAVIS, THOMAS NEIL

DAVIS, WENDI
HOLDER, NANCY L. JONES

DAVIS, WILLIAM
PRONZINI, WILLIAM JOHN
WALLMANN, JEFFREY M.

DAVIS, ZEKE
DAVIS, WILLIAM F.

DAVIS, [MARY] BERNICE
CURLER, [MARY] BERNICE

DAVISON, JULIE
DAVISON, JULIANNA

DAVITZ, J.R.
DAVITZ, JOEL ROBERT

DAVYDOVA, NATALIE
DAVYDOVA, MAII M.

DAVYS, SARAH
MANNING, ROSEMARY JOY

DAWE, FREDERICK
GETTINGS, FRED

DAWES, DOROTHY
COOPER, PARLEY J.

DAWLISH, PETER
KERR, JAMES LENNOX

DAWN, ADAM
MURRAY, WILLIAM P.

DAWSON, A.J.
DAWSON, ALEC JOHN

DAWSON, CLAY
LEVINSON, LEONARD [L]

DAWSON, ELIZABETH
GEACH, CHRISTINE

DAWSON, ELMER A.
STRATEMEYER, EDWARD

DAWSON, ERASMUS
DEVON, PAUL

DAWSON, FRANCINE
HUFF, URSULA

DAWSON, GERALYN
WILLIAMS, GERALYN DAWSON

DAWSON, JANE
CRITCHLOW, DOROTHY

DAWSON, JIM
DAWSON, JAMES LEE

DAWSON, LAWRENCE H.
LAWRENCE, DAVID HERBERT

DAWSON, MABEL LOUISE
CUSHING, ENID LOUISE

DAWSON, MICHAEL
BOYLE, JOHN HOWARD JACKSN

DAWSON, OLIVER
COXALL, JACK ARTHUR

DAWSON, PETER
FAUST, FREDERICK S.
GAYLORD, OTIS HEMMINGWAY
GLIDDEN, JONATHAN H.
GRAYLORD, OTIS

DAWSON, SARANNE
HOOVER, SARANNE

DAX, ANTHONY
HUNTER, ALFRED JOHN

DAY, ADRIAN
HARVEY, PETER NOEL

DAY, ADRIENNE
ANDERSEN, LINDA

DAY, ANNE
LOTHRINGER, ANNE & FRED

DAY, DERRICK
KOHR, DIETRICH

DAY, DONALD
HARDING, DONALD EDWARD

DAY, GENE
DAY, HOWARD E.

DAY, HARVEY
CLEARY, C.V.H.

DAY, HOUSTON
DAY, SAM HOUSTON

DAY, IRENE
ORME, EVE

DAY, JOCELYN
MCCOURTNEY, LORENA KNOLL

DAY, LILA
CHAFFIN, LILLIE D.

DAY, LIONEL
BLACK, LADBROKE LIONEL D.

DAY, LUCINDA
FLASSCHOEN, MARIE
SCHEIRMAN, MARIAM

DAY, MAX
CASSIDAY, BRUCE [BINGHAM]

DAY, MICHAEL
DEMPEWOLFF, RICHARD F.

DAY, PATIENCE
ZAWADSKY, PATIENCE

DAY, SAMANTHA
COURCELLES, SANDRA

DAY, WILLIAM
DERRINCOURT, WILLIAM

DAY-HELVIG, ANNE
LOTHRINGER, ANNE & FRED

DAYBREAK
GRAY, CLEMENT

DAYE, JOHN
ADYE, SIR JOHN

DAYLE, MALCOLM
HINCKS, CYRIL MALCOLM

DAYTON, LILY
HAMPTON, LINDA

DAYTON, PERRY
KALMUCZAK, ROLF

DAZAI, OSAMU
TSUSHIMA, SHUJI

DE ANDRADE, OSWALD
DE SOUSA, JOSE OSWALD

DE ANGELIS, NANCY
ANGELO, NANCY CAROLYN H.

DE ARAUGO-O'MULLANE, TESS
DE ARAUGO, TESS S.

PSEUDONYMS

DE BALKER, HABAKUK II
TER BALKT, HERMAN H.

DE BALLARD, JEAN
ROSKOLENKO, HARRY

DE BARRINKH, LENTZ
BERNDT, KARL-HEINZ

DE BARY, BRETT
NEE, BRETT DE BARY

DE BEAUREGARD, HENRI
CUMMING-SKINNER, DUGALD M

DE BEAUSABRE, JULIA M.
NAMIER, JULIA

DE BEAUSOBRE, IULIA
NAMIER, JULIA

DE BEKKER, JAY
WINCHELL, PRENTICE

DE BERGERAC, CYRANO
DE CYRANO, SAVINIEN

DE BOIS, HELMA
DE BOIS, WILHELMINA

DE BOLT, JOE
DE BOLT, JOSEPH WAYNE

DE BORCHGRAVE, ARNAUD
D'ALTENA, ARNAUD DE BORC.

DE BORCHGRAVE, ARNAUD
MOSS, ROBERT

DE BORN, EDITH
BISCH, EDITH

DE BOUT, JACQUES
GITTLER, LEWIS F.

DE BOVET, MARIE ANNE
DE BOIS-HEBERT, GUY [MAR]

DE BRISSAC, MALCOLM
DICKINSON, PETER

DE BROGLIE, L.
DE BROGLIE, LOUIS VICTOR

DE BURGH, A.
ALBOROUGH, EDWARD MORGAN

DE CAIRE, EDWIN
WILLIAMS, EDWIN ALFRED

DE CAMPOS, ALVARO
PESSOA, FERNANDO [A.N.]

DE CAMPOS, L.
DAHL, LINDA

DE CASSERES, BENJAMIN
SMITH, CLARK ASHTON

DE CASTRO, ADOLPHE
DE CASTRO, GUSTAF A.D.

DE CASTRO, LYNE
LYNE, CHARLES

DE CAUX, LEN
DE CAUX, LEONARD HOWARD

DE CESCO, FEDERICA
KITAMURA, FEDERICA

DE CHABRILLAN, CELESTE
CHABRILLAN, E. CELESTE DE

DE CHALON, PIERRE
SCHEER, KARL-HERBERT

DE CHARDIN, PIERRE TEILH.
TEILHARD DE CHARDIN, MARI

DE CHATELLERAULT, VICTOR
BEAUDOIN, KENNETH LAWR.

DE COSQUEVILLE, PIERRE
DE COSQUEVILLE STACEY, P.

DE COSTA, HENRY
POHL, FREDERIK

DE COTI, WERNER
KRUEGER, WERNER

DE CRESPIGNY, CHARLES
WILLIAMSON, ALICE M.L.
WILLIAMSON, CHARLES N.

DE CROISSET, FRANCIS
WIENER, FRANZ

DE CULWEN, DOROTHEA
HINES, DOROTHEA

DE DELORCA, FRANK
HARY, WILFRID A.

DE EXTRAMUROS, QUIXOTE
ESPINO, FEDERICO LICSI JR

DE FACCI, LIANE
DE BELLET, LIANE

DE FARNIENTE, BEAUREGARD
DE LATOUCHE, JACQUES CHAS

DE FLETIN, P.
FIELDEN, THOMAS PERCEVAL

DE FLUENT, AMELIE
GALLUP, LUCY

DE FONTCREUSE, MARQUIS
JAEGER, CYRIL KAREL S.

DE FORBES
FORBES, DELORES STANTON

DE FORD, MIRIAM ALLEN
SHIPLEY, MIRIAM ALLEN [D]

DE FORREST, JULIE
DEWITT, EDITH OPENSHAW

DE FOX, LUCIA UNGARO
LOCKERT, LUCIA [A.U.F.]

DE FRENZI, GIULIO
FEDERONZONI, LUIGI

DE GAMEZ, TANA
ALBA DE GAMEZ, CIELO CAY.

DE GRAEFF, W.B.
BLAUSTEIN, ALBERT PAUL
CONKLIN, [E.] GROFF

DE GRAFFE, RICHARD
ST. CLAIR, LEONARD

DE GRAMONT, SANCHE
MORGAN, TED

DE GRANAMOUR, A.
LITTLE, PAUL HUGO

DE GRASSE, WILL
FURNISS, WILLIAM

DE GRAVE, PHILIP
DE ANDREA, WILLIAM L.

DE GRAZIA
DE GRAZIA, ETTORE

DE GRAZIA, TED
DE GRAZIA, ETTORE

DE GUIMARAENS, ALPHONSUS
GUIMARAES, ALFONSO H.D.C.

DE GUY, LATTEUR
MOULIGNEAU, MICHEL

DE HAAN, MARGARET
FREED, MARGARET DE HAAN

DE HAHN, JULIA
SULLIVAN, ELEANOR

DE HAMEL, FELIX JOHN
HAMEL, FELIX JOHN

DE HAMONG, COUNT LEIGH
DE HAMONG, LOUIS

DE HART, ROBERT
HANZELON, ROBERT M.

DE HOSTOS, E.M.
DE HOSTOS, EUGENIO MARIA

DE HOSTOS, EUGENIO M.
DE HOSTOS, EUGENIO MARIA

DE IRALUCE, CECILIA
LAFUENTE ESTEFANIA, M.A.

DE JONG VAN HAGE, T.P.M.
REMPT, JAN DIRK

DE JONG-KEESING, ELISAB.
VAN TRICHT, ELISABETH E.

DE JOURLET, MARIE
LITTLE, PAUL HUGO

DE JOUVENEL, BERTRAND
DE JOUVENEL, EDUORD BERT.

DE JUAN, JAVIER
GALLARDOS MUNOZ, JUAN

DE KIEWIT, CORNELIS W.
DE KIEWET, CORNELIS WILL.

DE KIRILINE, LOUISE
DE KIRILINE LAWRENCE, L.

DE KLEINHANS, LAUREANA W.
WRIGHT, LAUREANA

DE KOVEN, BERNIE
DE KOVEN, BERNARD

PSEUDONYMS

DE L'ARBIN, BOB
HASSEL, SVEN

DE LA CORTINA, EL CONDE
DE LA CORTINA, JOSE GOMEZ

DE LA BRETE, JEAN
CHERBONNEL, ALICE

DE LA BRETONNE, RESTIF
RESTIF, NICHOLAS-ANNE-ED

DE LA BRETTONE, RATIF
DUVAL, MARTIN PAUL A.

DE LA CASA, JUAN
ZENO GANDIA, MANUEL

DE LA ESCOSURA, RAMON D.
MAY, KARL FRIEDRICH

DE LA GLANNEGE, R.M.
LEGMAN, GEORGE ALEXANDER

DE LA GLANNEGE, ROGER-MAX
LEGMAN, GEORGE ALEXANDER

DE LA MARAJA, XERES
BEGOVIC, MILAN

DE LA PARRA, TERESA
SANOJO, ANA TERESA PARRA

DE LA RAMEE, LOUISE
RAME, MARIE LOUISE

DE LA REE, GERRY
DE LA REE, GEREAUX DEFOR.

DE LA SALLE, JOHN
DAVIS, JOHN

DE LA TORRE, LILLIAN
MCCUE, LILLIAN BUENO

DE LA TORRE, TIRSO
MORALES CABRERA, PABLO

DE LA TORRE-BUENO, LILIAN
MCCUE, LILLIAN BUENO

DE LACY, LOUISE
HICKEY, MADELYN EASTLUND

DE LAFORET, JEAN
BOCKL, MANFRED

DE LAND, TRACY
LEETE, FREDERICK DE LAND

DE LANTAGNE, CECILE
CLOUTIER-WOJCIECH, CECILE

DE LAS CUEVAS, RAYMON
HARRINGTON, MARK R.

DE LAS LUNAS, CARMENCITA
TROCCHI, ALEXANDER

DE LAUBE
CARDENA, CLEMENT

DE LAUTREAMONT, COMTE
DUCASSE, ISIDORE LUCIEN

DE LEON, ANA LISA
MULLAN, CELINA RIOS

DE LEON, STUART
LYMAN, G.H.

DE LIMA, SIGRID
GREENE, SIGRID

DE LINT, CHARLES
HOEFSMIT, HENRI DIEDERICK

DE LIOST, GUERAU
BOFILL I. MATES, JAUME

DE LISSER, H.G.
DE LISSER, HERBERT GEORGE

DE LOGHE, SYDNEY
LOCK, FREDERICK SYDNEY

DE LOI, RAIMON
JAMESON, RAYMOND D.

DE LONG, JULIE
HAY, MILLICENT V.

DE LONGCLOTHES, NINON
HAIG, EMILY ALICE

DE LORA, JOANN S.
SANDLIN, JOANN S. DE L.

DE LORCA, FRANK
ANTON, UWE
BRAND, KURT
DOMBROWSKI, THEODOR
FRIEDRICHS, HOLGER
HARTSCH, GERHART
HELGATH, FRANC
HRDINKA, MICHAEL
HUNDSDORFER, GERHARD
KODELPETER, HANS P.
LUIF, KURT
SAUPE, DIETER
VON KOBLINSKI, HANS-JOACH

DE LOUNE, HENRY
POPHAM, PETER NICHOLAS H.

DE LUBANO, M.
GHNASSIA, MAURICE [J-H]

DE LYN, NICOLE
WOODLAND, EVA [EVE]

DE LYNN, EILEEN
HEILESEN, EILEEN DE LYNN

DE LYONNE, SUSAN
GROSS, SUSAN ELLEN

DE MAGRET, A.
GREEN, JULIAN [HARTRIDGE]
LEGRIS, JEAN

DE MAMMAIS, DRS. PIERRE
BERGLUND, E.P.

DE MAR, ESMERALDA
MELLEN, IDA MAY

DE MAR, PAUL
FOLEY, PEARL

DE MARQUAND, ALIX
SKINNER, MICHAEL

DE MENTON, FRANCISCO
CHIN, FRANK CHEW

DE MEXICO, N.R.
SHORE, LARRY

DE MILAN, SISTER JEAN
JEAN, GABRIELLE LUCILE

DE MILLE, AGNES
PRUDE, AGNES GEORGE

DE MILLE, NELSON
LEVINSON, LEONARD [L]

DE MIOMANDRE, FRANCIS
DURAND, FRANCOIS

DE MONT, POL
POLYDOOR, KAREL MARIA

DE MONTALVO, LUIS GALVEZ
DE AVALLE-ARCE, JUAN B.

DE MONTAUBAN, G.
GREENOUGH, WILLIAM PARKER

DE MONTFORT, GUY
JOHNSON, DONALD MCINTOSH

DE MONTTESSUY, LE ROY
LE ROY, MAX MARIE R.

DE MORNY, PETER
WYNNE-TYSON, ESME

DE MOTREUIL, GAETANE
BELANGOR-GILL, GEORGIANNA

DE MOURANT, GEORGE SOULI
BEDFORD-JONES, HENRY

DE NAGY, COURTH
FISCHER-ABENDROTH, WOLFD.

DE NAVERY, RAOUL
DAVID, MARIE DE SAFFRON
FULLERTON, GEORGIANNA

DE NORA, A.
NODER, ANTON ALFRED

DE ORCA, MARCO ANTONIO
MONTES DE ORCA, MARCO A.

DE P. FLINT, E.
FIELDING, THOMAS PERCEVAL

DE PAOLA, TOMIE
DE PAOLA, THOMAS ANTHONY

DE PAOR, RISTEARD
POWER, RICHARD

DE PAUL, EDITH
DELATUSH, EDITH

DE POLMAN, WILLEM
NICHOLS, DALE WILLIAM

DE PONT-JEST, RENE
DELMAS, LEON RENE

DE PONTAUMONT
LECANTEUR, M.E.

DE PRE, JEAN-ANNE
AVALLONE, MICHAEL

PSEUDONYMS

DE REYNA, JORGE
DE REYNA, DIANE DETZER

DE RICO, UL
DI TROPPENBURG, ULDERICO

DE RIVEL, ISA
CUEVAS, CLARA

DE ROSSO, H.A.
DE ROSSO, HENRY ANDREW

DE ROUTISIE, ALBERT
ARAGON, LOUIS

DE ROXAS, JUAN BARTOLOME
RUBIA BARCIA, JOSE

DE SAINT LUC, JEAN
GLASSCO, JOHN [S]

DE SAINT ROMAN, ARNAUD
ARAGON, LOUIS

DE SAINT-GALL, AUGUSTE A.
STRICH, CHRISTIAN

DE SAINT-LEON, REGINALD
DU BOIS, EDWARD

DE SAIX, TYLER
STACPOOLE, H. DEVERE

DE SALIGNAC, CHARLES
HASSON, JAMES

DE SAVALLO, DONA TERESA
WILLIAMSON, ALICE M.L.
WILLIAMSON, CHARLES N.

DE SCOTT, CARL
OBERMEIER, SIEGFRIED

DE SILVA, NINA
DE SILVA, ANGELITA H.

DE SOLA, JOHN
MORLAND, NIGEL

DE ST. CRISPIAN, CRISPIN
WAUGH, AUBERON

DE TEIVE, BARON
PESSOA, FERNANDO [A.N.]

DE TERAMOND, GUY
TERAMOND, EDMOND G.

DE TODANY, JAMES
BEAUDOIN, KENNETH LAWR.

DE TOLIGNAC, GASTON
GRIFFITH, DAVID LEWELYN W

DE TRABECK, SOPHIE
LAVRITCH, SOPHIE B.

DE VALLON, HENRI
DONGES, GUNTER

DE VERDI, MARIE
MENCKEN, HENRY LOUIS

DE VERE BEAUDERK, HELEN
BELLINGHAM, HELEN MARY D.

DE VERE, JANE
WATSON, JULIA

DE VERE, V.C.
VERE-HODGE, CONRAD C.R.

DE VILLIERS, RYNO B.
NIENABER, PETRUS JOHANNES

DE VILLIERS, VICTOR
HUGO, LEON HARGREAVES

DE VRIES, JORN
ALPERS, HANS JOACHIM

DE WINTERS, DANIELLE
TIMSON, KEITH

DE WITT, DENISE
SCHOEB, ERIKA

DE WITT, JAMES
LEWIS, MILDRED D.

DE WOHL, LOUIS
VON WOHL, LUDWIG

DE WOLFE, IVOR
HASTINGS, HUBERT CRONIN

DE WOLFE, IVY
HASTINGS, HUBERT CRONIN

DE WREDER, PAUL
HEMING, JOHN WINTON

DE ZAVALA, MARISA
MULLAN, CELINA RIOS

DE'BEUCLERK, LADY
DE VERE, [LADY] D.

DEACON, EILEEN
GEIPEL, EILEEN

DEACON, RICHARD
MCCORMICK, GEORGE DONALD

DEACTON, EUGENIA
LEWIS, ALETHEA BRERETON

DEAKIN, H.L.
DEAKIN, HILDA L.

DEAL, MASON
ELIOT, HENRY WARE

DEAL, SEFTON
KALMUCZAK, ROLF

DEALEY, TED
DEALEY, EDWARD MUSGROVE

DEAMER, DULCIE
GOLDIE, MARY E.K. DULCIE

DEAN EDNA
NORDSTROM, EDITH C.

DEAN, AMBER
GETZIN, AMBER DEAN

DEAN, CAROLE
SHEEHY, EDNA

DEAN, CHARLOTTE
FLETCHER, JOANNA L.G.

DEAN, DINAH
MAY, MAJORIE

DEAN, DONALD
HOPE, WILLIAM EDWARD S.

DEAN, DUDLEY
MCGAUGHY, DUDLEY DEAN

DEAN, EDNA
ADAMS, DOROTHY

DEAN, ELINOR
MCCANN, HELEN

DEAN, ELISABETH
BEILENSON, EDNA

DEAN, GREGORY
POSNER, JACOB D.

DEAN, HAYDON
HARDING, HARRY

DEAN, IDA
GRAE, IDA

DEAN, JOHN
BUMPPO, NATHANIEL JOHN B.

DEAN, LISA
JAMES, L[ANA] DEAN

DEAN, LYN
GARRETT, WINIFRED SELINA

DEAN, MRS. ANDREW
SIDGWICK, CECILY

DEAN, NELL MARR
RATZLAFF, NELL MARR DEAN

DEAN, PAMELA [C]
DYER-BENNET, PAMELA DEAN

DEAN, S.F.X.
SMITH, FRANCIS

DEAN, SHELLEY
SANDERS, DOROTHY LUCIE

DEAN, SPENCER
WINCHELL, PRENTICE

DEANE, LORNA
WILKINSON, LORNA H.K.

DEANE, NORMAN
CREASEY, JOHN

DEANE, SONIA
SOUTAR, GWENDOLINE AMY

DEANE, VESEY
MURRAY, ANDREW NICHOLAS

DEARBORN, ANDREW
GARDNER, LEWIS J.

DEARBORN, LAURA
PICTON, NINA

DEARMAND, DALE BURLISON
DEARMAND, DALE

DEAUVILLE, MAX
DUWEZ, MAURICE

DEAUXVILLE, KATHERINE
DAVIS, MAGGIE S.

DEBAL, SWAMI PUJI
KNIGHT, STEPHEN

DEBBS, LEO
ORNULF, GUNNAR

DEBILLE, GEORGE
CHENNEVIERE, GEORGES

DEBRETT, HAL
DRESSER, DAVIS
DRESSER, KATHLEEN ROLLINS

DEBROT, COLA
DEBROT, NICHOLAAS

DECATUR, WILLIAM
CAVE, HUGH B[ARNETT]

DECAUX, LUCILE
BIBESCO, MARTHE LUCILE

DECK, BRUNO
DECKER, HEINZ-BRUNO

DECKER, RALPH
KALMUCAZK, ROLF

DECLES, JON
STUDEBAKER, DONALD VALEN.

DECOLTA, RAMON
WHITFIELD, RAOUL

DECOVERLEY, ROGER
HATHAWAY, RONALD F.

DECREST, JACQUES
FAURE-BIGUET, JACQUES N.

DEDMON, EMMETT
DEADMAN, EMMETT

DEE, DARE
STEFFENS, ARTHUR JOSEPH

DEE, HENRY
TORBETT, HARVEY D.L.

DEE, JOHN
FANNING, D. CHRISTOPHER
TULLETT, DENIS JOHN

DEE, NICHOLAS
AIKEN, JOAN

DEE, R.K.
WOOD, JOHN JAMES O'HARA

DEE, REBECCA
CROSS, RENA
PATTINSON, LEE

DEE, ROGER
AYCOCK, ROGER DEE

DEE, RUBY
WALLACE, RUBY ANN

DEE, SHERRY
FLOURNOY, SHERYL HINES

DEE, SYLVIA
PROFFITT, JOSEPHINE MOORE

DEE, WILLIAM
DUNNE, RON

DEEGAN, FRANCIS M.
HAMLING, WILLIAM L.

DEEGAN, JOHN J.
TUBB, E.C.

DEEGAN, JON J.
BERRY, BRYAN
CAMPBELL, H[ERBERT] J.
RAYER, FRANCIS G.
SHARP, ROBERT GEORGE

DEELE, PHILIP F.
TOMPKINS, WALKER A.

DEEMING, RICHARD
DEMING, RICHARD

DEEN, DONALD
BEKESSY, JANOS

DEEP CHIN
GOULD, ALLAN MENDELL

DEEPS, FREDERICK
SPEED, FREDERICK MAURICE

DEER, M.J.
DEER, MARY J.
SMITH, GEORGE H[ENRY]
SMITH, MARY J. DEER

DEERE, PHILIP F.
BOSWORTH, ALLAN R.
FARRELL, A. CLIFFORD

DEERING, FREEMONT B.
GOLDFRAP, JOHN HENRY

DEEVER, BRIAN
WINTERMUTE, EDWIN H.

DEFOREST, BARRY
MANNING, WILLIAM HENRY

DEFOREST, JACQUES
ACKERMAN, FORREST J.

DEFOWE, WALTER
PLUMPIAN, PAUL

DEFRANCE, ANTHONY
DI FRANCO, ANTHONY MARIO

DEFREES, MADELINE
GILBERT, [SISTER] MARY

DEGAN, VON
RABE, ANN C.

DEGEN, VAN
RABE, ANN C.

DEGRAEFF, ALLEN
BLAUSTEIN, ALBERT PAUL

DEGROS, J.H.
VILLIARD, PAUL

DEHAN, RICHARD
GRAVES, CLOTILDE INEZ M.

DEIGHTON, LEN
DEIGHTON, LEONARD CYRIL

DEISS, JAY
WAGNER, ALICE

DEITZ, TOM
DEITZ, THOMAS FRANKLIN

DEJEANS, ELIZABETH
BUDGETT, FRANCES ELIZAB.

DEKA, CONNIE
LAUX, CONSTANCE

DEKALB, LORIMER
KNORR, MARIAN LOCKWOOD

DEKKER, CARL
HETHERINGTON, KEITH JAMES
JANES, GENE
LAFFIN, JOHN [ALFRED C.]
LYNDS, DENNIS

DEKKER, JOHNNY
ANGLOWITZ, MAURICE [MICK]

DEKOBRA, MAURICE
TESSIER, ERNEST MAURICE

DEL BERNIS, RIGOS
BOMKE, BERNHARD

DEL CASTILLO, RICHARD G.
GRISWOLD DEL CASTILLO, R.

DEL MAR, JUSTIN
ANDREWS, MERVYN

DEL MAR, MARIA
MOLT, ANGELA

DEL MARTIA, ASTON
FRANCES, STEPHEN D.

DEL MARTIA, ASTRON
FAWCETT, FRANK DUBREZ
FEARN, JOHN RUSSELL

DEL MONTE, FILOMENA
ZENO GANDIA, MANUEL

DEL OLMO, JULIO
PEREZ BLASCO, JULIO

DEL PIOMBO, AKBAR
RUBINGTON, NORMAN

DEL RAY, LESTER
FAIRMAN, PAUL W.
DANFORTH, ETHEL M.
UERDES, RAMON Y ALVAREZ

DELACORTA
ODIER, DANIEL

DELACORTE, SHAWNA
DENNISON, SHARON

DELACOUR, JEAN BAPTISTE
KURTH, HANNS

DELACOUR, MANFRED J.
KURTH, HANNS

DELACROIX, CLAIRE
COOKE, DEBORAH A.

DELAFIELD, E.M.
DE LA PASTURE DASHWOOD, E

DELAHANTY, RANDOLPH
DELEHANTY, RANDOLPH

DELAIRE, JEAN
BLAKE, MRS. MUIRSON

DELAISNE, JEAN
SOREIL, [JOSEPH] ARSENE

DELAMARTER, JEANNE
BONNETT, JEANNE

DELANCEY, ELIZABETH
TUNIS, ELIZABETH

DELAND, MARGARET
DELAND, MARGARETTA W.C.

DELANEY, BUD
DELANEY, FRANCIS JR.

DELANEY, CAROL
BLEECK, G.C.

DELANEY, CHIP
DELANY, SAMUEL R.

DELANEY, DENIS
GREEN, PETER MORRIS

DELANEY, FRANEY
O'HARA, JOHN [H]

DELANEY, GINA
ALSOBROOK, ROSALYN
WELLS, PATRICIA RAE

DELANEY, JOHN
ROWLAND, DONALD S.

DELANEY, MARSHALL
FULFORD, ROBERT

DELANEY, NED
DELANEY, THOMAS NICHOLAS

DELANEY, SAMUEL R.
DELANY, SAMUEL R.

DELANO, AL
LIVINGSTON, A.D.

DELANOE, PIERRE
LEROYER, PIERRE CHARLES

DELAPORTE, THEOPHILE
GREEN, JULIAN [HARTRIDGE]

DELARUE, JEAN
DREZE, JEAN

DELAVRANCEA, BARBU
STEFANESCU, BARBU

DELAY, CLAUDE
DELAY-TUBIANA, CLAUDE

DELDERFIELD, R.F.
DELDERFIELD, RONALD F.

DELEONE, RUTH
RANKIN, RUTH DELONE IRV.

DELFANO, M.M.
FLAMMONDE, PARIS

DELFT, WALTER
GEBAUER, WALTER LUDOLF

DELGADILLO, MONICO
YANEZ, AUGUSTIN

DELGADO, MANUEL S.
HAHN, RONALD M.

DELGADO, RYDER
EISELE, MARTIN
HOHLBEIN, WOLFGANG E.

DELHEID, BRIGITTE
ESCHBACH, JOSEF

DELIBES, MIGUEL
DELIBES SETIEN, MIGUEL

DELION, ELISABETH CHARL.
APPEL, LISELOTTE

DELL'ARCO, MARIO
FAGIOLO, MARIO

DELL, AMEN
MENDELL, IRVING

DELL, BELINDA
BOWDEN, JEAN

DELL, DUDLEY
GOLD, HORACE L.

DELL, ETHEL M.
SAVAGE, ETHEL MAE DELL

DELL, PAUL
BLAISDELL, PAUL

DELLA TORRE, RAOUL
MENCKEN, HENRY LOUIS

DELLA, LEW
DAWSON, GEORGE H.
MARTIN, THOMAS HECTOR

DELLAROSA, LUDWIG
GLEICH, JOSEPH ALOIS

DELMAR, ROY
WEXLER, JEROME

DELMONICO, ANDREA
MORRISON, EULA ATWOOD

DELMONT, JOSEPH
PICK, KARL

DELMORE, DIANA
NOLLETT, LOIS S.

DELORME, ANDRE
JULIEN, CHARLES-ANDRE

DELORME, EDMUND
GEORGE, STEFAN [ANTON]

DELORME, MICHELE
CRANSTON, METHILDE

DELORNE, CHARLES
RUMBALL, CHARLES

DELRAY, CHESTER
RAYER, FRANCIS G.

DELSEN, HARRY
KALMUCZAK, ROLF

DELTA
DENNETT, HERBERT VICTOR
HAZLEWOOD, REX
MOIR, DAVID MACBETH
TURNBULL, DORA AMY D.

DELVING, MICHAEL
WILLIAMS, JAY

DEMAINE, C.F.
TRUMBO, DONALD [DALTON]

DEMAINE, DON
DRINKALL, GORDON DON

DEMAREST, ANNE
BOND, FLORENCE DEMAREST F

DEMAREST, DOUG
BARKER, WILL

DEMARET, JIMMY
DEMARET, JAMES NEWTON

DEMARIS, OVID
DESMARAIS, OVID E.

DEMATHEWS, MO
DONALDSON, DALE C.

DEMBNER, RED
DEMBNER, S. ARTHUR

DEMBRY, R. EMMET
MURFREE, MARY NOAILLES

DEMERS, FRANS
BECKERS, FRANS

DEMI
HITZ, DEMI

DEMIC, WILLIAM
DONALDSON, DALE C.

DEMIJOHN, THOM
DISCH, THOMAS M.
SLADEK, JOHN

DEMILLE, ALEXANDRIA
DUBREUIL, ELIZABETH L.

DEMIN, MIKHAIL
TRIFONOV, GEORGII E.

DEMING, BOB
DEMING, ROBERT

DEMING, KIRK
DRAGO, HARRY SINCLAIR

DEMON, ROY
PUHLE, JOACHIM

DEMOTES, MICHAEL
BURGESS, MICHAEL ROY

DEMPSEY, HANK
HARRISON, HARRY

DEMPSEY, HENRY
HARRISON, HARRY

DEMPSEY, JACK
DEMPSEY, WILLIAM HARRISON

DEMPSTER, GUY
HEMING, DEMPSTER E.

DEN, PETR
RADIMSKY, LADISLAW

DENALI, PETER
HOLM, DONALD RAYMOND

DENBIE, ROGER
BRODIE, JULIAN PAUL
GREEN, ALAN [BAER]

DENBIGH, MAURICE
NUTBROWN, MAURICE

DENBOW, WILLIAM
STILES, GEORGE

DENBY, COLT
BLEECK, G.C.

DENDER, JAY
DEINDORFER, ROBERT GREENE

DENDERMONDE, MAX
HAZELHOFF, HENDRIK

DENE, ALAN
WIGNALL, T[REVOR] C.

DENE, HAMPTON
HOOK, SAMUEL CLARKE

DENELLA, UTTA
SCHNEIDER, UTTA [D]

DENES, ZSOFIA
SZALATNYAY, JOZEFNE

DENHAM, PETER
JONES, P.D.

DENHAM, SALLY
BUDD, MAVIS

DENHOLM, MARK
FEARN, JOHN RUSSELL

DENIS, CHARLOTTE
PLIMMER, CHARLOTTE
PLIMMER, DENIS

DENIS, JOHN
EDWARDS, JOHN
FROST, DENIS
OFFUTT, ANDREW J.

DENIS, JULIO
CORTAZAR, JULIO

DENISON, CORRIE
PARTRIDGE, ERIC [H]

DENMARK, HARRISON
ZELAZNY, ROGER

DENNING, A.T.
DENNING, ALFRED THOMPSON

DENNING, LAURENCE
SELLERS, CONNIE LESLIE

DENNING, MARK
STEVENSON, JOHN

DENNING, MELITA
BARCYNSKI, VIVIAN G.

DENNING, PATRICIA
WILLIS, CORINNE D.

DENNIS, BRUCE
O'BRIEN, DAVID WRIGHT

DENNIS, EVE
WORNUM, MIRIAM

DENNIS, PATRICK
TANNER, ED EVERETT III

DENNIS, STACEY
MORRIS, ESTHER

DENNISON, DOROTHY
GOLDEN, DOROTHY

DENNISON, MILO
CANTWELL, LOIS

DENNISON, PAULA
PYLES, DANNY

DENNY, ALMA
DENENHOLZ, ALMA

DENNY, BRIAN
DOUGHTY, BRADFORD

DENNY, CAROL
BRANDT, CAROL

DENNY, ROZ
FOX, ROSALINE
HAYDON, JUNE
SIMPSON, JUDITH [JUDY]

DENORRE, ROCHEL
DENNORE, ROBERTA

DENOVAN, SAUNDERS
HARVEY, WILLIAM

DENSLOW, W.W.
DENSLOW, WILLIAM W.

DENT, DENIS
WILLIAMS, GRAEME

DENT, GUY
DENNIS, GEOFFREY

DENT, LESTER
DONOVAN, LAURENCE

DENT, TOM
DENT, THOMAS COVINGTON

DENTINGER, STEPHEN
HOCH, EDWARD D.

DENTON, ANN
DEBORDE, SHERRY

DENTON, KATE
HAKE, CAROLYN
LAMBRIGHT, JEANIE

DENTON, REGINALD
HAWTHORNE, C.S.

DENTRY, ROBERT
WHITE, OSMAR [E.D.]

DENVER, BOONE
RENNIE, JAMES ALAN

DENVER, BRUCE
HOPE, WILLIAM EDWARD S.

DENVER, DRAKE C.
NYE, NELSON C[ORAL]

DENVER, JEFF
SCHRODER, RAINER M.

DENVER, JOHN
RELLERGERD, HELMUT

DENVER, LEE
GRIBBLE, LEONARD [R]

DENVER, MARK
APPEL, WALTER

DENVER, PAUL
ENEFER, DOUGLAS STALLARD

DENVER, ROBERT DALE
NAFZIGER, RAY

DENVER, ROD
EDSON, JOHN THOMAS

DENVER, SHAD
DUNN, DES R.
MEARES, LEONARD F.

DENVER, WALT
REDDING, ROBERT HULL
SHERMAN, JORY [T]

DENVERS, JAKE
EDGAR, ALFRED

DENYS, TERESA
BIANCHI, JACQUI

DENZER, ANN WISEMAN
WISEMAN, ANN [S]

DEPSTER, LUIS
MADSEN, BORGE

DEPWE, WALLY
DEPEW, WALTER WESTERFIELD

DERBY, MARK
WILCOX, HARRY

DERBYSHIRE, JANE
GREEN, MADGE

DEREK, LOGAN
ANTON, UWE
VOHL, U.

DEREKSON, DAVID
STACTON, DAVID DEREK

DEREN, MAYA
DEREN, ELEANORA

DERFALL, ART
KALINICH, WILLIAM

DERING, R.G.
BALFOUR, FREDERIC H.

DERMOTT, STEPHEN
BRADBURY, PARNELL

DERMOTT, VERN
FRYE, VERN D.

DERMOUT, MARIA
DERMOUT-INGERMANN, HELENA

DERN, DANIEL P.
SILVERBERG, ROBERT

DERN, EROLIE
DERN, E. PEARL GADDIS

DERN, PEGGY
DERN, E. PEARL GADDIS

DEROR, YEHEZKEL
DROR, YEHEZKEL

DERRICK, FRANCES
NOTLEY, FRANCES ELIZA M.

DERRICK, GRAHAM
RABY, DEREK GRAHAM

DERRICK, LIONEL
CUNNINGHAM, CHESTER GRANT
ROBERTS, MARK K.

DERRINGER, PETE
DUBINA, PETER

DERRY DOWN DERRY
LEAR, EDWARD

DERRY, GORDON
DEREVANCHUK, GORDON

DERSONNE[S], JACQUES
SIMENON, GEORGES [J.C]

DERTOLLE, JAIME
SHUTTE, JAMES E.

DES ESCORRES, CHARLES
CHARTRAND, JOSEPH DEMERS

DES ORMEAUX, J.J.
FORREST, ROSAIRE

DESANA, DOROTHY
TRENT, ANN

DESART, THE EARL OF
CUFFE, W.U.O'C.

DESCHAMPS, MARGUERITE
LAFONTANT-MEDARD, MICHEL.

DESCHNER, GUENTHER
DRESCHNER, HANS GUENTHER

DESMARAIS, BARBARA G.
TAYLOR, BARBARA G.

DESMOND
SPRATT, PHILLIP

DESMOND, CAROL
PUSCH, EDITH

DESMOND, HILARY
HAYS, LEE

DESMOND, HUGH
LINDSAY, KATHLEEN

DESMOND, WARREN
CARTER, DYSON

DESOR, RENE
WILKINSON, A.G.

DESPARD, LESLIE
HOWITT, J. LESLIE DESPARD

DESPLAINES, JULIE
JENNINGS, LESLIE NELSON

DESTINY, ARCHIBALD
SHAW, LAWRENCE TAYLOR

DESTRY, VINCE
NORWOOD, VICTOR [G.C.]

DETINE, PADRE
FREDRIKSEN, ERIK E.
OLSEN, IB SPANG

DETREME, TRISTAN
HUC, PHILIPPE

DETTER, INGRID
DELUPIS, INGRID

DETTMER, HANS
PANIZZA, OSKAR

DETZER, DIANE
DE REYNA, DIANE DETZER

DEUSE, ELSE
HUBNER, ELSE

DEUSEL, P.M.
BERTHOLD, WILL

DEUTSCH, EVA C.
COSTABEL, EVA DEUTSCH

DEUTSCH, KURT
DEUTSCHER, ISAAC

DEVAJEE, VED
GOOL, RESHARD

DEVAL, JACQUES
BOULARAN, JACQUES

DEVERAUX, EVE
BARNETT, PAUL LE PAGE

DEVEREAUX, JUDE
WHITE, JUDE GILLIAM

DEVEREUX, ROY
PEMBER-DEVEREUX, MARGARET

DEVERS, DELANEY
DAVIS, DIANE WICKER

DEVI, NILA
WOODY, REGINA JONES

DEVIL, RON
KUHNERT, JORG

DEVILBISS, PHILIP
MEBANE, JOHN [H]

DEVILLE, RENE
KACEWGARI, ROMAINE

DEVIN, FLANNA
JUNEMAN, KAREN

DEVIN, MARIUS
LANDAU, EDWIN MARIA

DEVINE, D.M.
DEVINE, DAVID MCDONALD

DEVINE, DAVID
ZETTERBORG, GABRIEL

DEVINE, DOMINIC
DEVINE, DAVID MCDONALD

DEVLIN, GEORGE
SMITH, GEORGE H[ENRY]

DEVLIN, OWEN
CHADWICK, CHARLES

DEVLIN, ROY P.
KELLEY, THOMAS P.

DEVON, ALEXANDRA
DIAL, JOAN MAVIS R.

DEVON, ANNE
RETTKE, MARIAN POPE

DEVON, D.G.
DEMOREST, STEPHAN
GROSS, MICHAEL ROBERT

DEVON, GARY
BLUM, GARY

DEVON, GEORGINA
HENTGES, ALISON J.

DEVON, H.T.
HODGE, THOMAS HOUNSELL

DEVON, JOHN ANTHONY
PAYNE, PIERRE S. ROBERT

DEVON, MARIAN
RETTKE, MARIAN POPE

DEVON, NICHOLAS
DOLPHIN, REGINALD C.

DEVON, NICOLA
BAKER, W.A. HOWARD
DOLPHIN, REGINALD C.

DEVON, SARAH
WALKER, EMILY KATHLEEN

DEVRIES, CON
SELLERS, CONNIE LESLIE

DEWALL, D.
FEARN, JOHN RUSSELL

DEWAR, EVELYN
WILCOCK, EVELYN

DEWDNEY, PETER
BROCK, ALAN [ST. HILL]

DEWEESE, GENE
DEWEESE, THOMAS EUGENE

DEWEESE, JEAN
DEWEESE, EUGENE

DEWES, SIMON
MURIEL, JOHN ST. CLAIR

DEWEY, JAMES
MCNEILLY, MILDRED MASTER.

DEWITT, ADDISON
NEWMAN, KIM [JAMES]

DEXTER, AL
POINDEXTER, CLARENCE A.

DEXTER, CATHERINE
MARTIN, CATHERINE DEXTER

DEXTER, CHARLES
LEVENSON, LOUIS

DEXTER, CLIFF
KALMUCZAK, ROLF

DEXTER, DON
HARSTEN, UWE

DEXTER, EDWIN
SHAVER, RICHARD S.

DEXTER, J.B.
GLASBY, JOHN S.

DEXTER, JOHN
BLOCK, LAWRENCE
BRADLEY, MARION ZIMMER
COLEMAN, JOHN
COX, ARTHUR JEAN
CURTIS, RICHARD [A]
HORNWOOD, HARVEY
JAMES, AL
KNOLES, WILLIAM [H]
MOSKOVITZ, JACK
PERICHITCH, MILO
PLOTNIK, ARTHUR
SILVERBERG, ROBERT
SMITH, GEORGE H[ENRY]
WESTLAKE, DONALD [EDWIN]
ZACHARY, HUGH

DEXTER, LEE
FALLON, MICHAEL

DEXTER, MARTIN
FAUST, FREDERICK S.

DEXTER, PETER
SHAVER, RICHARD S.

DEXTER, ROSS
REYNOLDS, JOHN EDMUND
STOKOE, E[DWARD] G[EORGE]

DEXTER, WILLIAM
PRITCHARD, WILLIAM THOMAS

DEY, HARYOT HOLT
DEY, HATTIE [H] CALHOON

DEY, MARMADUKE
DEY, FREDERIC VAN R.

DEZSERY, ANDRAS
DEZSERY, ENDRE ISTVAN

DHAN, DOROTHEE
MULLER, DOROTHEE [D]

DHU
MCALPINE, ROBERT W.

DI BASSETTO, CORNO
SHAW, GEORGE BERNARD

DI MARCO, GINO
WEISS, IRVING J.

DI MONTONE, N. BRACCIO
DE MAUNI, BARON ROGER

DI NATALE, FRANCINE
MALZBERG, BARRY [N]

DI POSITANO, RICO
LIEHR, HEINZ

DI SAVUTO, BARONESS
LA SPINA, FANNY GREYE

DI SAVUTO, BARONI
LA SPINA, FANNY GREYE

DI VAILLENT, FRANCOIS
HERSEY, HAROLD

DIAMANO, SILMANG
SENGHOR, LEOPOLD SEDAR

DIAMOND, ANN
MCLEAN, ANNE [JULIA]

DIAMOND, BRETT
BOUNDS, SYDNEY J.

DIAMOND, JACQUELINE
HYMAN, JACKIE DIAMOND

DIAMOND, JOHN
BAYLEY, BARRINGTON J.

DIAMOND, PETRA
SACHS, JUDITH

DIAMOND, REBECCA
SACHS, JUDITH

DIARA, SCHAVI M.
ALI, SCHAVI MALI

DIAS, B.H.
POUND, EZRA LOOMIS

DIBELL, ANSEN
DIBBLE, NANCY ANN

DICANT, V.L.
HEWETSON, SARA

DICK, ALEXANDRA
ERIKSON, SIBYL C. ALEX.

DICK, CAPPY
CLEVELAND, GEORGE

DICK, KAY
SCOTT, JEREMY

DICK, R.A.
LESLIE, JOSEPHINE A.

DICK, T.
OSLER, ERIC RICHARD

DICKBERRY, F.
BLAZE DE BURY, F.

DICKENS, FRANK
HULINE-DICKENS, FRANK W.

DICKENS, IRENE
COPPER, DOROTHY

DICKENS, MONICA
STRATTON, MONICA DICKENS

DICKENS, NORMAN
EISENBERG, LAWRENCE B.

DICKERSON, MARY A.
DONAHEY, MARY DICKERSON

DICKERSON-WATKINS, L.
ROURKE, LOUIS MUSGRAVE

DICKEY, LEE
BREMYER, JAYNE DICKEY

DICKEY, R.P.
DICKEY, ROBERT PRESTON

DICKINS, A.S.M.
DICKINS, ANTHONY STEWART

DICKINSON, DON
DICKINSON, DONALD PERCY

DICKINSON, ELIZABETH
MUGGESON, MARGARET E.

DICKINSON, FRANKIE
BROWNLEE, FRANCES

DICKINSON, MARTHA GILBERT
BIANCHI, MARTHA D.

DICKINSON, MIKE
HUTSON, SHAUN

DICKINSON, PETER
DE BRISSAC, MALCOLM

DICKINSON, RUBE
DICKINSON, WALTER S.

DICKSON, BOB
SORENSON, ERIK

DICKSON, CARR
CARR, JOHN DICKSON

DICKSON, CARTER
CARR, JOHN DICKSON

DICKSON, FRANK C.
DANSON, FRANK CORSE

DICKSON, HELEN
REYNOLDS, HELEN MARY G.C.

DICKSON, K.A.
DICKSON, KWESI ABOTSIA

DICTUM, STEVE
CRUMB, ROBERT

DIDELOT, MARIE
FORD, MARY ELIZABETH

DIEBOLD, JANET
SYLVESTER, JANET HART

DIEBOLD, JANET OLINE
SYLVESTER, JANET HART

DIEGO, GERARDO
DIEGO CENDOYA, GERARDO

DIEHNEL, ELLIE TATUM
DIEHNEL, TABITHA ELLEN

DIER, DEBRA
GOLDACKER, DEBRA DIER

DIERY, HERB
KALMUCZAK, ROLF

DIESCHEN, R.A.
MUHRMANN, WILHELM

DIESSEL, HILDEGARD
VON HALLER, HILDEGARD

DIETMER, HANS
CASTELLE, FRIEDRICH

DIETRICH, H.P.
BETHMANN, HORST

DIETRICH, HEINZ
HASSENSTEIN, DIETER

DIETRICH, JOHANN GOTTLIEB
BRAUN, HANNS MARIA

DIETRICH, ROBERT
HUNT, E. HOWARD

DIETRICH, WOLF
RUHEN, CARL

DIETZ, BETTY WARNER
DIETZ, ELISABETH [H]

DIETZENSCHMIDT
SCHMIDT, ANTON FRANZ

DIEZ, DORIS
BREHM, DORIS

DIFUSA, PATI
ALMODOVAR, PEDRO

DIGBY, GEORGE WINGFIELD
WINGFIELD DIGBY, GEORGE F

DIGGES, JEREMIAH
BERGER, JOSEF

DIGGS, IRENE
DIGGS, ELLEN IRENE

DIKSEN, BERND
DEMBSKI, WERNER

DIKTY, JUDY
DIKTY, JULIAN [C] MAY

DIL, ZAKHMI
HILTON, RICHARD

DILKE, LADY
STRONG, AMELIA FRANCIS

DILL, LIESBET
VON DRIGALSKI, ELISABETH

DILL, W.S.
MACBETH, MADGE HAMILTON

DILL, WALTER
THOMAS, WALTER DILL JR.

DILLARD, JAMES
SNOW, CHARLES H[ORACE]

DILLI, RICK
SELLERS, CONNIE LESLIE

DILLING, JUDITH
RHOADES, JUDITH GRUBMAN

DILLINGER, JAMES
BAKER, JAMES

DILLINGHAM, ROBERT B.
FOULKE, WILLIAM DUDLEY

DILLNOT, GEORGE
FROEST, FRANK

DILLON, CATHERINE
CORK, BARRY

DILLON, EILIS
O'CUILLEANAIN, EILIS D.

DILLON, LEO
DILLON, LIONEL J. & DIANE

DILLON, PATRICIA
DILLON, R. PATRICIA

DILLON, SHARON SASEEN
SASEEN, SHARON [DILLON]

DILLY, TANTE
BENSON, EDWARD FREDERIC

DIMDALE, C.D.
MEGROZ, R.L.

DIMEN-SCHEIN, MURIEL
DIMEN, MURIEL

DIMMOCK
HALL, HENRY

DIMOND, E. GREY
DIMOND, EDMUNDS GREY

DIMONT, PENELOPE
MORTIMER, PENELOPE [R]

DIMRECKIN, B. GRAYER
DE MILLE, RICHARD

DIMSON, WENDY
BARON, ORA WENDY

DINAHANDBU
ANDERSON, CHARLES FREER

DINESEN, ISAK
BLIXEN-FINEKE, KAREN

DINESEN, TANNE
BLIXEN-FENEKE, KAREN

DING LING
BINGZHI, JIANG
CHANG PIN-CHIN

DING, J.N.
DARLING, JAY NORWOOD

DINGLE, CAPT.
DINGLE, A. EDWARD

DINGLEBERRY, MR.
DINSDALE, TIMOTHY KAY

DINGWALL, PETER
FORSYTHE, ROBIN

DINN, MARY
FAID, MARY

DINNER, W. & W. MORUM
DINNER, WILLIAM

DINO
DINHOFER, ALFRED

DINWIDDY, J.R.
DINWIDDY, JOHN ROWLAND

DIOGENES
SALOLA, EEERO

DIOMEDE, JOHN K.
EFFINGER, GEORGE ALEC

DION, PETER
CHETWYND, LIONEL

DIOTIMA
WYNNE-TYSON, ESME

DIPI
DI PAOLA LEVIN, JORGE A.

DIPLOMAT
CARTER, JOHN FRANKLIN

DIPLOMATICUS
GUERRA Y SANCHEZ, RAMIRO
ZILLIACUS, KONNI

DIRAC, P.A.M.
DIRAC, PAUL ADRIEN M.

DIRK
GRINGHUIS, RICHARD H.

DIRK, R.
DIETRICH, RICHARD V.

DIRKS, WILLY
DIRKS, WILHELMINA

DISCH, TOM
DISCH, THOMAS M.

DISCHELL, JUDY
LALLI, JUDY

DISCIPLE OF THE MASTER, A
OUSELEY, GIDEON JASPER R.

DISCOBULUS
ALDOUS, DONALD WILLIAM

DISNEY, WALT
DISNEY, WALTER ELIAS

DISROBESON, KIN I.
STIVERS, MARK

DISTEL, PETER
KOCH, KURT EMIL

DITO UND IDEM
ELIZABETH, QUEEN, RUMANIA

DITTMAR, GABRIELE
KAFER, GRABRIELE

DITTON, JAMES
CLARK, DOUGLAS M.J.

DITTON, T.A.B.
DITTON, T.A. BELCHER

DIVER, JAMES FRANCIS
DWYER, JAMES FRANCIS

DIVER, MAUD
MARSHALL, KATHERINE H.M.

DIVERS HANDS
DERLETH, AUGUST [WILLIAM]

DIVINE, DAVID
DIVINE, ARTHUR DURHAM

DIVINSKY, N.J.
DIVINSKY, NATHAN [JOSEPH]

DIX, DOROTHY
CRANMER, HELEN WORDEN
GILMER, ELIZABETH M.

DIXEL, DELANO
LLIRO OLIVE, JOSE MARIA

DIXELIUS, HILDUR
DIXELIUS-BRETTNOR, HILDUR

DIXIE, MARMADUKE
HOWARD, GEOFFREY

DIXON, BINGHAM
BORLAND, WILLIAM ARMSTNG.

DIXON, CARTER
CARR, JOHN DICKSON

DIXON, DON
STEIN, J.H.

DIXON, FRANKLIN W.
ADAMS, HARRIET S.
ALBERT, SUSAN W. & BILL
BARRETT, NEAL JR.
MCFARLANE, LESLIE CHARLES
SVENSON, ANDREW E.
GOULART, RONALD JOSEPH
STRATEMEYER, EDWARD

DIXON, GEORGE
HATTON, CHARLES
WILLIS, TED

DIXON, LESLEY
VERNON, KATHLEEN R.

DIXON, MARK
BOYLL, RANDALL
MCDADE, CHARLES

DIXON, PAIGE
CORCORAN, BARBARA

DIXON, R.M.W.
DIXON, ROBERT MALCOLM W.

DIXON, REX
MARTIN, REGINALD ALEC

DIXON, RICHARD
WALKER, CLIFTON REGINALD

DIXON, ROSIE
WOOD, CHRISTOPHER [H]

DIXON, RUTH
BARROWS, [RUTH] MARJORIE

DIXON, WALLACE
CRONIN, BERNARD CHARLES

DJARV, JOHN
JERV, JONOTHAN

DJASSI, ABEL
CABRAL, AMICAR

DJIN DJIN
WILLIAMSON, J.C.

DNEPROV, ANATOLY
MITSKEVITCH, A.P.

DNIPROVA, CHAIKA
VASILEVSKA, LUDMYLA

DOAK
RANKIN, HUGH

DOAN, REECE
KING, ALBERT

DOANE, MARIAN S.
WOODWARD, GRACE STEEL

DOBELL, I.M.B.
DOBELL, ISABEL MARIAN B.

DOBKIN, KATHY
HAMEL PEIFER, KATHLEEN

DOBKIN, KAYE
HAMEL PEIFER, KATHLEEN

DOBLIN, ALFRED
DOEBLIN, ALFRED

DOBLING, MAXIMILIAN
FECHTNER, WOLFGANG

DOBREE, VALENTINE
DOBREE, GLADYS MAY M.

DOBSON, DENNIS
LEMIEUX, KENNETH

DOBSON, WILLIAM
BUTTERWORTH, MICHAEL

DOC
YAP, DIOSDADO M.

DOC ABRAHAM
ABRAHAM, GEORGE

DOCHERTY, JAMES L.
RAYMOND, RENE BRABAZON

DOCKER, THANE
KENT, JIM

DOCTOR BASEBALL
BJARKMAN, PETER CHRISTIAN

DOCTOR FUTUER
LYBURN, DR. ERIC FREDERIC

DODD, BELLA V.
DODD, MARIA ASSUNTA I.V.

DODD, DOUGLAS
FEARN, JOHN RUSSELL

DODD, MARTHA
STERN, MARTHA ECCLES D.

DODERER, HEIMITO
VON DODERER, HEIMITO

DODGE, DANIEL
DUBREUIL, ELIZABETH L.

DODGE, EMERSON
WHEELAHAN, PAUL

DODGE, FREEMONT
GRIMES, LEE

DODGE, GIL
HANO, ARNOLD

DODGE, LANGDON
WOLFSON, VICTOR

DODGE, MARY THURSTON
LE FEUVRE, AMY

DODGE, MICHAEL J.
FORD, JOHN M.

DODGE, STEVE
BECKER, STEPHEN [DAVID]

DOE, JOHN
THAYER, TIFFANY E.

DOE, JOHN JAMES
O'NOLAN, BRIAN

DOELY, SARAH BENTLEY
BENTLEY, SARAH

DOENIM, SUSAN
EFFINGER, GEORGE ALEC

DOERING, JEANNE
ZORNES, JEANNE DOERING

DOERMANN, FELIX
BIEDERMANN, FELIX

DOERNER, STEFAN
GUNTHER, HEINZ

DOESTICKS, Q.K. PHILANDER
THOMSON, MORTIMER

DOGBERRY
PHILLIPS, HUBERT

DOGBOLT, BARNABY
SILVETTE, HERBERT

DOGG, PROFESSOR R.L.
BERMAN, ED

DOGYEAR, DREW
GOREY, EDWARD ST. JOHN

DOHANEY, M.T.
DOHANEY, JEAN

DOHERTY, EDDIE
DOHERTY, EDWARD JOSEPH

DOHERTY, G.D.
DOHERTY, GEOFFREY DONALD

DOHL, FRANK
KRUNKE, HANS-WERNER

DOHL, STEFAN
SCHNEIDER, UTTA [D]

DOHRENBURG, THYRA
JAKSTEIN, THYRA [D]

DOHRN, MADELYN
DE VORE, MARY
DORNBUSH, JOAN

DOIMI DI DELUPIS, INGRID
DELUPIS, INGRID

DOLAN, BILL
WILLARD, TOM

DOLAN, DON
HARSTEN, UWE

DOLAN, WILLIAM
WILLARD, TOM

DOLBERG, ALEXANDER
BURG, DAVID

DOLBOKOV
DOLGOV, BORIS
WOODARD, WAYNE

DOLIN, ANTON
HEALEY-KAY, PATRICK

DOLINSKY, MIKE
DOLINSKY, MEYER

DOLITTLE, DR.
LOFTING, HUGH

DOLLAND, JOHN
PARSONS, H.F. DOLLAND

DOLLAR INVESTOR
D'AMBROSIO, CHARLES A.

DOLLAR, JIM
SHAGINYAN, MARIETTA S.

DOLLAR, JIMMY
SHAGINYAN, MARIETTA S.

DOLLEY, MARCUS J.
WATNEY, BERNARD MARTYN

DOLLEY, MICHAEL
DOLLEY, REGINALD HUGH

DOLLINGER, MARGARET
ERTTMANN, PAUL OSKAR

DOLPHIN, REX
DOLPHIN, REGINALD C.

DOLSON, FRANK
DOLSON, FRANKLIN ROBERT

DOLSON, HILDEGARDE
LOCKRIDGE, HILDEGARDE [D]

DOMAN, JUNE
BEVERIDGE, MERYLE SECREST

DOMANSKA, JANINA
LASKOWSKI, JANINA D.

DOMCIK, LUKAS
MODICK, KLAUS

DOMECQ, H. BUSTOS
BORGES, JORGE LUIS
BIOY-CASARES, ADOLFO

DOMIN, MICHAEL
VON CUBE, ALEXANDER

DOMINGUEZ, SERGIO ELIZON.
ELIZONDO, SERGIO D.

DOMINI, JON
LARUSSO, DOMINIC A.

DOMINI, REY
LORDE, ANDRE GERALDIN

DOMINIC, R.B.
HENISSART, MARTHA
LATSIS, MARY JANE

DOMINIC, SISTER MARY
GALLAHER, MARY DOMINIC

DOMINIE, [THE]
HUGHES, WILLIAM JESSE

DOMINIQUE
PROUST, [V-L-G-E] MARCEL

DOMINIQUE, MEG
SANFORD, ANNETTE [S]

DOMINO, JOHN
AVERILL, ESTHER [HOLDEN]

DOMMA, OTTOKAR
HAUSER, OTTO

DOMPO, KWESI
PARKES, FRANK KOBINA

DON
DIEKENGA, I.E.

DON BENITO
NIELSEN, BENT ROSENKILDE

DON CAMILLO
CELA, CAMILLO JOSE

DON QUIXOTE
ERSKINE, GLADYS SHAW

DON ROBERTO
CUNNINGHAME GRAHAM, R.B.

DON, A.
STEPHEN, LESLIE

DONAHUE, PHIL
DONAHUE, PHILLIP JOHN

DONALD, FRANK
BANZHAF, ERWIN

DONALD, R.V.
FLOREN, LEE

DONALD, VIVIAN
MACKINNON, CHARLES ROY

DONALDS, GORDON
SHIRREFFS, GORDON DONALD

DONALDSON, BRYNA
STEVENS, BRYNA

DONALDSON, JACK
NUETZEL, CHARLES A.

DONALDSON, P.J.
PFEIL, DONALD J.

DONAT, ANTON
DONART, ARTHUR C[HARLES]

DONATHAN, JEAN ANN
LEWIS, JEANE GILBERT

DONATUS, GEORG
KLEINE, ERWIN

DONAVAN, JOHN
MORLAND, NIGEL

DONEM, SUE
ROSS, STANLEY RALPH

DONETTA
CHESTER, TESSA ROSE

DONG, LEONIE
DOLL, HANELORE

DONKER, ANTHONIE
DONKERSLOOT, NICOLAAS A.

DONKEY, JOHN
ENGLISH, THOMAS DUNN

DONLEAVY, J.P.
DONLEAVY, JAMES PATRICK

DONNE, HAMILTON
LAZENBY, NORMAN A.

DONNE, JACK
BLOOM, DON JACK
ENCIMER, PAUL D.

DONNE, MAXIM
DUKE, MADELAINE

DONNELLY, A.
AITKEN, A. DONNELLY

DONNELLY, ESMOND
OBERDORF, CHARLES DONNELL

DONNER, GROVE
HARVEY, FLORENCE

DONNER, JAMES
JAMES, DONALD

DONNER, MIKE
KALMUCZAK, ROLF

DONNIGAN, DREGS
WEIRICH, BOB

DONOGHUE, MARTIN
GIBSON, WALTER B.

DONOGHUE, P.S.
HUNT, E. HOWARD

DONOHUE, MARTIN
GIBSON, WALTER B.

DONOSO, JOSE
YANEZ, JOSE DONOSO

DONOSTI, MARIO
LUCIOLLI, MARIO

DONOVAN, BONNIE
DONOVAN, BONITA R.

DONOVAN, CHAD
DELFS, RAINER

DONOVAN, CURT
LUTZ, GILES A.

DONOVAN, DICK
MUDDOCK, JOYCE E.P.

DONOVAN, JACK
DELFS, RAINER

DONOVAN, LOU
FITTOCK, R.J.

DONOVAN, RICK
DUNNE, RON

DONOVAN, SANDRA
DE SHA, SANDRA DONOVAN

DONOVAN, WILLIAM
BERKEBILE, FRED DONOVAN

DONRATH, MICHAEL
HORBACH, MICHAEL

DOOG, K. CAJ
GOOD, IRVING JOHN

DOOLARD, A. DEN.
SPOELSTRA, CORNELIUS

DOOLEY, EBON
EBON

DOOLEY, MARTIN
DUNNE, FINLEY PETER

DOOLEY, MR.
DUNNE, FINLEY PETER

DOOLING, DAVE
DOOLING, DAVID JR.

DOONE, JICE
MARSHALL, JAMES VANCE

DOOREN, INGRID V.
VAN DOOREN, INGRID

DOORN, JENS
MORITZ, PAUL

DOORSAGE, JEAN
SIMENON, GEORGES [J.C]

DOR, ANA
CEDER, GEORGIANA DORCAS

DOR, MILO
DOROSLAVIC, MILUTIN

DORANT, GENE
LENT, D[ORA] GENEVA

DORASAN, LUC
SIMENON, GEORGES [J.C]

DORCHATO, JEAN
BENTEIN, JEAN-MARIE G.J.

DORE, CHRISTY
PLAGAKIS, JIM

DORET, RICHARD
SHAVER, RICHARD S.

DORFY
SAMUELSON-SANDVID, DOROT.

DORGE, JEANNE EMILE MARIE
MARIE-ANDRE DU SC, SISTER

DORGELES, ROLAND
LECAVELE, ROLAND

DORIAN, HARRY
HAMILTON, CHARLES H.S.

DORIAN, PHILIP
PHILLIPS, DORIAN M.

DORLAND, HENRY
ASH, BRIAN

DORLIAE, SAINT
DORLIAE, PETER GONDRO

DORMAN, LUKE
BINGLEY, DAVID ERNEST

DORMER, DANIEL
CORDEAU, KATE MARIAN

DORMIE, M.A.
SHARROCK, MARIAN EDNA

DORMON, LUKE
BINGLEY, DAVID BINGLEY

DORN, ALEC B.
KALMUCZAK, ROLF

DORN, DEAN
MICHAEL, MORGAN

DORN, FRANK
DORER, FRANCIS CATHERINE

DORN, GEORG
HERING, GEO

DORN, GERTRUD
FUSSENEGGER, GERTRUD

DORN, I.
KALMUCZAK, ROLF

DORN, LISA
HUTTNER, DORALIES

DORNBERG, J.C.
GRUND, CARL-JOSEPH

DORNBERG, MICHAELA
PUSCH, EDITH

DORNE, PASCAL
GONDA, ADOLPHE

DORNER, PETER
DUBINA, PETER

DOROT, PETER
SHAVER, RICHARD S.

DOROTHY, R.D.
CHARQUES, DOROTHY [T]

DORPAT, CHRISTEL
PURRMANN, CHRISTEL

DORPH, JAN
MEYN, NIELS

DORRIE, DORIS
DOERRIE, DORIS

DORRIS, MICHAEL A.
DORRIS, MICHAEL [ANTHONY]

DORS, ALEXANDRA
MCKITTRICK, DOROTHY

DORS, DIANA
FLUCK, DIANA

DORSAINVIL, J.C.
DORSAINVIL, JUSTIN C.

DORSET, RICHARD
SHAVER, RICHARD S.

DORSET, RUTH
ROSS, WILLIAM E. DANIEL

DORSET, ST. JOHN
BELFOUR, HUGH J.

DORSETT, DANIELLA
DANIELS, NORMAN A.
DANIELS, DOROTHY

DOS
MADISON, JOHN RODRIGO

DOS PASSOS, JOHN
MADISON, JOHN RODRIGO

DOSSAGE, JEAN
SIMENON, GEORGES [J.C]

DOST, ZAMIN KI
ARMSTRONG, WILLIMINA L.

DOTSON, BOB
DOTSON, ROBERT CHARLES

DOTSON, DAVE
MUNRO, NORMAN L.

DOTTIG
GRIDER, DOROTHY

DOUARDO, WALDOMIRO AUTRAN
DOUARDO, AUTRAN

DOUBLE, LUKE
HYDE, THOMAS ALEXANDER

DOUBLEDAY, ROMAN
LONG, LILY AUGUSTA

DOUGHERTY, JOANNA FOSTER
FOSTER, JOANNA

DOUGHTY, C.M.
DOUGHTY, CHARLES MONTAGUE

DOUGHTY, FRANK
SENARENS, LUIS P.

DOUGHTY, NIGEL
WHITTINGTON-EGAN, RICHARD

DOUGLAS HOME, WILLIAM
HOME, WILLIAM DOUGLAS

DOUGLAS, ALBERT
ARMSTRONG, DOUGLAS A.

DOUGLAS, ALYSSA
CANADEO, ANNE

DOUGLAS, AMANDA HART
WALLMANN, JEFFREY M.

DOUGLAS, ANN C.
WELCH, ANN COURTENAY E.

DOUGLAS, ARTHUR
HAMMOND, GERALD [A.D.]
MORETON, DOUGLAS ARTHUR

DOUGLAS, BARBARA
LAKER, ROSALIND
OVSTEDAL, BARBARA

DOUGLAS, C.H.
GRIEVE, CHRIST. MURRAY

DOUGLAS, CASEY
CASEY, JUNE E.

DOUGLAS, CHRISTOPHER
NEILL, CHRISTOPHER H.D.

DOUGLAS, COLIN
CURRY, COLIN THOMAS

DOUGLAS, D.
WILKES-HUNTER, RICHARD

DOUGLAS, DAYLE
ADAMSON, EWART

DOUGLAS, DEAN
DE NEEN, DOUGLAS

DOUGLAS, DIANA
WILKES-HUNTER, RICHARD

DOUGLAS, DRAKE
ZIMMERMAN, WERNER

DOUGLAS, EDITH
BURNHAM, CLARA LOUISE

DOUGLAS, ELIZABETH
WILHITE, BETTIE MARIE

DOUGLAS, ELLEN
HAXTON, JOSEPHINE A.
WILLIAMSON, ELLEN DOUGLAS

DOUGLAS, FELICITY & HENRY
LEON, HENRY CECIL

DOUGLAS, FRANK
KALMUCZAK, ROLF
LANGLEY, F.E.

DOUGLAS, GARRY
KILWORTH, GARRY DOUGLAS

DOUGLAS, GEORGE
BROWN, GEORGE DOUGLAS
DEAN, GEORGE
DERRICK, HENRY
FERME, MRS. GEORGE
FISHER, DOUGLAS [GEORGE]

DOUGLAS, GLENN
DUCKETT, ALFRED A.
FRIEDRICHS, HOLGER

DOUGLAS, GLORIA
UPPER, GLORIA

DOUGLAS, GREGORY A.
CANTOR, ELI

DOUGLAS, HELEN BEE
BEE, HELEN L.

DOUGLAS, HUDSON
AITKEN, ROBERT

DOUGLAS, JAMES
BUTTERWORTH, WILLIAM E.

DOUGLAS, JEFF
BERRY, D[OUGLAS] BRUCE
OFFUTT, ANDREW J.

DOUGLAS, JOHN
LYNDS, DENNIS

DOUGLAS, JOYCE
MORETON, DOUGLAS ARTHUR

DOUGLAS, KATE
DOUGLAS, KATHLEEN

DOUGLAS, KATHRYN
EWING, KATHRYN

DOUGLAS, KIM
WOODFORD, [I] CECIL

DOUGLAS, LEONARD
BRADBURY, RAY [DOUGLAS]

DOUGLAS, LLOYD C.
DOYGLAS, LLOYD CASSEL

DOUGLAS, MALCOLM
SANDERSON, [R] DOUGLAS

DOUGLAS, MARY
TEW, MARY

DOUGLAS, MICHAEL
BRIGHT, ROBERT DOUGLAS
CRICHTON, DOUGLAS
CRICHTON, [JOHN] MICHAEL

DOUGLAS, NATHAN
YOUNG, NEDRICK

DOUGLAS, NOEL
CHELTHAM-STRODE, WARREN

DOUGLAS, O.
BUCHAN, ANNA

DOUGLAS, R.M.
MASON, DOUGLAS RANKINE

DOUGLAS, ROBERT
ANDREWS, [C] ROBERT D.

DOUGLAS, SCOTT
SMITH, WILLIAM SCOTT

DOUGLAS, SHANE
WILKES-HUNTER, RICHARD

DOUGLAS, THEO
EVERETT, MRS. H.D.

DOUGLAS, THORNE
HAAS, BENJAMIN LEOPOLD

DOUGLAS-HOME, ALEC
HOME, ALEXANDER FREDERICK

DOUGLAS-SCOTT-MONTAGU, ED
MONTAGU, EDWARD J.B.D.S.

DOUGLASS, BILLIE
DELINSKY, BARBARA R.

DOUGLASS, ELLSWORTH
DWIGGINS, ELMER

DOUGLASS, JESSICA
WALLERICH, LINDA H.

DOUGLASS, KEITH
KEITH, WILLIAM HENRY JR.

DOUGLASS, MARCIA KENT
DOTY, GLADYS

DOULOS, JAY
JOYCE, JON LOYD

DOURADA, WALDOMIRO AUTRAN
DOURADA, [W.F.] AUTRAN

DOURO, MARQUIS OF
BRONTE, CHARLOTTE

DOVER, BEN
ETCHISON, DENNIS WILLIAM

DOW, DOROTHY
FITZGERALD, DOROTHY DOW

DOW, ETHEL
KOHON, ETHEL [C]

DOWD, MAXINE
JENSEN, MAXINE DOWD

DOWD, T.B.
PORTER, WILLIAM SYDNEY

DOWDY, MRS. REGERA
GOREY, EDWARD ST. JOHN

DOWER, J.W.
DOWER, JOHN WILLIAM

DOWER[S], PENN
PENDOWER, THOMAS CURTIS H

DOWLEY, D.M.
MARRISON, LESLIE WILLIAM

DOWLEY, D.M.
MORRISON, LESLIE WILLIAM

DOWLING, TOM
DOWLING, THOMAS JR.

DOWNE, PATRICK
LASCELLES, WALTER

DOWNES, KATHLEEN
DOWNES, DEIRDRE K.

DOWNES, QUENTIN
HARRISON, MICHAEL
ROHAN, MAURICE DESMOND

DOWNEY, BILL
DOWNEY, WILLIAM LESLIE

DOWNING, CENTURY
PALMER, PAUL

DOWNING, J. MAJOR
DAVIS, CHARLES A.

DOWNING, MAJOR JACK
SMITH, SEBA

DOWNING, PAULA E.
KING, PAULA E. DOWNING

DOWNMAN, FRANCIS
OLDMEADOW, ERNEST JAMES

DOWNS, BILL
SELLERS, CONNIE LESLIE

DOWNS, ROBERT B.
DOWNS, ROBERT BINGHAM

DOYAN, RALPH
GERSTMAYER, HERMANN

DOYLE, A. CONAN
DOYLE, ARTHUR CONAN

DOYLE, ADRIAN M.C.
CONAN DOYLE, ADRIAN MALC.

DOYLE, CONAN
DOYLE, ARTHUR CONAN

DOYLE, DAVID
CARTER, DAVID CHARLES

DOYLE, DONOVAN
BOEGEHOLD, BETTY [DOYLE]

DOYLE, EMILY
HENRICHS, BETTY L.

DOYLE, EMMET
TRUMBO, DONALD [DALTON]

DOYLE, HAROLD EDMUND
STEARNS, HAROLD EDMUND

DOYLE, JERRY
DOYLE, GERALD A.

DOYLE, JOHN
ELLISON, HARLAN
GRAVES, ROBERT VAN RANKE

DOYLE, LYNN
MONTGOMERY, LESLIE ALEX.

DOYLE, MALCOLM
HINCKS, CYRIL MALCOLM

DOYLE, MIKE
DOYLE, CHARLES

DOYLE, SIR A.
DOYLE, ARTHUR CONAN

DOYLE, SIR ARTHUR CONAN
DOYLE, ARTHUR CONAN

DOZIER, ZOE
BROWNING, DIXIE [S.B.]

DR. A
ASIMOV, ISAAC
SILVERSTEIN, ALVIN & VIRG

DR. ACULA
ACKERMAN, FORREST J.

DR. ADDER
JETER, K[EVIN] W.

DR. COGGS
GIBERGA, OVIDIO

DR. DIOSCORIDES
HARTING, PIETER

DR. DREW
ARNESON, D.J.
TALLARICO, ANTHONY

DR. HIP
SCHOENFELD, EUGENE L.

DR. HIPPOCRATES
SCHOENFELD, EUGENE L.

DR. JUDY
KURIANSKY, JUDITH [A.B.]

DR. SCIENCE
COFFEY, DANIEL

DR. SEUSS
GEISEL, THEODOR SEUSS

DR. X
NOURSE, ALAN E.

DRACHLER, TRUMBULL
CREWS, JUDSON [C]

DRACHMAN, WOLF
ROSE, IAN

DRACO, F.
DAVIS, JULIA

DRAGER, GARY
EDENS, COOPER

DRAGO, SINCLAIR
DRAGO, HARRY SINCLAIR

DRAGOMIR, ASSENOV
MELAMED, ZHAK NISSUM

DRAGON, CAROLYN
DUBREUIL, ELIZABETH L.

DRAGPNAT, EDWARD
WILLIAMSON, THAMES ROSS

DRAIG, GLAS
JOHNSON, ARTHUR TYSILIO

DRAKE, ALISON
JANESHUTZ, PATRICIA MARIE

DRAKE, ALISON [CLAIRE]
MACGREGOR, PATRICIA M.J.

DRAKE, ASA
ANDERSSON, C. DEAN
ANDERSSON, NINA ROMBERG

DRAKE, BONNIE
DELINSKY, BARBARA

DRAKE, CONNIE
FEDDERSON, CONNIE

DRAKE, DREXEL
HUFF, CHARLES H.

DRAKE, FRANK
HAMILTON, CHARLES H.S.

DRAKE, GASTON V.
BANGS, JOHN KENDRICK

DRAKE, GLENN
HOBEIN, EUGEN

DRAKE, HAMILTON
HOFFENBERG, MASON

DRAKE, HARRY
KRAFT, ROBERT

DRAKE, JACK
TINE, ROBERT

DRAKE, JOAN
DAVIES, JOAN HOWARD

DRAKE, JOHN
BOSETZKY, HORST
GROSSMANN, HANS HUGO
HARTMANN, HELMUT HENRY
MOLSNER, MICHAEL

DRAKE, KIMBAL
GALLAGHER, RACHEL

DRAKE, LISL
BEER, ELOISE C.S.

DRAKE, MORGAN
BERRY, D[OUGLAS] BRUCE
FERGUSON, JAMES D.

DRAKE, RUPERT
BELFIELD, HARRY WEDGEWOOD

DRAKE, SHANNON
POZZESSERE, HEATHER G.

DRAKE, SUSAN
DUNN, SUSAN W.

DRAKE, W. ANDERS
ESHBACH, LLOYD ARTHUR

DRAKE, WINIFRED
BRYANT, DENNY

DRAPER, BLANCE A.
WEBB, BLANCHE A.

DRAPER, HASTINGS
JEFFRIES, RODERIC[GRAEME]

DRAPIER, M.B.
SWIFT, JONATHAN

DRAX, PETER
ADDIS, ERIC ELRINGTON

DRAXNER, WILL
PARRY-DRIXNER, WILLY

DRAYHAM, JAMES
MENCKEN, HENRY LOUIS

DRAYHAM, WILLIAM
MENCKEN, HENRY LOUIS
NATHAN, GEORGE JEAN

DRAYNE, GEORGE
MCCULLEY, JOHNSTON

DRAYSON, A.W.
WARWICK, SIDNEY

DRAYTON, LILLIAN R.
CORYELL, JOHN RUSSELL

DRAYTON, RICKY
BARNES, MICHAEL [L.G.]
GORELL, LETHBRIDGE

DREADSTONE, CARL
CAMPBELL, [JOHN] RAMSEY

DREPIER, M.B.
SWIFT, JONATHAN

DRESCHER-LEHMAN, SANDRA
DRESCHER, SANDRA

DRESSER, HELEN
MCCLOY, HELEN [CLARKSON]

DRESSMAN, DENNY
DRESSMAN, DENNIS LEE

DREW, CON
DREW, CONWAY

DREW, D'ARCY
MIVART, ST. GEORGE J.

DREW, ELEANOR
DAWES, EDNA

DREW, JENNIFER
ANDREWS, BARBARA
HANSON, PAMELA

DREW, KENNETH
COCKBURN, [FRANCIS] CLAU

DREW, LINCOLN
MCGAUGHY, DUDLEY DEAN

DREW, MARY ANNE
CASSIDAY, BRUCE [BINGHAM]

DREW, MORGAN
PRICE, ROBERT

DREW, NICHOLAS
HARLING, ROBERT

DREW, PATRICIA
KAYE, LLOYD S.

DREW, PATRICIA
PERCEVAL, JULIA

DREW, REGINALD
HOME-GALL, WILLIAM B.

DREW, SHERIDAN
FEARN, JOHN RUSSELL

DREW, SIDNEY
MURRAY, EDGAR JOYCE

DREWERY, MARY
SMITH, MARY

DREXEL, J.V.
PRONZINI, WILLIAM JOHN

DREXEL, JAY B.
BIXBY, JEROME L.

DREXLER, J.F.
PAINE, LAURAN BOSWORTH

DREYER, HARRY
PARRY-DRIXNER, WILLY

DREYFUS, FRED
ROSENBLATT, FRED

DRIAL, J.E.
LAIRD, JEAN E.

DRIBERG, TOM
DRIBERG, THOMAS EDWARD N.

DRIFTWOOD, PENELOPE
DE LIMA, CLARA ROSA

DRIGIN, S.
DRIGIN, SERGE R.

DRILLING, RICHARD W.
DONGES, GUNTER

DRINAN, ADAM
MACLEOD, JOSEPH [T.G.]

DRINCIC, SAVA
DJURICIC, ULADEN ST.

DRING, NATHANIEL
MCBROOM, R. CURTIS

DRINKROW, JOHN
HARDWICK, MOLLIE
HARDWICK, [J] MICHAEL [D]

DRISCOLL, ELI
KING, ALBERT

DRIVER, CYNTHIA C.
LOVIN, ROGER ROBERT

DRIVING HAWK, VIRGINIA
SNEVE, VIRGINIA D. HAWK

DRIVING, MAC
DONGES, GUNTER

DRIXNER, WILL
PARRY-DRIXNER, WILLY

DROGHEDA, EARL OF
MOORE, CHARLES GARRETT P.

DRONGO, LUKE
RIDDLESTON, CHARLES H.

DROP SHOT
CABLE, GEORGE WASHINGTON

DROPPER, H.
JENNINGS, LOUIS J.

DROSTE, LOTTE
BRUGMANN-EBERHARDT, LOTTE

DROWER, M.S.
HACHFORTH-JONES, MARGARET

DROZZA, PETER
ORZECHOWSKI, PETER

DRUCE, CHRISTOPHER
PULLING, CHRISTOPHER D.

DRUCKER, H.M.
DRUCKER, HENRY MATTHEW

DRUG, VICTOR
MORETTI, UGO

DRUID, THE
DIXON, HENRY HALL

DRUKKER, J.
PRESSER, [G] JACOB

DRUM, BOB
DRUM, ROBERT F.

DRUMM, D.B.
MONTELEONE, THOMAS F.
NAHA, ED
SHIRLEY, JOHN

DRUMMOND, ANTHONY
HUNTER, ALFRED JOHN

DRUMMOND, BRENNA
BRYER, JUDITH E.

DRUMMOND, CHARLES
GILES, KENNETH

DRUMMOND, EMMA
DAWES, EDNA

DRUMMOND, IVOR
LONGRIGG, ROGER [ERSKINE]

DRUMMOND, J.
CHANCE, JOHN NEWTON
HARRIS, JOHN WYNDHAM P.L.

DRUMMOND, JOHN
CHANCE, JOHN NEWTON

DRUMMOND, JOHN PETER
CUSHMAN, DAN
MULLEN, STANLEY

DRUMMOND, VIOLET HILDA
SWETENHAM, VIOLET HILDA

DRUMMOND, WALTER
SILVERBERG, ROBERT

DRUMMOND, WILLIAM
MARSHALL, ARTHUR C.

DRUON, MAURICE
DE REYNIAC, MAURICE DRUON
KESSEL, MAURICE

DRURY, CLARE MARIE
HOSKYNS-ABRAHALL, CLARE C

DRURY, REBECCA
BARRETT, NEAL JR.
DAMIO, WARD
HOLT, WILL
HUNT, GREG
LLOYD, ADRIAN
MYERS, BARRY
THOMPSON, ROBERT
TOOMBS, JANE [JENKE]
TREMBLAY, ERNEST A. II
ZACHARY, HUGH

DRY, ILONA
ROSENER, INGE

DRYASDUST
HERON-ALLEN, EDWARD

DRYDEN, JOHN
ROWLAND, DONALD S.

DRYDEN, KEITH
LANDELLS, RICHARD

DRYDEN, LENNOX
STEEN, MARGUERITE

DRYDEN, PAMELA
JOHNSTON, NORMA
ST. JOHN, NICOLE

DRYHAM, JAMES
MENCKEN, HENRY LOUIS

DRYHURST, EDWARD
ROBERTS, EDWARD DRYHURST

DRZEWIECKI, HENRY K.
ROSENBAUM, HERCEL

DU BLANC, DAPHNE
GROOM, ARTHUR WILLIAM

DU BOIS, CHARLES
COUNSELMAN, MARY ELIZAB.

DU BOIS, IRENE
LEIDING, FRIEDA

DU BOIS, JEAN
LEIDING, FRIEDA

DU BOIS, LEON
BATT, LEON

DU HALT, JEAN
GRINDEL, EUGENE

DU MAURIER, DAPHNE
BROWNING, DAPHNE DU MAUR.

DU MONT, DIETLIN NEVEN
GOLTZ, DIETLIND

DU NOUEY, PIERRE LECOMTE
LECOMTE DU NOUEY, PIERRE

DU PERRY, JEAN
SIMENON, GEORGES [J.C]

DU PLESSIS, PHIL
DU PLESSIS, JOHANNES

DU PRE, GABRIELLE
KLEINSCHMIDT, DIANNE M.
SMITH-WARE, SANDRA

DU PRES, HENRY
WEISS, JOE

DU VAUL, VIRGINIA C.
COFFMAN, VIRGINIA [E]

DUAN, LE
LE DUAN

DUANE, A.S.
LEACH, ANN

DUANE, ANDREW
BRINEY, ROBERT E.

DUANE, JIM
HURLEY, VIC

DUANE, TOBY
GANLEY, W. PAUL

DUBALL, MICHAEL
ALD, ROY ALLISON

DUBE, RODOLPHE
HERTEL, FRANCOIS

DUBH, SCIAN
MCCARROLL, JAMES

DUBIOUS, GARNER R.
GLICKSOHN, MIKE

DUBLIN, CONRAD PADRAIC
KIDD, WALTER EVANS

DUBOIS, ALAN
WOOD, CLEMENT

DUBOIS, BONNA LEE
COOK, BONNA LEE D.

DUBOIS, M.
KENT, ARTHUR WILLIAM C.

DUBOIS, PAUL
HAHN, ROLF

DUBOIS, ROCHELLE [L] HOLT
HOLT, ROCHELLE LYNN

DUBOIS, ROSEMARY
DURRANT, RITA D.

DUBOIS, SALLY
VINCENTNATHAN, LYNN

DUBREUIL, LINDA
DUBREUIL, ELIZABETH L.

DUBRONY, A.
DE BERMANS, A.

DUCA MINIMO
D'ANNUNZIO, GRABIELE

DUCHAMP, LAURA
DUCHAMP, L. TIMMEL

DUCHESNE, ANTOINETTE
PAINE, LAURAN BOSWORTH

DUCHESNE, JACQUES
SAINT-DENIS, MICHEL JACQ.

DUCHESS OF MARLBOROUGH
SPENCER-CHURCHILL, LAURA

DUCHESS OF WINDSOR
WINDSOR, BESSIE W.W.S.S.

DUCHESS, THE
HAMILTON, MARGARET WOLFE

DUCK, CAPTAIN
PINKWATER, DANIEL MANUS

DUCORNET, RIKKI
DUCORNET, ERICA

DUDGEON, ROBERT
ANDERSON, UELL STANLEY
EHRLICH, JOHN GUNTHER
FULLER, WILLIAM
GREENOP, FRANK S.
HANSON, VICTOR JOSEPH
ROHDE, ROBERT H.
STUART, WILLIAM LISTLE

DUDLEY, ARTHUR
BLAZE DE BURY, MARIE P.R.

DUDLEY, BIDE
DUDLEY, WALTER BRONSON

DUDLEY, DOROTHY
GOODRIDGE, MARY WILLIAMS

DUDLEY, ERNEST
COLTMAN-ALLEN, V. ERNEST

DUDLEY, FRANK
GREENE, WARD

DUDLEY, H.
HOPE-SIMPSON, JACYNTH

DUDLEY, HELEN
HOPE-SIMPSON, JACYNTH

DUDLEY, NANCY
COLE, LOIS DWIGHT

DUDLEY, OWEN
MCGAUGHY, DUDLEY DEAN

DUDLEY, ROBERT
BALDWIN, JAMES

DUDLEY, TREVOR
TREVOR, ELLESTON

DUDLEY-SMITH, T.
TREVOR, ELLESTON

DUELL, EILEEN-MARIE
PETRIE, RHONA

DUEREN, HANNA
ELZER, MARGARETE

DUFF, BELDON
SHARP, ETHEL

DUFF, HOWARD
BASNER, GERHARD

DUFF, HOWARD
GROSSMANN, HANS HUGO

DUFF, MAGGIE
DUFF, MARGARET K.

DUFFER, ALLAN
MAY, JOHN

DUFFIELD, ANNE
DUFFIELD, DOROTHY DEAN

DUFFY, BEN
DUFFY, BERNARD C.

DUFFY, JOHN
COOK, KENNETH
CROSS, RENA
ELLIS, DAVID

DUFFY, ROBERT M.
DIPRIMA, DIANE
MOLLOY, ALICE

DUFRECHOU, CAROL
MONROE, CAROL

DUGALL, H.L.
DURAND, LOUIS
GALLISSION, HENRI

DUGAN, JACK
BUTTERWORTH, WILLIAM E.

DUGAN, JOHN KEVIN
BUTTERWORTH, WILLIAM E.

DUGDALE, DOREEN
HARDY, HENRY

DUGDALE, ROBERT
HARDY, HENRY

DUGGAN, CHRIS
JORDAN, JAMES A.

DUGGANS, PAT
CONNOLLY, ROBERT DUGAN JR

DUGUID, ROBERT
PRING-MILL, ROBERT D.F.

DUHRING, NATHAN
COOPER, EVAN

DUHRKOPP, HERBERT
REINECKER, HERBERT

DUKA, IVO
DUCHACEK, IVO MARIA R.

DUKA, PETER
HERZOG, WILHELM PETER

DUKAINE, PAUL
DUKES, [SIR] PAUL

DUKAKIS, KITTY
DUKAKIS, KATHARINE

DUKE OF BEAUFORT
SOMERSET, HENRY HUGH A.F.

DUKE, DEREK
PHILLIPS, HORACE

DUKE, ELIZABETH
WALLINGTON, VIVIENNE

DUKE, HOBBY
KOHR, DIETRICH

DUKE, JIM
DUKE, JAMES A.

DUKE, JOHN
CHALMERS, FLOYD S.

DUKE, MADELAINE
MACFARLANE, E. MADL. DUKE

DUKE, MARGARET
DUNK, MARGARET

DUKE, PATTY
DUKE, ANNA MARIE

DUKE, RAOUL
THOMPSON, HUNTER S.

DUKE, WILL
GAULT, WILLIAM CAMPBELL

DUKELSKY, VLADIMIR
DUKE, VERNON

DUKES, PHILIP
BICKERS, RICHARD L.T.

DULIEU, JEAN
VAN OORT, JAN

DULOUP, VICTOR
VOLKOFF, VLADIMER

DUMAS, CLAIRE
VAN WEDDINGEN, MARTHE

DUMAS, CLAUDINE
MALZBERG, BARRY [N]

DUMBARTON, A.
MACAULEY, ROBIE [M]

DUMKEY, RAYMOND
BRAUN, WILBUR

DUMONT, JESSIE
FOLEY, DAVE

DUMPTY, HUMPTY S.
DENENBERG, HERBERT SIDNEY

DUN, MAO
YEN-PING, SHIN

DUNANT, PETER
BUSBY, PETER
DUNANT, SARAH

DUNBAR, ALICE
NELSON, ALICE RUTH M.D.

DUNBAR, ALICE MOORE
NELSON, ALICE RUTH M.D.

DUNBAR, DAVID
BAXTER, CRAIG

DUNBAR, EDWARD
SMITH, DAVID MACLEOD

DUNBAR, NOEL
INGRAHAM, PRENTISS

DUNBAR-NELSON, ALICE
NELSON, ALICE RUTH M.D.

DUNCAN, A.H.
CLEARY, C.V.H.

DUNCAN, ALEX
DUKE, MADELAINE

DUNCAN, ARL
BURGDORF, KARL-ULRICH

DUNCAN, BLANCHE
HEATH-MILLER, M. BLANCHE

DUNCAN, BRUCE
GREENFIELD, IRVING A.

DUNCAN, DAVID
GLIDDEN, JONATHAN

DUNCAN, DORA ISADORA
DUNCAN, ISADORA

DUNCAN, DUKE
RATHBORNE, ST. GEORGE

DUNCAN, GELIE
WALLACE, ELWYN

DUNCAN, GEORGE
DAVIDSON, GEOFFREY

DUNCAN, GREGORY
MCCLINTOCK, MARSHALL

DUNCAN, JAMES
HADATH, JOHN E.G.

DUNCAN, JANE
CAMERON, ELIZABETH JANE

DUNCAN, JOHN
KOBUSCH, JOACHIM

DUNCAN, JUDITH
MULHOLLAND, JUDITH

DUNCAN, JULIA COLEY
SATHER, JULIA COLEY D.

DUNCAN, JULIA K.
BENSON, MILDRED [A] WIRT
KARIG, WALTER
STRATEMEYER, EDWARD

DUNCAN, LOIS
ARQUETTE, LOIS S. DUNCAN

DUNCAN, LYNNE
BANKS, CAROLYN

DUNCAN, MURDOCK
DUNCAN, W. MURDOCK

DUNCAN, PETER
ATKINSON, B.M. JR.

DUNCAN, ROBERT
HARZER, KARL

DUNCAN, ROBERT [EDWARD]
DUNCAN, EDWARD HOWARD

DUNCAN, TERANCE
NOLAN, WILLIAM F.

DUNCAN, TERENCE
BARRETT, NEAL JR.
PUECHNER, BARBARA
REASONER, JAMES M.

DUNCAN, W.R.
DUNCAN, ROBERT L. & WANDA

DUNDEE, DOUGLAS
CUMMING-SKINNER, DUGALD M

DUNDEE, ROBERT
KIRSH, ROBERT R.

DUNDEE, WALT
GREENOP, FRANK S.

DUNHAM, BOB
DUNHAM, ROBERT

DUNHILL, JOE
RAHN, WOLFGANG

DUNKELMAN, BEN
DUNKELMAN, BENJAMIN

DUNLAP, JANE
DAVIS, ADELLE

DUNLOP, LON
MCCORMICK, WILFRED

DUNN, AIKEN
LATTO, THOMAS C.

DUNN, DETECTIVE
PEARCE, CHARLES E.

DUNN, ELEANOR
DUNTEMAM, ELEANOR ADELE

DUNN, ELIZA
NORTON, EDITH ELIZABETH A

DUNN, GERTRUDE
WEAVER, GERTRUDE RENTON

DUNN, HARRIS
DOERFFLER, ALFRED

DUNN, JAMES
WILKES-HUNTER, RICHARD

DUNN, JAMES A.
WILKES-HUNTER, RICHARD

DUNN, JOHN
ELLIS, DAVID

DUNN, JUDITH F.
BERNAL, JUDITH F.

DUNN, JUDY
SPANGENBERG, JUDITH DUNN

DUNN, KAYE
DUNHAM, KATHERINE

DUNN, LARRY
DONOVAN, LAURENCE

DUNN, MARY
WRIGHT, MARY MAUDE

DUNN, NELL
SANDERFORD, NELL MARY

DUNN, PAULINE
DUNN, DAWN PAULINE
HARTZELL, SUSAN KATHLEEN

DUNN, S.P.
DUNN, STEPHEN PORTER

DUNN, SAUL
DUNN, PHILIP M.

DUNNE, DESMOND
LEE-RICHARDSON, JAMES

DUNNE, J.W.
DUNNE, JOHN WILLIAM

DUNNE, JOHN T.
LOVECRAFT, H[OWARD] P.

DUNNE, LYELL
BUNDEY, ELLEN MILNE

DUNNE, MARY JO
DUNNE, MARY COLLINS

DUNNETT, DOROTHY
HALLIDAY, DOROTHY

DUNNING, EDWARD
GILBERT, ROBERT ANDREW

DUNNING, HAL
TOMPKINS, WALKER A.

DUNNINGER, JOSEPH
GIBSON, WALTER B.

DUNOYER, MAURICE
DOMERGUE, MAURICE

DUNSANY, LORD
PLUNKETT, EDWARD JOHN M.D

DUNSMUIR, AMY
OLEPHANT, MRS.

DUNSTAN, ANDREW
CHANDLER, A. BERTRAM

DUNSTAN, GREGORY
ROWE, JOHN GABRIEL

DUNSTONE, MAX
DUNSTONE, MAXWELL F.

DUPEA, BOBBY
CRAWLEY, TONY

DUPIN, AUGUST DUPONT
TAYLOR, JOHN A.

DUPLESSIS, BERTRAND
LEROUX, YVES

DUPLESSIS, YVES
DUPLESSIS, YVONNE
JAURAND, YVONNE

DUPLEX
HALLOWS, N.F.

DUPONT, KURT
RUELLAN, ANDRE

DUPONT, PAUL
FREWIN, LESLIE RONALD

DUPRE, HARRISON
FISHER, STEPHEN GOULD

DUPREE, MADRIS
DEPASTURE, MADRIS

DUPREE, MORRISON
GASS, SHERLOCK BRONSON

DUPRES, HENRI
FAWCETT, FRANK DUBREZ

DURAC, JACK
RACHMAN, STANLEY JACK

DURACK, MARY
MILLER, MARY

DURAND, CASS
PULLAN, RU

DURAND, G. FORBES
BURGESS, MICHAEL ROY

DURAND, LUCILE
BERSIANIK, LOUKY

DURAND, ORSON
GORHAM, CHARLES

DURANI, NADIR KHAN
ROMANOFF, ALEXANDER N.

DURANT, ARIEL
KAUFMAN, CHAYA

DURANT, CHERYL
IMBODEN, DURANT

DURANTE, JIMMY
DURANTE, JAMES FRANCIS

DURAS, MARGUERITE
DONNADIEU, MARGUERITE

DURATSCHEK, SISTER MARY C
DURATSCHEK, MARY CLAUDIA

DURFEE, JOHN
WARBURG, JAMES PAUL

DURHAM, ANNE
WALKER, EMILY KATHLEEN

DURHAM, DAVID
VICKERS, ROY

DURHAM, JOHN
PAINE, LAURAN BOSWORTH

DURHAM, MAE
ROGER, MAE DURHAM

DURIAN, SIBYLLE
BECHTLE-BECHTINGER, SIBYL

DURIAN, WOLF
BECHTKE, WOLFGANG

DURIE, LYNN
CHRISTIE, DOUGLAS

DURNING, ADDIS
RANZINI, ADDIS DURNING

DURR, FRED
DURR, FREDERICK ROLAND E.

DURRANT, SHEILA
GROVES, SHEILA

DURRANT, THEO
OFFORD, LENORE GLEN
WHITE, WILLIAM A.P.

DURRELL, JACQUIE
DURRELL, JACQUELINE S.R.

DURTAIN, LUC
NEPVEU, ANDRE

DUSENBURY, WINIFRED L.
FRAZER, WINIFRED LOESCH

DUSIC, STANKO
BEGOVIC, MILAN

DUSKIN, RUTHIE
FELDMAN, RUTH DUSKIN

DUSSERE, CAROL
DUSSERE, CAROLYN THOMAS

DUST, LIONEL
KALMUCZAK, ROLF

DUSTIN, CHARLES
GIESY, JOHN ULRICH

DUSTIN, SARAH
HOWELL, HANNAH D.

DUTCHMAN, KALAMU
ROSKAM, KAREL LODEWIJK

DUTTA, REX
DUTTA, REGINALD

DUTZ
DAVIS, MARY OCTAVIA

DUVAL, AIMEE
THURLO, AIMEE S.

DUVAL, HENRI
BURKE, NORA
FIRTH, NORMAN WESLEY
LEWIS, CLIFFORD
THOMAS, REGINALD GEORGE

DUVAL, JEANNE
COFFMAN, VIRGINIA [E]

DUVAL, KATHERINE
JAMES, ELIZABETH

DUVAL, MARGARET
ROBINSON, PATRICIA C.

DUVART, RENE
VAN DER BOURG, WERNER

DUVERNOISE, HENRI
SCHWABACHER, HENRI SIMON

DUX, DENNIS
BREUCKER, OSCAR HERBERT

DWEN, KARL
ERTTMANN, PAUL OSKAR

DWIGHT, ALLAN
COLE, LOIS DWIGHT
TAYLOR, TURNEY ALLAN

DWIGHT, OLIVIA
HAZZARD, MARY

DWORKIN, R.M.
DWORKIN, RONALD MYLES

DWYER, ARTHUR
CHAMBERS, [J.D] WHITTAKER

DWYER, DEANNA
KOONTZ, DEAN R.

DWYER, GALBRAITH WELCH
DWYER, JAMES FRANCIS

DWYER, K.R.
KOONTZ, DEAN R.

DWYER, WINIFRED
GROVER, WINIFRED POWELL

DWYNN, J.C.
DUENSING, JURGEN

DYCE, GILBERT
FITZGERALD, PERCY H.

DYCK, NORMAN
DICKMANN, ERNST GUNTER

DYE, ANNE G.
PHILLIPS, ANNE GARVEY

DYE, CHARLES
DYE, CHARLES
MACLEAN, KATHERINE

DYER, BRIAN
PETROCELLI, ORLANDO R.
ROTHERY, BRIAN

DYER, C. RAYMOND
DYER, CHARLES [RAYMOND]

DYER, ELINOR MARY BRENT
BRENT-DYER, ELINOR MARY

DYER, RAYMOND
DYER, CHARLES [RAYMOND]

DYER, RAYMOND J.
DYER, CHARLES [RAYMOND]

DYGAS
DYGASINSKI, TOMASZ ADOLF

DYKEMAN, WILMA
STOKELY, WILMA D.

DYKES, JACK
OWEN, JACK

DYKEWOMAN, ELANA
NACHMAN, ELANA

DYLAN, BOB
ZIMMERMAN, ROBERT ALLEN

DYMOKE, JULIET
DE SCHANSCHIEFF, JULIET D

DYMOND, ROSALIND
CARTWRIGHT, ROSALIND DYM.

DYMOV, OSIP ISIDOROVICH
PERELMAN, SIDNEY JOSEPH

DYOMIN, MIKHAIL
TRIFONOV, GEORGII E.

E., W.T.
EADY, W.T.

E.A.
ALEXANDER, ELEANOR JANE

E.B.
BAWDEN, EDWARD

E.B.W.
WHITE, ELWYN BROOKS

E.H.
HAIG, EMILY ALICE
HISCOCK, ERIC

E.H.W.M.
MEYERSTEIN, EDWARD H.H.

E.R.
ROSS, W.W. EUSTACE

E.V.B.
BOYLE, ELEANOR VERE G.

E.V.L.
LUCAS, BERYL LLEWELLYN
LUCAS, E[DWARD] V[ERRALL]

E.W.B.
BAARNHEIM, E.W.

E.W.M.
MARWICK, ERNEST W.

EADIE, ARLTON
EADY, LEONARD LEOPOLD

EADY, W.P.R.
GLASBY, JOHN S.

EAGER, MOLLY
EAGER, MARY ANN

EAGLE, JOHN
BIRD, WILLIAM HENRY F.

EAGLE, SARAH
HAWKES, SARAH

EAGLE, SOLOMON
SQUIRE, JOHN COLLINS

EAGLESFIELD, FRANCIS
GUIRDHAM, ARTHUR

EAGLETON, TERRY
EAGLETON, TERENCE [F]

EAKER, IRA
EAKER, IRA CLARENCE

EALLING, TILL
HERNANDEZ, EFREN

EAR, THE
MCLELLAN, DIANA

EARLE, AMBROSE
JONES, J.G.

EARLE, JEAN
BURGE, DORIS

EARLE, MARILEE
ZDEREK, MARILEE

EARLE, OLIVE L.
DAUGHTREY, OLIVE LYDIA

EARLE, W.J.
SENARENS, LUIS P.

EARLE, WILLIAM
JOHNS, WILLIAM EARLE

EARLEY, FRAN
WHEARLEY, BOB

EARLEY, MARTHA
WESTWATER, AGNES MARTHA

EARLIE, M[AY] A[GNES]
FLEMING, MAY AGNES [E]

EARLIN, SHELL
GENBERG, KJELL E.

EARLITON, ROBERT
SACCOMOMONO, MARYANNE

EARLL, TONY
BUCKLAND, RAYMOND

EARLSON, IAN MALCOLM
DORN, WILLIAM S.

EARLY, JACK
SCOPPETTONE, SANDRA

EARLY, JON
JOHNS, WILLIAM EARLE

EARLY, TOM
KELTON, ELMER
KNOTT, WILLIAM CECIL JR.
REASONER, JAMES M.
RODERUS, FRANK

EARP, F.R.
EARP, FRANK RUSSELL

EARP, VIRGIL
KEEVILL, HENRY J.

EAST, MICHAEL
WEST, MORRIS L.

EAST, ROGER
BURFORD, ROGER D'ESTE

EASTAWAY, EDWARD
THOMAS, PHILIP EDWARD

EASTERLING, RENE
EASTERLING, NARENA

EASTERLY, ROBERT
POTTER, ROBERT

EASTERMAN, DANIEL
MACEOIN, DENIS

EASTLUND, MADELYN
HICKEY, MADELYN EASTLUND

EASTMAN, G. DON
OOSTERMAN, GORDON

EASTON, EDWARD
MALERICH, EDWARD P.

EASTON, PAUL
PULLAN, RU

EASTWOOD, THOMAS
SICKLE, MILTON VAN

EATON, GEORGE L.
MONTANYE, HAROLD [MONTY]
VERRAL, CHARLES S [CHUCK]
WHEELER-NICHOLSON, MALCO.
WHITEHOUSE, ARTHUR G.T.

EATON, JANET
GIVENS, JANET E[ATON]

EATON, JOHN
BODINGTON, STEPHEN

EBAN, ABBA
SOLOMON, ABBA

EBAN, AUBREY
EBAN, ABBA SOLOMON
SOLOMON, ABBA

EBBETT, EVE
EBBETT, FRANCIS EVA

EBEL, SUZANNE
GOODWIN, SUZANNE

EBENSTEIN, ERICH
HRUSCHKA, ANNI

EBERHARDT, LOTTE
BRUGMANN-EBERHARDT, LOTTE

EBERHARDT, PETER
ADAMS, [FRANKLIN]

EBERHART, SHERI S.
TEPPER, SHERI S.

EBLIS, J. PHILIP
PHILLIPS, JAMES W.

EBN EL-NIL
ABDEL-MALEK, ANOUAR

EBNER, JEANNIE
EBNER-ALLINGER, JEANNIE

EBSEN, BUDDY
EBSEN, CHRISTIAN

ECCLES
WILLIAMS, FERELITH ECCLES

ECHO
PROUST, [V-L-G-E] MARCEL

ECKART, PETER
ECKERT, HERBERT

ECKBRECHT, ANDREAS
KAUS, GINA

ECKER, ERNST L.
QUANDT, ERNST

ECKERSLEY, JILL
BEAUMONT, HELEN

ECKFORD, HENRY
DE KAY, CHARLES

ECKHARDT, BOB
ECKHARDT, ROBERT CHRIST.

ECKMAN, J. FORRESTER
ACKERMAN, FORREST J.

ECKMAR, F.R.
DE HARTOG, JAN

ECLOV, SHIRLEY
PFOUTZ, SHIRLEY ECLOV

EDAR
ANTHONY, EDWARD

EDDIE
JONES, EDDIE

EDDISON, E.R.
EDDISON, ERIC RUECKER

EDDY, ALBERT
GALSBY, JOHN [S]

EDDY, C.M. JR.
EDDY, CLIFFORD MARTIN JR.

EDDY, CHARLES
ROSE, CHARLES E.

EDE, H.S.
EDE, HAROLD STANLEY

EDE, JIM
EDE, HAROLD STANLEY

EDEL, MARJORIE
SINCLAIR, MARJORIE JANE

EDELHARDT, MIKE
EDELHARDT, MICHAEL

EDEN, LAURA
HARRISON, CLAIRE [E]

EDEN, MARTIN
BOLSTAD, OIVIND
FARMER, PHILIP JOSE

EDEN, MATTHEW
NEWNHAM, DON

EDEN, ROB
BURKHARDT, EVE & ROBERT

EDENS, COOPER
DRAGER, GARY

EDGAR, ICARUS WALTER
BISHOP, S. WALTER EDGAR

EDGAR, JOSEPHINE
MUSSI, MARY

EDGAR, KEN
EDGAR, KENNETH FRANK

EDGAR, PETER
KING-SCOTT, PETER EDGAR

EDGEFIELD, PAUL
ILIFF, JOHN EDGAR

EDGREN, A.C.
LEFFLER, ANNE CHARLOTTE

EDGY, WARDORE
GOREY, EDWARD ST. JOHN

EDIANEZ, ANNA
FLEURIOT, Z. MARIE ANNE

EDILOG
ILOGU, EDMUND C.O.

EDINGTONS, [THE]
EDINGTON, ARLO & CARMEN

EDISON, JUDITH
PAUL, JUDITH EDISON

EDISON, THEODORE
STRATEMEYER, EDWARD

EDLER, TIM
EDLER, TIMOTHY

EDMOND, JAY
JONES, JACK

EDMONDS, CHARLES
CARRINGTON, CHARLES EDM.

EDMONDS, GEORGE
MERIWETHER, ELIZABETH [A]

EDMONDS, I.G.
EDMONDS, IVY GORDON

EDMONDS, JAE
EDMONDS, JAMES A.

EDMONDS, MARGOT
EDMONDS, MARGARET H.

EDMONDS, PAUL
KUTTNER, HENRY
MOORE, CATHERINE LUCILLE

EDMONDS, ROBIN
EDMONDS, ROBERT H.G.

EDMONDSON, G.C.
EDMONDSON Y COTTON, JOSE

EDMONDSON, GARRY C.
EDMONDSON Y COTTON, G.C.

EDMONDSON, WALLACE
ELLISON, HARLAN

EDMONS, ANN C.
WELCH, ANN COURTENAY E.

EDMUND, SEAN
PRINGLE, LAURENCE, P.

EDMUNDS, ALBERT
DUGGAN, EDMUND

EDMUNDS, BRENT
REYNOLDS, JOHN EDMUND

EDRIC, ROBERT
ARMITAGE, GARY EDRIC

EDSCHMID, KASIMIR
SCHMIDT, EDUARD

EDSON, GEORGE ALDEN
ERNST, PAUL FREDERICK

EDSON, HAROLD
HALL, ASA ZADEL

EDSON, J.T.
EDSON, JOHN THOMAS

EDUARDI, GUILLERMO
EDWARDS, WILLIAM B.

EDUARDO
HUNT, E. HOWARD

EDWA
EDWARDS, BILL

EDWARD, MARIE ELAINE
MOSLER, BLANCHE Y.

EDWARD, MAX
POHLMAN, MAX EDWARD

EDWARDES, ALLEN
KINSLEY, DANIEL ALLAN

EDWARDES, LAWRENCE
NEUBERG, VICTOR [B]

EDWARDS, ADRIENNE
KOLACZYK, ANNE & EDWARD

EDWARDS, AGNES
PRATT, AGNES ROTHERY

EDWARDS, AL
NOURSE, ALAN E.

EDWARDS, ALBERT
BULLARD, ARTHUR

EDWARDS, ALEXANDER
FLEISCHER, LEONORE

EDWARDS, ANDREA
KOLACZYK, ANNE & EDWARD

EDWARDS, BERTRAM
EDWARDS, HERBERT C.

EDWARDS, BOB
EDWARDS, ROBERT ALAN
SCHATZ, EDWARD R.

EDWARDS, BRONWEN ELIZAB.
ROSE, WENDY

EDWARDS, CHARLES F.
HOGLUND, KEN

EDWARDS, CHARMAN
EDWARDS, FREDERICK A.

EDWARDS, DOLTON
LAISING, W.K.
LESSING, WILFRED EDWARD

EDWARDS, DONALD EARL
HARDING, DONALD EDWARD

EDWARDS, ELEANOR LEE
VICTOR, MRS. M.V.

EDWARDS, ELI
MCKAY, FESTUS CLAUDIUS

EDWARDS, ELIZABETH
INDERLIED, MARY ELIZABETH

EDWARDS, ESTELLE
GREGORY, MARY LAWRENCE

EDWARDS, F.E.
NOLAN, WILLIAM F.

EDWARDS, FRANCIS
BRANDON, JOHNNY

EDWARDS, GAWAIN
PENDRAY, GEORGE EDWARD

EDWARDS, GERALD H.
HAMILTON-EDWARDS, GERALD

EDWARDS, HAL
NOBLE, HAROLD

EDWARDS, HAMM
EVANS, THELMA D. HAMM

EDWARDS, HANK
BROOMALL, ROBERT W.

EDWARDS, HARRY
EDWARDS, HENRY JAMES

EDWARDS, IRENE
BARR, ELIZABETH

EDWARDS, J.
WHITE, THEODORE EDWIN

EDWARDS, JAMES G.
MACQUEEN, JAMES WILLIAM

EDWARDS, JANE
CAMPBELL, JANE

EDWARDS, JIMMY
EDWARDS, JAMES KEITH O.

EDWARDS, JOHN
JOHNSON, THOMAS E.
MUCKLE, JOHN EDWARD

EDWARDS, JOHN MILTON
COOK, WILLIAM WALLACE
JENKS, GEORGE CHARLES

EDWARDS, JOHNSON
SHUTE, WALTER

EDWARDS, JOSH
LEVINSON, LEONARD [L]

EDWARDS, JULIA
CORYELL, JOHN RUSSELL

EDWARDS, JULIE
ANDREWS, JULIE
MCFARLANE, LESLIE CHARLES

EDWARDS, JULIE[A]
STRATEMEYER, EDWARD

EDWARDS, JUNE
BHATIA, JAMUNADEVI
FORRESTER, HELEN

EDWARDS, L.J.
LEITHEAD, J. EDWARDS

EDWARDS, LAURENCE
EDWARDS, FLORENCE

EDWARDS, LEE
LEVY, EDWARD J.

EDWARDS, LEO
LEE, EDWARD EDSON

EDWARDS, LEONARD
WILD, REGINALD

EDWARDS, MARIAN
JASTRZEMBSKI, MARIAN

EDWARDS, MAX
BENJAMIN, CLAUDE M.E.P.

EDWARDS, NORMAN
CARR, TERRY G.
WHITE, THEODORE EDWIN

EDWARDS, OLIVER
HALEY, WILLIAM JOHN

EDWARDS, OLWEN
GATER, DILYS

EDWARDS, OWEN
GATER, DILYS

EDWARDS, PATRICIA
WATTERS, PATRICIA

EDWARDS, PAUL
EIDEN, PAUL
LORY, ROBERT
STOKES, MANNING LEE

EDWARDS, PHOEBE
BLOCH, BARBARA

EDWARDS, R.M.
EDWARDS, ROSELYN

EDWARDS, R.T.
GOULART, RONALD JOSEPH

EDWARDS, RACHELLE
CASTLE, BRENDA

EDWARDS, ROBIN
GELINAS, ROBERT E.

EDWARDS, RUTH DUDLEY
DUDLEY EDWARDS, RUTH

EDWARDS, S.W.
SUBLETTE, WALTER EDWARDS

EDWARDS, SAMUEL
GERSON, NOEL B.

EDWARDS, SARAH
BILLS, SHARON & ROBERT

EDWARDS, STEPHEN
PALESTRANT, SIMON S.

EDWARDS, WALTER
SHUTE, WALTER

EDWARDS, WARD
RATHBORNE, ST. GEORGE

EDWARDS, WARREN
MANNING, WILLIAM HENRY

EDWARDS, WOODROW
WOOD, EDWARD D. JR.

EDWIN, BROTHER B.
ARNANDEZ, RICHARD

EDWINSON, EDMUND
SLOCUM, EDWARD MARK

EEEE
ACKERMAN, FORREST J.

EELA, H.P.
FREYBERG, HERMANN

EERFELD, B.
LE FEBER, DAVID

EFF, B.
CARNEY, JACK

EFJAY
ACKERMAN, FORREST J.

EFRON, MARINA IVANOVNA T.
TSVETAEVA, MARINA [I]

EFROT
EFROS, ISRAEL [ISAAC]

EFTALIOTIS, ARJRIS
MICHAILDIS, KLEANTHIS

EGAN, LESLEY
LININGTON, [B] ELIZABETH

EGBERT, H.M.
EMANUEL, VICTOR ROUSSEAU

EGBERT, VIRGINIA WYLIE
KILBORNE, VIRGINIA WYLIE

EGERTON, DENISE
DUGGAN, DENISE V.

EGERTON, GEORGE
BRIGHT, MARY C.D.

EGERTON, LUCY
MALLESON, LUCY BEATRICE

EGERTON, RANDOLPH
BESTWICK, HARRY

EGESTORFF, GEORG
VON OMPTEDA, GEORG

EGG-BENES, MARIA
EGG, MARIA

EGGER, ELLEN
MIRUS, LUDMILLA

EGGERT, JIM
EGGERT, PAT & JAMES E.

EGLESTON, JANET F.
DUNLEAVY, JANET EGLESTON

EGLINTON, JOHN
MAGEE, WILLIAM K.

EGOMET
FOWLER, HENRY WATSON

EGREMONT, MICHAEL
HARRISON, MICHAEL

EGREMONT, MICHAEL
ROHAN, MAURICE DESMOND

EGUISHEIM, RENE
LANGE, HANS O.

EGVINARDUS
MANLEY, MARY

EHLY, EHREN M.
EHLY, MOREEN

EHRENBOURG, ILYA [G]
EHRENBURG, ILYA G.

EHRENBURG, ILYO [G]
EHRENBURG, ILYA G.

EHRENCLOU, ADIL
KERFVE, AXEL

EHRLICH, COLLIS
COLLIS, ARTHUR
EHRLICH, ROSANNE

EHRLICH, JACK
EHRLICH, JOHN GUNTHER

EHRLICH, JAKE
EHRLICH, JACOB WILBURN

EIBEK
TASHMUKHAMEDOV, MUSA

EIBEN, ROBERT W.
EISFELD, RAINER

EICH, SEBASTIAN
KALMUCZAK, ROLF

EICHBERG, JAMES BANDMAN
GARFIELD, JAMES B.

EICHENHOF, MARTINA
EICHHOF, JOACHIM

EICHENHORST, GUSTAV
EIGENBRODT, CARL CHRIST.

EICHNER, WALTER
HEICHEN, WALTER

EICHTHAL, RUDOLF
PFERSMANN VON EICHTHAL, R

EIFION, WYN
WILLIAMS, ELISEUS

EIGK, CLAUS
BASTIAN, HARTMUT

EIGNER, LARRY
EIGNER, LAURENCE JOEL

EIKAN, THEO
BOLSTAD, OIVIND

EILER, HERMANN
HEICHEN, WALTER

EILERT, RICK
EILERT, RICHARD E.

EINAUDI, GIULIO
SCIASCIA, LEONARDO

EINHORN, VIRGINIA HILU
HILU, VIRGINIA

EIRELIN, GLENN
EVANS, GLEN

EIRENE
SEARLE, M.E.

EIRIK, SVEN O.
ERIKSSON, SVEN-OLOF

EIS, EGON & OSSO
EISLER, EGON & OSSO

EISEN, CAROL G.
RINZLER, CAROL EISEN

EISENBERG, LARRY
EISENBERG, LAWRENCE. B.

EISENHUTH, P.
HUBNER, HORST W.

EISLER, STEVEN
HOLDSTOCK, ROBERT P.

EISNER, SIMON
KORNBLUTH, C[YRIL] M.

EISNER, STEFAN
FERRARI, GUSTAV

EISNER, VIVIENNE
MARGOLIS, VIVIENNE

EITEMAL
DU PLOOY ERLANK, WILLEM J

EJE, ANDREAS
ESSEN, ANDERS AXEL HARALD

EK, EDGAR
KNUTSON, NILS

EKBLOM, PAL A.
BLOM, KARL ARNE

EKELOF, [BENGT] GUNNAR
EKELOEF, [BENGT] GUNNAR

EKSTROM, MARGARETA
EKSTROEM, [S] MARGARET

EKWENSKI, C.O.D.
EKWENSKI, CYPRIAN O.D.

EL BUNDUKHARI
DENT, ANTHONY AUSTEN

EL CARTUJANO
DE PADILLA, JUAN

EL CONDE DE CAMORS
CASAL, JULIAN DEL

EL CURIOSO PARLANTE
DE MESONERO ROMANO, RAMON

EL GALLO, ANICETO
ASCASUBI, HILARIO

EL HUITLACOCHE
KELLER, GARY D.

EL PARDO
CAMPO, ESTANISLAO DEL

EL POLLO, ANASTASIO
CAMPO, ESTANISLAO DEL

EL ROPO, SMOKESTACK
PERRY, CHARLES

EL SERENO
SARFATTI, MARGHERITA

EL SID
PERELMAN, SIDNEY JOSEPH

EL-SHABAZZ, EL-HAJI MALIK
LITTLE, MALCOLM

ELAINE
DUILLO, ELAINE

ELAINE
LEVERSON, ADA

ELAND, CHARLES
VON RIMANOCZY, CHARLES A.

ELBERGER, BERND
HOFE, GUNTER

ELBWART, WILM
VON ETZSCH, WOLF

ELCHAMO, JASON
CABALLERO, MANUEL

ELCHAMO, SEBASTIAN
CABALLERO, MANUEL

ELCLAIR, MOLLIE
SHAVER, RICHARD S.

ELDER, ART
MONTGOMERY, RUTHERFORD G.

ELDER, EVELYN
BURGE, M.R. KENNEDY

ELDER, LEON
YOUNG, NOEL

ELDER, MARC
TENDRON, MARCEL

ELDERDICE, J. RAYMOND
JUDSON, EDWARD Z.C.

ELDERSHAW, M. BARNARD
BARNARD, MARJORIE FAITH
ELDERSHAW, FLORA S.P.

ELDIN, RAYMOND
MORTON, JAMES SEVERS

ELDON, CLEO
KNOX, CLEO ELDON

ELDRED, BRIAN
BRADBURY, RAY [DOUGLAS]

ELEIGH, SEBASTIAN
GREENE, SIR HUGH

ELETHEA, ABBA
THOMPSON, JAMES W.

ELEUTER
IWASZKIEWICZ, JAROSLAW

ELEUTERO
PAGNINI, ANTONIO LUCA

ELEVE
STOWE, MRS. H.M.

ELFED
LEWIS, HOWEL ELVET

ELFENAU, W.
PRAMBERGER, ROMUALD

ELGAR, SINTON
HUGILL, ROBERT

ELGERS, PAUL
SCHMIDT-ELGERS, PAUL

ELGIN, MARY
STEWART, DOROTHY MARY
STEWART, WALTER

ELGIN, SUZETTE HADEN
ELGIN, PATRICIA SUZETTE

ELIA
LAMB, CHARLES

ELIAS, EILEEN
DAVIES, EILEEN WINIFRED

ELIN, FRED K.
KLEIN, FRED [FRITZ]

ELIN, PELIN
JOTOV, DIMITUR IVANOV

ELIN-PELIN
JOTOV, DIMITAR IVANOV

ELIOT, A.D.
JEWETT, [T] SARAH ORNE

ELIOT, ALICE [C]
JEWETT, [T] SARAH ORNE

ELIOT, ANNE
COLE, LOIS DWIGHT
CROMPTON, ANNE

ELIOT, ANNIE
TRUMBULL, ANNIE ELLIOT

ELIOT, C.S.
SELLERS, CONNIE LESLIE

ELIOT, DAN
SILVERBERG, ROBERT

ELIOT, JESSICA
BROWN, LOIS ANN
LEVY, BARBARA

ELIOT, MARC
PEDNEAU, DAVE

ELIOT[T], E.C.
MARTIN, REGINALD ALEC

ELIS, EGON
VAN EYSS, EDGAR

ELISHEVA
GIRKOVA, LISABETTA

ELITIS, ODISSEUS
ALEPUDELIS, ODISSEUS

ELIVAS, KNARF
SAVILE, FRANK [MACKENZIE]

ELIZABETH
BEAUCHAMP, MARY ANNETTE

ELIZABETH
RUSSELL, ELIZABETH MARY

ELIZABETH, ANNE
FLEUR, ANNE ELIZABETH

ELIZABETH, SUZANNE
WITTER, SUZANNE E.

ELIZABETH, VON S.
FREEMAN, GILLIAN

ELJENS, OLAF
JEHLE, ALFONS

ELKINS, H.V.
HINKLE, VERNON

ELKON, JULIETTE
ELKON-HAMELCOURT, JULIETT

ELLACOTT, S.E.
ELLACOTT, SAMUEL ERNEST

ELLANBEE, BOYD
BOYD, LYLE G. & WILLIAM C

ELLANBY, BOYD
BOYD, LYLE G. & WILLIAM C

ELLEN
NICHOLS, REBECCA S. REED

ELLEN, ELLEN
LEIBER, ELISABETH

ELLEN, JAYE
NIXON, JOAN LOWERY

ELLER, SCOTT
HOLINGER, WILLIAM JACQUES

ELLERHORST, PETRA
REUTER, RALPH

ELLERMAN, GENE
WELLS, BASIL [EUGENE]

ELLERRE
RUSSI, LUCIANO

ELLERS, MARJII
ELLERSIECK, MARJORIE

ELLERT, JOHN
GIBSON, WALTER B.

ELLERY, JAN
EWING, JAN

ELLICOTT, V.L.
ELLICOTT, VALCOULON MEMOY

ELLIN, E.M.
ELLIN, ELIZABETH MURIEL

ELLINGTON, DUKE
ELLINGTON, EDWARD KENNEDY

ELLIOT, ASA
BLINDER, ELLIOT

ELLIOT, BRIAN
APPEL, WALTER
BOCKL, MANFRED
FRIEDRICHS, HOLGER
HAHN, RONALD M.
HARY, WILFRIED A.
HELGATH, FRANC
HUNDSDORFER, GERHARD
KODELPETER, HANS P.
VON KOBLINSKI, HANS-JOACH

ELLIOT, BRUCE
HRDINKA, MICHAEL
SAUPE, DIETER

ELLIOT, DANIEL
FELDMAN, LEONARD

ELLIOT, EDITH
HOWARD, ANNA H.C.

ELLIOT, GERALDINE
BINGHAM, EVANGELINE M.

ELLIOT, LEE
HUGHES, DENNIS [TALBOT]

ELLIOT, LUCY
GREENMAN, NANCY A.

ELLIOTT, ALLAN
ELLIOTT, KENNETH ALLAN C.

ELLIOTT, BEN
HAAS, BENJAMIN LEOPOLD

ELLIOTT, BOB
ELLIOTT, ROBERT B.

ELLIOTT, BRUCE
STACY, WALTER
DERRICK, NEIL
FIELD, EDWARD

ELLIOTT, CHARLES
EWART-BIGGS, CHRISTOPHER

ELLIOTT, CHIP
ELLIOTT, ESCALUS E. III

ELLIOTT, CHRISTINE
DORSEY, CHRISTINE
ELLIOTT, ANNE

ELLIOTT, DON
WESTLAKE, DONALD [EDWIN]
SILVERBERG, ROBERT

ELLIOTT, ELLEN
ELLIOTT, NEIL
WESTMARLAND, ETHEL LOUISA

ELLIOTT, EMILIA
JACOBS, CAROLINE EMILIA

ELLIOTT, EMILY
MIMS, EMILY

ELLIOTT, G.R.
ELLIOTT, GEORGE ROY

ELLIOTT, JANE
MINER, PETER

ELLIOTT, JOHN MICHAEL
HAAS, BENJAMIN LEOPOLD

ELLIOTT, JUMBO
ELLIOTT, JAMES FRANCIS

ELLIOTT, LEE
BIRD, WILLIAM H.F.

ELLIOTT, NATHAN
EVANS, CHRIS[TOPHER D.]

ELLIOTT, RICHARD
ELLIOTT, ELTON T.
GEIS, RICHARD E.

ELLIOTT, ROBERT
GARFINKEL, BERNARD MAX

ELLIOTT, ROBIN
PICKART, JOAN ELLIOTT

ELLIOTT, WILLIAM
BRADBURY, RAY [DOUGLAS]

ELLIS, ALEXANDRA
REINGOLD, CARMEL B.

ELLIS, ALICE THOMAS
HAYCRAFT, ANNA

ELLIS, ANYON
ROWLAND-ENTWISTLE, A.T.

ELLIS, AUDREY
GELHAR, AUDREY P.A.

ELLIS, CRAIG
ROGOW, LEE
VERN, DAVID

ELLIS, E.S.
ELLIS, EDWARD S.

ELLIS, ELMO I.
ISRAEL, ELMO

ELLIS, HERBERT
WILSON, LIONEL

ELLIS, HILDA RODERICK
DAVIDSON, HILDA RODERICK

ELLIS, JOAN
ELLIS, JULIE M.

ELLIS, JOHN
BLEECK, G.C.
KNELLER, F.C.
MCKIBBON, J.E.

ELLIS, JULIAN
O'MAHONY, CHARLES K.

ELLIS, JULIE
RICHARD, SUSAN

ELLIS, KATHY
BENTLEY, MARGARET

ELLIS, LANDON
ELLISON, HARLAN

ELLIS, LEIGH
RUDEEN, ANNE & LOUISA

PSEUDONYMS

ELLIS, LOUISE
WALKER, EMILY KATHLEEN

ELLIS, LYN
ELLIS, GIN

ELLIS, MARILYN
ELLIS, JULIE M.

ELLIS, MICHAEL
LLEWELLYN, STEPHEN PETER

ELLIS, OLIVIA
WINTLE, ANNE

ELLIS, PATRICIA
MANGRUM, VALERIE

ELLIS, SCOTT
SCHORR, MARK

ELLIS, THELMA B.
ANDERSON, ALAN RITNER

ELLIS, WESLEY
BARRETT, NEAL JR.
WALLMANN, JEFFREY M.

ELLISON, EARL
BOUNDS, SYDNEY J.
FIRTH, NORMAN WESLEY
LAZENBY, NORMAN A.
WILLIS, ERNEST LISTER H.

ELLISON, ELLIS
SNELL, E.L.

ELLISON, GLENN "TIGER"
ELLISON, GLENN

ELLISON, HENRY LEOPOLD
ZERKHAUSEN, HENRY L.

ELLISON, MARJORIE
NORTON, MARJORIE

ELLMER, ARNDT
KEHL, WOLFGANG

ELLMER, MARCUS
MEYER-ESTNER, WERNER

ELLSEN, ELLIS
SNELL, E.L.

ELLSON, HAL
BREWER, GIL

ELLSWORTH, ELMER JR.
THAYER, TIFFANY E.

ELLSWORTH, PAUL
TRIEM, PAUL ELLSWORTH

ELLVINGER, BARBARA ANN P.
PRICE, BARBARA ANN ELLV.

ELLWOOD, EDITH E.
MUESING-ELLWOOD, EDITH E.

ELM, JONATHAN
SASSE, GERHARD

ELM, M.W.
WELLMAN, MANLY WADE

ELM, MICHAEL W.
WELLMAN, MANLY WADE

ELMORE, CAROLE
LUCY, THOMAS ELMORE

ELOUS, MARV
PROCTOR, GEO[RGE] W[YATT]
VARDEMAN, ROBERT E.

ELPHINSTONE, FRANCIS
POWELL-SMITH, VINCENT

ELPHINSTONE, MURGATROYD
KAHLER, HUGH [T] MACNAIR

ELPIDON
BALUCKI, MICHAL

ELROD, P.N.
ELROD, PAT

ELRON
HUBBARD, L. RON

ELSEY, J.J.
HERRON, ELSIE ELLERINGTON

ELSHEMUS, LOUIS M.
EILSHEMUS, LOUIS MICHAEL

ELSING, J.M.
BECKERS, FRANS

ELSNA, HEBE
ANSLE, DOROTHY PHOEBE

ELSON, LINDE
LINDE, PAUL

ELSON, R.N.
NELSON, RADELL FARADAY

ELSPET
LANGENHOVEN, CORNELIS J.

ELSPETH
BRAGDON, ELSPETH MACDUFF.

ELSSCHOT, WILLEM
DE RIDDER, ALFONS JOSEPH

ELSTAR, DOW
GALLUN, RAYMOND Z.

ELSTER, TOROLF
BR^CKENBERG, HANS

ELTEN, EVA
RIECK, ERIKA

ELTEN, THOMAS
FUCHS, ANTON

ELTON, BEN
ELTON, BENJAMIN CHARLES

ELTON, H.E.
HAYES, HERBERT E. ELTON

ELTON, JAMES T.
ACKERMAN, FORREST J.

ELTON, JOHN
MARSH, JOHN

ELTON, MAX
FEARN, JOHN RUSSELL

ELUARD, PAUL
GRINDEL, EUGENE

ELVIN, ANNE K. STEVENSON
STEVENSON, ANNE

ELVIN, DRAKE
BEHA, ERNEST

ELWART, JOAN POTTER
ELWART, JOAN FRANCES

ELWIN, WILLIAM
EBENSTEIN, WILLIAM

ELY, DAVID
LILIENTHAL, DAVID ELI

ELY, FREDERICK
KESSLER, JASCHA

ELY, JOHN WILTON
WILTON-ELY, JOHN

ELYSIAN, ANNE
WESTMORELAND, VERA GERTR.

EMANUEL, R.V.
EMANUEL, VICTOR ROUSSEAU

EMANUEL, V.R.
EMANUEL, VICTOR ROUSSEAU

EMBEY, PHILIP
PHILIPP, ELLIOT ELIAS

EMDEN, V.K.
BLISH, JAMES B.

EMEL
LANE, MARY LOUISA

EMENEGGER, BOB
EMENEGGER, ROBERT

EMERCE
CROWELL, MARY REED

EMERSON, ALICE B.
CREAGER, EUNICE WHAYNE
STRATEMEYER, EDWARD

EMERSON, CHERYL
DALE, CHERYL

EMERSON, EDWIN
ELLIS, EDWARD S.

EMERSON, H.O.
EMERSON, HENRY OLIVER

EMERSON, JILL
BLOCK, LAWRENCE

EMERSON, MARY LEE
KENNEDY, MARY

EMERSON, RONALD
SCOTLAND, JAMES

EMERY, DENISE
BEAUMONT, HELEN

EMF
FORSTER, EDWARD MORGAN

EMIN, GEVORK
MURADIAN, KORLEN GRIGOR

EMM, CATHERINE
MCMAHON, KAY

EMMANUEL, PIERRE
MATHIEU, NOEL JEAN

EMMBE
BERTIE, MARIE

EMMCKE, SUSANNE
BLOCH, SUSANNE [E]

EMMETT, ROBERT
WATERS, ROBERT E.

EMMONS, ELISE
EMMONS, ELIZABETH WALES

EMMOTT, BILL
EMMOTT, WILLIAM JOHN

EMOREY, N.
ELLISON, JEROME

EMPLOYEE X
FAUTSKO, TIMOTHY FRANK

EMPRINGHAM, TONI
EMPRINGHAM, ANTOINETTE F.

EMRICH, LOUIS
EMRICH, LUDWIG FRIEDRICH

EMSCHER, HORST
BOUTERWECK, OLAF

EMSH
EMSHWILLER, EDMUND A.

EMSH, ED
EMSHWILLER, EDMUND A.

EMSHLER
EMSHWILLER, EDMUND A.

EMSHWILLER, ED
EMSHWILLER, EDMUND A.

EMSLEY, CLARE
PLUMMER, CLARE [E]

EMSLIE, M.L.
SIMPSON, MYRTLE L.

ENCEL, SOL
ENCEL, SOLOMON

ENCHO
JIROKICHI, DEBUCHI

ENDE, RICHARD CHAFFEY V.
VON ENDE, RICHARD CHAFFEY

ENDERLE, JUDITH
ENDERLE, JUDITH [A] ROSS

ENDERS, ALFRED MICHAEL
HEBERER, ALFRED

ENDERS, RICHARD
FENSTER, ROBERT

ENDFIELD, MERCEDES
VON BLOCK, BELA [W]

ENDICOTT, CLEVE
BOND, LEE
BOSWORTH, ALLAN R.

ENDICOTT, STEPHEN
ROBERTS, W. ADOLPHE

ENERGLYN, LORD
EVANS, WILLIAM DANIEL

ENEY, DICK
ENEY, RICHARD HARRIS

ENFIELD, CARRIE
SMITH, SUSAN VERNON M.

ENFIELD, HUGH
HUGHES, GWILYM FIELDEN

ENG--, TOM
ENGELHARDT, THOMAS ALEX.

ENGEL, A.J.
ENGEL, ARTHUR JASON

ENGEL, ALAN
ENGELBERG, ALAN D.

ENGEL, ALAN M.D.
ENGELBERG, ALAN D.

ENGEL, DEL
VAN HORN, DALE R.

ENGELHARDT, FREDERICK
HUBBARD, L. RON

ENGELHARDT, TOM
ENGELHARDT, THOMAS ALEX.

ENGER, L.L.
ENGER, LEIF & LIN

ENGLAND, E. SQUIRES
BALL, SYLVIA PATRICIA

ENGLAND, E.M.
ANDERS, EDITH [M] ENGLAND

ENGLAND, EDITH
ANDERS, EDITH [M] ENGLAND

ENGLAND, JANE
JERVIS, VERA M.S.
MURDOCK, VERA

ENGLAND, NORMAN
WEBB, GODFREY EDWARD C.

ENGLAND, PIERS
KERSH, GERALD

ENGLE, ELOISE
PAANANEN, ELOISE KATHER.

ENGLEHART, BOB
ENGLEHART, ROBERT WAYNE

ENGLING, RICHARD
PATRICK, DAVID GEORGE

ENGLISH DETECTIVE
RUSSELL, WILLIAM

ENGLISH, ARNOLD
HERSHMAN, MORRIS

ENGLISH, BRENDA H.
RIDDOLLS, BRENDA HARK

ENGLISH, CHARLES
NUETZEL, CHARLES A.

ENGLISH, GENEVIEVE
PATTON, SARAH

ENGLISH, JUDITH
KELLY, JUDITH

ENGLISH, RICHARD
MURRAY, RICHARD
SHAVER, RICHARD S.

ENGREN, EDITH
MCCAIG, EDITH
MCCAIG, ROBERT JESSIE

ENGSTROM, ELIZABETH
ENGSTROM, BETSY LYNN G.

ENGSTROM, TED W.
ENGSTROM, THEODORE WILLH.

ENID
BANKS, ELIZABETH

ENIKI, AMIRAKHAN
ENIKEEV, AMIRKHAN N.

ENNIS, ROBERT D.
TUBB, E.C.

ENQUIRING LAYMAN
GRIERSON, WALTER

ENRIGHT, D.J.
ENRIGHT, DENNIS JOSEPH

ENRIGHT, ELIZABETH
GILLHAM, ELIZABETH W.

ENRIGHT, MAGINEL WRIGHT
BARNEY, MAGINEL WRIGHT

ENSE, WOLFGANG
FRANK, RUDOLF

ENSIGN, TOD
ENSIGN, THOMAS

ENTWISTLE, THEODORE ROWL.
ROWLAND-ENTWISTLE, A.T.

ENYS, SARAH L.
SLOGGETT, NELLIE

EPAFRODITO
WAGNER, CHARLES PETER

EPERNAY, MARK
GALBRAITH, JOHN KENNETH

EPHESIAN
ROBERTS, CARL ERIC B.

EPHRAIM, GAVRIEL BEN
BEN-EPHRAIM, GAVRIEL

EPP, JOVITA
EPP DE HARY, ELEONORE

EPPIE
NAISMITH, HELEN

EPSILON
BETJEMAN, [SIR] JOHN

EPSTEIN, ANN WHARTON
WHARTON, ANNABEL JANE

ERAMUS, M. NOTT
STUBER, STANLEY IRVING

ERASMUS, M. MOTT
STUBER, STANLEY IRVING

ERB, HEDWIG
KOCHER-ERB, HEDWIG

ERCKMANN-CHARTRIAN
CHARTRIAN, ALEXANDRE
ERCKMANN, EMILE

ERCKMANN-CHARTRIAN, M.M.
CHARTRIAN, ALEXANDRE
ERCKMANN, EMILE

ERCKMANN-CHATRAIN
CHATRIAN, ALEXANDRE

ERCOLI, ERCOLE
TOGLIATTI, PALMIRO

ERDSTELULOV
ACKERMAN, FORREST J.

ERENBURG, ILYA G.
EHRENBURG, ILYA G.

EREV
FLEISSNER, ROLAND

EREX
HASSLER, ADOLF OTTO

ERFURT, PETER
BIERSCHENCK, BURKHARD P.

ERGON, P.E.A.
HEYDA, ERNST

ERHART, ROLF
MAUERHARDT, ROLF

ERHART, WOLF
MAUERHARDT, ROLF

ERHOMAA, ESTER
ERHOLM, ESTER

ERIC
MONTEFIORE, CAROLINE L.

ERIC, KENNETH
HENLEY, ARTHUR

ERICH, OTTO
HARTLEBEN, OTTO ERICH

ERICK
BEST, [E] ALLENA CHAMPLIN

ERICKSON, LYNN
PELTONEN, CARLA F.

ERICKSON, STEVE
ERICKSON, STEPHEN M.

ERICKSON, TOR
OBERST, FREDERICK

ERICSON, JULIA
LEISY, JAMES FRANKLIN

ERICSON, SIBYL
ERIKSON, SIBYL C. ALEX.

ERICSON, WALTER
FAST, HOWARD [MELVIN]

ERIK, JAN
EIKERMANN, HELMUT

ERIKSEN, ANDREAS
VIGG, PELLE

ERIKSON, CHARLOTTE
ERIKSON, SIBYL C. ALEX.

ERIKSON, LYNN
SWANTON, MOLLY B.

ERIKSSON, BUNTEL
BERGMAN, ERNST INGMAR

ERIKSSON, LEIF
ESSEN, R^TGER THURESSON

ERIX, EINER
ERIKSSON, ERIK EINER

ERLANGER, BABA
TRAHEY, JANE

ERLAY, DAVID
ERLEI, HANS JOSEF

ERLINE, N.T.
RAGEN, NAOMI

ERMAN, JACK
ACKERMAN, FORREST J.

ERMAN, JACK DEFOREST
ACKERMAN, FORREST J.

ERMAN, JACQUES DEFOREST
ACKERMAN, FORREST J.

ERMAYNE, LAURAJEAN
ACKERMAN, FORREST J.

ERMINE, WILL
DRAGO, HARRY SINCLAIR

ERNE, NINO
ERNE, GIOVANNI BRUNO

ERNEST, BILL
PUHL, WILFRIED ERNST

ERNEST, JEANETTE
MARTIN, JUDY WELLS

ERNEST, PAUL
FAKENHEIM, PAUL ERNST

ERNEST, WILLIAM
BERKEBILE, FRED DONOVAN

ERNEST, [BROTHER]
RYAN, JOHN D.

ERNESTO
BREDBERG, ERNST C. JR.

ERNINGHAM, H.F.
HARMENING, WILHELM CHR.

ERNST, CLARA
BARNES, CLARA ERNST

ERNST, FRIEDRICH
PINKERT, ERNST FRIEDRICH

ERNST, HANNA
LUTZENBURGER, JOHANNA

ERNST, OTTO
SCHMIDT, OTTO ERNST

ERNST, WILLIE
PUHL, WILFRIED ERNEST

ERSKINE, ANDRA
MARTIN, JUDY

ERSKINE, DOUGLAS
BUCHAN, [JOHN] STUART

ERSKINE, FIRTH
ERSKINE, GLADYS SHAW
FIRTH, IVAN EUSTACE

ERSKINE, HELEN
SANTORI, HELEN

ERSKINE, MARGARET
WILLIAMS, MARGARET W.

ERSKINE, ROSALIND
LONGRIGG, ROGER [ERSKINE]

ERSKINE-GRAY
CORDES, THEODORE K.

ERTE
DE TIRTOFF, ROMAIN

ERTLER, FRITZI
ROITHMAIER, EMILIE

ERVIN, PATRICK
HOWARD, ROBERT E.

ERVIN, SUSAN
ERVIN-TRIPP, SUSAN MOORE

ERWIN, ANNABEL
BARRON, ANN FORMAN

ERWIN, GEORGE C.
GRUBER, FRANK

ERWIN, HOWARD W.
INGRAHAM, PRENTISS

ERWIN, WILL
EISNER, WILLIAM ERWIN

ESCH, A.
GOGOLIN, PETER

ESCH, L. IM
IMESCH, LUDWIG

ESCHBACH, LOTHAR
RAUSCH, LOTHAR

ESCHENBACH, WOLFRAM V.
VON ESCHENBACH, WOLFRAM

ESCHENLOH, WOLFGANG
HOHLBEIN, WOLFGANG E.

ESCHER, STEFAN W.
DRESCHER, WALTER

ESCOTT, JACK LEONARD
ESCOTT, JONATHAN

ESCRIVA, JOSEMARIA
ESCRIVA DE BALAGUER, JOSE

ESDAILE, DAVID
WALKER, DAVID ESDAILE

ESEKI, BRUNO
MOHAKLELE, EZEKIAL

ESHMEYER, R.E.
ESCHMEYER, REINHART ERNST

ESMOND, HARRIET
BURKE, JEAN
BURKE, JOHN [FREDERICK]

ESOHG, LAMA
GHOSE, AMAL

ESPERANCE
ARDAGH, ALICE MAUD

ESPINOZA, GUILLERMO
ROBINSON, WILLIAM I.

ESPINOZA, RUDY
ESPINOZA, RUDOLPH LOUIS

ESPRIELLA, DON MANUEL A.
SOUTHEY, ROBERT

ESSE, JAMES
STEPHENS, JAMES

ESSEX, CAPTAIN
STARR, RICHARD H.

ESSEX, FRANK
SIMMONDS, MICHAEL CHARLES

ESSEX, JON
WATFORD, JOEL ALBERT

ESSEX, LOUIS
ISAACS, LEVI

ESSEX, MARIANNA
VAN NUYS, JOAN

ESSEX, MARY
BLOOM, URSULA

ESSEX, RICHARD
STARR, RICHARD H.

ESSEX, WILLIAM
TIGGES, JOHN THOMAS

ESSLINGER, PAT M.
CARR, PAT M.

ESSOE, GABE
ESSOE, GABOR ATTILA

ESTEFANIA, M.L.
LAFUENTE ESTEFANIA, M.A.

ESTELLE
ELLIS-MORRIS, ESTHER

ESTERBROOK, TOM
HUBBARD, L. RON

ESTERGREEN, M. MORGAN
ESTERGREEN, MARIAN MORGAN

ESTERHAZY, LOUISE J.
FAIRCHILD, JOHN

ESTERRE, NEVILLE D'
LEE, ARCHIBALD EDWARD

ESTEVEN, JOHN
SHELLABARGER, SAMUEL

ESTIVAL
ESTIVAL, IVAN LEON

ESTORIL, JEAN
ALLAN, MABEL ESTHER

ESTRAGON, VLADIMIR
STOKES, GEOFFREY

ESZTERHAS, JOE
ESZTERHAS, JOSEPH A.

ETCHINSON, DENNIS
ETCHISON, DENNIS WILLIAM

ETHEL
GRAYSON, ALBERT VICTOR

ETIENNE
KING-HALL, STEPHEN

ETLON, TUMLEH
NOLTE, HELMUT

ETON, ROBERT
MEYNELL, LAURENCE WALTER

ETTER, LES
ETTER, LESTER FREDERICK

ETTINGER, L.D.
ETTINGER, LEOPOLD DAVID

ETTINGER, LEOPOLD D.
ETTINGER, LEOPOLD DAVID

ETTL, ALEXANDER
GOOCK, ROLAND

ETTRICK SHEPHERD
HOGG, JAMES

EUGENE
HUYGHUE, DOUGLAS S.

EULENSPIEGEL, ALEXANDER
SHEA, ROBERT [J]

EULERT, DON
EULERT, DONALD DEAN

EUPHAN
TODD, BARBARA EUPHAN

EUROPEAN
MOSLEY, OSWALD EMALD

EUSTACE, ALICE
THOMAS, MARY ALICE

EUSTACE, ROBERT
BARTON, ROBERT EUSTACE
RAWLINS, EUSTACE

EUSTIS, LAURETTE
MURDOCK, LAURETTE P.

EUSTIS, O.R.
EUSTIS, ORVILLE B.

EUWE, MAX
EUWE, MACHGIELIS

EVAN, CAROL
GOLDSMITH, CAROL EVAN

EVAN, EVIN
FAUST, FREDERICK S.

EVAN, PAUL
LEHMAN, PAUL EVAN

EVANOVICH, JANET
HALL, STEFFIE

EVANS, ALAN
STOKER, ALAN

EVANS, ANN
BAIR, ANN

EVANS, AUGUSTA JANE
WILSON, AUGUSTA JANE

EVANS, BENNETT
BERGER, IVAN [B]

EVANS, BILL
EVANS, WILLIAM HARRINGTON

EVANS, CARADOC
EVANS, DAVID

EVANS, CHERRY
DRUMMOND, CHERRY

EVANS, CLAIRE
DE LONG, CLAIRE

EVANS, DALE
ROGERS, DALE EVANS

EVANS, DEAN
KRULL, GEORGE

EVANS, DEE
EVANS, DARDANELLA LISTER

EVANS, ELAINE
BREWER, GIL

EVANS, ELLEN
DUBREUIL, ELIZABETH L.

EVANS, EMERALD
DUBREUIL, ELIZABETH L.

EVANS, EVAN
FAUST, FREDERICK S.

EVANS, F.M.G.
HIGHAM, FLORENCE MAY G.

EVANS, FRANCES
CARTER, FRANCES MONET

EVANS, FRANK
APPEL, WALTER

EVANS, G.B.
EVANS, GWYNNE BLAKEMORE

EVANS, G.R.
EVANS, GILLIAN ROSEMARY

EVANS, GWYN
EVANS, GWYNFIL ARTHUR
PHILIPS, GEORGE NORMAN
TEED, GEORGE HAMILTON

EVANS, GWYNNE B.
EVANS, GWYNNE BLAKEMORE

EVANS, HARRIS
EVANS, GEORGE BIRD
EVANS, KAY HARRIS

EVANS, HODGE
HUNTER, EVAN

EVANS, I.O.
EVANS, IDRISYN OLIVER

EVANS, IAN
WELLS, ANGUS

EVANS, JACKSON
FIRTH, NORMAN WESLEY

EVANS, JAMES
TUBB, E.C.

EVANS, JEAN
DEMETROPOULOS, NICHOLAS

EVANS, JESSICA
LOTTMAN, EILEEN [SHUBB]

EVANS, JOHN
BROWNE, HOWARD

EVANS, JONATHAN
FREEMANTLE, BRIAN [HARRY]

EVANS, LAUREL
WILSON, ELLEN

EVANS, LEE
FORREST, RICHARD S.

EVANS, LESLEY
BLOCK, LAWRENCE

EVANS, LINDA
APPEL, WALTER

EVANS, MARGARET
POTTER, MARGARET [N]

EVANS, MARGIAD
WHISTLER, PENELOPE
WILLIAMS, PEGGY EILEEN A.

EVANS, MARIANNE
DEMETROPOULOS, NICHOLAS

EVANS, MARY ANN
ELIOT, GEORGE

EVANS, MORGAN
DAVIES, LESLIE PERNELL

EVANS, PATRICIA HEALY
CARPENTER, PATRICIA [H.E]

EVANS, TABOR
CAMERON, LOU
KNOTT, WILLIAM CECIL JR.
MARSHALL, MEL[VIN]
REASONER, JAMES M.
WALLMANN, JEFFREY M.
WHITTINGTON, HARRY

EVANS, VICTOR G.
NORWOOD, VICTOR [G.C.]

EVARTS, ESTHER
BENSON, SALLY
BENSON, SARA MAHALA R.S.

EVE, BARBARA
REISS, BARBARA EVE

EVEARD, WALTER
GARRISH, HAROLD J.

EVELAND, BILL
EVELAND, WILBUR CRANE

EVELYN, A.W.
WILKES, W.

EVELYN, ROSE D'
BROEMEL, ROSE

EVENS, HODGE
MCGAUGHY, DUDLEY DEAN

EVENS, OWEN
MCGAUGHY, DUDLEY DEAN

EVER, MAC
EVERWIEN, MAX

EVERAGE, DAME EDNA
HUMPHRIES, BARRY

EVERARD, HENRY
SMITH, H. EVERARD

EVERARD, KATHERINE
VIDAL, [E] GORE LUTHER

EVERARD, MAURICE
BULLIVANT, CECIL H[ENRY]

EVEREST, HOPE
JAMES, W. MARTHA

EVERETT, EZA
EVERETT, ELIZABETH ABBEY

EVERETT, GAIL
ADAMS, TRACY
HALE, MARY ARLENE

EVERETT, KATHLEEN
WOOD, EDWARD D. JR.

EVERETT, MARY
KREY, LAURA LETTI

EVERETT, PAUL
LOVEJOY, CORNELIA

EVERETT, WADE
COOK, WILLIAM EVERETT
LUTZ, GILES A.

EVERHART, JIM
EVERHART, JAMES WILLIAM

EVERMAY, MARCH
EIKER, MATHILDE

EVERS, CRABBE
BRASHLER, WILLIAM
VAN TIL, REINDEER

EVERTIER, PAUL
BRINKMANN, JURGEN

EVERTON, FRANCIS
STOKES, FRANCIS W.

EVERTON, FRANK
MEARES, LEONARD F.

EVERTZ, FRANZ
BRORS, FRANZ

EVOE
KNOX, EDMUND GEORGE V.

EVTUSHENKO, EVGENIL A.
YEVTUSHENKO, YEVGENY A.

EWART, CHARLES
LYTE, CHARLES

EWERS, H.G.
GEHRMANN, HORST

EWIGK, TED
GIESA, WERNER K.

EWING, EDGAR
EWING, GEORGE M.

EWING, FRANK
NUETZEL, CHARLES A.

EWING, FREDERICK R.
SHEPHERD, JEAN
STURGEON, THEODORE

EWING, JENNY
BLUMENFELD, F. YORICK

EWING, TESS
SMILEY, VIRGINIA K.

EX JOURNALIST
LANIGAN, RICHARD

EX-PRIVATE X
BURRAGE, ALFRED M.

EX-R.S.M.
LINDSAY, HAROLD ARTHUR

EXALL, BARRY
NUGENT, JOHN PEER

EXCELLENT, MATILDA
FARSON, DANIEL NEGLEY

EXETASTES
HARAKAS, STANLEY SAMUEL

EXILE
DONALD, CHARLES HILLARD

EXPLORABILIS
HAYWOOD, ELIZA

EXZELSIOR
SCHULZE-GALLERA, DR. S.

EYEN, JEROME
EYEN, TOM

EYLES, MERLE
CROZIER, KATHLEEN MURIEL

EYLL, ORGE
FALK, HERMANN

EYNHARDT, GUILLERMO
QUIROGA, HORACIO [S]

EYRE, ANNETTE
WORBOYS, ANN[ETTE I.]

EYRE, DOROTHY
MCGUIRE, LESLIE SARAH

EYRE, MARIE
HUBBARD, RICHARD

EYSSEN, KURT
LLOP SELLARES, JUAN

EZEKI, BRUNO
MPHAHLELE, EZEHIEL

F.E.
HUBBARD, L. RON

F.F.
FYSH, FREDERICK

F.G.R.
ROE, F. GORDON

F.M.
LOCKARD, FRANCES M.

F.O.O.
STREET, CECIL JOHN C.

F.P.A.
ADAMS, FRANKLIN PIERCE

F.X., MICHAEL
BISCHOFF, DAVID F.

FABEL, RENATE
FISCHACH-FABEL, RENATE

FABER, ALFRED
FISCHER, ELSE

FABER, IMTRAUT
BOMKE, BERNHARD

FABER, MORTON
GIBSON, WALTER B.

FABER, WALTER
SCHMITZ, WALTER

FABIAN, FRANZ
MIELKE, FRANZ

FABIAN, RUTH
QUIGLEY, AILEEN

FABIAN, WARNER
ADAMS, SAMUEL HOPKINS

FABIO
LANZONI, FABIO
RILEY, EUGENIA

FABRIZIUS, PETER
FABRY, JOSEPH B.
KNIGHT, MAX

FACEY
FACEY, GERALD

FACEY, G.
FACEY, GERALD

FACIUS, ESTHER
PLATTEN, WILL

FACKLER, ELI
FACKLER, ELIZABETH

FACUNDO
DE CUELLAR, JOSE TOMAS

FADEYEV, A.
BULGYA, ALEXANDER A.

FADEYEV, ALEXANDER
BULGYA, ALEXANDER A.

FAG, FREDERICK
JOHNSON, JAMES WELDON

FAGAN BLACK, ALEXIS
VAN HISE, DELLA

FAGG, ELIZABETH
OLDS, ELIZABETH FAGG

FAGUS
FAILLET, GEORGES EUGENE

FAGYAS, MARIA
BUSH-FEKETE, MARIE ILONA

FAHLBERG, H.L.
FRICKE, HANS WERNER

FAID, MARY
DUNN, MARY ALICE

FAIN, C.C.
BENJAMIN, EGBERT

FAINE, CLAUDE
RUBAHN, HORST-GUNTER

FAINE, DJINN
RUSSELL, VIRGINIA FAINE

FAIR, A.A.
GARDNER, ERLE STANLEY

FAIR, J. MURRAY
HOISINGTON, MAY FOLWELL

FAIRBAIRN, ANN
TAIT, DOROTHY

FAIRBAIRN, ROGER
CARR, JOHN DICKSON

FAIRBANKS, NAT
PEARCE, CHARLES LOUIS

FAIRBANKS, SABRINA
EVERETT, ELIZABETH ABBEY

FAIRBARN, HELEN
SOUTHARD, HELEN FAIRBARN

FAIRBROTHER, NAN
MACKENZIE, NAN

FAIRBURN, A.R.D.
FAIRBURN, ARTHUR REX D.

FAIRCHILD, ELISABETH
GILMARC, DONNA

FAIRCHILD, KATE
AHEARN, PATRICIA

FAIRE, ZABRINA
STEVENSON, FLORENCE

FAIRFAX, ANN
CHESNEY, MARION G.

FAIRFAX, BEATRICE
MANNING, MARIE
MCCARROLL, MARION CLYDE
SCARBERRY, ALMA SIOUX

FAIRFAX, DICK
POWELL, OSCAR REGINALD

FAIRFAX, FELIX
GIBSON, WALTER B.

FAIRFAX, GWEN
TERRITO, MARY JO

FAIRFAX, KATE
ORD, IRENE

FAIRFIELD, CLARENCE
CHAMPLIN, EDWIN ROSS

FAIRFIELD, DARRELL
LARKIN, ROCHELLE R.

FAIRFIELD, HENRY W.A.
CORBIN, HAROLD STANDISH

FAIRFIELD, JOHN
LIVINGSTONE, HARRISON E.

FAIRLEIGH, CHRISTOPHER
PARCELL, NORMAN HOWE

FAIRLEIGH, RUNA
MORSE, LARRY ALLEN

FAIRLESS, MICHAEL
BARBER, MARGARET FAIRLESS

FAIRLEY, ALIDAIR
AIRD, ALISDAIR

FAIRMAN, P.W.
FAIRMAN, PAUL W.

FAIRMAN, PAULA
FAIRMAN, PAUL W.
VAUGHAN, ROBERT R.

FAIRSTAR, MRS.
HORNE, RICHARD HENRY

FAIRWAY, SIDNEY
DAUKES, SIDNEY HERBERT

FAITH, BARBARA
COVARRUBIAS, BARBARA F.

PSEUDONYMS

FAITH, WILLIAM ROBERT
FAGUE, WILLIAM ROBERT

FAKIR, FALSTAFF
WALLENGREN, AXEL

FALCK, ROBERT
KALMUCZAK, ROLF

FALCO, GIAN
PAPINI, GIOVANNI

FALCON
NESTLE, JOHN FRANCIS

FALCON, MARK
PICKERING, EILEEN MARION

FALCON, SALLY
HAWKES, SARAH

FALCONER, A.F.
FALCONER, ALEXANDER FRED.

FALCONER, COLIN
BOWES, COLIN RICHARD

FALCONER, DORA
LAWSON, LOUISA

FALCONER, JAMES
KIRKUP, JAMES

FALCONER, KENNETH
KORNBLUTH, C[YRIL] M.

FALCONER, LANOE
HAWKER, MARY ELIZABETH

FALCONER, LEE [N]
DIKTY, JULIAN [C] MAY

FALCONER, SOVEREIGN
STRETE, CRAIG [KEE]

FALK, ELISABETH
FALK, HERMANN

FALK, ELSA
ESCHERICH, ELSA FALK

FALK, HECTOR
KALMUCZAK, ROLF

FALK, LEE
COPPER, BASIL
GOULART, RONALD JOSEPH

FALK, ROBERT
KALMUCZAK, ROLF

FALK, TOBY
FALK, STEPHEN JOHN

FALK, VICTOR
HASSLER, ADOLF OTTO

FALKBERGET, JOHAN [P.]
LILLEBAKKEN, J.P.

FALKENDER, BARONESS MARCI
WILLIAMS, MARCIA

FALKENHAIN, JENS
PLOTZE, HASSO

FALKER, JAMES
HOBER, HEINZ WERNER

FALKIRK, RICHARD
LAMBERT, DEREK W.

FALKLAND
SCOTT, JOHN ROBERT

FALKLAND, FRANK
WILSON, G.L.

FALKLAND, SAMUEL
HEIJERMANS, HERMAN

FALKON, FELIX LANCE
SCITHERS, GEORGE

FALL, THOMAS
SNOW, DONALD CLIFFORD

FALLADA, HANS
DITZEN, RUDOLF WILHELM F.

FALLER, GERTH
EIPELDAUER, GERTRUDE

FALLERE, FELICIA
KNIST, F. EMMA

FALLON, GEORGE
BINGLEY, DAVID ERNEST

FALLON, JACK
FALLON, JOHN WILLIAM

FALLON, MARTIN
PATTERSON, HARRY

FALORP, NELSON P.
JONES, STEPHEN [PHILLIP]

FALSTAFF, JAKE
FETTER, ELIZABETH HEAD
FETZER, HERMAN

FALTAS YOUSSEF, EDWAR K.
AL-KHARRAT, EDWAR

FALUDY, GEORGE
FALUDY, GYORGY

FAMILY DOCTOR, A
HUTCHIN, KENNETH CHARLES

FANCHON, LISA
FLOREN, LEE

FANE, BRON
FANTHORPE, R.L.

FANE, VIOLET
CURRIE, LADY MARY M.L.

FANFARLO
STONIER, GEORGE

FANG, L.Z.
FANG LIZHI

FANGORN
BAKER, CHRIS

FANSHAW, CECIL
DENT, C.H.

FANSHAWE, CAROLINE
CUST, BARBARA

FANTAZY
GOMULICKI, WIKTOR

FANTONI, S.
JONES, EDDIE

FARADAY, M.M.
RORVIK, DAVID MICHAEL

FARALLA, DANA
FARALLA, DOROTHY W.

FARALLON, CERISE
CREWS, JUDSON [C]

FARB, PETER
FARB, STAN PETERS

FAREL, CONRAD
BARDENS, DENNIS [C]

FARELY, ALISON
POLAND, DOROTHY ELIZABETH

FAREWELL, NINA
COOPER, MAE [KLEIN]
KLEIN, GRACE

FARGE, MONIQUE
GREE, ALAIN

FARGO, DOONE
NORWOOD, VICTOR [G.C.]

FARGO, JOE
RIKHOFF, JAMES C.

FARGO, WES
DE SHORN, ROY

FARIDI, S.N.
FARIDI, SHAH NASIRUDDIN M

FARIGOULE, LOUIS
ROMAINS, JULES

FARINA, JOHAN
HANSEN, JURGEN

FARLAND, KATHRYN
FLADLAND, KATHRYN

FARLANE, JASON
MUNRO, [MACFARLAND] HUGH

FARLEY, ALAN
HERRINGTON, MRS. W. LEE

FARLEY, RALPH MILNE
HOAR, ROGER SHERMAN

FARMACEVTEN
HOLM, SVEN AAGE

FARMER JONES
JONES, BRYAN L.

FARMER, ARTHUR
JARDINE, JACK OWEN

FARMER, PATRICIA
LINES, MAUREEN

FARMER, PETER
LLOYD, JOHN IVESTOR

FARMER, R.L.
LAMONT, ROSETTE C.

FARMER, WENDELL
DAVIS, LAVINIA [R]

FARMINGTON, STONE T.
ACKERMAN, FORREST J.

FARNASH, HUGH
LUFF, STANLEY GEORGE A.

FARNDALE, JAMES
FARNDALE, W.A.J.

FARNDALE, JOHN
HARVEY, JOHN WILFRED

FARNHAM, BURT
CLIFFORD, HAROLD B.

FARNINGHAM, MARIANNE
HEARN, MARY ANN

FARNSBOROUGH
PEARCE, BRIAN LEONARD

FARNSWORTH, DUNCAN
O'BRIEN, DAVID WRIGHT

FARNSWORTH, JAMES
POHLE, ROBERT W. JR.

FARNSWORTH, MONA
NEWHALL, MURIEL

FARNUM, K.T.
RIPS, ERVIN M.

FARNWALD
STRUBBERG, FRIEDRICH ARM.

FARO, TEX
JENNISON, JOHN WILLIAM

FAROT, PIERRE
KALMUCZAK, ROLF

FARQUHARSON, CHARLIE
HARRON, DON[ALD]

FARQURHARSON, MARTHA
FINLEY, MARTHA

FARR, BILL
FARR, WILLIAM T.

FARR, C.
WILKES-HUNTER, RICHARD

FARR, CAROLINE
PATTINSON, LEE
RUHEN, CARL
WILKES-HUNTER, RICHARD

FARR, DOUGLAS
GILFORD, CHARLES BERNARD

FARR, FIONA
LEWIS, JUDITH BERESFORD

FARR, JOHN
WEBB, JACK RANDOLPH

FARR, SEBASTIAN
BLOM, ERIC WALTER

FARRA, MADAME E.
FAWCETT, FRANK DUBREZ

FARRADAY, ALICIA
ROSE, SHARON

FARRADAY, CHET
NORWOOD, VICTOR [G.C.]

FARRANT, SARAH
HARRIS, VALERIE

FARRAR, FRANCIS
FRANCIS, R.W.

FARRELL, AGNES
ADAMS, FRANCIS W.L.

FARRELL, B.A.
FARRELL, BRIAN ANTHONY

FARRELL, BEN
CEBULASH, MEL

FARRELL, CATHARINE
O'CONNOR, MARY CATHARINE

FARRELL, CLIFF
FARRELL, A. CLIFFORD

FARRELL, DAVID
SMITH, FREDERICK ESCREET

FARRELL, DESMOND
ORGAN, JOHN

FARRELL, FRANK
FARRELL, FRANCIS THOMAS

FARRELL, HENRY
HENRY, CHARLES

FARRELL, J.T.
FOGARTY, JONATHAN T.

FARRELL, JAMES T.
FARRELL, JAMES THOMAS

FARRELL, JOHN
MACDONALD, JOHN D.

FARRELL, JOHN WADE
MACDONALD, JOHN D.

FARRELL, JOHNNY
MAX, GEORGE

FARRELL, M.J.
KEANE, MARY NESTA S.

FARRELL, PATRICIA
ZELVER, PATRICIA [F]

FARRELL, SALLY
ODGERS, SALLY FARRELL

FARREN, DAVID
MCFERRAN, DOUGLASS DAVID

FARREN, RICHARD J.
BETJEMAN, [SIR] JOHN

FARREN, RICHARD M.
BETJEMAN, [SIR] JOHN

FARRER, E. MAXWELL
WILLIAMS, EDWARD JOHN

FARRERE, CLAUDE
BARGONE, FREDERIC C.P.E.

FARRINGTON, ANN
HUNDSDORFER, GERHARD

FARRINGTON, D.P.
FARRINGTON, DAVID P.

FARRINGTON, MAUDE
HICKEY, MADELYN EASTLUND

FARROW, J.
FONAROW, JERRY

FARROW, JAMES T.
TUBB, E.C.

FARWEST
ACKERMAN, FORREST J.

FASOLD, CHRISTIAN
CORDES, HEINRICH

FASSBINDER, CARLTON J.
YERKE, T. BRUCE

FASTLIFE
GROGAN, EMMETT

FATALIS, BRUDER
CASTELLI, IGNAZ FRANZ

FATHER OF THE TANK
SWINTON, ERNEST DUNLOP

FATIO, LOUISE
DUVOISIN, LOUISE

FAULCON, ROBERT
HOLDSTOCK, ROBERT P.

FAULKNER, COLLEEN
CULVER, COLLEEN

FAULKNER, FRANK
ELLIS, EDWARD S.

FAULKNER, JOHN
GALE, E.F.

FAULKNER, MARY
SEUFFERT, MURIEL

FAULKNER, NANCY
FAULKNER, ANNE IRVING

FAULKNER, WHITNEY
BISSELL, ELAINE

FAURE, JEAN
KILCHENSTEIN, MARY I.

FAUST, ALEXANDER
ALTSHULER, HARRY

FAVOR, ERIKA
TOBIN, LEE ANN

FAWCETT, BARBARA
UPSON, DOROTHY BARBARA

FAWCETT, BILL
FAWCETT, WILLIAM BRIAN

FAWCETT, C.
COOKSON, CATHERINE ANN

FAWCETT, CATHERINE
COOKSON, CATHERINE ANN

FAWCETT, MARION
SANDERSON, SABINA WARREN

FAWCETT, QUINN
FAWCETT, WILLIAM BRIAN
QUINN, CHELSEA Y

FAWKES, FARRAH
OFFUTT, ANDREW J.

FAWKES, GUY
BENCHLEY, ROBERT CHARLES

FAWLEY, WILBUR
FAULEY, WILBUR FINLEY

FAX
BARNUM, AUGUSTINE

FAXON, LAVINIA
RUSS, LAVINIA FAXON

FAY, DOROTHY
LINDHOLM, ANNA C.

FAY, ERICA
STOPES, MARIE [C] CARM.

FAY, MARY HELEN
FAGYAS, MARIA

FAY, NICHOLS
SHERREN, WILKINSON

FAY, SHIRLEY ANN
SHIVER, SHIRLEY T.

FAY, STANLEY
SHULMAN, FAY GRISSOM S.

FAYE, SHIRLEY
SHIVER, SHIRLEY T.

FAYRE, JILLIAN
DAGG, JILLIAN

FEAGLES, ELIZABETH
DAY, BETH [FEAGLES]

FEARING, ALDEN
DYER, WALTER ALDEN

FEARN, ELENA
SMITH, MARJORIE SEYMOUR

FEARN, JOHN
WANNAN, JOHN FEARN

FEARN, ROBERTA
HUTCHINSON, BARBARA BEAT.

FEATHERSTONE, D.
WARREN, DAVID

FEATHERSTONEHAUGH, FRANCI
MACG, ALASDAIR ALPIN

FEBRUARY, VERNIE A.
FEBRUARY, VERNON ALEXAND.

FECAMPS, ELISE
CREASEY, JOHN

FECHER, CONSTANCE
HEAVEN, CONSTANCE FECHER

FECHNER, HELGA
KLAMUCZAK, ROLF

FEDDEN, ROBIN
FEDDEN, HENRY ROMILLY

FEDERBUSCH, SMON
FEDERBUSH, SIMON

FEDERLI, F.
EISENPROBST, FERDINAND

FEDJA, FELIX
ESSEN, AXEL ANDERS H.

FEDOR
DOROSLAVIC, MILUTIN
FEDERMANN, REINHARD

FEEL, LAZARO
LOPEZ, RAFAEL

FEELIN', A. FELLOW
FULLER, HENRY STARKEY

FEELINGS, TOM
FEELINGS, THOMAS

FEHRENBACH, R.R.
FEHRENBACH, THOMAS REED

FEIGE, HERMANN ALBERT O.M
TORSVAN, BRUNO TRAVEN

FEIGELSON, NAOMI
CHASE, NAOMI FEIGELSON

FEIKEMA, FEIKE
MANFRED, FREDERICK [F]

FEILEN, JOHN
DIKTY, JULIAN [C] MAY

FEINBERG, BARBARA SILBER.
FEINBERG, BARBARA JANE

FELD, FRIEDRICH
ROSENFELD, FRIEDRICH

FELD, HEINRICH
CZERNIK, THEODOR

FELDER, PAUL
WELLEN, EDWARD [P]

FELDMAN, ANATOLE
FELDMAN, A. FRANCE

FELDMAN, ANATOLE FRANCE
FELDMAN, A. FRANCE

FELDON, HARRY
ASPERN-BUCHMEIER, ELISAB.

FELICJAN
FALENSKI, FELICJAN MEDARD

FELIX
VINCENT, FELIX

FELIX, CHARLES
RETCLIFF, JOHN

FELIX, CHRISTOPHER
MCCARGAR, JAMES GOODRICH

FELIX, PAUL
VON REZNICEK, FELICITAS

FELIX-TCHICAYA, GERALD
TCHICAYA, GERALD FELIX

FELL, ANDREW
ARTHUR, ROBERT

FELL, BARRY
FELL, HOWARD BARRACLOUGH

FELLINGE, H.L.
FELLINGE, HARRY LEE

FELLINGS, HENRY
FELLINGE, HARRY LEE

FELLMANN, FRIEDRICH M.
FELLMANN, MARIA

FELLNER, CLAUS
KALMUCZAK, ROLF

FELLOW, R.
SCUDDER, HORACE ELISHA

FELLOWES, ANNE
MANTLE, WINIFRED LANGFORD

FELMER, HELMUT
KURTH, HANNS

FELMERSHAM, MICHAEL
LEYLAND, ERIC

FELSEGG, ARCO v.
HEUER, WILHELM

FELSMANN, ERWIN
FELSINGER, EDWIN

FELTON, B.
BUFORD, ELMER

FEMORA
BRODEY, JIM

FEN, ELISAVETA
JACKSON, LYDIA [J]

FENELON, FANIA
GOLDSTEIN, FANIA

FENG, CHIN
LIU, SYDNEY [CHIEH]

FENIMORE, W.
MERRITT, ABRAHAM P.

FENIX, COMTE DE
CROWLEY, EDWARD ALEXANDER

FENN, LIONEL
GRANT, CHARLES L.

FENNEL, CONNIE
VAYSSE, CHARLES

FENNER, CAROL
WILLIAMS, CAROL ELIZABETH

FENNER, JAMES R.
TUBB, E.C.

FENNERTON, WILLIAM
MCDOUGALL, IAN CAMPBELL

FENNIMORE, STEPHEN
COLLINS, DALE

FENTON, BRUCE
KNELLER, F.C.

FENTON, FREDA
ROWLAND, DONALD S.

FENTON, JACK
MULLER, KURT

FENTON, JULIA
FENTON, ROBERT L.

FENTON, JULIE
FENTON, ROBERT L.

FENTON, MARK
NORWOOD, VICTOR [G.C.]

FENTON, SHANE
STARDUST, ALVIN

FENTON-BRICKS, MARK
ESSL, HERBERT

FENTY, PHILIP
FLEISCHER, LEONORE

FENWICK, E.P.
WAY, ELIZABETH FENWICK

FENWICK, ELIZABETH
WAY, ELIZABETH FENWICK

FENWICK, KAY
BEAN, KEITH FENWICK

FENWICK, PATTI
GRIDER, DOROTHY

FENWICK, PETER
HOLMES, PETER

FERBER, LUISA
FERVERS, LOUISE

FERDINAND
VONNEGUT, KURT JR.

FERDINAND, VALLERY III
SALAAM, KALAMU YA

FERGUS, DYJAN
FERGUSON, IDA MAY

FERGUSON, ANTHONY
READ, ANTHONY

FERGUSON, BOB
FERGUSON, ROBERT BRUCE

FERGUSON, BRAD
FERGUSON, BRADLEY MICHAEL

FERGUSON, DAN
BAJOG, GUNTHER

FERGUSON, EMILY
MURPHY, EMILY F.

FERGUSON, HELEN
EDMONDS, HELEN WOODS
KAVAN, ANNA

FERGUSON, MAGGIE
WILLIAMS, ANITA

FERGUTT, JAN
VAN DROOGENBROECK, JAN

FERKINSHAW, ALBERT
CUNLIFFE, DAVE

FERLAND, PAUL-HENRI
FRIEDLAENDER, PAVEL

FERLING
FERLINGHETTI, LAWRENCE M.

FERLING, LAWRENCE
FERLINGHETTI, LAWRENCE M.

FERLING, OTTO
FARBER, OTTO

FERMOR, PATRICK LEIGH
LEIGH FERMOR, PATRICK M.

FERN, EDNA
RICHTER, FERNANDE

FERN, EDWIN
CRYER, NEVILLE B.

FERN, FANNY
PARTON, SARA PAYSON W.

FERNANDES, CAROL
OATES, JOYCE CAROL

FERNEY, MANUEL
WELLMAN, MANLY WADE

FERNWALD, PAUL
BEKESSY, JANOS

FERNWAY, PEGGIE
BRAUN, WILBUR

FERRAND, GEORGINA
CASTLE, BRENDA

FERRANTE, DON
GERBI, ANTONELLO

FERRAR, GUL
SMITH, WILLIAM JOSEPH T.

FERRARELLA, MARIE [R]
RYDZYNSKI, MARIE R.

FERRARS, E.X.
BROWN, MORNA DORIS M.

FERRARS, ELIZABETH [X]
BROWN, MORNA DORIS M.

FERRAT, JACQUES JEAN
MERWIN, SAMUEL K. JR.

FERRA[-MIKURA], VERA
MIKURA, GERTRUD [F]

FERRER, F.L.
JOHN, FRIEDRICH LUDWIG

FERRER, JEAN-PIERRE
KALMUCZAK, ROLF

FERRER, JOE
BREUCKER, OSCAR HERBERT

FERRER, SISTER VINCENT
DOHERTY, BARBARA

FERRERIUS, BRUDER VINZENZ
GHERI, LEOPOLD

FERRES, ARTHUR
KEVIN, JOHN WILLIAM

FERRIER, HENRI
KALMUCZAK, ROLF

FERRIER, LUCY
PENZLER, OTTO

FERRING, DAVID
GARNETT, DAVID S.

FERRIS, ARTHUR
ROWE, JOHN GABRIEL

FERRIS, GINA
WILKINS, GINA

FERRIS, JAMES CODY
KARIG, WALTER
MCFARLANE, LESLIE CHARLES
STRATEMEYER, EDWARD

FERRIS, MONK
SHARKEY, JOHN MICHAEL

FERRIS, TOM
WALKER, PETER N[ORMAN]

FERRIS, VALERIE
FERRIS, ROSE MARIE

FERRIT, JAQUES JEAN
MERWIN, SAMUEL K. JR.

FERSTER, MARILYN B.
GILBERT, MARILYN B.

FERVAL, PAUL
BEDFORD-JONES, HENRY

FESENMEYER
LUXMORE, ROBERT

FETHALAND, JOHN
INKSTER, LEONARD

FETHERSTON, PATRICK
FETHERSTONHAUGH, PATRICK

FETTAMEN, ANN
HOFFMAN, ANITA

FEUR, D.C.
STAHL, FRED ALAN

FEVER, BUCK
ANDERSON, SHERWOOD

FEW, BETTY
FEW, EUNICE BEATTY

FEXTER, DONALD O.
RICHTER, FRITZ WALDEMAR

FEY, ANNELIESE
FEHRENBACH, ANNELIESE [F]

FEYDE, ANNE
SAPIEYEVSKI, ANNE LINDBG.

FEYDY, ANNE LINDBERG
SAPIEYEVSKI, ANNE LINDBG.

FEYNMAN, R.P.
FEYNMAN, RICHARD PHILLIPS

FEYNMAN, RICHARD P.
FEYNMAN, RICHARD PHILLIPS

FEYVEL, T.R.
FEIWELL, RAPHAEL JOSEPH

FFOLKES
DAVIS, BRIAN

FFOLKES, MICHAEL
DAVIS, BRIAN

FIACC, PADRAIC
O'CONNOR, PATRICK JOSEPH

FIALA, ERICH
MOLL, RUDOLF

FIAROTTA, NOEL
FICAROTTA, NOEL

FIAROTTA, PHYLLIS
FICAROTTA, PHYLLIS

FICKLING, G.G.
FICKLING, FOREST & GLORIA

FIDEL
GOYTORTUA, JESUS

FIDELIO
HUNT, EDGAR HUBERT

FIDELIS
MACHAR, AGNES MAUDE

FIDLER, JIMMIE
FIDLER, JAMES M.

FIDLER, KATHLEEN
GOLDIE, KATHLEEN ANNIE

FIEDENBERG, HARRY
GIBSON, WALTER B.

FIELD OFFICER
MADDEN, T.E.

FIELD, CHARLES
ROWLAND, DONALD S.

FIELD, CHRISTINE
LAURENCE, FRANCES ELSIE

FIELD, FRANK CHESTER
GLEMSER, BERNARD
ROBERTSON, FRANK CHESTER

FIELD, FREDERICK V.
FIELD, FREDERICK VANDER.

FIELD, GANS T.
WELLMAN, MANLY WADE

FIELD, HILL
FIELDING, MOLLY HILL

FIELD, JOANNA
MILNER, MARION BLACKETT

FIELD, LESLIE A.
SHEINFELD, LESLIE A.

FIELD, MARTYN
HORNER, FREDERIK WILLIAM

FIELD, MEDORA
PERKERSON, MEDORA F.

FIELD, MICHAEL
BRADLEY, KATHERINE H.
COOPER, EDITH EMMA

FIELD, PENELOPE
GIBERSON, DOROTHY D.

FIELD, PETER
CHENEY, S. LANCER
DRAGO, HARRY SINCLAIR
DRESSER, DAVIS
EAST, FRED
EMERSON, L.W.
HOBSON, FRANCIS THAYER
HOBSON, LAURA K.Z.
HOGAN, ROBERT J[ASPER]
MANN, EDWARD BEVERLY
MINES, SAMUEL
REPP, ED EARL

FIELD, RACHEL
PEDERSON, RACHEL FIELD

FIELD, RESHAD
FIELD, RICHARD TIMOTHY

FIELD, ROBERT A.
HAIG, EMILY ALICE

FIELD, ROBERT S.
EGLI, WERNER J.

FIELD, SANDRA
MACLEAN, JILL

FIELD, SARA BARD
WOOD, SARA BARD F.

FIELD, TEMPLE
WHITFIELD, RAOUL

FIELD, TONY
FELDMAN, A. FRANCE

FIELDHOUSE, W.L.
FIELDHOUSE, WILLIAM [L]

FIELDING, A.
FEILDING, DOROTHY

FIELDING, A.D.
ASH, EDWARD CECIL

FIELDING, A.E.
FEILDING, DOROTHY

FIELDING, A.W.
WALLACE, ALEXANDER FIELD.

FIELDING, ANN MARY
MOSTYN, ANITA MARY

FIELDING, ANTHONY
LEYLAND, ERIC

FIELDING, ARCHIBALD E.
FEILDING, DOROTHY

FIELDING, GABRIEL
BARNSLEY, ALAN G.

FIELDING, H.
HALL, HAROLD FIELDING

FIELDING, HOWARD
ANDERSON, G.J.B.
HOOKE, CHARLES W.

FIELDING, HUBERT
SCHONFIELD, HUGH JOSEPH

FIELDING, PETER
SCOTT, [PETER] HARDIMAN

FIELDING, WILLIAM H.
TEILHET, DARWIN L.

FIELDING, XAN
WALLACE, ALEXANDER FIELD.

FIELDINGS, HARRY LEE
FELLINGE, HARRY LEE

FIELDMAN, W.A.
ACKERMANN, WERNER

FIELDS, ALAN
DUPREY, RICHARD ALLEN

FIELDS, MORGAN
MORGAN, JILL M[EREDITH]

FIELDS, VINCENT
GREENFIELD, IRVING A.

FIELDS, W.C.
DUKINFIELD, WILLIAM CLAU

FIENNES, RICHARD
TWISLETON-W-F, RICHARD N.

FIFE, DUNCAN
ATKINSON, DOROTHY

FIFFORD, FRANK
GIFFORD, FRANCIS NEWTON

FIFIELD, MRS. JAMES C.
MERRIMAN, EFFIE

FIFO, RAY
GLAZAR, BOB

FIGHTER PILOT, A
JOHNSTON, HUGH ANTHONY S.

FIGHTON, GEORGE Z.
DE WEINDECK, U.M.C.W.

FIGUEROA, JOHN
FIGUEROA, JOHN [J] MARIA

FIGUEROA, LOIDA
FIGUEROA-MERCADO, LOIDA

FIGUEROA, MEDARDO
RAMIREZ, MEDARDO FIGUEROA

FIKKENS, J.
BRUNCLAIR, VICTOR J.

FILEMAN, NAN
ZIMMER, MAUDE FILES

FILIA ECCLESIAE
DORSEY, SARAH ANNE

FILMER, HENRY
CHILDS, JAMES RIVES

FILSTRUP, CHRIS
FILSTRUP, E. CHRISTIAN

FILSTRUP, JANE
MERRILL, JANE

FILSTRUP, JANE MERRILL
MERRILL, JANE

FINBAR, OWEN
SMITH, A. DE HERRIES

FINCH, ARIN
AMLER, IRENE

FINCH, CAROL
FEDDERSON, CONNIE

FINCH, JOHN
COOPER, JOHN

FINCH, MATTHEW
FINK, MORTON

FINCH, MERTON
FINK, MORTON

FINCHER, BETH
TRUMBO, DONALD [DALTON]

FINDER, MARTIN
SALZMANN, SIEGMUND

FINDLATER, RICHARD
BAIN, KENNETH B.F.

FINDLEY, FERGUSON
FREY, CHARLES WEISER

FINE, ESTELLE
JELINEK, ESTELLE C.

FINEMAN, A.
IZBITSKY, SAMUEL

FINK, BRAT
DAVIS, GWEN

FINK, STEVANNE AUERBACH
AUERBACH, STEVANNE

FINK, WILLIAM
MENCKEN, HENRY LOUIS

FINKELL, MAX
CATTO, MAX[WELL J.]

FINLAY, FIONA
STUART, VIOLET VIVIAN F.

FINLAY, MICHAEL
ROBERTS, EDNA

FINLAY, WILLIAM
MACKAY, JAMES [A]

FINLAY, WINIFRED
MCKISSACK, LINDSAY C.

FINLEY, GLENNA
WITTE, GLENNA FINLEY

FINLEY, SCOTT
CLARK, ROSY LEE W.C.

FINN MICKEY
JARROLD, ERNEST

FINN, ANNA E.
HOOPES, MARY HOWARD

FINN, ERIK
VON BORN, ERIC

FINN, HUCK
WIRTANEN, ATOS KASIMIR

FINN, R. WELDON
FINN, REGINALD P.A.W.

FINN, R.L.
FINN, RALPH LESLIE

FINN, REX WELDON
FINN, REGINALD P.A.W.

FINNEGAN, ROBERT
RYAN, PAUL WILLIAM

FINNEGAN, RUTH H.
MURRAY, RUTH HILARY

FINNERTY, ADAM DANIEL
CORSON-FINNERTY, ADAM D.

FINNERTY, DANIEL JOHN
CORSON-FINNERTY, ADAM D.

FINNEY, JACK
BARRAT, F.M.
FINNEY, WALTER BRADEN

FINNEY, MARK
MUIR, KENNETH [A]

FINNIGAN, JOAN
MACKENZIE, JOAN

FIORE DELLA NEVE
VAN LOGHEM, MARTINUS G.L.

FIOUN
WHYTE, HENRY

FIPS, SOCRATES
GERNSBACK, HUGO

FIRER, BEN ZION
FIRER, BENZION

FIRES, ALICIA
OGLESBY, JOSEPH

FIRESIDE, CAROLYN
BURGESS, JOANNA

FIRESTONE, TOM
NEWCOMB, DUANE G.

FIRTH, J.R.
FIRTH, JOHN RUPPERT

FIRTH, N. WESLEY
FIRTH, NORMAN WESLEY

FIRTH, SHEILA A.
FIRTH, NORMAN WESLEY

FIRTH, WESLEY
FIRTH, NORMAN WESLEY

FISCHEL, FLORENCE
HIRSCH, DORA

FISCHER, BOBBY
FISCHER, ROBERT JAMES

FISCHER, CORNELIUS
FISCHER, CLAUS

FISCHER, ELISABETH
FISCHER, ILSE [R]

FISCHER, ERNO
HARY, WILFRIED A.

FISCHER, FIONA
FLEGEL, SISSI

FISCHER, FRED
HALLACZ, KLAUS

FISCHER, MARIE LOUISE
KERNMAYR, MARIE LOUISE F.

FISCHER, RUTH
DICHTL, RUTH [v.M.]

FISCHER, URSULA
JUNIKE, ROLF

FISCHER, VERA K.
KISTIAKOWSKY, VERA

FISCHI, VIKTOR
DAGAN, AVIGDOR

FISH, JULIAN
CAMPBELL, BLANCHE

FISHER, A.E.
FISHER, EDWARD

FISHER, AGNES
MCEWEN, JESSIE EVELYN

FISHER, BOB
FISHER, ROBERT PERCIVAL

FISHER, CLAY
ALLEN, HENRY WILSON

FISHER, CYRUS T.
TEILHET, DARWIN L.

FISHER, DOROTHEA
FISHER, DOROTHY F.C.

FISHER, FRAN
COPELAND, FRANCES

FISHER, GEORGE
FISHER, DOUGLAS [GEORGE]

FISHER, JACOB
WOOD, SABINE W.

FISHER, KING
FISCHER, CLAUS

FISHER, LAINE
HOWARD, JAMES A[RCH]

FISHER, MARGOT
PAINE, LAURAN BOSWORTH

FISHER, R.A.
FISHER, RONALD AYLMER

FISHER, SAM M.
LLIRO OLIVE, JOSE MARIA

FISHER, STEVE
FISHER, STEPHEN GOULD

FISHER, SUZANNE
STAPLES, SUZANNE FISHER

FISHER, WADE
NORWOOD, VICTOR [G.C.]

FISHER, WILLIAM
FISCHER, HUGO WILHELM

FISK, CALLENE
CRAFTS, WILBUR FISK

FISK, NICHOLAS
HIGGINBOTTOM, DAVID LEE

FISKE, JOHN
GREEN, EDMUND FISK

FISKE, MAJORIE
LOWENTHAL, MAJORIE FISKE

FISKE, SHARON
HILL, PAMELA

FISKE, TARLETON
BLOCH, ROBERT [A]

FITCH, BOB
FITCH, ROBERT BECK

FITCH, CLARKE
SINCLAIR, UPTON BEALL

FITCH, ENSIGN CLARK USN
SINCLAIR, UPTON BEALL

FITCH, JOHN IV
CORMIER, ROBERT EDMUND

FITE, MACK
SCHNECK, STEPHEN
FREEMAN, KATHLEEN

FITZ-BERTH, WILLIAM
ARMING, FREDRICH WILHELM

FITZ-RANDOLPH, JANE [C]
CURRENS, JANE

FITZALAN
TREVOR, ELLESTON

FITZALAN, ROGER
TREVOR, ELLESTON

FITZBANCROFT, TERENCE
RENARD, JOSEPH

FITZGERALD, AMBER
SMITH, NANCY T.

FITZGERALD, BARBARA
NEWMAN, MONA ALICE JEAN
VALUE, BARBARA ANN

FITZGERALD, CAPT. HUGH
BAUM, L[YMAN] FRANK

FITZGERALD, CATHERINE
HINGSTON, MARY SANDRA

FITZGERALD, ELLEN
STEVENSON, FLORENCE

FITZGERALD, ENA
MACMILLAN, GEORGINA F.

FITZGERALD, ERIC
BREWER, GIL

FITZGERALD, ERROL
CLARKE, JOSEPHINE F.M.

FITZGERALD, HAL
JOHNSON, JOSEPH EARL

FITZGERALD, HUGH
BAUM, L[YMAN] FRANK

FITZGERALD, JACK
SHEA, JOHN GERALD

FITZGERALD, JOHN [D]
FAZZANO, JOSEPH E.

FITZGERALD, JULIE [JULIA]
WATSON, JULIA

FITZGERALD, JULIET
KALPAKIAN, LAURA ANNE

FITZGERALD, MAEVE
SEGER, MAURA

FITZGERALD, WILLIAM
JENKINS, WILLIAM FITZGER.

FITZPATRICK, JANIE
FRITZHAND, JAMES

FITZPATRICK, WILLIAM
JONES, DAVID

FITZRALPH, MATTHEW
MCINERNY, RALPH [M]

FITZROY, ROSAMOND
BRIGGS, DESMOND LAWTHER

FITZWILLIAM, MICHAEL
LYONS, JOHN BENIGNUS

FIVE OF CLUBS
PROCTOR, RICHARD H.

FIVE, BILLY
OBRECHT, JAS

FIX, PAUL
MORRISON, PAUL FIX

FIXX, JIM
FIXX, JAMES FULLER

FL*M*NG, I*N
CERF, CHRISTOPHER C.
FRITH, MICHAEL K.

FLACCUS
LEVY, NEWMAN

FLACK, JAMES
LINDSAY, NORMAN

FLAGG, FRANCIS
WEISS, HENRY GEORGE

FLAGG, JOHN
GEARON, JOHN

FLAGG, KENNETH
AYVAZIAN, L. FRED

FLAKE, OTTO
KOTTA, LEO F.

FLAKENHORST, C. v.
VON JEZEWSKI, STANISLAUS

FLAM, COSMUS
PIETSCH, JOSEF

FLAMANK, E.
HARPER, EDITH

FLAMBEAU, BLOSSOM
STOCKING, KATHLEEN

FLAMBERG, FRANZ PETER
GROSHOLZ, FRANZ

FLAMM, JERRY
FLAMM, GERALD ROBERT

FLAMMECHE, PIERRE
DAWSON, GEORGE H.

FLAMMENBERG, LORENZ
KAHLERT, KARL FRIEDRICH

FLAMMERBERG, LAWRENCE
KAHLERT, KARL FRIEDRICH

FLANAGAN, BUD
WINTHROP, BUD ROBERT

FLANAGAN, DOROTHY BELLE
HUGHES, DOROTHY BELLE

FLANDERS, JOHN
DE KREMER, JEAN RAYMOND

FLANDERS, REBECCA
BALL, DONNA
DANO, LINDA

FLANNEL, J.C.
FANTONI, BARRY [ERNEST]

FLANNER, HILDEGARDE
MONHOFF, JUNE HILDEGARDE

FLANNERY, SEAN
HAGBERG, DAVID [JAMES]

FLASSAN, MAURICE
BLAZE DE BURY, MARIE P.R.

FLAVIUS
HERON-ALLEN, EDWARD

FLECK, BETTY
PAINE, LAURAN BOSWORTH

FLECKNOR, RICHARD
ADCOCK, ARTHUR ST. JOHN

FLECNOC
ADCOCK, ARTHUR ST. JOHN

FLEET, CHARLES
VAN FLEET, CHARLES

FLEETWOOD, FRANK
FLEETWOOD, FRANCES

FLEIDEN, GEORG
KALMUCZAK, ROLF

FLEISCHER, JANE
OPPENHEIM, JOAN

FLEISCHMAN, A.S.
FLEISCHMAN, ALBERT SIDNEY

FLEISCHMAN, SID
FLEISCHMAN, ALBERT SIDNEY

FLEISSER, MARIELUISE
HAINDL, MARIELUISE

FLEMING, CARDINE
GRIEVESON, MILDRED

FLEMING, CAROLINE
GRIEVESON, MILDRED
MATHER, ANNE

FLEMING, CHARLES
KODELPETER, HANS P.

FLEMING, DANIELLE
MORSE, NANCY L.

FLEMING, GEORGE
FLETCHER, CONSTANCE

FLEMING, GERALDINE
CORYELL, JOHN RUSSELL

FLEMING, GUY
MASUR, HAROLD Q.

FLEMING, HARRY
BIRD, WILLIAM H.F.

FLEMING, IAN
AMIS, KINGSLEY [WILLIAM]

FLEMING, JANE
SMITH, STEVE

FLEMING, LEE
HAYMOND, GINNY

FLEMING, MACKLIN
STAINBACK, MACKLIN

FLEMING, NAN
BRAUN, WILBUR

FLEMING, OLIVER
MACDONALD, PHILIP
MACDONALD, RONALD

FLEMING, PETER
KODELPETER, HANS P.

FLEMING, REID
OBRECHT, JAS

FLEMING, RHODA
FLEMING, RONALD

FLEMING, STUART
KNIGHT, DAMON

FLEMING, WALDO
WILLIAMSON, THAMES ROSS

FLEMMING, HARFORD
MCCLELLAND, HARRIET [H]

FLEMMING, SARAH
GILDERDALE, MICHAEL

FLENSBURG, RUTH
HELD, CHRISTA

FLESCH, Y.
FLESCH, YOLANDE CATARINA

FLETA
DE STRATTON, ADAM

FLETCHER, ADAM
FLEXNER, STUART BERG

FLETCHER, ADRIAN
GUILEY, ROSEMARY ELLEN

FLETCHER, DAVID
BARBER, DULAN F.

FLETCHER, DIRK
CUNNINGHAM, CHESTER GRANT

FLETCHER, DONNA
CROW, DONNA FLETCHER

FLETCHER, FARIS
CUNNINGHAM, CHESTER GRANT

FLETCHER, FARRIS
FLETCHER, AARON
HUNSBURGER, H. EDWARD

FLETCHER, GEORGE U.
PRATT, [MURRAY] FLETCHER

FLETCHER, HARRY
WALTON, HARRY

FLETCHER, JOHN
FLETCHER, HARRY LUFT V.

FLETCHER, JOHN
KOBLINSKI, HANS-JOACHIM

FLETCHER, JOHN C.
CORBIN, HAROLD STANDISH

FLETCHER, LUCILLE
WALLOP, LUCILLE FLETCHER

FLETCHER, RICHARD
DODGE, WENDELL PHILLIPS

FLETCHER, RICK
FLETCHER, RICHARD E.

FLETCHER, SCOTT
PFEIFFER, C. BOYD

FLETCHER, SIR BANNISTER
FLETCHER, BANNISTER FLIG.

FLEUR, PAUL
POHL, FREDERIK

FLEUR, WILLIAM
GOSLING, WILLIAM FLOWER

FLEURE, H.J.
FLEURE, HERBERT JOHN

FLEURIDAS, ELLIE RAE
SHERMAN, ELEANOR RAE

FLEURY, DELPHINE
AMATORA, [SISTER] MARY

FLEURY, JACQUELINE
KJELLBERG, PAULINE A.

FLEXMAN, THEODORE
TRUMBO, DONALD [DALTON]

FLIEG, HELMUT
FLIEGEL, HELMUT

FLIGHT, FRANCIES
BIRCH, JACK ERNEST LIONEL
MURRAY, VENETIA PAULINE

FLINDERS, KARL
MILTON, SAUL

FLINDT, DAWN
MUNN, VELLA
THOMPSON, PAULA & MARCELA

FLINT, DICK
PERRY, STEVE

FLINT, HOMER EON
FLINDT, HOMER EON

FLINT, LUCY
FLINT-GOHLKE, LUCY

FLOOD, FLASH
ROBINSON, JAN M.

FLOOGLEBUCKLE, AL
SPIEGELMAN, ART

FLOORMAN, BERT
BODENSCHATZ, HERBERT
GRASMUCK, JURGEN
MIELKE, THOMAS R.P.

FLOR, CLUADE
KRABBE-FLOR, LIESE-LOTTE

FLORENS
VON EICHENDORFF, JOSEPH

FLORES, FRANCES
DE TALAVERA BERGER, FRAN

FLOURNOY, SHERYL
DEE, SHERRY

FLOWER, JOE
FLOWER, JOSEPH EDWARD

FLOWER, LUCAS M.
LINDHOLM, VALDEMAR

FLOWER, PAT
FLOWER, PATRICIA MARY B.

FLOWERDEW, PHYLLIS
KINGSBURY, PHYLLIS MAY

FLOWERS, T.J.
BELLINI, TINA

FLOYD, F. STRATFORD
LIST, JURGEN E.

FLOYD, HERBERT LEROY
FLOYD, R.H.

FLOYD, MORDIE
BRAGUNIER, MORDINA FLOYD

FLUGGE-KROENBERG, GERTRUD
FLUGGE, HANS-LUDOLF

FLUTE, MOLLIE
LOTTMAN, EILEEN [SHUBB]

FLYING OFFICER X
BATES, HERBERT ERNEST

FLYNN, CARTER
HUBNER, HORST W.

FLYNN, CASEY
FLINT, KENNETH C[OVEY]

FLYNN, CHARLES
BECKMAN, LEIF

FLYNN, DON
FLYNN, DONALD ROBERT

FLYNN, GEORGE
PAINE, LAURAN BOSWORTH

FLYNN, J.M.
FLYNN, JOHN [M]

FLYNN, JACKSON
BENSEN, DONALD R.
SHIRREFFS, GORDON DONALD

FLYNN, JAY
FLYNN, JOHN [M]

FLYNN, MARY
WELSH, MARY FLYNN

FLYNN, PETER
GIBSON, OWEN

FLYNN, T.T.
FLYNN, THOMAS THEODORE

FLYNN, VERONICA
LYONS, JACQUELINE

FLYNT, CATRIONA
FLYNN, KAREN
LEWIS, VIOLET

FLYNT, JOSHUA
WILLARD, JOSHUA FLYNT

FOBEL, JIM
FOBEL, JAMES M.

FOCK, EUGEN
BERENDT, KLAUS

FOCK, GORCH
KINAU, JOHANNES

FODA, ANN
FOXE, ARTHUR NORMAN

FODOR, NANDOR
CARRINGTON, HEREWARD

FOERSTER, EBERHARD
WEISENBORN, GUENTHER

FOGARTY, JONATHAN TITUL.
FARRELL, JAMES THOMAS

FOGEL, DANIEL
KAHN-FOGEL, DANIEL MARK

FOHREN, KLAUS
KLIPPEL, HERMANN

FOLEY, HELEN
FOWLER, HELEN ROSA H.

FOLEY, RAE
DENNISTON, ELINORE

FOLEY, SCOTT
DAREFF, HAL

FOLGORE, LUCIANO
VECCHI, OMERO

FOLKE, WILL
BLOCH, ROBERT [A]

FOLKERTS, MARTA
BUSCH, MARTA

FOLKESEN, SVEIN
TEIGE, LUDVIG

FOLLETT, EDWINA
FENTON, EDWARD

FOLLETT, KEN
FOLLETT, KENNETH [MARTIN]

FOLMAR, J. KENT
FOLMER, JOHN KENT

FOLSOM, JACK
FOLSOM, JOHN BENTLEY

FOLUP, FRANK
SIDIS, WILLIAM JAMES

FOMIN
GOLOMSTOCK, IGOR N.

FONG, C.K.
CASSIDAY, BRUCE [BINGHAM]

FONSALBA, PABLO MARIA
DE ALBINANA, ASUNCION I.

FONTAINE, PAULA
RICO, DON

FONTAYNE, OLIVIA
LAFUENTE, PATRICIA
OLIVER, PATRICIA

FONTENOY, MARQUIS DE
CUNLIFFE-OWEN, FREDERICK

FONTENOY, MYRA
LOUISE, DUCHESS OF ARGYLL

FONTEYN, MARGOT
FONTEYN DE ARIAS, MARGOT
HOOKHAM, MARGARET EVELYN

FOOTE, BUD
FOOTE, IRVING FLINT

FORAY, VERGE
MYERS, HOWARD L.

FORBAN, ANDRE
KRAMER, KARL EMERICH

FORBERG, ATI
FORBERG, BEATE GROPIUS

FORBES, ALECK
RATHBORNE, ST. GEORGE

FORBES, ALEXANDER
ANDERSON, WILLIAM

FORBES, ATHOL
PHILLIPS, ALEXANDER FORBE

FORBES, CABOT L.
HOYT, EDWIN P. JR.

FORBES, COLIN
SAWKINS, RAYMOND [H]

FORBES, COSMO
DRAGO, HARRY SINCLAIR

FORBES, D.F.
FORBES, DELORIS STANTON

FORBES, DANIEL
KENYON, MICHAEL

FORBES, GRAHAM B.
STRATEMEYER, EDWARD

FORBES, KARINE
MCLEAN, KATHRYN [A]

FORBES, KATHRYN
MCLEAN, KATHRYN [A]

FORBES, ROBERT
STRAUS, RALPH

FORBES, ROBERT ERSTONE
STRAUS, RALPH

FORBES, ROSITA
MCGRATH, JOAN ROSITA TORR

FORBES, STANTON
FORBES, DELORIS STANTON

FORBES, STEPHEN
FOX, STUART

FORBES-ROBERTSON, DIANA
SHEEAN, DIANA

FORD, ALBERT LEE
STRATEMEYER, EDWARD

FORD, BARRY
WHITFORD, JOAN

FORD, BETTY
FORD, ELIZABETH ANNE B.

FORD, BRIAN
TENKRAT, FRIEDRICH

FORD, BRYANT
BLANKFORT, MICHAEL [S]

FORD, COLLIER
FORD, JAMES LAWRENCE C.

FORD, COREY
VANCE, PHILO

FORD, D.M.
NORTHCROFT, DRORTHEA

FORD, DAVID
HARKNETT, TERRY W.

FORD, ELBUR
HIBBERT, ELEANOR BURFORD

FORD, ELIZABETH
BIDWELL, M. ELIZABETH

FORD, FLORENCE
NOVELLI, FLORENCE

FORD, FORD MADOX
HUEFFER, JOSEPH FORD M.

FORD, FRED
DOERFFLER, ALFRED

FORD, GARRET
CRAWFORD, MARGARET
CRAWFORD, WILLIAM [E]

FORD, HILARY
YOUD, CHRISTOPHER [S]

FORD, HILDEGARDE
MORRISON, VELMA FORD

FORD, J. MASSYNGBAERDE
FORD, JOSEPHINE MASSYNGB.

FORD, JEREMY
LEVINE, WILLIAM

FORD, JERRY
HACKMANN, KARL-HEINZ

FORD, JESSIE [HILL]
OSBORNE, JESSIE HILL

FORD, KIRK
SPENCE, W. JOHN DUNCAN

FORD, LANGRIDGE
COLEMAN-COOKE, JOHN C.

FORD, LESLIE
BROWN, ZENITH [JONES]

FORD, LEWIS
PATTEN, LEWIS B.

FORD, M.
FORD, MARY ELIZABETH

FORD, MARCIA
RADFORD, RUTH LORRAINE

FORD, MARIE
FORD, MARY ELIZABETH

FORD, NORREY
DILCOCK, NOREEN

FORD, PENDLETON
CHESHIRE, GIFFORD PAUL

FORD, QUINTON
POTHECARY, RAYMOND

FORD, ROBERT A.D.
FORD, ROBERT A[RTHUR] D.

FORD, WALLACE
KING, ALBERT

FORD, WEBSTER
MASTERS, EDGAR LEE

FORD, WHITEY
FORD, EDWARD CHARLES

FORDE, NICHOLAS
ELLIOTT-CANNON, ARTHUR

FORDEN, JAMES
BARLOW, JAMES HENRY S.

FORDWOOD, JACK
WOOLFOLK, JOSHUA PITTS

FORDWYCH, JACK
GARRISH, HAROLD J.

FORDWYCH, JOHN EDMUND
GARRISH, HAROLD J.

FOREMAN, BOB
FOREMAN, ROBERTO

FOREMAN, L.L.
FOREMAN, LEONARD LONDON

FOREMAN, LEE
KING, ALBERT

FOREMAN, LEN L.
FOREMAN, LEONARD LONDON

FOREST, DIAL
GAULT, WILLIAM CAMPBELL

FOREST, JIM
FOREST, HAMES H.

FOREST, SALAMBO
BELLINI, TINA

FORESTER, C.S.
SMITH, CECIL LEWIS T.

FORESTER, CECIL SCOTT
SMITH, CECIL LEWIS T.

FORESTER, FRANK
HERBERT, HENRY WILLIAM

FORESTIER, AUBER
MOORE, ANNIE A.W.

FORESTIER, GEORGE
KRAMER, KARL FRIEDRICH

FORESTIER, JOAN
FURSTAUER, JOHANNA

FORETHOUGHT, BACKSIGHT
SWINTON, SIR EDWARD

FOREZ
MAURIAC, FRANCOIS C

FORFEX ET HESTA
MORRIS, BESSIE C.
SPEAR, ANNIE B.

FORGE, ANDRE
DEIHL, EDNA GROFF

FORGE, JOHN
TWYMAN, HAROLD WILLIAM

FORIJAY
ACKERMAN, FORREST J.

FORIO, ROBERT
WEISS, IRVING J.

FORISHA, BARBARA L.
FORISHA-KOVACH, BARBARA L

FORJAK
ACKERMAN, FORREST J.

FORMAN, GINNY
ZACHARY, HUGH

FORMER RESIDENT OF HUB
BATCHELDER, JOHN

FORREST, ALLEN
SNOW, CHARLES H[ORACE]

FORREST, ANTONY
BROWN, ANTONY
MACKENZIE, NORMAN IAN

FORREST, CALEB
TELFER, DARIEL

FORREST, CAROL
TENNYSON, MARGARET

FORREST, CHELSEY
CUNNINGHAM, JAN

FORREST, CLARK
LLIRO OLIVE, JOSE MARIA

FORREST, COLONEL CHRIS
STODDARD, WILLIAM OSBORN

FORREST, DAVID
DENHOLM, DAVID
ELIADES, DAVID
FORREST-WEBB, ROBERT

FORREST, FELIX C.
LINEBARGER, PAUL M.A.

FORREST, GEORGE
WOOD, J.G.

FORREST, JULIAN
WAGENKNECHT, EDWARD [C]

FORREST, LEE
WOODS, CLEE

FORREST, MARK
MORTON, GUY [MAINWARING]

FORREST, MARY
FREEMAN, JULIA DEAN

FORREST, NORMAN
MORLAND, NIGEL

FORREST, SYBIL
MARKUN, PATRICIA MALONEY

FORREST, WILMA
FORREST, WILLIAM S.

FORRESTER, DEXTER J.
GOLDFRAP, JOHN HENRY

FORRESTER, E.
BATT, LEON

FORRESTER, GLEN
GALLARDOS MUNOZ, JUAN

FORRESTER, HELEN
BHATIA, JAMUNADEVI

FORRESTER, LEO
LEE, EDWARD EDSON

FORRESTER, MARIAN
SCHACHTEL, ROGER BERNARD

FORRESTER, MARY
HUMPHRIES, ELSIE MARY

FORRESTER, THORN
ALPERS, HANS JOACHIM
BUWERT, HARALD
HAHN, RONALD M.
MAXIMOVIC, GERD

FORS-WILLNER, LENA
GEDDES, CAROLA

FORSEY, PETER Q.
GARBUTT, JOHN L.

FORSMAN,, GUNNER
ORNULF, GUNNAR

FORST, GINO
VON MOELLWITZ, GINO F.

FORSTER, A.W.P.
PAFFRATH, ALFRED

FORSTER, CHRISTINE
FORTE, CHRISTINE

FORSTER, E.M.
FORSTER, EDWARD MORGAN

FORSTER, HILDE
FREUNDSBERGER, HILDEGARD

FORSTER, JOACHIM
ANGER, MARTIN

FORSTER, JOHN
KUNZE, ROLF

FORSTER, JOHN D.
MEYN, NIELS

FORSTER, MARK [ARNOLD]
ARNOLD-FORSTER, MARK

FORSTER, REBECCA
CZULEGER, REBECCA

FORSTER, WOLFGANG
MUHRMANN, WILHELM

FORSTNER, LUDWIG
MARGL, LUDWIG

FORSTO, MITRA
ACKERMAN, FORREST J.

FORSYTE, CHARLES
PHILO, GORDON

FORSYTH, JEAN
M'ILWRAITH, JEAN N.

FORSYTH, R.A.
JOHNSTON, ROBERT THOMSON

FORSYTHE, ANTHONY
BRAUN, WILBUR

FORSYTHE, IRENE
HANSON, IRENE FORSYTHE

FORSYTHE, JEAN
MCILWRAITH, JEAN NEWTON

FORSYTHE, PATRICIA
KNOLL, PATRICIA F.

FORSYTHE, ROBERT
CRICHTON, KYLE SAMUEL

FORT, PAUL
STOCKTON, FRANCIS R.

FORTEN, CHARLOTTE [L]
GRIMKE, CHARLOTTE L.F.

FORTHEMONEY, JUSTINIAN
SEDGEMORE, BRIAN CHARLES

FORTINA, MARTHA
CARSTENS, NETTA
LAFFEATY, CHRISTINA

FORTINI, FRANCO
LATTES, FRANCO

FORTNUM, PEGGY
NUTTALL-SMITH, MARGARET E

FORTRIDE, L.A.
APPEL, LISELOTTE

FORTRIDGE, ALLAN G.
JUNG, ROBERT

FORTUNE, DION
FIRTH, VIOLET MARY

FORTUNE, SPENCER
RANDISI, ROBERT J.

FORTUNIS
NIBOYET, [J.A] PAULIN

FORVE, GUY
CIMBALO, GUY

FORWARD, LUKE
PATRICK, JOHNSTONE G.

FOSCA, FRANCOIS
DE TRAZ, GEORGES

FOSS, JOHN
GORDON, JAMES

FOSSE, ALFRED
JELLY, GEORGE OLIVER

FOSSE, HAROLD C.
GOLD, HORACE L.

FOSTER, BLAIR
CLARK, BLAIR FOSTER
CLARK, SYLVIA

FOSTER, DELIA
WALKER, EMILY KATHLEEN

FOSTER, DIRK
FRANCES, STEPHEN D.
PARDOE, GEOFFREY

FOSTER, EVAN
KING, ALBERT

FOSTER, FAYE LOVE
DINWIDDIE, FAYE V.L.

FOSTER, FREDERICK
GODWIN, JOHN [F]

FOSTER, GEORGE
HASWELL, C. JOHN D.

FOSTER, GERRY
JENNISON, JOHN WILLIAM

FOSTER, GRANT
GARRISH, HAROLD J.

FOSTER, HAL
FOSTER, HAROLD RUDOLF

FOSTER, HARRY
PAINE, LAURAN BOSWORTH

FOSTER, IRIS
POSNER, RICHARD

FOSTER, J.A.
FOSTER, JAMES ANTHONY

FOSTER, JAKE
GORMAN, EDWARD [JOSEPH]
REASONER, JAMES M.

FOSTER, JEANNE
WILLIAMS, DOROTHY JEANNE

FOSTER, JOHN
HOBER, HEINZ WERNER

FOSTER, MARION
SHEA, SHIRLEY

FOSTER, P.T.
BOARD, PRUDENCE FOSTER T.

FOSTER, PRUDENCE
BOARD, PRUDENCE FOSTER T.

FOSTER, RICHARD
CROSSEN, KENDELL FOSTER

FOSTER, SARAH
BISHOP, ELIZABETH

FOSTER, SHEILA
BERNET, MICHAEL [STEVEN]

FOSTER, SIMON
GLEN, DUNCAN MUNRO

FOSTER, TONY
FOSTER, JAMES ANTHONY

FOSTER, W. BERT
FOSTER, WALTER BERTRAM

FOSTER, W.B.
FOSTER, WALTER BERTRAM

FOUGASSE
BIRD, [C] KENNETH

FOUGHT, CATHERINE ANN
HOSMER, CATHERINE ANN

FOULDS, E.V.
FOULDS, ELFRIDA VIPONT

FOULIS, HUGH
MUNRO, NEIL

FOUNTAIN, ARNOLD
OURSLER, [C] FULTON

FOUR CORNERS, GEORGE
VIERECK, GEORGE SYLVESTER

FOUREST, MICHEL
WYNNE-TYSON, JON

FOURNIER, FRANK
CHAPMAN, FRANK MONROE

FOURTH BROTHER, THE
AUNG, [MAUNG] HTIN

FOURTH, CLIFTON
MORSE, HENRY CLIFTON IV

FOWLE, ELEANOR CRANSTON
CAMERON, ELEANOR CRANSTON

FOWLER, DREW
OFFUTT, ANDREW J.

FOWLER, ELLEN THORNEYCROF
FELKIN, MRS. ELLEN [A]

FOWLER, GENE
FOWLER, EUGENE DEVLAN

FOWLER, HEATHER T.
REMOFF, HEATHER T[REXLER]

FOWLER, JIM
FOWLER, JAMES WILEY III

FOWLER, MARY JANE
WHEELER, MARY JANE

FOWLER, SYDNEY
WRIGHT, SIDNEY FOWLER

FOWLER, VIRGINIE
ELBERT, VIRGINIE FOWLER

FOWLES, JOHN
FOWLES, J.R.

FOX, ALICIA
CLEMENS-FOX, CAROL

FOX, ANTHONY
FULLERTON, ALEXANDER F.

FOX, BILL
FOX, WILLIAM

FOX, BRIAN
BALLARD, W. TODHUNTER

FOX, COL. VICTOR J.
WINSTON, ROBERT A.

FOX, DAVID
OSTRANDER, ISABEL EGENTON

FOX, ELEANOR
ST. JOHN, WYLLY FOLK

FOX, FRANCES MARGARET
FIELD, FRANCES FOX

FOX, FREEMAN
HAMILTON, CHARLES H.S.

FOX, GILL
FOX, GILBERT THEODORE

FOX, GRACE
ANDERSON, GRACE FOX

FOX, H.L.
HALL, HENRY

FOX, JAMES
KNIPSCHEER, JOHANNES M.W.

FOX, JAMES M.
KNIPSCHEER, JOHANNES M.W.

FOX, JOHN
TODD, JOHN M.

FOX, LAUREN
FOWLER, DENNIS & PENNY

FOX, LUCIA
LOCKERT, LUCIA [A.U.F.]

FOX, MARION
WARD, MARION INEZ

FOX, MEM
FOX, MERRION FRANCES

FOX, OWEN
FARMER, BERNARD J.

FOX, PETRONELLA
BALOUGH, PENELOPE

FOX, SEBASTIAN
BULLETT, GERALD WILLIAM

FOX, STEPHEN
FURTHMANN, JULIUS G.

FOX, TED
FOX, GILBERT THEODORE
FOX, THEODORE J.

FOX, V. HELEN
COUCH, HELEN FOX

FOX-LOCKERT, LUCIA
LOCKERT, LUCIA [A.U.F.]

FOXE, JASON
BUCHAN, [JOHN] STUART

FOXE, PAMELA
BUCHAN, [JOHN] STUART

FOXE, PRESTON
FEARN, JOHN RUSSELL

FOXHALL
SEAWELL, MOLLY ELLIOT

FOXX, ALEISTER
ANNAND, ALAN

FOXX, JACK
PRONZINI, WILLIAM JOHN

FOXX, ROSALIND
HAYDON, JUNE
SIMPSON, JUDITH [JUDY]

FOY, PETER
COOK, FRED GORDON

FRA ELBERTUS
HUBBARD, ELBERT

FRADDLE, FARRAGUT
MEARNS, DAVID CHAMBERS

FRAKE, WARNER
MUSCIANO, WALTER A.

FRAME, JANET
CLUTHA, JANET P. FRAME

FRAME, PATRICIA
WETHERELL, JUNE

FRANC, ERIC ARTUR
FRANZ, ERICH ARTHUR

FRANC, MAUD JEAN
EVANS, MATILDA JANE

FRANC-NOHAIN
LEGRAND, MAURICE-ETIENNE

FRANCE, ANATOLE
THIBAULT, JACQUES ANATOLE

FRANCE, CLAIRE
DORE, CLAIRE [MORIN]

FRANCE, EVANGELINE
FRANCE-HAYHURST, EVANGELN

FRANCE, VICTOR
JORDAN, PHILIP [F]

FRANCES, MICHEL
CATTAUI, GEORGES

FRANCES, MISS
HORWICH, FRANCES R.

FRANCES, SOPHIA
FRANCIS, SOPHIA L.

FRANCESCA, ROSINA
BROOKMAN, ROSINA FRANCESC

FRANCHI, EDA
VICKERS, ANTOINETTE L.

FRANCIS
GUTHRIE, THOMAS ANSTEY

FRANCIS, ANNE
BIRD, FLORENCE [B]
WINTLE, ANNE

FRANCIS, ARTHUR
GERSHWIN, IRA

FRANCIS, C.D.E.
HOWARTH, PATRICK [J.F.]

FRANCIS, CAT
FRANCIS, EMILE PERCY

FRANCIS, CHARLES
HOLME, BRYAN
PETERS, CHARLES FRANCIS

FRANCIS, D.
DEEGAN, FRANCIS M.

FRANCIS, DANIEL
CRANNY, TITUS FRANCIS

FRANCIS, DEE
HAAS, DOROTHY F.

FRANCIS, DICK
FRANCIS, RICHARD STANLEY

FRANCIS, E.A.
FRANZ, ERICH ARTHUR

FRANCIS, EMILY
ARTZ, EMILY
YARIV, FRANCIS POKRAS

FRANCIS, GREGORY
MACGREGOR, JAMES MURDOCH
PARNELL, FRANK H.

FRANCIS, H.G.
FRANCISKOWSKY, HANS GUNT.

FRANCIS, HANS G.
FRANCISKOWSKY, HANS GUNT.

FRANCIS, HAYWARD
SHEWRING, WALTER

FRANCIS, HEINZ G.
FRANCISKOWSKY, HANS GUNT.

FRANCIS, JAMES
ROSS, CHARLES

FRANCIS, JAMES R.
RABBIT, JAMES FRANCIS

FRANCIS, JEAN
GRACE, ANITA

FRANCIS, LEE
BROWNE, HOWARD
FAIRMAN, PAUL W.
HAMLING, WILLIAM L.
YERXA, LEROY

FRANCIS, M.E.
BLUNDELL, MRS. FRANCES

FRANCIS, MOTHER MARY
ASCHMANN, ALBERTA

FRANCIS, PAUL
ENGLEMAN, PAUL

FRANCIS, PHILIP
LOCKYER, ROGER WALTER

FRANCIS, RADFORD
FRANCIS, RADFIELD

FRANCIS, RICHARD H.
FRANCIS, RICHARD

FRANCIS, RICKI
HARDY, CARLENE

FRANCIS, ROBERT
MAXENCE, ROBERT

FRANCIS, ROBIN
FERRIS, ROSE MARIE

FRANCIS, SHARON
WARTSKI, MAUREEN A.C.

FRANCIS, STELLA M.
HONEYWELL, J. FRANK

FRANCIS, VICTOR
HAMMOND, LAWRENCE

FRANCIS, WILLIAM
URELL, WILLIAM FRANCIS

FRANCIS-WILLIAMS, BARON
WILLIAMS, EDWARD FRANCIS

FRANCISCO, H.G.
FRANCISKOWSKY, HANS GUNT.

FRANCK, DR.
ORTEA, FRANCISCO CARLOS

FRANCK, MONICA
STARFELT, VIVEKA

FRANCK, SEBASTIAN
JACOBY, HENRY

FRANCKEN, FRITZ
EDWARD, FREDERIK

FRANCOIS, YVES REGIS
BARBERO, YVES REGIS FRAN.

FRANCOISE
SEIGNOBOSC, FRANCOISE

FRANDERE
DES ROCHES, FRANCIS

FRANK, ARMIN
FREY, ANTON
HUBER, ARMIN OTTO

FRANK, AXEL
BERGER, PETER

FRANK, BEN
GRUND, CARL-JOSEPH

FRANK, BENNO
KOHLENBERG, KARL FRIEDR.

FRANK, DR. STEFAN
BENDER, ERICH F.
FECHTNER, WOLFGANG
HEBEL, PETER
KLEIN, DOROTHEE
PLOSSNER, JUTTA
RAUSCH, LOTHAR

FRANK, DR. STEFAN [CONT]
REISCH-NOWAK, CHRISTINE
SANKE, MARGIT

FRANK, GUNTHER
FRANCISKOWSKY, HANS GUNT.

FRANK, HELENE
VAUTIER, GHISLAINE

FRANK, JANET
DUNLEAVY, JANET EGLESTON

FRANK, LEE
GRIFFIN, ARTHUR J.

FRANK, LEO
MEYER, LEO

FRANK, PAT
HART, HARRY

FRANK, R. JR.
ROSS, FRANK [X] JR.

FRANK, T.C.
LAUGHLIN, TOM

FRANK, THEODORE
GARDINER, DOROTHEA FRANC.

FRANK, WILLIAM G.
FRANK, RUDOLF

FRANKE, JAN
FORSSBERG, LENNART

FRANKEN, BERT
BERTHOLD, WILL

FRANKEN, RENATE
KALZ, ELFRIEDE

FRANKLIN, A.
ARNOLD, ADLAI FRANKLIN

FRANKLIN, BENJAMIN
HASEK, JAROSLAV M.F.

FRANKLIN, CHARLES
USHER, FRANK HUGH

FRANKLIN, DONALD
NUETZEL, CHARLES A.

FRANKLIN, E.
HURT, EDWIN FRANKLIN

FRANKLIN, E.A.
REINHARD, WILHELM PETER

FRANKLIN, EDGAR
STEARNS, EDGAR FRANKLIN

FRANKLIN, EDWINA
MARKS, ARLENE

FRANKLIN, ELIZABETH
CAMPBELL, HANNAH

FRANKLIN, EUGENE
BANDY, [EUGENE] FRANKLIN

FRANKLIN, GRIFF
GRIFFEN, FRANK

FRANKLIN, HAROLD
FEIGENBAUM, HAROLD

FRANKLIN, JAY
CARTER, JOHN FRANKLIN

FRANKLIN, KEITH
FOY, KENNETH RUSSELL

FRANKLIN, KERRY
CALDWELL, STRATTON F.

FRANKLIN, L'ENGLE
FRANKLIN, MADELEINE L'ENG

FRANKLIN, LANCE
LANTZ, FRANCESS LIN

FRANKLIN, MAX
DEMING, RICHARD

FRANKLIN, MELISSA
MCCHESNEY, MARY F.

FRANKLIN, MILES
FRANKLIN, STELLA MARIA S.

FRANKLIN, NAT
BAUER, ERWIN A.

FRANKLIN, PAT
CADY, JACK [ANDREW]

FRANKLIN, PAUL
WALTON, BRYCE

FRANKLIN, ROGER
HARDY, CARLENE

FRANKLIN, STEVE
STEVENS, FRANKLIN

FRANKLYN, DONALD
NUETZEL, CHARLES A.

FRANKLYN, ROSS
HARDY, FRANK

FRANKS, ED
BRANDON, JOHNNY

FRANZ, ARNOLD
LIEBER, FRANCIS

FRANZ, GUNTER
PRAGER, HANS GEORG

FRANZ, ONKEL
EWERS, HANNS HEINZ

FRANZ, WILHELM
DREYSE, NIKOLAUS v.

FRANZERO, CHARLES MARIE
FRANZERO, CARLO MARIA

FRAPAN-AKUMAN, ILSE
LEVIEN, ILSE

FRASCATORO, GERALD
HORNBACK, BERT G[ERALD]

FRASER, ALEX
BRINTON, HENRY

FRASER, BERT
CRUICKSHANK, HAROLD F.

FRASER, BETTY
FRASER, ELIZABETH MARR

FRASER, DIANE L.
LYNCH-FRASER, DIANE

FRASER, ELIZABETH
GRANT, MAUDE MARGARET

FRASER, JAMES
WHITE, ALAN

FRASER, JANE
PILCHER, ROSAMUNDE

FRASER, JANET HOBHOUSE
HOBHOUSE, JANET

FRASER, JEFFERSON
WILDING, PHILIP

FRASER, KATHLEEN
BALL, MARGARET

FRASER, LAWRENCE
ABBOTT, LAWRENCE FRASER

FRASER, MARY
JAMES, LAURENCE

FRASER, MAXWELL
FRASER, DOROTHY MAY

FRASER, PETER
COLES, PHOEBE CATHERINE
WATT, ALEXANDER PETER F.

FRASER, RAY
FRASER, RAYMOND JOSEPH

FRASER, RONALD
TILTMAN, RONALD FRANK

FRASER, STUART
WOOD, JAMES [A.F]

FRAY, AL
SALAWAY, RALPH

FRAZEE, STEVE
FRAZEE, [CHARLES] STEPHEN

FRAZEN, BILL
FRANZEN, WILLIAM EDWARD

FRAZER, ALLISON
ROCHESTER, GEO[RGE] E.

FRAZER, ANDREW
MARLOWE, STEPHEN

FRAZER, FRED
AVALLONE, MICHAEL

FRAZER, GAIL
PULVER, MARY MONICA

FRAZER, MARGARET
BACON, GAIL
PULVER, MARY MONICA

FRAZER, MARK PETRIVICH
MACLEAN, DONALD DUART

FRAZER, MARTIN
CLARKE, PERCY A.

FRAZER, RENEE
FLEMING, RONALD

FRAZER, ROBERT CAINE
CREASEY, JOHN

FRAZER, SHAMUS
FRAZER, JAMES IAN ARBUTH.

FRAZER, WINIFRED DUSENB.
FRAZER, WINIFRED LOESCH

FRAZETTA, FRANK
FRAZZETTA, FRANK

FRAZIER, ARTHUR
BULMER, [HENRY] KENNETH
JAMES, LAURENCE

FRAZIER, F.M.
MORRIS, CHARLES [S]

FRAZIER, PAMELA
STEVENSON, FLORENCE

FRAZIER, SARAH
WIRT, WINOLA WELLS

FRAZIER, WALT
FRAZIER, WALTER

FREAIR, FRED
BANKS, RAYMOND E.

FRECKLES
DIETZ, HOWARD

FREDD, AL
CROUTCH, LESLIE A.

FREDERIC, AL
FRIEDRICHS, HOLGER

FREDERIC, MIKE
COX, WILLIAM ROBERT

FREDERICK, BARON CORVO
ROLFE, FREDERICK [W]

FREDERICK, BURT
FRIEDRICHS, HORST

FREDERICK, DICK
DEMPEWOLFF, RICHARD F.

FREDERICK, GERALD
BASNER, GERHARD

FREDERICK, JOHN
FAUST, FREDERICK S.

FREDERICK, KATE
BECKWITH, AUDREY

FREDERICK, LEE
NUSSBAUM, ALBERT F.

FREDERICK, ORLIN
TREMAINE, F. ORLIN

FREDERICK, OSWALD
SNELLING, O.F.

FREDERICK, THEA
KEILER, BARBARA

FREDERICKS, ARNOLD
KUMMER, FREDERICK ARNOLD

FREDERICKS, ERNEST
ERNST, PAUL FREDERICK

FREDERICKS, ERNEST JASON
ERNST, PAUL FREDERICK

FREDERICKS, FRANK
FRANCK, FREDERICK S.

FREDERICKS, FROHM
KERNER, FRED

FREDERICKS, HARRIET
LAURENTS, CLYDE
SMOCK, JAMES

FREDERICKS, VIC
FELL, FREDERICK VICTOR
MAJESKI, WILLIAM [BILL]

FREDERICS, JOCKO
FREDE, RICHARD

FREDERICS, MACDOWELL
FREDE, RICHARD

FREDMAN, IGON
DE PLANQUE, WALTER

FREDRICKS, P.C.
PRIMMER, PHYLLIS

FREDRICS, GEORGE
NUETZEL, CHARLES A.

FREE
HOFFMAN, ABBOTT [ABBY]

FREE, ROBERT H.F.
FELDMANN, HARRO

FREE, [MAJ.] MICKEY
ENTON, HARRY

FREED, BARRY
HOFFMAN, ABBOTT [ABBY]

FREED, CECIL V.
ROECKEN, KURT WALTER

FREED, PAUL
MCCUSKER, PAUL

FREEDLAND, NAT[HANIEL]
FRIEDLAND, NATHANIEL

FREELAND, JAY
MCLEOD, JOHN FREELAND

FREEMAN, BILL
FREEMAN, WILLIAM BRADFORD

FREEMAN, BJORN
PRATNEY, WILLIAM ALFRED

FREEMAN, CYNTHIA
FEINBERG, BEATRICE C.F.

FREEMAN, DAVE
FREEMAN, DAVID

FREEMAN, DAVIS
FRIEDMAN, DAVID F.

FREEMAN, H.W.
FREEMAN, HAROLD WEBBER

FREEMAN, J.L.
ST. JOHN, PERCY BOLLNGBRK

FREEMAN, JACK
FREEMAN, E.

FREEMAN, JAMES DILLET
FREEDMAN, JAMES DILLET

FREEMAN, JAY
HOLDING, JAMES [C.C.]

FREEMAN, LARRY
FREEMAN, GRAYDON LAVERNE

FREEMAN, M.E.
FREEMAN, MARY [E.W.]

FREEMAN, MARY E. WILKINS
WILKINS, MARY [E]

FREEMAN, PETER J.
CALVERT, PATRICIA

FREEMAN, R. AUSTIN
FREEMAN, RICHARD AUSTIN

FREEMAN, RHONDA
FRIESEN-MIELTITZ, FELICI.

FREEMAN, RITA
RICHTER-FRICH, OVRE

FREEMAN, THOMAS
FEHRENBACH, THOMAS REED

FREI, BRUNO
FRIESTADT, BENEDIKT

FREI, EDUARDO
FREI MONTALVA, EDUARDO

FREIBURGER, WALTER
JENS, WALTER

FREIER, GUSTAV
LAFONTAINE, AUGUSTUS H.J.

FREIRE, P.
FREIRE, PAULO

FREKSA, FRIEDRICH
FRIEDRICH-FREKSA, KURT
SCHMIDT-FREKSA, GERTRUD

FREMLIN, CELIA
GOLLER, CELIA MARGARET

FREMLIN, VICTOR
PHILIPS, GEORGE NORMAN

FREMONT, W.B.
BOWERS, WARNER FREMONT

FRENCH DETECTIVE
RUSSELL, WILLIAM

FRENCH, ARTHUR
NEUBERG, VICTOR [B]

FRENCH, ASHLEY
ROBINS, DENISE

FRENCH, DON
THODY, PHILIP MALCOLM W.

FRENCH, DORIS
SHACKLETON, DORIS [C]

FRENCH, ELLEN JEAN
ENGLISH, JEAN ELLEN

FRENCH, EMILY
KENNEDY, GERMAINE

FRENCH, FERGUS
FRIEDLANDER, PETER

FRENCH, JANINE
VAN-LOON, ANTONIO
FINKLESTEIN, RONI

FRENCH, KATHRYN
MOSESSON, GLORIA R.

FRENCH, PAUL
ASIMOV, ISAAC

FRENCH, ROSALIND
HARDY, CARLENE

FRENES, ALIX DU
FRENES-RILLA, ALIX E. DU

FRESCO, AL
KENWORTHY, CHARLES J.

FRESENUS, FRITZ
LOTTMANN, F.

FRESHFIELD, MARK
FIELD, M.J.

FRETAG, JOSEPH
COOPER, PARLEY J.

FRETAG, JOSEPHINE
COOPER, PARLEY J.

FRETTER, T.W.
ANDRE, [K] MICHAEL

FREUGON, RUBY
ASHBY, RUBY C.

FREUND, OTTO K.
KAHN-FREUND, OTTO

FREY, H.J.
FREYTAG, HANS-JURGEN

FREY, JAMES N.
WASHBURN, MARK

FREY, JULIAN
HYNAM, JOHN C.

FREY, KARL
FALKE, KONRAD

FREY, MARTYS
MAYFIELD, MARTYS

FREYER, ERICK
SHROYER, FREDERICK

FREYER, FREDERIC
BALLINGER, WILLIAM S.

FREYRE, RICARDO JAIMES
JAIMES FREYRE, RICARDO

FREYTAG, JOSEPHINE
COOPER, PARLEY J.

FRIAR TUCK
TUCKER, IRWIN ST. JOHN

FRICK, C.H.
IRWIN, CONSTANCE F.

FRICK, CONSTANCE
IRWIN, CONSTANCE F.

FRIDAY, BILL [B]
MANVILLE, WILLIAM HENRY

FRIDAY, JOE
WEBB, JACK RANDOLPH

FRIDAY, PETER
HARRIS, HERBERT

FRIDOLIN
CHRIST, ROBERT B.

FRIEBEL, G.
FRIEBEL-ROHRING, GISELA

FRIEBELUNG, MARGARETE
KUNZ-FROMEL, MARGARETE

FRIED, ELEANOR L.
FURMAN, ELEANOR L.

FRIEDEBURG, OSWALD
FREITAG, OTTO

FRIEDELL, EGON
FRIEDMANN, EGON

FRIEDENHAUS, FRIEDRICH
KLEINE, ERWIN

FRIEDENREICH, HARRIET P.
FREIDENREICH, HARRIET P.

FRIEDLAENDER, SAUL
FRIEDLAENDER, PAVEL

FRIEDLAENDER, SHAUL
FRIEDLAENDER, PAVEL

FRIEDLAND, CARL
GRUNERT, CARL H.

FRIEDMAN, ALAN
HOROWITZ, SHEL ALAN

FRIEDMAN, ARNOLD
BELLAH, JAMES WARNER

FRIEDMAN, ELIAS
FRIEDMAN, JACOB HORACE

FRIEDMAN, HAL
FRIEDMAN, HAROLD

FRIEDMAN, JERROLD DAVID
GERROLD, DAVID

FRIEDMAN, JOHN
FRIEDMAN, JACOB HORACE

FRIEDMAN, JOY TROTH
FRIEDMAN, JOSEPHINE TROTH

FRIEDMAN, MICKEY
FRIEDMAN, MICHAELE T.

FRIEDMAN, ROSEMARY
FRIEDMAN, EVE ROSEMARY

FRIEDMANN, WILL
PUHL, WILFRIED ERNST

FRIEDRICH, ANTON
STRICH, CHRISTIAN

FRIEDRICH, ERNST
PINKERT, ERNST FRIEDRICH

FRIEDRICH, HANNA
FURSTENBERG, HILDE

FRIEDRICH, HORST
LIST, HORST

FRIEDRICH, OSKAR H.
HOLESCH, OSKAR

FRIEDRICH, PAUL
HUBNER, PAUL FRIEDRICH

FRIEDRICH, TORBERG
KANTOR-BERG, FRIEDRICH

FRIEDRICHS, HANS FRANK
LEHMANN, HANS FRIEDRICH

FRIEND, A.
CLEVELAND, PHILIP JEROME

FRIEND, ED
WORMSER, RICHARD [E]

FRIENDLICH, DICK
FRIENDLICH, RICHARD J.

FRIENDS, JALYNN
ALSOBROOK, ROSALYN
HAUGHT, JEAN

FRIES, ERIKA
BEYFUSS, ERIKA

FRIESNER, ESTHER
STUTZMAN, ESTHER FRIESNER

FRIIS, BABBIS
FRII-BAASTAD, BABBIS E.

FRIKELL, SAMRI
BEDFORD-JONES, HENRY
OURSLER, [C] FULTON

FRIMAN, ROBERT
FREEMAN, RICHARD AUSTIN

FRIMBO, E.M.
WHITAKER, ROGERS E.M.

FRINDALL, BILL
FRINDALL, WILLIAM HOWARD

FRINGS, KETTI
FRINGS, KATHLEEN HARTLEY

FRISCHWASSER-RA'ANAN, H.F
RA'ANAN, URI

FRISCO, TOM
DIETSCH, WERNER
KUGLER, DIETMAR

FRISCO, TOM [CONT]
RAHN, WOLFGANG

FRITCH, ELIZABETH
FROHMAN, ELSA

FRITSCH, INA
PISCINI, INGRID

FRITTS, MARY BAHR
BAHR, MARY

FRITZ
FRAZZETTA, FRANK
MOSHER, FREDERICK C.
WHITEHALL, HAROLD

FRITZE, OTTOKAR
NERTH, HANS

FROEST, FRANK
DILNOT, GEORGE

FROHLAND, PETER
EGETEMEYR, PETER

FROHLICH, GUSTAV
FROEHLICH, GUSTAV

FROHLICH, SIGISMUND,
KOHR, DIETRICH

FROHMUT, A.
LOHR, ADOLF

FROLICH-BUME, LILLI
FROHLICH, CAROLINE LILLI

FROLLINE
FILLERON, ROGER-CHARLES

FROME, DAVID
BROWN, ZENITH [JONES]

FROME, FRIEDA
KRIEGER, FRIEDA FROME

FROME, NILES H.
BLISH, JAMES B.

FROMMHERZ, FLORIAN
ALBICKER, JOSEF

FRONTENAC, YVES
LEROUX, YVES

FRONTIER, TEX
MILLER, JAMES P.

FROST, ELEANOR
FROHMAN, ELSA

FROST, ERICA
SUPRANER, ROBYN

FROST, FREDERICK
FAUST, FREDERICK S.

FROST, G[RAHAM]
PAYNE, ROBERT LYLE

FROST, JACK
FROST, RUSSELL E.
OBSTFELD, RAYMOND
RAINEY, RICH[ARD]

PSEUDONYMS

FROST, JONI
PAINE, LAURAN BOSWORTH

FROST, MARTIN
SVEDELID, OLOV

FROST, MORGAN
HUNTINGTON, THOMAS W.

FROST, PAUL
CASTLE, ANTHONY PERCY

FROST, RYKER
FOSTER, RAYMOND KEITH

FROST, S. ANNIE
SHIELDS, MRS. S.A.

FROY, HERALD
DEGHY, GUY [S]

FROY, HERALD
WATERHOUSE, KEITH [S]

FRY, DAVID
ROPER, WILLIAM L.

FRY, JANE
DREW, JANE B.

FRY, PETE
KING, JAMES CLIFFORD

FRY, PLANTAGENET SOMERSET
SOMERSET FRY, P.G.R. PLA.

FRY, TOM
FRY, THOMAS FREDERICK

FRY, [E] MAXWELL
FRY, EDWIN MAXWELL

FRYBERG, JOHN
FREIBERG, HANS-JOACHIM

FRYDAG, WILL
FREYTAG, WILLI GUSTAV

FRYER, DONALD S.
SIDNEY-FRYER, DOANLD

FRYERS, AUSTIN
CLERY, WILLIAM EDWARD

FRYN
JESSE, F. TENNYSON

FUCHS, SONIA
SEEDO, SONIA

FUENTES, CARLOS
FUENTES MACIAS, CARLOS M.

FUENTES, GREGORIO LOPEZ Y
LOPEZ Y FUENTES, GREGORIO

FUEST, MILAN
FUERST, MILAN

FUFFMAN, PHYLLIS
ATWATER, PHYLLIS M.H.

FUFUKA, KARAMA
MORGAN, SHARON A.

FULKE, COMMISSIONER
LOMAX, WILLIAM JOSEPH

FULLBROOK, GLADYS
HUTCHINSON, PATRICIA

FULLER, ED
FULLER, HAROLD EDGAR

FULLER, IOLA
MCCOY, IOLA FULLER

FULLER, JARED
JARED, L.F.

FULLER, KATHLEEN
GOTTFRIED, THEODORE MARK

FULLER, LESTER
ROLFE, EDWIN

FULLER, MARGARET
OSSOLI, SARAH MARGARET F.

FULLER, MAUD
PETERSHAM, MAUD SYLVIA F.

FULLER, ROGER
TRACY, DON[ALD FISKE]

FULLER, RUTH
PERRY, RUTH FULLER

FULLER, SAM
FULLER, SAMUEL MICHAEL

FULLER, TIMOTHY
MARQUAND, JOHN P.

FULLERTON, GAIL PUTNEY
FULLERTON, GAIL JACKSON

FULMAN, AL
FULLER, HAROLD EDGAR

FULOP-MILLER, RENE
FUELOEP-MILLER, RENE

FULTON, LIZ
FULTON, ELIZABETH G.

FULTON, WARD
PRESTON, HARRY

FUNG, GONG
GOON, FOOK MUN

FUNK, TOM
FUNK, THOMPSON

FUQUA, ROBERT
TILLOTSON, JOSEPH W.

FURA, ERIK ASON
ANDERSSON, ERIK

FURBER, DOUGLAS
LEWIN, MICHAEL

FUREY, MICHAEL
WARD, ARTHUR HENRY S.

FURGURSON, PAT
FURGURSON, ERNEST BAKER

FURNEAUX, ROBIN
SMITH, FREDERICK W. ROBIN

FURNESS, ELIZABETH
UPSON, DOROTHY BARBARA

FURNEY, MAURICE
WILMOT, FRANK LESLIE T.

FURNIER, VINCENT DAMON
COOPER, ALICE

FURST, CARL
HARRINGTON, WILLIAM

FURTH, ALEX
SASULY, RICHARD

FURTH, CARLTON
GIBSON, JOE

FURTHMAN, JULES
FURTHMANN, JULIUS G.

FURY, NICK
PARRY, MICHEL P.

FURZE, BARTON
ROCHESTER, GEO[RGE] E.

FUSSENEGGER, GERTRUD
DIETZ, GERTRUD

FUTABATEI, SHIMEI
TATSUNOSUKE, HASEGAWA

FUTURE, STEVE
GILROY, STEVE

FUTURUS
NICKEL, TH.

FUVAL, PIERRE
FEVRIER, PAUL-HUBERT B.

FYFIELD, FRANCES
HEGARTY, FRANCES

FYODOROV, YEVGENY K.
FEDOROV, YEVGENY K.

FYSH
FISH, LEONARD G.

FYSON, J.G.
FYSON, JENNY GRACE [H]

FYVEL, TOSCO JOSEPH
FEIWEL, RAPHAEL JOSEPH

FYVEL, TOSCO RAPHAEL
FEIWEL, RAPHAEL JOSEPH

G-MAN
LANDSBOROUGH, GORDON H.

G., G.
HARPER, HENRY GEORGE

G., K.
GORDON, ACTHERINE J.B.

G.B.
BOAS, GUY HERMAN SIDNEY

G.B.S.
SHAW, GEORGE BERNARD

G.C.B.
BLEECK, G.C.

G.D.H.
COLE, GEORGE & MARGARET

G.E.
EISENKOLB, GERHARD

G.I.
ILIFF, GEORGE

G.K.C.
CHESTERTON, GILBERT KEITH

G.N.
KLOOS, WILLEM JOHAN TEOD.

GAATHON, A.L.
GAATHON, ARYEH LUDWIG

GABALDON, DIANA
GABALDON WATKINS, DIANA J

GABERG, GRETA
KURTH, HANNS

GABLE, J. HARRIS
GABLE, JACOB HENNY J.

GABLE, RUFE
LIVINGSTON, DON LESLIE

GABRIEL, JOHN
GABRIELSON, ERNEST L.
ROWE, JOHN GABRIEL

GABRIELLE
PARKS, GEORGINA

GABRYELLA
ZMICHOWSKA, NARCYZA

GADDES, PETER
SHELDON, PETER

GADDI, DARIO
GNOLI, DOMENICO

GADDIS, PEGGY
DERN, E. PEARL GADDIS

GADE, HENRY
PALMER, RAYMOND A.

GAELI, JOSETTE
GONDA, ADOLPHE

GAELIQUE, MORVEN LE
JACOB, [CYPRIEN] MAX

GAER, YOSSEF
GAER, JOSEPH

GAFRAN, KURT
VON GAGERN, KURT

GAGE, GERVAIS
RENTOUL, T. LAURENCE

GAGE, NICHOLAS
NGAGOYEANES, NICHOLAS

GAGE, WILSON
STEELE, MARY QUINTARD G.

GAHAGAN, HELEN
DOUGLAS, HELEN GAHAGAN

GAHAGAN, MARGARET
GAHAGAN, MARGUERITE

GAINES, BILL
GAINES, WILLIAM MAXWELL

GAINES, GARY
PATTERSON, VIRGINIA

GAINES, JACK
GAINES, JACOB

GAINES, ROBERT
SOMMERSCALES, ROWLAND

GAINHAM, SARAH
AMES, SARAH RACHEL S.

GAIR, MALCOLM
SCOTT, JOHN DICK

GAITE, FRANCIS
COLES, CYRIL HENRY
MANNING, ADELAIDE [F.O]

GAITSKELL, H.T.N.
GAITSKELL, HUGH TODD N.

GAJDUSEK, ROBIN
GAJDUSEK, ROBERT ELEMER

GAKOV, VLADIMIR
KOVALCHUK, MIKHAIL A.

GALA, RICO
ACKERMANN, WERNER

GALACTION, GALA
PISCULESCU, GRIGORE

GALAHAD, SIR
DIENER, BERTHA [E]

GALARZA, ERNEST
GALARZA, ERNESTO

GALAXAN, SOL
COPPEL, ALFREDO JOSE

GALDOS, BENITO PEREZ
PEREZ GALDOS, BENITO

GALE, ADELA
MARITANO, ADELE & GALE

GALE, ALAN
SEMPHILL, ERNEST

GALE, BOB
GALE, MICHAEL ROBERT

GALE, CHRISTOPHER
SUTTON, JEFFERSON HOWARD

GALE, FLOYD C.
GOLD, FLOYD

GALE, H. WINTER
MAITLAND, T.G. DOWLING

GALE, JOHN
OPENSHAW, G.H.
GAZE, RICHARD

GALE, SHANNON
AYLWORTH, SUSAN

GALE, WILLIAM C.
GILES, CARL H[OWARD]

GALEN, PHILIP
LANGE, KARL ERNST PHILIP

GALINDO, P.
HINOJOSA-SMITH, ROLANDO

GALL, AUGUSTE A. DE ST.
STRICH, CHRISTIAN

GALL, I.
GALL, INA

GALL, ROBERT
RUCH, HANS

GALLAGHER, GALE
OURSLER, WILL[IAM C.]
SCOTT, MARGARET

GALLAGHER, RICHARD
LEVINSON, LEONARD [L]

GALLAGHER, STEVE
GALLAGHER, STEPHEN

GALLANT, FELICIA
DANO, LINDA

GALLANT, JENNIE
SMITH, JOAN

GALLANT, PHOEBE
LAFARGE, ANNE

GALLARDO, GERVASIO
VILLASENOR, GERVASIO GAL.

GALLERITE, THE
BASON, FREDERICK THOMAS

GALLERY, DAN
GALLERY, DANIEL V.

GALLINGER, OSMA COUCH
TOD, OSMA GALLINGER

GALLISON, KATE
DUNN, KATHLEEN
GALLISON, KATHLEEN

GALLISTER, MICHAEL
BEDFORD-JONES, HENRY

GALLOIS, LUCIEN
DESNOS, ROBERT

GALLOWAY, LAURA
HILLMAN, DOROTHY ANN

GALLUP, RALPH
WHITEMORE, HUGH JOHN

GALT, JOSEPH R.
GALT, WILLIAM CAMPBELL

GALT, SERENA
DONALD, ANABEL

GALT, TOM
GALT, THOMAS FRANKLIN JR.

GALT, WILLIAM
GRIBBON, WILLIAM L.

GALTON, GWENDOLEN DOUGLAS
GASCOIGNE, GWENDOLEN G.T.

GALUBOK, VLADYSLAY
GOLUB, VLADYSLAY

GALUSSER, ROLAND
KRESSIG, ROLAND

GALWAY, HERBERT
TEAGUE, GEORGE HERBERT

GALWAY, NORMAN
GENTRY, BYRON B.

GALWAY, R.C.
MCCUTCHAN, PHILIP [D]

GALWAY, ROBERT CONNINGTON
MCCUTCHAN, PHILIP [D]

GAMBIER, KENYON
LATHROP, LORIN ANDREWS

GAMBLE, M.L.
NUCCIO, MARSHA L.

GAMBLE, MARY
MURRY, MARY MIDDLETON

GAME COCK
LOOKER, SAMUEL JOSEPH

GAMMA
GAMBLE, PAUL

GAMMAGE, BILL
GAMMAGE, WILLIAM LEONARD

GAN, INDEX
WILLIAMS, DAVID RHYS

GANDALAC, LENNARD
BERNE, ERIC [L]

GANDER, FATHER
LARCHE, DOUG

GANDHI, M.K.
GANDHI, MOHANDAS K.

GANDHI, MAHATMA
GANDHI, MOHANDAS K.

GANDVIK, LOKE
LINDBERG, GUSTAF BRYNOLF

GANNET, JAMES
GRIBBLE, LEONARD [R]

GANNOLD, JOHN
LANGDON, JOHN [F.C.]

GANPAT
GOMPERTZ, MARTIN LOUIS A.

GANT, CHUCK
GALUB, JACK

GANT, JONATHAN
ADAMS, CLIFTON H.

GANT, MATTHEW
HANO, ARNOLD

GANT, NORMAN
WOLK, GEORGE

GANT, RICHARD
FREEMANTLE, BRIAN [HARRY]

GANTER, CHRISTOPH ERIK
ELWENSPOEK, CURT

GANTOS, JACK
GANTOS, JOHN BRYAN JR.

GANZERT, ALBERT
HALBERT, ABRAM

GANZI, KURT
GAENZI, KURT FRIEDRICH

GAPERSONA, STAN
ACKERMAN, FORREST J.

GAR
GARCZYNSKI, J.

GAR, THE
GARFINKEL, CHARLES H.

GARAFALO, REEBEE
GARAFALO, ROBERT L.

GARAGIOLA, JOE
GARAGIOLA, JOSEPH HENRY

GARBE, RUTH MOORE
MOORE, RUTH ELLEN

GARBY, RALPH
BREUCKER, OSCAR HERBERT

GARCIA, E.
GARCIA SANCHEZ, JESUS

GARD, JANICE
LATHAM, JEAN LEE

GARD, JOYCE
REEVES, JOYCE

GARDEN, BRUCE
MACKAY, JAMES [A]

GARDEN, JOHN
FLETCHER, HARRY LUFT V.

GARDENER, HARRY J.
EVANS, E. EVERETT

GARDENER, HENRY
EVANS, E. EVERETT

GARDENER, HILDE
SCHAEFER, HILDEGARD

GARDINER, JOAN
BRIDGES, HILDA [MAGGIE]

GARDINER, MURIEL
BUTTINGER, MURIEL GARDIN.

GARDNER, ANNE
SHULTZ, GLADYS DENNY

GARDNER, B. WILSON
GARDNER, BENNIE WILSON

GARDNER, BARRY
GARDNER, BENNIE WILSON

GARDNER, DIC
GARDNER, RICHARD [M]

GARDNER, E.S.
GARDNER, ERLE STANLEY

GARDNER, ELSIE ANN
GRAFFAM, ELSIE ANN

GARDNER, JEFFREY
FOX, GARDNER F.

GARDNER, JEFFREY K.
FOX, GARDNER F.

GARDNER, JEREMY
GARDNER, JEROME

GARDNER, JOY
AUMENTE, JOY

GARDNER, KIT
GARLAND, KATHERINE MANN.

GARDNER, LAWRENCE
BRANNON, WILLIAM T.

GARDNER, LEE
GLADSON, LEE

GARDNER, MIRIAM
BRADLEY, MARION ZIMMER

GARDNER, NANCY
GARDNER, NANCY BRUFF

GARDNER, NOEL
KUTTNER, HENRY
MOORE, CATHERINE LUCILLE

GARDNER, RICHARD
ORTH, RICHARD MAURICA

GARDNER, ROGER
JENNISON, JOHN WILLIAM

GARDONS, S.S.
SNODGRASS, W.D.

GARE, FRAN
MANDELL, FRAN GARE

GARETH, MAX
JAMES, STUART

GARFIELD, FRANCIS
WELLMAN, MRS. MANLEY WADE

GARFIELD, PETER
LAZENBY, NORMAN A.

GARFIELD, SUSAN
LAZENBY, NORMAN A.

GARFINKEL, CHARLEY
GARFINKEL, CHARLES H.

GARFORTH, JOHN
HUSSEY, TONY

GARIOCH, ROBERT
SUTHERLAND, ROBERT GARIOC

GARLAND, BENNETT
GARFIELD, BRIAN F.W.
OLSEN, THEODORE VICTOR

GARLAND, BLANCHE
LESKO, RUTH

GARLAND, GEORGE
ROARK, GARLAND

GARLAND, JOHN
LEE, ALICE LOUISE

GARLAND, JOHNNY
GALLARDOS MUNOZ, JUAN

GARLAND, LAWRENCE
GARLAND, STEVEN
TOPPMAN, LAWRENCE

GARLAND, LISETTE
GIBBS, NORAH

GARLAND, LUKE
WHITSON, JOHN HARVEY

GARLAND, NICHOLAS
KATZ, HERBERT M.

GARLAND, RODNEY
HEGEDUS, ADAM

GARLAND, SHERRY
LAWRENCE, LYNN

GARN, JAKE
GARN, EDWIN JACOB

GARNE, GASTON
DOUGHTY, FRANCIS W.
SENARENS, LUIS P.

GARNER, ELIZABETH
NAPIER, ELMA

GARNER, GRAHAM
ROWLAND, DONALD S.

GARNER, HANS
DAMIAN, FRANZ

GARNER, KATHLEEN
ORR, KATHLEEN [KATHY]

GARNER, R.F.
DUBINA, PETER

GARNER, ROLF[E]
BERRY, BRYAN

GARNET, A.H.
SLOTE, ALFRED

GARNET, G.
ASHABRANNER, GERARD
ASHKENAZY, IRVIN

GARNETT, BILL
GARNETT, WILLIAM JOHN

GARNETT, CAPT. MAYN CLEW
HAINS, THORNTON JENKINS

GARNETT, DAV
GARNETT, DAVID S.

GARNETT, DAVID S.
RUSH, NOEL

GARNETT, ROGER
MORLAND, NIGEL

GARNIER, PIERRE
MAURRAS, CHARLES-MARIE-P

GAROFALO, REEBEE
GAROFALO, ROBERT L.

GARON, MARCO
HUGHES, DENNIS [TALBOT]

GAROS, STEPHANIE
KATZ, STEVE

GAROU, LOUIS P.
BOWKETT, STEPHEN

GARR, MULLIN
BOYNTON, WILLIAM DAVID

GARRARD, CHRISTOPHER
MILTON, JOHN R.

GARRARD, GENE
GARRARD, JEANNE SUE

GARRAT, TEDDIE
GARRAT, ALFRED

GARRET, GARET
GARRET, EDWARD PETER

GARRETT, BILL
BAJOG, GUNTHER

GARRETT, CHARLES C.
JAMES, LAURENCE
WELLS, ANGUS

GARRETT, EDWARD
MAYO, ISABELLA FYVIE

GARRETT, EILEEN J.
LYTTLE, EILEEN J.

GARRETT, FRANK
SCHMIDT, DAN

GARRETT, GORDON
GARRETT, RANDALL [P]

GARRETT, J.A.
GRASMUCK, JURGEN

GARRETT, PETER M.D.
PORTADIN, GARY

GARRETT, RUTH
MAYO, ISABELLA FYVIE

GARRETT, SALLY
DINGLEY, SALLY G[ARRETT]

GARRETT, STEVE M.
HARTSCH, GERHART

GARRETT, TOM
GARRETT, THOMAS SAMUEL

GARRETT, TRUMAN
JUDD, HARRISON
JUDD, MARGARET [H]

GARRETT, WENDY
HALEY, WENDY

GARRIK, PHIL M.
HACKL, LEOPOLD

GARRISON, ANET
WOODWARD, TENA GARRISON

GARRISON, FREDERICK
SINCLAIR, UPTON BEALL

GARRISON, JOAN
NEUBAUER, WILLIAM A.

GARRISON, PHIL
BRANDNER, GARY

GARRITY
GERRITY, DAVID JAMES

GARRITY, CALLI GORAN
GERRITY, DAVID JAMES

GARRITY, DAVE
GERRITY, DAVID JAMES

GARRITY, TERRY
GARRITY, JOAN THERESA

GARRON, MARCO
GRIFFITHS, DAVID ARTHUR

GARRON, ROBERT A.
WANDREI, HOWARD E.

GARROWAY, DAVE
GARROWAY, DAVID C.

GARROWAY, PETE
HANSON, VICTOR JOSEPH
USHER, [JOHN] GRAY

GARRY, MADELINE
DAVIS, MADELINE

GARRY, STEPHEN
STEVENS, HENRY CHARLES

GARRYOWEN
FINN, EDMUND

GARS, HENRY
EMSHWILLER, EDMUND A.

GARSKOF, MICHELE HOFNUNG
HOFFNUNG, MICHELE

GARSON, CLEE
FAIRMAN, PAUL W.
MCGIVERN, WILLIAM P.
O'BRIEN, DAVID WRIGHT

GARST, SHANNON
GARST, DORIS SHANNON

GARSTANG, BASIL
BRERETON, JOHN LE GAY

GARSTANG, JACK
GARSTANG, JAMES GORDON

GARSTON, GUY
HURREN, BERNARD JOHN

GARTH, ANDREW
ROTSLER, WILLIAM

GARTH, CECIL
CARLTON, GRACE

GARTH, ED
JOHNSTON, WILLIAM

GARTH, JACKSON
ELLIS, WILLIAM DONOHUE

GARTH, JOHN
GILES, JANET HOLT

GARTH, WILL
BINDER, EARL ANDREW
BINDER, OTTO
DANIELS, NORMAN A.
DERLETH, AUGUST [WILLIAM]
HAMILTON, EDMOND
KUTTNER, HENRY
MOORE, CATHERINE LUCILLE
SAMALMAN, ALEXANDER
WEISINGER, MORT
WELLMAN, MANLY WADE

GARTHWAITE, MALABY
DENT, ANTHONY AUSTEN

GARTNER, CHLOE
TRIMBLE, CHLOE MARIA

GARTNER, DAVIS
MEYN, NIELS

GARTON, D.K.
GARTON, DURHAM KEITH

GARUN, ALES'
PRUSHINSKI, ALEXANDER V.

GARVE, ANDREW
WINTERTON, PAUL

GARVEN, VIOLA
FROMMHOLZ, ALICE

GARVEY, KATHLEEN
BLUNDELL, JUDITH

GARVIN, TOM
GARVIN, THOMAS CHRISTOPH.

GARY, GENE
DES ORMEAUX, J.J.
ROSAIRE, FORREST

GARY, ROMAIN
KACEWGARI, ROMAIN

GARYS, WALTER
LUBARS, WALTER
WOONTEILER, GARY E.

GASCAR, PIERRE
FOURNIER, PIERRE

GASCOIGNE, ERIC
MOWBRAY, W.J.

GASCOIGNE, MARGUERITE
LAZARUS, MARGUERITE

GASCOIGNE, PETER
TOWNEND, PETER [R.G.]

GASCON, THE
MILLER, FREDERICK WALTER

GASH, JOE
GRANGER, BILL

GASH, JONATHAN
GRANT, JOHN

GASHBUCK, GRENO
GERNSBACK, HUGO

GASKELL, JANE
GASKELL DENVIL, JANE
LYNCH, JANE GASKELL

GASKELL, MRS.
GASKELL, ELIZABETH C.S.

GASKET, BAMBER
FANTONI, BARRY [ERNEST]

GASKIN, CATHERINE
CORNBERG, CATHERINE GASK.

GASPARRI, CHRISTIANE
BINDER-GASPER, CHRISTIANE

GAST, KELLY P.
COTTON, KELLY P. [J.M.G.]
EDMONDSON Y COTTON, JOSE

GAST, LISE
RICHTER, ELISABETH

GASTIT, HORACE DODD
BANGS, JOHN KENDRICK

GASTON, BILL
GASTON, WILLIAM JAMES

GASTON, WILBUR
GIBSON, WALTER B.

GASTPAR, MICHAEL
NEUFFER, MARTIN

GATE, A.G.
ANTHONY, EDWARD

GATER, DILYS
SINCLAIR, CLOVER

GATES, ALBERT
GLOTZER, ALBERT

GATES, MICHAEL
MACHUISDEAN, HAMISH

GATES, VIVIAN
HEDGE, CARO

GATH
TOWNSEND, GEORGE ALFRED

GATHERCOLE, ADRIENNE LOIS
KAEPPLER, ADRIENNE LOIS

GATHERIDGE, R. EDWARD
WILSON, ROBERT EDWARD

GATO, J.A.
KELLER, JOHN ESTEN

GATOW, GUNTER
NETSCH, GUNTER

GATTY, JULIANA HORATIA
EWING, JULIANA H. GATTY

GAUER, W.H.
BLOCH, ROBERT [A]

GAUGER, RICK
GAUGER, RICHARD C.

GAUL, GILBERT
DEMILLE, JAMES

GAULE, BEATRICE
O'NEILL, MARY AGATHA

GAULT, BILL
GAULT, WILLIAM CAMPBELL

GAULT, MARK
COURNOS, JOHN

GAULT, W.
GAULT, WILLIAM CAMPBELL

GAULTIER, BON
AYTOUN, WILLIAM E.
MARTIN, [SIR] THEODORE

GAUNT, GRAHAM
GRANT, JOHN

GAUNT, JEFFREY
ROCHESTER, GEO[RGE] E.

GAUNT, M.B.
HORSFIELD, RICHARD HENRY

GAUNT, MICHAEL
ROBERTSHAW, [JAMES] DENIS

GAUNT, PETER
ESHBACH, LLOYD ARTHUR

GAUNT, RICHARD
LANDELLS, RICHARD

GAUNTIER, GENE
LIGGETT, GENEVIEVE G.

GAUS, GEO. J.
FRITSCHEL, GEO[RGE] JOHN

GAUTHIER, GEORGES
MAUCKNER, WALTER G.

GAUTISOLO, MIGUEL
GILABERT, ANTONIO M. Y.

GAVELL, LILLEVI
STADENER, INGEGERD

GAVER, BECKY
GAVER, REBECCA

GAVIN, AMANDA
GIBSON-JARVIE, CLODAGH

GAVIN, BILL
GAVIN, WILLIAM S.

GAVIN, WILLIAM
HOUSTON, DOUGLAS NORMAN

GAWAIN
NEWTON, H. CHANCE

GAWSWORTH, JOHN
ARMSTRONG, TERANCE IAN F.
BATES, HERBERT ERNEST
FYTTON ARMSTRONG, T.I.

GAY, A. NOLDER
KOELSCH, WILLIAM A.

GAY, AMELIA
HOGARTH, GRACE W.A.

GAY, FRANCIS
GEE, HERBERT LESLIE

GAY, FRANK
GEE, HOWARD LESLIE

GAY, GREER
PAYNE, HAZEL BELLE

GAY, J. DREW
WELCH, EDGAR L.

GAY, NOEL
ARMITAGE, REGINALD

GAY, OLIVER
GOGARTY, OLIVER ST. JOHN

GAY, PETER [JACK]
FROELICH, PETER [JACK]

GAYE, CAROL
SHANN, RENEE

GAYLE, B.
REDMOND, BRENDA C.

GAYLE, EMMA
FAIRBURN, ELEANOR

GAYLE, HENRY K.
GAYLE, HAROLD

GAYLE, MARGARET
HAMILTON, GAIL

GAYLE, MARILYN
HOFF, MARILYN

GAYLE, NEWTON
DE MUNOZ MARIN, MUNA LEE
GUINESS, MAURICE C.

GAYLE, SUSAN
KASPER, GAYLE

GAYLL, ARTHUR
DONOHUE, FRANK

GAYLORD, BILLY
GAYLORD, WILLIAM GILBERT

GAYLORD, TIMAEUS
SMITH, CLARK ASHTON

GAYRE OF GAYRE, R.
GAYRE, GEORGE ROBERT

GAYRE OF GAYRE, ROBERT
GAYRE, GEORGE ROBERT

GAZDAG, ERZSI
GAZDAG, ERZSEBET

GAZDANOV, GEORGII
GAZDANOV, GAITO

GDANSKI, MAREK
THEE, MARK

GEARING-THOMAS, G.
NORWOOD, VICTOR [G.C.]

GEASLAND, JACK
GEASLAND, JOHN BUCHANAN

GEBHARDT, FRED J.
GEBHARDT, FRIEDRICH JOHAN

GEBHARDT, HANS
GRAF, JOHANN

GED, CAER
PROCTOR, GEO[RGE] W[YATT]
WYATT, LEE

GEDDES, HUGH
ATKINSON, HUGH

GEE, H.L.
GEE, HERBERT LESLIE

GEE, JEFF
GALBRAITH, F.

GEE, KENNETH F.
KAY, FREDERIC GEORGE

GEE, OSMAN
HINCKS, CYRIL MALCOLM

GEERLINK, WILL
HOFDORF, PIM

GEIGER-GOG, ANNI
HOF, ANNI [G]

GEISEL, EVA
BORNEMANN, EVA

GEIST, HANS
LERF, URS

GELL, FRANK
KOWET, DON

GELLER, EVELYN
GOTTESFELD, EVELYN

GELLER, RED
RELLERGERD, HELMUT

GELLERT, LEW
WELLEN, EDWARD [P]

GELLERT, ROGER
HOLMSTROM, JOHN ERIC

GELLES, SANDI
GELLES-COLE, SANDI

GELLINEK, JANIS LITTLE
SOLOMON, JANIS LITTLE

GELM, ROBERT
MUNTHE, GUSTAF LORENZ

GELMAN, WOODY
GELMAN, WOODROW

GELMAN-WAXNER, LIBBY
RUDNICK, PAUL

GELPERIN, L.
HALPERN, LEIVICK

GEMEL
MANUEL, GEORGE

GEMINI
GOODWIN, GEOFFREY

GEMMILL
KIRKPATRICK, MRS. HELEN

GENE, MARTA
POWELY, MRS. A.A.

GENERAL X
HOAR, ROGER SHERMAN

GENEROSO, MARC-ANTOINE
SCHWEIZER, MARC

GENET
FLANNER, JANET

GENEVIEVE, PIERRE
SCHWEIZER, MARC

GENIUS
BRONTE, CHARLOTTE

GENN, CALDER
GILLIE, CHRISTOPHER

GENNER, JULIUS
PFRAGNER, JULIUS

GENONE, HUDOR
ROE, WILLIAM JAMES

GENRTY, ARTHUR
SELLERS, CONNIE LESLIE

GENSAI, MURAI
HIROSHI, MURAI

GENT
LOVECRAFT, H[OWARD] P.

GENTER, HARRY
STACKLE-TREUTLEIN, FREDA

GENTIL, SPIRITO
HANNA, GEORGE W.

GENTLEWOMAN, A
MOORE, DORIS LANGLEY

GENTRY, CHRISTINE
RODRIGUEZ, CHRISTINE M.G.

GENTRY, GEORGINA
MURPHY, LYNNE

GENTRY, JANE
MALCOLM, JANE

GENTRY, PETER
NEWCOMB, KERRY
SCHAEFER, FRANK

GEOFF
DYSON, GEOFFREY HARRY G.

GEOFFREY, CHARLES
MULLER, CHARLES G.

GEOFFREY, THEODATE
WAYMAN, DOROTHY G.

GEORG, HANS
REINHARD, HANS GEORG

GEORG, JUSTUS
VON CONRING, FRIEDRICH

GEORG, REINHOLD
MULLER, ARTUR

GEORGE, BARBARA
KATZ, BOBBI[E]

GEORGE, BILL
GEORGE, WILLIAM FRANCIS

GEORGE, DANIEL
BUNTING, D.G.

GEORGE, DAVID
VOGENITZ, DAVID GEORGE

GEORGE, EDWARD
PROCTOR, GEO[RGE] W[YATT]
VARDEMAN, ROBERT E.

GEORGE, EDWARD [E]
VARDEMAN, ROBERT E.

GEORGE, ELIOT
FREEMAN, GILLIAN

GEORGE, EMILY
KATZ, BOBBI[E]

GEORGE, ERNEST
WISE, ERNEST GEORGE

GEORGE, EUGENE
CHEVALIER, PAUL EUGENE G.

GEORGE, G.S.
LEVIN, ABRAHAM

GEORGE, HERBERT
GUNSKE, GEORGE

GEORGE, JAY
STRACHAN, J. GEORGE

GEORGE, JONATHAN
BURKE, JOHN [FREDERICK]
THEINER, GEORGE

GEORGE, MARION
BENJAMIN, CLAUDE M.E.P.

GEORGE, MARION E.
BENJAMIN, CLAUDE M.E.P.
POHLMAN, MAX EDWARD

GEORGE, S.C.
GEORGE, SIDNEY CHARLES

GEORGE, STEVEN
HIRSHMAN, JACK

GEORGE, THEODORE
BERK, THEODORE GEORGE

GEORGE, VERNON
VERNON, GEORGE S.G.

GEORGE, VICKIE
COLLINGS, I.J.

GEORGE, VIRGINIA
AIKEN, GINNY

GEORGE, WILLIAM
FREBEL, ERNST

GEORGE, WILMA
CROWTHER, WILMA [BERYL]

GEORGES, GEORGE
SIMENON, GEORGES [J.C]

GEORGES, JEAN
BENTEIN, JEAN-MARIE G.J.

GEORGI, GEORG
GROH, GEORG ARTUR

GEORGIANNA, SISTER
TERSTEGGE, MABEL ALICE

GEORGUIS
GUIBOURG, GEORGES

GERAINT, GEORGE
EVANS, GEORGE

GERALD, DARYL
FITZGERALD, DESMOND

GERALD, LOUISE
DE LA COSTE, MATHILDE

GERALD, ZIGGY
ZEIGERMAN, GERALD

GERALDA, LADY
BRONTE, ANN

GERALDY, PAUL
LEFEVRE, PAUL

GERARD, ANDREW
GATTI, ARTHUR GERARD

GERARD, ELAINE
RYDER, EILEEN

GERARD, GASTON
OSTERGAARD, GEOFFREY

GERARD, MORICE
TEAGUE, JOHN JESSOP

GERARD, RON L.
RENAUD, RON

GERARDY
GERARD, EDWIN FIELD

GERBER, BOBBIE
GERBER, BARBARA [LIN]

GERDEN, FREDERICK PAUL
GREVE, FELIX PAUL B.F.

GERHARD, DIERK
PULS, DIERK

GERHARDI, WILLIAM
GAERHARDIE, WILLIAM

GERHARDI, WILLIAM ALEX.
GERHARDIE, WILLIAM ALEX.

GERHOLD, GERMAN
SCHMIDT, WILLY

GERIS, TOM ERWIN
WEISINGER, MORT

GERMAN, EDWARD
JONES, EDWARD GERMAN

GERMAN, GUNTHER
MEHL, ARNOLD

GERMANICUS
DUNNER, JOSEPH

GERMANY, JO
GERMANY, VERA JOSEPHINE

GERNOT, JURGEN
VON KLIMBURG, HANS-ULRICH

GEROELY, KALMAN
GABEL, JOSEPH

GEROME
THIBAULT, JACQUES ANATOLE

GERON, FRANK
GREENFIELD, IRVING A.

GERRARD, A.J.
GERRARD, JOHN

GERRARE, WIRT
GREENER, WILLIAM OLIVER

GERRISH, GEORGE
GARRISH, HAROLD J.

GERRITSEN, TESS
GERRITSEN, TERRY

GERROLD, DAVID
FRIEDMAN, DAVID JERROLD

GERSHON, KAREN
TRIPP, KAREN

GERSONI-STAVN, DIANE
GERSONI, DIANE

GERSTINE, JACK
GERSTINE, JOHN

GERTER, ELISABETH
AEGERTER-HARTMANN, ELISA.

GERTLER, DITTA
ADLER-GERTLER, DITTA

GERVAIS, C.H.
GERVAIS, CHARLES HENRY

GERVAIS, MARTY
GERVAIS, CHARLES HENRY

GERVASI, TOM
GERVASI, EUGENE MICHAEL

GESSNER, LYNNE
GESSNER, MERLYN C.

GETER, LENA
DAVENPORT, MARCIA

GETTLEMAN, SUSAN
BRAIMAN, SUSAN

GEWE, RADDORY
GOREY, EDWARD ST. JOHN

GEYER, FRANCIS
HARWOOD, GWEN

GEZI, KAL
GEZI, KALIL ISMAIL

GHALLOPING GOURMET, THE
KERR, GRAHAM

GHEON, HENRI
VANGEON, HENRI

GHEREA, ION
DOBROGEANU-GHEREA, ION

GHETTO POET
NOVACHOVITCH, LIPPE BENZ.

GHIL, RENE
GUILBERT,RENE

GHINE, WUNNAKYAWHTIN U O.
MAURICE, DAVID JOHN K.

GHOLSTON, J.N.
GHOLSTON, HOMER N.

GHOSE, SRI CHINMOY KUMAR
CHINMOY, SRI

GHOST, HENRY
ANTON, UWE
MIELKE, THOMAS R.P.

GIBB, LEE
DEGHY, GUY [S]
WATERHOUSE, KEITH [S]

GIBBARD, T.S.J.
VINTER, MICHAEL

GIBBON, LEWIS GRASSIC
MITCHELL, JAMES LESLIE

GIBBONS, BOB
GIBBONS, ROBERT

GIBBONS, HARRY S.
GIBBONS, HARRY SCOTT

GIBBONS, HELEN
GIBBONS, WILLIAM

GIBBONS, MARGARET
MACGILL, MARGARET

GIBBONS, WHIT
GIBBONS, J. WHITFIELD

GIBBS, HENRY
RUMBOLD-GIBBS, HENRY

GIBBS, JIM
GIBBS, JAMES ATWOOD

GIBBS, LEWIS
COVE, JOSEPH WALTER

GIBBS, MARY ANNE
BIDWELL, M. ELIZABETH

GIBBS, RAFE
GIBBS, RAPHAEL SANFORD

GIBBS, TONY
GIBBS, WOOLCOTT JR.

GIBNEY, HARRIET
HARVEY, HARRIET

GIBSON, BEN
GROSSMANN, HANS HUGO

GIBSON, CHARLES
GARVICE, CHARLES

GIBSON, FLOYD
KING, ALBERT

GIBSON, HARRY CLARK
HUBLER, RICHARD GIBSON

GIBSON, HENRY
BATEMAN, HENRY GIBSON

GIBSON, JOHN
GIBSON, JOE

GIBSON, JOSEPHINE
HINE, AL[FRED B.]
HINE, SESYLE JOSLIN

GIBSON, KATHARINE
WICKS, KATHARINE G.

GIBSON, MADELAINE
DUCKETT, MADELAINE G.

GIBSON, ROSEMARY
NEWELL, ROSEMARY

GICHON, MORDECHAI
GICHERMANN, MORDECHAI

GIDAL, NACHUM
GIDALEWITSCH, IGNAZ

GIDAL, TIM N.
GIDALEWITSCH, IGNAZ

GIDALEWITSCH, NACHUM
GIDAL, TIM NACHUM
GIDALEWITSCH, IGNAZ

GIDDINGS, LAUREN
GIDEON, NANCY

GIDEON, JOHN
HOKLIN, LONN

GIDEON, ROBIN
SEVERSON, K.D.

GIELGUD, GWEN BAGNI
DUBOV, GWEN BAGNI

GIERSCH, JULIUS
ARNADE, CHARLES W.

GIESY, J.U.
GIESY, JOHN ULRICH

GIFFARD, ANN
GREENHILL, ELIZABETH ANN

GIFFIN, FRANK
CARTER, ERNEST FRANK

GIFFORD, CLARK
BACON, DON

GIFFORD, MATT
KING, ALBERT

GIFFORD-JONES, W.
WALKER, KENNETH FRANCIS

GIFT, THEO
BOULGER, THEODORA HAVERS

GIGER, H.R.
GIGER, HANSRUEDI

GIJSEN, MARNIX
GORIS, JAN-ALBERT

GIL, DAVID G.
ENGEL, DAVID GEORG

GILBERT, ANN
TAYLOR, ANN

GILBERT, ANNA
LAZARUS, MARGUERITE

GILBERT, ANTHONY
MALLESON, LUCY BEATRICE

GILBERT, BEN
REOCH, J.S.

GILBERT, BRIAN
JENNISON, JOHN WILLIAM

GILBERT, BUTCH
GILBERT, C.H.

GILBERT, E. JAYNE
HUMPHREYS, ELIZA M.J.G.

GILBERT, ERNESTINE
CARET, ERNESTINE GILBERT

GILBERT, JOHN
HARRISON, JOHN GILBERT

GILBERT, JULIE GOLDSMITH
DANIEL, JULIE GOLDSMITH

GILBERT, MANU
WEST, JOYCE [T]

GILBERT, MIRIAM
PRESBERG, MIRIAM GOLDSTEN

GILBERT, NAN
GILBERTSON, MILDRED G.

GILBERT, RUTH GALLARD A.
AINSWORTH, RUTH GALLARD

GILBERT, SISTER MARY
DE FREES, MADELINE

GILBERT, WILLIE
GOMBERG, WILLIAM GILBERT

GILCHRIST, JOHN
GARDNER, JEROME

GILCRAFT
YOUNG, ERNEST A[VON]

GILDEN, K.B.
GILDEN, BERT & KATYA

GILDERSLEEVE, PROFESSOR
URNER, NATHAN DANE

GILES, BAXTER
OFFUTT, ANDREW J.

GILES, C.W. SCOTT
SCOTT-GILES, CHARLES WIL.

GILES, DOUGLAS
HALL, JAMES

GILES, ELIZABETH
HOLT, JOHN ROBERT

GILES, GEOFFREY
ACKERMAN, FORREST J.

GILES, GEOFFREY [CONT]
GILLINGS, WALTER H.

GILES, GORDON A.
BINDER, EARL ANDREW
BINDER, OTTO

GILES, JACK
FOSTER, RAYMOND KEITH

GILES, KRIS
NIELSEN, HELEN [B]

GILES, NORMAN
MCKEOWN, NORMAN ROBERT

GILES, RAY
HOLT, JOHN ROBERT

GILES, RAYMOND
HOLT, JOHN ROBERT

GILFORD, C.B.
GILFORD, CHARLES BERNARD

GILHOOLEY, JACK
GILHOOLEY, JOHN

GILL, ALAN
GILLESPIE, ALFRED

GILL, B.M.
TRIMBLE, BARBARA MARGARET

GILL, BARBARA
TRIMBLE, BARBARA MARGARET

GILL, BARTHOLOMEW
MCGARRITY, MARK

GILL, HUGH
HUGILL, ROBERT

GILL, JOHN
GILLIES, JOHN RUSSELL

GILL, PATRICK
CREASEY, JOHN

GILL, STANLEY
TAYLOR, ROLAND

GILLANE, MUCKY
DONGES, GUNTER

GILLEN, CATHY
THACKER, CATHY GILLEN

GILLEN, LUCY
STRATTON, REBECCA

GILLESPIE, DIZZY
GILLESPIE, JOHN BIRKS

GILLESPIE, JANE
SHAW, JANE

GILLESPIE, LINK
GILLESPIE, A. LINCOLN JR.

GILLESPIE, SUSAN
TURTON-JONES, EDITH C.B.

GILLETT, H.M.
GILLETT, HENRY MARTIN

GILLETTE, BOB
SHAW, BYNUM G.

GILLETTE, J. MICHAEL
GILLETTE, JAY MICHAEL

GILLETTE, LOUISA
FELDMAN, GILDA
RUGG, LESLIE

GILLHAM, BILL
GILLHAM, WILLIAM EDWIN C.

GILLIAN, JERRY
GILLIAM, TERRY [VANCE]

GILLIAN, KAY
SMITH, KAY NOLTE

GILLIAN, MICHAEL
EDGLEY, L.

GILLILAND, CHARLES
MULLER, CHARLES G.

GILLMER, TOM
GILLMER, THOMAS CHARLES

GILLMORE, INEZ HAYNES
IRWIN, INEZ HAYNES

GILMAN, DOROTHY
BUTTERS, DOROTHY GILMAN

GILMAN, GEORGE G.
HARKNETT, TERRY W.

GILMAN, J.D.
FISHMAN, JACK
ORGILL, DOUGLAS [W]

GILMAN, JAMES
GILMORE, JOSEPH [LEE]

GILMAN, LASALLE
STRASSMAN, TONI

GILMAN, ROBERT CHAM
COPPEL, ALFREDO JOSE

GILMAN, WENONA
SCHOEFFEL, FLORENCE B.

GILMAN, WINONA
ENTON, HARRY

GILMER, ALICE
ROSS, DON

GILMER, ANN
ROSS, WILLIAM E. DANIEL

GILMOOR, JOHN
KUGLER, DIETMAR

GILMORE, ANTHONY
HALL, DESMOND W.

GILMORE, CECILE
MACMILLAN, CECILE

GILMORE, MARIAN
DEY, FREDERIC VAN R.

GILMOUR, ANN
MCNAUGHT, ANN BOYCE

GILMOUR, ANTHONY
BATES, HARRY ARTHUR

GILMOUR, BARBARA
TRIMBLE, BARBARA MARGARET

GILPEN, JOANNA
MCGAURAN, JOANNA

GILRAY, J.D.
MENCKEN, HENRY LOUIS

GILRAY, JAMES
MADSEN, [MARK] HUNTER

GILROONEY
CASSIDY, ROBERT JOHN

GILROY, TOM
GILROY, THOMAS LAURENCE

GILSON, BARBARA
GILSON, CHARLES [J.L.]

GILSON, HIBBART
GILBART-SMITH, MARCUS M.T

GILTENE, JEAN
GELINET, CLAUDE

GINGER
SARGENT, GENEVIEVE

GINSBERG, JOANNE
SUMMERFIELD, JOANNE

GINZKEY, FRANZ KARL
HEGE, HEINRICH

GIPSON, FRED
GIPSON, FREDERICK BENJAM.

GIR
GIRAUD, JEAN

GIRARD, KATE
ROWE, MRS. GEORGE F.

GIRARD, PAUL
REED, PETER HUGH

GIRARDI, JOE
GIRARD, JOE

GIRARDIN, RAY
GIBSON, WALTER B.

GIRAUD, ALBERT
KAYENBERGH, MARIE EMIL A.

GIROUX, E.X.
SHANNON, DORIS

GIRTIN, TOM
GIRTIN, THOMAS

GIRTY, SIMON
KING, ALBERT

GIRUN, GIAN
CLAUVOT-GEER, URSINA

GISCARD, VALERIE
MESTA, EMILY

GISCARD, VALERY
GISCARD D'ESTAING, VALER.

GISELA, M.
MAY, KARL FRIEDRICH
GISH, JOE
SPRINGS, ELLIOTT WHITE

GITCHOFF, TOM
GITCHOFF, GEORGE THOMAS

GIULANI, ALDO
PALAZZESCHI, ALDO

GIZYCKA, ELEANOR M.
PATTERSON, ELEANOR MEDILL

GJALLANDI, PORGILS
STEFFANSSON, JON

GJALSKA, KSAVER SANDOR
BABIC, LJUBA

GLAD, PER
HORDAHL, KURT

GLADDEN, WASHINGTON
WASHINGTON, SOLOMAN

GLADSTONE, EVE
GLEIT, JOYCE
WERNER, HERMA

GLADSTONE, MAGGIE
GLADSTONE, ARTHUR M.

GLADWIN, WILLIAM Z.
ZOLLINGER, GULIEIMA

GLAGLA
GRAMS, BORIS

GLAMIS, WALTER
SCHACHNER, NATHAN

GLANDOUR, MAODEZ
FLOCH, LOEIZ AR

GLANVILLE, ALEC
GRIEVE, ALEX H. GLANVILLE

GLANZ, LEW
GLANZMAN, LOUIS

GLASBRENNER
FIELHAUSER, OTTO M.

GLASER, COMSTOCK
GLASER, KURT

GLASER, ELEANOR DOROTHY
ZONIK, ELEANOR DOROTHY

GLASER, FRANK
GLASER, FRANZ

GLASGOW, JACK
LARSON, DORAN

GLASHAN, JOHN
MACGLASHAN, JOHN

GLASKIN, G.M.
GLASKIN, GERALD MARCUS

GLASS, AMANDA
KRENTZ, JAYNE ANN

GLASS, JUSTINE [C]
CORRALL, ALICE ENID

GLASS, SANDRA
SHEA, ROBERT [J]

GLASS, WALTER
GIBSON, WALTER B.

GLASSCOCK, AMNESIA
STEINBECK, JOHN [E]

GLASSER, ALAN
GLASSER, ALLEN

GLASSEROW, MARIO N.
GLADNEY GLASSEROW, MARION

GLASSFORD, WILFRED
MCNEILLY, WILFRED G.

GLASSFORD, WILLIAM
MCNEILLY, WILFRED G.

GLASSMAN, JOYCE
JOHNSON, JOYCE

GLASTON, W.B.
LAZENBY, NORMAN A.

GLAZAROVA, JARMILA
PODIVINSKA, JARMILA

GLAZER, NONA Y.
GLAZER-MALBIN, NONA

GLEASON, GENE
GLEASON, EUGENE FRANKLIN

GLEIT, MARIA
HOFMANN, MARIA

GLEN, DOROTHY
GARLOCK, DOROTHY

GLEN, EUGENE
FAWCETT, FRANK DUBREZ

GLENDENNING, DONN
PAINE, LAURAN BOSWORTH

GLENDINNING, SALLY
GLENDINNING, SARA WILSON

GLENELG
FROST, J.W.

GLENN, ELIZABETH
GREGORY, MARTHA

GLENN, JAMES
PAINE, LAURAN BOSWORTH

GLENN, VICTORIA
DANN, VICTORIA

GLICK, ELMO
LEIBER, JERRY
STOLLER, MIKE

GLICK, PAULA BROWN
BROWN, PAULA

GLICKSOHN, SUSAN WOOD
WOODS, SUSAN [JOAN]

GLIDDEN, F.D.
GLIDDEN, FREDERICK D.

GLIDDEN, FRED
GLIDDEN, FREDERICK D.

GLINTO, DARCY
FRANCES, STEPHEN D.
KELLY, HAROLD ERNEST

GLOCKENHAMMER, WALKER
WELLS, H.G.

GLOGAU, HEINZ
HAMPEL, BRUNO

GLOPFHAISCHT
CHRIST, ROBERT B.

GLOSA, OTTO
MULLER, OTTO

GLOVER, BOB
GLOVER, ROBERT H.

GLUBB PASHA
GLUBB, JOHN BAGOT

GLUBOK, SHIRLEY
TAMARIN, SHIRLEY ASTOR

GLUD, DON
GLUT, DONALD F.

GLUECK, PETER
ASPERN-BUCHMEIER, ELISAB.

GLUTZ, AMBROSE
KNAPP, CLARENCE

GLUZMAN, BRIAN
GLUSS, BRIAN

GLYDE, PHILIP
FEARN, JOHN RUSSELL

GLYN, A.A.
GLYNN, ANTHONY ARTHUR

GLYN, ANTHONY
DAWSON, SIR GEOFFREY

GLYN, HARRISON
STEFFENS, ARTHUR JOSEPH

GLYN, MEGAN
PARRY, MARGARET G.

GLYN-FOREST, D.
LYNES, DAISY ELFREDA

GLYNN-WARD, H.
HOWARD, HILDA GLYNN

GLYNN-WARD, HILDA
HOWARD, HILDA GLYNN

GNADE, HEINZ
MEISNER, MICHAEL

GNAGY, JOHN
GNAGY, MICHAEL JACQUES

GNAGY, JON
GNAGY, MICHAEL JACQUES

GNIFFKE, RUDOLF
HARTMANN, RUDOLF A.

GNOSTICUS
WESCHCKE, CARL L.

GOAMAN, MURIEL
COX, EDITH MURIEL

GOANE, THOMAS
JAMES, LAURENCE

GOBBO, LANZELOT
BERENDT, KLAUS

GOBER, DON
NAZEL, JOSEPH G. JR.

GOBINAL, CHESTER
DONGES, GUNTER

GODDARD, ALFRED
HARPER, CAROL ELY

GODDARD, DARLENE
EGAR, RAUL

GODDEN, RUMER
FOSTER, MARGARET RUMER G.

GODE, ALEXANDER
GODE VON AESCH, ALEXANDER

GODEL, KURT
GOEDEL, KURT

GODEY, JOHN
FREEDGOOD, MORTON

GODFREY, CHARLES
WEBB, GODFREY EDWARD C.

GODFREY, ELIZABETH
BEDFORD, JESSIE

GODFREY, HAL
ECCLES, CHARLOTTE O.

GODFREY, JANE
BOWDEN, JOAN CHASE

GODFREY, MARCEL
ISAACS, MARCEL GODFREY

GODFREY, R.H.
TUBB, E.C.

GODFREY, WILLIAM
YOUD, CHRISTOPHER [S]

GODIN, AMELIE
LINZ, AMELIE SPEYER

GODLEY, JOHN
KILBRACKEN, JOHN [R.G]

GODLY, J.P.
PLAWIN, PAUL

GODWIN, FRANK
STARR, RICHARD H.

GODWIN, TONY
GODWIN, ANTHONY R.J.W.

GOEBBLES, JOSEF
GOEBBLES, [PAUL] JOSEPH

GOEBBLES, JOSEPH PAUL
GOEBBLES, [PAUL] JOSEPH

GOEN, TEX JR.
GOEN, RAYBURNE WYNDHAM JR

GOERING, HELGA
WALLMANN, JEFFREY M.

GOETCHINS, MARIE LOUISE
GIBSON, MARICE LOUISE

GOETSCH-TREVELYAN, KATHR.
TREVELYAN, KATHARINE

GOEWY, EDWIN A.
ASHTON, ADEN

GOFF, MADELEINE
WOODFORD, [I] CECIL

GOFFSTEIN, BROOKE
GOFFSTEIN, M.B.

GOFFSTEIN, M.G.
SCHAAF, MARILYN B.G.

GOFORTH, ELLEN
FRANCIS, DOROTHY BRENNER

GOG, P.D.
LAUTERBACH, CHARLES

GOGGIN, WILLIAM
GRUBER, FRANK

GOHAGEN, OMAR
MAVOR, ELINOR

GOHDE, HERMANN
HEER, FRIEDRICH

GOHM, D.C.
VAN DE GOHM, RICHARD

GOHM, DOUGLAS
VAN DE GOHM, RICHARD

GOING, MICKEL
HEMZELIUS, KARL-EVERT V.

GOITEIN, S.D.
GOITEIN, SHELOMO DOV

GOITEIN, SOLOMON DOB F.
GOITEIN, SHELOMO DOV

GOLAN, MATTI
GOLDWASSER, MATTI

GOLD, FRANK
DE CAMPOS, LUIS

GOLD, H.L.
GOLD, HORACE L.

GOLD, KID
JENNISON, JOHN WILLIAM

GOLD, KING
HOBER, HEINZ WERNER

GOLD, MICHAEL
GRANICH, IRVING

GOLD, PHYLLIS
GOLDBERG, PHYLLIS

GOLDBERG, FATS
GOLDBERG, LARRY

GOLDBERG, HYMAN
TALESE, GAETANO

GOLDBERG, JAN
CURRAN, JAN GOLBERG

GOLDBERG, LOUIS
GRANT, LOUIS THEODORE

GOLDBERG, RUBE
GOLDBERG, REUBEN LUCIUS

GOLDEN GORSE
WACE, M.A.

GOLDEN SILVER
STORM, HYEMEYOHSTS

GOLDEY
GOLDBERY, EDWARD

GOLDFEDER, CHERYL
PAHZ, CHERYL SUZANNE

GOLDFEDER, JAMES
PAHZ, JAMES ALON

GOLDFEDER, JIM
PAHZ, JAMES ALON

GOLDIE, TERRY
GOLDIE, TERRENCE W.

GOLDSCHMIDT, CLARA MALR.
MALRAUX, CLARA GOLDSCHMID

GOLDSMITH
MILLER, LYNNE ELLEN

GOLDSMITH, CELE
LALLI, CELE G.

GOLDSMITH, PETER
BILLAM, GEORGE
PRIESTLEY, JOHN BOYNTON

GOLDSTEIN, RHODA L.
BLUMBERG, RHODA L.G.

GOLDSZMIT, HENRYK
KORCZAK, JANUSZ

GOLDTHORPE, J.E.
GOLDTHORPE, JOHN ERNEST

GOLDTHWAITE, JAMES A.
FRANCIS, JAMES

GOLF, LOYAL E.
GOLV, LOYAL EUGENE

GOLIARD, ROY
SHIPLEY, JOSEPH TWADDELL

GOLL, IWAN
LANG, ISAAC

GOLLIN, GILLIAN LINDT
LINDT, GILLIAN

GOLLWITZER, JOSEF
HAMMERSCHMID, JOSEF

GOLODNYJ, MICHAIL
EPSTEIN, MICHAIL S.

GOLON, SERGEANNE
GOLON, SERGE & ANNE

GOMBOSSY, ZOLTAN
GABEL, JOSEPH

GOMPERTZ, [MAJ.] M.L.A.
GOMPERTZ, MARTIN LOUIS A.

GONSALES, DOMINGO
GODWIN, FRANCIS

GONZALES, JOHN
TERRALL, ROBERT

GONZALES, PANCHO
GONZALES, RICHARD ALONZO

GONZALEZ, N.V.M.
GONZALEZ, NESTOR VINCENTE

GOOCH, BOB
GOOCH, ROBERT MILETUS

GOOCH, G.P.
GOOCH, GEORGE PEABODY

GOOCH, MARY L.
GLASSCO, JOHN [S]

GOOCH, MARY S[HOMETTE]
GLASSCO, JOHN [S]

GOOCH, SILAS N.
GLASSCO, JOHN [S]

GOOCH, STAN
GOOCH, STANLEY ALFRED

GOOCH, STAN[LEY ALFRED]
ZUCH, STAN[LEY ALFRED]

GOOD, CHARLES H.
GOODRICH, CHARLES [H]

GOOD, EDWARD
OVED, M.

GOODALL, CEDRIC
DOUTHWAITE, L[OUIS] C.

GOODALL, J.S.
GOODALL, JOHN STRICKLAND

GOODALL, MELANIE
DRACHMAN, JULIAN M.

GOODALL, VANNE MORRIS
MORRIS-GOODALL, VANNE

GOODBODY, SLIM
BURSTEIN, JOHN

GOODBODY, [MR.] SLIM
BURNSTEIN, JOHN

GOODCHILD, GEORGE
DARE, ALAN

GOODE, ALICIA
WALLMANN, JEFFREY M.

GOODE, BILL
GOODYKOONTZ, WILLIAM F.

GOODEN, A.H.
GOODEN, ARTHUR HENRY

GOODENOUGH, EVELYN
PITCHER, EVELYN G.

GOODHART, A.L.
GOODHART, ARTHUR LEHMAN

GOODMAN, A.W.
GOODMAN, ADOLPH WINKLER

GOODMAN, HANNAH GRAD
SVERDIN, HANNAH GRAD

GOODMAN, JO
GASCOIGNE, TOSS
GOODMAN, JOSEPHINE CHARL.
TYRRELL, MARGOT

GOODMAN, OSCAR
KEATS, RICHARD STEPHEN

GOODMAN, SONYA
ARCONE, SONYA

GOODMAN, WINTHROP
GOODMAN, GEORGE [J.W.]
KNOWLTON, WINTHROP

GOODOVITCH, I.M.
GOODOVITCH, ISRAEL MEIR

GOODRICH, CLIFFORD
DANIELS, NORMAN A.
DONOVAN, LAURENCE
HATHWAY, ALAN

GOODRIDGE ROBERTS, THEODR
ROBERTS, GEORGE EDWARD T.

GOODSON, BILL
LUCAS, EDGAR ERNEST

GOODSPEED, J.M.
VESTAL, JEANNE

GOODSTEIN, R.L.
GOODSTEIN, REUBEN LOUIS

GOODWIN, DAVID
GOWING, SIDNEY [FLOYD]

GOODWIN, EUGENE D.
KAYE, MARVIN [NATHAN]

GOODWIN, FRANCIS
MULLALY, CHARLES

GOODWIN, GEORGE
GIBSON, WALTER B.

GOODWIN, HAL
GOODWIN, HAROLD LELAND

GOODWIN, HOPE
ARNOLD, LINDA

GOODWIN, JOHN
GOWING, SIDNEY [FLOYD]

GOODWIN, MARK
MATTHEWS, STANLEY GOODWN.

GOODWIN, SUZANNE
EBEL, SUZANNE

GOODYEAR, SUSAN
MATTHEWS, MARGARET BRYAN

GOONETILLEKE, D.C.R.A.
GOONETILLEKE, DEVAPRIYA C

GOOSEQUILL, GREGORY
TULLOCK, W.W.

GOOSSEN, AGNES
EPP, MARGARET A.

GOOTE, THOR
BERG, JOHANNES M.

GOPALEEN, MYLES NA
O'NOLAN, BRIAN

GORAN, CALLI
GERRITY, DAVID JAMES

GORDON
STOWE, D.A.
WALBROOK, LOUISE

GORDON, AD
HANO, ARNOLD

GORDON, ALEX
COTLER, GORDON

GORDON, ANGELA
PAINE, LAURAN BOSWORTH

GORDON, ARCHIE
GORDON, ARCHIBALD V.D.

GORDON, CAPT. CHARLES
HUBBARD, L. RON

GORDON, CLIVE
BLEECK, G.C.

GORDON, DAVID
GARRETT, RANDALL [P]

GORDON, DEBORAH
HASTINGS, BROOKE

GORDON, DIANA
ANDREWS, LUCILLA MATHEW

GORDON, DON
THOMAS, EDWARD LLEWELLYN

GORDON, DONALD
PAYNE, DONALD GORDON

GORDON, DOREEN
CHARD, JUDY

GORDON, FREDERICK
STRATEMEYER, EDWARD

GORDON, FRITZ
JARVIS, FREDERICK G.
VAN BEEVER, ROBERT F.

GORDON, GARY
EDMONDS, IVY GORDON

GORDON, GEOFREY
JONES, J.G.

GORDON, GEORGE
HASFORD, [JERRY] GUSTAVE

GORDON, GLENDA
BEADLE, GWYNETH GORDON

GORDON, GLENN
HABECK, FRITZ

GORDON, GORDON
CABRAL, WALTER A. GORDON

GORDON, HAL
GOODWIN, HAROLD LELAND

GORDON, HANS
REINHARD, HANS GEORG

GORDON, HARRY
GORDON, HENRY ALFRED

GORDON, HAVA
BUXTON, RAYMOND

GORDON, HORATIO
HUTCHINSON, HORACE GORDON

GORDON, IAN
FELLOWES-GORDON, IAN

GORDON, JANE
LEE, ELSIE

GORDON, JANET
WOODHAM-SMITH, CECIL

GORDON, JEAN
WICKHAM, JEAN

GORDON, JEFFIE ROSS
ENDERLE, JUDITH [A] ROSS
TESSLER, STEPHANIE GORDON

GORDON, JOHN
GESNER, CLARK
JENNISON, JOHN WILLIAM

GORDON, JULIEN
CRUGER, JULIE GRINNELL

GORDON, KATHARINE
PEARSON, KATHARINE

GORDON, KEITH
BAILEY, GORDON

GORDON, KEYNE
BEDFORD-JONES, HENRY

GORDON, KURTZ
KURTZ, C. GORDON

GORDON, LAURA
DEVRIES, LAURA LEE

GORDON, LESLEY
ELLIOTT, LESLEY

GORDON, LEW
BALDWIN, GORDON C.

GORDON, LUCY
FIOROTTO, CHRISTINE S.

GORDON, LUTHER
GIFFORD, JAMES NOBLE

GORDON, MARY
OSTLERE, MARY

GORDON, MARY EBBITT
WINTERS, CATHERINE [MARY]

GORDON, MAX
FODEN, FREDERICK [T]
LAZENBY, NORMAN A.

GORDON, MILLARD VERNE
WOLLHEIM, DONALD A.

GORDON, NANCY
HEINL, NANCY GORDON

GORDON, NATHANIEL
GASKO, GORDON

GORDON, NEIL
MACDONELL, A. GORDON

GORDON, OLIVER
EMERSON, HENRY OLIVER

GORDON, PETER
WILKES-HUNTER, RICHARD

GORDON, RAY
WAINWRIGHT, GORDON RAY

GORDON, REX
KODELPETER, HANS E.
HOUGH, STANLEY BENNETT

GORDON, RICHARD
MURRAY, ADRIAN
OSTLERE, GORDON STANLEY

GORDON, RICHARD A.
GORDON, [RICHARD] STUART

GORDON, ROBERT S.
ROECKEN, KURT WALTER

GORDON, S.S.
SHAW, STANLEY GORDON

GORDON, SELMA
LANES, SELMA G.

GORDON, SPIKE
BOYCE, DAVID
BUXTON, RAYMOND
FAWCETT, FRANK DUBREZ
FEARN, JOHN RUSSELL

GORDON, STANLEY
SHAW, STANLEY GORDON

GORDON, STEWART
SHIRREFFS, GORDON DONALD

GORDON, STUART
GORDON, [RICHARD] STUART

GORDON, SUSAN
CARBONI, SUSAN G.

GORDON, TOM
THOMAS, GORDON

GORDON, WILLIAM MURRAY
GRAYDON, WILLIAM MURRAY

GORDON, [COLONEL] H.R.
ELLIS, EDWARD S.

GORDONS, THE
GORDON, MILDRED & GORDON

GORE, MARY
SHANKS, WILLIAM F.G.

GORE, WILLIAM
GORDON, JAN

GORELL, LORD
BARNES, RONALD GORELL

GOREN, CHARLES H[ENRY]
VADAKIN, JAMES CHARLES

GORENKO, ANNA ANDREEVNA
AKMATOVA, ANNA

GORES, JOE
GORES, JOSEPH NICHOLAS

GORHAM, MICHAEL
ELTING, MARY
FOLSOM, FRANKLIN [B]

GORHAM, NICHOLAS
GERSON, NOEL B.

GORKI, MAKSIM
PESHKOV, ALEXEI M.

GORKY, MAXIM
PESHKOV, ALEXEI M.

GORLING, LARS
GOERLING, LARS

GORMAN, BETH
PAINE, LAURAN BOSWORTH

GORMAN, ED
GORMAN, EDWARD [JOSEPH]

GORMAN, GINNY
ZACHARY, HUGH

GORMAN, J.A.
GRASMUCK, JURGEN

GORMAN, MARK
LYNCH, W.

GORMAN, TERRY
POWERS, RICHARD M.

GORMAN, TOM
GORMAN, THOMAS DAVID

GORMANDER, DOKTOR
OHRLANDER, GUNNAR

GORNI, YOSEF
GORNY, YOSEF

GORNY, JOSEPH
GORNY, YOSEF

GORRISH, WALTER
KAISER, WALTER

GORSLINE, S.M.
GORSLINE, [SALLY] MARIE

GORT, SAM
BARRETT, GEOFFREY JOHN

GORTON, KAITLYN
EMERSON, KATHY LYNN

GORYAN, SIRAK
SAROYAN, WILLIAM

GOSFIELD, C. HEDDINGHAM
BROOKS, EDWY SEARLES

GOSLOVICH, MARIANNE
BROWN, MORRIS CECIL

GOSNELL, BETTY
GOSNELL, ELIZABETH DUKE T

GOSSAERT, GEETEN
GERRETSON, FREDERIK CAREL

GOSSIP, JOHN
CHAMPLIN, EDWIN ROSS

GOTAMA, RAMTA YOGI
BISSOONDOYAL, BASDEO

GOTIKE, MARIA
MELHARDT, TRUDE

GOTT, K.D.
GOTT, KENNETH DAVIDSON

GOTTANKA, HANS
EGGELKRAUT-GOTTANKA, HANS

GOTTESMAN, S.D.
KORNBLUTH, C[YRIL] M.
LOWNDES, ROBERT A.W.
POHL, FREDERIK

GOTTFRIED, TED
GOTTFRIED, THEODORE MARK

GOTTHELF, JEREMIAS
BITZIUS, ALBERT

GOTTSCHALK, ELIN TOONA
TOONA-ELIN, ELIN[-KAI]

GOTTSCHALK, LAURA RIDING
JACKSON, LAURA [RIDING]
REICHENTHAL, LAURA

GOTZ, IGNACIO
GOETZ, IGNACIO L.

GOUGE, ORSON
LARNER, JEREMY

GOUGH, BILL
GOUGH, WILLIAM JOHN

GOUGH, IRENE
HALL, IRENE

GOUGH, KATHLEEN
ABERLE, KATHLEEN GOUGH

GOULART, RON
GOULART, RONALD JOSEPH

GOULD, ALAN
BANKS, MICHAEL A.
CANNING, VICTOR

GOULD, ARTHUR LEE
LEE, ARTHUR S. GOULD

GOULD, BERNARD
PARTRIDGE, [SIR] BERNARD

GOULD, JOAN
KLEINBARD, JOAN GOULD

GOULD, JOY
BOYUM, JOY GOULD

GOULD, JUDITH
BIENES, NICHOLAS PETER
GALLAGHER, REA

GOULD, LETTIE
PAXSON, ETHEL

GOULD, MICHAEL
AYRTON GOULD, MICHAEL

GOULD, STEPHEN
BOGART, WILLIAM G.
FISHER, STEPHEN GOULD

GOULDER, GRACE
IZANT, GRACE GOULDER

GOULSON, CARY F.
GOULSON, CARLYN FLOYD

GOUTTIER, MAURICE
MORETTI, UGO

GOVINDA, LAMA ANAGARIKA
GOVINDA, ANAGARIKA B.

GOWANS, ELSA
WATT, ELSIE GOWANS

GOWAR, ANTONIO
DUNFORD, JUDITH
MARGOLIS, SUSANNA

GOWER, CRAVEN
HOSKEN, ERNEST CHARLES

GOWER, IRIS
DAVIES, IRIS

GOY, PHILIP
GOY, PHILLIPE

GOYA, FRED
DIAMANT, LINCOLN

GOYENECHE, GABRIEL
DE AVALLE-ARCE, JUAN B.

GRAAF, PETER
YOUD, CHRISTOPHER [S]

GRAAT, HEINRICH
WOLK, GEORGE

GRABE, REINHOLD TH.
BRENNER, HANS GEORG

GRABLE, MARSHA
BRAUN, WILBUR

GRABOWSKY, NICHOLAS
RANDERS, NICHOLAS

GRACCHUS
WINTRINGHAM, TOM

GRACE, ALICIA
GREENFIELD, IRVING A.

GRACE, ANITA
GREENFIELD, IRVING A.

GRACE, C.L.
DOHERTY, P.C.

GRACE, CAROL
CULVER, CAROL

GRACE, DEBORAH
WINER, DEBORAH GRACE

GRACE, JOSEPH
HORNBY, JOHN WILKINSON

GRACE, ROSEMARY
ALFONSI, ALICE

GRACQ, JULIEN
POIRIER, LOUIS

GRADUATE OF OXFORD, A
RUSKIN, JOHN

GRADY, LIZ
COUGHLIN, PATRICIA M.

GRADY, PETER
DANIELS, NORMAN A.

GRADY, TEX
WEBB, JACK RANDOLPH

GRAE, CAMARIN
GRACE, MARIAN

GRAEME, BRUCE
JEFFRIES, BRUCE GRAHAM M.

GRAEME, DAVID
JEFFRIES, BRUCE GRAHAM M.

GRAEME, LINDA
JEFFRIES, GAY

GRAEME, RODERIC
JEFFRIES, BRUCE GRAHAM M.
JEFFRIES, RODERIC[GRAEME]

GRAEY, JULIAN
GOLD, HORACE L.

GRAF, J.
EICHHORN, JOSY

GRAF, KARIN
KLEIN, DOROTHEE

GRAFE, FELIX
GREVE, FELIX PAUL B.F.

GRAFF, POLLY ANNE
COLVER, ANNE

GRAFFSHAGEN, STEPHAN
MULLER, KLAUS

GRAFTON, ANN
OWENS, THELMA

GRAFTON, GARTH
DUNCAN, SARA JEANETTE

GRAHAEM, JIM
GORDON, JAMES WILLIAM

GRAHAM, A.S.
GRAHAM, ALEXANDER STEEL

GRAHAM, BENJAMIN
GROSSBAUM, BENJAMIN

GRAHAM, BILLY
GRAHAM, WILLIAM FRANKLIN

GRAHAM, CARLOTTA
WALLMANN, JEFFREY M.

GRAHAM, CHARLES S.
TUBB, E.C.

GRAHAM, CHARLOTTE
BOWDEN, JOAN CHASE

GRAHAM, DAVID
WRIGHT, EVAN

GRAHAM, DON
GRAHAM, DONALD R.

GRAHAM, ELIZABETH
EDMONDS, ARTHUR DENIS
SCHATTNER, E.

GRAHAM, ENNIS
MOLESWORTH, MARY L.S.

GRAHAM, FELIX
BROWN, FREDRIC [WILLIAM]

GRAHAM, H.E.
HAMILTON, ERNEST GRAHAM

GRAHAM, HARRY
JONES, HARRY AUSTIN

GRAHAM, HARVEY
FLACK, ISAAC HARVEY

GRAHAM, HEATHER
POZZESSERE, HEATHER G.

GRAHAM, HOWARD W.
WANDREI, HOWARD E.

GRAHAM, HUGH
BARROWS, [RUTH] MARJORIE

GRAHAM, JAMES
PATTERSON, HARRY

GRAHAM, JANET
RANCE, JANET MAY

GRAHAM, JEAN
SCOTT, MARY E.

GRAHAM, JOHN
DOMBROWSKI, IVAN
PHILLIPS, DAVID GRAHAM
ROSE, GRAHAM

GRAHAM, JOHNSTON
SMITH, DAVID [L]

GRAHAM, KENNON
HARRISON, DAVID LEE

GRAHAM, LARRY
GRAHAM, LAWRENCE OTIS

GRAHAM, MATTHEW
ARNOLD, PETER

GRAHAM, NEILL
DUNCAN, W. MURDOCH

GRAHAM, PETER
LANGMAID, KENNETH [J.R.]

GRAHAM, PIPPIN
BAILEY, HILARY

GRAHAM, RAMONA
COOK, RAMONA GRAHAM

GRAHAM, ROBERT
HALDEMAN, JOSEPH WILLIAM

GRAHAM, ROBIN
RALEIGH-KING, ROBIN VICT.

GRAHAM, RUTH
EVANS, JEAN

GRAHAM, SCOTT
BLACK, HAZELTON

GRAHAM, SHIRLEY
DU BOIS, SHIRLEY GRAHAM

GRAHAM, SONIA
SINCLAIR, SONIA

GRAHAM, SUSAN
GRAHAM, MAUDE FITZGERALD

GRAHAM, TOM
LEWIS, [HARRY] SINCLAIR

GRAHAM, VANESSA
FRASER, ANTHEA

GRAHAM, VIRGINIA
GUTTENBERG, VIRGINIA

GRAHAM, VIVA
SOMERVILLE, EDITH A.O.

GRAHAM, W.S.
GRAHAM, WILLIAM SYDNEY

GRAHAM, WILLIAM
ASPERN-BUCHMEIER, ELISAB.

GRAHAM, WINIFRED
CORY, MATILDA WINIFRED G.

GRAHAM, [LT.] PRESTON
INGRAHAM, PRENTISS

GRAHAM-CAMERON, M.
GRAHAM-CAMERON, MALCOLM

GRAHAM-CAMERON, MIKE
GRAHAM-CAMERON, MALCOLM

GRAHN, JUDY
GARHN, JUDITH L.

GRAINGER, A.J.
GRAINGER, ANTHONY JOHN

GRAINGER, J.H.
GRAINGER, JOHN HERBERT

GRAINGERHILL, AMY M.
SCHIER, NORMA

GRAMMATICUS
BLAIKLOCK, EDWARD MUSGRV.

GRAMS, JAY
GRASMUCK, JURGEN

GRANADOS, PAUL
KENT, ARTHUR WILLIAM C.

GRANATSTEIN, J.L.
GRANATSTEIN, JACK LAWR.

GRANBERG, W.J.
GRANBERG, WILBUR JOHN

GRANBY, MILTON
WALLMANN, JEFFREY M.

GRAND, SARAH
MCFALL, FRANCES ELIZABETH

GRANDLIEN, DOCTOR
LAVADAN, LEON

GRANDMA
MULHEARN, WINIFRED

GRANDOWER, ELISSA
WAUGH, HILLARY B.

GRANDRITH, LORD
FARMER, PHILIP JOSE

GRANDVILLE, J.J.
GERARD, JEAN IGNACE I.

GRANDVILLE, JEAN IGNACE I
GERARD, JEAN IGNACE I.

GRANDVILLE, LOUISE
STREIB, DANIEL T.

GRANE, GUNNAR
KERFVE, AXEL

GRANGE, CHRIS
GNAEGY, CHARLES

GRANGE, ELLERTON
FRASER-HARRIS, D.

GRANGE, JOHN
BALLARD, W. TODHUNTER
BELLEM, ROBERT LESLIE

GRANGE, PETER
NICOLE, CHRISTOPHER ROBIN

GRANGER, ANN
HULME, ANN

GRANGER, BYRD HOWELL
HOWELL, BYRD

GRANGER, DARIUS JOHN
JAKES, JOHN [WILLIAM]
MARLOWE, STEPHEN

GRANGER, GEORGIA
GRANGER, GEORGE A.

GRANGER, GUY
GREEN, KAY

GRANGER, KATHERINE
SEDERQUEST, MARY F.F.

GRANGER, PEGGY
GRANGER, MARGARET JANE

GRANGER, STEWART
STEWART, JAMES L.

GRANIT, ARTHUR
GREENBERG, ARTHUR

GRANITE, TONY
POLITELLA, DARIO

GRANT, ALAN
CLARKE, GERALD
KENNINGTON, [G] ALAN

GRANT, ALLAN [ALLEN]
WILSON, JAMES GRANT

GRANT, ALLEN
SMITH, ARTHUR DOUGLAS H.

GRANT, AMBROSE
RAYMOND, RENE BRABAZON

GRANT, ANNA
MALCOLM, ANTHEA

GRANT, ANTHONY
CAMPBELL, JUDITH
PARES, MARION STAPYLTON

GRANT, BEN
GRANBECK, MARILYN

GRANT, C.B.S.
HAGA, ENOCH JOHN

GRANT, C.L.
GRANT, CHARLES L.

GRANT, CAROL
COPPER, DOROTHY

GRANT, CHARLES
LENGEL, WILLIAM CHARLES

GRANT, CHARLIE
RENNAU, JOACHIM

GRANT, DAVID
THOMAS, CRAIG [DAVID]

GRANT, DON
GLUT, DONALD F.

GRANT, DOUGLAS
MERLAND, OLIVER
OSTRANDER, ISABEL EGENTON

GRANT, E. GORDON
EDWARDS, ROBERT H.

GRANT, EVE
GRAY, K.E.

GRANT, FRANCIS
MAKGILL, [SIR] GEORGE

GRANT, GERALD
GRANT, GERTRUDE

GRANT, HILDA
GRANT, HILDA KAY

GRANT, J.B.
GRANT, JOHN BARNARD
GRANT, JACK
GRANT, JOHN BARNARD

GRANT, JAMES
CROWTHER, BRUCE [IAN]

GRANT, JANE
LEADER, [EVELYN] BARBARA

GRANT, JEANNE
CULBY, JILL ALISON HART

GRANT, JOAN
KELSEY, JOAN MARSHALL

GRANT, JOHN
BARNETT, PAUL LE PAGE
GROSSMANN, HANS HUGO
LANGFORD, DAVID [ROWLAND]

GRANT, KATHRYN
GRANT, KATHRYN ANNE P.

GRANT, KAY
GRANT, HILDA KAY

GRANT, KIRBY
HORN, MAURICE

GRANT, LANDON
GRIBBLE, LEONARD [R]

GRANT, LAURIE
CHAPPELYEAR, LAURIE
MILLER, LAURIE

GRANT, LINDA
WILLIAMS, LINDA V.

GRANT, MARGARET
CORYELL, JOHN RUSSELL
FRANKEN, ROSE [DOROTHY]
MELONEY, WILLIAM BROWN

GRANT, MARJORIE
COOK, MARJORIE GRANT

GRANT, MARK
BISCHOFF, DAVID F.
KING, BRUCE ALVIN
SULLIVAN, TIMOTHY ROBERT

GRANT, MARY
WILLANS, ANGELA

GRANT, MATTHEW G.
DIKTY, JULIAN [C] MAY

GRANT, MAXWELL
DAVIS, ROBERT HART
DENT, LESTER
ELLIOTT, BRUCE W.
GIBSON, WALTER B.
GRANT, JAMES TIMOTHY
LYNDS, DENNIS
TINSLEY, THEODORE

GRANT, NATALIE
GUSS, LINDA

GRANT, NEIL
MOUNTFIELD, DAVID

GRANT, NESTA
LEYLAND, ERIC

GRANT, RICHARD
CLARKE, JOSEPH CALVITT

GRANT, SABINA
GIBESON, JACQUELINE LA T.

GRANT, SARA
IRWIN, MARIANNE

GRANT, SKEETER
SPIEGELMAN, ART

GRANT, SUSAN
ESCHKOTTER, MARLENE

GRANT, VANESSA
OLTMAN, VANESSA

GRANT, WHITNEY
KEIF, AUBREY

GRANT, WILLIAM
REASONER, JAMES M.

GRANT, [MAJ.] A.F.
HARBAUGH, THOMAS C.

GRANT-ADAMSON, LESLEY
HEYCOCK, LESLEY

GRANTHAM, GERALD
WALLACE, JOHN

GRANTLAND, KEITH
TOMERLIN, JOHN E.
BEAUMONT, CHARLES

GRANVILLE, CHARLES
EGERTON, F. CHARLES G.

GRANVILLE-BARKER, HELEN
GATES, HELEN

GRAPE, OLIVER
WOOD, CHRISTOPHER [H]

GRAPHO
OAKLEY, ERIC GILBERT

GRASSE, JURGEN
GRASMUCK, JURGEN

GRATTON, THOMAS
HULME, THOMAS ERNEST

GRAU, ERNST
GURK, PAUL

GRAU, FRANZ
GURK, PAUL

GRAVE, STEPHEN
SCHOW, DAVID J.
YERKOVICH, ANTHONY

GRAVEL, FERN
HALL, JAMES NORMAN

GRAVELEY, GEORGE
EDWARDS, GEORGE G.

GRAVEN, NICHOLAS
DE KREMER, JEAN RAYMOND

GRAVES, KELLER
DAVENPORT, KATHRYN
ROGERS, EVELYN
GRAVES, TRICIA
GRAVERSON, PAT

GRAVES, VALERIE
BRADLEY, MARION ZIMMER

GRAVEY, FERNAND
MERTENS, FERNAND

GRAVEYARD, ALOYSIUS
THODY, PHILIP MALCOLM W.

GRAVIROS, RUTH
SULLIVAN, ELEANOR

GRAWOIG, SHEILA
RAESCHILD, SHEILA

GRAY, A.W.
BROWN, CROSSLAND

GRAY, ADRIAN
WILKES-HUNTER, RICHARD

GRAY, ALISON
MOSER, ALMA

GRAY, ANDREW
MURRAY, A.C.

GRAY, ANGELA
DANIELS, DOROTHY
DANIELS, NORMAN A.

GRAY, ANNABEL
COX, ANNE

GRAY, ANTHONY
GANN, ERNEST K.
SEARLS, HENRY HUNT JR.

GRAY, B.
BROOKS, EDWY SEARLES

GRAY, BERKELEY
BROOKS, EDWY SEARLES

GRAY, BETSY
POOLE, GRAY JOHNSON

GRAY, BILL
IDE, HEINO

GRAY, BLAKENEY
BANGS, JOHN KENDRICK

GRAY, CAPTAIN BILL
GRAY, WILLIAM BITTLE

GRAY, CARL
PARK, CHARLES CARROLL

GRAY, CAROLINE
BEERMAN, F.
NICOLE, CHRISTOPHER ROBIN

GRAY, CHARLES
TUBB, E.C.

GRAY, CHRIS[TOPHER]
USHER, [JOHN] GRAY

GRAY, DON
GRAYDON, ROBERT MURRAY

GRAY, DULCIE
DENNISON, DULCIE W.C.

GRAY, E. CONDER
JAPP, ALEXANDER HAY

GRAY, ELIZABETH JANET
VINNING, ELIZABETH GREY

GRAY, ELLINGTON
JACOB, NAOMI ELLINGTON

GRAY, ESCA
ADAMSON, FRANCES A.

GRAY, GALLAGHER
MUNGER, KATY

GRAY, GEOFFREY
MURRAY, C. GEOFFREY

GRAY, GEORGE P.
VOIGT, GUDRUN & KARL

GRAY, GINNA
GRAY, VIRGINIA

GRAY, HARRIET
ROBINS, DENISE

GRAY, J. RICHARD
GRAY, JOHN RICHARD

GRAY, JACK
DE KREMER, JEAN RAYMOND

GRAY, JANE
EVANS, CONSTANCE MAY

GRAY, JANET
RUSSELL, SYBIL

GRAY, JENNY
GRAY, GENEVIEVE S.

GRAY, JIM
RENNAU, JOACHIM

GRAY, JOHN
KUGLER, DIETMAR
RAFFETY, GORDON EDWARD

GRAY, JOHN LEE
JAKES, JOHN [WILLIAM]

GRAY, JONATHAN
ADAMS, HERBERT
TAYLOR, JACK

GRAY, KERRIE
GRAYBEAL, KATHRYN

GRAY, LINDA
BOYCE, DAVID

GRAY, MALCOLM
STUART, IAN

GRAY, MARCY
GRAY, LORI
GREGORY, MARTHA

GRAY, MARIAN
PIERCE, EDITH GRAY

GRAY, MARY LILIAN
DE KREMER, JEAN RAYMOND

GRAY, MAXWELL
TUTTIETT, MARY GLEED

GRAY, PATSEY
GRAY, PATRICIA [CLARK]

GRAY, PHILIP
PERLMAN, JESS

GRAY, ROBERTSON
RAYMON, ROSSITER W.

GRAY, ROD
FOX, GARDNER F.

GRAY, RUSSELL
FISCHER, BRUNO

GRAY, SIMON
DAVIDSON, SIMON

GRAY, SUZANNA
RICH, MARY LOU

GRAY, TONY
GRAY, GEORGE HUGH

GRAY, VANESSA
AEBY, JACQUELYN

GRAY, WALTER
MATTHAEI, CLARA

GRAY, WALTER T.
VICTOR, MRS. M.V.

GRAY, WIDETT
RAY, DEWITT GRINNELL

GRAY, WOODY
RAPUZZI, G.L.

GRAYDON, MARK
GRAYDON, ROBERT MURRAY

GRAYDON, W.
HUDSON, WILLIAM C.

GRAYLING, RONALD
GRAY, R.E.

GRAYN, MICHAEL
ENGLEBERT, MICHAEL

GRAYSON, ALICE BARR
GROSSMAN, JEAN SCHICK

GRAYSON, DAPHNE
GRAVELEY, G.C.

GRAYSON, DAVID
BAKER, RAY STANNARD

GRAYSON, DONALD
COOK, WILLIAM WALLACE

GRAYSON, ELIZABETH
CHADWICK, JOSEPH L.

GRAYSON, ENA
LEWIS, CLIFFORD

GRAYSON, GEOFFREY
FEARN, JOHN RUSSELL

GRAYSON, LAURA
WILSON, BARBARA

GRAYSON, LEANNE
WIETE, ROBIN LEANNE

GRAYSON, MARINA
ROGERS, ROSEMARY

GRAYSON, REX
CAMPBELL, RONALD GRAYSON

GRAYSON, RICHARD
GRINDAL, RICHARD

GRAYSON, ROGER
PRONZINI, WILLIAM JOHN
WALLMANN, JEFFREY M.

GRAYSON, [CAPT.] J.J.
WRIGHT, ELSIE N.

GRAYSTONE, LYNN
BRENNAN, JOSEPH [LOMAS]

GRAZHDANIN, MISHA
BURGESS, MICHAEL ROY

GREASEBALL JOE
HOGAN, ROBERT J[ASPER]

GREAT COMTE
HAWKESWORTH, ERIC

GREAVES, GILLIAN
MACVEAN, PHYLLIS

GREAVES, NORMAN
BROOKS, EDWY SEARLES

GREAVES, RICHARD
MCCUTCHEON, GEORGE BARR
SIMONDS, PETER

GREBENS, G.V.
GREBENSCHIKOV, GEORGE V.

GRECCO, JOHNNY
FRANCES, STEPHEN D.

GREEDERS, MIRIAM
BECKERS, MICHAEL

GREEDY WOMAN
PENNELL, ELIZABETH

GREELEY, MARY WILLIAMS
GOODRIDGE, MARY WILLIAMS

GREEN BAR BILL
BJERREGAARD, WILHEM

GREEN CROW, THE
O'CASEY, SEAN

GREEN, ADAM
WEISGARD, LEONARD JOSEPH

GREEN, ALEXANDER
GRINEVSKI, ALEK S.

GREEN, ANNA KATHARINE
ROHLFS, ANNA KATHARINE

GREEN, BENNY
GREEN, BERNARD

GREEN, BRIAN
CARD, ORSON SCOTT

GREEN, BRYAN
DAVIS, HORACE BANCROFT

GREEN, CHARLES M.
GARDNER, ERLE STANLEY

GREEN, CHARLES
GARDNER, ERLE STANLEY

GREEN, D.
CASEWIT, CURTIS [W]

GREEN, DON
KUGLER, DIETMAR

GREEN, F.L.
GREEN, FREDERICK LAWRENCE

GREEN, FRANCES
HORNWOOD, HARVEY

GREEN, GERALD
GREENBERG, GERALD

GREEN, GLINT
PETERSON, MARGARET [ANN]

GREEN, HANNAH
GREENBERG, JOANNA E.G.

GREEN, HENRY
YORKE, HENRY VINCENT

GREEN, I.G.
GREENBLATT, IRA

GREEN, J.C.R.
GREEN, JAMES C.R.

GREEN, JANET
MCCORMICK, VICTORIA

GREEN, JERRY
GREEN, JEROME FREDERIC

GREEN, JUDITH
GALBRAITH, JEAN
RODRIGUEZ, JUDITH G.

GREEN, JULI
CHILD, JUDITH
NEHER, LISA

GREEN, JULIEN
GREEN, JULIAN [HARTRIDGE]

GREEN, LINDA
COPPER, DOROTHY

GREEN, MARTYN
MARTIN-GREEN, WILLIAM

GREEN, O.O.
DURGNAT, RAYMOND [ERIC]

GREEN, OLIVE
REED, MYRTLE

GREEN, PETER
BULMER, [HENRY] KENNETH

GREEN, R.
WEIR, ROSEMARY

GREEN, ROBERT
SMITH, RICHARD REIN

GREEN, STEPHEN
SOUTHWOLD, STEPHEN

GREENAWAY, KATE
GREENAWAY, CATHERINE

GREENBERG, ARTHUR
GRANIT, ARTHUR

GREENBERG, JUDITH ANNE
AZRAEL, JUDITH ANNE

GREENBERGER, EVELYN BAR.
BARISH, EVELYN

GREENBLATT, M.H.
GREENBLATT, MANUEL HARRY

GREENE, A.C.
GREENE, ALVIN CARL

GREENE, ADAM
SCOTT, PETER DALE

GREENE, BOB
GREENE, ROBERT BERNARD JR

GREENE, FRED
CADET, JOHN

GREENE, HERBERT LESLIE[1]
BLOCK, LAWRENCE

GREENE, JANICE PRESSER
PRESSER, JANICE

GREENE, JENNIFER
CULBY, JILL ALISON HART

GREENE, JERRY
GREENE, CHARLES JEROME

GREENE, JOHNNY
GREENE, JOHN WILLIAM JR.

GREENE, L. PATRICK
GREENE, LOUIS MONTAGUE

GREENE, L.L.
GREENE, STEVEN
LEVINE, LARRY

GREENE, MABEL
BEAN, MABEL GREENE

GREENE, MILES
RABEN, HANS-JURGEN

GREENE, PAMELA
FORMAN, JOAN

GREENE, ROBERT
DEINDORFER, ROBERT G.

GREENE, SARA
STRONG, JUNE

GREENE, STEVEN
LUTZ, JOHN [T]

GREENE, YVONNE
FLESCH, YOLANDE CATARINA

GREENER, CARL
LOWNDES, ROBERT A.W.

GREENFIELD, BERNADETTE
DARBY, EDITH M.

GREENFIELD, DARBY
WARD, PHILIP

GREENFIELD, JERRY
GREENFIELD, JEROME

GREENFINGER, MR.
WALLS, IAN GASCOIGNE

GREENGOLD, JANE
STEVENS, JANE GREENGOLD

GREENGROIN, ARTIE
BROWN, HARRY PETER M.

GREENHALGH, KATHERINE
BOBIN, JOHN WILLIAM

GREENHILL, JACK
GREENBERG, JACK

GREENHORN, JOSEPH
BEDFORD, JOHN T.

GREENHOUGH, TERRY
LESTER, ANDREW
GREENHOUGH, TERENCE

GREENING, HAMILTON
HAMILTON, CHARLES H.S.

GREENLEA, DENICE
PIPKIN, DENICE

GREENOW, HELM
MILLIES, HELMUT

GREENSLADE, S.L.
GREENSLADE, STANLEY LAWR.

GREENSPAN, CAPPY PETRASH
GREENSPAN, CONSTANCE A.P.

GREENSPUN, H.M.
GREENSPUN, HERMAN MILTON

GREENSPUN, HANK
GREENSPUN, HERMAN MILTON

GREENSTOCK, H.T.
SCHIER, NORMA

GREENWALD, SHEILA
GREEN, SHEILA ELLEN

GREENWOOD, GRACE
LIPPINCOTT, SARA JANE

GREENWOOD, JOHN
HILTON, JOHN BUXTON

GREENWOOD, LEIGH
LOWRY, HAROLD

GREER, ART
GREER, ARTHUR ELLIS

GREER, FRANCESCA
JANAS, FRANCIS LEROY G.

GREER, JACK
BARRETT, GEOFFREY JOHN

GREER, PATRICK
MACRORY, PATRICK

GREER, RICHARD
GARRETT, RANDALL [P]
SILVERBERG, ROBERT

GREER, TOM
GREER, THOMAS

GREET, BEN
BARLING, PHILIP

GREET, T.Y.
GREET, THOMAS YOUNG

GREGG, ALAN
MALLETTE, GERTRUDE ETHEL

GREGG, GEORGE GREGORY
MCALPINE, ROBERT W.

GREGG, LARRY
LEIGHTON, LAUREN GRAY

GREGG, MARTIN
MCNEILLY, WILFRED G.

GREGOIRE, LEON
GOYAU, GEORGES

GREGOR, LEE
POHL, FREDERIK
ROTHMAN, MILTON A.

GREGOR, MANFRED
DORFMEISTER, GREGOR

GREGOR, NINA
FUSSER, ERIKA

GREGORIAN, JOYCE BALLOU
HAMPSHIRE, JOYCE BALLOU G

GREGORIUS, GREGOR A.
GROSCHE, EUGEN

GREGORY, CHARLES ALAN
DANIELS, NORMAN A.

GREGORY, CHUCK
GNAEGY, CHARLES

GREGORY, DANE
BRADBURY, RAY [DOUGLAS]
ROBBINS, ROB

GREGORY, DAVE
TAYLOR, W.T.

GREGORY, ELIZABETH
GILFORD, CHARLES BERNARD

GREGORY, GUY
WRIGHT, GUIER & GREGORY

GREGORY, H.
EDGAR, ALFRED

GREGORY, HARRY
GOTTFRIED, THEODORE MARK

GREGORY, HILTON
FERGUSON, CHARLES W.

GREGORY, HYLTON
LEWIS, JACK
HILL, HARRY EGBERT
POOLE, REGINALD H.

GREGORY, J. DENNIS
WILLIAMS, JOHN A.

GREGORY, JEAN
URE, JEAN

GREGORY, JILL
GREENBERG, JAN

GREGORY, JOHN
HOSKINS, ROBERT

GREGORY, JULIAN R.
KNOWLES, LEO

GREGORY, K.J.
GREGORY, KENNETH JOHN

GREGORY, KATE
CARRELL, LENORE K.C.G.

GREGORY, LISA
CAMP, CANDACE [PAULINE]

GREGORY, LYDIA
BRODEUR, DIANE & GREG

GREGORY, MARGARET
ERCOLE, VELIA

GREGORY, MARK
BURCH, MONTE G.

GREGORY, MARTY
GREGORY, MARTHA

GREGORY, MARY L.
GREGORY, MARY LAWRENCE

GREGORY, MASON
JONES, ADRIENNE
MEEK, DORIS

GREGORY, MOLLIE
GREGORY, MARY LAWRENCE

GREGORY, R.L.
GREGORY, RICHARD LANGTON

GREGORY, RICHARD CLAXTON
GREGORY, DICK

GREGORY, SEAN
HOSSENT, HARRY

GREGORY, STEPHAN
PENDLETON, DON[ALD E.]
PENZLER, OTTO

GREGORY, STEVEN
JONES, STEPHEN GREGORY

GREGORY, T.S.
GREGORY, THEOPHILUS S.

GREGORY, VERONICA
SHAKARJIAN, VICTORIA

GREGSON, PAUL
OAKLEY, ERIC GILBERT

GREIF, MARTIN
FREY, FRIEDRICH HERMAN

GREIF, RUDIGER
KUROWSKI, FRANZ

GREIG, CHARLES
CRUICKSHANK, CHARLES G.

GREIG, MAYSIE
GREIG-SMITH, JENNIFER M.

GREIMAS, A.J.
GREIMAS, ALGIRDAS JULIEN

GREINER, SUSY
BERGHAMMER, SUSANNE

GREKOVA
VENTZEL, ELENA

GRENANDER, M.E.
GRENANDER, MARY ELIZABETH

GRENDON, EDWARD
LESHAN, LAWRENCE L[EE]

GRENDON, STEPHEN
DERLETH, AUGUST [WILLIAM]

GRENELLE, LISA
MUNROE, ELIZABETH LEE

GRENFALL, JOHN
FLOYD, GILBERT

GRENVIL, WILLIAM
MARTYN, WYNDHAM

GRENVILLE, J.A.S.
GRENVILLE, JOHN ASHLEY S.

GRENVILLE, PELHAM
WODEHOUSE, PELHAM GRENV.

GRESHAM, ANTONY
RUSSELL, ROY

GRESHAM, GRITS
GRESHAM, CLAUDE HAM. JR.

GRESSER, SY
GRESSER, SEYMOUR

GRETEMAN, JIM
GRETEMAN, JAMES

GREV, WILLIAM
REUTER, RALPH

GREVE, ELSA
GREVE, FELIX PAUL B.F.

GREVELL, JULIE
GREVEN, HELGA

GREVEN, JULIANE
GREVEN, HELGA

GREVILLE, HENRY
DURAND, ALICE MARIE C.F.

GREVILLE, MINOR
SPENDER, JOHN ALFRED

GREW, WILLIAM
O'FARRELL, WILLIAM

GREWDEAD, ROY
GOREY, EDWARD ST. JOHN

GREX, LEO
GRIBBLE, LEONARD [R]

GREY OWL
BELANEY, ARCHIBALD S.

GREY, A.F.
NEAL, ADELINE PHYLLIS

GREY, ANTHONY
ASTON, BENJAMIN GWILLIAM
SCHILLER, HENRY CARL

GREY, BELINDA
MACKINLAY, LEILA A.S.

GREY, CARENNA JANE
KALPAKIAN, LAURA ANNE

GREY, CARLTON
BULLIVANT, CECIL H[ENRY]

GREY, CAROL
LOWNDES, ROBERT A.W.

GREY, CHARLES
TUBB, E.C.

GREY, DEAN
JENNISON, JOHN WILLIAM

GREY, DONALD
THOMAS, EUGENE

GREY, ELIZABETH
HOGG, ELIZABETH [T]

GREY, EVELYN
LESLIE, SUSAN

GREY, FANNIE
HUNDLEY, MRS. E.D.

GREY, GEORGINA
ROBY, MARY LINN

GREY, GILBERT
MARGERISON, JOHN S.

GREY, HAROLD
ARGLES, THEODORE EMILE

GREY, HARRY
GOLDBERG, HARRY

GREY, JACK
LLOP SELLARES, JUAN

GREY, JILLIAN
JULIAN, DONNA

GREY, JIM
RENNAU, JOACHIM

GREY, JOHN
KUGLER, DIETMAR

GREY, JUDSON
HARMON, JAMES JUDSON
HAYDOCK, RON

GREY, KATHARINE
SMITH, KATHARINE GREY

GREY, KITTY
ALLEN, MARY ELIZABETH

GREY, LINDSEY
PEEL, COLIN D[UDLEY]L

GREY, LLOYD ERIC
ESHLEMAN, LLOYD WENDELL

GREY, LOREN ZANE
MCGAUGHY, DUDLEY DEAN

GREY, LOUIS
GRIBBLE, LEONARD [R]

GREY, MAXWELL
TUTTIETT, MARY GLEED

GREY, MILLIE
GERGICH, MILLIE GREY

GREY, NAIDRA
COCKSHUT, NAIDRA

GREY, ROBIN
GRESHAM, ELIZABETH [F]

GREY, ROMER ZANE
BRANDNER, GARY
CURRY, THOMAS ALBERT
MATTHEWS, CLAYTON [H]
PRONZINI, WILLIAM JOHN
WALLMANN, JEFFREY M.

GREY, ROWLAND
BROWN, L. ROWLAND

GREY, SALIITHA
PATRICK, SUSAN M.

GREY, SAMANTHA
PERKINS, DEBORAH

GREY, STEELE
SMITH, G.M.

GREY, VIVIAN
ANDERSON, HARRY WALTER

GREY, WALT
GREILING, WALTER

GREY, WALTON
KUTTNER, HENRY

GREY, WALTON
MOORE, CATHERINE LUCILLE

GREY, ZANE
GREY, PEARL

GREYLAND, VALERIE
SIEBOND, VALERIE

GREYSTARK, CHON
ACKERMAN, FORREST J.

GREYSTONE, ALEXANDER A.
GOODAVAGE, JOSEPH F.

GREYSTROKE, LORD
FARMER, PHILIP JOSE

GREYSUN, DORIAC
BERTIN, EDDY C.

GREYWHISKERS, MRS. FIFI
HOSKIN, CYRIL HENRY

GRI
DENNEY, DIANA

GRICE, GRIMES
KAMP, IRENE KITTLE

GRICE, JULIA [H]
HAUGHEY, JULIA

GRIDBAN, VOLSTED
FEARN, JOHN RUSSELL
TUBB, E.C.

GRIDER, JAY
MILLER, JOHN GRIDER

GRIDLEY, AUSTIN
CONLON, BEN
DONOVAN, LAURENCE

GRIER, ROSEY
GRIER, ROOSEVELT

GRIER, SYDNEY C.
GREGG, HILDA CAROLINE

GRIERSON, JANE
WOODWARD, EDWARD E.

GRIEVE, C.M.
GRIEVE, CHRIST. MURRAY

GRIFF
BOYCE, DAVID
BUXTON, RAYMOND
FAWCETT, FRANK DUBREZ
FEARN, JOHN RUSSELL
MCKEAG, ERNEST LIONEL
NEWTON, WILLIAM [SIMPSON]
PATERSON, A.J. BLAIR

GRIFF, ALAN
SUDDABY, WILLIAM DONALD

GRIFFEN, DAVID
MAUGHAM, ROBERT CECIL R.

GRIFFEN, EDMUND
DUBREUIL, ELIZABETH L.

GRIFFEN, ELIZABETH L.
DUBREUIL, ELIZABETH L.

GRIFFEN, JEFF
GRIFFEN, JAMES JEFFERDS

GRIFFEN, W.E.B.
BUTTERWORTH, WILLIAM E.

GRIFFIN, A. ARTHUR
GANLEY, W. PAUL

GRIFFIN, A.H.
GRIFFIN, ARTHUR HAROLD

GRIFFIN, ANDREW
HECKLEMANN, CHARLES N.

GRIFFIN, ANDREW A.
POWERS, PAUL S.
TOMPKINS, WALKER A.

GRIFFIN, ANNE [J]
GRIFFIN, ARTHUR J.

GRIFFIN, C.F.
FIKSO, EUNICE CLELAND

GRIFFIN, C.S.
GRIFFIN, CLIFFORD STEPHEN

GRIFFIN, DAN
GRIFFIN, GEORGE DANIEL

GRIFFIN, EDWARD
GIBSON, WALTER B.

GRIFFIN, JOCELYN
SPARROW, LAURA

GRIFFIN, JOHN
CLAY, MICHAEL JOHN

GRIFFIN, JONATHAN
GRIFFIN, ROBERT JOHN T.

GRIFFIN, MEG
MORGAN, JILL M[EREDITH]

GRIFFIN, TOM
GRIFFIN, THOMAS E. JR.

GRIFFIN, W.E.B.
BUTTERWORTH, WILLIAM E.

GRIFFITH, BILL
GRANGER, BILL

GRIFFITH, D.W.
GRIFFITH, DAVID LEWELYN W

GRIFFITH, G.T.
GRIFFITH, GUY THOMPSON

GRIFFITH, GEORGE
GRIFFITH-JONES, GEORGE C.
MEYN, NIELS

GRIFFITH, GEORGE CHETWYND
GRIFFITH-JONES, GEORGE C.

GRIFFITH, JACK
GRIFFITHS, JACK

GRIFFITH, JASON
GRIFFITH, MR. & MRS. E.G.

GRIFFITH, JEANETTE
EVERLY, JEANETTE
GRIFFITH, VALERIE WINKLER

GRIFFITH, LAWRENCE
GRIFFITH, DAVID LEWELYN W

GRIFFITH, MORGAN
TILEY, VALERIE

GRIFFITH, ROSLYNN
PINIANSKI, PATRICIA
SWEENEY, LINDA

GRIFFITHS, G.D.
GRIFFITHS, EDITH GRACE C.
GRIFFITHS, GORDON DOUGLAS

GRIFFITHS, HELEN
SANTOS, HELEN

GRIFFITHS, MEL
GRIFFITHS, THOMAS MELVIN

GRIFFITHS, ROBERT L. III
PAUKER, JOHN

GRIFFITHS, STEVE
GRIFFITHS, STEPHEN GARETH

GRIGGS, BARBARA
VAN DER ZEE, BARBARA B.

GRIGGS, MARY
PHILLIPS, BLUEBELL S.

GRILE, DOD
BIERCE, AMBROSE

GRILEY, CHARLES
WHEELER, [C] GRILEY

GRIM, ANTHONY
LINECAR, ARTHUR

GRIMBLE, REV. CHAS. JAMES
ELIOT, T[HOMAS] S[TEARNS]

GRIMES, JOHN
CHANDLER, A. BERTRAM

GRIMES, W.H.
GRIMES, WILLIAM HENRY

GRIMETON, DOUGLAS
BJORILD, STEN DOUGLAS

GRIMM, BARON
MILLAIRD, M. ALBERT

GRIMM, BENJAMIN
LAMBERT, SPENCER

GRIMM, C.
GOLD, HORACE L.

GRIMM, CHARLIE
GRIMM, CHARLES JOHN

GRIMM, INGE MARIA
HASSLINGER, INGE MARIA

GRIMNER
HASSLER, ADOLF OTTO

GRIMSHAW, MARK
BELFIELD, HARRY WEDGEWOOD
MCKEAG, ERNEST LIONEL

GRIMSLEY, GORDON
GROOM, ARTHUR WILLIAM

GRIN, ALEKSANDR
GRINEVSKI, ALEK S.

GRIN, ELMAR
IAKIMOV, ALEKSANDR V.

GRINDLE, CARLETON
PAGE, GERALD W.

GRINGHUIS, DIRK
GRINGHUIS, RICHARD H.

GRINGOIRE
IRVING, NOEL

GRINNELL, DAVID
WOLLHEIM, DONALD A.

GRIP
WELCH, EDGAR L.

GRISE, JEANETTE
THOMAS, JEANETTE GRISE

GRISSOM, FAY
SHULMAN, FAY GRISSOM S.

GRISWOLD, GEORGE
DEAN, ROBERT GEORGE

GRIVA, ZHAN
FOLMANIS, ZHANIS K.

GRODE, REDWAY
GOREY, EDWARD ST. JOHN

GROENER, CARL
LOWNDES, ROBERT A.W.

GROH, ED
GROH, EDWIN CHARLES

GROHUS, MAXIMILIAN
HIERONIMUS, EKKEHARD

GROIA, PHIL
GROIA, PHILIP

GROLLER, BALDUIN
GOLDSCHEIDER, ALBERT

GROMA, PETER
GROMADECKI, JOSEF

GRONAU, HELMUT
MILLIES, HELMUT

GRONBERG, ERIK
SMEDS, BKJORN

GRONBJERG, KIRSTEN ANDER.
GROENBJERG, KIRSTEN ANDR.

GRONEWOLD, SUE ELLEN
GRONEWOLD, SUSAN ELLEN

GRONON, ROSE
BELLEFROID, MARTHA

GROPER, REINHARD
MULLER, EGBERT-HANS

GROSMONT, WESTON
GRONWALD, WERNER

GROSOFSKY, LESLIE
GROSS, LESLIE

GROSS, GENE
EDMONDS, IVY GORDON

GROSS, ROLF H.
GROSSHANS, ROLF H.

GROSS, SHELLY
GROSS, SHELDON HARVEY

GROSS, SUE
GROSS, SUSAN ELLEN

GROSS, SUE ELLEN
GROSS, SUSAN ELLEN

GROSSE, ANDREAS
FIELITZ, HANS PAUL

GROUPE, DARRYL R.
BUNCH, DAVID R.

GROVE, FRED
GROVE, FREDERICK HERRIDGE

GROVE, FREDERICK PHILIP
GREVE, FELIX PAUL B.F.

GROVE, MARJORIE
GROVE, MARTIN

GROVE, WILL O.
BRISTER, RICHARD

GROVELANDS, SARAH
SCHNEIDER, MYRA

GROVER, MADELEINE
GIBSON, WALTER B.

GROVER, MARSHALL
BLEECK, G.C.
MEARES, LEONARD F.

GROVES, GEORGINIA
SYMONS, DOROTHY GERALDINE

GROVES, H.E.
GROVES, HARRY EDWARD

GROVES, J.W.
GROVES, JOHN WILLIAM

GROVES, REG
GROVES, REGINALD

GROZNY, I.L.
BERGER, IVAN [B]

GRUBB
CRUMB, ROBERT

GRUBER, LUDWIG
ANZENGRUBER, LUDWIG

GRUELLE, JOHNNY
BARTON, JOHN

GRUELLE, JOHNNY
GRUELLE, JOHN BARTON

GRUEN, VON
HOLLOWAY, BRIAN W.

GRUENBAUM, LUDWIG
GAATHON, ARYEH LUDWIG

GRUMBLING GOURMET, THE
CHAPMAN, FRANK MONROE

GRUN, ANASTASIUS
AUERSPERG, ANTON ALEX. v.

GRUNBAUM, ADOLF
GRUENBAUM, ADOLF

GRUNDBERG, ANDY
GRUNDBERG, JOHN ANDREW

GRUNDT, OIVIND
GRAN, OYULV

GRUNDY, J.B.C.
GRUNDY, JOHN BROWNSDON C.

GRUNEBERG, HANS
GRUENEBERG, HANS

GRUNER-JUNGBLUT, ALICE
JUNGBLUT, ALICE

GRUNEWALT, PINE
KUNHARDT, EDITH

GRUNGE
CRUMB, ROBERT

GRUVER, REBECCA
GOODMAN, REBECCA GRUVER

GRYLLS, ROSALIE GLYNN
MANDER, M. ROSALIE G.G.

GUADALOUPE, BROTHER JOSE
MOJICA, JOSE

GUADO, SERGIO
GEROSA, GUIDO

GUARD, DAVE
GUARD, DAVID

GUARINO, DAGMAR
GUARINO, DEBORAH

GUBANE, BERNY
BERNDT, KARL-HEINZ

GUBBINS, NATHANIEL
MOTT, EDWARD SPENCER

GUBEN, BERNDT
BERNDT, KARL-HEINZ

GUDABUTSU
NATSUME, KINNOSUKE

GUDOI RICART, JOSE M.
GUDOI I RICART, JOSEP

GUDOI RICART, JOSEP
GUDOI I RICART, JOSEP

GUEHENNE, JEAN
GUEHENNO, JEAN MARCEL J.M

GUENTER, C.H.
GUNTHER, KARL HHEINZ

GUENTER, ERICH
EICH, GUENTER

GUERMANTES
BAUER, GERARD

GUERNSEY, H.W.
WANDREI, HOWARD E.

GUERNY, GENE
GURNEY, GENE

GUEST, A.G.
GUEST, ANTHONY GORDON

GUEST, DIANA
BIONDI, DIANNA R.G.

GUEST, HARRY
GUEST, HENRY BAYLY

GUETTE, EDITH
GROTKOP, EDITH

GUEVARA, CHE
GUEVARA SERNA, ERNESTO

GUGGENHEIM, PEGGY
GUGGENHEIM, MARGARET

GUGGISBERG, C.A.W.
GUGGISBERG, CHARLES A.W.

GUICCIOLI, [COUNTESS] T.
DE BOISSY, MARQUESE T.

GUIDO
KLOOS, WILLEM JOHAN TEOD.

GUIL, J.
GUILLEMONAT, JEAN

GUILDFORD, JOHN
HUNTER, BLUEBELL MATILDA

GUILFORD, J. PAUL
GUILFORD, JOY PAUL

GUILLEN, NICHOLAS
GUILLEN Y BATISTA, NICHOL

GUILLEVIC
GUILLEVIC, EUGENE

GUINNESS, OS
GUINNESS, IAN OSWALD

GUINNESS, OWEN
WILLIAMS, GUY RICHARD O.

GUIREC, JEAN
CHARTON, JEAN

GULDEN, BARBARA
GAA, EDEL

GULICK, BILL
GULICK, GROVER C.

GULL, RANGER
RANGER-GULL, C[YRIL A.E.]

GULLEMIN, JACQUES
SARTE, JEAN-PAUL

GULLIVER, JOHN
DESFONTAINES, PIERRE

GULLIVER, LEMUEL
FARRELL, MICHAEL
HASTINGS, MACDONALD
SWIFT, JONATHAN

GULLIVER, MARTIN
LAZENBY, NORMAN A.

GULLOIS, VALENTIN
DESNOS, ROBERT

GUMP, SALLY
STANFORD, SALLY

GUMPERT, JOACHIM S.
BECHTLE-BECHTINGER, JOAC.

GUN, WALTER
FEDDE, OVE

GUNBY, PETER
ERICSSON, THORE

GUNDOLF, FRIEDRICH
GUNDELFINGER, FRIEDRICH

GUNDY, H.P.
GUNDY, HENRY PEARSON

GUNN, BILL
GUNN, WILLIAM HARRISON

GUNN, ELIZABETH
GUNN, DIANA MAUREEN

GUNN, FRANK F.
SLATTERY, RAY

GUNN, S.J.
GUNN, STEVEN JOHN

GUNN, THOM
GUNN, THOMSON WILLIAM

GUNN, TOM
GRUBER, FRANK
MCDOWELL, SYL

GUNN, VICTOR
BROOKS, EDWY SEARLES

GUNNISON, LYNN
AMES, JOSEPH BUSHNELL

GUNNY, THE
PRONZINI, WILLIAM JOHN

GUNSTON, BILL
GUNSTON, WILLIAM TUDOR

GUNTHER, A.E.
GUNTHER, ALBERT EVERARD

GUNTRIP, HARRY
GUNTRIP, HENRY JAMES S.

GUNY, HANS
GRUNSKY, HANS

GUPTA, PRANATI SEN
SEN GUPTA, PRANATI

GURDAN, EMIL
BISCHOFF, EMIL

GURNARD, JOSEPH
STONIER, GEORGE

GURNEY, A.R.
GURNEY, ALBERT RAMSDELL

GURNEY, DAVID
BAIR, PATRICK

GURNEY, PETE
GURNEY, ALBERT RAMSDELL

GURNEY, PETER
GURNEY, ALBERT RAMSDELL

GUSEV, SERGEY IVANOVICH
DRABKIN, YAKOV D.

GUSIKOFF, LYNNE
HAWES, LYNNE GUSIKOFF S.

GUSTAFSON, JIM
GUSTAFSON, JAMES

GUSTAFSON, SARAH R.
RIEDMAN, SARAH R.

GUSTAFSON, SMITH
GUSTAFSON, JON
SMITH, DEAN WESLEY

GUSTAVE, JULES
NIELSEN, JULIUS

GUT, GOM
SIMENON, GEORGES [J.C]

GUT, SYLVIA
DENNEBORG, SILVIA [G]

GUTERSLOH, ALBERT PARIS
KIEHTREIBER, ALBERT KONR.

GUTHRIE, A.B.
GUTHRIE, ALFRED BERTRAM

GUTHRIE, A.B. JR.
GUTHRIE, ALFRED BERTRAM

GUTHRIE, ALAN
TUBB, E.C.

GUTHRIE, ARCHIBALD
SHAW, FRANK H.

GUTHRIE, BUD
GUTHRIE, ALFRED BERTRAM

GUTHRIE, DAVID
ALLEN, HUBERT RAYMOND

GUTHRIE, HUGH
FREEMAN, JOHN CROSBY

GUTHRIE, ISOBEL
GRIEVE, CHRIST. MURRAY

GUTHRIE, JOHN
BRODIE, JOHN

GUTHRIE, T.
GUTHRIE, WILLIAM TYRONE

GUTHRIE, WOODY
GUTHRIE, WOODROW WILSON

GUTT, DIETER
GUETT, DIETER

GUTTERIDGE, DON
GUTTERIDGE, DONALD GEORGE

GUY, JONATHAN
SMITH, GUY NEWMAN

GUY, RANDY
GEIS, RICHARD E.

GUZZO, LOU
GUZZO, LOUIS RICHARD

GWENDOLYN
BENNETT, [ENOCH] ARNOLD

GWINN, OMAR
BLAKE, ALAN

GWYN, EVANS
GRAYDON, ROBERT MURRAY
TEED, GEORGE HAMILTON

GWYN, W.B.
GWYN, WILLIAM BRENT

GWYNFRYN
MILLER, HARRIET MANN

GWYNNE, A.M.
GWYNNE, AGNES M.

GWYNNE, ARTHUR
EVANS, GWYNFIL ARTHUR

GWYNNE, FRED
GWYNNE, FREDERICK HUBBARD

GWYNNE, NELL
BOGGS, HELEN

GWYNNE, OSCAR A.
ELLIS, EDWARD S.

GWYNNE, OSWALD A.
ELLIS, EDWARD S.

GWYNNE, PAUL
SLATER, ERNEST

GYE, HAL
GYE, HAROLD FREDERICK N.

GYMIR, GERDA
MORRIS, GERDA

GYNCH, HENRY
GYMNICH, HEINZ

GYP
DE RIQUETTI MIRABEAU, SYB

H., T.W.
HANSHEW, THOMAS W.

H.A.K.
KENNEDY, H.A.

H.A.M.
MULLIGAN, HUGH A.

H.B.
BEALES, HELEN R. ABBOTT
BELLOC, [J] HILARY [P]

H.B.J.
BEDFORD-JONES, HENRY

H.D.
DOOLITTLE, HILDA

H.E.S.L.
LEECH, H.E.S.

H.F.E.
EVERETT-GREEN, EVELYN

H.H.
JACKSON, HELEN HUNT

H.J.M.
MASSINGHAM, HAROLD J.

H.L.G.
BENSON, ARTHUR CHRISTOPH.

H.M.S.
KIRK-GREEN, ANTHONY H.M.

H.M.W.
WANG, HUI-MING

H.T.
TUCKER, HERBERT

H.W.
HERAUD, JAVIER
WILLIAMS, HERBERT

H.W.L.
LUCY, HENRY WILLIAM

HA-AM, AHAD
GINZBERG, ASHER

HAAFTEN, JULIA V.
VAN HAAFTEN, JULIA

HAAM, ACHAD
GINZBERG, ASHER

HAAS, BEN
HAAS, BENJAMIN LEOPOLD

HAAS, CAROLA
CATALANI, VICTORIA

HABAKUK
FEILHAUSER, OTTO M.

HABBEMA, KOOS
HEIJERMANS, HERMAN

HABE, HANS
BEKESSY, JANOS

HABER, KAREN
SILVERBERG, KAREN HABER L

HABERGOCK, GUS N.
GERNSBACK, HUGO

HABERMAS, JURGEN
HABERMAS, JUERGEN

HABERSHAM, ELIZABETH
HARPER, ELIZABETH SHANNON
PORTER, MADELINE

HABERSHON, KEITH
MCCOMB, FREDERIC W.H.

HABERT, L.L.
HABERLER, LUCIA

HACH, ERIKA
HENGSBACH, ARNO

HACIKYAN, A.J.
HACIKYAN, AGOP J.

HACKEBEIL, MARGARETE
LEHMANN, MARGARETE

HACKER, BURT
STEIN, BEN

HACKETT, BUDDY
HACKER, LEONARD

HACKETT, LEE
ARKLEY, ARTHUR J[AMES]

HACKNEY, ROD
HACKNEY, RODERICK PETER

HACKO
GYE, HAROLD FREDERICK N.

HACKSTON, JAMES
GYE, HAROLD FREDERICK N.

HADDAM, JANE
PAPAZOGLOU, ORANIA

HADDIX, CECILLE
HADDIX-KONTOS, CECILLE P.

HADDO, OLIVER
PUECHNER, RAY

HADDOCK, ALBERT
HERBERT, SIR ALAN PATRICK

HADDON, CHRISTOPHER
PALMER, JOHN LESLIE

HADDON, PETER
TILSLEY, PETER

HADDON, SARAH
GREEN, MADGE

HADDOW, LEIGH
BEST, R. BRETON AMIS

HADERMAN, JANET H.
WALWORTH, JEANETTE R.

HADERMAN, JEANETTE
WALWORTH, JEANETTE R.

HADES, PROFESSOR
HADES, MICKEY

HADFIELD, E.C.R.
HADFIELD, [E] CHARLES [R]

HADFIELD, VIC
HADFIELD, VICTOR EDWARD

HADHAM, JOHN
PARKES, JAMES WILLIAM

HADITHI, MWENYE
HOBSON, BRUCE

HADLEY, FRANKLIN[T]
WINTERBOTHAM, RUSS[EL] R.

HADLEY, JOAN
HESS, JOAN E[DMISTON]

HADLEY, JOHN
HEMINGWAY, ERNEST

HADLEY, LEILA
SMITTER, ELIOTT-BURTON

HADLEY, ROBERT
SMITH, GEORGE H[ENRY]

HADRIAN, PHILIP
KETCHUM, PHILIP

HAEDREYI, ABGAD
DRUYANOV, ALTER

HAEFER, HANNA
CONDON, MADELINE B.

HAEL, KURT
LIPP, HERBERT

HAEM, A.
VON MELGUNOFF, ALEXANDER

HAFFNER, J. LILLIWHITE
SPEED, FREDERICK MAURICE

HAGAN, PATRICIA
HOWELL, PATRICIA HAGAN

HAGAR, GEORGE
DANFORTH, ETHEL M.
MARIA DEL REY, SISTER

HAGAR, JUDITH
POLLEY, JUDITH ANNA

HAGEL, JAN
ORTHOFER, PETER

HAGEN, BRETT
HUNTER, WILLIAM R.

HAGEN, C.J.
GIBSON, WALTER B.

HAGEN, CHRISTOPHER
STAMMEL, HEINZ-JOSEF

HAGEN, EVELYN
OLWITZ-TITZE, EVELYN

HAGEN, FRITZ
REINHARD, WILHELM PETER

HAGEN, LENI
KALZ, ELFRIEDE

HAGEN, LINDA
DUBREUIL, ELIZABETH L.

HAGEN, LORINDA
DUBREUIL, ELIZABETH L.

HAGEN, ROLF
KROEGER, WILLY

HAGEN, SABINE
DARNSTADT, HELGE

HAGENAU, GERDA
LEBER, GERDA

HAGERSTRAND, [S] TORSTEN
HAEGERSTRAND, [S] TORSTEN

HAGG, TOMAS
HAEGG, TOMAS

HAGGARD, PAUL
LONGSTREET, [H] STEPHEN

HAGGARD, WILLIAM
CLAYTON, RICHARD HENRY M.

HAGGERTY, P.E.
HAGGERTY, PATRICK EUGENE

HAGLER, SKEETER
HAGLER, ERWIN HARRISON

HAGON, PRISCILLA
ALLAN, MABEL ESTHER

HAGY, RUTH GERI
BROD, RUTH HAGY

HAHN, F.E.
HAHN, FRIEDRICH ERNEST

HAHN, FRED E.
HAHN, FRIEDRICH ERNEST

HAHN, FRED ERNEST
HAHN, FRIEDRICH ERNEST

HAHN, GLORIA
YOUNG, KIM RON

HAHN, STEVE
ROBINETT, STEPHEN [A]

HAHON, JAMES
SWIFT, PATRICK

HAIG, FENIL
FORD, FORD MADOX

HAIGAZ, ARAM
CHEKENIAN, ARAM HAIGAZ

HAIGH, RICHARD
JAMES, LAURENCE

HAIGHT, JAMES T.
ROSKOLENKO, HARRY
THWAITE, JEANNE

HAIGS, NORMA
SCHIER, NORMA

HAILE, H.G.
HAILE, HARRY GERALD

HAILEY, GAIL E.
ARNOLD, GAIL E.H.

HAILEY, J.P.
HALL, PARNELL

HAILEY, JOHANNA
HOWL, MARCIA Y.H.
JARVIS, SHARON [SYLVIA]

HAILSHAM OF ST. MARYLBONE
HOGG, QUINTIN MCGAREL

HAILSHAM, SECOND VISCOUNT
HOGG, QUINTIN MCGAREL

HAILWOOD, MIKE
HAILWOOD, STANLEY MICHAEL

HAIN, EGON
HAJEK, EGON

HAINDL, MARIELUISE
FLEISSER, MARIELUISE

HAINES, JACKSON
FIRTH, NORMAN WESLEY

HAINES, JOHN
RICHARDSON, GLADWELL G.

HAINES, JOHN S.
RICHARDSON, GLADWELL G.

HAINING, PETER
HARKNETT, TERRY W.

HAINSTOCK
ANDREWS, ELIZABETH

HAIR, P.E.H.
HAIR, PAUL EDWARD HEDLEY

HAKA, ROLF
KUNZE, ROLF

HAKUCHO, MASAMUNE
TADAO, MASAMUNE

HAL, DANE
MACFALL, CHAMBERS H.C.

HALACY, D.S. JR.
HALACY, DANIEL STEPHEN

HALACY, DAN
HALACY, DANIEL STEPHEN

HALAM, ANN
JONES, GWYNETH A.

HALCROW, PENELOPE
WALLACE, PENELOPE

HALDANE, R.A.
HALDANE, ROBERT ALYMER

HALDEMAN, H.R.
HALDEMAN, HARRY ROBBINS

HALDEMAN, JOE
HALDEMAN, JOSEPH WILLIAM

HALDEMAN-JULIUS, EMANUEL
JULIUS, EMANUEL

HALE, ALLISON
BLACKLEDGE, ETHEL H.

HALE, ANTOINETTE
STOCKENBERG, ANTOINETTE

HALE, ARLENE
ADAMS, TRACY

HALE, BOB
HALE, ROBERT DAVID

HALE, CHARLOTTE
ALLEN, CHARLOTTE HALE

HALE, CHRISTOPHER
STEVENS, FRANCES M.R.

HALE, CLEMENT
STEFFENS, ARTHUR JOSEPH

HALE, DOROTHEA
WELLER, DOROTHY

HALE, EUGENIA
WOOLSEY, MARY HALE

HALE, FORBES
CHALMERS, ISAAC

HALE, FRANCESCA
HALPERN, FRANCES JOY

HALE, GARTH
CUNNINGHAM, ALBERT B.

HALE, GLEN
WALKER, ROBERT WAYNE

HALE, HELEN
MULCAHY, LUCILLE BURNETT

HALE, HOPE
DAVIS, HOPE HALE

HALE, INNIS
HOOK, SAMUEL CLARKE

HALE, JADE
HYATT, BETTY HALE

HALE, JENNIFER
SMITH, FRANK ELLIS
TORREY [BUDLONG], WARE

HALE, KATHERINE
GARVIN, AMELIA WARNOCK

HALE, LAURA
HELLER, LORENZ

HALE, MADELINE
FELDMAN, GILDA
RUGG, LESLIE

HALE, MARGARET
HIGGONET, MARGARET R.

HALE, MARTIN
ROCHESTER, GEO[RGE] E.

HALE, MARY
ADAMS, TRACY
WOOLSEY, MARY HALE

HALE, MICHAEL
BULLOCK, MICHAEL HALE

HALE, PHILIP
EASTWOOD, CHARLES CYRIL

HALE, RANDOLPH
PERKINS, KENNETH

HALE, RAY
BREUCKER, OSCAR HERBERT

HALE, ROBERT
VARDEMAN, ROBERT E.

HALE, RUSSELL
BOGART, WILLIAM G.

HALE, WANDA
COUTARD, WANDA L. HALE

HALENZA, ADA
KOCH, MAGDA

HALER, W. KEITH
HALER, WILLIAM KEITH

HALES, ANN
HALES-TOOKE, ANN M.M.

HALES, JOYCE
COOMBS, JOYCE

HALES, NORMAN
YOUNG, VERNON

HALES, SMILER
HALES, ALFRED GREENWOOD

HALEVI, Z'EV BEN SHIMON
KENTON, WARREN

HALEY, ANDREA
PASCOE, IRENE M.

HALEY, CLAUD
TUBB, E.C.

HALEY, CLAUDE
FISH, LEONARD G.

HALEY, JACK JR.
HALEY, JOHN J. JR.

HALEY, JOCELYN
MACLEAN, JILL

HALEY, WENDY
GARRETT, WENDY

HALFENSTEIN, ERNEST
OAKES, ELIZABETH

HALFORD, LAURA
SPARROW, LAURA

HALIBURTON, HUGH
ROBERTSON, JAMES LOGIE

HALIBUT, EDWARD
WILSON, RICHARD

HALIDOM, M.Y.
HERON-ALLEN, EDWARD

HALIFAX, CLIFFORD
BEAUMONT, EDGAR

HALIFAX, [DF.] CLIFFORD
BEAUMONT, EDGAR

HALIVNI, DAVID
WEISS, DAVID

HALIVNI, DAVID WEISS
WEISS, DAVID

HALKET, ROBERTSON
PUNSHON, ERNEST ROBERTSON

HALKIN, SIMON
HALKIN, SHIMON

HALL, ADAM
TREVOR, ELLESTON

HALL, AKE
HALLBACK, SVEN AXEL

HALL, ANN
DUCKERT, MARY

HALL, AYLMER
HALL, NORAH E.L.

HALL, B.
GUNN, JOHN ANGUS L.

HALL, B.K.
MOSSER, ARNE J.

HALL, BORDEN
YATES, RAYMOND F.

HALL, CAMERON
DEL REY, LESTER
HARRISON, HARRY

HALL, CARYL
HANSEN, CARYL [HALL]

HALL, CLAUDIA
FLOREN, LEE

HALL, D.W.
HALL, DESMOND W.

HALL, ELIZA CALVERT
OBENCHAIN, ELIZA CAROLINE

HALL, ELLEN
HOLSTON, BARBARA
POLLACHER, ELLIN RENEE

HALL, ERNST
HASSLER, ERNST

HALL, EVAN
HALLERAN, EUGENE E.

HALL, GORDON LANGELY
SIMMONS, DAWN LANGLEY

HALL, H.W.
HALL, HALBERT WELDON

HALL, HOLWORTHY
PORTER, HAROLD E.

HALL, J. DE P.
MCKELWAY, ST. CLAIR

HALL, JAMES
KUTTNER, HENRY

HALL, JAMES
MOORE, CATHERINE LUCILLE

HALL, JEREMY
KEHL, WOLFGANG

HALL, JESSE
BOESEN, VICTOR

HALL, JOHN
POUND, EZRA LOOMIS

HALL, JOHN RYDER
ROTSLER, WILLIAM

HALL, KATE
MCMULLAN, KATE [HALL]

HALL, KATY
MCMULLAN, KATE HALL

HALL, KENDALL
HEATH, HARRY EUGENE JR.

HALL, LIBBY
HALL, OLIVIA M.

HALL, MARCIA
SELLERS, CONNIE LESLIE

HALL, MARJORY
YEAKLEY, MARJORIE HALL

HALL, MARK W.
HALLOWITZ, MARK W.

HALL, MARTYN T.
MORRIS, DAVID

HALL, O.M.
HALL, OAKLEY M.

HALL, OWEN
DAVIS, JAMES

HALL, PARIS
GELINAS, ROBERT E.

HALL, PATRICK
HALL, FREDERICK

HALL, RICHARD
BICKERS, RICHARD L.T.
HOLTON, WALTER H.

HALL, RUPERT
HOME-GALL, EDWARD REG.

HALL, RYDER JR.
ROTSLER, WILLIAM

HALL, SEA LION
HALL, CHARLES L.

HALL, SISSY
BRANDT, IRMENGARD

HALL, STEFFIE
EVANOVICH, JANET

HALL, STEPHANIE
SMITH, WILLIAM J.

HALL, STUART
TAYLOR, ROBERT

HALL, TONY
HALL, ANTHONY STEWART

HALL, WAGNER
KELLEY, THOMAS P.

HALL, WHYTE
RAYNER, AUGUSTUS ALFRED

HALL, [MIDSHIPMAN] TOM W.
INGRAHAM, PRENTISS

HALL-CLARKE, JAMES
ROWLAND-ENTWISTLE, A.T.

HALLA, CHRIS
HALLA, ROBERT CHRISTIAN

HALLAM
HUGHES, WILLIAM JESSE

HALLAM, JAY
RICE, JOAN

HALLARD, PETER
CATHERALL, ARTHUR

HALLARD, RUTH
TETZNER, RUTH

HALLAS, RICHARD
KNIGHT, ERIC MOWBRAY

HALLER, BILL
BECHKO, PEGGY ANNE

HALLER, ERNST
RATHMANN, OSWALD

HALLER, FRANK
ERNSTING, WALTER

HALLER, H.
ASPERN-BUCHMEIER, ELISAB.

HALLER, M.
DEINET, MARGARETHE

HALLER, MICHAEL
BARTHEL, MANFRED

HALLERAN, E.E.
HALLERAN, EUGENE E.

HALLEY, LAURENCE
O'KEEFE, LAURENCE

HALLIDAY, BEN
MANNING, WILLIAM HENRY

HALLIDAY, BRETT
ARTHUR, ROBERT
AVALLONE, MICHAEL
BLYTH, HAL
BRANDNER, GARY
BREESE, EDWARD Y.
BREWER, GIL
DEMING, RICHARD
DRESSER, DAVIS
DERVEER, MAX VAN
DEVEER, MAX VAN
GERMANO, PETER B.
HARTWICK, RICHARD
JOHNSON, WALTER RYERSON
KASSON, HELEN
LONG, FRANK BELKNAP
LYNDS, DENNIS
MATTHEWS, CLAYTON [H]
MAZROFF, DAVID
MERWIN, SAMUEL K. JR.
PRONZINI, WILLIAM JOHN
REASONER, JAMES M.
REASONER, JAMES & LIVIA
SWEET, CHARLES
TERRALL, ROBERT
WALLMANN, JEFFREY M.
WARREN, GEORGE

HALLIDAY, DOROTHY
DUNNETT, DOROTHY

HALLIDAY, ENA
BAUMGARTEN, SYLVIA

HALLIDAY, GUNN
DUNN, DES R.

HALLIDAY, JAMES
GRAY, SIMON [J.H.]
SYMINGTON, DAVID

HALLIDAY, MICHAEL
CREASEY, JOHN

HALLIDAY, SHIRLEY
BOBIN, DONALD E.M.

HALLOCK, G.R.F.
HALLOCK, GERARD BENJAMIN

HALLORAN, MARK
GUBERN RIBALTA, JORGE

HALLOW, GUS
HOPPE, ULRICH

HALLOWAY, JANE
DONAHEY, MARY DICKERSON

HALLOWELL, FLORENCE B.
GETCHELL, FLORENCE B.

HALLOWELL, TOMMY
HILL, THOMAS

HALLSTROM, PER [A.L.]
HALLSTROEM, PER [A.L.]

HALLSTROM, TOR
KERFVE, AXEL

HALLUS, TAK
ROBINETTE, STEPHEN [A]

HALMAR, AUGUSTO D'
THOMPSON, AUGUSTO GOEMINE

HALPER
HALPERN, LEIVICK

HALPERN, L.
HALPERN, LEIVICK

HALSBURY, EARL
GIFFARD, HARDINGE, GOULB.

HALSEY, STEWART N.
GRUBER, FRANK

HALSHAM, JOHN
SCOTT, G. FORRESTER

HALSTEAD, ADA L.
NEWHALL, MRS. LAURA E.

HALSTEAD, E. SINCLAIR
BROOKS, EDWY SEARLES

HALSTEAD, S.B.
BROOKS, EDWY SEARLES

HALSTOCK, MAX
CAULFIELD, MALACHY F.

HALSTON, CAROLE
HALL, CAROLYN

HALWARD, LESLIE
FIRTH, NORMAN WESLEY

HAMBERG, STEPHAN
KUGLER, DIETMAR

HAMBERG, STEVE
KUGLER, DIETMAR

HAMBLEDON, PHYLLIS
MACVEAN, PHYLLIS

HAMBLETONIAN
FAIRFAX-BLAKEBOROUGH, J.F

HAMEL DOBKIN, KATHLEEN
HAMEL PEIFER, KATHLEEN

HAMER, ISABEL
LEINS, ISABEL

HAMIL, TOM
HAMIL, THOMAS ARTHUR

HAMILL, ETHEL
WEBB, JEAN FRANCIS III

HAMILTON, ADAM
GRANBECK, MARILYN
MOORE, ARTHUR

HAMILTON, ALICE
CROMIE, ALICE HAMILTON

HAMILTON, ALISTAIR
BEATTIE, TASMAN

HAMILTON, AUDREY
POWELL, JAN HAMILTON

HAMILTON, BETSY
MOORE, IDORA [M]

HAMILTON, BUZZ
HEMMING, ROY

HAMILTON, CELESTE
POWELL, JAN HAMILTON

HAMILTON, CICELY
HAMILL, CICELY MARY H.

HAMILTON, CLARE
LAWLESS, BETTYCLARE H.

HAMILTON, CLIVE
LEWIS, CLIVE STAPLES

HAMILTON, DAVE
TROYER, BYRON L.

HAMILTON, ERNEST
GROSSMAN, JOSEPH. JUDITH

HAMILTON, FRANKLIN
SILVERBERG, ROBERT

HAMILTON, GAIL
CORCORAN, BARBARA
DODGE, MARY ABIGAIL

HAMILTON, GEORGE
TEED, GEORGE HAMILTON

HAMILTON, HERVEY
ROBINS, DENISE

HAMILTON, JACK
BRANNON, WILLIAM T.

HAMILTON, JESSICA
GREENHALL, KEN[NETH R.]

HAMILTON, JOHN
HAYDEN, STERLING

HAMILTON, JUDITH
LAWRENCE, DULCIE

HAMILTON, JULIA
WATSON, JULIA

HAMILTON, KATRINA
COCKRELL, BARBARA

HAMILTON, KAY
DE LEEUW, CATEAU W.

HAMILTON, KIRK
HETHERINGTON, KEITH JAMES

HAMILTON, LUCY
RHYNNE, JULIA A.

HAMILTON, MAX
HAMILL, CICELY MARY H.

HAMILTON, MICHAEL
CHETHAM-STRODE, WARREN
GLASBY, JOHN S.

HAMILTON, MOLLIE
KAYE, MARY MARGARET

HAMILTON, MURRAY
GRAYDON, ROBERT MURRAY
TEED, GEORGE HEBER

HAMILTON, NAN
BALL, NANONI PATRICIA M.H

HAMILTON, PAUL
DENNIS-JONES, HAROLD

HAMILTON, PRISCILLA
GELLIS, ROBERTA L.J.

HAMILTON, RALPH
STRATEMEYER, EDWARD

HAMILTON, ROBERT W.
STRATEMEYER, EDWARD

HAMILTON, ROGER
ROGERSON, JAMES

HAMILTON, RUFUS
GILMORE, RUFUS HAMILTON

HAMILTON, VICTORIA
DAVIS, PATRICIA

HAMILTON, VIRGINIA
ADOFF, VIRGINIA HAMILTON

HAMILTON, W.W.
HOFFMANN, OSKAR

HAMILTON, WADE
FLOREN, LEE

HAMILTON, WILLIAM
CANAWAY, W.H.

HAMILTON, WORLD SAVER
HAMILTON, EDMOND

HAMILTON-SYOCKFORD, JOAN
STOCKFORD, LELA E.

HAMILTON-WILKES, MONTY
HAMILTON-WILKES, EDWIN

HAMLET, OVA
LUPOFF, RICHARD A.

HAMLIN, DALLAS
SCHULZE, DALLAS

HAMLIN, KEN
ARD, WILLIAM [THOMAS]

HAMLIN, ROSCOE
OFFUTT, ANDREW J.

HAMLINE, DAVID
TAYLOR, KATHERINE

HAMM, T.D.
EVANS, THELMA D. HAMM

HAMM, THELMA D.
EVANS, THELMA D. HAMM

HAMMAIS, DR. PIERRE DE &
DEBILL, WALTER C. JR.

HAMMER, FRED
POETSCHKUS, HORST

HAMMER, JACOB
OPPENHEIMER, JOEL LESTER

HAMMER, ROBBY
KALMUCZAK, ROLF

HAMMERSLEY, CECIL
CROCOMBE, LEONARD CECIL

HAMMERTON, GRENVILLE
SHAW, FRANK H.

HAMMETT, DAVID
HAMMETT, DASHIELL

HAMMETT, LAFAYETTE
DOUGLAS, LALETTE

HAMMETT, MARY JANE
HAMMETT, DASHIELL

HAMMON, JEFF
GRASMUCK, JURGEN

HAMMOND, ANN
BAIR, ANN

HAMMOND, BRAD
KING, ALBERT

HAMMOND, CLARKE
MERWIN, SAMUEL K. JR.

HAMMOND, ELEANOR
CHADWICK, PAUL

HAMMOND, FRANCES
CROAL, FRANCES

HAMMOND, GIL
ERICHSEN, UWE

HAMMOND, JANE
POLAND, DOROTHY ELIZABETH

HAMMOND, KAY
DAVIES, KAY HAMMOND

HAMMOND, KEITH
BLOCH, ROBERT [A]
KUTTNER, HENRY
MOORE, CATHERINE LUCILLE

HAMMOND, MARY ANN
SLOJKOWSKI, MARY ANN

HAMMOND, PAUL
BOUNDS, SYDNEY J.

HAMMOND, RALPH
INNES, [RALPH] HAMMOND

HAMP, PIERRE
BOURILLON, PIERRE

HAMPSHIRE, JOYCE G.
GREGORIAN, JOYCE BALLOU

HAMPSON, JOHN
SIMPSON, JOHN HAMPSON

HAMPSON, ZENA
SHUMSKY, ZENA FELDMAN

HAMPTON, ANGELINE A.
KELLY, ANGELINE AGNES

HAMPTON, DAVID
FAIRCLOUGH, CHRIS

HAMPTON, JIM
HAMPTON, JOHN LEWIS

HAMPTON, JOHN
MADSEN, BORGE

HAMPTON, MARK
CHARLES, GEORGE
NORWOOD, VICTOR [G.C.]

HAMPTON, WILD
LLOP SELLARES, JUAN

HAMSON, C.J.
HAMSON, CHARLES JOHN

HAMSUN, KNUT
PEDERSON, KNUT

HAMSUND, KNUT PEDERSON
PEDERSON, KNUT

HAN SUYIN
COMBER, ELIZABETH

HANBURY, VICTOR
LOSEY, JOSEPH WALTON

HANCOCK, CAROL HELEN B.
HANCOCK, MORGAN

HANCOCK, FRANCES DEAN
JUDSON, JEANNE

HANCOCK, ROBERT
HOWELL, DOUGLAS NAYLER

HANCOCK, W.K.
HANCOCK, WILLIAM KEITH

HAND, JOHN
PIERSON, JOHN H.G.

HAND, PAT
COSTAIN, THOMAS

HANING, BOB
HANING, JAMES ROBERT

HANINGWAY, RALPH
HAHN, ROLF

HANKEY, ROSALIE A.
WAX, ROSALIE AMELIA H.

HANKINS, CLABE
MCDONALD, ERWIN LAWRENCE

HANKS, LINDSEY
CHESNUTT, LINDA
PIERCE, GEORGIA

HANLEY, ELIZABETH
DUBREUIL, ELIZABETH L.

HANLEY, HUGH
PRICE, EMERSON FIELD

HANLEY, MIKE
HANLEY, MICHAEL F. IV

HANLON, JOHN
KEMP, EARL
MITCHELL, JOHN HANLON

HANLON, JON
KEMP, EARL

HANMER, DAVINA
OURTNEY, NICHOLAS PIERS

HANN, DONALD
MACAULEY, KEN

HANNA, BILL
HANNA, WILLIAM

HANNA, EVELYN
DYNE, MICHAEL
FRANK, ETHEL

HANNA, PAUL
CAVE, HUGH B[ARNETT]

HANNAFORD, JUSTIN
FITZ-GERALD, S.J.A.

HANNAWAY, PATTI
HANNAWAY, PATRICIA H.

HANNIBAL
ALEXANDER, STANLEY WALTER

HANNIGAN, FRANCIS J.
SHELTON, RICHARD BARKER

HANNON, EZRA
HUNTER, EVAN

HANOS, JIM
HANOS, DMITRI [JAMES]

HANOUM, LEILA
PIAZZI, ADRIENNE

HANOVER, TERRI
HUFF, TANYA SUE

HANSA
HOEPNER, KAPT. A.D.

HANSBERRY, CARLENE
HARDY, CARLENE

HANSELL, ANTONINA
LOOKER, ANTONINA [H]

HANSEN, CAROL
FENICHEL, CAROL HANSEN

HANSEN, CECIL
HUFFAKER, CLAIR

HANSEN, CECIL DEAN
HUFFAKER, CLAIR

HANSEN, JAMES
HANOS, DMITRI [JAMES]

HANSEN, K.U.
BULTMANN KLAUS
KEHL, WOLFGANG

HANSEN, L. TAYLOR
HANSEN, LOUIS INGVALD

HANSEN, MICHAELA
KLEMME, CHRIS

HANSEN, PETER
MOLTKE-HANSEN, DAVID
PESCHKE, HANS

HANSEN, STEPHAN
GEISLER, HANS

HANSEN, VERN
HANSON, VICTOR JOSEPH

HANSHEW, HAZEL PHILLIPS
HANSHEW, MARY E.
HANSHEW, THOMAS W.

HANSHEW, T.W.
HANSHEW, THOMAS W.

HANSI
HIRSCHMANN, MARIA ANNE
WALTZ, JEAN JACQUES

HANSLEY, J.J.
GLASBY, JOHN S.

HANSON, FRANK
BARNES, MICHAEL [L.G.]
GORELL, LETHBRIDGE

HANSON, V. JOSEPH
HANSON, VICTOR JOSEPH

HANSON, V.J.
HANSON, VICTOR JOSEPH

HANSON, VIC J.
HANSON, VICTOR JOSEPH

HANSON, W.J.
HANSON, VICTOR JOSEPH

HANSRAJ BHATIA
OAK, PURUSHATTAM NAGESH

HANSSON, HANS
GRANATH, PER JOHAN W.

HAPI
JACK, ALEX

HARA, MONIQUE
HARRAH, MADGE

HARAH, PONJAY
GIBSON, WALTER B.

HARALD, ERIC
BOESEN, VICTOR

HARALD, LEO
GERSTMAYER, HERMANN

HARALDSSON, HARALD
HANSELL, PER TORE

HARAY, STUART BLUE
HARAY, KEITH

HARB, ALOY
HARBECK, ALOIS

HARBIN, JOEL
AMBROSE, WILLIAM

HARBIN, ROBERT
WILLIAMS, NED

HARBINSON, ROBERT
BRYANS, ROBERT HARBINSON

HARBORD, DAVIS J.
KOPP, WILHELM

HARBURG, YIP
HARBURG, EDGAR YIPSEL

HARCOURT, PALMA
TROTMAN, PALMA HARCOURT

HARCRAFT, ALICE B.
HARDING, ALLISON V.

HARD PAN
BONNER, GERALDINE

HARD, BORJE
NILSSON, SVEN-SRIK

HARD, FRANCIS
WRIGHT, FARNSWORTH

HARD, HEDWIG
REINHARD, HANS GEORG

HARD, RUDOLF
DAUMANN, RUDOLF HEINRICH

HARD, T.W.
HARD, EDWARD W. JR.

HARDCASTLE, CATHERINE
THATCHER, PHYLLIS

HARDECK, MARIANNE
ECKHARDT, ROSEMARIE

HARDEN, FRED
SASSE, GERHARD

HARDEN, HARALD
GORZ, HEINZ

HARDER, BEN
PIETRUSCHINSKI, HORST

HARDFORTH, CARNIE
BECKER, MAX O.

HARDIE, DAVID
MCLEAN, JOHN DAVID RUARI

HARDIN, CLEMENT
NEWTON, DWIGHT BENNETT

HARDIN, DAVE
HOLMES, L[LEWELLYN] P.

HARDIN, J.D.
BARRETT, NEAL JR.
RIEFE, ALAN
SHELDON, WALTER J.

HARDIN, LUKE
PULLAN, RU

HARDIN, MITCH
GERRITY, DAVID JAMES

HARDIN, PETER
VACZEK, LOUIS CHARLES

HARDIN, TOM
BAUER, ERWIN A.

HARDING, BERTITA
RADETZBY VON RADETZ, CTS.

HARDING, BRETT
STORY, JACK TREVOR

HARDING, CARL B.
BARKER, ELVER A.

HARDING, COLE
KRAUZER, STEVEN M.

HARDING, GEORGE
RAUBENHEIMER, GEORGE HARD

HARDING, KENNETH
LITTLE, PAUL HUGO

HARDING, LEE
HARDING, LEO

HARDING, MARIA
GOUDISS, MARIA A. D'ELIA

HARDING, MATT
FLOREN, LEE

HARDING, MATTHEW WHITMAN
FLOREN, LEE

HARDING, MICHAEL
HARMENING, WILHELM CHR.

HARDING, PAUL
DOHERTY, P.C.

HARDING, PETER
BURGESS, MICHAEL ROY

HARDING, RICHARD
BOULTON, A. HARDING
TINE, ROBERT

HARDING, STEVE C.
NAGEL, HERBERT CHRISTIAN

HARDING, TEX
PESCOLLER, HEINRICH

HARDING, TODD
REYNOLDS, DALLAS MCCORD

HARDING, WES
KEEVILL, HENRY J.

HARDINGE, E.M.
GOING, ELLEN MAUDE

HARDINGE, REX
HARDINGE, CHARLES WREXE

HARDNER, CARL
MEYN, NIELS

HARDNER, GUSTAV
MEYN, NIELS

HARDON, RONNY
BREUCKER, OSCAR HERBERT

HARDT, HANS
ALBRECHT, PAUL

HARDT, HELMUT
REINHARD, HANS GEORG

HARDT, MICHAEL
BREUER, GUSTAV J.
DAVENPORT, GWEN LEYS

HARDWICK, ADAM
CONNOR, JOHN ANTHONY

HARDWICK, HOMER
ROGERS, PAUL [PATRICK]

HARDWICK, J.M.D.
HARDWICK, [J] MICHAEL [D]

HARDWICK, SYLVIA
DOHERTY, IVY RUBY D.

HARDY, A.S.
STEFFENS, ARTHUR JOSEPH

HARDY, ADAM
BULMER, [HENRY] KENNETH
HARKNETT, TERRY W.

HARDY, ALICE DALE
STRATEMEYER, EDWARD

HARDY, ANTOINETTE
STOCKENBERG, ANTOINETTE

HARDY, ARTHUR S.
STEFFENS, ARTHUR JOSEPH

HARDY, ARTHUR SHERBURNE
STEFFENS, ARTHUR JOSEPH

HARDY, BOBBIE
HARDY, MARJORIE

HARDY, DOUGLAS
ANDREWS, [C] ROBERT D.

HARDY, JASON
OXLEY, WILLIAM

HARDY, LAURA
HOLLAND, SHEILA C.

HARDY, MARK
MAY, HERBERT RICHARD [D]

HARDY, RUSS
SNOW, CHARLES H[ORACE]

HARDY, STUART
SCHISGALL, OSCAR

HARDY, W.G.
HARDY, WILLIAM GEORGE

HARE, BILL
HARE, WILLIAM MOORMAN

HARE, BURTON
LLIRO OLIVE, JOSE MARIA

HARE, CYRIL
CLARK, ALFRED A.G.

HARE, MARTIN
GIRLING, ZOE

HARE, ROBERT
HUTCHINSON, ROBERT HARE

HARE, THOMAS BLENMAN
HARE, THOMAS WILLIAM

HARENG, ALEXIS
LINDEMANN, KELVIN

HARFORD, HENRY
HUDSON, WILLIAM HENRY

HARGIS, BARBARA
COCKRELL, BARBARA

HARGIS, PAULINE
DILLARD, POLLY HARGIS

HARGIS, POLLY
DILLARD, POLLY HARGIS

HARGRAVE, LEONIE
DISCH, THOMAS M.
VIDAL, [E] GORE LUTHER

HARGRAVES, THOMAS
AINSWORTH, THOMAS HARG.

HARGROVE, JIM
HARGROVE, JAMES

HARGROVE, MARION
SCHRODER, RAINER M.

HARI KARI
CARR, ELIAS F.

HARING, BERNHARD
HAERING, BERNHARD

HARK, MILDRED
MCQUEEN, MILDRED HARK

HARKAWAY, HAL
STRATEMEYER, EDWARD

HARKER, JONATHAN
LANSDALE, JOE R.
PRONZINI, WILLIAM JOHN
WALLMANN, JEFFREY M.

HARKINS, STERLING
PYLES, DANNY

HARKNESS, JACK
HARKNESS, JOHN LEIGH

HARKON, FRANZ
FEARN, JOHN RUSSELL

HARLAN
SHAW, WILLIAM HARLAN

HARLAN, GLEN
CEBULASH, MEL

HARLAN, ROSS
KING, ALBERT

HARLAND, MARION
TERHUNE, MARY VIRGINIA

HARLAND, PAUL
SMIT, JOHN-PAUL

HARLE, ELIZABETH
ROBERTS, IRENE W.

HARLEQUIN
REED, ALEXANDER WYCLIF

HARLEY, BRUCE
BOGART, WILLIAM G.
DONOVAN, LAURENCE

HARLEY, JOHN
MARSH, JOHN

HARLING, THOMAS
EASTHAM, THOMAS

HARLOW, JOHN
SNOW, CHARLES H[ORACE]

HARLOW, JUSTIN
BENNETT, LAURA

HARLOW, SHARON
GILLENWATER, SHARON

HARLOWE, JUSTIN
HARVEY, JEAN
MACKENZIE, TINA

HARLOWE, JUSTINE
BENNETT, LAURA

HARMAN, ALEC
HARMAN, RICHARD ALEXANDER

HARMAN, CLAIRE
SCHMIDT, CLAIRE HARMAN

HARMAN, JANE
HARKNETT, TERRY W.

HARMAN, R. ALEC
HARMAN, RICHARD ALEXANDER

HARMISTON, OLIVIA
WEBER, NANCY

HARMODIUS
JACKSON, C. PHILIP CASTLE

HARMON, ANNE
DI FRANCESCO, PHYLLIS
HERRMANN, NIRA

HARMON, DANELLE
COLSON, DANELLE F.

HARMON, GIL
KING, ALBERT

HARMON, H.H.
WILLIAMS, ROBERT MOORE

HARMON, JIM
HARMON, JAMES JUDSON

HARMS, CHRISTEL
HARMENING, WILHELM CHR.

HARMS, VALERIE
SHEEHAN, VALERIE HARMS

HARMSEN, C.W.
HARMENING, WILHELM CHR.

HARMSTON, DONALD
MATHESON, DONALD H.

HAROLD, CLIVE
HUTSON, SHAUN

HAROLDSON, WILLIAM
KING, HAROLD

HARPER, BILL
HARPER, WILLIAM ARTHUR

HARPER, CAROLINE
KORING-SCHETTGEN, HANNEL.

HARPER, CLYDE
HARPER, J. CLYDE

HARPER, DANIEL
BROSSARD, CHANDLER

HARPER, DAVID
CORLEY, EDWIN RAYMOND

HARPER, EDITH
HARRIS, WILLIAM

HARPER, ELAINE
HALLIN, EMILY WATSON

HARPER, F.E.W.
HARPER, FRANCES ELLEN W.

HARPER, KATE
HARPER, KATHERINE ERNA

HARPER, MADELINE
HARPER, ELIZABETH SHANNON
PORTER, MADELINE

HARPER, MARK
SHAW, CAPT. JOSEPH T.

HARPER, MARY WOOD
DIXON, JEANE

HARPER, MRS. F.E.W.
HARPER, FRANCES ELLEN W.

HARPER, OLIVE
D'APERY, HELEN B.G.

HARPER, TOM
HARPUR, THOMAS WILLIAM
RICHARTZ, HELMUTH

HARRAGAN, STEVE
CARSON, BART
MACONACHIE, WILLIAM

HARRALD, JON A.
SCHECHTER, HAROLD
SEMEIKS, GORMELY

HARRE, ROM
HARRE, HORACE ROMANO

HARRELL, ANNE
NEGGERS, CARLA A[MALIA]

HARRELL, SARA [J] GORDON
ANKS, SARA [J.G.H.]

HARRIETT
GINNINGS, HARRIETT W.

HARRIFORD, DAPHNE
HARRIS, MARION ROSE

HARRIGAN, CLARK
BREMER, SVEND AAGE

HARRIMAN, PRESTON
PRESTON, HARRY

HARRINGTON, ELIZABETH
FARMER, MINNIE ELIZABETH

HARRINGTON, EMMA
BROWN, VIRGINIA
HARRISON, MELINDA JANE

HARRINGTON, K.
BEAN, KEITH FENWICK

HARRINGTON, KAY
BEAN, KEITH FENWICK

HARRINGTON, LEE
BARKER, REGINALD C.

HARRINGTON, LYN
HARRINGTON, EVELYN DAVIS

HARRINGTON, RICK
KRUGER, BRUNO

HARRIOTT, TED
HARRIOTT, EDWIN THOMAS

HARRIS, AMY
BLOCK, LAWRENCE

HARRIS, ANDREA
CONNOLLY, VIVIAN
WALKER, IRMA [R.R.]

HARRIS, ANDREW
POOLE, FREDERICK KING

HARRIS, BILL
HARRIS, WILLIAM F.

HARRIS, BRIAN
KING, HAROLD

HARRIS, CATHERINE
AINSWORTH, CATHERINE H.

HARRIS, CHRISTOPHER
FRY, CHRISTOPHER

HARRIS, COLVER
COLVER, ANNE

HARRIS, DON
GALLARDOS MUNOZ, JUAN

HARRIS, FRANK
HARRIS, JAMES THOMAS
TROCCHI, ALEXANDER

HARRIS, HYDE
HARRIS, TIMOTHY [HYDE]

HARRIS, J.L.
MILSTEAD, JESSICA L[EE]

HARRIS, JED
HOROWITZ, JACOB

HARRIS, JESSICA L.
MILSTEAD, JESSICA L[EE]

HARRIS, JOANNA
BURGESS, JUSTINE

HARRIS, JOHN BENYON
HARRIS, JOHN WYNDHAM P.L.

HARRIS, JOHNSON
HARRIS, JOHN WYNDHAM P.L

HARRIS, KATHLEEN [M]
HUMPHRIES, ADELAIDE

HARRIS, LANE
HARRIS, MONICA

HARRIS, LARRY M.
HARRIS, LAURENCE MARK

HARRIS, LAVINA
JOHNSTON, NORMA

HARRIS, LAVINIA
ST. JOHN, NICOLE

HARRIS, LEE
LEAHY, SYRELL ROGOVIN

HARRIS, MACDONALD
HEINEY, DONALD WILLIAM

HARRIS, MARILYN
SPRINGER, MARILYN HARRIS

HARRIS, MARK
FINKLESTEIN, MARK
RUHEN, CARL

HARRIS, MELINDA
SNODGRASS, MELINDA

HARRIS, MRS. F.C.
HARRIS, CLARE WINGER

HARRIS, REP
HARRIS, ROBERT EUGENE P.

HARRIS, RINGO
OPPERMANN, HERMANN

HARRIS, ROBIN
SHINE, DEBORAH

HARRIS, ROGER
MOORCOCK, MICHAEL
WILSON, ROGER HARRIS

HARRIS, RONALD M.
HAHN, RONALD M.

HARRIS, SANDRA
YOUNG, SANDRA

HARRIS, SARA LEE
STADLEMAN, SARA LEE

HARRIS, STUART
FANTONI, BARRY [ERNEST]

HARRIS, THISTLE Y.
STEAD, THISTLE Y.

HARRIS, TOM
HARRIS, THOMAS CUNNINGHAM
ORNULF, HILDING KONSTANT.

HARRIS, VIVIAN
TICHENOR, VIVIAN H.

HARRIS, WILL
HARY, WILFRID A.

HARRISON, ALLIE
HARRIS, ALLISON

HARRISON, BILL
HARRISON, WILLIAM C.

HARRISON, BRUCE
PANGBORN, EDGAR

HARRISON, CHIP
BLOCK, LAWRENCE

HARRISON, CLAIRE
HARRISON, ELLEN

HARRISON, EDWIN
BALLARD, ERIC ALLEN

HARRISON, ELIZABETH
CAVANNA, ELIZABETH ALLEN

HARRISON, FRED
PAINE, LAURAN BOSWORTH

HARRISON, G.D.
HONEY, PHILIP

HARRISON, HARRY
DEMPSEY, HENRY MAXWELL
ENTON, HARRY

HARRISON, J.L.
BRAUNS-LEUTZ, ILSE

HARRISON, JENNIE
TOMKINS, JANE H.

HARRISON, JIM
HARRISON, JAMES THOM,AS

HARRISON, LEWIS
WATSON, LEWIS H.

HARRISON, MARY
RASH, NANCY

HARRISON, MICHAEL
ROHAN, MAURICE DESMOND

HARRISON, REX
HARRISON, REGINALD CAREY

HARRISON, TED
HARRISON, EDWARD HARDY

HARRISON, WHIT
WHITTINGTON, HARRY

HARRISON, WILLIAM
HARRISON, CHESTER WILLIAM

HARROD, FRANCES
FORBES-ROBERTSON, FRANCES

HARROWE, FIONA
HURD, FLORENCE S.

HARRY, M.
LEWIS, SASHA GREGORY

HARSCH, HILYA
JELLY, GEORGE OLIVER

HARSEN, SLEY
ELLISON, HARLAN
SLESAR, HENRY

HART, ALISON
CULBY, JILL ALISON HART
RUHEN, CARL
WILKES-HUNTER, RICHARD

HART, BARRY
BLOOM, HERMAN IRVING

HART, CAROLINE
GARVICE, CHARLES

HART, CAROLYN [G]
GARVICE, CHARLES

HART, CARRIE
JOYNER, CAROLYN

HART, CATHERINE
TIDD, DIANE

HART, DEREK
KLEIN, GERHARD

HART, ELLEN
BOEHNHARDT, PATRICIA

HART, ELLIS
ELLISON, HARLAN

HART, FRANCIS
PAINE, LAURAN BOSWORTH

HART, GERALD
IRVING, THOMAS J.

HART, H.W.
GECK, HEINZ

HART, HANS
MUNCH, HELLMUT-HUBERTUS

HART, HEINZ-BRUNO
DECKER, HEINZ-BRUNO

HART, HENRY
HARTMANN, HELMUT HENRY

HART, JEANNE
SCHRAGER, JEANNE HART

HART, JOHNNY
HART, JOHN LEWIS

HART, JON
HARVEY, JOHN [BARTON]

HART, KATE
KRAMER, ROBERTA

HART, LEONARD
BARNARD, ALFRED J.

HART, MARTIN
'T HART, MAARTEN

HART, MATTHEW S.
REASONER, JAMES M.

HART, MAX
URQUHARDT, MACGREGOR

HART, NICOLE
RUE, ROSINA F.

HART, PETER
HONEY, PHILIP

HART, R.W.
FERNEYHOUGH, ROGER EDMUND

HART, RAYMOND
DELFS, RAINER

HART, SHIRLEY
LARSON, SHIRLEY R.C.

HART, SUE
HART, SUSANNE

HART, SUSANNAH
GRAND, NATALIE

HART, SUSANNE
HARTHOORN, SUSANNE [W]

HART-DAVIS, PHYLLIDA
BARSTOW, PHYLLIDA

HARTE, BRYCE
NAMES, LARRY

HARTE, MARJORIE
MCEVOY, MARJORIE HARTE

HARTE, OLIVER
STAGG, JOHN REGINALD

HARTE, SAMANTHA
HOUSEBY, SANDRA LYNN

HARTEX, PIERRE
DAVIAULT, PIERRE

HARTFORD, VIN
DONSON, CYRIL

HARTLEY, CHRISTINE
THOMSON, CHRISTINE C.

HARTLEY, JAMES BUELL
LEITHEAD, J. EDWARDS

HARTLEY, L.P.
HARTLEY, LESLIE POLES

HARTLEY, MALCOLM
FEARN, JOHN RUSSELL

HARTLEY, TRAVIS
PAINE, LAURAN BOSWORTH

HARTLING, PETER
HAERTLING, PETER

HARTMAN, DANE
HORVITZ, LESLIE ALAN
MEYERS, RICHARD S.

HARTMAN, PATIENCE
ZAWADSKY, PATIENCE

HARTMAN, ROGER
MEHTA, RUSTAM JEHANGIR

HARTMANN, BETSY
HARTMANN, ELIZABETH

HARTMANN, CLAUS
LUIF, KURT

HARTMANN, LUKAS
LEHMANN, HANS RUDOLF

HARTSHORNE
BLUM, RICHARD H.

HARTWELL, NANCY
CALLAHAN, CLAIRE WALLIS

HARTWIG, W.H.
BLEY, WULF

HARTZELL, SUZY
HARTZELL, SUSAN KATHLEEN

HARVESTER, SIMON
RUMBOLD-GIBBS, HENRY

HARVEY, CAROLINE
POTTER, JOANNA

HARVEY, GENE
HANLEY, JACK

HARVEY, JAMES
FOX, GARDNER F.

HARVEY, JAMIESON
HARMON, JAMES JUDSON
KUHN, WILL

HARVEY, JIM
HARMON, JAMES JUDSON
KUHN, WILL

HARVEY, LYON
PORTER, EDWARD

HARVEY, MARIANNE
WILLIAMS, MARY

HARVEY, PAUL
AURANDT, PAUL HARVEY

HARVEY, PAULETT
TUMAY, PAULETT

HARVEY, RACHEL
BLOOM, URSULA

HARVEY, ROSS
HOOK, H. CLARKE

HARVEY, URSULA
BLOOM, URSULA

HARVEY, W.F.
HARVEY, WILLIAM FRYER

HARVOR, BETH
HARVOR, ERICA ELISABETH

HARWELL, ERNIE
HARWELL, WILLIAM EARNEST

HARWELL, SUSAN
HELLER, ALFRED

HARWICK, B.L.
KELLER, BEVERLY [L]

HARWIN, BRIAN
HENDERSON, LE GRAND

HARWOOD, GINA
BATTISCOMBE, ESTHER G.H.

HASBROUCH, LOUISE SEYMR.
ZIMM, LOUISE HASBROUCH

HASDUR, G.
GIESA, WERNER K.

HASDUR, MERLYN G.
GIESA, WERNER K.

HASELBUSCH, GUNTHER
GUNTHER, WILLY

HASELDEN, JOHN
FORRESTER, MARTYN JOHN

HASKELL, LEIGH
SHAHEEN, LEIGH

HASKELL, MARY
CURTIS, MARY HASKELL

HASKINS, BARBARA
STONE, BARBARA HASKINS

HASKINS, DICK
ANDRADE, H.

HASKINS, JIM
HASKINS, JAMES S.

HASLER, MARTIN
SHURLY, ERNEST WILLIAM

HASLETTE, JOHN
VAHEY, JOHN G. HAZLETTE

HASSEL, SVEN
PEDERSON, SVEN

HASSEN, SILAKI ALI
MIHALAKIS, ULYSSES G.

HASTING, WILLIAM
BLAYLOCK, JAMES P[AUL]
POWERS, TIM[OTHY THOMAS]

HASTINGS, ALAN
WILLIAMSON, GEOFFREY

HASTINGS, BEATRICE
HAIG, EMILY ALICE

HASTINGS, BEVERLY
BARKIN, CAROL
JAMES, ELIZABETH

HASTINGS, BROOK
EDGLY, LESLIE & MARY

HASTINGS, BROOKE
GORDON, DEBORAH

HASTINGS, ELIZABETH
SHERWOOD, MARGARET POLLOK

HASTINGS, GRAHAM
JEFFRIES, RODERIC[GRAEME]

HASTINGS, HARRINGTON
MARSH, JOHN

HASTINGS, HARRINGTON
SHEPHERD, FLORENCE

HASTINGS, HARRISON
MARSH, JOHN

HASTINGS, HUDSON
KUTTNER, HENRY

HASTINGS, HUDSON
MOORE, CATHERINE LUCILLE

HASTINGS, LAURA
SEGER, MAURA

HASTINGS, MARCH
LEVINSON, LEONARD [L]

HASTINGS, MICHAEL
BAR-ZOHAR, MICHAEL

HASTINGS, RODERIC
JEFFRIES, BRUCE GRAHAM M.

HASTINGS, VICTOR
DISCH, THOMAS M.
NAYLOR, CHARLES

HASTUR, G.
GIESA, WERNER K.

HASTWA, A.
CHIBBETT, H.S.W.

HASWELL, JOCK
HASWELL, C. JOHN D.

HASZARD, MRS.
MOYES, PATRICIA

HASZARD, PATRICIA MOYES
MOYES, PATRICIA

HATCH, GERALD
FOLEY, DAVE

HATCH, ROBERT
LEE, MANNING DE VILLEN.

HATEM, MOHAMED A.
HATIM, MUHAMMAD A.

HATFIELD, FRANK
STEVENS, JOHN

HATHAWAY, ANNE
INGHAM, MRS. W.A.

HATHAWAY, JAN
NEUBAUER, WILLIAM A.

HATHAWAY, LOUISE
METLOVA, MARIA

HATHAWAY, MAVIS
AVERY, IRA

HATHI
SMITH, [EDGAR] DENNIS

HATJE, JAN
DAHL, JURGEN

HATRED, PETER
DOUGLAS, KEITH

HATTEN, JIMMY
HANOS, DMITRI [JAMES]

HATTERAS, AMELIA
MENCKEN, HENRY LOUIS

HATTERAS, OWEN
MENCKEN, HENRY LOUIS
NATHAN, GEORGE JEAN

HATTERAS, OWEN III
MCDAVID, RAVEN I.

HATTON, CLIFF
MASON, SYDNEY CHARLES

HATTON, G. NOEL
CAIRD, ALICE MONA

HAUEISEN, KATHY
HAUEISEN, KATHRYN M.

HAUK, MAUNG
HOBBS, CECIL CARLTON

HAUS, LADOVIE
DELORME, REVE

HAUSEN, PETER
HODER, FRIEDRICH

HAUSER, KASPAR
TUCHOLSKY, KURT

HAUSER, MARGRIT
HINZELMANN, ELSA M.

HAUSERHOFF, ANNIE
KAYSER, ANNA

HAUSHOFER, MARLEN
HAUSHOFER, MARIE HELEN F.

HAUSMAN, GERRY
HAUSMAN, GERALD

HAUSRATH, A.
TAYLOR, GEORGE

HAUTALA, RICK
HAUTALA, RICHARD ANDREW

HAUTMAN, PETE
HAUTMAN, PETER

HAVARD, CHARLES
GIBBS-SMITH, CHARLES H.

HAVE, BURTON
LLIRO OLIVE, JOSE MARIA

HAVEL, JENNIFER
HAVILL, JUANITA

HAVENHAND, JOHN
COX, JOHN ROBERTS

HAVENS, STEWART
LEE, WAYNE CYRIL

HAVERS, DORA
BOULGER, THEODORA HAVERS

HAVIARAS, STRATIS
CHAVIARAS, STRATES

HAVIL, ANTHONY
PHILIPP, ELLIOT ELIAS

HAVILAND, DIANA
HERSHMAN, FLORENCE

HAVILAND, MEG
KETCHAM, HELEN

HAVILAND, [CAPT.] FERGUS
GODDARD, NORMAN M.

HAWES, LOUISE
JACOBSON, LOUISE HAWES

HAWK, AFFABLE
MACCARTHY, SIR DESMOND

HAWK, ALEX
BOUMA, JOHANOS L.
CHADWICK, JOSEPH L.
GARFIELD, BRIAN F.W.
KELTON, ELMER

HAWK, ALEX [CONT]
LUTZ, GILES A.
MCGAUGHY, DUDLEY DEAN

HAWK, JACK
SELLERS, CONNIE LESLIE

HAWK, PAT
HAWK, MARTIN R[AYMOND]

HAWK, PAUL
CHADWICK, PAUL

HAWK, RAY
HAWK, RAYMOND WALLACE

HAWKE, HARRIET
KRAMER, ARMIN

HAWKE, JESSICA
UPFIELD, ARTHUR C.

HAWKE, NANCY
NUGENT, NANCY

HAWKE, SIMON
YERMOKOV, NICHOLAS VALEN.

HAWKE, [CAPT.] ROBERT
O'MANT, HEDLEY P.A.

HAWKES, H.C.
HORNWOOD, HARVEY

HAWKES, ISAAC
HARBAUGH, THOMAS C.

HAWKES, JOHN
BURNE, CLENDENNIN TALBOT

HAWKES, ROBERT
OLDEN, MARC

HAWKEYE
CARLISLE, R.H.

HAWKIN, MARTIN
HAWKINS, MARTIN

HAWKING, S.W.
HAWKING, STEPHEN WILLIAM

HAWKINS, A. DESMOND
HAWKINS, ALEC DESMOND

HAWKINS, JACK
CAIN, NICHOLAS [COLORADO]
HAWKINS, JOHN EDWARD

HAWKINS, JOHN
CATCHPOLE, WILLIAM LESLIE
HAGAN, STELLA F.

HAWKINS, JOHN & WARD
CATCHPOLE, WILLIAM LESLIE

HAWKINS, SEKATARY
SCHULKERS, ROBERT FRANC

HAWKS, CHESTER
CHADWICK, PAUL

HAWKS, LEE
PEDNEAU, DAVE

HAWKSHAW
FRASER, JOHN ARTHUR

HAWKSHAW THE DETECTIVE
IRON, NATHANIEL COLV.

HAWKWOOD, ALLAN
BEDFORD-JONES, HENRY

HAWLEY, BEATRICE
JAGEL, BEATRICE HAWLEY

HAWLEY, FLORENCE M.
ELLIS, FLORENCE HAWLEY

HAWLEY, MABEL C.
STRATEMEYER, EDWARD

HAWORTH, MARY
YOUNG, MARY ELIZABETH R.

HAWTHORNE, ALAINA
RICHARDSON, ALAINA W.

HAWTHORNE, E.M.D.
DOLBEY, ETHEL & GEOFFREY

HAWTHORNE, ERNEST H.
DAWSON, WILLIAM HENRY

HAWTHORNE, J.R.H.
HOLDING, JOHN RICHARD

HAWTHORNE, MARX
GREENWOOD, A.E.

HAWTHORNE, RAINEY
RIDDELL, CHARLOTTE ELIZ.

HAWTHORNE, VIOLET
RAINONE, CHRISTOPHER

HAWTHORNE, [CAPTAIN] R.M.
ELLIS, EDWARD S.

HAY, CATHERINE
HUGHES, IVY

HAY, ELZEY
ANDREWS, ELIZA FRANCES

HAY, FRANCES
DICK-ERIKSON, CICELY S.
ERIKSON, SIBYL C. ALEX.

HAY, GEORGE
HAY, OSWYN ROBERT T.

HAY, IAN
BEITH, JOHN HAY

HAY, JOHN
DALRYMPLE-HAY, JOHN & BAB

HAY, MARIE
VON HINDEBURG, A.B. MARIE

HAY, NIGEL
NAGLE-HEALY, JAMES A.

HAY, STEPHEN
BRACK, WALTER

HAY, TIMOTHY
BROWN, MARGARET WISE
ROLLINS, MONTGOMERY

HAY, VICKY
HAY, MILLICENT V.

HAYDE, BERTL
HETMANEK, BERTA

HAYDEN, C. GERVIN
WICKER, RANDOLFE HAYDEN

HAYDEN, JAY
PAINE, LAURAN BOSWORTH

HAYDEN, JULIE
HAYDEN, JULIA ELIZABETH

HAYDEN, STIRLING
HAYDEN, STERLING

HAYDEN, TOM
HAYDEN, THOMAS EMMET

HAYDON, MONTY
HAYDON, PERCY MONTAGUE

HAYDON, ROBERT [EARL]
SHEFFEY, ASA

HAYES, ALEXANDER
COOPER, ROBERT ANDREW

HAYES, ALLISON
CODDINGTON, LYNN

HAYES, CLANTON
MASON, SYDNEY CHARLES

HAYES, EVELYN
BETHELL, MARY URSULA

HAYES, HENRY
KIRK, ELLEN WARNER O.

HAYES, IVOR
RANSOME, L.E.

HAYES, REX
REXHAUS, GUNTHER

HAYES, SALLY TYLER
HILL, TERESA

HAYES, TIMOTHY
FEARN, JOHN RUSSELL
RUBEL, JAMES LYON

HAYES, WILSON
GIBBS-WILSON, KATHRYN B.

HAYES, WOODY
HAYES, WAYNE WOODROW

HAYFORD, EUGENE
WILKINSON, RICHARD HILL

HAYFORD, LIEUT. HARLAN
KASER, ARTHUR LEROY

HAYFORD, TANIA
RUTHERFORD, PAT

HAYFORD, TARIA
HAYDON, JUNE

HAYMAN
PEEL, HAZEL MARY

HAYMON, S.T.
HAYMON, SYLVIA THERESA

HAYMOND, GINNY
FLEMING, LEE

HAYN, RALPH
HAHN, ROLF

HAYNES, ANNE
MADLEE, DOROTHY [H]

HAYNES, DOROTHY K.
GRAY, DOROTHY KATE

HAYNES, DOROTHY KATE
GRAY, DOROTHY KATE

HAYNES, HENRY HARRISON
ENTON, HARRY

HAYNES, JIM
HAYNES, JAMES ALMAND

HAYNES, JOHN ROBERT
WILDING, PHILIP

HAYNES, LINDA
SWINFORD, BETTY [J.W]

HAYNES, PAT
MCKEAG, ERNEST LIONEL

HAYNES-DIXON, RUMER GODD.
FOSTER, MARGARET RUMER G.

HAYNESWORTH, SUSAN
ROBERTSON, SUSAN E.

HAYSTEAD, WES
HAYSTEAD, WESLEY

HAYTHORNE, JOHN
PARSONS, [SIR] RICHARD

HAYWARD, DAGNEY
MAJOR, J.D.

HAYWARD, KEN
KAPPLER, HANNS-WALTER

HAYWARD, RICHARD
KENDRICK, BAYNARD H.

HAYWOOD, HARRY
HALL, HAYWOOD

HAYWORTH, EVELYN[E]
HEYMAN, EVAN LEE

HAZARD, FORRESTER
WILLIAMS, ALEXANDER [H]

HAZARD, HARRY
BADGER, JOSEPH E.

HAZARD, JACK
BOOTH, EDWIN

HAZARD, LAURENCE
BARR, PATRICIA

HAZEL, HARRY
JONES, JUSTIN

HAZEL, SVEN
HASSEL, SVEN

HAZEL, WILLIAM
ST. CLAIR, MARGARET

HAZELTINE, HORACE
WAYNE, CHARLES STOKES

HAZELTON, ALEXANDER
ARMSTRONG, WILLIAM A.

HAZELTON, CAPT.
WHITSON, JOHN HARVEY

HAZELTON, CAPT. JOSEPH P
BROCKETT, LINUS PIERPONT

HAZELTON, COL.
WHITSON, JOHN HARVEY

HAZELTON, HARRY
BADGER, JOSEPH E.

HAZELTON, MABEL
RAND, C.H.

HAZLETT, BILL
HAZLETT, WILLIAM SCOTT

HAZLITT, JOSEPH
STRAGE, MARK

HAZZARD, WILTON
ST. CLAIR, MARGARET

HEAD, ANN
MORSE, ANNE C.

HEAD, BESSIE
EMERY, BESSIE

HEAD, GAY
HAUSER, MARGARET L.

HEAD, MATTTHEW
CANADAY,JOHN

HEADAPOHL, B.R.
HEADAPOHL, BETTY R.

HEADE, REGINALD
WEBB, REGINALD CYRIL

HEADLEY, ELIZABETH
CAVANNA, ELIZABETH ALLEN

HEADON, JOHN
THOMPSON, JOHN H.

HEALD, EDITH
SHACKLETON, EDITH

HEALD, HAZEL
BISHOP, ZEALIA BROWN

HEALD, TIM
HEALD, TIMOTHY VILLIERS

HEALEY, B.J.
HEALEY, BENJAMIN J.

HEALEY, BEN
HEALEY, BENJAMIN J.

HEALEY, BROOKS
ALBERT, BURTON JR.

HEALY, JAMES H.
NAGLE-HEALY, JAMES A.

HEARD, GERALD
HEARD, HENRY FITZGERALD

HEARD, H.F.
HEARD, HENRY FITZGERALD

HEARN, EMILY
VALLEAU, EMILY

HEARN, SNEED
GREGG, ANDREW W.

HEARNE, BETSY GOULD
HEARNE, ELIZABETH GOULD

HEARST, PATTY
HEARST, PATRICIA CAMPBELL

HEART, HARDY
HAIMERL, OTTO

HEARTING, ERNIE
HERTZIG, ERNST

HEARTMAN, HAROLD
MEBANE, JOHN [H]

HEATH, BERNARD
SMITH, BERNARD

HEATH, CHARLES
RENAULD, RON

HEATH, ELDON
DERLETH, AUGUST [WILLIAM]

HEATH, ELIZABETH ALDEN
HOLTON, EDITH AUSTIN

HEATH, MICHAEL
HANNAY, D.

HEATH, MONICA
FITZGERALD, ARLENE J.

HEATH, NITA
KELLY, GWEN NITA

HEATH, PETER
FINE, PETER HEATH

HEATH, ROYSTON
WALLIS, GEORGE C.

HEATH, SANDRA
WILSON, SANDRA

HEATH, SHARON
RITCHIE, CLARE

HEATH, VERONICA
BLACKETT, VERONICA HEATH

HEATH, W. SHAW
WILLIAMSON, HENRY

HEATHCOTE, CLAUD
PANTING, JAMES HARWOOD

HEATHCOTT, MARY
KEEGAN, MARY HEATHCOTT

HEATON, PETER
STUART-HEATON, PETER

HEATON, TOM
HEATON, THOMAS PETER S.

HEAVEN, CONSTANCE
HEAVEN, CONSTANCE FECHER

HEBDEN, MARK
HARRIS, JOHN

HEBER, AUSTIN
POOLE, REGINALD H.

HEBER, REGINALD
POOLE, REGINALD H.

HECHT, HASSO
PLOTZE, HASSO

HEDAYAT, DASHIELL
LEGER, JACK-ALAIN

HEDEN, BALZAR
EDEN, ESKIL FRANS

HEDGE, RALPH WOLLSTONE.
FRIERSON, MEADE III

HEDGES, JOSEPH
HARKNETT, TERRY W.

HEDLEY, FRANK
BARKER, C. HEDLEY

HEFFERMAN, MICHAEL
FURGERSON, SAMUEL

HEFFERMAN, PATRICK
O'HEFFERMAN, PATRICK

HEFLIN, DONALD
WALLMANN, JEFFREY M.

HEFNER, PAUL
TABORI, PAL

HEGAN, ALICE CALDWELL
RICE, ALICE C. HEGAN

HEGARTY, SISTER M. LOYOLA
HEGARTY, ELLEN

HEGEDO, HERBERT G.
DOLL, HERBERT GERHARD

HEGESIPPUS
SCHONFIELD, HUGH JOSEPH

HEGGY, JOE P.
LANDSBOROUGH, GORDON H.
MANN, GEORGE PAUL

HEGMUN, IRA
MAGUIRE, H.N.

HEID, GWINNY
HEIDRICH, INGEBORG

HEIDBREDER, MARGARET ANN
EASTMAN, ANN HEIDBREDER

HEIDENS, PETER
CHRISTOPHS, BERNT

HEIKHENHOFF, PEER
HOFFMANN, GUNTHER

HEILBRUN, CAROLYN G.
HEILBRUN, CAROLYN GOLD

HEIM, HEIDE
MULLER, PAUL ALFRED

HEIMBERG, MARILYN MARKHAM
ROSS, MARILYN HEIMBERG

HEIMBORN, CARL
RUSS, PETER

HEIMBURG, WILHELMINE
VON BEHRENS, BERTHA

HEIMER, MEL
HERSHMAN, MORRIS

HEIMS, STEVE PAUL
HEIMS, STEVE JOSHUA

HEIN, GUNTHER
GUNTHER, HEINZ

HEINDORF, HEINER
RANK, HEINER

HEINE, IRVING
HUGHES, DENNIS [TALBOT]

HEINITZ, RALF
HYDEN, NILS

HEINKEL, STANFORD
HENNELL, STANFORD

HEINO, KYLLIKKI
POLVIANDER, ANNI K.

HEINRICH, CARL JOHANN
BRUGMANN, KARL

HEINRICH, VALENTIN
LUPESCU, VALENTIN

HEINZ, G.
GERARD-LIBOIS, JULES C.

HEINZ, K.
BERGER, KARL HEINZ

HEINZ, KARL
POPPE, KARL HEINZ

HEINZEN, MILDRED
MASTERS, MILDRED

HEISSENBUTTEL, HELMUT
HEISSENBUETTEL, HELMUT

HEITER, ERNST
LIST, HORST

HEITER, JEREMIAS
LASSWITZ, KURD

HEITZMANN, WM. RAY
HEITZMANN, WILLIAM RAY

HEIZMANN, GERTRUD
HEIMANN-HEIZMANN, GERTRUD

HELD, FRANZ
VON DER HEYDEN, FRIEDRICH

HELD, KARL
KABEL, WALTHER

HELD, KURT
KLABER, KURT

HELD, PETER
VANCE, JOHN HOLBROOK

HELDAU
LUBANSKI, JULES C.L.

HELDER, DOM
CAMARA, HELDER PESSOA

HELDERENBERG, GERY
BUYLE, HUBERT

HELDERS, MAJOR
KNAUSS, ROBERT

HELDING, CLAIR
ACKERMAN, FORREST J.

HELDT, JORG
KALMUCZAK, ROLF

HELFEN, OTTO J. MAENCHEN
MAENCHEN, OTTO JOHN

HELFENSTEIN, LOTHAR
HEICHEN, WALTER

HELFORTH, JOHN
DOOLITTLE, HILDA

HELGESSEN, LARS
BERGLUND, LARSS ERIK T.

HELIAS, PER JAKEY
HELIAS, PIERRE JACQUES M.

HELION, JO HANS
DRESSLER, JOHANNES

HELIOS, ALEXANDER
HERDEN, HERBERT

HELL, HELLAN
HANSTEIN, WOLFRAM v.

HELL, JON
THAULOW, HARALD

HELL, LISA
KRETSCHMAR, BRIGITTE

HELLBERG, WOLFGANG
BARTHEL, MANFRED

HELLBORN, KLAUS
RHEIN, EDUARD

HELLEN, ANDERS
GREEK, CARL GUSTAF L.

HELLENHOFFERN, VOJTECH
HASEK, JAROSLAV M.F.

HELLENS, FRANZ
VAN ERMENGEM, FREDERIC

HELLER
IRANEK-OSMECKI, KAZ.

HELLER, CORD
ROTSLER, WILLIAM

HELLER, FRANK
SERNER, MARTIN GUNNAR

HELLER, JEFF
FOLB, JAY
SLESAR, HENRY

HELLER, LARRY
HELLER, LORENZ

HELLER, MIKE
HANO, ARNOLD

HELLER, SHELLY
HELLER, RACHELLE SARA

HELLERLAMB, TONI
LAMB, ANTONIO

HELLEY, DENIS
ALLEN, HUBERT RAYMOND

HELLING, STEEN
MEYN, NIELS

HELLMAN, HAL
HELLMAN, HAROLD

HELLMAN, PETE
HEBEL, PETER

HELLMER, KLAUS
RHEIN, EDUARD

HELLRING, EVA
DREYSEL, DORE

HELLYER, A.G.L.
HELLYER, ARTHUR GEORGE L.

HELM, ERIC
RANDLE, KEVIN [DOUGLAS]
CORNETT, ROBERT

HELMAN, ALBERT
LICHTVELD, LOU A.M.

HELMERICKS, BUD
HELMERICKS, HARMON R.

HELMI, JACK
SANDS, LEO GEORGE

HELMI, PETER
HERZOG, WILHELM PETER

HELMS, TOM
HELMS, ROLAND THOMAS

HELMUTH, WILLIAM
WALFRIDSSON, WILLY

HELOISE
CRUSE, HELOISE
REESE, HELOISE BOWLES

HELT, ANDREAS
PFEIFFER-BELLI, ERICH

HELVICK, JAMES
COCKBURN, [FRANCIS] CLAUD

HELWIG, MAGGIE
HELWIG, SARAH MAGDALEN

HELY, ELIZABETH
YOUNGER, ELIZABETH HELY

HEMAN, NICHOLAS
HANSON, MICHAEL

HEMEL DOBKIN, KATHLEEN
HAMEL PEIFER, KATHLEEN

HEMEZE
CABALLERO, MANUEL

HEMEZE, SEBASTIAN
CABALLERO, MANUEL

HEMING, J.W.
HEMING, JOHN WINTON

HEMINGS, T.J.
REITER, VICTORIA KELRICH

HEMINGWAY, MUFFET
HEMINGWAY, JOAN

HEMLEY, ELAINE GOTTLIEB
GOTTLIEB, ELAINE

HEMMING, N.K.
HEMMING, NORA KATHLEEN

HEMMINGWAY, TAYLOR
RYWELL, MARTIN

HEMPEL, CARL G.
HEMPEL, CARL GUSTAVE

HEMPHILL, BETTY
HEMPHILL, ELIZABETH ANNE

HENBOS
BOSCH, HENRY GERARD

HENDERLEY, BROOKS
STRATEMEYER, EDWARD

HENDERSON, BETH
HENDERSON-DANIELS, BETH

HENDERSON, CHESTER
LIERSCH, ROLF WERNER

HENDERSON, COLT
MASON, SYDNEY CHARLES

HENDERSON, DONALD
LAUGHLIN, TOM

HENDERSON, F.C.
MENCKEN, HENRY LOUIS

HENDERSON, G.D.S.
HENDERSON, GEORGE DAVID S

HENDERSON, GEORGE
GLASBY, JOHN S.

HENDERSON, J. STANLEY
WILLETT, EDWARD

HENDERSON, M.R.
GRANBECK, MARILYN

HENDERSON, MARC ANTHONY
STRONG, GEORGE A.

HENDERSON, MARY
MAVOR, OSBORNE HENRY

HENDERSON, PAUL
FRANCE, RUTH

HENDERSON, SYLVIA
ASHTON-WARNER, SYLVIA C.

HENDERSON, WILLIAM
DETZER, KARL

HENDERSON-HOWAT, GERALD
HOWAT, GERALD MALCOLM D.

HENDRICKS, KAW
WOLFE, CHARLES KEITH

HENDRICKSON, EMILY
HENDRICKSON, DORIS E.

HENDRIK ADRIAAN MULDER
HESSELS, WILLEM

HENDRIK, ABBO
ABESSOR, RUDY

HENDRIKS, P.G.
PISTORIUS, PIETER

HENDRIKS, PAUL
HOOP, EDWARD

HENDRY, J.F.
HENDRY, JAMES FINDLAY

HENDRY, OLGA
FIRTH, NORMAN WESLEY

HENDRY, TOM
HENDRY, THOMAS

HENDRYX, HARRISON
HENDRYX, JAMES BEARDSLEY

HENEGE, THOMAS
GILLOTTI, ALBERT F.

HENFIL
DE SOUZA FILHO, HENRIQUE

HENKE, SHIRL
HENKE, SHIRL
REYNARD, CAROL

HENLEY, ART
HENLEY, ARTHUR

HENLEY, BETH
HENLEY, ELIZABETH BECKER

HENLEY, GAIL
OLSHESKI, GAIL

HENLEY, LIZ
DOOLEY, JANET M.
HENRY, LYDIA S.

HENLEY, P.A.
PROTHEROE, ERNEST

HENNER, CARL
NANNE, HENRIK

HENNESSEY, CAROLINE
VON BLOCK, BELA [W]
VON BLOCK, SYLVIA

HENNESSEY, HUGH
DONOVAN, JOHN

HENNESSY, MAX
HARRIS, JOHN

HENNING, D.L.
HENNING, DALE LEE

HENNING, KATJA
WEBBER, ANNE MARIE

HENREY, MRS. ROBERT
HENREY, MADELAINE

HENREY, ROBERT
HENREY, MADELAINE

HENRI, G.
CLEMENT, GEORGE H.

HENRICI, KARL HERBERT
HASSELBLATT, DIETER

HENRIES, DORIS
HENRIES, A. DORIS BANKS

HENRIETTE, CHRISTIANE
KREUTZER, CATHERINE

HENRIOT, EMILE
MAIGROT, EMILE

HENRIQUES, VERONICA
GOSLING, VERONICA

HENRY, ALAN
ORLOFF, A.H.
JAKES, JOHN [WILLIAM]

HENRY, ANNE
WALL, JUDITH H.

HENRY, ARTHUR
ANDERSON, ARTHUR HENRY

HENRY, BILL
HENRY, WILLIAM MELLORS

HENRY, CHARLES
FARRELL, HENRY

HENRY, CHARLES P.
BERGER, KARL HEINZ

HENRY, DANIEL
KAHNWEILER, DANIEL-HENRY

HENRY, DANIEL JR.
HOGBIN, HERBERT

HENRY, DAVID LEE
HILL, R. LANCE

HENRY, E. RAY
EISENHARDT, RAYMOND HENRY

HENRY, EDGAR
TOURGEE, ALBION WINEGER

HENRY, FRAN WORDEN
WORDEN, FRAN

HENRY, FRED
HARTMANN, HELMUT HENRY
TENKRAT, FRIEDRICH

HENRY, GEORGE
SMITH, GEORGE H[ENRY]

HENRY, HARRIET
DE STEUCH, HARRIET HENRY

HENRY, JOAN
THOMPSON, JOAN LEE

HENRY, LEWIS C.
COPELAND, LEWIS

HENRY, MARION
DEL REY, LESTER

HENRY, OLIVER
PORTER, WILLIAM SYDNEY

HENRY, ROBERT
HENREY, MADELAINE
MACDONALD, JOHN D.
POWELL, TALMAGE

HENRY, T.E.
ROWLAND-ENTWISTLE, A.T.

HENRY, WILL
ALLEN, HENRY WILSON

HENRY, WILLIAM
DIEZ, MRS. M.A.

HENRY,O.
PORTER, WILLIAM SYDNEY

HENSCHKE, ALFRED
KLABUND

HENSEN, HERWIG
MIELANTS, FLORENT C.A. JR

HENSEY, FRITZ
HENSEY, FREDERICK GERALD

HENSLEY, J.L.
HENSLEY, JOSEPH LOUIS

HENSLEY, JOE L.
HENSLEY, JOSEPH LOUIS

HENSON, JIM
HENSON, JAMES MAURY

HENSTELL, DIANA
SILBER, DIANA
LEVINE, DIANA

HENTON, COLLETT
BATCHELOR, RICHARD A.C.

HENTY, G.A.
HENTY, GEORGE ALFRED

HEPBURNE, MELISSA
BROUDE, CRAIG HOWARD

HEPPELL, BLANCHE
HEPPELL, MARY

HEPPLE, ANNE
DICKINSON, ANNE HEPPLE

HEPWORTH, MIKE
HEPWORTH, JAMES MICHAEL

HER
DEAL, BORDEN

HERALD, KATHLEEN
PEYTON, KATHLEEN WENDY
PEYTON, MICHAEL

HERBER, LEWIS
BOOKCHIN, MURRAY

HERBERGER, ERIKA
HENGSTENBERG, ERNST

HERBERT, ARTHUR
SHAPPIRO, HERBERT ARTHUR

HERBERT, CECIL
HAMILTON, CHARLES H.S.

HERBERT, FRANK
RANSOM, WILLIAM MICHAEL

HERBERT, HENRY K.
KNIBBS, H[ENRY] H[ERBERT]

HERBERT, JOHN
BRUNDAGE, JOHN HERBERT

HERBERT, KENNETH
KAHN, KENNETH

HERBERT, WALLY
HERBERT, WALTER WILLIAM

HERBERT, WILLIAM
CROLY, HERBERT DAVID

HERBERTSON, A.
BATT, LEON

HERBLOCK
BLOCK, HERBERT LAWRENCE

HERBRAND, JAN
HERBRAND, JANICE

HERBST, DANIEL
ALPERS, HANS JOACHIM
HAHN, RONALD M.

HERBSTENBURGER, TONI
VON OCHSENFELD, ANTON B-F

HERCO
OWAIN, OWAIN

HERDEGEN, HANS
DOHRING, KARL SIEGFRIED

HEREFORD, JOHN
FLETCHER, HARRY LUFT V.

HERFURTH, ALICE
REINHARD, WILHELM PETER

HERGE
REMI, GEORGES

HERGENHAN, LAURIE
HERGENHAN, LAURENCE THOM.

HERGESELL, PHILIPP
PHILIPP, JULIUS

HERIAN, V.
GREGORIAN, VARTAN

HERIAT, PHILIPPE
PAYELLE, RAYMOND GERARD

HERICAULT, CHARLES D'
DE RICAULT, CHARLES JOS.

HERITAGE, A.J.
ADDIS, HAZEL IRIS

HERITAGE, JOHN
SHAW, STANLEY GORDON

HERITAGE, MARTIN
HORLER, SYDNEY

HERKEN, CLARA
RICKE, EDELTRAUT

HERMAN, J.B.
HERMAN, JEANNIE M.

HERMAN, JACK
SANDS, LEO GEORGE

HERMAN, LOUIS
SELLERS, CONNIE LESLIE

HERMAN, WILLIAM
BIERCE, AMBROSE
HARCOURT, THOMAS A.

HERMANN, COMRADE
GIPPIUS, ZINAIDA N.

HERMANN, GEORG
BORCHARDT, GEORG HERMANN

HERMANN, SPRING
GALIARDI, SPRING

HERMANN, WALTER
WAGER, WALTER [HERMAN]

HERMANNS, PETER
BRANNON, WILLIAM T.

HERMES
CANAWAY, W.H.
FLAMMARION, N. CAMILLE
LIEDER, HERWIG
LUMLEY, BENJAMIN

HERMES, PAUL
THAYER, WILLIAM ROSCOE

HERMES, ROLF
MULLER, PAUL ALFRED

HERMLIN, STEPHAN
LEBER, RUDOLF

HERMON, ROPARZ
NEMO, L.P.

HERNANDEZ, VICTOR P.
RAPHAELA, CORNELIUS [N]

HERNE, ERIC
GARVEY, ERIC WILLIAM

HERNE, HUXLEY
BROOKER, BERTRAM

HERON, E.
PRICHARD, KATE O'BRIEN

HERON, H.
PRICHARD, HESKETH VERNON

HEROVIT, JONATHAN
FARMER, PHILIP JOSE

HERRICK, THORNECLIFF
BIXBY, JEROME L.

HERRICK, WALLACE
WARBURG, JAMES PAUL

HERRIES, NORMAN
HERSHMAN, NORMAN

HERRIGAN, JACKIE
MCDONALD, PAULA

HERRIGAN, JEFF
MCDONALD, RICHARD C.

HERRING, GUILLES
SOMERVILLE, EDITH A.O.

HERRINGTON, PAT
HERRINGTON, PATRICIA M.

HERRINGTON, TERRI
BLACKSTOCK, TERRI

HERRIOT, JAMES
WIGHT, JAMES ALFRED

HERRMANN, EUGEN
VON DEDENROTH, EUGEN H.

HERRMANN, KARL
BERGNER, KARLHERRMANN

HERRMANN, PHYLLIS
DI FRANCESCO, PHYLLIS
HERRMANN, NIRA

HERRMANN, TAFFY
HERRMANN, DOROTHY

HERRNSTEIN, BARBARA
SMITH, BARBARA HERRNSTEIN

HERROD, WALTER
LIGHT, WALTER HERROD

HERSCHOLT, WOLFE
BLEECK, G.C.
HAUSFELD, RUSSELL

HERSHEY, ED
HERSHEY, EDWARD NORMAN

HERSHEY, SHEAF
NEWELL, PETER

HERSHFIELD, HARRY
GIBSON, WALTER B.

HERTER, LORI
HERTER, LORETTA M.

HERTZ, GEORGE
HIRST, GEORGE STANLEY

HERTZ, JACKY
HERTZ, JACKOLINE G.

HERVE, JEAN-LUC
HUMBARACI, DEMIR ARSIAN

HERVENT, MAURICE
GRINDEL, EUGENE

HERVEY, EVELYN
KEATING, HENRY R.F.

HERVEY, JANE
MCGAW, NAOMI B.T.

HERVY, GRANT
COCHRANE, GEORGE HENRY

HERZ, JERRY
HERZ, JEROME SPENCER

HERZ-GARTEN, THEODOR
DE MATTOS, MRS.

HERZEN, ALEKSANDR
YAKOVLEV, ALEKSANDR I.

HERZOG, E.
HERZOG, EMILE S.

HERZOG, GABRIELE
GERICKE, GABRIELE

HERZOG, PAULUS
MULLER, GOTTFRIED

HESPRO, HERBERT
ROBINSON, HERBERT SPENCER

HESS, KATHARINA
MULLER-HESS, KATHARINA

HESS, MAJA
GERBER-HESS, MAJA

HESS, NORAH
BAGNARA, ELSIE POE

HESSELL, HENRY
TILTMAN, HUGH HESSELL

HESSING, DENNIS
DENNIS-JONES, HAROLD

HESTER, HELEN
KURTH, HANNS

HETMANN, FREDERIK
KIRSCH, HANS CHRISTIAN

HEUER, WILLIAM
HEUER, WILHELM

HEUSCHEN, MONIKA
ESCHBACH, JOSEF

HEVESI, LUDWIG
HIRSCH, LUDWIG

HEWATSON, BOB
PORTER, LANCELOT

HEWES, CADY
DEVOTO, BERNARD AUGUSTIN

HEWETT, ANITA
DUKE, ANITA

HEWITT, BEN
MITCHELL, ADRIAN

HEWITT, ELIZABETH
ABBOTT, MARY JEANNE

HEWITT, MARTIN
MORRISON, ARTHUR

HEXHAM, LIONEL J.
HAMEL, FELIX JOHN

HEXT, HARRINGTON
PHILLPOTTS, EDEN

HEXTALL, DAVID
PHILLIPS-BIRT, DOUGLAS

HEYDECKER, JUPP
BERENDT, KLAUS

HEYDORN, ELLEN
HOSS, MARGIT

HEYER, GEORGETTE
ROUGIER, GEORGETTE

HEYGK, RALPH
HEINECKE, RUDOLF

HEYM, STEFAN
FLIEGEL, HELLMUTH

HEYMANN, C. DAVID
HEYMANN, CLEMENS CLAUDE

HEYMANN, TOM
HEYMANN, THOMAS N.

HEYNEN, JIM
HEYNEN, JAMES

HEYST, AXEL
GRABOWSKI, Z. ANTHONY

HEYWARD, DOROTHY
KUHNS, DOROTHY HARTZELL

HEYWOOD, JOE T.
HEYWOOD, JOSEPH T.

HIAN
HIGGINSON, WILLIAM JOHN

HIAT, ELCHIK
KATZ, MENKE

HIATT, BRENDA
BARBER, BRENDA H.

HIBERNICUS
LECKY, WILLIAM EDWARD H.

HICHLER, LEOPOLD
EHRLICH, LEOPOLD

HICKEN, MANDY
HICKEN, MARILYN E.

HICKEY, H.B.
LIVINGSTON, HERB
LIVINGSTONE, BERKELEY

HICKEY, LYN
HICKEY, MADELYN EASTLUND

HICKEY, WILLIAM
DRIBERG, THOMAS EDWARD N.

HICKOK, WILL
HARRISON, CHESTER WILLIAM

HICKS, DAISY
ROE, M.S.

HICKS, ELEANOR [B]
COERR, ELEANOR BEATRICE

HICKS, HARVEY
STRATEMEYER, EDWARD

HICKS, J.L.
HICKS, JIMMY LYN

HICKS, JIM
HICKS, JIMMY LYN

HICKS, JOHN H.
FARIGOULE, LOUIS

HICKS, MARTHA
HIX, MARTHA R.

HIEK, PETE
KAPPEL, GUNTER

HIGGENS, MARTYN
SELLERS, CONNIE LESLIE

HIGGINGBOTHAM, ANNE T.
HIGGINGBOTHAM, ANNE D.

HIGGINGS, INK
WEISS, MORRIS S.

HIGGINS, DICK
HIGGINS, RICHARD CARTER

HIGGINS, JACK
PATTERSON, HARRY

HIGGINS, ZORASTER
EGGLESTON, EDWARD

HIGHAM, JON ATLAS
HIGHAM, JONATHAN HUW

HIGHAM, T.F.
HIGHAM, THOMAS FARRANT

HIGHET, HELEN
HIGHET, GILBERT
MACINNES, HELEN [CLARK]

HIGHLAND, DORA
AVALLONE, MICHAEL

HIGHLAND, LAWRENCE
LINFIELD, MARY B.

HIGHLAND, MONICA
ESPEY, JOHN
SEE, CAROLYN & LISA

HIGHMAN, FRANK
HICKMANN, FRANZ MARIA

HIGHTOWER, PAUL
COLLINS, THOMAS HIGHTOWER

HIGNON, ALBERT
JEURY, MICHEL
MARLSON, PIERRE

HIGSON, P.J.W.
WILLOUGHBY-HIGSON, PHILIP

HIGSON, PHILIP
HIGSON, PHILIP J. WILOBY.

HILARION
MACKELLAR, CAMPBELL

HILARY, RICHARD
BODINO, RICHARD
CONNORS, HILARY

HILBERSDORF, KARL
BOTTCHER, KARL

HILD, ALF
KNUTSEN, LALLI

HILD, JACK
BAETZ, WILLIAM
BOMACK, ALAN
CANON, JACK
GARSIDE, [CLIFFORD] JACK
GREEN, ROLAND [JAMES]
HARDY, ROBIN
MADEVILLE, JIM
PHILIPSON, ALAN
PRESTON, JOHN
RAINEY, RICH[ARD]
RANDISI, ROBERT J.
ROBERTS, JOE

HILDEBRAND
BEETS, NIKOLAAS

HILDEBRANDT, BROTHERS
HILDEBRANDT, TIM & GREG

HILDEBRANDT, DON
DEBRANDT, DON H.

HILDEBRANDT, KRIEMHILD
MAGYARI, KRIEMHILD

HILDEBRANDT, TIM
HILDEBRANDT, TIMOTHY

HILDEGARDE
HOSKINS, JOSEPHINE R.

HILDICK, E.W.
HILDICK, EDMUND WALLACE

HILDICK, WALLACE
HILDICK, EDMUND WALLACE

HILGENDORFF, HERMANN
MULLER, KURT

HILL, AB
HILL, ABRAM BARRINGTON

HILL, ALEXIS
CRAIG, MARY FRANCIS S.
GLICK, RUTH [BURTNICK]
TITCHENER, LOUISE

HILL, ANNE
MUSKETT, NETTA RACHEL

HILL, ARTHUR
TULLOCK, W.W.

HILL, BENNET
WINTER, BEVIS [PETER]

HILL, BOB
HILL, ROBERT CECIL
HILL, ROBERT L.

HILL, BUNKER C.
ABEL, ALAN [IRWIN]

HILL, D.W.R.
TUBB, E.C.

HILL, DAVE
HILL, DAVID CHARLES
HILL, DAVID JOHN

HILL, DEE
ZUCKER, DORIS MAE B.

HILL, DEVRA Z.
ZUCKER, DORIS MAE B.

HILL, DRAPER
HILL, LEROY DRAPER JR.

HILL, EILEEN
STACK, NICHOLETE MEREDITH

HILL, FIONA
PALL, ELLEN JANE

HILL, GRACE BROOKS
STRATEMEYER, EDWARD

HILL, GRIMES
NEBEL, [LOUIS] FREDERICK

HILL, H. HAVERSTOCK
WALSH, JAMES MORGAN

HILL, H.D.N.
DISSTON, HARRY

HILL, HEADON
GRAINGER, FRANCIS EDWARD

HILL, HEATHER
CARROLL, JOY

HILL, HELEN
MILLER, HELEN HILL

HILL, HYACINTHE
ANDERSON, VIRGINIA [R.C.]

HILL, JAMES
JAMESON, [MARGARET] STORM

HILL, JOE
HILLSTROM, JOSEPH

HILL, JOHN
KOONTZ, DEAN R.

HILL, JOHNSON
KUNHARDT, EDITH

HILL, K.F.
BAER, LUCY A.

HILL, KAY
HILL, KATHLEEN LOUISE

HILL, KING
GLEMSER, BERNARD
ROBERTSON, FRANK CHESTER

HILL, K[ATE] F.
BAER, MRS. LUCY A.

HILL, LEW
SKENE-MELVIN, DAVID

HILL, MEG
HILL, MARGARET [OHLER]

HILL, MEREDITH
CRAIG, MARY FRANCIS S.

HILL, MONICA
BAKER, AGNES MONICA
WATSON, JANE WERNER

HILL, MURRAY
HOLLIDAY, ROBERT CORTES

HILL, POLLY
HUMPHREYS, MARY E. HILL

HILL, PRUDENCE
MAXFIELD, PRUDENCE M.

HILL, RABIN
YOUNG, ROBERT

HILL, RICH M.
MEYN, NIELS

HILL, ROGER
PAINE, LAURAN BOSWORTH

HILL, ROWLAND
WALLACE-CLARKE, GEORGE

HILL, RUTH A.
VIGUERS, RUTH HILL

HILL, RUTH LIVINGSTON
MUNCE, RUTH HILL

HILL, SAM
TURNER, HARVEY S.

HILL, STRAWBERRY
WALPOLE, HORACE

HILL, W.M.
DODD, EDWARD HOWARD JR.

HILL, WELDON
SCOTT, WILLIAM RALPH

HILL,TOM
WOLFGANG, OTTO

HILL-LUTZ, GRACE L.
HILL, GRACE [LIVINGSTON]

HILLARY, ANNE
KOLACZYK, ANNE & EDWARD

HILLAS, JULIAN
DASHWOOD, ROBERT JULIAN

HILLCOURT, WILLIAM
BJERREGAARD, WILHEM

HILLENBURG, MARTIN
KALMUCZAK, ROLF

HILLER, FLORA
HURD, FLORENCE

HILLER, WILLIAM
HILLER, WILHELM

HILLERMAN, TONY
HILLERMAN, ANTHONY GROVE

HILLIARD, JAN
GRANT, HILDA KAY

HILLIARD, LATHAM
ROTSLER, WILLIAM

HILLIER, JIM
HILLIER, JAMES MARTIN

HILLIERS, ASHTON
WALLIS, HENRY MARRIAGE

HILLIG, WERNER
BOHLEN & HALBACH, BERNDT

HILLING, O.W.
KAPPLER, HANNS-WALTER

HILLMAN, MARTIN
HILL, DOUGLAS ARTHUR

HILLMAN, MAY
HIPSCHMAN, MAY

HILLS, BALDWIN
WOHL, BURTON

HILLS, DICK
HILLS, CHARLES RICHARD

HILLS, P.J.
HILLS, PHILIP JAMES

HILLS, TINA
HILLS, ARGENTINA SCHIFANO

HILLSON, BERT
KALMUCZAK, ROLF

HILLUS, WILHELM
HILLERS, HERMAN WILLIAM

HILLYER, RICHARD
STRANKS, CHARLES JAMES

HILSO, PAUL
MOTH-LUND, POUL

HILT, GEORGE
BENTZ, HANS GEORG

HILTEN, PETER
NEHER, FRANZ L.

HILTON, ALEC
CHESSER, EUSTACE
FULLERTON, ALEXANDER F.

HILTON, JACK
HARTMANN, HELMUT HENRY

HILTON, JOSEPH
ROBERTS, EDNA
SMYTH, JOSEPH HILTON

HILTON, MARGERY
WOODS, MARGERY

HILTON, MAUD
HOWARD, ADAH M.
WHICHER, FRANK

HILTON, NETTE
HILTON, MARGARET LYNETTE

HILTON, R.H.
HILTON, RODNEY HOWARD

HILTON, ROYCE
HITCHENS, A.

HILTON, SIBYLLE
GUGGENHEIM-WIESE, URSULA

HIM
DEAL, BORDEN

HIMROD, BRENDA
WILSON, BRENDA LEE E.

HIN ME GEONG
ARMITAGE, JOHN

HINCKLEY, HELEN
JONES, HELEN HINCKLEY

HINCKS, G. MALCOLM
HINCKS, CYRIL MALCOLM

HINDE, THOMAS
CHITTY, SIR THOMAS WILES

HINDIN, NATHAN
BLOCH, ROBERT [A]

HINDS, E.M.
HINDS, [EVELYN] MARGERY

HINE, MURIEL
COXON, MURIEL

HINES, CHARLOTTE
MCWILLIAMS, JUDITH

HINES, FATHA
HINES, EARL KENNETH

HINKSON, KATHARINE TYNAN
TYNAN, KATHARINE

HINO, ASHIHEI
TAMAI, KATSUNORI

HINOJOSA, ROLANDO
HINOJOSA-SMITH, ROLANDO

HINOJOSA-S, ROLAND R.
HINOJOSA-SMITH, ROLAND

HINTON, MILT
HINTON, MILTON JOHN

HINTON, RICHARD W.
ANGOFF, CHARLES

HINTON, S.E.
INHOFE, SUSAN ELOISE H.

HIPP, GEORGE
ABRAMS, GEORGE JOSEPH

HIPPIUS
GIPPIUS, ZINAIDA N.

HIPPIUS, ZINAIDA
GIPPIUS, ZINAIDA N.

HIPPOPOTAMUS, EUGENE H.
KRAUS, [HERMAN] ROBERT

HIRANO, MARSHA
HIRANO-NAKANISHI, MARSHA

HIRED MAN ON HORSEBACK
RHODES, EUGENE MANLOVE

HIRSCH, LEE
HIRSCH, DAVID LEON

HIRSCH, WILLIAM RANDOLPH
KITMAN, MARVIN

HIRSCH, WILLIAM RANDOLPH [CONT]
LINGEMAN, RICHARD R.
NAVASKY, VICTOR S.

HIRSCHLER, IVO
HIRSCHLER, ADOLF

HIRSCHMAN, A.O.
HIRSCHMAN, ALBERT O.

HIS SISTER
TRACY, ANN BROMFIELD

HISTORICUS
HARCOURT, WILLIAM VERNON
NOCK, ALBERT JAY

HITCHCOCK, ALFRED
ARTHUR, ROBERT
HAINING, PETER
MASUR, HAROLD Q.

HITCHCOCK, DEBORAH J.
JESSUP, DEBORAH HITCHCOCK

HITCHCOCK, KEITH
KENNETH, KEITH

HITT, ORRIE
WILLIAMS, BERNIE

HLYBINNY, VLADIMIR
SEDURO, VLADIMIR

HOA, NGUYEN-DINH
NGUYEN DINH HOA

HOARE, AGNES D.
HOARE, AGNES DOROTHEA M.

HOARE, DOROTHY M
HOARE, AGNES DOROTHEA M.

HOBART, ALICE TISDALE
HOBART, ALICE NOURSE

HOBART, BLACK
SANDERS, JAMES EDWARD

HOBART, ROBERTSON
LEE, NORMAN

HOBBES, JOHN OLIVER
CRAIGIE, PEARL MARY T.

HOBBS, ANNE
PURDY, ANNE S.

HOBBS, JACK
HORLER, SYDNEY

HOBBS, PERRY
BLACKMUR, RICHARD PALMER

HOBEL, PHIL
FANTHORPE, R.L.

HOBERG, MARIELIS
ROBERT, MARIELIS

HOBHOUSE, PENELOPE
MALINS, PENELOPE

HOBSON, B.
JAMES, BERT

HOBSON, FRANCIS
WINTERTON, FRANCIS DERYK

HOBSON, HANK
HOBSON, HARRY

HOBSON, POLLY
EVANS, JULIE RENDEL

HOCHGLEND, RUDOLF
EGER, RUDOLF

HOCHGRUNDLER, CHARLOTTE
HOFMANN, CHARLOTTE [H]

HOCHWALDER, FRITZ
HOCHWAELDER, FRITZ

HOCKABY, STEPHEN
MITCHELL, GLADYS [M.W.]

HOCKENBERRY, HOPE
NEWELL, HOPE HOCKENBERRY

HOCKER, KARLA
HOECKER, KARLA

HOCKETT, KATHRYN
HOCKETT, MARCIA KATHRYN

HOCKING, ANNE
MESSER, MONA [N. ANNE]

HOCKLEY, LEWIS
LONGHURST, PERCY WILLIAM

HODEMART, PETER
AUDEMARS, PIERRE

HODGE, E. CHATTERTON
HASTINGS, PHYLLIS DORA H.

HODGE, HARRY
HODGE, ALFRED HAROLD

HODGE, MERTON
HODGE, HORACE EMERTON

HODGE, P.K.
HODGE, PAUL WILLIAM

HODGE, P.W.
HODGE, PAUL WILLIAM

HODGE, T. SHIRBY
TRACY, ROGER SHERMAN

HODGE, TOBY
MCILVAINE, CHARLES

HODGEN, J.T.
HALE, ETHELA RUTH

HODGES, SHIRLEY M.
HAILL, ROBERT GODFREY

HODGES, TURNER
MOOREHEAD, ALBERT H.

HODGKIN, ROBIN A.
HODGKIN, ROBERT ALLASON

HODGKINS, DAVID C.
BUDRYS, ALGIRDAS JONAS

HODGSON, ANNE
CAPLAN, ANNE

HODGSON, D[AVID]
LEWIS, DAVID

HODGSON, MARGARET
BALLINGER, [V] MARGARET

HODGSON, NORMA
RUSSELL, NORMA HULL LEWIS

HODGSON, W.H.
HODGSON, WILLIAM HOPE

HODSDON, NICK
HODSDON, NICHOLAS EDWARD

HODSON, ARTHUR
NICKSON, ARTHUR [THOMAS]

HOE, LEE
TRIPP, H. ALKER

HOEST, BILL
HOEST, WILLIAM P.

HOFBAUER, FRIEDL
KAUER, FRIEDL

HOFBERG, NORBERT
KALMUCZAK, ROLF

HOFER, PETER
KORTNER, PETER

HOFER, PETRA
DIETSCH, WERNER

HOFF, ANNEGRET
GUMMERT, CHARLOTTE

HOFF, GERTRUD
MATTHAEI, CLARA

HOFF, H.S.
COOPER, WILLIAM
HOFF, HARRY SUMMERFIELD

HOFF, HARRY
HEIDSIECK, HANS

HOFF, SYD
HOFF, SYDNEY

HOFFMAN, ANDY
HOFFMAN, ANDREW JAY

HOFFMAN, ART
KING, ALBERT

HOFFMAN, D.T.
TENNOW, DOROTHY

HOFFMAN, LEE
HOFFMAN, SHIRLEY BELL

HOFFMAN, LOUISE
FITZGERALD, BERYL

HOFFMANN, ERNST THEODOR A
HOFFMANN, ERNST THEODOR W

HOFFMANN, KATE
HOFFMANN, MARGARET JONES

HOFFMANN, LIESELOTTE
VON ELTZ, LIESELOTTE [H]

HOFFMANN, PEGGY
HOFFMANN, MARGARET JONES

HOFFMANN-ALEITH, EVA
HEMPEL, EVA

HOFFNER, DOROTHY
DOANE, PELAGIE

HOFMAN, ANTON
HOLLO, ANSELM

HOFMANN, JO
MAHR, YVONNE

HOFMEYER, HANS
FLEISCHER, ANTHONY

HOFSOMMER, DON L.
HOFSOMMER, DONOVAN LOWELL

HOFSTEDE, GEERT
HOFSTEDE, GERARD HENDRIK

HOFSTEDE, GEERT H.
HOFSTEDE, GERARD HENDRIK

HOGAN, BEN
GENBERG, KJELL E.

HOGAN, D.C.
HOGL, DIETRICH

HOGAN, DAVID
GALLAGHER, FRANK

HOGAR, JACKSON
MOSKOVITZ, JACK

HOGARTH, CHARLES
BOWEN, [IVOR] IVAN
CREASEY, JOHN

HOGARTH, DOUGLAS
PHILLIPS-BIRT, DOUGLAS

HOGARTH, EMMETT
POLONSKY, ABRAHAM C.
WILSON, MITCHELL A.

HOGARTH, JOHN
FINNIN, [OLIVE] MARY

HOGARTH, JR.
KENT, ROCKWELL

HOGBOTEL, SEBASTIAN
GOTT, KENNETH DAVIDSON

HOGE, PHYLLIS
THOMPSON, PHYLLIS [HOGE]

HOGG, BETH [T]
HOGG, ELIZABETH [T]

HOGSTAD, OYVIND
HORNE, HERMOD

HOGUE, DOCK
HOGUE, WILBUR OWLINGS

HOHENOFEN, M.B.
BLANK, MATTHIAS

HOHENTHAL, KARL
MAY, KARL FRIEDRICH

HOHOFF, TAY
TORREY, THERESE V. HOHOFF

HOKE, HELEN [L]
WATTS, HELEN L. HOKE

HOLBACH, JUPP
ENGEL, ELMAR

HOLBEACH, HENRY
RANDS, WILLIAM BRIGHTY

HOLBERG, LEWIS
HOLBERG, LUDVIG

HOLBROOK, JACK
VANCE, JOHN HOLBROOK

HOLBROOK, JOHN
VANCE, JOHN HOLBROOK

HOLBROOK, PETER
GLICK, CARL CANNON

HOLBROOK, SABRA
ERICKSON, SABRA ROLLINS

HOLCOMBE
GODFREY, LIONEL ROBERT H.

HOLCOMBE, ARNOLD
GOLSWORTHY, ARNOLD

HOLCROFT, M.H.
HOLCROFT, MONTAGUE HARRY

HOLDE, MATTHEW
PARKINSON, ROGER

HOLDEN, ADELE
CECH, ADELE

HOLDEN, DALBY
HAMMOND, GERALD [A.D.]

HOLDEN, ELIZABETH RHODA
LAWRENCE, LOUISE

HOLDEN, GENEVIEVE
POU, GENEVIEVE LONG

HOLDEN, JOANNE
CORBY, JANE [IRENITA]
ROBERTS, WILLO DAVIS

HOLDEN, LARRY
HELLER, LORENZ

HOLDEN, LESLIE
HENSLEY, DENISE E.
MILLER, HOLLY G.

HOLDEN, MARC
HILL, LAWSON W.

HOLDEN, MONIQUE
HOLDEN, LISA

HOLDEN, W.C.
HOLDEN, WILLIAM CURRY

HOLDER, BOB N.
MULLARKY, TAYLOR

HOLDER, SAMANTHA
BURNS, CAROL
JONES, DEBORAH

HOLDRETH, LIONEL G.
GREG, PERCY

HOLIDAY, CECIL W.
HAGGOVIST, ARNE

HOLIDAY, GRANT
GARDNER, ERLE STANLEY

HOLIDAY, HOMER
DEBEAUBIEN, PHILIP FRANCI

HOLK, JAN
MULLER, PAUL ALFRED

HOLL, DR. STEFAN
FECHTNER, WOLFGANG

HOLLAND, BRUD
HOLLAND, JEROME HEARTWELL

HOLLAND, CLIVE
HANKINSON, CHARLES JAMES

HOLLAND, DELL
COONS, WILLIAM R.

HOLLAND, ELIZABETH
BAXTER, ELIZABETH

HOLLAND, JAN
VITRINGA, ANNES JOHAN

HOLLAND, JOYCE
MORICE, DAVE

HOLLAND, KATRIN
LOEWENGARD, HEIDI H.H.

HOLLAND, KEL
WHITTINGTON, HARRY

HOLLAND, LINDA
ROTSLER, WILLIAM

HOLLAND, LYS
GATER, DILYS

HOLLAND, MARCUS
CALDWELL, JANET TAYLOR

HOLLAND, MARTY
HOLLAND, MARY

HOLLAND, REBECCA
HORANSKS, RUBY

HOLLAND, ROSEMARY
PATTINSON, LEE

HOLLAND, RUTH
HOLLAND, EDITH

HOLLAND, TOM
KING, ALBERT

HOLLANDER, LESLIE
BERGER, ALBERT
NERAL, DIANNE

HOLLANDER, PAUL
SILVERBERG, ROBERT

HOLLBERG, JOHN
HALL, GUS

HOLLBURG, MARTIN
BURGDORF, KARL-ULRICH
EISELE, MARTIN
HOHLBEIN, WOLFGANG E.
LE BLANC, THOMAS

HOLLDOBLER, BERT
HOELLDOBLER, BERTHOLD K.

HOLLE, CHRISTIAN
BRINKMANN, KARL HERMANN

HOLLEGE, JAMES
WORKMAN, JAMES

HOLLERBOCHEN
BRADBURY, RAY [DOUGLAS]

HOLLIDAY, ARLENE
HODAPP, ARLENE S.

HOLLIDAY, DELORES
TABOR, DEE
VILE, DELORES HOLLIDAY

HOLLIDAY, DON
BLOCK, LAWRENCE
CASE, DAVID
DRESNER, HAL
KNOLES, WILLIAM [H]
PLOTNIK, ARTHUR

HOLLIDAY, JOE
HOLLIDAY, JOSEPH

HOLLING, H.P.
FROHLICH, HEINZ-PETER

HOLLINGER, MATT
GREEN, ROGER

HOLLINSHED, JUDITH
HAWTHORNE, JULIAN

HOLLIS, H.H.
RAMEY, BEN H.

HOLLIS, JIM
ROURKE, JAMES F.A.
SUMMERS, HOLLIS [S]
TRIMBLE, LOUIS P.

HOLLISTER, H.C.
NAGEL, HERBERT CHRISTIAN

HOLLISTER, RAINE
PHEGLEY, ANNA

HOLLOWAY, JEAN
TOBIN, JEAN HOLLOWAY

HOLLOWAY, TERESA
KOVACK, TERI S. [TERRY]

HOLLOWAY, TESS
KOVACK, TERI S. [TERRY]

HOLLRIEDE, HAGDIS
BRAKENHOFF, MARGARETHE

HOLLRIEGEL, ARNOLD
BERMANN, RICHARD ARNOLD

HOLLSTEIN, JOHANNES
GUMMERT, CHARLOTTE

HOLLY, J. HUNTER
HOLLY, JOAN CAROL

HOLLY, JOAN HUNTER
HOLLY, JOAN CAROL

HOLM, BILL
HOLM, OSCAR WILLIAM

HOLM, CORNELIA
KORN, ILSE

HOLM, DON
HOLM, DONALD RAYMOJND

HOLM, FRED
MOLL, RUDOLF

HOLM, HANNEBO
TENFJORD, JOHANNE MARIE

HOLM, HANS
HANDL, JOSEPH

HOLM, PETER
HOLMSTEN, GEORG

HOLM, RALF
GROSSMANN, HANS HUGO

HOLM, SAXE
JACKSON, HELEN HUNT

HOLM, STINE
MULLER-TANNEWITZ, ANNA

HOLMAN, BOB
HOLMAN, ROBERT

HOLME, CONSTANCE
PUNCHARD, CONSTANCE HOLME

HOLME, K.E.
HILL, [J.E.] CHRISTOPHER

HOLMES, A.R.
BATES, HARRY ARTHUR

HOLMES, ARNOLD W.
FRYEFIELD, MAURICE P.

HOLMES, B.P.
HOLMES, BRYAN JOHN

HOLMES, BUTCH
HOLMES, EMORY II

HOLMES, CAPT. HOWARD
HARBAUGH, THOMAS C.

HOLMES, CAROLINE
MASON, SYDNEY CHARLES

HOLMES, CLARE FRANCES
FRANCES, CLARE

HOLMES, DEE
BULK, NANCY HARWOOD

HOLMES, FRANCES
FRANCES, CLARE

HOLMES, GEOFFREY
WOOLRICH, DANIEL

HOLMES, GORDON
SHIEL, MATTHEW PHIPPS
TRACY, LOUIS

HOLMES, GRANT
KNIPSCHEER, JOHANNES M.W.

HOLMES, H.H.
WHITE, WILLIAM A.P.

HOLMES, JACK D.L.
LAZARUS, JACK DAVID

HOLMES, JAY
HOLMES, JOSEPH EVERETT

HOLMES, JOHN
SOUSTER, [HOLMES] RAYMOND

HOLMES, KENYON
DERLETH, AUGUST [WILLIAM]

HOLMES, L.G.
LANDSBOROUGH, GORDON H.

HOLMES, L.P.
HOLMES, L[LEWELLYN] P.

HOLMES, RAYMOND
SOUSTER, [HOLMES] RAYMOND

HOLMES, RICK
HARDWICK, RICHARD HOLMES

HOLMGREN, GEORGE ELLEN
HOLMGREN, HELEN JEAN

HOLMGREN, SISTER GEORGE J
HOLMGREN, HELEN JEAN

HOLMS, G. RANDOLPH
THOMPSON, RICHARD

HOLMS, HOLGER
ELLINGER, AUGUST

HOLMSEN, BJARNE P.
HOLZ, ARNO
SCHLAF, JOHANNES

HOLORENSHAW, HENRY
NEEDHAM, JOSEPH

HOLROYD, SAM
BURTON, SAMUEL HOLROYD

HOLST, LIANE
DREYSEL, DORE

HOLT, ANDREW
ANHALT, EDWARD

HOLT, ARAM
STANNARD, DAVID

HOLT, BRUCE
UTLEY, STEVEN

HOLT, CONRAD G.
FEARN, JOHN RUSSELL

HOLT, E. CARLETON
GUIGO, ERNEST PHILIP

HOLT, ELISABETH
GIBSON, LAVINIA

HOLT, ELIZABETH
KING, KAY

HOLT, GAVIN
RODDA, [P] CHARLES

HOLT, GEORGE
TUBB, E.C.

HOLT, GORDON
KELLY, HAROLD ERNEST

HOLT, HARMONY
ROTSLER, WILLIAM

HOLT, HELEN
PAINE, LAURAN BOSWORTH

HOLT, JOAN
WILSON, JOAN HOLT

HOLT, KARE
HOLT, KAARE

HOLT, MARGARET
PARISH, MARGARET HOLT

HOLT, MICHAEL
MARTIN, DAVID

HOLT, RACKHAM
HOLT, MARGARET VAN V.

HOLT, RICHARD
HOLTON, WALTER H.

HOLT, ROCHELLE L.
DU BOIS, ROCHELLE L. HOLT

HOLT, SAM
WESTLAKE, DONALD [EDWIN]

HOLT, SAMUEL
WESTLAKE, DONALD [EDWIN]

HOLT, STEPHEN
THOMPSON, HARLAN HOWARD

HOLT, TEX
HOPSON, WILLIAM L.
JOSCELYN, ARCHIE LYNN
RISTER, CLAUDE
SCOTT, ALEXANDER LESLIE

HOLT, TOM
HOLT, THOMAS CHARLES LOU.

HOLT, VICTORIA
HIBBERT, ELEANOR BURFORD

HOLTEN, FRITZ
KALTENBOECK, JOHANNES

HOLTON, H.B.
HOSSENT, HARRY

HOLTON, LEONARD
WIBBERLEY, LEONARD [P.O.]

HOLTZ, HANNELORE
KROLLPFEIFFER, HANNELORE

HOLYER, ERNIE
HOLYER, ERNA MARIA

HOLYOKE, ANNA
HOWARD, ANNA H.C.

HOLZ, DETLEV
BENJAMIN, WALTER

HOLZAPFEL, RUDI
HOLZAPFEL, RUDOLF PATRICK

HOLZEL, TOM
HOLZEL, THOMAS MARTIN

HOLZMAN, RED
HOLZMAN, WILLIAM

HOLZMAYR, SCHOLASTIKA
LAXANGER, GUSTL

HOLZNER, SEBASTIAN
HUNDSDORFER, GERHARD
REHFELD, FRANK

HOMBURGER, ERIK
ERIKSON, ERIK HOMBURGER

HOME GUARD
INGAMELLS, F.G.

HOME, MICHAEL
BUSH, CHARLIE CHRISTMAS

HOME, T.
HOME-GALL, WILLIAM B.

HOME-GALL, REGINALD
HOME-GALL, EDWARD REG.

HOMELY, JOSIAS
BRADFORD, JOHN

HOMER & ASSOCIATES
GALL, MICHAEL

HOMES, GEOFFREY
MAINWARING, DANIEL [G.H.]

HOMESLEY, LEATRICE
WYLIE, PHILIP

HOMEWOOD, HARRY
HOMEWOOD, CHARLES H.

HOMMY, BEG
HALL, THOMAS HENRY

HOMO, [DR.] ALI
HOMPF, ALOIS

HOMOSAP
NUTTALL, JEFF

HON MEMBER FOR X
DE CHAIR, SOMERSET S.

HONEYBEE
SMITH, ELIZABETH S.

HONEYCOMB, HENRY
HUNT, [J.H.] LEIGH

HONEYCOMBE, WILLIAM ESQ.
GARDINER, RICHARD

HONEYCUTT, RICHARD
HARDWICK, RICHARD

HONEYMAN, BRENDA
CLARKE, BRENDA M.L.H.

PSEUDONYMS

HONIGFELD, GILBERT
HOWARD, GILBERT

HONORIA N.
POWER, MARGUERITE A.

HOOD, JACK
HOOD-PHILLIPS, J.H.

HOOD, MARK
MACDONNELL, JAMES EDMOND

HOOD, SARAH
KILLOUGH, KAREN LEE

HOOD, STEPHEN
LEWIS, JACK

HOOKER, FRANCES
HOROVITZ, FRANCES MARGAR.

HOOKER, P.T.
KRAMER, PETER

HOOKER, RICHARD
HORNBERGER, H. RICHARD

HOOKS, GENE
HOOKS, GAYLOR EUGENE

HOOLEY, TERESA
BUTLER, TERESA MARY

HOOP, CECIL J.
REIF, IRENE

HOOPER, BETT
HOOPER, ELIZABETH EDNA

HOOPER, BIFF
OBRECHT, JAS

HOOPER, BYRD
ST. CLAIR, BYRD HOOPER

HOOPER, PETER
HOOPER, HEDLEY COLWILL

HOOS, SUZANNE
STOCKENBERG, ANTOINETTE

HOOSIER, HANK
MINER, VIRGINIA SCOTT

HOOSIER, HANNAH
MINER, VIRGINIA SCOTT

HOOT
VON ZITZEWITZ, HOOT

HOOTON, CHARLES
ROWE, VIVIAN C[LAUDE]

HOOVER, CAIL
LAUE, ALEXANDER

HOPE, AMANDA
LEWIS, JUDITH BERESFORD

HOPE, ANDREE
HARVEY, ANNIE JANE T.

HOPE, ANDREW
HERN, [GEORGE] ANTHONY

HOPE, ANTHONY
HAWKINS, ANTHONY HOPE

HOPE, ASCOTT R.
MONCRIEFF, ROBERT HOPE

HOPE, BRIAN
CREASEY, JOHN

HOPE, CAMILLA
THOMPSON, GRACE E.

HOPE, CECIL
SPERO, LEOPOLD

HOPE, DAVID
FRASER, DOUGLAS

HOPE, EDGAR
HOOK, SAMUEL CLARKE

HOPE, EDWARD
COFFEY, EDWARD HOPE, JR.

HOPE, ELIZABETH
MANCE, ELIZABETH HOPE

HOPE, ESTHER
ST. JOHN, PERCY BOLLNGBRK

HOPE, FELIX
WILLIAMSON, CLAUDE C.

HOPE, GRAHAM
HOPE, JESSIE

HOPE, JACQUELINE
HACSI, JACQUELINE

HOPE, JOHN FRANCIS
RANDALL, A.E.

HOPE, LAURA LEE
ADAMS, HARRIET S.
CREAGER, EUNICE WHAYNE
MCQUAY, MICHAEL DENNIS
STANLEY, GEORGE EDWARD
STRATEMEYER, EDWARD

HOPE, LAWRENCE
NICHOLSON, VIOLET

HOPE, MARGARET
KNIGHT, ALANNA
WICKSTEED, MARGARET HOPE

HOPE, MARK
MURRAY, EUSTACE C.G.

HOPE, NOEL
MOREWOOD, SARAH L.

HOPE, STANTON
STANTON-HOPE, W.E.

HOPE, WALTER
PHILLIPS, HORACE

HOPGOOD, ALAN
RUHEN, CARL

HOPKINS, A.T.
TURNGREN, ANNETTE

HOPKINS, HIRAM
SELTZER, CHARLES ALDEN

HOPKINS, JAMES
CLARKE, BODEN
NOLAN, WILLIAM F.

HOPKINS, LIGHTNIN'
HOPKINS, SAM

HOPKINS, LYMAN
FOLSOM, FRANKLIN [B]

HOPKINS, PRYNS
HOPKINS, PRYNCE [C]

HOPKINS, STANLEY
HOLT, HENRY

HOPKINS, STANLEY JR.
MORLEY, BLYTHE

HOPKINS, VIOLA
WINNER, VIOLA HOPKINS

HOPKINSON, TOM
HOPKINSON, HENRY THOMAS

HOPPEN, HARRIET
HOPPEN-RAM, HENDERIKA W.

HOPPER, HEDA
FURRY, ELDA

HOPPER, MAX
BELLINI, TINA

HOPPER, SAM
HASLAM, NICKY

HOPPLEY, GEORGE
WOOLRICH, CORNELL HOPLEY

HORATIO
PROUST, [V-L-G-E] MARCEL

HORATIO, JANE
CROWCROFT, PETER
CUDLIPP, EDYTHE

HORLA, ALEXANDER
FLECHTNER, HANS JOACHIM

HORLAK, E.E.
TEPPER, SHERI S.

HORMANN, MARKUS
BASIL, OTTO

HORN, ALFRED ALOYSIUS
SMITH, ALFRED ALOYSIUS

HORN, CHESTER
MASON, SYDNEY CHARLES

HORN, LUDWIG J.
BARANIECKI, ROBERT LEO

HORN, OTTO
BAUERLE, ADOLF-JOHANN

HORN, PETER
KUTTNER, HENRY
MOORE, CATHERINE LUCILLE
VERN, DAVID

HORN, PHYLLIS
HORNBUCKLE, PHYLLIS

HORN, R. de S.
JUDSON, EDWARD Z.C.

HORN, TRADER
SMITH, ALFRED ALOYSIUS

HORN, W.O. v.
OERTEL, FRIEDRICH W.P.

HORNA, HENRIK
HAAPAKOSKI, HENRIK

HORNBLOWER, HARRY C.
SHRIVER, HARRY C.

HORNBROOKE, OBADIAH
COMFORT, ALEXANDER

HORNBY, JOHN
HORNBY, JOHN WILKINSON

HORNE, HOWARD
PAYNE, PIERRE S. ROBERT

HORNE, PETER
REED, DAVID V.

HORNE, R. HENGIST
HORNE, RICHARD HENRY

HORNEM, HORACE ESQ.
BYRON, GEORGE GORDON NOEL

HORNER, J.C.
HORNER, JOHN CURWEN

HORNER, LANCE
HORNER, KENRIC LANCASTER

HORNIK, EDITH LYNN
BEER, EDITH LYNN

HORNIK-BEER, EDITH LYNN
BEER, EDITH LYNN

HORNSCHU, PAUL KARL
KETTLE, PAUL

HORNUNG, E.W.
HORNUNG, ERNEST WILLIAM

HORNUNG, EDWIN F.
BRAUN, WILBUR

HOROWITZ, AL
HOROWITZ, ISRAEL A.

HORSELY, RAMSBOTTOM
BERNE, ERIC [L]

HORSELY, T.J.
CURTIES, T.J. HORSELY

HORSLEY, DAVID
BINGLEY, DAVID ERNEST

HORSTEN, UDO
KALMUCZAK, ROLF

HORSTER, HANS-ULRICH
RHEIN, EDUARD

HORSTING, JESSIE
BUCHANAN, JESSIE HORSTING

HORSTMANN, ROSEMARY
WATERS, ROSEMARY ELIZAB.

HORTER, KRISTIN
LAHANY, KRISTIN E.E.

HORTON, FELIX LEE
FLOREN, LEE

HORTON, NAOMI
HORTON, SUSAN

HORTON, ROBERT J.
ROBERTS, JAMES

HORVITZ, LESLIE [ALAN]
HOROVITZ, LESLIE

HOSELITZ, BERT F.
HOSELITZ, BERTHOLD FRANK

HOSIER, PETER
CLARK, DOUGLAS M.J.

HOSKINS, PHILLIP
HOSKINS, ROBERT

HOSOKAWA, BILL
HOSOKAWA, WILLIAM K.

HOSTOS, E.M. DE
HOSTOS Y BONILLA, EUGENIA

HOSTOS, EUGENIA M. DE
HOSTOS Y BONILLA, EUGENIA

HOTSPUR
CURLING, BRYAN WILLIAM R.

HOTSPUR, PAUL
BIDSTON, LESTER

HOU, FU-WU
HOUN, FRANKLIN W.

HOUDINI, HARRY
EDDY, CLIFFORD MARTIN JR.
GIBSON, WALTER B.
LOVECRAFT, H[OWARD] P.
WEISS, EHRICH

HOUDINI, MERLIN X.
BORGMANN, DMITRI A.

HOUGAN, JIM
HOUGAN, JAMES RICHARD

HOUGH, DON
HUFF, DARRELL

HOUGHTON, CLAUDE
OLDFIELD, CLAUDE H.

HOUGHTON, ELIZABETH
GILZEAN, ELIZABETH H.B.

HOURANI, A.H.
HOURANI, ALBERT HABIB

HOURS-MIEDAN, MADELEINE
HOURS, MADELEINE

HOUSE, ANNE W.
MCCAULEY, ELFRIEDA BABNK.

HOUSE, BRANT
BITTNER, ARCHIBALD
CHADWICK, PAUL
FLEMING-ROBERTS, G.T.
SCOTT, ROBERT T. MAITLAND
TEPPERMAN, EMILE C.
ZAGAT, ARTHUR LEO

HOUSE, BRIAN
LUDLUM, ROBERT

HOUSE, PATRICIA
WHEEN, FRANCIS

HOUSE, R.C.
HOUSE, RICHARD CALVIN

HOUSEMAN, JULIAN
GIBSON, WALTER B.

HOUSEMAN, PHYLLIS
HOUSEMAN, JACK & PHYLLIS

HOUSEPIAN, MARJORIE
DOBKIN, MARJORIE HOUSEP.

HOUSSAYE, ARSENE
HOUSSET, ARSENE

HOUSTON, BRAD
GREEN, ROGER

HOUSTON, DAVID
LUMPKIN, HOUSTON FORCE

HOUSTON, HENRIETTA
LICHTE, PRUDENCE BINGHAM

HOUSTON, KILIAN
BRUNNER, JOHN [K.H.]

HOUSTON, R.B.
RAE, HUGH C[RAWFORD]

HOUSTON, WILL
PAINE, LAURAN BOSWORTH

HOUTON, KATHLEEN
KILGORE, KATHLEEN

HOUVILLE, GERARD D'
DE HEREDIA, MARIE-LOUISE

HOVELL, LUCY A.
HOVELL, LUCILLE A.P.

HOVEN, ERNIEST
HOOKER, FANNY

HOVORRE, M. AUBERRE
HOWARD, ALBERT WALDO

HOWARD, ALYSSA
BUCKHOLTZ, EILEEN [G]
GLICK, RUTH [BURTNICK]
MALES, CAROLYN
TITCHENER, LOUISE

HOWARD, BARBARA
CORYELL, JOHN RUSSELL

HOWARD, BILL
SHANNON, MIKE

HOWARD, BOB
STROUP, WILLIAM

HOWARD, BRUCE
DAY, GEORGE

HOWARD, CAPTAIN [POLICE]
SENARENS, LUIS P.

HOWARD, CARLETON
HOWE, CHARLES HORACE

HOWARD, CECIL
SMITH, CECIL HOWARD III

HOWARD, CHARLES
HARBAUGH, THOMAS C.

HOWARD, COLIN
SHAW, [COLIN] HOWARD

HOWARD, CONSTANCE
WHITE, CONSTANCE

HOWARD, CORALIE
COGSWELL, CORALIE NORRIS

HOWARD, CORRIE
JARDINE, JULIE ANN

HOWARD, DON
MENZEL, DONALD H.

HOWARD, ELEANOR
HODGSON, ELEANOR P.

HOWARD, ELIZABETH
MIZNER, ELIZABETH HOWARD
PAINE, LAURAN BOSWORTH

HOWARD, GEORGE
KAY, FREDERIC GEORGE

HOWARD, H.P.
DIEDRICH, KLAUS
HAHN, RONALD M.
PUKALLUS, HORST

HOWARD, HARRY
OGNALL, LEOPOLD HORACE

HOWARD, HARTLEY
OGNALL, LEOPOLD HORACE

HOWARD, HELEN
PENDOWER, THOMAS CURTIS H

HOWARD, J.T.
GILMORE, JOHN

HOWARD, JACK
RATHBORNE, ST. GEORGE

HOWARD, JAY
SAXTON, JOSEPHINE

HOWARD, JEAN
MACGIBBON, JEAN

HOWARD, JESSICA
MONROE, SCHERE
SCHERE, JEAN K. & MONROE

HOWARD, JILL
JAFFEE, SUSANNE

HOWARD, JOAN
GORDON, PATRICIA

HOWARD, JOHN
HEWITT, JOHN [HAROLD]
STIDWORTHY, JOHN

HOWARD, JOHN M.
HINCKS, CYRIL MALCOLM

HOWARD, JULIA
ADAMS-MANSON, PAT
CAMDEN, PATRICIA

HOWARD, KATHERINE
BLACK, MARGARET K.

HOWARD, KEBLE
BELL, JOHN KEBLE

HOWARD, KEN
LUMPKIN, HOUSTON FORCE

HOWARD, KEZ
HOUSTON, DAVID

HOWARD, LEE
LEE HOWARD, LEON A.

HOWARD, LEIGH
HOWARD, LEON A. LEE

HOWARD, LESLEY
ABBOTT, MONICA & STANLEY

HOWARD, LINDA
HOWINGTON, LINDA

HOWARD, LINDEN
MANLEY-TUCKER, AUDRIE

HOWARD, LOIS
GRUBER, FRANK

HOWARD, LYNDE
HOWARD, LYNETTE DELSEY

HOWARD, MARIE
LENA, MARIE HOWARD

HOWARD, MARK
RIGSBY, HOWARD [VECHEL]

HOWARD, MARY
MUSSI, MARY

HOWARD, NONA
LUXTON, LEONORA KATHRINE

HOWARD, PATRICK
HOWARD, ROBERT E.

HOWARD, PAUL
SPERRY, HENRY TREAT

HOWARD, PROSPER
DOWN, C. MAURICE
HAMILTON, CHARLES H.S.
HINTON, HERBERT ALLAN

HOWARD, ROLAND
CATCHPOLE, WILLIAM LESLIE

HOWARD, RONNALIE ROPER
ROPER, RONNALIE J.

HOWARD, SIDNEY
RAY, ANNA CHAOIN

HOWARD, TED
HOWARD, THEODORE KORNER

HOWARD, TOM
REID, JOHN T.H.

HOWARD, TROY
PAINE, LAURAN BOSWORTH

HOWARD, VECHEL
RIGSBY, HOWARD [VECHEL]

HOWARD, WARREN
GIFFORD, JAMES NOBLE

HOWARD, WARREN F.
POHL, FREDERIK

HOWARTH, JOHN
HARBINSON, WILLIAM ALLEN

HOWAT, JEAN
HERBERT, HELEN JEAN

HOWE, CLIFF
DENT, LESTER

HOWE, JOSEPHINE M.O.
O'CONNOR HOWE, JOSEPHINE

HOWE, M.A. DE WOLFE
HOWE, MARK ANTH. DE WOLFE

HOWE, MURIEL
SMITHIES, MURIEL

HOWE, SUSANNAH
THOMAS, BREE

HOWELL, JOHN
HALL, GUS

HOWELL, PATRICIA HAGAN
HAGAN, MARY PATRICIA

HOWELL, S.
STYLES, FRANK SHOWELL

HOWELL, SCOTT
KING, ALBERT

HOWELL, S[HOWELL]
STYLES, [FRANK] SHOWELL

HOWELL, VIRGINIA TIER
ELLISON, VIRGINIA HOWELL

HOWELLS, W.D.
HOWELLS, WILLIAM DEAN

HOWERD, GARETH
THOMAS, ROBERT RICHARD

HOWES, JANE
SHIRAS, WILMAR H.

HOWES, ROYCE B.
BLEAKERSTOWE, GEORGE H.

HOWES, ROYCE B.
BLY, BEVANS

HOWITZER, BRONSON
HARDMAN, RICHARDS LYNDEN

HOWLETT, LANCE
HILL, LANCE

HOWLEY, MARK
GREENWOOD, GEORGE A.

HOWORTH, M.K.
BLACK, MARGARET K.

HOWORTH, MARGARET
BLACK, MARGARET K.

HOY, DAVID
GIBSON, WALTER B.

HOY, ELIZABETH
CONARAIN, ALICE [NINA]

HOY, NINA
ROTH, ARTHUR JOSEPH

HOYAU, GEORGES
HEINDL, GOTTFRIED

HOYER, NIELS
HARTHERN-JACOBSON, ERNST

HOYLE, CORAL
TITUS, CORAL HOYLE

HOYLE, MARTHA BYRD
BYRD, MARTHA

HOYT, DON
GRANBECK, MARILYN
MOORE, ARTHUR

HOYT, HELEN
LYMAN, HELEN HOYT

HOYT, NELSON
KING, ALBERT

HOYT, W.M.
MANNING, WILLIAM HENRY

HOZJUSZ
DOBRACZYNSKI, JAN

HSIA, HSIAO
LIU, WU-CHI

HSIANG, YEH
LIU, SYDNEY [CHIEH]

HSU, K.
HSU, KENNETH JINGHWA

HSU, K. JINGHWA
HSU, KENNETH JINGHWA

HSU, K.J.
HSU, KENNETH JINGHWA

HSUN, LU
SHU-JEN, CHOU

HU, SHI MING
HU, SHU MING

HUAN YUE
SHEN CONGWEN

HUANG, FENG
GIBSON, WALTER B.

HUANG, PO-FEI
HUANG, PARKER PO-FEI

HUANZHULOUZHU
LI SHANJI

HUBBARD, ANNE MARGARET
PRILEY, MARGARET HUBBARD

HUBBARD, CAPT. L. RON
HUBBARD, L. RON

HUBBARD, JOAN
JACKSON, KATHRYN

HUBBARD, KIN
HUBBARD, FRANK MCKINNEY

HUBBARD, L. RON
HUBBARD, LAFAYETTE RONALD

HUBBARD, REGINA
HUBBARD, RICHARD

HUBBELL, BERNARD
HUBBARD, L. RON

HUBECK, JORG
PUPPA, GEORG

HUBELAIRE, JACOBUS
KELLER, DAVID H.

HUBELL, NED
HUBELL, LOUIS W.

HUBER, FLORENCE M.
HUBER, MARY FLORENCE

HUBERT, CAM
CAMERON, BARBARA ANNE

HUBERT, FRANK
SHAW, FRANK H.

HUBERT, JIM
HUBERT, JAMES LEE

HUBERT, TORD
LINDSTROM, TORD HUBERT

HUBY, FELIX
HUNGERBUHLER, EBERHARD

HUCHET, CLAIRE
BISHOP, CLAIRE HUCHET

HUDLESTON, JOHN
DENT, C.H.

HUDLESTON, ROBERT
DENT, C.H.

HUDSON, ABE
HOLMES, WILFRED JAY

HUDSON, ALEC
HOLMES, WILFRED JAY

HUDSON, ANNA
ALGERMISSEN, JO ANN

HUDSON, E.J.
JENNISON, JOHN WILLIAM

HUDSON, EDWARD S.
HALE, F.J.

HUDSON, HARRIET L.
SHALEEN, LEIGH

HUDSON, HARRY
HUNTER, HENRY

HUDSON, HELEN
LANE, HELEN

HUDSON, JACK
HUDSON, LAVASSA V.

HUDSON, JAN
HUDSON, JANECE OLIVER
SMITH, GEORGE H[ENRY]

HUDSON, JANIS REAMS
HUDSON, JANECE OLIVER

HUDSON, JEFFREY
CRICHTON, [JOHN] MICHAEL

HUDSON, MEG
KOEHLER, MARGARET [H]

HUDSON, MICHAEL
KUBE-MCDOWELL, MICHAEL P.

HUDSON, PEGGY
HERZ, PEGGY

HUDSON, STEPHEN
SCHIFF, SYDNEY

HUDSON, TED
FEY, JEREMY

HUDSON, W.H.
HUDSON, WILLIAM HENRY

HUEFFER, FRANCIS
HUEFFER, FRANZ

HUEL, FRITS
ELIZA, GODFRIED

HUEMER, DICK
HUEMER, RICHARD MARTIN

HUEPPER, FRANK
HUEFFER, FRANZ

HUERLIMANN, BETTINA
HUERLIMANN-KIEPENHEUER, B

HUETHER, ANNE FRANCES
FREEMAN, ANNE FRANCES

HUFF, T.E.
HUFF, TOM E.

HUFF, T.S.
HUFF, TANYA SUE

HUFMAN
GOFMAN, VICTOR V.

HUGER, A.R.
RAUSCH, ANNEGRET [H]

HUGGINS, ROY
BROWNE, HOWARD

HUGGINS, RUTH MABEL
ARTHUR, RUTH M.

HUGH, MACNAIR
KAHLER, HUGH [T] MACNAIR

HUGH, R.
HUG, ERNST-WALTER

HUGHES, ALISON
OLIVER, DORIS M.

HUGHES, BRENDA
COLLUMS, BRENDA

HUGHES, C.J. PENNETHORNE
HUGHES, CHARLES J. PENN.

HUGHES, CALLY
SMALL, LASS

HUGHES, COLIN
CREASEY, JOHN

HUGHES, DUSTY
HUGHES, RICHARD HOLLAND

HUGHES, EDEN
BUTTERWORTH, WILLIAM E.

HUGHES, ELIZABETH
ZACHARY, HUGH

HUGHES, HERBERT
GILLINGS, WALTER H.

HUGHES, JAMES PENNETHORNE
HUGHES, CHARLES J. PENN.

HUGHES, M. ALISON
STEED, MABEL A.

HUGHES, MATILDA
MACLEOD, CHARLOTTE [M.H.]

HUGHES, PHILLIP
PHILLIPS, HUGH

HUGHES, SAM
WILKS, BRIAN

HUGHES, SAMANTHA
HUFFORD, SUSAN

HUGHES, SARA
SAUNDERS, SUSAN

HUGHES, TED
HUGHES, EDWARD J.

HUGHES, TERRENCE
BEST, R. BRETON AMIS

HUGHES, TRACY
HERRINGTON, TERRI

HUGHES, VIRGINIA
CAMPBELL, HOPE
WALLIS, GERALDINE MCDONL.

HUGHES, ZACH
ZACHARY, HUGH

HUGHES, ZACHARY
ZACHARY, HUGH

HUGILL, STAN JAMES
HUGILL, STANLEY JAMES

HUGO, DON
LAZENBY, NORMAN A.

HUGO, ETIENNE
HUGO, LEON HARGREAVES

HUGO, GRANT
CABLE, JAMES

HUGO, IVAN
GUILER, HUGH

HUGO, RICHARD
HUCH, RICARDA

HUIDODRO, VINCENTE
HUIDODRO FERNANDEZ, VINC.

HULBECK, CHARLES R.
HULSENBECK, RICHARD

HULBERT, LLOYD
POPE, F.W.

HULDA
BJARKLIND, UNNUR B.

HULL, CHARLES
CHARLES, GORDON H.

HULL, E. MAYNE
VAN VOGT, ALFRED ELTON
VAN VOGT, EDNA MAYNE

HULL, E.M.
HULL, EDITH MAUDE

HULL, ERIC TRAVISS
HARNAN, TERRY

HULL, H. BRAXTON
JACOBS, HELEN HULL

HULL, JESSE REDDING
HULL, JESSIE REDDING

HULL, OPAL
LEHNUS, OPAL [HULL]

HULL, RICHARD
SAMPSON, RICHARD HENRY

HULLAR, LINK
HULLAR, LEONARD EARL

HULME BEAMAN, S.G.
HULME BEAMAN, SYDNEY G.

HULME, T.E.
HULME, THOMAS ERNEST

HULSEN, ADRIAN
RHEIN, EDUARD

HULTKRANTZ, AKE G.B.
HULTKRANTZ, AAKE G.B.

HUMANA, CHARLES
JACOBS, CHARLES

HUME, ARTHUR W.J.G.
ORD-HUME, ARTHUR W.J.G.

HUME, BASIL
HUME, GEORGE HALLIBURTON

HUME, BRIT
HUME, ALEXANDER BRITTON

HUME, DAVID
TURNER, J[OHN] V[ICTOR]

HUME, FERGUS
HUME, FERGUSON WRIGHT

HUME, FRANCES
BUCKLAND-WRIGHT, MARY

HUME, MICKEY
BEVARD, CAMILLE

HUMFREY, C.
OSBORNE, CHARLES H.C.

HUMILIS, HILAR
NIEDRIG, KURT-HEINZ

HUMMEL, MADELINE
MOORE, MADELINE ROBERTA

HUMMEL, SISTER MARIA I.
HUMMEL, BERTA

HUMPHREY, AILEEN
HYNE, AILEEN

HUMPHREYS, B.V.
SCHNEIDER, B.V.H.

HUMPHREYS, JOHN
OWAIN, OWAIN

HUMPHREYS, MRS.
GOLLAN, ELIZA MARGARET J.

HUMPHREYS, ROBIN A.
HUMPHREYS, ROBERT ARTHUR

HUMPHREYS, SUSAN L.
LOWELL, SUSAN

HUMPHRIES, GEOFFREY
HUMPHRYS, LESLIE GEORGE

HUMPHRIES, M.L.
HUMPHREYS, M.L.

HUNEFELD, HANNE
FRENZ, HANNELORE

HUNG LONG TOM
WILLIAMS, ROSWELL

HUNGERFORD, MRS
HAMILTON, MARGARET WOLFE

HUNGERFORD, PIXIE
BRINSMEAD, HESBA FAY

HUNGRY GULLIVER
WOLFE, THOMAS CLAYTON

HUNGRY WOLF, ADOLF
GUTOHRLEIN, ADOLF

HUNT, BARBARA
WATTERS, BARBARA HUNT

HUNT, BEVERLY
ALLEN, BEVERLY

HUNT, BOB
KOUF, MARVIN JAMES JR.

HUNT, CHARLOTTE
HODGES, DORIS MARJORIE

HUNT, CLARENCE
HOLMAN, [C] HUGH

HUNT, DAVE
HUNT, DAVID CHARLES H.

HUNT, DIANA
HUNT-BODE, GISELE

HUNT, DOROTHY
FELLOWS, DOROTHY ALICE

HUNT, EVE
HUNT, MARY EVE

HUNT, FRANCESCA
HOLLAND, ISABELLE

HUNT, FRANCIS
STRATEMEYER, EDWARD

HUNT, FREDERICK
KUHNER, HERBERT

HUNT, GILL
BRUNNER, JOHN [K.H.]
GRIFFITHS, DAVID ARTHUR
JENNISON, JOHN WILLIAM
TUBB, E.C.
HUGHES, DENNIS [TALBOT]

HUNT, HARRISON
BALLARD, W. TODHUNTER
DAVIS, NORBERT

HUNT, JENA
CONRAD, HELEN [MANAK]

HUNT, JOHN
PAINE, LAURAN BOSWORTH

HUNT, KYLE
CREASEY, JOHN

HUNT, MAURICE
PARSONS, B.

HUNT, NAN
RAY, NANCY LOUISE

HUNT, NIGEL
GREENBANK, ANTHONY HUNT

HUNT, NORMAMN C.
CROWTHER-HUNT, NORMAN C.

HUNT, NORMAN
HERSHMAN, MORRIS

HUNT, PENELOPE
NAPIER, PRISCILLA

HUNT, PETER
MARSHALL, CHARLES HUNT
YATES, GEORGE WORTHINGTON

HUNT, ROGER
ANDREWS, MERVYN
RILEY, L.W.
SLATTERY, RAY
WILKES-HUNTER, RICHARD

HUNT, STOKER
PIOTROWSKY, ANDREW

HUNTER, ALISON
HUNTER-BLAIR, NORMA

HUNTER, ANOLE
CRAWFORD, EVERETT LAKE

HUNTER, ANSON
ORRMONT, ARTHUR

HUNTER, CAPTAIN MARCY
ELLIS, EDWARD S.

HUNTER, CHRISTINE
HUNTER, MAUDE LILY

HUNTER, CLEMENTINE
KEYNES, HELEN MARY

HUNTER, CLINGHAM
ADAMS, WILLIAM TAYLOR

HUNTER, CLINGHAM M.D.
ADAMS, WILLIAM TAYLOR

HUNTER, DAWE
DOWNIE, MARY ALICE

HUNTER, E. WALDO
STURGEON, THEODORE

HUNTER, ELIZABETH
DE GUISE, ELIZABETH MARY

HUNTER, EVAN
LOMBINO, SALVATORE A.

HUNTER, GARY
HUNTER, GWEN F.
LEVEILLE, GARY

HUNTER, GEORGE
BALLARD, W. TODHUNTER

HUNTER, GEORGE E.
ELLIS, EDWARD S.

HUNTER, HALL
MARSHALL, EDISON [TESLA]

HUNTER, HILARY
YANOW, SHERRY

HUNTER, JEAN
HUNTER, ALFRED JOHN

HUNTER, JILLIAN
GARDNER, MARIA

HUNTER, JOAN
YARDE, JEANNE B.F.T.

HUNTER, JOE [J]
MCNEILLY, WILFRED G.

HUNTER, JOHN
BALLARD, W. TODHUNTER
HUNTER, ALFRED JOHN
HUNTER, CHRISTINE
HUNTER, MAUDE LILY

HUNTER, KAREN
FOX, GARDNER F.

HUNTER, LEIGH
ETCHISON, BIRDIE L[EE]

HUNTER, LEONA WESLEY
GREIF, MARTIN

HUNTER, M.O.
MABBOTT, THOMAS O.

HUNTER, MAC
HUNTER, HENRY MACGREGOR

HUNTER, MARGARET
SINGER, RONALD

HUNTER, MATTHEW
STONE, RODNEY

HUNTER, MICHAEL
TAYLOR, R.L.
SELLENGER, JOHN

HUNTER, MOLLIE
MCVEIGH, M. MOLLIE HUNTER

HUNTER, NEIL
LINAKER, MICHAEL

HUNTER, PAT
KEMPF, PAT

HUNTER, PAUL
WEAVER, BERTRAND

HUNTER, R.
WILKES-HUNTER, RICHARD

HUNTER, R. WILKES
WILKES-HUNTER, RICHARD

HUNTER, R.W.
WILKES-HUNTER, RICHARD

HUNTER, ROBIN
NEILLANDS, ROBIN

HUNTER, RODELLO
CALKINS, RODELLO

HUNTER, ROWLAND
CATCHPOLE, WILLIAM LESLIE

HUNTER, S.L.
MILAN, VICTOR [WOODWARD]
YERMAKOV, NICHOLAS VALEN.

HUNTER, TOM
BREUCKER, OSCAR HERBERT

HUNTER, VALANCY
MEAKER, ELOISE

HUNTER, VICKIE
HUNTER, VICTORIA ALBERT

HUNTER, VICKIE MACLEAN
HUNTER, VICTORIA ALBERTA

HUNTER, WILKES
WILKES-HUNTER, RICHARD

HUNTER, [LIEUT.] NED
ELLIS, EDWARD S.

HUNTINGDON, JOHN
PHILLIPS, GERALD WILLIAM

HUNTINGTON, HARRY
PENTELOW, JOHN NIX

HUNTLEY, CHET
HUNTLEY, CHESTER ROBERT

HUNTLEY, FRANCES E.
MAYNE, ETHEL COLBURN

HUNTON, MARY
GILZEAN, ELIZABETH H.B.

HUNVALD, HENRY
GROSS, HENRY H.

HURCH, CHARLES
ROCK, FRANK

HURKEY, ROOAN
HOLZAPFEL, RUDOLF PATRICK

HURLBA, ALTON
HOXIE, WALTER PALMER

HURLEY, ANN
SALERNO, ANN

HURLEY, BRUCE
FISHER, STEPHEN GOULD

HURLEY, MAXWELL
CRAWFORD, BETTY ANNE

HURLIMANN, BETTINA
HUERLIMANN-KIEPENHEUR, B.

HURLIMANN, RUTH
HUERLIMANN, RUTH

HURRICANE, RINGO
HELGATH, FRANC

HURST, ARDATH FRANCES
MAYHAR, ARDATH F.H.

HURST, BRIAN
SELLERS, CONNIE LESLIE

HUSER, VERNE
HUSER, LAVERNE CARL

HUSSERL, E.G.
HUSSERL, EDMUND GUSTAVE A

HUSSEY, LEONARD
PEARCE, BRIAN LEONARD

HUSSINGTREE, MARTIN
BALDWIN, OLIVER RIDSDALE

HUSTLE, HUGH
HALL, VERNER

HUSTON, FRAN
MILLER, RON S.

HUTCHINGS, BILL
HUTCHINGS, WILLIAM BRUCE

HUTCHINS, ANTHONY
MORLEY, LESLIE REGINALD

HUTCHINSON, A.S.M.
HUTCHINSON, ARTHUR S-M.

HUTCHINSON, ANNE
BURNETT, HALLIE

HUTCHINSON, PATRICIA
FULLBROOK, GLADYS

HUTCHINSON, R.C.
HUTCHINSON, RAY CORYTON

HUTH, MARY JO
HUTH, MARY JOSEPHINE

HUTTEN, HANS
LEITNER, RUDOLF

HUTTON, ANN
HUTTON, AUDREY GRACE W.

HUTTON, GINGER
HUTTON, VIRGINIA CAROL

HUXLEY, ALLAN
MADSEN, BORGE

HUXLEY, ELSPETH
GRANT, JOCELYN

HUY, NGUYEN NGOC
NGUYEN NGOC HUY

HUYGEN, WIL
HUYGEN, WILLIBRORD J.

HUYSMAN, J.K.
HUYSMAN, CHARLES H.G.

HUYSMAN, JORIS KARL
HUYSMAN, CHARLES M.G.

HVIEZDOSLAV
ORSZAGH, PAVOL

HYDE, CYNTHIA
SKINNER, MICHAEL

HYDE, D. HERBERT
CHAMBERS, DEREK HYDE

HYDE, E.A. WATSON
HYDE, ELIZABETH A[DSHEAD]

HYDE, ELEANOR
MUNTHE, FRANCES

HYDE, ELEANORE
COWEN, FRANCES

HYDE, HAWK
HYDE, DAYTON O[GDEN]

HYDE, ROBIN
WILKINSON, IRIS G.

HYDE, SHELLEY
REED, LILLIAN CRAIG

HYDE, TRACY ELLIOT
VENNING, COREY

HYLTON, SARA
UNSWORTH, LILIAN

HYMAN, MIRANDA
MILLER, MIRANDA

HYNDMAN, JANE LEE
WYNDHAM, LEE

HYNE, C.J. CUTCLIFFE
HYNE, CHARLES J CUTCLIFFE

HYNE, CUTCLIFFE
HYNE, CHARLES J CUTCLIFFE

I., CLARKUS
ERNSTING, WALTER

I.B.
BROWN, IVOR

I.O.
STREET, CECIL JOHN C.

I.S.
SCHNEIDER, ISADORE

IACOCCA, LEE
IACOCCA, LIDO ANTHONY

IAMS, JACK
IAMS, SAMUEL HARVEY JR.

IANNONE, JEANNE
BALZANO, JEANNE KOPPEL

IANNONE, RON
IANNONE, RONALD VINCENT

IASHEN, KAMIL
NUGMANOV, KAMIL

IBACH, LUTZ W.
RUMPFF, HEINRICH

IBARRA, CHRISOSTOMO
YABES, LEOPOLDO Y.

IBISTER, CLAIR
ISBISTER, JEAN SINCLAIR

IBIUS, ROBERT
HARRER, JOSEF ROBERT

IBRAHIM, SAMI
MOREH, SHMUEL

ICARUS
MOORCOCK, MICHAEL

ICONOCLAST
HAMILTON, MARY AGNES A.

IDAL, SVEINN
INDRIDASON, INDRIDI

IDEN, WILLIAM
GREEN, WILLIAM MARK

IDRIS
MEE, ARTHUR

IDSTROM, NILS
WIMMERMARK, KERSTEN

IFANS, GLYN
EVANS, GLYN

IGGENSEN, IGOR
RASCH, CARLOS

IGLAUER, EDITH
DALY, EDITH IGLAUER

IGNOTUS
BLASIUS, RICHARD
DE ELOLA Y GULIERREZ, JOE
FULLER, JAMES FRANKLIN
MULLER-GUTTENBRUN, ADAM
VEIGELSBERG, HUGO

IGNOTUS, AUCTOR
LEGG, W. DORR

IGNOTUS, MILES
LUTTWAK, EDWARD NICOLAE

IGNOTUS, PAUL
IGNOTUS, PAL

IKE
LANE, KATHERINE

IKER
KERNISKY, IVAN

ILE, TASMAN
PALAMOUNTAIN, ALAN

ILEISTER, CLAIR
ILEISTER, JEAN SINCLAIR

ILES, BERT
ROSS, Z. HELEN G.

ILES, FRANCIS
COX, ANTHONY BERKELEY

ILF, ILYA
FAINZIBERG, ILYA ARNOLD.

ILGERD, N.M.
DINGLER, MAX

ILLING, CLAIRE
HEIDRICH, INGEBORG

ILLIW-UEHRE, M.A. v.
HEUER, WILHELM

ILLUSTRATOR
FREY, OLIVER

IMM, GUNTHER
BISCHOF, HEINZ

IMMACULATA, SISTER
MAXWELL, SISTER MARY

IMRIE, RICHARD
PRESSBURGER, EMERIC

INCA-PABLO-OZOLLA
SEARS, ALFERD FRANCIS

INCHFAWN, FAY
WARD, ELIZABETH REBECCA

INCLEDON, PHILIP
WORNER, PHILIP A.I.

INCOGNITEAU, JEAN-LOUIS
KEROUAC, JEAN-LOUIS L.D.

INDIANA, KID
WEYGAND, JAMES LAMAR

INDICATOR
POYNTER, JAMES WILLIAM

INDRA
SPLINE, TRICIA

INDRANE, ILZE
FATIZIECE, UNDINE

INFANTE, G. CABRERA
CABRERA INFANTE, GUILLER.

INFUHR, HEINRICH
LAMMLE, RUDOLF

INGE, W.R.
INGE, WILLIAM RALPH

INGELBREKT, ALF
LARSEN, ALF

INGELOW, PAUL
DRAKE, J.B.

INGER, NAN
OESTMAN, NAN INGER

INGER, PETER
OSTMAN, NAN & PETER

INGERSLEY, R.M.
MARKLAND, RUSSELL

INGERSOL, JARED
PAINE, LAURAN BOSWORTH

INGHAM, COLONEL FREDERIC
HALE, EDWARD EVERETT

INGHAM, DANIEL
LAMBOT, ISOBEL [MARY]

INGHAM, FREDERIC[K]
HALE, EDWARD EVERETT

INGLESBY, LEONARD CRESWEL
GULL, C[YRIL A.E.] RANGER

INGOLDSBY, THOMAS
BARHAM, RICHARD HARRIS

INGRAM, BOWEN
INGRAM, M.R. BOWEN P.

INGRAM, HUNTER
LUTZ, GILES A.

INGRAM, MARTIN
CAMPBELL, ALICE ORMAND

INGRAM, TOM
INGRAM, THOMAS HENRY

INGRAM, WILLIS J.
HARRIS, MARK

INGRAMS, WILLIS J.
FINKLESTEIN, MARK

INGRID, CHARLES
VILOTT-SALSITZ, RHONDI A.

INGRISCH, LOTTE
VON EINEM, CHARLOTTE

INGULPHUS
GRAY, ARTHUR

INIGO, MARTIN
MILES, KEITH

INMAN, R.R.
MORRIS, CHARLES [S]

INMAN, ROBERT RANDOLPH
HARBAUGH, THOMAS C.
INGRAHAM, PRENTISS
MANNING, WILLIAM HENRY

INMERITO
JAVITCH, DANIEL GILBERT

INNES, ALAN/ALLAN
TUBB, E.C.

INNES, EVAN
ZACHARY, HUGH

INNES, HAMMOND
HAMMOND INNES, RALPH

INNES, JEAN
SAUNDERS, JEAN INNES

INNES, MICHAEL
STEWART, JOHN INNES M.

INNSBRUCKER, MICHAEL
OFFERGELD, FRIEDHELM

INSIGHT, JAMES
COLEMAN, ROBERT W.A.

INSPECTOR, F
RUSSELL, WILLIAM

INTELLIGENCE OFFICER
JAMES, LIONEL

INTRUS
KOEHLER, PAUL OSWALD

INYART, GENE
NAMOVICZ, GENE INYART

IONE
IONE, CAROLE

IONEL
RONN, YUVAL

IONICOS, ION
LESLIE, SIR SHANE

IOTA
CAFFYN, KATHLEEN M.

IPSE, HENRIK
HARTLEBEN, OTTO ERICH

IQUA
BORCHARD, RUTH

IRCHAN, MYROSLAV
BABJUK, ANDREY

IRELAND, BARON
SALSBURY, NATE

IRELAND, DAVID
GREEN, JULIAN [HARTRIDGE]

IRELAND, DOREEN
LORD, DOREEN MILDRED

IRELAND, JANE
POTTER, JACQUELINE

IRELAND, MAUDE
THOMPSON, JANE MAUDE [I]

IRELAND, MICHAEL
FIGGIS, DARRELL

IRELAND, NOELLE
GIBBS, NORAH

IRETON, ROLLO
SHIRLEY, RALPH

IRISH, WILLIAM
WOOLRICH, CORNELL HOPLEY

IRON THUNDERHORSE
SEKAXSU PETAKWONEXNAJUNK.

IRON, JOHN
CARLILE, JOHN CHARLES

IRON, RALPH
SCHREINER, OLIVE [E.A.]

IRONBARK
GIBSON, G.H.

IRONCLAD
ENTON, HARRY

IRONI
CZACZKES, SHMUEL YOSEF

IRONIC PROPHET
WEINSTEIN, NATHAN W.

IRONMASTER, MAXIMUS
WILKINSON, JOHN DONALD

IRONQUILL
WARE, EUGENE FITCH

IRONSIDE, JOHN
TAIT, E. MARGARET

IRONSIDE, MATTHEW
BOBIN, JOHN WILLIAM

IRVIN, BOB
IRVIN, ROBERT W.

IRVINE, LYN
NEWMAN, LYN LLOYD

IRVINE, R.R.
IRVINE, ROBERT RALSTONE

IRVINE, ROBERT
IRVINE, ROBERT RALSTONE

IRVING, ALEXANDER
FAHRENKOPF, ANNE
FOX [HUME], RUTH

IRVING, CHRISTOPHER
JOHNSTON, REGINALD FLEMNG

IRVING, CLIVE
BATES, CLIVE

IRVING, COMPTON
CARTER, JOHN L.J.

IRVING, H.B.
IRVING, HENRY BRODRIBB

IRVING, REGINALD
JOHNSTON, REGINALD FLEMNG

IRVING, ROBERT
ADLER, IRVING

IRWIN, AMY
KANTOR, HARRY

IRWIN, ANN
IRWIN, ANNABELLE BOWEN

IRWIN, CYNTHIA C.
IRWIN-WILLIAMS, CYNTHIA C

IRWIN, G.H.
PALMER, RAYMOND A.
SHAVER, RICHARD S.

IRWIN, HADLEY
HADLEY, LEE
IRWIN, ANNABELLE BOWEN

IRWIN, MARGARET E.
MONSELL, MARGARET E.

IRWIN, P.K.
PAGE, PATRICIA KATHLEEN

IRWIN, SARITA
ZACHARIA, IRWIN

IRWIN, VIOLET
DE WAAL, VIOLET MARY

ISAACS, EDITH J.R.
RICH, EDITH J.R.

ISAACS, JACOB
KRANZLER, GEORGE G.

ISAKOVSKY, MICHAIL VASIL.
ISAKOV, M.V.

ISAKSEN, MATHIS
AIKIO, MATTI

ISAMBARD
WILLIAMS, JACK LEWIS

ISBEL, URSULA
DOTZLER, URSULA

ISELER, JO
SCHAUMANN, JOCHEN

ISENBECK, ELSBETH
KOEBER, ELSBETH

ISHIKAWA, HAKUHIN
ISHIKAW, HAJIME

ISHIKAWA, TAKUBOKU
ISHIKAW, HAJIME

ISIS
TORBETT, HARVEY D.L.

ISKANDER
YAKOVLEV, ALEKSANDR I.

ISLAND, BERT F.
BREUCKER, OSCAR HERBERT

ISLAND, BERT F.
GUNTHER, KARL HEINZ
MULLER, PAUL ALFRED
SCHOLZ, WINFRIED

ISLAND, RICE
RISO, ALF

ISLAY, NICHOLAS
MURRAY, ANDREW NICHOLAS

ISLER, BETH
ISLER, ELIZABETH

ISLET, THEODORE OCEANIC
CROCKER, SAMUEL

ISLEY, DENT
CHAPMAN, JOHN STANTON H.
CHAPMAN, MARY HAMILTON

ISLEY, FLORA K.D.
DUNCAN, KUNIGUNDE

ISOU, ISIDORE
GOLDSTEIN, ISIDORE

ISRAEL, PETER
ISRAEL, J. LEON

ISSCHAR
STANFORD, JOHN KEITH

ITIM, TALANG
LAPENA-BONIFACIO, AMELIA

IVANOV, DIMITAR
JOTOV, DIMITAR IVANOV

IVANOV-RAZUMNIK
IVANOV, RAZUMNIK VASILY.

IVANS
VAN SCHEVICHAVEN, J.

IVENS, JORIS
IVENS, GEORG HENRI ANTON

IVERSON, BRETT
DUNN, DES R.

IVERSON, ERIC G.
TURTLEDOVE, HARRY

IVES, JOHN
GARFIELD, BRIAN F.W.

IVES, LAWRENCE
WOODS, FREDERICK

IVES, MORGAN
BRADLEY, MARION ZIMMER

IVES, SANDY
IVES, EDWARD D[AWSON]

IVEY, JIM
IVEY, JAMES BURNETT

IVNEV, RYURIK
KOVALEV, MIKHAIL ALEXAND.

IVORY, MARTIN
ULLMAN, JAMES MICHAEL

IZBAN, SAMUEL
IZBITSKY, SAMUEL

IZZO, J. JR.
DONALDSON, DALE C.

J
GARRITY, JOAN THERESA

J.A.H.
HAMMERTON, J.A.

J.C.
CROOK, JOEL
LAWRENCE, THOMAS EDWARD
MOORCOCK, MICHAEL

J.C.T.
TREWIN, J.C.

J.E.N.
NEILD, JAMES EDWARD

J.F-K.
FITZMAURICE-KELLY, JAMES

J.K.
LAMPTEY, JONATHAN KWESI

J.L.-M.
LEES-MILNE, JAMES

J.M.
MACGREGOR, JOHN

J.P.
PARKER, JOHN

J.R.D.
DILL, JAMES REID

J.R.R.T.
TOLKIEN, JOHN RONALD R.

J.R.S.
GOGARTY, OLIVER ST. JOHN

J.S.
DODGE, MARY ELIZABETH M.

J.S. OF DALE
GRANT, ROBERT
STIMSON, FREDERIC JESUP

J.S.H.
HUXLEY, JULIAN SORRELL

J.T.
BELL, ERIC TEMPLE

J.W.L.
LETHABY, J.W.

J.Z.
ZULAWSKI, JULIUSZ

JABBER, FUAD AMIN
JABBER, PAUL

JABEZ
NICOL, ERIC [P]

JAC, CHERLYN
BIGGS, CHERYL

JAC, LEE
MORTON, LEE JACK JR.

JACK
MADISON, JOHN RODRIGO

JACK FROST LADY
THOMPSON, JEAN M.

JACK THE RIPPER
CAMPOS, JOSE ANTONIO

JACK, GARRY
BRAND, KURT

JACK, J.W.
VAUGHAN, ROBERT R.

JACK, R.D.S.
JACK, RONALD DYCE SADLER

JACK, WARRIGAL
FURPHY, JOSEPH

JACKLIN, TONY
JACKLIN, ANTHONY

JACKS, L.P.
JACKS, LAWRENCE PEARSALL

JACKS, M.L.
JACKS, MAURICE LEONARD

JACKS, OLIVER
GANDLEY, KENNETH ROYCE

JACKSON, ALBINA
GEIS, RICHARD E.

JACKSON, ANNE
JACKSON, ANNA J.

JACKSON, BO
JACKSON, VINCENT EDWARD

JACKSON, CLARENCE J.L.
BULLIET, RICHARD WILLIAMS

JACKSON, DANIEL
WINGROVE, DAVID JOHN

JACKSON, DAVE
HONNEF, JOACHIM
JACKSON, J. DAVID

JACKSON, DON D.
JACKSON, DONALD DE AVILA

JACKSON, E.F.
TUBB, E.C.

JACKSON, ELAINE
FREEMAN, GILLIAN

JACKSON, EMORY
DUNN, JOSEPH ALLAN

JACKSON, EVERATT
MUGGESON, MARGARET E.

JACKSON, GILES
LEFFINGWELL, ALBERT

JACKSON, HOWARD
MCGRAW, J.H.
NUETZEL, CHARLES A.

JACKSON, INNES
HERDAN, INNES

JACKSON, J. AUSTIN
LAZENBY, NORMAN A.

JACKSON, J.P.
ATKINS, ARTHUR HAROLD

JACKSON, JIM
BAJOG, GUNTHER

JACKSON, JOYCE
CROUNSE, HELEN LOUISE

JACKSON, KELTER A.
LIST, JURGEN E.

JACKSON, LAURA [RIDING]
REICHENTHAL, LAURA

JACKSON, LEWIS
LEWIS, JACK

JACKSON, LISA
CROSE, SUSAN

JACKSON, LIVIA BITTON
BITTON JACKSON, LIVIA E.

JACKSON, LUCILLE
STRAUSS, M. LUCILLE J.

JACKSON, MARIAN J.A.
ROGERS, MARIAN H. JACKSON

JACKSON, MARK
KURZ, RON

JACKSON, NEVILLE
GLASKIN, GERALD MARCUS

JACKSON, NOEL
FEARN, JOHN RUSSELL

JACKSON, NORA
TENNANT, NORA JACKSON

JACKSON, O.B.
JACKSON, CAARY PAUL

JACKSON, R.E.
INNES, ROSEMARY E.J.

JACKSON, REGGIE
JACKSON, REGINALD MARTIN.

JACKSON, SALLY
KELLOGG, JEAN [D]

JACKSON, SAM
TRUMBO, DONALD [DALTON]

JACKSON, SARA
THOMAS, SARA SALLY
WINGROVE, DAVID JOHN

JACKSON, SCOOP
JACKSON, HENRY MARTIN

JACKSON, SHIRLEY
HYMAN, SHIRLEY JACKSON

JACKSON, STANLEY
JACKSON, SAMUEL

JACKSON, STEPHANIE
WERNER, VIVIAN

JACKSON, STEPHEN
STEVENSON, JOHN

JACKSON, W.A. DOUGLAS
JACKSON, WILLIAM ARTHUR D

JACKSON, WALLACE
BUDD, WILLIAM JOHN

JACKWOOD, JIM
WOOLFOLK, JOSHUA PITTS

JACKY, HELENE
LAVAGNINO-JACKY, HELENE

JACOB, HERBERT MATHIAS
DAVIES, D. JACOB

JACOB, J.R.
JACOB, JAMES R.

JACOBS, ALLEN S.
JACOBS, ALMA SYLVIA

JACOBS, JILL
BHARTI, MA SATYA

JACOBS, LEAH
GELLIS, ROBERTA L.J.

JACOBS, LINDA
ALTMAN, LINDA JACOBS

JACOBS, STEVEN
SELLERS, CONNIE LESLIE

JACOBS, SUSAN
QUINN, SUSAN

JACOBS, T.C.H.
PENDOWER, THOMAS CURTIS H

JACOBS, W.W.
JACOBS, WILLIAM WYMARK

JACOBSE, MUUS
HANZEN, KLAAS

JACOBSON, SPIDER
JACOBSON, ARTHUR

JACOBSON, STEVE
JACOBSON, STEPHEN A.

JACOBY, JEAN
EVANS, JEAN LORNA

JACOPETTI, ALEXANDRA
HART, ALEXANDRA

JACOT, B.L.
DE BOINOD, BERNARD L.J.

JACOT, BERNARD
DE BOINOD, BERNARD L.J.

JACQUELINE
CARPENTIER VALMONT, ALEJO
HOSKINS, JOSEPHINE R.

JACQUEMARD-SENECAL
SENECAL, JEAN-MICHAEL
JACQUEMARD, YVES

JACQUES
DUCHESNE, ALBERT

JACQUES, BEAU
HOUSE, RICHARD CALVIN

JADE, JACQUELINE
HYMAN, JACKIE DIAMOND

JADE, SYMON
ECKSTROM, MICHAEL

JADED OBSERVER
ZOLF, LARRY

JADWAY, J.J.
BERNET, MICHAEL [STEVEN]

JAEGER, C.K.
JAEGER, CYRIL KAREL S.

JAERVEN, OSCAR
AMUNDSEN, ENGEBRET

JAFFA, GEORGE
WALLACE-CLARKE, GEORGE

JAFFE, BETSY
JAFFEE, ELIZABETH LATIMER

JAFFE, ELSA
BARTLETT, ELSA JAFFE

JAFFEE, MARY L.
LINDSLEY, MARY FRANCES

JAGO, THOMAS
ERICHSEN, UWE

JAHN, MIKE
JAHN, JOSEPH MICHAEL

JAIS, SAFONE
PITT, STAN[LEY]

JALAN, EDI LEE
STIVENDER, ED

JALAP
DIAS, PATRICK WALTER

JALLANT, NORMAN C.
PALLANT, NORMAN C.

JAM, D.
MAY, KARL FRIEDRICH

JAMBON, JEAN
MACDONALD, J. HAY

JAMES, ADOBE
CARDWELL, JAMES M.

JAMES, ALLEN
ALLEN, JAMES LOVIC JR.

JAMES, AMALIA
NEGGERS, CARLA A[MALIA]

JAMES, ANDREW
KIRKUP, JAMES

JAMES, ANNA
HARPER, ELIZABETH SHANNON
PORTER, MADELINE

JAMES, ANTHONY
HANNA, DAVID

JAMES, ARLENE
RATHER, DEBORAH A.R.

JAMES, BERT
HOBSON, B.

JAMES, BILL
JAMES, GEORGE WILLIAM
TUCKER, [ALLAN] JAMES

JAMES, BRIAN
FOX, GARDNER F.
HIGH, HOPETON
THOMAS, GORDON
TIERNEY, JOHN LAWRENCE

JAMES, C.B.
COOVER, JAMES BURRELL

JAMES, C.L.R.
JAMES, CYRIL LIONEL R.

JAMES, C.W.
CUMES, JAMES WILLIAM C.

JAMES, CAPTAIN LEW
STRATEMEYER, EDWARD

JAMES, CARY
RICHARDSON, GLADWELL G.

JAMES, CHRISTINE
CROSS, RENA

JAMES, CY
WATTS, PETER CHRISTOPHER

JAMES, DAKOTA
JAMES, BERNARD JOSEPH

JAMES, DAN
SAYERS, JAMES DENSON

JAMES, DAVID
HAGBERG, DAVID [JAMES]

JAMES, DEANA
SIZER, MONA

JAMES, DEBORAH
BAILEY, DEBRA

JAMES, DIANA
GUNN, DIANA MAUREEN

JAMES, DYNELY
CAESAR, RICHARD DYNELY
MAYNE, WILLIAM [J.C.]

JAMES, EDWARD
MASUR, HAROLD Q.

JAMES, EDWIN
GUNN, JAMES E.

JAMES, ELLEN
CAIN, ELLEN JACOB

JAMES, ERNEST
PIKE, WILLIAM ERNEST

JAMES, FRANKLIN
GODLEY, ROBERT

JAMES, FREDERICK
MARTIN, WILLIAM

JAMES, GENE
JANES, GENE

JAMES, HALTON
KELLEY, THOMAS P.

JAMES, HARRISON
RUSK, JAMES JR.

JAMES, HENRY
KELLENBERGER, L.C.

JAMES, HENRY JAMES
ADAMS, ARTHUR HENRY

JAMES, JAMES
ADAMS, ARTHUR HENRY

JAMES, JOHN
LANGDON-DAVIES, JOHN

JAMES, JOSEPHINE
LINDSAY, BARBARA
STERNE, EMMA GELDERS

JAMES, JUDITH
JENNINGS, LESLIE NELSON

JAMES, KATHLEEN
HUTCHINSON, JOYCE

JAMES, KRISTIN
CAMP, CANDACE [PAULINE]

JAMES, L.F.
LITTLE, PAUL HUGO

JAMES, LEIGH FRANKLIN
LITTLE, PAUL HUGO

JAMES, LIVIA
REASONER, JAMES & LIVIA

JAMES, LLOYD E.
LAUGHLIN, TOM

JAMES, M.R.
JAMES, MONTAGUE RHODES
REASONER, JAMES M.

JAMES, MAC
DOBSON, JAMES

JAMES, MACK
KNELLER, F.C.

JAMES, MARGARET
BENNETTS, PAMELA

JAMES, MARTHA
DOYLE, MARTHA CLAIRE M.

JAMES, MARTIN
KISNER, JAMES [MARTIN JR]

JAMES, MARY
MEAKER, MARIJANE AGNES

JAMES, MATTHEW
LUCEY, JAMES DENNIS

JAMES, MAX
MCCORMICK, JAMES

JAMES, MONICA
NONHEBEL, CLARE

JAMES, P.D.
WHITE, PHYLLIS D. JAMES

JAMES, PAUL
WARBURG, JAMES PAUL

JAMES, PEREGRINE
SHEPHERD, WILLIAM JAMES

JAMES, PHILIP
BEARD, JAMES H.
CAWTHORN, JAMES
DEL REY, LESTER
MOORCOCK, MICHAEL

JAMES, POLICE CAPTAIN
VAN ORDEN, WILLIAM H.

JAMES, PRESTON
FEARN, JOHN RUSSELL

JAMES, R.
EDWARD, JAMES

JAMES, RACHEL
DANCYGER, IRENE

JAMES, REBECCA
ELWARD, JAMES JOSEPH

JAMES, ROBERT
HEITNER, IRIS

JAMES, ROBIN
CURTIS, SHARON & THOMAS

JAMES, RONALD
PRESTON, JAMES

JAMES, S.T.
SCUDDER, HORACE ELISHA

JAMES, SALLY
WILSON, JOYCE

JAMES, SAMANTHA
KLEINSCHMIDT, SANDRA

JAMES, SANDRA
KLEINSCHMIDT, SANDRA

JAMES, SARAH
JUSKEVICE, MILDRED H.

JAMES, SIMON
KUNEN, JAMES SIMON

JAMES, STANTON
FLEMMING, NICHOLAS COIT

JAMES, STEPHANIE
KRENTZ, JAYNE ANN

JAMES, SUSAN
GRIFFIN, ARTHUR J.

JAMES, SUSANNAH
MOODY, SUSAN [ELIZABETH]

JAMES, T.F.
FLEMING, THOMAS JAMES

JAMES, THOMAS N.
NEAL, JAMES THOMAS

JAMES, TREVOR
CONSTABLE, TREVOR JAMES

JAMES, VANESSA
BEAUMAN, SALLY

JAMES, VINCENT
GRIBBEN, JAMES

JAMES, VIOLA
PRONZINI, WILLIAM JOHN
WALLMANN, JEFFREY M.

JAMES, WALTER S.
SHELDON, WALTER J.

JAMES, WILL
DUFAULT, JOSEPH ERNEST N.

JAMES, WILL F.
JENKINS, WILLIAM FITZGER.

JAMES, WILLIAM
CRADDOCK, WILLIAM JAMES

JAMES, WILLIAM M.
HARKNETT, TERRY W.
HARVEY, JOHN [BARTON]
JAMES, LAURENCE

JAMES. WESTBROOK
WEYGAND, JAMES LAMAR

JAMESON, ERIC
TRIMMER, ERIC J.

JAMESON, JUDITH
NEYLAND, JAMES [E]

JAMESON, KEITH
PORGES, IRWIN

JAMESON, ROLAND
JAMESON, ROBERT

JAMESON, STORM
CHAPMAN, MARGARET STORM

JAMESON, TWIGGS
TWIGGS, JAMES

JAMESON, VERE
SHUTE, EVAN VERE

JAMIESON, BOB
JAMIESON, ROBERT JOHN

JAMIESON, IAN R.
GOULART, RONALD JOSEPH

JAMIESON, THOMAS
MOLLOY, EDWARD

JAMISON, AMELIA
SINGER, SALLY M.

JAMISON, KELLY
BUECHTING, LINDA

JAN
NOBLE, JOHN [A]

JANAKIEFF, DIMITER
INKIOW, [J] DIMITER

JANALAINE, ODETTE
DURRUA, ODETTE JEANNE

JANAS, FRANKIE-LEE
JANAS, FRANCIS LEROY G.

JANCE, J.A.
JANCE, JUDITH ANN

JANDA, N.L.
ALDANI, LINO

JANE, FRED T.
JANE, FREDERICK THOMAS

JANES, GENE
ARMITAGE, DOROTHY

JANES, GENE
WATKINS, MURIEL

JANES, JOSEPHINE
HELAND, VICTORIA J.R.

JANES, KATHLEEN
JAMIESON, KATHLEEN FLORN.

JANES, KATHLEEN F.
JAMIESON, KATHLEEN FLORN.

JANESHUTZ, TRISH
MACGREGOR, PATRICIA M.J.

JANET, LILLIAN
O'DANIEL, JANET
RESSLER, LILLIAN

JANICE
BRUSTLEIN, JANICE T.

JANIFER, LAURENCE M.
HARRIS, LAURENCE MARK

JANKA, JUDITH
PUSCH, EDITH

JANNAUSCH, DORIS
SCHMIDT, DOROTHEA MARIA

JANOSCH
ECKERT, HORST

JANS, EMERSON
BIXBY, JEROME L.

JANS, ZEPHYR
ZEKOWSKI, ARLENE

JANSEN, G.H.
JANSEN, GODFREY HENRY

JANSEN, JARED
CEBULASH, MEL

JANSEN, MICHEL
VAN HERP, JACQUES

JANSON, HANK
CARTER, REGINALD HERBERT
FRANCES, STEPHEN D.
HOBSON, HARRY
KELLY, HAROLD ERNEST
MOFFATT, JAMES
MONKHOUSE, BOB
MOORCOCK, MICHAEL
NEWTON, WILLIAM [SIMPSON]
NORWOOD, VICTOR [G.C.]
PARDOE, GEOFFREY
SIMPSON, COLIN

JANSSEN, JENS
BRENNECKE, JOCHEN

JANSSEN, KRISTA
POOLE, RHODA JANSSEN

JANTSANG, TANI
ROSE, PHYLLIS

JANTZEN, FRITZ
NUETZEL, CHARLES A.

JANUS
CLERY, REGINALD VALENTINE
EHRHARDT, PAUL GEORG

JANUS, GRETE
HERTZ, GRETE JANUS

JANUS, HIRAM
POUND, EZRA LOOMIS

JANUS, PAUL
WARBURG, JAMES PAUL

JANVIER, IVAN
BUDRYS, ALGIRDAS JONAS

JANVIER, PAUL
BUDRYS, ALGIRDAS JONAS

JAPONICA
HOLDAWAY, MARJORIE F.

JAPP, MATTHEW W.
FEARN, JOHN RUSSELL

JAPRISOT, SEBASTIEN
ROSSI, JEAN BAPTISTE

JAQUES
NEILD, JAMES EDWARD
STOTT, MARY

JARBER, E.
JARNES BERQUA, ENRIQUE

JARDIN, REX
BURKHARDT, EVE & ROBERT

JARDINE, CLAUDINE
BRISSON, CLAUDINE

JARDINE, WARWICK
BAYFIELD, WILLIAM J.
WARWICK, FRANCIS ALISTAIR

JAREED
FARIDI, SHAH NASIRUDDIN M

JARNFELDT, IVAN
LUNDBACK, IVAR

JAROCH, RANDY
JAROCH, FRANCES A. RANDY

JAROMIN, ROLF
GOOCK, ROLAND

JARON, LOU
SPENDER, LYNNE

JARRETT, AMANDA JEAN
AVALLONE, MICHAEL
GRANGER, GEORGE A.
SCAFIDEL, JAMES R.
STEELEY, ROBERT DEREK

JARRETT, JEANETTE
FISHER, LOIS JEANETTE

JARRETT, KAY
SAXON, SOPHIA

JARRETT, MIRANDA
SCOTT, SUSAN HOLLOWAY

JARRETT, ROXANNE
WERNER, HERMA

JARRIEL, TOM
JARRIEL, THOMAS EDWIN

JARVIS, E.K.
BLOCH, ROBERT [A]
ELLISON, HARLAN
FAIRMAN, PAUL W.
MCGIVERN, WILLIAM P.
SILVERBERG, ROBERT
WILLIAMS, ROBERT MOORE

JARVIS, LEE
HERNHUTTER, ALBERT

JASIENSKI, BRUNO
ZYSKIND, BRUNO

JASMIN, J.
JASINSKAS, JONAS

JASNER, W.K.
WATSON, JANE WERNER

JASON
CABALLERO, MANUEL
CRAINE, JOHN HENRY
MUNRO, [MACFARLAND] HUGH
STANNUS, [J] GORDON [D]

JASON, JERRY
SMITH, GEORGE H[ENRY]

JASON, JOHNNY
GLUT, DONALD F.

JASON, KEN
WHITE, VICTOR H.
NEWTON, DWIGHT BENNETT

JASON, N.V.
WOOD, EDWARD D. JR.

JASON, STUART
AVALLONE, MICHAEL
FLOREN, LEE
WILSON, OSCAR

JASON, VERONICA
JOHNSTON, VELDA

JASON, WILLIAM
MACHLIN, MILTON

JASPER, BOB
HOGAN, ROBERT J[ASPER]

JASSEM, KATE
OPPENHEIM, JOANNE

JASTRUN, MIECZYSLAW
AGALSTEIN, MIECZYSLAW

JATUES, AYRESOME
LOCKE, GEORGE [W]

JAUNIERE, CLAUDETTE
JAUNIERE, CLAUDE

JAVIER
GALLARDOS MUNOZ, JUAN

JAVLYN, GORDON
BUDRYS, ALGIRDAS JONAS

JAVOR, FRANK A.
JAWORSKI, FRANK ANTHONY

JAVOR, J.
VLCEK, BARTOS

JAVOROV, PEJU
KRACHALOV, PEJU

JAXON, MILT
KIMBRO, JOHN M.

JAY
JENNINGS, E.C.

JAY, CHARLOTTE
HALLS, GERALDINE [M. JAY]

JAY, DONALD
MEYER, CHARLES ROBERT

JAY, G.S.
HALLS, GERALDINE [M. JAY]

JAY, GERALDINE HALLS
HALLS, GERALDINE [M. JAY]

JAY, JOAN
DAVIES, EDITH

JAY, MARION
SPAULDING, RUTH

JAY, MEL
FANTHORPE, R.L.

JAY, MRS. W.L.M.
WOODRUFF, JULIA L.M.C.

JAY, RUTH JOHNSON
JAY, RUTH INGRID

JAY, SIMON
ALEXANDER, COLIN JAMES

JAY, THOMAS
KENDALL, STEPHEN

JAY, VICTOR
BANIS, VICTOR J[EROME]

JAY, WILLA
JOHNSTON, WILLIAM

JAYNE, FAITH
POWLEY, FAITH HINCKLEY

JAYNE, [LIEUT.] R.H.
ELLIS, EDWARD S.

JAYNES, CLARE
MAYER, JANE ROTHCHILD
SPIEGEL, CLARA GATZERT

JEAKE, SAMUEL JR.
AIKEN, CONRAD [P]

JEAN CHRISTOPHE
HUMBERT-DROZ, JULES

JEAN, EVE
BOESCHE, TILLY

JEAN-LOUIS
KEROUAC, JEAN-LOUIS L.D.

JEANETTE
NICHOLS, JEANETTE

JEANS, ANGELA
WATT, ESME VIOLET

JEANTY, NINETTE HELENE
RAVEN, NINETTE HELENE J.

JEDITZKA, MARIA
JERITZA, MARIA

JEEF, KALLE
TSHIAMALA, KABASELE

JEEMS, PIOUP
GORDON, JAMES

JEEVES, MAHATMA KANE
DUKINFIELD, WILLIAM CLAUD

JEFFCOATE, NORMAN
JEFFCOATE, SIR THOMAS

JEFFCOATE, T.N.A.
JEFFCOATE, SIR THOMAS

JEFFERIES, IAN
HAYS, PETER

JEFFERIES, JEFF
CURRY, THOMAS ALBERT

JEFFERIES, WILLIAM
DEAVER, JEFFREY WILDS

JEFFERS, ALBERT
CURRY, THOMAS ALBERT

JEFFERS, JEFF
CURRY, THOMAS ALBERT

JEFFERS, JO
JOHNSON, JOAN HELEN

JEFFERSON, BEN
WHEELAHAN, PAUL

JEFFERSON, HENRY LEE
CABELL, JAMES BRANCH

JEFFERSON, IAN
DAVIES, LESLIE PERNELL

JEFFERSON, JANET
MENCKEN, HENRY LOUIS

JEFFERSON, OMAR XAVIER
JEFFERSON, XAVIER T.

JEFFERSON, SARAH
FARJEON, ANNABEL
FARJEON, EVE

JEFFORD, BAT
BINGLEY, DAVID ERNEST

JEFFREY, CHRISTOPHER
LEACH, MICHAEL

JEFFREY, E. JEFFREY
MARSTON, J.E.

JEFFREY, RUTH
BELL, LOUISE PRICE

JEFFREY, WILLIAM
PRONZINI, WILLIAM JOHN
WALLMANN, JEFFREY M.

JEFFREYS, J.G.
HEALEY, BENJAMIN J.

JEFFRIES, HUGH
HEWELCKE, GEOFFREY

JEFFRIES, JEFF
BOATFIELD, JEFFREY

JEFFRIES, JESSICA
HERMANN, NANCY A.

JEFFRIES, JULIA
WARD, LYNDA C.M.

JEFFS, RAE
SEBLEY, FRANCES RAE

JEGE
NADASI, LADISLAV

JEHAN, NOOR
RATTRAY, HENRIETTA BARB.

JEKEL, PAMELA
JEKEL, P.L.

JELAKOWITCH, IVAN
HEIJERMANS, HERMAN

JELANOV
KOZAK, JUS

JELINEK, HENA M.
MAES-JELINK, HENA

JELLING, JORGEN
LINCK, MOGENS

JELLY, OLIVER
JELLY, GEORGE OLIVER

JEMYMA
HOLLEY, MARIETTA

JEN, GISH
JEN, LILLIAN

JENA, RUTH MICHAELIS
RATCLIFF, RUTH

JENKINS, C.B.
BAJOG, GUNTHER

JENKINS, HAL
JENKINS, HAROLD L.
JENKINS, WILLIAM FITZGER.

JENKINS, HERBERT
CHARBONNEAU, LOUIS

JENKINS, JOHN
MEYN, NIELS

JENKINS, KATE
JENKINS-NUTTING, LINDA

JENKINS, PHYLLIS
SCHWALBERG, CAROL[YN E.S]

JENKINS, WILL
JENKINS, WILLIAM FITZGER.

JENKINS, WILL F.
JENKINS, WILLIAM FITZGER.

JENNER, HEATHER
JAMES, HEATHER

JENNER, SUZANNE
JOHNSON, GRETCHEN
NETZEL, SALLY

JENNET, ANNA
HOWELL, HANNAH D.

JENNIFER
KENWARD, BETTY

JENNIFER, SUSAN
BENSEN, D.R.
HOSKINS, ROBERT

JENNINGS, CAYLIN
CLEMENTS, KAYE L.
TRINER, JEANNE

JENNINGS, DEAN
FRAZEE, [CHARLES] STEPHEN
FOX, GARDNER F.

JENNINGS, PATRICK
MAYER, SYDNEY LOUIS

JENNINGS, ROBERT
HAMILTON, CHARLES H.S.

JENNINGS, S.M.
MEYER, JEROME SYDNEY

JENNINGS, SARA
SEGER, MAURA

JENNISON, C.S.
STARBIRD, KAYE

JENSEN, JENS
BRENNECKE, JOCHEN

JENSEN, JO
PELTON, BEVERLY JO

JENSEN, JULIE
MCDONALD, JULIE

JENSEN, O.H.
GIBSON, WALTER B.

JENSEN, OLE KLINDT
KLINDT-JENSEN, OLE

JENSEN, PETER
WALLMANN, JEFFREY M.
PRONZINI, WILLIAM JOHN

JENSEN, V.N.
WOOD, EDWARD D. JR.

JENSI, MUGANWA NSIKU
SHORTER, ALYWARD

JENYNS, SOAMES
JENYNS, ROGER SOAME

JEPPSON, J.O
ASIMOV, JANET O. JEPPSON

JEPSON, RING
LATHAM, HENRY JEPSON

JEREMY, RICHARD
FOX, CHARLES

JERMAN, SYLVIA PAUL
COOPER, SYLVIA

JERMONTE
MOHAN, JOSEPHINE ELIZAB.

JEROME, FERRIS
JONES, ALICE I.

JEROME, FRED G.
DIETRICH, KARL A.

JEROME, GILBERT
JAMES, W.I.

JEROME, JOSEPH
SEWELL, BROCARD

JEROME, MARK
APPLEMAN, MARK JEROME

JEROME, OWEN FOX
FRIEND, OSCAR J[EROME]

JERROLD, BENTLEY
JENNISON, JOHN WILLIAM

JERROLD, PAMELA
RONNING, PAMELA

JERSEY, JOHN
BERNDT, KARL-HEINZ

JERSILD, P.C.
JERSILD, PER CHRISTIAN

JESKINS, RICHARD
STORY, ROSAMOND MARY

JESSE, MICHAEL
BALDWIN, MICHAEL

JESSE, TENNYSON
JESSE, F. TENNYSON

JESSELL, JOHN
WEINBAUM, STANLEY G.

JESSEN, ALF
BOHLMANN, ANNELIESE

JESSEY, CORNELIA
SUSSMAN, CORNELIA SILVER

JESSUP, FRANCES
VAN BRIGGLE, M. FRANCES J

JESSUP, KATHRYN
KOLACZYK, ANNE & EDWARD

JETER, JACKY
JETER, JACQUELYN I.

JEURY, MICHEL
HIGON, ALBERT

JEVONS, MARSHALL
BREIT, WILLIAM
ELZINGA, KENNETH GERALD

JEWESS, KATHLEEN
BURK, KATHLEEN

JEZ, TEODOR TOMASZ
MILKOWSKI, ZYGMUNT FORTU.

JGS
GOODALL, JOHN STRICKLAND

JIE, ZHANG
ZHANG JIE

JIG-SAW
MILNES, THOMAS WRAY

JIMENEZ MANTECON, RAMON
JIMENEZ [M], JUAN RAMON

JIMENEZ, RAMON
JIMENEZ [M], JUAN RAMON

JINGLE
GOLSWORTHY, ARNOLD

JIRA, JOHANN
GEISLER, HANS

JISKOGO
HARRINGTON, MARK R.

JLLING, HELLA
KRAUSE, HELGA

JOAN, MARY
PICKEN, MARY BROOKS

JOB, MODERN
TABER, CLARENCE WILBUR

JOBSON, SANDRA
DARROCH, SANDRA JOBSON

JOCELYN, RICHARD
CLUTTERBUCK, RICHARD

JOCUNDAS, FRATER
MULLER, WILHELM

JODY, J.M.
EDMUNDSON, JOSEPH

JOEL, BILLY
JOEL, WILLIAM MARTIN

JOHANNES, OTTO MARTIN
RADLEIN, JOHANNES

JOHANNES, R.
MOSS, ROSE

JOHANNESON, OLOF
ALFVEN, HANNES OLOF G.

JOHANSEN, HANNA
MUSCHG, HANNA

JOHANSON, ELISABETH
VERWER, JOHANNA ELISABETH

JOHANSSON, JOHAN FRIDOLF
FRIDEGARD, JAN

JOHN O' THE NORTH
BROWNE, HARRY T.

JOHN, A SUFFOLK HERD BOY
BRUNDLE, JOHN

JOHN, ADA
BOULET, ADA

JOHN, ALIX
JONES, ALICE I.

JOHN, ANTHONY
DE STEFANO, ANTHONY
LITTEL, JOHN S.

JOHN, B.
JOHN, ELIZABETH BEAMON

JOHN, BETTY
JOHN, ELIZABETH BEAMON

JOHN, CHRISTOPHER
BURGESS, CHRISTOPHER

JOHN, COLIN
HAGAN, CHET

JOHN, DANE
MAJOR, ALAN P.

PSEUDONYMS

JOHN, DON
INGELOW, JEAN

JOHN, EVAN
SIMPSON, EVAN JOHN

JOHN, J.F.
BURKE, JOHN [FREDERICK]

JOHN, JASPER
MUSPRATT, ROSALIE HELEN

JOHN, NANCY
SAWYER, JOHN & NANCY

JOHN, NAOMI
FLACK, NAOMI JOHN W.

JOHN, VERA P.
JOHN-STEINER, VERA POLGAR

JOHN-MARTIN
SHEPHERD, MORGAN

JOHNHETT
HETTINGER, JOHN

JOHNN, DAVID
ENGLE, JOHN DAVID JR.

JOHNS, AVERY
COUSINS, MARGARET

JOHNS, BLAIR
BLAIR, JOHN
PATERSON, A.J. BLAIR

JOHNS, FOSTER
SELDES, GILBERT VIVIAN

JOHNS, GEOFFREY
WARNER, G. GEOFFREY JOHN

JOHNS, GILBERT
STAGG, JAMES

JOHNS, HILARY
BARRAUD, E.M.

JOHNS, JACOB
JAKES, JOHN [WILLIAM]

JOHNS, JANETTA
QUIN-HARKIN, JANET

JOHNS, JUNE
JOHNS SMITH, JUNE

JOHNS, KAREN
KIMPEL-JOHNS, KAREN

JOHNS, KENNETH
BULMER, [HENRY] KENNETH
NEWMAN, JOHN

JOHNS, MARSTON
FANTHORPE, R.L.

JOHNS, RICHARD
SLATER, MONTAGUE

JOHNS, THOMPSON
THOMPSON, JOHN H.

JOHNS, W.E. [CAPT.]
JOHNS, WILLIAM EARLE

JOHNS, WHITEY
WHITE, JOHN IRWIN

JOHNS, WILLY
MEEKER, WILLY JOHNS

JOHNSON ABERCROMBIE, MIN.
ABERCROMBIE, MINNIE L.J.

JOHNSON, A.
JOHNSON, ANNABELL JONES

JOHNSON, A.E.
JOHNSON, ANNABELL JONES
JOHNSON, EDGAR RAYMOND

JOHNSON, ALAN
PHILLIFENT, JOHN T.

JOHNSON, ANNABEL
JOHNSON, ANNABELL JONES

JOHNSON, BENJ. F. OF BOO
RILEY, JAMES WHITCOMB

JOHNSON, BENJAMIN F.
RILEY, JAMES WHITCOMB

JOHNSON, BETSY
JOHNSON, EDITH

JOHNSON, BRIAN
WORTHY, BRIAN JOHNSON

JOHNSON, C. EDWARD
JOHNSON, CARL E[DWARD]

JOHNSON, C.F.
GOULART, FRANCES S.

JOHNSON, CARTER
GIBSON, WALTER B.

JOHNSON, CHARLENE
CRAWFORD, CHAR

JOHNSON, CHARLES S.
EDWARDS, WILLIAM B.

JOHNSON, CHARLOTTE BUEL
VON WODTKE, CHARLOTTE B.J

JOHNSON, CHUCK
JOHNSON, CHARLES R.

JOHNSON, COLIN
NAROGIN, MUDROOROO

JOHNSON, CROCKETT
LEISK, DAVID J.

JOHNSON, CURT
JOHNSON, CURTIS LEE

JOHNSON, DAVID
NUETZEL, CHARLES A.

JOHNSON, DICK
JOHNSON, RICHARD A.

JOHNSON, DUFF
FISHER, GRAHAM
HOSSENT, HARRY
MCCORMICK, JAMES
WHARTON, WILFRED G.

JOHNSON, E. HARPER
JOHNSON, EUGENE HARPER

JOHNSON, E. NED
JOHNSON, ENID

JOHNSON, EFFIE
RICHMOND, E. JOHNSON

JOHNSON, ELEANOR
SEYMOUR, DOROTHY JANE Z.

JOHNSON, EYVIND
WERNER, EYVIND OLOF

JOHNSON, FRANK
DANIELS, NORMAN A.

JOHNSON, FROSTY
JOHNSON, FORREST BRYANT

JOHNSON, GEORGE
LEOPOLD, NATHAN F.

JOHNSON, H.B.
WYMAN, WALTER F.

JOHNSON, HARPER
JOHNSON, EUGENE HARPER

JOHNSON, HENRY
HAMMOND, JOHN HENRY JR.

JOHNSON, J.R.
JAMES, CYRIL LIONEL R.

JOHNSON, JACK
JOHNSON, JOHN ARTHUR

JOHNSON, JAMES WELDON
JOHNSON, JAMES WILLIAM

JOHNSON, JANICE KAY
BACZEWSKI, JANICE K.J.

JOHNSON, JANN
JOHNSON, PAULA JANICE

JOHNSON, JIM
JOHNSON, JAMES ALLEN

JOHNSON, JINNA
JOHNSON, VIRGINIA

JOHNSON, JOEL
FIRTH, NORMAN WESLEY

JOHNSON, JOHN
FIGGE, MICHAEL

JOHNSON, KEN
JOHNSON, KENNETH R.

JOHNSON, LADY BIRD
JOHNSON, CLAUDIA ALTA T.

JOHNSON, LEE
JOHNSON, LILLIAN BEATRICE

JOHNSON, LEROY PETER V.
LEROY, PETER VERNON

JOHNSON, LESLIE T.
JOHNSON, LESLIE J.

JOHNSON, M.L.
ABERCROMBIE, MINNIE L.J.
MALZBERG, BARRY [N]

JOHNSON, MAGIC
JOHNSON, EARVIN JR.

JOHNSON, MARIGOLD
GILLES, DANIEL

JOHNSON, MARY LOUISE
KING, MARY LOUISE

JOHNSON, MEL
MALZBERG, BARRY [N]

JOHNSON, MIKE
SHARKEY, JOHN MICHAEL

JOHNSON, NATALIE
ROBISON, NANCY LOUISE

JOHNSON, RICHARD
RICHARDSON, JOHN
RICHEY, DAVID

JOHNSON, RICHARD TANNER
PASCALE, RICHARD TANNER

JOHNSON, ROB
JOHNSON, R.V.

JOHNSON, RUTH I.
JAY, RUTH INGRID

JOHNSON, RYERSON
JOHNSON, WALTER RYERSON

JOHNSON, SABINA THORNE
THORNE, SABINA

JOHNSON, SAINT
BURNETT, W.R.

JOHNSON, TOBY
JOHNSON, EDWIN CLARK

JOHNSON, VALERIE
JOHNSON, VICKIE

JOHNSON, W. BOLINGBROKE
BISHOP, MORRIS GILBERT

JOHNSSON, JOHN STEWART
ROOS, ERNST

JOHNSTON, AGNES CHRISTINE
DAZEY, AGNES J[OHNSTON]

JOHNSTON, CHRISTOPHER N.
SANDS, CHRIST. N. JOHNST.

JOHNSTON, HANK
JOHNSTON, HENRY

JOHNSTON, PORTIA
TAKAJIAN, PORTIA

JOHNSTON, TONY
JOHNSTON, SUSAN T.

JOHNSTONE, D. BRUCE
JOHNSON, DONALD BRUCE

JOHNSTONE, REX
CHAPMAN, FRANK MONROE

JOHNSTONE, TED
MCDANIEL, DAVID EDWARD

JOHNSTONE, WILLIAM
HOSKINS, ROBERT

JOHNSTONE, WILLIAM C.
WHITE, THEODORE EDWIN

JOHSSON, REIDAR
JOENSSON, REIDAR

JOK
WHITTET, GEORGE SORLEY

JOKAI, MAURUS
JOKAI, MOR

JOLAS, PIERRE
KALMUCZAK, ROLF

JOLI-OX
MANYASE, LENCHMAN T.

JOLLING, JACK
JUDD, ALFRED

JOLLY CHOLLY
GRIMM, CHARLES JOHN

JOLLY JACK
PRIESTLEY, JOHN BOYNTON

JOLLY, SUSAN
EDWARDS, FLORENCE

JOLO
OLSSON, JAN OLOF

JONAS, CLAUDIA
EITZERT, ROSEMARIE

JONAS-LICHTENWALLER, J.
JONAS, JOHANNA

JONATHAN
HASEBROEK, JOHANNES PETR.

JONCICH, GERALDINE
CLIFFORD, GERALDINE JONC.

JONES, ALICK
HYNE, CHARLES J. CUTLIFFE

JONES, ANNABEL
LEWIS, M. CHRISTIANNA M.

JONES, BILL
JONES, WILLIAM DAVID A.

JONES, BOB
JONES, ROBERT REYNOLDS JR

JONES, BOBBY
JONES, ROBERT TYRE JR.

JONES, BOBI
JONES, ROBERT MAYNARD

JONES, BRADSHAW
BRADSHAW JONES, MALCOLM

JONES, C.M.
JONES, CLARENCE MEDLYCOTT

JONES, CALICO
RICHARDSON, GLADWELL G.

JONES, CHUCK
JONES, CHARLES MARTIN

JONES, COURTWAY
JONES, JOHN ALLEN

JONES, D.F.
JONES, DENNIS FELTHAM

JONES, DUANE
JONES, DOROTHY HOLDER

JONES, E.B.C.
JONES, EMILY BEATRIX C.

JONES, E.D.
JONES, EVAN DAVID

JONES, EVERETT
DOMBROWSKI, THEODOR
FISCHER, CLAUS
GLOWACZ, HELMUT
NEUBERT, HELMUT
RELLERGERD, HELMUT

JONES, FAUSTINE CHILDRESS
JONES-WILSON, FAUSTINE C.

JONES, FRANK
FEARN, JOHN RUSSELL

JONES, G. WAYMAN
BURKHOLDER, EDWIN V.
CHAMPION, D'ARCY LYNDON
D'ARCY, JACK
DANIELS, NORMAN A.
DONOVAN, LAURENCE
FELDMAN, A. FRANCE
FLEMING-ROBERTS, G.T.
WINCHELL, PRENTICE

JONES, GILLINGHAM
HAMILTON, CHARLES H.S.

JONES, GONNER
JONES, P.F.G.

JONES, H. BEDFORD
FEARING, KENNETH

JONES, H.S.
MOLLOY, EDWARD

JONES, HAROLD
PAGE, GERALD W.

JONES, HARRIET
MARBLE, HARRIET CLEMENT

JONES, HELEN
HINCKLEY, HELEN

JONES, J. FARAGUT
STREIB, DANIEL T.

JONES, J. FARRAGUT
LEVINSON, LEONARD [L]

JONES, JACK
JONES, JAMES LARKIN

JONES, JAMES THOMAS
LESLIE, MARY

JONES, JAN
WELLES, CARON

JONES, JENNIFER
JOHNSON, ENID
LANE, MARGARET

JONES, JIMMY
JONES, CLARENCE MEDLYCOTT

JONES, JOANNA
BURKE, JOHN [FREDERICK]

JONES, JOHN J.
LOVECRAFT, H[OWARD] P.

JONES, K. WESCOTT
WESTCOTT-JONES, KENNETH

JONES, L.Q.
MCQUEEN, J.E.

JONES, LEROI
BARAKA, AMIRI
JONES, EVERETT LEROI

JONES, LLEWELLYN
ALLEN, HUBERT RAYMOND

JONES, LUKE
WATTS, PETER CHRISTOPHER

JONES, MACK
KNELLER, F.C.

JONES, MAJOR JOSEPH
THOMPSON, WILLIAM TAPPAN

JONES, MARGARET BOONE
ZARIF, MARGARET MIN'IMAH

JONES, MARTI
JONES, MARTHA

JONES, MCCLURE
JONES, DIANE MCCLURE

JONES, MELVILLE
BANDER, PETER

JONES, MIRIAM
SCHUCHMAN, JOAN

JONES, MRS. JANE
DIVER, JENNY

JONES, NANCY
HOLDER, NANCY L. JONES

JONES, NARD
JONES, MAYNARD BENEDICT

JONES, ORLANDO
LOOKER, ANTONINA [H]

JONES, PAT
JONES, VIRGIL CARRINGTON

JONES, PAUL
POND, PAUL

JONES, PHILLIPE
ROBERTS-JONES, PHILLIPE J

JONES, PLATO
HICKMAN, LYNN

JONES, RAY
MEYN, NIELS

JONES, SANDRA L.
IRELAND, SANDRA L. JONES

JONES, SANFORD W.
THORN, JOHN

JONES, TAD
JONES, THADDEUS B.

JONES, TED
JONES, THEADOR EDWARD

JONES, TERRY
JONES, TERENCE GRAHAM P.

JONES, TURKEL
MCKIMMEY, JAMES

JONES, VOLCANO
MITCHELL, ADRIAN

JONES, WEBB
HENLEY, ARTHUR

JONES, WILLIAM MONARCH
GUTHRIE, THOMAS ANSTEY

JONES, ZELDA
SCHUCHMAN, JOAN

JONES, [CAPT.] WILBER
EDWARDS, WILLIAM B.

JONES-JACKSON, PAT
JONES-JACKSON, PATRICIA

JONIUS, SUSANNA
KLEIN, DOROTHEE

JONQUIL
COLLINS, JOHN LAWRENCE JR

JONS, HAL
JONES, HARRY AUSTIN

JONTZA, GEORG
KRAMER, ARMIN

JOPP, HAL
JOPP, HAROLD DOWLING JR.

JORAT, BERT
HOCHHEIMER, ALBERT

JORDAN, ALEXIS HILL
GLICK, RUTH [BURTNICK]
TITCHENER, LOUISE

JORDAN, ALLIE
CHASTAIN, SANDRA

JORDAN, ANNE
CROUSE, ANNE D. JORDAN

JORDAN, BARBARA LESLIE
YELLOTT, BARBARA LESLIE

JORDAN, BILL
JORDAN, WILLIAM

JORDAN, BRYN
HENDERSON, JAMES MADDOCK

JORDAN, CARRIE
CUDLIPP, EDYTHE

JORDAN, DAVID
JONES, J.D.F.

JORDAN, GAIL
DERN, E. PEARL GADDIS

JORDAN, GILL
GILBERT, GEORGE

JORDAN, J.A.
JORDAN, JAMES A.

JORDAN, JANEANNE
SENA, JANEANNE

JORDAN, JOANNA
MORRIS, DEBRAH
SHAVER, PAT

JORDAN, KATE
VERMILYE, KATE

JORDAN, LAURA
BROWN, SANDRA [LYNN COX]
WARTSKI, MAUREEN A.C.

JORDAN, LEE ROY
EGLI, WERNER J.

JORDAN, LEE
SCHOLEFIELD, ALAN

JORDAN, LEONARD
LEVINSON, LEONARD [L]

JORDAN, MAGGIE
ROWE, MYRA

JORDAN, MATT
LINAKER, MICHAEL

JORDAN, MILDRED
BAUSHER, MILDRED JORDAN

JORDAN, MONICA
CARUBA, ALAN

JORDAN, NELL
BARKER, ELSA [M]

JORDAN, PENNY
HALSALL, PENNY

JORDAN, ROBERT
RIGNEY, JAMES OLIVER JR.

JORDAN, ROSEMARY
DAVIS, MARY JOHNSON
JORDAN, DEBORAH [DEBBIE]

JORDON, DON
HOWARD, VERNON L.

JORDON, NICOLE
BUSHYHEAD, ANNE

JORGENSEN, IVAR
BROWNE, HOWARD
ELLISON, HARLAN
FAIRMAN, PAUL W.
GARRETT, RANDALL [P]
SILVERBERG, ROBERT
SLESAR, HENRY

JORGENSEN, N & G
ELLINGTON, NORA & GEORGE

JORGENSON, ALLEN
STINE, HENRY EUGENE

JORGENSON, IVAR
ELLISON, HARLAN
GARRETT, RANDALL [P]

JORGENSON, THEODORE
NARVESTAD, JOERUND

JORGENSSON, A.K.
ROACH, ROBERT

JORRICKS, HANDON C.
SCHIER, NORMA

JOSE, ELLEN J.
WAYE, ELLEN JEANNE

JOSEPH, ANNE
COATES, ANNA
SCOTT, ANNA

JOSEPH, DON
HOLMES, DONALD JOSEPH

JOSEPH, FRANZ
SCHAUBELT, FRANZ JOSEPH

JOSEPH, JONATHAN
FINEMAN, IRVING

JOSEPH, M.K.
JOSEPH, MICHAEL KENNEDY

JOSEPH, R.F.
JOSEPH, ROBERT FARRAS

JOSEPH, ROBERT F.
JOSEPH, ROBERT FARRAS

JOSEPH, ROBIN
JOSEPH, ROBERT

JOSEPHS, ARTHUR
GOTTLIEB, ARTHUR

JOSEPHS, BERTRAND
BERCOVICI, JOSEPH

JOSEPHS, HENRY
LOWNDES, ROBERT A.W.

JOSEPHS, REBECCA
TALBOT, TOBY

JOSEPHS, STEPHEN
DOLMATCH, THEODORE BIELEY

JOSEPHSON, LAWRENCE
BLOCK, LAWRENCE

JOSH
CLEMENS, SAMUEL LANGHORNE

JOSIAH ALLEN'S WIFE
HOLLEY, MARIETTA

JOSLIN, SESYLE
HINE, SESYLE JOSLIN

JOSSA, HANS-MARTIN
PLATTEN, WILL

JOST, HANS
JONSSON, HJALMAR NILS

JOST, HERMANN
MOREL, HERMANN

JOTH, J.
ROTH, JERRY

JOTKATE, P.
KNODT, JOSEF

JOUBERT, DIAN
JOUBERT, DIRK DANIEL

JOUBERT, LINDA
GROVE, HENRIETTE

JOUDRY, PATRICIA
STEELE, PATRICIA M.V.

JOUHANDEAU, MARCEL
PROVENCE, MARCEL

JOURDAIN, E.F.
JOURDAIN, ELEANOR FRANCES

JOURNEYMAN
NOCK, ALBERT JAY

JOUVET, JEAN
STRICH, CHRISTIAN

JOY, ELIZABETH
DAVIS, ELIZABETH SWITZER

JOYAUX, PHILLIPPE
SOLLERS, PHILLIPPE

JOYCE, ADRIAN
EASTMAN, CAROL

JOYCE, BILL
JOYCE, WILLIAM

JOYCE, BRENDA
DWORMAN, BRENDA JOYCE

JOYCE, DEBORAH
BRYSON, DEBORAH
PORTER, JOYCE

JOYCE, JANE
YOUNG, ENA

JOYCE, JANET
BIEBER, JANET LYNN P.
THIES, JOYCE ANN S.

JOYCE, JENNA LEE
BIEBER, JANET LYNN P.
THIES, JOYCE ANN S.

JOYCE, JOANNA
IRWIN, DIANNE

JOYCE, JULIA
ANDRESEN, JULIA TETEL

JOYCE, MARIE
DEBERRY, VIRGINIA
GRANT, DONNA

JOYCE, THOMAS
CARY, JOYCE

JOYNER, TIM
JOYNER, TIMOTHY

JOYSTON, RALF
ANDERSEN, NILS

JOZK, WICKOV
HLOJZY, NAGEL

JUBRAN, KHALIL JUBRAN
GIBRAN, KAHLIL

JUCKER, IWAN
ISLER, URSULA

JUDD, ALAN
PETTY, ALAN

JUDD, CATHERINE
MARKS, KATHY

JUDD, CYRIL
GROSSMAN, JOSEPH. JUDITH
KORNBLUTH, C[YRIL] M.

JUDD, FRANCES K.
BENSON, MILDRED [A] WIRT
STRATEMEYER, EDWARD

JUDD, HARRISON
DANIELS, NORMAN A.

JUDGE, THE
SHARP, IAN

JUDKINS, PHIL
JUDKINS, PHILLIP EDWARD

JUDSON, WILLIAM
CORLEY, EDWIN [RAYMOND]

JUDY, STEPHEN
TCHUDI, STEPHEN N.

JUDY, STEPHEN N.
TCHUDI, STEPHEN N.

JUDY, WILL
JUDY, WILLIAM LEWIS

JUENGER, ERNST
JUNGER, ERNST

JUERGEN, ANNA
MUELLER-TANNEWITZ, ANNA

JUERGENSMEYER, JANE STU.
STUART, JESSICA JANE

JUEWO, DONGHAI
NIANCI, XU

JUGE, J.P.
RICHTER, HANS PETER

JUHASZ, LESLIE A.
SHEPARD, LESLIE ALBERT

JULIA
COX, JULIA

JULIAN, JANE
WISEMAN, DAVID

JULIAN, PETER
KORMENDI, FERENC

JULIAN, ROBERT
WERNICK, SAUL

JULIE
NETTZ, JULIE
ROBBINS, JUNE

JULIE OF COLORADA SPRINGS
ROBBINS, JUNE

JULIEN, DAVID
MACKAY, DAVID LORING
MACKAY, JOSEPHINE JULIA

JULIET
LEVY, JULIA ETHEL

JULINE, RUTH BISHOP
RITCHIE, RUTH

JULIUS
CURLING, BRYAN WILIIAM R.

JULOC
FISHER, D.H.

JUMPP, HUGO
MACPEEK, WALTER G.

JUN, TERAHATA
KIRKUP, JAMES

JUNE, CAROLINE SILVER
SMITH, LAURA ROUNDTREE

JUNE, JENNIE
CROLY, JANE CUNNINGHAM

JUNE, JENNY
CROLY, JANE CUNNINGHAM

JUNG, P.R.
KLING, BERNT

JUNG-STILLING, JOHANN H.
JUNG, JOHANN HEINRICH

JUNGBLUTH, ULRICH HERBERT
MULLER-JUNGBLUTH, ULRICH

JUNGEL, EBERHARD
JUENGEL, EBERHARD

JUNGER, ERNST
JUENGER, ERNST

JUNGHERR, VICTOR GEORG
JUNGFER, VICTOR

JUNGLE DOCTOR
WHITE, PAUL HAMILTON H.

JUNGT, ROBERT
BAUM, ROBERT

JUNIPER, ALEX
HOSPITAL, JANETTE TURNER

JUNIUS
LUXENBURG, ROSA

JUR, JERZY
LERSKY, GEORGE JAN

JURAT, BERT
HOCHHEIMER, ALBERT

JURGEN, ANNA
MULLER-TANNEWITZ, ANNA

JURGENSEN, HELKE
PETER, ALICE [J]

JURIJ, KLEN
BURGHARDT, OSWALD

JURNAK, SHEILA
RAESCHILD, SHEILA

JUSTICE, ANN
SCHMIDT, JO

JUSTICIAR
POWELL-SMITH, VINCENT

JUSTIFICUS
PAPPAS, GEORGE S.

JUSTIN, JENNIFER
WEST, JENNIFER

JUSTINUS, OTTO
COHN, OTTO JUSTINUS

JUTA, RENE
JUTA, JAN

JUTSON, MARY CAROLINE H.
GEORGE, MARY CAROLINE H.J

JUUL, ERIK
MEYN, NIELS

JUVENILIA
TAYLOR, ANN

JUVENIS
BOURNE, RANDOLPH S.

JYMES, ELIZABETH
ADAMS, BETSY

K-H NEWS SERVICE
KING-HALL, STEPHEN

K-TURKEL, JUDI
KESSELMAN-TURKEL, JUDI

K.M.
BEAUCHAMP, KATHLEEN M.

K.O.S.
DOMBROWSKI, KATRINA

K.R.
ROMANOV, CONSTANTINE

K.S.W.
WHITE, KATHARINE S.

KAAL, AIRA
HOUN, AIRA

KABAL, A.M.
BHABRA, H.S.

KABAPHES, KONSTANTINOS P.
KAVAFIS, KANSTANTINOS P.

KABASELE, JOSEPH
TSHIAMALA, KABASELE

KABDEBO, TAMAS
KABDEBO, THOMAS

KABIBBLE, OSH
JOBB, JAMIE

KABLER, KAPITAN WILLIAM
KABEL, WALTHER

KACEW, ROMAIN
KACEWGARI, ROMAIN

KADEN
BANDROWSKI, JULJUSZ

KADES, HANS
WERLBERGER, HANS

KAEMPFERT, WADE
DEL REY, LESTER
HARRISON, HARRY

KAFU
NAGAL SOKICHI

KAFU, NAGAI
SOKICHI, NAGAI

KAGEY, RUDOLF
STEEL, RUDOLPH HORNADAY

KAGG, PETER
SAMUELSSON, STURE

KAHANE, MARTIN
KAHANE, MEIR [DAVID]

KAHLE, KRISTIN
AHLSTRAND, KERSTIN

KAHLE, KRISTINA
KYHLE, LARS

KAHLER, WOODLAND
SAINT INNOCENT, MARQUIS

KAHN, BALTHAZAR
CARLISLE, THOMAS FISKE

KAHN, E.J. JR.
KAHN, ELY JACQUES

KAHN, OBIE
PROCTOR, GEO[RGE] W[YATT]
VARDEMAN, ROBERT E.

KAHN, PEGGY
KATZ, BOBBI[E]

KAHN, STEVE
KAHN, STEPHEN

KAHN-FOGEL, DANIEL
FOGEL, DANIEL MARK

KAHRAMAN, A.
KANATSIZ, NECATI

KAI, KIM
BECHTLE-BECHTINGER, SIBYL

KAILAND, ALEXANDER
KEILSON, HANS

KAIN, MALCOLM
OGLESBY, JOSEPH

KAIN, SAUL
SASSOON, SIEGFRIED [L]

KAIN, VICTOR
WORKMAN, JAMES

KAINE, GEORGE S.
MORRIS, CHARLES [S]

KAINE, MYRA
WALLMANN, JEFFREY M.

KAINEN, RAY
KAINULAINEN, RAY

KAININ, RAY
KAINULAINEN, RAY

KAINS, JOSEPHINE
GOULART, RONALD JOSEPH

KAISAN, NAKAZATO
YANOSUKE, NAKAZATO

KAISER WILHELM II
HOHENZOLLERN, FRIEDRICH W

KAISER, BILL
SUMNER, DAVID [W.K.]

KAISER, ELISABETH M.
BRAEM, ELISABETH M.

KAISER, JANICE
SUTCLIFFE, JANICE

KAISER, R.J.
KAISER, RONN & JANICE

KAJAR
BOWEN, RUBIN

KAKI
HEINEMANN, KATHERINE

KAKONEN, ULLA
ANOBILE, ULLA [K]

KAKONIS, TOM E.
KAKONIS, THOMAS E.

KAKUCHIN, MARTIN
BENCUR, MATEJ

KALBFLEISCH, E.C.
GIBSON, WALTER B.

KALE, ARVIND & SHANTA
GANTZER, HUGH

KALIN, JEREMIJA
DEBELJAK, TINE

KALIX, AXEL
SWEDIN, NILS-AXEL

KALL, EGON
CARLSSON, EGON

KALLBERG, STURE
KAELLBERG, STURE

KALLIO, SINIKKA
NEVANLINNA, SINIKKA SISKO

KALLIO-VISAPAA, SINIKKA
NEVANLINNA, SINIKKA SISKO

KALLMER, ULLRICH
DIETSCH, WERNER

KALMUS, AIN
MAND, EWALD

KALNEN, RAY
KAINULAINEN, RAY

KALPANA, MOHAN
LALLA, MOHAN BULCHAND

KAMBAN, GUDMUNDUR
HALLGRIMSON, JANSSON

KAMBU, JOSEPH
AMAMOO, JOSEPH GODSON

KAMEN, ISAI
STEIN, JESS

KAMENOVA, ANNA
STAYNOVA, ANNA

KAMERMAN, SYLVIA E.
BURACK, SYLVIA K.

KAMIN, NICK
ANTONICK, ROBERT J.

KAMP, FRIEDRICH
BOSKAMP, PAUL

KAMP, STEFFEN
DICKSCHAT, OTTO

KAMPF, AVRAM
KAMPF, ABRAHAM

KAN, KIKUCHI
HIROSHI, KIKUCHI

KANASAWA, ROGER
KANAZAWA, MASAKATA

KANATA, JAY
OLIVEROS TOVAR, MIGUEL

KANATSIZ, NECATI
ERDURAN, REFIK

KANE
MCKENZIE, C[ECIL] J[AMES]

KANE, AARNO
KAGAN, ANDREW

KANE, ALEX
LAZUTA, EUGENE MICHAEL

KANE, D.N.
KELLEY, THOMAS P.

KANE, JACK
BAKER, ALLEN ALBERT

KANE, JAMES
GERMANO, PETER B.

KANE, JULIA
ROBINS, DENISE

KANE, KASPER
MACISAAC, FRED[ERIC JOHN]

KANE, KATHLEEN
CHILD, MAUREEN

KANE, L.A.
MANNETTI, LISA

KANE, MARK
KING, ALBERT

KANE, PABLO
ZACHARY, HUGH

KANE, PAUL
SIMON, PAUL

KANE, PHILIP
CASE, JOHN FRANCIS

KANE, ROD
KANE, GERARD THOMAS MATT.

KANE, WILSON
BLOCH, ROBERT [A]

KANEMAN, SOL
TREDINNICK, WILLIAM JR.

KANGAROO, CAPTAIN
KEESHAN, ROBERT J.

KANILA, HILJA
JARNEFELT, ARVID

KANSIL, JOLI
GAINES, JOE DENNIS

KANTARIZIS, SYLVIA
KANTARIS, SYLVIA

KANTER, MARIANNE
KANTER, MARIANNE

KANTO, PETER
COLEMAN, JOHN
ZACHARY, HUGH

KANTOR, HAL
KANTOR, HARRY

KANTOR, MARIANNE
LIEBERMAN, RICHARD M.

KANZAWA, TOSHIKO
FURUKAWA, TOSHI

KAP-O-KASLO
WEST, G.A.

KAPEL, ANDREW
BURGESS, MICHAEL ROY

KAPLAN, DORIS
WILLENS, DORIS

KAPLAN, FRED M.
KAPLAN, FRED MICHAEL

KAPUSTA, PAUL
BICKERS, RICHARD L.T.

KAPUT
DARD, FREDERIC

KARA, GIORG
BRUHL, GUSTAV

KARAGEORGE, MICHAEL
ANDERSON, POUL [W]

KARASEK ZE LVOVIC, JIRI
KARASEK, JOSEF JIRI LVOV.

KARE, KAARINA
HONKANEN, HILJA L.V.

KARELIN, VICTOR
VON MICHALEWSKY, NIKOLAI

KAREN
ALDRICH, SANDRA PICKLSIM.

KAREN, ANNE
TENKRAT, FRIEDRICH

KARIG, WALTER
PATRICK, KEATS

KARIM, MUSTAI
KARISNOV, MUSTAFA S.

KARINA
GOUD, ANNE

KARISHKA, PAUL
HATCH, DAVID PATTERSON

KARJOT, JEK
KUCHARSKI, JAN EDWARD

KARK, NINA MARY [M]
BAWDEN, NINA MARY MABREY

KARKA, B.W.
KRAHNER, KARL

KARKALA, JOHN A.
ALPHONSO-KARKALA, JOHN B.

KARKALA, JOHN B.A.
ALPHONSO-KARKALA, JOHN B.

KARL, M.S.
SHUMAN, MALCOLM KARL

KARL, ROGER
TROUVE, ROGER

KARLIN, GEORGE
KROTKOV, YURI

KARLIN, MURIEL S.
TRACHMAN, MURIEL KARLIN

KARLOFF, BORIS
AVALLONE, MICHAEL
PRATT, WILLIAM HENRY

KARLOWNA, E.
LOBNER-FELSKI, ERIKA

KARNIEWSKI, JANUSZ
WITTLIN, THADDEUS ANDREW

KARNO, BROTHER
SUKARNO, AHMED

KARNO, BUNG
SUKARNO, AHMED

KAROL, ALEXANDER
KENT, ARTHUR WILLIAM C.

KAROL, K.S.
KEWES, KAROL

KAROLEVITZ, BOB
KAROLEVITZ, ROBERT F.

KAROV, RABBI
LEVINSKY, ELCHANAN LEIB

KARPAU, ULADZIMIR
KARPOV, VLADIMIR

KARPENKO-KARYJ, IVAN
TOBILEVICH, IVAN KARPOV.

KARR, HANS-PETER
JAHN, REINHARD

KARR, JILLIAN
GREENBERG, JAN
KATZ, KAREN A.

KARR, LEE
KARR, LEONA C.

KARRON, KRIS
NORRIS, CAROLYN B.

KARSHISH
CRESWELL, HARRY B.

KARTA, NAT
AMBLER, DAIL
CHARLES, GEORGE
CRESSWELL, DONALD
FEARN, JOHN RUSSELL
LAZENBY, NORMAN A.
NORWOOD, VICTOR [G.C.]
STANFORD, TERRY
WATSON, JOHN

KARX, PETER
SCHAUWECKER, EVA

KARY, EILZABETH [N]
GOW, KARYN WITMER

KARZ, EVA
SCHAUWECKER, EVA

KASCHNITZ, MARIE LUISE
VON KASCHNITZ-W., MARIE L

KASCHOWSKI, FRANZ
LERCH, HANSRUEDI

KASEY, MICHELLE
SEIDICK, KATHRYN A.

KASPAROV, G.K.
KASPAROV, GARY KIMOVICH

KASPAROV, GARI
KASPAROV, GARY KIMOVICH

KASPAROV, GARRY
KASPAROV, GARY KIMOVICH

KASSAK, FRED
HUMBLOT, PIERRE

KASSLER, J.C.
KASSLER, JAMIE CROY

KASSON, HELEN [W]
WEINBAUM, HELEN

KASSOW, GERT
HANSEN, ROBERT

KAST, PETER
PREISSNER, CARL

KASTEIN, DORIT
KLEIN, DOROTHEE

KASTEL, WARREN
GEIER, CHESTER S.
SILVERBERG, ROBERT

KASTELL, KATRIN
KLEIN, DOROTHEE

KASTNER, ERICH
KAESTNER, ERICH

KATAHN, MARTIN
KLEIN, MARTIN

KATAI, TAYAMA
ROKUYA, TAYAMA

KATAPHUSIN
RUSKIN, JOHN

KATCHA, VAHE
KATCHADOURIAN, VAHE

KATELEY, WALTER
JUNE, HAROLD

KATERLA, JOZEF
ZEROMSKI, STEFAN

KATH, LYDIA
KNOP, LYDIA

KATHRYN
SEARLE, KATHRYN ADRIENNE

KATI
REKAI, KATI

KATOLIQUE, A. DEFOUT
ACKERMAN, FORREST J.

KATSARAKIS, JOAN HARRIES
HARRIES, JOAN

KATZ, ALFRED
ALLAN, ALFRED K.

KATZ, BASHO
GATTI, ARTHUR GERARD

KATZ, HILDA
WEBBER, HULDA

KATZ, MARJORIE P.
WEISER, MARJORIE P.K.

KATZ, MICKEY
KATZ, MYRON MEYER

KATZ, SHMUEL
KATZ, SAMUEL

KATZ, STAN
CHAPMAN, FRANK MONROE

KAU, MICHAEL Y.M.
KAU, YING-MAO

KAUFFMAN, M.K.
NORBERG, MARCIA K.

KAUFMAN, IDA
KAUFMAN, CHAYA

KAUFMAN, SUE
BARONDESS, SUE K.

KAUFMANN, FRANZ K.
KUROWSKI, FRANZ

KAULITZ-NIEDECK, R.
ANDERSON, ROSA

KAUMANDI, KAVITA
ARNOLD, ELIZABETH

KAUNDA, K.D.
KAUNDA, KENNETH DAVID

KAUNDA, KENNETH D.
KAUNDA, KENNETH DAVID

KAUT, ELLIS
PREIS, ELISABETH

KAVAN, ANNA
EDMONDS, HELEN WOODS

KAVANAGH, CYNTHIA
DANIELS, DOROTHY

KAVANAGH, DAN
BARNES, JULIAN [P]

KAVANAGH, JACK
BLOCK, LAWRENCE

KAVANAGH, PAUL
BLOCK, LAWRENCE

KAVANAUGH, CYNTHIA
DANIELS, NORMAN A.

KAVANAUGH, IAN
HERSHMAN, MORRIS
WEBB, JEAN FRANCIS III

KAVENEY, ROZ
KAVENEY, ANDREW J.

KAVERIN, VENYAMIN
ZILLBERG, VENYAMIN ALEX.

KAVIFIS, KONSTANTINOS P.
KAVAFIS, KONSTANTINOS P.

KAY, BARBARA
KELLER, [Y] ETHEL MAY

KAY, CAMERON
VIDAL, [E] GORE LUTHER

KAY, CATHERINE
CROISSANT, KAY
DEES, CATHERINE

KAY, ELLEN
DEMILLE, NELSON [RICHARD]

KAY, GEORGE
LAMBERT, ERIC

KAY, GILBERT
GIBSON, WALTER B.

KAY, H.R.
KNOX, HUGH R.

KAY, HELEN
GOLDFRANK, HELEN [C]

KAY, JAY
KLEINHAUS, JULIUS

KAY, MARY
ASH, MARY KAY WAGNER

KAY, PAT
ALEXANDER, TRISHA

KAY, PHOEBE
MINER, VIRGINIA SCOTT

KAY, RONALD
KNOX-MAWER, RONALD

KAY, TERESA
DE KERPELY, THERESA

KAY, TERRY
KAY, TERENCE

KAY, WALLACE
ARTER, WALLACE E.

KAY, ZELL
KEMP, ROY ZELL

KAYE, ALAN
HOROWITZ, SHEL ALAN

KAYE, AMBER
HENTGES, ALISON J.

KAYE, BARBARA
MUIR, BARBARA K.

KAYE, EVELYN
EVANS, KATHLEEN

KAYE, GAYLE
KASPER, GAYLE

KAYE, H.B.
KAMPF, HAROLD BERTRAM

KAYE, H.R.
KNOX, HUGH RANDOLPH

KAYE, HAROLD B.
KAMPF, HAROLD BERTRAM

KAYE, JOANNE
PAYES, RACHEL C.

KAYE, JUDY
BAER, JUDY

KAYE, LORIN
KONSTAM, F.
LATHROP, LORIN ANDREWS

KAYE, LOUIS
NORMAN, NOEL WILSON

KAYE, M.M.
HAMILTON, MARY MARGARET

KAYE, MARX
BYRNE, STUART J.

KAYE, MARY MARGARET
HAMILTON, MARY MARGARET

KAYE, MELANIE
KAYE-KANTROWITZ, MELANIE

KAYE, MOLLIE
HAMILTON, MARY MARGARET

KAYE, PAMELA
ROBERTS, JANET LOUISE

KAYE, STEPHEN
SELTZER, CHARLES ALDEN

KAYE, TOM
KAYE, BARRINGTON

KAYE, WILMOT
TRENT, PAUL

KAYMOR, PATRICE MAGUILENE
SENGHOR, LEOPOLD SEDAR

KAYNE, MARVIN
FEARN, JOHN RUSSELL

KAYSER, DINAH
FRIEDRICH, ANITA

KAYSING, BILL
KAYSING, WILLIAM C.

KAZNAR, KURT
SERWICHER, KURT

KEANE, KAY
KEARNEY, KAY

KEANE, MOLLY
KEANE, MARY NESTA S.

KEARNEY, RUTH ELIZABETH
CARLSON, RUTH [E] KEARNEY

KEARNY, JILLIAN
GOULART, RONALD JOSEPH

KEAST, KAREN
CANFIELD, SANDRA

KEATING, BERN
KEATING, LEO BERNARD

KEATING, HENRY
KEATING, HENRY R.F.

KEATING, WALTER S.
ROSENBERG, HENRIETTA

KEATON, COREY
ENGELS, MARY TATE
THOMPSON, VICKI L.

KEATS, MYRON
STRONG, CHARLES STANLEY

KEATS, VIOLA
SMART, VIOLA

KEAVENY, JAMES R.
LANDIS, ARTHUR H.

KEBIN, JODY
LAWRENCE, JODI

KEBLA, WALTRAUD
KABEL, WALTHER

KEEFER, CATHERINE
OGAN, GEORGE & MARGARET

KEEFER, JANICE K.
KULYK KEEFER, JANICE

KEEGAN, CHRISTOPHER
GORMAN, EDWARD [JOSEPH]

KEEGAN, MARY CONSTANCE
KEEGAN, MARY HEATHCOTT

KEEL, FRANK
KEELER, RONALD F.

KEEL, JOHN A.
KIEHLE, JOHN ALVA

KEEL, LAURA
BERGE, CAROL

KEELING, E.B.
CURL, JAMES STEVENS

KEELYN, PATRICIA
VAN WIE, PATRICIA

KEEN, GERALDINE
NORMAN, GERALDINE [L]

KEEN, M.H.
KEEN, MAURICE HUGH

KEEN, ROBERT
POPPE, KARL HEINZ

KEEN, ROD
FARMER, PHILIP JOSE

KEENE, BURT
BICKERS, RICHARD L.T.

KEENE, CAROLYN
ADAMS, HARRIET S.
ALBERT, SUSAN WITTIG
ALBERT, SUSAN W. & BILL
AXELRAD, NANCY
BENSON, MILDRED [A] WIRT
KARIG, WALTER
MCFARLANE, LESLIE CHARLES
MCQUAY, MICHAEL DENNIS
STRATEMEYER, EDWARD
WAGNER, SHARON [BLYTHE]

KEENE, DAY
HJERTSTEDT, GUNARD

KEENE, FARADAY
JARRETT, CORA [H]

KEENE, FRANCES W.
CASMAN, FRANCES WHITE

KEENE, JAMES
COOK, WILLIAM EVERETT

KEENE, KING
BOMKE, BERNHARD

KEENE, LIEUT.
RATHBORNE, ST. GEORGE

KEENE, R.D.
KEENE, RAYMOND DENNIS

KEENE, RAY
KEENE, RAYMOND DENNIS

KEENE, SARAH
ATKINS, JANE

KEENEY, CHUCK
KEENEY, CHARLES JAMES

KEENY, S.M.
KEENY, SPURGEON MILTON

KEESING, NANCY
HERTZBERG, NANCY

KEFFERSTAN, JEAN
PEDRICK, JEAN

KEGLER, HANS
REINHOLD, KARL LUDWIG

KEHRET, PEG
KEHRET, MARGARET ANN

KEILLOR, GARRISON
KEILLOR, GARY [EDWARD]

KEIMBERG, ALLYN
KIMBRO, JOHN M.

KEIR, CHRISTINE
POPESCU, CHRISTINE

KEISLING, BILL
KEISLING, WILLIAM

KEISTER, ELINORE
DOBSON, ELINORE LUCILLE

KEITH X
ARMSTRONG, KEITH F.W.

KEITH, CARLTON
ROBERTSON, KEITH CARLTON

KEITH, COLIN
JAMESON, MALCOLM

KEITH, DAVID
STEEGMULLER, FRANCIS

KEITH, DONALD
MONROE, KEITH & DONALD

KEITH, HAMISH
CHAPMAN, JAMES KEITH

KEITH, HARRISON
CHAMBLISS, JOHN
CLARK, PHILIP

KEITH, J. KILMENY
MALLESON, LUCY BEATRICE

KEITH, JAMES
HETHERINGTON, KEITH JAMES

KEITH, JOHN
MASON, JOHN HOLLIS

KEITH, KATRIN
BECKER, MARIETTA

KEITH, LEE
SUNNERS, WILLIAM

KEITH, LEIGH
GOLD, HORACE L.

KEITH, LESLIE
JOHNSTON, GRACE L. KEITH

KEITH, MARIAN
MACGREGOR, MARY ESTHER

KEITH, MARION
MILLER, MARY ESTER

KEITH, MICHAEL
HUBBARD, L. RON

KEITH, ROBERT
APPLEBAUM, STAN

KEITH, SLIM
KEITH, NANCY

KEITH, VIVIAN
COPELAND, VIVIAN

KELASKER, HIVAR
KNEIFEL, HANNS

KELEM GIRL, THE
LIGGETT, GENEVIEVE G.

KELL, JOSEPH
WILSON, J ANTHONY BURGESS

KELLAR, VON
HUGHES, DENNIS [TALBOT]

KELLEM, RAY
NUETZEL, CHARLES A.

KELLER, ASAPH
SHAMIR, MOSHE

KELLER, B.L.
MALZBERG, BARRY [N]

KELLER, BRIGITTE
PFAFF, BRIGITTE

KELLER, DAN
KAUFMAN, LOUIS

KELLER, GAIL FAITHFULL
FAITHFULL, GAIL

KELLERMAN, DAN
SCHMIDT, DAN

KELLEY, AUDREY
ROOS, AUDREY [KELLEY]

KELLEY, BRYAN JAMES
ERNST, PAUL FREDERICK

KELLEY, DORSEY
ADAMS, DORSEY

KELLEY, LEO F.
KELLEY, LEO P[ATRICK]

KELLEY, RAY
PAINE, LAURAN BOSWORTH

KELLEY, RUBY M.
JOHNSON, RUBY KELLEY

KELLIER, ELIZABETH
KELLY, ELIZABETH

KELLINO, PAMELA
MASON, PAMELA OSTRER

KELLOCK, ARCHIBALD P.
MAVOR, OSBORNE HENRY

KELLOG, ERNEST P.
GROSSMANN, HANS HUGO

PSEUDONYMS

KELLOG, GRACE
GRIFFITH-SHAW, GRACE K.

KELLOG, JIM
VON KOBLINSKI, HANS-JOACH

KELLOG, ROBBIE
KALMUCZAK, ROLF

KELLOG, ROBERT
KALMUCZAK, ROLF

KELLOGG, GENE
KELLOGG, JEAN [D]

KELLOGG, GEORGE
HUBBARD, L. RON

KELLOGG, M. BRADLEY
KELLOGG, MARJORIE BRADLEY

KELLOW, KATHLEEN
HIBBERT, ELEANOR BURFORD

KELLWAY, MARY D.
HILLYARD, MARY DOROTHEA

KELLY IAN
KELLY, JOHN SPENCE

KELLY, A.A.
KELLY, ANGELINE AGNES

KELLY, BARBARA
FURSTAUER, JOHANNA

KELLY, C.M.O.
GIBBS, CECILIA MAY

KELLY, COMMANDO
KELLY, CHARLES E.

KELLY, DAVE
KELLY, DAVID MICHAEL

KELLY, FIONA
WELFORD, SUE

KELLY, GLENN
MCNEILLY, MILDRED MASTER.

KELLY, GUY
MOORE, NICHOLAS

KELLY, JACK
MULLER, KURT

KELLY, JAMES BRYAN
MACDONALD, GEORGE A.

KELLY, JEFF
KELLY, JEFFREY

KELLY, MARTY
KELLY, MARTHA ROSE

KELLY, PATRICK
ALLBEURY, THEODORE E.

KELLY, RALPH
GEIS, DARLENE STERN

KELLY, RAY
PAINE, LAURAN BOSWORTH

KELLY, RENYARD
DONALDSON, DALE C.

KELLY, RICHARD
LAYMON, RICHARD

KELLY, RON
GRASMUCK, JURGEN

KELLY, STAN
KELLY-BOOTLE, STAN

KELLY, VINCE
KELLY, VINCENT GATTON

KELLY, ZED
KELLEY, THOMAS P.

KELSEY, JANICE
KING, ALBERT

KELSO, CHUCK
GRIBBLE, LEONARD [R]

KELTON, ARYAN
KELTON, ARYON LEWIS

KELVIN, NED
KINGHORN, NORTON D.

KELWAY, CHRISTINE
GWINN, CHRISTINE M.

KEMMLER, URSULA
KOCHER-ERB, HEDWIG

KEMP, BERNARD
VAN VLIERDAN, BERNARD F.

KEMP, HANNES
KAPPLER, HANNS-WALTER

KEMP, HARRY
HERSEY, HAROLD

KEMP, JULIAN
KENT, JIM

KEMP, SARAH
BUTTERWORTH, MICHAEL

KEMPE, KARL
BOGERSHAUSEN, KARL-HEINZ

KEMPSTER, BERT
GIBBONS, H.H. CLIFFORD

KEMSLEY, VISCOUNT
BERRY, JAMES GOMER

KENDAL, GEOFFREY
BRAGG, RICHARD GEOFFREY

KENDAL, JUNE
STIFF, DOROTHY AILEEN

KENDAL, ROBERT
FORSTER, REGINALD KENNETH

KENDALL, GORDON
LEWITT, SHARIANN N.
SHWARTZ, SUSAN MARTHA

KENDALL, JACK
KALLMAN, MARY LOU
OSER, MARILYN

KENDALL, JANE
MARTENS, ANNE L.C.

KENDALL, JOHN
BRASH, MARGARET MAUDE
GLOWACZ, HELMUT

KENDALL, KATHERINE
APPLEGATE, KATHERINE

KENDALL, LACE
STOUTENBURG, ADRIEN [P]

KENDALL, MAY
GOLDWORTH, EMMA

KENDRAKE, CARLETON
GARDNER, ERLE STANLEY

KENDRICK, JOHN
BANGS, JOHN KENDRICK

KENDRICK, TERRY
TERRY, MAY

KENDRICKS, JAMES
CHADWICK, JOSEPH L.
FOX, GARDNER F.

KENDYL, SHARICE
CARSTENSEN, BERNICE
MICHELS, SHARRY

KENEALLY, TOM
KENEALLY, THOMAS MICHAEL

KENEALY, JIM
KENEALY, JAMES P.

KENECOTT, G.J.
VIKSNINS, GEORGE JURIS

KENEU
HAZLEWOOD, REX

KENIAN, PAUL ROGER
CLIFFORD, MARTIN

KENNAN, DAN
FALK, HERMANN

KENNAWAY, JAMES
PEEBLES, JAMES E.

KENNEALY, G.P.
KENNEALY, GERALD P.

KENNEALY, JERRY
KENNEALY, GERALD P.

KENNEALY, PATRICIA
MORRISON, PATRICIA K.

KENNEDY, ADAM
REDGATE, JOHN

KENNEDY, CHUCK
KENNEDY, CHARLES JOSEPH

KENNEDY, CLAY
JENNISON, JOHN WILLIAM

KENNEDY, CODY JR.
REESE, JOHN [HENRY]

KENNEDY, DIANA
DUGGLEBY, JEAN COLBECK

KENNEDY, EARL
CLINGAN, C.C.

KENNEDY, EDGAR REES
JENNISON, JOHN WILLIAM

KENNEDY, ELLIOT
GODFREY, LIONEL ROBERT H.

KENNEDY, GEORGE
SHELDON, WALTER J.

KENNEDY, GERALD STUDDERT
STUDDERT-KENNEDY, W.G.

KENNEDY, HOWARD
WOOLFOLK, JOSHUA PITTS

KENNEDY, JAMES
MONAHAN, JAMES HENRY F.
KENAFICK, JOSEPH

KENNEDY, JOHN PENDLETON
FOX, GARDNER F.

KENNEDY, LENA
SMITH, LENA K[ENNEDY]

KENNEDY, MILWARD
BURGE, M.R. KENNEDY

KENNEDY, NANCY [M]
KENNEDY, NANCY MACDOUGALL

KENNEDY, PHILIP
HERSEY, HAROLD

KENNEDY, R.C.
CORTEZ-COLUMBUS, ROBERT C

KENNEDY, ROBERT MILWARD
BURGE, M.R. KENNEDY
MACDONELL, ARCHIBALD G.

KENNEDY, ROSE
VICTOR, MRS. M.V.

KENNEDY, T.A.
KENNEDY, THERESA A.

KENNEDY, TED
KENNEDY, EDWARD MOORE

KENNEDY, X.J.
KENNEDY, JOSEPH CHARLES

KENNEDY, [CAPT.] J.L.
HARBAUGH, THOMAS C.

KENNEGGY, RICHARD
NETTELL, RICHARD GEOFFREY

KENNELLY, PATRICIA
BOECKMAN, PATRICIA

KENNER, LAURA
HAYDEN, LAURA

KENNETH, GORDON
BANZHAF, ERWIN

KENNETH, JOHN
KLEIN, WALTER J. JR.

KENNETH, JOHN H.
HOGLUND, KEN

KENNETH, MR.
MARLOWE, ALAN STEPHEN
MARLOWE, KENNETH

KENNEY, FRANK
LOBSACK, WILHELM

KENNEY, KATHRYN
SANDERLIN, OWENITA [H]

KENNEY, WIN
MARKS, WINSTON K.

KENNICOTT, MERVYN BRIAN
HAMER, GERTRUD [v.S.]

KENNIE, JESSIE
MACPHERSON, JESSIE INGRAM

KENNINGTON, ALAN
KENNINGTON, [G] ALAN

KENNY, CHARLES J.
GARDNER, ERLE STANLEY

KENNY, JEAN
FREEMAN, JEAN KENNY

KENNY, KATHLEEN
KRULL, KATHLEEN

KENNY, KATHRYN
BOWDEN, JOAN CHASE
KRULL, KATHLEEN
STACK, NICOLETE MEREDITH

KENNY, KEVIN
KRULL, KATHLEEN

KENNY, MARILYN
STACK, NICHOLETE MEREDITH

KENNY, NICK
KENNY, NICHOLAS NAPOLEON

KENNY, PAUL
LIBERT, JEAN
VANDENPANHUISE, GASTON

KENNY, STAN
GIGGAL, KENNETH

KENRICK, TONY
KENRICK, ANTHONY ARTHUR

KENSCH, OTTO
HAUSFELD, RUSSELL

KENSINGER, GEORGE
FICHTER, GEORGE S.

KENSLOW, VIC
BLEECK, G.C.

KENT, ALEXANDER
METHOLD, KENNETH [WALTER]
REEMAN, DOUGLAS [EDWARD]

KENT, AMANDA
HENRICHS, BETTY L.

KENT, ARDEN
MARION, FREIDA

KENT, BEVERLY
GANNON, E.J.

KENT, BILL
KENT, CARLETON VOLNEY JR.

KENT, BRAD
HUGHES, DENNIS [TALBOT]
HUGI, MAURICE G.
RUSSELL, ERIC FRANK

KENT, CASEY
MCINTOSH, KENNETH

KENT, CROMWELL
SPARSHOTT, FRANCIS EDWARD

KENT, DAVID
BIRNEY, HERMAN HOFFMAN
LAMBERT, DAVID [COMPTON]

KENT, ELIZABETH
ROCHESTER, GEO[RGE] E.

KENT, FORTUNE
TOOMBS, JOHN

KENT, GLORIA
FISHER, STEPHEN GOULD

KENT, GORDON
TUBB, E.C.

KENT, HELEN
POLLEY, JUDITH ANNA

KENT, JACK
KENT, JOHN WELLINGTON

KENT, JOHN
BALBERNIE, ARTHUR G.

KENT, KARLENE
NORTON, EDITH ELIZABETH A

KENT, KATHERINE
DIAL, JOAN MAVIS R.

KENT, KATHRYN
KENT, JEAN SALTER

KENT, KATIE
GREEN, KAY

KENT, KELVIN
BARNES, ARTHUR K.
KUTTNER, HENRY
MOORE, CATHERINE LUCILLE

KENT, LANE
BLEECK, G.C.

KENT, LARRY
DUNN, DES R.
HARING, DON

KENT, LYNETTE
BACON, CHERYL

KENT, MALLORY
LOWNDES, ROBERT A.W.

KENT, PAMELA
POLLOCK, IDA

KENT, PAUL
TOOMBS, JOHN

KENT, PETE
RICHARDSON, GLADWELL G.

KENT, PHILIP
BULMER, [HENRY] KENNETH

KENT, RICHARD
OWEN, FRANK
WILLIAMS, ROSWELL

KENT, ROBERTA
ROBERTS, DOREEN

KENT, ROY
APPEL, WALTER

KENT, SIMON
CATTO, MAX[WELL J.]

KENT, STEFFEN
FEIL, GEORG

KENT, STELLA
PHILLIPS, STELLA

KENT, TONY
CRECHALES, ANTHONY GEORGE

KENT, WARREN F.
MANNING, WILLIAM HENRY

KENT, WILLIS
COLLISON, WILSON

KENTIGERN, JOHN
VEITCH, THOMAS

KENTO, NOEL
KENTON, PAUL

KENTON, BERNARD J.
SIEGEL, JEROME

KENTON, L.P.
FANTHORPE, R.L.

KENTON, MAXWELL
HOFFENBURG, MASON
SOUTHERN, TERRY

KENWARD, JEAN
CHESTERMAN, JEAN

KENWOOD, NEIL
HOFFMANN, HORST

KENWORTHY, HUGH
WALKER, ROWLAND

KENYON, BERNICE
GILKYSON, BERNICE KENYON

KENYON, CORY
ENGELS, MARY TATE
THOMPSON, VICKI L.

KENYON, JOANNA
CLARKE, JANET K.

KENYON, KATE
ADORJAN, CAROL MADDEN
RANSOM, CANDICE F.

KENYON, LARRY
ENGEL, LYLE KENYON
LOUDERBACK, LEW

KENYON, ORR
CARTER, RUSSELL KELSOE

KENYON, PAUL
ENGEL, LYLE KENYON
FREEDLAND, NATHANIEL

KENYON, PAUL [CONT]
MOFFAT, DONALD
VARDEMAN, ROBERT E.

KENYON, ROBERT O.
KUTTNER, HENRY
MOORE, CATHERINE LUCILLE

KENYON, W.A.
KENYON, WALTER ANDREW

KEON, GRACE
DONOVAN, GRACE WALLACE

KEPAC, COIL
ACKERMAN, FORREST J.

KEPLER, UTTA
KEPPLER, GERTRUD

KEPPEL, CHARLOTTE
TORDAY, URSULA

KEPPEL, SONIA
CUBITT, SONIA ROSEMARY

KEPPS, GERALD
SPECK, GERALD EUGENE

KER, JILL
CONWAY, JILL KER

KERBY, SUSAN ALICE
BURTON, ALICE ELIZABETH

KERFIN, GERHARD
BIELICKE, GERHARD

KERHOUEL, GAETAN
VIGNE, PAUL

KERI, AMANDA
HARRIS, LIN
STOCKTON, ARTIE

KERKOW, HERBERT
LEWTON, VAL

KERLAY, ALLIS
ACKERMAN, FORREST J.

KERMAN, A.L.
GRUBER, FRANK

KERMAN, GERTRUDE
FURMAN, GERTRUDE L.K.

KERMIT, LANCE
GOODIS, DAVID
THOMPSON, THOMAS [TOMMY]

KERN, CANYON
RABORG, FREDERICK A.

KERN, E.R.
KERNER, FRED

KERN, ERICH
KERNMAYR, ERICH

KERN, GREGORY
ALPERS, HANS JOACHIM
FOX, GARDNER F.
HAHN, RONALD M.
PESCHKE, HANS
PUKALLUS, HORST
TUBB, E.C.

KERNEGGER, HANNES
REBCZEK, FRANZ

KERNER, KEITH
BENSON, ARNOLD
GALT, ALISTAIR

KEROUAC, JACK
KEROUAC, JEAN-LOUIS L.D.

KEROUAC, JAN
HACKETT, JAN MICHELE

KEROUAC, JOHN
KEROUAC, JEAN-LOUIS L.D.

KERR
PINNIX, HANNAH COURTNEY

KERR, ANDY
KERR, ALEX A.

KERR, BEN
ARD, WILLIAM [THOMAS]

KERR, CAROLE
CARR, MARGARET

KERR, FREDERICK
KERNER, FRED

KERR, JOHN O'CONNELL
WHITTET, GEORGE SORLEY

KERR, JOSIAH
SALMONSON, JESSICA A.

KERR, LAURA
HORNICKLE, LAURA

KERR, LENNOX
KERR, JAMES LENNOX

KERR, M.E.
MEAKER, MARIJANE [AGNES]

KERR, MICHAEL
HOSKINS, ROBERT

KERR, NORMAN D.
SIEBER, SAM DIXON

KERR, ORPHEUS C.
NEWELL, ROBERT HENRY

KERR, SHERRILL
MAGRUDER, JULIA

KERRIGAN, KATE LOWE
RICKETT, FRANCIS

KERRY, FRANCES
KERIGAN, FLORENCE

KERRY, LOIS
ARQUETTE, LOIS S. DUNCAN

KERSCHBAUMER, MARIE THER.
KURZ-G., MARIE-THERESE

KERSEY, JOHN
WARRINER, THURMAN

KERSHAW, PETER
LUCIE-SMITH, [J] EDWARD

KERSTEN, NICOLA
GREVEN, HELGA

KERSTEN, ROGER
SCHEER, KARL-HERBERT

KERSTETTER, JAMES
HORNWOOD, HARVEY

KERVERZHIOU
BERTOU, GWILHERM

KESS, ROLF
DIERKES, RUDOLF

KESSELMAN, JUDI R.
KESSELMAN-TURKEL, JUDI
ROSENTHAL, JUDI

KESSELMAN-TURKEL, JUDI
ROSENTHAL, JUDI

KESSLER, FRANK
KESSLER, FRANCIS PASCHAL

KESTEVEN, G.R.
CROSHER, GEOFFREY ROBINS

KESTREL, DAN
VEITCH, TONY

KESTREL, WARD
JUDGE, M.

KETCH, JACK
TIBBETTS, JOHN CARTER

KETCHAM, HANK
KETCHAM, HENRY KING

KETCHUM, CLIFF
PAINE, LAURAN BOSWORTH

KETCHUM, FRANK
PAINE, LAURAN BOSWORTH

KETCHUM, J.
FRENTZEN, JEFFREY

KETCHUM, JACK
PAINE, LAURAN BOSWORTH
MAYR, DALLAS WILLIAM

KETTENFEIER, PETRI
ROSEGGER, PETRI KETTENFR.

KETTER, PAM
BROWNING, PAMELA

KETTLE, JOCELYN
KETTLE, [JOCELYN] PAMELA

KETTLE, PETER
GLOVER, DENNIS JAMES M.

KEUNING, WILLEM DE
KEUNING, W.E.

KEVERN, BARBARA
SHEPHERD, DONALD LEE

KEVERNE, RICHARD
HOSKEN, CLIFFORD [J.W.]

KEVIN, JODI
LAWRENCE, JODI

KEVIN, KELLY
WIEMER, SUSANNE

KEVIN, LLOYD
SWEET, HAROLD G.

KEVIN, PETER
VISER, LON

KEWLEY, JENNIFER
DRASKAU, JENNIFER

KEY, L.J.
TAMKUS, DANIEL

KEY, SAMUEL M.
DE LINT, CHARLES [H.D.H.]

KEY, SEAN A.
COUGHLIN, WILLIAM J.

KEY, TED
KEY, THEODORE

KEY, UEL
KEY, SAMUEL WHITTELL

KEYBER, CONNY
FIELDING, HENRY

KEYEN, WERNER
MULLER, PAUL ALFRED

KEYES, NOEL
KEIGHTLEY, DAVID NOEL

KEYES, PETER
CONNORS, A.V.

KEYNE, GORDON
BEDFORD-JONES, HENRY

KEYS, DURHAM
GARTON, DURHAM KEITH

KEYSER, SARAH
MCGUIRE, LESLIE SARAH

KEYSTONE, OLIVER
MANTINBAND, JAMES M.

KGOSITSILE, ANEB
HOUSE, GLORIA

KHAI-HUNG
KHANH-GIU, TRAN

KHAKETLA, B.M.
KHAKETLA, BENNETT MAKALO

KHAN, HASSAN
ALI KHAN, SHIRLEY

KHAN, HASSINA
ALI KHAN, SHIRLEY

KHAN, KHALED
CROWLEY, EDWARD ALEXANDER

KHARMS, DANIIL
YUVACHOV, DANIIL IVANOVIC

KHATENA, JOE
KHATENA, JOSEPH

KHLEBNIKOV, VELIMIR
KHLEBNIKOV, VIKTOR VLAD.

KHOMEINI, AYATOLLAH
KHOMEINI, RUHOLLAH M.

KHOMEINI, IMAM
KHOMEINI, RUHOLLAH M.

KHORNAK, LUCILLE
KORNAK, LUCILLE

KHUMEINA, RUHOLLAH
KHOMEINI, RUHOLLAH M.

KIBALCHICK, VIKTOR
SERGE, VICTOR

KICHIZO, NAKAMURA
TSUNEHARU, NAKAMURA

KIDD, ELIZABETH
TRIEGEL, LINDA J.

KIDD, J. ROBY
KIDD, JAMES ROBBINS

KIDD, J.R.
KIDD, JAMES ROBBINS

KIDD, RUSSELL
DONSON, CYRIL

KIDDE, JANET
WOLK, GEORGE

KIEFER, BILL
KIEFER, TILLMAN W.

KIEFER, MIDDLETON
KIEFER, WARREN DAVID
MIDDLETON, HARRY

KIEMEL, ANN
ANDERSON, ANN KIEMEL

KIETREIBER, ALBERT CONRAD
GUETERSLOH, ALBERT PARIS

KIGI, TAKATARO
HAYASHI, TAKASHI

KIHL, ARMAND
ALD, ROY ALLISON

KIJIMA HAJIME
KOJIMA SHOZO

KILBOURN, MATT
BARRETT, GEOFFREY JOHN

KILBOURNE, FANNIE
SCHUBART, FANNIE KILBOURN

KILBURN, HENRY
RIGG, HENRY H. KILBURN

KILBURN, MILES
APPEL, WALTER

KILDARE, JOHN
KING, JOHN BOSWELL

KILDARE, MAURICE
RICHARDSON, GLADWELL G.

KILDARESON, MAURICE
RICHARDSON, GLADWELL G.

KILEY, JED
KILEY, JOHN GERALD

KILGORE, ALEX
AHERN, JEROME MORRELL
LAPORTE, SEAN
OBSTFELD, RAYMOND

KILGORE, JOHN
PAINE, LAURAN BOSWORTH

KILGORE, KATHLEEN
HOUTON, KATHLEEN KILGORE

KILGORE, WILLARD
BALLARD, W. TODHUNTER

KILINA, PATRICIA
WARREN, PATRICIA NELL

KILL HIM
DARD, FREDERIC

KILLDEER, JOHN
MAYHAR, ARDATH F.H.

KILLIAN, LARRY
WELLEN, EDWARD [P]

KILLOUGH, LEE
KILLOUGH, KAREN LEE

KILLREYNARD, EARL OF
BELL, CHARLES WENTWORTH

KILPATRICK, SARAH
UNDERWOOD, MAVIS EILEEN

KILRAIN, GEORGE
HEUMAN, WILLIAM

KILREON, BETH
MUIR, BARBARA K.

KIM
SIMENON, GEORGES [J.C]
SWEET, JOHN

KIM RONYOUNG
HAHN, GLORIA

KIM, TOMAS
MONTEIRO E GRILO, JOAQUIM

KIMBALL, ATKINSON
KIMBALL, GRACE & RICHARD

KIMBALL, CONRAD
BITTNER, ARCHIBALD
ROGERS, WAYNE

KIMBALL, FRANK
PAINE, LAURAN BOSWORTH

KIMBALL, NANCY
UPSON, NORMA

KIMBALL, RALPH
PAINE, LAURAN BOSWORTH

KIMBER, LEE
KING, ALBERT

KIMBERLEY, HUGH
MORLAND, NIGEL

KIMBERLY, GAIL
FRANCIS, GAIL KIMBERLY

KIMBRO, HARRIET
KOFALK, HARRIET

KIMBRO, JEAN
KIMBRO, JOHN M.

KIMBROUGH, COLLEEN
PORTERFIELD, KAY

KIMBROUGH, KATHERYN
KIMBRO, JOHN M.

KINBALL, CAPTAIN KIM
SCRIBNER, KIMBALL

KINCAID, ALAN
RIKHOFF, JAMES C.

KINCAID, D.
FIELDS, BERT

KINCAID, J.D.
DALGLEISH, JAMES CORTEEN

KINCAID, KATHARINE
DAOUST, PAMELA

KINCAID, NELL
CLARKE, JANET K.

KINDER, KATHLEEN
POTTER, KATHLEEN JILL K.

KINDLER, ASTA
HICKEN, UNA

KINEJI, MABORUSHI
GIBSON, WALTER B.

KINES, TOM
KINES, THOMAS ALVIN

KING OF THE BLACK ISLES
NICOLSON, JOHN URBAN

KING, ADAM
HOARE, ROBERT J[OHN]

KING, ALEC HYATT
KING, ALEXANDER HYATT

KING, ALFRED FITZMAURICE
LANGBRIDGE, FREDERICK

KING, ALISON
MARTINI, TERI

KING, AMES
KING, ALBERT

KING, AMON
KING, ALBERT

KING, ARTHUR
CAIN, ARTHUR H.
LAKE, KENNETH R[OBERT]

KING, BARRIE
KING, BARRINGTON

KING, BASIL
KING, WILLIAM BENJAMIN

KING, BERTA
KING, ALBERT

KING, BILLI
CAULDER, COLLINE

KING, CHARLES
AVENELLE, DONNE

KING, CHRISTOPHER
KING, ALBERT

KING, CLIFFORD
KING, JAMES CLIFFORD

KING, DAVID
PERHSON, HOWARD

KING, DIANE
KING, ELNORA
WALLACE, PAMELA D.

KING, DICKY
ENGSTROM, TOIVO ARMAS JO.

KING, ELIZABETH A.
ABRAVANEL, ELIZABETH

KING, EVAN
WARD, ROBERT SPENCER

KING, FLORENCE
BUCHANAN, LAURA

KING, FRANK
KING, FRANKLIN

KING, FRANK A.
KING, FRANKLIN ALEXANDER

KING, HENRY
KOEGEL, JOHANNES

KING, HILARY
DICKSON, JAMES GRIERSON

KING, JACK
DOWLING, ALLEN

KING, JOHN B.
BERNDT, KARL-HEINZ

KING, JOHN
MCKEAG, ERNEST LIONEL

KING, JOSIE
GERMANY, VERA JOSEPHINE

KING, JOYCE
CHING, JULIA CHIA-Y

KING, MARTIN
MARKS, STANLEY

KING, MICHAEL
BUSE, RENEE
KAHANE, MEIR [DAVID]

KING, NORMAN A.
TRALINS, [SANDOR] ROBERT

KING, O.B.
THAYER, TIFFANY E.

KING, OLIVER
MOUNT, THOMAS ERNEST

KING, PAUL
DRACKETT, PHILIP A.

KING, PAULA
KING, PAULA E. DOWNING

KING, PEGGY CAMERON
KING, MARJORIE CAMERON

KING, RANDALL
KRASNER, WILLIAM

KING, RAY
CUMMINGS, RAY[MOND KING]

KING, REEFE
BARKER, ALBERT W.

KING, RENEE
NEBEHAY, RENEE

KING, RICHARD
HUSKINSON, RICHARD KING

KING, ROBERT
SOHL, GERALD ALLEN

KING, ROBIN
RALEIGH-KING, ROBIN VICT.

KING, ROSCOE
WILLIS, ERNEST LISTER H.

KING, RUTH RODNEY
MANLEY, RUTH RODNEY KING

KING, SAM
WITT, OTTO

KING, SANDRA
BICKEL, ALICE

KING, SHERRY
KING, [R] SHERWOOD

KING, STEPHANIE
RUSSELL, SHIRLEY

KING, STEVE
KING, STEPHEN [EDWIN]

KING, T.W.
INGRAHAM, PRENTISS

KING, TERI
RATCLIFFE, PATRICIA

KING, THOROLD
GATCHELL, CHARLES

KING, VALERIE
BOSNA, VALERIE

KING, VERONICA
KING, FLORENCE

KING, VINCENT
VINSON, REX THOMAS

KING, W. SCOTT
GREENLAND, W. KINGSCOTE

KING, [MIDSHIPMAN] TOM W.
INGRAHAM, PRENTISS

KING-HALL, LOU
KING-HALL, LUISE OLGA E.

KINGHORN, A.M.
KINGHORN, ALEXANDER M.

KINGMAN, LEE
NATTI, MARY LEE

KINGSBURY, KATE
ROBERTS, DOREEN

KINGSFORD, GUY
MURRAY, C. GEOFFREY

KINGSLAND, PETER
TEED, GEORGE HAMILTON

KINGSLEY, ANNA
HANSHEW, MARY E.
HANSHEW, THOMAS W.

KINGSLEY, BETTINA
KAPLAN, BARRY JAY

KINGSLEY, CHARLOTTE MAY
HANSHEW, THOMAS W.

KINGSLEY, GEETA
KAKADE, GEETA M.

KINGSLEY, HAMILTON
MARTIN, W.

KINGSLEY, JOHANNA
MEYER, DONNA

KINGSLEY, KATE
DELK, KAREN

KINGSLEY, KATHERINE
KENDALL, JULIA JAY

KINGSLEY, LAURA
BENNETT, DOROTHY

KINGSLEY, MARY
KRUGER, MARY

KINGSLEY, ROBERT
CLARKE, JOHN

KINGSLEY, SIDNEY
KIESCHNER, SIDNEY

KINGSMILL, HUGH
LUNN, HUGH KINGSMILL

KINGSTEAD, JULIAN
CUNYNGHAME, FRANCES J.

KINGSTON, BRIAN
LONGHURST, PERCY WILLIAM

KINGSTON, CHARLES
O'MAHONY, CHARLES K.

KINGSTON, H.S.
BRAND, KURT

KINGSTON, JEREMY
BETANCOURT, JOHN GREGORY

KINGSTON, JOHN
ROBERTS, KEITH [J.R.]

KINGSTON, MEREDITH
BRUCKER, MEREDITH

KINGSTON, SYD
BINGLEY, DAVID ERNEST

KINKAID, MATT
ADAMS, CLIFTON H.

KINKAID, WYATT E.
JENNINGS, MICHAEL GLENN

KINKEAD, ELEANOR TALBOT
SHORT, ELEANOR [T.K.]

KINNEY, THOMAS
THOMAS, CURTIS

KINNOCH, R.G.B.
BARCLAY, GEORGE

KINOR, JEHUDA
ROTHMULLER, ARON MARKO

KINROSS, LORD
BALFOUR, J. PATRICK D.

KINSALE, FRED
BOCKL, MANFRED

KINSALE, LAURA
JAY, AMANDA MOOR

KINSBURN, EMART
HANKINS, ARTHUR PRESTON

KINSEY, ELIZABETH
CLYMER, ELEANOR

KINSEY-JONES, BRIAN
BALL, BRIAN N[EVILLE]

KINVER, RICHARD
VOGEL, HARRY BENJAMIN

KINZEL, DOTTIE
KINZEL, DOROTHY

KIPLINGER, DAVID
MINER, VIRGINIA SCOTT

KIPPAX, JOHN
HYNAM, JOHN

KIPROY, CHARLES
HERSEY, HAROLD

KIRATI, CEMILE
SCHIMMEL, ANNEMARIE BRIG.

KIRBY, ARTHUR
FRANCES, STEPHEN D.
MANN, GEORGE PAUL

KIRBY, DALLAS
GAMMON, DAVID J.

KIRBY, DAN
ASHABRANNER, GERARD
GALLARDOS MUNOZ, JUAN

KIRBY, JACK
KURTZBERG, JACK

KIRBY, JEAN
MCDONNELL, VIRGINIA B.
ROBINSON, CHAILLE HOWARD

KIRBY, JOHN
DELFS, RAINER
DUBINA, PETER

KIRBY, KATE
ELGIN, BETTY

KIRBY, KAY
BACZEWSKI, JANICE K.J.
JOHNSON, NORMA K. TADLOCK

KIRBY, MAC
CHADWICK, JOSEPH L.

KIRBY, MARGARET
BINGLEY, MARGARET [JANE]

KIRBY, MARK
FLOREN, LEE

KIRBY, SUSAN ALICE
BURTON, ALICE ELIZABETH

KIRCHMAYR, CHRISTA
REBNER-CHRISTIAN, DORIS

KIRK, ALEXANDRA
WOODS, SHERYL ANN

KIRK, DAVID
FODEN, FREDERICK [T]

KIRK, ELEANOR
AMES, ELEANOR MARIA

KIRK, IRINA
KIRK, IRENE

KIRK, JEREMY
POWELL, RICHARD PITTS

KIRK, LAURENCE
SIMSON, ERIC ANDREW

KIRK, MARGARET [P]
PRASNIEWSKI, MARGARET

KIRK, MARY
KILCHENSTEIN, MARY I.

KIRK, MARY ALICE
KILCHENSTEIN, MARY I.
RICHARDS-AKERS, NANCY

KIRK, MATTHEW
WELLS, ANGUS

KIRK, MICHAEL
KNOX, WILLIAM [BILL]

KIRK, PHILIP
LEVINSON, LEONARD [L]

KIRK, R.
DIETRICH, RICHARD V.

KIRK, RICHARD
HOLDSTOCK, ROBERT P.
WELLS, ANGUS

KIRK, RISA
FLORES, JANIS

KIRK, TED
BANK, THEODORE PAUL II

KIRK, WAYNE
KOCK, WINSTON E[DWARD]

KIRKE, EDMUND
GILMORE, JAMES ROBERT

KIRKHAM, MILO
DRUSSAI, GAREN

KIRKHAM, NELLIE
MYATT, NELLI

KIRKLAND, JACK
CALDWELL, ERSKINE

KIRKLAND, WILL
HALE, MARY ARLENE

KIRKUS, VIRGINIA
GLICK, VIRGINIA KIRKUS

KIRSCHNER, FRITZ
BICKERS, RICHARD L.T.

KIRSHA, ANTON
GIPPIUS, ZINAIDA N.

KIRSTEN-HERBST, RUTH
HERBST, RUTH

KIRTLAND, G.B.
HINE, AL[FRED B.]
HINE, SESYLE JOSLIN

KISH
LE RICHE, P.J.

KISH, ELY
KISH, ELEANOR MARY

KISH, G. HOBAB
KENNEDY, GERALD HAMILTON

KISNER, JACK
KISNER, JACOB

KITCHEN, BERT
KITCHEN, HERBERT THOMAS

KITE, LARRY
SCHNECK, STEPHEN

KITT, TAMARA
DE REGNIERS, BEATRICE S.

KITUOMBA
ODAGA, ASENATH BOLE

KJELGAARD, JIM
BLOCH, ROBERT [A]
KJELGAARD, JAMES ARTHUR

KLAASSEN, LEO H.
KLAASSEN, LEONARDUS HEND.

KLABUND
HENSCHKE, ALFRED

KLAINIKITE, ANNE
GEHMAN, BETSY HOLLAND

KLANSHENDEL, CHIRON
ROSE, WENDY

KLASS, HARRIET
KOSSOF, HARRIET

KLASS, JUDY
KLASS, JUDITH ALEXANDRA

KLASSEN, WALTER
KLAASSEN, WALTER

KLAVANS, J.K.
KLAVANS, JODIE KAY

KLAXON
BOWER, JOHN GRAHAM

KLEBE, GENE
KLEBE, CHARLES EUGENE

KLEIFUM, [FRA] MAGNEA
MAGNUSDOTTIR, MAGNEA

KLEIN, CHARLES
KLEIN, KARL FRIEDRICH

KLEIN, DORIS F.
JONAS, DORIS F.

KLEIN, JOE
KLEIN, JOSEPH

KLEIN, K.K.
TURNER, ROBERT H.

KLEIN, KARL
SALA, CHARLES

KLEIN-ROSSEL, A.
MIRO, FRANZ

KLEIN-WOLKEN, ERIKA
KLEIN, ERIKA

KLEINER, DICK
KLEINER, RICHARD ARTHUR

KLEINER, REX [ON COVER]
LAZENBY, NORMAN A.

KLEINFIELD, SONNY
KLEINFIELD, NATHAN RICH.

KLEINJAN
VAN BRUGGEN, JAN R.L.

KLENBORT, CHARLOTTE
SEMPELL, CHARLOTTE

KLETT, HAROLD
LORD, HALKLETT

KLEYMANN, KONNI
KROHNKE, FRIEDRICH

KLICHKA, BENJAMIN
FRAGNER, BENJAMIN

KLIMARIS, J.S.
KULILIUS, WALTER

KLIMIUS, NICHOLAS
HOLBERG, LUDVIG

KLIMO, JAKE
KLIMO, VERNON

KLINDT, ARNE
MEYN, NIELS

KLINE, STEVE
KLINE, STEPHEN EDWARD

PSEUDONYMS

KLINE, T.F.
HARWOOD, GWEN

KLINGSOR, TRISTAN
LECLERE, LEON

KLINICUS
VISSER, WILLEM J.C.

KLINT, JESPER
AHLSTEDT, IVAR

KLOBUCHAR, JIM
KLOBUCHAR, JAMES JOHN

KLONIS, N.I.
CLONES, NICHOLAS J.

KLOPFINGER, HERMAN III
DIAMANT, LINCOLN

KLOSE, NORMA CLINE
CLINE, NORMA

KLUEGER, RUTH
KLUGER, RUTH

KLUG, RON
KLUG, RONALD

KLUGE, HIDELORE,
OTT-KLUGE, HEIDELORE

KLUVER, BILLY
KLUVER, J. WILHELM

KLYCHKOV, SERGY
LESHENKOV, SERGY ANTONOV.

KNAPP, EDWARD
KUNHARDT, EDITH

KNAPP, ELLIS G.
GILBERT, KENNETH

KNAUFF, ELLEN RAPHAEL
HARTLEY, ELLEN R.

KNELLER, FRANK
WATT, JOHN F.

KNICKERBOCKER
DU SOLLE, JOHN S.

KNICKERBOCKER, CHOLLY
CASSINI, IGOR LOIEWSKI
PAUL, MAURY

KNICKERBOCKER, DIEDRICH
IRVING, WASHINGTON

KNIESE, JULIE
BOESS, JULIE

KNIFESMITH
CUTLER, IVOR

KNIGHT, ADAM
LARIAR, LAWRENCE

KNIGHT, ALICIA
WRIGHT, LUCRETIA

KNIGHT, ALLISON
KREIGER, MARTHA

KNIGHT, ARTHUR
ROSENHEIMER, ARTHUR

KNIGHT, BRIGID
SINCLAIR, KATHLEEN HENR.

KNIGHT, DAVID
PRATHER, RICHARD S.

KNIGHT, FRANK
KNIGHT, FRANCIS EDGAR

KNIGHT, FRIDA
KNIGHT, F. FRANCIS EMMA

KNIGHT, GARETH
WILBY, BASIL LESLIE

KNIGHT, HARRY ADAM
BROSNAN, JOHN RAYMOND
KETTLE, LEROY

KNIGHT, ISOBEL
LOCKIE, ISOBEL

KNIGHT, JAMES
SCHNECK, STEPHEN

KNIGHT, KATHRYN LASKY
LASKY, KATHRYN

KNIGHT, KIM
PERKINS, KENNETH

KNIGHT, KOBOLD
GIDDY, ERIC CAWOOD G.

KNIGHT, KRISTIE
KNIGHT, NANCY CHRISTOPHER

KNIGHT, MALLORY T.
HURWOOD, BERNHARDT J.

KNIGHT, REYNOLDS
KNIGHT, CLIFFORD REYNOLDS

KNIGHT, ROBERT
EVANS, CHRIS[TOPHER D.]

KNIGHT, SALI
SERAFINA, TINA

KNIGHT, TAYLOR C.
SNIDER, JOHN H.

KNIGHT, W. KOBOLD
GIDDY, ERIC CAWOOD G.

KNIGHT-JENKINS, VIVIAN
JENKINS, VIRGINIA C.

KNIGHT-PATTERSON, W.M.
KULSKI, WLADYSLAW WSZEBOR

KNIPPER, HEINZ
KALBFUSS, HEINRICH

KNISH, ANNE
FICKE, ARTHUR DAVIDSON

KNOBLOCH, HANS
KNOBLOCH, HILDA

KNOBLOCK, EDWARD
KNOBLAUCH, EDWARD

KNOCK, CHRISTOFFER
FEIL, GEORG

KNOCK, CHRISTOPHER
HUNGERBUHLER, EBERHARD

KNORR, K.E.
KNORR, KLAUS EUGENE

KNOTT, BILL
KNOTT, WILLIAM CECIL JR.
KNOTT, WILLIAM KILBORN

KNOTT, HERMANN
SMITH, WALTER CHALMERS

KNOTT, WILL C.
KNOTT, WILLIAM CECIL JR.

KNOTTS, RAYMOND
VOLK, GORDON

KNOWALL, GEORGE
O'NOLAN, BRIAN

KNOWLES, DAVID
KNOWLES, MICHAEL CLIVE

KNOWLES, MARTHA
DERN, E. PEARL GADDIS

KNOWLES, RUPERT
CAVE, HUGH B[ARNETT]

KNOWLES, THOMAS E.
MCLURE, R.

KNOWLES, WILLIAMSON
KNOLES, WILLIAM [H]

KNOX, BILL
KNOX, WILLIAM [BILL]
MACLEOD, ROBERT

KNOX, CALVIN M.
SILVERBERG, ROBERT

KNOX, CLEONE
KING-HALL, MAGDALEN

KNOX, GILBERT
MACBETH, MADGE HAMILTON

KNOX, JACKSON
HARBAUGH, THOMAS C.

KNOX, JAMES
BRITTAIN, WILLIAM E.

KNOX, LISBETH
WARD, ROSE ELIZABETH

KNOX, WINIFRED FRANCES
PECK, WINIFRED FRANCES

KNOX-JOHNSON, ROBIN
KNOX-JOHNSON, WILLIAM R.P

KNOX-MAWER, RONNIE
KNOX-MAWER, RONALD

KNUDSEN, R.R.
KNUDSEN, ROZANNE RUTH

KNUDSON, GRETA
KNUDSON, MARGRETHE

KNURRHAHN, KARL
NITZSCHE, KARL-WILLY

KNUTSEN, LALLI & FRIDTJOF
GERMANA, ALFHILD

KNUTSSON, PER
KALLEN, KNUT HILDING

KNUTT, A.P.
LIVANDAIS, AUGUSTUS

KNYE, CASSANDRA
DISCH, THOMAS M.
SLADEK, JOHN

KO, KANZEIN
ISOGAI, HIROSHI

KOCH, C.J.
KOCH, CHRISTOPHER JOHN

KOCSIS, J.C.
PAUL, JAMES

KOCSIS, ROBERT
KOSSEZ, ROBES

KODA ROHAN
KODA SHIGEYUKI

KODAK
O'FERRALL, ERNEST

KOEHLER, FRANK
PAINE, LAURAN BOSWORTH

KOEHN, ILSE
VAN ZWIENEN, ILSE C.K.

KOEHN, LALA
KOEHN-HEINE, LALA

KOENIGSWALDT, HANS
EINSLE, HANS

KOFOED, J.C.
LA SPINA, FANNY GREYE

KOFOED, JACK
KOFOED, JOHN C.

KOGAN, DEBORAH
KOGAN RAY, DEBORAH

KOGGEN, JAN
KURTH, HANNS

KOHAVI, Y.
STERN, JAY B[ENJAMIN]

KOHL, EVA MARIA
BENTZIEN, EVA MARIA

KOHLER, WOLFGANG
KOEHLER, WOLFGANG

KOHLHAAS, MICHAEL
FLUGGE, HANS-LUDOLF

KOHLS, R.L.
KOHLS, RICHARD LOUIS

KOHN, BERNICE
HUNT, BERNICE KOHN

KOHUT, LES
KOHUT, NESTER C.

KOI HAI
PALMER, [N] HUMPHREY

KOILPILLAI, DAS
KOILPILLAI, [J] CHARLES

KOIZUMI, YAKUMO
HEARN, [P] LAFCADIO [T.C]

KOJAK
APPEL, WALTER
BURKLE, ROLF A.
HEBEL, PETER
HELGATH, FRANC
VON KOBLINSKI, HANS-JOACH

KOKHANOVSHAYA
SOCKHANSKAYA, NADEZHDA S.

KOLBENHOFF, WALTER
HOFFMANN, WALTER

KOLBER, THOMAS
KALMUCZAK, ROLF

KOLBERG, WOLFGANG
FECHTNER, WOLFGANG

KOLBL, C.H.
KOBL, KONRAD

KOLDEWEY, MARTINA
LINDNER, HEDDA

KOLE, A.K.
LOVINGOOD, ALVIN

KOLIN, GUNNAR
VON KOBLINSKI, HANS-JOACH

KOLLEK, TED
KOLLEK, THEODORE

KOLLER, LARRY
KOLLER, LAWRENCE ROBERT

KOLLMAR, DICK
KOLLMAR, RICHARD TOMPKINS

KOLON, NITA
ONADIPE, [N] KOLAWOLE

KOLUNTSEV, FEDOR
BARKUDARIAN, TADEOS A.

KOLUPAEV, VICTOR
KOLUPAEV, VIKTOR D.

KOMED
LANGHER, ALFONS

KOMO, DELORES
KOMOROSKI, DELORES

KONA WORUK
HARRIS, [THEODORE] WILSON

KONADU, ASARE
KONADU, SAMUEL ASARE

KONADU, S.A.
KONADU, SAMUEL ASARE

KONG, KING
WAGER, WALTER [HERMAN]

KONIG, FRANZ
KOENIG, FRANZ

KONIG, FRITZ HANS
KOENIG, FRITZ HANS

KONIG, HANS
KONINGSBERGER, HANS

KONIG, RENE
KOENIG, RENE

KONIGSBERG, C.I.
KONIGSBERG, ISADORE

KONIGSBERG, E.L.
KONIGSBERG, ELAINE LOBL

KONNEBERG, DR. ERIC VON
EGLUND, E.P.

KONNER, ALFRED
KOENNER, ALFRED

KONRAD, GEORGE
KONRAD, GYOERGY

KONRAD, HERBERT
HUBNER, JALOB

KONRAD, JAMES
MACLEAN, CHARLES

KONSALIK, HEINZ G.
GUNTHER, HEINZ

KONTER, HEIN
GUNTHER, HEINZ

KONTOS, CECILLE
HADDIX-KONTOS, CECILLE P.

KOOIHER, LEONIE
KOOYKER-ROMIJN, JOHANNA M

KOOIMAN, HELEN W.
HOSIER, HELEN KOOIMAN

KOOMOTER, ZENO
MARNELL, JOSEPH

KOOSER, TED
KOOSER, THEODORE

KOOTMER, ZENO
MARNELL, JOSEPH

KOOYKER-ROMYN, JOHANNA M.
KOOYKER-ROMIJN, JOHANNA M

KOPERNICUS
LOERKE, GEORG

KOPEYKIN, CAPTAIN
KOJUHAROV, TUDOR

KOPLINKA, CHARLOTTE
LUKAS, CHARLOTTE KOPLINKA

KOPPEL, UTA
LEHR-KOPPEL, UTA

KORALOV, EMIL
DONCEV-KORALOV, EMIL

KORB, PETER
BROCK, RUDOLF

KORBEL, KATHLEEN
DREYER, EILEEN

KORCZAK, JANUSZ
GOLDSZMIT, HENRYK

KORDA, HANS
STITZ-ULRICI, ROLF

KORDA, LOTHAR
ROTSLER, WILLIAM

KORFF, ILKA
BOESCHE, TILLY

KORFF, WERNER JURGEN
DRIPKE, KARL-HANS

KORINETS, IURII I.
KORINETZ, YURI I.

KORN, PEGGY
LISS, PEGGY K[ORN]

KORN, PETER
GOOCK, ROLAND

KORNBLUTH, C.M.
KORNBLUTH, C[YRIL] M.

KORNEDEPLOV, MITYA
HERMAN, IRA H.

KORNER, STEPHAN
KOERNER, STEPHAN

KORNFELDER, J.D.
DUSCHEK, JOHANN

KORNHAUSER, JINCY
WILLETT, JINCY

KORNTHEUR, KONRAD
FARBER, SIGFRID

KOROLENKO, V.G.
KOROLENKO, VLADIMIR G.

KORT, AMELY
KLEIN, ERIKA

KORTE, MARY NORBERT
KOERTE, MARY NORBERT

KORTEN, INES
KAPPLER, HANNS-WALTER

KORTOOMS, TOON
KORTOOMS, ANTONIUS J.

KORZHAVIN, N.
MANDEL, NAUM M.

KOSARIK, DMITRII M.
KOVALENKO, DMITRII M.

KOSCH, ERICH
KOS, ERIH

KOSKA, JURGEN
KOCKA, JUERGEN

KOSKENMAKI, ROSALIE
MAGGIO, ROSALIE

KOSKENNIEMI, V.A.
FORSNAS, V.A.

KOSLOFF, MYRON
LITTLE, PAUL HUGO

KOSMAS
CASTELLI, IGNAZ FRANZ

KOSSELIN, TORSTEN
MUNCHOW, HEINZ

KOSTA, VICTOR
SIMENON, GEORGES [J.C]

KOSTKA, JEAN
DOINEL, JULES

KOTANI, ERIC
KONDO, YOJI
MACBRIDE, ROGER ALLEN

KOTCHEFF, TED
KOTCHEFF, WILLIAM THEODOR

KOTIN, ARMINE AVAKIAN
MORTIMER, ARMINE KOTIN

KOTTA, LEO F.
FLAKE, OTTO

KOTTE, MARGOT
BRARD, MARGOT

KOTZDE, WILHELM
KOTTENRODT, W.

KOUF, JIM
KOUF, MARVIN JAMES JR.

KOUFAX, SANDY
KOUFAX, SANFORD

KOURVETARIS, GEORGE A.
KOURVETARIS, YORGOS A.

KOUTOUKAS, H.M.
RIVOLI, MARIO

KOVARIK, BILL
KOVARIK, WILLIAM

KOVNER, B.
ADLER, JACOB

KOWITT, SYLVIA
CROSBIE, SYLVIA KOWITT

KOYO, OZAKI
TOKUTARO, OZAKI

KOZLOW, MARK
NEWTON, MICHAEL

KOZLOW, MARK J.
NEWTON, MICHAEL

KOZUMI, REI
SHIBANO, TAKUMI

KRABBLUND, FILIP
HOLZHAUSEN, CARL JOHAN

KRAFFT, HEINZ
DECKER, HEINZ-BRUNO

KRAFFT, JIM
KRAFFT, CONRAD JAMES

KRAFT, RUTH
BUSSENIUS, RUTH

KRAFT, WALTER ANDREAS
FRIEDLANDER, WALTER ANDR.

KRAGEN, JINX
MORGAN, JUDITH A.

KRAINY, ANTON
GIPPIUS, ZINAIDA N.

KRAMER, EDNA E.
KRAMER-LASSAR, EDNA E.

KRAMER, GEORGE
HEUMAN, WILLIAM

KRAMER, KARL
MORRIS, EDWARD A.

KRAMER, PROFESSOR
NAUBERT, CHRISTIANE B.E.

KRAMER, TED
STEWARD, SAMUEL M[ORRIS]

KRAMER-ROLLS, DANA
KRAMER, DANA

KRANIDAS, KATHLEEN
COLLINS, KATHLEEN

KRANTZ, D.
IZBITSKY, SAMUEL

KRANTZ, PHILIP
ROMBRO, JACOB

KRANZ, EDITH
RUSSELL, EDITH

KRANZLER, GERSHON
KRANZLER, GEORGE G.

KRAPIVA, KANDRAT
ATTRACHOVICH, KANDRAT

KRAPP, ANNEMARIE
MASCHLANKA, ANNEMARIE

KRAPP, R.M.
ADAMS, ROBERT MARTIN

KRASELCHIK, R.
DYER, CHARLES [RAYMOND]

KRASKO, IVAN
BOTTO, JAN

KRASNE, BETTY
LEVINE, BETTY K.

KRASNOHORSKA, ELISKA
PECHOVA, ELISKA

KRASSNOF, PETER N.
KRASNOV, PETR

KRATOS
POWER, NORMAN S.

KRAUS, H.P.
KRAUS, HANS PETER

KRAUSE, KNUT
EISENKOLB, GERHARD

KRAUSS, BOB
KRAUSS, ROBERT G.

KRAUSS, BRUNO
BULMER, [HENRY] KENNETH

KRAUSSE, K.
KRAUSSE, KAY

KRAUTTER, ELISA
BIALK, ELISA

KRAVCHENKO, ULIANA
SHNAIDER, JULIA

KRAVITZ, NATHAN
KREVITSKY, NATHANIEL I.

KRAVITZ, NATHANIEL
KREVITSKY, NATHANIEL I.

KREBB, JEREMY
OFFUTT, ANDREW J.

KREMER, RUDIGER
KREMER, RUEDIGER

KREMINOLOGIST
ZORZA, VICTOR

KREMNITZ, MITE
ELIZABETH, QUEEN, RUMANIA

KRESGE, GEORGE "KRESKIN"
GIBSON, WALTER B.

KRESKIN
KRESGE, GEORGE JOSEPH JR.

KREUGER, ELIZABETH
MCGUIRE, CHERYL KREUGER

KREUTER, MARGOT
KREUTER-TRANKEL, MARGOT

KREUTZENBERG, ALWIN
KRUEZMANN, GEORG

KREUZEMAN, MICHAEL
LAW, MICHAEL HALDANE

KREVITSKY, NIK
KREVITSKY, NATHANIEL I.

KRICH, A.M.
KRICH, ARON

KRIESTEN, HANS
RABL, HANS

KRIN, SYLVIE
FANTONI, BARRY [ERNEST]

KRISHNA, GOPI
SHIVPURI, GOPI KRISHNA

KRISLOV, ALEXANDER
HOWARD, LEON A. LEE

KRISTAN, GEORG R.
CORDTS, GEORG & RENATE

KRISTIAN, HANS
NEERSKOV, HANS KRISTIAN

KRITZ, HUGO MARIA
KRIZKOWSKY, HUGO

KRIYANANDA
WALTERS, J. DONALD

KRIYANANDA, SRI
WALTERS, J. DONALD

KRIYANANDA, SWAMI
WALTERS, J. DONALD

KROEPCKE, KAROL
KROLOW, KARL GUSTAV H.

KROGE, SUDS
WARDROP, DAVID

KROGER, ALEXANDER
ROUTSCHEK, HELMUT

KROLL, BURT
ROWLAND, DONALD S.

KRONDAL, ALVA
KERFVE, AXEL

KRONE, HERVOR
KERFVE, AXEL

KRONEN, ANDREI
HAAS, CARL-HELLMUTH

KRONIUK, LISA
BERTON, PIERRE

KRUGER, HARDY
KRUEGER, HARDY

KRUGER, LORENZ
KRUEGER, LORENZ

KRUGER, OVEN W.
NAGEL, HERBERT CHRISTIAN

KRUGER, PAUL
SEBENTHAL, ROBERTA E.

KRUGER, WOLF
HUTSON, SHAUN

KRULL, FELIX
WHITE, STANLEY

KRULL, MARIANNE
KRUELL, MARIANNE

KRUMB
CRUMB, ROBERT

KRUMWITZ
CRUMB, ROBERT

KRUPNIK, BARUCH
KARU, BARUCH

KRUSE, IRIS
RUBAHN, HORST-GUNTER

KRUSE, JUNE MILLICHAMP
ANDERSON, KAREN

KRUSS, JAMES
KRUESS, JAMES

KRUTZCH, GUS
ELIOT, T[HOMAS] S[TEARNS]

KRYMOV, YURI
BEKLEMISHEV, YURI SOLOM.

KRYPTON
GRAHAM, LLOYD M.

KRZYWAN, JOZEF
KROTKI, KAROL JOZEF

KUAN-SUO, DR.
HOSKIN, CYRIL HENRY

KUBE-MCDOWELL, MICHAEL P.
MCDOWELL, MICHAEL PAUL

KUBELKA, MARGARETE
KROHNKE, MARGARETE [K]

KUBILIUS, WALTER
KULILIS, WALTER

KUBLER-ROSS, ELISABETH
KUEBLER-ROSS, ELISABETH

KUBY, HANNS
KUBIAK, HANNS-KARL

KUCHARSKI, KASIMIR
KOCH, KURT EMIL

KUEHN, DOROTHY DALTON
DALTON, DOROTHY

KUHLMANN, SUSAN
LOHAFER, SUSAN

KUHN, HEINZ R.
KUEHN, HEINZ RICHARD

KUHN, MAGGIE
KUHN, MARGARET E.

KUHN, OTTO
ARNEMANN, M.F.
EISFELD, RAINER
KLEIM, HEINZ F.
LEDWIG, GERHARD
VAN DOORNICK, FRITZHEINZ

KUHN, URSULA
JAKUBCZYK, URSULA

KUHN, VOLKMAR
KUROWSKI, FRANZ

KUHNS, DOROTHY
HEYWARD, DOROTHY H. KUHNS

KUHNWALD, GERD
HEICHEN, WALTER

KUKLOS
WRAY, W. FITZWATER

KUKUCIN, MARTIN
BENCUR, MATEJ

KULICK, JOHN
PINCHOT, ANN KRAMER

KULKIN, MARY-ELLEN
SIEGEL, MARY-ELLEN KULKIN

KULL, A. STODDARD
KULL, ANDREW

KULL, STASI
ARTMANN, HANS CARL

KULLINGER, J.L.
DUCETTE, VINCE

KUMARA, SANANDANA
GRAHAM, ROGER P.

KUMBEL
HEIN, PIET

KUMMERLY, WALTER
KUEMMERLY, WALTER

KUMPA
BARBERIS, JUAN CARLOS

KUNCEWICZOWA, MARIA
KUNCEWICZ, MARIA S.

KUNG, HANS
KUENG, HANS

KUNG, TOR
GILBERT, JACK
MCLEAN, JEAN

KUNIKIDA, DOPPO
TETSUO, KUNIKIDA

KUNSTLER, MORTON
KUENSTLER, MORTON

KUNZUR, SHEELA
GEIS, RICHARD E.

KUPALA, JANKA
LUCEVICH, IVAN DAMINIK.

KUPER, YURI
KUPERMAN, YURI

KUPFERBERG, TULI
KUPFERBERG, NAPHTALI

KUPPORD, SKELTON
ADAMS, J.

KURDSEN, STEPHEN
NOON, BRIAN

KUROWSKI, EUGENIUSZ
DOBRACZYNSKI, JAN

KURT, K.S.
SOBOTTA, KURT

KURT, ROBERT
HANGEKORB, KURT

KURTIS, BILL
KURTIS, WILLIAM HORTON

KURTIS, GORDON
AALBORG, GORDON K.

KURTS, ALFRED
FORAN, STEVE

KURTZ, MELCHIOR
KASTNER, ERICH

KURZ, ARTHUR R.
SCORTIA, THOMAS N.

KURZ, HANS
ALPERS, HANS JOACHIM

KUSCHE, LARRY
KUSCHE, LAWRENCE DAVID

KUTHUMI
FLEISHMANN, HELLE

KUTTNER, HENRY
CARTMILL, CLEVE

KUYLE, ALBERT
KUITENBROUWER, LOUIS M.A.

KVARAN, EINAR
HJORLEIFSSON, KVARAN EIN.

KWABENA NKETIA, J.H.
NKETIA, JOSEPH H. KWABENA

KWANT, R.C.
KWANT, REMIGUS C.

KWANT, REMY C,
KWANT, REMIGUS C.

KWOLEK, CONSTANCE
PORCARI, CONSTANCE KWOLEK

KYD, THOMAS
HARBAGE, ALFRED B.

KYLE, DUNCAN
BROXHOLME, JOHN FRANKLIN

KYLE, EGLETON
VICKERS, ROY

KYLE, ELIZABETH
DUNLOP, AGNES MARY R.

KYLE, GEOFFREY
MOORE, ARTHUR

KYLE, MARLAINE
HAGER, [WILMA] JEAN [L]

KYLE, ROBERT
TERRALL, ROBERT

KYLE, SEFTON
VICKERS, ROY

KYLE, SUSAN S.
KYLE, SUSAN E. SPAETH

KYLLBURG, HERBERT
PFRETZCHNER, HERBERT

KYOKA, IZUMI
KYOTARO, IZUMI

KYPRIANOS, IOSSIF
SAMARAKIS, ANTONIS

L'AMOUR, LOUIS
LAMOORE, LOUIS [DEARBORN]

L'ARRONGE, ADOLF
AARON, ADOLF

L'AUBANELENCO
DRUTEL, MARCELLE L.M.

L'ENGLE, MADELEINE
FRANKLIN, MADELEINE L'ENG

L'ESTOILO, PIERRE
HOUSSET, ARSENE

L'ESTRANGE, ANNA
ELLERBECK, ROSEMARY A.L.

L*NG, L*Z*R*S
JACOBSON, SUSANNA

L., G.
LUDLUM, GEORGE

L., X.
FIELD, JULIAN OSGOOD

L.A.C. BREYDOR, B.
WELSH, KEN

L.L.
SMITH, GEORGE

L.Y.
YERXA, LEROY

LA BAN, L.E.
KIRBY, LAURAINE

LA BARR, CREIGHTON
VON BLOCK, BELA [W]

LA COLERE, FRANCOIS
ARAGON, LOUIS

LA DESHABILLEUSE
SIMENON, GEORGES [J.C]

LA FONTAINE, BLANCHE
SCHWALBERG, CAROL[YN E.S]

LA FONTAINE, HENRI
HILL, ROY

LA MARA
LIPPERT, CLARISSA START
LIPSIUS, MARIE

LA MERI
HUGHES, RUSSELL MERIW.

LA MESSINE
ADAM, JULIETTE

LA PLANTE, SANDRA
LYONS, LUELLA B.

LA POINTE, PIERROT
ORTHOFER, PETER

LA REYNIERE
COURTINE, ROBERT

LA ROCCA, ED
LIERSCH, ROLF WERNER

LA SALLE, VICTOR
EVANS, GERALD
FANTHORPE, R.L.
FISH, LEONARD G.
GLASBY, JOHN S.
WADE, THOMAS W.

LA THORNE, JEAN
DILKS, JOHN M.

LA TOURETTE, JACQUELINE
GIBESON, JACQUELINE LA T.

LA VERN, SHERRY
DEMING, RICHARD

LAAR, CLEMENS
KOEBSEL, EBERHARD

LABORDE, RENE
NEUFFER, IRENE LABORDE

LABRADOR, JAMES
HAMEL PEIFER, KATHLEEN

LABRADOR, JUDY
HAMEL PEIFER, KATHLEEN

LABRONIO, G.
MARRADI, GIOVANNI

LACEY, ANNE
CORSON, MARTHA

LACEY, JOHN
ALEXANDER, BOYD

LACEY, UNA
LEWIS, CLIFFORD

LACH-SZYRMA, REV. W.S.
LACH-SZYRMA, W.S.

LACHLAN, EDYTHE
CUDLIPP, EDYTHE

LACHMAN, MARV
LACHMAN, MARVIN

LACHNIT, XAVER
LINSINGER, PERT

LACKEY, MERCEDES
DIXON, LARRY

LACKS, CISSY
LACKS, CECILIA

LACKSEY, G.A.
GIBSON, WALTER B.

LACLOS, MICHEL
FRANCOIS, [JACK] MICHEL

LACOLERE, FRANCOIS
ARAGON, LOUIS

LACOMBE, MARIE
BRUCKNER, MARIE

LACOSTE, LILLY
HARRIS, YVONNE L.

LACROIX, LOUISE
SWIFT, HELEN C[ECILIA]

LACROIX, RAMON
MCKEAG, ERNEST LIONEL

LACROIX, RAMON [RAYMOND]
LAZENBY, NORMAN A.

LACY, CHARLES
HIPPISLEY COXE, ANTHONY D

LACY, ED
ZINBERG, LEONARD S.

LACY, TIRA
ESTRADA, RITA

LADAME, CATHRYN
BALDWIN, CATHY-JO LADAME

LADANY, L.
LADANY, LASZIO

LADD, CATHRYN
BALDWIN, CATHY-JO LADAME

LADD, JUSTIN
REASONER, JAMES M.

LADD, VERONICA
MINER, JANE CLAYPOOL

LADEN, JANIS
SHIFFMAN, JANIS LADEN

LADENBURG, MAX
HEYMANN, ROBERT

LADIS, MARIO
RYBARCZYK, MARIO

LADNEK, ODLAW
KENDALL, CARLTON

LADNER, KURT
DEMILLE, NELSON [RICHARD]

LADURIE, EMMANUEL LE ROY
LE ROY LADURIE, EMMANUEL

LADWICK, MARTY
KIRBY, DEREK AMOS

LADY GREGORY
GREGORY, ISABELLA A.P.

LADY GUSTINE
WEAVER, GUSTINE COURSON

LADY OF MANITOBA, A
FRANK, MRS. M.J.

LADY OF QUALITY, A
BAGNOLD, ENID

LADY PACKER
PACKER, JOY

LADY WILDE
WILDE, JANE FRANCESCA S.

LADY, A
TAYLOR, ANN

LADYLIFT
HUTCHINSON, JOHN

LAERTES, JOSEPH
SALZMAN, JOSEPH

LAEVASTU, TAIVO
GRANFELT, TAIVO

LAFARGUE, PHILIP
PHILPOT, JOSEPH HENRY

LAFAYETTE, CARLOS
BOILES, CHARLES LAFAYETTE

LAFAYETTE, RENE
HUBBARD, L. RON

LAFEUILLE, STEFAN
HAACKE, WILMONT

LAFFEATY, CHRISTINA
CARSTENS, NETTA

LAFFERTY, R.A.
LAFFERTY, RAPHAEL ALOY.

LAFIT, GASTON
KURTH, HANNS

LAFITTE, JEAN
DELFS, RAINER
ERICHSEN, UWE
FISCHER, CLAUS

LAFITTE, [COL.] LEON
INGRAHAM, PRENTISS

LAFOREST, SERGE
STEWART, TERRY

LAFORGE, EDWIN
FEARN, JOHN RUSSELL

LAGER, CLAUDE
LAPP, CHRISTIANE GERMAIN

LAGERKVIST, PAR
LAGERKVIST, PAER FABIAN

LAGEVI, BO
BERTHELIUS, JENNY
BLOM, KARL ARNE
BOLINDER, JEAN
GENBERG, KJELL E.
HAKANSSON, JAN
HAMMENSKOG, STURE
MOEN, JAN

LAHR, MAXIMILIAN
RICHTER, HANS

LAIDLAW, A.K.
GRIEVE, CHRIST. MURRAY

LAINE, ANNABEL
TANNAHILL, REAY

LAINE, GLORIA
HANNA, DAVID

LAING, ANNE C.
SCHACHTERLE, NANCY [L]

LAING, KENNETH
LANGMAID, KENNETH [J.R.]

LAING, MARTHA
CELESTINO, MARTHA LAING

LAING, PATRICK
LONG, AMELIA REYNOLDS

LAINI, SAFISHA
EASTON, CAROL D.

LAIR, HELENE
BIRTI, HELENE

LAIRD
LOWTHER, ARMSTRONG JOHN

LAIRD, ANDREW
BRADLEY, W.H.

LAIRD, BAILEY
GOODWIN, RICHARD NARADHOF

LAIRD, DAVID
LAIRD, WILBUR DAVID JR.

LAIRD, DOROTHY
CARR, DOROTHY STEVENSON

LAIT, JACK
LAIT, JACQUIN

LAKATOS, IMRE
LIPSCHITZ, IMRE

LAKE, ALLEN
KELLEY, THOMAS P.

LAKE, BABETTE ROSMOND
LAKE, LEONARD M.
ROSMOND, BABETTE

LAKE, BARRY
LAKE, JOE BARRY

LAKE, HARRIET
TAYLOR, PAULA [WRIGHT]

LAKE, M.D.
SIMPSON, JAMES ALLEN

LAKE, ROBERT
RANDISI, ROBERT J.

LAKE, ROZELLA
LEIGH, ROBERTA

LAKE, SARAH
WEINER, MARGERY

LAKE, SIMON
GRANT, CHARLES L.

LAKEN, BOB
HOLMAN, ROBERT

LAKER, ROSALIND
OVSTEDAL, BARBARA

LAKHU
KHUBCHANDANI, LACHMAN M.

LAKLAN, CARLI
LAUGHLIN, VIRGINIA CARLI

LAKOTTA, CONSILIA MARIA
LAKOTTA, ANNELIESE

LAKS, S.
IZBITSKY, SAMUEL

LALITA
JOHNSON, MAUD LALITA

LAMANCUSA, KATHERNE C.
KOOP, KATHERINE C.

LAMAR, ASHTON
SAYLER, HARRY L.

LAMARSH, JUDY
LAMARSH, JULIA VERLYN

LAMB, CHARLOTTE
HOLLAND, SHEILA C.

LAMB, HELEN B.
LAMONT, HELEN LAMB

LAMB, LADY CAROLINE
FREEMANTLE, ANNE

LAMB, MILTON T.
POWELL, TALMAGE

LAMB, WALLY
LAMB, WALTER

LAMB, WILLIAM
JAMESON, [MARGARET] STORM

LAMBEC, ZOLTAN
KIMBRO, JOHN M.

LAMBER, JULIETTE
ADAM, JULIETTE

LAMBERT, ARTHUR
WIDNER, ARTHUR L.

LAMBERT, BETTY
LAMBERT, ELIZABETH MINNIE

LAMBERT, CHRISTINE
LOEWENGARD, HEIDI H.H.

LAMBERT, ELIZABETH
ORTIZ, ELIZABETH LAMBERT

LAMBERT, FRANK
KALMUCZAK, ROLF

LAMBERT, HAL
NUETZEL, CHARLES A.

LAMBERT, KRISTIN
FRTEYBE, HEIDI HUBERTA

LAMBERT, LYDIA
ZUCKERMANN, LYDIA

LAMBERT, MARION
PERRY, MONTANYE

LAMBERT, RICKY C.
LLIRO OLIVE, JOSE MARIA

LAMBERT, S.H.
SOUTHWOLD, STEPHEN

LAMBERT, TOM
HUTSON, SHAUN

LAMBERT, TONY
KALMUCZAK, ROLF

LAMBERT, WILLA
LAMBERT, W[ILLIAM J.] III

LAMBOURNE, JOHN
LAMBURN, JOHN B. CROMPTON

LAMBRO
NIEMOJEWSKI, ANDRZEJ

LAMIA
AUSTIN, ALFRED

LAMMERT, CHARLOTTE
CALIF, RUTH

LAMOND, GASTON
LAZENBY, NORMAN A.

LAMONT, DUNCAN
TUBB, E.C.

LAMONT, FRANCES
JOURDAIN, ELEANOR FRANCES

LAMONT, GIL
LAMONT, GILVAN DERWENT

LAMONT, MARIANNE
RUNDLE, ANNE

LAMONT, N.B.
BARNITT, NEDDA L.

LAMONT, NEDDA
BARNITT, NEDDA L.

LAMONT, PETER
FRANCES, STEPHEN D.

LAMONT, ROBERT
ANTON, UWE
APPEL, WALTER
BRAND, KURT
BRANDHORST, ANDREAS
DECKER, ANDREAS
DUENSING, JURGEN
FRIEDRICHS, HOLGER
FRIEDRICHS, HORST
GIESA, W.K.
HAHN, RONALD M.
HARTSCH, GERHART
HARY, WILFRID A.
HELGATH, FRANC
HOHLBEIN, WOLFGANG E.
HRDINKA, MICHAEL
KUBIAK, MICHAEL
MAHN, TRAUTE
MAURER, KURT
MICHAEL, ROLF
NEUHAUS, WOLFGANG
RELLERGERD, HELMUT
SAUPE, DIETER
VON KOBLINSKI, HANS-JOACH

LAMONT, WOOD C.
SEWALL, ROBERT

LAMOUR, ANDRE
FIRTH, NORMAN WESLEY
GRAHAM, EILEEN WILMOT
THOMAS, REGINALD GEORGE

LAMOUR, DOROTHY
BURKE, NORA
KAUMEYER, DOROTHY

LAMPLAUGH, LOIS
DAVIS, LOIS CARLILE

LAMPMAN, CAROLYN
BRUBAKER, CAROLYN

LAMPREY, A.C.
FISH, ROBERT L.

LAMPTON, AUSTIN
DENT, ANTHONY AUSTEN

LAMPTON, CHRIS
BISCHOFF, DAVID F.
LAMPTON, CHRISTOPHER

LAN
DE LANCEY LANDON, MELVILL

LAN, GRET
LANE, MARGRET

LANARK, DAVID
MARTEN, JON CHISHOLM

LANCASTER, A.F.
FLEUR, ANNE ELIZABETH

LANCASTER, CAPT.
HOOK, SAMUEL CLARKE

LANCASTER, DAVID
HEALD, TIMOTHY VILLIERS

LANCASTER, EVELYN
SIZEMORE, CHRISTINE COST.

LANCASTER, F. DONALD
FREDRIKSSON, DON

LANCASTER, G.B.
LYTTLETON, EDITH J.

LANCASTER, JOAN
ANDERSON, MARLENE J.

LANCASTER, LISA
LANE, ELIZABETH Y.

LANCASTER, LYDIA
MEAKER, ELOISE

LANCASTER, SHEILA
HOLLAND, SHEILA C.

LANCASTER, VICKY
ANSLE, DOROTHY PHOEBE

LANCASTER, WILLIAM
WARREN, JOHN BYRNE L.

LANCE, LESLIE
CHARLES, THERESA
SWATRIDGE, CHARLES J.

LANCER, JACK
LAWRENCE, JAMES DUNCAN
STRATEMEYER, EDWARD

LANCING, GEORGE
HUNTER, BLUEBELL MATILDA

LANCOUR, GENE
FISHER, GENE L.

LANCOUR, JEANNE
FISHER, GENE L.

LAND
LANDRY, ROBERT JOHN

LAND, JANE & ROSS
BORLAND, KATHRYN KILBY
SPEICHER, HELEN ROSS

LAND, JANE
BORLAND, KATHRYN KILBY

LAND, ROSINA
HASTINGS, PHYLLIS DORA H.

LANDAU-ALDANOV, MARK A.
LANDAU, MARK ALEC

LANDELS, D.H.
HENDERSON, DONALD [L]

LANDELS, STEPHANIE
HENDERSON, DONALD [L]

LANDER, DANE
CLARKE, PERCY A.

LANDER, HANNS
BURMESTER, ALBERT KONRAD

LANDERS, ANN
LEDERER, ESTHER PAULINE

LANDES, MARIE GISELE
LANDES-FUSS, MARIE-GISELE

LANDGRAVE OF HESSE
ROSEN, MICHAEL

LANDI, STEFANO
PIRANDELLO, STEFANO

LANDING, JERRY
DONGES, GUNTER

LANDIS, MARIE
EDWARDS, MARIE A. LANDIS
HERBERT, BRIAN

LANDMANN, MICHAEL
NAGULA, MICHAEL

LANDMANN, ROBERT
ACKERMANN, WERNER

LANDON, HILARY
BELLAIRS, GEORGE
BLUNDELL, HAROLD

LANDON, JEANNE
LANDIS, JILL MARIE

LANDON, LOUISE
HAUCK, LOUISE PLATT

LANDON, NANCY
BERLAND, NANCY

LANDRESS, ELEE
PENNINGTON, JACQUELINE E.

LANDSMAN, SANDY
LANDSMAN, SAMUEL N.B.

LANE, ALLISON
RHODES, EVAN

LANE, ARNOLD
LAZENBY, NORMAN A.

LANE, ARTHUR
TREMAINE, F. ORLIN

LANE, CHARLES
GATTI, ARTHUR GERARD

LANE, EDWARD
DICK, KAY

LANE, ELIZABETH
FARMERS, EILEEN ELIZABETH

LANE, FEARNLEY
LANE, THOMAS H.

LANE, GERALD
FANNING, D. CHRISTOPHER

LANE, GRANT
BOGART, WILLIAM G.
FISHER, STEPHEN GOULD

LANE, HELEN
LACKS, HENRIETTA

LANE, JANE
DAKERS, ELAINE KIDNER

LANE, JERRY
GOFF, JERRY M. JR.
MARTIN, PATRICIA MILES

LANE, JOHN
HUGHES, DENNIS [TALBOT]
MACDONALD, JOHN D.

LANE, KAMI
SMITH, ELAINE C.

LANE, KENDALL
CARROLL, SIDNEY

LANE, LEX
GROSSMANN, HANS HUGO
KRATOCHWIL, JOSEF

LANE, MARVYN
PRICE, JEREMIE

LANE, MARY D.
DELANEY, MARY MURRAY

LANE, MEGAN
WILSON, BRENDA LEE E.

LANE, R.
VANDERBILT, CORNELIUS JR.

LANE, RICHARD
RICHARDSON, MAURICE

LANE, ROUMELIA
GREEN, KAY
LEIGH, ROBERTA

LANE, SHERRY
SMITH, RICHARD REIN

LANE, TEMPLE
LESLIE, MARY ISABEL

LANG, ANTHONY
VAHEY, JOHN G. HAZLETTE

LANG, DON
WHITNEY, WALTER LANGDON

LANG, ELMY
DILLENBURGER, ELMY

LANG, EVE
LANGAN, RUTH

LANG, FRANCES
MANTLE, WINIFRED LANGFORD

LANG, GRACE
FLOREN, LEE

LANG, GREGOR
BIRREN, FABER

LANG, HEATHER
BAKER, DARLENE

LANG, HILARY
LONG, GABRIELLE M.V.C.

LANG, JIM
SELLERS, CONNIE LESLIE

LANG, KING
GRIFFITHS, DAVID ARTHUR
HAY, OSWYN ROBERT T.
HOLLOWAY, BRIAN W.
JENNISON, JOHN WILLIAM
TUBB, E.C.

LANG, MARIA
LANGE, MARIA DAGMAR

LANG, MARTIN
BIRREN, FABER

LANG, MAUD
WILLIAMS, CLAERWEN

LANG, NANCY M.
MACE, NANCY LAWSON

LANG, NED
SHECKLEY, ROBERT

LANG, PETER
FEARN, C. EATON

LANG, REX
LYTTLE, RICHARD

LANG, RUPERT
TURNER, ERNEST SACKVILLE

LANG, SIMON
HARTMAN, DARLENE

LANG, STEWART
MUIR, WARDROP OPENSHAW

LANG, T.T.
TAYLOR, THEODORE

LANG, THEO
LANGBEHN, THEO

LANGART, DARREL[L] T.
GARRETT, RANDALL [P]

LANGDALE, EVE
CRAIG, EVELYN QUITA

LANGDALE, STANLEY
MOORHOUSE, SYDNEY

LANGDON, MARY
PIKE, MARY HAYDEN G.

LANGE, JOHN
CRICHTON, [JOHN] MICHAEL

LANGE, KURT
KERFVE, AXEL

LANGE, OLIVER
WADLEIGH, JOHN

LANGELL, SEARS
GLASSER, ALLEN

LANGELY, DOROTHY
KISSLING, DOROTHY HIGH

LANGENFELD, JOHANNES
KREIN, DANIELA

LANGER, ALFRED
LEHEN, TUURE

LANGER, BORIS
BERGER, MARGOT

LANGER, MARYN
SMITH, MARYN LANGER

LANGFORD, JANE
MANTLE, WINIFRED LANGFORD

LANGFORD, JEROME J.
LANGFORD, JAMES R.

LANGGASSER, ELISABETH
HOFFMANN, ELISABETH

LANGGASSER, ELISABETH [M]
LANGGAESSER, ELISABETH M.

LANGGUTH, A.J.
LANGGUTH, ARTHUR JOHN

LANGHARDT, HETTY
DEPPE, HETTY

LANGHOLM, A.D
DAVIDSON, ALAN

LANGHOLM, NEIL
BULMER, [HENRY] KENNETH
JAMES, LAURENCE

LANGLAND, WILLIAM
MUNTZ, [ISABELLE] HOPE

LANGLEY, HELEN
ROWLAND, DONALD S.

LANGLEY, JOHN
MASON, SYDNEY CHARLES

LANGLEY, JOHN PRENTICE
RATHBORNE, ST. GEORGE

LANGLEY, LEE
LANGLEY, SARAH

LANGLEY, PETER
FLEMING, RONALD

LANGLEY, TANIA
ARMSTRONG, TILLY

LANGLEY, WARD
HARING, DON

LANGNER, NOLA
MALONE, NOLA LANGNER

LANGREN, CHRISTIAN G.
HERCHENRODER, JAN

LANGRENUS, MANFRED
HECHT, FRIEDRICH

LANGSTAFF, JOSEPHINE
HERSCHBERGER, RUTH M.

LANGSTAFF, LAUNCELOT
IRVING, WASHINGTON

LANGSTER, SAM
HOBER, HEINZ WERNER

LANGTRY, ELLEN
ELLIOTT, NANCY

LANGWAY, HUGO
LANG, ANDREW

LANGWORTHY, YOLANDE
READE, FRANCES LAWSON

LANHAM, CHERYL
ARGUILE, CHERYL

LANI, CHRISTINA
NIAL, CHRISTINA RUT

LANIN, E.B.
DILLON, EMILE JOSEPH

LANNE, WILLIAM F.
LEOPOLD, NATHAN F.

LANSBURY, ANGELA
SHAROT, ANGELA

LANSDALE, NINA
SOREL, MARILYN MEESKE

LANSEL, PIEDER
DERIN, P.L.

LANSING, HENRY
ROWLAND, DONALD S.

LANSING, JESSICA
RITZ, DAVID

LANSING, JOHN
ANDREWS, PATRICK E.

LANSKY, IRENE
ROTTENSTEINER, FRANZ

LANSTAFF, TRISTRAM
LORD, WILLIAM WILBERFORCE

LANT, HARVEY
ROWLAND, DONALD S.

LANTRY, MIKE
GLYNN, ANTHONY ARTHUR
TUBB, E.C.

LANTZ, FRAN
LANTZ, FRANCESS LIN

LANUZA, PEDRO
GUBERN RIBALTA, JORGE

LANZA DEL VASTO, JOSEPH J
TRABIA-BRANCIFORTE, GIUS.

LANZA, SILVERO
AMOROS, JUAN BATISTA

LANZER, ELISABETH
FREUNDLICH, ELISABETH

LANZOL, CESARE
LANDELLS, RICHARD

LAO SHE
SHU CH'ING-CH'UN

LAODES, FRIEDRICH
LOMLER, FRIEDRICH WILHELM

LAOIDE, SEOSAMH
LLOYD, JOSEPH H.

LAON
LE SEUR, W.D.

LAPAQUELLERIE, YVON
BIZARDEL, YVON

LAPIDE, PHINN E.
LAPIDE, PINCHAS E.

LAPOUSE, MICHELIN
ZUCKERMANN, LYDIA

LAPP, CHUCK
LAPP, CHARLES LEON

LAPPIN, BEN
LAPPIN, BERNARD WILLIAM

LARA
GRIFFITH-JONES, GEORGE C.

LARA, JAN
HINKEMEYER, MICHAEL T.

LARAMEE, COLE
GRIBBLE, LEONARD [R]

LARAMY, FRANK
KANN, ALBRECHT PETER

LARDNER, RING
LARDNER, RINGGOLD W.

LAREDO, BETTY
CODRESCU, ANDREI

LAREDO, JOHNNY
CAESAR, [EU]GENE [LEE]

LAREDO, KID
HARTSCH, GERHART

LARGO, LOU
ARD, WILLIAM [THOMAS]
JAKES, JOHN [WILLIAM]

LARIAR, LAWRENCE
ROSENBLUM, LAWRENCE

LARISTA, PEPE
SCHWEIZER, MARC

LARK, J.C.
ACKERMAN, FORREST J.

LARK, JODY
SELLERS, CONNIE LESLIE

LARKIN, AMY
BURNS, OLIVE ANN

LARKIN, ELINOR
LEFER, DIANE

LARKIN, MAIA
WOJCIECHOWSKA, MAIA [T]

LARKIN, R.T.
LARKIN, ROCHELLE R.

LARKIN, SARAH
LOENING, SARAH [E] LARKIN

LARNACH, RUPERT
NEVILL, BARRY ST. JOHN

LARNEUIL, MICHEL
BATBEDAT, JEAN

LAROCHE, REBECCA
MAHN, TRAUTE

LAROCHE, RENE
MCKEAG, ERNEST LIONEL

LAROQUE DE ROQUEBRUNE, R.
ROQUEBRUNE, ROBERT

LARRIMORE, LIDA
TURNER, LIDA LARRIMORE

LARRING, GLENN
DONGES, GUNTER

LARRY
PARKES, TERENCE

LARSEN, EGON
LEHRBURGER, EGON

LARSEN, FRED
HUBER, ARMIN OTTO

LARSEN, JORGEN
HASSEL, SVEN

LARSEN, KNUT
KRAFT, ROBERT

LARSEN, PETER
LEHRBURGER, PETER

LARSEN, TOM
KURTH, HANNS

LARSEN, VIOLA
HAHN, ANNELY [M.-B.]

LARSON, EVE
ST. JOHN, WYLLY FOLK

LARSSEN, PEDAR
MALLETTE, GERTRUDE ETHEL

LARSSEN, TIM
FUHSE, GEORG FEODOR

LARSSON I BY, CARL
LARSSON, CARL FILIP

LARTEGUY, JEAN
OSTY, LUCIEN PIERRE JEAN

LASALLE, C.E.
ELLIS, EDWARD S.

LASALLE, CHARLES A.
ELLIS, EDWARD S.

LASALLE, GEORGE E.
ELLIS, EDWARD S.

LASCELLES, ALISON
PARRIS, JOHN

LASCELLES, [LADY]CAROLINE
MAXWELL, MARY ELIZABETH B

LASELL, FEN H.
LASELL, ELINOR H.

LASH, LARRY
BOMKE, BERNHARD

LASKA
LASKA, PETER JEROME

LASKI, MARGHANITA
HOWARD, MARGHANITA LASKI

LASKY, KATHRYN
KNIGHT, KATHRYN LASKY

LASLEY, JACK
LASLEY, JOHN WAYNE III

LASLY, WALT
POHL, FREDERIK

LASS, E.G.
BRENNECKE, JOCHEN

LASSANG, IWAN
LANG, ISAAC

LASSE-MAJA
MOLIN, LARS

LASSEN-WILLEMS, JAMES
WILLEMS, J. RUTHERFORD

LASSERRE, SONJA
CHEVALLIER, SONJA

LASSEZ, M.
BEDFORD-JONES, HENRY

LASSITER, ADAM
KRAUZER, STEVEN M.

LASSITER, MARY
HOFFMAN, MARY MARGARET

LAST, JEF
LAST, JOSEPHUS CAREL F.

LATEEF, TOLEN S.
SANDERS, CLINTON R.

LATHAM, MAVIS
CLARK, MAVIS THORPE

LATHAM, MURRAY
LATHAM, ALISON & ESTHER

LATHAM, O'NEILL
O'NEILL, ROSE CECIL

LATHAM, PHILIP [PHILLIP]
RICHARDSON, ROBERT S.

LATHEN, EMMA
HENISSART, MARTHA
LATSIS, MARY JANE

LATHROP, FRANCIS
LEIBER, FRITZ REUTER JR.

LATIMER, HONDO
APPEL, WALTER

LATIMER, JOANNA
PHILLIPS, JILL META

LATIMER, RUPERT
MILLS, ALGERNON VICTOR

LATNER, PAT WALLACE
STROTHER, PAT WALLACE

LATOUCHE, JOHN
CRAWFURD, OSWALD J.F.

LATREAUMONT
MAY, KARL FRIEDRICH

LATREAUMONT, PRINZ MUHAM.
MAY, KARL FRIEDRICH

LATTA, MARGUERITE
GREENBILL, MARJORIE BARST

LATTIMORE, JESSIE
DRESSER, NORINE
FONTES, MONTSERRAT

LATTIN, ANN
COLE, LOIS DWIGHT

LATTISSIONER, JOHN
JEFFERYS, WILLIAM H.

LAU, CHARLEY
LAU, CHARLES RICHARD

LAUBENSTEIN, VERENA
HAMANN, BARBEL

LAUDER, AFFERBECK
MORRISON, ALISTAIR A.

LAUDER, GEORGE
DICK-LAUDER, GEORGE A.

LAUDER, TOOFIE
LAUDER, MARIA ELISE T.

LAUFFER, PIERRE
MARTES, JOSE ANTONIO

LAUGHLIN, P.S.
SHEA, PATRICK

LAUGHLIN, TOM
HENDERSON, DONALD [L]

LAUGIER, R.
CUMBERLAND, MARTEN

LAUKKO, ESKO
KORPELA, TUULA
SARIOLA, MAURI

LAULER, MICHAEL
OSENBURG, RICHARD

LAUNAY, ANDRE
DE LAUNAY, ANDRE JOSEPH

LAUNAY, DROO
DE LAUNAY, ANDRE JOSEPH

LAUNKA, OKINBA
OSOFISAN, FEMI

LAURA
HUNTER, EILEEN

LAURAC, SERGE
SCHWEIZER, MARC

LAURANCE, ALFRED D.
TRALINS, [SANDOR] ROBERT

LAURANCE, ALICE
HAYWOOD, LAURA ALICE W.

LAURAT, LUCIEN
MACHL, OTTO

LAURE, ETTAGALE
BLAUER, ETTAGALE

LAUREEN, PATRICIA
SCHAFER, ROBERT

LAUREN, LINDA
BUNCE, LINDA SUSAN S.

LAURENCE, ANNE
PFISTERER, SALLY

LAURENCE, BETHEL
KALIS, BETTY

LAURENCE, CLARICE
SADLER, CLARICE LAURENCE

LAURENCE, DON
DONOVAN, LAURENCE

LAURENCE, JOHN
PRITCHARD, JOHN LAURENCE

LAURENCE, LEILA
DOBSCHA, LEILA LAURENCE

LAURENCE, RICHARD
BARTLE, L.E.

LAURENCE, ROBERT
FISCHER, MATTHIAS JOSEPH

LAURENCE, WILL
SMITH, WILLARD L.

LAURENT, JACQUES
LAURENT-CELY, JACQUES

LAURI
SALOLA, EEERO

LAURI, PIKKU
SALOLA, EEERO

LAURIE, ANDRE
GROUSSET, PASCHAL

LAURIE, ANNIE
BLACK, WINIFRED
SCARBERRY, ALMA SIOUX

LAURIE, HARRY L.
CAHN, ZVI

LAURIE, JESSICA
GRANBECK, MARILYN

LAURIER, DON
SIZER, LAURENCE

LAURIN, ANNE
MCLAURIN, ANNE

LAURIN, FRIEDRICH
ERDMANSDORFFER, FRIEDRICH

LAUSCHER, HERMANN
HESSE, HERMANN

LAUTER
CHAMSON, ANDRE J.

LAUTERBACH, HERMANN O.
OTTO, HERMANN

LAVANT, CHRISTINE
HABERNIG, CHRISTINE

LAVELLE, MARC
WILLIS, ERNEST LISTER H.

LAVELLE, MARK
JENNISON, JOHN WILLIAM

LAVEN, J.C. MARTI
O'LAIMHIN, J. MARTI LAVEN

LAVEN, MARTI
O'LAIMHIN, J. MARTI LAVEN

LAVERTY, DONALD
BLISH, JAMES B.
KNIGHT, DAMON

LAVIGNE, MARK
LEOPOLD, EMMANUEL FLAVIA

LAVIN, MARY
WALSH, MARY

LAVINGTON, HUBERT
CARRINGTON, HEREWARD

LAVINSON, JOSEPH
KAYE, MARVIN [NATHAN]

LAVOIX, JEAN
SAUVAGEAU, JUAN

LAVOND, PAUL DENNIS
DOCKWEILER, JOSEPH HAROLD
KORNBLUTH, C[YRIL] M.
LOWNDES, ROBERT A.W.
POHL, FREDERIK
WOLLHEIM, DONALD A.

LAW, ELIZABETH
PETERS, MAUREEN

LAW, JANICE
TRECKER, JANICE LAW

LAW, M.R.
LAULETTA, MICHAEL

LAW, MARJORIE J.
LIDDELOW, MARJORIE JEAN

LAW, SIMONE
RUHEN, CARL

LAW, VIRGINIA W.
SHELL, VIRGINIA LAW

LAW-ABIDING REVOLUTIONIST
WELLMAN, BERT

LAWFORD, PAULA JANE
MARTYR, PAULA [JANE]

LAWLESS, ANTHONY
MACDONALD, PHILIP

LAWLOR, PAT
LAWLOR, PATRICK ANTHONY

LAWRENCE
STEVENS, LAWRENCE STERNE

LAWRENCE OF ARABIA
LAWRENCE, THOMAS EDWARD

LAWRENCE, A.R.
FOFF, ARTHUR R[AYMOND]

LAWRENCE, ALLISON
BRYER, JUDITH E.

LAWRENCE, AMY
SCHENK, JOYCE

LAWRENCE, ARIADNE
LING, AMY

LAWRENCE, B.L.
BLOCK, LAWRENCE

LAWRENCE, CHESTER
CAMPBELL, SYDNEY GEORGE

LAWRENCE, D.H.
LAWRENCE, DAVID HERBERT

LAWRENCE, DAVID
MORRIS, DAVID ST. LAWREN.

LAWRENCE, DON
DONOVAN, LAURENCE

LAWRENCE, E.S.
BRADBURNE, ELIZABETH S.

LAWRENCE, EDDIE
EISLER, LAWRENCE

LAWRENCE, EDMOND
DE BRA, LEMUEL LAWRENCE

LAWRENCE, EDWARD
EISLER, LAWRENCE

LAWRENCE, FRED
FELDMAN, FRED

LAWRENCE, GIL
GEIS, GILBERT L.

LAWRENCE, H.L.
LAWRENCE, HENRY LIONEL

LAWRENCE, HILDA
KRONEMULLER, HILDA

LAWRENCE, IRENE
MARSH, JOHN

LAWRENCE, J.A.
BLISH, JUDITH ANN LAWREN.

LAWRENCE, J.D.
LAWRENCE, JAMES DUNCAN

LAWRENCE, J.T.
ROWLAND-ENTWISTLE, A.T.

LAWRENCE, JACK
FITZGERALD, LAWRENCE P.

LAWRENCE, JAMES
TAMES, RICHARD LAWRENCE

LAWRENCE, JIM
LAWRENCE, JAMES DUNCAN

LAWRENCE, JOCK
LAWRENCE, JUSTUS BALDWIN

LAWRENCE, JOHN
LAWRENCE, JODI

LAWRENCE, JUDITH ANN
BLISH, MRS. JAMES

LAWRENCE, KARL
FOFF, ARTHUR R[AYMOND]

LAWRENCE, KATY
MARTIN, LARRY JAY

LAWRENCE, KATY [KATHY]
MARTIN, KATHLEEN KELLY

LAWRENCE, KENNETH G.
RINGGOLD, GENE

LAWRENCE, LARRY
DOW, LAWRENCE T.

LAWRENCE, LARS
STEVENSON, PHILIP EDWARD

LAWRENCE, LESLEY
LEWIS, LESLEY

LAWRENCE, LINDA
HUNT, LINDA LAWRENCE

LAWRENCE, LOUISE
HOLDEN, ELIZABETH RHODA

LAWRENCE, LYNN
GARLAND, SHERRY

LAWRENCE, MARGERY
TOWLE, MRS. A.E.

LAWRENCE, MARTIN
GREIF, MARTIN
GROW, LAWRENCE

LAWRENCE, MARY
YOUNG, MARY LOU DAVES

LAWRENCE, MELINDA
WEINHOUSE, BETH

LAWRENCE, MICHAEL
LARIAR, LAWRENCE

LAWRENCE, NANCY
STARTS, NANCY

LAWRENCE, P.
TUBB, E.C.

LAWRENCE, RAE
LIEBMANN, RUTH E.

LAWRENCE, RICHARD
EDWARDS, LAWRENCE

LAWRENCE, RICHARD A.
LEOPOLD, NATHAN F.

LAWRENCE, ROBERT
BEUM, ROBERT LAWRENCE

LAWRENCE, STEPHEN
STEPHENS, LAWRENCE STERNE

LAWRENCE, STEVEN C.
MURPHY, LAWRENCE A.

LAWRENCE, SUSANNAH
HARTMAN, JAN & LORIE

LAWRENCE, T.E.
LAWRENCE, THOMAS EDWARD

LAWRENCE, TERRY
LAWRENCE, MARY TERESE

LAWRENCE, THOMAS
ROBERTS, THOMAS SACRA

LAWRENCE. SIMON
LARGENT, R. KARL

LAWSON, CHET
TUBB, E.C.

LAWSON, CHRISTINE
WALKER, EMILY KATHLEEN

LAWSON, DINK
BLEECK, G.C.

LAWSON, DR. PHILIP
TRIMMER, ERIC J.

LAWSON, H. LOWE
LAWSON, HORACE LOWE

LAWSON, HENRY HERTZBERG
LARSEN, HENRY H.

LAWSON, JACOB
BURGESS, MICHAEL ROY

LAWSON, JOHNNY
NEWTON, DWIGHT BENNETT

LAWSON, M.C.
LAWSON, HORACE LOWE

LAWSON, MICHAEL
RYDER, MICHAEL LAWSON

LAWSON, PATRICK
EBY, LOIS CHRISTINE

LAWSON, STEVE
TURNER, ROBERT H.

LAWSON, SUSAN
MOORE, ROGER E[LWOOD]

LAWSON, W.B.
INGRAHAM, PRENTISS
JENKS, GEORGE CHARLES
RATHBORNE, ST. GEORGE
STRATEMEYER, EDWARD

LAWSON, WARREN J.
BOBIN, DONALD E.M.

LAWSRENCE, STEVEN C.
MURPHY, LAWRENCE A.

LAWTON, CAPT. WILBUR
GOLDFRAP, JOHN HENRY

LAWTON, CHARLES
HECKLEMANN, CHARLES N.

LAWTON, DENNIS
FAUST, FREDERICK S.

LAWTON, MANNY
LAWTON, MARION RUSSELL

LAXNESS, HALLDOR
GUDJONSSON, HALLDOR KIJAN

LAYMON, CARL
LAYMON, RICHARD

LAYNE, BOBBY
LAYNE, ROBERT LAWRENCE

LAYNE, JIM
CHADWICK, JOSEPH L.

LAYNE, LAURA
KNOTT, WILLIAM CECIL JR.

LAYNE, MARION MARGERY
PAPICH, MARGERY
TORKELSON, LAYNE
WOOLF, MARION

LAYNHAM, PETER
GLASBY, JOHN S.

LAYTON, ANDREA
BANCROFT, IRIS M. NELSON

LAYTON, EDITH
FELBER, EDITH

LAYTON, F.G.
LAYTON, FRANK GEORGE

LAZARE, JERRY
LAZARE, GERALD JOHN

LAZARUS, FELIX
CABLE, GEORGE WASHINGTON

LAZARUS, HENRY
SLAVITT, DAVID RYTMAN

LAZENBY, N.A.
LAZENBY, NORMAN A.

LAZENBY, NAT
LAZENBY, NORMAN A.

LAZEROWITZ, MORRIS
LAIZEROWITZ, MORRIS

LAZLO, KATE
ANGUS, SYLVIA

LAZUTA, GENE
LAZUTA, EUGENE MICHAEL

LE BARON, GRACE
UPHAM, GRACE LE BARON

LE BARON, MARIE
URIE, MARY LE BARON [A]

LE BEAU, ROY
SMITH, MITCHELL

LE BRETON, AUGUSTE
MONTFORT, AUGUSTE

LE BRETON, MRS. JOHN
MURRAY-FORD, ALICE MAY

LE BRETON, THOMAS
FORD, T. MURRAY

LE CAGAT, BENAT
WHITAKER, RODNEY W.

LE CARON, HENRY
BEACH, THOMAS MILLER

LE CHANOIS, JEAN-PAUL
DREFUS, JEAN-PAUL ETIENNE

LE CLAIR, TOM
LE CLAIR, THOMAS

LE COQ, MONSIEUR
SIMENON, GEORGES [J.C]

LE FANU, J. S[HERIDAN]
DERLETH, AUGUST [WILLIAM]

LE FEVRE, WILLIAM
FOSTER, BENNETT

LE GRYS, WALTER
NORGATE, WALTER

LE GUIN, U.K.
LE GUIN, URSULA K.

LE JEMLYS
JELLY, SYMMES M.

LE JOHN, KEVIN
RELLERGERD, HELMUT

LE MARQUE, MICHEL
SCAMMEL, MICHAEL

LE MON, LYNN
WERT, LYNETTE L.

LE MOYNE, ROY
HERSEY, HAROLD

LE MOYNE, SEYMOUR
HERSEY, HAROLD

LE NOIRE, FELICIA
BLISS, LENA EDITH

LE NORMAND, MICHELLE
DESROSIERS, MARIE A.T.

LE PAGE, RAND
BIRD, WILLIAM H.F.
GLASBY, JOHN S.
HUGHES, DENNIS [TALBOT]
O'BRIEN, DAVID WRIGHT
ROBERTS, ARTHUR O.

LE QUESNE, A.L.
LE QUESNE, ALFRED L.

LE QUESNE, LAURENCE
LE QUESNE, ALFRED L.

LE REVELER
ARTAUD, ANTONIN

LE ROY, DAVE
LE ROY, LEMUEL DAVID

LE ROY, IRENE
SVEE, SALLY

LE SIEG, THEO
GEISEL, THEODORE SEUSS

LE VARRE, DEBORAH
VARLINSKY, DEBORAH

LE VERT, LIBERTE E.
BLEILER, EDWARD F.

LE VOLEUR
CAREY, ROSA NOUCHETTE

LE VOYEUR, PIERRE
FEARN, JOHN RUSSELL

LE, IVAN
MOISIA, IVAN LEONTEVICH

LE, JOHN
PUHLE, JOACHIM

LEA, JOAN
LOWRY, JOAN [CATLOW]

LEA, JOHN
NEUFELD, JOHN [ARTHUR]

LEA, RICHARD
LEA, ALEC

LEA, TIMOTHY
WOOD, CHRISTOPHER [H]

LEACH, E.R.
LEACH, EDMUND RONALD

LEACROFT, ERIC
YOUNG, ERIC BRETT

LEADER, CHARLES
SMITH, ROBERT CHARLES

LEADERMAN, GEORGE
ROBINSON, RICHARD B.

LEAN, PATRICK
SALMONSON, JESSICA A.

LEANDER, CATHERINE
KREUTZER, CATHERINE

LEANDER, ED
RICHELSON, GERALDINE

LEAR, PETER
LOVESEY, PETER [HARMER]

LEASOR, JAMES
BAJOG, GUNTHER
LEASOR, THOMAS JAMES

LEAST HEAT MOON, WILLIAM
TROGDON, WILLIAM

LEATHER, GEORGE
SWALLOW, NORMAN

LEAVER, RUTH
TOMALIN, RUTH

LEAVIS, Q.D.
LEAVIS, QUEENIE DOROTHY

LEAVITT, RUBY R.
ROHRLICH, RUBY

LEBA, W.K.
KABEL, WALTHER

LEBAR, JOHN
WRIGHT, GILBERT MUNGER
WRIGHT, HARRY BELL JR.

LEBARON, ANTHONY
LAUMER, [JOHN] KEITH

LEBARON, JOSEPH
SMYTH, JOSEPH HILTON

LEBENSON
KAHN, YITZHAK

LEBERECHT, PETER
TIECK, JOHANN LUDWIG

LEBERT, RANDY
BRANNON, WILLIAM T.

LEBIES, RENE
SEIBEL, WERNER

LEBKA, WALLY
KABEL, WALTHER

LEBO, DELI
LEBO, DELL

LEBREO, STEWART
WEINER, STEWART

LEBRETON, THOMAS
FORD, T. MURRAY

LEBRUN, GAUTIER
GIBSON, WALTER B.

LECALE, ERROL
MCNEILLY, WILFRED G.

LECARRE, JOHN
CORNWELL, DAVID J.M.

LECAVELE, L.
LECAVELE, ROLAND

LECAVELE, ROLAND
DORGELES, ROLAND

LECHON, JAN
SERAFINOWICZ, LESZEK JO.

LECKIE, PETER
HOPEGOOD, PETER

LECLAIRE, DAY
SMITH, DAY TOTTON

LECLERC, VICTOR
PARRY, ALBERT

LEDD, PAUL
RANDISI, ROBERT J.

LEDER, RUDOLF
HERMLIN, STEPHEN

LEDGARD, JAKE
MASON, SYDNEY CHARLES

LEDNER, ERNST
RICHTER, JOSEFINE

LEDUC, CLAUDINE
LINDSAY, SADI

LEE, A.R.
ASH, RENE LEE

LEE, AGNES
FREER, MARTHA AGNES R.

LEE, ALYSSA
LEE, LINDA FRANCES

LEE, AMANDA
BAGGETT, NANCY
BUCKHOLTZ, EILEEN [G]
GLICK, RUTH [BURTNICK]

LEE, AMBER
CUTHRELL, FAITH B.

LEE, ANDREA
TOONA-ELIN, ELIN[-KAI]

LEE, ANDREW
AUCHINCLOSS, LOUIS S.

LEE, ANNE S.
MURPHY, MABEL ANSLEY

LEE, BABS
LEE, MARION [V.D.M.]
SAUNDERS, CLARE CASTLER

LEE, BETTY
LAMBERT, ELIZABETH MINNIE

LEE, BILL
LEE, WILLIAM SAUL

LEE, BOB
MCGRATH, ROBERT L.

LEE, BONNIE
HOVLAND, BONNIE L.

LEE, CAROL
FLETCHER, HELEN JILL

LEE, CAROLINE [CAROLINA]
DERN, E. PEARL GADDIS

LEE, CECILE
LEE, MARY EMILY

LEE, CHARLES
GRAHAM, ROGER P.
LEVY, CHARLES

LEE, CHARLES C.
ROSE, MARTHA EMILY

LEE, CHARLES H.
STORY, ROSAMOND MARY

LEE, CONRAD
DOEHMEL, FRIEDRICH

LEE, CORA
ANDERSON, CATHERINE CORL.

LEE, DAVID
GARNETT, DAVID S.

LEE, DEVON
POHLE, ROBERT W. JR.

LEE, DON L.
MADHUBUTI, HAKI R.

LEE, DORIAN
MOORE, ISABEL

LEE, EDWARD
FOUTS, EDWARD LEE
SEYMOUR, LEE EDWARD

LEE, ELSIE
SHERIDAN, ELSIE LEE

LEE, ERIC
BLITCH, FLEMING LEE
LEE, FLEMING
PAGE, GERALD W.

LEE, FLEMING
BLITCH, FLEMING LEE

LEE, FRANK
LEBER, EMIL

LEE, GEORGE B.
HARBAUGH, THOMAS C.

LEE, GEORGE LESLIE
LEE, BROTHER BASIL LEO

LEE, GYPSIE ROSE
HOVICK, ROSE LOUISE
RANDOLPH, GEORGIANNA ANN

LEE, HARRY
FELLINGE, HARRY LEE

LEE, HERBERT D'H
KASTLE, HERBERT D.

LEE, HOLME
PARR, HARRIET

LEE, HOWARD
GOULART, RONALD JOSEPH
MALZBERG, BARRY [N]

LEE, JAE GARDINER
LEE, PALI JAE

LEE, JENNIE
LEE, JANET

LEE, JESSE
MASON, SYDNEY CHARLES

LEE, JUDY
CARLSON, JUDITH LEE

LEE, JULIAN
LATHAM, JEAN LEE

LEE, KATHERINE
JENNER, KATHERINE LEE

LEE, KAY
KELLY, KAREN

LEE, LARRY
LEE, LAWRENCE

LEE, LINDA
GOODWIN, HOPE

LEE, LOUISE CARTER
JENKINS, WILLIAM FITZGER.

LEE, LUCY
TALBOT, CHARLENE JOY

LEE, LYDIA
LIMA, ROSE MARIE

LEE, MAC
HEYMANN, ROBERT

LEE, MANFRED B.
LEPOFSKY, MANFORD

LEE, MARIAN
CLISH, [LEE] MARIAN

LEE, MARK
ROWLAND, MARCUS L.

LEE, MARTIN
WEBB, VICTORIA

LEE, MATT
MERWIN, SAMUEL K. JR.

LEE, MILDRED
SCUDDER, MILDRED LEE

LEE, MINNIE MARY
WOOD, JULIA AMANDA

LEE, MURIEL
LANE, MARY LOUISA

LEE, NATA
FRACKMAN, NATHALINE

LEE, PARKER
TURNER, ROBERT H.

LEE, PATRICK
ANDREWS, PATRICK E.
FIELDHOUSE, WILLIAM [L]
ROBERTS, MARK

LEE, POLLY JAE
LEE, PALI JAE

LEE, RACHEL
CIVIL, SUSAN

LEE, RANGER
SNOW, CHARLES H[ORACE]

LEE, RAYMOND
MARTIN, E. LE BRETON

LEE, ROBERT [EGGERT]
FAIRMAN, PAUL W.

LEE, ROBERTA
MCGRATH, ROBERT L.

LEE, RONNY
LEVENTHAL, RONALD

LEE, ROSIE
AIKEN, JOAN

LEE, ROWENA
BARTLETT, MARIE

LEE, ROY
HOPKINS, CLARK

LEE, S.C.
AKENS, DAVID STRODE

LEE, SAMANTHA
WEBB, MAGGIE

LEE, SANDRA
GONDA, ADOLPHE
SMITH, SANDRA LEE

LEE, SIR SIDNEY
LEVY, SOLOMAN LAZARUS

LEE, SPIKE
LEE, SHELTON JACKSON

LEE, STAN
LEIBER, STANLEY MARTIN

LEE, STEVE
PARRY, MICHEL P.

LEE, TAMMIE
TOWNSEND, THOMAS L.

LEE, TED
LEAVY, HERBERT

LEE, THOMAS
KROEGER, WILLY

LEE, THORNE
SHIVELEY, THORNTON

LEE, TOM
LEE, TOMMY L.

LEE, VERNON
PAGET, VIOLET

LEE, VERONICA
WOODFORD, [I] CECIL

LEE, W. STORRS
LEE, WILLIAM STORRS

LEE, W.W.
LEE, WENDI

LEE, WILLIAM
BURROUGHS, WILLIAM S.

LEE, WILLY
BURROUGHS, WILLIAM S.

LEE, [SIR] SIDNEY
LEVY, SOLOMAN LAZARUS

LEECH, RICHARD
MCCLELLAND, RICHARD L.

LEEK, MARGARET
BOWEN-JUDD, SARA HUTTON

LEEMING, JO ANN
LEEMING, JOSEPH

LEES, HANNAH
BACHMAN, LAWRENCE P.
FETTER, ELIZABETH HEAD

LEES, JOHN MORTON
MIDDLETON, ELLIS

LEES, MARGUERITE
BAUMANN, MARGARET

LEESON, BOB
LEESON, ROBERT [ARTHUR]

LEESON, R.A.
LEESON, ROBERT [ARTHUR]

LEFEVRE, GUI
BICKERS, RICHARD L.T.

LEFFLAR, ERIKA
VON LOEWIS OF M., ERIKA

LEFY, NORA
RUSSELL, HANORA MARY

LEGER, ALEXIS
LEGER, [M.-R. A.] ALEXIS

LEGER, SAINTLEGER
LEGER, [M.-R. A.] ALEXIS

LEGGETT, ERIC
RIMEL, DUANE [W]

LEGIONAIRE 14830
HUBBARD, L. RON

LEGMAN, G.
LEGMAN, GEORGE ALEXANDER

LEGRAEME, D.A.
GRAHAM, DALE

LEGRAND
HENDERSON, LE GRAND

LEGRANDE, LOUIS MD
VICTOR, MRS. M.V.
VICTOR, ORVILLE J.

LEGRANDE, SYBIL
BYINGTON, KAA

LEGRIS, JEAN-LUC
DONALDSON, WILLIAM

LEGRU, SEIKO
VAN DE WETERING, JANWILL.

LEHMAN, WALTER
HARWOOD, GWEN

LEHMANN, R.C.
LEHMANN, RUDOLF C.

LEHNE, FR.
BUTENSCHON, HELENE

LEHNERT, H.P.
PLEHN, HEINZ

LEHOVICH, EUGENIE O.
OUROUSSOW, EUGENIE

LEHRER, JIM
LEHRER, JAMES CHARLES

LEHRER, TOM
LEHRER, THOMAS ANDREW

LEHRMANN, CHANAN
LEHRMANN, CHARLES CUNO

LEIBACH, OSKAR
HARBECK, ALOIS

LEIBENGUTH, CHARLA ANN
BANNER, CHARLA ANN L.

LEIBER, VIVIAN
PRESSER, ARLYNN LEIBER

LEICHT, MARKUS
LEGER, JEAN-MARC

LEIGH, ANA
BAIER, ANNA LEE

LEIGH, BARBARA
JONES, BARBARA L.

LEIGH, CATHERINE
DONICH, CATHERINE LEIGH
WOLTHAUSEN, LINDA S.

LEIGH, CYNTHIA
WARTSKI, MAUREEN A.C.

LEIGH, DAVE
POWELL, TALMAGE

LEIGH, DR. HENRY
RICH, H. THOMSON

LEIGH, ELIZABETH
BOURNE, CAROLINE
HANCOCK, DEBBIE BARR

LEIGH, EUGENE
SELTZER, LEON E[UGENE]

LEIGH, HART
DENNY, JOHN THOMAS

LEIGH, HOWARD
JOHNS, WILLIAM EARLE

LEIGH, IONE
MASSADA, IONE

LEIGH, JACKIE
SMITH, DEBORAH

LEIGH, JANET
MORRISON, JEANETTE HELEN

LEIGH, JO
KRAMER, JOLIE

LEIGH, JOHANNA
SAYERS, DOROTHY L[EIGH]

LEIGH, KATHY
KILLOUGH, KAREN LEE

LEIGH, LORI
CARLTON, LORI

LEIGH, MATTHEW ANDREW
CHERVOKAS, JOHN VINCENT

LEIGH, MEREDITH
KENYON, BRUCE

LEIGH, MICAH
GEE, D. EVELYN H.
MERRITT, EMMA

LEIGH, OLIVIA
CLAMP, HELEN M.E.

LEIGH, PALMER
PALMER, PAMELA LYNN

LEIGH, PETRA
LING, PETER

LEIGH, ROBERTA
LINDSAY, RACHEL

LEIGH, ROBIN
HATCHER, ROBIN LEE

LEIGH, RUTH
SCLATER, RUTH LEIGH

LEIGH, TAMARA
SCHAMSKI, TAMMY

LEIGH, URSULA
GWYNN, URSULA GRACE

LEIGH, VERONICA
BARUFELD, R.

LEIGH, VICTORIA
ERBSCHLOE, VICTORIA LEIGH
SPENSER, EMMA JANE

LEIGH, W. RYE
RILEY, WILLIE

LEIGH, [CAPT.] ARTHUR
STEFFENS, ARTHUR JOSEPH

LEIGHTON, ANN
SMITH, ISADORE L.L.

LEIGHTON, EDWARD
BARRETT, GEOFFREY JOHN

LEIGHTON, FLORENCE
PFALZGRAF, FLORENCE L.

LEIGHTON, J.G.
COLE, JOHN

LEIGHTON, LEE
MERRIMAN, CHAD
OVERHOLSER, WAYNE D.
PATTEN, LEWIS B.

LEIGHTON, LEN
PATTEN, LEWIS B.

LEIGHTON, TED
LEVINSON, LEONARD [L]
LINK, WILLIAM

LEIMBACH, MARTI
LEIMBACH, MARTHA R.

LEINO, EINO
LOENNBOHM, ARMAS EINO L.

LEINSDORF, ERICH
LANDAUER, ERICH

LEINSTER, MURRAY
JENKINS, WILLIAM FITZGER.

LEISURELY SAUNTERER
EGGLESTON, EDWARD

LEITCH, LAVINIA
HYND, LAVINIA LEITCH

LEITH, ELIZABETH
JULYAN, LOUISE ELIZABETH

LEITICH, ANN TIZIA
KORNINGEN, ANN TIZIA

LEIVICK, H.
HALPERN, LEIVICK

LEIVICK, HALPER
HALPERN, LEIVICK

LEJEUNE, ANTHONY
THOMPSON, EDWARD ANTHONY

LELAND, SIDNEY
HOLMES, ERIC

LEMAGE, GASPARD
TACHE, JEAN CHARLES

LEMAISTRE, JOHN
MURRY, JOHN MIDDLETON

LEMBO, DIANA L.
SPIRT, DIANA LOUISE

LEMERCIER, JUSTINE & JULE
BUSH, JOSEF
WRAY, PHOEBE

LEMERY, ALYSSE
RASMUSSEN, ALYSSE

LEMESURIER, PETER
BRITTON, PETER EWART

LEMIR, ANDRE
RIMEL, DUANE [W]

LEMKE, HENRY E.
TOOKER, RICHARD [PRESLEY]

LEMOINE
DIDIER, EUGENE LEMOINE

LEMOINE, ERNEST
ROY, EWELL PAUL

LEMON PEEL, NORMAN
HIRSH, PHIL

LEMON, GREY
GRAY, LINDSAY RUSSELL N.

LEMOTT, JUSTIN G.T. III
GEBAUER, WILLIAM
MCGOWAN, RAYMOND

LENA
LATHROP, MARY TORRANS

LENANTON, C.
OMAN, CAROLA MARY A.

LENANTON, CAROLA MARY A.O
OMAN, CAROLA MARY A.

LENCY, C.
TRAIN, ARTHUR

LEND, PERT
LINSINGER, PERT

LENGEL, FRANCES
TROCCHI, ALEXANDER

LENIN, N.
LENIN
ULYANOV, VLADIMIR ILICH

LENIN, NIKOLAI
LENIN

LENIN, V.I.
LENIN

LENIN, VALDIMIR ILYICH
LENIN

LENIN, VLADIMIR I.
LENIN

LENNAR, ROLF
PILZ, ROLF

LENNARD, H.K.
GLASBY, JOHN S.

LENNART, MARK
ANTONI, FRIDE [E.R.]

LENNERT, NIKOLAUS
POCHE, KLAUS

LENNON, FRANK
WOOD, EDWARD D. JR.

LENNON, HELEN M.
GOULART, FRANCES S.

LENNOX, JACQUELINE
SMITH, DEBORAH

LENNOX, JOCELYN L.
HERMANN, GUNTHER

LENNOX, JOHN
BESTER, ALFRED

LENNOX, PETER
HOLENSTEIN, PETER

LENNOX, SUSAN
WORLEY, DOROTHY

LENNOX, TERRY
HARVEY, JOHN [BARTON]

LENOIR, JACQUES
LARAQUE, PAUL

LENOIR, PIERRE
KAGAN, GEORGE

LENORE, LISA
BROUDE, CRAIG HOWARD

LENOTRE, G.
GOSSELIN, LOUIS LEON T.

LENOTRE, GEORGES
GOSSELIN, LOUIS-LEON-TEO.

LENOX, PETER
HOLENSTEIN, PETER

LENS, CONNY
HITZBLECK, FRIEDRICH

LENSEN, W.
KABEL, WALTHER

LENTON, ANTHONY
NUTTALL, ANTHONY

LENZ, BEATE
KANIES, GERTIE

LENZ, CAROLINE RUTH S.
SWIFT, CAROLYN RUTH

LENZ, MAX WERNER
RUSSENBERGER, MAX

LEO, BESSIE
MURRAY, LESLIE

LEODHAS, SORCHE NIC
ALGER, LECLAIRE GOWANS

LEON, FELIPE
GALICIA, LEON FELIPE CAM.

LEON, FRANCES
SWADESH, FRANCIS LEON

LEON-FELIPE
CAMINO Y GALICIA, LEON-F.

LEONA
BUTTON, MARGARET

LEONARD, A.B.
ALDRICH, EARL AUGUSTUS

LEONARD, CHARLES L.
HEBERDEN, M[ARY V.]

LEONARD, DUTCH
LEONARD, ELMORE

LEONARD, FRANK
WOOD, EDWARD D. JR.

LEONARD, HUGH
BYRNE, JOHN KEYES

LEONARD, J.S.
LEONARD, JAMES S.

LEONARD, JASON
ESCOTT, JONATHAN

LEONARD, LEONARD L.
LEVINSON, LEONARD [L]

LEONARD, PHYLLIS
ORTEGA, ISABEL

LEONARD, PHYLLIS G.
ORTEGA, ISABEL

LEONE, LAURA
RESNICK, LAURA

LEONE, SCOTT
BONNELL, KENNETH

LEONG, GOR YUN
ELLISON, VIRGINIA HOWELL

LEONHARDT, THOMAS
KERNMAYR, HANS GUSTL

LEONHART, RAPHAEL W.
WYBRANIEC, PETER F.

LEONID
BOSWORTH, WILLAN GEORGE

LEOPOLD, CHRISTOPHER
SYNGE, ALLEN

LEOPOLD, GUY
LETTS, BARRY
SLOMAN, ROBERT

LEPAGE, RAND
HOLLOWAY, BRIAN W.
PROTHEROE, CYRIL

LEPEL, H.
GUTSTER, EUGENE

LEPETIT, CHARLES
SALA, CHARLES

LEPKO, E.
KOPELEV, LEV Z.

LEPPOC, DERFLA
COPPEL, ALFREDO JOSE

LERHMAN, LIZA
WILLIAMS, LIZA

LERNET-HOLENIA, ALEXANDER
VON HOLLENIA, ALEXANDER

LERNIER, LUKE
LEIGHTON, F.S.

LEROUX, ANDRE
TASCA, ANGELO

LEROUX, ETIENNE
LEROUX, S.P.D.

LEROYD, RAYMOND
WADE, THOMAS W.

LERROVITCH
HERSEY, HAROLD

LERTETH, OBAN
FANTHORPE, R.L.

LERTETH, OBEN
FANTHORPE, R.L.

LES ANGELEANO
ACKERMAN, FORREST J.

LESBIA
LEWIS, LYDIA T.

LESIZWE, ILIZWI
LEE, FRANZ JOHN T.

LESKO, WENDY
SCHAETZEL, WENDY

LESLEY, BLAKE
DUCKWORTH, LESLIE BLAKEY

LESLEY, COLE
COLE, LEONARD LESLIE

LESLEY, PAUL
MACAULEY, KEN

LESLIE, A.
SCOTT, ALEXANDER LESLIE

LESLIE, A. SCOTT
SCOTT, ALEXANDER LESLIE

LESLIE, A.L.
LAZARUS, ARNOLD LESLIE

LESLIE, ANN
CAMERON, LESLIE GEORGIANA

LESLIE, ANNE
LESLIE, ANITA

LESLIE, ARTHUR
GRIEVE, CHRIST. MURRAY

LESLIE, BLAKE
DUCKWORTH, LESLIE BLAKEY

LESLIE, COLIN
ROOME, GERALD ANTHONY

LESLIE, DORIS
FERGUSON-HANNAY, DORIS

LESLIE, EDWARD
SELLICKS, LESLIE EDWARD

LESLIE, EMMA
DIXON, MRS.

LESLIE, FRANK
LESLIE, MIRIAM FLORENCE

LESLIE, HENRIETTA
SCHUTZE, GLADYS H.

LESLIE, JANE
COADE, JESSIE

LESLIE, JOHN
HOWITT, J. LESLIE DESPARD

LESLIE, LAWRENCE
RATHBORNE, ST. GEORGE

LESLIE, LILIAN
HOOD, ARCHER
PERKINS, VIOLET LILLIAN

LESLIE, LYNN
BODINE, SHERRILL
SIMA, ELAINE

LESLIE, MARGOT
LANG, MIRIAM

LESLIE, MIRIAM
KETCHUM, PHILIP
ROSS, WILLIAM E. DANIEL

LESLIE, NICOLE
BLEECK, G.C.

LESLIE, O.H.
SLESAR, HENRY

LESLIE, RICHARD
BICKERS, RICHARD L.T.

LESLIE, ROBERT
ROBERTS, LEE

LESLIE, ROBERT B.
WOOLEY, JOHN [S]

LESLIE, ROCHELLE
DIAMOND, GRAHAM

LESLIE, SAN
CROOK, BETTE JEAN

LESLIE, SARAH
MCGUIRE, LESLIE SARAH

LESLIE, SCOTT
SCOTT, ALEXANDER LESLIE

LESLIE, SHANE
LESLIE, JOHN RANDOLPH

LESLIE, VAL
KNIGHTS, LESLIE DOUGLAS

LESLIE, WARD S.
WARD, ELIZABETH HONOR

LESLIE-MELVILLE, JOCK
LESLIE-MELVILLE, JOHN D.

LESMAN, B.
LESMIAN, BOLESLAW

LESOURD, CATHERINE
MARSHALL, [S] CATHERINE

LESSER, ANTHONY
WHITBY, ANTHONY CHARLES

LESSER, DERWIN
HORNIG, CHARLES D.

LESSER, MILTON
MARLOWE, STEPHEN

LESSING, BRUNO
BLOCK, RUDOLPH

LESTER, A.H.
LEHMANN, ARTHUR-HEINZ

LESTER, ANDREW
GREENHOUGH, TERENCE

LESTER, FRANK
USHER, FRANK HUGH

LESTER, FRANK B.
USHER, FRANK HUGH

LESTER, GENE
MERCER, JEAN

LESTER, IRVIN
PRATT, [MURRAY] FLETCHER

LESTER, JACK
MEYN, NIELS

LESTER, JAMES
BLAKE, LESLIE JAMES

LESTER, JANE
WALKER, EMILY KATHLEEN

LESTER, JOHN
WERNER, VIVIAN

LESTER, MARK
RUSSELL, MARTIN [JAMES]

LESTER, SAMANTHA
ROPER, LESTER

LESTER, TERI
PATTINSON, LEE
WILKES-HUNTER, RICHARD

LESTER-RANDS, A.
JUDD, FREDERICK CHARLES

LESTRANGE, PAUL
BURKE, NORA
FIRTH, NORMAN WESLEY
LAZENBY, NORMAN A.
LEWIS, CLIFFORD
THOMAS, REGINALD GEORGE

LESUEUR, DANIEL
LAPAUZE, JEANNE LOISEAU

LETHBRIDGE, OLIVE
BANBURY, OLIVE L.

LETHBRIDGE, REX
MEYERS, ROY [LETHBRIDGE]

LETROMACHE, MAENG
LEE, FRANZ JOHN T.

LETRUSCO
MARTINI, VIRGILIO

LETT, ANTHONY
TRIPP, MILES [BARTON]

LEUCHTENBERG, CARL JOHANN
DE MENDELSSOHN, PETER

LEUCI, BOB
LEUCI, ROBERT

LEUTZ, ILSE
BRAUNS-LEUTZ, ILSE

LEVADA, A.
KOSIAK, ALEKSANDR S.

LEVENAX, DAVID
BECKETT, C.E.

LEVER, J.W.
LEVER, JULIUS W.

LEVER, JAY
HEBEL, PETER

LEVER, WALTER
LEVER, JULIUS W.

LEVI, ARISTOTLE
SCHOEB, ERIKA

LEVI, ELIPHAS
CONSTANT, ALPHONSE LOUIS

LEVICKIJ, ANTON
JADVIGIN, ANTON

LEVIEN, SONYA
HOVEY, SONYA

LEVIN, EDWINA
MACDONALD, EDWINA LE VIN

LEVINE-FREIDUS, GAIL
PROVOST, GAIL LEVINE

LEVINREW, WILL
LEVINE, WILLIAM

LEVINSON, CHIP
LEVINSON, CHARLES

LEVINSON, IRENE
ZAHAVA, IRENE

LEVINSON, LEN
LEVINSON, LEONARD [L]

LEVIS
VON HOFMANNSTHAL, HUGO

LEVITINE, GEORGE
LEVITIN, GEORGE

LEVITT, I.M.
LEVITT, ISRAEL MONROE

LEVON, FRED
AYVAZIAN, L. FRED

LEVY, LORELEI
SCHWALBERG, CAROL[YN E.S]

LEVY, NORMA
RUSSELL, HANORA MARY

LEWALD, FANNY
STAHR, FANNY [LEWALD]

LEWEES, JOHN
STOCKTON, FRANCIS R.

LEWELLYN, LEW
PAINE, LAURAN BOSWORTH

LEWESDON, JOHN
DANIELL, ALBERT SCOTT

LEWIN, C.L.
BRISTER, RICHARD

LEWIS, BEN
SMOLAR, BORIS

LEWIS, C.S.
LEWIS, CLIVE STAPLES

LEWIS, CALEB
LEWIS, EDWIN HERBERT

LEWIS, CANELLA
RICHARDS, JONATHAN

LEWIS, CAROLINE
BEGBIE, [EDWARD] HAROLD
RANSOME, J. STAFFORD
TEMPLE, M.H.

LEWIS, CARSON
MILTON, JOHN R.

LEWIS, CATHERINE
ALLEN, FELICITY

LEWIS, CHARLES
DIXON, ROGER
ROWE, JOHN GABRIEL

LEWIS, CLIFFORD
FEARN, JOHN RUSSELL

LEWIS, D.B.
BIXBY, JEROME L.

LEWIS, D.B. WYNDHAM
LEWIS, DOMINIC BEVAN W.

LEWIS, DAN
LAFUENTE ESTEFANIA, M.A.

LEWIS, DAVID
PATTON, DAVID LEWIS

LEWIS, DAVID MARSHALL
COOK, MICHAEL LEWIS

LEWIS, DEBORAH
GRANT, CHARLES L.

LEWIS, ERIC
NEBEL, [LOUIS] FREDERICK

LEWIS, ERNEST
VESEY, ERNEST BLAKEMAN

LEWIS, ETHEL G.
LEWINE, ETHEL

LEWIS, FRANCINE
WEINSTOCK, HELEN

LEWIS, FREDERICK
COLLINS, FREDERICK LEWIS

LEWIS, HERSHELL G.
MURPHY, MICHAEL

LEWIS, J.R.
LEWIS, JOHN ROYSTON

LEWIS, JANET
WINTERS, JANET LEWIS

LEWIS, JERRY
LEVITCH, JOSEPH

LEWIS, JON
FORD, MARY ELIZABETH

LEWIS, JUAN
LEWIS, JOHN WOODRUFF

LEWIS, LANGE
BENYON, JANE

LEWIS, LEON
LEWIS, JULIUS WARREN

LEWIS, LUCIA Z.
ANDERSON, LUCIA LEWIS

LEWIS, MARY
LEWIS, M. CHRISTIANNA M.

LEWIS, MERVYN
FREWER, GLYN M.L.

LEWIS, PAUL
GERSON, NOEL B.

LEWIS, PETE
CROWN, PETER J.

LEWIS, PHIL
LOMAX, PHIL

LEWIS, PHYLIS
LEWIS, JACK

LEWIS, ROGER
ZARCHY, HARRY

LEWIS, ROY
LEWIS, JOHN ROYSTON

LEWIS, STEPHEN
WHITE, TERI

LEWIS, SUFORD
LEWIS, SUSAN M HEREFORD

LEWIS, SYLVAN R.
ARONSON, VIRGINIA

LEWIS, TONY
LEWIS, ANTHONY R.

LEWIS, VOLTAIRE
RITCHIE, L. EDWIN

LEWITON, MINA
SIMON, MINA LEWITON

LEWITT, S.N.
LEWITT, SHARIANN N.

LEWTAN, MEG
SPLINE, TRICIA

LEWTON, VAL
LEVENTON, VLADIMIR IVAN

LEY, BREA R.
MCCALMENT, MAEBELLE [B]

LEYKAM, CHRISTINE
KAUFMANN, CHARLOTTE

LEYNARD, MARTIN
BERGER, IVAN [B]

LEYTON, E.K.
CAMPBELL, [JOHN] RAMSEY

LEYTON, ELLIOTT [HASTNGS]
LEVSON, ELLIOT [HASTINGS]

LEYTON, SOPHIE
WALSH, SHEILA

LEZAMA, JOSE
LIMA, JOSE LEZAMA

LIBBY, BILL
LIBBY, WILLIAM B.

LICHT, HANS
BRANDT, PAUL

LICHTENAU, ERIK-ALFONS
LIPKE, ERIK-ALFONS

LICKS, H.E.
MERRIMAN, MANSFIELD

LIDDELL, C.H.
KUTTNER, HENRY
MOORE, CATHERINE LUCILLE

LIDIN, VLADIMIR GHERMANO.
GOMBERG, V.

LIE, ROMIE
LIECHTI-MOSER, ROSE-MARIE

LIEF, N.H.
BAYES, RONALD H[OMER]

LIENAU, RENATE
LERBS-LIENAU, RENATE

LIENHART, HERMANN
GERSTMAYER, HERMANN

LIEPELT, KARIN
AFZALI, KARIN

LIESENBERG, LEOPOLD
HOGHRAIN, HELMUT

LIFE, JOHN
CHADWICK, CHARLES

LIFTON, MIKE
LIFTON, WALTER MICHAEL

LIGGETT, HUNTER
PAINE, LAURAN BOSWORTH

LIGHT, CAROLINE
HYNNES, LUCETTA L.

LIGHTFOOT, D.J.
SIZEMORE, DEBORAH LIGHTF.

LIGHTNER, A.M.
HOPF, ALICE MARTHA L.

LIGHTNER, ALICE
HOPF, ALICE MARTHA L.

LIKHODEEV, LEONID I
LIDES, LEONID I

LILIENTHAL, NORA
GOTHA, LESTER L.

LILL, PETER
FRANK, PETER

LILLEY, TOM
LILLEY, THOMAS WILLIAM

LILLY, RAY
CURTIS, RICHARD [A]

LIMA, ROSE MARIE
LEE, LYDIA

LIME, HARVEY F.
LIST, HORST

LIMNELIUS, GEORGE
ROBINSON, LEWIS [GEORGE]

LIMNER, LUKE
LEIGHTON, JOHN

LIN, FRANK
ATHERTON, GERTRUDE [F]

LIN, SHAO-YANG
JOHNSTON, REGINALD FLEMNG

LINCKENS, HENDRIK P.
LINCKENS, PAUL H.

LINCOLN, E.R.
VAN HORN, DALE R.

LINCOLN, GEOFFREY
MORTIMER, JOHN [CLIFFORD]

LINCOLN, HOWARD
HARBAUGH, THOMAS C.

LINCOLN, JOHN
CARDIF, MAURICE

LINCOLN, LILLIAN
HAZARD, BARBARA

LIND, EINAR
HYDEN, NILS

LIND, HILTRUD
ARNOLD, HILDEGARD-GERTRUD

LIND, JAKOV
LANDWIRTH, HEINZ

LIND, MARIA-MADDALENA
ELLINGER, INGEBURG

LIND, PAMELA
HOOVER, SARANNE

LINDALL, EDWARD
SMITH, EDWARD ERNEST

LINDARS, BARNABUS
LINDARS, FREDERICK C.

LINDBERG, ANNE
SAPIEYEVSKI, ANNE LINDBG.

LINDBERG, MICHAEL
ARMER, KARL MICHAEL

LINDEMANN, ELSA
JUNG, ELSE

LINDEN, CHRISTA
LEPKE, FRIEDA-HERTHA

LINDEN, DEANNA
PUGH, DANA RAE

LINDEN, HANNE
FURSTENBERG, HILDE

LINDEN, INA
HEPPNER, WALTHER

LINDEN, OLIVER
ABRAHAMS, DORIS CAROLINE

LINDEN, SARA
BARTLETT, MARIE

LINDENAU, ERIK
DOLEZAL, ERICH

LINDER, D. BARRY
DUBREUIL, ELISABETH [L]

LINDER, STEVEN
KERN, STEVEN

LINDHOLM, M[EGAN]
OGDEN, MEGAN

LINDHORST, HARM
BAHRS, HANS

LINDLEY, ERICA
QUIGLEY, AILEEN

LINDLEY, GERARD
PILLEY, PHIL

LINDLEY, MEREDITH
BRUCKER, MEREDITH B.

LINDNER, D. BERRY
DUBREUIL, ELIZABETH L.

LINDNER, ELISABETH
LINSINGER, PERT

LINDNER, KARL
LINSINGER, PERT

LINDRODER, WOLFGANG
HOFFMANN-HARNISCH, WOLFG.

LINDSAY, D. BARRY
DUBREUIL, ELIZABETH L.

LINDSAY, DAVID
WALLS, IAN GASCOIGNE

LINDSAY, DEVON
HUNT, CYNTHIA WRIGHT

LINDSAY, H.
HUDSON, H. LINDSAY

LINDSAY, HARRY
HUDSON, H. LINDSAY

LINDSAY, JOHN
MURIEL, JOHN ST. CLAIR

LINDSAY, JOSEPHINE
STORY, ROSAMOND MARY

LINDSAY, KATHLEEN
FAULKNER, MARY

LINDSAY, LEE
BARRE, JEAN

LINDSAY, M.
NONHEBEL, CLARE

LINDSAY, MARK
HAHN, RONALD M.

LINDSAY, MARY
NONHEBEL, CLARE

LINDSAY, NICOLE
WOODLAND, EVA [EVE]

LINDSAY, PERRY
DERN, E. PEARL GADDIS

LINDSAY, RACHEL
LEIGH, ROBERTA

LINDSEY, DAWN
DIMICK, CHERYLLE LINDSEY

LINDSEY, TERRI
WILHELM, TERRI LYNN

LINDSTROM, ALF
LUNDHOLM, ANJA

LINE, DAVID
DAVIDSON, LIONEL

LINESMAN
GRANT, M.H.

LINGARD, J.M.
LETTENMAIR, JOSEF

LINKE, POOT
DOEBLIN, ALFRED

LINKLATER, J[OSEPH] LANE
WATKINS, ALEX

LINLEY, JULIAN
PEARSON, ALEC GEORGE

LINLEY, MARK
SAMWAYS, GEORGE R.

LINN, BILL
LINN, WILLIAM JOSEPH

LINNANKOSKI, JOHANNES
PELTONEN, JUHO VIHTORI

LINSLEY, LADD E.
SELLERS, CONNIE LESLIE

LINSON
TOMLINSON, JOSHUA LEONARD

LINTNER, GRACE
INGRAHAM, ELLEN M.

LINTON, A.H.
HOPKINS, ALPHONSO A.

LINTON, DUKE
FAWCETT, FRANK DUBREZ
FRANCES, STEPHEN D.
HANSON, VICTOR JOSEPH
LAZENBY, NORMAN A.
USHER, [JOHN] GRAY

LINUS
CHRISTIN, PIERRE

LINZ, CATHIE
BAUMGARDNER, CATHIE L.

LINZ, MARIA
PUSCH, EDITH

LIONEL, ROBERT
FANTHORPE, R.L.

LIPPINCOTT, SARA
RICHARDS, SARA LIPPINCOTT

LIPTON, DEAN
LIPSITZ, DEAN

LIPTON, MRS. LAWRENCE
RANDOLPH, GEORGIANNA ANN

LIQUORI, SAL
CRAWFORD, BETTY ANNE

LIRA, FELIPE
ALVAREZ, MIGUEL N. LIRA

LIRIO
BRUNCLAIR, VICTOR J.

LISENIUS, MICHAEL
LIESEN, HEINZ

LISKY, I.A.
FUCHS, SUMMER

LISLE, MARY
CORNISH, DORIS MARY

LISLE, MICHAEL
WILLIS, ERNEST LISTER H.

LISLE, SEWARD D.
ELLIS, EDWARD S.

LISSAR, FRANK
LIPP, WOLFGANG

LISTER, PAUL
MADSEN, BORGE

LISTER, RICHARD
WORSLEY, T.C.

LISTON, B.E.
LIVINGSTONE, BERKELEY

LISTON, E.J.
LIVINGSTON, BERKELEY

LISTON, JACK
MALONEY, RALPH LISTON

LITCHFIELD, FRANK JOHNSON
BOSWORTH, ALLAN R.
FARRELL, A. CLIFFORD

LITE, JAMS
SCHNECK, STEPHEN

LITTLE BOBBIE
FAUST, FREDERICK S.

LITTLE, A. EDWARD
KLEIN, AARON E.

LITTLE, BYRD
LOMAX, E. VICTORIA

LITTLE, CONYTH
LITTLE, CONSTANCE/GWENYTH

LITTLE, FRANCES
MACAULAY, FANNIE CALDWELL

LITTLE, KENNETH
SCOTLAND, JAMES

LITTLE, PAUL HUGO
LITWINSKI, PAUL H.

LITTLE, PAULA
LITTLE, PAUL HUGO

LITTLE, SYLVIA
LEYLAND, ERIC

LITTLEBOY, SHEILA M.
ARY, SHEILA M.L.

LITTLEFIELD, HAZEL
SMITH, HAZEL G. LITTFIELD

LITTLEJOHN, JON R.
KLEINHOUSE, THEODORE JOHN

LITTLEWIT, HUMPHREY
LOVECRAFT, H[OWARD] P.

LITTLEWOOD, S.R.
LITTLEWOOD, SAMUEL ROB.

LITWOS
SIENKIEWICZ, HENRYK

LIU NGO
LIU E.

LIU T'IEH-YUN
LIU E.

LIU, YONG
LIU, WILLIAM T.

LIUTOV, KIRIL
BABEL, ISAAC E.

LIVELY, WALTER
ELLIOTT, BRUCE W.

LIVERMORE, OSCAR K.
GRUBER, FRANK

LIVIA, ANNA
BRAWN, ANNA LIVIA JULIAN

LIVINGSTON, GRACE
HILL, GRACE [LIVINGSTON]

LIVINGSTON, JACK
NUSSER, JAMES L.

LIVINGSTON, KENNETH
STEWART, KENNETH LIVINGST

LIVINGSTON, M. JAY
LIVINGSTON, MYRAN JABEZ

LIVINGSTON-MATTHEWS, ASEN
LESHER, PHYLLIS

LIVINGSTONE, MARGARET
FLYNN, MARY

LIVINGSTONE, MARK J.
PELLA, JUDITH
PHILLIPS, MICHAEL J.

LIZASO, FELIX
LIZASO Y GONZALES, FELIX

LJUNG, TOM
LOFGREN, EMANUEL

LLEWELLYN, CAROLINE
CHAMPLIN, CAROLINE L.

LLEWELLYN, EDWARD
LLEWELLYN-THOMAS, EDWARD

LLEWELLYN, RICHARD
LLOYD, RICHARD DAVID V.L.

LLEWELYN, T. HARCOURT
HAMILTON, CHARLES H.S.

LLEWMYS, WESTON
POUND, EZRA LOOMIS

LLEYON, GUTTO
JONES, GRIFFITH ROBERT

LLOYD OF HAMPSTEAD, BARON
LLOYD, DENNIS

LLOYD, CHARLES
BIRKIN, CHARLES L.

LLOYD, E. JAMES
JAMES, ELIZABETH

LLOYD, HERBERT
FEARN, JOHN RUSSELL

LLOYD, JAMES
JAMES, ELIZABETH

LLOYD, JANE
ROBERTS, JOHN S[TORM]

LLOYD, JOHN
COOPER, JOHN

LLOYD, JOSEPH M.
PURVES, FREDERICK

LLOYD, LEVANAH
PETERS, MAUREEN

LLOYD, MARTA
BUCKHOLDER, MARTA

LLOYD, NIGEL
TUBB, E.C.

LLOYD, ROBERT
TUBB, E.C.

LLOYD, RONALD
FRIEDLAND, RONALD LLOYD

LLOYD, STEPHANIE
GOLDING, MORTON JAY

LLOYD, WALLACE
ALGIE, JAMES

LLOYD, WILLSON
DENNISON, ENID

LO MEDICO, BRIAN T.
MONTELEONE, THOMAS F.

LOBEL, BRUNI
HAGEN, BRUNHILDE MELITTA

LOBSANG, T. RAMPA
HOSKIN, CYRIL HENRY

LOBSTER, RIF H.
SCHIER, NORMA

LOCHARD, DOC
LOCHARD, METZ T.P.

LOCHLONS, COLIN
JACKSON, CAARY PAUL

LOCHTE, DICK
LOCHTE, RICHARD S.

LOCK, THOMAS
LAND, GEORGE THOMAS LOCK

LOCKE, CLINTON W.
STRATEMEYER, EDWARD

LOCKE, JOSEPH
GARTON, RAY

LOCKE, MARTIN
DUNCAN, W. MURDOCH

LOCKE, PETER
MCCUTCHAN, JOHN WILSON

LOCKE, W.J.
LOCKE, WILLIAM JOHN

LOCKE, WILLIAM J.
LOCKE, WILLIAM JOHN

LOCKHARD, LEONARD
HARNESS, CHARLES [L]
THOMAS, THEODORE L.

LOCKHART, JOHN
BIERACH, ALFRED

LOCKHART, LYNN
JORDAN, MARILYN

LOCKHART, MAX
MEREDITH, DORIS R.

LOCKHART, T.C.
STAMMEL, HEINZ-JOSEF

LOCKRIDGE, NORMAN
ROTH, SAMUEL

LOCKWOOD, KAREN
FINNIGAN, KAREN

LOCKWOOD, MARY
SPELMAN, MARY

LOCKWOOD, THOMAS
BRANDHORST, ANDREAS

LODE, REX
BOYLAND, BOYD
GOLDSTEIN, WILLIAM ISAAC

LODER, VERNON
VAHEY, JOHN G. HAZLETTE

LODEWYK
MULDER, LODEWIJK

LODGE, JOHN
LEYLAND, ERIC

LODGE, MAUREEN ROFFEY
ROFFEY, MAUREEN

LODGER, THE
IVESTER, LLOYD J.

LOEWEN, ROBERT
KALMUCZAK, ROLF

LOEWENGARD, HEIDI H.H.
FREYBE, HEIDI HUBERTA

LOEWENTHAL, KAREN
TRIPP, KATHLEEN

LOFTY
ISAACS, MARCEL GODFREY

LOGAN, AGNES
ADAMS, AGNES

LOGAN, ANNE
COLLEY, BARBARA

LOGAN, BENNY
LAZENBY, NORMAN A.

LOGAN, BRYN
KELLY, HAROLD ERNEST

LOGAN, CAIT
KLEINSASSER-TESTERMAN, L.

LOGAN, DAISY
ORWIG, SARA

LOGAN, DAN
LYNCH, W.

LOGAN, DON
CRAWFORD, WILLIAM [E]

LOGAN, FORD
NEWTON, DWIGHT BENNETT

LOGAN, FRANK
GALLARDOS MUNOZ, JUAN

LOGAN, JACK
HARTSCH, GERHART

LOGAN, JAKE
BAVOUSETT, GLEN B[YRON]
BICKHAM, JACK [JOHN M.]
EDMONDSON Y COTTON, JOSE
KNOTT, WILLIAM CECIL JR.
KREPPS, ROBERT WILSON
MCCAIG, DONALD
MILAN, VICTOR [WOODWARD]
PERHSON, HOWARD
RIEFE, ALAN
RIFKIN, SHEPARD
SMITH, MARTIN WILLIAM
VARDEMAN, ROBERT E.

LOGAN, JESSICA
FOSTER, LAWRENC & PAULINE

LOGAN, KRISTINA
FREETHY, BARBARA

LOGAN, LEANDRA
SCHULTZ, MARY

LOGAN, MARK
NICOLE, CHRISTOPHER ROBIN

LOGAN, MATT
WHITEHEAD, DAVID [HENRY]

LOGAN, SARA
HAYDON, JUNE
SIMPSON, JUDITH [JUDY]

LOGAN, WILLIAM
HARRIS, LAURENCE MARK

LOGROLLER
LE GALLIENNE, RICHARD

LOHDE, CLARISSA
BOTTICHER, CLARISSA [L]

LOHRMAN, PAUL
FAIRMAN, PAUL W.
SHAVER, RICHARD S.

LOIKAJA, THOMAS
SCHATTSCHNEIDER, PETER

LOIS, JOHN
KORSELL, JOHN

LOM, JOSEPHINE
LOMNICKA, JOSEPHINE

LOMAN, ERIC
MOOLMAN, VALERIE

LOMAS, FRANK T.
TUBB, E.C.

LOMAS, STEVE
BRENNAN, JOSEPH [LOMAS]

LOMAX, BLISS
DRAGO, HARRY SINCLAIR

LOMAX, JEFF
MASON, SYDNEY CHARLES

LOMBARD, HELEN
VISHER, HELEN [C] CARUSI

LOMBARD, NAP
JOHNSON, PAMELA HANSFORD
STEWART, NEIL

LOMBARDI, CYNTHIA
LOMBARDI, GEORGINA M.

LOMBART, CHRISTIAN
LLOP SELLARES, JUAN

LOME, MIKE
PINKWATER, DANIEL MANUS

LOMOSIA, ANDREW
STERN, JAY B[ENJAMIN]

LONDON, ANNE
GORDON, ROBERT I.
MILLER, ANN

LONDON, CAIT
KLEINSASSER-TESTERMAN, L.

LONDON, HILARY
SAWYER, JOHN & NANCY

LONDON, JACK
CHANEY, WILLIAM HENRY
FISH, ROBERT L.
LONDON, JOHN GRIFFITH

LONDON, JANE
GEIS, DARLENE STERN

LONDON, JOHN GRIFFITH
CHANEY, JOHN GRIFFITH

LONDON, LAURA
CURTIS, SHARON & THOMAS

LONDON, LISA
MARTIN, GLORIA ANN

LONDON, ROBERT
GORDON, ROBERT I.

LONDON, R[USTY] KENT
LOBSENZ, IRVING LOUIS

LONDONER
BARRON, OSWALD

LONG, ANN MARIE
JENSEN, PAULINE MARIE

LONG, ELLIOTT
BENNETT, REGINALD G.S.

LONG, EMMETT
LEONARD, ELMORE

LONG, GERRY
LARKINS, WILLIAM F.

LONG, HELEN BEECHER
STRATEMEYER, EDWARD

LONG, JOY
SALMONSON, JESSICA A.

LONG, JUDY
LONG, JUDITH ELAINE

LONG, KARAWYNN
HENRY, KAREN RAYE

LONG, LUCILE
BRANDT, LUCILE [L.S.]

LONG, LYDA BELNAP
LONG, FRANK BELKNAP

LONG, MYLES
FLANAGAN, JAMES

LONG, NAOMI CORNELIA
MADGETT, NAOMI LONG

LONG, PETER
FOWLER, EUGENE DEVLAN
HECHT, BEN

LONG, SHIRLEY
LONG, LEONARD

LONG, WESLEY
SMITH, GEORGE O.

LONG, WILLIAM STUART
STUART, VIOLET VIVIAN F.

LONGBAUGH, HARRY
GOLDMAN, WILLIAM

LONGBEARD, FREDERICK
LONGYEAR, BARRY B[ROOKES]

LONGDON, GEORGE
RAYER, FRANCIS G.

LONGFIELD, JO
HOWARD, FELICITY

LONGFORD, LINDSAY
MOREL, JIMMIE L.

LONGLEY, JOHN
DENTON, JOHN

LONGLEY, W.B.
RANDISI, ROBERT J.

LONGMAN, IRWIN
LOCKWOOD, INGERSOLL

LONGMAN, MARLENE
SILVERBERG, ROBERT

LONGSWORD, JOHN
LONG, JOHN FREDERICK LAW.

LONGWAY, A. HUGE
LANG, ANDREW

LONSDALE, FREDERICK
LEONARD, LIONEL FREDERICK

LONSDALE, JERRY
DONGES, GUNTER

LOOG, BUSTER
AARONS, EDWARD S.
CUSHMAN, DAN

LOOKER, O.N.
URNER, NATHAN DANE

LOOKOUT
NOBLE, JOHN [A]

LOOMIS, RAE
STEGER, SHELBY

LOONIE, JANICE HAYS
HAYS, JANICE NICHOLSON

LOOS, IRMA
HAIN, IRMA

LOOSLEY, WILLIAM ROBERT
LANGFORD, DAVID [ROWLAND]

LOOTHMANN, HARRO
HEYCK, HANS

LOPATE, CAROL
ASCHER, CAROL

LOPEZ, HANK
LOPEZ, ENRIQUE

LORA, JOSEPHINE
ALEXANDER, JOSEPHINE

LORAC, E.C.R.
RIVETT, EDITH CAROLINE

LORAINE, PHILIP
ESTRIDGE, ROBIN

LORAN, MARTIN
BAXTER, JOHN
SMITH, RON

LORCA, FREDERIC H.
LIST, HORST

LORD ASTOR OF HEVER
ASTOR, GAVIN

LORD COMMISSIONER
MCCOY, JOHN

LORD GILHOOLEY
SEYMOUR, FREDERICK HENRI

LORD PRIME
REYNOLDS, WALTER DOTY

LORD, ALEXANDRA
SEIBERT, CATHERINE
WILLIAMS, PATRICIA A.

LORD, ALISON
ELLIS, JULIE M.

LORD, DOUGLAS
COOPER, DOUGLAS
LORD, DOREEN MILDRED

LORD, GARLAND
GARLAND, [MARY] ISABEL
LORD, MINDRET

LORD, GLENN
KREBS, ALFRED

LORD, GORDON
TREAT, LAWRENCE

LORD, JEFFREY
ELLIS, JULIE M.
ENGEL, LYLE KENYON
GREEN, ROLAND [JAMES]
NELSON, RADELL FARADAY
STOKES, MANNING LEE

LORD, JEREMY
REDMAN, BEN RAY

LORD, LONNIE
HAYDOCK, RON

LORD, MOIRA
LYNCH, MIRIAM

LORD, NANCY
TITUS, EVE

LORD, SHELDON
BLOCK, LAWRENCE
DRESNER, HAL
PERICHITCH, MILO

LORD, SHIRLEY
ANDERSON, SHIRLEY LORD

LORD, VIVIAN
STROTHER, PAT WALLACE

LORE, ELANA
SULLIVAN, ELEANOR

LORE, PHILIPS
SMITH, TERENCE LORE

LOREL, CLAIRE
DE JONG, DAPHNE

LOREL, PHIL
DE PIETRO, ALBERT

LORENS, M.K.
KEILSTRUP, MARGARET

LORENZ, FREDERICK
HELLER, LORENZ

LORENZ, MICHAEL
HAUSCHILD, REINHARD

LORENZ, SARAH E.
WINSTON, SARAH

LORETTA, JOSCHI
REUTER, RALPH

LORIMER, ADAM
WATSON, WILLIAM LORIMER

LORIN, AMII
HOHL, JOAN M.R.

LORINER
WILLIAMS, DORIAN

LORING, ANDREW
LATHROP, LORIN ANDREW

LORING, J.M.
CROZETTI, RUTH G.W.L.

LORING, JENNY
SANS, MARTHA

LORING, JULES
MACKAYE, DAVID & JULIA

LORING, PETER
SHELLABARGER, SAMUEL

LORIOT
VON BULOW, VICCO

LORIS
VON HOFMANNSTHAL, HUGO

LORM, HIERONYMUS
LANDESMANN, HEINRICH

LORNA
STODDARD, JANE T.

LORNE, CHARLES
BRAND, CHARLES NEVILLE

LORNE, DAVID
HOOF, DAVID L.

LORNING, RAY
BRALY, MALCOLM

LORNQUEST, OLAF
RIPS, ERVIN M.

LORRAINE, ALDEN
ACKERMAN, FORREST J.

LORRAINE, ANNE
ALAN, JANE
CHISHOLM, LILLIAN MARY

LORRAINE, JEAN
DUVAL, MARTIN PAUL A.

LORRAINE, LILITH
WRIGHT, MARY MAUDE

LORRAINE, MARIAN
HORTON, MARIAN L.

LORRAINE, PAUL
BIRD, WILLIAM H.F.
FEARN, JOHN RUSSELL
GLASBY, JOHN S.
ROBERTS, ARTHUR O.

LORRIMER, CLAIRE
CLARK, PATRICIA D.R.

LOS, GEORGE
AMABILE, GEORGE

LOSSIUS, ROBERT
JUHLING, JOH.

LOT, PARSON
KINGSLEY, CHARLES

LOTHAR, ERNST
MULLER, ERNST LOTHAR

LOTHAR, FRANK M.
FRANK, LOTHAR-MATHIAS

LOTHROP, AMY
WARNER, ANNA BARTLETT

LOTI, PIERRE
VIAUD, LOUIS MARIE

LOTT, NOAH
HOBART, GEORGE VERE

LOTT, S. MAKEPEACE
MAKEPEACE-LOTT, STANLEY

LOTTING, EVA
COHN, ELSE

LOTTMAN, EILEEN
WILLIS, MAUDE

LOU
LEATHAM, LOUIS S.

LOUIS
HUMBERT-DROZ, JULES

LOUIS, CARLA
HESPOS, LISELOTTE

LOUIS, FATHER M.
MERTON, THOMAS JAMES

LOUIS, JACQUELINE
HACSI, JACQUELINE

LOUIS, JEAN
KEROUAC, JEAN-LOUIS L.D.

LOUIS, PAT
FRANCIS, DOROTHY BRENNER

LOUISBURGH, SHEILA BURNFD
BURNFORD, SHEILA [P.C]

LOUISE, HEIDI
EDRICH, LOUISE & HEIDI

LOURIE, HELEN
STORR, CATHERINE [COLE]

LOUVIER, PIERRE
LUCAS, GERALD

LOUVIGNY, ANDRE
RUELLAN, ANDRE

LOUYS, PIERRE
LOUIS, PIERRE

LOVAN, THEA
KING, CHRISTINE

LOVE, ARTHUR
LIEBERS, ARTHUR

LOVE, CHARLES K.
SWICEGOOD, THOMAS L.P.

LOVE, DAVID
LASKY, JESSE LOUIS JR.

LOVE, E.M.
HOLT, ELIZABETH

LOVECHURCH, LEONARD
SMITH, GEORGE

LOVECRAFT, H.P.
LOVECRAFT, H[OWARD] P.

LOVECRAFT, LINDA
PARRY, MICHEL P.

LOVEGOOD, JOHN
GRANT, WATSON
WATSON, ELLIOT GRANT

LOVEGROVE, PETER
RAY, JOHN PHILIP

LOVEGROVE, PHILIP
RAY, JOHN PHILIP

LOVEHILL, C.B.
BEAUMONT, CHARLES

LOVELACE, JANE
MCKEONE, DIXIE

LOVELACE, LINDA
BOREMAN, LINDA

LOVELL, ARTHUR
LOVELL-WILLIAMS, DAVID A.

LOVELL, INGRAHAM
BACON, JOSEPHINE D.

LOVELL, MARC
MCSHANE, MARK

LOVELL, MARK
TOLLEMACHE, DAVID

LOVEQUIST, GWENDOLYNN
STAFFORD, LINDA

LOVESMITH, JANET
FAIRMAN, PAUL W.

LOVITT, WILL U.
LEVESQUE, PAUL

LOW, DOROTHY MACKIE
LOW, LOIS DOROTHEA

LOW, GARDNER
RODDA, [P] CHARLES

LOW, HANNES
TRALOW, JOHANNES

LOW, IVY
LITVINOV, IVY

LOW, LOIS
MCCORQUODALE, BARBARA H.C

LOW, RACHAEL
WHEAR, [DR.] RACHAEL

LOWAM, RON
TUBB, E.C.

LOWE, ALFONSO
LOEWENTHAL, LEONARD J.A.

LOWE, EDITH
KOVAR, EDITH MAE

LOWE, JAY JR
LOPER, JOHN JOSEPH

LOWE, KENNETH
LOBAUGH, ELMA K.

LOWE, MARJORIE G.
LOWE, MARJORIE GRIFFITHS

LOWE, SUSAN L.
LOWE, SUSAN [CLAIRE] L.

LOWE, VICTORIA LINCOLN
LINCOLN, VICTORIA

LOWE-PORTER, H.T.
LOWE, HELEN PORTER

LOWELL, ANNE HUNTER
BOIES, JANICE

LOWELL, ELAINE
COVERT, ALICE LENT

LOWELL, ELIZABETH
MAXWELL, ANN & EVAN

LOWELL, J.R.
LOWELL, JAN & ROBERT

LOWENBRUCK, OLIVER
SCHOW, DAVID J.

LOWENZAHN, LEO
HAGN, HUGO

LOWERY, LYNN
HAHN, [MONA] LYNN L.

LOWING, ANNE
GEACH, CHRISTINE

LOWITT, E.L.
ELLIOTT, WILLIAM J.

LOWNDES, DOC
LOWNDES, ROBERT A.W.

LOWNDES, GEOFFREY
HIRSHMAN, JACK

LOWNDES, GEORGE
DAWSON, WILLIAM HENRY

LOWNDES, R.A.W.
LOWNDES, ROBERT A.W.

LOWNDES, R.W.
LOWNDES, ROBERT A.W.

LOWNDES, SUSAN
MARQUES, SUSAN LOWNDES

LOWO, HANS
LINDEN, ERIK HUGO E.

LOWRY, NAN
MACLEOD, RUTH

LOXLEY, RAYMOND
MURRAY, C. GEOFFREY

LOXSMITH, JOHN
BRUNNER, JOHN [K.H.]

LOXTON, [CHARLES] HOWARD
LOXSTON, [CHARLES] HOWARD

LOY, DIANA
COHEN, RHODA

LOY, MINA
LOWRY, MINA GERTRUDE

LOYD, NORMAN
GROSSMANN, HANS HUGO

LOYSON-BRIDET
SCHWARTZ, [MAYER] MARCEL

LRE
EISENHOWER, LEROY R.

LU, K'UAN-YU
LUK, CHARLES

LU-CH'IAO
WU, NELSON I.

LUARD, L.
LUARD, WILLIAM BLAINE

LUBER, JET
MEULENBELT-LUBER, HENRIET

LUBINGER, EVA
MIESS, EVA

LUBON, W.
LOZINSKI, WLADYSLAW

LUCAS, BARBARA
WALL, BARBARA

LUCAS, CURTIS
URELL, WILLIAM FRANCIS

LUCAS, E.V.
LUCAS, E[DWARD] V[ERRALL]

LUCAS, EMILY BEATRIX C.
JONES, EMILY BEATRIX C.

LUCAS, F.L.
LUCAS, FRANK LAWRENCE

LUCAS, GEORGE
FOSTER, ALAN DEAN

LUCAS, J.K.
PAINE, LAURAN BOSWORTH

LUCAS, MAYO
LUCAS, MARY M.

LUCAS, ROBERT
EHRENZWEIG, ROBERT

LUCAS, VICTORIA
PLATH, SYLVIA

LUCCHESI, ALDO
VON BLOCK, BELA [W]

LUCERO, ROBERTO
MEREDITH, ROBERT C.

LUCIFER
MICHAELIS, PAUL

LUCIO
PHILLIPS, GORDON

LUCKLESS, JOHN
BURKHOLTZ, HERBERT
IRVING, CLIFFORD MICHAEL

LUCRECE
DANIELS, CORALIN

LUCULLUS
BENNIS, WESSEL JOHANNES

LUDLOW, GEOFFREY
MEYNELL, LAURENCE WALTER

LUDLOW, GEORGE
KAY, ERNEST

LUDLOW, IAN
GOLDBERG, LEE
PERDUE, LEWIS

LUDLOW, JOHN
PALMER, CECIL

LUDLOW, JOHNNY
WOOD, ELLEN PRICE

LUDLUM, MABEL CLELAND
WIDDEMER, MABEL CLELAND

LUDOVICI, L.J.
LUDOVICI, LORENZ JAMES

LUDWELL, BERNICE
STOKES, MANNING LEE

LUDWIG, EMIL
COHN, EMIL

LUELLEN, VALENTINA
POLLEY, JUDITH ANNA

LUENN, NANCY
JONES, NANCY E.

LUERSSEN, MARGARETHE
BOHLEN & HALBACH, HERTHY

LUGAR, HANS
BLAIR, JOHN
FARRELL, JOHNNY
MAX, GEORGE
PATERSON, A.J. BLAIR
QUINN, SEABURY

LUGAR, KEITH
OLIVEROS TOVAR, MIGUEL

LUGMAN, ABDULLAH
SWAFFORD, JOHNNY C.

LUGO, J. PEREZ
CABANAS, JOAQUIN R.

LUHAN, MABLE DODGE
LUHAN, MABLE GANSON

LUIGI
PELLETIER, ALEXIS

LUIGI, BELLI
BLEECK, G.C.

LUIMARDEL
MARTINEZ-DELGADO, LUIS

LUK, CHARLES
LU KUAN YU

LUK-OIE, OLE
SWINTON, ERNEST DUNLOP

LUKAS, MANFRED
KLAUS, MICHAEL

LUKE, THOMAS
MASTERTON, GRAHAM

LUKENS, ADAM
DE REYNA, DIANE DETZER

LULL, SUSAN
FORWARD, ROBERT L[ULL]

LUM, PETER
CROWE, [BETTINA] LUM

LUMAS, GORDON C.
LLIRO OLIVE, JOSE MARIA

LUMBERJACK
LAMBERT, T.H.

LUMINUS
MELLING, LEONARD

LUMLEY, BOB
MOORCOCK, MICHAEL

LUMLEY, R.
MOORCOCK, MICHAEL

LUMLEY, ROBERT
MOORCOCK, MICHAEL

LUMLEY, ROBERT S.
MOORCOCK, MICHAEL

LUMPP, JAMES W.
LAMPP, JAMES W.

LUNA, KRIS
O'BRIEN, DAVID WRIGHT

LUNA, KRIS [CHRIS]
BIRD, WILLIAM H.F.

LUNAR, DENIS
MUNGO, RAYMOND

LUNATIC, SIR HUMPHREY
GENTLEMAN, FRANCIS

LUNCHBASKET, ROGER
REEVE-JONES, ALAN EDMUND

LUND, JAMES
STONEHOUSE, JOHN [T]

LUNDBERG, KAI
POTTHOFF, MARGOT MARIA

LUNDY, MIKE
BAIN, DONALD
KELLY, TOM

LUNG, CHANG
RIGNEY, JAMES OLIVER JR.

LUNT, LOIS
METZ, LOIS LUNT

LUNTZ, HEINRICH
MAXIMOVIC, GERD

LUPIN, ARSENE
BOILEAU, PIERRE
NARCEJAC, THOMAS

LUPOFF, DICK
LUPOFF, RICHARD A.

LURGAN, LESTER
KNOWLES, MABEL WINIFRED

LURIE, ALLISON
BISHOP, ALLISON

LUSIN
SHU-JEN, CHOU

LUSKA, SIDNEY
HARLAND, HENRY

LUSSNIGG, MARIA
MULLER, MARIA

LUTETIUS
STEARNS, HAROLD EDMUND

LUTHER, MARTIN
LEY, ARTHUR GORDON
LEY, ROBERT ARTHUR

LUTHER, RAY
LEY, ARTHUR GORDON

LUTHER, RENATE K.
KRAACK, RENATE

LUTZ, ADRON
GOOCK, ROLAND

LUTZ, HARRO
LUDWIG, HELMUT

LUX
JONES, LUCY M.

LUX, HARRY
DERFOLDY-LUX, WILHELM

LYALL, DAVID
MATHEWS, ELLEN B.
REEVES, HELEN BUCKINGHAM
SWANN, ANNIE S.

LYALL, EDNA
BAYLY, ADA ELLEN

LYASKO, NIKOLAY
LYASHCHENKO, NIKOLAY NIK.

LYCURGUS, SOLON
CLEMENS, SAMUEL LANGHORNE

LYDECKER, J.J.
COLTMAN-ALLEN, V. ERNEST

LYDECKER, JOHN
GALLAGHER, STEPHEN

LYFICK, WARREN
REEVES, LAWRENCE F.

LYKKE, ANNE
MEYN, NIELS

LYKKE, TILL
ALBERT, MAX

LYKOFF, PIERRE
RITTER, WOLFPETER

LYMINGTON, JOHN
CHANCE, JOHN NEWTON

LYNAES, KAI
MEYN, NIELS

LYNAM, SHAWN
LYNAM, JOAN

LYNCH, BRIAN
LIDDY, JAMES [D.R.]

LYNCH, DAN
LIPSKY, ELEASAR
SILVERBERG, ROBERT

LYNCH, DAVIS
BIOY-CASARES, ADOLFO
BORGES, JORGE LUIS

LYNCH, ERIC
BINGLEY, DAVID ERNEST

LYNCH, FRANCES
COMPTON, DAVID GUY

LYNCH, GREY
DORWORTH, ALICE GREY

LYNCH, JAMES
ANDREYEV, LEONID N.

LYNCH, LAWRENCE L.
VAN DEVENTER, EMMA MURD.

LYNCH, M.C.
WALLACE, MARY

LYNCH, MIRIAM
WALLACE, MARY

LYNCH, MIRIAM C.
WALLACE, MARY

LYNCH, WILLIAM
THOMAS, EUGENE

LYNDALE, SYDNEY M.
MOORHOUSE, SYDNEY

LYNDE, H.H.
HUNTINGTON, HELEN

LYNDELL, CATHERINE
BALL, MARGARET

LYNDON, AMY
RADFORD, RICHARD F.

LYNDON, BARRE
EDGAR, ALFRED

LYNDON, DIANA
ANTONIO, DIANE

LYNGSETH, JOAN
DAVIES, JOAN HOWARD

LYNK, WARDER
BOWMAN, GERALD [MOORE]

LYNLEY, ELINOR
LINSLEY, JUDITH
RIENSTRA, ELLEN

LYNN, ANN
HARLOW, NANCY
PARADISO, KAREN

LYNN, BARBARA
MACKINNON, CHARLES ROY

LYNN, BECKY
ZAWADSKY, PATIENCE

LYNN, CAROL
GOETCHEUS, CAROLYN

LYNN, ESCOTT
LAWRENCE, CHRISTOPHER G.H

LYNN, FRANK
LEISY, JAMES FRANKLIN

LYNN, GODWARD
HARZER, KARL

LYNN, IRENE
ROWLAND, DONALD S.

LYNN, KAREN
MAXFIELD, KAREN
TAYLOR, LYNN

LYNN, LESLIE
BODINE, SHERRILL
SIMA, ELAINE

LYNN, MARGARET
BATTYE, GLADYS STARKEY

LYNN, MARY
BROKAMP, MARILYN

LYNN, MAX
ANDERSON, G.J.B.

LYNN, PATRICIA
WATTS, MABEL PIZZEY

LYNN, ROBIN
LATHAM, ROBIN

LYNN, SHERYL
MANUS, JAYE W.

LYNN, STEPHEN
BRADBURY, PARNELL

LYNN, TERRI
WILHELM, TERRI LYNN

LYNN, VIRGINIA
BIANCHI, VIRGINIA BROWN

LYNNETTE
BRADLEY, LURA LYNNETTE

LYNRVN, N.S.
LYNRAVN, NORMAN SOREN

LYNSON, JAN
SMITH, LYNNE A.

LYNSON, JANE
SMITH, LYNNE A.

LYNTON, ANN
RAYNER, CLAIRE B.

LYNX
FAIRFIELD, CECILY ISABEL

LYNX, LARRY
LOTINGA, W.

LYON, BUCK
PAINE, LAURAN BOSWORTH

LYON, ELINOR
WRIGHT, ELINOR BRUCE

LYON, JESSICA
DE LEEUW, CATEAU W.

LYON, JOHN
BURNS, JIM
DEAN, MARTYN
EVANS, CHRIS[TOPHER D.]

LYON, KATHERINE
MIX, KATHERINE LYON

LYON, LYMAN R.
DE CAMP, L[YON] SPRAGUE

LYON, MARJORIE
MEREDYTH-STORMER, MARJORY

LYON, WINSTON
WOOLFOLK, WILLIAM

LYONS, DELPHINE C.
SMITH, EVELYN E.

LYONS, ELENA
FAIRBURN, ELEANOR

LYONS, J.B.
LYONS, JOHN BENIGNUS

LYONS, JAMES
LOEWEN, JAMES W.

LYONS, LEILA
CONAWAY, JAMES C.

LYONS, MARCUS
BLISH, JAMES B.

LYONS, SOPHIE
BURKE, SOPHIE VAN E.L.

LYRE, PINCHBECK
SASSOON, SIEGFRIED [L]

LYS, CHRISTIAN
BREBNER, PERCY [JAMES]

LYSING, HENRY
NANOVIC, JOHN L.

LYSSAC, LISA
LISSACK, LISA

LYTE, RICHARD
WHELPTON, [GEORGE] ERIC

LYTTON, EDWARD
MORRIS, CHARLES [S]

LYTTON, JANE
CLARKE, PERCY A.

LYTTON, LORD
BULWER-LYTTON, EDWARD G.

M'CRIB, THEOPHILUS
LEE, HENRY BOYLE

M'GOVAN, JAMES
HONEYMAN, WILLIAM C.

M'GROOM, HECTOR
NORWOOD, VICTOR [G.C.]

M'INTOSH, J.T.
MACGREGOR, JAMES MURDOCH

M'QUADE, TEX
BOYCE, DAVID

PSEUDONYMS

M.
MILNER, ALFRED VISCT.

M., A.
MURDOCH, JAMES

M., C.E.
MARTIN, CHARLES E.

M.A.C.
CURSHAM, MARY ANN

M.B.
FAUST, FREDERICK S.

M.E.B.
MAXWELL, MARY ELIZABETH B

M.E.R.
ROTHMANN, MARIA ELIZABETH

M.E.S.
SEARLE, M.E.

M.H.S.
SPIELMANN, MARION H.A.

M.M.D.
DODGE, MARY ELIZABETH M.

M.P.
BIELECKI, CZESLAW

M.R.J.
JAMES, MONTAGUE RHODES

M.T.C.W.
HERR, MICHAEL

M.T.F.
PORTER, CALLIE RUSSELL

M.W.
WILSON, MILES

MAARTENS, MAARTEN
SCHWARTZ, JOOST VAN DER P

MABLE, PETER
WIEDENBECK, EMILIE AGNES

MAC
MACMANUS, SEUMAS
MCCANCE, JAMES LAW

MAC A'GHOBHAINN, IAIN
SMITH, IAIN CRICHTON

MAC A'GHOBHAINN, SEAMUS
SMITH, IAIN CRICHTON

MAC A'GHREIDHIR, G.
GRIEVE, CHRIST. MURRAY

MAC AN BHARD, SENGHAN
WARD, JOHN C.

MAC FEE, MAXWELL
RENNIE, JAMES ALAN

MAC GAN, WALL
LLOP SELLARES, JUAN

MAC ORLAN, PIERRE
DUMARCHAIS, PIERRE

MAC-TU, HAN
TRONG-TRI, NGUYA

MACADAM, EVE
LESLIE, CECILE

MACADAM, IAN
ADAMSON, IAIAN BEATON

MACADAMS, TOBIN
CREWS, JUDSON [C]

MACALAN, PETER
ELLIS, PETER BERRESFORD

MACALLAN, ANDREW
LEASOR, THOMAS JAMES

MACALPIN, RORY
MACKINNON, CHARLES ROY

MACANDREW, RENNIE
ELLIOT, ANDREW GEORGE

MACAO, MARSHALL
MEARES, LEONARD F.
TULEJA, THADDEUS V.F.

MACAODHAGON, EAMON
EGAN, EDWARD WELSTEAD

MACAPP, C.C.
CAPPS, CARROLL M.

MACARTHUR, BURKE
BURKS, ARTHUR J.

MACAULAY, CLARENDON
ADAMS, WALTER MARSHAM

MACAULEY, DOUGLAS
BRADLEY, W.H.

MACAW
HANNAYS, KITTY

MACBETH, KEN
MOORCOCK, MICHAEL

MACBRIAN, JAMES
CURTIS, RICHARD [A]
FOLEY, DAVE

MACBRIDE, MELCHIOR
QUINTON, JOHN P.

MACCALL, ISABEL
BOYD, ELIZABETH

MACCALL, LIBBY
MACHOL, LIBBY

MACCARGO, J.T.
RABE, PETER

MACCOLLA, FIONN
MACDONALD, THOMAS DOUGL.

MACCONNELL, COLUM
ROSSEN, STEVE
SMITH, MITCHELL

MACCREIGH, JAMES
POHL, FREDERIK

MACDANIEL, CHARLES
GARRISON, CHARLES M.

MACDIARMID, HUGH
GRIEVE, CHRIST. MURRAY

MACDONALD, AENEAS
THOMSON, GEORGE MALCOLM

MACDONALD, ANDREW
PIERCE, WILLIAM LUTHER

MACDONALD, ANSON
HEINLEIN, ROBERT A.

MACDONALD, BLACKIE
EMRICH, DUNCAN [B.M.]

MACDONALD, ERIC
ALLAN, F. CARNEY

MACDONALD, FRANK
NUETZEL, CHARLES A.

MACDONALD, FRED
NUETZEL, CHARLES A.

MACDONALD, FREDA
NUETZEL, CHARLES A.

MACDONALD, GOLDEN
BROWN, MARGARET WISE

MACDONALD, JOHN
MILLAR, KENNETH

MACDONALD, JOHN R.
MILLAR, KENNETH

MACDONALD, JOHN ROSS
MILLAR, KENNETH

MACDONALD, MALCOLM
ROSS-MACDONALD, MALCOLM J

MACDONALD, MARCIA
HILL, GRACE [LIVINGSTON]

MACDONALD, MARY
GIFFORD, GRISELDA

MACDONALD, NINA HANSELL
LOOKER, ANTONINA [H]

MACDONALD, ROSLYN
CLARK, LOUISE

MACDONALD, ROSS
MILLAR, KENNETH

MACDONALD, SKRANTON
LLOP SELLARES, JUAN

MACDONNAILL, BRIAN
MCDONALD, BERNARD

MACDONNELL, J.E.
MACDONNELL, JAMES EDMOND

MACDONNELL, MEGAN
STEVENS, SERITA DEBORAH

MACDOUALL, ROBERTSON
MAIR, GEORGE B.

MACDOUGAL, JOHN
BLISH, JAMES B.
LOWNDES, ROBERT A.W.

MACDUFF, ANDREW
FYFE, H.B.

MACDUFF, ILKA
LIST, ILKA KATHERINE

MACE, HELEN
HALL, M. HELEN

MACE, MARGARET
LAWRENCE, DULCIE

MACE, MERLDA
MCCOY, MADELEINE

MACENRI, SEAGHAN
HENRY, JOHN PATRICK

MACEY, CARN
BARRETT, GEOFFREY JOHN

MACEY, CLARK
LAZENBY, NORMAN A.

MACFARLAND, ANNE
MACDONALD, SUSANNE

MACFARLAND, GEORGE R.
LEITHEAD, J. EDWARDS

MACFARLANE, KENNETH
WALKER, KENNETH MACFARLD.

MACFARLANE, STEPHEN
CROSS, JOHN KEIR

MACFHIOUNLASICH, PEADOR
MACGINLEY, PETER T.

MACGILL, MRS. PATRICK
MACGILL, MARGARET

MACGOWAN, JONATHAN
THURLOW, DAVID MICHAEL

MACGREGOR, MARY
JAMESON, MALCOLM

MACGREGOR, RICHARD
URQUHARDT, MACGREGOR

MACGREGOR, T.J.
MACGREGOR, PATRICIA M.J.

MACGRIAN, MICHAEL
WEST, ANTHONY

MACHAYE, ERIC
ROCHE, ARTHUR SOMERS

MACHEN, ARTHUR
JONES, ARTHUR LLEWELLYN

MACHIAVELLI
MCCREADY, WARREN T.

MACHLIS, JOSEPH
SELCAMM, GEORGE

MACINNES, ANDREW
LOONEY, PETER

MACIRE, ESOR B.
AMBROSE, ERIC [S]

MACIVER, SHARON
IHLE, SHARON J.

MACIVERS, SARAH
DEVANEY, ROBERT

MACK BRIDE, JOHNNY
MCGEOUGH, JOHN

MACK, AMANDA
ADELSON, JEAN

MACK, BREARLY
MCCALMENT, MAEBELLE [B]

MACK, DOROTHY
MCKITTRICK, DOROTHY

MACK, EVALINA
MCNAMARA, LENA BROOK[E]

MACK, JERRY
JOHNSON, JERRY MACK

MACK, JIM
MCCORMICK, JAMES

MACK, JOHNNY
MCCORMICK, JAMES

MACK, KIRBY
MCEVOY, HARRY K.

MACK, MAEBELLE
MCCALMENT, MAEBELLE [B]

MACK, MARJORIE
DIXON, MARJORIE [MACK]

MACKAIL, J.W.
MACKAIL, JOHN WILLIAM

MACKAY, AMANDA
SMITH, AMANDA JOAN MacK.

MACKAY, LORING
MACKAY, DAVID LORING
MACKAY, JOSEPHINE JULIA

MACKAY, MARY
MACKAY, MINNIE

MACKEEVER, MAGGIE
CLARK, GAIL

MACKELLAR, SINCLAIR
YATES, ALAN GEOFFREY

MACKENDRICK, LOUISE
THOMSEN, FREIDA
FOX, GARDNER F.

MACKENZIE, COLIN
TURNER, COLIN

MACKENZIE, GORDON
PRIEST, CHRISTOPHER [M]

MACKENZIE, JONATHAN BLAKE
GARRETT, RANDALL [P]

MACKENZIE, SEAFORTH
MACKENZIE, KENNETH

MACKENZIE, STEVE
RANDLE, KEVIN [DOUGLAS]

MACKENZIE, [DR.] WILLARD
STRATEMEYER, EDWARD

MACKEY, ERNAN
MCINERNY, RALPH [M]

MACKIE, ALICE
CUMMINS, MARY WARMINGTON

MACKIE, JOHN
LEVINSON, LEONARD [L]

MACKIE, MARON
MCNEELY, JEANETTE

MACKIE, PAULINE BRADFORD
HOPKINS, PAULINE MACKIE

MACKIN, ANITA
DONSON, CYRIL

MACKIN, EDWARD
MCINERNY, RALPH [M]

MACKIN, RICK
KASNER, WILLIAM MICHAEL

MACKLEWORTH, R.W.
MACKLEWORTH, RONALD W.

MACKS, BERT
MACKENROTH, ALBERT

MACKSEY, [MAJOR] K.J.
MACKSEY, KENNETH J.

MACKWORTH
RHONDDA, MARGARET HAIG

MACLAGAN, BRIDGET
BORDEN, MARY

MACLAREN, IAN
WATSON, JOHN

MACLAREN, JAMES
GRIEVE, CHRIST. MURRAY

MACLAY, CHARLOTTE
LOBB, CHARLOTTE

MACLEAN, ART
SHIRREFFS, GORDON DONALD

MACLEAN, ARTHUR
MANN, GEORGE PAUL
TUBB, E.C.
WEBB, C.P.

MACLEAN, BARRY
CHOSACK, CYRIL

MACLEAN, CHRISTINA
CASEMENT, CHRISTINA

MACLEAN, JAN
MACLEAN, ANNE & JILL

MACLEAN, R.D.
MACLEAN, REZIN DONALD

MACLEOD, AUSTIN
RAINE, WILLIAM MACLEOD

MACLEOD, FIONA
SHARP, WILLIAM

MACLEOD, ROBERT
KNOX, WILLIAM [BILL]

MACLEOD, SHEILA
JONES, SHEILA MACLEOD

MACMADISON
REUTER, RALPH

MACMANN, ELAINE
WILLOUGHBY, ELAINE M.

MACMANUS, JAMES
MACMANUS, SEUMAS

MACMILLAN, ANNABELLE
QUICK, ANNABELLE

MACNAMARA, BRINSLEY
WELDON, A.E.
WELDON, JOHN

MACNAUGHTAN, RICHARD
YOUNG, RICHARD

MACNEE, PATRICK
LESLIE, PETER

MACNEIL, ANNE
SEGER, MAURA

MACNEIL, DUNCAN
MCCUTCHAN, PHILIP [D]

MACNEIL, NEIL
BALLARD, W. TODHUNTER

MACNEILL, JANET
MCNEELY, JEANETTE

MACNELL, JAMES
MACDONNELL, JAMES EDMOND

MACNIB
MACKIE, ALBERT DAVID

MACOKAY, A.
KADOW, MANES

MACOMBER, DARIA
ROBINSON, PATRICIA C.
STEVENSON, FERDINAN

MACPATTERSON, F.
ERNSTING, WALTER

MACPHERSON, DONALD
MACTAVISH, GEORGE

MACPHERSON, SELINA
MCCLAFFERTY, SUSAN

MACPIARAIS, PADRAIC
PEARSE, PATRICK HENRY

MACQUEEN, JAY
MINTO, MARY

MACRAE, HAWK
BARKER, ALBERT W.

MACRAE, HERBERT
FEARN, C. EATON

MACRAE, MASON
RUBEL, JAMES LYON

MACRAE, TRAVI
FEAGLES, ANITA MACRAE

MACRAE, TRAVIS
FEAGLES, ANITA MACRAE

MACREADY, R.J.
HUTSON, SHAUN

MACROSS, ROSS
REACH, JAMES
TAGGART, TOM [BARNARD]

MACSHOVES, BAAL
ELIASHIV, ISIDORE

MACSTIOFAIN, SEAN
STEPHENSON, JOHN E.D.

MACTAGGART, MORNA
BROWN, MORNA DORIS M.

MACTHOMAS, RUARAIDH
THOMSON, DEREK S.

MACTYRE, PAUL
ADAMS, ROBERT JAMES

MACUMBER, MARI
SANDOZ, MARI[E SUSETTE]

MACVEIGH, SUE
NEARING, ELIZABETH CUSTER

MACWILLIAMS, SARAH
MAYHAR, ARDATH F.H.

MACY, DORA
OURSLER, GRACE P.

MADDEN, DICK
SELLERS, CONNIE LESLIE

MADDEN, E.S.
MADDEN, EDWARD STANISLAUS

MADDEN, JACK
MOSKOVITZ, JACK

MADDEN, WARREN
CAMERON, KENNETH NEILL

MADDERN, AL[AN]
ELLISON, HARLAN

MADDERN, STAN
MASON, SYDNEY CHARLES

MADDOCK, LARRY
JARDINE, JACK OWEN

MADDOCK, STEPHEN
WALSH, JAMES MORGAN

MADDOX, CARL
TUBB, E.C.

MADDOX, LESTER
GALLARDOS MUNOZ, JUAN

MADDOX, MAX
JEANS, HERBERT

MADDUX, RACHEL
BAKER, RACHEL MADDUX

MADEOC
ROBINSON, H.

MADHAVIKUTTY
DAS, KAMALA

MADISON, DOLLY
PAUL, MAURY

MADISON, FRANK
HUTCHINS, FRANCIS GILMAN

MADISON, HANK
ROWLAND, DONALD S.

MADISON, JANE
HORNE, HUGH ROBERT

MADISON, JOYCE
MINTZ, JOYCE LOIS

MADISON, MARY
PICKEN, MARY BROOKS

MADISON, REX
BROOKS, EDWY SEARLES

MADISON, RICK
BOUNDS, SYDNEY J.
WILLIS, ERNEST LISTER H.

MAE, EYDIE
HUNSBERGER, EDITH MAE

MAEL, PETER/PIERRE
CAUSSE, CHARLES
VINCENT, CHARLES

MAEPANN, HUGH
KUTTNER, HENRY
MOORE, CATHERINE LUCILLE

MAEPANN, K.H.
KUTTNER, HENRY
MOORE, CATHERINE LUCILLE

MAGAFAN, SOPHIA
MULLEN, SOPHIA

MAGALI
CORRADOT, JEANNE E.M.J.

MAGENHEIMER, KAY
MAGENHEIMER, CATHRYN C.

MAGILL, MARCUS
GILES, JOANNA ELDER
HILL, BRIAN [MERRIKEN]

MAGILL, RORY
FAULKNER, DOROTHEA M.

MAGLIORE, FRANCIS L.
SEJOUR-MAGLIORE, FRANCIS

MAGNER, LEE
TATARA, ELLEN LEE M.

MAGNUS, GERALD
BOWMAN, GERALD [MOORE]

MAGNUS, JOHN
ELLISON, HARLAN

MAGNUS, PHILIP
MAGNUS-ALLCROFT, PHILLIP

MAGNUSSON, ORWAR
NILSSON, SVEN-ERIK

MAGOON, CAREY
CAREY, ELIZABETH
MAGOON, MARIAN AUSTIN

MAGRISKA, HELEN
BROCKIES, ENID FLORENCE

MAGRON, VECTOR
FRANKLYN, JULIAN

MAGROON, VECTOR
FEARN, JOHN RUSSELL

MAGUEN, DAVID
MARKISH, DAVID

MAGUIRE, ANNE
MUNN, MERYL LUCILE
NEARING, PENNY

MAHAN, PAT
WHEAT, PATTE

MAHAN, PATTE WHEAT
WHEAT, PATTE

MAHDEN, MAC
BERG, DANIEL

MAHEN, JIRI
VANCURA, ANTONIN

MAHMOUD, MOUSTAFFA
MAHMUD, MUSTAFA

MAHNSFELD, EUGEN
KLATT, CONRAD

MAHONE, COLT
LAZENBY, NORMAN A.

MAHOOD, LOIS
GRUBER, FRANK

MAHR, KURT
MAHN, KLAUS

MAHR, RUD.
MOLL, RUDOLF

MAI, MANFRED
MAIER, MANFRED

MAIDOFF, ILKA LIST
LIST, ILKA KATHERINE

MAIK, HENRI
HECHT, HENRI JOSEPH

MAILER, CECIL O.
MAHN, KLAUS

MAIN, ERIC CHARLES
MCILWAIN, DAVID

MAINE, C.E.
MCILWAIN, DAVID

MAINE, CHARLES ERIC
MCILWAIN, DAVID

MAINE, DAVID
AVICE, CLAUDE-PIERRE

MAINE, MASTERLING
MASON, SYDNEY CHARLES

MAINE, TREVOR
CATHERALL, ARTHUR

MAINSAIL
DUFF, DOUGLAS VALDER

MAIR, G.H.
MAIR, GEORGE HENRY

MAIR, H. ALLEN
MURRAY, FRANCIS EDWIN

MAIR, MARGARET
CROMPTON, MARGARET NORAH

MAIRENA, ANA
DE ALBINANA, ASUNCION I.

MAIS, S.P.B.
MAIS, STUART PETRE

MAISON, DELLA
KATZ, BOBBI[E]

MAISTER, MAX
FEDDE, OVE

MAITLAND, MARGARET
DUBREUIL, ELIZABETH L.
FOX, GARDNER F.
WALLMANN, JEFFREY M.

MAITLAND, REGINALD T.
SCOTT, REGINALD T. MAITL.

MAITRE
DES ESSAUT, M. DAVRELLE

MAIZEL, C.L.
MAIZEL, CLARICE M.

MAIZEL, LEAH
MAIZEL, CLARICE M.

MAIZIE
ROSE, MARY H.

MAJA X
ALVING, FANNY

MAJEROVA, MARIE
TUSAROVA, MARIE

MAJOR, ANN
CLEAVES, MARGARET MAJOR

MAJOR, DAGNEY
MAJOR, J.D.

MAJOR, GERRI
MAJOR, GERALDINE H.

MAJOR, H.M.
BUCKLEY, KATHLEEN
JARVIS, SHARON [SYLVIA]

MAJORS, SIMON
FOX, GARDNER F.

MAKANOWITSKY, BARABRA
NORMAN, BARBARA

MAKARY
IRANEK-OSMECKI, KAZ.

MAKEPEACE, JOANNA
YORKE, MARGARET E.

MAKEWRIGHT, GEORGE W.
CAHILL, FRANK

MAKSIMOV, MARK D.
LIPOVICH, MARK D.

MALACHY, FRANK
MCAULIFFE, FRANK

MALAPARTE, CURZIO
SUCKERT, CURZIO

MALAPONTE, MARCO
RABE, PETER

MALCOLM X
LITTLE, MALCOLM

MALCOLM, ALEEN
MALCOLM, AILEEN

MALCOLM, ANTHEA
GRANT, JOAN & TRACY

MALCOLM, CHARLES
HINCKS, CYRIL MALCOLM

MALCOLM, DAN
SILVERBERG, ROBERT

MALCOLM, GRANT
HUGHES, DENNIS [TALBOT]

MALCOLM, HONEY
ROTSLER, WILLIAM

MALCOLM, JAMES
FLYNN, JOHN [M]

MALCOLM, JOHN
ANDREWS, JOHN MALCOLM
UREN, MALCOLM JOHN LEGGOE

MALCOLM, MARGARET
KUETHER, EDITH LYMAN

MALCOLM, MARINA
DOUGLAS, CHARLOTTE

MALCOLM, RONALD
HINCKS, CYRIL MALCOLM

MALCOLM, ROY
MALCOLM, DONALD
ROY, ARCHIBALD EDMISTON

MALCOLM, SCOTT
KELLEY, THOMAS P.

MALCOLMSON, ANNE
VON STORCH, ANNE B.

MALET, LUCAS
HARRISON, MARY ST. LEGER

MALET, ORIEL
VAUGHAN, LADY AURIEL R.M.

MALIN, PETER
CONNER, PATRICK REARDON

MALISZEWSKA, MARIA
BEYLIN, KAROLINA

MALL, VIKTOR
BESKOW, BO

MALLERY, AMOS
GELB, NORMAN

MALLERY, SUSAN
MACIAS, SUSAN W.

MALLEY, ERN
MCAULEY, JAMES PHILLIP
STEWART, HAROLD

MALLIEUX, HOLM
MILLIES, HELMUT

MALLINSON, RUSSELL
STANNARD, RUSSELL

MALLOCH, PETER
DUNCAN, W. MURDOCH

MALLOCK, W.H.
MALLOCK, WILLIAM H.

MALLORY, C.H.
CABOS, LEW M.

MALLORY, DREW
GARFIELD, BRIAN F.W.

MALLORY, JAY
CAREY, JOYCE

MALLORY, LEE
FALLON, M.

MALLORY, MARK
HERSHMAN, MORRIS
REYNOLDS, DALLAS MCCORD

MALLOWAN, A.C.
CHRISTIE, AGATHA [M.C.]

MALLOY, LESTER
MEARES, LEONARD F.

MALLOY, ROBERT
HAMILL, PETE

MALM, GUN MAJ.
ESSEN, AXEL ANDERS H.

MALM, MARGARETHA
PETTERSON, H. BERTIL

MALONE, EDWARD DUNN
WELLMAN, MANLY WADE
WELLMAN, WADE

MALONE, LOUIS
MACNIECE, LOUIS

MALONE, PAUL
NEWTON, MICHAEL

MALONE, RUTH E.
RANDOLPH, GEORGIANNA ANN

MALONE, RUTH
RANDOLPH, GEORGIANNA ANN

MALONE, SHERRY
BLOCH, ROBERT [A]

MALONEY, MACK
KELLEHER, BRIAN

MALONEY, PAT
MARKUN, PATRICIA MALONEY

MALONEY, TIGHE
MACBEATH, INNIS [S]

MALORNY, RALPH
HARTSCH, GERHART

MALPEDE, KAREN
TAYLOR, KAREN MALPEDE

MALPOTT, VIRGULE
GHNASSIA, MAURICE [J-H]

MALSER, HANS
ROSEGGER, PETRI KETTENFR.

MALTEN, MARGARETE
ASPERN-BUCHMEIER, ELISAB.

MALTEN, THEA
JAHN, DOROTHEA

MALU
LUBIN, MAURICE A.

MALVERN, HUGH
DONALDSON, DALE C.

MALVILLE, KIM
MALVILLE, JOHN MCKIM

MALWYN
A'BECKETT, SIR WILLIAM

MAMA G.
DAVIS, GRANIA

MAMIN, SIBERIAK
MAMIN, DMITRI N.

MAMPEL, ANNE-MARIE
BARTEL, ANNE-MARIE [S]

MANCHECOURT
LAVADAN, HENRI L.E.

MANCHESTER, IVY
CARPENTER, CARLETON

MANCINI, PAT MCNEES
MCNEES, PAT

MANCLAIR, CAMILLE
FAUST, CAMILLE

MAND, CYRIL
HAHN, GEORGE R.
LEVIN, RICHARD

MANDAN DIAZ, ANTONELLA
MANDAN, ANTONIO

MANDE, ELIZABETH ERIN
FRIEDMAN, STUART

MANDELIK, NINA
HAJDA, NINA JANA

MANDER, MATTHIAS
MANDL, HARALD

MANDERS, HARRY "BUNNY"
FARMER, PHILIP JOSE

MANDERS, JOHN F.
SANDFIELD, LAURENCE

MANDEVILLE, D.E.
COATES, ANTHONY

MANDEVILLE, SIR JOHN
DE BOURGOGNE, JEHAN

MANETTI, FANNY
SMITH, FANNY

MANFRED, FREDERICK F.
FEIKEMA, FREDERICK

MANFRED, IGO
DE PLANQUE, WALTER

MANFRED, ROBERT
MARX, ERICA ELIZABETH

MANGIONE, JERRE
MANGIONE, GERLANDO

MANING, KYLE
ALEXANDER, DAVID

MANJON, MAITE
MANJON-ALONSO, MARIA T.

MANLEY, MARK
ZWINGELBERG, MARK

MANLY, MARLINE
RATHBORNE, ST. GEORGE

MANN, A. PHILO
ALD, ROY ALLISON

MANN, A. SUFFERAN
BANGS, JOHN KENDRICK

MANN, ABBY
GOODMAN, ABRAHAM

MANN, ABEL
CREASEY, JOHN

MANN, AVERY
BREETVELD, JAMES PATRICK

MANN, CHARLES
GRAHAM, ROGER P.
HECKLEMANN, CHARLES N.

MANN, CHUCK
HECKLEMANN, CHARLES N.

MANN, D.J.
FREEDMAN, JAMES DILLET

MANN, DANIEL
LEUKEFELD, PETER

MANN, DEBORAH
BLOOM, URSULA

MANN, E.B.
MANN, EDWARD BEVERLY

MANN, GEOFFREY M.
WALLMANN, JEFFREY M.

MANN, JACK
CANNELL, CHARLES HENRY
VIVIAN, E[VELYN] CHARLES

MANN, JAMES
HARVEY, JOHN [BARTON]
JAMES, LAURENCE

MANN, JIM
MANN, JAMES ANTHONY

MANN, JOHN
STEVENS, HENRY CHARLES

MANN, JOSEPHINE
PULLEIN-THOMPSON, JOSEPH.

MANN, MATTHIAS
HEINEMANN, ERICH

MANN, MILTON
GRAHAM, ROGER P.

MANN, P. GUNTER
GUNTERMANN, PAUL

MANN, PATRICIA
EARNSHAW, PATRICIA

MANN, PATRICK
WALLER, LESLIE

MANN, PEGGY
HOULTON, PEGGY MANN

MANN, PETER
MAN, PITER

MANN, STANLEY
MASON, SYDNEY CHARLES

MANN, W. BERG
BERGMAN, WERNER

MANN, W.L.
HAUSMANN, WOLFGANG L.

MANNERING, JULIA
BINGHAM, MADELEINE

MANNERING, MAY
NOWELL, HARRIETT P.

MANNERS, ALEXANDRA
RUNDLE, ANNE

MANNERS, GORDON
FULLERTON, MARY ELIZA

MANNERS, JULIA
GREENAWAY, GLADYS

MANNERS, MISS
MARTIN, JUDITH SYLVIA

MANNES, MARYA
BLOW, MRS R. [MARYA M.]

MANNIGIAN, PETER
MONGOR, IFOR DAVID

MANNING, DAVID
FAUST, FREDERICK S.

MANNING, HILDA
REACH, JAMES

MANNING, JACK
MOSKOVITZ, JACK

MANNING, JO
ROBINSON, IRENE

MANNING, JOHN SPENCER
ASSAEL, SOL

MANNING, JOHN SPENCER [CONT]
NAHUM, MICHAEL

MANNING, JUNE
MANOFF, RUTH

MANNING, LEE
STOKES, MANNING LEE

MANNING, LEO
HALLBING, KJELL KARL

MANNING, MARSHA
GRIMSTEAD, HETTI

MANNING, MARTIN
SMITH, REGINALD DONALD

MANNING, MARY LOUISE
CAMERON, LOU

MANNING, ROSEMARY
COLE, MARGARET ALICE

MANNING, ROY
REACH, JAMES
EAST, FRED

MANNING, VAL
MILLER, VAL

MANNINGHAM, BASIL
HOMERSHAM, BASIL H.

MANNOCK, JENNIFER
MANNOCK, LAURA

MANNON, M.M.
MANNON, MARTHA & MARY E.

MANNON, WARWICK
HOPKINS, KENNETH

MANON, MADELEINE
HAFT, ELLI

MANOR, JASON
HALL, OAKLEY M.

MANS, ADRIENNE
LUDERS-KNEGTMANS, ANNEKE

MANSBRIDGE, PAMELA
COURSE, PAMELA MARY

MANSELL, C.R.
PAYNE, EILEEN MARY

MANSFELD, MICHAEL
HEINZ, ECKHARD

MANSFIELD
MEE, HUAN

MANSFIELD, ELIZABETH
SCHWARTZ, PAULA REIBEL

MANSFIELD, KATHERINE
BEAUCHAMP, KATHLEEN M.

MANSFIELD, LIBBY
SCHWARTZ, PAULA REIBEL

MANSFIELD, N.
GLADDEN, EDGAR NORMAN

MANSFIELD, PAUL H.
SCHWARTZ, PAULA REIBEL

MANSON, MARGARET
ALDISS, MARGARET [C]

MANSON, WILL
FREEDMAN, COLE
LEROY, HOWARD

MANSOR, A.L.
BOSKAMP, PAUL

MANT, RICHARD
HEARNE, G. RICHARD MANT

MANTEL, FELIX
KUSCHE, LOTHAR

MANTHEY, JUTTA
MEYER, JUTTA

MANTLE, W.
MANTLE, WINIFRED LANGFORD

MANTON, JO
GITTINGS, JO [G] MANTON

MANTON, PAUL
WALKER, PETER N[ORMAN]

MANTON, PETER
CREASEY, JOHN

MANTU, LUCIA
NADEJDE, CORNELIA

MANTZ, LEW
MARTIN, THOMAS HECTOR
MCCORMICK, JAMES

MANUEL, ARTHUR
MEYER, ARTHUR EMANUEL

MANUGUPTA
SHASTRI, PRITHVINATH

MANVILLE, GEORGE
FENN, GEORGE MANVILLE

MANVILLE, W.H.
MANVILLE, WILLIAM HENRY

MAO-TUN
YEN-PING, SHEN

MAORI
INGLIS, JAMES

MAPES, MARY A.
ELLISON, VIRGINIA HOWELL

MAPLESDEN, RAY
PEARCE, RAYMOND

MARA, BARNEY
ROTH, ARTHUR JOSEPH

MARA, BERNARD
MOORE, BRIAN

MARA, JEANETTE
CEBULASH, MEL

MARA, THALIA
MAHONEY, ELIZABETH

MARALTO, ONAPHRIO
WALPOLE, HORACE

MARAS, KARL
HAWKINS, PETER
BULMER, [HENRY] KENNETH

MARASMUS, SEYMOUR
RIVOLI, MARIO

MARATH, LAURIE
ROBERTS, SUZANNE

MARATH, SPARROW
ROBERTS, SUZANNE

MARATHON
MCNISH, JAMES THOMAS

MARBACH, MICHAEL
BELZ, FRED GOTTHILF

MARBROOK, DEL
MABROUK, DJELLOUL

MARCEAU, FELICIEN
CARETTE, LOUIS ALBERT

MARCELLINO
AGNEW, EDITH J.

MARCELLINUS, ANIMIANUS
NADEL, AARON

MARCH HARE
WALMSLEY, LEO

MARCH, ANNE
WOOLSON, CONSTANCE F.

MARCH, EMMA
STUBBS, JEAN

MARCH, HILARY
ADCOCK, ALMEY ST. JOHN
GREEN, LALAGE ISOBEL

MARCH, JERMYN
WEBB, DOROTHY ANNA

MARCH, JESSICA
AFRICANO, LILLIAN

MARCH, MARJORIE
LIEBICH, AUGUSTA

MARCH, MAXWELL
CARTER, MARGERY L.A.
ALLINGHAM, MARGERY LOUISE

MARCH, STELLA
MARSHALL, MARGUERITE M.

MARCH, WILLIAM
CAMPBELL, WILLIAM MARCH

MARCHANT, BESSIE
MARCHANT, ELIZABETH

MARCHANT, CATHERINE
COOKSON, CATHERINE ANN

MARCHANT, R.A.
MARCHANT, REX ALAN

MARCHANT, ROMANO ISABEL
COLBRON, GRACE ISABEL

MARCHBANKS, SAMUEL
DAVIES, [W] ROBERTSON

MARCHMONT, ROSS
HOME, SCOTT

MARCO
MOUNTBATTEN, LORD LOUIS

MARCO, GUY A[NTHONY]
MONGELLUZZO, GUY ANTHONY

MARCO, LOU
GOTTFRIED, THEODORE MARK

MARCOMBE, EDITH MARION
SHIFFERT, EDITH [M]

MARCONETTE
MARCHIONI, MARK

MARCOTT, JAMES
SCHERMERHORN, DUANE R.

MARCOY, PAUL
DE SAINT CRICQ, LORENSO

MARCUS, AURELIUS
PADLEY, WALTER

MARCUS, BENJAMIN
KEATS, RICHARD STEPHEN

MARCUS, BERESFORD
BRANDEL, MARC

MARCUS, JOANNA
ANDREWS, LUCILLA MATHEW

MARCUS, ROY
MIELKE, THOMAS R.P.

MARDLE, JONATHAN
FOWLER, ERIC

MARDON, DEIRDRE
MARDON, ALLAN

MAREK, MAX
DIETSCH, WERNER

MAREK, WALDO
MAUCKNER, WALTER G.

MARETH, GLENVILLE
GILBERT, WILLIE

MARGARET
KENT, ELLEN LOUISA MARG.

MARGARET, KARLA
ANDERSDATTER, KARLA M.

MARGERSON, DAVID
DAVIES, DAVID MARGERISON

MARGRAF, MIRIAM
LEWIN, HANNAH-MIRIAM

MARGRET, ANN
GEISSLER, MARGARETE

MARGULIES
MOSKOWITZ, SAM

MARHOLM, LAURA
HANSSON, LAURA MOHR

MARIA
ENGLISH, ANASTASIA MARY

MARIA, IGNA
JUNEMANN, IGNA MARIA

MARIANA
FOSTER, MARIAN CURTIS

MARICHAUD, ALPHONSE
WILSON, FLORENCE R.M.

MARIE, JEANNE
WILSON, MARIE BEATRICE

MARIE-LOUISE
SHARE, MARIE-LOUISE

MARIE-VICTORIN, FRERE
KIROUAC, JOSEPH LOUIS C.

MARIELLA, [SISTER]
GABLE, MARY

MARILUE
JOHNSON, MARILUE CAROLYN

MARIN, A.C.
COPPEL, ALFREDO JOSE

MARIN, ALFRED
COPPEL, ALFREDO JOSE

MARINER, DAVID
SMITH, DAVID MACLEOD

MARINER, SCOTT
KORNBLUTH, C[YRIL] M.
POHL, FREDERIK

MARINO, NICK
DEMING, RICHARD
OURSLER, WILL[IAM C.]

MARINO, SUSAN
ELLIS, JULIE M.

MARINONI, ROSA ZAGNONI
ZAGNONI, ROSA

MARINUS
MARTIN, JACQUES

MARION, HENRY
DEL REY, LESTER

MARION, S.T.
LAKRITZ, ESTHER

MARISA
NUCERA, MARISA LONETTE

MARITZ, EMPIE
MARITZ, MAGDALENA P.

MARIUS
BENEDICT, STEVE

MARIUS, CLAUDE
DUPLANY, CLAUDE MARIUS

MARJORAM, J.
MOTTRAM, RALPH HALE

MARK ALAN, ROY
MALAN, RENATA MARCO

MARK, ALANE
JESSUP, MARY ALANE

MARK, ARTHUR
WESTBERG, SIGURD

MARK, DAVID
BUITENKANT, NATHAN

MARK, EDWINA
FADIMAN, EDWIN JR.

MARK, JAN
MARK, JANET MARJORIE

MARK, JON
DUBREUIL, ELIZABETH L.

MARK, MATTHEW
BABCOCK, FREDERICK

MARK, POLLY
MARK, PAULINE [D]

MARK, TED
GOTTFRIED, THEODORE MARK

MARK, WILLIAM
KANN, ALBRECHT PETER

MARKAM, ROBERT
AMIS, KINGSLEY [WILLIAM]

MARKANDAYA, KAMALA
TAYLOR, KAMALA

MARKEN, WOLFGANG
MARDICKE, FRITZ

MARKER, CLARE
WITCOMBE, RICK

MARKET MAN
LAKE, KENNETH R[OBERT]

MARKFIELD, RALPH
RODRIGUEZ, DENNIS

MARKHAM, HORD
ROTSLER, WILLIAM

MARKHAM, PATRICIA
CARRO, PATRICIA

MARKHAM, PAULINE
MCMAHON, MARGARET [H]

MARKHAM, RUSS
HALL, STEVE

MARKHAM, STEVE
FRANCES, STEPHEN D.

MARKIN, MAIA
WOJCIECHOWSKA, MAIA [T]

MARKINS, W.S.
JENKINS, MARIE M.

MARKKLEEBERG, P.A.
MULLER, PAUL ALFRED

MARKLAND, PETER
SCHEUTZ, TORSTEN V.
SCHULMAN, ALLAN

MARKLIN, MEGAN
HARRINGTON, WILLIAM

MARKOOSIE
PATSAUQ, MARKOOSIE

MARKOVA, ALICIA
MARKS, LILLIAN ALICIA

MARKS, ALAN
ANNAND, ALAN

MARKS, HANNAH K.
TRIVELPEACE, LAUREL

MARKS, JASON
HIGHWATER, JAMAKE M.

MARKS, JOANNA
DARBY, JOANNA

MARKS, MICHAEL
HOHLBEIN, WOLFGANG E.

MARKS, NORA
ATKINSON, ELEANOR [S]

MARKS, PAT R.
FEINMAN, JEFFREY

MARKS, PETER
SMITH, ROBERT KIMMEL

MARKS, STAN
MARKS, STANLEY

MARKS, T.W.
BRAND, KURT

MARKS-HIGHWATER, J.
HIGHWATER, JAMAKE M.

MARKSMAN, A.M.
HOLMBERG, NILS

MARKUS
LEHEN, TUURE

MARKUS, MARIO
REIS, KURT

MARKUS, URS
HEFTRICH, ECKHARD

MARKWALDER, MARGA
CORRODI-HORBER, MARGRIT

MARKWELL, MARY
HAYES, CATHERINE E.

MARKWICK, EDWARD
JOHNSON, EDWARD MARHWICK

MARL, WALTER DEN
MADEL, WALTER

MARLBOROUGH
OAKSEY, JOHN GEOFFREY T.

MARLE, T.B.
LAMBERT, HUBERT STEEL

MARLIN, HENRY
GIGGAL, KENNETH

MARLIN, HILDA
VAN STOCKUM, HILDA

MARLIN, ROY
ASHMORE, BASIL NORTON

MARLITT, E.
JOHN, EUGENIE
JOHN, FRIEDERIKE C.H.

MARLITT, E.P.
JOHN, EUGENIE

MARLOT, RAYMOND
ANGREMY, JEAN-PIERRE

MARLOW, EDWINA
HUFF, TOM E.

MARLOW, JOYCE
CONNOR, JOYCE MARY

MARLOW, LOUIS
WILKINSON, LOUIS U.

MARLOW, MAX
BACKMAN, DIANA
NICOLE, CHRISTOPHER ROBIN

MARLOW, PHYLLIS
MASON, SYDNEY CHARLES

MARLOW, SIDNEY
COGGINS, PASCHAL HESTON

MARLOWE, AMY BELL
STRATEMEYER, EDWARD

MARLOWE, ASTON
PRONZINI, WILLIAM JOHN
WALLMANN, JEFFREY M.

MARLOWE, CHARLES
JAY, HARRIETT

MARLOWE, DELPHINE
SINGER, RONALD

MARLOWE, GREG
BARNARD, LESLIE T.
MCCORMICK, JAMES

MARLOWE, HUGH
PATTERSON, HARRY

MARLOWE, MARCH
STOKES, MANNING LEE

MARLOWE, MARY
SHANAHAN, MARGARET MARY

MARLOWE, PIERS
GRIBBLE, LEONARD [R]

MARLOWE, REX
BOUNDS, SYDNEY J.

MARLOWE, STEPHEN
LESSER, MILTON

MARLOWE, TERRY
ABSHIRE, RICHARD
CLAIR, BILL

MARLOWE, TESS
GLICK, RUTH [BURTNICK]
TITCHENOR, LOUISE

MARLOWE, WEBB
MCCOMAS, J. FRANCIS

MARMADUKE, T.
THOMPSON, MARMADUKE

MARMORA, DAGOBERTO
BOBADILLO Y LUNAR, EMILIO

MARNAIS, PHILIP
NORDEN, ERIC

MARNEK, M.
MARHEINEKE, MARIA

MARNER, FRANK
ERDMANN, FRANZ

MARNER, ROBERT
BUDRYS, ALGIRDAS JONAS

MARNEY, SUZANNE
JOHNSTON, MABLE ANNESLEY

MARO, JUDITH
JONES, JUDITH ANASTASIA

MARONIS
MACIULIS-MACIULEVICIUS, J

MAROSSI, RUTH
KREFETZ, RUTH

MAROT, MARK
KOCH, KURT EMIL

MARQUAND, JOSEPHINE
GLADSTONE, JOSEPHINE

MARQUIS, DON
PERRY, ROBERT

MARR, ANNE
RATZLAFF, NELL MARR DEAN

MARR, N.J.
JOHNSON, NANCY MARR

MARR, NANCY J.
JOHNSON, NANCY MARR

MARR, REED
REED-MARR, P.J.

MARRECO, ANNE
WIGNALL, ANNE

MARRIC, J.J.
BUTLER, WILLIAM A. VIVIAN
CREASEY, JOHN

MARRIOT, JOHN
ELLIOT, CHRISTOPHER

MARRIOTT, BUCK
MEAGHER, M.

MARRIOTT-WATSON, E.B.
MARRIOTT-WATSON, H.B.

MARRIOTT-WATSON, ETHELL
MARRIOTT-WATSON, H.B.

MARROQUIN, PATRICIO
MARKUN, PATRICIA MALONEY

MARRYAT, CAPT.
MARRYAT, FREDERICK

MARRYAT, FLORENCE
LEAN, FLORENCE MARRYAT C.

MARS, A.
GILLESPIE, A.C.

MARS, DIANA
MARLISS, DEANNA

MARS, E.C.
MAZANI, ERIC C.F.N.

MARS, JEAN PRICE
PRICE-MARS, JEAN

MARS, KASEY
MARTIN, KATHLEEN KELLY

MARS, W.T.
MARS, WITOLD TADEUSZ J.

MARSAL, UNA
LIXFIELD, URSULA

MARSANO, RAMON
DINGES, JOHN [CHARLES]

MARSCHALL, HANNS
ICKES, JOHANNES

MARSCHALL, RUDOLF
RING, LOTHAR

MARSDEN, ANTONY
SUTTON, [ERIC] GRAHAM

MARSDEN, JAMES
CREASEY, JOHN

MARSDEN, JUNE
INGRAM-MOORE, ERICA

MARSH, CAROL
ANKERSON, CAROL
MCHAM, MARCIA

MARSH, EDWIN
SCHORB, EDWIN MARSH

MARSH, ELLEN TANNER
JOHNSON, RENATE

MARSH, GEOFFREY
GRANT, CHARLES L.

MARSH, HENRY
SAKLATVALA, BERAM

MARSH, J.E.
MARSHALL, EVELYN

MARSH, JAMES J.
MARSHALL, JOSEPH R.

MARSH, JEAN
MARSHALL, EVELYN

MARSH, JERI
LEE-HOSTETLER, JERI

MARSH, JOAN
MARSH, JOHN

MARSH, LILLIAN
FRANKEL, RUBY

MARSH, PATRICK
HISCOCK, LESLIE

MARSH, PAUL
HOPKINS, KENNETH

MARSH, PETER
MARCHAND, FIRMIN PIERRE

MARSH, REBECCA
NEUBAUER, WILLIAM A.

MARSH, RICHARD
HELDMAN, RICHARD B.

MARSHALL ALAN
COONS, WILLIAM R.
HENDERSON, NEDRA
HORNWOOD, HARVEY
MOSKOVITZ, JACK
OFFUTT, ANDREW J.
WESTLAKE, DONALD [EDWIN]

MARSHALL, ANDREA
CRAWFORD, KAREN

MARSHALL, ARCHIBALD
MARSHALL, ARTHUR H.

MARSHALL, BEVERLEY
HOLROYD, ETHEL MARY

MARSHALL, BEVLYN
KAUKAS, BEVLYN M.

MARSHALL, BILL
WARD, BILL

MARSHALL, CATHERINE
DUBREUIL, ELIZABETH L.

MARSHALL, DOUGLAS
MCCLINTOCK, MARSHALL

MARSHALL, E.P.
MONTGOMERY, RUTHERFORD G.

MARSHALL, EDMUND
HOPKINS, KENNETH

MARSHALL, EDWARD
MARSHALL, JAMES [EDWARD]

MARSHALL, EMILY
HALL, BENNIE CAROLINE

MARSHALL, GARY
SNOW, CHARLES H[ORACE]

MARSHALL, H.H.
JAHN, JOSEPH MICHAEL

MARSHALL, JACQUELINE
AUSTIN, DEBORAH

MARSHALL, JAMES
BOUNDS, SYDNEY J.
RISTER, CLAUDE

MARSHALL, JAMES VANCE
PAYNE, DONALD GORDON

MARSHALL, JEFF
LAYCOCK, GEORGE [EDWIN]

MARSHALL, JOANNE
RUNDLE, ANNE

MARSHALL, JOCK
MARSHALL, ALAN JOHN

MARSHALL, JOHN
PEPPER, FRANK S.

MARSHALL, JOSEPH
KRECHNIAK, JOSEPH MARSHAL

MARSHALL, KIM
MARSHALL, MICHAEL [KIM]

MARSHALL, LLOYD
WILDING, PHILIP

MARSHALL, LOVAT
DUNCAN, W. MURDOCH

MARSHALL, MARGUERITE M.
DEAN, MARGUERITE M.M.

MARSHALL, PERCY
YOUNG, PERCY MARSHALL

MARSHALL, RAYMOND
RAYMOND, RENE BRABAZON

MARSHALL, STEVE
LEWIS, ORT

MARSHALL, WILLIAM
WALPOLE, HORACE

MARSHALLIK
ZANGWILL, ISRAEL

MARSLAND, BISHOP OF
DUNCAN, RONALD [F.H]

MARSLAND, MAJ. GEN.
DUNCAN, RONALD [F.H]

MARSON, JO
LOBSACK, WILHELM

MARSTEN, RICHARD
HUNTER, EVAN

MARSTON, EDWARD
MILES, KEITH

MARSTON, MILDRED
SCOTT, ANNA

MART, DONOVAN
MARTIN, E. LE BRETON

MARTEL, AIMEE
THURLO, AIMEE S.

MARTEL, CHARLES
DELF, THOMAS

MARTELL, CLAUDIA
WOLFF, VIRGINIA

MARTELL, DAVID
MASON, DAVID

MARTELL, GUNTER
BECKER, KURT

MARTELL, JAMES
BINGLEY, DAVID ERNEST

MARTEN, ERICH
DE MARTINI, EMIL

MARTEN, MARION
RIECK, ERIKA

MARTENS, ADEMAR
DE GHELDERODE, MICHEL

MARTENS, FRED
ENGELSBERGER, BERTA
ENGELSBERGER, JOSEF

MARTENS, PAUL
SOUTHWOLD, STEPHEN

MARTHA, HENRY
FINKLESTEIN, MARK

MARTIG, SINA
BACHMANN-MARTIG, SINA

MARTIN, A.E.
MARTIN, ARCHIBALD EDWARD

MARTIN, ABE
HUBBARD, FRANK MCKINNEY

MARTIN, ALBERT
MEHAN, JOSEPH ALBERT

MARTIN, ALBERTO N.
NUSSBAUM, ALBERT F.

MARTIN, ANDRE
JACOBY, HENRY

MARTIN, ANN
BEST, CAROL ANN

MARTIN, ANTHONY
GLYNN, ANTHONY ARTHUR
ZEHNDER, MEINRAD

MARTIN, AXEL
HAAKE, JURGEN

MARTIN, BRUCE
PAINE, LAURAN BOSWORTH

MARTIN, CARL
NUSSBAUM, ALBERT F.

MARTIN, CAROLA
PUSCH, EDITH

MARTIN, CHIP
MARTIN, STODDARD [H] JR.

MARTIN, CHRIST
ANDRESEN, THOMAS

MARTIN, CHRISTOPHER
HOYT, EDWIN P. JR.

MARTIN, CHUCK
MARTIN, CHARLES M.

MARTIN, CORT
SHERMAN, JORY [T]

MARTIN, DAVID
SMITH, MARTIN

MARTIN, DONALD
HONIG, DONALD

MARTIN, DOROTHEA
HEWITT, KATHLEEN DOUGLAS

MARTIN, ELLIS
RYAN, MARAH ELLIS

MARTIN, EUGENE
DE VAUX, BARON
STRATEMEYER, EDWARD

MARTIN, FRANCIS
REID, CHARLES [STUART]

MARTIN, FRANKLIN H.
ERNST, PAUL FREDERICK

MARTIN, FREDERIC
CHRISTOPHER, MATTHEW F.

MARTIN, FREDERICK
STERN, FREDERICK MARTIN

MARTIN, G.A.
MARTIN, GLORIA ANN

MARTIN, GEORGE
MARTIN, JORGE

MARTIN, GIGI
HUPPERTZ, MARGOT

MARTIN, GIL
OVERY, JILLIAN P.J.

MARTIN, HART E.
GREENOP, FRANK S.

MARTIN, IVOR
SMITH, BERNARD

MARTIN, JACK
ETCHISON, DENNIS WILLIAM

MARTIN, JANET
GARFINKLE, BERNARD

MARTIN, JAY
GOLDING, MORTON JAY

MARTIN, JEREMY
LEVIN, MARCIA OBRANSKY
LEVIN, MARTIN P.

MARTIN, JOHN
TATHAM, LAURA

MARTIN, JOHN R.
WADE, THOMAS W.

MARTIN, JUNE HALL
MCCASH, JUNE HALL

MARTIN, KAT
MARTIN, KATHLEEN KELLY

MARTIN, KAY
MARITANO, ADELE

MARTIN, KEN
HUBBARD, L. RON

MARTIN, L.W.
MARTIN, LINCOLN WILLIAM

MARTIN, LEE
DELFS, RAINER
WEBB, [MARTHA] ANNE G.

MARTIN, LES
SCHULMAN, LESTER MARTIN

MARTIN, LEVIN
PELTON, ROBERT W.

MARTIN, LOUISA
FEJMERT, ELSA

MARTIN, LUCIEN
GABEL, JOSEPH

MARTIN, MARCIA
LEVIN, MARCIA OBRANSKY

MARTIN, MARY STEICHEN
CALDERON, MARY S.

MARTIN, MATTHIAS
FROBA, KLAUS

MARTIN, MICHAEL
KALMUCZAK, ROLF

MARTIN, MONICA
BETZ, INGRID

MARTIN, MR.
BURROUGHS, WILLIAM S.

MARTIN, NANCY
SALMON, ANNIE ELIZABETH

MARTIN, OCTAVE
MAURRAS, CHARLES-MARIE-P

MARTIN, OLIVER
DAVIES, ERNEST
SMITH, REGINALD DONALD

MARTIN, OTTO
FISCHER, MARTIN

MARTIN, PAT
HAWK, MARTIN R[AYMOND]

MARTIN, PAUL
DEALE, KENNETH EDWIN LEE
RADE, PAUL MARTIN

MARTIN, PETE
MARTIN, WILLIAM THORNTON

MARTIN, PETER
CHAUNDLER, CHRISTINE
LECKIE, PETER MARTIN

MARTIN, PRUDENCE
LICHTE, PRUDENCE BINGHAM

MARTIN, R. JOHNSON
MEHTA, RUSTAM JEHANGIR

MARTIN, R.J.
MEHTA, RUSTAM JEHANGIR

MARTIN, RAIMUND
MARTINEK, RAIMUND

MARTIN, REX
MARTIN, REGINALD ALEC

MARTIN, RICHARD
EHARMAN, RICHARD
CREASEY, JOHN

MARTIN, ROBERT
MARTIN, REGINALD ALEC

MARTIN, ROBERT W.
PELTON, ROBERT W.

MARTIN, RUSS
MARTIN, RUSSELL W.

MARTIN, RUTH
RAYNER, CLAIRE B.

MARTIN, SALLY
PFISTERER, SALLY

MARTIN, SAM
MOSKOWITZ, SAM

MARTIN, SCOTT
MARTIN, REGINALD ALEC

MARTIN, SHANE
JOHNSTON, GEORGE HENRY

MARTIN, STELLA
HEYER, GEORGETTE

MARTIN, TOM
PAINE, LAURAN BOSWORTH

MARTIN, VICKEY
STOREY, VICTORIA CAROLYN

MARTIN, WEBBER
SILVERBERG, ROBERT

MARTIN, WENDY
MARTINI, TERI

MARTINDALE, SPENCER
WOLFF, WILLIAM DEAKIN

MARTINE
WOOLFOLK, JOANNA MARTINE

MARTINEE, RAOUL
MARTINEK, RAIMUND

MARTINES, JULIA
O'FAOLAIN, JULIA

MARTINETZ, V.L.
MARTINETZ, VIVIAN L.

MARTINEZ, BENITO
BAJOG, GUNTHER
DELFS, RAINER
DUENSING, JURGEN
HEBEL, PETER
HUBNER, HORST W.
PRIESS, KARL-HEINZ
VON KOBLINSKI, HANS-JOACH

MARTINEZ, J.D.
PARKHILL, FORBES

MARTINI, ANDREA
LIGENSA, ELFIE

MARTINI, LILLI
BLUM, LILLI [M]

MARTINI, STEVE
MARTINI, STEVEN PAUL

MARTINI, THERESE
MARTINI, TERI

MARTINSEN, MARTIN
FOLLETT, KENNETH [MARTIN]

MARTINSON, HANS
BEMMANN, HANS

MARTINSON, MOA
SWARTZ, MARIA HELGA

MARTON, FRANCESCA
BELLASIS, MARGARET ROSA

MARTON, SANDRA
MYLES, SANDRA

MARTYN, DON
BARBOLLA, BARBARA MARTYN

MARTYN, HENRY
PERRY, MARTIN HENRY

MARTYN, MILES
ELLIOTT-CANNON, ARTHUR

MARTYN, OLIVER
WHITE, HERBERT OLIVER

MARTYN, PHILLIP
TUBB, E.C.

MARTYN, WYNDHAM
GBRENVIL, WILLIAM

MARUKAS, KAZIS
KRASAUKAS, MARIONAS I.

MARUT, RET
FEIGE, HERMANN ALBERT O.M

MARVEL, IK
MITCHELL, DONALD GRANT

MARVELL, ANDREW
DAVIES, HOWELL

MARVELL, HOLT
MASCHWITZ, ERIC

MARVIK, JAN
KNUTSEN, LALLI

MARVIN, F.S.
MARVIN, FRANCIS SYDNEY

MARVIN, JAMES W.
JAMES, LAURENCE

MARVIN, RICHARD
ELLIS, JULIE M.

MARVIN, SUSAN
ELLIS, JULIE M.

MARVIN, W.R.
CAMERON, LOU

MARWERT, MICHAEL
HEINDEL, GOTTFRIED

MARX, JEAN
DE LINVAL, PAUL CASSIUS

MARX, MAGDALEINE
PAZ, MAGDALEINE

MARX-LINDNER, LO
HOCKER, CHARLOTTE

MARY ALFREDA
ELSENSOHN, EDITH M.

MARY ALPHONSA
LATHROP, ROSE [H]

MARY ANGELITA
STACKHOUSE, MARY AGNES

MARY CONSOLATA
CARROLL, ALICE VIOLA

MARY FRANCIS
ASCHMANN, ALBERTA

MARY SALESIA [SISTER]
POGGEL, MARY

MARY SCHOLASTICA
JENKINS, MARIE M.

MARY, ANDRE
MONNIOT, JEAN-VORLE

MARY, ESTELLE
CASALANDRA, ESTELLE

MARYANNA
CHILDS, MARYANNA

MARYNEN, JOANNES
MATTYSSEN, JOHANNES

MARZIK, TRUDE
MARCZIK, EDELTRUD

MAS, CHRISTEL
HAAKE, JURGEN

MASCALL, MARGERY D.
NETHERCLIFT, BERYL C.

MASHA
STERN, MARIE

MASKOFF, JOZEF
KORWIN-PIOTROWSKA, GABRL.

MASON, ADRIAN
LEE, [REV] ALBERT

MASON, ANDREW
WELSH, KEN

MASON, CARL
KING, ALBERT

MASON, CHUCK
ROWLAND, DONALD S.

MASON, DAVID
MASON, SAMUEL

MASON, ERNEST
POHL, FREDERIK

MASON, ERNST
POHL, FREDERIK

MASON, F.V.W.
MASON, F. VAN WYCK

MASON, FRANK W.
MASON, F. VAN WYCK

MASON, FRANK
BUDRYS, ALGIRDAS JONAS

MASON, GREGORY
JONES, ADRIENNE
MEEK, DORIS

MASON, HARRY
STRATEMEYER, EDWARD

MASON, HILARY
MASON, EDITH HELEN
RODDICK, BARBARA M.

MASON, HOWARD
RAMAGE, JENNIFER

MASON, JOHN
TUBB, E.C.

MASON, LEE W.
MALZBERG, BARRY [N]

MASON, MICHAEL
SMITH, EDGAR

MASON, R.
REASONER, JAMES M.

MASON, R.A.K.
MASON, RONALD ALISON KELL

MASON, RAY
KNELLER, F.C.
WATT, JOHN F.

MASON, RAYMOND
MASON, CLARENCE RAY

MASON, ROGER
VERE-HODGE, CONRAD C.R.

MASON, S.C.
MASON, CHARLES

MASON, STUART
MILLARD, CHRISTIAN SCLATR

MASON, TALLY
DERLETH, AUGUST [WILLIAM]

MASON, TEX
GROSSMANN, HANS HUGO

MASON, TYLER
MASON, MADELAINE

MASON, VAL
HACKLEMAN, WAUNETA

MASON, WILLIAM
JOHNSTONE, WILLIAM W.

MASOVIUS, WERNER
MIALKI, W.

MASS, WILLIAM
GIBSON, WILLIAM

MASSA, JACK
MASSA, JOHN ANDREW

MASSAN, FR.
LEMKE, KARL

MASSARY, ISABEL
RAMSAY-LAYE, ELIZABETH

MASSEY, CHARLOTTE
CAPRIANA, VINCENT

MASSEY, JAMES
DE PATOT, SIMON TYSSOT

MASSEY, JESSICA
CULBY, JILL ALISON HART

MASSEY, RUTH
TOVELL, RUTH MASSEY

MASSOGLIA, MARTY
MASSOGLIA, MARTIN FRANK

MASSON, GEORGINA
JOHNSON, MARION GEORGINA

MASTERO STORYTELLER
SAHER, PETER J.

MASTERS, BAT
BULEY, BERNARD

MASTERS, DOUG
REY, PIERRE

MASTERS, J.D.
YERMAKOV, NICHOLAS VALEN.

MASTERS, KAY
MEISTER, KNUD

MASTERS, MELISSA
DENT, ROXANNE

MASTERS, PAUL
SAMWAYS, GEORGE R.

MASTERS, ROBERT V.
BOEHM, DAVID ALFRED

MASTERS, ROY
GIBSON, WALTER B.

MASTERS, STEVE
MASON, SYDNEY CHARLES

MASTERS, W.W.
MASTERS, WILLIAM WALTER

MASTERS, WILLIAM
COUSINS, MARGARET

MASTERS, ZEKE
BENSEN, DONALD R.
GOULART, RONALD JOSEPH

MASTERSON, J.B.
EDMONDSON Y COTTON, JOSE

MASTERSON, LOUIS
HALLBING, KJELL KARL
WALLMANN, JEFFREY M.

MASTERSON, WHIT
MCILWAIN, DAVID
MILLER, BILL[Y]
WADE, ROBERT [BOB]

MASTON, T.B.
MASTON, THOMAS BUFFORD

MASTRI, PIETRO
MASETTI, PIRRO

MASUDA, TAKESHI
ASKA, WARABE

MASUR, ERIKA
HORN, ERIKA

MASUR, H.Q.
MASUR, HAROLD Q.

MASUR, HAL
MASUR, HAROLD Q.

MASUR, HAROLD A.
MASUR, HAROLD Q.

MATA, DAYA
WRIGHT, FAYE

MATELOT
UREN, MALCOLM JOHN LEGGOE

MATHE, ALBERT
CAMUS, ALBERT

MATHER, ANNE
GRIEVESON, MILDRED

MATHER, BERKLEY
DAVIES, JOHN E.W.

MATHER, MELISSA
BROWN, MELISSA MATHER

MATHER, VIRGINIA
LIEBELER, JEAN MAYER

MATHERS, HELEN
MATHEWS, ELLEN B.

MATHESON, CHRIS
MATHESON, RICHARD CHRIST.

MATHESON, HUGH
MACKAY, HUGH LEWIS

MATHESON, JOAN
TRANSUE, JACOB

MATHESON, SYLVIA A.
SCHOFIELD, SYLVIA ANNE

MATHETES
JONES, JOHN

MATHEWS, DENISE
HRIMAK, DENISE
MATTHEWS, PATRICIA [BRIS]

MATHEWS, JAN
MILELLA, JAN

MATHEWS, KEVIN
FOX, GARDNER F.

MATHEWS, LOUISE
TOOKE, LOUISE MATHEWS

MATHEWS, MICHELLE
CROSE, SUSAN

MATHIESON, RICHARD
MATHESON, RICHARD [B]

MATHIESON, UNA COOPER
GIBSON, AMANDA M.T.

MATHIEU, JOE
MATHIEU, JOSEPH P.

MATHISON, RICHARD
MATHESON, RICHARD [B]

MATIASON, K.G.
LILJENFORS, BENNIE M.C.

MATLOCK, ALEX
COOPER, ROBERT ANDREW

MATRE, HERO
MAYER-TREES, HILDEGARD

MATSON, DR.
BREDBERG, ERNST C. JR.

MATSUNO, MASAKO
KOBAYASHI, MASAKO MATSUNO

MATT
SANDFORD, MATTHEW

MATTEO, P.B. JR.
RINGGOLD, GENE

MATTHESON, RODNEY
CREASEY, JOHN

MATTHEWMAN, PHYLLIS
SURREY, KATHRYN

MATTHEWS, ANN
MARTIN, ANN M[ATTHEWS]

MATTHEWS, ANTHONY
BARKER, DUDLEY

MATTHEWS, BAY
RICHARDS, PENNY

MATTHEWS, BRAD
DEMILLE, NELSON [RICHARD]

MATTHEWS, BRANDER
MATTHEWS, JAMES BRANDER

MATTHEWS, JACK
MATTHEWS, JOHN HAROLD JR.

MATTHEWS, JACKLYN MEEK
MEEK, JACKLYN O'HANLON

MATTHEWS, KEVIN
FOX, GARDNER F.

MATTHEWS, LAURA
ROTTER, ELIZABETH N.W.

MATTHEWS, PHOEBE
JONES, DIANE MCCLURE

MATTHEWS, WEBB
STANNARD, DAVID

MATTHEY, A.
ARNOULD, ARTHUR

MATTOX, AUSTIN
MADDOX, AUSTIN

MATURA, MUSTAPHA
MATHURA, MUSTAPHA

MATUSOW, MARSHALL
MATUSOW, HARVEY MARSHALL

MATUTE, ANA MARIA
GOICOECHEA, ANA MARIA M.

MAUGHAM, DIANA
MARR-JOHNSON, DIANA

MAUGHAM, ROBIN
MAUGHAM, ROBERT CECIL R.

MAULE, TEX
MAULE, HAMILTON BEE

MAURER, G.
MULLER, PAUL ALFRED

MAURER, OTTO
MASON, EUDO COLECESTRA

MAURICE, ALFRED
GIBSON, WALTER B.

MAURICE, FURNLEY
WILMOT, FRANK LESLIE T.

MAURICE, JACQUES
MORRIS, JAMES W.

MAURICE, MICHAEL
SKINNER, CONRAD ARTHUR

MAURICE, RENE LOUIS
FOLLETT, KENNETH [MARTIN]

MAURICE, ROGER
ASSELINEAU, ROGER [M]

MAURICE, WALTER
BESANT, [SIR] WALTER

MAURINA, ZENTA
RAUDIVE-MAURINA, ZENTA

MAUROIS, ANDRE
HERZOG, EMILE S.

MAUSER, MAX
LIE, JONAS JR.

MAUZY, PETER
BURGESS, MICHAEL ROY

MAVERICK, RANDY
RAHN, WOLFGANG

MAVIN, JOHN
GARMAN, DOUGLAS MAVIN
RICKWORD, [JOHN] EDGELL

MAVITY, HUBERT
BOND, NELSON S.

MAWATANI, NANATA
ALTEN, INGRID

MAWBY, JANET
GARTON, JANET

MAX, BARBARA
VALENTI, JUSTINE

MAX, NICHOLAS
ASBELL, BERNARD

MAX, RAYMOND
HART, CYRIL CHARLES

MAXAM, MIA
CREWS, ETHEL MAXAM

MAXFIELD, ELIZABETH
MILLER, ELIZABETH MAXFLD.

MAXHIM, TRISTAN
JONES, [MAX HIM] HENRY

MAXIME, A.
BRIE, ALFRED

MAXINE
FORTIER, CORA B.

MAXON, ANNE
BEST, [E] ALLENA CHAMPLIN

MAXON, J.G.
GOODWIN, JUNE
SCHIFF, BEN

MAXWELL, A.E.
MAXWELL, ANN [ELIZABETH]
MAXWELL, EVAN

MAXWELL, ALLAN
BAYFIELD, WILLIAM J.

MAXWELL, ANN
PATTINSON, LEE

MAXWELL, C. BEDE
MAXWELL, VIOLET S.

MAXWELL, CLIFFORD
LEON, HENRY CECIL

MAXWELL, EDWARD
ALLAN, TED
POLLOCK, COURTENAY

MAXWELL, EMILY
SCHWAB, LINDA J.

MAXWELL, ERICA
PYKE, LILLIAN MAXWELL

MAXWELL, GORDON
SHUTE, WALTER

MAXWELL, GRANT
RICHARDSON, GLADWELL G.

MAXWELL, HELEN K.
DENNISTON, ELINORE

MAXWELL, HERBERT
LOMAX, WILLIAM JOSEPH
WYMAN, WALTER F.

MAXWELL, JACK
MCKEAG, ERNEST LIONEL

MAXWELL, JOHN
FREEMANTLE, BRIAN [HARRY]

MAXWELL, JOHN C.
GLASBY, JOHN S.

MAXWELL, JOSLYN
IRELAND, M.J.

MAXWELL, KATHLEEN
GRANT, KATHRYN ANNE P.

MAXWELL, MARY
HEATON, JEN M.
OSBURN, MICKY K.

MAXWELL, MARY M.
BANKS, ELIZABETH

MAXWELL, PETER
CAVE, PETER [LESLIE]

MAXWELL, RONALD
SMITH, RONALD GREGOR

MAXWELL, SILVESTER
DORNER, CLAUS S.

MAXWELL, THOMAS
GIFFORD, THOMAS [E]

MAXWELL, VICKY
WORBOYS, ANN[ETTE I.]

MAXWELL, W.B.
MAXWELL, WILLIAM BABINGTN

MAXXE, ROBERT
ROSENBLUM, ROBERT J.

MAY, BERNICE
CROSS, ZORA BERNICE MAY

MAY, COLIN
TUBB, E.C.

MAY, FLORISSA
GREEN, KAY

MAY, HELEN
JACKSON, EILEEN V.

MAY, IDA
PIKE, MARY HAYDEN G.

MAY, JANINE
ANDONIAN, JEANNE

MAY, JONATHAN
JAMES, LAURENCE
WOOD, CHRISTOPHER [H]

MAY, JULIAN [C]
DIKTY, JULIAN [C] MAY

MAY, MARGERY LAND
FOSTER, MARGERY LAND MAY

MAY, ROBERTA E.
DAVIDSON, EDITH MAY

MAY, ROBIN
MAY, ROBERT STEPHEN

MAY, SOPHIE
CLARKE, REBECCA SOPHIA

MAY, WYNNE
KNOWLES, MABEL WINIFRED
MAY, WINIFRED JEAN

MAYBURY, ANNE
BUXTON, ANNE

MAYER, AHGATHA
MAHER, RAMONA

MAYER, HERBERT
GIBSON, WALTER B.

MAYER, SUZANNE
MEIER, LINDA SUSAN

MAYFAIR, BERTHA
RABORG, FREDERICK A.

MAYFAIR, FRANKLIN
MENDELSOHN, FELIX JR.

MAYFIELD, ANNE
GRANT, KATHRYN ANNE P.

MAYFIELD, JACK
COOPER, PARLEY J.

MAYFIELD, JULIA
HASTINGS, PHYLLIS DORA H.

MAYFIELD, M.I.
HIRSHFIELD, HENRY I.
MATEYKO, G.M.

MAYFIELD, MARLYS
FREY, MARLYS

MAYFIELD, SERENA
BENTHAM, JOSEPHINE

MAYHEW, ELIZABETH
BEAR, JOAN E.

MAYNARD, CHRIS
MAYNARD, CHRISTOPHER

MAYNARD, JACK
MOSKOVITZ, JACK

MAYNARD, R.T.
CAVE, HUGH B[ARNETT]

MAYNC, SUSY
LANGHANS-MAYNC, SUSY

MAYNE, ARTHUR
BATCHELOR, RICHARD A.C.

MAYNE, CORA
WALKER, EMILY KATHLEEN

MAYNE, H.H.
WILSON, HELEN HELGA

MAYNE, RUTHERFORD
WADDELL, SAMUEL

MAYNE, SHARON
MOEHN, SHARON DULING

MAYNES, DR. J.O. ROCKY
MAYNES, J. OSCAR JR.

MAYNES, J.O. ROCKY JR.
MAYNES, J. OSCAR JR.

MAYNWARING, ARCHIBALD
LOVECRAFT, H[OWARD] P.

MAYO, ARNOLD
MEREDITH, KENNETH LINCOLN

MAYO, JAMES
COULTER, STEPHEN

MAYO, JIM
LAMOORE, LOUIS [DEARBORN]

MAYO, MARK
LANE, YOTI

MAYO, NICK
MARTOFF, NICKOLI

MAYOE, MARIAN & FRANKLIN
ROSEWATER, FRANK

MAYRANT, DRAYTON
SIMON, KATHERINE DRAYTON

MAYS, SPIKE
MAYS, CEDRIC WESLEY

MAYSI, KADRA
SIMON, KATHERINE DRAYTON

MAYY
ZIYADAH, MARIE

MAZ
MAZURE, ALFRED LEONARDUS

MAZAL TOV
CZACZKES, SHMUEL YOSEF

MAZE, EDWARD
MAZZOCCO, EDWARD

MCADAM, PRESTON
MCADAM, DOUG
PRESTON, JOHN

MCADAMS, CHARLES
RICHARDSON, GLADWELL G.

MCALISTAIR, AMANDA
DOWDELL, DOROTHY [F.K.]

MCALISTER, IAN
ALBERT, MARVIN H.

MCALLISTER, AMANDA
MEAKER, ELOISE
HAGER, [WILMA] JEAN [L]

MCALLISTER, ANNE
SCHENCK, BARBARA

MCALLISTER, ANNIE LAURIE
CASSIDAY, BRUCE [BINGHAM]

MCALPIN, GRANT
MCCULLEY, JOHNSTON

MCANDREW, CASS
TAYLOR, MARY ANN

MCANDREWS, JOHN
STEWARD, SAMUEL M[ORRIS]
WISE, ARTHUR

MCBAIN, ED
HUNTER, EVAN

MCBRIDE, AENEAS
MACKAY, FULTON

MCBRIDE, ARTHUR
GRUBER, FRANK

MCBRIDE, CAITLIN
ALLEN, DANICE

MCBRIDE, HARPER
WEAVER, JUDITH

MCBRIDE, JULE
MOORE, JULIANNE RANDOLPH

MCBRIDE, MARY
MYERS, MARY

MCBRIDE, PATRICIA
BARTZ, PATRICIA MCBRIDE

MCBROWN, JOE
VON KOBLINSKI, HANS-JOACH

MCC
MCCANCE, JAMES LAW

MCC, J.L.
MCCANCE, JAMES LAW

MCCABE, CAMERON
BORNEMAN, ERNEST [W.J.]

MCCABE, CORD
FITTOCK, R.J.

MCCABE, RORY
GREENWOOD, T.E.

MCCABE, SUNDOWN
GREEN, ROGER

MCCAFFERY, LARRY
MCCAFFERY, LAWRENCE FLOR.

MCCAFFREE, SHARON
SHALLENBERGER, SHARON MC.

MCCAFFREY, MARY
SZUDEK, AGNES SUSAN F.

MCCAIG, MORGAN
TAYLOR, R.L.

MCCAIG, SNEE
MCCAIG, DONALD

MCCALL, ANTHONY
KANE, HENRY

MCCALL, CLINT
ASHLEY, JIM
HETHERINGTON, KEITH JAMES

MCCALL, JOHN COREY
MORLAND, NIGEL

MCCALL, K.T.
ARMITAGE, AUDREY
WATKINS, MURIEL

MCCALL, KATHLEEN
DRYMON, KATHLEEN

MCCALL, SIDNEY
FENELLOSA, MARY MACNEIL

MCCALL, VINCENT
MORLAND, NIGEL

MCCALL, WENDELL
PEARSON, RIDLEY

MCCANN, ARTHUR
CAMPBELL, JOHN W[OOD]

MCCANN, COOLIDGE
FAWCETT, FRANK DUBREZ

MCCANN, EDSON
DEL REY, LESTER
POHL, FREDERIK

MCCANN, HEATHER
GRACE, LAURA

MCCARTER, JODY
DE MELIKOFF, JODI
MCCARTER, VERMILLE

MCCARTHY, JANE
SEARS, RUTH MCCARTHY

MCCARTHY, SHAUN
MCCARTHY, SHAUN LLOYD

MCCARY, REED
RYDBERG, ERNIE

MCCAUGHEY, ELLEN
KOSHLAND, ELLEN

MCCAUGHREAN, GERALDINE
JONES, GERALDINE

MCCAULEY, BARBARA
JOEL, BARBARA

MCCAULL, M.E.
BOHLMAN, EDNA MCCAULL

MCCLARY, THOMAS [CALVERT]
GIBSON, WALTER B.

MCCLEAN, KATHLEEN
HALE, KATHLEEN

MCCLEARY, ELEANOR
PICKEN, MARY BROOKS

MCCLELLAN, TIERNEY
MCCAFFERTY, BARBARA TAYL.

MCCLELLAN, WILLIAM
STRONG, CHARLES STANLEY

MCCLINTOCK, MIKE
MCCLINTOCK, MARSHALL

MCCLOUD, JASON
HOHLBEIN, WOLFGANG E.

MCCLOUD, JED
FEARN, JOHN RUSSELL

MCCLOUD, VAN
LUTZ, JOHN [T]

MCCLURE, ANNA
SORRELS, ROY

MCCONNELL, CHAN
SCHOW, DAVID J.

MCCONNELL, FRANK
MCCONNELL, FRANCIS DEMAY

MCCONNELL, JAMES
MCCONNELL, JAMES D.R.

MCCONNELL, LISA
MCCOURTNEY, LORENA KNOLL

MCCONNELL, WILL
SNODGRASS, W.D.

MCCORD, CLAY
ROTSLER, WILLIAM

MCCORD, GUY
REYNOLDS, DALLAS MCCORD

MCCORD, WHIP
NORWOOD, VICTOR [G.C.]

MCCORMACK, CHARLOTTE
ROSS, WILLIAM E. DANIEL

MCCORMICK, BROOKS
ADAMS, WILLIAM TAYLOR

MCCORMICK, CLAIRE
LABUS, MARTA HAAKE

MCCORMICK, INSPECTOR
GROSSMANN, HANS HUGO

MCCORMICK, ROSE M.
MCCORMICK, MARY

MCCORMICK, THEODORA
DU BOIS, THEODORA

MCCOY, ANDREW
JUTE, ANDREW

MCCOY, ARCH
MILLER, VICTOR [B]

MCCOY, CATHLYN
BAKER, FRAN

MCCOY, CLIFF
KRAMER, PETER

MCCOY, HANK
MARTIN, REGINALD ALEC

MCCOY, MALACHY
CAULFIELD, MALACHY F.

MCCOY, MARSHALL
MEARES, LEONARD F.

MCCOY, MICK
FEARN, JOHN RUSSELL

MCCOY, ROSEANNA
NORWOOD, VICTOR [G.C.]

MCCOY, STEVE
ERICHSEN, UWE

MCCOY, TEX
JENNISON, JOHN WILLIAM

MCCOY, TRENT
BOYCE, DAVID

MCCRACKEN, MIKE
LANDSBOROUGH, GORDON H.

MCCREADY, JACK
POWELL, TALMAGE

MCCREIGH, JAMES
POHL, FREDERIK

MCCULLOCH, JOHN TYLER
BURROUGHS, EDGAR RICE

MCCULLOCH, SARA[H]
URE, JEAN

MCCULLOUGH, COLEEN
MCCULLOUGH-ROBINSON, COL.

MCCULLY, EMILY ARNOLD
ARNOLD, EMILY

MCCURRY, BETSY
MOORE, BERTHA B.

MCCURTIN, PETER
HAYES, RALPH EUGENE
SMITH, GEORGE H[ARMON]

MCCUTCHEN, ANN
BROOMHEAD, ANN [ALLEDA]

MCCUTCHEON, JAMES
LUNDGREN, PAUL ARTHUR

MCDANIEL, DAVID
JOHNSTONE, TED

MCDANIEL, LARAINE
BELL, LARAINE

MCDERMOT, LT. THOMAS
GIBSON, WALTER B.

MCDERMOTT, DENNIS
MCDERMOTT, PAUL
MILLER, P. SCHUYLER

MCDERMOTT, ROBERT
HAWLEY, DONALD THOMAS

MCDEVITT, JACK
MCDEVITT, JOHN CHARLES

MCDOLE, CAROL
FARELY, CAROL

MCDONALD, DIANNA
SHOMAKER, DIANNA

MCDONALD, JAMIE
HEIDE, FLORENCE PARRY

MCDONALD, JO
MCDONALD, MARGARET J.

MCDONALD, KATHY
WALLIS, GERALDINE MCDONL.

MCDONALD, RAYMOND
LEGER, RAYMOND A.
MCDONALD, EDWARD R.

MCDONALD, ROBERT
LEACH, ANN

MCDONNELL, JINNY
MCDONNELL, VIRGINIA B.

MCDOUGAL, STAN
DIAMANT, LINCOLN

MCDOW, GERALD
SCORTIA, THOMAS N.

MCDOWELL, CROSBY
FREEMAN, JOHN CROSBY

MCDOWELL, EMMETT
MCDOWELL, ROBERT EMMETT

MCDOWELL, JOHN
PARKS, TIMOTHY HAROLD

MCDUFF, E.M.
MCDUFF, EILEEN MAY

MCDUNN, GARRY
BISCHOFF, MARIANNE [E]

MCELFRESH, ADELINE
MCELFRESH, ELIZABETH A.

MCELROY, LEE
KELTON, ELMER

MCELROY, WINSTON
WALLMANN, JEFFREY M.

MCERLEAN, SHEILA
LYNDS, DENNIS

MCFERRAN, ANN
TOWNSEND, DORIS M.

MCFERRAN, DORIS
TOWNSEND, DORIS M.

MCGANN, MICHAEL
NAHA, ED

MCGARRITY, MARK
GILL, BARTHOLOMEW

MCGAVIN, MOYRA
CRICHTON, ELEANOR

MCGAW, J.W.
MORRIS, JOHN

MCGEE, T.D.
SAVAGE, TERESA

MCGEORGE, DR. M. ERNEST
BREDBERG, ERNST C. JR

MCGHEE, EDWARD
HARPER, EDWARD M.

MCGILL, IAN
ALLEGRO, JOHN MARCO

MCGILL, JOYCE
WEST, CHASSIE

MCGILL, MARCI
BALTERMAN, MARCIA R.

MCGILL, NANCY
RICHARDS, TAD & JONATHAN

MCGILLICUDDY, MR.
ABISCH, ROSLYN KROOP

MCGINN, MAUREEN ANN
SAUTEL, MAUREEN ANN

MCGINNIS, E.L.
VON BLOCK, BELA [W]

MCGINNIS, K.K.
PAGE, GROVER JR.

MCGIRR, EDMUND
GILES, KENNETH

MCGIVENY, MAURA
DE BETS, JULIE

MCGLINN, DWIGHT
BRANNON, WILLIAM T.

MCGLYNN, CHRISTOPHER
GINDER, RICHARD

MCGORGO
BEUMELBURG, WERNER

MCGORIAN, GLADYS
DRESSLER, GLADYS M.

MCGOWAN, D.C.
GRAHAM, ROGER P.

MCGOWAN, INEZ
GRAHAM, ROGER P.

MCGOWAN, JAN
MCGAURAN, JOANNA

MCGOWEN, TOM
MCGOWEN, THOMAS E.

MCGRATH, DOYLE
SCHORB, EDWIN MARSH

MCGRATH, MARY
MURRANKA, MARY

MCGRATH, MORGAN
RAE, HUGH C[RAWFORD]

MCGREAL, ELIZABETH
YATES, ELIZABETH

MCGREEVEY, JOHN [W]
BROWNE, HOWARD
HAMLING, WILLIAM L.

MCGREGOR
HURLEY, DORAN

MCGREW, FENN
FENN, CAROLINE K.
MCGREW, JULIA

MCGUINNESS, BRIAN
MCGUINNESS, BERNARD

MCGUIRE, JENNY
FLEMING, KATE
MORGAN, NANCY

MCGUIRE, MOLLY
GOLDENBAUM, SALLY

MCGUIRE, NICHOLAS
MELIDES, NICHOLAS

MCGUIRE, PATRICK O.
MITCHELL, JAMES [W]

MCGURK, SLATER
ROTH, ARTHUR JOSEPH

MCHART, GEORGE
HARTSCH, GERHART

MCHUGH, HUGH
HOBART, GEORGE VERE

MCHUGH, JAY
MACQUEEN, JAMES WILLIAM

MCHUGH, STUART
ROWLAND, DONALD S.

MCILVAINE, JANE
MCCLARY, JANE STEVENSON

MCINTOSH, J.T.
MACGREGOR, JAMES MURDOCH

MCINTOSH, LOUIS
JOHNSON, CHRISTOPHER

MCINTYRE, HOPE
TUCKER, RUTH B.

MCIVER, N.J.
HOWARD, ALAN

MCIVOR, IVOR BEN
WELSH, CHARLES

MCKAY, ANDREW
ERICHSEN, UWE

MCKAY, CHARLES
DUENSING, JURGEN
HUBNER, HORST W.
PRIESS, KARL-HEINZ

MCKAY, CLAUDIA
LAMPERTI, CLAUDIA J. MCK.

MCKAY, ERNAN
MCINERNY, RALPH [M]

MCKAY, JOHN
MOSKOVITZ, JACK

MCKAY, KELVIN
STRONG, CHARLES STANLEY

MCKAY, KENNETH R.
KANE, HENRY

MCKAY, RENA
MCCOURTNEY, LORENA KNOLL

MCKAY, SIMON
NICOLE, CHRISTOPHER ROBIN

MCKEAG, EILEEN
MCKEAG, ERNEST LIONEL

MCKEE, JAN [JANICE]
MCKEE, JANICE

MCKEEN, CAPT.
ST. JOHN, PERCY BOLLNGBRK

MCKEEVER, MARCIA
LAIRD, JEAN E.

MCKENNA, A. DANIEL
FINNERTY, ADAM DANIEL

MCKENNA, EVELYN
JOSCELYN, ARCHIE LYNN

MCKENNA, LINDSAY
NAUMAN, EILEEN

MCKENNA, MARY LAWRENCE
MCKENNA, MARGARET MARY

MCKENNA, R.M.
MCKENNA, RICHARD MILTON

MCKENNA, ROSE ANNE
PINIANSKI, PATRICIA

MCKENNA, TATE
ENGELS, MARY TATE

MCKENZIE, DONALD J.
YOUNG, ERNEST A[VON]

MCKENZIE, KATE
CROISSANT, KAY
DEES, CATHERINE

MCKENZIE, MELINDA
SNODGRASS, MELINDA

MCKENZIE, PAGE
BLOOD, MARJE

MCKENZIE, RAY
SILVERBERG, ROBERT

MCKEONE, LEE
MCKEONE, DIXIE

MCKERN, PAT
WILLETT, FRANCISCUS

MCKETTRIG, SEATON
GARRETT, RANDALL [P]

MCKINLEY, BRETT
WHEELAHAN, PAUL

MCKINLEY, KAREN
RUNBECK, MARGARET LEE

MCKINNEY, D.J.
COOPER, PARLEY J.

MCKINNEY, GEORGIA
POTEET, ARDIA

MCKINNEY, JACK
DALEY, BRIAN C.
LUCENO, JAMES

MCKINNEY, MEAGAN
GOODMAN, RUTH

MCKNIGHT, JENNA
SCHWEISS, V.M.

MCKRACKEN, JAMES A.
RAHMAN, G. ARTHUR

MCLAGLEN, JOHN J.
HARVEY, JOHN [BARTON]
JAMES, LAURENCE

MCLANE, JACK
CRIDER, [ALLEN] BILL[Y]

MCLAREN, GORDON
PATTEN, WILLIAM GEORGE

MCLAUGHLIN, BILL
PHILLIPS, JAMES R.

MCLEAN, CARA
BARRETT, ELIZABETH

MCLEAN, DAVIDA
SKOV, DAVID A.

MCLEAN, J. SLOANE
GILLETTE, VIRGINIA M.
WUNSCH, JOSEPHINE M.

MCLEAN, SALLY PRATT
GREENE, SARA PRATT M.

MCLEISH, DOUGAL
GOODSPEED, DONALD JAMES

MCLEISH, GAREN
STINE, WHITNEY WARD

MCLELLAN, WILLIAM B.
STRONG, CHARLES STANLEY

MCLEOD, FINLAY
WOOD, JAMES [A.F]

MCLEOD, KIRSTY
HUDSON, [MARGARET] KIRSTY

MCLEOD, MARGARET VAIL
HOLLOWAY, TERESA BRAGUNIE

MCLINN, PATRICIA
MCLAUGHLIN, PATRICIA

MCLOCIARD, GEORGE
LOCKE, CHARLES F.

MCLOUD, SCOTT
MCLEOD, SCOTT WILLARD

MCLOUGHLIN, R.B.
MENCKEN, HENRY LOUIS

MCLOWERY, FRANK
KEEVILL, HENRY J.

MCLURE, SCOTT
VEITCH, TONY

MCMAHON, GEORGE
HAENSEL, HUBERT

MCMAHON, PAT
HOCH, EDWARD D.

MCMAHON, PATRICK
HOCH, EDWARD D.

MCMAN, MARC
MIELKE, THOMAS R.P.

MCMASTER, ALISON
BAKER, MARJORIE

MCMEEKIN, CLARK
CLARK, DOROTHY [PARK]
MCMEEKIN, ISABEL [M]

MCMILLAN, STEVE
MAAG, GEORG

MCMUD, DOK
MCLACHLAN, DAN

MCMULLAN, KATY HALL
MCMULLAN, KATE [HALL]

MCMULLEN, CATHERINE
COOKSON, CATHERINE ANN

MCMULLEN, KATIE
COOKSON, CATHERINE ANN

MCMULLEN, MARY
WILSON, MARY REILLY

MCMURDIE, ANNIE LAURIE
CASSIDAY, BRUCE [BINGHAM]

MCNAB, CLAIRE
CARMICHAEL, CLAIRE

MCNAB, OLIVER
FREDE, RICHARD

MCNAIR, CHRISTY
GARRARD, DOROTHY

MCNAIR, RON
RAYMOND, BENN

MCNAUGHT, JUDITH
SMITH, JUDITH SPAETH M.

MCNEILL, ELISABETH
TAYLOR, ELISABETH D.

MCNEILL, JANET
ALEXANDER, JANET

MCNEILLY, WILFRED
BAKER, W.A. HOWARD

MCNEISH, NEIL
SCHIER, NORMA

MCNORTH, JACK
MCLAREN, JACK

MCNUTT, CHARLES
BEAUMONT, CHARLES

MCPATTERSON, FRED
ERNSTING, WALTER

MCPHERSON, HUGO
MCPHERSON, HUGH [A]

MCQUAY, MICHAEL D.
MCQUAY, MICHAEL DENNIS

MCQUAY, MIKE
MCQUAY, MICHAEL DENNIS

MCRAE, LINDSAY
SOWERBY, A. LINDSAY

MCRAE, ROY
BULEY, BERNARD

MCRITCHIE, HAL
RICHARTZ, HELMUTH

MCROBERTS, AGNESANN
MEEK, PAULINE PALMER

MCS, DEWI
SKOV, DAVID A.

MCTAVISH, PAULINE
DONALDSON, DALE C.

MCVEAN, JAMES
LUARD, NICHOLAS

MCVICKER, CHUCK
MCVICKER, CHARLES TAGGART

MEABEY, LEONARD
GANDER, LEONARD

MEAD, MATT
RICHARDS, ROSS

MEAD, RUSSELL
KOEHLER, MARGARET [H]

MEAD, SHEPHERD
MEAD, EDWARD

MEADE, ELLEN
RODDICK, ELLEN

MEADE, L.T.
BARTON, ROBERT EUSTACE
DOUGLAS, ROBERT K.
HALIFAX, CLIFFORD
SMITH, ELIZABETH THOMASIN

MEADE, RICHARD
HAAS, BENJAMIN LEOPOLD

MEADMORE, SUSAN
SALLIS, SUSAN DIANA

MEADOWCROFT, ENID LAMONTE
WRIGHT, ENID M.

MEADOWES, ALICIA
ZEIG, JOAN

MEADOWS, ADRIAN
ALEXANDER, MARK [MARSHA]
BURAK, LINDA [GALLINA]

MEADOWS, PAULINE
MEGROS, PHYLLIS

MEADOWS, PETER
LINDSAY, JACK

MEAKER, M.J.
MEAKER, MARIJANE [AGNES]

MEANS, EVIL
PROWELL, SANDRA WEST

MEARE, EDNA
MIER, EDNOR

MEARS, LADY
TEMPEST, MARGARET MARY

MEASDAY, GEORGE
SODERBURG, PERCY MEASDAY

MECHLER, ULRICH
FIELITZ, HANS PAUL

MECK, BARBARA
CINAR-MECK, BARBARA

MECS, LASZLO
MARTONCSIK, LASZLO

MEDARD, YVES
LABUCHIN, RASSOUL

MEDHURST, JOAN
LIVERTON, JOAN

MEDICA
GRAHAM, DR. JOAN

MEDICANT, ARCH
ALDISS, BRIAN [WILSON]

MEDICUS
MACLAREN, JAMES PATERSON

MEDILL, ROBERT
MCBRIDE, ROBERT MEDILL

MEDLEY, ANNE
BORCHARD, RUTH

MEDLOCK, MARILYN
AMMAN, MARILYN MEDLOCK

MEDUSA, KARL
BARNES, MICHAEL [L.G.]
GORELL, LETHBRIDGE

MEDVEDER, PAVEL
BAKHTIN, MIKHAIL M.

MEE
SCHUBE, PURCELL G.

MEE, MARY
DEAN, MARY

MEEK, JOSEPH
PERLBERG, CHARLEY W.
RANDISI, ROBERT J.

MEEK, MARGARET
SPENCER-MEEK, MARGARET

MEEK, S.P.
MEEK, STERNER ST. PAUL

MEEKER, JASON
KUROWSKI, FRANZ

MEEKER, RICHARD
BROWN, FORNAN

MEEROPOL, MICHAEL
ROSENBERG, MICHAEL

MEES, STEVE
FLEXNER, STUART BERG

MEGO, AL
ROBERTS, ARTHUR O.

MEIDINGER-GEISE, INGE
MEIDINGER-GEISE INGEBORG

MEIER, LISI
LOCHER-WERLING, EMILIE

MEIER, SUSAN
MEIER, LINDA SUSAN

MEIER-KNILBENDORFF, RALF.
REIMANN, GERO

MEIKLE, CLIVE
BROOKS, JEREMY

MEINERT, ANNALIESE
PENKALA, ALICE

MEINHARDT, PETER
MANDT, GEORGE

MEINHART, RODERICH
MULLER-GUTTENBRUNN, RODER

MEINIKOFF, PAMELA
HARRIS, PAMELA

MEIRING, DESMOND
RICE, DESMOND CHARLES

MEISE, EDITHA
FROBOSE, EDITHA

MEISTER, KARL
LELAND, CHARLES G.

MELBORNE, IVOR
RANSOME, L.E.

MELBOURNE, IDA
RANSOME, L.E.

MELDE, G.R.
HUGHES, DENNIS [TALBOT]

MELDRUM, HELEN MYERS
SCOTT, HELEN MYERS

MELDRUM, JAMES
BROXHOLME, JOHN FRANKLIN

MELENA, ELPIS
VON SCHWARTZ, MARIE E.

MELIKOW
VON HOFMANNSTHAL, HUGO

MELLALIEU, JAMES S.
MARGERISON, JOHN S.

MELLINA, GLORIA
KUROWSKI, FRANZ

MELLING, O.R.
WHELAN, GERALDINE

MELLOR, MICHAEL
SPOONER, PETER ALAN

MELLORS, SAMANTHA
LOTTMAN, EILEEN [SHUBB]

MELMOTH
TULLETT, DENIS JOHN

MELONEY, FRANKEN
FRANKEN, ROSE [DOROTHY]
MELONEY, WILLIAM BROWN

MELROSE, ANDREA LASONDE
ANASTOS, ANDREA LASONDE M

MELSHIN, L.
YAKUBOVICH, PETER FILIP.

MELTON, GEORGE
MENTZEL, GEORG

MELVIER, LARENT
LUCAS, GERALD

MELVILLE, ALAN
CAVERHILL, W. MELVILLE

MELVILLE, ANNE
POTTER, MARGARET [N]

MELVILLE, JAMES
MARTIN, ROY PETER

MELVILLE, JEAN
CUMMINS, MARY WARMINGTON

MELVILLE, JENNIE
BUTLER, GWENDOLINE W.

MELVILLE, LEWIS
BENJAMIN, LEWIS SAUL
HARGREAVES, REGINALD C.

MELWOOD, MARY
LEWIS, E.M.

MENA, MARIA CRISTINA
CHAMBERS, MARIA CRISTINA

MENANDER
MORGAN, CHARLES

MENASCO, JOHN
SELLERS, CONNIE LESLIE

MENASCO, NORMAN
GUIN, WYMAN

MENCER, D.J.
KNELLER, F.C.

MENCET, D.R.
WATT, JOHN F.

MENCKEN, H.L.
MENCKEN, HENRY LOUIS

MENDEL, JO
BOND, GLADYS BAKER
GILBERTSON, MILDRED G.

MENDELE, MOCHER SFORIM
ABRAMOVICH, SHOLEM JACOB

MENDL, GLADYS
SCHUTZE, GLADYS H.

MENDONCA, SUSAN
SMITH, SUSAN VERNON M.

MENEN, AUBREY
MENON, S. AUBREY CLARENCE

MENEX, YANN
MENAIS, BRUNO

MENG, WU WU
BEILES, SINCLAIR

MENK, F.
DITTMARSCH, KARL

MENKEN, HANNE
HOF, ANNI [G]

MENSCH, H.L.
COHEN, ERIC
ETCHISON, DENNIS WILLIAM

MENTER, A.
MENZER, CLARA

MENTOR
JONES, FRANK H.
LAKE, KENNETH R[OBERT]
URNER, NATHAN DANE

MENTZEL, DONALD H.
MENZEL, DONALD H.

MENZ, ABI
KOSTER-LJUNG, HANNA

MENZ, GISELA
MANSS, GISELA

MENZEL, JOHANNA
MESKILL, JOHANNA MENZEL

MEONIO, CLEARCO
PAGAZA, ARCADIO

MEPLATS, ISIDORE
TACHE, JEAN CHARLES

MERAK, A.J.
GLASBY, JOHN S.

MERCADER, ENRIQUE
COROMINAS, PERE

MERCEIN, ELEANOR
KELLY, ELEANOR MERCEIN

MERCER, FRANCES
HILLS, FRANCES E.

MERCHANT, PAUL
ELLISON, HARLAN

MERCURY
ALLEN, CECIL J.
EAMES, HELEN MARY

MEREDITH, ANNE
BRUNER, BRENDA A.
BRUNER, BUREEDA
MALLESON, LUCY BEATRICE

MEREDITH, ARNOLD
HOPKINS, KENNETH

MEREDITH, D.R.
MEREDITH, DORIS R.

MEREDITH, DAVID WILLIAM
MIERS, EARL SCHENCK

MEREDITH, DEAN
DEAN, EDITH M.

MEREDITH, HAL
BLYTH, HARRY

MEREDITH, NICHOLETE
STACK, NICHOLETE MEREDITH

MEREDITH, OWEN
LYTTON, ROBERT BULWER

MEREDITH, PETER
WORTHINGTON-STUART, BRIAN

MEREK, JACK
ANDERSON, DENNIS

MEREZHKOVSKY, ZINAIDA
GIPPIUS, ZINAIDA N.

MERGEN, KIREI
KIREEV, AKHNIAF N.

MERIN, PETER
BIHALJI-MERIN, OTO

MERINGOFF, LAURENE KRASNY
BROWN, LAURENCE KRASNY

MERITON, PETER
HUNTER, ALFRED JOHN

MERITT, CADE C.
FRANCISKOWSKY, HANS GUNT.

MERIVALE, MARGARET
FROST, KATHLEEN MARGARET

MERIWETHER, KATE
AHEARN, PATRICIA

MERKLE, JUDITH A.
RILEY, JUDITH [A] MERKLE

MERLE, PETE
BLEECK, G.C.

MERLIN, CHRISTIE[A]
MCGAURAN, JOANNA

MERLIN, CHRISTINA
HEAVEN, CONSTANCE FECHER

MERLIN, DAVID
MOREAU, DAVID

MERLIN, JAN
WASCJLEWSKI, JAN

MERLING, MAJA
AMERLING, MAJA

MERLINI, [THE] GREAT
RAWSON, CLAYTON

MERLINO, MERLIN MESMER
CARPENTER, DONALD G.

MERLYN, ARTHUR
BLISH, JAMES B.

MERRELL, BARBARA
GIBBONS, HARRY

MERRICK, DR. MARK
RATHBORNE, ST. GEORGE

MERRICK, HUGH
MEYER, HAROLD ALBERT

MERRICK, JIM
FEARN, C. EATON

MERRICK, LEONARD
MILLER, LEONARD

MERRICK, SPENCER
MASON, SYDNEY CHARLES

MERRICK, VAL
MILAN, VICTOR [WOODWARD]

MERRICK, WILLISTON
FORD, WILLISTON MERRICK

MERRIDEW, ARTHUR
GASKOIN, CHARLES JACINTH

MERRIL, J.
GROSSMAN, JOSEPH. JUDITH

MERRIL, JUDITH
GROSSMAN, JOSEPH. JUDITH

MERRILL, DICK
MERRILL, HENRY TINDALL

MERRILL, LYNNE
GIBBS, NORAH

MERRILL, MANDY
WOOD, EDWARD D. JR.

MERRILL, P.J.
ROTH, HOLLY

MERRILL, PHIL
MERRILL, JANE

MERRILL, TONI
MERRILL, ANTOINETTE JUNE

MERRIMAN, ALEX
SILVERBERG, ROBERT

MERRIMAN, CHAD
CHESHIRE, GIFFORD PAUL

MERRIMAN, HENRY SETON
SCOTT, HUGH STOWELL

MERRIMAN, MAURICE
HOOK, SAMUEL CLARKE

MERRIMAN, PAT
ATKEY, PHILIP

MERRIT, KATARIN MARKOV
ACKERMAN, FORREST J.

MERRITT, A.
MERRITT, ABRAHAM P.
WOODARD, WAYNE

MERRITT, AIME
ACKERMAN, FORREST J.

MERRITT, E.B.
WADDINGTON, MIRIAM

MERRITT, JACKIE
JOYNER, CAROLYN

MERRITT, SI
HOYER, MILDRED N.

MERRIWELL, FRANK
WHITSON, JOHN HARVEY

MERRY FELLOW, DICK
GARDINER, RICHARD

MERTEN, GERDA
ROCHSTROH, ERNST

MERTEN, [T] K.
KURTH, HANNS

MERTON, GILES
CURRAN, MONA ELISA

MERTZ, STEVE
MERTZ, STEPHEN

MERWIN, SAM JR.
MERWIN, SAMUEL K. JR.

MERWIN, W.S.
MERWIN, WILLIAM STANLEY

MERYON, EDWARD
WEBB, EDWARD MERYON

MERZ, CARL
CZELL, CARL

MERZ, KONRAD
LEHMANN, KURT

MESCALERO, JEFF
PETERS, HERMANN

MESSER, MONA
HOCKING, [MONA N.] ANNE

MESSMAHL, SIGNEUR
GRIMMELSHAUSEN, HANS JAK.

METCALF, GEORGE
JOHNSON, GEORGE METCALF

METCALF, NORM
METCALF, NORMAN

METCALF, SUZANNE
BAUM, L[YMAN] FRANK

METCALFE, FRANCIS
EGERTON, J.K.

METCALFE, WHITAKER
METCALFE, FELICIA

METCALFE, [CAPT.] W.C.
LAWRENCE, CHRISTOPHER G.H

METESKY, GEORGE
HOFFMAN, ABBOTT [ABBY]

METHUEN, JOHN
BELL, JOHN KEBLE

METLER, ALF
FANGMEIER, NORBERT

METRESS, JAMES P.
METRESS, SEAMUS P.

METSANURK, MAIT
HUBEL, EDUARD

METZNER, KATHE
KREUTZER, CATHERINE

MEUER, CARSTEN
ANTON, UWE

MEUNIER, FRANCOIS
MILLER, FRANCIS TREVELYN

MEURICE, BLANCA
VON BLOCK, BELA [W]

MEURON, SKIP
SANDS, LEO GEORGE

MEWBURN, MARTIN
HITCHIN, MARTIN MEWBURN

MEYEN, GERTRUD v.
KURTH, HANNS

MEYER, ED
DIERKES, RUDOLF

MEYER, H.A.
MERRICK, HUGH

MEYER, H.K. HOUSTON
MEYER, HEINRICH

MEYER, HENRY J.
HIRD, NEVILLE

MEYER, JUNE
JORDAN, JUNE

MEYER, LYNN
SLAVITT, DAVID RYTMAN

MEYER, OLGA
BLUMENFELD-MEYER, OLGA

MEYER-MEYRINK, GUSTAV
MEYER, GUSTAVE

MEYERS, JULIE
MEYERS, JUDY BLACKWELL

MEYERS, MAAN
MEYERS, MARTIN & ANNETTE

MEYERS, RAY
MEYERS, ROY [LETHBRIDGE]

MEYERS, RIC
MEYERS, RICHARD S.

MEYERS, SUSAN
FALK, SUSAN MEYERS

MEYERSTEIN, E.H.W.
MEYERSTEIN, EDWARD H.H.

MEYRINK, GUSTAVE
MEYER, GUSTAVE

MIALL, ROBERT
BURKE, JOHN [FREDERICK]

MICHAEL X
DE FREITAS, MICHAEL

MICHAEL, ALBERT
LYONS, A. NEIL

MICHAEL, ANTHONY
ROECKEN, KURT WALTER

MICHAEL, JOHN
SEMPHILL, ERNEST

MICHAEL, JUDITH
BARNARD, JUDITH
FAIN, MICHAEL

MICHAEL, KAREL
BUKSA, PAVEL

MICHAEL, MANFRED
WINTERFELD, HENRY

MICHAEL, MARIE
RYDZYNSKI, MARIE R.

MICHAEL, PAUL
SEMPHILL, ERNEST

MICHAEL, PETER
MICHAEL, SIMON
ROSENBERG, JOEL

MICHAEL, Z.M.
ZUROY, MICHAEL

MICHAELHOUSE, JOHN
MCCULLOCH, JOSEPH

MICHAELIS, KARIN
STANGELAND, KATHARINA

MICHAELIS, KARINA
STRANGELAND, KATHARINA M.

MICHAELS, BARBARA
MERTZ, BARBARA GROSS

MICHAELS, CAROLYN LEOPOLD
LEOPOLD, CAROLYN CLUGSON

MICHAELS, DALE
RIFKIN, SHEPARD

MICHAELS, ELIZABETH
STANTON, JEANNE M.

MICHAELS, ELIZABETH ANN
SPROULL, MARIE

MICHAELS, FERN
ANDERSON, ROBERTA
KUCZKIR, MARY

MICHAELS, GRANT
MESROBIAN, MICHAEL

MICHAELS, IRENE
JURCZYK, MARY IRENE D.

MICHAELS, JACK
DOLAN, MIKE

MICHAELS, JAN
MILELLA, JAN

MICHAELS, JOANNE LOUISE
TEITELBAUM, MICHAEL

MICHAELS, JOE
SALZMAN, JOSEPH

MICHAELS, KASEY
SEIDICK, KATHRYN A.

MICHAELS, KRISTIN
CHOATE, GWEN PETERSON
CORSON, MARTHA
TUCKER, SUE LONG
WILLIAMS, DOROTHY JEANNE

MICHAELS, LEIGH
LEMBERGER, LE ANN

MICHAELS, LINDA
ELLIS, JULIE M.

MICHAELS, LORNA
ZIRKELBACH, THELMA

MICHAELS, LORNE
LIPOWITZ, LORNE

MICHAELS, LYNN
SMITH, LYNNE A.

MICHAELS, M.M.
GOLDING, MORTON JAY

MICHAELS, MARGIE
MCDONNELL, MARGIE P.

MICHAELS, MICHELLE
O'HARA, GERRY

MICHAELS, NEAL
TEITELBAUM, MICHAEL

MICHAELS, NEIL
GIBSON, WALTER B.

MICHAELS, PETER
JACKSON, CAROL

MICHAELS, PHILIP
VAN RJNDT, PHILIPPE

MICHAELS, RALPH
FILICCHIA, RALPH

MICHAELS, SKI
PELLOWSKI, MICHAEL JOSEPH

MICHAELS, STEVE
AVALLONE, MICHAEL

MICHAELS, THERESA
DIBENEDETTO, THERESA

MICHE, JOSEF
BOCHENSKI, JOSEPH M.

MICHEL, MAX
MARX, MICHAEL

MICHELL, JAN
GEIGER, ERICH

MICHELLE, SUZANNE
LARSON, SUSAN
MICHELS, BARBARA

MICHELMORE, SUSAN
HARVEY, MARGARET SUSAN J

MICHELS, CAROL
QUINTO, CAROLE

MICHELS, CHRISTINE
MICHELS, S.C.

MICKEY THE MAGICIAN
HADES, MICKEY

MICKLEMANN, HENRY
SIEBERT, WILLA

MICROS
CAMPO, ANGEL DEL

MIDDLE WALLOP
SPRAKE, LESLIE

MIDDLEBROOK, DAVID
ROSENUS, ALAN [H]

MIDDLETON, ARTHUR
O'BRIEN, EDWARD JOSEPH H.

MIDDLETON, DON
STRIKER, FRAN

MIDGETT, WINK
MIDGETT, ELWIN

MIDLING, PERSPICACITY
MILLWARD, PAMELA

MIDNITE, CAPT.
SMITH, THOMAS

MIECZYSLAWA
RADZYMINSKA, JOZEFA

MIGGY, MRS.
KRENTEL, MILDRED WHITE

MIGNON, AUGUST
DARLING, JOHN A.

MIKALOWITCH, NICHOLAI
MICHELS, NICHOLAS A.

MIKAN, BARON
BARBA, HARRY

MIKE
DONNET, MICHAEL G.L.M.

MIKELEITIS, EDITH
EHLERS, EDITH

MIKELS, JENNIFER
KUHLIN, SUZANNE J.

MIKES, GEORGE
MIKES, GYORGY

MIKHAILOV, A.
SCHELLER, ALEKSANDRO K.

MIKRO
KUHN, CHRISTOFFEL HERM.

MILAN, ANGEL
LYNN, MARY ELIZABETH N.

MILANO, RICARDO
HOLLAND, STEVE

MILBILLER, PROFESSOR
NAUBERT, CHRISTIANE B.E.

MILBROOK, JOHN
MCFADDEN, GERTRUDE V.

MILBURN, CYNTHIA
BROOKS, ANNE TEDLOCK

MILBURN, ELLEN
SMITH, MILBURN

MILECETE, HELEN
JONES, SUSAN CARLETON

MILES
SOUTHWOLD, STEPHEN

MILES, CARA
MASON, CONNIE

MILES, CASSIE
BERGSTROM, KAY

MILES, DAVID
CRONIN, BRENDAN LEO

MILES, ELLIOT
LUDVIGSEN, KARL [E]

MILES, HOWARD SCOTT
ROTSLER, WILLIAM

MILES, HUGH
MULLER, HEINZ

MILES, JOHN
BICKHAM, JACK [JOHN M.]
DELFS, RAINER

MILES, KEITH
TRALINS, [SANDOR] ROBERT

MILES, MISKA
MARTIN, PATRICIA MILES

MILES, PATRICIA A.
MARTIN, PATRICIA MILES

MILES, PETER
PERREAU-SAUSSINE, GERALD

MILES, RICHARD
PERREAU-SAUSSINE, GERALD

MILES, SUSAN
ROBERTS, URSULA

MILES, SYLIA
MILES, DORIEN KLEIN
MULARCHY, SYLVIA

MILES, YUKON
CUSHMAN, DAN

MILETUS, REX
BURGESS, MICHAEL ROY

MILITANT
SANDBERG, CARL [AUGUST]

MILK, CORNELL
DARD, FREDERIC

MILK, LOUIS G.
GARCIA LECHA, LUIS

MILKY WHITE
EMERSON, ERNEST

MILL, C.R.
CRNJANSKI, MILOS

MILL, GARRETT
MILLER, MARGARET

MILL, IAN ST. JOHN
MILLER, TERRY KENNETH

MILLAR, F.N.
MILLAR, FLORENA N.

MILLARD, ALICE
BULLIVANT, CECIL H[ENRY]

MILLARD, JOE
MILLARD, JOSEPH [JOHN]

MILLBANK, [CAPT.] H.R
ELLIS, EDWARD S.

MILLBURN, CYNTHIA
BROOKS, ANNE TEDLOCK

MILLE, RICHARD
HOLLAND, STEVE

MILLER, A.G.
KERNMAYR, HANS GUSTL

MILLER, ALICE DUER
MILLER, MRS. HENRY WISE

MILLER, BENJ[AMIN]
LOOMIS, NOEL [MILLER]

MILLER, BRINHILD
AYDT, BRUNHILD

MILLER, BROOKE
MILLER, VICTOR [B]

MILLER, BUZI
MILLER, BORIS I.

MILLER, CHUCK
MILLER, CHARLES FRANKLIN

MILLER, CISSIE
COY, STANLEE MILLER
NICHOLS, CAROLYN

MILLER, CONRAD
STRUNG, NORMAN

MILLER, DORIS R.
MOSESSON, GLORIA R.

MILLER, DOROTHY
RYAN, DOROTHY [BARGER]

MILLER, E.F.
POHLE, ROBERT W. JR.

MILLER, EDDIE
MILLER, EDWARD

MILLER, ELLEN
PATTINSON, LEE

MILLER, EUGENIA
MANDELKORN, EUGENIA M.

MILLER, EVELYN
BERGER, EVELYN MILLER

MILLER, FRANK
LOOMIS, NOEL [MILLER]

MILLER, G.R.
JUDD, FREDERICK CHARLES

MILLER, GABRIELLE
MULLER, GABRIELE

MILLER, HAL
MULER, HELMUT

MILLER, ISABEL
ROUTSONG, ALMA

MILLER, J.P.
MILLER, JAMES P.

MILLER, JAN
MEYN, NIELS

MILLER, JIM
COLLINS, JAMES L.

MILLER, JOAQUIN
MILLER, CINCINNATUS H.

MILLER, JOHN
LANE, WILLIAM
SAMACHSON, JOSEPH

MILLER, JON
MILLER, JOHN GORDON

MILLER, KAREN
CROSS, RENA
SLATTERY, RAY
WORKMAN, KAREN

MILLER, KENNETH
MILLAR, KENNETH

MILLER, LANORA
WELZENBACH, LANORA

MILLER, LAWRENCE
ALAIS, ERNEST W.

MILLER, MARC
BAKER, MARC[EIL GENEE K.]

MILLER, MARCUS
PERICHITCH, MILO

MILLER, MARGARET J.
DALE, MARGARET J.M.

MILLER, MARGERY
WELLES, MARGERY MILLER

MILLER, MARTHA
BAKER, MARC[EIL GENEE K.]
IVAN, MARTHA MILLER

MILLER, MARY
NORTHCOTT, WILLIAM CECIL

MILLER, MAX
JOHNSSON, [K.O.] HARALD

MILLER, OLIVE THORN
MILLER, HARRIET MANN

MILLER, PATRICK
MACFARLANE, GEORGE GORDON

MILLER, R.S.
MILLER, RON S.

MILLER, RICHARD
PIETSCHMANN, RICHARD JOHN

MILLER, RUTH WHITE
WHITE, RUTH C.

MILLER, SANDY
MILLER, SANDRA

MILLER, THOS. KENT
MILLER, THOMAS KENT

MILLER, WADE
WADE, ROBERT [BOB]
MILLER, BILL[Y]

MILLER, WARNE
RATHBORNE, ST. GEORGE

MILLETT, E.B.
HEBEL, PETER

MILLICENT
JORDAN, MILDRED ARLENE

MILLIGAN, SPIKE
MILLIGAN, TERENCE ALAN

MILLIGAN, WILLIAM
SLOANE, WILLIAM MILLIGAN

MILLS, A.V.
MILLS, ALGERNON VICTOR

MILLS, ADAM
STANLEY, GEORGE EDWARD

MILLS, ALLAN
MILLER, ALBERT

MILLS, D.F.
MILLS, DEANIE FRANCIS

MILLS, DOROTHY
HOWARD, DOROTHY GRAY

MILLS, EDDIE
REUTER, EALPH

MILLS, HARRY
GOODE, GEORGE W.

MILLS, JOHN
JENNISON, JOHN WILLIAM

MILLS, MARTIN
BOYD, MARTIN A. BECKER

MILLS, OSMINGTON
BROOKS, VIVIAN COLLIN

MILLS, RUTH
TEAGUE, RUTH [T. MILLS]

MILMAN, HARRY DU BOIS
CORYELL, JOHN RUSSELL

MILNA, BRUNO
PAINTING, NORMAN

MILNE, A.A.
MILNE, ALAN A.

MILNE, EWART
MILNE, CHARLES

MILNE, RICHARD
SHARPLES, RICHARD MILNE

MILNER, GEORGE
HARDINGE, GEORGE

MILNER, MICHAEL
COOPER, SAUL

MILONAS, ROLF
MYLLER, ROLF

MILOSZ
DE LUBICZ-MILOSZ, OSCAR W

MILSEN, OSCAR
MENDELSOHN, OSCAR

MILTON, DAVID
WIND, DAVID MILTON

MILTON, JACK
KIMBRO, JOHN M.

MILTON, MARK
PELTON, ROBERT W.
SHEPPARD, S. ROSSITER

MILTON, TED
NAGEL, HERBERT CHRISTIAN

MILVERTON, CHARLES A.
PENZLER, OTTO

MIMBI
KEIM, FRIEDRICH

MIMEI, OGAWA
KENSAKI, OGAWA

MINDE-BONITZ, GRETE
BONITZ, CLEMENTINE

MINDEN, BERTE-EVE
HUMPEL, ELKE

MINER, MATTHEW
WALLMANN, JEFFREY M.

MINERVE
DURRUA, ODETTE JEANNE

MINGSTON, R. GRESHAM
STAMP, ROGER G.

MINGSTON, R.G.
STAMP, ROGER G.

MINICAM
RUSSELL, HENRY GEORGE

MINIER, NELSON
BAKER, LAURA NELSON
STOUTENBURG, ADRIEN [P]

MINK MOLE
GIBSON, WILLIAM [FORD]

MINNAAR-VOS, ANNA
VOS, ANNA BEYERA

MINOR, LASKER
LASKER, EDWARD

MINSKY, N.
VILENKIN, NIKOLAY MAXIM.

MINTO-COWEN, FRANCES
MUNTHE, FRANCES

MINTON, PAULA
LITTLE, PAUL HUGO

MINTON, T.M.
BADE, THOMAS MICHAEL
STEVENSON, ROBIN

MINTURN, EDWARD
URNER, NATHAN DANE

MIRANDA, JAVIER
BIOY-CASARES, ADOLFO

MIRBEAU, KEN
WEISS, JOE

MIRBEAU-FRANCOIS
WEISS, JOE

MIRMUKHSIN
MIRSAIDOV, MIRMUKHSIN

MIRUS-KAUBA, LUDMILLA
MIRUS, LUDMILLA

MIRYAM
YARDUMIAN, MIRYAM

MISER, ABEL
JESCHKE, WOLFGANG

MISES, DR.
FECHNER, GUSTAV THEODOR

MISHA
CHOCHOLAK, MISHA

MISHIMA, YUKIO
HIRAOKA, KIMITAKE

MISS X
GOODRICH-FREER, ADELA

MISTER ROGERS
ROGERS, FRED MCFEELY

MISTRAL, BENGO
LAZENBY, NORMAN A.
WARD, B.

MISTRAL, GABRIELA
DE ALCAYAGA, LUCILA GODOY

MITCHAM, GILROY
NEWTON, WILLIAM [SIMPSON]

MITCHEL, JACKSON
MATCHA, JACK

MITCHELL, ALBERT PAGE
MITCHELL, EDWARD PAGE

MITCHELL, ALLISON
BUTTERWORTH, WILLIAM E.

MITCHELL, CARLTON
MARSHALL, MEL[VIN]

MITCHELL, CHARLES
MARTINEZ, CARLOS MIGUEL

MITCHELL, CLYDE T.
ELLISON, HARLAN
GARRETT, RANDALL [P]
SILVERBERG, ROBERT
SLESAR, HENRY

MITCHELL, ERICA
POSNER, RICHARD

MITCHELL, EWAN
JANNER, GREVILLE EWAN

MITCHELL, GENE
HOADLEY, H. ORLO

MITCHELL, JACK
SELLERS, CONNIE LESLIE

MITCHELL, JAY
ROBERSON, JENNIFER

MITCHELL, JENNIFER
O'GREEN, JENNIFER M.R.

MITCHELL, K.I.
LAMB, ELIZABETH SEARLE

MITCHELL, KERRY
PATTINSON, LEE
SLATTERY, RAY
WILKES-HUNTER, RICHARD

MITCHELL, MAGGIE
MITCHELL, MARGARET JULIA

MITCHELL, MARGARET
MARSH, MARGARET M.M.

MITCHELL, PAIGE
GINNES, JUDITH S.

MITCHELL, SCOTT
GODFREY, LIONEL ROBERT H.

MITCHELL, V.E.
GUSTAFSON, VICTORIA E.M.

MITCHELL, [JUDITH] PAIGE
SEGEL, JUDITH

MITCHUM, HANK
KNOTT, WILLIAM CECIL JR.
NEWTON, DWIGHT BENNETT
REASONER, JAMES M.
SHERMAN, JORY [T]

MITTON, G.E.
SCOTT, GERALDINE EDITH

MIXON, VERONICA
WESTON, NIGELLA

MIZZEN, MATT
WILLIAMS, HENRY LLEWELLYN

MLAD-MILTIJAD
DJURICIC, ULADEN ST.

MO, MANAGER
CASSITY, JUNE

MOAMRATH, M.M.
PUMILIA, [JOSEPH L.] JOE
WALLACE, BILL

MOBACHUS, VESALIUS
DE VEER, HENDRIK

MOBERLY, C.A.E.
MOBERLY, CHARLOTTE ANNE

MOBIUS, MARTIN
BIERBAUM, OTTO JULIUS

MOBLEY, WALT
BURGESS, MICHAEL ROY

MOCATTA, FRANCES
MOCATTA, DOROTHY ALLEN

MOCZAR, MIECZYSLAW
DEMKO, MIKOLAY

MODEAN, MARY
MOON, MODEAN

MODELL, MIRIAM
PIPER, EVELYN

MODENA, MARIA
KREIS, ERMA

MODERN BURNS
GRIEVE, CHRIST. MURRAY

MODESTA
DICHTL, RUTH [v.M.]

MOEBIUS
GIRAUD, JEAN

MOERIS, ROBERT
GRUN, ROBERT

MOFFATT, GEO. ALLAN
BOGART, WILLIAM G.
CONLON, BEN

MOFFATT, GEORGE ALLAN
BURKHOLDER, EDWIN V.

MOFFETT, JULIE
CZECHOWSKI, JULIE

MOFFIT, JACK
STOCKTON, FRANCIS R.

MOFFUSAILLITE
LANG, THOMAS

MOG, JAN
HASSENSTEIN, DIETER

MOGADOR, CELESTE
MORETON DE CHABRIL., ELIZ

MOHAN, P. NATH
SHASTRI, PRITHVINATH

MOHOAO
FAIRBAIRN, EDWIN
JOSEPH, MARIE

MOHR, FREDERICK
LEIDHOF, CHARLES

MOINEAU, MAX
SPARROW, MALCOLM W.

MOIRA, MARTIN
BERTHOLD, WILL

MOKO
MEAD, SIDNEY MOKO

MOLE, OSCAR
SEAVER, RICHARD

MOLE, WILLIAM
YOUNGER, WILLIAM A.

MOLENDO, GASPAR
ZENO GANDIA, MANUEL

MOLESWORTH, VOL
MOLESWORTH, VOLTAIRE

MOLIN, CHARLES
MAYNE, WILLIAM [J.C.]

MOLINARO, URSULE
HERNDON, URSULE MOLINARO

MOLITOR, JAN
MULLER-MAREIN, JOSEF

MOLLER, NIKOLAJ
MEYN, NIELS

MOLNAR, IMRE
LIPSCHITZ, IMRE

MOMORUS
NUTTALL, JEFF

MONAHAN, JOHN P
BURNETT, W.R.

MONAHAN, THOMAS P.
KELLEY, THOMAS P.

MONCK, TRISTAM K.
MAITLAND, T.G. DOWLING

MONCRIEFF, WILLIAM THOMAS
THOMAS, WILLIAM GEORGE

MONDAY, MICHAEL
GINDER, RICHARD

MONDELLE, WENDAYNE
ACKERMAN, WENDAYNE

MONDRAGON, MAGDALENA
AGUIRRE, MAGDALENA M.

MONET, LIREVE
MURPHY, EVERIL WORRELL

MONET, NICOLE
MCCUE, NOELLE BERRY

MONETT, LIREVE
WORRELL, EVERIL

MONGO, MARCOS
DOMBROWSKI, THEODOR

MONGO, MARCUS
RAHN, WOLFGANG

MONIG, CHRISTOPHER
CROSSEN, KENDELL FOSTER

MONIQUE
BENOIT, ALICE P.

MONITOR
LEVINE, ISAAC DON

MONJO, F.N.
MONJO, FERDINAND N.

MONK, ALAN
KENDALL, WILMORE

MONKLAND, GEORGE
WHITTET, GEORGE SORLEY

MONKSHOOD, G.F.
CLARKE, WILLIAM JAMES

MONMOUTH, JACK
PEMBER, WILLIAM L.

MONNOW, PETER
CROUDACE, GLYNN

MONOD, RENE
KOCH, KURT EMIL

MONORBY, EBERHARD
MOES, EBERHARD

MONRO, GAVIN
MONRO-HIGGS, GERTRUDE

MONROE, CAROLYN
GREENE, CAROLYN

MONROE, DANIEL
HAHN, RONALD M.

MONROE, DON
GIBSON, WALTER B.

MONROE, FRANK
CHAPMAN, FRANK MONROE

MONROE, LYLE
HEINLEIN, ROBERT A.
WENTZ, ELMA

MONS, MARTIN
MONSMA, HILDEGARD S.

MONTAG, MARCUS
HAHN, RONALD M.

MONTAGU OF BEAULIEU, 3RD
MONTAGU, EDWARD J.B.D.S.

MONTAGUE, J.J.
KENNAN, JAMES

MONTAGUE, JEANNE
YARDE, JEANNE B.F.T.

MONTAGUE, JOSEPH
DUNN, JOSEPH ALLAN

MONTAGUE, LISA
SHULMAN, SANDRA DAWN

MONTAGUE, MERYL ST. JOHN
SANDFIELD, LAURENCE

MONTAGUE, ROBERT
HAMDEN, JOHN

MONTANA, PAT
MCCANDLESS, PATRICIA A.

MONTANA, ZED
KELLEY, THOMAS P.

MONTANUS, DOLF
LEBER, EMIL

MONTANYE, C.S.
MONTANYE, CARLETON S.

MONTCLAIR, DENNIS
SLADEN, NORMAN ST. BARBE

MONTCLAIR, J.W.
WEIDEMEYER, JOHN WILLIAM

MONTE, JILL
ELLIS, JULIE M.

MONTEITH, HAYTON
MITTERMEYER, HELEN

MONTEITH, OWEN
HOOK, SAMUEL CLARKE

MONTERDO, JORGE
RAVINES, EUDOCIO

MONTEREY, ELIZABETH
BANIS, VICTOR J[EROME]

MONTES, FABIAN
ELZABURU, MANUEL

MONTGOMERY, BETTINA
CUDLIPP, EDYTHE

MONTGOMERY, CONSTANCE
CAPPELL, CONSTANCE

MONTGOMERY, DEREK
SIMMONS, J.S.A.

MONTGOMERY, ELIZABETH
JULESBERG, ELIZABETH R.M.

MONTGOMERY, ELIZABETH R.
JULESBERG, ELIZABETH R.M.

MONTGOMERY, L.M.
MACDONALD, LUCY MAUDE M.

MONTGOMERY, MARIANNE
ALLEN, D.H.

MONTGOMERY, MAX
DAVENPORT, GUY M.

MONTGOMERY, YVONNE
EWEGEN, YVONNE

MONTIEL, GUSTAVO
LAGUERRE, ENRIQUE A.

MONTROSE, DAVID
GRAHAM, CHARLES ROSS

MONTROSE, GRAHAM
MACKINNON, CHARLES ROY

MONTROSE, JAMES ST. DAVID
APPLEMAN, JOHN ALAN

MONTROSE, SARAH
BOSNA, VALERIE

MONTROSS, DAVID
BACKUS, JEAN LOUISE

MOODIE, EDWIN
WILLIAMS, EDWIN ALFRED

MOODY, G.F.
HAMEL PEIFER, KATHLEEN

MOOLB, LEINAD
BLOOM, DANIEL HOWARD

MOOLSON, MELUSA
SOLOMON, SAMUEL

MOON, LINDA
LEWIS, CLIFFORD

MOON, LORNA
LEWIS, CLIFFORD

MOONCHILD
FOX, GARDNER F.

MOONDYNE JOE
JONES, JOSEPH BOLITHO

MOONEY, TED
MOONEY, EDWARD

MOOR, EMILY
DEMING, RICHARD

MOOR, ERNESTINE
MORKEPUTZ-ROOS, ERNA

MOORCOCK, MICHAEL
BAILEY, HILARY
BAYLEY, BARRINGTON J.

MOORE, AL
CURRY, THOMAS ALBERT

MOORE, AMOS
HUBBARD, GEORGE [BARRON]

MOORE, ANDREW
BINDER, FREDERICK MOORE

MOORE, ANON
GALLOWAY, JAMES M.

MOORE, ARTHUR
MATTHEWS, CLAYTON [H]

MOORE, AURORA
MOORE, ARTHUR

MOORE, AUSTIN
MUIR, CHARLES AUGUSTUS C.

MOORE, BARBARA
LEE, BARBARA [MOORE]

MOORE, BERYL
SMITH WOODS, DOROTHY BER.

MOORE, C.L.
MOORE, CATHERINE LUCILLE

MOORE, CAROLINE
STRACHAN, MARGARET P.

MOORE, CHARLES
MOORE, REGINALD CHARLES A

MOORE, CHARLOTTE
LOBB, CHARLOTTE

MOORE, CLAYTON
BRANDNER, GARY
GRANBECK, MARILYN
MATTHEWS, CLAYTON [H]

MOORE, COLLEEN
MESSMANN, JON [JOHN]

MOORE, CORY
STURGEON, WINA

MOORE, DIANA
MARLISS, DEANNA

MOORE, DICK[IE]
MOORE, JOHN RICHARD

MOORE, EDWARD
MUIR, EDWIN

MOORE, ELIZABETH
ATKINS, MARGARET ELIZAB.

MOORE, FENWORTH
STRATEMEYER, EDWARD

MOORE, FRANCES SARAH
MACK, ELSIE FRANCES

MOORE, FRANCIS
MACISAAC, FRED[ERIC JOHN]

MOORE, GERALD
BOWMAN, GERALD [MOORE]

MOORE, GWYNETH
BANNISTER, PATRICIA V.

MOORE, HARRIS
HARRIS, ALFRED
MOORE, ARTHUR

MOORE, KENNETH
LA DUE, HUBERT

MOORE, LANDER
FENSCH, THOMAS

MOORE, LISA
CHATER, ELIZABETH EILEEN

MOORE, LORRIE
MOORE, MARIE LORENZ

MOORE, MARGARET
WILKINS, MARGARET

MOORE, MICHAEL
HARRIS, HERBERT

MOORE, N. HUDSON
MOORE, HANNAH H.

MOORE, NICHOLAS
NICOLAEFF, ARIADNE

MOORE, PATTI
DALEY, MARGARET K.R.

MOORE, PAULA
VAUGHAN, ROBERT R.

MOORE, PHILIPS
MOORE, DORIS O.
PHILIPS, MARY ALICE

MOORE, REG
MOORE, REGINALD CHARLES A

MOORE, REGINA
DUNNE, MARY COLLINS

MOORE, ROBERT
MARTIN, RUSSELL W.
WILLIAMS, ROBERT MOORE

MOORE, ROBIN
HARPER, EDWARD M.
MOORE, ROBERT LOWELL

MOORE, ROSALIE
BROWN, ROSALIE G.M.

MOORE, RUDIN
SMITH, GARY

MOORE, WALLACE
CONWAY, GERARD F.

MOORE, WENTWORTH
MALLOCK, WILLIAM H.

MOORE-BENTLY, MARY ANN
LING, MRS. H.H.

MOORES, DICK
MOORES, RICHARD ARNOLD

MOORHOUSE, CATHERINE
ALLEN, CATHERINE
JENSEN, DOROTHEA

MOORHOUSE, E. HALLAM
MEYNELL, ESTER H.

MOORHOUSE, HOPKINS
MOORHOUSE, HERBERT JOSEPH

MOOROCK, MICHAEL
MOORCOCK, MICHAEL

MOORSHEAD, HENRY
PINE, LESLIE GILBERT

MOPOKE
POLLARD, JAMES

MORA, HEDWIG
MORAWETZ, HEDWIG

MORALES, SEBASTIAN
LUTZ, GILES A.

MORAN, DANIEL
VARDEMAN, ROBERT E.

MORAN, J-L
WHITAKER, RODNEY W.

MORAN, J.L.
WHITAKER, RODNEY W.

MORAN, JUDY
SELLERS, CONNIE LESLIE

MORAN, MIKE
ARD, WILLIAM [THOMAS]

MORAND, ERIC
BREUCKER, OSCAR HERBERT

MORAVIO, ALBERTO
PINCHERLE, ALBERTO

MORAWA, MICHAEL
MENZEL, RODERICH

MORAY, DAVID
CUMMING-SKINNER, DUGALD M

MORAY, JOHN S.
CAZAURAN, AUGUSTUS R.

MORAYNS, JACQUES
GONDA, ADOLPHE

MORCK, PAAL
ROELVAAG, OLE EDVART

MORDAUNT, ELINOR
WIEHE, EVELYN M.C. MORD.

MORE, ANDREAS
ROGLER, AUGUST

MORE, ANTHONY
CLINTON, EDWIN M.

MORE, ATHERTON
CHILD, HERBERT

MORE, CAROLINE
CONE, MOLLY [L]

MORE, DENNIS
TAYLOR, KEITH

MORE, EUSTON
BLOOMER, ARNOLD E.M.

MORE, J.J.
MOFFATT, JAMES

MOREAU, EMIL
WOOD, EDWARD D. JR.

MOREAU, HELENE
MORAY, HELGA

MORECK, CURT
HAEMMERLING, KONRAD

MOREHEAD, JEFF
OFFUTT, ANDREW J.

MOREL, DIGHTON
WARNER, KENNETH LEWIS

MOREL, ED
BANZHAF, ERWIN

MORELAND, PEGGY
MORSE, PEGGY BOZEMAN

MORELL, CHARLES
RIDLEY, JAMES

MORELL, JUANA
GYMNICH, HEINZ

MORELL, WALLACE
GARRISH, HAROLD J.

MORELLI, SPIKE
NEWTON, WILLIAM [SIMPSON]

MORELY, SUSAN
CROSS, JOHN KEIR

MORENO, BENTO
DE QUEIROS, FRANCISCO TE.

MORENO, FILIPP
MEISTER, FRIEDRICH

MORENO, MARTIN
SWARTZ, HARRY

MORENO, PHIL
KALMUCZAK, ROLF

MORESBY, LOUIS
BECK, ELIZA LOUISA M.

MORESBY, L[OIS]
BECK, ELIZA LOUISA M.

MORETON, JOHN
COHEN, MORTON N.

MORETTE, EDGAR
FEZANDIE, HECTOR

MOREY, CHARLES
FLETCHER, HELEN JILL

MORGAN, ALLAN
GRANBECK, MARILYN

MORGAN, ALYSSA
DELATUSH, EDITH

MORGAN, ANGELA
PAINE, LAURAN BOSWORTH

MORGAN, ARLENE
PAINE, LAURAN BOSWORTH

MORGAN, BAILEY
BREWER, GIL

MORGAN, BASSETT
MORGAN, GRACE JONES

MORGAN, BRYAN
MORGAN, BRIAN STANFORD

MORGAN, CAROL MCAFEE
APPLEBY, CAROL MCAFEE

MORGAN, CLAIRE
HIGHSMITH, PATRICIA

MORGAN, D.
JENNISON, JOHN WILLIAM
MORGAN, DELORES MILLER

MORGAN, DE WOLFE
WILLIAMSON, THAMES ROSS

MORGAN, DEAN
FISHER, GRAHAM

MORGAN, DIANA
GOODMAN, IRENE
KAMAROFF, ALEX

MORGAN, ELLEN
BUMSTEAD, KATHLEEN MARY

MORGAN, EMANUEL
BRYNNER, WITTER

MORGAN, FAYE
MALEK, DOREEN OWENS

MORGAN, FRANK
PAINE, LAURAN BOSWORTH

MORGAN, G.J.
ROWLAND, DONALD S.

MORGAN, GLEBE
ROWLAND, DONALD S.

MORGAN, GWLADYS M.
LYLE, GWLADYS M.

MORGAN, GWYNETH
BEAL, GWYNETH MORGAN

MORGAN, HANS
HEUER, WILHELM

MORGAN, HARRIET
MENCKEN, HENRY LOUIS

MORGAN, HELEN TUDOR
MORGAN, HELEN G.L.

MORGAN, J.M.
MORGAN, JILL M[EREDITH]

MORGAN, JANE
COOPER, JAMES FENIMORE
MOREN, SALLY M.

MORGAN, JASON
FRISSELL, WILLIAM DONALD

MORGAN, JENNIFER
HORBACH, URSULA [S]

MORGAN, JINX
MORGAN, JUDITH A.

MORGAN, JOHN MEDFORD
FOX, GARDNER F.

MORGAN, JOHN
PAINE, LAURAN BOSWORTH

MORGAN, JUSTINA
FREEMAN, JEAN TODD

MORGAN, KRISTIN
VEILLON, BARBARA LANTIER

MORGAN, LEE
HALLBING, KJELL KARL

MORGAN, LESLIE
MILLER, ANN

MORGAN, LOUISE
MORGAN, HELEN G.L.

MORGAN, LT. SCOTT
BOWEN, ROBERT SIDNEY
DANIELS, NORMAN A.
HUBBARD, L. RON
REICHNITZER, F.E.

MORGAN, MARJORIE
CHIBNALL, MARJORIE MCCAL.

MORGAN, MARK
OVERHOLSER, WAYNE D.

MORGAN, MAX
PFEFFER, HEINRICH

MORGAN, MAYBETH
RONAL, PETER

MORGAN, MEMO
AVALLONE, MICHAEL

MORGAN, MICHAEL
CARLE, C.E.
DORN, DEAN M.

MORGAN, MICHAELA
BASILE, GLORIA VITANEA

MORGAN, MICHEL
MORGANSTERN, DAN M.

MORGAN, NICHOLAS
MORGAN, THOMAS BRUCE

MORGAN, PATRICK
SNYDER, GEORGE

MORGAN, PHYLLIS
THOMPSON, PHYLLIS [HOGE]

MORGAN, RAYE
CONRAD, HELEN [MANAK]

MORGAN, ROBERT
TURNER, ROBERT H.
HENDERSON, C.J.

MORGAN, SCOTT
KUTTNER, HENRY
MOORE, CATHERINE LUCILLE

MORGAN, SHIRLEY
KIEPPER, SHIRLEY MORGAN

MORGAN, STEPHEN
MURRAY, THOMAS C.

MORGAN, TED
DE GRAMONT, SANCHE

MORGAN, TOM
MUELLER, JOHN HENRY

MORGAN, TRACY
PRIMM, TRACYE

MORGAN, VALERIE
PAINE, LAURAN BOSWORTH

MORGAN, VIRGINIA
MUNDIS, HESTER JANE

MORGAN, WESKY
BENNETT, ISADORA

MORGAN, WYNN L.
BREEN, PHILLIP
KRONE, CHESTER

MORGEN, JORG
DECKER-VOIGT, HANS-HELMUT

MORGEN, JURGEN
DECKER-VOIGT, HANS-HELMUT

MORGEN, KEITH
FURSTAUER, JOHANNA

MORGENSTERN, S.
GOLDMAN, WILLIAM

MORICE, ANNE
SHAW, FELICITY

MORICH, STANTON
GRIFFITH-JONES, GEORGE C.

MORIN, CLAIRE
DORE, CLAIRE MORIN

MORIN, MICHEL
RIEGEL, WILHELM MICHAEL

MORINE, HODER
CONROY, JOHN WESLEY

MORISON, ELIZABETH
MOBERLY, CHARLOTTE ANNE

MORISON, FRANK
ROSS, ALBERT HENRY

MORITZ, CORDULA
BOLLING-MORITZ, CORDULA

MORK, PAUL BADURA
THUNSTROM, GORAN

MORKIM, I.B.
GRONWALD, WERNER

MORKOVIN, BELA V.
MORKOVIN, BORIS V.

MORLAND, CATHERINE
SCHUBERT, JOHN D.

MORLAND, DICK
HILL, REGINALD [CHARLES]

MORLAND, LYNETTE
O'CONNELL, KAREN

MORLAND, PETER HENRY
FAUST, FREDERICK S.

MORLEY, ARTHUR SPENCER
BANGS, JOHN KENDRICK

MORLEY, BRIAN
BRADLEY, MARION ZIMMER

MORLEY, KELL
WILKES-HUNTER, RICHARD

MORLEY, RALPH
HINTON, HOWARD

MORLEY, WILFRED OWEN
LOWNDES, ROBERT A.W.
ACKERMAN, FORREST J.

MORLOCK, MARTIN
GOERCKE, GUNTHER

MORNAU, WILJA
MORNAU, WILLI

MORNING, ALICE
HAIG, EMILY ALICE

MORNINGTON, EDOR
ROBERTS, CECIL EDRIC M.

MOROJO
DOUGLAS, MYRTLE R.

MORPHY, COUNTESS
FORBES, MARCELLE AZRA

MORRAH, DAVE
MORRAH, DAVID WARDLAW JR.

MORRELL, JOHN
OLSEN, THOMAS CARL M.

MORREN, THEOPHIL
VON HOFMANNSTHAL, HUGO

MORRICE, KEN
MORRICE, JAMES KENNETH

MORRILL, RICHARD
SCHRECK, EVERETT M.

MORRIS, CHRIS
MORRIS, CHRISTOPHER C.
MORRIS, JANET E[LLEN]

MORRIS, CLAUDE
ILMER, WALTHER

MORRIS, CLYDE
BIEGE, KARL HEINZ

MORRIS, DAN
VON MELGUNOFF, ALEXANDER

MORRIS, DAVE
RELLERGERD, HELMUT

MORRIS, ELIZABETH
FAVORS, JEAN

MORRIS, G.A.
MACLEAN, KATHERINE

MORRIS, IRA J.
JEFFERIES, IRA

MORRIS, JACK
BAJOG, GUNTHER
MODIN, UNO
MEYN, NIELS

MORRIS, JAN
MORRIS, JAMES HUMPHREY

MORRIS, JANE
ARDMORE, JANE KESNER

MORRIS, JOHN
CARGILL, MORRIS
HEARNE, JOHN EDGAR C.

MORRIS, JULIAN
WEST, MORRIS L.

MORRIS, KATHLEEN
BRINGLE, MARY HANFORD B.

MORRIS, M.
THIBAUDEAU, COLLEEN

MORRIS, MATTHEW
GRUBER, FRANK

MORRIS, MYRON
STEARNS, MYRON MORRIS

MORRIS, NOBUKO
ALBERY, NOBUKO

MORRIS, RUTH
WEBB, RUTH ENID B.M.

MORRIS, SARA
BURKE, JOHN [FREDERICK]

MORRIS, WINIFRED
SCHECTER, WINIFRED MORRIS

MORRISON, C.T.
MORRISON, CHARLES THEODRE

MORRISON, EDWARD
HUNPHREY, PAUL

MORRISON, G.F.
BERNSTEIN, GERRY

MORRISON, GERT W.
STRATEMEYER, EDWARD

MORRISON, HENRI
BOTHE-PELZER, HEINZ

MORRISON, J. STRANG
THOM, WILLIAM A. STRANG

MORRISON, JO
STAFFORD, JO LEE

MORRISON, MISCHA
HAHN, RONALD M.

MORRISON, MISKA
ALPERS, HANS JOACHIM

MORRISON, PEGGY
MORRISON, MARGARET MACKIE

MORRISON, RICHARD
LOWNDES, ROBERT A.W.

MORRISON, ROBERT
LOWNDES, ROBERT A.W.

MORRISON, ROBERTA
WEBB, JEAN FRANCIS III

MORRISON, TONI
MORRISON, CHLOE ANTHONY

MORRISON, VICTOR
GLUT, DONALD F.

MORRISON, WILLIAM
SAMACHSON, JOSEPH

MORRISS, J.H.
GHNASSIA, MAURICE [J-H]

MORRISSON, LINDA
MICHAEL, PETRA & ROLF

MORROW, BETTY
BACON, ELIZABETH

MORROW, CHARLOTTE
KIRWAN, MOLLEY [M]

MORROW, HONORE WILLSIE
MORROW, HONORE MCCUE

MORROW, VAN
MILAN, VICTOR [WOODWARD]

MORROW, W.C.
MORROW, WILLIAM CHAMBERS

MORSE, BENJAMIN [DR.]
BENJAMIN, MORTON J.

MORSE, CAROL
YEAKLEY, MARJORIE HALL

MORSE, DR. BENJAMIN
BLOCK, LAWRENCE

MORSE, L.A.
MORSE, LARRY ALLEN

MORT, VIVIAN
CROMIE, ALICE HAMILTON

MORTELMANS
MORTELMANS, EDWARD

MORTIMER, CARROL
BORNSTROEM-RUNDE, UWE

MORTIMER, CHAPMAN
CHAPMAN-MORTIMER, CHARLES

MORTIMER, CHARLES
CHAPMAN-MORTIMER, CHARLES

MORTIMER, GEOFFREY
GALLICHAN, WALTER M.

MORTIMER, GLENN
KOBUSCH, JOACHIM

MORTIMER, JANUARY
GALLICHAN, WALTER M.

MORTIMER, JUNE
RYDER, VERA

MORTIMER, MARY H.
COURY, LOUISE ANDRE

MORTIMER, PETER
ROBERTS, DOROTHY JAMES

MORTIMER, PHILIPP
BRAND, KURT

MORTMAIN, MORTIMER
RAHN, WOLFGANG

MORTON, ANTHONY
CREASEY, JOHN

MORTON, ELEANOR
STERN, ELIZABETH G.

MORTON, GLEN
LAZENBY, NORMAN A.

MORTON, GUY MAINWARING
DUNSTAN, GUY MAINWARING

MORTON, J.B.
MORTON, JOHN BINGHAM

MORTON, JACK
APPEL, WALTER
BAJOG, GUNTHER
GROSSMANN, HANS HUGO
KRUG, FRANZ
RELLERGERD, HELMUT

MORTON, JOHN
GLASBY, JOHN S.

MORTON, JOSEPH
RICHMAN, AL

MORTON, LEAH
STERN, ELIZABETH G.

MORTON, MIRIAM
MOORE, EULA & MIRIAM

MORTON, MONICA
MCCULLEY, JOHNSTON

MORTON, PATIENCE
GOVAN, [MARY] C.N.

MORTON, PATRICIA
GOLDING, MORTON JAY

MORTON, STANLEY
FREEDGOOD, MORTON

MORTON, WILLIAM
FERGUSON, WILLIAM B.M.

MORUM, WILLIAM
DINNER, WILLIAM
SMITH, SURREY

MORUS, CENYDD
MORRIS, KENNETH

MORWOOD, PETER
SMITH, ROBERT PETER

MOSCA, FRANK
DALGLEISH, OSCAR

MOSCOVIT, ANDREI
EFIMOV, IGOR M.

MOSER, DON
MOSER, DONALD BRUCE

MOSES, RUBEN
WURMBRAND, RICHARD

MOSKOWSKI, IVAN
DE PEREYRA, MARIA E. Y R.

MOSKVITIN, JURIJ
HANSEN, JURIJ

MOSS, CHERRY
BRAND, KURT

MOSS, DUNCAN
AMBROSE, MICHAEL E.

MOSS, JACK
MOSKOVITZ, JACK

MOSS, JERRY
RASCH, CARLOS

MOSS, NANCY
MOSS, ROBERT ALFRED

MOSS, PETER
FRITCH, CHARLES E.

MOSS, ROBERTA
MOSS, ROBERT ALFRED

MOSSIG, HANK A.
WHITTINGTON, HARRY

MOSSMAN, BURT
KEEVILL, HENRY J.

MOSSOP, IRENE
SWATRIDGE, IRENE M.M.

MOST PROLIFIC WRITER, THE
HAMILTON, CHARLES H.S.

MOSTAR, GERHART HERRMANN
HERRMANN, GERHARD

MOSTYN, SYDNEY
RUSSELL, WILLIAM CLARK

MOSTYN-OWEN, GAIA
SERVADIO, GAIA

MOTH
FLEMING, PETER

MOTHERWELL, HIRAM
MODERWELL, HIRAM K.

MOTLEY, MARY
DE RENEVILLE, MARY M.M.S.

MOTTE, NEL
HARRISON, MRS. E.E.

MOTTE, PETER
HARRISON, RICHARD [MOTTE]

MOTTRAM, R.H.
MOTTRAM, RALPH HALE

MOULTON, CARL
TUBB, E.C.

MOULTON, CHARLES
MARSTON, WILLIAM MOULTON

MOUNDS, MONICA
PROCTOR, GEO[RGE] W[YATT]
VARDEMAN, ROBERT E.

MOUNT, CHARLES MERRILL
SUCHOW, SHERMAN MERRILL

MOUNT, PITT
BERGER, PETER

MOUNT, TOM E.
CODY, STONE

MOUNTAIN, ALICE
WISEBERG, MARIAN ALICE

MOUNTAIN, JULIAN
COWIE, DONALD

MOUNTAIN, ROBERT
MONTGOMERY, RAYMOND A.

MOUNTBATTEN, RICHARD
PRONZINI, WILLIAM JOHN
WALLMANN, JEFFREY M.

MOUNTFIELD, DAVID
GRANT, NEIL

MOUNTJOY, DESMOND
CHAPMAN-HUSTON, D.M.

MOUNTJOY, ROBERTA [JEAN]
SOHL, GERALD ALLEN

MOUSSE, ALFRED
HOUSSET, ARSENE

MOUTHPIECE
PORTER, MAURICE

MOWAT, ROBIN
MOWAT, ROBERT CASE

MOWBRAY, JOHN
VAHEY, JOHN G. HAZLETTE

MOWERY, DOROTHY
DUNSING, DEE

MOYER, CAROLYN
SWAYZE, CAROLYN NORMA

MOYES, PATRICIA
HASZARD, PATRICIA MOYES

MOYES, ROBIN
BATEMAN, ROBERT MOYES

MOYLAN, TOM
MOYLAN, THOMAS P.

MOZANS, H.J.
ZAHM, JOHN AUGUSTINE

MR. M____
MASON, CHARLES W.

MRABET, MOHAMMED
EL-HAJJAN, MOHAMMED CHAIB

MUDDOCK, J.E.
MUDDOCK, JOYCE E.P.

MUDE, O.
GOREY, EDWARD ST. JOHN

MUDGEON, APEMAN
MITCHELL, ADRIAN

MUDGETT, HERMAN W.
WHITE, WILLIAM A.P.

MUELLER, GERHARDT
BICKERS, RICHARD L.T.

MUELLER, H.C.
MULLER, KURT

MUHAMMAD-I MAS'UD
DIHATI, MUHAMMAD-I MAS'UD

MUHLBACH, LOUISA
MUNDT, KLARA

MUHLENFELD, ULRICH
HAUSCHILD, REINHARD

MUHLGRABNER, MARIA
KAESEN, MARIA

MUHLHOFER, INGE[BORG]
PURNER, INGE

MUIR, ALAN
MORRISON, THOMAS J.

MUIR, DEXTER
GRIBBLE, LEONARD [R]

MUIR, JAMES A.
WELLS, ANGUS

MUIR, JANE
PETRONE, JANE MUIR

MUIR, JOHN
MORGAN, THOMAS C.

MUIR, LUCY
MOORE, LUCILE

MUIR, WILLA
MUIR, WILHELMINA JOHNSTON

MUKS, ROBERTS
AVERS, ROBERTS

MULDOON, OMAR
MATUSOW, HARVEY MARSHALL

MULDOR, CARL DE
MILLER, CHARLES HENRY

MULESKO, ANGELO
OGLESBY, JOSEPH

MULGAN, CATHERINE
GOUGH, CATHERINE

MULIER
HIGGINS, CHARLES ELI

MULKEEN, ANNE
MARCUS, ANNE M.

MULKOR, PIOTER
HLOJZY, NAGEL

MULLEN, DORE
MULLEN, DOROTHY

MULLEN, RICHARD
GIBSON, WALTER B.

MULLER, ALFRED
MULLER, PAUL ALFRED

MULLER, BILLEX
ELLIS, EDWARD S.

MULLER, HEINZ W.
HOBER, HEINZ WERNER

MULLER, HEINZ WERNER
HOBER, HEINZ WERNER

MULLER, JOHANN FRIEDR. W.
NAUBERT, CHRISTIANE B.E.

MULLER, JOHN E.
FANTHORPE, R.L.
GLASBY, JOHN S.
GLYNN, ANTHONY ARTHUR

MULLER, JORG
MUELLER, JOERG

MULLER, PAUL
KING, ALBERT

MULLER, W.
KORNER, HEINZ

MULLER-BECK, EDITH
BERGMANN, EDITH

MULLER-MARKKLEEBERG, A.
MULLER, PAUL ALFRED

MULLER-MURNAU, P.A.
MULLER, PAUL ALFRED

MULLER-ROLAND, HARALD
HAUSCHILD, REINHARD

MULLIN, CHRIS
MULLIN, CHRISTOPHER JOHN

MULLINS, ANN
DALLY, ANN G.M.

MULOCK, DIANA
CRAIK, DINAH MARIA MULOCK

MULOCK, DINA MARIA
CRAIK, DINAH MARIA MULOCK

MULTON
VOORT, H. VOL

MUMFORD, TEX
HECKLEMANN, CHARLES N.

MUMMS, HARDEE
MCLELLAN, DIANA

MUN
LEAF, [WILBUR] MUNRO

MUNBY, A.N.L.
MUNBY, ALAN NOEL L.

MUNCHAUSEN, BARON
GERNSBACK, HUGO

MUNCHAUSEN, KARL F.H.F. v
RASPE, RUDOLF ERICH

MUNDAS, JAKOB
VETSCH, JAKOB

MUNDY, MAX
SCHOFIELD, SYLVIA ANNE

MUNDY, TALBOT
GRIBBON, WILLIAM L.

MUNDY, V.M.
CUNNINGHAM, VIRGINIA MYRA

MUNGER, AL
UNGER, MAURICE ALBERT

MUNI, NARAD
AMAND, MULK RAJ

MUNIN, HANS
ERTTMANN, PAUL OSKAR

MUNK, CHRISTIAN
WEISENBORN, GUENTHER

MUNK, GEORG
BUBER, PAULA [W]

MUNK, KAJ
PETERSON, KAJ HARALD L.

MUNKEPUNKE
MEYER, ALFRED RICHARD

MUNN, HART
HARDY, C. COLBURN

MUNN, VELLA
THOMPSON, PAULA & MARCELA

MUNNICH, MAGDA
HESS, MAGDA

MUNO, JEAN
BURNIAUX, ROBERT

MUNRO, ARN
MAHRLEIN, GOTTLIEB

MUNRO, C.K.
MACMULLAN, CHARLES W.K.

MUNRO, C.R.
BRAND, KURT

MUNRO, CHARLES KIRKPATRIC
MCMULLAN, CHARLES WALDEN

MUNRO, CHRISTY
TAVES, ISABELLA

MUNRO, DAVID
DEVINE, DAVID MCDONALD

MUNRO, H.H.
MUNRO, HECTOR HUGH

MUNRO, JAMES
CAVE, RODERIC K.G.J.M.
MITCHELL, JAMES [W]

MUNRO, MARY
HOWE, DORIS KATHLEEN

MUNRO, RONALD EADIE
GLEN, DUNCAN MUNRO

MUNROE, DUNCAN H.
RUSSELL, ERIC FRANK

MUNROE, R.
CHEYNE, JOSEPH LISTER W.

MUNSHI
SOOMRO, M.I.

MUNSHI, SKEHNAAZ
MUNSHI, KIKI SKAGEN

MUNTER, HERRMANN
ARNESEN, DAVID DIETRICH

MUNTHE, FRANCES
MINTO, FRANCES

MUNTZ, JAMES
CROWCROFT, PETER

MUNTZ, JAMES Z.
CROWCROFT, PETER

MUNZER, HARALD
BURGDORF, KARL-ULRICH

MURAT, ROLF
GRASMUCK, JURGEN
MAUERHARDT, ROLF

MURCH, MEL
MANES, STEPHEN
SOMERSON, PAUL

MURCH, MEL & WARD STARR
MANES, STEPHEN

MURDOCH, H.J.
M'INTOSH, JIM
MACGREGOR, JAMES MURDOCH

MURDOCK, FRANK
HITCHCOCK, FRANCIS

MURGATROYD, MATTHEW
JONES, JAMES ATHEARNE

MURGEL, MUSAGET
PFEFFER, HEINRICH

MURI, EBERHARD
MUHRMANN, WILHELM

MURON, JOHANNES
KECKEIS, GUSTAV

MURPHY, AGATHA
MURPHY, CHARLOTTE A.

MURPHY, ANTHONI G.
GONZALES MORALES, ANTONIO

MURPHY, AUDIE JR.
MELTZER, R.

MURPHY, BILL
BAJOG, GUNTHER

MURPHY, C.L.
MURPHY, CHARLOTTE A.
MURPHY, LAWRENCE A.

MURPHY, DENNIS JASPER
MATURIN, CHARLES ROBERT

MURPHY, HAUGHTON
DUFFY, JAMES HENRY

MURPHY, JOHN
GRADY, RONAN CALISTUS

MURPHY, LOUIS J.
HICKS, TYLER GREGORY

MURPHY, MARIO
EDMONDSON Y COTTON, JOSE

MURPHY, PAT
MURPHY, EMMETT JEFFERSON
MURPHY, PATRICE ANNE

MURPHY, TOM
MURPHY, THOMAS BASIL JR.

MURPHY, WARREN
MURPHY, MOLLY COCHRAN
HUNSBURGER, H. EDWARD
JOY, WILLIAM "TED"
MEYERS, RICHARD S.
MURRAY, WILLIAM P.
RANDISI, ROBERT J.

MURR, JAN
SACHSE, WILLI RICHARD

MURR, KATER
BIRNBAUM, ERNST

MURR, STEFAN
HORSTMANN, BERNHARD

MURRAY, A.A.
MURRAY, AUDREY ALISON

MURRAY, ADRIAN
CURRAN, MONA ELISA

MURRAY, ANNABEL
MURRAY, MARIE

MURRAY, BEATRICE
POSNER, RICHARD

MURRAY, BILL
MURRAY, WILLIAM P.

MURRAY, CAITLIN
AHEARN, PATRICIA

MURRAY, CROMWELL
MORGAN, MURRAY C.

MURRAY, D.L.
MURRAY, DAVID LESLIE

MURRAY, EDNA
ROWLAND, DONALD S.

MURRAY, FIONA
BEVAN, GLORY ISOBEL

MURRAY, FRANCES
BOOTH, ROSEMARY FRANCES

MURRAY, GERALDINE
MURRAY, BLANCHE

MURRAY, GILBERT
WYCHERLEY, RICHARD N.

MURRAY, GORDON W.
KRATOCHWIL, JOSEF

MURRAY, INSPECTOR
BAILIE, ALEXANDER DUKE

MURRAY, IRENE
WITHERSPOON, IRENE MURRAY

MURRAY, JILL
WALKER, EMILY KATHLEEN

MURRAY, K.F.
CARLISLE, FRED

MURRAY, KEN
TURNER, ROBERT H.

MURRAY, LT. M.M.
BALLOU, MATURIN M.

MURRAY, MAX
MURRAY, MAXWELL

MURRAY, MICHAEL
MCLAREN, MORAY DAVID SHAW

MURRAY, PETER
HAUTMAN, PETER

MURRAY, ROBERT
GRAYDON, ROBERT MURRAY
TWYMAN, HAROLD WILLIAM

MURRAY, ROSALIND
TOYNBEE, ROSALIND

MURRAY, SINCLAIR
SULLIVAN, EDWARD ALAN

MURRAY, T.C.
MURRAY, THOMAS C.

MURRAY, W.P.
MURRAY, WILLIAM P.

MURRAY, WILL
MURRAY, WILLIAM P.

MURRAY, WILLIAM
GRAYDON, WILLIAM MURRAY

MURRELL, GLENN
MEARES, LEONARD F.

MURRELL, SHIRLEY
SCOTT-HANSEN, OLIVE

MURRILL, RAY W.
MURRAY, WILLIAM P.

MURRILL, WRAY
MURRAY, WILLIAM P.

MURRY, COLIN MIDDLETON
MURRY, JOHN MIDDLETON

MURRY, COLIN
MURRY, JOHN MIDDLETON

MURRY, WILLIAM
MORRIS, CHARLES [S]

MUSGRAVE, JACQUELINE
MUSGRAVE, DAVID & MARG

MUSIKARA
PARIKH, RASIKLAL C.

MUSKATEER
BARKER, ARTHUR JAMES

MUSKETOEREN
WIRTANEN, ATOS KASIMIR

MUSSEY, VIRGINIA T.H.
ELLISON, VIRGINIA HOWELL

MUTZ
KUNSTLER, MORTON

MWAMBA, PAL
ROBERTS, JOHN S[TORM]

MWANGA
STARK, CLAUDE ALAN

MY
BARBERIS, JUAN CARLOS

MYATT, NELLIE
KIRKHAM, NELLIE

MYDDLETON, ROBERT
HEBBLETHWAITE, PETER

MYERS, F.W.H.
MYERS, FREDERIC

MYERS, HARRIET KATHRYN
WHITTINGTON, HARRY

MYERS, JUDY [JULIE]
MYERS, JUDITH BLACKWELL

MYERS, L.H.
MYERS, LEOPOLD HAMILTON

MYERS, WALTER M.
MYERS, WALTER DEAN

MYKEL, A.W.
ANDALORO, MICHAEL

MYLER, LOK
MULLER, PAUL ALFRED

MYLES, DEVERA
ZUCKER, DORIS MAE B.

MYLES, SABRINA
WALKER, LOIS ARVIN

MYLES, SIMON
FOLLETT, KENNETH [MARTIN]

MYNONA
FRIEDLANDER, SALOMO

MYRIAM
GONDA, ADOLPHE

MYRNYJ, PANAS JAKOVICH
PANAS, RUDCENKO

MYRON, PAUL
LINEBARGER, PAUL M.W.

MYRTLE, ANNIE
CHESTER, ANNIE M.

MYRTLE, MINNIE
DYER, MINNIE THERESA

MYRTLE, NAY
HOLDEN, MARIA

MYSELF AND ANOTHER
CASWELL, EDWARD A.

MYSTERIOUS TRAVELER
ARTHUR, ROBERT

McCARRICK, CHRIS SHEA
GORMAN, EDWARD [JOSEPH]

McCARTHY, CORMAC
MCCARTHY, CHARLES

McCLARY, T.C.
MCCLARY, THOMAS CALVERT

McCOLLAM, JIM
MCCOLLAM, JAMES G.

McCONNELL, CHAN
SCHOW, DAVID J.

McCOY, ANDREW
JUTE, ANDREW

McCRAY, MIKE
MCDOWELL, MICHAEL
PRESTON, JOHN

McCURTIN, PETER
HAYES, RALPH EUGENE

McDONALD, PAUL CHEROKEE
CWALINSKI, PAUL

McGOWAN, TOM
MCCOWAN, THOMAS E.

McINTOSH, J.T.
O'DONNELL, PETER

McIVER, N.J.
HOWARD, ALAN

McKENNA, K.C.
CRIDER, [ALLEN] BILL[Y]

McKINLEY, DEAN
BOSWORTH, ALLAN R.

McKINNEY, JACK
LUCENO, JAMES

McLENNAN, WILL
GORMAN, EDWARD [JOSEPH]
WISLER, G[ARY] CLIFTON

McM. DOUGLAS, JAMES
BUTTERWORTH, WILLIAM E.

McMAHON, ROBERT
WEVERKA, ROBERT

McNAB, CLAIRE
CARMICHAEL, CLAIRE

McPHEE, JAMES
JAMES, LAURENCE

McROBERTS, CAPT. KERRY
JUDSON, EDWARD Z.C.

McROBERTS, KERRY
DANIELS, NORMAN A.

N.D.H.
DICK-HUNTER, NOEL

N.H.D.
DOLE, NATHAN HASKELL

N.W.
LEWIS, CLIVE STAPLES

NA GCOPALEEN
O'NOLAN, BRIAN

NA GCOPALEEN, MYLES
O'NOLAN, BRIAN

NA GOPALEEN
O'NOLAN, BRIAN

NA GOPALEEN, MYLES
O'NOLAN, BRIAN

NAAGGI, TILLA
RABER, HANS

NABER, CHARLES R.
HALL, FRANK RICHARDS

NABOR, FELIX
ALLMENDINGER, KARL

NABUCO, JOAQUIM
DE ARAUJO, JOACHIM A.B.N.

NACNAB, JOHN
GATES, DAVID EDGERLEY

NACRAY, J.-B.
DANIEL PENNAC, JEAN-BERN.
RAYNARD, PATRICK

NADA, JOHN
LANGDON-DAVIES, JOHN

NADAR
TOURNACHON, FELIX

NADARR, ABU
MORROUGH, E.R.

NADER, OWEN & SEENA
ACKERMAN, FORREST J.

NADIR, A.A.
ROMANOFF, ALEXANDER N.

NADIR, MOISHE
REIZ, YITZCHOK

NADLER, THEODORE [TEDDY]
GIBSON, WALTER B.

NADZHMIR, NAZAR
NAZMUTDINOV, NAZAR M.

NAGENDA, MUSA
HOWARD, MOSES L.

NAGLE, ARTHUR
SULLIVAN, EDMUND

NAGOL
LOGAN, LILLIAN MEE
LOGAN, VIRGIL GLEN

NAIPAUL, SHIVA
NAIPAUL, SHIVADHAR S.

NAISMITH, HORACE
HELMER, WILLIAM

NAJAM
SHASTRI, PRITHVINATH

NAKANISHI, MARSHA
HIRANO-NAKANISHI, MARSHA

NAKOVSKI, ATANAS
NAKOV, ATANAS FOTINOV

NAM SUK
AHN, SOO-GIL

NAMBOKU, TSURUYA
INOSUKE, TSURUYA

NAMLEREP, SIDNEY
PERELMAN, SIDNEY JOSEPH

NANCY, A.P.F.
CLAUDE, ANNE P.F.

NANKIVELL, JOICE M.
LOCH, JOICE NANKIVELL

NANSUI, SUDO
MITSUTHERU, SUDO

NAPIER, GEOFFREY
GLEMSER, BERNARD

NAPIER, GERALDINE
GLEMSER, BERNARD

NAPIER, MARK
LAFFIN, JOHN [ALFRED C.]

NAPIER, MARY
WRIGHT, MARY PATRICIA

NAPIER, WILLIAM
SEYMOUR, WILLIAM NAPIER

NAPJUS, JAMES
NAPJUS, ALICE JAMES

NARAYAN
TAGORE, SAUMYEND

NARAYAN, K.
NARAYAN, RASIPURAM K.

NARAYANA, HARI
ESSEN, AXEL ANDERS H.

NARCEJAC, THOMAS
AYRAUD, PIERRE

NARSANMOR
SANCHEZ, MORALES NARCISCO

NASH, CHANDLER
HUNT, KATHERINE CHANDLER

NASH, DANIEL
LEADER, WILLIAM REGINALD

NASH, ENO
STEVENS, AUSTIN N.

NASH, GARRY
NETSCH, GUNTER

NASH, GORDON
KOBUSCH, JOACHIM

NASH, JEAN
SUTHERLAND, JEAN

NASH, LINELL
SMITH, LINELL NASH

NASH, NEWLYN
HOWE, DORIS KATHLEEN
HOWE, MURIEL

NASH, NOREEN
SIEGEL, NORABELLE ROTH

NASH, NORMAN
SUTHERLAND, DOUGLAS

NASH, PADDER
SEWART, ALAN

NASH, SIMON
CHAPMAN, RAYMOND

NASH, THURLOE
GIDDINGS, JOHN

NASS, WALDEMAR
LOEST, ERICH

NAST, ELSA RUTH
WATSON, JANE WERNER

NATHAN, DANIEL
DANNAY, FREDERIC

NATHENSON, JOSEPH
ST. JOHN, CHERYL

NATIONS, OPAL L.
HUMM, MARTIN J.

NATSUME, SOSEKI
NATSUME, KINNOSUKE

NAUGHTON, BILL
NAUGHTON, WILLIAM J.F.

NAUNDORF, PETER
DASCHKOWSKI, OTTO

NAUTICUS
CLOWES, WILLIAM LAIRD
SEAMAN, SIR OWEN
WALTARI, MIKA [T]

NAV ESIH, ALLED
VAN HISE, DELLA

NAVA, FRANZ
RIMBAULT, EDWARD FRANCIS

NAVAL, FREDERIK
BRUSTAT-NAVAL, FRITZ

NAVARCHUS
VAUX, PATRICK
WOODS, JAMES
YEXLEY, LIONEL

NAYDENOV, S.
ALEXEYEV, SERGEY ALEXAND.

NAYLOR, ELIOT
FRANKAU, PAMELA

NAYLOR, GRANT
GRANT, ROB
NAYLOR, DOUG

NAZARIAN, NIKKI
NICHOLS, CELIA FAWN

NAZEL, JOE
NAZEL, JOSEPH G. JR.

NEAL, GAVIN
TUBB, E.C.

NEAL, HARRY
BIXBY, JEROME L.

NEAL, HILARY
NORTON, OLIVE MARION

NEAL, MICHAEL
TEITELBAUM, MICHAEL

NEALE, ARTHUR
GIBSON, WALTER B.

NEANISKOS
SMITHERS, LEONARD

NEARING, PENNY
MUNN, MERYL LUCILE

NEBAN, HUGH
MANN, EDWARD BEVERLY

NEBEL, CASPAR
ORTHOFER, PETER

NEBEL, MIMOUCA
NEBEL, GUSTAVE E.

NEBRENSKY, ALEX
COOPER, PARLEY J.

NEBY, AL
JOHNS, WALTER T.

NECKAR, HEINRICH
KOCHER, HUGO

NED, NEVADA
TILBURN, E.O.

NEE, DAVE
NEE, DAVID CHIN-KUO

NEEF[E], ELTON T.
FANTHORPE, R.L.

NEEL, JANET
COHEN, JANET

NEEPER, CARY
NEEPER, CAROLYN A.

NEERA
ZUCCARI, ANNA RADIUS

NEETHLING, J.S.
NEETHLING, JACOBUS STEPH.

NEETHLING, KOBUS
NEETHLING, JACOBUS STEPH.

NEETIX, TRAUTCHEN
HAEFS, GABRIELE

NEFF, HILDEGARD
KNEF, HILDEGARD

NEGGERS, CARLA A[MALIA]
JEWEL, CARLA AMALIA N.

NEGULESCO, BRIAN
AUCHINCLOSS, BAYARD

NEHER, FRANK
NEHER, FRANZ L.

NEIBOR, ELIZABETH
LYNN, MARY ELIZABETH N.

NEIGHBOUR, RHONA M.
MARTIN, RHONA

NEIL, BARBARA
SHERROD, BARBARA

NEIL, FRANCES
GEACH, CHRISTINE

NEIL, GEOFFREY
BELLAH, JAMES WARNER

NEIL, MARTIN
BELLAH, JAMES WARNER

NEILSON, KOEF
KOEFED-NIELSON, CARL

NEILSON, MARGUERITE
TOMKINS, JULIA MARGUERITE

NEILSON, MAX
CAVE, HUGH B[ARNETT]

NEISH, DUNCAN
ALLAN, F. CARNEY

NEKKEPEN, EKKE
KUHLEMANN, PETER

NELL
HANNA, NELL[IE L.]

NELL, LUKAS
HARRER, JOSEF ROBERT

NELSON, ANNIE GREENE
PLUNKETT, ANNIE E.

NELSON, BARDY
THOMAS, REGINALD GEORGE

NELSON, CHRIS
HUNT, DARRELL

NELSON, ELIZABETH
LYNN, MARY ELIZABETH N.

NELSON, GERTRUDE
BOBIN, JOHN WILLIAM

NELSON, HEINRICH
KUMPMANN, KARL

NELSON, HENRY
NEUBERT, HELMUT

NELSON, INGRID
BANCROFT, IRIS M. NELSON

NELSON, JOHNNY
MEARES, LEONARD F.
BLEECK, G.C.

NELSON, JOSEPH
MITCHELL, ISAAC

NELSON, LOIS
NORTHAM, LOIS EDGELL

NELSON, MARGUERITE
FLOREN, LEE

NELSON, MARK
JOHNSTON, RONALD

NELSON, MILDRED
SILVERBERG, ROBERT

NELSON, NINA
NELSON, ETHEL FLORENCE

NELSON, PETER
SOLOW, MARTIN

NELSON, R. FARADAY
NELSON, RADELL FARADAY

NELSON, R.F.
NELSON, RADELL FARADAY

NELSON, RAY
NELSON, RADELL FARADAY

NELSON, RAY FARADAY
NELSON, RADELL FARADAY

NELSON, REX
MEYN, NIELS

NELSON, ROY
NELSON-SMITH, ALAN ROY V.

NELSON, STEVE
BOBIN, JOHN WILLIAM

NELSON, VICTOR
BOBIN, JOHN WILLIAM

NEMCOVA, BETTY
NEMCOVA, BOZENA

NEMI, ORSOLA
VEZZANI, FLORA

NEMO
DOUGLAS, ARCHIBALD C.

NEMO, OMEN
REHM, WARREN S.

NEMOURS, PIERRE
GUILEMOT, PIERRE

NEMOV, ALEXANDER
NESMANSKY, FRIEDRICH
TOPOL, EDUARD

NEREV, ADELAIDE
HARKSEN, VERENA C.

NERI TANFUCIO
FUCINI, RENATO

NESBIT, EDITH
BLAND, EDITH NESBIT

NESBIT, TROY
FOLSOM, FRANKLIN [B]

NESS, EVALINE [M]
BAYARD, EVALINE

NESS, K.T.
GRANT, DONALD
WILSON, WILLIAM

NESS, THOMAS
KALMUCZAK, ROLF

NESS, TOM T.
THIENES, THOMAS L.

NETTERVILLE, LUKE
O'GRADY, JAMES STANDISH

NETTLETON, ARTHUR
GAUNT, ARTHUR NETTLETON

NETTSON, KLAUS
JAMES, LAURENCE

NETZEN, KLAUS
JAMES, LAURENCE

NEUBERG, A.
LEHEN, TUURE

NEUENKIRCH, RAINER
LAUXMANN, LONI

NEUERT, H.
PANY, LEONORE

NEUGEBAUER, RALF
LIEDER, HERWIG

NEUHOFER, W.
KABEL, WALTHER

NEUNER, ROBERT
KASTNER, ERICH

NEUSCHUB, WALTHER
KABEL, WALTHER

NEUWERT
NOWACZYNSKI, ADOLF

NEVE, FIORE DELLA
VAN LOGHEM, MARTINUS G.L.

NEVEROT, ALEXANDER
SKOBELEV, ALEXANDER SERGE

NEVILLE, ANNA
FAIRBURN, ELEANOR

NEVILLE, ANNE
VINEY, JANE

NEVILLE, C.J.
FRANKLIN, CYNTHIA

NEVILLE, MARGOT
GOYDER, MARGOT
JOSKE, ANNE GOYDER

NEVILLE, MARY
WOODRICH, MARY NEVILLE

NEVILLE, ROBERT
HUTSON, SHAUN

NEVIN, EVELYN C
FERGUSON, HELEN

NEVINS, KATE
MALKIND, MARGARET

NEVINS, MIKE
NEVINS, FRANCIS JR.

NEVINSON, H.W.
NEVINSON, HENRY WOODD

NEWARK, ELIZABETH
DINNEEN, BETTY

NEWBURY, WILL
COTTON, WILLIAM

NEWBY, P.H.
NEWBY, PERCY HOWARD

NEWCOMB, NORMA
NEUBAUER, WILLIAM A.

NEWCOMBE, COLIN
YOUNG, FRED W.

NEWCOMBE, ELLSWORTH
KENNY, ELLSWORTH N.

NEWCOMBE, JACK
NEWCOMBE, EUGENE A.

NEWCOMBE, LOUIS
STOBBS, J. LOUIS NEWCOMBE

NEWELL, CROSBY
BONSALL, CROSBY B. NEWELL

NEWHOME, W.H.
NEUHAUS, W.

NEWKIRK, FOSTER
TUCKER, JOHN F.

NEWKIRK, NEWTON
NEWKIRK, CLYDE C.

NEWLAND, N.M.
HARRISON, CHESTER WILLIAM

NEWMAN, BARBARA
NEWMAN, MONA ALICE JEAN

NEWMAN, ERNEST
ROBERTS, E.N.
ROBERTS, WILLIAM

NEWMAN, FRANK
ABRAMS, SAM

NEWMAN, GAVIN
SMITH, GUY NEWMAN

NEWMAN, JOHN
BLUMER, HENRY KENNETH

NEWMAN, MARGARET
POTTER, MARGARET [N]

NEWMAN, ODETTE
ABRAMS, BARBARA

NEWMAN, ROBERT
NORTON, ROGER HOWARD

NEWTON, CLARKE
HARMON, JAMES JUDSON

NEWTON, D.B.
NEWTON, DWIGHT BENNETT

NEWTON, DAVID C.
CHANCE, JOHN NEWTON

NEWTON, FRANCES
DENISON, MURIEL [G]
HOBSBAWM, ERIC JOHN ERN.

NEWTON, MACDONALD
DONALDSON, FRANCIS
NEWTON, WILLIAM [SIMPSON]

NEWTON, MIKE
NEWTON, MICHAEL

NEXTER, GLENN
NETSCH, GUNTER

NEY, ELISABETH
ASPERN-BUCHMEIER, ELISAB.

NEY, JOHANNES
REIBER, JOHN N.

NEY, WOLFGANG
HARRANTH, WOLF

NGUGI, WA THIONGIO
NGUGI, J.T.

NGUYEN SA
TRAN BICH LAN

NHAT, LINK
NGUYEN, TUONG TAN

NI FHAIRCHEALLAIGH, UNA
O'FARRELLY, AGNES

NIALL, IAN
MCNEILLIE, JOHN

NIALL, MICHAEL
BRESLIN, HOWARD

NIALL, SEAN
MANGAN, [J.J] SHERRY

NIBOR, KAY
TUCKER, ROBIN

NIC LEODHAS, SORCHE
ALGER, LECLAIRE GOWANS

NICHOLAS, DEBORAH
MARTIN, DEBORAH

NICHOLAS, F.R.E.
FREELING, NICHOLAS

NICHOLAS, WILLIAM
JOHNSON, WILLIAM O.
THIMMESCH, NICHOLAS P.

NICHOLLS, ANTHONY
PARSONS, ANTHONY

NICHOLLS, MARK
FREWIN, LESLIE RONALD

NICHOLS, CHARLOTTE
KNOLL, PATRICIA F.
WILLIAMS, BARBARA

NICHOLS, DAVE
FROST, HELEN

NICHOLS, FAN
HANNA, FRANCES NICHOLS

NICHOLS, JANE
SCALES, LISA

NICHOLS, JASON
WOOD, EDWARD D. JR.

NICHOLS, JESS
GIBSON, WALTER B.

NICHOLS, LEIGH
KOONTZ, DEAN R.

NICHOLS, MATT
DUBINA, PETER

NICHOLS, PAMELA
PATTINSON, LEE

NICHOLS, PETER
YOUD, CHRISTOPHER [S]

NICHOLS, SARAH
HAYS, LEE

NICHOLS, SCOTT
SCORTIA, THOMAS N.

NICHOLS, SUZANNE
STAPLEBROEK, MARLYS

NICHOLS, T. NICKLE
NICHOLS, THOMAS

NICHOLSON, C.R.
NICOLE, CHRISTOPHER ROBIN

NICHOLSON, CHRISTINA
NICOLE, CHRISTOPHER ROBIN

NICHOLSON, JANE
STEEN, MARGUERITE

NICHOLSON, JOHN
PARCELL, NORMAN HOWE

NICHOLSON, KATE
FAY, JUDITH

NICHOLSON, KATHERINE
FAY, JUDITH

NICHOLSON, ROBIN
NICOLE, CHRISTOPHER ROBIN

NICHOLSON, SAM
NIKOLAISEN, SHIRLEY

NICHOLSON, VICTORIA MARY
SACKVILLE-WEST, VITA M.

NICKELS, MERYL
UNICKEL, MARTHA

NICKERSON, BETTY
NICKERSON, ELIZABETH

NICKOLAE, BARBARA
GERSTNER, NICKOLAE
PRONIN, BARBARA

NICODEMUS
PEARCE, MELVILLE CHANING

NICOL, ANN
TURNBULL, ANN [C]

NICOLAS
MORDVINOFF, NICOLAS

NICOLE, CLAUDE
MESSMANN, JON [JOHN]

NICOLE, CLAUDETTE
MESSMANN, JON [JOHN]

NICOLE, CLAUDIA
MESSMANN, JON [JOHN]

NICOLE, MARIE
RYDZYNSKI, MARIE R.

NICOLI, C.L.R.
CLAIR, COLIN

NIDDEN, CHRISTOPHER
BEHRENDT, ERWIN

NIELS, OLIVER
KEPPNER, GERHARD

NIELSEN, JENS C.
LIEPMAN, HEINZ

NIELSEN, VIRGINIA
MCCALL, VIRGINIA NIELSEN

NIELSON, VERNON
CLARKE, PERCY A.

NIELSSEN, ERIC
LUDVIGSEN, KARL [E]

NIEMAND, O.
EFFINGER, GEORGE ALEC

NIEMANN, DORA
PESSLER-ADAM, DORA

NIEMOLLER, ARA
LLERENA, MARIO

NIENACKI, ZBIGNIEW
NOWICKI, ZBIGNIEW

NIENKAMP, HEINRICH
KLIEMKE, ERNST

NIG, CAPT'N
SWAFFORD, JOHNNY C.

NIGG, JOE
NIGG, JOSEPH EUGENE

NIGHT, KIM
PERKINS, KENNETH

NIGHTINGALE, CHARLES
DUDDINGTON, CHARLES L.

NIGHTINGALE, URSULA
LITCHMAN, FRANK

NIGHTRATE, EMIL
SPIELMANN, PETER JAMES

NIHIL
MILLER, P. SCHUYLER

NIININEN, MARGIT
TOERNUDD, MARGIT

NIK
LEE, FRANCIS NIGEL

NIK-UHERNIK
CAIN, NICHOLAS [COLORADO]

NIKOLAEVA, GALINA EVGENEV
VOLYANSHAYA, GALINA EVG.

NIKOLAUS, GEORG
POCHE, KLAUS

NIKOLI, BORIS
GUNTHER, HEINZ

NILE, DOROTHEA
AVALLONE, MICHAEL

NILSON, BEE
NILSON, ANNABEL RHODA

NIMBLE, JACK B.
BURGESS, MICHAEL ROY

NINA V.
VICKERS, ANTOINETTE L.

NINESPOT
PHILLIPS, HUBERT

NISTER, DER
KAHANOVITCH, PINHAS

NITGENOCKLE
GALT, WILLIAM H.

NITRAM, H.
MARTIN, HANS

NITRAM, HANS
MARTIN, HANS

NITSUA, BENJAMIN
AUSTIN, BENJAMIN FISH

NIVEN, LARRY
NIVEN, LAURENCE VAN COTT

NIVEN, MARIAN
ALSTON, MARY NIVEN

NIVEN, VERN
GRIER, BARBARA G.D.

NIXON, K.
NIXON, KATHLEEN IRENE

NIXON, KATHLEEN
BLUNDELL, V.R.

NO NAME
JACKSON, HELEN HUNT

NO, DR.
MANY, SETH E[DWARDS]

NOACK, WERNER
FIELITZ, HANS PAUL

NOBEL, PHIL
FANTHORPE, R.L.
MANSFIELD, HARRY O.

NOBLE, CHARLES
PAWLEY, MARTIN EDWARD

NOBLE, EMILY
GIFFORD, JAMES NOBLE

NOBLE, JOHN
GRIFFIN, FRANK
HUBBLE, LESLIE ARTHUR B.

NOBODY NOTHING OF NOWHERE
YOUNG, JAMES ALEXANDER

NOBODY, NICK N.
GEIST, RUDOLF

NOBODY, UNUS
BREUCKER, OSCAR HERBERT

NOCENI, EARL
SELLERS, CONNIE LESLIE

NODSET, JOAN L.
LEXAU, JOAN M.

NOEL, ATANIELLE ANNYN
NOEL, RUTH HELEN SWYCAF.

NOEL, EUGENIO
MUNOZ, EUGENIO

NOEL, JOHN
BIRD, DENNIS LESLIE

NOEL, L.
BARKER, LEONARD NOEL

NOEL, RUTH S.
NOEL, ANTANIELLE ANNYN

NOESTLINGER, CHRISTINE
NOSTLINGER, CHRISTINE

NOHAIN, FRANC
LE GRAND, FRANC

NOIR, JEAN
CASSOU, JEAN

NOIR, L'ANGE
DARD, FREDERIC

NOLAN, CHRISTOPHER
JAMES, LAURENCE

NOLAN, CHUCK
EDSON, JOHN THOMAS

NOLAN, FREDERICK
BAJOG, GUNTHER
BECK, FLORIAN
BIRNER, OTTO
BOCKL, MANFRED
DUENSING, JURGEN
HEBEL, PETER
HELGATH, FRANC
KOBUSCH, JOACHIM
NEUBERT, HELMUT
VON KOBLINSKI, HANS-JOACH

NOLAN, JENNY
YOUNG, MARY JO

NOLANE, RICHARD D.
RAYNAUD, OLIVIER

NOLDEN, ARNOLD
PFERDEKAMP, WILHELM

NOLDEN, SUSANNE
LIGENSA, ELFIE

NOLDREN, MARK
PFANDLER, MARCEL

NOLL, BINK
NOLL, LOU BARKER

NOLL, MARTIN
BUXBAUM, MARTIN

NOMAD, MAX
NACHT, MAX

NONAME
ENTON, HARRY
SENARENS, LUIS P.

NONG
LOBLEY, ROBERT

NONNI
SVENSON, JON STEFAN

NOON, ED
AVALLONE, MICHAEL

NOON, T.R.
NORTON, OLIVE MARION

NOONE, CARL
CHESTER, CHARLIE

NOONE, EDWINA
AVALLONE, MICHAEL

NOORDEN, RUTH
NICKEL, RUTH

NOORDUNG, HERMANN
POTOCNIK, CAPTAIN

NOR, A.C.
KAVAN, JOSEF

NORAH
MCDOUGALL, MARGARET

NORBERT, W.
WIENER, NORBERT

NORBURN, MARTHA
MEAD, MARTHA NORBURN

NORCROSS, ELIZABETH
GLADSTONE, ARTHUR M.

NORCROSS, JOHN
CONROY, JOHN WESLEY

NORCROSS, LISABET
GLADSTONE, ARTHUR M.

NORD, F.R.
HORN, ROBERT W.

NORD, PIERRE
BROUILLARD, ANDRE

NORDAU, MAX SIMON
SUDFELD, MAX SIMON

NORDAY, MICHAEL
WEISS, JOE

NORDEN, CHARLES
DURRELL, LAWRENCE [G]

NORDEN, NICK
VON MICHALEWSKY, NIKOLAI

NORDEN, TIM
KALMUCZAK, ROLF

NORDHAUSEN, K.L.
LUTGE, KARL

NORDICUS
SNYDER, LOUIS L.

NORDMANN, FRITZ
ASPERN-BUCHMEIER, ELISAB.

NORFOLK, WILLIAM
FARMER, PHILIP JOSE

NORGAY, TENZING
WANGDI, NAMGYAL

NORHAM, GERALD
JAMES, J.W.G.

NORK, F.
KOHN, SELIGMANN
KORN, FRIEDRICH

NORMA, NICOLA
GREVEN, HELGA

NORMAN, ART
GIESA, WERNER K.

NORMAN, CHARLES
BLOOM, CHARLES

NORMAN, CHET
JENNISON, JOHN WILLIAM

NORMAN, COLEEN
BROWN, ELIZABETH D.

NORMAN, DAVID
DANIELS, NORMAN A.

NORMAN, DEE
LOPEZ, DEE
WILLIAMS, NORMA

NORMAN, DONALD N.
HORAN, DON
STAHL, NORMAN

NORMAN, EARL
THOMSON, NORMAN

NORMAN, ELIZABETH
KUMMANN, WILLIAM

NORMAN, ERIC
OLSON, EUGENE E.

NORMAN, JAMES
SCHMIDT, JAMES NORMAN

NORMAN, JAY
ARTHUR, ROBERT

NORMAN, JOE
HEARD, J. NORMAN

NORMAN, JOHN
LANGE, JOHN FREDERICK, JR

NORMAN, LOUIS
CARMAN, BLISS

NORMAN, MICK
JAMES, LAURENCE

NORMAN, NESTA
LAZENBY, NORMAN A.

NORMAN, NICOLE
CUDLIPP, EDYTHE

NORMAN, PEGGY
NAUMANN, MARGOT

NORMAN, PHILIP
PHILLIPS, GEORGE NORMAN

NORMAN, REIDAR
RICHTER-FRICH, OVRE

NORMAN, ROB
QUINN, SEABURY

NORMAN, STEVE
PASHKO, STANLEY

NORMAN, VICTOR
RANSOME, L.E.

NORMAN, W.S.
WILSON, NORMAN SCARLYN

NORMAN, WYNN
WILLIAMS, NORMA

NORMAN, YVONNE
SEELY, NORMA YVONNE

NORMANDIE, ROGER
HITT, ORRIE [EDWIN]
WEISS, JOE

NORMYX
DOUGLAS, ELSA F.
DOUGLAS, GEORGE NORMAN

NORNE, THOMAS
SANDBERG, DANNIS

NORRELL, MARJORIE
NORTON, MARJORIE

NORRIS, CAROL[YN]
NORRIS, CAROLYN B.

NORRIS, FRANK
NORRIS, BENJAMIN F. JR.

NORRIS, GIL
NETSCH, GUNTER

NORRIS, MAUREEN
CUDLIPP, EDYTHE

NORRIS, P.E.
CLEARY, C.V.H.

NORRIS, S.D.
MASTORAKIS, NICO

NORST, JOEL
MITCHELL, KIRK [JOHN]

NORTH STAFFS
HULME, THOMAS ERNEST

NORTH, ANDRE
NORTON, ANDRE ALICE

NORTH, ANDREW
NORTON, ANDRE ALICE

NORTH, ANISON
WILSON, MAY

NORTH, ANTHONY
KOONTZ, DEAN R.

NORTH, BARCLAY
HUDSON, WILLIAM C.

NORTH, CAPTAIN GEORGE
STEVENSON, ROBERT LOUIS

NORTH, CAROL
NORTH-MONTFORT, GRACE M.

NORTH, CHARLES
JOHNSON, GERALD WHITE

NORTH, CHARLES W.
BAUER, ERWIN A.

NORTH, COLIN
BINGLEY, DAVID ERNEST

NORTH, ERIC
CRONIN, BERNARD CHARLES

NORTH, GENE
NEILS, GRANT JR.

NORTH, GENE JR.
GRANT, NEILS JR.

NORTH, GEOFFREY
HORNE, GEOFFREY

NORTH, GERRY
ARMITAGE, AUDREY
WATKINS, MURIEL

NORTH, GIL
HORNE, GEOFFREY

NORTH, GRACE MAY
NORTH-MONTFORT, GRACE M.

NORTH, HOWARD
TREVOR, ELLESTON

NORTH, INGOLDSBY
URNER, NATHAN DANE

NORTH, JACK
PENTELOW, JOHN NIX

NORTH, JAMES
SWANSON, DAN

NORTH, JESSICA
MACDONALD, JESSICA NORTH
SOMERLOTT, ROBERT

NORTH, LEIGH
PHELPS, ELIZABETH STEWART

NORTH, LIONEL
NORTHCROFT, GEORGE J.H.

NORTH, MARILLA
WILSON, MARILLA

NORTH, MARK
MILLER, WRIGHT

NORTH, MILOU
DORRIS, MICHAEL [ANTHONY]
EDRICH, LOUISE

NORTH, MIRANDA
AUSTIN, NANCY
KEVERN, MARY

NORTH, PEARSON
PEARSON, T.E.

NORTH, RICK
BONANNO, MARGARET WANDER
BRENNER, MAYER ALAN
LEWITT, SHARIANN N.
PEEL, JOHN [RONALD]

NORTH, ROBERT
WITHERS, CARL A.

NORTH, SARA
HAGER, [WILMA] JEAN [L]
BONHAM, BARBARA THOMAS

NORTH, VALENTINE
KELLEY, THOMAS P.

NORTHAN, IRENE
LOWTHER, ELIZABETH

NORTHCOTE
BOULTING, SYDNEY
COTES, PETER

NORTHE, MAGGIE
LEE, MAUREEN

NORTHERN, LESLIE
LONG, FRANK BELKNAP

NORTHERNER
HUGHES, WILLIAM JESSE

NORTHRUP, CAPT. B.A.
HUBBARD, L. RON

NORTHUMBIAN GENTLEMAN
TEGNER, HENRY

NORTON, ANDRE
NORTON, ANDRE ALICE

NORTON, ANDRE ALICE
NORTON, ALICE MARY

NORTON, BESS
NORTON, OLIVE MARION

NORTON, BROWNING
NORTON, FRANK R.B.

NORTON, CHARLES ELIOT
DAY-LEWIS, CECIL

NORTON, GERALD
NETSCH, GUNTER

NORTON, JED
LAZENBY, NORMAN A.

NORTON, JOHN
NETSCH, GUNTER

NORTON, RICHARD
SIEURIN, SVEN

NORTON, S.H.
RICHARDSON, MARY KATHLEEN

NORTON, SYBIL
COURNOS, HELEN

NORTON, VICTOR
DALTON, GILBERT LAWFORD

NORVIL, MANNING
BULMER, [HENRY] KENNETH

NORWAY, KATE
NORTON, OLIVE MARION

NORWOOD, ELLIOTT
KENSDALE, W.E.N.

NORWOOD, JOHN
STARK, DELBERT RAYMOND

NORWOOD, V.G.C.
NORWOOD, VICTOR [G.C.]

NORWOOD, VICTOR
CHARLES, GEORGE

NORWOOD, WARREN C.
ODOM, MEL[VIN LEWIS III]

NORWOOD, WARREN G.
NORWOOD, WARREN C.

NOSGOROV, SHAN
MULLEN, STANLEY

NOSILLE, NALRAH
ELLISON, HARLAN

NOSNER, FRIEDRICH
CSALLNER, ALFRED

NOSTALGIA
BENTLEY, JAMES W.B.

NOSTRADAMUS
NOTREDAME, MICHEL DE

NOSTRODAMUS, MERLIN
COBBE, FRANCIS POWER

NOTLEP, ROBERT
PELTON, ROBERT W.

NOTT, BARRY
HURREN, BERNARD JOHN

NOTTINGHAM, POPPY
DUNAWAY, PATTI

NOUS-TERRE, JEAN
GRATIANT, GILBERT

NOUS-TOUS, JEAN
GRATIANT, GILBERT

NOV, J.M.
KOTHNER, PAUL

NOVAK, HELGA M.
KARLSDOTTIR, MARIA

NOVAK, JERZY
KOSINSKI, JERZY

NOVAK, JOHN LUTHER
PRIEST, CHRISTOPHER [M]

NOVAK, JOSEPH
KOSINSKI, JERZY

NOVAK, ROBERT
LEVINSON, LEONARD [L]

NOVELIST OF CATTLE KINGDM
RHODES, EUGENE MANLOVE

NOVELLO, IVOR
DAVIES, IVOR NOVELLO

NOVICUS, ALOYSIUS
LOGAN, JOHN DANIEL

NOVY, KAREL
NOVAK, KAREL

NOX, OWEN
CORY, CHARLES BARNEY

NOXIUS, FRED
SCHADLICH, GOTTFRIED

NOXIUS, FRIED
SCHADLICH, GOTTFRIED

NRE, HITTIER
WHITTINGTON, HARRY

NU'AIMAH, MIKHA'IL
NAIMY, MIKHAIL

NUDLEMAN, NORDYK
GLASBY, JOHN S.

NUDNICK
NERNEY, PATRICK W.

NUED, D.E.
MURRAY, WILLIAM P.

NUELLE, HELEN [SHEARMAN]
NUELLE, HELEN SHEARMAN

NUKI
MILLSAPS, DANIEL W. III

NULPE, H.C.
KOCH, RICHARD

NUNLEY, MAGGIE RENNERT
RENNERT, MAGGIE

NURAINI
SIM, KATHARINE [T]

NURENBERG, THELMA
GREENHAUS, THELMA NURENB.

NUSBAUM, N. RICHARD
NASH, N[ATHAN] RICHARD

NUSS, EMMA
MAHNER-MONS, EMMA

NUSS, EMMERICH
MAHNER-MONS, EMMA

NUSSBAUM, AL
NUSSBAUM, ALBERT F.

NUTCHUK
OLIVER, SIMEON

NXELEAFRIKA, MNGUNI
JAFFEE, HOSEA

NYE, CASSANDRA
DISCH, THOMAS M.

NYE, HAROLD G.
HARDING, LEE [JOHN]

NYNCH, STEPHANIE J.
CAULDER, COLLINE

NYOZEKAN, HASEGAWA
MANJIRO, HASEGAWA

NYSSEN, ERNST WILHELM
HELLWIG, ERNST

O CEALLAIGH, SEAN
O'KELLY, JOHN J.

O CEALLAIGH, THOMAS
O'KELLY, THOMAS

O DUBH, CATHAL
DUFF, CHARLES ST. LAWREN.

O DUBHGHAILL, SEAMUS
DOYLE, JAMES J.

O HAODHA, TOMAS
HAYES, THOMAS

O'BANYON, CONSTANCE
GEE, D. EVELYN H.

O'BEIRNE, BRIAN
DONN-BYRNE, BRIAN OSWALD

O'BLATHER, COUNT
O'NOLAN, BRIAN

O'BRAWES, TARNEL
LA BARRE, WESTON

O'BREY, KATHLEEN
MOTH-LUND, POUL

O'BRIAN, EVE
BRYER, JUDITH E.
HELLER, ARNIE

O'BRIAN, FRANK
GARFIELD, BRIAN F.W.

O'BRIAN, TED
KOBUSCH, JOACHIM

O'BRIEN, BERNADETTE
HIGGINS, MARGARET

O'BRIEN, CLANCY
SMITH, GEORGE H[ENRY]

O'BRIEN, DEAN D.
BINDER, EARL ANDREW
BINDER, OTTO

O'BRIEN, DEE
BRADLEY, MARION ZIMMER

O'BRIEN, DEIRDRE
MCNALLY, MARY ELIZABETH

O'BRIEN, E.G.
CLARKE, ARTHUR C.

O'BRIEN, FLANN
O'NOLAN, BRIAN

O'BRIEN, FRANK
GARFIELD, BRIAN F.W.

O'BRIEN, JEFF
MARZINEK, WILHELM

O'BRIEN, JOHN
HARTIGAN, PATRICK JOSEPH

O'BRIEN, KATHLEEN
PYNN, KATHLEEN

O'BRIEN, LARRY CLINTON
O'BRIEN, CLIFFORD EDWARD

O'BRIEN, LEE
WARD, CANDACE

O'BRIEN, RALEY
MCCULLEY, JOHNSTON

O'BRIEN, ROBERT C.
CONLY, ROBERT LESLIE

O'BRIEN, SALIEE
JANAS, FRANCIS LEROY G.

O'BYRNE, DERMOT
BAX, SIR ARNOLD

O'CARROLL, RYAN
MARKUN, PATRICIA MALONEY

O'CATHASAIGH, DONAL
CASEY, DANIEL J.

O'CLEANER, JAMES
BRESLAUER, HANS KARL

O'CONNELL, PEG
AHERN, MARGARET MCCROHAN

O'CONNELL, R.F.
VAN DE GOHM, RICHARD

O'CONNELL, ROBERT FRANK
GOHM, DOUGLAS CHARLES

O'CONNELL, STEVE
REITCI, JOHN GEORGE

O'CONNER, ELIZABETH
MCNAMARA, BARBARA WILLARD

O'CONNOR, BERT
PAINE, LAURAN BOSWORTH

O'CONNOR, CLINT
PAINE, LAURAN BOSWORTH

O'CONNOR, DERMOT
NEWMAN, TERENCE

O'CONNOR, FRANK
O'DONOVAN, MICHAEL

O'CONNOR, JACK
O'CONNOR, JOHN WOOLF

O'CONNOR, LIAM
LIDDY, JAMES [D.R.]

O'CONNOR, LYNN
RUSSELL, WALTER

O'CONNOR, PATRICK
WIBBERLEY, LEONARD [P.O.]

O'CONNOR, PHILIP
BANCROFT, MARIE C.

O'CONNOR, W.
GUBERN RIBALTA, JORGE

O'CONNOR, WILLIAM
BAJOG, GUNTHER

O'DAIR, STAN
MATTHEWS, CLAYTON [H]

O'DARE, KERRY
STARR, RICHARD H.

O'DOHERTY, NED
DOHERTY, EDWARD JOSEPH

O'DONNELL, DICK
LUPOFF, RICHARD A.
THOMPSON, DON[ALD ARTHUR]

O'DONNELL, DONAT
O'BRIEN, CONOR CRUISE

O'DONNELL, JODI
RADNOR, JODE

O'DONNELL, K.M.
MALZBERG, BARRY [N]

O'DONNELL, KATE
GARCIA, NANCY

O'DONNELL, LAWRENCE
KUTTNER, HENRY
MOORE, CATHERINE LUCILLE

O'DONNEVAN, FINN
SHECKLEY, ROBERT

O'DONOHOE, NICK
O'DONOHOE, NICHOLAS BENJ.

O'DONOVAN, GERALD
O'DONOVAN, JEREMIAH

O'DOWD, DARBY
LUBY, KATE

O'DREAMS, JOHN
WALLACE, HENRY

O'FAOLAIN, SEAN
WHELAN, JOHN

O'FINN, THADDEUS
MCGLOIN, JOSEPH THADDEUS

O'FLYNN, JIMMY
GRAYDON, ROBERT MURRAY

O'FLYNN, PETER
FANTHORPE, R.L.

O'GORMAN, JOHN
MACGILL, PATRICK

O'GRADA, SEAN
O'GRADY, JOHN PATRICK

O'GRADY, FELIX
HADATH, JOHN E.G.

O'GRADY, ROHAN
SKINNER, JUNE M. O'GRADY

O'GRADY, TONY
CLEMENS, BRIAN

O'GREEN, JENNIFER
ROBERSON, JENNIFER

O'GREEN, JENNIFER ROBERS.
ROBERSON, JENNIFER

O'HALLION, SHEILA
ALLEN, SHEILA ROSALYND

O'HANLON, JACKLYN
MEEK, JACKLYN O'HANLON

O'HANNEGAN, LARRY
O'HARRIS, LEE

O'HARA FAMILY
BANIM, JOHN & MICHAEL

O'HARA, DALE
GILLESE, JOHN PATRICK

O'HARA, DAN
REMUS, MICHAEL

O'HARA, DAVID
SNELL, ROY JUDSON

O'HARA, DONN
CHIDSEY, DONALD BARR

O'HARA, FRANK
SLATTERY, RAY

O'HARA, KENNETH
WALTON, BRYCE
MORRIS, MARGARET JEAN

O'HARA, KEVIN
CUMBERLAND, MARTEN

O'HARA, MARY
ALSOP, MARY O'HARA
STURE-VASA, MARY

O'HARA, SCOTT
MACDONALD, JOHN D.

O'HARA, SHAUN
MARTIN, THOMAS HECTOR

O'HARRIS, PIXIE
PRATT, RHONA OLIVE

O'HEARN, MARIAN
MACDONALD, JOHN D.

O'HEFFERNAN, PATRICK
HEFFERNAN, PATRICK

O'KEY
RADWANSKI, PIERRE A.

O'LAITHAIN, SESU
LYONS, JOHN MAGUIRE

O'LAOGHAIRE, LIAM
O'LEARY, LIAM

O'LEARY, CHESTER F.
KUEHNELT-LEDDIHN, ERIK v.
VON KUEHNELT-LEDDIH, ERIK

O'LOAGHAIRE, PEADAR
O'LEARY, PETER

O'LONDON, JOHN
LYND, ROBERT
WHITTEN, WILFRED

O'MAHONEY, RICH
CROZETTI, RUTH G.W.L.

O'MAHONY, PATRICK
MAHONY, PATRICK

O'MAILLE, MICHAEL
O'MALLEY, MICHAEL

O'MALLEY, FRANK
O'ROURKE, FRANK

O'MALLEY, KEVIN
HOSSENT, HARRY

O'MALLEY, PATRICK
O'ROURKE, FRANK

O'MARA, JIM
FLUHARTY, VERNON L.

O'MARA, JON
O'MARA, JOHN

O'MARA, PAT
O'MARA, TIMOTHY JOSEPH

O'MORE, PEGGY
BLOCKLINGER, PEGGY O'MORE

O'NAIR, MAIRI
EVANS, CONSTANCE MAY

O'NEAL, BLACKIE
O'NEAL, CHARLES

O'NEAL, KATHLEEN M.
GEAR, KATHLEEN [M] O'NEAL

O'NEAL, REAGAN
RIGNEY, JAMES OLIVER JR.

O'NEAL, REGGIE
O'NEAL, REGINA

O'NEDDY, PHILOTHIE
DONDAY, AUGUSTE MARIE

O'NEIL, KERRY
MACINTYRE, JOHN T[HOMAS]

O'NEILL, ARCHIE
HENAGHAN, JIM

O'NEILL, C.M.
BLEECK, G.C.
WILKES-HUNTER, RICHARD

O'NEILL, EGAN
LININGTON, [B] ELIZABETH

O'NEILL, JUDE
BLUNDELL, JUDITH

O'NEILL, KATHLEEN
GOETZ, AUSTIN B.

O'NEILL, KERRY
MACINTYRE, JOHN [THOMAS]

O'NEILL, MOIRA
SKRINE, AGNES HIGGINSON

O'NEILL, NOREEN
ARMSTRONG, THOMAS

O'NEILL, PAMELA
MOHAN, PAMELA L. O'NEILL

O'NEILL, SCOTT
SCOTT, PEG O'NEILL

O'NERVA, L.
MADETOJA, ONERVA

O'NUALLAIN, BRIAN
O'NOLAN, BRIAN

O'QUILL, MAURICE
DENSLOW, MARTIN VAN B.

O'QUILL, SCARLETT
MOSSMAN, DOW

O'QUINN, ALLEN
QUINTER, A.S.

O'QUINN, VITHALDAS
SANTESSON, HANS STEFAN

O'QUINN, VITHALDAS H.
SANTESSON, HANS STEFAN

O'RANDA, JACK
STONE, ENA MARGARET

O'RANE, PATRICIA
DARK, ELEANOR

O'REILLEY, JACKSON
RIGNEY, JAMES OLIVER JR.

O'REILLY, MONTAGU
ANDREWS, WAYNE

O'REILLY, SEAN
DEEGAN, PAUL JOSEPH

O'RELL, MAX
BLOUET, PAUL

O'RIAIN, LIAM P.
RYAN, WILLIAM PATRICK

O'RILEY, WARREN
RICHARDSON, GLADWELL G.

O'ROURKE, ISRAEL
CAPON, ELLIOTT
O'BRIEN, G.M.

O'SHEA, SEAN
TRALINS, [SANDOR] ROBERT

O'SHEEL, SHAEMAS
SHEILDS, JAMES

O'SULLIVAN, SEUMAS
STARKEY, JAMES SULLIVAN

O'SULLIVAN, VINCENT
O'SUILLEABHAIN, SEAN

O'TOOLE, KATE
MONTAGUE, BRUCE [ALEX.]

O'TOOLE, REX
TRALINS, [SANDOR] ROBERT

O'TRIGGER, SIR LUCIUS
HORNE, RICHARD HENRY

O'TYNE, NICHOLAS
FOSTER, LEROY A.

O.P.
ECCLESHARE, COLIN

O.S.
SEAMAN, SIR OWEN

OAKES, VANYA
OAKES, VIRGINIA

OAKLAND, HARRY
NOBLE, HAROLD

OANA, KAY D.
OANA, KATHERINE D.

OBERG, ULLA
GUSTAFSSON, LISA

OBERHANSLI, TRUDI
SCHLAPBACH-OBERHANSLI, T.

OBERHOLTZER, PETER
BRANNON, WILLIAM T.

OBOE, PETER
JACOBS, WALTER DARNELL

OBOLENSKY, ILKA
LIST, ILKA KATHERINE

OBSERVER
VELIKOVSKY, IMMANUEL

OBUKHOVA, LYDIA
OBUKHOVA, LIDIIA ALEKS.

OBUTUNDE, IJIMERE
BEIER, ULLI

OCEAN, JULIAN
DE MESNE, EUGENE [F]

OCH, ARMIN
OCHS, ARMIN

OCTAVIA
IVES, MARY ALICE

OCTOBER, JOHN
PORTWAY, CHRISTOPHER [J]

OCTOPUS
DRACHMAN, JULIAN M.

ODDEY, JAMES D.
SUTTON, DAVID A.

ODDIE, E.M.
O'DONOGHUE, ELINOR MARY

ODELL, CAROL
FOOTE, CAROL

ODELL, GILL
FOOTE, CAROL
GILL, TRAVISS

ODEM, J.
RUBIN, JACOB A.

ODINTSOV, ARNOLD BORISOV.
ODER, ARNOLD B.

ODYSSEUS
ELIOT, CHARLES

OFFERE, M.
SHAMIR, MOSHE

OFFERMANN, HEINZ
KURTH, HANNS

OGAI, MORI
RINTARO, MORI

OGAN, M.G.
OGAN, GEORGE & MARGARET

OGDEN, C.K.
OGDEN, CHARLES KAY

OGDEN, CHRISTOL
ENGLISH, THOMAS DUNN

OGDEN, CLINT
KING, ALBERT

OGDEN, H.B.
ASIMOV, ISAAC

OGDEN, RUTH
IDE, FRANCIS OTIS [A.L.]

OGNEV, N.
ROSANOV, MIKHAIL G.

OGNEV, NIKOLAY
ROZANOV, MICHAIL GRIGORV.

OHIYESA
EASTMAN, CHARLES A.

OHL, HANS
KUSENBERG, KURT

OHNET, GEORGES
HENOT, GEORGES

OHON
BANKS, HARRY

OK
NOVIKOV, OLGA

OKADA, HIDEKI
GLASSCO, JOHN [S]

OKE, RICHARD
MILLET, NIGEL STAMBURG

OKE, SIMON
VANN, GERALD

OKER, EUGEN
GEBHARDT, FRIEDRICH JOHAN

OKONSKI, WLADYSLAW
SWIETOCHOWSKI, ALEKSANDER

OLBRACHT, IVAN
ZEMAN, KAMIL

OLD BOY
HUGHES, THOMAS

OLD BROADBRIM
RATHBORNE, ST. GEORGE

OLD CONTRIBUTOR
LEWIS, HARRIET NEWELL
LEWIS, JULIUS WARREN
OLD COYOTE, ELNORA A.

OLD DETECTIVE
ROLFE, MARO ORLANDO

OLD DOG
CUNNINGTON, CHARLES L.

OLD FAG
BELL, ROBERT STANLEY W.

OLD HUTCH
ADAMS, O.L.

OLD SETTLER, THE
LYMAN, ALBERT ROBINSON

OLD SLEUTH
HALSEY, HARLAN PAGE
HARBAUGH, THOMAS C.

OLD STAGER
GORE, JOHN FRANCIS

OLD TIMER
MERRILL, JAMES MILFORD

OLDCASTLE, ALICE
MEYNELL, ALICE [C.G.T.]

OLDCASTLE, JOHN
MEYNELL, WILFRID

OLDCASTLE, JONATHAN
MEYNELL, WILFRID

OLDEST AUTHORESS
POLLOCK, ALICE

OLDFELD, PETER
BARTLETT, VERNON
JACOBSSON, PER

OLDHAM, HUGH R.
WHITFORD, JOAN

OLDMEADOW, E.J.
OLDMEADOW, ERNEST JAMES

OLDSTYLE, JONATHAN
IRVING, WASHINGTON

OLE-LUK-OIE
SWINTON, ERNEST DUNLOP

OLEMY, P.T.
BAKER, GEORGE

OLENDORF, BILL
OLENDORF, WILLIAM

OLESKY, WALTER
OLEKSY, WALTER

OLGA
PHILLIPS, OLGA SOMECH

OLGIN, M.J.
NOVOMISKI, MOISHE

OLIPHANT, B.J.
TEPPER, SHERI S.

OLIPHANT, MRS.
OLIPHANT, MARGARET

OLIVANE, MARY
ANSLE, DOROTHY PHOEBE

OLIVER, CHAD
OLIVER, SYMMES CHADWICK

OLIVER, DR. N.T.
TILBURN, E.O.

OLIVER, EDITH
GOLDSMITH, EDITH

OLIVER, FRANCES
SCHNEIDER, MONICA MARIA

OLIVER, GAIL
SCOTT, MARIAN GALLAGHER

OLIVER, GAY
OWEN, GARNET

OLIVER, GEORGE
ONIONS, OLIVER

OLIVER, JAN
HUDSON, JANECE OLIVER

OLIVER, JANE
REES, HELEN CHRISTINA E.

OLIVER, L.
BROWN, LAURENCE OLIVER

OLIVER, LAURENCE
BROWN, LAURENCE OLIVER

OLIVER, MARIE
MARRIS, KATHERINE

OLIVER, MARK
TYLER-WHITTLE, MICHAEL

OLIVER, OWEN
FLYNN, SIR J.A.

OLIVER, RICHARD
KAISER, HANS K.

OLIVER, ROBERT
CARRIER, DICK
DICK, OLIVER LAWSON

OLIVER, ROY
WALKER, ROY

OLIVER, RUPERT
MATTHEW, RUPERT O[LIVER]

OLIVER, TEMPLE
SMITH, JEANIE OLIVER

OLIVER, TESS
KOVACK, TERI S. [TERRY]

OLIVES, RICARDO
KURTH, HANNS

OLIVIA
BUSSY, DOROTHY

OLLIVER, TOM
GRAYDON, WILLIAM MURRAY

OLMSTED, CHARLOTTE
KURSH, CHARLOTTE OLMSTED

OLNERS, KJENNE
OLNERS, ARNE

OLNERS, SAM
OLNERS, ARNE

OLNEY, OLIVER
DES VOIGNES, JULES VERNE

OLSEN, BOB
OLSEN, ALFRED JOHANNES

OLSEN, D.B.
HITCHENS, DELORES B.

OLSEN, HERB
OLSON, HERBERT VINCENT

OLSEN, JAMES P.
HITCHENS, DELORES B.
HUBBARD, L. RON

OLSON, ANGIE
VON KOBLINSKI, HANS-JOACH

OLYMIAS
GRONSTEDT, JOHAN

OLYMPIC
HUTTON, ANDREW NEILSON

OM
GOREY, EDWARD ST. JOHN

OMAHUNDRO, J.B.
INGRAHAM, PRENTISS

OMAN, CAROLA
LENANTON, LADY

OMCHERY
PILLAI, N.N.

OMEGA
BRADBURY, RAY [DOUGLAS]
ZENO GANDIA, MANUEL

OMRE, ARTHUR
ANTONISEN, O. ARTHUR J.

ONADIPE, KOLA
ONADIPE, [N] KOLAWOLE

ONATEYAC
BELTRAN, CAYETANO R.

ONDREJOV, LUDO
MISTRIK, LUDO

ONE OF HER SONS
LEGGE, ALFRED OWEN

ONE OF THE BUNGLERS
ORD, LEWIS REDMON

ONEAL, ZIBBY
ONEAL, ELIZABETH

ONEIROPOLOS
JOHNSTON, CHARLES

ONIONS, BERTA
OLIVER, AMY ROBERTA

ONIONS, OLIVER
OLIVER, GEORGE

ONKEL TOM
HEVESI, LUDWIG

ONKEL, ADAM
WETTERBERG, CARL ANTON

ONLOOKER
GRANGE, CYRIL
GRANT, WILLIAM
PARSONS, EDWARD
RUSSELL, GEORGE WILLIAM

ONN, CARRIE
PROCTOR, GEO[RGE] W[YATT]
VARDEMAN, ROBERT E.

ONSLOW, KATHERINE
DENNYS, ELISABETH

ONWARD, MAC
HAUSCHILD, ALBIN WALDEMAR

ONYX
WARD, STUART

OOGAM, LE ROI
SMITH, LE ROI TEX

OOIMAN, JO ANN
ROBINSON, JO ANN OOIMAN

OOM WARDEN
VERMEULEN, EDWARD

OPATOSHU, JOSEPH
OPATOVSKY, JOSEPH

OPDYKE, OLIVER
OPDYCKE, JOHN BAKER

OPERATOR 1384
HARVEY, JOHN HENRY

OPHIEL
PEACH, EDWARD

OPP, FRANCIS
OPPENHEIMER, FRANCIS J.

OPTIC, OLIVER
ADAMS, WILLIAM TAYLOR
STRATEMEYER, EDWARD

ORAM, JOHN
THOMAS, JOHN ORAM

ORAN, JACK
SBURNIK, YAKOFF

ORB, CLAY
CONROW, HERBERT

ORBAN, MARCUS T.
MIELKE, THOMAS R.P.

ORBIS, VICTOR
POWELL-SMITH, VINCENT

ORBISON, KECK
KECK, MAUDE
ORBISON, OLIVE

ORCHARD, EVELYN
SWANN, ANNIE S.

ORCHARDS, THEODORE
PALMER, [CHARLES] STUART

ORCHELLA, R.L.
SCHEFFAUER, HERMÁN GEORGE

ORCUTT, STEPHEN HOPKINS
NEW, CLARENCE HERBERT

ORDE, A.J.
TEPPER, SHERI S.

ORDERLY SERGEANT
MURRAY, WILLIAM WALDIE

ORDON, A. LANG
GORDON, ALAN BACCHUS

ORDWAY, ROGER
PAUKER, JOHN

ORE, REBECCA
BROWN, REBECCA BARD

ORESHNIK, A.F
MARLOWE, DAN J.
NUSSBAUM, ALBERT F.

ORFORD, ELLEN
DELLIGAN, WILLIAM F.

ORGA, ATES
D'ARCY-ORGA, ATES

ORGAN, PERRY
CARROLL, PERRY ORGAN

ORIANO, JANINE
BOISSARD, JANINE

ORIEL
SANDES, JOHN

ORIEL, ANTRIM
MOORE, ARTHUR

ORIOL, LAURENCE
LORIOT, NOELLE

ORIOLO, JOE
ORIOLO, JOSEPH

ORION
BROOKS, ERN
TULLOCK, W.W.

ORKAN, WLADYSLAW
SMRECZYNSKI, FRANCISZEK

ORLANDO, CHRIS
KEIM, FRIEDRICH

ORLANDO, PIETRO
SCARNE, JOHN

ORLEV, URI
ORLOWSKI, JERZY HENRYK

ORLIK, HENRY
KALMUCZAK, ROLF

ORLIK, JENS
KALMUCZAK, ROLF

ORLOFF, FRANK
KALMUCZAK, ROLF

ORLOFF, MAX
CROWCROFT, PETER

ORLOFF, WERA
FALK, HERMANN

ORLOFF, WOLF
BURESCH, WOLFGANG

ORME, ALEXANDRA
BARCZZA, ALICJA

ORME, BENJAMIN
JAPP, ALEXANDER HAY

ORME, ROWAN
ROWAN-HAMILTON, SYDNEY O.

ORMES, JACKIE
ORMES, ZELDA J.

ORMISTON, MARGARET
CURLE, M.O.

ORMISTON, ROBERTA
FLETCHER, ADELE

ORMOND, FREDERIC
DEY, FREDERIC VAN R.

ORMSBEE, DAVID
LONGSTREET, [H] STEPHEN

ORN, RICHARD
MEYN, NIELS

ORNFJELL, STIG
LARSSON, KARL ADOLF

ORNIG, GRAEG
ACKERMAN, FORREST J.

ORNIS
WINCHESTER, CLARENCE

ORNULF, GUNNAR
ORNULF, HILDING KONSTANT.

ORPET, FRED
EAST, FRED

ORR, A.
SPRAGUE, ALICE INGRAM ORR

ORR, FRANKLIN
RAHT, CARLYSLE GRAHAM

ORR, KATHY [KATHLEEN]
ORR, KATHLEEN [KATHY]

ORR, MARY
DENHAM, MARY ORR

ORRIS
INGELOW, JEAN

ORSI, ROBERT
PALLENBERG, CORRADO

ORSINI, GIULIO
GNOLI, DOMENICO

ORT, IVAN
DODGE, OSSIAN E.

ORT, MIK
DEZORT, MIREK

ORTH, BENNINGTON
HOAR, ROGER SHERMAN

ORTH, RICHARD
GARDNER, RICHARD [M]

ORTIZ DE MONTELLANO
ORTIZ DE MONTELLANO, B.

ORTMAN, ELMER JOHN
ORTMAN, E. JAN

ORTNER-ZIMMERMAN, TONI
ORTNER, TONI

ORTON, JOE
ORTON, JOHN KINGSLEY

ORTWIG RAMIN, FR. D.
DAUM, FRITZ

ORTWIG, F.D.
DAUM, FRITZ

ORVIS, KENNETH
LEMIEUX, KENNETH

ORWELL
SMITH, WALTER CHALMERS

ORWELL, GEORGE
BLAIR, ERIC ARTHUR

OSBORN, LYNN
OSBORN, LINCOLN

OSBORN, REUBEN
OSBERT, REUBEN

OSBORNE, BETSY
BOSWELL, BARBARA

OSBORNE, DAVID
SILVERBERG, ROBERT

OSBORNE, GEORGE
SILVERBERG, ROBERT

OSBORNE, HELENA
MOORE, GEORGINA MARY G.

OSBORNE, MAGGIE
OSBORNE, MARGARET ELLEN

OSBORNE, MARK
BAYFIELD, WILLIAM JOHN
BOBIN, JOHN WILLIAM

OSBORNE, O.O.
KOFOED, WILLIAM H.
LIEFERSAND, HENRY

OSBURN, JESSE
RANSOME, CANDICE F.

OSCEOLA
BLIXEN-FENEKE, KAREN

OSGOOD, IRENE
HARVEY, IRENE

OSKAR, THEODOR
CORTE, WILHELM

OSORGIN, M.A.
ILLYIN, M.A.

OSORIO, GRIS
MURRAY, WILLIAM P.

OSSIT
DESLANDES, MADELAINE A.E.

OSSLINGER, KURT
ALLEN, BOB

OSTEN, FRANZISKA
KOSTER-LJUNG, HANNA

OSTEN, I.S.
BRAND, KURT
HAHN, RONALD M.

OSTEN, LUDWIG
MARDICKE, FRITZ
REESE, WILHELM F.C.

OSTEN, MICHAEL
GOLDSTEIN, MORITZ

OSTEN, PETER
GORZ, HEINZ

OSTERBURG, DAISY
MUHRMANN, WILHELM

OSTRANDER, ISABEL EGENTON
LAMB, ISABEL OSTRANDER

OSURGIN, MIKHAIL A.
ILYIN, MIKHAIL A.

OSWALD, SYDNEY
LOMER, SYDNEY FREDERICK M

OSWALT, SABINE
MACCORMACK, SABINE G.

OTIS, G.H.
GAYLORD, OTIS HEMMINGWAY

OTIS, GEORGE
MELLEN, IDA MAY

OTIS, JAMES
KALER, JAMES OTIS

OTRTHOFER, HILDA
KNOBLOCH, HILDA

OTT, E. HARRISON
WILKINSON, RICHARD HILL

OTT, MAGGIE GLENN
OTT, VIRGINIA

OTT, PETER
VON HILDEBRAND, DIETRICH

OTTEN, HEINRICH
HEDERICH, JOHANNES

OTTO, FRANZ
FREITAG, OTTO

OTTO, OTTO
BEISSEL, RUDOLF

OTTO, SVEND
SOERENSEN, SVEND OTTO

OTTUM, BOB
OTTUM, ROBERT K.

OUBO, IRAC
LOHIER, MICHEL

OUDEIS
DARBY, CHRISTOPHER LOVETT

OUIDA
DE LA RAMEE, MARIE LOUISE

OUN, GABRIEL
HEPBURN, THOMAS NICOLLSET

OUSELY, GIDEON
GOGARTY, OLIVER ST. JOHN

OUSPENSKY, P.D.
USPENSKII, PETR

OUTI
HONKANEN, HILJA L.V.

OUTLAW, THE
L'HOTELLIER, ALF

OUTSIDER
HAAPAKOSKI, HENRIK

OUVARD, JACQUES
GUICHARDAN, ROGER

OVALOV, LEV S.
SHAPOVALOV, LEV S.

OVERLACK, JAMES
HALLER, HANS

OVERTON, MAX
KNOX, CLEO ELDON

OVERY, CLAIRE MAY
BASS, CLARA MAY

OVERY, MARTIN
OVERY, JILLIAN P.J.

OVESEN, ELLIS
SMITH, SHIRLEY M[AE]

OWEN, BOB
GEIS, RICHARD E.

OWEN, CAROLINE DALE
SNEDECKER, CAROLINE D.P.

OWEN, CATHERINE
NITSCH, HELEN ALICE [M]

OWEN, CLIFFORD
HAMILTON, CHARLES H.S.

OWEN, DEAN
MCGAUGHY, DUDLEY DEAN

OWEN, DILYS
GATER, DILYS

OWEN, DUDLEY
MCGAUGHY, DUDLEY DEAN

OWEN, EDMUND
TELLER, NEVILLE

OWEN, EVENS
MCGAUGHY, DUDLEY DEAN

OWEN, FRANK
WILLIAMS, ROSWELL

OWEN, GEOFFREY
HANSEN, ROBERT

OWEN, HEDLEY
O'MANT, HEDLEY P.A.

OWEN, HUGH
FAUST, FREDERICK S.

OWEN, J. BRADLEY
GRAINGER, STEPHNEE KAY

OWEN, JOHN PICKARD
BUTLER, SAMUEL

OWEN, MAGGIE
WADELTON, MAGGIE JEANNE

OWEN, MARGO
MACSHANE, MARY

OWEN, MARK
CARLISLE, NORMAN

OWEN, MICHAEL
MCKENZIE, C[ECIL] J[AMES]
WATKINS, ALLAN
WILKES-HUNTER, RICHARD

OWEN, NORMAN
WALTERS, J.

OWEN, PHILIP
PHILIPS, JUDSON P.

OWEN, R.N.
GEIS, RICHARD E.

OWEN, RAY
KING, ALBERT

OWEN, RICHARD
FAWCETT, DENNIS
NOTT, DAVID
ROBERTS, EDNA

OWEN, ROBERT N.
GEIS, RICHARD E.

OWEN, RODERIC
FENWICK-OWEN, RODERIC

OWEN, TOM
WATTS, PETER CHRISTOPHER

OWEN, VINCENT
COOK, FRED GORDON

OWENS, ALBERT
HERSEY, HAROLD

OWENS, BARBARA
WEIMAN, BARBARA OWENS

OWENS, FANNIE
BURKE, SOPHIE VAN E.L.

OWENS, MARISSA
O'CALLAGHAN, MAXINE

OWENS, TED
KALMUCZAK, ROLF

OWENS, TOM
KELTON, ELMER

OWINGS, MARK
CHALKER, JACK

OWL EYES
LARDNER, RINGGOLD W.

OWL, SEBASTIAN
THOMPSON, HUNTER S.

OWLGLASS, DR.
BLAICK, HANS ERICH

OXENHAM, ELSIE JEANETTE
DUNKERLY, ELSIE JEANNETTE

OXENHAM, JOHN
DUNKERLEY, WILLIAM ARTHUR

OXFORD, JANE
WILLIAMS, ELMA MARY

OXFORD, JOHN BARTON
SHELTON, RICHARD BARKER

OXLEY, KATE
WHITEHEAD, KATE

OXON, M.B.
WALLACE, LEWIS ALEXANDER

OY-VIK
HOLMVIK, OYVIND

OYVED, MOYSHEH
GOOD, EDWARD

OZ, AMOS
KLAUSNER, AMOS

OZY
ROSSET, BENJAMIN CHARLES

P., K.U.
PARROTT, KATHERINE URSULA

P.C.
JACKSON, C. PHILIP CASTLE

P.I., O.
OUSTABASIDAS, PETER

P.I.X.
HALLAM, DOUGLAS

P.K.
ROSEGGER, PETRI KETTENFR.

P.L.K.
KIRK-GREEN, ANTHONY H.M.

P.O., D.
DONOVAN, PETER

P.Q.
QUENNELL, PETER COURTNEY

P.R.S.
SHERIDAN, PHIL R.

PA-CHIN
FEI-KAN, LI

PAAR, ANGELICA
PAPAZOGLOU, ORANIA

PAASCHE, JOHAN FREDRIK
AMUNDSEN, JOHAN FREDRIK

PAATZ, HERBERT
FIEBRANDT, H.

PAB
BLOOMAN, PERCY A.

PABLO, MIGUEL
JENNISON, JOHN WILLIAM

PACE, LAUREL
WOJHOSKI, BARBARA M.

PACE, PETER
BURNETT, DAVID

PACKARD, CINDY
RICHMOND, CINDY PACKARD

PACKER, VIN
MEAKER, MARIJANE AGNES

PACKETT, LUKE
MASTERS, EDGAR LEE

PACO, CARY
JENNISON, JOHN WILLIAM

PADESON, MARY
MAGRAW, BEATRICE IRENE

PADGET, MEG
TORREY [BUDLONG], WARE

PADGETT, DESMOND
VON BLOCK, BELA [W]

PADGETT, LEWIS
KUTTNER, HENRY
MOORE, CATHERINE LUCILLE

PADMORE, GEORGE
NURSE, MALCOLM IVAN MERE.

PAEMENTO
LOPEZ PINILLOS, JOSE

PAGAN, ROBERT
PLOMER, WILLIAM C.F.

PAGE, ABRAHAM
HOLT, JOHN SANDERS

PAGE, ALAIN
CONIL, JEAN-EDMOND

PAGE, BETSY
WILHITE, BETTIE MARIE

PAGE, BILL
PAGE, WILLIAM REESE

PAGE, EILEEN
HEAL, EDITH

PAGE, ELEANOR
COERR, ELEANOR BEATRICE

PAGE, EMMA
TIRBUTT, HONORIA

PAGE, G.S.
GALBRAITH, GEORGIE S.

PAGE, H.A.
JAPP, ALEXANDER HAY

PAGE, HENRI
DUCKETT, WILLIAM

PAGE, JAKE
PAGE, JAMES KEENA JR.

PAGE, JUAN
FISH, ROBERT L.

PAGE, LORNA
ROWLAND, DONALD S.

PAGE, MARCO
KURNITZ, HARRY

PAGE, MARY
HEAL, EDITH

PAGE, STANTON
FULLER, HENRY BLAKE

PAGE, THOMAS
JONES, ROBERT PAGE
STREIB, DANIEL T.

PAGE, VICKI
AVERY, RUBY D.

PAGERY, FRANCOIS
CALIXTE, HERVE
KLEIN, GERARD

PAGET, JOHN
AIKEN, JOHN [KEMPTON]

PAGET, MARGARET
MEDLICOTT, MARGARET P.

PAGET-LOWE, HENRY
LOVECRAFT, H[OWARD] P.

PAHHALA, TEUVO
FROSTERUS, OSKAR

PAHL, JOACHIM
PUHLE, JOACHIM

PAHLEN, HENRY
GUNTHER, HEINZ

PAHZ, CHERYL SUZANNE
GOLDFEDER, CHERYL SUZANNE

PAHZ, JAMES ALON
GOLDFEDER, [K] JAMES

PAIGE, DAVID
WHITTINGHAM, RICHARD

PAIGE, JUAN
GORDON, RICHARD M.

PAIGE, LAURIE
HALL, OLIVIA M.

PAIGE, LEO
COCHRANE, WILLIAM E.

PAIGE, LESLIE
RUBINGTON, NORMAN

PAIGE, RICHARD
KOONTZ, DEAN R.

PAIGE, ROBIN
ALBERT, SUSAN W. & BILL

PAIN, BARRY
GUTHRIE, P.R.

PAINE, GUTHRIE
TREMAINE, F. ORLIN

PAINE, HAMMOND
HOOK, H. CLARKE

PAINE, J. LINCOLN
KRAMISH, ARNOLD

PAINE, L.B.
PAINE, LAURAN BOSWORTH

PAINE, MICHAEL
CURLOVICH, JOHN

PAINE, NICKY
PAINE, LESLIE HAROLD W.

PAINTER, DANIEL
BURGESS, MICHAEL ROY

PAISLEY, REBECCA
ROSAS, REBECCA BOADO

PAISLEY, TOM
BETHANCOURT, T. ERNESTO

PALADAN, JOSEPHINE
PELADAN, JOSEPH [JOSEPHIN

PALAZZESCHI, ALDO
GIURLANI, ALDO

PALAZZO, TONY
PALAZZO, ANTHONY D.

PALEAU, ROGER
MOSKOVITZ, JACK

PALEN, ADELINE
DUDLEY, LOUISE POWELSON

PALEY, FRANK
PALESCANDOLO, FRANK

PALEY, MORTON D.
BIXBY, JEROME L.
MERWIN, SAMUEL K. JR.

PALINURUS
CONNOLLY, CYRIL VERNON

PALLIDINI, JODI
ROBBIN, [J] LUNA

PALM, GENE
PALMISANO, LUIGI

PALMER, CARA
FOX, GARDNER F.

PALMER, DIANA
KYLE, SUSAN E. SPAETH

PALMER, DON
BENSON, MILDRED [A] WIRT

PALMER, EDGAR A.
POSSELT, ERIC

PALMER, HALLECK
WATSON, EVELYN MABEL

PALMER, HELEN [MARION]
GEISEL, HELEN

PALMER, JOE
WHITTINGTON, HARRY

PALMER, JOHN
PALMER, JOHN LESLIE
WATTS, EDGAR JOHN PALMER

PALMER, L.D.
ANTON, UWE

PALMER, LEW
REAHM, THELMA L.

PALMER, LILLI
PEISER, MARIA LILLI

PALMER, LUCILE
THOMPSON, MRS. ALFRED H.

PALMER, LYNDE
PEEBLES, MARY LOUISE

PALMER, PAUL
GODDARD, GLORIA

PALMER, PETE
PALMER, EDGAR POOLE JR.

PALMER, PETER
PALMER, ELSIE PAVITT

PALMER, RACHEL
POTTS, RUTH

PALMER, ROY
FRIEDRICHS, HOLGER

PALMER, TOBIAS
WEATHERS, WINSTON

PALMER, TOM
LEIRD, HENRY J.
PALMER, THOMAS

PALMER, WARREN
GIBSON, WALTER B.

PALMIERI, MARINA
CAMPBELL, MARILYN

PALOMAR, NATAL DEL
ALMAZAN, PASCUAL

PALTENGHI, MADELEINE
ANDERSON, MADELEINE P.

PAMJEAN, LOUIS
BEDFORD-JONES, HENRY

PAN
BERESFORD, LESLIE

PAN PETER
KNUTSEN, LALLI & FRIDTJOF

PAN, GEORGE
JENNISON, JOHN WILLIAM

PANBOURNE, OLIVER
ROCKEY, HOWARD

PANC, PETRO JOSYPOVICH
PANCHENKO, PETR IOSIFOVIC

PANCH, PETR
PANCHENKO, PETR IOSIFOVIC

PANDORA
MACCHETA, BLANCHE R.
MOORE, MARY MCLEOD

PANK, WERNER
GREINER, FRANZ

PANLAKE, RICHARD
SALMON, P.R.

PANSY
ALDEN, ISABELLA MACDONALD
DONISTHORPE, IDA M.L.

PANTELL, S.F.
MCGREGOR, ELLEN

PANTER, PETER
TUCHOLSKY, KURT

PANTOPUCK
PHILPOTT, ALEXIS ROBERT

PAOLO, PETER MARIA
BERNARD, KARL

PAOLOTTI, JOHN
WILSON, GUTHRIE EDWARD

PAPE, D.L.
PAPE, DONNA LUGG

PAPERMAKER, PETER
THOMAS, PETER & DONNA

PAPERNY, MYRA
GREEN, MYRA

PAPPAZISIS, EVANGELOS
PAPPAS, ANGELOS

PAPPILON, HENRI
CHARRIERE, HENRI

PAPRIKA
HOLMVIK, OYVIND

PAPUS
ENCAUSSE, GERARD [A.V.]

PARABELLUM
GRAUTHOFF, FERDINAND H.

PARADIJS, CORNELIS
VAN EEDEN, FREDERIK

PARADISE, LUKE
QUINN, SEABURY

PARADISE, MARY
EDEN, DOROTHY E.

PARAGRAPH
STUCHA, PETER

PARAMENY, K.
KEMPE, ANNE

PARASARA
DE SILVA, DAVID

PARATUS, VICTOR
GAST, EMIL

PARDOE, GEOFFREY
FRANCES, STEPHEN D.

PARIOS
LEE, HENRY DAVID COOK

PARIS, ANN
PAPAZOGLOU, ORANIA

PARIS, FIRMIN
HUDSON, MAXINE

PARIS, JOHN
ASHTON-GWATKIN, FRANK T.A

PARIS, JUSTINE
JOHNSTON, PAUL

PARISH, GLENN
GARCIA LECHA, LUIS

PARISH, JED
BRAUN, WILBUR

PARISH, PEGGY
PARISH, MARGARET CECILE

PARISH, TOWNSEND
PIETSCHMANN, RICHARD JOHN

PARK, BILL
PARK, W[ILLIAM] B[RYAN]

PARK, D.W.
WOODS, CLEE

PARK, ELM
DUNBAR, CHARLES STUART

PARK, JORDAN
KORNBLUTH, C[YRIL] M.
POHL, FREDERIK

PARK, MAEVA
DOBNER, MAEVA PARK

PARK, RUTH
NILAND, ROSINA RUTH PARK

PARKER, ANN
NEAL, ANN PARKER

PARKER, ANTHONY
TULL, ANTHONY

PARKER, BEATRICE
HUFF, TOM E.

PARKER, BERT
ELLISON, HARLAN

PARKER, DAVID
MEYN, NIELS

PARKER, DEE
PARKER, DAVID L.

PARKER, DOROTHY
RITHCHILD, DOROTHY

PARKER, FRANK
RICHARDSON, GLADWELL G.

PARKER, FRED
KALMUCZAK, ROLF
ORNULF, HILDING KONSTANT.

PARKER, GEORGE
MENTZEL, GEORG

PARKER, JAMES
NEWBY, GEORGE ERIC

PARKER, JOHN
WYATT, JOHN

PARKER, LAURA
CASTORO, LAURA ANN

PARKER, LESLIE
THIRKELL, ANGELA

PARKER, M.E. FRANCES
BELLERBY, [M.E] FRANCES

PARKER, MORTON
ATKINSON, TERRY

PARKER, NORAH
HODGSON, ELEANOR

PARKER, PAMELA
LAEDTKE, INGRID

PARKER, ROBERT
BOYD, WALDO T.

PARKER, SETH
LORD, PHILLIPS H.

PARKER, SHARON
BLEECK, G.C.

PARKER, TOM
PARKER, JOHN THOMAS

PARKER, VALENTINE
GILLINGS, WALTER H.

PARKER, WILL S.
PORTER, WILLIAM SYDNEY

PARKER, WILL[IAM]
NOFFKE, FRITZ

PARKES, LUCAS
HARRIS, JOHN WYNDHAM P.L.

PARKES, WYNDHAM
HARRIS, JOHN WYNDHAM P.L.

PARKHILL, JOHN
COX, WILLIAM ROBERT

PARKS, RON
GUARIENTO, RONALD

PARKSMITH, GEORGE
BUSH, GEORGE S[IDNEY]
SMITH, PARK

PARLACH, ALEXANDER
KUBY, ERICH

PARLANTE CURIOSO
MESONERO Y ROMANOS, ROMAN

PARLEY, PETER
GOODRICH, SAMUEL G.

PARLIN, JOHN
GRAVES, CHARLES PARLIN

PARMA, CLEMENS
MENZEL, RODERICH

PARMER, J.N.
PARMER, JESS NORMAN

PARNASS, ROY
HOBEIN, EUGEN

PARNELL, FRANCIS
PRAGNELL, FESTUS

PARNELL, KEITH
PALMER, P.K.

PARNELL, MIKE
MIELKE, THOMAS R.P.

PARR, ROBERT
GARDNER, ERLE STANLEY

PARRIS, LAURA
MAGNER, LAURA

PARRISH, BARNEY
WOLK, GEORGE

PARRISH, EUGENE
HARDING, DONALD EDWARD

PARRISH, FRANK
LONGRIGG, ROGER [ERSKINE]

PARRISH, JEAN J.
CHURCH, ELSIE

PARRISH, LAURA
GRAHAM, ELIZABETH

PARRISH, MARY
COUSINS, MARGARET

PARRISH, PATT
BUCHEISTER, PATT

PARRISH, WENDAL
MERRILL, JAMES MILFORD

PARRY, HANS-HEINZ
PARRY-DRIXNER, WILLY

PARRY, JOHN
WHELPTON, [GEORGE] ERIC

PARRY, PERCY
PARRY-DRIXNER, WILLY

PARRY, ROCK
REUTER, RALPH

PARSIVAL, PETER
FRANKE, HERBERT W.

PARSONS, BRIDGET
COX, EUPHRASIA EMELINE

PARSONS, ELLEN
DRAGONWAGON, CRESCENT

PARSONS, PAUL
HASLAM, NICKY

PARSONS, TOM
MACPHERSON, THOMAS GEORGE

PARTINGTON, F.H.
YOXALL, HARRY W.

PARTINGTON, MRS.
AVERY, SAMUEL PUTNAM

PARTRIDGE, ANTHONY
OPPENHEIM, E. PHILLIPS

PARTRIDGE, KATHLEEN
WOODERIDGE, KATHLEEN M.

PARTRIDGE, SYDNEY
PARTRIDGE, KATE MARGARET

PARY, C.C.
GILMORE, CHRISTOPHER COOK

PASCAL
FREDERICHS, HANS-JURGEN

PASCAL, FRANCINE
ALBERT, SUSAN WITTIG

PASCALL, JEREMY
ZUPRINGER, JEREMY JAMES

PASCHAL, NANCY
TROTTER, GRACE V.

PASCUAL
GARCIA SANCHEZ, EDUARDA

PASCUDNIAK, PASCAL
LUPOFF, RICHARD A.

PASDELOUP, JEAN-MARIE
DURBEN, WOLFGANG J.M.

PASQUALI, SELENE
ANDREWS, MERVYN

PASSANTE, DOM
FEARN, JOHN RUSSELL

PASSER, ARNOLD v. d.
HOFFMANN, F.C.

PASSES, ALAN
PAZOLSKI, ALAN

PASSES-PAZOLSKI, ALAN
PAZOLSKI, ALAN

PASSMORE, AILEEN E.
GRIFFITHS, AILEEN ESTHER

PASSMORE, EILEEN ESTHER
GRIFFITHS, EILEEN ESTHER

PASTNOR, PAUL
MORRIS, CHARLES [S]

PASTON, GEORGE
SYMONDS, EMILY MORSE

PASTOR, FELIX
LOCKHART, ARTHUR JOHN

PASTOR, TONY
HALSEY, HARLAN PAGE

PASTOR, VERBENA
PASTOR, BEN

PAT
KENNY, P.D.

PATANNE, MARIA
LA PIETRA, MARY

PATCHETT, M.E.
PATCHETT, MARY O. ELWYN

PATER, ELIAS
FRIEDMAN, JACOB HORACE

PATER, ROGER
HUDLESTON, GILBERT ROGER

PATERSON, A.B.
PATERSON, ANDREW BARTON

PATERSON, ANNE
EINSELEN, ANNE FRANCIS

PATERSON, BANJO
PATERSON, ANDREW BARTON

PATERSON, HUNTLEY
LUDOVICI, ANTHONY M.

PATERSON, JUDITH
JONES, JUDITH PATERSON

PATIENT OBSERVER, THE
STRUNSKY, SIMEON

PATON WALSH, JILL
PATIN WALSH, GILLIAN H.M.

PATON, JOHN
BATEMAN, F. JOHN ALFORD

PATRICE, ANN
GALBRAITH, GEORGIE S.
KAY, PATRICIA A.

PATRICK, BRENNAN
MONNINGER, JOSEPH

PATRICK, DE ANN
CORCORAN, DOROTHY
SLOJKOWSKI, MARY ANN

PATRICK, DIANA
WILSON, DESEMEA

PATRICK, FRED
KAPPEL, GUNTER

PATRICK, JOHN
GOGGAN, JOHN PATRICK

PATRICK, KEATS
KARIG, WALTER

PATRICK, LEAL
STONE, PATTY [PATTI]

PATRICK, LILIAN
KEOGH, LILIAN GILMORE

PATRICK, LYNN
PINIANSKI, PATRICIA
SWEENEY, LINDA

PATRICK, MAX
MCCORMACK, JAMES

PATRICK, MAXINE
MAXWELL, PATRICIA ANNE P.

PATRICK, Q.
ASWELL, MARY LOUISE W.
KELLEY, MARTHA MOTT
WEBB, RICHARD WILSON
WHEELER, HUGH C.

PATRICK, ROSLYN
PINIANSKI, PATRICIA
SWEENEY, LINDA

PATRICK, VICTOR
JOHNSON, VICTOR L.

PATRIGE, SYDNEY
STONE, KATE MARGARET

PATRIOT, A.
DU MAURIER, GUY

PATROCLUS
LYALL, JAMES ROBERT

PATROLMAN
MCWALTERS, GEORGE S.

PATTEN, GIL
PATTEN, WILLIAM GEORGE

PATTEN, GILBERT
PATTEN, WILLIAM GEORGE

PATTEN, J.
COBB, CLAYTON W.

PATTEN, WYOMMING BILL
PATTEN, WILLIAM GEORGE

PATTERSON, ALISTAIR
BLAIR, JOHN

PATTERSON, DUKE
LEYLAND, ERIC

PATTERSON, HENRY
PATTERSON, HARRY

PATTERSON, INNIS
PATTERSON, ISABELLA INNIS

PATTERSON, JANE
BRITTON, MATTIE LULA C.

PATTERSON, MARGARET
GRANT, MAUDE MARGARET

PATTERSON, OLIVE
ROWLAND, DONALD S.

PATTERSON, ROD
KNELLER, F.C.

PATTERSON, SHOTT
RENFREW, A.

PATTISON, RUTH
ABBEY, RUTH

PATTON, FRANK
PALMER, RAYMOND A.
SHAVER, RICHARD S.

PATTON, GLENN
BAJOG, GUNTHER
FALK, HERMANN

PATTON, HARVEY
PESCHKE, HANS

PATTON, MARION
WALDRON, MARION PATTON

PATTOU, EDITH
EMERY, EDITH PATTOU

PATURI, FELIX R.
MINDT, HEINZ R.

PATYN, ANN
CARLI, AUDREY

PAUL, ADRIAN
MCGEOGH, ANDREW

PAUL, AUREN
URIS, AUREN

PAUL, BARBARA
OVSTEDAL, BARBARA

PAUL, CHARLOTTE
REESE, CHARLOTTE PAUL

PAUL, DANIEL
KESSEL, LIPMANN

PAUL, DANIELLE
MITTERMEYER, HELEN

PAUL, ELIZABETH
CROW, DONNA FLETCHER

PAUL, EMILY
EICHER, [ETHEL] ELIZABETH

PAUL, ERNEST
FOCKE, ERNEST

PAUL, F.W.
FAIRMAN, PAUL W.

PAUL, GENE
CONANT, PAUL

PAUL, HUGO
LITTLE, PAUL HUGO

PAUL, JAMES
WARBURG, JAMES PAUL

PAUL, JEAN
RICHTER, JOHANN PAUL F.

PAUL, JOANNA
JONES, PAULINE

PAUL, JOHN
WEBB, CHARLES HENRY

PAUL, PAULA
PAUL, PAULA G.

PAUL, PIERRE ET
DE LOUDONIEX, PAUL

PAUL, ROBERT
ROBERTS, JOHN GAITHER

PAUL, SANDRA
CHOVOSTAL, SANDRA NOVY

PAUL, SHERI
RESNICK, SYLVIA [SAFRAN]

PAUL, WILLIAM
EICHER, [ETHEL] ELIZABETH

PAULDING, FREDERICK
DODGE, FREDERICK

PAULL, JESSICA
BURGER, ROSAYLMER
PERCEVAL, JULIA

PAULOWSKI, E.
VARGA, JENO [EUGEN]

PAULSEN, PAULA
HOFMANN, IRMELA

PAULSEN, ROBERT
GLUCHOWSKI, BRUNO
KALMUCZAK, ROLF

PAULSON, JACK
JACKSON, CAARY PAUL

PAULY, NICK
PUTZ, PAUL

PAUSACKER, JENNY
PAUSACKER, JENNIFER

PAVITRA
SAINT-HILAIRE, P.B.

PAVLENKO, PIOTR
PAVLENKO, PETR ANDREVITCH

PAVOLOVIC, IVAN
COLAKOVIC, RODOLJUB

PAWLIKOWSKA
JASNORZEWSKA, MARIA

PAWNEE BILL
LILLIE, GORDON W.

PAXTON, DR. JOHN
LAWTON, SHERMAN P.

PAXTON, JACK
LAWTON, SHERMAN P.

PAXTON, JEAN
POWERS, MARTHA [JEAN]

PAXTON, LOIS
LOW, LOIS DOROTHEA

PAYE, ROBERT
LONG, GABRIELLE M.V.C.

PAYER, ERIK N.
PICKLER, EBERHARD

PAYNE, ALAN
JAKES, JOHN [WILLIAM]

PAYNE, ALMA SMITH
RALSTON, ALMA

PAYNE, CHARLOTTE
O'NEAL, CHARLES

PAYNE, CRUTCHLEY
EVANS, FRANK HOWELL

PAYNE, EMMY
WEST, EMILY GOVAN

PAYNE, F.M.
ENGLISH, THOMAS DUNN

PAYNE, HAROLD
KELLY, GEORGE C.

PAYNE, NATHANIEL
ALBERT, SUSAN W. & BILL

PAYNE, RACHEL ANN
JAKES, JOHN [WILLIAM]

PAYNE, ROBERT
PAYNE, PIERRE S. ROBERT

PAYNE, STEPHEN
JAKES, JOHN [WILLIAM]

PAYSON, [LT.] HOWARD
GOLDFRAP, JOHN HENRY

PAYZANT, JESSIE MERCER K.
SHANNON, TERRY

PAZ, A.
GOLDFEDER, [K] JAMES
PAHZ, JAMES ALON

PAZ, ZAN
GOLDFEDER, [K] JAMES
PAHZ, CHERYL SUZANNE

PEABODY, MRS. MARK
VICTOR, MRS. M.V.

PEACE, FRANK
COOK, WILLIAM EVERETT

PEACHUM, THOMAS
OXMAN, PHILIP

PEAD, D.
PESLER-ADAM, DORA

PEAKE, MERVYN
JONES, LANGDON

PEAL[E], CONSTANCE F.
STINE, WHITNEY WARD

PEARCE, A.H.
QUIBELL, AGATHA HUNT

PEARCE, ANN PHILIPPA
CHRISTIE, ANN PHILIPPA P.

PEARCE, DONN
PEARCE, DONALD

PEARCE, PHILIPPA
CHRISTIE, ANN PHILIPPA P.

PEARL, ERIC
ELMAN, RICHARD M.

PEARL, ESTER E[LIZ]
RITZ, DAVID

PEARL, IRENE
GUYONVARCH, IRENE CECILIA

PEARL, JACK
PEARL, JACQUES BAIN

PEARLMAN, MOSHE
PEARLMAN, MAURICE

PEARSE, PADRAIC
PEARSE, PATRICK HENRY

PEARSON, ALEX O.
FEARN, JOHN RUSSELL

PEARSON, DIANE
MCCLELLAND, DIANE MARGAR.

PEARSON, HARVEY
PESCHKE, HANS

PEARSON, LON
PEARSON, MILO LORENZ

PEARSON, MARTIN
KORNBLUTH, C[YRIL] M.
WOLLHEIM, DONALD A.

PEARSON, SHEPHERD
HADATH, JOHN E.G.

PEARY, DANNY
PEARY, DANNIS

PEARY, MARIE AHNIGHITO
KUHNE, MARIE

PEASE, LT. JOHN
HOAR, ROGER SHERMAN

PECCADILLE
DOUBLED, VICTOR

PECCAVI
HOLDEN, BEATRICE [P]

PECK, ABE
PECKOLICK, ABE

PECK, LEONARD
HARDY, C. COLBURN

PECK, MAGGIE
PRICE, MARJORIE

PECKHAM, RICHARD
HOLDEN, RAYMOND P[ECKHAM]

PEDERAK, SIMON
THOMAS, PETER

PEDERSON, BORGE V.R.
HASSEL, SVEN

PEDLER, KIT
PEDLER, CHRISTOPHER M.H.

PEDRICK, GALE
PEDRICK-HARVEY, GALE

PEEBLES, ANNE
GALLOWAY, PRISCILLA

PEEKNER, RAY
PUECHNER, RAY

PEEL, JESSE
PERRY, STEVE

PEEL, NORMAN LEMON
HIRSCH, PAUL

PEEL, WALLIS
PEEL, HAZEL MARY

PEESLAKE, GAFFER
DURRELL, LAWRENCE [G]

PEET, BILL
PEET, WILLIAM BARTLETT

PEET, WILLIAM BARTLETT
HOPKINS, WILLIAM BARTLETT

PEFF
PEFFER, SAM

PEGDEN, HELEN
MACGREGOR, MIRIAM

PEGLER, BUD
PEGLER, [JAMES] WESTBROOK

PEGLER, PEG
PEGLER, [JAMES] WESTBROOK

PEGLER, WESTY
PEGLER, [JAMES] WESTBROOK

PEGLER, WRONG WESTBROOK
PEGLER, [JAMES] WESTBROOK

PELADAN, MERODACK SAR
PELADIN, JOSEPH [JOSEPHIN

PELHAM, ANTHONY
HOPE, CHARLES E. GRAHAM

PELHAM, RANDOLPH
LANDELLS, RICHARD

PELHAM, ROCK
MIANDER, HARRY NILS O.H.

PELICAN, A.
GERARD, JAMES WATSON

PELIN, ELIN
JOTOV, DIMITAR IVANOV

PELKIE, J[OE] W[ALTER]
PALMER, RAYMOND A.

PELKONEN, ELINA
HONKANEN, HILJA L.V.

PELL, FRANKLYN
PELLIGRIN, FRANK E.

PELL, ROBERT
HAGBERG, DAVID [JAMES]

PELLICANE, PATRICIA
HAUGHT, JEAN

PELLUME, NOAM D.
CARD, ORSON SCOTT

PELLY, SMELLY
PELLY, WILLIAM DUDLEY

PELTIER, FLORENCE
LEONARD, FLORENCE PELTIER

PEMBERTON, NAN
PYKARE, NINA ANN COOMBS

PEMBERTON, RENFREW
BUSBY, F.M.

PEMBERTON, RONALD
BOLBJERG, ALFRED

PEMBROKE, KENNETH
PAGE, GERALD W.

PEMBROKE, THOMAS
HOPKINSON, HENRY THOMAS

PEMBURY, BILL
GROOM, ARTHUR WILLIAM

PEMBURY, GROSVENOR
HAYDON, N.G.

PEMBURY, MONTAGUE
MOON, GEORGE P.

PEMJEAN, LUCIAN
BEDFORD-JONES, HENRY

PEMSTEEN, HANS
MANES, STEPHEN

PEN, ALFRA
PREINERSTORFER, ALOIS

PENALURICK, JAN
DE LINT, CHARLES

PENARTH, WYM
PLUMMER, CLARE [E]

PENDARVES, G.G.
TRENERY, GLADYS GORDON

PENDENNIS, ARTHUR ESQ.
THACKERAY, WILLIAM MAKEP.

PENDENYS, ARTHUR
HUMPHREYS, ARTHUR LEE

PENDER, LAURA
ANDERSON, DANA

PENDER, LEX
PENDOWER, THOMAS CURTIS H

PENDER, MARILYN
PENDOWER, THOMAS CURTIS H

PENDLE, NICHOLAS
BIRTILL, GEORGE ARTHUR

PENDLETON, CONRAD
KIDD, WALTER EVANS

PENDLETON, CONRAD PADRAIC
KIDD, WALTER EVANS

PENDLETON, DON
ARNETT, TOM
BOMACK, ALAN
BREWER, GIL
CHURCHILL, E. RICHARD
CUNNINGHAM, CHESTER GRANT
DANFORTH, LES
DELANEY, KENT
FURST, CARL
JAGNINSKI, TOM
KRAUZER, STEVEN M.
LESLIE, PETER
LORD, JAMES
LYNDS, DENNIS
MCDADE, CHARLES
MCQUAY, MICHAEL DENNIS
MERTZ, STEPHEN
NEARY, PATRICK
NEWTON, MICHAEL
OBSTFELD, RAYMOND
ODOM, MEL[VIN LEWIS III]
RANDLE, KEVIN [DOUGLAS]
SANSON, KIRK
SCHMIDT, DAN
STIVERS, DICK
STONE, GAYLE
VAN COOK, JERRY
WERNICK, SAUL

PENDLETON, FORD
PATTEN, LEWIS B.

PENDLETON, GRACE
MANN, MARGARET BOYER

PENDLETON, TOM
VAN ZANDT, EDMUND

PENDOWER, JACQUES
PENDOWER, THOMAS CURTIS H

PENDRAGON, ERIC
PARRY, MICHEL P.

PENDRAY
EDWARDS, GAWAIN

PENFIELD, CORNELIA S.P.
LATHROP, CORNELIA

PENGREEP, WILLIAM
PEARSON, W.T.

PENHOLDER
EGGLESTON, EDWARD

PENKLUB
LANG, CARL GUSTAVE A.

PENMARE, WILLIAM
NISOT, MAVIS ELIZABETH

PENN, ANNE
PENDOWER, THOMAS CURTIS H

PENN, ARTHUR
MATTHEWS, JAMES BRANDER

PENN, CHRISTOPHER
LAWLOR, PATRICK ANTHONY

PENN, JOHN
TROTMAN, JACK H. & PALMA

PENN, MICHAEL
PERICHITCH, MILO

PENN, RACHEL
WILLARD, CAROLINE MCCOY

PENN, RICHARD
SPROAT, IAIN MACDONALD

PENN, RUTH BONN
ROSENBERG, ETHEL [C]

PENNAGE, E.M.
FINKEL, GEORGE [I]

PENNE, AGILE
AIKEN, ALBERT W.

PENNEBAKER, D.A.
DYLAN, BOB

PENNIBB
SIBLEY, INEZ K.

PENNINGTON, PATIENCE
PRINGLE, ELIZABETH WATIES

PENNINGTON, PENNY
GALBRAITH, GEORGIE S.

PENNINGTON, STUART
GALBRAITH, GEORGIE S.

PENNOT, PETER
ROUND, WILLIAM M.F.

PENNY, F.E.
PENNY, FANNY EMILY FARR

PENNY, MRS. FRANK
PENNY, FANNY EMILY FARR

PENNY, PRUDENCE
GOLDBERG, HYMAN

PENNY, RICHARD
LASSER, DAVID

PENNY, RUPERT
THORNETT, ERNEST BASIL C.

PENO
OAK, PURUSHATTAM NAGESH

PENROSE, MARGARET
STRATEMEYER, EDWARD

PENT, KATHERINE
SHANN, RENEE

PENTECOST, HUGH
PHILIPS, JUDSON P.

PENTECOST, MARTIN
HEARN, JOHN

PENTLAND, FRANK
HABISREUTINGER, RUDOLPH D

PENTREATH, PAUL
NEUBERG, VICTOR [B]

PENZIK, IRENA
NARELL, IRENA

PEPIN, F.
FROSCHL, JOSEF G.

PEPPER, BILL
PEPPER, CURTIS G.

PEPPER, DAN
MORHEIM, LOUIS

PEPPER, JOAN
ALEXANDER, JOAN
WETHERELL-PEPPER, JOAN A.

PEPPER, K.N.
MORRIS, JAMES M.

PEPPER, MARTIN
KRICH, JOHN

PEPPERPOD, PIP
STODDARD, CHARLES WARREN

PEPPLER, ALICE STOLPER
STOLPER, ALICE

PERA, IRA
SCHATZLER-PERASINI, GEBH.

PERCH, PHILEMON
JOHNSTON, RICHARD MALCOLM

PERCIVAL, NORMAN
PARCELL, NORMAN HOWE

PERCY, BRIGHTON
SHERWOOD, ROBERT EMMET

PERCY, CHARLES HENRY
SMITH, DOROTHY GLADYS

PERCY, EDWARD
SMITH, EDWARD PERCY

PERCY, KAREN
PERSHING, KAREN

PERDUE, ANN
CARROLL, WILLIAM JOSEPH

PERDURABO, FRATER
CROWLEY, EDWARD ALEXANDER

PEREGOY, CALVIN
MCCLARY, THOMAS CALVERT

PEREGOY, GEORGE WEEMS
MENCKEN, HENRY LOUIS

PEREGRINE
DEUTSCHER, ISAAC

PERELLI, NICK
WILLIS, ERNEST LISTER H.

PERELMAN, S.J.
PERELMAN, SIDNEY JOSEPH

PERERA, PADMA
HEJMADI, PADMA

PEREVALOV, NIKOLAI I
KOLESNIKOV, NIKOLAI I.

PEREY, LUCIEN
HERPIN, CLARA ADELE LUCE

PEREZ, FAUSTINO
HOFFENBERG, MASON

PEREZ, JUAN
WELLMAN, MANLY WADE

PEREZ, WALTER
JOSEPH, JAMES HERZ

PERGARTH, PETER
GODDARD, NORMAN M.

PERIL, MILTON R.
JONES, FRANCIS A.

PERIWINKLE, PAUL
ST. JOHN, PERCY BOLLNGBRK

PERKINS, ABIGAIL
KALER, JAMES OTIS

PERKINS, BILLY
ERTTMANN, PAUL OSKAR

PERKINS, ELI
DE LANCEY LANDON, MELVILL

PERKINS, ELIZABETH
DE LANCEY LANDON, MELVILL

PERKINS, FAITH
BRAMER, JENNIE PERKINS

PERKINS, GRACE
OURSLER, GRACE P.

PERKINS, VIRGINIA CHASE
CHASE, VIRGINIA

PERLACH, MARK
CONRADS, DIETRICH

PERNER, FRITZ
MAY, KARL FRIEDRICH

PERONNE
THOMPSON, ELLEN PERRONET

PEROWNE, BARRY
ATKEY, PHILIP

PERPESSICIUS
PANAITESCU, D.

PERRELLI, NICK
DAWSON, GEORGE H.
MARTIN, THOMAS HECTOR

PERRI, LESLIE
WILSON, DORIS MARIE

PERRIMAN, COLE
COLEMAN, WIN
PERRIN, PAT

PERRIN, CLYDE
O'BRIEN, HOWARD VINCENT

PERRIN, NEIL
KELLEY, THOMAS P.

PERRIWILS, G.W.
PERRY, GEORGETTE
WILSON, WILLIAM J.

PERROT, GERVASE
JONES, ARTHUR LLEWELLYN

PERRY, ANNE
HULME, JULIET

PERRY, BARBARA FISHER
FISHER, BARBARA

PERRY, BERNARD
GIBSON, WALTER B.

PERRY, BRIGHTON
BENCHLEY, ROBERT CHARLES

PERRY, CAROL DUNCAN
DUNCAN, CAROL S.

PERRY, CLAY
PERRY, CLAIR WILLARD

PERRY, HARRY DENNIES
INGRAHAM, PRENTISS

PERRY, L.J.
PERICHITCH, MILO

PERRY, MAX
OSTER, JERRY

PERRY, ROGER
COWERN, ROGER WILLIAM

PERRY, RUFUS
GIBSON, WALTER B.

PERRY, WILL
WEATHERBY, WILLIAM JOHN

PERSHING, MARIE
SCHULTZ, PEARLE HENDRKSN.

PERSIS
HAIME, AGNES IRVINE CONS.

PERSON, NIKLAS
BOLDING, PER OLOF

PERTH, ALY
PREINERSTORFER, ALOIS

PERTH, JACK
PREINERSTORFER, ALOIS

PERTINAX
GERAUD, ANDRE
GERAULT, CHARLES
HAWS, DUNCAN

PERTRUP, BERT
RUPPERT, WALTER

PERTUIS, MAURICE
SIMENON, GEORGES [J.C]

PERUS-CUEVA, FRANCOISE
PERUS, FRANCOISE

PESTUM, JO
STUMPE, JOHANNES

PETERKIEWICZ, JERZY
PIETRKIEWICZ, JERZY

PETERMANN, A.G.
RANK, HEINER

PETERS, A.F. JR.
BASNER, GERHARD
DUBINA, PETER

PETERS, ALAN
SPOONER, PETER ALAN

PETERS, ALEX
HARKNETT, TERRY W.

PETERS, ALEXANDER
HOLLANDER, ZANDER

PETERS, ANNE
HANSEN, ANNE

PETERS, BARNEY
BAUER, ERWIN A.

PETERS, BILL
MCGIVERN, WILLIAM P.

PETERS, BRIAN
STOKOE, E[DWARD] G[EORGE]

PETERS, BRYAN
GEORGE, PETER [BRYAN]

PETERS, CAROLINE
BETZ, EVA KELLY

PETERS, CLARICE
KWOCK, LAUREEN

PETERS, CLAUS
BASNER, GERHARD

PETERS, DAVID
DAVID, PETER [ALLEN]

PETERS, DR. T.K.
WOOD, EDWARD D. JR.

PETERS, ELIZABETH
MERTZ, BARBARA GROSS

PETERS, ELLIS
PARGETER, EDITH [MARY]

PETERS, EVELYN
JOOST, EVELYN

PETERS, FRITZ
PETERS, ARTHUR A.

PETERS, GEOFFREY
PALMER, MADELYN
TRIPPE, PETER

PETERS, HANS-HEINZ
PARRY-DRIXNER, WILLY

PETERS, HENNI
NADOLNI-S., BARBARA

PETERS, JACK C.
GIBSON, WALTER B.

PETERS, JOCELYN
OAKESHOTT, EDNA

PETERS, L.T.
KLAINER, JO-ANN & ALBERT

PETERS, LANCE
LICHTENSTEIN, PETER

PETERS, LANE
LAPIDUS, ELAINE

PETERS, LAWRENCE
DAVIES, LESLIE PERNELL

PETERS, LINDA
CATHERALL, ARTHUR

PETERS, LUDOVIC
BRENT, PETER [LUDWIG]

PETERS, NATASHA
CLEAVER, ANASTASIA

PETERS, NOEL
HARVEY, PETER NOEL

PETERS, OTHELLO F.
DONALDSON, DALE C.

PETERS, PIT
BRAND, KURT
MUNCH, HELLMUT-HUBERTUS

PETERS, ROY
NICKSON, ARTHUR [THOMAS]

PETERS, S.H.
PORTER, WILLIAM SYDNEY

PETERS, S.T.
BRANNON, WILLIAM T.

PETERS, STEPHEN
GEISER, ROBERT L.

PETERS, SUE
CARSON, ANGELA

PETERSEN, HELLY
MAYER, HELLY

PETERSEN, KAY JENS
LYS, GUNTHER

PETERSEN, PETER
KURTH, HANNS

PETERSEN, PETRA
JUNIKE, ROLF

PETERSHAM, MISKA
PETERSHAM, P.M.

PETERSON, CARRIE
PARANYA, FLORENCE J.

PETERSON, CHRISTMAS
CHRISTMAS, JOYCE
PETERSON, JON

PETERSON, INGO
PORSCH, F.E.

PETERSON, JAMES
ZEIGER, HENRY A.

PETERSON, JEANNE WHITEH.
WHITEHOUSE, JEANNE

PETERSON, JIM
CRAWFORD, WILLIAM L.

PETERSON, KEITH
KLAVAN, ANDREW

PETERSON, MAUDE HOWARD
HOOPES, MARY HOWARD

PETERSON, SIMONE
THOMSON, DAISY HICKS

PETERSUNNE, RODDY RON
LAW, JULIAN SIMON

PETIT, VICTOR
ALTENHOFER, LUDWIG

PETO
WHITE, STANLEY

PETO, JAMES
WHITE, STANLEY

PETRIE, JODRA
BURGER, PIXIE
PERCIVALL, JULIA

PETRIE, JOHN
HEWISON, ROBERT JOHN P.

PETRIE, RHONA
BUCHANAN, EILEEN-MARIE D.

PETRONIUS
LARSEN, ERIK

PETRONSKY, BORIS
BEAUCHAMP, KATHLEEN M.

PETROV
RASKALNIKOV, FEDOR F.

PETROV, EVGENY PETROVICH
ARNOLDOVICH, ILYA
KATEYEV, EVGENY

PETROV, IVAYLO
KYUCHOUKOV, PRODAN

PETROVSKAYA, KYRA
WAYNE, KYRA PETROVSKAYA

PETROVSKY, N.
POLTORATSKY, N.P.

PETTIT, MIKE
PETTIT, AUBREY L. JR

PEURONE, JOYCE
DRAGO, HARRY SINCLAIR

PEYO
CULLIFORD, PIERRE

PEYTON, GREEN
WERTENBAKER, G. PEYTON

PEYTON, K.M.
PEYTON, KATHLEEN WENDY
PEYTON, MICHAEL

PFEIFER, TILL
ARNOLD, TIM

PFEIL, FRED
PFEIL, JOHN FREDERICK

PFNISS, MARIA
PLENK, ELEONORA

PHANDERSON, BO
SIEGBAHN, BO

PHEE, HUGH
MCPHEE, HUGH

PHELAN, JEREMIAH
KING, C. DALY

PHELIX
BURNETT, HUGH

PHELPS, ELIZABETH STUART
WARD, STUART

PHELPS, FREDERIC
MCCULLEY, JOHNSTON

PHILIPP, FLORIAN
DELFS, RAINER

PHILIPP, FRANK
DELFS, RAINER

PHILIPPE, EDOUARD
WEISS, JOE

PHILIPPO, MARK
BENDER, ARNOLD

PHILIPS, PAGE
SCARBOROUGH, GEORGE

PHILIPS, THOMAS
DAVIES, LESLIE PERNELL

PHILISTINE
SPENDER, JOHN ALFRED

PHILLIMORE, FRANCES
MEYNELL, ALICE [C.G.T.]

PHILLIPS, AILEEN PAUL
PAUL, AILEEN

PHILLIPS, ALAN
STAUDERMAN, ALBERT P.

PHILLIPS, BETTY
PHILLIPS, ELIZABETH M.A.

PHILLIPS, BETTY LOU
PHILLIPS, ELIZABETH LOU.

PHILLIPS, D.J.
PHILLIPS, DENNIS JOHN A.

PHILLIPS, DENNIS
PHILLIPS, DENNIS JOHN A.

PHILLIPS, DOROTHY
GARLOCK, DOROTHY

PHILLIPS, FRANK
NOWLAN, PHILLIP FRANCIS

PHILLIPS, H.C.
HONEY, PHILIP

PHILLIPS, IRV
PHILLIPS, IRVING W.

PHILLIPS, J.B.
PHILLIPS, JOHN BERTRAM

PHILLIPS, JACK
SANDBURG, CARL [AUGUST]

PHILLIPS, JAMES R.
JENNETT, RICHARD P.

PHILLIPS, JEAN
SWANN, FRANCIS

PHILLIPS, JILL M.
PHILLIPS, JILL META

PHILLIPS, JOHANNA
GARLOCK, DOROTHY

PHILLIPS, JOHN
MARQUAND, JOHN P.

PHILLIPS, KING
PERKINS, KENNETH

PHILLIPS, LEON
GERSON, NOEL B.

PHILLIPS, LYN
SCAFIDEL, JAMES R.

PHILLIPS, MAC
PHILLIPS, MAURICE J.

PHILLIPS, MARK
GARRETT, RANDALL [P]
HARRIS, LAURENCE MARK

PHILLIPS, MICHAEL
BEAUMONT, CHARLES
NOLAN, WILLIAM F.

PHILLIPS, MICKEY
PHILLIPS, ALAN MEYRICK K.

PHILLIPS, OSBORNE
BARCYNSKI, LEON ROGER

PHILLIPS, PAT
PHILLIPS, PATRICIA SONIA

PHILLIPS, PETER
BROWNE, HOWARD

PHILLIPS, R.B.
BRADLEY, RODRICK

PHILLIPS, RICHARD
DICK, PHILIP K.

PHILLIPS, ROG
GRAHAM, ROGER P.

PHILLIPS, SONIA
PHILLIPS, PATRICIA SONIA

PHILLIPS, STEVE
WHITTINGTON, HARRY

PHILLIPS, TOM
DROTNING, PHILLIP T.
RAMIREZ, THOMAS P.

PHILLIPS, TONY
BAGDON, PAUL
CUNNINGHAM, CHESTER GRANT
READ, JOHN

PHILLIPS, W.
DODGE, WENDELL PHILLIPS

PHILLIPS, WARD
LOVECRAFT, H[OWARD] P.

PHILMORE, R.
HOWARD, HERBERT EDMUND

PHILO
FREND, WILLIAM HUGH C.

PHIN
THAYER, ERNEST LAWRENCE

PHINEAS
HANIFIN, JOHN M.

PHIPPS, MARGARET
TATHAM, LAURA

PHIPSON, JOAN
FITZHARDINGE, JOAN M.

PHIZ
BROWNE, HABLOT KNIGHT

PHOENICE, J.
HUTCHINSON, JULIET MARY F

PHOOKY, FRED H.
POKATSKY, HORST

PHUCHER, ITOTHE
CHITTENDEN, HIRAM MARTIN

PHUSIN, KATE
RUSKIN, JOHN

PHYLOS THE TIBETIAN
OLIVER, FREDERICK S.

PHYPPES, HYACINTH
GOREY, EDWARD ST. JOHN

PIANO, CELESTE
LYKIARD, ALEXIS [C]

PICA, PETER
ALDISS, BRIAN [WILSON]

PICARD, SAM
COPP, DEWITT S.

PICCIRILLI, TOM
PICCIRILLI, THOMAS EDWARD

PICHLER, ELISABETH
BALASSA, ILONA

PICKARD, JOHN Q.
BORG, PHILIP ANTHONY JOHN

PICKEM, PETER
STEARNS, HAROLD EDMUND

PICKERING, PERCIVAL
STIRLING, ANNA MARIA D.W.

PICKERING, R.E.
PICKERING, ROBERT EASTON

PICKLE, PEREGRINE
UPTON, GEORGE PUTNAM

PICOU, ALPHONSE
GHNASSIA, MAURICE [J-H]

PICTON, BERNARD
KNIGHT, BERNARD

PIED PIPER
WILLIAMS, DORIAN

PIED PIPER, THE
MALLALIEU, J.P.W.

PIERCE, GLENN
DUMKE, GLENN S.

PIERCE, JESSICA
MORGAN, JILL M[EREDITH]

PIERCE, JO
MANNING, WILLIAM HENRY
MORRIS, CHARLES [S]

PIERCE, KATHERINE
ST. JOHN, WYLLY FOLK

PIERCE, MATTHEW
LUCEY, JAMES DENNIS

PIERCE, MIRNA
PEREZ-VENERO, MIRNA

PIERMARINI
MALACRIDA, MARCHESE

PIERRE, PAUL
CALLE, PAUL

PIERREPOINT, ALBERT
ANDREWS, ALLEN

PIERS, ASHDOWN
FREEMAN, RICHARD AUSTIN
PITCAIRN, JOHN JAMES

PIERS, PETRA
HOFFMANN, HANS

PIERSON, WALTER
MCCULLEY, JOHNSTON

PIETRKIEWICZ, JERZY
PETERKIEWICZ, JERZY

PIG, EDWARD
GOREY, EDWARD ST. JOHN

PIGOT, F.
ARNOLD, FREDERICK

PIKE, BOB
PIKE, ROBERT MARVIN

PIKE, CHARLES R.
BULMER, [HENRY] KENNETH
HARKNETT, TERRY W.
WELLS, ANGUS

PIKE, MORTON
PARRY, DAVID HAROLD

PIKE, ROBERT L.
FISH, ROBERT L.

PIKKUMOLLIAINEN, LEENA
PENNANEN, LEA A.

PILE
MORENO, VIRGINIA

PILGRIM
WRIGHT, MARJORY BEATRICE

PILGRIM, A
ARGLES, THEODORE EMILE

PILGRIM, ADAM
WEBSTER, OWEN

PILGRIM, ANNE
ALLAN, MABEL ESTHER

PILGRIM, DAVID
PALMER, JOHN LESLIE
SAUNDERS, HILARY A.

PILGRIM, DERRAL
ZACHARY, HUGH

PILGRIM, PETER
BIRD, ROBERT M.

PILIO, GERONE
WHITEFIELD, JOHN HUMPHREY

PILKINGTON, CYNTHIA
HORNE, CYNTHIA MIRIAM

PILNYAK, BORIS
VOGAU, BORIS ANDREYEVICH

PILNYAK, BORIS ANDREYEVIC
VOGAU, BORIS ANDREYEVICH

PIMM, FRITZ
GRAAS, FRITZ

PIN, OSCAR
PERDIGUERO PEREZ, FERNAND

PINCKNEY, CALLAN
PINCKNEY, BARBARA B.P.

PINDELL, JON
PAINE, LAURAN BOSWORTH

PINDER, CHUCK
DONSON, CYRIL

PINE, E. THEODORE
HASSE, HENRY
PETAJA, EMIL

PINE, M.S.
FINN, SISTER MARY PAULINA

PINE, WILLIAM
HARKNETT, TERRY W.

PING-HSIN
WAN-YING, HSIEH

PINKERTON, FRANK
PINKERTON, A. FRANK A.

PINKNEY, J. BRIAN
PINKNEY, [JERRY] BRIAN

PINKPANK, PETER
PIJET, GEORG W.

PINKWATER, D. MANUS
PINKWATER, DANIEL MANUS

PINKWATER, DANIEL M.
PINKWATER, DANIEL MANUS

PINKWATER, MANUS
PINKWATER, DANIEL MANUS

PINNER, JOMA
WERNER, HERMA

PINO, E.
WITTERMANS, ELIZABETH

PINOAK, JUSTIN WILLARD
PROSSER, HAROLD LEE

PINSCHER, MICHEL
BERNDT, KARL-HEINZ

PINTO, PETER
BERNE, ERIC [L]

PIONEER
YATES, RAYMOND F.

PIPER, A.G.
LEWIS, JULIUS WARREN

PIPER, EVELYN
MODELL, MERRIAM

PIPER, H. BEAM
PIPER, HORACE BEAM

PIPER, PETER
LANGBEHN, THEO

PIPER, ROGER
FISHER, JOHN [O.H.]

PIPER, THEO
LANGBEHN, THEO

PIPER, WATTY
BRAGG, MABEL CAROLINE

PIRAT, FRITZ
VON CZIFFRA, GEZA

PIRIE-GORDON, C.H.C.
PIRIE-GORDON, HARRY

PISCATOR
LASCELLES, ROBERT

PISMIRE, OSBERT
HIVNOR, ROBERT

PITAWALL, ERNST
VON DEDENROTH, EUGEN H.

PITCAIRN, FRANK
COCKBURN, [FRANCIS] CLAUD

PITCHFORD, HARRY RONALD
EBBS, ROBERT

PITIGRILLI
SEGRE, DINO

PITT, JEREMY
WYNNE-TYSON, JON

PITT, PAUL
ERTTMANN, PAUL OSKAR

PITT, VALERIE
HALL, VALERIE

PLAIDY, JEAN
HIBBERT, ELEANOR BURFORD

PLAIN, JOSEPHINE
MITCHELL, ISABEL
MITCHELL, MARY

PLAIN, WARREN
OEHMKE, THOMAS HAROLD

PLAISTED, MAX
BINDER, JACK
BINDER, OTTO

PLANCHE, MATILDA ANNE
MACKARNESS, MATILDA ANNE

PLANE, ANNIE
SEYMOUR, MARJORIE F.

PLANET PRINCE
HAGGARD, J. HARVEY

PLATANOV, ANDREI
KLIMENTOV, ANDREI PLATON.

PLATTS, A. MONMOUTH
COX, ANTHONY BERKELEY

PLAUT, MARTIN
MARTINN, PAUL

PLAYER, ROBERT
JORDAN, ROBERT FURNEAUX

PLEDGER, P.J.
TONKIN, C.B.

PLESS, E.W.
VOSS, WILLI

PLEYDELL, GEORGE
BANCROFT, GEORGE PLEYDELL

PLEYDELL, SUSAN
SENIOR, ISABEL JANET C.S.

PLICK ET PLOCK
SIMENON, GEORGES [J.C]

PLIMPTON, PRUFROCK
PLIMPTON, GEORGE [AMES]

PLINY THE YOUNGEST
WILSON, STANLEY KIDDER

PLOGAU, FRED
KALMUCZAK, ROLF

PLOWMAN, STEPHANIE
DEE, STEPHANIE

PLOWSHARE, JOHN
SHARPLES, ALFRED

PLUM, J.
WODEHOUSE, PELHAM GRENV.

PLUM, JENNIFER
KURLAND, MICHAEL

PLUMB, BEATRICE
HUNZICKER, BEATRICE PLUMB

PLUMM, NORMAN D.
HORNBACK, BERT G[ERALD]

PLUMMER, BEN
BINGLEY, DAVID ERNEST

PLUMMY
DELLBRIDGE, JOHN

PLUNKETT, JAMES
KELLY, JAMES PLUNKETT

PLUTONIUS
MEHTA, RUSTAM JEHANGIR

POCOCK, H.R.A.
POCOCK, [HENRY] ROGER [A]

POCOCK, ROBERT
POCOCK, [HENRY] ROGER [A]

POCRATES, DR. HIP
SCHOENFELD, EUGENE L.

PODMARSH, ROLLO
SALTER, DONALD P.M.

PODMORE, PERIWINKLE
BANGS, JOHN KENDRICK

POE, BERNAND
HAUSMAN, LEON AUGUSTUS

POE, EDGAR
LEVINE, PHILIP

POGE, N. WOOTEN
PAGE, NORVELL W[OOTEN]

POGGI, JACK
POGGI, EMIL J.

POGO
GRAY, PATRICIA [CLARK]

POINTON, ROBERT
ROOKE, DAPHNIE [MARIE]

POLA
WATSON, PAULINE

POLDER, MARKUS
KRUESS, JAMES

POLDYS, CAROL
RADWANER, LEOPOLD

POLESKI
BIELECKI, CZESLAW

POLITICUS
KULSKI, WLADYSLAW WSZEBOR

POLITIS, KOSMAS
TAVELUDI, P.

POLITZER, HEINZ
POLITZER, HEINRICH

POLLACK, RACHEL [GRACE][1
POLLACK, RICHARD A.

POLLARD, A.F.
POLLARD, ALBERT F.

POLLARD, A.W.
POLLARD, ALFRED WILLIAM

POLLARD, JOHN X.
BROWNE, HOWARD
FAIRMAN, PAUL W.

POLLARD, SIDNEY
POLLAK, SIDNEY

POLLMER, EMMA
MAY, KARL FRIEDRICH

POLLOCK, MARY
BLYTON, ENID

POLLOCK, TED
POLLOCK, THEODORE MARVIN

POLLOTTA, NICK
POLLOTTA, NICHOLAS ANGELO

POLO, GEORG
POLOMSKI, GEORG

POLONI, HELENA
STADENER, INGEGERD

POLTROON
BUTLER, FRANCIS
JOHNSTON, ALASTAIR

POLTROON, MILFORD
BASCOM, DAVID

POLVA, ANNI
POLVIANDER, ANNI K.

POLWARTH, G. MARCHANT
POLWARTH, GWENDOLINE M.

POMEROY, EUGENE
DONNELLY, THOMAS F.

POMEROY, FLORENCE MARY
POWLEY, FLORENCE MARY P.

POMEROY, HUB
CLAASEN, HAROLD

POMEROY, PETE
ROTH, ARTHUR JOSEPH

POMFRET, BARON
DAME, LAWRENCE

POMFRET, JOAN
TOWNSEND, JOAN

PONCHARDIER, DOMINIQUE
DOMINIQUE, ANTOINE

PONDER, PATRICIA
MAXWELL, PATRICIA ANNE P.

PONG, HOY PING
TUCKER, [ARTHUR] WILSON

PONT
LAIDLER, GRAHAM

POOK, PETER
MILLER, J.A.

POOL, BILL
PUHL, WILFRIED ERNST

POOLE, JOSEPHINE
HELYAR, JANE P. JOSEPHINE

POOLE, MICHAEL
POOLE, REGINALD H.

POOLE, RICHARD
WELLS, LEE EDWIN

POOLE, SETH
RIEMER, GEORGE

POOLE, VIVIAN
JAFFEE, GABRIEL

POOR SCHOLAR
REID, [THOMAS] MAYNE

POORTVLIET, RIEN
POORTVLIET, MARIEN

POOT, LINKE
DOBLIN, ALFRED

POOTER
HAMILTON, ALEXANDER

POPE, ANN
ZAVALA, ANN

POPE, LEE
ZAVALA, ANN

POPE-HENNESSY, J.W.
POPE-HENNESSY, JOHN W.

POPULUS
COLE, GEORGE D.H.

PORATH, ELLEN
SEVERSON, ELLEN DODGE

PORCHE, SIMONE [BRENDA]
PORCHE, PAULINE

PORLOCK, MARTIN
MACDONALD, PHILIP

PORT, WYMAR
JUDY, WILLIAM LEWIS

PORTAL, ELLIS
POWE, BRUCE

PORTE-THOMAS, BARBARA ANN
PORTE, BARBARA ANN

PORTER, ALVIN
ROWLAND, DONALD S.

PORTER, DONALD CLAYTON
GERSON, NOEL B.

PORTER, GENE
STRATTON-PORTER, GENE

PORTER, GENE STRATTON
STRATTON, GENEVA GRACE

PORTER, KATHERINE ANNE
PORTER, CALLIE RUSSELL

PORTER, KATHRYN
SWINFORD, BETTY [J.W]

PORTER, KEN
GEHRMANN, HORST

PORTER, LEX
BRAND, KURT

PORTER, MARK
LECKIE, ROBERT [H]

PORTER, NEIL
PETERS, HERMANN

PORTER, NINA
PYKARE, NINA ANN COOMBS

PORTER, R.E.
HOCH, EDWARD D.

PORTER, SHEENA
LANE, SHEENA PORTER

PORTER, SUE
LIMB, SUE

PORTIPHAR
MARRACK, J.F.

PORTOBELLO, PETRONELLA
ANDERSON, [LADY] FLAVIA

PORTSEA
MACKENZIE, SIR EDWARD

POSNER, ALICE
FINS, ALICE

POSSE, G. PETER
MEISCHKE, WOLFGANG

POSSENDORF, HANS
MAHNER-MONS, HANS

POSSUM, PETER
ROWE, RICHARD

POST, J.B.
POST, JERRY BENJAMIN

POST, MAVERIC
MAPES, VICTOR

POST, MORTIMER
BLAIR, WALTER

POSTMA, MINNIE
POSTMA, MAGDALENA J.

POTIPHAR
HERN, [GEORGE] ANTHONY

POTOMAC, PETER
HOOPES, ROY

POTTER, BEATRIX
HEELIS, BEATRIX

POTTER, FAITH
TOPEROFF, SAM

POTTER, JAY HILL
HANSON, VICTOR JOSEPH

POTTER, RONALD
LEOPOLD, GUNTHER

POUM ET ZETTE
SIMENON, GEORGES [J.C]

POUND, SINGLETON
MERLAND, OLIVER

POWELL, A.M.
MORGAN, ALFRED P[OWELL]

POWELL, EMMETT J.
OVERHOLSER, WAYNE D.

POWELL, ERSHAW
EHNEBOM, PAR BIRGER

POWELL, FERN
SAMMAN, FERN

POWELL, FRANCIS
CASE, FRANCIS POWELL

POWELL, FRANK
INGRAHAM, PRENTISS

POWELL, MASON
STUDEBAKER, DONALD VALEN.

POWELL, NEELY
POWELL, JAN HAMILTON

POWELL, NEIL
INNES, BRIAN

POWELL, RICHARD STILLMAN
BARBOUR, RALPH HENRY

POWELL, SONNY
BESTER, ALFRED

POWER, ARTHUR
DUDDEN, ARTHUR P.

POWER, CATHERINE
DUBREUIL, ELIZABETH L.

POWER, CECIL
ALLEN, [CHARLES] GRANT B.

POWER, NELSON
JUDD, ALFRED

POWER, REX
LANGLEY, ROGER

POWERS, ANNE
SCHWARTZ, ANNE POWERS

POWERS, BARBARA HUDSON
DUDLEY, BARBARA HUDSON

POWERS, DICK
SELLERS, CONNIE LESLIE

POWERS, GEORGE
INFIELD, GLENN [B]

POWERS, J.F.
POWERS, JOHN F.

POWERS, J.L.
GLASBY, JOHN S.

POWERS, JOHN
BOYCE, DAVID
ENEFER, DOUGLAS STALLARD

POWERS, JOHN R.
POWERS, JOHN J.

POWERS, L.C.
TUBB, E.C.

POWERS, M.L.
TUBB, E.C.

POWERS, MARGARET
HEAL, EDITH

POWERS, NORA
PYKARE, NINA ANN COOMBS

POWERS, R.T.
COLLINS, ANDREW J.

POWERS, RALPH
FISHER, STEPHEN GOULD
GRUBER, FRANK

POWYS, EDWARD
MOORCOCK, MICHAEL

POWYS, J.C.
POWYS, JOHN COWPER

POWYS, STEPHEN
WODEHOUSE, PELHAM GRENV.

POWYS, T.F.
POWYS, THEODORE FRANCIS

POY
FEARON, PERCY

POYER, D.C.
POYER, DAVID C.

POYER, JOE
POYER, JOSEPH JOHN

POYNTZ, LAUNCE
WHITTAKER, FREDERICK

POZZESSERE, GRAHAM
POZZESSERE, HEATHER G.

PRAED, MRS. CAMPBELL
PRAED, CAROLINE MARY-PR.

PRAED, ROSA
PRAED, CAROLINE MARY-PR.

PRAGER, HANSJORG
JESCHKE, WOLFGANG

PRAIZE, ANN
BLEWETT, DOROTHY EMILE

PRATE, KIT
HOWELL, DOROTHY

PRATNEY, WINKIE
PRATNEY, WILLIAM ALFRED

PRATT, CORNELIA ATWOOD
COMER, CORNELIA ATWOOD

PRATT, HARPER
EGLI, WERNER J.

PRAVDA, FRANTISEK
HLINKA, VOJTECH

PRAY, PAUL
WILKINSON, RICHARD HILL

PREBLE, AMANDA
TAYNTOR, CHRISTINE B.

PREECE, CHARLES M.
PRIESS, KARL-HEINZ

PREEDY, GEORGE [R]
LONG, GABRIELLE M.V.C.

PREMANCANDA
SRIVASTAVA, DHANPAT RAI

PREMONT, BROT. JEREMY
WILLETT, BROT. FRANCISCUS

PRENDER, BART
KING, ALBERT

PRENTICE, AMY
KALER, JAMES OTIS

PRENTIS, RICHARD
AGATE, JAMES

PRENTISS, CHARLOTTE
BRAME, WILLIAM
PLATT, CHARLES [M]

PRENTISS, KARL
PURDY, KEN WILLIAM

PRESCOTT, CALEB
BINGLEY, DAVID ERNEST

PRESCOTT, CASEY
MORRIS, CHRIS[TOPHER C.]

PRESCOTT, DOROTHY
POOR, AGNES BLAKE

PRESCOTT, DRAY
BULMER, [HENRY] KENNETH

PRESCOTT, JIM
RELLERGERD, HELMUT

PRESCOTT, JOHN
LUCCHETTI, ANTHONY

PRESCOTT, JULIAN
BUDD, JOHN

PRESLAND, JOHN
BENDIT, GLADYS WILLIAMS
SKELTON, GLADYS

PRESSLEY, HILDA
NICKSON, HILDA

PRESTO, C.
CARSJENS, GERHARD

PRESTON, ARTHUR
HANKINS, ARTHUR PRESTON

PRESTON, ARTHUR H.
HANKINS, ARTHUR PRESTON

PRESTON, FRED
PROBST, ALFRED

PRESTON, GEORGE F.
WARREN, JOHN BYRNE L.

PRESTON, HILLARY
NICKSON, HILDA

PRESTON, HUGH
WILSON, DEREK ALAN

PRESTON, JACK
BUSCHLEN, JOHN PRESTON

PRESTON, JAMES
UNETT, JOHN

PRESTON, JANE
THOMAS, REG

PRESTON, PAUL
MORRIS, CHARLES [S]

PRESTON, RICHARD
LINDSAY, JACK

PRESTON, WALFORD
TOWNLEY, HOUGHTON

PRETORIUS, HERTHA
KOUTS, HERTHA PRETORIUS

PREVOST, FRANCIS
PREVOST BATTERSBY, H.F.

PREVOST, MARCEL
MARCEL, EUGENE

PREZIHOV, VORANC
KUHAR, LOVRO

PRIAM
COLLINS, CHARLES JAMES

PRICE, ASHLAND
CARLSON, JANICE

PRICE, EVADNE
SMITH, HELEN ZENNA

PRICE, JENNIFER
HOOVER, HELEN D.B.

PRICE, KERRY
PERSHING, KAREN

PRICE, LAURA
CARLSON, JANICE

PRICE, LELAND
GEORGE, CHARLES

PRICE, LUCIE LOCKE
LOCKE, LUCIE

PRICE, LYNN [LINDA]
PURVIANCE, CHERYL LYNN

PRICE, NANCY
MAUD, LILLIAN NANCY

PRICE, RHYS
PRICE, GEORGE [H]

PRICE, WILL
GRUND, CARL-JOSEPH

PRICE-BROWN
PRICE-BROWN, JOHN

PRICHARD, K.
PRICHARD, KATE O'BRIEN

PRIEST, CARL
PRIESS, KARL-HEINZ

PRIESTLEY, J.B.
PRIESTLEY, JOHN BOYNTON

PRIESTLEY, ROBERT
WIGGINS, DAVID

PRIME, C.T.
PRIME, CECIL THOMAS

PRIMITIF, GEORGES
WEISS, JOE

PRIMM, BROT. ORRIN
WILLETT, BROT. FRANCISCUS

PRIMROSE, JANE
CURRY, WINIFRED J.P.

PRINCE, J.H.
PRINCE, JACK HARVEY

PRINCE, MARGOT
PRICE, MARJORIE

PRINS, JAN
SCHEPP, CHRISTIAAN LOUIS

PRINS, PIERRE
LINDHOLM, FREDRIK

PRIOR, HARRY
KNIGHTLEY, D.G.

PRIOR, JAMES
KIRK, JAMES PRIOR

PRITCHETT, ARIADNE
GRACE, ANITA

PRITCHETT, V.S.
PRICTHETT, VICTOR SAWDON

PRIVATE 19022
MANNING, FREDERIC

PRIYAMVADA, USHA
NILSSON, USHA SAKSENA

PRO-ROK
SLONIMSKI, ANTONI

PROBAZKI, BORIS
DEKKER, MAURITS RUDOLF J.

PROBERT, LOWRI
JONES, ROBERT MAYNARD

PROBSTING, BEATE
ILGERT, BEATE

PROBYN, ELISE
MCKIBBON, J.E.

PROBYN, HUGH
MCKIBBON, J.E.

PROBYN, JOHN E
MCKIBBON, J.E.

PROCTOR, EVERITT
MONTGOMERY, RUTHERFORD G.

PROCTOR, IDA
HARRIS, IDA FRASER

PROCTOR, PAUL
SAMWAYS, GEORGE R.

PROCTOR, WALTER. G.
CORBIN, HAROLD STANDISH

PROFESSOR X
BOORSTIN, DANIEL JOSEPH
FAULK, ODIE B.

PROLE, LOZANIA
BLOOM, URSULA
EADE, CHARLES

PRONZINI, BILL
PRONZINI, WILLIAM JOHN

PROPHET JAMES, THE
BUCK, JAMES SMITH

PROSKAUER, JULIAN J.
GIBSON, WALTER B.

PROSPER, JOHN
BURANELLI, PROSPER
FARRAR, JOHN C.

PROSPER, LINCOLN
CANNON, HELEN

PROSPERO & CALIBAN
PIRIE-GORDON, HARRY
ROLFE, FREDERICK [W]

PROTEUS
WHITAKER, PETER

PROTHERO, JOLEN KEITH
CHESTERTON, ADA ELIZABETH

PROUDFOOT, WALTER
VAHEY, JOHN G. HAZLETTE

PROUT, DENTON
PHILLIPS, CHARLES WALTER

PROVENCE, MARCEL
JOUHANDEAU, MARCEL H.

PROWLER, HARLEY
MASTERS, EDGAR LEE

PROWSE, R.O.
PROWSE, RICHARD ORTON

PRUDHOMME, SULLY
PRUDHOMME, RENE FRANCOIS

PRUITT, ALAN
ROSE, ALVIN EMANUEL

PRUNING KNIFE
ALLEN, HENRY FRANCIS

PRUS, BOLESLAW
GLOWACKI, ALEKSANDER

PRUTKOV, KOZMA
SNODGRASS, W.D.

PRYCE, MELINDA
SHERTZER, LINDA K.

PRYDE, ANTHONY
WEEKES, A[GNES] R[USSELL]

PRYE, CHRISTOPHER
FRY, DANIEL

PRYOR, ADEL
WASSEFALL, ADELL

PRYOR, NATALIE
PYKARE, NINA ANN COOMBS

PRYOR, PAULINE
ROBY, MARY LINN

PRYOR, ROBERT STONE
HOLLAND, CECELIA [A]

PRYOR, VANESSA
YARBRO, CHELSEA QUINN

PRZYJACIEL
NOWACZYNSKI, ADOLF

PSEUDOMAN, AKKAD
NORTHRUP, EDWIN FITCH

PSIGOLOOG
VISSER, WILLEM J.C.

PSYCHO ANN
BARROWS, [RUTH] MARJORIE

PTACEK, KATHY
GRANT, KATHRYN ANNE P.

PTELEON
GRIEVE, CHRIST. MURRAY

PUBLIUS
PANIZZA, OSKAR

PUCK, PETER
REINHARD, WILHELM PETER

PUCK, Y.U.
ANDRE, [K] MICHAEL

PUGANIGG, INGRID
ROTH-KAPELLER, INGRID

PULEO, NICOLE
MILLER, NICOLE PULEO

PULLEIN-THOMPSON, CHRIST.
POPESCU, CHRISTINE

PULLEIN-THOMPSON, DIANA
FARR, DIANA PULLEIN-THOMP

PULLING, PIERRE
PULLING, ALBERT VAN SILER

PULVAR, MARY MONICA
KUHFELD, MARY MON. PULVAR

PULVERTAFT, LALAGE
GREEN, LALAGE ISOBEL

PUMPERNICKLE
WEINSTEIN, SOL

PUNDIT, EPHRAIM
LOOKER, SAMUEL JOSEPH

PUNSHON, E.R.
PUNSHON, ERNEST ROBERTSON

PURCAL, JOHN T.
PURACAL, JOHN T.

PURDELL, REGINALD
GRASDORF, REGINALD

PURDOM, C.B.
PURDOM, CHARLES B.

PURDOM, TOM
PURDOM, THOMAS EDWARD

PURDY
MILLER, EMILY

PURDY, AL
PURDY, ALFRED W.

PURDY, [CAPT.] JIM
GILLILAN, G. HOWARD

PURE, SIMON
SWINNERTON, FRANK ARTHUR

PURLEY, JOHN
THOMAS, REGINALD GEORGE

PURVIS, CLEMENT
FOX, GARDNER F.

PUSHCHIN, LEV
GIPPIUS, ZINAIDA N.

PUTINAS
MYKOLAITIS, VINCAS

PUTMAN, ARTHUR LEE
ALGER, LECLAIRE GOWANS
ALGER, HORATIO JR.

PUTNAM, ISRA [EZRA]
LA SPINA, FANNY GREYE

PUTNAM, J. WESLEY
DRAGO, HARRY SINCLAIR

PUTNAM, JOHN
BECKWITH, BURNHAM PUTNAM

PUTNAM, KATE
O'SHEA, PATRICK J.
OSGOOD, KATE PUTNAM

PUTNAM, KENNETH
KLASS, PHILIP J.

PUTNEY, GAIL J.
FULLERTON, GAIL JACKSON

PUTRA, KERALA
PANIKKAR, K. MADHAVA

PUTTER, POLLY
ADOMEIT, RUTH E.

PYATT, ROSINA
BEAUMONT, ANNE

PYKARE, NINA
PYKARE, NINA ANN COOMBS

PYLES, AITKEN
MCDAVID, RAVEN I.

PYNE, NICHOLAS
NEUBERG, VICTOR [B]

PYRRHO
MCCABE, RALPH

PYTCHELY, R.F. ST. B.
COWIE, DONALD

PYTHAGOROLUNISTER
DEFOE, DANIEL

PYTHON, MONTY
CHAPMAN, GRAHAM
CLEESE, JOHN [MARWOOD]
GILLIAM, TERRY [VANCE]
IDLE, ERIC
JONES, TERENCE GRAHAM P.
PALIN, MICHAEL EDWARD

Q
QUILLER-COUCH, ARTHUR

Q, JOHN
QUIRK, JOHN EDWARD
KELLEY, MARTHA MOTT

QROLL
ANDERSSON, STIG

QUAD, M.
LEWIS, CHARLES BERTRAND

QUAESTOR
BYFORD-JONES, WILFRED

QUARRY, NICK
ALBERT, MARVIN H.

QUARTERLY, MILTON
CORYELL, JOHN RUSSELL

QUARTERMAIN, JAMES
LYNNE, JAMES BROOME

QUASIMOTO
GORSKI, ARTHUR

QUEDNAU, WALTER
GANLEY, W. PAUL

QUEEN, ELLERY
BREWER, GIL
DANNAY, FREDERIC
DAVIDSON, AVRAM
DEMING, RICHARD
FAIRMAN, PAUL W.
HOCH, EDWARD D.
LEE, MANFRED B.
MARLOWE, STEPHEN
POWELL, TALMAGE
RUNYON, CHARLES W.
SMITH, GEORGE H[ENRY]
STURGEON, THEODORE
VANCE, JOHN HOLBROOK

QUEEN, ELLERY JR.
DANNAY, FREDERIC
HOLDING, JAMES [C.C.]
LEE, MANFRED B.

QUEN, THORA-ELLEN
ELLINGER, INGEBURG

QUENTIN, PATRICK
WEBB, RICHARD WILSON
WHEELER, HUGH C.

QUEST, ERICA
SAWYER, JOHN & NANCY

QUEX
NICHOLS, GEORGE HERBERT F

QUICK, AMANDA
KRENTZ, JAYNE ANN

QUICK, DOROTHY
MEYER, DOROTHY QUICK
STRAUB, MARGARET ROGERS

QUICK, PHILIP
STRAGE, MARK

QUICK, W.T.
ALLAN, MARGARET

QUICKENS, QUARLES
ENGLISH, THOMAS DUNN

QUIDAM
WEINTRAUB, WIKTOR

QUIEN SABE
HERO, NUMA C.

QUIEN-SABE
GREGORY, JACKSON

QUILEBET
FOWLER, HENRY WATSON

QUILIBET, PHILIP
POND, GEORGE EDWARD

QUILL
GRANGE, CYRIL
PUDDEPHA, DEREK

QUILL, BARNABY
BRANDNER, GARY

QUILL, JOHN
CLARK, CHARLES HEBER

QUILL, MONICA
MCINERNY, RALPH [M]

QUILLER, ANDREW
BULMER, [HENRY] KENNETH
JAMES, LAURENCE

QUILLER, ARTHUR
JAMES, LAURENCE
WELLS, ANGUS

QUILLET
FOWLER, HENRY WATSON

QUILP, JOCELYN
SUTCLIFFE, HALLIWELL

QUILTER, EDDIE
WOODMAN, THOMAS

QUILTY, RAFE
WHITCOMBE, RICK TRADER

QUIN
LEWIS, ALFRED HENRY

QUIN, DAN
LEWIS, ALFRED HENRY

QUIN, MIKE
RYAN, PAUL WILLIAM

QUIN, SHIRLAND
GUEST, ENID

QUINCE, PETER
DAY, GEORGE HAROLD
THOMPSON, J.W.M.

QUINCE, PETER LUM
RITCHIE, [HARRY] WARD

QUINCY, HAL
MASUR, HAROLD Q.

QUINLAN, RED
QUINLAN, STERLING C.

QUINLAN, WILLIAM
LASH, WILLIAM QUINLAN

QUINN, COLLEEN
BOSLER, COLLEEN Q.

QUINN, ELIZABETH
BARNARD, ELIZABETH QUINN

QUINN, ETHEL
RUSSELL, LINDSAY PATRICIA

QUINN, HENRY
ANTON, UWE
ZUBEIL, RANIER

QUINN, JAKE
CONAWAY, JAMES C.

QUINN, JOHN
RODRIGUEZ, DENNIS
WOOD, EDWARD D. JR.

QUINN, JULIA
GARDNER, DARLENE HROBAK

QUINN, MARTIN
SMITH, MARTIN WILLIAM

QUINN, SAMANTHA
BULLINGER, MAUREEN

QUINN, SIMON
SMITH, MARTIN WILLIAM

QUINN, SUSAN
JACOBS, SUSAN

QUINN, TARA TAYLOR
REAMES, TARA LEE

QUINN, VERNON
QUINN, ELISABETH

QUINPOOL, JOHN
REGAN, JOHN WILLIAM

QUINT, NEAL
OCHSNER, NEAL

QUINT, ROBERT
EPPERS, EVA

QUINT, ROBERT [CONT]
GIESA, WERNER K.
ZUBEIL, RAINER

QUINTANA, FRANCES
SWADESH, FRANCES LEON

QUINTANILLA, MARIA ALINE
GRIFFITH, MARIA ALINE

QUINTIN, REX
HARDINGE, CHARLES WREXE

QUIRK
SQUIBBS, H.W.Q.

QUIROULE, PIERRE
SAYER, WALTER WILLIAM

QUIST, FELICIA
HOBSON, LAURA K.Z.

QUIST, TORNER
BLUME, HORST-M.

QUITMAN, WALLACE
PALMER, RAYMOND A.

QUIZ, ROLAND
QUITTENTON, RICHARD M.H.

QUIZ, ROLAND JR.
QUITTENTON, BERTRAM

QUOD, JOHN
IRVING, JOHN TREAT

QUONDAM
STEVENS, CHARLES M.

QUOOS-RABE, R.C.
FRANCISKOWSKY, HANS GUNT.

QUYTH, GABRIEL
JENNINGS, GARY

R.A.K.
KNOX, RONALD A.

R.C.W.
WATERSTON, WILLIAM

R.D.A.
HERBERT, ROBERT DUDLEY S.

R.H.S.
SPRING, HOWARD

R.M.B.
BULL, REINA M.

R.P.
WALKER, R.

R.R.
BURGESS, MICHAEL ROY
IYENGAR, K.R.

R.S.
PALTOCK, ROBERT
ZINSSER, HANS

R.S.L.
MOORCOCK, MICHAEL

R.T.L.
VINING, CHARLES A.M.

RA'ANAN, URI
FRISCHWASSER, HEINZ FELIX

RABASSEIRE, HENRY
PACHTER, HENRY M.

RABBIE
TOWERS, MAXWELL

RABBIT, PETER
LONG, WILLIAM JOSEPH

RACE, PHILIP
PARSONS, ELMER M.

RACHEL
FERGUSON, RACHEL

RACHILDE
VALLETTE, MARGUERITE

RACHMANOWA, ALJA
VON HOYER, GALINA

RACINA, THOM
RAUCINA, THOMAS FRANK

RACINE, JOHN
RAUCINA, THOMAS FRANK

RACKHAM, JOHN
PHILLIFENT, JOHN T.

RADAN, G.T.
LENGYEL, ALFONZ
RADAN, GEORGE T.

RADCLIFFE, GARNETT
TRAVERS, STEPHEN

RADCLIFFE, JANETTE
ROBERTS, JANET LOUISE

RADCLIFFE, JOCELYN
BEARDSLEY, CHARLES N.

RADCLIFFE, VIRGINIA
HURST, VIRGINIA RADCLIFFE

RADD, RALPH
NORTH, WILLIAM

RADEBRECHT, F.
FIENHOLD, WOLFGANG

RADEBRECHT, R.
FIENHOLD, WOLFGANG

RADEK, KARL BERNARDOVICH
SOBELSOHN, KARL

RADEMACHER, HEIKE
ANTON, UWE

RADFORD, JOHN P.
BENTLEY, WILLIAM

RADHA
SMITH, MARY

RADIO PADRE
WRIGHT, RONALD SELBY

RADLEY, SHEILA
ROBINSON, SHEILA M.

RADMUS, G.
RAWSON, ALBERT L.

RADNER, SIDNEY H.
GIBSON, WALTER B.

RADNOR, ALAN
LEWIS, RICHARD

RADSCHA
AMINOFF, IVAN T.E.

RADWAY, ANN
GEIS, RICHARD E.

RADYR, TOMOS
STEVENSON, JAMES PATRICK

RAE, DORIS
RAE, MARGARET DORIS

RAE, RICCARDA
EDON, MARGRET RICCARDA

RAE, RUSTY
RAG, MILFORD ANDERSON

RAE, SCOTT
HAMILL, CICELY MARY H.

RAEF, LAURA C.
RAEF, LAURA G. CAUBLE

RAESCHILD, SHEILA
GRAWOIG, SHEILA

RAESIDE, JUKS
RESIDE, W.J.

RAFFERTY, CARIN
KICHLINE, LINDA

RAFFERTY, S.S.
HURLEY, JOHN JEROME

RAFFI
CAVOUKIAN, RAFFI

RAFFLES
HORNUNG, ERNEST WILLIAM
LISTER, LORD

RAFFT, BJORN
ARNESEN, DAVID DIETRICH

RAG MAN
BURROWS, HERMANN

RAGATZY, ANTON
PARR, JULIAN F.

RAGGED STAFF
COLEY, REX

RAGGED, HYDER
BIRON, SIR HENRY CHARTRES
DE MORGAN, JOHN

RAGLAN, BARON
RAGLAN, FITZROY

RAGLAND, LORD
RAGLAN, FITZROY

RAGNAR REDBEARD
DESMOND, ARTHUR

RAGSDALE, LULAH
RAGDALE, TALLULAH

RAHA, GEORGE
ROBINSON, LEWIS [GEORGE]

RAHMAN, ABDUL
WAYMAN, TONY RUSSELL

RAHV, PHILIP
GREENBERG, IVAN

RAI, NAVAB
SRIVASTAVA, DHANPAT RAI

RAIKES, ROBERT
HAYDEN, ERIC WILLIAM

RAILIE, ARTHUR LYON
WARREN, EDWARD PERRY

RAIMOND, C.E.
ROBINS, ELIZABETH

RAINBOW, JASON
MURRAY, WILLIAM P.

RAINBOW-WIND, SHANDOR
WEISS, [PAUL] SHANDOR

RAINE, ALLEN
ADALISA, ANNE

RAINE, MAC
FIRTH, NORMAN WESLEY

RAINE, NICOLE
GELLES-COLE, SANDI

RAINE, RICHARD
SAWKINS, RAYMOND [H]

RAINE, WILLIAM MACLEOD
OVERHOLSER, WAYNE D.

RAINER, GEORGE
GREENBERGER, INGRID E.

RAINER, JEROME
GOODE, GERALD

RAINER, JULIA
GOODE, RUTH

RAINEY, BUCK
RAINEY, BILL S.

RAINEY, W.B.
BLASSINGAME, WYATT RAINEY

RAINEY, WILLIAM B.
BLASSINGAME, WYATT RAINEY
GRUBER, FRANK

RAINHAM, THOMAS
BARREN, CHARLES MCKINNON

RAINIS, JAN
PLIEKSANS, JAN

RAINTREE, LEE
SELLERS, CONNIE LESLIE

RAJARAM
IYENGAR, K.R.

RAKOSI, CARL
RAWLEY, CALLMAN

RALE, NERO
BURGESS, MICHAEL ROY

RALEIGH, ALAN
BROWN, ELIJAH

RALEIGH, CECIL
ROWLANDS, CECIL

RALEIGH, RICHARD
LOVECRAFT, H[OWARD] P.

RALEY, ROWENA
MCCULLEY, JOHNSTON

RALLENTANDO, H.P.
SAYERS, DOROTHY L[EIGH]

RALPH 124E41
ACKERMAN, FORREST J.

RALPH, NATHAN
GOLDBERG, NATHAN RALPH

RALSTON, JAN
DUNLOP, AGNES MARY R.

RAMAL, WALTER
DE LA MARE, WALTER

RAMALA, PRATAP ROY
BHOSALE, YESHWANTRAO

RAMBAM, MYRIAM
RAMBAM, CYVIA

RAMBERT, MARIE
RAMBAM, CYVIA

RAME, DAVID
DIVINE, ARTHUR DURHAM

RAME, MARIE LOUISE
DE LA RAMEE, MARIE LOUISE

RAMEAU, JEAN
LABAIGT, LAURENT

RAMEAUS, LEON
MAURRAS, CHARLES-MARIE-P

RAMEAUT, MAURICE
MARTEAU, F.A.

RAMIN, MONIKA
RENNAU, JOACHIM

RAMIN, TERESE
RAMIN, TEREY DALY

RAMM, CARL
WHITE, RANDY

RAMON, BORIS
HAWKINS, PETER

RAMPLING, ANNE
RICE, ANNE

RAMPO, EDOGAWA
HIRAI, TARO

RAMSAY, DIANA
BRANDES, RHODA

RAMSAY, FAY
EASTWOOD, HELEN B.

RAMSAY, GRACE
O'MEARA, KATHLEEN

RAMSAY, JACK
CHAPMAN, MATTHEW
ROBINSON, BRUCE

RAMSAY, JAY
CAMPBELL, [JOHN] RAMSEY

RAMSDEN, E.H.
RAMSDEN, HARTLEY

RAMSDEN, LEWIS
DOWDING, A.L.

RAMSEY, ERIC
HAGBERG, DAVID [JAMES]

RAMSEY, LILA
KRETSCHMER, JOHN & JOAN C

RAMSEY, MARK
ROBERTS, JOHN MADDOX

RAMSEY, MICHAEL
GREEN, T.

RAMUS, PIERRE
BAROCHE, JACQUES ANTOINE

RAN, KIP
RANDOLPH, LOWELL KING

RANA, J.
BHATIA, JAMUNADEVI
FORRESTER, HELEN

RANCE, JOSEPH
HOYLE, TREVOR
ONO, RYUNOSUKE
SATO, JUNYA

RAND, AYN
ROSENBAUM, ALISSA

RAND, BRETT
NORWOOD, VICTOR [G.C.]

RAND, JAMES S.
ATTENBOROUGH, BERNARD G.

RAND, JOHN
REACH, JAMES

RAND, KIRK
DANIELS, NORMAN A.

RAND, LEW
PULLAN, RU

RAND, LOU
HOGAN, LOU RAND

RAND, MAT
HECKLEMANN, CHARLES N.

RAND, MATT
STRANGE, THOMAS OLIVER

RAND, R.H.
HOLLAND, JAMES R.

RAND, REX
LAZENBY, NORMAN A.

RAND, ROBERT E.
MEARES, LEONARD F.

RAND, STEVE
BENNETT, JAY

RAND, SUZANNE
BRAND, DEBRA

RAND, WILLIAM
ROOS, WILLIAM

RANDA, LUIGI
BELLOMI, ANTONIA

RANDAL, JUDE
WILNER, JUDE

RANDALL, BOB
GOLDSTEIN, STANLEY B.

RANDALL, CLAY
ADAMS, CLIFTON H.

RANDALL, CLINT
ROTSLER, WILLIAM

RANDALL, DIANA [DIANE]
ROSS, WILLIAM E. DANIEL

RANDALL, ELIOT
WALLACH, LEAH

RANDALL, FLORENCE E.
RANDALL, FLORENCE ENGEL

RANDALL, J.R.
RENNAU, JOACHIM

RANDALL, JANET
YOUNG, JANET & ROBERT

RANDALL, JEAN
HAUCK, LOUISE PLATT

RANDALL, JOSHUA
RANDISI, ROBERT J.

RANDALL, LINDSAY
ANDERSON, SUSAN M.

RANDALL, ROBERT
SILVERBERG, ROBERT
GARRETT, RANDALL [P]

RANDALL, ROLF
RENNAU, JOACHIM

RANDALL, RONA
SHAMBROOK, RONA [GREEN]

RANDALL, ROSS
KALMUCZAK, ROLF

RANDALL, STEVE
ANDREWS, CLARENCE A.

RANDALL, WILLIAM
GWINN, WILLIAM R.

RANDELL, BEVERLY
PRICE, BEVERLY JOAN

RANDELL, MIKE
BREUCKER, OSCAR HERBERT

RANDEN, RONALD
HENCKELL, JURGEN

RANDOLPH, ARTHUR C.
GREENE, ALVIN CARL

RANDOLPH, BARRY
HUBBARD, L. RON

RANDOLPH, CRAIG
JACOBSON, EJLAR & EDITH

RANDOLPH, ELISE
LOWE, SUSAN [CLAIRE] L.

RANDOLPH, ELLEN
ROSS, DON
ROSS, WILLIAM E. DANIEL

RANDOLPH, GEOFFREY
ELLIS, EDWARD S.

RANDOLPH, GORDON
VON BLOCK, BELA [W]
VON BLOCK, SYLVIA

RANDOLPH, JANE
ROSS, WILLIAM E. DANIEL

RANDOLPH, JERRY
BRANNON, WILLIAM T.

RANDOLPH, MARION
RODELL, MARIE F.

RANDOLPH, MELANIE
RAGOSTA, MILLIE J.

RANDOLPH, NANCY
ROBB, INEZ [C]

RANDOLPH, RICHARD
PENTELOW, JOHN NIX

RANDOLPH, [LIEUT.] J.H.
ELLIS, EDWARD S.

RANDOLPHE, ARABELLA
JONES, RUSS

RANDOM, ALAN
KAY, ERNEST

RANDOM, ALEX
ROWLAND, DONALD S.

RANDOM, RICK
HARRISON, HARRY

RANGELEY, E.R.
ZACHARY, HUGH

RANGELY, OLIVIA
ZACHARY, HUGH

RANGER, KEN
CREASEY, JOHN

RANGER, L.S.
BOMKE, BERNHARD

RANGER, SETH
PIERCE, FRANK RICHARDSON

RANGER-GULL, C.
RANGER-GULL, C[YRIL A.E.]

RANJE
KNUTSEN, LALLI

RANJEE
SHAHANI, RANJEE

RANK, CLIFTON
DAVIES, COURTMAN

RANKINE, DOUGLAS
MASON, DOUGLAS RANKINE

RANKINE, JOHN
MASON, DOUGLAS RANKINE

RANL, CLIFTON
DAVIES, COURTMAN

RANSOM, BILL
RANSOM, WILLIAM MICHAEL

RANSOM, DANA
GIDEON, NANCY

RANSOM, DANIEL
GORMAN, EDWARD [JOSEPH]

RANSOM, KATHERINE
SEDERQUEST, MARY F.F.

RANSOME, BARBARA
RANSOME, L.E.

RANSOME, CHARLES A.
ROWE, JOHN GABRIEL

RANSOME, STEPHEN
DAVIS, FREDERICK [CLYDE]

RANT, TOL E.
LONGYEAR, BARRY B[ROOKES]

RANZETTA, V.
RANZETTA, LUAN

RAOUL
THOMPSON, RALPH J.

RAOUL, ANTHONY
WILMOT, ANTHONY

RAPER, JACK
RAPER, JULIUS ROWAN

RAPHAEL
KOTHNER, PAUL

RAPHAEL, JAY
JOSEPHS, RAY

RAPHAEL, RAB
RAPHAEL, CHAIM

RAPHAEL, [FATHER] M.
GOLDGRABER, KENNETH

RAPPAPORT, SEMEN A.
RAPPAPORT, SOLOMON SAMUEL

RASEY, RUTH M.
SIMPSON, RUTH MARY

RASKIN, ELLEN
FLANAGAN, ELLEN

RASMUS-BRAUNE, JOACHIM
BRAUNE, JOACHIM

RASMUSSEN, ANDR.
MEYN, NIELS

RASMUSSEN, STYRMAND
MEYN, NIELS

RASNIC, STEVE
TEM, STEVE RASNIC

RASTHOLF, J.
FABER, ELSE

RASTHOLF, JORGEN
JANSEN, ERIK B. VOLMER

RASTHOLT, JORGEN
FABER, ELSE
JENSEN, ERIK B. VOLMER

RASUL, RZA
RZAEV, RASUL IBRAGIM

RATATOSKR
BLAICK, HANS ERICH

RATCLIFFE, JAMES P.
MENCKEN, HENRY LOUIS

RATH, E.J.
BRAINERD, EDITH RATHBONE

RATHBONE, JAMES
PARKHILL-RATHBONE, JAMES

RATHER, LOIS
RODECAPE, MARJORIE FOSTER

RATJEN, HANS HARDER
BIERMANN-RATJEN, HANS H.

RATTRAY, SIMON
TREVOR, ELLESTON

RAU, CHRISTINE
HAAKE, JURGEN

RAU, DAVID
HAAKE, JURGEN

RAU, SANTHA RAMA
BOWERS, SANTHA RAMA RAU

RAUER, INGE
RADZIWILL, ANNA INGE

RAULT, WALTER
GORHAM, MAURICE ANTHONY C

RAUTEN, L.C.
REPPERT-RAUTEN, LOTHAR v.

RAUTER, JOE
MCCHESNEY, MARY F.

RAUTH, RAINER
LETTENMAIR, JOSEF

RAUTTER, CHRISTIANE
HOCKER, KARLA

RAVEN, ANTHONY
RUPP, AUGUSTUS

RAVEN, DANIEL
LAZUTA, EUGENE MICHAEL

RAVEN, HOWARD
BELLAH, JAMES WARNER

RAVENDRO, RAVI
DOHRING, KARL SIEGFRIED

RAVENGLASS, HAL
WOOD, [SAMUEL] ANDREW

RAVENSBERG, MICHAEL
HOLMSTEN, GEORG

RAVENSCROFT, ROSANNE
RAVENSCROFT, JOHN R.

RAVENSTOCK, CONSTANCE
CASEY, JUNE E.

RAVENSWOOD, FRITZEN
FRITZHAND, JAMES

RAVI, BISON
VIAN, BORIS

RAW COSMIC
GLASBY, JOHN S.

RAWFORD, W.C.
CRAWFORD, WILLIAM [E]

RAWICZ, WACLAW
BERENT, WACLAW

RAWLE, HENRY
FEARN, JOHN RUSSELL

RAWLINGS, J.R.
MCCULLOCH, J.H.

RAWLINGS, LOUISA
BAUMGARTEN, SYLVIA

RAWLINGS, MARJORIE KINNAN
BASKIN, MARJORIE RAWLINGS

RAWLINGS, PETER
CHALLON, DAVID

RAWLS, PHILIP
LEVINSON, LEONARD [L]

RAWSON, TABOR
SHULMAN, IRVING

RAXIN, ALEXANDER
KOHLHOFER, ALEXANDER

RAY, A.A.
NETSCH, GUNTER

RAY, DEBORAH
KOGAN RAY, DEBORAH

RAY, IRENE
SUTTON, MARGARET BEEBE
SUTTON, RACHEL IRENE B.

RAY, JEAN
DE KREMER, JEAN RAYMOND

RAY, LINDE
LARSSON, LINDA

RAY, NICHOLAS
KIENZLE, RAYMOND N.

RAY, OPHELIA
MCMURTRY, LARRY

RAY, OSCAR
FARKAS, ALADAR A.

RAY, RENE
CREESE, IRENE

RAY, ROBERT
BERNSTEIN, AL

RAY, VIOLET
IRVINE, EDWARD JAMES

RAY, WESLEY
GAULDEN, RAY

RAY-ATKINSON, JOHN
ARNOLD, HAMNS

RAYCRAFT, STAN
SHAVER, RICHARD S.

RAYE, LINDA
TURNER, LINDA RAY

RAYLE, GEOFFREY
MCLEAN, ERIC W.

RAYMOND, ALEX
CASSIDAY, BRUCE [BINGHAM]

RAYMOND, ALICE
SALVATO, SHARON ANNE

RAYMOND, CHARLES
KOCH, CHARLOTTE
KOCH, RAYMOND

RAYMOND, DEREK BALLAN.
COOK, ROBERT [W.A.]

RAYMOND, E.V.
GALLUN, RAYMOND Z.

RAYMOND, G. ALISON
LANIER, ALISON RAYMOND

RAYMOND, HUGH
MICHEL, JOHN B.

RAYMOND, JAMES
SCAFIDEL, JAMES R.

RAYMOND, JOHN
BROSNAN, JOHN RAYMOND
DEL REY, LESTER
FANTHORPE, R.L.
FISH, LEONARD G.

RAYMOND, JOSEPH H.
LE FONTAINE, JOSEPH [R]

RAYMOND, LEE
HILL, MARY RAYMOND

RAYMOND, MARY
KEEGAN, MARY HEATHCOTT

RAYMOND, P.K.
SHEA, CORNELIUS

RAYMOND, P.L.
GIBSON, WALTER B.

RAYMOND, PAT
HAWK, RAYMOND & MARTIN

RAYMOND, RENE
RAYMOND, RENE BRABAZON

RAYMOND, RICK
PORTER, GIL

RAYMOND, ROBERT
ALTER, ROBERT EDMOND

RAYNER, OLIVE PRATT
ALLEN, GRANT

RAYNER, RAY
RAHNER, RAYMOND W.

RAYNER, RICHARD
MCILWAIN, DAVID

RAYSON, PAUL
JENNINGS, LESLIE NELSON

RAYTER, JOE
MCCHESNEY, MARY F.

RAZZI, JIM
RAZZI, JAMES

READ, BRIAN
AHIER, BRIAN

READ, JACK
DOMBROWSKI, THEODOR

READ, JAN
READ, JOHN HINTON

READ, MISS
SAINT, DORA JESSIE

READE, HAMISH
GRAY, SIMON [J.H.]

READE, JOHN
BOTNER, PHIL

READE, ROLF S.
ROSE, ALFRED

REAGAN, THOMAS
REAGAN, THOMAS B.

REALIST, B.A.
BENFORD, GREGORY ALBERT

REAMY, TOM
REAMY, THOMAS EARL

REARDON, JOSEPH
MILLER, TEVIS

REAVES, J. MICHAEL
REAVES, JAMES MICHAEL

REAVES, MICHAEL
REAVES, JAMES MICHAEL

REAY, TREVACE
POND, S.T.R.

REBEL
EGGLESTON, GEORGE CARY

REBEL, ADAM
ROAN, TOM

REBELO, MARQUES
DIAS DA CRUZ, EDDY

REBERG, ALEX
BURMESTER, ALBERT KONRAD

RECHLIN, EVA
BARTOSCHEK, EVA [R]

RECHNITZER, REX
RECHNITZER, F.E.

RECK, ALEXANDER
SILBERMAN, ALEX

RECKE, CONRAD
RIEDEL, CURT

RECOUR, CHARLES
BOTT, HENRY

RECTEZ, IAN
WEISINGER, MORT

RED BUTTERFLY
LAURITSEN, JOHN [P]

RED CROSS
GRANT, CHARLES L.

RED WING
POND, FREDERICK E.

REDCAM, TOM
DERMOT, THOMAS AH.

REDDER, GEORGE
DRUMMOND, JACK

REDDINGTON, LARRY
CASE, ROBERT ORMOND

REDDOCH, JENNIFER
MCNEILL, GEORGE

REDFERN, JOHN
PARGETER, EDITH [MARY]

REDFIELD, JENNIFER
HOSKINS, ROBERT

REDFIELD, MARTIN
BROWN, ALICE

REDGATE, JOHN
KENNEDY, ADAM

REDMAN, JOSEPH
PEARCE, BRIAN LEONARD

REDMAYNE, BARBARA
HOWE, MURIEL

REDMAYNE, JOHN
GOODSPEED, DONALD JAMES
WOOD, HERBERT FAIRLIE

REDMON, ANNE
NIGHTINGALE, ANNE REDMON

REDNERS
DENT, W. REDNERS

REDSHAW, JAMES FRANCIS
KELLEY, THOMAS P.

REDSTONE, SYLVIA
HONNOR, SYLVIA CROFTS

REDWAY, RALPH
HAMILTON, CHARLES H.S.

REDWAY, RIDLEY
HAMILTON, CHARLES H.S.

REDWING, MORRIS
MERRILL, JAMES MILFORD

REDWOOD, ALEC
MILKOMANE, G. ALEXIS M.

REDWOOD, RALPH
HOLDEN, J.G.P.

REDWOOD, ROSALINE
STAPLES, MARJORIE CHARLT.

REDZICH, CONSTANTIN
FALKENHEYN, EGON

REECE, JEAN
KISTLER, MARY

REED, ALLAN
EISFELD, RAINER
ROHR, WOLF DETLEF

REED, CYNTHIA
NOLAN, [VIOLET] CYNTHIA

REED, DANA
BERKMAN, EDWINA

REED, DAVID V.
KNOX, CLEO ELDON
VERN, DAVID

REED, ELIOT
AMBLER, ERIC
RODDA, [P] CHARLES

REED, EMMETT X.
KING, FLORENCE

REED, JACKSON
EDER, GEORGE JACKSON

REED, KIT
REED, LILLIAN CRAIG

REED, LOU
FIRBANK, LOUIS

REED, MARK
DANIELS, NORMAN A.

REED, PAUL
HUSTOFT, PAUL

REED, PETER
MACDONALD, JOHN D.

REED, SIMON
BOSTOCK-SMITH, COLIN
DANBY, MARY HEATHER
DICKENS, DORIS

REED, VAN
HUGHES, DENNIS [TALBOT]

REED, WALLACE
STRACH, JOSEPH GEORGE

REED, WILLIAM
ALEXANDER, DAVID

REED, Z.B.
BISHOP, ZEALIA BROWN

REEDER, COL. RED
REEDER, RUSSELL P. JR.

REELHEW, RIBLEW
WHEELER, WILBER

REENS, MARY
SINGLETON, BETTY

REEP, DIANE
ALLEN, EMILY JOAN
REEP, DIANE

REES, DAVID
WIGNALL, T[REVOR] C.

REES, DILWYN
DANIEL, GLYN [EDMUND]

REES, J. LARCOMBE
LARCOMBE, JENNIFER GERAL.

REES, MERIEL
LAMBOT, ISOBEL [MARY]

REES, RICHARD
MONTAGUE, LODOWICK EDWARD

REESE, BOB
REESE, ROBERT A.

REESE, WILLY
REESE, WILHELM F.C.

REEVE, CHRISTOPHER
WEBB, ANNE

REEVE, JOEL
KENNICOTT, DONALD
COX, WILLIAM ROBERT

REEVES, AMBER
BLANCO WHITE, AMBER

REEVES, BARBARA
KOLASKI, BARBARA REEVES

REEVES, DANIEL
LIDDY, JAMES [D.R.]

REEVES, JAMES
REEVES, JOHN MORRIS

REEVES, JOYCE
GARD, JOYCE

REEVES, PHILIP
KIESTER, EDWIN JR.

REEVES, RUTH ELLEN
RANNEY, AGNES V.

REEVES, SAM
SALTER, ALAN

REFUGITTA
HARRISON, CONSTANCE CARY

PSEUDONYMS

REGA, FRANCESCA
VON BOSELAGER, ADA

REGALIA, NANZI
COLLINS, NANCY A.

REGAN, BRAD
NORWOOD, VICTOR [G.C.]

REGAN, CASS
BARNARD, LESLIE T.

REGAN, JERRY
HARRIS, HERBERT

REGAN, LARRY
STRONG, CHARLES STANLEY

REGAN, REX
REXHAUS, GUNTHER

REGAN, WADE
GORDON-COOKE, N.

REGARD, PAUL
SHEEHAN, PERLEY POORE

REGER, ERIK
DANNENBERGER, HERMANN

REGESTER, SEELEY
VICTOR, MRS. M.V.

REGINALD, R. [ROBERT]
BURGESS, MICHAEL ROY

REGINALD, REGINALD R.
BURGESS, MICHAEL ROY

REGIO, JOSE
PEREIRA, JOSE MARIA D.R.

REGIS, ANCILLA
LAKOTTA, ANNELIESE

REGIS, JULIUS
PETTERSON, JULIUS

REGNAL, F.
D'ERLANGER, FREDERIC A.

REHN, JENS
LUTHER, OTTO JENS

REHN, VIKTORIA
KOHN-BEHRENS, CHARLOTTE

REI, KOSUMI
SHIBANO, TAKUMI

REIBEL, PAULA
SCHWARTZ, PAULA REIBEL

REICH, ALI
KATZ, BOBBI[E]

REICH, BODO
FISCHER, CLAUS

REICHARDT, FRANK
APPEL, WALTER

REICHERT, MICKEY ZUCKER
REICHERT, MIRIAM ZUCKER

REICKE, ILSE
VON HULSEN, ILSE

REID BANKS, LYNNE
BANKS, LYNNE REID
STEPHENSON, LYNNE REID B.

REID, CHRISTIAN
TIERNAN, FRANCIS C.

REID, DESMOND
BAKER, W.A. HOWARD
BOUNDS, SYDNEY J.
BROWNE, NOEL
BURKE, JOHN [FREDERICK]
CAHILL, A.
CAWTHORN, JAMES
CHAMBERS, PHILIP
CHANCE, JOHN NEWTON
DOLPHIN, REGINALD C.
DOUSE, ANTHONY
ELLIOTT, ROBERT COWELL
FRANCES, STEPHEN D.
GARSTIN, A.
GLYNN, ANTHONY ARTHUR
HALL, S.
HANSON, VICTOR JOSEPH
HEBER, GEORGE
LAMBE, FRANK
LOWDER, CHRISTOPHER
MANN, GEORGE PAUL
MARTIN, A.L.
MCARDLE, BRIAN
MCNEILLY, WILFRED G.
MOORCOCK, MICHAEL
RICHARDS, ROSS
PLAYER, EDDIE
RICHARDS, ROSS
ROBERTS, LEE
ROBERTSON, COLIN
SOWMAN, GORDON
STAGG, JAMES
STORY, JACK TREVOR
STORY, ROSAMOND MARY

REID, ELEANOR
SMITH, CONSTANCE ISABEL

REID, FRANK
VENNARD, ALEXANDER VINDEX

REID, GRACE
GREEN, GRACE

REID, LESLIE
JURIN-REID, BARBARA

REID, MARGARET ANN
SCHOENWEISS, SALLY

REID, MARSHALL
MCBRIDE, ROBERT MEDILL

REID, PHILIP
INGRAMS, RICHARD REID
OSMAN, ANDREW [P.K.]

REID, SALLY HELEN
PLES, SALLY R.

REID, V.S.
REID, VICTOR STAFFORD

REID, WALLACE Q.
GOODCHILD, GEORGE

REIHER, ROLF
KALMUCZAK, ROLF

REILING, NETTY
RADVANYI, NETTY REILING

REILLY, MARY
WILSON, MARY REILLY

REILLY, WILLIAM K.
CREASEY, JOHN

REIMER, HANS
KRILL, HANS RUDOLF

REIMEVA, ESTHER
HAJAK, EVA-JOHANNA

REIN, RICHARD
SMITH, RICHARD REIN

REINEL, FRITZ
MULLER, FRITZ

REINER, H.G.
GREINER-MAI, HERBERT

REINER, MAX
CALDWELL, [JANET] TAYLOR
REBACK, MARCUS

REINERS, CHRIS
BISCHOFF, MARIANNE [E]

REINHARDT, MADGE
RITTER, MADGE REINHARDT

REINHART, E.W.A.
EGGERT, REINHART

REINHOLD, FRITZ
GROMMER, HELMUT

REINHOLD, KARL LUDWIG
KEGLER, HANS

REINLEIN, M.
HERTEL, JOHANN GEORG

REINOW, HANS
REINOWSKI, HANS J.

REINSMITH, RICHARD
SMITH, RICHARD REIN

REIS, ERNST LUDWIG
KURTH, HANNS

REIS, RICARDO
PESSOA, FERNANDO [A.N.]

REISBACHER, HERMAN
HAGN, HUGO

REISER, HENRY
MACDONALD, JOHN D.

REISER, W.G.
GREISSER, WOLFGANG

REIT, SY
REIT, SEYMOUR

REITBOCK, ELISABETH
FISCHER, ILSE [R]

REITBOCK, ILSE
FISCHER, ILSE [R]

REITERLEIN, HANNES
MUNCH, HELLMUT-HUBERTUS

REITH, MARION
AMFT, MARION JANET

REITTER, NIKOLAUS
HERZBRUCH, ARND

REJJE, E.
HYDE, EDMUND ERROL CLAUD

RELDNIK, C.E.
KINDLER, OTTO

RELGIS, EUGENE
SIEGLER, EUGENE

RELHAM, HEDWIG
COURTHS-MAHLER, HEDWIG

RELING, JAN
DAVIS, HORACE BANCROFT

RELIS, HARRY
ENDORE, [SAMUEL] GUY

RELL, BERT W.
FIEDLER, ARIBERT

REMARQUE, ERICH MARIA
REMARD, ERICH PAUL

REMBACK, WILLIAM
VALIGURSKY, ED

REMENHAM, JOHN
VLASTO, JOHN ALEXANDER

REMICK, BRANT
NUETZEL, CHARLES A.

REMINGTON, MARK
BINGLEY, DAVID ERNEST

REMPLE, SIMON
KALMUCZAK, ROLF

REMY, ILLA
COLLIGNON, ILSE

REMY, PIERRE-JEAN
ANGREMY, JEAN-PIERRE

RENA
CROSSLEY, LOUISE RODGERS

RENA, SALLY
RENA, SARAH MARY

RENARD, MADELEINE
HOHOFF, MARGARETE

RENAULD, PIERRE
REUTER, RALPH

RENAULT
LAURENT, EMMANUEL

RENAULT, MARY
CHALLANS, MARY

RENAULT, RICK
PRONZINI, WILLIAM JOHN
WALLMANN, JEFFREY M.

RENCELAW, BRIAN
RUSSELL, RAY

RENDRAG, NITRAM
GARDNER, MARTIN

RENE, GASTON
SCHATZLER-PERASINI, GEBH.

RENE, HANS EVERT
RENERIUS, HANS-EVERT

RENEGADE
MOORCOCK, MICHAEL

RENICH, JILL
RENICH, HELEN T.

RENIER, ELIZABETH
BAKER, BETTY DOREEN F.

RENIN, PAUL
GOYNE, RICHARD

RENN, CHRIS
LYLE, JOHN

RENN, LUDWIG
VON GOLSSENAU, ARNOLD F.V

RENN, ROLF
RENNAU, JOACHIM

RENNA, G.
RAPUZZI, G.L.

RENNAU, ROLF
RENNAU, JOACHIM

RENNEL, KAJ
ERIKSSON, LENNART

RENNER, PIT
REESE, WILHELM F.C.

RENNIE, CHRISTOPHER
AMBROSE, ERIC [S]

RENNIE, JACK
SPOONER, PETER ALAN

RENO, CLINT
BALLARD, W. TODHUNTER

RENO, JOHN
HONNEF, JOACHIM

RENO, MARK
KEEVILL, HENRY J.

RENOLD, MARTIN
PFANDLER, MARCEL

RENSIE, WILLIS
EISNER, WILLIAM ERWIN

RENTON, CAM
ARMSTRONG, RICHARD

RENTON, JULIA
COLE, MARGARET A.

RENTZLOW, BRITTA
COLLIGNON, JETTA

RENWICK, WALT
DUNN, DES R.

RENZELMAN, MARILYN
FERGUSON, MARILYN

REPP, ED EARL
BLACKBURN, TOM W.
BONHAM, CECIL FRANCIS

REQUEL, LEYNE
SCHIER, NORMA

RESKIND, JOHN
WALLMANN, JEFFREY M.

RESNICK, MIKE
RESNICK, MICHAEL DIAMOND

RESSIEB, GEORGE
REACH, JAMES

RESSING, RON
HESSING, JAKOB

RESSOM, J. ARNE
MOSSER, ARNE J.

RESTLESS, JIMMY
HULL, JAMES

RESURGAM
PETTIT, CHARLES

RETCLIFFE, SIR JOHN
GOEDSCHE, HERMANN O.F.
HEYMANN, ROBERT

RETLA, ROBERT
ALTER, ROBERT EDMOND

RETLAW, HENRY
ELLIOTT, WILLIAM J.
RAWLE, HENRY

RETNUH X
HUNTER, WILLIAM F.

RETORT, JACK
HUNT, ISAAC

REUBENI, AARON
SHIMSHELEVITZ, AARON

REUBENS, AIDA
RAWKINS, ADA

REUTER, JAN
NYSTRAND, FOLKE

REUTIN, GEORG
FRANK, PETER

REVAL, JAMES
LAVER, JAMES

REVEL
VOLLEAU, ADOLPHE

REVEL, JAQUES
LAVER, JAMES

REVELL, HARRY
FLOYD, GILBERT

REVELL, LOUISA
SMITH, ELLEN HART

REVENA
WRIGHT, BETTY REN

REVERE, JOHN D.
BENNETT, HAL

REVERE, M.P.
WILLIAMSON, ALICE M.L.
WILLIAMSON, CHARLES N.

REVERE, PAUL
ABARBANELL, JACOB RALPH

REVERMORT, J.A.
CRAMB, JOHN ADAM

REVILO
CHRISTIANSSON, OLIVER

REVO, L.
MACHL, OTTO

REVOIR, AU
MULLER, ARTHUR

REVSBECH, VICKI
LIESTMAN, VICKI

REX, ARNE
MEYER-KOENIG, ERNA

REY, HANS AUGUSTO
REYERSBACH, HANS AUGUSTO

REY, RUSSELL
HUGHES, DENNIS [TALBOT]

REYAM
MAYER, CHARLES LEOPOLD

REYAM, LORAC
MAYERS, CARROLL

REYHER, BECKY
REYHER, REBECCA HOURWICH

REYMOND, LOUIS
DAUDET, ERNEST

REYMONT, LADISLAS
REYMONT, WLADYSLAW S.

REYNOLDS, ADRIAN
LONG, AMELIA REYNOLDS

REYNOLDS, ANN
MARTENS, ANNE L. COULTER

REYNOLDS, ANNE
BLY, CAROLYN
STEINKE, ANN E.R.

REYNOLDS, BAILLIE
REYNOLDS, GERTRUDE M.R.

REYNOLDS, CAPT. HUMBERT
HUBBARD, L. RON

REYNOLDS, CATHERINE
NICKENS, CATHERINE A.

REYNOLDS, DICKSON
REYNOLDS, HELEN MARY G.C.

REYNOLDS, DON
BRADBURY, RAY [DOUGLAS]

REYNOLDS, ELIZABETH
STEINKE, ANN E.R.

REYNOLDS, HUMBERT
HUBBARD, L. RON

REYNOLDS, JACK
JONES, JACK

REYNOLDS, JOHN
FEAR, WILLIAM H.
WHITLOCK, RALPH

REYNOLDS, KAY
REYNOLDS, KATHLEEN N.

REYNOLDS, L. MAJOR
LEIPIAR, LOUISE

REYNOLDS, LIGGET
SIMON, ROBERT ALFRED

REYNOLDS, LIONEL
KINAST, LEOPOLD

REYNOLDS, MACK
REYNOLDS, DALLAS MCCORD

REYNOLDS, MADGE
WHITLOCK, RALPH

REYNOLDS, MAXINE
REYNOLDS, DALLAS MCCORD

REYNOLDS, MRS. BAILLIE
REYNOLDS, GERTRUDE M.R.

REYNOLDS, PETER
CRAWFORD, WILLIAM L.
LONG, AMELIA REYNOLDS

REYNOLDS, TED
REYNOLDS, THEODORE A

RHEA, NICHOLAS
WALKER, PETER N[ORMAN]

RHEE, DENA
BRAUER, DEANA

RHIANNON
MACKWORTH, CECILY

RHINE, RICHARD
SILVERSTEIN, ALVIN

RHINEHART, LUKE
COCKCROFT, GEORGE POWERS

RHOADES, JONATHAN
OLSEN, JOHN EDWARD [JACK]

RHOADES, NINA
RHOADES, CORNELIA HARSEN

RHODAN, FORRY
ACKERMAN, FORREST J.

RHODE, ARVID
BREKKE, PAAL EMANUEL

RHODE, AUSTEN
FRANCIS, BASIL [HOSKINS]

RHODE, JOHN
STREET, CECIL JOHN C.

RHODE, WINSLOW
ROE, F. GORDON

RHODES, DANIEL
MCMAHON, NEIL

RHODES, LAURA
ROBINSON, LISA

RHODES, LELAND
PAINE, LAURAN BOSWORTH

RHOME, ADA
SUMNER, ADA

RHONE, FRANKIE
HUBBARD, L. RON

RHOSCOMYL, OWEN
VAUGHAN, OWEN

RHUDDLAU, JOHN
BLANDEN, CHARLES G.

RHUE, MORTON
STRASSER, TODD

RHYDDERCH, IENAN
JONES, EVAN DAVID

RHYS, FRANK
REES, CLAIR [FRANCIS]

RHYS, JEAN
REES, ELLA GWENDOLEN

RHYS, JOAN
REES, JOAN BOWEN

RHYS, MEGAN
WILLIAMS, DOROTHY JEANNE

RIBBER, JACK D.
BANKS, JEFF

RIBERA, LUCAS
CABRERA, LUIS

RICARD, W.
MACKAY, WILLIAM R.

RICCI, LEWIS ANSELM DA C.
DE COSTA RITCHIE, LEWIS A

RICE, ADAM
MOMMERS, HELMUTH W.
VLCEK, ERNST

RICE, ALBERT
LEVENTHAL, ALBERT RICE

RICE, ALLISON
ALLISON, RUTH
RICE, JANE

RICE, ANNE
O'BRIEN, HOWARD ALLAN F.
RICE, HOWARD ALLAN F.O.

RICE, CRAIG
RANDOLPH, GEORGIANNA ANN

RICE, ELINOR
HAYS, ELINOR RICE

RICE, ELMER
REIZENSTEIN, ELMER

RICE, ELMER L.
REIZENSTEIN, ELMER

RICE, MOLLY
SCHUCK, MARILYN D.

RICE, PAT
RICE, PATRICIA

RICE, R.B.
CHAPMAN, FRANK MONROE

RICH
FAIRFIELD, RICHARD IVAN

RICH, BARBARA
GRAVES, ROBERT VAN RANKE
GRAVES, SUSAN
REICHENTHAL, LAURA

RICH, C.B.
LEWIS, LEO RICH

RICH, D. COLEMAN
RICHARDSON, DARRELL C.

RICH, HARRIET
RICHLEY, MARGARET

RICH, HENRY K.
GODDARD, NORMAN M.

RICH, JEAN
RINKOFF, BARBARA

RICH, ROBERT
TRUMBO, DONALD [DALTON]

RICHARD, BILL
VAN HORN, DALE R.

RICHARD, FRANK
BEKESSY, JANOS
HOOK, H. CLARKE
WOOD-SMITH, NOEL

RICHARD, GEORGE
STUBBS, HARRY CLEMENT

RICHARD, JAMES ROBERT
BOWEN, ROBERT SYDNEY

RICHARD, KARL
BLASIUS, RICHARD

RICHARD, KENT
CROSSEN, KENDELL FOSTER

RICHARD, LOUIS
MICHEL, JOHN B.

RICHARD, R.J.
KAISER, HANS K.

RICHARD, SUSAN
ELLIS, JULIE M.

RICHARD-BESSIERE, F.
BESSIERE, RICHARD
RICHARD, FRANCOIS

RICHARDS, AL
SHUBIN, SEYMOUR

RICHARDS, ALAYNA
POSNER, RICHARD

RICHARDS, ALLEN
ROSENTHAL, RICHARD A.

RICHARDS, ANN
MERKT, FRANKIE

RICHARDS, CHARLES
MARVIN, JOHN T.

RICHARDS, CINDA
REAVIS, CHERYL

RICHARDS, CLARE
MALES, CAROLYN
TITCHENER, LOUISE

RICHARDS, CLAY
CROSSEN, KENDELL FOSTER

RICHARDS, CURTIS
CURTIS, RICHARD [A]

RICHARDS, CYNDI
RICHESON, CENA GOLDER

RICHARDS, DAVID
BICKERS, RICHARD L.T.

RICHARDS, DENISE
SHREFFLER, KIM

RICHARDS, DUANE
HURLEY, VIC

RICHARDS, EDWARD
TUBB, E.C.

RICHARDS, EMILIE
MCGEE, EMILIE R.

RICHARDS, EUGENE
CLAYTON, RICHARD

RICHARDS, FRANCIS
LOCKRIDGE, FRANCIS & DICK

RICHARDS, FRANK
AUSTIN, STANLEY
BARNARD, RICHARD INNES
BROOKS, EDWY SEARLES
CATCHPOLE, WILLIAM LESLIE
COOK, FRED GORDON
DAVIS, A.W.
DOWN, C. MAURICE
DUFFY, MICHAEL FRANCIS
GIBBONS, WILLIAM
HAMILTON, CHARLES H.S.
HINTON, HERBERT ALLAN
HOPE, WILLIAM EDWARD S.
KIRKHAM, REGINALD S.
NEWMAN, KENNETH E.
O'MANT, HEDLEY P.A.
PENTELOW, JOHN NIX
PIKE, WILLIAM ERNEST
RANSOME, L.E.
SAMWAYS, GEORGE R.
SHEPPARD, S. ROSSITER
TWYMAN, HAROLD WILLIAM

RICHARDS, HARVEY D.
SAINSBURY, NOEL E.

RICHARDS, HENRY
MORRISEY, JOSEPH LAWRENCE
SAXON, RICHARD

RICHARDS, HILDA
HAMILTON, CHARLES H.S.
WHEWAY, JOHN W.

RICHARDS, J.M.
RICHARDS, JAMES MAUDE

RICHARDS, JOEL
FRUCHTMAN, JOEL RICHARD

RICHARDS, K.
KOCH, RICHARD

RICHARDS, KAY
BAKER, SUSAN CATHERINE

RICHARDS, KEL
RICHARDS, KELVIN BARRY

RICHARDS, LARRY
RICHARDS, LAWRENCE O.

RICHARDS, LEE
WELLS, LEE EDWIN

RICHARDS, LESLIE
GREEN, RICHARD

RICHARDS, M.R.
HEINZ, M.R.

RICHARDS, MARK
FRISCHWASSER, HEINZ FELIX

RICHARDS, NAT
RICHARDSON, JAMES NATHANL

RICHARDS, PAUL
BUDDEE, PAUL
CUNNINGHAM, CHESTER GRANT
MESSMANN, JON [JOHN]
SNYDER, GEORGE
STREIB, DANIEL T.

RICHARDS, PETER
MONGER, IFOR DAVID

RICHARDS, PHYLLIS
AUTY, PHYLLIS

RICHARDS, SERENA
COPPULA, SUSAN CARROLL

RICHARDS, STANLEY
ALBERT, JERRY

RICHARDS, STELLA
STARR, RICHARD H.

RICHARDS, THOMAS
BERGMAN, RICHARD T.

RICHARDS, TODD
SUTPHEN, RICHARD C.

RICHARDS, VANESSA
MOFFETT, PAULA

RICHARDS, WILLIAM
COOK, WILLIAM EVERETT
HJERTSTEDT, GUNARD

RICHARDS, WM. [WILLIAM]
KEENE, DAY

RICHARDSON, ARLETA
WRIGHT, ARLETA

RICHARDSON, BETH
GUTCHEON, BETH R.

RICHARDSON, EVELYN
WHEALLER, CYNTHIA

RICHARDSON, FLAVIA
THOMSON, CHRISTINE C.

RICHARDSON, FRANCIS
BARTLE, L.E.
PARNELL, FRANK H.

RICHARDSON, GRACE LEE
DICKSON, NAIDA

RICHARDSON, HENRIETTA
RICHARDSON, ETHEL FLOREN.

RICHARDSON, HENRY HANDEL
ROBERTSON, ETHEL FLORENCE

RICHARDSON, HUMPHREY
GALL, MICHAEL

RICHARTZ, W.E.
BEBENBURG, WALTER ERICH v

RICHES, PHYLLIS
SUTTON, PHYLLIS MARY

RICHLER, JOHN
BEKESSY, JANOS

RICHMOND, AL
RICHMAN, AL

RICHMOND, CLARE
MALES, CAROLYN
TITCHENER, LOUISE

RICHMOND, DONALD
DANEHY, DONALD

RICHMOND, E.J.
RICHMOND, E. JOHNSON

RICHMOND, FIONA
HARRISON, JULIA

RICHMOND, GEORGE
BRISTER, RICHARD
SAMWAYS, GEORGE R.

RICHMOND, GRACE
MARSH, JOHN

RICHMOND, HUGH
YOUNG, GORDON [RAY]

RICHMOND, MARY
LINDSAY, KATHLEEN

RICHMOND, ROD
GLUT, DONALD F.

RICHMOND, ROE
RICHMOND, ROALDUS F.

RICHMOND, WILLIAM
FELL, WILLIAM RICHMOND

RICHTER, ANDREAS IGEL
RICHTER, ALFRED

RICHTER, EUGENE
RICHTER, EUGEN

RICHTER, HANNES
ANDREAS-DRANERT, PETER W.

RICHTER, HELGA
JUNIKE, ROLF

RICHTER, JOSEFINE
BOHNE, JOSEFINE

RICHTER, VALENTIN
PICK, ROBERT

RICHTER, VERNON
HUTCHCROFT, VERA

RICKARD, COLE
BARRETT, GEOFFREY JOHN

RICKARD, JESSIE LOUISA
RICKARD, MRS. VICTOR

RICKERT, CORINE HOLT
SAWYER, CORINE HOLT

RIDDELL, JOHN
FORD, COREY

RIDDELL, MRS. J.H.
RIDDELL, CHARLOTTE ELIZ.

RIDEAMUS
OLIVEN, FRITZ

RIDER, BERT
LACHER, HERBERT E.

RIDER, BRETT
GOODEN, ARTHUR HENRY

RIDER, ELISE B.
DE GUISE, ELIZABETH MARY

RIDER, J.W.
STEVENS, SHANE

RIDER, JANE
LYONS, LUELLA B.

RIDER, SAMANTHA
RUHEN, CARL

RIDGEWAY, ALGERNON
WOOD, ANNA COGSWELL

RIDGEWAY, JASON
MARLOWE, STEPHEN

RIDGWAY, JIM
RIDGWAY, JAMES M.

RIDING, LAURA
GOTTSCHALK, LAURA RIDING
REICHENTHAL, LAURA

RIDLEY, NAT JR.
STRATEMEYER, EDWARD

RIDLON, MARCI[A]
BALTERMAN, MARCIA R.

RIED, CAROLIN
HEUERT, EVA

RIED, FRANZISKA
GREITHER, MARGIT

RIEFE, A.R.
RIEFE, ALAN

RIEFE, BARBARA
RIEFE, ALAN

RIEGL, CARL
REINECKE, WALTER

RIENZI
TASCA, ANGELO

RIESEK, ROLAND
EILERS, KONRAD

RIFLE, JOHN
BRAND, KURT

RIFT, VALERIE
BARTLETT, MARIE

RIGAN, BRAD
NORWOOD, VICTOR [G.C.]

RIGG, H.K.
RIGG, HENRY H. KILBURN

RIGG, JENNIFER
SCOTT, GENEVIEVE

RIGHT, P.M.
BRANDT, PAUL MARTIN

RIGISEPP
CAMENZIND, JOSEF MARIA

RIIS, DAVID ALLEN
HORVITZ, LESLIE ALAN

RIKER, ANTHONY
REEDS, F. ANTON

RIKKI
DUCORNET, ERICA

RILEY, DICK
RILEY, RICHARD ANTHONY

RILEY, EUGENIA
ESSENMACHER, EUGENIA R.

RILEY, FRANK
RYHLICK, FRANK

RILEY, LEN
SULLIVAN, TONY

RILEY, TEX
CREASEY, JOHN

RIMMER, W.J.
ROWLAND, DONALD S.

RINALDINI, ANGIOLO
BATTISI, EUGENIO

RING, ADAM
REED, BLAIR

RING, BASIL
BRAUN, WILBUR

RING, DOUGLAS
PRATHER, RICHARD S.

RING, GEORG
VON IHERING, GEORG ALBR.

RING, LAURA
REICHENTHAL, LAURA

RING, THOMASINO
MORTON, TAMMYE RING

RINGDALH, MARK
LONGYEAR, BARRY B[ROOKES]

RINGELNATZ, JOACHIM
BOETTICHER, HANS

RINGER, F.A.
MEYER, FRIEDRICH-ALBERT

RINGMASTER
MENCKEN, HENRY LOUIS

RINGO, JOHNNY
BASNER, GERHARD
KEEVILL, HENRY J.

RINGOLD, CLAY
HOGAN, [ROBERT] RAY

RINGUET
PANNETON, PHILIPPE

RINGWOOD
PRICE, EDWIN WATHER

RINK, HERMANN
MIELKE, OTTO

RINPACHE
CHOGYAM TRUNGPA

RIORDAN, DAN
COOK, WILLIAM EVERETT

RIOS, TERE
VERSACE, MARIE TERESA R.

RIOTI, REX
STORY, JACK TREVOR

RIPLEY, ALVIN
KING, ALBERT

RIPLEY, JACK
WAINWRIGHT, JOHN [W]

RIPLEY, JULIA C.
DORR, JULIA CAROLINE

RIPLEY, KAREN
URHAUSEN, MARY K.

RIPOSTE, A.
MORDAUNT, EVELYN MAY

RIPY, MARGARET
DALEY, MARGARET K.R.

RIQ
ATWATER, RICHARD TUPPER

RISCO, MAX
MARTIN, THOMAS HECTOR

RISENHOOVER, C.C.
RISENHOOVER, CARMEL C.

RISER, HENRY
MACDONALD, JOHN D.

RISSMAN, ART
SUSSMAN, SUSAN

RISSMAN, SUSAN
SUSSMAN, SUSAN

RISSOW, NILS
NEHLS, RUDOLF

RISTARE, BO
LINDEN, ERIK HUGO E.

RITA
HUMPHREYS, ELIZA M.J.G.

RITCHIE, BILL
EDGAR, FRANK TERRELL R.

RITCHIE, CLAIRE
GIBBS, NORAH

RITCHIE, JACK
REITCI, JOHN GEORGE

RITCHIE, LEWIS
DE COSTA RITCHIE, LEWIS A

RITCHIE, RITA
REITCI, RITA KROHNE

RITCHIE, SIMON
FODDEN, SIMON R.

RITCHIE-CALDER, PETER R.
CALDER, PETER RITCHIE

RITER, D.
MILLER, BORIS I.

RITSON, JOHN
BABER, DOUGLAS GORDON

RITSOS, GIANNES
RITSOS, YANNIS

RITTER, FELIX
KRUESS, JAMES

RITTER, INA
JUNIKE, ROLF

RITTER, KURT
REIS, KURT

RITTER, LINA
POTYKA, LIN

RITTER, ROBERT
ALBRECHT, FRITZ

RITVALA, M.
WALTARI, MIKA [T]

RIVAS, GUILLERMO
PHILLIPS, HOWARD

RIVERA, DON
BERCKHAN, ORTRUD

RIVERA, PICO
ESSEX, HARRY
SAUL, OSCAR

RIVERE, ALEC
NUETZEL, CHARLES A.

RIVERINA
WINTER, C.H.

RIVERS, DEE
BRADLEY, MARION ZIMMER

RIVERS, DOROTHY
MACKESY, LEONORA

RIVERS, GAYLE
BROOKS, RAYMOND

RIVERS, GEORGIA
CLARK, MARJORIE

RIVERS, NIKKI
EDWIN, SHARON

RIVERS, RONDA
SVEINSSON, SOLVEIG

RIVERS, STU
NUETZEL, CHARLES A.

RIVERS, TEX
LEWINS, C.A.

RIVERSIDE, JOHN
HEINLEIN, ROBERT A.

RIVERTON, STEIN
ELVESTAD, SVEN CHRISTOFER

RIVES, AMELIA
TROUBETZKOI, PRINCESS

RIVES, LEIGH
SEWARD, WILLIAM W. JR.

RIVETT, CAROL
RIVETT, EDITH CAROLINE

RIVOLI, MARIO
KOUTOUKAS, H.M.

RIX, DONNA
ROWLAND, DONALD S.

RIXON, ANNIE [LOUISA]
STUDDERT, ANNIE LOUISE

RIZA, ALI
ORGA, IRFAN

ROACH, BRONWYN
FOLEY, ALAN

ROACH, PORTIA
TAKAJIAN, PORTIA

ROAN, PAUL
COLLINS, ANDREW J.

ROANE, PETER
CAMPBELL, C. SAMUEL

ROB ROY
MACGREGOR, JOHN

ROB-JON
JONAS, ROBERT

ROBARD, JACKSON
WALLMANN, JEFFREY M.

ROBAT
BUCKLAND, RAYMOND

ROBB, CHRISTINE
GOOLD, CHRISTINE R.

ROBB, JO ANN
ROSS, JO ANN

ROBB, JOHN
ROBSON, NORMAN

ROBB, T.N.
MACGREGOR, ROB

ROBBE, MICHELE
SEAMAN, LUCY

ROBBE, MICHELLE
SEAMAN, LUCY

ROBBINS, ANDREA
ALBANO, PETER

ROBBINS, BURCH
REITMAN, BOB

ROBBINS, C.A.
ROBBINS, CLARENCE AARON

ROBBINS, DOROTHY B.
ROBBINS-MOWRY, DOROTHY B.

ROBBINS, HAROLD
RUBIN, HAROLD

ROBBINS, HENRY
SLAVITT, DAVID RYTMAN

ROBBINS, JANE
ROBBINS-CARTER, JANE [B]

ROBBINS, JO ANN
ROSS, JO ANN

ROBBINS, KAY
HOOPER, [GLENDA] KAY

ROBBINS, RALEIGH
HAMILTON, CHARLES H.S.

ROBBINS, REBECCA
HACKING, ROBIN

ROBBINS, RUTH
SCHEIN, RUTH ROBBINS

ROBBINS, TOD
ROBBINS, CLARENCE AARON

ROBBINS, TOM
ROBBINS, THOMAS EUGENE

ROBBINS, TONY
PASHKO, STANLEY

ROBBINS, W. WAYNE
GREGORY, ORMOND

ROBBINS, WAYNE
COX, WILLIAM ROBERT

ROBBY, ALEX
KALLAHNE, GUNTHER

ROBE, ALEXANDER
CAP, FRIEDL[INDE]

ROBER, KARL
MARTIN, KARL

ROBERSON, JENNIFER
O'GREEN, JENNIFER M.R.

ROBERT
BEDFORD, JOHN T.

ROBERT, HENRY
PUKALLAS, HORST

ROBERT, LESLIE
FRANKS, NORMAN

ROBERT, MATI
ROBERT, MARIELIS

ROBERT, PAUL A.
ROUBICZEK, PAUL [ANTON]

ROBERTI, EDUARDO
SCHATZ, EDWARD R.

ROBERTS, ADRIAN
JOHNSTON, NORMA

ROBERTS, ANTHONY
WATNEY, JOHN B.

ROBERTS, DAN
ROSS, WILLIAM E. DANIEL

ROBERTS, DAVID
COX, JOHN ROBERTS

ROBERTS, DELL
FENDELL, BOB

ROBERTS, DESMOND
BEST, R. BRETON AMIS

ROBERTS, DON
ROSS, DON

ROBERTS, E.E.
ECKELS, ROBERT EDWARD

ROBERTS, EDD
BRINEY, ROBERT E.

ROBERTS, EDITH
ROBERTS, ELIZABETH K.

ROBERTS, FRED
HEYMANN, ROBERT
HEYMANN, ROBERT JR.

ROBERTS, GILLIAN
GREBER, JUDITH A.

ROBERTS, GRANT
PRONZINI, WILLIAM JOHN
WALLMANN, JEFFREY M.

ROBERTS, H.G.
BAJOG, GUNTHER

ROBERTS, HOLT
DRAPER, BEN

ROBERTS, I.M.
ROBERTS, IRENE W.

ROBERTS, IVOR
ROBERTS, IRENE W.

ROBERTS, J.R.
RANDISI, ROBERT J.

ROBERTS, JAMES HALL
DUNCAN, ROBERT LIPSCOMB

ROBERTS, JANE
BUTTS, JANE ROBERTS

ROBERTS, JIM
BATES, BARBARA S.

ROBERTS, JOE
SALZMAN, JOSEPH

ROBERTS, JOHN
PIERCE, JOHN ROBINSON
BINGLEY, DAVID ERNEST

ROBERTS, JULIAN
BARDENS, DENNIS [C]
JEFFRIES, RODERIC[GRAEME]

ROBERTS, K.
LAKE, KENNETH R[OBERT]

ROBERTS, KELSEY
POLLERO, RHONDA

ROBERTS, KEN
LAKE, KENNETH R[OBERT]

ROBERTS, KENNETH
DENT, LESTER

ROBERTS, KENNETH L.
LAKE, KENNETH R[OBERT]

ROBERTS, L.R.
JUNG, ROBERT

ROBERTS, LAWRENCE
FISH, ROBERT L.

ROBERTS, LEE
MARTIN, ROBERT [LEE]

ROBERTS, LEIGH
SMITH, LORA [ROBERTS]

ROBERTS, LILLIAN
WALLACH, IRA

ROBERTS, LIONEL
FANTHORPE, R.L.

ROBERTS, LISA
TURNER, ROBERT H.

ROBERTS, LOWELL
MOORE, ROBERT LOWELL

ROBERTS, MACLEAN
MACHLIN, MILTON

ROBERTS, MACLENNAN
TERRALL, ROBERT

ROBERTS, MARK
SCHATZLER-PERASINI, GEBH.

ROBERTS, MARSHALL
MARSH, DONALD

ROBERTS, MURRAY
GRAYDON, ROBERT MURRAY

ROBERTS, NORA
ROBERTSON, ELEANOR

ROBERTS, PAULA
HOHL, JOAN M.R.

ROBERTS, PEGGY
HANCHAR, PEGGY

ROBERTS, RINALDA
CUDLIPP, EDYTHE

ROBERTS, RINALDO
CROWCROFT, PETER

ROBERTS, ROY
BRINCHMANN, ALEXANDER

ROBERTS, SALLY
JONES, SALLY ROBERTS

ROBERTS, TERENCE
SANDERSON, IVAN TERENCE

ROBERTS, TOM
THOMAS, R. MURRAY

ROBERTS, TREV
TREVATHAN, ROBERT E.

ROBERTS, URSULA
MILES, SUSAN

ROBERTS, VIRGINIA
RATZLAFF, NELL MARR DEAN

ROBERTS, WAYNE
OVERHOLSER, WAYNE D.

ROBERTSON, ALEX
RATHBORNE, ST. GEORGE

ROBERTSON, AMY
COOPER, ROBERT ANDREW

ROBERTSON, DIRK R.
HARDT, HEINZ

ROBERTSON, E. ARNOT
ROBERTSON, EILEEN A.

ROBERTSON, ELLIS
ELLISON, HARLAN
SILVERBERG, ROBERT

ROBERTSON, ELSPETH
ELLISON, JOAN AUDREY

ROBERTSON, H. RICHARDSON
ROBERTSON, ETHEL FLORENCE

ROBERTSON, HELEN
EDMISTON, HELEN [J.M.]

ROBERTSON, JAMES
GEISLER, HANS
KNELLER, F.C.

ROBERTSON, JENNY
ROBERTSON, JENNIFER SIN.

ROBERTSON, JOHN
BENSINK, JOHN ROBERT
KNELLER, F.C.

ROBERTSON, MUIRHEAD
JOHNSON, HENRY

ROBERTSON, STEPHEN
WALKER, ROBERT WAYNE

ROBERTSON, VINCENT
WADE, THOMAS W.

ROBESON, KENNETH
BOGART, WILLIAM G.
DANIELS, NORMAN A.
DAVIS, HAROLD A.
DENT, LESTER
DONOVAN, LAURENCE
ERNST, PAUL FREDERICK
GOULART, RONALD JOSEPH
HATHWAY, ALAN
JOHNSON, WALTER RYERSON
MURRAY, WILLIAM P.
SALE, RICHARD [B]
TEPPERMAN, EMILE C.

ROBIE, ANNE A.
ROLFE, MARO ORLANDO

ROBIN
ROBERTS, ERIC

ROBIN, COMMODORE
HARDING, WILLIAM

ROBIN, KANAGAKI
BUNYO, NOZAKI

ROBINET, LEE
BENNETT, ROBERT AMES

ROBINS, ELIZABETH
PARKS, ELIZABETH ROBINS

ROBINS, FENTON
GAMMON, DAVID J.

ROBINS, G.M.
REYNOLDS, GERTRUDE M.R.

ROBINS, GINA
FEDDERSON, CONNIE

ROBINS, HAROLD
KANE, FRANCIS

ROBINS, PATRICIA
CLARK, PATRICIA D.R.
LORRIMER, CLAIRE

ROBINS, PATRICIA DENISE
ROBINS-CLARK, PATRICIA D.

ROBINS, ROLLO
ELLIS, EDWARD S.

ROBINS, SEELIN
ELLIS, EDWARD S.

ROBINSON
PHILSTRAND, RAGNAR

ROBINSON, AGNES MARY F.
DUCLAUX, AGNES MARY F.

ROBINSON, ALAN
SMITH, GEORGE H[ENRY]

ROBINSON, BUDD
ROBINSON, DAVID

ROBINSON, KATHLEEN
ROBINSON, CHAILLE HOWARD

ROBINSON, KAY
MAHN, TRAUTE

ROBINSON, LLOYD
SILVERBERG, ROBERT

ROBINSON, SHARI
MCGUIRE, LESLIE SARAH

ROBINSON, SPIDER
ROBINSON, PAUL

ROBINSON, SUZANNE
ROBINSON, LYNDA S.

ROBINSON, TED
ROBINSON, EDWIN MEADE

ROBINSON, VINCE
NEWTON, MICHAEL

ROBION, JEAN
LANIER, CLEMENT

ROBSON, DIRK
ROBINSON, DEREK

ROC, JOHN
NICHOLSON, DAVID

ROCAFUERTE, JOS MARIA
KAUTER, KURT

ROCCO, RODOLFO
FECHTNER, WOLFGANG

ROCHARD, HENRI
CHARLIER, ROGER H.

ROCHDALE, THOMAS
HIND[E], ALFRED

ROCHE, A.K.
ABISCH, ROSLYN KROOP
KAPLAN, BOCHE

ROCHE, ERIC
ROCHESTER, GEO[RGE] E.

ROCHE, HESTER
ROCHESTER, GEO[RGE] E.

ROCHE, JOHN
LE ROI, DAVID DE R.

ROCHE, TERRY
POOLE, PEGGY

ROCK, C.V.
ROECKEN, KURT WALTER

ROCK, DALBY
WEBB, ETHEL

ROCK, JAMES
PATTEN, CLINTON A.

ROCK, PAM
ANDREWS, BARBARA
HANSON, PAMELA

ROCK, PHILIP
FINK, R.M.

ROCK, RICHARD
MAINPRIZE, DON[ALD C.]

ROCKER, FERRY
ESCHNER, LENA
WORM, EBERHARD

ROCKET, CAPTAIN
MACHADO, PAULO SERGIO M.

ROCKFERN, DANIELLE
NOLAN, FREDERICK

ROCKINGHAM, MONTAGUE
NYE, NELSON C[ORAL]

ROCKLYNNE, ROSS
ROCKLIN, ROSS L.

ROCKWELL, KEITH
ROTHROCK, KENNETH

ROCKWELL, MATT
ROWLAND, DONALD S.

ROCKWOOD, HARRY
HALSEY, HARLAN PAGE
YOUNG, ERNEST A[VON]

ROCKWOOD, KARL
ROTHROCK, KENNETH

ROCKWOOD, ROY
GARIS, HOWARD R.
MCFARLANE, LESLIE CHARLES
STRATEMEYER, EDWARD

RODA RODA, ALEXANDER F.L.
ROSENFELD, ALEXANDER F.L.

RODA, ALEXANDER RODA
ROSENFELD, SANDOR FRIEDR.

RODDA, EMILY
ROWE, JENNIFER JUNE

RODDENBERRY, GENE
RODDENBERRY, EUGENE WES.

RODDY THE ROVER
DE BLACAM, HUGH [A]

RODEN, ROBERT
FOCKEN, HANS

RODGERS, FRANK
INFIELD, GLENN [B]

RODGERS, M.J.
JOHNSON, MARY

RODIN, ARNOLD
SROOG, ARNOLD

RODISSI
RINGGOLD, JACOB

RODMAN, EMERSON
ELLIS, EDWARD S.

RODMAN, ERIC
SILVERBERG, ROBERT

RODMAN, MAIA
WOJCIECHOWSKA, MAIA [T]

RODNEY, BOB
RODRIGO, ROBERT

RODNEY, BRYAN
EDGELEY, CYRIL

RODNEY, HENRY [HANK]
GIBSON, WALTER B.

RODNEY, M.
REDMAYNE, MARY PRIESTLEY

RODOS, HANS
STITZ-ULRICI, ROLF

ROE, CLEEVE
DALEY, VICTOR

ROE, DOROTHY
LEWIS, DOROTHY ROE

ROE, HARRY MASON
STRATEMEYER, EDWARD

ROE, M.S.
THOMSON, DAISY HICKS

ROE, OWEN
YATES, LIONEL [PEEL]

ROE, RICHARD
COWPER, FRANCIS

ROE, TIG
ROE, ERIC

ROEBUCK, C.M.
ROTHSTEIN, ANDREW

ROEDER, PAT
ELLISON, HARLAN

ROELVAAG, O.E.
ROELVAAG, OLE EDVART

ROERICH, WILLIAM
ROEHRICH, WILLIAM

ROESSEL-WAUGH, C.C.
WAUGH, CAROL-LYNN ROESSEL
WAUGH, CHARLES G.

ROESSNER, MICHAELA
ROESSNER-HERMAN, MICHAELA

ROEST, RUST
ELKAN, SOPHIE

ROFFMAN, JAN
SUMMERTON, MARGARET

ROFFMAN, SARA
HERSHMAN, MORRIS

ROGAN, DON
BUXTON, RAYMOND

ROGER, FRANK
DE CUYPER, FRANK ROGER

ROGER, NOELLE
PITTARD, HELENE [D]

ROGERS, ANNE
SERAILLIER, ANNE

ROGERS, BEN
PUGH, ROGER

ROGERS, DON
DEGLER, CLAUDE

ROGERS, DOUG
BRADBURY, RAY [DOUGLAS]

ROGERS, FLOYD
SPENCE, W. JOHN DUNCAN

ROGERS, GARET
MILLER, MARGARET ROGERS

ROGERS, GAYLE
BROWN, GAYLE ROGERS

ROGERS, HARRY, D.D.
EMANUEL, VICTOR ROUSSEAU

ROGERS, JOHN
ROGERS, THOMAS PERCY

ROGERS, KEITH
HARRIS, MARION ROSE

ROGERS, KERK
KNOWLTON, EDWARD ROGERS

ROGERS, LANNY
FISH, LEONARD G.

ROGERS, LEE
ROGERS, ROBERT LEE

ROGERS, LESLEY
GREEN, ROGER

ROGERS, MARYLYLE
LISLE, MARY

ROGERS, MELVA
GRAHAM, ROGER P.

ROGERS, MICK
GLUT, DONALD F.

ROGERS, PAT
PORGES, ARTHUR

ROGERS, PHILLIPS
IDELL, ALBERT E.

ROGERS, RACHEL
REDMON, LOIS

ROGERS, ROBERT
HAMILTON, CHARLES H.S.

ROGERS, STEVE
CLARKE, PERCY A.

ROGERS, W.G.
ROGERS, WILLIAM GARLAND

ROGERS, WADE
MADLEE, DOROTHY [H]

ROGERS, WAYNE
BITTNER, ARCHIBALD

ROGERSOHN, WILLIAM
HUGHES, DENNIS [TALBOT]

ROGGENDORF, UTA
BALZER, UTA

ROH, URSULA
RASSAERTS, URSULA

ROHAN, CRIENA
CASH, DEIRDRE

ROHAN, KODA
SHIGEYUKI, KODA

ROHAN, MIKE SCOTT
ROHAN, MICHAEL SCOTT

ROHDE, HEDWIG
OELZE, HEDWIG MARIE

ROHDEN, ERNST
EBEL, WILLI

ROHL, WOLF DETLEF
EISFELD, RAINER

ROHLFS, MRS. CHARLES
ROHLFS, ANNA KATHERINE

ROHMER, ELIZABETH SAX
WARD, ROSE ELIZABETH

ROHMER, SAX
WARD, ARTHUR HENRY S.

ROHRLICH-LEAVITT, RUBY
ROHRLICH, RUBY

ROJAN
ROJANKOVSKY, FEODOR S.

ROKA, TOKUTOMI
KENJIRO, TOKUTOMI

ROKESMITH, JOHN THAMES
COX, ARTHUR JEAN

ROKEYA, BEGUM
BEGUM, ROKEYA S, HOSSAIN

ROLAND, BETTY
MACLEAN, ELIZABETH

ROLAND, DAVID
FRANCES, STEPHEN D.

ROLAND, GEORGES
BAUDISCH, PAUL

ROLAND, HENRY
PUKALLAS, HORST

ROLAND, JOHN
OLIVER, JOHN RATHBONE

ROLAND, KENT
ROTHROCK, KENNETH

ROLAND, MARY
LEWIS, M. CHRISTIANNA M.

ROLAND, MICHELLE
FERRIS, ROSE MARIE

ROLAND, NIC
NICKEL, ROLAND

ROLAND, NICHOLAS
WALMSLEY, ARNOLD ROBERT

ROLAND, OTTO
LECHLE, OTTO

ROLAND, PETER
GOOCK, ROLAND

ROLAND, STEPHEN
ROOS, ELNA

ROLANT, RENE
FANTHORPE, R.L.
MANSFIELD, HARRY O.

ROLEINE, ROBERTE
ROLEINE, ROBERTA

ROLF, O.
WALGREN, OTTO ROLF

ROLFE, FATHER
ROLFE, FREDERICK [W]

ROLFE, SERGEANT
ROLFE, MARO ORLANDO

ROLKER, A.W.
ROLFE, MARO ORLANDO

ROLLS, ANTHONY
VULLIAMY, COLWYN EDWARD

ROLPH, C.H.
HEWITT, CECIL ROLPH

ROLVAAG, O.E.
MORCK, PAAL

ROLYAT, JANE
MCDOUGALL, E. JEAN

ROMAINE, DALLAS
GIBBS, NORAH

ROMAINE, LINTON
LEE, [REV] ALBERT

ROMAINES, JULES
FARIGOULE, LOUIS

ROMAINS, JULES
FARIGOULE, LOUIS

ROMAN, DANIEL
ROMANOW, DANIEL DAVID

ROMAN, FRIEDRICH
ROSCHMANN, KURT

ROMAN, PETER
RAMAGE, BRUCE

ROMAN, VIC
DI LORENZO, EDWARD

ROMAN, WILLIAM
WILLS, GARY ANTHONY A.

ROMANO, CLARE
ROSS, CLARE ROMANO

ROMANO, DON
EIDEN, PAUL
NIXON, ALLAN
TURNER, ROBERT H.

ROMANO, MIGUEL
OLIVEROS TOVAR, MIGUEL

ROMANO, PAOLO
ALATRI, PAOLO

ROMANONES, COUNTESS OF
DE QUINTANILLA, MARIA A.

ROMANY
EVENS, GEORGE BRAMWELL

ROMAY, ROMAN
LAUSSERMAYER, ROMAN

ROMBERG, HANS
SOBCZYK, RUDOLF

ROMBERG, JENNY
BRESSLAUER, HANS KARL

ROMBERG, NINA
ANDERSSON, NINA ROMBERG

ROME, ALGER
BIXBY, JEROME L.
BUDRYS, ALGIRDAS JONAS

ROME, ANTHONY
ALBERT, MARVIN H.

ROME, DAVID
BOUTLAND, DAVID

ROME, ELAINE
BARBIERI, ELAINE

ROMEN, ROBERT
APPEL, WALTER

ROMER, JONATHAN
MAYO, WILLIAM STARBUCK

ROMERO, GERRY
NEYLAND, JAMES [E]

ROMILUS, ARN
HOLLOWAY, BRIAN W.
HUGHES, DENNIS [TALBOT]

ROMLEY, DEREK
ROMLEY, FREDERICK J.

ROMMY, THOMAS
MAUERHARDT, ROLF

ROMNEY, A.B.
RAMBAUT, A. BEATRICE

ROMNEY, STEVE
BINGLEY, DAVID ERNEST

ROMUN, ISAK
BENNETT, GORDON

RONALD, E.B.
BARKER, RONALD [ERNEST]

RONCKENDORFF, EDDA
JANUS, EDDA [R]

RONDA, TRISTAN
LAGUERRE, ENRIQUE A.

RONECK, ELEONORE
BRUCKNER, ELEONORE

RONEY, RUTH ANNE
MCMULLEN, RUTH R.

RONKEN, HARRIET
LYNTON, HARRIET RONKEN

RONN, S.
AARONS, EDWARD S.

RONNBECK, ROLAND
SMEDS, BJORN

RONNS, EDWARD
AARONS, EDWARD S.

RONSMAN, M.M.
NOWAK, MARITTE

RONSON, L.F.
KNUTSEN, LALLI

RONSON, MARK
ALEXANDER, MARC [ELWARD]

ROOD, JACK
VAN HORN, DALE R.

ROOINEK
BOWLER, LOUIS P.

ROOKE, DENNIS
ROTHERRAY, GEOFFREY NEVL.

ROOME, DOUGLAS DEREK
EMPRINGHAM, DOUGLAS R.

ROOME, HOLDAR
MOORE, HAROLD WILLIAM

ROOP, CONNIE
ROOP, CONSTANCE BETZER

ROOS, HANS
MEISSNER, HANS-OTTO

ROOS, KELLEY
ROOS, AUDREY & WILLIAM

ROOS, REBECCA
OLJELUND, THEA

ROOSDORP, FRITS
SCHRODER, FREDERIK CORN.

ROOSEVELT, BLANCHE
MACCHETA, BLANCHE R.

ROOSEVELT, ELLIOTT
HARRINGTON, WILLIAM

ROOT, HENRY
DONALDSON, WILLIAM

ROOTE, MIKE
FLEISCHER, LEONORE

ROPS, DANIEL
PETIOT, HENRI JULES C.

ROPSHIN
SAVINKOV, BORIS VIKTOR.

ROPSHIN, V.
SAVINKOV, BORIS VIKTOR.

ROQUELAIRE, A.N.
RICE, ANNE

ROS, AMANDA MCKITTRICK
MCKITTRICK, ANNA MARGARET

ROSA
JEFFREY, ROSA VERTNER

ROSA, VICKI
RAWKINS, ADA

ROSAS, JULIO
PUIG Y DE LA PUENTE, FRAN

ROSCOE, CHARLES
ROWLAND, DONALD S.

ROSCOE, JANET
PRIOR, MOLLEY

ROSCOE, MIKE
ROSCOE, JOHN
RUSO, MICHAEL

ROSE, A.N. MOUNT
JAPP, ALEXANDER HAY

ROSE, ALLISON
ALLISON, RUTH
ROSE, JANE

ROSE, ANNA PERROT
WRIGHT, ANNA MARIA L.P.

ROSE, BILLY
ROSENBERG, WILLIAM S.

ROSE, FELICITAS
MOERSBERGER, ROSEFELICITA

ROSE, FLORELLA
CARLSON, VADA F.

ROSE, FRANCIS
FEARN, JOHN RUSSELL

ROSE, FRANK
FEARN, JOHN RUSSELL

ROSE, HILARY
MACKINNON, CHARLES ROY

ROSE, J.H.
ROSE, JOHN HOLLAND

ROSE, JEANNE
PINIANSKI, PATRICIA
SWEENEY, LINDA

ROSE, JENNIFER
WEBER, NANCY

ROSE, LAWRENCE F.
FEARN, JOHN RUSSELL

ROSE, MARCIA
KAMIEN, MARCIA
NOVAK, ROSE

ROSE, NANCY A.
SWEETLAND, NANCY A[NN]

ROSE, PHYLLIS
THOMPSON, PHYLLIS [HOGE]

ROSE, ROBERT
ROSE, IAN

ROSEDALE, VALERIE
HARRON, DON[ALD]

ROSEGGER, P.K.
ROSEGGER, PETRI KETTENFR.

ROSEGGER, PETER
KETTENFEIER, PETER
ROSEGGER, PETRI KETTENFR.

ROSEMOOR, PATRICIA
PINIANSKI, PATRICIA

ROSEN, HAIIM B.
ROSENRAUCH, HEINZ ERIC

ROSENBERG, GILL
KOSTLER, GISELA MARIA

ROSENFELD
CASTELLI, IGNAZ FRANZ

ROSENKO, MIKHAIL LENINEST
COLAKOVIC, RODOLJUB

ROSENTHAL, M.L.
ROSENTHAL, MACHA LOUIS

ROSENTHAL, RICHARD A.
RICHARDS, ALLEN

ROSENWALL, PH.
RAUSCHNIK, GOTTFRIED PET.

ROSMANITH, OLGA L.
WOOD, FERNEY

ROSMER, JEAN
DE BRAHM, JEANNE I.A.

ROSMOND, B.
ROSMOND, BABETTE

ROSNA
ROSMAN, ALICE GRANT

ROSNER, HANS
GRAF, JOHANN

ROSNY, J.H. [AINE]
BOEX-BOREL, JOSEPH

ROSNY, J.H. [JU]
BOEX-BOREL, JUSTIN

ROSS
MARTIN, VIOLET FLORENCE

ROSS, ADRIAN
ROPES, ARTHUR REED

ROSS, ALAN
WARWICK, ALAN ROSS

ROSS, ALAN O.
ROSENMEYER, ALAN OTTO

ROSS, ALBERT
GOLDSTEIN, ARTHUR D.
PORTER, LINN BOYD

ROSS, ALLEN V.
ROSKOLENKO, HARRY

ROSS, ANGUS
GIGGAL, KENNETH

ROSS, BARNABY
DANNAY, FREDERIC
LEE, MANFRED B.

ROSS, BERNARD L.
FOLLETT, KENNETH [MARTIN]

ROSS, BEVERLEE
COUILLARD, BEVERLEE

ROSS, BRADLEY
WILKES-HUNTER, RICHARD

ROSS, CARL
HORNWOOD, HARVEY

ROSS, CARLTON
BROOKS, EDWY SEARLES

ROSS, CATHERINE
BEATY, BETTY

ROSS, CLARISSA
ROSS, WILLIAM E. DANIEL

ROSS, COLIN
ROSKOLENKO, HARRY

ROSS, DALLAS
REYNOLDS, DALLAS MCCORD

ROSS, DAN
ROSS, WILLIAM E. DANIEL

ROSS, DANA
ROSS, WILLIAM E. DANIEL

ROSS, DANA FULLER
GERSON, NOEL B.
REASONER, JAMES M.

ROSS, DEBORAH
STOFFER, EDITH G.

ROSS, DIANA
DENNEY, DIANA

ROSS, DONALD
MACISAAC, FRED[ERIC JOHN]

ROSS, ERIN
TALLMAN, SHIRLEY BENNETT

ROSS, FRANK
EWINGS, MICHAEL
NORTHWAY, COLIN

ROSS, GENE
NEWTON, WILLIAM [SIMPSON]

ROSS, GEORGE
MORGAN-GRENVILLE, GERARD
ROSS, ISAAC

ROSS, H. WILLIAMSON
HOPE, WILLIAMSON

ROSS, HELAINE
DANIELS, DOROTHY
DANIELS, NORMAN A.

ROSS, HELENA
YOUNG, PATRICIA HELENA

ROSS, IAN
ROSSMAN, JOHN F.

ROSS, IVAN T.
ROSSNER, ROBERT

ROSS, J.H.
LAWRENCE, THOMAS EDWARD

ROSS, JAKE
HUBNER, HORST W.

ROSS, JAMES
BOUNDS, SYDNEY J.
DARRINGTON, HUGH
HALLIWELL, TONY

ROSS, JEAN
HEWSON, IRENE DALE

ROSS, JOE
ROSS, A. JOSEPH

ROSS, JOHN
JONES, RUDOLPH CLIFFORD
WINNINGTON, RICHARD

ROSS, JOHN HUME
LAWRENCE, THOMAS EDWARD

ROSS, JONATHAN
ROSSITER, JOHN

ROSS, JOSEPH
WROCZ, JOSEPH

ROSS, KATHERINE
WALTER, DOROTHY BLAKE

ROSS, KATHLEEN
STORY, ROSAMOND MARY

ROSS, LAURA
MINCIELI, ROSE LAURA

ROSS, LAURENCE
HYLAND, ANN

ROSS, LEAH
WEBB, MARY HAYDN

ROSS, LEONARD Q.
ROSTEN, LEO [CALVIN]

ROSS, MAGGIE
BERMANGE, MAURINE J.L.

ROSS, MALCOLM
ROSS-MACDONALD, MALCOLM J

ROSS, MARILYN
ROSS, DON
ROSS, WILLIAM E. DANIEL

ROSS, MARTIN
MARTIN, VIOLET FLORENCE

ROSS, MARY ADELAIDE EDEN
PHILLPOTTS, ADELAIDE

ROSS, MICHAEL D.H.
ROSENTHAL, MICHAEL D.H.

ROSS, MORGAN
MONROE, ELIZA

ROSS, NANCY
DEROIN, NANCY

ROSS, PATRICIA
WOOD, PATRICIA E.W.

ROSS, PAUL
AMIDON, WILLIAM VINCENT
CRAWFORD, WILLIAM [E]
FREEDLAND, NATHANIEL
STREIB, DANIEL T.

ROSS, PHILIP
ECK, PHILIP R.

ROSS, REBECCA
DONALDSON, DALE C.

ROSS, REGINA
MACKINTOSH, MAY

ROSS, RONALD
KLINGLER, HERMANN

ROSS, SUSAN
JAMISON, SUSAN RAU

ROSS, SUTHERLAND
CALLARD, THOMAS HENRY

ROSS, W.E. DAN
ROSS, WILLIAM E. DANIEL

ROSS, W.E.D.
ROSS, WILLIAM E. DANIEL

ROSS, WARD
FEARN, JOHN RUSSELL

ROSS, Z.H.
ROSS, Z. HELEN G.

ROSS-MACDONALD, MALCOLM J
MACDONALD, MALCOLM JOHN R

ROSSA, BARBA
ROTHENBURG, WALTER

ROSSE, IAN
STRAKER, J[OHN] F[OSTER]

ROSSE, SUSANNA
CONNOLLY, VIVIAN

ROSSEAU, HELENE
ROTHCHILD, DOROTHY

ROSSER, G.
GROSSER, KARL-HEINZ

ROSSETTI, MINERVA
ROWLAND, DONALD S.

ROSSI, A.
TASCA, ANGELO

ROSSI, BRUNO
HOFRICHTER, PAUL
LEVINSON, LEONARD [L]
MCCURTIN, PETER
REARDON, DAN
SMITH, RUSSELL
STEVENSON, JOHN

ROSSITER, IAN
WILLIAMSON, HUGH ROSS

ROSSITER, JANE
ROSS, DON
ROSS, WILLIAM E. DANIEL

ROSSITER, OSCAR
SKEELS, VERNON H.

ROSSITER, SAM
DELFS, RAINER

ROSSMAN, EVELYN
ROTHCHILD, SYLVIA

ROSSNER, MICHAELA
HERMAN, MICHAELA ROSSNER

ROSTAND, ROBERT
HOPKINS, ROBERT S.

ROSTOV, MARA
BUCKETTE, HILDAGARDE

ROSTOV, STEFAN
HUTSON, SHAUN

ROSTREVOR, GEORGE
HAMILTON, SIR GEORGE R.

ROSTRON, P.R.
HULBERT, JOAN MARGERY

ROSTRON, PRIMROSE
HULBERT, JOAN MARGERY

ROSZEL, RENEE
WILSON, RENEE

ROTARIUS
KEREKES, TIBOR

ROTH, ALEXANDER
DUNNER, JOSEPH

ROTH, JILLIAN
LADD, LINDA [KING]

ROTH, KAREN
SELLERS, CONNIE LESLIE

ROTH, MICHAEL
DORTENWALD, RUDOLF

ROTH, PAMELA
TOTH, PAMELA

ROTH, ROBERT
SELLERS, CONNIE LESLIE

ROTH, SUSANNE
GREITHER, MARGIT

ROTHBERG, GERT
JAHNE, GERTRUD

ROTHBERG, WINTERSET
ROETHKE, THEODORE

ROTHE, GRETA
KURTH, HANNS

ROTHEN, HANS
FEIGEL, HANS-DIETER

ROTHERY, AGNES EDWARDS
PRATT, AGNES ROTHERY

ROTHFELD, OTTO
ROTHFIELD, OTTO

ROTHMAN, CHUCK,
ROTHMAN, CHARLES WARREN

ROTHMAN, JUDITH
PETERS, MAUREEN

ROTHMAN, SARA
HERSHMAN, MORRIS

ROTHWELL, ANNIE
CHRISTIE, ANNIE ROTHWELL

ROTTER, ELIZABETH
WALKER, ELIZABETH NEFF

ROUNDTREE, OWEN
KITTREDGE, WILLIAM
KRAUZER, STEVEN M.

ROURKE, JAMES
HECKLEMANN, CHARLES N.
TRIMBLE, LOUIS P.

ROURKE, THOMAS
CLINTON, DANIEL JOSEPH

ROUSSEAU, J.J.
NIENABER, PETRUS JOHANNES

ROUSSEAU, V.
EMANUEL, VICTOR ROUSSEAU

ROUSSEAU, VICTOR
EMANUEL, VICTOR ROUSSEAU

ROUVEROL, JEAN
BUTLER, JEAN ROUVEROL

ROVALI, CARLO
REUBEL-CIANI, THEO

ROVER
GIBSON, ALFRED

ROVER, MAX
MURRAY, EDGAR JOYCE

ROVIN, ALEX
RUSSO, ALBERT

ROWAN, BARBARA
POLLOCK, IDA

ROWAN, DEIRDRE
WILLIAMS, DOROTHY JEANNE

ROWAN, HESTER
ROBINSON, SHEILA M.

ROWAN, M.M.
ROWAN, MARIE

ROWANS, VIRGINIA
TANNER, ED EVERETT III

ROWE, ALICE E.
ROWE, JOHN GABRIEL

ROWE, MARTIN
ZETTERLUND, GOSTA

ROWE, MELANIE
BROWNING, PAMELA

ROWE, STEPHEN
STARES, JOHN EDWARD S.

ROWEL, M.
THISTED, VALDEMAR ADOLPH

ROWLAND, GREY
ROWLAND-BROWN, LILIAN

ROWLAND, HENRY
GEORGE, CHARLES

ROWLAND, IRIS
ROBERTS, IRENE W.

ROWLANDS, EFFIE ADELAIDE
ALBANESI, EFFIE A. MARIA

ROWLANDS, LESLEY
ZUBER, MARY E.L.

ROWLANDS, PETER
LOVELL, MARK

ROWLEY, AMES DORRANCE
LOVECRAFT, H[OWARD] P.

ROWLEY, RICHARD
WILLIAMS, RICHARD V.

ROWLEY, THOMAS
PAUKER, JOHN

ROWSE, A.L.
ROWSE, ALFRED LESLIE

ROY, ARCHIE
ROY, ARCHIBALD EDMISTON

ROY, BRANDON
BARCLAY, FLORENCE L.C.

ROY, CLAUDE
ORLAND, CLAUDE

ROY, GORDON
WALLACE, HELEN

ROY, JULIEN
MACINNES, TOM

ROY, LIAM
SCARRY, PATRICIA [M]

ROY, PERCY GORDON
WOLFGANG, OTTO

ROY, RALPH
BADGER, JOSEPH E.

ROY, RAMALA PRATAP
BHOSALE, YESHWANTRAO

ROYAL, BRIAN JAMES
FOX, GARDNER F.

ROYAL, D.
DUBREUIL, ELIZABETH L.

ROYAL, DAN
BARRETT, GEOFFREY JOHN

ROYAL, RALPH
ABARBANELL, JACOB RALPH

ROYAL, ROSAMOND
HINES, JEANNE MCNEILL

ROYALL, VANESSA
HINKEMEYER, MICHAEL T.

ROYAN, ROY
BERGER, OTTO

ROYCE, E.R.
HUGHES, DENNIS [TALBOT]

ROYCE, KENNETH
GANDLEY, KENNETH ROYCE

ROYCROFT, JAMES
FRIEDRICHS, HORST

ROZAN, S.J.
ROSAN, SHIRA

RUBENS, BERNICE
NASSAUER, BERNICE RUBENS

RUBENSTEIN, ROBERTA
LARSON, ROBERTA RUBENSTN.

RUBICON
LUNN, SIR ARNOLD

RUBIN, HAROLD
KANE, FRANCIS

RUBIN, SEP
BARTH, OSKAR

RUBIOS, JOSE
MALONEY, F.J. TERENCE

RUBUNIN, LIONEL
BOHLIEN, GUENTHER

RUBY
KAVANAGH, ROSE

RUBY, B.F.
PRATT, [MURRAY] FLETCHER

RUCK, AMY ROBERTA
OLIVER, AMY ROBERTA

RUCK, BERTA
OLIVER, AMY ROBERTA

RUCKER, RUDY
RUCKER, RUDOLF VON BITTER

RUDD, MARGARET
NEWLIN, MARGARET

RUDD, STEELE
DAVIS, ARTHUR HOEY

RUDERSBERG, PETER
KRAMER, PETER

RUDHYAR, DANE
CHENNEVIERE, DANIEL

RUDI
COLAKOVIC, RODOLJUB

RUDLOFF, LEO
VON RUDLOFF, ALFRED FELIX

RUDOLPH, GEORG
EGER, RUDOLF

RUDOMIN, ESTHER
HAUTZIG, ESTHER

RUDOR, JACK
DORTENWALD, RUDOLF

RUEDI, NORMA PAUL
AINSWORTH, NORMA

RUELL, PATRICK
HILL, REGINALD [CHARLES]

RUF, ADAM
BRAUN, REINHOLD

RUFER, WILFRIED
BUHNEMANN, HERMANN

RUFFIAN, M.
HASEK, JAROSLAV

RUFFLES
TEGNER, HENRY

RUGE, SIMON
KUMMERT, WOLFGANG

RUHENI, MWANGI
MEIRAGURI, NICHOLAS

RUITER, JAN
REUTER, RALPH

RUKHI
ALIEV, AKPER

RUKUZA, E.W.
RUKUJZO, RON

RUMPLEFORESKIN
KRASSNER, PAUL

RUNARSSON, HADAR
ESSEN, AXEL ANDERS H.

RUNCIMAN, JOHN
ALDISS, BRIAN [WILSON]

RUNCIMAN, STEVEN
RUNCIMAN, JAMES C.S.

RUNE, BERT
FORSSBERG, LENNART

RUNE, K.G.
BRINGEMAN, GUSTAF

RUNYAN, JOHN
PALMER, BERNARD

RUNYON, DAMON
RUNYON, ALFRED DAMON

RUPPERT, CHESTER
GRAHAM, ROGER P.

RURIC, PETER
SIMS, GEORGE CARROL

RUSETSKIE, ALEXSEI S.
BURDELEV, ALEKSEI S.

RUSETT, O.X.
SCHIER, NORMA

RUSH, JOSHUA
PEARLSTEIN, HOWARD J.

RUSH, MALLORY
RUPPRECHT, OLIVIA

RUSH, PHILIP
HUNTER, IAN MCLELLAN
LARDNER, RINGGOLD W.

RUSH, ROBERT
BARBER, DULAN F.W.

RUSHING, PATRICK
COLLINS, MAX ALLAN

RUSHKIN, ARIANE
BATTERBURY, ARIANE R.

RUSHOLM, PETER
POWELL, ERIC

RUSHTON, CHARLES
SHORTT, CHARLES RUSHTON

RUSSEL, ALBERT
BIXBY, JEROME L.

RUSSEL, J. [RUSSEL]
BIXBY, JEROME L.

RUSSELL, ALAN K.
LEVENTHAL, LIONEL

RUSSELL, AMANDA
FELDMAN, ELLEN [BETTE]

RUSSELL, ARTHUR
GOODE, ARTHUR RUSSELL

RUSSELL, BERTRAM
HARDINGHAM, L.H.

RUSSELL, CHARLES
GIBSON, WALTER B.
KELLY, TERENCE

RUSSELL, CHARLOTTE
RATHJEN, CARL HENRY

RUSSELL, CLINTON
RATHJEN, CARL HENRY

RUSSELL, ERLE
WILDING, PHILIP

RUSSELL, G.W.E.
RUSSELL, GEORGE WILLIAM

RUSSELL, JAMES
HARKNETT, TERRY W.

RUSSELL, JIM
RUSSELL, JAMES

RUSSELL, JOHN
FEARN, JOHN RUSSELL

RUSSELL, LINDSAY
STONEHOUSE, PATRICIA ETHL

RUSSELL, LUCY MAY
CORYELL, JOHN RUSSELL

RUSSELL, NORMA
RUSSELL, HANORA MARY

RUSSELL, OSCAR GEORGE
RUSSELL, G. OSCAR

RUSSELL, PATRICK
SAMMIS, JOHN

RUSSELL, RALF
HANSELL, PER TORE

RUSSELL, RAY
BALFOUR, WILLIAM

RUSSELL, RAYMOND
BALFOUR, WILLIAM
FEARING, LILLIAN B.

RUSSELL, RENEE
HERMANN, NANCY A.

RUSSELL, REX
LANGDON, JOHN [F.C.]

RUSSELL, SARAH
LASKI, MARGHANITA
WRIGHT, MABEL OSGOOD

RUSSELL, SCOTT
JENNISON, JOHN WILLIAM

RUSSELL, SHANE
NORWOOD, VICTOR [G.C.]

RUSSELL, THOMAS
LASLETT, PETER

RUST, ALBERT OTTO
ANSCHUETZ, A.O.

RUSTAM, SULIEMAN
RUSTAMNASADE, SULIEMAN

RUSTESCH, GERHARD
KRAMER, KARL FRIEDRICH

RUSTICUS
JENKINS, MACGREGOR
MARTIN, BRIAN P[HILIP]

RUSTLER, ROBIN
MACLEAN, JOHN

RUSTYFACE
CUNNINGTON, CHARLES L.

RUTHERFORD, DOUGLAS
MCCONNELL, JAMES D.R.

RUTHERFORD, EDWARD
WINTLE, FRANK EDWARD

RUTHERFORD, MARK
WHITE, WILLIAM HALE

RUTHERFORD, WARD
RUTHERFORD, EDWARD JAMES

RUTHIN, MARGARET
CATHERALL, ARTHUR

RUTLAND, ARTHUR
ADCOCK, ARTHUR ST. JOHN

RUTLAND, DODGE
SINGLETON, BETTY

RUTLAND, ELIZABETH
FEARN, JOHN RUSSELL

RUTLEDGE, ADAM
REASONER, JAMES M.

RUTLEDGE, BRETT
PAUL, ELLIOT [H]

RUTLEDGE, DOM DENYS
RUTLEDGE, EDWARD WILLIAM

RUTLEDGE, MARYSE
HALE, MARIE LOUISE G.

RUTTE-DIEHN, ROSEMARIE
DIEHN, ROSMARIE

RUTTING, BARBBARA
VON EINSIEDEL, WALTRAUD I

RYAN, AL
GARTON, DURHAM KEITH

RYAN, ALLYSON
KICHLINE, LINDA

RYAN, BETSY
RYAN, ELIZABETH ANNE

RYAN, COURTNEY
WOOD, TONYA [TONIA]

RYAN, DETECTIVE PATRICK
PINKERTON, A. FRANK A.

RYAN, J.M.
MACDERMOTT, JOHN RICHARD

RYAN, JEANETTE MINES
MINES, JEANETTE MARIE

RYAN, JENNA
GOFF, JACQUELINE

RYAN, MARK
SILVERBERG, ROBERT

RYAN, NAN [NANCY]
RYAN, NAN HENDERSON

RYAN, RACHEL
BROWN, SANDRA [LYNN COX]

RYAN, SABRINA
MACDONALD, ELIZABETH

RYAN, SGT.
CORYELL, JOHN RUSSELL

RYAN, TEX
FEARN, JOHN RUSSELL

RYAN, TIM
DENT, LESTER

RYBOT, DORIS
PONSONBY, DORIS ALMON

RYCON
SAVERY, CONSTANCE W.

RYDELL, FORBES
FORBES, DELORIS STANTON
RYDELL, HELEN B.

RYDELL, SIERRA
ROLLE-BERG, RAMONA

RYDELL, WENDELL
RYDELL, WENDY

RYDEN, ARNOLD
FEARN, JOHN RUSSELL

RYDER, CLIFTON
WALLMANN, JEFFREY M.

RYDER, JAMES
PATTINSON, JAMES

RYDER, JOHN F.
GRUBER, FRANK

RYDER, JONATHAN
LUDLUM, ROBERT

RYDER, M.L.
RYDER, MICHAEL LAWSON

RYDER, THOM
HARVEY, JOHN [BARTON]

RYE, ANTHONY
YOUD, CHRISTOPHER [S]

RYERSON, JAMES PAUL
ROTHWEILER, PAUL R.

RYERSON, LOWELL
VAN ATTA, WINFRED L.

RYKER, MONTY G.
GIESA, WERNER K.

RYLAND, CLIVE
PRIESTLEY, CLIVE RYLAND

RYLAND, LEE
ARLANDSON, LEONE

RYLAND, TEX
FRANCES, STEPHEN D.

RYLE, RANDOLPH
PENTELOW, JOHN NIX

RYMAN, RAS
BROWN, JAMES D.

RYMANN, CHET
MULLER-REYMANN, WERNER

RYS, JAN
NERLICH, MARCEL

S, ELIZABETH VON
FREEMAN, GILLIAN

S-RINGI, KJELL
RINGI, KJELL ARNE S.

S., G.G.
SMALL, GEORGE

S., R. ESQ.
SICKLEMORE, RICHARD

S., SVEND OTTO
SOERENSEN, SVEND OTTO

S.A.M.
VESTAL, HERMAN BEESON

S.B.
WELLS, H.G.

S.H.M.
CHANDLER, A. BERTRAM

S.H.S.
SPENDER, STEPHEN

S.L.S.
STRACHEY, JOHN ST. LOE

S.M.D.
DAVIS, SARAH MATILDA

S.S.
SASSOON, SIEGFRIED [L]
WELLS, H.G.

S.V.
HALCOMB, RUTH

S.V.F.G.
FITZGERALD, SEYMOUR VESEY

SAAL, JOCELYN
SACHS, JUDITH

SAAR, LILLI
KOLB, ULRIKE

SABATTIS
GILL, T.M.

SABBAH, HASSAN I
BUTLER, ERNEST ALTON

SABE, QUIEN
BATES, HARRY ARTHUR

SABEN, GREGORY
BURKITT, FREDERICK EVELYN

SABER, LEE
SLESAR, HENRY

SABER, ROBERT O.
OZAKI, MILTON K.

SABIAD
WHITE, STANHOPE

SABIN, GREGORY
SABEN, GERTRUDE C.S.

SABIN, MARK
FOX, NORMAN A.

SABRE, DIRK
LAFFIN, JOHN [ALFRED C.]

SABU, FRANK
KONADU, SAMUEL ASARE

SABUROWA, IRINA
VON ROSENBERG, IRINA

SABUSO
PHILLIPS, IRVING W.

SACA BONA
GRIMSHAW, IVAN GEROULD

SACASTRU, MARTIN
BIOY-CASARES, ADOLFO

SACHS, JETTA
COLLIGNON, JETTA

SACHS, MAURICE
ETTINGHAUSEN, MAURICE

SACKERMAN, HENRY
KAHN, HAROLD S.

SACKETT, HARRY
DIXON, ANDREW

SACKETT, SUSAN
STERN, SUSAN

SACKVILLE-WEST, V.
SACKVILLE-WEST, VITA M.

SADAR, SAHIB
NIELSEN, ISAK

SADBALLS, JOHN
MATUSOW, HARVEY MARSHALL

SADDENS, ANNE
JOYCE, MARIANNE

SADDLER, ALLEN
RICHARDS, RONALD CHARLES

SADEH, PINHAS
FELDMAN, PINHAS

SADEN, MAURICE
WEISS, JOE

SADEUR, JAQUES
DE FOIGNY, GABRIEL

SADLEIR, MICHAEL
SADLER, M.T.H.

SADLER, GEOFF
SADLER, GEOFFREY WILLIS

SADLER, JEFF
SADLER, GEOFFREY WILLIS

SADLER, K. ALLEN
RICHARDS, RONALD CHARLES

SADLER, MARK
LYNDS, DENNIS

SAETONE
CAMUS, ALBERT

SAFIAN, JILL
JACOBS, JILL

SAFIRE, BILL
SAFIR, BILL

SAGAN, FRANCOISE
QUOIREZ, FRANCOISE

SAGE OF BALTIMORE
MENCKEN, HENRY LOUIS

SAGE, DANA
ALLVINE, GLENDON

SAGE, JESSIE BELL
BITTNER, F. ROSANNE

SAGE, JETT
JURGENS, JAMES

SAGE, JUNIPER
BROWN, MARGARET WISE
HURD, EDITH THATCHER

SAGE, RUE
JOHNSTONE, W.H.

SAGE, SHERYL
MCTAGGART, SHERYL
SAGE, PENNY

SAGITARIOUS
KATZIN, OLGA

SAGITTA
MACKAY, JOHN HENRY

SAGOLA, MARIO J.
KANE, HENRY

SAHARIEN
PICHLER, ERNST

SAHDAS, GERD
DOLL, HERBERT GERHARD

SAHLSTAEDT, BERTIL E.
HASSELBLATT, DIETER

SAHM, OSKAR T.
HAEFS, GISBERT

SAID, LAILI
ABOU, SAIF LAILI

SAIDA
LEMAIR, HENRIETTE WILLEB.

SAINT ANDE, MAGLIORE
MAGLIORE, CLEMENT

SAINT GIL, PHILIPPE
GILLET, PHILIPPE CLAUDE

SAINT LAURENT, CECIL
LAURENT-CELY, JACQUES

SAINT PATRICE
HARDEN-HICKEY, JAMES

SAINT ROBERT
VIARD, FELIX

SAINT-ALBAN, DOMINIQUE
TOURNIER, JACQUES

SAINT-AUBIN, HORACE DE
BALZAC, HONORE DE

SAINT-CLAIR, M.
VAN RYSSELBERGHE, MARIA

SAINT-CLAIRE, SYBIL
DE MARCO, JOANNE

SAINT-EDEN, DENNIS
FOSTER, DON

SAINT-HELIER, MONIQUE
BRIOD, BETTY [E]

SAINT-JOHN-PERSE
LEGER, [M.-R. A.] ALEXIS

SAINT-LAMBERT, PATRICK
DE LONGUEVILLE, M.THERESE

SAINT-LAURENT, CECIL
LAURENT-CELY, JACQUES

SAINT-PIERRE, LAURA
HENCKELL, JURGEN

SAINTE FOY
POTVIN, DEMASE

SAINTINE, XAVIER
BONIFACE, JOSEPH XAVIER

SAISON, JACQUES
SOMER, DERK

SAITO, MICHIKO
FUJIWARA, MICHIKO

SAKHARNOV, S.
SAKHARNOV, SVYATOSLAV

SAKI
MUNRO, HECTOR HUGH

SAKS, ELMER ELIOT
FAWCETT, FRANK DUBREZ

SALACIOUS, GRACE
WESTLAKE, DONALD [EDWIN]

SALADIN
ROSS, WILLIAM STEWART

SALAMANCA, D.F. SE
INGRAM, JOHN H.

SALAMANCA, DON FELIX DE
INGRAM, JOHN H.

SALAMATULLAH
ULLAH, SALAMAT

SALAVINA
SAVANE, VIRGILE

SALDONS, PER
OLNERS, ARNE

SALECK, JEAN-CHARLOT
BREITBACH, JOSEPH

SALESKI, BUFFY
SALESKI, KATHLEEN

SALIK, KONRAD
BRENNEISEN, WOLFGANG

SALISBURY, CAROLA
BUTTERWORTH, MICHAEL
JULIEN, [CAROLA] ISOBEL

SALISBURY, JOHN
CAUTE, DAVID

SALISBURY, ROBERT
HUNT, E. HOWARD

SALMONSON, JESSICA AMANDA
SALMONSON, JESSIE AMOS

SALOP, LYNNE
HAWES, LYNNE GUSIKOFF S.

SALSITZ, R.A.V.
VILOTT-SLASITZ, RHONDI A.

SALT, JOHN
NEVILLE, DEREK

SALT, JONATHAN
NEVILLE, DEREK

SALT, SARAH
HOBSON, CORALIE[VON WERN]

SALT, TITUS
EDMOND, JAMES

SALTAR THE MONGOL
WILLIAMSON, THAMES ROSS

SALTEN, FELIX
SALZMANN, FELIX
SALZMANN, SIEGMUND

SALTER, CEDRIC
KNIGHT, FRANCIS EDGAR

SALTER, MARGARET LENNOX
DONALDSON, MARGARET

SALTER, MARY D.
AINSWORTH, MARY D. SALTER

SALZER, L.E.
WILSON, LIONEL

SAMAROW, GREGOR
MEDING, OSKAR

SAMOILOFF, LOUISE CRIPPS
CRIPPS, LOUISE LILIAN

SAMOILOV, DAVID S.
KAUFMAN, DAVID S.

SAMPSON, RICHARD HENRY
HULL, RICHARD

SAMS, VEANIE
SAMS, JESSIE BENNETT

SAMTER, LINDA BANTEL
BANTEL, LINDA
FLEXNER, JAMES THOMAS

SAMUEL, ATHANASIUS
SAMUEL, YESHUE

SAMUELS, BACON
SAMUELS, PHILIP FRANCIS

SAMUELS, E.A.
TIFFANY, E.A.

SAMUELS, VICTOR
BANIS, VICTOR J[EROME]

SAN ANTONIO
DARD, FREDERIC

SANBORN, B.X.
BALLINGER, WILLIAM S.

SANCHEZ ALZADA, JUAN
JOSEPH, JAMES HERZ

SANCHEZ DE ALMODOVAR, B.T
DEL MONTE Y APONTE, DOMIN

SANCHEZ, FEDERICO
SEMPRUN, JORGE

SANCTION
JOHNSTON, REGINALD FLEMNG

SAND, DAVE
NEWTON, DWIGHT BENNETT

SAND, GEORGE
DUDEVANT, AMANDINE AURORE
TREVOR, ELLESTON

SAND, KIRSTIN
SANDBERG, KERSTIN

SAND, PETER
BOYCE, DAVID

SAND, WARREN B.
TREMAINE, F. ORLIN

SANDARS, HARRY
STANNARD, WILLIAM JOHN

SANDAVAL, JAIME
MARLOWE, DAN J.
NUSSBAUM, ALBERT F.

SANDBERG, BERENT
BERENT, MARK
SANDBERG, PETER LARS

SANDBERG, CHARLES
SANDBERG, CARL [AUGUST]

SANDBERG, CORINNA
APPEL, WALTER

SANDBURG, CHARLES A.
SANDBURG, CARL [AUGUST]

SANDBURG, HELGA
CRILE, HELGA SANDBURG

SANDEL, CORA
FABRICIUS, SARA

SANDER, FRANK
NEITSCH, OTTO

SANDER, SIMON
KLINGLER, HERMANN

SANDERS, BRETT
BARRETT, GEOFFREY JOHN
MCGAUGHY, DUDLEY DEAN

SANDERS, BRUCE
GRIBBLE, LEONARD [R]

SANDERS, BUCK
ADCOCK, THOMAS LARRY
FRENTZEN, JEFFREY

SANDERS, DAPHNE
RANDOLPH, GEORGIANNA ANN

SANDERS, DOROTHY LUCY
WALKER, LUCY

SANDERS, ED
SANDERS, JAMES EDWARD

SANDERS, GEORGE
BRACKETT, LEIGH
RANDOLPH, GEORGIANNA ANN

SANDERS, GLENDA
KACHELMEIER, GLENDA S.

SANDERS, JEANNE
RUNDLE, ANNE

SANDERS, KENT
WILKES-HUNTER, RICHARD

SANDERS, LIA [LISA]
JACKSON, ANGELA & SANDRA

SANDERS, MADELYN
DAY, DIANNE

SANDERS, PHIL E.
KOHR, DIETRICH

SANDERS, RICARDO
SANDERS, RICHARD

SANDERS, SUZETTE
HERDER, EDELTRAUT

SANDERS, W. FRANKLIN
WILLEFORD, CHARLES [RAY]

SANDERS, WINSTON P.
ANDERSON, POUL [W]

SANDERSON, JILL
BEAUMONT, HELEN

SANDERSON, MARGARET LOVE
SAMPSON, EMMA K. SPEED

SANDERSON, MR. DE
BIGNON, JEAN PAUL

SANDFORD, JANE
CUSHMAN, JANE

SANDFORD, JOHN
CAMP, JOHN

SANDHURST, B.G.
GREEN, CHARLES HENRY

SANDIFER, LINDA P.
SANDIFER, LINDA PROPHET

SANDISON, JANET
CAMERON, ELIZABETH JANE

SANDOIZ, ALBA
AE ALBINANA, ASUNCION I.

SANDON, J.D.
HARVEY, JOHN [BARTON]
WELLS, ANGUS

SANDOR, ALFRED
SANDWINA, ALFRED HEYMANN

SANDOR, JEAN
SIMENON, GEORGES [J.C]

SANDOVAL, ARMANDO
MORENO BERNET, MANUEL

SANDOW, GERD
PUHLE, JOACHIM

SANDOW, GERT
PUHLE, JOACHIM

SANDOW, J.B.
PUHLE, JOACHIM

SANDOWN, MARGARET
STONE, ENA MARGARET

SANDRE, THIERRY
MOULIE, CHARLES

SANDS, BEDWIN
RAFFALOVITCH, GEORGE

SANDS, DAVE
WALTON, BRYCE
POWELL, TALMAGE

SANDS, GLENDA
KACHELMEIER, GLENDA S.

SANDS, JOHN
HUTCHINSON, WILLIAM

SANDS, LEONARD
SELLERS, CONNIE LESLIE

SANDS, MARTIN
BURKE, JOHN [FREDERICK]

SANDY, STEPHEN
SANDYS, STEPHEN

SANDYS, ELSPETH
PURCHASE, ELSPETH [S]

SANDYS, GEORGE WINDLE
CRAWFURD, OSWALD J.F.

SANDYS, OLIVER
EVANS, MARGUERITE H.J.

SANDYS, PETE
JENNISON, JOHN WILLIAM
BOYCE, DAVID

SANFORD, JOHN B.
SHAPIRO, JULIAN L.

SANFORD, URSULA
CARDONA-HINE, ALVARO

SANGERSON, MARGARET LOVE
BEDFORD-JONES, HENRY

SANGODARE AKANJI, OMIDIJI
BEIER, ULLI

SANGSTER, ANN
SHENNAN, VICTORIA

SANSHI, TOKAI
SHIRO, SHIBA

SANSOM, JOHN
EDGAR, ALFRED
LYNDON, BARRE
SANGSTER, JIMMY

SANTA MARIA
POWELL-SMITH, VINCENT

SANTEE, COLLIER
FLEXNER, STUART BERG

SANTEE, WALT
KING, ALBERT

SANTESSON, H.S.
SANTESSON, HANS STEFAN

SANTIAGO, DANNY
JAMES, DANIEL LEWIS

SANTOS ZAPATA, EMILIANO
LLOP SELLARES, JUAN

SANTOS, ALFRED
TREMAINE, F. ORLIN

SANTOS, DOMINGO
DOMINGO, PEDRO

SANTREY, LOUIS
SABIN, LOUIS

SANZARA, RAHEL
BLESCHKE, JOHANNA

SAPIN, RUTH
HURWITZ, RUTH [SAPIN]

SAPPER
FAIRLIE, GERARD
MCNEILE, HERMAN CYRIL

SAPTE, W.
EDWARDS, ROBERT H.

SAR
PELADAN, JOSEPH [JOSEPHIN

SARA
BLAKE, SALLY MIRLISS
DE LA ROCHE ST ANDRE, ANN

SARA, [COL.] DELLE
AIKEN, ALBERT W.

SARAC, ROGER
CARAS, ROGER ANDREW

SARASIN, J.G.
SALMON, GERALDINE GORDON

SARASIN, JENNIFER
SACHS, JUDITH

SARASON, MARTIN
MEYERS, MARTIN

SARAZEN, NICHOLAS
COOPER, RICK
DAVIS, MARK
MARK, DAVIS

SARBAN
WALL, JOHN W.

SARBROW, CEPRE
BARROW, P.S.

SARD, ERASMUS
BLACKBURN, DOUGLAS

SARDOUX, LEON
WERNBERG, HJALMAR

SARDUCCI, GUIDO
NOVELLA, DON

SARG, TONY
SARG, ANTHONY FREDRICK

SARGEANT, ADELINE
SERGEANT, [E.F.] ADELINE

SARGENT, CRAIG
STACY, JAN

SARGENT, J.
FEARN, JOHN RUSSELL

SARGENT, JOAN
JENKINS, SARAH LUCILLE

SARGESON, FRANK
DAVEY, MORRIS FRANK

SARI
FLEUR, ANNE ELIZABETH

SARIS, RHET
GIESA, WERNER K.

SARMIENTO, CAMILO
ZENO GANDIA, MANUEL

SARNE, MICHAEL
PLUMMER, T. ARTHUR

SARR, KENNETH
REDDING, KENNETH SHIELS

SARTO, BEN
FAWCETT, FRANK DUBREZ
JORDAN, JAMES A.
NEWTON, WILLIAM [SIMPSON]
NORWOOD, VICTOR [G.C.]
PATERSON, A.J. BLAIR

SARTON, ELEANOR MARIE
SARTON, [ELEANOR] MAY

SARTORIUS, E.
SCHNEIDER, HEINRICH EMIL

SARVER, HANNAH
NIELSEN, JEAN SARVER

SASHUN, SIGMUND
SASSOON, SIEGFRIED [L]

SATANE, PAUL
HAILL, ROBERT GODFREY

SATANE, R.P.
HAILL, ROBERT GODFREY

SATINWOOD, DEBORAH
BUSSE, DEBRA

SATIVA, MARY
RUDAHL, SHARON

SATOMI
HIDEO, YAMANOUCHI

SATPREM
ENGINGER, BERNARD

SATTERFIELD, CHARLES
DEL REY, LESTER
POHL, FREDERIK

SATTERLY, WESTON
SUNNERS, WILLIAM

SATURN, SERGEANT
MERWIN, SAMUEL K. JR.
WEISINGER, MORT

SAUCIER, DONNA
SCHOMBERG, DONNA

SAUER, MURIEL S.
STAFFORD, MURIEL

SAUL, OSCAR
HALPERN, OSCAR SAUL

SAUNDERS, ABEL
POUND, EZRA LOOMIS

SAUNDERS, AMY ELIZABETH
TUCKER, AMY

SAUNDERS, ANNE
ALRED, MARGARET

SAUNDERS, CALEB
HEINLEIN, ROBERT A.

SAUNDERS, CARL MCK.
KETCHUM, PHILIP

SAUNDERS, DAVID
SONTUP, DANIEL

SAUNDERS, DIANA
COFFMAN, VIRGINIA [E]

SAUNDERS, IONE
COLE, MARGARET ALICE

SAUNDERS, JOHN
NICKSON, ARTHUR [THOMAS]

SAUNDERS, LAWRENCE
DAVIS, BURTON & CLARE O.

SAUNDERS, MACK
KETCHUM, PHILIP L.

SAUNDERS, MARSHALL
SAUNDERS, MARGARET MARSH.

SAUNDERS, RUSSELL
WILEY, CARL A.

SAUNDERS, WES
BOUNDS, SYDNEY J.

SAUNDERS, WILT
LYNCH, W.

SAUVAGE, FRANCK
HORN, MAURICE

SAUVAGE, FRANCOISE
HORN, MAURICE

SAVA, GEORGE
MILKOMANE, G. ALEXIS M.

SAVAGE, ADRIAN
SERANO, JOE

SAVAGE, ALAN
NICOLE, CHRISTOPHER ROBIN

SAVAGE, BLAKE
GOODWIN, HAROLD LELAND

SAVAGE, CHRISTINA
NEWCOMB, KERRY
SCHAEFER, FRANK

SAVAGE, DAVID
HOSSENT, HARRY

SAVAGE, IAN
GIGGAL, KENNETH

SAVAGE, J.J.
KEENAN, JAMES

SAVAGE, JOAN
WEISMAN, JOAN

SAVAGE, LES JR.
SAVAGE, LESLIE H. JR.

SAVAGE, LESLIE
DUFF, DOUGLAS VALDER

SAVAGE, MARK
GALLARDOS MUNOZ, JUAN

SAVAGE, MARY
DRESSER, MARY

SAVAGE, OSCAR
MONTAGUE, BRUCE [ALEX.]

SAVAGE, RICHARD
SINCLAIR-WOOD, R.
ROE, IVAN

SAVAGE, ROTH
KEHRER, DANIEL M[ARK]

SAVAGE, STEVE
GOODAVAGE, JOSEPH F.

SAVAGE, THOMAS
SAVAGE, LESLIE H. JR

SAVARIN
COURTINE, ROBERT

SAVERY, JEANNE
CASSTEVENS, JEANNE S.

SAVI, E.W.
SAVI, ETHEL WINIFRED B.

SAVIC, RANN
SINCLAIR-WOOD, R.

SAVINO, ALBERTO
DE CHIRICO, ANDREA

SAVIOZZI, ADRIANNA
MAZZA, ADRIANNA

SAVOY, MARK
TURNER, ROBERT H.

SAVOY, SUZANNE
STERN, SUSAN

SAWLEY, PETRA
MARSH, JOHN

SAWTELLE, WILLIAM CARTER
GRAHAM, ROGER P.

SAWYER
WIRTANEN, ATOS KASIMIR

SAWYER, JOHN
FOLEY, [CEDRIC] JOHN

SAWYER, LEE
SANS, MARTHA

SAWYER, MARK
GREENHOOD, [C] DAVID

SAWYER, MERYL
UNICKEL, MARTHA

SAWYER, RUTH
DURAND, MRS. ALBERT C.

SAX, ANDRE
KINNEY, JAMIE
SOITOS, STEPHEN

SAXBY, H.M.
SAXBY, [HENRY] MAURICE

SAXE, ISOBEL
RAYNER, CLAIRE B.

SAXO-NORMAN
YVELIN, ALBERT

SAXON
MATTHEWS, EDWIN J.

SAXON, ALEX
PRONZINI, WILLIAM JOHN

SAXON, ANTONIA
SACHS, JUDITH

SAXON, BILL
WALLMANN, JEFFREY M.

SAXON, CARL
DAY, A. GROVE

SAXON, GRANT TRACY
RAUCINA, THOMAS FRANK

SAXON, JOHN
GIFFORD, JAMES NOBLE
RUMBOLD-GIBBS, HENRY

SAXON, JOHN A.
BELLEM, ROBERT LESLIE

SAXON, PETER
BAKER, W.A. HOWARD
BOUNDS, SYDNEY J.
DOLPHIN, REGINALD C.
FRANCES, STEPHEN D.
MARTIN, THOMAS HECTOR
MCNEILLY, WILFRED G.
RICHARDS, ROSS

SAXON, RICHARD
MORRISSEY, JOSEPH LAWREN.

SAXON, VAN
GRANBECK, MARILYN
MOORE, ARTHUR

SAXON, VIN
HAYDOCK, RON

SAXON, WILLIAM
MAYLEAS, WILLIAM

SAXTON, JUDITH
TURNER, JUDY

SAYA, PETER
PETERSON, ROBERT E.

SAYER, WAL
SAYER, WALTER WILLIAM

SAYLER, H.L.
SAYLER, HARRY L.

SAYLES, TED
SAYLES, EDWIN BOOTH

SAYRE, GORDON
WOOLFOLK, JOSHUA PITTS

SAZANAMI, IWAYA
SUEO, IWAYA

SCALLY, M.A.
SCALLY, MARY PAULINE

SCALLY, [SIS]MARY ANTHONY
SCALLY, MARY PAULINE

SCAMPINGTON, DUKE OF
MURRAY, EUSTACE C.G.

SCANLON, C.K.M.
CHURCHILL, ED
DANIELS, NORMAN A.
DENT, LESTER
DONOVAN, LAURENCE
ELIOT, G.F.

SCANLON, C.K.M.
ELLIOT, GEORGE FIELDS
GRUBER, FRANK
KUTTNER, HENRY
MOORE, CATHERINE LUCILLE
WEBB, JEAN FRANCIS III
WINCHELL, PRENTICE

SCANLON, HERBERT
BLOCH, ROBERT [A]

SCANNELL, JAN
SCANNELL, JOHANNES PETRUS

SCAPEL, AESULAPIUS
BERDOE, EDWARD

SCARBOROUGH, CHUCK
SCARBOROUGH, CHARLES B.

SCARF, MAGGI
SCARF, MAGGIE

SCARFF, WILLIAM
BUDRYS, ALGIRDAS JONAS

SCARLET, WILL
MEEHAN, FRANCIS JOSEPH
REDMAN, WILLIAM XAVIER

SCARLETT, ROGER
BLAIR, DOROTHY
PAGE, EVELYN

SCARLETT, SUSAN
STREATFIELD, [MARY] NOEL

SCARPETTA, FRANK
HOFRICHER, PAUL
MCCURTIN, PETER
SMITH, GEORGE H[ARMON]
SMITH, RUSSELL

SCARPETTI, FRANK
FLETCHER, AARON

SCARPI, N.O.
BONDY, FRITZ

SCARROT, MICHAEL
FISHER, A. STANLEY T.

SCARRY, HUCK
SCARRY, RICHARD JR.

SCARRY, PATSY
SCARRY, PATRICIA [M]

SCHAAK, JEAN
HOCHRAIN, HELMUT

SCHAAKE, URSULA
HORBACH, URSULA [S]

SCHACHNER, NAT
SCHACHNER, NATHAN

SCHADEK, PETER
KALMUCZAK, ROLF

SCHAEFFER, ROBIN
MALZBERG, BARRY [N]

SCHAEFFNER, GEORG
KOLATSCHEWSKY, VALERIUS

SCHAELING, MARIANNE
AMFT, MARION JANET

SCHAFFER, E.
RING, LOTHAR

SCHAFFER, MICHEL
REIMESCH, FRITZ HEIN

SCHAIBLE, ELISABETH
DUNKELSBUHLER, ELISABETH

SCHALIN, ELISABETH
BOLINDER, JEAN

SCHALLES, LOTTE
BOTSCH, CHARLOTTE

SCHAMI, RAFIK
FADEL, SUHEIL

SCHARY, JILL
ROBINSON, JILL

SCHAW, RUTH
DRUMMOND, ALISON

SCHEEL, MARIANNE
GRAEF, MARIANNE

SCHEER, K.H.
SCHEER, KARL-HERBERT

SCHEER, MAXIMILLIAN
SCHLIEPER, WALTHER

SCHEERBART, PAUL
KUFER, BRUNO

SCHEFFLER, FRIEDEL
OEHLE, SOPHIE

SCHELL, BURNY
SCHELL, ROLFE F.

SCHELL, WALTER
PUSCHEL, WALTER

SCHELLE, WERNER
LEZYNSKI, WERNER J.

SCHELLE-NOETZEL, A.H.
BRONNEN, ARNOLT

SCHELLER, NIKOLAUS
FRANK, PETER

SCHENCK, BURKHARD
BIERSCHENCK, BURKHARD P.

SCHENCK, SIBYLLE
BECKMANN, MARIA [N]

SCHIAP
SCHIAPARELLI, ELSA

SCHIEFER, HERMANN
AYREN, ARMIN

SCHILLER, MAYER
SCHILLER, CRAIG

SCHILLER, ROSE LEIMAN
GOLDEMBERG, ROSE L.

SCHIOLDBRAND, GRAN
JOHNSSON, [K.O.] HARALD

SCHIPPER, ULRICH
ENGELKES, GUSTAV G.

SCHIRE
GARDNER, E.D.

SCHIRMANN, LI
GEBERT, LI

SCHIRMERHORN, CLINT
RIEMER, GEORGE

SCHLAGETER, JEANNE
DUNKY-SCHLAGETER, JOHANNA

SCHLEMIHL, PETER
THOMA, LUDWIG

SCHLINK, [MOTHER] BASILEA
SCHLINK, KLARA

SCHLITZ, PAUL M.
FEY, JEREMY

SCHLOSBERG, H.J.
MAY, HENRY JOHN

SCHLUTOW, W.
NEUMANN-REINHARD, LUCIE

SCHMIDT-ELLER, BERTA
KUNZELL, BERTA

SCHMIDTBONN, WILHELM
SCHMIDT, WILHELM

SCHMITZ, VIRGINIA
PASLEY, VIRGINIA SCHMITZ

SCHMUERZ, ADOLPH
VIAN, BORIS

SCHNEIDER, BASTIAN
BRESLAUER, HANS KARL

SCHNEIDER, J.
EISENPROBST, FERDINAND

SCHNEIDER, LAURIE
ADAMS, LAURIE

SCHOCK, GEORGE
LOOSE, KATHERINE R.

SCHOENER, KARL
MURRAY, WILLIAM P.

SCHOFIELD, PAUL
TUBB, E.C.

SCHOLASTICA, SISTER MARY
JENKINS, MARIE M.

SCHOLEFIELD, A.T.
SCHOLEFIELD, ALAN

SCHOLEFIELD, EDMUND O.
BUTTERWORTH, WILLIAM E.

SCHOLL, JERRY
SCHUTZ, JOSEPH W.

SCHOLTIS, AUGUST
BOGEN, ALEXANDER

SCHOLZ, FERDINAND
RAVEN, ACHIM

SCHONBECK, MARIANNE
KLEINER-SCHONBECK, MARIA.

SCHONENBERGER, ELISABETH
HASLER-SCHONENBERGER, E.

SCHONERMARK, J.
SCHADE-HADICKE, JOSEFINE

SCHORN, L.B.
PUHLE, JOACHIM

SCHOSTACK, RENATE
KUHNERT-SCHOSTACK, RENATE

SCHOTTE, PAULAS
ELBOGEN, PAUL

SCHRAUT, MAX
KABEL, WALTHER

SCHRECK, JOACHIM
BECHTLE-BECHTINGER, JOAC.

SCHREIBER, JUTTA
MEYER, JUTTA

SCHREIBER, RAINER
PIRWITZ, HORST

SCHREINER, LEE
SCHREINER, GEORGE F.

SCHROEDER, MARKUS
MUNSTER, CLEMENS

SCHROEDTER, BILLA
CWOJDZINSKA, SELMA

SCHUBIN, OSSIP
KIRSCHNER, ALOISIA

SCHUCK, F.H.P.
SCHUCK, FREDERICK H.P.

SCHUDER, ROSEMARIE
HIRSCH, ROSEMARIE [S]

SCHUGGE, M.E.
KABEL, WALTHER

SCHULTZ, CACILE
RITTER, VERA

SCHULTZE, PAUL
LANGER, ALFONS

SCHULZ, JOH.
KUROWSKI, FRANZ

SCHUMANN, EDZAR
EHLERS, EDITH

SCHURRER, UTE
ERB, UTE

SCHUYLER, JUDY
ESHBACH, LLOYD ARTHUR

SCHWAB, ANTON
LOB, WILHELM HERMANN

SCHWABE, WILLIAM
CASSIDY, WILLIAM L.

SCHWARTZ, S.
STARR, S[TEPN.] FREDERICK

SCHWARZ, ALEXANDRA
SCHWINDT, EDELTRAUT

SCHWARZ, ALICE
GARDOS, ALICE

SCHWARZ, BRUNO
MANN, GEORGE PAUL

SCHWARZ, ERICA
DEGLMANN, ERICA

SCHWARZ, JACK
SCHWARZ, JACOB

SCHWARZE, PETER
FALK, HERMANN

SCHWARZER, ANNALIESE
ESCHBACH, JOSEF

SCHWATTZ, MURIEL A.
ELIOT, T[HOMAS] S[TEARNS]

SCHWEIDLER, MARY
MEINHOLD, WILHEIM

SCHWEITZER, BYRD BAYLOR
BAYLOR, BYRD

SCHWEITZER, FRANK
LUKAS, JOSEF

SCHWEIZER, H.
BRANDECKER, WALTER G.

SCHWENK, KARL EMIL
BOHM, ALBERT

SCHWENN, GUNTHER
FRANZKE, GUNTHER

SCHWERTENBACH, WOLF
MEYER, PAUL E.

SCHWINDT, BARBARA
SCHWINDT, EDELTRAUT

SCIENCE INVESTIGATOR
SPECK, GERALD EUGENE

SCIPIO
WATSON, ADAM

SCLANDERS, DOORN
FEARN, JOHN RUSSELL
JENNISON, JOHN WILLIAM

SCOBEY, MARION
COOMBS, JOYCE

SCOFIELD, JONATHAN
BUSBEE, JAMES JR.
CAMERON, LOU
GRANGER, GEORGE A.
HEYMAN, EVAN LEE
LEVINSON, LEONARD [L]
MYERS, BARRY
RITHWEILER, DOROTHY
ROTHWEILER, PAUL R.
SCAFIDEL, JAMES R.
STREIB, DANIEL T.
TOOMBS, JOHN
VAN ZWIENEN, JOHN
VAUGHAN, ROBERT
WINSTEN, STEPHEN

SCOFIELD, LEE
SCHMIDT, RUTH

SCOLLAN, E.A.
O'GRADY, ELIZABETH ANNE

SCOLOPAX
GRANT, M.H.

SCORPIO
TUCKER, WILLIAM JOSEPH

SCOT, A.F.
JAPP, ALEXANDER HAY

SCOT, CHESMAN
BULMER, [HENRY] KENNETH

SCOT, MICHAEL
ROHAN, MICHAEL SCOTT
SCOTT, ALLAN

SCOT, NEIL
GRANT, LADY SYBIL

SCOT-BERNARD, P.
BERNARD, PATRICIA SCOT

SCOTLAND, JAY
JAKES, JOHN [WILLIAM]

SCOTT, A.G.
GRONMARK, SCOTT

SCOTT, ADRIENNE
WILLIAMS, LAURIE

SCOTT, AGNES NEILL
MUIR, WILHELMINA JOHNSTON

SCOTT, ALICIA
BAUMGARTNER, LISA

SCOTT, ALISTAIR
ALLEN, KENNETH S.

SCOTT, ALLAN
KAPPLER, HANNS-WALTER

SCOTT, AMANDA
SCOTT-DRENNAN, LYNNE

SCOTT, ANNJEANETTE
WRIGHT, SCOTT

SCOTT, ANTHONY
DRESSER, DAVIS

SCOTT, ANTONIA
RIGDON, CHARLES

SCOTT, ARABY
BROUSE, BARBARA

SCOTT, ARCHER G.
LARBALESTIER, PHILIP GEO.

SCOTT, BILL
SCOTT, WILLIAM NEVILLE

SCOTT, BRADFORD
CURRY, THOMAS ALBERT
SCOTT, ALEXANDER LESLIE

SCOTT, BRUCE
MCCARTNEY, R.J.

SCOTT, CAL
LAZENBY, NORMAN A.
JENNISON, JOHN WILLIAM

SCOTT, CASEY
KUBIS, PAT

SCOTT, CATHERINE
EHRENBERG, GOLDA

SCOTT, CHARLES
LEMKE, KARL

SCOTT, CHESMAN
BOLMER, [HENRY] KENNETH

SCOTT, CHURCHILL
JACKSON, JOSEPH [F.A]

SCOTT, CRAIG
MERWIN, SAMUEL K. JR.

SCOTT, DAN
BARKER, S. OMAR
STRATEMEYER, EDWARD

SCOTT, DANA
ROBERTSON, CONSTANCE N.

SCOTT, DEBORAH
SNIPES, DEBORAH

SCOTT, DENIS
SAUNDERS, THEODORE
MEANS, MARY

SCOTT, DIXON
SCOTT, WALTER [SIR]

SCOTT, DOUGLAS
THORPE, JOHN

SCOTT, ELIZABETH
CAPSTICK, ELIZABETH

SCOTT, ERNEST
GROVES, WILLIAM E.

SCOTT, EVELYN
DUNN, ELSIE

SCOTT, FRANCES V.
WING, FRANCES

SCOTT, GENEVIEVE
RIGG, JENNIFER

SCOTT, GRACE
CLARK, GAIL

SCOTT, GROVER
KING, ALBERT

SCOTT, HAMILTON
O'MANT, HEDLEY P.A.

SCOTT, HEDLEY
O'MANT, HEDLEY P.A.
YOUNG, FRED W.

SCOTT, HENRY C.
ARNOLD, WALTER

SCOTT, HENRY O.
FALK, HERMANN

SCOTT, J.W. ROBERTSON
SCOTT, JOHN W. ROBERTSON

SCOTT, JACK S.
ESCOTT, JONATHAN

SCOTT, JAMES
MCEWAN, MARCIA

SCOTT, JANE
MCELFRESH, ELIZABETH A.

SCOTT, JANEY
LEIGH, ROBERTA
LINDSAY, RACHEL

SCOTT, JEAN
MUIR, MARIE AGNES

SCOTT, JEFFREY
USHER, SHAUN

SCOTT, JEREMY
DICK, KAY

SCOTT, JOHN
NEARING, JOHN SCOTT

SCOTT, JOHN-PAUL
FARQUHAR, JESSE CARLTON

SCOTT, JULIA
O'BRIEN, MARY

SCOTT, KERRY
SWANSON, HAROLD NORLING

SCOTT, KRISTAL LEIGH
DEBORDE, SHERRY

SCOTT, LAUREN
FRENTZEN, JEFFREY

SCOTT, LEADER
BAXTER, LUCY C.

SCOTT, LES
SCOTT, ALEXANDER LESLIE

SCOTT, LESLIE
SCOTT, ALEXANDER LESLIE

SCOTT, LISA
SCOTT, DELORAS

SCOTT, MAITLAND
SCOTT, ROBERT T. MAITLAND

SCOTT, MALCOLM
KELLEY, THOMAS P.

SCOTT, MARCO
CHARLIER, ROGER H.

SCOTT, MARIANNE DE JAY
SNIPES, DEBORAH

SCOTT, MARTIN
GEHMAN, RICHARD BOYD

SCOTT, MAXWELL
STANIFORTH, JOHN WILLIAM

SCOTT, MELISSA
THIES, JOYCE ANN S.
RING, ELIZABETH

SCOTT, MILDRED
RAYER, FRANCIS G.

SCOTT, MILTON
MICHEL, MILTON SCOTT

SCOTT, MILWARD
RAYER, FRANCIS G.

SCOTT, NATALIE ANDERSON
SOKOLOFF, NATALIE B.

SCOTT, NICK
ERIKSSON, GUSTAF RUNE

SCOTT, NORFORD
ROWLAND, DONALD S.

SCOTT, O.R.
GOTTLIEBSEN, RALPH JOSEPH

SCOTT, P.T.
POAGE, SCOTT T.

SCOTT, R.T.M.
SCOTT, REGINALD T.M.
SCOTT, ROBERT T. MAITLAND

SCOTT, RACHEL
MULLAN, CELINA RIOS

SCOTT, RALPH
ATKINSON, GEORGE SCOTT

SCOTT, RICHARD
RENNART, RICHARD SCOTT

SCOTT, ROBIN
WILSON, ROBIN SCOTT

SCOTT, RONEY
GAULT, WILLIAM CAMPBELL

SCOTT, ROWENA
CRAGO, CLARA

SCOTT, SAMANTHA
HERMANN, NANCY A.

SCOTT, STUART
AITKEN, WILLIAM RUSSELL

SCOTT, TARN
SZOT, WALTER
TARNOR, PETER G.

SCOTT, TED
FRANCISKOWSKY, HANS GUNT.
HOFFMANNS, W.P.
PETERS, HERMANN
PUHLE, JOACHIM

SCOTT, THURSTON
LEITE, GEORGE THURSTON
SCOTT, JODY

SCOTT, TOM
HOBEIN, EUGEN

SCOTT, TONY
SCOTT, JOHN ANTHONY

SCOTT, VALERIE [X]
ROWLAND, DONALD S.

SCOTT, WALTER
CHESTNUTT, EDGAR B.

SCOTT, WARWICK
TREVOR, ELLESTON

SCOTT, WILL
SCOTT, W.H.

SCOTT, WILLIAM
REYBURN, WALLACE [M]

SCOTT, [CAPT.] RUSSELL
PEARSON, ALEC GEORGE

SCOTT, [MAJ.] S.S.
HARBAUGH, THOMAS C.

SCOTT-GILES, C.W.
SCOTT-GILES, CHARLES WIL.

SCOTT-JAMES, R.A.
SCOTT-JAMES, ROLFE ARNOLD

SCOTT-MORLEY, A.
OAKLEY, ERIC GILBERT

SCOTTI, ANNA
COATES, ANNA

SCOUT, TED
BRAND, KURT

SCOVEL, JUY
FONTANA, JEAN PIERRE

SCRAM, ARTHUR N.
GUILD, LEO

SCRIMGEOUR, G.J.
SCRIMGEOUR, GARY JAMES

SCROPE, MASON
MASON, ARTHUR CHARLES

SCRUTATOR
MEASOR, CHARLES PENNELL

SEA-LION
BENNETT, GEOFFREY MARTIN

SEA-WRACK
CREBBIN, EDWARD HORACE

SEABAUGH, CAROLYN
MATTHEWS, CAROLYN SEAB.

SEABORN, CAPT. ADAM
SYMMES, JOHN CLEVES

SEABRIGHT, IDRIS
ST. CLAIR, MARGARET

SEABRIGHT, JOHN
TUBB, E.C.

SEABROOK, JOHN
HUBBARD, L. RON

SEABROOKE, DAVID
BEDFORD-JONES, HENRY

SEABROOKE, JOHN PAUL
CHAPIN, ANNA ALICE
LUEHRMANN, ADELE

SEABURY, DON A.
RAYNAUD, OLIVIER

SEAFARER
BARKER, C. HEDLEY
RUSSELL, WILLIAM CLARK

SEAFORD, CAROLINE
COOK, MARJORIE GRANT

SEAFORTH
FOSTER, GEORGE C.
SKUES, GEORGE EDWARD

SEAFORTH, A. NELSON
CLARKE, GEORGE SYDENHAM

SEAGAR, JOAN
FEARN, JOHN RUSSELL

SEAGRAVE, BARBARA ANN G.
JACKSON, BARBARA A.G.S.

SEAL, BASIL
BARNES, JULIAN [P]

SEALE, SARA
MACPHERSON, MRS. A.D.L.

SEALIS, HATHERLY
FOSTER, CHARLES FREEMAN

SEALSFIELD, CHARLES
POSTL, KARL ANTON

SEAMARK
SMALL, AUSTIN J.

SEARCH, JOHN
MURSELL, ARTHUR

SEARCH-LIGHT
FRANK, WALDO DAVID

SEARCHLIGHT
EARDLEY-WILMOT, R. ADM

SEARE, NICHOLAS
WHITAKER, RODNEY W.

SEARIGHT, ELLEN
STUART, DORIS

SEARLS, HANK
SEARLS, HENRY HUNT JR.

SEARS, DEANE
RYWELL, MARTIN

SEATON, BERYL
PLATTS, BERYL

SEATTLE, FRANK
DUBREUIL, ELIZABETH L.

SEBASTIAAN, SR.
KLOOS, WILLEM JOHAN TEOD.

SEBASTIAN, ANNIE
SHAPIRO, KAREN

SEBASTIAN, JEAN
NEWSOME, ARDEN J.

SEBASTIAN, JOHN
HARRINGTON, CURTIS

SEBASTIAN, LEE
SILVERBERG, ROBERT

SEBASTIAN, MARGARET
GLADSTONE, ARTHUR M.

SEBASTIAN, MARY
GLADSTONE, ARTHUR M.

SEBASTIAN, TILL
BERENDT, KLAUS

SEBESTYEN, IGEN
SEBESTYEN, OUIDA

SEC
MANNES, MARYA

SECONDSIGHT, SOLOMON
MCHENRY, JAMES

SECREST, MERYLE
BEVERIDGE, MERYLE SECREST

SECRIST, KELLIHER
SECRIST, W.G.
KELLIHER, DAN T.

SECUNDUS, NOE
DIETL, FRANZ

SECUTOR
SLATER, JOHN HERBERT

SEDGES, JOHN
BUCK, PEARL [S]

SEDGEWICK, ANNE DOUGLAS
DE SELINCOURT, ANNE

SEDGEWICK, MODWENA
GLOVER, MODWENA

SEDOLIN, STURE
HALLSTROM, CARL

SEDYCH, ANDREI
ZWIBAK, JACQUES

SEEBORD, G.R.
SODERBURG, PERCY MEASDAY

SEED, JENNY
SEED, CECILE EUGENIE

SEEDO, SONIA
FUCHS, SONIA HUSID

SEEDY, ALFRED
ROWCROFT, CHARLES

SEEFELDER, ANDREAS
JOHN, FRIEDRICH LUDWIG

SEEKER, A.
EAGAN, FRANCES W.

SEEL, JOCHEN
ESSL, HERBERT

SEELEY, CHARLES SUMNER
MUNDAY, JOHN WILLIAM

SEELMANN, KURT E.
BIEGER, MARCEL

SEESTUM
GRAUTHOFF, FERDINAND H.

SEEVER, R.
REEVES, LAWRENCE F.

SEFERIS, GEORGE
SEFERIADES, GIORGOS [S]

SEFFENZOFF, PAUL
HASSLER, ADOLF OTTO

SEFTON, CATHERINE
WADDELL, MARTIN

SEGELCKE, JOHANN PETER
GUNTHER, HANS

SEGERCRANTZ, GOSTA
PALMCRANTZ, GOSTA

SEGHERS, ANNA
RADVANYI, NETTY REILING

SEGOVIA, PHIL
GONDA, ALEXANDER

SEGUNDO, BART
ROWLAND, DONALD S.

SEHLER, TOM
BURNS, REX RAOUL S.S.

SEIDMAN, SY
GIBSON, WALTER B.

SEIDNER, DIANE
SEIDE, DIANE

SEIFERT, ELIZABETH
GASPAROTTI, ELIZABETH S.

SEINFEL, RUTH
GOODE, RUTH

SELBER, MARTIN
MERBT, MARTIN

SELBY, CURT
PISERCHIA, DORIS

SELBY, ROBIN ANNE
FOX, GARDNER F.

SELCAMAN, GEORGE
MACHLIS, JOSEPH

SELDEN, GEORGE
THOMPSON, GEORGE SELDEN

SELDON-TRUSS, LESLIE
TRUSS, [LESLIE] SELDON

SELINKO, ANNEMARIE
KTISTIANSEN, ANNEMARIE S.

SELKIRK, JANE
CHAPMAN, JOHN STANTON H.
CHAPMAN, MARY HAMILTON

SELL, FRED
GIESEL, MANFRED-GERHARD

SELL, JOSEPH
HALEY, WILLIAM [JOHN]

SELL, PETER
LEHMANN, ARTHUR-HEINZ

SELLEN, GUSTAV
ALVENSLEBEN, KARL LUDWIG

SELLERS, CON
SELLERS, CONNIE LESLIE

SELLERS, CONNIE
SELLERS, CONNIE LESLIE

SELLERS, MARY
SELLERS, CONNIE LESLIE

SELLERS, NAOMI JOHN
FLACK, NAOMI JOHN W.

SELLINGS, ARTHUR
LEY, ARTHUR GORDON
LEY, ROBERT ARTHUR

SELLNER, ERIKA
KURTH, HANNS

SELMARK, GEORGE
TRUSS, [LESLIE] SELDON

SELMERGEDETH, HARALD
ORN, WERNER AUGUST

SELWYN
WATSON, SELWYN VICTOR

SELWYN, CHUCK
SELLERS, CONNIE LESLIE

SELWYN, FRANCIS
THOMAS, DONALD

SEMENOV, JULIAN
LYANDRES, YULIAN SEMENOV

SEMENOV, YULIAN
LYANDRES, YULIAN SEMENOV

SEMINOFF, VERA
AGUIRRE, MAGDALENA M.

SEMKIEV, VIRYANA
BISHOP, TETIANA KROITOR

SEMKIW, VIRLYANA
BISHOP, TETIANA KROITOR

SEMLOH
HOLMES, PEGGY

SEMPLE, GORDON
NEUBAUER, WILLIAM A.

SEMPLE, JESSE B.
HUGHES, [JAMES] LANGSTON

SEMYNOV, JULIAN
LYANDRES, YULIAN SEMENOV

SEMYONOV, YULIAN
LYANDRES, YULIAN SEMENOV

SEN, ELA
REID, ELA

SENACOURT, ROBERT
GEORGE, ROBERT ESMONDE G.

SENARENS, LU
SENARENS, LUIS P.

SENFTBAUER, E.
JESCHKE, WOLFGANG

SENNACHIE
WHYTE, DONALD

SENNETT, TED
SINITSKY, TED

SENTRY, JOHN A.
BUDRYS, ALGIRDAS JONAS

SEON, SIGGI
KALMUCZAK, ROLF

SEPHERIADES, GEORGIOS
SEFERIADES, GIORGOS [S]

SEPIA
HOLMVIK, OYVIND

SEPTAMA, ALDARA
REEVES, JUDSON

SEPTON, STANFORD
KASELLI, JOHAN EMANUEL

SEQUOIA, ANNA
SCHNEIDER, ANNA

SERAFIAN, MICHAEL
MARTIN, MALACHI

SERAFIMOVICH, ALEXANDER
POPOV, ALEXANDER SERAFIM.

SERAFIN, DAVID
MICHAEL, IAN

SERANNE, ANN
SMITH, MARGARET RUTH

SERANUS
HARRISON, SUSIE FRANCES

SERENY, GITTA
SERENYI, GITTA

SERGEANT SATURN
FRIEND, OSCAR J[EROME]

SERGHI, CELLA
SERGHI BOGDAN, CELLA

SERIEL, JEROME
VALLEE, JACQUES

SERJEANT, RICHARD
VAN ESSEN, W.

SERLING, ROD
DICKSON, GORDON R[UPERT]

SERNER, MAC
MELLVIG, CARL FOLKE S.

SERNICOLI, DAVIDE
TRENT, ANN

SERNINE, DANIEL
LORTIE, ALAIN

SERRA
TASCA, ANGELO

SERRA, DIANA
CARY, PEGGY-JEAN M.

SERRA, RALPH
ILLNER, WOLFGANG

SERRIFILE, F.O.O.
HOLMES, WILLIAM KERSLEY

SERRY, VICTOR
SEREBRIAKOFF, VICTOR

SERVANS
RICHTER-FRICH, OVRE

SERVATIUS, VICTOR
BERNARD, FRITS

SERVISS, GARRETT P.
ACKERMAN, FORREST J.

SESYLE, JOSLIN
HINE, SESYLE JOSLIN

SETH, ANDREW
PATTISON, ANDREW SETH P.

SETH, MARIE
LEXAU, JOAN M.

SETH-SMITH, ELSIE K.
MURRELL, ELSIE K.

SETHI, DENIS
SETHI, NARENDRA KUMARMES

SETON, ANYA
CHASE, ANYA SETON

SETON, ERNEST THOMPSON
THOMPSON, ERNEST EVAN S.

SETON, GRAHAM
HUTCHISON, GRAHAM SETON

SETTLE, EDITH
ANDREWS, WILLIAM L.

SEUBERLICH, H. GRIT
HEBSAKER, GRIT

SEUFFERT, MUIR
SEUFFERT, MURIEL

SEVEN, JOHN
MCEWAN, MARCIA

SEVERAC, PAUL
GONDA, ADOLPHE

SEVERANCE, FELIX
LAUMER, MARCH

SEVERINE
REMY, CAROLINE

SEVERN, BILL
SEVERN, WILLIAM IRVING

SEVERN, DAVID
UNWIN, DAVID STORR

SEVERN, DONALD
NOLAN, FREDERICK [W]

SEVERN, JEAN PAUL
MCEWAN, MARCIA

SEVERN, RICHARD
EBBS, ROBERT

SEVERNYAK, SERAFIM
SERAFIMOV, SERATIM N.

SEVERS, JEROME
WOOLEY, JOHN [S]

SEVERYANIN, IGOR
LOTAREV, IGOR VASILYEVICH

SEVREY, OPAL IRENE
MINER, OPAL IRENE F.S.

SEWARD, PROF. ALFRED FRAN
GIBSON, WALTER B.

SEWELL, ARTHUR
WHITSON, JOHN HARVEY

SEWELL, CAPT. ALBERT
EMANUEL, VICTOR ROUSSEAU

SEWER
MACIEJOWSKI, IGNACY

SEYDELL, MILDRED
SEYDEL, MILDRED [W]

SEYMOUR, A.J.
SEYMOUR, ARTHUR JAMES

SEYMOUR, ALAN
WRIGHT, SIDNEY FOWLER

SEYMOUR, ANA
BRACHO, MARY

SEYMOUR, EDWARD
HISCOCKS, RICHARD

SEYMOUR, HENRY
HARTMANN, HELMUT HENRY

SEYMOUR, JOHN
TURBAYNE, JOHN

SEYMOUR, MIRANDA
SINCLAIR, MIRANDA JANE

SEYMOUR, SAMANTHA
STEPHENS, BARBARA

SEYMOUR, WAYNE
HARTMANN, HELMUT HENRY

SEYTON, MARION
SAXON, GLADYS RELYEA

SHACKLETON, C.C.
ALDISS, BRIAN [WILSON]

SHACOCHIS, BOB
SHACOCHIS, ROBERT G.

SHADOW, MARK
SNEDDON, ROBERT W.

SHADOW, MIKE
EISELE, MARTIN
GIESA, WERNER K.
GRANDT, GUIDO
HARY, WILFRID A.
KUHNERT, JORG
ROSENBAUER, ROLAND
WEINLAND, MANFRED

SHADWELL, THOMAS
SULLIVAN, TIMOTHY ROBERT

SHALIMAR
HENDRY, FRANK COUTTS

SHALLOW, ROBERT
ATKINSON, FRANK

SHALTER, BRUNO
GUBERN RIBALTA, JORGE

SHAMGAR
SHAMIR, MOSHE

SHAN
MCMORDIE, JOHN ANDREW

SHAND, CAPTAIN
FLOYD, GILBERT

SHANE
RICHARDSON, EILEEN

SHANE, BART
ROWLAND, DONALD S.

SHANE, J.E.
JUHNKE, JOE

SHANE, JOHN
DURST, PAUL

SHANE, MARK
NORWOOD, VICTOR [G.C.]
OZAKI, MILTON K.

SHANE, NEVIS
SHEARER, SONIA M.

SHANE, RHONDO
NORWOOD, VICTOR [G.C.]

SHANE, SANDI
CANFIELD, SANDRA

SHANE, STEVE
GRIBBLE, LEONARD [R]

SHANE, SUSANNAH
ASHBROOK, HARRIETTE CORA

SHANE, V. BAXTER
NORWOOD, VICTOR [G.C.]

SHANE, VICTOR
NORWOOD, VICTOR [G.C.]

SHANE, YOUNG E.
JUHNKE, JOE

SHANER, CARL
MURRAY, WILLIAM P.

SHANN, RENEE
GAGE, CAROL

SHANNON, A. DONNELLY
AITKEN, A. DONNELLY

SHANNON, BESS
THOMPSON, ALLYN

SHANNON, BRAD
HANSON, VICTOR JOSEPH

SHANNON, CARL
HOGUE, WILBUR OWINGS

SHANNON, COLE
FALLON, M.

SHANNON, COLLEEN
JESKE, COLLEEN

SHANNON, DELL
LININGTON, [B] ELIZABETH

SHANNON, EVELYN
WARTSKI, MAUREEN A.C.

SHANNON, FRANK
SHINE, DENNIS FRANCIS J.

SHANNON, FRED
RUBEN, WILLIAM S.

SHANNON, ISBELL
ISBELL, SHANNON

SHANNON, LEONARD
SELLERS, CONNIE LESLIE

SHANNON, LYTLE
SHANNON, MARY JANE

SHANNON, MARK
GROSSMANN, HANS HUGO

SHANNON, MONICA
KATCHAMAKOFF, ATANAS

SHANNON, ROBERT
FECHTNER, WOLFGANG
WIEDER, ROBERT S.

SHANNON, STEVE
BOUMA, JOHANNES L.
GARST, DORIS SHANNON

SHANNON, TERRY
MERCER, JESSIE

SHANWA
HAARER, ALEC ERNEST

SHAPCOTT, REUBEN
WHITE, WILLIAM HALE

SHAPIRO, CORA
MAUCKNER, WALTER G.

SHAPIRO, ELIZABETH KLEIN
KLEIN, ELIZABETH

SHAPIRO, TERI
KOVACK, TERI S. [TERRY]

SHAPPIRO, HERBERT
JENKINS, WILLIAM FITZGER.

SHARD, DIANA
STEARNS, PETER N.

SHARK, GILL
GILLESE, JOHN PATRICK

SHARK, ROLF
KOIZAR, KARL HANS

SHARKEY, JACK
SHARKEY, JOHN MICHAEL

SHARMAN, ALISON
LEONARD, ALISON

SHARMAN, MIRIAM
BOLTON, MAISIE SHARMAN

SHARMAN, NICK
GRONMARK, SCOTT

SHARON, DONNA HAYE
SCHARLEMANN, DOROTHY H.

SHARON, ROSE
GROSSMAN, JOSEPH. JUDITH

SHARP, GUSTAVUS
RUSSELL, WILLIAM

SHARP, HELEN
PAINE, LAURAN BOSWORTH

SHARP, HOOKER
GROSSMANN, HANS HUGO

SHARP, JAMES
KINGHORN, ALEXANDER M.

SHARP, LUKE
BARR, ROBERT

SHARP, MARGERY
CASTLE, MARGERY SHARP

SHARP, SIDNEY
MAPES, VICTOR

SHARPE, C.
HOUGH, CLARA SHARPE

SHARPE, FRANKLIN
RICHARDSON, GLADWELL G.

SHARPE, JACK
RATHBORNE, ST. GEORGE

SHARPE, JON
KNOTT, WILLIAM CECIL JR.
MESSMANN, JON [JOHN]
RANDISI, ROBERT J.
WALLMANN, JEFFREY M.
BAVOUSETT, GLEN B[YRON]

SHARPE, LUCRETIA
BURGESS, MICHAEL ROY

SHARPE, RICHARD D.
SHAVER, RICHARD S.

SHARPE, SHANE E.
MEARES, LEONARD F.

SHATI, BENT EL
ABDEL-RAHMEN, AISHA

SHATTUCK, RICHARD
SHATTUCK, DORA [RICHARDS]

SHAUKI, AHMAD BEY
SHAUQI, AHMAD

SHAUKI, AHMED
SHAUQI, AHMAD

SHAUL, FRANK
ROWLAND, DONALD S.

SHAW, ADELAIDE
O'SHAUGHNESSY, MARJORIE

SHAW, ANDREW
BLOCK, LAWRENCE
COONS, WILLIAM R.
WESTLAKE, DONALD [EDWIN]

SHAW, BARTON
DRUMMOND, PATRICK HAMILTN

SHAW, BOB
SHAW, ROBERT

SHAW, BRIAN
HOLLOWAY, BRIAN W.
O'BRIEN, DAVID WRIGHT

SHAW, BRIAN [BRYAN]
FEARN, JOHN RUSSELL
GRIFFITHS, DAVID ARTHUR
TUBB, E.C.

SHAW, DAVID
GRIFFITHS, DAVID ARTHUR

SHAW, DAWN
SHAW, THELMA

SHAW, DICK
OPENSHAW, G.H.

SHAW, DUSTIN
OPENSHAW, G.H.

SHAW, ELIZABETH
PRANCE, JUNE E.

SHAW, FLORA LOUISA
LUGARD, FLORA LOUISA S.

SHAW, FLOYD
HAYES, MARRIJANE & JOSEPH

SHAW, GEORGE
BICKHAM, JACK [JOHN M.]

SHAW, IRENE
ROBERTS, IRENE W.

SHAW, JANE
EVANS, JEAN BELL SHAW

SHAW, JILL A.
KEELING, JILL ANNETTE

SHAW, JOSEPHINE
CLARKE, DOROTHY JOSEPHINE

SHAW, LARRY T.
SHAW, LAWRENCE TAYLOR

SHAW, LAURA
MOTHERAL, NANCY

SHAW, MARTIN
MARTIN, E. LE BRETON

SHAW, P.B.
SHAW, PATRICIA

SHAW, ROBERT SANDERS
MOSKOWITZ, SAM

SHAW, SUGARWOLF
SHAW, RUFUS JR.

SHAW, T.D.W.
SHAW, THELMA

SHAW, T.E.
LAWRENCE, THOMAS EDWARD

SHAW, THOMAS EDWARD
LAWRENCE, THOMAS EDWARD

SHAW, VIVIAN
SELDES, GILBERT VIVIAN

SHAW, WILENE
HARRISON, VIRGINIA M.

SHAWN, CLYDE B.
MEARES, LEONARD F.

SHAWN, FRANK S.
GOULART, RONALD JOSEPH

SHAY, LACEY
SCHODER, JUDITH
SHEBAR, SHARON S.

SHAYNE, GORDON
WINTER, BEVIS [PETER]

SHAYNE, MAGGIE
BENSEN, MARGARET

SHAYNE, NINA
GIBBS, NORAH

SHEA, TIMOTHY
KNIPE, ALDEN ARTHUR

SHEAFFER, LOUIS
SLUNG, LOUIS SHEAFFER

SHEARD, VIRNA
SHEARD, VIRGINIA [S]

SHEARER, JOHNNY
SMITH, WARREN B.

SHEARING, JOSEPH
LONG, GABRIELLE M.V.C.

SHEDLEY, ETHAN I.
BEIZER, BORIS

SHEEDY, ALLY
SHEEDY, ALEXANDRA ELIZAB.

SHEEHAN, PATRIC AUGUSTINE
O SIOCHAIN, P.A.

SHEFFER, H.R.
ABELS, HARRIETTE SHEFFER

SHEIL, M.P.
SHEIL, MATTHEW PHIPPS

SHELBOURNE, CECILY
EBEL, SUZANNE
GOODWIN, SUZANNE

SHELBY, BRIT
GRADY, JAMES [THOMAS]

SHELBY, COLE
KING, ALBERT

SHELBY, SUSAN
KINNICUTT, SUSAN SIBLEY

SHELDON, ALICE
SHELDON, ALICE H. BRADLEY

SHELDON, ANN
STRATEMEYER, EDWARD

SHELDON, C.M.
SHELDON, CHARLES MONROE

SHELDON, GEORGE E.
STAHL, LE ROY

SHELDON, JOHN
BLOCH, ROBERT [A]

SHELDON, LEE
LEE, WAYNE CYRIL

SHELDON, MRS. GEORGIE
DOWNS, SARAH ELIZABETH F.

SHELDON, RACCOONA
SHELDON, ALICE H. BRADLEY

SHELDON, ROY
BERRY, BRYAN
BRUNNER, JOHN [K.H.]
CAMPBELL, H[ERBERT] J.
HAY, OSWYN ROBERT T.
TUBB, E.C.

SHELDON, SCOTT
WALLMANN, JEFFREY M.

SHELDON, WALT
SHELDON, WALTER J.

SHELLEY, A. FISH
GERARD, JAMES WATSON

SHELLEY, ELIZABETH
CICHANTH, ELAINE
SCHAAL, ELIZABETH

SHELLEY, LILLIAN
KOPPEL, LILLIAN & SHELLEY

SHELLEY, PETER
DRESSER, DAVIS

SHELLEY, RICK
SHELLEY, RICHARD MICHAEL

SHELLEY, SUSAN
PERSHALL, MARY

SHELLY, FRANCES
WEES, FRANCIS SHELLEY

SHELLY, LAUREN
TEDDER, LORNA

SHELLY, NARY
GODWIN, MARY W.

SHELLY, PAUL
HUDSON, LAVASSA V.

SHELTON, BARKER
SHELTON, RICHARD BARKER

SHELTON, COLE
GREEN, ROGER

SHELTON, LINK
FRANCES, STEPHEN D.

SHELTON, LOLA
KLAUE, LOLA SHELTON

SHELTON, MICHAEL
DE COSQUEVILLE STACEY, P.

SHELTON, MILES
KNOX, CLEO ELDON

SHEM, SAMUEL
BERGMAN, STEPHEN JOSEPH

SHENLEY, JOHN D.
LIST, HORST

SHEPARD, FERN
STONEBRAKER, FLORENCE

SHEPARD, LESLIE ALBERT
JUHASZ, LESLIE ALBERT

SHEPARD, MARY
KNOX, [MARY] ELEANOR J.

SHEPARD, SAM
ROGERS, SAMUEL SHEPARD

SHEPARD, SHEP
WHITTINGTON, HARRY

SHEPARD, STRATTON
VAN DEURS, GEORGE

SHEPHERD, CONRAD
SCHAEF, CONRAD C.

SHEPHERD, DOROTHEA ALICE
PRATT, ELLA ANN

SHEPHERD, JOAN
BUCHANAN, BETTY JOAN

SHEPHERD, JOHN
BALLARD, W. TODHUNTER

SHEPHERD, MICHAEL
LUDLUM, ROBERT

SHEPHERD, NEAL
MORLAND, NIGEL

SHEPHERD, PERDITA
GRISANTE, MARY LEE

SHEPHERD, SHEP
WHITTINGTON, HARRY

SHEPPARD, DON
HAYDOCK, RON

SHEPPARD, ELI
YOUNG, MARTHA

SHEPPARD, SHEP
WHITTINGTON, HARRY

SHEPPARTON, PAUL
LUTZ, JOHN [T]

SHERARD, BRIAN
FRIEDRICHS, HORST

SHERASHEVSKI, BORIS
BROWN, JOHN J.

SHERATON, NEIL
SMITH, NORMAN EDWARD M.

SHERIDAN, ADORA
HONG, JANE FAY

SHERIDAN, ADORA [CONT]
PAVLIK, EVELYN MARIE

SHERIDAN, ELSIE
LEE, ELSIE

SHERIDAN, JANE
WINSLOW, PAULINE GLEN

SHERIDAN, JIM
ERICHSEN, UWE

SHERIDAN, JOHN
BLOCH, ROBERT [A]

SHERIDAN, LEE
LEE, ELSIE
SHERIDAN, MICHAEL

SHERIDAN, TERESA
RONALDS, MARY TERESA

SHERIDAN, THOMAS
GILLINGS, WALTER H.

SHERIDAN, WALT
GALLARDOS MUNOZ, JUAN

SHERIFF BEN
JEIER, THOMAS

SHERMAN, CHARLOTTE A.
SHERMAN, JORY [T]

SHERMAN, DELIA
SHERMAN, CORDELIA CAROLN.

SHERMAN, ELIZABETH
FRISKEY, MARGARET RICHARD

SHERMAN, GAIL
DERN, E. PEARL GADDIS

SHERMAN, GEORGE
MORETTI, UGO

SHERMAN, JOAN [JANE]
DERN, E. PEARL GADDIS

SHERMAN, NANCY
ROSENBERG, NANCY SHERMAN

SHERMAN, ROGER
PLUMMER, ROGER S.

SHERMAN, [PETER] MICHAEL
LOWNDES, ROBERT A.W.

SHERRIFF, R.C.
SHERRIFF, ROBERT CEDRIC

SHERRILL, KEVIN
KING, BRUCE ALVIN

SHERRILL, SUZANNE
WOODS, SHERYL ANN

SHERROD, JANE
SINGER, JANE SHERROD

SHERRY, GORDON
SHERIDAN, H.B.

SHERRY, OLIVER
LOBO, GEORGE EDMUND

SHERWIN, STERLING
HAGEN, JOHN MILTON

SHERWOOD, ELIZABETH
SPROULL, MARIE

SHERWOOD, HENRY
SEITZ, EBERHARD

SHERWOOD, JONATHAN
LONDON, JONATHAN [PAUL]

SHERWOOD, MICHAEL
WEATHERS, PHILIP JOSEPH

SHERWOOD, NELSON
BULMER, [HENRY] KENNETH

SHERWOOD, R.E.
SHERWOOD, ROBERT EMMET

SHERWOOD, ROBERT E.
SHERWOOD, ROBERT EMMET

SHERWOOD, VALERIE
HINES, JEANNE MCNEILL

SHESTOV, LEV
SCHWARZMANN, LEV ISAAKOV.

SHEVCHUK, TETIANA
BISHOP, TETIANA KROITOR

SHEW, ROLAND
FLYNN, MICHAEL F[RANCIS]

SHI, MUI
WEI, JI

SHIEL, M.P.
SHIEL, MATTHEW PHIPPS

SHIEL-MARTIN
OLD, PHYLLIS MURIEL ELIZ.

SHIELS, BARBARA
ADAMS, BARBARA JOHNSTON

SHIGERO TSUYNKI
KIRKUP, JAMES

SHIKI, MASAOKA
TSUNENORI, MASAOKA

SHINKLE, TEX
SHINKLE, JAMES D.

SHIPPEN, ZOE
VARNUM, ZOE SHIPPEN

SHIPPEY, TOM
SHIPPEY, THOMAS A.

SHIVE, THOMAS
EGAR, RAUL

SHOCK, JULIAN
WILLIAMSON, GERALD NEAL

SHOCKENHAMMER, WALTER
WELLS, H.G.

SHOCKER, DAN
ANTON, UWE
DUENSING, JURGEN
GRASMUCK, JURGEN
HARY, WILFRIED A.

SHOCKER, DAN [CONT]
LAUE, ALEXANDER
NAGULA, MICHAEL
ROSENBAUER, ROLAND

SHOLS, W.W.
SCHOLZ, WINFRIED

SHOMRONI, REUVEN
VON BLOCK, BELA [W]

SHONE, PATRIC
HANLEY, JAMES

SHOONOVER, WINSTON
SEVILLA, CHARLES

SHORE, ANNE
SANFORD, ANNETTE [S]

SHORE, FRANCINE
WARTSKI, MAUREEN A.C.

SHORE, JULIET
HAYE, JAN

SHORE, NORMAN
SMITH, NORMAN EDWARD M.

SHORE, PHILIPPA
HOLBECHE, PHILIPPA

SHORE, VALERY
VISER, LON

SHORR, ANNE
SCHMIDT, ANNA

SHORT, FRANCIS
HARRIS, MRS. HERBERT

SHORT, FREDERIC
FRIEDRICHS, HORST

SHORT, JACKSON
HOCHSTEIN, PETER

SHORT, LEW
GLIDDEN, FREDERICK D.

SHORT, LUKE
GLIDDEN, FREDERICK D.

SHORT, MALCOLM
DUPERRAULT, DOUG

SHORT, ROGER
ARKIN, ALAN [WOLF]
EYEN, TOM

SHORTER, CARL
SCHWALBERG, CAROL[YN E.S]

SHORTHOUSE, REBECCA
LEA, CONSTANCE NICHOLSON

SHOTT, ABEL
FORD, T.W.

SHOTWELL, RAY P.
CUMMINGS, RAY[MOND KING]

SHOYO
YUZO, TSUBOUCHI

SHOYO, TSUBOUCHI
YUZO, TSUBOUCHI

SHRAKE, BUD
SHRAKE, EDWIN

SHRAKE, BUDD
SHRAKE, EDWIN

SHREWSBURY, RALPH
JAMIESON, LELAND S.

SHRIVIDHATA
MISHA, VIDHATA

SHROEDER, BINETTE
NICKL, BARBARA ELISABETH

SHUBAEL
PURDY, JENNIE BOUTON

SHUBIK, IRENE
HAYLES, BRIAN

SHUFFLE, RUBE
HEATON, AUGUSTUS G.

SHULBERG, ALAN
WILKES-HUNTER, RICHARD

SHULL, PEG
SHULL, MARGARET ANNE W.

SHULMAN, NEIL M.D.
HIAASEN, CARL
JACOBS, HAL

SHUMAN, M.K.
SHUMAN, MALCOLM KARL

SHURA, MARY FRANCES
CRAIG, MARY FRANCIS S.

SHUSEI, TOKUDA
MATSUO, TOKUDA

SHUTE, NEVIL
NORWAY, NEVIL SHUTE

SHY, TIMOTHY
LEWIS, DOMINIC BEVAN W.
SEARLE, RONALD W.F.
WYNDHAM LEWIS, D.B.

SIBIRIAK
MAMIN, DMITRI N.

SIBLEY, LEE
LANDELLS, ANNE

SIBLEY, SUSAN
KINNICUTT, SUSAN SIBLEY

SIBSON, CAROLINE
DRACUP, ANGELA

SIDDON, BARBARA
BRADFORD, BARBARA
SIDDON, SALLY

SIDEN, CAPTAIN
VAIRASSE, DENIS

SIDETRACKED HOME EXECUTV.
JONES, PEGGY
YOUNG, PAM

SIDNEY, EDWARD WILLIAM
TUCKER, BEVERLEY

SIDNEY, FRANK
WARWICK, ALAN ROSS
WARWICK, FRANCIS ALISTAIR
WARWICK, SIDNEY

SIDNEY, MARGARET
LOTHROP, HARRIET M.

SIDNEY, NEILMA
GANTNER, NEILMA

SIDNEY, SAMUEL
SOLOMON, SAMUEL

SIDOBRE, ANDRE
SCHUMANN, MAURICE

SIDONS, C.
POSTL, KARL ANTON

SIEBENBRODT, DOROTHEE
FANGK, DOROTHEA

SIEBENPUNKT, AMADEUS
DOERRSCHUCK, HUBERT

SIECK, HEIDE
HEIDSIECK, HANS

SIEGEL, HELEN
SIEGL, HELEN

SIEGEL, STEVE
DUBINA, PETER

SIEGENTALER, PETER
HOFFMANN, HANS

SIEGMUND, HEINRICH
DEPTA, SIEGMUND

SIEGWART, ALFRED
BIENENGRABER, ALFRED

SIEVEKING, L. DE GIBERNE
SIEVEKING, LANCELOT DE G.

SIEVEKING, LANCE
SIEVEKING, LANCELOT DE G.

SIEVERT, JAN
ALEXANDER, DAVID
SYVERTSEN, RYDER [OTTO]
STACY, JAN

SIGFUSDOTTIR, GRETA
SIGFUSDOTTIR, LARA MARGAR

SILANGAN, MANUEL
YABES, LEOPOLDO Y.

SILAS
MCCAY, WINSOR

SILBER, DIANA
HENSTALL, DIANA

SILBERMAN, DAVID
HEIDEN, KANRAD

SILENT, WILLIAM T.
JACKSON, JOHN W.

SILESIUS, EDUARD
VON BADENFELD, EDUARD

SILINGSBY, MAURICE
URNER, NATHAN DANE

SILK, STAFFORD
COTTON, LESTER

SILL, PETER
SCHAFER, MAX

SILLER, HILDA
VAN SILLER, HILDA

SILLER, VAN
VAN SILLER, HILDA

SILLS, JENNIFER
LEWIS, STEPHEN

SILLY, E.S.
KRAUS, [HERMAN] ROBERT

SILONE, IGNAZIO
TRANQUILLI, SECONDO

SILURIENSIS, LEOLINUS
JONES, ARTHUR LLEWELLYN

SILVA, BEN
HELGATH, FRANC

SILVA, JOSEPH
GOULART, RONALD JOSEPH

SILVANUS, P.W.
STRASSER, TODD

SILVE, CLAUDE
DE LA FOREST-DIVONNE, P.

SILVER, NICHOLAS
FAUST, FREDERICK S.

SILVER, PAT
CARLETON, BARBARA

SILVER, RICHARD
BULMER, [HENRY] KENNETH

SILVER, RUTH
CHEW, RUTH

SILVERBIRD, CORD
CLINGAN, C.C.

SILVERLEAF
LLOYD, JESSIE GEORGINA

SILVERLOCK, ANNE
TITCHENER, LOUISE

SILVERWOOD, JANE
TITCHENER, LOUISE

SILVESTER, CLAUS
DORNER, CLAUS S.

SILVESTER, FRANK
BINGLEY, DAVID ERNEST

SILVESTRE, DINO
BIRON, GEORG

SILVONIUS, A.J.
WILSON, ANDREW J.

SIM, GEORGES
SIMENON, GEORGES [J.C]

SIMA, CARIS
MOUNTCASTLE, CLARA H.

SIMALO
LOINGER, SILVIA MARY

SIMBEAUX, L.L.
SELLERS, CONNIE LESLIE

SIMEON, SCOTT
BROWN, EDWIN SCOTT

SIMMON, KENNETH
GOLDGRABER, KENNETH

SIMMONDS, MIKE
SIMMONDS, MICHAEL CHARLES

SIMMONS, BLAKE
WALLMANN, JEFFREY M.

SIMMONS, CATHERINE
DUNCAN, KATHLEEN

SIMMONS, DAWN LANGLEY
HALL, GORDON LANGLEY

SIMMONS, DEBORAH
SIEGENTHAL, DEBORAH

SIMMONS, KIM
DUNCAN, KATHLEEN

SIMMONS, MARK
FOSTER, BRAD
LANSDALE, JOE R.

SIMMONS, MARY KAY
FREED, MARY KAY S.

SIMMONS, PETER
PUNNETT, IVOR

SIMMONS, RAY
LLIRO OLIVE, JOSE MARIA

SIMMONS, SUZANNE
GUNTRUM, SUZANNE

SIMMONS, WM. MARK
SIMMONS, WILLIAM MARK

SIMMS, CHARLOTTE
CHIN, CHARFA
KIDDER, JANE

SIMMS, NORTON
LLOP SELLARES, JUAN

SIMMS, SUZANNE
GUNTRUM, SUZANNE

SIMON
BURFORD, ROGER D'ESTE
BLAKESTON, OSWELL

SIMON, ANGELA
MAHONEY, IRENE

SIMON, CHARLIE MAY
FLETCHER, CHARLIE MAY H.

SIMON, GEORGE
CARLSON, WADE

SIMON, IRVING
HAENSEL, HUBERT

SIMON, JO ANN
BRUCE, JOANNA H. CAMPBELL

SIMON, JOE
SIMON, JOSEPH H.

SIMON, KATHARINA
KRUSE, MAX

SIMON, KATJA
HAMANN, BARBEL

SIMON, MADELAINE
SIMON, MORRIS

SIMON, MINA LEWITON
LEWITON, MINA

SIMON, ROBERT
MUSTO, BARRY

SIMON, S.J.
SKIDELSKY, SIMON JASHA

SIMON, TED
JONES, DENNIS

SIMONE
PORCHE, PAULINE

SIMONE, MADAME
PORCHE, PAULINE

SIMONE, SONIA
SIMONE-ROSSNEY, SONIA

SIMONS, HENRY
MOORCOCK, MICHAEL

SIMONS, LES
GRANT, KATHRYN ANNE P.

SIMONS, ROGER
PUNNETT, IVOR & MARGARET

SIMONS, STUART
STANLEY, GEORGE EDWARD

SIMONSON, MARY JANE
WHEELER, MARY JANE

SIMPKIN
WEBB, ARTHUR PATTERSON

SIMPLE, PETER
HERBERT, JOHN
HOGG, MICHAEL
WELCH, COLIN
WHARTON, MICHAEL

SIMPLEX, SIMON
MIDDLETON, HENRY CLEMENT

SIMPSON, ALBERTA
BERCOVICI, ALFRED

SIMPSON, ALLEN
SIMPSON, JAMES ALLEN

SIMPSON, HARRIETTE
ARNOW, HARRIETTE [L]

SIMPSON, J.A.
SIMPSON, JAMES ALLEN

SIMPSON, LEW
ADAMS, NORMAN

SIMPSON, MAGGIE
MASTEN, MARGARET
POOL, SANDRA

SIMPSON, MARIA
CAHILL, FRANK

SIMPSON, PAMELA
SIMPSON, CARLA
WALLACE, PAMELA D.

SIMPSON, RONALD
TILLY, RONALD SUGDEN

SIMPSON, WARWICK
RIDGE, WILLIAM PETT

SIMS, D.N.
SIMS, DENISE NATALIE

SIMS, JOHN
HOPSON, WILLIAM L.

SIMS, LT. A.K.
WHITSON, JOHN HARVEY

SINBAD
DINGLE, A. EDWARD

SINBALDI, FOSCO
KACEWGARI, ROMAINE

SINBETH, LESLY
BENOIT, ALICE P.

SINCLAIR, ALASDAIR
CLYNE, DOUGLAS

SINCLAIR, ALBERTA
GRAZIA, THERESA

SINCLAIR, ANNA
MOFFATT, MRS. LEN

SINCLAIR, BOWER
RICHARDSON, GLADWELL G.

SINCLAIR, BROOKE
BROOKS, KANDIUS

SINCLAIR, CLOVER
GATER, DILYS

SINCLAIR, CYNTHIA
WARTSKI, MAUREEN A.C.

SINCLAIR, DENNIS
YATES, ALAN GEOFFREY

SINCLAIR, DUNCAN
DUNNETT, ALISTAIR M.

SINCLAIR, ELIZABETH
SMITH, MARGUERITE

SINCLAIR, EMIL
HESSE, HERMANN

SINCLAIR, GAVIN
MACARTHUR, D[AVID] WILSON

SINCLAIR, GRACE
WALLMANN, JEFFREY M.

SINCLAIR, GRANT
DRAGO, HARRY SINCLAIR

SINCLAIR, HEATHER
JOHNSTON, WILLIAM

SINCLAIR, HELENE
LEHR, HELENE

SINCLAIR, IAN
FOLEY, [CEDRIC] JOHN

SINCLAIR, JAMES
STAPLES, REGINALD THOMAS

SINCLAIR, JO
SEID, RUTH

SINCLAIR, KATHERINE
DIAL, JOAN MAVIS R.

SINCLAIR, MAY
SINCLAIR, MARY AMELIA

SINCLAIR, MICHAEL
SHEA, MICHAEL [S.M.]

SINCLAIR, OLGA
DANIELS, OLGA

SINCLAIR, OLIVIA
LANGFORD, SANDRA

SINCLAIR, PULIAN
SINCLAIR, MARY AMELIA

SINCLAIR, REBECCA
VIALL, PATRICIA F.

SINCLAIR, ROSE
SMITH, SUSAN VERNON M.

SINCLAIR, TRACY
SCHULTZ, JANET

SINDERBY, DONALD
STEPHENS, DONALD RYDER

SINGER, A.L.
LERANGIS, PETER

SINGER, ADAM
KARP, DAVID

SINGER, AMANDA
BROOKS, JANICE YOUNG

SINGER, BANT
SHAW, CHARLES

SINGER, BURNS
SINGER, JAMES HYMAN

SINGER, ERNEST
KRAPP, ERNST

SINGER, I.J.
SINGER, ISRAEL JOSHUA

SINGER, KURT
DEUTSCHER, ISSAC

SINGER, KURT D[EUTSCH]
DEUTSCHER, ISAAC

SINGER, PHYLIS
MORRISON, PHYLLIS

SINGER, SHELLEY
SINGER, ROCHELLE

SINGLETON, LEONARD
BATT, LEON

SINGMASTER, ELSIE
LEWARS, MRS. HAROLD

SINJIN
JOHN, ELIZABETH BEAMON

SINJOHN, JOHN
GALSWORTHY, JOHN

SINUSS, Z.
SKUJINS, ZIGMUNDS

SIOGVOLK, PAUL
MATHEWS, ALBERT

SION, MARI
JONES, ROBERT MAYNARD

SIR TOPAZ
AGATE, JAMES

SIRIN, V.
NABOKOV, V.V.

SIRIUS
MARTYN, EDWARD

SIROTA, MIKE
SIROTA, MICHAEL BARRY

SIRROM, WES
WEISS, MORRIS S.

SISE, ANNIE
REID, PHILLIPA

SISTER DORA
PATTISON, DOROTHY W.

SISTER MARY JEAN
DORCY, MARY JEAN

SISTER MARY THEODORE
HEGEMAN, MARY THEODORE

SITTY, BASIL
LAZENBY, NORMAN A.

SITZFLEISCH, VLADIMIR
SPIRER, HERBERT F.

SIU SIN FAR
EATON, EDITH

SIWAARMILL, H.P.
SHARP, WILLIAM

SIX, JUPP
BODENSTEDT, HANS

SIXT, PETER
MECKEL, EBERHARD

SIZEMORE, CHRIS COSTNER
SIZEMORE, CHRISTINE COST.

SJOBERG, ARNE
BRINKMANN, JURGEN

SKAFTE, KATRIN & ERIK
PETERZEN, ELISABETH

SKAGEN, KIKI
MUNSHI, KIKI SKAGEN

SKALD
CRAY, EDWARD

SKALDASPILLIR, SIGFRIOUR
BROXON, MILDRED DOWNEY

SKEEVER, JIM
HILL, JOHN ALEXANDER

SKELTON, C.L.
SKELTON, C. LISTER

SKENE, ANTHONY
PHILIPS, GEORGE NORMAN

SKETCHLEY, ARTHUR
ROSE, GEORGE

SKIMPOLE, HAROLD
HUNT, [J.H.] LEIGH

SKINFLINT, OBEDIAH
HARRIS, JOEL CHANDLER

SKINNER, AINSLEE
GOSLING, PAULA

SKINNER, ARNO
DOMBROWSKI, THEODOR

SKIPPER, BETTY
BARR, BETTY

SKITALETS
PETROV, STEPAN G.

SKOOG, MALTE
MOPP, MICHAEL

SKOOKUM CHUCK
CUMMING, ROBERT DAZIEL

SKORPIOS, ANTARES
BARLOW, JAMES WILLIAM

SKOTE, Z.
SKUJINS, ZIGMUNDS

SKRAN, UDO
LLOP SELLARES, JUAN

SKRATTHULT, SVEN I
KERFVE, AXEL

SKRINE, MARY NESTA
KEANE, MARY NESTA S.

SKRINE, MOLLY
KEANE, MARY NESTA S.

SKURDENIS, JULIEN V.
SKURDENIS-SMIRCICK, JULIN

SKY, FRANK
FRANCISKOWSKY, HANS GUNT.

SKY, KATHLEEN
GOLDIN, KATHLEEN MCKINNEY

SKYE, CHRISTINA
HELMER, ROBERTA

SLACK
PASSINGHAM, KENNETH

SLACK, SOLOMAN
MUIR, JOHN RAMSEY BRYCE

SLADE, BERNARD
NEWBOUND, BERNARD SLADE

SLADE, GURNEY
BARTLETT, STEPHEN

SLADE, JACK
APPEL, WALTER
BAJOG, GUNTHER
BALLARD, W. TODHUNTER
BECK, FLORIAN
BOCKL, MANFRED
DELFS, RAINER
DUENSING, JURGEN
ERICHSEN, UWE
FRIEDRICHS, HOLGER
FRIEDRICHS, HORST
GERMANO, PETER B.
HAAS, BENJAMIN LEOPOLD
HARTSCH, GERHART
HEBEL, PETER
HELGATH, FRANC
KUGLER, DIETMAR
MAUERHARDT, ROLF
MAURER, KURT
MCGAUGHY, DUDLEY DEAN
MICHAEL, ROLF
NEUBERT, HELMUT
PRIESS, KARL-HEINZ
RAHN, WOLFGANG
RELLERGERD, HELMUT
ROMHILD, HELMUT
VON KOBLINSKI, HANS-JOACH

SLADE, MICHAEL
BANKS, JOHN
CLARKE, JAY
CLARKE, LEE
COVELL, RICHARD

SLADE, TED
ANTON, UWE
HAHN, RONALD M.

SLADE, TRINA
EGAR, RAUL

SLAGG, GLENDA
FANTONI, BARRY [ERNEST]

SLANGE, LENNART
WAGNER, HARALD

SLATE, JOHN
FEARN, JOHN RUSSELL

SLATER, ELIZABETH ANNE
NORTON, ALICE MONTGOMERY

SLATER, JIM
SLATER, JAMES DERRICK

SLATER, JOHN
HARDY, CARLENE
RUHEN, CARL
SLATTERY, RAY
TAYLOR, R.L.

SLATER, PATRICK
MITCHELL, JOHN

SLATER, RAY
LANSDALE, JOE R.

SLAUGHTER, ANSON
ATHANAS, WILLIAM VERNE

SLAUGHTER, DOCTOR
THEROUX, PAUL EDWARD

SLAUGHTER, JEAN
DOTY, JEAN SLAUGHTER

SLAUGHTER, JIM
PAINE, LAURAN BOSWORTH

SLAVIC, ROSALIND WELCHER
WELCHER, ROSALIND

SLAVUTYCH, YAR
ZHUCHENKOV, YAR

SLEASAR, HENRY
SLESAR, HENRY

SLICK, SAM JR.
AVERY, SAMUEL PUTNAM

SLIER, DEBBY
SHINE, DEBORAH

SLIM, ICEBERG
BECK, ROBERT

SLINGSBY, JONATHAN FREDE
WALLER, JOHN FRANCIS

SLINGSBY, RUFUS
PEEL, FREDERICK
SIDDLE, CHARLES

SLOAN, CHRISTOPHER
LUPIANO, VINCENT

SLOAN, JOHN
WADE, THOMAS W.

SLOANE, BEN
COX, STEPHEN R.

SLOANE, ERIC
HINRICHS, EVERARD J.

SLOANE, SARA
BLOOM, URSULA

SLOBUCK, J. MILTON
BIERCE, AMBROSE

SLOCUM, HI
CLEMENS, SAMUEL LANGHORNE

SLOKUMB, SI
CHEEVER, HENRY P.

SLOPER, MACE
LELAND, CHARLES G.

SLOSBERG, MIKE
SLOSBERG, MYRON

SLY, CHRISTOPHER
NEILD, JAMES EDWARD

SMALACOMBE, JOHN
MACKAY, LOUIS ALEXANDER

SMALL, AUSTIN J.
MAJOR, AUSTIN SMALL

SMALL, ERNEST
LENT, BLAIR

SMALL, WILLIAM
EVERSLEY, DAVID E.C.

SMALLWOOD, JASON
KISNER, JACOB

SMEATON, FRED
COOK, FRED GORDON

SMEATON, OLIPHANT
SMEATON, WILLIAM HENRY

SMEE, WENTWORTH
BURGIN, G.B.

SMEED
TAYLOR, DEEMS

SMEED, FRANCES
LASKY, JESSE LOUIS JR.

SMILE, R. ELTON
SMILIE, ELTON R.

SMILEY, JIM
SPEARS, RAYMOND S.

SMITH , ELLERY
QUEEN, ELLERY

SMITH, A.C.H.
GUNNARSSON, THORINN

SMITH, A.J.M.
SMITH, ARTHUR JAMES M.

SMITH, ACH
SMITH, ANTHONY CHARLES

SMITH, ADAM
GOODMAN, GEORGE [J.W.]
KNOWLTON, WINTHROP

SMITH, ALANA
SMITH, RUTH ALANA

SMITH, ANGELA
HOHLBEIN, WOLFGANG E.

SMITH, ARTEGALL
NORTON, PHILIP

SMITH, ARTEMIS
MORPURGO, ANNA SELMA
TAULMAN, BILLIE

SMITH, ASHTON CLARK
CASS, DE-LYSLE FERREE

SMITH, BOBBI
WALTON, ROBERTA F. SMITH

SMITH, C. BUSBY
SMITH, JOHN

SMITH, C. PRITCHARD
HOYT, EDWIN P. JR.

SMITH, CAESAR
TREVOR, ELLESTON

SMITH, CARLTON
ROCKLIN, ROSS L.

SMITH, CARMICHAEL
LINEBARGER, PAUL M.A.

SMITH, CHARLES
HECKLEMANN, CHARLES N.

SMITH, CHARLES MERRILL
SMITH, TERRENCE LORE

SMITH, CHRISTOPHER MARTIN
FORBES, CABOTT L[OWELL]

SMITH, CLYDE
SMITH, GEORGE

SMITH, CORDWAINER
LINEBARGER, PAUL M.A.

SMITH, D. MacLEOD
SMITH, DAVID MacLEOD

SMITH, DANA WARREN
BROWN, A.L.
BROWN, LISA G.

SMITH, DOC
SMITH, EDWARD ELMER

SMITH, DODIE
SMITH, DOROTHY GLADYS

SMITH, DON
SMITH, DONALD TAYLOR

SMITH, DR. EDWARD E.
SMITH, EDWARD ELMER

SMITH, E. GRAHAM
WALLACE, EDGAR

SMITH, E.E.
SMITH, EDWARD ELMER

SMITH, E.E. "DOC"
ESHBACH, LLOYD ARTHIUR

SMITH, EDITH LILLIAN
WEBSTER, EDITH SMITH

SMITH, ELVET
MARSHALL, MARGARET

SMITH, ESSEX
HOPE, FRANCES ESSEX T.

SMITH, F.E.
FARRELL, DAVID
SMITH, FREDERICK ESCREET

SMITH, F.J.
SMITH, F. JOSEPH

SMITH, FENTON
PRATT, LEONARD E.

SMITH, FORD
FRIEND, OSCAR J[EROME]

SMITH, FRANC
SMITH, FRANCIS DENNIS

SMITH, GEORGE
SMITH, GEORGE H[ENRY]

SMITH, GEORGE H.
SMITH, GEORGE H[ARMON]
SMITH, GEORGE H[ENRY]

SMITH, GEORGE HUDSON
SMITH, GEORGE H[ENRY]

SMITH, GUY N.
SMITH, GUY NEWMAN

SMITH, HAMILTON
ROCHESTER, GEO[RGE] E.

SMITH, HARRIET
SCOTT, HILDA R.

SMITH, HELEN ZENNA
PRICE, EVADNE

SMITH, HOGAN
MORGAN, ALLEN D.

SMITH, J.C.S.
SMITH, JANE S.

SMITH, JACK
SMITH, BERNARD

SMITH, JAN
SMITH, GEORGE H[ENRY]

SMITH, JEAN
SMITH, FRANCES C.

SMITH, JESSICA
PENWARDEN, HELEN

SMITH, JESSIE
KUNHARDT, EDITH

SMITH, JOHN
HERRICK, MARVIN THEODORE
HUDSON, HOYT
LEWIS, JOHN DELAWARE

SMITH, JOHNSTON
CRANE, STEPHEN [TOWNLEY]

SMITH, JOSEPH
FLETCHER, JOSEPH SMITH

SMITH, JULIA CLEAVER
CLEAVER, DIANE
SMITH, NICHOLS

SMITH, L.K.
SMITH, LENA K[ENNEDY]

SMITH, LAFAYETTE
HIGDON, HAL

SMITH, LARRY
BOUNDS, SYDNEY J.

SMITH, LAWRENCE
BOUNDS, SYDNEY J.

SMITH, LEE
ALBION, LEE SMITH

SMITH, LEW
FLOREN, LEE

SMITH, LOUIS
BARZINI, LUIGI G.

SMITH, MARION
COLLINS, MARION SMITH

SMITH, MARTIN
SMITH, MARTIN WILLIAM

SMITH, MARTIN CRUZ
SMITH, MARTIN WILLIAM

SMITH, MARY
ADKINS, AVA VERLEA

SMITH, MAXWELL
CAVE, HUGH B[ARNETT]

SMITH, MIKE
SMITH, MARY ELLEN

SMITH, NAOMI
VINTER, HELEN

SMITH, NAOMI G.
ROYDE-SMITH, NAOMI

SMITH, PATRICK D.
SMITH, PATRICK DAVID

SMITH, RED
SMITH, WALTER [W]

SMITH, RICHARD E.
SMITH, RICHARD REIN

SMITH, ROBERT RUSSELL
GIBSON, WALTER B.

SMITH, ROBIN LEIGH
SMITH, KENN

SMITH, ROSAMOND
OATES, JOYCE CAROL

SMITH, S.S.
WILLIAMSON, THAMES ROSS

SMITH, SACHEVERELL
DARLING, WILLIAM YOUNG

SMITH, SARAH
STRETTON, HESBA

SMITH, SARAH STAFFORD
SMITH, DOROTHY [S]

SMITH, SHELLEY
BODINGTON, NANCY H.

SMITH, SHERWOOD
LOWENTROUT, CHRISTINE I.S

SMITH, SHIRLEY
CURTIS, E.J.

SMITH, SOSTHENES
WELLS, H.G.

SMITH, SPARTUCUS
JOHNSTON, ALEXANDER

SMITH, STEVIE
FLORENCE, MARGARET SMITH
SMITH, FLORENCE MARGARET

SMITH, SURREY
DINNER, WILLIAM
MORUN, WILLIAM

SMITH, SUSAN
SMITH, SUSAN VERNON M.

SMITH, T. CARLYLE
BANGS, JOHN KENDRICK

SMITH, T.D.
TREVOR, ELLESTON

SMITH, THORNE
MATSON, NORMAN [H]

SMITH, VERONICA
MIHOLOVICH, VERONICA

SMITH, W.J.
SMITH, WALTER JAMES

SMITH, WADE
SNOW, CHARLES H[ORACE]

SMITH, WARD
GOLDSMITH, HOWARD

SMITH, WAYLAND
BAYLEY, VICTOR

SMITH, WINSTON
FRITCH, CHARLES E.

SMITH, WOODROW WILSON
KUTTNER, HENRY
MOORE, CATHERINE LUCILLE

SMITH, Z.Z.
WESTHEIMER, DAVID

SMITHFIELD, ARTHUR P.
MOORE, ARTHUR

SMITHSON, I.
SMITH, RUSSELL

SMITS, TEO
SMITS, THEODORE R.

SMITTS, MR.
LINDS, MARK PRAGER

SMYLES, L.E.
JELLEY, SYMMES W.

SMYTHE, ALICE M.
HADFIELD, ALICE M.

SMYTHE, JAMES P.
MCGARRY, WILLIAM RUTL

SNAFFLES
PAYNE, CHARLES J.

SNAPP, ORVILLE
BRAUN, WILBUR

SNIFF, MR.
ABISCH, ROSLYN KROOP

SNODGRASS, THOMAS JEFFER.
CLEMENS, SAMUEL LANGHORNE

SNOOKS, EPAMINONDAS
MASON, C.P.

SNOW BABY
KUHNE, MARIE

SNOW, ASHLEY
CLAGUE, MARYHELEN

SNOW, C.P.
SNOW, CHARLES PERCY

SNOW, EBONI
MCGEE, GWYN

SNOW, FRANCIS COMPTON
ADAMS, HENRY BROOKS

SNOW, LUCY
AUBERT, ROSEMARY

SNOW, LYNDON
ANSLE, DOROTHY PHOEBE

SNOW, TERRY
WOOLSEY, MARY HALE

SNOWDEN, KEIGHLEY
SNOWDEN, JAMES

SNUT, HEIN
SACHSE, WILLI RICHARD

SNYDER, E.V.
SNYDER, EUGENE VINCENT

SNYDER, GENE
SNYDER, EUGENE VINCENT

SO, BERNAT
RUTT KAY, ARNOLD

SOA, IMANU E.K.
KNIGHT, ETHERIDGE

SOBERGK, CORA
HOGEL, LISA

SOBLE, JENNIE
CAVIN, RUTH BRODIE

SOFTLY, EDWARD
LOVECRAFT, H[OWARD] P.

SOHEI, MORITA
YONEMATSU, MORITA

SOHL, JERRY
SOHL, GERALD ALLEN

SOKOL, BILL
SOKOL, WILLIAM

SOKOLOV, SASHA
SOKOLOV, ALEXANDER V.

SOLBER, ARNE
MEYN, NIELS

SOLBERT, RONNI
SOLBERT, ROMAINE

SOLITAIRE, M.
NURNBERGER, WOLDEMAR

SOLMUND, OLAV
KRINGS, CARL

SOLO, FRANCO
ERICHSEN, UWE
FISCHER, CLAUS
RELLERGERD, HELMUT

SOLO, JAY
ELLISON, HARLAN

SOLOGUB, FEDOR
TETERNIKOV, FEDOR K.

SOLOMONS, IKEY ESQ. JR.
THACKERAY, WILLIAM MAKEP.

SOMBRE, SAMUEL
GERARD, JAMES WATSON

SOMERS, BART
FOX, GARDNER F.

SOMERS, J.L.
STICKLAND, LOUISE ANNIE B

SOMERS, JANE
LESSING, DORIS

SOMERS, JONATHAN SWIFT
FARMER, PHILIP JOSE

SOMERS, PAUL
WINTERTON, PAUL

SOMERS, SUZANNE
DANIELS, DOROTHY
DANIELS, NORMAN A.

SOMERSET, FITZROY RICHARD
RAGLAN, FITZROY

SOMERSET, PERCY
HOLLIS, CHRISTOPHER

SOMERVILLE
MAUGHAM, W. SOMMERSET

SOMERVILLE & ROSS
MARTIN, VIOLET FLORENCE
SOMERVILLE, EDITH A.O.

SOMERVILLE, H.B.
MCCOMAS, I.V.

SOMES, JETHRO
PAUKER, JOHN

SOMMERER, THEA
DETLEFSEN, THEA

SOMMERS, DAVID
SMITH, HOWARD VAN
VAN SMITH, HOWARD

SOMMERS, FRANK
NIEHAUS, WERNER

SOMMERS, JANE R.
JONES, CORNELIA

SOMMERS, JEANNE
MYERS, BARRY

SOMTOW, S.P.
SUCHARITKUL, SOMTOW PAP.

SONAMA, GERDA
MORRIS, GERDA

SONDERLAND, NILS O.
WILLIAMSON, JOHN STEWART

SONDERS, MARK
BERLYN, MICHAEL [STEVEN]

SONERO, DEVI
PELTON, ROBERT W.

SONGWEAVBER, CERIN
DE LINT, CHARLES

SONICA
MCALPINE, ROBERT W.

SONNTAG, USCHI
WIEGAND, URSULA

SONTUP, DAN
SONTUP, DANIEL

SOPHIA, MEVROUW
MACLEOD, MEVROUW SOPHIA

SORACE, RICHARD
WILLIAMSON, LYDIA BUCKLN.

SOREL, BYRON
YATRON, MICHAEL

SOREL, JULIA
DREXLER, ROSALYN

SORENSEN, BEVERLY
ROTSLER, WILLIAM

SORENSEN, SVEND, OTTO
SOERENSEN, SVEND OTTO

SORGE, BIRGIT
HEIDEMANN, LENI

SORTOR, TONI
SORTOR, JUNE ELIZABETH

SOSEKI
KINNOSUKE, NATSUME

SOSEKI, NATSUME
KINNOSUKE, NATSUME

SOSKIN, V.H.
ELLISON, VIRGINIA HOWELL

SOSTHENES
COAD, FREDERICK R.

SOUDLEY, HENRY
WOOD, JAMES PLAYSTEAD

SOULI, CHARLES GEORGE
BEDFORD-JONES, HENRY

SOUTH, BARBARA
STEPHENS, BARBARA

SOUTH, CLARK
SWAIN, DWIGHT V[REELAND]

SOUTH, GRACE
CLARK, GAIL

SOUTH, M.A.
ATWOOD, MARY ANN

SOUTH, MARTIN
JENSEN, ERIK B. VOLMER

SOUTHARD, J.H.
MORRIS, CHARLES [S]

SOUTHERLAND, MYRTELLA
HARKNESS, EDITH MYRTELLA

SOUTHERN CROSS
HILL, MRS. E.E.

SOUTHERN, JACK
SOUTHWORTH, JOHN VAN D.

SOUTHWOLD, STEPHEN
CRITTEN, STEPHEN HENRY

SOUTHWORTH, LOUIS
GREALEY, THOMAS LOUIS

SOUTTER, FRED
LAKE, KENNETH R[OBERT]

SOUVARINE, BORIS
LIFCHITZ, BORIS

SOUZA, ERNEST
DUNN, ELSIE
SCOTT, EVELYN

SPACE, PHILLIP
MURRAY, WILLIAM P.

SPADE, DANNY
AMBLER, DAIL

SPADE, MARK
BALCHIN, NIGEL MARTIN

SPADE, RUPERT
PAWLEY, MARTIN EDWARD

SPAIN, JOHN
ADAMS, CLEVE F.

SPAIN, NICHOLAS
SKINNER, MICHAEL

SPAIN, TERRY
STRATTON, JOHN THEODORE

SPALDING, JOSEPH
TAGGART, TOM [BARNARD]

SPALDING, KEITH
SPALT, KARL HEINZ

SPALDING, LUCILLE
JAY, MARION

SPALDING, NEIL J.
KNELLER, F.C.

SPALDING, WILLIAM
BRADBURY, RAY [DOUGLAS]

SPALT, KARL HEINZ G.
SPALDING, KEITH

SPANNER, VALERIE
GRAYLAND, VALERIE MERLE

SPARK, MURIEL
STANFORD, MURIEL S. SPARK

SPARKMAN, WILLIAM
ROPER, WILLIAM L.

SPARKROCK, FRED
PROCTOR, GEO[RGE] W[YATT]
VARDEMAN, ROBERT E.

SPARKS, CHRISTINE
FIOROTTO, CHRISTINE

SPARKS, MERLA JEAN
MCCORMICK, MERLA JEAN

SPARLING, NED
SENARENS, LUIS P.

SPARLING, W.
SPRATLING, WALTER NORMAN

SPARROW, PHILIP
STEWARD, SAMUEL M[ORRIS]

SPARSHOTT, F.E.
SPARSHOTT, FRANCIS EDWARD

SPARTACUS, DEUTERO
FANTHORPE, R.L.

SPARTICUS, TERTIUS
BURGESS, MICHAEL ROY

SPAT, KONRAD
GERLE, WOLFGANG ADOLF

SPATZ, H. DONALD
ESHBACH, LLOYD ARTHUR

SPAULDING, DOUGLAS
BRADBURY, RAY [DOUGLAS]

SPAULDING, LEONARD
BRADBURY, RAY [DOUGLAS]

SPAULDING, LUCILE
SPAULDING, RUTH

SPAULDING, NEIL J.
KNELLER, F.C.

SPAVERY
AVERY, SAMUEL PUTNAM

SPECHT, BARBARA
VAN POORTVLIET, BARBARA

SPECTATOR, MR.
HUBBARD, L. RON

SPECTOR, ROBERT D.
SPECTOR, ROBERT DONALD

SPEED, DONALD
HAMILTON, ALEXANDER

SPEED, F. MAURICE
SPEED, FREDERICK MAURICE

SPEED, NELL
SAMPSON, EMMA K. SPEED

SPEKTOR, [DR.] ADAM
GLUT, DONALD F.

SPELLMAN, ROGER G.
COX, WILLIAM ROBERT

SPENCE, AINSLIE
MURPHY, IDA MARY

SPENCE, BETTY E.
TETTMAR, BETTY EILEEN

SPENCE, BILL
SPENCE, W. JOHN DUNCAN

SPENCE, CYNTHIA
EBLE, DIANE

SPENCE, DUNCAN
SPENCE, W. JOHN DUNCAN

SPENCE, HUBERT
LONGHURST, PERCY WILLIAM

SPENCE, J.A.D.
ELIOT, T[HOMAS] S[TEARNS]

SPENCER & WEST
WOOD, EDWARD D. JR.

SPENCER, CANDACE
SCHULER, CANDACE L.

SPENCER, CAPT.
TUITE, HUGH

SPENCER, CATHERINE
ORR, KATHLEEN [KATHY]

SPENCER, CHERYL
PURVIANCE, CHERYL LYNN

SPENCER, CLARK
BRAND, KURT

SPENCER, CORNELIA
YAUKEY, GRACE S.

SPENCER, EDWARD
MOTT, EDWARD SPENCER
STARES, JOHN EDWARD S.

SPENCER, ELIOT
SCHOENEBECK, WILLI

SPENCER, GEOFFREY
WILSON, ALEXANDER [D.C.]

SPENCER, HANK
FAWCETT, FRANK DUBREZ
NEWTON, WILLIAM [SIMPSON]
PATERSON, A.J. BLAIR

SPENCER, JAKE
KAPLUN, JACOB

SPENCER, JOHN
VICKERS, ROY

SPENCER, LEONARD G.
FAIRMAN, PAUL W.
GARRETT, RANDALL [P]
SILVERBERG, ROBERT

SPENCER, MARGARET
MEEK SPENCER, MARGARET [D

SPENCER, MARY
LIMMING, MARY SPENCER

SPENCER, PARKE
WRIGHT, SEWELL PEASLEE

SPENCER, ROLAND
PROUT, GEOFFREY
WARWICK, FRANCIS ALISTAIR

SPENCER, WARREN
LENGEL, WILLIAM CHARLES

SPENCER, [DR.] BRUCE
ABEL, ALAN [IRWIN]

SPENDER, J.A.
SPENDER, JOHN ALFRED

SPENDER, J.M.
SPENDER, JEAN MAUDE

SPENSER, EMILY
ELKINS, CHARLOTTE

SPENSER, JAMES
GUEST, FRANCES HAROLD

SPENSER, JULIAN
DRAFFIN, PETER

SPERRY, J.E.
EISENSTAT, JANE SPERRY

SPERRY, JANE
EISENSTAT, JANE SPERRY

SPERRY, RAYMOND JR.
STRATEMEYER, EDWARD

SPHINX, THE
LEVERSON, ADA

SPICER, DOROTHY
FRASER, DOROTHY G. SPICER

SPIDER, JOHN
ANTON, UWE
APPEL, WALTER
ROSENBAUER, ROLAND

SPIDER, JOHN
VAN HEESE, DIETHARD

SPIEL, HILDIE
DE MENDELSSOHN, HILDE

SPIELBERG, STEPHEN
WALLER, LESLIE

SPIELMANN, M.H.
SPIELMANN, MARION H.A.

SPIELMANN, WERNER
MARDICKE, FRITZ

SPIELMANNS, JORG
LUIF, KURT

SPIES, OLIVER
SLOTKIN, JOSEPH

SPILLANE, MICKEY
BROWNE, HOWARD
SPILLANE, FRANK MORRISON

SPINELLI, MARCOS
SPINELLI, GRACE

SPINGFIELD, DAVID
LEWIS, JOHN ROYSTON

SPINIFLEX
MARTIN, DAVID

SPINNER, ALICE
FRASER, AUGUSTA ZELIA

SPINOSSIMUS
WHITE, WILLIAM

SPIRIDION
LOBOWSKI, EDWARD

SPIRIT, GORDON
BAJOG, GUNTHER

SPIT, SAM
SCHNECK, STEPHEN

SPITZNAGEL, D. KILIAN Z.
DOEHNEL, KARL FRIEDRICH

SPOONBILL
REANEY, JAMES CRERAR

SPOT, RYHON
POST, HENRY

SPOTSWOOD, JOHN
STANNARD, JOHN D.S.

SPRAGUE, CARTER
MERWIN, SAMUEL K. JR.

SPRAGUE, MORTIMER
BRAUN, WILBUR

SPRAGUE, W.D.
VON BLOCK, BELA [W]
VON BLOCK, SYLVIA

SPRAT, JOHN
HUNT, [J.H.] LEIGH

SPRIEL, STEPHEN
PILOTIN, MICHAEL

SPRIGEL, OLIVER
AVICE, CLAUDE-PIERRE

SPRING, DAN
SPAULDING, HENRY D.

SPRING, PHILIP
DOBSON, E. PHILIP

SPRING, RACHEL
HAILL, ROBERT GODFREY

SPRING, TONY
FAFUENTE ESTEFANIA, M.A.

SPRINGER, RUDOLF
RENNER, KARL

SPROSTON, JOHN
SCOTT, PETER DALE

SPROULE, WESLEY
SPROULE, HOWARD

SPROUT, MR.
WHITEING, RICHARD

SPRUNG, RENATE
RICHTER, ROSEMARIE

SPUN YARN
LOOMIS, ALFRED F.

SPURR, CLINTON
ROWLAND, DONALD S.

SPYDER, I.M.
MURRAY, WILLIAM P.

SQUARE, A.
ABBOTT, EDWIN A.

SQUARE, CHARLOTTE
HALDANE, ROBERT AYLMER

SQUEAKER'S MATE
BAYNTON, BARBARA

SQUERENT, WILL
BRADBURY, WILLIAM

SQUIER, LUCITA
WILLIAMS, LUCITA SQUIER

SQUIRE, J.C.
SQUIRE, JOHN COLLINS

SQUIRE, MIRIAM
SPRIGGE, ELIZABETH

SQUIRE, MIRIAM F.
LESLIE, MIRIAM FLORENCE

SQUIRES, PATRICIA
BALL, NANONI PATRICIA M.H

SQUIRES, PHIL
BARKER, S. OMAR
BOSWORTH, ALLAN R.
BRAGG, WILLIAM FREDERICK

SR. VRAIN, [MAJ.] E.L.
MANNING, WILLIAM HENRY

SRI-RAJPUTRA
BERA, SUDHIU

ST, GEORGE, EDITH
DELATUSH, EDITH

ST. AIME, GEORGES
PELLETIER, ALEXIS

ST. ALCORN, LLOYD
MEYER, DAVID N. II

ST. ANBECK, ROLAND
BECK, ROLAND STANLEY

ST. AUBYN, ALAN
MARSHALL, FRANCIS B.

ST. BARBE
SLADEN, DOUGLAS

ST. BRIAVELS, JAMES
WOOD, JAMES PLAYSTEAD

ST. CLAIR
FORD, WILLIAM

ST. CLAIR, CECIL
CLARK, SUSIE CHAMPNEY

ST. CLAIR, CLOVIS
SKARDA, PATRICIA LYN

ST. CLAIR, DEXTER
WINCHELL, PRENTICE

ST. CLAIR, ELIZABETH
COHEN, SUSAN HANDLER

ST. CLAIR, ERIC
PFLAUM, GEORGE A.

ST. CLAIR, EVERETT
MANSELL, MRS. C.B.

ST. CLAIR, JEANANNE
HASSLER, KENNETH L.

ST. CLAIR, KATHERINE
HUFF, TOM E.

ST. CLAIR, MIKE
RETCHKIN, NORMAN

ST. CLAIR, PHILIP
HOWARD, MUNROE

ST. CLAIR, STEPHANIE
MAAS, DONALD

ST. CLAIRE, ERIN
BROWN, SANDRA [LYNN COX]

ST. CLAIRE, YVONNE
HALL, EMMA

ST. CYR, CYPRIAN
BERNE, ERIC [L]

ST. CYR, MELANIE
SCHLEICHER, GISELA

ST. DARE, JULIAN
PATTEN, WILLIAM GEORGE

ST. DAVID, IVY
DUPONT, ELLEN

ST. DAVID, JOHN
WALSH, DAVID JOHN

ST. EBBAR
RABBETS, THOMAS G.

ST. FELIX, MARIE
LYNCH, HARRIET LOUISE

ST. GEORGE, ARTHUR
PAINE, LAURAN BOSWORTH

ST. GEORGE, DAVID
MARKOV, GEORGII IVANOV
PHILLIPS, DAVID ATLEE

ST. GEORGE, GEOFFREY
HART, JEFFREY

ST. GEORGE, HARRY
RATHBORNE, ST. GEORGE

ST. GEORGE, JOSEPH
JOSEPH, GEORGE ISRAEL

ST. GEORGE, MARGARET
OSBORNE, MARGARET ELLEN

ST. GERMAIN, GREGORY
WINTER, PATRICK
WALLMANN, JEFFREY M.

ST. GIRAUD
KNOTT, WILLIAM CECIL JR.

ST. HERETICUS
BROWN, ROBERT MCAFEE

ST. IVEN, W.
STRIVEN, WILLIAM

ST. JAMES, ANDREW
STERN, JAMES

ST. JAMES, BERNARD
TREISTER, BERNARD WILLIAM

ST. JAMES, BLAKELY
GOTTFRIED, THEODORE MARK
PLATT, CHARLES [M]

ST. JAMES, IAN
TAYLOR, DON CAMBRIDGE

ST. JAMES, JESSICA
HOY, CHARLOTTE
PALMER, LINDA VARNER

ST. JAMES, SCOTNEY
HOY, CHARLOTTE
PALMER, LINDA VARNER

ST. JOHN BATHE, MARGARET
DULLARD, MARGARET

ST. JOHN, ANDREA
HOWARD, DONALD M.

ST. JOHN, BETH
JOHN, ELIZABETH BEAMON

ST. JOHN, CHERYL
LUDWIGS, CHERYL
NATHENSON, JOSEPH

ST. JOHN, CHRISTOP. MARIE
MARSHALL, CHRISTOBEL

ST. JOHN, DAVID
HUNT, E. HOWARD

ST. JOHN, ELIZABETH
JOHN, ELIZABETH BEAMON

ST. JOHN, EUGENIA
BERRY, MARTHA EUGENIA

ST. JOHN, GAIL
GRACE, ANITA
GREENFIELD, IRVING A.

ST. JOHN, GENEVIEVE
GLADSON, LEE

ST. JOHN, HENRY
COOPER, [C] HENRY ST JOHN
CREASEY, JOHN

ST. JOHN, JOHN
SALE, RICHARD [B]

ST. JOHN, LEONIE
BAYER, WILLIAM
HARMON, NANCY

ST. JOHN, LISA
SANFORD, ANNETTE [S]

ST. JOHN, NICOLE
JOHNSTON, NORMA

ST. JOHN, P.B.
ST. JOHN, PERCY BOLLNGBRK

ST. JOHN, PHILIP
DEL REY, LESTER

ST. JOHN, WARREN
ST. JOHN, PERCY BOLLNGBRK

ST. KAYNE, HUMPHREY
CRAWFURD, OSWALD J.F.

ST. LOUIS, ROBERT
NATHAN, ROBERT

ST. LUZ, BERTHE
ROBERTSON, ALICE A.

ST. MARS, F.
ADKINS, FRANK HOWARD
ATKINS, FRANK JR.

ST. MARS, F. JR.
ATKINS, FRANCIS HENRY

ST. MARTIN, THOMAS
LINCOLN, PETER

ST. MICHAELS, DONELLE
RICO, DON

ST. MOORE, ADAM
DOUYAN, JACQUES

ST. MOX, E.A.
ELLIS, EDWARD S.

ST. MYER, NED
STRATEMEYER, EDWARD

ST. PAUL, STERNER
MEEK, STERNER ST. PAUL

ST. PIERRE, LISANN
VERGE, LISA ANN

ST. REYNARD, GEOFF
KREPPS, ROBERT WILSON

ST. TAMARA
KOLBA, TAMARA

ST. THOMAS, ROBIN
BADE, THOMAS MICHAEL
STEVENSON, ROBIN

ST. VIVANT, M.
BIXBY, JEROME L.

ST.CLAIR-ERSKINE, SELINA
FORBES, [LADY] ANGELA

STAB, JAKOB
DESSAUER, FRIEDRICH

STABILE, STICKUM
STABLEFORD, BRIAN M.

STABLES, DR. GORDON, RN
STABLES, [WILLIAM] GORDON

STACEY, JO ANN
MORRIS, DEBRAH
SHAVER, PAT

STACEY, PAUL
SAVILL, ROY

STACEY, SUSANNAH
STAYNES, JILL
STOREY, MARGARET

STACK, ANDY
RULE, ANN

STACY, BRUCE
ELLIOTT, BRUCE W.

STACY, DONALD
POHL, FREDERIK

STACY, EILEEN
STACY, KATHY

STACY, JAN
ADAMS, CLIFTON H.

STACY, JOEL
DODGE, MARY ELIZABETH M.

STACY, O'CONNOR
ROLLINS, WILLIAM STACY

STACY, RYDER
STACY, JAN
SYVERTSEN, RYDER [OTTO]

STACY, TERRY
LEA, TERREA

STACY, WALTER
ELLIOTT, BRUCE W.

STADLEMAN, S.L.
STADLEMAN, SARA LEE

STAFF, JACK
HARRIS, JAMES HENRY

STAFFANS, K.G.
LAGERSTROM, BERTIL AKE G.

STAFFORD, ANNE
PEDLER, ANNE I. STAFFORD

STAFFORD, CAROLINE
WATJEN, CAROLYN L.T.

STAFFORD, JOHN K.
BROUGHTON, F. LUSK
BYRNES, EDWARD GAINES
DRUID, DAVID
GRANT, MAJOR A.F.
MORRIS, ANTHONY P.
RATHBORNE, ST. GEORGE
SHARP, JACK
SMART, HAWLEY
TOZER, ALFRED B.
WILLIAMS, M.H.
WINCH, WILL

STAFFORD, JUDITH
CHRISTENBERRY, JUDITH [R]

STAFFORD, PETER
TABORI, PAL

STAGG, ANNE
PENDOWER, THOMAS CURTIS H

STAGG, DELANO
EIDEN, PAUL
SABRE, MEL R.

STAGG, JAMES
JOHNS, GILBERT

STAGG, JAMES
PENDOWER, THOMAS CURTIS H

STAGGE, JONATHAN
WEBB, RICHARD WILSON
WHEELER, HUGH C.

STAHL, ACHIM
HAHN, ROLF

STAHL, HERBERT
KAUFMANN, CHARLOTTE

STAHL, MARE
KAUFFMANN, MARE

STAHL, P.J.
HETZEL, PIERRE JULES

STAHL, RAY
HOSSENT, HARRY
MACONACHIE, WILLIAM

STAHL, SUE
MOSIMAN, BILLIE SUE

STAHLE, STEIN
VON HIRSCH, TRYGVE EINAR.

STAHLFELDT, STINA
QVARNSTROM, INGRID

STAICAR, TOM
STAICAR, THOMAS EDWARD

STAINES, TREVOR
BRUNNER, JOHN [K.H.]

STAINTON, AUDREY
NOHRA, AUDREY

STAIR, VIRGINIA
RUSSELL, WINIFRED BRENT

STAIRS, GORDON
AUSTIN, MARY H.

STAMBLER, HELEN
LATNER, HELEN [S]

STAMES, WARD
STEWARD, SAMUEL M[ORRIS]

STAMPER, ALEX
KENT, ARTHUR WILLIAM C.
MCCORMICK, JAMES

STANCLIFFE, ELAINE
STONE, ELISA

STAND, MARGUERITE
STICKLAND, M.E.

STANDAGE, VIRGINIA
SHAMBROOK, RONA [GREEN]

STANDARD, PATTI
STANDARD-CRONK, PATTI

STANDBY
PORTEOUS, RICHARD SYDNEY

STANDING BEAR, CHIEF
STANDING BEAR, LUTHER

STANDISH, BUCK
PAINE, LAURAN BOSWORTH

STANDISH, BURT L.
MCFARLANE, LESLIE CHARLES
PATTEN, GILBERT
PATTEN, WILLIAM GEORGE
WHITSON, JOHN HARVEY

STANDISH, CAROLE
KOEHLER, MARGARET [H]

STANDISH, CAROLINE
READ, LORNA

STANDISH, HOLT
SMITH, GEORGE H[ENRY]

STANDISH, O.J.
HORLER, SYDNEY

STANDISH, PETER
CHAMBERS, DEREK HYDE
LAZENBY, NORMAN A.

STANDISH, RICHARD
GOYNE, RICHARD

STANDISH, ROBERT
GERAHTY, DIGBY GEORGE

STANDISH, WINN
SAWYER, WALTER LEON

STANEV, ERUILIAN
STANEV, NIKOLA [S]

STANFIELD, ANN
COFFMAN, VIRGINIA [E]

STANFORD, LARA
HOPPE, SIGRID

STANG, JUDY
STANG, JUDIT

STANHOPE OF CHESTER
NORMAN, C.H.

STANHOPE, DOUGLAS
DUFF, DOUGLAS VALDER

STANHOPE, ERIC
HAMILTON, CHARLES H.S.

STANHOPE, JOHN
LANGDON-DAVIES, JOHN

STANHOPE, LAVINA
SCHEIN, MIRIAM

STANISLAVSKI
ALEKSEYEV, KONSTANTIN S.

STANLEY FRANCIS
CROCCHIOLA, FRANCIS STAN.

STANLEY, ALIXIE RUSSELL
GRANT, MAUDE MARGARET

STANLEY, ARTHUR
MEGAW, ARTHUR STANLEY

STANLEY, BENNETT
HOUGH, STANLEY BENNETT

STANLEY, BETH
AMERSKI, BETH

STANLEY, BOB
YERGER, ROBERT

STANLEY, CAROL
WHITE, CAROL

STANLEY, CHUCK
STRONG, CHARLES STANLEY

STANLEY, DAVE
DACHS, DAVID

STANLEY, DR.
FURSTAUER, JOHANNA

STANLEY, F.
CROCCHIOLA, STANLEY FRAN.

STANLEY, FRANK
GIBSON, MARY W. STANLEY

STANLEY, HEXER
MUGGENBURG, HANS J.

STANLEY, J.F.
FURSTAUER, JOHANNA

STANLEY, MARGARET
MASON, SYDNEY CHARLES

STANLEY, MARGE
WEINBAUM, STANLEY G.

STANLEY, MICHAEL
HOSIE, STANLEY WILLIAM

STANLEY, OLIN
HONEYWELL, E.L.

STANLEY, PHIL
IND, ALLISON

STANLEY, RAY
ENGEL, LYLE KENYON

STANLEY, ROBERT
HAMILTON, CHARLES H.S.

STANLEY, T. LLOYD
SMITH, RICHARD MORRIS

STANLEY, WARWICK
HILTON, JOHN BUXTON

STANLI, SUE
MEILACH, DONA Z.

STANNARD, LANE
TAURASI, JAMES V. SR.

STANSBURY, ALEC
HIGGS, ALEC S.

STANSTEAD, JOHN
GROOM, ARTHUR WILLIAM

STANTON, ANNA
BEAUMONT, HELEN

STANTON, BORDEN
WILDING, PHILIP

STANTON, CARL
HOLT, GLEN

STANTON, CHUCK
SELLERS, CONNIE LESLIE

STANTON, CORALIE
HOSKEN, ALICE C.S.
HOSKEN, [E.C.] HEATH

STANTON, EDWARD
HUNTINGTON, E. STANTON

STANTON, JAMES S.
TUBB, E.C.

STANTON, JOHN
WALLIS, GEORGE C.

STANTON, KEN
STOKES, MANNING LEE

STANTON, MARJORIE
PHILLIPS, HORACE

STANTON, PAUL
BEATY, [ARTHUR] DAVID

STANTON, REX
RANDISI, ROBERT J.

STANTON, SCHUYLER
BAUM, L[YMAN] FRANK

STANTON, VANCE
AVALLONE, MICHAEL

STANTON, WILL
HOPE, WILLIAM EDWARD S.

STANTON, WILLIAM
HOPE, WILLIAM EDWARD S.

STANWOOD, BROOKS
KAMINSKY, HOWARD & SUSAN

STANYA, F.
JESCHKE, WOLFGANG

STAPLETON, D & D
STAPLETON, DOROTHY & DOUG

STAPLETON, D.
STAPLETON, DOROTHY & DOUG

STAPLETON, KATHERINE
KANE, HENRY

STAPLETON, MAURICE
PURCELL, J.S.

STAR, CATHY HAIG
SCHIER, NORMA

STAR, ELISON
COMBER, ROSE

STAR, JEAN
LUBANSKI, JULES C.L.

STAR-MAN'S PADRE
PATRICK, JOHNSTONE G.

STARCROSS, ROGER
POPE, CHARLES HENRY

STARFORTH, ASTROEA
FEARN, JOHN RUSSELL

STARHAWK
SIMOS, MIRIAM

STARK, INSPECTOR
BROUGHTON, F. LUSK
COX, STEPHEN ANGUS D.
GRANT, MAJOR A.F.
HOWARD, JACK
JAMES, W.I.
MORRIS, ANTHONY P.
RATHBORNE, ST. GEORGE
SMART, HAWLEY

STARK, JAMES
GOLDSTON, ROBERT C.

STARK, JOHN
GODWIN, JOHN [F]
KORSELL, JOHN
STOKOE, E[DWARD] G[EORGE]

STARK, JONATHAN
MARSHALL, H.P.

STARK, JOSHUA
OLSEN, THEODORE VICTOR

STARK, MICHAEL
LARIAR, LAWRENCE

STARK, RICHARD
WESTLAKE, DONALD [EDWIN]

STARK, SIGGE
BJORNBERG, SIGNE

STARKE, HENDERSON
NEVILLE, KRIS [O]

STARKE, R.
KRAFT, ROBERT

STARNE, PETER L.
BRAND, KURT

STARR, ADDISON
GALLARDOS MUNOZ, JUAN
LAFUENTE ESTEFANIA, M.A.

STARR, ANNE
SANFORD, ANNETTE [S]

STARR, CLAY
MARTIN, CHARLES M.

STARR, H.W.
WARD, HAROLD

STARR, HENRY
BINGLEY, DAVID ERNEST

STARR, JOHN
AYCOCK, ROGER DEE
CUSHMAN, DAN

STARR, JOHN A.
GILLESE, JOHN PATRICK

STARR, JUDY
GELFMAN, JUDITH S.

STARR, KATE
DINGWELL, JOYCE

STARR, LEONORA
MACKESY, LEONORA

STARR, MARK
KLEIN, GERARD

STARR, MARTHA
GORDON, MARTHA STARR

STARR, MORGANA
ORR, ALICE HARRON

STARR, ROLAND
ROWLAND, DONALD S.

STARR, WARD
MANES, STEPHEN
SOMERSON, PAUL

STARR, WARD & MEL MURCH
MANES, STEPHEN

STARRET, WILLIAM
MCCLINTOCK, MARSHALL

START, CLARISSA
LIPPERT, CLARISSA START

STASEK, ANATAL
ZEMAN, ANTONIN

STATON, ANNA LLOYD
ENGLISH, DORIS S.
ROCKER, JUDY S.

STATTEN, VARGO
FEARN, JOHN RUSSELL

STAUFFER, DON
BERKEBILE, FRED DONOVAN

STAVELEY, ROBERT
CAMPBELL, R.O.

STAVROS, NIKO
KING, FLORENCE

STAWELL, AUGUSTUS
LEGGE, ALFRED OWEN

STEADMAN, [CAPT.] DICK
HARBAUGH, THOMAS C.

STEAMER
NASON, LEONARD HASTINGS

STEARNS, ALBERT
STEARNS, EDGAR FRANKLIN

STEARNS, E.F.
STEARNS, EDGAR FRANKLIN

STEBELSKI, JULIAN
STOBERSKI, ZYGMUNT JULIAN

STEBER, A.R.
GRAHAM, ROGER P.

STEBER, A[LFRED] R.
PALMER, RAYMOND A.

STECHER, L.J.
WESLEY, JOSEPH

STED, RICHARD
THACKREY, THEODORE OLIN

STEDMAN
DODGE, ELIZABETH C.
KINNEY, ELIZABETH C.

STEED, NEVILLE
SHARAM, NORMAN

STEEL, ADDISON
WHITSON, JOHN HARVEY

STEEL, DANIELLE
TRAINA, DANIELLE STEEL

STEEL, DAVE
FRANCES, STEPHEN D.

STEEL, DAVID
FRANCES, STEPHEN D.

STEEL, DOUGLAS
HANOS, DMITRI [JAMES]

STEEL, HOWARD
HAYTER, CECIL G.
MARSHALL, ARTHUR C.
SYMONDS, FRANCIS A.

STEEL, JACK
LEGER, JEAN-MARC

STEEL, KURT
KAGEY, RUDOLF H.
STEEL, RUDOLPH HORNADAY

STEEL, MARJORY
FEARN, JOHN RUSSELL

STEEL, ROBERT
WHITSON, JOHN HARVEY

STEELE, ADDISON
LUPOFF, RICHARD A.

STEELE, BEN
GARDNER, BENNIE WILSON

STEELE, BLUE
NORWOOD, VICTOR [G.C.]

STEELE, BYRON
STEEGMULLER, FRANCIS

STEELE, CHARLES
SELLERS, CONNIE LESLIE

STEELE, CHESTER K.
STRATEMEYER, EDWARD

STEELE, CURTIS
BITTNER, ARCHIBALD
DAVIS, FREDERICK [CLYDE]
ROGERS, WAYNE
TEPPERMAN, EMILE C.

STEELE, DALE
GLUT, DONALD F.

STEELE, DANIEL
CHADWICK, CHARLES

STEELE, DERWENT
STEWARD, DONALD WILLIAM
STUART, DONALD

STEELE, DIRK
PLAWIN, PAUL

STEELE, ERSKINE
HENDERSON, ARCHIBALD

STEELE, FLETCHER
CHIDSEY, DONALD BARR

STEELE, FRITZ
STEELE, FRED I.

STEELE, GUNNISON
GARDNER, BENNIE WILSON

STEELE, HOWARD
STEELE, HARWOOD ELMES R.

STEELE, JACLEN
STEELE, JACK & HELEN

STEELE, LINDA
UZQUIANO, LINDA STEELE

STEELE, MONTE
TAYLOR, ROBERT

STEELE, MORRIS J.
LIVINGSTONE, BERKELEY
PALMER, RAYMOND A.

STEELE, SAMANTHA
RUHEN, CARL

STEELE, SHARON
FERH, RICHARD
MULVEY, WILLIAM

STEELE, TEX
ROSS, WILLIAM E. DANIEL

STEELE, V.M.
FIRTH, MARY VIOLET

STEEL[E], RUDOLF
KAGEY, RUDOLF H.

STEEMAN, A.S.
STEEMAN, S.S. ANDRE

STEEN, ALBERT
ALBERT, MAX

STEEN, FRANK
FELSTEIN, IVOR

STEEN, I.V.
MULLER, PAUL ALFRED
SCHMIDT, HELMUT K.

STEEN, KARL
DAUDET, JULIE R.C.

STEEN, MIKE
STEEN, MALCOLM HAROLD

STEENBERG, SVEN
DOELLERDT, ARTUR

STEER, CHARLOTTE
HUNTER, CHRISTINE
HUNTER, MAUDE LILY

STEERS, HELEN
BURGESS, HELEN STEERS

STEFFAN, JACK
STEFFAN, ALICE JACQUELINE

STEFFAN, SIOBHAN R.
GOULART, FRANCES S.

STEFFANSON, CON
CASSIDAY, BRUCE [BINGHAM]
GOULART, RONALD JOSEPH

STEIGER, BRAD
OLSON, EUGENE E.

STEIN, ADAM
SPRINGER, ROBERT

STEIN, BAKER
BAKER, CAROL
STEIN, LANA

STEIN, BARBARA
HAFT, ELLI

STEIN, BERNARD
KAHLERT, KARL FRIEDRICH

STEIN, CHARLES
SCHWALBERG, CAROL[YN E.S]

STEIN, CLAUS
KALMUCZAK, ROLF

STEIN, DUFFY
BERGER, MELVIN H.

STEIN, F.N.
ALLRED, JOE

STEIN, FLORIAN
HAAKE, JURGEN

STEIN, FRANK N.
KUBIAK, MICHAEL

STEIN, GREGOR
GREGOIRE, PIERRE

STEIN, J.J.
RICHARDS, SARA LIPPINCOTT

STEINART, ARMIN
LOOFS, FRIEDRICH A.

STEINBACH, ELLEN
KOPPENBERG, ELLEN

STEINBERG, JILL
RIELAU, URSULA

STEINBRUNNER, CHRIS
STEINBRUNNER, PETER CHRIS

STEINEMANN, FRITZ
BRAUN, HANS

STEINER, ALEXIS
ROTHSTEINER, ALOIS

STEINER, CONRAD C.
HAHN, RONALD M.

STEINER, JUTTA
MUHRMANN, WILHELM

STEINER, K. LESLIE
DELANY, SAMUEL R.

STEINER, KURT
RUELLAN, ANDRE

STEINER, ROBERT O.
QUEISER, HANS R.

STEINHAUSEN, H.
GURSTER, EUGENE

STEINMANN, ELSA
BANCHINI, ELSA

STEINMETZ, EULALIE
ROSS, EULALIE STEINMETZ

STELLA
IRON, MRS. N.C.
KING, STELLA

STELLIER, KILSYTH
SUMMERS, A. WELBOURNE

STEMP, ISAY
STEMPNITSKY, ISAY

STENDAL, GERTRUD
VON BROCKDORFF, GERTRUD

STENDHAL
BEYLE, HENRI

STENHAGEN, JAN-JORAN
TOLLET, GUNNAR

STENUS
HUXLEY, HERBERT HENRY

STEPHAN, AGNES
KREUTER-TRANKEL, MARGOT

STEPHANI, MARION
GEISLER, HANS

STEPHEN, CHARLES B.
BEYLIN, KAROLINA

STEPHENS, ANN
STEVENSON, ANDY

STEPHENS, ARTHUR
AGNEW, STEPHEN

STEPHENS, BLYTHE
WAGNER, SHARON [BLYTHE]

STEPHENS, CASEY
WAGNER, SHARON [BLYTHE]

STEPHENS, CHARLES
GOLDIN, STEPHEN

STEPHENS, DANNY
FRANCES, STEPHEN D.

STEPHENS, EVE
WARD-THOMAS, EVELYN B.P.S

STEPHENS, FRANCES
BENTLEY, MARGARET

STEPHENS, I.M.
PRATT, INGA STEPHENS

STEPHENS, JEANNE
HAGER, [WILMA] JEAN [L]

STEPHENS, JENNIFER
JENKS, KATHLEEN

STEPHENS, JOHN
SANTESSON, HANS STEFAN

STEPHENS, KAY
STEPHENS, DOREEN

STEPHENS, KENNETH
AGNEW, STEPHEN

STEPHENS, KIT
STEPHENS, CHARLES A.

STEPHENS, LON
MULLER, HERMANN

STEPHENS, MARK
FRANCES, STEPHEN D.

STEPHENS, REED
DONALDSON, STEPHEN R.

STEPHENS, S.J.
PALICKAR, STEPHEN J.

STEPHENS, SHANE
STEVENS, SHANE

STEPHENS, SHARON
CAMP, CANDACE [PAULINE]

STEPHENS, SUZANNE
KIRBY, SUSAN E.
WHITTINGTON, HARRY

STEPHENSEN, A.M.
MANES, STEPHEN

STEPKA, MILAN
BENES, JAN

STEPNIAK
KRAVCHINSKI, SERGEI M.

STEPTOE, LYDIA
BARNES, DJUNA

STERLAND, CARL
NEWQUIST, ROY

STERLING, ANTHONY
CAESAR, [EU]GENE [LEE]

STERLING, BARRY
LIPTON, ROBERT

STERLING, BRETT
BRADBURY, RAY [DOUGLAS]
HAMILTON, EDMOND
MORRISON, WILLIAM
SAMACHSON, JOSEPH

STERLING, DOROTHY
GEORGE, CHARLES

STERLING, EDGAR T.
ROECKEN, KURT WALTER

STERLING, HANK
SNYDER, HARRY

STERLING, HELEN
HOKE, HELEN L.

STERLING, KAREL
PEREZ BLASCO, JULIO

STERLING, MARIA S[ANDRA]
FLOREN, LEE

STERLING, ROBERT
MEYN, NIELS

STERLING, SANDRA
FLOREN, LEE

STERLING, STEWART
WINCHELL, PRENTICE

STERLING, VAL
MEARES, LEONARD F.

STERLING, WARD
WARD, HAROLD

STERLING-JONES, M.
JONES, MARY R.

STERN, ADOLPH
ERNST, ADOLPH

STERN, DUNCAN
OPENSHAW, G.H.

STERN, ELIZABETH
UHR, ELIZABETH

STERN, G.B.
HOLDSWORTH, GLADYS BRONS.

STERN, JOHN
STEARN, JOHN THEODOR

STERN, MATT
PRESTON, HARRY

STERN, MAX
BARRETT, GEOFFREY JOHN

STERN, PAUL FREDERICK
ERNST, PAUL FREDERICK

STERN, SEBASTIAN
KALMUCZAK, ROLF

STERN, STUART
RAE, HUGH C[RAWFORD]
UNGAR, S.

STERNBACH, RICK
STERNBACH, RICHARD MICHL.

STERNE, BILL
LEIBL, ERNST

STERNE, JULIAN
WEBSTER, NOSTRA H.

STERNE, KARL
DAUDET, JULIE R.C.

STERNER, WILLIAMS
RENERTZ, KAJ

STERNIG, LARRY
GAULT, WILLIAM CAMPBELL

STETSON, CHARLOTTE PERKIN
GILMAN, CHARLOTTE PERKINS

STETTNER, ERIK
KALMUCZAK, ROLF

STEUART, GLEN
ROBERTSON, LILLIAN MAY

STEUNE, GEORGES
SCHONESTEIN, DAVID

STEUSSY, MARTI
STEUSSY, MARTHA JANE

STEVENS, AMANDA
AMANN, MARILYN MEDLOCK

STEVENS, ANDY
DANBY, MARY HEATHER
STICKLEE, E.

STEVENS, BLAINE
WHITTINGTON, HARRY

STEVENS, BRYN
DONALDSON, BRYN STEVENS

STEVENS, CARL
OBSTFELD, RAYMOND

STEVENS, CHRISTOPHER
ROCHEFORT, JULIAN
TABORI, PAL

STEVENS, CURTIS
CURTIS, RICHARD [A]
STEVENS, PAUL

STEVENS, DAN J.
OVERHOLSER, WAYNE D.

STEVENS, E.S.
DROWER, ETHEL STEFANA MAY

STEVENS, FAE HEWSTON
STEVENS, FRANCES ISTED

STEVENS, FRANCES
BENNETT, GERTRUDE BARROWS

STEVENS, GREG
COOK, GLEN

STEVENS, GUS
STEVENS, CLARENCE A.

STEVENS, HAROLD
NEUBERG, VICTOR [B]

STEVENS, J.D.
ROWLAND, DONALD S.

STEVENS, JANICE
BACZEWSKI, JANICE K.J.

STEVENS, JENNIFER
HANCHAR, PEGGY

STEVENS, JILL
MOGRIDGE, STEPHEN

STEVENS, JOHN
KELTON, ELMER
TUBB, E.C.

STEVENS, LEE
LEIGH, STEPHEN W.

STEVENS, LINDA
HAMILTON, STEVE & MELINDA

STEVENS, LYNSEY
HOWARD, LYNETTE DELSEY

STEVENS, MAURICE
WHITSON, JOHN HARVEY

STEVENS, PETER
GEIS, BERNARD & DARLENE S

STEVENS, R.L.
HOCH, EDWARD D.

STEVENS, R.T.
STAPLES, REGINALD THOMAS

STEVENS, S.P.
PALESTRANT, SIMON S.

STEVENS, SHIRA
STEVENS, SERITA DEBORAH

STEVENS, SIBYLLE
OBRIST-STRENG, SIBYLLE

STEVENS, SUSAN
MACKIE, MARY

STEVENS, TRISHA
PEARL, JACQUES BAIN

STEVENS, WARD M.
POWERS, PAUL S.

STEVENSON, ALEXANDER
KUGLER, DIETMAR

STEVENSON, ANNE
ELVIN, ANNE KATHARINE S.

STEVENSON, CHRISTINE
KELLY, ELIZABETH

STEVENSON, D.E.
STEVENSON, DOROTHY EMILY

STEVENSON, J.P.
HALDANE-STEVENSON, JAMES

STEVENSON, JOHN [P]
GRIERSON, EDWARD [D]

STEVENSON, KATE
WILLIAMS, KATHLEEN F.

STEVENSON, RICHARD
LIPEZ, RICHARD

STEVENSON, ROBERT
NAISMITH, ROBERT STEVENS.

STEVENSON, ROBERT LOUIS
BALFOUR, ROBERT LOUIS

STEWARD, ADA
SUMNER, ADA

STEWART, A.C.
STEWART, AGNES CHARLOTTE

STEWART, ALAN W.
EKLUND, GORDON

STEWART, ANDREW
DAKERS, ANDREW H.

STEWART, CATHERINE
ZEIGLE, KATE M.

STEWART, CHARLES
ZURHORST, CHARLES [S]

STEWART, COCHRANE
STEWART, KENNETH

STEWART, DAN
LINAKER, MICHAEL

STEWART, DAVID
POLITELLA, DARIO

STEWART, DICK
JAMES, W.I.
MILLER, WARREN
RATHBORNE, ST. GEORGE
TOZER, ALFRED B.
WILLIAMS, M.H.
WINCH, WILL

STEWART, ELIZABETH GREY
REED, ELIZABETH STEWART

STEWART, EVE
NAPIER, PRISCILLA

STEWART, FRANCIS
WILMOT, JAMES R.

STEWART, GORDON
RATHBORNE, ST. GEORGE

STEWART, J.I.M.
STEWART, JOHN INNES M.

STEWART, JAY
PALMER, [CHARLES] STUART

STEWART, JEAN
NEWMAN, MONA ALICE JEAN

STEWART, JO
SCHENK, JOYCE

STEWART, JUDITH
POLLEY, JUDITH ANNA

STEWART, JUDITH ANNE
MACIEL, JUDI[TH ANNE]

STEWART, KAYE
HOWE, DORIS KATHLEEN

STEWART, KERRY
STEWART, LINDA

STEWART, LOGAN
WILDING, PHILIP
SAVAGE, LESLIE H. JR.

STEWART, LOIS
NOLLETT, LOIS S.

STEWART, MARGARET
WILSON, MARGARET C.

STEWART, MARJORIE
HUXTABLE, MARJORIE

STEWART, NATACHA
ULLMAN, NATACHA

STEWART, RATTRAY
MACBEATH, INNIS [S]

STEWART, RUTH
SCANTLIN, BEA

STEWART, SAM
STEWART, LINDA

STEWART, SCOTT
ZAFFO, GEORGE J.

STEWART, W.T.
STEWART, WILLIAM THOMAS

STEWART, WENDELL
EKLUND, GORDON [STEWART]

STEWART, WILL
WILLIAMSON, JOHN STEWART

STEWART-HARGREAVES, E.H.I
WHITE, FRANK JAMES

STEWER, JAN
COLES, ALBERT JOHN

STEWERT, PAUL
YOUNG, GORDON [RAY]

STICHLING, CASPAR
DOLL, HERBERT GERHARD

STIERWELL, JAY
SWICEGOOD, THOMAS L.P.

STIG, STURE
WAGMAN, FRANS OSCAR

STIGSON, ARNE
MALMBERG, ARNE

STILLE, C.A.
CASTELLI, IGNAZ FRANZ

STILLER, KARL
DE MARTINI, EMIL

STILLFRIED, FELIX
BRANDT, ADOLF

STINE, HANK
STINE, HENRY EUGENE

STINE, JEAN MARIE
STINE, HENRY EUGENE

STINE, JOVIAL BOB
STINE, ROBERT L.

STINE, R.L.
STINE, ROBERT L.

STIRLING, A.M.W.
STIRLING, ANNA MARIA D.W.

STIRLING, ARTHUR
SINCLAIR, UPTON BEALL

STIRLING, ELAINE K.
AUSTIN, DEBORAH

STIRLING, GLENN
DIETSCH, WERNER

STIRLING, JESSICA
COGHLAN, PEGGIE
RAE, HUGH C[RAWFORD]

STIRLING, PETER
STERN, DAVID

STIRLING, S.M.
STIRLING, STEPHEN MICHAEL

STIRLING, STELLA
RANSOME, L.E.

STIRLING, TOM
RANSOME, L.E.

STIRLING, VEDA
DRUMMOND, EDITH VICTORIA

STIRNAGEL, ALOIS
ERNSTING, WALTER

STITCH, WILHELMINA
COLLIE, RUTH

STIVENS, DAL
STIVENS, DALLAS GEORGE

STIVERS, DICK
ARNETT, TOM
CAIN, NICHOLAS [COLORADO]
FROST, G.H.
HOFRICHER, PAUL
LIND, LARRY
NORTH, DAVID
PAYNE, L.R.
PENNINGTON, ROD
POWELL, LARRY
RENAUD, RON
ROGERS, CHUCK
ROSE, KEN
SHIAO, C.J.
WINSKI, NORMAN

STOCKBRIDGE, GRANT
BITTNER, ARCHIBALD
CORMACK, DONALD G.
GRUBER, FRANK
PAGE, NORVELL W[OOTEN]
ROGERS, WAYNE
SCOTT, REGINALD T. MAITL.
SCOTT, ROBERT T. MAITLAND
TEPPERMAN, EMILE C.
WINCHELL, PRENTICE

STOCKER, PAUL
MULLER, PAUL ALFRED

STOCKLEY, CYNTHIA
WEBB, LILIAN JULIAN

STOCKTON, F.R.
STOCKTON, FRANCIS R.

STOCKTON, FRANK R.
STOCKTON, FRANCIS R.

STOCKWELL, GAIL
STOCKWELL, GRACE

STODDARD, CHARLES
KUTTNER, HENRY
MOORE, CATHERINE LUCILLE
STRONG, CHARLES STANLEY

STODDARD, SANDOL
WARBURG, SANDOL STODDARD

STODDARD, [MAJ.] HENRY B.
INGRAHAM, PRENTISS

STODELLE, ERNESTINE
HENOCH, ERNESTINE

STOHR, PETRA
SABOTT, EDMUND

STOKER, BRAM
STOKER, ABRAHAM

STOKES, CEDRIC
BEARDMORE, GEORGE CEDRIC

STOKES, EDWARD
KNELLER, F.C.

STOKES, MANNING
STOKES, MANNING LEE

STOKES, SIMPSON
FAWCETT, FRANK DUBREZ

STOLL, URSULA
JUNIKE, ROLF

STOLLE, FERDINAND
ANDERS, LUDWIG FERDINAND

STOLP, HANNS PETER
LOB, WILHELM HERMANN

STOLZ, MARY
JALESKI, MARY S. STOLZ

STONE, ALAN
STRATEMEYER, EDWARD
SVENSON, ANDREW E.

STONE, ANDY
STONE, ANDREW

STONE, CHARLOTTE
JAKUBOWSKI, MAXIM

STONE, EDDIE
HOLLANDER, CARLTON

STONE, ELISA
STANCLIFFE, ELAINE

STONE, EUGENE
SPECK, GERALD EUGENE

STONE, GENE
STONE, EUGENIA

STONE, HAMPTON
STEIN, AARON MARC

STONE, IDELLA PURNELL
PURNELL, IDELLA

STONE, IKEY
PURNELL, IDELLA

STONE, IRVING
TANNENBAUM, IRVING

STONE, JOHN MACK
MCCULLEY, JOHNSTON

STONE, JOSEPHINE RECT.
DIXON, JEANE

STONE, KASSI
RICHTER-TERSIK, OSWALD

STONE, KATE
HOLMES, SARA K. STONE

STONE, LESLIE F.
SILBERBERG, LESLIE F.

STONE, MIKE
BERGER, MEL

STONE, MIRIAM
HARWOOD, GWEN

STONE, NATALIE
GOLDENBAUM, SALLY
STAFF, ADRIENNE

STONE, OLETA
LAROCQUE, RUTH

STONE, RAYMOND
STRATEMEYER, EDWARD

STONE, RICHARD
DELANEY, JACK

STONE, RICHARD A.
STRATEMEYER, EDWARD

STONE, ROSETTA
FRITH, MICHAEL K.
GEISEL, THEODOR SEUSS

STONE, RUFUS
COWIE, DONALD

STONE, SALLY
BULGARELLI, SALLY STONE

STONE, SIMON
BARRINGTON, HOWARD

STONE, THOMAS H.
HARKNETT, TERRY W.

STONE, THOMAS P.
HARKNETT, TERRY W.

STONE, ZACHARY
FOLLETT, KENNETH [MARTIN]

STONEBRIDGE, JOANNE
HANSELL, FRANZ T.

STONEBRIDGE, JOE
HANSELL, FRANZ T.

STONECLINK
DALE, THOMAS F.

STONER, BERT
BRAUN, WILBUR

STOOKEY, AARON W.
BEATTY, JEROME

STOPPARD, TOM
STRAUSSLER, TOM

STOPPELMAN, FRANCIS
STOPPELMAN, FRANS

STOREY, ALICE
SHANKMAN, SARAH

STOREY, RHODA LYS
SCHIER, NORMA

STORM, ANTHONY
ROBERTS, JOHN S[TORM]

STORM, BRIAN
HOLLOWAY, BRIAN W.

STORM, CHRISTOPHER
OLSEN, THEODORE VICTOR

STORM, DUNCAN
FLOYD, GILBERT

STORM, ELIZABETH
SANDSTROM, EVE K.

STORM, ERIC
BECK, ED
TUBB, E.C.

STORM, HARRISON
FISCHER, BRUNO

STORM, IVAN
THOMAS, REGINALD GEORGE

STORM, JACK
DANIELS, NORMAN A.
FISHER, STEPHEN GOULD
DONOVAN, LAURENCE

STORM, JANNICK
JORGENSEN, J.S.

STORM, JASON F.
FISCHER, BRUNO

STORM, LESLEY
CLARK, MABEL MARGARET C.

STORM, MALLORY
FAIRMAN, PAUL W.

STORM, MICHAEL
SEMPHILL, ERNEST
RYAN, WALTER C.

STORM, OMAR
KORSELL, JOHN

STORM, RUPERT
SEMPHILL, ERNEST

STORM, RUSSELL
WILLIAMS, ROBERT MOORE

STORM, VIRGINIA
SWATRIDGE, IRENE M.M.

STORMCROW
TALIFERO, GERALD

STORME, JED [ON TITLE PG]
LAZENBY, NORMAN A.

STORME, MICHAEL
SHARP, ROBERT GEORGE

STORME, PETER
STERN, PHILIP VAN DOREN

STORM[E], MICHAEL
DAWSON, GEORGE H.

STORR, ROBERT
MALY, ANTON JOHANN

STORY, JOSEPHINE
LORING, EMILIE [B]

STORY, RICHARD
GOLD, HORACE L.

STORY, SYDNEY A. JR.
PIKE, MARY HAYDEN G.

STOTT, DOT
STOTT, DOROTHY M.

STOTTER, MIKE
STOTTER, MICHAEL JAMES

STOWE, ROSETTA
OGAN, GEORGE & MARGARET

STOWERS, SANDRA
STOWERS, WALTER G.

STRACHEY, BARBARA
HALPERN, BARBARA STRACHEY

STRADLEY, MARK
SMITH, RICHARD REIN

STRADLING, MATTHEW
MAHONY, MARTIN FRANCIS

STRAFFORD, MURIEL
SAUER, MURIEL STRAFFORD

STRAITON, EDDIE
STRAITON, EDWARD CORNOCK

STRAKER, PHILIP
SEYMOUR, LEE EDWARD

STRAKOSCH, AVERY
DENHAM, AVERY S.

STRAND, PAUL E.
PALESTRANT, SIMON S.

STRANG, HERBERT
ELY, GEORGE HERBERT
L'ESTRANGE, C.J.

STRANGE, DILLON
NORWOOD, VICTOR [G.C.]

STRANGE, ELWIN
LUTZ, JOHN [T]

STRANGE, ERIC
HAKANSSON, JAN

STRANGE, HARRY
SHAW, STANLEY GORDON

STRANGE, JOHN STEPHEN
TILLETT, DOROTHY S.

STRANGE, JOSEPH
CRAWFURD, OSWALD J.F.

STRANGE, KEMBLE
MCENVOY, C.N.

STRANGE, MARK
STEPHEN, ADRIAN LESLIE
STEPHEN, KARIN COSTELLOE
STRACHEY, MARJORIE COLV.
STRACHEY, RACHEL COSTELL.

STRANGE, MICHAEL
OELRICHS, BLANCHE MARIE L

STRANGE, NORA K.
STANLEY, NORA K.B.S.

STRANGE, OLIVER
STRANGE, THOMAS OLIVER

STRANGE, PHILLIPA
COURY, LOUISE ANDRE

STRANGER, BERT
PETERS, HERMANN

STRANGER, JOYCE
WILSON, JOYCE M.

STRANGER, RALPH
JUDSON, RALPH

STRANGER, THE
JANSON, CHARLES WILLIAM
LIEBER, FRANCIS

STRANGEWAY, MARK
LEYLAND, ERIC

STRASSER, HEIDI
DALLMAYR, ILSE

STRATEGICUS
O'NEILL, HERBERT CHARLES

STRATFORD, KAREN
FINNIGAN, KAREN

STRATFORD, MICHAEL
CASSIDAY, BRUCE [BINGHAM]

STRATFORD, PHILIP
BULMER, [HENRY] KENNETH

STRATHEARN-HAY
ROBERTSON, WILLIAM

STRATHERN, WILLIAM
JOBSON, HAMILTON

STRATTON, CHRIS
HUBBARD, RICHARD

STRATTON, HENRY
NELSON, MICHAEL HARRINGT.

STRATTON, JEFF
BARNARD, LESLIE T.

STRATTON, JOHN
ALLDRIDGE, JOHN STRATTON

STRATTON, REBECCA
GILLEN, LUCY

STRATTON, TED
STRATTON, JOHN THEODORE

STRATTON, THOMAS
COULSON, ROBERT
DEWEESE, EUGENE

STRATTON-PORTER, GENE
STRATTON, GENEVA GRACE

STRATYNER, BARBARA
COHEN-STRATYNER, BARBARA

STRAUB, OTTO
SOBOTTA, KURT

STRAVOLGI, BARTOLOMEO
TUCCI, NICCOLO

STRAYER, E. WARD
STRATEMEYER, EDWARD

STREAMER, COL. D.
GRAHAM, HARRY

STREEBECK, NANCY
STRIEBECK, NANCY

STREET, A.G.
STREET, ARTHUR GEORGE

STREET, BRADFORD
HINE, AL[FRED B.]

STREET, C.J.C.
STREET, CECIL JOHN C.

STREET, EMMETT
BEHAN, BRENDAN

STREET, HARRY
LLOP SELLARES, JUAN

STREET, JAY
SLESAR, HENRY
STREET, GEORGE SLYTHE

STREET, KELLY
TUCKER, JOY

STREET, LEE
HAMPTON, KATHLEEN

STREET, LEROY
HOPPER, MILLARD

STREET, LESLIE
FREEMANTLE, BRIAN [HARRY]

STREET, OCTAVIA
BYINGTON, KAA

STREET, ROBERT
THOMAS, GORDON

STREFF, ERNST
NIEBERGALL, ERNST ELIAS

STRETTON, CHARLES
DYER, CHARLES [RAYMOND]

STRETTON, HESBA
SMITH, SARAH

STRETTON, RENSLAW
DYER, CHARLES [RAYMOND]

STREUVELS, STIJN
LATEUR, FRANK

STRIBE, DAN
STREIB, DANIEL T.

STRIBLING, T.S.
STRIBLING, THOMAS S.

STRICK, MARV
PIKE, ROBERT MARVIN

STRICK, MARVIN
PIKE, ROBERT MARVIN

STRICKLAND, BRAD
STRICKLAND, WILLIAM BRAD.

STRICKLAND, BRADLEY
STRICKLAND, WILLIAM BRAD.

STRICKLAND, JEROME
WRIGHT, LAN

STRICKLAND, JEROME
WRIGHT, LIONEL PERCY

STRIEB, DAN
STREIB, DANIEL T.

STRIKE, JEREMY
RENN, THOMAS EDWARD

STRIKER, RANDY
WHITE, RANDY

STRINGER, ARTHUR
STRINGER, JOHN ARBUTHNOTT

STRINGER, DAVID
ROBERTS, KEITH [J.R.]

STRINGER, KEITH
ROBERTS, KEITH

STRIPPER
WILSON, JOHN

STRIX
FLEMING, PETER

STRODE, MARY
SAUNDERS, CICELY

STROM, LESLIE WINTER
WINTER, LESLIE

STRONG'TH'ARM, C.
ARMSTRONG, CHARLES W.

STRONG, BEN
ELLIS, WILLIAM SR.
HULME-BEAMAN, EMERIC

STRONG, CHARLES
EPSTEIN, BERYL [WILLIAMS]
EPSTEIN, SAMUEL

STRONG, DAVID
MCGUIRE, LESLIE SARAH

STRONG, ERIC
SILBERSCHLAG, EISIG

STRONG, HARRINGTON
MCCULLEY, JOHNSTON

STRONG, HARRY
KRAFT, ROBERT

STRONG, HERO
JONES, CLARA AUGUSTA

STRONG, J.J.
STRONG, JEREMY

STRONG, JOHN B.
DUNN, JOSEPH ALLAN

STRONG, LENNOX
GRIER, BARBARA G.D.

STRONG, PAT
HOUGH, RICHARD ALEXANDER

STRONG, PITT
ASPERN-BUCHMEIER, ELISAB.

STRONG, SPENCER
ACKERMAN, FORREST J.

STRONG, SUSAN
REES, JOAN

STRONG, ZACHARY
MANN, EDWARD BEVERLY

STRONGBLOOD, CASPER
WEBSTER, DAVID ENDICOTT

STROUD, ALBERT
BUDRYS, ALGIRDAS JONAS

STROUD, LUKE
KINNES, J.

STROVER, DOROTHEA
TINNE, DOROTHEA

STRUAN, FRANK
FISHER, GRAHAM

STRUBBERG, ACHIM F.
HUBER, ARMIN OTTO

STRUG, ANDRZEJ
GALECKI, TADEUSZ

STRUNZ, PETER
ASPERN-BUCHMEIER, ELISAB.

STRUTHER, JAN
MAXTONE-GRAHAM, JOYCE

STRUTTON, BILL
STRUTTON, WILLIAM HAROLD

STRYDOM, LEN
ROUSSEAU, LEON

STRYFE, PAUL
NEWMAN, JAMES ROY

STRYJKOWSKI, JULIAN
STARK, PESACH

STRYKER, DANIEL
MORRIS, CHRISTOPHER C.
MORRIS, JANET E[LLEN]
STUMP, JANE [BARR]

STRYKER, DEV
MURPHY, MOLLIE COCHRAN
MURPHY, WARREN

STRYKER, HAL
SMITH, GEORGE H[ENRY]

STRYKER, HANK
SMITH, GEORGE H[ENRY]

STUART, ALAN
WEIGHTMAN, ARCHIBALD JOHN

STUART, ALEX
STUART, VIOLET VIVIAN F.

STUART, ALEX R.
GORDON, [RICHARD] STUART

STUART, ANNE
OHLROGGE, ANNE K. STUART

STUART, ANTHONY
HALE, J. ANTHONY STUART

STUART, BECKY
BUCHAN, [JOHN] STUART

STUART, BLAIR
EWINGS, MICHAEL

STUART, BRIAN
WORTHINGTON-STUART, BRIAN

STUART, C.F.
FLAISCHLEIN, CASAR

STUART, CASAR
FLAISCHLEIN, CASAR

STUART, CASEY
BULLARD, ANN ELIZABETH

STUART, CHARLES
MACKINNON, CHARLES ROY
REID, CHARLES [STUART]

STUART, CLAY
WHITTINGTON, HARRY

STUART, DAVID
HOYT, EDWIN P. JR.

STUART, DEE
STUART, DORIS

STUART, DIANA
TOOMBS, JANE [JENKE]

STUART, DON A.
CAMPBELL, JOHN W[OOD]

STUART, DONALD
STEWARD, DONALD WILLIAM

STUART, ELEANOR
CHILDS, ELEANOR STUART
PORTER, ELEANOR [H]

STUART, ELIZABETH
BEACH, ELIZABETH
PRATT, ELIZABETH STUART

STUART, ESME
LEROY, AMELIA CLARE

STUART, FAY
LEONARD, NELLIE MABEL

STUART, FLORENCE
STONEBRAKER, FLORENCE

STUART, FREDERICK
TOMLIN, ERIC

STUART, GERALD
STUART, DONALD

STUART, GORDON
BEDFORD-JONES, HENRY
SAYLER, HARRY L.
WOOD, JAMES [A.F]

STUART, IAN
GRIERSON, DAVID
MACLEAN, ALISTAIR STUART

STUART, JAN
SCHULTZ, JANET

STUART, JAY ALLISON
TAIT, DOROTHY

STUART, JOHN ROY
MCMILLAN, DONALD

STUART, KENNETH
COX, PATRICK BRIAN

STUART, KENNETH [CONT]
KOHLER, ROLF
WESANDER, BJOERN K.

STUART, LESLIE
MARLOWE, ALAN STEPHEN
MARLOWE, KENNETH

STUART, LOGAN
WILDING, PHILIP

STUART, LYLE
SIMON, LIONEL

STUART, MARGARET
PAINE, LAURAN BOSWORTH

STUART, MATT
HOLMES, L[LEWELLYN] P.

STUART, MEGAN
WILLIAMS, DOROTHY JEANNE

STUART, MICHAEL
THOMAS, REGINALD GEORGE

STUART, MIRANDA
THOMPSON, MURIEL STUART

STUART, ROBYN
STUART, VIOLET VIVIAN F.

STUART, RONALD
STUART, DONALD

STUART, SHEILA
BAKER, MARY GLADYS

STUART, SIDNEY
AVALLONE, MICHAEL

STUART, TONNY
BOMKE, BERNHARD

STUART, V.A.
STUART, VIOLET VIVIAN F.

STUART, VIVIAN
MACKINNON, CHARLES ROY
STUART, VIOLET VIVIAN F.

STUART, W.J.
MACDONALD, PHILIP

STUART, WARREN
MACDONALD, PHILIP

STUART-VERNON, CHARLES
MACKINNON, CHARLES ROY

STUCLEY, ELIZABETH
NORTHMORE, ELIZABETH F.

STUKELEY, SIMON
SAVERY, HENRY

STULTIFER, MORTON
CURTIS, RICHARD [A]

STUMPKE, HARALD
STEINER, GEROLF

STURDY, CARL
STRONG, CHARLES STANLEY

STURE-VASA, MARY
ALSOP, MARY O'HARA

STURGEON, KENNETH
BULMER, [HENRY] KENNETH

STURGEON, THEODORE
WALDO, EDWARD HAMILTON

STURGIS, COLIN
COLE, LESTER
STURGIS, MELVIN

STURGIS, J.B.
BASTIN, JOHN

STURM, DELIA
LEITNER, HILDEGARD

STURROCK, JEREMY
HEALEY, BENJAMIN J.

STURTON, HUGH
JOHNSTON, HUGH ANTHONY S.

STUTLEY, S.J.
STUTLEY, SYDNEY JAMES D.

STUYVESANT, ALICE
WILLIAMSON, ALICE M.L.
WILLIAMSON, CHARLES N.

STUYVESANT, POLLY
PAUL, MAURY

STYLITES, SIMEON
CALDWELL, WILLIAM A.
LUCCOCK, HALFORD EDWARD

SUARES, ANDRE
SCANTREL, FELIX-ANDRE-YVE

SUAREZ LYNCH, B.
BIOY-CASARES, ADOLFO
BORGES, JORGE LUIS

SUBHADRA-NANDAN
DAS, PRAFULLA CHANDRA

SUBOND, VALERIE
GRAYLAND, VALERIE MERLE

SUDBURY, RICHARD
GIBSON, CHARLES HAMMOND

SUE, EUGENE
JOSEPH, MARIE

SUFFLING, MARK
ROWLAND, DONALD S.

SUIXON, G.F.W.
SCHADLICH, GOTTFRIED

SUK, RATIBOR
VASEK, VLADIMIR

SUKRON, S.N.
GAREIS, HERBERT

SULIMAN, RUSTAM
RUSTAMNASADE, SULIEMAN

SULLIVAN, EDWARD S.
GIBSON, WALTER B.

SULLIVAN, ERIC HARRISON
HICKEY, MADELYN EASTLUND

SULLIVAN, PAT
MESSMER, OTTO

SULLIVAN, REESE
LUTZ, GILES A.

SULLIVAN, REX
BOOTH, EDWIN

SULLIVAN, SEAN MEI
SOHL, GERALD ALLEN

SULLIVAN, TIM
SULLIVAN, TIMOTHY ROBERT

SULLIVAN, TOM
SULLIVAN, THOMAS JOSEPH

SULLIVAN, VERN
VIAN, BORIS

SULLIVAN, VERNON
VIAN, BORIS
WEISS, JOE

SULTAN, MARTINA
PICKER, RITA

SUMIKO
DAVIES, SUMIKO

SUMMER, BRIAN
DUBREUIL, ELIZABETH L.

SUMMER, MIKE
REMUS, MICHAEL

SUMMERFOREST, IVY B.
KIRKUP, JAMES

SUMMERHAYES, PRUDENCE
ALAN TURNER, V. PRUDENCE

SUMMERHILL, J.K.
SCHERE, MONROE

SUMMERS, ASHLEY
ASHLEY, FAYE

SUMMERS, BLUE PETER
SUMMERS, J.C.

SUMMERS, CHLOE
CONNELL, SUSAN

SUMMERS, COLIN
AGNEW, STEPHEN

SUMMERS, D.B.
BARRETT, GEOFFREY JOHN

SUMMERS, DENNIS
BARRETT, GEOFFREY JOHN

SUMMERS, DIANA
GOTTFRIED, THEODORE MARK
SMITH, GEORGE H[ENRY]

SUMMERS, ESSIE
SUMMERS, ETHEL NELSON

SUMMERS, FAYE
ROHR, PAULA M.

SUMMERS, GERALD
KARNAOOKH, GEORGE

SUMMERS, GORDON
HORNBY, JOHN WILKINSON

SUMMERS, IRIS
KNIGHT, JOAN GEIZEY
KUCZKIR, MARY

SUMMERS, JOHN A.
LAWSON, HORACE LOWE

SUMMERS, LEO RAMON
MOREY, LEO

SUMMERS, REY
SUMMERS, AUGUSTUS MONTAG.

SUMMERS, ROWENA
SAUNDERS, JEAN

SUMMERS, TRUE
CAMPBELL, HOPE

SUMMERSCALES, ROWLAND
GAINES, ROBERT

SUMMERVILLE, MARGARET
WILSON, BARBARA & PAMELA

SUMNER, OLIVIA
TOOMBS, JANE [JENKE]

SUN, ANNALISE
MAXWELL, ANN [ELIZABETH]

SUNBEAM, SUSIE
MACKARNESS, MATILDA ANNE

SUNDARAM
LUHAR, TRIBHUVANDAS

SUNDOWN, WILL
SANDERS, WILLIAM

SUNDOWNER
TICHBORNE, HENRY

SUNESON, VIC
LUNDQUIST, SUNE

SUNNA
LARUSDOTTIR, ELINBORG

SURAGLE, PIERRE
PELOT, PIERRE

SURANSKY, VALERIE POLAKOW
POLAKOW, VALERIE [S]

SURBANK, EVAN
KALMUCZAK, ROLF

SURCINGLE
BOAKE, BARCROFT

SURD, ABE
SIDEBOTTHAM, PETER

SURGEON SCOUT
POWELL, [DAVID] FRANK

SURREY, KATHRYN
MATTHEWMAN, PHYLLIS

SURREY, RICHARD
BROOKER, BERTRAM

SURYA, G.W.
GEORGIEWITZ-WEITZER, DEM.

SUSAN
GRAHAM, SUSAN

SUSSEX, GORDON
VOLK, GORDON

SUTHERLAND, ELIZABETH
MARSHALL, ELIZABETH M.

SUTHERLAND, JEAN
NASH, JEAN

SUTHERLAND, JOAN
KELLY, JOAN COLLINGS

SUTHERLAND, KARI
SMITH, KAREN ROSE

SUTHERLAND, MORRIS
MORRIS, G. SUTHERLAND

SUTHERLAND, PEG
ROBARCHEK, PEG

SUTHERLAND, ROY
SOUTHER, HUGH

SUTHERLAND, WILLIAM
COOPER, JOHN MURRAY

SUTTER, LARABIE
SAVAGE, LESLIE H. JR.

SUTTON, ANDREW
TUBB, E.C.

SUTTON, HENRY
SLAVITT, DAVID RYTMAN

SUTTON, I.M.
COAD, FREDERICK R.

SUTTON, JEAN
SUTTON, EUGENIA

SUTTON, JEFF
SUTTON, JEFFERSON HOWARD

SUTTON, JEFFERSON H.
SUTTON, JEFFERSON HOWARD

SUTTON, JOHN
TULLETT, DENIS JOHN

SUTTON, MARGARET
SUTTON, RACHEL IRENE B.

SUTTON, MARGARET BEEBE
SUTTON, RACHEL IRENE B.

SUTTON, PENNY
CARTWRIGHT, JUSTIN
WOOD, CHRISTOPHER [H]

SUTTON, RACHEL B.
SUTTON, RACHEL IRENE B.

SUTTON, STACK
SUTTON, MAURICE LOUIS

SUTTON, THOMAS
REACH, JAMES

SUYIN, HAN
CHOU KUANG HU

SUZANNE, JAMIE
HAWES, LOUISE
LANTZ, FRANCESS LIN

SVAREFF, COUNT VLADIMIR
CROWLEY, EDWARD ALEXANDER

SVEINSSON, ASLAKUR
INDRIDASON, INDRIDI

SVENSEN, KNUT
HOLMBERG, ERIK

SVENSKE, TOR
KERFVE, AXEL

SVENSON, BOB
NICKEL, RUTH

SVENSSON, SVEN
BOLAY, KARL-HEINZ

SVETLA, KAROLINA
MUZAKOVA, JOHANNA

SVEVO, ITALO
SCHMITZ, ETTORE

SWAHN, CHRISTER
WICKSTROM, VICTOR HUGO

SWAIN, E.G.
SWAIN, EDMUND GILL

SWAIN, MARK
CLEMENS, SAMUEL LANGHORNE

SWAIN, MIRIAM
MASON, MIRIAM EVANGELINE

SWAN, ANNIE S.
BURNETT-SMITH, ANNIE S.

SWAN, EDGAR
WHISHAW, FRED[ERICK J.]

SWAN, MARIE
BARTLETT, MARIE

SWAN, PEGGY
GEIS, RICHARD E.

SWAN, REBECCA
ROGERS, ELIZABETH J.

SWANHOLM, BIRGIT
GREVEN, HELGA

SWANSEA, CHARLEEN
SWANZEY, CHARLEEN

SWANSON, LOGAN
MATHESON, RICHARD [B]

SWANSON, MARK
SKINNER, MICHAEL

SWANSTROM, NILS
BRANNON, WILLIAM T.

SWANZA, H.J.
PETAJA, EMIL

SWATRIDGE, IRENE MAUDE
CHARLES, THERESA

SWAYNE, GEOFFREY
CAMPION, SIDNEY RONALD

SWAYNE, MARTIN [LUTRELL]
NICOLL, H. MAURICE D.

SWEENEY, KAREN O'CONNOR
O'CONNOR, KAREN

SWEENEY, R.C.H.
SWEENEY, CHARLES

SWEET, SARAH [C]
JEWETT, [T] SARAH ORNE

SWEETLAND, NANCY ROSE
ROSE, NANCY A.

SWENSON, PEGGY
GEIS, RICHARD E.

SWEVEN, GODFREY
BROWN, JOHN MACMILLAN

SWIFT, ANTHONY
FARJEON, J. JEFFERSON

SWIFT, AUGUSTUS T.
LOVECRAFT, H[OWARD] P.

SWIFT, BENJAMIN
MCKIMMEY, JAMES

SWIFT, BENJAMIN
PATERSON, WILLIAM ROMAINE

SWIFT, BRIAN
KNOTT, WILLIAM CECIL JR.
WISE, ARTHUR

SWIFT, BRYAN
KNOTT, WILLIAM CECIL JR.

SWIFT, DAVID
KAUFMAN, JOHN

SWIFT, JULIAN
APPLIN, ARTHUR

SWIFT, LEWIS J.
GARDNER, LEWIS J.

SWIFT, MERLIN
LEEMING, JOSEPH

SWIFT, RACHELL
LUMSDEN, JEAN

SWIFT, STELLA
WHISH, VIOLET E.

SWINFORD, BOB
SWINFORD, BETTY [J.W]

SWINTON, E.D.
SWINTON, ERNEST DUNLOP

SWITHEN, JOHN
KING, STEPHEN [EDWIN]

SWITHIN, ANTHONY
SARJEANT, W.A.S.

SYDNEY
SEAWELL, MOLLY ELLIOT

SYDNEY, CYNTHIA
TRALINS, [SANDOR] ROBERT

SYDNEY, FRANK
WARWICK, FRANCIS ALISTAIR

SYDNEY, GEORGE
BOUNDS, SYDNEY J.

SYDOW, MARIANNE
BISCHOFF, MARIANNE [E]

SYGRIANUS
DE BOLOGNE, MICHELE

SYLVA, CARMEN
ELIZABETH, QUEEN, RUMANIA

SYLVAN
PROCTOR, RICHARD W.

SYLVESTER, ANTHONY
LAVRENCIC, KARL

SYLVESTER, HELGE
BORNSTROEM-RUNDE, UWE

SYLVESTER, JOHN
HAWTON, HECTOR

SYLVESTER, MICHAEL
BLUME, HORST-M.

SYLVESTER, PHILIP
WORNER, PHILIP A.I.

SYLVIN, FRANCES
SCHWARTZ, FRANCES

SYLVIN, FRANCIS
SEAMAN, SYLVIA S.

SYMMES, ROBERT EDWARD
DUNCAN, EDWARD HOWARD

SYMONS, A.J.A.
SYMONS, A. JAMES ALBERT

SYMONS, ALBERT JAMES A.
SYMONS, A. JAMES ALBERT

SYNGE, DON
EDELSTEIN, HYMAN

SYNGE, J.M.
SYNGE, JOHN M.

SYNOPTICUS
RENNER, KARL

SYNTAX
ASH, EDWARD CECIL

SYNTAX, JOHN
DENNETT, HERBERT VICTOR

SYRIL, BINNIE
BRAUNSTEIN, BINNIE SYRIL

SYRUC, J.
MILOSZ, CZESLAW

SZAJKOWSKI, ZOSA
FRYDMAN, SZAJKO

SZCZUCKA
KOSSAK, ZOFIA

SZILLAGHY, IRMA
HARDT, HEINZ

SZTYRMER, ELEONORA
SZTYRMER, LUDWIK

SZYDLOW, JARL
SZYDLOWSKI, MARY V.

SZYMANSKI, RICHARD
SYMANSKI, RICHARD

T.
THORP, JOSEPH

T.-E., CHARLES ROY EARL
ELLINGER, AUGUST

T.B.
BENSON, ARTHUR CHRISTOPH.

T.B.D.
JAMES, WILLIAM MILBOURNE

T.E.
ERSKINE, THOMAS

T.M.
MARTIN, [SIR] THEODORE

T.N.T.
THOMAS, CORNELIUS D.

T.P.
O'CONNOR, THOMAS POWER

T.S.
SECCOMBE, THOMAS

TAAFFE, MICHAEL
MAGUIRE, ROBERT A.J.

TABARD, GEOFFREY
MCNELLY, WILLIS E.

TABARD, PETER
BLAKE, LESLIE JAMES

TABARIN
DUVAL, GEORGES

TABLET, HILDA
SWANN, DONALD [I]

TABORI, PAUL
TABORI, PAL

TAD
DORGAN, THOMAS ALOYSIUS

TADLOCK, NORMA
JOHNSON, NORMA K. TADLOCK

TADRACK, MOSS
CARYL, WARREN H.

TAE-YONG, RO
RUTT, RICHARD

TAFFRAIL
DORLING, HENRY TAPRELL

TAFFY
LLEWELLYN, D[AVID] W.

TAGGART, BEN
GREEN, ROGER

TAGGART, DEAN
KING, ALBERT

TAGGERT, JOHN
BREUCKER, OSCAR HERBERT

TAHLAQUAH, DAVID
LEMOND, ALAN

TAHNEY, C.G.
GREEN, CHARLES

TAINE, JOHN
BELL, ERIC TEMPLE

TAK YUSSUF HOFF
SASSOON, SIEGFRIED [L]

TAKI
THEODORACOPULOS, PETER

TALAGRANDE, JACQUES LOUIS
MAULNIER, THIERRY

TALBOT, CARL
HIPKINS, CHARLES HAMMOND

TALBOT, HAKE
NELMS, HENNING CUNNINGHAM

TALBOT, HENRY
ROTHWELL, HENRY TALBOT

TALBOT, HUGH
ALINGTON, ARGENTINE F.
CHETWYND-TALBOT, EDWARD H

TALBOT, KATHERINE
ASHTON, KATHERINE
BARKER, ILSE EVA L.

TALBOT, KAY
ROWLAND, DONALD S.

TALBOT, LAWRENCE
BRYANT, EDWARD W.

TALESE, GAY
TALESE, GAETANO

TALIS, GERD
FRIEDE, GERHARD

TALKE, HELGA
BROZA-TALKE, HELGA

TALKER, T.
RANDS, WILLIAM BRIGHTY

TALKIN, GIL
ROSENTHAL, ALAN

TALL, STEPHEN
CROOK, COMPTON N[EWBY]

TALLARICO, TONY
TALLARICO, ANTHONY

TALLIS, ROBYN
COVILLE, BRUCE [F]
DOYLE, DEBRA
LOWENTROUT, CHRISTINE I.S
MACDONALD, JAMES D.
MAGON, JYMN

TALLIS, ROBYN [CONT]
ZAMBRENO, MARY FRANCES

TALLY, JUDD
DANIELS, NORMAN A.

TALMAGE, ANNE
POWELL, TALMAGE

TALMEY, ALLENE
PLAUT, ALLENE TALMEY

TALVIO, MAILA
MIKKOLA, MARIA WINTER

TAMAS, LAJOS
TREML, LAJOS

TAMMSAARE, A.H.
HANSEN, ANTON

TAMMSAARE, ANTON
HANSEN, ANTON

TAMOR, CASPIPINI
DUCHI, JACOB

TAN
BOGORAZ, LLADIMIR GERM.

TAN YUN
LIN, ADET J[USU]

TANDEM, CARL FELIX
SPITTELER, CARL

TANFUCIO, NERI
FUCINI, RENATO

TANGENT, PATRICK Q.
PHELPS, GEORGE H.

TANIA B.
BLIXEN-FENEKE, KAREN

TANIS
DAVIES, HILDA A.

TANIYA, KYN
QUINTANELLA, LUIS

TANNENBAUM, IRVING
STONE, IRVING

TANNER, BARBEL
HOLLWERTH, HILDE

TANNER, CLAY
PROCTOR, GEO[RGE] W[YATT]

TANNER, JAKE
MUSEO, LAURA
SCHERMERHORN, STEPHEN

TANNER, JOHN
MATCHA, JACK

TANNER, STEPHEN
HABISREUTINGER, RUDOLPH D

TANNER, WILLIAM
AMIS, KINGSLEY [WILLIAM]

TANNER-RUTHERFORD, C.
WINCHESTER, CLARENCE

TANNWEBER, MILLA
BOHNE, JOSEFINE

TANTRIST
WESANDER, BJOERN K.

TANZER, MARTIN
KALMUCZAK, ROLF

TAO MULIAN
TOTTEN, GEORGE O. III

TAPER
LEVIN, BERNARD

TAPIO, PAT DECKER
KINES, PAT DECKER

TAPPEN, ROY
LANGFORD, DAVE

TAPSELL, R.F.
TAPSELL, ROBERT FREDERICK

TAR, JACK
BRUSTAT-NAVAL, FRITZ

TARA, JOHN
MICHEL, JOHN B.

TARASC, GILBERT
BEST, THARRATT GILBERT

TARDE, GABRIEL
DE TARDE, JEAN GABRIEL

TARIO, FRANCISCO
PELAEZ, FRANCISCO

TARLOW, NORA
COHEN, NORA

TARN, SHIRLEY
NEUBERG, VICTOR [B]

TARNACRE, ROBERT
CARTMELL, ROBERT

TARNE, ROSINA
FEARN, JOHN RUSSELL

TAROKATH, CARMUTH
TREDINNICK, WILLIAM JR.

TARR, HANNO
BRAND, KURT

TARR, MICHAEL
KARNOW, MICHAEL

TARRANT, ELIZABETH
LEYLAND, ERIC

TARRANT, JOHN
EGLETON, CLIVE F.

TARRANT, WILMA
SHERMAN, JORY [T]

TARTARUGA, U.
EHRENFREUD, EDMUND OTTO

TASHRAK
ZEVIN, ISRAEL JOSEPH

TASMA
COUVEUR, JESSIE

TATE, ELLALICE
HIBBERT, ELEANOR BURFORD

TATE, MARY
ADAMS, TRACY

TATE, MARY ANNE
HALE, MARY ARLENE

TATE, RICHARD
MASTERS, ANTHONY

TATE, ROBIN
FANTHORPE, R.L.
MANSFIELD, HARRY O.

TATHAM, CAMPBELL
ELTING, MARY

TATRAY, ISTVAN
RUPERT, RAPHAEL RUDOLPH

TATTERSALL, IVAN
HODGKINSON, IVAN T.

TAUNTON, ERIC
JONES, KENNETH WESTCOTT

TAURUS
HONEY, PHILIP

TAUSCHECK, CARINA
PFAEFFLI, CARINA

TAVARES, BRAULIO
NETO, BRAULIO F. TAVARES

TAVEREL, JOHN
HOWARD, ROBERT E.

TAVIS, ALEC
DUNNETT, ALISTAIR M.

TAVO, GUS
IVAN, GUSTAVE E.
IVAN, MARTHA MILLER

TAVY, PETER
HEMERY, ERIC

TAWNY, T.V.
GREEN, CHARLES

TAY PAY
O'CONNOR, THOMAS POWER

TAYLOR, ABRA
BROUSE, BARBARA

TAYLOR, ANN
BRODEY, JIM
SMITH, RICHARD REIN

TAYLOR, ANTHONY
VELEY, CHARLES

TAYLOR, BRAD
SMITH, RICHARD REIN

TAYLOR, BRUCE
YIN, LESLIE CHARLES B.

TAYLOR, DANIEL
SCHNEIDER, DANIEL EDWARD

TAYLOR, DAY
PARKINSON, CORNELIA M.

TAYLOR, DAY [CONT]
SALVATO, SHARON ANNE

TAYLOR, DAYNA
HOBBS, DAVID B.
PARKINSON, CORNELIA M.

TAYLOR, DIANNE
TAYLOR, JANELLE [W]

TAYLOR, DOMINI
LONGRIGG, ROGER [ERSKINE]

TAYLOR, DUNCAN
SMITH, DONALD TAYLOR

TAYLOR, ELLIS [TYLER?]
KING, ALBERT

TAYLOR, FRANK
HUTSON, SHAUN

TAYLOR, GEORGE
PARULSKI, GEORGE R.

TAYLOR, H. BALDWIN
WAUGH, HILLARY B.

TAYLOR, J.R.
MOORCOCK, MICHAEL

TAYLOR, JAYNE
KRENTZ, JAYNE ANN

TAYLOR, JEROME
KREJCI, JEROME

TAYLOR, JESSIE
AMIDON, WILLIAM VINCENT

TAYLOR, JIM
MOORCOCK, MICHAEL

TAYLOR, JOHN
MAGEE, JAMES
MIELKE, THOMAS R.P.

TAYLOR, JOHN ROBERT
TAYLOR, ANDREW JOHN ROBT.

TAYLOR, JUDSON R.
HALSEY, HARLAN PAGE

TAYLOR, JUDY
HOUGH, JUDY TAYLOR

TAYLOR, L.A.
SPARER, LAURIE A. TAYLOR

TAYLOR, LOIS DWIGHT COLE
COLE, LOIS DWIGHT

TAYLOR, MIKE
HARSTEN, UWE

TAYLOR, NANCY
ROSENBERG, NANCY TAYLOR

TAYLOR, NED
RATHBORNE, ST. GEORGE

TAYLOR, NORMAN
WOOD-SMITH, NOEL

TAYLOR, R.W.
TAYLOR, RONALD WILLIAM

TAYLOR, RON W.
TAYLOR, RONALD WILLIAM

TAYLOR, SAM
GOODYEAR, STEPHEN FREDRK.

TAYLOR, SAM S.
ZANE, LEHI

TAYLOR, SELMAN
SELMAN, ELSIE EMILY

TAYLOR, SNIP
QUINN, SEABURY

TAYLOR, SUSAN
CUMMINS, MARY WARMINGTON

TAYLOR, TIM
TAYLOR, HOWARD LANGDON

TAYLOR, TOSO
TAYLOR, THOMAS HILHOUSE

TAYLOR, VALERIE
TATE, VELMA

TAYLOR, WALKER
TAYLOR, PHILIP N. WALKER

TAYLOR, WILLIAM
JUHLING, JOH.

TAYLOR, [CAPT.] ALFRED B.
INGRAHAM, PRENTISS

TCHAADAIEFF
SOROKIN, PITIRIM ALEXAND.

TE SELLE, SALLIE MCFAGUE
MCFAGUE, SALLIE

TEAGUE, BOB
TEAGUE, ROBERT

TEARLE, CHRISTIAN
JAQUES, EDWARD TYRRELL

TEED, HAMILTON
TEED, GEORGE HAMILTON

TEED, JACK
LOWDER, CHRISTOPHER

TEED, JACK HAMILTON
LOWDER, CHRISTOPHER

TEFFI, NADEZHDA
LOKHVITSKAYA, NADEZHDA A.

TEFFY
BUCHINSKAYA, NADEZHDA AL.

TEG, TWM
VULLIAMY, COLWYN EDWARD

TEGERN, THOMAS
GESKE, MATTHIAS

TEHUDI, STEPHEN N.
STEPHEN, JUDY

TEICHERT, PETRA
LAMP, PETRA

TEJN, MICHAEL
KLAEHR, MOGENS

TELESCOPE, TOM
NEWBERY, JOHN

TELFAIR, NANCY
DUBOSE, LOUISE JONES

TELFAIR, RICHARD
JESSUP, RICHARD

TELFORD, STAN
GROSSMANN, HANS HUGO

TELLAR, MARK
COLLINS, VERE HENRY

TELLET, ROY
EVANS, ALBERT EUBULE

TELMANN, KONRAD
ZITELMANN, KONRAD

TELSTAR
GOODWIN, GEOFFREY

TEMBORN, KLAUS
ERTTMANN, PAUL OSKAR

TEMPEST, EVELYN
CUMING, EDWARD WILLIAM D.

TEMPEST, JAN
SWATRIDGE, IRENE M.M.

TEMPEST, JOHN
SPILLSBURY, JULIAN

TEMPEST, SARAH
PONSONBY, DORIS ALMON

TEMPEST, THERESA
KENT, LOUISE ANDREWS

TEMPEST, VICTOR
PHILIPP, ELLIOT ELIAS

TEMPKA, ZYGMUNT
NOWAKOWSKI, ZYGMUNT

TEMPLAR, JOHN
GARBUTT, JOHN L.

TEMPLAR, MAURICE
GROOM, ARTHUR WILLIAM

TEMPLE, ANN
MORTIMER, PENELOPE [R]

TEMPLE, ARTHUR
NORTHCOTT, WILLIAM CECIL

TEMPLE, DAN
NEWTON, DWIGHT BENNETT

TEMPLE, EDITH
MURRELLS, JOSEPH

TEMPLE, JAMES
BELL, ERIC TEMPLE

TEMPLE, LEAH
PATTON, LEAH & CLIFF

TEMPLE, PAUL
DURBRIDGE, FRANCIS H.
MCCONNELL, JAMES D.R.

TEMPLE, RALPH
ALEXANDER, ROBERT W.

TEMPLE, ROBIN
WOOD, [SAMUEL] ANDREW

TEMPLE, RUTH
ALEXANDER, ROBERT W.

TEMPLE, SARAH
ARGUILE, CHERYL

TEMPLE-ELLIS, N.A.
HOLDAWAY, NEVILLE A.

TEMPLETON, HERMINIE
KAVANAGH, HERMINIE T.

TEMPLETON, JANET
HERSHMAN, MORRIS

TEMPLETON, JESSE
GOODCHILD, GEORGE

TENGAL, KOSUGI
TAMEZO, KOSUGI

TENN, WILLIAM
KLASS, PHILIP J.

TENNANT, CARRIE
KELLY, MRS. T.

TENNANT, CATHERINE
CROZIER, KATHLEEN MURIEL

TENNANT, KYLIE
RODD, KATHLEEN TENNANT

TENNESHAW, S.M.
BEAUMONT, CHARLES
GARRETT, RANDALL [P]
GEIER, CHESTER S.
HAMILTON, EDMOND
HAMLING, WILLIAM L.
MARLOWE, STEPHEN
SILVERBERG, ROBERT

TENNESS, GEORGE
DELK, ROBERT CARLTON

TENNOV, DOROTHY
TENNOW, DOROTHY

TENT, NED
DENNETT, HERBERT VICTOR

TENTH EARL OF BESSBOROUGH
PONSONBY, FREDERICK E.N.

TEOFILUS
LOENNQUIST, CARL A.

TERANUS
ZAPP, ARTHUR

TERBERG, HUGO
MUENSTERBERG, HUGO

TEREGO, A.L.
GEIS, RICHARD E.

TERENZ, GABRIELE
FROMMHOLZ, ALICE

TERESA MARGARET, [SISTER]
ROWE, MARGARET [KEVIN]

TERESAH
UBERTIS, CORINNA TERESA G

TERGIT, GABRIELE
REIFENBERG, ELISE

TERJE, SEVED
VEGENOR, SVERRE

TERKEL, STUDS
TERKEL, LOUIS

TERME, HILARY
HAY, JACOB

TERRENCE, FREDERICK J.
HAYES, JOHN F.

TERRID, PETER
RITTER, WOLFPETER

TERRIDGE, ERNEST
RICHTER, ERNST H.

TERRY
MALONEY, F.J. TERENCE

TERRY, BEVERLY
HAAF, BEVERLY T.

TERRY, C.V.
SLAUGHTER, FRANK GILL

TERRY, CAROL
TALBOT, CAROL TERRY

TERRY, HENRY MACHU
IMBERT-TERRY, HENRY MACHU

TERRY, MARGARET
DUNNAHOO, TERRY

TERRY, NOEL
WOOD-SMITH, NOEL

TERRY, SARALEE
KAYE, MARVIN [NATHAN]

TERRY, WILLIAM
HARKNETT, TERRY W.

TERSON, PETER
PATTERSON, PETER

TERTZ, ABRAM
SINIAVSKII, ANDREI D.

TERVAPAA, JUHANI
WUOLIJOKI, HELLA MARIA

TERZIN, GERO
LEWIN, GEORG

TESCH, MICHAEL
MYER-PAYSAN, DIETER

TESSENDORF, K.C.
TESSENDORF, KENNETH C.

TETEL, JULIE
ANDRESEN, JULIA TETEL

TETON, DON
RICHARDSON, GLADWELL G.

TETZNER, INGEBORG R.
REINTSCH, INGEBORG

TETZNER, LISA
KLABER, LISA [T]

TEVIS, WALTER S.
TEVIS, WALTER STONE

TEW, MARY
DOUGLAS, MARY

TEX, WILLIAM
MULLER, KURT

TEXAS DOLL LADY
WEAVER, GUSTINE COURSON

TEXAS RANGER
WALLACE, JOHN

TEXAS-REITER
PUTZ, PAUL

TEXTU
DUPREY DE LA RUFFINERE, P

TEY, JOSEPHINE
MACKINTOSH, ELIZABETH

THACKER, SHELLY
MEINHARDT, SHELLY THACKER

THACKERAY, NORMAN
HUBNER, HORST W.

THACKERY, C.T.
AMBROSE, MICHAEL E.

THACKERY, NORMAN
RAHN, WOLFGANG

THALER, DORA
FINALY, DOROTHEA [D]

THALER, M.N.
KERNER, FRED

THALER, MIKE
THALER, MICHAEL C.

THAMES, C.H.
JAKES, JOHN [WILLIAM]
MARLOWE, STEPHEN

THAMES, CHRISTOPHER H.
MARLOWE, STEPHEN

THAMES, JACK
RYAN, JOHN FERGUS

THAN, JOHN A.
LYNCH, JOHN A.

THANE, ELSWYTH
BEEBE, ELSWYTH

THANET, NEIL
FANTHORPE, R.L.

THANET, OCTAVE
FRENCH, ALICE

THARAUD, JEROME & JEAN
THARAUD, CHARLES & ERNEST

THARP, JEFFREY
GIRARD, JAMES PRESTON

THATCHER, AMELIA
MINER, VIRGINIA SCOTT

THATCHER, JULIA
BENSEN, DONALD R.
HOSKINS, ROBERT

THAXTER, NIGEL
NORWOOD, VICTOR [G.C.]

THAYER, GERALDINE
DANIELS, DOROTHY
DANIELS, NORMAN A.

THAYER, JANE
WOOLLEY, CATHERINE

THAYER, LEE
THAYER, EMMA REDINGTON L.

THAYER, PATRICIA
WRIGHT, PATRICIA

THAYER, PETER
WYLER, ROSE

THAYER, ROSE
WYLER, ROSE

THAYER, URANN
ROLLINS, WILLIAM STACY

THE AUTHOR OF CHERRY AMES
GIBSON, WALTER B.

THE BUTTE BASHKIRTEFF
MACLANE, MARY

THE LODGER
LLOYD, JOHN IVESTOR

THE PHELONS
PHELON, MIRA M. & W.P.

THE RAMBLER
DEUTZMAN, LAWRENCE

THE SNAKE MAN
DITMARS, RAYMOND LEE

THE WESTERN SPY
DILLON, JOHN M[YLES]

THEATES
WEINTRAUB, WIKTOR

THEBEN, ERIKA
HORN, ERIKA

THEIR WELLWISHER
IDE, SIMEON

THEO, ION
TEODORESCU, ION N.

THEOBALD
LOVECRAFT, H[OWARD] P.

THEOBALD, LEWIS [LOUIS]
LOVECRAFT, H[OWARD] P.

THEOBALDUS
LOVECRAFT, H[OWARD] P.

THEODAMUS
GLASS, THEODORE

THEODOR, PETER
KRAMER, PETER

THEODORE, BROTHER
GOTTFRIED, THEODORE MARK
KAYE, MARVIN [NATHAN]

THEOPHANY
TOFANI, LOUISE E.

THEOSOPHO & ELLORA
OUSELEY, GIDEON JASPER R.

THERIDION, PAUL
KNOLL, HAROLD

THERION, MASTER
CROWLEY, EDWARD ALEXANDER

THERIVE, ANDRE
PUTHOSTE, ROGER

THERSITES
WHIBLEY, CHARLES

THES, P.R.
PERTHES, HANS

THETA, ERIC MARK
HIGGINSON, HENRY CLIVE

THEUER, MARTIN MINOR
MILDNER, THEODOR

THEVENIN, DEVIS
DUHAMEL, GEORGES

THEYDON, JOHN
JENNISON, JOHN WILLIAM

THIELE, MARGARETE
ABSHAGEN, MARGARETE

THIERY, HERMAN
DAISNE, JOHAN

THINN, AXEL
VON KLIMBURG, HANS-ULRICH

THIRLMERE, ROWLAND
WALKER, JOHN

THISBY
GENOVESE, VINCE
TURNER, DONNA M.

THISTLETON, HON. FRANCIS
FLEET, WILLIAM HENRY

THIUSEN, ISMAR
MACNIE, JOHN

THOENE, PETER
BIHALJI-MERIN, OTO

THOLE, KAREL
THOLE, CAROLUS A.M.

THOMAN, EGBERT S.
ELLIS, EDWARD S.

THOMAS, ALLISON
FLEISCHER, LENORE

THOMAS, ANDREA
BORNSTROEM-RUNDE, UWE
HILL, MARGARET [OHLER]

THOMAS, ANTHONY
POOLE, REGINALD H.

THOMAS, BREE
HOWE, SUSANNA

THOMAS, BRUCE
PAINE, LAURAN BOSWORTH

THOMAS, CARL H.
DOERFFLER, ALFRED

THOMAS, CAROLYN
DUNCAN, ACTEA CAROLYN

THOMAS, COGSWELL
COGSWELL, THEODORE
THOMAS, THEODORE L.

THOMAS, DAN
SANDERS, LEONARD M. JR.

THOMAS, DANIEL B.
BLUESTEIN, DANIEL THOMAS

THOMAS, DEREK
BOGDANOVICH, PETER

THOMAS, DIANNE
MORRIS, DEBRAH
SHAVER, PAT

THOMAS, DICEY
COCKS, PAMELA P.

THOMAS, DORIS
VANCEL, DORIS

THOMAS, DOROTHY
THOMASHOWER, DOROTHY

THOMAS, EDDY
JOHNSON, THOMAS E.

THOMAS, ELTON
FAIRBANKS, DOUGLAS SR.

THOMAS, G.K.
DAVIES, LESLIE PERNELL

THOMAS, GERRARD
KEMPINSKI, TOM

THOMAS, GOUGH
GARWOOD, GODFREY THOMAS

THOMAS, H.C.
KEATING, LAWRENCE A.

THOMAS, HENRY
SCHNITTKIND, HENRY THOMAS

THOMAS, J. BISSELL
STEPHEN, JOYCE ALICE

THOMAS, J.F.
FLEMING, THOMAS JAMES

THOMAS, JIM
REAGAN, THOMAS B.

THOMAS, JOAN GALE
ROBINSON, JOAN M.G.T.

THOMAS, JOANNA
HARDY, CARLENE

THOMAS, JODI
KOUMALATS, JODI

THOMAS, JULIAN
JAMES, JOHN STANLEY

THOMAS, K.
FEARN, JOHN RUSSELL

THOMAS, K.H.
KIRK, THOMAS HOBSON

THOMAS, KATE
BULL, KATHERINE T.J.
HUDGINS, CATHERINE

THOMAS, KATHRIN
AMLER, IRENE
DARNSTADT, HELGE

THOMAS, LATELY
STEELE, ROBERT V.P.

THOMAS, LEE
FLOREN, LEE

THOMAS, M.L.
JEIER, THOMAS

THOMAS, MANFRED
PFEFFER, HEINRICH

THOMAS, MANUEL
MULLER-HARLIN, WOLFGANG

THOMAS, MARK L.
JEIER, THOMAS

THOMAS, MARTIN
MARTIN, THOMAS HECTOR

THOMAS, MERVYN
CURRAN, MONA [ELISA]

THOMAS, MICHAEL
WILKS, MICHAEL THOMAS

THOMAS, MOLLY
TEMTE, MYRNA

THOMAS, MURRAY
RAGG, THOMAS MURRAY

THOMAS, NEAL
THOMAS, CORNELIUS D.

THOMAS, PAUL
COOK, WILLIAM EVERETT
MISRAKI, PAUL

THOMAS, PENELOPE
THOMAS, P.J.

THOMAS, PIRI
THOMAS, JOHN PETER

THOMAS, TAY
THOMAS, MARY

THOMAS, TED
THOMAS, THEODORE L.

THOMAS, VICTORIA
DEWEESE, EUGENE
KUGI, CONNIE

THOMPSON, A.C.
MEYNELL, ALICE [C.G.T.]

THOMPSON, A.L.B.
THOMPSON, ARTHUR LEONARD

THOMPSON, BUCK
PAINE, LAURAN BOSWORTH

THOMPSON, CHESWICK J.
THOMPSON, CHARLES J.S.

THOMPSON, CHINA
LEWIS, M. CHRISTIANNA M.

THOMPSON, CHRISTINE PULL.
PULLEIN-THOMPSON, CHRIST.

THOMPSON, DAVID
ROBBINS, DAVID LAWRENCE

THOMPSON, DIANA PULLEIN
PULLEIN-THOMPSON, DIANA

THOMPSON, EILEEN
PANOWSKI, EILEEN JANET T.

THOMPSON, FRANCIS CLEGG
MENCKEN, HENRY LOUIS

THOMPSON, FRED
NIGGEMANN, GUNTER
PUTZ, PAUL

THOMPSON, FREIDA
FOX, GARDNER F.

THOMPSON, GARY
THOMPSON-MORAGA, GARY A.

THOMPSON, GENE
LUTZ, GILES A.
THOMPSON, EUGENE ALLEN

THOMPSON, J.J.
THOMPSON, JESSE JACKSON

THOMPSON, JAMES
THOMPSON, JAMES [MYERS]

THOMPSON, JAMES H.
FREEMAN, GRAYDON LAVERNE

THOMPSON, JIM
THOMPSON, JAMES [MYERS]

THOMPSON, JONATHAN H.
ROE, M.S.

THOMPSON, JOSEPHINE
PULLEIN-THOMPSON, JOSEPH.

THOMPSON, MADELINE
GREIG-SMITH, JENNIFER M.

THOMPSON, MAGGIE
THOMPSON, MARGARET CURTIS

THOMPSON, MIKE
TURNER, ROBERT H.

THOMPSON, PAMELA
THOMPSON, PAULA & MARCELA

THOMPSON, RALPH L.
FUCHS, JAKOB

THOMPSON, RUSS
PAINE, LAURAN BOSWORTH

THOMPSON, STEPHEN
DELL, DRAYCOT MONTAGU

THOMPSON, TOBY
TURNER, ROBERT H.

THOMPSON, WILLIAM C.L.
EDWARDS, WILLIAM B.

THOMPSON, WOLF
THOMPSON, ERNEST EVAN S.

THOMSON, A.A.
THOMSON, ARTHUR ALEX.

THOMSON, AUDREY
GWYNN, AUDREY

THOMSON, D.H.
THOMSON, DAISY HICKS

THOMSON, DAISY
ROE, M.S.

THOMSON, EDWARD
TUBB, E.C.

THOMSON, JOAN
CHARNOCK, JOAN PADGETT

THOMSON, JONATHAN H.
THOMSON, DAISY HICKS

THOMSON, NEIL
JOHNSON, HENRY T.

THOOK, GARRY
MAUERHARDT, ROLF

THOPMAS, IVOR
BULMER-THOMAS, IVOR

THOR, JOHANNES
LANG, ISAAC

THOR, TERRY
SHAW, LAWRENCE TAYLOR

THOR, TRISTAN
LANG, ISAAC

THORBURN, JOHN
GOLDSMITH, JOHN THORBURN

THORBY, MARIANNE
NYBERG, MARIANNE

THORER, KONRAD
GREVE, FELIX PAUL B.F.

THORMANBY
DIXON, W. WILLMOTT

THORN, BARBARA
PAINE, LAURAN BOSWORTH

THORN, ISMAY
POLLOCK, EDITH CAROLINE

THORN, KATE
JONES, CLARA AUGUSTA

THORN, RONALD SCOTT
WILKINSON, RONALD

THORNDIKE, HELEN LOUISE
ADAMS, HARRIET S.

THORNDYKE, ALAN
GLASBY, JOHN S.

THORNDYKE, HELEN LOUISE
STRATEMEYER, EDWARD

THORNE, ALEXANDRA
THORLEIFSON, ALEX

THORNE, B.K. TED
THORNE, BLISS KIRBY

THORNE, BELLA
JARRETT, BELLA

THORNE, BRADLEY D.
GLUT, DONALD F.

THORNE, EDOUARD
GREVE, FELIX PAUL B.F.

THORNE, EMILY
JUDSON, JEANNE

THORNE, GUY
RANGER-GULL, C[YRIL A.E.]

THORNE, HART
CARHART, ARTHUR H.

THORNE, IAN
DIKTY, JULIAN [C] MAY

THORNE, JEAN WRIGHT
DIKTY, JULIAN [C] MAY

THORNE, JED
HUBER, FREDERICK V [FRED]

THORNE, JOY
HUBER, FREDERICK V [FRED]

THORNE, KENT
CODY, STONE

THORNE, LUCIFER
EISENBERG, ERNEST

THORNE, NICOLA
ELLERBECK, ROSEMARY A.L.

THORNE, P.
SMITH, MARY PRUDENCE [W]

THORNE, RAMSAY
CAMERON, LOU

THORNE, ROGER
RUSSELL, RAY

THORNE, STERLING
FULLER, DOROTHY MASON

THORNE, WHYTE
WHITEING, RICHARD

THORNET, TERESA A.
HOLLOWAY, ANNA

THORNTON, CAROLYN
STROMEYER, CAROLYN

THORNTON, EDWARD
BROOKS, EDWY SEARLES

THORNTON, ELIZABETH
GEORGE, MARY

THORNTON, HALL
SILVERBERG, ROBERT

THORNTON, HAROLD
OFFARD, CECIL

THORNTON, JERRY
THORNTON, EMMA SHORE

THORNTON, MAYSIE
JEFFREY-SMITH, MAY T.

THORNTON, W.B.
BURGESS, THORNTON W.

THORP, MODWENA
ROBERTSON, MARGERY ELLEN

THORPE, CHARLES J.
PACHTER, JOSH

THORPE, DICKSON
CARR, WOODA NICHOLAS

THORPE, DOBBIN
DISCH, THOMAS M.

THORPE, E.G.
THORPE, GEORGE

THORPE, ELLEN
ROBERTSON, MARGERY ELLEN

THORPE, FRED
STEARNS, ALBERT

THORPE, J.K.
NATHANSON, LAURA WALTHER

THORPE, KAMPA
BELLAMY, ELIZABETH WHITF.

THORPE, LEE
GREENOP, FRANK S.
MEARES, LEONARD F.

THORPE, SYLVIA
THIMBLETHORPE, J. SYLVIA

THORPE, TREBOR
KEMP, ERNEST

THORPE, TREBOR [TREVOR]
FANTHORPE, R.L.

THORSTEIN, ERIC
GROSSMAN, JOSEPH. JUDITH

THORVALL-FALK, KERSTIN
THORVALL, KERSTIN

THORWALD, JURGEN
BONGARTZ, HEINZ

THORWANG, JULIANE
HAFT, ELLI

THRASHER, L.L.
BATY, LINDA LEA

THRIBB, E.J.
FANTONI, BARRY [ERNEST]
INGRAMS, RICHARD REID

THRICE, LUKE
RUSSELL, JOHN

THUMBTACK, TOM
SQUIRES, FREDERICK

THUNDERBOLT, CAPT.
WARD, FREDERICH

THUNDERCLOUD, KATHERINE
WITT, SHIRLEY HILL

THURLAND, BILBERRY
HOOTEN, CHARLES

THURLEY, NORGROVE
STONEHAM, C. THURLEY

THURLOW, ROBERT
GRIFFIN, ROBERT JOHN T.

THURMAN, STEVE
CASTLE, FRANK

THURN, FRITZ
FOREGGER, F.

THURSTON, HOWARD
GIBSON, WALTER B.

THURSTON, OLIVER
FLANDER, HENRY

THYNN, ALEXANDER
GEORGE, VISCOUNT WEYMOUTH

THYNNE, ALEXANDER
THYNN, ALEXANDER GEORGE

THYROW, CHRISTIANE
BRAUNS-LEUTZ, ILSE

THYS, FRANK
REHFELD, FRANK

THYSELIUS, THORA
BEHRENS-THYSELIUS, THORA

THYSON, A.C.
AITCHISON, GEORGE

TIBBER, ROBERT
FRIEDMAN, EVE ROSEMARY

TIBBER, ROSEMARY
FRIEDMAN, EVE ROSEMARY

TIBBERTS, WILLIAM
BRANNON, WILLIAM T.

TICHEBURN, CHEVIOT
AINSWORTH, WILLIAM HARR.

TICK-TACK
CAMPO, ANGEL DEL

TIEMPO, CESAR
ZEITLIN, ISRAEL

TIFTON, LEO
PAGE, GERALD W.

TIGAR, CHAD
LEVI, PETER

TIGER LILY
.BLAKE, LILLIAN DEVEREAUX

TIGER OF THE SNOWS
WANGDI, MANGYAL

TIGER, DERRY
ELLISON, HARLAN

TIGER, JACK
PUECHNER, RAY

TIGER, JOHN
WAGER, WALTER [HERMAN]

TIGER, THEOBALD
TUCHOLSKY, KURT

TIGRINA
EIDE, EDYTHE

TIHOTI
CALDERON, GEORGE

TIKHONOV, VALENTIN
PAYNE, PIERRE S. ROBERT

TIKTIN, CARL
TUCKACHNISKY, CARL

TILBURNE, LEE
TILBURNE, A.R.

TILBURY, QUENNA
WALKER, EMILY KATHLEEN

TILLEY, GENE
TILLEY, E.D.

TILLMAN, ROLLE
STAHLSTROM, ROLLE

TILLOT, W.E.
ELLIOTT, WILLIAM J.

TILLRAY, LES
GARDNER, ERLE STANLEY

TILLY
KANNAN, LAKSHMI

TILLYARD, E.M.W.
TILLYARD, EUSTACE M.W.

TILMAN, H.W.
TILMAN, HAROLD WILLIAM

TILMAN, TILO
HENCKELL, JURGEN

TILMS, RICHARD A.
SLADEK, JOHN

TILTON, ALICE
TAYLOR, PHOEBE ATWOOD

TILTON, RAFAEL
TILTON, MADONNA ELAINE

TIM
MARTIN, TIMOTHY

TIME, MARK
IRWIN, H.C.

TIMMS, E.V.
TIMMS, EDWARD VIVIAN

TIMON, JOHN
MITCHELL, DONALD GRANT

TIMOTHY, A COUNTRY BOY
MELLICK, HENRY GEORGE

TIMOTHY, ARTHUR
VAHEY, JOHN G. HAZLETTE

TIMOTHY, ARTHUR N.
VAHEY, JOHN G. HAZLETTE

TIMRAVA
SLANCIKOVA, BOZENA

TIMSOL, ROBERT
BIRD, FREDERIC MAYER

TINA
TINA, DOROTHY LES

TINA, BEATRICE
HAIG, EMILY ALICE

TINCROWDER, LEO QUEEQUEQ
FARMER, PHILIP JOSE

TING-LING
PING-CHIH, CHIANG

TINKER, BEAMISH
JESSE, F. TENNYSON

TINKER, JOSEPH
GARRETT, RANDALL [P]

TINNE, DOROTHEA
STROVER, DOROTHEA

TINNE, E.D.
STROVER, DOROTHEA

TINY ALICE
RAMIREZ, ALICE

TIPTREE, JAMES JR.
SHELDON, ALICE H. BRADLEY

TIREBUCK, W.
SHARP, WILLIAM

TISH TASH
TASHLIN, FRANK

TISSANT-BERNAC, MATHIEU
MACBEATH, INNIS [S]

TISTE, R.
WILLIAMS, ARTHUR

TITAN, EARL
FEARN, JOHN RUSSELL

TITANIA
BLIXEN-FENEKE, KAREN

TITMARSH, MICHAEL ANGELO
THACKERAY, WILLIAM MAKEP.

TITTERTON, W.R.
TITTERTON, WILLIAM R.

TIVEYCHOC, A.
LORDING, ROWLAND EDWARD

TIVOLI
BLEAKLEY, HORACE WILLIAM

TJORNSEN, ALF
RUDAT, RICHARD J.

TOBBY, TIM
PEHLEN, KARL

TOBER, SIXT
LAUXMANN, LONI

TOBIAS, KATHERINE
GOTTFRIED, THEODORE MARK

TOBY, LIZ
MINSKEY, BETTY JANE

TOBY, M.P.
LUCY, HENRY WILLIAM

TODD, ANNE OPHELIA
DOWDEN, ANNE OPHELIA TODD

TODD, BRENDA
HAMILTON, BRENDA

TODD, ELIZABETH
RASLEY, ALICIA TODD

TODD, ERIC
DUBREUIL, ELIZABETH L.

TODD, H.E.
TODD, HERBERT EATON

TODD, MIKE
GOLDBOGEN, AVROM

TODD, OWEN L.
GRASMUCK, JURGEN

TODD, PAUL
POSNER, RICHARD

TODD, PETER
HAMILTON, CHARLES H.S.

TODD, SARAH MANNING
FREEMAN, JEAN TODD

TODD, W.
KRAMER, PETER

TODHUNTER, PHILIPPA
BOND, GRACE

TOGESEN, VOBBER
ROSENDORFFER, HERBERT

TOHUNGA
LANE, WILLIAM

TOIL, CUNNIN
LEHMANN, R.C.

TOKKO, RI
DEXHEIMER, LUDWIG

TOKLAS, ALICE B.
STEIN, GERTRUDE

TOLBY, ARTHUR
INFIELD, GLENN [B]

TOLD, GUSTAV
ARNOLD, TIM

TOLER, BUCK
KELLY, HAROLD ERNEST

TOLHURST, GEOFFREY
CROSS, RENA

TOLIVAR, ROBIN
BISHOP, LESLIE
OAKSON, PAT C.

TOLIVER, GEORGE
MASSELINK, BEN

TOLKIEN, J.R.R.
TOLKIEN, JOHN RONALD R.

TOLLEIS
TOLKIEN, JOHN RONALD R.

TOLLER
LYBURN, DR. ERIC FREDERIC

TOLLER, KATE CAFFREY
CAFFREY, KATE

TOLMAN, GUY
BROWN, WENZELL

TOLMAN, HILDEGARDE
TEILHET, HILDEGARDE TOLMN

TOLNAI, KAROLY
DE TOLNAY, CHARLES E.

TOLNAI, LAJOS
HAGYMASSY, LAJOS

TOLNAI, VAGUJHELYI KAROLY
DE TOLNAY, CHARLES E.

TOLNAY, TOM
TOLNAY, THOMAS

TOLSTOY, LEO
TOLSTOY, LEV NIKOLALEVICH

TOLZ, NICK
SLOTKIN, JOSEPH

TOM, HUNG LONG
OWEN, FRANK

TOMAN, ALFRED
GIBSON, WALTER B.

TOMASITO, DON
ROBERTSON, THOMAS ANTHONY

TOMERLIN, J.E.
ACKERMAN, FORREST J.

TOMFOOL
FARJEON, ELEANOR

TOMKINS, JASPER
BATEY, TOM

TOMKINSON, CONSTANCE
WEEKS, CONSTANCE T.

TOMLINE, F.
GILBERT, WILLIAM S.

TOMLINE, F. LATOUR
GILBERT, WILLIAM S.

TOMLINSON, H.M.
TOMLINSON, HENRY MAJOR

TOMPKINS, JULIET WILBOR
POTTLE, JULIET W.T.

TOMPKINS, WALKER A.
CURRY, THOMAS ALBERT

TONASHI
HARRINGTON, MARK R.

TONDER, ERIK
MEYN, NIELS

TONKONGY, GERTRUDE
FRIEDBERG, GERTRUDE

TONSON, JACOB
BENNETT, [ENOCH] ARNOLD

TONVUS, HEINZ
KLOSTERMEYER, ANTON

TOOK, BELLADONNA
CHAPMAN, VERA

TOOKER, DICK PRESLEY
TOOKER, RICHARD [PRESLEY]

TOOLE, PETER
PUSCH, HARALD

TOOLE, REX
TRALINS, [SANDOR] ROBERT

TOOMBS, HARRY
WALLEY, DAVID GORDON

TOOMER, EUGENE
TOOMER, NATHAN P.

TOOMER, JEAN
TOOMER, NATHAN P.

TOOMER, N[ATHAN] JEAN
TOOMER, NATHAN P.

TOONDER, MARTIN
GROOM, ARTHUR WILLIAM

TOPAZ, JACQUELINE
HYMAN, JACKIE DIAMOND

TOPICUS
GOODWIN, GEOFFREY

TOPOL, EDWARD
TOLPOLBERG, EDMON

TOR, REGINA
SHEKERJIAN, REGINA TOR

TORAL, JUDITH
DAVIS, JUDITH L.

TORBERG, FRIEDRICH
KANTOR-BERG, FRIEDRICH

TORGA, MIGUEL
DE ROCHA, ADOLFO CORREIA

TORGOIS, VERPERTINA
ACKERMAN, FORREST J.

TORGOSI, KARLON
ACKERMAN, FORREST J.

TORLEY, LUKE
BLISH, JAMES B.

TORPARE, TORD
SANDBLAD-HANESON, E.C.S.

TORQUEMADA
MATHERS, EDWARD POWYS
MOORCOCK, MICHAEL

TORR, DOMINIC
PEDLER, JOHN B.S.

TORR, I.
MACKINNON, CHARLES ROY

TORR, IAIN
MACKINNON, CHARLES ROY

TORRANCE, LEE
SADGROVE, SIDNEY HENRY

TORRES, TERESKA
TORRES-LEVIN, TERESKA [S]

TORREY, MARJORIE
CHANSLOR, MARJORIE TORREY
HOOD, TORREY

TORRIE, MALCOLM
MITCHELL, GLADYS [M.W.]

TORRIS, CHRISTIANE v.
REBNER-CHRISTIAN, DORIS

TORRO, PEL
ANDREWS, PETER J.
FANTHORPE, R.L.
MANSFIELD, HARRY O.

TORROLL, G.D.
LAWSON, ALFRED

TORSI, TRISTAN
LANG, ISAAC

TORSTEN, LARS
BRAND, KURT

TORSTEN, THEA
EBLE, THEA

TORWEGGE, CLAUDIA
EISELE, MARTIN

TOSON, SHIMAZAKI
HARUKI, SHIMAZAKI

TOTH, LAZLO
NOVELLA, DON

TOTHAM, MARY
BREINBERG, PETRONELLA

TOTIUS
DU TOIT, JACOB DANIEL

TOTOLOCHE
MURILLO, JOSEFA

TOTTERMAN, ALICE
UNNERSTAD, EDITH ALICE

TOUCAN, JOHN
BIRD, WILLIAM H.F.

TOUCHSTONE, TOM
BURY, THOMAS

TOULMIN, DAVID
REID, JOHN

TOURNET, JEAN JACQUES
GEISLER, HANS

TOURNYINPARTE, ALESSANDRA
GINZBERG, NATALIE

TOUSSAINT, JACKIE
LOURENS-KOOP, ADRIANA L.K

TOUSSEUL, JEAN
DEGEE, OLIVIER

TOUZALIN, ROBERT
REED, ROBERT

TOVARDS, JOHN
SASS, EUGEN v.

TOWARS, IVAR
KORNBLUTH, C[YRIL] M.

TOWER, DIANA
SMITH, RICHARD REIN

TOWERS, IVAR
KORNBLUTH, C[YRIL] M.
WILSON, RICHARD

TOWERS, REGINA
PYKARE, NINA ANN COOMBS

TOWERS, TRICIA
IVISON, ELIZABETH

TOWNE, MARY
SPELMAN, MARY

TOWNE, PETER
NABOKOV, PETER [F]

TOWNE, STUART
RAWSON, CLAYTON

TOWNLEY, CAROL
TOWNLEY-PARKER, CAROLINE

TOWNSEND, ERIC W.
MCLEAN, ERIC W.

TOWNSEND, MARK
PRONZINI, WILLIAM JOHN
WALLMANN, JEFFREY M.

TOWNSEND, TIMOTHY
ROBEY, TIMOTHY LESTER

TOWNSEND, TOM
TOWNSEND, THOMAS L.

TOWNSHEND, RICHARD
BICKERS, RICHARD L.T.

TOWRY, PETER
PIPER, DAVID TOWRY

TRACEY, ANN
BROMIGE, IRIS

TRACEY, GRANT
NUTTALL, ANTHONY

TRACEY, HUGH
EVANS, KAY & STUART

TRACY, CATHERINE
STORY, ROSAMOND MARY

TRACY, LELAND
TRALINS, [SANDOR] ROBERT

TRACY, MARGARET
KLAVAN, ANDREW
KLAVAN, LAWRENCE

TRACY, MARILYN
LECOCQ, TRACY

TRACY, POWERS
WARD, DON

TRACY, SUSAN
MARINO, CAROLYN FITCH

TRAFFORD, F.G.
RIDDELL, CHARLOTTE ELIZ.

TRAFFORD, JEAN
WALKER, EDITH

TRAFT, RINGO
NAGEL, HERBERT CHRISTIAN

TRAHERNE, MICHAEL
WATKINS-PITCHFORD, D.J

TRAHNA, EBBA
ORNULF, HILDING KONSTANT.

TRAIL, ARMITAGE
COONS, MAURICE

TRAILL, PETER
MORTON, GUY [MAINWARING]

TRAILRIDER
HYLAND, ANN

TRAIN, ADAM
FISCHER, BRUNO

TRAINE, GYPSEY
LOVEJOY, MARY EVELYN

TRAINER, RUSSELL
TRALINS, [SANDOR] ROBERT

TRAINOR, RICHARD
TRALINS, [SANDOR] ROBERT

TRAINOR, SANDY
TRALINS, [SANDOR] ROBERT

TRAINOR, STARR
TRALINS, [SANDOR] ROBERT

TRAKEHNEN, ERIKA
HITZ, ERIKA

TRALINS, BIG BOB
TRALINS, [SANDOR] ROBERT

TRALINS, BOB
TRALINS, [SANDOR] ROBERT

TRAMIN, A.G.
MARTIN, GLORIA ANN

TRAMIN, ED
MARTIN, GLORIA ANN

TRAMIN, LISA
MARTIN, GLORIA ANN

TRAMP, TILBURY
LEVER, CHARLES [JAMES]

TRANK, WERNER
PURKART, WALTER

TRANKEL, MARGOT
KREUTER-TRANKEL, MARGOT

TRANSUE, JACOB
MATHESON, JOAN

TRANT, ERICA
ALLEN, AGNES [B]

TRANT, MARTIN
WHITE, TRENTWELL MASON

TRANTER, NIGEL [GODWIN]
TREDGOLD, NYE

TRAPROCK, WALTER E.
CHAPPELL, GEORGE S.

TRASK, HELEN
LOWELL, JOAN

TRASK, JONATHAN
LEVINSON, LEONARD [L]

TRASK, KATRINA
TRASK, KATE NICHOLS

TRASK, MERRILL
BRAHAM, HAL
COLTON, MEL

TRASS, EUGEN
BERENDT, KLAUS

TRAUBE, RUY
TRALINS, [SANDOR] ROBERT

TRAUSTI, JON
MAGNUSSON, GUOMUNDUR

TRAVEN, B.
TORSVAN, BRUNO TRAVEN

TRAVEN, BEATRICE
GOLDEMBERG, ROSE L.

TRAVEN, DIANA
CHURS, GUNTER

TRAVER, ROBERT
VOELKER, JOHN DONALDSON

TRAVERS, COL J.M.
RATHBORNE, ST. GEORGE

TRAVERS, GRAHAM
TODD, MARGARET

TRAVERS, HUGH
MILLS, HUGH [TRAVERS]

TRAVERS, KENNETH
HUTCHIN, KENNETH CHARLES

TRAVERS, STEPHEN
RADCLIFFE, [H] GARNETT

TRAVERS, W.A.
HARY, WILFRID A.

TRAVERS, WILL
ROWLAND, DONALD S.

TRAVERS, [COL.] J.M.
RATHBORNE, ST. GEORGE

TRAVIS, GERRY
TRIMBLE, LOUIS P.

TRAVIS, GORDON
SCHAAKE, ERICH

TRAVIS, GRETCHEN
MOCKLER, GRETCHEN

TRAVIS, JACK
MADDEN, JERRY DAVID

TRAVIS, LAWRENCE
DEUTZMAN, LAWRENCE

TRAVIS, WILL
KEEVILL, HENRY J.

TRAWLE, MARY ELIZABETH
ELWART, JOAN FRANCES

TRAYNOR, ALEX
LAGERWALL, EDNA

TRAYNOR, J. RICHARD
BOLEN, R. KEATING

TRE, HERRAR
HASSELBLATT, EMIL ALERIK
HOMAN, OLOF
SODERHIELM, HENNING

TREACLE, UNCLE
MITCHELL, ADRIAN

TREAT, LAWRENCE
GOLDSTONE, LAWRENCE A.

TREBIZSKY, VACLAV BENES
BENES, VACLAV

TREBONIUS, R.
VON HANSTEIN, OTFRID

TREBOR, SNIVIG C.
GIVINS, ROBERT C.

TREDGOLD, NYE
TRANTER, NIGEL [G]

TREDINICK, BILL & KANEMAN
TREDINNICK, WILLIAM JR.

TREE, CORNELIA
NICHOLS, NINA DE VINCI

TREE, GREGORY
BARDIN, JOHN FRANKLIN

TREEVES, KATHLEEN
WALKER, EMILY KATHLEEN

TREFOR, EIRLYS
WILLIAMS, EIRLYS O.

TREFOSSA
DE ZIEL, HENRI FRANS

TREGALLIS, JOHN
GOWING, SIDNEY [FLOYD]

TREGARTHEN, ENYS
SLOGGETT, NELLIE

TREHEARNE, ELIZABETH
ALBRITTON, CAROL
MAXWELL, PATRICIA ANNE P.

TREHUNE, MORGAN
SMITH, GEORGE H[ENRY

TREHUNE, MORGANA
SMITH, GEORGE H[ENRY]

TRELAWNEY, HUBERT
TUITE, HUGH

TRELOS, TONY
CRECHALES, ANTHONY GEORGE

TREMAINE, BOB
STEINDLER, ROBERT A.

TREMAINE, HERBERT
DEUCHAR, MAUDE

TREMAINE, JENNIE
CHESNEY, MARION G.

TREMAINE, JENNY
CHESNEY, MARION G.

TREMAINE, LINDA
MORGAN, DIANA

TREMAYNE, HARTLEY
ARMOUR, R. COUTTS

TREMAYNE, JONATHAN
FORREST-WEBB, ROBERT

TREMAYNE, PETER
ELLIS, PETER BERRESFORD

TREMAYNE, SYDNEY
COOKSON, SYBIL ELEANOR T.

TREMONT, PHILIP
EIDEN, PAUL

TREMONTE, JULIA
DELLIGAN, WILLIAM F.

TRENCK, PETER
VON CZIFFRA, GEZA

TRENK, PETER
KALMUCZAK, ROLF

TRENT, BRENDA
WILSON, BRENDA LEE E.

TRENT, CLIVE
EMANUEL, VICTOR ROUSSEAU

TRENT, DANIELLE
TRENT, DAN & LYNDA

TRENT, DICK
WOOD, EDWARD D. JR.

TRENT, GREGORY
WILLIAMSON, THAMES ROSS

TRENT, LAWRENCE
SELLERS, CONNIE LESLIE

TRENT, LEE
NUTTALL, ANTHONY

TRENT, LEO
SELLERS, CONNIE LESLIE

TRENT, LYNDA
TRENT, DAN & LYNDA

TRENT, MARTHA
SMITH, DOROTHY WHITEHILL

TRENT, OLAF
FANTHORPE, R.L.

TRENT, PAUL
PLATT, EDWARD

TRENT, PETER
NELSON, [HUGH] LAWRENCE

TRENT, TIMOTHY
MALMBERG, CARL

TRENTON, OLSH
ANTON, UWE
GEISA, WERNER K.
WEINLAND, MANFRED

TRENTWORTH, FISHER
ACKERMAN, FORREST J.

TRES, L.
BAKER, BERNHARD

TRESILIAN, LIZ
GREEN, ELIZABETH SARA

TRESS, ARTHUR
PINKWATER, DANIEL MANUS

TRESSAL, ROBERT
NOONAN, ROBERT

TRESSIDY, JIM
NORWOOD, VICTOR [G.C.]

TRESSILIAN, CHARLES
ATCHESON, RICHARD

TREVANIAN
HASHIAN, JAMES T.
WHITAKER, RODNEY W.

TREVARTHEN, HAL P.
HEYDON, JOSEPH KENTIGERN

TREVELYAN, JULIA
DELLIGAN, WILLIAM F.

TREVELYAN, PERCY
THOMAS, CHARLES

TREVELYAN, ROBERT
FORREST-WEBB, ROBERT

TREVENA, JOHN
HENHAM, ERNEST GEORGE

TREVERANUS, PETRUS
KNODT, JOSEF

TREVISION, TORQUAY
BEDFORD-JONES, HENRY

TREVOR, A.C.
PULSFORD, NORMAN GEORGE

TREVOR, CHARLOTTE
ROBERTS, SONYA LESLIE

TREVOR, DAN
MELDAL-JOHNSEN, TREVOR B.
SHERMAN, DANIEL MICHAEL

TREVOR, ELLESTON
DUDLEY-SMITH, TREVOR

TREVOR, GLEN
HILTON, JAMES

TREVOR, JAMES
BOLAND, BERTRAM J[OHN]

TREVOR, JOY
LINSKILL, DORIS JOY

TREVOR, JUNE
CASEY, JUNE E.

TREVOR, MERIOL
TREVOR, LUCY MERIOL

TREVOR, RALPH
WILMOT, JAMES R.

TREVOR, WILLIAM
COX, WILLIAM TREVOR

TREW, CECIL G.
EHRENBORG, MRS. C.G.

TREW, DIGHTON
JONES, J.G.

TREY, STEPHAN
GEISLER, HANS

TREYMAINE, D. LERIUM
BRADBURY, RAY [DOUGLAS]

TREZ
TREDEZ, ALAIN

TREZ, ALAIN
TREDEZ, ALAIN

TREZ, DENISE
TREDEZ, DENISE [LAUGIER]

TRIBUNE
ARMSTRONG, DOUGLAS A.

TRICE, BOROUGH
ALLEN, ARTHUR BRUCE

TRIFORMIS, D.
HAIG, EMILY ALICE

TRIGGER, GEORGE
HUTCHISSON, W.H. FLORIO

TRIGLIA, JUNE
CASEY, JUNE E.
TRIGLIA, JOAN

TRIMBALL, W.H.
MENCKEN, HENRY LOUIS

TRIMBLE, BJO
TRIMBLE, BETTY JOANN C.

TRINER, JEANNE KAYE
CLEMENTS, KAYE L.
TRINER, JEANNE

TRING, A. STEPHEN
MEYNELL, LAURENCE WALTER

TRINIAN, JOHN
MARKO, ZEKIAL

TRIOLET, ELSA
BLICK, ELSA

TRIPP, C.E.
MORRIS, CHARLES [S]

TRIPP, JOHN
MOORE, JOHN TRAVERS

TRIPP, KAREN
GERSHON, KAREN

TRISTAN
LINDSTROM, SIGFRID

TRITTON, DUKE
CROYDON, HAROLD PERCY

TRIX, MO
HAYMAN, SHEILA

TROIS, ETOILES
MURRAY, EUSTACE C.G.

TROJAN, EVE
BOESCHE, TILLY

TROLL, HENRY
GEYER, HANS-JOACHIM

TROLLE, BIRGER
KERFVE, AXEL

TROLLEY, JACK
ARDIES, TOM

TROLLOPE, JOANNA
POTTER, JOANNA

TROOPER BLUE-GUM
HOGUE, OLIVER

TROOPER GERARDY
GERARD, EDWIN FIELD

TROSSAU, BURKHARD ASTL
ASTL, JARO

TROTSKY, LEON
BRONSTEIN, LEV DAVYDOVICH

TROTT-THOBEN, TILLY
HEINKEN, MATHILDE [T]

TROTTA, GERI
TROTTA, GERALDINE

TROTTE, THURE
ORNULF, HILDING KONSTANT.

TROTTER, SALLIE
CRAWFORD, SALLIE

TROTWOOD
MOORE, JOHN TROTWOOD

TROTWOOD, JOHN
MOORE, JOHN TROTWOOD

TROUT, KILGORE
CURREY, L.W.

TROUT, KILGORE [CONT]
FARMER, PHILIP JOSE
HARTWELL, DAVID G.

TROY, ALAN
HOKE, HELEN L.

TROY, AMANDA
KAHN, MARY

TROY, KATHERINE
BUXTON, ANNE

TROY, SIMON
WARRINER, THURMAN

TROYAT, HENRI
TARASSOV, LEV

TRUDEAU, GARRY B.
TRUDEAU, GARRETSON BEEKM.

TRUDIX, MARTY
TRUMAN, RUTH

TRUEBLOOD, THOMAS
SHERER, MICHAEL L.

TRUESDELL, SUE
TRUESDELL, SUSAN G.

TRUNDLETT, HELEN B.
ELIOT, T[HOMAS] S[TEARNS]

TRUSCOTT, BRUCE
PEERS, EDGAR ALLISON

TRUTH, HANSEL
HERZOG, JOHANN ADOLF

TRY-DAVIES, J.
HENSLEY, SOPHIA MARGARET

TSATSOS, JEANNE
TSATSOS, IOANNA

TSCHIFFELY, A.F.
TSCHIFFELY, AIME FELIX

TSG
GUELLETTE, THOMAS SIMON

TUBALCAIN
WATSON, MARY [FRANCES]

TUBBY, I.M.
KRAUS, [HERMAN] ROBERT

TUCK, DOROTHY
MCFARLAND, DOROTHY TUCK

TUCKER, ANN
GIUDICI, ANN COUPER

TUCKER, BEN
BAJOG, GUNTHER

TUCKER, BOB
TUCKER, [ARTHUR] WILSON

TUCKER, CAROLINE
NOLAN, JEANETTE COVERT

TUCKER, DELAINE
CAMP, DEBORAH ELAINE

TUCKER, ELAINE
CAMP, DEBORAH ELAINE

TUCKER, GINA
TUCKER, GEORGINA

TUCKER, LAEL
WERTENBACKER, LAEL TUCKER

TUCKER, LES
MOSKOVITZ, JACK

TUCKER, LINK
BINGLEY, DAVID ERNEST

TUCKER-FETTNER, ANN
GIUDICI, ANN COUPER

TUGENDHAT, JULIA
DOBSON, JULIA LISSANT

TUGLAS, FRIEDEBERT
MIHKELSON, FRIEDEBERT

TULLY, PAUL
GARDNER, JEROME

TULLY, TOM
SELLERS, CONNIE LESLIE

TUMANNYI, DIR
PANOV, NIKOLAI N.

TUOHY, JOHN FRANCIS
TUOHY, FRANK

TURBOJEW, ALEXEJ
SCHEER, KARL-HERBERT

TUREK, IAN FRANCIS
BINDER, EARL ANDREW
BINDER, OTTO

TUREK, IONE FRANCES
BINDER, EARL ANDREW
BINDER, OTTO

TUREK, WILL
BERNDT, KARL-HEINZ

TURK, KAY
BRAND, KURT

TURK, MIDGE
RICHARDSON, MIDGE TURK

TURKEL, PAULINE
ROSENTHAL, JUDI

TURNER, ALEXANDER FREKE
CRAWFURD, OSWALD J.F.

TURNER, ALLAN
KALMUCZAK, ROLF

TURNER, BILL
TURNER, WILLIAM PRICE

TURNER, C. JOHN
WHITEMAN, WILLIAM MERED.

TURNER, CLAY
BALLARD, W. TODHUNTER

TURNER, E.S.
TURNER, ERNEST SACKVILLE

TURNER, ELIZABETH
OUST, GAIL

TURNER, ELLIOT
GALLARDOS MUNOZ, JUAN

TURNER, ETHEL
CURLEWIS, ETHEL S. [T]

TURNER, F.H.
TURNER, FLORENCE

TURNER, JACK
NUETZEL, CHARLES A.

TURNER, JOSIE
CRAWFORD, PHYLLIS

TURNER, L.A.
LATURNER, HANS JURGEN

TURNER, LEN
FLOREN, LEE

TURNER, LYNN
WATSON, MARY [FRANCES]

TURNER, MARY
LAMBOT, ISOBEL [MARY]

TURNER, PAGE
MURRAY, WILLIAM P.

TURNER, PETER PAUL
JEFFERY, GRANT

TURNER, ROBERT
DWYER, JAMES FRANCIS
NEBEL, [LOUIS] FREDERICK

TURNER, SHEILA
ROWBOTHAM, SHEILA

TURNER, SHEILA R.
SEED, SHEILA TURNER

TURO, BISHOP OF
LEONARD, GRAHAM DOUGLAS

TURREK, SAM
FALK, HERMANN

TURVEY, WINSOME
RUSTERHOLTZ, WINSOME LUCY

TUSTIN, ELIZABETH
WHITE, CELIA

TUTTLE, W.C.
TUTTLE, WILBUR COLEMAN

TUVARI, TESSA
VON EINEM, CHARLOTTE

TUYUCHI
LEITO, ARTURO

TWAIN, MARK
CLEMENS, SAMUEL LANGHORNE

TWAIN, MINERVA MARK
MITCHELL, CHARLOTTE G.

TWAIN, QUARTER
CLEMENS, SAMUEL LANGHORNE

TWEED, J.H.
KNIGHT, VICK R.

TWEEDALE, J.
BICKLE, JUDITH BRUNDRETT

TWEEDSMUIR, BARON
BUCHAN, JOHN

TWEIGGY
HORNBY, LESLEY

TWELKER, THOMAS
KLINGLER, HERMANN

TWICE, VINCENT
WHITE, VICTOR H.

TWIST, ANANIAS
NUNN, WILLIAM CURTIS

TWIST, PETER
HEWITT, C.P.

TWO EAST LONDENERS
NASH, VAUGHAN
SMITH, LLEWELLYN

TWO FRIENDS
HOWELLS, WILLIAM DEAN
PIATT, JOHN JAMES

TWO WOMEN OF THE WEST
JONES, ALICE I.
MARCHANT, ELLA

TYBERG, SON
TYBERGIAN, SONIA

TYDEUS
WALPOLE, HORACE

TYERS, KATHY
TYERS, KATHLEEN L.M.

TYLER, A.E.
ARMSTRONG, ELIZABETH

TYLER, ALISON
TITLE, ELSIE

TYLER, ANNE
MODARESSI, ANNE TYLER

TYLER, ANTONIA
WOLF, SUSAN WHITTLESEY

TYLER, CLARKE
BROOKES, EWART STANLEY

TYLER, ELLIS
KING, ALBERT

TYLER, J.E.A.
TYLER, J.E. ANTHONY

TYLER, JAY
LOWNDES, ROBERT A.W.

TYLER, JO
KIRBY, BRYAN

TYLER, MARTIN WALLACE
O'DELL, J.W.

TYLER, THEODORE
ZIEGLER, EDWARD WILLIAM

TYLER, TONY
TYLER, J.E. ANTHONY

TYLER, W.T.
HAMRICK, SAMUEL J. JR.

TYLER, ZEKE
MARSHALL, MEL[VIN]

TYNAN, KATHARINE
HINKSON, KATHARINE TYNAN

TYPIST, TOPSIE
MINER, ENOCH NEWTON

TYRO
WELLS, H.G.

TYRONE, PAUL
NORWOOD, VICTOR [G.C.]

TYSON, ARNOLD
HERSEY, HAROLD

TYSON, TELLO
MCFARLANE, DAVID

TYTLER, SARA
KEDDIE, HENRIETTA

UBERZWERCH, WENDELIN
FUSS, KARL

UBIQUE
GUGGISBERG, CAPT SIR F.

UDDE, T.
TUDEER, ERIK

UDEN, HORST
KUTHE, EUGEN

UENO, NORIKO
NAKAE, NORIKO

UENTZE, HERTHA
KANNENGIESSER, GERTRUD

UFFELMAN, F.C.
GEHMAN, RICHARD BOYD

UGAMA, LE ROI
SMITH, LE ROI TEX

UHERNIK, NICK
CAIN, NICHOLAS [COLORADO]

UHL, YVONNE
MAHN, TRAUTE

UHLENBRUCK, DIETER
EBEL, WILLI

UIGUN
ATAKUZIEV, RAKHMATULLA

ULF, HAERVED
STRINDBERG, JOHAN AUGUST

ULISSE
LAJOLO, DAVIDE

ULLER, TYLL
DUYSEN, PAUL

ULLMAN, BARBARA
SCHWALBERG, CAROL[YN E.S]

ULLMAN, ROBRT
EGLI, WERNER J.

ULLMANN, URBAN
KLINGLER, HERMANN

ULLRICH, LUISE
CASTELL, LUISE zu

ULMER, FLORIAN
HIPP, RUDIGER

ULMER, ROGER EUGENE
ULMER, ROBERT EUGENE

ULRICH, CHARLES JR.
GALT, WILLIAM H.

ULRICH, THOMAS
HAUSCHILD, REINHARD

ULRICI, ROLF
STITZ-ULRICI, ROLF

ULSTER IMPERIALIST
WILSON, ALEC

ULTIMUS, ROMANORAM
WALPOLE, HORACE

ULYSSES, MOHAMMED
GERNSBACK, HUGO

UNADA
GLIEWE, UNADA G.

UNCLE GORDON
ROE, F. GORDON

UNCLE GUS
REYERSBACH, HANS AUGUSTO

UNCLE HENRY
WALLACE, HENRY

UNCLE JAKE
MCALPINE, ROBERT W.

UNCLE JONATHAN
BADGLEY, JONATHAN

UNCLE KWESI
LAMPTEY, JONATHAN KWESI

UNCLE MAC
MCCULLOCH, DEREK

UNCLE MONTY
HAMILTON-WILKES, EDWIN

UNCLE RAY
COFFMAN, RAMON PEYTON

UNCLE REG
WOODCOCK, E. PAGE

UNCLE REMUS
HARRIS, JOEL CHANDLER
KAVANAGH, ROSE

UNCLE SHELBY
SILVERSTEIN, SHEL[BY]

UNCLE TOM'S NEPHEW
DRIVER, THOMAS

UNCLE WILL, V.M.
CRAFTS, WILBUR FISK

UNCUT CAVENDISH
MEARES, JOHN WILLOUGHBY

UNDERCLIFFE, EARL
CAMPBELL, [JOHN] RAMSEY

UNDERHILL, CHARLES
HILL, REGINALD [CHARLES]

UNDERHILL, PETER
SODERBURG, PERCY MEASDAY

UNDERWOOD, KEITH
SPOONER, PETER ALAN

UNDERWOOD, LEWIS GRAHAM
WEGNER, C. PETER

UNDERWOOD, MICHAEL
EVELYN, JOHN MICHAEL

UNDERWOOD, MILES
GLASSCO, JOHN [S]

UNDINE, P.F.
PAINE, LAURAN BOSWORTH

UNENGE, JAN
OLLESSON, OLLE

UNGARO DE FOX, LUCIA
LOCKERT, LUCIA [A.U.F.]

UNGERER, TOMI
UNGERER, [JEAN] THOMAS

UNICUS
JOERGENSEN, JOHANNES

UNKNOWN
BISHOP, WILLIAM HENRY

UNOFFICIAL OBSERVER
CARTER, JOHN FRANKLIN

UPCHURCH, BOYD
UPCHURCH, BOYD BRADFIELD

UPDIKE, JAMES
BURNETT, W.R.

UPFIELD, ARTHUR C.
PRICE, J.L.
STRANGE, DOROTHY

UPPER, JOSEPH
HARRIS, JOSEPH UPPER

UPSHAW, HELEN
STARR, HELEN UPSHAW

UPTON, MARK
SANDERS, LAWRENCE

UPTON, MUNRO R.
ERNSTING, WALTER
KUMMING, WALDEMAR
REINECKE, WALTER
SCHOLZ, WINIFRIED
VOM SCHEIDT, JURGEN

UQSOR, EL
BORGMANN, DMITRI A.

URBAN, SEPTIMUS
URNER, NATHAN DANE

URE, JEAN
MCCULLOCH, SARA[H]

URIEL, HENRY
FAUST, FREDERICK S.

URN, ALTHEA
FORD, CONSUELA URISARRI

UROYAN, LUIS
LAGUERRE, ENRIQUE A.

URQHARDT, PAUL
BLACK, LADBROKE [L.D.]

URQUHART, GUY
MCALMON, ROBERT

URREA, LIC. BLAS
CABRERA, LUIS

URSPRUNG, WOLFRAM
MULLER, WOLFRAM

URSULA, SANNA
HONKANEN, HILJA L.V.

URSUS
BIERCE, AMBROSE

USDERMARK, HANS F.L.
LEHMAN, HANS FRIEDRICH

USHER, H.P.
ANTON, UWE
GEISA, WERNER K.
HARY, WILFRID A.
KUHNERT, JORG
ROSENBAUER, ROLAND

USHER, MARGO SCEGGE
MCHARGUE, GEORGESS

USIKOTA
BRINITZER, CARL

UTLEY, RALPH
CAIRNS, HUNTINGTON

UTTAM
OAK, PURUSHATTAM NAGESH

UTTLEY, ALISON
UTTLEY, ALICE JANE T.

UWESON, ULF
DUFOUR, LOUIS

UZAIR, SALEM BEN
HORNE, RICHARD HENRY

V. ESCHEN, M.
VON ESCHSTRUTH, MATHILDE

V.C.C.W.
WILLIAMS, VIVIAN CLAUD C.

V.V.V.
LUCAS, BERYL LLEWELLYN

VACE, GEOFFREY
CAVE, GEOFFREY
CAVE, HUGH B[ARNETT]

VAETH, MARTIN
KUMMER, FREDERICK ARNOLD

VAGABOND
BLAKE, GEORGE
JAMES, JOHN STANLEY

VAGRANT
DUFFUS, LOUIS GEORGE
LEHMANN, RUDOLF C.

VAID, SANFORD
LES TINA, DOROTHY
TUCKER, [ARTHUR] WILSON

VAIDON, LAWDOM
WOOLMAN, DAVID S.

VAIL, AMANDA
MILLER, WARREN

VAIL, CHRISTINA
HARVEY, LINDA

VAIL, JOHN
CARSE, ROBERT

VAIL, LINDA
HAMILTON, STEVE & MELINDA

VAIL, PHILIP
GERSON, NOEL B.

VAIZGANTAS
TUMAS, JUOZAS

VAJANSKY
HURBAN, SVETOZAR

VAJANSKY, SVETOZAR HURBAN
HURBAN, SVETOZAR

VALCOE, H. FELIX
SWARTZ, HARRY

VALCOUR, VANESSA
CONAWAY, JAMES C.

VALDEZ, PAUL
GLENNING, RAYMOND
YATES, ALAN GEOFFREY

VALDING, VICTOR
BENSON, ALLAN INGVALD
PETERSON, JOHN VICTOR

VALE, KEITH
CLEGG, PAUL

VALE, LEWIS
OGLESBY, JOSEPH

VALE, MARTIN
VEILLER, MARGUERITE

VALENCAK, HANNELORE
MAYER, HANNELORE [K]

VALENIN, PETER
BROGGER, WALDEMAR

VALENTIN, URSULA
GENAZINO, URSULA

VALENTINE
PECHEY, ARCHIBALD THOMAS

VALENTINE, ALEC
ISAACS, ALAN

VALENTINE, DAVID
LUDOVICI, ANTHONY M.

VALENTINE, DOUGLAS
WILLIAMS, GEORGE VALENT.

VALENTINE, HENRY
POOLE, REGINALD H.
PROUT, GEOFFREY
WARWICK, FRANCIS ALISTAIR

VALENTINE, JO
ARMSTRONG, CHARLOTTE

VALENTINE, ROGER
DUKE, DONALD NORMAN

VALENTINE, VICTOR
EATON, BENJAMIN V.

VALERAN, A.B.
STARR, S[TEPN.] FREDERICK

VALERIY, IVAN
TARSIS, VALERII I.

VALHOPE, CAROL NORTH
MARX, OLGA

VALID, BATYR
VALIDOR, BATYR K.

VALLE
TASCA, ANGELO

VALLEE, RUDY
VALLEE, HUBERT PRIOR

VALLEY, MEL
ZEIGLER, MEL

VALLIENT, FRANCOIS DI
BROADWELL, CLYDE

VALMONT, GUY DE
MAUPASSANT, GUY DE

VALNAY, RAOUL
HERVE, AIME MARIE EDUOARD

VALOIS, GEORGES
GRESSENT, ALFRED GEORGES

VALOIS, JEAN PAUL
BELL, GEORGE
GARRETT, ALBERT EDWARD
JENNISON, JOHN WILLIAM
WILLIS, ERNEST LISTER H.

VALTIN, JAN
KREBS, RICHARD JULIUS

VALTNA, ATS
HELMS, KARL-HEINZ

VALUR
FRIDRIKSSON, THEODOR

VAMBA
BERTELLI, LUIGI

VAMBERG, ARMIN
BAMBERGER, HERMAN

VAMDEVA, VISHNUDAYAL
BISSOONDOYAL, BASDEO

VAN ALPEN, ERNEST
HALPER-SZIGETH, ERNST AL.

VAN AMEIDE, TH
LABBERTON, JOHN HENRDRIK

VAN ANROOY, FRANS
VAN ANROOY, FRANCINE

VAN ARNAM, DAVE
VAN ARNAM, DAVID G.

VAN ARSDALE, WIRT
DAVIS, MARTHA WIRT

VAN AVOND, JAN
SLATER, FRANCIS CAREY

VAN BERG, STEFANIE
LIGENSA, ELFIE

VAN BERGEN, DETLEF
ROHR, WOLF DETLEF

VAN BERKEN, TINE
WITMOND-BERKHOUS, ANNA C.

VAN BRUNT, H.L.
VAN BRUNT, [HOWELL] LLOYD

VAN BUREN, ABIGAIL
PHILLIPS, PAULINE ESTHER

VAN CALCAR, ELISE
VAN CALCAR-SCHIOTLING, E.

VAN CAMPEN, KARL
CAMPBELL, JOHN W[OOD]

VAN CORSTANJE, AUSPICIUS
VAN CORSTANJE, CHARLES

VAN DALL, HAROLD
BUDRYS, ALGIRDAS JONAS

VAN DAM, HENRY
KONIG, HANS H.

VAN DAM, J.
PRESSER, [G] JACOB

VAN DER GRAFT, GUILLAUME
BARNARD, WILHELMUS

VAN DER LOEWEN, P.
MAY, KARL FRIEDRICH

VAN DER STRAETEN, EMIEL
DELRUE, EMIEL

VAN DER ZEE, KAREN
KILMER, WENDELA

VAN DER, WILLEM
VAN LEPENDAAL, WILLEM

VAN DEWALL, JOHANNES
KUHNE, AUGUST

VAN DEYSSEL, LODEWIJK
THIJM, KAREL JAN L.A.

VAN DINE, S.S.
WRIGHT, WILLARD H.

VAN DOREN, DIRCK
DEY, FREDERIC VAN R.

VAN DORNE, R.
PRONZINI, WILLIAM JOHN
WALLMANN, JEFFREY M.

VAN DOVSKI, LEE
LEWANDOWSKI, HERBERT

VAN DUINKERTEN, ANTON
ASSELBERGS, WILLEM JAN M.

VAN DYKE, JULIUS
EDWARDS, FREDERICK A.

VAN DYKE, MARK
DICK, PHILIP K.

VAN DYNE, EDITH
BAUM, L[YMAN] FRANK

VAN EEMLANDT, W.H.
HAASSE, WILLEM HENDRIK

VAN ELRO, H.
HOUWINK, ROEL

VAN EYK, PIET
KOCH, EDMUND P.

VAN FLEET, JOHNNY
LLOP SELLARES, JUAN

VAN GIESON, JUDITH
WOODRUFF, JUDY

VAN GOEL, LOTHAR
GOEBEL, GUNTHER

VAN GREVELINGEN, H.
VERHAGE, JOHANNES W.C.

VAN HAREN, WOUTER
KOLFF, ROELOF COENRAAD

VAN HASSEN, AMY
WILES, DOMINI

VAN HAZINGA, CYNTHIA
KUTZ, CYNTHIA VAN HAZINGA

VAN HEELU, JAN
VAN LEEUWE, JAN

VAN HELLER, MARCUS
COLEMAN, JOHN
MOORE, ARTHUR
STANNARD, DAVID
STEVENSON, JOHN
YERGER, ROBERT
ZACHARY, HUGH

VAN HELSING, KURT
KLEIN, T.E.D.

VAN HOLK, FREDER
MULLER, PAUL ALFRED

VAN HOREN, THEO
VAN LOOY, JACOBUS

VAN ITERSON, S.R.
VAN ITERSON, SINY ROSE

VAN ITH, LILY
FRIEDLI, EMILIE IDA

VAN JOHST, J.J.
BERNDT, KARL-HEINZ

VAN KESSEL, ROLF
DONGES, GUNTER

VAN LHIN, ERIK
DEL REY, LESTER

VAN LIERDE, PETER C.
VAN LIERDE, JOHN

VAN LODEN, EARL
WILLIS, ERNEST LISTER H.

VAN LODEN, ERLE
WILLIS, ERNEST LISTER H.

VAN LOENE, GABRIELLE
VAN SCHAILK-WILLING, JEAN

VAN LOON, PIT
MUHRMANN, WILHELM

VAN LOOT, CORNELIUS O.
ROBERTS, KENNETH [L]
TARKINGTON, BOOTH

VAN LORNE, WARNER
TREMAINE, F. ORLIN
TREMAINE, NELSON

VAN MATRE, PAZ
THOMPSON, ARIADNE

VAN NESS, LIKA
SULLIVAN, ELEANOR

VAN NIEKERK, I.R.
NIENABER, PETRUS JOHANNES

VAN OEVERE, WILLIAM
VAN GROENINGEN, AUGUST P.

VAN ONDERE, JOCHEM
VITRINGA, ANNES JOHAN

VAN OUDSHOORN, J.
FEYLBRIEF, J.K.

VAN RENSBURG, JACO
VAN RENSBURG, ROELOG J.J.

VAN RENSBURG, ROELF
VAN RENSBURG, ROELOG J.J.

VAN REY, E.W.
REYLE, WILHELM

VAN RIJN, IGNATIUS
INGRAM, FORREST L[EO]

VAN RODENBACH, ZOE
SACHER-MASOCH, LEOPOLD

VAN SAANEN, MARIE LOUISE
GIBSON, MARICE LOUISE

VAN SICKLE, V.A.
CARHART, ARTHUR H.

VAN SLYKE, HELEN
ELWARD, JAMES JOSEPH

VAN SMITH, S.
ENGUIDANOS USACH, PASCUAL

VAN SOMEREN, LIESJE
LICHTENBERG, ELISABETH J.

VAN STEEN, PETRA
GLUCK, ANNA [S]

VAN TIJN, MAARJE
VAN TIJN, MIJNJE L.

VAN TUYL, ZAARA
VAN TUYL, ROSEALTHEA

VAN VOGT, A.E.
VAN VOGT, ALFRED ELTON

VAN WAGENINGEN, J.
PRESSER, [G] JACOB

VAN WERTH, RUDOLF
BERNDORFF, HANS-RUDOLF

VAN WIERAN, MONA
KILMER, WENDELA

VAN WIEREN, JAN
DURIBREUX, GASTON

VAN WINKLE, RIP
JACKSON, HELEN HUNT

VAN WORMER, JOE
VAN WORMER, JOSEPH EDWARD

VAN WOULDE, JOHANNA
WERMESKERKE-JUNIUS, SOPH.

VAN YZEREN-LOON, WILLEM
MUHRMANN, WILHELM

VAN ZANDT, E.F.
CROWCROFT, PETER
CUDLIPP, EDYTHE

VAN ZEYCK, KARIN
HOBER, HEINZ WERNER

VAN'T SANT, MIEN
VAN'T SANT-VAN BOMMEL, A.

VAN, GENE
TUTTLE, GENE VAN

VAN, HARRY
VAN SCHREINER, HARRY

VANARDY, VARICK
DEY, FREDERIC VAN R.

VANCE, EDGAR
AMBROSE, ERIC [S]

VANCE, ETHEL
STONE, GRACE ZARING

VANCE, GALE
VAN HORN, DALE R.

VANCE, GERALD
FAIRMAN, PAUL W.
GARRETT, RANDALL [P]
GEIER, CHESTER S.
GRAHAM, ROGER P.
MCGIVERN, WILLIAM P.
SILVERBERG, ROBERT
SLESAR, HENRY

VANCE, JACK
VANCE, JOHN HOLBROOK

VANCE, RAY
MACAULEY, KEN

VANDA, JOHN P.
BOCKL, MANFRED

VANDAL, CAMERON
THORNE, BLISS KIRBY

VANDEN, DIRK
FULLMER, RICHARD

VANDENBERG, JESSE C.
NAGEL, HERBERT CHRISTIAN

VANDENBERG, PHILIPP
HARTEL, KLAUS DIETER

VANDERGRIFT, MARGARET
JANVIER, MARGARET T.

VANDERVEEN, BART H.
VANDERVEEN, BARELD H.

VANDON, GEORGE
JOHNSTON, GEORGE HARCOURT

VANDOR, CYRIL
SURMELIAN, LEON

VANDREY, BORIS
BOGERSHAUSEN, KARL-HEINZ

VANE, BRET
KENT, ARTHUR WILLIAM C.

VANE, BRETT
FODEN, FREDERICK [T]
GRIFFITHS, DAVID ARTHUR
JENNISON, JOHN WILLIAM
LAZENBY, NORMAN A.
PETHICK, PHILIP M.

VANE, DEREK
EATON-BACK, MRS. B.

VANE, MICHAEL
HUMPHRIES, SYDNEY

VANE, NIGEL
STEWARD, DONALD WILLIAM
STUART, DONALD

VANE, NORMAN THADDEUS
DANIELS, NORMAN A.

VANE, PHILLIPPA
MACVEAN, PHYLLIS

VANE, ROLAND
MCKEAG, ERNEST LIONEL

VANE, VIOLET
HOWELL, JANE L.

VANECKEREN, GERARD
ESSER, MAURITS

VANEER, WILLIAM
LAMPP, JAMES W.

VANEK, C.S.
CASTBERG, CHRIS

VANGEN, STYRK
KORSELL, JOHN

VANNER, JOHN
NORTH, WILLIAM

VANNY, JIM
VAN NAME, E.J.

VANSITTART, JANE
MOORHOUSE, H. VANSITTART

VAPCAROV, NIKOLA
JONKOV, NIKOLA

VARANGE, ULICK
YOCKEY, FRANCIS PARKER

VARANI, MARIO
REUTER, RALPH

VARAS, FLORENCIA
OLEA, MARIA FLORENCIA

VARBERGER, FRITZ
FORSSBERG, LENNART

VARDE, LESLIE
DAVIES, LESLIE PERNELL

VARDEL, CLAUDIO
GOYTORTUA, JESUS

VARDON, RICHARD
O'BRIEN, DAVID WRIGHT

VARDON, ROGER
DELAFOSSE, FREDERICK M.

VARENNE, ALBERIC
LAURENT-CELY, JACQUES

VARGA, JUDY
STANG, JUDIT

VARGAS, GRAF EDOUARD ROM.
GROSSE, CARL FRIEDRICH A.

VARLEY, JOHN PHILIP
MITCHELL, LANGDON ELWYN

VARNER, LINDA
PALMER, LINDA VARNER

VASE, GILLAN
NEWTON, ELIZABETH

VASILI, [COMTE] PAUL
ADAM, JULIETTE

VASILIKOS, PETROS
CHATZOPULOS, KOSTAS

VASILOS, FREDA
VASILOPOULOS, FREDA

VASILOS, TINA
VASILOPOULOS, FREDA

VASISTHA, MOHAN
SHASTRI, PRITHVINATH

VASSI, MARCO
VASSI, FRED

VASSILEV, ORLIN
VASSILEV, HRISTO PETKOV

VASSILI, [COUNT] PAUL
RADZIWILL, CATHERINE

VASUDEVA, VISHNUDAYAL
BISSOONDOYAL, BASDEO

VAUGHAN, DUDLEY
JOHNSON, DUDLEY VAUGHAN

VAUGHAN, GARY
BOGGIS, DAVID

VAUGHAN, LEO
LENDON, KENNETH HARRY

VAUGHAN, VIVIAN
VAUGHAN, JANE

VAUGHN, CARTER A.
GERSON, NOEL B.

VAUGHN, EVELYN
JOCKS, YVONNE

VAUGHN, HILDA
MORGAN, HILDA CAMPBELL

VAUGHN, JASON
BARBOUR, H.W.

VAUGHN, KATE
KESTIN, HELEN

VAUGHN, RICHARD
THOMAS, ERNEST LEWIS

VAUGHN, TONI
DUBREUIL, ELIZABETH L.

VAUTRIN, JEAN
HERRMANN, JEAN

VAYLE, VALERIE
BROOKS, JANICE YOUNG
BROOKS-JANOWIAK, JEAN

VEDDER, JOHN K.
GRUBER, FRANK

VEDETTE
FITCHETT, W.H.
WILLIAMS, GEORGE VALENT.

VEDEY, JULIAN
ROBINSON, JULIEN LEWIS

VEE, ROGER
VOSS, VIVIAN

VEHEYNE, CHERRY
WILLIAMSON, ETHEL

VEIIAN, ANDRIS
KALNACH, DONAT G.

VEITCH, TOM
PADGETT, RON

VEITS, ULF
LINDBERG, KARL SIEVERT

VELATUS, L.
LASSWITZ, KURD

VELLE, FREDERIQUE
HEBRARD, FREDERIQUE

VELLER, R.A.
KURTH, HANNS

VENABLE, LYN
VENABLE, MARILYN

VENCE, GERALD
VANCE, GERALD

VENERDI, MARCELLO
KALMUCZAK, ROLF

VENET, MICHELL
RASLEY, ALICIA TODD

VENEZIS, ILIAS
MELLOS, ILIAS

VENI VIDI
CROLY, JANE CUNNINGHAM

VENIR, A.
GROTEWOLD, CHRISTIAN S.

VENISON, ALFRED
POUND, EZRA LOOMIS

VENN, MARY ELEANOR
JORGENSEN, MARY VENN

VENNER, J.G.
LEWIS, JOHN NOEL CLAUDE

VENNING, MICHAEL
RANDOLPH, GEORGIANNA ANN

VENNINGS, HUGH
VAN ZELLER, CLAUDE HUBERT

VENTURA, JEFFREY
FEINMAN, JEFFREY

VEQUIN, CAPINI
QUINN, ELISABETH

VERCORS
BRULLER, JEAN MARCEL

VERCORS, J. BRULLER
BRULLER, JEAN MARCEL

VERDAD, S.
KENNEDY, JOHN MCFARLAND

VERDE, CAMPO
GREENFIELD, IRVING A.

VERDON, DOROTHY
TRALINS, [SANDOR] ROBERT

VERDU, MATILDE
CELA, CAMILLO JOSE

VERE, MARGARET
LONG, GABRIELLE M.V.C.

VEREB, JANOS
BRAND, KURT

VERELART, MYNDART
SALTUS, EDGAR EVERTON

VEREN, GILBERT
KEVEREN, A.G.

VERESAYEV, VIKENTI
SMIDOVICH, VIKENTY VIK.

VERETT, E.
EVANS, E. EVERETT

VERETT, H.E.
EVANS, E. EVERETT
EVANS, THELMA D. HAMM

VERETTE, JOYCE
PETRATUR, JOYCE

VEREY, [REV] C.
CROWLEY, EDWARD ALEXANDER

VERHAGEN, BRITTA
ROMMEL, ALBERTA

VERIN, VELKO
INKIOW, [J] DIMITER

VERITAS
MCWALTERS, GEORGE S.

VERITE SANS PEUR
PROUTING, FREDERICK JAMES

VERLANGER, JULIA
TAIEB, HELIANE

VERNE, CHARLES
HITT, ORRIE [EDWIN]

VERNE, JULES
OLEHEWITZ, L.M.

VERNER, GERALD
STEWARD, DONALD WILLIAM
STUART, DONALD

VERNES, HENRI
DEWISME, CHARLES

VERNEY, SARAH
HOLLOWAY, BRENDA WILMAR

VERNOM, JACK
HOHLBEIN, WOLFGANG E.

VERNON, ALDA
DICKINSON, SUSAN E.

VERNON, CLAIRE
BOON, AUGUST

VERNON, KAY [R]
VERNON, KATHLEEN R.

VERNON, LEE M.
VON BLOCK, BELA [W]

VERNON, MARJORIE
RUSSELL, SHIRLEY

VERNON, MAX
KELLOGG, VERNON L.

VERNON, OLIVIA
BRONTE, ANN

VERNON, PETER
HUDDLESTON, SISLEY

VERNON, SUSAN
SMITH, SUSAN VERNON M.

VERNON, VAIL
HERSEY, HAROLD

VERNOR, D.
CASEWIT, CURTIS

VERONIQUE
FISHER, VERONICA SUZANNE

VERR, HARRY COE
KUNHARDT, EDITH

VERSATILE, VAL
ENTON, HARRY

VERSEAU, DOMINIQUE
GUIEU, JIMMY

VERVAL, ALAIN
GREENWOOD, THOMAS
LANDE, LAWRENCE MONTAGUE

VERWER, HANS
VERWER, JOHANNA ELISABETH

VERYAN, PATRICIA
BANNISTER, PATRICIA V.

VESELIN
VLAJKOV, TODOR GENCOV

VESEY, ARTHUR H[ENRY]
VEYSEY, ARTHUR HENRY

VESEY, PAUL
ALLEN, SAMUEL WASHINGTON

VESPER, TERRA
SCHIOLER, CARSTEN

VESTAL, STANLEY
CAMPBELL, WALTER STANLEY

VESTER, SASKIA
FLORKE, SASKIA

VET, T.V.
STRAITON, EDWARD CORNOCK

VETERAN
STUCHA, PETER

VETTER, LOUIS
FEDDERSEN, JOHANNES

VEVAY, PAUL
ROUND, WILLIAM M.F.

VEXILLUM
BANNER, HUBERT STEWART

VEZELAY, EDITH
DAVIS, EDITH VERZOLLES

VEZHINOV, PAVEL
GUGOV, NIKOLA

VIAL, GION
DEPLAZE, GION

VIALIO, G.
SIMENON, GEORGES [J.C]

VIALIS, GASTON
SIMENON, GEORGES [J.C]

VIATOR, SCOTUS
SETON-WATSON, ROBERT W.

VIATOR, VACUUS
HUGHES, THOMAS

VICAR, HENRY
FELSEN, HENRY GREGOR

VICARION, COUNT PALMIRO
LOGUE, CHRISTOPHER

VICARY, DOROTHY
RICE, DOROTHY MARY

VICKER, ANGUS
FELSEN, HENRY GREGOR

VICKERS
KAUFMAN, WALLACE

VICKERS, AL
POPOV, ALEXANDER

VICKERY, KATE
KENNEDY, TERESA A.

VICKERY, KATHERINE
KRAMER, KATHRYN LYNN

VICKYBIRD
NEUBERG, VICTOR [B]

VICTOR, CHARLES B.
PUECHNER, RAY

VICTOR, CYNTHIA
KATZ, CYNTHIA
SKURNICK, VICTORIA

VICTOR, F.M.
MEISTER, FRIEDRICH

VICTOR, SAM
HERSHMAN, MORRIS

VICTOR, VANESSA
VALENTI, JUSTINE

VICTORIA, M.
DANFORTH, ETHEL M.

VICTORINE, OMAR
WALLMANN, JEFFREY M.

VIDAL, GORE
VIDAL, [E] GORE LUTHER

VIDENS
MUMFORD, A.H.

VIENUOLIS
ZUKAUSKAS, ANTANAS

VIERECK, G.S.
VIERECK, GEORGE SYLVESTER

VIESER, DELORES
AICHBICHLER, WILHELMINE M

VIETON, PETER T.
ALPERS, HANS JOACHIM

VIGA, DIEGO
ENGEL, PAUL

VIGAN, LUC
RUELLAN, ANDRE

VIGIL, LAWRENCE
FINNIN, [OLIVE] MARY

VIGILANS
PARTRIDGE, ERIC [H]
RICE, BRIAN K.

VIGILANT
DIXON, SYDENHAM

VIGILANTES
ZILLIACUS, KONNI

VIGILIANTE, MARY
SZYDLOWSKI, MARY V.

VIGNANT, JEAN FRANCIS
BELIARD, JEAN

VIGNE, D'OCTON
VIGNE, PAUL

VIKING, TED
LOUWEN, JAN

VILDE, IRINA
DROBIAZKO, DARIA D.

VILDRAC, CHARLES
MESSAGER, CHARLES

VILKS, EVALD
LATSIS, EVALD M.

VILLAIN, JEAN
BRUN, MARCEL

VILLAIN, REGARDANT
TOZER, BASIL JOHN JOSEPH

VILLARD, HENDRIK
KEHL, WOLFGANG

VILLARD, HENRY
HILDGARD, HEINRICH GUSTAV

VILLARET, WALTRAUT
HENSCHEL, WALTRAUT

VILLARS, ELIZABETH
FELDMAN, ELLEN [BETTE]

VILLER, FREDRIK
SPARRE, CHRISTIAN

VILLETTE, ALLIS
ACKERMAN, FORREST J.

VILLIERS, ELIZABETH
THORNE, ISABEL MARY

VILLNER, OLLE
BLOMBERG, STIG

VILLUN, K.
FLOGSTAD, KJARTAN

VILOTT, RHONDI
VILOTT-SALSITZ, RHONDI A.

VINCAM, FRATER OMNIA
NEUBERG, VICTOR [B]

VINCENT
NAPOLI, VINCENT

VINCENT, CLAIRE
WALLACE, MARY
LYNCH, MIRIAM

VINCENT, CLARE
ALLEN, CHARLOTTE VALE

VINCENT, E.L.
MORRIS, CHARLES [S]

VINCENT, ELLERTON
LOGAN, M.C.

VINCENT, FRANK
KIRKHAM, REGINALD S.

VINCENT, HARL
SCHOEPFLIN, HARL VINCENT

VINCENT, HEATHER
WALKER, EMILY KATHLEEN

VINCENT, HONOR
WALKER, EMILY KATHLEEN

VINCENT, J. HARRY
TAURASI, JAMES V. SR.

VINCENT, JAMES
NAPOLI, VINCENT

VINCENT, JIM
FOXALL, P.A.

VINCENT, JOAN
WESOLOWSKY, JOAN

VINCENT, JOHN
DEL REY, LESTER
EEL, JOHN [RONALD]
FARROW, R.

VINCENT, MARY KEITH
ST. JOHN, WYLLY FOLK

VINCENT, STAN
SILVERBERG, ROBERT

VINCER, RACHEL
BRUCE-THOMAS, CAROL
MCCARTHY-ANDERSON, DEBRA

VINDICATOR
HOPKINSON, HENRY THOMAS

VINE, BARBARA
RENDELL, RUTH [B]

VINE, KERRY
OXLEY, GILLIAN

VINE, SARAH
ROWLAND, DONALD S.

VINE, WILLIAM
YOUD, CHRISTOPHER [S]

VINEGAR, TOM
GREGG, ANDREW W.

VINEST, SHAW
LONGYEAR, BARRY B[ROOKES]

VINGE, JOAN D.
FRENKLE, JOAN [C] D[ENN.]

VINING, ELIZABETH GRAY
GRAY, ELIZABETH JANET

VINING, JACK
MCKENNA, GEORGE

VINOKUR, GRIGORY
WEINRAUCH, HERSCHEL

VINSON, ELAINE
ROWLAND, DONALD S.

VINSON, KATHRYN
WILLIAMS, KATHRYN VINSON

VINTON, ALDIN
LINTON, ADELIN S.B.

VINTON, ANNE
HAYE, JAN

VINTON, V.V.
DALE, MRS. R.J.

VIOLA
WORTHLEY, R.G.

VIOLIS, G.
SIMENON, GEORGES [J.C]

VIP
PARTCH, VIRGIL FRANKLIN

VIPONT, CHARLES
FOULDS, ELFRIDA VIPONT

VIPONT, ELFRIDA
FOULDS, ELFRIDA VIPONT

VIRAKAM, SOROR
STURGES, MARY D'ESTE

VIRDEN, KATHERINE
SOUTHERLAND, KATHERINE V.

VIRGINIA, DAISY
VAN HORN, DALE R.

VIRGINIA, JULIA
LAENGSDORFF, JULIA V.

VIRGINIUS
CONNETT, EUGENE VIRGINIUS

VIRLUP, A. KVAZAU
ACKERMAN, FORREST J.

VIRMONNE, CLAUDE
AGARD, ESTELLE

VIRMONNE, CLAUDETTE
AGARD, ESTELLE

VIRTUOUS, CARD SHARK
SCARNE, JOHN

VISAN, TANCREDE DE
BIETRIX, VINCENT

VISCHER, GEORG ALFRED
FISCHER, KARL

VISI, BARON
VIAN, BORIS

VISIAK, E.H.
PHYSICK, EDWARD HAROLD

VISSER, WILLIE
VISSER, WILLEM J.C.

VITESSE, GRANDE
WALKERLEY, RODNEY L.

VITEZOVIC, TOMISLAV
KUEHNELT-LEDDIHN, ERIK v.

VITKA, VASIL
KRYSKO, TIMOFEI V.

VIVA
WILSON, VIVA

VIVELO, JACKIE
VIVELO, JACQUELINE J.

VIVIAN
MOYNIHAN, CORNELIUS

VIVIAN, DAISY
KENYON, BRUCE

VIVIAN, E. CHARLES
CANNELL, CHARLES HENRY

VIVIAN, FRANCIS
ASHLEY, ARTHUR ERNEST

VIVIER, COLETTE
DUVAL, COLETTE

VIZARD, STEPHEN
JAMES, DAVID BURNETT S.

VLADIMOV, GEORGII N.
VOLOSEVICH, GEORGII N.

VLASIC, BOB
HIRSCH, PHIL

VLOTHO, FRIEDRICH
RINTELEN, FRITZ MARTIN

VLOTO, OTTO
PARKHILL, FORBES

VOER, JON UR
JONSSON, JON

VOGEL, HANS
WATSON, JOHN
LAZENBY, NORMAN A.

VOGGENBERGER, RESA
HUTZINGER, THERESA

VOGH, JOHN
SLADEK, JOHN

VOIGT, JO [IO]
VOIGT, GUDRUN

VOIGT-ROTHER, ERNA
VOIGT, ERNA

VOITIN, AL
VOITNOVICI, ALEXANDRU

VOLDEZ, PAUL
VALDEZ, PAUL

VOLKER, HEINZ
FALK, HERMANN

VOLNEY, DEX
MATHIESON, VOLNEY

VOLNOV, IVAN
VLADIMIROV, IVAN EGORROV.

VOLOSHINOV, VLADIMIR
BAKHTIN, MIKHAIL M.

VOLTAIRE
DE VOLTAIRE, FRANCIS M.A.

VOLYNSKY, AKIM L'NOVICH
FLEKSER, A.L.

VON ALTAN, STEFFI
FRITSCH, STEFFANIE

VON ALTENAU, EDITH
HERDER, EDELTRAUT

VON ALTENBURG, OLGA ELIS.
JAGOUTZ, OLGA ELISABETH

VON AMBESSER, AXEL
OESTERREICH, AXEL EUGEN v

VON AMYNTOR, GERHARD
VON GERHARDT, DAGOBERT

VON ARX, EDITH KATHARINA
DRILHON-VON ARX, KATHAR.

VON ASCHENBACH, GUSTAVE
FARMER, PHILIP JOSE

VON AUKAMP, PETER
KUHLEMANN, PETER

VON BARUTH, FRIEDRICH
MEISTER, FRIEDRICH

VON BELLINGEN, BARBARA
PARADIS-SCHLANG, ILKA

VON BERN, H.
BERNDT, KARL-HEINZ

VON BERNECK, ALRUN
MUHRMANN, WILHELM

VON BERNFELD, ELEONORE
BRUCKNER, ELEONORE

VON BIRKENBURG, MORITZ
HOMANN, WALTER

VON BLANKENSEE, THEO
BLANK, MATTHIAS

VON BOLANDER, KONRAD
BISHOFF, JOSEPH E.K.

VON BRANDT, LUISE
RUNGE, LUISE LILY

VON BRENCKEN, JULIA
COLLIGNON, JETTA

VON BRITZEN, ANGELA
VON ENGEL, SABINE

VON BUCHEN, ALIX
LIST, ELLEN ERNA

VON BULOW, JOACHIM
BULAU, J.v.

VON CASTELHUN, FRIEDL
MARION, FREIDA

VON DANSDORF, CHRYSILLA
SANDFORD, CHRISTOPHER

VON DER CLANA, HEINRICH
WEISS, ALBERT MARIA

VON DER EICHEN, M.
VON ESCHSTRUTH, MATHILDE

VON DER GROTH, FRANZ
KAISER, OSCAR

VON DER MEHDEN, HEILWIG
AHLERS, HEILWIG [M]

VON DER RELL, PITER
FREPPERT, PETER

VON DETTEN, LEONORE
PINKERT, ERNST FRIEDRICH

VON DIEKEN, MANFRED
KLEFF, THEODOR

VON DREY, HOWARD
WANDREI, HOWARD E.

VON DUROW, JOACHIM
VON MEDEM, IDA

VON EHRENFELS-MEIR., ERIC
JUNG, HERMANN

VON EICHENBERG, ARMIN
EISFELD, RAINER
ERNSTING, WALTER

VON ESCHWEG, CORNELIA
JUNIKE, ROLF

VON FALKENBERG, FRANK
BEHM, WILHELM

VON FALKENBURG, CARL
CASSAU, CARL

VON FUGSHAIM, MELCHIOR S.
GRIMMELSHAUSEN, HANS JAK.

VON GOLDMAR, JON
VON ROMMEL, THEODORE

VON GRAU, WERNHER
SCHOEB, ERIKA

VON GREIFENSHOLM, ERICH S
GRIMMELSHAUSEN, HANS JAK.

VON GRIMM, VERA
EGGERT, VERA

VON GROSSE, MARQUIS
GROSSE, CARL FRIEDRICH A.

VON HAGEN, GRAF LEO
KRAFT, ROBERT

VON HARTENFELS, SIMON L.
GRIMMELSHAUSEN, HANS JAK.

VON HELMHOLTZ, BASTIEN
POUND, EZRA LOOMIS

VON HILGENDORFF, GERTRUD
FELKL, GERTRAUD

VON HIMMEL, ERNST
PETERSILEA, CARLYLE

VON HIRSCHFELT, SAMUEL G.
GRIMMELSHAUSEN, HANS JAK.

VON HOCHRIED, INA
EICHHOF, JOACHIM

VON HOHENBERG, LIANE
VON BLUCHER, RUTH

VON HOHENFELS, GUENTHER
VON HANSTEIN, OTFRID

VON HOLLANDER-LOSOW, ELSE
VON LOSSOW, ELSE

VON HOLSTEIN, KARL
GUNTHER, KARL HEINZ

VON HOLT, UTA
HEPPNER, WALTHER

VON HOLTEN, LORE
EICHHOF, JOACHIM

VON HORVATH, ODON
VON HORVATH, OEDOEN

VON HUGENFELS, ISRAEL F.
GRIMMELSHAUSEN, HANS JAK.

VON HUTTEN, BETTINA
RIDDLE, BETSY

VON ILMENAU, CARL
CASSAU, CARL

VON JOSTEN, JUTTA
SANKE, MARGIT

VON KALTENBERG, HANS
KESSLER, HELENE

VON KASELLA, KONRAT
GARCIA LECHA, LUIS

VON KIESLING, ANGELA
FAEHNDRICH, MARGARITA

VON KIRCHSTEIN, DAGMAR
ARNOLD, WALTER
VON KOBLINSKI, HANS-JOACH

VON KLOPP, VAHRAH
MALVERN, GLADYS

VON KNOBELDORFF-B, NATALY
VON ESCHSTRUTH, NATALY

VON KONNEBERG, DR. ERIC
DEBILL, WALTER C. JR.

VON KRIES, GERDA
PREUSS, GERDA

VON LAMBBE, COL. SPIRO RT
MARTIN, RUSSELL W.

VON LANGENN, VENDLA
VON DER BRUGGEN, VENDLA

VON LENZBURG, A.
VON KRIESCH, AUGUSTE

VON LILIENCRON, DETLEV
LILIENCRON, FREDRICH A.

VON LINDEN, E.
MAY, KARL FRIEDRICH

VON LINDEN, ERNST
MAY, KARL FRIEDRICH

VON MARROTH, BENNO
GUNTHER, HEINZ

VON MAYENBURG, RUTH
DICHTL, RUTH [v.M.]

VON MEYERN, WILHELM-FR.
MEYER, WILHELM-FRIEDRICH

VON MORL, LEA
RUKAVINA-MORL, LEA

VON MOTTEN, FRIEDE
HOFBAUER, ELFRIEDE

VON MUELLER, KARL
MILLER, CHARLES DEAN

VON MUNDE, SWEA
KABEL, WALTHER

VON NACHSTEBRECK, ELMAR
HAHN, RONALD M.

VON NEMMERSDORF, FRANZ
VON REITZENSTEIN, FRAN.

VON NEUEN, RUTH
NEUEN, RUTH

VON NEUHOF, W.
KABEL, WALTHER

VON OERTZEN, MARGARETE
FUNFGELD, MARGARETE

VON ORLOWSKI, AXEL
REIS, KURT

VON OSTAU, RUTH
VON BRANDENSTEIN, RUTH O.

VON OSTEN, RENATE
REESE, WILHELM F.C.

VON PERCHA, IGOR
SENTJURC, IGOR

VON PRAUNHEIM, ROSA
MISCHWITSKY, HOLGER

VON RACHEN, KURT
HUBBARD, L. RON

VON RAVEN, IRIS
FRANZ, ERIKA

VON REHREN, LUDMILLA
VON HEYMER, L.

VON RIENZIEHAUSEN, BORCH.
REESE, WILHELM F.C.

VON ROBERTUS, GERDA
BORNGRABER, GERTRUD

VON ROEDER-GNADBERG, KATE
FEURSTEIN, KATE

VON ROEDERN, JOACHIM
MOHR, ADRIAN

VON ROM, THE
VON ROMMEL, THEODORE

VON ROMMEL, THEA
VON ROMMEL, THEODORE

VON ROTENBURG, W.
KORNER, HEINZ

VON ROTHENFELS, EMMY
VON INGERSLEBEN, EMILIE

VON SAWERSKY, MARIA
BECCE, EMMA [W]

VON SCHENCKENDORFF, C.E.
CARROLL, CARLA-ELISABETH

VON SCHWARZFELD, GERTRUDE
DE ALENCAR, GERTRUDE E.L.

VON SEBETTENDORF, R.F.
GLAUER, RUDOLF

VON SEBOTTENDORF, RUDOLF
GLAUER, RUDOLF

VON SEHNSTORFF, MICHAEL R
GRIMMELSHAUSEN, HANS JAK.

VON SONNENBERG, JUTTA
L.VON SONNENBERG, JUTTA

VON SONNHOF, MARIA
BRANOWITZER-RODLER, MARIA

VON SPIELBERG, HANNS
VON ZOBELTITZ, HANNS

VON STARK, BARBARA
KUHL, BARBARA

VON STERNAU, THEO
HEUER, WILHELM

VON STOCKHAUSEN, JULIANA
VON GATTERBURG, JULIANA

VON STREERBACH, ALBERT
VON JANTSCH-STREERBACH, A

VON SUDORF, FINGAL
ROSENQUIST, FINGAL

VON SULSFORT, GERMAN S.
GRIMMELSHAUSEN, HANS JAK.

VON SUMAROW, ROTISLAW
HURT, ROLF

VON TAACK, MERETE
KURTZ-SOLOWJEW, MERETE

VON TANNMARK, ETTA
HARDT, HEINZ

VON TARNOWITZ, WILHELM
BREHM, WILHELM JOHANN

VON TESSIN, BRIGITTE
KUGELMULLER v. TESSIN, B.

VON TIPPELSKIRCH, WILHELM
LLOP SELLARES, JUAN

VON TWERNE, ERLIK
MICHAEL, ROLF

VON URBANITZKY, GRETE
PASSINI, GRETE [v. U]

VON WACHENDORF, F. LOHR
ETTIGHOFER, PAUL COELEST.

VON WAU WAU, RALPH
FARMER, PHILIP JOSE

VON WIESE, CHRISTIANE
KASHIN, CHRISTIANE

VON WIESE, URSULA
GUGGENHEIM-WIESE, URSULA

VON WITTINGHAUSEN, WERNER
FILEK-WITTINGHAUSEN, WER.

VON WITZLEBEN, UTA
VON KARDORFF, HUBERTA S.

VON ZIEGLER, MARIANNE
VON RUMMEL, MARIANNE [Z]

VONDREY, MARTIN
KALMUCZAK, ROLF

VOORHIS, JERRY
VOORHIS, HORACE JEREMY

VORANC, PREZIHOV
KUHAR, LOVRO

VOS, TONNY
VOS-DAHMER VON BUCHOLZ, T

VOSK, D.M.
SKOV, DAVID A.

VOSS BARK, CONRAD
BARK, CONRAD VOSS

VOUAGEUR
ALLEN, CECIL J.

VOUREKA, AMALIA
FLEMING, AMALIA

VOVCHOK, MARKO
MARKOVICH, MARIA ALEXAND.

VOX
AMINOFF, IVAN T.E.

VOX, AGNES MARY
DUFFY, AGNES MARY

VOYANT, CLAIR
ACKERMAN, FORREST J.

VOYLE, MARY
MANNING, ROSEMARY JOY

VOYNICH, E.L.
VOYNICH, ETHEL L.B.

VREEB, ARTEMIS
SCHWEITZER, DARRELL

VREPONT, BRIAN
TRUEBRIDGE, BENJAMIN A.

VUKOVIC
COLAKOVIC, RODOLJUB

VUYK, BEB
DE WILLIGEN, ELISABETH

VYVYAN, NIGEL
NEVILL, BARRY ST. JOHN

W.B.
BESANT, [SIR] WALTER

W.E./W.J.E.
ELLIOTT, WILLIAM J.

W.E.B.
MOORCOCK, MICHAEL

W.E.P.
PIDGEON, WILLIAM EDWIN

W.G.
GARDNER, WILLIAM

W.G.L.
MENCKEN, HENRY LOUIS

W.M.
JENNINGS, RICHARD

W.W.
BLOOM, WILLIAM
FORTUNE, MARY HELENA W.

WA SHA-QUON-ASIN
BELANEY, ARCHIBALD S.

WABUN
JAMES, MARLISE ANN

WACE, W.E.
NICOLL, WILLIAM ROBERTSON

WACO, G.F.
BASNER, GERHARD

WADDEN, HELMUT
GOBELS, HUBERT

WADE, ALAN
VANCE, JOHN HOLBROOK

WADE, BILL
BARRETT, GEOFFREY JOHN

WADE, CARLSON
WOOD, EDWARD D. JR.

WADE, DAVID
DANIELS, NORMAN A.

WADE, GARRISON
HARDING, WADE GARRISON

WADE, HENRY
AUBREY-FLETCHER, HENRY L.

WADE, HERBERT
WALES, HUGH GREGORY

WADE, JENNIFER
WEHEN, JOY DEWEESE

WADE, JOANNA
BERKMANN, EVELYN [D]

WADE, KIT
CARSON, XANTHUS

WADE, ROBERT
MCILWAIN, DAVID

WADE, T.W.
WADE, THOMAS W.

WADE, THOMAS
LOOKER, SAMUEL JOSEPH

WADE, TOM
WADE, THOMAS W.

WADELTON, MAGGIE-OWEN
WADELTON, MAGGIE JEANNE

WADEY, VICTOR
WADE, THOMAS W.

WAELE, ELISABETH
GONDA, ADOLPHE

WAGHORN, H.L.
HORN, HOLLOWAY

WAGNER, DENSON
IANNELLI, RICHARD

WAGNER, HARRY
SASSE, GERHARD

WAGNER, JOHANNES
DARBOVEN, ANNA-MARIA

WAGNER, PEGGY
WAGNER, MARGARET DALE

WAGS, TWA
BANGS, JOHN KENDRICK
SHERMAN, FRANK DEMPSTER

WAHLOO, PETER
WAHLOO, PER

WAIFE, MARIE
WAIFE-GOLDBERG, MARIE

WAINER, CORD
DEWEY, THOMAS B.

WAINWRIGHT, DAVID
STANFIELD, RICHARD H.

WAINWRIGHT, KEN
TUBB, E.C.

WAINWRIGHT, RICHARD ASHTN
HANCOCK, HARRIE I.

WAITE, VICTOR
MAKGILL, [SIR] GEORGE

WAKE, G.B.
HAYNES, JOHN HAROLD

WAKEFIELD, ELIZABETH
MONTGOMERY, MAMIE ELIZAB.

WAKEFIELD, HANNAH
BURTON, SARAH
HOLLAND, JUDITH [JUDY]

WAKEFIELD, JEAN L.
LAIRD, JEAN E.

WAKEFIELD, R.I.
WHITE, GERTRUDE MASON

WAKEMAN, ANNIE
LATHROP, ANNIE W.

WAKEMAN, EVANS
WAKEMAN, FREDERIC EVANS

WAKING, ELIZABETH
CLAGETT, SUE HARRY

WAKO, MDOGO
NAZURETH, PETER

WALDECK, HEINRICH SUSO
POPP, AUGUSTIN

WALDEN, FRANK
GLOSSNER, HARRY

WALDEN, H.
GLEICH, JOSEPH ALOIS

WALDER, J.
EICHHORN, JOSY

WALDMUELLER, ROBERT
DUBOC, EDOUARD

WALDMULLER, ROBERT
DUBOC, EDOUARD

WALDNER, IRENE
FEDERLE, ELISABETH

WALDO, CEDRIC DANE
WOLFF, CECIL DRUMMOND

WALDO, DAVID
CLARKE, DAVID WALDO

WALDO, E. HUNTER
STURGEON, THEODORE

WALDOR, FRANK
HORDAHL, KURT

WALDRON, D'LYNN
WALDRON-SHAH, DIANE L.

WALDRON, SIMON
KING, ALBERT

WALDTHAUSEN, SEBASTIAN
BEST, WALTER

WALES, HUBERT
PIGGOTT, WILLIAM C.

WALES, KIRK
RONALD, JAMES

WALES, NYM
SNOW, HELEN FOSTER

WALFORD, CHRISTIAN
DILCOCK, NOREEN

WALKER, BARBARA
MIDDLETON, MAUD BARBARA

WALKER, BRAZ
WALKER, JAMES BRAZELTON

WALKER, ELIZABETH
ROTTER, ELIZABETH N.W.

WALKER, ELIZABETH NEFF
ROTTER, ELIZABETH N.W.

WALKER, FREDERICK
SCHULTZ, FREDERICK WALTER

WALKER, HARRY
WAUGH, HILLARY B.

WALKER, HOLLY BETH
BOND, GLADYS BAKER

WALKER, HUGH
STRASSEL, HUBERT

WALKER, IRA
WALKER, IRMA [R.R.]

WALKER, J.
CRAWFORD, JOHN RICHARD

WALKER, JEAN BROWN
WALKER, EDITH

WALKER, JOSEPH
MCSPADDEN, JOSEPH WALKER

WALKER, LUCY
SANDERS, DOROTHY LUCIE

WALKER, MAX
AVALLONE, MICHAEL

WALKER, MILDRED
SCHEMM, MILDRED WALKER

WALKER, REEVE
TOMPKINS, WALKER A.
HECKLEMANN, CHARLES N.

WALKER, RUTH
WALKER, IRMA [R.R.]

WALKER, SHEL
SHELDON, WALTER J.

WALKER, THOMAS P.
PAGE, THOMAS

WALKER, W.H.
RANKEN, GEORGE

WALKHAM, WALTER
IVORY, JAMES HARVEY T.

WALKINSHAW, COLIN
REID, JAMES MACARTHUR

WALL, CHRISTIAN
STROMBERG, SIGGE NATANAEL

WALL, MAX
LORIMER, MAXWELL

WALL, ROBERT E.
WALL, ROBERT EMMET JR.

WALLACE, AGNES
KING, ALBERT

WALLACE, ARTHUR
ARMER, FRANK

WALLACE, BETTY
WALLACE, ELIZABETH VIRG.

WALLACE, BILL
WALLACE, WILLIAM KEITH

WALLACE, C.H.
BURGER, ROSAYLMER
PERCIVAL, JULIA

WALLACE, CLIFFORD
BOUNDS, SYDNEY J.

WALLACE, DAISY
CUYLER, MARGERY S.

WALLACE, DEXTER
MASTERS, EDGAR LEE

WALLACE, DOREEN
RASH, DORA EILEEN AGNEW

WALLACE, EDGAR
GERARD, FRANCIS
WALLACE, RICHARD H. EDGAR

WALLACE, F.L.
WALLACE, FLOYD L.

WALLACE, GORDON
SHAW, STANLEY GORDON

WALLACE, IAN
PRITCHARD, JOHN WALLACE

WALLACE, JAMES
BARRETT, GEOFFREY JOHN

WALLACE, JOHN
DAVIS, WILL R.

WALLACE, MARY
LYNCH, MIRIAM

WALLACE, MICHAEL
HERWEY, MICHAEL

WALLACE, NIGEL
HAMILTON, CHARLES H.S.

WALLACE, PAT
STROTHER, PAT WALLACE

WALLACE, PATRICIA
ESTRADA, PATRICIA WALLACE

WALLACE, RAY
HAWK, RAYMOND W[ALLACE]

WALLACE, RICHARD
IND, ALLISON

WALLACE, ROBERT
BALLARD, W. TODHUNTER
BOWEN, ROBERT SIDNEY
BURKHOLDER, EDWIN V.
BURKS, ARTHUR J.
CAMERON, DONALD A.
CHAMPION, D'ARCY LYNDON
CUMMINGS, RAY[MOND KING]
DANIELS, NORMAN A.
DENT, LESTER
DONOVAN, LAURENCE
FELDMAN, A. FRANCE
FLEMING-ROBERTS, G.T.
GREEN, CHARLES
HOPSON, WILLIAM L.
JOHNSON, WALTER RYERSON
KUTTNER, HENRY
MACDONALD, GEORGE A.

WALLACE, ROBERT [CONT]
MONTANYE, CARLETON S.
OPPENHEIM, RALPH
TEPPERMAN, EMILE C.
WALLACE-CRABBE, ROBIN
WELLMAN, MANLY WADE
WINCHELL, PRENTICE

WALLACE, ROGER
CHARLIER, ROGER H.

WALLACE, TRENT
TOMPKINS, WALKER A.

WALLACE, WAYNE
HARRIS, FRANK G.

WALLATZE, EDGAR
FIENHOLD, WOLFGANG

WALLDORF, HANS
LOEST, ERICH

WALLECHINSKY, DAVID
WALLACE, DAVID

WALLEK, LEE
JOHNSON, CURTIS LEE

WALLENTIN, GEORG
HERBST, HANS

WALLER, BROWN
FRASER, WALLER BROWN

WALLER, JOHN
CROFTS, FREEMAN WILLS

WALLER, LESLIE
MANN, PATRICK

WALLER, M.E.
WALLER, MARY ELLA

WALLER, MAX
WARLOMONT, MAURICE

WALLEY, BRYON S.
CARD, ORSON SCOTT

WALLIN, AMOS
KUNICZAK, W.S.

WALLING, R.A.J.
WALLING, ROBERT ALFRED J.

WALLIS, A.S.C.
VON ANTAL, ADELE SOPHIA C

WALLIS, B.
WALLIS, GEORGE C.

WALLIS, B. & G.C.
WALLIS, GEORGE C.

WALLIS, G. MCDONALD
CAMPBELL, HOPE

WALLIS, JOHN
NYLEN, INGEBORG

WALLIS, PENNY
MORRISON, MARY JANE

WALLMANN, JEFFREY N.
WALLMANN, JEFFREY M.

WALMSLEY, BUCK
WALMSLEY, HAINES

WALRAVEN
KALER, JAMES OTIS

WALRAVEN, E.G.
JONES, EMMA GARRISON

WALSBY, CHARNOCK
HEALD, LESLIE V.

WALSER, MARGRET
GREITHER, MARGIT

WALSER, SAM
HOWARD, ROBERT E.

WALSH, J.M.
WALSH, JAMES MORGAN

WALSH, JAMES
ROBINSON, FRANK M.

WALSH, KELLY
WALSH, V.P.

WALSTER, ELAINE
HATFIELD, ELAINE [C]

WALSTER, ELAINE HATFIELD
BERSCHEID, ELLEN
HATFIELD, ELAINE [C]

WALSTON, JOSEPH
WALSTON, MARIE

WALTER, ERICH
HEICHEN, WALTER

WALTER, ERNST
HEYDA, ERNST

WALTER, HENRY
ROECKEN, KURT WALTER

WALTER, JUDITH
GAUTIER, JUDITH

WALTER, KATHERINE
WALTER, DOROTHY BLAKE

WALTER, KAY
WALTER, DOROTHY BLAKE

WALTER, R.
BLANK, MATTHIAS

WALTER, VILLIAM CHRISTIAN
ANDERSON, HANS CHRISTIAN

WALTER, W.E.C.
LOVELING, VIRGINIE

WALTERS, CHAD
SMITH, RICHARD REIN

WALTERS, GORDON
LOCKE, GEORGE [W]

WALTERS, HUGH
HUGHES, WALTER LLEWELLYN

WALTERS, LINDA
RICE, LINDA & WALTER

WALTERS, NELL
MUSE, PATRICIA [ALICE]

WALTERS, RICK
ROWLAND, DONALD S.

WALTERS, SELDON
SHELDON, WALTER J.

WALTERS, SHELLY
SHELDON, WALTER J.

WALTERS, T.B.
ROWE, JOHN GABRIEL

WALTERS, W.G.
STEFFENS, ARTHUR JOSEPH

WALTERS, WARREN
MANNING, WILLIAM HENRY

WALTERSCHEID, WALTER C.
WALTERSCHEID, EDWARD C.

WALTHER, KARLA
KABEL, WALTHER

WALTHER, TOM
WALTHER, THOMAS A.

WALTIMORE, IAIN
WALTMAN, WILLIAM JOHN

WALTON, EVANGELINE
ENSLEY, W. EVANGELINE W.

WALTON, FRANCIS
HODDER, ALFRED

WALTON, LUKE
HENDERSON, BILL

WANDERER
D'AVIGDOR, ELIM HENRY
DIXON, WILLIAM SCARTH
GILBERT, JEAN
SMITH, LILY

WANG, STEIN
KALMOE, ALF HALVOR

WANGARA, HARUN KOFI
LAWRENCE, HAROLD G.

WANK, THOMAS
KALMUCZAK, ROLF

WANNAMAKER, BRUCE
MONCURE, JANE BELK

WANNON, BILL
WANNON, WILLIAM FIELDING

WANSTALL, KEN
GREEN-WANSTALL, KENNETH

WARBLER, J.M.
COCAGNAC, A.M.

WARBOROUGH, MARTIN LEACH
ALLEN, GRANT

WARBRIDGE, C.W.
WOODS, CLEE

WARD, A. SARSFIELD
WARD, ARTHUR HENRY S.

WARD, ARTEMUS
BROWNE, CHARLES FARRAR

WARD, B.
WARD, EDWARD

WARD, BARBARA
JACKSON, BARBARA W[WARD]

WARD, BRAD
PEEPLES, SAMUEL A.

WARD, CHARLES DEXTER
TAYLOR, JOHN A.

WARD, CHARLOTTE
CHESNEY, MARION G.

WARD, E.C.
WARD, ELIZABETH CAMPBELL

WARD, E.D.
GOREY, EDWARD [ST. JOHN]
LUCAS, E[DWARD] V[ERRALL]

WARD, ELIZABETH C.
WARD, ELIZABETH CAMPBELL

WARD, EVELYN
EVERETT-GREEN, EVELYN

WARD, HENRY
VIARD, HENRI LOUIS LUC

WARD, HERBERT B.S.
MOLLOY, EDWARD

WARD, HUGO A.
GARNETT, DAVID S.

WARD, IRELAND
WIDDEMER, IRENE

WARD, JANICE
HARTMAN, RACHEL FRIEDA

WARD, JONAS
ARD, WILLIAM [THOMAS]
COX, WILLIAM ROBERT
GARFIELD, BRIAN F.W.
SILVERBERG, ROBERT

WARD, JONATHAN
STINE, WHITNEY WARD

WARD, KATE
CUST, BARBARA

WARD, KIRWAN
KIRWAN-WARD, BERNARD

WARD, LINDA
REISCH-NOWAK, CHRISTINE

WARD, MAISIE
WARD, MARY JOSEPHINE

WARD, MELANIE
CURTIS, RICHARD [A]
LYNCH, MARILYN

WARD, OLIVER
GANLEY, W. PAUL

WARD, PETER
FAUST, FREDERICK S.

WARD, R. PATRICK
HOLZAPFEL, RUDOLF PATRICK

WARD, R.H.
WARD, RICHARD HERON

WARD, REBECCA
WARTSKI, MAUREEN A.C.

WARD, ROB
SCHATZ, EDWARD R.

WARD, ROBERT
HOWARD, ROBERT E.

WARD, STEVE
ROSENTHAL, NORMAN

WARD, TAYLOR
HYDE, ALAN

WARD, TOM
SELLERS, CONNIE LESLIE

WARD, WILLIAM
WOOD, H[ARRY] F[REEMAN]

WARDDEL, NORA HELEN
HERON-ALLEN, EDWARD

WARDE, MARAGRET
DUNTON, EDITH KELLOGG

WARDE, WILLIAM F.
NOVACK, GEORGE [EDWARD]

WARDELL, DEAN
PRINCE, JACK HARVEY

WARDEN, FLORENCE
JAMES, FLORENCE ALICE P.

WARDEN, FRANCIS
HARRISON, MARY BENNETT

WARDEN, GERTRUDE
JONES, GERTRUDE WARDEN

WARDLE, DAN
SNOW, CHARLES H[ORACE]

WARDLE, JANE
HUEFFER, OLIVER MADOX

WARE, JUDITH
TORREY [BUDLONG], WARE

WARE, L.L.
WARD, LEW

WARE, MONICA
MARSH, JOHN

WARE, WALLACE
KARP, DAVID

WARFIELD, SELENA
BAITAILLE, DIANE

WARGAR, KURT
RUELLAN, ANDRE

WARING, BETH
ROTSLER, WILLIAM

WARING, BRETT
MEARES, LEONARD F.

WARING, BRETT
HETHERINGTON, KEITH JAMES

WARING, MAIN
HUGHES, W.T. MAINWARING

WARING, MARCUS H.
MANNING, WILLIAM HENRY

WARING, SONIA
BOYCE, DAVID

WARLAND, ALLEN
WOLLHEIM, DONALD A.

WARLOCK, PETER
HESELTINE, PHILIP ARNOLD

WARNE, LEONA
BATT, LEON

WARNEFORD, LIEUTENANT
RUSSELL, WILLIAM

WARNEFORD, LOJNANT ROBERT
GUNTHER, ARCH. CLAVERING

WARNER, DOUGLAS
CURRIE, JOHN DESMOND
WARNER, ELIZABETH

WARNER, DR
KRAFT, ROBERT

WARNER, ESTHER S.
DENDEL, ESTHER [S.W]

WARNER, FRANK
RICHARDSON, GLADWELL G.

WARNER, FRANK A.
STRATEMEYER, EDWARD

WARNER, HANNAH
JEWETT, JOHN HOWARD

WARNER, JACK
WATERS, JOHN

WARNER, LEE
BATTIN, BRINTON WARNER

WARNER, LEIGH
SMITH, LILLIAN M.

WARNER, MATT
FICHTER, GEORGE S.

WARNER, REX
WARNER, REGINALD ERNEST

WARNER, WARREN
RUSSELL, WILLIAM
WARREN, SAMUEL

WARNER-CROZETTI, R.
CROZETTI, RUTH G.W.L.

WARNOFRIED
KIRCHHEIM, KARL WILHELM

WARRE, MARY DOUGLAS
GREIG-SMITH, JENNIFER M.

WARREGO, PAUL
WENZ, PAUL

WARREN, ALAN
ZIEGENFUSS, ALAN JOHN

WARREN, ALAN J.
ZIEGENFUSS, ALAN JOHN

WARREN, ANDREW
ROSENTHAL, ANDREW
TUTE, WARREN [S]

WARREN, BEN
GRONWALD, PETER

WARREN, BETSY
WARREN, ELIZABETH AVERY

WARREN, BILL
WARREN, WILLIAM BOND

WARREN, BILLY
WARREN, WILLIAM STEPHEN

WARREN, CHRISTOPHER
BROWN, WILLIAM F.

WARREN, EARL
APPEL, WALTER

WARREN, ELIZABETH
SUPRANER, ROBYN

WARREN, FRANK
RAWSON, CLAYTON

WARREN, HANS
REINHARD, HANS GEORG
REINHARD, WILHELM PETER

WARREN, HUGH
MANNING, WILLIAM HENRY

WARREN, J.T.
MANNING, WILLIAM HENRY

WARREN, LINDA
APPEL, WALTER

WARREN, MARY DOUGLAS
GREIG-SMITH, JENNIFER M.

WARREN, NED
MANNING, WILLIAM HENRY

WARREN, PAULETTE
FAIRMAN, PAUL W.

WARREN, RED
WARREN, ROBERT PENN

WARREN, ROY
SMITH, GEORGE H[ENRY]

WARREN, TONY
SIMPSON, ANTHONY MCVAY

WARREN, V.S.
MANNING, WILLIAM HENRY

WARREN, VERNON
CHAPMAN, GEORGE W.V.

WARREN, WALTERS
RAYMOND, GEORGE LANSING

WARREN, WAYNE
BRAUN, WILBUR

WARREN-HOLM, HANS
REINHARD, WILHELM PETER

WARRICK, LON
BAJOG, GUNTHER

WARRINGTON, DAN
REED-SMITH, IDA

WARRINGTON, GEORGE
AGATE, JAMES

WARRINGTON, MARIS
BILLINGS, EDITH S.

WARSH
WARSHAW, JERRY

WARSHOFSKY, ISAAC
SINGER, ISAAC BASHEVIS

WARUNG, PRICE
ASTLEY, WILLIAM

WARWICK, ANNE
CRANSTON, RUTH

WARWICK, CHESTER
LUPTON, LEONARD

WARWICK, DOLORES
FRESE, DOLORES WARWICK

WARWICK, EDEN
JABET, GEORGE S.

WARWICK, ELSIE
FULLILOVE, MRS. E.J.

WARWICK, GEORGE
DEEPING, GEORGE WARWICK

WARWICK, JARVIS
GARNER, HUGH

WARWICK, PAULINE
DAVIES, BETTY EVELYN

WASH, R.
COWLISHAW, RANSON

WASHBURN, L.J.
REASONER, LIVIA & JAMES
REASONER, LIVIA J.W.

WASHBURN, LIVIA J.
REASONER, LIVIA J.W.

WASHINGTON C.
PHARR, ROBERT D.

WASHINGTON, ALEX
FINKLESTEIN, MARK

WASHINGTON, BERWELL
CABELL, JAMES BRANCH

WASHINGTON, BOOKER T.
TALIAFERRO, BOOKER

WASHINGTON, PAT BEAUCHAMP
WASHINGTON, M. BEAUCHAMP

WASON, BETTY
HALL, ELIZABETH WASON

WASSILEWSKA, WANA
VASILEVSKAYA, VANDA

WAST, HUGO
ZUVIRIA, GUSTAVO MARTINEZ

WAT, ALEKSANDER
CHWAT, ALEKSANDER

WATANNA, ONOTO
BABCOCK, WINIFRED

WATCHMAN
DRAPER, WARWICH HERBERT

WATER, SILAS
LOOMIS, NOEL [MILLER]

WATERHOUSE, ARTHUR
FEARN, JOHN RUSSELL

WATERS
RUSSELL, WILLIAM

WATERS, C.
RUSSELL, WILLIAM

WATERS, CHRIS
WATERS, HAROLD A.

WATERS, LUCY
WILKES-HUNTER, RICHARD

WATERS, THOMAS
RUSSELL, WILLIAM

WATKINS, A.C.
WATKINS, ALAN CLARENCE

WATKINS, A.T.L.
WATKINS, ARTHUR T.L.

WATKINS, FRANCES ELLEN
HARPER, FRANCIS E.W.

WATKINS, GERROLD
MALZBERG, BARRY [N]

WATKINSON, VALERIE
ELLISTON, VALERIE MAE W.

WATKYN, ARTHUR
WATKINS, ARTHUR T.L.

WATSON & REES
REES, ARTHUR JOHN
WATSON, JOHN REAY

WATSON, ANDREW
WATSON, ALBERT ERNEST

WATSON, B.S.
TEITELBAUM, MICHAEL

WATSON, BILLY
STURGEON, THEODORE

WATSON, DR. JOHN
OSTWALD, THOMAS

WATSON, DR. JOHN H.
COLLINS, RANDALL
ESTLEMAN, LOREN D.

WATSON, ELIZABETH
PRONZINI, WILLIAM JOHN
WALLMANN, JEFFREY M.

WATSON, FRANCES
WATKINSON, BRENDA F.

WATSON, FRANK
AMES, FRANCES H.

WATSON, FREDERICK
PORTER, FREDERICK

WATSON, GAYLE HUDGENS
HUDGENS, A[LICE] GAYLE

WATSON, IRVING S.
MENCKEN, HENRY LOUIS

WATSON, J.
TOWNSEND, LARRY

WATSON, JOHN H. MD
DOYLE, ARTHUR CONAN
WELLMAN, MANLY WADE
WELLMAN, WADE
FARMER, PHILIP JOSE

WATSON, RICHARD F.
SILVERBERG, ROBERT

WATSON, ST. JOHN
CLARKE, PERCY A.

WATSON, WILL
FLOREN, LEE

WATT, JON
WATT, JOHN F.

WATT, SEBASTIAN
WOLK, GEORGE

WATT, WILLIAM
SCOTT, W.H.

WATT-EVANS, LAWRENCE
EVANS, LAWRENCE WATT

WATTERS, BARBARA H.
HUNT, BARBARA

WATTIE, MARGARET
ESPINASSE, MARGARET

WATTS, EPHRAIM
HORNE, RICHARD HENRY

WATTS, HELEN L. HOKE
HOKE, HELEN L.

WATTS, JOHN
MILLER, HUGH

WATTS, PETER
WATTS, PETER CHRISTOPHER

WATTS-DUNTON, THEODORE
WATTS, WALTER THEODORE

WAUD, ELIZABETH
TATTERSALL, MURIEL JOYCE

WAUGH, ALEC
WAUGH, ALEXANDER RABAN

WAUGHBURTON, RICHARD
BYRON, ROBERT
SYKES, CHRISTOPHER

WAVERLEY, JOHN
SCOBIE, STEPHEN ARTHUR C.

WAVERLY, SHANNON
SHANNON, KATHLEEN

WAY, WAYNE
HUMPHRIES, ADELAIDE

WAYDE, BERNARD
CARLTON, GERALD

WAYER, FRED M.
WEGENER, MANFRED

WAYFARER
COSENS, ABNER

WAYLAN, MILDRED
HARRELL, IRENE B.

WAYLAND, PATRICK
O'CONNOR, RICHARD

WAYNE, ALICE
RESSLER, ALICE

WAYNE, ANDERSON
DRESSER, DAVIS

WAYNE, DONALD
DODD, WAYNE DONALD

WAYNE, DOROTHY
SAINSBURY, NOEL E.

WAYNE, FRANCIS
WEDGE, FLORENCE

WAYNE, H.
ZINGLERSEN, Z.

WAYNE, HEATHER
GIBBS, NORAH

WAYNE, J.H.
VON KOBLINSKI, HANS-JOACH

WAYNE, JOANNA
WEST, JOANN

WAYNE, JOHN
CAVE, HUGH B[ARNETT]

WAYNE, JOSEPH
OVERHOLSER, WAYNE D.
PATTEN, LEWIS B.

WAYNE, LOIS
GARRARD, DOROTHY

WAYNE, MARCIA
BEST, CAROL ANN
MCEWAN, MARCIA

WAYNE, MARSHA
MCEWAN, MARCIA

WAYNE, RICHARD
DECKER, DUANE

WAYNE, RICK
OBER, NORMAN

WAYNE, ROCHELLE
MULVIHILL, ROCHELLE A.

WAYNE, WALTER
DONOVAN, LAURENCE

WAYSTAFF, SIMON
SWIFT, JONATHAN

WAZYK, ADAM
WAGMANN, ADAM

WEALE, ANNE
BLAKE, ANDREA

WEALE, [B] PUTNAM
SIMPSON, BERTRAM L.

WEARE, RALSTON B.
LA BARRE, WESTON

WEARY, OGDRED
GOREY, EDWARD ST. JOHN

WEATHERBY, W.J.
WEATHERBY, WILLIAM JOHN

WEATHERCOCK, THE
ROMAINE, LAWRENCE B.

WEAVER, INGRID
CARIS, INGRID

WEAVER, KITTY
WEAVER, KATHERINE GREY D.

WEAVER, MATEMAN
GREENE, ALVIN CARL

WEAVER, NICKY
HITT, ORRIE [EDWIN]

WEAVER, WARD
MASON, F. VAN WYCK

WEB, DAN
MILLSAPS, DANIEL W. III

WEBB, A.C.
WEBB, AUGUST CAESAR

WEBB, ALEX
LYLE-SMYTHE, ALAN

WEBB, ANTHONY
WILSON, NORMAN SCARLYN

WEBB, BOB
FORREST-WEBB, ROBERT

WEBB, CHRISTOPHER
WIBBERLEY, LEONARD [P.O.]

WEBB, CY
WEBB, REGINALD CYRIL

WEBB, CYRIL
WEBB, REGINALD CYRIL

WEBB, FORREST
FORREST-WEBB, ROBERT

WEBB, LILIAN JULIAN
STOCKLEY, CYNTHIA

WEBB, LIONEL
HERSHMAN, MORRIS

WEBB, LUCAS
ELLIOT, JEFFREY M.

WEBB, LUCAS [CONT]
BURGESS, MICHAEL ROY

WEBB, NEIL
ROWLAND, DONALD S.

WEBB, PETER
LAZENBY, NORMAN A.

WEBB, ROBERT FORREST
FORREST-WEBB, ROBERT

WEBB, RON
WEBB, SHARON LYNN

WEBB, SPIDER
GOHMAN, FRED JOSEPH

WEBB, W.T.
WEBB, WILLIAM THOMAS

WEBBER, BERT
WEBBER, EBBERT T.

WEBBER, STAWFORD
PILE, D.W.

WEBER, ANNEMARIE
LORENZEN, ANNEMARIE

WEBER, KARIN
JUNIKE, ROLF

WEBER, LUCIAN
EMMERICH, JOSEPH FRIEDR.

WEBER, RUBIN
RUBENSTEIN, SAMUEL L.
WEAVER, ROBERT G.

WEBER, VEIT
WAECHTER, GEORGE P.L.

WEBLEY, JONATHAN
BATT, LEON

WEBLEY, PELAGIAN
MORGAN, WILLIAM SACHEUS

WEBSTER, FRANK V.
STRATEMEYER, EDWARD

WEBSTER, GARY
GARRISON, WEBB BLACK

WEBSTER, HARRY
BREUCKER, OSCAR HERBERT

WEBSTER, JEAN
WEBSTER, ALICE JANE C.

WEBSTER, JESSIE
CASSILL, RONALD VERLIN

WEBSTER, NOAH
KNOX, WILLIAM [BILL]

WEBSTER, ROBERT N.
PALMER, RAYMOND A.

WEBSTER, SAM
HAAS, BENJAMIN LEOPOLD

WEDDING, ALEX
WEISKOP, GRETE

WEDGELOCK, COLIN
PRIEST, CHRISTOPHER [M]

WEDGWOOD, [DAME] C.V.
WEDGWOOD, CECILY V.

WEER, WILLIAM
KAUFMAN, ISADORE

WEEROONA
SIMPSON, MARY

WEES, WENDY ADRIAN
SCHULTZ, WENDY ADRIAN

WEETWOOD, E.M.
TETLEY, EDITH MADELINE

WEGO, G.F.
BASNER, GERHARD

WEHR, WERNER
GARTMAN, HEINZ

WEI WU WEI
GRAY, TERENCE J.S.

WEIBER, JOHN
LLOP SELLARES, JUAN

WEIGHT, FRANK
TUBB, E.C.

WEIKERSHEIM, MATTHIAS
DOLL, HERBERT GERHARD

WEIL, BARRY
ROBERT, DEREK

WEIL, JERRY
O'MARA, JOHN

WEILENMANN, E.
KURTH, HANNS

WEILER, ANDREAS
BRANDHORST, ANDREAS
BURGDORF, KARL-ULRICH

WEIN, LEN
WEIN, LEONARD NORMAN

WEINBAUM, HELEN
KARU, BARUCH
KASSON, HELEN WEINBAUM

WEINBERG, JANET HOPSON
HOPSON, JANET L[OUISE]

WEINBERG, LARRY
WEINBERG, LAWRENCE E.

WEINER, HENRI
LONGSTREET, [H] STEPHEN

WEINER, SKIP
WEINER, STEWART

WEINER, WILLIAM M.
MOSKOWITZ, SAM

WEINERT-WILTON, LOUIS
WEINERT, ALOIS

WEIR, ALICE M.
MCLAUGHLIN, EMMA MAUDE

WEIR, EVANGELINE
WEIDNER, E.H.

WEIR, JOHN
CROSS, COLIN JOHN

WEIR, JONNET
NICHOLSON, JOAN

WEIR, LOGAN
PERRY, JAMES BLACK

WEIR, MORDRED
LONG, AMELIA REYNOLDS

WEIRING, KATJA
BANDILLA, MARGRIT

WEISS, MIRIAM
SCHLEIN, MIRIAM

WELBURN, VIVIENNE
FURLONG, VIVIENNE CAROLE

WELCH, CHARLES SCOTT
SMITH, LE ROI TEX

WELCH, PAULINE
BODENHAM, HILDA ESTER

WELCH, RONALD
FELTON, RONALD OLIVER

WELCH, ROWLAND
DAVIES, LESLIE PERNELL

WELCOME, JOHN
BRENNAN, JOHN N.H.

WELDEN, REX [D]
RIMEL, DUANE [W]

WELDON, REX
RIMEL, DUANE [W]

WELDON, WALLACE
GIBSON, WALTER B.

WELL, ALAN STEWART
SEWART, ALAN

WELL-WISHER TO KING & CTY
WHALLEY, DOROTHY

WELLAND, COLIN
WILLIAMS, COLIN

WELLE, STEIN
KNUTSEN, LALLI & FRIDTJOF

WELLER, FREDDY
BURKHARDT, OTTO BRUNO
KLEIN, FRED [FRITZ]

WELLER, FREDY
GERSTMAYER, ALFRED

WELLER, PHILIPP
LOB, WILHELM HERMANN

WELLES, ALYSSA
BERGER, NOMI

WELLES, CARON
JONES, JAN

WELLES, ELIZABETH
ROBY, MARY LINN

WELLES, KERMIT
STOKES, MANNING LEE

WELLES, PATRICIA
ROGERS, PATRICIA

WELLES, RACHEL
ROGERS, PATRICIA

WELLES, ROSALIND
WASHINGTON, ELSIE

WELLESLEY, LORD CHARLES
BRONTE, CHARLOTTE

WELLING, RENATE
GUGGENHEIM-WIESE, URSULA

WELLINGTON, ANDREW
WEED, TRUMAN A.W.

WELLINGTON, ANNE
HEWETT, ANITA

WELLINGTON, JOHN
FARNILL, BARRIE

WELLINGTON, KATE
SCHULZE, HERTHA

WELLMAN, WADE
WELLMAN, WADE

WELLS, ANGELA
BOSTWICK, ANGELA

WELLS, BARRY
RICHARDS, DALE
RICHARDS, DICK

WELLS, BRAXTON
WOLLHEIM, DONALD A.

WELLS, CATHERINE
DIMENSTEIN, CATHERINE WE.

WELLS, CHARLIE
WELLS, CHARLES HARDING

WELLS, CHUCK
WELLS, CHARLES HARDING

WELLS, DEE
AYER, ALBERTA CONSTANCE

WELLS, FRANK
PLOTZE, HASSO

WELLS, H.G.
WELLS, HERBERT GEORGE

WELLS, H.S. [#]
WELLS, H.G.

WELLS, HAMPTON
WELLMAN, MANLY WADE

WELLS, HELEN
GIBSON, WALTER B.
WALLIS, GERALDINE MCDONL.
WEINSTOCK, HELEN

WELLS, HONDO
WHITTINGTON, HARRY

WELLS, HUBERT GEORGE
ACKERMAN, FORREST J.

WELLS, J. WELLINGTON
DE CAMP, L[YON] SPRAGUE

WELLS, J.W.
DE CAMP, L[YON] SPRAGUE

WELLS, JANE WARREN
PICKEN, MARY BROOKS

WELLS, JESSICA
BUCKLAND, RAYMOND

WELLS, JOHN JAY
BRADLEY, MARION ZIMMER
COULSON, JUANITA [R.W.]

WELLS, JOHN WARREN
BLOCK, LAWRENCE

WELLS, JUNE
SWINFORD, BETTY [J.W]

WELLS, LISA
RAUCINA, THOMAS FRANK

WELLS, MICHAEL
MULLINS, RICHARD

WELLS, SUSAN
SIEGEL, DORIS

WELLS, TIM
KALMUCZAK, ROLF

WELLS, TOBIAS
FORBES, DELORIS STANTON

WELLS, TRACEY
NUTTALL, ANTHONY

WELLS, WADE
WELLMAN, MANLY WADE

WELLSLEY, JULIE
BAKER, W.A. HOWARD
DOLPHIN, REGINALD C.
MCNEILLY, WILFRED G.
RICHARDS, ROSS

WELSH, JEAN-LOUISE
KEMPTON, JEAN WELCH

WELTEN, HEINZ
PHILIPSOHN, MARTIN

WELTHORPE, EDNA
ORTON, JOHN KINGSLEY

WELTY, S.F.
WELTY, SUSAN

WELZ, MARTIN
KALMUCZAK, ROLF

WELZ, STEFAN
KALMUCZAK, ROLF

WELZ, THOMAS
KALMUCZAK, ROLF

WELZENBACH, LANORA F.
MILLER, LANORA

WENCK, LENE
KARO, HELENE

WENDEL, OTTOKAR
PFEFFER, HEINRICH

WENDELBURG, OTTO M.
MIELKE, OTTO

WENDELESSEN
DE LINT, CHARLES

WENDELIN, R.
VON DEDENROTH, EUGEN H.

WENDER, THEODORA
WENDER, DOROTHEA

WENDHOFER, TONI
JOHN, FRIEDRICH LUDWIG

WENDLAND, HEIDE
HEROLD, ANNEMARIE

WENDLAND, MARTIN
STRUBE, WILHELM

WENDOLIN
DURBEN, WOLFGANG J.M.

WENDT, JULIA
DONGES, GUNTER

WENDT, KATHE
KABEL, WALTHER

WENGEN-BERGER, K.
KAPPLER, HANNS-WALTER

WENGROV, CHARLES
WENGROVSKY, CHARLES

WENK, RUDOLF
CZERWENKA, RUDI

WENKART, HENRI
WENKART, HENNY

WENTWORTH, BARBARA
PITCHER, GLADYS

WENTWORTH, CHARLES
SHUTE, WALTER
STEFFENS, ARTHUR JOSEPH

WENTWORTH, HERBERT
JAMES, HERBERT WENTWORTH

WENTWORTH, JOHN
CHILD, PHILIP A.G.

WENTWORTH, PATRICIA
TURNBULL, DORA AMY D.

WENTWORTH, RICK
SILVERBERG, ROBERT

WENTWORTH, ROBERT
HAMILTON, EDMOND

WENTWORTH, WALTER
GILMAN, BRADLEY

WENZEL, SOPHIE LOUISE
ELLIS, SOPHIE WENZEL

WERATA, TOTA
GADD, DAVID BERNARD H.

WERDENBERG, HEIDI
NOLL-WERDENBERG, HEIDI

WERNER, E.
BURSTENBINDER, ELISABETH

WERNER, EDWARD
LUNDGREN, NILS

WERNER, ELSA JANE
WATSON, JANE WERNER

WERNER, GEORGE
SCOTT, PETER T.

WERNER, ISAIAH
DOUGLASS, ELLSWORTH

WERNER, JANE
WATSON, JANE WERNER

WERNER, K.
CASEWIT, CURTIS

WERNER, KATHARINA
GOTZ, GERD

WERNER, M.R.
WERNER, MORRIS ROBERT

WERNER, PATRICIA
WERNER, PATRICIA BARNES

WERNER, PETER
BOOTH, PHILIP ARTHUR

WERNER, PETRA
GENTZ-WERNER, PETRA

WERNER, THOMAS
BLOM, KARL ARNE
LARSSON, JANERIK

WERNHEIM, JOHN
FEARN, JOHN RUSSELL

WERNING, ANDREAS
BRANDHORST, ANDREAS

WERO
ROTHENBURG, WALTER

WERPER, BARTON
SCOTT, PEG O'NEILL
SCOTT, PETER T.

WERRERSON, TALBOT
ROBERTSON, WALTER GEORGE

WERTHAM, FREDERIC
WERTHEIMER, FREDERICK I.

WERTNER, HEINZ
HINTZ, WERNER

WERY, ERNESTINE
FENTSCH-WERY, ERNA

WESBURY, MICHAEL
JONES, LANGDON

WESCOTT, SERENA LOUISE
TAYLOR, R.L.

WESLAGER, C.A.
WESLAGER, CLINTON ALFRED

WESLEY, ALISON
BARNES, MICHAEL [L.G.]

WESLEY, ART
GRENNELL, DEAN A.

WESLEY, ELIZABETH
MCELFRESH, ELIZABETH A.

WESLEY, JAMES
RIGONI, ORLANDO JOSEPH

WESLEY, MARY
EADY, MARY ALINE
SIEPMANN, MARY

WESSEL, OKTAVIA
CWOJDZINSKA, SELMA

WESSEX REDIVIVUS
DEWAR, HUBERT STEPHEN L.

WESSEX, MARTIN
LITTLE, D.F.

WESSLING, M. v.
BLANK, MATTHIAS

WESSO, [H.W]
WESSOLOWSKI, HANS W.

WESSON, JOAN
PITTOCK, JOAN [H]

WEST COUNTRY
DAWSON, CHARLES KENNETH

WEST, ANNA
EDWARD, ANN

WEST, BARBARA
PRICE, OLIVE

WEST, BUXTON
CHAMPLIN, EDWIN ROSS

WEST, C.P.
WODEHOUSE, PELHAM GRENV.

WEST, CAROL
WAKEVAINEN, CLARA A.

WEST, CHRISTINE
BAKER, CHRISTINE

WEST, DAVID
STACTON, DAVID DEREK

WEST, DOROTHY
BENSON, MILDRED [A] WIRT

WEST, DOUGLAS
TUBB, E.C.

WEST, EDGAR
CARR, GORDON

WEST, EDWIN
WESTLAKE, DONALD [EDWIN]

WEST, EMMY
WEST, EMILY GOVAN

WEST, FRANCES
WARREN, LINDA

WEST, FRANK H.
WEST, FRANCIS HORNER

WEST, GEOFFREY
WELLS, GEOFFREY H[ARRY]

WEST, HARALD
ASPERN-BUCHMEIER, ELISAB.

WEST, JAMES
WITHERS, CARL A.

WEST, JAMIE
VINES-HAINES, BEVERLY

WEST, JAY
NUETZEL, CHARLES A.

WEST, JENNIFER
JUSTIN, JENNIFER

WEST, JERRY
STRATEMEYER, EDWARD
SVENSON, ANDREW E.

WEST, JESSAMYN
MCPHERSON, MRS. H.M.

WEST, JOHN
PENTELOW, JOHN NIX
ARTHUR, ROBERT

WEST, JULIAN
MULLER, ERNST

WEST, KEITH
LANE, KENNETH WESTMACOTT

WEST, KENYON
HOWLAND, FRANCES LOUISE

WEST, KIRKPATRICK
HARRIS, F. BRAYTON

WEST, LAURA M.
HYMERS, LAURA M.

WEST, LINDSAY
WEBER, NANCY

WEST, MARK
HUNT, DARRELL
RUNYON, CHARLES W.

WEST, MARVIN
GOLDFRAP, JOHN HENRY

WEST, MARY
ROCHESTER, GEO[RGE] E.

WEST, MICHAEL
DERLETH, AUGUST [WILLIAM]

WEST, NANCY RICHARD
WESTPHAL, WILMA ROSS

WEST, NATHANIEL
WEINSTEIN, NATHAN W.

WEST, NIGEL
ALLASON, RUPERT

WEST, OLIVER
HOGBERG, ERIK YNGVE

WEST, OWEN
KOONTZ, DEAN R.

WEST, PAMELA [ELIZABETH]
KATKIN, PAMELA E. WEST
RUBENSTEIN, SAMUEL L.

WEST, PAT
STROTHER, PAT WALLACE

WEST, PEP
WEINSTEIN, NATHAN W.

WEST, REBECCA
ANDREWS, CECILY ISOBEL

WEST, ROGER
WATSON, VIRGINIA CRUSE

WEST, TERRY
SLATTERY, RAY

WEST, TOKEN
HUMPHRIES, ADELAIDE

WEST, TOM
EAST, FRED
REACH, JAMES

WEST, TRUDY
WEST, GERTRUDE IDA

WEST, V.C.
WOOLACOTT, LESLIE LOVAL

WEST, WARD
BORLAND, HAROLD GLEN

WESTA, THOMAS
NOGLY, HANS

WESTALL, LORNA
HOUSEMAN, LORNA

WESTBURY, HUGH
FARRIE, HUGH

WESTCOMBE, CHARLES
CARR, GORDON

WESTCOTT, KATHLEEN
ABRAHAMSEN, CHRISTINE E.

WESTCOTT-JONES, K.
JONES, KENNETH WESTCOTT

WESTERHAM, JULIA
ORMHAUG, ELLA GRIFFITHS

WESTERHAM, S.C.
ALINGTON, CYRIL A.

WESTERKAMP, THOMAS M.
ADAM VAN EYCK, HERBERT

WESTERLY, DANIEL
DONABEDIAN, BAIRJ

WESTERMIER, DAVID L.
WOOD, EDWARD D. JR.

WESTERN, BARRY
EVANS, GWYNFIL ARTHUR

WESTERN, MARK
CRISP, ANTHONY THOMAS

WESTERN-HOLT, J.C.
HEMING, JACK C.W.

WESTFLAG, FLETCHER
ROTSLER, WILLIAM

WESTHAVEN, MARGARET
HANSEN, PEGGY M.

WESTIN, JEAN
WESTIN, JEANNE EDDY

WESTLAND, LYNN
JOSCELYN, ARCHIE LYNN

WESTLAW, STEVEN
PYKE, JOHN

WESTLEY, KIRK
STOKES, MANNING LEE

WESTMACOTT, MARY
CHRISTIE, AGATHA [M.C.]

WESTMANN, HARALD
ASPERN-BUCHMEIER, ELISAB.

WESTMINSTER, AYNN
MUNDIS, HESTER JANE

WESTON, ALLEN
HOGARTH, GRACE W.A.
NORTON, ANDRE ALICE

WESTON, ANN
PITCHER, GLADYS

WESTON, BARRY
EVANS, GWYNFIL ARTHUR

WESTON, COLE
RANDISI, ROBERT J.

WESTON, HELEN GRAY
DANIELS, DOROTHY
DANIELS, NORMAN A.

WESTON, JOHN
DAVIES, JOHN E.W.

WESTON, MATT
PERHSON, HOWARD

WESTON, PATRICK
HAMILTON, GERALD

WESTON, WARREN
GALE, LINN A.E.

WESTON, WILLIAM [G]
MILSOM, CHARLES HENRY

WESTPHAL, JUTTA
SCHAFFER, JUTTA [W]

WESTRIDGE, HAROLD
AVERY, HAROLD

WESTWOOD, GORDON
SCHOFIELD, MICHAEL

WESTWOOD, JENNIFER
CHANDLER, JENNIFER [W]

WESTWOOD, N.J.
MILLARD, JOSEPH [JOHN]

WESTWOOD, PERRY
HOLMES, L[LEWELLYN] P.

WETCHECK, J.L.
FEUCHTWANGER, LION

WETHERELL, ELIZABETH
WARNER, SUSAN BOGERT

WETZEL, LOUIS
KING, ALBERT

WEYMOUTH, ANTHONY
COBB, IVO GEIKIE

WEYMOUTH, LALLY
WEYMOUTH, ELIZABETH G.

WHALEN, GARY
BLEECK, G.C.

WHARF, MICHAEL
WELLER, GEORGE [ANTHONY]

WHARTON, ANTHONY
MCALLISTER, ALISTER

WHARTON, EDITH
JONES, EDITH NEWBALD

WHARTON, JAMES
MENCKEN, HENRY LOUIS

WHARTON, VIRGINIA
RATIGAN, ELEANOR ELDRIDGE

WHARTON, WILLIAM
DU AIME, ALBERT

WHEAT-LIEBER, PATTE
WHEAT, PATTE

WHEATLEY, CHRIS
JORDAN, JAMES A.

WHEATLEY, G.W.
BEER, GUSTAVE

WHEATLEY, H.B.
WHEATLEY, HENRY BENJAMIN

WHEDON, JULIA
SCHICKEL, JULIA WHEDON

WHEELAN, ARTHUR
FISHER, STEPHEN GOULD

WHEELER, CAPTAIN
ELLIS, EDWARD S.

WHEELER, CHRIS
MACOWEN, ARTHUR H.

WHEELER, JANET D.
STRATEMEYER, EDWARD

WHEELHOUSE
SEMPLE, DUGALD

WHEELS, H.G.
WELLS, H.G.

WHEELTON, BROOKE
SLADEN, DOUGLAS

WHEEZY
HOUNSFIELD, JOAN

WHETTER, LAURA
MANNOCK, LAURA

WHILK, NAT
LEWIS, CLIVE STAPLES

WHIM WHAM
CURNOW, ALLEN

WHISENAND, VAL
WHISENAND, VALERIE

WHISNANT, CHARLEEN
SWANZEY, CHARLEEN

WHISTLER, MARY
POLLOCK, IDA

WHISTLER, REX
WHISTLER, REGINALD JOHN

WHITAKER, RAY
DAVIES, JOHN

WHITAKER, ROD
WHITAKER, RODNEY W.

WHITBREAD, J.R.
LEVIN, JANE WHITBREAD

WHITBREAD, JANE
LEVIN, JANE WHITBREAD

WHITBY, SHARON
PETERS, MAUREEN

WHITE BEAVER
POWELL, [DAVID] FRANK

WHITE EAGLE
CARTER, PETE

WHITE ELK, MICHAEL
WALKER, T. MICHAEL

WHITE FOX
HARGRAVE, JOHN

WHITE FRIAR
SABINE, WILLIAM HENRY

WHITE, ANDY
WHITE, ELWYN BROOKS

WHITE, BABINGTON
BRADDON, MARY ELIZABETH

WHITE, CECIL B.
CHRISTIE, WILLIAM H.

WHITE, DALE
PLACE, MARIAN T.

WHITE, E.B.
WHITE, ELWYN BROOKS

WHITE, EDMUND
PATTON, JAMES BLYTHE

WHITE, EN
WHITE, ELWYN BROOKS

WHITE, G.A.
MILLAR, JAMES P.M.

WHITE, GEORGE H.
ENGUIDANOS USACH, PASCUAL

WHITE, GEORGE M.
WALSH, JAMES MORGAN

WHITE, HARRY
WHITTINGTON, HARRY

WHITE, HEATHER
FOSTER, JESS MARY MARDON

WHITE, HENRY
LLOP SELLARES, JUAN

WHITE, JAMES DILLON
WHITE, STANLEY

WHITE, JAMES S.
RENNAU, JOACHIM

WHITE, JANE
BRADY, JANE FRANCES

WHITE, JONATHAN
HARVEY, JOHN [BARTON]

WHITE, LEONARD
FARJEON, J. JEFFERSON
QUINN, SEABURY

WHITE, LOFTUS
HORSCHELT, THEODOR

WHITE, LORIMER
COLLINS, ANDREW J.

WHITE, MARY
TALBOT, MARY WHITE

WHITE, MAURINE
MILLER RIIS, MAUREEN

WHITE, MAX
WHITE, CHARLES WILLIAM

WHITE, PALMER
SPRY, THEODORE JAMES

WHITE, PARKER
WHITE, WILLIAM A.P.

WHITE, RAMY ALLISON
STRATEMEYER, EDWARD

WHITE, ROBIN
WHITE, WILLIAM ROBINSON

WHITE, ROLD
NEUBERG, VICTOR [B]

WHITE, SALLY JOY
WHITE, SARA ELIZABETH

WHITE, STEVE
MCGARVEY, ROBERT

WHITE, SYLVIA
FURSTAUER, JOHANNA

WHITE, TED
WHITE, THEODORE EDWIN

WHITE, TIFFANY
EBERHARDT, ANNA

WHITE, WILLY
JAREMKO, NESTOR

WHITE, ZITA
DENHOLM, TERESE MARY ZITA

WHITEBAIT, WILLIAM
STONIER, GEORGE

WHITEFRIAR
HISCOCK, ERIC

WHITEHEAD, JANET
WHITEHEAD, DAVID [HENRY]

WHITEHORN, KATHARINE
LYALL, KATHARINE ELIZAB.

WHITEHOUSE, ARCH
TAYLOR, W.T.

WHITEHOUSE, ARCH[IBALD]
WHITEHOUSE, ARTHUR G.T.

WHITEHOUSE, PEGGY
CASTLE, FRANCES MUNDY

WHITELAND, SATHERLEY
SATHERLEY, DAVID

WHITELY, T.K.
WELLMAN, MANLY WADE

WHITFIELD, ISABEL
GRANAHL, TAMARA

WHITINGER, R.D.
PLACE, MARIAN T.

WHITLEY, GEORGE
CHANDLER, A. BERTRAM

WHITLEY, MARY ANN
SEBREY, MARY ANN

WHITLEY, REID
ARMOUR, R. COUTTS

WHITLEY, SHARON
PETERS, MAUREEN

WHITMAN, JOHN
FRIEDRICHS, HORST

WHITMORE, CILLA
GLADSTONE, ARTHUR M.

WHITNELL, BARBARA
HUTTON, AUDREY GRACE W.

WHITNEY, ALEC
WHITE, ALAN

WHITNEY, DIANA
HINZ, DIANA

WHITNEY, ELLIOTT
BEDFORD-JONES, HENRY
DOCKWEILER, JOSEPH HAROLD
KUMMER, FREDERICK ARNOLD
SAYLER, HARRY L.

WHITNEY, HALLAM
WHITTINGTON, HARRY

WHITNEY, J.L.H.
TRIMBLE, JACQUEL. WHITNEY

WHITNEY, JAMISAN
BROWNLIE, NOREEN

WHITNEY, LUCIA
KELLER, [Y] ETHEL MAY

WHITNEY, MARYLOU
WHITNEY, MARIE LOUISE S.H

WHITNEY, PHYLLIS
GARNER, PHYLLIS A.

WHITNEY, SPENCER
BURKS, ARTHUR J.

WHITSON
WARREN, PETER WHITSON

WHITSTABLE, GEORGE
LISSENDEN, GEORGE B.

WHITTIER, HENRI
WHITTINGTON, HARRY

WHITTINGTON, HARRY
LAMPP, JAMES W.

WHITTINGTON, PETER
MACKAY, JAMES [A]

WHITTLE, TYLER
FRASER, GEORGE MACDONALD
TYLER-WHITTLE, MICHAEL

WHITTLEBOT, HERNIA
COWARD, NOEL [PIERCE]

WHITTON, BARBARA
CHITTY, MARGARET HAZEL

WHITTON, DANIEL
POMEROY, JOHN H.

WHIZ, WALTER
JOHNSON, CURTIS LEE

WHTIEHAND, SATHERLEY
WHITEHAND, JAMES

WHYE, FELIX
DIXON, ARTHUR

WHYMER, MAC
WIMMER, MAX

WHYTE, SIBLEY
STEIN, HENRY EUGENE
STINE, GEORGE HARRY

WHYTE, VIOLET
STANNARD, HENRIETTA ELIZ.

WIAT, PHILIPPA
FERRIDGE, PHILLIPPA

WICK, CARTER
WILCOX, COLLIN

WICK, STUART MARY
FREEMAN, KATHLEEN

WICKER, TOM
WICKER, THOMAS GREY

WICKES, MARTHA
CHASE, JOSEPHINE

WICKHAM, ANNA
HEPBURN, EDITH ALICE M.

WICKING, G.W.
WICKING, GEORGE WALTER

WICKLOE, PETER
DUFF, DOUGLAS VALDER

WIDBORG, MICHAEL
LEUKEFELD, PETER

WIDDEMER, MARGARET
SCHAUFFLER, MARGARET WID.

WIDE, GUSTAF
KERFVE, AXEL

WIDE, LENNART
FORSSBERG, LENNART

WIDGERY, JAN
WIDGERY, JEAN-ANNE

WIDMANN, W.L.
HAUSLEITNER, INES HERMINE

WIDMARK, HAKAN
BENGSTON, HAKAN

WIDOC, E.N.
PETRY, ERNEST

WIEBEL, MARION
KURTH, HANNS

WIEBSCHER, LALT
LEIBSCHER, WALT

WIED, ANN
GLUCK, ANNA [S]

WIEDEN, ERIKA
JANSEN, ERIKA [W]

WIEDEN, RUTH
DICHTL, RUTH [v.M.]

WIEDERUMP, TROTZHARD
STEINER, GEROLF

WIEN, ALEXANDER
KOLB, KARL

WIENER, RALPH
ECKE, FELIX

WIENER, SAM
DOLGOFF, SAM

WIESEL, ELIE
WIESEL, ELIEZER

WIESNER, PORTIA
TAKAKJIAN, PORTIA

WIEST, GRACE L.
DELOUGHERY, GRACE L.

WIETIG, ANNEMARIE
BUNTE, ANNEMARIE

WIGAN, CHRISTOPHER
BINGLEY, DAVID ERNEST

WIGG, T.I.G.
MCCUTCHAN, PHILIP [D]

WIGGEN, HENRY J.
FINKLESTEIN, MARK

WIGGEN, HENRY W.
HARRIS, MARK

WIGGS, SUSAN
CHILDRESS, SUSAN

WIGNELL, EDEL
WIGNELL, EDNA

WIJK, KAARE
LAGERVIST, ULF

WIJNSTROOM, CHRISTY
HOPPEN-RAM, HENDERIKA W.

WIKSTROM, LENNART
SODERHJELM, HENNING
SODERSTROM, OLE

WILBER, RICK
WILBER, RICHARD ARNOLD

WILBRAHAM, JOHN
POTTER, ROBERT

WILBURN, LEN
BURGE, JERRY
PAGE, GERALD W.

WILBY, JANE
HAMPSON, ANNE

WILBY, R. HUNT
EYSTER, WILLIAM REYNOLDS

WILCOX, DON
KNOX, CLEO ELDON

WILCOX, HANNAH SIMS
MINER, VIRGINIA SCOTT

WILCOX, JESS
HERSHMAN, MORRIS

WILCOX, JESSICA
HERSHMAN, MORRIS

WILD HICKORY NUT
GIBBONS, EUELL

WILD HORSE ANNIE
JOHNSTON, VELMA B.

WILD SCOTCHMAN, THE
MACPHERSON, ALPIN

WILD, HAMPTON
LLOP SELLARES, JUAN

WILDBERG, BODO
DICKINSON-WILDBERG, HEINO

WILDE, D. GUNTHER
HURWOOD, BERNHARDT J.

WILDE, EDWARD
VILDE, EDUARD

WILDE, HILARY
BOON, AUGUST
BRETON-SMITH, CLARE

WILDE, JENNIFER
HUFF, TOM E.

WILDE, JIMMY
CREASEY, JOHN

WILDE, JOCELYN
TOOMBS, JOHN

WILDE, KARIN
RASENBERGER-KOCH, ERIKA

WILDE, KATHEY
KING, PATRICIA

WILDE, LAUREN
REDD, JOANNE

WILDE, LESLIE
BEST, R. BRETON AMIS

WILDE, NIALL[E]
RUSSELL, ERIC FRANK

WILDE, OSCAR
WILLS, FINGAL O'FLAHERTIE

WILDE, RITA
HAYDOCK, RON
NUETZEL, CHARLES A.

WILDEBLOOD, JOAN
MURRAY, JOAN

WILDEN, HARRY F.
PESCHKE, HANS

WILDENVEY, HERMAN
PORTAAS, HERMAN

WILDER, ALLEN
JAKES, JOHN [WILLIAM]

WILDER, CHERRY
GRIMM, CHERRY BARBARA L.

WILDER, JOAN
LANIGAN, CATHERINE

WILDER, ROSE
LANE, ROSE WILDER

WILDER, STEPHEN
MARLOWE, STEPHEN

WILDER, WILLIAM WEST
PATTEN, WILLIAM GEORGE

WILDERNESS, DAVID O.
BRODY, PETER S.

WILDERS, JULIANE
GREVEN, HELGA

WILDING, ANN
BUDD, MAVIS

WILDING, ERIC
TUBB, E.C.

WILDING, ERNEST
MOLLOY, JOSEPH FITZGERALD

WILDING, KARL
HEICHEN, WALTER

WILDING, KAY
HICKS, JOAN WILSON

WILDING, PAT
DONGES, GUNTER
NETSCH, GUNTER

WILDING, STEN
LILJENFORS, BENNIE MADS C

WILDMAN, FAYE
DAGG, JILLIAN

WILDWOOD
WINSON, J.W.

WILDWOOD, WILL
POND, FREDERICK E.

WILEY, GERALD
BARKER, RONNIE

WILEY, JOHN
GRAHAM, ROGER P.

WILEY, LAURA
MATTHEWS, PATRICIA [BRIS]

WILEY, MARGARET L.
MARSHALL, MARGARET L.W.

WILFORD, HARRY
HARY, WILFRID A.

WILHELM am BERGER, CARL
AMBERGER, CARL WILHELM

WILHELM, LAMBERT
LAMBERT, W[ILLIAM J.] III

WILHELMI, HELMA
HUBLER-WILHELMI, CHARLOT.

WILHELMSON, FRANCESKA
SANDELL, ULLA

WILKE, DIRK
AHLBORN-WILKE, DIRK

WILKERSON, CYNTHIA
LEVINSON, LEONARD [L]

WILKINS, J.H.
HARMON, JAMES JUDSON
KUHN, WILL

WILKINS, MARNIE
WILKINS, MARILYN R.

WILKINS, MARY E.
FREEMAN, MARY [E.W.]

WILKINS, ROBINSON
JOHNSSON, [K.O.] HARALD

WILKINSON, L.
MACMANUS, YVONNE

WILKINSON, LEE
MACMANUS, YVONNE

WILKINSON, LYDIA
MACMANUS, YVONNE

WILKINSON, TIM
WILKINSON, PERCY FRANCIS

WILKINSON, WINIFRED
HAUSMANN, WINIFRED

WILKOW, MICHAEL
KALMUCZAK, ROLF

WILKS, MIKE
WILKS, MICHAEL THOMAS

WILL
LIPKIND, WILLIAM

WILL, RUTH
GLASER, MARTHA

WILLARD, C.D.
DIFFIN, CHARLES WILLARD

WILLARD, CHARLES
ARMSTRONG, JOHN BYRON

WILLARD, PORTMAN
NORWOOD, VICTOR [G.C.]

WILLBERG, HEINO
BLANVALET, LOTHAR

WILLE, EDRIKA
JANSEN, ERIKA [W]

WILLER
EMSHWILLER, EDMUND A.

WILLETTS, R.F.
WILLETTS, RONALD F.

WILLEY, ROBERT [ROBBERT]
LEY, WILLIE

WILLHELM, KATE
KNIGHT, KATIE G.M.WILHELM

WILLIAM CHURN OF STAFFDSH
PAGET, FRANCES EDWARD

WILLIAM, ARNOLD
MEADOWCROFT, ERNEST [W]

WILLIAMS, A.P.
PLOTNIK, ARTHUR

WILLIAMS, AGNES
PRONZINI, WILLIAM JOHN
WALLMANN, JEFFREY M.

WILLIAMS, ANN
MYERS, PEGGY A.

WILLIAMS, ANNE
STEINKE, ANN E.R.

WILLIAMS, ARTHUR
MILES, JOHN

WILLIAMS, BERYL
EPSTEIN, BERYL [WILLIAMS]

WILLIAMS, BILL
CRAWFORD, WILLIAM [E]
WILLIAMS, WILLIAM H.

WILLIAMS, BRONWYN
BROWNING, DIXIE [S.B.]
WILLIAMS, MARY

WILLIAMS, CHARLES
COLLIER, JAMES L.

WILLIAMS, CHESTER
SCHECTER, WILLIAM

WILLIAMS, CHRIS
KLEMME, CHRIS

WILLIAMS, COE
HARRISON, CHESTER WILLIAM

WILLIAMS, D.
RONALD, DAVID WILLIAM

WILLIAMS, DAVID
SROOG, ARNOLD

WILLIAMS, E.C.
WILLIAMS, ERIC CYRIL

WILLIAMS, E.N.
WILLIAMS, ERNEST NEVILLE

WILLIAMS, F. HARALD
ORDE-WARD, F.W.

WILLIAMS, FRANCES
HARDTER, FRANCES

WILLIAMS, FRANCIS B.
BROWIN, FRANCES WILLIAMS

WILLIAMS, FRANK
WILLIAMS, EDWARD FRANCIS

WILLIAMS, FRED J.
SMITH, BERNARD

WILLIAMS, GATENBY
GUGGENHEIM, WILLIAM

WILLIAMS, HAROLD WORKMAN
WILSON, HALSEY WILLIAM

WILLIAMS, HAWLEY
HEYLIGER, WILLIAM

WILLIAMS, HENRY
MANVILLE, WILLIAM HENRY

WILLIAMS, J. WALKER
WODEHOUSE, PELHAM GRENV.

WILLIAMS, J.R.
WILLIAMS, DOROTHY JEANNE

WILLIAMS, J.X.
JAKES, JOHN [WILLIAM]
JAMES, JORDAN
KNOLES, WILLIAM [H]
LUDWIG, MILES ERIC
MOSKOVITZ, JACK
OFFUTT, ANDREW J.
PERICHITCH, MILO
SMITH, GEORGE H[ENRY]
WOOD, EDWARD D. JR.

WILLIAMS, JEANNE
WILLIAMS, DOROTHY JEANNE

WILLIAMS, JOEL
JENNINGS, JOHN [E]

WILLIAMS, JOHN BARRY
LUTZ, JOHN [T]
MALZBERG, BARRY [N]
PRONZINI, WILLIAM JOHN

WILLIAMS, JON
WILLIAMS, WALTER JON

WILLIAMS, LAURIE
SCOTT, ADRIENNE

WILLIAMS, LEE
MERRIT, WILLIAM
WILLIAMS, LEIGH ANNE

WILLIAMS, LEIGH ANNE
MERRIT, WILLIAM

WILLIAMS, LYNN
ADAMS, TRACY
HALE, MARY ARLENE

WILLIAMS, MARGERY
BIANCO, MARGERY WILLIAMS

WILLIAMS, MAX
KNOLES, WILLIAM [H]

WILLIAMS, MICHAEL
ST. JOHN, WYLLY FOLK

WILLIAMS, PATRICK J.
BUTTERWORTH, WILLIAM E.

WILLIAMS, PATRY
PATRY, M.
WILLIAMS, D.F.

WILLIAMS, PAULA
DARRINGTON, PAULA

WILLIAMS, PEGGY
MYERS, PEGGY A.

WILLIAMS, PETE
FAULKNOR, CLIFF[ORD V.]
REACH, JAMES

WILLIAMS, RENDALL
RIDELL, WILLIAM RENWICK

WILLIAMS, REX
WEI, REX YUE-TIEN

WILLIAMS, RICHARD
BAKER, W.A. HOWARD

WILLIAMS, RICHARD
CHAMBERS, PHILIP
DOLPHIN, REGINALD C.
FRANCES, STEPHEN D.
FRANES, S.O.
HOSKINS, ROBERT
HOPKINS, B.
HOPKINS, ROBERT S.
MANN, GEORGE PAUL
MARQUIS, MAX
REACH, JAMES
STORY, JACK TREVOR

WILLIAMS, ROSE
ROSS, WILLIAM E. DANIEL

WILLIAMS, ROSEANNE
SLATTERY, SHEILA

WILLIAMS, ROSWELL
OWEN, FRANK

WILLIAMS, ROTH
ZILLIACUS, KONNI

WILLIAMS, RUSSELL
WHITSON, JOHN HARVEY

WILLIAMS, SHIRLEY
WILLIAMS, SHERLEY

WILLIAMS, SLIM
WILLIAMS, CLYDE C.

WILLIAMS, SPEEDY
SMITH, L.H.

WILLIAMS, TAD
WILLIAMS, ROBERT PAUL

WILLIAMS, TENNESSEE
WILLIAMS, THOMAS LANIER

WILLIAMS, URSULA MORAY
MORAY WILLIAMS, URSULA

WILLIAMS, VIOLET M.
BOON, VIOLET MARY

WILLIAMS, WETHERBY
WILLIAMS, MARGARET W.

WILLIAMS, WRIGHT
WRIGHT, WATKINS E.

WILLIAMS, WYNN
WILLIAMS, NORMA

WILLIAMSON, A.M.
WILLIAMSON, ALICE M.L.

WILLIAMSON, C.N.
WILLIAMSON, CHARLES N.

WILLIAMSON, CHET
WILLIAMSON, CHESTER C.

WILLIAMSON, J.N.
WILLIAMSON, GERALD NEAL

WILLIAMSON, JACK
WILLIAMSON, JOHN STEWART

WILLIAMSON, MRS. HARCOURT
WILLIAMSON, ALICE M.L.

WILLIAMSON, PAUL
BUTTERS, PAUL

WILLIAMSON, PENELOPE
LAMBERT, ELIZABETH MINNIE

WILLIAMSON, SHERMAN
SHERMAN, DANIEL MICHAEL
WILLIAMSON, ROBIN

WILLIBALD, GRAF
DURBEN, WOLFGANG J.M.

WILLIE, ALBERT FREDERIC
LOVECRAFT, H[OWARD] P.

WILLIE, FREDERICK
LOVECRAFT, H[OWARD] P.

WILLINGHAM, CALDER
THOMPSON, JAMES [MYERS]
WILLINGHAM, CALDER

WILLIS, SAMUEL
PARKER, HERSHEL

WILLIS, CHARLES
CLARKE, ARTHUR C.

WILLIS, CONNIE
WILLIS, CONSTANCE ELAINE

WILLIS, LISLE
WILLIS, ERNEST LISTER H.

WILLIS, LOWELL E.
DAVIS, HORACE BANCROFT

WILLIS, MAUD
LOTTMAN, EILEEN [SHUBB]

WILLIS, TED
WIESLER, ROLF
WILLIS, EDWARD HENRY

WILLIUS, T.F.
TAMMINGA, FREDERICK WILL.

WILLOUGHBY, BARRETT
O'CONNER, BARRETT WILL'BY

WILLOUGHBY, CASS
OLSEN, THEODORE VICTOR

WILLOUGHBY, HUGH
HARVEY, NIGEL

WILLOUGHBY, LEE DAVIS
AVALLONE, MICHAEL
BEARDSLEY, CHARLES N.
BRANDNER, GARY
CAMERON, LOU
D'ANDREA, WILLIAM L.
DAMIO, WARD
DE ANDREA, WILLIAM L.
DEMING, RICHARD
FLETCHER, AARON
GRANGER, GEORGE A.
HUNT, GREG
JAHN, JOSEPH MICHAEL
KELLEY, LEO P[ATRICK]
LAWRENCE, KATHLEEN
LAYMON, RICHARD
MCMAHAN, IAN
MEYER, KARL ERNEST
MYERS, BARRY
RICHARDS, TAD
ROTHWEILER, JOAN & PAUL
RYAN, GEORGE
SCAFIDEL, JAMES R.
STREIB, DANIEL T.
SUFRIN, MARK
TOOMBS, JANE [JENKE]
TOOMBS, JOHN
VAN ZWIENEN, JOHN
VAUGHAN, ROBERT
WAGER, WALTER [HERMAN]
WEBB, JEAN FRANCIS III
WINSTEN, STEPHEN
ZACHARY, ELIZABETH

WILLOUGHBY-HIGSON, PHILIP
HIGSON, PHILIP J. WILOBY.

WILLRECHT, WALDO
ALBICKER, JOSEF

WILLS, ANN MEREDITH
WILLS, BETTY JO
WILLS, MARALYS

WILLS, CHESTER
SNOW, CHARLES H[ORACE]

WILLS, GEOFFREY
STAAL, CYRIL

WILLS, RONALD
THOMAS, RONALD WILLS

WILLS, THOMAS
ARD, WILLIAM [THOMAS]

WILLSON, WINGROVE
LIGHT, WALTER HERROD

WILLY
GAUTHIER-VILLARS, HENRY

WILMA, DANA
FARALLA, DOROTHY W.

WILMER, DALE
WADE, ROBERT [BOB]
MILLER, BILL[Y]

WILMORE, JOHN
LUNFBERG, IVAR CARL-ALF.

WILMOT, EILEEN
GRAHAM, EILEEN WILMOT

WILMOT, [MAJ.] WALT
HARBAUGH, THOMAS C.

WILSDEN, CLEMENSFORD
WICKHAM, JOHN

WILSON, A.G.
HARRISON, W.G.A.

WILSON, ABIGAIL
YOUNG, SANDRA

WILSON, ANGUS
JOHNSTONE, FRANK

WILSON, ANN
BAILEY, FRANCES EVANS

WILSON, ANNE
WEALE, ANNE

WILSON, B.L.
WILSON, BRENDA LEE E.

WILSON, BARBARA
HARRIS, LAURENCE MARK
WILLIAMS, BARBARA

WILSON, BARBARA KER
TAHOURDIN, BARBARA KER W.

WILSON, CAMMY
WILSON, CAMILLA JEANNE

WILSON, CAROLE
WALLMANN, JEFFREY M.

WILSON, CARYL
WILSON, CAROL

WILSON, CHARLES
STILSON, CHARLES BILLINGS

WILSON, CHRISTINE
GEACH, CHRISTINE

WILSON, CLARK S.
HEIDE, HARRY F.

WILSON, CRANE
O'BRIEN, CYRIL C.

WILSON, DAVE
FLOREN, LEE

WILSON, DAVID
MACARTHUR, D[AVID] WILSON

WILSON, DIRK
POHL, FREDERIK

WILSON, EDWINA H.
BROOKMAN, LAURA L.

WILSON, ELIZABETH
IVISON, ELIZABETH

WILSON, F.P.
WILSON, FRANK PERCY

WILSON, FRAN
WILSON, FRANCES ENGLE

WILSON, G.L.
FEARN, JOHN RUSSELL

WILSON, GABRIEL
CUMMINGS, GABRIELLE
CUMMINGS, MR. & MRS. RAY
CUMMINGS, RAY[MOND KING]

WILSON, GAR
FIELDHOUSE, WILLIAM [L]
HOSKINS, ROBERT
LINAKER, MICHAEL
MARLOWE, DAN J.
NEUMAN, PAUL GLEN
RAMIREZ, THOMAS P.
STREIB, DANIEL T.
SWENSON, REX

WILSON, GAYLE
THOMAS, MONA GAY

WILSON, GWENDOLINE
EWENS, GWENDOLINE WILSON

WILSON, H.W.
WILSON, HALSEY WILLIAM

WILSON, HAL
HOBEIN, EUGEN

WILSON, HOLLY
WILSON, HELEN

WILSON, IRIS HIGBIE
ENGSTRAND, IRIS W.

WILSON, J. ARBUTHNOT
ALLEN, [CHARLES] GRANT B.

WILSON, JANE
BADERI, JUNE

WILSON, JAYE
WILSON, DOROTHY JEAN

WILSON, JOHN BURGESS
WILSON, J ANTHONY BURGESS

WILSON, JOYCE
JAMES, SALLY

WILSON, JUSSEN
WILSON, NELLY

WILSON, KATE
BURKE, SOPHIE VAN E.L.

WILSON, LEE
LEMMON, LAURA ELIZABETH

WILSON, MARGERY
STRAYER, SARA BARKER

WILSON, MARJORIE
WILSON, BUDGE

WILSON, MARK
GIBSON, WALTER B.

WILSON, MARTHA
MORSE, MARTHA WILSON

WILSON, MARY
BURKE, SOPHIE VAN E.L.
ROBY, MARY LINN

WILSON, PENELOPE COKER
HALL, PENELOPE C.

WILSON, REG
THOMAS, REGINALD GEORGE

WILSON, ROMER
MUIR, FLORENCE ROMA

WILSON, SANDY
GALBRAITH, ALEXANDER

WILSON, SHAWN
WILLIAMSON, SHARON

WILSON, SNOO
WILSON, JAMES ANDREW

WILSON, YATES
WILSON, ALBERT W.

WILTE, L.T.J.
ELLIOTT, WILLIAM J.

WILTON, HAL
PEPPER, FRANK S.

WILTON, [CAPT.] MARK
MANNING, WILLIAM HENRY

WINCH, EVELYN M.
WINCH, MARIE ELIZABETH A.

WINCH, JOHN
LONG, GABRIELLE M.V.C.

WINCHESTER, JACK
FREEMANTLE, BRIAN [HARRY]

WINCHESTER, KAY
WALKER, EMILY KATHLEEN

WINCHEVSKY, MORRIS
NOVACHOVITCH, LIPPE BENZ.

WIND, DAVID
WIND, DAVID MILTON

WIND, RUTH
SAMUEL, BARBARA

WINDER, MAVIS
WINDER, MAVIS ARETA

WINDHAM, BASIL
WODEHOUSE, PELHAM GRENV.

WINDHAM, KIT
HICKS, JOAN WILSON

WINDMULLER, ILSE
PLOOG, ILSE

WINDOR, ANNIE
SHULL, MARGARET ANNE W.

WINDSOR, CLAIRE
HAMERSTROM, FRANCES

WINDSOR, FRANK
BIRNAGE, DEREK A.W.

WINDSOR, PAMELA
MESSMANN, JON [JOHN]

WINDSOR, REX
ARMSTRONG, DOUGLAS A.

WINE, DICK
POSNER, RICHARD

WINFIELD, ALLEN
STRATEMEYER, EDWARD

WINFIELD, ARTHUR M.
STRATEMEYER, EDWARD

WINFIELD, DICK
PERRY, DICK

WINFIELD, EDNA
STRATEMEYER, EDWARD

WINFIELD, LEIGH
YOUNGBERG, NORMA IONE

WING, JAMES EGERTON
BAYFIELD, WILLIAM JOHN

WINGATE, ANNE
WEBB, MARTHA [ANNE] G.

WINGATE, WILLIAM
GRBICH, RONALD IVAN

WINGE, PETER
FREY, AKE

WINGE, STEIN
GRAN, OYULV

WINGERT, HEINER
BEMME-WINGERT, HEINZ

WINGFIELD, SUSAN
REECE, ALYS [TRACY]

WINGRAVE, ANTHONY
WRIGHT, SIDNEY FOWLER

WINGRAVE, JOSH
SOWMAN, GORDON

WINGS, MARY
GARBER, ERIC
GELLER, MARY LEE

WINGSHOT, LEO
MCKENNA, EDWARD LAWRENCE

WINHELLER, CHARLOTTE
FRANKE, CHARLOTTE [W]

WINIKI, EPHRAIM
FEARN, JOHN RUSSELL

WINKLER, DIETER
REHFELD, FRANK

WINKLER, JOHANNES
WALLNER, CHRISTIAN J.

WINN, ALISON [O.]
WHARMBY, MARGOT

WINN, PATRICK
PADLEY, ARTHUR

WINNARD, FRANK
TUBB, E.C.

WINNER, THOMAS G.
WIENER, THOMAS G.

WINNEY, KEN
MARKS, WINSTON K.

WINNIFRED
GIBSON, MARY FRANCES

WINSLOW, DONALD
ZOLL, DONALD ATWELL

WINSLOW, DORIAN
STRASBERG, DAOMA WINSTON

WINSLOW, ELLIE
ELIOT, WINSLOW

WINSLOW, JOAN
BUDLONG, WARE TORREY
TORREY [BUDLONG], WARE

WINSLOW, LAUREL
SEGER, MAURA

WINSLOW, MARTHA
RICKETT, FRANCIS

WINSLOW, PAUL
MULLALY, CHARLES

WINSLOWE, JOHN
RICHARDSON, GLADWELL G.

WINSLOWE, JOHN R.
RICHARDSON, GLADWELL G.

WINSOR, THOMAS
GIBSON, WALTER B.

WINSTAN, MATT
NICKSON, ARTHUR [THOMAS]

WINSTEAD, REBECCA NOYES
MERWIN, SAMUEL K. JR.

WINSTON, ANNE MARIE
RODGERS, ANNE MARIE

WINSTON, DAOMA
STRASBERG, DAOMA WINSTON

WINSTON, F.S.
HARBAUGH, THOMAS C.

WINSTON, LENA
CHAFFIN, LILLIE D.

WINSTON, MIKE
KING, FLORENCE

WINSTON, PETER
EIDEN, PAUL
BOWSER, JIM

WINTER BOTTOM, RUSS
WINTERBOTHAM, RUSS[EL] R.

WINTER, ABIGAIL
SCHERE, MONROE

WINTER, CORINNA
LIGENSA, ELFIE

WINTER, DETLEV G.
HORN, DETLEV

WINTER, H.G.
BATES, HARRY ARTHUR
HALL, DESMOND W.

WINTER, HARRY
BOJERUD, STELLAN

WINTER, HELGA
JUNIKE, ROLF

WINTER, JOHN STRANGE
STANNARD, HENRIETTA ELIZA

WINTER, R.R.
WINTERBOTHAM, RUSS[EL] R.

WINTER, THOMAS R.
BERNARD, KARL

WINTER, TURK
OFFUTT, ANDREW J.

WINTERS, BAYLA
WINTERS, BERNICE

WINTERS, DANIEL
HARTLEY, WILLIAM

WINTERS, DEENA
DE MARCO, JOANNE

WINTERS, J.C.
CROSS, GILBERT B.

WINTERS, JON
CROSS, GILBERT B.

WINTERS, LOGAN
LEDERER, PAUL JOSEPH

WINTERS, MALORI
RENSHAW, LISA M.

WINTERS, MARJORIE
HENRI, FLORETTE

WINTERS, MARY K.
HART, CAROLINE HOROWITZ

WINTERS, MICK
WOLFE, RON
WOOLEY, JOHN [S]

WINTERS, RAE
PALMER, RAYMOND A.

WINTERS, REBECCA
BURTON, REBECCA

WINTERTON, GAYLE
ADAMS, WILLIAM TAYLOR

WINTHROP, ELIZABETH
MAHONY, ELIZABETH WINTHRP

WINTON, HARRY
HARBAUGH, THOMAS C.
PRATT, JOHN

WINTON, VAL
HEMING, JOHN WINTON

WINTON, [CAPT.] WALT
HARBAUGH, THOMAS C.

WINWAR, FRANCES
GREBANIER, MRS. B.D.N.
VINCIGUERRA, FRANCESCA

WINWOOD, BRET
DENNY, JOHN THOMAS

WINWOOD, EILEEN
PUTMAN, EILEEN

WINZER, FELIX
GORLITZ, WOLF-DIETER

WIRT, ANN
BENSON, MILDRED [A] WIRT

WIRT, MILDRED A.
BENSON, MILDRED [A] WIRT

WIRT, W.
TEPPERMAN, EMILE C.

WISDOM, JOHN
MOORCOCK, MICHAEL

WISDOM, KENNY
GROGAN, EMMET

WISDOM, PENELOPE
STUART, PENELOPE

WISDOME, THOMAS
DUNBAR, CHARLES STUART

WISE, ROBERT A.
GEBHARDT, FRIEDRICH JOHAN

WISELY, CHARLOTTE
HASTINGS, CHARLOTTE

WISER, H. FRED
FRIEDMAN, HARRY & LINDA

WISHART, HENRY
SHEPHERD, ROBERT HENRY W.

WISLER, G.C.
WISLER, GENE CHARLES

WISNER, BILL
WISNER, WILLIAM L.

WITHERBY, DIANA
COOKE, DIANA

WITHERS, E.L.
POTTER, GEORGE WILLIAM

WITHERSPOON, J.J.
WYMAN, WALTER F.

WITHERSPOON, NAOMI LONG
MADGETT, NAOMI LONG

WITHERUP, ANNE WARRINGTON
BANGS, JOHN KENDRICK

WITKOWICKI, KAROL
BEYLIN, KAROLINA

WITLEY, A.F.
FORBAT, SANDOR

WITTE, GEORGE H.
ENGUIDANOS USACH, PASCUAL

WITTENBOURG, JACOB
WERREMEIER, FRIEDHELM

WITTGEN, TOM
SIEBENSTADT, INGEBURG

WITTIG, SUSAN
ALBERT, SUSAN WITTIG

WITTINGHAM, SARA
GIBBS, NORAH

WITTINGHAUSEN, ARTY
FILEK-WITTINGHAUSEN, WER.

WITWATERSRAND
SCULLY, WILLIAM CHARLES

WITZIG, ANNELIE
LOCHER-WERLING, EMILIE

WIWJORRA, ERNST OTTO
ELLERMANN, ROLF

WIZARD, MR.
HERBERT, DON

WODAK, HERMANN
KADOW, MANES

WODEHOUSE, P.G.
WODEHOUSE, PELHAM GRENV.

WODEN, GEORGE
SLANEY, GEORGE WILSON

WODGE, DREARY
GOREY, EDWARD ST. JOHN

WOHLMUTH, HANS
PITTIONI, HANS

WOJHOSKI, B.
WOJHOSKI, BARBARA M.

WOLDECK, HANS
VON GAUDECKER, HANS

WOLF, ALEXANDER
ROSLER, K. HERBERT

WOLF, FREDERICK
DEMPEWOLFF, RICHARD F.

WOLF, HENRY
BURGDORF, KARL-ULRICH
HOHLBEIN, WOLFGANG E.

WOLF, RAINER
KRAUSNICK, MICHAILL

WOLF, ROMAN
RICHTER, WOLFGANG

WOLF, S.K.
WOLF, SARAH [ELIZABETH]

WOLF, STEFAN
KALMUCZAK, ROLF

WOLFE, AARON
KOONTZ, DEAN R.

WOLFE, CEDRIC
ALAIS, ERNEST W.

WOLFE, ELIZABETH
LEDERER, PAUL JOSEPH

WOLFE, MICHAEL
WILLIAMS, GILBERT M.

WOLFE, PHILIP
KERKOFF, JOHNSTON D.

WOLFENBERG, PETER
KNUTH, PETER WALDEMAR

WOLFENDEN, GEORGE
BEARDMORE, GEORGE CEDRIC

WOLFF, KLAUS
OSTEN-SACKEN, KLAUS v DER

WOLFF, SEBASTIAN
ALTENHOFF, WOLFGANG

WOLFF, SONIA
LEVITIN, SONIA [WOLFF]

WOLFF-SASSE, HERMANN
ANTON, UWE

WOLFFE, KATHERINE
SCOTT, MARIAN GALLAGHER

WOLFGANG, BRUNO
PROCHASKA, BRUNO

WOLFGANG, HANS
BEKESSY, JANOS

WOLFGARTEN, BERT
KALMUCZAK, ROLF

WOLFRAM, HELLMUT
HOFMANN, HELMUT W.

WOLFSHAGEN, G. v.
CASSAU, CARL

WOLICK, PETER
BROLL, WOLFGANG W.

WOLLER, HERMANN
HOPPE, HERMANN

WOLLETT, LEOPOLD J.
ELLIOTT, WILLIAM J.

WOLLF, NICK
FEARN, JOHN RUSSELL

WOLLONOVER, FRED
MOSKOWITZ, SAM

WOLNY, P.
JANECZKO, PAUL B.

WOLSELEY, FAITH
TOWER, STELLA [MARY H.]

WOLTER, FRANK
BREUCKER, OSCAR HERBERT

WOLTER, HANS-JOACHIM
CHOLLET, HANS-JOACHIM

WOLTER, WERNER
GRONWALD, WERNER

WOLVERTON, DAVE
WOLVERTON, JOHN DAVID

WONDER, JAL
FERGUSON, PETER K.

WONDER, WILLIAM
KIRWAN, THOMAS

WONGAR, B.
BOZIC, SRETEN

WOOD, CATHERINE
ETCHISON, BIRDIE L[EE]

WOOD, DEBORAH
BREUER, SANDRA

WOOD, ERIC
CAMPLING, FRANK KNOWLES

WOOD, ESTHER
BRADY, ESTHER WOOD

WOOD, GEOFFREY
RUSSELL, C.

WOOD, GLEN
TURNER, ROBERT H.

WOOD, H.F. WILBER
WOOD, H[ARRY] F[REEMAN]

WOOD, HARVEY
HORNWOOD, HARVEY

WOOD, J. CLAVERTON
CARTER, THOMAS

WOOD, KERRY
WOOD, EDGAR ALLARDYCE

WOOD, KIRK
STAHL, LE ROY

WOOD, LAURA N.
ROPER, LAURA WOOD

WOOD, MARK L.
JEIER, THOMAS

WOOD, MARY
BAMFIELD, VERONICA

WOOD, MRS. HENRY
WOOD, ELLEN PRICE

WOOD, NURIA
NOBISSON, JOSEPHINE

WOOD, QUALITY
WOOD, VIOLET

WOOD, ROBIN
WOOD, ROBERT PAUL

WOOD, S. ANDREW
WOOD, [SAMUEL] ANDREW

WOOD, SERRY
FREEMAN, GRAYDON LAVERNE

WOOD, STANLEY
TULLBERG, SIGURD

WOOD, TED
WOOD, EDWARD JOHN

WOOD, URSULA
VAUGHN WILLIAMS, URSULA

WOOD, VALENTINE
BAILEY, GEORGE T.

WOOD, VALENTINE
MCMULLEN, DYSART
MILTON, PAUL R.
ROBERTS, W.A.
TOMPKINS, WALKER A.

WOODBURY, FRANK
CHAPMAN, FRANK MONROE

WOODBURY, LEONORA
KELMAN, ELLEN

WOODCOTT, KEITH
BRUNNER, JOHN [K.H.]

WOODFERN, WINNIE
GIBSON, MARY W. STANLEY

WOODFORD, CECIL
TARKINGTON, BOOTH

WOODFORD, JACK
WOOLFOLK, JOSHUA PITTS

WOODFORD, JILL
WOOLFOLK, JOSHUA PITTS

WOODHOUSE, C.M.
WOODHOUSE, CHRISTOPHER M.

WOODLEY, WINIFRED
HEDDEN, WORTH TUTTLE

WOODROFFE, DANIEL
WOODS, MRS. J.C.

WOODROOK, R.A.
COWLISHAW, RANSON

WOODRUFF, CLYDE
VERN, DAVID

WOODRUFF, MARIAN
GOUDGE, EILEEN

WOODRUFF, PHILIP
MASON, PHILIP

WOODRUFF, ROBERT W.
MENCKEN, HENRY LOUIS

WOODS, CONSTANCE
MCCOMB, KATHERINE WOODS

WOODS, ELEANOR
ROGERS, ELEANOR WOODS

WOODS, JACK
O'NEAL, WILLIAM B.

WOODS, JONAH
WOODS, OWEN SPENCER

WOODS, LAURENCE
MICHEL, JOHN B.

WOODS, LAWRENCE
LOWNDES, ROBERT A.W.
WOLLHEIM, DONALD A.

WOODS, LELAND
DETZER, KARL

WOODS, NAT
MCFARLANE, LESLIE CHARLES
STRATEMEYER, EDWARD

WOODS, P.F.
BAYLEY, BARRINGTON J.

WOODS, PETER
BAYLEY, BARRINGTON J.

WOODS, ROSS
STORY, ROSAMOND MARY

WOODS, SARA
BOWEN-JUDD, SARA HUTTON

WOODS, SHERRYL
WOODS, SHERYL ANN

WOODS, STOCKTON
FORREST, RICHARD S.

WOODS, STUART
LEE, STUART

WOODSMAN, DAVID
GIBSON, WALTER B.

WOODSON, JACK
WOODSON, JOHN WADDIE JR.

WOODSON, JEFF
OFFUTT, ANDREW J.
OGLESBY, JOSEPH
WOODSON, JEFF

WOODVILLE, JENNIE
STABLER, JAMIE LATHAM

WOODWARD, L.T. MD
SILVERBERG, ROBERT

WOODWARD, LILLIAN
MARSH, JOHN

WOODWARD, MEL
DRABER, UWE

WOODY, WILLIAM
FAGETTE, WOODBURY WILLIAM

WOOLF, F.X.
ENGEL, HOWARD
HAMILTON, JANET

WOOLF, VICTORIA
HOLLAND, SHEILA C.

WOOLLAND, HENRY
WILLIAMS, GUY RICHARD O.

WOOLRICH, CORNELL
WOOLRICH, CORNELL HOPLEY

WOON
WOTHERSPOON, RALPH

WORBOYS, ANNE E. EYRE
WORBOYS, ANN[ETTE I.]

WORCESTER, DONALD E.
MAKEMSON, DON E.

WORCESTER, ROLAND
RAYER, FRANCIS G.

WORDEN, HELEN
CRANMER, HELEN WORDEN

WORRELL, EVERIL
MURPHY, EVERIL WORRELL

WORTH, AMY
KELLER, DAVID H.

WORTH, DAN
CRUGER, PAUL

WORTH, JOHN
KURTH, HANNS

WORTH, MARGARET
ARVONEN, HELEN
STRICKLAND, MARGOT

WORTH, MARTIN
WIGGLESWORTH, MARTIN

WORTH, MAURICE
BOSWORTH, WILLAN GEORGE
MASH, MAURICE H.B.

WORTH, NICHOLAS
PAGE, WALTER HINES

WORTH, NIGEL
WRIGHT, NOEL

WORTH, PETER
GEIER, CHESTER S.
GRAHAM, ROGER P.

WORTH, VALENTINE
KELLEY, THOMAS P.

WORTH, VALERIE
BAHLKE, VALERIE WORTH

WORTHING, TEMPLE
HUNTER, ALFRED JOHN

WORTHY, KEN
WOOD, EDWARD D. JR.

WOTHE, ANNY
MAHN, ANNY

WOTMAN, JOHN
LLOP SELLARES, JUAN

WOUIL, GEORGE
SLANEY, GEORGE WILSON

WRAITH, JOHN
APPS, EDWIN
DEVANEY, PAULINE

WRAY, I.
PALLISER, IRIS

WRAY, REGINALD
HOME-GALL, WILLIAM B.

WRAY, ROGER
MARRIOTT, JAMES WILLIAM

WREFORD, JAMES
WATSON, JAMES WREFORD

WREN, JENNY
CRUTTENDEN, NELLIE

WREN, M.K.
RENFROE, MARTHA KAY

WREN, P.C.
WREN, PERCIVAL CHRISTOP.

WREN, THOMAS
THOMAS, THOMAS T[HURSTON]

WREXE, CHARLES
HARDINGE, CHARLES WREXE

WRIGHT, AMOS
MAGOUN, FREDERICK ALEX.

WRIGHT, ANSON
MAGOUN, FREDERICK ALEX.

WRIGHT, CYNTHIA
HUNT, CYNTHIA WRIGHT

WRIGHT, DAMON
ACKERMAN, FORREST J.

WRIGHT, DON
WRIGHT, DONALD K.

WRIGHT, ELNORA A.
OLD COYOTE, ELNORA A.

WRIGHT, FRANCES J.
CROTHERS, JESSIE F.

WRIGHT, FRANCESCA
ROBINS, DENISE

WRIGHT, FRANKLIN
FARMER, HENRY

WRIGHT, GENE
WRIGHT, EUGENE ALDEN

WRIGHT, GLOVER
GLOVER-WRIGHT, GEOFFREY

WRIGHT, JACK R.
FINKLESTEIN, MARK

WRIGHT, JOSEPHINE
WEAVER, HARRIET SHAW

WRIGHT, JUDITH GROVNER
BULL, LOIS

WRIGHT, KATRINA
GATER, DILYS

WRIGHT, KENNETH
DEL REY, LESTER

WRIGHT, LAN
WRIGHT, LIONEL PERCY

WRIGHT, PHILIP
HUBBLE, LESLIE ARTHUR B.

WRIGHT, ROBERT
ACKERMAN, FORREST J.
LOWNDES, ROBERT A.W.

WRIGHT, ROWLAND
WELLS, CAROLYN

WRIGHT, RUTH
KAUFFMAN, RUTH [H]

WRIGHT, S.P.
WRIGHT, SEWELL PEASLEE

WRIGHT, SALLY
OLD COYOTE, ELNORA A.

WRIGHT, STEVE
WRIGHT, STEPHEN WILLIAM

WRIGHT, TED
WRIGHT, GEORGE T.

WRIGHT, WADE
WRIGHT, JOHN

WRIGHT, WEAVER
ACKERMAN, FORREST J.

WRIGHTFRIERSON
WRIGHT-FRIERSON, VIRGINIA

WROBEL, IGNAZ
TUCHOLSKY, KURT

WROXHAM, CECIL
BELFIELD, HARRY WEDGEWOOD

WRYDE, DOGEAR
GOREY, EDWARD [ST. JOHN]

WSL-S
LACH-SZYRMA, W.S.

WTATT, B.D.
ROBINSON, PAUL

WUEST, GRITLI
LOCHER-WERLING, EMILIE

WUL, STEFAN
PAIRAULT, PIERRE

WUNDER, ERASMUS
BERGK, JOHANN ADAM

WUNDT, WILHELM
DE MILLE, RICHARD

WURDEMANN, AUDREY
AUSLANDER, AUDREY WURDE.W

WURF, KARL
SCITHERS, GEORGE

WURTS, JANNY
WURTS[Z], JANICE

WYANDOTTE, STEVE
THOMAS, STANLEY C.

WYATT, BEN
YOUNG, FRED W.

WYATT, ESCOTT
LEYLAND, ERIC

WYATT, JAMES
ROBINSON, LOUIE JR.

WYATT, JANE
BRADBURY, BIANCA [R]

WYATT, LEE
PROCTOR, GEO[RGE] W[YATT]

WYATT, MOLLY
BRADBURY, BIANCA [R]

WYCLIFFE, JOHN
BEDFORD-JONES, HENRY

WYETH, GILLIAN
WOLFE, LOIS

WYETH, N.C.
WYETH, NEWELL CONVERS

WYKEHAMICUS, FRIEDRICH
GALE, FREDERICK

WYKHAM, HELEN
EVANS, PAMELA

WYLCOTES, JOHN
RANSFORD, OLIVER

WYLDE, HAZEL
HOTCHKISS, ELLA A.

WYLDE, KATHARINE
COLVILLE, HELEN HESTER

WYLER, RICHARD
LINAKER, MICHAEK

WYLER, ROSE
AMES, ROSE WYLER

WYLIE, DIRK
DOCKWEILER, JOSEPH HAROLD
KORNBLUTH, C[YRIL] M.
POHL, FREDERIK

WYLIE, I.A.R.
WYLIE, IDA ALEXA ROSS

WYLIE, JEFF
WYLIE, FRANCIS E.

WYLIE, JONATHAN
SMITH, JULIA [MARY WYLIE]
SMITH, MARK [JONATHAN A.]

WYLIE, LAURA
MATTHEWS, PATRICIA [BRIS]

WYLIE, LAURIE
MATTHEWS, PATRICIA [BRIS]

WYLWYNNE, KYTHE
HYLAND, M.E.F.

WYMAN, OLIVE
HOLMES, OLIVE & WYMAN

WYN, A.A.
WEINSTEIN, AARON

WYNDER, MAVIS ARETA
WINDER, MAVIS ARETA

WYNDHAM, ESTHER
LUTYENS, MARY

WYNDHAM, JOHN
HARRIS, JOHN WYNDHAM P.L.

WYNDHAM, LEE
HYNDMAN, JANE ANDREWS

WYNDHAM, ROBERT
HYNDMAN, ROBERT UTLEY

WYNDHEIM, VICTOR
KLAGES, VICTOR

WYNES, PATRICIA
RITTER, WOLFPETER

WYNES, PATRICK
RITTER, WOLFPETER

WYNGARD, RHODA
TRUAX, RHODA

WYNMAN, MARGARET
DIXON, ELLA HEPWORTH

WYNN, ALFRED
BREWER, FRED

WYNN, PATRICIA
RICKS, PATRICIA W.B.

WYNNE, ANTHONY
WILSON, ROBERT MCNAIR

WYNNE, BRIAN
GARFIELD, BRIAN F.W.
MCGAUGHY, DUDLEY DEAN

WYNNE, FRANK
GARFIELD, BRIAN F.W.

WYNNE, PAMELA
SCOTT, WINIFRED MARY

WYNNTON, PATRICK
RICHARDSON, ANTHONY T.S.C

WYNYARD, JOHN
HARRISON, J.H.

WYNYARD, TALBOT
HAMILTON, CHARLES H.S.

WYSEMAN, DEMETRIUS
DICKE, WILLIS

WYTSKE
NEDERVEEN HENDRIKS, WIETK

WYVIS, BEN
MUNRO, [MACFARLAND] HUGH

WYZEWA
DE WYZEWSKI, TEODOR

X
FAWKES, FRANK ATTFIELD

X, MR.
HOCH, EDWARD D.

X.
FOX-DAVIES, ARTHUR CHAS.
O'MANT, HEDLEY P.A.
WARE, WILLIAM
WOLLHEIM, DONALD A.

X.X.
STREET, CECIL JOHN C.

X.Y.Z.
TILSLEY, FRANK

X.Y.Z. CLUB
LIVEN, DOUGLAS A.
PETTES, GEORGE W.
SAXE, JOHN GODFREY

XANTHUS, XAVIER
LAUMER, MARCH

XANTIPPE
MEISER, EDITH

XARIFFA
TOWNSEND, MARY ASHLEY

XAVIER, [FATHER]
HURWOOD, BERNHARDT J.

XELA
SCHOMBURG, ALEX

XENIUS
D'ORS Y ROVIRA, EUGENIO

XENO
LAKE, KENNETH R[OBERT]

XENOPHON XIII
MAURRAS, CHARLES-MARIE-P

XERXES, B.T.H.
ALDISS, BRIAN [WILSON]
BOARDMAN, THOMAS VOLNEY

XIMENEZ, MAIN
BENITEZ, MIGUEL ANGEL OS.

XOCHITL
MURILLO, JOSEFA

XUAN VIET
NGHIEM XUAN VIET

Y.L.G.
GORDON, YEHUDA LEIB

Y.Y.
LYND, ROBERT

Y.Z.
BAKER, BERNHARD

YAEGER, BARTD
STRUNG, NORMAN

YAFFE, ALAN
YORINKS, ARTHUR

YAKOVETIC, JOE
YAKOVETIC, JOSEPH SANDY

YALE, REX
BANZHAF, ERWIN

YAMA
SUR, ATUL KRISHNA

YAMBO
NOVELLI, ENRICO

YAN, MAXI
DE ECHEVARRIA, MARIA F.Y.

YAN, V.
YANCHEVETSKY, VASILY

YANCEY, WES
LAZENBY, NORMAN A.

YANKAS, LAUTARO
MORALES, MANUEL SOTO

YARBO, STEVE
KING, ALBERT

YARNALL, SOPHIA
JACOBS, SOPHIS YARNALL

YASHIMA, TARO
IWAMATSU, JUN ATSUSHI

YATES, A.G.
YATES, ALAN GEOFFREY

YATES, ALAN
YATES, ALAN GEOFFREY

YATES, DAVID O.
WOMACK, DAVID A.

YATES, DORNFORD
MERCER, CECIL WILLIAM

YATES, JUDITH
YODER, JUDITH

YATES, PETER
YATES, ALAN GEOFFREY
LONG, WILLIAM

YATES, ROSCOE
BUCKLES, ELEANOR

YBARRA, T.R.
YBARRA, THOMAS R.

YEATES, MABEL
PEREIRA, HAROLD BERTRAM

YEATMAN, R.J.
YEATMAN, ROBERT JULIAN

YEATS-BROWN, F.C.
YEATS-BROWN, FRANCIS C.C.

YELLING, DAN
BOMKE, BERNHARD

YENSID, RETLAW
DISNEY, WALTER ELIAS

YEOVIL, JACK
NEWMAN, KIM [JAMES]

YEREX, CUTHBERT
CUTHBERT, ESTELLA Y

YERKE, T,B,
YERKE, T. BRUCE

YERMAKOV, NICHOLAS
LARSON, GLEN A.
YERMAKOV, NICHOLAS VALEN.

YERRICK, H.
HOGBERG, ERIK YNGVE

YERUSHALMI, CHAIM
LIPSCHITZ, CHAIM

YERUSHALMI, GERSHON
HARKAVY, ZVI

YES TOR
ROCHE, THOMAS

YESTER, BURT
BREUCKER, OSCAR HERBERT

YETSKA
IRONSIDE, JETSKE

YEXLEY, LIONEL
WOODS, JAMES

YIDDISH MARK TWAIN
ZEVIN, ISRAEL JOSEPH

YLLA
KOFFLER, CAMILLA

YOE, SHWAY [SCHWAY]
SCOTT, JAMES GEORGE

YOGLI, BUKKI BEN
KATZNELSON, YEHUDA LOEB

YOLA, YERIMA
KIRK-GREEN, ANTHONY H.M.

YOLEN, JANE
STEMPLE, JANE H. YOLEN

YONGE, REMINGTON
DOHERTY, ROBERT R.

YORICK
IVENS, MICHAEL WILLIAM

YORICK, A.P.
TINDALL, WILLIAM YORK

YORK, ALISON
NICOLE, CHRISTOPHER ROBIN

YORK, AMANDA
DIAL, JOAN MAVIS R.

YORK, ANDREW
NICOLE, CHRISTOPHER ROBIN

YORK, GEORGIA
HOFFMAN, SHIRLEY BELL

YORK, HELGA
ESCHBACH, JOSEF

YORK, JEREMY
CREASEY, JOHN

YORK, PAULINE
HOWL, MARCIA Y.H.

YORK, PETER
WALLIS, PETER

YORK, REBECCA
BUCKHOLTZ, EILEEN [G]
GLICK, RUTH [BURTNICK]

YORK, ROBERT
ESTRIDGE, ROBIN

YORK, SIMON
HEINLEIN, ROBERT A.

YORK, VICKIE
PATTISON, BETTY ANN

YORK, WESLEY SIMON
PLATT, KIN

YORKE, ANTHONY
REILLY, BERNARD JAMES

YORKE, ANTON
ZAGAT, ARTHUR LEO

YORKE, CARAS
MARSHALL, ARTHUR C.

YORKE, CURTIS
LEE, SUSAN RICHMOND

YORKE, ERIN
HEALY, CHRISTINE
YANSICK, SUSAN MCGOVERN

YORKE, KATHERINE
ELLERBECK, ROSEMARY A.L.

YORKE, MARGARET
NICHOLSON, MARGARET B.L.

YORKE, PRESTON
KELLY, HAROLD ERNEST

YORKE, ROGER
BINGLEY, DAVID ERNEST

YORKE, SUSAN
TELENGA, SUZETTE

YORK[E], ELIZABETH
YORK[E], MARGARET E.

YOUD, C.S.
YOUD, CHRISTOPHER [S]

YOUD, SAMUEL
YOUD, CHRISTOPHER [S]

YOUNG BROADBRIM
RATHBORNE, ST. GEORGE

YOUNG, A.S.
YOUNG, ANDREW S.N.

YOUNG, AGATHA
YOUNG, AGNES

YOUNG, AXEL
MCDOWELL, MICHAEL
SCHUETZ, DENNIS

YOUNG, BOB
YOUNG, JANET & ROBERT
YOUNG, ROBERT W.

YOUNG, BRITTANY
YOUNG, SANDRA

YOUNG, CARRIE
YOUNG, AHDELE CARRINE

YOUNG, CARTER TRAVIS
CHARBONNEAU, LOUIS

YOUNG, CHESLEY V.
GIBSON, WALTER B.

YOUNG, CLARENCE
STRATEMEYER, EDWARD

YOUNG, COLLIER
BLOCH, ROBERT [A]

YOUNG, DOC
YOUNG, ANDREW S.N.

YOUNG, E.H.
YOUNG, EMILY HILDA

YOUNG, EDWARD
REINFELD, FRED

YOUNG, ELAINE L.
SCHULTE, ELAINE L.

YOUNG, FRANK W.
YOUNG, FRED W.

YOUNG, G.M.
YOUNG, GEORGE MALCOLM

YOUNG, GORDON
JUNG, RICHARD

YOUNG, GORDON R.
YOUNG, GORDON [RAY]

YOUNG, JAN
YOUNG, JANET & ROBERT

YOUNG, JIM
YOUNG, JAMES MAXWELL

YOUNG, KAREN
REEDER, DAVE
STONE, KAREN

YOUNG, KENDAL
YOUNG, PHYLLIS BRETT

YOUNG, NACELLA
TATE, VELMA

YOUNG, NEDRICK
BESSIE, ALVAH

YOUNG, PAUL
JENNISON, JOHN WILLIAM

YOUNG, PHILIP
STEWARD, SAMUEL M[ORRIS]

YOUNG, RAYMOND A.
JONES, VERNON H.

YOUNG, ROBERT
PAYNE, PIERRE S. ROBERT

YOUNG, ROGER FLINT
GRAINGER, PETER

YOUNG, ROSE
HARRIS, MARION ROSE

YOUNG, THOMAS
YOSELOFF, THOMAS

YOUNG, VIVIEN
GATER, DILYS

YOUNG, WARWICK
PARSONS, B.

YOUNG, WILL
HOME-GALL, WILLIAM B.

YOUNG, WILSON
TIPPETTE, GILES

YOUNGER, JACK
KRAFT, DAVID ANTHONY
JONES, RUSS

YOURCENAR, MARGUERITE
DE CRAYENCOUR, MARGUERITE

YOWA
MCMURRAY, NANCY A.

YPSEN, UDO
BREUCKER, OSCAR HERBERT

YU-HO, TSENG
YU-HO ECKE, BETTY TSENG

YUILL, P.B.
WILLIAMS, GORDON M.
VENABLES, TERRY

YUKON, BILL
HAYES, CATHERINE E.

YULYA
WHITNEY, JULIE

YUMA, DAN
DUNHAM, ROBERT

YUN, TAN
JUSULIN, ADET

YUNQUE, ALBERTO
LAGUERRE, ENRIQUE A.

YURKA, BLANCHE
JURKA, BLANCHE

YUTANG, LIN
YU-T'ANG, LIN

YUU, HEE FOO
GIBSON, WALTER B.

YVER, COLETTE
HUZARD, ANTOINETTE DE B.

Z, HASSE
ZETTERSTROM, HANS HARALD

Z.Z.
ZANGWILL, LOUIS

ZACHARIA, DAN
NOVAK, C. DAN ZACHARIA

ZACHARY, ELIZABETH
ZACHARY, ELIZABETH
ZACHARY, HUGH

ZACHARY, LEO
MEEHAN, FRANCIS JOSEPH

ZACHERLEY
ZACHERLE, JOHN C.

ZACK
KEATS, GWENDOLINE

ZAIDYS, PRANAS
GAIDA-GAIDAMAVICIUS, PRA.

ZAKI, NURI
NURETDINOV, ZAKI S.

ZAMACOIS, EDUARDO
DE ZAMACOIS Y QUINTANA, E

ZAMBOCK, GEORGE
GLASSER, ALLEN

ZAMETKIN, LAURA K. HOBSON
HOBSON, LAURA K.Z.

ZANDERBERGEN, GEORGE
DIKTY, JULIAN [C] MAY

ZANDTT, CULPEPER
NEW, CLARENCE HERBERT

ZANE, CAROLYN
PIZZUTI, CAROLYN

ZANE, LEHI
TAYLOR, SAM S.

ZANTA, C.C.
KURTH, HANNS

ZAPOLSKA, GABRIELA
KORWIN-PIOTROWSKA, GABRL.

ZARA, LOUIS
ROSENFELD, LOUIS ZARA

ZARINS, JOYCE AUDY
DOS SANTOS, JOYCE AUDY

ZARO, BUKKO BE
MCCABE, BILL

ZAROVITCH, PRINCESS VERA
LANE, MARY E.

ZASCHKE, ANNA
KOTULLA, ANNEMARIE

ZASTROW, ERIKA
MASSEY, ERIKA

ZATLIN-BORING, PHYLLIS
ZATLIN, PHYLLIS

ZAULA, ONDREK
SOULEN, HENRY J.

ZAYNE, VALERIE
SHALEEN, LEIGH

ZEBRA, A.
SCOLTOCK, JACK

ZEBROWSKI, GEORGE [THAD.]
ZEBROWSKI, JERZY TADEUZ

ZECHT, BERNHARD
ASPERN-BUCHMEIER, ELISAB.

ZECK, GERRY
ZECK, GERALD ANTHONY

ZED
DIENES, ZOLTAN PAUL

ZED, DR.
PENROSE, GORDON

ZEEMANN, DOROTHEA
HOLZINGER, DOROTHEA

ZEHLEN, OTTO
VON HANSTEIN, OTFRID

ZEHLEN, W.I.
KABEL, WALTHER

ZEIGFREID, KARL
FANTHORPE, R.L.
GLASBY, JOHN S.
WADE, THOMAS W.

ZEIT, CALVIN
BARASCH, MARC IAN
DRESCHER, HENRIK

ZELL, IRA
ROOSEVELT, ROBERT BARNWLL

ZELLAN, AUDREY PENN
PENN, AUDREY

ZELLER, LIESL
VON KOBLINSKI, HANS-JOACH

ZEMAITE
BENIUSEVICIUTE-Z, JULIJA

ZENA, REMIGIO
INVREA, GASPARE

ZENOBIA, ALEXANDRIA
BRONTE, ANN

ZERLIN, WALTER JR
CONWAY, ROBERT

ZERO
RAMSAY, ALLAN

ZETA
COPE, VINCENT ZACHARY

ZETFORD, TULLY
BULMER, [HENRY] KENNETH

ZEVERIL, HUBERT
MURRAY, A.C.

ZHI, YU
ZHISHAN, YE

ZIEGLER-STEGE, ERIKA
KLEIN, ERIKA

ZIEMANN, MARTINA
KURTH, HANNS

ZIF, JAY JEHIEL
SILBERSTEIN, JAY JEHIEL

ZIGIS
SKUJINS, ZIGMUNDS

ZILIOX, MARC
FICHTER, GEORGE S.

ZILLAH
MACDONALD, ZILLAH K.

ZILSO, PAUL
MOTH-LUND, POUL

ZIMMER, ASTARA
BRADLEY, MARION ZIMMER

ZIMMER, JILL SCHARY
ROBINSON, JILL

ZIMMER, MARION
BRADLEY, MARION ZIMMER

ZIMMERMANN, MARIA
HORTI, MARIA

ZIMMETH, MARY
SCHOMAKER, MARY Z.

ZINBERG, LEN
ZINBERG, LEONARD S.

ZINER, FEENIE
ZINER, FLORENCE

ZINGARA, PROFESSOR
LEEMING, JOSEPH

ZINKEN
HOPP, SIGNE

ZINNER, HEDDA
ERPENBECK-ZINNER, HEDDA

ZINOVIEV, ALEXANDER
ZIONOVIEV, ALEKSANDR A.

ZINTH, SIRMIONE
HARTMANN, EDITH

ZMAJ
JOVANOVIC, JOVAN

ZMOGAS
RODZIEWICZOWNA, MARIA

ZOGENREUTH, G.H.
HERING, GEO

ZOHAR, ATTILA
HOLLEDGE, JAMES

ZOILUS
LOVECRAFT, H[OWARD] P.

ZOLAR
KING, BRUCE ALVIN

ZOLINE, PAMELA
LIFTON-ZOLINE, PAMELA

ZOLLER, ARNO
LIERSCH, ROLF WERNER

ZOLNY, NORMAN
BRANDNER, GARY

ZOLOTOV, ELLEN
DRAGONWAGON, CRESCENT

ZONIK, ELEANOR DOROTHY
GLASER, ELEANOR DOROTHY

ZOOK, DEBORAH
GREEN, DEBORAH

ZOOL, M.H.
ADYE, TIM
BISHOP, MATTHEW
BRAY, JOHN
COHEN, MALCOLM
COX, ADRIAN
CRAY, PAUL
DYMOND, MELANIE
HEAL, PENELOPE
HOLKAR, MO
MARROW, PAUL
MCLEISH, SIMON
OXFORD SFI GROUP

ZOOL, M.H. [CONT]
TOWLSON, IVAN
TRINGHAM, NEAL

ZORE, HYMAN
AMESBURY, JAMES E.
BARNES, MICHAEL [L.G.]
GORELL, LETHBRIDGE
WATSON, JOHN
WINTER, BEVIS [PETER]
HANSON, VICTOR JOSEPH
KEDDELL, SCUD
LAZENBY, NORMAN A.

ZORRO
MORRIS, EDWARD P.
STARR, H.W.
STERLING, WARD
WARD, HAROLD

ZORRO, JOSE
DIETSCH, ARTHUR

ZU MONDFELD, WOLFRAM
LOWENSTEI-W-F, WOLFRAM ZU

ZUCCOLI, LUCIANO
VON INGENHEIM, LUCIANO

ZUPA, G. ANTHONY
ZECK, GERALD ANTHONY

ZUROMISKIS, DIANE
STANLEY, DIANE

ZVEREV, ILIA
SAMDBERG, IZOLD I.

ZVI, H.
HARKAVY, ZVI

ZWEIG, ALLEN
POHL, FREDERIK

ZWEIT, ADAM
LOVIN, ROGER ROBERT

ZWEYDORN, PETER
HASSELBLATT, DIETER

ZYCH, MAURYCY
ZEROMSKI, STEFAN